Kabbalah and Eco-theology

Jewish mysticism is fundamentally concerned with cosmology and cosmogony, the origins and the process of creation, and the holism of creation in all its aspects, as well as the processes within divinity that sustain the world. Jewish mysticism has taken many forms throughout history, but the tradition we call Kabbalah became fully crystallized in the thirteenth century with the publication of the *Zohar* ("The Book of Radiance"). Kabbalistic literature spans many centuries and is incredibly diverse and complex; here the focus will be on themes within Kabbalah relevant to eco-theology.

While the literature of Kabbalah is vast, certain themes are persistent. Kabbalah is founded on the idea that the commandments of the Torah are given for the sake of restoring or healing the whole cosmos and reuniting it with the Infinite. As such, Kabbalah is the primary thread within Jewish tradition that imagines a purpose for the Jewish covenant, and hence, an intention within the divine will that embraces the more-than-human world, beyond both Israel and humanity. As Seth Brody wrote, "The kabbalist's goal is to become a living bridge, uniting heaven and Earth, so that God may become equally manifest above and below, for the healing and redemption of all" (1993: 153).

Two fundamental kabbalistic principles provide a strong foundation for Jewish eco-theology. One is that "there is no place empty of God," (*leyt atar panui miney*) that is, the presence of God can be found in every single creature and being. The other is that "the whole world is blessed because of us" (*kula alma m'varkhin b'ginan*) that is, the actions of the righteous bring blessing to the whole of creation and to the Earth and all its creatures, as well as to God. Moshe Cordovero (1522–1570, Palestine) elucidated the meaning of this principle in his work *Or Ne'erav* ("Sweet Light"):

> Being involved in this wisdom, a person sustains the world and its life and its sustenance. And this is what Rabbi Shimon bar Yochai [the main protagonist of the *Zohar*] explained in saying that "the world is blessed because of us" ... for involvement with divinity causes cleaving, and when the human cleaves to the One who flows/guides the world, he causes the flow [of divine energy] necessarily, and ... causes to flow upon the world a great flow (1965: 32).

One of Cordovero's most popular works, *Tomer D'vorah* ("The Palm Tree of Deborah"), sums up the human task as follows: "This is the principle: he should cause life to stream forth to all" (from the Hebrew, 1969: 21; see also 1974: 82). While there are many approaches to understanding Kabbalah, if one focuses on this principle, one finds a fertile ground in which to root contemporary Jewish eco-theology.

In addition to this foundation there are also several areas in Kabbalah which may be drawn upon for developing an ecological ethics, including views regarding the ethical treatment and moral standing of other animals and other species, the contemplation of the natural world as a revelation of divine presence, and the extension of the idea of God's image from humanity to creation itself.

On the cosmological level, a number of characteristics of Kabbalah are equally significant for contemporary ecological thought. The holographic complexity that characterizes most kabbalistic texts is resonant for any theology of nature that attempts to account for contemporary science. For ecofeminism, the kabbalistic emphasis on balancing or uniting male and female at all levels, and the acknowledgement of the feminine aspect of the divine, are also intriguing, even though these texts generally maintain gender hierarchy. Finally, the sensuous way that Kabbalah understands cosmogony is echoed in the significance attributed to playfulness in contemporary ecopsychology.

Sefirotic Play

The *Sefer Bahir* ("Book of Brightness," ca. twelfth century), the earliest articulation of what later came to be called Kabbalah, declares in a parable that when the king began building his palace (that is, when God began creating the world), a spring gushed forth. When he saw the spring, he said, "I will plant a garden, then I will delight (or "play") in it, and so will all the world" (§5, Kaplan 1989: 3). Creation is seemingly both God's act of delight or play, and a gift of delight to all the creatures.

The playful garden that the king planted is described later in the *Bahir* as the Tree of Life. This Cosmic Tree is defined in later Kabbalah as a particular pattern called the *Sefirot* (singular: *Sefirah*), which are together the image of God, or what Gershom Scholem (1991) called "the mystical shape of the Godhead." The *Sefirot* are regarded alternatively as divine attributes, essence, emanations, instruments or vessels; different perspectives are emphasized by different kabbalists. The kabbalists in general found God by tracing back the pattern of God's unfoldment (to borrow David Bohm's term) through the levels of emanation, from one *Sefirah* to the next, and from one world to the next. These levels represent the way in which divine energies such as love and judgment, male and female, hidden and manifest, and so on, are balanced and made manifest. Everything has within it the essence and image of those supernal levels. The unifying concept in Kabbalah is that the structure of each "holon" manifests the *Sefirot* and so bears witness to the image of God. ("Holon" is Ken Wilber's term for the way the nature of every being reflects the whole of what he calls "the Kosmos.") At each level and within each entity, the kabbalists saw the pattern of the *Sefirot*, in a manner that we might call fractal or holographic.

Holism

Kabbalah embraced a holistic view of the universe which called for the expansion of divinity into the physical world. Kabbalah represents the theological science (in the medieval sense of the term) that draws all the worlds, including dimensions of God and nature, into one realm, one whole. "Implicit is a notion of sacred cosmology . . . The kabbalists' faith involves a hierarchy of worlds that are ontologically higher than the material world" (Krassen 1999: 137). The work of the kabbalist is to draw the higher worlds into the lower and to unite the lower with the higher.

This tendency is most pronounced in the radical cosmogony that some texts propose: the universe is regarded as the shards of an original creation that shattered while it was still in the realm of the divine, carrying "sparks" of divinity into what became the physical realm. Each of these sparks is some part of the divine that has been alienated from its root. Human beings provide the vehicle to repair this brokenness and reunite the sparks with the whole. Equally important, the process that begins creation is understood to be a contraction of God, called *tzimtzum*, which makes space for the world to emerge. Isaac Luria (1534–1572, Palestine) in particular used images of birth to describe this process, suggesting quite literally that the universe or nature is somehow commensurable with God in the way that a child is with its mother.

These tropes teach that the human purpose in creation is to unify all realms of being with and within the divine. The *kavanot* or opening incantations that kabbalists added to their prayers expressed this purpose: "for the sake of the unification of the Holy One and the *Shekhinah*." One of the most beautiful expressions is found in the remarkable opening prayer of the original *Tu biSh'vat seder* (a kabbalistic ritual meal in honor of the Mishnaic New Year for the trees, interpreted as the cosmic Tree), which is found in the book *Chemdat Yamim* ("Treasure of Days", seventeenth century):

O God who makes, and forms, and creates, and emanates the upper worlds, and in their form and pattern you created their model on the Earth below; You made them all with wisdom, upper ones above and lower ones below, to join together the tent to become one . . . And this day is the beginning of your works, to ripen and renew . . . May it be Your will that the merit of our eating the fruit, and meditating on the secret of their roots above, you will bless them, flowing over them the flow of desire and energy, to make them grow and bloom, for good and for blessing, for good life and for peace . . . And may the Whole return now to its original strength . . . and may all the sparks that were scattered by our hands, or by the hands of our ancestors, or by the sin of the first human against the fruit of the tree, be returned to sustain in might and majesty the Tree of Life. "Then the trees of the forest will sing out," and the tree of the field will raise a branch and make fruit . . . (translated and abridged by the author; for a complete translation see Krassen 1999: 148–51).

The purpose of wisdom, i.e., Kabbalah, is to both recognize and reestablish the pattern of the divine image, called here "joining the tent to become one." One way to understand the holism of Kabbalah in modern terms is to consider the idea of the "more-than-human world." This terminology was coined by David Abram to keep reminding us that "Nature" is not "out there" but also within, and that human society is part of the natural world. Conceptually, both God and nature are more-than-human; in certain moments, the distinction between the two is dissolved in the overwhelming power of being. This happens in Kabbalah through the sanctification of the world around us by holy acts. Every deed is an act of compassion for creation, as well as a fulfillment of *tzorekh gavoha*, the "need on high," in the divine realm.

The Earth or Cosmos as Divine Body and Image

There are several themes in Kabbalah that relate to the idea that nature as a whole participates in divinity. *Shekhinah*, the "indwelling presence" which is the feminine dimension of divinity, is also called "the image which includes all images," that is, the images of all creatures above and below (*Zohar* 1:13a). The *Shekhinah*, as the source of all divine *shefa* or overflow that reaches the lower worlds, is the image of God that is closest to the Earth:

R' Eliezer said to him: Father, didn't they learn above that there is no body and no substance? He said to him: My son, about the world-to-come it was said, for that is a supernal [i.e., purely immaterial] mother, but below there is the body of this world, which is the *Shekhinah* below (*Tikuney Zohar* §70, 131a).

The *Shekhinah* in some sense represents "Nature." The Kabbalah's conception of nature, however, is vastly different from both science and Gaia-spirituality. Compared to classical scientific determinism, nature in Kabbalah is potentially free and self-willing. But, unlike what one finds in the neo-pagan celebration of nature as Mother-Goddess, nature *Shekhinah* must become united with the worlds above and hence with the transcendent. Hence nature is creative but it is not self-creating. According to some texts, this unification ends with the feminine being reabsorbed into the masculine, while others depict the feminine attaining equal stature, "eye-to-eye" with the masculine.

Whatever these images mean on a practical level, they imply an ambivalent relation to the natural world, which is insufficient in itself and needs to be redeemed. For this reason, Elliot Wolfson (2002) doubts whether Kabbalah has value for eco-theology. Seth Brody, Daniel Matt, Arthur Green, among others, however, find these tropes to be powerful grounds for creating an "eco-Kabbalah."

Kabbalah conceptualized the cosmos as both tree and as *Adam Qadmon* ("primordial human," sometimes translated "divine *anthropos*"), thereby connecting the divine image, the tree, and the cosmos itself through Adam. While some texts connect *Adam Qadmon* primarily with the upper or originary realms only (especially with the crown *Sefirah, Keter*), others see it as the macrocosm which inscribes the divine image onto the whole of creation. The former dualistic perspective (discussed below) and the latter holistic perspective can sometimes be found in the same text. This complexity suggests that a wholesale adoption of kabbalistic cosmology into a theology of nature cannot work without a re-reading of the texts.

Nevertheless, there were particular authors who consistently emphasized the inclusion of the Earth and the creatures in the divine image. Yosef ben Shalom Ashkenazi (fourteenth century Spain), for example, calls this "the secret of *Adam HaGadol* (the great Adam)", explaining:

> The human being should be called a small world, for in his form he is like all [the creatures of the world] – the human, formed of "the dirt of the ground" [Gen 2:8], included in himself the seal and structure and likeness and image of all ten *Sefirot* and all that is created and formed and made from them (1984: 36).

The Earth itself includes the seal and structure and image of God that became part of Adam. God's image in Adam not only unites the whole of creation, but also carries within itself each created species and individual, that is, the entire diversity of creation. Isaiah Horowitz (1562–1630) similarly taught that God's purpose in creating humanity was to unite the diversity of creation with God's image: "'The end of the thing' [Eccl. 12:13] is Adam, who was created last ... Adam was created at the end so that he could include everything in his image and likeness" (1996: 216).

God's Image in the World

If the *Sefirot* are the soul of the world, then the substance of creation is sometimes treated as the body: "The ten *Sefirot* ... are clothed in ten things that were created on the first day, and these are: skies and land, light and darkness, abyss and chaos, wind and water, the measure of day and the measure of night" (*Tikuney Zohar* §70:120a–b). At the same time, the pattern of the *Sefirot* at the highest level is the guarantor that every subsequent level is also an image of God. For example, the *Sefirot*, the angels, the animals of the Ezekiel's chariot (human, lion, eagle, and ox), and the four elements are seen as manifestations of the same pattern at different levels (Horowitz 1996: 152).

Kabbalah also uses the letters of *Yod Heh Vav Heh* (which spell the holiest name for God, also known as the Tetragrammaton) to represent the structure of the *Sefirot*. Seeing these letters in a thing expresses the idea that God's image or presence is manifest through that thing. For example, in *Tikuney Zohar* (a series of meditations on the first verses of Genesis, written in the style of the *Zohar*) each limb of the human body is an image of this name; each human being as a whole person is understood to be an image; and the diversity of humanity as one species is also an expression of God's image, mapped on to *YHVH* (146a).

This trope was not limited to the human realm. The human species as a whole is further seen as one letter in the name formed by the spectrum of animal species represented in the chariot. Similar correspondences were drawn with respect to the bodies of other creatures like birds and fruit trees, and to other dimensions of the physical and supernal worlds like the colors of the rainbow, thereby relating various senses, spectrums and dimensions to *YHVH*. In general, those creatures which were seen as uniting the upper and lower worlds represent an image of God in the world, along with those symbols of human culture whose explicit purpose was to create unification, like the Torah and the *Mishkan* or Tabernacle.

On the largest scale, the four letters of the name *YHVH* were seen as corresponding to the multi-level process of emanation, becoming well-defined in the Kabbalah of Moses Cordovero according to four worlds or stages of being: emanating (*Y*), creating (*H*), shaping (*V*) and acting (*H*). From this perspective, the entirety of creation, embracing all the levels, is conceived to be an image of God. While in general all creation is in some sense part of God, some texts emphasize that the lower creatures are essentially part of God's name. For example, the *Zohar* (in a later strata) explains:

In the secret of the ten *Sefirot*, all is included in this image of *Heh*. In this secret were created and fixed all these lower beings, and for this [reason] it's written, "Elohim said: Let us make/*N'SH* in our image as our likeness" [Gen. 1:27] – literally "let us make/*N'S* the letter *Heh*, with all these that are existing below and are united in her, in her image, truly (*Zohar Chadash, Sitrey Otiyot B'reishit*, "Secrets of the Letters of Creation").

When the physical dimension of being is not conjoined with the higher levels, then the final letter of God's name, the *Heh*, is as it were missing, and the image of God is diminished. While Kabbalah mostly focused on specific manifestations of the *Sefirot* and God's image, the image of God ultimately embraced the breadth and diversity of creation.

Rabbinic Roots and Modern Branches

Many elements found in Kabbalah are rooted in classical rabbinic texts. The raw material for kabbalistic cosmology includes the midrashic idea that the upper beings or heavens were created in God's image, as well as the idea that the human body is a complete microcosm of the Earth. A second-century esoteric teaching, a tradition known as *Shiur Qomah*, delved into ("The Measure of the Body") and held that God's body was similar in structure to the human body but measured in the ancient equivalent of light-years. This tradition provided a critical element that allowed Kabbalah to make a connection between God's image and the physical cosmos. Even the expression "there is no place empty of God" is Talmudic in origin.

The classical texts, however, never made a connection between the structure of the cosmos, the human microcosm, and the image of God, and they explicitly stated that the lower beings or the creatures of the Earth were not created in God's image. Kabbalah, on the other hand, penetrated the boundaries between heaven and Earth and between upper and lower realms, projecting the image of God, either directly or through various analogues, onto the "lower beings."

Contemporary scholars such as Green and Seth Brody understand these texts to be the product of imaginations that embraced the diversity of creation; a paradigmatic text from the *Zohar* related to this theme has been translated by Matt (1996: 134). Krassen explains,

> Nature is neither a source to be exploited for utilitarian benefits nor a sentimental vestige of the past to be romanticized by poets and naturalists. It is rather an ultimate link in a chain of divine manifestation that directly emerges from the divine source of life (137).

Other scholars like Hava Tirosh-Samuelson doubt that the intention of Kabbalah goes beyond the play of textuality and linguistic interpretation. While the author of this essay supports the former view, in either case, Kabbalah provides a powerful model for any contemporary theologian wanting to express the religious meaning of our encounter with the diversity of life. Applying these principles to eco-theology, as Green and Arthur Waskow do, if the image of God is an image of the diversity of life, then God's image is diminished every time human beings cause another extinction.

Dualism and Repairing the Cosmos

According to some cosmologies, especially within Lurianic Kabbalah, the human of the Genesis story is born into an already shattered universe. This perspective led some kabbalists to a dualistic understanding of creation in which the connection between the Earth and *imago dei* is rejected. For example, in one *Zohar* passage, we read, "*Adam Qadmon*, even though his body is made from dirt, it's not from the dirt here ... *Adam Qadmon* has nothing from this world at all" (*Zohar* 3:83a).

This cosmology could be characterized as a "dual Earth" theory, where the element from which the primordial human is created is entirely derived from an anti-physical (or ante-physical) Earth. Nevertheless, even though the image of God is not expressed through the originary physical universe, our human bodies still have the potential to express the divine pattern, and this can only happen in completeness in the physical world. (This position radically divided Kabbalah from medieval Jewish philosophy.) In Lurianic doctrine, this is called raising the sparks to their root in divinity and purifying them from their materiality, and is called *berur han'tzotzot*. Through this process, the original brokenness of creation could be repaired; this is seen as the purpose of our existence. Thus, whereas rejection of the natural world is a possible consequence of Gnostic dualism, even within the most dualistic interpretations of Kabbalah, the purpose of humanity is to be engaged with the physical world and to bring redemption to the entirety of creation.

Ethics

Because Kabbalah saw the redemption of the cosmos as something that could happen through every interaction with the world, some kabbalists developed an acute sensitivity toward other creatures, asserting for example that only one knowledgeable in Torah and engaged in the deepest contemplation of raising the sparks should be allowed to eat meat.

One of the foundations of kabbalistic ethics is that all creatures deserve and require respect. One seminal concept in Kabbalah is the idea of reincarnation; for many kabbalists this included the possibility that human beings could reincarnate as animals. But the seeds for this idea of respect are independent of the concept of reincarnation and can be found already in the classical rabbinic idea that everything has a place and one must despise nothing in the world. Cordovero, who developed this principle further than any other kabbalist, wrote:

> One should train himself... to honour the creatures entirely, in whom he recognizes the exalted nature of the Creator who in wisdom created man. And so all creatures, the wisdom of the Creator is in them ... It is evil, too, in the eyes of the Holy One if any one of His creatures are despised. It is therefore written: "How great/*rabu* [diverse] are your works" [Ps. 104:24] – [this means] very important/*rav* ... (Cordovero 1974: 78; see also 71, 83–5).

Cordovero stressed that showing mercy and respect and bringing beneficence upon every aspect of creation is what it means to become like the Creator: "One's mercy should extend to all creatures, neither destroying nor despising any of them. For the Supernal Wisdom is extended to all created things – silent, growing, moving and speaking [i.e., mineral, plant, animal and human]" (Cordovero 1974: 83).

The wisdom of the Creator is found in the pattern of the *Sefirot*. When a person imitates this pattern, they allow the influx of divinity to reach each and every being, according to Cordovero. He wrote that this principle has strong practical implications:

> One should not uproot anything which grows, unless it is necessary, nor kill any living thing, unless it is necessary. And he should choose a good death for them, with a knife that has been carefully examined, to have pity on them as far as possible (Cordovero 1974: 84; see also 78).

Differing broadly from normative *halakhah* or Jewish law, Cordovero understood other creatures not in terms of human need, but rather in terms of the need of each living thing to fulfill its divine purpose. Human use must "elevate them higher and higher ... for [only] then is it permitted to uproot the plant and kill the animal ..." (Cordovero 1974: 78).

This deep understanding of ethics extended even to the interpretation some kabbalists gave to the prohibition against idolatry. Yosef Ashkenazi, who was quoted above, explained that the sin of idolatry is that it separates the worshipped thing from the divinity that comprises the whole:

> Since all the existences, from the upper ones and the lower ones, all of them are tied into his great, mighty and awesome name, blessed and holy be, therefore he warned [Israel] to not worship them in separation from his name – only in the name of *YHVH* [as] one ... (1984: 148, 41b).

Here as elsewhere, the unity of being, which is concomitant with the presence of divinity in all being, is the root of the extraordinary proto-ecological sensibility displayed in Kabbalah.

Contemplation and Ritual

Kabbalists reconciled the unity of being with the diversity of creation by seeing every aspect of the world as simultaneously cloaking and revealing the divine. They found the *Sefirot* and the letters of God's explicit name everywhere, and reached the spiritual dimension of things by engaging with the traces of the divine in the physical world. This engagement happened mostly through the projection of language and text onto the world, and thus focused on ideas at least as much as it focused on phenomena. However, the Lurianic doctrine of raising the sparks also focused the mystic's consciousness on the depth within real physical things. Elevation of the sparks required direct contact with the physical world, through ritual and mystical intentions in any physical act. It engendered a deeper respect for the intrinsic value of other creatures and things than one finds in normative Judaism.

The implication of kabbalistic theurgy (ritual or magic which operates on or affects divinity) was that proper intention and consciousness could reveal the divinity underlying all phenomena and unify phenomena with their source. The potential to create a phenomenology of holiness was made manifest by Chasidism in the eighteenth century. These ideas also inspired many Jewish thinkers, both in the Renaissance and the early modern period, to use Kabbalah to reconcile theology and science.

Some modern kabbalists gave full expression to the power of contemplating and understanding nature that is hinted at in Kabbalah. Abraham Isaac Kook (1865–1935, Palestine) wrote:

> Contemplate the wonders of creation, the divine dimension of their being, not as a dim configuration that is presented to you from the distance but as the reality in which you live. Know yourself and your world ... find the source of your own life, and of the life beyond you, around you, the glorious splendor of the life in which you have your being. The love that is astir in you – raise it to its basic potency and its noblest beauty, extend it to all its dimensions, toward every manifestation of the soul that sustains the universe ... (1978: 207).

For Kook, the meaning of Kabbalah was found within the lived experience of the natural world. He wrote that from the knowledge of God, "there radiates ... a love for the world, for all worlds, for all creatures, on all levels of their being. A love for all existence fills the hearts of the good and kindly ones among creatures, and among humans" (1978: 226). Kook's theology may even be called biocentric, in the broadest sense, as further evidenced by his encomiums on the theory of evolution. Kook gave a directive to his students to embrace the natural world in the words quoted above, a directive that may be realized in part by contemporary work that unites Kabbalah with ecology.

Conclusion

Looked at over the course of its entire history, Kabbalah is a process which has led to an increasing embrace of the more-than-human world as divine in all its aspects. No particular text or moment in the history of Kabbalah completes the manifestation of this potential, but the trajectory of Kabbalah's evolution points in this direction. The cosmogonic, ethical and spiritual dimensions of Kabbalah are all fundamental to any eco-theology or theology of nature in Judaism.

David Mevorach Seidenberg

Further Reading

Ashkenazi, Yosef ben Shalom. Moshe Hallamish ed. *Perush L'parshat B'rei'shit* (Commentary on Creation in Genesis). Jerusalem: Magnes Press, 1984 (Hebrew).

Brody, Seth. "Human Hands Dwell in Heavenly Heights: Contemplative Ascent and Theurgic Power in Thirteenth Century Kabbalah." In R. Herrera, ed. *Mystics of the Book: Themes Topics and Typologies*. New York: Peter Lang, 1993, 123–58.

Cordovero, Moshe. *The Palm Tree of Deborah*. Louis Jacobs, trans. New York: Sepher Hermon Press, 1974.

Cordovero, Moshe. *Tomer D'vorah* (Palm Tree of Deborah). Jerusalem: Or Yiqar, 1969 (Hebrew).

Cordovero, Moshe. *Or Ne'erav* (Sweet Light). Jerusalem: Kol Y'hudah, 1965 (Hebrew).

Elon, Ari, Naomi Hyman and Arthur Waskow, eds. *Trees, Earth and Torah: A Tu B'Shvat Anthology*. Philadelphia: Jewish Publication Society, 1999, 113–62.

Green, Arthur. *EHYEH: A Kabbalah for Tomorrow*. Woodstock, VT: Jewish Lights, 2002.

Green, Arthur. "A Kabbalah for the Environmental Age." In Tikkun 14: 5, 33–40. Revised in Hava Tirosh-Samuelson, ed. *Judaism and Ecology*. Cambridge: Harvard University Press, 2002, 3–15.

Horowitz, Isaiah. *The Generations of Adam*. Miles Krassen, trans. New York: Paulist Press, 1996.

Kaplan, Aryeh, trans. *The Bahir*. York Beach, ME: Weiser, 1989.

Kook, Abraham Isaac. *Abraham Isaac Kook*. Ben Zion Bokser, trans. New York: Paulist Press, 1978.

Krassen, Miles. "Peri Eitz Hadar: A Kabbalist Tu B'shvat Seder." In Ari Elon et al., eds. *Trees, Earth, and Torah: A Tu B'Shvat Anthology*. Philadelphia: Jewish Publication Society, 1999, 135–53.

Matt, Daniel C. *God and the Big Bang: Discovering Harmony Between Science & Spirituality*. Woodstock, VT: Jewish Lights, 1998.

Matt, Daniel C., ed. *The Essential Kabbalah*. San Francisco: HarperCollins, 1996.

Matt, Daniel C., ed. & trans. *Zohar: The Book of Enlightenment*. New York: Paulist Press, 1983.

Scholem, Gershom. *On the Mystical Shape of the Godhead*. Joachim Neugroschel, trans. New York: Schocken Books, 1991.

Seidenberg, David. "The Cosmic Tree and the Human Body." In Ari Elon and others, eds. *Trees, Earth and Torah: A Tu B'Shvat Anthology*. Philadelphia: Jewish Publication Society, 1999, 263–75.

Seidenberg, David. "Crossing the Threshold: God's Image in the More-Than-Human World." Doctoral Dissertation. Jewish Theological Seminary, 2002.

Tirosh-Samuelson, Hava. "The Textualization of Nature in Jewish Mysticism." In Hava Tirosh-Samuelson, ed. *Judaism and Ecology*. Cambridge: Harvard University Press, 2002, 389–96.

Wolfson, Elliot. "The Mirror of Nature Reflected in the Symbolism of Medieval Kabbalah." In Hava Tirosh-Samuelson, ed. *Judaism and Ecology*. Cambridge: Harvard University Press, 2002, 305–31.

See also: Depth Ecology; Eco-kabbalah; Hassidism and Nature Mysticism; Holism; Israel and Environmentalism; Judaism; Jewish Environmentalism in North America; Paganism and Judaism; Perennial Philosophy; Vegetarianism and Judaism (adjacent to Vegetarianism and Kabbalah); Vegetarianism and Rabbi Abraham Isaac Kook; Waskow, Rabbi Arthur; Wilber, Ken.

Kalash Culture (Northwestern Pakistan)

Numbering approximately three thousand people, the Kalash are refugees scattered throughout roughly fifteen hamlets in the northwestern corner of Pakistan. Descending from the Indo-Europeans, they have dwelled in the mountains of the Hindu Kush for at least four millennia and have maintained indigenous pagan traditions. Through Muslim oppression at the end of the nineteenth century, most pagan people in Afghan's Kafiristan (formerly Nuristan – *kafir* meaning "infidel") either perished or adopted the majority religion. Among the three communities that now inhabit the last Kalash valleys in Pakistan, the Chitralis and the Katis both converted to Islam. It is the Kalash alone who still maintain original festivals and customs that relate to spiritual perceptions embedded in the environment.

According to one Kalash myth that indicates the value placed in nature, it is said that at the beginning, a very long time ago, gods, spirits, humans, animals and plants lived together and spoke the same language. This is the Kalash way of portraying the interrelation between humans, nature and the gods as co-dependent. The interconnection between humanity and the environment is expressed through the idea of an original common language shared by all.

Kalash polytheism is centered on ten central figures: their father-god Koda (Sajigor or Imra), a war-god Gish/Guisch, Imra's messenger Moni, a fortune-god Bag(u)isht, the god of peace Arom, the rain-god S(o)uteram, the wine-god Inthr, the grain-goddess Dizane who also protects men in battle, the fecundity goddess Nirmali who protects pregnant women, and the goddess Kshumay/Kshoumaï who presides over the fertility of the goats. Through the gods' essential identity with nature, Kalash polytheism suggests a form of pantheism in which everything is considered divine, and life is not understood as something separate from nature.

However, for the Kalash the sacred is understood vertically with a value scale that concerns each domain of life determined by the people's mountainous habitat. At the top are the gods who dwell in the sky. They are followed by the mountain's summit where the fairies live. It is these who intervene in human life and allow the shamans to predict the future. For instance, through dreams they indicate where the hunter will find game. Various tales concern the intercourse between fairies and human beings, and a person who displays strange behavior may be considered to have been born from a human–fairy union. The mountain's mid-regions are understood as an intermediary domain in which the sacred and the profane are mixed. Women are forbidden, and possibly this is a more recent custom that develops from Muslim influence. Nevertheless, women are still respected; they have rights and are free, even though they appear to have lost their former status. It is in this more liminal region where men engage in hunting and erect altars for the gods. Finally, as the lowest level, valleys represent the impure world par excellence. Here are the places for cemeteries and menstrual houses. While husbandry is the men's preserve and occurs in the higher habitats, the agriculture of the valleys is more the concern of women and is comparatively depreciated. The subterranean regions associated with roots, graves and, further, underground caves represent pollution in contrast to the ethereal heavens, so that the deeper one goes into the Earth, the more impure a state of being is involved.

This conception also determines the nobility of animals and vegetables themselves. For instance, goats are considered more sacrosanct than cows as they graze farther in the heights. The Kalash refuse to eat eggs and beef because of their impurity. These criteria are equally applied to the houses: chimneys are the most sacred place in a house as they are constructed in a wall which is built against the mountain. Similarly, the roof is the most sacred place of the goatshed. While the Kalash celebrate a great number of festivals, the spring celebration of Joshi in May is the most important. This is a time when men can reach the top of the mountain, kept by fairies during the winter, and try to obtain their benevolence. The *dehar* or shamans are said to have taught this code to men during the Golden Age.

The mountaintop is also the final this-worldly destination of the post-mortem soul. From here, fairies raise a bridge so that a horse may take the soul across to live in a golden house. It is difficult to know when this myth originated and whether it was influenced by Islamic culture. It is, however, reminiscent of some European developments, for instance the myth of Asgard in German and Scandinavian mythology.

In the importance of sacrifice to the Kalash, nature often plays a significant role. The chief sacrifice for the gods is the goat. From among the natural register, two plants are particularly important: the juniper, which is the only easily combustible plant that grows in the mountains, and the oak, which is considered holy. The oak's persistence and presence in the heights links it with the gods. It is used in fumigation and purification rituals.

For the Kalash, nature is central to their relationship with the sacred. They read the signs and portents embedded within the landscape as if it were itself a divine book. Their concept of religion is that of an open contract, and every year each individual renews his or her engagement with the gods of nature during the winter solstice. This renewal is not prescribed through inherited dogma but constitutes a voluntary act through which the individual accepts a personal responsibility for the community's relationship with the divine. Among the more important characteristics of individual life is the person's social behavior, with one of life's aims being the development of a generosity that future generations will recall.

The Kalash, however, are today in danger. Apart from the inroads of Islam, which has already influenced their culture, myths and customs, the Kalash must also face modernism and its accompanying ecological imbalance. The future of this small community is uncertain.

Anne Ferlat

See also: Faerie Faith in Scotland; Pantheism; Polytheism.

Kaphirintiwa – The Place of Creation (Central Africa)

According to Chewa and Nyanja tradition from Malawi and Zambia:

High above the clouds lived God Chiuta (the Big Bow), the only High God. Down below, the Earth was dry and sterile as there was no rain.

God Namalenga (the Creator) gathered the clouds together and covered the sky. God Mphambe (the

Lightning) made a flare of fire in the sky and thunder roared in the mountains of Dzalanyama. The lightning hit the rocks and broke them into pieces. The wind and rain swept the mountain top leaving a clean and soft surface; stones rolled down the mountain and sat at its foot to witness God's power.

Then God Chiuta lit the rainbow across the sky, touching the clouds. In the pouring rain, with the sky wide open, God himself came down with man and woman and all the animals. They descended at Kaphirintiwa. They stepped gently onto the soft surface and walked on the Earth for the first time. Later this surface hardened and became rock and their footprints were left on the stones as witness for the generations to come ... Plants and trees grew big and strong and so was formed the dense thicket of bush of Kasitu, the sacred grove in which the mother shrine of the Chewa prospered (Boucher 2003; for other versions of this story see Werner 1906: 70–1; Ntara 1973: 8–9; Schoffeleers and Roscoe 1985: 19–20).

Schoffeleers and Roscoe have argued that this is the most ancient of the central African creation stories. Subsequent writers have suggested that it may have been passed down to farmer communities from the autochthonous hunter-gatherers. This could indeed be the case as oral traditions state that there was an ancient hunter-gatherer settlement at Kaphirintiwa and surface archeological observations have confirmed this. Kaphirintiwa has therefore been a special sacred place for as far back into prehistory as we are able to see. The Kaphirintiwa creation myth is filled with symbolic messages and observations upon how the current social order came to be. Schoffeleers and Roscoe have discussed these meanings, while here I focus on the place of Kaphirintiwa itself.

The site of Kaphirintiwa is not simply a mythical place. It lies on top of the Dzalanyama mountain range near to the border of Malawi and Mozambique. Kaphirintiwa itself is just inside Mozambique. When approaching the site from Malawi, about two kilometres before Kaphirintiwa is a sacred forest with a sacred pool. This is known as "the gateway." Here offerings must be left and only those who meet the conditions necessary for visiting Kaphirintiwa may pass beyond this point. The traditional conditions are that one should not have washed, shaved or engaged in sexual relations for seven days before the visit (the period of time may have been longer in the past).

Proceeding beyond "the gateway" the landscape opens up to a long upward slope of undulating rock. At the top of this slope is a second sacred forest known as Kasitu. Tradition states that it was in this forest that the first great central African rain shrine was founded on the site of an ancient BaTwa settlement (the BaTwa were the former hunter-gathering Pygmy inhabitants of the region). The shrine is no longer maintained and its exact original location within the forest is now forgotten. What is known is that the shrine persisted here for many centuries before it was moved down the mountain to Msinja in the fourteenth or fifteenth century. As at Msinja, there is a sacred pool near to Kasitu. Today, a traditional custodian still looks after the place and it is not unusual in times of trouble for people to travel to Kasitu today to make offerings.

Immediately below Kasitu to the west, on the Mozambiquan side of the Dzalanyama range, is a flat platform of rock with a group of egg-shaped rock monoliths at its centre. This is the place where it is believed that God, all the living creatures and the first human couple fell to Earth in the great thunderstorm. The platform of rock is pitted with shallow holes and it is these features that are said to be the impressions made when all of the feet fell into the soft rock. These imprints are evoked in the name Kaphirintiwa, which is translated "the hill that leaves traces behind" by Ntara (1973: 8).

B.W. Smith

Further Reading

Boucher, Claude. *Digging our Roots: The Chamare Frescoes.* Mua: KuNgoni Art Crafts Centre, 2003.

Ntara, Samuel J. *The History of the Chewa (Mbiri Ya Achewa).* Weisbaden: Frank Steiner, 1973 (originally published in 1950).

Schoffeleers, J. Matthew and Adrian Roscoe. *Land of Fire: Oral Literature from Malawi.* Limbe: Montford Press, 1985.

Werner, Alice. *The Natives of British Central Africa.* London: Constable, 1906.

See also: Creation Myths in the Ancient World; Makewana the Rainmaker (Central Malawi); Rock Art – Chewa (Central Africa).

Kapu in Early Hawaiian Society

Hawaiians were aware of the breeding seasons and the biological diversity of the fauna of their islands. This required keen observational powers and ability to recognize the importance of what was seen. These observational powers may have grown out of necessity. There is evidence that the first Polynesian settlers in Hawai'i had a negative impact on the ecology and landscape of the islands. These perturbations included extinction, presumably by overhunting (impossible to verify since Hawaiians brought with them the dog and the Polynesian rat). Thus of 11 species of large flightless birds of the Family Anatidae (ducks) only one remains today. Although many forest birds used for feather cloaks have also gone extinct since 1848, (e.g., yellow and black mamo for feather capes, yellow and black oʻo used for feathered cloaks) these did so only after the introduction of mosquitoes and avian malaria which continues to drive native bird declines in the islands today. Techniques to take feathers but leave the birds alive had been developed and used for decades if not centuries.

Still, it is under the scenario of natural resource decline and loss that the *hoʻo kapu* and Kahuna systems are likely to have coevolved. The importance of *kapu* is seen in the meaning of the original Royal Hawaiian coat of arms, on which are two *kapu* signs; two *poloulou* or taboo sticks (white balls with staffs) and a triangular flag (*puela*) lying across two *alia* or spears which is a sign of tabu and protection.

By the late sixteenth century, burgeoning native population densities of the islands (between 500,000 and 800,000 depending on the model used) required innovation to feed their masses. The only way to avoid further biological extinction problems was to enhance dependence on agriculture, aquaculture, marine resources and placement of strong *kapu* on taking of those resources to stop over harvest.

The *kapu* system of prehistoric Hawaiian culture served as a control on action. The term has the dual meaning of taboo on the one hand and sacred on the other. It is likely that the *kapu* system of prohibitions taught by the Kahuna arose for reasons concerning control of the common people, a need to provide warning about attitudes or behaviors considered dangerous to health or society in general, and a need to control access to the natural resource base of economic and survival importance.

The Kahuna were priest educators, overseers of what was passed on to the next generation and innovators of new technologies when called for. The Kahuna system of prehistoric Hawaiʻi served as an educational and technical arm of the culture similar to how technical schools serve modern Western Society. Examples are seen in the Kahuna who taught canoe building, *hale* (house) building, navigation, and farming or fishing techniques among others. Associated with each endeavor were specific gods to whom one had to pay tribute, thought and prayer.

The spiritual taboo on activities important to everyday survival of the people and the culture gives insight into the strictness and rigidity of thought, and the harsh environmental conditions that had to govern the minds, spirit and bodies of those who created it. The conservation of this thought would occur through time if encoded and passed on from one generation to the next in chants, dances and as a part of the spoken folklore. Because it worked well to protect the culture against actions by members that hurt the tribe at large (e.g., overharvesting of fish), and because the island microcosm as the known physical universe of the tribe could be just as unforgiving, such finality of thought and decision seems justified. Remote and isolated island systems afford no easy escape so a loss of the culture or a significant portion of it might take place if the *kapu* were not observed rigorously over time.

Agriculture and aquaculture required a system to pass techniques and technology to the next generation. To verbally codify this knowledge system into the religious order of the day and frame it within *kapu* restrictions ensured its survival. Linking daily activities to *kapu*-based systems could do this. Examples are seen with regard to activities that followed the 29½-day Hawaiian lunar calendar. Planting, fishing, harvesting and even cloth making and prayer were observed on strict schedules. Thus, pre-contact Hawaiian culture became highly structured, governed by strict religious customs that helped protect the natural and political environment. For example, some days were simply "off limits" (*kapu*) for fishing. Upon fear of death, dismemberment and scattering of one's *iwi* (bones) preventing one from finding peace as a *kupuna* or revered ancestor of the family, one did not fish on *kapu* days at all. Some months were also *kapu*, fishing was avoided in April and May for specific species. Only eight of the days in any month would be considered good for fishing. An exception occurred during the *Makahiki* (the winter months celebration for the primary god *Lono* and the period when the Chiefs collected the tribute as a form of taxation) when fishing in general was avoided. These harvest restrictions occurred during spawning periods, enabling the resource to reproduce and replenish itself, providing a continual food source.

The Kahuna related this special knowledge to the gods and to natural elemental forces the gods controlled. Examples can be seen in the teaching of the daily and monthly *kapu* and maintaining the rituals, and in special dietary restrictions such as the *kapu ʻohiʻa*, which forbade eating from certain food patches during a famine (were these seed sources that needed protection?). Women were generally under many more *kapu* than men, including many food restrictions considered to be embodiments of the primary male gods Kane and Kanaloa (pig, most bananas (*kapu maiʻa*), many fish, coconuts, most foods used sacrificially). Women could not enter *Heiau* (places of public ceremony) or even household shrines, could not participate in central religious practices, and could not prepare or grow *kalo* (taro). Many *kapu* were set aside during the Makahiki along with war, sailing on the ocean, making of cloth (*tapa*), drum playing, and farming. Even the *kapu* of the lunar cycle were set aside, *heiau* were closed and religious services were suspended.

But the dual *kapu-kuhuna* system collapsed in the post-contact world after the discovery of the islands by Captain James Cook in 1779. The collapse was driven by the introduction of Western cultural ways, including Western religions proselytized by priests who did not appreciate the unique cultural function of either the Kahuna or the *kapu* systems. The Hawaiian people themselves may have come to distrust the *kapu* system when they noticed that the breaking of strict rules by foreigners had no apparent consequence. In addition, foreign gods seemed stronger since foreigners had better technologies, clothing and tools. The reliance on Western law grew to dominate the culture.

Today, Hawai'i struggles with the loss of the culture and the *kapu* system and what this loss has meant for Hawaiian marine and terrestrial resources. There is no replacement of the religious context in which Hawaiian resource use and conservation took place. The result is a disconnection between conservation of limited resources, the current system of Western-based laws, and the growth potential and anthropogenic impact of large human populations. This has resulted in the Hawaiian Islands becoming known as a "hotspot" in scientific circles for species loss. Fully 28 percent; of all United States Endangered Species Act listings occur in Hawai'i, which is now a microcosm of what is happening in the world.

William Steiner

Further Reading

Abbott, Isabella Aiona. *La'au Hawai'i: Traditional Hawaiian Uses of Plants*. Honolulu: Bishop Museum Press, 1992.

Johnson, Rubellinte Kawena. *Kumulipo: The Hawaiian Hymn of Creation*. Honolulu: Topgallant Publishing Co., 1981.

Kamakau, Samuel Manaiakalani. *Tales and Traditions of the People of Old*. Honolulu: Bishop Museum Press, 1991.

Kent, Harold W. *Treasury of Hawaiian Words*. Honolulu: University of Hawai'i Press, 1986.

Lawrence, Mary Stebbins. *Old-Time Hawaiians*. Honolulu: Patten Publishing Co., 1939.

Pukui, Mary K. and Alfons L. Korn, trs. *The Echo of our Song: Chants and Poems of the Hawaiians*. Honolulu: University of Hawai'i Press, 1973.

See also: Hawai'i; Pacific Islands; Polynesian Traditional Religions; Surfing; Volcanoes.

Kasama Spirit Sites (Northern Zambia)

Kasama town sits on top of a low sandstone ridge a few hundred meters above the forested plains of northern Zambia. Immediately east and west of the town, along this ridge, are areas of massed boulders. In places these boulders are so massed that they form a labyrinth of small and winding passageways. The densest areas of rock each have a name and these names refer to a series of spirits who are believed to dwell in the rocks, in the water sources and unusual natural features in the area. The Bemba who live in this area today refer to these spirits collectively as *ngulu*. There are more than a dozen *ngulu* living within a thirty-kilometer radius of Kasama town.

Beliefs in general spirits of natural forces and ancestral spirits are almost universal amongst Bantu-speaking groups throughout central Africa, but the *ngulu* are somewhat different. As noted by Andrew Roberts, these are not forces of nature or spirits of dead people: rather they represent the land in which they have their abode. The unusual nature of these spirit creatures may reflect an ancient origin. The Bemba say that they found these spirits already living in the area when they arrived (probably some time in the first millennium). If this is correct then the beliefs may have been passed down from the autochthonous hunter-gatherers of the area: the Batwa (or Pygmies). Some support for this comes from the fact that this area has more Batwa rock art sites than the whole of the rest of central Africa taken together.

Whatever their origin, each *ngulu* has a particular site of residence. Where this is a rock, it is usually in a group of boulders with a dark crevice between them. People will visit these places to speak with the spirits and it is believed that the spirits often answer. The reason for visiting the spirit is usually to ascertain and overcome the reason for illnesses within the family or for misfortunes. There is a hierarchy to the spirits, with some recognized as more powerful than others. The less powerful spirits, such as Mwankole, Sumina, Chama and Kaponyansuli can be approached with little preparation, but, to approach the more powerful ones such as Mwela, Changa and Mulenga (and formerly Chishimba), extensive preparations are needed. Traditional preparations include not shaving, not washing and abstaining from sex for a period of a week before the visit.

When visiting an *ngulu* people traditionally wear white cloth and bring white gifts such as flour, traditional beer, white beads and white clay called *mpemba*. Sometimes a white chicken will also be slaughtered. The descriptions of what happens when one consults with an *ngulu* vary from person to person. Many people describe how, when they approach those *ngulu* who dwell in the rocks, the rocks will open up and they go inside and speak with the spirit. Sometimes people say that the *ngulu* appears in the form of an animal, bird or lizard. The python and other large snakes are among the most common forms described. All agree that particular *ngulu* do not stick to one form, each can take a variety of forms. Sometimes only the voice of the *ngulu* is heard. On other occasions *ngulu* may fail to appear at all.

The power of the *ngulu* is believed to extend beyond its place of residence. People are sometimes spoken to by the *ngulu* in dreams and, on rare occasions, people may be possessed by the *ngulu*. This reaching out of the power of the spirit is particularly true of the strongest spirits such as Changa. Today people continue to come from many hundred of kilometers away to give offerings to and to consult with the spirits around Kasama. One particular spirit, Mwankole, has become a place of pilgrimage for those afflicted with AIDS. In the mid-1990s a former Minister of Tourism was possessed by Mwankole and, following tradition, he went to the dwelling place of the spirit, cleaned it, and built a small grass-roofed structure in the site. Under this structure he placed a range of offerings to spirits. Sometimes such offerings will appease the spirit and the possession will end. At other times, as in this case, the possession leads to death.

As well as the personal interactions with the *ngulu* there is (or was) also a formal curatorial structure for the Kasama spirits. Each *ngulu* had a keeper who looked after its dwelling places, sweeping the area clean and so on. Only a few *ngulu* have keepers today. These local custodians fell under a spirit priest with the title of Kamima. Kamima was a key spiritual adviser to the Bemba paramount chief Chitimukulu. The position was inherited according to the matrilineal principle, and the village of the Kamimas is known even today by the name of the title. Kamima was charged with looking after all the *ngulu* and, before the rains each year, he had to conduct rituals at each spirit site in order of importance, culminating at Changa. The last time that these ceremonies were performed in their traditional manner was in the 1950s. Today the Kamima performs rituals only in times of particular need, or if requested by the Chitimukulu.

B.W. Smith

Further Reading

Roberts, Andrew D. *A History of the Bemba*. London: Longman, 1973.

Sheane, J.H. West. "Some Aspects of Awemba Religion and Superstitious Observances." *Journal of the Royal Anthropological Institute* 36 (1906), 150–8.

Smith, Benjamin W. *Zambia's Ancient Rock Art: The Paintings of Kasama*. Livingstone: National Heritage Conservation Commission, 1997.

See also: Rock Art – Batwa/Pygmies (Central Africa).

Kawabata, Yasunari (1899–1972)

Kawabata Yasunari was a Japanese novelist, short-story writer, literary critic, and aesthetic theorist. His youth was filled with loneliness and death. Both parents died when he was young, then the grandmother he lived with passed away, as did his sister, leaving him with his blind grandfather. At first he wanted to become a painter, but in school he studied Western and Japanese literature. His early story *Izu Dancer* (1927) was highly regarded, and *Snow Country*, his most celebrated book, was published in 1938 (and revised ten years later). In 1968, he became the first Japanese writer to win the Nobel Prize for literature. Four years later he died of an apparent suicide.

Kawabata's novels are distinctive in many ways. Perhaps more than any other Japanese writer, he fused traditional Japanese aesthetics with a modern sensibility of alienation, ennui, and even depravity. His works display an exquisite sensibility to both nature's beauty and its spiritual dimension. His descriptions of the natural world are highly sensual, detailed, and realistic, yet they also have an ethereal character that suggests a deeper dimension: a metaphysical immensity and stillness that encompasses the human drama and elicits yearning and inexplicable sorrow. Much of the rich meaning in his novels is found in the mood and atmosphere evoked (as in the classical *nō* drama) as much as the plot or characters. Commentators often note that the characters in his novels tend to merge with nature. At the same time, the characters often remain distant from each other, suggesting paradoxically both the failings of modern relationships and an ideal of a pure love heightened by yearning and unsullied by physical consummation. Indeed, one of his central themes is purity. But perhaps most of all, his writings are characterized by the joining of beauty and sadness (the title of one of his novels), both in his depictions of love and his aesthetic metaphysics.

In his Nobel Prize acceptance speech, *Japan, the Beautiful, and Myself*, Kawabata offered insight into his own aesthetics by commenting on qualities of classical Japanese literature and art. He praised the *Shinkokinshū*, the great thirteenth-century poetry collection, for its "elements of the mysterious, the suggestive, the evocative and inferential, elements of sensuous fantasy that have something in common with modern symbolist poetry" (1969: 44), words that astutely describe his own novels. This aesthetic is closely related to the ideal of *yūgen* ("mystery and depth"). Originally a Chinese Daoist term for the essential color of the universe (deep purple), it suggests the subtle and melancholy beauty of a reality that exceeds our grasp. This metaphysical dimension is not a separate realm: the natural world of form and color is never negated or transcended but rather is enriched by a deeper reality to which it is always connected (similar to the Daoist notion of non-being).

In his Nobel speech, Kawabata extolled the classical aesthetic of *mono-no-aware*, a tranquil sorrow at the transience of what is beautiful and fragile, a sentiment found in his own works. He also pointed to the asymmetrical aesthetic of Japanese gardens as an art form that can suggest the vastness of nature. So too, the small, spare room used for the tea ceremony evokes limitless space, as well as the austere elegance of *wabi*. Throughout the speech, Kawabata also highlighted the significance of Zen Buddhism to traditional Japanese aesthetics and to his own.

His metaphysics of nature is seen in the famous opening scene of *Snow Country*, in which the protagonist, Shimamura, is startled to see the eye of a beautiful woman reflected in the window. Her eye merges with the mountainous background "into a sort of symbolic world ..." (1956: 15). The train moves through a long, dark tunnel into that world as "the depths of night turned white with snow." Whiteness, the traditional Shinto color for the ideal of purity, permeates the novel and is significant in part because "White is the cleanest of colors, it contains in itself all the other colors" (1969: 51). At one point the purity of white is set off against the color of *yūgen*, displaying Kawabata's ability to evoke simultaneously the erotic and the metaphysical: "The brightness of the snow was more intense, its seemed to be burning icily. Against it, the woman's hair became a clearer black, touched with a purple sheen" (1956: 48).

Kawabata's sense of the beauty of nature, the intimate relationship of humans to nature's metaphysical dimension, and his use of classical literature are revealed in the final scene of *Snow Country*. A building is in flames amid the night snow. As the sparks rise to the sky, Shimamura gazes at the "terrible voluptuousness" (1956: 134) of the River of Heaven (the Milky Way), which the poet Bashō had made famous in a haiku. From the building, Shimamura's lover Komako carries out another beauty who had entranced Shimamura from a distance. At that moment, "his head fell back, and the Milky Way flowed down inside him with a roar" (1956: 142).

David Landis Barnhill

Further Reading

Gessel, Van C. *Three Modern Novelists: Sōseki, Tanizaki, Kawabata*. Tokyo: Kodansha, 1993.

Kawabata, Yasunari. *Beauty and Sadness*. Howard Hibbett, tr. New York: Knopf, 1975.

Kawabata, Yasunari. *Japan, the Beautiful, and Myself*. Edward G. Seidensticker, tr. Tokyo: Kodansha, 1969.

Kawabata, Yasunari. *Thousand Cranes*. Edward G. Seidensticker, tr. New York: Knopf, 1958.

Kawabata, Yasunari. *Snow Country*. Edward G. Seidensticker, tr. New York: Knopf, 1956.

See also: Aesthetics and Nature in China and Japan; Buddhism – East Asia; Daoism; Japanese Love of Nature; Japanese Religions; Zen Buddhism.

Keepers of Lake Eyre (South Australia)

The Keepers of Lake Eyre (KOLE) are an intercultural collective maintaining an anti-uranium protest enclave at Lake Eyre in the South Australian desert. Part of a re-enchantment-seeking radical ecology movement, KOLE members are generally young eco-pilgrims committed to the rights of Aboriginal peoples and the natural environment. Acting under the authority of inspirational Arabunna elder "Uncle" Kevin Buzzacott, their enclave (otherwise known as the Arabunna Coming Home Camp) is situated 180 kilometers north of Roxby Downs where Western Mining Co (WMC) work one of the world's largest copper/uranium deposits. KOLE oppose WMC's operation which constitutes a major threat to both arid lands ecology and Aboriginal culture in the Lake Eyre region. WMC's growing demands on underground water sources in one of the driest regions on the planet has had a devastating impact on Aboriginal peoples (especially Arabunna and Kokatha) since such sources feed the precious springs around the Lake Eyre region essential for their cultural survival.

In 1997, the South Australian government handed WMC control of Aboriginal Heritage (sacred sites) over 1.5 million hectares of the state – in a region (Billa Kalina – the area between Coober Pedy, Maree and Woomera) already suffering the consequences of experiments conducted at the start of the nuclear era (atomic weapons testing in the 1950s), and sited to become a nuclear dumping ground (the planned national radioactive waste dump). Buzzacott's Going Home camp was established on 26 March 1999 to coincide with the official opening of WMC's Olympic Dam Expansion Project – a project licensed to draw up to 42 million litres of water per day from the Great Artesian Basin.

Water, bored by WMC to mine and mill uranium, lies at the heart of the matter. According to the KOLE website (www.lakeeyre.green.net.au):

Arabunna tell of a time, not long ago, when the springs flowed strong and there was enough water for everyone. Now the Land is getting drier and drier, the Kangaroos and Emus are scarce, there are fewer Custodians than ever and the Sacred Springs are dying, some have already gone.

As for Buzzacott, Lake Eyre "is hurting and it's calling ... If you feel strong in spirit to save the Old Lake then be there. We invite you to come with your strong spirit." Responding to the call, hundreds of inspirited activists bestowed with the title "Keepers of Lake Eyre," have gravitated to the region surrounding the vast inland salt lake. KOLE formed in Adelaide in early 1999. Again, their web-site states that Keepers are "very recent additions to a long line of Custodians and Protectors of Lake Eyre," and that their goal is to "support and further the upkeep of Arabunna Law [which] demands the protection of Arabunna Country, Culture, Spirituality and People." Furthermore, Keepers are said actively to perform "the responsibilities we all have for Mother Earth and her life giving resources."

Under the authority of Arabunna elders, proactive non-Aboriginal "custodians" are thus educated about the culturally significant Mound Springs, engaging in activities – blockades, vigils, fund raisers and educational workshops – through which their identification with, and attachment to, this threatened region is enacted. Through their rites and communities of protest, they commit to defending country that they have come to know and experience as sacred.

As an intriguing dimension to this story, the sacrality attributed to the region by inhabitants from diverse backgrounds, is extended to uranium itself – a reality reminiscent of other sites of environmentalist/Aboriginal solidarity, such as that which transpired at the now stalled Jabiluka project in Kakadu National Park opposed by the Mirrar. In these cases, far from being evil or malign, uranium is considered sacred – which is true so far as it remains untouched, "pure." In such circumstances dialogue occurs between local mining, beleaguered indigenes attempting to maintain obligations toward country, and non-indigenous environmentalists who believe that unearthing uranium constitutes the violation of an environmental taboo. For both, uranium's unearthing is dangerous – amounting to *desecration*. Possessing a mixture of science and Aboriginal religion, they hold the view that uranium should not be tampered with, it must "stay in the ground" – its disturbance, removal and milling presaging disaster, sickness and ruin.

KOLE is one of many new intercultural alliances evidencing post-colonialist sensibilities in Australia. With their proactive ecologism effected under indigenous cultural and religious authority, the political and spiritual dimensions of their opposition to existing practices are inseparable. For non-indigenes, a level of custodianship is conferred. Activist Rufus describes his experience at the camp in 1999:

> Every day we would sit around the fire and Uncle Kev would describe his vision of the future, or what he thinks are the steps we need to take to create the future that we want to live in. His ideas were progressive in the sense that anyone who comes out here to this bit of land and feels the spirit of the old lake and dances on the land, they're welcome. And you feel the call to defend it (Interview with the author, May 2000).

Dwelling beside the Lake on and off since its inception, doing "whatever it takes to look after the land," young environmentalists Marc and Izzy have become "Keepers of Lake Eyre." According to "Uncle Kevin," says Marc,

> Lake Eyre is calling, and it's calling us back. The old spirits are calling us to come and protect the country and look after the country. So we need to be there to make sure nobody comes in and stuffs up the country. So basically we sit on our hill that overlooks Lake Eyre. We keep an eye on Lake Eyre (Interview with the author, May 2000).

Such activists have come to identify closely with threatened nature – establishing, through ethical action, a legitimate right to belong.

Graham St John

See also: Aboriginal Dreaming (Australia); Australia; Mother Earth.

Kenya Green Belt Movement

The Green Belt Movement (GBM) is an innovative, community-based, development and environmental organization with a focus on community mobilization and empowerment for sustainable development and especially for environmental conservation. The movement seeks to improve the livelihoods of communities, alleviate poverty, and promote the rights of women, and it has done so by focusing especially on tree planting and environmental conservation. Professor Wangari Maathai founded the GBM in 1977. Her work and the movement received international acclaim when in 2004, at the age of sixty-four, she was awarded the Nobel Peace Prize.

Maathai initiated the movement under the auspices of the National Council of Women of Kenya, where she interacted much with rural women. During these interactions she realized that women were faced with a problem of insufficient fuel wood after years of woodland destruction to pave the way for cash-crop farming. It was therefore easy to craft together Green Belt Movement and work with rural women on a project that addressed their immediate need for fuel wood.

Wangari Maathai on Reforesting Kenya
Editor's note: This excerpt from the 2004 recipient of the Nobel Peace Prize shows that her nature-related spirituality is an important part of her identity and motivation.

> All of us have a God in us, and that God is the spirit that unites all life, everything that is on this planet. It must be this voice that is telling me to do something, and I am sure it's the same voice that is speaking to everybody on this planet – at least everybody who seems to be concerned about the fate of the world ...
>
> Poverty and need have a very close relationship with a degraded environment ... to break the cycle, one has to start with a positive step, and I thought that planting a tree is very simple, very easy – something positive that anybody can do.

Quoted in: Suzuki, David. *The Sacred Balance: Rediscovering our Place in Nature*. Vancouver, British Columbia: The Mountaineers, 1997, 227.

After 25 years of working with the Green Belt Movement, the founder/coordinator of the movement, Professor Wangari Maathai, was elected to parliament after the December 2002 elections. She was then appointed Assistant Minister for Environment, Natural Resources and Wildlife. The renowned environmentalist has gained world acclaim through her selfless contribution to local, national and global issues on environmental concern. She has been working very closely with other global greens and by the time of her appointment to the government, she was (and still is) a member of Mazingira Green Party which she helped to found. The Green Belt Movement is currently nurturing the Society of Greens project, through which it is working hard to capture the prevailing environmental awareness in Kenya.

The primary energy behind the movement is rural women, who work to save and protect their immediate natural environment and especially biological diversity of plants and animals threatened with extinction. Although women are the main driving force, men and children are also involved in the planting and caring of trees, especially on school compounds. Even then, men plant trees more as an economic investment for the future, while women and children plant trees to meet the currently felt needs of communities. These needs include wood-fuel, fencing and building materials, fruits for better health – especially for children – shade and aesthetic beauty. Traditionally, trees and nature in general were highly valued in African religion. In my community, with which I am very familiar, use of biodiversity was a specialized discipline where men and women had distinct relationships with all the various life forms. For instance, when building or fencing, branches of trees or coppices of coppicing trees were cut by men, but not the whole tree. Women would only collect dead dry wood for firewood. *Ficus* spp. is especially valued for spiritual purposes and would not be cut down under whatever circumstances. A variety of other species were regarded as peace trees and therefore conserved for these purposes. Parts of these trees would be used in peace building, especially during tribal or clan conflicts.

Unfortunately, these cultural environmental ideals were lost during the colonial period when traditional religion was effectively phased out and replaced with the conventional religions. Most Kenyans today are Christians, and members of the GBM constituency are almost 100 percent Christian. It is for this reason that GBM uses the biblical story of creation to reach out to the hearts of communities and show them that God, after all, created human beings after all the other members of the living and non-living community because human beings could not survive without them. All vegetation, animals and birds, waters and the atmosphere can do very well without human beings. But human beings cannot live without each of these. This approach helps in enabling people to understand that even though the Bible says that human beings were given *dominion* over the rest of the creation, they must be disciplined in using the resources they have been endowed with since their eventual exhaustion means eventual death to human beings. And this effectively prepares people for a change in mindset from dominion to stewardship of God's creation. This again introduces a new jurisprudence where human beings consider themselves as co-creations of God with vegetation, animals and birds, and relearn to accord them due respect. This new jurisprudence is rooted in the indigenous way of life where people respected nature and viewed themselves as part of the greater whole of the universe. They controlled the way they extracted resources from their immediate environment and had their way of life (including spirituality) woven closely together with the environment. Although global warming is not a well-known issue or motivation among the rural women, trees also contribute as a carbon sink for greenhouse gases.

The religious teaching of the Green Belt Movement is informed by the fact that close to 90 percent of Kenyans are Christians, these having closed their eyes to their culture and embraced Christian spirituality completely. The dominant Catholic, Anglican and Presbyterian denominations are promisingly receptive to the teachings on environment and actually preach this in their churches. They also encourage their adherents to participate in activities that heal the Earth like planting trees in church compounds and on their farms. However, there has been marked indifference in some of the evangelical churches, who view the Green Belt Movement as controversial because it encourages people to think about the Earth as they think about heaven! Again this attitude is slowly waning as people are confronted by the harsh ecological realities of their actions embodied in constant droughts and famines, floods and landslides. All of these calamities are contributing to much destruction and loss of life.

GBM Approach to Development

The community-based approach of GBM enables it to address all people in the community, and in that way development efforts become a truly communal effort. Project implementation is done in close partnership with communities, which are provided with the financial and training back-up they need to improve their capacity. GBM also monitors, evaluates and reports on the progress of the project to donors and friends. Members of local communities provide labor, local expertise, knowledge and follow-up, which are valuable aspects of community involvement in project management. Communities are also partly responsible for the sustainability of projects.

Vision and Mission

The vision of the Green Belt Movement is to create a value-driven society of grassroots people who consciously work for continued improvement of their livelihoods. The mission is to mobilize community consciousness for self-determination, equity, justice, environmental conservation and improved livelihood securities (food, shelter, education, health, employment, and human rights), using both civic and environmental education and tree-planting projects as the entry point.

One of the unique attributes of the Green Belt Movement is that it is a value-driven organization committed to the principles and values of sound environmental management. Such values are well articulated by the Earth Charter, which resulted from the efforts of many sectors of civil society in the years after the United Nations "Earth Summit" in Rio de Janeiro in 1992. Many of the principles of the Earth Charter reflect the values and ethical philosophy of GBM. That is partly why GBM was happy to accept an invitation to promote the Charter in the African region. The values of GBM include: working to achieve accountability, integrity, commitment, transparency, reverence for life, and intergenerational responsibility. Others are the spirit of volunteerism and service to the common good, a deep desire for self-fulfillment and dignity, and a love for a greener, cleaner environment. Through its educational seminars, the organization also encourages a strong motivation for self-betterment, a thirst for self-knowledge and self-empowerment, and a desire to improve oneself. Other values include a personal commitment and dedication to serve communities. These values are not new; they are also shared by many organizations committed to development and societal transformation.

Core Projects

To achieve its vision and mission, GBM developed a program that incorporates Four Core Projects:

Tree planting on public lands

The objective of this project is to inculcate, within community members, the culture of planting trees as well as protecting local biological diversity of plants and animals and commonly owned resources such as forests, green open spaces, riparian and road reserves, wildlife and sites of cultural significance.

Promotion of food security at household level

The objective of this project is to assist communities in analyzing and understanding the threats to their food security as well as learning and practicing simple agricultural techniques. This would enable them to consistently provide adequate farm-sourced food of high nutrient value and variety to their households. The project aims at enhancing farmers' knowledge of local biodiversity, indigenous dietary principles, indigenous crops and their role in food security, organic farming and other techniques for improving productivity and food processing.

Advocacy and networking

The objective of this project is twofold. First, to bring actions of poor governance and abuse of the environment into the national and international limelight; secondly, to rally resistance against such anti-environmental actions and thereby stop violation of environmental rights. There is a strong synergy between advocacy and civic and environmental education, and therefore GBM adopts an integrated approach in the implementation of the two projects. When individuals and communities understand the causes and consequences of injustices (through civic and environmental education) they are driven to advocate a more equitable order – be it social, economic or political. Advocacy and networking is done both at the local and international levels. Within Africa, a Pan African Green Network has been formed, partly to promote green consciousness in the region. GBM has reached 36 organizations in 15 African countries where it is hoped that a strong environmental movement will eventually emerge, especially in Eastern and the Horn of Africa regions.

Civic and environmental education

The objective of this project is to raise awareness concerning primary environmental care so as to enhance knowledge, attitudes and values that support sustainable grassroots socio-economic and ecological welfare. The aim is to make people more responsible in matters affecting their livelihoods as well as those of the wider community. The course emphasizes the responsibility of the current generation to those in the future, the need for a self-regulatory jurisprudence and the principles articulated in the Earth Charter. This project also attempts to show the connection between culture and spirituality and environmental conservation.

Successes

The GBM has empowered local communities to implement activities such as mass action events to protest destruction of forests, privatization of open public green spaces in urban centers and the destruction of watershed areas. GBM has recorded much success in advocacy work, especially in saving public open lands including Karura Forest, Uhuru Park, Gevanjee Gardens and Kamukunji grounds in Kenya. Local green belt womens' groups have also saved many local open spaces in the rural areas. GBM's persistent and consistent advocacy work partly contributed to the government's decision to introduce an Environment Management and Coordination Act (1999), which is a new law to protect the environment. A Forest Bill has been drafted and a Land Commission, which has finished its report and handed it over to the president, was established to look into Kenyan land laws and make recommendations.

At the end of 1998, GBM commenced an organizational development process and produced a strategic plan

(2000–2002). With that, Phase I (1977–1999) was closed. Phase I had facilitated the establishment of 6000 women tree nursery groups throughout the country, especially among farming communities. The groups mobilized over 100,000 rural women, who in turn mobilized their communities to plant trees, especially on their farms.

One of the major achievements of GBM in Phase I was mass planting of twenty million trees. Other achievements include the fact that many women no longer need to walk long distances to collect firewood since it is now produced on their own farms. Some women have also adopted energy-saving cook-stoves to promote family health and energy conservation. Such technologies particularly reduce respiratory tract diseases. The planting of many fruit trees has contributed to the betterment of nutrition and health, especially among children. Therefore, a firm foundation has been laid on which GBM will further achieve community development. For their extension work during Phase II, women will continue to be financially compensated by GBM, but this will be done through purchase of seedlings surviving after transplanting on public lands. This will generate some income for the women extension workers.

Conservation of Local Indigenous Biodiversity: The Current Focus

GBM decided to focus on planting of trees on public lands because these can easily be conserved to become *in situ* seed and gene banks. Also, the GBM emphasizes the benefits of conservation of biological diversity and effective carbon sinks. Since much of the local biological diversity is on public lands such as forests, local hills, riverbeds, highways, etc., it becomes necessary to educate the public that, contrary to popular opinion (influenced by system of governance), public lands, and the biological diversity in them, are a common heritage. These resources should therefore be protected and conserved and not allowed to be extracted or privatized by greedy and corrupt individuals at the expense of the common good of communities and future generations. To address the threat of lost biological diversity, soil erosion and seeds of food crops, GBM has encouraged women groups to form community networks, which are a culmination of many years of training and empowering communities, to take charge of their environment and their livelihoods. The networks represent a unique way of empowering communities so that they can protect forests and sources of biological diversity near them, collectively. Training of these networks has encouraged many communities to get involved in the protection of sites of interest near them, such as sacred forests, watersheds, catchment areas, indigenous food crops and wildlife. Kaya Forests on the Kenyan coast are one example of such sacred forests. The local people protect the forests with the assistance of the government, but the essential principles underlying the protection bid are cultural/spiritual. The local people still practice their spiritual and other cultural activities in the forests and these form the basis of the protection of the forests. Besides these networks, GBM also trains local leaders like the clergy (mainly from the Anglican and Presbyterian churches), progressive farmers, and teachers, so that they can work alongside the women networks. Activities of these networks also contribute toward poverty reduction, especially since poverty has become both a symptom and a cause of environmental degradation.

During Phase I, and despite GBM's persistent appeal to plant indigenous trees, plants and food crops, many farmers opted for exotic species of trees. This was because they perceived indigenous trees as having a disadvantage of delayed material benefits, due to slow growth. Communities also felt that some indigenous trees create large canopies that take up too much arable space on farms. Besides, farmers felt that indigenous trees are not as easily commercialized as the exotic trees introduced during the colonial era for quick commercial exploitation. Even then, this disadvantage is compensated by the value of the rich biological diversity, which indigenous species encourage under their canopy. Therefore, indigenous trees have a higher environmental conservation benefit. GBM continues to concentrate on planting them on public lands.

GBM has a great capacity to mobilize large numbers of community members to work for the environment on a voluntary basis, and indeed it is impossible to compensate women groups for all the extension work that they do. But much of that work is done through the spirit of volunteerism by the networks and tree nursery groups. In mobilizing thousands of people in the rural areas, GBM commits a lot of energy to environmental conservation and improvement of livelihoods.

Each network is being encouraged to establish a Community Environment Fund (CEF), which will sponsor environmental activities. Activities will include the local demonstration center, renewable energy-saving technologies, purchase of seeds and vegetative stocks, exchange visits, farm work and provision of water and other inputs. The network would also be able to facilitate training and exchange of information and advice among other actors. The CEF could also serve as a source of capital for innovative economic initiatives started by the members of the network. This would be cheaper than bank loans, which are often inaccessible to women and the poor without collaterals.

Conclusion

Individuals and communities can change their world by the little they can do to contribute to the greater whole. Green Belt Movement was recognized as a case of good practice in Johannesburg during the United Nation's 2002 World Summit on Sustainable Development. Through the film, *A Quiet Revolution*, the work of the

Green Belt Movement was further acknowledged, along with other initiatives in the world, for its capacity to mobilize the masses and their human resources to focus on changing their world for the better. In the decades to come the profile and influence of Wangari Maathai and the Green Belt model will certainly grow and spread even more widely as a result of the international attention brought on by the Nobel Peace Prize.

Gathuru Mburu

Further Reading

Maathai, Wangari. "Bottlenecks of Development in Africa." A paper presented at the 4th UN World Women's Conference in Beijing, China. 30 August–15 September, 1995.

Maathai, Wangari. "The Green Belt Movement: Sharing the Approach and the Experience." Nairobi, Kenya: Environmental Liaison Centre International, 1988.

The World Commission on Environment and Development. *Our Common Future*. Oxford: Oxford University Press, 1988.

See also: African Religions and Nature Conservation; Christian Environmentalism in Kenya; Earth Charter; Sacred Groves of Africa.

Khoisan Religion

The Khoisan peoples of southern Africa are click language-speaking foragers and herders, who have been in the region and have interacted with each other culturally and genetically for thousands of years. As a result, any clear ethnic, cultural or linguistic distinctions between the two groupings that comprise them – the hunting-gathering band-organized Bushmen (or San) and the cattle-keeping, clan-organized Khoekhoe (or "Hottentots" as they used to be called, pejoratively) – have become difficult to draw. A number of the Bushman groups speak either Khoe or Khoe-derived languages, such as the Hai// om of Namibia, who speak Nama (a Khoe language), or the Nharo (Naro) of Botswana, whose San language has pervasive Nama influences. A number of historical Khoekhoe groups of the Cape, who have now all disappeared, lost their cattle through ecological and political pressures and assumed a hunting-gathering economy and mode of production. Conversely, some Bushman groups of northern Namibia and Angola have acquired cattle. In the past, San also used to work as servants and herders for cattle-keeping Khoekhoe.

Religion is one of the cultural domains of the Khoisan peoples that reveals how closely interrelated the San and Khoekhoe have become over the course of their long-standing association. Here similarities and convergences outnumber differences, the latter reflective, in significant ways, of the two diverse socio-economic patterns of the herders and foragers. Thus, Khoekhoe ritual and myth include a concern with cattle; for instance, myths tell of how cattle were acquired by the Khoe people's ancestors (and lost to the Bushmen) and fresh cattle dung was used in death purification ceremonies by the Nama (who had a strong concern with taboos and ritual danger). Khoekhoe myths also tell of early chiefs and warring clans, a theme absent from Bushman myth and belief wherein the concern is more with game animals and ritual aspects of hunting. The large, meat-rich game animals, the eland, gemsbok or giraffe, are the animals that are most prominent in San rock paintings and they stand at the symbolic and ritual center of the initiation ceremonies of numerous Bushman groups, as well as the trance-curing dance, as the source of n/om (the healing potency employed by the shaman-curer).

Despite such divergences in content and emphasis, however, the two people share one religious system. This is evident, more than anywhere else, in the two groups' supernatural beliefs and in their myths and folklore, which, in her recent comprehensive catalogue of Khoisan folktales, the German folklorist Sigrid Schmidt treats as one oral tradition. The preeminent figure on the Khoisan mythological landscape is the trickster, who may be a human-like being – such as Haiseb (or Haitsi-aibib) of the Nama or Paté of the Nharo – or he may bear the traits of an animal. He may assume these either sporadically, when he transforms himself into an animal – for instance, into a mantis, such as Kaggen (Cagn) of the /Xam – or his animalian traits may be a permanent aspect of his being, such as the pan-Khoisan Jackal, who is especially prominent in Khoe folklore. The Khoisan trickster was an ambiguous blend of mischievous or evil prankster, culture hero, protector and even god. In the last capacity he stood opposed to the Khoisan-wide creator god, whom the Nama called Tsui-//goab ("Wounded Knee") and the Nharo N!adi (or Hise) and for whom the !Kung had as many as eight different names, each associated with different attributes. He is associated with the sky and the rain and, according to a widespread traditional Khoisan belief, his "village in the sky" is the destination of the souls of the dead.

The principal protagonists of the trickster were the people of the mythological past, who were either the early humans or animals with human traits and capabilities. They were beset by such social problems and moral shortcomings as food, greed, marital strife and in-law tensions. These converged in the widespread "woman-as-meat" story plot, that is, of a man coming to realize that his wife is a game antelope – that he has "married meat" – and subsequently killing and eating her for her meat, with the collusion of his relatives. This Khoisan-wide story is an expression of the symbolic equivalence of hunting with sex and marriage. The moon and other stellar bodies were frequently personified in Khoisan myths and were mystically charged, and the portentous story of the angry moon, who punished the hare-child for disbelieving and distorting the moon's message to humankind of immortality, is one of the key myths in Khoisan mythology. Another shared story myth motif, and the basis for elaborate and especially melodramatic and frightful tales, is cannibalistic ogres threatening, chasing, killing and devouring humans, especially maidens.

In the sphere of ritual, male and female initiation rites are found among all of the Khoisan groups, although the degree to which they are ritually elaborated varies, with Khoekhoe favoring the male rite, through greater ritual elaboration, and Bushman groups favoring the female one. (Again, we may perhaps explain this difference in economic terms, as herding and foraging are economic patterns in which men and women, respectively, play the more prominent roles.) While the trance-curing dance appears to be exclusive to the Bushmen, its basic ritual and mystical modus operandi, of calling on the aid of the spirits of the dead, is pan-Khoisan. So is the transformation of spirits and humans into animals, a trait that is especially well developed in Bushman ritual and belief (and reflective of their closeness and their spiritual attunement, as hunters, to animals).

Commonality of the Khoisan religious tradition is evident also when one compares it to that of their Bantu-speaking neighbors. Here one notes two striking differences: the absence, in Khoisan religion, of witchcraft and sorcery beliefs and practices, and of any forms of ancestor worship; indeed, instead of worship, what one finds is an attitude of wariness or aversion toward dead persons, and proscriptions about uttering their names. Also absent are totemistic beliefs, which are found among some Bantu-speaking peoples (for instance, the various Tswana tribes, neighbors to many Kalahari Bushman groups).

We should note, however, that some Bushman groups have adopted one or another of these elements of Bantu ritual and mythology, and the Nama-speaking peoples today, despite having retained their myths and tales and many beliefs, are all Christians (and have been for many generations). This reveals a basic structural element of Khoisan religion, resilience and adaptability, along with a certain lack of orthodoxy and tolerance of other beliefs. These traits are consistent with the structural qualities of flexibility, openness and resilience, which Khoisan – especially Bushman – societies have displayed for centuries and millennia.

Mathias Guenther

Further Reading

Barnard, Alan. "Aspects of Khoisan Religious Ideology." In Alan Barnard. *Hunters and Herders of Southern Africa: A Comparative Ethnography of the Khoisan Peoples*. Cambridge: Cambridge University Press, 1992.

Bleek, Wilhelm H.I. *Reynard the Fox in South Africa, or, Hottentot Fables and Tales*. London: Trübner & Co., 1864.

Hahn, Theophilus. *Tsui-//goam: The Supreme Being of the Khoi-khoi*. London: Trübner & Co. 1881.

Schapera, Isaac. *The Khoisan Peoples of South Africa: Bushmen and Hottentots*. London: George Routledge and Sons, 1930.

Schmidt, Sigrid. *Catalogue of the Khoisan Folktales of Southern Africa*, 2 vols. Hamburg: Helmut Buske Verlag, 1989.

See also: San (Bushmen) Apocalyptic Rock Art; San (Bushmen) Religion (and adjacent, San (Bushmen) Rainmaking).

Kimbanguism (Central Africa)

Kimbanguism originated in the Democratic Republic of the Congo (formerly Zaire), and has now spread to many countries in Africa and beyond. The movement takes its name from the founder Simon Kimbangu who was born in 1889 at N'Kamba, a small and isolated village in the Lower Congo, some 200 miles from the capital Kinshasa. He grew up in a church founded by the British Baptist Missionary Society. But in 1918 Kimbangu believed he received a call from God to go and look after his people, for God was telling him that the Europeans had been unfaithful to the call of Christ. On 6 April 1921 Kimbangu began his ministry of healing, and extraordinary scenes followed, with vast numbers flocking to N'Kamba to hear his message and to be healed. Kimbangu healed in the name of Jesus Christ, and stood up against local sorcerers. But the large numbers pouring into N'Kamba were too much for the Belgian colonial power, which feared a political uprising. A state of emergency was declared and in September 1921 Kimbangu was arrested, flogged, and sent into exile in Lubumbashi: 1500 miles from his home. He died in solitary confinement on 12 October 1951. The persecution of Kimbanguists was severe, but through trials and tribulations their following grew. The movement is now officially known as The Church of Jesus Christ on Earth through his Special Envoy Simon Kimbangu and is a member of the World Council of Churches.

According to his followers, Simon Kimbangu taught a very close respect for nature. Independent witnesses tell a variety of stories which substantiate this claim, and provide evidence that Simon Kimbangu's approach was distinctive. Kimbangu stressed that human beings are themselves a part of nature. Flora and fauna are a part of the environment to which humans belong. As such, a special respect for nature is required. Animals are seen as close neighbors whilst plants are to be used with due deference. The indiscriminate destruction of the natural environment is not permitted.

Nowhere is Kimbangu's own attitude to nature more clearly seen than in his teachings on the primate cousins of human beings. Kimbangu strictly forbade any of his followers from killing or eating other primates. The reasons he gave for this edict, which remain strictly enforced among his followers to this day, are instructive, and, while we must always guard against the dangers of anachronism, they mark him as a prophet in the area of primate conservation. Kimbangu used several arguments to support his claim that primates are our cousins. In the first place, he taught that we share a common ancestry with other primates. To kill a primate is to kill a cousin and such an act would be intolerable: indeed tantamount to murder. Second, Kimbangu pointed to the way that, when left to fend for ourselves in the forest, we mimic the activities of our primate cousins. We are forced in survival to forage like them: indeed to become as them. This demonstrates, said Kimbangu, our commonality. Thirdly, he said that nowhere is the human-like quality of the primate world seen more clearly than when human beings, in their sinful activity, point a rifle at primates. For when this happens, primates look the hunter in the eyes, cower, bow down, and whimper in distress. They act, in other words, as humans. Fourth, Kimbangu taught that it is part of God's plan to unify humans and animals. One day we will lie down with the lion in peace, and this cautions us against treating nature as a servant instead of cousin. For all these reasons, Kimbangu strictly forbade the killing of primates. It is particularly interesting to note a predominantly nature-based, rather than theological, reasoning of Kimbangu in this regard. In a region well known for its eating of primate meat, Simon Kimbangu's teaching is all the more remarkable, and the taboo extends into the life of his estimated ten million followers today. Kimbanguists today are found in central west Africa, as well as Kenya, in the United States, and in the United Kingdom, Belgium, and France.

If the teaching and practice of Kimbanguists toward primates is unusual and instructive, then further examples of their positive attitude to nature can be seen. The holy mountain of N'kamba in the Belgian Congo is an example, seen elsewhere in African religions, of the importance of sacred place. Shortly after Kimbangu's death in 1951, his followers began constructing a temple on the site where his ministry had begun. The 37,000-capacity temple that now stands on the holy mountain was built with the help of ordinary believers, many of whom literally carried rocks and stones several kilometers to the site. At the same time as the building program, Kimbanguist followers went to strenuous efforts to maintain the environmental surrounds of the village. A number of sacred trees, important sites in Kimbangu's own ministry, and sacred groves, were preserved. And while there is an element of subjectivity in such remarks, N'kamba is a remarkable place: quiet and peaceful, full of lush trees, and a gentle breeze. Small wonder then that Kimbanguists themselves today proudly call the village "N'kamba New-Jerusalem." The village receives large numbers of visitors. Many of them go to bathe in a site where they believe there is holy water: and both this water, and the very soil from N'Kamba, is taken elsewhere for healing. This material dimension is thus an important theme of the movement. The whole site of N'kamba is seen as holy ground by the Kimbanguists and, as such, shoes are always removed around the village complex: a sign of respect not only for the prophet and his God, but also for the very land on which he and his followers walked. In this Kimbanguists mirror some traditional African religious attitudes to nature in which land and belief were inextricably linked. The fact that such an approach is now cause for some wonderment is testament to the severe environmental crisis now reaching Africa.

Another example of the close relationship of Kimbanguists to nature can be seen in their headquarters in Kinshasa. In the compound humans move alongside animals in a curious harmony: a stark contrast to the huge, bustling, and now pollution-ridden city of Kinshasa. A crane lives in the compound, for no other apparent reason than that it looks beautiful and is an animal cousin. Other animals fare likewise. There are ponds with fish, which are regularly fed and which, it seems, are only used as a supply of food if necessary. A sermon preached by one of Kimbangu's sons, Papa Diangenda Kuntima, extolled the virtues of looking after animals. One day, stopping at a pond at the headquarters in Kinshasa, he began to throw bread into the pond to the fish, saying how important it was to feed and preserve the livelihood of fish and other creatures. Such attitudes are most unusual in modern Africa, particularly so in a country which has seen much of its population on the edge of starvation for a decade or more.

Faith Warner
Richard Hoskins

Further Reading
Hoskins, Richard. *Kimbanguism*. London: Hurst & Co., 2003.
Martin, Marie-Louise. *Kimbangu: A Prophet and His Church*. London: Blackwell, 1975.
See also: African Independent Churches (South Africa); African Religions and Nature Conservation; Congo River Watershed; Sacred Groves of Africa.

Kline, David (1945–)

David Kline, an Amish dairy farmer and writer, lives in Holmes County, Ohio. His vision of nature is rooted in the Anabaptist heritage which he describes in an essay: "God's Spirit and a Theology for Living," in *Creation & the*

Environment: An Anabaptist Perspective on a Sustainable World. Kline says:

> If one's livelihood comes from the Earth – from the land, from creation on a sensible scale, where humans are a part of the unfolding of the seasons, experience the blessings of drought-ending rains, and see God's spirit in all creation – a theology for living should be as natural as the rainbow following a summer storm (2000: 69).

Kline's first book, *Great Possessions: An Amish Farmer's Journal* (1990), is a collection of natural history essays he wrote originally for *Family Life* magazine, an Amish journal read mainly within Amish communities. The essays, which describe wildlife on and around Kline's 120-acre farm, are grounded, he says, in a belief "in nurturing and supporting all our community – that includes people as well as land and wildlife" (xxi).

Scratching the Woodchuck: Nature on an Amish Farm (1997), like the earlier book, includes short essays that explore the varied life forms on the Kline farm. In addition, Kline describes the joy he finds in the shared farm-work of a community made up of non-Amish neighbors, as well as the families in his own congregation. The exchange of labor that makes possible a kind of farming that does not depend on expensive technology reminds Kline, he says, "of a river – serene and beautiful, yet within its gentle flow is great strength" (204).

Kline's writing examines the joys of simple living, informed by "plain" Amish values. He joined with friends, family members, and neighbors in the spring of 2001 to begin *Farming Magazine: People, Land, and Community*. In the magazine's first editorial, "Letter from Larksong," named for the Kline farm, he says, "the true test of a sustainable agriculture will be whether we can romance our children into farming." To accomplish that, Kline says, farms must be profitable, farmers must not be overwhelmed with work, and farming must be fun. Much of Kline's writing explores this fun, grounding his faith and hope in the songs of birds, the changing seasons, and the fellowship found in work done together for a common good. With his two books and *Farming Magazine's* growing circulation, as well as increasingly frequent speaking engagements, Kline's call for a spiritually-grounded, sustainable agriculture has begun to reach well beyond Amish communities.

William Nichols

Further Reading
Kline, David. "God's Spirit and a Theology for Living." In Calvin Redekop, ed. *Creation & the Environment: An Anabaptist Perspective on a Sustainable World*. Baltimore: Johns Hopkins University Press, 2000.
Kline, David. *Scratching the Woodchuck: Nature on an Amish Farm*. Athens, Georgia: The University of Georgia Press, 1997.
Kline, David. *Great Possessions: An Amish Farmer's Journal*. SanFrancisco: North Point Press, 1990.
See also: Christianity (6c3) – Anabaptist/Mennonite Traditions.

Klingenthal Symposia

In October 1995, Pax Christi, France, through its Commission on the Protection and Management of the Creation chaired by Dr. Jean-Pierre Ribaut, also Director of the Environment Division at the Council of Europe, organized the first in a series of symposia on Ecology, Ethics and Spirituality at the Klingenthal Castle in Alsace, France. These symposia aimed for a dialogue between scientists and representatives of different spiritual and ethical approaches, and were remarkable for the breadth of different perspectives they brought together, including Christian, Muslim, Jewish, Buddhist, Hindu, Shintoist, Bahá'í, Australian Aborigine, African Animist, Native Canadian, Brazilian and Peruvian Indian, Finish Sami, Materialistic-Universalist and Masonic. Leading scientists shared their views and explored common interests with those on the spiritual side, or sometimes combined the two. The first symposium issued the Klingenthal Appeal calling for united efforts to inspire respect for nature and sustainable management of resources, harmonizing scientific, aesthetic and spiritual approaches. This first symposium was followed by a series of more thematic Klingenthal Symposia applying the same approach, on water, source of life (1997), soil, cultures and spiritualities (1998), trees and forests (1999), and animals and fauna (2001). Each explored the environmental and scientific challenges under the theme and the perspectives and contributions that each form of spirituality could bring to those challenges. The proceedings of the symposia have been published by the Charles Leopold Mayer Foundation for the Progress of Humanity.

Arthur Dahl

Further Reading
Bourguinat, Élisabeth and Jean-Pierre Ribaut. *L'Arbre et la Forêt: Du Symbolisme Culturel à . . . l'Agonie Programmée?* Charles Léopold Mayer, ed. *Dossiers pour un Débat No. 111*. Paris, 2000.
Caïs, Marie-France, Marie-José Del Rey and Jean-Pierre Ribaut. *L'Eau et la Vie: Enjeux, Perspectives et Visions Interculturelles*. Charles Léopold Mayer, ed. *Dossiers pour un Débat No. 97*. Paris, 1999.
Lamar, Rabah and Jean-Pierre Ribaut. *Sols et Sociétés: Regards Pluriculturels*. Charles Léopold Mayer, ed. *Dossiers pour un Débat No. 116*. Paris, 2001.

Ribaut, Jean-Pierre and Marie-José Del Rey. *The Earth Under Care: Spiritual and Cultural Approaches to the Challenges for a Sustainable Planet. The Klingenthal Appeal and Contributions from the October 1995 Symposium.* La Librairie FPH, *Dossiers pour un Débat No. 73 bis*. Paris, June 1997.

Knowledge, Knowing and Nature

Among the complex interrelations between religion and nature a dynamic currently being recognized connects "knowledge," "knowing" and "nature." Three factors, 1) what is known at any time, 2) how we know it (epistemology) and 3) how we participate consciously in what we know, are all interconnected with the ongoing changes in the physical world. Knowing is dynamic and has efficacy.

Recent philosophy of science has generated epistemologies (theories of knowledge) relating to how we know nature as seen from the perspective of the natural sciences. Religion acknowledges that in some ways we can know the divine and also the inmost reaches of the human person, as well as the outside world that we know as nature, so there are theological epistemologies. In recent developments "spirituality" has begun to be distinguished from "religion" as relating more centrally to the inner experiences of the self and the divine from which the religious traditions have arisen and on which their dogmas and institutions are based; thus a major focus within the academic discipline of contemporary spirituality concerns moment-by-moment experience of life, meaningfulness, wholeness and energy. Investigation of the kind of knowledge involved in this expanded knowledge base, along with how we know it, is leading to the recognition of spiritual epistemologies. Each type of epistemology corresponds to a view of the world, of nature, and of how we humans are related to nature: depending on the worldview held, so will be our implicit attitude and explicit action toward nature.

The Modern Period, through the dominant influence of the natural sciences from Newton onwards, has inculcated in us the sense that we know nature as outside of ourselves and as other than ourselves. This worldview is currently associated with much exploitation of nature. Faced with the now life-threatening issue of how to sustain a world that is ecologically unsustainable, many are reexamining the concept of nature and finding it not only more complex but more all-encompassing than had been assumed within the Newtonian worldview. The academic study of spirituality, still a relatively new field in 2003, is playing an important part in defining what nature is. The examination of the concept of nature is itself a factor in changing how we deal with nature. "Nature" is coming to be known as not only the external, physical/material environment, as investigated by the techniques of the natural sciences, but also as a much more complex reality with manifold depths and relationships yet to be discovered. There is increasing acknowledgement that we humans are part of nature, not separate from it: we are integral to nature and therefore inseparable from its future. Ecology recognizes this, highlights human responsibility for caring for nature and emphasizes that whatever degradation we inflict on nature impacts back on us. Theological worldviews and epistemologies on the whole corroborate this ecological perspective and it is becoming incorporated into popular thinking. But there is an urgent need to go beyond this and some have done just that. It is being recognized that between ourselves and nature there are not only the now obvious external and physical connections but also equally important interior relationships and activities. These internal relations are not superficially evident; they are not visible or detectable by what we know as objective "scientific" investigation. To know what nature is from the inside and so to understand and work with our internal connections with nature, we have to investigate who we are and what we can know of ourselves not only on the physical, biological, mental and psychological levels but also as spiritual beings. It is with this deeper investigation that spiritual epistemologies are generated, first in the form of modes of knowing the deeper levels of the human self and then, integrated with this, as modes of knowing the cosmic order. The results of such investigation "from the inside" are expressed in an expanded concept of nature, for nature itself is multidimensional, while the concept of "nature" is seen to be a human construct which changes in relation to what we know about it.

Western science has been successful in mapping, as it were, the configurations of nature, according to what it acknowledges as the physical world and using methods appropriate to that. Western psychology, up to and not including the Transpersonal Movement, has mapped the levels of the human person according to what it acknowledges as its field. These levels are seen now, from within this new field known as Transpersonal Studies, as the lower, or less-evolved levels of the human being. In the East primarily – although there are some striking Western examples also – the higher domains of the human person have been mapped meticulously by pioneers who have been there (i.e., the mystics, seers and sages, who have based their theories and teachings on their own experience). Significantly, there are criteria of verification appropriate to these teachings on a par with the verification criteria accepted within the scientific community. Data coming from these sources not only can, but now also needs to be, integrated with the Western "scientific" findings on the outer nature, to present a more complete, deeper and fuller understanding of what "nature" is.

According to the particular worldview or theory of existence one holds, so one will act toward the goal envisaged in that theory. Believing that material nature is the only reality (as in Western science), the goal, psychologically, is the development of the individual. Accordingly, the ego and its security (particularly the egos of dominant groups) are being prioritized, along with what appear to be the best social and material structures and institutions to support that goal. In the adult egocentric mode of existence, which is where most of us are, other persons and nature will by definition be experienced as other, as "not-self," as potentially threatening and to be defended against, dominated, and eventually overcome; hence further division, exploitation and the prospect of self-destruction. By contrast, from a center of consciousness higher than the ego, as in the case of the explorers of the higher domains, other persons and nature are experienced as not other than the self. From the higher levels of awareness the lower levels and domains can be integrated, and their structures and energies used consciously as instruments of the higher.

Integrating the findings of spiritual investigation, intelligence and creativity with the findings of the natural and human sciences extends the notion of consilience (E.O. Wilson) to open up new horizons and latent possibilities. With such a reciprocally enhancing and integrated worldview, knowing who we are in relation to nature, knowing what we know and participating consciously in what we know, we can identify where change is needed in ourselves and in what we are doing to nature. Articulating this next stage in the religion/nature dynamic itself generates both strategies for change and energy to implement them.

Felicity Edwards

Further Reading

Wilber, Ken. *Sex, Ecology, Spirituality: Spirit in Action*. Boston and London: Shambhala Press, 1995.

Wilson, E.O. *Consilience: Unity of Knowledge*. New York: Vintage Books, 1998.

See also: Conservation Biology; Wilber, Ken; Wilson, Edward O.

Kogi (Northern Colombia)

High in the folds of the world's largest coastal mountain massif, the Sierra Nevada de Santa Marta, on Colombia's Caribbean coast, live three Chibcha-speaking Amerindian groups: the Ijka (or Arhuacos); the Sanka (or Arsario or Wiwa); and the Kogi (more properly called Kaggaba). Of these, the Kogi/Kaggaba have remained the most "unacculturated," true to their traditions and beliefs, and pursuing an environmentally aware and instructive spirituality. They are, however, under increasing pressure from the outside world, yet they retain an intense commitment to isolation.

The Sierra (called Gonavindua, or "snowfields" by the Kogi) is a vast, three-sided pyramid, starting at sea level and rising to a staggering 5770 meters. Situated near the Equator, it has minimal seasonal temperature and rainfall variation. Altitude determines almost everything, from tropical rainforest below to snowfields and glaciers at its peaks. It is rather like the world in miniature, encompassing almost every known kind of natural environment – at each particular level. For the Kogi, this vast territory (covering 12,000 km^2 above a 300-meter level) becomes more sacred the higher one goes.

The 6000–7000 Kogi live a slightly austere and rigorous, but profoundly content and rewarding life. They reside in isolated settlements in the 1000 to 2000-meter levels, with even more isolated homesteads at other levels, where they care for their sloping garden-fields of (depending upon altitude) plantains/bananas, beans, cucumbers, manioc, corn, and fruit trees. Animal protein consumption is minimal. Cotton is grown for their white garments; men weave the clothes, women weave baskets (for everyday carrying purposes as well as sacred ones). No shoes are worn as footwear is forbidden. The regular but tightly controlled use of the leaves of the sacred coca plant is a marker of manhood, a method of spiritual communication, and the mark of "civilization." (Chewing coca leaves as the men do has only a weak chemical affect, much like betel nut, and helps them to stave off hunger, handle altitude sickness, and supplement their diet).

This extremely self-sufficient lifestyle – with only carefully considered inputs (such as iron blades and spades) from the "outside" world – sustains the Kogi population, who are ruled by hereditary lords and sacred priests. The latter, the *Máma(s)*, the enlightened ones, are the focal point of life: the populace gear their lives and thoughts to assist them. The *Máma(s)* exist to look after them, but more importantly, to pursue the arduous and unremitting religious tasks of ensuring harmony and the continuation of all plant, animal and human life on Earth and indeed, the continuation of Earth (as a living entity) itself.

The *Máma(s)* follow the Law of Hába Gaulchováng (the Great Mother), who created all things in Alúna ("Thought," a pre-conscious/conscious state that all *Máma(s)* aspire to regularly attain) in the depths of the vast primordial sea before Munsá (the "Dawning"/Creation). The material world, pre-created by the Thoughts of the Great Mother before the Dawning, must follow her laws of Nulúka/Yulúka ("harmony," "balance") to continue. Acutely aware of the interrelationships between the weather, climate, plants, animals and humans, the *Máma(s)*, from their vast cosmos that is still nonetheless a miniature at the heart of the larger world, pursue regular and profound deprivation to attain the required levels of consciousness and purity. Such pursuit is necessary to perform the incessant prayer, oration and ritual gift-giving that ensure the protection and continuation of harmony and balance on Earth. The

Kogi sometimes call themselves the "Elder Brothers," and assume that the innumerable societies of "Younger Brothers" outside of the Sierra around the rest of the conceived world know that their priests, the *Máma(s)*, are dedicated to essential tasks on behalf of all.

Learning to become a *Máma* is possibly the most arduous priesthood training of any society on Earth. Preferably chosen by divination, the young candidate (usually male but sometimes female) is ideally taken at birth (and certainly before reaching the age of five) and raised in almost complete darkness in a cave or specially constructed darkened hut, for two consecutive nine-year periods. Some, wanting to go deeper, may continue for a third nine-year period. Raised in a re-creation of the world of Alúna in a womb-like dark sea, the young *kuívi* (initiate, "abstinent") is taught the Laws of the Great Mother, the rules and balances of the non-material and material worlds, and the *sewá* ("alliance" gifts/prestations) necessary for required harmonies.

Ritual postures, movements, chants, lineages, geography and the natural "sciences," botany, biology, astronomy, meteorology, cosmogony and cosmology, religious and spiritual analogy, history, divination, confession procedures, ethics, dream interpretation, plant growth, animal behavior, sensory deprivation, healing, curing, medicine, time-cycle manipulation, ritual language – and many more topics – are taught and learnt. All of this occurs while seeing almost nothing and living on a special diet not far removed from perpetual starvation. Much of this intense training is likened to the Great Mother's pre-creation in the darkness of Alúna of the kalguashija ("model," "essence," "image") of all living things before their actual physical creation with the Dawning. But those who emerge from this training are very special, often gifted beyond normal human abilities and expecting to live to 90 years, which they believe is their allotted span. Coming out of their training darkness, once they make adjustments to the shock of the material world, another *Máma* will now present the young male with his *poporo* (the small gourd to contain slaked lime to accompany the taking of coca leaves), which is also a symbol of manhood and with profound religious significance that he must have with him at all times. He can then take a wife, and his life's work can begin, not just for his people, but for all things in the world.

Kogi/Kaggaba society seems to stand slightly apart from many traditions of northern South America, and they themselves feel that they should remain so because of their strongly held beliefs in their unique and special position with regard to the essential balancing of elements necessary for the continuation of life on Earth. Although forming a fascinating amalgam of ancient pre-Colombian Tairona cultures from the coastal areas of northern Colombia, the Spanish conquest and eventual domination and destruction of the Tairona cultures in the sixteenth century forced survivors to retreat higher into the Sierra (around 1600), and into areas already peopled by Chibcha-speaking cultures. Tairona priests, *Noamas*, linked up with sacred *Máma(s)* high in the Sierra, and a modified sacred culture was developed, under the latter's control, which eschewed material cultural trappings, and hid golden objects from the intruding Spaniards.

In Kogi belief, disregard shown by the "Younger Brother" for the Laws of the Mother equals disrespect for maintaining the living world in good health. This disrespect and greed makes the *Máma's* work more difficult, and may lead, if not stopped, to the end of the world. This end could come in the form of fiery Teiku – a burning, sun-like fire/heat (Teiku is also the sun, who is also a *Máma*) which will create immense destruction (analogous to one early Kogi story which relates that some of the first ancestors appeared in the Sierra to escape an earlier fiery end). Today, the Kogi are under pressure of Christian missionization, but they still deliberately retreat into isolation in the belief that, through their life-way, they sustain the whole cosmos.

Kirk Huffman

Further Reading
Alan Ereira, A., *The Elder Brothers: Heart of the World*. New York: Vintage, 1993.
Reichel-Dolmatoff, Gerardo. *The Sacred Mountain of Colombia's Kogi Indians*. Leiden: E.J. Brill, 1990.
Reichel-Dolmatoff, Gerardo. "The Great Mother and the Kogi Universe: A Concise Overview," *Journal of Latin American Lore* 13:1 (1987), 73–113.
See also: Ecology and Religion; Reichel-Dolmatoff, Gerardo – and Ethnoecology in Columbia; Tukanoan Indians (Northwest Amazonia); U'wa Indians (Columbia).

Koliada Viatichei

The Viatichi cultural center was established in Moscow in 1995 through the initiative of N. Speransky (a Ph.D. in physics and math), who goes by the pagan name Velimir. In the fall of 1998, the small Viatichi community, comprised of well-educated Moscow intellectuals, united with the Koliada community to form the larger Koliada Viatichei community. This is a faction within Russian neo-paganism which strives to recreate a pre-Christian Slavic wisdom that avoids any alien influences and borrowings.

Speransky rejects as unacceptable for Slavs the esotericism and Eastern flavor of the popular teachings of Nikolai and Elena Rerikh. Likewise, he rejects Christianity for its historical connection to the "Semitic ideology." Yet, unlike some other Russian neo-pagans, Koliada Viatichei is negative toward Nazism and criticizes it for its esoteric and occult bias. It also censures anti-Semitism as destructive. Speransky is skeptical toward any primeval "Aryan civilization," treats Vedic literature as an alien heritage (while some Russian neo-pagans look to it as part of their own Slavic-Aryan roots), and rejects the *Book of Vles* as a forgery.

In their concerns for Russian traditional culture the Viatiches demonstrate a strong sense of Russian nationalism, alongside a conspiratorial view of the non-Russian world. They reject Western "technocratic civilization" as "destructive" and oppose it with Russian ancestral values and an ecological worldview. Paganism is identified as an ecophilic ideology which should be promoted at the state level. Speransky argues that salvation is to be gained through the maintenance of a careful and healthy relationship with the natural environment and through preserving the cultural heritage of one's ancestors. Critical of high technology and consumerism, he foretells a collapse of Western civilization, followed by a clash between "white" and "yellow" races in the twenty-first century, and calls for a struggle against both Eastern teachings and Christianity in favor of a renewed Russian pagan faith. He praises "Russian folk Christianity" for its break away from the "Semitic ideology," a break that is considered to have cleansed the "Russian faith" and made it healthy once again. Accordingly, this faith is destined to a final victory over Christianity, a victory which will lead Russia to a great future.

The Viatichi teaching is based on the Manichean idea of an eternal struggle between Good (Belbog) and Evil (Chernobog). Curiously, both gods are thought to have made a contribution to the creation of man, Chernobog building his body, and Belbog awarding him an everlasting soul. Hence, the belief is that humans have an inherently dual and divided nature.

Speransky recognizes variability in Slavic pagan beliefs, with each tribe having its own gods and sacred places. He argues that great thinkers have periodically managed to integrate these beliefs into a uniform pantheon of Pan-Russian deities, but that this has always been followed by a collapse and dissolution. He believes that a new era is coming which calls for a restoration of a uniform system of Slavic beliefs. But this system should be polytheistic, to account for the complexity of the world with its multitude of good and evil forces. Nevertheless, a Russian "Great Goddess" – "Mother Earth" – is at the center of his teaching. Borrowed from Russian folklore, this idea of a close relationship between humans and a nourishing native soil is said to call up deep emotions toward the land and a willingness to defend it by all means. This Great Goddess is identified with the "Motherland-Russia."

More recently, Speransky has developed an appreciation for Lithuanian neo-paganism and has begun advocating its teaching of "*Darna*," or "life in accordance with the Earth and with the ancestors, which provides a feeling of happiness and is welcomed by the gods." Accordingly, he has revised his earlier dualistic views from seeing the polar forces as conflicting to a view that recognizes them as complementary and mutually reinforcing. His appreciation for prehistoric peoples and "folk culture" approaches a romantic conception of the "noble savage," and he advocates self-restriction, refusal of consumerism, and a rural lifestyle, as the way to find a new balance between humans and nature. Not avoiding politics, however, he continues to warn that "Russia is pressed by a fatal evil," and points out that pagans have to defend the Russian land, finding strength and energy in tradition and in the old Slavic gods who will ultimately determine the future.

Victor A. Shnirelman

Further Reading
Shnirelman, Victor A. "Perun, Svarog and Others: The Russian Neo-Paganism in Search of Itself." *Cambridge Anthropology* 21:3 (1999–2000), 18–36.

See also: Neo-paganism and Ethnic Nationalism in Eastern Europe; Oshmarii-Chimarii (Mori El Republic, Russia); Russian Mystical Philosophy.

Korean Mountains

The Korean peninsula is a rugged mountainous land, looking from the sky more like a storm-tossed ocean than a placid lake. The rivers that tumble out of those mountains usually do not have very far to go before they reach the ocean. The traces of their short journeys across the peninsula's rocky surface are much less impressive than the broad floodplains left behind by the rivers that shaped the civilizations of China and India. Mountains, more than waterways, have dominated the physical landscape the Korean people have inhabited for centuries. Mountains have dominated the religious landscape as well, shaping Korean concepts of nature and of how they should interact with it.

When Koreans look at mountains, they see not only mountains but also the sky behind and above them. Those mountains and the sky above them have inspired both reverence and apprehension in those who lived beneath them. Koreans believed that nature was filled with willful entities which could, for example, provide or deny rain when crops needed it and could send diseases to afflict humanity or cure those already afflicted. Since mountains and the heavens were the features of nature that Koreans found most impressive, it is the behaviors of mountain spirits and heavenly spirits that Koreans have been most anxious to influence through ritual. The oldest accounts of religious activity on the peninsula, going back almost two millennia, describe rituals honoring and imploring spirits in the heavens above and the mountains below.

Koreans have traditionally assigned different functions to terrestrial and celestial spirits. Mountain spirits, including not only mountain gods but also mountain-dwelling tigers and even particularly impressive trees or stones found on or near mountains, have often been enlisted to serve as tutelary gods for villages. Even today, despite the changes wrought by decades of modernization, it is still possible to find a rope placed around a particularly old and large tree on the edge of a village, or an informal altar formed from a pile of stones off to the side of a mountain path, to signal the presence of a guardian spirit. Moreover, most Buddhist temple complexes still include a small shrine to the local mountain spirit behind the main worship hall.

Until Christianity introduced Koreans two centuries ago to the notion of a God in heaven who cared for those on the Earth below, celestial spirits have tended to be viewed as too far above the human realm to be interested in maintaining an ongoing protective relationship with an individual human community. Though a few villages have adopted celestial spirits as tutelary deities, the gods of heaven, including such celestial bodies as the sun, the moon, the planets, and certain constellations, have usually been conceived more as judges and administrators than as protectors. The Big Dipper gods, for example, collectively determine how long human beings will live as well as whether an unborn child will be male or female. There is often a shrine to the Big Dipper gods not far from the shrine to the mountain god in a Buddhist temple, but the Big Dipper shrine is for individual petitions for a change in fate and does not provide the same general protection to the shrine precincts that the mountain spirit shrine does.

Korea's folk religion assumes that rituals and prayers can persuade planets and stars, or at least the spirits they represent, to change a decision in a petitioner's favor. Neo-Confucianism, which began to dominate upper-class culture in Korea from the fifteenth century, denied that objects moving through the heavens possess the ability to make decisions. It also denied conscious intent to mountains, trees, and rocks. Nevertheless, Neo-Confucianism agreed that there is a strong link between the way humans and nature behave.

Neo-Confucian philosophers insisted that human beings were an integral part of the natural world and therefore human behavior affected the behavior of other natural objects and natural forces. If human beings acted in accordance with the patterns of harmonious interaction, which constituted the natural order, then nature would function in predictable and beneficial ways. On the other hand, if human beings pursued individual self-interest at the expense of the common good, they injected disharmony into the universe. The result would be natural disasters such as earthquakes, floods, and droughts. The impact individual behavior could have on nature varied according to the political status of the individual actor. A king's selfish behavior was more likely to cause natural disasters or ominous phenomena such as an unpredicted comet or meteor shower than was the inappropriate behavior of a peasant.

In addition to providing spirits to be cajoled and worshipped, and portents to warn against inappropriate behavior, nature also provides settings for some religious activities. The indigenous Korean belief in mountain spirits combined with the imported Chinese belief in geomancy to make mountains a favored location for spiritual cultivation. Geomancy holds that there are invisible channels of energy beneath the Earth and that certain locations have particularly high concentrations of that energy. By the ninth century, Koreans were building Buddhist temples in foothill locations believed to be best situated to tap into that underground energy as well as gain the favor of particularly powerful mountain spirits. Though Neo-Confucians claimed to be skeptical of the power of mountain spirits, when they began establishing rural academies in the sixteenth century they too often selected locations on the lower reaches of mountain slopes. In the twentieth century, two mountains with particularly strong geomantic properties and guardian spirits, Mt. Kyeryong in the center of South Korea and Mt. Moak in the southwest, have attracted adherents of new religions in large enough numbers to concern the government.

These new mountain-based religions have not expressed much explicit concern over the state of the environment that surrounds them. Instead, Buddhists and Christians living in Korea's crowded cities (South Korea is now over 80 percent urban) have been at the forefront of the environmental protection movement. Since the early 1980s, Buddhists emphasizing the traditional Buddhist respect for all forms of life and Christians emphasizing respect for all that God has created have joined forces with secular activists in a broad coalition called the Federation of Environmental Movements. Their focus has been less on protecting mountains *per se* than on protecting the waters that flow from those mountains and that are lifelines for all city-dwelling creatures.

Not all the gods Koreans worship are deified natural objects. Nor do all Korean religious activities take place in a forested mountainside. Nevertheless, any account of Korean religion that neglected the worship of stars and mountain spirits, the reliance on astronomical phenomena for moral guidance, or the appeal of mountain settings to the devout would be incomplete and misleading.

Don Baker

Further Reading

Chang, Chong-ryong. "Patterns and Practices of Village Rites." In Korea Foundation, ed. *Korean Cultural Heritage, Vol. II: Thought and Religion*. Seoul: Korea Foundation, 1996, 166–73.

Choe, Chang-jo. "Study of How Koreans View and Utilize Nature." *Korea Journal* 32:4 (Winter 1992), 26–45.
Keum, Jang-tae. "Mountains in Korean Thought." In Korea Foundation, ed. *Korean Cultural Heritage, Vol. II: Thought and Religion*. Seoul: Korea Foundation, 1996, 36–41.
Mason, David A. *Spirit of the Mountains: Korea's San-Shin and Traditions of Mountain-Worship*. Seoul: Hollym, 1999.
Park, Seong-rae. *Portents and Politics in Korean History*. Seoul: Jimoondang, 1998.
See also: Mt. Hiei (Japan); Sacred Mountains.

Krishnamurti, Jiddhu (1895–1986)

Krishnamurti was a religious teacher whose life reads like a legend, but is well documented. Born in a lower-middle-class traditional Brahmin family in a small town called Madanapalle in Andhra Pradesh (India), he was picked up in 1909 by the leaders of the international Theosophical Society in Adyar, Chennai. Mrs. Annie Besant, the then President of the society, predicted that Krishnamurti would be a world-teacher who would give a new interpretation of religion for the scientific age. She adopted him and sent him to England for education.

In 1922, Krishnamurti had his first spiritual awakening under a pepper tree in Ojai, California in the form of a mystic experience in which he felt one with everything around him. This mysterious "process" went on intermittently throughout his life and has been a subject of much conjecture. From 1922 to 1932 Krishnamurti went through an intense period of inquiry, questioning all the Theosophical teachings he had accepted until then and dropping what appeared to him to be false. In 1929, he dissolved the organization set up around him and returned all the properties donated for his work, saying, "I maintain that Truth is a pathless land, and you cannot approach it by any path whatsoever, by any religion, by any sect" (in Lutyens 1990: 78). The essential philosophic difference lay in Krishnamurti's perception that there is no path to truth, which contradicted the Theosophical belief that all religions were paths to the same truth. Ironically, despite this parting of ways with the Theosophical Society, Krishnamurti became a world-teacher, lecturing and holding dialogues worldwide to convey his teachings until his death in Ojai, California in 1986. He also started schools for children to realize his vision of education. To him science and religion were two complimentary quests of humanity, the former for discovering the order that manifests itself in nature, and the latter for discovering order within our consciousness.

To Krishnamurti, religion is not belief in some concept of God, acceptance of a code of morality, or the performance of rituals; it is the flowering of virtue in the consciousness of a human being. Virtue is order in consciousness in which there is love, compassion, peace, nonviolence, happiness, joy and beauty. Since virtue is a state of consciousness, it cannot be practiced through will and decision. It arises, naturally, through the ending of the disorder that human beings experience as violence, fear, sorrow, and conflict. This disorder has a cause that can be perceived and eliminated since it is based on illusions created by our own memory and imagination. It can be ended through the perception of what is true and what is false. But truth is not merely an idea – it comes into being through a deep, undistorted and holistic perception of reality. This quest for truth is the essence of religion, for without it there is no wisdom or virtue. Wisdom requires freedom from illusion, which comes from self-knowledge and not through the acceptance of ideas. In his words, "The ignorant man is not the unlearned but the one who does not know himself" (1955: 17).

Truth does not come from an intellectual quest, but mysteriously, in a flash of insight. That is why it is pathless and is not dependent on a Guru. A Guru can point out the truth but cannot create perception in the disciple. The individual is both the teacher and the student and totally responsible for her or his own learning. Further, since truth is the unknown, it cannot be pursued or sought or spread through the word. One must keep the mind open and not block insight. This requires living with questions, without any conclusions, observing everything keenly like a true student wanting to learn about life by watching it, without interfering with what is taking place or judging it and without creating boundaries of what is possible and what is not possible. He called such a learning state one of choiceless awareness. It starts from the ground of not knowing and can be shared with fellow-inquirers in what he termed the art of dialogue.

Krishnamurti had a deep love for nature, which he considered an essential part of a truly religious mind. All Krishnamurti schools and centers are located in sites of tremendous natural beauty, because contact with nature creates a sensitivity which is conducive to a religious quality in the human mind. Krishnamurti maintained that there is a universal consciousness which connects all of nature, but we separate ourselves from it by living in a self-created, narrow, limited world of our own thoughts. To realize our oneness with nature, it is necessary to understand the thinking process and not let it become self-centered. He talked about the need to live with a silent mind which uses thought only when it is necessary and is not driven by it. He taught that there is an order and intelligence everywhere in nature and that the observer can learn to live in harmony with that order if he does not separate himself from the observed. There is disorder only in human consciousness and it originates from an ego-process that can be ended through self-knowledge. With the ending of disorder comes a natural order which is not enforced. The religious quest can thus be regarded as a quest for discovering what it means to live with a consciousness that is in complete harmony with the order of nature. He called it the art of living. Commenting on our relationship with nature, Krishnamurti wrote:

> We never seem to have a feeling for all living things on the Earth. If we could establish a deep abiding relationship with nature we would never kill an animal for our appetite, we would never harm, vivisect, a monkey, a dog, a guinea pig for our benefit. We would find other ways to heal our wounds, heal our bodies. But the healing of the mind is something totally different. That healing gradually takes place if you are with nature, with that orange on the tree, and the blade of grass that pushes through the cement, and the hills covered, hidden by the clouds. This is not sentiment or romantic imagination but a reality of the relationship with everything that lives and moves on the Earth ... If we could, and we must, establish a deep long abiding relationship with nature ... then we would never slaughter another human being for any reason whatsoever (Krishnamurti 1987: 80).

Krishnamurti pointed out that all disorder that we see in human society is a projection of the disorder in our consciousness and there can be no fundamental transformation in society unless the individual transforms his or her consciousness. Therefore self-knowledge is an essential requirement for all human beings and not merely a specialization for the religious person. Religion to him was something integral to daily life, which when separated from it becomes an escape:

> It is our Earth, not yours or mine or his. We are meant to live on it helping each other, not destroying each other. This is not some romantic nonsense but the actual fact. But man has divided the Earth hoping that in the particular he is going to find happiness, security, a sense of abiding comfort. Until a radical change takes place and we wipe out all nationalities, all ideologies, all religious divisions and establish a global relationship – psychologically first, inwardly, before organizing the outer – we shall go on with wars. If you harm others, if you kill others, whether in anger or by organized murder which is called war, you, who are the rest of humanity, not a separate human being fighting the rest of humanity, are destroying yourself (Krishnamurti 1987: 60).

P. Krishna

Further Reading

Holroyd, Stuart. *Krishnamurti – The Man, the Mystery and the Message.* Rockport, MA: Element, 1991.
Jayakar, Pupul. *Krishnamurti.* New York: Harper & Row, 1986.
Krishnamurti, J. *Krishnamurti to Himself.* New York: Harper & Row, 1987.
Krishnamurti, J. *Freedom from the Known.* London: Gollancz, 1972.
Krishnamurti, J. *The Education and Significance of Life.* London: Gollancz, 1955.
Lutyens, Mary. *The Life and Death of Krishnamurti.* London: John Murray, 1990.
Sanat, Aryel. *The Inner Life of Krishnamurti.* Wheaton, IL: Quest Books, 1999.
Skitt, David, ed. *Questioning Krishnamurti.* London: Thorsons, 1996.

See also: Huxley, Aldous; Hinduism; India; Theosophy.

Kropotkin, Peter (1842–1921)

The Russian prince Pyotr Alexeyevich Kropotkin was one of the leading geographers of his time and a central figure in the history of anarchist thought. His ideas have had an enduring influence on decentralism, regionalism, and alternative technology, and later thinkers such as Patrick Geddes, Lewis Mumford and Paul Goodman have looked to him for inspiration. More recently, he has been recognized for his influence on the radical environmental movement and more specifically as the most important theoretical forefather of green anarchism. Kropotkin's most famous concept is the idea that evolutionary advances throughout the natural world are promoted best through mutual aid, cooperation, and symbiosis. His social theory, including his view of religion and other institutions, is grounded in this view of nature.

Kropotkin sought to refute the Social Darwinist idea that social inequalities are the result of a competitive "struggle for survival" that is inescapable because it is rooted in nature. He observed that animals have social instincts with evolutionary value, and that symbiotic activity is more useful for survival than competitive and antagonistic behavior. Similarly, he saw the "struggle for survival" in human society as being primarily a cooperative social project of adapting successfully to the challenges of the environment. Mutual aid is thus a "factor of evolution" both in nature and in human society. In effect, the social instincts of animal communities are raised to the level of rational action and moral choice in humanity. Ethics therefore has a naturalistic basis, for ideas of good and evil relate ultimately to that which either contributes to or threatens the survival and well-being of the community.

For evidence of the efficacy of social cooperation, Kropotkin cites the practices of tribal societies, free cities and cooperative communities over the ages. This history inspires his anarchism, which has as its goal a system of social cooperation free from the state, capitalism, and other forms of hierarchical, concentrated power. He envisions a future cooperative society rooted in a scientific understanding of nature and society that understands mutual aid between human beings as a continuation of the larger tendencies of natural evolution. He recognizes the destructive instincts of humanity as being every bit as natural as the cooperative ones, but he considers them to be anti-evolutionary forces whose effects should be minimized through benign environmental influences.

Kropotkin applies these ideas concerning evolution, science and ethics in his analysis of religion. He sees religion as having two opposed dimensions. On the one hand, it has expressed the human tendency toward mutual aid and solidarity, thus furthering social evolution. He sees the religious precept of doing to others as one would have them do to oneself as only the developed form of the ethics that pervades nature. In his view, both Buddhism and Christianity differed from all previous religions by replacing cruel and vengeful gods with "an ideal man-god" who taught a religion of love. He credited Shakyamuni Buddha with introducing such concepts as universal compassion and kindness, love for one's enemies, sympathy for all living beings, contempt for wealth, and the equality of all human beings. He saw Christianity as a very similar but "higher" teaching than Buddhism, noting that Jesus (unlike Buddha, who was a Prince) came from among the ordinary people, and early Christianity showed a strong identification with the oppressed. He also argued that although Buddhism and Christianity were a break with previous religions, they were merely universalizing principles that were practiced within tribal religion, which applied principles of love, equity, and disinterested generosity within the bounds of the tribe, and which had their natural basis in the evolutionary value of mutual aid.

Kropotkin saw the other, anti-evolutionary dimension of religion in its role providing powerful (albeit declining) support for the system of domination, particularly in the case of Christianity. He contends that Jesus' original message of universal love and social equality was de-emphasized and thereby undermined by his later followers and scriptural interpreters and eventually destroyed with the establishment of a hierarchical Church (thus paralleling similar developments in Buddhism). Thus, Christianity was originally a revolt against the Roman Empire, but the Empire triumphed. Despite the egalitarian and communist tendencies of early Christianity, the Church became the avowed enemy of all such tendencies. In Kropotkin's view, Roman law and the hierarchical Church were the two forces that undermined the spirit of the freedom and instilled authoritarianism in European culture.

At the same time, according to Kropotkin, Christianity profoundly shaped the European view of nature. In his view, the religions of Egypt, Persia and India (except Buddhism) saw nature as a conflict between good and evil. He contended that this dualistic "Eastern" idea influenced Christianity and contributed to the belief in a moral battle between good and evil within the person and in society. Such beliefs, he says, reinforced tendencies toward repression and persecution. Moreover, the Church condemned the scientific study of nature and supported revelation, as opposed to nature, as the sole source of moral guidance. Kropotkin conceded that within Christianity the importance of human social instincts and human reason in the discovery of moral truth were recognized in Thomas Aquinas' philosophy, in Renaissance religious thought, and in other tendencies. However, he contended that on the whole the Church continued to stress the evil, fallen quality of both nature and human nature, and the need to look to God and revelation for salvation from them.

For Kropotkin, religion plays either a positive evolutionary role, to the extent that it continues tendencies in nature toward mutual aid and solidarity, or an anti-evolutionary one, to the extent that it allies itself with systems of domination. Furthermore, he saw a strong connection between the social functions of religions and their conceptions of nature. Religions that emphasize universal love and social equality generally have a positive view of the natural world, whereas religions that are allied with social hierarchy and domination propagate highly negative views of nature and justifications for dominating it.

John P. Clark

Further Reading
Kropotkin, Peter. *Mutual Aid: A Factor of Evolution.* London: Freedom Press, 2002.
Kropotkin, Peter. "Anarchist Morality" and "Modern Science and Anarchism." In *Kropotkin's Revolutionary Pamphlets.* New York: Dover Publications, 1970.
Kropotkin, Peter. *Ethics: Origin and Development.* New York and London: Benjamin Blom, 1968.
See also: Anarchism; Anarcho-Primitivism and the Bible; Bioregionalism and the North American Bioregional Congress; Earth First! and the Earth Liberation Front; Green Politics; Radical Environmentalism; Social Ecology; Snyder, Gary.

Krueger, Fred (1943–)

Fred Krueger is an Eastern Orthodox Christian who has been deeply involved in creating numerous Christian environmental organizations, coordinating interreligious conferences on nature and the environment, writing on

Christianity's ecological perspective, lobbying congress on forest issues, and facilitating workshops and backpacking trips in nature.

Krueger became involved in eco-theology through his involvement with a Californian new religious movement turned Orthodox quasi-monastic order, the Holy Order of MANS (HOOM), and a sub-group, the Eleventh Commandment Fellowship (ECF) dedicated to what the order's leader, Vincent Rossi, deemed the 11th Commandment: "The Earth is the Lord's and the fullness thereof: Thou shalt not despoil the Earth, nor destroy the life thereon" (see Nash 1989: 97 for a 1939 version of the 11th Commandment). Inspired by the ecological insights present in Eastern Christianity, the ECF's mission was to stimulate ecological thinking and action throughout Christianity. The group played a significant role in the first North American Conference on Christianity and Ecology (NACCE) in 1987, of which Krueger was a founding member. Following the conference, much of Krueger's (and the ECF's) energies were shifted to building NACCE as an organization.

Krueger left his role as executive director of NACCE and editor of their magazine *Firmament* in 1993 and became the director of the Christian Society of the Green Cross, a ministry of Evangelicals for Social Action in order to promote ecological concern among conservative Christians. Krueger was also part of the editorial board for the group's quarterly, *Green Cross*. When *Green Cross* became a part of the Evangelical Environmental Network, Krueger moved on to develop Opening the Book of Nature (OBN), a program whose roots lay in earlier ECF wilderness backpacking trips led by Krueger. Convinced that direct experiences of nature would help people of faith recover a lost spiritual heritage and convert them to an ecological viewpoint, these trips became the framework for OBN, one of Krueger's current projects. OBN programs (workshops, weekend wilderness retreats, ten-day backpacking trips) are designed to help Christians "discover the spiritual lessons in creation" (*OBN Newsletter*) and the value of wilderness.

Another Krueger-led group, the primarily Jewish and Christian Religious Campaign for Forest Conservation (RCFC), is the activist arm for OBN. Founded in 1998 it has supported forest conservation legislation, lobbied Congress, created important religious statements on the value of wilderness in conjunction with the Wilderness Society, and worked with the World Bank to protect the world's forests.

Krueger also publishes environment-related resources gathered from the pope, the Green Patriarch Bartholomew, and other religious figures. Through his publications and organizations, by drawing on nature-experiences as well as scripture, historical theology, early Christian figures, Orthodox saints, and "prophets" like George Washington Carver and John Muir, Krueger has spread the Christian ecological message to a wide range of Christians from self-identified "tree-hugging, Jesus freak" evangelicals and Pentecostals, to urban Episcopalian psychiatrists, to an array of Catholics, Protestant, and Orthodox Christians.

Laurel Kearns
Matthew Immergut

Further Reading

Krueger, Fred, ed. *A Nature Trail through the Bible: An Ecological Tour of Key Passages*. Santa Rosa, CA: Religious Coalition for Forest Conservation, 2004.

Krueger, Fred, ed. *Why the Ecological Crisis is a Moral Crisis: Pope John Paul II and the Environment*. Santa Rosa, CA: Religious Coalition for Forest Conservation, 2003.

Krueger, Fred, ed. *Orthodox Patriarchs and Bishops Articulate a Theology of Creation*. Santa Rosa, CA: Religious Coalition for Forest Conservation, 2003.

Krueger, Fred, ed. *A Cloud of Witnesses: The Deep Ecological Legacy of Christianity*. Santa Rosa, CA: Religious Coalition for Forest Conservation, 2002 (4th edn).

Nash, Roderick. *The Rights of Nature: A History of Environmental Ethics*. Madison, WI: University of Wisconsin Press, 1989.

See also: Christianity (6b1) – Christian Orthodoxy; Eleventh Commandment Fellowship; Evangelical Environmental Network; North American Conference on Christianity and Ecology [and the] North American Coalition on Religion and Ecology; Religious Campaign for Forest Conservation; Sierra Treks.

Krutch, Joseph Wood (1893–1970)

During the 1950s and 1960s, Joseph Wood Krutch gained recognition as a nature essayist. His best-known books include *The Twelve Seasons, The Desert Year*, and *Voice of the Desert*. These writings marked a vocational shift for Krutch, who had previously distinguished himself as a theater reviewer and a Professor of English at Columbia University. Depicting a profound yet fragile spiritual kinship among living things, they also culminated a personal spiritual pilgrimage.

Krutch was born into a nominally Episcopalian family in Knoxville, Tennessee, in 1893. By his teen years, he was an agnostic with a budding interest in science. This interest flagged during Krutch's undergraduate years at the University of Tennessee because he increasingly sensed a conflict between scientific materialism and the values that Western humanistic traditions upheld as foundations of meaningful existence, such as individuality and free will. He turned to literature as a means of resisting scientific reductionism.

Krutch vigorously defended humanistic values while building his career as an essayist following graduate study at Columbia. In his first book, *The Modern Temper* (1929), Krutch asserted that to affirm the reality of consciousness, morality, and free will was to "live spiritually" in an age when traditional religion had apparently failed. This endeavor seemingly entailed alienation from other beings, as Krutch also wrote there that it was "better to die as men than to live as animals" (Krutch 1956: 169).

Krutch's spiritual vision soon became more expansive. Regular visitors from New York to the Connecticut countryside after 1925, he and his wife settled there in 1932 and became avid observers of animals and landscapes. The region inspired Krutch's first nature book, *The Twelve Seasons* (1949), which introduced his belief in the kinship of life with a recollection of perceiving an inscrutable but unmistakable joyfulness in the songs of frogs on a spring evening. This experience suggested to Krutch that evidence of the kind of mental life he valued exists throughout creation, and that humans and other animals "belong equally to something more inclusive than ourselves" (Krutch 1949: 10).

The Krutchs relocated to Tucson, Arizona in 1952, and most of Krutch's subsequent books treated environments of the American southwest. These works further developed the idea that manifestations of consciousness, emotion, and purposefulness in different creatures form a variegated sacred center in nature, which may redeem a robust sense of human potential.

Though Krutch called his faith "a kind of pantheism," it falls short of pantheism because creatures whose lives appeared unconscious and programmed – notably ants and dandelions – fall outside this sacred center. The prevalence of these creatures underscored for Krutch the tenuousness of mindful qualities and the need for their continual affirmation.

Krutch's faith is an anthropocentric naturalism that identifies the sacred not with nature's otherness or unity, but with parts of nature that sustained a cherished (and culturally specific) vision of humanity. His beliefs parallel some strands of modern naturalistic theology (especially as developed by empirical theologians of the Chicago School), and despite their limitations, present a suggestive contrast to the holistic spirituality of many nature writers.

Paul Wise

Further Reading

Krutch, Joseph Wood. *The Modern Temper: A Study and A Confession*. New York: Harcourt, Brace, and World, 1956 (1929).

Krutch, Joseph Wood. *The Twelve Seasons: A Perpetual Calender for the Country*. New York: William Sloane, 1949.

Margolis, John D. *Joseph Wood Krutch: A Writer's Life*. Knoxville, TN: University of Tennessee Press, 1980.

McClintock, James I. *Nature's Kindred Spirits*. Madison: University of Wisconsin Press, 1994.

See also: Abbey, Edward; Pantheism.

Labyrinth

An ancient and pre-Christian symbol, taking the form of the serpent, spiral, cross, or knot, the labyrinth has recently experienced a resurgence of interest among New Age spiritual groups. Labyrinths are physical and metaphorical, favored by civilizations in Greece, Egypt, India, and Indonesia. They are also a favorite image of modernist writers, particularly philosopher Freidrich Nietzche and Louis Borges. Lima de Freitas notes that, in modern times, the labyrinth represents "the existential dilemmas of modern urban man, who finds himself trapped in a prison-like world and condemned to wander aimlessly therein" (1987: 411). The labyrinth symbolizes a path through which the soul must find its way. In *Geography of the Imagination*, Guy Davenport calls the labyrinth "a life symbol" for the twentieth century.

Labyrinths are found in a variety of physical settings; they are found as stone patterns and drawings in caves, entrenched into hillsides, cut into turf-mazes or trimmed hedges, carved into stone obelisks, and set into the floors of medieval churches and cathedrals. One of the most famous labyrinths is in the floor of Chartres cathedral in France, which has proved to be the basis for a special eponymous design, the Chartrain, a maze of four quadrants, eleven paths, and a center rosette set within a circle. The labyrinth can also be traced to the familiar Celtic knot design. The Hopi of the American southwest use the labyrinth in their Man in the Maze symbol to represent life's journey.

While labyrinths are constructed by humans, they symbolize and explain natural processes that have been celebrated in ritual for centuries: birth, death, fertility, the sunrise and sunset, planting and harvest. They also are tied to female Earth deities, as the center of the labyrinth is a hole, an empty space that is filled when the penitent walks the path. It thus represents the womb.

In his study of maze imagery, Craig Wright points out that there are two basic maze designs: the *multicursal*, those mazes where a choice of path is necessary, and the *unicursal*, those with only a single path leading to the center (2001: 3). Like the cathedrals in which many of the Christian labyrinths are found, the labyrinth itself employs principles of sacred geometry in its construction and connotation. As George Lesser points out, sacred geometry presumes that the universe is created by God as a rational system "and therefore mathematical conception, the highest manifestation of divine wisdom, is imitated, in a mystic way, by the sacred building and its precinct which thus become a reflection of divine order, harmony, and beauty" (1957: 3). Geometric figures, such as the circle, the polygon, and the five-pointed star, are sacred because they refer to mystical numbers and symbolic concepts in numerology. The basic shape of the labyrinth is a circle divided into four quadrants. These represent the cardinal directions north, south, east, and west. In the symbolic cross labyrinth, the vertical axis links the underworld to heaven. As with the cross in traditional Christian iconography, in the labyrinth the cross "reconciles opposed directions and divided drives at its center" (de Freitas 1987: 417). The Christian maze, found primarily in naves of French and Italian medieval churches, was approached and entered from the west. The penitent moves eastward, and the symbolism is potent – east is the dawning of the day, the spiritual rebirth in the faith (Wright 2001: 19). Typically, the Christian labyrinth contains eleven tracks within its circumference, symbolizing "sin, dissonance, transition, and incompleteness" (Wright 2001: 23). "It extends beyond the number of the Commandments," writes Wright, "yet does not attain that of the Apostles or of the months of the year" (2001: 23). The center rosette is often construed to be a symbol of the Virgin Mary, writes Lauren Artress (1995: 58).

The knot shape represents Ariadne's thread and memory. In Greek myth, Ariadne helped Theseus to escape the labyrinth of the Minotaur at Crete. When the thread is knotted, it must be unwound, thus it illustrates the difficulties that must be overcome in the soul's movement toward salvation. The serpent shape, often found on prehistoric rock drawings, is most directly related to pathways and the promise of freedom or release at the end of the journey. The spiral labyrinth illustrates two basic movements, inward and outward. It can be associated with life processes of ingestion and energy. The spiral is also a powerful archetype that represents time, the cycle of the seasons, and the arc of life. Lauren Artress stresses that the spiral is "the whole." Neo-pagan religions, such as Wicca, revere the circle in ritual. Women's dream quests make use of dancing, chanting, dreaming, healing, and blessing inside the circle, often using candles, incense, or flower petals to connect to nature and her ancient and sacred powers.

The introduction to Wiccan teachings composed by Starhawk (Miriam Simos), *Spiral Dance* (1979), takes its name from the ritual clockwise cyclic dance around the perimeter of a sacred circle. Helen Raphael Sands writes that the spiral dance most often associated with the labyrinth is performed in a group in which the dancers link hands. Called "*Tsankonikos*, meaning 'from Tsakonia,' a town in the Peloponnese," the dance is "connected with the labyrinth and *Geranos*, the Crane Dance that Ariadne is said to have taught Theseus on the island of Naxos after their escape from Crete" (Sands 2001: 70). Thus, it is clear from Artress, Starhawk, and Sands that the ancient symbol of the labyrinth has taken on a new life in women's religious practices.

Marguerite Helmers

Further Reading
Artress, Lauren. *Walking a Sacred Path: Rediscovering the Labyrinth as a Spiritual Tool*. New York: Riverhead, 1995.
Davenport, Guy. *Geography of the Imagination*. New York: Pantheon Books, 1992.
de Freitas, Lima. "Labyrinth." *The Encyclopedia of Religion*, vol. 8. Mircea Eliade, ed. New York: Macmillan, 1987, 411–19.
Lesser, George. *Gothic Cathedrals and Sacred Geometry*, 2 vols. London: Alec Tiranti, 1957.
Sands, Helen Raphael. *The Healing Labyrinth: Finding Your Path to Inner Peace*. Hauppauge, NY: Barron's, 2001.
Starhawk. *The Spiral Dance: A Rebirth of the Ancient Religion of the Great Goddess*. San Francisco: Harper & Row, 1979.
Wright, Craig. *The Maze and the Warrior: Symbols in Architecture, Theology, and Music*. Cambridge, MA: Harvard University Press, 2001.
See also: Epic of Evolution; (and adjacent, Epic Ritual); Reclaiming; Spirit and Nature Walking Paths; Starhawk.

Ladakh Buddhism

The harvest lies in golden stacks in the terraced fields. Rooftops are bright orange with apricots drying in the sun. Across the valley, a monastery clings to the side of a mountain. Above, rocky slopes rise to the snows of a glacier. This is Ladakh or "Little Tibet." I first came to this remote region in the Indian Himalayas in 1975. I found a culture so harmonious, so attuned to the needs of people and the environment, that it was unlike anything I had ever known. The Ladakhis exhibited an exceptional sensitivity in managing their environment and a keen awareness of their place in the natural order.

I had never before met people who seemed so emotionally healthy, so secure as the Ladakhis. The reasons are, of course, complex and spring from a whole way of life and worldview. But I am sure that the most important factor was the sense of being part of something much larger than oneself, of being inextricably connected to others and to one's surroundings. The Ladakhis belonged to their place on Earth. They were bonded to that place through intimate daily contact, through knowledge about their immediate environment with its changing seasons, needs and limitations. They were aware of the living context in which they found themselves. The movement of the stars, the sun and moon were familiar rhythms that influenced their daily activities.

This sense of interconnectedness, in large part, emanated from the Ladakhis' Buddhist beliefs and practice. Even today, everything in Ladakh reflects its religious heritage. The landscape is dotted with walls of carved prayer stones and *chortens*, fluttering flags whisper prayers to the winds and always, on some distant height, rise the massive white walls of a monastery. Buddhism has been the traditional religion of the majority of Ladakhis since approximately 200 B.C.E. Today all sects of Tibetan Mahayana Buddhism are represented, under the overall spiritual leadership of His Holiness the Dalai Lama.

The villages where I have lived are Buddhist, but in the capital almost half the population is Muslim. In addition, there is a small group of Christians numbering a few hundred. Relations among these three groups have changed in recent years, but when I arrived in 1975 they all showed profound mutual respect and an easygoing tolerance.

Emptiness and Interdependence
One of the central elements of Buddhism is the philosophy of *sunyata*. The use of the term "emptiness" or "nothingness" to define *sunyata* has led many Westerners to think of Buddhism as nihilistic. Yet, we are not being asked to deny the "existence" of the world, but to alter our perception of it. Tashi Rabgyas, one of Ladakh's leading scholars, explained it to me like this:

> Take any object, like a tree. When you think of a tree, you tend to think of it as a distinct, clearly defined object, and on a certain level it is. But on a more important level, the tree has no independent existence; rather, it dissolves into a web of relationships. The rain that falls on its leaves, the wind that causes it to sway, the soil that supports it – all form a part of the tree. Ultimately, if you think about it, everything in the universe helps make the tree what it is. It cannot be isolated; its nature changes from moment to moment – it is never the same. This is what we mean when we say things are "empty," that they have no independent existence.

It is said that the universe is like an endless river. Its totality, the unity, does not change, yet at the same time it is in constant motion. The river as a whole exists, but you cannot say what it consists of; you cannot stop the

Ladakh Project

In 1975, Helena Norberg-Hodge established the Ladakh Project to help counteract the negative effects of conventional development in Ladakh. She eventually founded the International Society for Ecology and Culture (ISEC), which now has branches in the United States, United Kingdom, Germany and Ladakh. ISEC acts as the parent organization for the Ladakh Project, while also running a number of other programs aimed at promoting locally based alternatives to the global consumer culture.

The Ladakh Project has worked with thousands of Ladakhis in hundreds of villages to help strengthen and rebuild the local economy and cultural self-esteem. ISEC provides Ladakhi leaders with information about the impact of conventional development on other parts of the world while exploring more sustainable patterns of development in Ladakh itself, based on the use of local resources and indigenous knowledge. Genuine information exchange between cultures is part of what Norberg-Hodge calls "counter-development" – countering development myths with accurate information about its impacts.

ISEC's "counter-development" work includes collaborating with a number of Ladakhi organizations, many of which ISEC helped to establish. With the Ladakh Ecological Development Group (LEDG), ISEC set up one of the largest renewable energy projects in the "developing world." Through establishing the Centre for Amchi Medicine and assisting The Amchi Association, ISEC also been helping Ladakh's traditional doctors, or *amchis*, to keep their ancient knowledge alive. ISEC also works closely with the Women's Alliance of Ladakh (WAL), a rural women's organization, which now has over 5000 members from around the region.

During the tourist season ISEC runs daily workshops as part of the Tourist Education Programme. The workshops are focused around a showing of the film *Ancient Futures* (an award-winning film based on the book by Norberg-Hodge) followed by a facilitated discussion. These workshops help tourists to see beyond surface impressions of Ladakh and associate the changes they see in their own communities with the same economic forces that are eroding Ladakhi culture and sustainability. ISEC also sponsors Ladakhi community leaders to come to the West on "Reality Tours," which serve to balance the glamorized image of modern, urban life that is spread through advertising, television and tourism.

ISEC's Ladakh Farm Project offers the opportunity for foreigners of all nationalities to live and work with Ladakhi families for a month during the summer. For participants, the project provides invaluable insights into both the strengths of the traditional culture and the forces threatening to undermine it. For Ladakhis, having foreigners show such interest in their way of life reinforces a sense of pride in their culture, which, because of the widespread images of the Western consumer culture, many now look up upon as primitive and backward.

Similarly, these foreigners often reveal a growing interest in the West in spiritual values which also helps to strengthen Ladakhi self-respect. This work encourages the young people of Ladakh to maintain respect for their own religion, which in turn helps to counteract feelings of alienation and inferiority.

In part because of ISEC's work, a new sense of confidence has emerged in Ladakh and development is now seen in a different light; while in the world outside, the story of Ladakh helps to highlight some of the foundations necessary for a sustainable future for us all.

Helena Norberg-Hodge

---

flow and examine it. Everything is in movement and inextricably intertwined.

Living Religion

In traditional Ladakh, religion permeated all aspects of life, inseparable from art and music, culture and agriculture. People were deeply religious. Yet, from a Western point of view, they appeared strangely casual about it. This apparent paradox struck me particularly strongly in 1976 when his holiness the Dalai Lama came for a visit – the first one in many years. For months before, the sense of anticipation grew. People painted their houses, printed prayer flags, and stitched new clothes, they even dismantled their elaborate headdresses washing the turquoises and corals and refurbishing the felt backing with bright red cloth. It was to be the Great Wheel, or Kalachakra, Initiation, performed on the banks of the Indus. Long before the event, villagers from all over Ladakh started streaming in, some coming by bus or truck, thousands more walking or riding for days to reach the capital.

By the middle of the week-long teaching, the numbers had swelled to forty thousand. The air was charged with intense devotion, and yet amazingly at the same time there was almost a carnival atmosphere. One minute the man in front of me was lost in reverence, his gazed locked on the Dalai Lama; the next he would be laughing at a neighbor's joke; and a while later he seemed to be somewhere else, spinning his prayer wheel almost absent-mindedly. During this religious teaching – for many of those present, the most important event in their lifetime – people came and went, laughing and gossiping. There were picnics and everywhere children – playing, running, calling out to each other.

Attending the ceremonies was a young Frenchman named Mcleod Ganj who had studied Buddhism in Dharamsala, the Dalai Lama's residence in exile. He took his new religion very seriously and was shocked by the Ladakhis. "These people are not serious. I thought they were supposed to be Buddhists," he said scornfully. Even though I knew there was something wrong about his reaction, I was not sure how to respond. I too had grown up in a culture in which religion was separated from the rest of life. It was something a small minority did on Sunday mornings, solemnly and seriously, but that was all.

In Ladakh on the other hand, the entire calendar is shaped by religious beliefs and practices. The day of the full moon, which always falls on the fifteenth of the Tibetan lunar month, is when the Buddha was conceived, attained enlightenment and died. Every other week of the month also has religious significance. The tenth day, for instance, marks the birthday of Guru Rinpoche, who brought Buddhism to Tibet from India. On this day villagers gather in one another's houses to eat and drink while reading religious texts. For *nyeness*, in the first month of the Tibetan calendar, people assemble to fast and meditate together in the *gongpa*, or monastery. On holy days, the family often prints new prayer flags. Cloth in the five holy colours – red, blue, green, yellow and white – is pressed onto inked carved wooden blocks. The new flags are placed on top of the old, which are never removed, but left slowly to disintegrate, spreading their message on the winds.

Every house is filled with reminders of the region's Buddhist heritage. The kitchen stove is decorated with *spallbi*, an elaborate knot with no beginning and no end – the knot of prosperity. It is one of the eight lucky symbols of Tibetan Buddhism, which are often depicted in frescos in the guest room. In addition to the prayer flags strung from corner to corner on every rooftop, there is often a large flagpole in front of the house. This *tarchen* signifies that the house chapel contains all sixteen volumes of the basic Mahayana text, the *Prajnaparamita*, or books of "perfect wisdom." On one of the exterior walls, you may also see a little balcony with three *chortens* (stupas) – one orange, one blue, and one white – symbolizing wisdom, strength and compassion.

Symbols from earlier indigenous religions have also been incorporated into present-day Buddhism. On the roof is a *lhato*, a little chimney of mud topped with a bunch of willow branches and a wooden arrow. This is for the protective deity of the house. It contains a vessel filled with grains, water and precious metals that are changed every New Year to assure continued prosperity.

The Role of Monasteries

On a broad societal level, monasteries provided "social security" for the community, ensuring that no one went hungry. If an individual family found itself with too many mouths to feed, any number of sons – usually the younger ones – became monks. In the monastery they were provided for by the community in exchange for religious services. The process of give and take between the monastery and village sustained a rich cultural and religious tradition.

On a number of occasions throughout the year, the monasteries are home to important ceremonies and festivals involving several days, even weeks of ritual and prayer. During Yarnas, which takes place in summer, the monks stay indoors for up to a month, to avoid unwillingly treading on and killing insects. One of the biggest events of the year is the Cham dance, during which the basic teachings of Vadjrayana Buddhism are enacted in theatrical form and an effigy of the enemy of all people – the ego – is ceremoniously killed. Hundreds, sometimes thousands, of villagers from all around would come to watch the monks dancing in splendidly colourful masks, representing various figures of the Tibetan pantheon, all of which have a deeper symbolic meaning.

Wisdom and Compassion

For me, the most profound expression of Buddhism in traditional Ladakh lay in the more subtle values and attitudes of the people, from the simplest farmer to the most educated monk. The Ladakhi attitude to life – and death – seemed to be based on an intuitive understanding of impermanence and a consequent lack of attachment. Again and again I was struck by this attitude in my Ladakhi friends. Rather than clinging to an idea of how things should be, they seemed blessed with the ability to actively welcome things as they are. The conception of reality was circular, one of constant returning. There was not the sense that this life is the only opportunity. Death is as much a beginning as an end, a passing from one birth to the next, not a final dissolution. Unlike in the West, "good and bad," "fast and slow," "here and there" were not seen as sharply different qualities. In the same way, Ladakhis did not think in terms of fundamental opposition, for instance between mind and body or reason and intuition. Ladakhis experience the world through what they call their *semba*, best translated as a cross between "heart" and "mind." This reflects the Buddhist insistence that Wisdom and Compassion are inseparable.

Modernization

When I first arrived in Leh, the capital of Ladakh, it was a lovely town. It had only two paved streets and a motor vehicle was a rare sight. Cows were the most likely cause of congestion. The air was crystal clear, so clear that the snow peaks on the far side of the valley, 30 kilometres away, seemed close enough to touch. Within five minutes' walk in any direction from the town centre were barley fields, dotted with large farmhouses. Though it was a district capital of 5000 people, Leh had the feeling of a village; everyone greeted each other.

In the last three decades I have watched the capital of Ladakh turn into an urban sprawl. Now the streets are choked with traffic, and the air tastes of diesel fumes. "Housing colonies" of soulless, cement boxes have eaten into the green fields and spread into the dusty desert, punctuated not by trees but by electricity poles. Piles of rusty metal, broken glass and discarded plastic packaging fill the gutters. Billboards advertise cigarettes and powdered milk. The once pristine streams are polluted, the water undrinkable. For the first time, there are homeless people in Ladakh and crime is increasing.

This sudden modernization of Ladakh brought many economic changes which led to an increasingly centralized and urban society, and in which job opportunities became scarce and power was in the hands of a few. Competition for jobs and political representation therefore increased and this started to divide the previously peaceful Ladakhi society. Ethnic friction between local Buddhists and Muslims – unheard of previously – escalated to open violence in 1989.

The influx of Western influence also brought with it glamorized images in the media of a Western consumer culture. The impressions from films and advertisements were of a life with almost infinite wealth and leisure. This one-dimensional view caused young people to feel that their rural lifestyles were shameful and backward. This led to a rejection of their own culture and a desire to imitate the consumer culture.

In traditional Ladakh I knew a society in which there was neither waste nor pollution, a society in which crime was nonexistent, communities were healthy and strong, and a teenage boy was never embarrassed to be gentle and affectionate with his mother or grandmother. As that society begins to break down under the pressures of modernization, the lessons are of relevance far beyond Ladakh itself. We urgently need to steer toward a sustainable balance – a balance between urban and rural, male and female, culture and nature. The Buddhism that has shaped the culture of Ladakh – teachings of interdependence and wisdom and compassion – can help lead us in the right direction toward a more sustainable and harmonious future.

Helena Norberg-Hodge

Further Reading

Badiner, Alan. *Dharma Gaia: A Harvest of Essays in Buddhism and Ecology*. Berkeley: Parallax Press, 1990.

Norberg-Hodge, Helena. *Ancient Futures: Learning from Ladakh*. London: Rider Books: 2000.

Sivaraksa, Sulak. *Seeds of Peace: A Buddhist Vision for Renewing Society*. Berkeley: Parallax Press, 1992.

Watts, Jonathan, Alan Senauke and Santikaro Bhikkhu, eds. *Entering the Realm of Reality: Towards Dhammic Societies*. Bangkok: Suksit Siam, 1997.

See also: Bon (Tibet); Dalai Lama; Tibet and Central Asia.

LaDuke, Winona (1959–)

Winona LaDuke is an enrolled member of the Bear Clan Mississippi Band of the Anishnabeg. Author, environmental activist, and two-time Green Party vice-presidential candidate, all of her numerous roles are directly informed by Anishnabe religion and culture. Hers is a land-based understanding of the world, and her particular land base is that of the forest of the White Earth Reservation in Northeastern Minnesota (USA). From her successful struggle against James Bay's hydro-electric development in the 1980s, to her ongoing reclamation of lost land for White Earth Reservation, LaDuke has become an international voice for indigenous environmental activism.

Born in 1959, in East Los Angeles, to Vincent (a.k.a. Sun Bear) and Betty (Bernstein) LaDuke, she left the west coast to get her Bachelor's degree from Harvard University in Native Economic Development, later receiving a Master's in Rural Development from Antioch College. It was at Harvard, at the age of 18, that she encountered and became active in Native American political activism. She is her father's daughter in terms of her identity and culture; she moved to the White Earth Reservation, where her father was born and raised, in 1981, where she has since remained, and immediately became involved in the community and its struggles. She eventually founded the Honor the Earth Fund, an organization that funds indigenous environmental activism, and the White Earth Land Recovery Project. Sun Bear became a spiritual guru of sorts, attracting a mostly white audience, while receiving criticism from some Native Americans who resented his capitalizing on their sacred ways. Like her father, she serves as a conduit between native and white cultures, most obviously as Green Party Vice-Presidential candidate in 1996 and 2000, and as a representative of indigenous communities around the world to white society. Yet, unlike her father, LaDuke believes that each culture and community must develop its own ways and stay true to them. While not explicit in any criticism of Sun Bear, LaDuke's own philosophy and practices betray a clear deviation from and disapproval of his behavior; for LaDuke, different communities can and should work together yet must always remain distinct.

LaDuke and the Anishinabe see the need for a diversity of perspectives; there is not even a single Native American perspective. To maintain its integrity and power, each community must have its own ways, which must be based on the land on which that community lives. LaDuke's religion and culture are directly related to her activism; she asks: How can a forest culture exist without a forest? As an Anishinabe, she believes activism should be community-based, that is, it should be land-based, a point argued in *All Our Relations: Native Struggles for Land and Life* (1999). As the title indicates, LaDuke and the Anishinabe believe the entire natural world is related to humankind and is animate (i.e., alive and with spirit) and should be treated accordingly.

For LaDuke, indigenous worldviews and ways of life are fundamentally different from the dominant contemporary American worldview. The native worldview asserts the authority of what she calls "Natural Law," which is the highest law, trumping all others. This "Natural Law" is cyclical and dictates a state of balance that results in sustainability, whereas "Industrial Law" is linear and ultimately destructive. In contrast to industrial society's treating of symptoms alone, "Natural Law" advocates a systemic approach that searches out the sources of problems and recognizes the interconnectedness of all things. LaDuke sees the contemporary source of environmental and social problems as industrial culture's insatiable consumption, and works to turn society away from that accumulation-based thought and conquest-driven behavior toward a system of conservation and harmony governed by "Natural Law."

LaDuke is an advocate of decision making based on the teachings of the Six Nations Iroquois Confederacy, which stipulate that all actions should be considered in light of their impact on the seventh generation from now. The influence of this can be found in her own environmental activism and observed in her novel *Last Standing Woman* (1997), a recounting of seven generations of Anishnabeg.

Becky O'Brien

Further Reading

LaDuke, Winona. *All Our Relations: Native Struggles for Land and Life*. Cambridge, MA: South End Press, 1999.

LaDuke, Winona. "Learning from Native Peoples." In Greg Ruggiero and Stuart Sahulka, eds. *The New American Crisis: Radical Analyses of the Problems Facing America Today*. New York: The New Press, 1995, 150–65.

South End Press Collective, ed. *Talking About a Revolution: Interviews*. Cambridge, MA: South End Press, 1998, 67–79.

Taylor, Bron. "Earthen Spirituality or Cultural Genocide: Radical Environmentalism's Appropriation of Native American Spirituality." *Religion* 17 (1997), 183–215.

See also: Anishnabeg Culture; Black Mesa; Devils Tower, *Mato Tipi*, or Bears Lodge; G-O Road; Holy Land in Native North America; Law, Religion, and Native American Lands; Manifest Destiny; The Sacred and the Modern World; Sacred Geography in Native North America.

Lake Pergusa (Sicily)

In the center of the Italian island of Sicily, in a place that was known in antiquity as Sicily's "navel," lies one of the world's most remarkable natural and cultural wonders: Lake Pergusa. A salinated body of water, it has turned deep red approximately every 15 to 20 years during the past century as a part of a dramatic biochemical cleansing process. Its reedy banks also serve as a major resting place for migrating and wintering birds coming from all over Europe.

Hailed in the literature for more than two thousand years as a marvel of flora and fauna, the lake was considered by the Romans to be the mythological spot where the goddess Persephone was abducted into the underworld, and was the site of an important religious center dedicated to the grain deity Demeter and her daughter Persephone during the period of Greco-Roman colonization of the island. Today, Lake Pergusa faces an environmental threat from an auto racetrack that has been built around its entire three-mile perimeter.

Natural History

Located in the Province of Enna, five miles from the mountain town of Enna in a vast grain-growing region of Sicily, Lake Pergusa is one of only two natural lakes that remain on an island that was famed in antiquity for its wetlands. From a geological standpoint, Pergusa's basin is tectonic in origin, meaning that it formed eons ago due to the sudden sinking of the Earth's rock layers. The lake is fed only by rainwater and tricklings coming from the subterranean levels, which carry minerals that make its waters slightly salinated and sulfurous. Italian scientist Sergio Angeletti has noted, "This lake represents a marvelous example in microcosm ... of the formation of the ocean four to five million years ago" (Angeletti in Cimino 1985: 1).

The lake periodically undergoes a remarkable reddening phenomenon due to the presence of a red, sulfur-oxidizing bacteria (*Thiocapsa roseopersicina*) that lives in its waters. During summer months of years in which the sulfur content reaches a critical level, the bacteria proliferate to such an extent that the lake's waters turn either partially or entirely a deep red color. Over a period of several weeks, the bacteria act to reduce the sulfur level; they, in turn, are eaten by a tiny, transparent crustacean, and the lake returns to its normal color. The phenomenon, which has only been documented since the twentieth century, was studied in 1932 by Italian scientist Achille Forti, who dubbed Pergusa "the lake of blood" (Forti 1932: 36–86). Sicilian environmentalists are not sure whether this occurrence is part of the lake's natural cleansing process or a response to environmental distress, therefore it is not known how long the reddening has been taking place.

Lake Pergusa is a major wet zone in central Sicily and an important resting and wintering spot for migratory birds from all over the Mediterranean. The lake is the most important area in Sicily for the wintering of ducks and coots, hosting, on average, approximately 50 percent of the total number of water birds found in all other Sicilian natural lakes and artificial basins. Swans, herons, flamingos, and cranes, are among the many other water species that have made Lake Pergusa their home.

Religious History

The discovery of the archeological site known as Cozzo Matrice, whose name means "Hill of the Mother," has provided abundant evidence that Lake Pergusa was once the location of an important religious center dedicated to female deities going back at least as far as the Bronze Age. This plateau, located less than a quarter of a mile from the lake, has revealed ceramic material dating to as early as 4000 B.C.E., as well as a settlement featuring circular and elliptical huts overlooking the lake, dating to 2500 B.C.E. Such circular kinds of enclosures, which archeologist Marija Gimbutas has noted were constructed throughout Paleolithic and Neolithic Europe for ritual purposes to symbolize the "womb" of the female divinity, suggest that this site was probably sacred to a goddess or goddesses from very early times. A Bronze Age layer (ca. 1700–1300 B.C.E.) has furnished a great deal of cult-related material.

A later Greek layer, dating to the fifth century B.C.E., during the height of the Greek colonization of the island, has revealed the stone remains of a sanctuary and statuettes of the goddess Demeter, or possibly Persephone, as well as other sacred objects. At other villages near the lake – Zagaria, Juculia, and Jacobo – statuettes representing Demeter and Persephone have also been found dating from the sixth to third centuries B.C.E. The religion dedicated to these two goddesses was characterized by elaborate festivals celebrating Sicily's agricultural cycle, particularly as it related to the production of wheat and barley, as well as mystery rites centering on the human seasons of birth, growth, death, and reincarnation. While Demeter was the goddess of growth and abundance, Persephone was a goddess of both budding spring and death/the underworld. Archeologists generally agree that the indigenous Sicilians at Lake Pergusa, and up in the nearby mountain town of Enna, easily adopted this Greek religion because it probably resembled their own native tradition.

In antiquity, Lake Pergusa was only one of many craters of water fed by underground streams that were a unique part of the Sicilian landscape. Regarded with fascination, such craters were associated with the underworld. The religious connection between Lake Pergusa and the nether realms is particularly strong in the work of Ovid, who, writing in the first century during the period of Roman occupation of the island, named it as the precise place where the goddess Persephone (the Roman Proserpina) was separated from her mother, Demeter (the Roman Ceres), abducted by Hades (the Roman Pluto and lord of the underworld), and taken to his subterranean abode, where she became his bride.

In *The Metamorphoses*, Ovid further described Lake Pergusa as a remarkable place filled to profusion with water birds and wildly blooming flowers. The historical veracity of his description is confirmed by Enna's historian Enrico Sinicropi, who as recently as the 1950s similarly described the lake as "an Eden ... part of a powerfully enchanted panorama where dream is easily confused with reality" (Sinicropi 1958: 72).

Many of Lake Pergusa's natural characteristics – its subterranean streams, water birds, and flowers – undoubtedly had deep religious significance for the ancient dwellers of Sicily, and provide clues as to why Lake Pergusa was probably considered a sacred spot associated with female divinity and the underworld from very early times. The water bird, in its various species, was considered an epiphany of female divinity going back to the Paleolithic and Neolithic periods all over the world. Flowers have also long been associated with the sacred feminine. Moreover, if the lake had been turning red in antiquity, it most likely would have been seen as a living manifestation of the "menstruation" of the female deity, much as appearances of red in nature have been perceived the world over from time immemorial. This element may have led to the lake's association with Persephone, a goddess also of young womanhood and menarche, or first menstruation.

Furthermore, sulfur, one of the minerals in the lake's waters, was considered by the Greeks to be a magical substance associated with the underworld that would drive away the spirits of disease. Sicilian commentator Francesco Potenza Lauria, writing in 1858, noted that Pergusa's waters had many medicinal qualities and could be used to treat afflictions such as hemorrhoids, rheumatism, and skin lesions. Since antiquity, sulfurous bodies of water all over the world have been bathed in and ingested by sick people to treat a host of maladies. One can therefore imagine that Lake Pergusa was similarly used as a pilgrimage site for healing and healing-related rituals.

Environmental History

Today, Lake Pergusa hardly resembles the Eden it once was. In 1957, the Province of Enna began constructing an auto racetrack, known as the Autodrome, around the lake's entire perimeter. Such a project violated laws prohibiting construction so close to a body of water. The concrete and asphalt barrier of the structure prevents the lake from expanding and contracting naturally.

Additionally, waters from the rock layers that would otherwise go to fill the lake basin are continually being drained by two large wells that were built by local authorities in 1963, as well as numerous wells from private houses that have been illegally constructed around the lake in the last several decades. The lake has progressively become filled with sediment, vegetative residue, and polluting run-off from the Autodrome. Every year, it continues to dry up. Before 1860, its maximum depth was approximately twenty-one feet; today it is less than three. Its perimeter, which measured five miles at the beginning of the nineteenth century, is now less than three. Lake Pergusa is disappearing.

The wildlife around the lake is also in decline. Pollution, along with hunting and fishing, have resulted in the profound diminution of the populations of aquatic birds that nest there, as well as most of the species of fish that once filled its waters. Many of the species once found in and around the lake have disappeared.

A crusade to save Lake Pergusa began in 1980, when Maria Cimino, a Sicilian native and long-time resident of Enna, founded the Enna chapter of the World Wildlife Fund. Cimino has been working tirelessly to see that the lake is restored and that the Autodrome is removed from its banks, despite political resistance from the racetrack's promoters, who include local political decision-makers and – many citizens privately contend – those involved in organized crime. She has received anonymous phone calls threatening her with death unless she ceases her environmental activism, and has been the subject of unflattering graffiti on public walls.

Cimino successfully campaigned to have hunting prohibited at the lake and, in 1991, to have the lake and its environs declared a "natural reserve" of the highest status. However, for every victory she and a handful of environmental allies have achieved, there have been new setbacks. For example, in 1995, the regional government of Enna downgraded the status of the reserve from "total" to "special" in order to bypass certain laws. Illegal activity involving building around the lake has continued to be authorized by local politicians, and the regional Minister of the Environment has frequently neglected to intervene, despite protest by activists. Proposals that Cimino has submitted suggesting activities and projects for turning Lake Pergusa into an eco-tourist attraction have been ignored.

"I believe that Lake Pergusa is an immensely sacred place," Cimino said to reporter Sylvia Poggioli, in a story on Lake Pergusa that ran on America's National Public Radio in March 2001. Cimino herself is a practicing Buddhist, as are several other activists working to save the lake. This small group has conducted several *Sur Ngo* ceremonies – Tibetan Buddhist offerings to the local spirits – on behalf of the lake over the past several years. Since 1996, a growing number of Americans of Sicilian descent who are involved in the neo-pagan and women's spirituality movements have become interested in the lake as a sacred locale, as well, and have similarly conducted prayers for the lake's survival both on site and at various places in the United States. Among these individuals are Italian Americans who practice "stregoneria," or Italian witchcraft, which many claim to be a survival of Italy's pre-Christian religions dedicated to Demeter, Persephone, and other Greco-Roman deities. One American scholar, Marguerite Rigoglioso, has organized an activist campaign on the lake's behalf in the United States and has created a website to support the environmental effort.

Meanwhile, Cimino has persisted in her activism. In 2001, she created a "Scientific-Technical Committee to Save Lake Pergusa," which includes experts from many disciplines whose expertise could be applied to an eventual restoration project. The World Wildlife Fund Enna has submitted a request to the European Community to provide international funds for the lake's restoration, and Cimino's committee has solicited proposals from the Italian and international scientific and technical communities for projects to remove the racetrack and restore the lake basin and its vegetation. The committee is now seeking government approval and public and private funding to enact these projects.

The total desiccation of Lake Pergusa would be an environmental catastrophe for an agriculturally important island that, in the past two centuries, has already experienced the loss of many of its lakes, rivers, and springs – as well as much of its rainfall – due to deforestation. As Pergusa continues to shrink, the most important event taking place at the Autodrome may well be the race against time. Meanwhile, Persephone's sacred lake, which may well be claimed in part by the Mafia, serves as a striking living metaphor for the "abduction" of nature at the hands of the contemporary "underworld."

Marguerite Rigoglioso

Further Reading

Cimino, Maria. "Che cos'e' il Lago di Pergusa" (What is Lake Pergusa?). Report presented to the Assessore Regional al Territorio e Ambiente, Enna, Sicily, 5 March 1985.

Finley, M.I. *A History of Sicily: Ancient Sicily to the Arab Conquest*. London: Chatto & Windus, 1968.

Forti, Achille. "Il lago di sangue a Pergusa in Sicilia e la prima piaga d'Egitto." *Il Naturalista Siciliano* 8 (1932) 36–86.

Gimbutas, Marija. *Civilization of the Goddess*. San Francisco: HarperSanFrancisco, 1991.

Gimbutas, Marija. *Language of the Goddess*. San Francisco: HarperSanFrancisco, 1989.

Grahn, Judy. *Blood, Bread and Roses: How Menstruation Created the World*. Boston: Beacon Press, 1993.

Kingsley, Peter. *Ancient Philosophy, Mystery, and Magic: Empedocles and the Pythagorean Tradition*. Oxford: Clarendon Press, 1995.

Ovid. *The Metamorphoses*. Mary M. Innes, tr. Middlesex, England: Penguin Books, 1955 (1970).

Rigoglioso, Marguerite. *Mysticism, Mother Worship, and Misogyny in the Navel of Sicily: A Spiritual History of Enna, Lake Pergusa, Demeter, and Persephone*. Ann Arbor, MI: Bell & Howard Information and Learning, 2001.

Sinicropi, Enrico. *Enna nella stora nell'arte e nella vita*. Palermo: Antonio Renna, 1958.

See also: Gimbutas, Marija; Greco-Roman World; Ovid's Metamorphoses; Roman Natural Religion; Sacred Space/Place.

Lakota

The Lakota, (known historically as the Teton, Sioux and Dakota) are composed of seven tribes: Oglala (They Scatter Their Own), Sicangu (Burned Thighs, also know as Brule), Oohenunpa (Two Kettles), Itazipco (Sans Acrs, Without Bows), Hunkpapa (End of the Camp Circle), Sihasapa (Blackfeet), and Mnicowojou (Planters by the Water). As they moved west out of Minnesota, they became nomadic hunter-gatherers whose resource base included a large number of game animals, particularly the buffalo, but also elk, deer, and other mammals, as well as seeds, fruits, roots, and tubers. They also traded or raided for agricultural products such as corn and squash with the native peoples to the east. The appropriation of the horse after European incursion to the Americas extended their geographical range and increased their food supply. Rifles increased successful hunting of fur-bearing mammals and allowed the Lakota to engage in the fur trade as early as the second half of the eighteenth century. This trade expanded as late as the 1850s.

Anthropology and Lakota oral tradition provide a variety of explanations for the origins of the Lakota and their geographical location on the Plains. According to Lakota oral history, the Lakota emerged from under the Earth in the Black Hills, the spiritual center of their universe, and were the first people in existence. The Black Hills, along with other locations, are therefore part of a sacred geography that encodes Lakota oral and written history and to which important pilgrimages continue to be made.

According to archeology, linguistics and ethnohistory, the Lakota, not yet differentiated into their current political configuration, came to the western Plains from what is now southern Wisconsin, southeastern Minnesota, and northeastern Iowa. They migrated to the Plains by the latter 1700s. The western migration of the Lakota was a response to European immigration that pushed tribes such as the Anishnabe (Ojibwa) further west as well as an attraction to abundant game, especially the buffalo, a key spiritual and nutritional resource with which they have a special relationship. The decline of buffalo numbers, as well as of other game and vegetal resources, was due to overhunting, deliberate destruction of food resources to restrict the movement of the Lakota and other Plains groups, and disruption of habitat and loss of grazing land through European immigration and then settlement.

This decline was apparent by the 1840s, and the buffalo all but disappeared from the Western plains by the time of the last hunt in 1883. At the same time the United States began restricting the Lakota to reservations in violation of earlier treaty agreements. Lakota lands were further diminished through government legislation (the Allotment Act), which assigned specific amounts of land to individual Lakota and sold off "surplus" lands. This policy continued up until the 1930s.

The Lakota have no word for religion. Belief in and interaction with the sacred are not restricted to certain times, places, or activities, in contrast to Western belief systems in which sacred and profane are important binary oppositions. The Lakota held and continue to hold that all is sacred (wakan), although certain objects, activities, and even persons are imbued with more of this sacrality than others. This sacrality can also be sought and obtained by such means as prayer, fasting, self-sacrifice, and generosity. Thus, all of nature is sacred, while certain places, events, and relationships may be more sacred than others. Thus many contemporary Americans see the world in terms of sacred times and non-sacred times and attempt to draw a careful distinction between Church and state while Lakota do not make these divisions. To express these different worldviews, some Lakota say that Whites have "religion" while Lakota have "spirituality."

The Lakota believed and continue to believe that maintaining moral bounds, expressed as doing things "in a good way" is key to success in hunting and in all of life's endeavors. The Lakota did not and do not live in a world of total ecological harmony or mystical participation with all beings: rather they seek balance in the world through reciprocity. At the same time the Lakota remain highly pragmatic in determining causes for disasters in the world, such as the near-extinction of the buffalo, and seek remedies that will serve the needs of future generations.

According to Lakota oral history, the Lakota were granted their spiritual and social organization from a sacred person, the White Buffalo Calf Woman, who gave the people, at a time of starvation, the sacred pipe along with a promise to teach them the rituals and morality required for living as a united group. This pipe links the Lakota to the buffalo as generous relatives who would give their very lives to sustain their kin. The Lakota's buffalo relatives would express familial generosity by providing food and many other useful products.

Religious revelation through personal quest, dreams, and visions remains an important part of this highly charismatic belief system. Thus Lakota spirituality is not a static set of dogma and precise rituals, locked in a past that can only be duplicated. Rather, it is a dynamic belief system, respectful of and linked to past practices but highly adaptive in addressing contemporary needs. Spiritual leadership comes through the spiritual and life experiences of individuals who take up these roles for the good of the community. Their authority is affirmed by their success in prayer, their good lives, and the allegiance of others who also seek the "wakan" (holy) through their leadership. While the belief system is unified by a common set of rituals and key symbols, there is freedom for individual variation and innovation, always monitored by elder spiritual leaders and general participants.

The key metaphor for Lakota culture is kinship or relatedness. Thus the term "to pray" is also the term used to address someone as a relative. The Lakota see their relationship to their relatives, whether through blood, marriage, or adoption as a sacred responsibility. This kinship extends not just to humans but, most importantly, to the entire universe. Ritually, the Lakota re-create the sacred cosmos that is coterminous with the natural and supernatural world through marking out and praying toward the cardinal directions, the heavens and grandmother Earth (unci maka). Colored flags and the arrangement of participants in a circle make physical this cosmic map. Rituals call on "wakan" entities to help the participants in various tasks and trials. Voluntary suffering and flesh offerings are offered in exchange for this divine patronage. Lakota stress that spirituality should not be used to enhance one's own prestige. Rather, spirituality and ritual should benefit relatives, and indeed the entire universe. One frequently hears prayers for the protection of creation, the cessation of pollution, the survival of endangered species, peace in troubled areas of the world, and harmony in the universe. Lakota will also frequently stress that all peoples pray to the same God, and, while maintaining their distinctive beliefs and rituals, also see a unity of all spiritual traditions expressed in their own spiritual hospitality. Lakota prayers are ended with "Mitakuye Oyasin," a prayer for "all my relatives," which includes the cosmos.

Lakota do not treat these religious aspirations as poetic spiritual expressions. Spiritual commitment must be carried out through action. They disdain outsiders who come to the reservation to engage in romantic spiritual escapism, because such outsiders are not enveloped in the Lakota kinship network sewn together by complex ceremonial and practical obligations and exchanges.

"Ecology" is a relatively recent formulation that does not appear as a social and spiritual movement in the early descriptions and transcriptions of Lakota beliefs as such. Throughout their history and especially during the period of White contact, the Lakota were certainly and acutely aware of issues now labeled as ecological. Some of the issues they faced were conservation of faunal and floral resources, and, with the coming of Whites, new catastrophic diseases, diminution of their land base, reacquisition of resources such as water, timber and land, preservation of spiritual resources, and care for a rapidly increasing population.

The Lakota recognize that their beliefs and rituals have diffused to other native and non-native groups. In contemporary discussions of their own culture, Lakota move between the poles of universalism and particularism in dealing with the spread of their beliefs. For example, the four colors used in rituals to symbolize and mark out the four directions of the universe are also interpreted today to represent the four "races" of humanity: red, white, yellow and black. At the same time there is lively debate over how far non-Lakota and especially non-Indians should enter into the ritual life of the Lakota. Universalists argue that because the four colors are included in a sun dance or a sweatlodge or a yuwipi all people must be welcome; others hold that these "ways" were given particularly to the Lakota and can only properly be used by the Lakota. Particularists point to numerous examples of exploitation of Lakota rituals for money or individual prestige. Between the poles of exclusion and inclusion, particularist and universalist, there is a gradient: many Lakota welcome non-Indians provided they are respectful, do not try to assume leadership roles or try to control the ceremonies, and do not begin conducting the ceremonies on their own. Some Lakota will give ceremonial leadership for specific rituals to non-Indians: others maintain a total prohibition of non-Indian involvement, excluding even the observation of spiritual events. Essential for participating in Lakota ceremonies are the relationships one has developed with the praying community. When one is welcomed at a ceremony, it is because of relationships that have already been established and which all parties wish to be strengthened.

Lakota spirituality is not restricted to interaction with spiritual beings or the classic rituals so well known to the outside world: sun dance, sweatlodge, vision quest, yuwipi, keeping of the soul, making relatives, lowanpi, throwing of the ball, buffalo sing. Belief extends to medicinal practices that combine practical cures with spiritual inspiration, to hunting, and even to warfare. Interaction with family members is a sacred duty; children, the elderly, and the disabled are traditionally highly sacred personages and are to be reverently cared for. Treaties, especially the Fort Laramie Treaty of 1868 are considered sacred, as are certain geographical locations. The illegal confiscation of the Black Hills cannot be compensated for by the U.S. government's offer of a monetary settlement; contemporary Lakota are to regain territory that is rightfully theirs, not because of its real-estate value but because of its spiritual meaning.

Participation in Lakota spirituality is increasing in visibility and number of participants as more and more

Lakota leave Christian denominations to return to Lakota practices or publicly combine both Lakota and Christian beliefs. The complex set of Lakota beliefs generally referred to as "traditional" stresses the connectedness of all reality and the importance of respect and generosity in dealing with a universe of relatives and relationships. At the same time, contemporary Lakota have inherited a daunting set of challenges including the traumatic legacy of nineteenth-century warfare; the loss of land and subsequent restriction to diminished reservation areas; forced assimilation and loss of language promoted by Church and state; and an increased population suffering from poverty, poor diet, new diseases, and alcoholism, with very little healthcare.

To address such challenges, Lakota spirituality incorporates not only rituals and prayer but also legal action by tribal agencies and grassroots groups dealing with sovereignty, environmental protection, forestry, water purity, and restoration of buffalo herds on reservation lands. Protests, political action, and alliances with individuals and groups who can assist them, provide an ongoing reinvigoration of Lakota spirituality and culture (elements which Lakota do not separate) on its path to wholeness. Today, the spiritual force of Lakota traditional practice combines with the pursuit of sound ecological practice to produce a sense of connectedness with and responsibility to a universe of interrelationships that should be honored and fulfilled with generosity. The goal of these interrelationships is summed up by the Lakota term Wolakota: to be in right relationship with all of creation. Through relationship the Lakota pursue a future of ecological integrity that is, at root, a spiritual endeavor to care for all relatives with generosity.

Mitauye Oyasin

Raymond A. Bucko

Further Reading

Deloria, Vine, Jr. *Red Earth, White Lies: Native Americans and the Myth of Scientific Fact.* New York: Scribner, 1995.

DeMallie, Raymond J. "Sioux until 1850." In Raymond J. DeMallie, ed. *Handbook of North American Indians: Plains Volume*, vol. 13. Washington, D.C.: Smithsonian Institution, 2001, 718–60.

DeMallie, Raymond J. "Teton." In Raymond J DeMallie, ed. *Handbook of North American Indians: Plains Volume* vol. 13. Washington, D.C.: Smithsonian Institution, 2001, 794–820.

DeMallie, Raymond J., Jr. and Douglas R. Parks, eds. *Sioux Indian Religion: Tradition and Innovation.* Norman: University of Oklahoma Press, 1987.

Ostler, Jeffrey. " 'They Regard Their Passing as Wakan': Interpreting Western Sioux Explanations for the Bison's Decline." *Western Historical Quarterly* 30:4 (1999), 475–98.

Powers, William K. *Oglala Religion.* Lincoln: University of Nebraska Press, 1975.

Swagerty, William R. "History of the United States Plains Until 1850." In Raymond DeMallie, ed. *Handbook of North American Indians*, vol. 13. William Sturtevant, ed. Washington, D.C.: Smithsonian Institution, 2001, 256–79.

Wedel, Waldo R. and George Frison. "Environment and Subsistence." In Raymond J. DeMallie, ed. *Handbook of North American Indians*, vol. 13. Washington, D.C.: Smithsonian Institution, 2001, 44–60.

See also: Bison Restoration and Native American Traditions; Black Elk; Indigenous Environmental Network; Indra's Net; Holy Land in Native North America; Lakota Sun Dance.

Lakota Sun Dance

Lakota people gathering for the annual Sun Dance of the Wakpamni Lake community on Pine Ridge Reservation in South Dakota would not be likely to say the words "nature," "environment," or "ecology." These words would be perceived as terms belonging to the discourse of the dominant culture, and it would be routine for traditional Lakota people to suspect that such words would be employed to extend and maintain colonizing policies toward indigenous peoples and their plant and animal relatives. While Sun Dancers at Wakpamni clearly recognize that they are participating in a ceremony once belonging to nineteenth-century ancestors who lived as prosperous buffalo hunters on the northern plains, their participation in the Wakpamni Lake Sun Dance is no nostalgia trip, no reenactment of a once-glorious past. It is an intense engagement with the present in which their ancestral relatives such as the eagle nation and buffalo nation, along with the rock people and tree people, are fully interactive with the human community gathered for this renewal of life's fundamental relationships. These contemporary-traditional Lakota people also know implicitly that the utilitarian ethos of the dominant culture, which is founded on the paired belief in individualist subjectivity and an objectified "natural" world, represents an outlook that is decidedly antithetical to the ceremonial meaning of Sun Dance. Therefore, Sun Dancing is an act of cultural and political resistance to the aggressive force of the dominant culture in the present moment, and it represents continuity with many past moments of such resistance.

The dominant North American culture perceives Lakota Sun Dancing as so utterly "other" that it serves as a primary signifier of an indigenous difference that is both exotically fascinating and fundamentally threatening.

Both Canadian and United States governments took legal steps to suppress Sun Dancing in the late nineteenth century, and full liberty to practice Lakota Sun Dancing was not regained until after the mid-twentieth century. Sun Dance represents the clash between the colonizing ("civilizing") interests of European-derived cultures bent on conquest of the "land" and the holistic outlook of indigenous peoples focused on keeping kinship with their plant and animal relatives. The extraordinary revival of Lakota Sun Dancing since the 1960s indicates that this conflict between two lifeways is far from over.

Suppression of the Sun Dance in the 1880s and opposition to its renewal in the 1960s centered on the practice of piercing as ethically objectionable to the dominant culture – it was considered barbaric. Piercing is performed most commonly on the flesh of the upper chest or of the upper back of male dancers and wooden or bone skewers are inserted through the pierced flesh. Thongs at the end of a rope are attached to the skewers and the rope is connected to the central tree (when piercing the chest) or to one or more buffalo skulls (when piercing the back). To dance until the flesh gives way is understood by the dancers to be a voluntary act by which a ritual reciprocity with the spiritual powers of the universe is carried through so that life-enhancing benefit ensues for the entire kinship system of the dancers – recognizing that such a system extends eventually to the whole created order. Lakota holy men told James R. Walker in 1896 that female dancers were not pierced. "A man or a woman or a child may dance. But for women and children the dance is done differently. They are not attached to . . . the pole as men are" (Walker 1991: 181). Contemporary female dancers often participate in the reciprocity of piercing by making a "flesh offering" of very small slices of skin taken from the upper arms and ritually presented at the sacred tree in the center.

The piercing of Sun Dancers dramatizes the "otherness" of the Sun Dance, and this "otherness" both attracts outsiders who wish to appropriate an exotic ritual for their own subjective adventures, and offends those for whom religion and ethics are cultural categories of European origin and for whom praying is not a matter of dancing and piercing but of thoughts and rhetoric. The implicit parallelism between the piercing of Sun Dancers and the crucifixion of Jesus as paired instances of vicarious suffering was apparent to nineteenth-century Lakota people, but abhorrent to the culture-bearers of a European Christianity representing the leading edge of "civilizational progress."

The ethical character of piercing derives from a traditional understanding of hunting as a ritual transaction between related "peoples." The buffalo people give away their lives to their relatives, the hunters, and the hunters are obligated to emulate their relatives, the buffalo people, with similar acts of generosity, including the ritual reciprocities enacted in the annual Sun Dance. The voluntary flesh-and-blood sacrifice of buffalo relatives is ritually acknowledged by the voluntary flesh-and-blood sacrifice of the Sun Dancers – the wounding of the piercing is a kind of death and the release from the skewers brings regenerative power to the community. Chased-by-Bears, a leader of nineteenth-century Lakota Sun Dances, told Frances Densmore in 1911, "A man's body is his own, and when he gives his body or his flesh he is giving the only thing which really belongs to him" (in Densmore 1992: 96). Environmental ethics might be construed to be truly compatible with an ethic of piercing that keeps kinship with all the relatives of the environing world. Nevertheless, traditional Lakota people can readily suspect that the acquisitive voice of the dominant culture with its concern about strategies to preserve its dominance may govern even environmental discourse in the form of analyses, calculations, and predictions which are subjective projections by humans regarding orders of being perceived as dependent and subordinate. Unless this voice is perceived by Sun Dancers as the language of kinship or give-away, it is not understood to be truly ethical. To become ethical it must acknowledge that plant and animal relatives have their own moral voice, and this implies an awareness of the sacredness of such kinship relations and a willing participation in the ritual acts which give embodied expression to this awareness and which sustain the interpersonal bonds of those kinship relations on a cosmic scale.

The ethics of kinship expressed in the give-away of piercing is crucially connected to the noetic dimension of visions and dreams. The classic instance of a Lakota dream-vision is related by Nicholas Black Elk to John Neihardt who published it in *Black Elk Speaks* in 1932. Black Elk's "great vision" came to him at age nine in connection with an illness. His dream-vision takes the form of a shamanic journey to a sky world above the mundane world of earthly existence. Dreams and visions are generically characterized by the power of metamorphosis through which beings and elements in the visionary experience change form in dramatic and revelatory ways. Black Elk's dream-vision is stocked with extraordinary metamorphoses. In an early episode he meets six "grandfathers" who embody the powers of the four quarters of the world along with sky above and Earth below. Each of the six instructs Black Elk, gives him gifts of power, and undergoes metamorphosis into an animal form – the sixth changing into a likeness of Black Elk himself.

In one of his dream-vision episodes, Black Elk describes how the camp of people he is leading transforms into "buffalo and elk and even fowls of the air" (in DeMallie 1984: 126). In an aside to his narrative, Black Elk explains to Neihardt that this metamorphosis means "that the Indian generations have dreams and are like unto the animals of this world. Some have visions about elks, birds, and even gophers or eagles. People will be like the animals – take the animals' virtues and strengths" (1984: 127). Not only Lakota persons but all humans dream, and the universality of dreaming consciousness with its characteristic signature of metamorphosis fosters the recognition that our kinship relations extend well beyond the strictly human community. Lakota Sun Dancers understand that Sun Dancing engages these kinship reciprocities and opens the door of dreaming consciousness to a psychic depth beyond the merely human.

Many traditional Lakota people are concerned about the diffusion of their Sun Dance to locations beyond their reservations, so that the ceremony is being held in contexts outside the rootedness of a specific Lakota community. Another concern is the inclusion of people whose ancestry and cultural identity is European-derived. Such persons are politely but routinely excluded from becoming Sun Dancers at the Wakpamni Lake Sun Dance, whereas persons with indigenous ancestry from other North American peoples are readily accepted into the ceremony as Sun Dancers. These distinctions point to the way Sun Dance continues to sustain Lakota identity. Despite the end of buffalo hunting by the 1880s and the federal prohibitions instituted at that time, Sun Dance was such a critical factor for Lakota survival that it was maintained clandestinely for most of a century. Today, Sun Dancers continue to dance in the real world of kinship relations and of give-away reciprocities, so that the sacred relatedness of all the powers in the world is renewed. Moreover, Sun Dancing is a way of resisting the unreality of the world of commerce, industrial pollution, commodification of plant and animal relatives, and corporate claims of responsible environmentalism. To permit persons of the dominant culture to participate as dancers in this ceremony would confuse the resistance character of Sun Dance and dilute its clarity as a cultural signifier.

Dominant-culture persons are not rejected altogether from the ceremony. At the Wakpamni Lake Sun Dance there are a number of roles that are open to male and female persons of European ancestry, including ritual roles. One of these is the handling and smoking of the sacred pipe handed out to the community from the dancers at intervals throughout the ceremony and which signifies the dancer-generated benefit being given away to the larger kinship circle. Another is the opportunity to make a "flesh offering" at the time that community members who are not dancers may offer sacrifice of themselves in the same form as with female dancers which involves small slices of skin taken from the upper arms and presented at the sacred tree in the center. In these ways, the universal scope of kinship relations expressed by the Sun Dance is ritually extended even to dominant-culture persons whose identity is potentially destructive for the kinship relations being renewed.

In an attempt to represent here the voice of Lakota Sun Dancers, it should be noted that they would, on grounds of sound historical precedent, suspect that the discourse operative in the *Encyclopedia of Religion and Nature* will more likely resemble that of the dominant culture than that of an indigenous culture. It follows from this assumption that a voice representing Sun Dance may be expected to justify in these pages its relevance to the environmental issues of said discourse. A suitable rejoinder to this expectation comes from Black Elk in another of his side comments to John Neihardt in 1931.

They [the white men] couldn't get along with us and they did not look after us. The birds and other animals are the only race that we really get along with. We, [the] Indian race, and the beings on this Earth – the buffalo, elk, and birds in the air – they are just like relatives to us and we get along fine with them, for we get our power from them and from them we live. The white people came on this continent and put us Indians in a fence and they put another fence somewhere else and put our game into it. When the buffalo and elk are gone, the Great Spirit will look upon the whites for this and perhaps something will happen (in DeMallie 1984: 127).

Traditional Lakota people would likely conclude that the dominant culture's addiction to a materialist trajectory featuring economic "growth" signifies a profound religious emptiness. Their prescription for this condition, following the religious and ethical logic of Sun Dance, would be a turning to new (or old) dreams and to give-away dances in the hope of recovering kinship relations and the renewal of the world.

Dale Stover

Further Reading

DeMallie, Raymond J. *The Sixth Grandfather: Black Elk's Teachings Given to John G. Neihardt.* Lincoln: University of Nebraska Press, 1984.

Densmore, Frances. *Teton Sioux Music and Culture.* Lincoln: University of Nebraska Press, 1992.

Mails, Thomas E. *Sundancing at Rosebud and Pine Ridge.* Sioux Falls, SD: Center for Western Studies, 1978.

Stover, Dale. "Postcolonial Sun Dancing at Wakpamni Lake." *Journal of the American Academy of Religion* 69:4 (2001), 817–36.

Walker, James R. *Lakota Belief and Ritual.* Raymond J. DeMallie and Elaine A. Jahner, eds. Lincoln: University of Nebraska Press, 1991.

See also: Dance; Lakota; Black Elk; Devils Tower, *Mato Tipi*, or Bears Lodge; Ghost Dance; Sun Worship.

Land Institute

For more than 25 years, the Land Institute has pioneered research in sustainable agriculture, attempting to address (as their publications like to say) the problem *of* agriculture, as opposed to the problems *in* agriculture. That is to say, the Land Institute has been dedicated to the question of how to switch from an agriculture based upon extraction of the Earth's resources to an agriculture based upon preserving those resources.

Co-founded by Wes and Dana Jackson in 1976, the Land Institute's original research project is located on 28 acres of native Kansas prairie, near the city of Salina. Various areas of research include an internship program, a 150-acre Sunshine Farm project neighboring the Land's headquarters, a Rural Community Studies Project at Matfield Green (120 miles southeast of Salina), the annual Prairie Festival, as well as the institute's original and ongoing research in Natural Systems Agriculture. Recent grants in the 1990s have allowed the Land institute to become the center for a Natural Systems Agriculture project that will have worldwide reach.

Natural Systems Agriculture (NAS) looks to the "wisdom of nature" to provide clues for developing a sustainable form of agriculture. On the Kansas prairie, NAS attempts to mimic the natural polyculture of perennial grasses by cultivating plots of perennial grains that have been bred to produce seed yields comparable to monocultural annuals such as wheat and corn. This polycultural approach preserves the prairie ecosystem: it supplies its own nitrogen, eliminating the need to add petroleum-based fertilizers; it preserves moisture in the soil; it minimizes vulnerability to damage caused by insects and disease, eliminating harmful chemical controls; and it reduces soil erosion. In a word, NSA is a paradigm shift that moves away from the model of extractive economy to that of cooperation with and imitation of nature's wisdom. As the Land's website says (pun surely intended), "Natural Systems Agriculture would leave the ground unplowed for years and use few or no chemicals, solving many environmental problems at their root."

The goal of the Sunshine Farm is to run a productive farm, as much as possible, on the sun's energy. This is done by producing the energy needed to run the farm (e.g., electricity, fuel for tractors, and fertilizers), using wind, bio-diesel, and other solar energy sources on the farm itself, rather than importing energy produced by an extractive economy. One interesting dimension of this experiment is that the farm carefully monitors the amount of energy that goes into and out of the land in order to provide a truer accounting of the farm's environmental and economic impacts.

The Rural Community Studies program is conducted at Mattfield Green, a small town in tall-grass prairie country of Chase County, Kansas. Using a refurbished elementary school, the Institute hosts meetings and conferences to explore "ecological community accounting" that monitors the extent of reliance upon an extractive economy versus reliance upon an ecologically sustainable economy. In addition, the Rural Community Studies program has also developed "place-based" curricula that are being implemented in a consortium of three school districts, involving over 180 teachers and 2000 students.

The annual Prairie Festival is a public celebration and educational outreach event that invites scientists, environmentalists, philosophers, religionists, artists, and writers, to reflect upon and celebrate the meaning of the prairie in its agricultural, cultural, and spiritual dimensions. Many visitors camp at the Land Institute for the weekend and attend lectures, workshops, performances, dances, and an evening bonfire where all are invited to "meet, visit, and make music" together.

The underlying vision of the Land Institute can be found in its mission statement, which says in part,

> When people, land, and community are as one, all three members prosper . . . By consulting Nature as the source and measure of that membership, The Land Institute seeks to develop an agriculture that will save soil . . . while promoting a community life . . .

Consciously shaped by the religious ideals of people like Aldo Leopold, E.F. Schumacher, and Wendell Berry, the Land Institute's vision is one of the mutual interrelatedness of humanity and nature that affirms the intrinsic value of the ecosystem and human responsibility to learn from, honor, and preserve that value. Significantly, the Land Institute has been a major model and inspiration for other bioregional movements and their attendant spiritualities.

Paul Custodio Bube

Further Reading

Jackson, Wes, Wendell Berry and Bruce Colman, eds. *Man and the Environment; New Roots for Agriculture, Meeting the Expectations of the Land.* San Francisco: Friends of the Earth, 1980.

The Land Report (published three times a year by The Land Institute).

See also: Back to the Land Movements; Berry, Wendell; Conservation Biology; Jackson, S. Wesley "Wes"; Leopold, Aldo; Restoration Ecology and Ritual; Schumacher, Ernest Friedrich.

Landscapes

Landscapes that reflect religious beliefs do not easily lend themselves to categorical definitions. Part of the difficulty is that the words "religion" and "landscapes" each possess a long history and many meanings. Further, there is a wide range of phenomena to which the phrase "religious landscapes" may refer. Yet, if any universal traits exist, it is that such places tend to be material and express values embedded in them by individuals and groups. Values are generally transmitted and maintained through story. Many of these stories pertain to beliefs about the nature of the universe and the human place or role within it.

The term "religion" has been and remains notoriously difficult to define. Tylor and Frazer described it as a belief system. Freud saw it as illusion, while to Durkheim it was the source of social cohesion. Otto focused on the *mysterium tremendum et fascinans*. Here, the root of religion was understood to be "the holy," something experienced by people through emotions of both fearful awe and reverent attraction. Geertz framed religion as a cultural system of meaning. Scholars have offered other definitions in addition to these.

A similar problem exists with "landscapes." The word originated among Germanic peoples in medieval times or earlier, when *landschaft* were tracts of land primarily distinguished one from the other on the basis of kinship relations and customary law regarding land-use rights. This sense of community and connection to particular places was incorporated into paintings after the 1600s. While retaining traces of these earlier meanings, landscape generally came to refer to a picture of natural inland scenery or to the presence of such scenery in the background of a portrait or figure-painting. It was sometimes applied to intangible settings such as those of dreams or visions as well.

Religious landscapes may be comprised of natural features, built features, or a combination of the two. Some may be understood in terms of the sacred and profane, and some cannot. Some act as *axis mundi*, and some do not. This was a term frequently used by historian of religion Mircea Eliade to describe the idea of a center, generally conceived as a pole or line linking upper, earthly, and lower realms. Religious landscapes commonly link the local to the cosmological. They may be geographically fixed or mobile. Their scale may range from that of a country or region down to a household ritual space. Some, but not all, are the sites of contested identities. Here, in the process of struggling for dominance, groups may attempt to control the physical appearance of a specific place, including its symbolic content and meaning. And some religious landscapes, but certainly not all, express primarily religious beliefs.

Such landscapes may be comprised of natural features like rivers, groves of trees, mountains, or caves. There are Hindu conceptions of the Ganges, wooded locales important to "New Agers," Shinto and Buddhist places associated with Mt. Fuji, and the subterranean labyrinth of paleolithic Lascaux, just to name a few. Lascaux dates from approximately 27,000 years ago, and is famous for its wall paintings depicting animals and humans apparently participating in ritualistic trance-states. Other landscapes, like those presented by temples, mosques, and churches, are fully fashioned by humans. Alternatively, natural and built elements may be interwoven, as at Stonehenge and Hua Shan, the latter of which is a mountain range in China with ancient and ongoing Daoist and Buddhist associations.

Sites may be designated as sacred in contrast to the rest of the landscape, which is considered profane. The word "sacred" derives from the Latin "sacer," translated as meaning "to set apart." "Profane," also derived from Latin, refers to that which is in front of, and thus outside of a temple; due to its location beyond holy precincts, it is by definition not sacred. The ideas of Mircea Eliade play a key role here too. Drawing from work by scholars like Durkheim, he claimed that a dialectic or creative tension exists between the sacred and the profane, and that these categories of understanding and experiencing the world are common to all people. However, understandings derived from this particular cultural tradition cannot necessarily be generalized to other contexts. In most, if not all, Native American traditions prior to Euro-American contact there is no sense of sacred separate from profane; the entire world is suffused with spirit and/or permeated with spirits. A lack of division between sacred and profane exists in conceptions of Buddha-nature, the Dao, and Brahman, among others.

The overwhelming majority of religious landscapes manifest symbols of cosmological truths that are communicated through story, and many of these places serve as *axis mundi*. Winchester Cathedral is a geographically fixed site. Shaped like a Latin cross, its architecture is suggestive of the Trinity. It is also reminiscent of situations that unfolded upon Calvary Hill in Jerusalem – a city that serves as an *axis mundi* for Jews, Christians, and Muslims. One might look to the Lakota traditions for another example.

Tipis were traditionally set in circles called *tipospaye*, and each tipi itself was circular. The circle represented community, the cycle of seasons, the great dome of the sky, and the cycle of life. Although unlike Winchester in their mobility, each tipi and *tiyospaye* was similar to it in that each was homologous to an *axis mundi*. It is important to note here that not all religious landscapes act as *axis mundi*. In *To Take Place* (1987), Jonathan Z. Smith convincingly challenges Mircea Eliade's assertions in this regard by undertaking a telling examination of Australian Aboriginal myths and Mesopotamian ziggurats.

All landscapes by definition, and thus all religious landscapes, present a vista or scene to the eye. Their scale may vary widely. Ancient Chinese understood the vast territory they inhabited to be sacred. Across that land were mountains, altars, and other features associated with ontological beliefs. Nested within this widespread landscape were regional landscapes, and smaller places yet were framed within those. The Imperial City of any given time period contained its landscapes of cosmological beliefs, as did towns and villages. Households, too, encompassed religious landscapes. Typically these took the form of family shrines dedicated to ancestors.

Some places testify to contested identities. The Javanese temple of Borobodur stands as a case in point. It was built by a Hindu dynasty, with a layout and symbolic content reflecting its cosmology and social structure. When Buddhists kings succeeded in taking control of the area, they transformed the temple into a wonder of Buddhist iconography. However, the original edifice was not entirely destroyed in the process. Today, elements of both religious systems remain visible, literally etched in stone.

There are religious landscapes that do not necessarily reflect embedded values about the nature of the cosmos and the human place within it. What about when secular or profane space becomes sacred, as it has at former Nazi concentration camps, at places like Gettysburg and Wounded Knee, at the Oklahoma City or New York Towers terrorism sites, or when a mountain is transformed into a sculpture of famous American presidents? These are all deemed special and set aside as sacred, but not necessarily on the basis of spiritual experiences or ideas.

Religious landscapes are highly complex phenomena. Categorical definitions are problematic, and hence must be applied with caution. Taken as a whole, however, they may be generally understood as physical sites, as expressing convictions about the nature of the universe through story, and as sites of related human activities.

Joel Geffen

Further Reading

Capps, Walter H. *Religious Studies: The Making of a Discipline*. Minneapolis: Fortress Press, 1995.

Eliade, Mircea. *The Sacred and the Profane*. Willard R. Trask, tr. New York: Harcourt Brace Jovanovich, Publishers, 1959.

Holm, Jean and John Bowker, eds. *Sacred Place*. Themes in Religious Studies. London: Pinter Publishers, 1994.

Olwig, Kenneth. "Recovering the Substantive Nature of Landscape." *Annals of the Association of American Geographers* 86:4 (1996), 630–53.

Smith, J.Z. *To Take Place*. Chicago: The University of Chicago Press, 1987.

See also: Anthropologists; Eliade, Mircea; Sacred Geography in Native North America; Sacred Mountains; Sacred Space/Place; Stonehenge; Trees – As Religious Architecture.

Law, Religion, and Native American Lands

The appropriation of North American native lands has been accomplished, as well as contested, over the last five centuries by means of complex culturally embedded assumptions concerning law, religion, and nature. While military conquest and outright theft have certainly played an important part in the loss of tribal lands, even more crucial have been the various legal and religious traditions animating the worldviews and negotiating positions of both colonizers and native peoples.

In the twentieth century, opposition to the legally secured control of native lands increased significantly. Tribal governments, individuals and intertribal groups frequently challenged the historic loss of native lands, employing strategies arising out of Congressional legislation, changes in the political climate, and their own marshalling of legal, political, cultural and economic resources. Since the passage of the American Indian Religious Freedom Act in 1978, a variety of claims invoking the sacredness of traditional lands have been brought both to the bar and into the channels of public opinion. These challenges to the means of American territorial expansion, or to what the Court of Claims in *United States v. Sioux Nation* (1975) referred to as "rank and dishonorable" action on the part of the government, have achieved limited success. Nevertheless, they raise a number of ongoing issues for the federal as well as tribal governments, not to mention the constituents they represent.

America's legal expropriation of native lands has its roots in the worldview of Renaissance Europeans. When Christopher Columbus first reached the island he called San Salvador in 1492, he was careful to display the royal standards, offer a prayer of thanksgiving, and secure witness from his first officers that he "was taking possession of this island for the King and Queen." The efficacy of the brief ritual employed to claim the island for his Castilian sovereigns depended on two assumptions about the Christian Church's station in the world. First, since the Church was universal in scope – there being no other means by which humans could gain salvation – Catholic thinkers such as Pope Innocent IV also claimed that the Church held a universal authority over temporal affairs. This doctrine had already served in efforts to subordinate European political power to that of the Church, and during the crusades it gave justification to the conquest of Muslim lands by Christians.

Second, since Christians had a duty to reclaim Muslim lands in order to extend the domain of the Christian religion, they also had a duty to bring the religion to those in the newly discovered regions of the world, a point that Nicholas V emphasized well before Columbus' first voyage. In *Romanus Pontifex* (1455), Nicholas connected the Church's goal of universal salvation with Portugal's exploration of new territory along the western coast of Africa.

> This we believe will more certainly come to pass, through the aid of the Lord, if we bestow suitable favors and special graces on those Catholic kings and princes, who, like athletes and intrepid champions of the Christian faith, as we know by the evidence of facts, not only restrain the savage excesses of the Saracens and of other infidels, enemies of the Christian name, but also for the defense and increase of the faith vanquish them and their kingdoms and habitations, though situated in the remotest parts unknown to us, and subject them to their own temporal dominion (in Davenport 1967: 21).

For many Christian Europeans, although conquest was not in itself a just form of war, the retaking of the holy lands from the Muslims, and the spread of the gospel, were. Thus territory to be gained through crusade would be land reincorporated into Christian civilization.

As European exploration led to the Americas, this same doctrine of the Church as the provider of universal salvation shaped articulation of the "law of discovery." The only limiting factor, Alexander VI said in *Inter Caetera* (1493), on the claiming of land by one "Christian prince," was whether the land was already in "actual temporal possession of any Christian owner" (in Davenport 1967: 62). Even such staunch opponents of Spanish lust for gold as Bartolemé de Las Casas and Francisco de Vitoria understood the need for the extension of the Christian message to the New World by Christian princes. Vitoria, whose views appeared posthumously in *De Indis et De Iure Belli Relectiones* – "Lectures on the American Indians and the Justness of War" (1557) – was successful at least in countering prevailing views enough to persuade emperor Charles V that the Spanish should treat (negotiate) with Indians, rather than launch war against them upon failure to heed the *requerimiento* to convert to Christianity, as had been the case in the decades after Columbus' first landfall.

Undergirding the theory of the spread of Christian political power was also a theory of human nature, evident in the thinking of Spanish and Portuguese Catholics, but perhaps even more explicit among their Protestant English rivals – who made use not only of Christian ideas but also of the Germanic land laws inherited from the Anglo-Saxons. On this theory, the role of humans in a sinful world is to rise above their sinful inclinations through the discipline of work. Both biblical tradition and natural law theory endorsed the human transformation of nature. Columbus took pains to describe the people of the Indies as indolent, a point that continually frustrated him in his attempts to employ Indians as laborers in the gold streams, and evidently to minimize for him the horror of native loss of life as the islands underwent their rapid depopulation.

Although the Catholic French held much of North America for two hundred years, their own colonizing strategy, or lack of it, bypassed the acquisition of native land in favor of a general claim to royal title and offers of protection for the tribes, by which they maintained their dependence on native hunters and trappers. North America's English colonizers, however, did employ the theory of the Christian use of nature, though glossing it in decidedly non-Catholic ways.

John Locke, in his *Second Treatise of Government* (1689), drew on both biblical exegesis and the Germanic freehold tradition that shaped the view of private property found in English common law, explaining that land was free, held in common and without explicit title, until it had been transformed by labor. This transformation by labor gave both right to the laborer and value to labor's results. As Locke expressed the Christian use of nature, labor also functioned as a divine mandate.

> God, when he gave the world in common to all mankind, commanded man also to labor, and the penury of his condition required it of him. God and his reason commanded him to subdue the Earth, i.e. improve it for the benefit of life, and therein lay out something on it that was his own, his labor (Locke 1948: 17).

Thus, permanent occupancy, the transformation of natural resources into wealth through the application of systematic labor, and the individual holding of particular parcels of land, all became the normative markers of title in North America. The English accordingly saw nothing in the life-ways and subsistence economies of native tribes that gave them claim against the appropriation of land under the colonizer's flag.

In the early years of the American republic, a mixture of laws and practices kept the process for taking native land legally uncertain. Following the Revolution, New York State treated with the Oneida and other members of the Iroquois confederacy for the acquisition of several million acres in the western half of the state. Individuals also acquired land on their own, while the Trade and Intercourse Acts (1790–1802) mandated that states and individuals could not bypass the federal government's role in regulating trade with Indians. The discovery of gold in Georgia in the aftermath of the Redstick War (1813–1814), and the influx of white settlers onto Muskogee (Creek) land, created a social crisis in the south that spurred the development of legal doctrines having lasting effects on native land. Although the Northwest Ordinance (1787) had earlier held that "the utmost good faith shall always be observed towards the Indians, and their lands and property shall never be taken without their consent," the confusion of law and the public's desire for southern land made Indian consent a malleable constraint.

On the one side, President Andrew Jackson – who defeated the Redstick Creeks in the 1814 Battle of Horseshoe Bend, and ended Muskogee resistance to white encroachment in the southeast – championed the right of the states to deal with Indian tribes as they saw fit. Jackson also employed a heavy hand in articulating the old doctrine of the Christian use of land. In his "Second Annual Address to Congress" (1830), for instance, while explaining the rationale for removing the Choctaws from their Georgia lands, he asked

> What good man would prefer a country covered with forests and ranged by a few thousand savages to our extensive Republic, studded with cities, towns, and prosperous farms, embellished with all the improvements which art can devise or industry execute, occupied by more than 12,000,000 happy people, and filled with all the blessings of liberty, civilization, and religion? (in Richardson 1901: 521).

In the hands of the populist Jackson, legitimating native lands appropriation thus became a simple exercise of common sense.

On the other side, Chief Justice John C. Marshall – often regarded as setting out an Indian doctrine antithetical to that of Jackson – played a singular role in establishing the legal mainstay of U.S. and tribal relations. Rather than championing Indian interests, however, as a strong federalist, he was most concerned to weaken the states rights position advanced by the Jacksonian Democrats.

In *Johnson v. McIntosh* (1823), which concerned conflicting claims to land acquired from the Piankeshaw tribe of Illinois, Marshall made clear that the English monarch's title to native land based on the doctrine of discovery had been taken over by the United States. The idea of Christian discovery acknowledged that natives at the time of discovery were sovereign nations, but this sovereignty was limited as a claim to title, since tribes did nothing more than occupy their lands. They thus fell short of the criteria for the possession of property that Locke and other Christians deduced from the Bible and natural reason. For Marshall, falling short of title still gave Indians rights of use and occupancy, but these rights were circumscribed, since

> their rights to complete sovereignty, as independent nations, were necessarily diminished, and their power to dispose of the soil at their own will, to whomsoever they pleased, was denied by the fundamental principle that discovery gave exclusive title to those who made it (in Cohen 1971: 292).

In trying to systematize the contending frameworks of law concerning Indians inherited by the United States, Marshall certainly could have reflected on the adequacy of the doctrine of discovery's theological underpinnings. He explicitly chose to avoid this task, however, saying "It is not for the Courts of this country to question the validity of this title, or to sustain one which is incompatible with it." Instead,

> if the principle has been asserted in the first instance, and afterwards sustained; if a country has been acquired and held under it; if the property of the great mass of the community originates in it, it becomes the law of the land and cannot be questioned (in Cohen 1971: 292).

As legal scholar Peter d'Ericco has commented, Marshall wound up "allowing power to justify itself" (d'Ericco 2000: 28). Marshall concludes as a legal positivist – encouraging subsequent Indian jurisprudence to rest complete with a narrow consideration of the constitutionality of government action.

In the years of national expansion the United States entered into 370 treaties with tribes, which Marshall framed in his second consideration of Indian lands as "domestic dependent nations" (*Cherokee Nation v. Georgia*, 1831). Marshall's oxymoronic term carried important implications. The federal government was to negotiate with tribes as it did with foreign, sovereign nations, but at the same time the federal government played the superior role in determining the interests and needs of its dependents, or "wards" in Marshall's terms.

Some 60 percent of the treaties ratified by the Senate provided for the transfer of lands. Although the superiority of Christian use slipped into the background as the explicit legal justification for these transfers, the sentiments were never really submerged among the American public, nor from the worldviews of those Americans administering the western reservations on which posttreaty Indians were confined after the Civil War. In restricting tribes to reservations, reform-minded whites had long hoped to instill Christian values, a national task Congress first undertook in the Civilization Fund Act (1819).

In the 1870s, this desire became explicit federal policy when President Ulysses S. Grant authorized the administration of western reservations by the various denominations. Virtually all Americans at the time saw the "Indian problem" as the perpetuation of Indian cultural patterns and land use incompatible with those of the larger society. One eager editorialist for the *Yankton Press and Dakotan* appealing to the broad public sentiment in favor of the 1874 gold rush into the Black Hills, wrote of the Lakotas:

> What shall be done with these Indian dogs in our manger? They will not dig the gold, nor let others

dig it ... They are too lazy and too much like animals to cultivate the fertile soil, mine the coal, develop the salt mines, bore the petroleum wells or wash the gold. Having all these things in their hands, they prefer to live as paupers, thieves and beggars; fighting, torturing, hunting, gorging, yelling and dancing all night to the beating of old tin kettles (Jackson 1966: 8–9).

Reformers – unlike editorialists who advocated extermination or imprisonment for native tribes – believed that through education, technical training and religious indoctrination, the clash of civilizations could be ended, and the loss of life diminished. As Colonel Richard Henry Pratt – who oversaw the first post-Civil War experiments in Indian boarding schools – put it, reformers would need to "kill the Indian to save the man." The complete intermixture of religious indoctrination with the development of agrarian and capitalist individualism common to the reformers' aims is evident in the words of Congregational minister Lyman Abbott, who argued in 1885 at the third of the Lake Mohonk Conferences of Friends of the Indian that "The post office is a Christianizing institution; the railroad, with all its corruptions, is a Christianizing power, and will do more to teach the people punctuality than schoolmaster or preacher can" (Prucha 1978: 35).

The normative notion of the industrious, individual owner of property had its culminating impact on the loss of tribal lands in 1887, when Congress approved Massachusetts Senator Henry Dawes's General Allotment Act. The act – which did not, initially at least, affect the lands of certain tribes, notably those of the Lakota (Sioux) on the Plains, the Cherokees and others removed to Oklahoma in the 1830s, nor the Pueblos in the Southwest – gave the president authority to subdivide treaty-designated communal lands on a fee-simple basis. Accordingly, following a 25-year agricultural apprenticeship, heads of household were entitled to 160 acres – the same size plot available to whites (following a five-year apprenticeship) under the 1862 Homestead Act – while other Indian individuals received smaller plots. The enormous surplus of tribal lands remaining after subdivision was then offered to the American public. In theory the Dawes Act would promote the productive enterprise of Indian individuals and incorporate them into the life-ways of civilized society. In practice, within a short time it led to even greater land loss and impoverishment, as land-holders were pressured to lease non-used fee-simple lands to non-Indians, a practice resulting in the checkerboard patterns of use and ownership visible on many reservations today. Before Congress abandoned the allotment system in 1934, the act diminished treaty land by 86 million acres, some 60 percent of Indian lands held in 1887.

The tribes were certainly not passive in contesting the loss of their land base, and just as the encroaching whites employed in addition to organized violence a synthesis of religious worldview and legal mechanisms in order to gain control of native land, tribes relied upon a variety of symbolic, ritual and legal strategies to cope with that encroachment. Law itself was an arena in the conflict of native and European culture, and although in some places law governing land emerged through a process of translation between tribes and colonizers – as in the *pays d'en haut* of the upper Great Lakes prior to the Revolution – for the most part tribes found themselves required to accept, and to function within, the imposition of European legal philosophy. The mixture of Roman, Saxon and Christian traditions was being secularized by the seventeenth-century colonial era, and the emerging positivism conflicted greatly with tribal assumptions about law as consensus, as sacred, and as shaper of tribal identities and resource economies.

As Europeans made initial contacts with North American tribes, many engaged the colonizers with rituals of incorporation. By bringing gifts and offering hospitality, they extended to the newcomers the web of family relationships governing so many of their own tribes. Interesting to note, Columbus, who received numerous gifts from the Tainos and other islanders, consistently misrepresented these acts in his journals, often ascribing the native willingness to give to simplicity of mind, acknowledgement of a socially inferior position, or a child-like ignorance of the real value of both resources, such as gold, and the land itself.

Two crucial elements of the European and American notion of title: exclusive use and alienation through contract, proved quite foreign to the traditions of native tribes. Tribal lands were generally held in common, although members of more permanently settled Eastern or Southwestern tribes passed their cultivated fields on to individual family members – as among the Iroquois women who were the primary users of fields.

Crucial features of tribal cosmologies linked communal and individual well-being to the land. Tribes rehearsed their rightful occupation of particular territory through sacred accounts, which might depict – as with the Hopi – their ancestors' migration or emergence from under the Earth, or their creation from pieces of the Earth by a superhuman being – such as the Anishinabeg (Ojibwa) hero Nanabozho. Once given land on which to dwell, the ancestors in these stories are also often given instruction on how to uphold social relations and how to make a living on the land, instructions that emphasize the people's continued dependence on the benevolence of other life forms or superhuman powers. Frequently, these instructions came from ancient figures, such as the Cheyenne prophet Sweet Medicine, or Deganawidah – the Iroquois Peacemaker – who brought from the Creator the constitution establishing the Haudenosaunee confederacy.

Tribes also developed a wide variety of rituals in order to mark these relations of dependence upon the land, which established or renewed their bonds when broken by human action, the passage of time, or mysterious causes. In addition, tribal members observed elaborate systems of proscription – taboos – governing the essential activities of hunting, planting and harvesting, and ensuring that individuals would not disturb the web of agreements by which animals and plants consented to offer themselves up to meet human needs. Through traditions of myth, ritual, community identity and moral action, then, tribes were often not easily inclined to see themselves in positions to sell land or extinguish title to other human beings, but rather as dependent upon the greater-than-human power embodied in the land.

Treaties for land transfer were typically troubled affairs, given the coercive tactics white negotiators frequently adopted in order to acquire signatures from some segment of a tribal community, and – by the 1820s – considering the military superiority that generally backed the U.S. design upon land. Only a small faction of the Cherokees, for instance, approved the signing of The Treaty of New Echota (1835), which divested them of their lands in Georgia, and resulted in their removal west of the Mississippi.

At the same time, tribes often took steps to incorporate treaties within their understanding of the sacred obligations binding them to the land. The Haudenosuanee wampum belt marking such treaties as the first one signed at Fort Stanwix, New York (1768), extended to the British membership in the confederacy's "covenant chain." The widespread formalizing of treaty negotiations through the smoking of pipes, for the native participants at least, carried the promises aloft as prayers. Even contentious treaties, such as The Treaty of Medicine Lodge Creek (1867) with the Kiowas and Comanches, and The Fort Laramie Treaty (1868) with the Lakotas and Arapahos, came to define particular treaty-defined territory as a crucial aspect of tribal identity.

Apart from *Cherokee Nation v. Georgia* (1831), in which arguably the most successfully acculturated of the tribes failed to obtain the Marshall Supreme Court's protection from white encroachment on treaty lands, Indians were generally unable to make good use of nineteenth-century courts to counter land loss. In addition to the cultural barriers impeding western tribal members' mastery of legal arcana, in 1863 Congress also prohibited the Federal Court of Claims from hearing treaty-related suits. This required tribes to seek redress directly from Congress itself, which was seldom interested in reversing itself on questions of land, or in giving up its "sovereign immunity."

Instead, tribes and factions in large numbers engaged in religious renewal to provide strategies to cope with the devastating consequences of land loss. Prophetic movements arose across the country between the Revolutionary era and the early twentieth century, inspiring political leadership and animating occasional militant campaigns. The prophetic movements, such as those of the Delaware Neolin in the 1760s, or the Shawnee Tenskwatawa in the early 1800s, were grounded in the visionary experience of individuals who had learned from sacred beings that white domination did not necessarily entail the tribes' permanent alienation from traditional life-ways and territory. Military leaders such as Pontiac, Tecumseh, and Blackhawk, were inspired by these movements to resist encroachment, and in some cases formed broad pan-tribal alliances to stem the tide of settlers into the Ohio River valley and other contested eastern regions.

Others preached coexistence or isolation, and drew – like the Seneca prophet Handsome Lake at the beginning of the nineteenth century – on visions to help them articulate a revamping of traditional religious and cultural practices. In some cases, these movements targeted aspects of traditional culture: witchcraft, or women's leadership; in others they focused on white influence as the source of contemporary social turmoil and loss of land. Many, as with Wovoka – the Walker Lake Paiute leader of the Ghost Dance whose teachings spread across western reservations in the 1880s – blended traditional tribal theology with aspects of Christianity. As in the dominant society, apocalyptic visions were widespread, in which world-transforming floods or fires restore Indians and animals and sweep away the whites too numerous for Indian bullets. In some cases prophetic teachings about the erosion of land or the loss of game animals could be incorporated within traditional individual and communal understandings of ritual. Since one function of rituals related to important agricultural or hunting resources was to petition for the annual return of the resource, some religious leaders turned to ritual solutions to restore land or game lost to American expansion. In other cases, such as that of Handsome Lake, although preservation of tribal lands was key to his message and politics, it receded under the power of his apocalyptic vision, where he foresaw believers in his *Gaiwiio* – the "Good Word" – ascending to heaven following the destruction of the Earth.

In one of the last of these renewal movements, the Crazy Snakes, the charismatic Muskogee orator Chitto Harjo urged his militant followers to retain traditional culture and reject allotment. In addition to engaging federal troops in 1901, and the Oklahoma National Guard in 1909, Harjo's group also undertook legislative campaigns, Washington lobbying, and succeeded in securing a U.S. Senate investigation of allotment efforts in Oklahoma, though not in halting the subdivision of Muskogee land.

The legal status of Indians, as individuals and as members of distinct political communities, changed over the course of the twentieth century in ways that affected land questions. The Supreme Court held in *Lone Wolf v. Hitchcock* (1903) – in which Kiowa and Comanche plaintiffs complained that allotment could not proceed without the approval of three quarters of the adult male tribal members – that Congress had always exercised "plenary authority" over Indians. This absolute power was "a political one, not subject to be controlled by the judicial arm of the Government" (in Prucha 1990: 203). Thus Congress certainly had power to make and break treaties as it determined necessary, and this exercised power confirmed that the Allotment Act's subdivision of treaty lands was constitutional. In 1920 however, in acknowledgment of Indian service in the First World War, Congress did approve jurisdictional acts for many tribes, waiving sovereign immunity concerning treaty claims, and offering tribes some theoretical means of redress before the Court of Claims.

Contradictory impulses shaped federal Indian lands policy making during the twentieth century. One was an explicit overturning of the Christian assumptions that had led to the acquisition of native lands and the dissolution sought for native cultures. The 1934 Wheeler-Howard Indian Reorganization Act, with its roots actually in the Hoover administration, mandated the most systematic reversal in Indian policy in American history. Under John Collier – President Franklin Delano Roosevelt's appointment to head the Bureau of Indian Affairs – the federal government first advanced as goals the protection of tribal lands and culture. The Indian Reorganization Act ended allotment, restored surplus tribal lands not yet sold off to the public, and allowed for the purchase of additional tribal lands. Collier, who through exposure to the Pueblos had become a forceful advocate of Indian religious liberty and the necessity of preserving traditional cultures, saw tribal lands as a key ingredient to the health of Indian societies.

The "Indian New Deal" was contested by whites and by many tribes – such as the Navajos, who refused to implement some of its provisions – and subsequently judged harshly by those who argued that it remained a form of tribal domination. Nevertheless, it set the stage for a serious revision of the conditions under which Indians had been living since their first confinement to reservations, and sparked greater effort by Indians to master the legal and political machinery used to control their land.

The second impulse animating twentieth-century Indian policy was far more consistent with historical trends than was Collier's New Deal. In the era after World War II, first the Eisenhower and then other Republican administrations replaced Collier's policies of cultural preservation with "termination" or "emancipation." For tribes such as the Klamath, Menominee and Potawatami, Congress made use of its plenary power to abolish trustee/ward relationships, dissolve tribal status and end federal responsibility for Indian people – resulting in the "urban relocation" of one quarter of the native population by the mid-1960s.

The primary means Congress offered tribes to contest acquisition of their lands reflected both trends in federal policy. Collier's hope to address the injustice of tribal land expropriation bore fruit only following his departure, when, in 1946, President Harry S. Truman approved the creation of the Indian Claims Commission (ICC) to make a final disposition of land claims. Tribes readily took the opportunity to bring their grievances forward. By the end of the commission's original five-year mandate, all 176 federally recognized tribes and bands had filed at least one claim. By 1978, when the commission finally dissolved, it had examined nearly four hundred, and authorized restitution in over one-third of these.

While the ICC focused national attention on native land grievances, and the $818 million it awarded the tribes was a significant sum in total if not per tribe or per capita, its very purpose – to settle grievances through financial compensation – conflicted with the land-restoration goals of many tribes. Unlike the seventeenth-century Manhattans, who supposedly gave up their island for a few trinkets, tribal treaty negotiators often appreciated the value of the dollar – Cornplanter and Red Jacket, for instance, the Seneca rivals to Handsome Lake – each received cash grants and annuities as personal compensation for signing The Treaty of Big Tree in 1797. Others, like the Lakota Red Cloud, who argued to his dying days that the Black Hills were worth far more than any government official was prepared to offer him, held out for the largest sums possible for their people. Nevertheless, most Indians did not see the swap of land for money as an ideal market transaction. Many tribes took up the opportunity to file with the Commission because it was the only means available for addressing their concerns, and in hopes that it would be simply a first step toward restoration of some portion of their land base.

The case of the Western Shoshones illustrates the limitations facing tribes as they dealt with the Commission and the courts. The Western Shoshones' Treaty of Ruby Valley, signed in 1863, was primarily a treaty of "peace and friendship," in which the Shoshones agreed to allow the U.S. to develop telegraph and rail lines, establish outposts and engage in mining and farming on their lands – nearly 25 million acres comprising most of Nevada, and adjacent lands in Utah, Idaho and California. The treaty remains the only formal agreement worked out between the government and the Western Shoshones for the disposition of their land, yet clearly omits any provisions for limiting territory, qualifying title or establishing reservation boundaries. In spite of subsequent resource and urban development, the majority of Shoshone land remains within the public domain, since the federal government administers 87 percent of the state of Nevada's land base.

Under advisement of the Bureau of Indian Affairs, members of the Temoak band filed the original Shoshone claim with the ICC in 1951 (*Western Shoshone Identifiable Group v. US*). The claim – which sought compensation for the "taking" of tribal land – remained unendorsed by most Shoshones and their tribal councils throughout its history, since they were not party to the claim, and the Temoak plaintiffs had no authority to represent other Shoshones. In 1962, the ICC ruled that although the U.S. had not signed any agreement dealing with the issue of Shoshone title, a history of "gradual encroachment of whites, settlers and others" had effectively deprived the Shoshones of any valid claim to continuing title. Accordingly, the Commission awarded the Shoshones, without interest, a figure based on an 1872 valuation of the land – a date with no significance in Shoshone history, but one that allowed the government to overlook the payment of royalties related to mining claims filed in the area under the 1872 General Mining Law.

Although the ICC lacked the necessary jurisdiction to settle questions of title, the courts have generally held subsequently that the ICC award for "taking" created the presumption that the land was actually taken. Shoshone organizers created the Western Shoshone Sacred Lands Association in 1974 in order to pursue the title question directly. In a ruling on the related case of Shoshone ranchers Mary and Carrie Dann (*United States v. Dann*, 1984), the federal district court held that Shoshone "aboriginal" title remained good until the final 1979 Court of Claims hearing on the ICC award. For the Supreme Court in 1985, the only issue needing adjudication was simply whether or not the Shoshones – who had refused the award – had actually been paid and the government's obligations therefore discharged. The Kafkaesque course of the Shoshone claim through the judicial system was acknowledged by the Court of Claims itself, which noted that "if the Indians desire to avert the extinguishment of their land claims by final payment, they should go to Congress" (*Temoak Band v. United States*, 1979).

The procedural focus in the courts' consideration of the Shoshone land claim – or those of most other North American tribes, for that matter – have sharply limited the extent to which tribes can expect an adequate weighing of their arguments for a just solution to the appropriation of their lands. In the case of the Dann sisters – who have, since 1973, been charged with violating the Taylor Grazing Act (by not obtaining livestock grazing permits) on land their family has made exclusive use of since "time immemorial" – the courts have been content to reemphasize the assumptions about the relation of native people to their lands contained in Marshall's "doctrine of discovery" and the Dawes Act, assumptions dependent upon the Christian worldview for their plausibility. The high courts' legal positivism is an interpretive mechanism that has obscured the Christian grounding of federal Indian law, without abandoning it, or bringing it into any critical juxtaposition with the worldviews of Indian plaintiffs.

Another legal front in the contest over tribal territory opened in the aftermath of the civil rights era, one focused specifically on native claims about the sacredness of land. In 1978, as the ICC ended its work, Congress passed – with little debate and by a large majority – a law that seemed to many to open the door to some form of land control for tribes, and even its potential return. The American Indian Religious Freedom Act (AIRFA) noted the long history of religious persecution that had accompanied the U.S. policy of civilizing Indians and opening their lands, and required federal agencies to report on how they could ensure that they were not prohibiting Indians from the "free exercise" of their religion. The act specifically underscored the prominent role that land plays in native religious life; its promoted authors – like John Collier in the preceding generation – the belief that this was a role the federal government should respect as part of its trustee relationship to the tribes.

Although AIRFA's sponsor in the House, Rep. Morris Udall, cautioned the leery that the law would have "no teeth," many tribes and interested parties quickly filed land-related suits under the act. These cases reflected a broad range of concerns: prohibited access to ritually significant sites, resource development of sacred areas, insensitive administrative and management priorities. Some, such as the Navajo Medicine Men's Association in *Badoni v. Higginson* (1980), the Eastern Cherokees in *Sequoyah v. Tennessee Valley Authority* (1980), and both the Navajos and Hopis in *Wilson v. Block* (1983), sought to constrain federal land agencies from damaging specific sacred sites; others – as with a group of Lakota and Cheyenne religious leaders in *Fools Crow v. Gullet* (1983) – aimed to prevent states from controlling Indian religious practitioners. Common to all these cases, Indian plaintiffs argued that fundamental features of their religious liberty were threatened by government policy.

In some cases the land concerned – administered by a state parks department, or the National Park Service – was small in scale, and the impact of protecting Indian religious practice could be weighed against the interests of other visitors to the park. *Sequoyah*, however, with its challenge to the TVA's flooding of the Little Tennessee River, and *Wilson* – in which Navajo and Hopi medicine men were concerned about the Forest Service developing a ski resort in the San Francisco Peaks – showed that AIRFA-fueled challenges might have a significant economic impact, and raised red flags on the part of development-minded politicians and resource industry groups, especially in the western states with their large acreages of multiple-use public land.

While AIRFA aided traditional Indian religious practice in some ways, the courts in general have rejected its ability to dictate land agencies' management of "what, after all, is the government's land," as Justice Sandra O'Connor concluded in *Lyng v. Northwest Indian Cemetery Protective*

Association, 1988 (489 U.S. 439, 454). In the AIRFA land cases the courts have consistently chosen to read "religion" and "religious liberty" in a very restrictive sense. In *Sequoyah* the court concluded that Cherokee claimants were motivated by "cultural" and not religious concerns – in spite of the fact that the Tellico dam would destroy both a burial ground, and the ceremonial center of Cherokee life – the place of their emergence in this world. *Sequoyah* also established the courts' practice of narrowing sacred land claims by maintaining that government infringement on religious liberty must stem from a directly coercive intent.

In First Amendment case law the courts have historically relied on several tests to determine whether government infringes on religious liberty: whether the affected religion is genuine, whether belief is sincere, whether government action causes a burden, and whether government exercises a "compelling interest" to override religious liberty. Traditionally, the courts have found indirect infringement sufficient to rule in favor of claimants, but in AIRFA cases – and not simply in the land cases – the courts have declined to restrict government infringement, even when – as O'Connor also noted in *Lyng* – it would so clearly destroy an Indian religion.

Observers have remarked that the high court holds a normative view of religion as something best exemplified by Christianity, which consistently prevents it from recognizing the legitimacy of native religious practices and understandings foreign to mainstream American culture. In *Badoni*, for instance, the court held that Navajo rituals performed at Rainbow Bridge were not essential to Navajo religious life because they were held infrequently, and not attended by sufficient numbers of Navajos – as though weekly church services provided the justices with their template for viewing ritual. Perhaps the most telling expression of this majoritarian bias to advocates of Indian rights was Justice Scalia's admission in *Employment Division v. Smith* (1990),

> It may fairly be said that leaving accommodation [of Indian religious practice] to the political process will place at a relative disadvantage those religious practices not widely engaged in, but that unavoidable consequence of democratic government must be preferred to a system in which each conscience is a law unto itself (494 U.S. 872, 891).

With the courts so frequently unable to aid Indians seeking control of sacred places or the return of traditional lands, tribal and pan-tribal organizations have turned to political forums. The Shoshones, the Lakotas and others have approached Congress in the last couple of decades, with little result. In the Shoshone case, although Congress could consider the transfer of public lands back to the Shoshones, it has been unwilling to do so, given concerns for precedent, for the enormous wealth which modern gold mining has extracted from tribal land, and for the vast spaces necessary for Department of Defense and Department of Energy activities in Nevada.

Likewise, following the Supreme Court ratification of the Lakota ICC award for the taking of the Black Hills (*United States v. Sioux Nation*, 1980) – the ICC's largest single award – the Lakotas were also unsuccessful in generating sufficient interest on the part of Congress. Black Hills Steering Committee coordinator Gerald Clifford was able to get a bill to Congress, sponsored by New Jersey Democrat Senator Bill Bradley, in 1985 and again in 1987. For Clifford and many other Lakotas, the return of the Hills was a religious cause. "Our first priority," he said of the committee's work "must be to keep faith with our sacred traditions. The Lakotas were placed around the Black Hills for a purpose by God ... and it is a moral imperative that we reject the selling of land" (Lazarus 1991: 416). Bradley also framed his support in religious terms of embracing the nation's highest values and respecting Lakota traditions, which many had come to say accounted for their origins as a people from beneath the Hills. The bill provided for the creation of a Sioux Nation National Park on public lands as well as for compensation in addition to the ICC award of $106 million. Although the bill received the co-sponsorship of Senator Daniel Inouye, chair of the Senate's Select Committee on Indian Affairs, Inouye said it would also need support of home state legislators in order for him to bring it to the committee, a support never provided in deference to non-Indian constituents interested in preserving the existing Forest Service multiple-use policy. Western states' opposition to both the Shoshone and Lakota claims invoked the ironic threat of what Justice O'Connor framed as "de facto beneficial ownership of some rather spacious tracts of public property" (485 U.S. 439, 454) should Indians become able to dictate public lands policy to the larger society.

On a few occasions tribes have been successful in obtaining the return of sacred lands from the federal government, but this has generally required strong presidential endorsement of legislation, or the issuing of an executive order. President Richard Nixon, who replaced "termination" with "self-determination" as the goal of federal Indian policy in 1970 – prompted in part by Indian activists' eighteen-month occupation of Alcatraz Island – responded to Yakama Nation appeals for the return of a portion of Mount Adams, in 1972. The Washoe, Navajo, Havasupai and Warm Springs tribes also benefited from the reversal of government policy during the Nixon era.

Most widely noted at the time, Nixon intervened on behalf of the Taos Pueblo in their long-running struggle to regain control of Blue Lake, issuing a presidential order for its return in October, 1970. The lake – from which the Taos people emerged onto this world in mythical times, and which is the site of yearly pilgrimages, had been included in the Kit Carson National Forest, created by President Theodore Roosevelt in 1906. Its return – and Nixon's personal interest in land restoration – encouraged native grassroots activists, tribal leaders and legal advocacy groups to persevere in the use of legal and political channels in spite of the ongoing obstacles presented by the courts and Congress. Nevertheless, tribes have found presidential support as difficult to obtain as congressional. The 500 thousand acres of land actually restored in the last few decades, when measured against the 110 million lost just due to allotment, might fairly suggest that the tribes face insurmountable hurdles in resolving the issue to their satisfaction.

In the years since Nixon, one finds even fewer bright spots. Congress did approve creation of the Zuni Heaven Reservation in 1984 (Public Law 98–498). President William J. Clinton was willing to use his authority – enacting Executive Order 13007, "Indian Sacred Sites" – to protect Indian land-based religious practice, although the courts have not yet weighed in on its ability to provide injunctive relief for sacred lands or to legitimate additional land-return campaigns. In addition, Congress has passed several laws in the wake of the judicial defeats trailing the AIRFA cases, such as the Native American Graves Protection and Repatriation Act (1990), the Religious Freedom Restoration Act (1994), and the National Historic Preservation Act (1996), which have offered some oblique protection, and if not land return, at least some potential of greater tribal participation in the management of sacred sites on public land.

Increasingly, though, tribes and native organizations have employed three additional strategies to promote land return, in an effort to bypass the limits of their ward-like reliance upon the federal legislative and judicial systems. First, native people have been able to marshal the post-1960s shift in popular culture to build a larger public consensus around the idea of land return. The Romanticist underpinnings of the 1960s counterculture and the 1970s environmental movement – invoking the noble savage tradition of real Indians as model human beings closer to nature than their alienated, urban Indian and non-Indian counterparts – provided native activists and cultural leaders with an opportunity to address wider and more sympathetic forums than in earlier periods. This has often merely resulted in the politics of celebrity gesture – such as Marlon Brando's refusal of his 1972 Academy Award for "The Godfather," in solidarity with the American Indian Movement's occupation of Wounded Knee, South Dakota. Nevertheless, tribes have also been able to advance their arguments through celebrity-endorsed media ventures, as in Robert Redford's narration of the two documentaries on the Western Shoshone claim, "Broken Treaty at Battle Mountain" (1974) and "To Protect Mother Earth" (1991).

Alliances with environmental groups have also developed in the last twenty years, overcoming some of the initial resistance to native land-use issues held by groups such as the Sierra Club. The Shundahai Network, for instance, coordinated by Shoshone elder Corbin Harney, is a grassroots organization combining the energies of west coast anti-nuclear advocates with proponents of Ruby Valley treaty rights, and devoted to civil disobedience, education and advocacy efforts at federal nuclear facilities such as the proposed Yucca Mountain waste repository site located in the middle of Shoshone territory.

In southern Arizona, members of the San Carlos Apache reservation in 1989 enlisted the "Apache Survival Coalition," a broad network of outside support, to assist them in their opposition to the Mount Graham International Observatory – sponsored by the University of Arizona, and by international research institutions such as the Vatican Observatory, the Arceti Observatory and the Max Planck Institute. Conflicting agendas, and differing perceptions of what makes Mount Graham sacred among supporting groups and within the San Carlos tribe kept this network from providing sufficient unified political pressure to cancel the project, which the Apache Survival Coalition maintained would disturb the Gaans, elemental powers of the universe residing within the mountain (Taylor 1995; Williams 1998).

A second front has emerged as tribes and pan-tribal groups have obtained international attention. Bucking Justice Marshall's presumption in *Johnson v. McIntosh* that tribal sovereignty does not extend to relations with foreign powers, delegates from the Iroquois, the Lakota, Western Shoshone and other tribes have appealed directly to international law in appearances before such institutions as the European Parliament and the World Court. As part of an emerging global movement of indigenous peoples, American Indians have also appealed to the Organization of American States and the United Nations – which has provided support for the development of non-governmental organizations, such as the American Indian Movement's International Indian Treaty Council. Appearances before the UN Commission on Human Rights have led to the publication of scathing incictments of federal Indian policies. A 2000 ruling by the OAS's Inter-American Commission on Human Rights finds the United States in violation of several counts of international human rights law in regard to its dealings in the Western Shoshone Dann sisters. However, the limited extent to which the United States wishes to acknowledge the authority of international bodies over its internal affairs indicates the questionable short-term utility of these efforts. Should the global indigenous movement gain increasing international support, however, the United States may prove more amenable to tribal claims – just as it had to accommodate 1950s demands for civil rights in order to present itself as a principled opponent of communist totalitarianism.

More immediate as a strategy for land restoration, though less satisfying as a measure of justice, is the willingness of tribes to make increased use of the real-estate market. Alaska tribes since the early 1970s have fashioned themselves as corporations and used money obtained through the Alaska Native Lands Settlement Act (1971) to purchase additional lands, and to develop their resources. Other tribes have also used ICC awards to purchase at current market values historically or culturally significant acreages. Eastern tribes were able to argue that the original Trade and Intercourse Acts made invalid land transfers, as the Penobscott and the Passamoquoddy did in 1980 against the state of Maine.

Nationally, the development of nonprofit land trusts has also served the aims of tribes. Organizations such as the White Earth Land Recovery Project in Minnesota, The Cultural Conservancy and the Trust for Public Land have provided the nexus of capital and real-estate experience to enable tribes to recover historically significant portions of their traditional lands. The Nez Perce have purchased traditional sacred lands in Oregon's Wallowa Mountains to provide the basis for a tribally managed wildlife preserve. Other tribes, such as the Mashpee at Bufflehead Bay, are engaged in joint administration of refuge lands with state and federal authorities. In northern California the Sinkyone Intertribal Wilderness Area involves eleven coastal tribes, along with state conservation agencies and a land trust, in the creation of the nation's first intertribal land reserve. While these reserves are all small in scale, they speak to the seriousness of tribal aims, and to the long-term nature of tribal goals. In the most fundamental way, they are testimony to the failure of United States policy, which hoped through the instillation of Christian values and the insertion of native individuals into the marketplace to abolish tribal links to the land.

Students of Indian law have formed conflicting evaluations of the history of tribal land loss. For some, such as Wilcomb Washburn, the legacy of this history is not, when the American story is compared with those of other colonial powers, as bleak as it may seem on first count. Resistance, opposition, and some success in the courts and legislative halls of the conqueror show that the tribes have faced a more enlightened foe than they might have done. Others, such as Felix Cohen – famous for his comment that Indians, like Jews in Nazi Germany, function as "canaries in the coal mine" of the legal order – offer a somewhat darker reading of the tradition. On both of these accounts, however, the tribes remain dependent on the good graces of those outside their communities. That land remains a significant motivating force within these communities, however, is due less to public largess or legal achievement and more to the determination of the tribes themselves to retain the animating spirit they have long found in land.

Matthew Glass

Further Reading

Brodeur, Paul. *Restitution: The Land Claims of the Mashpee, Passamaquoddy, and Penobscot Indians of New England.* Boston: Northeastern University Press, 1985.

Cohen, Felix. *Handbook of Federal Indian Law.* Albuquerque: University of New Mexico Press, 1971 (1942).

Columbus, Christopher. *The Voyage of Christopher Columbus: Columbus's Own Journal of Discovery, Newly Restored and Translated.* London: Weidenfeld & Nicolson, 1992.

Cornell, Stephen. *The Return of the Native: American Indian Political Resurgence.* New York: Oxford University Press, 1988.

Crum, Steven J. *The Road on Which We Came: A History of the Western Shoshone.* Salt Lake: University of Utah Press, 1994.

Davenport, Frances Gardiner. *European Treaties Bearing on the History of the United States and its Dependencies to 1648.* Gloucester, MA: 1967 (1917).

Department of the Interior. *Implementation Report, Executive Order 13007 – Indian Sacred Sites.* Washington, D.C.: GPO, 1997.

d'Errico, Peter. "John Marshall – Indian Lover?" *Journal of the West* 39:3 (Summer 2000), 19–30.

Deloria, Vine, Jr. and Raymond J. DeMallie *Documents of American Indian Diplomacy: Treaties, Agreements and Conventions, 1775-1979.* Norman: University of Oklahoma Press, 1999.

Deloria, Vine, Jr. and Clifford M. Lytle. *American Indians, American Justice.* Austin: University of Texas Press, 1983.

Dowd, Gregory Evans. *A Spirited Resistance: The North American Indian Struggle for Unity, 1745–1815.* Baltimore: Johns Hopkins University Press, 1992.

Dussias, Allison M. "Squaw Drudges, Farm Wives, and the Dann Sisters Last Stand: American Indian Women's Resistance to Domestication and the Denial of Their Property Rights." 77 *North Carolina Law Review* 637, 1999.

Fixico, Donald. *Termination and Relocation: Federal Indian Policy, 1945-1960.* Albuquerque: University of New Mexico Press, 1986.

Gordon-McCutchan, R.C. *The Taos Indians and the Battle for Blue Lake.* Santa Fe: Red Crane, 1991.

Gulliford, Andrew. *Sacred Objects and Sacred Places: Preserving Tribal Traditions.* Boulder: University of Colorado Press, 2000.

Hanscom, Greg. "Tribes Reclaim Stolen Lands." *High Country News*, 3 August 1988.

Hargrove, Eugene C. "Anglo-American Land Use Attitudes." In *Ethics and the Environment*. Donald Scherer and Tom Attig, eds. Englewood Cliffs, NJ: Prentice-Hall, 1983, 97–113.

Irwin, Lee. "Freedom, Law, and Prophecy: A Brief History of Native American Religious Resistance." *The American Indian Quarterly* 21:1 (1997), 35–55.

Jackson, Donald D. *Custer's Gold: The United States Cavalry Expedition of 1874*. New Haven: Yale University Press, 1966.

Jacobs, Wilbur. *Dispossessing the American Indian: Indians and Whites on the Colonial Frontier*. Norman: University of Oklahoma, 1985.

Johnson, Troy. *The Occupation of Alcatraz Island*. Urbana: University of Illinois Press, 1996.

Jorgensen, Joseph. "Land is Cultural, So is a Commodity: The Locus of Difference among Indians, Cowboys, Sod-busters and Environmentalists." *Journal of Ethnic Studies* 12:3 (1985).

Kelley, Klara Bonsack and Harris Francis. *Navajo Sacred Places*. Bloomington: Indiana University Press, 1994.

Lazarus, Edward. *Black Hills/White Justice: the Sioux Nation Versus the United States, 1775 to the Present*. New York: HarperCollins, 1991.

Locke, John. *Second Treatise of Government*. J.W. Gough, ed. Oxford: Basil Blackwell, 1948.

Martin, Joel. *Sacred Revolt: The Muskogee's Struggle for a New World*. Boston: Beacon Press, 1991.

Michaelsen, Robert S. "Dirt in the Court Room: Indian Land Claims and American Property Rights." In David Chidester and Edward Tabor Linenthal, eds. *American Sacred Space*. Bloomington: Indiana University Press, 1995, 43–96.

Newcomb, Steven T. "The Evidence of Christian Nationalism in Federal Indian Law: The Doctrine of Discovery, *Johnson v. McIntosh*, and Plenary Power." *New York University Review of Law and Social Change* 20:2 (1993).

Oakes, Jill, et al., eds. *Sacred Land: Aboriginal World Views, Claims and Conflicts*. Winnipeg: Canadian Circumpolar Institute Press, 1998.

Prucha, Francis Paul, ed. *Documents of United States Indian Policy*. Lincoln, Nebraska: University of Nebraska Press, 1990.

Prucha, Francis Paul. *The Great Father: The United States Government and the American Indians*. Lincoln: University of Nebraska Press, 1984.

Prucha, Francis Paul. *Americanizing the American Indians: Writings by the "Friends of the Indian," 1880–1900*. Lincoln: University of Nebraska Press, 1978.

Richardson, James D. *A Compilation of Messages and Speeches of the Presidents, 1789–1897*. Volume II. Washington, D.C.: Government Printing Office, 1901.

Rosenthal, Harvey D. *Their Day in Court: A History of the Indian Claims Commission*. New York: Garland, 1990.

"Sioux Nation Black Hills Act: Hearing Before the Select Committee on Indian Affairs." United States Senate, Ninety-ninth Congress, Second Session on S. 1453, 16 July 1986. Washington, D.C.: U.S. Government Printing Office, 1986.

Sutton, Imre. *Irredeemable America: The Indians' Estate and Land Claims*. Albuquerque: University of New Mexico Press, 1985.

Taylor, Bron. "Resacralizing Earth: Pagan Environmentalism and the Restoration of Turtle Island." In David Chidester and Edward T. Linenthal, eds. *American Sacred Space*. Bloomington: Indiana University Press, 1995, 97–151.

Vecsey, Christopher, ed. *Handbook of American Religious Freedom*. New York: Crossroad, 1991.

Vecsey, Christopher and William A. Starna, eds. *Iroquois Land Claims*. Syracuse: Syracuse University Press, 1988.

Wallace, Anthony F. C. *The Death and Rebirth of the Seneca*. New York: Random House, 1969.

Washburn, Wilcomb E. *Red Man's Land/White Man's Law: A Study of the Past and Present State of the American Indian*. New York: Charles Scribner's Sons. 1971.

Wilkinson, Charles. *American Indians, Time and the Law*. New Haven: Yale University Press, 1987.

Williams, Robert A. "Large Binocular Telescopes, Red Squirrel Pinatas and Apache Sacred Mountains: Decolonizing Environmental Law in a Multicultural World." In *Readings in American Indian Law: Recalling the Rhythm of Survival*. Jo Carrillo, ed. Philadelphia: Temple University Press, 1998.

Williams, Robert A., Jr. *The American Indian in Western Legal Thought: The Discourses of Conquest*. New York: Oxford University Press, 1990.

See also: Anishnabeg Culture; Black Elk; Black Mesa; Bison Restoration and Native American Traditions; Casas, Bartolomé de las; Devils Tower, *Mato Tipi*, or Bears Lodge; Ghost Dance; G-O Road; Haudenosaunee Confederacy; Holy Land in Native North America; Indigenous Environmental Network; LaDuke, Winona; Lakota; Lakota Sun Dance; Manifest Destiny; Miwok People; Mother Earth; Peoyte; The Sacred and the Modern World; Sacred Geography in Native North America; Shoshone (Western North America); Spirit of Sage Council; Yakama Nation; Yuchi Culture and the Euchee (Yuchi) Language Project.

Le Guin, Ursula K. (1929–)

Ursula K. Le Guin is known primarily for her science fiction and fantasy novels, but she also has written children's books, poetry, translation, and essays. These literary interests were formed by the intellectual and multicultural environment of her youth: her father was the famous anthropologist Alfred L. Kroeber who with her mother wrote the classic ethnography, *Ishii in Two Worlds* (1961).

Her writings exhibit some of the standard themes of science fiction and fantasy: the heroic quest, the possibilities and problems of technology, and the potential of magic and paranormal consciousness. But her work is distinctive and significant in a variety of ways. The imaginary worlds she creates have an uncommon anthropological richness. She is more concerned with detailing social psychologies and the intricacies of culture than presenting technological marvels. Indeed, she has described her work as "social science fiction."

But it is more accurate to call it "ecosocial" science fiction because Le Guin is a master at revealing the relationship between culture and nature. She makes clear how the specifics of the natural world shape the societies that inhabit them, although not in a simplistic, deterministic way. Similarly, the political ideologies and social values of a society are shown to be directly related to their conception of and behavior toward the Earth. Her imaginary worlds exhibit a wide range of connections between nature and culture, and frequently her novels present two or more cultures in conflict over their relationship with nature. The reader thus comes to recognize various possibilities for healthy and destructive correlations between nature and culture.

The result has been numerous incisive critiques of contemporary social structures and their ideologies of nature. The most explicit critique is found in *The Word for the World is Forest*, written in response to the Vietnam War. In it, an aggressive and ultimately self-destructive Captain Davidson attempts to exploit an Eden-like setting populated by smaller native humans that live in harmony with nature.

In her view of nature and culture, Le Guin has been deeply influenced by Daoism. References to the *Daodejing* (*Tao te ching*) and the *Zhuangzi* (*Chuang Tzu*) are used to illustrate her view of natural harmony, her anarchist political philosophy, and themes such as dream and unreality. In *City of Illusions*, which takes place in future North America, the "Old Canon" that helps guide the protagonist is the *Daodejing*. There is also a "New Canon," Thoreau's *Walden*, and people who follow the teachings of the two canons are called "Thurro-dowists."

Feminism has been increasingly important to Le Guin's thought. She has been fascinated by the complexities of gender, most famously in *The Left Hand of Darkness*. In that work, the Gethenian people are neuter until they undergo "kemmer" (estrus), at which time they may become either male or female. Since then Le Guin has become more deeply and outspokenly feminist, seen especially in *Buffalo Gals and Other Animal Presences* and her collection of essays *Dancing at the Edge of the World*.

Feminism has influenced Le Guin's concern with the issue of the "Other." Her work celebrates diversity in both nature and culture while at the same time recognizing continuity within "the community of all life." Both a sense of absolute otherness and the denial of difference lead to destruction. Instead she affirms both difference and connection – among humans and between humans and nature. This is seen, for instance, in "Buffalo Gals," in which Myra, a girl, is adopted by the First People (animals, particularly Coyote). She ultimately takes on a double personality in which both her human identity and her "animal" identity are retained.

This concern with otherness is tied to her "ethic of communication." Communication with others, including those in the natural world, is possible and necessary. In particular, we need to overcome our "deafness" to those who have been given no voice, including women, children, so-called primitive people, and the wilderness (see "Women/Wilderness" in *Dancing* and the introduction to *Buffalo Gals*).

Her pacifist, anarchist social philosophy is found in a number of works. *Always Coming Home*, set in the future in California, is a pseudo-anthropological presentation of the Kesh, a simple, egalitarian society living in relative harmony with nature. In *The Eye of the Heron*, the People of Peace organize their society along explicitly Quaker principles. Le Guin has described her utopian views as *yin* compared to the *yang* of Western civilization ("A Non-Euclidean View of California as a Cold Place to Be," in *Dancing*). Such a utopia is based on a sense of communal identity rather than rational structure. Neither static nor progressing toward some end, it manifests organic and unpredictable process. It arises not from power centers but from margins. Imperfect, it is full of potential. As the subtitle of *The Dispossessed* makes plain, it is an "ambiguous" utopia.

Her Daoist, ecofeminist, and anarchist views are ultimately rooted in a vision of nature as deeply interrelated. Coyote, perhaps, captures this best in *Buffalo Gals*, where she sings "one of the endless tuneless songs that wove the roots of trees and bushes and ferns and grass in the web that held the stream in the streambed and the rock in the rock's place and the Earth together" (Le Guin 1987: 56).

David Landis Barnhill

Further Reading

Armbruster, Karla. "Blurring Boundaries in Ursula Le Guin's 'Buffalo Gals, Won't You Come Out Tonight': A Poststructuralist Approach to Ecofeminist Criticism." *ISLE: Interdisciplinary Studies in Literature and Environment* 3:1 (1996), 17–46.

Le Guin, Ursula K. *Dancing at the Edge of the World: Thoughts on Words, Women, Places.* New York: Grove Press, 1989.

Le Guin, Ursula K. *Buffalo Gals and Other Animal Presences.* Santa Barbara: Capra Press, 1987.

Le Guin, Ursula K. *Always Coming Home.* New York: Harper, 1985.

Le Guin, Ursula K. *The Eye of the Heron.* New York: Harper & Row, 1978.

Le Guin, Ursula K. *The Word for the World is Forest.* New York: Berkley, 1976.

Le Guin, Ursula K. *The Dispossessed: An Ambiguous Utopia.* New York: Harper & Row, 1974.

Le Guin, Ursula K. *The Left Hand of Darkness.* New York: Ace Books, 1969.

Walker, Charlotte Zoe. "Ursula K. Le Guin." *Dictionary of Literary Biography,* 2003.

See also: Anarchism; Bioregionalism; Daoism; Ecofeminism; Snyder, Gary; Trickster.

Leary, Timothy (1920–1996)

Timothy Leary is most famous for his promotion of the "nature religion" interpretation of psychedelic experiences. After earning a doctorate in psychology (UC Berkeley, 1950) and authoring a highly innovative and influential theoretical system (Interpersonal Diagnosis of Personality, 1957), Leary was appointed Lecturer at Harvard in 1959. Ambitious, idealistic, eager for an intellectual revolution, the brilliant young psychologist found his calling while summering in Mexico in 1960, when he ingested psilocybin mushrooms and underwent the first of his several hundred psychedelic voyages. Leary's intellectual contributions were obscured by the social tumult that ensued, including Harvard's controversial firing of Leary and his collaborator Richard Alpert in 1963, their subsequent campaign to "turn on" the world, arrests and legal battles, a dramatic escape from prison, exile abroad, and recapture, to name just some.

In brief, Leary believed that psychedelic drugs bring into consciousness neurological information that is ordinarily filtered from awareness. This information, encompassing all levels of structural organization within the nervous system (sensory, cellular, molecular, atomic), has existed for thousands, millions, even billions of years and retains an historical record that can reach awareness during psychedelic experience. For example, Leary proclaimed that on LSD one could experientially recapitulate biological evolution (encoded in neural DNA) back to life's origin, and physical evolution (encoded in neural atoms) back to the Big Bang. Thus, psychedelic users could experience subjectively the same phenomena that scientists study objectively.

Leary contended that mystics who lived in pre-scientific times interpreted such experiences with non-scientific concepts. In a manner later popularized and developed by Fritjof Capra and others, Leary proclaimed that religious mysticism and scientific method often arrived at identical conclusions – with mystics using the language of supernaturalism. For example, whereas mystics interpreted past-life recall as reincarnation, Leary explained this as recollection of one's evolutionary past archived in DNA. (Leary himself actually charted a family tree based upon LSD-induced past-life experiences.)

Resisting the temptation "to impose old models, premature theories," Leary endeavored to modernize such models with the language of science. In this spirit, he "translated" the *Tibetan Book of the Dead* and the *Tao Te Ching* using the naturalistic concepts of science. His 1966 psychedelic version of the Tao, for example, included such poems as "The Serpent Coil of DNA" and "Prehistoric Origins of DNA," and others paying homage to experiences of atomic energy and the sense organs.

When psychedelic drug use exploded into a mass phenomenon around 1964, it became clear that the drugs would soon be outlawed. Preparing a legal challenge to protect psychedelic drug use under the First Amendment right to free exercise of religion, Leary deliberately embraced the supernaturalistic language that previously he had resisted. Setting the stage for a legal showdown, Leary founded a religious organization (League for Spiritual Discovery), produced public "religious celebrations" in which he ceremoniously enacted the roles of Jesus and the Buddha, and wrote books and essays brazenly trumpeting supernaturalism.

Ironically, although Leary's promotion of supernaturalism failed to persuade the jurors for whom it was intended – his legal strategy, used to defend himself against marihuana charges, failed in 1966 and, on appeal, in 1967 – it did persuade legions of impressionable young seekers to imbibe the sacrament and interpret their experiences with the language, if not the concepts, of supernaturalism. Ultimately, Leary's charismatic influence further enshrined psychedelic experience in the mysticism, occultism, and anti-scientific primitivism from which he had initially labored to wrest it.

Having failed to win legal protection on grounds of religious freedom, and disappointed at what he regarded as the anti-intellectual supernaturalism promoted partly by his own rhetoric, Leary upon release from prison in 1976 pointedly abandoned supernatural rhetoric and struck an almost confrontational scientism in his return to the public eye. Ever the prolific author, lecturer, and media celebrity, Leary helped popularize life extension, space colonization, and the computer revolution in his championing of his new calling, Science.

Although Leary never promoted activism to protect the natural environment, he blamed urban-industrialism not only for aesthetic and environmental pollution but also for alienating city-dwellers from the "cellular wisdom" he believed psychedelics revealed. Consistent with his style of addressing problems with elements of both avoidance (passive) and approach (active), Leary's favored remedy involved the theme of exodus. At the height of his influence in the mid-1960s, for example, Leary's new religion counseled initiates to "drop out" of urban-industrial culture, adjoin as tribal colonies in intentional rural communities, supporting themselves through handicraft. The drop-outs would thus occupy a social-environmental niche left vacant by "Man's lemming-like rush to the cities" and "the insane society of adults around you rushing to enslave itself to machines." With his colleagues and friends, Leary attempted to establish colonies in Millbrook, New York, in Zijuatanejo, Mexico, and in several Caribbean island nations, but each project, opposed by government or imploding onto itself, was short-lived. (Upon release from prison in 1976, Leary transmuted the exodus theme in championing the cause of space migration, which involved leaving Earth to inhabit colonies in outer space.)

How history will judge Timothy Leary remains yet to be determined. In life, he often was condemned by conservatives as an irresponsible Pied Piper emblematic of all that was threatening about the cultural changes of the 1960s, dismissed by political leftists as unserious and irrelevant to their cause of Socialist Revolution, and even distrusted by many in the otherwise sympathetic counterculture who suspected that his flamboyance and media savvy signified insincerity, attention-seeking, or snake-oil salesmanship. But the cultural changes of "The Sixties" have largely been assimilated, making Leary's "radicalism" seem relatively mild by contemporary standards; with the fall of the Soviet Union and the left's increased recognition of the practical challenges of maintaining a socialist cure that is clearly better than the capitalist ills for which it is prescribed, the leftist movements that promised imminent Revolution in the 1960s seem unserious and irrelevant themselves; and the personal demeanor that aroused excessive veneration in some and excessive doubt in others in the counterculture will exert diminishing impact, biasing posthumous judges less strongly than it biased Leary's contemporaries and thus allowing his ideas to receive a fairer trial in the future.

Joseph Kasof

Further Reading

Horowitz, Michael, Karen Walls and Billy Smith. *An Annotated Bibliography of Timothy Leary*. Hamden, CT: Archon Books, 1988.

Leary, Timothy. *Flashbacks: An Autobiography*. Los Angeles, CA: J.P. Tarcher, 1983.

Leary, Timothy. *The Politics of Ecstasy*. New York: Putnam, 1968.

Leary, Timothy. *Psychedelic Prayers after the Tao te Ching*. Kerhonkson, NY: Poets Press, 1966.

Leary, Timothy, R. Metzner and R. Alpert. *The Psychedelic Experience: A Manual Based on the Tibetan Book of the Dead*. New York: Citadel Press, 1964.

See also: Ayahuasca; Beat Generation Writers; Entheogens; Ethnobotany; Huxley, Aldous; New Age; Perennial Philosophy; Peyote.

Left Biocentrism

Left biocentrism or left ecocentrism (the two terms are used interchangeably), is a theoretical tendency which has been unfolding within the deep ecology movement since the mid-1980s. It has been called "the left wing" of the deep ecology movement. Left biocentrists (left bios) support the eight-point Deep Ecology Platform drawn up by Arne Naess and George Sessions. They see this Platform as a key component of the existing deep ecology movement, which should therefore not be subject to unilateral changes by any individual deep ecologist. Necessary changes to the Platform, so that it can evolve, must be sorted out collectively within the movement. Left bios see their work as endeavoring to strengthen the deep ecology movement. "Left" as used by left biocentrists, means anti-capitalist and anti-industrialist, but not necessarily socialist. Industrialism is seen as having a capitalist or a socialist face. The future economic and political organization of an ecocentric society is seen as a subject of necessary and ongoing discussions.

Many left biocentrists (myself included) came to this perspective from a left-wing background. As we became aware of deep ecology we saw the importance of moving beyond the human-centered values (anthropocentrism) of the anarchist, social democratic, communist, and socialist traditions, and became aware of the need to put the Earth first. This meant to identify and express solidarity with all life. Some within this group of people had been working on a broadly defined "left" deep ecology path, but were using different names to describe it (e.g., "deep green theory" (Richard Sylvan), "radical ecocentrism" (Andrew McLaughlin), "revolutionary ecology" (Judi Bari), "green fundamentalism" (Rudolf Bahro), "revolutionary ecocentrism" (Ken Wu), etc.). All these left deep ecology supporters, and others not mentioned, would believe that although deep ecology pointed us in the needed new philosophical direction, it had yet to evolve a practical political program in opposition to industrial capitalism.

Others drawn to left biocentrism were responding to the theoretical and practical work done in its name, or were drawn to it because they opposed the "accommodating" stance of much deep ecology toward industrial capitalism. The influence of the internet has been important, not only for the dissemination and exchange of writings, but also for making possible a "left bio" discussion group, which in 1998 collectively produced a ten-point Left Biocentrism Primer. The Primer provides a starting point for left biocentrism, but it is also a work in progress, like that of deep ecology itself.

Left bios believe that the Earth belongs to no one and should be a non-privatized Commons. They call for a global redistribution of wealth, oppose economic growth and consumerism, and practice voluntary simplicity. There is a bioregional not a global focus. Social ecology, eco-Marxism, and ecofeminism have important insights, left bios believe, but are nevertheless seen as unduly human-centered in orientation.

To facilitate collaboration left bios distinguish between "primary" and "secondary" contradictions. The primary contradiction resides in anthropocentric industrial capitalist society. Secondary contradictions over other issues, such as vegetarianism, remain but are accepted so that people can unite and focus on the primary contradiction.

Spirituality is also critical in left biocentrism. Point six of the Primer states:

> Left biocentrism holds that individual and collective spiritual transformation is important to bring about major social change, and to break with industrial society. We need inward transformation, so that the interests of all species override the short-term self-interest of the individual, the family, the community, and the nation.

Left biocentrists believe that, in order to try and turn around the ecological "Armageddon" and to prevent the coming social disaster, a profound transformation is required in our relationship to the Earth. This will include resacralizing nature so that people come to see the Earth as alive and part of themselves. A future Earth-centered society will need to be organized around an ecocentric morality that has an essential spiritual or sacred dimension and is not based on economics.

The discussions among left biocentrists about what it means to advocate the resacralization of nature are ongoing and contentious. Some left bios, including myself, have been influenced by atheism or the Marxist tradition that sees organized religion as an "opiate," while other left bios have some kind of relationship to various institutional religions. Left bios usually draw a distinction between "institutional religion" and "spirituality." Resacralizing the Earth is seen as a concern with spirituality, not with establishing some new institutional religion.

Left biocentrism is interested in what should be our relationship to the spiritualities of Aboriginal cultures, in particular animism. The basic idea that the Earth is alive, and that plants and animals have their own intrinsic spirits and values, has in the past acted as a restraint on human exploitation. However, animism, which sustained hunter/gatherer societies over thousands of years, was still ultimately human-centered, perhaps a form of "deep stewardship," and this did not prevent the now documented extinctions of fauna in the Americas, Polynesia, New Zealand, and Australia.

Deep ecology, which is not human-centered, must build on but go beyond an animistic "seventh generation" consciousness to resacralize *all* species on Earth.

Millions of people around the world use religion as their ethical guide. These religions help shape how people interact with the natural world through different cultures, and the place of humankind within these cultures. Religions differ in this regard and an important part of any deeper ecological work is endeavoring to understand this, so as ecologically to engage with existing religions. There are ongoing discussions on the differences between, as well as within, the Abrahamic and the Vedic religions in regard to ecological consciousness. Within deep ecology, for example, a number of writers have been influenced by Buddhism. The concern with self-realization in deep ecology seems analogous to the Buddhist sense of the interconnected self with the universe. E.F. Schumacher, himself a Catholic, outlined in the early 1970s in his book *Small is Beautiful* what he called a "Buddhist economics," seeking to move societies away from capitalist consumerism as a false identity basis, to an identity based on the cultivation of personal inner growth. The theoretical tendency of institutional religions is a concern for left biocentrism and has come more to the foreground with the prominence of a variety of religious fundamentalisms (e.g., Islamic, Christian, Jewish, Hindu) that seem lacking in any ecological awareness. Religious fundamentalists want to resacralize human societies, not the natural world.

In order for industrial capitalism to commodify the Earth, Earth-based spirituality had to be undermined. Left biocentrists believe that addressing this is a crucial part of any engaged green politics in the twenty-first century.

David Orton

Further Reading

Bahro, Rudolf. *Avoiding Social & Ecological Disaster: The Politics of World Transformation*. Bath, UK: Gateway Books, 1994.

McLaughlin, Andrew. *Regarding Nature: Industrialism and Deep Ecology*. Albany, NY: State University of New York Press, 1993.

Naess, Arne. *Ecology, Community and Lifestyle*. Cambridge, UK: Cambridge University Press, 1989.

Sylvan, Richard and David Bennett. *The Greening of Ethics: From Human Chauvinism to Deep-Green Theory*. Cambridge, UK: The Whitehorse Press; Tuscon, AZ: The University of Arizona Press, 1994.

Taylor, Bron, ed. *Ecological Resistance Movements: The Global Emergence of Radical and Popular Environmentalism*. Albany, NY: State University of New York Press, 1995.

See also: Anarchism; Bioregionalism; Bioregionalism and the North American Bioregional Congress; Deep Ecology; Earth First! and the Earth Liberation Front; Radical Environmentalism; Schumacher, E.F.; Social Ecology; Snyder, Gary.

Leibniz, Gottfried Wilhelm (1646–1716)

Leibniz lived in a time of great revolutions. It was a time that brought about the fundamental paradigm shift related to the mechanistic theory of Isaac Newton. Leibniz, likewise, was striving for a scientific and even mechanistic model for interpreting nature, but he combined this attitude in an interesting manner with less deterministic and more organistic explanations. Because Leibniz's system of thought is scattered in many small texts that are not sufficiently edited even today; and because Hegel had dismissed Leibniz's philosophy as arbitrary, haphazard, and incomplete – in fact, it is often said that Hegel's philosophy is the completion of Leibniz's – his thoughts have long been underrated, and it is only today that his ideas are newly appreciated.

At the center of his thinking lies the so-called *philosophy of monads*. The term "monad," which Leibniz most likely took from cabbalist and vitalist Franciscus Mercurius von Helmont and Giordano Bruno, reflects the non-material essence of any living creature: God, the angels and every human's soul, the sensual ability of animals and plants, even microorganisms, are monads. Every monad is singular and different; there are no identical monads. Thus, Leibniz's fundamental idea is not a general one like "spirit" or "matter" but the individual itself. The individual monads are the only inseparable units of life and they follow their own plans. Leibniz says, "The monads do not have windows" (Leibniz 1898: 219) which means that they cannot be influenced from outside. The monads are, in a way, spiritual entities that are capable of developing and acting. What we see in the material world is not reality but mere illusion. The monadic reality lies hidden behind the empirically sensible. But since the monad owns a body, this body is a perfect representation of the hidden entity.

No monad can be distinguished or separated from its bodily appearance; even if the body dies, the monad lives on, at least in a sleeping form. The harmonic and exact relationship between monad and body connects Leibniz's metaphysics and his philosophy of nature. Thus, the Cartesian dualism of *res cogitans* and *res extensa* is overcome. Furthermore, the cosmos is conceptualized as a living creature, or, in Leibniz's words, "There is nothing deserted, nothing sterile, nothing dead in the universe" (Leibniz 1898: 257).

Another of Leibniz's conclusions is imperative: according to his theory, space and time do not exist independently of one another. Instead, they are idealized patterns of thought, imagined in order to organize the material world. In contrast to Newton's axiom of deterministic and reliable patterns of space and time, Leibniz thus argues for a philosophical doctrine that became prominent in twentieth century thought under the name "philosophy of life."

Kocku von Stuckrad

Further Reading
Jolley, Nicholas, ed. *The Cambridge Companion to Leibniz*. Cambridge: Cambridge University Press, 1995.
Leibniz, Gottfried Wilhelm. *The Monadology and Other Philosophical Writings*. Robert Latta, tr., ed. London: Oxford University Press, 1898.
Rutherford, Donald. *Leibniz and the Rational Order of Nature*. Cambridge: Cambridge University Press, 1995.
Savile, Anthony. *Routledge Philosophy Guidebook to Leibniz and Monadology*. New York: Routledge, 2000.
See also: Perennial Philosophy; Philosophy of Nature.

Leopold, Aldo (1887–1949)

In a 1947 address, "The Ecological Conscience," conservation scientist and writer Aldo Leopold succinctly identified the dilemma facing those who understood the cultural significance of the emerging ecological worldview.

> No important change in human conduct is ever accomplished without an internal change in our intellectual emphases, our loyalties, our affections, and our convictions. The proof that conservation has not yet touched these foundations of conduct lies in the fact that philosophy, ethics, and religion have not yet heard of it (in Flader and Callicott 1991: 338).

Leopold would soon thereafter incorporate the passage, in modified form, in his landmark essay, "The Land Ethic," the capstone of his posthumously published *A Sand County Almanac*. "In our attempt to make conservation easy," he would add, "we have made it trivial" (Leopold 1949: 210).

In a post-World War II world harshly awakened to the social and environmental impacts of new technologies, Leopold's statement resonated with clarity. The conservation movement of the early twentieth century was roughly understood to be a response to destructive and inequitable resource-use practices, driven by short-sighted economics and lax (or nonexistent) governmental policies. Looking forward, Leopold identified the need to deepen that movement, to "touch the foundations of conduct." In defining his land ethic Leopold sought to expand conservation's scope, and so preclude its marginalization. For Leopold, conservation entailed more than just smarter resource management. It posed a fundamental challenge. It sought a closer "harmony" between people and nature, informed by science, woven into culture, inspired by ethics and spiritual insight. In the very act of compiling "The Land Ethic," Leopold defined this challenge and broadened the conversation about the ethics of the human–nature relationship.

In the decades after its publication, "The Land Ethic" became a core text and starting point for those concerned with the ethical and spiritual dimensions of conservation and environmentalism. There is irony in the fact. Aldo Leopold was not a philosopher or theologian, and well appreciated his own limitations in posing such essential questions. Trained as a forester, founder of the then-new field of wildlife management, an innovative thinker in land management and conservation planning, Leopold only occasionally ventured into the higher conceptual realms of his work. When he did, however, he brought to the task his vast field experience, scientific understanding, extensive reading, abiding interest in history, and strong personal commitment to land stewardship. Reticent on matters of the spirit, his life work as a conservationist and teacher nonetheless led him to the ultimate expression of "The Land Ethic."

In his extensive published and unpublished corpus, Leopold rarely alluded to his personal religious beliefs. He grew up in Burlington, Iowa, in an ostensibly Lutheran family of German descent, but he was not a churchgoer. His wife, Estella, whom he met while working as a young forester in the American Southwest, was a devout Catholic, but the Church played a minor role in their married life and the lives of their children. How is it, then, that one of the key progenitors of environmental ethics came to develop such acute sensitivity to the moral aspects of conservation?

The biographer can only connect scattered dots: Leopold as a boy hunter along the Mississippi River in the 1890s, absorbing lessons of responsibility and respect for game from his father Carl (whom Leopold later memorialized as "a pioneer in sportsmanship"); Leopold as a student, struck by the statement of a Native American speaker, that "Nature is the gate to the Great Mystery" ("The words are simple enough, but the meaning unfathomable") (Meine 1988: 35); Leopold as a young forester, watching the "green fire" dying in the eyes of a mother wolf that he and his colleagues had just shot, and sensing "something new to me in those eyes – something known only to her and to the mountain" (Leopold 1949: 130).

Late in Leopold's life, his youngest daughter asked him directly about his belief in God.

> He replied that he believed there was a mystical supreme power that guided the universe, but this power was not a personalized God. It was more akin to the laws of nature. He thought organized religion was all right for many people, but he did not partake of it himself, having left that behind him a long time ago (in Meine 1988: 506–7).

His son corroborated this view. "I think he . . . was kind of pantheistic. The organization of the universe was enough to take the place of God, if you like . . . The wonders of nature were, of course, objects of admiration and satisfaction to him" (in Meine 1988: 506–7).

Perhaps the closest Leopold came in print to describing his own spiritual stance came in an early essay, "Goose Music." He asked, "What value has wildlife from the standpoint of morals and religion?" His answer referred obliquely to

> a boy . . . who was brought up an atheist, [but who] changed his mind when he saw that there were a hundred-odd species of warblers, each bedecked like the rainbow, and each performing yearly sundry thousands of miles of migration about which scientists wrote wisely but did not understand. No "fortuitous concourse of elements" working blindly through any number of millions of years could quite account for why warblers are so beautiful. No mechanistic theory, even bolstered by mutations, has ever quite answered for the colors of the cerulean warbler, or the vespers of the woodthrush, or the swansong, or – goose music. I dare say this boy's convictions would be harder to shake than those of many inductive theologians (Leopold 1953: 171).

Leopold did not identify himself as "this boy"; he did not have to.

Although such expressions surfaced only occasionally in Leopold's writing, this abiding regard for the beauty, diversity, and healthy functioning of the natural world suffused his work as a resource manager, scientist, writer, and teacher over a forty-year professional career. As a product of the Progressive Era conservation movement, he caught the spirit of the times – the connecting of ethics and governmental policy though political reform, the respect for the role of science in the management of resources, the blending of social responsibility and personal commitment. As he advanced in the new U.S. Forest Service, Leopold had his youthful idealism tested and tempered. But he also found that work to be a rich source of insight, along with his broad-ranging literary interests.

By the mid-1920s, Leopold was working out his first extensive considerations of conservation philosophy. He was influenced in particular during these years by the Russian philosopher Pyotr Ouspensky, whose book *Tertium Organum* Leopold specifically drew upon in framing his own emerging ecological worldview. Ouspensky's near-vitalist notion of a living Earth (" 'Anything indivisible is a living being,' says Ouspensky") (Ouspensky 1920: 201) dovetailed well with Leopold's field-based appreciation of the complex interrelations of the landscape of the American Southwest. Fusing Ouspensky's holism with insights from his own ecological research, Leopold gave expression to his latent biocentrism:

> Possibly, in our intuitive perceptions, which may be truer than our science and less impeded by words than our philosophies, we realize the indivisibility of the Earth – its soil, mountains, rivers, forests, climate, plants, and animals, and respect it collectively not only as a useful servant but as a living being, vastly less alive than ourselves in degree, but vastly greater than ourselves in time and space – a being that was old when the morning stars sang together, and when the last of us has been gathered unto his fathers, will still be young (in Flader and Callicott 1991: 95).

Leopold delivered these thoughts in a 1923 manuscript entitled "Some Fundamentals of Conservation in the Southwest." Over the next 25 years he would return to the broader dimensions of conservation philosophy, intermittently but steadily, in a series of published and unpublished essays and addresses. Their titles provide a sense of the progression and extension of his thoughts in these years: "The Conservation Ethic" (1933), "Conservation Economics" (1934), "Land Pathology" (1935), "Engineering and Conservation" (1938), "Conservation Esthetic" (1938), "A Biotic View of Land" (1939), "Ecology and Politics" (1941), "Conservation: In Whole or In Part" (1944), "The Ecological Conscience" (1947). Weaving and reweaving themes involving the interrelated social, economic, political, and cultural aspects of conservation, and demonstrating the practical limits of the dominant utilitarian and anthropocentric approach to conservation, these writings were points along the way toward the synthesis of "The Land Ethic." In these writings, Leopold rarely alluded directly to the religious "foundations of conduct." Only with that final synthesis did he expressly issue his challenge to philosophers and theologians to join the effort.

Even as he was defining and testing his conservation philosophy, Leopold was putting it into practice as a scientist, teacher, policy-maker, and practitioner. Over the last twenty years of his life, he made basic contributions in a number of applied conservation fields. He brought ecological perspectives into the established fields of forestry, agriculture, range management, and soil conservation. He was the preeminent leader in the then-new field of wildlife management. He laid important foundations for the future practice of ecological restoration in both his professional work at the University of Wisconsin and in his personal commitment on his "sand county" farm. Of the latter he wrote:

> On this sand farm in Wisconsin, first worn out and then abandoned by our bigger-and-better society, we try to rebuild, with shovel and axe, what we are losing elsewhere. It is here that we seek – and still find – our meat from God (Leopold 1949: viii).

Following publication of "The Ecological Conscience," Leopold received a response to the essay from an academic colleague, Max Otto, a prominent Unitarian thinker with whom Leopold was acquainted in Madison, Wisconsin, where both lived. Otto's remarks spoke well for a new generation of leaders, from varied faiths, beginning to focus on the same post-war dilemmas that Leopold identified in his essay.

> I value . . . a quality in your paper which I can only call *spiritual*. You have a *philosophy of wildlife management* which is itself a philosophy of life . . . I'm sure that your argument is sound, and I wish religious people – *church* people, I mean – could see it to be part of religion to enlist in your cause. I'm afraid most of them do not see life in these terms (in Meine 1988: 500).

In the decades that followed Leopold's death in 1948, more and more "religious people" would come to see "life in these terms" and would enlist in the cause of promoting closer harmony between people and the larger community of life. Into this conversation, Leopold injected insights from the revolutionary new science of ecology, while pointing out in clear terms the essential role that philosophy and ethics had to assume. With the publication of "The Land Ethic" in *A Sand County Almanac*, Leopold provided a bulwark against the trivialization of conservation.

Curt Meine

Further Reading

Callicott, J. Baird. *In Defense of the Land Ethic*. Albany, New York: State University of New York Press, 1989.

Flader, Susan and J. Baird Callicott, eds. *The River of the Mother of God and Other Essays by Aldo Leopold*. Madison, WI: University of Wisconsin Press, 1991.

Leopold, Aldo. *Round River: From the Journals of Aldo Leopold*. New York: Oxford University Press, 1953.

Leopold, Aldo. *A Sand County Almanac and Sketches Here and There*. New York: Oxford University Press, 1949.

Meine, Curt. *Aldo Leopold: His Life and Work*. Madison, WI: University of Wisconsin Press, 1988.

Ouspensky, Pyotr. *Tertium Organum: The Third Canon of Thought, a Key to the Enigmas of the World*. Nicholas Bessaraboff and Claude Bragdon, trs. Rochester, NY: Manas Press, 1920.

See also: Biocentric Religion – A Call for; Callicott, Baird; Conservation Biology; Darwin, Charles; Earth First! and the Earth Liberation Front; Environmental Ethics; Gaia; Marshall, Robert; Natural History as Natural Religion; Ouspensky, Pyotr Demianovich; Pantheism; Radical Environmentalism; Restoration Ecology and Ritual; Watson, Paul – and the Sea Shepherd Conservation Society; Wilderness Society.

Levertov, Denise (1923–1997)

Denise Levertov's lifelong concern with the experience of mystery began in childhood. Educated at home, Denise, and her older sister Olga, came of age in an eclectic religious atmosphere. Her father, a Hassidic Jew from Russia, converted to Christianity and immigrated to England to become a priest in the Anglican church. Her mother, raised a Welsh Congregationalist, descended from the Welsh tailor and mystic Angel Jones of Mold.

In 1948, Levertov immigrated to the United States and became a distinctive voice in the tradition of American poetry during the second half of the twentieth century. In the late 1960s, Levertov's active participation in the anti-war movement led to poetry explicitly engaged with the collective awareness of the war in Vietnam. In the 1970s, Levertov struggled to balance the drama of public injustice with an emerging interest in the affinities between her religious and ecological concerns.

Asked what the term "religious" meant to her (in a 1971 interview with William Packard) Levertov pointed to a sense of awe: "The felt presence of some mysterious force, whether it be what one calls beauty, or perhaps just the sense of the unknown" (in Wagner 1990: 19). During the 1980s, in a phase of her career devoted to a meticulous and sophisticated development of organic form, Levertov refigures this force in terms of the elusive but persistent mystery of the Christian Incarnation.

In the final books of poems – *Evening Train* (1992), *Sands from the Well* (1996) and the posthumous *This Great Unknown: Last Poems* (1999) – Levertov's celebration of the nonhuman world is inextricable from the intensity of her religious faith. As she insists in one of her essays from this period, "to witness nature is not simply to observe, to regard, but to do these things in the presence of a god" (Levertov 1992: 249). Levertov works toward a "conscious attentiveness to the non-human" as well as to "a more or less conscious desire to immerse the self in that larger whole" (Levertov 1992: 6). Eschewing the American impulse to recreate the self by returning to its primal source in nature – a position that, for Levertov, reinforces an inward, individualistic, and exclusive ethos – Levertov seeks mystical surrender. With art understood as an ongoing affirmation of faith in the unknown, Levertov suggests that the creative act of poetry affirms the possibility of *living with* the natural world.

Mark C. Long

Further Reading

Gelpi, Albert, ed. *Denise Levertov: Selected Criticism*. Ann Arbor: University of Michigan Press 1993.

Levertov, Denise. *The Stream & the Sapphire: Selected Poems on Religious Themes*. New York: New Directions, 1997.

Levertov, Denise. *The Life Around Us: Selected Poems on Nature*. New York: New Directions, 1997.

Levertov, Denise. *New & Selected Essays*. New York: New Directions, 1992.

Sakelliou-Schulz, Liana. *Denise Levertov: An Annotated Primary and Secondary Bibliography*. New York: Garland, 1989.

Wagner, Linda Welshimer. *Critical Essays on Denise Levertov*. Boston: Twayne, 1990.

Wagner, Linda Welshimer. *Denise Levertov: In Her Own Province*. New York: New Directions, 1979.

Wagner, Linda Welshimer. *Denise Levertov*. New York: Twayne, 1967.

See also: Christianity (6c4) – Anglicanism; Memoir and Nature Writing; Wonder toward Nature.

Lilburn, Tim (1950–)

Tim Lilburn is a Canadian poet, essayist, and teacher of philosophy. Born into a Protestant working-class family in Regina, Saskatchewan, he was profoundly affected in his early twenties by the anonymous Middle English book of mysticism *The Cloud of Unknowing* and other classics of "negative contemplation." He taught in Nigeria, worked for social-action projects, and became a Jesuit. In the late 1980s he left the Jesuit order, distancing himself from Catholicism but continuing to adapt ideas and terminology from its contemplative texts. He worked as a farm laborer for three years, and later became a teacher of philosophy and literature at St. Peter's College in Saskatchewan.

Colorful, buoyant, wide-ranging from the vernacular and the hyperbolic to the lyrical and the elegiac, the poems in Lilburn's three earlier collections show influences as diverse as Gerard Manley Hopkins and the Beats. In his next three collections, *Moosewood Sandhills* (1994), *To the River* (1999), and *Kill-site* (2003), his exploration of human struggles to interact with the natural world moves into the foreground. As dramatized in *Moosewood*

Sandhills, Lilburn spent two years living on the land, where he dug a root garden, slept in coyote dens and deer beds, wandered and watched. Themes of this book and his two subsequent collections have been elaborated upon in Lilburn's collection of essays, *Living in the World as If It Were Home* (1999).

A key to Lilburn's writing is a conviction that infinitude has wrongly been seen as belonging to divinity alone; for him a single blade of grass is also beyond comprehension, infinitely complicated. Moreover, our longing for the "stupendous manyness" and "apparently limitless play" of nature is analogous to our longing for divinity. "The eros for the world, I believe," Lilburn has written, "unfolds in the same way as dialectic and the eros for God have been understood to unfold" (Lilburn 1999: ix). Lilburn sees *naming* as an inevitable part of an erotic longing for the world, but also as something to be doubted, truncated, and deemed incomplete, before it resumes. Steeped in the thought of Plato, the Desert Fathers, Gregory of Nyssa, and Gregory of Nazianzus, Lilburn has adopted a vocabulary from such sources (*ascesis, apophasis, penthos*), but he also often employs phrases such as "unspeakable otherness," "intentionless idiosyncrasy," "astounding particularity," "fretful proximity," "muted, protean regard," "carefully attentive befuddlement," "insistent and adoring incomprehension." His poems and his essays are unique in their blend of fecund natural detail and radically adapted contemplative language. While their focus is not on particular environmental issues, they are fueled by a strong questioning of dangerous assumptions about human power and knowledge, and by an underlying advocacy of our need to move beyond centuries of error-fraught interactions with nature. "Looking with care and desire," Lilburn says in a note to *Moosewood Sandhills*, "seemed a political act" (Lilburn 1994: 9).

Lilburn has also served a valuable role in editing two anthologies of prose by poets poised on the intersections among literature, nature, ecology, and philosophy: *Poetry and Knowing: Speculative Essays and Interviews* (1995) and *Thinking and Singing: Poetry and the Practice of Philosophy* (2002).

Brian Bartlett

Further Reading
Lilburn, Tim. "The Provisional Shack of the Ear." Interview with Shawna Lemay. In Tim Bowling, ed. *Where the Words Come From: Canadian Poets in Conversation*. Roberts Creek, British Columbia: Nightwood, 2002.
Lilburn, Tim. *Living in the World As If It Were Home*. Dunvegan, Ontario: Cormorant, 1999.
Lilburn, Tim. *Moosewood Sandhills*. Toronto: McClelland and Stewart, 1994.
See also: Canadian Nature Writing.

Linnaeus, Carl (1707–1778)

Often called the "father of taxonomy," Carl Linnaeus was a Swedish naturalist whose monumental *Systema Naturae* (multiple editions starting in 1735) established the basic strategy for the naming and classification of plants and animals used by Western science. He is thus one of the key figures in the development of modern biology. His philosophy of nature was strongly marked by the natural theology of his era (i.e., he understood nature as a comprehensive rational system that had been designed by an intelligent and benevolent God). Thus his prodigious efforts to collect and catalogue various species from around the globe, as important as they were to the scope and conceptual organization of modern biology, were regarded by him as profound acts of piety.

The son of a Lutheran minister, from an early age Linnaeus demonstrated an exceptional ability to observe and catalog details about natural phenomena. While preparing for a medical career, he began to study botany and aggressively pursued the collection and classification of European specimens. In 1735 he completed his medical degree and published the first version of what would become his most important work, *Systema Naturae*. A few years later, he became a professor at Uppsala where he practiced medicine among the Swedish aristocracy, expanded his studies of plants and animals, and developed elaborate gardens that illustrated his ideas. Students and admirers often assisted this process by sending him exotic specimens from their travels around the world. Although Linnaeus published books and essays on a wide range of topics, his most important works concerned classification. He would revise and supplement *Systema* over much of the rest of his life – notably adding materials on animals and non-European materials as they became available to him. Eventually, it became a multi-volume work that established Linnaeus as one of the leading naturalists of Europe.

Linnaeus' famed system aimed to simplify the existing practice of using long Latin descriptions for plants and animals by substituting a shorthand strategy that consisted of a generic name and a specific modifier – or "binomial nomenclature." Linnaeus also believed that the naming of species should be integrated into a larger system of natural order based upon common physical characteristics. To do so he created a multileveled system of classification that moved from the general to the specific. With some modifications and additions, this is still the basic classification system used by biologists today: Kingdom, Phylum, Class, Order, Family, and the two that name the organism, Genus and Species.

Like many of the era's naturalists, Linnaeus was an enthusiastic exponent of natural theology and would bracket his published works with biblical quotes and paeans to the Almighty. Typically, Linnaeus linked theology to the legitimization of natural science, the task of classification, and hopes for a better future. For example, in the preface to a 1753 study of plant species, he noted,

> the WORLD is the Almighty's theater ... we must research these creations by the creator, which the Highest has linked to our well-being in such a way that we shall not need to miss anything of all the good things we need ... [E]ach object ought to be clearly grasped and clearly named, for if one neglects this, the great amount of things will necessarily overwhelm us and, lacking a common language, all exchange of knowledge will be in vain (Linnaeus in Koerner 1999: 93).

Yet in spite of his Lutheran heritage and dutiful church-going, he was not orthodox in terms of belief. The theological faculty at Uppsala often accused him of conflating God and nature in ways that approached pantheism, and private writings exhibit doubts about doctrines such as the atonement, resurrection, and an afterlife. Thus he is perhaps best understood as a transitional figure whose rhapsodic theism in published works gives way to private doubts and naturalistic views of humanity that are in many ways decidedly modern.

For example, while Linnaeus largely recapitulated the medieval view that human beings stood at the head of the "Great Chain of Being" (i.e., the top of the hierarchy of organic life), he was a significant player in the process through which philosophical and theological concern for the "rational animal" (i.e., in classical and scholastic thought) became the study of a type of particularly clever ape under the aegis of natural history. In the tenth edition of *Systema Naturae* (1758), he introduced three of the enduring terms in the taxonomy of human beings – *Homo sapiens*, *Mammalia*, and *Primates*. Implicit in these categories was Linnaeus' conviction, articulated throughout his later writings, that there were no significant physical characteristics that distinguished human beings from apes. In a letter to a friend, he noted, "If I were to call man ape or vice versa, I should bring down all the theologians on my head. But perhaps I should do it according to the rules of science" (Linnaeus in Frangsmyr, et al. 1983: 172). Although more cautious than later biologists, his classification strategy ultimately took aim on one of the inherited conceits of the Western tradition, that human beings were outside of the natural system by virtue of their rational or spiritual qualities.

Subsequent generations have hailed Linnaeus as one of the great "system builders" in biological science whose achievements are analogous to Newton's influence on physics. In Sweden this reverence has been even more pronounced. During the nineteenth century, reverential biographers and public celebrations of his achievements elevated him to the status of national hero, and more recently, the country has undertaken the careful restoration of his beloved gardens in Uppsala. In England and America various Linnaean Societies continue to advance the study of nature. And of course, every student in a basic biology class pays a kind of tribute to Linnaeus by learning to name and categorize species using the basic principles that he established. In terms of religion, the legacy of Linnaeus is more ambiguous. The theological beliefs that sustained his philosophy of nature would be deemed largely irrelevant to subsequent generations of biologists, particularly after the Darwinian revolution. Some religious conservatives, however, still invoke his ideas on the fixity of species to bolster their attacks on evolutionary concepts. On the more liberal side of things, the spirit of Linnaeus' natural philosophy is perhaps more influential than the content. At once scientifically rigorous and theologically reverent, his efforts remain a source of inspiration for at least a few *Homo sapiens* that also fancy themselves *Homo religiosus*.

Lisle Dalton

Further Reading

Frangsmyr, Tore, Sten Lindroth, Gunnar Eriksson and Gunnar Broberg, eds. *Linnaeus: The Man and His Work*. Berkeley: University of California Press, 1983.

Koerner, Lisbet. *Linnaeus: Nature and Nation*. Cambridge: Harvard University Press, 1999.

See also: Darwin, Charles; Science

Lopez, Barry (1945–)

Born in New York in 1945, Barry Holstun Lopez spent most of his first ten years in California, returning to the West after college at Notre Dame for graduate studies in folklore in Oregon. Deciding for a life of writing rather than an academic career, he settled on the McKenzie River in western Oregon. His writing is primarily in the genres of short stories and natural history essays; he has received literary awards for both and is one of the leading U.S. contemporary ecological writers.

Best known among his non-fiction works are *Of Wolves and Men*, *Arctic Dreams*, and the collection of essays, *Crossing Open Ground*. His fiction includes *Desert Notes*, *River Notes*, *Field Notes*, and *Winter Count*. Central to all his work is the landscape – whether of Oregon or other parts of the U.S. West or the Americas, the Arctic or Antarctic. Whatever the location, his work aims to create a palpable awareness of a landscape that is rich in details and in mystery, in facts and in meaning. In "Landscape and Narrative" he describes an external and an internal landscape.

The external landscape is the one we see – not only the line and color of the land and its shading at different times of the day, but also its plants and animals in season, its wealth, its geology, the record of its climate and evolution" (Lopez 1989: 64).

Both the external and internal landscapes become comprehensible only by understanding the relationships between and within them, which requires sensuous participation as well as mental reflection. It is the patterns that he believes inhere in these relationships that create a meaningful, trustworthy universe.

To draw the reader into the experience of a particular landscape, Lopez fills his books with scientific information about geography, plants, and animals, including their migration and socializing patterns; as well as information about humans: their mythic stories and artistic creations and their differences (e.g., between Eskimo and European orientations), their scientific research and technological developments, their expeditions – and his reflections on all of these. A *New York Times* review of *Arctic Dreams* said that it is "a book about the Arctic North in the way that *Moby-Dick* is a novel about whales" (Kakutani 1986). I think there are many ways in which this is not true. Although Lopez's goal is certainly to discover more about humans through his explorations of the land, the landscape does not serve primarily as a springboard to reflect on human meaning; rather, it is only by deeply understanding the whole process of which humans are an interrelated part that they can come to understand themselves. He reports that as he traveled through the Arctic, he came to the realization "that people's desires and aspirations were as much a part of the land as the wind, solitary animals, and the bright fields of stone and tundra. And, too, that the land itself existed quite apart from these" (Lopez 1986: xxii). Humans can be understood, then, only as part of the landscape.

This land that exists apart from humans can be approached imaginatively, though not definitively. Lopez could be accused of anthropomorphism as he imagines what it would be like to be a wolf or when he says of migrating geese, "They flew beautifully each morning in the directions they intended, movements of desires . . . In that hour their lives seemed flush with yearning" (Lopez 1986: 158). However, rather than collapsing animals into humans, what he is trying to do is open our human imaginings to the full and rich *Umwelt*, or life-world, that a wolf has quite beyond our imaginings (Lopez 1978: 285) and enable us to allow for the mystery that geese too may have desires, not known by us.

Lopez seldom speaks directly about religion in relation to this quest for openness to the world, though his works are filled with a sense of "something more" (as Williams James defined religion), which one comes upon in the landscape, even though it remains elusive. Nor do his works invite a translation into religious tenants. Such categorization loses the rich reality of humans fully living in and with the landscape, within which the sacred reveals itself. He says he hopes his writing will "contribute to a literature of hope" (Lopez 1998: 14), which seems to depend on humans beings recognizing their place in and responsibility to the whole and the spiritual meaning that is rooted in the whole, which lies beyond human ability to comprehend or control.

> Whatever evaluation we finally make of a stretch of land . . . no matter how profound or accurate, we will find it inadequate. The land retains an identity of its own, still deeper and more subtle than we can know. Our obligation toward it then becomes simple: to approach with an uncalculating mind, with an attitude of regard . . . To intend from the beginning to preserve some of the mystery within it as a kind of wisdom to be experienced, not questioned. And to be alert for its openings, for that moment when something sacred reveals itself within the mundane, and you know the land knows you are there (Lopez 1986: 228).

Lynn Ross-Bryant

Further Reading
Aton, Jim. "Interview with Barry Lopez." *Western American Literature* (Spring 1986).
Kakutani, Michiko. "Review." *New York Times* 12 February 1986, C21.
Lopez, Barry H. *About This Life: Journeys on the Threshold of Memory.* New York: Vintage Books, 1998.
Lopez, Barry. *Crossing Open Ground.* New York: Random House, 1989.
Lopez, Barry H. *Arctic Dreams: Imagination and Desire in a Northern Landscape.* New York: Charles Scribner's Sons, 1986.
Lopez, Barry H. *Of Wolves and Men.* New York: Charles Scribner's Sons, 1978.
See also: Memoir and Nature Writing.

Lost Worlds

Remote, unexplored or allegedly "disappeared" regions of the natural and cultural world have been prominent subjects of mytho-poetic discourses throughout human history. The multifarious conceptions concerning "sunken cities," "islands," or "continents," and similar "lost worlds," have been (and still are) prominent examples for the construction of "utopias," "paradises," and "El Dorados." They have led to influential motifs in colonial expansion or exotic imaginations about foreign countries and civilizations, and in many instances, evolutionary myths with historical, geographic or socio-political facets come into play.

In his dialogues *Timaios* and *Kritias*, the Greek philosopher Plato presented the famous account of a mythic island called "Atlantis," using it mainly as an elucidation for certain socio-political ideals set in a once perfect and abundant commonwealth (Plato indeed used to incorporate mythic illustrations in his philosophical writings). Following this paradigmatic story, which includes a final destruction of the island with its spiritually declined population by nature catastrophes (flood and earthquakes), Atlantis gradually surfaced as one of the most popular mytho-geographical and nature-historical images in the utopian genres of the West. Following the corresponding literary output of modern Theosophic/esoteric "visionaries" like Helena P. Blavatsky (*The Secret Doctrine* [1888]), Edgar Cayce (various clearvoyant "Readings" related to Atlantis) or James Churchward (*The Lost Continent of Mu, The Children of Mu*, both in 1931), and others, many of today's esoteric traditions have incorporated the idea of sunken islands into their mythic topography and history of Earth's past and future. Culture heroes of primordial times (the "Builders") are associated with these sunken islands, and in many esoteric eschatologies Atlantis is supposed to "return" again one day from the bottom of the "Atlantic" Ocean (as well as its legendary companion "Lemuria" or "Mu" in the Pacific Ocean), when a millenarian harmony is finally to be restored on "Mother Earth".

As in the case of Ignatius Donnelly's prominent *Atlantis: the Antediluvian World* (1882), and up to the present time, countless attempts have been made to identify and locate Atlantis, and to relate the Atlantis-legend to other mythic accounts of various religious traditions in order to prove its historical truth – for example, to the mythic "Aztlan" of the Aztec mythic records about the origin of the "Mexicans." Sometimes, the "lost world" mythology of Atlantis, Mu, Thule, and the like, is combined with the global dissemination of the whole human race – or at least certain "superior" parts of it, as in some strands of (Neo-) Nazi esotericism. A similar nativistic reconstruction of a "lost world" can be found in revisionist strands of Neo-Hindu thought, when the ancient Indus Valley civilization is presented as "the" grand culture-giving (and supposedly "Vedic") source for all humanity – with high technologies, and the like. Until today, innumerable books and web-pages are devoted to such "lost worlds" – themes or aspects thereof – including ideas about living subterranean or submarine remnants of the legendary "Atlanteans," or even quite anomalistic ideas about an inhabited "hollow Earth" (cf. Childress & Shaver).

In the modern Space Age, however, the "lost world" idea is expressed not only in such "earthly" terms, but also on an interplanetary or even intergalactic level – especially in the modern fantasy (cf. H.P. Lovecraft) and science-fiction genres. Obviously, the frontiers of today's "terrae incognitae" have moved more and more into outer space. However, Lucian's (Lukianos of Samosata; ca. 120–180) eye-twinkling "records" in his *True Stories* – a collection of biting satires on the Greek utopian genre – relate miraculous "travels" by sailing ship to some kingdoms of the solar system and, thus, display quite an ancient prototype for contemporary science-fiction utopias and Star Wars-scenarios up in the skies.

With their spiritual reinterpretation of the Space Age cosmology, contemporary religious ufologies clearly display a postmodern "re-enchantment" of the heavenly reigns with "Angels in space suits" (see Clark 1998). Here, the earthly Atlantis/Mu-theme is often reappearing in particular association with "extraterrestrial" Space Aliens as primordial culture heroes who supposedly colonized these mundane regions with the use of superior technologies (space and air travel, genetic engineering, etc.), unknown energies, and paranormal faculties (cf. the once relatively famous Californian "Sunburst" community around Norman Paulsen in the 1980s). The impact of Charles Fort's *Book of the Damned* (1919; with three follow-up volumes), propounding the idea that "we are property" of some superior Alien race, has additionally shaped this line of thought which is still very popular in modern religious ufologies (cf. "Ashtar Command" or Claude Vorilhon's "Raëlian Religion") and in various other esoteric cosmologies and "channelings," as well as in the so-called "Ancient Astronauts" theories or "paleo-SETI" discourses of Erich von Däniken, Robert Charroux and similar "fringe" archeologists and "Fortean" students.

However, this seemingly contemporary tie between a superior scientific or technological control over nature and the Atlantis-theme (e.g., E. Cayce) can already be found in Francis Bacon's *Nova Atlantis* (1626/27), where he describes a utopian island with an ideal commonwealth: in a wonderful socio-political setting, the scientists of "Bensalem" developed devices for "flying in the air," as well as "ships and boats for going under water"; they also used scientific experiments to breed "new animals" and "perfect creatures" by hitherto unknown means, all in service to the inhabitants' utilitarian needs ("Happy are the people of Bensalem"). Combining pious recourse to transcendence with an empirical and rational pursuit of truth, spiritually and scientifically "enlightened" reason is presented to serve "perfect" human hedonistic control over nature.

In a similar vein, most of the "lost world" myths idealize the "perfect society" in all dimensions – comprising justice on the societal and individual plane, economic well-being and abundance, scientific and spiritual enlightenment, control *over* nature, and, at the same time, harmony *with* nature, as well as the use of advanced, but ecologically harmless ("green") technologies and "free energies." Despite apparently "modern" technological issues, this alludes strongly to the archetypal "once upon a time" image of the paradisiacal "Garden": Its representation by mytho-logic is a ubiquitous religious method to stage important human ideals, norms, hopes, as well as paradigmatic warnings – even if the mythic reappearance of the lost paradise is put into an imminent, or distant, millenarian future.

In the end, therefore, the most successful search for Atlantis and its alleged siblings, once "forgotten" and "sunken" during the course of Earth's natural history, will locate these "lost worlds" not so much topographically somewhere on the globe, but rather in the religious, mythic and utopian creativity of the human mind.

Andreas Gruenschloss

Further Reading
Bacon, Roger. "The New Atlantis" (*Nova Atlantis*, 1627). In *The Harvard Classics*, vol. 4. New York: Collier, 1909 (also available on the internet).
Charroux, Robert. *Forgotten Worlds*. New York: Walker, 1973.
Childress, David Hatcher and Richard Shaver. *Lost Continents and the Hollow Earth*. Kempton, IL: Adventures Unlimited Press, 1999 (reprint).
Clark, Jerome. *The UFO Book. Encyclopedia of the Extraterrestrial*. Detroit: Visible Ink Press, 1998.
De Camp, Lyon Sprague. *Lost Continents: The Atlantis Theme in History, Science, and Literature*. New York: Dover, 1970 (1954).
Donelly, Ignatius. *Atlantis – The Antediluvian World*. New York: Dover, 1976 (1882).
Goodrich-Clark, Nicholas. *Black Sun: Aryan Cults, Esoteric Nazism and the Politics of Identity*. New York: New York University Press, 2002.
Paulsen, Norman. *Sunburst: Return of the Ancients*. Goleta, CA: Sunburst, 1980.
See *also*: Earth Mysteries; Fascism; Proto-Indo-Europeans.

Lovelock, James (1919–)

James Lovelock, a professional research biologist and Fellow of the Royal Academy, is best known as the author of the Gaia hypothesis, a proposal that the Earth be viewed as a single physiological system. Lovelock began to develop the Gaia hypothesis in 1965 while he was working with NASA to test for life on Mars. Realizing that the lack of atmosphere was evidence of a lifeless Mars led him to recognize the vital importance of life in maintaining the improbable chemical balance of the Earth's atmosphere. Working out the details of this insight, he published a full argument for his hypothesis in his 1979 book, *Gaia: A New Look at Life on Earth*. The initial response from the scientific community was mixed – some, such as the evolutionary biologist Richard Dawkins, denounced the hypothesis as unscientific. However, the effect on the popular imagination was strong, and the name Gaia quickly became identified with the emerging environmental movement – especially as it sought to address global issues. Lovelock continued to work on Gaia, using computer modeling to simulate global processes; and he set forth the complete theory in his 1988 book, *The Ages of Gaia: A Biography of Our Living Earth*. From the beginning he has had a number of allies in developing Gaia theory including the microbiologist Lynn Margulis, who identified the specific role of microbial life in maintaining homeostasis of the planetary system. Gaia theory has persisted and refined itself, and now has many adherents amongst other biological scientists in spite of its initial poor reception.

Gaia has had a particular appeal to religious thinkers. Lovelock reports that two-thirds of his mail related to Gaia theory asks about the relationship between Gaia and God. While Lovelock has been supportive of theologians and other religious thinkers using Gaia theory, he has personally taken a more reserved stance. He identifies himself as an agnostic and does not support the idea that Gaia theory provides warrant for the existence of a particular divinity. However, he has argued that the holistic aspects of Gaia theory inspire a sense of wonder and devotion to the Earth system and an understanding of the human role within it.

Lovelock is above all an independent thinker, as displayed by his often tense relationship with the environmental movement. Environmentalists have expressed concern that Gaia theory undermines the magnitude of the environmental crisis by suggesting that the self-regulation of the system will compensate for human destruction. Lovelock actually suggested that Gaia theory gives insight into how human actions disrupt not only local environments, but also the global regulation system itself. However, Lovelock has distanced himself from environmentalists who display suspicions of science and technology, himself advocating primarily technological responses to environmental problems. He often credits the environmental movement with a dogmatism that undermines the free inquiry of science. While he was one of the first scientists to identify the quantity of chlorofluorocarbons (CFCs) in the Southern atmosphere, he found himself initially on the industry side of the ozone debate of the late twentieth century. As a result, he was cast as a lackey of industry. Although Lovelock later embraced the environmentalist side of that debate, he holds that he was motivated by clear science rather than political commitments.

Grant Potts

Further Reading

Lovelock, James. *Homage to Gaia: The Life of an Independent Scientist.* Oxford: Oxford University Press, 2000.

Lovelock, James. *Gaia: A New Look at Life on Earth.* Oxford: Oxford University Press, 2000 (3rd edn).

Lovelock, James. *The Ages of Gaia: A Biography of Our Living Earth.* New York: W.W. Norton and Company, 1988.

Margulis, Lynn and Dorian Sagan. *Slanted Truths: Essays on Gaia, Symbiosis, and Evolution.* New York: Copernicus, 1997.

See also: Epic of Evolution; Gaia; Gaia Foundation and Earth Community Network; Gaian Mass; Gaian Pilgrimage.

Luo (Kenya) – See Hyenas – Spotted; Snakes and the Luo of Kenya.

Lyons, Oren (1930–)

As Faithkeeper of the Turtle Clan of the Onondaga Nation, Oren Lyons has been a clear, persistent, and respected voice for the Haudenosaunee (Iroquois Confederacy), and for indigenous people throughout the world. He has effectively carried the message of an environmental crisis facing indigenous ways of life to larger human communities. His personal life story spans a wide diversity of experiences including athletics, hunting, fishing, painting, public speaking, activism, writing and serving as a traditional leader. He has had several careers including a tour of duty in the army, a commercial artist, a professor, and an ambassador to the United Nations for the Haudenosaunee.

Lyons, whose clan name is Joagquisho, was born in 1930. He was raised on the Onondaga Nation Territory in upstate New York. During his youth he learned Haudenosaunee ceremonial practices, which included their game of lacrosse. He also learned to hunt, fish and live fully with respect for the natural world. From 1951–1953 he was a member of the 82nd Airborne Division of the US Army. In 1957 he was the goalie for the undefeated lacrosse team at Syracuse University and made the All American Lacrosse Team, playing with Jim Brown, who would go on to pro-football fame. After receiving his Bachelor of Fine Arts from Syracuse University in 1958, he moved to New York City to pursue a career as a freelance commercial artist. During this time he also worked for Norcross Greeting Cards, Inc., supervising 250 artists and technicians.

In 1967, at the request of Clan-mothers, he gave up his career and returned to the Onondaga Nation to be raised as a Faithkeeper of the Turtle Clan. The Onondaga Nation Territory, near Syracuse, is the Central Fire of the Iroquois (or "Haudenosaunee") Confederacy. The Haudenosaunee are the last remaining traditional indigenous government, still in charge of their lands, that is recognized by the United States. It is still run by the Longhouse system of clans, which are overseen by Clan-mothers, Clan-chiefs, sub-chiefs, and male and female Faithkeepers. From 1971 until the present he has been a Professor of American Studies at the State University of New York in Buffalo.

Lyons has been present at many of the most significant recent events for indigenous people. In 1972 he accompanied a peace delegation of the Haudenosaunee to the Bureau of Indian Affairs (BIA) headquarters in Washington, D.C., which had been taken over by the American Indian Movement (AIM). In 1973 he led a Haudenosaunee delegation to the Lakota Nation during the standoff at Wounded Knee. In 1977 he was instrumental in organizing a group of Native American leaders to speak at the United Nations in Geneva, Switzerland. This momentous event is the subject of the book *Basic Call to Consciousness*. He has continued his work at the UN and helped to establish the Working Group on Indigenous Populations in 1982. He serves on the Executive Committee of the Global Forum of Spiritual and Parliamentary Leaders on Human Survival. He is a co-founder of the Traditional Circle of Indian Elders and Youth, which is an annual council of traditional grassroots leadership of Native American nations. In 1990 he was a negotiator between the governments of Canada, Quebec, New York State, and the Mohawk Nation over the crisis at the Mohawk community of Oka. He then led a delegation of seventeen American Indian leaders to meet with President Bush in Washington in 1991. In 1992 he organized a Haudenosaunee delegation to attend the United Nations Conference on Environment and Development in Rio de Janeiro. Lyons was a founder of the Haudenosaunee Environmental task force. In 2000, along with co-chair Henry Lickers, he won the EDA, Region 2-Environmental Quality Award of the U.S. Environmental Protection Agency. Also in 2000 he was a plenary speaker in the Global Environmental Youth Convention held in Lund, Sweden.

Oren Lyons has been featured in many important media events. In 1992 he was the subject of a one-hour documentary by Bill Moyers titled "Faithkeeper." He has appeared as a major speaker before the U.N. in New York and Geneva. He has appeared on Larry King Live and the Charlie Rose show and has been a featured speaker on various film projects including the acclaimed series "The Native Americans" produced by TBS in 1992. He wrote the story and script for the film *Hidden Medicine* that debuted at the Sundance Film Festival in 1999. In 2001 he sat down in public with the famous author and friend Peter Matthiesson to discuss "Perspectives on Spiritual Law and Human Responsibility" at the SUNY College of Environmental Science and Forestry and Syracuse University. Lyons is well known to some of the most respected entertainers in the film and music industry. He consistently uses his visibility to emphasize those things most urgent to him; namely the survival of indigenous people, their traditions and the perpetuation of creation.

He is known also for his lifelong commitment to the game of lacrosse. It was originally a Haudenosaunee game and is still played as a healing game among the Longhouse people. Since 1983 Lyons has helped organize the Iroquois Nationals Lacrosse Team, which has competed in the World Games. Over the last twenty years the Iroquois Nationals have steadily risen in the world rankings. The effect of their performance among the world's top teams has been an increasing pride among the Haudenosaunee youth. In 1993 he was inducted into the Lacrosse National Hall of Fame. In 1998 he was inducted into the Ontario Lacrosse Hall of Fame. In 2003 he was inducted into the International Scholar-Athlete Hall of Fame at the University of Rhode Island's Institute for International Sport.

In 1992 Lyons, along with John Mohawk, published his most important scholarly work titled *Exiled in the Land of the Free*. Through his efforts in educating America's leaders the U.S. Senate passed resolution #76 in 1987 which formally acknowledges the "contribution of the Iroquois Confederacy of Nations to the development of the United States Constitution." Founding Fathers Thomas Jefferson, George Washington and Benjamin Franklin counseled with Haudenosaunee leaders to discuss effective governmental structures. Resolution #76 goes on to reaffirm the continuing government-to-government relationship between Indian tribes and the U.S. In 1992 he was formally recognized in the U.S. Senate for his work.

Lyons was awarded two honorary doctorates. The first in 1987 by the City University of New York Law School at Queens College, and the second in 1993 by Syracuse University. In 1994 he was given the First Annual National Museum of the American Indian Art and Cultural Achievement Award by the Smithsonian Institution. In 1995 he was given The Elder and Wiser Award for "Selfless efforts on behalf of the human family," which was presented to him by Rosa Parks at the Rosa Parks Institute for Human Rights and Self-Development. For many years Lyons has been working with the business and government leaders in Sweden on their ambitions to become the leading nation in Europe on sustainable development. For his efforts in Sweden he was named Honorary Adult Friend of The World's Children's Prize for the Rights of the Child in 2002.

Lyon is currently Chairman of the Honoring Nations Advisory Board, which is a granting agency administered through the Harvard Project on American Indian Economic Development. He is also board-member of The American Indian Law Alliance; The American Indian Institute: the Traditional Circle of Elders and Youth; The International Lacrosse Federation (ILF); The Iroquois Nationals Lacrosse; The Global Forum of Spiritual and Parliamentary Leaders; The Institute for the Preservation of the Original Languages of the Americas; and the American Indian Ritual Object Repatriation Foundation.

Oren Lyons has spoken to world-famous environmentalists, artists, academics, businessmen, politicians, entertainers, and athletes in world forums. He is equally well known to traditional leaders among various indigenous communities all over the world. He has traversed this world with a critical eye on all that serves to degrade and destroy the natural world. His message of peace is that human beings can no longer afford to act irresponsibly toward creation; nor can people of the First World continue to disregard the messages coming from indigenous people. Lyons has listened to indigenous people from all parts of the Earth and his conclusion is that we have a very short time in which to turn our world from its present destructive path. Human beings are routinely defying the natural laws of creation – something that they can no longer afford to do. It will inevitably lead to our own destruction unless we can find a suitable response to the present malaise of the human spirit.

Philip P. Arnold

Further Reading

Lyons, Oren and John Mohawk, eds. *Exiled in the Land of the Free: Democracy, Indian Nations and the U.S. Constitution*. Santa Fe, NM: Clear Light Press, 1992.

See also: Haudenosaunee Confederacy; Holy Land in Native North America; Law, Religion, and Native American Lands; Mother Earth; Religious Studies and Environmental Concern; Sacred Geography in Native North America; United Nations' "Earth Summits".

M

Maasai (Tanzania)

Historically, Maasai were semi-nomadic pastoralists who lived in Tanzania and Kenya. Nature and its elements have been and remain central to Maasai religion, even as Maasai lives and livelihoods have changed in response to colonialism, nationalism, development interventions, Christian evangelization, education and other processes. These processes have also exacerbated regional, social, cultural and thus religious variations among and within Maasai sections (large territorial groupings). Moreover, although many Maasai, in addition to keeping livestock, now cultivate small farms, work for wages, and pursue other modes of economic diversification, most still remember and uphold their long-standing history and ideals as semi-nomadic pastoralists. Their close customary relationship to and dependence on the environment for their sustenance and social reproduction was expressed in many aspects of their religious beliefs and practices, including: their concept of their deity (*Eng'ai*), their sacred symbols and colors, their holy mountains and trees, their attitudes toward wild and domestic animals, and their prayers and praise songs. Although many of their beliefs and practices continue today, this entry is written in the past tense to acknowledge the changing circumstances of their lives.

Maasai believed in one deity, Eng'ai (also spelled Ng'ai, Nkai, and Enkai), who was understood primarily, although not exclusively, in feminine terms as the divine principle that created and nurtured life on Earth. Eng'ai also meant "rain" and "sky," and was addressed through many metaphors such as *Noompees*, ("She of the growing grasses") and *Yieyio nashal inkilani* ("My mother with the wet clothes") that emphasized wetness, darkness, motherhood and growth, and thus reinforced the association of Eng'ai with fertility and femaleness. According to most myths and proverbs, Eng'ai resided in and was one with the sky, and had a dialectical relationship of mutual dependency with *enkop*, the land or the Earth: *Kerisio Eng'ai o Enkop*, "Eng'ai and the Earth are equal." Together, Eng'ai and humans, the Sky and Earth, created and nurtured life; there was a necessary unity and complementarity between them. All natural phenomena, especially those concerned with the weather, were attributed to the interventions of Eng'ai and read as expressions of divine power and judgment – rain as blessing, drought as displeasure, thunder and lightening as anger, rainbows as approval, and comets as portents of bad luck.

Both Eng'ai and humans had the ability, through their actions, to alter their relationship. This agency is evident in one set of myths that describe how, because of human jealousy and greed, Eng'ai ended the flow of cattle to Maasai from the sky and distanced (but did not separate) herself from them. The dynamic relationship between humans and Eng'ai also shaped how Maasai understood and invoked Eng'ai in their daily lives, and the almost complete lack, at least historically, of a distinction between the sacred and secular worlds. Although most Maasai men tended to pray only on special occasions to Eng'ai, Maasai women prayed throughout the day, from the early morning when they milked their cattle to their last waking moment at night. During their prayers, women sprinkled some milk on the ground for Eng'ai, raised their arms and heads to the sky (sometimes clutching grass in their hands), and entreated her for continued protection, preservation, expansion and prosperity of the family and herds. Women also sang prayer and praise songs to Eng'ai when gathered together for chores and rest, or at ceremonies and celebrations. Through their prayer and songs, women maintained a daily, ongoing relationship with Eng'ai, and took responsibility for ensuring that Eng'ai bestowed continued blessing and bounty on their households.

In addition to the constant intercessions of women, Maasai also tried to influence and understand Eng'ai's actions through their *iloibonok* (*oloiboni*, singular), male ritual leaders who had the powers of prophecy and divination. According to Maasai myths, iloibonok were direct descendants of Eng'ai, beginning with the first *oloiboni*, Kidongoi, who became the apical ancestor of their sub-clan, Inkidong'i. They were always seen as "outsiders" to some extent, and their powers were viewed with a mixture of fear and fascination. There were major Iloibonok who had superior powers of prophecy and divination and large followings. They were called upon to appeal to Eng'ai in times of great crisis such as prolonged drought, warfare, or sickness, and some even served as Maasai "chiefs" during the early colonial period. In contrast, the minor Iloibonok usually did not prophesy, but performed divinations at the request of individual clients to investigate more mundane, everyday problems such as the occasional ill health of people and livestock. The primary method of divination was to shake stones and other objects from a gourd or horn, then analyze them with the complex Maasai numerology of auspicious and inauspicious numbers. Iloibonok also provided charms and amulets for various purposes such as to ward off sickness or to ensure the success of a cattle raid by junior men.

Finally, in times of crisis and concern, Maasai men and women held elaborate ceremonies to entreat Eng'ai for help. These usually involved prayer and praise song-dances, the ritual slaughter, roasting and consumption of cattle, the brewing and imbibing of honey beer, and special prayers using elements of nature associated with Eng'ai such as milk, honey, grass, and water (discussed below).

As pastoralists, Maasai were concerned with having sufficient grass and water to feed their livestock. Not surprisingly, then, grass and certain liquids (milk, spittle and honey) featured in their religious entreaties, practices and ceremonies as near-sacred symbols of and gifts from Eng'ai. Grass was a sign of welcome and peace. It was often held in the hands, tied as a sprig to one's clothing, placed in the neck of a calabash, or draped on someone's shoulders as they were being blessed. Milk, like cattle, was a gift from Eng'ai, and symbolically associated with women (who produced, processed and controlled its distribution) and fertility. It was sprinkled on the ground at the beginning of each milking, on humans from a calabash with grass in its mouth for blessing, and offered to family, visitors, and even strangers. To spit on a person (usually their head or hands) or a thing (such as a gift) was to bless them or express reverence. New-borns were spat on constantly, elders spat into the hands of juniors to bless them and wish them well, and ritual participants often spat a mixture of milk and water on whoever was being honored, prayed for, or blessed. Honey signified the sweetness of Eng'ai, and honey beer was also often spat on people as a sign of blessing.

These and other natural elements were associated with and expressed in the meaning and use of colors in the Maasai religious cosmology. White (of milk, animal fat, and the white cumulus clouds that appear after a rain storm) was a sign of blessing, peace and contentment. White chalk was often used to draw special protective designs on the face, legs or torso of certain ritual participants; they were also sometimes anointed with animal fat. Maasai spoke of *Eng'ai Naibor*, the "White God," or the "God with the white stomach." A stomach was white and content from being filled with the milk that was Eng'ai's gift to Maasai. White beads also featured in Maasai beadwork.

Black (of the dark rain clouds) was a particularly holy color. Black cloth used to be worn by fertile women, and is still worn by people in holy or liminal states (such as newly circumcised boys and girls, or prophets and prophetesses) to entreat Eng'ai's special protection. Eng'ai was referred to as *Eng'ai Narok*, the "Black God," when she was being helpful, kind and compassionate. Black bulls were required for the sacrifices made at major age-set ceremonies and the dark blue beads (which were categorized as black) worn by married men and women marked the sanctity of their marital bonds. Charcoal was often used to make symbolic black markings and designs.

The meaning of red (of blood and ochre) was somewhat contradictory. On the one hand red clothing (formerly leather rubbed with ochre, now red cloth) and skin (achieved by rubbing a mixture of ochre and cow fat) were considered a distinctive marker of Maasai ethnic identity. As the color of blood, red signified kinship, life and vitality. On the other hand, red could express anger and destruction. When the actions of Eng'ai were seen as harmful and vengeful, she was called *Eng'ai Nanyokie*, the "Red God." Red was also associated with fire and the relentless heat of the dry season. Red for Maasai was, it seems, the color of power, which had the potential to be creative or destructive, or even both – destroying in order to create. Finally, many other nature-associated colors – the blue of the sky, the green of the grass, the orange of the sun – appeared in meaningful patterns and arrangements in the elaborately beaded ornaments, jewelry and clothing crafted by Maasai women. Thus Eng'ai was sometimes referred to as *Parmuain*, "Multicolored God."

Maasai also symbolically associated trees and mountains with Eng'ai. Trees and shrubs were called *olcani*, which also meant "medicine." The roots, bark and leaves of certain trees and shrubs were used as medicine to treat specific diseases. Since disease and death, like health and birth, were derived from Eng'ai, the power of olcani to heal and protect was understood as a divine intervention mediated through human knowledge and practice. In addition, *oreteti*, a species of parasitic fig tree, was believed to be particularly sacred. The oreteti tree spreads and grows by lodging its seeds in the cracks and crevices of other trees. As a result, its branches extend in all directions and its many roots entangle and hang down in coils from the host tree from sometimes-great heights. Oreteti often have water in their trunks and fissures, its sap is a reddish color, and its leaves contain a milky white substance. Maasai saw these vertical thickets as links growing from the sky and Eng'ai down to the Earth and humans; they were therefore considered holy places where people could be closer to Eng'ai. Maasai men and women visited these holy trees either alone or in groups to pray, worship, and plead to Eng'ai for rain and other blessings. The leaves, bark and branches of the oreteti tree were also used in religious ceremonies and prayers.

Certain mountains also figured in Maasai religious cosmology and stories as the homes of Eng'ai or her descendants. Oldoinyo Orok, the "Black Mountain" (Mt. Meru) was recognized as holy and a home of Eng'ai. Oldoinyo Oibor, the "White Mountain" (snow-capped Mt. Kilimanjaro), was sometimes referred to as the home of the first human, Naiterukop ("She who creates the earth"). Oldoinyo Leng'ai, the "Mountain of God," is an active volcano that still spouts smoke and ash in the Rift Valley.

Its occasional eruptions signaled the wrath of Eng'ai. Nonetheless, ritual delegations of barren Maasai women (*olamal*), led by elder men, regularly visited Oldoinyo Leng'ai to pray to Eng'ai to bless them with children.

As part of their reverence for nature as Eng'ai's creation, Maasai also treated wild and domestic animals with respect. Cattle, of course, were prized as the primary source of food, social worth and Maasai identity. Each animal was distinguished by name, based on its colors, size, and other physical features. Goats and sheep were also marked as individuals, although with less fanfare and prestige. Historically, Maasai did not hunt or eat wild animals, including the large herds of wildebeest and zebra that roamed their plains. Lions, however, were hunted by junior men for protection and prestige. Snakes were usually left alone, and there was a belief that certain very prominent men returned as black pythons. Birds were never eaten, but certain species were killed so that their bodies and feathers could be used to create elaborate headdresses for newly circumcised boys.

Nature and all of its elements, as described above, were reflected and expressed in Maasai prayers and praise songs. As an example, take a woman's dance song recorded by Jan Voshaar and transcribed in his book *Maasai, Between the Oreteti-Tree and the Tree of the Cross*. The chorus invoked both Eng'ai and the Earth: "We pray to Eng'ai and Earth, iyioo. God of many qualities. O Multicolored God, let me (us) pass where the calf was slaughtered for rain, give me also someone to sit with." The ensuing verses mentioned sitting under shady trees, begged Eng'ai to give children to all women, and invoked "The oreteti tree of the white clay so sweet; Sweet at the time of ritual." One verse asked Eng'ai to "Give me that which is yellow and that which is white," referring to the first milk and the last milk of both mothers and cows. Another series of verses spoke of the duality and complementarity of Eng'ai and the Earth: "To the two expanses I pray; I pray to God's expanses that comes as equals" (1998: 226–7).

In conclusion, Eng'ai's relationship to humans was seen in and understood through nature. Since Maasai had no concept of the afterlife, they focused on leading good and holy (*sinyati*) lives in the present so that Eng'ai would be pleased and bless them with good health, children and cattle. The focus of their religious beliefs and practices was thus on maintaining the complementarity between Eng'ai and humans, between the sky (or heavens) and the Earth, and correcting – through daily prayers and ritual ceremonies – any transgressions or disturbances that occurred to this relationship.

In recent years, this relationship has been more difficult to maintain as the tremendous, cumulative losses of land and key water supplies to game parks, commercial agriculture, and settlers have converged with a long history of inappropriate development interventions to undermine pastoralism as a viable livelihood and to force Maasai to seek other ways of supporting themselves. Moreover, these colonial and post-colonial interventions have also privileged Maasai men as economic and political actors, thereby disenfranchising Maasai women from their historical rights and powers. In response to these dislocations, many Maasai women have embraced Christianity as a way to enhance their spiritual powers and critique what they perceive as the increasingly materialistic, secular and amoral practices of Maasai men. Maasai religious beliefs and practices have been encouraged, modified, disparaged, or prohibited, depending on the denomination and attitude of the missionaries and church involved.

Dorothy L. Hodgson

Further Reading
Århem, Kaj. "A Folk Model of Pastoral Subsistence: The Meaning of Milk, Meat, and Blood in Maasai Diet." In Anita Jacobson-Widding and Walter Van Beek, eds. *The Creative Communion: African Folk Models of Fertility and the Regeneration of Life*. Stockholm: Almqvist & Wiksell, 1990, 201–31.

Århem, Kaj. "Why Trees are Medicine: Aspects of Maasai Cosmology." In Anita Jacobson-Widding and David Westerlund, eds. *Culture, Experience and Pluralism*. Stockholm: Almqvist & Wiksell, 1989, 75–84.

Galaty, John. "Ceremony and Society: The Poetics of Maasai Ritual." *Man* 18:2 (1983), 361–82.

Hodgson, Dorothy L. *Once Intrepid Warriors: Gender, Ethnicity and the Cultural Politics of Maasai Development*. Bloomington: Indiana University Press, 2001.

Hodgson, Dorothy L. "Engendered Encounters: Men of the Church and the 'Church of Women' in Maasailand, Tanzania, 1950–1993." *Comparative Studies in Society and History* 41:4 (1999), 758–83.

Hollis, Alfred C. *The Masai: Their Language and Folklore*. Freeport, NY: Book for Libraries Press, 1905.

Olsson, Tord. "Philosophy of Medicine among the Maasai." In Anita Jacobson-Widding and David Westerlund, eds. *Culture, Experience and Pluralism*. Stockholm: Almqvist & Wiksell, 1989, 235–46.

Voshaar, Jan. *Maasai: Between the Oreteti-Tree and the Tree of the Cross*. Kampen, Netherlands: Kok Publishers, 1998.

See also: Sacred Mountains; San (Bushmen) Religion; (and adjacent, San (Bushmen) Rainmaking); Volcanoes.

Maathi, Wangari – *See* Kenya Green Belt Movement.

MacGillis, Sister Miriam – *See* Genesis Farm.

Macy, Joanna (1929–)

One of the outgrowths of social and environmental activism in the late twentieth and early twenty-first centuries has been a reevaluation and reappropriation of the various religious traditions of the world. "Engaged Buddhism" utilizes Buddhist concepts such as co-dependent co-arising (in Sanskrit, *Pratîtya Samutpâda*), compassion (*karunâ*) and wisdom (*prajñâ*) as a basis for ethical action in the world. Many Buddhist practitioners understand their relationship with the natural world in terms of interconnectedness and mutuality of being. These ideas are used to describe both experiences of unity with the natural world, as well as to provide an impetus for action on behalf of it.

Joanna Macy, one of the founders of the Institute for Deep Ecology, combines Buddhist teaching and practices with General Systems Theory in workshops and classes that she leads around the world in order to facilitate personal and social transformation, especially in regard to environmental issues. She promotes what she refers to as the "Great Turning," from an industrial growth society, to a life-sustaining civilization.

Through working with Tibetan refugees, she became acquainted with Tibetan Buddhist monks and was formally introduced to Buddhist thought and practice. After returning to the United States, she pursued and completed a doctoral degree in which she explored the relationship between Buddhist notions of interdependence and mutual causality and systems thought (Macy 1991). She spent several years in Sri Lanka where she worked with Theravadan Buddhists of the Sarvodaya Shramadana Movement who were engaged in efforts to help rural villagers to become communally and ecologically self-sustaining. Buddhist insights and practices are found throughout her work.

Macy began to do what she came to call Despair and Empowerment work as a result of her involvement with the Nuclear Freeze and Disarmament campaigns of the 1960s through 1980s (Macy 2000). She developed group exercises and role-playing scenarios that were designed to enable people to acknowledge and express their pain, grief and despair for the world and then to harvest that passion and compassion to bring about the changes necessary to diminish or rid the world of those things which threatened it. Her book, *Despair and Power in the Nuclear Age*, as well as its revision (with Molly Young Brown), *Coming Back to Life: Practices to Reconnect Our Lives, Our World*, grew out of this work and contains a collection of these exercises and role-playing scenarios, as well as an explanation of some of the principles behind Despair and Empowerment work.

In Macy's work, the notion of interconnectedness is what enables persons to feel pain for the world and one another, and is also the source of strength for addressing the crises facing the world:

> I have been deeply inspired by the Buddha's teaching of dependent co-arising. It fills me with a sense of connection and mutual responsibility with all beings. Helping me understand the non-hierarchical and self-organizing nature of life, it is the philosophic grounding of all my work (Macy, www.joannamacy.net).

In Buddhism, the practice of meditation is to break through the illusions the mind creates about the nature of reality. Macy's work builds upon this idea through the use of role playing and exercises designed to help workshop participants to see the world as it is, not only its interconnectedness, but also the destruction of the environment and species extinctions. Her work is designed to cut through the illusions constructed by the individual mind and society that serve to deny the reality of the environmental crisis. But that practice is an engaged practice, addressing environmental and other social issues:

> The vitality of Buddhism today is most clearly reflected in the way it is being brought to bear on social, economic, political, and environmental issues, leading people to become effective agents of change. The gate of the Dharma does not close behind us to secure us in a cloistered existence aloof from the turbulence and suffering of samsara, so much as it leads us out into a life of risk for the sake of all beings. As many Dharma brothers and sisters discover today, the world is our cloister (Macy, www.joannamacy.net).

Macy uses the imagination in the form of role playing and rituals in order to look closely at the actual conditions of the world. This use of the imagination is a way to move people beyond mental numbness to experience the reality of the global environmental situation. One example of this is the Council of All Beings, which Macy and John Seed developed to ritually reconnect human beings with other species and natural forces.

Craig S. Strobel

Further Reading

Macy, Joanna. *Widening Circles*. Gabriola Island, BC, Canada: New Society Publishers, 2000.

Macy, Joanna. *Mutual Causality in Buddhism and General Systems Theory: The Dharma of Natural Systems*. Albany: State University of New York Press, 1991.

Macy, Joanna. *Despair and Power in the Nuclear Age*. Philadelphia, PA: New Society Publishers, 1983.

Macy, Joanna and Molly Young Brown. *Coming Back to Life: Practices to Reconnect Our Lives, Our World.* Gabriola Island, BC, Canada: New Society Publishers, 1998.

Seed, John, Joanna Macy, Pat Fleming and Arne Naess. *Thinking Like a Mountain: Towards a Council of All Beings.* Philadelphia, PA and Santa Cruz, CA: New Society Publishers, 1988.

Strobel, Craig. *Performance, Religious Imagination and the Play of the Land in the Study of Deep Ecology and Its Practices.* Unpublished dissertation. Berkeley, CA: Graduate Theological Union, 2000.

See also: Buddhism – Engaged; Buddhism – North America; Council of All Beings; Deep Ecology; Deep Ecology – Institute for; Epic of Evolution; Gandhi, Mohandas; Re-Earthing; Sarvodaya Shramadana Movement (Sri Lanka); Seed, John.

Magic

Magic is, broadly speaking, an attempt to violate the natural exchange of energy. It seeks an operative shortcut, the getting of more for an output of less. In this sense, the practice of magic appears to be anti-nature – especially the "demonic" magic of the medieval grimoires that seeks to suspend the laws of nature and accomplish superhuman ends. Traditionally, magic represents a category of attempts to tamper with the natural flow. In this sense, it has an affinity with the efforts of technological engineering and civilization's wish to tame or harness the natural world as a resource for exploitation.

But if magic represents a violation of the natural order, a transgression of the linear laws of equal exchange, contemporary science's emergent theories of complexity argue that the cosmos is more alinear than linear. Complexity theory studies retrodictively the processes by which something becomes more than merely the sum of its constituent parts. In like manner, as magic seeks to generate power through ritual and spells, in principle the word when correctly spoken becomes more than itself. In the fullest sense, the word expresses the physical being or essence of the thing it describes. Consequently, magic may be thought of as a "science of the word" – a notion that appears to its fullest in the *logos* prologue to the gospel of St. John.

Another understanding of magic, apart from illusion for the purpose of entertainment, posits it as the production of effects in the world by means of invisible or supernatural causation. It may also be considered as action that is based on belief in the efficacy of symbolic forms. But once again, the essential idea remains the notion of securing something of greater value in exchange for something whose intrinsic worth is less. This need not necessarily involve the supernatural. For instance, for a nominal outlay of electrical energy and telephonic financial charges, two people on different sides of the planet can engage in conversation and as such may be considered involved in an act of magic. This allows recognition of how technology itself represents a violation of the natural law of exchange. For the Greeks, *techne* referred to the "art of craft," and magic and technology were both the patronages of the god Hermes. As French theologian Jacques Ellul explains, *technique* is not only a reference to machines but also to "the logic of manipulation and gain that lay behind machines" (in Davis 1998: 144).

In its traditional sense, magic has limited concerns. These include the healing and preventing of disease, the finding of lost or stolen articles, identifying thieves and witches, gaining vengeance and the warding off of evil influences. An early distinction was made between magic and religion – with magic operating by constraint; religion, through supplication. Following a structural-functionalist approach, the French sociologist Émile Durkheim (1858–1917) accepted a radical distinction between religion as a communal matter and magic as a non-congregational affair between a practitioner and a client. But Marcel Mauss (1872–1950), following a different line of structural-functional theory, in his *A General Theory of Magic* (1902), reasoned that magic is indeed a social phenomenon but one that makes use of a universal force or *mana*, an available spiritual power. In other words, for Mauss, magic or *mana* refers to the genuine effectiveness of things.

In contrast, and following what Graham Cunningham (1999) considers an emotionalist approach, Bronislaw Malinowski (1884–1942) denied Mauss and considered magic not as a universal force but as a power located within the individual magician. It amounts to a substitute technology in primitive society in which scientifically established knowledge is otherwise unavailable. Consequently, for Malinowski, magic is primarily a question of psychology: where knowledge or technology is lacking, it offers psychological relief. Malinowski also distinguished between religion and magic in which the Church is understood as the central community and magic as what exists on the fringes of communal activity. He argued that magical acts are expressions of emotion – particularly emotions that are connected to either possession or powerlessness. Such acts or emotions for Malinowski are in reality mental obsessions.

It is, however, the English anthropologist James G. Frazer (1854–1941), classified within the intellectualist school, who developed the distinction between magic and religion into one of progressive historical stages. For Frazer, magic is part of the earliest level of human development and arises from the human desire to control nature. It is, however, formulated on fallacious understandings of cause and effect. The successive stage of understanding reputedly develops with the realization concerning the ineffectiveness of magical rites and that the laws of magic do not really exist. Control of nature was then placed under the jurisdiction of supernatural beings (gods or spirits) beyond human control. Frazer called the moment when humanity turns to supplication of such forces as the beginning of the stage of religion. However, he posits a third stage, that of science, which is marked by the discovery of the correct laws of nature. As an evolutionist, Frazer expected that both magic and religion would cease to exist as science continues to develop.

Frazer argued that the two laws of magic are imitative and contagious. Imitative or homeopathic magic operates according to the "law" of similarity, that is, the belief that like produces like. Results are achieved through mimicry. In contrast, contagious magic is governed by the "law" of contact – the use of materials that have been in contact with the object of magic. Here, we find the belief that people can be influenced even by remote touch. To these two "categories" of magic, Frazer added a third, namely, the use of items that symbolize the intended object.

Another emotionalist discussed by Cunningham in theorizing magic is Sigmund Freud (1856–1939). One of the clearest contemporary articulations of the Freudian position is that of Faber (1996) who insists that magic in the hands of an adult signifies a regression to infantile fantasy. Belief in magic is seen to root in what is considered the "primary narcissism" of the symbiotic stage of individual development. It amounts accordingly to a form of regressive fusion to the time of unconditional love between mother and child. However, in contrast to this psychological approach is that of the symbolists. Mary Douglas, in *Purity and Danger* (1966), claims that the tendency to dismiss ritualistic sacramental religions as magical and consequently not truly religious is a prejudice that selects the prophetic-Protestant model of inner experience as the paradigm of authentic religiosity. But symbolists consider that magic offers a workable framing of experience in a local context. Nevertheless, modern Western culture has shown an increasing tendency to distrust ritual or symbolic activity of any kind – including magic.

Interest and belief in magic have been present since the beginnings of Western culture. Manuals of magical recipes were formulated in the Middle Ages under the name of grimoires. These sought to conjure demonic entities in order to achieve ends that are beyond ordinary human means. Essentially, grim moiré magic seeks to suspend the laws of nature. This, in turn, developed during the Renaissance into hermetic magic in which a spiritual endeavor was added to the efforts of the magician who now sought to develop an internally personal divine nature. The modern history of magic begins with the late eighteenth century through the rise in Western Europe of dilettante interest in occultism and interaction with Freemasonry as well as the emergence of publicly recognized magical groups. Three literary works became seminal at this time: Ebenezer Sibley's *Celestial Sciences* (1784), Francis Barrett's *The Magus* (1801), and a work published by Count de Gebelin that connected the Tarot with the Egyptian *Book of Thoth*. Barrett's work functioned as the textbook for the group that had gathered around him. It in turn influenced an ex-Catholic seminarian, Alphonse-Louis Constant, who, under the name of Eliphas Levi, published in the 1850s *Dogma and Ritual of High Magic*, *History of Magic* and *Key of the Great Mysteries* that purportedly revived the entire Western magical tradition. Levi invented the terms *occultisme* ("hidden wisdom") and *haut magie* ("high magic") and claimed for magic both antiquity and potency. He insisted that magic is the only universally valid religion. Levi is responsible for rediscovering both the Kabbalah and the Tarot, and he is a foundational inspiration for Rosicrucians, ritual magicians and contemporary witches.

Levi had adopted the Freemasonic idea that the human race had been created as part of the divine. Consequently, the divine nature is arguably still present and something one can contact – chiefly by going back into the past, foremost to Egypt. In other words, Levi changed the concept of old magic that sought the gods into a search for self-knowledge and self-empowerment. His ideas, along with those of Freemasonry, Rosicrucianism and the magical formulas of Barrett, coalesced with the founding of the Hermetic Order of the Golden Dawn in the 1880s. This last, under the leadership of Samuel Liddell MacGregor Mathers, who assumed leadership in 1897, developed a ritualistic worldview system of Western *magick*. The Golden Dawn promoted the Hermetic principle of correspondence between the microcosm as the human being and the macrocosm as the universe. Its standard practices involved invocation (the "calling down" into the self of a cosmic force) and evocation (the "calling up" of magical forces from the depth of the self). The Order taught that the trained will is capable of achieving anything, and this led to the contemporary understanding of magic as the changing of consciousness according to will (usually attributed to Dion Fortune). The Golden Dawn's most famous member was Aleister Crowley (1875–1947) who formulated Thelemic Magic (from Greek *thelema* "will").

Most modern magical groups have been inspired from the Knights Templar (a quasi-monastic, magical fraternity formed in 1118 to protect Jerusalem for Christian pilgrims) and the kabbalists (developing from ancient Hebrew sources in Babylon in the early Middle Ages and culminating with Moses de Leon's thirteenth-century *Book of Zolar*). A third influence comes through the fourteenth-century *tarrochi* cards (Tarot). As a system of popular divination, Levi, Crowley and A.E. Waite combined the Tarot's modern form with kabbalistic symbolism. Contemporary Western magic seeks the production of desired effects at will through harnessing hidden forces within the universe. Sybil Leek understands magic as the employment of various techniques (e.g., incantations) by which human beings can control and manipulate supernatural agencies and/or the forces of nature to produce a desired effect or result. Magicians and magical groups inevitably employ ritual as a tool to focus the concentration and power of the individual or group. They maintain an essential secrecy or "social invisibility," employ hidden ancient wisdom, and retain roots in the pre-Christian world.

Implicit in much of the Western magical tradition is an anti-nature bias, the violation of the natural law of exchange or the laws of nature. Magical endeavor can be seen as the human wish to tamper with the natural flow. In principle, it differs little from the manipulation and control of technology – allowing the nature/culture or nature/technology or nature/magic divide that has been articulated by Freud in his *Civilization and Its Discontents*. Nevertheless, a counter-tradition can be traced again to the Middle Ages that understood "natural magic" in distinction to "demonic magic" – including the manipulation of people through curses (i.e., black magic). Consequently, opposed to demonic magic of both nefarious and exalted ends is the domain of natural magic – essentially, operation within the "laws of nature" as they are found and encountered. Del Rio, in his *Disquisitiones Magicae* of 1606, explained natural or physical magic as none other than knowledge of the deepest secrets of nature. In the Middle Ages, natural magic was essentially the science of the day.

Most traditional magical practice descends from Neo-Platonism as a system of spiritual development that can be traced through the Martinists, the Illuminati, the Rosicrucians, the Freemasons and the Golden Dawn. In contrast, many modern-day Witches and neo-pagans do not link magic with the supernatural. It is instead viewed primarily as a series of techniques that alter consciousness in order to facilitate psychic activity. Magic has become a psychological endeavor rather than a supernatural one. Along with modern-day ceremonial or thelemic magic(k), a more recent development is that of Chaos Magick (Peter Caroll, Phil Hine) that employs a chaos paradigm and the individual image to obtain a state of gnosis.

In the cultural matrix of the West, the magician can assume the role of magus, wizard, sorcerer, thaumaturge and, more recently, shaman. The etymological origins of these various designations and their different historic trajectories allow us to understand a variety of different emphases. The magus or magician *per se* is concerned with power and its development *vis-à-vis* people, nature and spirit. The wizard, by contrast, pursues wisdom or knowledge rather than controlling or manipulating force in and of itself. The sorcerer is a "caster of lots," which he or she engineers through techniques of enchantment or incantation. In many respects the sorcerer or enchanter is similar to the shaman – both engage with the other-world and its denizens, and both may do "battle" with spirit beings. But the shaman's pursuit is always social and ultimately on behalf of his or her grounding community. With the sorcerer, on the other hand, magical work is solitary and motivated by self-interest. It is the thaumaturgist, however, who, as a "worker of wonders" is less the seeker after power, wisdom, control or conflict but essentially after the miraculous. And in contrast to *techne* or achieving psychological states of mind, *thauma* or the miracle reveals a further dimension of magic and one that opens it to the natural that may not automatically be apparent with the technological.

While the Greek term *thauma* is of obscure origin, its English equivalent "marvel, miracle" and cognates ("smile," "mirror" and "admire") reveal an underlying dynamic of appreciative reflection. The miraculous is not a denial or transgression of the natural but its mirror image. It introduces the possibility that the magical can be an integral part as well as counterpart to nature rather than an operative that contravenes fundamental natural laws. And as the etymological root behind the "miracle" complex suggests, magic as the miraculous engenders "smiling"; it is an occasion for "laughter."

Michael York

Further Reading

Cunningham, Graham. *Religion and Magic: Approaches and Theories*. New York: New York University Press, 1999.

Davis, Erik. *TechGnosis: Myth, Magic and Mysticism in the Age of Information*. New York: Harmony/Crown, 1998.

Douglas, Mary. *Purity and Danger*. Harmondsworth: Pelican Books, 1970 (1966).

Faber, M.D. *New Age Thinking: A Psychoanalytic Critique*. Ottawa: University of Ottawa Press, 1996.

Freud, Sigmund. *Civilization, Society and Religion: Group Psychology, Civilization and Its Discontents and Other Works*. The Penguin Freud Library 12. London: Penguin, 1991.

Greenwood, Susan. *Magic, Witchcraft and the Otherworld: An Anthropology*. Oxford/New York: Berg, 2000.

Hutton, Ronald. *Triumph of the Moon: A History of Modern Witchcraft*. Oxford: University Press, 1999.

Levi, Eliphas. *History of Magic*. A.E. Waite, tr. London: Rider, 1913.

Mathers, Samuel Liddell MacGregor. *The Key of Solomon the King (Clavicula Solomonis)*. New York: Kegan Paul, 1909 (1888).

Spence, Louis. *Encyclopaedia of Occultism*. New Hyde Park, NY: University Books, 1960.

Waldrop, M. Mitchell. *Complexity: The Emerging Science at the Edge of Order and Chaos.* New York: Touchstone, 1992.

See also: Complexity Theory; Ecology and Religion; Magic, Animism, and the Shaman's Craft; New Age; Paganism – Contemporary; Shamanism (various); Wicca.

SP Magic, Animism, and the Shaman's Craft

Animism and Perception

Although the term "animism" was originally coined in the nineteenth century to designate the mistaken projection of humanlike attributes – such as life, mind, intelligence – to nonhuman and ostensibly inanimate phenomena, it is clear that this first meaning was itself rooted in a misapprehension, by Western scholars, of the perceptual experience of indigenous, oral peoples. Twentieth-century research into the phenomenology of perception revealed that humans never directly experience *any* phenomenon as definitively inert or inanimate. Perception itself is an inherently relational, participatory event; we say that things "call our gaze" or "capture our attention," and as we lend our focus to those things, we find ourselves affected and transformed by the encounter – the way the blue sky, when we open our gaze to it, reverberates through our sensing organism, altering our mood and even the rhythm of our beating heart. When we are walking in the forest, a particular tree may engage our awareness, and if we reach to feel the texture of its bark we may find that our fingers are soon being tutored by that tree. If the bark is rough and deeply furrowed our fingers will begin to slow down their movements in order to explore those ridges and valleys, while if the trunk is smooth, like a madrone, even the palm of our hand will be drawn to press against and caress that smooth surface. Maurice Merleau-Ponty, in his classic work, *Phenomenology of Perception*, suggests that the primordial event of perception is always experienced as a reciprocal encounter between the perceiver and the perceived, an open dialectic wherein my sensing body continually responds and adjusts itself to the things it senses, and wherein the perceived phenomenon responds in turn, disclosing its nuances to me only as I allow myself to be affected by its unique style, its particular dynamism or active agency.

Merleau-Ponty's careful analyses of perception revealed, contrary to our common ways of speaking, that the perceiving self is not a disembodied mind but rather a bodily subject entirely immersed in the world it perceives. His later work underscored the reciprocity of perceptual experience by pointing out the obvious (yet easily overlooked) fact that the eyes, the visual organs by which we gaze out at and explore the visible field, are themselves entirely a part of that field; they have their own colors, like the color of the sky or the grass. Similarly, the hands with which we touch things are entirely a part of the tactile field that they explore – since, of course, the hand has its own textures, its own smooth or rough surfaces. Hence, when we are touching another being, feeling the texture of a tree-trunk, or caressing a boulder with our fingers, we may also, quite spontaneously, feel our hand being touched *by* that tree, or our fingers felt *by* that stone. Similarly, when we step outside in the morning and gaze across the valley at a forested hillside, if we attend mindfully to the vision we will sense our own visibility, will feel ourselves *exposed to* those trees, perhaps even feel ourselves *seen by* that forested hillside. Perception, according to Merleau-Ponty, is nothing other than this reciprocity, this mutual reverberation and blending in which the surrounding terrain is experienced by me only to the extent that I feel myself caught up within and *experienced by* those surroundings.

Such a description neatly echoes the discourse of many indigenous peoples, such as the Koyukon people of central Alaska, who claim that they live "in a world that watches, in a forest of eyes" (Nelson 1983: 14). Oral, indigenous peoples from around the world – whether hunters or rudimentary horticulturalists – commonly assert that the land itself is alive and aware, that the local animals, the plants, and the earthly elements around them have their own sensitivity and sentience. They claim that the earthly world we experience also *experiences us*. And hence that we must be respectful toward that world, lest we offend the very ground that supports us, the winds and waters that nourish us.

If the phenomenological study of perception is correct, however, then these claims need not be attributed to a "projection" of human awareness onto an ostensibly inanimate and objective world; they are simply a way of speaking more in accord with our most direct and spontaneous experience of the perceptual cosmos. Far from being a distortion of our actual encounter with the material world around us, the animistic discourse of so many indigenous, place-based peoples is likely the most practical and parsimonious manner of giving voice to the earthly world as that world discloses itself to humankind in the absence of intervening technologies.

When the natural world is perceived not from the spectator-like position of a detached or disembodied intellect, but rather from an embodied position situated entirely *within* that world, one encounters no aspect of that world that is definitively inert or inanimate. "Animism" remains a useful term for this highly embodied, and *embedded*, mode of perception. In this sense, "animism" may be said to name a primordial mode of perception that admits of no clear distinction between that which is animate and that which is inanimate. Rather, every phenomenon that draws our attention is perceived, or felt, to be at least potentially animate. Each perceived thing has its own rhythm and style, its own interior animation. Everything moves – although, clearly, some things move much slower than other things, like the mountains, or the ground underfoot.

A short, haiku-like poem by Gary Snyder neatly illustrates this style of awareness:

As the crickets' soft, autumn hum
is to us
so are we to the trees
as are they
to the rocks and the hills.

Each entity in this poem has its own dynamism, its own rhythm – and yet each rhythm is vastly different, in the pace of its pulse, from the others. Nevertheless each entity is also listening, mindful of the other rhythms around it.

To such an embodied, and embedded, perspective, the enveloping world is encountered not as a conglomeration of determinate objects, but as a community of subjects – as a relational field of animate, active agencies in which we humans, too, are participant.

Magic and Shamans

Such an understanding of the animistic style of perception common to indigenous, oral cultures is necessary for comprehending the vital role played by shamans, the indigenous magic practitioners endemic to such place-based cultures. For if awareness is not the exclusive attribute of humankind – if, indeed, every aspect of the perceivable world is felt to be at least potentially alive, awake and aware – then there is an obvious need, in any human community, for individuals who are particularly adept at communicating with these other shapes of sensitivity and sentience. The shamans are precisely those persons who are especially sensitive and susceptible to the expressive calls, gestures and signs of the wider, more-than-human field of beings, and who are able to reply in kind. The shaman is an intermediary, a mediator between the human community and the more-than-human community in which the human group is embedded. This wider community consists not only of the humans, and the other animal intelligences that inhabit or migrate through the local terrain, but also the many plant powers that are rooted in the local soils – the grasses, and herbs (with their nourishing and medicinal characteristics, their poisonous and mind-altering influences), the trees with their unique personalities, and even the multiform intelligence of whole forests; it consists as well of the active agency and expressive power of particular land forms (like rivers, mountains, caves, cliffs), and of all the other elemental forces (the winds and weather-patterns, the radiant sun and the cycling moon, storm clouds and seasonal patterns) that influence, and effectively constitute, the living landscape.

The magic skills of the shaman are rooted in his or her ability to shift out of his common state of awareness in order to contact, and learn from, these other powers in the surrounding Earth. Only by regularly shedding the accepted perceptual logic of his culture can the shaman hope to enter into relation with other species on their own terms; only by altering the common organization of her senses is she able to make contact and communicate with the other shapes of sentience and sensitivity with which human existence is entwined. And so it is this, we might say, that defines a shaman: the ability to readily slip out of the collective perceptual boundaries that define his or her culture – boundaries held in place by social customs, taboos, and especially the common language – in order to directly engage, and negotiate with, the multiple non-human sensibilities that animate the local Earth.

As a result of his or her heightened receptivity to the meaningful solicitations of the wider community of beings, the shaman tends to dwell at the very periphery of the human settlement, at the very outskirts of the village or the camp. The indigenous magician's acute sensitivities often render him unable to dwell, or even linger, in the midst of the human hubbub; only at the edge of the community is he able to attend to the exigencies of the human world while living in steady contact with the wider, and wilder, field of earthly powers. The shaman is thus an edge dweller, one who tends the subtle boundary between the human collective and the wild, ecological field of intelligence, ensuring that that boundary stays a porous membrane across which nourishment flows in both directions – ensuring that the human community never takes more from the living land than it returns to the land, not just materially, but with prayers, with propitiations, with spontaneous and eloquent praises. To some extent, every adult in the human community is engaged in the process of listening and attuning to the other presences that surround and influence daily life. Yet the shaman is the exemplary voyager in the intermediate realm between the human and more-than-human worlds, the primary strategist and negotiator in any dealings with these earthly powers. By his constant rituals, trances, ecstasies, and "journeys," the shaman ensures that the relation between the human and more-than-human realms remains balanced and reciprocal; that the living membrane between these realms never hardens into a static barrier shutting out the many-voiced land from the deliberations of the human collective.

Further, it is only as a result of continually monitoring and maintaining the dynamic equilibrium between the human and the more-than-human worlds that the shaman typically derives his or her ability to heal various illnesses arising within the human community. Disease is commonly conceived, in such animistic cultures, as a kind of disruption or imbalance within a particular person, and yet the source of this disequilibrium is assumed to lie not in the individual person but in the larger field of relationships within which that person is entwined. A susceptible person, that is, may become the bearer of a *disease* that belongs not to her but to the village as a whole. Yet the ultimate source of such community disequilibrium will commonly be found in an imbalance between the human community and the larger system of which it is a part. Hence the illnesses that beset particular individuals can be healed, or released, only if the healer is simultaneously tending, and "healing" the relative balance or imbalance between the human collective and the wider community of beings. The shaman's primary allegiance, then, is not to the human community, but to the earthly web of relations in which that community is embedded – it is from this that his or her power to alleviate human illness derives – and this sets the local shaman apart from most other persons.

The term "shamanism" is regularly used, today, to denote the belief system, or worldview, of such cultures wherein the shaman's craft is practiced. Yet this term is something of a misnomer, for it implies that the person of the shaman stands at the very center of the belief system and of the culture itself; it suggests that the shaman is revered or perhaps even worshipped by the members of such a culture. Yet nothing could be farther from the case. We have seen that the shaman is quintessentially an edge-dweller, a marginal figure, one who straddles the boundary between the culture and the rest of animate nature. It is not the *shaman* who is central to the beliefs of that culture, but rather the *animate natural world* in all its visible and invisible aspects – the expressive power and active agency of the sensuous and sensate surroundings. And thus the worldview of such a culture is not, properly speaking, "shamanistic," but rather "animistic." It is first and foremost in *animistic* cultures – cultures for whom any aspect of the perceivable world may be felt to have its own active agency, its own interior animation – that the craft of the magician first emerges, and it is in such a context that the shaman (the indigenous magician) finds his or her primary role and function, as intermediary between the human and more-than-human worlds.

The Contemporary Magician

Finally, a few words should perhaps be said, here, about the role of the magician in modern, technological societies. After all, the modern conjuror's feats with rabbits, doves, or tigers hearken back to the indigenous shaman's magical rapport with other species. Indeed, virtually all contemporary forms of magic may be shown to derive, in various ways, from the animistic mode of experience common to all of our indigenous, hunting and foraging ancestors – to the experience, that is, of living within a world that is itself alive. Moreover, it is likely that this participatory mode of sensory experience has never really been extinguished – that it has only been buried beneath the more detached and objectifying styles of perception made possible by a variety of technologies upon which most moderns have come to depend, from the alphabet to the printing press, from the camera to the computer. In the course of our early education, most of us learn to transfer the participatory proclivity of our senses away from the more-than-human natural surroundings toward our own human symbols, entering into an animistic fascination with our own humanly generated signs and, increasingly, with our own technologies. And as we grow into adulthood, our instinctive yearning for relationship with an encompassing sphere of life and intelligence is commonly channeled beyond the perceptual world entirely, into an abstract relation with a divine source assumed to reside entirely outside of earthly nature, beyond all bodily or sensory ken.

Yet even a contemporary sleight-of-hand magician still makes use of our latent impulse to participate, animistically, with the objects that we perceive. Magicians – whether contemporary sleight-of-hand conjurors or indigenous tribal shamans – have in common the fact that they work with the participatory power of perception. (Perception is the magician's medium, as pigments are the medium for a painter.) Both the modern sleight-of-hand magician and the indigenous shaman are adept at breaking, or disrupting, the accepted perceptual habits of their culture. The indigenous shaman practices this in order to enter into relation and rapport with other, earthly forms of life and sentience. The modern magician enacts these disruptions merely in order to startle, and thereby entertain, his audience. Yet if contemporary conjurors were more aware of the ancient, indigenous sources of their craft (if they realized, for instance, that indigenous shamans from many native cultures already used sleight-of-hand techniques in their propitiatory and curative rituals), then even these modern magicians, too, might begin to realize a more vital, ecological function within contemporary culture.

In an era when nature is primarily spoken of in abstract terms, as an objective and largely determinate set of mechanisms – at a time when eloquent behavior of other animals is said to be entirely "programmed in their genes," and when the surrounding sensuous landscape is referred to merely as a stock of "resources" for human use – it is clear that our direct, sensory engagement with the Earth around us has become woefully impoverished. The accelerating ecological destruction wrought by contemporary humankind seems to stem not from any inherent meanness in our species but from a kind of perceptual obliviousness, an inability to actually notice anything outside the sphere of our human designs, a profound blindness and deafness to the more-than-human Earth. In such an era, perhaps the most vital task of the sleight-of-hand magician is precisely to startle the senses from their slumber, to shake our eyes and our ears free from the static, habitual ways of seeing and hearing into which those senses have fallen under the deadening influence of abstract and overly objectified ways of speaking and thinking.

Yet perhaps such magic is also, now, the province of all the arts – the province of music, of painting, of poetry. Perhaps it falls to all our artists, today, to wield their pigments and their words in such a way as to loosen the perceptual habits that currently keep us oblivious to our actual surroundings. In any case, the craft of magic is as necessary in the modern world as it was for our indigenous ancestors. For it is only by waking the senses from their contemporary swoon, freeing our eyes and our ears and our skin to actively participate, once again, in the breathing cosmos of wind and rain and stone, of spider-weave and crow-swoop and also, yes, the humming song of the streetlamp pouring its pale light over the leaf-strewn pavement, that we may have a chance of renewing our vital reciprocity with the animate, many-voiced Earth.

David Abram

Further Reading
Abram, David. *The Spell of the Sensuous: Perception and Language in a More-than-Human World*. New York: Vintage, 1997.
Duerr, Hans Peter. *Dreamtime: Concerning the Boundary Between Wilderness and Civilization*. Oxford: Basil Blackwell, 1985.
Kane, Sean. *Wisdom of the Mythtellers*. Peterborough, Ontario: Broadview Press, 1994.
Lame Deer, John and Richard Erdoes. *Lame Deer, Seeker of Visions*. New York: Simon & Schuster, 1972.
Merleau-Ponty, Maurice. *The Visible and the Invisible*. Evanston, Illinois: Northwestern University Press, 1968.
Merleau-Ponty, Maurice. *Phenomenology of Perception*. Colin Smith, tr. London: Routledge & Kegan Paul, 1962.
Nelson, Richard. *Make Prayers to the Raven: A Koyukon View of the Northern Forest*. Chicago: University of Chicago Press, 1983.
Phillippi, Donald L. *Songs of Gods, Songs of Humans*. San Francisco: North Point Press, 1982.
Prechtel, Martin. *Secrets of the Talking Jaguar: Memoirs from the Living Heart of a Mayan Village*. New York: Tarcher/Putnam, 1999.
Snyder, Gary. *No Nature: New and Selected Poems*. New York: Pantheon, 1992.
Snyder, Gary. *The Practice of the Wild*. San Francisco: North Point Press, 1990.
Thomas, Elizabeth Marshall. *Reindeer Moon*. Boston: Houghton Mifflin, 1987.

See also: Anarchism; Animism; Animism – A Contemporary Perspective; Bioregionalism and the North American Bioregional Congress; Earth First! and the Earth Liberation Front; Eco-Magic; Hundredth Monkey; Radical Environmentalism; Snyder, Gary.

Maimonides (1135–1204)

Maimonides (Rabbi Moshe ben Maimon, also known as Rambam) is arguably the premier philosopher and theologian of Jewish history. As one of the most influential thinkers, Jewish, Christian or Muslim, of the medieval period, not only in theology but also in medicine and law, the ecological profundity of his work, long overlooked, is only beginning to be understood. Maimonides, uniquely in Jewish thought, challenged the primacy of humanity within the order of creation, asserted that there is complete equivalence between human and animal emotions, and believed that creation as a whole is the only dimension of being which has intrinsic value.

In his most important work, *The Guide for the Perplexed*, Maimonides suggested a model of the cosmos that is parallel to the Gaia hypothesis. Maimonides admonished his reader, "Know that this whole of being is one individual and nothing else," adding that the whole of creation is "a single being which has the same status as Zayid or Omar," in other words, endowed with a heart and a soul (1:72, 184). In keeping with Aristotelian cosmology, Maimonides emphasized that all of the spheres of the heavens were "living beings, endowed with a soul and an intellect" (2:4, 259), yet with respect to the entirety of being, all the other spheres were seen by him as mere organs of the whole, while the outermost sphere was the heart of the cosmos.

For Maimonides, the idea that the universe was an organic whole was a fundamental scientific fact. This, according to Maimonides, led to a direct understanding of God's relation to the world, for "[t]he One [God] has created one being" (1:72, 187; see also 2:1, 251). Maimonides believed that in order to develop the intellect "in God's image," one needed to understand this truth scientifically by studying the more-than-human world.

> I have already let you know that there exists nothing except God, may He be exalted, and this existent world, and that there is no possible inference proving his existence, may He be exalted, except those deriving from this existent taken as a whole and from its details (1:71, 183).

Maimonides' emphasis on natural theology laid the foundation for the development of scientific method in the West. In contrast with the Kalam school and with most theologians of his time, Maimonides asserted that "demonstrations . . . can only be taken from the permanent nature of what exists, a nature that can be seen and apprehended by the senses and the intellect" (1:76, 231; see also 1:71, 179).

For Maimonides, this perspective also had direct metaphysical and ethical implications, for "the individuals of the human species, and all the more so the other species, are things of no value at all in comparison with the whole [of creation] that exists and endures" (3:13, 452). His ideas about the wholeness of creation profoundly influenced the Church, especially Thomas Aquinas, as can be seen in *Summa Theologica* (1a, q.47, art.1, 1:246) and *Summa Contra Gentiles* (part 1, ch. 64, 3:213, paragraph 10; also 3:212, paragraph 9).

Maimonides rejected the idea that humanity was the final end of creation, rejecting also the idea that other creatures exist to serve human pleasure: "It should not be believed that all the beings exist for the sake of the existence of man. On the contrary, all the other beings too have been intended for their own sakes . . ." (3:13, 452). In this respect, his thought contrasts sharply with most other medieval Jewish thinkers, like Sa'adyah Ga'on or Bachya ibn Paquda. Maimonides held that this was the view delineated within Genesis itself, explaining the word "good" used in chapter one of Genesis to mean that each creature has something like intrinsic value (3:13, 453). The phrase "very good" (Gen. 1:31), indicates the overwhelming value of "the whole."

Maimonides arrived at this interpretation after concluding that there can be no *telos* for creation: "[E]ven according to our view holding that the world has been produced in time, the quest for the final end of all the species of beings collapses" (3:13, 452). In a later chapter, he derived a remarkable conclusion from this idea: "[T]he entire purpose [of God's actions] consists in bringing into existence the way you see it everything whose existence is possible . . ." (3:25, 504). This formulation, fundamentally congruent with Spinoza's cosmology, is also compatible with those who understand evolution to be "directed" toward diversity.

Maimonides held that animals and humans were equal in their capacity to feel and imagine. This understanding was integral to his interpretation of the commandments:

> It is forbidden to slaughter [an animal] and its young on the same day, this being a precautionary measure to avoid slaughtering the young animal in front of its mother. For in these cases animals feel very great pain, there being no difference regarding this pain between [humanity] and the other animals. For the love and the tenderness of a mother for her child is not consequent upon reason, but upon the activity of the imaginative faculty, which is found in most animals just as it is found in [humanity] . . . (3:48, 599; see also 1:75, 209 and 2:1, 245).

Some modern interpreters have downplayed this passage by emphasizing another passage where Maimonides states that the prohibition against causing pain to animals is meant to create good habits in people (3:17). However, he is clear in that passage as well that compassion is enjoined for individual animals. In general, and in contrast with other philosophers and theologians, Maimonides minimized the differences between humanity and other animals. Maimonides also explained that instrumental reason by itself merely makes human beings into very dangerous animals (1:7, 33). He further taught that the instruction to "dominate" in Genesis 1 was neither a commandment nor an imperative, but merely a description of human nature (3:13, 454).

For Maimonides the uniqueness of human nature is found in the capacity to apprehend the divine. This is humanity's perfection (1:1-2, 23-4) which only a few individuals reach. Yet even this quality, along with the "hylic intellect" (1:72, 190-1), makes human beings "merely the most noble among the things that are subject to generation," since the spheres and the heavens far surpass humanity in their capacities (3:12, 443).

Much in Maimonides is also problematic for contemporary thinkers. As an Aristotelian, Maimonides had a strongly negative attitude toward the sense of touch (2:56, 371; 3:8, 432-3), which is incompatible with the phenomenological approach to the Earth that is taken by many eco-philosophers. In the same vein, he rejected imagination as inferior and espoused an intellectual elitism that remains controversial. Nonetheless, his rejection of anthropocentrism and espousal of a holistic cosmology are starting points for any eco-theology based on the biblical traditions. As we say in the world of traditional Jewish study, "From Moses [the prophet] to Moses [Maimonides], there is no one like Moses."

David Mevorach Seidenberg

Further Reading
Maimonides, Moses. *The Guide for the Perplexed*. Moses Friedlander, tr. New York: Dover Books, 1980.
Maimonides, Moses. *The Guide for the Perplexed*, vol. 1 & 2. Shlomo Pines: University of Chicago Press, 1963.
See also: Animals; Animals in the Bible and Qur'an; Aquinas, Thomas; Holism; Judaism; Spinoza, Baruch.

Makapansgat Cobble

What can be regarded as the world's oldest known "art object" was found in 1925 in a cave at Makapansgat, South Africa. This small waterworn cobble of ironstone was clearly brought into the site from some distance away, and one can only assume that the Australopithecine (a type of fossil hominid) who did this around three million years ago was attracted not only by the cobble's reddish color – red is the color most attractive to both apes and humans (as was shown by Desmond Morris' experiments with Congo, the chimpanzee who liked to paint) – but also and especially by its entirely natural resemblance to a human face: one side has two symmetrically placed small cavities in it, like a pair of sunken eye-sockets, above a simple mouth. This "face" was in no way artificially manufactured, but its accidental resemblance to a face is so striking that it seems certain the object was noticed and brought back to a dwelling place as an important possession. This was a giant step for hominids – apparently they were seeing a face that was not a face, they were responding to an image, they were indulging in a primitive form of symbolism. The discoverer of the cobble, Wilfred Eitzman, a schoolmaster, speculated that it might have been "the god of these early people" or "their god or fetish."

In most primates, a direct stare denotes self-confidence and the possible prelude to an attack by an aggressive individual, so that monkeys become disturbed when they are stared at or even just presented with drawings of two eyes. Chimpanzees have been known to avoid looking at a toy with large black eyes, while gorillas see the twin discs of binoculars as a threat. In other words, the face pattern with two staring eyes has specific meanings. Where humans are concerned, it is known that up to the age of three months, an infant has a tendency to smile when presented with a full human face, even that of a stranger.

In experiments, copies of the Makapansgat cobble have failed to elicit any significant response from apes; but apes are not Australopithecines, and since even chimpanzees have been observed to wear blades of grass and to paint parts of their bodies with white clay, as well as to hoard objects and carry single stones for several days, one can hardly doubt that Australopithecines were capable of similar behavior and much more. It can never be proved that that they saw a face in the Makapansgat cobble, but the balance of probability is surely that this stone was indeed seen as significant, since it was brought into the site; and that significance is most likely to have come not only from its color and shape, but also and primarily from its natural resemblance to a human face.

Paul G. Bahn

Further Reading

Bahn, Paul G. "Face to Face with the Earliest 'Art Object.' " In Matthias Strecker and Paul Bahn, eds. *Dating and the Earliest Known Rock Art*. Oxford: Oxbow Books, 1999, 75–7.

Dart, Raymond A. "The Waterworn Australopithecine Pebble of Many from Makapansgat." *South African Journal of Science* 70 (1974), 167–9.

See also: Art; Paleolithic Art; Paleolithic Religions; Rock Art (various).

Makewana the Rainmaker (Central Malawi)

Makewana – literally meaning the mother of children, but intended to convey the meaning: mother of all people – was among the most powerful of central African rainmakers. Makewana presided over a rain/shrine complex that spread across much of central Malawi. Makewana was seen as having direct access to God; without her it was believed that there would be no rain and women would be barren. It is said that she could never cut hair because to do so would be to "cut the rain." Her powers were so highly regarded that during the early part of the nineteenth century she received annual tribute from as far as modern Zimbabwe. The tribute was in the form of precious materials such as ivory, and it said that Makewana slept on a bed of ivory tusks that was covered with dark cloths to hide its whiteness. Nothing near Makewana could be white as this would affect the coming of the rain.

Oral traditions state that the first Makewana was a priestess named Mangadzi Banda who is said to have been the mother of Mwali, the wife of one of the early Karonga chiefs. It is said that Mangadzi stayed at Msinja. If we accept this, we can put a tentative date on the time of Mangadzi. The Karonga chiefs were of the Phiri clan, a clan who are credited with founding the first Malawi state. A combination of oral traditions, chiefly lineages and archeological evidence, has been used to argue that the Phiri clan were a group who arrived in Malawi from Luba country (in the Democratic Republic of Congo) in the fourteenth or fifteenth century. Mangadzi must therefore have lived at least five hundred years ago.

Matthew Schoffeleers has argued that the rain shrine complex was already well established by this time and has made the compelling argument that, for many centuries before the arrival of the Phiri clan, a rain shrine system had existed under the control of Mangadzi's Banda clan. This could take the founding of the rain shrine complex as far back as the later centuries of the first millennium. Oral traditions state that the first rain shrine was on a mountaintop known as Kaphirintiwa and that it was only after many centuries that the shrine was moved down to the plain near Msinja where Mangadzi is said to have stayed. We can be sure that at Kaphirintiwa there would also have been a rain shrine and a rain priestess who would have conducted similar rites to those conducted in more recent times by Makewana, but we cannot be sure that these ancient Banda clan rain-priestesses were known by the name Makewana. I will confine myself here to what we know about the Makewanas who lived at Msinja in recent times, but I expect that much of this will hold true even for the early Banda clan rain priestesses.

Makewana was a spirit medium, the keeper of the Msinja rain shrine and a prophetess. When one Makewana died, the people would wait, sometimes for many years,

Mbiriwiri – The Sacred Rainmaking Drum

Mbiriwiri – literally the drum of good tidings – is a sacred drum that was fundamental to the practices of rainmaking in the central Malawi rain shrine system.

There are a number of accounts of the origins of the drum. Almost all agree that it originally belonged to the BaTwa – the former Pygmy inhabitants of central Africa. Some say that it was taken from the BaTwa by force in battle, others that it was found lying near the sacred pool of Malawi a few kilometres from the shrine of Msinja. That it is extremely old is beyond question.

Mbiriwiri is a cylinder-shaped double-ended drum. It is made of wood and its tympanums are made from monitor lizard skin (*Varanus* sp.). The monitor skin is symbolically important: the creature is associated with and shares the name of the supreme god – Chiuta. It is believed to live in the sky above the clouds and its falling to Earth brings thunder, lightning and rain. Half way between the tympanums is a hole that is closed with a plug. The sides of the drum are decorated with geometric designs that are not understood today. The designs echo those in the BaTwa rock paintings of the area.

The traditional keeping place for mbiriwiri was a special hut at the Msinja rain shrine, in central Malawi. In this it was stored resting on two poles and covered with dark (ideally black) cloth. Each year it was covered with reddish oil. The drum was only taken out of the shrine to be beaten at the start of the rainmaking ceremony or for repairs. Only a special functionary called Tsang'oma – meaning the beater of the drum – was allowed to handle the drum. Another functionary, Kapanga Banda, was charged with providing new monitor lizard skin for the drum when needed.

To start the rainmaking ceremonies, Tsang'oma (which is here an inherited title and does not refer to a traditional healer) would be called upon to beat mbiriwiri. The ceremonies would then last some days and if rain had not fallen by the end of the ceremonies then Tsang'oma would be blamed. He would be taken to a rock called Dzanzi several miles from the Msinja shrine, bound and his head wrapped in a black cloth so that he could not see. He would then be placed in a natural hole in the rock and a sharpened stake of hardwood would be driven into the top of his skull and down as far as his chest or sometimes right through his body. A tooth was taken from the body and placed in mbiriwiri through the hole in its side. It is said that the drum makes a distinctive noise when moved and that this is the sound of many teeth rattling inside it. The rattle is likened to the name: mbiriwiri.

When Ngoni invaders sacked the shrine at Msinja in the 1860s it is recalled that the Tsang'oma of the time fled with Mbiriwiri to a place inside Mozambique. While it was in Mozambique it seems that he had a squabble and this led to the drum being thrown down onto a large flat rock and broken. The man who broke the drum was executed. The drum was repaired and the teeth were replaced inside it. Today the drum is kept at a new shrine at a village called Tsang'oma, in Malawi. Today the drum is still kept on poles and covered in a dark cloth. It is never brought out into the open as it is said that the drum has become too powerful, and that if it were taken out there would be no rain.

B.W. Smith

Further Reading

Ntara, Samuel J. *The History of the Chewa (Mbiri Ya Achewa)*. Weisbaden: Frank Steiner, 1973 (originally published in 1950).

Rangeley, William H. "Two Nyasaland Rain Shrines." *Nyasaland Journal* 5:2 (1952), 31–50.

Van Breugel, J.W.M. *Chewa Traditional Religion*. Blantyre: Kachere Monograph 13, 2001.

See also: Pygmies (Mbuti foragers) & Bila Farmers of the Ituri Forest; Rock Art – Batwa/Pygmies (Central Africa); Rock Art – Chewa (Central Africa); San (Bushmen) Rainmaking.

---

until another woman appeared at Msinja who was clearly possessed, who uttered strange prophesies and who could answer a set of secret questions. No Makewana could ever marry, as Makewana was the wife of God (Chiuta). When God came down to Earth to visit Makewana he would do so in his snake manifestation: Thunga. It is believed that Thunga most often took the form of the python and therefore pythons were kept in baskets within the shrine of Msinja. Once a year, at the culmination of the girl's puberty rituals (*chinamwali*), Thunga would ceremonially sleep with Makewana and thereby bring fertility to the young maidens. In this ceremony a man named Kamundi Mbewe would stand in for Thunga. Kamundi also could never marry. Makewana could never become pregnant as to bear a human child would prove her infidelity to Thunga. Any Makewana who became pregnant was therefore killed.

Makewana's hut was near the Msinja spirit shrine. The spirit shrine was a small round hut made out of grass that is said to have been a replica of the original shrine at Kaphirintiwa. Between the hut of Makewana and the spirit shrine was the hut of the sacred drum: Mbiriwiri. Around this sacred area was a large village made up of a network of functionaries who all serviced the shrine. It is said that no one at Msinja planted crops or worked so as to provide for their own needs; their sole job was to service the shrine. Their needs were provided for out of the tribute that was brought to the shrine.

Makewana was assisted in her duties by the Matsano – literally meaning the chief's wives. The Matsano were a group of girls or women (oral sources disagree) who had felt the call to join Makewana. They lived in a series of huts behind the hut of Makewana. They were also known as the wives of God and were also not allowed to marry. Any man caught sleeping with a Matsano was put to death. Beyond the Matsano was the hut of Tsang'oma: the beater of the drum. It was the task of Tsang'oma to beat Mbiriwiri upon receiving Makewana's command. This would be the signal for all to gather to witness Makewana prophesy or make rain.

The rainmaking ceremony was known as Mgwetsa. In this ceremony Makewana would go to a nearby pond called the pool of Malawi and she would submerse herself in the pool for three days. The area around the pool was sacred and only Makewana could go there. The trees around the pool could not be cut and no one was allowed to fish in the pool, drink or wash in it. All animals and birds around the pool were also sacred and protected. This pool is sometimes called the pool of the ancestors and it was thought to be one of the places where Thunga could appear. In the public part of the Mgwetsa ceremony Makewana and the Matsano (the exact role of the Matsano is contested) would dance and throw water into the air. Offerings, such as black animals, would be made at the shrine. It is said that there would be a torrential downpour even before the ceremony was complete. If rain did not fall then Tsang'oma would be blamed and killed.

The shrine complex declined in power in the late nineteenth century after it was ransacked by Ngoni invaders. Livingstone records that Msinja was in a very poor state in 1867 after repeated raids. At this time Makewana fled to the north. In the colonial period attempts to restore the shrine faced difficulties because the old tribute system that sustained Msinja could not be reestablished. A Makewana named Kandiwona is said to have appeared, but failed the tests and was therefore driven away. She remained in the area and married, but soon after burnt herself to death in her hut. Msinja is still a functioning shrine today though its influence is now limited and local. It becomes important only in times of drought. A recent keeper is a widow but she does not consider herself to be Makewana.

B.W. Smith

Further Reading

Morris, Brian. *Animals and Ancestors: An Ethnography.* Oxford: Berg, 2000.
Ntara, Samuel J. *The History of the Chewa (Mbiri Ya Achewa).* Weisbaden: Frank Steiner, 1973 (originally published in 1950).
Rangeley, William, H. "Two Nyasaland Rain Shrines." *Nyasaland Journal* 5:2 (1952), 31–50.
Schoffeleers, J. Matthew. *Guardians of the Land, Essays on Central African Territorial Cults.* Salisbury (Harare): Mambo Press, 1978.

See also: Kaphirintiwa – The Place of Creation (Central Africa); Pygmies (Mbuti foragers) & Bila Farmers of the Ituri Forest); San (Bushmen) Rainmaking.

Måldhåris of Gujaråt (India)

A Måldhåri (pronounced as Maa-l-thaa-ri, "th" as in *the*) is a semi-tribal pastoralist. The Måldhåris are primarily based in the arid to semi-arid regions of Sauråshtra and Kutchchh, including the protected Gir wildlife sanctuary area, in the state of Gujaråt, India. *Mål* connotes precious wealth; here, it is implied for the wealth of livestock – mainly buffaloes, cows, sheep, goats, camels, and horses – and *dhåri* means the one who has, keeps, or raises such wealth. There are nomadic, semi-nomadic, and settled (non-nomadic) Måldhåris. They have been known for raising high-quality and drought-resistant breeds of buffaloes and cows for their milk and its by-products.

The Chåran, the Rabåri, the åhir, the Bharwåd, the Mér, and the Kåthis are the major Hindu Måldhåris. There are also a few Muslim Måldhåris, such as the Makaråni and the Siddi, groups who earn their livelihood as Måldhåris. They all have diverse beliefs, myths, rituals, and festivals. Thus, the Måldhåris are primarily an occupational community rather than a singular religious or cultural group. However, it is this occupation and the resulting kinship, tangible and intangible relationship with livestock, spatial and biophysical transactions with place, traditional ecological knowledge, and myths that seem to tie them together. These themes also help us understand the relations between their religion (beliefs and values) and ecology.

While a large percentage of the Måldhåris engaged with livestock rearing are illiterate, most of them, especially those living in the Gir wildlife sanctuary's forest area and its fringes, are very knowledgeable about the region's natural patterns and processes. Sharing of skills, stories, and social norms takes place through intergenerational interactions around daily chores and simple acts of leisure like sitting and conversing around bonfires in late evenings. Everyone in the household plays a significant role in subsistence activities and maintaining cultural traditions. Through such lifestyle they have developed a strong bond with their *mål*, family, kin, other Måldhåris, the land, and the plants and animals found in their local area. Such interactions and the resulting bond often translates into reverence for both their cherished *mål* and nature, upon which their own way of life closely depends.

Different Måldhåri groups share many religious traits. There are references of them in the Hindu volumes of the Vedas, the Puråṇas, the Råmåyana, and the Mahåbhårat. They mainly worship and attend rituals and festivities related to the Goddess *Durgå* or *Bhawåni* who is worshipped in many different forms of local deities. They also worship Lord Krishna and, especially celebrate with grandeur his birth-date, *Janmåshtami*. In religious and cultural festivals they perform with devotional songs, group dance called *garbå*, and couple-group dance of *rås*. Their prayers and *aarti* (devotional offering) also acknowledge their reverence and gratitude for Mother Earth. For many Måldhåris *bhom* or *bhoomi* (the land, Earth) is a very dear entity. They worship and value it; they understand that their socio-economic worth is dependent upon it.

Myths and stories surround the origins of this people. It is commonly believed that the ancestors of the Måldhåris came to Gujaråt and particularly to the Sauråshtra region along with Lord Krishna when he moved from Vrindåvan-Mathurå area (in the state of Uttar Pradesh in India) and established his rule with Dwårkå as its capital (in the western tip of the Sauråshtra peninsula). This is significant since many Måldhåris worship Lord Krishna (whose was also known as *Gopål* – the protector and keeper of cows) as their *thåkur* (lord or figurehead) or *kul-guru* (clan or ancestral teacher). Another story claims that the Måldhåris, as cattle herders, precede the times of Lord Krishna. It explains why they also worship Lord Shiva and Goddess Pårvati (or Bhawåni). According to this myth, Lord Shiva and Goddess Pårvati needed a keeper for their camel. Goddess Pårvati created a person out of clay under a *Samadi* (a Prosopis) tree and Lord Shiva gave life to it and was called *Såmod*. He was married to an angel named Rai and their descendents are the Måldhåris, particularly the Rabåris.

The underlying significance here is the deep-rooted, life-giving association with land and the nurturing capacity of trees or vegetation with the mythical overtones of gods, goddesses, and angels. Such myths provide a basis for reverence and continued faith in nature and power of supreme beings in giving life and sustenance. Such faith and values are then celebrated by the community in the folk-dances, especially *garbå* and *rås*, performed with gaiety and music around an idol of the goddess during the nine-night festival of *Navaråtri*. Such faith in and connection with nature are also reflected in daily religious performance (*pujå*) or family events around the year. Some Måldhåris, especially the Chårans, are bards and folk-singers. They share much of their wisdom and experience through folklores and folk-songs. Many of these expressions also have mythological and spiritual dimensions revealing their veneration for nature and God.

As Hindus they follow the lunar calendar and associate their religious practices with the full or new moon and changing seasons. Such association with temporal cycles also link them to the cosmic events that help them remember their place and role in the larger universe. Based on their experience with natural and human-created calamities and change, they believe that the ecological crisis results from lack of faith and immoral ways. At the same time they also believe that in this impermanent world, only their good *karma*, the fruits of well-performed duties, will go with them (their soul) when they die. Such grand perspectives are often manifested in their reverential attitudes and ethical behavior toward land, animals, people, and life.

From cultural celebrations and rituals to social traditions and economic practices they link their *mål*, the land, and gods or goddesses in a very intimate and often sacred manner. Often, they are seen as one and the same. What the Måldhåris believe from a "religious" point of view is often reflected in their views on nature and its quality. In a study on the Gir's resource management issues and landscape quality, when asked about their views on nature, they typically described "Nature" as mother, their "very own soul" and acknowledged that "everything" is due to her. They are especially captivated by the Gir's natural beauty and other values which, in turn, add to their respect for the land and attachment to their way of life. Many Måldhåris often pay respect to smaller shrines, trees, rocks, and some water-bodies of religious and cultural significance. A notable aspect of this relationship is their view that nature's diversity is key to their very survival and emotional bond with the place. This is often manifested in their folklores as well as daily rituals. Such bonding needs to be understood better as it may prove to be vital for nature conservation.

All these rich cultural, social, and spiritual traditions and beliefs do not necessarily reduce the issues that the Måldhåris engaged with pastoral activities today face. They are similar to other pastoralists like the Gaddis in the lower Himalayas of North India or the Maasai pastoralists of East Africa. With increased focus on industrialization and urbanization, harsh climatic patterns, financial debts, and lack of insurance or extension facilities, their way of life is being marginalized. Many Måldhåris continue to abandon their traditional pastoral vocation and, willingly or otherwise, adjust and survive in an urban-industrial economy that is alien and often degenerating to them. This often leads to social and kin disintegration. Women and children usually get the rough end of the deal.

The world is facing many resource problems as well as spiritual perturbation, and these seem to be linked. The microcosmic life and times of pastoralists in general and the Måldhåris in particular reflect this reality. The Måldhåris' way of life may also show a way out. Pastoralism brings these people in close contact with structure and functions of nature and nonhuman living beings. Time, intergenerational interactions, community interdependencies, stories and myths, rituals and festivals, disasters, uncertainties, simple joys, majestic settings, temporal rhythms, and relationship with the local and regional landscapes are the forces that hone their very body, mind, and soul. Therefore, a unique worldview and

Shishir R. Raval

Further Reading
Desai-Abdi, Roopa. *Maldharis of Saurashtra – A Glimpse into Their Past and Present*. Bhåvnagar, Gujaråt, India: Excel Industries Pvt. Ltd. and Suchitrå Offset, 1993.
Grim, John A. "Indigenous Traditions and Ecology." *Earth Ethics* 10:1 (1998).
Raval, Shishir R. *Perceptions of Resource Management and Landscape Quality of the Gir Wildlife Sanctuary and National Park in India*. Unpublished Doctoral Dissertation. Ann Arbor: University of Michigan, 1997.
Vorå, Vasudev, S. Gadhavi and R. Vorå. (In Gujaråti) *Måldhåri ni Vimåsan* (The Dilemma of Måldhåri). Lok Yatra Series 10. Råjkot, Gujaråt, India: Hind Swaråj Mandal, 1990.
Wilberforce-Bell, Harold. *The History of Kathiawad from the Earliest Times*. London: W. Heinemann, 1916.
See also: Hinduism; India; San (Bushmen) Religion.

Malthus, Thomas Robert (1766–1834)

Thomas Robert Malthus was an Anglican clergyman, educator, and essayist whose ideas have exerted a powerful influence on Western thought in a number of areas, most notably demography, political economy, and biology. His most famous and controversial work, *Essay on the Principle of Population* (first edition, 1898), is considered one of the seminal sources of classical economics and strongly influenced other disciplines as well, notably evolutionary biology. At the heart of Malthus' thought was a vision of nature that emphasized inevitable limits and persistent suffering, and as a clergyman he was obliged to contemplate the religious implications of this harsh conclusion. He did so by developing a distinctive theodicy, grounded in utilitarian thought, as well as an ethics of moral restraint aimed at controlling population pressures. And while some of Malthus' views reflect the parochial concerns of his church and era, his general interest in the relationship between nature and religion resonate in contemporary debates about environmentalism, economic development, and human values.

The Principle of Population, Nature, and Society
Malthus' most famous and enduring idea, the population principle, starts from two simple postulates. First, that food is necessary to human existence. Second, that the "passion between the sexes" stays at a constant level throughout human history. Recognizing that sexuality quickly begets children that must be fed, Malthus quickly builds to his famous principle – "the power of population is indefinitely greater than the power in the earth to produce subsistence for man" (1976: 21). Put in mathematical terminology, "population, when unchecked, increases in a geometric ratio ... [s]ubsistence increases only in an arithmetic ratio" (1976: 118). Critics charged that Malthus did not have the statistical evidence to warrant such a precise mathematical equation, but his main point was well taken. Any population is naturally beset by a "struggle for existence" as various individuals and groups vie for limited resources. In human societies, Malthus argued that the principle of population frustrated any attempts at a comprehensive amelioration because population would always be racing ahead of society's ability to nourish itself. For even the most civilized nations, especially at the lower strata, life was beset by "checks" – disease, vice, starvation, natural disasters, and other forms of misery – that painfully brought population back to levels that could be fed. Malthus thus opposed the optimistic hopes of reformers such as William Godwin, who felt that society free of crime, war, poverty, and disease could be achieved.

While Malthus believed that the population principle was a universal natural law, he recognized that its severity varied somewhat according to historical circumstances. In some societies, it brought on spectacular cycles of boom and bust, whereas in others it might only impact the lower classes during severe economic downturns. Ultimately, he hoped that his *Essay* would help decision-makers (government officials, parents, educators, etc.) put policies into place that would soften and reduce the checks, even though he felt very strongly that no society could completely eliminate them.

Nature then, for Malthus, was essentially composed of contradictory forces that vexed human existence (later thinkers like Darwin would apply this reasoning to all organic existence). On the one side was an expansive tendency linked to sexual reproduction that increased populations. On the other was limiting tendency (a finite food supply, the diminishing capacity of land to produce food) that led to deprivations, competitive struggle, and for many, early mortality. Small wonder that Thomas Carlyle would dub the classical economics that built from Malthus "the dismal science." At the most fundamental level, nature guaranteed suffering and pain that even the most civilized and orderly societies could not eliminate.

The prescriptions to reduce suffering that Malthus offered made him a controversial and often reviled figure. He asserted that direct efforts to help the poor (welfare payments, etc.) were in vain because recipients tended to use the resources to have more children who ultimately would be vulnerable to the checks. Instead, he argued that the English poor laws should be reduced or eliminated and that "moral restraint" (sexual abstinence) ultimately would be a better curb to the population principle because it addressed the root of the problem.

Malthus and Religion

Malthus was educated during an era when many prominent British natural historians were Anglican clergymen. Although some of his early teachers came from dissenting traditions, his primary education (at Cambridge) and career (as a country minister in Surrey) were steeped in Anglican orthodoxy. Malthus' thought was strongly marked by the era's natural theology that argued "through nature up to nature's God." In the most general sense, natural theologians maintained that the natural world was the harmoniously and intelligently designed masterwork of a benevolent, caring, providential God.

But how could one reconcile the pain and suffering that extend from the population principle with the "power, goodness, and foreknowledge of the Deity"? Especially now that the scope of natural evil had been enlarged to include all populations, all societies? Malthus was much troubled by this problem and devoted two chapters of his *Essay* and later writings to developing a theodicy that encompassed the population principle.

According to Malthus, "The original sin of man is the torpor and corruption of the chaotic matter in which he may be said to be born" (1976: 118). Furthermore, life was to be considered

> the mighty process of God ... for the creation and formation of mind, a process necessary to awaken inert, chaotic matter into spirit, to sublimate the dust of the Earth into soul, to elicit an ethereal spark from the clod of clay (1976: 118).

Thus the pressure articulated by the population principle was part of a great series of "excitements and impressions" by which the Creator, acting through "general laws;" awakened "sluggish existence." At the level of human society, the cruel "checks" so seemingly incongruent with theism were the very means by which a benevolent God elicited thoughtfulness, preparation, diligence, moral excellence, compassion, and ingenuity – in short, those habits of mind and behavior that secured improvement. Ultimately, the rational thought and exertion developed to alleviate the "partial evils" brought by the population principle resulted in an "overbalance of good" that benefited society.

Malthus linked his theological views to a utilitarian philosophy holding that a good society maximizes pleasure and eliminates pain for the greatest number. Like other utilitarians, Malthus saw the gratification of passion and desire as the foundation of human happiness, and thus entirely natural and good, except when overindulged. Typical of Anglican utilitarianism of his era (which had little regard for birth control), Malthus felt that the greatest scope for pleasure would be secured by restraining and/or redirecting passion until sufficient resources could be secured to safely enjoy the pleasures of life, chiefly, family and moderate consumption. Thus throughout his writings, Malthus endorsed moral restraint, "dictated by the light of nature and expressly enjoined by revealed religion," as the best means of addressing the population principle (1826: IV, 2, 19).

Anti-Malthusianism

Malthus' ideas, particularly after they were used to legitimize the rolling back of legal reforms designed to ameliorate the condition of the poor, became anathema to a variety of religious and political movements that championed the less fortunate. Radicals like Marx and Engels argued that Malthusianism was not so much a natural principle as a political ideology that inhibited the development of a more just, caring, and egalitarian society. According to this perspective, poverty and want were not rooted in "natural" conditions but in the greed and political shortsightedness of the more privileged classes. Liberal responses were more complicated. While most joined the radicals in rejecting Malthus' pessimism about comprehensive social amelioration, many, following the lead of John Stuart Mill, acknowledged Malthus' basic diagnosis of the human condition. Thus many liberals differed from Malthus only insofar as they held out greater hopes for increasing the production of food and/or regulating population through birth control and family planning – thereby tempering and perhaps eliminating the cycles of misery that plagued human history.

The relationship of religion to these anti-Malthusian trends is varied and complex. Many of the radicals dismissed traditional religion (revealed and supernatural) and Malthusianism as allied forms of reactionary political ideology – and perhaps could look to the popularity of Malthus among socially conservative Anglican clergy as suggestive evidence of this alliance.

Others, especially Christian socialists and religious liberals, insisted upon the rejection or modification of Malthusian pessimism in the name of ethical duties to help the poor and reduce human suffering. Likewise, much anti-Malthusianism sentiment emerges out of the loosely codified faith in progress that emerged during the Enlightenment. Thus in various utopian schemes and economic philosophies, poverty and want are not permanent social conditions but technical problems that can be solved or market inefficiencies that can be corrected – thereby transforming a suffering world into a place of peace, plenty, opportunity, and surplus.

Malthusianism and Environmentalism

With the rapid increases in human population over the course of the twentieth century (and projections for the twenty-first) many economists, environmentalists, and policy specialists, especially in the "limits to growth" camp, have revisited Malthus' ideas and used them to frame contemporary discussions of overpopulation and food supply. Although these efforts generally include a strong emphasis on birth control and eschew explicit theological content, they are often infused with a moral and prophetic urgency, reminiscent of Malthus. For example, American biologists Paul and Anne Erhlich have repeatedly argued that the world is overpopulated and that food production in many regions is already at full capacity or environmentally unsustainable. They contend that the basic solutions to this potentially disastrous situation will entail a fundamental shift in human values and attitudes, especially those that concern reproductive behavior, economic growth, technology, the environment, and conflict resolution. In a more general way, writers like John Rohe and Garrett Hardin use Malthus to introduce contemporary discussions of natural limits, overpopulation, economic planning, and environmental management.

Malthus' ideas are still widely discussed and debated by environmentally concerned people of diverse religious faiths. Perhaps his views remain current because his population principle framed some of the central concerns of human existence in ways that are easily grasped, yet powerful in their implications. The causes of human suffering, the limits to population, the consequences of sexuality, and the hope for a just and sustainable economic system all find articulation in his writings. A conscientious prophet for some, a reactionary ideologue for others, Malthus continues to cast a long shadow over discussions of religion and nature in the modern era.

Lisle Dalton

Further Reading

Hardin, Garrett. *Living Within Limits*. New York: Oxford University Press, 1993.

Malthus, Thomas Robert. *An Essay on the Principle of Population*. London: John Murray, 1826. Sixth edition, based upon the second edition of 1803. Available online at http://www.econlib.org/library/Malthus/malPlong1.html; accessed 28 May 2003.

Malthus, Thomas Robert. *An Essay on the Principle of Population: Text, Sources, and Background Criticism*. Philip Appleman, ed. New York: W.W. Norton & Company, 1976.

Rohe, John F. *A Bicentennial Malthusian Essay: Conservation, Population and the Indifference to Limits*. Traverse City, MI: Rhodes and Easton, 1997.

Winch, Donald. *Malthus*. New York: Oxford University Press, 1987.

See also: Abortion; Breeding and Contraception; Environmental Justice and Environmental Racism; Fertility and Abortion; Fertility and Secularization; Judaism and the Population Crisis; Population and Consumption – Contemporary Religious Responses; Population, Consumption, and Christian Ethics.

Mammy Water (West Africa)

Mammy Water is a Pidgin English name with different spellings (e.g., *Mami Wata, Mammywater, Mami Wota*, etc.) in West African coastal areas and near major bodies of water (e.g., rivers, lakes, and lagoons). The people refer to their highly localized divine waters as Mammy Water (e.g., Nigeria's late Igbo novelist, Flora Nwapa, and the Yoruba musician and artist, Twins 77). A scholar, Mrs. Chinwe Achebe, wife of the Nigerian author and Nobel Prize nominee, Chinua Achebe, asserted that:

> *Nne Mmiri* is a female deity with variants of local names, e.g., *Idemili* ... With the arrival of Europeans to this part of the world, "*Nne Mmiri*" became known as "*Mami Wota*" – a translation which enabled the local inhabitants to communicate the existence and exploits of this female deity to foreigners (Achebe 1986: 15).

Foreigners were slow to accept the notion of a water goddess. The conquerors of territories were more interested in the Earth than in water. Together with the English name, a chromolithograph depicting a woman with long hair and snakes was introduced in the 1920s, spread quickly, gained popularity and is commonly identified as Mammy Water. Furthermore, native artists utilize the foreign image, an African icon, in their own renderings of water spirits, adding to an academic controversy.

The Academic Discourse on Mammy Water

A psychiatrist indebted to Judeo-Christian and Freudian interpretations of the icon's snakes first explored connections between Mammy Water and mental illness in Liberia while unaware of indigenous links between Mammy Water and healing. Art historians largely ignored ethnographic detail, focused on the history of art objects, overlooked the existence of local water divinities, and following Salmons' influential article, speculated on the "cult's" foreign origins, pointed to the icon's importation, pondered on European or Indian affinities, and even considered possible New World sources (e.g., Vodun). Some social anthropologists have translated the snake symbolism into Marxist interpretations of socio-economic structures, or interpreted the religious practices as indigenous responses to modernity. Others emphasize African agency, literature, art, cosmology and cultural contexts, taking their clues primarily from African ethnography and meanings of the components: snake, woman, long hair, and color symbolism.

The Python

Mammy Water's serpents are loaded with Judeo-Christian and European-American gender symbolism. This, in turn, has distracted from alternative views. Comparative and historical studies of myth, ritual, iconography and symbolism reveal the snake as an ancient, significant, and recurrent theme, near-universally imbued with polar meanings (e.g., in the primordial snake of Babylon, the Egyptian hieroglyph, *djet*, classic Greek mythology, and Africa where pythons in particular are often linked to creation, mythical origins of the world, and regarded as sacred).

In South-East Nigeria, the python, imbued with religious symbolism, is regarded as a messenger of the gods (e.g., the lake goddess). An avenger of the divine ire, the python punishes an offender in Chinua Achebe's novel, *Anthills of the Savannah* (1986). A circle represents the python's association with death, but also circular time, reincarnation and eternity, in a chalk drawing by Palmer, a herbalist and water deity priest of *Egbema*, signaling the impending death of his patient moving to another stage of the eternal cycle of life and death.

Woman and the Color White

Africans sometimes say that Mammy Water is "white", "yellow", or "very beautiful." This has encouraged speculations on the foreign origins of not only the icon, but also associated beliefs in *The Spirit of the White Woman*. Mammy Water priests, instead, insist on healing, teaching to dance, and reconciling their clients with custom. The color white has special significance in West Africa: whiteness metaphorically indicates spirit involvement (e.g., in a new-born baby, or a dying person). White chalk cools the possessed mind and the feverish body, is awesome, mysterious, beautiful, and a symbol of femininity.

The color white signals birth and death, the transition from life to death, and vice versa in the eternal cycle of life, death and rebirth, delineating circular time. *Nzu*, white limestone/ chalk, found underwater, or white powder, is used in initiation ceremonies involving symbolic death and rebirth, to dedicate a person, or a body, as a medium to communicate with deities, and mark the crossroads between humans and spirits. A priest or diviner's eyes and the front heads of the congregation are painted white. White chalk is blown to the spirits, sprinkled on the ground in prayers and sacred Nsibidi drawings, and disperses like women leaving their ancestral home. Both water and whiteness are associated with childbirth, female fertility, transitions, and mobility. White (chalk) is a gift of the lake goddess and her favorite color: she prefers white in costume and sacrifice. Mammy Water's lightness and the portions of her dress and poster seen as white indicate spirit involvement. Initiates read the icon's gender and whiteness as "female divine water" – not to be mistaken for a racial feature.

Red and White

The white color is significant not only by itself, but also in combination with red. Yellow chalk, *edo*, defined as red, complements *nzu* and symbolizes virility. The combination of red and white in ritual expresses the complementary dualism of male and female, procreative powers, and the ideal balance of divine creation. The desired equilibrium of gender is embodied in divine pairs (e.g., in the shrine sculptures for the river goddess, Ava and her husband, near Nsukka) and expressed in the Igbo proverb, "If something stands, something else stands besides it" (Obioma Nnaemeka, personal communication).

Mammy Water's dress contrasts red and white, recalling the important theme of complementary gender, ritually symbolized (e.g., in the stark contrast of red blood on white chalk, of yellow and white chalk, and in costume). The combined use of the female icon and a chromolithograph of an Indian deity with three heads representing the male Mammy Water, or the water goddess' husband, further emphasizes the dualism of male and female.

Long Hair

One striking feature of the Mammy Water icon is her long, uncut, unbraided, and wavy hair. Foreigners read racial features into this hairstyle. But in West Africa, unkempt and uncut "long hair" has its own significance. African hairstyles are highly developed and diverse, an essential part of the ideals of feminine beauty and male grooming. Great care is applied to coiffure, an intrinsic part of personal grooming.

Classic African sculptures represent humans as well balanced, composed, and well groomed. Images of humans with wild, long, or unkempt hair are rare. Yet, in real life, not everybody is as composed as in artistic imagery. Though rarely represented, people with dreadlocks are known as *Dada* and Ajali in Yoruba and Igbo. Their long hair transcends social norms of controlled beauty and signals danger, disease, death, witchcraft, forces of wilderness, water, or spirit dedication.

Yoruba children with dreadlocks, *Omolokun*, (children of the sea), are considered related to water spirits. The Igbo link a person's dreadlocks to his destiny and extraordinary state of mind. A *Dada* is thought to be either "mad", or a "prophet", in touch with nature spirits outside of human society, often living an unusual life (e.g., as did Sunday, no longer cutting his hair, leaving it long, forever unkempt). More than a mere fashion, *Dada* is an expression of profuse existential crisis, physical, emotional, or both, at the brink of death, close to the spirit world, apart from ordinary human life. This may afflict anyone at any time in their life, even a child (e.g., when the river god Urashi re-incarnated a baby boy). Wild hair signals wilderness spirit involvement, the opposite of the human civilization and its well-groomed, cut, or shaven hair in men, and braided, plaited, cut, or combed hair in women. Long hair characterizes the water goddess herself.

Women with "Wild," Long Hair

Long, "wild" hair, or dreadlocks have added significance for African women. A young maiden is adored, praised and flirted with. Adulthood and entry into womanhood mark a shift of ideals of beauty to that of a mature woman, a matron who acts, looks, and is looked at differently from an adolescent girl. This transition is often marked through initiation and a time in the fattening house. The "fattening house" or "fattening room" is a term used in South Eastern Nigeria and other parts of West Africa where large size rather than skinny women idealize traditions of female beauty. The "fattening house/room" refers to a part of female initiation (from girl to woman) whereby a maiden entering the stage of mature womanhood stays in a special hut, or room, for a period of time (e.g., a week) groomed and is given special, rich food, special education and training in housekeeping, female and child healthcare, hygiene, etc., in some societies accompanied by female circumcision (female genital mutilation), and initiation camp.

The move is not easy and not every woman lightheartedly identifies with the ideals of mature beauty, constraints of adult womanhood, marriage arrangements, and other social pressures. Some women are unable to meet gender norms (e.g., are barren, have lost all of their children, suffer, or revolt against life, marriage, a job, training, or other social expectations). They may trade ordinary life for esoteric involvement and dedication to Mammy Water. In Igbo cosmology, changing one's destiny is possible with the aid of the water goddess who controls the crossroads between life and death, and in turn, requires religious commitment.

Mammy Water's long hair is synonymous with a particular splendor, the "killer" beauty of *Ogbuide*, "She who kills with excess," the gorgeousness of a young maiden, ephemeral as white chalk, yet equally powerful. Mammy Water's long hair signals fertility, beauty, female power, dedication to divine waters, and often an inability or refusal to live an ordinary life.

The Deities and Their Priesthood

While the icon known as Mammy Water is clearly indebted to foreign influences, there is no doubt in this author's mind that the deities collectively referred to as Mammy Water are indigenous, highly localized, and historically rooted in African cosmologies.

These divinities customarily have their own hereditary priests (e.g., via entitlement by virtue of seniority in a clan). But despite this prerogative, personal achievement must be qualified. Spirit calling, possession, or vocation are alternate avenues to individuals whose lineage does not own a title. Some have attained their status through vocation or possession, personal misfortune, sickness, healing and initiation. They are locally known as Mammy Water priests/esses.

Mammy Water and the Monotheistic Religions

The ideas of female divinities, multiple gods, divine nature, reincarnation and circular time are alien to the Abrahamic religions, some of which are competing for the souls of the natives. As a result, Mammy Water and other indigenous beliefs and arts are under attack.

Sabine Jell-Bahlsen

Further Reading

Achebe, Chinwe. *The World of the Ogbanje*. Enugu: Fourth Dimension Publishers, 1986.

Achebe, Chinua. *Anthills of the Savannah*. New York: Anchor Books, 1986.

Anderson, Martha and Christine M. Kreamer. *Wild Spirits, Strong Medicines: African Art and the Wilderness*. New York: The Center for African Art, 1989.

Becoming A Woman in Okrikra (Nigeria) (video). Filmmakers Library, NYC.

Boone, Sylvia, A. *Radiance from the Waters: Ideals of Feminine Beauty in Mende Arts*. New Haven: Yale University Press, 1986.

Drewal, Henry. "Performing the Other: Mami Wata Worship in West Africa." *The Drama Review* 118 (1988), 160–85.

Fabian, Johannes. "Popular Culture in Africa. Findings and Conjectures." *Africa* 48 (1978), 315–34.

Henderson, H.K. *The King in Every Man*. New Haven: Yale University Press, 1972.

Horton, Robin. "African Traditional Thought and Western Sciences." *Africa* 3 (1967), 150–81.

Jell-Bahlsen, Sabine. "Female Power: Water Priestesses of the Oru Igbo." In Obioma Nnaemeka, ed. *Sisterhood, Feminisms, and Power*. Trenton, NJ: Africa World Press, 1998.

Jell-Bahlsen, Sabine. "An Interview With Flora Nwapa." In Marie Umeh, ed. *Emerging Perspectives on Flora Nwapa*. Trenton, NJ: Africa World Press, 1998.

Jell-Bahlsen, Sabine. "Eze Mmiri di Egwu – The Water Monarch is Awesome: Reconsidering the Mammy Water Myths." In Flora E. Kaplan, ed. *Queens, Queen Mothers, Priestesses and Power: Case Studies in African Gender*. New York: Academy of Sciences, 1997.

Jell-Bahlsen, Sabine. "Dada-Rasta-Hair: The Hidden Messages of Mammy Water in West Africa." A Paper presented at the *African Studies Association Meeting*, 1995.

Jell-Bahlsen, Sabine. *Mammy Water: In Search of the Water Spirits in Nigeria* (video). Berkeley: University of California Extension Center for Media and Independent Learning, 1991.

Jenkins, Della. "Mamy Wata." In Chike Aniakor and Herbert Cole, eds. *Igbo Arts: Community and Cosmos*. Los Angeles: Museum of Cultural History, 1984.

Magnin, André, ed. *Okhai Ojeikere Photographs*. New York: Scalo, 2000.

Nevadomsky, Joseph and Charles Gore. "Practice and Agency in Mammy Water Worshipping in Southern

Nigeria." A Paper Presented at the *African Studies Association Meeting*, 1993.
Nwapa, Flora. *Mammywater*. Enugu: Tana Press, 1979.
Nwapa, Flora. *Efuru*. London: Heinemann, 1966.
Oha, Obododimma. "The Rhetoric of Nigerian Christian Videos: The War Paradigm of '*The Great Mistake.*'" Nigerian Video Films. Jonatha Haynes, ed. Jos: Nigerian Film Corporation, 1997.
Parrinder, Geoffrey. *African Mythology*. London: Hamlyn, 1967.
Paxon, Barbara. "Mami Wata: Ideas and Images of a New World Transcendent Being." M.A. Thesis. Seattle: University of Washington, 1980.
Salmons, Jill. "Mammy Water." *African Arts* 10 (Spring 1977), 8–15.
Schwartz, Nancy. "From Freudian Mutations and Christian Diabolization to Africanist and Feminist Herpetology: Some Luo Views on Snakes and Pythons." Paper Presented at the *African Studies Association Meeting*, 2002.
Thompson, Robert F. *Flash of the Spirit*. New York: Vintage Books, 1983.
Warburg, Abby. "A Lecture on Serpent Rituals." *Journal of the Warburg Institute* II (1938–1939), 222–93.
Wendl, Tobias and Wiese Wendl. *Mami Wata: The Spirit of the White Woman*. (Video) Goettingen, Germany: Institute for Scientific Film, 1991.
Wintrob, Ronald M.D. "Mammy Water: Folk Beliefs and Psychotic Elaborations in Liberia." *Canadian Psychiatric Association Journal* 15:2 (1970), 143–57.

See also: Divine Waters of the Oru-Igbo (Southeastern Nigeria); Sea Goddesses and Female Water Sprits; Serpents and Dragons; Water Spirits and Indigenous Ecological Management – South Africa; Yoruba Culture (West Africa).

Mandailing People (Sumatra)

The Mandailing people in the northwest island of Sumatra are a clan-based society with an indigenous tradition of representative and consultative governance. They are well known for their ancient tree-bark books, their contribution to modern Malaysian and Indonesian literature as well as their ritualistic music of the Nine Great Drums. They practice an indigenized brand of Islam where customs and customary usage is considered close to religion. Their habitat ranges from well-irrigated highlands with volcanoes to marshy lowlands. Their tropical rainforest is rich in biodiversity with, among others, Sumatran tigers, rhinoceroses, serows and Rafflesia flowers. Their productive economy is based on paddy, rubber, palm sugar, cinnamon, coffee and gold mining. "Mandheling Coffee" is famous amongst coffee connoisseurs today. There are over 300,000 Mandailings in their homeland in Sumatra, with about equal numbers throughout the rest of Indonesia and an estimated 200,000 or so, in Malaysia. The Mandailing homeland is today called the regency of Mandailing-Natal (Madina), in the province of North Sumatra, Indonesia.

The environmental worldview of the Mandailing people is embedded in its language, folklore and cultural heritage. The great epic of the Mandailing people speaks of the elements, the sky and the Earth. The recitation of the epic invokes the Earth, water and habitat guardian. The storyteller employs five different types of languages to transmit the oral tradition, including that of the camphor-gatherers as well as proverbs and maxims.

The epic begins with, "Once upon a time in the primordial past, the plant kingdom flourished and its flowers and fruits were abundant . . ." The symbolism used in the epic which forms the essence of Mandailing ethics and governance point to a way of life that is intimately bound to the forest and natural habitat.

This close connection to the habitat they lived in is also reflected in place-names, which are named after rivers, trees, mountains and such. Names of soil types also reflect an intimate relationship with "nature." For example, a fertile land is called green land.

Mandailing tradition defined the classical role of the Mandailing leader in naturalistic terms. The Mandailing nobleman is likened to the *baringin* tree, a place of shelter; its spreading roots a place of protection, its canopy a cover for the head. The nobleman's acute sense of hearing is likened to the rhinoceros.

Traditional Mandailing society has a few key concepts on division of land resources, territoriality and jurisdiction, and the management of resources. Central to these are the notion of a politically unified territory held together by customary law that secures territorial integrity as well as control over resources.

This set-up has a defined territory, citizen and jurisdiction, governed by a council of nobles and elders representing clans, nobility, religious functionaries headed by a chief. The strong connection of a Mandailing to his or her territoriality is testified to by the fact that when two Mandailings meet, they first and foremost ask which territoriality the other is from.

Elements representing the animal kingdom feature prominently in the houses of the nobles and elders called "house with horns" or "house of ornaments." The horns symbolize the sacrificial buffalo, sacrificed during ceremonial and ritualistic occasions.

In a typical Mandailing settlement, the chief's dwelling and the council hall are far more important and significant than the mosque. These two customary buildings reflect the status of the settlement as an autonomous entity.

In the chief's dwelling, the sacred Nine Great Drums are placed. They are played at customary ceremonies such as weddings and installations, and ceremonies to mark the death of the nobleman. The death of a tiger, described as the king of the forest, is similarly commemorated.

In Mandailing society, the management of the environment is tied to the origin of clans and settlement, social structure, system of land tenure, governance and sense of territory. Mandailing society in the past and up to this day is a rural, agrarian and pastoral society. The main agricultural activity is paddy planting. Ownership of a plot of paddy land is critical to Mandailing social life as it defines one's standing and status in society.

In the Mandailing perspective, a territorial unit is only complete when it constitutes land and water. The land and water in a settlement is communally owned and its usage has to conform to the customs as well as the sanction of the council of nobles and elders.

The water systems in Upper Mandailing are a feat of traditional water management and engineering. An extensive irrigation system provides for religious, domestic, agricultural and other uses. As such, settlements are strung all along the streams and river banks, traversed by path and canals leading to the paddy fields. One can hear the water flowing twenty-four hours a day in a typical Mandailing settlement.

Mandailing settlements are always located near a spring, stream or a river, which is used for domestic, agriculture, fisheries and religious/ritualistic purposes. Each territorial unit has its own protected forest area, where agriculture, hunting and harvesting of forest products are prohibited. These are usually watershed areas, believed to be where the spirits lived.

Inspired by the traditional concept of protected areas, local communities in the Mandailing homeland have been overseeing the implementation of a river-protection program. The practice prohibits the harvesting of fisheries' resources close to human settlements for a stipulated period. Implemented in seventy settlements, Mandailing has the largest river-protection scheme in the province of North Sumatra.

The income derived from the harvesting of river resources is used to pay for the development of social facilities such as schools, roads and mosques, providing educational scholarships and administrative salaries, charity toward orphans, the poor and invalids, etc. The income generated by this community-based ecological resource-management program benefits the community directly.

Both mother and child "village republics" are autonomous in implementing their system of governance. The general rule is that the chief of the Nasution clan rules settlements in Lower Mandailing while the nobleman of the Lubis clan rules settlements in Upper Mandailing, but there are exceptions.

The Mandailing nobleman governs in council, in that he acts in concert with his counselors. The nobles and elders jointly carry out their duties and obligations of governance and customary laws, which cover not only social and ceremonial matters such as marriage but also matters of local governance such as division of new paddy lands, rights of water and pastoral land, and so forth.

Although the territorial units were terminated by the Japanese imperial army in the 1940s, which meant that the nobles and elders lost their territoriality and powers to function effectively in Mandailing society, it did not wipe them out of existence, and to this day, the nobles and elders still play a recognized role as arbiters of the customs, although their authority is circumscribed.

Abdur-Razzaq Lubis

Further Reading
Harahap, Basyral Hamidy. "The Political Trends of South Tapanuli and its Reflection in the General Elections (1955, 1971 and 1977)." In Rainer Carle, ed. *Cultures and Societies of North Sumatra*. Dietrich Reimer Verlag, 1989.
Harahap, Basyral Hamidy. "Islam and Adat among South Tapanuli Migrants in Three Indonesian Cities." In Rita Smith Kipp and Susan Rodgers, eds. *Indonesian Religions in Transition*. Tucson, AZ: The University of Arizona Press, 1987, 221–37.
Kartomi, Margaret. *"Lovely When Heard From Afar": Mandailing Ideas of Musical Beauty in Five Essays on the Indonesian Arts – Music, Theatre, Textiles, Painting and Literature*. Monash, Australia: Monash University, 1981.
Lubis, Abdur-Razzaq. "Transformation of Mandailing Cultural Identity and Leadership." *Journal of the Malaysian Branch of the Royal Asiatic Society (JMBRAS)* 76 (2003), part 1.
Lubis, Abdur-Razzaq and Khoo Salma Nasution. *Raja Bilah and the Mandailings in Perak, 1875–1911*, (Monograph No. 35). Kuala Lumpur: MBRAS, 2003.
Lubis, Dr. Z. Pangaduan. "Ideas of Governance in the Built Heritage of Mandailing, Sumatra." *Asia & West Pacific Network for Urban Conservation (AWPNUC) Newsletter* 5:3 (1999), 7–9.
Traditional Buildings of Indonesia, Batak Simalungun and Batak Mandailing, vol. 3. Bandung: United Nations, Regional Housing Centre, ESCAFE, 1973.
Tugby, Donald. *Cultural Change and Identity: Mandailing Immigrants in West Malaysia*. St. Lucia, Australia: University of Queensland Press, 1977.
Tugby, Donald J. "The Social Function of *Mahr* in Upper Mandailing, Sumatra." *American Anthropologist* 61:4 (1959), 631–40.

Manifest Destiny

Coined by New York journalist John O'Sullivan in 1845, the term "manifest destiny" played an important, contentious role in American territorial expansion during the nineteenth century, and has had a lasting but equally fractious impact on American self-understanding in years since. Components of the idea of manifest destiny have a long and influential history in the United States, appearing in the guises of religious and political discourse, as well as in both elite and popular culture before and after their constellation within O'Sullivan's editorial work supporting American annexation of Texas and Oregon. In its various usages, the term encompasses nature, geography and race as key determiners of American values and institutions. For its proponents, it has typically served to attribute a sacred quality to American lands, one achieved through the work of subduing both raw nature and "inferior" peoples.

The oldest, and perhaps most crucial, component to the idea of manifest destiny is millennial. Early European colonists, most consistently the Puritans of New England, drew frequently on the Bible's millennial traditions in order to frame both their own colonizing agendas, and their view of the new world landscape to which they had migrated. As a sacred enterprise, their establishment of Massachusetts settlements was an analogue of the Israelites' exodus from Egypt to the land of milk and honey. The *New Canaan*, to which God led English Puritans as his newly chosen people, was an appropriation of widely embraced English Protestant ideas correlating the Israelite and English monarchies. Thus the Puritans did not so much coin the analogy as they deprived England's establishment of the analogy's "proper" use. But while Church of England expositors had to make biblical language of the wilderness and the heathen tribes metaphors for papal power, the New England Puritans were able to carve out a Christian beachhead in real wilderness, "full of wilde beasts and wilde men," as the Plymouth colony's first governor William Bradford put it. Just as the establishment of Israel was necessary for the history of redemption culminating in the life of Jesus of Nazareth, New Englanders came to see their own wilderness enterprise as crucial to redemption's second phase. In a kind of divine balance of history, since – as theologian Jonathan Edwards calculated – the "other continent hath slain Christ, and has from age to age shed the blood of the saints and martyrs of Jesus," it was reasonable to conclude that God would use the newly settled one to bring history to its glorious end (in Cherry 1971: 56).

In the meantime, New Englanders transformed their physical surroundings, guided by the biblical injunctions of Genesis 1:26, and the Arcadian vision of a subdued and bountiful nature subject to human enterprise. At times, as in judge Samuel Sewall's 1697 musings on New England's millennial role, this vision of New World abundance stressed a notable harmony between humans, nature, and divine intention: "as long as nature shall not grow old and dote, but shall constantly remember to give the rows of Indian corn their education by pairs: so long shall Christians be born there, and being first made meet, shall from thence be translated . . ." (in Miller 1956: 215). By contrast, the wilderness itself was often cast as a satanic realm where the divine aim was subverted.

Following the revolution, America's millennial role of playing host to the divine work expanded from providing the example of right religion practiced in the testing ground of the wilderness, to encompass the development of divinely approved political and cultural institutions as well. When earlier Puritans drew on the Mosaic covenant to speak about God's blessing of New England with abundance, that blessing was dependent upon their maintenance of right religious doctrine. In his 1795 Thanksgiving sermon, preacher Thomas Barnard – with little of the Puritan's ground for self-doubt – could simply assert that "we (Americans) are a people peculiarly favoured of Heaven." Such "favour" was most visible in the many "publick blessings" of prosperity obtained from still-fertile lands along the Atlantic seaboard (in Tuveson 1968: 31). The agricultural, industrial and technological achievement of the early republic over nature – for millennialists such as theologian Samuel Taylor Hopkins – was evidence of America's unique place in the economy of salvation. Americans, he urged, should expect such divinely sponsored advance that in the days to come

> a very little spot will then produce more of the necessities and comforts of life, then [sic] large tracks do now. And in this way, the curse which has hitherto been upon the ground, for the rebellion of man, will be in a great measure removed (in Tuveson 1968: 61–2).

For Congregational minister Joseph Emerson (cousin of famed Transcendentalist Ralph Waldo Emerson), in 1818 the future promised such an easy marriage of human technology and divine intent in ensuring agricultural advancement that the chemist might little think "how much his labors conduce to bring on that happy state of things, that shall distinguish the Millennial period" (in Tuveson 1968: 68).

As Americans turned their territorial gaze across the Appalachians, they augmented biblical millennialism with Enlightenment ideas. Nature as the product of a rational deity justified their interest in the Mississippi River and its terminus in the Gulf of Mexico, in the peninsula of Florida, and even in Canada. As Samuel Adams put it in 1778: "We shall never be upon a solid Footing till Britain cedes to us what Nature designs we should have, or till we wrest it from her" (in Weinberg 1958: 22). Nature's intent for human beings, which Thomas Jefferson in the "Declaration of Independence" (1776) had framed as individual rights to life, liberty and the pursuit of happiness, could be expanded upon at the national level to include independence and security from the harmful plotting of other nations, such as France and Spain. For residents of Kentucky this meant "the natural right of the inhabitants of this country to navigate the Mississippi" and to develop the region's agricultural potential in accordance "with the immense designs of the Deity" (in Weinberg 1958: 25–6), and for Jefferson himself, natural right offered a sufficiently elastic basis for delimiting expansion. When nature intended Americans use of the Mississippi, it must also have intended them a port, he said, since "the right to use a thing, comprehends a right to the means necessary to its use" (in Weinberg 1958: 27). Such elastic rights, to some, suggested the reduction to absurdity of arguments based on natural design. Nevertheless, they enabled Americans to envision themselves within the first few decades of the nineteenth century as a continental power, and – as geographic knowledge replaced myths of the "Great American Desert" – to brush aside the constraints of western mountain ranges and arid lands. Thus the idea that nations were created within natural limits found little to recommend it until Americans had stretched themselves "from sea to shining sea," as a patriotic hymn put it later in the century.

Publisher John O'Sullivan's phrase, "manifest destiny," coined in his mid-1840s *Democratic Review* editorials favoring annexation of Texas and Oregon, quickly gained great rhetorical power as a wide range of politicians, religious leaders, land speculators and others took it up. Opponents of the notion were themselves divided about America's course. Unitarian minister William Ellery Channing considered the original Texas revolt of 1836 "an act of criminality" in itself, but also a precedent, he wrote to Senate leader Henry Clay, since "we cannot seize upon or join to ourselves that territory, without manifesting and strengthening the purpose of setting no limits to our empire" (in Graebner 1968: 48). A decade later, diplomat Albert Gallatin, Ralph Waldo Emerson and a number of Eastern liberals opposed war with Mexico, but most were slow to term manifest destiny simply "political clap-trap," or to deny its underlying view of Providence, as did the *National Intelligencer* (in Graebner 1968: 239). Congressional opponents, such as Representative Charles Goodyear, who in 1846 spoke of manifest destiny being a "robber's title," were basically intent on averting war with England, and softening U.S. claims to western Canada above the 49th parallel.

Ralph Waldo Emerson himself celebrated the energies expended in continent spanning, seeing "a sublime and friendly Destiny" guiding the human race across America, the future "home of man" (in Graebner 1968: 11). The construction of national railroads, binding people of one region with another, Emerson said, "introduced a multitude of picturesque traits into our pastoral scenery. The tunneling of mountains, the bridging of streams ... the blowing of rocks, explosions all day ..." were signs of national promise and potential, making it possible for the race to tap the vastness of the land, which would be "physic and food for our mind, as well as our body" (in Graebner 1968: 6–7). Even Henry David Thoreau, opposed to so many of his fellow-citizens' endeavors, felt "Nature's magnetism" pulling him along the same continental trajectory. "Eastward I go only by force," he famously acknowledged, "but westward I go free" (Thoreau 1975: 667–8).

The biblical arguments remained effective political justifications throughout the period – and seemed by many expansionists to have been thought sufficient to make England abandon its own interest in Oregon. Former president John Quincy Adams argued in Congress that since England was a Christian nation, it was bound to respect the relevance of Genesis 1:26–28 as the surest foundation of title. Whereas England only wanted Oregon for its Hudson Bay Company trappers, Americans claimed Oregon, Adams concluded, in order to "make the wilderness blossom as the rose, to establish laws, to increase, multiply and subdue the Earth, which we are commanded to do by the first behest of God Almighty" (in Graebner 1968: 109). But even those expansionists who did not draw upon biblical or Transcendentalist mandates spoke of America's continental destiny with religious, ecstatic, fervor.

William Gilpin, first territorial governor of Colorado, was perhaps foremost – certainly most energetic – among expansion's intellectual advocates. Gilpin's writings, dependent upon the theories of the German explorer and naturalist Alexander von Humboldt, melded his scientific postulating about the "isothermal zodiac" – the global climatic belt within which empires had developed and moved ever-westward – with enthused descriptions of the American continent and the "pioneer army" he saw pushing across the Rocky Mountains in search of gold and fertile soil. The pioneer, for Gilpin, spearheads the vital portion of the "human current," which

> bears with it the immortal fire of civilization revealed to man. This central current has reached the Plateau of America, up which it will ascend to plant the sacred fires over its expanse and shine upon the world with renewed effulgence. Such is the resplendent era and the gorgeous promise unveiled to humanity. The arrival of this is *now* announced by the indefinite gold production and pastoral power of the interior, domestic region of our continent and country (Gilpin 1974: 53).

Manifest destiny's advocates could only go so far in making religious or scientific appeals, however. If the English and the Americans might be expected to establish consensual readings of scripture, ponder the isothermal lesson, or merely to submit to diplomatic resolution of the

Oregon dispute – which President Polk achieved in 1846 despite Democrats' desire to war with England – this possibility was less expected of others who stood in the way of American expansion. In American dealings with Mexico, native tribes, and later with both Cuba and the Philippines, race thus became the key factor in determining the direction of achieving manifest destiny, and violence its often justified means.

As early as the 1820s, when Americans pushed into Cherokee and Choctaw lands, Christian land use seemed a practice that only Anglo-Saxons were capable of employing. Confronted by arguments that Indians were mere occupiers of the soil, and hence lacking any legal title to it, Cherokees and other southern tribes vigorously embraced the agricultural lifestyle and religion of encroaching Americans, and were then sued by the gold-hungry Georgians who wanted their lands – for violating treaty terms. As Governor Troup noted to the Georgia legislature during the debates leading up to passage of the 1830 federal Indian Removal Bill – which eventually solved the problem to the Georgians' satisfaction – "by changing the mode of life of the aboriginals upon the soil of Georgia," by causing "her lands to be separately appropriated for the purpose of tillage," and by promoting "every encouragement to fixed habits of agriculture," the federal government and the Cherokees "violated the treaties in letter and spirit, and did wrong to Georgia" (in Weinberg 1958: 87). Efforts to "civilize" tribes were thus violations of "the laws of nature," as one Georgia legislator put it, which "have fixed an insuperable barrier between the moral condition of the savage and the Christian" (in Weinberg 1958: 88).

The belief in Anglo-Saxon moral superiority gained ground as it was deployed not only in the taking of tribal lands, but also in conflicts with Mexico. Some supporters of the 1846 invasion of Mexico and the conquest of California envisioned Mexican citizens greeting American forces as liberators, and perhaps melding into the American population as their lands experienced the regenerative rule of republican institutions and the development of mineral and agricultural resources. The more prominent tendency after the war, as Florida's Senator Westcott complained in 1848, was to reject the idea that the U.S. should

> receive not merely the white citizens of California and New Mexico, but the peons, negroes, and Indians of all sorts, the wild tribes of Camanches [sic], the bug-and-lizard-eating "Diggers" and other half-monkey savages in those countries as equal citizens of the United States (in Horsman 1981: 276).

By the end of the nineteenth century, carving out national boundaries and dispossessing tribes from their lands ceased to figure in forward-looking American imaginations. The wilderness-transforming energy that white Americans attributed to their Anglo-Saxon roots – and which historian Frederick Jackson Turner's 1893 essay "The Significance of the Frontier in American History" and President Theodore Roosevelt's *Winning of the West* (1907) claimed was defining of national character – seemed to have reached a terminus. However, Anglo-Saxon manifest destiny continued to shape American life. The push to open trade with Asia – key to Senator Thomas Hart Benton's imperial vision as early as the 1820s – and even to acquire Asian colonies, spread widely. By the century's end the vision was commonly accompanied by a racial justification of U.S. dominance in the Pacific. America's 1898–1901 war in the Philippines against first Spain, and then insurgent Filipino nationalists, was cast by its supporters in the McKinley and Roosevelt administrations as a repetition of the frontier struggle. For Roosevelt, Filipinos were "Apaches," playing the same role in thwarting national destiny as Geronimo (in Slotkin 1992: 121). For Senator Albert J. Beveridge, opponents of U.S. military operations in the Philippines – arguing that whites could not successfully live in tropical environments – erred in concluding that the Anglo-Saxon race therefore had no obligations there. On the contrary, he told the Republican National Convention in 1900, "the general welfare of the world" demanded American rule, otherwise

> this land, rich in all that civilized man requires, and these people needing the very blessings they ignorantly repel, should be remanded to savagery and wilderness. If you say this, you say that barbarism and undeveloped resources are better than civilization and the Earth's resources developed (in Cherry 1971: 142).

The need to subdue nature, in the course of the twentieth century, lost some of its focus as a theme in American discussions of national aims. Manifest destiny, however, did continue to be invoked, as in the arguments of President Woodrow Wilson for American participation in the First World War, and Franklin Delano Roosevelt for the Second. These weighings of America's unique responsibility had less to do with the conquest of nature, though, and more with what Wilson framed as the moral mission of American democracy. Nevertheless, America's mobilization in both wars was also nature's, since the country's abundant natural resources provided American factories with the material necessary to achieve victory. Although twentieth-century Americans did at times contest the implications of natural abundance, as in the conservation movement's debates about "finite" resources during the Gifford Pinchot era and then again in the 1970s, very few seriously advocated an overturning of the economic order that had been built on the basis of manifest destiny. Which is to say that Beveridge's 1900 challenge to anti-imperialists – that consistency would require them to give "Australia back to its Bushmen, and the United States to its

Indians" – has rarely been accepted, other than by tribal advocates themselves (in Cherry 1971: 148).

But if subduing nature became a given in the twentieth century, popular culture has provided an enduring context in which the task can be reappropriated, its urgency rekindled and its achievements often commemorated. The American landscape is full of memorials to manifest destiny, none more striking than Colorado's Mount of the Holy Cross, which journalist Samuel Bowles was first to proclaim as a divine seal of approval upon American enterprise in *The Switzerland of America: A Summer Vacation in the Parks and Mountains of Colorado* (1869), and which Yellowstone explorer and artist William Henry Jackson first photographed in 1873. Made a national monument in 1929, the mountain's deep snow-filled couloirs offered several generations of pilgrims confirmation that nature itself spoke the gospel in America. Although its remoteness kept visitation at such low levels that the federal government removed it from the list of national monuments in 1955, and the permanent snowfields have subsequently melted in part, reproductions of the Jackson photograph and numerous paintings of the mountain circulated widely for long afterwards, and Climbers for Christ offered cyberspace images of the mountain at their website.

The remembered past, embodied in works of art and architecture, or in numerous historical and recreational sites, also preserves the vision of manifest destiny. Emmanuel Leutze's gigantic mural "Across the Continent, Westward the Course of Empire Takes its Way" (1864) hangs in the U.S. Capitol. Mass circulation prints of Fanny Palmer's "Emigrants Crossing the Plains" (1868), or John Gast's "Westward Ho" (1872) linked technology, American determination and divine inspiration – in Gast's case by means of a gigantic, gauzy-gowned Goddess of Liberty floating above westward-moving citizens, telegraph wire and law book in her hands. The homes of westward-pushing or western-raised heroes such as Daniel Boone and Abraham Lincoln, battle sites such as Wounded Knee, the Little Bighorn, and the Alamo; monuments such as the Jefferson Arch and Mount Rushmore; and consumer theme parks such as Disneyland; are all centers at which tourists absorb the spirit of manifest destiny. Innumerable annual "Pioneer Day" celebrations – such as the "Laura Ingalls Wilder Days" in DeSmet, South Dakota – offer small-town and big-city residents the chance to connect heroic ancestral deeds with their communities' needs of the present and hope for the future.

The preeminent icon of manifest destiny in the twentieth century was Hollywood's archetypal American hero and most popular actor, John Wayne, who built much of his career reenacting the drama of manifest destiny. A brief consideration of his films shows the link between nature and national mission in twentieth-century guise. In Wayne's westerns and war films, manifest destiny is represented as the just and overarching aim of the American people, while Wayne serves as its closed-mouth and hard-fighting but morally virtuous agent. The Wayne persona is most at home on horseback, passing confidently across the land, or nestled rifle-at-the-ready, against rock, tree or sand – though as Gary Wills (1997) points out, he also fills the frame of the interior shots in *Stagecoach* (1939) with the ease of a man of nature. He has enough experience with indigenous people to be on speaking terms with them, and to know their habits and aims, but generally avoids familiarity, and even when preventing imperial violence – as in *Rio Grande* (1950) – he upholds the aim of civilizing the savage and making the land into a secure home for Americans. As a heroic figure he rarely approves of run-of-the-mill religious expression, telling the whore in *Sands of Iwo Jima* (1949) – with whom he drinks but doesn't sleep – "Don't get religion on me" when she offers to pray for him, and ridiculing the preaching of Ward Bond in *The Searchers* (1958). Nevertheless, he embodies the muscular Christianity advocated by Theodore Roosevelt for urban Americans growing soft in the aftermath of frontier conquest. He casually refers to God as "Sir" in *Rio Grande*, and "the man upstairs" in *Sands of Iwo Jima*. At the center of his character is duty, and rarely does it lead him into conflict with official American power. His most conventional religious gesture is his performance of perfunctory but heartfelt funeral services, in which he returns to the Earth either unfortunate subordinates or enemies fallen in his conflicts over soil.

Though Wayne worked with several directors, and played a variety of heroic roles, these portraits cohere in ways that consistently underscore the centrality of manifest destiny to his persona and to an understanding of America as an ideal. Consider, for example, the thematic overlap between *Red River* (1948) for Howard Hawks, his *Rio Grande* trilogy for John Ford (1948–50), his self-produced *The Alamo* (1960), and such war films as *Flying Tigers* (1942), *The Fighting Seebees* (1944), *They Were Expendable* (1945), and *The Sands of Iwo Jima*. The westerns emphasize the righteousness of Wayne's violence against Indians and Mexicans; the Pacific-based war films present racially uncomplicated portraits of the American fight against Japanese aggressors. But Wayne and his directors erase the historical gap between western conquest and Pacific war by a spatial assimilation; Texas, Arizona, a Pacific island, these separate pieces of Earth are the same under the sweep of Wayne's gun. Overwhelmingly, Wayne's violence – even that which is clearly brutal – fulfills a fundamentally religious function, providing what Richard Slotkin (1992) calls "regeneration." In *They Were Expendable* – the story of U.S. Navy patrol torpedo boats in the opening days of World War II – the western and war story mix to provide a historical, or mythical, gloss on American possession of the Philippines. In one scene, when American defeat before the Japanese invasion appears certain, Wayne's Lt. Rusty Ryan talks with Dad Knowland, an old boat-builder who refuses to flee. He sits on the front step of his tropical homestead, rifle and whiskey bottle in hand, and tells Ryan: "I worked forty years for this, son. If I leave it they'll have to carry me out," while the background music provides a chorus of "Red River Valley" – a folk-song from the end of the nineteenth century that helped romanticize the American annexation of Texas lands south of the Red River. Music also underscores the righteousness of the American cause in the final scene, as the Civil War's "The Battle Hymn of the Republic" helps reconcile viewers to a shot of Wayne's boatless crew marching ragtag off to sacrifice themselves in the jungle. The familiar hymn enables viewer consent to the extension of America's redemptive role in the Pacific, as the land appropriated by one generation of manifest destiny advocates, and defended by another, is made meaningful through connection with the most important example of regenerative violence in American history – the chastened killing and massive dying that Lincoln declared "hallowed" at Gettysburg.

Howard Hawks' *Red River* connects the Western adventure with the biblical account of the Israelites crossing the Red Sea, a point which Hawks' screenwriter, novelist William Faulkner, emphasized obliquely to a journalist in 1955 during the filming of *Land of the Pharaohs*. According to Faulkner "It's 'Red River' all over again. The Pharaoh is the cattle baron, his jewels are the cattle, and the Nile is the Red River" (in Hillier and Wollen 1996: 2). In "Red River," Wayne, playing the historic cattleman Tom Dunson, blazer of the Chisholm Trail, establishes his claim to land below the river by shooting without clear provocation or much explanation a Mexican *vaquero*, who challenges Dunson's presence on land his boss had received as a grant from the King of Spain. Justification comes from sidekick Walter Brennan (Groot), who remarks "That's too much land for one man. Why it ain't decent. Here's all this land aching to be used and never has been. I tell you, it ain't decent." The perfunctory killing, the *vaquero*'s brief burial, over which Dunson presides, and the branding of their small stock of cattle are sufficient to mark the land as home for the forward-looking Dunson, who plans to raise the largest herd in Texas and satisfy the American family needs for an abundance of beef.

In both films, American land, wherever it is, is home to American enterprise, violence establishes or maintains its original – and contextless – Anglo-Saxon appropriation, and American identity is framed as relentless, forward-looking and violence-bestowing determination to hold this land in the face of threats from non-Anglos. These twin themes of appropriation and defense of the land overshadow almost any other in Wayne's films, to the extent that his muscular Christian hero rarely appears as a mere worker of the land. And in an age where manifest destiny is already an accomplished fact, his hero is out of step, harkening back to the time when nature's abundance was not yet assured, or still threatened by the nation's demonic foes.

Wayne's normative nostalgia often served to revive American ideals in challenging times, especially in films produced in the midst of the Second World War, or under the cloud of Cold War uncertainty, as were so many of his westerns. Their frequent reliance upon manifest destiny to establish the meaning of America's mission in the past and its role in the present ran up against the wall of defeat in Vietnam, however, a war which Wayne sought to reinvigorate in familiar terms with *The Green Berets* (1968). But the nature presented by southeast Asian jungles offered little that Wayne could depict as home for American enterprise. Sacrifice for soil comes through more successfully, however, as the Special Forces unit Wayne commands fights off a massive Vietcong siege of their central highlands compound, reversing the outcome of Mexican General Santa Ana's famous 1836 siege of the Alamo. Soil, sacrifice and the example of history mattered as well to President Lyndon Johnson, a Texan whose grandfather may have died at the Alamo, and to whom Wayne wrote in 1965 in support of Johnson's deployment of U.S. troops. For Wayne, the causes were the same, enabling him to use the justification his "Alamo" character, Davy Crockett, offered. "We don't want people like Kosygin, Mao Tse-tung, or the like" Wayne told Johnson, " 'gorin' our oxes' " (in Wills 1997: 228).

In the decades since, American popular culture has apparently abandoned Wayne's faith in manifest destiny and America's overcoming of geography through violence, though he remains Hollywood's most popular figure. Certainly the western saga, as a story of righteous conquest or personal and social redemption achieved through Anglo-Saxon subduing the land, has ceased to animate culture producers. Likewise, Anglo-Saxon racialism has lost its resonance as a public justification for resource extraction. Since Vietnam, Hollywood cameras have often captured war itself through a cynical lens. But the taming of the American landscape – the domestication of nature – that western expansionists first envisioned as the divinely commissioned destiny of the American people is reaffirmed through their endless journeying – moving, working, vacationing – over the country's vast transportation network, and their absorption of natural resources into the needs and designs of their daily lives. Bound by duty to wield a gun in defense of American enterprise, Wayne's characters rarely had time to share in the absorption of nature which this enterprise enables.

Perhaps this absorption has been secularized. However the forthright James Watt, Secretary of the Interior under President Ronald Reagan from 1981 to 1983, certainly viewed America's consumption of nature within a decidedly traditional religious framework. In telling Congress that "my responsibility is to follow the Scriptures, which call upon us to occupy the land until Jesus returns," he brought back into public life the millennial assumptions regarding the American land and the American mission that had so shaped the idea of manifest destiny to begin with (Klein 1981: 22). By the century's end that orientation had not lessened among the general public, though it was anathema to left-leaning journalists and environmental activists. In addition, the equation of moral purpose and political power that has guided America's role on the twentieth-century international frontier was still leading early twenty-first century American policy-makers to sound biblical echoes, as it led Albert J. Beveridge in 1900, to wonder "When nations shall war no more without the consent of the American Republic: what American heart thrills not with pride at that prospect?" (in Cherry 1971: 153).

Matthew Glass

Further Reading

Cherry, Conrad, ed. *God's New Israel: Religious Interpretations of American Destiny*. Englewood Cliffs, NJ: Prentice-Hall, 1971.

Gilpin, William. *Mission of the North American People: Geographical, Social and Political*. New York: Da Capo, 1974 (1873).

Graebner, Norman A., ed. *Manifest Destiny*. New York: Bobs-Merrill, 1968.

Hillier, Jim and Peter Wollen, eds. *Howard Hawks: American Artist*. London: British Film Institute: 1996.

Horsman, Reginald. *Race and Manifest Destiny: The Origins of American Racial Anglo-Saxonism*. Cambridge: Harvard University Press, 1981.

Klein, Jeffrey. "Man Apart: James Watt and the Making of God's Green Acres." *Mother Jones* 6:6 (August 1981), 20-7.

Miller, Perry, ed. *The American Puritans: Their Prose and Poetry*. New York: Anchor, 1956.

Slotkin, Richard. *Gunfighter Nation: The Myth of the Frontier in Twentieth-Century America*. New York: Atheneum, 1992.

Thoreau, Henry David. *Selected Works of Henry David Thoreau*. Walter Harding, ed. Boston: Houghton Mifflin, 1975.

Tuveson, Ernest Lee. *Redeemer Nation: The Idea of America's Millennial Role*. Chicago: University of Chicago Press, 1968.

Weinberg, Albert K. *Manifest Destiny: A Study in Nationalist Expansion in American History*. Gloucester, MA: P. Smith, 1958 (1935).

Wills, Gary. *John Wayne's America: The Politics of Celebrity*. New York: Simon & Schuster, 1997.

See also: Book of Nature; Disney Worlds at War; Emerson, Ralph Waldo; Holy Land in Native North America; Indigenous Environmental Network; Native American Languages; Nature Religion in the United States; Thoreau, Henry David.

A Manifesto to North American Middle-Class Christians

Preamble

It is time for an Ecological Reformation. The Protestant Reformation and Vatican II brought the importance of the human individual to the attention of Christians. It was a powerful revolution with many impressive religious and political results. But our current version of this model – the individualistic market model, in which each of us has the right to all we can get – is devastating the planet and making other people poor. This model is bankrupt and dangerous. We now need a new model of who we are in the scheme of things and therefore how we should act in the world.

The Individualistic Model

The model of human being as individual is deeply engrained in North American culture. Its goal is oriented to *individuals* – to their rights and desires. North American Christianity has also been focused on individual well-being, either as salvation of believers or comfort to the distressed. This model of human life supports that we are a collection of individuals who have the right to improve our own lives in whatever ways we can. We see ourselves as separate from other people, while acknowledging the right of others to improve themselves. But this is not a description of "the way things are"; it is a model, a *way* of seeing ourselves and nature. It is a way that is proving to be harmful to most of the world's people and to nature.

There is very little public discussion of the key consequences of this model: climate change (global warming), the increasing gap between the rich and the poor, the extinction of other species, and the rapid decline in natural resources. We are being kept in denial about the seriousness of these major global issues by powerful business lobbies and timid politicians, *but also* by our own reluctance to disrupt the most comfortable lifestyle that any people on Earth have ever enjoyed.

The Ecological Model

The individualistic market model has failed us: it has limited religious viability and it is proving to be dangerous to our planet. We need another model of human life: we need an Ecological Reformation. An Ecological Reformation would base its model of human life on how reality is understood in our time. The picture of reality emerging from cosmology, evolutionary biology, and ecology today focuses on relations and community, not on individuals and objects. *We are all related*: we all came from the same beginning.

This story also provides us with a new model of human life. In this story, human beings are not individuals with the power to use nature in whatever ways they wish. Rather, we are *dependent* on nature and *responsible* for it. In a sharp reversal, we do not control nature, but rely utterly on it. The rest of nature does not, however, depend on us; in fact, if human beings were to disappear from the Earth tomorrow, all plants and animals would be better off.

Our radical dependence on nature means that we are also responsible for it. As the species currently laying waste the planet – and aware that we are doing so – we must accept responsibility for our actions. The ecological model of human life tells us not only who we are but also what we must do: it gives us guidelines on how we should act. In other words, it is a *functional* creation story, one that has practical implications for how we live at personal and public levels.

We could call these implications our new "house rules." The common creation story tells us that the Earth is our home – it is where we evolved and where we belong. It also tells us what we must do for all of us to live decently and happily here. House rules are what one pins on the refrigerator as guidelines for sharing the space, the food, the resources of the home. The basic rules are: take only your share, clean up after yourself, and keep the house in good repair for future occupants. The ecological model comes with some definite house rules, clearly seen in the fact that "ecology" and "economics" come from the same word root having to do with laws for living in a household. The basic rule is that if everyone is to have a place at the table, the limits of planetary energy must be acknowledged. The house rules of our home set limits to growth – both of our consumer desires and the size of the human population. We need, then, to become "ecologically literate," to learn what we can and cannot do if our home is to continue to exist in a sustainable way. We must fit our little economy into the Big Economy, Earth's economy, if our economy is to survive.

Christianity and the Ecological Model

As Christians we need to do all this and more. This new model, which could be summarized by a version of Irenaeus' watchword – the glory of God is every creature fully alive – provides Christians with new ways to say that God is *with* us on the Earth and that God is *for* us, especially the oppressed. This new model suggests to Christians that the way to picture God's presence with us is the eschatalogical banquet to which all are invited, all people and all other creatures.

The ecological model, then, suggests a new vision of the "abundant," the good life. We must envision models of the abundant life based not on material goods, but on those things that really make people happy: the basic necessities of food, clothing, and shelter; medical care and educational opportunities; loving relationships; meaningful work; an enriching imaginative and spiritual life; and time spent with friends and in the natural world. In order to move toward this good life, we will need to make changes at every level: personal, professional, and public – how we live in our houses, how we conduct our work lives, and how we structure economic and political institutions. It is a life that for us North Americans may well involve limitation and significant change in our level of comfort. Christians might see it as form of discipleship, a cruciform life of sacrifice and sharing burdens.

A Call to Action

The Ecological Reformation is the great work before us. The urgency of this task is difficult to overstate. We do not have centuries to turn ourselves around and begin to treat our planet and our poorer brothers and sisters differently. We may not even have the next century. But the scales are falling from our eyes and we see what we must do. We must change how we think about ourselves and we must act on that new knowledge. We must see ourselves as both radically dependent on nature and as supremely responsible for it. And most of all, we North American privileged people who are consuming many times our share at the table must find ways to restructure our society, our nation, and the world toward great equitability. Christians should be at the forefront of this great work – and it is a *great* work. Never before have people had to think about the well-being of the entire planet – we did not ask for this task, but it is the one being demanded of us. We Christians must participate in the agenda the planet has set before us – in public and prophetic ways – as our God "who so loved the world" would have us do.

Sallie McFague

See also: Christianity (7d) – Feminist Theology; McFague, Sallie.

Manser, Bruno (1954–2000) and the Penan of Sarawak

Born into a devout Protestant family in Basel, Switzerland, Bruno Manser was one of the foremost global campaigners for the indigenous Penan nomads of Sarawak, Malaysia, until his suspicious disappearance in Sarawak, on or around 25 May 2000. With a worldview centered on communal harmony and the veneration of nature, Manser was a firm believer and active practitioner of nonviolent civil disobedience. Gaining wide fame and attention in Europe, Manser and the nonprofit, Swiss-based Bruno Manser Fonds (in English, the Bruno Manser Foundation) campaigned fiercely and relentlessly for two decades to stop the decimation of tropical forests, to defend and institutionalize the rights of indigenous peoples to autonomy and self-determination, and to document egregious violations of basic human rights.

Manser was primarily focused on saving the indigenous Penan and their communal forests on the island of Borneo, and in this pursuit he was a formidable self-taught ethnographer, ethnobotanist, artist, writer, linguist, craftsman and photographer. His informal medical studies ensured his self-treatment and recovery from a lethal bite of a red-tailed pit viper while living in remote Penan territories in 1989.

One of three boys and two girls born to a factory worker, Manser's parents wanted him to become a doctor. Surrounded and nourished by the tempered wilderness of the Swiss Alps, Manser early on challenged the epistemological dictates of "civilization." An independent thinker from the start, at nineteen years old Manser spent three months in a Lucerne prison for conscientious objection to Switzerland's compulsory military service. While he was known to be aware of the Gandhian philosophy of Satyagraha, the extent of Manser's familiarity with the non-violent ideologies of Tolstoy, Thoreau or Martin Luther King is less certain.

Leaving prison in 1973, Manser lived for twelve years as a cowherd in a secluded Swiss alp, where he laid bricks, carved leather and kept bees. He wove, dyed and cut his own clothes and shoes. Mountaineering and technical climbing were regular pursuits. Foreshadowing later solo wilderness expeditions in Malaysia, Mexico, Congo (Zaire) and Alaska, Manser ventured alone into the Swiss mountains for long periods.

In 1984 Manser traveled with an English spelunking expedition to explore the Gunung Mulu National Park in Borneo. Afterward he traveled deep into the interior of Sarawak to find and live with the Penan. "In my search to understand the deep essence of our humanity," Manser said, "there grew in me the desire to learn from a people who still live close to their source. At Swiss libraries I found almost nothing about the Penan of Sarawak, and so I said 'I want to go there'" (personal communication, 1993).

From 1984 to 1989 Manser lived intimately with the Penan, mastering the Penan language, documenting the ethnology of the Penan and their natural environment. Manser adopted the Penan way of life absolutely, dressing in a loincloth, hunting with a blowpipe and bow and arrows, eating primates and snakes and the staple sago palm of the Penan diet. Manser's respect and sensitivity for the Penan gained him an unprecedented status in the egalitarian and non-hierarcrhical community of the last several hundred nomadic Penan.

Bruno Manser's total immersion in the Penan lifestyle became a source of much derision, humor and ridicule in the West, and his experience was often dismissed as "pure Hollywood" foolishness. "They called me 'white Tarzan,' 'medical school drop-out,' 'short-time hero'; they even said I had taken two Penan wives," said Manser (personal communication, 1993).

To those who investigated or knew his story, Bruno Manser was venerated. He was known and respected by Hindu, Buddhist, Islamic and Christian leaders, whom he often met with, at home and abroad. Manser's nonviolent protests (especially prolonged public fasts) drew the attention of Switzerland's churches: Catholic and Protestant leaders in Switzerland regularly dedicated services to Manser. An exemplary citizen, respected for his efforts to mitigate Penan suffering, Manser grew in stature, often portrayed as a moral beacon for religious stories, themes and dedications; for church services and celebrations (especially Confirmation); and for protracted rites where Bruno Manser was chosen as the focus of prolonged meditations. After his disappearance, the veneration of Bruno Manser increased significantly: school and church groups frequently request(ed) information from the BMF.

Absent any judicial recourse to the unrestricted logging that was increasingly devastating the remaining indigenous forests of Borneo, the Penan in the early-1980s instituted nonviolent blockades of logging operations, blockades that continued over subsequent decades. While their plight was mostly ignored and marginalized, the Penan persisted in attempting to further their indigenous rights to autonomy and self-determination through international forums, local actions and the efforts of Penan leaders both resident and exiled.

Bruno Manser's role in Penan blockades is uncertain. Living amongst the Penan from 1984 to 1990, a fugitive remaining in Malaysia without a visa, Manser catapulted the Penan story onto the world stage. He did not participate in logging blockades but the Malaysian and Sarawakian government nonetheless blamed him for Penan actions. In 1990 he left the Penan to campaign in Europe, Japan and North America to stop the logging of Penan territories. Manser correctly perceived that the economic policies of the already industrialized nations would determine the future of indigenous people like the Penan.

In December 1992 Manser led a twenty-day hunger strike in front of Marubeni Corporation headquarters in downtown Tokyo, Japan. In 1993 he led a sixty-day fast, supported by forty hunger-strikers in front of the Swiss Parliament. In 1996, Manser and Jacques Christinet hung huge banners on the auxiliary cable of the Swiss Kleinmatterhorn aerial cable car, a risky action for which Manser was criticized by some supporters. There were countless lesser actions, meetings with parliaments and corporate executives, and appearances at international conferences and before the United Nations. By 2000, Bruno Manser Fonds raised over $10,000 to establish a mobile dental clinic for the Penan but the Malaysian government refused to cooperate and rejected the project.

In 2000, Manser privately confirmed that success in Sarawak had been "less than zero" (personal communication). He was deeply saddened.

Academics, newspapers and officials widely criticized and derided Manser, although the U.S. press ignored the Bruno Manser and Penan story altogether. Malaysian officials were hardened by Manser's presence in Sarawak. Some environmental groups blamed Manser for inflaming the Malaysian government. Prime Minister Mahathir Mohammed blamed Manser for disrupting law and order. In a personal letter to Manser, Mahathir wrote:

> As a Swiss living in the laps of luxury with the world's highest standard of living, it is the height of arrogance for you to advocate that the Penans live on maggots and monkeys in their miserable huts, subjected to all kinds of diseases (Mahathir, 3 March 1992).

Mahathir responded to Penan blockades with the designation of Biosphere Reserves for the Penan (subsequently logged illegally). Dr. Mahathir in 1987 invoked Malaysia's State Security Act to jail critics of the regime. The Act was also used to neutralize the Penan campaign: at the time of writing, over 1200 people had been arrested for challenging the logging; up to 1500 Malaysian soldiers and police had stormed barricades, beaten and arrested people; bulldozers had leveled nomadic camps; and the Sarawak government tolerated criminal gangs hired by logging firms to intimidate the indigenous people.

The government of Sarawak's Chief Minister Tan Sri Abdul Taib Mahmud responded with military operations targeting Manser. Through his embarrassing investigations and reports, Manser gained the wrath of many timber companies. He evaded Malaysian security on numerous occasions to visit the Penan. Soldiers in Malaysia hunted him, and he was captured by soldiers, and escaped under gunfire, twice. Declared "enemy of the state number one," a $50,000 word-of-mouth bounty was rumored and widely believed to have been placed on Manser's head: the source of the bounty remains unconfirmed.

Manser's expedition to document the effects of logging and war on the Ituri pygmies in the rainforest of Congo (Zaire) in 1995 occurred amid widespread political upheaval and terror. Manser returned to Switzerland with a massive body of moving ethnographic photographs, later shown at expositions around Europe. His efforts to defend the Penan never ceased.

In 1999 Manser entered Sarawak illegally, and was arrested and deported after landing a motorized glider on the property of Sarawak's Chief Minister Taib Mahmud, where a group of Penan leaders, never welcome, were waiting to get a meeting with the Chief Minister. On 22 May 2000, on what became his last mission to Sarawak to meet with Penan friends besieged by logging, Bruno Manser disappeared without a trace on or after 25 May 2000. He was last seen by a Penan friend within two days' walk from the village of Bario, Sarawak, not far from the base of Batu Lawi, the venerated limestone spire. Within a year, the pristine forest where Manser disappeared was logged.

Throughout his life Manser quietly rejected the dogmatism of religion, especially his native Christianity. In contradistinction, Manser found his personal beliefs confirmed in alignment with aspects of Buddhism, Islam, Hinduism, Christianity and animism that he considered noble and sacred. Manser's spiritual coherence with nature was born in his youthful and mostly solitary explorations of the alpine environment; his coherence with animism was keenly furthered through his deep association with the Penan. Manser believed in following one's dreams, no matter the impediments or implications. With a very poignant understanding of the commonality of hopes and fears of human beings, Manser lived life in respect of all beings, and in respect of the unseen world, which he considered the base of all life.

In the Penan cosmology, Manser was known as *lakei Penan* – Penan man – signifying the respect the Penan held for their adopted brother. Manser's drawings and stories collected during his stay with the Penan are richly elaborated with tales of animal and nature spirits, and the concomitant superstitions and taboos. Manser documented oral histories from Penan elders and recorded and translated their interpretations of self, tribe and nature.

Manser's documentation of the Penan way was intimate and unprecedented. Sense of place is paramount in the Penan cosmology, where the geomorphology is intimately known and all natural objects (trees, rivers, animals, etc.) have creation stories or fables associated with them. Penan social and gender roles attest to a deeply spiritual and respectful cosmology absent of hierarchy. Manser's intimacy with, and acceptance by, the Penan enabled him to transcend the arrogance and ethnocentricity that characterize and inform (detrimentally) much anthropological research. He was painstaking in his efforts accurately to interpret the metaphysical and practical symbology of the Penan. Manser claimed that in his six years with the Penan he never witnessed an argument or expression of violence of any kind. He often spoke of the peace and violence of the forest, and the joys and sorrows of the Penan way.

In January 2002, hundreds of Penan gathered for a private commemoration of Manser with the ritual *tawai* ceremony ("think fondly of someone or something that is not here"). With taboos against speaking the names of the dead, the Penan will forever address Manser as *lakei tawang* ("man who has become lost") and *lakei e'h metat* ("man who has disappeared").

Keith Harmon Snow

Further Reading

Davis, Wade, Ian Mackenzie and Shane Kennedy. *Nomads of the Dawn: The Penan of the Borneo Rainforest*. Pomegranate Books, 1995.

Manser, Bruno. *Voices from the Rainforest: Testimonies of a Threatened People*. Basel, Switzerland: Bruno Manser Fonds & INSAN, 1996.

Manser, Bruno. *Tong Tana: Journal on Rainforests, Indigenous Rights and the Timber Trade*. Basel, Switzerland: Bruno Manser Fonds, 1998.

High Stakes: The Need to Control Transnational Logging Companies – A Malaysian Case Study. World Rainforest Movement (Uruguay) and Forests Monitor Ltd. (U.K.), 1998.

Snow, Keith Harmon. "Bruno Manser: Man Who Has Disappeared." *Kyoto Journal* 53 (March 2003).

See also: Penan Hunter-Gatherers (Borneo).

Marshall, Robert (1901–1939)

Robert Marshall was an Alaskan explorer, a relentless advocate for preserving samples of American wilderness, and the primary founder of the Wilderness Society. Marshall had a lifelong fascination with the exploration of unmapped wilderness and the enjoyment of the wilderness experience. This resulted in his exploration and initial mapping of the Central Brooks Range of Northern Alaska. As early as his undergraduate college days at the School of Forestry at Syracuse University, Marshall expressed sadness at the loss of wild conditions throughout North America. By the time he earned his doctoral degree in plant physiology, in 1930, he believed that if something were not done soon, no significant samples of American wilderness would remain. Thus, in 1935, with several others (most notably, Aldo Leopold and Benton MacKaye, the "father of the Appalachian Trail"), he founded the Wilderness Society, whose mission was to save as much American wilderness as possible. Marshall also financed nearly all of the Wilderness Society's activities from 1935 to 1939.

Most of Marshall's wilderness preservation arguments were designed to appeal to utilitarian values. He often referred to wilderness as a "resource," and argued that a "balanced" approach to resource planning would have to include large amounts of undeveloped landscape. Perhaps this is not surprising because Marshall was trained as a forester and scientist, and had mainly to convince foresters and scientists. Like any effective communicator, he spoke in the language of his audience. As a result, his best arguments advocate wilderness for providing a unique human experience rather than for its value independent of humans.

On the other hand, there are important streaks of pantheism in Marshall, perhaps not well recognized even by himself. Most importantly, he viewed wild places as sacred. He was brought up in the Jewish faith, and once, at age 24, he took a long reflective walk in the mountains of Idaho for Yom Kippur, the Day of Atonement. On this hike, he spent three hours sitting on a rock in quiet contemplation. The setting, he reported, was conducive to the purpose, for "there was no wandering of thoughts to the chance of the Pirates in the World Series ... nor even to the less frivolous subjects of pine production or the political situation." He thus found himself

> forced to confess that in Temple ... it has in the past been impossible to banish [trivial] thoughts from my mind, and, at best, fasting, hard seats and dull sermons are not conducive to deep thought. Therefore, I feel that my celebration of Yom Kippur, though unorthodox, was very profitable (Glover 1986: 81).

Wild nature, in other words, was Marshall's temple, his sacred space. And the spiritual value of wilderness to him explains much about his enormous drive to preserve it. In one of his most telling statements, he observed that, for people like himself, the wilderness experience "is absolutely essential to happiness. In the wilderness they enjoy the most worthwhile and perhaps the only worthwhile part of life" (Glover 1986: 96).

Thus Marshall's religion, if he had one, was nature. A short statement he made to a friend after the death of his father, Louis Marshall, tells as much about his religious philosophy as he ever revealed.

> Fortunately, I suppose due to the general philosophy I have about life and death I didn't take [my father's] passing as emotionally as you imagine. The significance read into death is of course an individual matter. Between the most glorious conceptions of heaven and the unbearable ideas about hell there is infinite room for divergence. Personally, I do not believe in any hereafter and my guess is that death means oblivion. Yet it is a perfectly inevitable event, and nothing which is inevitable seems tragic (Glover 1986: 110).

Death, in other words, though sad, was perfectly natural to Marshall, who spent enough time in wild nature to recognize the role of death in the natural, "inevitable" unfolding of events, and to realize, surely, that without death there is no life. All of which would be unremarkable had Marshall not lived in a culture obsessed with removing itself from nature by, among other things, denying death.

Still, Marshall's spirituality remains obscure, hidden behind his rejection of the Judeo-Christian conception of God, his non-belief in an afterlife, his activism in secular issues like politics and civil liberties, his human-centered arguments for wilderness as a "resource," and the perception that he was always in a hurry to get things done (as if he knew he had less than 39 years to live).

Perhaps, had he lived longer, he might better have articulated for himself and others the intuitive feeling of sacredness that drove him hard to defend wild places – even if his culture demanded he do so mostly in the language of human-centered, scientific rationalism.

James M. Glover

Further Reading

Glover, James M. "Romance, Recreation, and Wilderness: Influences on the Life and Work of Bob Marshall." *Environmental History Review* 13:3–4 (1990), 23–40.

Glover, James M. *A Wilderness Original: The Life of Bob Marshall*. Seattle: The Mountaineers, 1986.

Glover, James M. and Regina Glover. "Robert Marshall: Portrait of a Liberal Forester." *Journal of Forest History* 30:3 (1986), 112–19.

Marshall, Robert. "The Problem of the Wilderness." *The Scientific Monthly* (February 1930), 141–8.

See also: Leopold, Aldo; Muir, John; Pinchot, Gifford; Wilderness Religion; Wilderness Society.

Martial Arts

> Caution: "Those who know do not talk, and talkers do not know"
> Lao Tzu, *Tao Te Ching* 56 (R.B. Blakney, tr.).

The quasi-mythical origins of many Asian martial arts enfold them within a religious context and tradition. This is clear whether they are traced to Bodhidharma in the sixth century – who, legend has it, traveled from India to teach Buddhism in China and found the monks in such pathetic physical condition that he invented exercises to improve their health and self-defense capabilities – or linked to Cheng San-Feng, a thirteenth-century monk who introduced taijiquan as a "grand ultimate" method of internal martial art among Shaolin monks. From the beginning, the fundamental practices found in these martial arts bear a strong family resemblance in terms of ritual, discipline, and psychophysical effects to the fundamental practices of nearly every world religion.

Many Asian martial arts are explicit regarding their spiritual goals (enlightenment, embodying eternal principles in the apparent finitude of physical life) and methods (meditative standing and ritualized movement designed to produce spiritual insight). This is especially true of the so-called "internal" styles from China (like taijiquan, baguazhang, and xing yi) or Japan (like aikido and those which emphasize the perfection of character over fighting skills). In "harder" or "external" styles, which include Chinese "kung fu" forms probably best known to the West through popular stereotypes from martial art movies with names like *Preying Mantis, Tiger, Dragon*, and *White Crane*, the spiritual dimension is more implicit. The complex family trees of Okinawan karate and many of the Korean styles are included in this category. These styles stress fighting skills – but even those emphasizing the most brutal physicality eventually turn inward to consider, as integral to mastery, the psychospiritual aspects of their training. Whether internal or external, these martial arts achieve their physical aim (self-defense) and their spiritual aim (insight into the ground of existence) in the same way; by exhorting practitioners to move, and to exist, *naturally*.

Nearly all ritual practices in the Asian martial arts are informed by symbolic heuristics derived from nature. Typically, one begins by learning the series of movements characteristic of the particular martial art – just as in a monastery one begins to learn the correct postures for mediation, to bow in a specific way, to perform cycles of movement in yoga postures, or walk mindfully. The movements themselves often carry the names of animals or natural phenomena and these provide a kind of symbolic representation for the physical postures the practitioner attempts to emulate. In Tiger style the hands often imitate a tiger's claws. The stance and finger placement in Preying Mantis resemble a preying mantis as she stalks and then grasps her prey. Movements in taijiquan like Dragon Spits Out Pearl or Stork Cools Wings seem to adopt something of the animal to which they refer. "Long boxing" exhorts its practitioners to imagine striking with the pent-up force, the inertial density, of a great river (the name refers to the "long" distance the energy travels from ground, to leg, waist, shoulder, arm, hand, and finally into the opponent – as if with the "long" weight of a great river). But while the outward forms may bear some relation to animals, the identification is made for psychological ends.

Consider Wave Hands As Clouds – a movement common to most forms of taijiquan (in some topological configuration it is common to every martial art). There may be some sense in which the hands look like clouds waving back and forth but the name is more of an instruction to the mind than to the body. It is a kind of iconic template that brings body and mind together. Identification with the icon allows the practitioner to absorb the deeper significance for which the icon is a conduit or veil. Cloud Hands tells you to move fluidly and in rounded motions. This psychological suggestion – "wave my hands like clouds" – is exactly how the martial arts appropriate nature in order to cultivate, first, sound biomechanical techniques, second, effortless technique in movement, and then, as if by infection, effortless effort in every corner of life.

Animals and natural phenomena inform the physical and psychospiritual practices in most Asian martial arts but the religious end of identification with these structures lies in cultivating the internal energy called *qi* (or, under the old Wade-Giles system of transliteration, *ch'i*). The concept of *qi* requires an encyclopedia of its own but, just as many kinds of yoga attempt to cultivate and then use *prana* for spiritual attainment, the aim of most Asian martial arts is to cultivate and then apply *qi*. Cultivating one's *qi* is the first step toward a spiritual understanding of one's relation to one's self and to the rest of the universe. In the language of meditative technique, identifying with the heuristics derived from nature makes it possible to cultivate *qi* because of the focus and concentration this identification creates.

Identification with these metaphors and beginning the process of developing one's *qi* is a first step toward proper form. In martial arts practice, in sparring or grappling for instance, proper form means greatest biomechanical efficiency. Biomechanical efficiency makes it possible to relax or loosen the muscles, and the mind that moves them, and allow *qi* to flow. Once the *qi* is accumulated and put to work informing one's movements the practitioner finds him or herself stronger and faster than any opponent. Using internal energy is said to be infinitely greater than mere physical strength. Oddly, cultivating and using *qi* is said to be possible only when the practitioner is completely relaxed or loose. *Qi* cannot "flow properly" when the practitioner is tensed or exerting him/herself physically.

Here we run into the kind of paradox that seems ever present in Asian thinking – the internal energy that makes you strong only works when you loosen your muscles completely or, to put this in even more obscure language: one can only be strong through yielding, one can only advance by retreating, etc. It is, in other words, nearly impossible to express the physiological effects of this looseness using mere language – as Lao Tzu wisely noted in our opening quote – but it is quite easy, and often dramatic, to *experience* the effects in practice. The tension between the rational and experiential modes of understanding of these ideas suggests something about the futility and even the danger of attempting to describe, in language, experiences that seem to transcend language. Experiencing can be hard enough; understanding is harder still; but describing these effects in words turns out to be nearly impossible.

A humorous aside: a lot has been written about *qi*, not all of it useful. There is a "*ch'i/qi*-whiz" factor associated with this aspect of martial arts practice. In the same way that novices practicing meditation sometimes mistake their early experiences for Enlightenment, it is not surprising to hear novice martial artists discuss their sudden and astonishing facility with the mysterious powers of *qi*; in both cases this is almost always the sign of an over-enthusiastic beginner. The martial arts thus carry the same hazards as any other spiritual practice. Pride, envy, attachment, overestimation of advancement, and all the other Sirens call to the ego from every side. Short of tying yourself to the mast of your ship, like Odysseus, humor is the next-best prophylaxis. The most direct and pithy comment this author has ever heard on the matter was at a seminar in Green Bay, Wisconsin, some years ago when I had the good fortune to meet Nate Defensor, an instructor in Philippine martial arts. I asked Nate why I had not heard any mention of *qi* development in Filipino martial arts. Nate grinned and said, "Oh, we were too poor to have *qi*. We had rice instead."

Describing *qi* is fraught with dangers but the experiential effects of proper form are relatively easy to describe. Performing the movements incorrectly (when sparring or grappling) is difficult and requires a great deal of physical exertion. Performing the movements properly by using internal energy or *qi* instead of one's mere physical strength – having properly assimilated the ideas of naturalness, in other words – is startlingly easy: it is, in fact, effortless. Martial artists call this "good technique" and it begins to explain why smaller, much older, men and women can defeat one or more younger and apparently stronger opponents. Efficient technique, properly applied, can offset uninformed, merely physical strength.

We could describe this seeming effortlessness as the result of habituating and employing proper biomechanics along with the complementary psychological conditioning, but it seems to be more than this. It is, in fact, the physical correlate of the naturalness and ease that lies at the heart of Daoism and the meditative practices of Hinduism and Buddhism. The effortlessness of good physical technique requires a thorough understanding of the truth of your position, balance, and relation to the world around you. The psychological aspect of this is to see beyond the apparent distinction between yourself and your opponent, or yourself and the world, to an underlying unity that grounds both. The spiritual aspect, when physical and psychological come together, is effortless effort, or *wu wei*. Effortless technique is thus a physical manifestation of properly assimilating and understanding *wu wei*. Here the circle of training the body turns out to be the circle that trains the spirit.

Every mystical practice depends on quieting the ego-consciousness, whether by spinning the prayer wheel of a mantra, through the fire of aspiring passions, or completing a complex series of physical movements. Once the drunken-monkey brain of everyday consciousness is quieted (either by being occupied with its exercises or through an identification with the animal or natural form), the practitioner can begin to perceive reality and their place in it *as it is* – as a whole rather than as the broken and fleeting sensations of daily consciousness. To borrow the traditional metaphor, we can imagine that the universe is a great lake and the mind a wind blowing across it. If we could stop this wind from fracturing the surface into a cracked glaze of wavelets, then the lake would become smooth and allow the soul to see its true reflection. Martial arts calms these waters like any other yogic or spiritual practice. Quieting the mind is required for *wu wei* and for the effortlessness that characterizes excellent technique.

Considered in a religious context we might argue that martial arts is a branch of raja yoga; the yoga of psychophysical experimentation. The physical exercises harness their practitioners to a spiritual grindstone. Eventually the circle of training they tread produces religious effects. The practices themselves are a yoke of physical and psychological ritual – in all Asian martial arts this means learning a series of complex movements which, in principle, contain the combat applications specific to different styles. These movement sets are learned and internalized to the point that they become habitual. Like a prayer wheel or mantra, these physical movements become an axle of focus, concentration, and meditation. Achieving facility with these movements requires concentration, attention to increasingly minute details, a concomitant increase in alert mindfulness, and the cultivation of effortlessness. This mindfulness maps directly into the kind of psychological state required for practice in any meditative exercise – whether Zen, tantric, or Jesuitical. Learning the physical movements is only the beginning. The mere choreography of taijiquan or karate, for instance, can be learned in a few months; mastery, achieved through the integration of physical and spiritual dimensions, requires a lifetime. Effortlessness is easy; achieving effortlessness is hard.

If martial arts is a branch of raja yoga, the methods and effects should look the same. The end or eventual purpose of such an exercise is *samadhi*, union with the object of your meditation. Whether yantric line drawings or iconic representations of saints and deities, the end point of spiritual exercise is union with that object. Martial arts, at the advanced levels, seeks the same kind of union. If one reads the traditional stories about the fights and feats of great taijiquan or Shaolin masters, one is always struck by the way combat is couched in terms of uniting with the adversary in order to borrow their own strength and use it against them or, a bit more esoterically perhaps, helping the enemy accomplish their own deepest desire – to find the ground of their being. Ueshiba Morihei, founder of Aikido, built his entire style on the philosophy that you must blend with your opponent so as to overcome the difference between you. Even in harder styles like hapkido this means joining with your opponent's intentions, whether to help them head-first into the floor or, more compassionately, into an understanding of their own needlessly aggressive tendencies. Union with your adversary requires a profound insight into the existential nature of conflict, of difference, and dialectical resolution – physically and intellectually.

Thus, if we may at last fall back on the language of thought to describe what lies beyond it, underlying the physical gestures of breaking boards, fighting, or cultivating one's character is a complex dialectic of self and other. This dialectical encounter creates an ambient religious context and religious potential; a teleology as spiritual as combative. For the philosophically minded, Hegel's dialectic of self and other should come to mind or perhaps Socratic method as a therapeutic style of dialectical remediation. For the religious, wrestling with God, loving your enemies, or liberating your self by defeating your own self-generated fears, are equally sound analogies. Appropriating naturalness to open the door to effortlessness in movement, in thought, and in our relationships, lifts humans out of the fixed and fixated ego-consciousness which prevents us from an adequate mediation with our surroundings and so, finally, with ourselves.

Mark C.E. Peterson

Further Reading
Dang, Tri Thong. *Toward the Unknown*. Rutland, VT; Tokyo, Japan: Charles E. Tuttle, 1997.
Dang, Tri Thong. *Beyond the Known*. Rutland, VT; Tokyo, Japan: Charles E. Tuttle, 1993.
Donahue, John J. *Herding the Ox*. Hartford: Turtle Press, 1998.
Fauliot, Pascal. *Martial Arts Teaching Tales of Power and Paradox*. Rochester, VT: Inner Traditions, 2000.
Leggett, Trevor. *Zen and the Ways*. Rutland, VT: C.E. Tuttle Co., 1987.
Morris, Glenn. *Martial Arts Madness: Light and Dark in the Esoteric Martial Arts*. Berkeley, CA: Frog, Ltd. (Distributed by North Atlantic Books), 1998.
Shoshin Nagamine. *Tales of Okinawa's Great Masters*. Patrick McCarthy, tr. Boston: Charles E. Tuttle Publishers, 2000.
Ueshiba, Morihei. *Budo: Training in Aikido*. Larry E. Bieri and Seiko Mabuchi, trs. Tokyo: Japan Publications (New York: distributed by Kodansha America), 2001.
Ueshiba, Morihei. *Budo: Teachings of the Founder of Aikido*. John Stevens, tr. New York: Kodansha America, 1991.
See *also*: Chinese Traditional Concepts of Nature; Daoism; Yoga and Ecology.

Mary in Latin America

Throughout Latin America the Virgin Mary gains specific abilities and qualities as she interacts with the cultural history and natural forces of a particular place. Her elevated position within the Catholic Church as the Mother of God combined with the traditional iconography associated with Mary facilitates her versatile connection with powerful indigenous and African female deities; reproduction and fertility; earth and agriculture; the moon; serpents; water and the sea. Agricultural festivals that celebrate planting, first-fruits, and harvest frequently coincide with a local *fiesta* honoring a specific manifestation of the Virgin and combine ritual observance of both the moon in its different phases and the nourishing sacred soil. Alternately, manifestations of the Virgin preside over coastal festivals honoring the life-giving and life-taking powers of the sea. In order to understand the specific ways that Marian devotion engages indigenous and African Diaspora interpretations of nature throughout Latin America, we will concentrate first on Andean representations of Mary in colonial iconography and postcontact mythology, and then turn briefly to similar examples in Meso-America, Brazil, and the Caribbean.

In the Andes, the Virgin is alternately associated with Quilla, the moon and corresponding water forces such as rain, rainbows, springs and waterfalls. She is also associated with Pacha Mama, "the earth which is our mother" and accordingly, with specific volcanic mountains. In the colonial period, paintings of Mary by the Cuzco School reveal how indigenous painters attributed the Virgin's authority to her Andean connections to nature. Traditional European iconography associated with the Virgin of the Immaculate Conception drew from the Book of the Revelation of John, which describes "a woman, adorned with the sun, standing on the moon, and with the twelve stars on her head for a crown." For Native Andean painters this iconography took on new physical shape and symbolic resonance. Artists inscribed the astronomical emblems with Andean meanings and depicted Mary as a triangular statue, a shape that linked her to the Andean volcanoes, sacred living beings that contain and control the circulation of agricultural produce, livestock and minerals. Painters enhanced this depiction of fundamental alliance to the sacred land by embellishing the Virgin's clothing with ritual meaning. Andean robes decorated with flowers and feathers associated the Virgin with Inca nobility, direct descendants of the sun and moon. Pearl necklaces linked her to the moon and the sea, and gold dangling earrings with emeralds linked her to the sun and the mountains. While her gold and jewel encrusted halo replicated Incaic representations of the sun, the crescent moon at Mary's feet reinforced her association to the Coya, the sister/wife of the Inca and daughter of the moon. This iconography unveiled the ways that Native Andeans viewed the Virgin Mary's authority as rooted in the sacred land and animated by astronomical forces. It also affirmed her authority through Andean forms of ritual expression, thereby maintaining traditional Andean social structures of sacred power.

In the Andes, post-colonial origin myths attribute Mary's authority directly to her alliances with the Andean land. Typically, these stories recount how a local manifestation of the Virgin appeared at a sacred spring, river, waterfall or ravine. The origin stories parallel pre-Colombian accounts of the birth of the *w'akas* – indigenous nature deities who became the ancestors and later transformed into mountains, springs, rivers, ravines, trees or stones. In Southeast Ecuador, for example, *Nuestra Señora del Rosario de Agua Santa de Baños* is known for presiding over healing thermal pools and for protecting the town of Baños from the violent eruptions of the nearby Volcano Tungurahua. Local myths relate that this Virgin, born from a sacred waterfall, leaves the basilica's altar at night in order to bathe in Tungurahua's springs. In the Andes, ritual bathing in sacred springs, which are viewed as the eyes of the living mountain body, can impart spiritual authority to *yachajs* or shamans granting them the power to heal and to negotiate with mountain spirits. Accordingly, the mythic explanation for the Virgen de Agua Santa's abilities to heal and protect her devotees arises directly from the *yachaj*-like pact that she makes with Tungurahua through bathing. In this agricultural region the primary festivals honoring the Virgen de Agua Santa fall alternately in October, a month of drought, and February, a month of excessive rains.

Throughout Mesoamerica, Marian devotion engages the specific geomythic and ritual history of the Aztecs, Mayas, Otomis, Huichols, and Tzutujils, among others. Mexico's most renowned Virgin, La Virgen de Guadalupe, appeared on 9 December 1531 to the Indian Juan Diego on Tepeyac hill near a shrine to the Aztec fertility goddess, Cihuacoatl-Tonantzin. Aztec pilgrimages to Tepeyac had formed part of pre-Colombian rainmaking rituals that consisted of travel to water-holding hills around Tenochtitlan. Aztecs referred to Cihuacoatl-Tonantzin as "Our Lady Mother" and believed that she had helped to create the human race. They associated Cihuacoatl or Snake Woman with deer and adversity. The dark skinned Virgin told Juan Diego her name was María Coatlalopeuh. *Coatl* is the Nahuatl name for serpent and *lopeuh* means "the one who has dominion over serpents." Today in central Mexico, devotees still refer to images of the Virgin Mary as Tonatzin. In other parts of Mexico devotees associate the Virgin with Chalchiuhuitlicue, the goddess of water; Xilonen, the goddess of tender maize, a symbol for fertility and rejuvenation; and Chicomecoatl, the goddess of sustenance. In the uplands of Morelos, native ritualists plant crosses, which they associate with Mary and maize, as a means of attracting rain to their crops. This contemporary cult of the crosses parallels pre-Colombian celebrations for Chicomecoatl.

In Brazil and the Caribbean, Catholic devotees of the African diaspora associate the Virgin Mary with a variety of African goddesses. Practitioners of Candomblé and Santería correlate Mary Star of the Sea, Our Lady of Regla, and Our Lady of the Immaculate Conception, to Yemaya the Mother of Waters, fish, and all of the *orisha*. As the goddess of the ocean, Yemaya represents creativity and ancient wisdom and, as such, is associated with the full moon and the planet Neptune. Like Mary her colors are sky blue and white. She is associated with silver and is symbolically represented by a six-pointed star or an open shell. In Brazil, on New Year's Eve, Candomblé practitioners create elaborate beach-front altars with food and candles. As the ocean waves consume the offerings, Yemaya accepts her devotees' gifts and washes away their troubles with the waters of creation.

For Cuban practitioners of Santería, the Yoruban *orisha* Ochún appears in cross-dress as Nuestra Señora de la Caridad de Cobre, Cuba's patron saint. In 1628 a wooden image of La Virgen de la Caridad first appeared to *los tres Juanes*, two Native Cubans and an African slave rowing in a storm. The statue was taken to a church but continually disappeared and reappeared under an orange tree in the copper-mining town of Cobre. Ochún, the *orisha* linked to La Virgen de la Caridad, is the *orisha* of sweet water and the goddess of love, marriage and motherhood. She is associated with the new crescent moon and the planet Venus, with the metals copper and gold, and the color yellow. To celebrate Ochún/La Virgen de la Caridad, devotees make offerings of honey, cinnamon or oranges on riverbanks or near waterfalls.

In Haiti, Vodou practitioners link Mary to a group of female love spirits known as Ezili who express and amplify different aspects of Mary. Lasyrenn, one of the Ezili, is Queen of the Ocean and appears as a mermaid or whale and, like Ochún, appears as La Virgen de la Caridad. As mistress of the underwater world, Lasyrenn "links ancient African senses of woman power and water power" (McCarthy Brown 1991: 220–25).

Lisa Maria Madera

Further Reading

Carrasco, David. *Religions of Mesoamerica: Cosmovision and Ceremonial Centers*. New York: Harper Collins Publishers, 1990.

Damian, Carol. *The Virgin of the Andes: Art and Ritual in Colonial Cuzco*. Miami Beach: Grassfield Press, 1995.

Ingham, John M. *Mary, Michael and Lucifer: Folk Catholicism in Central Mexico*. Austin: University of Texas Press, 1986.

Madera, Lisa Maria. *The Virgin and the Volcano: Healing Alliances in the Ecuadorian Andes*. Dissertation. Emory University, 2002.

McCarthy Brown, Karen. *Mama Lola: A Vodou Priestess in Brooklyn*. Berkeley: University of California Press, 1991.

See also: Andean Traditions; Aztec Religion – Pre-Columbian; Cihuacoatl; Mesoamerican Deities; Serpents and Dragons; Virgin of Guadalupe; Volcanoes.

Masons, Fraternal Order of

The Fraternal Order of Masons is an international mutual-aid association of men dedicated to ethical refinement. Masons are organized locally as "lodges," into which prospective Masons are initiated. More commonly known as "Freemasonry," the order includes a wide number of organizations, some of whom have rival claims to the tradition. Freemasonry's likely origins are in the medieval guilds of builders and stoneworkers. Masonic lore also claims origin in the Knights Templar, a medieval military and religious order that was suppressed in the early fourteenth century by the Roman Church under charges of heresy, and a tradition going back to the original Temple of the Hebrew Scriptures. Scholars locate the genesis of the contemporary fraternal order with the founding of the London Grand Lodge in 1717. The London Grand Lodge bound together several other British lodges, and eventually became the defining body for orthodox Freemasonry around the world. Importantly, it presented to the world an association of gentlemen rather than a craft guild, and carried specific ethical and spiritual teachings, as well as the basic initiations that define most Masonry to date.

The historian Margaret Jacob argues strongly for the importance of Freemasonry in creating the culture of the eighteenth century. This is less because of membership in the Order by some Enlightenment philosophers as because Freemasonry helped foster a social milieu of popular adherence to that philosophical movement. With its mythology based around the building of the Temple of Solomon, it envisioned God as a grand architect who constructed the world as a monument to his glory. This coordinated well with the Newtonian mechanistic understanding of the world that had become popular within the Enlightenment and through the scientific revolution. Masons saw a spiritual order to nature that they felt should be the foundation for an ethical life of harmony and virtue. This was a spiritual life lived in the world, not apart from it. While the environmental results of this mechanistic worldview brought it into question by the late twentieth century, Newtonian science and the Enlightenment undeniably turned toward nature as inspiration for ethical behavior rather than as a source of sin. Freemasonry developed a body of lore, communicated in its rituals and lectures that carried these ideas to a wide population and ensured their persistence.

Freemasonry also aligned with the Enlightenment in its concept of universal human brotherhood and coordinate emphasis on religious tolerance. Although charity was initially directed toward other Masons, its focus quickly broadened to include non-Masons as well. At the same time, the notion of Masonic brotherhood as emblematic of a more universal brotherhood between humans grew in popularity. While Masonry carries religious and spiritual teachings, it maintains that Masons are free to participate in whatever religion they feel called to. Masons are discouraged from discussing their religious convictions within the Lodge to avoid internal division. Both of these attributes echo the Enlightenment universalism that created the context for ethics of global unity that remains with us in the twenty-first century. As with the spread of naturist ideas of order, Masonry helped propagate these Enlightenment ideals beyond a small cadre of intellectuals.

The esoteric aspects of Western spirituality were also transmitted through Freemasonry. While the London Grand Lodge held a Stoic, Newtonian understanding of the world, esoteric traditions like Rosicrucianism were incorporated in seventeenth-century Scottish Freemasonry, the "Ancient" wing of eighteenth-century British Freemasonry, and continental Freemasonry. These esoteric traditions of Freemasonry shared with the Newtonians an admiration of the harmony and order of nature, but they taught a more alchemical and vitalistic understanding of that order. With their roots in ancient cosmology and Neoplatonism, the esoteric traditions visualized the world as a living inspired organism rather than as a mechanical construction. During the eighteenth century, continental esoteric Masonry grew in two strains – one following a mythology of Templar origin and the other of Rosicrucian mysticism. Both sets of traditions developed by adding "upper" degrees of initiation over the three basic initiations of Masonry (commonly known as "Blue Lodge" degrees). The exemplar of the Templar rites was "Strict Observance" Masonry, which carried the romantic grandeur of medieval knighthood and mystical Christian symbolism. The leading Rosicrucian tradition, called the Order of the Golden and Rosy Cross, arose in the mid-eighteenth century in Germany. In contrast to Templar Masonry, it gravitated to a more alchemical and magical mysticism, and was stripped of chivalric mythology. While the order eventually died off, many of its teachings were subsumed into other initiatic societies (the Golden Dawn's heritage is in the Golden and Rosy Cross) which preserved the vitalistic traditions of Western science and magic by creating a social context for their study and pursuit apart from the increasingly popular mechanized cosmology of the scientific revolution. Esoteric freemasonry provided a key component to the occult revival of the twentieth century and its transmitting of a vitalistic cosmology to movements like contemporary Paganism and naturopathic medicine.

Although Masonry continues in the contemporary world, it serves primarily as a conservative social force. While its teachings of tolerance and harmony remain, the more radical aspects of its spirituality have been taken up by other popular and philosophical movements. Having suffered heavy persecution throughout its history for its supposed overinvolvement in politics, today Freemasonry primarily serves as a social fraternity emphasizing its core values of fraternity and ethical refinement among its members. By all accounts, the focus of Masonic ethics remains on charity and civic works. Despite the Masonic part in spreading the ideologies that would foster respect for nature in the West, Masons have yet to play a substantial role in the contemporary environmental movement.

Grant Potts

Further Reading

Faivre, Antoine. *Access to Western Esotericism*. Albany, NY: State University of New York Press, 1994.

Jacob, Margaret. *Living the Enlightenment: Freemasonry and Politics in Eighteenth-Century Europe*. New York: Oxford University Press, 1991.

McIntosh, Christopher. *The Rose Cross and the Age of Reason: 18th-century Rosicrucianism in Central Europe and Its Relationship to the Enlightenment*. Leiden, Netherlands: E.J. Brill, 1992.

Stevenson, David. *The Origins of Freemasonry: Scotland's Century 1590–1710*. Cambridge: Cambridge University Press, 1988.

See also: Deism; Golden Dawn; Paganism – Contemporary; Western Esotericism.

Masowe Wilderness Apostles

The *Masowe* Apostolic movement is made up of many religious communities that originated in colonial Southern Rhodesia during the 1930s and have become widely known in southern and central Africa. Distinguished by white robes and worshipping in open-air venues that they call *masowe*, meaning "wilderness," these African Apostles can be seen anywhere in fringe places by the roadside, behind factories, on the edge of fields, on hilltops, near lakes, on rock surfaces, in grasslands, underneath trees, etc. Buildings are avoided for ritual purposes because of the belief that the Holy Spirit comes through the wind and must blow freely through the atmosphere. Today, this form of vernacular Christianity has a membership of approximately five million people in southern and central Africa alone.

Through the symbolic act of going to pray out-of-doors, the Wilderness Apostles also see themselves as stepping outside *zvinhu zvechirungu*, meaning symbols of Western culture that they associate with human folly and immoral behavior. Although toilets and fences are becoming common features that gradually bring about a sense of the permanence of the sacred wilderness, the general pattern has been to declare the quest for freedom of the human spirit in sacred venues that contrast with the European missionary model of Church.

In addition to the tradition of spending long hours praying in the open air as a way of registering discontent with a modernity supported by missionary Christianity that believers are forced to grapple with in wider society, Wilderness Apostles are known for migrating from the country of their origins in Zimbabwe, to South Africa, Botswana, Zambia, Tanzania and Kenya. Werbner describes this trend in the African Apostles thought pattern as a way of using the biblical idea of "exile" to communicate a quest for liberation from an oppressive social order. He relates the experience of oppression to the quest for freedom and transcendence through an insistence on prayers held in fringe places bereft of any enclosure and lacking permanence.

Such is the social reality in Africa today, however, that it is imperative to see beyond the stories of African protest against colonialism and biblical imagery. Women and children are so visible in the sacred wilderness that it is important to articulate the nature of their oppression and their language of resistance in relation to the landscape. Jules-Rosette has drawn attention to ritual activities among the Maranke Apostles originating from the same setting, but with its own history. She observed as I have subsequently done among the Masowe Apostles that women are the ceremonial leaders because they exercise certain important mystical powers and spiritual gifts. This argument can be taken a stage further by relating the ceremonial function of women to their experiences and conceptual understanding of nature.

For a start, the open air is the most natural environment for women to pray and exercise mystical powers. Women spend many long hours each day working in the fields, fetching water and firewood, collecting fruit and vegetables and so on in the background culture. These chores explain not only the marginality of women through a relationship forged with nature, but also the existence of a female-oriented knowledge system whereby nature is held sacred as the Mother of all living creatures. The sacred wilderness thus takes on a special meaning for women who experience oppression by being subjugated as if they were a part of nature and are filled with a quest for transcendence based on an understanding of nature as sacred.

However, patriarchal attitudes are so pervasive in southern and central Africa that, even in this movement of liberation, men refuse to consider women for official leadership. At the same time, they respect their vital role as mediators of divine truths and executors at healing ceremonies. The male clientele of the Wilderness movement also join women in their special quest for emancipation from the male ancestors. For instance, all members of the sacred wilderness drop their lineage names and call each other by their first names only. This is to avoid invoking the ancestors and to allow for a greater sense of equality among believers in the agreement that the ancestors are ignorant of the ways of God and, as a result, are to be exorcised through prayer. The rejection of the ancestors, who are the pillar of the man-led traditional family, and the burden it puts on women in the background culture as crop-producers, child-bearers, and hunter-gatherers roaming the rivers and forests, prompted this new definition of the sacred wilderness as being in some profound sense associated with women despite the official leadership.

It is not surprising that women who have always worked closely with the elements of nature to please the patrilineal ancestors are attracted to a movement that dramatizes resistance to oppression and even rejects the ancestors to whom women are beholden subjects by having rituals in the open air. Daneel observed that in the Mwari (high god) religion among the Shona, Earth is not just a place for men to have dominion, but in creation mythology Earth is feminine and divine, with her creative power being that of generating and nurturing life through the rains which is equated with women giving birth to children. The soil, water and the wind and the woman's womb are key ideas used in creation myths to interpret the coming to being of living creatures in a world that begins with all living creatures coexisting harmoniously. Women are thus attracted to the Wilderness movement because their quest for transcendence takes them beyond the colonialists, missionaries, and the male ancestors to a spiritual freedom that respects the pre-Christian conceptualization of Earth as feminine in the Mwari religion.

Consequently, Masowe women in the sacred wilderness excel as healers (i.e., people filled with the spirit that restores life and causes barren women to give birth again while encouraging good morals and peaceful living). Furthermore, the use of earthenware bowls filled with water, stones, clay or leaves, milk and sometimes oil, is consistent with them as children made in the image of Mother Earth. These objects, held in association with the manifestation of the Holy Spirit during healing ceremonies and exorcisms of evil spirits among the Wilderness Apostles are direct reminders of Earth as Mother and lifegiver in Shona mythology.

Finally, the Apostles hold the Earth sacred and their venues of prayer are usually chosen because they are deemed uninhabited – open and not as yet spoiled by man. One of the reasons that the communities disappear from the landscape in a city such as Harare, and reappear elsewhere, is largely determined by the wish for prayer in environments where human beings have not destroyed trees and grasslands by putting up buildings. Although it is again becoming common to see toilets built for sanitation purposes, and pressure is being put on Apostles to build churches and thus to bureaucratize, the Apostles could teach us about preserving life on Earth. By using the landscape to construct a sacred wilderness in which one leaves the trees, grass and rivers flowing is a beautiful illustration of how human beings could rethink their relationship to nature as one of sharing, rather than manipulating and destroying. Occasionally, the Apostles have been known to destroy rock paintings when they have gone into the mountains to pray (Domboshava, Harare). This is because they see rock paintings as direct reminders of the ancestors whom they regard as evil, and are therefore at war with, in the sacred wilderness. Otherwise, the Wilderness movement is guardian to an ecotheology that has yet to be fully articulated.

In summary, somewhere in the background world of Masowe believers is a religious heritage whereby Earth is gendered, divine, and necessarily part of any discourse on religion and nature. In the vernacular Christianity represented by the Masowe Apostles the sacred wilderness is filled with large numbers of female adherents and fewer men, where lessons are taught about the uses of space by people who have always had an intimate relationship with nature and who have shown their discontent with colonialism and traditional African patriarchal culture, and who continue to wrestle with the effects of both in today's world.

Isabel Mukonyora

Further Reading

Aschwanden, Hebert. *Karanga Mythology: An Analysis of the Consciousness of the Karanga in Zimbabwe.* Gweru: Mambo Press, 1989.

Daneel, Martinus. *God of the Matopo Hills: An Essay on Mwari.* The Hague: Mouton Press, 1970.

Dillon-Malone, Clive. *The Korsten Basketmakers: A Study of the Masowe Apostles, An Indigenous African Religious Movement.* Manchester, England: University of Manchester Press, 1978.

Jules-Rosette, Benadette. *African Apostles: Ritual and Conversion in the Church of John Maranke.* Ithaca, NJ: Cornell University, 1975.

Mukonyora, Isabel. "Marginality and Protest: A Study of the Role of Women in Shaping the *Masowe* Thought Pattern." Harare: *Southern African Political and Economics Journal (SAPEM)*, 2004.

Mukonyora, Isabel. "Women and Ecology in Shona Religion." *Word & World, Luther Seminary Journal* (Summer 1999), 276–84.

Werbner, Richard. "The Argument of Images: From Zion to the Wilderness in African Churches." In Wim van Binsbergen and Matthew Schoffeleers, eds. *Theoretical Exploration of African Religion.* London: Routledge & Keegan Paul, 1985, 253–86.

See also: African Independent Churches (South Africa); Zimbabwe Spirit Mediums; Zimbabwe's Matopos Hills.

Matsuo Bashō (1644–1694)

Matsuo Bashō, a Japanese writer, is generally considered to be the greatest haiku poet. He was also a significant writer of literary travel journals and poetic prose (*haibun*), and his poetics continue to be central to Japanese aesthetic theory. In the West, he is probably the most famous and influential literary figure from pre-modern Asia. He spent much of the last ten years of his life traveling through Japan, and his writings and poetics are filled with references to the natural world. Part of the richness of his view of nature comes from the multiplicity of traditions he drew from: Buddhism (both elite and popular), Daoism, Neo-Confucianism, Shinto, the Chinese literary tradition, and Japanese literature and art. As a result, his writings manifest a complex view of nature that differs from those found in the West.

Bashō's view of nature was dominated by the notion of change. One type of change is found in the "Creative" (Japanese: *zōka*; Chinese: *zaohua*), an idea he adopted from the Chinese. *Zōka* is sometimes translated as "nature," but it refers not to nature as scenery or as individual beings but rather the creativity that brings them forth and leads them through ongoing transformations. It is also sometimes translated as the "Creator," but *zōka* is not a being separate from nature. Rather it is nature's own spontaneous and wondrous skill at creating and reshaping beauty. We can translate *zōka* as "the Creative," which makes what we call nature a continuously renewing work of art within which we live.

Another form of change is the turning of the seasons. Japanese literature, especially haiku, involves sensitive attunement to the particular season and to the process of seasonal change. We never experience "nature," but always nature in and of a particular season. Thus all haiku poems are supposed to have a "season word" that indicates the time of year. While *zōka* involves creative and unpredictable change, this seasonal change is an ordered pattern, a yearly recurrence that can be anticipated and even conventionalized in "season words," poetic words that indicate the season of the poem.

A third type of change found in Bashō's writings was heavily influenced by Buddhism. *Mujō*, "impermanence," suggests the inevitable passing away of things. *Mujō–kan*, the "feeling of impermanence," was sorrowful but at the same time tranquil, because it resulted from a realization and acceptance of the nature of the universe. It is a condition all things share and so we all are wayfarers through life. His great travel journal, *The Narrow Road to the Deep North*, begins,

> Months and days are wayfarers of a hundred generations, the years too, going and coming, are wanderers. For those who drift life away on a boat, for those who meet age leading a horse by the mouth, each day is a journey, the journey itself home (Imoto, et al. 1972: 341).

For Bashō, nature is vitalistic. Just as the natural world as a whole is characterized by change, individual things are alive with *qi* (the Chinese notion of the vitality of things) and have "feelings." We too have *qi* and feelings, and this enables us to experience a union with the natural world. Part of the poet's task is to lose the sense of a separate self and become intimate with the object to be written about. In *The Red Booklet*, written by his disciple Tohō (1657–1730), Bashō is quoted as saying, "the mind's movements merge with the object . . . [which] is taken in its nature, without obstruction . . . Learn of the pine from the pine, learn of the bamboo from the bamboo." Tohō explained this notion of "learning" as follows: "In other words, one must become detached from the self . . . To learn means to enter into the object and feel the subtlety that is revealed there." As a result, "the color of the mind becomes the object" and one "can identify with the feelings of the things in nature . . ." (Ijichi, et al. 1973: 547–8).

While individual things have their own subtle feelings, the universe as a whole is characterized by an essential quality, *sabi* ("loneliness") that a true poet is able to experience. The universe is immense in both space and time, and *sabi* refers to a feeling of being small and fleeting within a vast cosmos. Like *mujō-kan*, this feeling is characterized by inner tranquility, for it grounds us in the fundamental condition of reality shared by all.

Bashō's notion of nature also differs from ours because of its conventional nature. Like any other poet in Japan, he saw the natural world through the eyes of culture. Particularly important are what we might call "imbedded associations." A bush warbler, for instance, is considered a bird of early spring because it is one of the first birds to sing in the new year (i.e., the lunar year, which normally began around early February). As such it is also associated with another image of early spring, plum blossoms. In addition its song is not only considered beautiful but is said to sound like the title of the Lotus Sutra (*Hokke-kyō*). All of these meanings are embedded in the one word, *uguisu*. However, the bush warbler is actually a common year-round resident throughout Japan, and it sings in other seasons beside early spring.

Such a conventionalized view has led to the conclusion that Bashō and other Japanese poets did not write of "real" nature but only an artificial, culturalized version of nature. However, we need to realize that different assumptions about nature are at work in Bashō's writings. One is that plants, animals, and even natural scenes have a "true nature," just as humans do. A bush warbler, a pine, a moment of late-autumn dusk when the light fades behind silhouetted trees: they are not mere objects but are characterized by certain qualities that make them distinctive. One can appreciate the true nature of a bush warbler most fully as it sings in early spring with the plum blossoms in bloom; if we want to see the true nature of a pine we should look to an aged pine on a cliff-edge; and a scene of late dusk in autumn (*aki no kure*) is by its nature lonely.

The Japanese held to an idea of "poetic essences" (*hon'i*) that captured the true nature of a thing and could be handed down in the literary tradition. Similarly there were *utamakura*, famous places that were characterized by certain qualities and even a particular season, and references to those places were expected to refer to those accepted associations.

A second assumption is that the natural world and the experience of nature are not wholly distinct: our objective–subjective distinction does not hold. A true poet is one who has cultivated his sensibility to the point that his "subjective" feelings match the "objective" feelings in the scene being experienced. *Sabi*, for instance, is a quality inherent in a scene as well as a feeling experienced by the refined poet.

A third assumption is that there are authoritative experiences of nature. Some experiences of nature are "truer" – more deeply insightful of the essential nature of things – than others. We can look to the experiences of great poets of the past and to literary conventions derived from them as guides for what can and should be experienced when we see a bird, tree, or scene.

A fourth assumption is that nature and culture are deeply interrelated. Bashō's sense of this interrelationship can be seen in the famous passage in which he says that:

> One thread runs through all the artistic Ways. And this aesthetic spirit is to follow the Creative (*zōka*), to be a companion to the turning of the four seasons. Nothing one sees is not a flower, nothing one imagines is not the moon. If what is seen is not a flower, one is like a barbarian; if what is imagined is not a flower, one is like a beast. Depart from the barbarian, break away from the beast, follow the Creative, return to the Creative (Imoto, et al. 1972: 311–12).

The barbarian and beast are those without culture. They are also those who have lost contact with nature's creativity. Highly refined culture such as poetry is at root a natural expression of human feelings. Poetry is not essentially different from birdsong and is, in fact, our own form of *zōka*. This will happen only, however, if artists create out of their deepest nature, in concert with the creativity of nature itself. So poetry must arise spontaneously out of authentic feelings and our true nature. It is culture that allows this to take place. The greatest poet, then, is not only the most cultured but also the most natural, because to be fully cultured is to follow the processes of nature. It is "barbarians and beasts" – those devoid of culture – that are far from nature. "Culturized nature," perceived with deep cultural insight into nature, is "true nature."

David Landis Barnhill

Further Reading

Barnhill, David. "Of Bashōs and Buddhisms." *Eastern Buddhist* 32:2 (Fall 2000), 170–201.

Barnhill, David. "Impermanence, Fate, and the Journey: Bashō and the Problem of Meaning." *Religion* 16 (1986), 323–41.

Hamill, Sam, tr. *The Essential Bashō*. Boston: Shambhala, 1999.

Ijichi Tetsuo, Omote Akira and Kuriyama Riichi, eds. *Rengaron shū, Nōgakuron shū, Hairon shū. Nihon koten bungaku zenshū*, vol. 51. Tokyo: Shogakkan, 1973.

Imoto Nōichi, Hori Nobuo and Muramatsu Tomotsugu, eds. *Matsuo Bashō shū. Nihon koten bungaku zenshū*, vol. 41. Tokyo: Shogakkan, 1972.

Shirane, Haruo. *Traces of Dreams: Landscape, Cultural Memory, and the Poetry of Bashō*. Stanford, CA: Stanford University Press, 1998.

Ueda, Makoto, tr. *Bashō and His Interpreters: Selected Hokku with Commentary*. Stanford, CA: Stanford University Press, 1991.

Ueda, Makoto. *Matsuo Bashō*. Tokyo: Kodansha, 1982 (New York: Twayne, 1970).

See also: Aesthetics and Nature in China and Japan; Buddhism – East Asian; Chinese Traditional Concepts of Nature; Daoism; Japanese Gardens; Japanese Love of Nature; Japanese Religions; Zen Buddhism.

Matthiessen, Peter (1927–)

Peter Matthiessen is a novelist and essayist born and raised in New York City in an affluent family. After graduating from Yale in 1950, he moved to Paris, where he co-founded the *Paris Review*. In 1953 he returned to the U.S. and became a commercial fisherman for several years before becoming a full-time writer. He has traveled extensively on nature expeditions while making his home in Long Island, New York.

Matthiessen's writings evidence four major concerns: wild nature, particularly threatened species and ecosystems; cultures rooted in nature but marginalized by encroaching civilization; contemporary issues of social justice, particularly with regard to Native Americans; and Zen Buddhist spirituality. While the majority of his works are non-fiction, he also has published eight novels, his preferred genre. His combination of nature writing, anthropological inquiry, social critique, and spirituality is reminiscent of Gary Snyder's works, although social criticism rarely enters into his nature writing. Matthiessen's writings project a deep sense of the value of biological and cultural diversity and an underlying tone of melancholy concerning the devastation brought by encroaching civilization. He also avoids a romantic view. Traditional peoples of various cultures exhibit widely different characters, some of which are far from anyone's ideal. And nature can be dreary, difficult, and dangerous.

Matthiessen's range of interests leads to various types of writing. Some works are clearly natural history (e.g., *Wildlife in America* and *The Shorebirds of North America*), which may either be a narrative of personal experience of nature or a more objective account. Many of his works are in the tradition of travel literature (e.g., *Cloud Forest* and *The Tree Where Man Was Born*), which often include a sense of adventure as he learns about nature and cultures in foreign lands. Still other works (e.g., *Sal Si Puedes* and *In the Spirit of Crazy Horse*) are social criticism. Spiritual autobiography is found in *The Snow Leopard* and *Nine-headed Dragon River*.

Matthiessen is also an accomplished novelist. His early fiction (*1954–61: Race Rock, Partisans, and Raditzer*) were *bildungsroman* about coming of age. From the 1960s to the 1980s he published primarily in non-fiction, but in that period he produced arguably his finest, and most ecological, novels: *At Play in the Fields of the Lord* (1965) and *Far Tortuga* (1975). *At Play* takes place in South America (and was informed by the same trip that lead to *Cloud Forest*). In the novel, Protestant missionaries battle the Catholics, the jungle, and the natives in their disastrous attempt to convert local Indians. The rainforest functions as a major actor in the narrative as well as an abiding presence that dwarfs the tragicomic human play. *Far Tortuga* explores the lives of a disappearing breed of turtle fishermen in the Caribbean who try to extract an old-style living in the face of modernization. *Far Tortuga* is an experimental novel influenced by Zen and haiku poetics in the extreme spareness of presentation and the use of empty spaces in the text. In the 1990s Matthiessen has again focused on fiction with a trilogy set primarily in the Everglades: *Killing Mr. Watson, Lost Man's River*, and *Bone by Bone*.

The Snow Leopard (1978), which won the National Book Award, is generally considered his most significant work. In 1973 Matthiessen journeyed to Nepal with the zoologist George Schaller, not long after his wife and fellow Zen Buddhist had died. Schaller's research centered on the Himalayan blue sheep, but both Schaller and Matthiessen were fascinated by the elusive Snow Leopard. Matthiessen's book chronicles the extremely challenging expedition in which the presence of the great cat was felt but never directly encountered, like Buddhist enlightenment itself. He combined natural history and cultural observations, exquisite descriptions of austere beauty (often using haiku-like techniques in his prose), and reflections on his spiritual pilgrimage. At times Matthiessen achieves a state of "transparency," in which the self and the world are no longer separate and the true meaning of mountains and rivers is revealed as their simple but absolute presence within the moment. What is required – and so difficult – is to lose desires, fears, and expectations and to let go of clinging, including attachment to spiritual achievement. In moments of open stillness, the "ringing silence" that permeates the natural world can be experienced. After finishing this book, Matthiessen continued his Zen practice and received official recognition as an enlightened master.

David Landis Barnhill

Further Reading

Matthiessen, Peter. *Birds of Heaven: Travels with Cranes.* New York: North Point Press, 2001.

Matthiessen, Peter. *Sal Si Puedes (Escape If You Can): Cesar Chavez and the New American Revolution.* Berkeley: University of California, 2000 (New York: Random House, 1971).

Matthiessen, Peter. *The Snow Leopard.* New York: Viking, 1978.

Matthiessen, Peter. *The Tree Where Man Was Born.* New York: Dutton, 1972.

Matthiessen, Peter. *At Play in the Fields of the Lord.* New York: Random House, 1965.

See also: Autobiography; Memoir and Nature Writing; Zen Buddhism.

Maya Religion (Central America)

The culture that we now call Maya still occupies the southern states of Mexico (Chiapas, Campeche, Yucatan and Quintana Roo), and the territories of Belize, Guatemala and Honduras. The Mayans are well known to the world because of their cultural, religious and scientific achievements in ancient times. The best-known period is the Classic Maya, which comprises various centuries of history (250–900). It is from the Classic Maya that we have received most of the information about ancient religion and spirituality in the Mesoamerican region. No doubt, much of this religious belief system was destroyed during the Spanish conquest and subsequent colonization of the Mayas. Fortunately, not everything was lost, since Maya leaders maintained their spirituality passing on their religious beliefs to new generations through the oral tradition. This is how the *Popol Vuh*, the most important and sacred book of the Mayas, was written immediately after the conquest.

The Classic Maya have been studied extensively and from these anthropological and religious studies we have a better understanding of this great civilization. Unfortunately, the Mayas lost their written tradition when the last ones who knew how to read and write hieroglyphic texts were punished by Spanish missionaries during the early sixteenth century. Fortunately, some of the sacred texts were memorized by the spiritual leaders and this is how the Maya ceremonies and prayers have continued until now. For example, among the Tzotzil Maya, the recitation of sacred texts during their religious ceremonies and festivals is still common today, while there is resistance by those converted to Protestantism.

We can argue that the Mayas may have had a state religion during the Classic Maya period because of the abundance of sacred sites in the Maya region. Also, there is an abundance of written religious texts such as the works of the *Chilam Balam* or Jaguar Priest in Yucatan. Most of the iconography at the sacred Maya sites show the connection of rulers with mythical ancestors and the supernatural world. Referring to these sacred sites, the Temple of the Cross in Palenque is a major shrine which is considered the center of the world and where the Lacandon Maya have continued to perform sacred ceremonies in modern times (Perera 1982).

Despite the existence of many hieroglyphic texts explaining these events, we cannot fully interpret these messages. Thus, from the writing of early missionaries we learned that Maya spirituality was condemned as witchcraft or the teaching of the devil, so it had to be eradicated. Even in modern times, epigraphers have misinterpreted and confused Maya spirituality with animism. Thus the worldview of indigenous people in which they see Earth as a living entity and plants and animals as having the spirit of creation is seen as evidence of a lack of rationality among the Indians.

On the other hand, the bishop of Yucatan Diego de Landa (1566) also mentioned the Maya sciences and the religious training of spiritual leaders before the conquest. According to Landa, the Maya priests or *Ah-q'inh* were in charge of teaching and guiding the people in their sciences, writing, divination and the interpretation of signs from the sky and the natural world for their prophecies.

Also, the Maya priests were experts in the Maya calendar and the counting of the days, months and the years. They played the role of scholars, teachers and spiritual leaders who promoted Maya knowledge and the appropriate ways of acting and dealing with the supernatural and the natural world. The celebration of a series of festivities in accordance with the Maya calendar has continued until now, sometimes as a syncretic religious practice. For example, the present cult of the patron saints in Maya towns and villages is central to Maya religion today. The persistence of religious beliefs among contemporary Mayas shows us the deep spirituality that they have inherited from their ancestors.

In terms of the relationship between humans and their natural environment, the Maya creation myths in the *Popol Vuh* provide us with complex religious and philosophical ideas. According to the Mayas, the Earth and heaven were connected and the divinity, too, was not separated from humans and the environment. Thus, for the present Mayas, there are sacred places, such as mountains, lakes, caves and rivers where humans can pray for their ancestors and be connected with the supernatural world. In other words, Maya cosmology does not separate religion from agriculture, education, mathematics or other forms of knowledge, since everything is interrelated. Thus, each part of creation, plants, animals and humans enjoy the spirit of creation, and humans must respect and not abuse plants and animals with whom they coexist.

Similarly, the account in the *Popol Vuh* referring to the creation of the sky and the Earth is very important in understanding the nature of the Creator or God who is a totality, male and female. This Creator is,

> He who gives breath and thought, she who gives birth to the children, he who watches over the happiness of the people, he who meditates on the goodness of all that exists in the sky, on the Earth, in the lakes and in the sea (Goetz and Morley 1983: 80).

Maya creation myths explain the integration or interrelationship that must exist between humans, plants and animals for their collective survival. For this reason, most indigenous scholars make a distinction between religion and spirituality. What we know today is that the natural world has been the focal point of Mayan spirituality. Mayas; as with other indigenous people of the continent, have developed sacred ceremonies for an appropriate relationship with Earth and the supernatural world.

One of the major continuities in Maya religion or spirituality is the use of the sacred Maya calendar. The calendar was used extensively during the Classic Maya period as it is exemplified in the codices and other hieroglyphic written materials of the Mayas. The practice did not disappear, but was continued; sometimes secretly because of the persecution of the religious Maya leaders by Church authorities in the past. The uses of the Maya calendar were related to the omens and prophecies of the day and the different time cycles such as the *tun* (year) and the *k'altun*, or prophetic cycle of twenty years. The calendar was also related to agriculture, as the Mayas were very respectful of the natural world and needed to perform ceremonies before cutting the trees and preparing the land for planting.

In modern Maya communities there are experts in divination and in the uses of the calendar. These experts or spiritual leaders are called *ajq'ij*, currently known as Maya priests. Their role in modern Maya culture is to maintain the sacred tradition of counting the days, divining the best time to perform rituals and for the giving of names to new-born children. The *ajq'ij* have been persecuted in recent times as they are still carrying the sacred knowledge of the past. During the past decade (1990s), the *ajq'ij* organized themselves openly in a National Association of Maya Priests or *ajq'ijab*. After remaining secluded and performing their rituals almost secretly, they have decided to bring to light their knowledge and religious practices. They needed to continue their sacred mission, despite the criticism by Catholic and Protestant missionaries who accuse them of continuing paganism and idolatry. Truly, the sacred tradition of the Mayas and the role of the *ajq'ij* have not been understood properly until now.

In this religious practice that includes the natural world we can mention the Mayas' concern for corn. Corn was perhaps the most important product of the Mayas; peasants still believe that corn has a spirit and it has to be treated with respect as a gift from the ancestors. Among the Jakaltek Maya, corn is called "*komi' ixim*," (mother corn) since it gives life and nourishment to humanity. Many people wrongly suppose that the Maya have multiple gods and that corn is also a god. But for the Mayans, each part of creation such as plants and animals have their own spirit and they contribute to the existence of the whole. In this way, the corn plant provides nourishment to humans and it has been the source of their strength and life. According to the *Popol Vuh*, the first four fathers created were made of white and yellow corn. "The corn used to create the first men was found in the place called Paxil and K'ayala'. *Yak* the wildcat, *Utiu* the coyote, *K'el* the parrot and *Joj* the crow, were the creatures who discovered this food" (*Popol Vuh*, Montejo 2000).

It is appropriate to mention that in most Mayan linguistic communities, there are still traditionalists who continue to practice their ceremonies following the counting of the days from the Maya calendar There are good and bad omen days, as well as days that are appropriate to pray for human health, for nature and animals, as well as for giving thanks to the Creator for the gift of life and the beauty of Earth that we humans enjoy and must protect.

The calendar was also used to commemorate the ancestors in each Maya community, so among the Jakaltek maya, Imox and Q'ana' are two day names, but they are also the names of the ancestors, or first Mother and Father, of the Jakaltek Maya. In ancient Maya religion, the pilgrimages to the shrine of the ancestors have been practiced by the tribes according to the *Popol Vuh*. Similarly, among the Jakaltek Maya of highland Guatemala there has been a continuous pilgrimage to the sanctuary of B'alunh Q'ana and Imox. In most recent times, this has become a symbolic practice during the Maya New Year, during which the spirits of the children and the adults are thought to go to salute the ancestors in their shrine, located at the edge of the Blue River in the Cuchumatan Mountains.

The continuity of Maya religion is then evident in the religious practice called Waxajib Batz or Maya New Year among the Mayas of highland Guatemala, particularly the Kaqchikel and K'iche. This is the sacred time of renewal when the new fire is lighted, recharging life on Earth and the universe. The Waxajib Batz has become one of the most important ceremonies of the modern Mayas, reaffirming their continuous presence and practice of their ancient sacred heritage.

During the colonial time, the Mayans were persecuted because of this religious practice. Some *ajq'ij* were jailed and persecuted by religious and civilian authorities. Just as Diego de Landa burned the books of the Mayas in Yucatan and punished the practitioners of the ancient Maya religion, the religious leaders of the Mayan communities were also persecuted and punished up until the first half of the twentieth century. In most places the eradication of the Maya ceremonies was successful as Maya spiritual leaders were jailed and fiercely persecuted by the Catholic Church and Protestant missionaries.

Most of Maya religion and spirituality practiced today is a syncretic expression or mixture of Maya beliefs and Christian religion. Most of these Christian elements were integrated into Maya beliefs and ceremonies because they were similar to those that Mayas were already practicing. For example the cult for the saints brought to Mayan communities by Catholic missionaries was similar to that of the owners or guardians of the hills. The Mayans considered that the hills and the mountains had spiritual owners who were the guardians of animals and plants inhabiting the mountains. The cult to these spirit guardians was strong, so when the Spanish priests brought the saints to the Mayan communities as patron saints, they were easily accommodated within the Maya worldview and religious beliefs.

Perhaps the relationship between religion and the natural world is the most important attribute of Maya religion. In the case of the cross, before cutting a big tree for the purposes of making a cross, the tree is interviewed or consulted by the *ahb'eh* or diviner. The tree will respond if he or she is ready or not to fulfill a mission to protect a whole community. The cross, then, talks and acts as a "person," according to Maya beliefs. This is quite different from the concept or meaning of the cross as a sacred symbol in Catholic religion.

Similarly, before cutting the trees for cultivating corn, the farmer will burn candles and ask permission to the owner or spirit of the hill for his forgiveness. According to Maya religious beliefs, *Witz*, the owner of the hills, is placed there by God to protect and be the guardian of plants and animals. Thus, humans do not have the supremacy or total freedom to do whatever they want against nature. The rivers too are considered roads to heaven and humans must not pollute them. Anyone who does so pays the penalty of not being accepted into heaven when they die. The spirit will be sent back to Earth to search for the dirt that the person has thrown into the river thus polluting it or the ocean. These are ecological myths that reinforce human behaviour and respect for nature as a sacred part of creation.

These ecological knowledge and practices still exist among the Mayans in modern times. Some of this traditional knowledge is being sought by ecologists or members of the environmental movement. While the researchers look for the sacred knowledge of the Mayas for ecological purposes, they certainly do not understand the deep spiritual belief of the indigenous people who have been living in close contact with and respectfully toward their environment.

Currently, the traditional religious leaders are worried that some foreigners who appropriate Maya knowledge of the sacred, such as the Maya calendar, are becoming shamans themselves. These are members of the New Age movement and are currently called by some indigenous people "white-shamans" or "plastic medicine men and women." In this case, instead of destroying Maya spirituality, as early foreign missionaries did, these New Age people appropriate it for the purpose of making a profit, as they claim to be experts of Maya religion.

In the current revitalization of Maya culture, the role of religion and Maya spirituality has been very significant. Mayan priests *or ajq'ij* are showing the world that their beliefs are still alive and that they are not ashamed to practice their spirituality. Despite being persecuted for centuries, and criticized or condemned as devil-worshippers and promoters of idolatry, the Maya priests are now performing their ceremonies in public places. They are reclaiming their rights to practice their religion at the sacred sites, such as Tikal, Copán, Palenque, etc., as they revitalize Maya religion and spirituality.

Lately, some Protestant groups have entered into Mayan communities and condemned the practices of Maya religion. During the armed conflict in Guatemala in the early 1980s, some fundamentalist religious believers came to Maya communities arguing that the Mayans would be safer if they abandoned Catholicism and were "born again." This was the religion of the Chief of State at that time, General Efrain Ríos Montt, who stands accused of allowing massacres of entire communities in 1982. While the army persecuted the Catholic priests and catechists, the guerrilla movement too contributed to the destruction of Maya religion and spirituality. The religious roles of the elders or *Principales* were changed as they were seen as traditionalists and an obstacle to expansion of the guerrilla movement. Also, Catholic Action, which had a very revolutionary agenda, got rid of the traditional authorities and imposed a new form of liberation theology preached by the Church through Catholic Action.

Now, the Maya religious and spiritual leaders are revising their role as guides and leaders of the communities and are refining their role as Maya priests. Most importantly, with the signing of the peace accords on 26 December 1996, which promised freedom to practice Maya spirituality and access to sacred sites, the revitalization of Maya religion and spirituality has been strengthened.

Currently, Mayan priests are working on the standardization of their religious canons and the uses of religious symbols and paraphernalia. Not all of them are in agreement, since some are more inclined to the practice of Maya traditional religion as attached to Catholicism. In other words, the Maya priests are also Catholics and they practice both traditions equally since they believe that Maya religion complements Catholicism. Maya religion or spirituality is not something separated from Mayas' daily life, but it pervades all Maya activities. The cyclical religious festivals and ceremonies organized by the *Cofradías*, or religious brotherhoods, are very good examples of the syncretic continuities of Maya religion and spirituality.

Maya religion is now going through a process of reconstruction and there are Mayans who call themselves Catholics and reject Maya *costumbres* or traditional religious practices, while there are also Mayas who are recognizing the need to go back to the roots of their spirituality, which though not in opposition to Christian beliefs is different because of its holistic connection to the natural and supernatural world.

Maya religion is now viewed by the government and some other religious traditions, such as Catholicism, as a shamanistic reminiscence of an ancient past. Others, mainly fundamentalist Protestants, argue it represents the continuation of paganism and idolatry, which must be eradicated to save the soul of these poor Indians. But for Mayan religious leaders, the practice of Maya ceremonies and rituals is the appropriate way of giving thanks for the life that we enjoy on this Earth. It is the continuation of the first acts of creation and responsibilities of human beings continuously to give thanks for the gift of life given to them by the Creator, according to the *Popol Vuh*.

This is why the attitude of indigenous people toward the environment is religious or *quasi*-religious, and this is what non-indigenous people must learn from indigenous people: to be more compassionate toward the creatures with whom we share our world, thinking of ourselves and the future of our generations. This is the main message of the Maya priests to their followers, and this practice will continue as part of the revitalization of Maya religion and spirituality in the Maya region, particularly Guatemala.

Victor Montejo

Further Reading

Carlsen, Robert S. *The War for the Heart & Soul of a Highland Maya Town*. Austin: University of Texas Press, 1997.

Cook, Garrett W. *Renewing the Maya World: Expressive Culture in a Highland Town*. Austin: University of Texas Press, 2000.

Gates, William. *Yucatan Before and After the Conquest*. New York: Dover Publications Inc., 1978.

Goetz, Delia and Sylvanus Morley. *Popol Vuh: The Sacred Book of the Ancient Quiche Maya*. Norman: University of Oklahoma Press, 1983.

Gossen, Gary H. *Telling Maya Tales: Tzotzil Identities in Modern Mexico*. New York: Routledge, 1999.

La Farge, Oliver and Douglas Byers. *The Year Bearer's People*. Middle American Research Series, Publication No. 2. New Orleans: Tulane University, 1931.

Montejo, Víctor D. *Popol Vuh: A Sacred Book of the Mayas*. Toronto: Groundwood Books, 2000.

Montejo, Víctor D. "The Road to Heaven: Jakaltek Maya Belief, Religion, and the Ecology." In John Grim, ed. *Indigenous Traditions and the Ecology*. Cambridge, MA: Harvard University Press, 2001.

Perera, Victor and Robert D. Bruce. *The Last Lords of Palenque: The Lacandon Mayas of the Lacandon Forest*. Boston: Little Brown and Company, 1982.

Stoll David. *Is Latin America Turning Protestant? The Politics of Evangelical Growth*. Berkeley: University of California Press, 1990.

Tedlock, Dennis. *Popol Vuh: The Definitive Edition of the Maya Book of the Dawn of Life and the Glories of Gods and Kings*. New York: Touchstone Books, 1996.

Warren, Kay B. *The Symbolism of Subordination: Indian Identity in a Guatemalan Town*. Austin: University of Texas Press, 1978.

Wilson, Richard. *Maya Resurgence in Guatemala: Q'eqchi' Experiences*. Norman: University of Oklahoma Press, 1995.

See also: Harmonic Convergence. Maya Spirituality (Guatemala Highlands); Mesoamerican Deities.

Maya Spirituality (Guatemala Highlands)

The Guatemala highlands, ribbed with volcanic-formed mountain ridges, fertile plains and canyons, are carved by multiple rivers in the west and deposits of limestone terrain built up in the east. This backbone of mountain ridges varying from 4000 to over 14,000 feet in elevation, framed on both sides by a piedmont, extends from Guatemala City north and west to the Mexican border. These physically and ecologically diverse high plateaus of the western highlands, isolated valleys, and pockets of the piedmont are the geography in which the earliest entry occurred, perhaps as early as 15,000 B.C.E.; about 1500 B.C.E., sedentary village life was a cultural reality. From steep, rocky mountains to the depths of the gorges where freshwater springs tumble down, pine forests rise to meet the sky. Mists envelop mountains, enshrouding volcanic peaks. Sulfur springs steam along riverbanks; winds high in the altiplano swing through forests, knocking against the rocks. Cultivated mountainsides appear as a patchwork of green and brown striped squares, the deeply furrowed brown Earth giving birth to verdant cornfields, the long leaves and tassels tossing in the wind. Within these natural environments, inhabitants, interacting with the celestial cycles and with the land, configured the sky and the Earth not only as a spatial territory or cultural landscape, but also as sacred and living. In this natural environment, humans have shaped consciousness, behaviors and religious systems.

Archeological sites, hieroglyphic texts, creation accounts recorded in *Popol Vuh*, the Ki'che' Maya lineage and creation account, and in *Chilam Balaam*, the lowland Maya account, in living stories and traditions, all reveal that humans living in this region have perceived that Earth and heaven are connected, and that a dynamic, animated reciprocal interaction occurs between the two. As narrated in *Popul Vuh*, the nature of the Creator is an enlightened being, a totality in duality, with multiple manifestations: great knowers and great thinkers in their being; Mother and Father; *Alom k'ajolom*, the Bearer and the Begetter; *B'itol Tz'akol*, the Maker, the Modeler, who amass and give form to the materials that make up the Earth, plants, animals and humans. In the account in the *Popol Vuh* referring to the creation of the sky and of the Earth, as genius Heart of Sky and Sovereign Plumed Serpent, who work by means of words, genius and sacrifice, think, converse, worry, and agree, they establish a rhythm of gestation deep in time, setting off the formation of the Earth, of all creation, toward their goal – the completion of their work in the human design. The work of humans is to speak, name and pray to the Heart of Sky and Sovereign Plumed Serpent, and keep the days so the Maker and Modeler will be invoked and remembered on the face of the Earth. The alive, natural world is the source, fulcrum and channel of this human work, this work of Maya spirituality. In the natural environment there is an understood interrelationship and harmony of humans, animals, and plants. Universal laws rule each living being; each creature is temporal and its period of life varies depending upon the mission that has been commissioned within the cosmos. Each being fulfills a cycle of life, to come and go, to be born and to die. While humans share the same category of creature, they have a superior being, and thus take on the responsibility to look after all, as a guardian, as an older brother or sister. The genealogy of their spirituality establishes a human position of reciprocity, gratitude and responsibility, based on observations of celestial and Earth cycles and of interrelationships in nature, ordered in rounds of time.

In trading and migrating, settling and working the land to cultivate corn, beans, and squash, inhabitants developed a relationship with their environment. Predecessors configured terrestrial landscapes, spatial cartography, and mythic narratives to mirror the celestial events of the night sky. From 250–850, architects mapped astronomical space and laid over it geography, aligning architecture, settlement patterns and ritual practice with solar, planetary and lunar events. As in other areas of Mesoamerica, the construction and layout of temple-mountains in the highlands (Abaj Takalik, Utatlán, Uaxactún, and Zaculeu) and other cities present strikingly literal maps of the sky on dates associated with the Maya creation or with important events in each polity's history. Time, observed, recorded on agricultural and sacred calendars, and remembered in ritual practice, was given primordial importance so that it organized social, agricultural, and religious life. Dawn, dusk, the equinoxes and the solstices at specific geographical locations were viewed as sacred; these time/spaces provided entrance to the sacred. At these sites, at designated times, people performed rituals interlocking themselves with cosmic cycles.

Human response in this lush, ecologically diverse natural environment was one of reciprocity. Material legacy, in architecture, settlement patterns, agricultural ways and ritual practice, bears witness "to repeated or recrafted strategies for acknowledging the Earth, for honoring and working with its vital forces" (Brady and Ashmore 2000: 126). Large quantities of incense burners found in caves indicate that the elite and peasants made pilgrimages to caves, considered portals to the underworld, to make offerings for rain and the fertility of the Earth. Religious practitioners smeared the blood of the victims on the face of the (stone) idols with the idea that the deities needed to be strengthened. There has been an assumed connection between bodily sacrifice – bloodletting and human sacrifice rituals – and the continuation of life processes on Earth. Precious substances such as copal incense, maize dough, rubber and jade contained soul and were burned in huge braziers where they converted to smoke, the form of sustenance the deity could understand (Freidel, Schele and Parker 1993: 204). In the K'iche' creation account, *Popol Vuj*, ancestors offered blends of copal honoring the first dawn.

Many of the Ki'che', Kaqchikel, Tz'utujtil, Jakaltek and Mam Maya communities residing in the highlands have maintained continuities of ancestral systems of belief and spiritual practices, distinct in each village, but in broad terms quite uniform. Beliefs and rituals of reciprocity framed within a sacred calendar system of 260 days survived the Catholic colonial period and subsequent centuries of persecution and repression in the Guatemalan highlands through strategic appropriations of Catholic practices, through clandestinely maintained rituals, but in most cases transformed through syncretism; continuities survived, in great part, because of geographical inaccessibility. Since the mid-1980s, transformed continuities of these spiritual practices have emerged publicly and have been reclaimed and revitalized.

Foundational to understanding reciprocity with the natural environment is translation of the concept "nature." In Ki'che', the indigenous language spoken by over one million highland inhabitants, the word *chomb'al juyub' tay'j*, (*chomb'al* = it's alive; *juyub'* = mountain; *tay'aj* = lowland), or "nature" in English, is interpreted as "a place of much happiness and energy" or "the happy house where I live" or "the green of the earth." These renderings reflect the aliveness of the environment, the underpinning construction of duality (high/low) and the warm, heartfelt affections emanating from a people's relationship to place. *Popul Vuj* recounts the response of the first four humans when they first saw everything under the sky, "Truly now, double thanks, triple thanks that we've been formed . . ." (Tedlock 1996: 147).

In a traditional highland Maya perspective, the Earth is a territory maintained by the Owner, Ajau, (*rajaw juyub* "mountain owner"), who owns the land and everything on its surface. Ethnographic work concurs: "The face of this earth is not ours. We are just renting it for a while. We just pass through it, then we are gone" (Molesky-Poz 1999: 257). This perspective is shared among other highland people. According to the traditional Tz'utujiles around Lake Atitlan, Mam (the Earth Lord) is a proliferate sacred being that is as much "felt" by his people as an animistic presence as he is known to them as their Lord of the Earth (Stanzione 2000). Other Maya refer to the earth as *our mother*. "The earth is our mother. She gives us corn, fruits, flowers. Her waters wash us clean. At the end of our life, she opens her entrails and receives our bodies. So she must be respected and loved" (Molesky-Poz 1999: 274). Whether the Earth is understood as a *territory*, maintained by Ajau, the Owner, the Earth Lord, or as a *mother*, the land is alive and needs to be cared for, to be respected, to be fed. Maya belief that the universe sustains us and that as humans we have a transitory passage on Earth informs their relationship to the land. Men and women not only cultivate the Earth, but also in ritual practice, offer aromatic gifts, thanksgivings and petitions to maintain a reciprocal relation with the sacred Earth. This concept of reciprocity – that to receive something of value, you must give something of value – permeates Maya values.

As a farmer plants kernels of corn, he first exhales on the palm of his hand a "huh" prayer, asking permission to open the Earth. Before the exhumation of a mass grave to identify village members who disappeared or were murdered during the late 1970s and early 1980s, an *Ajq'ij'* asks permission to open the Earth. Before a family constructs a house, the family speaks with the Earth, asking permission, explaining to the Earth their need to dig holes, to plant poles in her surface for the house's foundation. They address the Earth,

> We are just passing through this life, but we need shelter. We need a place to sleep, to be protected from the rains and from the dangers of night. Please understand us, that we are asking permission to change your face, the face of the Earth. We are only passing through (Molesky-Poz 1999: 279).

Further embedded in this worldview are beliefs concerning how particular offerings accomplish certain tasks. For example, in Cantel, people bury the hooves of a sacrificed goat in each of the four corners of the house and the head of the goat in the center as a present to the Owner of the Earth, that the foundation of the house will be stable and strong. Traditionalists of Santiago at Lake Atitlan believe that as long as the Flowering Mountain Earth is "fed," it will continue to provide sustenance. Rituals like burning copal, dancing sacred bundles, or praying can feed the ancestral form.

Foundational to understanding the spirituality emergent in the highlands is the interpretation of the word *faith* in Ki'che'. *Faith* is translated as the verb *kojonik*, which can be rendered in two meanings: *to put on* and *to believe*. The first meaning of *kojonik*, *putting it on*, is doing the ritual work of sacrifice, of placing aromatic materials (*copal* and *pom* incense, tallow candles, chocolate, sesame, flowered water, alcohol) in the fire and through them of giving thanks, of asking pardon and permission, of petitioning Ajau. The second mien of *kojonik* is "to believe" or more carefully rendered, "the center where we connect to trust." That is, one's disposition, one's faith, informed by an inner determinateness, facilitates a connection and mutual love with *B'itol Tz'akol*, the Maker, the Modeler, who is manifest in the animate potentiality of the universe, yet who is also transcendent. One way of connecting to this center is through the ceremony on a designated day on the Maya sacred calendar and at a selected sacred site.

Among the highland Maya, the *Ajq'ij* is a woman or man who understands one's particular spiritual capacity and destiny, undergoes training, offers petitions and thanksgiving in rituals, serves their community and advises according to the sacred calendar of 260 days. Non-Maya scholars have identified them as Daykeepers, priest-shamans and shaman-priests, working people or ritual specialists who illuminate according to the Maya calendar and worldview. *Ajq'ijab* guard the values and knowledge of the calendar, their spiritual base, and transmit it in ceremonies, in divinations with *tz'ite* seeds (*Erthrina coallordendron*) or through discerning in the "lightening in their blood," and in conversations with persons who seek their counsel. *Ajq'ijab'* who understand their lives in terms of service and responsibility to their communities, explain that ceremonies are necessary to maintain the tremendous energy that they carry and control. In the current revitalization of Maya culture, people have turned to the *Ajq'ijab'* and public ceremonies as sources of identity, community, cultural, and spiritual growth.

The 260-day calendar, the Sacred Calendar, which the Ki'che' call the *Cholq'ij*, refers to two continuous repeating cycles, the count of thirteen days and the set of twenty day-names. Each of the twenty day-names designates an attribute, an element of life; each of the numbers from one to thirteen carries a particular characteristic. The combination of a particular day-name and a particular number designate the quality of that day.

This 260-day calendar was common to many parts of Mesoamerica, called the *tonalamatl* by the Aztec, identified as the *tzolkin* by some Maya and Western scholars. Written evidence for the use of this calendar goes back to the sixth century B.C.E. While its origin is not known, it is suggested that the numbers 13 and 20 relate to the various segments of the lunar cycle. This calendar, imaged in signs in the lowlands and Peten, but as day-names in the highlands, remains the spiritual foundation for ceremonies, divination, and understanding personal capacities. Contemporary *Ajq'ijab'* utilize the *Cholq'ij* as an orientation instrument so that people can live in harmony with the universe.

Geological formations such as volcanoes, mountains, convergences of mountain ranges, springs of water, and particularly caves, are linked with ancestral traditions and possess spiritual qualities. Each geological formation and place has a distinct *Uk'ux*, heart, owner, *nawal* or guardian spirit, and possesses some determined energy, making communication with the sacred accessible; thus distinct places are portals to the sacred. Some sites are designated for curing and healing, others for economic well-being, or to resolve a problem. Maya speak of sacred places as *encantos*, places where one is more likely to encounter a spirit or where a specific, personalized, maybe anthropomorphic manifestation shows itself, and of *altars* (*kojb'al* = "a place where you go to give something") where one offers prayers, but does not necessarily perform a ceremony. However, both *encantos* and altars are places of contact and communication with Ajau, and with the ancestors.

Central and most sacred to the *Ajq'ijab'* is the natural element of fire. The ceremonial arena, prepared of aromatic materials and designed to mirror the Maya quatrefoil microcosm in images, colors and spatial designs, becomes the ritual space, set apart in geography and time. Here, the aromatic materials are consumed in the flames; the fire becomes the conduit between heaven and Earth, between humans and the Heart of the Sky, Heart of the Earth. In the legacy of the first humans, the great wise ones, the great thinkers, penitents, and sacrificers in *Popul Vuh*, who unwrapped their copal incense, offer their copal and pom with great thanksgiving. In this ritual, positive and negative forces of the animating energy are brought into harmony.

Oh, Ajau,
Heart of the Sky, Heart of the Earth.
Hidden treasure, which fills the four corners of the
    universe
Only peace and tranquility surround you.
(Prayer of *Ajq'ijab'* of Zunil)

As transnational, national, and local companies or families privatize land and natural resources for profitable development, *Ajq'ijab'* find their access or right of entry to sacred places barred, at some sites their safety threatened. On a larger level, Maya agricultural workers confront serious questions as the processes of transnational agribusiness have established a dependency on imported chemical sprays, fertilizers, factory farms, and non-reproducible seeds, which yield marketable crops in a shorter period of time, but in the long run, deplete the Earth's nutrients. Farmers find that after years of using chemical fertilizers and pesticides, the Earth no longer produces. The farming population is torn between immediate economic survival and a long-term sustainable relationship with the land. Some local Maya communities are developing agricultural projects that investigate and cultivate diverse species of edible, medicinal, and aromatic plants native to the region, which combine agricultural practices with forest habitations, utilize organic products, and develop and share seeds unique to the region for the purpose of developing a sustainable, ecological relationship with the land. At the same time, unexplored and untapped wealth, especially in terms of petroleum, minerals, and hydro-electric power, and subject to Ladino colonization and state-foreign economic activity, such as dams, roads, oil exploration and cattle production in the Franja Transverals del Norte and in the Peten, are being developed. These recent projects have displaced tens of thousands of Maya during the civil war (1978-1985); more recently Maya communities and ecological support groups have begun questioning and protesting these projects, such as the oil drilling in Lake Petén Itzá. Communities question the damage to the beauty and ecological balance of the land, the depletion of natural resources, and the displacement of indigenous communities. The ancestral philosophy of reciprocity and care of the Earth is foundational to Maya responses to this nascent and emerging resistance. Some local groups, often motivated by *Ajq'ijab'*, are beginning to cultivate medicinal gardens, clinical dispensaries of natural medicine, and small organic agricultural projects; however, to date, *Ajq'ijab'* who are not an organized, institutionalized body, have not responded to these concerns systematically nor publicly. Local Maya communities are beginning to understand and confront the consequences of transnational, global agricultural projects, and the consequent depletion of their natural resources and the economic and biological loss to their communities.

Jean Molesky-Poz

Further Reading
Brady, James E. and Wendy Ashmore. "Mountains, Caves, Water: Ideational Landscapes of the Ancient Maya." In Wendy Ashmore and A. Bernard Knapp, eds. *Archaeologies of Landscape: Contemporary Perspectives*. London: Blackwell Publishers, 2000, 124-45.

Carlsen, Robert S. *The War for the Heart and Soul of a Highland Maya Town.* Austin: University of Texas Press, 1997.
Freidel, David, Linda Schele and Joy Parker. *Maya Cosmos.* New York: Quill, 1993.
Kading, Terrance W. "The Guatemalan Military and the Economics of La Violencia." *Canadian Journal of Latin American and Caribbean Studies* 24:47 (1999), 57–91.
Lovell, W. George. *Conquest and Survival in Colonial Guatemala: A Historical Geography of the Cuchumatán Highlands, 1500–1821.* London: McGill-Queen's University Press, 1992.
Molesky-Poz, Jean. *The Public Emergence of Maya Spirituality in Guatemala.* Dissertation, Graduate Theological Union, Berkeley, 1999.
Stanzione, Vicente. *Rituals of Sacrifice.* Western Highlands of Guatemala: Stanzione, 2000.
Tedlock, Barbara. *Time and the Highland Maya.* Albuquerque: University of New Mexico Press, 1982.
Tedlock, Dennis. *Popul Vuh: The Definitive Edition of the Mayan Book of the Dawn of Life and the Glories of Gods and Kings.* New York: Simon & Schuster, 1996.

See also: Harmonic Convergence; Maya Religion (Central America); Mayan Catholicism; Mayan Protestantism; Mayan Spirituality and Conservation (Western Highlands, Guatemala); Mesoamerican Deities.

Mayan Catholicism

Christianity came to the Mayas during the early sixteenth century, as the "spiritual conquest" comprised a central element of the Spanish subjugation of present-day Mexico and Guatemala. In Yucatan, Chiapas, and Guatemala, friars from the Franciscan, Dominican, Augustinian, and the Jesuit orders endeavored to convert indigenous souls and to extirpate pre-Christian Mayan religion with some, but by no means complete, success. By the middle of the seventeenth century, the Roman Catholic Church had established a firm institutional presence in southern Mexico and Guatemala. Nevertheless, pre-hispanic religion proved resilient, as Mayan people grafted Christian beliefs onto their traditional worldview. In many parts of Mesoamerica (southern Mexico, Yucatán, and highland Guatemala) today, Mayan spirituality still coexists alongside Catholic religion.

Folk Catholicism

In modern times, most Mayans consider themselves to be Christian, even though they may simultaneously subscribe to a Mayan, as opposed to Western, view of the temporal world and the cosmos. This simultaneous adherence to what might appear to be otherwise contradictory belief systems is possible in part because many Maya consider their spirituality to be not so much a "religion" *per se*, based on dogma, as a "way of being" that is integrated into and helps determine the conduct of everyday life. As such, Mayan spirituality is generally focused around three central elements: peace with the natural world that sustains life, peace with other people (including the dead), which is negotiated within the sacred space of the ancient Mayan calendar cycle, and peace with the deity/ies (saints).

The relationship with nature in Mayan Catholicism is especially strong, as the Maya believe that the essence of divinity is present in significant land forms, plants and animals. Corn is a sacred element to the Maya, not only as the primary source of food, but also as the literal source of life itself, as described in the creation myth of the Ki'che' Maya holy book, the *Popol Vuh*. As Catholics, the Maya share a belief in a monotheistic creator God, but they also pray to many saints/gods. These divine beings are considered to be present in spatial geography, especially in mountains, which provide a sacred landscape visible in nearly every corner of Guatemala. Sacred landforms include not only mountains, but also caves, *cenotes*, and other notable but transient natural features such as earthquakes. These elements are believed to embody divine energy and power, and demand consideration, offerings, and propitiation.

Secondly, the environmental aspect of Mayan folk Catholicism is evident in the dual-gendered nature of God. In this hermeneutics, the motherness of God is in the form of the Earth (*tierra*), and the Earth is considered to be the feminine face of God. As such the Earth exhibits multiple facets of God's divine maternity, as the source of life, and, like a mother, "protects, cures, punishes, and suffers for her children" (Ak'Kutan 1994: 58). Thus, the Earth is not only a material symbol of God's benevolence and amplitude, but it is also considered sacred as a physical entity.

In the scholarly literature, the commingling of two or more religious systems has been defined as "religious syncretism," or, more specifically to the Mayan context, "folk Catholicism" (Wallace 1956: 81) or, most recently, "religious creolization" (Seibers 1999: 272). All three of these terms refer to the fusion of Mayan spirituality with Catholic belief, ritual, and practice. This body of creolized religious practices is commonly referred to as "*costumbre*," (custom). *Costumbre*, which incorporates not only religious belief in practice, but also day-to-day concerns such as language use, mode of dress, gender relations, relations with the natural environment, and locationality, has traditionally formed the nexus of Mayan social identity. Because the Catholic saints, ritual and liturgical cycle are integral to *costumbre*, there has long been a strong historical association between this type of Catholicism and Mayan ethnic identity.

Catholic Action

In the early decades of the twentieth century, the Catholic Church initiated a program known as Catholic Action to bring centrifugal groups, such as workers, youth and others, back within the broad authority of the Church. In Guatemala, this resulted in the entry of missionary clergy to reintroduce orthodox Roman Catholic dogma and liturgy into Mayan parishes. A particular focus of Catholic Action was to try to uncouple Catholic practices from their long association with the Mayan sacred landscape. A second focus was to attempt to divest the practice of "everyday" Mayan spirituality – associated with divination, fertility, the planting and harvesting of corn, and interaction with the natural world (plants, animals, Earth, and cosmos) – of its Catholic symbolism. Finally, Catholic Action has also sought to diminish the importance that Mayan Catholics places on the traditional Mayan calendar cycle, by redirecting liturgical performance toward the Western Catholic liturgical calendar.

Virginia Garrard-Burnett

Further Reading

Ak'Kutan, Centro. *Evangelio y Culturas en Verapaz*. Cobán, Guatemala: Centro Ak'Kutan, 1994.

Clendinnen, Inga. *Ambivalent Conquests: Maya and Spaniard in Yucatán, 1517–1570*. Cambridge: Cambridge University Press, 1987.

Ricard, Robert. *The Spiritual Conquest of Mexico*. Los Angeles: University of California Press, 1966.

Seibers, Hans, "Globalization and Religious Creolization and the Q'eqchi'es of Guatemala." In Christian Smith and Joshua Prokopy, eds. *Latin American Religion in Motion*. New York: Routledge, 1999.

Wallace, Anthony F.C. "Revitalization Movements." *American Anthropologist* 58 (1956), 264–81.

Warren, Kay. *The Symbolism of Subordination: Indian Identity in a Guatemalan Town*. Austin: University of Texas Press, 1989.

Watanabe, John. *Mayan Saints and Souls in a Changing World*. Austin: University of Texas Press, 1992.

Vogt, Evon Z. *Tortillas for the Gods: A Symbolic Analysis of Zinacanteco Rituals*. Norman: University of Oklahoma Press, 1993.

See also: Christianity (6a) – Roman Catholicism; Maya Religion (Central America); Maya Spirituality (Guatemala Highlands); Mayan Protestantism; Mayan Spirituality and Conservation (Western Highlands, Guatemala); Mesoamerican Deities.

Mayan Protestantism

Protestantism came to the Mayan areas of Guatemala and Mexico in the late nineteenth century in the form of missionaries from mainline Protestant denominations from the United States. In addition to their evangelizing project, these early missionaries enjoyed close ties to the Guatemalan and Mexican governments, which saw missionaries as "civilizing agents" who would advance Liberal social interests such as education. Although Protestant missionaries did create a significant social presence in Mayan communities, where they established schools, health clinics, literacy training, and the first modern orthographies for the transcription of Mayan languages, their religious influence in the communities was practically nil for at least the first half of the twentieth century.

This situation changed dramatically, however, in the second half of the twentieth century. Changes within the Roman Catholic Church, particularly the introduction of Catholic Action, which sought to eliminate "folk" and traditionalist Mayan religious practices from Catholicism in Guatemala and southern Mexico, and economic changes, began to challenge the spiritual hegemony of Catholicism. At the same time, in the late 1950s, new types of Protestant missionaries from the United States, offering what they called a "spiritual alternative to communism," began actively to evangelize in Guatemala, although to a lesser extent in Mexico, where their efforts were stymied by strong anti-clerical legislation. It was, however, a natural disaster, the catastrophic earthquake of 1976, that propelled the growth of Protestantism in Guatemala, as people flocked to churches for spiritual solace and for the emergency relief that critics referred to as "*amina por lámina*," or a "soul for plastic roofing."

The post-earthquake period marked the beginning of large-scale conversion of Mayan people from Catholicism to Protestantism, and specifically to Pentecostalism, a highly experiential, ecstatic form of worship in which believers experience what they call the "baptism in the Holy Spirit." Conversions to Protestantism continued to increase in the late 1970s and 1980s, particularly during the period known as *la violencia* (the violence), when the Guatemalan army's war of counterinsurgency against the guerrillas destroyed hundreds of Mayan villages and their inhabitants, displacing tens of thousands of people from their geographic and familial homelands. In southern Mexico, Protestantism began to advance among the Maya of Chiapas in the 1980s, during a period of increasing political and economic pressure in the region. In Chiapas, tension between Mayan Protestants and Mayan traditionalists has resulted in interethnic violence and the expulsion of Protestants from their villages, a situation that has been exacerbated by the political and economic crises that provoked the emergence of the Zapatista armed movement in 1994. Some scholars have suggested that the physical displacement of Mayan people from their traditional sacred landscapes may have opened a social space for Protestantism, which is less dependent than "folk Catholicism" on sacred geography, such as specific mountains or the cycles of nature, for its symbolism and meaning.

Pentecostalism

Mayan Pentecostals eschew such "traditionalist" practices as the adoration of the saints/deities, the rituals associated with the sacred days of the Mayan calendar, and divination, all of which they condemn as both "pagan" and, simultaneously, as "Catholic." Yet Mayan Protestants argue that the form and substance of Pentecostal worship does, in some regards, valorize critical aspects of Mayan culture. Because leadership in a congregation comes from personal revelation and public affirmation, the pastorate of such churches is largely Mayan and pastors tend to reflect the common experience, worldview, including the relations between humans and their environment, and language as the members of their congregations. The liturgical practices of Pentecostalism – the testimonies, demonstrations of "gifts of the Spirit" (speaking in tongues, faith healing, prophecy) – may bear more of a structural linkage to the other-worldly practices of Mayan shamanism (healing, speaking to and by inanimate objects, divination) than they do to either traditional Catholicism or mainline (non-Pentecostal) Protestantism. Since the 1980s, a Catholic analog to Pentecostalism, known as *Renovación católica*, or "Catholic Renewal" has also been a dynamic force in Mayan areas, suggesting that the appeal of pneumatic religion transcends denominational considerations.

Because Mayan Protestants eschew the ritual and material elements of worship such as the use of pine resin incense, astrology, and pilgrimages to mountain shrines that are found in folk Catholicism, there is not as strong a tie to the natural world in Mayan Protestantism or Pentecostalism as there is in Mayan Catholicism. Nevertheless, because many Mayan Protestants are *campesinos* (rural peasants), they are still closely tied to their environment and to the cycles of nature, particularly as they relate to planting and harvest, even to the extent of offering special prayers and offerings at critical times during the agricultural cycle. While Mayan Protestants officially subscribe to the biblical teaching that God gave humankind dominion over the Earth (Genesis 1:28), Mayan Protestants are likely to interpret this "dominion" as a benign guardianship.

Virginia Garrard-Burnett

Further Reading

Garrard-Burnett, Virginia. *Protestantism in Guatemala: Living in the New Jerusalem*. Austin: University of Texas Press, 1998.

Martin, David. *Tongues of Fire: The Explosion of Protestantism in Latin America*. London: Basil Blackwell, 1990.

Sherman, Amy. *The Soul of Development: Biblical Christianity and Economic Transformation in Guatemala*. New York: Oxford, 1997.

See also: Maya Religion (Central America); Maya Spirituality (Guatemala Highlands); Mayan Catholicism; Mayan Spirituality and Conservation (Western Highlands, Guatemala); Mesoamerican Deities.

Mayan Spirituality and Conservation (Western Highlands, Guatemala)

Indigenous peoples comprise two-thirds of the 11 million inhabitants of Guatemala, most of them of Maya origin. Evidence has demonstrated the presence of human population in the territory occupied today by Guatemala since 11,000 B.C.C., according to Michael Coe. With time and the domestication of several important crops, like maize, beans and squashes, the Maya evolved into one of the most developed civilizations of the ancient world, building large cities and sophisticated waterworks, and inventing a hieroglyphic writing system, and a very precise calendar based in deep astronomical knowledge.

The Maya, as other indigenous peoples, have a belief system deeply rooted in nature, which they consider sacred. For the Maya the relationship with the cosmos and the community is framed in terms of reciprocity, which means that people should always be grateful and respectful for what they receive. Although poverty, discrimination, technology and cultural change have all modified the relationship of the Maya with nature, they still have a basic ethic and attitude different from mestizo peoples, who have received more Western influence.

After three decades of civil war and military repression that mainly affected Mayan peoples, Guatemalan society is slowly looking for better ways to relate among its constituents. The Peace Agreements signed in 1996 opened a new era for the country, and the Mayan organizations were able to articulate a specific agreement that deals with their identity and rights, including their right to practice their spirituality. On the other hand, Mayan spirituality is experiencing an unprecedented revival, especially among young intellectuals and professionals who look for ways to differentiate themselves from mainstream society and reaffirm their Mayan identity.

The Significance of Sacred Sites

Rituals are the visible cornerstone of Mayan spirituality. They are the visible component of the reciprocal relationship that Mayas try to maintain with nature. The rationale behind this is that if nature is providing them with good soil, water, wood, medicinal plants, and animals to hunt, they should be grateful for this generosity. In a different sense, several Mayan groups consider that the "owners" of natural resources are local guardians. Consequently, everybody should always ask permission from local guardians in order to slash the forest for agriculture, cut a tree for construction or firewood, or hunt an animal for subsistence.

Rituals are performed in natural settings, mainly on the summit of high mountains, close to cave entrances, and on a few occasions, at the border of lagoons and rivers. Ancient Maya cities and Catholic churches built on top of ancient temples are also important sacred sites. Their location is usually indicative of an in-depth sensibility to natural beauty and the search for quietness and intimacy with *Ajaw*, the Lord, and with nature. The cultural landscape of Guatemala has plenty of sacred sites, several of them located in groups of four around the main historical towns, and representing the four corners of the universe.

Actual Status of Sacred Sites

After the arrival of the Spaniards, several Maya sacred sites were "christianized" by building churches, or at least a cross, on top of them. Actual ownership of sacred sites depends on the history of each particular region of the country. In the western highlands, most sacred sites are located in communal or municipal lands, while in the Pacific Coast and the Verapaces, several sacred sites are nowadays privately owned. In several cases, private ownership has created problems of access to some sacred sites, especially when the owner has become an evangelical Christian. Often sacred sites are located in areas important for biodiversity conservation, which opens opportunities for the building of alliances with conservationists.

Several sacred sites have fallen into decay, due to increased deforestation in the surrounding landscapes, forest fires and non-biodegradable garbage. In the Maya-Popti' territory of western Huehuetenango some exceptions to this rule are found. There, local Maya spiritual guides, together with the municipality and the Academy of Mayan Languages, have organized to take care of them. They clean and fence the sacred sites, ask for respect from visitors, and build structures where pilgrims can take shelter from sun and rain while praying. The Ministry of Culture is taking care of Ancient Maya cities such as Zaculeu, Iximche', and Chiantla Viejo, although sometimes specific sacred sites within an archeological park are polluted with garbage, as is the case in Iximche'. On the other hand, other important ancient Maya cities are totally abandoned, with no management responsibility from the central government, municipalities or local spiritual guides.

The Commission of Sacred Sites

A Commission of Sacred Sites, formed with spiritual guides and government representatives, was created as a result of the Peace Agreements signed between the Guatemalan Government and the leftist insurgency after 36 years of civil war ended in 1996. After several months of deliberations the commission was dismantled, however, without reaching agreement. The main source of controversy was the non-negotiable position of the indigenous representatives that only an indigenous organization of spiritual leaders has the right to manage ancient Maya cities. These indigenous organizations believe mestizo organizations, including the government, should only manage colonial monuments.

Despite the long history of government harassment, Mayan people at a number of ancient Maya cities have conducted rituals without interruption throughout colonial, republican and modern times. Ritualizing at other sites, such as Tikal, Dos Pilas, Naj Tunich, and Cancuén in Petén, has restarted recently. Permanent altars for Maya religious ceremonies have been built in the ancient Maya cities of Takalik Abaj and Tikal, much to the dismay of most archeologists. Some archeologists believe that building permanent structures for altars distorts the original meaning of the site and deleteriously impact on the original layout, and that some have been located in places where previously there was no ceremonial use.

The Chicabal Volcano and Lagoon

The case of Chicabal volcano, however, shows that a dialogue between Maya spiritual guides and protected area managers is possible, at least at the local level, and that it can lead to the protection of sacred sites.

Chicabal, which means "good or sweet place" in the Maya-Mam language, is a volcano with a lagoon in its crater. It is located at the municipality of San Martín Sacatepéquez, department of Quetzaltenango in western Guatemala. Chicabal is occupied by the Maya-Mam, one of the four largest indigenous groups in the country. The area is located within the cloud forests of the southern slope of the volcanic chain of western Guatemala, an important region for conservation due to its endemism, water production, tourism potential, and role as winter refuge and stopover for migratory birds.

Chicabal is the most important sacred site for the Maya-Mam, especially for those in western Quetzaltenango. Spiritual guides report that there were more than 80 altars in the past, although by the early twenty-first century, only 26 altars appear to be used, and most of these are situated around the lagoon or near the summit of the crater, called *Popb'il*. The altars are visited all year round, following the sacred Maya calendar, which provides for appropriate dates according with the intended praying. However, what makes Chicabal outstanding is the annual "praying for the rains" ceremonies, drawing more than 6000 visitors from the surrounding region and beyond. This special day coincides with the Catholic celebration of Jesus' Ascension to heaven. Besides people following Mayan spirituality, Catholic priests and pilgrims from the region climb to Chicabal the day before the Maya celebration in order to hear Mass at the border of the lagoon. This is part of a widespread movement within the Catholic Church that calls for the "inculturation" of the Christian message into the indigenous cultures. Although evangelicals generally consider Maya spirituality to be diabolic, they also visit the lagoon to fast and pray, a legacy that can, perhaps, be considered to be the result of cultural inertia. As a sign of respect, Maya spiritual guides give Chicabal the treatment of *Q'txu*, which means mother or lady. Other important days for Mayan rituals at Chicabal are the Day of the Cross (3 May) and the *Waxaqib' B'atz*, the first day of the sacred Maya calendar.

Management as Protected Area

In 1956 the entire Chicabal area was declared, together with all the volcanoes in Guatemala, to be a "no-hunting zone," but the law had little impact in the field. Chicabal was also included in the list of archeological monuments in June 1972. In spite of its legal status, Chicabal has been managed as a protected area by ASAECO (Asociación de Agricultores Ecológicos), a local organization formed by the actual landowners of most of the lagoon and the crater. All of them are Maya-Mam farmers from the nearby community of Toj Mech who bought the area in 1986 from a non-indigenous woman who had bought it from the first non-indigenous owner.

The farmers now associated in ASAECO bought the area to increase their farmland, mainly for potato and maize crops. They slashed the forest in several areas for agriculture and built a road to the lagoon in order to transport their agricultural produce. However, the terrain proved to be very steep, sandy and prone to erosion. Recognising the difficulties in farming the area, the municipality of San Martín Sacatepéquez and Helvetas, a Swiss NGO, approached the landowners in 1996. They offered them technical and financial assistance if they would declare and manage their terrain as a protected area, indicating they would help them to develop its tourism potential. The technical studies required to create a protected area have been presented to the national Congress and a completed management plan will likely be established by 2004.

The Sacred Dimension is Taken into Account

When active management and protection of the area started in 1999, spiritual guides were afraid that their traditional rituals would be prohibited. Gradually they realized that ASAECO, Helvetas and the municipality wanted to prevent the environmental degradation of the area, and promote and regulate public use of the area. María Victoria García, the former director of the municipal department of protected areas; started a process of dialogue with spiritual guides from the surrounding areas. As a starting point, several Mayan ceremonies were performed in Chicabal and other sacred sites, in essence, seeking harmony and the conservation of nature in the protected areas. As confidence grew, spiritual guides were asked for suggestions for the management of Chicabal. They requested that visitors should not be allowed to bathe, swim and fish in the lagoon, in order to respect its sacredness, and this desire was incorporated into the current area management plan, further building trust between the spiritual guides and the management authorities of the protected area.

Several additional actions have further built respect for and promoted the site's sacred status. First, the area is being characterized in the welcoming signs as "Center of the Maya-Mam worldview," while other signs at the entrance ask the visitor to respect the Maya altars. Furthermore, a complete interpretation of the Maya calendar was posted in the most visited area of the lagoon. Park guards and guides from ASAECO ask visitors to respect the area as a sacred site, not to leave any garbage and to avoid making a noise when Mayan ceremonies are being performed.

As a result, spiritual guides are satisfied that Mayan altars and nature are being protected. They feel, however, that the many members of ASAECO, being evangelical Christians, do not fully respect Maya spirituality and the Chicabal lagoon as a sacred site. These guides would like to have more formal participation in the protected area management and even greater consideration of its sacredness.

The Chicabal case suggests that protected areas, managed by local authorities, are more likely to incorporate respect for indigenous religious practices performed by their own people. However, some distrust remains when authorities follow a different religion and do not participate in Mayan ceremonies. Nonetheless, it is clear that a fruitful dialogue with indigenous spiritual guides is possible as part of the management of protected areas. As this is one of the very few examples where Mayas themselves are managing a protected area, a great deal can be learned from its evolution and development.

Estuardo Secaira

Further Reading
Coe, Michael. *The Maya*. London and New York: Thames and Hudson, 1987.

See also: Indigenous Activism and Environmentalism in Latin America; Maya Religion (Central America); Maya Spirituality (Guatemala Highlands); Mesoamerican Deities; Traditional Ecological Knowledge; Volcanoes.

McDonagh, Sean (1944–)

Sean McDonagh, a renowned ecological theologian, was born in Nenegh, Ireland, studied for the priesthood in Navan (ordained 1969), and was sent as a Columban missionary father to Mindanao Island, the Philippines, the same year. After working among the lowland people in Oroqueita City, Misamis Occidental, Mindanao for four years, he studied linguistic anthropology in the USA. On returning from Washington, D.C., he taught at the Mindanao State University in a predominantly Muslim area, and then moved to Lake Sebu to work among the mountain people called the T'boli.

In response to the destruction of local forest in T'boli country, McDonagh began his ecological activism, which culminated in the pioneering book *To Care for the Earth* (1985), though it took three years to find a publisher because the connection between ecology and theology was not well known. *To Care for the Earth* called for a new theology which would give at least as much prominence to creation as to redemption. McDonagh argued that the grammar of this new creation theology ought to be the findings of modern science. McDonagh believed this new cosmology, developed from the insights of Teilhard de Chardin and Thomas Berry, ought to become the guiding myth for modern humankind, especially in the way we relate to the Earth and other creatures.

In 1990 this volume was followed by *The Greening of the Church*, which revealed that, while Catholic teaching was strong on social issues, it needed to promulgate a supplementary message about the destruction of God's creation. The focus this time was on developing a theology of creation from the resources of the biblical tradition to complement the cosmological approach. The book also dealt with the thorny (at least from a Catholic perspective) issue of population. The chapter "Are There Too Many Mouths to Feed?" revisited the population question but from an ecological rather than philosophical-theological perspective. McDonagh argued that notion of "carrying capacity" puts limits on the human population levels on the planet. He pointed out that the notion of carrying capacity was not addressed by Pope Paul IV in the encyclical *Humanae Vitae*. The book was well received in environmental circles but strongly criticized by prominent bishops in both Ireland and the Philippines.

McDonagh's second book, moreover, contained the first environmental pastoral letter of any Catholic Conference of Bishops. Entitled *What is Happening to our Beautiful Land?*, the book had a major impact on the Philippine Church. Social justice programs are no longer confined to addressing human rights abuses or working for a more equitable society. They now include concern for the environment. In the Philippines this means protecting what is left of the tropical forests, mangroves and coral reefs. The pastoral letter was also printed and distributed by the Philippine Department of the Environment and Natural Resources (DENR). McDonagh was the main drafter of this document, which was published in 1988.

Passion for the Earth (1995) contains a critique of multilateral lending and trading bodies (World Bank, IMF, GATT-WTO) and their effects on development and the environment. Third World debt was his particular focus. In 1999 *Greening the Christian Millennium* appeared. It reflects on the ethical and ecological implications of genetic engineering in the plant world and on the patenting of life. McDonagh argued that a human-centered ethical framework, which has dominated Western thought for almost 2000 years, was unsuitable for discussing issues like genetic engineering. While supporting laboratory research in genetic engineering, he maintained that current field trials and the commercial planting of genetically engineered crops breached the precautionary principle and posed a danger to human health and the environment. Furthermore, he opposed patenting living organisms such as seeds or animals, viewing this as a new form of colonialism whereby the North, which is financially rich but poor in biodiversity, is able to commandeer the rich species and genetic resources of the South.

His most recent book *Why Are We Deaf to the Cry of the Earth?* looks at environmental challenges facing Ireland today after six years of unprecedented economic growth.

Garry W. Trompf

Further Reading
McDonagh, Sean. *Why Are We Deaf to the Cry of the Earth?* Dublin: Veritas, 2001.
McDonagh, Sean. *Greening the Christian Millennium.* Dublin: Dominican Publishers, 1999.
McDonagh, Sean. *Passion for the Earth.* Maryknoll, NY: Orbis, 1995.
McDonagh, Sean. *The Greening of the Church.* Maryknoll, NY: Orbis, 1990.
McDonagh, Sean. *To Care for the Earth.* London: Chapman & Sons, 1985.
See also: Ireland; The Philippines.

McFague, Sallie (1933–)

"The world is our meeting place with God . . . as the body of God, it is wondrously, awesomely, divinely mysterious" (McFague 1993: vii). Sallie McFague ends her book *Models of God* and begins her book *The Body of God* with these words. For several decades McFague probed the language, specifically the metaphorical models used for God, in Christian doctrine and offered alternative models for what she calls an "ecological, nuclear age." Her basic premise is that the patriarchal, transcendent models that have dominated Christian theology, liturgy, and devotional life for generations contribute to the destructive, dominating relationship that, primarily, Christian cultures have assumed toward nature. McFague's alternative models include God as mother, lover, and friend and the world or universe as God's body.

McFague's first two books, *Speaking in Parables* and *Metaphorical Theology*, focused on the intersection of literature and theology. She takes seriously the impact of theological language on belief systems and practices, then questions the ontological claims made by such theological language (metaphors/models). The connections between patriarchal, transcendent metaphorical language and environmental theology emerge in her book *Models of God: Theology for an Ecological, Nuclear Age*. In this book, which received the American Academy of Religion's Award for Excellence, she claims that the destruction of Earth, our only home, is tantamount to the most grievous of sins. It is this direction that she follows in *The Body of God*. Here McFague claims that Christianity, while often equated with a world-negating and body-hating belief system, is actually "the religion of the incarnation par excellence" (1993: 14). With that claim in mind, she questions the "abhorrence and loathing" of at least some "bodies" by Christianity. McFague then suggests that Christianity consider the "use of the model of body as a way of interpreting everything that is." In a world that constructs reality differently, "one that took the ecological context as the primary one," McFague suggests that "the body would be an appropriate model of God" (1993: 21). This is the challenge she offers to Christian theology.

Her final two books, *Life Abundant* and *Super, Natural Christians* are intended for audiences outside of academia, and for Christian lay audiences in particular. She proposes that "Christian nature spirituality should be based on a subject–subjects model of being, knowing, and doing in place of the subject–object model of Western culture" (1997: 2).

Sallie McFague received her B.A. from Smith College, her B.D., M.A. and Ph.D. from Yale University. Her degrees are in literature and theology. She taught at Vanderbilt University's Divinity School for over thirty years, holding the positions of Carpenter Professor of Theology and serving as Dean of the Divinity School. She is Distinguished Theologian in Residence at Vancouver School of Theology.

Laura Hobgood-Oster

Further Reading

McFague, Sallie. *Life Abundant: Rethinking Theology and Economy for a Planet in Peril*. Philadelphia: Fortress, 2000.

McFague, Sallie. *Super, Natural Christians: How We Should Love Nature*. Philadelphia: Fortress Press, 1997.

McFague, Sallie. *The Body of God: An Ecology Theology*. Philadelphia: Fortress Press, 1993.

McFague, Sallie. *Models of God: Theology for an Ecological, Nuclear Age*. Philadelphia: Fortress Press, 1987.

McFague, Sallie. *Metaphorical Theology: Models of God in Religious Language*. Philadelphia: Fortress Press, 1982.

McFague, Sallie. *Speaking in Parables: A Study in Metaphor and Theology*. Philadelphia: Fortress Press, 1975.

See also: Christianity (7d) – Feminist Theology; Ecofeminism; Manifesto for North American Christians.

McKenna, Terence (1946–2000)

Terence McKenna was perhaps the most prominent spokesperson of the post-rave neo-psychedelic movement. McKenna's writing challenges the reader to investigate ecstatic states empirically in order to judge whether his often very broad "repertoire of operational constructs" is "... in Wittgenstein's wonderful phrase, 'True enough'" (McKenna and McKenna 1994: xxv) Indeed, many of McKenna's ideas are contentious: for instance, the notion of an Edenic "Ur culture" in humanity's past; the simplistic typology of "partnership" *versus* "dominator" societies; and the theory that ingestion by early hominids of psilocybin mushrooms (provided by extraterrestrials) catalyzed human evolution. However, these polemical concerns are less pertinent to the reception of McKenna's writings than they would be for studies that fall more conventionally within the sciences and humanities. Like the nineteenth-century Romanticists, Terence McKenna's writing conveys a revelation of a primary, poetic, revolutionary consciousness where, for those drawn to them, fantasy, hallucination, and dream are varieties of data that are as real as any other.

In 1975 Terence and his brother Dennis McKenna – an ethnobotanist and psychopharmacologist – published the recondite *The Invisible Landscape: Mind, Hallucinogens and the I Ching*, recounting the hyperdimensional adventures and eschatological ideas resulting from an expedition to the Amazon in 1971. The goal of this expedition was to learn from *ayahuasqueros* – shamans who use the entheogenic potion *ayahuasca* to obtain ecstatic trance. The model of nature presented in *Invisible Landscape* is that of a complex mystery emanating as an organized fractal sequence from a unified, sentient, and abstract field: a model resonant with the newly simulated "virtual realities" of early 1990s cyberculture.

That symbioses between psychedelic plants and people can lead to deeper cultural and ecological awareness is a central theme of Terence McKenna's work. McKenna advocated naturally occurring psychoactive substances, especially psilocin-containing mushrooms, DMT, and the tryptamine-containing entheogens of the Amazon, as ways of transcending the constraints of "dominator culture" and obtaining a vision of a more integrative, archaic and geocentric sociality. These themes are extensively developed in *The Archaic Revival* (1991) and *Food of the Gods: The Search for the Original Tree of Knowledge* (1992).

The visible manifesting of language is another recurrent theme in Terence McKenna's writing. Appropriately, his (counter)cultural significance extended beyond his writings and charismatic spoken-word performances to multimedia collaborations, ethnobotanical conservation, and fundraising for environmental groups. He was a co-founder of Botanical Dimensions – an organization for the conservation of plants that have traditional ritual and medicinal uses. His work and memory provide an enduring social-cohesive force within the neo-psychedelic community.

Des Tramacchi

Further Reading

McKenna, Terence K. *True Hallucinations: Being an Account of the Author's Extraordinary Adventures in the Devil's Paradise*. New York: HarperSanFrancisco, 1993.

McKenna, Terence K. *Food of the Gods: The Search for the Original Tree of Knowledge: A Radical History of Plants, Drugs, and Human Evolution*. New York: Bantam Books, 1992.

McKenna, Terence K. *The Archaic Revival: Speculations on Psychedelic Mushrooms, the Amazon, Virtual Reality, UFOs, Evolution, Shamanism, the Rebirth of the Goddess and the End of History*. New York: HarperSanFrancisco, 1991.

McKenna, Terence K. and Dennis J. McKenna. *The Invisible Landscape: Mind, Hallucinogens, and the I Ching*. New York: HarperSanFrancisco, 1994 (1975).

McKenna, Terence K., Ralph Abraham and Rupert Sheldrake. *Trialogues at the Edge of the West*. Albuquerque: Bear & Co., 1992.

Oss, O.T., O.N. Oeric, I.T. Obscure and Kat (pseudonymously written by Jeremy Bigwood, Katherine Harrison McKenna, Dennis J. McKenna and Terence K. McKenna). *Psilocybin: Magic Mushroom Grower's Guide*. Berkeley: And/Or Press, 1976.

See also: Ayahuasca; Entheogens; Ethnobotany; Leary, Timothy; New Age; Peyote; Psychonauts; UFOs and Extraterrestrials.

Media

"Mediated Spectacular Nature" is a catch-all phrase for a wide assortment of nature-themed media presentations. In the past, the term "spectacular" has been used to characterize venues in which natural phenomena have been separated from their place on the Earth and presented as freestanding spectacles, often for entertainment and/or economic gain. Critics have found fault with this practice, warning that failure to account for the interconnectivity of all things will eventually lead to environmental ruin. However, *mediated* spectacular nature – magazines, films, and television programs – have done more than simply inform and entertain. The media genre may also be playing a prominent role in the central meaning systems of those who use its presentations.

The findings that led to these conclusions emerged from the Symbolism, Media, and the Lifecourse Project at the University of Colorado-Boulder's School of Journalism and Mass Communication. The multi-year audience-research project employed qualitative interview techniques better to understand how people meaningfully exist in the world, and specifically, how media play a role in the process of meaning-making. In almost all cases, the profound and mundane acts of daily life now involve interaction with the symbols and meanings of the media sphere. Over time, with the decline of the influence of traditional religious institutions, mediated meanings and the *realm* of commodity culture can be thought of as a religious sphere.

There are indications that the texts of mediated spectacular nature, located at the nexus of media, religion, and culture, have religious significance for many of those who use them. For example, one mother, a 43-year-old Native American spiritualist, described the way *National Geographic* magazines and specials capture the essence of her connection to the Earth:

> It provides, for me, physically, solitude and quietness and contemplation and smallness, or just a small piece of this Earth. And I think that *National Geographic* catches that in the land, which I can relate to. It's that *stillness*. They're beautiful.

These sorts of interpretations were not exclusive to those aligned with Earth-centered belief systems. A discussion of mediated spectacular nature brought a similar response from a woman who subscribed to a religiously conservative Christian belief system. The connection between her religiosity and mediated spectacular nature emerged as a result of her reports of favorite family activities. One involved family members gathering together to view rented wildlife films and watch nature programming on the *Discovery Channel* and *Animal Planet* (she especially liked the show *Crocodile Hunter*). The mother explained that even the violence has a place in the meaning of life:

> . . . it's terrible to watch that kind of thing, so when (her youngest daughter) cries I want to reassure her that . . . I don't know why it has to be so violent, but it has to be because of "the circle of life" and all the balance and all this and that. And so I'm constantly pointing those things out, especially the religious aspect . . . the God aspect when she's crying about it or upset, and so I bring that into, "That's the reason, honey, because God needed this to happen, we have to have the balance."

Clearly, not all of the families interviewed presented such rich evidence. Other parents considered mediated spectacular nature to be merely a safe location for entertaining and informing their families. But enough of the families shared the convictions of the women quoted above to warrant further understanding of a media genre with deep historical roots in the Western world and recent explosive growth.

A starting point for mediated spectacular nature has been traced back to the late nineteenth century with the developments of field biology and the movie camera. Edward Muybridge was the first to study animal locomotion with a series of cameras, and later filmed a tiger attacking a tethered buffalo at the Philadelphia Zoo. Public popularity of Muybridge's pioneering work, and the work of others, prompted a steady growth of wildlife film production at the turn of the century with public exhibitions becoming commonplace. Soon, images of animals (often purchased from the growing libraries of the wildlife film-makers) also found their way into travelogues and Hollywood adventure movies. The development was not restricted to motion pictures. The rise of mass journalism and technologies enabling photoengraving, along with the increasing public interest in science and the growing desire in the Western world to better understand itself by considering the "other" (human, animal, and land) fueled the slow but steady growth of *Natural Geographic* magazine. Over the twentieth century, the success of *National Geographic* spawned a variety of similar publications.

A pair of identifiable styles of mediated spectacular nature developed. The first, the "British model," put more emphasis on scientific research and less on narrative entertainment. It tended to have more descriptive close-ups than action-packed wide shots. The American tradition has followed the lines of what would later be known as the "classic" wildlife film: emphasizing drama, action, a strong story, and in more recent times, anthropomorphized animal characters. To capture dramatic action, practitioners of the American model have found it necessary to film in controlled settings, such as enclosures, and even zoos. Dramatic events are often set up, provoked, or pieced together in the editing room, sometimes using unrelated film and sequences.

Quintessential examples of each form have existed. Walt Disney's wildly popular and heavily distributed *True Life Adventure* movies produced through the 1950s and 1960s embodied the American model. Meanwhile, David Attenborough's work with the British Broadcasting Corporation's (BBC) wildlife film-making projects has always been carefully attentive to the spirit of the British model. But most examples of mediated depictions of the natural world have presented a blending of the two. In *Mutual of Omaha's Wild Kingdom*, the Natural Geographic Society's specials and magazines, Jacques Cousteau's undersea adventures, and countless other wildlife films and TV productions, one can detect the influence of both approaches.

Another important development that contributing to the importance of the meaningful potential of this genre, has been its meteoric expansion. After having watched the success of cable channels such as Home Box Office and ESPN, John S. Hendricks launched the Discovery Channel with a niche format that attracted viewers interested in programming about the natural world. By investing in its own original programming, funding expeditions around the world, and recouping hefty costs by dubbing the narrations for a global audience, the channel has grown to be one of the most popular in the world. Discovery Communications has spun-off the popular Animal Planet channel, while the United States Public Broadcasting Service (PBS), a haven for wildlife film-makers and home to the successful *Nature* series, has seen a boost in ratings in recent years. The American television network ABC has presented nature programming in an agreement with ABC World of Discovery executive producer Dennis B. Kane, and competitor NBC's return of *National Geographic* specials to prime-time commercial TV in the mid-1990s all enjoyed solid ratings. In January of 2001, National Geographic Television went after lucrative market share when it launched its own National Geographic Channel. Combined with a growing array of nature shows aimed at children on the network and cable channels, mediated spectacular nature has become a pervasive presence in American media.

The examples of meaningful relationships of audience members with mediated spectacular nature, combined with an ever-more pervasive presence in the media market, indicate that the use of mediated spectacular nature may have reached the status of popular religious practice. Charles Lippy presented a number of characteristics of meaningful practice that would designate it popular religiosity, including: a private character; a lack of organization; a tendency to syncretically blend worldviews, drawing from well-established, central-social beliefs, as well as newer, at times even ephemeral, ideas; a sense of sanctuary from chaotic existence; and access to the power of the supernatural, or what lies beyond the here-and-now. While activities such as body building, or spending time at Starbucks may constitute similar, meaningful popular religious activity for individuals in a relatively small group, the number of people experiencing mediated spectacular nature and the rich potential for the possibilities of that experience indicate that a substantial collectivity, indeed what we may one day be able to demonstrate as *global* in scope, may be using mediated spectacular nature as an inventory of contemporary symbols and values. Indeed, we could say it is a religion of nature.

If people are utilizing such presentations as *National Geographic* magazine and Animal Planet's *Crocodile Hunter* for their symbols and meanings, why is this happening now? One might point to the technological and market forces that prompted the explosive growth of mediated spectacular nature (i.e., it is what is there, so people will eventually find it meaningful). That is undoubtedly part of it, but there is also something else. Humans need vivid stories that they can tell themselves to make sense of the contradictions of existence. As we have become more aware of the degradation resulting from our burdensome resource usage, we have filled out these stories with the symbols and meanings of the natural world. Mass communication serves as a prominent vehicle in the telling and retelling of these stories. Mediated spectacular nature has come to stand at the intersection of media, religion, and nature – a representative example of a contemporary, nature-related, religious cultural production.

Joseph G. Champ
Stewart M. Hoover

Further Reading
Champ, Joseph. G. *Media, Identity, and the Environment: Spectacular Nature and Popular Religiosity*. University of Colorado, Ph.D. Dissertation, 2001.
Cronon, William, ed. *Uncommon Ground, Rethinking the Human Place in Nature*. New York: W.W. Norton and Company, 1995.
Davis, Susan. *Spectacular Nature: Corporate Culture and the Sea World Experience*. Berkeley: University of California Press, 1997.
Hoover, Stewart and Knut Lundby, eds. *Rethinking Media, Religion, and Culture*. Beverly Hills: Sage, 1997.
Lippy, Charles. *Being Religious American Style: A History of Popular Religiosity in the United States*. Westport, CT: Greenwood Press, 1994.
Lutz, Catherine A. and Jane L. Collins. *Reading National Geographic*. Chicago and London: The University of Chicago Press, 1993.
Price, Jennifer. *Flight Maps: Adventures with Nature in Modern America*. New York, NY: Basic Books, 1999.
See also: Disney; Disney Worlds at War; Mother Nature Imagery; Motion Pictures; Social Construction of Nature and Environmental Ethics.

Melanesia – Eco-Missiological Issues

The impact of Christianity on Melanesia has been immense, over 90 percent of its population identifying with one denomination or another. Marshaling the moral powers of this universal tradition for environmental care has become an urgent imperative to curb irresponsible actions toward forests, waterways and oceans. With the continuing effects of international business enterprises, the onset of new national or regional governments, and pressures from the foreign policies of stronger powers, tropical environments have been made vulnerable, and high standards of environmental safeguarding are needed. Christian appeals to care for God's creation take on a crucial significance when the churches play such a potentially potent role to instill common values and insist on national protection against outsiders. Unfortunately, however, foreigners' purchasing power – a taste of the "Cargo" – can too easily tempt local communities to part with precious resources, while levels of corruptibility among the new elites (especially in complex Papua New Guinea) have made for many underhand exploitations of forestland. Exposure of the issues by defenders of the environment (in parliaments, the press, churches, etc.) are too often made after disasters have occurred.

The up-and-coming elite, however, have received exposure to ecological issues through the writings of environmental philosophers and eco-theologians, and this is generating a climate of wiser decision making. The most famous of these thinkers in the region are Bernard Narokobi, who has been Minister for Justice and Speaker of the House of Parliament, Papua New Guinea, and the late Jean-Marie Tjibaou, who was the leading radical opponent to French colonialism in New Caledonia, and head of the *Front de liberation nationale kanake et socialiste* (FLNKS).

Narokobi has questioned whether Western concepts of private property rights and crown land concepts should be imposed on traditional peoples, and, combining traditional and Christian insights, he has also called for a radical re-visioning of Oceania's environmental future – to forestall damage coming through foreign exploitation. His influence has been greater on post-Independence Ni-Vanuatu policies than in his native Papua New Guinea.

Narokobi's fellow Catholic, former priest Tjibaou, has worked against alienation of tribal lands by colonial settlers and massive scarring of mountain faces through nickel mining. He knew that political self-determination for the islanders (kanaks) was fundamental for obtaining environmental security.

Tjibaou was aware of the dangers of hand-out development from the French Government and bitterly opposed France's nuclear explosion trials in the eastern Pacific. Apropos hand-out development, his position has been expanded upon by Protestant churchman Pothin Wete, who teaches that state financial concessions to the kanaks has come at the expense of the indigenous people's souls, along with the constant temptation to sell land for ready-at-hand cash. As for the nuclear question, this has also been taken up by a Protestant woman theologian, Suliana Siwatibau of Fiji, who cooperated with expatriate David Williams to produce the best popular handbook about the dangers of nuclear testing. Siwatibau used the biblical prophetic tradition as the basis for her ethical stance and for urging the preservation of creation. (The handbook was re-published by Greenpeace, yet without the insightful references to biblical prophetism).

Other indigenous eco-theologians of note are Choiseul Islanders Rev. Leslie Boseto (former Moderator of the United Church of Papua New Guinea and the Solomon Islands), who has sponsored the World Council of Churches' values for the "Integrity of Creation," and Esau Tuza, who perceived the significance of the independent Christian Fellowship Church (CFC) on New Georgia as a model of defense against environmental piracy. This church is one among a variety of independent groups, started by indigenous leaders that have split off from the mission churches during Melanesia's history. The CFC, led by a prophet called the "Holy Mama," successfully prevented Lever Brothers' irresponsible rainforest logging in the 1980s. Job Dudley, the son of this prophet, kept up the same pro-conservationist stance as a minister in the Solomonese government (although independent Korean loggers later subverted the local people with bribes).

In Papua New Guinea, the Tolai priest ToVagira (from New Britain) has produced an important resource book on land and mineral rights in his nation. Meanwhile, Tolai public servant and United Church layman Paulias Matane spearheaded work to create the Melanesian Environment Foundation in 1984, a national Melanesian Council of Churches project trying to integrate traditional and Christian values in a unified environmental policy for Papua New Guinea.

Generally speaking, interdenominational church voices had become somewhat muted by 2000, but Christian appeals to the integrity of creation are likely to become more effective as Melanesia's environmental vulnerability becomes more obvious. The Evangelical Lutheran Church of New Guinea, for instance, declared an active policy of land restoration in 2001 in order that – after a history of church-run plantations – the land be restored to its original inhabitants, along with their choice of its utilization. Another example is found in Aitape (a western Sepik district), where the Catholic Justice and Peace Commission for the Diocese has published popular materials to deter people from spoiling their lands and selling off rainforest to logging interests.

Various other voices and eco-theological impetuses could be noted. Expatriate influences are involved. The longest-standing residential protagonist for environmentalism and a nuclear-free Pacific in Papua New Guinea is Elizabeth Johnson, a poetess influenced by Quakerism and creation spirituality. Agricultural advisers with church connections have also long been monitoring soil erosion on sugar cane plantations owned by Fijians. All these voices have affected government and local action to place restraints on environmental exploitation in Melanesia, which, because of huge forest areas in inaccessible valleys, still remains one of the least environmentally damaged regions on Earth.

Garry W. Trompf

Further Reading

Ole, Ronnie Tom. "Making Sense of the Oneness of Life: A Melanesian Christian View of Creation." *Melanesian Journal of Theology* 6:2 (1990), 33–41.

Siwatibau, Suliana and David Williams. *A Call to a New Exodus: Anti-Nuclear Primer for Pacific Peoples*. Suva: Pacific Council of Churches, 1982.

ToVagira. *Land and Mineral Rights for Indigenous People in Papua New Guinea: A Quest for Justice, Peace and Integrity of Creation*. Rome: Pontificia Universitas Lateranensis, 1990.

Trompf, Garry W., ed. *The Gospel is Not Western: Black Theologies from the Southwest Pacific*. Maryknoll, NY: Orbis, 1987.

See also: Melanesian Traditions; Surfing.

Melanesia – New Religious Movements

In the Melanesian region different kinds of new religious movements have emerged during the colonial and postcolonial periods. These include "cargo cults," neo-traditionalist movements, and independent churches. Of these; cargo cults are by far the best-known response to social change: their leaders and adjutants seek to persuade villagers that the strange new (Western-style) goods, which they have difficulty acquiring, will soon arrive in remarkable quantities. These goods were seen as coming from the hands of their returning ancestors, or of Jesus in his second advent, or by some other spiritually significant means. These apparently bizarre expectations often arise because, when not knowing the source of internationally marketed commodity items, villagers apply ritual techniques to acquire them, just as they invoked the spirits to make their gardens produce and their livestock increase. Prima facie, these responses to rapid social change look "environmentally unfriendly," translating the Melanesians' well-known "materialist" attentions from their own organic products to consumer items. In various outbursts of collective conviction that a great day of blessing (some scholars say "millennium") is coming, gardens have been deliberately ruined and pigs killed in great numbers.

Thus traditional life-ways or modes of production have been abandoned while people waited for ships and planes to bring new riches from the great beyond. Makeshift airstrips and wharves have sometimes been built to receive the goods, dreams of miraculous transformations being especially fueled by the presence of the American forces, with their startling equipment and intense activity in the Pacific during World War II. Many Mengan people, for instance, who have joined a movement in East New Britain called the Pomio Kivung movement, currently share such high cargoist hopes. They believe that the returning ancestors will have the power to create, by a mere wish, a city the size of New York on Jacquinot Bay.

On the other hand, various cargo cults are protests against unequal access to "the Cargo" in favor of the white people or of foreigners generally, and in the course of time they can inspire effective opposition against colonial intrusion, including land alienation and desecration. Bougainville, an island to the far north-east of Papua New Guinea, provides an important example. There the mining of Mt. Panguna by an Australian company resulted in a cluster of cargo-cultist responses, one of them backing the local war to keep the mine closed down by upholding an ideology that the whole island is sacred (*mekamui*) and its environment requiring protection. It is a fallacy, however, to overlook other kinds of Melanesian religious responses that cannot easily be dubbed cargoist. These include neo-traditionalist movements and independent (or indigenously originated) churches.

Neo-traditionalist movements call for a rejection of outsider influences and a return to ancestral ways of life (even if these are almost always inevitably modified to preclude warriorhood activity). Some cargo cults have certainly taken on this aspect. Yali of Singina in the Madang area (New Guinea), for instance, organized a large movement that turned its back on "Mission and Administration" after World War II and performed innovative rituals to the ancestors to get the Cargo. Because the Cargo has not come in any grand miraculous fashion, though, the movement now tends to encourage old village ways rather than cash-cropping and business. Other collective neo-traditionalist responses are not cargoist. The leaders of the Moro movement on Guadalcanal (Solomon Islands), for example, simply teach – albeit with writing and use of blackboards in small schools – that the followers should avoid the introduced ways and keep up traditional practice, which will conserve the environment.

Melanesian independent churches, like their black counterparts in Africa, often synthesize indigenous with Christian outlooks. Led by local prophet-founders, such churches have been known to take up environmental causes. The NaGriamel movement, for example, founded by Jimmy Stevens on Espiritu Santo and also known as the NaGriamel Church of Christ, gained popularity and eventually pre-independence political clout for its opposition to massive (especially French settler-generated) land alienation in the New Hebrides (renamed Vanuatu). The movement's subversive qualities were used as an excuse to clinch Vanuatu's independence, with the British and French leaving their former colonial Condominium at exactly the same time, to allow the Papua New Guinea Defense Force (PNGDF) to land on Espiritu Santo, and to put down Stevens' activities in the so-called "Coconut War" (1980). This legitimated the new indigenously led national government at Port Vila. Ironically, the leader of the PNGDF received a plantation on Espiritu Santo as a prize. Such vulnerability in environmental struggle is also illustrated by the Christian Fellowship Church of New Georgia (Solomons), which successfully opposed American logging interests in the 1980s only to find the villagers succumbing to persistent Korean pressures a decade later.

Overall, each new Melanesian movement requires examination to see the extent to which any "nativistic pull" produces an impetus toward environmental security or pushes toward embracing modernity.

Garry W. Trompf

Further Reading
Loeliger, Carl E. and Garry W. Trompf, eds. *New Religious Movements in Melanesia*. Port Moresby and Suva: Institute of Papua New Guinea Studies and Centre for South Pacific Studies, 1985.
Trompf, Garry W. *Payback: The Logic of Retribution in Melanesian Religions*. Cambridge: Cambridge University Press, 1994.
Trompf, Garry W. "Independent Churches of Melanesia." *Oceania* 54:1 (1983), 51–72; 54:2 (1983), 122–32.
See *also*: Bougainville (Papua New Guinea); Melanesian Traditions; Papua New Guinea.

Melanesian Traditions

Melanesia, stretching from the Bird's Head in the west of the great New Guinea island across to Fiji, and including West Papua (Irian Jaya), Papua New Guinea, the Solomon Islands, New Caledonia, and Vanuatu, carries more discrete religions than any other region on Earth. With very general configurations discussed under "Pacific Islands, Religion and Nature," here we make sense of the great complexity of over 1500 small-scale and "stone age" cultures with some guarded generalities. Lexical equivalents for religion and nature are generally lacking in traditional vocabularies, but words for worship and world are found virtually everywhere, although "world" almost always denotes some small geographical encompassment, with Melanesians tending to conceive their cosmoses horizontally rather than vertically.

Thus creator beings are very often already part of the landscape, as we see in Tolai belief with the great volcanoes of Ia Kupia (great Mother) and her relatives near Rabaul, East New Britain, and as we also find with collective culture-bearing deities or heroes that come along the coasts or over the mountains in "mythic times" with their gifts of skills (to garden, hunt, etc.) or useful objects (canoes, weapons, etc.). Sometimes sky gods are present, such as Aitawe, the sustainer of all things (in the western highland Enga people's worldview), and the sun and moon treated as deities, thought to lay "eggs" on the Earth in the form of black stones (used for cultic purposes, as with the southern highland Huli). But the landscape-connected deities predominate in the whole region, along with place spirits (*tok pisin: masalai*) living in dangerous lairs, sickness-bearing spirits, sprites or tricksters, and the dead. The dead are usually conceived as going to places more or less laterally positioned: to the mountaintops where they are buried (western highland Wahgi); down in caves at the end of rivers (lower highland Daribi); to the distant west (the coastal Papuan Toaripi); or to an isle of the blessed called Tuma (Papuan Trobriand islanders, the last two cultures with Austronesian languages).

The understanding of place and its meanings will vary with local features and culturo-linguistic inheritances. Take the Austronesian Sentani, for instance, living around the great Lake Sentani in northern Irian Jaya (West Papua). The world is described as Above-Below (*bumana-ana*), and might seem vertically oriented, but in practice horizontal preoccupations dictate all. The root of the cosmic Waringin tree may have broken in heaven, but it tumbles onto the island of Ayauwo on the lake and takes root, generating the primal village of Abar in the earth, which, along with other villages, is dug up by the spirit-being Uaropo. Creative energies are more associated with the lake and its surroundings, and these potencies are taken over the mountains to coastal places. The lake and its bay sustain all life and bear many meaningful implications for human livelihood. There is no word for nature, or a sense of responsibility for it, but only a givenness of the locale with signs from it recognized through ancestral lore. Every year (in our late December), for instance, the lake turns yellow and yields up many struggling fish, and villages wait for the right time to kill them in plenty before they die. Among other phenomena, strange turbulences near a village presage the death of a chief (*ondoforo*); a great deal of fish dying in one spot foreshadows the death of a great personage; a child dying in the lake or the bay becomes a fish relative, and in this sense a totem, such as a swordfish (and though no word for totem is present, a proscription against eating it applies). Environmental attitudes are not independent of concerns for group prosperity and social explanations.

In a mountainous region, the feel will be very different. Take the Papuan highland Fuyughe, in a world of steep mountains and few wide valleys. Each cluster of related and allied hamlets live beneath a recognized mountainous configuration, that in turn is protected by a place spirit (called *sila*) guarding the heights. No one gardens the heights, it is dangerous to enter them alone, the presence of a *sila* being recognized by a hunting party, let us say, through the appearance of a giant python. Gardening, trading expeditions, feasting, and fighting are all done on a "medial strip," just before valleys drop steeply into ravines. The respect for *sila* prevents the possibility of unchecked surprise raids by enemies, because no war party will ever take a secret route through the high forest for fear of trespassing on one's foes' protected area. While the mountains deeply condition their picturing of the world, the Fuyughe are unusual for having some sense of every "species" needing to survive. Every named type of living thing – a winged bird type, cassowaries, pigs, opossums, reptiles, and also people – possesses an *utam[e]*, that is, a special instance of it (it seems at times like a Platonic form!) that, if killed, would result in the death of the whole of a given [species-]group. Members of each hamlet learn the signs and contexts in which the possibility of making such a mistake would occur. Never kill a snake, for example, on a tribal borderland, where animal life is apparently prolific anyway. The most important *utam* of all was that of the chiefs (*amende*), and he could never leave his tribal area without fear of his group's cosmos collapsing. Environmental sensitivities, in any case, are never separated from concerns for military and social survival.

Generally, as is the strong implication of these examples, Melanesians found maximum security in their places of habitation (house lines, hamlets, villages), some in their gardens, and the least security in the forest. Yet the forest was usually conceived as sacred for being the habitation of the spirits, the very epitome of horizontal orientations. What can be translated as the sacred, though, is not always positive. The central highlander Faiwolmin, for instance (straddling Irian Jaya and Papua New Guinea), talk both of the good sacred (*anang awem*) – of ancestral sites and initiatory seclusion centers in "the bush," men's houses, cult objects, and great leaders in the hamlets – and of the bad sacred (*awem tem*) – for masalai places, ghosts, and the enemies' appropriations of spirit powers. (On further central highlands variations, cf. Papua New Guinea.) Where dependency on a lake or the sea is involved, a spirit-being lies behind the cycles of plenty (cases from from Sentani to Oavulu, Fiji).

Other themes to note concern naming the environment (with gender associations, for instance, so that dry places are male, wet places, such as valleys, female); fertility cults, some with goddesses (e.g., Timbehes on Nissan Island); sanctions against greed and personal prestige accrued from sharing and generosity; and a sense of interconnectedness with animals (men as birds; sorcerers entering creatures to strike, etc.). A debate also surrounds whether feasting, especially the large-scale pig killing in the highlands, is determined by ecological factors, such as the need to kill off a surplus of pigs (see A. Vayda and R. Rappaport 1968) rather than on group/human will. One certainly needs to appreciate that groups exercise their organizing power when they see circumstances (including environmental ones) allowing for it, but of course they can err in their judgments.

These religio-environmental values persist in group consciousness throughout Melanesia, but they are always in danger of being subverted in a new world of individual

Melanesian entrepreneurs and greedy politicians. Each small society tends not to hold the values of their neighbors or other groups in any esteem, so it has been necessary, in nationalist rhetoric and eco-theological discourse, to appeal in the modern context to spiritual and conservationist values that transcend cultural particularities.

Garry W. Trompf

Further Reading

Hirsch, Eric and Michael O'Hanlon, eds. *The Anthropology of Landscape: Perspectives on Place and Space*. Oxford: Clarendon Press, 1995.

Lawrence, Peter and Mervyn J. Meggitt, eds. *Gods, Ghosts and Men in Melanesia*. Melbourne: Melbourne University Press, 1965.

Salisbury, Richard F. "Non-Equilibrium Models of New Guinea Ecology: Possibilities of Cultural Extrapolation." *Anthropologica* (New Series) 17 (1975), 128–47.

Trompf, Garry W. *Melanesian Religion*. Cambridge: Cambridge University Press, 1991.

Vayda, Andrew P., ed. *Environmental and Cultural Behavior: Ecological Studies in Cultural Anthropology*. American Museum Sourcebooks in Anthropology 11. New York: Natural History Press, 1965.

Vayda, Andrew P. and Roy A. Rappaport. "Ecology, Cultural and Non-cultural." In *Introduction to Cultural Anthropology*. James A. Clifton, ed. Boston: Houghton Mifflin, 1968.

See also: Polynesian Traditional Religions.

Memoir and Nature Writing

A memoir (from the French "to remember") is essentially a record of specific times and places kept alive through recall and based primarily on first-hand knowledge rather than research. Nature narratives that also explore deeply felt issues through the lens of personal experience may then be grouped as memoirs for fruitful consideration. Historically, the range of materials that inform memoirs, or that share similar preoccupations, includes: letters, diaries, journals or biographical sketches, as well as personal essays and spiritual autobiographies. The act of writing, too, is significant; since composing one's memoir serves as a rite of return, the writing becomes a place apart, a circumscribed landscape as it were, where the author gains a footing, fresh perspective and not a little consolation.

Where loss colors a work, an elegiac tone separates the memoir from more pragmatic strains of nature writing. By definition, memoirs are a less pragmatic vehicle; their primary orientation is the self and its relations with the world. While self-absorption may be inherent in the task, memoir writing is actually a powerful antidote to narcissism once an author learns how to adapt this literary form to the genuine search for self-knowledge. Annie Dillard's *Pilgrim at Tinker Creek* and Terry Tempest Williams's *Refuge* are classic nature memoirs that succeed in balancing deeply personal questions with nuanced inquiry into broader cultural issues. This willingness to admit to rigorous self-examination, which has so shaped spiritual autobiography in Western literature, suggests that the nature memoir is also heir to a similar quest. However distant Augustine's *Confessions* seem from nature writing, it is important to recall the formative influence religious figures have played in contemplating the self's relationship to nature and the vitality of even their most misguided conclusions. From the Waters of Prayer in Teresa of Avila's *A Life* to Thomas Merton's *Seven Storey Mountain*, Western confessional classics are redolent with spiritual images drawn from nature's palate.

Religious roots are also evident in nature writing's earliest classics. Gilbert White's *The Natural History and Antiquities of Selborne* (1789) faithfully reconciles Christian belief with scientific inquiry. White and naturalist theologians such as John Ray were not the least conflicted in confirming the divine order behind nature's complexities. A more controversial follower of Linnaeus, Jean-Jacques Rousseau was no nature writer, yet his final collection of confessional essays, *Reveries of the Solitary Walker* (1782), still echo in today's wistful testimonials about finding solace in the natural world.

With European expansion in North America, the overwhelming power of uncolonized nature was commonly exploited, feared, or decried as moral wilderness. By the nineteenth century, Romantic recommendations of nature's salutary effects (as opposed to the corrupting influences of civilization and excessive domesticity) diverged sharply from pioneer struggles to conquer nature and to wrest a decent living from its grasp. This tension between hostile and benevolent visions of nature cropped up in the recollections of Transcendentalists and immigrants alike. However, consider the bold assurances in Emerson's "Nature" and Thoreau's *Walden* alongside ambivalent accounts of rearing children in the woods. Susannah Moodie (*Roughing it in the Bush, or, Life in Canada*, 1852) and her sister, Catherine Parr Traill (*The Backwoods of Canada*, 1836), were English gentlewomen who pioneered in Upper Canada (now central Ontario). Warning ostensible colonists abroad about the joys and hazards of surviving in the wild, their works soon became classics – astute observations of natural detail tempered with Victorian clarity on the moral dimensions of wilderness beauty, usefulness and danger.

Eventually, nature memoirs with a confessional bent lost ground to writings with a more secular ring. Sporting narratives, for instance, unencumbered by religious agendas, offered a haven from "softer" naturalist leanings that veered off into cosmology. Thanks to recent authors who have elevated the fish tale to mythic proportions, avid anglers and mystics alike are again dipping into the same stream (Norman Maclean, *A River Runs through It*; David James Duncan, *My Story as Told by Water*).

Memoirs of exotic places (Bruce Chatwin, *Songlines*; Peter Matthiessen, *The Tree Where Man was Born*) have always been popular, but musings on domestic landscapes have also had a loyal following. Garden autobiographies, which originated in the 1850s, quickly became a celebrated genre that fused cultural, personal and natural histories (see Douglas Chambers, *Stonyground: The Making of a Canadian Garden*). Often written in highly evocative prose with a pronounced mythological cast, early examples plumbed Genesis to Milton in search of the model garden and, by extension, the model relationship between humans and nature. Not unlike wilderness parks, gardens were viewed as sacred landscapes that instructed humans about the right relationship between people and place. Strong moral preoccupations informed these inquiries, reasoning that, if Eden was the primordial scene of order, then the garden was nature properly tended.

Often the product of a mature writer's lifelong preoccupations (Barry Lopez, *About This Life*), the memoir reflects highly charged personal as well as cultural associations. Common themes include numinous experiences in either strange or familiar landscapes (Sharon Butala, *The Perfection of the Morning*) and similar encounters with animals (Rick Bass, *The Ninemile Wolves*). Land as text is also a significant, if problematic, theme, as memoirs try to render human experience and place mutually intelligible. The memoir allows a writer – and, by extension, a reader – the luxury of exploring place through stories about wild inhabitants and the varieties of human experience fostered in a particular landscape. The storied landscape is an important theme that informs our search for morals, as contemporary naturalists consistently call for right living, instead of seeking the rare uplifting encounter with the wild (Alison Deming, *The Edges of the Civilized World*). Over the past decades, shifts in cultural and religious values have made memoirs increasingly important records that chart this evolving dialogue in nature ethics.

With this lofty mandate, do memoirs have pitfalls? Yes, the writerly danger is that natural forces are simply reduced to symbols or totems that bear the burden of human yearning. Even with the best of intentions, the tendency to use nature for the purposes of the writer's own personal inquiry is a hazard. Literary sins range from anthropomorphizing and sentimentalizing to just plain missing the obvious. The tendency to reduce wildness to meditations on human feelings about wildness invariably flaws otherwise good nature writing, yet the hunch that wildness is our rightful partner in the search for self-knowledge is not misguided. Problems occur when the approach becomes a conceit rather than a discipline. Nature writing requires humility, attentiveness, and detachment from self-serving digressions. At its best, the memoir is an exercise in studied looking and an avenue to finely tuned contemplation. This is Lopez at the river "with no intention but to sit and watch"; this is Dillard's "stalking."

These values, in particular, suggest that nature memoirs share more religious undercurrents than is commonly recognized. Conventional and unconventional pieties have influenced the spiritual and artistic formation of naturalists for generations. Authors who see the world as the site of contemplation (Wendell Berry) or conversion (John Muir, Mary Sojourner) often turn to explicitly religious language to convey their experiences. Indeed, religious language is often the only way to communicate ineffable experiences, intuitions and that instinctual, dreaming knowledge that a mechanical culture invariably tries to suppress. Yet the question goes beyond that of language. Understanding religious roots and spiritual leanings allows us to appreciate a whole worldview. Those who can steer through statistics to a discerning evaluation of the facts possess a strong moral compass – a compass we turn to again and again. Consider the Calvinistic restraint echoed in Dillard, Berry and Lopez, which continues to provide powerful moral ballast in these darkening times.

Nature memoirs may convey astonishing revelations or prophecies about the natural world, but they must be authentic and authoritative to be trusted. The adventurer who risks returning to the past to retrieve riches for the tribe is a valuable culture-bringer, but is he or she committed to watching and to listening over the course of a lifetime? If memoirs are a reliable gauge of an author's integrity, they seem to tell us that the finest guides make no pretensions to exhaustive knowledge at all. Rather, they urge the acquisition of knowledge in order to develop (or submit to) the discipline of seeing, witnessing, and attending to the thing itself. If anything, these individuals are expert at not knowing – what in mysticism is referred to as the apophatic way – and at grappling with the holy limits of all forms of knowledge.

The nature of that commitment makes the memoir a powerful spiritual and imaginative tool for writers, let alone for readers, who are instructed by places, actual and imagined, that most of us may never see.

Susan L. Scott

Further Reading

Austin, Mary. *The Land of Little Rain*. Boston: Houghton Mifflin, 1903.

Berry, Wendell. *Recollected Essays 1965–1980*. San Francisco: North Point Press, 1983.

Melloy, Ellen. *The Anthropology of Turquoise: Meditations on Landscape, Art, and Spirit*. New York: Pantheon, 2002.

Muir, John. *The Mountains of California*. New York: Century, 1894.
Sojourner, Mary. *Bonelight: Ruin and Grace in the New Southwest*. Reno, NV: University of Nevada Press, 2002.
Stegner, Wallace. *Wolf Willow: A History, A Story, and a Memory of the Last Plains Frontier*. New York: Viking, 1962.

See also: Autobiography; Berry, Wendell; Dillard, Annie; Emerson, Ralph Waldo; Lopez, Berry; Muir, John; Thoreau, Henry David; Williams, Terry Tempest.

Men of the Trees (East Africa)

One of the pioneering movements in social forestry was Men of the Trees, now known as the International Tree Foundation, founded by Richard St. Barbe Baker (1889–1982) among the Kikuyu in Kenya in 1922, when he was Assistant Conservator of Forests for the British Colonial Office. Members of Men of the Trees committed to planting ten trees every year and to protecting trees everywhere. The organization was a response to widespread forest destruction and soil loss leading to desertification. St. Barbe, as he was known to his friends, was a deeply spiritual man with a profound respect for traditional cultures and peoples and a long-standing membership in the Bahá'í Faith. After a further forestry assignment in Nigeria, he began to travel the world writing and lecturing about forest conservation and turning Men of the Trees into a global organization based in England. A journal was published starting in 1929, as well as a Tree Lover's Calendar. Invited to Palestine by the High Commissioner in 1929, he brought representatives of the major religions together to commit to a plan of reforestation of desert areas, and helped to make the traditional *Tu Bi'Shvat* (Feast of Trees) a national tree-planting day. The first life member of Men of the Trees was Shoghi Effendi, the Guardian of the Bahá'í Faith. St. Barbe reached many prominent people with his message, and influenced such world leaders as Nehru and Franklin D. Roosevelt, leading the latter to establish the Civilian Conservation Corps. He worked to save the redwoods of California starting in 1930, and launched a desert reclamation program in Africa that became the Sahara Reclamation Program and the Green Front. His Royal Highness the Prince of Wales became patron of the International Tree Foundation in 1979.

In 1946, at St. Barbe's instigation, the First World Forestry Charter Gathering was held in London. The aim was to provide an opportunity for the exchange of ideas on forest conservation between diplomatic representatives from many countries. Such gatherings continued through the 1950s and 1960s, and inspired a number of efforts at global environmental cooperation. They were revived in 1989, the hundredth anniversary of St. Barbe Baker's birth, at the initiative of the Bahá'í International Community Offices of the Environment and Public Information. The 1994 Gathering held at St. James's Palace in London in July, was addressed by His Royal Highness Prince Philip, Duke of Edinburgh, and by Amatu'l-Bahá Rúhíyyih Khánum, leading dignitary in the Bahá'í Faith.

All of the work of St. Barbe Baker, including Men of the Trees, was inspired by his global and holistic perspective on forests and forestry. He viewed the planet as a living organism long before the Gaia theory, and saw the complex interactions within the forest as a mirror of the organization of all life. He saw forests as a vital organ within the whole self-regulating life-sustaining ecosphere. Removing too many trees disrupted the ecosystem, and planting trees could begin a cycle of regenerative recovery. His view of forests was simultaneously scientific, aesthetic and spiritual. His extensive writings shared the wonder, beauty and sacredness of nature while teaching ecological principles and respect. By integrating science and religion, he saw the potential for a mature planetary civilization based on ecological and spiritual principles.

Arthur Dahl

Further Reading
Gridley, Karen, ed. *Man of the Trees: Selected Writings of Richard St. Barbe Baker*. Willits, CA: Ecology Action, 1989.
Locke, Hugh C. "Richard St. Barbe Baker, O.B.E. 1889–1982." In *The Bahá'í World: An International Record*, Volume XVIII, 1979–1983. Haifa: Bahá'í World Centre, 1986, 802–5.

See also: Bahá'í Faith; Druids and Druidry; Green Man.

Men's Movement

In the wake of late twentieth-century feminist challenges to prevalent understandings and practices of gender in modern Western societies, a number of men within these societies undertook to fashion, individually and collectively, responses to feminism's wide-ranging critiques. Beginning in the 1970s, "movements" of these men arose, some in conscious alliance with contemporary feminist goals and methods (e.g., "profeminist men"), others in more or less hostile reaction against them (e.g., "men's rights" groups). Some of these "men's movements" linked their gender concerns with a spiritual or religious focus and a stated interest in relations with the natural world.

Of these latter groups, the most widely publicized exemplar was the "mythopoetic men's movement," which attained its greatest popularity in the decade or so surrounding the 1990 publication of its formative text, the poet Robert Bly's *Iron John: A Book about Men*, an extended exegesis of a fairytale collected by the Grimm brothers. As its name implies, this movement looked to myth and ritual as primary sources for the sort of self-transformation its adherents – primarily heterosexual Euro-American men of at least moderate means – sought. Through the medium of paid workshops and multi-day retreats (generally held in "wilderness" settings), Bly and other teachers advanced the theory that contemporary men in industrialized societies, having escaped stultifying 1950s-style masculinity only to become mired in a debilitating "softness" attributable, at least in part, to feminism, were in need of a distinctly masculine spirituality. And this, Bly argued, was available to them through connection with the "deep masculine," an archetypal force personified in the mythic figure of the "wildman." "What I'm suggesting," he wrote, ". . . is that every modern male has, lying at the bottom of his psyche, a large, primitive being covered with hair down to his feet. Making contact with this Wild Man is the step the Eighties male or the Nineties male has yet to take" (Bly 1990: 6). Bly was explicit about the religious dimensions of this quest for a fundamental masculinity: "Getting in touch with the wildman means religious life for a man in the broadest sense of the phrase" (in Thompson 1987: 180).

For men who embraced this path, the mythopoetic leaders offered a "practice" composed of guided interpretations of (primarily European) myths and folk-tales, participation in (primarily Native American- and African-derived) "initiation" rituals, and group-therapy-style personal sharing, all of which was intended to bring men into experiential contact with the primal "wildness" that Bly and his colleagues identified as essentially masculine. Undergirding the entire mythopoetic approach was a neo-Jungian belief in transhistorical, gender-appropriate archetypes (e.g., wildman, king, warrior) to be embraced on the way to healthy manhood in the late twentieth century. Through deeply felt, ritualized engagement with these designated "masculine" figures, within the context of an all-male group, participants hoped to be initiated into a more vital, self-assured gender identity.

As already noted, "wildness" was a term of value in the mythopoetic men's movement's vocabulary – both the wildness believed to be at the heart of "deep masculinity" and the wildness that characterized the natural settings in which much of the ritual work of initiation took place. Bly considered it necessary for men to reach beneath and beyond civilized society, into a wider realm of nature encompassing the more chaotic – yet more fruitful – elements of the human psyche: "The Wild Man is not opposed to civilization; but he's not completely contained by it either" (Bly 1990: 8). Accordingly, mythopoetic men's groups convened in outdoor settings at some remove from civilized "confinements"; there, they engaged in communal drumming sessions, sweatlodges, and other ritual practices designed to promote intragroup bonding and a feeling of connection with such "natural" manifestations of masculinity as "fierce" animals (e.g., bears, wolves). Although it is unclear whether such ritual use of "wild" settings ever went beyond a sort of nature-as-backdrop approach, to the point of actual connection and conscious interaction with a specific place, there was, among at least some men in the mythopoetic movement, a stated generalized concern for the well-being of the Earth: "Men have traditionally been the guardians of the earth . . . It's time for men to wake up and take this historical role again. We need to define the new warriors. Men are called to be warriors for the earth" (Craver 1996: 69). Here, characteristically, the call for male ecological responsibility was couched in terms of the traditional archetype of the warrior.

Frequently ridiculed by the mass media – the spectacle of middle-class white men taking to the woods to beat on drums and "get in touch with their inner wildman" provided an easy target – the mythopoetic men's movement attracted more substantive criticism from feminists, profeminist men, and Native American observers. Feminists condemned the reliance of Bly and others on an essentialist account of "natural" gender difference – the unproblematized (and inevitably prescriptive) linking of specifically delineated "masculine" and "feminine" modes of being with biologically male and female human beings, respectively, despite the wide cultural and individual variation displayed by actual men and women, boys and girls. Feminists and profeminist men objected no less strongly to this men's movement's indifference to – if not outright denial of – persisting power differentials between men and women. Noting the generally privileged constituency of this movement – "those [men] who quietly benefit from patriarchy without being militant in its defence" – sociologist R.W. Connell characterized it as a form of "masculinity therapy" whose consequence would be nothing more than "an adaptation of patriarchal structures through the *modernization* of masculinity" (Connell 1995: 210, 211; italics in original). Finally, Native American criticism of the mythopoetic men's movement focused especially on its arguably neo-colonialist appropriation of indigenous spiritual practices: ". . . to play at ritual potluck is to debase all spiritual traditions, voiding their internal coherence and leaving nothing usably sacrosanct as a cultural anchor for the peoples who conceived and developed them" (Churchill 1996: 371).

With the fading of this men's movement from cultural prominence, questions concerning existing and desirable relations among men, gender, religion, and nature remain to be explored. A number of men influenced by ecofeminism, including J. Michael Clark, Seth Mirsky, and John Rowan, have produced work in this area suggestive of alternative future possibilities for a men's movement.

Seth Mirsky

Further Reading

Bly, Robert. *Iron John: A Book about Men*. Reading, MA: Addison-Wesley, 1990.

Churchill, Ward. "Indians 'R' Us? Reflections on the 'Men's Movement.' " In Ward Churchill. *From a Native Son: Selected Essays in Indigenism, 1985–1995*. Boston: South End Press, 1996, 367–408.

Clark, J. Michael. *Beyond Our Ghettos: Gay Theology in Ecological Perspective*. Cleveland: Pilgrim Press, 1993.

Connell, R.W. *Masculinities*. Berkeley: University of California Press, 1995.

Craver, Forrest. "Finding Our Place on Earth Again: An Interview with John Stokes." In Cass Adams, ed. *The Soul Unearthed: Celebrating Wildness and Personal Renewal through Nature*. New York: Jeremy P. Tarcher/Putnam, 1996, 63–70.

Hagan, Kay Leigh, ed. *Women Respond to the Men's Movement: A Feminist Collection*. San Francisco: HarperSanFrancisco, 1992.

Krondorfer, Björn, ed. *Men's Bodies, Men's Gods: Male Identities in a (Post-) Christian Culture*. New York: New York University Press, 1996.

Mirsky, Seth. "Men and the Promise of Goddess Spirituality: Reflections along the Way." In Stephen B. Boyd, W. Merle Longwood and Mark W. Muesse, eds. *Redeeming Men: Religion and Masculinities*. Louisville: Westminster/John Knox Press, 1996, 197–208.

Rowan, John. *The Horned God: Feminism and Men as Wounding and Healing*. London: Routledge & Kegan Paul, 1987.

Thompson, Keith. "What Men Really Want: An Interview with Robert Bly." In Franklin Abbott, ed. *New Men, New Minds: Breaking Male Tradition*. Freedom, CA: Crossing Press, 1987, 166–81.

See also: Feminist Spirituality Movement; Green Man; Indigenous Religions and Cultural Borrowing; Jung, Carl Gustav; Plastic Medicine Men; Radical Environmentalism.

Merchant, Carolyn (1936–)

As one of the first prominent environmental historians, Carolyn Merchant weaves ecofeminist methodologies into her philosophical, ethical and historical inquiry. Her approach focuses on the interrelationships between productive and reproductive forces, in both human and nonhuman history, as well as the metaphoric connections between women and nature. Merchant integrates the history of science, ecology (which she views as a "subversive science") and cultural studies in order to present a holistic environmental history.

In 1980, Merchant published *The Death of Nature: Women, Ecology and the Scientific Revolution*. She begins this groundbreaking work with the statement: "The world we have lost was organic" (1980: 1). From there she examines the formation of a worldview and science focused on the domination of both nature and women. Thus, as "Western culture became increasingly mechanized in the 1600s, the female earth and the virgin earth spirit were subdued by the machine" (1980: 2). Focused initially on pastoral imagery, this shifting worldview assumed women and nature to be nurturing and passive, benevolent and willingly manipulated. Functionally, however, perceptions of nature as female did limit certain abusive practices (i.e., it was a "violation of Mother Earth" to engage in mining) (1980: 32). Merchant sees Bacon's publication *A New Atlantis*, with its "mechanistic utopia," as a symbolic of a turning point. Bacon writes from the perspective of paralleling mechanical devices to interrogate suspected witches and the mechanical torture of nature by science. His idea of scientific progress focused on control of nature as a way to remedy the "Fall" and return to paradise in the Garden of Eden. This is a metaphorical construct that Merchant continues to analyze in *Reinventing Eden: Women, Nature, and Narrative*.

Merchant proceeds to trace the influence of mechanistic modeling in society as a whole. She contends that the "brilliant achievement of mechanism" is its "reordering of reality around two fundamental constituents of human experience – order and power" (2003: 216). God becomes a clockmaker, the world becomes a machine comprised of inert particles. Order and power form the basis for patriarchal structures throughout society. By analyzing the whole, thus subverting the very societal model she addresses, Merchant's work helped shape the core issues of ecofeminist dialogue, including discussions of problematic essentialisms in connecting women and nature.

Merchant's contributions extend into analysis of, and participation in, environmental activism. Her examination of the contradictions between production, ecology and reproduction suggests that these dynamics have contributed to the global ecological crisis of the late twentieth century. She argues that policy shifts cannot respond adequately to the rapidly increasing ecological stress. Radical alternatives – spiritual, economic, scientific – are requisite. Merchant emphasizes the reality and promise of diverse visions and actions arising in different parts of the world (see *Radical Ecology*). She also helps to delineate various ecofeminisms, such as socialist, radical, liberal and cultural, thus reemphasizing the fact that myriad voices contribute to this complex movement.

Merchant received her doctorate in the History of Science from the University of Wisconsin, Madison and is Professor of Environmental History, Philosophy and Ethics at the University of California, Berkeley. She has written or edited seven books, published myriad articles and helped to establish the American Society for Environmental History.

Laura Hobgood-Oster

Further Reading

Merchant, Carolyn. *Reinventing Eden: Women, Nature, and Narrative.* New York: Routledge, 2003.

Merchant, Carolyn, ed. *Green Versus Gold: Sources in California's Environmental History.* Washington, D.C.: Island Press, 1998.

Merchant, Carolyn. *Earthcare: Women and the Environment.* New York: Routledge, 1996.

Merchant, Carolyn, ed. *Ecology: Key Concepts in Critical Theory.* Atlantic Highlands, NJ: Humanities Press, 1994.

Merchant, Carolyn. *Radical Ecology: The Search for a Livable World.* New York: Routledge, 1992.

Merchant, Carolyn. *Ecological Revolutions: Nature, Gender and Science in New England.* Chapel Hill, NC: University of North Carolina Press, 1989.

Merchant, Carolyn. *The Death of Nature: Women, Ecology and the Scientific Revolution.* San Francisco: Harper & Row, 1980.

See also: Descartes, René, and the Problem of Cartesian Dualism; Dualism; Ecofeminism; Eden and Other Gardens; Fall, The; Feminist Spirituality Movement; Holism; Radical Environmentalism; Women and Animals.

Merwin, W.S. (William Stanley) (1927–)

In an early poem, "The Wilderness," from *Green with Beasts* (1956), the American poet W.S. Merwin wrote:

> Remoteness is its own secret. Not holiness,
> Though, nor the huge spirit miraculously avoiding
> The way's dissemblings . . . (Merwin 1988a: 33).

By way of example, these lines indicate how carefully Merwin's poetry approaches the relation between religion and nature. Separating himself from claims that God resides in nature, through his poems Merwin pursues personal religiosity animated by the longing for a revelation of self and a sense of totality. Yet Merwin's poetry hinges on the idea that at best one can perceive only discrete parts of physical reality. This view of the person–nature relationship places Merwin's poetry in proximity to the tradition of Henry David Thoreau, especially in its fascination with the details of careful observation.

While Merwin's poetry renders nature as fragments – like hands or feet, or in his later poetry the particulars of the biological world – it also represents an intense awareness of a kind of absence run through with meaning. And where there is absence there is also a sense of loss. In this way, Merwin's poetry suggests a relationship to nature that is elegiac, yet in a relative sense, static, asserting that wherever we are, we are surrounded by where we are not. This sort of absence acquires value to the extent that it is sought out, yet remains unknown.

Frequently, it is Merwin's careful rendering of the natural cycles of life and death that leads toward self-discovery. In this sense, Merwin's poetic vision places substantial attention on autobiography. He grew up as the son of a Presbyterian minister, and in later life he studied Zen Buddhism. In the books that follow *The Lice* (1967), the sense of the continuity of life becomes increasingly expansive and considerably less anthropocentric, as the poems represent life in more fundamentally biological terms. Later, the short poems of *Finding the Islands* (1982) represent a union of aesthetic and spiritual experience similar to that found in early haiku writers like Bashō.

Parallel to their focus on natural cycles, some of Merwin's poems harshly render humankind's urge to plunder nature, thus creating discontinuity in the form of ecological disaster. Reflecting a keen awareness of the influence both Linnaeus and Charles Darwin had on twentieth-century attitudes toward the natural world, Merwin's poetry presents, especially from *The Lice* onward, a fine-tuned ecopoetic sensibility that becomes increasingly pervasive in his poetry. In *The Rain in the Trees* (1988) Merwin's ecopoetics reached a high point at which he combined the rhetoric of absence that fueled his early writing with an elegiac sensibility associated with environmental degradation. At one point, he asserted that nature is wiser than humans: "I will have to decipher the language of the insects" (1988b: 50). Through the 1990s, Merwin's poetry focused on horticultural and autobiographical matters, allowing the poems to continue exploring the border area that links the world of nature to the mystery of human religious experience.

James Kraus

Further Reading

Merwin, W.S. *Selected Poems.* New York: Atheneum, 1988a.

Merwin, W.S. *The Rain in the Trees.* New York: Atheneum, 1988b.

See also: Autobiography.

Mesoamerican Deities

Mesoamerican deities wield natural powers, live in the natural world, and follow natural processes. Moreover, while deities control natural forces, natural entities control deified forces. All deities embody the powers of various natural forces such as rain, lightning, wind, growth, death and decay that allow them to interact with and affect other beings. Likewise, natural entities such as celestial objects, mountains, streams, plants, animals, and humans can embody powers that give them life, deify them, allowing them to interact with and affect other beings. Because all these beings – deities with natural powers and deified natural entities – are considered living, they are born into actual places within which they live. There they grow and transform as they eat and defecate, and willfully act according to their particular capacities in ways that impinge on others' lives. Almost all also live for appropriate lifespans and then die, their bodies becoming food for others. Biologically natural metaphors involving processes of creation and destruction that continually transform living beings from birth until death's beyond govern much of Mesoamerican theological thinking.

Mesoamerica stretches roughly from what is now northern Mexico into Nicaragua. Its long history began with hunter-gatherers in the Paleoindian era (ca. 25,000–7000 B.C.E.). This period was followed by six more: the Archaic (ca. 7000–2000 B.C.E.); the Preclassic (ca. 2000 B.C.E.–250 C.E.); the Classic (ca. 250–1000); the Postclassic (ca. 1000–1521); the era of Spanish Conquest and Colonialism (ca. 1521–1808); and the era of Independence to the present (beginning ca. 1808). The Archaic was marked by the slow development of agriculture and more settled life. By the Preclassic, the first urban centers had developed. While many of these pre-Conquest cities claimed no more than 30,000–40,000 inhabitants, some contained very large populations. Tenochtitlan (ca. 1350–1521), the center of the Aztec (more properly Mexica) domain, held approximately 250,000 inhabitants within its island borders; around one million more lived in villages and other urban centers throughout the Valley of Mexico where Tenochtitlan was located (Mexico City's several million inhabitants now sit on Tenochtitlan's remains). Besides countless deified beings with which each center's inhabitants interacted, a patron deity governed each city, giving it life and strength, thereby creating a distinctive ritual and pilgrimage center. Each center constituted a complex, stratified yet flexible society of many groups ranging from governing elite, to religious professionals, warriors, traders, educators, healers, craftspeople, and farmers. Moreover, these urban centers often competed for power creating a situation of shifting alliances among them.

Four major cultural areas dominated Mesoamerica from early pre-Conquest times: the Olmec (ca. 2250–300 B.C.E.); Oaxaca (ca. 1400 B.C.E.–present); the Mexican highland peoples (ca. 1200 B.C.E.–present); and the Maya (ca. 1400 B.C.E.–present). Two of these, the Olmec and Mexican highland peoples, at times wielded great influence and sometimes considerable direct power over extensive geographic expanses. The other two, the Maya and those living in Oaxaca, have tended toward more regional forms of influence; nevertheless, their contributions to Mesoamerican life in general have proven considerable through time. While all four areas share key cultural traits, each also claims its own characteristics and distinctive spins on those traits.

The Spanish Conquest (1521) brought major changes to Mesoamerica on all fronts from political to social. Nevertheless, all pre-Conquest forms of life did not simply disappear, for the conquest was not complete on any level, including the spiritual. Religious conversions to Catholicism occurred so rapidly and often under such coercive conditions that superficiality proved inevitable. Long periods of isolation for many indigenous peasants also weakened the Church's oversight.

As a result, often the converts understood their new religion in idiosyncratic ways having little to do with what the Church fathers thought they were teaching them. The indigenous folk likely saw Jesus as the victor over their now defeated patron deities; and because in pre-Conquest times patron deities often returned to power as competing cities shifted their alliances, the same expectation sometimes existed after the Conquest. Throughout the following centuries, patron deities in diverse, imaginative forms – pre- and post-Conquest gods, indigenous and Christian, or blends thereof – rose to lead various peasant groups in rebellion against an often oppressive governing elite. Everyone, from the Feathered Serpent God and the long-dead Maya leader Can Ek to the Virgin Mother Guadalupe, has led revolts in the last 500 years. Moreover, today many earthly and celestial topographies have come to house either or both local deities and saints (some of whom Rome has never heard of); the Devil has set up housekeeping in the wet underground; many a cook blesses the four quarters of the cosmos as she grills the day's first tortilla; and one may sacrifice a chicken following ancient traditions to celebrate Christian communion. Some view indigenous and Christian traditions as mutually contradictory, others as one unified tradition. Through both continuity and invention, pre-Conquest theological conceptions have remained alive and well throughout Mesoamerica's long history up to the present.

Today as before, deities' lives and personalities often closely reflect the particular environment within which they dwell. Mesoamerica enjoys a diverse geography and climate. This ranges from deserts to tropical and mountainous regions, which boast both active and inactive volcanoes. However, in spite of its jungles and rainforests, from the Archaic era on, Mesoamerica has lived with a mostly semi-arid climate, making water scarce. By the Archaic, two major seasons had come to dominate the year: a rainy period from roughly June–October; and a dry one from November–May. Moreover, even in the tropical zones during the rainy season, water comes at a premium because much of the area rests on a limestone base. Water tends to disappear quickly beneath the surface through the porous stone, lacing the area with sink-holes, caves, and underground rivers; while the surface remains largely dry, the underground retains most of the water.

It makes sense that many deities and deified natural entities concern themselves with water and related natural forces. Water is needed for agriculture, and corn – one of the most ancient and thirsty crops – forms a basic metaphor for human sustenance. Beings must drink and eat to sustain life; and since humans drink water and eat corn, these two natural entities have come to symbolize life itself. For some nonhuman beings, the blood and flesh of humans and other animals is the symbolic life-sustaining equivalent of water and corn for humans. For centuries, sacrifice has symbolized a natural feeding exchange in which beings ate and fed each other. Ritual sacrifice formed the heart of pre-Conquest religious practice; and although humans no longer serve as offerings, it continues today in altered, often Christian forms.

Local environments also form symbolic, deified celestial and earthly topographies. Each town marks space beginning with its center: in pre-Conquest days, where the temple stood; today, where the church or town plaza stands. From there, the four cardinal directions are marked, each supported by a cosmic tree, mountain, bird, rain god, saint, or any combination thereof. The center rests on Earth's Surface, which takes the form of a four petaled flower, one petal for each direction. People, animals, and plants live on dry Earth's Surface, which some myths describe as the back of a great monster. The Olmec said this monster was a giant fish floating in the sea, the Mexica described it as a crocodilian beast whom Quetzalcoatl and Tezcatlipoca twisted in two. One half became the sky, the other created plants, flowers, trees, springs, caves, mountains and valleys. But the beast was so hurt by her destruction that she cried out, and would not be quieted unless fed human hearts as a debt-payment for her own sacrifice.

In many towns, actual mountains mark the cardinal directions, and real caves, springs, or underground rivers mark entrances to the cavernous Underworld lying beneath Earth's Surface. The mountains at the four corners, and sometimes the center, are viewed as deified pots whose underworld innards contain water and seeds that produce corn and other edible plants. The rain gods guard these giant pots, thunderously striking them open with their lightning bolts when it comes time to release rain. But, not all moisture is good. An Oaxacan story says that one of these mountain-pots contained good flower-producing rain; but a second, volcanic fiery rain; a third, fungus-producing rain; a fourth, wind-storm rain; and a fifth, icy flint-blade rain. For the Mexica, one pot brought drought.

Below in the Underground, everything is opposite from life on Earth's Surface. Below it is wet, above it is dry; below things point downward, above things point upward toward the sky. The Underworld beings, delightful characters bearing names like Lord and Lady of Death (Mexica), or Pus and Jaundice Masters, Bone and Skull Scepters, or Bloody Teeth and Bloody Claws (K'iché Maya), eat rotting and dead things such as tortillas of fungi, beans of fly larvae, and corn paste of decayed human flesh. The Panajachel Maya said that, if one partook of such pseudo-human food, one would be forced to remain there forever. They also said that the Devil lived there and ate food made of blood collected by his vampire bat cook. Because everyone does at least some bad things during life, upon death one spends time there before going to heaven; rich landowners who treated their workers poorly, however, were so bad they never got out. Nevertheless, no matter how forbidding the Underworld is, life cannot live without its destructive, corruptive forces. Corn grows on Earth's Surface, but pushes its roots into the Underworld to feed on its watery, decaying excrement. And the Sun and all other celestial objects move through its underground passages on a daily basis. When the Sun rises from the beast's bowels at dawn, the Moon is just entering its mouth; and when it is day above, it is night below.

The Sky soars above Earth's Surface, and like the Underworld it too is a watery realm. Water completely surrounds the Mesoamerican cosmos, trapping the dry air bubble in which people live on Earth's Surface. The Sky forms the liquid walls of a great house, while Earth's Surface serves as both a floor of this house and that of the upside-down Underworld. Like Earth's Surface and the Underworld, the Sky is divided into quadrants. The Mexica said that Quetzalcoatl and Tezcatlipoca met at the celestial crossroads to create the cosmos, and the K'iché say that four roads move out from the center: a red road moves east; a black, north; a white, west; and a yellow, south. The colonial Yucatec Maya said that four gods called the Bacabs planted the four cosmic trees holding up the Sky. Others say that the Sky moves up seven steps like a pyramid, and six down; this motion is reversed as one moves into the Underworld, seven steps down and six up.

But unlike the Underworld, living people do not enter the Sky, perhaps because they cannot fly. Nonhuman beings and dead ancestors pass along the Sky's watery passages like boaters navigating a great river. The sun, moon and stars all follow the Sky's particular currents; and birds fly through the air bubble above Earth's Surface to the Sky, sometimes also swooping into the Underworld through its cave-doors. Some also say that dead ancestors move to the Sky becoming stars, clouds, birds, or butterflies. Once the Panajachel have paid for their sins by doing time working for the Devil in the Underworld, they go as stars to a great heavenly city to live with God the Sun, all the apostles, the saints and their dead ancestors. Moreover, it is God who makes it rain by rippling his hand over the Sky's watery surface; to make storms, God wildly splashes the water.

Many tell tales about animals and their various antics. Opossums – those odd little holdovers from the Cenozoic era – become the protagonists in many a creation story. Opossum is often said to have brought fire, having stolen it from the old fire-god or the first people to have discovered it. Today's Huichol tell how once upon a time Opossum was cold and asked if she could spend the night near the only fire around. Although the fire's owners did not trust her, they agreed. In the morning when she was ready to leave, they searched her, but did not find the little coal she had tucked into her pouch. When they discovered a coal was missing, they pursued her, caught her, and beat her into many pieces, leaving her for dead. But Opossums "play possum," and can take a great deal of physical abuse. When they had left, she regained consciousness, and began thinking about the problem. She put all her pieces back in place: her skin, hair, sandals, hands, top of her head, brains, everything. Then she thought, "My goodness! Suppose they grabbed that little piece I hid in my pocket!" But looking into her pouch, she found it still there. Taking it, she began to blow it gently into life – wiwiwiwiwiwi. This is the reason the Huichol never eat opossums; without her, they would never have had fire.

And so stories go on, spinning new-old tales about deities' natural powers and deified natural entities. A long creative, continuity can be traced to the earliest of times; and root metaphors speaking of creation from destruction and natural forces flow through most of these tales. The Earth Monster eats the Sun each evening, only to emit it out in the morning; things growing on Earth's Surface eat the Underworld's moist decay, and death's living beyond moves through both the Underworld and the Sky. Even fire comes from a clever little creature who reconstituted herself after having been destroyed. If one observes natural processes closely, all this comes clearer. Deities control such forces as water, wind, and death, and deified natural entities hold water in their innards, support the sky, and steal fire. And so life goes on, and on, and on.

Kay A. Read

Further Reading
Friedel, David, Linda Schele and Joy Parker. *Maya Cosmos: Three Thousand Years on the Shaman's Path.* New York: William Morrow, 1993.
Joralemon, Peter David. "In Search of the Olmec Cosmos: Reconstructing the World View of Mexico's First Civilization." In Elizabeth P. Benson and Beatriz de la Fuente, eds. *Olmec Art of Ancient Mexico.* Washington, D.C.: National Gallery of Art, 1996, 51–9.
López-Austin, Alfredo. *The Myths of the Opossum: Pathways to Mesoamerican Mythology.* Bernard Ortiz de Montellano and Thelma Ortiz de Montellano, trs. Albuquerque: University of New Mexico Press, 1993.
Popul Vuh: The Definitive Edition of the Mayan Book of the Dawn of Life and the Glories of Gods and Kings. Dennis Tedlock, tr. New York: Simon & Schuster, 1985.
Read, Kay Almere and Jason J. González. *Handbook of Mesoamerican Mythology.* Santa Barbara, CA: ABC-CLIO, 2000.
Sahagún, Fray Bernardino de. *The Florentine Codex: A General History of the Things of New Spain.* Arthur J. O. Anderson and Charles E. Dibble, trs. Monographs of the School of American Research, No. 14. Santa Fe & Salt Lake City: School of American Research, University of Utah Press, 1953–1982.

See also: Aztec Religion – Pre-Colombian; Cihuacoatl – Aztec Snakewoman; Maya Religion (Central America); Maya Spirituality (Guatemala Highlands); Mesoamerican Sacrifice; Virgin of Guadalupe.

Mesoamerican Sacrifice

Ancient Mesoamerican sacrifice nourished the world's beings, thereby supporting life and growth. A natural, biological metaphor shaped sacrifice. To live, one must eat; and to eat one must kill something, which also must kill to eat to live. Moreover, ancient Mesoamericans considered almost all things to be living. Hence, ritual sacrifice formed a feeding exchange among various living beings of the cosmos including gods, humans, animals, plants, celestial objects like the sun, and even earthly entities like mountains and streams. All these living entities both killed to eat and died to feed other beings. Performing a sacrificial ritual meant one was paying one's debt to the various forces in the universe; since various beings of the cosmos sacrificed themselves so one might eat, one needed to return the favor by feeding them. No free lunch existed.

Moreover, this natural sacrificial eating exchange seems to have been symbolically linked with another natural metaphor involving transformative cycles of creation and destruction. When one is born, one can do two things: eat and defecate. As one eats and defecates, one grows and transforms from a baby into a child, an adolescent, an adult with children of one's own, a mature person, an elder, and finally one dies. To sustain one's life between birth and death, one eats corn, which also moves through a natural life cycle. One consumes corn that has matured in the fields, and then one defecates the digested corn back in the fields to fertilize more new corn plants. The corn feeds people, and people feed corn. Finally, at death one's body disintegrates, becoming the natural food of small insects and creatures living in the underworld. Such naturally creative-destructive, transformative cycles of birth, eating, defecation, feeding, growth and death continually shaped all existence.

While most are aware that the Aztecs (ca. 1350–1521) performed human sacrificial rituals, such sacrifice actually claims a long history in Mesoamerica. Splintered bones found in refuse deposits in the Preclassic Olmec site of San Lorenzo, Veracruz (ca. 1200–900 B.C.E.) suggest cannibal practices, and similar bone deposits have appeared at Teotihuacan in the Valley of Mexico (ca. 400–600). The Preclassic Maya site of Cuello (Belize, ca. 400 B.C.E.–250 C.E.) boasts a burial with the sacrificial remains of 32 young men of warrior age in its main plaza. Cannibalism and war both have long histories as forms of sacrifice. Cannibalism makes sense, for if sacrifice constitutes an exchange, then cannibalism is no more than the human end of that eating exchange. And if sacrifice demands that something be caught and killed in order to eat it, then war becomes one of the ways in which meals are hunted, caught and killed. Still not all sacrifice involved human comestibles, or war.

Sacrificial rites could be extraordinarily varied, and most sacrifices were not even human. A huge variety of sacrificial meals were offered up using just about anything edible. Many considered the first tortilla of the day a sacrificial meal. Other offerings could include quail, fish, jaguars, crocodiles, snakes, salamanders, and amaranth cakes. Ritual bloodletting was one of the most common forms; small amounts of blood were offered on numerous ceremonial occasions, from family naming ceremonies of new-born Aztec babies to the high state ceremonies of Maya rulers.

Sacrificial techniques were equally varied. Extreme forms of human sacrifice included heart extraction, decapitation, drowning, and shooting with arrows or poison darts. Rituals involved both willing and unwilling participants, native and foreign born, from all segments of society, both male and female and of all ages. Who or what became the offering depended on who required sustenance at any particular moment. Hence, sacrificial rituals were performed for diverse reasons. Large state sacrifices usually were associated with war and political hegemony, the need to sustain the state. But, other sacrifices were associated with agricultural cycles; offered to celestial recipients such as the sun, moon and stars; or more earthly foci such as the earth monster, or water deities taking the forms of mountains, or streams.

Some have claimed that sacrifice's origins rest in a protein deficiency resulting from a lack of domesticated animals. But this theory cannot account for the protein-rich diet already available to most Mesoamericans. They ate just about anything that walked, crawled, flew or swam; and studies now indicate that the natural Mesoamerican diet was a good one. Moreover, in Aztec times, very little of the sacrificial offerings were eaten, and that by only a few people who did not really need it at a time of year when food was most plentiful. Therefore, most scholars now accept that sacrifice's purpose was to sustain various cosmic beings, not to make up for a nutritional deficiency.

With the Spanish Conquest (1521), a new form of sacrifice appeared in Mesoamerica: the one-time sacrifice of Jesus Christ. Many Spanish found human sacrifice an abomination. The Eucharistic celebration of Christ's own last supper and sacrifice substituted bread and wine for human flesh and blood; it did not require actually killing anyone. Other forms of sacrifice proved more acceptable to the conquerors. Penitential practices involving fasting and offerings of food, birds and animals meshed more easily with medieval European practices. For their part, Mesoamericans quickly blended Christian sacrificial practices with their own traditions. Today, the sacrifice of chickens and other animal and plant comestibles in Christian ceremonies is quite common; and many faithful women still offer a meal's first tortilla to the four quarters of the cosmos. Christian rituals also continue to celebrate various points of life's transitions; agricultural cycles, birth, coming of age, and death all are commemorated now with a Christian sacrificial communion.

Kay A. Read

Further Reading
Durán, Fray Diego. *Book of the Gods and Rites and the Ancient Calendar*. Doris Heyden and Fernando Horcasitas, trs. Norman, OK: University of Oklahoma Press, 1971.
Landa, Diego de. *Yucatan Before and After the Conquest* (Relación De Las Cosas De Yucatán). William Gates, tr. New York: Dover Publications, 1978.
Ortiz de Montellano, Bernard R. *Aztec Medicine, Health, and Nutrition*. New Brunswick: Rutgers University Press, 1990.
Popul Vuh: The Definitive Edition of the Mayan Book of the Dawn of Life and the Glories of Gods and Kings. Dennis Tedlock, tr. New York: Simon & Schuster, 1985.
Read, Kay A. *Time and Sacrifice in the Aztec Cosmos*. Bloomington: Indiana University Press, 1998.
Sahagún, Fray Bernardino de. *The Florentine Codex: A General History of the Things of New Spain*. Arthur J. O. Anderson and Charles E. Dibble, trs. Monographs of the School of American Research, No. 14. Sante Fe, Salt Lake City: School of American Research, University of Utah Press, 1953–1982.

See also: Maya Religion (Central America); Maya Spirituality (Guatemala Highlands); Maya Spirituality and Conservation (Western Highlands, Guatemala); Mayan Catholicism; Mayan Protestantism; Mesoamerican Deities.

Mesopotamia – Ancient to 2000 B.C.E.

The development of a complex set of beliefs and practices over the millennia in Mesopotamia, the land between the two great rivers of the Euphrates and the Tigris, seems to have had as its primary aim the explanation, understanding and control of this environment by humans. The early evidence for any kind of ritual or "religious" behaviour is extremely scanty. There is no evidence at all from south Mesopotamia in the Paleolithic or pre-pottery-using Neolithic phases as the area seems to have been uninhabited. A very limited number of finds have, however, been made in the north of the region which date to the eighth/seventh millennia and which seem to point to the importance of wild animals and birds to the hunter-gatherers of the period. Wing bones from the skeletons of huge birds of prey have been found at a site called Zawi Chemi Shanidar piled together in such a way as to raise the possibility that the wings may originally have been specially preserved. The wing bones are associated with the skulls of wild sheep or goats. The excavator suggested that both were deliberately selected and may have been used to adorn the participants in rituals whose nature is unknown, but which may have been intended to placate the forces of nature and ensure the survival of the group. The importance of birds of prey and other wild animals to the hunter-gatherers who were the first people to live in the region is supported by remarkable new finds from Turkey of sculpted pillars showing these creatures in low relief at sites such as Nevali Çori in Eastern Turkey. In north Mesopotamia some remarkable small sculptures showing the heads of raptors from Nemrik, an early Neolithic site in northern Iraq, also point in the same direction. There are no traces of ritual buildings or of sacred artifacts during this early period, but the deliberate interment of human beings, sometimes with a few grave goods, may already indicate a belief in an afterlife.

By the sixth millennium B.C.E., when agriculture was well established in north Mesopotamia, we begin to find representations of men and women, though we do not know if these were gods or men. In some cultures at least, such as the so-called Halaf culture, their faces seem to be of little significance, and are often represented merely by blobs of clay. Such figurines are usually female and show women with huge thighs and a marked accumulation of fat on the buttocks. It can be suggested that they represent a generic concept of fertility rather than individuals. The fertility of animals and crops was of paramount importance to these early farmers while children provided useful additions to the workforce. In contrast to this, paintings on contemporary Samarra pottery from further south show heavily scarified faces, while the bodies are not shown. It is tempting to suggest that the scars represent group identifiers as in many traditional societies today, although of course, there could be other explanations. If this is the case then these are the first realistic representations of the human face in Mesopotamia. Remarkable human figurines in alabaster of similar date have been found in graves at the site of a fortified village near Baghdad called Tell es Sawwan, but their purpose is again unknown.

There are a range of burial rites from these early periods, which include cremation and burial of all or part of the body, probably pointing to a range of beliefs among the different groups in society, all concerned in their different ways with the proper disposal of the dead.

The evolving and transitional nature of beliefs at this time is striking. It is illustrated in south Mesopotamia by a number of human figurines with strange lizard-like heads modeled from clay. These figures are usually, but not exclusively female, some suckle babies, while one male figure carries what looks like a scepter. They date to the late sixth/early fifth millennium B.C.E. in the so-called Ubaid period and are found widely distributed in domestic settings as well as in graves. It is by no means certain that they represent supernatural beings, but such composite creatures could in no way be described as naturalistic representations and we may ask if they represent an intermediate step in the anthropomorphizing of natural forces, a process which was complete by the fourth millennium. It is also in the Ubaid period that the first cult buildings or temples appear in southern Iraq. Religious belief seems to be crystallizing and the divinities are represented as at least partially human for the first time. Burial rites also become more standardized and inhumation becomes the norm.

These developments coincide with the moment when human beings were first able to exert a measure of control over the forces of nature by the introduction of agriculture itself, and then of simple irrigation and storage techniques which gave them a small measure of control over the resources on which they depended for survival. As the impersonal natural forces of sun, wind, and storm, which had held early hunter-gatherers to ransom, became less all-powerful it is suggested that such forces began to appear more comprehensible and so could, for the first time, be visualized in human form. Once in human form it was possible, by analogy, to understand them better and to suggest ways in which they might be manipulated in order to maintain their favor, thus ensuring survival. The struggle by humans to control their environment had another weapon in its armory.

By the late fourth/early third millennium B.C.E. a fully urban civilization with irrigation systems and centralized storage of agricultural produce had emerged in the potentially fertile southern plains of Mesopotamia, the area which today lies between Baghdad and the head of the Arabian Gulf. People exerted more control over their environment than ever before, although it was recognized that this control was extremely tenuous. The humanization of natural forces continued and for the first time we have texts in the ancient cuneiform script, which allow us to reconstruct the names and personalities of the major deities. Archeology also enables us to rebuild their temples and reconstruct some of the rites that took place in them. The major deities represent natural forces or observed features in the landscape. Initially they have Sumerian names as most of the population seems to have spoken this language, then many acquired Semitic ones as the linguistic composition of the population changed. The great gods include Anu the sky, Shamash the sun, Sin/Nannar the moon, Enlil the air/wind; all powerful forces in a flat desert landscape where temperatures can reach 50 degrees centigrade in high summer. It is no surprise in this sort of landscape that the god seen as the particular friend of humanity is the god of sweet water, Ea/Enki, a cunning and wise god who saves humankind from a great flood in a story that is the precursor of the biblical story of Noah. (It is curious that the great rivers on which the region depended for survival do not seem to have been deified.) Among the goddesses Ninhursag represented fruitfulness and Inanna/Ishtar was the capricious goddess of sexual love and of war. Many other less important deities represented other aspects of the natural world and the new skills and crafts such as writing and metallurgy. Anu, the sky god, ruled them all and humankind was created to look after the pantheon as the servants of often extremely demanding and irrational masters.

The composition of the pantheon was extremely flexible, reflecting perhaps the fact that there are few geographical boundaries in Mesopotamia so that new peoples often infiltrated the great plains. Their gods were frequently either added to the existing roll call or amalgamated with older deities. The Semitic Ishtar is amalgamated with her Sumerian predecessor Inanna, while Sumerian Anu becomes of less and less significance during the third millennium and Marduk the god of Babylon rises up the hierarchy to rule the gods, just as his city comes to dominate the political scene. With the advent of city states, politics as well as the environment began to play a role in religious thought.

A cosmology can be reconstructed from texts of the second millennium B.C.E., which also tells us how the ancient Mesopotamians saw their world. The gods inhabited the heavens, which were separated from Earth by the air. The Earth itself was flat and floated on a sea of sweet water. Heaven and Earth were formed from the corpse of a female monster called Tiamat, who had been slaughtered in mortal combat by Marduk. Each deity was responsible for a particular city and its prosperity depended on the goodwill of that god and on his or her advocacy in the assembly of the great gods where major decisions were taken about the future of humankind. From this it followed that the first duty of every person was to care for the god or goddess of his or her city in order to retain their goodwill. This duty fell most heavily on the priests who were charged with the day-to-day business of feeding, clothing and entertaining the deity in his temple or palace.

Rulers were chosen by the gods and were often said to have been suckled by goddesses, or like the great hero Gilgamesh, to be semi-divine themselves. Their main task was to oversee all the needs of their patron deity, building new temples when instructed to do so, providing lavish gifts, dedicating booty after a successful campaign, and where appropriate acting as the husband of the goddess in a sacred marriage, so ensuring the fertility of the land. Where the patron deity was male a high priestess apparently fulfilled this duty. Agriculture was the foundation of the region's prosperity so that the link between environment and religion remained fundamental. Kingship was regularly withdrawn by the gods from one city and passed to another. Divine goodwill might be withdrawn for ritual infringements or because of neglect or other wrongdoing.

The underworld seems to have been a mirror image of the heavens; it was a gray, bleak place below the ground ruled by a ferocious queen called Erishkigal, a sister of Ishtar/Inanna who had at her command a court of demons and other officials who carried out her bidding as Anu did in heaven. The dead had little comfort and little to look forward to unless they had a large surviving family who would make offerings of food and drink to them in perpetuity.

We have already noted that each god had his or her own city in which s/he was thought to live, residing like the earthly ruler in his/her own temple or palace often accompanied by other members of the divine family and with a fully staffed court of officials. Gods were fed, clothed and entertained by their priests as if they had been human kings or queens. The buildings in which these ceremonies took place were of different plans and different sizes, ranging from the great central temples with adjacent stepped ziggurats, to small neighborhood chapels. They all have a number of features in common whatever their size; access was limited, the statue of the living god on his or her altar was shielded from the eyes of all but a few priests and senior officials, while major festivals were celebrated in the courtyard of the shrine so that ordinary people might participate in a limited manner. Initially these patron divinities were thought to own all the land and all the people of their city. The temple was the economic hub of the settlement too and the manufacturing industries, trade and agriculture were all centered in it. It was also the administrative center of the city with judicial and welfare functions. It is important to realize that the people of Mesopotamia made no distinction between religious and secular, between church and state; society was seen as a single entity, a concept perhaps closer to that of Islam than of Christianity.

By the end of the third millennium B.C.E. the initially simple agricultural technology of the region had developed into a centralized, state-run system of considerable sophistication, which gave people a far greater degree of control over their environment than ever before, although natural forces could still wreak havoc. Other factors now come into play in the evolution of religious thought, notably changes in the political environment, which saw the first territorial state emerge in the region.

The same period saw another major change in the political environment with the establishment of a dynasty of rulers in the city of Agade and, slightly later, in the ancient southern city of Ur, who declared themselves divine. To bolster their position these self-proclaimed divinities seem to have made a deliberate attempt to transfer power into their own hands at the expense of the old temple institutions thus undermining the power of the priesthood. Changes in the plans of temples, the appearance of shrines in private houses and the occurrence of large numbers of quasi-religious clay plaques in domestic contexts all seem to suggest this. It seems that men and women no longer needed the services of a priest to make an approach to the gods, but did so through the mediation of a personal god or "guardian angel" who becomes of increasing importance. The scene of a man or woman being introduced into the presence of one of the great gods by such a personal god is the most common theme of the glyptic art of the period.

This increasing control over the environment, though far from complete, seems to have made the gods appear less terrifying and less capricious, although their goodwill was never assumed. The texts of the period speak of an assembly of the gods at which major issues were discussed and decisions taken. Perhaps it is this relative rationality among the gods that led to the emergence of the first indications of a concept of a rational judgment of the individual according to his deserts by the gods after death. By extension the notion emerged of personal responsibility among men and women for their actions. It was shortly after this that the texts began to speak of the dilemma presented by the harsh treatment, on occasion, of the so-called just person by the gods, a dilemma exemplified by the story of Job in the Old Testament.

In the course of around four thousand years the people of ancient Mesopotamia seem to have moved from the worship of untamed natural forces to a state-sponsored religion where each person had a personal god or goddess who guarded and guided them through life, procuring favours from the great gods and protecting them from illness and other forms of bad luck. In addition, each individual was increasingly seen as responsible for their own actions to a divine judge whose decision would decide their fate in the afterlife. These major intellectual developments can be correlated with changes in the relationship between humans and their physical and political environment. As human beings' control of the natural forces, which had originally determined their survival or death, improved, so human beings' perception of the nature of those forces changed. First they were given human forms and human characteristics, but were seen as capricious and unpredictable; gradually they were seen as more rational; and the pantheon might be said to have begun to grow up by about 2000 B.C.E.

Harriet Crawford

Further Reading

Black, Jeremy and A. Green. *Gods, Demons and Symbols of Ancient Mesopotamia.* London: British Museum Publications, 1992.

Cauvin, Jean and Trevor Watkins, trs. *The Birth of the Gods and the Origins of Agriculture.* Cambridge: Cambridge University Press, 2000.

Frankfort, Henri. *Kingship and the Gods.* Chicago: University of Chicago, 1948.

George, Andrew. *The Epic of Gilgamesh.* New York: Penguin, 2000.

Jacobsen, Thorkild. *Treasures of Darkness.* New Haven: Yale, 1976.

See also: Creation Myths of the Ancient World; Creation Story in the Hebrew Bible; Egypt – Ancient; Greece – Classical; Roman Natural Religion.

Michell, John (1933–)

John Michell is a prolific British writer and artist concerned with what he sees as the recovery and further elaboration of sacred principles of living. He combines interests in, for example, architecture, art, astrology, geomancy, geometry, gematria, music, and numerology with a wide engagement of archeological and historical literature and sites. This is even more impressive when one notes that Michell's knowledge of geomancy includes traditions and practices originating not only in China (e.g., Fengshui), but also in Europe and elsewhere. Furthermore, his writings arise from and provoke a passionate participation in the present realities and future possibilities of the world. When he writes about Jerusalem, for example, he is deeply concerned not only with ancient architecture, geometry and history, but with something far more than a Middle-East peace settlement. The words "sacred" and "harmony" are leitmotivs in all he has written about humanity, the world and the cosmos.

Since its first publication in 1967, his book *The View Over Atlantis* has had a significant impact on the study and practise of "Earth Mysteries." Others might map lines (leys) across landscapes and argue about UFOs, ancient civilizations, and Earth energies. Michell proffers a glorious vision of a global civilization that once tapped some enormous but subtle energy and channelled it through a vast astronomically and artistically perfect system to enhance harmony and beauty. The discovery of alignments and the understanding of ancient megalithic sites, for example, are related to a greater purpose than the production of a gazetteer of obscure facts. Michell encourages people to "bring human ways into harmony" with the place and the world in which they live. Science and imagination combine in underscoring a visionary but practical encounter with a nature that is itself the manifestation of perfect and balanced proportions.

His many publications are hard to summarize briefly. But if *View over Atlantis* is about Earth Mysteries, *Twelve Tribe Nations* concerns ideal social structures, *Euphonics* is a sonic and musical primer, *Traveller's Guide to Sacred England* is a walking tour guide, *The Earth Spirit* catalogs artistic representations of Earth energies, and his many newspaper and internet articles discuss popular theories about a sacred but damaged world. Even a full list of Michell's publications along these lines would fail to do them or their author justice any more than would describing Michell as a popularizer of Platonic and Pythagorean theories.

Michell's combination of precise measurement, careful argument, impassioned advocacy, and confident eccentricity have probably won him as many admirers as they have lost him credibility in various academic circles. Conversely, perhaps, his advocacy of monarchy and priestly authority may be ignored by those enchanted by the geometrically and artistically pleasing structures he adduces in diverse landscapes and localities. However, a better test of the appeal of Michell's work is that it has influenced both mystics and eco-activists, romantics and pragmatists. It can perhaps be summed up as a continuing quest for the reconciliation of the intrinsic patterns discernible in literally all sensual, material forms, thereby elucidating cosmic principles for harmonious living for all.

Graham Harvey

Further Reading

Michell, John. *Sacred England*. Glastonbury: Gothic Image, 1996.

Michell, John. *Euphonics*. Glastonbury: Gothic Image, 1995.

Michell, John. *The New View over Atlantis*. London: Thames and Hudson, 1986.

Michell, John. *The Earth Spirit*. London: Thames and Hudson, 1975.

Michell, John and C. Rhone. *Twelve Tribe Nations*. Kimball, MI: Phanes Press, 1991.

See also: Earth Mysteries; Geomancy; Lost Worlds; Stone Circles; UFOs and Extraterrestrials.

Middle Earth

The "Middle Earth" is the setting for J.R.R. Tolkien's (1892–1973) mythopoetic book *The Lord of the Rings*, as well as his earlier children's book *The Hobbit*. It is inhabited by a number of different "races," only one of which is human. The elves, masters of lore and art, are immortal; dwarves are secretive, hardy and hard-working; and hobbits, Tolkien's own unique invention, are a short and sociable people, shrewd if not intellectual. There are also corrupted opposites of the elves and dwarfs – orcs and trolls.

In Tolkien's tale, Frodo the hobbit comes into possession of a magic ring which turns out to be the One Ring of Power, forged by Sauron, the evil lord of Mordor and the most powerful ruler in Middle Earth. Sauron is looking for his Ring, which would enable him to complete his conquest. So Frodo, accompanied by a Company comprised of two men, an elf, a dwarf, three hobbits and an Odinic wizard named Gandalf, is obliged to try to take it back to the furnace in Mordor where it was forged, which is the only place it can be destroyed, and which is the only way that harmony can be restored to the Middle Earth. This pursuit constitutes the story of *The Lord of the Rings*.

Each of the races exists in interdependence with the places where they naturally live: the hobbits in the Shire, with its villages and fields, bounded by woods and streams; the dwarves in the vast heights and depths of the mountains, where they live and mine; and the elves in forests. As one character remarks of the last, "Whether they've made the land, or the land's made them, it's hard to say . . ." Their relationship is that of living in place – bioregional rather than proprietorial. As someone says to Frodo, "all things growing or living in the land belong each to themselves."

Much of Tolkien's story centers on the struggle of good against evil. Among his most memorable creations are the Ents, who are sentient trees who walk and talk. And when Fangorn, the chief Ent, is asked whose side he is on in the War of the Ring, he replies, "I am not altogether on anybody's side, because nobody is altogether on my side, if you understand me: nobody cares for the woods as I care for them . . ."

The Ents eventually do go to war against Sauron's allies. But the natural world in Tolkien's story has an importance, and a degree of autonomy, that is striking in a modern work. At least sixty-four kinds of non-cultivated plants are mentioned, plus eight of his own invention. Trees especially stand out: not only the four major forests, each with its own particular character, but individual trees as well. As Tolkien noted in a letter late in life, "In all my works I take the part of trees as against all their enemies" (in a letter printed in *The Daily Telegraph*, 4 July 1972).

Indeed, Middle Earth itself is a kind of character in its own right. Although a secondary creation, Middle Earth is clearly, as Tolkien insisted, *our* Earth in a different time. One of its roots lies in ancient Northern myth, in which Middle Earth was so called because it hung between the heavens and the underworld, and between the land of ice to the North and the land of fire to the South. The other root was, as Tolkien himself said, "my wonder and delight in the earth as it is, particularly the natural earth" and its weather, geology, ecology, flora and fauna, stars and lunar phases (in Resnik 1967: 41).

As befits a character, Middle Earth is capable of intelligence and emotion. A mountain causes blizzards to block the Company's way; when a king dies, a great rain weeps on the battlefield; and the summer following royal nuptials is unsurpassed for its fecundity. In short, it is a premodern animistic and pagan world, where personality and agency is not reserved for humanity alone, and the Earth is alive. Tolkien does not romanticize nature; much of Middle Earth is dangerously hard or hostile, and tragic in its history. But the only place which is dead, or nearly so, and where the land is ruthlessly subdued to industrial production, is Mordor.

By the same token, the natural world in Middle Earth is not divorced from religion. There is no organized religion there as such, but the worship that takes place is of deities that are coeval with elemental powers and natural phenomena (stars, trees, etc.). And its continuity, in Tolkien's world, depends on narratives: the collective, ritualized stories of divine, human and nonhuman beings that constitute myth.

For Tolkien himself, this aspect of his work presented certain problems; it existed in complex tension with his deep personal commitment to Roman Catholicism. On the one hand, the latter's tolerance of intermediary spirits (unlike Protestantism) permitted him to draw on the pagan mythology he also loved. And this has ethical implications, for example, reflected in Frodo's experience of the intrinsic value of a tree in the Elvish forest of Lorien: "He felt a delight in wood and the touch of it, neither as forester nor as carpenter; it was the delight of the living tree itself." On the other hand, Christian theism insists on the ultimate dominance of the one transcendent God, and there is a corresponding Christian stewardship ethic in the hobbit Sam's responsibility for renewing the post-war Shire.

Readers have responded to Tolkien's work in diverse ways, shaped by their own time. Since the 1970s – a time of global ecological crisis – the story is increasingly appropriated as an environmental story. As Fangorn puts it, "it seems that the wind is setting East, and the withering of all woods may be drawing near." And at the center of that storm is the Ring of Power, which some readers liken to technological society and what Lewis Mumford called "the megamachine" (Mumford 1964: 263).

More specifically, the *The Lord of the Rings* was an inspirational book for the late David McTaggart, founder of Greenpeace. It circulated widely in *samizdat* form among the underground resistance (environmental as well as political) in the USSR and communist Central Europe. And it has become a part of the green spirituality of radical environmentalists in the United States fighting deforestation who took Fangorn as a symbol of their biocentrism, and in Britain, among activists resisting the imposition of new roads.

Tolkien's work is thus a modern myth about a world not yet disenchanted and commodified, and it tells the story of how that world was saved. In apparently looking back to a lost world, it offers readers hope for this one through what Fraser Harrison termed "radical nostalgia" (1984: 170). As a significant cultural contribution to a much-needed re-enchantment of the world, Tolkien's Middle Earth has never been more relevant, and new generations of appreciative readers – and as of the early twentieth century, motion picture afficionados as well – will continue to find inspiration there.

Patrick Curry

Further Reading

Curry, Patrick. *Defending Middle-Earth: Tolkien, Myth & Modernity*. New York: St. Martin's Press and Edinburgh: Floris Books, 1997; London: HarperCollins, 1998.

Harrison, Fraser. "England, Home and Beauty." In Richard Mabey, Susan Clifford and Angela King, eds. *Second Nature*. London: Jonathan Cape, 1984, 162–72.

Kane, Sean. *Wisdom of the Mythtellers*. Peterborough: Broadview Press, 1994.

Mumford, Lewis. *The Pentagon of Power, vol. 2: The Myth of the Machine*. New York: Harcourt Brace Javonovitch, 1964.

Resnik, Henry. "An Interview with Tolkien." *Nieklas* 18 (Spring 1967), 41.

Shippey, Tom. *J.R.R. Tolkien: Author of the Century*. London: HarperCollins, 2000.

Veldman, Meredith. *Fantasy, the Bomb, and the Greening of Britain: Romantic Protests 1945–1980*. Cambridge: Cambridge University Press, 1994.

See also: Disney; Disney Worlds at War; Dragon Environmental Network (United Kingdom); Earth First! and the Earth Liberation Front; Fantasy Literature; Greenpeace; Motion Pictures; Paganism (various).

Minakata, Kumagusu (1867–1941)

Kumagusu Minakata was called "a neglected Japanese genius" by Carmen Blacker, a specialist in Japanese shamanism, in her Presidential Address to the Folklore Society in England in 1982. Born a year before the initiation of the Meiji Period, Minakata became an exemplar of the Meiji renaissance intellectual, traveling to the United States and England as a young man, educating himself in a variety of subjects, and writing articles in Japanese and English on biology, folklore, ethnology, psychology, and religion. He is receiving renewed attention today in Japan particularly because of his "Anti-Amalgamation of Shrines Movement," according to Sadamichi Kato.

In his opposition to two laws passed by the Meiji government, the first in 1888 and the second in 1906, which first attempted to consolidate villages into larger political units and then sought to limit official religious shrines to one per political unit, Minakata formulated his arguments by melding together ecological and religious arguments. In so doing, he sought to uphold vernacular spiritual practices in opposition to centralized religion and to defend the local shrines and their surrounding woods as places that not only generated a reverential attitude toward nature, but also supported local flora and fauna on sacred ground and provided a focal point for community self-regulation. True to his localist emphasis, Minakata fought for the preservation of specific shrines, such as the Oyama Shrine to which his family was historically attached, and was jailed at one point for his protests. In 1920 the Japanese government abandoned the contested ordinances. Although none of Minakata's writings have been translated into English, volume ten and the appendix to volume one of *Minakatq Kumagusu Zenshu* do contain English-language pieces that he authored.

Patrick D. Murphy

Further Reading

Blacker, Carmen. "Minakata Kumagusu: A Neglected Japanese Genius." *Folklore* 94 (1983), 139–52.
Kato, Sadamichi. "The Three Ecologies in Minakata Kumagusu's Environmental Movement." *Organization and Environment* 12:1 (1999), 85–98.
Minakata, Kumagusu. *Minakata Kumagusu Zenshu*, 12 vols. Shinobu Iwamura, ed. Tokyo: Heibonsha, 1971–1975.

See also: Japanese Religions.

Mitchell, Elyne (1913–2002)

A poetically descriptive essayist on environmental issues, Sibyl Elyne Keith Mitchell (born Melbourne, Australia; daughter to Sir Harry Chauvel) was the first Australian to place the condition of her country's soil in the context of comparative civilization and ecology. Most of her life was spent on a station in the upper reaches of the Murray River, in southernmost New South Wales. While writing more aesthetically oriented works – *Australia's Alps* (1942), *Speak to the Earth* (1945), and *Images in Water* (1947) – her most famous work is on the need to preserve ecological balance. In *Soil and Civilization* (1946) she plots the paths of civilization away from an earlier ecological unity and a spiritual awareness that the whole of life rested in God. The same error of neglecting this unity, and showing irresponsibility toward the soil above all, brought trouble to Sumeria, Persia, Egypt, China and India, Greece and Rome, Western Europe, [and] the Mayas, with Westerners repeating the same errors in the Americas and South Africa. Her prophetic goal was to save a vulnerable Australia from the same fate, by (re-)extolling the soil as the divinely ordained matrix of our being, which has to be rebuilt, where damaged, with patient research and wise water conservation. Supporting images from the world of comparative religion are prolific, if more often than not utilized as rather poetic invocations.

Garry W. Trompf

Further Reading

Green, Henry M. *A History of Australian Literature: Pure and Applied*, vol. 2. Sydney: Angus and Robertson, 1961.
Hyde, William H., Joy Hooker and Barry Andrews, eds. *The Oxford Companion to Australian Literature*. Oxford: Oxford University Press, 1994 (2nd edn).

See also: Australia.

Miwok People

Miwok (alternatively Miwuk, Mewuk, and Me-wan) is a modern designation which groups innumerable small nations of California Indians according to broad-based linguistic and cultural similarities. The Miwokan subgroup of the Utian language family (Penutian stock) consists of seven such cultural nationalities: Coast, Lake, Bay, Plains, Northern Sierra, Central Sierra, and Southern Sierra Miwok. While these categories provide a useful comparative framework, for most of their history Miwok peoples lived as members of independent, relatively egalitarian, multi-village tribes, each one with distinct territorial boundaries and control of the resources within those territories. The landscapes Miwok peoples inhabited varied from coastal baylands and inland hills to higher-elevation foothills and mountains in the Sierra Nevada. Today, eleven federally recognized tribes have Miwok membership; others are still seeking federal recognition.

For Miwok peoples, nature, culture, and religion did not exist as separate categories, but as blended elements of day-to-day life. As the underpinning of Miwok religious systems, creation narratives provided people with a sense of identity, rules of appropriate behavior and a context for evaluating life's most meaningful experiences. They described the actions of the "First People," supernatural personages with both human and animal attributes, and, at times, the attributes of natural phenomenon, such as stars and hail. The Miwok referred to the First People by the names of the present-day animals and natural phenomenon into which they transformed themselves after they created humans and provided "everything, everywhere" humans would need to live. Miwok narratives describe how the First People created human beings from crow, goose, raven, and turkey vulture feathers placed on or planted into the ground, or from wood and mud. One contemporary Bodega Miwok/Dry Creek Pomo woman sees the creation from feathers as confirmation that humans comprise "both earth and a spirit that soars" (Kathleen Smith, personal communication, 2002).

As a gift of the First People, the animals of today serve as a tangible reminder of myth-time, and Miwok cultures and spiritual values incorporated proscriptions for the responsible, respectful use of those same animals. According to Central, Northern, Southern and Coast Miwok sacred narratives, the very shape of people's hands was an outcome of the wise foresight of a Lizard personage. Northern, Central, Coast and Lake Miwok peoples variously attributed the red breast of robins, red throat of hummingbirds, and the ability to make fire from buckeye and incense cedar, as an outcome of the theft of fire by Robin and Hummingbird personages in myth-time, when they brought heat and light to an otherwise cold and dark world. Mount Diablo, Mount Konocti, Sonoma Peak, and the sites of other events during myth-time, all served as awe-inspiring reminders of creation, and became places of prayer and sources of spiritual power.

As with many other North American Indians, the birth imagery of a world flood permeates the creation narratives of the Southern, Central, and Coast Miwok. In Sierra Miwok versions, Frog, Hummingbird, and Dove, all male personages, obtain sand and mud from which to create (re-birth) the flooded world. Dundes (1984) has conducted a comparative study of psycho-symbolic elements of this distinctly male creation, which has cognates in several parts of the world.

Another mythic event that interconnected nature, culture, and religion among the Miwok featured a world fire. The Miwok were well aware of the regenerative qualities of fire, which they used as a horticultural tool, in a carefully managed way, to return nutrients to the soil, eliminate disease organisms from it, improve seed harvests, and bring about the growth of young, herbaceous plant material which provided browse for deer, elk and antelope, which they in turn used for food, clothing and tools. Regular burning caused the growth of long, straight shoots needed to make shapely baskets and a variety of other objects. It also eliminated the accumulation of fuel in the form of decaying plant material and other plant debris on the ground, thereby preventing the occurrence of the type of uncontrolled, destructive fire which spread across the world in myth-time.

Not only did the Miwok manage the land in a way that acknowledged their relationship with it and their responsibility to it, but they also ascribed consciousness to inanimate objects, as well as plants and animals. They viewed the world as comprised of an interconnected system of powerful, usually ambivalent, supernatural forces, including spirits associated with air, wind, and water, ghosts, and other beings, which existed as an integral part of daily experience. The world had the potential for both good and bad – not necessarily in the moral or ethical sense of right and wrong, but as an expression of harmonious and inharmonious elements. These component forces were good (in harmony) when under control, but had the potential for bad (illness or catastrophe) if uncontrolled.

Supernatural sanctions, ritual, ceremony, and cultural rules served to control and stabilize a potentially unstable world. They provided an affirmation of, and check on, natural forces. So it was that Miwok peoples kept the world harmonious (balanced) through prayerful thoughts, actions, and offerings, adherence to rules of proper behavior, fasting, and the observance of spiritual dances on a seasonal cycle.

The most sacred dances, as visual prayers, gave thanks to the Creator and served to maintain the world's spiritual balance, thereby ensuring the health and well-being of the group, protecting people from natural disasters, and creating the conditions necessary for an abundant harvest. The Miwok also held less sacred dances for doctoring, to dedicate and give thanks for the autumn acorn harvest, to initiate economic activities appropriate to a given time of year, to commemorate important events, and for mourning.

Throughout north-central California a roundhouse served as the center of religious observances. The earliest roundhouses were semi-subterranean, earth-covered structures supported by posts and secondary rafters, their shape reminiscent of the Miwok conception of the cosmos as a sky dome resting on the Earth; their central smokehole reminiscent of an opening, recognized by at least some Miwok, as existing at the top of the sky dome. Beyond this dome, and below the Earth, supernatural beings existed who conducted activities which affected the Miwok, such as creating earthquakes and moving the sun from east to west. The womb-like darkness and tunneled entrances of roundhouses evidence birth symbolism.

The roundhouse provided the locale for the observance of the Kuksu religious system, a system shared by people in the San Francisco Bay area, the Sacramento and northern San Joaquin Valleys, and adjacent hill areas.

Kuksu observances were characterized by a male secret society and, at times, a similar female secret society. The society members were chosen on the basis of their social, political or economic status. They underwent formal initiation rites and special instruction before receiving leadership positions. In their role as religious specialists, initiates administered the cycle of Kuksu ceremonies, which included singing, dancing, and curing. Through ritual observances, the dancers "recreated sacred time and in one way or another restored their people to the unsullied state that had prevailed at the time of creation" (Bean and Vane 1978: 665). In the most important and elaborate ceremonies, dancers represented supernatural spirits and beings, often the same as those prominent in creation accounts. The words of a Central Sierra Miwok lileusi dance expresses well the transformation from human to spirit that the dancers undergo: "This is what he [the spirit] said when he came. He came from Mt. Diablo

[Supemenenu]. The dancers get just like this fellow when they start to be this kind of a dancer" (Gifford 1955: 277). In undergoing this transformation, the dancers accepted tremendous responsibility. They adhered to stringent rules lest illness or catastrophe result from improper conduct of the dances.

The dancers wore elegant feathered regalia, comprised of flicker quill headbands, hairnets, headdresses, hairpins, belts, earrings and cloaks, which served as "a symbol of great wealth and prestige" (Bates 1982: 1). Because of the intense supernatural power associated with the dance and regalia, the latter had to be properly produced, manufactured, handled, and cared for. The makers sang special songs and made food offerings. Construction details, such as feather arrangements, showed the maker's respect for the birds from which they come. The finest examples demonstrated the tremendous technical ability and care needed to trim, cut, and secure the materials for a grand appearance. During the ceremonies, the actions of the dancers, firelight reflecting against their regalia in the otherwise dark roundhouse, the sounds of shell pendants and beads moving with their rhythmic steps, and the voices of the singers, accompanied by whistles, split-stick rattles, and a footdrum, all helped to transport the dancers and audience into the spiritual realm, and provided a visible affirmation of their day-to-day relationship with nature and the supernatural.

Spanish, Mexican, Russian and American intrusions onto Miwok lands irrevocably altered that relationship. Miwok peoples variously grappled with missionization, introduced disease, enforced servitude, displacement, massacres, separation in boarding schools, and social marginalization, at the same time that trapping, building, mining, logging, ranching, agriculture, and the elimination of Miwok land-management practices caused rapid environmental deterioration. The Miwok economy shifted from one based on foraging and horticultural techniques, to one based on a cash economy. Many Miwok converted to Christian religions, seeing elements of the older beliefs in the new religions. Where the older religious systems continued to be practiced, they underwent changes due to the implementation of the prophesies, visions, and dreams of new religious leaders, and the new and closer contracts established between tribes in wider geographical areas than the past. Some of this change may have been generated by the spread of the Ghost Dance movement into north-central California in 1870, with its hope for a return to the "peaceful and prosperous conditions" that existed prior to non-Indian intrusion.

Those Miwok who continued to dance began substituting cloth, buttons, glass beads, yarn, commercial cordage, and non-native feathers for some of the harder to obtain and make materials used in the older regalia, especially the raptor feathers of old, which the federal government, in an effort to prevent extinctions, made illegal to possess, except by special permit. Although many old-time traditions had declined or fallen into disuse by the early 1900s, some Miwok people fought to keep the dances going. Notable among these efforts was that of the late Bill Franklin, who, in the 1940s collaborated with Sierra Miwok and Nisenan traditionalists to form what is now called the Miwuk Dance Group. Franklin also helped establish Chaw'se (Indian Grinding Rock State Park), where a roundhouse was established, and an annual big time, which brings together several Central California Indian dance groups, occurs. He was also instrumental in the establishment of a Miwuk Indian Roundhouse at Westpoint.

Some Coast Miwok dance with their Pomo relatives in a roundhouse established at Point Reyes National Seashore. Other Miwok people participate in dances at a roundhouse built at Yosemite National Park, where old-style ceremonies are hosted as well as an annual Bear Dance, a new tradition borrowed from the Mountain Maidu. Whether public or private, such dances provide an affirmation of Miwok peoples determination to ensure the health and well-being of their people and culture into the future.

Some of the older values and beliefs which bound nature, culture and religion together in Miwok life have undergone a renaissance in other areas as well. Those Miwok who continue to gather some of the native foods, such as acorn and manzanita, and natural materials from which to make cultural objects, such as basketry, still pray and leave offerings when they do. Miwok and other basketmakers are actively working with officials associated with National Forests and other public and private landholders to urge the discontinuation of herbicide spraying, ensure access to native foods and materials, and seek the reintroduction of native plants and ancient land-management techniques, especially burning. Contemporary Miwok peoples also seek protection of their sacred sites.

Beverly Ortiz

Further Reading
Barrett, S.A. "Myths of the Southern Sierra Miwok." *University of California Publications in American Archaeology and Ethnology* 16:1 (1919), 1–28.

Bates, Craig. "Feathered Regalia of Central California: Wealth and Power." In James Dotta, ed. *Occasional Papers of the Redding Museum, Paper No. 2*. Redding: Redding Museum and Art Center, 1982, 1–30.

Bean, Lowell John and Sylvia Brakke Vane. "Cults and Their Transformations." In Robert Heizer, ed. *The Handbook of North American Indians, Volume 8, California*. Washington, D.C.: Smithsonian Institution, 1978, 662–72.

Bibby, Brian. "Still Going: Bill Franklin and the Revival of Miwuk Traditions." *News from Native California* 7:3 (1993), 21–35.

Blackburn, Thomas C. and Kat Anderson, eds. *Before the Wilderness, Environmental Management by Native Californians*. Menlo Park: Ballena Press, 1993.

Callaghan, Catherine. "Lake Miwok." In Robert Heizer, ed. *The Handbook of North American Indians, Volume 8, California*. Washington, D.C.: Smithsonian Institution, 1978, 264–73.

Collier, Mary and Sylvia Thalman, eds. "Interviews with Tom Smith and Maria Copa, Isabel Kelly's Ethnographic Notes on the Coast Miwok Indians of Marin and Southern Sonoma Counties, California." *MAPOM Occasional Papers Number 6*. San Rafael: Miwok Archeological Preserve of Marin, 1991.

Du Bois, Cora. "The 1870 Ghost Dance." *Anthropological Records* 3:1 (1939), 1–151.

Dundes, Alan. "Earth-Diver: Creation of the Mythopoeic Male." In Alan Dundes, ed. *Sacred Narrative: Readings in the Theory of Myth*. Berkeley: University of California Press, 1984, 270–94.

Gayton, A.H. "The Ghost Dance of 1870 in South-Central California." *University of California Publications in American Archaeology and Ethnology* 28:3 (1930), 57–82.

Gifford, Edward Winslow. "Central Miwok Ceremonies." *Anthropological Records* 14:4 (1955), 261–318.

Gifford, Edward Winslow. "Miwok Cults." *University of California Publications in American Archaeology and Ethnology* 18:3 (1926), 391–408.

Heizer, Robert F. "Natural Forces and Native World View." In Robert Heizer, ed. *The Handbook of North American Indians, Volume 8, California*. Washington, D.C.: Smithsonian Institution, 1978, 649–53.

Kelly, Isabel. "Coast Miwok." In Robert Heizer, ed. *The Handbook of North American Indians, Volume 8, California*. Washington, D.C.: Smithsonian Institution, 1978, 414–25.

Levy, Richard. "Eastern Miwok." In Robert Heizer, ed. *The Handbook of North American Indians, Volume 8, California*. Washington, D.C.: Smithsonian Institution, 1978, 398–413.

Loeb, E.M. "The Western Kuksu Cult." *University of California Publications in American Archaeology and Ethnology* 33:1 (1932), 1–137.

Merriam, C. Hart. *The Dawn of the World, Myths and Tales of the Miwok Indians of California*. Lincoln: University of Nebraska Press, 1993 (1910).

Rooth, Anna Birgitta. "The Creation Myths of the North American Indians." In Alan Dundes, ed. *Sacred Narrative: Readings in the Theory of Myth*. Berkeley: University of California Press, 1984, 166–81.

See also: Harmony in Native North America; Holy Land in Native North America; Mother Earth; Muir, John; National Parks and Monuments (United States); Sacred Geography in Native North America; Sierra Club; Spirit of Sage Council; Wilderness Religion.

Miyazawa, Kenji (1896–1933)

Kenji Miyazawa was a Japanese agronomist, poet, and writer. Through his writing we see how the knowledge of the scientist, the intuition of the poet, and the Buddhist's sense of compassion as well as understanding of the interdependence of all phenomena, can nurture attitudes rooted in "deep ecology" and promote the growth of a bioregional consciousness. Miyazawa's collected works include poems, songs, plays and tales (*dowa*). Although *dowa* refer to children's tales, his stories have earned international recognition as literary masterpieces, offering multiple levels of interpretation.

Miyazawa grew up in a struggling agricultural community in Iwate Prefecture, about 300 miles north of Tokyo. At age eighteen he embraced the teachings of the Lotus Sutra, a doctrine of co-enlightenment that preaches the essential unity of all phenomena over time and space, offering hope for Buddhahood to all, regardless of species or gender. Miyazawa was deeply influenced by this sutra, which calls upon the reader to act out the sutra with his or her body and mind, following the example of the various bodhisattvas who are prepared to come to the aid of all beings, whether man or woman, human or nonhuman.

Miyazawa studied at Morioka College of Agriculture in order to share his knowledge with local farmers. He also taught at an agricultural high school. During breaks from regular work in class and field, Kenji would lead his students up the volcanic slopes of Mt. Iwate, or take them to the local riverbed to dig for fossils. As they walked, he would tell them about the relationships over space and time between rocks, soil, plants, and animals. He was a pioneer of environmental education.

Although Miyazawa devoted his life to the local farm community, he was saddened to see wild lands destroyed for further development. In his poem "A Recitative on Irises by a Young Surveyor from the Land Cultivation Bureau," our surveyor decries as "original sin" the destruction of a lovely green highland with its dense clusters of irises, soon to be plowed under and converted to dreary humus (Miyazawa 1980: v.5, 198–200).

From early childhood Miyazawa enjoyed hiking over the plains and into the mountains of Iwate. His joy, bordering on ecstasy, is expressed in "Ippongi no" (One-tree Plain):

I am the beloved of forest and field.
When I walk through rustling reeds
Green messages, bashfully folded,
Slip into my pockets;
When I enter the shade of the woods,
Crescent-shaped lipmarks
Cover my elbows and trousers (Miyazawa 1980: v.2, 260–2).

In "Taneyama Heights," the poet goes beyond rapport to complete identification with nature, as he looks out from a high plateau, over layers of mountain ridges: "I am the water and the light and the wind" (Miyazawa 1980: v. 3, 419). In contrast to the traditional literary view that sought to bring external nature into one's spiritual universe and internalize it – the so-called "miniature garden tendency" – we find that Miyazawa's inner world flows outward, merging with the universe.

Rooting his poems and stories in the landscape of Iwate Prefecture, Miyazawa provides the intimacy necessary to establish a sense of place, while simultaneously transcending time and space, to supply the modern myths that will reconnect us to the Earth. Themes characterizing Miyazawa's tales are the virtues of humility, the equality of all phenomena, harmonious coexistence, balance and compromise, the aesthetics of untamed nature, and science that benefits life. Many tales illustrate the cyclical nature of natural systems, and at the same time explore the deeper philosophical issues of karma and cycles of life and death. Miyazawa's tales seem to convey "the will of the universe" as expressed to the poet through the sounds of nature, particularly the voice of the wind. Miyazawa, as artist, is a modern-day shaman, interpreting the divinity in nature. Miyazawa, as scientist, brings to us a detailed view of a local ecosystem. His words unfold as an ecology of sacred space.

If Miyazawa Kenji has become an almost mythical figure in contemporary Japan, it is because he has provided through both his literary work and lifestyle some of the guidelines that could help us create a better world. As the child Giovanni says in Miyazawa's *Night of the Milky Way Railroad*, ". . . we've got to create a better place than heaven, right here" (Miyazawa 1980: v.12, 152).

Karen Colligan-Taylor

Further Reading

The Lotus Sutra. Burton Watson, tr. New York: Columbia University Press, 1993.

Miyazawa, Kenji. *Masterworks of Miyazawa Kenji*. Sarah Strong and Karen Colligan-Taylor, trs. Tokyo: International Foundation for the Promotion of Languages and Culture, 2002.

Miyazawa, Kenji. *Crossing the Snow*. Karen Colligan-Taylor, tr. Tokyo: International Foundation for the Promotion of Languages and Culture, 2000.

Miyazawa, Kenji. *Once and Forever: The Tales of Miyazawa Kenji*. John Bester, tr. New York: Kodansha International, 1993.

Miyazawa, Kenji. *A Future of Ice, Poems and Stories of a Japanese Buddhist*. Hiroaki Sato, tr. San Francisco: North Point Press, 1989.

Miyazawa, Kenji. *Shinshu Miyazawa Kenji zenshu*, 16 vols. Tokyo: Chikuma Shobo, 1980.

See also: Buddhism – East Asia; Deep Ecology; Japanese Love of Nature; Japanese Religions; Sacred Space/Place.

Moltmann, Jürgen (1926–)

Jürgen Moltmann is widely regarded as the foremost Protestant theologian of the last forty years. Moltmann was a professor of systematic theology at the University of Tübingen from 1967 until 1994. He was an early proponent of "political theology" which stresses the Church's public mission to promote social justice. His first major book, the *Theology of Hope* (1964), won wide acclaim for its forceful affirmation that an eschatological "openness to the future" must be at the core of Christian proclamation. This openness, he argued, sustains hope for liberation and societal transformation. In *The Crucified God* (1973), Moltmann secured his international stature by developing a "theology of the cross" that understands the inbreaking of the future of God's kingdom in the midst of Christ's and the world's suffering. In the mid-1970s he began to introduce ecological concerns into his theological reflection. In *The Future of Creation* (1979) he sought to integrate his eschatological emphasis on history with an ecological understanding of the natural world. He described creation as a "still open, creative process" in which God enlivens and sustains the community of life. Instead of the biblical charge to "subdue the earth," Moltmann holds we must "free the earth through fellowship with it" (Moltmann 1979: 119, 129).

In 1980 Moltmann began to publish a major series in systematic theology titled *Messianic Theology*. His second volume, *God in Creation* (1985), developed his integration of eschatological transformation with an ecologically informed theology of creation. Moltmann is a broadly ecumenical thinker and he developed his views in close conversation with Jewish, Catholic, and Orthodox sources as well as ones drawn from the Protestant traditions. Moltmann stressed the role of the Holy Spirit dwelling in, and sustaining, the world of creation. He understood creation as being transformed by the kingdom of God that renews all things. He concluded, too, that genuine human liberation requires living in peace with nature. Against Western anthropocentric traditions, Moltmann called for a theocentric view that understands the natural world as God's creation, not as mere property subject to any human use. Moltmann drew on the Jewish kabbalistic doctrine of the *zimsum* that holds that God first created space for the world of natural creation by withdrawing into him or herself. For Moltmann, this notion of divine self-limitation reminds us helpfully that God creates in major part "by letting-be, by making room" (Moltmann 1985: 86–8). Rejecting Christianity's long-standing view that the human is the "crown of creation," Moltmann followed the

Jewish belief that the Sabbath is creation's true crown (Moltmann 1985: 31). The Sabbath is a "feast of creation" for it marks God's resting with, and immanent presence within, the natural world, and it suggests to Moltmann that the path of ecological responsibility lies in an ethic of dwelling within and respecting creation, rather than one of mastery and domination.

While Moltmann's views on creation have been generally applauded, some fear that he pushes an eschatological sense of nature's "openness" too far. They worry that his description of creation as an "open system" might unwittingly play into the hands of those who lose no sleep over the onrush of humanity's transformation of nature. If nature is so "open," are there then no stable balances, ordered relationships, or relatively fixed requirements for species flourishing that must not be transgressed? Despite such concerns, Moltmann deserves recognition for his important contribution in developing an ecological theology of creation. Many theologians and lay-people, who had before dismissed ecological concerns as marginal ones for the Christian churches, have come to a new appreciation of their significance under Moltmann's prodding. Moltmann's international stature allowed him to draw the attention of a wide range of theologians and lay-people to ecological concerns in a way that few other theologians were able to do.

William French

Further Reading

Bouma-Prediger, Steven. *The Greening of Theology: The Ecological Models of Rosemary Radford Ruether, Joseph Sittler, and Jürgen Moltmann*. Atlanta: Scholars Press, 1995.

Lorenzen, Thorwald, "Jürgen Moltmann." In Donald W. Musser and Joseph L. Price, eds. *A New Handbook of Christian Theologians*, Nashville: Abingdon Press, 1996, 304–16

Meeks, W. Douglas. "Jürgen Moltmann's Systematic Contributions to Theology," *Religious Studies Review* 22:2 (1996), 95–102.

Moltmann, Jürgen. "The Adventure of Theological Ideas," *Religious Studies Review* 22:2 (1996), 102–5.

Moltmann, Jürgen. *God in Creation: A New Theology of Creation and the Spirit of God*. Margaret Kohl, tr. San Francisco: Harper & Row, 1985.

Moltmann, Jürgen. *The Future of Creation*. Margaret Kohl, tr. Philadelphia: Fortress Press, 1979.

See also: Christianity (7b) – Political Theology; Christianity (7c) – Liberation Theology; Christianity (7d) – Feminist Theology.

Mongolian Buddhism and Taimen Conservation

I became interested in the impact of religious belief while visiting a church in Louisiana in 2000, on the edge of what is referred to as "cancer alley" in Louisiana; an area crowded with refineries. A group of African-American women garnered spirited community support through their church, mixing rallies with gospel music and bridge-building with Southern-fried righteousness. As a director of the national Sierra Club at that time, I was there to support legislation to limit levels of dioxin getting dumped into the Gulf of Mexico and surrounding communities. This blending of local culture and religion with conservation demonstrated surprising muscle, attracting the support of regional conservation groups and the national Sierra Club. Through this experience, I became intrigued with religion-based conservation activism.

In September of 2000, the Mongolian nonprofit organization Taimen Conservation Fund initiated a taimen conservation project, the Uur River Project. A taiman is a Mongolian fish that can attain a length of more than seven feet and can weigh up to 230 pounds. In addition to fisheries research, the Taimen Conservation Fund recently received funding from the World Bank to rebuild a Buddhist monastery as part of the overall restoration strategy. A collaborative effort between the Buddhist community and conservationists has been forged to ensure protection for one of the last places on Earth with a healthy taimen population. My role is to assist both parties in creating an outreach program on rivers and taimen. Outreach derived from a bridge between the conservation goals and Buddhist beliefs will help to enlist local support as well as make the message palatable to the general public. By working within existing cultural precepts, river protection and taimen preservation has a greater chance of success.

During my stay in Hvolsgul, I interviewed several residents of the Uur River Valley who practice a faded blend of Lamist Buddhism and Shamanism. My project entails research and discussion on the nexus of Buddhism and conservation. The goals of the Uur project are: to create a regional Buddhist outreach program on the importance of the river and the fisheries; to restore the Dayan Derkh monastery; to work with the community to manage taimen conservation; to curtail taimen poaching; and to strengthen bonds between the Buddhist and conservation communities. The Uur River flows past the remnants of the toppled Dayan Derkh monastery, winding through a golden larch forest, spilling into the interior of an ancient empire that once stretched from Beijing to the Caspian Sea. Within this body of water lives a giant fish named the taimen, believed by locals to be river god's daughter. To watch this fish explode from calm waters is to know why the taimen is also called the river wolf by the fly-fishing community.

Mongolia's Uur River Valley, one of the most isolated and pristine in Eurasia, attracted the shaman Dayan Derkh to live on the banks of its cold waters during the thirteenth century. It was here, as legend has it, that the feisty shaman got crossways with Genghis Khan and turned himself to stone to escape the Khan's wrath. Vexed by his behavior, the great Khan called upon the Dalai Lama in Tibet to deal with this stubborn stone. The Dalai Lama sent over seven monks to build a Buddhist monastery under the shaman's cave. It was while listening to the monks' prayers that Dayan Derkh converted to Buddhism. The monastery became a school housing 150 monks and taught a thousand students before it was destroyed.

In 1937, under the influence of Russia's leader Joseph Stalin, the Mongolian government slaughtered more than 17,000 monks in Mongolia. (No records are available and some reports indicate as many as 200,000 were killed.) Dayan Derkh monastery was locked and the Uur Valley was left without spiritual leadership. After three generations, the residents' beliefs began to blur and lose power. The monastery was looted and torn down. Today, all that is left are the weathered foundation posts tied with blue ribbons, leaning beside scattered piles of gifts left for Dayan Derkh and Buddha.

Like many resource-rich habitats, the Uur Valley is experiencing overhunting, timber and mineral extraction and habitat destruction. Taimen are poached and sold in regional markets to urbanites and foreigners. It is illegal to kill taimen and this trend in poaching is a modern issue. Residents once guided by the regional religious beliefs, which considered the fish the river god's daughter, left the taimen unharmed. Eating fish in this culture remains taboo. Nevertheless, in recent years, the river god's daughters have felt the pressure of poaching.

In 1998, Jeff and Dan Vermillion, brothers from Livingston, Montana, opened up catch-and-release fly fishing in this region and in conjunction with the Mongolian government, hired local men to patrol the river and issue citations. The fine for poaching taimen, however, was less than what the taimen sell for and the poaching patrol failed. Vermillion, who has a vested interest in keeping the taimen fishery healthy, underwrote a grant with the Taimen Conservation Fund to fund a team of aquatic scientists to study and make conservation recommendations for the Uur fishery.

The aquatic research component was only half of the envisioned project. Vermillion wants to work with the Khambo Lama, Mongolia's head lama. As scientists conduct fish counts to establish data sets and create conservation management recommendations, the Buddhist monastery restoration can help to restore cultural perceptions of the environment. Every resident I spoke with was excited about the restoration of Dayan Derkh. It served for centuries as an important cultural and spiritual center. Despite the fact that the monastery was destroyed, the site is still a very vital place in this valley.

Construction on the monastery began in 2004, the aquatic research in 2003. Plans are underway for an educational film, narrated in the Mongolian language, on taimen poaching. Meanwhile, Buddhist leaders are helping to develop the message and a regionwide outreach plan. As the project advances I will track shifting attitudes, changes in poaching practices, and taimen population recovery.

At a time when religion is fueling hatred elsewhere in the world, can religion, religious texts and dogma help humans better connect and care for their Earth? As a conservationist, I have worked for years looking for opportunities to encourage local investment in the protection of natural resources. I think exploring the marriage of Buddhist ecological thought and conservation in Mongolia could provide a promising example that could spawn many such efforts in the future.

Betsy Gaines

Further Reading
Crane, George. *Bones of the Master: A Journey to Secret Mongolia*. Bantam Books, 2000.
Hessig, Walther. *The Religions of Mongolia*. London: Routledge and Kegan Paul, 1980.
Kaza, Stephanie and Kenneth Kraft. *Dharma Rain, Sources of Buddhist Environmentalism*. Boston: Shambala Publications, 2000.
Meyhew, Bradley. *Mongolia*. Lonely Planet Publications, 2001.
Middleton, Nick. *The Last Disco in Outer Mongolia*. Guernsey, Channel Islands, Great Britain: Guernsey Press Co. Ltd, 1992.
Novick, Rebecca. *Fundamentals of Tibetan Buddhism*. Freedom, CA: Crossing Press, Freedom, 1999.
Palmer, Martin and Victoria Finlay. *Faith in Conservation: New Approaches to Religions and the Environment*. Washington, D.C.: The World Bank, 2003.

See also: Bon (Tibet); Buddhism – Engaged; Buddhism – Tibetan; Fly Fishing; Tibet and Central Asia; Yunnan Region (Southwest China and Montane Mainland Southeast Asia).

Mora, Pat (1942–)

Pat Mora, a native of El Paso, Texas, first established herself as a poet, then as an author of children's books, and, more recently, of essays and a memoir. Nicolás Kanellos has claimed that she has one of the widest audiences of any Hispanic poet in the U.S. Kanellos, Anya Achtenberg, and other critics have noted that Mora's poetic voice exudes a tone and spirit of healing. Such healing is both physical and spiritual and repeatedly is tied to a healthy relationship between people and place, culture and environment. Throughout her work, whether writing for children or adults, she integrates place, spirit, and personal development, into an interanimating process of achieving wholeness. The southwestern landscape, the environment of her own life and her heritage, as a particular aspect of the natural world is represented not only as life-giving but also as alive. Thus, Kanellos speaks of Mora's interest in shamanism, while others might view her metaphysics as distinctly animistic. The term shamanism specifically refers to Mora's interest in and depiction of *curanderos/curanderas*, herbal and spiritual healers. It also includes her less frequent depiction of the *curandera*'s opposite, the *bruja*, witch. This attention comes out clearly in poems in her first three books, *Chants*, *Borders*, and *Communion*, in which to a large extent the Southwest remains not only the primary setting but also the primary subject of individual pieces.

Before publishing another volume of poetry, Mora brought out *Nepantla: Essays from the Land in the Middle*. In these short pieces, she relates her strong sense of a living, spiritually informing nature to her *mestizaje*, her mixed ethnic heritage, with particular emphasis on the native side of that heritage. She clarifies that, for her, conserving natural diversity and conserving cultural diversity go hand in hand. She explores these notions further in her next book of poetry, *Agua Santa: Holy Water*. Playing on the clear allusion to the Catholic heritage of most Mexican Americans, Mora immediately links this sacred water to its earthly origins, including amniotic fluid, in the first two sections of the book titled "Old Sea" and "Rivers." Inverting the anti-body, anti-sensuality stereotypes promoted by patriarchal tradition she celebrates the embodied spirituality of mother–daughter relationships. In the process she links together all of the religious traditions of her heritage invoking various goddesses along the way. While the "pagan" predominates in *Agua Santa*, a vernacular Catholicism is humorously and lovingly portrayed in her most recent poetry collection, *Aunt Carmen's Book of Practical Saints*, which is lavishly illustrated. These illustrations link her poems to the popular Northern New Mexico village tradition of saint carving. In the same year that *Practical Saints* appeared, 1997, Mora also published *House of Houses*, a family memoir, in which the dead and the living intermingle and share the space of the family homestead. Memory, cultural preservation, spirituality, and healing are all blended in this loving tribute in which every day is treated like The Day of the Dead.

Patrick D. Murphy

Further Reading
Mora, Pat. *House of Houses*. Boston: Beacon Press, 1997.
Mora, Pat. *Aunt Carmen's Book of Practical Saints*. Boston: Beacon Press, 1997.
Mora, Pat. *Agua Santa: Holy Water*. Boston: Beacon Press, 1995.
Mora, Pat. *Nepantla: Essays from the Land in the Middle*. Albuquerque: University of New Mexico Press, 1993.
Mora, Pat. *Communion*. Houston: Arte Público Press, 1991.
Mora, Pat. *Borders*. Houston: Arte Público Press, 1986.
Mora, Pat. *Chants*. Houston: Arte Público Press, 1984.
See also: Autobiography; Animism; Memoir and Nature Writing; Shamanism (various).

Moro Movement (Guadalcanal, Solomon Islands)

The Moro Movement of Guadalcanal, in the Solomon Islands, is a custom (*kastom*) movement that promotes a traditional way of life instead of embracing mission ways or modernization. The age of the movement's founder, the famed Moro, is not known, but he is a man long respected across the whole Guadalcanal community. He worked as a carrier for the Americans during and after World War II, in a conflict that had profound social consequences for islanders throughout the Pacific. In 1957, he initiated his movement after a spiritual experience. As he has put it:

One day I got sick and died at six in the morning. The village cried for me and began preparing my funeral. In the evening my heart started to beat again. As I became conscious again I had a vision: I had to take my people back to a traditional way of life – especially clothing, houses, fishing and gardens (author interview).

Children are taught both the custom values attached to the Movement while also attending traditional school classes like the rest of the country. There are several Christian churches within the area and people are free to practice. There is no conflict between Christianity and Moro's followers. Moro expressed the platform of the movement and its environmentalist implications in 2000:

Before Jesus there were spirits of land and sea and forbidden (*tambu*) places. Missionaries destroyed our totems and dispelled bad spirits. People accepted it mostly and now believe their life is a mix of Christianity and traditional life. We are not devil people. We don't worship any bad spirits. We are Christians but we want to keep our traditional way of life. This means no development or spoiling of our environment. The trees and gardens and rivers give us life and we must keep them. The land is our mother . . . our life . . . our future (conversation with author).

Guadalcanal, like many Melanesian societies, is matrilineal – the women are the traditional landowners. To visit the 8000 people who live under Moro's influence in a string of villages along the southern Weathercoast of Guadalcanal, is to glimpse a people who have effectively rejected the Cargo or modern commodities of the modern world and who seek a *Kastom* way of life. The men wear a bark loincloth called a *kabilato* and spend their days fishing and building canoes and huts. The women wear only grass skirts and work in the sweet potato gardens and raise children. Among the few concessions to modern technology are some fiberglass banana boats with outboard engines, solar-powered radios at home, and blackboards.

For Moro and his followers, the relationship between nature and themselves is a holistic one and not divided into the worship of particular animals, plants or nature spirits. Their concern is for the preservation of their natural environment which is in some ways linked to the preservation of a harmonious society. The movement's relative isolation helps to reinforce this. Moro was clearly affected by the battles of Guadalcanal during the Second World War. The killing machines which destroyed human beings and nature may well have influenced Moro's vision effectively to disengage from the modern world and rely on the certainties of a *kastom* life and the sanctity of nature. The movement has recently become embroiled in the two-year civil war on Guadalcanal. Moro claims that he never supported the Guadalcanal militants who began evicting Malaitan and other squatters from around the capital Honiara in 1998, which triggered the war and claimed at least 100 lives. An uneasy truce is currently holding, with peacekeeping forces from Australia, New Zealand, and Fiji monitoring a ceasefire. But several attacks by the rival Malaitan Eagle Force, who successfully launched a coup there in May 2000 against Moro and those villages loyal to him, have marked Moro as the "spiritual leader" of the Guadalcanal militants and thus his movement remains under threat.

Ben Bohane

Further Reading

Bohane, Ben. "Shades of Bougainville: The Battle for Paradise." *Australian Style* (November 2000), 99–105.

Davenport, William and Gulbun Coker. "The Moro Movement of Guadalcanal, British Solomon Island Protectorate." *Journal of the Polynesian Society* 76 (1967), 123–75.

Trompf, Gary W. *Melanesian Religion.* Cambridge: Cambridge University Press, 1991.

See also: Bougainville (Papua New Guinea); Melanesian Traditions.

Mother Earth

The existence of an American Mother Earth, the bountiful giver of life, seems common knowledge. As the nurturing sustainer of American Indian communities and individuals, as a reference within ordinary language, as a trope in advertising and popular culture, as a motivating symbol in the public discourse of environmental groups, and as the subject of commentary in scholarly publications – in more forms than might be readily traced, recognition of Mother Earth's influence seems nearly universal. Following the publication of University of Colorado professor Sam Gill's *Mother Earth: An American Story* in 1987, however, common knowledge was attacked, defended and reformulated in ways that have subsequently affected the study of religion and nature in native North America.

Consider perhaps the single most widely spread image of Mother Earth, the globally televised opening ceremony of the 2002 Winter Olympics in Salt Lake City, Utah. Drum circles representing Utah's five native nations, drumming what the announcer explained as the 'heartbeat of Mother Earth," and accompanying music composed by Canadian Mohawk rock musician Robbie Robertson merged into the Olympic symbol (Frost 2003). Gill would claim that the satellite-conveyed unity of the Olympic Mother Earth bears little to no relation to the traditional beliefs and practices of any American native culture. Instead, Mother Earth only came into the worldviews of American Indians during the nineteenth century as they responded to the expansion of white society across their homelands.

In order to grasp Mother Earth's historical status, Gill argues against reading her numerous contemporary references back into the past, and for explaining any apparently earlier reference in terms of its own original source and context. In performing the kind of "source-criticism" familiar to biblical scholars, Gill winds up claiming that the entire body of ethnographic literature is invalid evidence, since the assumptions regarding Mother Earth in that literature are themselves based on only a few historical accounts. Of these, the two most common are attributed to the Shawnee political and military leader, Tecumseh, and the Wanapum prophetic figure Smohalla.

Tecumseh, in an 1810 meeting with General – and later U.S. President – William Henry Harrison to discuss settlement of Wabash River lands, made the statement: "The Earth is my mother – and on her bosom I will repose." Except that Gill claims he probably did not, since the earliest accounts of their meeting at Vincennes (Indiana), including Harrison's diary, make no mention of Tecumseh's words. Instead, the quote proliferated rapidly following the 1825 publication of Henry Ward Schoolcraft's *Travels in the Central Portions of the Mississippi Valley.* For Gill, the historical record shows that even if Tecumseh spoke these words, they cannot be evidence of native belief in a Mother Earth goddess, since the earliest texts making use of them do so to remark on Tecumseh's heroic character, or even merely to describe the seating arrangements at his tense meeting with Harrison. Gill insists that at best Tecumseh's language was metaphorical and strategic – deployed in an effort to deflect American designs on native land – not theological.

The paucity of historical documentation, Gill also claims, calls into question the scholarship of mainstay figures in the history of religion. Figures such as E.B. Tylor, Mircea Eliade and Ake Hultkrantz, each drew broad conclusions about American Indian religions from the single statements of Tecumseh or Smohalla – whose "shall I take a knife and tear my mother's bosom?" suffers from the same flimsy documentary pedigree as Tecumseh's statement, while also being derivative in its Victorian euphemism. Accordingly, such pronouncements as Eliade's that the "emotions that we feel when we hear (Smohalla's words) is our response to what they evoke with their wonderful freshness and spontaneity – the primordial image of the Earth-Mother" (in Gill 1987: 116) reflect far more about the theoretical desires and cultural needs of twentieth-century intellectuals than they do of the traditional worldviews of native North Americans.

Contemporary cultural needs, Gill claims, have also encouraged American Indians to embrace Mother Earth language in their efforts to maintain their distinctive cultural and personal identities over against the assimilationist influence of the dominant culture, and to provide symbolic capital in their ongoing political struggles. As Gill considers recent Indian references to Mother Earth, he is most struck by the ways in which she "is identified with the most fundamental concerns of all Indian peoples, the retention of lands" (Gill 1987: 147–8). She is thus, he thinks, a crucial contemporary symbol for pan-tribal concerns. He suspects, however, that this same broad-based sense of Indian-ness formed around Mother Earth serves the countercultural needs of many within the dominant culture today; just as, he argues, it served the needs of earlier generations of Americans in helping to form their own national identity. Mother Earth "expresses the civilizing, building, transforming aspects of Americans. Yet it also permits expression of the male, conquering, destructive, defiling aspects of the American character" (Gill 1987: 155).

Reaction to Gill's book, which he himself saw as "heretical" (Gill 1987: 156), was sharp. Several scholarly reviews were quite critical. Jordan Paper noted the widespread reference in Latin America among Amazon Basin tribes to Mother Earth figures, and in Peru to "Pachamama" – citing sixteenth-century Spanish sources to that effect – as well as telling linguistic and archeological evidence from Great Lakes Algonquians and other tribes (Paper 1990: 5, 14). Dan Merkur found Gill's work marred by a logical flaw – in concluding that an absence of evidence is evidence of absence – and therefore irrelevant (Merkur 1993: 178), and also noted the widespread distribution among the Inuit of a figure conforming to Gill's expectations of Mother Earth. J. Baird Callicott found Gill employing the same sort of archetypal category of interpretation, "goddess," that Gill found Tylor, Eliade, Hultkrantz and other "top-down" historians of religion imposing on their test cultures (Callicott 1989: 317).

More intense was the reaction among American Indian readers. The most heated came from Ward Churchill, Gill's colleague at the University of Colorado and a member of the American Indian Movement, whose criticism appeared in several forums in the years following the book's publication. As had other scholars, Churchill faulted Gill for arguing against a "straw man" (Churchill 1998: 110), and – more than most – attacked his reading of the historical evidence. For Churchill, the "obvious conclusion to be drawn" from Gill's source reading "is that so many people refer to the Tecumseh statement for the simple reason that this is what the man said" (Churchill 1998: 113).

While disagreements in reading strategies might be glossed as "merely academic," what set Churchill's reaction apart from other reviews was his explanation for Gill's historical treatment of Mother Earth. Gill's problem is not simply one of faulty reasoning from evidence to claim, but rather of intent. Churchill sees in Gill, and in a variety of New Age and environmentalist appropriations of Indian religious traditions popular at the time, the same historical revisionist ideology that animates "the sordid neonazi [sic] sentiments" of Holocaust deniers such as Arthur Butz. Thus Gill's "scholarly disgrace" is "a continuation and perfection of the twin systems of colonization and genocide which have afflicted Native America for 500 years" (Churchill 1998: 117). If Mother Earth is the giver and sustainer of life in American Indian communities, the "disgrace" of *Mother Earth* lay in how it seemed to take away what Churchill phrased as "the rights of American Indians to any modicum of cultural sanctity or psychological sanctuary" (Churchill 1998: 116).

In the aftermath of Churchill's response, and a series of "letters of outrage from community leaders" among Denver-area Indians to University of Colorado administrators (Churchill 1998: 107) seeking some formal action against Gill, the campus was tense with, as one Canadian scholar visiting there on academic leave put it: "a highly charged stand-off that no one talks much about" (Grimes 2000: 79). According to another Canadian, the controversy "was simmering all across North America" (Parkhill 1997: 1) and had expanded from a focus on the merits of Gill's claims to a more general conflict about the competence of those teaching native religions, the role of scholarship, and the continued legacy of colonialism within the academic world.

In light of these far-ranging debates, what might be said about Mother Earth herself? A first consideration is Mother

Earth's puzzling historical presence. Were historians experimental scientists, they might confirm or dismiss Gill's claims about Mother Earth's illusive existence in the documents by a repetition of his research. As it stands, few besides Churchill have argued against his suspicious reading of the Tecumseh story, and several reviewers found it impressive detective work. However, even if Mother Earth in print is more a shadow figure than the clearly framed textual center of American Indian understandings of the sacred, what exactly to conclude about her sketchy documentary existence is still subject to some debate. Though print may create the surest sort of knowledge, and establish the most real of identities, it did not then have the power to travel persuasively – as Schoolcraft's "on the bosom of my mother" statement must have if Gill is right – across the tribal hinterlands of both American continents in the short space of a few decades, or at most of little more than a century. Gill's reading of history seems as hard to accept as the pronouncements of Eliade.

A second consideration is how Mother Earth might best be conceptualized, assuming she can be attested to either in documents or through cultural tradition. Gill sought a singular "goddess," and in not finding one, or in finding one only recently invoked, concluded that Mother Earth had not been central to pre-contact traditions. Is Mother Earth a goddess, though? Issues of category translation arise here, as Osage theologian George Tinker acknowledged in a consideration of Gill's work posted on the internet after the initial controversy had receded. No "Native American language . . . even has a word for 'god' or a word that can be easily and appropriately translated as 'god' in the English language sense" (Tinker 2003). Like "Great Spirit," which Tinker calls "a popular white man's formula," the English expression "Mother Earth" is a term arising out of the exigencies of crosscultural contact, negotiation and conflict.

Gill's succumbing to the tendency among many European and American interpreters of Indian religious life to impose contestable categories derived from Western traditions has an instructive parallel in James Walker's *Lakota Myth*. Walker recorded numerous testimonies about traditional Lakota beliefs from several Lakota religious authorities between 1896 and 1914, and then tried to arrange their accounts of Lakota myth in ways that reflected "the work of a systematic European mind," as the Yankton Dakota ethnologist and linguist Ella Deloria wrote in 1938 to her Columbia University employer, anthropologist Franz Boas (in Walker 1983: 24).

Deloria noted that the Lakota people to whom she read Walker's mythical narrative frequently could not recognize many of the characters, actions or ideas presented in Walker's narrative, framed as they were through Greco-Roman mythology and the language of the Christian Church.

I have a feeling always that . . . ecclesiastical language was very much part of Walker's thinking, and that he explained what he thought the Dakotas said, in terms he knew best. But the Indians who heard all this were mildly amused and sometimes impatient with it (in Walker 1983: 396).

Likewise, in keeping Mother Earth as metaphor separate from Mother Earth as theology, Gill employs controlling assumptions about theology that are unvoiced, and perhaps with good reason, not easily shared among American Indian expressers of Mother Earth. If Walker constructed his cycle of Lakota stories with the aid of culturally foreign conceptions, Gill seems to have deconstructed native religions as a whole, aided by an equally alien conception of theology. This may account for the reaction among Indian *Mother Earth* readers so similar to the "amused" and "impatient" responses of those who heard Deloria read Walker.

A third consideration is that Mother Earth also gives rise to irony. Gill's primary concern is to undercut the "top-down" study of religion (Gill 1987: 157), yet he repeats its absolute pronouncements and employs its universal categories of interpretation. More ironic is that Mother Earth's defenders such as Churchill attack Gill for holding the same basic reading of colonialism in North America as they do themselves. On Gill's account, Mother Earth has provided American Indians since Tecumseh's day with enough common language and common concerns to forge a variety of movements, organizations and habits of thought to resist the dominant society's assimilation goals. Through such responses Mother Earth became an important bridge between tribal cultures, and has helped establish a common sense of "Indian" identity augmenting that of tribal affiliation

Churchill argues that Gill's sins "of commission" include trying to prove that "the adoption of a belief in Mother Earth has led contemporary American Indians away from their traditional tribal/cultural specificity and towards a homogeneous sort of 'pan-Indianism,' " which he says is simply "a variation on the standard rationalization that Indian rights no longer exist as such because Indians in the traditional sense no longer exist" (Churchill 1998: 112). This is surely an over-reading of Gill, however.

Gill highlights two periods during which public Indian articulation of Mother Earth furthered pan-tribal interests. During the 1890–1920s era, western tribes confined to reservations played the role of negative other to significant American land-use values. During the post-1968 civil rights era, Indians were able to reassert land claims, argue for increased sovereignty and make important political advances. Public figures such as first, the Santee Dakota author Charles Eastman, and later, American Indian Movement national director Russell Means, drew on Mother Earth during these periods in order to argue their respective positions regarding Indian survival before both Indians and the larger American public, and in Means's case, to international audiences as well. In both periods, Mother Earth enabled these and other Indian public figures to gain some moral high ground and to build solidarity within and across Indian communities in support of their critiques of American policy. Churchill's evident denial of this impact seems disingenuous, especially since his own role in the American Indian Movement – as an associate member of the United Keetowah Cherokee Band concerned about issues on Lakota land – illustrates Gill's point.

Also troubling, is that Churchill seems to share Gill's reading of the multisided history of Mother Earth's role in political rhetoric. In part her success is dependent upon – and her assistance in advancing tribal goals endangered by – the spread of Romanticist images of the noble savage lying at the heart of late twentieth-century American culture. In spite of his condemnation of Gill's work, he would, by virtue of his own fundamental concerns, have to agree with Gill that the Mother Earth who aids in marketing consumable spirituality, prompts easy alignment with environmentalist agendas, and spreads through the literary works of those Gill calls "White Indians," bears little resemblance to the one who might emerge in "balanced and informed presentations of Native American cultures and their religions" (Gill 1987: 148).

Matthew Glass

Further Reading

Callicott, J. Baird. "Review of *Mother Earth: An American Story*." *Religious Studies Review* 15:4 (October 1989), 316–19.

Churchill, Ward. "A Little Matter of Genocide: Colonialism and the Expropriation of Indigenous Spiritual Tradition in Contemporary Academia." In *Fantasies of the Master Race: Literature, Cinema and the Colonization of American Indians*. San Francisco: City Lights, 1998, 99–120.

Frost, Kenny. "The 2002 Winter Olympics: A Tribal Member's View." Canku Ota webpage, accessed 16 August 2003.

Gill, Sam. *Mother Earth: An American Story*. Chicago: University of Chicago Press, 1987.

Grimes, Ron. "This May be a Feud, but it is Not a War: An Electronic, Interdisciplinary Dialogue on Teaching Native Religions." In Lee Irwin, ed. *Native American Spirituality*. Lincoln: University of Nebraska Press, 2000, 78–96.

Merkur, Dan. "Review of *Mother Earth: An American Story*." *Journal of Ritual Studies* 7:1 (Winter 1993), 177–9.

Paper, Jordan. "Through the Earth Darkly: The Female Spirit in Native American Religions." In Christopher Vecsey, ed. *Religions in Native North America*. Moscow: University of Idaho Press, 1990, 3–19.

Parkhill, Thomas C. *Weaving Ourselves into the Land: Charles Godfrey Leland, "Indians" and the Study of Native American Religions*. Syracuse: State University of New York Press, 1997.

Tinker, George. "God, Gods, Goddesses and Indians." Northern California Osage Association website, accessed 10 August 2003.

Walker, James R. *Lakota Myth*. Elaine A. Jahner, ed. Lincoln: University of Nebraska Press, 1983.

See also: American Indians as "First Ecologists"; Gaia; Hinduism; Indigenous Environmental Network; Mother Nature Imagery; Noble Savage; Plastic Medicine Men; Religious Environmentalist Paradigm; Romanticism and Indigenous People; Savages; United Nations' "Earth Summits".

Mother Earth and the Earth People (Trinidad)

The Earth People are an antinomian and "neo-pagan" community settled on the north coast of Trinidad in the Caribbean which originated in the visions of their leader Mother Earth (Jeanette MacDonald, 1934–1984). From 1975 until 1976, she had experienced a series of revelations: she came to understand that the Christian teaching of God the Father as Creator was false and that the world was the work of a primordial Mother, whom she identified with the African ancestors, with Nature and with the Earth. Nature gave birth to a race of black people, but her rebellious Son (God) reentered his Mother's womb to gain her power of generation and succeeded by producing (or forcing her to create) white people. The Whites, the Race of the Son, then enslaved the Blacks and have continued to exploit them. The Way of the Son is that of Science – of cities, clothes, schools, factories and wage labor. The Way of the Mother is the Way of Nature – a return to the simplicity of the Beginning, a simplicity of nakedness, cultivation of the land by hand and with respect, and of gentle and non-exploiting human relationships.

The Son, in a continued quest for the power of generation, has recently entered into a new phase. He has now succeeded in establishing himself in Trinidad's Africans and Indians and is also on the point of replacing humankind altogether with computers and robots. Nature, who has borne all this out of love for the whole of her creation, has finally lost patience. The current order of the Son will end in a catastrophic drought and famine, nuclear war, or a heating up of the Earth, a destruction of the Son's work through his own agency, after which the original state of Nature will once again prevail.

Jeanette herself is a partial manifestation of the Mother who will fully enter into her only at the End. Her task at the time of initial ethnographic fieldwork (1980–1982) was to facilitate the return to Nature by organizing the community known as Hell Valley, the Valley of Decision, to prepare for the return to the Beginning and to "put out the life" to her people, the Black Nation, the Mother's Children. She has to combat the false doctrines of existing religions which place the Son over the Mother and to correct the distorted teaching of the Bible where she is represented as the Devil (hence "Hell Valley"). She stands for Life and Nature, in opposition to the Christian God who is really the Son, the principle of Science and Death. As the Devil she is opposed to churches and prisons, education and money, contemporary morals and fashionable opinions. Because God is "right" Mother Earth teaches the Left, and the Earth People interchange various conventional oppositions: "left" for "right;" "evil" or "bad" for "good." Seeming obscenities are only Natural words for She Herself, who is the Cunt, the origin of all life.

The exact timing of the End was uncertain but it was expected in Jeanette's physical lifetime. Then time would end, sickness would be healed and the nation would speak one language. The Son will be exiled to his planet, the Sun, really the Planet of Ice which is currently hidden by Fire placed there by the Mother: Fire which will eventually return to where it belongs, back to the heart of the nurturant Earth.

Mother Earth's revelations ceased in 1975–1976 after an episode called the Miracle in which she brought the sun closer to the Earth. At this time her family was still living with her in a deserted village some fifteen miles from the nearest settlement, and they were joined by an assortment of young men, mostly old friends and neighbors of hers from Port-of-Spain, together with Rastafarians attracted by a newspaper article written about a family going naked in the bush. Her ideas were now consolidated in reflection and debate. By 1978 her title of "Mother Earth" was adopted, possibly after a recent carnival masquerade which had portrayed a large, fecund Earth Mother. Mother Earth continued to have visions in her dreams but these were similar to those of other members: premonitions and answers to the immediate organizational problems on which her attention was now focused.

While around sixty people have been active Earth People at different times, in October 1981, twenty-two were resident in the Valley, with perhaps twenty sympathizers and occasional members in town. There were annual naked marches into Port-of-Spain which sometimes ended in arrests with brief stays in the state psychiatric hospital for Mother Earth (with a variety of diagnoses), together with raids on the settlement by social workers which resulted in confinement of the younger children to an orphanage: Mother Earth's youngest son escaped and trekked back to the community across the mountains. There were, however, supportive articles in two local periodicals, *Ras Tafari Speaks* and *The Bomb*. Trinidad's first prime minister had recently died and the government was preoccupied with an election: those in the Hell Valley group were left to themselves.

Only one other member of the group was female, with 16 young male followers between 18 and 33, most previously associated with the local cults of Rastafari or Spiritual Baptism, besides Mother Earth and her immediate family. The reason they gave for joining (to the visiting anthropologist in 1981) was the corruption and spiritual decay associated with the post-independence government, and a wish to return to a simpler natural lifestyle. In opposition to the *material* world, the group all went naked, sleeping out on the bare ground, and maintained themselves through fishing and cultivation of the land using only cutlasses.

The center of the community was the old wooden house of the deserted village into which Mother Earth had moved in 1972, together with some added "African" huts. For about half a mile in each direction, the secondary bush and scrub of the seasonal rainforest had been cleared and a variety of trees and perennial cultigens were grown: medicine bushes; trees and plants for cordage and wrapping and for basketry and calabashes; timber for building; plantain and banana; roots like cassava, sweet potatoes, dasheen, yam, tannia; aubergine, pineapple, tomato, pigeon peas, callaloo, okra; Indian corn, pumpkin, ginger, sugar cane, christophene; trees bearing oranges, grapefruit, guava, nuts, mango, avocado, pawpaw, pomerac, tamarind and breadfruit; garlic and bushes with pepper, shadobenny and other herbs. Above the settlement, reaching into the lower reaches of the mountains of the northern range, were cocoa and coffee, cannabis and tobacco. In the nearby bush were cress and watermelon, mauby bark, mammy apple, passion fruit, star apple, nutmeg and soursap, while along the coast grew coconut and almond. The variety of crops, virtually every Trinidad food plant, perhaps justified the boast of the Earth People that they were living in the original Eden.

Although all members accepted Mother Earth's role as the Original Mother, the group was "this worldly" in their emphasis on present cultivation of the land and on the preparation and consumption of food. Daily agricultural labor ended with a swim in the sea and Mother Earth ritually dealing out the cooked vegetable food to the group. The central "rite of synthesis" (as anthropologists would put it) was this daily meal. The evening was passed with the smoking of cigars and ganja spliffs, and communal drumming and dancing with singing of their favorite anthems "Beat them Drums of Africa," "The Nation It Have No Food" and "We Going Down Town to Free Up the Nation."

Each new member took a "fruit name" – like Breadfruit, Coconut, Cassava or Pumpkin. Relations between members were fairly egalitarian, and not especially "religious," generally recalling those of the average Trinidad working-class family. Supposedly the group was living in the Beginning of the End, a run-up to the eventual, very physical, end of the world, but little time was spent on millennial speculation. Painted words on the main house proclaimed "Fock [sic] God" – a sentiment in accord with the group's opposition to Christianity and Islam (although there was a more sympathetic attitude toward Rastafari and Shango Baptism as being "half-way there").

In 1982, with disputes in the group relating to differences in practical authority, and Mother Earth's continued illness, relations deteriorated, splits occurred and the settlement was burned. Mother Earth died in 1984, and by the late 1990s, the Earth People were split into four groups, one on the original site. For all four, what has remained central is less Mother Earth's personal messianic vision than some sense of a more "natural" and "African" style which her own life had embodied.

Roland Littlewood

Further Reading

Chevannes, Barry, ed. *Rastafari and Other African-Caribbean Worldviews*. London: Macmillan, 1995.

Littlewood, Roland. *Pathology and Identity: The Work of Mother Earth in Trinidad*. Cambridge: Cambridge University Press, 1993.

See also: Caribbean Cultures; Mother Earth; Rastafari.

Mother Nature Imagery

Mother Nature is a central theme in religion and ecology. The notion that the natural environment is, either metaphorically or literally, a mother to all humanity is an ancient and influential one. Mother Nature imagery speaks directly to the experience many people have of the environment providing both physical and spiritual refueling, two things that the real "good ol' Mom" often provided as well. People frequently report wilderness experience – even a stroll in a city park – to be rejuvenating, transformative, and spiritually fulfilling. But the notion of Mother Nature is also controversial, as seen from the various perspectives of gender studies, environmentalism, and religious faith. A feminist perspective asks about the negative effects on mothers and on women in general of using her as a "fuel source." Environmentalists add the argument that casting nature as mother can easily compound ecological problems if nature is then viewed as a never-ending source of energy and resources. And people of varying religious faiths disagree as to whether nature is properly understood, either metaphorically or literally, as a divine goddess and whether such a view is justified as a corrective to patriarchal theism.

An Ancient Tradition of Imagery in Western Religion and Culture

The sense of the environment as bountiful female participates in a long and powerful tradition of association. The Mother Nature image, or that of nature as the Great Mother, appears to be almost timeless. It is found in figurines, cave paintings, and burial practices that date back to early human prehistory. Nature as the Great Mother may, indeed, be *the* oldest human religious idea. Paleolithic peoples regarded nature as the Great Mother who nurtured them much like a mother feeds and cares for her infant child. The Goddess of Laussel, one of the earliest such images we have, was sculpted from a rock face at the entrance to the cave of Cap Blanc, near Les Eyzies in the valley of the Dordogne, France. It dates back about 21,000 years. This Paleolithic figure holds up a notched bison horn, believed to represent the crescent moon and the thirteen-month lunar calendar. Her rounded, fleshy buttocks and belly are common among the goddess figurines of the time. The rock relief is painted with red ochre, symbolizing the powerful color of birth and menstruation.

The Classical Greeks revered the Earth Goddess Gaia – in a usage currently resurrected by some scientists, environmentalists, and neo-pagans – as "Mother of All." The Romans sang a hymn to the holy goddess Tellus Mater (Mother Earth), Mother of Living Nature. This second century Roman hymn reads in part:

> The food of life
> Thou metest out in eternal loyalty
> And, when life has left us,
> We take our refuge in Thee.
> Thus everything Thou dolest out
> Returns into Thy womb (Getty 1990: 10).

In the first century, the Alexandrian Jewish scholar Philo identified nature with mother and with food-provider. This example helps make the important point that Mother Nature imagery is part of a larger association in Western religion and culture that links together women and nature. The imagery not only functions to portray the environment as maternal, but also to reinforce common cultural notions that women are "nature-like" or closer to nature than men. Philo, for example, sees Earth and women alike as sharing a "teeming" fertility and a bountifulness that they offer freely to all offspring:

> Nature has bestowed on every mother as a most essential endowment teeming breasts, thus preparing in advance food for the child that is to be born. The earth also, as we all know, is a mother, for which reason the earliest men thought fit to call her "Demeter," combining the name of "mother" with that of "earth"; for as Plato says, earth does not

imitate women, but woman earth ... Fitly therefore on earth also, most ancient and most fertile of mothers, did Nature bestow, by way of breasts, streams of rivers and springs, to the end that both the plants might be watered and all animals might have abundance to drink (in Glacken 1967: 14).

While in these examples, Mother Earth willingly "metest out the food of life," in another version of the theme, humans violently take that sustenance from her. Here we see that Mother Nature imagery portrays the environment not only as a life-giving female who is beneficent toward humanity and beloved in return (the Good Mother), but also as one who is wounded or conquered by humans (the Hurt Mother or Bad Mother). All three motifs play an important part in Mother Nature imagery.

Mother Nature as Good, Bad, and Hurt
The Hurt Mother motif emerges as early as ancient Rome, where strictures against mining (in comments by Pliny, Ovid, and Seneca, later repeated in the Renaissance) expressed concern about violating Mother Earth by stripping precious metals from her womb in a process that despoils the Earth's surface and fuels human avarice and war. "When will be the end of thus exhausting the earth?" asked Pliny in worried lament (in Merchant 1980: 30). Mother Nature is also sometimes wounded because her conquest by humans is held to be justified and rightful. A famous chorus from Sophocles's play *Antigone* (ca. 441 B.C.E.) celebrates man's conquest over nature:

Oh, Earth is patient, and Earth is old,
And a mother of Gods, but he breaketh her,
To-ing, froing, with the plough-team going,
Tearing the soil of her, year by year.

Nature is still a fertile mother who provides for humanity, but now that bounty is taken by force. This example highlights the ancient identification of the female and the plowed earth that forms an important part of the woman–nature association. The identification reoccurs later in the play when Antigone's uncle Creon – a character seemingly obsessed with the need for men to control women – defends his decision to kill his rebellious niece, betrothed to his son, with the contemptuous line, "There are other fields for him to plow." In these examples, neither nature nor woman is in control of her fertility, but is depicted as tamed and mastered by man/humans.

The Bad Mother motif of nature as a recalcitrant or withholding mother intensifies with the Scientific Revolution of the sixteenth and seventeenth centuries. Historian Carolyn Merchant argues that the image of nature changes in this period from "active teacher and parent" to "mindless, submissive [female] body" (1980: 190). The language of the new experimental science and its mechanistic worldview is often that of sexual mastery, of enslavement and rape, as in Francis Bacon's promise in *The Masculine Birth of Time*: "I am come in very truth leading to you nature with all her children to bind her to your service and make her your slave" (in Merchant 1930: 170). Baconian imagery of domination over nature includes references to mining as wresting hidden secrets and goods from nature's withholding womb, and how through use of anvil and forge, nature can be "forced out of her natural state and squeezed and molded" (in Merchant 1980: 171).

Both the Hurt Mother and Bad Mother motifs became more frequent as ecological damage mounted in modern Western culture. Smohalla, a Native American of the Columbia Basin Tribes and leader of a small group resisting settlement and treaty, spoke out famously against European-American attitudes to the land around 1885. Making skillful use of maternal metaphor to contrast the impact of his people's traditional root gathering, Smohalla told a visiting cavalry officer:

We no more harm the earth than would an infant's fingers harm its mother's breast. But the white man tears up large tracts of land, runs deep ditches, cuts down forests, and changes the whole face of the earth ... Every honest man knows in his heart that this is all wrong (in Gill 1987: 54)

And from the dustbowl crisis of the 1930s, American painter Alexandre Hogue created powerful art that despairs over the damage of land erosion. His oil painting *Mother Earth Laid Bare* (1938) shows a woman's naked body outlined in the barren ground, stripped of all topsoil. Hogue describes her as "raped by the plow and laid bare" (DeLong 1984: 120). More recently and with equal imagistic verve, Jim Morrison, vocalist and songwriter for the 1960s rock group, The Doors, inquires in their 1967 song "When the Music's Over": "What have they done to the earth?/What have they done to our fair sister?" (I take Morrison here to be drawing on 1960s counterculture egalitarian language of "sister/brother" in order to make an environmentalist point about solidarity with the plight of "Mother Earth.") His answer is a graphically violent image of the Hurt Mother, spoken over chaotic drumbeat and disintegrating guitar riffs:

Ravaged and plundered
and ripped her and bit her.
Stuck her with knives
in the side of the dawn
and tied her with fences
and dragged her down.

The modern environmental movement draws heavily on this ancient tradition of imagery depicting nature as our loving but wounded mother, who now suffers from the human pressures of population, technology, and disrespectful practice. Reflecting an activist agenda, the imagery features humans as her/its healers. For example, Turner Broadcasting has a successful children's cartoon series called "Captain Planet and the Planeteers" and "The New Adventures of Captain Planet" in which five children from around the world work with the environmental superhero Captain Planet to protect Gaia, the spirit of the Earth and our "archetypal mother." The well-known environmental slogan "Love Your Mother" fits in this same category, with its implicit message that we must now help and heal she whom we have harmed.

Bad Mother Nature imagery continues to thrive as well. It is found perhaps most commonly today in references to the "wrath of Mother Nature" in everyday conversation and professional reporting about the weather and such natural disasters as floods, hurricanes, and volcanoes. The imagery is also often used by advertisers trying to sell their products by evoking a deep emotional response about the pleasure of human victory over the threats of nature. A recent campaign for the Nissan Pathfinder, for example, claimed Mother Nature was using fierce weather to try – unsuccessfully – to drown, burn, and blow away the human tucked securely and triumphantly into his SUV.

Given the radically different cultural contexts of all these examples, what accounts for the transmission of "Mother Nature" as a cultural trope across cultures and centuries? Why does it endure, and in forms similar enough to be recognizable from the Paleolithic, or at least the classical period, to today? For some, the apparent "naturalness" of the metaphor itself – based on the fertility of the Earth and on woman's biological role as childbearer – is a sufficient explanation. From this perspective, nature, to the extent that it produces and provides for all life, simply seems like a mother. Others root the prevalence and longevity of the metaphor not so much in nature, as in culture: they focus on women's childrearing role and supposedly greater capacity for nurturance as social constructions that only appear natural within patriarchal societies that assign women these roles. The social constructions that label childcare and nurturing in general to be "women's work" then make the life-giving environment appear to be maternal also, since it too is expected to serve human needs.

Ecofeminist Critique

Ecofeminists have been the scholars most active in these debates documenting and deconstructing the meanings of Mother Nature imagery. Their most basic claim is that gender matters. A cursory study of Western culture, or even of current television weather forecasting, reveals "Mother Nature" to be a major motif in conceptualizing nature. Because of this prevalence, gender analysis and ecofeminism help get to the heart of how societies construct concepts of nature and how they structure human–nature relations. Furthermore, ecofeminist scholarship documents the function of the woman–nature link and demonstrates how women in patriarchal contexts tend to suffer from it. Sherry Ortner, an anthropologist, was one of the first to frame this problem. She argued that women are crossculturally perceived to be closer to nature than men and claimed that this perception accounts for women's universal subordination, since nature is itself universally devalued. Others – such as Dorothy Dinnerstein, Annette Kolodny, Carolyn Merchant, Elizabeth Dodson Gray, Rosemary Radford Ruether, and Susan Griffin – responded and contributed to the debate.

Their argument is that, in patriarchal culture, when women are symbolically associated with nature, or seen as having a particular affinity with nature that surpasses that of men, then women are seen as less fully human than men. Mother Nature imagery works to associate the feminine more with the carnal, the emotional, and the physical and to associate the masculine with the cultural and the intellectual. Susan Griffin, for example, in her passionate and poetic book *Woman and Nature: The Roaring Inside Her* (1978), illustrates how this traditional association contributes to women's voicelessness and powerlessness by assigning woman the roles of passive and obedient reproducer and nurturer (in her chapter entitled "Cows"), obstinate and dull-witted drudge, bred for labor the breeders do not wish to do (in the "Mules" chapter), and well-trained and well-groomed gratifier of her master ("The Show Horse"). One way to put this point reveals the connection between woman-as-nature and nature-as-mother: in patriarchal culture, women are under-personified and nature is over-personified. Women are perceived to merge with nature as a servile resource, Dinnerstein says, as "an asset to be owned and harnessed, harvested and mined" (1976: 36). Even when women are exalted as purer than men, as less bestial, and as the "guardians of culture and morals," Ortner points out that these seeming inversions merely place women above instead of below culture and that women, in both cases, remain excluded from the realm of culture. The consequences here for both women and nature can be noxious. Both are seen as an endless source of succor, who, if she fails to provide what we want, is cruelly withholding it, so justifying our exploitation or plunder.

Nature Spirituality

Although ecofeminists share these concerns about imaging nature as mother in any society still shaped by patriarchal devaluations of women and nature, they and others with interests in religion and ecology agree there is nevertheless a positive role to be played by Mother Nature imagery. The imagery remains compelling, important, and apt, especially if its patriarchal cultural context can be critiqued and resisted. For example, popular ecological slogans like "Love Your Mother" could become more effective if "mother" meant less exclusively the self-sacrificing, ever-giving nurturer. Maternal metaphors do express the environmental truth that nature provides all life and sustenance, as does the childbearing mother. Christian mystic Hildegard of Bingen's endorsement from the twelfth century rings equally true today for many eco-theologians and practitioners of nature-based spirituality: "The earth is at the same time mother. She is mother of all that is natural, mother of all that is human. She is the mother of all, for contained in her are the seeds of all" (Fox 1988: 11, 13). Such language makes much intuitive sense to feminists and nonfeminists alike and can serve the important environmentalist role of facilitating people's sense of connection with nature.

The Earth has functioned as a very powerful and ancient center for worship and for seeing the divine as female, a resource important for many feminist theologians. Such meanings and ritual practices are revived today in various forms of syncretistic nature religion: neo-paganism, Wicca, ecofeminist spirituality, and eco-theology. Artist Judith Anderson, for example, combines commitments to environmentalism and woman-centered spirituality in a powerful etching entitled "Missa Gaia: This is My Body" (1988). Here the Great Mother sits in a birthing position. The world's animals flow from her and merge with her, boundaries of self and other barely discernible. Anderson describes her Great Mother as embodying "both celebration and profound grief and anger" (Middlebury symposium 1990). This Mother, in other words, is at once Good and Bad and Hurt. In such contexts of religious experimentation and renewal, women might well sometimes see themselves as "closer to nature," as when celebrating their bodies, their ability to create new life, or the interrelation of all species. Indian feminist theologian Aruna Gnanadason suggests that "the fear of what is being done to the earth is giving women the urgent imperative to assert their connectedness with nature ... more specially in the Third World where the struggle for survival is the most acute" (1996: 77–78). Mother Nature imagery thus has the power to evoke a whole range of both patriarchal and feminist notions of what "mother" means and projects these meanings onto the environment, with consequences both oppressive and liberatory.

Significance of Mother Nature Imagery

The present human situation is one of ecological imperilment, and Mother Nature imagery, in some ways, seems only to render matters worse. Images of the Good Mother make environmental destruction appear less of a problem, for the bounty of nature is then inexhaustible. And when the Bad Mother is invoked, striking back against nature becomes a good. Mother Nature imagery is hardly the sole means by which the environment is represented in the cultural imagination. It is, however, popular, pervasive, widespread, and immediately understood. That groups as diverse as environmental organizations and auto manufacturers use it for their ends indicates that this imagery elicits powerful and conflicting responses in a large and varied audience. The imagery holds sway from shared and deep recesses of personal and cultural fantasy.

The remarkable diversity of emotional response in the Mother Nature imagery – sometimes loving and respectful, sometimes condescending and controlling, sometimes suspicious and fearful, and sometimes downright violently adversarial – is significant in itself. It suggests a fundamental ambivalence toward nature. The imagery reveals not simply connection, but complex, ambivalent tendencies toward both violent control and loving repair in human relations toward nature. Mother Nature imagery yields insight into these tensions that, while probably intensified by the present hyperconsumerism of American culture, seem generally characteristic of Western modernity. The imagery suggests that many people may resist and refrain from a committed environmentalism because it is easy and comforting to imagine that nature's provisions are ever-abundant and guaranteed. Overall, imagery of Mother Nature – even when putatively environmentalist – can portray a response toward nature that is ambiguous and uneasy and can undermine its own activism.

That such ambivalent passions are found in Mother Nature imagery is not surprising. The imagery is so rich, so provocative, so imagistically intense, precisely because it seems to embody central riddles or universal problems about human identity and experience. Part of what it means to be human is to confront the meaning of our "creatureliness," the riddle of our existence as beings within the context and constraints of a natural environment. One perennial way we do this is through Mother Nature imagery that tells us the relation is one of familial dependence or interdependence. The imagery also serves a cultural purpose of exploring the riddles of gender difference and of the problem of evil. In all societies, although in different ways, gender acts as a significant lens for structuring social relations: why is this the case and why do patterns of subordination result (paralleling patterns of ecological degradation)? Why do we hurt one another (including the Earth) and how can we establish communities of care? Is the metaphor of mother (or parent) and child the answer?

Catherine M. Roach

Further Reading

Anderson, Judith. "Missa Gaia: This is My Body." Etching, 1988, in Steven C. Rockefeller and John C. Elder, eds. *Spirit and Nature: Why the Environment is a Religious Issue.* Boston: Beacon Press, 1992.

DeLong, Lea Rosson. *Nature's Forms/Nature's Forces.* Tulsa: University of Oklahoma Press, 1984.

Dinnerstein, Dorothy. *The Mermaid and the Minotaur: Sexual Arrangements and Human Malaise.* New York: Harper & Row, 1976.
Getty, Adele. *Goddess: Mother of Living Nature.* London: Thames & Hudson, 1990.
Gill, Sam D. *Mother Earth: An American Story.* Chicago: University of Chicago Press, 1987.
Glacken, Clarence. *Traces on a Rhodian Shore.* Berkeley: University of California Press, 1967.
Gnanadason, Aruna. "Toward a Feminist Eco-Theology for India." In Rosemary Radford Ruether, ed. *Women Healing Earth: Third World Women on Ecology, Feminism, and Religion.* Maryknoll, NY: Orbis Books, 1996.
Gray, Elizabeth Dodson. *Green Paradise Lost.* Wellesley: Roundtable Press, 1979, 1981.
Griffin, Susan. *Woman and Nature: The Roaring Inside Her.* New York: Harper & Row, 1978.
Merchant, Carolyn. *The Death of Nature: Women, Ecology, and the Scientific Revolution.* San Francisco: Harper & Row, 1980.
Ortner, Sherry B. "Is Female to Male as Nature is to Culture?" In Michelle Zimbalist Rosaldo and Louise Lamphere, eds. *Woman, Culture, and Society.* Stanford: Stanford University Press, 1974.
Ruether, Rosemary Radford. *Gaia and God: An Ecofeminist Theology of Earth Healing.* HarperSanFrancisco, 1992.

See also: Ecofeminism; Gaia; Mother Earth.

Motion Pictures

In the past two decades, humanity's interaction and relationship with the natural world has become a notable theme in many popular feature films. These films present different stories and interpretations of how nature can be viewed and how humanity should respond to it. Whether based on true events or fictionalized dramas, film narratives present us with concepts and images about reality and the way the world does or could function (Turner 1999). Since films often function on a series of storytelling formulas and electronic stereotypes, this enables us easily to identify dominant perceptions of nature in popular culture. Identifying these themes might also lead to a need to reinterpret these conceptions, especially as they relate to spiritual relationships between the material, natural and non-material worlds. As Martin and Ostwalt claim, "Films do much more than simply entertain [they] have the potential to reinforce, to challenge, to overturn, or to crystallize religion's perspectives, ideological assumptions and fundamental values" (Martin and Ostwalt 1995: vii). Therefore it is important to recognize the power of film to inform our views and values concerning how we perceive and treat the natural world as it relates to spiritual themes. Three common themes dealing with religion and nature presented through motion pictures are: nature as an instrument of God, nature as a metaphysical realm, and nature as a religious storyteller.

Nature as an Instrument of God

Humanity's conflict with nature is a common theme in films. This conflict often centers on human attempts to control nature. When humanity fails and nature is proved to be more commanding, this is often interpreted in religious terms. Nature is viewed as a spiritual force directed by the "hand of God." Biblical language and apocalyptic pictures often emerge in these characterizations.

This is most clearly demonstrated in films dealing with weather where humanity only has the ability to respond. Nature is unpredictable at best, destructive at its worst. Two recent examples of this are *Twister* (1996) and *The Perfect Storm* (2000); both stress the fury of nature and humanity's vulnerability. *Twister* is based around the storm-chasing researchers who spend their days pursuing tornadoes in an attempt to study and refine their ability to predict these natural phenomena. Tensions rage as former partners are reunited to race against time and a competing research team as they try out their new storm-measuring technology. While humans attempt to map and comprehend the tornadoes, they cannot control their path of destruction. The "finger of God" blows where it wills. There is a sense of awesomeness and divine beauty in the chaos, that no matter what technology or means are employed, the fury of nature can only be adapted to but not controlled. The characters progressively come to terms with the fact that nature has a power beyond the human level.

Similarly in *The Perfect Storm* a fishing crew is overwhelmed by the unpredictability of nature, when a dying tropical hurricane from Bermuda collides with a cold front from the Great Lakes resulting in the "Perfect Storm." The captain and crew's determination to take advantage of the last good fishing run of the season puts them in the midst of the worst storm in history. While skill, teamwork and determination do help the ship's crew to maneuver through several near-fatal experiences, in the end, nature's fury proves greater. One can question whether it was greed or desperation that put them in the situation to begin with, yet no matter the reason the outcome would have been the same as seen by the plight of others trapped in the storm. The ending scene brings us to a church where people remember the lost crew. Peace that comes after the storm appears to be found in the acknowledgment of a Higher Being.

Humanity's attempts to control natural phenomena are displayed as futile in films. Therefore in these circumstances nature is to be feared and connected with the unknown, uncontrollable God. This is illustrated again in *Volcano* (1997) where the erupted stream of lava is equated to the "wrath and will of God" and the city planner who built a subway system on a fault line is described with the biblical reference as "the foolish man who built his house upon the sand." Since competing with God is futile, humanity only wins when it either accepts the majestic power of nature or when it fights to protect it.

Nature as a Metaphysical Realm
Another religious theme in nature-based motion pictures can be characterized as the metaphysics of interrelatedness, spiritual descriptions of nature's internal interactions. Here films focus on communal narratives and the physical and spiritual linking of different spheres of the created order.

Many animation films have portrayed these relationships and conflicts in playful ways, yet dealing with serious religious worldviews. In *The Lion King* (1994) this spiritual connection is described as the "circle of life" dealing with tension between species as well as themes of redemption and restoration. It presents a coming-of-age tale, as a lion cub becomes "King of the Jungle" and is a mix of African folk-tales and classical myths. Simba's journey into adulthood begins with him facing the tragic death of his father King Mufasa. Simba's rejection of the past brings decimation to the "Pride land" where plant and animal life are on the verge of extinction. This film focuses on the idea that all life is connected. This relates not only to ideas about the natural order, but also to the idea that within nature spiritual ideas are transferred. From nature comes wisdom, as illustrated by the spirit of the King speaking through the stars and a shamanic baboon advising Simba through nature-based illustrations. Redemption comes through Simba's battle to confront the past and reestablish order. A depressed and ravaged natural environment represents evil. When the balance of good (i.e., Simba becoming king) is restored, the jungle and animal kingdom almost immediately returns to a state of splendor. This film interprets the world in terms of animistic spirituality, ancestor worship, and the spirit world speaking through nature.

Another film which focuses on the mystical interconnection of nature through an animistic worldview is the Disney animated feature *Pocahontas* (1995). In the film, nature is portrayed as possessing a voice that has the ability to speak to the heart. The voice of nature comes to Pocahontas through her mentor, Grandma Willow, a tree which encourages Pocahontas to listen with her heart to the voices of the forest who will direct her. She is "led" to a white man who falls in love with her. A clash of cultures and intentions results, yet love prevails and the Indians and English seemingly come to a peaceful truce. Thus nature's voice leads those who listen to it toward their destiny. This portrayal of nature having a spirit is basically animistic. Those who acknowledge the voice and spirit of nature as Pocahontas are seen as enlightened and wise while the Englishmen who focus on gold are seen as shallow, selfish and destructive. Peace is equated with harmony with nature. This is a retelling of a traditional American myth highlighting a modified Native American understanding of nature.

Nature's interaction with human society through spiritual channels is also represented in films dealing with myth and nature, often utilizing classic myths of the battle of good versus evil. In the animated production *Fern Gully: The Last Rainforest* (1992) the spirit and natural world appear intertwined. Everything is peaceful in Fern Gully until the intrusion of a clear-cutting logging crew, which wreaks havoc on the spiritual and physical balance of the rainforest. Young fairy Crysta saves the life of one of the logging crew, Zac, by shrinking him to her own size. Zac in turn learns the ways of the forest and helps the fairies battle evil spirits and logging destruction in an attempt to preserve this last bit of the rainforest. The myth expresses the conviction that goodness is based on a desire to nurture the environment while evil seeks to destroy it. Not every spirit in the forest is good, as seen by the demon Hexxus who seeks to destroy not only the fairies, but also the environment itself. The film infers that nature is not alone in maintaining its balance, but relies on the aid of the spirit world. While based in a fantasy realm, this idea of the need for spiritual intervention in the battle against environmental destruction is a prevalent theme.

Nature as a spiritual realm where religious themes guide the interactions of animal and plant systems is demonstrated through the above-mentioned films. Relationships within the animal kingdom seem to mirror the struggle portrayed between humans and nature. Yet, instead of an external God-figure guiding the outcomes and effects of the natural world, it is spiritual forces within, be they animistic or magical, that guide the cycles of nature. The focus in these films is not one of power as it appears on the surface, but often of good versus evil.

Nature as Religious Storyteller
Films about nature also deal with underlying stories of meaning; narratives that seek to make sense of the world and share that sense with others. Often this searching uncovers various spiritual beliefs. John May (1997), in his analysis of a religious approach to film, states that film narratives can provide archetypal patterns, images and elements that frame meaning and mythic orientation, central values that illustrate human drives to live, love and transcend self. These patterns and myths can deal with very different religious persuasions or worldviews.

Engaging with the natural world can be portrayed in films as a path to the divine. Even in times of stress, the natural world possesses the ability to bring about spiritual revelation. The movie *Alive* (1993) features the underlying story of how one survivor "found God on the mountain" while chronicling the true events of the 1972 plane crash of an Uruguayan rugby team. As rations run low the moral dilemma arises of whether eating the remains of their former companions is acceptable if they are to survive. *Alive* begins and ends with spiritual musings of one of the survivors about the nature of God and purposes to life. There are glimpses of the moral dilemma as to whether the ends (meaning survival) justify the means (inferring cannibalism). In the midst of this battle for survival of the fittest, which involves fighting starvation, avalanches, and winter storms, praying the rosary and moments of reflection provide peace between storms. Those who survive, and are seemingly hailed as heroes, are those who do not let morals take precedence over the need for food. The film represents a traditional/theistic religious worldview. Nature brings death, but it also bring space for epiphany as it forces the survivors to engage that which is bigger than themselves, namely God, in order to survive and find hope.

The classic conflict of science versus religion has also been articulated in films that deal with the seen and unseen natural world. *Contact* (1997), based on a Carl Sagan novel, portrays science and discovery as forms of a spiritual quest. The central character is Ellie, a scientist who searches radio waves of space looking for life outside our solar system. She and the rest of her team hope their quest will lead to a message from another world ... and it does. The researchers are soon overwhelmed as political, scientific and religious figures rally to assert their positions and have a part in this new discovery. Through the struggles, Ellie receives support from a spiritual advisor to the White House who urges her to accept the existence of a higher life-force. The film portrays classic tensions between science and religion. Religious faith is portrayed in a broad, fairly relativistic sense with the only really theological strongpoint being a belief in a higher power. Experience defines reality and spiritual engagement, representing a postmodern form of spirituality. At first Ellie rejects the idea of a God she cannot see, but changes her position after having an "alien" encounter she cannot prove to others. She asserts that because she knows she experienced it, then it must be real. While dealing with cosmic themes rather than natural sciences, the film relays the potential for science to engage with and possibly accept the idea of a "g/God" that cannot be seen.

The *Lord of the Rings: Fellowship of the Rings* (2001) also deals with religious themes as a classic fantasy tale based on J.R.R. Tolkien's trilogy. It centers on the "one ring" which holds the potential to manipulate dark powers and enslave the world. The Hobbit keeper of the ring, along with a band of elves, dwarfs and humans, must travel to the land of Mordor where it was created and can alone be destroyed. This journey through a dark environment is also a sort of spiritual quest. Tension between free will and providence are highlighted by Frodo's choice to accept the quest to return the ring and at the proclamation by the wizard Gandalf that other forces are at work guiding our fate. Temptation surrounds the ring in a mystique that challenges even the purest of intentions of Frodo's protectors. In the midst of this there is hope as fellow journeymen fight to protect Frodo and his quest. In *The Two Towers* (2002) there also is Fangorn, who demonstrates traits of druidic spirituality, as he summons his fellow tree protectors and raises them as troops to fight, if only partly, in response to the destruction of his forest.

The mythical environment is a shell for a deeper purpose. The journey through this environment seems as important as the destination. This film represents a complex system of myth- and magic-based beliefs. Here there is no higher being representing an ultimate good; the central battle against evil is a fight against the evil within the self and in various levels of the represented created order.

Investigating this theme of nature as a religious storyteller demonstrates how films can present traditional/theistic, postmodern spiritual, and mythical and magical views of the natural world. Numerous other films could be mentioned for the other religious or ideological interpretations of nature that they present: for instance, *The Matrix* (1999) using a combination of Greek mythology, Christianity and Buddhism to describe a world destroyed by humanity and dominated by a new biotechnological order; *Planet of the Apes* (2001) introducing an adapted postmodern, civil religion in which apes are the highest form of the created order; or *Signs* (2002) where crop circles and alien attack are designed to lead characters toward the recovery of a traditional Christian faith. In these and other films traditional images and myth orientations are used to point the viewer to a spiritual narrative. Archetypal framing of the characters and scenes and implied ideals of the film's underlying theme craft the overall message.

Recognizing the stories films tell us about nature can be an insightful way to identify beliefs and conceptions found in popular culture regarding our natural world. This also provides us the opportunity to reinforce, challenge, overturn or even crystallize the images and religious interpretations these stories pose. Images portrayed express the spiritual and physical perceptions of reality and projections of how the world could be. More than just visual stories, these films become texts of the religious mindset of our current culture. Film narratives can also be used as teaching tools and illustrations for inspiring environmental action, or at least, reinforcing responsible caring and stewardship of the natural world.

Heidi Campbell
Heather Elmatti

Further Reading

Ingram, David. *Green Screen: Environmentalism and Hollywood Cinema.* Exeter: University of Exeter Press, 2000.

Johnston, Robert K. *Reel Spirituality: Theology and Film in Dialogue.* Grand Rapids, MI: Baker Books, 2000.

May, John, ed. *New Image of Religious Film.* Kansas City: Sheed & Ward, 1997.

Martin, Joel and Conrad Ostwalt, eds. *Screening the Sacred: Religion, Myth, and Ideology in Popular American Film.* Boulder: Westview Press, 1995.

Turner, Graeme. *Film as Social Practice.* (3rd edn). London and New York: Routledge, 1999.

Films

Alive. Frank Marshall (Director). USA: Buena Vista, 1993.

Contact. Robert Zemeckis (Director). USA: South Side Amusement/Warner Brothers, 1997.

Fern Gully: The Last Rainforest. Bill Kroyer (Director). USA/Australia: 20th Century Fox/Youngheart Productions, 1992.

The Lion King. Roger Allers and Robert Minkoff (Directors). USA: Buena Vista, 1994.

Lord of the Rings: The Two Towers. Peter Jackson (Director). New Zealand: WingNut Films, 2002.

Lord of the Rings: Fellowship of the Rings. Peter Jackson (Director). New Zealand: WingNut Films, 2001.

The Matrix. Andy Wachowski and Larry Wachowski (Directors). USA: Groucho II Film Partnership/Silver Pictures/Village Roadshow Pictures, 1999.

The Perfect Storm. Wolfgang Petersen (Director). USA: Baltimore Pictures/Radiant Films/Spring Creek Pictures, 2000.

Planet of the Apes. Tim Burton (Director). USA: Zanuck Company, 2001.

Pocahontas. Mike Gabriel and Eric Goldberg (Directors). USA: Buena Vista/Walt Disney Productions, 1995.

Signs. M. Night Shyamalan (Director). USA: Blinding Edge Pictures/Kennedy/Marshall/Touchstone Pictures, 2002.

Twister. Jan de Bont (Director). USA: Universal/Warner Brothers, 1996.

Volcano. Mick Jackson (Director). USA: 20th Century Fox/Moritz Original, 1997.

See also: Disney; Disney Worlds at War; Middle Earth; Theme Parks.

Mount Nyiro and the Samburu (East Africa)

The Samburu nomadic pastoralists occupy a semi-arid region in north-central Kenya with a complex topography of lowlands and highlands. The lowlands are dry regions of sparse savannah vegetation, while the forested mountains receive slightly higher rainfall, serving as dry-season grazing while the lowlands are used for wet-season grazing. The region has few permanent water sources but is crossed by seasonal streams. The local people dig sand wells in the river beds to obtain water for their livestock and personal use; there are also springs around the lower mountain slopes. Rainfall totals and annual distribution are highly variable and severe droughts that kill large numbers of livestock usually occur at least once in a decade.

Like the other pastoral regions of Kenya, the Samburu homeland has been characterized by the slow pace of modernization, partly attributed to limited interaction with the more developed high potential areas of the country and the influences of the Western world. The Samburu have generally maintained their traditional way of life with little change over the years; indigenous religious beliefs and practices are still strongly held, especially among the older generation. These beliefs and practices have contributed significantly to the conservation of their environmental resources. As pastoralists, they are totally dependent on pasture, water and plants for livestock keeping. The Samburu, therefore, have an intimate relationship with their environment which is interwoven in their traditional religious beliefs and practices. They are a deeply religious people, as is demonstrated through their understanding and relationship with their God. To them, God is an essential part of their existence; indeed, the Samburu name for God is also the word for rain, *Nkai*. Just as rain is the most important climatic element for their existence, as it determines the pasture and water necessary for their systems of livestock keeping, so is the Samburu God of vital importance to them.

The Samburu have a strong religious attachment to mountains. To some extent, all the mountains and highland masses within their territory are considered special areas with religious significance, as they believe that God has a preference for highland areas. However, Mount Nyiro is considered a special sacred site for the Samburu people, for it is here that God resides. They have even a specific location on Mount Nyiro where he lives, called Kosikosi. Though *Kosikosi* is not the peak of the mountain, it is a strikingly distinct peak and an important high point, where God is believed to have his seat at a particular rock, called Ndadapoi. In many ways, Mount Nyiro symbolizes God's presence among the Samburu.

The Samburu believe that God has human characteristics, including sensory attributes. God can hear and see just like human beings and has the ability to know. However, it is important to note that the Samburu recognize that God has qualities superior to those of human beings. They believe God has absolute power and is omnipotent and therefore knows everything that happens even in secret and even before it happens. When a person is seen wanting to do evil, he is warned with the words "*mintining Nkai nemintodol*" (let God not hear or see what you are planning to do). This means that God can read people's thoughts and can punish you. The Samburu use these attributes of God to control their moral behavior, including behavior related to environmental conservation. They believe that God is offended and angered by people's unacceptable actions such as misuse of the environmental resources.

The Samburu God is also perceived to have human features, which the Samburu use to express their total dependence on God for existence and, therefore, the need to please him. The most significant are God's back, armpits and the belly, which depict God's ability to provide shelter, protection, security and love to humans. This is vividly described in this Samburu prayer:

> *Nkai ai, tanapa iyioo* – God carry us on your back, as a mother does with her baby
> *Nkai ai, tejapa iyioo te nkitikit inono* – My God, hide us or secure us with your armpits
> *Nkai ai, tipika iyioo atua Nkosheke ino* – Place us inside your belly
> *Nkai ai, imbung'a iyioo te atua nkosheke ino* – Keep us inside your belly
> *Nkai ai, irrita iyioo to nkosheke naibor* – Pasture us with a white belly with love (Lolarrarri 2000).

The well-watered mountain and highland areas are a constant reminder to the Samburu of their God who sits on Mount Nyiro. It is still strongly believed among the Samburu that God gives the rain or withholds it. This could explain why God is equated to rain, which expresses God's actions and demonstrates his vitality and power. Rain is a direct manifestation of God's benevolence to humankind as through the giving of rain he replenishes the Earth by watering the dry ground and satisfies the thirst and hunger of the people.

The Samburu believe that God predetermines everything and that the only role people can play on Earth is to complement God's efforts and will. This is expressed as "*Materetore Nkai*" which literally means, "let us work together with God and not against him." This could be interpreted to mean working and living in harmony with the natural environment. Destruction of the environment can anger God who is able to punish the people. One of the worst punishments from God seems to be the withholding of rain, which means life and death to the Samburu.

Prayers, sacrifices and incense are offered to God from Mount Nyiro. Any Samburu will always face Mount Nyiro in prayer regardless of where they may be within their extensive grazing territory, signifying their unity of culture despite different exposures and interactions with other communities. They always face the direction of Mount Nyiro when praying, just as the Muslims face Mecca. Mount Nyiro is where most sacrifices and prayers are performed at *Lorian le kosikosi*. Lorian refers to open grassland with a permanent stream, often high on a mountain; such areas are often settlement sites. This is "the open space up the mountain at Kosikosi." God communicates to the Samburu people about impending calamities or current disasters from Mount Nyiro. These messages are delivered to the people through God's appointed messengers who live at the foot of the mountain. Many of the Samburu astrologers, dreamers/messengers, the rope interpreters and intestine readers are found around Mount Nyiro. These special messengers provide religious and cultural leadership to the community.

The Samburu people perform a number of sacrifices to their God. The sacrifices are done using livestock along with incense from a mixture of leaves and branches of special sacred tree species which are put together and burnt. The Samburu believe that God accepts their sacrifice when mixed with incense as represented in the saying: "*Keing'uaya Nkai Lasar*" ("God smells the sacrifice"). "*Kelo nkuama e Lasar netii Nkai*" ("The smell of the sacrifice goes where God is").

The sacrificial animal is slaughtered and blessed with milk mixed with water, and with words "*Torropilo, taalorian, taa Lmalmal matan iyie ana ntasim namunyak*" ("be sweet smelling, smell like the olive tree, smell like incense, that you may be eaten as a blessed sacrifice"). These religious rites cannot be complete without the use of specific environmental resources. Sacrifices offered on Mount Nyiro are considered very special and sacred events. The Samburu offer sacrifices to God for different purposes, but the most important is to appease God when calamities befall them, as they believe these are the result of their wrongdoing. Calamities such as drought, famine, sickness, war, infant death, or female infertility require propitiatory sacrifices. Sacrifices are also offered for thanksgiving in recognition of blessings or good fortune that have come people's way, or to invoke God's guidance and protection. For example, young men of a certain age get together and offer sacrifices asking God to guide them as they start adult life.

Mount Nyiro provides a number of the environmental resources used in Samburu religious sacrifices and prayers. Due to their religious and cultural significance, the Samburu have established a complex system to ensure their conservation and sustainable use. This system is embodied within their religious and traditional practices. The resources are:

a) Water: Mount Nyiro is a source of seven important springs which are a lifeline for people and livestock on the different sides of this sacred mountain. The Samburu understand that the water from these springs is life to them which must be handled in a sacred manner, and they protect the sources using taboos and curses. Water is commonly used as *Nkarrer* (a mixture of water and milk) in blessings and prayers. The water used in these rituals is obtained specifically from one of the Mount Nyiro springs.

b) Plants: A number of plants from Mount Nyiro are used for burning incense and for other religious practices. For example, the bamboo has religious and cultural significance among the Samburu. The bamboo is closely linked to God. Samburu often refer to *kosikosi* as the place of the "talking bamboo," and it is a place for offering prayers such as "the God of the talking bamboo, I pray to you" (Lolarrarri 2000). A number of taboos are used which have been instrumental in the conservation and sustainable use of the bamboo. Bamboo can only be cut when there is a full moon. This helps to control the harvesting period. The sacredness of the bamboo is also maintained through restrictions on its uses; for example, the fact that it must never be used as a stick to discipline children. Several other tree species used in burnt offerings are found only on the mountains.

c) Green grass is a symbol of peace and wealth and has a direct link to livestock, the Samburu source of wealth. When green grass is plentiful, the livestock will be healthy and strong. The Samburu use green grass as a mark of regret and repentance; the person asking for forgiveness pulls a handful of green grass and shows it to the other person while pleading for another chance. During traditional ceremonies such as circumcision and in traditional prayers, green grass is used variously to signify peace and as part of the prayers.

Mount Nyiro also has considerable ethnobotanical significance as the source of certain medicinal plants, which cannot be found anywhere else in Samburu District. As many as 135 species of trees and shrubs have been identified by the Samburu as having medicinal value. Recent studies have shown that most of the ethnomedicinal and ethnoveterinary remedies are plant-based. Surveys show that most of these materials are obtained from mountain areas. One particularly important mountain plant is *Seketet* (*Myisine africana*), which is widely used for both humans and livestock as a de-wormer. It is probably the most commercially used medicinal plant in the district and beyond.

Mount Nyiro has for generations served as a fortress to the Samburu people against raids from neighboring communities. The Samburu believe that they owe their existence partly to this mountain, as they have frequently saved themselves and their livestock by escaping to Mount Nyiro where God gives them protection. Animals from the lowlands are moved to the safety of Mount Nyiro whenever there is a threat of attack. Even the Turkana, the main enemies of the Samburu, dread climbing Mount Nyiro to stage an attack.

Mount Nyiro also provides security to the Samburu people from ecological disasters such as severe droughts. With its greater environmental resources of pasture and water, the mountain is an important dry-season grazing area. The seven permanent springs that flow from the different sides of the mountain provide the only source of water to the surrounding areas at a time when it is most desperately needed. It is of special significance as it provides both physical security from raids, which escalate with drought intensity, as well as pasture and water.

In order to safeguard the use of Mount Nyiro and other exclusive grazing areas, the Samburu use their religious and traditional practices to enforce the controls. One of these is the curse which can be pronounced by the elders. It is called *Ldeket le loip* (the curse of the shade), referring to the shade tree where elders gather to exchange news or discuss specific issues. This is pronounced when a person misbehaves and disregards the warnings of the elders. It is an important cultural control with regard to grazing rights and exploitation of other environmental resources. Mount Nyiro has also benefited from legal protection from the Kenya Government through its designation as a state forest under the Forestry Department. The Samburu people have been given exclusive rights to grazing on the mountain.

Despite both traditional and modern forms of protection, the future of Mount Nyiro as a sacred mountain to the Samburu people is threatened by a number of factors. These are mainly manmade as a result of the dynamic changes taking place within the Samburu community and from outside. Growing insecurity among neighboring pastoral communities has seriously affected the Samburu's traditional use of Mount Nyiro. With the frequent raids, the Samburu are spending more time with their livestock on the mountain than is ecologically sustainable. This problem has also been aggravated by the frequent severe droughts, which necessitate longer periods on the mountain than the normal dry-season grazing period. This has resulted in overutilization of the mountain resources. Fires set by people to smoke out bees while harvesting honey in the forest have also been instrumental in degrading the environment. Development activities in the Mount Nyiro vicinity are also a potential threat. Human populations are increasing and settlement is becoming more permanent, creating an increased demand for resources such as timber, fuel wood and water. Mount Nyiro is also the site of an "ecotourism" lodge which was constructed against the wishes of the local people, who consider it a desecration of the holy mountain.

While it is true that the traditional religious beliefs and practices of the Samburu reflect a strong influence on the way they utilize and conserve environmental resources, these valuable practices and knowledge are rapidly being eroded. This could perhaps be considered one of the most important internal threats to Mount Nyiro, as its historical basis for conservation is being undermined. The young people are increasingly being alienated from the pastoralist way of life because they have to go to school and later take up formal employment in urban areas away from the influence of their culture and traditional beliefs. The older generation of Samburu are concerned that God is unhappy with the people because they are not offering sacrifices as they should. This is being attributed to the weakening of their religious beliefs and traditional practices. As one elder put it "God must have moved because there are no fresh bones at the Rock of *Kosikosi* of late" (personal communication with local elder Lengaur Lelait, in 2000).

Despite these threats however, the traditional beliefs and practices must be appreciated for the role they have played in the past in the preservation of environmental resources. Revival of these cultural values and the involvement of local communities must be seen as important elements in any future conservation efforts at sacred sites such as Mount Nyiro.

Asenath Omwega
Leina Mpoke
Jacob Wanyama

Further Reading

Fratkin, Eliot. "Traditional Medicine and Concepts of Healing among Samburu Pastoralists of Kenya." *Journal of Ethnobiology* 16:1 (1996), 63–97.

Kihumba, Roseline. *Samburu Culture and Natural Resources Management: A Desk Literature Study.* Consultancy report, Intermediate Technology Development Group – Eastern Africa. Nairobi, Kenya, 1999.

Lanasunya, Pat. "Market Survey on Traditional and Modern Livestock Remedies in Samburu." Consultancy report, Intermediate Technology Development Group – Eastern Africa. Nairobi, Kenya, 2000.

Lolarrarri, Melgu. "The God of the Talking Bamboo, I Pray to You." Recording of a song made in Samburu, Kenya, 2000.

Owuor, Bernard. "Veterinary Medicinal Plant Resource Survey and Training Needs Assessment in Baragoi and Nyiru Divisions of Samburu District." Consultancy report, Intermediate Technology Development Group – Eastern Africa. Nairobi, Kenya, 2000.

Pendezini, Fr. Egidio. *"Ana ninye Nkai ang": The Samburu Traditional View of God.* Maralal, Kenya: J. Allamano Pastoral Center Publications, 1996.

Wanyama, Jacob. *Confidently Used Ethnoveterinary Knowledge among Pastoralists of Samburu, Kenya.* Book 1. Nairobi, Kenya: Intermediate Technology Kenya, 1997.

See also: African Religions and Nature Conservation; Ethnobotany; Sacred Groves of Africa; Sacred Mountains; Traditional Ecological Knowledge.

Mount Rushmore

Mount Rushmore, a 6000-foot-tall schist and pre-Cambrian granite peak, sits close to the center of South Dakota's Black Hills, just shy of the geographical center of the North American continent. Gigantic visages of four American presidents rest on the summit, gazing off to the east across the prairies, carved out by Gutzon Borglum (1867–1941) and a host of federally subsidized workers between 1927 and 1941. In the decades since South Dakota historian Doane A. Robinson (1856–1946) first advocated patriotic mountain carving in the Black Hills' Harney Peak area, Mount Rushmore National Memorial has become an internationally recognized icon of American nationalism, a curious blend of nature, art, politics and piety.

For Doane Robinson, the link between sculpture and the Harney Peak region of the Black Hills was obvious, given the extensive collection of naturally carved pinnacles left there from millions of years of erosion. Carving into their surface heroic figures of Western exploration and conquest – such as Buffalo Bill, Jedidiah Smith or Lewis and Clark – would, he thought, help preserve the memory of the virtuous pioneers who had struggled to transform the Great Plains from prairie and near-desert into productive farm and rangeland. For Robinson, as for many Americans in the nineteenth and early twentieth centuries, what animated those pioneers was not simply human aspiration, but rather the "mystic dynamic of the universe," which compelled them onward "to do deeds of miracle" (in Glass 1995: 157).

Robinson first broached the idea to an association of South Dakota innkeepers and roadside businessmen in 1923. His effort to memorialize the miraculous transformers of the west met considerable opposition, however, as Dakota newspaper editors – and their readers – took aim at his fundamental contention that the Hills were insufficiently beautiful as they stood. "Why should we add to, or rather, desecrate, the work of nature with the puny work of man?" Hills resident Maude Hoover wanted to know (in Glass 1995: 158).

Robinson's reply, offered in correspondence, editorials and a campaign's worth of speeches at business luncheons across the state, highlighted his theological conviction that nature, God's creation, required something more from humans than mere romantic appreciation. "God did not quite complete his job in the Harney district, but left it for man ... to finish ... developing the seed of beauty which God has planted" (in Glass 1995: 158).

Although the romantic lovers of natural beauty who objected so strongly to Robinson may have been large in number, their suspicion that mountain carving was an act of desecration largely gave way over the next year. Perhaps Robinson got the best of the argument because Dakotans recognized that they too saw nature as something that required human transformation in order to be perfected. Many were also susceptible to his argument that such a memorial would bring considerable economic benefit to the hard-scrabble state.

Sculptor Gutzon Borglum, whom Robinson eventually approached – and himself the child of pioneers – saw the possibility of setting a larger drama in stone than simply that of settlers, explorers and army heroes. For Borglum, the size of the Black Hills outcroppings called forth a vision of the largest possible national scope. "American history itself shall march along that skyline," Borglum reportedly burst out when first seeing the top of Rushmore in 1924 (in Smith 1985: 33). The busts of Washington and Lincoln (and later Jefferson and T. Roosevelt) seemed to him far more fitting than western heroes, since their achievements and commitments were what made America possible to begin with.

Like Robinson, Borglum also shared the idea that nature itself prompts the transformations which human artistic, economic and political achievements require. Borglum's writings are rife with purple prose extolling the Anglo-Saxon spirit embodied in American institutions, which he saw as the product of both a natural and divine momentum. "America," he wrote, was "sired by aeons of upward struggle out of hair and leaves, out of mud and fear, out of slavery in galleys and cells" (in Glass 1994: 268).

Rushmore's stone, already nearly as old as the Earth itself, was the most fitting embodiment for the symbolic visages of the greatest American leaders. On many occasions Borglum told visitors admiring his progress that the faces were already present within the mountain. His drills, explosive caps and dynamite merely "relieved ... from the head" excess granite (in Glass 1994: 274). In its apparent agelessness the granite would preserve, as well as art could insure, the virtues of American character and civilization. Rushmore's "wondrous cenotaphs" – as one anonymous poet put it – signaled in the social and political tumult of the early twentieth century that America might not suffer the fate of other nations.

That the memorial serves to give America a natural foundation is evident in the descriptions of the four presidents often found in promotional literature developed for visitors by the National Park Service, philanthropic associations and individual citizens. Washington, as the "father of his land," is often portrayed as the seminal figure. Jefferson, who saw political rights deriving from the laws of nature itself, is also memorialized for his purchase of the western half of the continent from Napoleon, making possible the great western expansion that Americans thought of as their God-given, natural destiny. Lincoln, who shepherded the nation through war, in his own words framed that war's massive spilling of blood as the nutritive means for national rebirth – in essence grounding America's future in the natural process of death. Roosevelt, something of a problematic figure for the memorial's early proponents, was the great western outdoorsman who "upon these Black Hills hunted" and also perfected nature's design by linking Atlantic and Pacific together in the Panama Canal.

In the late 1930s Robinson claimed to detect among the American public "a growing tendency to confer on the project a sort of mystical, semi-religious connotation," which he thought would only grow to become a "worshipful reflex" over time (in Glass 1995: 161). Certainly, he was correct to a significant extent.

In the decades since work ceased Americans have gathered at the memorial for Easter sunrise services, and since the Vietnam War for annual POW/MIA memorial services. Americans have married there, and some have wanted to be buried there – and at least a few have had their ashes scattered there. All of these activities conjoin the nation's political history with the natural phenomena of death and rebirth.

On numerous occasions concern about the commercial and inappropriate use of the Rushmore image has led to charges of desecration, perhaps most notably during the controversy caused by Alfred Hitchcock's filming of *North by Northwest*'s climactic chase scene in 1958–1959. Hitchcock's murder and mayhem was widely viewed as an unsuitable linking of the memorial with the reality of death.

Robinson hoped that the worshipful reflex would be conducive to social harmony and greater "devotion to America." That this hope has not been completely realized is evident from the ways in which the memorial has become a kind of countersymbol. To some romantics, the original objections still seem right. To some it is merely kitsch. Some have campaigned to include the profiles of other significant Americans, such as feminist Susan B. Anthony.

Since the late 1960s many Native American activist groups have used the memorial as a focal point for protest. Although many sorts of political concerns have been raised there, what made the memorial seem especially appropriate for native protesters was the original underlying equation of natural beneficence and the spread of the American political order. Members of the Lakota nation in particular have generally remained skeptical that Rushmore's linkage of nature and nationalism is due to its sacred status. Their right to the Hills – acknowledged by Congressional treaty in 1868, and given moral legitimacy by the 1980 Supreme Court award of reparations which culminated the longest-running court battle in American history – has sparked continuing Lakota political effort to regain control of the Hills. In that effort Rushmore stands as an indictment of what scholars have come to call "civil religion."

Matthew Glass

Further Reading

Glass, Matthew. "Alexanders All: Symbols of Conquest and Resistance at Mount Rushmore." In David Chidester and Edward Tabor Linenthal, eds. *American*

Sacred Space. Bloomington: Indiana University Press, 1995, 152–86.
Glass, Matthew. "Producing Patriotic Inspiration at Mount Rushmore." *Journal of the American Academy of Religion* LXX:2 (1994), 265–83.
Schama, Simon. *Landscape and Memory.* New York: Vintage, 1995.
Smith, Rex Alan. *The Carving of Mount Rushmore.* New York: Abbeville, 1985.
See also: Devils Tower, *Mato Tipi*, or Bear's Lodge; Manifest Destiny; National Parks and Monuments (United States); Nature Religion in the United States.

Mountaineering

Mountaineering can be generally addressed as an encounter of humans and nature, as a relationship between human and mountain. Although this relationship can take on quite different qualities – from domination to sacralization – there is an implicit tendency to personalize and thus to ontologize the mountain as an individual entity. The climbing of a mountain has always been part of religious devotion, but it is only in early modern times that *overcoming* the difficulties related to high mountain walking became a symbol either of controlling the power of nature or of connecting spiritually with the transcendent realms high mountain areas stand for. A watershed in this regard was Petrarca's climbing the Mont Ventoux (France) on 26 April 1336, which he described as an overwhelming experience that felt like being carried from space into time. He was the first in recorded Western history to have climbed a mountain for the mere longing to see the land from above and – as he told in his report – from a new perspective.

"Mountain," like "nature" in general, is not a neutral term. Its aesthetic perception is fundamentally prefigured by mental dispositions and ideas that generate the object of experience in the first place. The mountains can be personalized as enemies, representing the dangerous and threatening aspects of nature that humans are about to conquer in a risky fight, or as a revelator of spiritual wisdom. The latter personalization talks of mountains as "father" or "mother" that care for their children on their spiritual path. Often mountaineering connects both forms of relationship.

The dominating aspect of climbing is of paramount importance for the Western relationship to mountains. This can be proven by a cornucopia of documents from the sixteenth century through today. But one has to point at the ambivalence of this engagement with mountains. On the one hand nature is the degraded "wild," and the mountains symbolize the purest and most powerful manifestations of nature's threatening that man struggles to overcome (one may think, for instance, of the mythical descriptions of expeditions to K2, Mount Everest, or the Eiger north face). On the other hand climbing a mountain means to overcome the dangers and weaknesses *inside* a person, thus mountaineering is a means to transgress the borders of bodily exhaustion in order to gain a fuller awareness of one's own psychical or spiritual capacities. Reinhold Messner, who climbed each 8000 meter peak and experienced a lot of emotionally touching situations (like cutting off his dead brother from the rope), time and again makes sure that climbing is a way to the inner self. Here, outer domination is mirrored by an internal conflict. This sheds light on the discussion of Messner's meeting the "Yeti" or "Big Foot." Whether or not this giant animal exists in the Himalayas, this story is definitely a transference of "the hero's journey" (on which the climber meets the "dragon") from internal into material realms.

Another aspect of mountaineering is its being depicted as revelation. Romantic authors often describe their meeting with mountains as an epiphany of nature's sacred dimensions. Many nineteenth-century authors both from North America and from Europe could be mentioned here, from Johann Wolfgang Goethe and Novalis to Ralph Waldo Emerson and Henry David Thoreau. In this perspective, the mountain reveals the living beauty of nature and initiates a feeling of universal connectedness in the human climbing it. In modern environmentalism and the U.S. National Park movement, it was especially the mountains that (contradictorily) symbolized both the unconquered wilderness and the American project of universal salvation.

In the last three decades, mountaineering has been closely related to new developments within the "outdoor" scene. Although the disparate free-climbing movement is difficult to address generally and many climbers are not interested in ecological or even spiritual aspects of their sport, there is an undeniable relation between deep-ecological activities and the romanticized picture of free-climbing. A number of mountain climber-intellectuals are drawn to deep ecology because of spiritual experiences they have made outdoors, many of them being influenced by Arne Naess' earliest environmental philosophy. Naess himself was an experienced climber and the first to ascend Tirich Mir (7690 meters; 25,230 feet), the highest peak in the Hindu Kush, in 1950.

Founders of internationally successful outdoor and climbing companies participate in grassroots deep ecological activities not only for advertisement reasons, but also as a consequence of their personal experiences that are often spiritually colored. This is true in particular for Doug Thompkins (founder of "The North Face" and "Esprit"), who funded the "Foundation for Deep Ecology," the "EcoForestry Institute," and the "El Pumalin Bosque Foundation," which ambitiously supports the idea of Pumalin National Park in Chile ("Pumalin" means "where Pumas live"). Yvonne Chouinard (founder of "Patagonia"

Messner on Everest and Cosmos

Reinhold Messner and Peter Habeler were the first two climbers to ascend Mount Everest without the use of oxygen. In his report of the expedition Messner wrote:

> I have not come here to ascend Everest at any price. I wished to get to know it, in all its might, difficulty, and severity. And I was resolute to renounce the peak, should I not be able to climb it without a breathing mask: With that modern oxygen apparatus one simulates at the Everest a level of 6,000 meters. But to experience that level, I need not go to Everest. To acknowledge, to sense, and to feel the Everest's power, I have to climb it without technical tricks. Only then I know what a man undergoes there, which new dimensions will open before him, and if he can arrive at a new relationship to the cosmos (1978: 162).

Finally standing at the peak of Everest, Messner described his feelings thus:

> Standing in the diffuse light, with the wind in the back, I suddenly have a feeling of all-inclusiveness (*Allgefühl*) – not the feeling of success and of being stronger than all those who came here before us, not a feeling of reaching the ultimate point, not omnipotence. Just a touch of happiness deep inside my head and breast. The peak that suddenly seemed to me like a resting place. As if I hadn't expected a resting place up here. At the sight of those steep, sharp ridges beneath us [we experience] the imagination that later we really would have come too late. Everything we say to each other now, we say in mere embarrassment. I don't think any more. While in a trance-like state I get the tape out of the backpack, switch it on, and try to speak a few reasonable sentences, my eyes are immediately filled with tears. "Now we are at Everest's peak; it is so cold that we cannot take photos," I later start the conversation with the tape recorder switched on. But right away crying again shakes me. I neither can talk nor think, but I feel this deep emotional commotion which throws me into a new balance. Only a few meters below the peak the exhaustion would have been the same, also the anxiety and the pain suffered; such a burst open of emotions, though, is only possible at the peak.
>
> Everything that is, everything I am, is marked by the knowledge that I reached the final destination. The peak – at least temporarily – as naïve, intuitive answer to the question of being (1978: 180).

Kocku von Stuckrad

Further Reading
Messner, Reinhold. *Everest: Expedition zum Endpunkt*. Kocku von Stuckrad, tr. Munich: BLV Verlagsgesellschaft, 1978.

and "Black Diamond") spends a fixed part of the company's budget on grassroots environmental projects, many with a biocentric, radical environmental approach. Reinhold Messner (affiliated with "Salewa") is a member of the European Parliament for the Green Party; and "Jack Wolfskin" (founded by the German Wolfgang Dausien) supports environmental projects around the world. Many of those brands explicitly refer to U.S. climbing romanticism (especially Yosemite Park), even when such relations are artificial, like in the "Think Pink" case, which was founded in Italy.

Kocku von Stuckrad

Further Reading
Bonington, Chris. *The Climbers: A History of Mountaineering*. New York: BBC/Parkwest Publications, 1992.
Keay, John. *When Men and Mountains Meet: The Explorers of the Western Himalayas, 1820–1875*. Karachi: Oxford University Press, 1993 (1977).
Neate, Jill. *Mountaineering Literature: A Bibliography of Material Published in English*. Milthorpe: Cicerone Press, 1986.
Peters, Ed, ed. *Mountaineering, the Freedom of the Hills*. Seattle, WA.: Mountaineers, 1982.
Scott, Chick. *Pushing the Limit: The Story of Canadian Mountaineering*. Calgary: Rocky Mountain Books, 2000.

See also: Deep Ecology; Earth First! and the Earth Liberation Front; Fly Fishing; Naess, Arne; Radical Environmentalism; Rock Climbing; Sacred Mountains; Surfing.

Mountains and Rivers Sutra by Japanese Soto Zen Master Dogen Kigen (1200–1253)

The Sanskrit term *sutra* has been reserved throughout the Buddhist tradition for what is taught by a Buddha. Its use in the title of this text immediately suggests the extraordinary nature of Dogen's 1240 address to a monastic assembly, written as a powerful attempt to combine the broad rhetorical sweep and spiritual depth of Chinese

Buddhist Huayan concepts with a deeply personal vision of portraying the Soto practice of enlightenment ("to actualize the ways of ancient Buddhas"). Dogen was the founder of the Japanese Soto Zen school, its most sophisticated master, one of the greatest of native philosophers, and an unusually skilled writer of classical Chinese and Japanese. (This text is one chapter among nearly a hundred stemming from his massive life work, the *Shobogenzo* or *Treasures of the Essentials of the True Dharma*.)

Dogen supposes numerous religious images from Song dynasty (960–1279) Chinese culture: mountains as a primary *yang* expression of hardness, height, brightness, etc., as sacred pilgrimage sites, as Buddhist and Daoist training centers and retreats, as wilderness unsullied and uncontrolled by secular political authority; waters as the penultimate Daoist "flowing" reality, as a primary *yin* expression of softness, darkness, adaptability, nurture basic to life, etc. Mountains and waters is the common Chinese character compound *shan-shui* for "nature" as totality, for its depiction as landscape in ink-wash painting and literature, and for suggesting the *yin/yang* dynamic of extending upward toward the heavens versus running downward into Earth as well as immediacy of flow versus long-term solidity and stability. These are combined with a Japanese religious awareness of mountains as sacralized abodes of *kami* (or as *kami* themselves). (*Kami* are the archaic, indigenous Japanese conception of any being with powers beyond the human.) In addition, both of the major classical Heian period (eleventh–twelfth centuries) esoteric Buddhist schools were located in mountains – the Tendai school on the Mt. Hiei range northeast of Kyoto, and the Shingon school on the Mt. Koya range in traditional Kii province (modern Wakayama prefecture). (Dogen trained as a Tendai novice among the hundreds of temples on Mt. Hiei.) Indigenous Japanese religion carried a contamination/purity moral basis that saw waters as a primary means of purification in the removal of defilement (*tsumi*) caused by physical acts (i.e., death, killing, birth, menstruation) and by damaging emotions (i.e., jealousy, hatred, greed, etc.).

What is so powerful in Dogen's vision is that here mountains and waters are viewed as Buddhas, as living enlightenment in a continuous practice of wisdom and compassion. Mountains and waters are alive; they exist in complete ease in their phenomenal circumstances, they express enlightenment, they realize inexhaustible "spiritual power" (as do Buddhas and ancestors).

Not only are mountains always moving (forward and backward, more swiftly than the winds), but they also flow (like waters), travel on water, ride the clouds, and their toes splash through waters – in other words they practice wisdom and compassion and actualize enlightenment. ("If movement stops, Buddhas and ancestors will not emerge.") Mountains are uncommon territory ("although as a rule, mountains belong to nations, mountains belong

---

Dogen Kigen's *Mountains and Rivers Sutra* [excerpts]

The mountains and waters of this very moment actualize the ways of the ancient Buddhas. Both settle in their phenomenal circumstances, yet realize perfect virtue. Because they existed before the kalpa of empty space had disappeared, they are alive at precisely this very moment. Because they had a uniqueness before forms had come about, they are emancipation.

The many virtues [spiritual powers] of a mountain expand, the virtues of riding the clouds are always reached from a mountain, and the mysterious power of soaring on the winds comes freely from a mountain . . .

A mountain can never be wanting in the virtues that it needs, so it always settles in ease and it is always moving. One of the first things to be examined in detail should be the virtues of this movement. Because a mountain moves just like a human moves, never doubt that a mountain is moving simply because it does not seem to move the way a human being does.

What the Buddhas and the patriarchs have explained points to movement – this is the basis. Penetrate this "always moving" described to the assembly.

Because they are always moving, the motion of green mountains is swifter than the winds, but a person in the mountains does not realize or understand this. "In the mountains" is the blossoming of the entire universe. Someone who is away from the mountains does not realize or understand this. The people who cannot see a mountain appearing right before their eyes, cannot realize, cannot know, cannot see, and cannot hear it just as it is. If someone doubts the movement of a mountain that person does not even understand one's own movement; if you do not know your own movement, then you will have to know the movement of a green mountain.

Green mountains are not sentient and they are not non-sentient. A person is not sentient and is not non-sentient. Right now there can't be anyone who doubts the movements of green mountains.

Translated by Dennis Lishka

---

to the people who love them") because they are the places of retreat for great sages and saints. Thus mountains literally love people of virtue and continually absorb such virtues – they are the "heart/minds" of such people. The positive karma continually developing from actualizing enlightenment is the spiritual power (Japanese: *kudoku*), which is the "name-and-form" and the life-force of such mountains. Here the ordinary does not apply; absent are secular authority ("not places where imperial virtue reaches"), social custom (where rulers bow to saints), and human conceptualization ("do not understand mountains using standards of human thinking"). Here as well, to the enlightened, typical individuals do not meet because human ordinariness is "disconnected in the mountains." Such mountains are everywhere – virtual treasures hidden in the air, in swamps, and in mountains. To Dogen, mountains are a dynamic practice (actualizing enlightenment according to the precise circumstances of the present moment), they are Buddhist reality (an interrelated "universe-as-the-Dharma" [Sanskrit: *dharmadhatu*]), and they are Buddhas and ancestors teaching the unenlightened in each new moment in every way ("investigate the mountains hidden in 'hiddenness' ").

Dogen immediately divests waters of common human-conceived properties. These are neither wet nor dry, strong nor weak, hot nor cold, still nor in motion, existent nor nonexistent, deluded nor enlightened. Images of water conceived during perception by various beings are included – heavenly beings seeing waters as spectacular flowers and jewelry, dragons and fish seeing waters as palaces and towers, greed-reborn hungry ghosts seeing waters as raging fire, pus, or blood. Waters are not simply the characteristics of its perceived forms (characteristics of element and color, concepts like gravitational flow, evaporation, etc.) to Dogen. He asks how different beings perceiving waters results in different images of the same perception, and if so, where lies the reality of water? ("This should not be investigated only when we see the waters of humans and heavenly beings, this is investigating how waters see waters.") Waters attract human settlement – and sages and saints; thus, there are many kinds of "catching" – catching fish, attracting followers, catching the Way (Chinese: *tao*). ("In addition, one should catch the self, one should catch catching, one should be caught by catching, one should be caught by the Way.") Like mountains, waters practice and authenticate; their Buddhist flowing penetrates what human-conceived waters commonly do not: flames, conceptualizing, memory, discrimination, and the awareness of Buddha-nature. Ordinary properties of water such as its essential nourishment to life, flow, adaptability, permeability, etc. are reinvested to depict the all-encompassing nature of Buddhist teaching as practice ("Places where waters penetrate are always the actualization of Buddhas and ancestors. According to this, Buddhas and ancestors continually touch water to make it their bodies, their hearts/minds, and their deliberations.").

It is easy to misapprehend what Dogen is doing from major Western viewpoints of monotheism, Enlightenment philosophies, political and Romantic individuality, scientific materialism, and post-structuralism. In purely Buddhist terms, he advances the common East Asian Mahayana position of the "universe-as-the-Dharma" of the Chinese Huayan or "Wreath of Flowers" School, now as the foundation of a flexible, adaptive, present-oriented Zen practice (where the practitioner's awareness as a separated being disappears into an ever-changing total community of beings). This involves the totality of all sentient existence explained as: (1) the karmic interdependency of all beings, (2) the interrelationship of all beings such that the uniqueness of each being in form and function is harmonized with its functional contributions to totality, (3) the interpenetration of all beings as (A) how any being at any instant and any point in space provides the context for the practice of wisdom and compassion that affects all beings, and (B) how the time and space of distinct beings may be superseded (from the standpoint of an individual being) or merged (from the standpoint of totality). Yet to Dogen and to many in Japanese religion, "sentient beings" conceptualized still limits this totality by exclusion, so the term "entities" (or "non-carbon life forms") is more appropriately encompassing. What enables such expansive spiritual influence is the tremendous potential of positive karma resulting from the actualization of enlightenment as a Buddha's practice of wisdom and compassion. Karma drives the engine of suffering that is the Buddhist ignorant, ever-changing self (Sanskrit *anatman*), but it is transformed in the Mahayana into strong soteriological capacity as Enlightenment is practiced (this is the Japanese term *kudoku* that I have rendered as "spiritual power"). Western interpreters often reduce this vision to an impoverished pantheism, animism, animitism, etc., but Dogen's portrayal of Soto Zen experience as the actualization of one's inherent Buddha-nature during each new instant of practice dissolves sacred/profane, subject/object, distinct parts/one whole conceptual dichotomies plus typical comprehension of distinct entity time/space conceptual integrity – as he often described his own realization in Song China, a complete "dropping away of body and mind."

Dennis Lishka

Further Reading
Dogen Kigen. "Mountains and Waters Sutra." In Kazuaki Tanahashi, ed. *Moon in a Dewdrop*. San Francisco: Northpoint Press, 1985, 97–107.
Stambaugh, Joan. *Impermanence is Buddha-nature: Dogen's Understanding of Temporality*. Honolulu: University of Hawai'i Press, 1990.
See also: Japanese Love of Nature; Japanese Religions; Sacred Moutains; Zen Buddhism.

MOVE

In the early 1970s, Vincent Leaphart, who later took the name John Africa, began to work out a philosophy of nature that respected all life, even to the point of refusing to repel or eradicate rodents or insects from inhabited buildings. In 1973, he and a group of associates moved into a house near the University of Pennsylvania campus in West Philadelphia, vocally advocating a total separation from the evils of modern society. They took the name MOVE, which was not an acronym but a word simply chosen to communicate dynamism. In an undated manifesto, members wrote, "MOVE's work is to stop industry from poisoning the air, the water, the soil, and to put an end to the enslavement of life – people, animals, *any* form of life."

MOVE members, mostly African Americans, saw themselves as a radical back-to-nature movement – a "Sierra Club with guns," as one observer called it. They dressed in blue denim and did not bathe with soap or cut their hair. They rejected hospitals, doctors, and veterinarians. The MOVE women delivered several babies themselves, biting off and eating their umbilical cords and licking them clean. Unvaccinated pets roamed the premises, which were also infested with cockroaches, termites, and rats. Members used loudspeakers in the yard to blare out John Africa's teachings and denounce, with great vitriol, those who disagreed with them.

The police raided the premises in 1978, arresting several members and bulldozing the wretched house. Those remaining, however, moved to another home and continued as before. After more years of conflict, the police dropped an explosive device onto the house from a helicopter and burned down most of the city block on which the MOVE house was located. Eleven members were killed in the fire and a battle with the police that accompanied the action. A few members survived, but have since avoided public attention. To some radical environmentalists, MOVE has continued to be an important symbol of resistance to consumerist society.

Timothy Miller

Further Reading

Anderson, John and Hilary Hevenor. *Burning Down the House: MOVE and the Tragedy of Philadelphia*. New York: Norton, 1987.

Boyette, Michael. *"Let it Burn": The Philadelphia Tragedy*. Lincolnwood, IL: Contemporary Books, 1989.

See also: Anarchism; Environmental Justice and Environmental Racism; New Religious Movements; Radical Environmentalism.

Mt. Hiei (Japan)

Japanese fondly identify Mt. Hiei (h. 848m) as Hieizan. Hieizan has become a mountain monastic center since Saicho's (767–822) arrival there in 788 B.C.E. and his carving of a statue of the medicine Buddha, Yakushi Nyorai. The Hieizan monastic complex, Enryakuji, is located between Lake Biwa in Shiga Prefecture and the northeast side of Heian capital Kyoto. Japanese believe that "northeast" is an "inauspicious" direction called "devil's gate" (*kimon*) and to prevent dangers entering into the capital, religious specialists were required to perform religious rites there. Thus the purpose of Saicho's establishment of a monastic complex on the mountain was to protect the emperor and the new capital. The birth of this monastic center serves an important role in understanding the relationship that exists between Buddhism and the Japanese state.

The monastic complex on Mt. Hiei is the headquarters of the Tendai branch of Japanese Buddhism. It was a site of over 3000 temples before Oda Nobunaga's destruction in 1581 and still contains many temples scattered around the mountain.

As a traditional center of learning, its reputation is attested by the very fact that several Kamakura reformers such as Honen (1133–1212), Eisai (1141–1215), Shinran (1173–1262), Dogen (1200–1253), and Nichiren (1222–1282) who gave birth to several important Japanese Buddhist schools had their initial monastic training in Mt. Hiei.

On Saicho's return from China in 805, Hieizan became the center of Tendai Buddhism with emphasis on one vehicle of the *Lotus Sutra*. In addition, its multitude of religious practices historically have embraced a wide range of syncretic rites deriving from Shinto and Japanese native religions. Its complex esoteric practices, the *nembutsu*, *sutra* chanting, and meditation, have had a great influence on Japanese religiosity.

For Tendai monks, Mt. Hiei is a place for religious austerity in which seclusion on the mountain is a deep spiritual practice important in developing spiritual insight. Even today, all prospective abbots in Mt. Hiei are required to live in seclusion on the mountain for at least 100 days practicing austerities. As a prominent Buddhist learning center, it still continues to support rigorous monastic practices such as the twelve-year ascetic retreat (*rozangyo*) and the one-thousand-day mountain pilgrimage (*kaihogyo*).

The *Kaihogyo* practice is a daily pilgrimage of a few rare ascetic monks who walk through the forests and hills of Hieizan for 100 days or 1000 days over a period of seven years to perfect themselves to Buddhahood so that they can be vessels of solace for those immersed in the problems of the mundane world, exemplifed in busy Japanese city life. Modern ascetic practitioners have followed two ascetic pilgrimage routes extending over 35 kilometers through the hills of Mt. Hiei. Mt. Hiei's strong association with nature is very clear both in its walking pilgrimage through the hills and the practice of waterfall austerities by ascetic monks such as Sakai Yusai and Hakozaki Bunyo. As an essential part of their pilgrimage, without any religious discrimination, the ascetic monks pray and chant esoteric *mantras* at 260 Buddhist and Shinto sacred sites including the objects of nature. This practice demonstrates the inclusive nature of the Japanese religious world, which embraces the worship of trees, rocks, and waterfalls and holds the belief that the natural world is a locus for spiritual existence. In conversations with devotees, the preeminent ascetic monk Sakai Yusai frequently expresses his immense gratitude for the natural world, stating that "even the rain" that hinders his pilgrimage is a cause for gratitude since it helps crops to grow and thus people may have plenty of food to eat.

Within this devotional religiosity, there is a great emphasis on the mountain, the forest and nature. Positive attitudes toward nature and the close relationship between Japanese religions and nature appear clearly in both the Japanese religious worldview and Tendai monasticism. In 1999, when I stayed with a group of students at Saikyoji for five weeks, the abbot of Saikyoji explained the Tendai attitude toward nature and the symbolism attached to the mountain. In particular, their attitude toward monkeys is rather striking since they regard them as animals with deep spirituality. According to the abbot, when monks arrived at Saikyoji after Nobunaga's destruction, they witnessed monkeys playing the bell while repeating the *nembutsu*. To remember that event today Saikyoji still rings the bell daily. On the whole, the pilgrimage and other practices at Mt. Hiei combine Japanese religious attitudes toward nature by creating a nature-friendly religiosity coupled with contemplative aspects of Buddhist monasticism.

Mahinda Deegalle

Further Reading

Deegalle, Mahinda. "Asceticism: Buddhist Perspectives" and "Marathon Monks." In William M. Johnston, ed. *Encyclopedia of Monasticism*. Chicago and London: Fitzroy Dearborn Publishers, 2000, 88–92, 821–2.

Groner, Paul. *Saicho: The Establishment of the Japanese Tendai School*. Berkeley: University of California Press, 1984.

Stevens, John. *The Marathon Monks of Mount Hiei*. Boston: Shambhala, 1988.

Swanson, Paul L., ed. "Tendai Buddhism in Japan." *Japanese Journal of Religious Studies* 14:2–3 (1987).

See *also*: Japanese Religions; Mountaineering; Sacred Mountains.

P Muhammad, The Prophet of Islam (570–632)

Muhammad, son of Abd Allah was born in 570 in Mecca, Arabia. He belonged to a noble tribe of Qu'raysh of the city of Mecca, and was orphaned at an early age. He developed into a sober and responsible young man, known for his trustworthiness. When he received the first revelation, he was forty years old. In the year 622 B.C.E., the Prophet decided to leave Mecca, where he had lived in some danger. He migrated to Yathrib, later called Madina al-Nabi (The City of the Prophet). A decade later, Muhammad was able to return to Mecca, clear the sacred shrine (Qa'ba) of idols, and establish worship of the one real God. After his death in 632, his message spread north of the peninsula to North Africa, Spain, and India.

Muslims generally believe that Muhammad is the archetypal true man, representing in his life and person an example all Muslims should aspire to follow. So, the best example of Islamic environmental awareness, if there is any, may be seen in the life and attitudes of Muhammad toward the environment, which may set an ideal for Muslim generations. Since every good Muslim is expected to emulate the behavior of the Prophet, the following case is a good example of how he changed the worldview of his milieu regarding animals. One of his companions was seen crumbling up bread for some ants with the words, "They are our neighbors and have rights over us" (Johnson-Davies 1994: xvii).

To understand Muhammad's attitude toward the environment, it is necessary to highlight the Qur'anic *Weltanschauung*/worldview which provided a comprehensive, integrated, and holistic worldview that is based on the unity of Reality (i.e., *tawhid*). Thus, the purpose of the Qur'an, is "to awaken in man the higher consciousness of his manifold relations with God and universe" (Iqbal 1958: 8–9). The Qur'an, for example, speaks of trees, gardens, and orchards so frequently that it is not difficult for any attentive reader of the Qur'an to develop an appreciation for them. Since nature is not out there just by accident, as a result of the process of evolution or chaotic configurations, it must have some meaning and purpose. The Qur'an suggests that if any human being ponders over and scrutinizes the very structure of natural phenomena, he/she can deduce the existence of a Creator, who is All-Powerful, All-Knowing, and All-Merciful. Nature reflects, just like a mirror, the power, beauty, wisdom and mercy of its Creator. Therefore, the Islamic worldview does not endorse any view of humanity's viceregency of the Earth that destroys and spoils the ecological balance of nature.

Muhammad can be seen as the first example of the Qur'anic viceregency. He attached great importance, in his own practice and sayings (*hadiths*), not only to public worship, civil law, and social etiquette, but also to planting trees, preserving forests, and conserving the environment. The following sayings are instructive in giving clues about his environmental concerns:

If you have a sapling, if you have the time, be certain to plant it, even if Doomsday starts to break forth (*Musnad* 183–4, 191, III).

There is none amongst the believers who plants a tree, or sows a seed, and then a bird, or a person, or an animal eats thereof, but is regarded as having given a charitable gift [for which there is great recompense] (Muslim, *Musakat* 9, 12, II. 1188–9).

Muhammad, exemplifying in his personality the Qur'anic viceregency and being a man of Arabian deserts, was aware of the integrity of the ecosystem and the importance of water, greenery, and forests.

On migrating to Medina, Muhammad organized the planting of trees and date groves. He made forests and green spaces conservation areas, where every sort of living creature could live unmolested. Within these "inviolable zones," which are called sanctuaries (*hima*), neither trees, nor shrubs, nor vegetation could be cut, nor could any wild animal be hunted or even disturbed. Around Medina, a strip of land approximately twelve miles wide was proclaimed a sanctuary and made a conservation area by Muhammad. Likewise, he declared other areas, similar to the one in this example, as sanctuaries. Most importantly, when Muhammad established these sanctuaries, he said he was following the example of the prophet Abraham, who declared Mecca a sanctuary. Today these sanctuaries, with the addition of new ones, are still intact.

Muhammad insisted on the protection and kind treatment of animals. He taught with his deeds and sayings that Muslims should act kindly toward all living beings. He said: "The Most Merciful One is merciful towards those who are merciful. Act kindly to those on the earth so that those in the heavens [the angels] will be merciful to you" (Tirmizi, *Birr* 16). Muhammad commanded that birds' nests should not be disturbed or the eggs or chicks stolen. He ordered someone who had filled his bag with fledglings stolen from nests, brought to town, to return them to their nests immediately.

Furthermore, he said: "If without good reason anyone kills a sparrow, or a creature lesser than that even, the living creature will put his plaint to God on the Day of Judgment, saying: 'So-and-so killed me for no purpose'" (Nasai, *Dahaya* 42, VII. 239). He warned Muslims against mistreating animals, "a woman was sent to Hell because she tied up her cat and neither gave it food nor allowed it free to hunt the cockroaches" (Bukhari, *Adhan* 90 I. 181–2; Muslim, *Birr* 133, III. 2022). Muhammad tells a story of a man who was walking along a road and felt thirsty. Finding a well, he lowered himself into it and drank. When he came out he found a dog panting from thirst and licking at the earth. He therefore went down into the well again, and filled his shoe with water and gave it to the dog. For this act God forgave him his sins. Muhammad was then asked whether man had a reward through animals, and he replied: "In everything that lives there is a reward" (Bukhari, *Musakat* 9, III. 77). So, while treating animals well is one means for a person to enter Paradise, mistreatment of animals may be the cause of a person going to Hell. The Prophet banned hunting, especially the arbitrary hunting of animals for pleasure. While hunting is permitted in principle, it might become prohibited depending on the conditions. Islam permits eating meat; however, it gives instructions to ensure humane slaughter, with as little pain to the victim as possible. The main counsel of Islam in the slaughter of animals for food is to do it in the least painful manner.

Another aspect of Muhammad's environment-related concern is his insistence on private cleanliness. This is considered to be one of the fundamentals of Islamic belief. Muhammad says, "cleanliness is half of belief" (Muslim, *Taharah* 1, I. 203). When going to the mosque, to visit someone, or when in the company of others, he was always careful to wear clean and presentable clothes, to rub fragrant scents on his body, and not eat things like onions and garlic, which would have an unpleasant smell.

In spite of Muhammad's insistence on protecting the environment and exemplary treatment of animals, the signs of environmental crisis can be seen in nearly every Muslim country. One reason may be, as Seyyed Hossein Nasr has argued,

the Islamic world is not totally Islamic today and much that is Islamic lies hidden behind the cover of Western cultural, scientific, and technological ideas and practices emulated and aped to various degrees of perfection, or rather one should say of imperfection, by Muslims during the past century and a half (Nasr 1992: 87).

In short, the Prophet Muhammad was very conscious of his environment and developed a spirit of love and care toward the creatures of God. If Muslims examine the life of Muhammad with a "green" eye, they may discover new insights for developing an environmental ethic.

Ibrahim Ozdemir

Further Reading

Armstrong, Karen. *Muhammad: A Biography of the Prophet*. San Francisco: HarperSanFrancisco, 1992.

Bukhari. *Sahih*. Muhammad Muhsin Khan, tr. Chicago: Kazi Publications, 1979.

Guillaume, A. *The Life of Muhammad*. (A translation of Ishaq's *Sirat rasul Allah*). Oxford; New York: Oxford University Press, 2001.

Haykal, Muhammad Husayn. *The Life of Muhammad*. Isma'il al- Raci, tr. London: Shorouk, 1983.

Iqbal, Muhammad. *The Reconstruction of Religious Thought in Islam*. Lahore: The Ashraf Press, 1958.

Johnson-Davies, Denys. *The Island of Animals, Adapted from an Arabic Fable*. Austin: University of Texas Press, 1994.

Lings, Martin. *Muhammad: His Life Based on the Earliest Sources*. New York: Inner Traditions International, 1983.

Nasr, Seyyed Hossein. *Islam and Environmental Crisis*. In Steven C. Rockefeller and John C. Elder, eds. *Spirit and Nature*. Boston: Beacon Press, 1992.

Rahman, Fazlur. *Major Themes of the Qur'an*. Minneapolis: Bibliotheca Islamica, 1994.

See also: Islam; Islam, Animals, and Vegetarianism; Islam on Man and Nature (and adjacent, Hadith and Shari'a on Man and Nature).

Muir, John (1838–1914)

Generations of nature lovers in America and the world have been thrilled and inspired by John Muir's accounts of his youthful experiences in the mountains of California – swaying atop a storm-blown spruce tree, communing with a favorite plant in the spray of a waterfall, or gazing upon the glories of his beloved Yosemite Valley. Over the same period, Muir's political career has served as a model of ethical and political commitment to an entire tradition of environmental activists. Both sides of Muir's life and work – the experiential and the activist – are expressions of a fundamentally religious orientation toward the natural world. Although the exact character of this religiousness has proven difficult for later interpreters to formulate in conceptual terms, the figure of Muir himself continues to serve as an icon of nature religion – a window through which individuals and communities can see their own relationships with nature in a deeper and more profound light.

John Muir was born on 21 April 1838 in Dunbar, Scotland, the first son of a middle-class family that would eventually include seven siblings. While Muir's mother Ann nurtured him with the delights of backyard flowers, his father Daniel (a lifelong Protestant seeker) expressed his version of Christian love by using scriptural injunction backed by physical punishment to keep the sometimes-headstrong boy from sin. Thus, contrasting currents of maternal affirmation and paternal restriction fueled the child's own capacities for sensual and imaginative contact with nature, infusing Muir's escapes to the surrounding Scottish coastline, moors, and hills with a profound and complex religious sensibility.

In 1849, when he was 11, Muir's family immigrated to America. On the Wisconsin frontier, Muir experienced the beauty and glory – as well as the hardship and danger – of wild nature with a greater intensity than ever before; in the human realm, he learned to balance his father's increasing harshness with an increased reliance upon his siblings, on the evangelical figure of Jesus as comforter and companion, and on his own sense of personal achievement in his work as farmhand, mechanic, and inventor. Finally leaving home in 1860, at age 22, Muir encountered more liberal strands of nineteenth-century American Protestantism, including a religiously informed openness to modern scientific, evolutionary, and humanitarian thought that would inform his outlook throughout his life. Entering the University of Wisconsin at Madison in 1861, Muir was introduced by professors such as Ezra Carr to the latest research and theory in disciplines such as geology and chemistry, while Carr's wife Jeanne stood at the center of a social circle stitched together by the bonds of Christian love – love which was expressed and embodied in the intimacies of everyday domestic life as well as in a shared passion for amateur botany.

By late 1867, when Muir (inspired by explorers such as Alexander von Humboldt) left on a long botanical journey through the American South, he had moved decisively away from conservative Protestantism's devaluation of nature:

The world, we are told, was made especially for man – a presumption not supported by all the facts ... Why should man value himself as more than a small part of the one great unit of creation? And what creature of all that the Lord has taken the pains to make is not essential to the completeness of that unit – the cosmos? (Muir 1997: 825–6)

After falling ill with some unknown fever in Florida, Muir continued his journey not to the Amazon but to California, where work as a sheepherder allowed him ample time to observe the works of God both on the plains and in the mountains. Shaped by increasingly intimate letters to and from Jeanne Carr, Muir's religious experience of a welcoming nature became ever more sensual and energetic, even erotic, especially after he entered the Yosemite Valley in 1869: "Last Sabbath I was baptized in the irised foam of the Vernal & in the divine snow of the Nevada [falls], and you were there also & stood in real presence by the sheet of joyous rapids beneath the bridge" (Muir in Holmes 1999: 213). His earlier intellectual revaluation of the relationship between humanity and nature broke through to a more bodily, experiential level: "I'm in the woods woods woods, and they are in *me-ee-ee!*" (Muir in Holmes 1999: 220). Moreover, this communion with nature was an opening into communion with the divine: "I will fuse in spirit skies. I will touch naked God" (Muir in Holmes 1999: 238).

Perhaps understandably, Muir could not sustain in his everyday life the level of naturalistic ecstasy expressed in his letters and journals; as early as 1873 he had moved from Yosemite down to the San Francisco Bay area, where he would live for most of the rest of his life and from which he would take increasingly long botanical and scientific travels throughout California, the West, Alaska, and eventually the world. Casting about for a career during the 1870s, Muir wrote influential geological articles on the glacial origins of Yosemite Valley, travel articles for local newspapers, and scientific studies of Californian trees; in 1879 he married Louie Strentzel, with whom he had two daughters (Helen and Wanda), soon settling into the life of a farmer in Martinez, California. By the end of the 1880s, financially successful but tired of farming, Muir resumed his literary career with travel writing on the West and Alaska. A pair of articles in *Century Magazine* in 1890 and 1891 represented his first foray into political waters, in support of federal control of Yosemite Valley; his success in influencing public opinion led to national prominence as a conservationist, through his work as co-founder and president of the Sierra Club, his numerous books and articles popularizing wilderness recreation and protection, and his friendships with important leaders such as Teddy Roosevelt and Gifford Pinchot. However, despite numerous successes in protecting wild nature through the system of national parks and forests and other efforts during the Progressive era, defeats such as the damming of the Hetch Hetchy Valley for a reservoir in 1913 helped lend an apocalyptic and tragic element to an otherwise confident American conservation movement. Muir died in 1914.

Although undeniably grounded in the Christian Bible and in specifically Protestant theology and piety (both evangelical and liberal), Muir's nature religion has been interpreted by later scholars in the light of a wide array of ideas and images: Transcendentalism, mysticism, Daoism, Buddhism, pantheism, and others. However one describes it, at the heart of Muir's religiousness is 1) the importance of *direct experience* of nature and of the divine – experience that in all cases combines bodily, emotional, cognitive, and spiritual elements. Such experience reveals 2) the *ecological interconnections* between all beings, as captured in one of his most famous aphorisms: "When we try to pick out anything by itself, we find it hitched to everything else in the universe" (Muir 1997: 245). Out of this direct experience of interconnection comes 3) an attitude of *reverence* toward the world – reverence expressed through the pursuit of scientific knowledge as well as by a joyous humility before the mysterious and the unknown. Such reverence leads Muir to 4) a *biocentric* worldview, in which all living things, human or non-human, are valued as children of God; indeed, Muir goes further, consistently expanding the bounds of biocentrism to include "inanimate" objects such as rocks and rain as living elements of the divine creation. Finally, Muir reformulates the prophetic spirit of the Old Testament and the moralism of the New into 5) a call and demand for *political and personal action* on behalf of threatened nature, expressed most fully not in ethical theory but in his own public career as conservationist and activist. Indeed, it has been through his actions as much as his words, his public figure and legend as much as his own writings, that Muir's legacy has brought these religious elements of direct experience, ecological interconnection, reverence, biocentrism, and activism to an ever-widening audience of environmentalists, nature lovers, scholars, scientists, and politicians.

At the same time, looking beneath the mythic figure, a critical perspective on Muir's biocentrism reveals an unexpected philosophical and social hierarchy, as his valuation of wild, untouched nature over humanly transformed landscapes was paralleled by a preference for middle-class, white tourists and adventurers over working people and non-white inhabitants. On the one hand, this outlook has served to justify the removal of Native Americans and other indigenous peoples in the process of *creating* "pure wilderness" out of formerly inhabited landscapes (as in many national parks, such as Yosemite and Yellowstone in the U.S.); on the other hand, Muir's influence helped allow the American conservation movement to virtually ignore inhabited and working landscapes (such as cities and farms) as objects of environmental concern over most of the twentieth century. Thus, Muir's wilderness ideals must be understood and critiqued as products of their cultural context at the same time as they may be valued as important and invigorating historical tools in the attempt to forge a larger and better vision of humanity in harmony with nature. Patron saint of modern environmentalism and intellectual forerunner of the philosophy of deep ecology, Muir has been influential beyond these specialized movements in making a religiously grounded appreciation of and concern for wild nature a part of modern society and culture in general, in America and throughout the globe.

Steven J. Holmes

Further Reading

Cohen, Michael P. *The Pathless Way: John Muir and American Wilderness.* Madison: University of Wisconsin Press, 1984.

Holmes, Steven J. *The Young John Muir: An Environmental Biography.* Madison: University of Wisconsin Press, 1999.

Muir, John. *Nature Writings.* William Cronon, ed. New York: Library of America, 1997.

Spence, Mark David. *Dispossessing the Wilderness: Indian Removal and the Making of the National Parks.* New York: Oxford University Press, 1999.

Turner, Frederick. *Rediscovering America: John Muir in His Time and Ours.* New York: Viking, 1985.

Williams, Dennis C. *God's Wilds: John Muir's Vision of Nature.* College Station: Texas A&M University Press, 2002.

See also: Animism (various); Biocentric Religion – A Call for; Deep Ecology; Miwok People; National Parks and Monuments (United States); Pinchot, Gifford; Scotland; Sierra Club; Wilderness Religion.

Müller, Friedrich Max (1823–1900)

Friedrich Max Müller, a German-born linguist who settled in Oxford, England at the age of 26, pioneered the development of comparative Indo-European mythology. A student of the philologist Franz Bopp, the basis of Müller's approach was the study of the Vedas and the piecing together of etymological identities. He argued that the original proto-Indo-Europeans were "mythopoeic" and could express abstract notions only through analogy. This Romantic view of language conceived primitive speech as not yet having developed a propensity for abstract nouns. Accordingly, the earliest Indo-European *Ursprache* employed only concrete references – foremost those of natural phenomena. In Müller's understanding, the sky and sun became the preeminent religious symbols.

Müller argued that the process of myth-making involves a "disease of language" in which metaphors redevelop meaning apart from what they were first used to express. In other words, after the migrations from the Indo-European homelands and the subsequent emergence of separate daughter languages from the parent, the original significances of the names and epithets of the Aryan gods were forgotten and new comprehensions were invented for them. To understand this view from our present perspective, Müller must be placed within the context of nineteenth-century Germany and Victorian Age Britain. Central to the Romantic thought of the time was an alleged intimate original relationship between humanity and nature. Müller's discovery of a naturalistic base to the original spiritual formulations of European ancestors follows in this line of Romantic reinterpretation. But even today, despite its persistent idealization, nature remains an informing metaphor and foundation for Romantic and quasi- or neo-Romantic positions that oppose the rational and the mechanical when posited as exclusive concerns. In the wider "tug-of-war" between the Greco-Roman foundations of Western civilization, on the one hand, and Judeo-Christian reallocations, on the other, the search for cultural origins has taken root. Müller inaugurated much of this process, although he himself sought to develop a science of religion which, at the end of the day, would find the kernel of "true" religion as distinct from the myths and fables that develop around it.

The chief contemporary criticism of Müller is that a time in which abstraction could only be expressed through concrete metaphors did not exist. The other criticisms include rejections of the notion of a "disease of language" as a biased concept, Müller's exclusive use of linguistic methodology, and his assumption that the Vedic Aryans were the proto-Indo-Europeans. Though perhaps now entering its twilight period, the current fashion in Indo-European Studies is George Dumézil's tripartite functionalism that, following Durkheim, denies the validity of any definition of religion in terms of the supernatural and also rejects both "naturalism" and "animism" as providing adequate explanations of religious origins. However, a counter-argument to the Dumézilian rejection of Müller is that Müller is in need of updating rather than dismissal. In Müller's defense, the professor denied that all mythology has a solar origin. It is instead simply one process among many. While several of the specific Greek-Vedic equations on which Müller's comparative mythology and presentation of Eurocentric root-spirituality are based are now recognized as faulty and incorrect, new understandings of phonological change nevertheless allow us to appreciate the essentials of the methodology. While the proto-Indo-European may have been fully capable of abstract thought, he/she nevertheless took his/her primary religious metaphors from the natural environment. This reaffirmation of Müller resituates the consideration of Western spirituality as a development from humanity's earliest interactions with the most prominent elements and rhythms of nature.

Michael York

Further Reading

Müller, F. Max. *Chips from a German Workshop*, vol. 2. New York: Scribner, Armstrong, 1872.

Müller, F. Max. *Lectures on the Science of Language*. New York: Scribner, Armstrong, 1869.

York, Michael. *The Divine Versus the Asurian: An Interpretation of Indo-European Cult and Myth*. Bethesda, MD: International Scholars Publications, 1996.

See also: Anthropologists; Ecological Anthropology; Ecology and Religion; Proto-Indo-Europeans; Religious Studies and Environmental Concern; Sun Worship.

Murie, Olaus J. (1889–1963)

Olaus J. Murie was a renowned field zoologist, environmental writer, and wilderness preservationist. As a field scientist he conducted landmark 'life history" studies of the Alaskan caribou herds and of the Jackson Hole, Wyoming, elk herd. While doing so, he spent months at a time, over several decades, traveling and living in many remote wilderness areas. He developed a nearly mystical reverence for nature, and an opinion that preserving wilderness was important for the protection of certain animal species that required large acreages of habitat, such as wolves, mountain lions, grizzly bears, elk and caribou. He also came to believe, through his own experience, that wilderness was worth saving for humans to enjoy as a counterpoint to modern civilization.

Murie's spiritual connection to the Earth and its natural processes was well expressed in a letter he wrote in 1920 to his then-fiancé, Margaret Thomas, while he was following the Denali caribou herd. "I guess I am still enrolled in the Lutheran Church at home" [Moorehead, Minnesota] he said, "but there is no one creed or church as far as I know with which I fully agree. For one thing, I am crazy about Nature, and almost worship it, but isn't Nature the direct work of God?" (in Glover 1989: 33).

Murie worked for the U.S. Bureau of Biological Survey during the decades when that agency spent millions of dollars on its campaign to eliminate large predators and raptors from North America. Murie was a nearly lone internal dissenter against this campaign. In an argument with a fellow scientist, he wrote,

> I am very fond of all our native mammals, amounting almost to a passion . . . I believe the cougar is Nature's masterpiece in physical fitness. The big cats are infinitely beautiful. The wolf is a noble animal with admirable cunning and strength . . . I would utilize every opportunity to let them live . . . (in Glover 1989: 36).

In 1945, tired of battling the agency he worked for, Murie resigned and became half-time director of the Wilderness Society. In that role he traveled widely around the U.S., showing slides of the American wilderness and its fauna, and urging people to support preservation. In the early 1950s, he led a campaign to preserve the coastal plain and mountains of northeastern Alaska that comprise the range of the Porcupine caribou herd. This resulted in the eventual establishment of the Arctic National Wildlife Refuge.

By this later stage of his career, Murie's actions and viewpoint might best be described as Taoist (today this is more often translated Daoist), even though he may never have read or heard much about that ancient Chinese tradition. He was acutely aware of the constant flow of natural processes. He believed humans should live in harmony with those processes, and stand in humility before them. Indeed, he saw humility as one of the highest virtues, and constantly advocated its cultivation by both individuals and nations.

What he saw instead was a culture growing increasingly arrogant, especially toward nature. Examples, for Murie, were everywhere: in the effort to do away with "harmful" forms of wildlife, in the construction of enormous dams to "control" wild rivers, in the spraying of chemical pesticides from airplanes all over the cattle country of the west, in the usurpation of wildlands by a rapidly growing military.

Murie was especially opposed to the relatively harmless practice of naming natural features after human beings. Similarly, he opposed the construction of human monuments, especially in places where the much greater power and mystery of natural processes was on display. This resulted in an ironic situation when he died, in the fall of 1963. Admirers wanted to build a rather large monument to Murie in Jackson, Wyoming. His widow, Margaret, had to argue strenuously to prevent them from doing so, knowing that it would violate one of Olaus' strongest beliefs.

Murie's religious attitude may best be illustrated by his reaction to a proposal by the National Park Service, in the early 1950s, to build a church on the south rim of the Grand Canyon. The sacredness of that place, he argued,

> cannot be enhanced by architectural gymnastics. The Grand Canyon and the other beautiful and meaningful dedicated portions of our wonderful earth, should not be cluttered with manmade contrivances . . . And we modern human beings should forget our modern exaltation in material progress and approach the Grand Canyon with humility, in the hope that we can improve ourselves (in Glover 1989: 40).

James M. Glover

Further Reading

Glover, James M. "Thinking Like a Wolverine: The Ecological Evolution of Olaus Murie." *Environmental [History] Review* 13 (Fall/Winter 1989), 29–45.

Kendrick, Gregory D. "An Environmental Spokesman: Olaus J. Murie and a Democratic Defense of Wilderness." *Annals of Wyoming* 50 (Fall 1978), 213–302.

Little, John J. "A Wilderness Apprenticeship: Olaus Murie in Canada, 1914–15, and 1917." *Environmental History* 5:4 (2000), 531–4.

See also: Conservation Biology; Leopold, Aldo; Marshall, Robert; Wilderness Religion; Wilderness Society.

Music

The power of music to draw us in to states of spiritual openness and oneness with the world of surrounding nature has been known to humanity for thousands of years. Because of its inherent abstraction and allusion to a more pure world of resonances, tones, and frequencies, music has more than any art been understood as inherently sacred, able to lift its listeners and performers up to levels of higher consciousness. If religion is the belief that there are powers beyond our control that help give meaning and purpose to the world, then for many, music is the proof that such powers exist.

There are at least two ways the spiritual power of music can address nature, dependent on the contradictory meanings the word "nature" can have. On the one hand, music can lift us out from and above the mundane particularities of the obvious, base, material world of everyday life, toward some kind of harmony that encompasses inner human essence and the outer physical purpose, holding the world together and assuring humanity a place within it. The whole thing could be called nature, with "speculative music" our route to inhabiting it correctly. As Athaneseus Kircher (1601–1680) wrote,

> The chord of the soul must be aligned with the chord of the Hierarchy, and that of the body with the celestial one of the stars, and you will penetrate the secret of secrets, the absolute knowledge of things divine and human, as St. John says, "You have been anointed by the Holy One, and know all things" [I John 2:20] (in Godwin 1993: 284).

Thus nature has been described as a music of the spheres, all the way back to Pythagoras, some perfect Platonic song that human music or conduct can only aspire to. The more spiritual the music, the closer it is to such heavenly structured ecstasy.

On the other hand, music can easily seduce us *away* from a higher calling, and into a nature that is beautiful, immediate, and, according to some spiritual traditions, nothing but base amusement. As Hunayn (808–873) wrote in his *Maxims of the Philosophers*,

> The soul sings plaintive melodies, whereby it reminds itself of its own superior world. As soon as Nature sees this, and becomes aware of it, she presents herself by all sorts of her images (sensuous beauties) introduced one by one, to the soul, until finally she succeeds in recapturing it. The soul will soon forsake that which constitutes its own essence, and will become with all of its faculties entirely submerged in the *ocean of nature* (in Godwin 1993: 93).

It may be Marsilio Ficino (1433–1499) who best described how music works upon the player or listener to draw us out of ourselves and unto a larger place:

> By purified air music excites the aerial spirit which is the bond of body and soul – by meaning it works on the mind – by the conformity of its quality it floods us with wonderful pleasures "by its nature, both spiritual and material, it at once seizes man in his entirety" (in Rowell 1983: 71).

If the Western traditions suggest that the immortal music of the universe is a direct line from the human soul up from nature into the pure other world, then remember, this is not the only way. Hazrat Inayat Khan writes of the Sufi path, where God is in the living world all around us.

> The more widely one observes nature, the more it appeals to one's soul. Why? Because there is a music there. One sees more deeply into life and observes life more widely, one listens to more and more music, the music which answers the whole universe. Even a piano of a thousand octaves cannot produce the variety that nature represents (in Rothenberg and Ulvaeus 2001: 19).

The music of nature is *infinitely greater* than anything humanity can measure up to. Hinduism speaks of *Nada Brahma* – God is Sound, or the World is Sound. As Joachim-Ernst Berendt explains in his book of the same name, "before we make music, the music makes us" (1991: 12). Sound pulses through all of the universe, and through actual and ideal music, humanity can find an artful way into the whole. Alexandra David-Neel met a Tibetan lama on her travels who was a master of sound who told her this: "In the beginning was the wind. This wind sounded, thus it was sound which formed matter. The sound brings forth all forms and all beings. The sound is *that through which we live*" (Berendt 1991: 178).

The music that is considered spiritual is generally thought to have greater clarity of purpose than mere enjoyment or entertainment. Does this require certain specifically musical qualities? Some identify repetition, solemnity, and intensity as pushing the limits of musicality toward intoxication and trance. Ludwig van Beethoven found his greatest inspiration through walks in the woods. He writes, "My bad hearing does not trouble me here. In the country, every tree seems to speak to me, saying 'Holy! Holy!' In the woods, there is enchantment which expresses all things" (in Glesner 2001). His Symphony no. 6, the Pastorale, is his homage to the romantic power of the countryside.

Just as words are transformed into magic syllables in mantra, melodies and harmonies become larger than their musical selves inside spiritual compositions and improvisations. Spiritual music transforms the listener and performer, with the intent of getting us to look beyond ourselves to a greater sense of Oneness. Free jazz saxophonist Ornette Coleman says that he has always been guided by "the universal sound, the sound of the universe" (in Berendt 1991: 56). If this unity draws us into the environment around us, not apart from it, then nature is approached, not denied. Listening to the natural world around us is part of the discipline.

Music may imitate nature, learn from nature, but the hardest thing may be to find the best way for humanity to fit into nature. This too is a spiritual quest. A few ethnographies document various cultures with specifically musical views of the universe and the people's place within it. The Kalapalo of Brazil's Upper Xingu River sing of times when we were closer to the world: "at the beginning, the Birds' language was our language. We lived on the Other Side of the Sky" (in Guss 1985: xi). The birds' language is still like music, while ours has moved away from melody and we have lost the spiritual connection to nature around us. The Kaluli of New Guinea have a special word for the way their songs and society fit into the surrounding rainforest, *dulugu ganalan*, "lift-up-over sounding," the definition of a musical ecology where the highest goal is not something far away, but immediately accessible to those who are prepared to listen.

Their music does not simply define their culture in terms of nature but grounds them very precisely in a particular place. Steven Feld asked the singer Ulahi if the Kaluli learned how to fit their music so well into the surroundings by copying the ornate songs of the forest birds, but she said, "Oh no, they learned from us" (in Feld 1990: 211). (As someone who has learned much from playing music live with birds and insects myself, I have to admit that when contact between species happens this way, I feel much closer to some secret art that resounds across all life forms than before.)

Some traditions preach a kind of ultimate musical humility where we mere human musicians must stop singing and playing in order fully to attend to the more powerful music of the spirits, spheres, or of nature. "You cannot capture God's choir," says nature sound expert Bernie Krause, "in a recording" (in Rothenberg and Ulvaeus 2001: 223). Hazrat Inayat Khan eventually had to give up music, because he was called to a higher, more pure and austere life of prayer and devotion. Perhaps the suspicion that music is more fun than spiritual practice should be always lurks inside us even when we succumb to its power.

Common to many visions of the spiritual power of sound is a realization that music possesses us, can sweep over our being to pull us up in its wake toward a place in nature we cannot quite reach but know we must strive for. Gilbert Rouget explains how the music of trance leads the body to take on a whole new identity. If music is deep enough, it cannot be explained. It pushes us forward, toward a better destination. "We sing," says the Lubavicher Rebbe, "when we have tasted joy and are climbing it to the heavens" (Lubavicher 2001). The Midrash speaks of ten songs of the history of Israel. Nine are in the Bible, but the tenth is still ahead, the

> "New Song" of ultimate redemption, a redemption that is global and absolute, that will annihilate all suffering, ignorance, jealousy and hate from the face of the Earth, with a completely new musical vocabulary to capture the voice of Creation's ultimate striving (Lubavicher 2001).

So the perfect music may not be some pure unattainable ideal, but something humans might, or *must* find, somewhere still to come. "Listen," writes composer Pauline Oliveros, "not with your ears, with your blood. Listen! Not with your ears, with your ancestors. Listen! Not with your ears, with your futures" (in Rothenberg and Ulvaeus 2001: 247). This most spiritual of musics will not run from nature, but delve into nature, hear nature, and fit into nature in a way greater than any previous music has yet been able to achieve. The human music that truly enters into nature is still in our future, part of the purpose of progress that we can never quite pin down.

David Rothenberg

Further Reading
Basso, Ellen. *A Musical View of the Universe: Kalapalo Myth and Ritual Performances*. Philadelphia: University of Pennsylvania Press, 1985.
Berendt, Joachim-Ernst. *The World is Sound: Nada Brahma*. Helmut Bredigkeit, tr. Rochester, VT: Destiny Books, 1991.
Eisenberg, Evan. *The Recording Angel*. New Haven: Yale University Press, 2003 [1986].
Feld, Steven. *Sound and Sentiment: Birds, Weeping, Poetics, and Song in Kaluli Expression*. Philadelphia: University of Pennsylvania Press, 1990.
Glesner, Elizabeth. "Ludwig Beethoven, Symphony no. 6." http://w3.rz-berlin.mpg.de/cmp/beethoven_sym-6.html (2001).
Godwin, Joscelyn. *The Harmony of the Spheres: A Sourcebook of the Pythagorean Tradition in Music*. Rochester, VT: Inner Traditions, 1993.
Guss, David. *The Language of the Birds*. San Francisco: North Point Press, 1985.
Lubavicher, Rebbe. "Miriam's Song." http://www.chabad.org/Parshah/Article.asp?AID=2744. (2001).
Mâche, François-Bernard. *Music, Myth, and Nature*. Susan Delaney, tr. Chur: Harwood Academic, 1992 [1983].
Rothenberg, David and Marta Ulvaeus, eds. *The Book of Music and Nature*. Middletown: Wesleyan University Press, 2001.
Rouget, Gilbert. *Music and Trance*. Chicago: University of Chicago Press, 1985.
Rowell, Lewis. *Thinking about Music*. Amherst: University of Massachusetts Press, 1983.
Sullivan, Lawrence, ed. *Enchanting Powers: Music in the World's Religions*. Cambridge, MA: Harvard University Press, 1997.
See also: Dance; Indian Classical Dance; Music and Eco-activism in America; Music and its Origins; Music of Resistance; Tree Music.

Music and Eco-activism in America

Since music has often served both as a marker of cultural organization and as a means for the dissemination of information and social commentary, it is not a surprise that music has accompanied the growth and organization of environmentalism in the Americas. Since the 1960s, environmental themes have been tied by musicians to countercultural protest, as in Joni Mitchell's anthem "Woodstock." Notions of a "return" to nature and the preservation or protection of the natural environment were reflected in popular music.

By the 1980s, this general compatibility of environmentalism and countercultural music gave rise to the explicit support of musicians who performed benefit concerts and tours for such established environmentalist organizations as Greenpeace. These activities continued through the 1990s and into the early twenty-first century; for example, in the early 1990s artists such as U2, REM, Midnight Oil, and Sonic Youth contributed tracks to the Greenpeace album "Alternative NRG." Other charitable organizations formed alongside and with the cooperation of rock groups, including the Grateful Dead's Rex Foundation and Phish's Waterwheel Foundation. Since these organizations were not alliances between musicians and existing external organizations, they reflected the beliefs of the bands and their fans directly, and raised funds for a variety of smaller local environmental causes.

In addition to these forms of interactions, activists themselves have created their own musical forms. In recent decades, radical environmental activist music has proliferated rapidly in the United States. Such music connects the nature religion of this movement with evocative and persuasive artistic expressions. Rooted in and similar to other forms of popular American music, the music of the radical environmental movement is distinguished by its lyric content, but also by its cultural location, and social and spiritual functions. Activist songs spread messages of environmentalism to a wider audience and also teach and reinforce these messages within the community of activists. They serve both to evoke and reinforce proper spiritual perceptions of the natural world but also to convey messages of eco-apocalypticism and the urgency of immediate action.

Just as environmentalism itself springs from diverse streams in American culture, environmental activist music emerges from a number of musical traditions. It is a genre dominated by integrative forms of artistic expression that effectively mobilize an eclectic mix of cultural capital. Such forms are well suited to a movement that values beauty and simplicity, but demands worldly utility and eschews the bourgeois or decadent. Musical influences have included the folk and protest music traditions in the United States. Many traditions that are part of the folk canon in U.S. culture, including old-time fiddle, bluegrass, blues, Cajun/zydeco, and Celtic, have left an audible mark on activist songs. Activists have adopted the community dance setting in which many of these forms of music are played as well.

Overtly religious forms of music, including Native American musical traditions, New Age and neo-pagan songs, and Christian gospel traditions, have also influenced style and content of activist songs. Elements of the hippie aesthetic have been sparingly appropriated, although environmental activists are often critical of perceived escapism in some countercultural musical communities, particularly that surrounding the Grateful Dead. Other cultural traditions from which activist music has drawn include American religious revivalism and political protest movements, including the labor and civil rights movements. More clearly religious forms of environmentalist music have developed in parallel at neo-pagan gatherings and festivals.

The "road shows" that activists, including but not limited to Earth First! activists, undertake to raise consciousness about environmental threats and inspire action against them, are an important means for disseminating the message of radical environmentalism. These shows usually involve performances, musical and otherwise. They aim both to gain supporters on the "outside" of the movement, and to bring new individuals "inside" the movement. But these interests spring from more than a simply political agenda; they evoke and promote a perception of the sacredness of the Earth and its living systems. Activist musician Alice DiMicelle, for example, explained that since "the wilderness is my church," her role as artist is to bring those attending road shows "experientially into the wilderness" in order to perceive its sacrality (in Taylor 2001a: 227). The road shows combine the practical environmental concerns of the movement with its spiritual orientation in expressive forms that are seen mystically to connect the two.

Expressive forms are also central to the various gatherings of activists that occur regularly; these include regional wilderness meetings, camps, and trainings as well as the larger national "rendezvous." Among activists, expressive and artistic forms in general and song in particular help reinforce activism and spirituality as well as cement the communal bond between them. While the often light-hearted character of these gatherings is reflected in the songs, rowdiness and joking occur in the context of an assumption that the gatherings are important on both temporal and spiritual levels. Music is central to the fulfillment of these purposes. The themes of radical environmentalism are woven into lyrics and music and provide points of entry for the themes of community and spirituality. Activist music in this context suggests and encourages a spiritually proper perception of wilderness that is connected to a sense of the urgency of radical action.

Well-known environmental activist singer/songwriters include Alice DiMicelle, Danny Dolinger, Robert Hoyt, Timothy Hull, Dana Lyons, Peg Millett, Casey Neill, Jim Page, Joanne Rand, Walkin' Jim Stoltz, and John Trudell. Stylistically, these artists' recordings integrate a broad range of eclectic influences into a primarily acoustic setting. Radical activist music contributes to the production of coherent narratives within which activists' religious sensibilities and communal needs can be nurtured. The primary contents of their songs frequently address specific environmental issues, and the songs meaningfully tie environmental activism to a broader cultural setting, in terms of the familiar categories "sacred" and "profane."

Activist songs often fuse environmentalism with overtly religious themes. While the movement is not formally tied to any institutional religion, radical environmentalism encourages a range of pagan or pantheistic spiritualities. Many such traditions are woven together by activist musicians in innovative ways, bringing disparate elements together in a bricolage of previously unassociated elements. An example is Timothy Hull's "Indigenous Time," which links environmental activism to respect for native peoples and religions. Another recurring theme in activist songs, popularized by Walkin' Jim Stoltz, mirrors the common radical environmentalist contrast between "desecrated" destroyed forests and "sacred" intact ecosystems. Casey Neill's "May Day" leverages the coincidence of the pagan festival Beltane and the international worker's holiday to create a celebration of joy, deity, physical gratification, and social change. Subtle but effective musical juxtapositions are mirrored by the ideological ones; activist themes are placed beside Pagan ones. In the chorus, Neill claims that their Pagan and activist rejoicing will destroy the political status quo.

Environmentalist songs also juxtapose overtly activist themes with the "everyday" or "profane." These songs are playful, satirical, and humorous; they contrast activist life with the "mainstream" and place "everyday" things (such as romance, travel, humor) in the context of radical environmentalism. These themes, however, are tied to an eco-apocalypticism that urges immediate, radical action. These clever songs model how "normal" life continues even under radical circumstances and the all-encompassing life-changes required by them.

Folksinger/songwriter Danny Dolinger has several such songs, which fuse jovial and clever lyrics on "everyday" topics with a serious activist message, including "If I Had a Dollar" and "Hillbilly Hippie."

These functions are not necessarily genre-specific. In recent years, as environmental activists have found common cause with activists for human rights and social justice and the anti-war and anti-globalization movements, the music associated with these movements have also found new audiences. As boundaries between activisms blur, the hip-hop, punk, and electronic music brought into environmentalist circles is understood, as are the movements themselves, to reflect a shared ethos.

Thus, activist song and music occupy several important roles. They serve the vitally important role of community-building. Music also occupies a central place in radical environmentalist ritualizing. The road shows and wilderness gatherings serve a religious function in concretizing and reinforcing spiritual ideals of the community, and connecting them to play, humor, and art. Activist music often seeks to evoke and reinforce a proper spiritual perception of the natural world. The playful interpolation of seemingly disparate ideas, traditions, and aspects of life is part and parcel of expressive and religious life in the movement. Through this process of creative juxtaposition, disparate parts of a difficult activist life are sewn together to make this sort of life cohesive and *possible* for participants. The "ordinary" parts of life are drawn into the activist world, and the activist world is normalized for its participants. At the same time, however, the urgency of radical environmental action is stressed by the themes of eco-apocalypticism. These forms of artistic freedom and innovation in the music reflect and are a product of the movement's critique of capitalism and power structures. Further, the musicians understand their music to be one form of their activism and their most important contribution to the community.

Masen Uliss

Further Reading

Albanese, Catherine L. *Nature Religion in America: From the Algonkian Indians to the New Age.* Chicago: University of Chicago Press, 1990.

Pike, Sarah. *Earthly Bodies, Magical Selves: Contemporary Pagans and the Search for Community.* Berkeley and Los Angeles: University of California Press, 2001.

Taylor, Bron. "Earth and Nature-Based Spirituality: From Deep Ecology to Radical Environmentalism" (part I). *Religion* 31:2 (2001b), 175–93.

Taylor, Bron. "Earth and Nature-Based Spirituality: From Earth First! and Bioregionalism to Scientific Paganism and the New Age" (part II). *Religion* 31:3 (2001a), 225–45.

Taylor, Bron. "Resacralizing Earth." In David Chidester and Edward T. Linenthal, eds. *American Sacred Space.* Bloomington and Indianapolis: University of Indiana Press, 1995.

Taylor, Bron. "Evoking the Ecological Self." *Peace Review* 5:2 (1993), 225–30.

See also: Diggers and Levelers (and adjacent, Diggers Song); Drums, Drumming, and Nature; Earth First! and the Earth Liberation Front; Music of Resistance; Music and its Origins; Radical Environmentalism; Tree Music.

Music and its Origins

The origins of human-created music, and perhaps language itself, can be traced to the mimicry of bird songs and animal sounds. One of the oldest artifacts ever discovered is a bone whistle, found in a cave in northern Spain. Rhythm is likely an innate quality, sequenced to the cycles of day and night, the four seasons, fulfillment and hunger. Thus even the most synthetic modern music has indisputable roots in the natural world, and in humankind's capacity for empathy and expression, wonder and delight. Music was a way to preserve and pass down information prior to the advent of writing, and for tens of thousands of years it has served as a means for enhancing religious sensibilities and spiritual states.

The Lilloets of southern British Columbia sang a deep lament over the body of any bear killed, thus winning, they believed, the continued favors of the bear people. The Ona of Tierra del Fuego, on the far southern tip of South America, believed that a child who sings in its sleep or a teen who breaks unconsciously into song will become a shaman. To this day music remains an integral component of the spiritual teachings and practices of most indigenous, land-based peoples. The White Mountain Apaches have songs for every season and situation, as well as for essential social and religious rituals. These include planting and harvest songs, songs for birth and death, victory and courtship, the onset of puberty, the honoring of cronehood, and shamanic rites. The Aboriginal peoples of Australia navigate the overlapping natural and spiritual landscapes by following "songlines," auditory guide maps made up of ancestral place-based compositions, performed at each point along the way.

Shamans from Ecuador to Siberia use music as a transportive vehicle, arresting rational thought and suspending "imagined separation." Their power songs are intended to put them in touch with their magical allies, and chants and drumbeats assist their journey through the spirit world, to function as an aural bridge between what is known and what can be. The result of this connectedness can be enhanced sensitivity, lucid dreaming, "intrasensory perception" and clairvoyance. In this condition they access the wisdom of the ancestors and the gifts of the spirits, returning to normal consciousness with crucial prophecies and cures. Tuvan throat-singing and Vietnamese Buddhist chants share a common purpose, putting the singer in deeper contact with the experience and reality of spirit.

Similarly, music continues to be employed to help people get out of their "left-brain" minds and into the intuitive, responsive self away from what many participants in Western civilization see as a paradigm of artifice, and "back to nature." Hand-carved flutes are played reverentially by hikers in the wilderness, while back in the city altered states are encouraged by the rhythmic trance dancing popularized by groups like Gabrielle Roth & The Mirrors. Singing and drumming are core elements of women's circles and covens, as well as men's groups inspired by the archetypal Green Man or the works of writers like Robert Bly. Drum circles provide a sense of sacred space and communality for the several thousand "brothers and sisters" of the counterculture Rainbow Tribe, and they often use a drum to announce important councils at their gatherings. Chants (or "rounds") strengthen the communities and empower the rituals of contemporary Earth-worshipping Pagans (Wiccan, Neo-druid, Gaian, Pantheist).

Some of the most emotive Western classical pieces have been inspired by or are meant to evoke the color, drama or peace of the natural world, such as "The Grand Canyon Suite" and "Four Seasons." Mendelssohn tried to capture the sound of the ocean surf in his "Fingal's Cave," and the flute parts in Vivaldi's "Goldfinch" were written to approximate the sounds of the birds themselves. Attempting the same effect are the various examples of modern atmospheric or "New Age" music, usually combining recorded nature sounds such as rain, surf and bird song with electronic washes. The use of synthesizers in "environmental music" has been criticized by a number of academics and musicians including the Greek pianist Sakis Papadimitriou:

Today, playing the flute, congas, piano, saxophone, becomes an ecological protest. Sound emerges from within the musical instruments, directly from their source. And you hold this source in your hands, in your lap, in your arms, around your neck. Vibrations warm you. The sound touches you. It is not coming at you from a different, distant and mechanical point. Synthesizers do not emit music. They are faulty. They do not vibrate. The sound takes a digital walk first and then jumps into the loudspeakers. These sounds are ignorant of the earthly environment. They do not possess the elementary quality of surviving in Nature (Lone Wolf Circles 1991).

While a large percentage of environmental music is relaxing, some is intended to stir its listeners to action instead. In North America, following the example of civil rights and anti-war activists, the biocentric singer-songwriters such as "Walkin' Jim" Stoltz, Dana Lyons, Joanne Rand and Darryl Cherney helped to reinvigorate the American environmental movement in the 1980s and 1990s. Anglo eco-activist Lone Wolf Circles joined Native American John Trudell in performing spoken-word poetry to live world beat and rock music. On "Tribal Voice" Trudell chants to the beat of a tom-tom, "The generations surge together to meet the reality of power. Mother Earth embraces her children in natural beauty, to last beyond oppressor's brutality," and more simply, "Without Earth, there is no heaven." Born of rebellion and protest, Rock and Roll has contributed a few eco-paeans including the 1960s hit "In The Year 2525" and Barry Maguires' "Eve of Destruction," with their decidedly environmental message. In 1970 the group Spirit sang "It's nature's way of telling you something's wrong, it's nature's way of telling you with a song." In the 1990s the California family band Clan Dyken took their mix of socially conscious rock and reggae on the road with a mobile solar-powered stage, raising funds for the protection of remnant old-growth redwoods. Both the Canadian Bruce Cockburn and Georgia-based Indigo Girls have incorporated Native American spiritual sensibilities in pieces performed live, in tours spotlighting environmental and native rights issues.

The commercial country music of the 1930s–1950s often waxed sentimental about beautiful western landscapes and wide-open spaces, but within twenty years had developed a rock flavor and began catering to a largely urban audience. Country superstar John Anderson nonetheless contributed several songs addressing environmental concerns, and his "Seminole Wind" evokes a spiritual dimension in its paean to the vanishing Florida Everglades. In the 1970s Charlie Daniels sang about "The Last Lonely Eagle" passing over fields of destruction below, endlessly circling without a single standing forest left to land in. In "Coyote" new traditionalist Don Edwards laments the disappearance not only of old-time outlaws and Indians, but also the red wolf, the noble buffalo and the ineffable spirit of the land.

American Country music is derived in part from the Celtic ballads brought over by the English and Irish immigrants of the eighteenth and nineteenth centuries. The Scotch and Irish in particular came with a rich history of songs intended to deepen its people's connection, loyalty and devotion to the land that sustains them. In albums including *Real Estate* and *Indigenous* the popular Celtic folk musician Dougie Maclean celebrates sense of place in original pieces about what it means to belong, as true "care-takers" of the Earth. A continent away Geoffrey Oryema of the Ivory Coast writes songs that honor Africa's soulful countryside, and the Sami songstress Mari Boine calls forth the spirits of her Nordic land. The Aboriginal's connection to nature comes across strong in songs by native Australian Archie Roach, whose albums like MacLean's, Boine's and Oryema's are now distributed worldwide.

Not all examples of music, of course, move one closer to the meaning or experience of nature. Those that do tend to reform the ways in which we hear, define and relate to the natural world. Rather than substituting for nature, they draw the listener outside and into direct engagement with the more-than-human world. Of special interest are acoustic compositions recorded outside in a natural setting, such as those by jazz musicians Paul Winter, James Newton and Paul Horn. On the albums *Prayer for the Wild Things* and *Canyon*, Winter plays not *over* the sounds of nature but *with* them, enjoying an active melodic exchange with wind and willow, river and raven. With his project "Interspecies Communication" activist and musicologist Jim Nollman has taken this cross-species interaction one step further, employing music as a common language for the sharing of emotion and information between humans and other animals, especially orcas. In this way not only is the intelligence of cetaceans affirmed, but so also is the human penchant to reach out and connect through the "magic" of music.

Every expression of nature offers instruction as well as inspiration, setting an example of authentic and undiluted being. Like the echolation of whales and dolphins, the sharing of music is a way of probing the world for like-minded and like-hearted individuals, for sustenance, reciprocity and insight in a practice that ethnomusicologist Charlie Keil calls "deep echology." Being consciously "at one with the Earth" is compared to adjusting our pitch for perfect harmony, as people of every race and culture seek to find their part in the greater earthen song.

Jesse Wolf Hardin

Further Reading
Hardin, Jesse Wolf. "The Whole Earth Soundtrack." In *Kindred Spirits: Sacred Earth*. Wisdom, NC: Raven & Co., 2001, 59–65.
Hardin, Jesse Wolf. "Deep Echology: A Quarter Century of Earth Minstrelsy." *Humboldt Journal of Social Relations* (April 1995), 95–109.
Lone Wolf Circles. "The Deep Ecology Soundtrack: Music as a Vehicle of Awakeness." *The Trumpeter; Journal of Ecosophy* 10:4 (Fall 1993), 162–3.
Lone Wolf Circles (interview). "The Maestro's Baton: Music, Direct Action & Deep Ecology." *Echology: A Green Journal of Theoretical & Applied Sociomusicology* 4 (1991), 40–4.
Rothenberg, David and Marta Ulvaeus, eds. *The Book of Music & Nature*. Middletown, CT: Wesleyan University Press, 2001.

See also: Drums, Drumming, and Nature; Music; Music and Eco-activism; Music of Resistance; Pagan Music; Winter, Paul.

[P] Music of Resistance

Humankind has long rallied to evocative religious and secular music, from the chants of our ancestral cave dwellers or a melodic prayer for alignment with the spirits of nature to the arboreal anthems at the close of the twentieth century, emboldening a community of tree-sitters obstructing highway construction in some of England's most revered hardwood groves. While music has been employed by ruling states to unite their populations around a particular vision of patriotism and comportment, the protest movements that inevitably rise to oppose the status quo use the mood and metaphor of song to excite reconsideration and resistance. For both, music proves a powerful means of defining a shared group identity, deepening solidarity, evoking emotion and inspiring response. Whether a martial composition or a softly sung anti-war ditty, music fortifies the courage of the participants by sentimentalizing what they hold most dear, rhythmically reiterating what's at stake, reminding them that they are not alone in their efforts, fortifying their wills in the face of often unknowable odds.

In the summer of 1988, 24 Earth First! protesters blockading a logging road in the Kalmiopsis Forest, Oregon, U.S.A., were rounded up and placed in the back of a paddy wagon with barred windows. Rather than being taken at once to the jail, they were left in their sweltering confines to watch the falling of the giant old-growth fir trees they had come to protect. One by one they joined in singing the few words they remembered of an old protest song popularized by performers such as Walkin' Jim Stoltz and Si Kahn, "There is power, there is power, in a band of folks who care . . ." The vehicle rocked back and forth as they sang louder and louder, the music not so much a healing balm as fuel to keep their struggle and hopes alive.

Forty years earlier, the women of certain villages in Northern India banded together to stop the cutting of remnant Himalayan forests, chanting their sacred songs as they climbed the slopes to confront the government loggers. In statements they cited not only the increasing erosion and floods, and their dependence on a continuous supply of firewood, but also the offense to the Devas: spirits embodied in the threatened trees, as in all living things. They placed themselves at grave risk as they threw their arms around the trunks, their songs rising above the cacophony of saws. In this way, their growing forest protection campaign became known as the "Chipko" movement, a word meaning literally "to embrace."

From "I Feel the Forests," on Oregon native Cecelia Ostrow's 1985 album:

> There is a power dwelling in this land, a power deep
>   as it is old,
> Now you remember when you cut these trees,
>   that spirit cannot be bought or sold.
> I feel the forest swaying over me,
> I feel the flowing mountain streams,
> I smell the forest's breezes sweet and pure –
>   and I start to remember who I am.

The kinds of people who risk their credibility, jobs, freedom and even lives in defense of the last wild places are almost without exception inspired by more than the escalating extinction of species worldwide. While they may not always classify it as spiritual, they usually act out of a deep bond with the more-than-human world dating back to some formative childhood experience. Their pain is rooted in the loss or denigration of those childhood playgrounds, the places of refuge and belonging, the sources of their sensitivity, interdependency and epiphany.

"That townhouse used to be my tree fort" the eco-activist Dana Lyons sings on his album "Animal" in a song with the apocalyptic title "Time Bomb": "That highway used to be the wood. That building used to be the beach. That brown haze used to be the sky. Oh say goodbye!"

Lyric metaphor and melodic inference can help focus one's attention on their relationship to the natural world. Even more so, active listening and singing-along are integrative practices that connect a person in an immediate way to their physical and spiritual environs. Even singing songs that make no mention of the natural world can contribute to one's engagement through the transcendence of the intellect, the awakening of bodily senses and the stirring of the feeling heart. Songs with decidedly non-spiritual lyrics, or with no words at all, can nonetheless lead to individual and group experiences that are essentially spiritual in nature.

In the ecosophy and music of the environmental movement, human political concepts such as dignity and freedom have been broadened to include the more-than-human world, the fabric of life and non-life that make up the interactive Gaian whole. In this way, a new contemporary culture has been developing with a musical intentionality and religiosity more akin to their early indigenous counterparts than what they often refer to as "the dominant paradigm." Many of the most radical environmental activists in the U.S. and abroad have been motivated by "deep ecology" and the various strains of paganism and "New Age" spirituality in which the natural world is held to have not only a practical and evolutionary worth but also an intrinsic sacred value as well. Regardless of lyric content, music employed in the struggle to save what are held to be sacred lands and inspirited species could be said to serve a liturgical function.

In the 1980s and 1990s, American ecotroubadors performing on the environmental and college circuit included Joanne Rand, Alice DiMicele, Walkin' Jim Stoltz, Greg Keeler and Katie Lee. The political implications and outright danger that green performers face was driven home by what may have been the attempted assassination of Judi Bari and Darryl Cherney, when a pipe bomb exploded beneath them while they were driving to their next performance in the bay area of Northern California. The notable Australian activist and musician John Seed, co-founder of the Australia-based Rainforest Information Centre, spoke about the importance of an ecocentric (Earth-centered) spirituality while touring around the world raising money for the very practical purpose of rainforest preservation.

In 1985, I launched the first of 24 "Deep Ecology Medicine Show" tours, encouraged by Dave Foreman, co-founder of the radical environmental movement Earth First! Like earlier EF! road shows (featuring Foreman, Mike Roselle and Bart Kohler) the Medicine Shows were politicized rallies incorporating both live topical music and motivational speeches. Both were intended to gather new adherents to the cause of wilderness preservation, often resulting in the formation of new groups around local issues, or civil disobedience "direct actions" the day after a show. The Medicine shows differed in two fundamental ways: the various musicians and bands performed pieces with me rather than separately, symbiotically dramatizing my stories, provocations and prayers. We blended overtly emotive and spiritual elements into the shows endeavoring to create a tribal experience for a caring and sensitized audience. University and community center performances characteristically began and concluded with prayer, often contributed by Native American, Buddhist and other spiritual teachers drawn from the regions we traveled through. During these performances a band came forward and played, and my words were set to some jazz improvisation, bracketed between Country Western stanzas, propelled by a reggae skank, or buoyed by the lilt of a Syrian love song. In these performances I spoke of a litany of extinct plants and animals and provided a paean to those in danger of being lost, while teasing the audience with tales of my canyon home. These performances provided wilderness fundamental revival, a deep ecology Chautauqua proffering Gaian canticles and melodic manna for the would-be heroes of a wilder Earth.

There may be no more dramatic an example of the religious dimensions of eco-activist music than the "Tribal Jams," a long-time component of the Sage Brush Rally, at the annual Earth First! Round River Rendezvous. Following a host of speakers, humorists and performers, the Tribal Jam redirected the energy of those gathered – toward heightened presence, primal mindfulness, sentience, sense of place, and a palpable experience of an inclusive, Earth-embodied Spirit/God. During these rallies the crowd of professors and litigants, students and outlaws, often doff their clothes, paint one another's faces with red-mud war paint, and hoot and howl like the owls and wolves they spend much of their lives trying to save.

"Ease out of your minds," I would urge them, "and down into your intuitive, instinctual animal bodies." Anchored by archaic drum rhythms and colored with flute and guitar, an incantation floats out of the speakers and over and through them, as clouds of mountain dust rise moon-bound from beneath the dancers' busied feet. I chant to chant down the walls, chant open the hearts, chant us all back to authentic self and a whole-ly healed planet.

"Only one cause. One job. One people. One Earth. One Love. Gaia, Gaia, Gaia . . ."

Jesse Wolf Hardin

Further Reading

Hardin, Jesse Wolf. "The Whole Earth Soundtrack." In *Kindred Spirits: Sacred Earth Wisdom*. North Carolina: Swan, Raven & Co. 2001, 59–65.

Hardin, Jesse Wolf. "Deep Echology: A Quarter Century of Earth Minstrelsy." *Humboldt Journal of Social Relations* (April 1995), 95–109.

"The Deep Ecology Soundtrack: Music and Activism." *Talking Leaves* 47 (Fall 1993), 3–4.

Lone Wolf Circles. "Earthen Griots." Interview by Beth Bosk. *The New Settler Review* (Spring 1993).

Lone Wolf Circles. "Shaman." Interview by Beth Bosk, Mendocino County, CA, 16 December 1986. *The New Settler Review* (Spring 1993), 4–6.

Lone Wolf Circles. "The Maestro's Baton: Music, Direct Action & Deep Ecology." Interview. *Echology: A Green Journal of Theoretical & Applied Sociomusicology* 4 (1991), 40–4.

Taylor, Bron. "Evoking the Ecological Self: Art as Resistance to the War on Nature." In *Peace Review: the International Quarterly of World Peace* 5:2 (June 1993), 225–30.

See also: Deep Ecology; Earth First! and the Earth Liberation Front; Music and Eco-activism; Pagan Music; Tree Music.

Muti and African Healing

Muti (spelling variation Muthi) is a word describing a range of practices connected with the medicinal use of plants, animals, and occasionally humans in African and African-derived religions. It is one of the most widely known, yet misunderstood, concepts.

The word "muti" comes from the Zulu peoples of South Africa and originally means "medicine." This is important, because some of the negative associations of muti reported in recent years tend to ignore that, in itself, muti is a morally neutral practice, although there are ethical issues surrounding the extraction methods of plant and animal material.

In essence muti centers on the belief that many plant and animal parts have intrinsic power. This power can be harnessed through the careful preparation of potions and medicines. Thus, certain plants are believed to have special powers, and usually particular plants will be associated with different types of curative power. Likewise, the use of certain body parts may be associated with the healing of different types of illness. The power may be used for either good or bad purposes depending on the intention of those making, or commissioning, the particular medicine.

Some of the ingredients in muti are said by allopathic curers to have proven healing properties. *Prunus Africana* is believed to help the prostate; *Ocotea bullata* (black stinkwood), a drink, steam bath or general tonic is used for a whole range of skin problems; *Agathosma betulina* (buchu), is given as a diuretic and antiseptic; and the *Hypoxis* family is used to boost the immune system. Some pharmaceutical companies have been in running disputes with traditional healers over muti "patents," with the latter accusing the drug companies of "ethnopiracy" – the theft of traditional knowledge for their own financial gain.

The largest muti market in the world is to be found at Durban in South Africa's KwaZulu Natal province, closely followed by the Faraday muti market in Johannesburg. Here one can encounter a huge range of medicinal goods – from plants through to animal parts. A remarkable 4000 tons of plant material passes through KwaZulu Natal province every year destined for muti use, and the figure rises nationally to 20,000 tons. There are over 700 plant species throughout South Africa that are known to be used in muti medicine. Demand for muti is so high that many wild species are now threatened with extinction. Some species have already become extinct: for example wild ginger (*Siphonochilus aethiopicus*) and the pepper-bark tree (*Warburgia salutaris*) have become extinct outside of protected areas in KwaZulu Natal. One of the problems has been lack of cultivation of indigenous muti plants, partly through lack of horticultural knowledge and resources, as well as lack of foresight. It is estimated that there are over 27 million consumers of muti in South Africa, with an astonishing 4–6 percent of annual householder budgets being spent on them. This is lucrative business, and the plants and animals do not figure as top in the priorities of those who are making financial gain. Here, then, muti medicine and so-called allopathic medicine have more in common than might at first glance seem apparent.

In response to some of the serious environmental issues surrounding the use of muti, a few nurseries have sprung up in South Africa dedicated to helping "farm" supplies; to educate those involved in the trade; and to protect endangered species. One of the foremost examples of this is the Silverglen Nature Reserve in Chatsworth, South Africa, which contains over 200 medicinal plant species in its nursery. Another important educational establishment, with a small adjoining muti garden, is to be found in the KwaMuhle Museum, Durban.

To be trained to handle muti medicines properly is not something anyone can simply take up on an ad hoc basis, although there are undoubtedly charlatans at work. The training of a proper priest to do the task (usually known in South Africa as a sangoma) may take up to seven years, and involves time dwelling in rural areas under the tutelage of a senior priest. Not that muti should in any sense be seen as a rural practice in contrast to an urban allopathic practice. Sangomas are thriving in the towns and cities of South Africa, often operating out of "back street" style apartments and terraces where they are regularly visited by poor and rich alike.

The most controversial aspect of muti concerns the use of animal, and occasionally human, body parts. Different parts of the body are often associated with particular healing properties: thus a cure for infertility or impotence may be the use of genitalia (a commonly used part); emotional problems may involve the use of the heart; the need for discernment the eyes; or social issues parts of the brain. Particular parts of the body are thought to be especially powerful – notably parts of the spine (especially the top vertebrae); the genitals, finger nails, hair, and teeth. Some animals are thought to be more powerful than others and properties of certain animals relate to the need: so, for example, a leopard may be used in medicine for courage; a snake for guile; an elephant for power.

But the most controversial aspect of all in muti involves the use of human beings. By no means in all cases are people killed for muti – rather those who have already died may have body parts removed for use in such medicine. While raising ethical problems, this is not killing for muti, but this does, however, also exist. The most gruesome aspect of the use of animal and human body parts in muti concerns the extraction of parts while the victim is still alive, usually in the belief that the parts are thereby empowered by being fresh – especially if the victim screams. The extraction from a living victim thus makes the medicine more efficacious and "powerful." This author has encountered young bonobos (*par. Paniscus*) in central Africa with missing digits, hair, and teeth – all extracted in the name of muthi while the bonobos were still alive. There are several similar cases of human parts being removed while the victims were still alive.

Muti is now a global phenomenon. Long gone are the days where an academic purist could refer to muti as an exclusively South African, or even Zulu, practice. Both the concept, and even the terminology, now exists throughout Africa, and beyond, in cities such as London and New York. The use of animal and plant materials in medicines has long been recorded throughout Africa by anthropologists, but the term "muti" is also now regularly replacing local words as the sole descriptor for what are sometimes disparate practices.

Richard Hoskins

Further Reading

Mander, M. "Marketing of Indigenous Medicinal Plants in South Africa: A Case Study in KwaZulu-Natal: Summary of Findings." The Food and Agricultural Organisation of the United Nations, Forest Products Division, 1999.

See also: African Religions and Nature Conservation; Muti Killings.

Muti Killings

Muti killings (variation "Muthi") are those in which the victim has died as a result of the extraction of body parts for medicine or "muti." Thus a muti killing normally differs from cases of sacrifice, in which the purpose of the murder is a propitiation, or offering, to a deity or ancestor.

While there may be overlaps in some of the practices, the key aspect of a muti killing is that it is one in which the killing occurs as a by-product of the primary intent to extract body parts for medicine.

Just as certain plants are believed by practitioners of African and African-derived religions to have innate powers, so too it is believed that certain animal, and even human, body parts have intrinsic power. Their extraction for use in muti is therefore routinely practiced in South Africa, and elsewhere in African and African-derived religions. However, it is important to differentiate between several different issues here.

The removal of animal and human body parts for muti *after they are already dead from other causes* may raise ethical issues, but is not killing for muti *per se*. Many of the body parts on sale in muti markets in South Africa have been acquired in this way, and there is evidence of "black market" activity around morgues and crematoriums.

However, practitioners of muti more frequently believe that the provenance of their medicine is of importance to its empowerment. It is unusual, though not unknown, for muti to be extracted from older or ailing victims, while conversely, the young and healthy make for prime candidates. Among the animals there are favorite candidates: primates and the big cat family are at the top of the list.

Similarly, it is widely believed that the removal of parts while the victim is still alive renders the medicine more powerful. This is partly to be explained as "keeping the medicine fresh." But it is also because some believe that the screams of the victim empower the medicine. There are several gruesome cases, mainly in South Africa, where the extraction of body parts has taken place over several hours while the victim remained alive throughout. Some victims have thus been discovered missing parts of their anatomy, yet still alive. In one particularly brutal case in the Transkei province a woman was skinned alive and her genitals, breast, feet, and hands were removed all while she was kept alive (she died later). The body parts in this case were intended for empowerment in fertility and sexual healing. In many cases parts are sold off to different customers – each buying a part that relates to their own particular need for empowerment. Contract muti killings are not unknown – the murder of an innocent victim as part of a commissioning of certain body parts.

Some body parts are believed to be more powerful than others. It is normal, though not always the case, that genitals will be removed. Similarly, the eyes, parts of the brain, finger nails, hair, and internal organs such as the top vertebra, the heart, and spleen are all highly prized for muti.

While there may be overlaps with instances of sacrifice, it is important to recognize that in the latter the victim is usually killed quickly and the central empowerment occurs through the blood, rather than the body parts, the pouring of which acts as a libation to an ancestor or deity. Sacrifice of animals in this way is routinely practiced throughout sub-Saharan Africa.

The killing of human beings, whether for sacrifice or muti killing, is regarded by the majority of practitioners as a deviation of African religious practices, and the vast majority of Africans utterly condemn this. It is likewise important to remember that deviants kill in the name of religion in all cultures. But this does not mean it never occurs in African and African-derived religions. The 2001 discovery of the torso of a young West African boy in the River Thames, London, led police officers through cultural advice to the extraordinary realization that he had been sacrificed as part of a ritual killing. Such sacrifices are relatively frequent in parts of West Africa. Muti killings meanwhile remain relatively common in South Africa, with some estimates stating that as many as 300 occur every year. With HIV and AIDS infection rates soaring in many parts of Africa, life is deemed to be cheap. In addition, unscrupulous healers often proclaim miracle cures for life-threatening illnesses such as AIDS by the use of muti.

Richard Hoskins

See also: African Religions and Nature Conservation; Muti and African Healing; Zulu (amaZulu) Culture, Plants and Spirit Worlds.

Mutwa, Credo (1921–)

Attending an international conference on transpersonal psychology in Kyoto, Japan, during 1985, the great Zulu shaman, Credo Vusamazulu Mutwa, began his plenary address by remarking that he was delighted to be among people who revered mountains, because he was so fat that he was often mistaken for one. In this humorous observation, Credo Mutwa indicated not only that he was familiar with a recurring feature of Japanese folk religion but also that he felt a certain sense of solidarity with indigenous Japanese religious life. As he later explained, the Zulu and Japanese languages share many common words. The two languages supposedly have a cognate vocabulary, which enabled his wife to communicate effectively by speaking Zulu to Japanese shopkeepers. According to Mutwa, this shared vocabulary ultimately pointed to an underlying commonality of indigenous religion, whether that religion was referred to in Japanese as *Shinto*, "the way of the gods," or in Zulu as *Sintu*, "the way of man." By preserving their indigenous religion, the Japanese had established a model for the Zulu, according to Credo Mutwa, that would "make the black people of our culture as respected and powerful as the Japanese."

As guardian of tribal traditions, Mutwa had the responsibility of preserving the Zulu past. But he also claimed to know the future. At the 1985 conference in Kyoto, Credo Mutwa indicated that the future was in the stars. Asked to explain the significance of a bronze object he wore around his neck, Mutwa recounted, "in Africa we have a tradition that there are extraterrestrial intelligences watching the Earth. Do you not have reports in Japan of what are called 'Flying Saucers' ...?" According to Mutwa, aliens from outer space, known in Zulu as *abahambi abavutayo*, the "fiery visitors," featured prominently in the myths and legends of Zulu tradition. With increasing frequency, these extraterrestrial beings in flying saucers were visiting the Earth. Mutwa explained the significance of his necklace: "These ritual ornaments are intended so that when one of these vehicles comes to Earth, and extraterrestrial beings, who wish to establish contact with humanity, emerge, they will know the right person to talk to!" (Mutwa 1996: xiv, 163, xxix, xv–xvi). By his own account, Credo Mutwa – guardian of Zulu tradition; shaman, teacher, and healer of Africans; and prophet of the world's future – was exactly the right person.

The case of Credo Mutwa raises a crucial problem in the study of folk religion, the problem of authenticity. I have no intention of solving this problem. Instead, I want to think about some of the processes through which authenticity is produced, appropriated, and mobilized under the sign of folk religion, popular religion, or indigenous religion. In other words, I want to highlight the dilemma of artificial authenticity in the study of folk religion, and in so doing, will illustrate some ways in which nature is deployed in the service of authenticity.

Although folk religion might be regarded as a residual category, designating relations with gods, spirits, and sacred places that are left over when "world religions" have been factored out of the religious landscape, the very category of folk religion was produced out of a range of intellectual interests in the authenticity of the primitive, the savage, or the exotic. As historian of religions Charles Long has demonstrated, the notion of folk, popular, or indigenous religion has carried an aura of authenticity because it evokes the organic religious life of the rural peasantry rather than the urban citizenry, the lower class rather than the elite, the ordinary people rather than the clergy. In the process of its production as a category, however, folk religion was appropriated, reproduced, and arguably reinvented by urban, literate elites within modern societies to lend an aura of authenticity to emerging nationalisms. These "invented traditions" transformed folklore into "fakelore" in the service of national interests.

In the study of religion we occasionally have to confront outright frauds. During the eighteenth century in London, for example, the literary conman, George Psalmanaazaar, produced an entirely fake account of the society, culture, and religion of the island of Formosa. As anthropologist Rodney Needham argued, the temporary success of this fraud can be explained by the fact that Psalmanaazaar managed to make his fake account of the religion of Formosa look very much like a recognizable religion, or at least a religion that would fit expectations of an "exotic" religion among his readers in England. Such productions of authenticity require a careful mediation between extraordinary accounts, which cannot be independently confirmed or disconfirmed, and ordinary expectations about the primitive, the savage, or the exotic. In this work of mediation, successful frauds in the study of religion have acted as intercultural brokers speaking in the name of silent partners who bear the burden of authenticity. In some cases, these intercultural mediations of authenticity are relatively easy to expose as fraudulent, as in Eugen Herrigel's representations of the Zen Master Kenzo Awa or Carlos Castanada's account of the Yaqui shaman Don Juan Matus. Both are transparently fake. In other instances, however, the mutual complicity of reporter and informant in the production of indigenous authenticity has made the exposure of fraud extremely difficult if not impossible. If we critically review the exchanges between John Neihardt and Black Elk or between Marcel Griaule and Ogotemelli, for example, we have to conclude that these accounts of indigenous religion were produced out of specific intercultural mediations rather than through any extraordinary, unmediated access to authentic Sioux or Dogon religion.

Against this background, Credo Mutwa poses an extremely difficult problem. Speaking for himself, as well as for Africa, Credo Mutwa asserts an indigenous authenticity that has been acknowledged all over the world. In his native South Africa, however, he has often been described in the popular media as a fake, a fraud, and a charlatan. "He has been called an old fraud, a charlatan," journalist Angela Johnson observed (Johnson 1997). Alluding to Mutwa's complicity with apartheid, the apartheid regime of the National Party, and apartheid structures of South African Bantustans, journalist Hazel Friedman reported that Credo Mutwa has been widely regarded as "a charlatan and opportunist who consorted with the enemy" (Friedman 1997). Within South Africa, therefore, Credo Mutwa has not always represented indigenous authenticity. In fact, when he has not been entirely ignored, Mutwa has primarily appeared in popular media stories about his failed predictions as a false prophet who nevertheless continues to predict the future. But how does such a fake produce real effects in the real world? How has Credo Mutwa emerged globally, if not locally, as the supreme bearer of South African indigenous authenticity?

During the 1990s Credo Mutwa was celebrated not only as a Zulu shaman but also as an environmentalist, healer, prophet, teacher, and authority on aliens from outer space.

The new religious space opened up by the internet has been crucial to this development. On his own website, he appears in cyberspace as "Credo Mutwa, A Small Ray of Hope for Africa." On many other websites, however, he appears as one of the world's most important shamans, the High Sanusi of the Zulu nation of South Africa. In what follows, I review the historical production of this indigenous authenticity.

African Origins
Born in 1921 in the South African province of Natal, Credo Mutwa grew up in a household that was religiously divided between his father's Roman Catholicism and his mother's adherence to African traditional religion. In 1935 his father converted to Christian Science, the American church founded in the nineteenth century by Mary Baker Eddy, who understood God as "Divine Mind" responsible for healing the body, mind, and spirit. Undergoing a serious illness, Mutwa was forbidden conventional medicine in keeping with the avoidance of modern medical practice among Christian Scientists. Instead, his father read to him from the book *Science and Health*, by the "American holy woman" (Mutwa 1996: 3). Rejecting his father's "holy woman," Mutwa turned to his mother's family during his crisis. Under their tutelage, he learned that his illness was not an illusion, as the teachings of Christian Science held, but an entry into a new and special role within African indigenous religion. As Mutwa later recalled, his initiatory sickness signaled his calling to become a *sangoma*, an indigenous healer, diviner, and seer.

In 1954 Credo Mutwa found employment in a curio shop in Johannesburg that specialized in providing African artifacts for the tourist market. Mutwa's employer, A.S. Watkinson, relied upon him to authenticate these objects of African art. Besides developing detailed interpretations of the meaning of African artifacts, Mutwa emerged as a gifted and imaginative storyteller, recounting elaborate tales that he insisted were drawn from the authentic repository of Zulu tribal history, legends, customs, and religious beliefs. Sponsored by Watkinson and edited by A.S. Brink, an academic with the Institute for the Study of Man in Africa at the University of the Witwatersrand, a collection of Credo Mutwa's stories was published in 1964 under the title, *Indaba, My Children*. A second volume, *Africa Is My Witness*, was published in 1966. As editor Brink explained, the term, *indaba*, referred to a Zulu tribal council at which different views were presented "to have their authenticity or acceptability evaluated" (Mutwa 1964: xv). Ostensibly, therefore, Mutwa's stories were presented to the reading public to test their authenticity. In making such an assessment, however, the historical and ethnographic record provided no help, since the wild, extravagant, and imaginative poetry and prose of these texts bore little if any relation to anything previously recorded in print about Zulu religion. Nevertheless, rendering his own judgment, Brink advised that these tales were authentic because they revealed the "strange workings of the mind of the African" (Mutwa 1964: xv). Three decades later, reviewing the British republication of *Indaba, My Children*, Randolph Vigne could only agree that the entire point of Credo Mutwa's account of Zulu tradition seemed to be "to project an African culture wholly alien to and unassimilable with any other, least of all that of the Europe-descended millions who share South Africa" (Vigne 1999).

This construction of indigenous authenticity certainly fits with the tribalism of apartheid during the 1950s and 1960s. Under the auspices of its policy of separate development, the ruling National Party tried to create new African nations, with their own traditions, histories, languages, cultures, and religions, which would reinforce the establishment of separate homelands or Bantustans that were geographically within the territory of South Africa but legally outside of the Republic of South Africa. In the case of Zulu nationalism, the Department of Native Affairs, under the direction of apartheid ideologue H.F. Verwoerd and anthropologist W.M. Eiselen, sponsored the first Shaka Day in 1954 to celebrate Zulu tradition. They convinced the Zulu King Cyprian to dress up in a traditional costume of leather loin covering, leopard skin, feathers and beads that neither Cyprian nor his father, King Solomon, had ever worn before. For this recovery of tradition, they had to refer to an illustrated book about Africans that had been published in 1855. In this context, indigenous authenticity was constructed as a tribal continuity with a traditional past that allegedly prevented Africans from integrating into modern South Africa.

Although Credo Mutwa has claimed to have an "unashamedly unpoliticized conscience," his writings in the 1960s clearly reinforced apartheid, a political system that legally excluded all black Africans from citizenship within the Republic of South Africa, but incorporated them as exploitable labor. Like the architects of apartheid in the National Party, Mutwa argued that apartheid was not racial discrimination but racial separation that was consistent with divine and natural law. "Discrimination is to distinguish and decide which is best," Mutwa wrote. "Apartheid is to distinguish without deciding which is best" (1966: 318). Insisting that Africans in South Africa actually wanted apartheid and were not interested in equal rights, Mutwa declared, "Apartheid is the High Law of the Gods! It is the highest law of nature!" (1966: 319). Racial integration, according to Mutwa, "is as abhorrent as extermination" (1966: 319). Praising H.F. Verwoerd, who by then had become president of South Africa, Credo Mutwa maintained that the

> White men of South Africa are only too right when they wish to preserve their pure-bred racial identity.

And what is good enough for them is good enough for us, the Bantu . . . Separate Development . . . is the clearest hope that the Bantu have thus far had" (Mutwa 1966: 323).

Under apartheid, Verwoerd's National Party promised to protect independent African homelands from "Communists or militant Bantu rebellion-mongers" such as the African National Congress (ANC). Into the 1980s, Mutwa continued to lend his support to the apartheid regime, even writing the foreword to a book published in 1989 arguing that the United States should not impose sanctions on South Africa. Instead, the U.S. should embrace South Africa and consider making the country its fifty-first state. As he argued in the 1960s, Mutwa insisted that such protection would save Africans from communists, militants, or rebels such as "the ANC terrorists" (1989: 13). Under the apartheid regime of the 1960s or the neo-apartheid regime of the 1980s, Credo Mutwa was only concerned that Africans should be free to preserve their distinctive tribal customs and their traditional way of life.

In his publications of the 1960s, Credo Mutwa declared himself the guardian of Zulu tribal tradition. Referring to himself as a Zulu witchdoctor, Mutwa related a bewildering array of traditional tales, which Mutwa himself characterized as "a strange mixture of truth and nonsense," showing a remarkable facility of literary invention. Mutwa's presentation drew its authority from a careful balance of transparency and secrecy. On the one hand, Mutwa claimed that he was relating common African folk traditions, the familiar "stories that old men and old women tell to boys and girls seated with open mouths around the spark-wreathed fire in the center of the villages in the dark forests and on the aloe-scented plains of Africa" (1964: 429). If this assertion were true, then the authenticity of these stories could presumably be confirmed by every African man, woman, and child. On the other hand, Mutwa claimed to be relating secrets that were only revealed during the initiation of a witchdoctor. "If ever you pass what you are about to be told today on to the ears of the aliens," his instructor had warned him during his own initiation, "a curse shall fall upon you" (1964: xiii). By publishing these stories, including a word-for-word account of all the secrets conveyed during his initiation, Credo Mutwa had clearly broken his sacred tribal oath of secrecy. As Mutwa put it, he had made a "terrible choice to betray my High Oath as a Chosen One" (1964: 455). Although this betrayal apparently violated the dual source of his authority – shared tradition, secret initiation – Credo Mutwa nevertheless asserted his role as traitor as if it underwrote the authenticity of his accounts of Zulu folk religion.

In the 1960s, calling himself a Zulu witchdoctor, Credo Mutwa traced his lineage back to his maternal grandfather, who served as the "High Witchdoctor" under the Zulu King Cetshwayo (ca. 1836–1884). During the 1990s, biographies of Credo Mutwa traced his lineage back to his great-grandfather, the High Sanusi of Zulu King Dingaan (ca. 1745–1840), and observed that in 1963 Credo Mutwa had been "officially declared" or "officially proclaimed" the High Sanusi of the Zulu people (Ringing Rocks Foundation 2001, Payback Press 2001). As Mutwa noted in 1964, the term, sanusi, which designated an "Unmarried High Witchdoctor," was etymologically related to the Sanskrit sanyassin, an "Unmarried Holy Man" (Mutwa 1964: 439). Nevertheless, he eventually appropriated this title for an inherited role transmitted from his maternal grandfather. Although the "official" structures through which this title was bestowed upon Credo Mutwa have never been specified, in 1963 they could only have been official apartheid structures, such as the Department of Native Affairs, which was busy installing new chiefs and traditional leaders for the Bantustans. Unlike the public declaration of Shaka Day in 1954, however, there is no evidence of any public ceremony proclaiming Credo Mutwa as the High Sanusi of the Zulu people. Instead, capitalizing on his reputation as an author and building on the authority of his texts, Mutwa found a public role in South Africa as an African tourist attraction.

Culture and Nature

During the 1970s, Credo Mutwa was employed by the South African National Parks Board as the attendant of a traditional African tourist village located in the black township of Soweto outside of Johannesburg. Designed for the entertainment of foreign visitors, this display of authentic African religion, culture, and traditions was generally ignored by Africans. Above the entrance, Mutwa inscribed the warning: "ALL LIARS, ATHEISTS, SKEPTICS AND FOOLS MUST PLEASE KEEP OUT!" As journalist Joseph Lelyveld observed, anyone who passed through the entrance found "a shrine that seemed to derive its inspiration partly from the cult of the avenging Hindu goddess Kali and partly from Disney World" (Lelyveld 1986: 249). Struck by the eclectic and idiosyncratic symbolism on display, Lelyveld called into question the authenticity of this tourist attraction. Like his writings, Mutwa's African village in Soweto evoked the strangeness of Africa. During the black-consciousness uprising of 1976, African students attacked Credo Mutwa's shrine, burning its huts, carvings, and other artifacts, because they saw his tourist village as promoting the tribalism of apartheid and separate development. Although Mutwa eventually had to abandon his shrine and leave Soweto in 1978, the Credo Mutwa Village remained on the tourist itinerary into the 1990s with its burned and blackened features.

During the 1980s, Credo Mutwa established a larger and more ambitious tourist attraction within the South African Bantustan of Bophuthatswana, an African nation that was not recognized by any other nation in the world, except by the apartheid regime in South Africa. At Lotlamoreng Dam Cultural Park, beginning in 1983, Mutwa supervised the construction of small adobe villages, each representing the traditional culture of one of South Africa's tribal African peoples. Traditional villages were built for Tswana, Zulu, Ndebele, Xhosa, and Southern Sotho groups. Around these displays, Mutwa erected clay statues of African deities, most prominently a twenty-foot-tall African goddess. Praising Lucas Mangope, the president of Bophuthatswana, Credo Mutwa declared that "Anyone who gives me the opportunity to rebuild the African past knows what he is doing" (Republic of Bophuthatswana 1987: 19). Following the first democratic elections of 1994 and the reincorporation of Bophuthatswana into South Africa, the cultural park was deemed to belong to the National Parks Board. Credo Mutwa was expelled. By August 1995, as anthropologists Jean and John Comaroff found, the cultural village had become an informal settlement in which people lived in and around the various tribal displays.

Moving to the Eastern Cape, Credo Mutwa was employed by the Shamwari Game Reserve, near Port Elizabeth, where he sold African artifacts, such as sacred necklaces, headdresses, icons, and implements used in rituals. "In the Zulu tradition," according to the publicity for the reserve, "each of these artifacts must be kept alive by being used in a sacred way on a regular basis." Accordingly, Credo Mutwa was charged with the responsibility of performing the rituals that would keep these objects alive for the tourist market. In addition to authenticating African artifacts, Mutwa presided over a traditional African Arts and Culture Village, Khaya Lendaba, the "Place of Enlightening Talk," which was next to the Shamwari Born Free Conservation and Education Center. Once the cultural village was built, however, Credo Mutwa was forced to leave. By 2000, the cultural center was run by the Rev. Mzwandile Maqina, featuring a one-hour show of song, dance, and stories depicting rituals of love, marriage, birth, and circumcision and the daily lives of traditional rural village. Although this traditional village came to be operated by a Christian minister, who had been identified by South Africa's Truth and Reconciliation Commission as responsible for working with the apartheid regime in fomenting violence against Africans in the Eastern Cape during the 1980s, the merger of indigenous African culture and nature continued to attract foreign tourists.

Although he left under uncertain circumstances, the merger of culture and nature at Shamwari defined a new role for Credo Mutwa as an indigenous environmentalist. In August 1997, Mutwa received the Audi Terra Nova Award for his contribution to wildlife conservation at the Shamwari Game Reserve. The patron of the award, the conservationist Ian Player, identified Credo Mutwa as the "sole surviving Sanusi, the highest grade of spiritual healer" (Audi 1997). As this indigenous authority was appropriated by conservationists, Mutwa lent his support to various environmental causes. During 1997, Credo Mutwa spoke at the sixth international Whale and Dolphin conference, sponsored by the International Cetacean Education Research Centre, in Queensland, Australia, relating African traditions about the special relationship between Africans and whales and dolphins. During 1999, he spoke at the Living Lakes Conference, sponsored by the U.S. Forest Service at the Mono Lake Visistor's Center, Lee Vining, California, recounting indigenous African traditions about sacred lakes. Proponents of animal rights found in Credo Mutwa an indigenous African defender of animals. "Apartheid is dead," he observed, "but 'separatism' is alive and well," an apartheid-like separation between human beings and animals (Mutwa 1997). For environmentalists, conservationists, and animal-rights activists, therefore, Credo Mutwa lent an aura of authenticity that could be appropriated in the service of a variety of popular causes.

During the 1990s, the new medium of the internet changed the terrain for promoting cultural tourism. While an announcement was made in 2001 that Credo Mutwa, the "visionary behind the venture," planned to construct a new cultural village, Kwavezitemba, featuring a Zulu hut, a Pedi-Tswana hut, a Dokodo healing hut, and a Digoja-Star hut, he had already established a prominent place in cyberspace. For example, Mutwa's account of Zulu traditions was featured on the Kwa-Natal Tourism site; his explanation of the meaning of indigenous symbolism featured on a site, "Living Symbols of Africa," that exported a range of African artifacts; and his artwork decorated TheAfrican.Com, the "website of the African diaspora," which claimed two patrons, the ancient Egyptian hawk-deity Heru and the Yoruba deity Shango, who was depicted on the website in a painting by "His Holiness Credo Mutwa, Zulu Sanussi [sic] of South Africa." In these sites on the internet, Mutwa's indigenous authenticity was employed to invite tourists to South Africa and to sell tourist artifacts from South Africa. As indicated by the website of TheAfrican.Com, Credo's Mutwa's indigenous authenticity had become global on the internet as he provided religious legitimation for an indigenous culture supposedly shared by Africans all over the world. Although he had presided over a series of failed cultural villages in South Africa, Credo Mutwa now played an important role in a new global cultural village on the internet.

Indigenous Knowledge

At the heart of his claim to authenticity, Credo Mutwa insisted that he possessed specialized indigenous knowledge that could be used in healing, divination, education, and social transformation. Following the democratic elections of 1994, the new government in South Africa supported a number of initiatives that involved recovering "indigenous knowledge systems" as the basis for an African Renaissance. Throughout Africa, largely in response to the AIDS pandemic, new interest was shown in the indigenous knowledge and human resources of traditional healers. At a meeting of traditional healers and representatives of the World Health Organization held in 1997 in Kampala, Uganda, Credo Mutwa defended the importance of indigenous knowledge about healing in Africa. Recognition of indigenous healers by the WHO, Mutwa proposed, "will show the scientists that our people are not just a bunch of superstitious savages. If the world accepts many of our herbal medicines, this will help to ensure the survival of our traditional healers" (Cohen 1997). At the thirteenth International AIDS Conference meeting in Durban, South Africa, in 2000, Credo Mutwa appeared wearing a sacred healing necklace. As a member of the executive committee of the Nyangazizwe Traditional Healers Organization of South Africa, Mutwa promoted the use of an indigenous herb, *Sutherlandia* (*Kankerbos*, in Afrikaans), as a cure for AIDS. Instead of relying upon expensive foreign pharmaceuticals, medical practitioners could find an effective treatment in South Africa. "It's there in the violated plains of my fatherland," Credo Mutwa declared. "It is being ploughed up as a weed" (*Cape Times* 15 March 2001). Like this indigenous herb, traditional healers were generally being ignored by the scientific medical profession in South Africa.

Alternative medicine, including spiritual healing, is a central preoccupation of New Age spirituality. Under the editorship of Bradford P. Keeney, who has been described as a psychologist, medicine man, and shaman, a book on the healing wisdom of Credo Mutwa was published in the United States in the series, "Profiles in Healing." Keeney apparently recommended Mutwa to the attention of the directors of the Ringing Rocks Foundation, which was established in Philadelphia in 1995 with the mission "to explore, document, and preserve indigenous cultures and their healing practices" (Ringing Rocks Foundation 2001). As its first project, the foundation decided to sponsor Credo Mutwa with a lifetime stipend that would "allow this treasure to live out his days free to create as he chooses" (Ringing Rocks Foundation 2001). Recognizing him as the High Sanusi of the Zulu, the foundation bestowed another title upon Credo Mutwa, Ringing Rocks Foundation's "Distinguished Artist and Teacher of African Traditional Culture." On the foundation's website, Mutwa would be given space to transmit his indigenous knowledge to others. The directors of the foundation seemed to imagine their website as the culmination of Mutwa's long career of establishing cultural villages in South Africa since they intended to compile a retrospective profile of those sites on the website. "We hope to spend time with him at each of the sites he has built," they stated, "recording through pictures and his own words the background for his cultural and healing villages" (Ringing Rocks Foundation 2001). Although he had no secure place in South Africa, the Ringing Rocks Foundation in the United States promised to provide Credo Mutwa with a healing center in cyberspace.

In keeping with the eclecticism of New Age spirituality, the African healing practiced by Credo Mutwa was equated with the healing systems of other indigenous cultures. Increasingly, he operated at the intersection of African and Native American traditions. In 1997, for example, Credo Mutwa, the "well-known Zulu prophet," and Roy Little Sun, a Native American healer who had been born in Indonesia as Roy Steevenz, but was reportedly adopted by the Hopi, performed a ceremony entitled, "Healing the African Wound." At the Wonderboom, the "Tree of Life," in Pretoria, these indigenous healers took two feathers, one from an American golden eagle representing the sky, the other from an African guinea fowl representing the Earth, and tied them together to signify the healing of Africa through the sacred union of Earth and sky, indigenous Africa and Native America. Unfortunately, since they included the feather of an endangered species, the healing feathers were confiscated by U.S. custom officials at the Atlanta airport when Roy Little Sun returned to America. Although his campaign to recover the feathers, including appeals to President Bill Clinton, failed to secure their return, Roy Little Sun returned to South Africa for another ceremony in 2000 to reaffirm the healing connection between the indigenous people of America and Africa.

The indigenous authenticity represented by this fusion of African and Native American spirituality was also attractive to some white South Africans. During 2001, for example, a New Age event in the Eastern Cape of South Africa was advertised as "A Tribal Gathering," not a gathering of indigenous African tribes, but a festival attracting primarily white South African enthusiasts for Native American spirituality. Living in a Tipi Circle, participants at this gathering would celebrate Mother Earth, enter a sweatlodge, and perform the ceremonies of the Medicine Wheel. Promising that African ritual specialists, *sangomas*, from the local village would also visit the gathering, the advertising for the event certified the merger of African and Native American spirituality by featuring a photograph of Credo Mutwa at the Medicine Wheel. In the United States, New Age enthusiasts tended to assume the basic equivalence of all indigenous spirituality. For example, the Heart Healing Center in Denver, Colorado, hosted a conference in 2001 of "Indigenous Earth Healers." At this gathering of indigenous healers from all over the world, Africa was represented by the High Sanusi of the Zulu, Credo Mutwa. Unable to attend in person, Mutwa was replaced on the program by his student, C.J. Hood, a "white Zulu" from Port Elizabeth in the Eastern Cape, who played a videotaped message by Credo Mutwa and performed a traditional Zulu dance. Praising his Zulu teacher, Hood declared that "Credo Mutwa will go down in history as a man who was able to bridge a gap between white and black South Africans and start a healing process" (Heart Healing Center 2001). By invoking the indigenous authenticity of the Zulu healer, C.J. Hood was able to find a New Age audience in the United States for his message, as reported in the *Wellness Journal*, "Respect all that is around us, accept all cultures as they are, and go back to our traditions" (Wellness 2001).

Back home in South Africa, new applications were being discovered for African indigenous knowledge. As a prophet, seer, and master of African techniques of divination, Credo Mutwa remained a target of ridicule in the popular press. "Soothsayer Credo Mutwa got it wrong last year," as the *Sunday Times* observed in January 2000, a feature discrediting the prophet that seemed to run at the beginning of every year. Nevertheless, Mutwa lent his credibility to divination workshops, often designed for business executives, to teach indigenous African techniques for contacting and communicating with ancestors, divining through mediumship or sacred objects, and making long-term regional and global predications.

Alien Encounters

In his writings of the early 1960s, Credo Mutwa referred to "aliens" and "the Strange Ones" who came from outside of Africa. Beginning with the ancient Phoenicians, the "Strange Ones" arrived in unfamiliar ships from unknown lands across the sea. European colonizers, also referred to as the "Strange Ones," had established alien empires in Africa. In the post-colonial era, as Mutwa advised, Africans had to resist the "schemes of the Strange Ones," which included communism and parliamentary democracy, but apparently not the divine and natural law of apartheid, by maintaining indigenous African traditions. In these terms, indigenous authenticity was established in opposition to the aliens and Strange Ones who came from outside of Africa.

During the 1990s, however, Credo Mutwa used the term aliens for beings from outer space, those extraterrestrials that supposedly featured prominently in African myths, legends, and traditions. According to Mutwa, Africans have long known about many species of extraterrestrials. Some are evil, bringing harm to human beings, such as the *Muhondoruka*, fifteen-foot high, cylindrical, column-like creatures who cause violence, or the *Mutende-ya-ngenge* (also known as *Sekgotswana* or *Puhwana*), green creatures, with large heads, chalk-white faces, and large green eyes, who capture people, cut them up, and put them back together again. The most dangerous aliens, however, were the *Mantindane*, who are "star monkeys" and "tormenters," the powerful extraterrestrial reptiles known as the Chitauri, and the Greys, the small servants of the Chitauri.

The Chitauri's evil schemes to harm humanity included supporting institutionalized religions. "They like religious fanatics," he observed. "Ones who are burdened with too much religion are very popular with the Chitauri" (Martin 1999). Working through institutionalized religions, the evil Chitauri seek to divide and conquer human beings.

By contrast to these dangerous aliens, other extraterrestrials are good. The *Mvonjina* are three-foot high creatures, looking like a "caricature of a white person," who act as "a messenger of the gods" by bringing knowledge to humanity. Other races of beneficent extraterrestrials frequently appearing in Africa included the friendly *Sikasa*, the timid *Mmkungateka*, the beloved *Nafu*, and the ape-like *Mbembi*. Besides trying to communicate with human beings, these aliens from outer space have often mated with African women. "There have been many women throughout Africa in various centuries who have attested to the fact that they have been fertilized by strange creatures from somewhere" (Mutwa 1996: 152). Although apartheid had criminalized interracial relations in South Africa, aliens from outer space were apparently engaging in interspecies sexual relations throughout Africa.

By his own account, Credo Mutwa has experienced many encounters with extraterrestrial beings. As early as 1951, in what is now Botswana, he witnessed a falling star, a strange vehicle in the sky, and two alien creatures disappearing into the spaceship. In the bush where the spaceship had landed, these aliens had left behind extraterrestrial rubbish. Along with the local people who witnessed this event, Mutwa made sure that the rubbish was buried. "That is the African tradition," he explained (1996: 135). He also encountered a variety of aliens from outer space in Kenya, Zimbabwe, and Zambia during his travels in the 1950s. Besides seeing extraterrestrials, he also claimed to have eaten them, describing the smell and taste of their cooked flesh. According to Credo Mutwa, the ritual consumption of extraterrestrial flesh was common in Africa, sometimes causing severe illness, but sometimes resulting in mind-altering experiences of great beauty, harmony, and transcendence.

Visiting what is now Zimbabwe in 1959, however, Credo Mutwa underwent his most dramatic encounter with extraterrestrials. While digging for medicinal herbs, he was suddenly confronted by five "little fellows," strange, unfamiliar beings, small dull-gray creatures, with large heads, but thin arms and legs, who captured him and took him to a metallic room, shaped like a tunnel, where they probed and tested his body. The aliens then forced him to have sex with a female of their species, an experience that Mutwa reported as cold, clinical, and humiliating. "I felt like a victim at a sacrifice," he recalled (1996: 142). After this ordeal, he was deposited back on Earth, with his clothing torn, only to discover that he had been missing for three days.

Based on these encounters, Credo Mutwa emerged as an authority on extraterrestrial beings. In a book on alien abductions, Professor John Mack of Harvard University devoted a chapter to Credo Mutwa's meetings with beings from outer space. Although he recounted his humiliating treatment by his extraterrestrial tormentors, Mutwa stressed the positive potential of human exchanges with aliens. "I just get furious," he declared, "because the people from the stars are trying to give us knowledge, but we are too stupid" (Mutwa in Mack 1999: 57, see also 198–218). As confirmation of his global recognition as an authority on aliens from other worlds, Credo Mutwa was invited to deliver the keynote address at an international "Conference on Extraterrestrial Intelligence" in Australia during March 2001.

In establishing Credo Mutwa as an African authority on extraterrestrials, the New Age conspiracy theorist, David Icke, played a significant role. A former sports broadcaster in Great Britain, Icke developed a distinctive blend of personal spirituality and political paranoia that he promoted through books, public lectures, and an elaborate website. Although he seemed to embrace every conspiracy theory, David Icke identified the central, secret conspiracy ruling the world as the work of shape-shifting reptilians from outer space. As Icke revealed in his book, *The Biggest Secret*, these extraterrestrial reptiles interbred with human beings, establishing a lineage that could be traced through the pharaohs of ancient Egypt, the Merovingian dynasty of medieval Europe, the British royal family, and every president of the United States. Although they plotted behind the scenes in the secret society of the Illuminati, the aliens of these hybrid blood-lines were in prominent positions of royal, political, and economic power all over the world. Occasionally shifting into their lizard-like form, these aliens maintained a human appearance by regularly drinking human blood, which they acquired by performing rituals of human sacrifice. In *The Biggest Secret*, David Icke invoked the indigenous African authority of Credo Mutwa to confirm this conspiracy theory about blood-drinking, shape-shifting reptiles from outer space. Reportedly, Mutwa declared, "To know the Illuminati, Mr. David, you must study the reptile" (Icke 2001; see also Icke 1999). In two videos produced and distributed by David Icke, "The Reptilian Agenda: Volumes 1 and 2," Credo Mutwa confirmed that extraterrestrials, the Chitauri, were a shape-shifting reptilian race that has controlled humanity for thousands of years. Icke and Mutwa appeared together on a popular American television program, "Sightings," to explain the alien reptile conspiracy. In his lectures in the United States, Icke insisted that Credo Mutwa provided proof for his conspiracy theory, as one observer noted, in the "pure voice of a primitive belief system." In Credo Mutwa, therefore, David Icke found indigenous authentication for an alien conspiracy, and of course, this is also about nature, understood as the order of the universe.

Folk Religion, Fake Religion

In retracing his long journey from Zulu witchdoctor to New Age shaman, I have highlighted Credo Mutwa's ongoing reinvention of himself in relation to different appropriations of his authority. As we have seen, during the 1950s Mutwa was used to authenticate African artifacts for a curio shop in Johannesburg. Through his writings in the 1960s, his tourist attraction in Soweto in the 1970s, and his cultural village in Bophutatswana in the 1980s, he was used to authenticate the racial, cultural, and religious separations of apartheid. During the 1990s, as he acquired the label, shaman, through the interventions of Bradford Keeney, Stephen Larsen, David Icke, and other exponents of New Age spirituality, Credo Mutwa's authority was invoked to authenticate a diverse array of enterprises in saving the world from human exploitation, environmental degradation, epidemic illness, endemic ignorance, organized crime, or extraterrestrial conspiracy. In all of these projects, the indigenous authenticity of Credo Mutwa added value, credibility, and force because he represented the "pure voice," untainted by modernity, of an unmediated access to primordial truth.

These appropriations of Credo Mutwa raise important problems for any assessment of authenticity in the study of folk religion. In conclusion, I would like to highlight only two issues that require further reflection as we wrestle with the ordeal of authenticity. Let us say, for the sake of argument, that Credo Mutwa is a fake, a fraud, and a charlatan, as the South African media would have it, rather than the authentic voice of indigenous African religion as he appears in cyberspace. Even if he is a fake, we are still faced with the problem of analyzing what Credo Mutwa has really been doing in the field of indigenous African folk religion. Even a fake, as I will suggest in conclusion, can be doing something authentic.

First, even if fake, a fake religion can draw upon recurring, enduring motifs of indigenous folk religion. Folk religion is often assumed to be timeless, deriving its authenticity from the faithful repetition of discourses and practices that have persisted from time immemorial. Like any form of religious life, however, folk religion has reformers, reformulators, and innovators. Credo Mutwa, it might be argued, is precisely such an innovator in African folk religion. Like the eighteenth-century English poet William Blake, who adapted recurring pagan and Christian mythic motifs to create his own innovative, creative, and idiosyncratic religious mythology, Credo Mutwa has drawn upon recurring patterns and processes of indigenous African religious life to produce an innovative mythology that ranges from the original earth goddess to the ultimate encounters of human beings with aliens from outer space. Certainly, neither the goddess nor the extraterrestrials in this mythology simply preserve African folk religion. Instead, against the background of an indigenous religious landscape, these mythological inventions create new possibilities for African religion in the contemporary world. During the 1990s, widespread enthusiasm for these inventions has been evident on the internet. In cyberspace, any line that might divide folk religion from fake religion has been blurred. As a religious figure representing both indigenous authenticity and innovative applications, Credo Mutwa is perfectly suited, even if he is a fake, for playing a significant role in the emerging productions of different forms of folk religion, including nature-related ones.

Second, even if fake, a fake religion can do real religious work by establishing the kinds of relations among superhuman beings, subhuman beings, and human beings that are worked out in any folk religion. In the case of Credo Mutwa, these classifications have been central to his ongoing creative work in redefining African indigenous religion. As a religious innovator, he has constantly called attention to the importance of these basic classifications not by reifying them but by emphasizing the creative exchanges among them. Although the basic distinction among superhuman deities, subhuman animals, and human beings might seem stable, Mutwa has always worked to put those fundamental classifications at risk. Speaking at the Whale and Dolphin Conference in Australia in 1997, for example, he urged his listeners to rethink these classifications.

> Some time during the long journey of human history, there comes a time when human beings must stop thinking like animals, must stop thinking like perishable beings, must stop thinking out of greed, fear and ignorance. The time has come for all of us to think like Gods, to act like Gods, to speak like Gods, but to remain humanly humble (Mutwa in Haecker 1998).

Although he exhorted human beings to be like superhuman gods, Credo Mutwa also insisted that representatives of Western civilization, who had consistently treated Africans as if they were a subhuman species, as he noted during the 1960s in *Indaba, My Children*, had falsely arrogated to themselves a supremely superhuman status. "The entire Western civilization is based upon a blatant lie," as Mutwa told Harvard researcher John Mack, "the lie that we human beings are the cocks of the walk in the world, the lie that we human beings are the highest evolved forms in this world, and that we are alone and that beyond us there is nothing" (Mack 1999: 215–16). Mutwa's reports about extraterrestrials, therefore, might be regarded as reinforcing this challenge to the "superhuman" status of Western human beings. Consistent with any measure of authenticity within folk religion, therefore, Credo Mutwa was doing real religious work by mediating among superhuman, subhuman, and human beings in the world.

These classifications, like any religious classifications, represent religious mediations that can be situated in history. As I have tried to suggest, Credo Mutwa's innovations in African folk religion can be located in a history that stretches over fifty years from the enforced separations of apartheid to the fluid connections of the internet. Briefly reviewing that history, I have only been able to raise the problems involved in adjudicating the authenticity of this self-proclaimed representative of African indigenous religion. If we assume that he is the real thing, we might conclude that Credo Mutwa is an exemplar of indigenous African folk religion in South Africa that has been misappropriated in the global fake religion on the internet. However, recalling that he has been generally dismissed within South Africa as a fake, a fraud, and charlatan, we must recognize that Credo Mutwa has achieved a greater aura of authenticity in cyberspace than in Africa. At every stage in his personal history, Credo Mutwa has found that his indigenous authenticity had to be certified by aliens, from apartheid ideologues to environmentalists to New Age conspiracy theorists, who have appropriated his aura of indigenous authenticity for their own projects. Throughout the long career of Credo Mutwa, the line between folk religion and fake religion has been consistently blurred through this ongoing interchange between indigenous inventions and alien appropriations of authenticity. In the end, these exchanges suggest that Credo Mutwa has been most authentic when he has been used, claimed, or even abducted by aliens.

David Chidester

Further Reading

Arnold, Philip P. "Black Elk and Book Culture." *Journal of the American Academy of Religion* 67 (1999), 85–111.

Audi. "Audi Honours Credo Mutwa." WildNet Africa News Archive 21 August (1997), available online at http://wildnetafrica.co.za/bushcraft/dailynews/1997arcive_3/archive19970821_audi.html.

Castaneda, Carlos. *The Teachings of Don Juan: A Yaqui Way of Knowledge.* Berkeley: University of California Press, 1968.

Cohen, Tom. "WHO Acknowledges African Healers." *Associated Press* 18 October (1997).

de Mille, Richard. *The Don Juan Papers: Further Castaneda Controversies.* Santa Barbara, CA: Ross-Erikson, 1980.

de Mille, Richard. *Castaneda's Journey: The Power and the Allegory.* London: Sphere Books, 1978.

Dorson, Richard M. *Folklore and Fakelore: Essays Toward a Discipline of Folk Studies.* Cambridge, MA: Harvard University Press, 1976.

Dorson, Richard M. "Folklore and Fakelore." *American Mercury* 70 (1950), 335–49.

Dundes, Alan. "Nationalistic Inferiority Complexes and the Fabrication of Fakelore: A Reconsideration of the *Ossian*, the *Kinder- und Hausmärchen*, the *Kalevala*, and Paul Bunyan." *Literature and Foklore* 22:1 (1985), 5–18.

Friedman, Hazel. "Of Culture and Visions." *Mail and Guardian* (27 March 1997).

Griaule, Marcel. *Conversations with Ogotemelli: An Introduction to Dogon Religious Ideas*. Oxford: Oxford University Press, 1975.

Haecker, Diana. "Requiem for the Whales." *New World* 1 (1998).

Heart Healing Center. "Earth Healers." Available online at http://www.hearthealincenter.com/earth-healers.htm, 2001.

Herrigel, Eugen. *Zen in the Art of Archery*. R.F.C. Hull, tr. London: Routledge & Kegan Paul, 1953.

Icke, David. "The Reptilian Brain." (2001). Available online at http://www.davidicke.com/icke/articles2/reptbrain.html.

Icke, David. *The Biggest Secret*. London: Bridge of Love Publications, 1999.

Johnson, Angela. "The Angela Johnson Interview." *Mail and Guardian* (18 July 1997).

Keeney, Bradford, ed. *Vusamazulu Credo Mutwa: Zulu High Sanusi*. Stony Creek, CT: Leete's Island Books, 2001.

Lelyveld, Joseph. *Move Your Shadow: South Africa, Black and White*. New York: Random House, 1986.

Long, Charles H. "Popular Religion." In Mircea Eliade, ed. *Encyclopedia of Religion*. New York: Macmillan, 1995.

Mack, John E. *Passport to the Cosmos*. New York: Crown, 1999.

Makgoba, Malegapuru William, ed. *African Renaissance*. Sandton: Mafube, 1999.

Martin, Rick. "Great Zulu Shaman and Elder Credo Mutwa: A Rare, Astonishing Conversation." *The Spectrum Newspaper* (1999).

Mutwa, Vusamazulu Credo. "Apartheid is Dead – But 'Separatism' is Alive and Well." Available online at http://home.intekom.com/animals/orgs/animalvoice/97aprjul/separatism.html, 1997.

Mutwa, Vusamazulu Credo. *Song of the Stars: The Lore of a Zulu Shaman*, ed. Stephen Larsen. Barrytown, NY: Station Hill Openings, 1996.

Mutwa, Vusamazulu Credo. "Foreword." In Stefano Ghersi and Peter Major, *South Africa, the 51st State*. Randburg: Fastdraft, 1989.

Mutwa, Vusamazulu Credo. *Africa Is My Witness*. Johannesburg: Blue Crane Books, 1966.

Mutwa, Vusamazulu Credo. *Indaba, My Children*. Johannesburg: Blue Crane Books, 1964.

Needham, Rodney. *Exemplars*. Berkeley: University of California Press, 1985, 75–116.

Neihardt, John. *Black Elk Speaks*. Lincoln, NE: University of Nebraska Press, 1961.

Niman, Michael I. *People of the Rainbow: A Nomadic Utopia*. Knoxville: University of Tennessee Press, 1997, 131–48.

Payback Press. "Indaba, My Children." Available online at www.canongate.net†payback/pbp.taf?-p=3059, 2001.

Republic of Bophuthatswana. *A Nation on the March*. Melville: Hans Strydom Publishers, 1987.

Ringing Rocks Foundation. "Welcome to the Ringing Rocks Foundation." Available online at http://www.ringingrocks.org/index.html, 2001.

van Beek, Walter E.A. "Dogon Restudied: A Field Evaluation of the Work of Marcel Griaule." *Current Anthropology* 12 (1991), 139–67.

Vigne, Ralph. "Why It Isn't All Black and White." *Mail and Guardian* (9 February 1999).

Wellness. 2001. *Wellness eJournal*. Available online at http://www.compwellness.com/eJournal/2001/0131.htm.

See also: Animism (various); Castaneda, Carlos; Harner, Michael – and the Foundation for Shamanic Studies; New Age; Shamanism (various); Somé, Malidome Patrice; UFOs and Extraterrestrials.

Naess, Arne (1912–)

In a lecture in Bucharest in 1972 the Norwegian philosopher Arne Dekke Eide Naess made the now famous distinction between the shallow ecology movement and the deep, long-range ecology movement. He has since remained one of the major international voices of deep ecology. Naess originally gained his reputation in philosophy from work in semantics, but he has also published several books on Gandhi, and on Spinoza, skepticism and philosophy of science. Naess identified, on the one hand, a shallow ecology movement that fought against pollution and resource depletion for anthropocentric reasons. Pollution and resource depletion were wrong because they threatened human health and affluence. The deep ecology movement, on the other hand, favors some form of biocentric egalitarianism as a guideline for environmental action. This distinction between anthropocentric and biocentric environmentalism is at the heart of deep ecology. Deep ecology therefore is a critique of a commonly held doctrine that the natural world has value only insofar as it is useful to humans.

Naess' main eco-philosophical work was published in 1989 as *Ecology, Community and Lifestyle*, which was based on the Norwegian *Økologi, samfunn og livsstil*, issued in 1976. Naess has also contributed to the development of environmental philosophy in numerous articles and speeches and through action. The political program of deep ecology was formulated in the Deep Ecology Platform formulated by Arne Naess and George Sessions in 1985.

Because deep ecology questioned a dominating cultural paradigm, that of excessive anthropocentrism, it could claim to rely on a deeper level of argumentation than shallow ecology, that is, on the level of religion and philosophy. A worldview that can support the deep ecology platform is called an ecosophy, a term coined by Naess. A variety of religions and philosophies can have this function, but many are probably too anthropocentric. Naess' personal ecosophy is called Ecosophy T. T stands for his mountain cottage, Tvergastein, and points to the personal nature of ecosophies. Naess himself ascribes the origin of central values of his ecosophy to important childhood experiences. He used to spend hours at the age of four observing the ecosystem on the coastline, and at the age of eight he became attached to a particular mountain. What he calls shore-life philosophy values "richness, diversity, multiplicity, equivalence, equivalidity, egalitarianism, peacefulness, cheerfulness" and also skepticism (Naess 1983: 211). The mountain became for him a symbol of a "benevolent, equiminded, strong 'father'"(Naess 1983: 212). The love of this mountain "reduced the need for anything supernatural," and he learned to value austerity, toughness, distance and aloofness (Naess 1983: 213).

Early on, Naess came under the influence of the ethics of nonviolence of Mahatma Gandhi, and the Gandhian influence on Ecosophy T is significant. Naess' ecological views are based on childhood experiences but they are shaped by, and a continuation and further development of, his Gandhian beliefs. The key concept of Naess' ecosophy is self-realization. Self-realization is the ultimate norm of his eco-philosophical system. According to Ecosophy T, all living beings are capable of self-realization. The concept of self-realization in Naess' philosophy has developed from his lifelong engagement with the philosophy of Gandhi. In one of his many books on Gandhi, Naess explains that, according to Gandhi, self-realization was the final goal of life. This was attained by a gradual perfection. All that humans do, say and think should have this self-realization as its goal. Gandhi also believed in the unity of life. To explain the central concept of self-realization and the mature experience of oneness in diversity in his ecological writings, Naess quotes the famous Hindu text Bhagavadgita, verse 6.29. Bhagavadgita was Gandhi's most sacred book, a source of wisdom he turned to whenever he needed to solve ethical dilemmas. Naess' use of the Bhagavadgita has to be understood in this Gandhian context. Verse 6.29 describes the yogin who "sees himself as in all beings and all beings in himself" (or "self" according to Naess) and who "sees the same everywhere." Bhagavadgita 6.29 sums up, according to Naess, the maximum of self-realization. It expresses the idea that all is connected to everything else and therefore that the self-realization of any living being is part of the self-realization of each one of us.

The ecosophy of Arne Naess as it is presented in his writings draws on the close connection between non-violence (*ahimsa*), the philosophy of oneness (*advaita*) and the goal of self-realization (*moksha*) in the religious thought of Gandhi. Naess understands the Bhagavadgita to say that solidarity with all beings and nonviolence depends on widening one's identification and that to see the greater self means to expand one's identification to include all living beings as one's self.

Naess finds the same doctrine of self-realization and unity of life expressed also in the philosophy of Spinoza. According to Spinoza's philosophy, every living being tries to realize its potential, its power or essence. Unity of nature means that everything is connected to everything else and that therefore the self-realization of one living being is part of the self-realization of all other beings. Naess uses Gandhian concepts to exemplify the similarity between Spinoza's philosophy and Gandhian thought. Naess argues that "adherence to Spinoza's system is consistent with being a *karma-yogi*" (Naess 1980: 323). *Karma-yogi* is here a concept borrowed from Gandhi. Vivekananda, who was a great influence on how Hinduism was received in the West, held that the Hindu ascetics should perform social service (*seva*). This new ideal he called *karma-yoga*. Gandhi was a foremost practitioner of this new ideal. He made social service a necessity for self-realization. Ecosophy T combines twentieth-century reinterpretations of Hindu asceticism by Gandhi and Vivekananda, the philosophy of Spinoza, and a belief in the world as the ultimate concern typical of religious environmentalism. This philosophy is further blended with traditional and twentieth-century Norwegian attitudes to nature and the outdoors, and the concept of solidarity with the weaker segments of society that is at the foundation of the Scandinavian welfare state system.

Gandhi lived before environmentalism and the environment was not his main concern. He is nevertheless recognized as the father of the environmental movement in India. Gandhi's famous statement that "the Earth has enough for everyone's need, but not for anyone's greed," is a slogan for contemporary environmentalism. Gandhi is more than any other, probably, the father of the father of deep ecology. But in spite of the close relationship between the ecosophy of Arne Naess and Gandhi, the Indian environmentalist Ramachandra Guha has argued that the concerns of deep ecology are foreign to, harmful to or, at best, irrelevant to the people of India. Guha argues that in India the deep ecology idea of wilderness and natural parks is a threat to people living in the wilderness areas and that environmentalism in poor countries needs to be anthropocentric in order to address the gruesome living conditions of the urban slums and the many human tragedies caused by poverty. Naess argues that Guha misrepresents deep ecology (Witoszek and Brennan 1999). Naess actually defends weak anthropocentrism; Ecosophy T is a critique only of excessive anthropocentrism, a point often misunderstood by followers of deep ecology. Ecosophy questions the wisdom of emulating the economic growth and development path of rich countries and argues that alternative ways, such as Gandhi's vision of India as a village-based economy, still need to be explored.

Knut A. Jacobsen

Further Reading
Barnhill, David and Roger Gottlieb. *Deep Ecology and World Religions*. Albany, New York: State University of New York Press, 2000.
Drengson, A. and Y. Inoue, eds. *The Deep Ecology Movement: An Introductory Anthology*. Berkeley, California: North Atlantic, 1995.
Jacobsen, Knut A. "Bhagavadgita, Ecosophy T and Deep Ecology." In Eric Katz, Andrew Light and David Rothenberg, eds. *Beneath the Surface: Critical Essays in the Philosophy of Deep Ecology*. Cambridge: The MIT Press, 2000, 231–52.
Johns, David. "Practical Relevance of Deep Ecology to the Third World." *Environmental Ethics* 12:3 (1990), 233–52.
Katz, E., A. Light and D. Rothenberg, eds. *Beneath the Surface: Critical Essays on Deep Ecology*. Cambridge, MA: MIT Press, 2000.
McLaughlin, A. *Regarding Nature: Industrialism & Deep Ecology*. New York: State University of New York Press, 1993.
Naess, Arne. *Ecology, Community and Lifestyle*. David Rothenberg, tr. Cambridge: Cambridge University Press, 1989.
Naess, Arne. "How My Philosophy Seemed to Develop." In André Mercier and Maja Svilar, eds. *Philosophers on Their Own Work*, vol. 10. Bern: Peter Lang, 1983.
Naess, Arne. "Environmental Ethics and Spinoza's Ethics. Comments on Genevieve Lloyd's Article." *Inquiry* 23 (1980), 313–25.
Naess, Arne. *Gandhi and Group Conflict: An Exploration of Satyagraha: Theoretical Background*. Oslo: Universitetsforlaget, 1974.
Sessions, George, ed. *Deep Ecology for the Twenty-first Century*. Boston: Shambhala, 1995.
Witoszek, Nina and Andrew Brennan, eds. *Philosophical Dialogues: Arne Naess and the Progress of Ecophilosophy*. Lanham: Rowman & Littlefield, 1999.
See also: Ahimsa; Bhagavadgita; Biocentric Religion – A Call for; Council of All Beings; Deep Ecology; Deep Ecology Institute; Earth First! and the Earth Liberation Front; Ecosophy T; Environmental Ethics; Friluftsliv; Gandhi, Mohandas; Hinduism; Left Biocentrism; Mountaineering; Radical Environmentalism; Re-Earthing; Religious Studies and Environmental Concern; Rock Climbing; Seed, John; Spinoza, Baruch; Yoga and Ecology.

Narmada Bachao Andolan (Save the Narmada Movement) – *See* Amte, Baba; India.

Naropa University

Naropa University (formerly the Naropa Institute) is a private, non-sectarian, accredited university inspired by its Buddhist heritage to integrate contemplative learning, intellectual rigor, and active engagement with the world. It offers bachelor's degrees, master's degrees, and certificate programs through on-campus and online courses, study-abroad programs, and continuing education workshops. Its academic programs include degrees in Buddhism and other religions, environmental studies, Transpersonal Counseling Psychology, education, writing and poetics, and fine arts, and offers certificates in ecopsychology, and other areas.

Naropa University was founded in 1974 by Chogyam Trungpa, a Tibetan scholar and meditation teacher. Born in Tibet in 1940, Trungpa Rinpoche was a lineage holder in both the Kagyu and Nyingma Buddhist traditions. In 1959, he escaped the Chinese invasion of Tibet. Later, he studied comparative religion, philosophy, and fine arts at Oxford University. A scholar and artist as well as meditation master, he became widely recognized as a teacher of Buddhism in the West. With the founding of the Naropa Institute, he realized his vision of creating a university that would combine contemplative studies with traditional Western scholastic and artistic disciplines. Since the death of Trungpa in 1987, Naropa University has continued to grow and integrate teachings from a variety of spiritual wisdom traditions. Joining intellect and intuition in an atmosphere of mutual appreciation and respect for different contemplative traditions has become the University's ongoing inspiration.

At the core of Naropa's contemplative learning approach is the cultivation of awareness through intellectual, artistic, body-centered, and meditative disciplines. In the view of contemplative learning, such awareness provides the basis for continued development of openness, communication, intellect, creativity, and intuition. These qualities, in turn, are the foundation for building and deepening a community of learners and for service to the world. While it has been inspired by Buddhist traditions, Naropa University seeks to remain true to its founder's vision as a setting in which diverse views can come together in an environment of respect and authentic dialogue.

Naropa University's vision and orientation is evident in its programs in environmental leadership, ecopsychology, and wilderness studies. These programs are grounded in a core principle of both ecology and many spiritual wisdom traditions, which exemplify the nonduality of interconnection. They integrate academic inquiry, spiritual wisdom, contemplative practice, and skilled engagement. Both during their educational programs and after, students practice critical and creative thinking, meditative disciplines, and active service in the world. Many of these programs also integrate intensive wilderness experiences. The aim of these programs is to promote wise, just, effective, and compassionate action in a number of arenas, including environmental policy, environmental restoration, community development (understood as an aspect of environmental restoration), horticulture, wilderness therapy, and ecotherapy.

John Davis

See also: Buddhism – Tibetan; Ecopsychology; Transpersonal Psychology; Wilderness Rites of Passage.

Nasr, Seyyed Hossein (1933–)

Hossein Nasr (b. Tehran, Iran; "Seyyed" is an honorific title designating a descendant of the Prophet Muhammad) is widely considered to be one of the most significant contemporary Iranian philosophers. Muslim in background but educated in both Iran and the United States, Nasr is a proponent of the perennial philosophy associated with Frithjof Schuon, Titus Burckhardt and Rene Guenon, in which timeless truths are seen as being expressed in a variety of historical cultural and philosophical traditions. His work thus blends traditional Islamic with modern Western approaches.

Nasr was among the first scholars to draw attention to the spiritual dimensions of the environmental crisis, and the first contemporary Muslim to do so. He first introduced his perspective in a 1965 essay, going on to develop it in a series of lectures at the University of Chicago the following year, several months prior to Lynn White, Jr.'s famous address before the American Academy of Arts and Sciences (published in *Science* as "The Historical Roots of Our Ecologic Crisis"). While Nasr agrees with White that the desacralization of nature in Enlightenment Europe laid the groundwork by which the dominating tendencies of the modern technological worldview would be justified, he argues that in Islam science never lost its sacred character. Nasr goes on to point out that much of the contemporary Muslim world is no longer "Muslim" in the traditional sense, implicitly suggesting that environmental degradation is a Western product that has been subsequently exported to other cultures.

Widely cited by both Muslims and non-Muslims alike, Nasr's thought has provided the foundation for much of the current discussion on Islam and the environment. As such, he is considered by many as the "founding father" of contemporary Islamic environmentalism.

Richard C. Foltz

Further Reading
Nasr, Seyyed Hossein. *Man and Nature: The Spiritual Crisis in Modern Man.* Chicago: Kazi Publishers, 1997 (1967).

Nasr, Seyyed Hossein. *Religion and the Order of Nature.* New York: Oxford University Press, 1996.

Nasr, Seyyed Hossein. *An Introduction to Islamic Cosmological Doctrines*. Boulder: Shambala Publications, 1978 (rev. edn).

Nasr, Seyyed Hossein. *Science and Civilization in Islam*. Cambridge, MA: Harvard University Press, 1968.

Nasr, Seyyed Hossein. "The Meaning of Nature in Various Intellectual Perspectives in Islam." *The Islamic Quarterly* 9:1–2 (1965), 25–9.

See also: Islam; Religious Studies and Environmental Concern; White, Lynn – Thesis of.

National Council of Churches, Eco-Justice Working Group (USA)

The Eco-Justice Working Group (EJWG) of the National Council of Churches (NCC) provides a mechanism for NCC-member Protestant and Orthodox denominations to work together on issues affecting care of the Earth. The Group began in 1983 when the Joint Strategy and Action Coalition (JSAC) merged into the NCC. The Responsible Lifestyle Task Force of JSAC, which had begun work on issues of energy, organic food and food sufficiency with the participation of American Baptists, Presbyterians, Methodists and Lutherans, formed the core for the EJWG.

Early discussion in the group and a report from the United Church of Christ formulated the term environmental justice, denoting the impact on poor and minority communities in regards to environmental issues. Environmental justice includes a broader set of social and economic issues than the word environmental used alone.

In 1986 the EJWG sponsored a seminal conference at Stony Point, New York. The "Eco-Justice Agenda: Loving the Earth and People" brought together 150 people including denominational representatives, clergy, lay and a wide variety of community groups. The conference was a major turning point for increased activity that included a wider justice agenda with environmental issues. Discussions that began at the conference sparked denominations to take action that included the adoption of policy statements. Concerns from community groups at the conference led to a reorganization in 1988 that included full participation by a wide variety of groups not affiliated directly with a religious group. The wider membership continued until the late 1990s when another reorganization brought in Orthodox participation, but excluded community groups. Stories of environmental poisoning in local communities told at the conference led to the production of an early video on the topic, *For Our Children*.

In 1992 several representatives from the EJWG participated in the United Nations' conference on Environment and Development in Rio de Janeiro, leading to increased awareness of eco-justice in congregations. From 1985 until 1995 the EJWG published the *EGG*, a journal of eco-justice, in cooperation with the Eco-Justice Project at Cornell. Its articles provide a good summary of major eco-justice issues of the day.

The production of resources and the generation of program ideas to help local congregations focus on ecological issues has been a major part of the work of the EJWG in recent years. Present programs include the Environmental Justice Covenant Program and the Interfaith Global Climate Change Program. A biennial national conference held in 1997, 1999 and 2001 brought together persons working on the local level. The EJWG also sponsors a resource center where a wide variety of materials are available for local congregations.

The EJWG is a partner in the National Religious Partnership for the Environment. The other partners are: The U.S. Catholic Conference, the Evangelical Environmental Network and the Coalition on the Environment and Jewish Life. As part of the Partnership, the group produced *God's Earth: Our Home*, Shantilal Bhagat (Eco-Justice Work Group, NCC, 1995) as a resource for local congregations.

J. Andy Smith, III

See also: World Council of Churches and Ecumenical Thought.

National Parks and Monuments (United States)

Travelers in the hundreds of millions make the national parks and monuments spread across the modern American map focal points of their annual journeys. By 2002 these public centers of recreation, education and inspiration numbered more than 350 and covered some 84 million acres. During the last several decades they have been exported abroad as a conservation ideal, but threatened continually at home by conflicts over their meaning and purpose, as well as over more mundane concerns such as funding, boundaries and maintenance. Frequently heralded as sacred places and deployed globally as evocative images of a unique American nature and history through works of art and the mass media, the national parks and monuments remain embedded deep within the nation's culture.

Prior to war with Mexico in 1846, Americans more cultivated than the ones who French traveler Alexis de Tocqueville found hacking down Ohio River valley forests in 1831 – or those who Emerson in *Nature* (1836) chastised as blind to the beauty of their own fields and farms – voiced a frequent note of doom as they reflected on the nation's prospects. The sweeping floods of early nineteenth-century religious and social reform had tangled together conflicting cultural anxieties over matters of race, capital, technology, the body, and women's role in society. These anxieties, as historian Robert Abzug has shown, also centered around competing views of what was sacred, and what profane, to a people bent on constructing a distinctly new nation. In the midst of the continent's rapid transformation, Emerson's poetic sort of American – if few others, initially – found in the vanishing form of landscape "something more dear and connate than in streets or villages" (1836: 13), and thus came to seek in wilderness a sacred antidote to the young republic's many ills.

Although Americans turned forests into woodlots at a remarkable rate, by the 1830s those who saw in still-uncivilized land something greater than profit or utility were sufficient in number to support the preservation from resource development of various natural prominences – such as New York's Niagara Falls or Kentucky's Mammoth Cave – and to embrace scenic wilderness travel as a form of cultural education and spiritual renewal. Nevertheless, as is evident in such paintings as Thomas Cole's "The Oxbow" (1836) – with its stormy change on the horizon – and most especially in his five-panel "The Course of Empire" (1834–1836), the wilderness available to eastern travelers often proved melancholic in inspiration, and they worried along with Cole that an empire devoted to nature could not help but decay over the ages. By far a better painter than poet, Cole still gave this melancholy a pointed gloss, writing "Each hill and every valley is become / An altar unto Mammon, and the gods / Of man's idolatry – its victims we" (in Hughes 1997: 146). To be expected, perhaps, eastern efforts at preservation quickly succumbed to commercial impulses, so much so that Tocqueville in 1831 was urging that friends hurry to Niagara Falls, since he wouldn't "give the Americans ten years to establish a saw or flour mill at the base of the cataract" (in Runte 1987: 6).

Western lands obtained from Mexico under the Treaty of Guadalupe Hidalgo (1848) thus offered America's cultural elite a distinct solution to the vexing problem of the new nation's identity. For those who, with Cole, felt a post-revolutionary inadequacy in relation to Europe, no amount of light irradiating an eastern scene, nor the steady bragging of politicians Jefferson and Jackson or novelist James Fenimore Cooper about the virtues of the eastern countryside, could obscure what America lacked: a storied past, an aristocratic imprint on the land and spirit of the people, great cathedrals connecting the generations to heaven and Earth, and the Alps.

In the west, description also outran the reality of the landscape, but the landscape ran close enough. Journalist Horace Greeley, for instance, traveling in the Sierra Nevada in 1859, wrote his eastern readers, after a walk among the Mariposa Grove sequoias, that they were "of substantial size when David danced before the ark, when Solomon laid the foundations of the Temple, when Theseus ruled in Athens, when Aeneas fled from the burning wreck of vanquished Troy" (Greeley 1860: 311–12). No matter their precise age, the giant sequoias did constitute a living antiquity – one would not even need to read to absorb their wisdom of ages. The western scale of nature's architecture provided sources of culture and the sacred that Europeans themselves would envy. At times, Americans were even able to acknowledge the antiquity of the west's first people, as when they flocked in the late 1830s and 1840s to see George Catlin's traveling "Indian Gallery" of portraits from the upper Missouri – his Mandans, Arikaras and Pawnees so vivid in their ceremonial garments and paint that they looked at times realer than real, and rather similar in pose to noble Romans.

The raw western topography – all granite peaks, basalt outcrops, red oxide soils and sedimentary gashes – seemed specially made for those who sought a visual and natural embodiment of powerful, nation-forming divinity at work, an embodiment that easily surpassed the achievements of European culture and the sublimity of its landscape. Admittedly, no one besides George Catlin imagined that the complex of tribes, herds and open spaces might be significant as whole: "a *nation's Park*, containing man and beast, in all the freshness of nature's beauty" (in Chittenden 1895: 78). Instead, what seemed most worth preserving were nature's monumental artifacts. The earliest parks – Yosemite, which Congress granted to the state of California in 1864, and Yellowstone, established as the first truly national park in 1872 – were both preserved because the landscape contained gigantic wonders, challenges to the American imagination, whether orthodox, scientific or aesthetic, and natural testimonies to Providential purpose. Each park seemed to call forth different poetic impulses from their proponents and publicists – Yosemite most often glossed as "nature's cathedral," and Yellowstone ("Colter's Hell," originally) framed less comfortably as a "wonderland" of the grotesque. In both cases, however, Americans could find in the extravagant creations of wild nature confirmation of their world-historical destiny.

American proponents of national parks drew on available social and cultural resources in order to persuade the public and Congress that preservation was in the national interest. Their strategic efforts helped Americans define national parks as sacred environments, and created the paradigmatic practices of veneration and recreation that have since been employed within them.

Common to the presentation of Yosemite and Yellowstone as centers of sublime nature was the reliance upon both verbal and visual prompters, as early interpreters made use of traditional religious language and the Romantic practice of landscape painting to promote interest among Easterners and Europeans. Lafayette Bunnell, physician to the Mariposa Battalion – the white militia that first came upon the Yosemite Valley while chasing Tenaya's band of Ahwaneechee Miwoks in 1851 –

enthused on his first descent into the secret valley while worrying about his scalp: "If my hair is now required, I can depart in peace, for I have here seen the power and glory of a Supreme being, the majesty of His handy-work is in that 'Testimony of the Rocks' " (Bunnell 1880: 56). With less regard to orthodoxy: "Granite is great, and the Yo-Semite is its prophet," wrote Unitarian minister Thomas Starr King in 1861 (in Sears 1989: 127), several years before John Muir himself began placing the template of gospel metaphor over his mystical wanderings through California's mountains.

Muir was perhaps at heart a pagan pantheist. "We are now in the mountains, and they in us, kindling enthusiasm, making every nerve quiver, filling every pore and cell of us," he wrote of his first view of the high country approaching Yosemite (Muir 1911: 20). Nevertheless, he drew incessantly on biblical religion to marshal support for the preservation of Yosemite (1890), Mt. Rainier (1899), Glacier (1910) and other western parks, and styled himself as the gospel of beauty's John the Baptist. To the "business-tangled," so "burdened with duty that only weeks can be got out of the heavy-laden year," he preached seemingly-easy sermons. A month in wilderness, such as at Montana's Lake MacDonald, and "never more will time seem short or long, and cares never again fall heavily on you, but kindly and gently as gifts from heaven" (Muir 1901: 17, 19).

Visual art played a crucial role in disseminating iconic presentations of the early parks' overwhelming and varied landscapes. Thomas Ayres went into Yosemite with San Francisco editor – and shortly thereafter Yosemite innkeeper – James Mason Hutchings in 1855, four years after its discovery by whites. Within less than a decade, painters such as Albert Bierstadt and Thomas Hill, and photographers Carleton Watkins and Eadward Muybridge, were exhibiting to audiences as far from California as New York and London. Yellowstone's most famous artists, Thomas Moran and photographer William Henry Jackson, accompanied F.V. Hayden – director of the U.S. Geological Survey – on the first scientific expedition into Yellowstone, in 1870. The work of these artists, widely viewed in exhibits and in the press, emphasized a transcendent – and at times imaginary – landscape absent the human presence, and certainly absent the evidence of Civil War carnage that had recently so weighted the landscape familiar to Americans back east.

Not all subscribed to the sublime notion that God was granite, however. Mark Twain, for instance, poked at Bierstadt's 1867 "The Domes of the Yosemite," saying that while the various components of the picture looked natural enough, the atmosphere was "altogether too gorgeous," more "the atmosphere of Kingdom-Come than California" (in Anderson 1990: 91). Working-class squatters and homesteaders, as well as tribal members living near the parks, were also particularly uninterested in public administration and religious veneration of country that held necessities of survival. The only reason for Indians even to be in Yellowstone, wrote Superintendent Philetus Norris in 1878, was "for the purposes of plunder, or of concealment after bloody raids upon the ranchmen, pilgrims, or tourists" (in Jacoby 2001: 90).

Others failed to accept that nature was best understood in Romantic terms. Muir's evangel that preserved wilderness as "full of charming company, full of God's thoughts . . ." (Muir 1901: 78) sounded a false note to some, such as Truman Everts – Yellowstone survivor of 39-days' separation from the 1870 Washburn party. For Everts, who relayed his experience to readers of *Scribners* in 1871, the terror of wilderness, especially as part of a divine order, was only too real. Forced by circumstance to endure as much of nature's rawness as Muir chose to, Everts could only gloss the harrow of his experience with a Ben Franklin-ish admonition. "Put your trust in Heaven. Help yourself and God will help you" (Everts 1871: 11).

Parks might have remained the preserve of cultural elites under the influence of Muir, but for his use of publisher Robert Underwood Johnson's *The Century* to spread his message, and but for the interests of the railroads, who were early supporters of both Yellowstone and Yosemite. To underscore the irony – Muir was adamant in seeing the parks as antidotes to capitalist civilization. They would preserve divine nature from forces bent on its destruction in the name of profit. On the other hand, railroads such as the Northern Pacific took on the task of promoting Yellowstone with all the sophistication and resources of a modern advertising campaign. A wide range of brochures, lecture tours and artwork portrayed an American future in which rail-accessible nature functioned just as Muir hoped wild nature would, to restore the souls of citizens. Northern Pacific director Colgate Hoyt confessed a vision for his railroad, in 1878: a West filled with homes, wheatfields and cattle.

> And I thanked God that right in the middle of all this noise and wrestless [sic] life of millions a wise Government had forever set apart that marvelous region as a National Park . . . where the worn, the sick, and jaded could even find rest, and refreshment, and opportunity to study the Master's hand in nature (in Magoc 1999: 21).

Another NP executive, Olin Dunbar Wheeler, played up the importance of scenic wilderness to a democratic populace by linking Yellowstone's redemptive promise with that of the Hebrew prophet Isaiah:

> the common run of humanity, the *hoi polloi*, will see a vision – a picture that causes them to stand in awe and silence, and caring less as to the why and wherefore of such amazing results, "shall see of the

travail of their souls and be satisfied" (in Magoc 1999: 102).

Although Muir certainly took opportunity to lambaste the railroads in *Our National Parks*, he also had to acknowledge that the mobility they provided made possible for others their own mystical immersions in nature.

Thus from their inception national parks as nature's emblems of high national purpose, or as wild antidotes to the baseness of capitalist civilization, were not only dependent upon capitalist energies, but were also embodiments of capitalist achievement. This irony complicates any effort to understand the preservationist impulse in American conservation by means of easy distinctions drawn between public and private, or sacred and secular intentions regarding wilderness. Although – as Tocqueville's 1831 reaction to Niagara Falls demonstrates – Romantic devotees of wild nature have long complained about the inappropriate reach of commercial culture into sacred sites supposedly preserved from just that sort of reach, the outrage of a Muir, Thoreau, or a Cole, let alone a European aristocrat like Tocqueville, is not evidence of a broader public consensus. In opening the parks up to Wheeler's *hoi polloi* – the democratic masses – park creators had to contend with the broad range of readings Americans brought to the term "sacred."

Perhaps the best way to assess the religious role of the national parks in American life is to follow the lead of historian Lawrence Moore, who in *Selling God: Religion in the Marketplace of American Culture* (1994) captured the peculiar dynamic between sacred (religion) and profane (economy) that permeates American history – including the history of American conservation. For Moore, the religious and the economic are not contradictory impulses. As he shows, commercial culture emerged in the nineteenth century largely through the agency of Protestant religious leaders attempting to retain control of a society reinventing itself. Crucial features of nineteenth- and twentieth-century American economic life: the rise of consumption, the growth of leisure, the birth of advertising and mass media, all carried sacred meanings and practices for the majority of Americans, and all affected their use and appreciation of the parks. Furthermore, the capitalist culture that so dominated post-Civil War American life gained its sway by absorbing those movements or values that first appeared as countercultural alternatives. For Moore then, the Protestant ethic that really triumphed was not one of work alone, but also of play.

By the early twentieth century administration of the parks was piecemeal, but development of the infrastructure to sustain travelers within America's "Playgrounds for the People" was in full surge. Rail lines, hotels and inns, some – such as Yellowstone's Old Faithful Inn (1903) – quite regal, and – most fatefully – roads, were all constructed under private leases or with inadequate Congressional appropriations. In 1916, Congress authorized the Interior Department to create the National Park Service (NPS), to coordinate administration at all parks and national monuments – which first were established under the 1906 Antiquities Act, as well as battlefields and other historic sites administered originally by the War Department. The Park Service Organic Act mandated that the NPS "conserve the scenery and the natural and historic objects and the wildlife therein" and "provide for the enjoyment of the same in such manner and by such means as will leave them unimpaired for future generations" (in Runte 1987: 104). The latitude of this mandate appears in a 1916 proposal regarding Yellowstone from the first NPS director, Stephen T. Mather. "Golf links, tennis courts, swimming pools and other equipment for outdoor pastime and exercise should be provided by concessions, and the park should be extensively advertised as a place to spend the summer instead of five or six days of hurried sight seeing" (in Ise 1961: 198). As many have noted, the service has often struggled to balance "conserve the scenery" with "provide for the enjoyment." Nevertheless, reading them as opposites stems from overlooking how deeply the democratic and sacred pursuit of leisure has shaped all aspects of modern American life.

Perhaps nothing symbolizes and ritualizes that pursuit more than the automobile, which was first permitted at Mount Rainier in 1908 and in Yosemite in 1913, where within five years it was bringing in five times as many visitors as the recently completed railroad, which itself, according to one correspondent, was chastised by "the athletic rich" as degenerating the valley into "a mere picnic-ground with dancing platforms, beery choruses and couples contorting in the two-step" (in Runte 1987: 156). The railroad did remain an elite institution though, while the automobile exploded across the national parks by the 1920s.

Early proponents of roads through the parks emphasized the automobile's role in instilling an appropriate American spirit in travelers, as *The American Motorist* in "A Motorist's Creed" put it in 1917:

> I believe that travel, familiarity with the sights and scenes of other parts of the country, first hand knowledge of how my fellow-men live, is of inestimable value to me and will do more to make me patriotic and public spirited than daily intimacy with the Declaration of Independence (in Shaffer 2001: 1917).

Groups such as the Daughters of the American Revolution lobbied relentlessly for the construction of highways linking sights of historic or scenic interest, in the process providing a high-brow justification for auto travel as a necessary ritual for inculcating patriotic spirit and civic virtue. Others emphasized the fun of free-wheeling travel to the parks, as "sagebrushing" – automobile camping – brought waves of independent visitors, each prepared to "cut loose from all effeteness" and let "his adventurous, pioneering spirit riot here in the mountain air" (in Runte 1987: 157).

In either case, twentieth-century parks visitors took on the role of pilgrims inherited from early wonder-struck travelers, but augmented this with a recapturing of the true American spirit. The auto tourist used modern technology not simply to witness the divine stamp on the Grand Canyon or Crater Lake, but to claim the purifying effects of immersion in the frontier experience – which historian Frederick Jackson Turner in 1893 had said was defining of the American character – as his or her own. Thus while Americans across the board responded to automotive technology as a mythical power, in the national parks, as sacred preserves of a nearly vanished era, they were able to use the automobile to propel themselves into the primordial past, and to return home inspired in ways that would assist them in creating the urban, industrial future.

For campers this reimmersion in Paradise or Eden meant a temporary life of physical exertion on a par with that of their ancestors, which reformers such as President Theodore Roosevelt, Boy Scouts of America founders Ernest Thompson Seton and William D. West, or organizations such as the Young Man's Christian Association (YMCA), had for some time been urging on urban Americans as their bodies' and even spirits' means of redemption from the debilitating effects of office and factory life. Campers slept under the stars or in canvas tents, cooked over open fires, endured primitive means of sanitation, as well as exercised on steep mountain trails or swam in bracing waters. Some parks proponents, such as U.S. Geological Survey chief topographer Robert Marshall, even saw the parks as martial training ground for modern warriors, where young men could

> forget something of the rush and jam of modern life ... and build up their bodies by being next to nature. Then, should there be a general call to arms, the dwellers of the city canyons will be able to meet the physical needs of a strenuous field service (in Runte 1987: 96).

As a symbolically powerful means of personal freedom, and as the provider of ritualized immersion in nature, automobiles had a drastic effect on the parks. By 1919 nearly 98,000 were reported to have passed through park boundaries. Even in the early years, some foresaw with alarm their ultimate impact, though officials such as NPS Director Stephen Mather regarded their presence as inevitable and positive, claiming in 1924 that auto touring eroded "sectional prejudice through the bringing together of tourists from all sections of the country." Only through the "the medium of an automobile, and camping out in the open" could "people learn what America is" (in Shaffer 2001: 119). British ambassador to the U.S. and lover of Yosemite, James Bryce, however, cautioned as early as 1912 that

> If Adam had known what harm the serpent was going to work, he would have tried to prevent him from finding lodgment in Eden; and if you were to realize what the result of the automobile will be in that incomparable valley, you will keep it out (in Runte 1987: 159).

Even during the Depression, visitation continued to climb dramatically, declining briefly during World War II, with only one to two percent of visitors relying upon public transportation. In the aftermath of the war – with union jobs turning the two-week vacation into an American right – park use doubled every ten to fifteen years, a trend continuing through the 1990s. In these decades the system as a whole also expanded, more than tripling in acreage between 1960 and the century's end. At the same time, debates over the purpose of the national parks also increased, often in terms consistent with the contradiction inherited from the Park Service's original 1916 mandate: enjoyment versus preservation – each functioning for its devotees as a principle for constructing the parks as sacred environments. The most notable of these debates was the one surrounding Mission 66, the Eisenhower-era infusion of capital into park infrastructures, already overburdened in 1955 by twice as many visitors than the system could accommodate. The resulting construction of visitor centers, campgrounds and improved roads – enthusiastically supported by the American Automobile Association – seemed to post-war preservationists proof that the NPS gave priority to providing for visitor enjoyment. For naturalist Joseph Wood Krutch, Mission 66 placed a fundamental value on technology over nature. Instead of "valuing the automobile because it may take one to a national park, the park comes to be valued because it is a place the automobile may be used to reach" (in Runte 1987: 175)

Preservationist concerns over Mission 66, and even more long-standing management choices, received an influential voice in 1963, when the research team of zoologist A. Starker Leopold (son of Aldo Leopold) released their *Wildlife Management in the National Parks*, a scathing survey of ecological situation in the parks. The officially commissioned report urged the NPS to adopt an environmentally based management philosophy, informed by scientific principles regarding biotic communities, habitat, and plant succession, and to restore park environments to their pre-nineteenth-century conditions. Given the shifts in cultural values that occurred in the 1960s, preservationist goals finally found significant

NPS support. Over the next 25 years park management moved often toward an ecological model, as seen in the prescribed- and let-burn policies adopted first for Yosemite sequoias and then in the fire-based plant communities of other parks, in the reintroduction of predators, and in the development of such concepts as the Greater Yellowstone Ecosystem. Though these policies, and their advocacy by environmentalists, were framed in scientific language, they also invoked Muir-like expressions of how to understand the sacred within the national parks.

Unfortunately for wilderness preservationists, long-range ecological management policies had a difficult time surviving when Americans rejected the 1960s resurgence of Romanticism with the election of Ronald Reagan in 1981. The urge to privatize based on increasing distrust of federal bureaucracy and to focus on facilities over habitat increasingly shaped executive branch goals for the NPS. Perhaps the most fitting symbol of the era is the 1988 Yellowstone fire – which engulfed some 40 percent of the park in what *Time* called an "environmental Armageddon" (Magoc 1999: 174), and about which many Americans expressed their sense that environmentalists had defiled the "crown jewel" of the nation's parks through their misguided let-burn policies. Wyoming Senator Malcolm Wallop catalyzed this anti-bureaucrat sentiment by angrily calling for Park Service director William Penn Mott's resignation.

In the same years the NPS found itself in the middle of the widely spread culture wars, as its historic battlefields were subjected to competing efforts to commemorate ground "hallowed," as President Lincoln put it, by the shedding of blood. At Gettysburg, the Little Big Horn, Pearl Harbor and many other parks' various parties challenged the nation's legacy on race, westward expansion, the conduct of its wars, or the presence of commercial interests at such sites. Others, such as veterans groups, military reenactors, and Custer buffs, objected to the historical "revisionism" they saw influencing shifts in Park Service site management and interpretation. Just as American wilderness sparked apparently competing conceptions of the sacred within park boundaries, American history yielded lasting conflicts over appropriate commemoration of significant events, a limitless possible "affront to the living as well as the dead," as columnist George F. Will complained regarding construction of Gettysburg's observation tower (in Linenthal 1993: 115). In the 1990s, concerns over desecration of historic grounds culminated in controversy surrounding Walt Disney Corporation's plans to build an American history theme park in rural Virginia, near Manassass, Antietam and several other Civil War battlefields.

Common to the parks as a whole has been the desire to retain the unsullied past, whether in the wonder-evoking beauty of the natural landscape or in the sense of historical immediacy that led a young General George S. Patton in 1909 to recall a Gettysburg sunset moment at the site of Pickett's charge when "I could almost see them coming, growing fewer and fewer while around and behind me stood calmly the very cannons which had so punished them" (in Linenthal 1993: 117). The "objective of every national park and monument" claimed Leopold in his 1963 report, should be the creation of a "reasonable illusion of primitive America" (Leopold et al. 1963). What makes these "reasonable illusions" of virgin land or the presence of the past obtainable – what gives them value and form, is the culture of leisure consumption that has so shaped American society over the last century. Parks are simply one more option available to those engaged in leisure pursuits, as a 1995 issue of *Glamour* suggested: "Everyone should see Manhattan, the Grand Canyon, Walt Disney World . . . Yellowstone National Park, Beverly Hills . . ." (in Magoc 1999: 168). Whether one sees Mt. Rainier on a brief pass through the park on the way to somewhere else, stays several days at the volcano's base in a motor home, pumps up the road on a touring bike, or camps near the summit in a four-season tent, the park functions as a set of nature-options available for consumers to enjoy. And whether consumption entails a rejection of the search for sacred, or its transformation, it has certainly taken on the forms and language of traditional American religion.

Although some commentators have argued that contemporary tourist experience has abandoned the sacred visions of nature and nation sought by earlier generations of travelers, the intensity of conflict over the meanings, means of administration, and practices of the sacred available at national parks, and their steady increase in use, suggests that they do still retain a great hold on American imaginations as democratic hallmarks of both nature and nationhood.

Matthew Glass

Further Reading

Abzug, Robert. *Cosmos Crumbling: American Reform and the Religious Imagination*. New York: Oxford University Press, 1994.

Anderson, Nancy and Linda Ferber. *Albert Bierstadt: Art and Enterprise*. New York: Hudson Hills, 1990.

Bunnell, Lafayette H. *Discovery of the Yosemite, and the Indian War of 1851 which Led to that Event*. Freeport, NY: Books for Free Libraries, 1971 (1880).

Chittenden, Hiram Martin. *The Yellowstone National Park*. Norman: University of Oklahoma Press, 1964 (1895).

Emerson, Ralph Waldo. *Nature*. Boston: Beacon Press, 1985 (1836).

Everts, Truman. "Thirty-seven Days of Peril." *Scribner's Monthly* 3:1 (November 1871), 1–17.

Greeley, Horace. *An Overland Journey from New York to San Francisco in 1859*. San Francisco: H.H. Bancroft and Co., 1860.

Hughes, Robert. *American Visions: The Epic History of Art in America*. New York: Alfred A. Knopf, 1997.

Ise, John. *Our National Park Policy: A Critical History*. Baltimore: Johns Hopkins Press, 1961.

Jacoby, Karl. *Crimes against Nature: Squatters, Poachers, Thieves and the Hidden History of American Conservation*. Berkeley: University of California Press, 2001.

Leopold, A.S., et al. *Wildlife Management in the National Parks: The Leopold Report*. Washington: GPO, 1963.

Linenthal, Edward Tabor. *Sacred Ground: Americans and Their Battlefields*. Champaign/Urbana: University of Illinois Press, 1993.

Magoc, Chris J. *Yellowstone: The Creation and Selling of an American Landscape, 1870–1903*. Albuquerque: University of New Mexico Press, 1999.

Miller, Perry. "Nature and the National Ego." In *Errand into the Wilderness*. Cambridge: Harvard University Press, 1956, 204–16.

Moore, Lawrence. *Selling God: American Religion in the Marketplace of Culture*. New York: Oxford University Press, 1994.

Muir, John. *My First Summer in the Sierra*. Boston: Houghton Mifflin, 1911.

Muir, John. *Our National Parks*. Boston: Houghton Mifflin, 1901.

Runte, Alfred. *National Parks: the American Experience*. Lincoln: University of Nebraska Press, 1987.

Sears, John F. *Sacred Places: American Tourist Attractions in the Nineteenth Century*. New York: Oxford University Press, 1989.

Shaffer, Susan. *See America First: Tourism and National Identity, 1880–1940*. Washington, D.C.: Smithsonian Institution, 2001.

See also: Biosphere Reserves and World Heritage Sites; Disney Worlds at War; Earth First! and the Earth Liberation Front; Holy Land in Native North America; G-O Road; Krutch, Joseph Wood; Law, Religion, and Native American Lands; Marshall, Robert; Miwok People; Muir, John; Nature Religion in the United States; Pinchot, Gifford; The Sacred and the Modern World; Sacred Geography in Native North America; Sierra Club; Wilderness Society; Wise Use Movement; World Heritage Sites and Religion in Japan.

National Religious Partnership for the Environment

The National Religious Partnership for the Environment (NRPE) advocates for the environment within national Christian and Jewish organizations and through individual congregations in the United States. An "umbrella" organization, NRPE has four component groups, the National Council of Churches' Eco-Justice Working Group (EJWC), the eco-justice program at the United States Catholic Conference (USCC), the Evangelical Environmental Network (EEN), and the Coalition on the Environment and Jewish Life (COEJL). Their purpose is to promote environmental causes in church and temple teaching, in management practices, and in public policy. They argue for religious protection of the environment as part of reverence for God and God's works, an outlook some participants have labeled environmental stewardship (invoking the fiscal stewardship that has long been part of church process).

NRPE grew out of ideas formulated in the 1960s and 1970s by numerous commentators, some religious, some not. Professor Lynn White's 1967 paper on ecology and Christianity, "The Historical Roots of Our Ecological Crisis," was a starting point cited by many involved. Others tried to integrate ideas from Eastern thinking, particularly Zen Buddhism, or from Celtic and other "minority" traditions in Christianity. Early leaders in this movement included California State Senator Tom Hayden, members of the Lindisfarne Association, Dr. James Parks Morton (now-retired Dean of St. John the Divine Cathedral (Episcopalian), New York City), Catholic priest Thomas Berry, and evangelical professor of biology, Dr. Calvin DeWitt. These figures and others pressured religious authorities to take up environmental issues and tried to get ordinary Americans to think religiously about environmental issues. By the early 1980s, a number of religious environmental organizations had formed, most notably the Eco-Justice Working Committee of the National Council of Churches.

NRPE emerged to coordinate official religious environmentalism in the US during the years 1991–1993. It was not founded (as has often been claimed) as a result of the 1990 exchange of "official" letters between clerics and scientists on the global environmental "crisis" organized by James Parks Morton, Paul Gorman, and, surprisingly, the outspoken atheist scientist Carl Sagan. The letter exchange marked instead a turning point after which church and temple hierarchies publicly recognized the crisis. Much of the credit goes to Gorman, then a staff member working for Morton at the Cathedral of St. John the Divine, now director of the organization. The component groups were at different levels of development. Gorman organized them under one umbrella using the carrot of funding. Initial and subsequent funding came from liberal foundations such as Ford and Pew. The NRPE agreed to disseminate money on an equal basis to each component group.

The NRPE quickly organized and disseminated information to congregations that represented each group's understanding of the relevant Jewish and Christian teachings on justice, social ethics, and the creation. In the mid-1990s, over 125,000 literature packets were distributed to churches and temples. Numerous conferences and other kinds of meetings were held. The NRPE's teachings carried extra authority stemming from the proclamations of church leaders, including Pope John Paul II, the respective NCC synods, presbyteries, and general meetings, and the four Jewish rabbinical seminaries.

Official recognition would be more difficult for the EEN, which aims to influence the evangelical-fundamentalist religious bloc. Evangelical and fundamentalist Christianity in America comprises smaller church organizations and individual churches without any particularly national group that could offer official endorsement. The EEN made up for this with advocacy and public relations, particularly their *Evangelical Declaration on the Care of the Creation*, supported by Billy Graham's magazine *Christianity Today*. Also noteworthy was the 1996 congressional lobbying in support of the Endangered Species Act reauthorization, for which conservative representatives and senators, particularly those influenced or supported by the New Christian Right, were unprepared. EEN and other religious groups demonstrated that conservative Christians did not speak with one voice on the issue. The ESA was successfully reauthorized.

All four NRPE member groups have held educational meetings and conferences, reinforcing the effect of their information packets on congregational leaders and clerics with face-to-face discussion of the various issues involved. Among the issues discussed has been climate change, ozone depletion, loss of species, natural resource policy, development policy for the South, and so on. Thousands of small environmental groups and many local projects have been started by individual churches as a result. NRPE ran a TV advertisement campaign in support of the Kyoto Accords on climate-change policy. In 2003, NRPE leaders pointedly asked Detroit automobile manufacturers, "What would Jesus drive?" and began a television campaign to press the question.

A conservative backlash, led by vociferous elements of what was known as the "Wise Use" movement, has attempted to delegitimize the movement, specifically targeting the new organizations in the press. An opposition group, the Interfaith Council for Environmental Stewardship, was formed for this purpose. The writings and speeches of some opposition leaders have included derogatory language; many can be dismissed as polemical and provocative. One exception might be a more principled opposition that is found within the evangelical-fundamentalist community itself, led by professors at evangelical-fundamentalist colleges and universities. This opposition from "Wise Users" and academics is marginalized to the libertarian right and the evangelical-fundamentalist bloc and has little or no penetration within mainstream U.S. churches and temples. Recent news articles, however, suggest some influence within the presidential administration of George W. Bush and in the U.S. Congress.

How far can the new U.S. religious environmental movement led by NRPE really go? Some of the answers to this question obviously require the use of quantitative social science technique, work that has yet to be conducted. A movement that successfully recruits American Jewish and Christian congregations would be a considerable addition to the secular environmental movement, but there is little evidence to suggest that this recruitment has or will take place. While the thousands of "green" congregations and associated environmental groups now in existence certainly denote successful organizing within the churches, environmental thinking has not become a way of life for those congregation members not directly involved, and is certainly not a major factor in voting behavior for the great majority of American Christian and Jews touched by the movement.

NRPE is thus not an arm of secular environmentalism, but rather a different kind of movement, perhaps, its leaders argue, more analogous to nineteenth-century church concerns with slavery, or twentieth-century concerns with civil rights and the war in Vietnam. The movements for abolition, civil rights, and to end the Vietnam War were elevated to public prominence first by direct action, the work of more extreme activists, before mainstream religions were willing to get involved. When they did, a revision of ordinary morality took place in the churches, which allowed mainstream politicians outside the activist cause to embrace the aims of the movement without losing votes. This may be the pathway that allows this movement to succeed.

Mick Womersley

Further Reading
White, Lynn Jr. "The Historical Roots of Our Ecological Crisis." *Science* 155 (10 March 1967), 1203–7.
Womersley, Michael William. *A Peculiar American Green: Religion and Environmental Policy in the United States*. Doctoral dissertation, School of Public Affairs, University of Maryland, 2002.
See also: Au Sable Institute; Berry, Thomas; Biblical Foundations for Christian Stewardship; Christianity (7i) – An Evangelical Perspective on Faith and Nature; Evangelical Environmental Network; Interfaith Council for Environmental Stewardship; Jewish Environmentalism in North America; North American Conference on Christianity and Ecology [and the] North American Coalition on Religion and Ecology; Religious Campaign for Forest Conservation; White, Lynn – Thesis of.

Native American Church – *See* Peyote.

Native American Languages (North America)

Indigenous peoples of the continent now called North America have suffered enormous losses under the processes of colonial assault and exploitation: the loss of population at the rate of 90 percent for most areas through the interplay of disease and genocide; the theft of the land and its resources, and destruction of animal species and plant habitats; the loss of traditional lifeways through aggressive assimilationist policies, including the loss of ceremonial vitality through systematic and legal proscription via government agencies and church institutions. All of these have been devastating for indigenous nations. Yet the greatest loss is perhaps only now coming into full effect. After withstanding an intensive siege throughout recent centuries the indigenous languages are now quickly falling silent in rapid succession. With them the indigenous cultures, religions, and the environments they inhabit are, once again, and in some ways more so than ever, in peril. The intricate knowledge of local ecosystems and the complex relations to the environment that grow out of indigenous languages are now jeopardized.

Whereas as much as half the world's known languages were lost over the previous 500 years of colonial expansion, the losses are now accelerating dramatically. The next twenty years could witness the demise of half of the world's approximately 6700 languages. A century from now, at present rates of loss, as much as 90 percent of human linguistic diversity will succumb to silence. Globally, one language disappears on average every two weeks according to the United Nation's education and science arm, UNESCO. Of course, the great majority of these endangered and disappearing languages are carried by indigenous peoples. Within the present area of the United States, over 73 percent of the remaining indigenous languages are spoken only by the grandparents' generation. Numbers such as these give stark clarity to the extremely limited time for addressing the global language crisis. And the magnitude of the loss of language for an indigenous heritage must be measured by the immense value of language to a multitude of diverse and rich cultures in their complex relations to their living environment. As Chris Jocks, a Mohawk scholar from Kanawake in southeastern Canada, has written:

> There is no way to decide which is more devastating: the loss of practical knowledge in such realms as history, natural science, and social organization; the loss of stories and jokes and all the richness of human experience they carry; the loss of skills of perception trained by Indigenous linguistic structures; or the loss of depth in our relationships with Other-than-human beings (Jocks 1999: 219).

To appreciate the difficulties involved in keeping alive the linguistic and cultural heritage of indigenous nations requires an understanding of the genocidal assault they have sustained. Waves of physical decimation were followed by generations of systematic cultural genocide in which enormous resources were expended in efforts to break traditional continuity between the culture-rich elders and the youth who were taken out of their homes and sent to government and church boarding schools and later public education facilities. The Dawes Allotment Act of 1887, which divided lands previously held in common by native nations into individual holdings, was devastating to indigenous languages. It led to the isolation of the remaining indigenous-language speakers in many communities, leaving them separated by miles of rural countryside.

Land Loss and Language Loss

This link between land and language loss represents more than just another indicator of the social and economic assault on traditional communities. For indigenous peoples the deep life-connection between their languages and their land are real and powerful. Grounded in the conviction that knowing the Earth's own language is essential for sustaining life, Jeanette Armstrong of the Okanagan in British Columbia has insisted:

> The language spoken by the land, which is interpreted by the Okanagan into words, carries parts of its ongoing reality. The land as language surrounds us completely, just like the physical reality of it surrounds us. Within that vast speaking, both externally and internally, we as human beings are an inextricable part – though a minute part – of the land language.
>
> In this sense, all indigenous peoples' languages are generated by a precise geography and arise from it. Over time and many generations of their people, it is their distinctive interaction with a precise geography which forms the way indigenous language is shaped and subsequently how the world is viewed, approached, and expressed verbally by its speakers (1998: 178–9).

Indigenous languages intertwine with the living environment at many levels. The languages connect an intricate web of complex relations between land, climate, plants, ceremonies, social structures, and living history in particular landscapes. For many communities certain classes of stories are only to be uttered during designated seasons of the year. Snow should be on the mountains for the Diné of Arizona and New Mexico to relate bear stories. The utterance of indigenous speech is understood to effect the physical world. Traditional Kiowas of the southern plains rise early to pray the sun up. Traditional hunters of the northeast utter ceremonial words of thanksgiving in order to ensure a relationship of reciprocity and a continued supply of game animals. Careful sensibilities of observation are carried in the languages. For the Micmac of Newfoundland and Labrador, names ascribed to trees change from season to season as the sound of the wind blowing through them shifts over time (Nettle and Romaine 2000: 16). Even the sense of the physical self is mediated by the landscape and articulated through language. For Wintu speakers of northern California, the "right" arm is not identified according to an orientation taken from the center of the individual human body. Instead, it is spoken of in terms of the person's orientation to the surrounding land, so that the "west arm" and the "east arm" could both refer to the same right arm as one changes directions within the landscape (in Hinton 1994: 58).

A complex cultural interplay between geography and indigenous language can also be expressed within a society. The language of the Western Apache in the American southwest situates them within a landscape and traditional history through the naming of the land, which acts as a guide to appropriate moral and social behaviors. This is a cultural world born by a language in which storytellers are hunters using stories about the names in the land to stalk their fellow community members. As Lewis Benson expressed it:

> I think of that mountain called *Tséé Łigai Dah Sidilé* (White Rocks Lie Above In A Compact Cluster) as if it were my maternal grandmother. I recall stories of how it once was at that mountain. The stories told to me were like arrows. Elsewhere, hearing that mountain's name, I see it. Its name is like a picture. Stories go to work on you like arrows. Stories make you live right. Stories make you replace yourself (Basso 1996: 38).

Endangered Languages, Endangered Species

Scholarly attention to linkages between species endangerment and patterns of language loss among indigenous peoples took shape in the early 1990s – including the terminology of language endangerment itself. The academic discussion was spurred by an article from Michael Krauss. He classified those languages that were no longer being learned by children in the home as moribund, a condition beyond endangerment, "for, unless the course is somehow dramatically reversed, they are already doomed to extinction, like species lacking reproductive capacity" (Krause 1992: 4). He provided viability statistics for Alaska, where only 2 of 20 languages are being learned by children, leaving 90 percent of the languages moribund. For the entire USA and Canada he listed over 80 percent of the 187 indigenous languages as already moribund with no natural means of reproducing themselves. Even Navajo, which had over 100,000 speakers a generation ago, he concluded, had "an uncertain future" (Krause 1992: 7). The situation remained uncertain in 2004; only about 30 percent of Navajo children began their formal education speaking Navajo. The patterns of language retention among other indigenous nations suggests that all indigenous languages within the boundaries of Canada and the U.S.A. are endangered.

Krauss went on to compare the pattern of global language loss to that of endangered and threatened mammal and bird species, where the percentages considered to be in danger of extinction were much lower. He contrasted the lack of attention to indigenous language endangerment to the greater levels of public concern for endangered species and argued for increased valuing of human languages:

> Any language is a supreme achievement of a uniquely human collective genius, as divine and endless a mystery as a living organism. Should we mourn the loss of Eyak or Ubykh any less than the loss of the panda or California condor? (Krause 1992: 8).

Scholarly interest in relationships between language and natural environments has expanded and includes some aspects of the new sub-field, ecolinguistics. In 1996 the non-governmental organization Terralingua was founded to preserve linguistic diversity and explore connections between linguistic and biological diversity. Though some scholars remain dismissive of connections between language loss and environmental degradation – the majority working in this area hold that there is a strong correlation between ecosystem decline and the erosion of indigenous cultures and their religions – and that the vitality of languages is an especially important variable.

The most compelling discussion to date has been presented by Daniel Nettle and Suzanne Romaine, who contend that the connections of indigenous peoples to environments are intense, ancient and unique. They demonstrate the remarkable overlap between regions with high concentrations of biological and linguistic diversity, and they argue that losses for both domains are due to the same underlying causes, namely, powerful forces controlled by social elites. Their expansive discussion of "biolinguistic diversity" foregrounds the detailed classification systems demonstrated by many indigenous languages, which provide "verbal botanies" useful for categorizing the natural environment. They argue that indigenous languages offer potentially rich contributions to scientific theories and to such problems as land management, marine technology, plant cultivation, and animal husbandry. They offer a sophisticated theory of the "ecology of language" where a language is understood to be enmeshed within a social and a geographical matrix that can be valuable to the project of sustainable development:

There is now widespread agreement that the problem of sustainable development is more likely to be solved if indigenous systems of knowledge and languages are valued and brought into play . . . Delicate tropical environments [for example] must be managed with care and skill. It is indigenous peoples who have the relevant practical knowledge, since they have been successfully making a living in them for hundreds of generations. Much of this detailed knowledge about local ecosystems is encoded in indigenous languages and rapidly being lost (Nettle and Romaine 2000: 166).

Indeed, the demise of any indigenous language represents a double loss. At a primary level, language loss severely jeopardizes the irreplaceable storehouse of richly detailed knowledge of plants, soils, terrains, sacred loci in the land, animal behaviors, and patterns of fish, bird, and insect life. Such knowledge has been developed and refined for thousands of years and integrated within a gendered human society in relation to the larger cosmos, seasons, and spirit worlds. Beyond this loss of knowledge associated with particular plants and local environments, which have been meshed with superb technologies, sophisticated medicinal practices, and elaborate social structures and religious traditions, the very process of indigenous knowledge development has been arrested.

Beginning in the waning years of the twentieth century, native nations took up the challenge to revitalize their languages. By so doing they endeavor to keep alive their unique and fertile epistemologies and thus their languages' essential role in the ceremonial life of their communities, as well as in promoting ecological knowledge and environmentally sustainable lifeways.

Richard A. Grounds

Further Reading
Abley, Mark. *Spoken Here: Travels Among Threatened Languages*. Boston: Houghton Mifflin, 2003.
Armstrong, Jeannette C. "Land Speaking." In Simon J. Ortiz, ed. *Speaking for the Generations: Native Writers on Writing*. Tucson, AZ: University of Arizona Press, 1998.
Basso, Keith H. *Wisdom Sits in Places: Landscape and Language Among the Western Apache*. Albuquerque: University of New Mexico Press, 1996.
Jocks, Christopher. "Living Words and Cartoon Translations: Longhouse 'Texts' and the Limitations of English." In Lenore A. Grenoble and Lindsay J. Whaley, eds. *Endangered Languages: Language Loss and Community Response*. New York: Cambridge University Press, 1999.
Hinton, Leanne. *Flutes of Fire: Essays on California Indian Languages*. Berkeley, California: Heyday Books, 1994.

Krauss, Michael, "The World's Languages in Crisis." *Language* 68 (1992), 4–10.
Nettle, Daniel and Suzanne Romaine. *Vanishing Voices: The Extinction of the World's Languages*. Oxford: Oxford University Press, 2000.

See also: Traditional Ecological Knowledge; Yuchi Culture and the Euchee Language Project.

Native American Spirituality

Native American spirituality is a hybrid form of religion that is clearly different from the highly specific beliefs and rituals that identify particular tribal religions and distinguish them from one another. Native American spirituality is a pan-Indian phenomenon involving native peoples from many different tribes. It is also a religious movement that thousands of people without any native ancestry identify with. Because of its syncretic character and fairly recent origin, Native American spirituality is sometimes regarded as inauthentic. However, most scholars of religion recognize that living religions are always changing and subject to reinterpretation and reinvention. From that perspective, Native American spirituality is as "authentic" as many other forms of religious life.

Native American spirituality first emerged in the nineteenth century as native people from different cultures found new areas of common ground, and as reverence for nature developed as an important force within both native and Euro-American cultures. Native religious leaders and non-native admirers alike pointed to an underlying spirituality of nature characteristic of all Native American cultures. This emphasis on a common nature spirituality underlying different native religions contributed to cooperation among native groups and challenged Western tendencies to view native religions as forms of heathenism that ought to be left behind if not actively suppressed. During the late twentieth century, respect for Native American spirituality became widespread as part of a general increase in ecological sensitivity throughout American religious life.

The historical development of Native American spirituality can be described in terms of an evolving conversation between Native Americans and Westerners about religious respect for the Earth. In the early nineteenth century, the Shawnee leader Tecumseh referred to the Earth as his mother in an effort to explain to a U.S. Army officer his resistance to the seizure of Indian lands and his understanding of the difference between instrumental Western ideas about land and native ideas about the spiritual powers inherent in local environments and forces. Later in the century, the Sahaptin leader Smoholla described the Earth as the mother of mankind and spoke against forcing native groups in the northwest basin to plow arid land for farming with figures of speech that pictured plowing the Earth as tearing a mother's bosom and digging under her skin for bones. The eloquence of these Indian leaders caught hold among Euro-Americans drawn to Romantic ideas about nature as a source of religious inspiration as well as among Native Americans struggling to define the strength and beauty of their traditions in the context of Euro-American colonization. Eager to recast Romantic ideas into an American idiom, American writers and artists such as Henry David Thoreau, George Catlin, and Edward Westin portrayed the Indian's relationship to the Earth as a powerful symbol of human virtue, simplicity, and purity. In the twentieth century, under the influence of European ideas about primitive religions as an antidote to the alienation from nature associated with Western civilization, both Indians and whites looked back to traditional native cultures as repositories of ancient wisdom and vitality. In the context of this search for the recovery of spiritual meaning, Mother Earth became a full-fledged goddess revered by neo-pagans of Euro-American ancestry as well as by many Native Americans themselves.

The Oglala holy man Black Elk and his interpreters played important roles in the development of Native American spirituality in the twentieth century. John Neihardt's popular recounting of Black Elk's visions and life journey in *Black Elk Speaks* countered any idea that native religions were simple. It also confirmed Romantic belief in the fundamental opposition between native reverence for nature and Western commercialism and greed. As the original transcripts of Black Elk's story show, Niehardt exaggerated Black Elk's sense of despair about the survival of native cultures.

In the 1960s, *Black Elk Speaks* served as an important source of religious education for participants in the American Indian Movement, many of whom had grown up in urban environments without much traditional religion. Because many of these Indian readers had ancestral ties to groups other than Sioux, *Black Elk Speaks* contributed to the development of a pan-Indian spirituality, grounded to a considerable extent in Sioux beliefs as Black Elk and his interpreters reconstructed them.

Black Elk also figured importantly in the thought of people without native ancestry who wanted to incorporate Native American beliefs about spiritual forces within nature as part of their own religions. Hyemhyosts Storm, Jamake Highwater, Sun Bear and several other New Age writers caused controversy and resentment by claiming Native American identity and promoting themselves as teachers of Native American spirituality; others inspired by native reverence for nature made no such claims.

Black Elk's ideas about nature appealed to many Christians seeking environmentally sensitive interpretations of their own religious tradition. The discovery that Black Elk had been a Roman Catholic catechist as well as an Oglala holy man contributed to Christian appropriation of his ideas, and Black Elk himself viewed native spirituality as a needed supplement to Christianity. In identifying the rituals of the sacred pipe as seven rites in which divine presence became manifest in nature, he reconstructed Sioux religious practice in a way that paralleled and enhanced the sacraments of the Catholic Church. Black Elk's conceptualization of Native American spirituality, along with his respect for Christianity, helped inspire the greening of American Christian thought in the late twentieth century and increased interest in and respect for Native American spirituality.

Amanda Porterfield

Further Reading
Brown, Joseph Epes, ed. *The Sacred Pipe: The Seven Rites of the Oglala Sioux*. Norman: University of Oklahoma Press, 1953.
Clifton, James A., ed. *The Invented Indian: Cultural Fictions & Government Policies*. New Brunswick: Transaction Publishers, 1996.
Gill, Sam D. *Mother Earth: An American Story*. Chicago: University of Chicago Press, 1987.
Holler, Clyde, ed. *The Black Elk Reader*. Syracuse: Syracuse University Press, 2000.
Niehardt, John G. *Black Elk Speaks: Being the Life Story of a Holy Man of the Oglala Sioux*. Lincoln: University of Nebraska Press, 1961 (1932).
See also: American Indians as "First Ecologists"; Black Elk; Black Mesa; Cosmology; Holy Land in Native North America; Indigenous Religions and Cultural Borrowing; Mother Earth; Nature Religion in the United States; Religious Environmentalist Paradigm; Romanticism and Indigenous People; Plastic Medicine Men; Seattle (Sealth), Chief; Snyder, Gary.

Natural History and Indigenous Worldviews

Beliefs about the relationship between humans and the natural environment are expressed through worldviews. A worldview is a mechanism *system or complex of ideas* through which the world makes cultural sense. As deeply seated belief systems, worldviews illuminate the ecological priorities and concepts of various peoples.

All traditional societies that have managed resources well over time have done so in part through religion and worldview – by the use of cultural symbols that reinforce particular management strategies. Many of these religious beliefs and cultural practices, while seeming unscientific, are based in part on long and careful observation of nature.

Natural history is the integrated study of the relationships between the biological, the physical, and the sensual (personal). It integrates keen observation of the natural world with an acknowledgement – indeed, an affirmation – that humans are sentient beings. Hence, natural history mixes the scientific perspective with elegant, heartfelt and intelligent responses to science. It mixes the social sciences and humanities with ecology, and it entails a breaking down of the normative barriers between the scientific and the poetic. It blends tradition with innovation and engages us in informed discussions of conservation efforts to reveal useful approaches to our environmental crises. Natural history personalizes science and enlivens it with meaning; a naturalist is one who has the eyes of a scientist and the vision of a poet; one who confronts evocative ideas, and is respectful of both facts and mysteries. By taking an ecological approach to the study of worldviews, we can gain greater understanding of critical interactions between humans and the natural world.

Worldviews are situated in the landscape, and indigenous cosmologies function as storehouses of critical knowledge of the natural world. At the heart of research on worldviews and natural history is an exploration of creation stories and how they inform and explain cultural understanding of the more-than-human world. Such research strives to result in ethnographic information and theoretical explication of some cultural understandings of ecological relations.

Mythologies provide explanation as to why the physical world is the way it is. The Cahuilla people of the Sonoran Desert in southern California, as one example among thousands, have elaborate myths detailing how the landscape of their territory came to be. In Cahuilla stories, Coyote is held in esteem because he is said to have brought mesquite seeds down from the mountains. Mesquite seedpods were a staple food for traditional Cahuilla, and continue to be an important plant, and because of Coyote's actions Cahuilla held coyotes sacred and never killed them. The Cahuilla version of how mesquite colonized the arid valleys is likely a literal one; because coyotes feed on mesquite beans but do not digest the seeds, it is likely that the plant was spread from the higher elevations to the lowlands in coyote scat.

All traditional societies have myths that explain why things are the ways they are. Ingeniously encoded in these symbolic systems are often profound understandings of ecological relationships. Indigenous worldviews, as explicated through myths, are often extremely sophisticated and of considerable practical value.

Numerous scholars have overlooked the ecological dimension of cosmologies or worldviews, while writing at length about native understandings of "supernatural" entities. We can attribute much of this oversight to a modern worldview that holds that natural world is largely determinate and mechanical, and that that which is regarded as mysterious, powerful, and beyond human ken must therefore be of some other, non-physical realm above nature (i.e., supernatural). But in oral indigenous cultures, the physical world itself is the dwelling place of the gods, of the numinous powers that can sustain or extinguish life.

Worldviews reflect, among other things, attitudes toward nature. These attitudes are expressed through conceptions, uses, and manipulations of the land. Aspects of cultural ecology are expressed through belief systems, and investigations of the intersection between the external world and cultural constructions of that world are providing fruitful insights into the relationship between nature and the human mind.

Paul Faulstich

Further Reading

Abram, David. *The Spell of the Sensuous: Perception and Language in a More-Than-Human World.* New York: Pantheon Books, 1996.

Anderson, E.N. *Ecologies of the Heart: Emotion, Belief, and the Environment.* Oxford: Oxford University Press, 1996.

Nabhan, Gary Paul. *Cultures of Habitat: On Nature, Culture, and Story.* Washington, D.C.: Counterpoint, 1997.

Rose, Deborah Bird. *Dingo Makes Us Human.* Cambridge: Cambridge University Press, 1992.

Shepard, Paul. *The Others: How Animals Made us Human.* Washington, D.C.: Island Press, 1996.

Suzuki, David and Peter Knudtson. *Wisdom of the Elders.* New York: Bantam Books, 1992.

See also: Cosmology; Magic; Magic, Animism, and the Shaman's Craft; Native American Spirituality; Natural History as Natural Religion; Shepard, Paul; Storytelling and Wonder; Trickster.

SP Natural History as Natural Religion

In my opinion, the seminal document that spawned the academic exploration of environmental ethics – and dialectically, the greening of religion, as I latterly explain – was "The Historical Roots of Our Ecological Crisis," by Lynn White, Jr., published in *Science* in 1967. I was especially primed to resonate with its message. I grew up in a lower-middle-class neighborhood in Memphis, Tennessee, the son of a poor artist, struggling to raise a family and find time to paint on an instructor's salary in a municipally funded art school. He took me to the Unitarian Church – there was then only one in Memphis – because it offered freedom of belief and welcomed everyone from Enlightenment-style deists to Emersonian Transcendentalists to Theosophists, which was my father's peculiar and ardent persuasion. All my classmates seemed to be Southern Baptists and I was, in their opinion, a damned (literally) infidel – worse even than a Catholic – the object of pity, ridicule, and contempt. Thus my childhood and teenage relationship to the only Christianity I then knew was problematic at best and painful at worst. The weekend Unitarian-youth community was my refuge from weekday religious persecution and social ostracism. When I was a highschooler I wanted to become a Unitarian minister (and shortly found what I was truly called to do in my first philosophy course during my sophomore year of college). So, when I read "Historical Roots" as a young philosophy instructor, I was very ready to believe that the ultimate blame for our ecologic crisis lay at the doorstep of Christianity.

In retrospect, that claim is of course both jejune and cavalier. Its lurid brashness, however, obscured another, far more general claim worthy of serious consideration. It must have registered on me back then – the late 1960s – only subliminally because it was fully a quarter-century later that I began consciously to ponder critically its significance. Four or five times throughout the infamous article, White reiterates the claim that what we do depends on what we think, and thus that if we are to effect any lasting changes in what we do in and to the natural environment, we must first effect fundamental changes in our environmental attitudes and values. This then became for me personally a mandate and an agenda – and, I dare say, it was for many of the other "pioneers" (as we are sometimes called, though the irony is not lost on me) of environmental philosophy. Only we philosophers and theologians (for White had also equated "beliefs about our nature and destiny" with "religion") could save the world from destruction by the juggernaut of "modern technology," which, in White's opinion, was forged in the crucible of Western Medieval Christendom. And Christianity, according to White, "is the most anthropocentric religion the world has seen" (with the minor exception, he curiously notes, of "perhaps" Zoroastrianism). That was the mandate. The agenda was twofold.

First, raise for critical attention the rest of the intellectual legacy of the West from the new perspective of environmental crisis. White himself portrayed Greek and other forms of European paganism as nature-friendly, but the Olympic religion of ancient Greece (and copycat Rome) was long dead – whether nature-friendly or not is of course moot. The Greco-Roman legacy that shaped modern Western civilization is the legacy of ancient Greek and Roman philosophy and proto-science, the legacy of Plato and Aristotle, of Democritus and Lucretius. A virtual cottage industry of critical environmental philosophy sprang up almost overnight. In addition to Plato and Aristotle, Descartes was routinely hacked and flayed, as were a number of other historically influential thinkers in the Western canon.

Second – and much more ambitious, if not utterly hubristic – think up a new nature-friendly philosophy (and perhaps a sympatico new religion) and somehow infuse it into the cultural ether, so as to transform popular consciousness in the West. How preposterous! But that's how it all started and, amazingly, the project is still ongoing and, indeed, gaining momentum and enjoying some modest success. But it is a tricky business. Just how do you go about thinking up a new nature-friendly philosophy (and religion)? Not from scratch; to be convincing such a philosophy must have continuity with the past and must seem inevitably to flow – however dialectically and revolutionarily – from the past into the present and future with the force of a historic tide. Just as futile as starting from scratch, some environmental philosophers were at first inclined to take a neglected past philosophy off the historical shelf, burnish it up, and try to sell it anew. If we all became Heracliteans, Spinozists, Whiteheadians, Heideggerians ... our ecologic crisis could be overcome. This approach to phase two of the environmental philosophy agenda, set by White, was perhaps presaged by his own suggestion – which he quickly and wisely rejected as culturally unrealistic – that if we all became Zen Buddhists our ecologic crisis could be overcome.

I myself proceeded with this forward-looking and creative – as opposed to backward-looking and critical – phase-two agenda of environmental philosophy on the basis of an interesting and portentous relationship of cognitive domains in the two most profoundly dialectical and revolutionary moments in the intellectual history of the West. Natural philosophy is first philosophy; it precedes and appears to precipitate changes in moral philosophy.

During the sixth and fifth centuries B.C.E., in ancient Greece, the first philosophers, the PreSocratics, mainly asked and boldly answered questions about nature. What is the stuff of which the world is composed? What forces move that stuff around? What are the laws of nature which govern those motions or otherwise give order to the world? The most elegant and persuasive answers to these questions were provided by the atomists. In the late fifth century, natural philosophy (along with other emergent phenomena, such as urbanization and democratization) had created an ethical and social crisis that diverted a considerable portion of the intellectual capital of philosophers into moral and political questions. The nearly universal moral and political philosophy of the time (Socrates seems to have been the only notable dissenter) was the generic social contract theory – each "sophist" playing a specific variation on this common theme. At the core of social contract theory is egoism and enlightened self-interest. The individual human agent is, as it were, a social atom. The inertial motions of the physical atoms cause them to collide chaotically with one another in Euclidian physical space; analogously the desires and aversions that move the social atoms cause them to collide chaotically with one another in the amoral and pre-political "state of nature" (or Euclidian social space). And, although here the analogy is imperfect, just as (perhaps God-ordained) natural laws govern the behavior of the physical atoms, so ethico-political laws were humanly ordained to govern the behavior of the social atoms – to bring them into a political order, and to reduce the hurtful and destructive collisions among them that occur in the emptiness of pre-contract social space.

Following the lead of Socrates, Plato and Aristotle rejected atomism (in natural philosophy) and the social contract theory (in moral philosophy) in favor of teleology (in both domains of philosophy, natural and moral). Their influence lingered over Western thought for more than a thousand years. The Modern "scientific revolution" initiated by Copernicus and completed by Newton revived atomism in Western natural philosophy. And, lo and behold, that was followed, as night follows day, by the revival of the social contract theory in Western moral philosophy, most notably by Thomas Hobbes, John Locke, and Jean-Jacque Rousseau. In the early twentieth century a second scientific revolution occurred. And although contemporary physicists still blithely talk about "particles," the ancient and Modern classical atom, conceived by Democritus and Newton as a solid materio-mathematical corpuscle that fills a tiny volume of space, is as dead an idea in contemporary natural philosophy (now coincident with the high theoretical end of the natural sciences) as is the idea of phlogiston. In its place we have what? Quarks? Super strings? I'm not sure anyone yet knows, but it seems that the ultimate stuff of the world is more energetic than material and more internally related (or systemic) and mutually defining than externally related and reductive.

Correlative to – or at least coincident with – the emergence of the new physics at the dawn of the last century was the emergence of ecology. Ecology, too, offered a picture of middle-sized organic nature – the scale at which we human beings live between the micro-scale of dancing electrons and photons and the macro-scale of fleeing galaxies and black holes – that is material to be sure, but organized systemically by the flux of solar energy. And the living components of ecosystems also seem to be internally related and mutually defining; certainly they are mutually dependent.

Here we have the makings of a new worldview, a new natural philosophy. If the historical pattern that has characterized Western thought from the beginning holds through the current revolutionary era – change in moral philosophy following, after about a century's lag time, change in natural philosophy – what will the moral philosophy of the twenty-first century be like? We shall have to wait and see how it fully and unpredictably unfolds. I think, however, that contemporary environmental ethics, which developed exponentially over the last quarter of the twentieth century, is the harbinger of things to come – to the extent that it is informed by ecology and evolutionary biology. I myself have followed the lead of the person who seemed clearly to grasp all these things before anyone else, Aldo Leopold.

Leopold even anticipated White's blaming the Judeo-Christian worldview for our contemporary environmental malaise – a dubious distinction. In the foreword to his *chef d'oevre, A Sand County Almanac*, Leopold writes "Conservation is getting nowhere because it is incompatible with our Abrahamic sense of land. We abuse land because we regard it as a commodity belonging to us. When we see land as a community to which we belong, we may begin to use it with love and respect." The Whitean despotic reading of the biblical worldview surfaces again in *Sand County*'s climactic essay, "The Land Ethic": "Abraham knew exactly what the land was for: it was to drip milk and honey into Abraham's mouth."

Opposed to this caricature of the Judeo-Christian worldview is the evolutionary-ecological worldview, the representation and implications of which is the principal burden of the *Almanac*. From an evolutionary point of view, *Homo sapiens* is just another animal – the most recent and perhaps the most complex and sophisticated of evolution's random mammalian experiments, but just another animal nevertheless. We are therefore a part of nature, not set apart – for better or worse – from nature, from an evolutionary point of view. From an ecological point of view the human economy is but a small and utterly dependent subset of the economy of nature; and the human community is embedded in the larger biotic community.

The stage is thus set for the derivation of the land ethic. Darwin himself, in the *Descent of Man*, had explained how ethics could have arisen among *Homo sapiens* through natural selection. Human beings are quintessentially social animals. Primitive human societies could not have endured if the internecine competition among their members were untempered and if their members were disinclined to cooperate in provisioning and defending themselves. Individuals who were incapable of social integration and cooperation were expelled from society to fend for themselves as solitaries. Lacking the increased efficiency of cooperative gathering, hunting, and defense, they quickly succumbed to starvation or predation. Thus their anti-social tendencies were winnowed from the human gene pool. When the naturally selected social instincts and sympathies were augmented by acute intelligence, vivid imagination, and true language, ethics proper eventually evolved. As Darwin writes, "No tribe could hold together if murder, robbery, treachery, were common; consequently such crimes are branded with everlasting infamy, but excite no such sentiment beyond these bounds." From a Darwinian point of view, ethics is, as it were, the glue that holds human societies together.

Next Darwin envisioned a gradual evolution of human

societies and the ethics correlative to them by the controversial process of group selection. Larger, better organized groups of *Homo sapiens* would out-compete smaller, less well-organized groups in the now collective or corporate struggle for existence. Clans thus merged into tribes, tribes into national confederacies, these eventually merged to form nation-states, and now – under our very noses – supranational entities, such as Europe and NAFTA are evolving, loosely integrated by transportation and communications technologies and very loosely governed by such multinational parliaments as the United Nations. Corresponding to each of these stages in social evolution is a corresponding stage in ethical evolution. Corresponding to the nation-stage stage of social evolution is the emergent virtue of patriotism. Corresponding to the emergence of the global village is the declaration of universal human rights. As Darwin summarized it, "As man advances in civilisation, and small tribes are united into larger communities, the simplest reason would tell each individual that he ought to extend his social instincts and sympathies to all the members of the same nation, though personally unknown to him." Darwin even anticipated the present stage of ethico-social evolution: "This point being once reached there is only an artificial barrier to prevent his sympathies being extended to all the nations and races."

To cook up the land ethic, Leopold simply took over this Darwinian recipe for the origin and development of ethics, correlative to the origin and development of society or community, and added an ecological ingredient. Ecology represents plants and animals that live together on a landscape (or in a waterscape) as members of a "biotic community." The British ecologist, Charles Elton, a friend of Leopold's, had most vividly portrayed the biotic community as an economic analog of human society. Just as we have division of labor and specialization in the human economy – doctors, lawyers, butchers, bakers, candlestick makers – so in the economy of nature, evolution has sorted producers, consumers, and decomposers of the biotic community into myriads of professions or niches. If, following Darwin, our response to perceived community membership is an extension of our social instincts and sympathies – an extension in some modified form of our ethics – then general recognition of the existence of a biotic community should be followed by a land ethic. As Leopold succinctly put it, "All ethics so far evolved rest upon a single premise: that the individual is a member of a community of interdependent parts." Ecology, Leopold goes on to note, "simply enlarges the boundaries of the community to include soils, waters, plants, and animals, or collectively: the land." The upshot is "a land ethic [that] changes the role of *Homo sapiens* from conqueror of the land community to plain member and citizen of it." At the heart of such an ethic is "respect for ... fellow-members and also for the community as such."

Elton had characterized ecology as "scientific natural history." In addition to a land ethic, Leopold also derived spiritual sustenance from ecology and evolutionary biology. One might fairly say that *A Sand County Almanac* is a book of scripture for a new religion of natural history. Certainly the rhetorical devices of *Sand County* are markedly biblical. Its second most famous essay, "Thinking Like A Mountain" records a road-to-Damascus-like experience. In it Leopold and his Forest-Service comrades kill a she-wolf and arrive in time to watch a "fierce green fire dying" in her eyes. Leopold "saw something new ... in those eyes – something known only to her and to the mountain." This knowledge forms the foundation of an inevitable question, but a question that Leopold's artistic sensibility requires him to leave his readers, whether consciously or subconsciously, to ask for themselves on behalf of the dying wolf: "Why persecutest thou me?"

In other passages, the contours of Leopold's religion of natural history are more explicit. "Marshland Elegy" is about evolutionary time. "A sense of time lies thick and heavy on such a place" as a crane marsh. Here he confronts directly what seems to many to be one of two main obstacles to the theory of evolution being taken as a spiritual, indeed a religious resource.

> An endless caravan of generations has built of its own bones this bridge into the future, this habitat where the oncoming host [a word loaded with religious significance] again may live and breed and die. To what end? Out on the bog a crane, gulping some luckless frog, springs his ungainly hulk into the air and flails the morning sun with mighty wings. The tamaracks re-echo his bugled certitude. He seems to know.

I once argued with another Leopold scholar about the meaning of this passage. He thought that Leopold was actually stating that the answer to this question was for the crane to *know* and for us to find out. But I think that Leopold is challenging – in his typically ironic, understated style – the importance of the question itself. Evolution is resolutely anti-teleological. There is no end, goal, or purpose at which it aims; hence to this and the related questions, "Why are we here?," and "What is the meaning of life?" the answers are "For no reason," and "There is none," respectively. If, to live fully and robustly in the present, cranes need no answers to such questions, then why should we? Further, because evolution *per se* may have no goal does not imply that we cannot select lofty ends to give transcendent meaning to our personal and communal lives.

The other obstacle to a religion of natural history thrown up by the theory of evolution is the apparent cosmic demotion of humanity from a form of being created in the image of God – "half animal, half angel," in

John Muir's turn of phrase – to simply and utterly an animal. Leopold confronts this obstacle indirectly throughout the whole of *Sand County*, in which humankind's animal and plant fellow members of the biotic community are portrayed with affection and respect for their dignity and particular virtues. More directly confronting it in "On a Monument to the Pigeon," Leopold writes:

> It is a century now since Darwin gave us the first glimpse of the origin of species. We know now what was unknown to all the preceding caravan of generations: that men are only fellow-voyagers with other creatures in the odyssey of evolution.

The use of "odyssey" here suggests once more an ateleological voyage and "only" addresses the present point. Should "this new knowledge" be an occasion for depression and spiritual despair? Not at all, "it should have given us, by this time, a sense of kinship with other creatures; a wish to live and let live . . ." After all, being "lord man" – I echo Muir again – is a lonely job. And given what we learn about many of our fellow-voyagers in the odyssey of evolution from all that we have read in the *Almanac*, far from being debased, we are gladdened and ennobled by our kinship with them. And this new knowledge should also have given us, finally and most importantly, "a sense of wonder over the magnitude and duration of the biotic enterprise." What a paltry world, temporally speaking, we have inherited from the Judeo-Christian tradition, one only some 6000 years old. Think about it! From the point of view of the theory of evolution, life has been metamorphosing and colonizing and transforming Earth for 3.5 billion years. We are its latest manifestation and carry within our DNA the genetic legacy of this immense journey.

In "On a Monument to the Pigeon," Leopold, despite all this, agrees with traditional Judeo-Christian belief that human beings occupy a privileged place in the cosmos. The pigeon in this essay is the extinct passenger pigeon and the monument mourns its demise. "Had the funeral been ours," Leopold soberly reflects, "the pigeons would hardly have mourned us. In this fact, rather than Mr. Dupont's nylons or Mr. Vannevar Bush's bombs, lies objective evidence of our superiority over the beasts." We are superior to other creatures, Leopold ironically suggests, not because we have the technological power to fulfill the biblical injunction to subdue them and the Earth itself, but because we have the moral capacity to include them within the compass of our ethics.

Meanwhile, Lynn White seems to have presented environmentally concerned members of the Judeo-Christian community with a hard choice: their environmentalism or their religion. In White's own words, the choice is "to find a new religion" – such as the then-popular Zen Buddhism – "or rethink our old one."

Choosing the latter is by far the more realistic, not to mention the more palatable course. White himself recommends the (heretical?) theology of Saint Francis of Assisi as a start for rethinking our old religion. And in the last sentence of his article, he proposes that Francis be named the patron saint of ecologists, which, as I recall, Pope John Paul has now done. However, the actual response was not to make Christianity over in the mold of Francis' theology – official designation of Francis the patron saint of ecologists notwithstanding. Rather, it was to challenge White's reading of the Bible and, from a more plausible alternative reading, to develop an environmental ethic out of the same biblical resources that White had lambasted. The result is what I call the Judeo-Christian Stewardship Environmental Ethic.

Here are its basic elements. In several passages in Genesis prior to those (1:26–28) that White had focused on exclusively, God declares his daily acts of creation to be good. That can be read as declaring that the creation has intrinsic value, in the jargon of secular environmental ethics. Moreover, what is declared good (or in possession of intrinsic value) are various wholes, not individuals – species not specimens, whales not Moby Dick or the one that swallowed Jonah. In the jargon of secular environmental ethics, the Judeo-Christian Stewardship Environmental Ethic is thus holistic. And the good (or intrinsically valuable) creation in Genesis is represented as bringing forth abundantly and teeming with life – fishes in the sea; fowl in the firmament; and cattle, creeping things, and other beasts of the field being fruitful and multiplying, *each after its kind*. We may, therefore, in good conscience harvest the surplus and live on the usufruct of the creation as long as we preserve a fitting abundance of each kind. Then in chapter of 2 of Genesis (ignoring the fact that there we find another and substantially different and independent account of creation) key passages indicate that man (for exegetical purposes represented by Adam) is put into the Garden of Eden (which we may construe to represent the whole creation) to dress and keep it – that is, to be its steward. Now with these passages as book ends, we return to those that White made seem so damning environmentally. We may interpret man's created exclusively in the image of God as bestowing unique responsibility as well as unique privilege. And we may interpret God's giving man "dominion" over the Earth as a mandate for responsible management – that is, stewardship – not as a mandate for despotic exploitation and destruction. Now, finally, the Fall, described in Genesis 2, is invoked to mute God's command in Genesis 1 to go forth and subdue the Earth. Whatever stewardly thing God meant by that, fallen man has perverted and depraved it.

Thus did White dialectically spawn the greening of religion. If so powerful and so persuasive (to believers in its premises, for example, that God exists and created the world) an environmental ethic could be teased out of the very texts that White had made seem so environmentally anathematic, surely environmental ethics could be teased out of the sacred texts of other religions. Judaism is already covered, because the texts in question belong to the Hebrew Bible. Islam is in the same Abrahamic family of religions, and, sure enough, various passages of the Qur'an can be given a stewardship spin. Hinduism and Buddhism share the concept of *ahimsa*, or non-injury to all living beings. In the Chinese traditions of Confucianism and Taoism, we find such nature-friendly concepts as *fengshui*, *wu wei*, and the injunction to follow the *Dao*, or way of nature. Common to American Indian and other indigenous worldviews is a sense of embeddedness in and dependence on an animate and communicative nature – which people must respect, in order to continue to be blessed by its generosity of spirit.

It would be nice to think that the current greening of these and many other religions were a spontaneous and wonderfully coincidental process. But the greening-of-religions phenomenon is, in my opinion, a response to and an implicit affirmation of the more scientific evolutionary and ecological worldview so elegantly and attractively expressed by Aldo Leopold. If it weren't for ecology we would not be aware that we have an "ecologic crisis." If it weren't for the theory of evolution we would be both blind and indifferent to the reduction in global biodiversity. The world's newly green religions thus tacitly orbit around the evolutionary-ecological worldview. I myself consider most religions – especially the Abrahamic family of religions – to be grounded in primitive superstition and ignorance. (In "Monument to the Pigeon," Leopold says that such ideas as God creating man in his own image "arose from the simple necessity of whistling in the dark.") I am, however, immensely grateful for the greening-of-religions phenomenon and have modestly contributed to its development. The religious potential of natural history that Leopold so beautifully tapped but only scarcely explored is perhaps centuries away from its full actualization. But while a true – that is, an epistemically sound and scientifically compatible – religion gestates, people now have to be reached where they are with some kind of environmental ethic. And for most people, their religion seems to be among the most compelling of motives. If the popular traditional religions can be marshaled to achieve a better fit between global human civilization and the natural environment in which it is embedded, I shall not worry their green apologists, expositors, and theologians with logical and philosophical quibbles.

J. Baird Callicott

Further Reading

Albanese, Catherine L. *Nature Religion in America: From the Algonkian Indians to the New Age*. Chicago: University of Chicago Press, 1990.

Berry, Thomas. *The Dream of the Earth*. San Francisco: Sierra Club Books, 1990.

Berry, Thomas and Brian Swimme. *The Universe Story: From the Primordial Flaring Forth to the Ecozoic Era – A Celebration of the Unfolding of the Cosmos*. San Francisco: HarperSanFrancisco, 1994.

Black, John. *The Dominion of Man: The Search for Ecological Responsibility*. Edinburgh: Edinburgh University Press, 1970.

Callicott, J. Baird. *Earth's Insights: A Multicultural Survey of Ecological Ethics from the Mediterrainean Basin to the Australian Outback*. Berkeley: University of California Press, 1994.

Callicott, J. Baird and Roger T. Ames, eds. *Nature in Asian Traditions of Thought: Essays in Environmental Philosophy*. Albany: SUNY Press, 1989.

Hargrove, Eugene C., ed. *Religion and Environmental Crisis*. Athens: University of Georgia Press, 1986.

Oelschlaeger, Max. *Caring for Creation: An Ecumenical Approach to the Environmental Crisis*. New Haven: Yale University Press, 1994.

Rolston, Holmes III. *Genes, Genesis, and God*. Cambridge: Cambridge University Press, 1999.

Spring, David and Eileen Spring. *Ecology and Religion in History*. New York: Harper & Row, 1974.

See also: Biocentric Religion – A Call for; Conservation Biology; Darwin, Charles; Ecology and Religion; Environmental Ethics; Evolutionary Biology, Religion, and Stewardship; Leopold, Aldo; Religious Environmentalist Paradigm; Religious Studies and Environmental Concern; Restoration Ecology and Ritual; Social Construction of Nature and Environmental Ethics; White, Lynn – Thesis of; Wilderness Religion.

SP Natural Law and Natural Rights

The natural law is not a single or simple theory. It is rather a dynamic and diverse tradition, with both philosophical and religiously grounded expressions. Prominent among the historical variety of versions are those of Cicero, Seneca, Aquinas, Hooker, Grotius, Locke, and Blackstone. While embraced in Christian thought by most Catholic and at least some Protestant ethicists, versions of the natural law can also be found among thinkers in other religious traditions, including Confucianism, Judaism, and Islam. The natural law has been used both to condemn and to commend democracy, imperialism, slavery, and gender equality, as well as to sanctify and to vilify some cultural institutions. This diversity reflects how, despite aspirations to moral universalism, particular theories, like all human constructs, are shaped in part by ideological assumptions, religious values, and cultural contexts.

The natural law is not "law" in the sense of socially enacted or declared legal codes, usually called positive law. Nor is it "law" in the sense of the order known to physics, such as the law of gravity or other "laws of nature." Rather, it is "law" in the sense of a rational order of moral norms and obligations – a presumed "higher" standard that has often provided a basis for challenging and reforming cultural conventions and positive laws.

Similarly, the natural law is not "natural" in the sense of being instinctive or self-evident standards – even though many in the tradition have asserted that humans, as rational and relational beings, appear to have innate moral capacities and inclinations, which can be culturally cultivated or corrupted. Instead, "natural" means that moral values and norms are discerned in "nature," specifically the human condition. They are also rooted in, rather than externally imposed upon, that condition. Moreover, these values and norms are discovered through "natural" reasoning capacities, without benefit of privileged revelations. In Christian history, the "natural" was often contrasted with the "supernatural." The "two books" of morality were the "natural" and the "divine" or "revealed" law. The natural was accessible to all rational beings, and the divine – usually clarifying, confirming, and completing the natural – was known mainly through scripture. The two are still seen as complements in some Christian circles, but as alternative, even competing, methods in some inter-religious epistemological controversies.

Natural law affirms a universal moral order. This order is not necessarily built into the structure of the universe, though it is in most religious interpretations. But it is at least built into the essential constitution of humans as rational and relational beings. Against moral relativism, natural law proponents argue that moral norms are factual claims about the human condition and can be evaluated as objectively true or false. Moreover, in the form of ethical naturalism, which characterizes most, but not all, modern interpretations, natural law ethics depends on empirical data to justify what humans ought to be and to do, in view of the values and virtues, rights and responsibilities, principles and practices that contribute to the well-being of our kind – and one can add, other kinds of creatures – in relationships. Respecting the natural law then is not "following nature" in the imitative manner of Social Darwinists, but rather practicing the norms of our nature, the conditions necessary for interdependent flourishing.

The mainstream of the natural law tradition, especially since the Enlightenment, has followed a rational-experiential method. Experience is usually defined broadly so that nothing, in theory, is excluded as irrelevant data for ethical reflection (though, in fact, moral conclusions were often deductions from philosophical or theological assumptions about human nature). Reason is not an autonomous source of moral truth in this approach. Instead, moral reasoning is critical reflection on the givenness of experience in search of the norms of our nature. These norms are discovered only gradually and imperfectly through the trials and errors of historical experience. Such discovery depends on receptivity to the fullness of cultural wisdom, including all the empirical disciplines from psychology to ecology, as well as religious insights.

Ironically, however, most natural law theorists have ignored the bulk of nature. Like the rest of Western philosophy and theology, natural law ethics has been predominantly anthropocentric and dualistic, focusing exclusively on human interests and segregating humanity from the rest of nature. It has generally been oblivious to the fact that humans are not only social but also ecological animals, and must, therefore, reflect and act on questions of the good and rightness in our ecological relationships. Viable versions of the natural law, some environmental critics contend, depend on giving due consideration not only to human experience and values but also to the whole of biotic experience and values.

One of the great values of the natural law tradition to its religious supporters is that it can be interpreted as compatible with important affirmations of faith and yet simultaneously independent of these affirmations. In these views, the natural law reflects the moral character of the Ultimate. It is part of the rational, moral order of the universe and humanity's moral constitution, as created by God. The human capacity for moral reasoning, moreover, is often seen as a dimension of the image of God. The natural law is not an alternative to revelation in this view; it is divine revelation – a natural revelation, open to all rational beings, and, therefore, a "common grace" of God. Still, the viability of the natural law as a universal moral claim depends on logical independence from particular confessions of faith. It must be open in principle to all, whatever their ultimate commitments. In the midst of moral diversity, from imperial Rome to contemporary globalization, the prospect of universal norms universally accessible has always been one of the natural law's primary appeals. The tradition represents an abiding aspiration, and increasingly a practical necessity, for some shared standards of global ethics to enable the world's citizens to confront global social and ecological problems in global solidarity.

On the normative substance of the natural law, the tradition has covered a wide spectrum of views. Interpretations of this law have ranged from precise precepts to general principles, like the Golden Rule, and have included a variety of virtues and values, dues and duties. One of the enduring elements from this tradition, however, is the concept of *natural rights*.

These rights are "natural" in the sense that they allegedly inhere in human nature, applying equally and universally to human beings in respect for their intrinsic value. They exist as moral facts independent of, though demanding embodiment in, positive law. Moreover, they are discernible and defensible by reason reflecting on human experience, apart from any special revelations. The term human, rather than natural, rights is more common today, partly to suggest that such claims can be justified on grounds other than the natural law. The two terms, however, are usually synonyms.

Natural or human rights are specifications of just dues. They are strong moral claims for the imperative conditions of human well-being in community. They are not usually absolute; but they can be overridden only for compelling cause and only to the extent necessary for a fuller and fairer balance of rights. Though classical interpretations generally had a narrow range of rights, some modern versions of natural rights embrace a breadth of provisions, including the following categories: basic economic needs, physical security, religious and moral autonomy, educational and cultural development, environmental sustainability and integrity, equal political participation in shaping the common good, legal ground rules for fair and equal treatment, and the common good as a right in itself to a caring, collaborative order and as the precondition of all other rights. Which rights ought to be recognized has been an important but implicit political question, because rights logically define our social responsibilities in justice to one another, locally and globally.

Environmental rights are a newly emerging category of moral entitlements, prompted by diverse forms of environmental degradation. Since humans are not only social but also ecological animals, one of the essential conditions of human well-being is ecological integrity. In an interdependent biosphere, the sustainability of socio-economic systems depends on the sustainability of ecosystems. Indeed, the possibility of realizing every other natural right, environmental advocates argue, depends on the realization of environmental rights. These claims include the right to protections of the soils, air, water, and atmosphere from various forms of pollution; the right to the preservation of biodiversity in healthy habitats; and the right to governmental regulations ensuring the fair and frugal use of environmental goods.

But environmental rights for humans are not sufficient, according to some critics of the natural law tradition's almost exclusively humanistic focus. For those committed to redefining responsible human relationships with the rest of the planet's biota, and grounding those responsible relationships not only in utility and generosity but also in distributive justice, the moral claims of other life forms on the human community should be considered as part of the natural law and as a demand for fair treatment from moral agents. Most rights theorists acknowledge that some human rights must be restricted to protect the same or other moral claims of other parties in situations of conflicting claims. Thus, if other life forms – as individuals, populations, and species – are goods for themselves or otherwise moral claimants, then limits on the exercise of some human rights are warranted to respect the imperative conditions for the well-being of these life forms. Given currents threats to biodiversity, advocates argue, the moral claims of other species for healthy habitats and fair shares of planetary goods demand limits on economic production and human reproduction.

Natural rights are sometimes criticized as impositions of Western values on other cultures. Some expressions may be. Rights proponents must constantly struggle to avoid universalizing cultural relativities. But this grievance is increasingly hard to sustain in most cases in the light of strong international support for these claims, notably in the United Nations covenants. It is a striking fact that oppressive governments regularly condemn human rights as an alien idea, while oppressed peoples commonly appeal to these rights as the central moral standards in their struggles.

James A. Nash

Further Reading
Cogley, John, et al. *Natural Law and Modern Society.* Cleveland: World Publishing Co., 1962.
Curran, Charles E. and Richard A. McCormick, eds. *Readings in Moral Theology, No. 7: Natural Law and Theology.* New York: Paulist Press, 1991.
Finnis, John. *Natural Law and Natural Rights.* Oxford: Clarendon Press, 1980.
Freeden, Michael. *Rights.* Minneapolis: University of Minnesota, 1991.
George, Robert P., ed. *Natural Law Theory: Contemporary Essays.* Oxford: Clarendon Press, 1994.
Nash, James. "Seeking Moral Norms in Nature: Natural Law and Ecological Responsibility." In Dieter T. Hessel and Rosemary Radford Ruether, eds. *Christianity and Ecology: Seeking the Well-Being of Earth and Humans.* Cambridge: Harvard University Press, 2000.
Pennock, Roland and John W. Chapman, eds. *Human Rights: Nomos 7.* New York: New York University, 1981.
Porter, Jean. *Natural and Divine Law: Reclaiming the Tradition for Christian Ethics.* Grand Rapids, MI: Eerdmans, 1999.
See also: Book of Nature; Christianity (9) – Christianity's Ecological Reformation; Environmental Ethics.

Natural Law Party

The Natural Law Party was founded in 1992 as an alternative American political party. Dr. John Hagelin has been the party's candidate for the presidency in each election since 1992.

This party bases its platform on the idea of "natural law" which is described as "the order, the intelligence of the universe." According to Dr. Hagelin, science has shown us that the laws of nature are the orderly principles governing life throughout the physical universe. When people violate these laws, problems such as disease, pollution, and poor quality of life result. The NLP describes a program for bringing modern life into harmony with the laws of nature, using scientific and medical studies as evidence for many of its ideas.

The party takes a strong environmental position. It argues that U.S. dependence on fossil fuels causes greater harm than benefit. The harm comes not only from pollution, which leads to health problems and creates an unpleasant living environment, but also from the waste of money and loss of lives in global conflicts centered on fuel resources. To solve this problem, the party advocates research and development of renewable fuel technologies and increasing energy efficiency. This does not mean giving up the present standard of living, but actually raising it through developing technologies that are in harmony with nature. It also requires educational programs that promote "pollution-free" behavior.

Education is a major focus for the NLP. This is not just a matter of basic school skills, but the broader idea that people must be given the ability to see how their individual lives fit into the natural order so they can make wise choices. Education must enlighten people so that they will want to live in accord with natural law. This will, of course, lead to better care of the environment. It may also lead to better care of the self, greater harmony in families, a more orderly society and, eventually, global peace. Behavior that is in accord with natural law should not create problems for society or the environment.

To teach this awareness, the NLP advocates Transcendental Meditation. This is not prayer directed outward to a god, but a turning inward to find the inner self which is part of the whole unified cosmos. With this awareness of unity, people see themselves as part of society and the world, rather than selfish individuals. The party cites medical studies that show TM practitioners handle stress better and thus are healthier, less prone to violence, and happier in their lives.

The NLP considers stress the primary cause of many world problems. Stress causes drug use, crime, health problems like hypertension, and even wars. Several studies have shown that meditation reduces stress. The party argues that teaching meditation in schools can help children handle life so that they avoid bad habits, teaching it in prisons can reduce crime, and teaching it to the military can help alleviate global tensions. The latter idea is based on the TM theory that if a small percentage of a population meditates, it has an affect on the stress levels of the larger community. This concept is supported by research published in peer-reviewed articles in respected venues such as the *Journal of Conflict Resolution*. Thus, a group of people could be sent into a high-tension area to meditate and bring the people into harmony with natural law.

Cybelle Shattuck

Further Reading

Dillbeck, M.C. and K.L. Cavanaugh, et al. "Consciousness as a Field: The Transcendental Meditation and TM-Siddhi Program and Changes in Social Indicators." *The Journal of Mind and Behavior* 8 (1987), 67–104.

Orme-Johnson, D.W. and C.N. Alexander, et al. "International Peace Project in the Middle East: The Effect of the Maharishi Technology of the Unified Field." *Journal of Conflict Resolution* 32 (1988), 776–812.

Roth, Robert. *The Natural Law Party: A Reason to Vote*. New York: St. Martin's Press, 1998.

See also: Hundredth Monkey; Transcendental Meditation.

Nature Fakers Controversy

At first glance, the Nature Fakers Controversy was a light-hearted literary debate over whether or not wild animals can reason and teach their young to hunt and avoid traps, or a fox can ride a sheep across a field to avoid pursuing hounds. On a deeper level, it embodied an increasingly urbanized United States public's efforts to reconcile Darwinian, humanitarian and Edenic visions of nature and wildlife.

The controversy spanned four years of magazine and newspaper articles, book prefaces and a full editorial page of the *New York Times*. John Burroughs, America's preeminent literary naturalist, began the debate in 1903 with an *Atlantic Monthly* article accusing a number of prominent nature writers of what he called "sham natural history." Ernest Thompson Seton, William J. Long, Charles G.D. Roberts and others, he claimed, fabricated and overly dramatized the lives of wild animals in order to sell books to a burgeoning, lucrative national market of gullible nature lovers.

These writers were practitioners of a new genre, the realistic wild animal story. Such stories presented events from the perspective of their animal protagonists. This was a radical shift in perspective, one that emphasized non-anthropocentrism. A fox hunt, for example, is a very different story when viewed from the point of view of the fox, rather than the hunter. Inevitably, the authors often read their own expectations and biases into the minds and behaviors of their animal heroes The psychology of the day tended to explain behavior in terms of either reason or instinct, with little ground in between. Facing such options, the authors accused of nature faking granted their subject the gift of reason.

Seton and Roberts did not defend themselves publicly and emerged relatively unscathed. Long, however, mounted a vigorous defense and became the lightning rod of the debate. A Connecticut Congregationalist minister whom some accused of Unitarian tendencies, Long received his Ph.D. from the University of Heidelberg in 1897. He was no stranger to controversy. He attended Andover Theological Seminary shortly after it had been attacked for teaching "higher criticism" of the Bible. In 1898, Long became pastor of the North Avenue Church in Cambridge, Massachusetts. However, the Cambridge Council refused to ordain him because of his liberal theology, which included a belief in universal salvation. This drew national attention in Congregational circles. Long resigned after serving only two months, but was praised for his religious conviction and integrity.

Long was an experienced woodsman and close observer of nature. Although he often misinterpreted what he saw, he did not intentionally fabricate his natural history "facts." His vigorous defense of himself and his books, while principled and philosophically sophisticated, was misguided by his poor understanding of inductive science. Long rejected Darwinism and scientific rationalism, arguing that animals experience no struggle for survival. He believed that all minds, be they human or not, are reflections of the Creator's. Thus, he relied on empathy as the key to understanding animal psychology.

John Burroughs' existential view of nature had no place for a God, although he felt a deep emotional bond with nature. Many of those accused of nature faking, on the other hand, viewed nature in spiritual terms. For example, Ernest Thompson Seton, who later became a founder of the Boy Scouts of America, rejected Christianity and adopted a Native American-styled pantheism. William J. Long argued that animals are capable of religious experience. His *Brier-Patch Philosophy* (1906), an unsung classic in animal-rights literature, is one of the fullest statements of Long's views.

Finally, in 1907 President Theodore Roosevelt publicly spoke out against Long. He was especially upset that books written by Long and other fakers were used in the public schools. He shifted the focus of debate from errant writers to irresponsible publishers and school committees. In response, they paid greater attention to the accuracy of nature books. Following Roosevelt's attack, Long turned to writing books about American and English literature. Nevertheless, his publisher and fellow Congregationalist Edwin Ginn, a proponent of world peace and opponent of hunting, kept his books in print for years.

The controversy helped to set standards of accuracy for nature writers, while it also underscored the American public's discomfort with "cold science" and eagerness for an emotionally and spiritually satisfying vision of the natural world.

Ralph H. Lutts

Further Reading

Lutts, Ralph H. *The Nature Fakers: Wildlife, Science & Sentiment*. Golden, CO: Fulcrum, 1990; Charlottesville: University Press of Virginia, 2001.

Lutts, Ralph H., ed. *The Wild Animal Story*. Philadelphia: Temple University Press, 1998.

Lutts, Ralph H. "John Burroughs and the Honey Bee: Bridging Science and Emotion in Environmental Writing." *ISLE: Interdisciplinary Studies in Literature and Environment* 3:2 (Fall 1996), 85–100.

See *also*: Burroughs, John; Indian Guides; Native American Spirituality; Scouting.

Nature Religion

The term "nature religion" was introduced into contemporary discourses of the study of religion by Catherine Albanese's *Nature Religion in America* (1990). Albanese uses the term to interpret a wide variety of phenomena not previously considered in terms of religion. However, subsequent to her study, the academic use of the term has been largely confined to research into contemporary Paganism and New Age spiritualities, notably in the collection *Nature Religion Today* (Pearson, Roberts and Samuel 1998). It is appropriate to restore Albanese's broader understanding of the term, since the term has a more general currency historically and geographically, appearing not only in contemporary Paganism before Albanese's work, but also in Germany in the late eighteenth and early nineteenth centuries. Like Robert Bellah's notion of civil religion, Albanese's idea of nature religion can help make visible practices in popular culture and political activity of all religions as religious expressions, and thus broaden the understanding of religion beyond its most identifiable institutional expressions, and help religionists more easily to understand religious activities that do not easily correspond to categories of study derived from religious institutions like churches and scriptures.

Albanese does not explicitly define "nature religion" in *Nature Religion in America*, but indicates that she uses the term as a construct to describe a religion or type of religion found in the United States, which takes nature as its sacred center. She describes it as a religion, in the singular, but also says that it occurs in variants as nature religions. What the variants have in common is that in these phenomena, nature is the symbolic center. Albanese describes a chronological development of major variants of nature religion in North America. Forms and movements discussed include Algonquian spirituality and Native American traditions more broadly, seventeenth- and eighteenth-century Puritanism, Freemasonry, Gaia consciousness, conservation and preservation movements, as well as Emersonian idealism, ecofeminism and feminist spirituality, and various New Age phenomena.

Albanese's work is indispensable in its extension of the purview of religion beyond what is considered religion proper in the academic study of religion. It facilitates, for example, the study of phenomena within environmentalism as religious activity, as in Bron Taylor's research on practitioners of deep ecology and bioregionalism. Closer to the study of religion proper, Albanese's use of the term "nature religion" enables examination of nature-oriented non-institutional religion on its own terms.

The term "nature religion" has probably been adopted most readily in the study of contemporary Paganism because it already had some currency within the groups Margot Adler began researching in 1972, for her study of North American Paganism *Drawing Down the Moon* (1979). Adler's first use of the term in print equates "contemporary nature religions" with "Neo-Pagans," without comment or explanation of the term. In the groups Adler studied, practitioners of contemporary Paganism already regarded themselves as practitioners of nature religion or nature religions, which they conceived as ancient European shamanistic religion, devoted to variants of a Mother Earth goddess and/or various other gods and goddesses of nature, making no distinctions between the spiritual and the material world.

Adler cites two published references to nature religion preceding the publication of her study. In 1974, Frederick Adams published an article called "Feraferia for Beginners" in *Earth Religion News*, in which he refers to the need to look to the "original root-systems of Nature Religion" for inspiration and education (Adams 1974: 51). Adler also cites Tim Zell's use of the term in the early 1970s. In an undated Church of All Worlds tract, "An Old Religion for a New Age, Neo-Paganism," Adler reports, Zell distinguished between "philosophical religions" and "natural religions." These natural religions Zell identified with indigenous, folk, and Pagan religions that evolve naturally, in contrast to what he saw as the artificially constructed philosophical religions.

Zell made the distinction between natural and philosophical religion at least as early as 1972, using "Pagan" and "natural religion" to refer to folk, indigenous, and non-institutionalized religion, in an article titled "Paganism & Neo-Paganism: The Old Religion & the New," published in *Green Egg*. Zell's polarization of natural and philosophical religion strikingly parallels Hegel's use of these terms, but follows the Romantics' valuation of the natural over the philosophical.

Hegel, Schlegel, Schelling, and their early nineteenth-century contemporaries in Germany, were in agreement that all peoples had a common origin in a first religion and culture, but Hegel disagreed with Schlegel and Schelling in that he identified the original religion as primitive, savage and evil, whereas they felt it expressed a state of innocence, a golden age. In *Lectures on the Philosophy of Religion*, Hegel calls this first religion "nature religion."

For Hegel, nature religion is crude and simple, the lowest form of religion, in which Spirit is perceived in nature, rather than transcendent of nature as in philosophical religion, epitomized by Christianity. Hegel indicates that nature religion continues to influence the "higher" forms of religion, through belief in magic, citing the practice of witchcraft within Christianity.

Ideas of "nature religion," "natural religion," and "religion of nature" were circulating in German thought in the late eighteenth and early nineteenth centuries. Kant, for example, argued that there are two kinds of religion: the religion of nature, and the religion of ethics. Schelling believed that the first religion of humanity was the best, a natural religion. In a 1796 letter to Hegel, Schelling suggested that a new religion was necessary, one that did not reject mythology in favour of reason. In his novel *Lucinde*, Friedrich Schlegel identifies this new religion with "the old religion" of nature. Schlegel champions a religion of nature, of the imagination, and of poetry, as a religion that prizes women and the ideal feminine, passivity, and the natural as opposed to the artificial, especially in terms of social norms. For Schlegel, this religion of nature is the primordial religion, the religion of the Garden before the Fall, a religion of innocence, without shame. It is polytheistic in a sense familiar to contemporary Pagans, as the god/desses do not definitively either "really exist" or exist only in the imagination. There is no equivocal distinction between the two in this expression of nature religion, because, in Schlegel's terms, the imagination is the faculty humans have for perceiving divinity.

In the German Idealist, and Romantic traditions to an extent, nature religion was contrasted with Christianity, as everything that Christianity was held not to include. Albanese, however, instructs that nature religion should not be taken simply as the opposite of the "Judeo-Christian religions of history." Nature religion is not opposite to the religions of history or of ethics, but is a type of religion that can be found within the practices of Christianity and other mainstream religions as well as marginal traditions. Albanese's understanding of nature religion is vital for its implicit recognition that any religion can be expressive of nature religion, not only indigenous and contemporary Pagan religion. Expanding the use of the term beyond its expression in North America, nature religion can then be applied to any religion.

Using the term "nature religion" in the singular is appropriate for applying the concept to various religious traditions, since it suggests that nature religion is a type of religion or tendency to be found within and running across different religions. To use the term in the singular indicates that nature religion is not restricted to one group of religions in opposition to another group of religions that are not nature religion. While the use of the plural "nature religions" may aim to be inclusive, it suggests that some religions are never expressive of nature religion, or categorically cannot be expressive of it. To use the term in the singular allows it to be applied to any religious group, on the basis of criteria that are not dependent on any particular religion.

Nature religion can be distinguished from other religion on the basis of its understanding of transcendence. Nature religion can then be constructed as a type of religion in which nature is the milieu of the sacred, and within which the idea of transcendence of nature is unimportant or irrelevant to religious practice. By this definition, not only contemporary Paganism and indigenous traditions, but practices and beliefs of any religion can be expressive of nature religion. This definition recognizes that a religion can be expressive of nature religion without being exhaustively defined by nature religion. For example, not all contemporary Pagan religious traditions are expressive of nature religion by this definition, since some posit divinity transcendent of nature, as in the panentheism of Gus diZerega (2001).

Transcendence, in nature religion, tends to be lateral rather than vertical. Spirits and deities are of this world rather than beyond it, and can be contacted through the natural world. Nature religion is this-worldly religion. Contemporary expressions of nature religion are often explicitly this-worldly, with the hope that a valuation of this world and none beyond it will encourage us to respect and preserve it. In nature religion it is more often culture than nature that is transcended. This is to be expected in phenomenon that are often seen as countercultural, as are many of the phenomenon of nature religion, such as the Christian folk singers discussed by Albanese, and modern British witchcraft as described by Ronald Hutton (1999).

The usefulness of the term "nature religion" lies in the broadness of its applicability. It is limited in being applied only to the United States, or only to contemporary Pagan religious traditions. It is useful to look at wider social and cultural developments in terms of nature religion, and to look for expressions of nature religion in mainline religious traditions, such as creation spirituality in Christianity, and Thich Nhat Hanh's practices in engaged Buddhism, and to look for this-worldly expressions of mainstream traditions. However, it remains to be seen how useful the term might be in understanding indigenous traditions. There have been no in-depth studies of specific groups or spiritual traditions in indigenous cultures in terms of nature religion, probably in part because "nature religion" is yet another Western category, but also because it is a relatively new area of research in the study of religion.

Barbara Jane Davy

Further Reading

Adams, Frederick. "Feraferia for Beginners." *Earth Religion News* 1:5 (1974), 51.

Adler, Margot. *Drawing Down the Moon: Witches, Druids, Goddess-Worshippers, and Other Pagans in America Today*. Boston: Beacon Press, 1986 (1979).

Albanese, Catherine L. *Nature Religion in America: From the Algonkian Indians to the New Age*. Chicago: University of Chicago Press, 1990.

Bellah, Robert N. "Civil Religion in America." In *Beyond Belief: Essays on Religion in a Post-Traditional World*. Berkeley: University of California Press, 1970, 168–89.

diZerega, Gus. *Pagans & Christians: The Personal Spiritual Experience*. St. Paul, Minnesota: Llewellyn Publications, 2001.

Hegel, Georg Wilhelm Friedrich. *Lectures on the Philosophy of Religion*, vol. II. Peter C. Hodgson, ed., R.F. Brown et al., trs. Berkeley: University of California Press, 1987.

Hutton, Ronald. *The Triumph of the Moon: A History of Modern Pagan Witchcraft*. Oxford: Oxford University Press, 1999.

Pearson, Joanne, Richard H. Roberts and Geoffrey Samuel. *Nature Religion Today: Paganism in the Modern World*. Edinburgh: Edinburgh University Press, 1998.

Schelling, F.W.J. *On University Studies*. E.S. Morgan, tr. Athens, OH: Ohio University Press, 1966.

Schlegel, Friedrich. *Lucinde and the Fragments*. Peter Firchow, tr. Minneapolis: University of Minnesota Press, 1971.

Taylor, Bron. "Nature Religion and Ecology" (Ecology and Religion Section). In Lindsay Jones, Editor-in-Chief. *The Encyclopedia of Religion*. New York: Macmillan, 2005 (2nd edn).

Taylor, Bron. "Earth and Nature-Based Spirituality (Part II): From Earth First! and Bioregionalism to Scientific Paganism and the New Age." *Religion* 31:3 (July 2001), 225–45.

Taylor, Bron. "Earth and Nature-Based Spirituality (Part I): From Deep Ecology to Radical Environmentalism." *Religion* 31 (2001), 175–93.

Zell, Tim. "Paganism & Neo-Paganism: The Old Religion & the New." *Green Egg* V:48 (1972).

See also: Bioregionalism; Bioregionalism and the North American Bioregional Congress; Celestine Prophecy; Deep Ecology; Earth First! and the Earth Liberation Front; Nature Religion in the United States; Paganism (various); Radical Environmentalism; Religious Studies and Environmental Concern; Romanticism (various); Snyder, Gary.

Nature Religion in the United States

(This article is adapted from material previously published in Catherine L. Albanese, *Reconsidering Nature Religion* (Harrisburg, PA: Trinity Press International, 2002) and is used with the permission of the publisher.)

What does it mean to speak of nature religion? For a general audience in the Western and English-speaking world, probably the first reference that comes to mind is land-based and environmental. Nature means grass and trees, panoramas and vistas, mountains and lakes and oceans. So nature religion means beliefs and practices that involve turning to God in nature or to a nature that is God. For a smaller, largely self-identified group in the same Western and English-speaking world, nature religion signals Goddess more than God, and nature is the principal trope for a religiosity that calls itself pagan or, alternately, neo-pagan. To invoke nature religion becomes a way to call attention to one's pagan/neo-pagan spirituality and, also, group commitment. For still others who have a familiarity with Western religious and theological history, the term nature religion is teasingly close to two others – natural religion and natural theology.

These last are designations that arose in an eighteenth-century Enlightenment context under the guiding star of deism. For the Enlightenment, natural religion made sense in contradistinction to supernatural religion – the revealed religion of Christianity based on the inspired word of scripture. Natural religion therefore meant the religion of reason alone; or, in tandem with human reason, the religion that looked to nature as its holy book of inspiration. It ranked inferior or superior to Christianity, depending on prior belief commitment and point of view. Still more, if it was counted superior, it was thought to be grounded in the essential order of the universe and of all things. In a distinctly Christian understanding, natural theology became the system of religious thought constituting knowledge of God and divine things that one could obtain by reason alone. It was suspect and generally rejected in Protestant theological circles of Reformation provenance (because of their view of the fallen nature of humanity) but more warmly received by Roman Catholics and, later, by liberal Protestants.

In light of all of the above, what other way or ways can there be to invoke nature religion, and that in a United States historical context? The answer to this question (or, really, set of questions) leads as far back as the early coalescence of the culture that later came to flourish in the United States, and it leads, too, through a multiple canon of religious meanings, ranging from Idealist philosophical statements that show clear marks of European influence to popular cultural practices that have come together in new ways in our own time. The answer leads us, too, to an extremely fragile world – a world that is deconstructing itself even as it comes to be.

As an Idealist philosophical statement at its broadest, consider the definition announced by Ralph Waldo Emerson (1803–1882) in his Transcendentalist manifesto *Nature*:

Philosophically considered, the universe is composed of Nature and the Soul. Strictly speaking, therefore, all that is separate from us, all which Philosophy distinguishes as the NOT ME, that is, both nature and art, all other men and my own body, must be ranked under this name, NATURE.

Here Emerson invoked "both nature and art" to define nature, and then he went on to explain that the term had both a "common" and a "philosophical import." "*Nature*, in the common sense," he wrote, "refers to essences unchanged by man; space, the air, the river, the leaf. *Art* is applied to the mixture of his will with the same things, as in a house, a canal, a statue, a picture." Yet of this latter – of "art" – Emerson was dismissive. Human operations collectively considered were "so insignificant, a little chipping, baking, patching, and washing, that in an impression so grand as that of the world on the human mind, they do not vary the result" (Emerson: 1971, 8). Many, of course, would be less speedy to relegate human constructions to a cosmic recycle bin. Yet in the space between Emerson's two definitions – his "philosophical" sense and his "common" one, there stands an American definitional and historical territory that may fruitfully be explored under the rubric of nature religion.

Since the rubric is distinctly nature *religion* and not simply nature *theology*, let it be clear that any American historical survey must move beyond beliefs regarding nature, however reverent and profound. Rather, the rubric must encompass cultural practice that is intimately connected with belief both in condensed symbolic settings (i.e., in ritual and devotional situations) and in more broad-gauged and general ones (i.e., in everyday behaviors that act out ethical stances and convictions). It helps to remember, too, that to engage in such an American historical survey of nature religion is hardly a minor exercise or an add-on from the point of view of the Western religious tradition. With theology or religious thought as its strong suit, this tradition has placed nature near the top of its short list of major categories by which to make sense of religion. God and humanity comprise the first two categories. Nature, however culturally diffuse and evanescent, forms the third.

Shaped then by an Emersonian space between philosophy and common usage and a Western religious space, in which nature counts for major consideration, what does a hypothetical cultural narrative regarding nature religion in the United States look like? We are back, in effect, at a more reflective version of the initial question: how do we speak with definitional and historical inclusiveness of nature religion in the United States? How do we name and narrate nature religion? And, again, what are the limits of such speaking? How, in other words, do we construct a past that may be useful in the twenty-first century? The beginning of an answer and a narrative may be found in the seventeenth century – in the time when the different players who would assume leading roles initiated the series of contacts and exchanges that produced the dominant culture of the land.

Among these players, Anglo-Protestants assumed hegemonic importance in terms of a public and religiously inspired culture, but their views and behaviors were affected subtly (and sometimes not so subtly) by other groups with whom they shared space. Numbered among them were Native Americans and native Africans, English and French Catholics, continental European immigrants of both Protestant and Roman Catholic backgrounds in general, even a small community of Jews when the Dutch New Amsterdam colony became New York. Of all of these groups, it was Native Americans (or American Indians) who engaged in the series of cultural attitudes and activities that could be most clearly linked to nature religion. Working on the bases of accounts that must be pieced together from hostile English sources, from archeologically derived remnants, and from narratives collected as much as several centuries later, the general lines of an encompassing religion of nature may be sketched. Ironically, this religion of nature was never identified as such by native Indian peoples: in Indian cultural circles and communities there was no abstract "nature" to which or whom to relate. To say this another way, both word and abstraction are Western European designations for referents named and understood differently among Native Americans and also among others. Yet considered generally and collectively Native American beliefs and practices point to sacred objects and subjects residing in, or manifest as, aspects of the material world that Europeans have called nature.

With spatially oriented and environmentally shaped perception, Native Americans have honored their kinship with sacred Persons – e.g., thunder grandfathers, spider grandmothers, corn mothers, and the like – who represent (and, for them, are) the powers of nature. They have elaborated etiquettes of relationship with these Beings, for instance, when killing game and/or harvesting crops. Indians have noted their own placement on land-based terrains by paying acute attention to directional points in ritual practice and by according symbolic and theological import to the directions (for example, seeing the east as associated with sunrise, the color yellow, and new life and growth, while the west was linked to sunset, darkness, and death). Although Indians have certainly been aware of the vicissitudes of the seasons and the uncertainties of the weather, overall they have found a harmony in nature that, historically, they chose to imitate in practical ways. This meant everything from taking cues from nature in the construction of housing and bodily adornment to living out convictions that Western Europeans would regard as ethical directives.

When Africans entered what Europeans claimed was the "new world" in the early seventeenth century as indentured servants or – very quickly the norm – as slaves, they, too, brought nature-based forms of religiosity with them. West African tribes, from whom blacks had been forcibly separated, revered their ancestors but, also, revered Persons who came out of nature – again, without a generalized overarching concept of the same. While exception must be made for a significant number of Muslims among these native Africans, the local religions of West Africa tended to support theological visions of distant creator deities but also of other spirit powers and gods who were seen as close at hand. These nearer sacred beings embodied the elements of nature and could come intimately close to the bodies of devotees in rituals of trance and possession. They functioned at the center of religious life and tied their devotees to a sense of self and environment alive and holy.

Among Roman Catholics both from England and the Continent, nature occupied a relatively prominent place in theology and ritual practice as well. By the thirteenth century, scholasticism had reached new clarity in the work of Dominican friar Thomas Aquinas (ca. 1225–1274) and had articulated a comprehensive understanding of natural law, based on older Greek categories but reordering them in Christian terms. Nature here was not only land-based but encompassed, too, the orderly pattern of the heavens and the stars as well as the inner and mysterious workings of animal (including human) and vegetable bodies. Moreover, nature stood at the core of cultural practice within the Church both in a natural-law ethic that arose from the scholastic category and in a sacramental system culminating in the mysteries of the Eucharist. In this sacramental understanding, pieces of the material world became force-filled conduits for spiritual power, so that as representational signs they themselves were transmuted into the sacredness they signified. In the most graphic illustration of the proposition, the bread and wine of the Eucharistic sacrificial meal at the Mass became, for medieval and modern Catholics, the actual physical body of Jesus the Lord. Nature was exalted, indeed, as it became the body of God.

Nor was the religious importance of the material world lost on the small Jewish community residing on American shores. Jewish religious practice, in fact, privileged natural categories and sites. Much more than in versions of Christianity, for example, the home functioned at the center of Jewish ritual life – to the degree that it stood beside the synagogue as sacred space. The liturgy of Shabbat, or the Sabbath, took place in the home and featured agricultural products transmuted into food and family fare, in a ritual that accorded women places of ritual honor and also clearly connected natural life and products to transcendent sacred meanings. Jewish religiosity put its premium on the embodied spirituality of ritual and of ethical directives for life in this world, in relation to human communities. Jewish notions of the afterlife, by contrast, came off as vague and trailing – afterthoughts and underthoughts in Jewish theological explication. That there were no ordained Jewish rabbis and few synagogues in the Atlantic colonies only emphasized these general tendencies in Jewish belief and practice.

What did all of this mean for Anglo-Protestants in the British North Atlantic colonies? On arrival, literate New England Puritans alternately feared the wild country of their new landscape as a wilderness in which their souls and spirits would be tested and, by contrast, celebrated it as a garden of God's good, especially when planted in new Puritan towns. Meanwhile, in the common culture that elites shared with others, English country tradition already supported a world of cunning women and men who used the products of nature in magical practices that existed alongside of and, sometimes, intermixed with Protestant church ritual. If colonial libraries can be taken as evidence, alongside these cultural manifestations an elite magical and metaphysically oriented tradition, influenced by continental Hermeticism that had been subsumed into Paracelsan, Rosicrucian, and Jewish Kabbalistic forms, flourished in early America.

Although we know all too little regarding the interactions of the dominant Anglo-Protestant culture with Indians and blacks as well as with Catholics and Jews, we gain brief and provocative glimpses as, for example, in the much-recorded Salem witchcraft epidemic of 1692. Here Tituba, a female Caribbean slave from Barbados of African or, more probably, South American Arawak Indian ancestry, stood accused of corrupting a group of young Puritan girls by introducing them to pagan practices of sorcery. In a well-known narrative, this was only the beginning of a series of "discoveries" of practicing witches in and around Salem. The communication of cultural practice, of which Tituba stood accused, must have occurred many times over in the informal connections and exchanges between Anglo-Protestant elites and their servants. In her book *The World They Made Together: Black and White Values in Eighteenth-Century Virginia* (Princeton, 1987), Mechal Sobel explored the process for whites and blacks in eighteenth-century Virginia, demonstrating the subtle ways that blacks helped to shape white planter culture, as for example in attitudes toward space and the natural world. Meanwhile, among elites themselves of different religious backgrounds, there was often more social interaction than might at first be expected. In her doctoral dissertation "Early Modern English Women, Families, and Religion in the New World" (University of Rochester, 1997), for instance, Debra Meyers has documented the culture of intermarriage between Catholics and Arminianized (stressing free will) Anglicans in the Maryland colony from 1634 to 1713, and she has also shown the parallel track that Quakers followed compared to these first two groups. For all three, when "nature" meant human nature it could be more or less trusted given the prior work of Christ, so that these groups tended to support more egalitarian family structures and downplayed patriarchy and hierarchy in general.

Examples such as these, of course, add up only to tantalizing suggestions of what common sense already argues. At any rate, by the late eighteenth century and the time of the American Revolution, nature became explicitly linked by elites who were establishing the new political culture with their expansive republican venture. They understood nature in at least three senses, and each of the ways of signifying nature led to the patriotic ideology they promoted (suggesting already a nature religion in the process of unraveling?). First, nature meant "new-world" innocence – a freedom from the corruptions of old England that was symbolized in the purity of country living beside clear streams and fertile soil and also symbolized in the lack of social formalism and affectation among new Americans. Such new-world innocence brought with it a reinvigoration of the social and political project unlike what patriots viewed as the tired and effete political culture of old England with its stilted hierarchies and aristocracies.

This sense of collective freshness and vigor led to a second meaning of nature, which came with distinctly Enlightenment credentials. Akin to the affirmations that accompanied natural religion and deism, this meaning of nature pointed away from Earth and toward the heavenly bodies in order to make its point for the Earth. Nature now meant the law that turned sun and stars in their orbits, ordering the regular motion of the planetary bodies. Brought back to Earth, this universal law became the ground for all human rights and, among them especially, for political rights. Like the planets in their contained and lawful motions, the individual states that comprised the new United States would operate in their individual orbits but also cooperate in a grand symmetry of order and form. So, too, would individual human beings: nature pointed toward the egalitarian social and political patterns that were idealized in the "new order of the ages" the patriots aimed to create.

Finally, as a third meaning accompanying patriotic affirmations, nature signaled the growing practice of venerating a distinctly American landscape. Already in the late Puritan culture before the American Revolution, thoughtful religious leaders like Jonathan Edwards (1703–1758) and Cotton Mather (1663–1728) had, in different ways, found God in nature. After the war, in prose and poetry that linked the republican experiment with, literally, the ground that supported and accommodated it, nature became a new aesthetic trope. The "spacious skies" of the young nation, the seeming boundlessness and expansiveness of its landscape, became the divine benediction on its political project. America as a place in nature was bigger and better than anything European because its political experiment was bigger and better. More than that,

American nature evoked the Kantian "sublime" as mediated through the writings of English philosopher Edmund Burke. In his *Philosophical Enquiry into the Origin of Our Ideas of the Sublime and Beautiful* (1757), Burke had distinguished the sublime from the beautiful because of the capacity of the former to cause astonishment, awe, and even a species of horror. Americans felt the presence of hierophany in the landscapes they observed, as Thomas Jefferson when he gazed at Natural Bridge; and they acknowledged a sacred splendor in what they beheld – in ways that redounded to their new political system. America was physically grand and awesome, and so was its political project.

These estimates turned ugly by the Jacksonian era, as territorial aggrandizement became justified in terms of the grandeur of the political project. Cherokee Indians and others walked their trail of tears to make room for white farmers. By the middle of the nineteenth century, nature religion became the justification for manifest destiny, and imperialism rode strong on nature's back. Earlier, however, even as Andrew Jackson was exporting Cherokee Indians to the Oklahoma Territory, the New England Transcendentalists were busy creating a thoroughly self-conscious and ethically high-minded endorsement of the religion of nature. (Emerson and his friends, for example, protested the forcible eviction of the Cherokees from Georgia and became stalwart anti-slavery advocates.) The Transcendental gospel itself was stated canonically in Emerson's little book *Nature*, with its declaration of profound correspondences between nature and humanity. The Emersonian declaration was accomplished in the context of the combinative English Hermetic tradition that by then was emphasizing Neoplatonism, and in concert with a then-contemporary admiration of the work of the Swedish mystic and scientist Emanuel Swedenborg (1688–1772). The new declaration was contained, too, in a decidedly literary consciousness, but a consciousness that pushed literature strongly into the realm of the religious. For Emerson and his followers, words were signs of natural facts, which were symbols of spiritual facts. And all nature was the symbol of the spiritual.

Emerson himself preached more than he practiced. But his younger friend Henry David Thoreau (1817–1862) did both. He built his well-remembered cabin on Emerson's land at Walden Pond outside of Concord, Massachusetts, and wrote his classic *Walden; or Life in the Woods* (1854) about his sojourn there. He also tramped the Maine woods, climbed local mountains like Mount Katahdin, and befriended Indian guides. Out of his experiences he pushed Emerson's religio-philosophical convictions regarding self-reliance in still more radical (and expressive) directions that led him into active anti-slavery work shielding runaway slaves and into at least one night in jail. To be natural, for Thoreau, meant to keep one's conscience free, to preserve the integrity of the self in face of the compromises that society – especially in organized political form – sought to impose. Thoreau's fondness for South Asian Indian religious philosophy, when he discovered it in the late 1830s, grew out of his sympathy with Indian mystical notions of unity of Self and world. If, as the Indian texts affirmed, Atman (Self) really was Brahman (the all-power in the universe), if This was That, then Thoreau's nature religion led to fellow beings and their rescue from inequity.

The Transcendentalist moment in American religious history enjoyed its heyday through the 1840s and 1850s. As an elite statement of a complex and many-faceted form of nature religion (at least in germ), it produced a lasting template for what might count as nature religion in the United States. Unlike the earlier folklorized occult and metaphysical religion of colonial America, Transcendental nature religion took religious ideas about human correspondences with an almighty Nature into new and more public directions. It acted, as it were, as a conduit from the seventeenth- and eighteenth-century past into a nineteenth-century and later American future. In terms of nature religion itself, that future moved in at least three, and possibly four, major directions.

First, one major form of nature religion in the nation led out from the Transcendentalism of Emerson and, especially, Thoreau in the direction of environmentalism. The often-celebrated John Muir (1838–1914) carried writings by the two of them in his saddlebags, and he clearly revered them as spiritual mentors. Muir himself, who as a young boy had emigrated from Scotland with his family, left the family and the conventional life behind and trekked far and wide, eventually reaching California's Sierra Nevada Mountains. There he felt that he had come home to nature and to himself, a "higher self" that directed him with inner wisdom and even mystical forms of intuition. In Muir's own writings, it is clear that he worshipped a nature that was alive and sentient, resplendent with sacramental manifestations that fed his spirit to the point of inebriation. But Muir combined the earlier Transcendental veneration of the panorama of the land (Emerson) and the details of its construction and inhabitants (Thoreau) with a sense of social activism and public accountability. In this, he was not unlike Henry David Thoreau, but more than Thoreau, Muir's cause became nature itself. That he founded the Sierra Club, the nation's first environmental lobby, and that he worked at the forefront of the national-park movement that gave the United States Yosemite in 1890 are uncompromising statements to his moral conviction and its social enactment.

Muir had found a public rhetoric to connect private delight in wilderness and religious reverence for it with a domain of political practice. After him, and even alongside him, there were others, Aldo Leopold (1887–1948), Professor of Game Management at the University of Wisconsin, important among them. Leopold's enormously influential *Sand County Almanac* (1949) gave voice to a religious and ethical valuation of nature not tied to conventional Western biblical themes. In fact, turning self-consciously away from what he called an "Abrahamic concept of land," Leopold called for a land ethic based on an affirmation of the land as a community in which humans were members. As community, the land was alive – not a mechanized and commodified other – and humans who understood its life could express love and regard for it, with its encompassing channels of energy that flowed in circuits bringing life and death to individuals.

Leopold's work made a major impact on a then-emerging twentieth-century discourse in environmental ethics, and it also provided resources for the near-mystical spirituality of many who embraced a radical form of environmentalism by the later part of the century. His haunting vision of the dying green fire in the eyes of a mother wolf that as a young man he had hunted down became a catalytic sign and emblem of the death of nature at human hands. Between Leopold's green fire, as it kept burning among those committed to radical action in movements like Earth First! and Greenpeace, and the more law-bound environmentalism of established lobbies like the Sierra Club and the Wilderness Society, twentieth-century environmentalism continued into the twenty-first. It became increasingly clear that the wellspring for the passion that drove public speech and action on behalf of the environment was in large part religious and ethical. Environmentalism, in short, had become one version of nature religion in the lingering shadow of American Transcendentalism.

The Transcendentalists functioned, however, as a switching station for a second form of American nature religion as well. The metaphysical nature religion of the past, encoded in a series of cultural practices that ranged from dowsing, to the casting of magical spells, to the pursuit of astrology, to a plethora of folk behaviors involving correspondences with nature still continued even as it was transformed. Based at least in part on the new religious language that Emerson and the other Transcendentalists helped to make familiar to Americans, this metaphysical form of nature religion was now shaped by more urbanizing and middle-class times, reaching out to embrace an Enlightenment rhetoric of reason and science. All the same, it still encompassed a rural and poorer past. And it encompassed, as well, a moral logic similar to the one that had compelled Thoreau and other Transcendentalists, including Emerson, in anti-slavery directions. By the second half of the nineteenth century, the results were visible in spiritualism, both in its practical and speculative varieties.

Spiritualism flourished in popular and what has become known as "phenomenal" (practical or spirit-manifesting) form after 1848, the year that two upstate New York girls, Kate and Maggie Fox, claimed that they were in contact with a murdered peddler whose remains were buried in the cellar of the ramshackle house their family rented. Along with spiritualist phenomena and practice came elaborate theories of how its seeming miracles were produced: spirits, it turned out, were part of nature. They represented a more refined version of matter, and in certain situations (séances), with the aid of gifted professionals (mediums, who were usually but not always female), their material refinement was visible to grosser human eyes and senses.

The more speculative version of spiritualism, from its inception in 1847 – one year before the fabled communications of the Fox sisters – had from the first provided a self-conscious and sophisticated theology to explain spiritualist phenomena and manifestations. Under the banner of the "harmonial philosophy," Andrew Jackson Davis (1826–1910) and others supplied their own theoretical frame for the ghostly life of phenomenal spiritualists. They did so by means of Enlightenment thought that met and married a metaphysical theory of correspondence in the absence of Christianity. Davis, especially, became an important culture broker, bringing together a Swedenborgian doctrine of correspondence with the "magnetic" or mesmeric theory and practice of Austrian physician Franz Anton Mesmer (1734–1815), based on the belief that there was a universal fluid with mysterious tides operating in all of space.

In effect, harmonialism linked these European concepts to an American popular culture shaped in part by notions of the power of Reason and Right inherited from public discourse in the context of the American Revolution and from a folklorized metaphysicalism that had been handed down. It linked the European concepts, too, to a popular culture shaped in part by the Transcendentalist discourse of correspondence – through the popular speaking tours of Emerson and others, the ubiquitous newspaper reports about them, and the stream of publications by them that kept coming. Harmonialism stressed reform and, in the name of nature, radically equalized the playing field between women and men, even as it also posited something like eternal progress. Always though, nature, not the supernature of Christianity, was God and goal.

Howard Kerr and Charles L. Crow underline the significance of spiritualism for what followed, noting that as conventional religion became subject to a growing fear that it was "untenable," spiritualism itself became a "historical hourglass" through the channel of which "the sands of witchcraft, popular ghost lore, mesmerism, Swedenborgianism, and scientism" poured, "then to disperse into Theosophy and parapsychology" (Kerr and Crow 1983: 4). And, it could be added for a century later in the 1970s, into the New Age movement. Theosophy arose as a spiritualist reform movement in 1875, the year after Russian immigrant Helena P. Blavatsky (1831–1891) and American Colonel Henry S. Olcott (1832–1907) met at a

Vermont farm where they both had gone to investigate reported spiritualist phenomena. The Theosophical Society, which the two founded along with William Q. Judge (1851–1896) and others, announced its object in its bylaws as the collection and diffusion of knowledge concerning the laws of the universe. That in itself sounded scientific enough, except that the preamble to the document advanced the hope of going beyond science into ancient esoteric philosophy. Indeed, the religious character of the theosophical enterprise was clarified even further three years later when leaders of the society articulated two new goals in the context of their now-involvement with Asian religions. Theosophy aspired to promote universal "brotherhood" and to promote as well the study of comparative religions. Theosophists understood all three of their goals in light of an esoteric vision of the secrets of nature, the further reaches of which they were seeking to understand and to make productive in their lives.

It requires only a brief foray into the history of connection between the late nineteenth-century Theosophical Society and the century-later New Age movement to notice the line between earlier Theosophical teachers and later interpreters of the New Age. Moreover, clear lineages aside, the continuity of subject and theme between the two movements points to both as strongly linked and related expressions of the metaphysical form of nature religion. In a context that is linked to this, the small but growing neo-pagan movement of the late twentieth and early twenty-first centuries needs to be noted here. In Wicca and related movements, nature – become personified in the Goddess and her consort – led her devotees into a religious world of both ritual ecstasy and ethical practice that looked to nature as law and guide. Significantly, for all of these movements, the secrets that humans would uncover in nature were secrets with practical application. None of the movements has aimed at knowledge for knowledge's sake. Rather, all of them have looked to metaphysical knowledge of nature as a vehicle of power, as the source of cultural practice to repair and enhance lives. And nowhere did that practice become more urgent and insistent by the late twentieth- and early twenty-first century than in the domain of healing.

This last observation brings us to the third major form of nature religion that was advanced by and in the Transcendentalist milieu. In keeping with Emersonian claims for the powers of nature and, also, for the realized Self, nature religion came to stand for the physicality of the human body itself. Here, in one religious logic, matter remained subject to universal natural laws, the violations of which automatically brought disease and ill health and the observances of which, by contrast, guaranteed health and blessing. The often-repeated dictum "Early to bed, early to rise, makes a man healthy, wealthy, and wise" was, in fact, a tenet of this version of nature religion. Or, at the same time and often for the same people, matter became at once the plastic substance that could be shaped and changed by the power of Mind (with the American Vedanta of oneness proclaiming the ability of the Self to cure disease and attract wealth and blessing).

One version of the logic, therefore, leads to immersion in a series of healing practices that valorize natural law and its results. Thomsonian herbal healing, inherited Native American herbalisms, and related Euro-ethnic herbalisms, all of which preceded the Transcendentalists already expressed this form of conviction, and various forms of herbalism have continued from early America into our own times. Perhaps even more graphic in their physicality and their appeal to the laws of an almighty nature have been the late nineteenth-century modalities of osteopathy and chiropractic. Indeed, early osteopathy arose out of an Enlightenment discourse strongly inflected with mechanistic accents, so that the clockwork regularity of nature as expressed in the bones and their manipulation became testimonies to the God of Reason and Law. And chiropractic, for its part, explained its healing work in language about freeing a mysterious energy called Innate, blocked and trapped in the body through spinal misalignments and subluxations. All the same, both Andrew Taylor Still (1828–1917), the founder of osteopathy, and D.D. Palmer (1845–1913), the founder of chiropractic, knew spiritualism intimately, and they also spoke in an American colloquial style that reflected the ideology of the Enlightenment. Both, significantly, had been magnetic doctors, whose goal was the unblocking of the trapped energies of nature. But both, finally, embraced the optimistic and perfectionist style that Transcendentalism expressed and encouraged, and both, even in their emphasis on physicality, looked to the ultimate powers of Mind. Their century seemingly everywhere made similar connections. Healing modalities from the vegetarianism of Sylvester Graham to the hydrotherapy of a small army of water-cure advocates like Russell T. Trall and Mary Gove Nichols pointed to nature, but also led to speculations about "mind" and, as the late twentieth and twenty-first century would say, about consciousness.

Consciousness itself came to be increasingly understood as part of nature, as a mysterious energy that could be tapped, in effect, as a refined version of matter. Paradoxically, for many, nature was now functioning as a bridge to the immateriality of spirit. A classic paradigm for the situation, and for the new cultural practice of nature religion, exists in homeopathy. As formulated by German physician Samuel Hahnemann (1755–1843), homeopathy, then as now, represented a form of what today would be called "energy medicine," and that in a Western context. As Hahnemann experimented with his new healing modality, he constructed a theoretical frame to explain it based in part on the ancient notion of correspondence, which – as we have already seen – was alive and well in nineteenth-century metaphysical circles. Hahnemann's law of similars, as articulated in his *Organon* (1810), taught that a substance that produced somatic results in a healthy person that were similar to the disease symptoms in a sick individual was the very substance that could heal the disease. Like, in other words, cured like. However, "like" worked according to a second law, Hahnemann's law of infinitesimals. The German doctor and his followers used increasingly greater dilutions or, as they said, "potentizations" of the substance that they were employing in order to heal. Indeed, the potentizations were so zealously executed – for example, up to one-thirtieth of one-millionth of a remedy – that in present-day terms not even a molecule of the original substance remained in the homeopathic medicine. What was it then that remained? An energy trace? An electromagnetic field? Some kind of spiritual signature that interacted with a disease? And how did the remedy actually work? Was it a mysterious spiritual vaccination that operated in a murky halfway land between matter and spirit, between body and cosmic Mind?

Whatever the answers to the theoretical questions, homeopathy developed a series of "provings" for its medicines and, also, an anecdotal trail to demonstrate claims that patients were getting better under homeopathic regimes. It began to gain a following in the United States from the 1830s and as the century progressed became almost the preferred healing modality in the nation, used by perhaps half of the population at a time when the heroic medicine of bleeding, blistering, and calomel, or chloride of mercury (a deadly poison) was the orthodox alternative. Especially important here, homeopathy helped to forge a path for Americans into increasingly "mental" forms of cure. In a tradition beginning with the one-time magnetic doctor Phineas P. Quimby (1802–1866), a self-conscious cadre of healers announced the power of Mind to cure the body – in an American melting pot in which homeopathy, spiritualism, Swedenborgianism, and mesmerism had been blended and stirred well.

Quimby, the clockmaker become mesmerist become mental healer, drew to himself the patients-turned-students who brought to Americans the new religious orientations of Christian Science and New Thought. Quimby, in his lifetime, had at least once invoked the term "Christian science" in the context of discussing his healing practice. But it was the chronically ill Mary Baker Eddy (1821–1910), so thoroughly dependent on his healing influence before his death, who discovered her independence from Quimby through a new emphasis on the Christian gospel, recited for her and others in the late nineteenth century in a different key. Under a platonized Christian rubric that denied the reality of matter, she taught that contact with divine truth and transformation by it could alter the ailing "appearance" of a sick individual; that is, could effect "healthy" changes in the perceived matter of the body. But even as Eddy denied the reality of matter, she exalted nature as the place where Spirit resided. She thought of "man" as the body of God, and continued to identify natural with spiritual laws.

Among Quimby's other patient-students, Warren Felt Evans and Julius and Annetta Dresser moved in a different direction from Eddy, and their form of interaction with the religion of nature came eventually to be known as New Thought. In a movement that greatly admired Emerson and that celebrated the metaphysical doctrine of correspondence, the power of mind to alter nature meant, not an idealism that denied matter, but – in the long shadow of Transcendentalist thinking and of the spiritualist-Swedenborgian-mesmerist model – a vision of mind as continuous with matter. The mental "image" or idea shared real space and time with the afflicted body and could change it for the better. Affirming health was key to *being* health. Conceptions such as this and the plethora of cultural practices that arose from them continued well past the late nineteenth- and early twentieth-century heyday of Christian Science and New Thought. Under the banner of positive thinking and, later, of other versions of visualization and affirmation in the service of healing, the generalized American self-help movement spread widely, seemingly everywhere, into the twenty-first century. A flourishing New Thought movement became only the tip of the cultural iceberg. Popular bookstore sales told the greater story, and so did television talk shows, newspaper feature articles, and popular magazine subjects and sales. Always, mind and thought were (more powerful) parts of nature, and always they could change the embodied state of humans who only saw and practiced the connection. The body, the news was, could be well. And even if its grosser material failed to respond on a cellular level, gifts of spiritual and psychic integration and personal peace could, in their own ways, alter appearances. The nature of nature was, in the ultimate sense, bliss and joy.

The complex Transcendental model of nature religion had led, then, in three different directions, with lines and connections among them. Environmentalism, metaphysical religion, and the physical religion of healing the body had all taken cues from this elite nineteenth-century religious and cultural movement. But, arguably, a fourth direction remained for nature religion, and this direction returns us to the eighteenth-century Enlightenment world of old Europe and the new United States. This world that preceded the Transcendentalists was addressed by them in a new rhetoric and was subsequently transformed by later lineages of American philosophers. Ironically enough perhaps, then, this fourth major direction for the nature religion that followed the Transcendental moment in American religious history returns us to a world of natural religion and theology. In his *Emerson Handbook* (1953; reprint, New York, 1967), literary scholar Frederick Ives Carpenter long ago noticed the connection between

Emerson and the pragmatism of William James (1842–1910), and in *American Religious Thought: A History* (Chicago, 1973), so did religious studies scholar William A. Clebsch. Calling James "the American who would ... refine Emerson's new religious consciousness to the extent of making God essentially man's deity and of making man at home with his humanity" (124), Clebsch read the pragmatic philosopher in ways that underlined that nature, as distinct from supernature, was James' controlling concern. The historical connections were real: Emerson had known James' father, the Swedenborgian theologian Henry James (1811–1882), and had even visited the James household. But the connections of thought and idea, for Clebsch (as for Carpenter), were central. As Emerson before him stressed the overriding importance of direct experience, in religion as in all of life, so, too, did James. With his corridor theory of truth, in which truth opened a route to a series of "rooms" filled with experiences and beliefs that enabled people to live successfully in an often chaotic and even catastrophic world, James hailed religion and its "overbeliefs" when they worked to support human projects and goals. In effect, therefore, the Jamesian stance toward religion saw it as a natural project. It was no accident that James had begun as a medical doctor, had moved from physiological to mental considerations, and had then steered his psychological concerns toward a version of natural religion.

Without James' medical-psychological background, later pragmatic philosophers agreed about natural religion or – in the language invoked here – nature religion. Charles Sanders Peirce (1839–1914), a mathematician and scientist, who before James had used the term pragmatism and propounded an earlier version of the pragmatic philosophy, had been a supernaturalist. The same was clearly not the case, however, for the Spanish-born poet and philosopher George Santayana (1863–1952) who became James's Harvard colleague. Even as he emphasized the rational and imaginative prowess of the mind, Santayana situated it squarely in the physicality of the body and spoke of "animal faith." In his *Realms of Being* (1942; reprint, New York, 1972), he argued that the home of spirit lay in matter, for spirit "must be the spirit of some body, the consciousness of some natural life" (843). Meanwhile, John Dewey (1859–1952), who – as Sydney E. Ahlstrom reported in *Theology in America* (Indianapolis, 1967) – had once hailed Emerson as "the one citizen of the New World fit to have his name uttered in the same breath with that of Plato" (59) brought to his philosophy of instrumentalism a new and uncompromising statement of natural religion. With his conviction that truth was an evolutionary phenomenon and a tool for human labor, in his classic work *A Common Faith* (1934; reprint, New Haven, 1975). Dewey argued strenuously against supernaturalism and constructed in its stead a natural religion that, as Emerson and the earlier pragmatists had done, worked to bring idealism down to Earth. Under the banner of the American democratic ideal, he thought that natural piety could "rest upon a just sense of nature as the whole of which we are parts, while it also recognizes that we are parts that are marked by intelligence and purpose" (25).

Evolutionary thinking became a still more explicit path into natural religion in the series of late nineteenth-century thinkers who took on the Darwinian manifesto. After the appearance of Charles Darwin's *Origin of Species* (1859) and its subsequent permeation of intellectual discourse, the theory of evolution through natural selection provided a frame for conceptions that privileged organicism and turned distinctly away from metaphysics. Liberal philosophers and theologians alike worked out intellectual strategies to come to terms with the new prestige of evolutionary science, and in so doing they resituated themselves in what distinctly looked like the world of nature religion. The philosopher, historian, and scientific popularizer John Fiske (1842–1901), as a leading example, was deeply impressed by English evolutionist Herbert Spencer who had promoted a popularization of the Darwinian thesis that totalized it to interpret human (social) history as well as the history of nature. Fiske's *Outlines of Cosmic Philosophy* (1874) argued subsequently for an immanent God who was manifest in the life of the phenomenal world. Nature, for Fiske, was the revelation of God that could be considered true, and for him the perfection of humankind was the goal of natural evolution. Others, however, articulated cosmologies that slid them into agnosticism, free thought, and the ideological humanism that came to be known, as in the Free Religious Association after 1867, as the "Religion of Humanity."

With a self-conscious anti-Christian and antimetaphysical stance, members of the FRA, along with adherents to similar groups such as the Society for Ethical Culture and the National Liberal League, sounded in many ways like Enlightenment deists. America's most famous freethinker Robert Ingersoll (1833–1899), the Congregational minister's son who earned himself the epithet "the great agnostic," turned the earlier Emersonian proposition that nature was all that was "not me" upside down. Nature meant human nature, and the religion of nature, including the landscape delights that surrounded humans and their built environments, ended in humankind. Yet even as he pronounced, in ringing terms, his rhetorical trinities of "Liberty, Fraternity, and Equality," of "Observation, Reason, and Experience," and of "Man, Woman, and Child," like nature religionists from Puritan times to the present, he could find the biblical book that lay outside the mind and in the environment, and he declared in favor of nature in sometimes lyrical terms.

The inclusion of Enlightenment-style natural religion and natural theology under the rubric of nature religion, of course, presents its share of difficulties. For one problem, religion on an Enlightenment model tends to lack strong practical expression. Natural theology has mostly been the province of philosophers and theologians who have sought to clarify belief and thought. As cultural practice, it has been diffuse. We can point, for example, to only a few humanist and freethinking organizations that promote it in organizational terms, and – unlike other phenomena surveyed here (for example, environmentalism, magical practice, various healing modalities) – its symbolic expression in ordinary cultural life is hard to demonstrate. Thus, as *religion* it limps. For another problem, natural theology as an enterprise arises out of a negative characterization of the supernatural more than out of a positive preoccupation with nature itself. In other words, it comes trailing a long history of Christian ideology and antipathy to it. Yet the nod to the Enlightenment, with its natural religion and theology, has its compensating value for any survey of American nature religion. Its glaring weakness regarding institutional forms – its absence of nature "churches" – is only a stronger version of a glaring weakness that may be found repeatedly in this narrative. Cultural practice may be pointed to aplenty, but how and when does it stop being useful to describe it as religious? Where, in fact, does the definitional line end? Where does religion stop and something else begin?

The nod to the Enlightenment, however, has another value. It offers a useful caveat regarding the easy and exclusive identification of nature religion with benign landscapes and/or environmental activism. Like the other great theological terms that have haunted the Western mind – "God" and "man" – nature has no clearly visible boundaries. The history of nature religion, from the time of the seventeenth-century multicultural contact culture that later became the United States to our own time, is a contested history. Both the contest and the undervisibility of the boundaries argue for the wisdom of being content with the broad-gauged Transcendental model as an interpretive trope for making hypothetical sense of nature religion. Neither purely environmental, nor simply neo-pagan, Goddess-oriented, and/or metaphysical, nor primarily deistic and rationalistic in an Enlightenment anti-supernaturalistic framework, this model suggests that to invoke the rubric of nature religion encompasses all of the above and very much more.

Perhaps the concept itself makes the most sense in a political context, and this in the end may be the strongest argument for continuing to employ the term despite the fragility of the phenomenon. Put simply, nature religion is a *bon mot* that has arisen in the very multicultural late twentieth and early twenty-first century as a sounding center for civil discourse. It offers a "common" that can be shared – both as a concept and as a condition that all must deal with, whatever their multicultural pasts and presents. Contra a "civil religion" that looks to a Jewish-Christian biblical revelation and a European Enlightenment ideology – both of them the historic domain of a privileged Anglo-Protestant leadership community – and contra a "public religion" that secularizes the terms of that discourse to offer a mediating ethical restatement of Christian and Enlightenment values, nature religion begins not with history but with what stands over against it. The "against-ness" is there for all, as a something that must be seriously confronted, something requiring – demanding – response. Nature religion, as an idea and phenomenon, reiterates democratic values, to be sure, by acknowledging the essential similarity and equality of human experience embedded in the reality that constitutes nature. But it also acknowledges forces and factors that delimit the human project – aspects of life over which humans, literally, have no control and before which they must bow. Bowing, of course, is one central and important act of worship. Bowing can also promote acts of public and communal reconciliation.

Catherine L. Albanese

Further Reading
Adler, Margot. *Drawing Down the Moon: Witches, Druids, Goddess-Worshippers, and Other Pagans in America Today*. Boston: Beacon Press, 1986 (rev. edn).

Albanese, Catherine L. *Reconsidering Nature Religion*. Harrisburg, PA: Trinity Press International, 2001.

Albanese, Catherine L. *Nature Religion in America: From the Algonkian Indians to the New Age*. Chicago: University of Chicago Press, 1990.

Boller, Paul E., Jr. *American Thought in Transition: The Impact of Evolutionary Naturalism, 1865–1900*. Chicago: Rand McNally, 1965.

Cohen, Michael P. *The Pathless Way: John Muir and American Wilderness*. Madison: University of Wisconsin Press, 1984.

Emerson, Ralph Waldo. *Nature* (1836). In Ralph Waldo Emerson. *The Collected Works of Ralph Waldo Emerson*, vol. 1. *Nature, Addresses, and Lectures*. Alfred R. Ferguson, et al., eds. Cambridge: Harvard University Press, Belknap Press, 1971.

Fuller, Robert C. *Alternative Medicine and American Religious Life*. New York: Oxford University Press, 1989.

Jefferson, Thomas. *Notes on the State of Virginia* (1784). New York: Harper & Row, Harper Torchbooks, 1964 (reprint edition).

Kerr, Howard and Charles L. Crow, eds. *The Occult in America: New Historical Perspectives*. Urbana: University of Illinois Press, 1983.

Leopold, Aldo. *A Sand County Almanac and Sketches Here and There* (1949). Oxford: Oxford University Press, 1981 (reprint edition).

Nash, Roderick. *Wilderness and the American Mind*. New Haven: Yale University Press, 1932.

Thoreau, Henry D. *Walden.* J. Lyndon Shanley, ed. Princeton, NJ: Princeton University Press, 1971.

See also: Bioregionalism; Bioregionalism and the North American Bioregional Congress; Book of Nature; Celestine Prophecy; Deep Ecology; Deism; Earth First! and the Earth Liberation Front; Emerson, Ralph Waldo; Environmental Ethics; Greenpeace; Leopold, Aldo; Muir, John; Native American Spirituality; Nature Religion; New Age; Paganism (various); Radical Environmentalism; Religious Studies and Environmental Concern; Romanticism (various); Sierra Club; Snyder, Gary; Thoreau, Henry David; Transcendentalism; Wicca; Wilderness Society.

Ndembu Religion (South-central Africa)

With *The Forest of Symbols: Aspects of Ndembu Ritual* and subsequent ethnographies of the ritual life of the Ndembu of Zambia, British anthropologist Victor Turner embarked on what is still to this day one of the most innovative series of symbolic analyses in anthropology. Turner especially focused on rituals of initiation, divination, hunting and therapeutic rituals, and other religious processes in the context of the savannah cultures of South Central Africa. As indicated by the title of Turner's monograph which is itself taken from *Correspondances*, a poem on nature by Baudelaire, the natural environment plays a very important part in the lives and ritual cycles of the Ndembu.

The Ndembu of Northwest Zambia (formerly Northern Rhodesia) are part of a larger Lunda-related cultural complex that spreads out over the southern part of the Democratic Republic of Congo (formerly Zaïre), Angola and Zambia. This Lunda world has its core in *Kool*, the historical Lunda (Ruund) heartland in the province of Katanga, Congo. The Lunda, Ndembu, and other related groups, live in a varied environment of multiple microecological niches: plateau soils of clay, sand plains and rolling hills of wooded savannah, grass plains, shrub lands, woodlands, and gallery forests that grow along the numerous streams and rivers. Nature, in its rich variety, is an omnipresent fact of Lunda life. It constitutes the environmental horizon of Lunda experience, it patterns the social activities, the practical knowledge and the gendered labor divisions that rhythm daily life; it structures the individual life cycle from birth to death; and it offers the raw material that is "good to think with" in the production of symbolic and practical knowledge that is generated in ritual activities. As such, the natural environment provides a topological, projective space, both structured by and structuring the way in which the Lunda perceive their own body, their social relations, and their relations with the surrounding environment and cosmos.

Animals, but to an even greater extent also trees, offer a rich lived-in model to symbolize and signify essential Lunda notions of individual (gendered) health and social well-being, of the union and mediation of male and female in regenerative sexuality, of social reproduction through the creation and sustaining of kinship categories and lineage continuity, and of the political realities of the Lunda world. An example of the rich symbolism provided by trees among the Ndembu is offered in Turner's classic analysis of the "milk tree" (*mudyi* in Ndembu, *muwudi* in Lunda vernacular; Apocynaceae, Dyplorrynchus condilocarpon). The milk tree, conspicuous for its white latex, plays a crucial role in girls' puberty ritual (*Nkang'a*). Ndembu women attribute several meanings to this tree: it stands for human breast milk and thus highlights the metaphorical patterning of the female body, symbolizing the nurturing bond between mother and child. Secondly, Ndembu women describe the milk tree as "the tree of a mother and her child," thus shifting the biological reference of breast-feeding to a wider social tie of profound significance in domestic relations and in the structure of the larger Ndembu community, namely the principle of matriliny (itself denoted by the word *ivumu*, womb) with its underlying notions of unity and inclusiveness. Beyond that, the milk tree also symbolizes the total system of interrelations between groups and persons that make up Ndembu society. At its highest level of abstraction, therefore, the milk tree stands for the unity and continuity of Ndembu society as a whole.

Trees, however, do not only signify female physical and social reproductive qualities. Among the Lunda, the central metaphor of the tree may also express masculinity and male life-giving powers through references to a tree's more vertical qualities of erectness, hardness, stiffness and rootedness (and its manifold associations with the rising sun, the rooster, the hunter's trap, the bow and other "masculine" features). In growing toward the status of senior elder, one becomes more tree-like, rooted in one place. The process of becoming an elder goes together with the acquiring of wisdom, exemplified by the qualities of erectness and immobility that are so typical of a tree. The tree-like immobility of the elder, most fully embodied by the royal title-holder, makes present the ideologically important unchanging continuity of the societal order, over and against the transformations of society as it is lived in everyday life. This is also one of the meanings implied by the invocations that Lunda ritual therapists make to the *kapwiip* tree (Leguminosae, *Swartzia madagascariensis*). In addressing this shrub-like tree, considered to be "the elder of all trees" because of its "bridging" qualities between male and female, left and right, red and white, Lunda therapists address the unchanging fixed normality to which the tree – and the elder – testifies through its immobility. This is also the reason why the Lunda king, as ultimate elder, as living ancestor and as both father *and* mother to his people, is identified with the *kapwiip* tree. In Lunda and Ndembu culture political title-holders, like this tree, are both root and fruit, male and female, phallus and womb, genitor and genitrix. As such, they also exemplify the structural tension which lies embedded in the complementary opposition between men and women, masculine and feminine, agnatic and uterine, virilocality and matrilineage, that underpins Lunda society as a whole. Therefore, the image of the tree, and the image of the elder as tree, is deeply political: through its similar capacity to bridge between the complementary oppositions that pervade Lunda society, the royal body, like trees, assures the interjoining of individual, social group, and cosmos and thereby maintains and perpetuates the ideal cultural order.

At the same time the image of the tree and, by extension, the land, becomes the means by which one's place in the social landscape is not only "rooted" in an ancestral space-time but also in a material historicity. The tree and, in particular, the *muyoomb* tree (Amnacardiaceae, *Lennea welwichii*), planted as a living ancestral shrine in the center of villages, seems to be one of the Lunda's preferred means for the production of historically situated locality. Trees do not only convey meanings of immobility or qualities of bridging and joining. The tree simultaneously conveys the *combination* of the idea of a central and static nexus with images of interconnection, knotting, and hence, mobility (as spatialized in the pathways leading into and away from each village). Therefore, in a seeming paradox, the Lunda notion of "place" (*pool*), although drawing on a pool of meaning related to rootedness, fixity, bridging, tying, and knotting, allows for movement through space, as the centuries-long Lunda history of migration and conquest exemplifies. Although place and a sense of locality and belonging are strongly situated in socially and spatially defined communities, they are also in a sense transportable and repetitive. As such, locality can be moved through space, recreated, or repeated in different spaces by planting new *miyoomb* trees and thus creating or growing memory, history, and belonging. Physical and metaphorical roots can thus emerge out of any social and material landscape, thereby allowing the transformation of forest into village, turning the subjects of newly conquered, dominated space into localized (i.e., Lunda) subjects and rooting the present place into the ancestral past while tying it to Lunda history. Simultaneously, the image of the tree strongly suggests that the production of culture and history is underpinned by a history of natural rhythm and processes of gestation, germination, and growth.

Filip De Boeck

Further Reading

De Boeck, Filip. "The Rootedness of Trees: Place as Cultural and Natural Texture in Rural Southwest Congo." In Nadia Lovell, ed. *Locality and Belonging*. London: Routledge, 1998, 25–52.

De Boeck, Filip. "Of Trees and Kings: Politics and Metaphor Among the Aluund of Southwestern Zaire." *American Ethnologist* 21:3 (1994), 451–73.

De Boeck, Filip and René Devisch. "Ndembu, Luunda and Yaka Divination Compared: From Representation and Social Engineering to Embodiment and Worldmaking." *Journal of Religion in Africa* 24:2 (1994), 98–133.

Kopytoff, Igor. "The Internal African Frontier: The Making of African Political Culture." In Igor Kopytoff, ed. *The African Frontier: The Reproduction of Traditional African Societies*. Bloomington and Indianapolis: Indiana University Press, 1987, 3–84.

Pritchett, James A. *The Lunda-Ndembu: Style, Change, and Social Transformation in South Central Africa*. Madison, WI: The University of Wisconsin Press, 2001.

Turner, Victor. *Revelation and Divination in Ndembu Ritual*. Ithaca and London: Cornell University Press, 1975.

Turner, Victor. *The Drums of Affliction: A Study of Religious Processes among the Ndembu of Zambia*. Oxford: Oxford University Press, 1968.

Turner, Victor. *The Forest of Symbols: Aspects of Ndembu Ritual*. Ithaca and London: Cornell University Press, 1967.

See also: Anthropologists; African Religions and Nature Conservation; Congo River Watershed; Nyau – A Closed Association (Central Africa); Pygmies (Mbuti foragers) and Bila Farmers of the Ituri Forest (Democratic Republic of the Congo); Ritual; Ritualizing and Anthropology; Traditional Ecological Knowledge.

Neo-paganism and Ethnic Nationalism in Eastern Europe

Neo-paganism in Eastern Europe is based on a wide range of religious, cultural and political ideas and practices. In Russia it is represented by numerous, mainly urban, small-size ethnic Russian groups and cultural associations (in Moscow, the Moscow Slavic Pagan community, the "Russian Warriors," the Koliada Viatichei community, the Church of Nav', the Satja-Veda Aryan community; in St. Petersburg, the Union of Veneds, the Tezaurus Spiritual Union, the School of Wolves; and the Sviatogor Warrior Center in Kolomna, the Kaluga Slavic community in Kaluga, Jiva Temple of Ingliia in Omsk, the Tur pagan community in Izhevsk, among others). There are also neo-pagan communities and organizations among certain ethnically non-Russian peoples in republics within the Russian Federation: these include the "Oshmarii-Chimarii" community in the Mari El Republic, the "Udmurt Vos" community in Udmurtiia, the "Erzian Master" political party in Mordovia, the "Chuvash National Religion" in Chuvashia, the Tengrianist movement in Tatarstan, and groups in the Komi Republic and Northern Ossetia-Alaniia. The Native Ukrainian National Faith (RUNvira) is a network of communities in Ukraine which competes with many other autonomous neo-pagan communities like "Pravoslavie" in Kyiv, the Community of the Pagan Faith in Kharkiv, and others. The "Latvju dievturu sadraudze" is an umbrella neo-pagan organization in Latvia, and the "Romuva" community in Lithuania. Several neo-pagan communities and cultural organizations are also known in Belarus.

In Russia, Ukraine, Belarus and Latvia, most neo-pagan groups represent a radical form of the associated ethnic nationalist movements. In contrast to their Central and West European counterparts, local neo-pagans are mainly concerned with revitalizing traditional folk cultures, languages and identities, which are threatened with disappearance due to Russification, globalization, or both processes. Hence, there is an emphasis on the notion of "cultural ecology," an approach that takes as its primary value the maintenance of the "purity" of ethnic or national culture. East European neo-pagans (Lithuanians aside) aspire to develop ethnic nationalist self-awareness ("Russianness" among Russians, "Ukrainianness" in Ukraine, etc.) and to spread it to the general public through fiction, religious literature, the mass media, and school curricula. Well-educated urban intellectuals (poets, writers, linguists, folklorists, philosophers, archeologists, ethnographers) play a prominent role among the leadership of neo-pagan groups, systematizing folk beliefs and developing consistent religious teachings which can be presented as the primordial ethnic or national religions. They also introduce new religious rituals, establish their own sacred sites and sanctuaries, and serve the rites and holidays which they represent as old and authentic ones. Besides references to local historical sources which are usually scarce and fragmentary, East European neo-pagans borrow from Celtic, German and Scandinavian folk traditions, Zoroastrianism, Vedic traditions of ancient India, as well as occultism and Theosophy. Russian and Ukrainian neo-pagans highly appreciate the "Book of Vles" which they treat as an authentic pre-Christian Slavic chronicle. After a paleographic examination, the document has proved to be a fake. It was fabricated by Russian emigres (assumedly by the chemical engineer Yuri P. Miroliubov) in California in the early 1950s: they did their best to identify the Slavic ancestors with the prehistoric "Aryan" (i.e., Indo-European) pastoralists who roamed throughout the Eurasian steppe between Mongolia and the Carpathian Mountains led by the forefather Oryi, according to the "Book of Vles."

A widespread component of contemporary East-European neo-pagan movements is their hostility toward universal cosmopolitan religions, which they accuse of authoritarianism, intolerance toward cultural variability, anthropocentrism, and responsibility for the destruction of the natural environment and of traditional culture. Participation in a green movement, however, remains limited: neo-pagans are nationalists more than environmentalists, and they emphasize cultural survival most of all. There is still no major shift toward activity for the protection of the natural environment although such concern is sometimes expressed. Russian and Ukrainian neo-pagans often treat Christianity as an evil ideology introduced by "the Jews" to subjugate all peoples, and especially Russians and Ukrainians. Similarly, Finnish- and Turkic-speaking Chuvash neo-pagans in the Middle Volga River region view Russian Orthodoxy as an ideology of enslavement (the same attitude is expressed by the Tatar Tengrianists toward Islam). Yet, while rejecting Western Christianity, certain Russian neo-pagans are willing to reconcile themselves with Russian Orthodoxy, which they treat as a younger branch of the primordial Russian religion.

At the same time, neo-pagans have been influenced by the universal religions to the extent that some of them are seeking to develop ethnic monotheist traditions, such as Dievturiba in Latvia, RUNVira in Ukraine, or the Russian Religion developed by Viktor Kandyba in Russia. Others (such as Koliada Viatichei) retain polytheistic beliefs; but many reject local variability in an attempt to create a uniform ethnic faith (sometimes also monotheist, for example, in Chuvashia). This trend is especially evident in the Republics of the Middle Volga Region.

Sometimes a "cultural ecology" orientation is taken to an extreme, resulting in biological and cultural racisms such as the "Aryan ideology" popular among some ethnic Russian, Ukrainian, Belorussian and Latvian groups. There is a close relationship between a neo-Nazi-like political extremism and this sort of neo-paganism which promotes "cultural ecology" at the expense of practical environmentalism and feminism, albeit an articulation of a "healthy way of life" and of harmony with nature is common to all the neo-pagan groups. Certain militant Russian, Ukrainian and Belorussian neo-pagans have also established schools for "warrior training" where they teach wrestling and battle skills, both with and without traditional weapons (sword, battle-ax, shield, and the like).

Some of them are obviously in contact with and borrow a lot from the Nordic neo-pagans such as Odinists and Ásatrú people (Aryan identity, Arctic homeland, runic magic, et al.). Julius Evola's and Herman Wirth's ideas are also highly appreciated and adapted to the Russian environment by the radical neo-pagan Russian nationalists.

By contrast, the less nationalistic and more liberal the movement, the more it tends to promote feminism and environmentalism. The latter are especially characteristic for the Lithuanian neo-pagans, in part because ethnic Lithuanians make up a dominant majority in Lithuania and see no threat to their culture and language from anywhere. Such nature-oriented values are shared by the Tezaurus Spiritual Union among ethnic Russians and, especially, by the Middle Volga Region neo-pagan movements. Harmony with nature and rejection of consumerism are central to the Koliada Viatichei faith, the teaching of Dobroslav (a form of Russian neo-paganism which is based on national socialism), the Ukrainian "Pravoslavia" movement, and some others. Certain movements focus mainly on human health and self-treatment; the Porfirii Ivanov's "Detka" teaching is the most popular of them comprising a few dozen thousand followers.

Victor A. Shnirelman

Further Reading

Shnirelman, Victor A. " 'Christians, Go Home!' " A Revival of Neo-Paganism between the Baltic Sea and Transcaucasia (an overview)." *Journal of Contemporary Religions* 17:2 (2002), 197–211.

Shnirelman, Victor A. "Perun, Svarog and Others: The Russian Neo-Paganism in Search of Itself." *Cambridge Anthropology* 21:3 (1999–2000), 18–36.

Shnirelman, Victor A. "Russian Neo-Pagan Myths and Antisemitism." *Analysis of Current Trends in Antisemitism* 13. Jerusalem: The Hebrew University of Jerusalem, 1998.

Vovina, Olessia P. "Building the Road to the Temple: Religion and National Revival in the Chuvash Republic." *Nationalities Papers* 28:4 (2000), 695–706.

See also: Fascism; Heathenry – Ásatrú; Neo-Paganism in Ukraine; Odinism; Oshmarii-Chimarii (Mari El Republic, Russia); Paganism and Judaism; Paganism – A Jewish Perspective; Russian Mystical Philosophy.

Neo-Paganism in Ukraine

Though interest in pre-Christian religion can be found throughout the pre-Soviet and Soviet eras, modern neo-paganism, or contemporary Ukrainian "native faith," emerged in Ukraine in the aftermath of Gorbachevan *perestroika* and has undergone its most dramatic growth since the early and mid-1990s. Ukrainian *ridnovira* (literally, "native faith") includes such groups as *Pravoslavia* (Orthodoxy, or Right-worship), *Obiednannia Ridnoviriv Ukraïny* (Association of Ukrainian Native-Faithers), *Sobor Ridnoï Ukraïnskoï Viry* (Synod of the Native Ukrainian Faith), *Triitsia* (Trinity), *Perunova Rat'* (Perun's Host), *Ladovira*, and devotees of the goddess Berehynia. Many, though not all, of these identify themselves as *yazychnyks*, the term customarily used for pre-Christian animist and polytheist ("pagan" or "heathen") practices.

Ukrainian neo-paganism and native faith derive from several general sources, including 1) folkloristics, ethnography, and the study of traditional music, arts, and medicine; 2) the study of Ukrainian prehistory, including speculations on prehistoric cosmology and astroarcheology, debates about the ethnocultural affiliation of the Trypillian, Scythian, and proto-Indo-European or "Aryan" archeological cultures, and writings on controversial texts such as the *Book of Veles*; and 3) the neo-pagan revivalism of émigré writers Volodymyr Shaian and Lev Sylenko. The majority of Ukrainian neo-pagans take their modern founder to be Lviv University Sanskritologist Volodymyr Shaian (1908–1974), author of *Faith of Our Ancestors*, who in the 1930s began advocating the revival of Ukrainian paganism and who worked toward that goal, with minimal success, in Britain and later Canada. Shaian saw Ukrainians, alongside other Slavs, as the central branch of the "Aryan race" and called for a "pan-Aryan renaissance" opposed to the Germanocentric Aryan theories informing Hitler's Reich. The best-known leader of contemporary Ukrainian neo-paganism is Halyna Lozko (*Volkhvynia Zoreslava*), a philologist, folklorist, and university lecturer in religious studies. Lozko and her associates founded the Svitovyd Center for the Rebirth of Ukrainian Culture, the School of the Native Faith (in 1995), the journal *Svaroh*, and, in 1998, the Native Faith Association of Ukraine (ORU). The ORU has been prominent in the effort to recognize the *Book of Veles* (*Velesova Knyha*) as an authentic pre-Christian text, despite its dismissal as a late-modern forgery by most scholars. Many neo-pagans claim the *Book of Veles* as their holy writ, seeing in it an ancient manual of hymns and prayers, myths, sermons, theological tracts, political invectives, and fragments of historical narrative covering the movements of the ancestors of the "Rusyches" or "Oriians" across vast territories between the Indian sub-continent and the Carpathian mountains over some fifteen centuries. The text's emphasis on ethnic or cultural identity amidst a world of enemies has arguably resulted in a deemphasis (for neo-pagans) of the ecological concerns that marked the upsurge of Ukrainian ethnic nationalism in the post-Chornobyl late 1980s. Neo-pagans such as Lozko see the assertion of Ukrainian ethnic identity as equal, if not greater, in importance to the preservation and defense of nature. The two are seen as inherently intertwined and equally threatened by economic and cultural globalization, cosmopolitan Westernization, and the legacies of "Sovietization," Russification, and several centuries of "Christianization." The ORU thus works to prevent the "ruination of the ethnosphere," which is seen as a necessary component of the Earth's biosphere.

A related stream of native faith is *RUNVira*, an acronym for the Native Ukrainian National Faith. *Runvists* consider themselves a "reformed" native faith, a transformation and completion of the original Ukrainian polytheism in favor of a scientifically grounded monotheism, or panentheistic monism, centered around

Dazhboh, an impersonal representation of the life-giving energy of the cosmos. Founded in North America by Lev Sylenko, a one-time member of Shaian's Order of the Knights of the Solar God, RUNVira takes as its bible Sylenko's 1427-page *Maha Vira*, which purports to be an 11,000-year history of Ukraine and a prophetic message for a new era. Small groups of *runvists* appeared in the 1960s and 1970s in Ukrainian émigré communities in North America, Britain, and Australia, and the "Oriiana" Temple of Mother Ukraine was established as the religion's center in New York State's Catskill mountains. The first RUNVira congregation in Ukraine was registered by Kyiv authorities in 1991, and by the end of the 1990s there were about fifty officially registered and at least another dozen unregistered RUNVira congregations across the country, ranging in size from a few families to over a hundred members. A split within the international RUNVira movement has resulted in the existence of rival associations of Ukrainian *runvists*, with some moving towards a more generic and eclectic form of Ukrainian native faith while others have retained a strict interpretation of the writings of the founder. Sylenko himself remains alive but in poor health in New York State.

An assortment of other nature-centered, cosmo-ecological, and theosophical movements overlap with the native faith milieu. These include the Ukrainian Spiritual Republic (*Ukraïns'ka Dukhovna Respublika*), founded by science-fiction writer and mystic Oles' Berdnyk; the followers of nature mystic and teacher Porfyrii Korniiovych Ivanov, founder of a system of natural health and philosophy which has spread from rural eastern Ukraine to other parts of the former Soviet Union; a large but diffuse "Vedic" movement; and a range of writers and publications, sometimes called "Aryosophists," who have been propagating the (scientifically unsupported) theory that Ukrainians are the most direct descendants of prehistoric "Aryans."

Ukrainian neo-paganism and native faith finds its main base of adherents among nationally oriented ethnic Ukrainians of higher than average educational levels. Sociologists suggest there are over 90,000 Ukrainian neo-pagans and *ridnovirs* (or 0.2 percent of the population), though active community membership appears much smaller. There is a broader interest in topics related to paganism and Ukrainian prehistory, and in the revival of folk calendar customs connected to pre-Christian practices (such as the midwinter Koliada celebrations and midsummer Kupala rites), which frequently take place within a Christian context but are now being reclaimed as pagan festivals. Membership in neo-pagan and native faith groups overlaps with that of folk and traditional music revival groups, Cossack associations, traditional martial arts groups, and nationalist and ultra-nationalist political groups. Though environmental activism is rare among Ukrainian neo-pagans (as it is among Ukrainians more generally), a concern for nature is often voiced as a primary motivating factor for the conversion to a native faith perspective. This concern manifests as a general desire to return to a time when people lived in direct relationship and harmony with nature, rooted in the land and in a sense of communal honor and self-respect, familial and community ritual, and responsibility toward one's ancestors.

Adrian Ivakhiv

Further Reading
Ivakhiv, Adrian. "In Search of Deeper Identities: Neo-paganism and Native Faith in Contemporary Ukraine." *Nova Religio* (forthcoming, 2004).
Shnirelman, Victor A. " 'Christian! Go home!': A Revival of Neo-Paganism between the Baltic Sea and Trans-caucasia." *Journal of Contemporary Religion* 17:2 (2002), 197–211.

See also: Druids and Druidry; Fascism; Heathenry – Ásatrú; Odinism; Oshmarii-Chimarii (Mori El Republic, Russia; Neo-paganism and Ethnic Nationalism in Eastern Europe; Paganism (various); Russian Mystical Philosophy.

Neo-Wessex Archeology

Neo-Wessex (named after a region of southern England rich in Neolithic monuments) is a term used to distinguish a number of archeologists who advocate the interpretation and recovery of the mental states of past peoples, especially in relation to prehistoric ideas of place, or landscape. These archeologists consider the landscape within which prehistoric peoples once dwelt, along with the built monuments it contained, to have not only reflected those people's belief systems and social structures, but also to have played an active role in their ongoing creation and perpetuation. Influenced by the hermeneutics of philosophers such as Martin Heidegger, Hans-George Gadamer and Paul Ricoeur, as well as by theoretical currents within archeology that attempt to interpret the past in ways transcending a purely materialistic framework, Neo-Wessex archeology emerged in the early 1990s advocating a more emphatic, less "scientistic," approach to material culture. This interpretative approach, which includes attempting to "read" the past subjectively as well as actively engage with the cognitive (even experiential) states of prehistoric peoples, has resulted in a number of methodological experiments that are open to the recovery of past religious experience, meaning, and change.

This approach rests upon the assumption that the landscape in prehistory held a cognitive dimension, a collection of meanings (myths, rituals, normative precedents, etc.), which extended its value far beyond concerns with land usage of a solely utilitarian or materialist nature. In addition, it is hypothesized that such an infused understanding of the surrounding world was the cognitive framework through which all of life's activities were played out, be they primarily environmental, biological, socio-political, or religious. Hence, this ritualistic understanding filtered and permeated each and every daily action. As the landscape was modified by human activity, through the creation of monuments, graves, paths, and places of habitation, etc., its form was molded to further reflect and reinforce the preexisting layers of meaning. However, such modifications to the surrounding landscape necessarily affected its cognitive reading, and therefore not only did the modified environment reflect extant social forms and belief systems, but over time it also came to exert additional new elements of its own. As the landscape changed and people developed new ways of interacting with their surroundings, the meanings it held for its inhabitants changed also and, in turn, these reinterpretations were projected back onto the lived geography.

One of the aims of the Neo-Wessex archeologists is the hermeneutical recovery of this process, arrived at through the examination of a prehistoric people's material remains, the ancient geography they existed within, and possible relationships between the two. The interpretive tools used to establish such elusive meaning extend far beyond the hard sciences and include generalized anthropological and humanistic principles, comparative ethno-historical evidence, and even personal emphatic insight. The imaginative hypotheses that are critically applied to the material culture thus have their own history, especially the comparative ethno-historical analogies all of which come from their own historical contexts. This is especially true of the founding premise that prehistoric space was mediated and ritualized space, existentially significant and permeating all other cultural and environmental relations, an idea appropriated partly from ethnographic research on the Australian Aborigines.

One result of this stress on the importance of systems of belief and perception in the interpretation of all aspects of past culture has been a growing awareness of the central part religion played in the worldview and actions of past peoples. It is the realization that for many traditional cultures social and spiritual meaning was contained within the lived landscape and permeated all experience that has caused purely environmental and economically functional explanations of why people acted and why culture changed to be deemed insufficient. Economy, biology, and politics are seen as having been indistinguishable from the essentially religious systems of meaning that encompassed them. Accordingly, the Neo-Wessex approach allows a reconciliation of the polarity between functional/environmental utility and systems of belief/ideology that archeologists have often been wont to project backwards in time onto the cultures they study. Advocates of the new perspective attempt to free modern reconstructions of the past from just such an overly rationalistic bias based upon modern premises of secularization, materialism, and functionalism and to produce less limited, more imaginative visions of prehistoric culture: visions perhaps more true to how those people may have once perceived themselves.

The researchers following a Neo-Wessex approach to landscape are varied in both their focus and the degree to which they commit themselves to the rather abstract outline given above. The classic Neo-Wessex approach to landscape is provided by Christopher Tilley.

Julian Droogan

Further Reading
Barrett, John. *Fragments from Antiquity: An Archaeology of Social Life in Britain, 2900–1200 BC*. Oxford: Blackwell, 1994.
Bradley, Richard. *The Significance of Monuments*. London: Routledge, 1998.
Edmonds, Mark. *Ancestral Geographies of the Neolithic: Landscape, Monuments and Memory*. London: Routledge, 1999.
Tilley, Christopher. *A Phenomenology of Landscape: Places, Paths and Monuments*. Oxford: Berg Publishers, 1994.
Tilley, Christopher. *Material Culture and Text: The Art of Ambiguity*. London: Routledge, 1991.

See also: Paleolithic Art; Paleolithic Religions; Stone Circles; Stonehenge; Trees – as Religious Architecture.

Nepal

A pervasive and misleading mythology about religion and nature in Nepal – and the interrelationship between the two – has developed in "Western" popular culture over the last three or four decades. This particular vision usually depicts Nepal as a natural and spiritual paradise, in which a profoundly devout people with deep spiritual links to nature live in blissful harmony with the surrounding near-pristine environment.

Whilst many Nepalese are indeed deeply religious and the beauty and power of their natural surroundings is ubiquitous, the realities of the situation are nonetheless typically very different to those sketched above. In many places deforestation and pollution have sorely degraded the environment, a circumstance that reflects ambivalence toward the natural world on the part of many Nepalese. This ambivalence is arguably also evident in certain of their core religious beliefs, and appears to have evolved from the often far from idyllic character of the Nepalese peoples' actual experience of nature.

Altitude and climate severely limit the scope for agriculture in much of the country, and although 90 percent of the population is estimated to be involved in agriculture, this is largely on a subsistence basis, with famine a constant specter for many. For mountain and hill dwellers freezing temperatures and avalanche are a genuine source of danger in the winter, whilst monsoon mud and landslide take an annual toll in the hillside villages. Although not as prone to dramatic cataclysm, the jungles of the Terai were – until recent massive chemical sprayings – malarial death-traps, and a variety of tropical diseases still take an alarming toll among the region's inhabitants.

Many Nepalese therefore experience the natural environment as a powerful and potentially hostile "other" with which they must make some accommodation to ensure their own survival. Whilst it remains a fundamentally alien realm, it is (with certain exceptions) perceived as available for human exploitation, provided appropriate ritual preconditions have been met.

This vision of the forces of nature as potentially inimical – yet still available for exploitation – has had the consequence of allowing significant environmental degradation. It is a perspective which is deeply ingrained in the folk religions of Nepal, and these in turn have had a considerable influence on the Hindu and Buddhist religions which have largely supplanted them.

The folk religions date from remote antiquity, and are probably a fusion of the beliefs of the original indigenous inhabitants with those of the Tibeto-Burman and Indo-Aryan tribes who (many millennia apart) came as settlers to the region. Being preliterate cultures it is impossible to identify their beliefs with certainty, but available evidence suggests that they practiced a form of animism: that is they believed that every aspect of the phenomenal world, from crops, weather and mountains, to fertility and disease, was the consequence – or even the actual manifestation – of an extraordinary variety of supernatural beings.

These gods, demons, and spirits – and therefore nature itself – had a multiplicity of responses to humanity, some hostile, some welcoming and many simply ambivalent. Although invisible in normal context, they were perceived as ever-present and easily prone to taking offense, the consequences of which might be felt in any manner of natural catastrophe such as landslide, drought, fire, or illness. Conversely their cooperation was regarded as essential to the successful outcome of many endeavors, from constructing a house, to growing crops, to safely completing a journey through the mountains. Rituals were developed to deal with certain common situations: a symbolic offering would be left as thanks for the cooperation of the attendant deity when a mountain pass had been safely crossed, prayers and offerings would be made to placate the Earth spirits when turning soil in a particular area for the first time, and so on.

Given that the supernatural beings had their main existence in a world beyond the mundane, a specially skilled intermediary was required when more complex transactions with them were required. These specialists commonly displayed the attributes which we would associate with the word "Shaman," entering a supranormal state of consciousness, either trance or ecstatic, to communicate with the being in question. He or she would thereby determine the actions necessary to placate or win the cooperation of the entity, which would usually require some form of offering or sacrifice. Interestingly, most animals do not appear to have had any status in this hierarchy aside from their value as commodities, and were themselves often offered as a sacrifice.

The welfare of the people was obviously regarded as dependent upon the success of the intermediary, and as such they held a valued and powerful position in Nepalese popular religion. Indeed they remain an ever-present feature in rural (particularly tribal) societies throughout Nepal, where they are often known as Jahkri or Dhami. While many confine their activities to the traditional role as intermediaries between the human and spirit worlds, some also perform the function of village priest or religious specialist. Those of the Limbu tribes, for example, have expanded their duties so that they include not only communication with gods, demons and spirits, soothsaying and healing, but also the performance of religious rituals, prayers, and sacrifice when not under direct "spirit control."

In some Nepalese communities – among certain of the aforementioned Limbu tribes for example – the folk religion remains predominant. In most cases it has been supplanted by Hinduism, whose roots go back to the Indo-Aryan tribes who settled in Nepal approximately three millennia ago. They had brought with them some distinctive customs – including the recitation of a group of hymns called the Vedas – with their emphasis on the gods of nature, Agni, fire, Varuna, water, and Vayu, wind, presided over by the rain-god, Indra. The wrathful goddess Durga retains great popularity, and is worshipped in all her manifestations during Dashain, the largest of the Nepalese annual festivals, but the principal gods of the modern era are the triad of Shiva, Vishnu (conceived as having entered the world in the human form of Rama and later Krishna) and Brahma. Hindu philosophers explain that all gods are aspects of the one Brahman, a transcendent, unifying all-pervading deity, and that the world is governed by the principles of karma.

The broader relationship of Hinduism with nature – as it is experienced globally – is discussed in a separate entry, but in local context it clearly has much in common with aspects of Nepalese folk religion. Again there is a sacred element to the forces of the natural world, which are to be treated cautiously but are still available for human exploitation provided that the appropriate ritual conditions are met.

These often find their place in the large, spectacular festivals for which Nepal is renowned, many of which have connections to the seasons, climate, agriculture or harvest, or some other form of natural resource management. Amongst the more obvious examples of this is the Indrajatra, usually celebrated in August/September, which appeals to Indra to provide the rain necessary for the harvest of the rice crop.

Nepalese Hinduism and folk religion also find common ground in that both continue to perform animal sacrifice, a custom which has been abandoned by most other Hindus as contrary to the precept of *ahimsa* (nonviolence). The practice is common throughout Nepal, although the Dakshinkali temple on the outskirts of Kathmandu is famous for the numbers of chickens, pigs, goats and other animals which are slaughtered every Saturday on behalf of pilgrims. Such sacrifice can be traced to Hinduism's roots in Vedic society, where it was offered either as a way of providing sustenance for the dead, or – as it is usually performed in the Nepalese folk tradition – as an act of exchange or offering to spirits or gods, from whom some reciprocal boon was expected.

It is in the character of this latter form of offering that most contemporary animal sacrifice seems to take place, although more sophisticated adherents of the practice have justified it as ultimately being a kindness to the animal, which is thus released from a life of suffering, and brought one step closer to a more fortunate rebirth as a human being. This perspective could be seen as reflecting the tradition, which emphasizes the illusory nature of the material world (*maya*) and asserts the importance of transcendence, but it seems likely that – on a popular level at least – it is the widespread belief in the efficacy of the practice that explains its persistence rather than more abstract concerns for the creature's spiritual welfare.

A rejection of animal sacrifice – and indeed the unnecessary killing of any living creature – is of course one of the hallmarks of the other numerically significant religion in Nepal: Buddhism. The Buddhism practiced in Nepal is largely that of the Mahayana school, commonly associated with Tibet. The Buddhist perspective on nature is a complex one: the phenomenal world has ambivalent status as it is characterized by suffering, but it is also the ground from which the enlightened attitude of compassion is developed, as the Buddhist's ultimate wish is to attain enlightenment so as to bring all beings to enlightenment. The concept of interdependent origination is also important. This emphasizes the connectedness of everything and gives significance to all life.

While such perspectives are embraced and understood by a small, educated elite, the majority of Nepalese Buddhist practitioners appear to follow more simple precepts, such as refraining from killing animals personally, because the Buddha stressed the importance of compassion. Otherwise their perception of the natural world is that of the local folk beliefs: hardly surprising given their shared cultural history. Thus they also regard the natural world as alive with spirits, and when necessary call upon the priest or lama – and in some cases the local Jahkri – to mediate on their behalf. The belief in these spirits is strong at all levels of Buddhist society. Testament to this are the local rNying-ma lamas of the Jomsom area, who volubly maintain that the destruction by landslide of their monastery several decades ago was the result of the wrath of a local mountain deity who was affronted by a foreign mountaineering party which had stayed with them, but failed to undertake the appropriate rituals of permission before venturing up its slopes.

Perhaps the best-known festival of the Kathmandu valley is that of the Red Machchendranath: the local god of rain and fertility. Originally a local Newar and Buddhist festival, Machchendranath is regarded as the deity who brings the all-important monsoon rains to the region, and as such is now worshipped by virtually the whole populace irrespective of religion or caste.

The Nepalese perspective on nature has been problematic in its effects. While it encourages people to respect the environment and reflect upon their interaction with it, it also inclines the popular imagination toward the view that the environment is a commodity which can be exploited heedless of other consequences once the requisite ritual actions have been performed (the exception being actions that are specifically taboo such as the killing of cattle by Hindus, or the defilement of any site deemed sacred). This has left the path clear for the extraordinary environmental damage that has been wrought throughout the country in the latter half of the twentieth century.

In the last few decades there have been increasing attempts to tackle the problems of environmental degradation. Initially these took place under the auspices of foreign aid bodies, but there has been a growing local awareness of the problem. This has inspired a movement within Hindu and Buddhist circles actively to promote the idea of the sacred totality of nature as expressed in their religions as an alternative to the exploitative model. In practical terms this has also led to the creation by religious leaders and groups of a variety of societies, projects and trusts with ecologically "friendly" objectives.

Keith Richmond

Further Reading
Dowman, Keith. *Power Places of Kathmandu: Hindu and Buddhist Holy Sites in the Sacred Valley of Nepal.* London: Thames & Hudson, 1995.
Hitchcock, John T. and Rex L. Jones. *Spirit Possession in the Nepal Himalayas.* New Delhi: Vikas Publishing House, 1994.

Levy, Robert I. *Mesocosm: Hinduism and the Organization of a Traditional Newar City in Nepal*. Berkeley: University of California Press, 1991.

Slusser, Mary Shepherd. *Nepal Mandala: A Cultural Study of the Kathmandu Valley*, 2 vols. Princeton, NJ: Princeton University Press, 1982.

See also: Buddhism – Tibetan; Hinduism; Mongolian Buddhism and Taimen Conservation; Mountaineering; Sacred Mountains; Tibet and Central Asia.

Network on Conservation and Religion

In September 1986, to commemorate its 25th anniversary, the World Wide Fund for Nature (WWF) founded a Network on Conservation and Religion. At the initiative of the then-president of the WWF, Prince Philip of the UK, and Martin Palmer, director of ICOREC (the International Consultancy on Religion, Education and Culture), a strange mix of environmentalists, including grassroot environmentalists, prominent officers of WWF-International, and representatives from the five so-called world religions (Buddhism, Christianity, Hinduism, Islam and Judaism) undertook a pilgrimage to Assisi, Italy, the birthplace of St. Francis, the Roman Catholic saint whom the Vatican had in 1979 given official status as a heavenly protector for environmentalists.

The final session was staged as a religious ceremony in the basilica raised above the grave of St. Francis, and included apologies to First Peoples represented by a Maori warrior. Representatives of the religious traditions read their declarations on religion and nature and pledged themselves to cooperate with each other and the WWF in order to help save the planet, Mother Earth, from ecological disaster. The WWF Network on Religion and Conservation (sometimes also called The New Alliance), was thus formally established. Other religions joined the network in subsequent years, including Bahá'í, Sikhism, Jainism and Daoism.

The ideas behind the Network can be summarized as follows: the religious traditions, with their spiritual and ethical values as well as their billions of adherents and their impact on substantial geographical and cultural areas all over the world, can cooperate with conservationists to make a substantial and durable contribution to environmental thinking and practice. Though recognizing that the religions in the past have not always contributed in a positive way to the conservation of the natural environment, the Network sees them as an alternative to a purely materialistic, dualistic, anthropocentric and utilitarian worldview which has been partly responsible for creating the environmental crisis.

The event in Assisi, and the issuing of the declarations (published by WWF-International as *The Assisi Declarations on Religion and Nature: Interfaith Ceremony,* WWF 1986) set the standard for the activities (interfaith meetings, celebrations of specially designed ceremonies like Harvest rituals, environmental projects run by religious communities in collaboration with scientists and the WWF, publication of more declarations) of the Network from 1986–1995. During this time, the WWF Network on Conservation and Religion published a periodical *The New Road*, and in cooperation with WWF-International and ICOREC it helped pave the way for several other publications, including among others the series *World Religions and Ecology* published by Cassell. In 1995, the WWF Network on Conservation and Religion was subsumed by the Alliance of Religion and Conservation, ARC.

Tim Jensen

See also: Alliance of Religion and Conservation; World Wide Fund for Nature (WWF).

New Age

The New Age movement is an amorphous association of people who identify primarily as spiritual explorers. Many if not most feel that humanity is at the dawn of entering into a new form of consciousness. The new Age of Aquarius, unlike its Piscean predecessor, is to be a time for balance between male and female qualities, the elimination of aggression and power obsessions, and a civilization more in tune with the rhythms of nature and based on a more equitable development of human potential. New Age adherents or associates, inevitably characterized by various forms of spiritual syncretism, are seekers after what they believe to be truth and peace. With this protean mix of nuance and the bizarre, the New Age itself remains among the more difficult of contemporary spiritual developments to comprehend and portray, but as a "religion of commodification," it parlays with any number of alternative medical or psychological methods ranging from meditation, acupuncture, homeopathy, aromatherapy, astrology, environmentalism, Hermetic practice, Esoteric Christianity and Goddess Worship.

Beneath the popular image of New Age, its antecedents derive from various venerable aspects of what Colin Campbell terms the "cultic milieu." Among these we find the Spiritualist, New Thought and Theosophical traditions of the nineteenth century. From these particular orientations, New Age inherits its practice of channeling spirits or entities from other dimensions, its belief that both illness and poverty are illusions or diseases of the mind, and its understandings of karma and reincarnation. The "cultic milieu" is itself a mix of non-mainstream spiritual and esoteric ideas imported from the East and blended with Western occult and pagan notions. The bedrock New

Age spiritual position is Gnostic or Transcendental and seeks divine truth as something masked by the physical phenomenal world. From this perspective, nature is considered ultimately an illusion and something that must be penetrated to gain access to "higher understandings."

In the 1960s, at the Esalen Institute in Big Sur, California, the Jewish-German ex-patriot Fritz Perls introduced his Group Gestalt Therapy with its stress on the value of immediate, authentic experience within a framework that takes the mind/body as a holistic organism rather than a Cartesian dichotomy. Perls, along with such seminal thinkers as Wilhelm Reich, Otto Rank, Kurt Lewin, and Carl Rogers and such complementary practices as Abraham Maslow's Self-Actualization and Roberto Assagioli's Psychosynthesis, launched the field of humanistic psychology from which the Growth and Human Potential movements took their birth. Beginning in California and quickly spreading beyond, Human Potential intertwined with the American psychedelic heritage and spawned numerous self-help/psychophysical therapeutic practices. As these became increasingly integrated with the "cultic milieu," the New Age as a self-conscious spiritual movement began to evolve.

Following the emergence of transpersonal psychology from humanistic psychology and concern with the transcendent potential of the individual in self-actualization, New Age represents the spiritualization of the Human Potential movement. Placing relationship with divinity into a holistic worldview, any development of an ecology of self eventually includes an ecology of the planet and the potential for cross-fertilization with the concerns of deep ecology. Succinctly, and grounded by the astrological consideration that we are leaving an age of Pisces for the new age of Aquarius, the New Age is an expectation of individual change that will coalesce into a quantum leap of collective consciousness. Following current theories of complexity that study spontaneous self-organization in which the whole becomes more than simply the sum of its parts, New Age continues the idealism of the counterculture of the 1960s as a modification if not refutation of contemporary cynical trends by affirming the reality of magic as it relates to self-transformation, communal development and progressive global change.

While New Age derives from specific cultural or subcultural trends (Theosophy, spiritualism, humanistic and later transpersonal psychologies), it is nevertheless a disparate conglomerate of different movements and/or religions. Sociologically, it remains difficult to grasp. It is neither a traditional church, identifiable sect, mainstream denomination, nor a single unorthodox cult. There is no institutional mechanism for determining membership or countenancing expulsion, no one who can speak for the movement as a whole, there is no list of creeds, and there is no register of membership. It is instead a loose series of networks, often cellular and replicate, with a constantly shifting rostrum of spokespeople, therapists and teachers. In short, its fluid organization or even non-organization makes it more of a consumer phenomenon than anything that could be understood as traditionally religious. In fact, New Agers frequently proclaim that they are not religious but spiritual. This non-institutional nature and marketing choice of New Age appears to be its underlying appeal. The New Age represents *a* if not *the* spiritual consumer supermarket that is steadily superseding the appeal of traditional religion in the Western world. In the present-day context of rapid social change, New Age may be cited as an affirmation and celebration of spiritual choice. But this in turn leads to severe accusations of cultural appropriation – especially from identity-endangered peoples such as Native Americans and the Aboriginal peoples of Australia. As a rebuttal, New Age insists that the multi-cultural register is now public domain and accessible to everyone.

In short, an inordinate amount of criticism is directed against its varied practices and more prominent beliefs. Foremost is the critique that dismisses New Age spirituality as essentially narcissistic. The self-preoccupation that has to do with "me" only is described as touchy-feely, airy-fairy, intellectually vapid and eclectically woolly. For many, New Age is described as cheaply false, spiritually kitsch, and a mumbo-jumbo mash that is pastel-colored and lavender-scented. Its central purpose is frequently understood by the non-sympathetic as little more than an effort to make money from those reputedly foolish enough to purchase the many gimmicks and psychophysical therapies that are marketed under the widely embracing label of New Age.

The New Age response to anti-religion criticism accepts that religions have their roots in early practicalities and anxieties but argues that uncertainty and the need for pragmatic solutions is no less a part of our ever-changing and increasingly complicated world. The New Ager is also as likely to retort that if Christianity, Buddhism and the other major religions are now established, they were not always so but were once themselves essentially new religious spiritualities. Despite the wide range of beliefs and practices that might fall under the general rubric of "New Age," as a religious perspective, New Age is no less a shared attempt to understand what constitutes the world, humanity and the supernatural and the relationships between them in ways that give meaning to participants' lives and help them determine what is valuable within some sort of workable framework. The heart of New Age is not such superficial peripherals as candles, crystals and incense, but is instead the increasing awareness in today's world of individual difference and cultural multiplicity that religious choice is a personal decision. Insisting that religious truth is no longer the monopoly of private elites or esoteric cabals, New Age religion may be said to represent a democratization of spirituality within the emergent information age that validates universal suffrage to spiritual prerogative.

Consequently, the shallow, scented and evasive proclivities of what is termed characteristically New Age are primarily a media-induced creation. The press has tended to sensationalize the practice of channeling, use of crystals and the reputation for "flakiness," but New Age itself may be something more than these. As holistic theoretician Marilyn Ferguson describes it, there is an "Aquarian conspiracy" that endeavors and promotes humanitarian and ecological consciousness. The problem for New Age in gaining a respectable public image perhaps lies more with the fact that decentralist empowerment policies, citizen diplomacy missions, ecological and educational reform, and integral thought do not sell newspapers. Apart from the unresolved issue of cultural "theft," New Age's deepest problem is a public relations issue.

Nevertheless, New Age appropriation from a truly holistic perspective might constitute the movement's Achilles' heel. Inasmuch as New Age facilitators exploit indigenous culture for financial profit and self-gratification, they remain largely insensitive to the suppression, denial and socio-economic constraint under which the traditional holders of such culture have labored. They also appear to be callous with regard to the damage and destruction they cause to the heritage of people whose identity and potential for survival are intimately connected to their own spirituality. For those for whom knowledge is something that is privileged and not simply a marketable commodity, the unscrupulous and ruthless exploiter of "sacred knowledge" becomes simply a fraud, charlatan, liar and cheat. The "plastic" shaman and New Age wannabe who claim that practicing native spirituality is "their right" are condemned by those who feel robbed as seeking "a quick-fix or religious Band-Aid." If it were true that spiritual property can no longer be privately owned, New Agers have consistently demonstrated a flagrant lack of sensitivity to the broader consequences of this issue.

Analytically, New Age may be broken down into three distinguishable and often overlapping orientations: occult, spiritual and social. Occult or esoteric New Agers accept the supernatural as a real and intervening force in human and terrestrial affairs. Frequently there is in this orientation an expectation of violent or even apocalyptic Earth changes (storms, famine, earthquakes, pole shift, plagues) that will constitute the transition into the new era. There is general acceptance of a *deus ex machina* or divine intervention as the instigator if not designer of collective consciousness emergence. By contrast and unlike the media-promoted occult side of New Age with its associations of spirit guides, channeling, crystal meditation and appropriation of symbols from different cultures, the spiritual and social dimensions of New Age place their emphasis on human effort rather than supernatural intervention. The former stresses spiritual development of the individual – whether through meditation, yogic practice, shamanism, personal discipline, human potential and/or psychophysical therapy. The rationale is based on the belief that as individuals develop and transform, so too will both global society and the human biosphere. Personal enlightenment in enough numbers will bring about collective enlightenment (i.e., a new age). The social dimension of New Age, on the other hand, is epitomized in Ferguson's 1980 publication of *The Aquarian Conspiracy*. Here the emphasis is on social service and pragmatic work in the areas of educational, institutional, environmental and remedial change. The concern is neither with the self nor with transcendental or magical assistance but with concrete work that brings about empirical transformation. The social-service wing of New Age preoccupies itself with charity work and both humanitarian and ecological reform.

When critics ignore the more serious and less sensational sides of New Age, they tend to dismiss it as little more than a fad. New Age becomes accused of being shallow, self-indulgent, escapist and superstitious – offering little more than a potpourri equivalent of snake-oil cures. But once again, even to the degree that such accusations may contain an element of accuracy, faddism is simply New Age's means and not its goal. New Age uses the currently popular to explore, test and digest each religion's symbols, images, objects and "spiritual truths" as resources to understand their validity and usefulness. While to date much of this pursuit can accurately be labeled uncritical and insensitive, New Age's insistence on the undemanding and pleasant is simply a reflection of present-day consumer-society mores. The critic accuses New Age of adopting the position that "anything goes," but the reality of New Age experimentation is that everything is tried and sampled. There are no restrictions. This is the way it seeks to uncover meaning and value within a religious framework that applies as much to the individual as it might also to various collectivities, communities, society or the planet.

Despite the great disparities of practice and pursuit encountered throughout the broad range of what can be labeled as New Age, we find certain common denominators of belief. Among these there is the acceptance that we have all lived previously; that our present life is not our first or only life. This attitude is largely to be traced to Eastern ideas of reincarnation that New Age inherited from Theosophy. It is predicated upon the essentially Gnostic belief that the cycle of rebirth is something from which to escape and transcend. In this sense, New Age contrasts strongly with contemporary forms of Western Paganism that embrace the world as a desirable and welcome reincarnation as offering a means for the return to earthly life. The corollary to this, therefore, is that New Age is less likely than Western Paganism to promote environmental activism.

From its Spiritualist legacy, on the other hand, New Age accepts that we can communicate with the dead. Once again, this possibility relates to the idea that this life is not all that there is. With or without reincarnation, or at least between successive incarnations, there is, to use the Spiritualist designation, Summerland – the realm of spirits in the beyond. Spiritualism insists that we can communicate with our deceased family members and loved ones for guidance, knowledge and confirmation. New Age has tended to take this further and, especially through its Theosophical affinities, is less interested in the departed as it is in contacting spiritual masters or mahatmas, extraterrestrial beings or space-brethren, and extra-dimensional discarnates. New Age is not concerned with Spiritualism's desire to *prove* the existence of life after death but rather with the acquisition of "higher wisdom" to assist one's spiritual development in the here and now. At the same time, as environmental alarm increases in the world at large, New Age channeled messages have revealed a growing turn toward more "green" issues.

From its origins in New Thought, New Age assumes that evil is an illusion of the mind. It seeks therefore to eradicate both illness and penury for the individual – at least the evolved individual who comes to understand the almost limitless power of the human brain and its relationship to ultimate universal energy. For New Age, this translates into the doctrine that we can heal ourselves. Its many Human Potential therapies from Rolfing, yoga, Reiki, shiatsu, reflexology, t'ai chi, gestalt, encounter, bioenergetics, iridology, *est*, Zen, Aikido, neo-shamanism, Transactional Analysis and Transcendental Meditation are simply different vehicles through which the New Ager seeks self-healing. In other words, these techniques aim to assist the individual toward actualizing the implicit assumption that the negative is simply a figment of the imagination. As New Age shaman Jonathan Horwitz perceives the healing consequences of the illusory nature of evil, the challenge arises from this to "network nature" and halt the "slaughter of the environment" – using the powers of the universe in the optimum way for the planet and all its inhabitants.

The Human Potential aspect of New Age also relates directly to what could be identified as a fourth New Age belief, namely, that we are in charge of our lives. This attitude, along with the belief that the negative or evil of illness and deprivation is an illusion, comprises the singular uniqueness of New Age: its insistence on the positive and utter denial of hindrance. In this sense alone, New Age is an affirmation that demands the world to be as it wishes. Concepts of retribution, original sin and punishment become completely alien in the New Age context, and however naive and foolish such an attitude might be judged to be, New Age represents a daringly courageous spirituality that affirms the power of positive thinking as a means to obtaining progressive ends. If there is one spiritual principle that distinguishes New Age from the world's other major religions, it is probably this. To the degree that the "negative is encountered," it is seen simply as an "opportunity" for spiritual progress.

And, finally, in keeping with its place in the Gnostic lineage, New Age is the belief that spiritual truth comes from within. Insight is not a product of revelation or external acquisition, but one of inner development and discovery. In this complete valorization of self-experience, New Age affirms its belief in both seekership and the validation of private experience. In this sense, New Age offers a Gnostic form of mysticism – not a mysticism of escape as we find in Hinduism and Buddhism, nor quite the mysticism of union with God that occurs with esoteric Christianity or Sufism, but a mysticism of *becoming* a god. Authority and validity belong to the inner, private individual where, for New Age, lies the source of truth.

All these essential New Age beliefs – that we have lived before, that we can communicate with discarnate forms of consciousness, that we can heal ourselves and are in charge of our lives, and that spiritual truth is something to be discovered within the sanctity of the self rather than in a sacred text, or from a pulpit, or through an ecclesiastical sacrament or via an act of external or transcendental grace – resonate with the contemporary forms of spirituality that appear increasingly to be turning away from traditional institutional forms. In our world of today, spirituality is about choice – perhaps reflecting our increased valuing of the consumer and the right to make decisions that reflect personal needs and desires as apart from automatically following the dictates of established authority.

Because of its Gnostic and Theosophical heritage, there is an underlying bias throughout New Age to consider the environment a secondary concern. At the same time, however, the nature-as-illusion versus nature-as-real dichotomy has not been clearly articulated within much if not most New Age expression. Through such collective efforts as Findhorn, The Farm and Esalen or such communal centers as Glastonbury, Sedona and Ojai, New Age community efforts develop immediate awareness of – and have direct impacts on – their local environments and have tended thereby to emerge as vanguard ecological models for the global audience. Experimentation and incorporation of organic farming methods, renewable energy sources, conservation techniques, vegetarianism, home-spun textiles, alternative technology, cottage industries and cost-efficient production have shown that where New Age types of spirituality meet the Earth, they are fully capable of developing a sustainable environmental equilibrium. Consequently, despite New Age's affinity and continuation of Gnosticism, the movement's overall paradoxical nature as well as its interface with paganism and shamanism encourage a holistic inevitability that encompasses not only whatever other concerns there are with self and transcendence but also the well-being of the planet as a place upon which "to walk gently."

Michael York

Further Reading

Bloom, William, ed. *Holistic Revolution: The Essential New Age Reader*. London: Allen Lane/Penguin, 2000.

Bloom, William, ed. *The New Age: An Anthology of Essential Writings*. London: Rider, 1991.

Brown, Michael. *The Channeling Zone: American Spirituality in an Anxious Age*. London: Harvard University Press, 1997.

Campbell, Colin B. "The Cult, the Cultic Milieu and Secularization." In Michael Hill, ed. *A Sociological Yearbook of Religion in Britain* 5. London: SCM Press, 1972, 119–36.

Ferguson, Marilyn. *The Aquarian Conspiracy: Personal and Social Transformation in Our Time*. Los Angeles: J.P. Tarcher, 1987.

Grayling, Anthony C. and Michael York. "Should We Treat New Age Beliefs with Respect?" *The Guardian: Saturday Review* (6 February 1999).

Hanegraaff, Wouter. *New Age Religion and Western Culture*. Leiden: E.J. Brill, 1997.

Heelas, Paul. *The New Age Movement: The Celebration of the Self and the Sacralization of Modernity*. Oxford: Blackwell, 1996.

Lewis, James R. and J. Gordon Melton, eds. *Perspectives on the New Age*. Albany: SUNY, 1992.

Mears, Daniel P. and Christopher G. Ellison. "Who Buys New Age Materials? Exploring Sociodemographic, Religious, Network, and Contextual Correlates of New Age Consumption." *Sociology of Religion* 61:3 (2000), 289–313.

York, Michael. "New Age and the Late Twentieth Century." *Journal of Contemporary Religion* 12:3 (1997), 401–19.

York, Michael. *The Emerging Network: A Sociology of the New Age and Neo-pagan Movements*. Lanham, Maryland: Rowman & Littlefield, 1995.

See also: Aboriginal Spirituality and the New Age in Australia; Astrology; California Institute of Integral Studies; Celestine Prophecy; Cetacean Spirituality; Channeling; Dolphins and New Age Religion; Earth Mysteries; Ecopsychology; Ecotopia; Esalen Institute; Findhorn Foundation/Community (Scotland); Harmonic Convergence; Rainbow Family; Re-Earthing; Rustlers Valley (South Africa); Shamanism – Neo; Steiner, Rudolf – and Anthroposophy; Theosophy; Transpersonal Psychology; Unitarianism; UFOs and Extra-terrestrials; Western Esotericism; Whales and Whaling.

New Religious Movements

The expression "new religious movement" (NRM) is a term of convenience designed to circumvent the negative connotations that, sometimes correctly but perhaps more often erroneously, have accrued in the public mind to such sociological constructs as the "cult" and "sect." More accurate terminology might be "marginal religious movements" or "alternative religious movements." These terms avoid the question of when ought a group no longer be classified as new, but "NRM" has emerged in the academic *lingua franca* as the currently accepted and pragmatic designation.

Among the higher-profile NRMs are the Church of Scientology, the Unification Church (the Moonies), ISKCON (International Society for Krishna Consciousness or the Hari Krishnas), The Family (formerly, the Children of God) and Rastafarianism. Others more contentious in the past but now generally less so, either through internal transformations or through changes in external perception, include Maharishi Mahesh Yogi's Transcendental Meditation, Guru Maharaj Ji's Divine Light Mission (now Elan Vital), followers of Rajneesh/Osho, Ananda Marga, Summit Lighthouse/Church Universal and Triumphant, *est*/the Forum or Centres Network and Subud. On the other hand, certain groups have demonstrated various degrees of violence – either self-directed against themselves (Jim Jones' Peoples Temple of Guyana; Heaven's Gate in San Diego; the Solar Temple in both Switzerland and Canada) or engineered against others (Aum Shin Rikyo in Japan) or as themselves the recipients of external violence (David Koresh's Branch Davidians in Waco, Texas). Less prominent groups that come under the label of new religious movements include the Aetherius Society, Raëlians, Brahma Kumaris, Sahaja Yoga, Sri Chinmoy, ECKANKAR, Church of the Movement of Spiritual Inner Awareness (MSIA)/Insight Transformational Seminars and Nicheren Shoshu Buddhism/Soka Gakkai. In general, NRMs that can be located as or through identifiably organized groups derive chiefly from the traditions of Christianity, various forms of Eastern spirituality (Hindu, Buddhist, Jain, Sikh or Sufi) or the more secular Human Potential Movement (including UFO groups). Nevertheless, other influences and innovations found throughout the general alternative-spirituality market that Colin Campbell referred to as the cultic milieu continue to modify and shape Christian, Eastern and secular NRMs. In addition, less organized, structured and/or totalitarian religious expressions have also emerged, namely, the more amorphous New Age and Contemporary Western Pagan movements.

Many of the "older" NRMs developed as counter-responses to the 1960s counterculture in which radical experimentation and rejection of established social mores led to disorientation, polarization, hostility, confusion and anomie for many, and the emerging new religions may have served as vehicles toward either social reintegration or increased but structured marginalization and status as outsiders. For others, however, NRMs are part of a perennial exploration of new and different spiritual parameters that has always been a feature of Western civilization. In virtually all cases, NRMs represent various forms of protest and efforts toward either social withdrawal or social change. These are understood by Roy Wallis to be either world-rejecting, world-affirming or world-accommodating.

Charles Glock and Rodney Stark see religion more broadly as providing various forms of compensation to economic, social, organismic, ethical and/or psychic deprivations. Individuals or groups that are not equally valued by a society resort to the Church as a logically religious response. Those, however, who suffer from a disadvantaged economic position turn instead to the sect. On the other hand, the resolution for those who perceive mental or physical disability (organismic deprivation) – both objective and subjective – is the healing movement. If healing becomes the exclusive concern of the religious movement, the group will tend to conform to the cult-type. Ethical deprivation refers to holding values that are in conflict with prevailing norms, while psychic deprivation is that which is experienced by people who do not possess a system of meaningful values by which to interpret and organize their lives. The response to both psychic and ethical disequality may be either religious or secular. Movements that arise through ethical deprivation tend to be ephemeral, faddish and reformist. In contrast, psychic deprivation finds its religious resolution in the extreme cult and/or occult milieu (New Age, UFO groups, Theosophy and New Thought), but if this deprivation is accompanied by economic disadvantage, one likely outcome is the radical political movement (e.g., the more violent protest activities directed against the World Trade Organization). For Glock and Stark, either the cult succeeds and comes to set the prevailing social norm or it fades away. In their typology, protest against industrial pollution and environmental degradation is a response of ethical deprivation, but to the degree that it is also a healing and remedial effort it is an organismically derived response as well.

In contrast to Glock and Stark's understanding of organizational resolutions based on the various types of subjective deprivations that people experience relative to others, Bryan Wilson has refined the broad sectarian response to encompass what he terms conversionist, adventist or revolutionist, introversionist, Gnostic or manipulationist, thaumaturgical (miracle-working), reformist and utopian ideal-types. To understand the relationships of new religious movements to nature, Wilson's typology along with an understanding of the theological tradition in which any specific NRM emerges allows the most fruitful analysis. But at the same time, the sectarian response as understood by Wilson conforms in its range of possibilities to the specific attitude toward the world shared by the holders of any given response. Those who reject the world take little or no interest in its preservation, and those who simply accommodate their own agendas to something that is regarded as either intrinsically or indifferently valueless have no rationale toward making any concrete and sustainable engagement or reformist effort. Consequently, it is largely those who religiously, spiritually and/or secularly affirm the world as something real and valuable who are the ones who become involved with holistic concerns, ecological reforms and political protest on behalf of the environment and protection of nature.

From Wilson's perspective, the sectarian movement always exists in some kind of tension with the world, rejecting the orthodox or dominant religious tradition and generally seeking salvific goals in ways that differ from the means provided by the prevailing socio-cultural institutional facilities. Wilson's typology is meant to provide a measuring of standard ideal-types rather than to be a system of classification. This means that any specific group might approximate to more than one type, although usually more to one particular ideal over the others. Wilson's conversionist sect is exemplified by Christian evangelism, orthodox fundamentalism and pentecostal sectarianism. A classic example is the Salvation Army and, among NRMs, The Family, the Jesus Army (the Jesus Fellowship Church) and the International Church of Christ (the "Crosslands Movement") in which the primary concern is the experience of emotional conversion and transformation. This change of heart as the central feature becomes the proof of an individual's transcending the world's evils and his or her ultimate unconcern with decay, death and worldly well-being. This conversionist response differs from the revolutionist one that holds instead that only the destruction of the world will be sufficient for human salvation. This is usually expected imminently and through divine action. Believers may participate directly in the revolutionary process, but in general they are more passive and rely on faith for the new dispensation of supernatural intervention and apocalyptic upheaval. The classic examples here are Jehovah's Witnesses and Christadelphians and, among NRMs, the Branch Davidians, the Unification Church and again to some extent The Family.

The most developed anti-worldly position from Wilson's perspective is his introversionist response that sees the world as irrevocably evil and calls for withdrawal from it as the only possible route to salvation. Some of the Holiness movements conform to this response as do conservative Quakers and the Amana Society, but here too we find many of the Eastern-inspired or -derived groups such as the Hari Krishnas, Brahma Kumaris and to some extent Mataji Nirmala Devi's Sahaja Yoga. More extreme than the introversionist position but at the same time less anti-worldly is the utopian response that seeks to reconstruct the world according to some divinely inspired plan – usually by establishing a communal model. Some examples include the Mennonite, Amish, Hutterite and/or Brüderhof groups, Koreshan Unity and the Oneida community as well as the more contemporary collectives such as Stephen Gaskin's The Farm, Esalen in Big Sur, California, Findhorn in Forres, Scotland and the various communities of the Emissaries of Divine Light. The reformist response is less radical than the utopian, concerned with accommodation to the world but is centered on making efforts toward the gradual improvement of society and terrestrial life. While some of the New Age manifestations may be seen as reformist, much of the neo-pagan and related spiritualities are concerned with amending the world through motivations of social conscience if not also spiritual connection. Especially for contemporary Western Paganism, reformation may be either dictated through supernaturally inspired insight or via secularly rational deduction. To the degree reformist orientation conforms to this last, it essentially bypasses the Wilsonian typology that restricts itself to the positing of a supernatural factor in its sectarian response to the world. If, on the other hand, we allow that the supernatural may or may not be regarded as an operative, Wilson's ideal-types are applicable to the contemporary range of new religious movements. The revolutionist, thaumaturgical and conversionist responses are the ones that specifically emphasize the autonomous operation of the supernatural: the first expects it to overturn the world, the last expects change through divine Providence to be internal, and the magical expects certain concrete or demonstrable dispensations and miracles to occur.

In Wilson's understanding, the conversionists are subjectivists, but the "overturning" revolutionists, the "abandoning" introversionists, the "amending" reformists and the "reconstructing" utopians are all objectivists who focus one way or another on the world itself. Both thaumaturgists and manipulationists he refers to as relationists, and while the latter is close to the subjectivist position in that they expect a change of perception through the supernatural, it is at the same time more intellectual and less emotional, other-worldly and transcendental. But again, both these relational responses are implicitly this-worldly: the thaumaturgical in seeking local, immediate healing, restoration, reassurance, foresight, consolation and magical guarantee; the manipulationist in seeking everyday well-being and improvement. It is this last which essentially informs most of the New Age, Contemporary Western Pagan and Human Potential/Self-Help movements as well as such specific identities as Christian Science, New Thought, Scientology, *est*, Raëlianism, Transcendental Meditation, Rajneeshism, Elan Vital, Sri Chinmoy, Subud, ECKANKAR, MSIA, Eternal Flame Foundation and Soka Gakkai. At its heart is the obtaining of gnosis or inner wisdom through intellectual acquisition, mental hygiene or physical regimen that in turn becomes the tool by which to change one's perception of the world and achieve both objective achievement and psychic reassurance. By contrast, the thaumaturgical consideration of the supernatural as an external force that can exert tangible influence on the world is most at home, along with the revolutionist movement, in less-developed societies. It persists in the West through Spiritualism, such orientations as the "I AM" Religious Activity and the Church Universal and Triumphant, or New Age channeling. On the other hand, the contemporary Pagan and esoteric practices of Ceremonial and other forms of Magic(k) tend to work with psychological and internal constructs of the mind rather than with what are considered to be objective and self-existing magical entities. In other words, they conform more to the manipulationist than thaumaturgical positions.

Consequently, NRMs can be focused on individual salvation or universal concerns or both. To the degree that they follow a Gnostic or Transcendental theology of one sort or another, they exhibit less interest with the world and its reform and transformation. But inasmuch as NRMs are grounded in a this-worldly pagan theological understanding, religion and nature become fused as a central concern – especially as industrial imbalance and random unconscious exploitation continues to put the very viability and future of the planet into a perceived and/or real jeopardy. New religions that engage with nature rather than some transcendental reality to which nature is merely a foil, impediment or at best subservient will tend to be reformist, utopian or manipulationist and, to a lesser extent, thaumaturgical. Those that are either conversionist, revolutionist or introversionist will tend to see nature as an illusion or worthless or both and have little foundation or desire for a dynamic and holistic engagement with the organic dimension.

Michael York

Further Reading

Barker, Eileen. *New Religious Movements: A Practical Introduction*. London: Her Majesty's Stationery Office, 1989.

Campbell, Colin B. "The Cult, Cultic Milieu and Secularization." In Michael Hill, ed. *A Sociological Yearbook of Religion in Britain* 5. London: SCM Press, 1972.

Glock, Charles Y. and Rodney Stark. *Religion and Society in Tension*. Chicago: Rand McNally, 1965.

Hill, Michael. *A Sociology of Religion*. London: Heinemann, 1973.

Kaplan, Jeffrey and Heléne Lööw. *The Cultic Milieu: Oppositional Subcultures in an Age of Globalization*. Lanham, MD: Altamira, 2002.

Stark, Rodney and William Sims Bainbridge. *The Future of Religion: Secularization, Revival and Cult Formation.* Berkeley: University of California Press, 1985.

Wilson, Bryan R. "A Typology of Sects." In Roland Robertson, ed. *Sociology of Religion: Selected Readings.* Harmondsworth, England: Penguin, 1969, 361–83.

Wilson, Bryan R. *Magic and Millennium.* London: Heinemann, 1973.

York, Michael. *The Emerging Network: A Sociology of the New Age and Neo-pagan Movements.* Lanham, MD: Rowman & Littlefield, 1995.

See also: Cetacean Spirituality; Church of Nazareth, KwaZulu-Natal, Deep Ecology; Dolphins and New Age Religion; Ecopsychology; Emissaries of Divine Light; Esalen Institute; The Family (Children of God); The Farm; Findhorn Community (Scotland); Gush Emunim; Harmonic Convergence; Hippies; Kimbanguism (Central Africa); Koliada Viatichei; Masowe Wilderness Apostles; Mother Earth and the Earth People (Trinidad); MOVE; New Age; Radical Environmentalism; Rainbow Family; Redwood Rabbis; Scientology; Soka Gakkai and the Earth Charter; Steiner, Rudolf – and Anthroposophy; Transcendental Meditation; Transpersonal Psychology; UFOs and Extraterrestrials; Western Esotericism.

New Zealand

New Zealand is a nation-state composed of three major islands in the southern Pacific approximately 1000 miles (1750 km) southeast of Australia. Its remote geographic location contributed to its unique ecology, which included flightless birds such as the moa. The moa ranged in height from four to ten feet and was hunted to extinction by Maori inhabitants centuries before Captain James Cook claimed the islands for Britain in 1769.

Stretching nearly 1000 miles from north to south, New Zealand has a temperate climate, characterized by semi-tropical fern-tree forests in the north and hardwood beech forests in the uninhabited fjordlands of the South Island. The indigenous Maori population migrated south in a series of canoe journeys from "Hawaiki" in Eastern Polynesia from the ninth to the fourteenth centuries. The Maori introduced exotic mammals, the dog and the rat, and the kumara (a sweet potato cultivated in the southern Pacific region). Maori history has been divided into an "archaic moa-hunting culture" (ca. 900–1300) and a "classic" Maori culture (ca. 1300–present).

Religion in pre-contact New Zealand has been reconstructed with great difficulty, due to the aggressive colonization and Christianization of the Maori by European settlers and missionaries beginning in 1814. Most of the missionaries were British Anglicans and Methodists who regarded the Maori as the "children of Shem," descendants of the "lost" ten tribes of Israel. Subsequent Maori prophets alleged that Jehovah was brought to the islands by their Jewish ancestors, forgotten for centuries, and rediscovered by them in their dreams and visions.

Missionaries required converts to renounce *mana* and *tapu* as things of the devil. Mana is an extra-human power that inheres in certain people, places, objects, and collectives. It can be gained or lost. *Tapu* refers to any place, object, or person that is set apart as prohibited or sacred. *Tapu* rules regulated Maori society, just as civil law imposes order in Western cultures. Loss of *mana* and *tapu* contributed to social disorder and the rise of Maori renewal movements that challenged colonization and Christianization. Followers of the "good and peaceful" movement received *mana* from wind spirits, led by the Angel Gabriel. The King movement united the central North Island tribes under the *mana* of a Maori king and established a *tapu* boundary around their ancestral lands. Today, the Maori practice a variety of Christian religions, some of which, such as Anglicanism, Methodism, and Mormonism, are imports, and a few of which, such as Ringatu and Ratana, were initiated by nineteenth-and twentieth-century visionaries.

The European impulse to missionize the Maori was millenarian. New Zealand was the geographical antipode of the British Isles. The Christianization of the Maori tribes fulfilled the command to carry the Gospel to the "end of the Earth" (Acts 1:8) before the Savior would reappear in the thousand-year reign of God. The enterprise of colonization was regarded as the fulfillment of a prophecy that "God shall enlarge Japhet and he shall dwell in the tents of Shem" (Buddle 1873: 5). Japhet was presumed to be the white race, "enlarged" by its technological superiority and parliamentary system and destined to rule over the other biblical races delineated in Genesis, chapters 9 and 10.

The rise of Maori new religious movements in response to colonization and Christianization sparked the epic series of Land Wars from 1858 to 1872 that forged the modern state of New Zealand, a "new Albion" in which pastures and orchards replaced native forests, and commercial enterprises replaced fishing and horticulture. During the wars, tribes lost their lands through punitive confiscations and special legislation that divided tribal holdings into private parcels. In the North Island, Aboriginal forest remains primarily in the Urewera National Park – contested ground between conservationists and the Tuhoe tribe that claims the totara tree of the creator god, Tane Mahuta, and ancestral burial caves in the sacred mountain fished from the sea by the creator god, Maui. The South Island was inhabited only in the north by the Kai Tahu people, who controlled the trade in greenstone, which was used to fashion sacred objects. The Kai Tahu land was acquired under extreme duress in 1848 by the imperial government, which sold it to settlers for sheep stations.

New Zealand is now an independent commonwealth nation, a largely biracial state that remains divided over ultimate claims to the land. The Treaty of Waitangi, a founding document signed by some Maori chieftains and representatives of the British in 1840, is so ambiguously worded that Maori and Pakeha (New Zealanders of European descent) both claim that their sovereignty over the land is upheld by the treaty's language. The extraordinary Waitangi Tribunal, set up in 1985, has since fostered the payment of reparations and the restoration of land and fishing rights to specific North and South Island tribes, including the Kai Tahu.

According to Maori custom, land is an inalienable possession of the tribe and cannot be sold. The Maori word for "land" and "placenta" are one and the same. A new-born's umbilical is buried in the Earth in a special ceremony. Sacred places are the central feature of Maori religion, and the land is regarded as essential to the life-force of the people. It is noteworthy that the Maori population suffered its greatest decline in the latter half of the nineteenth century when tribes were being separated from ancestral lands. A prophet who received God's call to save his people, responded: "If your wish is for me to save only people, I won't help, but if it is to save the land, then I will carry out this task" (Webster 1979: 158).

According to the Christian creation myth, from the beginning man (not woman) was granted dominion over the Earth and its creatures. This myth has been cited time and again by British agents and settlers to justify their takeover of Maori "waste lands." The official who drafted the English version of the Treaty of Waitangi argued against Aboriginal rights, asserting that the only "natural right of a man to land" was over land "which he had subdued from the forest, to the uses of man." He compared this right to "that instinctive sense of right which a man possesses in his own children" (Busby 1860: 10). The tension over what the Maori call "mana over the land" and the Pakeha call property rights underlies the cultural conflict between the government and the tribes regarding specific places and ecological resources. These contesting worldviews are derived from each people's creation myths.

New Zealand has been cited as one of the least religious (i.e., church-attending) countries on Earth. Jokingly, the religion of New Zealand has been called "rugby, racing, and beer." Neither assertion has much validity, because religion is that which symbolically binds a distinct people together in a common religious identity. Myths of the origin of a tribe's world and people, and its oral recitation of the names of ancestors and significant events that happened at specific places, reveal what is of ultimate concern to a self-identified group. Statistics regarding church affiliation or attendance are insufficient measures of religion. What is most sacred to both races in New Zealand is the land itself, which is not surprising considering that islands are finite territories wherein an expanding population must negotiate the use of its most important and dwindling resource: space. Viewed as the paramount religious sacrality, the land of these beautiful islands is the chief protagonist in the history of New Zealand.

To New Zealanders of European descent the land is also dear. No longer regarded as terra incognita, the Anglicized landscape of New Zealand provides recreation (literally, re-creation) for a largely urban population. Sheep stations and coastal or lakeside cabins are handed down as familiar places of refuge and rest. They are places infused with meaning, where ancestors and present inhabitants are connected via remembrance and story.

The Southern Alps and Fjordland National Park in the South Island are world-class tourist destinations. The Pakeha conservationist ethic may be interpreted as a benign extension of the Genesis myth of domination and enterprise when it succeeds in establishing wild lands as an economic base for outdoor sports and tourism. Conversely, the Maori struggle to regain their ancestral places may be interpreted as an extension of tribal creation stories that establish certain trees, waters, stones and mountains as tapu treasures (taonga) that provide for the continued wholeness and life of the community.

In 1991 after extensive public review, the New Zealand parliament passed the Resource Management Act, a "greenprint" for the islands' ecological health. It divided the country into sixteen bioregions based on watersheds. Elected regional authorities are responsible for implementing the goal of the RMA: comprehensive planning of sustainable management of natural resources. Utilizing a Nash Equilibrium approach, business interests have rallied around the RMA as the optimal means of securing each company's self-interest (Johnson 1995: 68–87). The RMA seems to have combined the Pakeha myth of human management of natural resources and the Maori myth of human dependence on Earth as sustainer of life in a rational program to protect the environment of New Zealand. One may regard the RMA as an expression of an emerging transnational religious consciousness of the doctrine of ecological sustainability. Only New Zealand and The Netherlands have committed themselves to such a far-reaching political, social, and environmental plan. This cannot be accidental. Religion in New Zealand is pre-eminently oriented to landscape, which is the "homescape," of Maori and Pakeha, both of whom have established their lives and those of their descendants upon their contrasting but equally sacred orientations to the land and its treasures.

Jean E. Rosenfeld

Further Reading

Buddle, Thomas. "Christianity and Colonisation among the Maoris." Supplement to the *Nelson Evening Mail*. 23 and 30 August 1873.

Busby, James. "Remarks upon a Pamphlet Entitled 'The Taranaki Question,' by Sir William Martin, D.C.L., Late Chief Justice of New Zealand." Auckland: Philip Kunst, The *Southern Cross* Office, 1860.
Johansen, J. Prytz. "Studies in Maori Rites and Myths." *Historisk-filosofiske Meddelelser* 37:4 (1958), 66–102.
Johnson, Huey D. *Green Plans: Greenprint for Sustainability*. Lincoln, Nebraska and London: The University of Nebraska Press, 1995.
Kawharu, I.H., ed. *Waitangi: Maori & Pakeha Perspectives of the Treaty of Waitangi*. Auckland: Oxford University Press, 1989.
Rosenfeld, Jean E. *The Island Broken in Two Halves: Land and Renewal Movements among the Maori of New Zealand*. University Park, PA: The Pennsylvania State University Press, 1999.
Sorrenson, M.P.K. "Land Purchase Methods and Their Effect on Maori Population, 1865–1901." *Journal of the Polynesian Society* 65:3 (1956), 183–99.
Stokes, Evelyn, J. Wharehuia Milroy and Hirini Melbourne. *Te Urewera Nga Iwi Te Whenua Te Ngahere: People, Land and Forests of Te Urewera*. Hamilton: University of Waikato, 1986.
Walker, Ranginui. *Ka Whawhai Tonu Matou: Struggle without End*. Auckland: Penguin Books, 1990.
Webster, Peter. *Rua and the Maori Millennium*. Wellington: Victoria University Press, 1979.

See also: Australia.

Nhat Hanh, Thich (1926–)

Thich Nhat Hanh is a Vietnamese Zen monk trained in both Zen and Theravada practices. He was nominated for the Nobel Peace Prize by Dr. Martin Luther King, Jr. for his peace work during the Vietnam War. He lives in exile in France, is a prolific writer and retreat leader, and is one of the most influential Buddhist teachers in the West.

The heart of Thich Nhat Hanh's teaching consistently has been healing and reconciliation. Nhat Hanh offers tools to heal and reconcile not only human communities, but also human relationships with our bodies and the natural world. For Nhat Hanh, if we could heal our relationship with nature, if we could "be peace" with respect to nature, knowing that we are in no way separate from it, the actions that naturally arose from that condition would spontaneously be respectful, loving and generous toward the natural world.

The healing and reconciliation of our relationships with the natural world are rooted in mindful awareness, in particular, mindfulness of "interbeing." Nhat Hanh uses two favorite mindfulness practices for this healing purpose: eating meditation and walking meditation. In eating meditation, one simply eats something, for example, an orange, very slowly and with full attention given to the present moment of peeling, smelling, chewing, tasting, salivating, swallowing, etc., with no silent verbal commentary. Such a meditation may take as much as an hour. In addition, one may be asked to contemplate the interconnections that have made the orange possible – the sun without which the orange could not exist, the rain-producing cloud, the minerals, the farmer. One may be invited to see the sun and the cloud within the orange and, ultimately, all things within the orange. Thus, one is invited to see how the orange, the sun, oneself, and all things "inter-are," producing visceral awareness of the non-separation of all life.

Whereas in traditional Buddhist walking meditation, one is asked to focus one's attention exclusively on the internal physical sensations of very slow walking, in Nhat Hanh's walking meditation one is invited to look out at the world, to feel the warmth of the sun on one's face, the gentle touch of the breeze, to see the beauty of the flower, the greenness of the leaves – all in mindfulness, one attention focus at a time, in a relaxed and unhurried manner, with internal silence.

These meditations are deceptively simple; for their practitioners, they do many things. They help them to feel themselves alive in and through their bodies. For those in the modern, urban, technological world, this is a necessary first step. Secondly, these meditations put their bodies in the world: they make real in a tangible, physical way using all their senses, their connection and continuity with the world, and ultimately their non-separation from it. From their experiential awareness of their connectedness with the natural world, practitioners' will to care for the world springs naturally.

In addition to his creative work in adapting traditional meditation practices, Nhat Hanh has also creatively expanded the traditional Five Precepts, the five minimal ethical practices, of Buddhism. Whereas the traditional first precept invited all people to avoid destroying life (by which sentient life was meant), Nhat Hanh's expanded first precept reads:

Aware of the suffering caused by the destruction of life, I vow to cultivate compassion and learn ways to protect the lives of people, animals, plants, and minerals. I am determined not to kill, not to let others kill, and not to condone any act of killing in the world, in my thinking, and in my way of life (1993: 3).

Here Nhat Hanh has enlarged the traditional first precept in four ways. The precept: 1) now includes all forms of life, "people, animals, plants, and minerals"; 2) has moved from passive (avoiding killing) to active (actively protect life); 3) calls for nonviolence in one's thinking and way of life, in addition to one's acts; and 4) calls for the individual to intervene in the acts of others, not only to guard his/her own actions. In support of this precept, Nhat Hanh cites both instrumental motives based on interbeing ("We humans are made entirely of nonhuman elements, such as plants, minerals, Earth, clouds, and sunshine") and deep ecology reasons ("Minerals have their own lives, too"). In Buddhist monasteries, we chant, 'Both sentient and nonsentient beings will realize full enlightenment' " (1993: 14). Both are rooted in the awareness of interbeing produced by mindfulness practice: "We feel in permanent and loving touch with all species on Earth" (1993: 18).

Without advocating any particular approach, Thich Nhat Hanh encourages his students directly to face the suffering of the Earth and then take action to care for the Earth and its beings. Consequently, his students are found throughout the environmental movement. They lead efforts to end radioactive waste, intervene to prevent the cutting of redwood forests, teach environmentalism, lobby and work legally on behalf of the Earth, promote the protection of endangered species, hold leadership positions in national environmental organizations, promote alternative energies, work to protect the rainforest and strive to protect animals from suffering, among other things.

Sallie B. King

Further Reading

Nhat Hanh, Thich. *For a Future to Be Possible: Commentaries on the Five Wonderful Precepts.* Berkeley, CA: Parallax Press, 1993.

Nhat Hanh, Thich. *Present Moment, Wonderful Moment: Mindfulness Verses for Daily Living.* Berkeley, CA: Parallax Press, 1990.

Nhat Hanh, Thich. "The Last Tree." In Allan Hunt Badiner, ed. *Dharma Gaia: A Harvest of Essays in Buddhism and Ecology.* Berkeley, CA: Parallax Press, 1990, 217–21.

Nhat Hanh, Thich. *The Sun My Heart.* Berkeley, CA: Parallax Press, 1988.

See also: Buddhism – Engaged; Payutto, Phra Dhammapitaka; Siam's Forest Monasteries; Sivaraksa; Sulak; Thai Buddhist Monks.

Nietzsche, Friedrich (1844–1900)

In a now famous article written in 1967, Lynn White, Jr. traced the roots of our present ecological crisis to Christianity and other monotheistic religions, while arguing that the solution of this crisis requires that we adopt a new religion or radically rethink our old one. In the years since the publication of this article, there has been much debate over White's position. Some philosophers have attempted to defend monotheistic religions by claiming that these religions suggest that humans are to be stewards or caretakers of nature, not despots of nature as White had claimed. While the view that humans are despots is clearly incompatible with ecologically oriented thinking, these critics of White believe that the position of humans as stewards is consistent with the principles and aims of reform environmentalism.

Other thinkers, however, especially those who have been identified with the movement known as deep ecology, have whole-heartedly adopted White's call for a new religion or way of thinking. These thinkers argue that, even if monotheistic religions are consistent with the principles and aims of reform environmentalism, these principles and aims are inadequate to resolve our current ecological crisis.

In carefully examining the views of the nineteenth-century German philosopher Friedrich Nietzsche (1844–1900), it is apparent that Nietzsche's philosophy is relevant to this recent debate over the merits of White's position. Indeed, Nietzsche not only anticipates many of White's criticisms of Christianity and monotheistic religion, but the development of his thinking also shows a movement from what can be described as a reform environmentalist position to a position that has many affinities with the views of the deep ecologists.

While anyone acquainted with the philosophy of Nietzsche will no doubt be aware of his antipathy for Christianity and monotheistic religion – one of his last books was entitled *The Anti-Christ* – they may not be aware that one of Nietzsche's principal lines of criticism of Christianity is almost identical to the line of criticism that was later developed by White. Like White, Nietzsche criticizes Christianity for divorcing humans from the natural world, for elevating humanity above nature, for denigrating the Earth by instilling in humans the feeling that they are the crown of creation and thus lords over other creatures. In other words, for Nietzsche as for White, traditional Western religious thinking has tended to ascribe a disproportionate importance to the human species, thereby providing a religious framework for the domination of the natural world.

Moreover, by tracing the development of Nietzsche's thinking, we can see that he was gradually working his way toward the new type of thinking that White envisioned. In his first book, *The Birth of Tragedy*, Nietzsche identified a type of human experience (Dionysian experience) that would allow us to discover what he calls "wild and naked nature." However, it was in one of his *Untimely Meditations*, "Schopenhauer as Educator," that Nietzsche's early views on humanity's relation to nature are most fully developed. In this work, Nietzsche describes nature in decidedly anthropomorphic terms. He says that nature has certain goals or intentions, but that these goals are usually thwarted because nature is imperfect, misguided, wasteful, inexperienced, a "bad economist." Because of this misguidedness, Nietzsche argues that nature needs humanity (or at least the highest types of humanity – the philosopher, saint, and artist) to correct its mistakes and to set it on its proper course. Although Nietzsche's views differ in important respects from White's critics, it should be evident that his position here falls within the humanity-as-steward tradition that they were defending. Also, while most reform environmentalists would assign the task of correcting or perfecting nature to the scientist rather than to the philosopher, saint, or artist, Nietzsche's early views are consistent with the assumptions of reform environmentalism.

However, in his later writings, Nietzsche attacks human arrogance and pride, and argues that humanity must be reimmersed into nature. Rather than viewing themselves as lords over nature, or as enlightened perfecters of nature, Nietzsche claims that humans must realize that they are only one species among many, that they are, to use Aldo Leopold's terminology, plain members of the biotic community. Indeed, Nietzsche states that his task in *Beyond Good and Evil* is to "translate man back into nature" (1966: 161), and his later writings are filled with passages, like the following one from *The Anti-Christ*, that attempt to undermine human arrogance and pride:

Man is absolutely not the crown of creation: every creature stands beside him at the same stage of perfection ... And even in asserting that we assert too much: man is, relatively speaking, the most unsuccessful animal, the sickliest, the one most dangerously strayed from its instincts (1968: 124).

The flip side of Nietzsche's attempt to undermine human arrogance and pride is his recognition that the values and perspectives of nonhuman life forms must be taken into consideration. On a symbolic level, this is shown by the fact that Zarathustra's companions are animals, an eagle and a serpent, and by the fact that it is the eagle and serpent who first state Nietzsche's doctrine of the eternal return in *Thus Spake Zarathustra*. On a theoretical level, it is demonstrated by Nietzsche's epistemological position, known as *perspectivism*, in which he rejects epistemological anthropocentrism and explicitly acknowledges the views and values of nonhuman creatures. Stating in a note collected in *The Will to Power* that the attempt to privilege human interpretations and values is "one of the hereditary madnesses of human pride" (1969: 305), Nietzsche goes on to say that this privileging of human knowledge and values is directly linked to the attempt to "maintain and increase human constructs of domination" (1969: 14). However, in rejecting epistemological anthropocentrism and thereby deconstructing the human constructs of domination that have resulted from it, Nietzsche's later philosophy opens the way for a non-exploitative relationship of humanity with nature. Instead of viewing themselves as the crowns of creation and/or the masters of the nonhuman world, humans become plain members of the biotic community.

In addition to reimmersing humans into nature and thus rejecting epistemological anthropocentrism, Nietzsche is also one of the first modern Western thinkers to recognize two key concepts of contemporary ecological thinking: the interdependency of all living things, and the importance of environmental factors for the quality of both human and nonhuman life. In the *Twilight of the Idols*, Nietzsche coins the term "life-collective" (*Gesammt-Lebens*) to express the interdependency of human and nonhuman life forms, and in a note collected in *The Will to Power* he says clearly that "man is not only a single individual but one particular line of the total living organic world" (1969: 359–60). In other notes, he defines life as a system of interdependent forces that are connected by a common mode of nutrition (suggesting a view of the natural world similar to Aldo Leopold's land pyramid), and he describes the world as an energy system in which there is "contiguous and concurrent dependence" (1969: 340). Indeed, while Nietzsche's notion of the will to power has been variously interpreted, there is a clear sense in which the will to power serves as a concept that explains change immanently, a concept that comes close to the ecosystem approach of modern ecologists.

Like modern ecologists, moreover, Nietzsche is well aware of the way in which our theoretical views about the natural world can impact the quality of both human and nonhuman life. While Nietzsche's perspectivism contains an implicit call for the preservation of endangered species (since the values and perspectives of all life forms have epistemological significance), several passages in his writings and letters discuss the practical implications of our philosophical thinking about the world in which we live. One example of this is found in the following passage from *The Will to Power*: "The way our streets are paved, good air in our room, the soil, the wells not poisoned, food – we grasp their value; we have taken the necessities of existence seriously" (1969: 525).

"We have taken the necessities of existence seriously" – these simple words provide a key to understanding Nietzsche's significance to the topic of nature and religion. For as we have seen, Nietzsche not only relentlessly attacks those types of thinking that are other-worldly and anti-natural, he also repeatedly urges us to remain faithful to the Earth. In other words, one important thrust of Nietzsche's thinking, a thrust that has decidedly ecological implications, is to extend an invitation to us to return home – home to the Earth and to the joys of this-worldly existence. While this invitation reverberates throughout Nietzsche's later writings, it is already forcefully expressed in the following passage from *Human, All Too Human*, where he describes the "aftereffect" of philosophical thinking.

Finally one would live among men and with oneself as in *nature*, without praise, reproaches, overzealousness, delighting in many things . . . that one formerly had only to fear. One would . . . no longer feel the goading thought that one was not simply nature, or that one was more than nature (1984: 37).

This invitation for us to return home to the Earth, this call for us to live fully in the natural world, becomes even more pronounced in Nietzsche's later writings. Indeed, this invitation not only stands behind one of Nietzsche's most life-affirming concepts, the concept of *amor fati* (love of fate), it also becomes one of the principal motifs of Nietzsche's best-known work, *Thus Spake Zarathustra*. For whereas the concept of amor fati serves as a concept through which one is finally able to view the natural world without praise, reproaches, or overzealousness, one of the fundamental goals of Zarathustra's teaching is to lead us away from other-worldly hopes and back to the Earth. In other words, one of the primary thrusts of Nietzsche's thinking is to make it possible for each of us to leave our caves of ignorance and despair, as Zarathustra himself does, "glowing and strong as a morning sun that comes out of dark mountains" (1966: 327). But if we are to do so, Nietzsche tells us that we must learn the simple, yet difficult, lesson that the ugliest man learns from Zarathustra – we must learn to love the Earth and earthly existence.

Max O. Hallman

Further Reading

Drenthen, Martin. "The Paradox of Environmental Ethics: Nietzsche's View of Nature and the Wild." *Environmental Ethics* 21 (Summer 1999), 163–75.

Hallman, Max O. "Nietzsche's Environmental Ethics." *Environmental Ethics* 13 (Summer 1991), 99–125.

Langer, Monika. "The Role and Status of Animals in Nietzsche's Philosophy." In H. Peter Steeves, ed. *Animal Others: On Ethics, Ontology, and Animal Life*. Albany: State University of New York Press, 1999, 75–92.

Moles, Alaistair. *Nietzsche's Philosophy of Nature and Cosmology*. New York: Peter Lang, 1990.

Nietzsche, Friedrich Wilhelm. *The Portable Nietzsche*. Walter Kaufmann, tr. New York: Viking Penguin, 1982.

Nietzsche, Friedrich Wilhelm. *The Will to Power*. Walter Kaufmann and R.J. Hollingdale, trs. New York: Vintage Books, 1969.

Parkes, Graham. "Human/Nature in Nietzsche and Taoism." In J. Baird Callicott and Roger J. Ames, eds. *Nature in Asian Traditions and Thought*. New York: State University of New York Press, 1989, 79–97.

See also: Deep Ecology; Leopold, Aldo; Philosophy of Nature; White, Lynn – Thesis of.

Nile Perch

Sometimes called the world's largest freshwater fish, Nile perch (*Lates niloticus*) are not as big as White or Beluga sturgeon, Yangtze paddlefish, Amazonian pirarucu, or Mekong and Wels catfish. They are Africa's largest freshwater fish. Some have exceeded 6 feet in length and 500 pounds in weight. Remains pointing to rituals involving land and water animals, including Nile perch, have been found at ancient Egypt's Hierakonpolis-Nekhen ceremonial complex (ca. 4000–3100 B.C.E.). Nile perch are known fiercely to battle capture yet few Hierakonpolis-Nekhen skeletal materials belong to "small" perch (under 3.5 feet). One was 7 feet long. Nile perch burials dominated the fish section of Egypt's Gurob animal cemetery (ca. 1290-1190 B.C.E.). More attention was given to their preservation–mummification than with other fish, oxen, or sheep. Artifacts linked to Seth, a god connected to violence, and Sobek, the Crocodile God, were also found at Gurob, along with a pottery dish showing a Nile tilapia-lotus motif.

Greeks named the city of Esna "Latopolis" for the prominence that the Nile perch (*latos*-fish) held in the city's religious practices. Neith, who had Nile perch as a sacred symbol, was one of the deities the town's inhabitants worshipped. Archeologists have found coins and art with the venerated *latos*-fish and many mummified Nile perch there. A painting of Anubis, the jackal-headed god of the dead, embalming a Nile perch, appears at Luxor on the walls of the tomb of Khabekhnet, a tomb-builder for Rameses II (ca. 1290–1224 B.C.E.). Neith and the nome-sign of Latopolis are depicted, linking Luxor to Latopolis' spirituality. Other Luxor-area tomb art shows Menna, "Scribe of the Fields of Lord" under Tuthmosis IV (ca. 1400–1390 B.C.E.) and Amenhotep III (ca. 1390–1353 B.C.E.), thrusting a spear into waters with a Nile perch and Nile tilapia inside. The Nile perch has been interpreted as symbolizing the turbulent stage of the journey of the deceased; the Nile tilapia the calmer. Nile perch and Nile tilapia were often paired in Egyptian art. Symbolism joined what ecology gave some separation. Nile perch have preferred the Nile's deeper waters; tilapia the shallower. The two could come into conjunction in ways inimical to tilapia. Some Egyptian fish spears were tipped with Nile perch bone. Tilapia flesh served as bait for Nile perch.

Neith/Nit, a goddess whose importance to Upper and Lower Egypt was long-standing and who had the epithet "Terrifying One," was associated with Nile perch. Neith was associated with blessing warriors' and hunters' weapons and with mortuary rituals. As a creator deity, she cast her saliva into the primal waters, producing Apep/Apophis, the water-serpent, sometimes identified with the python, Africa's largest and most aquatic snake. Apep's attempt to swallow everything in the created world and send it into non-existence was continually battled by other deities. Apep was the nemesis of Neith's son Re/Ra, the Sun God. Neith also had the epithet "Nurse of Crocodiles." Neith's other son Sobek/Sebek took the shape of *Crocodylus niloticus*, reputedly Africa's greatest eater of humans, and a killer of large wild and domesticated animals. Neith sometimes took the form of the fierce *latos*-fish which was believed to swim beside Neith on her journeys. Neith's more benign activities included controlling floods and protecting marriages. Neith was generally thought of as an independent virgin-goddess; sometimes Seth was called her spouse.

Ancient Egyptians accorded Nile perch some beneficent attributes. Oil in which its dorsal fin had been cooked was used to increase milk flow in lactating mothers. Egyptian children and young women wore apotropaic fish pendants, including those of Nile perch, to avert drowning. When it came to beauty, however, Nile tilapia dominated on perfume containers and zoomorphous palettes which held cosmeceuticals used to protect and beautify eyes, like kohl. Mouth-brooding tilapias take their dependent young into their mouths to protect them, releasing them when danger passes. Tilapia/tilapia-lotus motifs signified rebirth in Egypt's religious art. Nile perch devoured this affirmative symbol.

Seth/Set was a deity of evil, hunger, destruction, wastelands, and the unclean. Seth slew, dismembered, and cast the body of Osiris, his brother, into the Nile. Most sources name the elephant snout fish (the *Oxyrhynchus* fish, *Mormyrus kannume*), seabream, eel, mudfish, or tiger fish (the *Phagrus*), and Nile carp (the Lepidotus fish, *Barbus bynni*), as the fish that ate Osiris' phallus. A few sources place Nile perch in this group. The elephant snout fish, with which the Nile perch is most often misidentified in these presentations, actually feeds upon insects and midge larvae, while the Nile perch is almost fully carnivorous-piscivorous. Nile perch were among the fish trampled and burned in some areas of Egypt in a ritual repudiating opponents of divine-royal order. In some places, tomb inscriptions have fish hieroglyphics which appear to have been made and then deliberately damaged, following "homeopathic magic," to prevent dangerous fish from injuring the deceased.

Nile perch is a misnomer in ichthyogeographical terms. It is not a true perch but a snook, and is indigenous to other waters, including some in Benin, Chad, Côte d'Ivoire, Ghana, Guinea, Guinea-Bissau, Liberia, Mali, Niger, Nigeria, Senegal, Sierra Leone, and Togo. While Nile perch fossils dating to the Miocene have been found on Rusinga Island in Lake Victoria, the lake was later drained by geological faulting. In its current form, Lake Victoria arose 12,000–12,400 years ago as a shallow but vast water. A rich and diverse variety of cichlid fishes proliferated in the absence of Nile perch. In the 1950s, Nile perch were introduced into the lake with catastrophic consequences. Had more attention been paid to the biological observations embedded in Egyptian religious beliefs about Nile perch, British plans for the world's second largest freshwater lake might not have gone so awry. Destruction, devouring, and death were symbols made quite concrete when this large predator was taken from waters where it was endemic and placed elsewhere.

Plantations, pesticides, pollution, and population growth around Lake Victoria had led to decline of its indigenous cichlids (tilapias and haplochromines) by the 1950s. In response, the British put Nile tilapia (*nyamami*: *Oreochromis/Tilapia niloticus*), which grow to a little over two feet, into Lake Victoria. Other introduced tilapia, ranging from one and a half feet to nine inches did not catch on well. Placed into the lake, Nile perch exploded in numbers. Many of Lake Victoria's indigenous cichlids were unable to survive the onslaught of the voracious, prolific Nile perch. At present, 65–85 percent of the estimated 350–500 or more indigenous species, many unique to Lake Victoria, are said to have died out, or become rare. Nile perch ate fish which helped control malaria, schistosomiasis, detritus, anoxia, and the diseases algal blooms-cyanobacteria bring. Indigenous tilapias (*ngege*: *Oreochromis esculenta*, *ngege/mbiru*: *Oreochromis variabilis*) can be sun-dried. Nile perch are too big and oily; they have to be wood-smoked for local preservation without refrigeration. Further deforestation, eutrophication, and disease ensued. Lake conditions contributed to proliferation of water hyacinth (*Eichhornia crassipes*), "the beautiful blue devil." It prevented even large boats from leaving some ports, blocked irrigation canals, and led to human displacement when clogged areas of the lake flooded. This "curse" can form masses so extensive that ordinary people can "walk on water" where it flourishes. Mechanical removal, hand removal, chemicals, biological agents, and indigenous doctor-diviners have been set against it, but the resurgent "devil" eludes defeat.

Scientists have documented these details, lamented fish extinction, and then considered this extinction "an event as exciting as it is depressing" to observe (Kaufman 1992: 846). Terms like "fish genocide" and a "green holocaust" are scarce, perhaps because they question why the mass extinction of nonhuman animals has not evoked the widespread revulsion associated with human genocides, particularly those in Europe. Some local and foreign sources even portray Nile perch as a "Savior" (*Mkombozi*) of the lake-basin economy, and a "successful predator" by capitalistic calculus. Yet it is national and foreign elites rather than local people who are the main beneficiaries of the Nile perch takeover of Lake Victoria. Independent fishermen who used small boats when they fished offshore, and women who had processed and traded sun-dried fish and done some riverbank fishing lost out to an industry predicated on big boats, unrelated workers, refrigeration, and mostly foreign-funded processing plants concerned with export of Nile perch fillets, hides, and other by-products to Israel, Europe, Asia, Australia, and the USA. Proponents note Nile perch is protein-rich with high levels of Omega-3 fatty acids. Many Luo claim its fatty, oily character makes it difficult to digest. Some studies show it absorbs more mercury than other fish, making it unhealthy in the long term, especially for women and children. With a high percentage of fillets sent overseas, poor people get smoked, leftover scraps. Protein export coexists with protein deficiency diseases.

Having eaten its way through many cichlid species, Nile perch are increasingly feeding on their young or small shrimp (*Caridina nilotica*). With changing international tastes for less fatty foods, remaining juveniles are being exported. By the 1980s, while 500-lb "giants" were still reported, most Nile perch caught ranged from 110–220 lbs. Presently, it is said the average size may be a tenth of that. This fish with predatory appetites seems itself threatened by global capitalism and its appetites.

Scientists, the Ugandan, Tanzanian, and Kenyan governments, the UN, and NGOs have produced a vast literature on Nile perch's impact on Lake Victoria's ecosystem. The religious response has not been proportionate. A number of NGOs have religious help in funding projects to "save" the lake. However, Henry Sindima, a Presbyterian minister-scholar from Malawi, is one of the few commentators to mention Nile perch's impact on Lake Victoria, link it to ecological theology, and critique development "experts" who fail to acknowledge the "spiritual intelligence" of African peoples (1990: 140, 142). Many Western missionaries working around Lake Victoria consider eating Nile perch an "authentic" African experience. Some Christians assert that the fish connected with Jesus' miracles was the Egyto-African Nile perch, although Nile tilapia ("St. Peter's fish") is a more likely candidate. Exponents of Afrocentric theology and Theosophy tend to present Nile perch positively, though close attention to Egyptian religious history shows it was an ambivalent symbol. Evangelist Billy Graham's parable of "God's Provision in a Fish"/"Keys in an African Fish," a popular sermon topic, displays no awareness of Nile perch's historical trajectory in Africa.

Many Africans living around Lake Victoria know it as more than nature endangered. Baganda have called it *Nalubaale*, "Mother of the Gods." For Kenya Luo, it is *Nam Lolwe*, "The Endless Lake." They take their identity from it, calling themselves *Jonam*, "people of the lake." Indigenous Luo religion had rituals for making boats and fishing implements, for recognizing the spiritual personality and maintaining the sanctity of boats, for setting out to fish. A death out on *Lolwe* was "like one kinsman killing another" (Ocholla-Ayayo 1980: 123). For Luo, *Lolwe* has been home to powerful possession spirits. What the Nile perch introduction has irreparably harmed is not the nature of positivistic and "dismal" sciences – it is nature imbued with spirituality, peoplehood, political economy, and passions.

Legio Maria, the largest African-instituted church in sub-Saharan Africa showing Roman Catholic influence, began among Kenya Luo circa 1963. It has a long list of potential food prohibitions. Legios believe that the Holy Spirit can provide personal release from some prohibitions or move an individual toward stricter observance. Prohibitions are placed upon things seen as polluting the body, "the tabernacle of God." Alcohol, tobacco, and goat-meat prohibitions are the most likely to be observed. Nile perch is next for many Legios. Many will not drink unboiled water, bathe in open water, eat chyme or meat from livestock that has not been slaughtered but is found dead, believing these harm the body-as-tabernacle. One reason Legios reject goat, quail, and wild greens/edible botanicals is their association with doctor-diviners, who work with indigenous spirits rather than the Holy Spirit. A number of prohibitions follow from Leviticus 11 (e.g., pork, hare, flying "white ants"/termites, fish without scales). Many Legios consider all fish with "snake-like" appearance, "ugly snouts," or bottom-feeding habits abominations, whether or not they have scales, and reject lungfish (*Protopterus aethiopicus*), elephant-snout fish (*Mormyrus kannume*), mudfish (*Bagrus bajad, B. domac*), and various catfish (*Arius africanus, Clarias spp, Amphilius jacksonii, Schilbe spp. Synodontis spp.*). Bony fish which can choke people and the Holy Spirit may be on Legios' lists of rejected food. *Omena* (*Rastrineobola argentea*) are on lists because these 1.75 inch "little sardines" are equated with swarming insects, because the mounds these insects build for homes are equated with graves, and because cooking *omena* sends a smell upwards deemed offensive to the Holy Spirit. Children are allowed to "grow into the Spirit." Some eat foods a parent rejects. Cheap *omena* rather than smoked Nile perch bits are the fish-protein many Legio children now get to eat.

Most tabooed fish have declined in numbers with Nile perch predation but Legios are not favorably inclined toward the killer of "abominable" fish. The most common reason Legios give for considering Nile perch an utter abomination is its cannibalism of fish, fishermen, and others who fall into *Lolwe*. Legios have also spoken against the harm it brings to the body-as-tabernacle, particularly their experience of intestinal and skin problems. Legios view it as anomalous in size and behavior. It is blamed for causing tragedy, trouble, and death in *Lolwe*. Nile perch are anti-charismatic megafauna for Legios.

Legios reject the multicolored garment (*law mokiko*) saying it creates an environment the Holy Spirit does not want to enter. A synonym for "mixed-up" clothing is

"Nile perch clothing" (*law mbuta*). Many diviner-doctors, especially those who work with lake-dwelling possession spirits, share Legios' dislike of Nile perch. Doctor-diviners claim their spirits strongly protest against it,

> Mumbo is a spirit whose ways I know well. The spirits want Nile perch to be stopped – it is a thing of today. That is why the Mumbo-spirit rumbled, making a loud sound that reached from Kadenge to the lake. It was the sound "Dududududuu," sounds like that (Schwartz 1989: 206).

At a Legio church in the 1980s, the Voice of the Holy Spirit, speaking through a woman congregant, was explicit in its odium, "All of you curse Nile perch, my friends!" (*Kuoug'euru mbuta, yawa*). The congregation responded back resoundingly, "*Wakuong'e*, 'We curse it' " (Schwartz 1989: 308–10). A few Legio women, driven to sell smoked Nile perch for needed income at local markets, reported having nightmares afterwards. The local unacceptability of Nile perch has been strong and spirited.

Nancy Schwartz

Further Reading

Barlow, George W. *The Cichlid Fishes: Nature's Grand Experiment in Evolution.* Cambridge, Massachusetts: Perseus Publishing, 2000.

Brewer, Douglas and Renee Friedman. *Fish and Fishing in Ancient Egypt.* Warminster, England: Aris and Phillips, 1990.

Kaufman, Les. "Catastrophic Change in Species-Rich Freshwater Ecosystems: The Lessons of Lake Victoria." *Bioscience* 42:11 (1992), 846–58.

Ocholla-Ayayo, A.B.C. *The Luo Culture.* Wiesbaden: Franz Steiner, 1980.

Pitcher, Tony and Paul Hart, eds. *The Impact of Species Changes in African Lakes.* London: Chapman and Hall, 1995.

Schwartz, Nancy. *World Without End: The Meanings and Movements in the History, Narratives and "Tongue-Speech" of Legio Maria of African Church Mission Among Luo of Kenya.* Unpublished dissertation. Princeton University, 1989.

Sindima, Henry. "Community of Life: Ecological Theology in African Perspective." In *Liberating Life: Approaches in Ecological Theology.* Charles Birch, William Eaken, and Jay McDaniel, eds. Maryknoll, NY: Orbis Books, 1990, 137–47.

Stoneman, J. "Burden or Blessing for Lake Victoria?" *Geographical Magazine* 60:10 (1990), 28–42.

See also: Egypt (both); Fishers; Snakes and the Luo of Kenya.

Noble Savage

"Primitivism" is a belief that arose during the European Romantic Movement which held that people who live in a natural setting are closer to God and thus live purer lives. The primitivist prefers the "natural," tribal life to highly urbanized social orders, and reveres impulsiveness, free expression and passion over the dictates of reason, rules and the restrictions of form. The motif of the "Noble Savage" is an idealized stereotype of indigenous people as primitive in this sense. Its two main elements are a reverence for people in the rural environment, and a simplistic representation of indigenous morality, including the assignment of high-minded virtue to pastoral peoples. The motif is connected with the belief that goodness, dignity and nobility have to do with a primitive and free state that existed in innocent prototypical people like Adam and Eve in the Garden of Eden. It came into existence largely as a reaction against the onslaught of capitalism, industrialization and materialism in the later half of the eighteenth century and early nineteenth century.

The phrase "Noble Savage," was first expressed in the eighteenth century by Jean Jacques Rousseau (1712–1778) in his famous essay, "The Social Contract," (1762) where he stated that humanity in a state of nature does not know good and evil, but their independence, along with "the peacefulness of their passions, and their ignorance of vice," keeps them from wickedness. To Rousseau, the Noble Savage represented the "natural man," uncorrupted by contact with the structures of society, or the evil effects of civilization including political organization and technology. This idea is reiterated in *Emile* (1762) where Rousseau writes, "Everything is well when it comes fresh from the hands of the Maker . . . everything degrades in the hands of Man" (pages vary by edition).

Since Rousseau, the "Noble Savage" has become a stereotypical romanticization of indigenous people in general, particularly in pre-European America and Africa, especially the Zulu's and Maasai when allied with militaristic idealization, but not limited by those territorial boundaries. Examples of the motif stretch back to antiquity, but are readily identifiable in Michel Eyuemde Montaigne (1533–1592) in his Essay "Of Cannibals" (1580), later in Dryden's play *The Conquest of Granada* (1670) and more famously in Aphra Behn's *Oroonoko: or the History of the Royal Slave* (1688). This motif has special significance in America where the concept of the Noble Savage is integral to the early nineteenth-century fascination with North American Aboriginal peoples. The romanticized American Aborigine personified the spirituality assigned to humanity in a natural state, uncorrupted by European society, thus reinforcing the established links between primitivism and the "Noble Savage."

Rousseau's contrast between natural and social existence attests to the underlying elevation of "White" civilization in the noble savage myth: "Although, in this state [civil society], he deprives himself of some advantages which he got from nature, he gains in return others so great, his faculties are stimulated and developed" (Rousseau 1993: Book I, section 8). However, Rousseau's Eurocentrism paled in comparison to some xenophobic commentators. Charles Dickens wrote

> I beg to say that I have not the least belief in the Noble Savage. I consider him a prodigious nuisance, and an enormous superstition. His calling rum fire-water, and me a pale face, wholly fail to reconcile me to him. I don't care what he calls me. I call him a savage, and I call a savage a something highly desirable to be civilised off the face of the Earth (Dickens 1850: pages vary by edition).

Although the motif of the "Noble Savage" is primarily associated with the nineteenth century, its antecedents are still with us today. The main tropes of the motif still embrace a belief in the superiority of the person in a rural setting and an associated spiritual superiority or closeness to God in nature, but now also include an associated ecological soundness romanticized as the indigenous worldview.

John Senior

Further Reading

Barnett, Louise K. *The Ignoble Savage: American Literary Racism 1790–1890*. Westport, CT: Greenwood Press, 1975.
Dickens, Charles, ed. *Household Words [serial]*. London: Bradbury and Evans, 1850–1859.
Lovejoy, Arthur and George Boas. *Primitivism and Related Ideas in Antiquity*. Baltimore: Johns Hopkins University, 1997.
Hammond, Dorthy and Alta Jablow. *The Africa that Never Was*. Prospect Heights, IL: Waveland Press, 1992.
Rousseau, Jean-Jacques. *Emile ou de l'éducation/Jean-Jacques Rousseau; introduction et bibliographie par Tanguy L'Aminot; établissement du texte, notes et index par François et Pierre Richard*. Edition illustrée. Paris: Classiques Garnier, 1999.
Rousseau, Jean Jacques. *The Social Contract; and, Discourses*. G.D.H. Cole, tr. London: J.M. Dent; Rutland, VT: C.M. Tuttle, 1993.

See also: American Indians as "First Ecologists"; Eden and Other Gardens; Mother Earth; Religious Environmental Paradigm; Romanticism and Indigenous People; Rousseau, Jean-Jacques; Savages.

Noble, David F. (1938–)

David Noble is a historian of technology whose body of work has explored how technology has more often been used to reinforce hierarchy than to deliver humans from drudgery. In *The Religion of Technology* Noble traced the role that spiritual investiture plays in driving and rationalizing centralized technological development. Understanding technology as a religion can help explain why so many have embraced rapid technological change despite its human and ecological costs, he has argued.

For over 1000 years in Western Europe the "useful arts" have been closely associated with notions of salvation, driving technological innovation, by Nobel's account. Innovation is primarily driven by interest, he says: it is the means by which some people and societies control and subjugate others. But cultural justification is necessary, and for those benefiting from technology the religious impulse cloaks self-interest, justifies the technological world, and comforts those who suffer from it. Noble finds his earliest evidence among ninth-century Benedictines who embraced knowledge of the useful arts as something akin to godliness. Charlemagne's heirs were influenced by Benedictines. Joachim of Fiore (twelfth century), Noble reports, saw the development of technology as a means toward reunification with God. The thirteenth-century Franciscans and Roger Bacon believed humans had lost the knowledge of God's creation with the Fall and could regain it by increasing humanity's knowledge of the world, technology being a primary means. It was the sixteenth century's Francis Bacon, however, heir to the Rosicrucian revival of an earlier era, who most fully developed the theme of reclaiming the garden through application of the useful arts. Noble argues that Bacon saw the useful arts as the path to heaven and as marking human uniqueness. He quotes Bacon: "We are agreed, my sons, that you are men. That means, as I think, that you are not animals on their hind legs, but mortal gods" (Bacon in Noble 1977: 51). This hubris, Noble argues, combined with early capitalism, was an irresistible historical force that accelerated the pace of technological innovation in the face of injury and criticism.

The founders of the early modern scientific academies further developed the religious view of technology, Noble argues, viewing science and technology as indistinct. The knowledge necessary for and generated by technological innovation not only helped the faithful know God's creation, but also allowed them to know the mind of the Great Architect. Scientists considered science the pursuit of divine knowledge and held it sacred, Noble argued, in *A World Without Women*. As late as the early nineteenth century, Noble documents scientists declaring that the truths of science and religion could never conflict. Darwin, he reminds us, changed all that, and because science and technology formally disengaged into separate spheres by the mid-nineteenth century, this enabled technological faith to continue while science challenged religious orthodoxy and even belief in a Creator.

Noble argues that three of the twentieth century's major technological projects have a powerful religious component: space travel, artificial intelligence, and genetic engineering. From the early days of the missile program to NASA at present, Noble argues, religiosity has permeated the space program. Werner Von Braun spoke of taking the gospel to other worlds; astronauts have spoken of flight bringing them closer to God. Noble quotes Lewis Mumford: "Only a mixture of adventurous impulses and religious convictions of the deepest sort would persuade normal warm-hearted human beings, such as many astronauts seem to be, to take part in such a life-denying ritual" (Mumford in Noble 1997: 137).

Noble admits that the project to create a thinking machine has not been explicitly religious in the way the space program has been. But he argues that the project is nonetheless imbued with an extreme dualism characteristic of much Western religious thought: the animal is a degrading fetter on the spirit. By stripping away the body, reason and spirit approach god-like perfection. Noble quotes Danny Hill of the Massachusetts Institute of Technology: "[W]hat's good about humans is the idea thing. It's not the animal thing" (Hill in Noble 1997: 162–3).

Genetic engineering is seen by many practitioners, Noble says, as providing the opportunity to join with God and become co-creators of life. Genetic engineers see their applied knowledge as God's gift, allowing them to redeem humanity by reprogramming evolution's haphazard programming. Since they believe genetics can only alter the body and not the soul, Noble says, they believe nothing can go terribly wrong.

Critics have puzzled at Noble's failure to address more directly the effects of the marriage of technology and religion on the natural world. Keith Thomas, the British historian, noted that Noble's argument doesn't account for the many other, non-Christian and secular cultural milieus in which technology has developed; nor do his arguments acknowledge that Christianity was far from monolithic, at times ignoring or opposing technological development.

David Johns

Further Reading

Noble, David F. *The Religion of Technology, The Divinity of Man and the Spirit of Invention*. New York: Knopf, 1997.

Noble, David F. *A World Without Women: The Christian Clerical Culture of Western Science*. New York: Knopf, 1992.

Noble, David F. *America by Design: Science, Technology and the Rise of Corporate Capitalism*. New York: Knopf, 1977.

Thomas, Keith. "God in the Computer." 45 *New York Review of Books* 20 (1998), 78–80.

See also: Astronauts; Space Exploration.

Noble Savage and the "Ecologically Noble" Savage

Since the Greeks and Romans of classical antiquity, but most of all from the age of European geographic exploration and colonization, usually the "savage" has represented the primitive condition of humans in nature prior to the domestication of plants and animals. Both the earliest stage of prehistoric cultural evolution, and contemporary hunter-gatherers as supposed analogues, have been viewed in two diametrically opposed ways, in essence as either positive or negative.

More than anyone, philosopher Jean-Jacques Rousseau (1712–1778) is usually credited with the positive view, but not necessarily accurately. The 'noble savage" was envisioned as enjoying a life of harmony within society and between it and nature. This is the romantic image of the "primitive" as superior in freedom, innocence, simplicity, generosity, goodness, purity, and peacefulness. Also this society was conceived as an egalitarian community with property held in common rather than privately. Such an ideal or utopian society supposedly thrived in a natural paradise during a golden age.

By the eighteenth century those Europeans ascribing to this cult of exoticism pursued the critical analysis of their own society and its morality and politics by glorifying the "savage" in contrast to degenerate civilization, the ideology of primitivism. Indeed, primitivists would even go so far as to reject civilization, at least in their discourse although almost never in practice. In theory the "noble savage" offered alternative possibilities for European society, having been identified variously as archetypal primitive communists, ecologists, environmentalists, conservationists, spiritualists, healers, philosophers, and pacifists.

For primitivists, these societies are not simply a more desirable human condition, but also are closer to nature, most living in wilderness. A correlate is that such societies practice various kinds of nature religion or eco-spirituality. Accordingly, implicitly if not explicitly, the societies and religions of civilization are critiqued as unnatural and environmentally destructive. Environmental organizations from the Sierra Club to Earth First! have stereotyped indigenes as guardians of nature – "green primitivism." The so-called "ecologically noble savage" and nature religions have often found common ground in New Age spiritualities like neo-paganism and their antecedents.

The "noble savage" was popularized much more than anywhere else through the arts (poetry, novels, drama, opera, art, music), but occasionally surfaced in philosophy and eventually in the social sciences. Among the better known examples in literature are Daniel Defoe's *Robinson Crusoe* (1719), Jonathan Swift's *Gulliver's Travels* (1726), James Fenimore Cooper's *Last of the Mohicans* (1826), and William H. Hudson's *Green Mansions* (1904). Hollywood's *Dances with Wolves* (1989) expressed this idea, and the movie's widespread popularity indicates that the idea of the "noble savage" remained attractive in the late twentieth century.

Within anthropology, primitivism is more of a personal and private emotional attitude than any overt and examined philosophical, intellectual, or theoretical stance, according to William Y. Adams. Nevertheless, elements of primitivism can be detected in the writings of many anthropologists, some more explicitly than others, including Franz Boas, Margaret Mead, Ruth Benedict, Paul Radin, Claude Lévi-Strauss, Stanley Diamond, Marshall Sahlins, Elman R. Service, John Bodley, and Gerardo Reichel-Dolmatoff. Primitivism is also reflected in the life of several notable anthropologists who have actually "gone native" while living in an indigenous culture for many years or even decades, including Frank Hamilton Cushing with the Zuni, Jacques Lizot with the Yanomami, Kurt Nimuendaju with several Amazonian societies, and Patrick Putnam with the Pygmies of the Congo. Some outstanding ethnographic examples of the "noble savage" are Ishi of the Yahi, Kayapo, Kogi, Koyukon, Kuna, Mbuti, Semai, Tahitians, and Tasaday. In the first textbook on spiritual ecology, David Kinsley (1995) portrays the Ainu, Australian Aborigines, Mistassini Cree, and Koyukon, all hunter-gatherers, as ecologically noble by virtue of their nature religions which tend to promote sustainable subsistence economies and green cultures.

The opposite of this romantic view, the "ignoble savage," is commonly attributed to philosopher Thomas Hobbes (1588–1679). Hobbes imagined "savage" life as poor, nasty, brutish, and short. This negative view considers "primitive" life to be permeated by disharmony, conflict, and violence, both socially and ecologically. Ritualized violence, such as blood sacrifice and cannibalism, is another common correlate.

Paradoxically, in the writings of a single individual, the prominent British anthropologist Colin Turnbull (1961, 1972), both extremes are found, the Mbuti Pygmies of the Ituri forest in the heart of Africa described as "noble savages," and the Ik in the rugged mountains of Uganda as "ignoble savages." He depicted the Ik as former foragers, forced by the government to relocate, sedentarize, and farm; and, as a result, a degenerate and dehumanized society without sociality, culture, morality, and religion. Not surprisingly, Turnbull was severely criticized for his explicit negativity regarding the Ik, but not for his positive view of the Mbuti.

As described by Turnbull, the Mbuti are the epitome of the "noble savage" in the way their society and religion are embedded in nature. For millennia they have lived as an integral part of the forest in all of its beauty, goodness, and mystery. Their profound dependence, understanding, respect, and affection regarding the forest is best expressed in the words of one Mbuti: "The forest is a father and mother to us . . . and like a father or mother it gives us everything we need – food, clothing, shelter warmth . . . and affection" (Turnbull 1961: 89).

The Mbuti commune with the forest not only in their daily subsistence activities, but also in their sacred music which embraces singing, chanting, and dancing around the camp fire at night in a ritual called the molimo. In particular, they use a long wooden or bamboo trumpet (molimo) to sing through, or to make naturalistic imitations of the voices of forest animals, such as the leopard and the elephant which respectively symbolize life and death. The trumpet for this ritual is retrieved from high in a tree where it is usually stored, then bathed in a stream, and brought into the camp late at night. If this ritual is to be repeated the next night, then during the day the trumpet is hidden in a streambed. Women and children are not supposed to see the molimo, they hide in the huts when the sounds of the trumpet become audible as it is played by men approaching camp. While men take turns using the trumpet, the distinctive effect seems to transcend any human noise to become an awesome sound invoking the great spirit of the forest.

If the Mbuti suffer bad luck in hunting, illness, death, social tensions, or other problems, then they believe that the spirit of the forest has fallen asleep and must be awakened by the molimo so that it will again protect and nourish them. The molimo sounds awaken the forest and make it happy, and thereby the Mbuti are empowered with its trust and love. Thus, for the Mbuti, the forest is their benevolent deity, their religion is the worship of nature, and this is celebrated through the sounds of the molimo. In sum, Turnbull writes:

> They were a people who had found in the forest something that made their life more than just worth living, something that made it, with all its hardships and problems and tragedies, a wonderful thing full of joy and happiness and free from care (1961: 17).

In conclusion, whether it is the relationship of "savages" to one another within or among societies, or with nature, Westerners tend to emphasize either the positive or negative image. That is, "savages" exemplify a life of harmony socially and ecologically far more than any other culture, or else they are antithetical to sociality and nature. In reality, however, the world is far more complicated, varied, and variable than to sustain such all-or-none and always-or-never postures. Either pole, the "noble savage" or the "ignoble savage," is simplistic, dualistic, reductionist, and essentializing. Extremists ignore the tremendous variations among and within the up to 7000 distinct cultures extant today. It is far more scholarly and scientific to consider this great diversity through particular cases, rather than to over-generalize in either idealistic or derogatory excess. Both the noble and the ignoble representations of the "primitive" need to be scrutinized for the possiblity of a hidden agenda and its consequences as well as deconstructed and thereby demystified. Nevertheless, often indigenous cultures can provide profound wisdom and insights for realizing the place of humans in nature in spiritual and other ways.

Leslie E. Sponsel

Further Readings

Adams, William Y. "Primitivism." In *The Philosophical Roots of Anthropology*. Stanford, CA: CSLI Publications (Center for the Study of Language and Information, Leland Stanford Junior University), 1998, 75–112.

Albanese, Catherine L. *Nature Religion in America: From the Algonkian Indians to the New Age*. Chicago, IL: University of Chicago Press, 1990.

Barnard, Alan. "Images of Hunters and Gatherers in European Social Thought." In Richard B. Lee and Richard H. Daly, eds. *The Cambridge Encyclopedia of Hunters and Gatherers*. New York, NY: Cambridge University Press, 1999, 375–83.

Buege, Douglas J. "The Ecologically Noble Savage Revisited." *Environmental Ethics* 18:18 (1996), 71–88.

Edgerton, Robert B. *Sick Societies: Challenging the Myth of Primitive Harmony*. New York, NY: Free Press, 1992.

Ellen, Roy F. "What Black Elk Left Unsaid: On the Illusory Images of Green Primitivism." *Anthropology Today* 2:6 (1986), 8–12.

Ellingson, Ter. *The Myth of the Noble Savage*. Berkeley, CA: University of California Press, 2001.

Grinde, Donald A. and Bruce E. Johansen. "Native Americans: America's First Ecologists?" In *Ecocide of Native America: Environmental Destruction of Indian Lands and Peoples*. Santa Fe, NM: Clear Light Publishers, 1995, 22–55.

Harvey, Graham. *Contemporary Paganism: Listening People, Speaking Earth*. New York, NY: New York University, 1997.

Jahoda, Gustav. *Images of Savages: Ancient Roots of Modern Prejudice in Western Culture*. New York, NY: Routledge, 1999.

Kinsley, David. *Ecology and Religion: Ecological Spirituality in Cross-Cultural Perspective*. Englewood Cliffs, NJ: Prentice-Hall, 1995.

Narby, Jeremy and Francis Huxley. *Shamans Thought Time: 500 Years on the Path to Knowledge*. New York: Jeremy P. Tarcher/Putnam, 2001.

Pandian, Jacob. "The Mythology of the Savage Other in the Western Tradition." In his *Anthropology and the Western Tradition: Toward an Authentic Anthropology*. Prospect Heights, IL: Waveland Press, Inc., 1985, 62–9.

Turnbull, Colin M. *The Mountain People*. New York, NY: Simon & Schuster, 1972.

Turnbull, Colin M. *The Forest People*. Garden City, NY: Doubleday & Co., 1961.

See also: American Indians as "First Ecologists"; Anarchism; Anthropologists; Anthropology as a Source of Nature Religion; Earth First! and the Earth Liberation Front; Ethnobotany; Ethnoecology; Mother Earth; Pygmies (Mbuti foragers) & Bila Farmers (Ituri Forest); Radical Environmentalism; Reichel-Dolmatoff, Gerardo and Ethnoecology in Columbia; Romanticism and Indigenous Peoples; Rousseau, Jean-Jacques; Savages; Sierra Club; Traditional Ecological Knowledge.

North American Conference on Christianity and Ecology [and the] North American Coalition on Religion and Ecology

The North American Conference on Christianity and Ecology (NACCE) was one of the early organizations in the United States founded to motivate Christians toward ecological action. Founded in 1986 by Al Fritsch, David Haenke and Fred Krueger, it originally attempted to bring together activists from across the Christian theological spectrum. The desire was to bring everyone together to "elucidate Christianity's ecological dimension," as the motto on their symbol, the North American continent surrounded by crosses, reads.

Toward this end, the organization held a major conference in 1987 at a Methodist camp in North Webster, Indiana, attended by over 500 people. This was a significant turnout considering that the idea of Christian ecology was still relatively new in the U.S. and Canada. One stated goal of the conference/organization was to help "Christians become ecologists." But even before the conference took place, tensions concerning this goal erupted during the initial planning, as the organizers argued over whether to solely focus on Christianity. The decision was made that a conference on Christianity still left room for participants from other traditions. Tensions were also evident at the conference between the more interfaith, cosmologically oriented theology of Thomas Berry and the more biblically oriented theology of the evangelical and Orthodox members, especially as delegates worked together to articulate a statement of Christian ecology. No statement was ever approved by everyone at the conference, although a version was published in the proceedings of the conference. This was in part because of objections from the Berry advocates who complained of an over-reliance in the document on biblical references, while on the other side, conservative Christians charged that creation spirituality was pagan and all references to creation spirituality should be excluded. From reports in their magazine, *Epiphany*, members of the Orthodox Eleventh Commandment Fellowship, one of the organizing groups, were particularly offended by the "beyond Christianity" approach of Thomas Berry and adherents of the creation spirituality associated with Matthew Fox. In one statement, they called Fox a "wolf in sheep's clothing." They also objected to Berry's suggestion to put the Christian Scriptures temporarily on "the shelf" in order to learn from the revelation of the "new story" found in the evolution of the universe and his view that the future lay in developing a common religious ecological worldview, a common creation story, that went beyond the exclusivity of many religious traditions. Put simply, the differences in definitions of Christianity and theology, as well as the future direction of outreach – whether to be solely focused on Christians – were too great to be overcome for the group to present a unified Christian voice.

By 1989, after a bumpy two years, the outcome of the tensions led to two separate organizations – NACCE: the North American Coalition (or Conference) on Christianity and Ecology, and NACRE, the North American Coalition on Religion and Ecology. The confusing similarity of the names highlights the tension of the split. While their differences were great in the beginning (even though Thomas Berry's brother, James, was the president of NACCE), with the diminished influence of those associated with the Eleventh Commandment Fellowship, and with the growth and diversification of the religious environmental movement, the two organizations were not so far apart a decade later.

In the early years and up until 1991, NACCE published a magazine entitled *Firmament*. With the departure of its editor, Fred Krueger, the group started publishing a simpler newsletter entitled *Earthkeeping News* under the long-term guidance of Elizabeth Dyson. In its initial stages, NACCE was associated with James Berry, Fred Krueger (later of the Religious Campaign for Forest Conservation) and the Eleventh Commandment Fellowship, Cal DeWitt and the Au Sable Institute, and NACCE soon merged with Wesley Granberg-Michaelson's New Creation Institute. Grandberg-Michaelson, author of several eco-theology books in the 1980s, served on the World Council of Churches and played a significant role at the 1992 Earth Summit in Rio de Janiero, Brazil. Granberg-Michaelson's theology in many ways summed up the stewardship or earthkeeping approach of the organization. This eco-theological position was premised on the Genesis commandment (said by many eco-stewards to be God's first commandment) for humans to till and keep the "garden" or Earth.

Despite the anthropocentric implications of the "Earthkeeping" name, NACCE's approach involves more than stewardship, or the human care for God's creation and resources. The pages of *Earthkeeping News* demonstrate the group's commitment to issues of environmental justice and its support for a wide range of activities and theologies. The organization's mission even speaks of "a loving relationship with Earth" that includes "reverence for God's creation, with the understanding that humans are embedded in the natural world," as well as "the study of ecological issues in the context of biblical theology and contemporary science." NACCE has sponsored several noteworthy conferences, and has worked to promote earthkeeping circles, once termed eco-churches, both within and outside of individual congregations. NACCE is now a broad and mainstream Christian (Catholic, Protestant and Orthodox) ecological membership organization that has moved far beyond some of its conservative Christian roots. It represents a broad spectrum of Christians, from evangelicals to Quakers, with an openness to interfaith work. NACCE is active in the Earth Charter movement, and was a significant religious ecological presence at the second World Parliament of Religions in 1993, where it offered six environment-related workshops.

NACRE, or the North American Coalition on Religion and Ecology, was founded by Catholic Don Conroy (a member of NACCE) in part, as the name change reflects, in order to pursue a more interfaith approach. The schism of the two groups was not amicable, for NACRE took with it a recently awarded World Wildlife Fund grant to organize the 1990 Earth Day ceremony at the Episcopal National Cathedral in Washington, D.C. The WWF was sponsor of the Assisi Declarations on Religion and Nature, made by representatives of the world religions in 1986. The WWF approach embodied the perspective of Berry, who had been influential at the Assisi conference. The schism was also the result of power struggles for influence within NACCE. For a while, there was talk of lawsuits and charges about not forwarding mail to the correct organization, but both organizations survived the split. Even NACRE's vision, as summed up in the phrase "Caring for Creation," is similar in focus to NACCE's emphasis on "earthkeeping."

NACRE, however, pursued this vision in a different manner than NACCE, for its central focus is the advocacy of the "Eco3 Solution" of getting "ecologists, economists, and ecumenists to have," as Conroy describes it, a "trialogue, in which religion, science and society clarify and come to share values for a new global ethic which promotes sustainability at all levels" (email correspondence with author, 24 June 2003). Although NACRE briefly attempted to become a membership organization and tried to produce a newsletter, the organization's focus, under Conroy's continuing leadership, has always been on forming partnerships for education and specific projects. In 1990, it produced a religious study guide to accompany the 1990 Public Broadcasting Service television series, "Race to Save the Planet," and during the 1990s, NACRE worked with the United States Environmental Protection Agency both on climate-change education, and with its "Solar Stewardship Initiative" in an effort to enlist 340,000 faith-based congregations and organizations. NACRE is listed on websites concerning genetically engineered food, the treatment of animals, sustainability, solar energy, and the Earth Charter, which illustrates how it has sought to work outside religious circles and closely with environmental organizations. NACRE, along with its international arm, ICORE, is listed as part of Earthvoice, which describes itself as the "Global Environmental Arm of the United States Humane Society" and also as "the chairman" of ICORE. It is through Earthvoice that NACRE has worked to promote the Earth Charter.

Laurel Kearns

Further Reading

Conroy, Donald B. and Rodney L. Petersen, eds. *Earth At Risk: An Environmental Dialogue Between Religion and Science.* Amherst, NY: Humanity Books, 2000.

Granberg-Michaelson, Wesley. *Redeeming the Creation: The Rio Earth Summit: Challenges for the Churches.* Geneva: World Council of Churches, 1992.

Kearns, Laurel. "Noah's Ark Goes to Washington: A Profile of Evangelical Environmentalism." *Social Compass* 44 (3 September 1997), 349–66.

Kearns, Laurel. "Saving the Creation: Christian Environmentalism in the United States." *Sociology of Religion* 57:1 (Spring 1996), 55–70.

See also: Au Sable Institute; Biblical Foundations for Christian Stewardship; Berry, Thomas; Christianity (7i) – An Evangelical Perspective on Faith and Nature; Earth Charter; Eco-Church movement; Eleventh Commandment Fellowship; Evangelical Environmental Network; Fox, Matthew; Religious Campaign for Forest Conservation; Stewardship; United Nations' "Earth Summits".

Nursi, Said (1877–1960)

Said Nursi, also known as Bediuzzaman, was born in 1877 in eastern Turkey and died in 1960. Nursi's eventful life can be divided into three major periods. The first is informal learning. It was as a result of these feats of learning that he was given the name of Bediuzzaman (Wonder of the Age) by one of his masters. He witnessed the collapse of the Ottoman Empire, following World War I, which led to the birth of the modern Republic of Turkey. He was actively involved in politics before the collapse of the Ottoman Empire, which he referred to in his later writings as the "Old Said" period.

The second period, the "New Said," began after World War I. It coincided with the founding of the Turkish Republic. In this period, he devoted his life to interpreting the Qur'an afresh. As he was by nature a lover of solitude, he would retire into seclusion to devote himself to worship and meditation. The last ten years of Nursi's life witnessed the emergence of a "Third Said," which differed from the New Said in so far as Nursi once again took a closer interest in social and political matters.

Nursi on Nature and God

The adorned animals, decorative birds, fruit-bearing trees, and flowering plants are miracles of His knowledge, wonders of His art, gifts of His munificence, propitious signs of His grace. The blossoms smiling at the embellished fruits, the birds twittering in the breezes of the early morn, the pattering of the rain on the petals of the flowers, the tender affection of mothers for their infants and young, all show to jinn and men, and spirits and living creatures, and angels and spirit beings a Loving One making Himself known, a Merciful One making Himself loved, a Tenderly Kind One bestowing His mercy, a Gracious Bestower manifesting His kindness.

Bediuzzaman Said Nursi
Ibrahim Ozdemir

Further Reading

Hatip, Abdulaziz. *Risale-i Nur'dan Dualar.* (Supplication from Risale-i Nur Collection). Istanbul: Gençlik Yayinlari, 1993, 57–9.

Nursi was a religious scholar of the highest standing, who was unusual in his breadth of learning of both religious and modern sciences. He was well aware of the challenges posed by the modern worldview to religious thought. Aware of this global challenge, he invited members of the Abrahamic religions to develop a spirit of dialogue and establish a common ground against the spread of secular values and their implications in the 1940s. On the other hand, he devoted his life to the revival of the traditional Islamic understanding of the universe and its moral implications. It is here, that his cosmological views come to the fore. In his emphasis on the spiritual aspects of Islam, Nursi is regarded as a modern representative of the great saintly tradition embodied in the life of such figures as al-Ghazali (d. 1111) and Rumi (d. 1273). He once said that he regarded his works as a modern rendering of Rumi's great *Masnawi*. To overcome the challenge of "mechanical" modernity, Nursi developed a God-centered view of the universe. He underlines the Qur'anic notion of stewardship in his system of thought.

Nursi had a great passion for nature. He contemplated both the manifest and hidden wonders of nature, and linked nature's secrets to the omnipotence and omnipresence of the divine. In his daily life he formed relations of a very different sort with the universe and with everything around him – from dogs to ants – based on wisdom, compassion, and kindness.

For example, he would give the cats and pigeons that came to him part of his own food. Once, he rebuked one of his students who killed a lizard, saying, "Did you create it?" While in prison, he was most upset when the flies were killed by spraying, and wrote a short piece called *The Treatise on Flies*. In all the places he stayed, he had close ties, almost at the level of friendship, with all the creatures around him and called them "my brethren." When going for excursions in the countryside, Nursi would study "the Great Book of the Universe," and urge his disciples to read it "in the Name of the Sustainer Who created." The hallmark of Nursi's *magnum opus, Risale-i Nur* (*The Epistle of Light*) is that it never compromises its rule of taking the Qur'an as its guide and explains what, why, and how the universe should be seen and read.

Nursi examined nature through the Beautiful Names of God. For example, the Most Holy (Quddus), one of the Most Beautiful Names of God, means being exempt from all fault and defect; most sacred; deficient in absolutely nothing; pure and clean. Nursi likens the universe and the Earth to a vast factory, guest-house, or hostel. He draws attention to its cleanliness and explains that everything – the clouds, rain, flies, crows, wolves, worms, ants, insects, the red and white corpuscles in a person's body – all manifest the Name of Most Holy and perform their cleansing duties. He points out that the cleansing of the soil is done in the Name of Most Holy. For if all the corpses of all the animal species and the debris of dead vegetation on the land and in the seas were not cleaned up by the carnivorous cleansing officials of the sea and those of the land like the eagles, and even maggots and ants, the Earth would have become uninhabitable.

Nursi regards animals as divine officials, which act as mirrors, and glorify God and mention his Name. For example, all sorts of beings from microbes and ants to rhinoceroses, eagles, and planets are diligent officials of the Pre-Eternal Sovereign; he regards these animals as cleansing and public health officials which collect the corpses of wild animals, and since they act as mirrors to and have a relation with that Sovereign, the value of all things infinitely surpasses their individual value ... (paraphrased from Nursi 1995: 397). According to him,

> everything, from the heavens to the Earth, from the stars to flies, from angels to fishes, and from planets to particles, prostrates, worships, praises and glorifies Almighty God. But their worship varies according to their capacities and the Divine Names that they manifest; it is all different (Nursi 1998: 361).

Nursi suggests that if the natural world were observed through the Qur'anic lens, then everything would turn to a book and a letter which could be read and understood by any careful student of the Qur'an.

Thus, Nursi reads the universe as a book. He says that "one page of this mighty book is the face of the Earth" and

> one word of the line is a tree which has opened its blossom and put forth its leaves in order to produce its fruit. This word consists of meaningful passages lauding and praising the All-Glorious Sapient One to the number of orderly, well-proportioned, adorned leaves, flowers, and fruits (Nursi 1995: 404–5).

Nursi, therefore, calls the universe "the mighty Qur'an of the universe" and he repeats this in many places. Also, a noteworthy point is his emphasis on the order and balance in the universe. While he considers this order and balance as indicating God's existence, he also draws people's attention to the preservation of this order and balance. For example, he argues that "there is no wastefulness, futility, and absence of benefits in the nature of things. Wastefulness, in fact, is the opposite of the Name of Wise" (Nursi 1995: 410). So, when he argues that humanity should take lessons from ecosystems and lead a wise and frugal life, he also keeps in mind the Qur'anic verse: "Eat and drink, but waste not in excess" (7:31). According to him, there is no contradiction between the teachings of the Qur'an and the book of nature.

Thus, in Nursi's metaphysics, the universe, as a whole, is meaningful, full of art, lovable, and comprised of numerous benefits. Moreover, it makes known to us its Creator together with His Beautiful Names. Nature, as a sacred book, is full of symbols and signs and therefore has some far-reaching implications for Nursi. As Muslims hold the Qur'an in respect and awe and do not touch it unless purified by ablutions, they also must treat the book of the universe respectfully and lovingly.

Nursi encourages human beings to take nature seriously by pursuing a meaningful life. He rebukes those who see the order, harmony, and measure in the universe, yet do not draw the necessary lessons and moral implications from it. In a nutshell, Nursi's cosmology is based on the Qur'anic *Weltanschauung* and demands an environmentally friendly life.

Ibrahim Ozdemir

Further Reading

Abu-Rabi', Ibrahim, ed. *Islam at the Crossroads: On the Life and Thought of Bediuzzaman Said Nursi*. Albany: SUNY, 2003.

Mardin, Serif. *Religion and Social Change in Modern Turkey: The Case of Bediuzzaman Said Nursi*. Albany: SUNY Press, 1989.

Nursî, Bediüzzaman Said. *Epitomes of Light: Mathnawi al-Nuriya, The Essentials of Risale-I Nur*. Ali Unal, Izmir: Kaynak, 1999.
Nursî, Bediüzzaman Said. *The Words*. Sukran Vahide, tr. Istanbul: Sözler Publications, 1998.
Nursî, Bediüzzaman Said. *The Rays Collection*. Sukran Vahide, tr. Istanbul: Sözler Publications, 1998.
Nursî, Bediüzzaman Said. *Letters 1928–1932*. Sukran Vahide, tr. Istanbul: Sözler Publications, 1997.
Nursî, Bediüzzaman Said. *The Flashes*. Sukran Vahide, tr. Istanbul: Sözler Publications, 1995.
"Said Nursi and Turkish Experience." *The Muslim World* 89:3–4 (July–October 1999), special issue.
Vahide, Sükran. *The Author of the Risale-i Nur, Bediüzzaman Said Nursî*. Istanbul: The Sözler Publications, 1998.

See also: Islam; The Qur'an; Rumî, Jalaluddin.

Nyau – A Closed Association (Central Africa)

Often referred to as a secret society and described by locals as a religion, nyau belongs to the Chewa, Nyanja and Mang'anja peoples of eastern Zambia, central and southern Malawi and neighboring parts of Mozambique. Nyau is one of a group of closed associations spread across central Africa. The origins of these associations can be traced to the Katanga Region of what is now the Democratic Republic of the Congo and to the time of the Lunda and Luba kingdoms. These associations therefore have a history extending back at least one thousand years. When one asks, "What is nyau?," the most common answer received is "Nyau is an animal." Animal power and animal symbolism lie at the heart of nyau.

Nyau membership is open only to men and entry is gained near the time of puberty through a boys' group initiation ceremony. For the ceremony, the boys are taken off for up to one month and taken to a place called the "dambwe." Today this is usually in the graveyard, but in the past it might have been any thickly forested place. At the start of the initiation each boy is engulfed by a large basketwork animal figure known as kasiyamaliro. As noted by Claude Boucher, when lifted up, the base of this figure has the form of the womb. The symbolism of all the parts of kasiyamaliro is explicitly female. Inside kasiyamaliro the boy learns the greatest secrets of nyau and, when he comes out, he is metaphorically reborn as an adult. Boys who do not go through this ceremony are never considered to become to men.

Both members and non-members refer to nyau as Gule wamkulu – meaning the greatest dance – and dance is key to nyau activity. Nyau dances occur at three main ceremonies: the funerary ritual (maliro), the commemorative celebrations for the deceased (m'meto) and the girls' initiation ceremony (chinamwali). In all of these dances elaborate costumes and masks are used. There are, essentially, two types of masks: face-masks and mobile structures. All represent animals and spirits. Face-masks are most commonly made of wood and then painted, but a few are made out of cloth, feathers or mud. The rest of the body is covered with bits of cloth, grass and leaves. Where skin can be seen, it is disguised with white ash. The mobile structures comprise a wickerwork wooden frame, covered by an ornate shell of tied maize husks, grass and pieces of cloth. Concealed dancers animate these structures from inside. The majority of structures take the form of particular animals or birds. Kasiyamaliro is the most important of all the structures. The animal that it represents is contested, but most believe that it is the eland.

Non-initiates are meant to believe that the nyau characters are real animals and spirits; that they are not, is the greatest secret of nyau. The majority of nyau dancing occurs in an open arena on the edge of the village known as the "bwalo." When nyau perform in the bwalo they are accompanied by vigorous drumming by special nyau drums. The rhythms of the drums reflect the unique identity and character represented by each mask. Each nyau figure has its own name and its own dance and, when it appears, women will sing its own particular song. Most of the dances and songs carry a strong instructive message; they remind people of societal norms and taboos and they warn of the dire consequences that result from bad behavior.

Today there are many hundreds of different masks, but it appears that this multiplicity may be comparatively recent. Many of the masked characters, such as the Pope, the Colonial Officer, the Car, former President of Malawi Dr. Hastings Kamuzu [d. 1997] Banda, current Malawian President Bakili Muluzi, are demonstrably recent. New masks continue to be developed: a recent one is Edzi – meaning AIDS. Kasiyamaliro – meaning the one that delivers the funeral – is probably among the most ancient of all nyau figures. Kasiyamaliro dances at all important rites of passage and thereby oversees the transformation of boys into men, girls into women and the dead into ancestral spirits. Its appearance marks the climax point of most nyau ceremonies.

Despite nearly a century of suppression from the 1860s until the 1960s when nyau came into conflict with Ngoni invaders, the early Christian Church, and the Colonial administration, nyau continues to thrive. In the operations of nyau we see a key historical force that has made Chewa, Nyanja and Mang'anja society strongly resilient to unwelcome intruding forces. Its masks caricature and mock intruding forces and reaffirm traditional ways and values. The cow mask, ng'ombe, for example, was developed in the 1860s to mock the incoming Ngoni invaders who, as with other Ngoni groups, built their villages around the cattle kraal and buried their male dead within the kraal. The ng'ombe mask lampooned this behavior and thereby served to undermine Ngoni authority.

The masked figures do not just represent animals and spirits, they are perceived by society to be animals and spirits. They are above the law and they cannot be prosecuted. In the final years of Dr. Banda's government this allowed nyau to be a powerful force in advocating multiparty democracy, even at the time when all other avenues for political dissent were closed. Nyau figures continue to parody what is perceived as the poor behavior of societal leaders and thereby play a key role in the sometimes troubled democratic processes of the region.

B.W. Smith

Further Reading

Birch de Aguilar, Laurel. *Inscribing the Mask: Interpretation of Nyau Masks and Ritual Performing among the Chewa of Central Malawi.* Freiburg: University Press, 1996.

Schoffeleers, J. Matthew. "Nyau Societies: Our Present Understanding." *Society of Malawi Journal* 29 (1976), 59–68.

Smith, Benjamin W. "Forbidden Images: Rock Paintings and the Nyau Secret Society of Central Malawi and Eastern Zambia." *African Archaeological Review* 18:4 (2001), 187–212.

Yoshida, Kenji. "Masks and Transformation among the Chewa of Eastern Zambia." *Senri Ethnological Studies* 31 (1992), 203–73.

See also: African Religions and Nature Conservation; Congo River Watershed; Dance; Drums, Drumming and Nature; Ritual; Rock Art – Batwa/Pygmies (Central Africa); Rock Art – Chewa (Central Africa); Nature; Saro-Wiwa, Kennle Beeson – and the Ogoni.

Odinism

Odinism refers to the modern reconstruction and revival of pre-Christian Germanic heathenism centered on the pantheon of ancient northern deities in which the god Odin (variously called Óđinn, Woden, Wodan, etc., in the different older Germanic languages) is a principal figure. Odinism is only one of a number of generic designations that might be used by practitioners to describe their beliefs; the term Ásatrú ("loyalty to the gods," a modern coinage derived from Old Norse) is in equally widespread use today. Odinism may in some instances refer to a less ritual-oriented and more philosophical variant of Germanic heathenism than Ásatrú, or one that places a marked importance on racialism, but such distinctions are rarely consistent or precise within a sub-culture that generally eschews dogmatism.

Odinism is a polytheistic religious system that also emphasizes the reverence of past ancestors, the acknowledgment of archaic wisdom contained in mythological tales, respect for ethnic heritage and the continuance of folk traditions, and the maintenance of a heroic bearing toward life's challenges. Some prominent practitioners have described Odinism as a "nature religion"; this is not surprising given that in all its important aspects – cosmology, outlook, and practice – strong connections to the natural world and its forces are evident.

A central feature in Odinist cosmology is Yggdrasil, the World Tree (usually conceived of as an ash or yew), which symbolically connects the nine worlds that are variously inhabited by gods, giants, humans, and other beings. A number of animals also live within the tree; their activities seem mythically to represent the dynamic interactive forces of what could be termed the greater "multiverse." It was also on the tree of Yggdrasil that Odin hung himself in a ritual of self-sacrifice, thereby gaining his powerful understanding of the mysteries of the runes: primordial Germanic linguistic, cultural, and magical symbols, many of which directly relate to aspects of the physical world (various rune names refer to trees, animals, and natural phenomena). In Germanic creation mythology, the first human beings were created when Odin and his brothers took two trees, Askr and Embla, and bestowed consciousness upon them.

Odinism posits a cosmos full of divine and natural energies, operating both within Midgard (from Old Norse, *Miđgarđr*), the world inhabited by humans, as well as in transcendent domains where the gods and other non-human entities reside. The gods travel freely between these worlds and thus can and do interact with humans. Gods and humans are also subject to their position within both a personal and a collective *Wyrd* (from Old Norse *urđr*), or "fate"; this does not predetermine every lesser action, but rather exerts influence upon the overall course of life. Although it is believed that the distinctive essence or soul of a human being will depart for another realm after death (various specific possibilities are described in the mythological literature), the primary emphasis of the religion is not other-worldly; instead it focuses upon right conduct in the here-and-now. Virtues such as honor, courage, and hospitality are highly valued, and an awareness of humankind's place in the natural world is also cultivated.

While there are differing beliefs as to the exact nature of the gods, the latter are generally seen as real and knowable, and their mythological depictions simply as means to illustrate or understand various aspects of their character and function. The primary deities fall into two clans or groups, the Æsir and the Vanir. The Æsir consist of Odin, Frigga, Thor, Tyr, Balder, and others; they are often associated with important societal functions such as war, sovereignty, and law. Certain atmospheric events may also be associated with these deities (e.g., the thunder and rain caused by Thor wielding his mighty hammer in the heavens, hence his importance to the peasantry as both a defensive protector and a fertility god). Of the Vanir gods, Frey and Freyja are the best known. These deities generally exhibit stronger connections to "earthly" realms of fertility and sensuality, both of which are important categories to many Odinists. Fertility is not only recognized in relationship to agricultural crops and a healthy natural environment, but also in the continuance of familial lineages which are central in a religion emphasizing ancestral culture and ethnic heritage. Sensuality is welcomed as a vital and stimulating ingredient for the full enjoyment of human existence.

In addition to gods and humans, other entities such as elves, dwarves, and land-wights (from Old Norse *landvættir*) receive important consideration. These beings may be acknowledged in rituals, and in some cases offerings of food or drink are made to ensure their good favor. Land-wights are the unseen residents of a given geographical location, capable of bestowing blessings or misfortune on the humans who live in their proximity. In the Viking period in Iceland their importance was such that an early law ordered boats to remove the fearsome carved dragon heads from their prows as they approached shore, so as not to frighten these spirits; a modern vestige of this tradition still exists whereby ships entering Icelandic harbors are officially requested briefly to lower their flags as a gesture of respect to the land spirits.

In addition to living in harmony with the ethical principles of the religion, organized rituals and feasts are celebrated by Odinists at varying times throughout the year. The primary religious festivals can be located at specific points of the seasonal solar or agricultural calendar; these include mid-winter (Yule) and mid-summer, as well as specialized occasions in the spring and fall. Other formal rituals are performed for specific purposes, or to honor specific deities. The general term *blót* (from the Old Norse word for "sacrifice") is used to refer to any one of the aforementioned ceremonies. Such a sacrifice is frequently symbolic in nature, and usually features a libation in the form of mead or ale. The most appropriate location for major ceremonies is generally considered to be outdoors, a tendency that resonates with historical accounts of various ancient Germanic tribes practicing their rites in "sacred groves." The implements utilized in Odinist rituals – drinking horns, hammers (potently connected to Thor; many Odinists also wear a talismanic hammer pendant to indicate their allegiance to the religion), carved wooden staffs, wooden or metal bowls – are fashioned from natural materials, ideally by the practitioners themselves. A small branch cut from a living tree is commonly used to sprinkle mead as a blessing on the participants of a ceremony, and at the conclusion of a ritual any remaining libation will often be poured onto the ground as an offering of respect for the land-wights. A further ceremony is a *sumbel*, a structured session of ritualized drinking in which participants offer up toasts to deities, heroes, human ancestors, or spiritual principles. It might also be an occasion for making personal boasts or oaths. While the formats of rituals vary between groups, generally they are studiously reconstructed from archaic references in older Germanic literature (usually Old Norse and Scandinavian sources, as these contain the largest body of pre-Christian lore), often combined with aspects of folk traditions that have survived into more recent times and appear to have a basis in older beliefs.

A balanced scholarly study of the emergence of Odinism in the modern era has yet to be written, but various stages can be discerned. Although the revival of interest in ancient Germanic culture can already be seen in the seventeenth-century Swedish Storgoticist movement and the figure of Johannes Bureus (1568–1652), more concrete indications are evident in late eighteenth-century Germany, when specific efforts were made to stir popular interest in the newly rediscovered religion of Odin and the elder Germanic deities. Among *Sturm und Drang* intellectuals, the philosopher J.G. Herder (1744–1803) extolled the legacy of the pre-Christian Germanic north as an important ingredient for building an organic national culture. A 1775 book called *Wodan, der Sachsen Held und Gott* (*Wodan, the Hero and God of the Saxons*) by H.W. Behrisch (1744–1825) declared Odin the "light of the world" and loftiest exemplar for the modern Germans of Saxony, and urged them to rediscover the true nature of their beginnings in the "sacred darkness of the northerly forests." A century later, the burgeoning Germanic national romanticism coalesced into pan-Germanist and *völkisch* movements with visible alternative religious elements. By the early 1900s, overtly neo-heathen groups had established themselves. These included the Armanenshaft, led by the Austrian mystic and author Guido von List (1848–1919), and the Germanische Glaubens-Gemeinschaft, led by the German painter Ludwig Fahrenkrog (1867–1952). This flowering was relatively short-lived, however, as the incipient National Socialist regime would eventually curtail or forbid nearly all such groups, forcing them to go underground or disband.

An Australian lawyer and writer, Alexander Rud Mills (1885–1964), appears to have been the first person publicly to promote Odinism in the English-speaking world. By the 1930s Rud Mills was advocating a movement firmly opposed to Christianity and featuring a strident anti-Jewish component, and in 1936 he published a substantial handbook detailing the philosophy and rituals of this highly idiosyncratic "Anglecyn Church of Odin." Despite issuing publications over a period of three decades, Rud Mills never found any significant support for his efforts, and his work has largely faded into obscurity.

In the aftermath of World War II, with lingering public perceptions that National Socialism had been a "pagan" movement (an inaccurate perception, as official Third Reich policy endorsed "positive Christianity"), over twenty years would pass before Germanic neo-heathenism began to flourish again, and now in new areas. In the United States a number of small groups emerged unbeknown to one another, such as the Odinist Fellowship, formed by Else Christensen in 1971 (and influenced to some degree by the preceding efforts of Rud Mills), the Viking Brotherhood, formed by Stephen A. McNallen in 1971–1972, and the Northernway, founded by Robert and Karen Taylor in 1974. The Viking Brotherhood would later develop into the Ásatrú Free Assembly, the first national Odinist organization to gain any momentum in America. During the mid-1980s the A.F.A. went into a hiatus – out of which emerged two significant and still active groups, the Ásatrú Alliance and the Ring of Troth – before reconstituting itself as the Ásatrú Folk Assembly. In England similar initiatives had arisen independently, such as the Committee for the Restoration of the Odinic Rite (later shortened to the Odinic Rite) established in 1973 by John Yeowell; a variety of other groups have also sprung up there over the last quarter-century. In Iceland, the home of the Old Norse sagas, Sveinbjörn Beinteinsson (1924–1993) formed the Ásatrúarfélag in 1973 and succeeded in having heathenism legally recognized. Other small groups have been active since at least the 1970s in most Scandinavian countries. Beyond the growing list of national Odinist organizations, many smaller, localized independent associations exist, as do untold numbers of solitary practitioners.

Odinism remains largely a sub-cultural phenomenon, although in recent decades it has gained increasing recognition in the wider landscape of neo-paganism and new religious movements. In contrast to some other branches of neo-paganism, Odinist groups may tend toward traditionalist viewpoints, and in certain instances this can include strong racial beliefs. A number of organizations believe that the religion is most suited for the descendants of its original, ancient practitioners; this has been described as "ethnic" or "folkish" Odinism or Ásatrú, and does not generally imply supremacist notions. Other groups are vocally universalistic, and would not concede the legitimacy of any ethnic criterion in regard to prospective members. Distanced from both views are those who interpret the religion foremost as a racial, or even racist, vehicle. In order to draw a distinction from mainstream Odinist or Ásatrú groups, some racially motivated practitioners may refer to themselves as "Wotanists" (according to racialist ideologue David Lane, the name Wotan is an acronym for "Will of the Aryan Nation"). Groups associated with this hard-line position have a constituency consisting primarily of incarcerated males, and tend to be volatile and incapable of maintaining significant longevity.

Most mainstream heathen groups avoid taking overt political positions, and will tolerate a wide range of personal beliefs among their membership. Libertarian values of personal freedom are commonly found among practitioners, and are often viewed as being in line with older Germanic attitudes. Most groups promote ecological awareness; some have encouraged their members to become involved with environmental activities, or have organized campaigns to protest the destruction of historic sites in England and elsewhere. Although the religion is sometimes viewed as heavily emphasizing "masculine" deities and virtues, the importance of and lore concerning the female goddesses is often underscored in contemporary Odinist literature, and a number of women have taken on leadership roles in both the U.S. and Iceland in recent years. These developments, along with the diversity of socio-political beliefs found among its practitioners, all point toward the long-term viability of Odinism or Ásatrú in the postmodern age.

Michael Moynihan

Further Reading
Behrisch, Heinrich Wolfgang. *Wodan, der Saxon Held und Gott*. Dresden: Hilscher, 1775. English edition: Waterbury Center, VT: Dominion, 2005.

Flowers, Stephen E. "Revival of Germanic Religions in Contemporary Anglo-American Culture." *Mankind Quarterly* XXI: 3 (1981), 279–94.
Gardell, Mattias. *Gods of the Blood*. Durham: Duke University Press, 2003.
Harvey, Graham. *Contemporary Paganism*. New York: New York University Press, 1997.
Kaplan, Jeffrey. *Radical Religion in America*. Syracuse: Syracuse University Press, 1997.
McNallen, Stephen A. *Rituals of Ásatrú*, 3 vols. Breckenridge, TX: Ásatrú Free Assembly, 1985; Payson, AZ: World Tree, 1992.
Turville-Petre, E.O.G. *Myth and Religion of the North*. New York: Holt, Rinehart and Winston, 1964.

See also: Elves and Land Spirits in Pagan Norse Religion; Fascism; Heathenry – Ásatrú; Neo-paganism and Ethnic Nationalism in Eastern Europe; Paganism and Judaism; Paganism – A Jewish Perspective; Paganism – Contemporary; Trees (Northern and Middle Europe); Trees – Sacred.

Oikos

Oikos is a Greek word used to describe a variety of often overlapping structures and the basis for a number of compound words central to classical Western thinking. Its basic translation is "house." In ancient texts it can refer to a physical dwelling, but also to a family, clan, a smaller economic unit including land, owners, animals, slaves and servants, as well as products. Ancient Greek sources often oppose it to or distinguish it from the term *polis*, which describes a more "public," potentially urban relational civic structure. In most ancient sources, though gender roles could at times involve some slippage, the *polis* was often described as the designated realm for masculine civic and legal activity and the *oikos* as the proper realm for women's activity, dedicated to the production and management of land, humans, animals, food. It is important to remember that *oikos* in those times did not refer to a one family nuclear household, but is better compared to a small family business that was often overseen by a woman.

The compound *oikonomos* signifies a steward or manager of the system of the *oikos*, who would often be a slave (see for example Jesus' parables). This term has found application both in the Christian notion of (creation) stewardship and in modern economic science. *Oikonomia* can describe any kind of management structure or plan, on large and smaller scales. Thus it could refer to ancient state management, the notion of a divine plan within creation (*oikonomia theou*), as well as the management of a variety of economic units. The term's application is clearly anthropocentric, centering on human structures of organization of communal and civic life and anthropomorphic concepts of divine agency.

Ecology, the anglicized version of a neo-Greek compound *oikologia* is not a classical Greek term and has come into its own only in the twentieth century. Though the idea of relational being of natural systems is ancient, ecology as a science or conceptual framework is a latecomer.

In some recent theological and ethical texts the term *oikos, oikonomia, oikumene* (the known inhabited world) and ecology have been redefined so as to refer to the community of all creation. Writers have employed it as a tool for the necessary rethinking of what stewardship of creation in times of ecological crisis might mean. Countering the narrowing of modern capitalist notions of "economy" reduced to market dynamics, these texts attempt to recast *oikonomia theou*/divine economy (linked to the notion of the kingdom of God) as congruent with the ecology of the planet. If the household of God's creation includes all planetary life, it should be lived in with reverence. Though at bottom an anthropocentric theological concept, authors employ it to urge humans to see themselves less as the "crown of creation" than as parts of a divinely created whole that cannot be endangered without seriously compromising life as we know it on planet Earth.

Marion Grau

Further Reading

McFague, Sallie. *The Body of God: An Ecological Theology.* Minneapolis: Fortress Press, 1993.

Meeks, Douglas. *God the Economist: The Doctrine of God and Political Economy.* Minneapolis: Fortress Press, 1989.

Torjesen, Karen. *When Women Were Priests: Women's Leadership in the Early Church and the Scandal of their Subordination in the Rise of Christianity.* San Francisco: HarperSanFrancisco, 1993.

See also: Christianity (2) – Jesus; Haeckel, Ernst.

Olson, Sigurd F. (1899–1982)

Sigurd F. Olson was one of America's most beloved nature writers and most influential conservationists of the twentieth century. Best known as the author of *The Singing Wilderness* and eight other books, Olson also played an important role in the preservation of a number of national parks, seashores, and wilderness areas.

Born in Chicago on 4 April 1899, Olson spent most of his childhood and youth in northern Wisconsin, where he discovered a love of nature. He was the second of three sons raised by the Reverend Lawrence and Ida May Olson, Swedish immigrants who met and married in the United States. His parents were devout Swedish Baptists, and Olson was raised in a strict household. One time, for example, Lawrence Olson discovered Sigurd and another son playing with a chess set, and he threw it into the fire.

While attending college at the University of Wisconsin in Madison at the end of World War I, Olson nearly committed himself to becoming a missionary. The night before he was publicly to declare his intent, however, he climbed the roof of the YMCA building where he lived, stared out over Lake Mendota, and struggled with his decision. He realized that his interest in becoming a missionary had more to do with exploring wild places than with saving souls; in the morning he resigned from the church organization he had been chosen to lead, and in effect broke from the faith of his parents.

For years afterward, Olson was obsessed with discovering a sense of meaning and mission to replace what he had lost. Eventually, he found what he was looking for in the wilderness canoe country of northern Minnesota and Ontario. He moved to Ely, Minnesota in 1923, and taught in the local high school and junior college, eventually becoming dean of the college. During the summers he guided canoe parties through the wilderness, and he noticed that the wilderness often had as profound an effect on his clients as it did on him. They laughed more, sang songs, played practical jokes. They watched the sunset and the moonrise, and listened to the roar of rapids and the soft sighs of wind in the trees. Like Olson, they became re-connected to the grand, eternal mystery of creation.

Olson came to believe his mission in life was to share with others what he had found in the wilderness, and to help lead the fight to preserve it. Science, technology and materialism were turning many people away from the religious truths and practices that had given spiritual sustenance, he argued, and offered nothing in their place. The result was a widespread, if often vague, discontent, partially hidden underneath fast-paced lives, yet also nourished by that same fast pace that left little time for reflection. Olson believed that the silence and solitude and noncivilized surroundings of wilderness provide a physical context in which people can more easily rediscover their inner selves. Just as important, wilderness gives people a chance to feel the presence of a universal power that science can never explain, but that brings meaning to their lives. "Wilderness offers [a] sense of cosmic purpose if we open our hearts and minds to its possibilities," he said at a national wilderness conference in 1965.

> It may come in . . . burning instants of truth when everything stands clear. It may come as a slow realization after long periods of waiting. Whenever it comes, life is suddenly illumined, beautiful, and transcendent, and we are filled with awe and happiness (Olson 1966: 218).

Olson spread his philosophy in nine books, in many magazine and newspaper articles, and in countless speeches and conversations across the United States and Canada. He read and thought deeply about the works of others who were searching for meaning in the modern world – such as Pierre Teilhard de Chardin, Lewis Mumford, Aldous Huxley, Josef Pieper, and Pierre Lecomte du Noüy – but was able to get across his deep message about the spiritual values of wilderness mostly by writing about simple things: the sound of wings over a marsh, the smell of a bog, the memories stirred by a campfire, the movement of a canoe.

By the 1970s Olson was a beloved environmental figurehead whose name and image invoked strong feelings. Often photographed with a pipe in his hand and a warm, reflective expression on his weathered face, he was not just a hero but an icon. His books were read on public radio, his portrait was taken by Alfred Eisenstaedt for *Life* magazine, he received the John Burrough's award for nature writing, and earned the highest honors of four of the major national environmental groups for his leadership role in preserving wilderness across the United States and Canada. He died of a heart attack on 13 January 1982, while snowshoeing near his home.

David Backes

Further Reading

Backes, David. *A Wilderness Within: The Life of Sigurd F. Olson*. Minneapolis, MN: University of Minnesota Press, 1997.

Olson, Sigurd F. "The Spiritual Need." In Bruce M. Kilgore, ed. *Wilderness in a Changing World*. San Francisco: Sierra Club, 1966, 212–19.

See *also*: Huxley, Aldous; National Parks and Monuments (United States); Teilhard de Chardin, Pierre; Wilderness Religion.

Open Land Movement

Open land has been a dream of back-to-nature visionaries at least since the time of the Diggers and Levelers in England. Proponents of that dream have often envisioned a nature-oriented society far from the degradation of urban life, one in which all would thrive in a state of nature. Often the vision has taken form as an open-door intentional community and in many cases that has led to inundations of problematic residents. One of the first open-land communities was Celestia, founded in Sullivan County, Pennsylvania, in 1850 by Peter Armstrong, who opened the land to all seeking refuge from the sinful world in a place where they could await the Second Coming of Christ, which was understood to be imminent. A half-century later the Christian Commonwealth Colony (1896–1900), in Georgia, flung its doors open to all; its founders sought to establish a perfect Christian socialist society on Earth in an agricultural setting, but the colony never could rise out of poverty.

In the 1960s and early 1970s, dozens, perhaps hundreds, of open-land communities appeared. Gorda Mountain, in the Big Sur region of California, was opened to all by its owner Amelia Newell in 1962 and grew to a population of around 200 before pressure from neighbors brought it to a close in 1968. In the meantime, Huw Williams and others had opened Tolstoy Farm in Washington, and the flamboyantly countercultural Drop City, founded outside Trinidad, Colorado, in 1965, welcomed all who would share its egalitarian poverty. The following year Lou Gottlieb threw open his Morning Star Ranch in northern California, believing that people have an inherent deep spiritual relationship with the Earth and thus should live close to the land, to nature; it attracted hundreds of residents and became the focus of extended battles with the local authorities who finally succeeded in bulldozing its makeshift structures in the early 1970s, although Gottlieb preached the gospel of open land for the rest of his life. Experiments in open land have endured, as many other 1960s-era and later communes have continued to embrace all who would come

Timothy Miller

Further Reading

Fairfield, Richard. *Communes USA: A Personal Tour*. Baltimore: Penguin, 1972.

Miller, Timothy. *The 60s Communes*. Syracuse: Syracuse University Press, 1999.

See *also*: Back to the Land Movements. Diggers and Levelers (and adjacent, Diggers Song); Hippies; New Age; New Religious Movements.

Ortiz, Simon J. (1941–)

Simon J. Ortiz, Acoma Pueblo, was recognized in 1993 with a Lifetime Achievement Award for literature at the Returning the Gift Festival of Native Writers. In addition to his own work as a poet, fiction writer, and essayist, he has edited books and journals devoted to promoting contemporary native writing. Throughout his work, and in the course of promoting the work of others, Ortiz has remained emphatic about the relationship of contemporary native literature to oral tradition, defining it as a form of cultural and spiritual continuity. In 1981, in "Towards a National Indian Literature," Ortiz defined contemporary native writing as an element of native oral tradition, linking it with ceremony, song, and prayer narratives as cultural acts of "bringing about meaning and meaningfulness." Invariably, this linkage with tradition, ritual and ceremony, also requires for him a recognition of an indigenous ecological worldview that sees the people and the land as a single entity. In his introduction to *Speaking for Generations* he stated,

The young are frequently reminded by their elders: these lands and waters and all elements of Creation are a part of you, and you are a part of them . . . This belief is expressed time and time again in traditional song, ritual, prayer, and in contemporary writing (1998).

In 1976 and 1977, Ortiz published *Going for the Rain* and *A Good Journey* as two separate volumes of poetry, but actually they comprised parts of a 400-page manuscript of poems he had already written by that time. Another piece, *Fight Back*, combining poems and prose narratives was published in 1980. Finally, in 1992, these three texts were united in *Woven Stone* with an extensive introduction by the author. This volume best represents Ortiz's explicit themes outlined above, as well as the range of his poetics. The first section contains numerous "songs," coyote stories, and ceremonial poems celebrating birth, all life on the planet, and the relationship of a person to place. The second section returns to coyote, as well as other animals treated as guides and spiritual brothers. Ortiz also includes poems specifically designated as "prayer." But perhaps most significantly, Ortiz depicts the poet-traveler as becoming increasingly unhealthy in both body and spirit the farther he journeys away from home, with a psychic, spiritual, and physical reintegration occurring not only for him but for other tribal people upon homecoming. In the third section, "Fight Back: For the Sake of the People, for the Sake of the Land," Ortiz opens with "Mid-American Prayer" and then divides the poems and prose narratives of this section into two parts: "Too Many Sacrifices" and "No More Sacrifices." While reciting the destruction of native peoples and their lands, Ortiz also emphasizes endurance and the possibility of change and rebirth based on the reintegration of all people with the living land. Ortiz continued this life's work theme in *After and Before the Lightning* in 1994, focusing on the land and the people, not in the warm climate of the Pueblo region, but in the snow and ice of the Rosebud Reservation in South Dakota.

Patrick D. Murphy

Further Reading

Ortiz, Simon J., ed. *Speaking for the Generations: Native Writers on Writing*. Tucson: The University of Arizona Press, 1998.

Ortiz, Simon J. *After and Before the Lightning*. Tucson: The University of Arizona Press, 1994.

Ortiz, Simon J. *Woven Stone*. Tucson: The University of Arizona Press, 1992.

Ortiz, Simon J. "Towards a National Indian Literature: Cultural Authenticity in Nationalism." *MELUS* 8:2 (1981), 7–12.

See also: Lakota; Memoir and Nature Writing; Trickster.

Oshmarii–Chimarii (Mari El Republic, Russia)

A revival of indigenous nature religion in the Volga River region in the 1990s was spearheaded by Mari religious organizations in the Mari El Republic (one of twenty-one republics within the Russian Federation). The Mari are a Finno-Ugric people who make up less than half of the population of some 780,000 in this Central Volga basin republic. The neo-pagan community *Oshmarii-Chimarii* (White Mari – Pure Mari) was established in 1991 with a center in the republic's capital, Yoshkar-Ola. Though its founders had intended it to become an All-Mari religious organization, the community has so far failed in this ambition, but it continues to sponsor and arrange various public events, and a Council of *Karts* (Mari priests) holds its meetings under its auspices.

The revival of Mari paganism developed hand in hand with the growing nationalist movement of the 1980s and early 1990s. The largest Mari nationalist organization, the Mari Democratic Union (*Marii Ushem*), was formed with the goal of reviving and promoting Mari language and culture throughout Russia, but by 1992 the union's leaders were advocating an enlargement of Mari representation in republican and local power structures. In early 1991, a radical faction of this movement, *Kugeze Mlande* (Ancestors' Land), initiated a revival of Mari paganism. This faction was dissolved in March 1995 and replaced by *Sorta* (Candle), an educational neo-pagan organization led by academics and intellectuals. These urban activists have tended to combine their religious goals with political aspirations aimed at national consolidation and resistance to Russification. Some have tried to systematize and unify pagan teachings in order to develop a consistent national religion, free of those elements (such as animal sacrifice) that seem less attractive to the general public.

In contrast to the intellectual-led and politically motivated urban-centered paganism, the revival of Mari paganism in the countryside was led by local priests (*karts*), some of whom could claim to have maintained an unbroken connection to ancestral traditions. Large public rituals had in fact been conducted by Maris as late as the 1880s, and family and communal prayers were kept up in sacred groves and ritual knowledge transmitted into recent decades, despite persecution in the Soviet era.

Traditional Mari paganism comprises a mosaic of locally based beliefs and practices. Mari paganism holds environmental awareness and "harmony with nature" among its central moral imperatives. A 1991 act of legislation has resulted in the protection of some three hundred sacred groves and prayer sites by the republican authorities, and public prayers involving sacrifice of horses, bulls, rams, and fowl, have been conducted at these groves since that time. Prayers and rituals have been conducted in many Mari villages and at the grave of the sixteenth-century Mari hero, prince, and priest Chimblat in Kirov province. An All-Mari harvest festival gathering occurs every five years. Nowadays, Maris pray for protection of their culture, natural environment, health, and "the people's spirit." A similar movement has been growing among Maris outside the Mari El Republic, especially in neighboring Bashkortostan.

According to a 1994 sociological survey, "pure pagans" account for 7.9 percent of the Mari people in the Mari El Republic, while another 20.7 percent practice both paganism and Christianity. The proportion of pagans among Mari in the Urals region, Bashkortostan, and Tatarstan, where they had fled from forcible Christianization, are even higher. Women dominate among the pagans and the dual-believers (respectively, 69.2 and 63.6 percent). Many dual-believers also attend pagan services. By contrast, Mari intellectuals frequently view Christianity with hostility, seeing it as a "religion of slaves." Yet both old and new Mari pagan beliefs integrate certain Christian ideas, such as apocalypticism and references to Christian prophets (such as Elias), apostles (Peter and Paul), and even Jesus Christ and the Virgin Mary, in their prayers.

A restoration of pagan traditions in the Mari El Republic is patronized by both the republican and local authorities. The republican Ministry of Education approves school textbooks which teach traditional Mari folklore. Certain Mari scholars represent the Mari El Republic as an oasis of pagan traditions. They advocate making the republic a "culture-historical reserve," which would involve the establishment of a center for the study of folk culture, the organization of folklore festivals, arrangement of scientific-practical conferences, promotion of traditional arts and crafts, support for ethnographic folklore groups, and the like. Plans are underway to build the main All-Mari religious sanctuary in a suburb of Yoshkar-Ola, together with an ethnographic museum, educational center, and hotel. A guidebook published by the republican authorities claims that the "Maris are the only people in Europe who maintained the pure faith of their ancestors and did not renounce their old gods." It argues that devotion to the traditional spirituality has been responsible for Mari national self-awareness and for the maintenance of the Mari language and ethnic customs.

Victor A. Shnirelman
Adrian Ivakhiv

Further Reading

Cordier, Bruno de. "The Finno-Ugric peoples of Central Russia: Opportunities for Emancipation or Condemned to Assimilation?" *Central Asian Survey* 16:4 (1997), 587–609.

See also: Neo-paganism and Ethnic Nationalism in Eastern Europe; Paganism-Mari (Mari El Republic, Russia); Russian Mystical Philosophy.

Otherworlds

Religions are often understood to be concerned with realms beyond everyday life. "Spiritual," "heavenly" or "supernatural" realities are sometimes considered central to definitions and experiences of religion. The location of matters of central importance (perhaps 'ultimate reality") beyond everyday life is definitive for some theologically understood religions. Similarly, in translating other people's religious language with words like "spirit" or "sacred" it is often implied, at least, that religion concerns transcendent realities and states. That is, according to some religious and academic authorities, "religion" is about spirituality not embodiment, heaven not Earth, divine will not human desire. Whether or not such systematizations of religions reflect the understanding, experience and motivations of "ordinary" religionists may be debated. Certainly, however, all cosmologies indicate concerns both about ultimate concerns and about "nature" or "this world." For example, classical Christian teachings about heaven, purgatory, Earth and hell imply a range of daily and ceremonial interactions with the "mundane" or "secular" world that are worthy of consideration, especially in our attempt to understand the meaning and role of nature in Christian and Western thought and experience.

In a wide range of worldviews and lifeways, this world and the relationships that take place here are of central importance. The terms "otherworld" and "otherworlds" (sometimes capitalized) might seem to similarly privilege the extra-ordinary, supernatural, or transcendent above the ordinary, natural or daily. However, close exploration of discourses of other-worldly reality challenge such understandings. Even if the otherworld is the home of ancestors, elves, fairy-folk or "spirits," such locations are neither distant nor alien. Ancestors are neighbors, and sometimes more intimate than that: a wide variety of indigenous peoples consider children to be ancestors reborn. Even saints remain in communion with the faithful, but, unlike ancestors, seem less interested in family life. The realm of faery – and its various inhabitants (elves, gnomes, dwarves, boggarts as well as fairies themselves) – are otherworlds contiguous with "ordinary" nature. For example, in W.B. Yeats' evocative poem "The Stolen Child," the clear difference and opposition between human and other-worldly realities, moralities and desires is firmly located in the recognizable geography of Ireland's County Sligo. The otherworlds of Irish and Norse cosmologies are the alterities of the everyday – as inseparable and as near/far as one's own shadow. Perhaps the otherworld is also like those metaphorical or psychological "shadowy" parts of our own inner lives: necessary to a full understanding of ourselves but rarely referred to explicitly. It might also contribute to debates about cosmologies in which the world is divided into "human domains" and "elsewhere" (e.g., the forest, bush, wilderness in which "wild" animals and wilder "spirits" are in control). Indeed, "wilderness" is constructed (not found) very differently in urban modernity than elsewhere, especially as a romantic location for awesome and/or holistic rather than demonic and purifying experiences.

The otherworld is part of the "ecology of souls" – if this phrase can be used as Terence McKenna intends (i.e., without evoking a duality in which body is denigrated in favor of disembodiment). Instead it should suggest the interdependent coexistence of all manner of living persons (e.g., trees, birds, animals, humans, "the little people," and sometimes rocks and clouds). Irving Hallowell's dialogue with Ojibwe led him to refer to the relationships of human and other-than-human persons. As the alterity of the ordinary, of everyday nature, or of the taken-for-granted world, otherworlds define the world as a richer place than the realm of daily life. They enchant, and require responses that maintain and even reinforce the boundaries between "here" and "there." They also enable understandings of events as intentional acts rather than allegedly impersonal, mechanical or accidental processes. Thus the enchantment of otherworlds permits and generates "magic" and "fate." That is, for example, seeming accidents may be considered to result from insults to otherworld persons.

Some otherworlds are post-mortem destinations for humanity. These include not only the various heavens or hells (or transcendent realms) but also those neighboring spaces, contiguous to this world, which might also be home to deities and others. The "land of youth" and the "land of women" are locations for particular after-lives, but can be visited by the living (heroes or fools at least). More generally, however, otherworlds are the specific homes of other-than-human persons such as elves, faeries, dwarves, giants, and so on. They too might visit this-world, sometimes for less than neighborly purposes. Even the rich and diverse ecologies of "middle Earth" do not exhaust the nations of living beings.

Academic discussion of otherworlds and their inhabitants often assumes the unreality of otherworlds and proceeds to wonder why humans invent such places and inhabitants, such fantasies and fears. Sometimes they interpret alleged encounters with otherworld visitors as references to psychological process. More recently, however, scholars such as Edith Turner have been willing to accept the reality of encounters with "spirits" in healing rituals at face value, and then struggled to find appropriate ways to tell academic colleagues that "native" or insiderly cosmologies and discourses have validity.

So what are faeries, dwarves and so on? Some people will insist that they are exactly what they are said to be. A popular contemporary understanding is that such beings were once more widely encountered, but retreated into wildernesses in the face of either Christian demonization or of more recent industrialization. In many cultures worldwide, reference is made (in narrative, ritual, iconography or conversation) to "little people." Eschewing the Victorian notion that such beings evidence memories of earlier "races," and their literalist diminishment into childhood fantasies, it is clear that such beings are generally spoken of circumspectly. "Little people" avoids naming persons who might otherwise visit, and who might be far from cute and diminutive. Thus we are thinking of feared persons, or at least those who are less than welcome everyday. If nothing else, this indicates that the world is not always encountered as a nurturing place. We are confronted by much that challenges our own needs and desires. Otherworlds are areas of life that resist human control, even in imagination. Meanwhile, that offerings are made to them suggests that respect is necessary and rewarded, indicating that otherworlds are enticing and seductive, and that life can be more than it seems.

Graham Harvey

Further Reading
Hallowell, A. Irving. "Ojibwa Ontology, Behavior, and World View." In S. Diamond, ed. *Culture in History*. New York: Columbia University Press, 1960, 19–52. Reprinted in Graham Harvey, ed. *Readings in Indigenous Religions*. London: Continuum, 2002, chapter 1.
McKenna, Terence and Zuvaya McKenna. *Dream Matrix Telemetry*. Gerrards Cross: Delerium Records, 1993, DELEC CD2012.
Purkiss, Diane. *At the Bottom of the Garden: A Dark History of Fairies, Hobgoblins and Other Troublesome Things*. New York: New York University Press, 2000.
Turner, Edith. "A Visible Spirit from Zambia." In David E. Young and Jean-Guy Goulet, eds. *Being Changed: The Anthropology of Extraordinary Experience*. Peterborough: Broadview Press, 1994, 71–95. Reprinted in Graham Harvey, ed. *Readings in Indigenous Religions*. London: Continuum, 2002, chapter 6.

See also: Faerie Faith in Scotland; Lost Worlds; Magic; Middle Earth; Polytheism.

Ouspensky, Pyotr Demianovich (1878–1947)

P.D. Ouspensky is known today chiefly as the author of *In Search of the Miraculous*, his definitive account of fellow Russian mystic and esoterist G.I. Gurdjieff's teaching which has subsequently become a classic of late twentieth-century mystical literature. In it Ouspensky documents his first meeting with Gurdjieff in Moscow 1915, their relationship through the years of war and revolution which marked the period, to his break from Gurdjieff in 1918, which began a process of separation as both fled from Russia, becoming refugees in Turkey until Ouspensky came to London in 1921, where he stayed until the outbreak of World War II, when he settled in the United States.

Although best known for this work, Ouspensky was in his own right a leading Theosophist who was at the center of the philosophical and occult subcultures that flourished in pre-revolutionary St. Petersburg. His pre-Gurdjeffian publications, especially *Tertium Organum*, synthesized and popularized late nineteenth-century Russian mystical and literary traditions in early twentieth-century Russia. Written in 1911 and published in New York in 1922 it quickly became a bestseller and gave him a worldwide reputation. Outside Russian artistic circles, it also influenced many American writers, including Jean Toomer, Waldo Frank, Gorham Munson, and Kenneth Burke, and through them modern literature. Most significantly, his notion of "the living world is an *entire* organism" shaped Aldo Leopold's important ethical argument for conservation (Ouspensky 1949: 299).

In *Tertium Organum* Ouspensky outlined a suprarational logic that was meant to surpass the *Organon* of Aristotle and the *Novum Organum* of Francis Bacon, and help lead to mystical insights. The key to this effort was his contention that "in mysticism there is a new method" (Ouspensky 1949: 230) and his identification of mysticism with "knowledge received under conditions of expanded receptivity" (Ouspensky 1949: 251).

Indeed, Ouspensky later wrote that he believed he had gained access to mystical states through experiments in yoga, prayer, fasting, and breathing nitrous oxide and ether (Ouspenksy 1930: 315). It was during the period of these experiments that *Tertium Organum* was written (Ouspensky 1930: 323–4). Central to his perception was his experience of a "world in which everything is connected, in which nothing exists separately" (Ouspensky 1930: 315–16), and where all things "were dependent on one another, all things lived one another" (Ouspensky 1930: 323).

As a consequence, he believed, "in this world, there is nothing dead, nothing inanimate, nothing that did not think, nothing that did not feel, nothing unconscious. Everything was living, everything was conscious of itself" (Ouspensky 1930: 323). Ouspensky concluded, "our world is merely our incorrect perception of the world: the world seen by us through a narrow slit" (Ouspensky 1949: 242).

Grounded on this perception, Ouspensky urged his contemporaries to "regard the different forms of consciousness in different divisions and strata of living nature as belonging to one organism and performing different, but related functions, than as separate, and evolving from one another" (Ouspensky 1949: 299). This led to an understanding similar to that found in the more holistic ecological positions of today. Such ecological descriptions of natural systems (for example, a forest – "in which there are trees of different kinds, grass flowers, ants, beetles, birds, beasts – this is a living thing too, living by the life of everything composing it, thinking and feeling for all of which it consists" (Ouspensky 1949: 186)) – is one of many found throughout *Tertium Organum*. While his understanding has become common coin in later environmental movements through the agency of Leopold, for Ouspensky it was only a small part of a more complex relationship between two interdependent entities, Man and Nature.

He encapsulated his mystical perception in one of the most lyrical passages of *Tertium Organum*, a passage which exemplified Ouspensky's dictum that "in all conditions of encompassing nature ... lies ... the sensation of a compete oneness with nature" (Ouspensky 1949: 275):

... in the procession of the year; in the iridescent leaves of the autumn, with their memory-laden smell; in the first snow, frosting the fields and communicating a strange freshness and sensitiveness to the air; in the spring freshets, in the warming sun, in the awakening but still naked branches through which gleams the turquoise sky; in the white nights of stars – in all these are the thoughts, the emotions, the forms, peculiar to itself alone, of some great consciousness: or better, all this is the expression of the emotions, thoughts, and forms of consciousness of a mysterious being – Nature (Ouspensky 1949: 179).

However, Ouspensky argued that only in " 'man' this unity is apparent" (Ouspensky 1949: 298). In later publications, he introduced a less-influential image of nature which built upon and clarified this earlier vision, that of the "Great Laboratory which controls the whole of life" (Ouspensky 1930: 44). Ouspensky argued that "*all* the work of the Great Laboratory had in view one aim – the creation of *Man*" (Ouspensky 1930: 51), and that out of the preliminary experiments and the refuse of the production there were formed the animal and vegetable kingdoms.

What was meant in this instance was something other than a justification of anthropocentrism, for what Ouspensky meant by this was that the "task of the Laboratory was to create a 'form' evolving by itself" (Ouspensky 1930: 50). Indeed, Nature "made attempts at creating self-evolving beings before man" (Ouspensky 1930: 59); Ouspensky thought that "both ants and bees came from the Great Laboratory and were sent to Earth with the privilege and the possibility of evolving" (Ouspensky 1930: 60) but failed when they having "begun to alter their being, their life and their form ... severed their connection with the laws of Nature" (Ouspensky 1930: 62).

All this implied that our species too may fail and be disposed of by nature unless the directive of evolution was pursued. "All forms of consciousness in him can exist simultaneously" (Ouspensky 1949: 298) – to transform this from a possibility to an actuality is what in a broad sense Ouspensky meant by "evolution." Yet it was precisely because with us was "everything from a mineral to a God" (Ouspensky 1930: 118) that such self-evolving beings have failed, for in uniting in potential the single organism of living nature, self-evolving beings had to contend with the eternal cycle of recurrence and the continuation of being through which nature perpetuates itself.

Paradoxically, nature's aim of the creation of self-evolving beings is underpinned by impeding that evolutionary effort, so that movement from potentiality to actuality must be in a sense "anti-nature." Here, as in other publications after *Tertium Organum*, it is difficult to distinguish where Gurdjieff ends and Ouspensky begins, and it could be argued that Ouspensky's greatest influence lies in his popularization of Gurdjieff's teaching as he received it. Nevertheless, when Ouspensky wrote, "the desire of God in man ... is based on his separating himself from the world, on his opposing to the world his own 'I' and on his recognizing as reality all apparent forms and divisions" (Ouspensky 1930: 18), he outlined not only his own vision of the interdependent relationship between nature and man and their respective roles, but also sought to bring together his sometime contradictory imagery of nature.

David Pecotic

Further Reading

Carlson, Maria. *"No Religion Higher Than the Truth": A History of the Theosophical Movement in Russia, 1875-1922*. Princeton, NJ: Princeton University Press, 1993.

Ouspensky, P.D. *Tertium Organum: The Third Canon of Thought - A Key to the Enigmas of the World*. Nicholas Bessarboroff and Claude Bragdon, trs. London: Routledge & Kegan Paul, 1949 (1st edn, 1920).

Ouspensky, P.D. *A New Model of the Universe: Principles of the Psychological Method in its Application to Problems of Science, Religion, and Art*. London: Routledge & Kegan Paul, 1930.

Reyner, J.H. *Ouspensky: The Unsung Genius*. London: George Allen & Unwin, 1981.

See also: Alchemy; Gurdjieff, Georges Ivanovitch; Leopold, Aldo; Russian Mystical Philosophy; Western Esotericism.

Ovid's Metamorphoses

Greek and Roman poets and philosophers shared a concern for the permeable boundaries that divide nature, humankind, and god. This theme can be found in Homer, where gods become human and humans are transformed into animals, and in Plato, where the human task is to resolve the conflict between animal and divine potentialities within the self. The interplay between nature, humankind, and god is seen most vividly in Ovid's masterpiece, *The Metamorphoses* (published in the year 8). In these stories the Roman poet Ovid (43 B.C.E.–17 C.E.) wove together a large number of Greco-Roman myths around the theme of change: "All things are mutations – Heaven and Earth and all that grows within it, and we among the changes in creation" (Ovid, Book XV: 427–8). The *Metamorphoses* is a cosmological poem aiming to "tell the shifting story of the world from its beginning to the present hour" (Ovid, Book I: 31). Stories from Ovid's encyclopedia of transformation have become standard parts of Western culture, showing up in the visual artists, in poetry, in psychology, and even in the natural sciences.

The transformative power of nature was recognized by Epicurean natural philosophy through observation of developmental processes in nature. However, Ovid expanded the idea of transformation far beyond the boundaries of Epicurean empiricism. The stories he presented include transformations across the differences separating god, humankind, and nature. Often these tales explain natural phenomena by providing mythological stories about the origin of things.

In Ovid, metamorphoses often happen as punishments or rewards that fit the deeds of the one transformed. For example, Semele, the lover of Jupiter, was burned to ashes by the power of Jove's love; self-loving Narcissus was turned into a plant; and the arrogant Niobe was turned into a stone. In addition to punishment or reward, the transformative power of desire provides the motive force for Ovid's stories of meddlesome gods and immodest humans.

Like Euripides and the Athenian tragedians, Ovid was fascinated by the destructive power of Dionysus. But Dionysus (or Bacchus), associated by Ovid with Liber, the god of wine, is only one of the gods who had the power to transform. Ovid also focused on the power of Jupiter (Jove), Juno, and Apollo. But Ovid was perhaps most interested in the transformative power of Venus, goddess of love. Venus is of further importance because she was the mother of Aeneas, founder of Rome, whose story was most famously told by Ovid's predecessor, Virgil.

Selected Myths Synopses:

Deucalion and the Flood

Jove's anger against the tyrant Lycaon led him to become angry with the whole human race. Jove and Neptune covered the Earth with water, killing all humans except Deucalion and his bride, Pyrrha. Deucalion and Pyrrha then created the new race of humans by transforming stones into flesh.

Daphne and Apollo

Apollo, the archer, insulted Cupid, whose arrows were the cause of love. In retaliation, Cupid shot Apollo with an arrow of desire, while also causing Daphne to have no desire for man or god. Apollo pursued Daphne, who vigorously resisted his advances. As Apollo chased her, Daphne prayed to her father, the river god Peneus, to be saved from Apollo's ardor. Peneus transformed Daphne into a tree, the laurel tree. Apollo still loved Daphne and ordained that the laurel leaf would be his symbol.

Io and Jove

Jove bewitched and raped Io, a young virgin. However, Juno, Jove's consort, suspected Jove of philandering. To conceal Io, Jove transformed her into a cow. Juno demanded that the beautiful cow be given to her. She then appointed Argos, who had 100 eyes, to guard the cow so that Jove could not reclaim her. Jove dispatched Mercury to put Argos to sleep with the enchanting sound of music. Mercury then killed Argos. Juno commemorated her hero by placing the image of his eyes on the tail-feathers of the peacock. Io, the cow, now freed, ran all the way to the Nile. Jove managed to persuade Juno to forgive him and to cease punishing Io. Finally, Io was transformed back into a human and was then further transformed into Isis, the Egyptian goddess.

Europa and Jove

In order to possess the beautiful Europa, Jove transformed himself into a bull. Europa fell in love with the beautiful beast. She hung a garland of flowers around his neck and eventually mounted him. Jove then took Europa out to sea.

Echo and Narcissus

Everyone loved the beautiful boy Narcissus. But Narcissus tempted and rejected everyone. Echo, a beautiful girl who had been cursed by Juno for her dalliance with Jove, also fell in love with Narcissus. Juno's curse was that Echo was only able to repeat the last few words she had heard. Narcissus rejected Echo's love and she faded away out of sorrow, only leaving her voice behind. Meanwhile another spurned lover of Narcissus prayed that Narcissus would only love himself and yet fail in that love. Nemesis agreed to punish Narcissus by creating a pond in which Narcissus found his reflection. He fell in love with his own image but was always unable to possess this image. Eventually he died, was mourned by Echo, and was transformed into a flower.

Apollo and Hyacinthus

Apollo loved the boy Hyacinthus. They practiced discus throwing together. Unfortunately, the discus thrown by Apollo ricocheted off a rock and struck Hyacinthus in the face, killing him. To commemorate Hyacinthus, Apollo wrote "ai, ai," (syllables reminiscent of Hyacinthus' name) on the petals of a purple flower.

Pygmalion

Pygmalion was a clever artist who carved a beautiful woman out of stone and fell in love with the statue. He prayed to Venus that his creation would come to life. Venus granted his wish. Pygmalion's sculpture came alive and became his wife.

Cinyras and Myrrha

Myrrha was the daughter of Pygmalion's grandson, Cinyras. She was in love with her father and tricked him into sleeping with her by coming to his bed in the dark of night. When Cinyras finally discovered that he had slept with his own daughter he chased her out of his country. She prayed to become a thing that neither lives nor dies. Some nameless god granted her wish and transformed her into the myrrh tree, whose tears are famous.

Venus and Adonis

Adonis was the beautiful male offspring of Myrrha and Cinyras. He gestated within the myrrh tree and upon his birth was adopted by Venus. His brother, Cupid, accidentally scratched their mother, Venus, with one of his arrows and as a result Venus fell in love with Adonis. Venus consorted with Adonis, hunting with him in the woods. In order to warn him of the dangers of the wild animals in the wood, Venus told Adonis the story of how Atalanta and Hippomenes were transformed into lions because they were ungrateful toward the gods. However, Adonis did not heed her warning and was killed by a wild boar. Venus commemorated Adonis with a fragile flower the color of blood, the anemone.

Ovid's Influence

Ovid's *Metamorphoses* had a strong influence on Roman culture of the first and second centuries of the Common Era among poets and writers such as Seneca and Lucan. However, with the rise of Christianity, Ovid's text was either suppressed along with other pagan literature or was interpreted allegorically in an attempt to align the Ovidian myths with Christian stories and themes. Ovid's myths were eventually celebrated both for their Latin style and for the psychological, moral, and cosmological value of their themes. Medieval romances and love poetry borrowed themes from Ovid. Ovid's importance can be seen in Dante's *Divine Comedy*, where Ovid can be found in the first circle of Hell. By the time of the Renaissance, Ovid was celebrated both for his imagery and for his basic moral sentiment. Other authors who were influenced by Ovid include Petrarch, Chaucer, Shakespeare, Milton, Cervantes, Calderon, La Fontaine, and Corneille. In the visual arts, themes from Ovid's *Metamorphoses* were taken up by artists such as Raphael, Corregio, Titian, Michelangelo, Bernini, Rubens, and Poussin. Almost any visual or literary artist of the last 500 years of Western culture who took up a theme from ancient mythology derived this theme either directly or indirectly from Ovid.

Besides his influence on art and literature, Ovid's myths have found their way into other parts of Western culture including common words such as narcissism, echo, and Adonis. Zoologists have utilized Ovid's language in naming creatures such as the Argus pheasant, the python, the Icarus butterfly, the Atalanta butterfly, and the Io and Polyphemus moths. Flowers like the Hyacinth bear Ovidian names. Astronomers make use of the language of ancient myths in naming celestial objects. For example, the names Galileo gave to the moons of Jupiter were derived from the characters described by Ovid as consorts of the god Jupiter: Io, Europa, Ganymede, and Callisto. Psychologists such as Freud have identified and discussed character traits such as narcissism. And popular culture has adopted themes such as Cupid's arrows, Midas' gold touch, and the story of Pygmalion.

Ovid is an important contributor to the set of myths that form the background of Western culture. His myths display a world of flux in which there is an open interface between humans, gods, and nature. Ovid's *Metamorphoses* provides us with narratives about the origins of many natural features that also serve as cautionary tales about the disruptive power of desire, certainly one of nature's great transformational forces. Ovid's universe is one in which natural objects such as flowers and birds are given significance by acts of the gods. It is also one in which desire makes it possible for humans and gods to cross the borders that separate them from each other and from natural objects.

Andrew Fiala

Further Reading

Brewer, Wilmon. *Ovid's Metamorphoses in European Culture.* Boston: Cornhill Publishing, 1933.

Galinsky, Karl G. *Ovid's Metamorphoses: An Introduction to the Basic Aspects.* Berkeley: University of California Press, 1975.

Ovid. *The Metamorphoses.* Horace Gregory, tr. New York: Viking Press, 1958.

Tissol, Garth. *The Face of Nature: Wit, Narrative, and Cosmic Origins in Ovid's Metamorphoses.* Princeton, NJ: Princeton University Press, 1997.

See also: Delphic Oracle; Greco-Roman World; Greece – Classical; Greek Landscape; Greek Paganism; Lake Pergusa (Sicily); Roman Natural Religion; Roman Religion and Empire; Western Esotericism.

P

Pacific Islands

Oceania, or the Pacific Islands region, includes Melanesia (the islands of black peoples), Polynesia (many islands), and Micronesia (small islands) over a vast area covering one third of the globe, running from Vogelkop at the western end of the great New Guinea island across to Hawai'i and Easter Island, nearer the Americas.

Almost a quarter of the known distinct religions of humanity are found in these islands, with the most complex ethnic scene on Earth being found in Papua New Guinea (where over 750 living languages and cultures have been identified). In Melanesia the variations of religious life are remarkable, with very many land-locked groups lying in the mountain ranges that form the spine of New Guinea, the world's second largest island. The religious scenes of Polynesia and Micronesia, by comparison, have much more cultural unity about them, and the so-called Austronesian (or "Malayo-Polynesian") family of languages predominates there.

The peoples of Oceania generally lack terms for religion and nature, but normally have lexical equivalents for worship and world. Their lifeways before any extensive exposure to the outside world were almost exclusively small-scale and their technologies based on stone. Only Polynesia's Tonga is known to have attempted a far-flung (quasi-)empire, stretching to the west as far as New Caledonia, and iron-working was known only along the coasts of Vogelkop through interaction with the Sultanate of Tidore. Thus the descriptors primitive or primal, indigenous, tribal, and traditional, have been conventionally used in research to refer to pre-contact Oceanic cultures religions. In imagings of the European mind, however, the presence of religion has generally been acknowledged for Polynesia and Micronesia, because their societies are generally hierarchical, under chiefly rule – even famous monarchies in Hawai'i and Tonga – with priests often making up a special caste. Melanesia, on the other hand, has a reputation for magic, or less developed forms of (magico-) religious life, because the societies there appear less structured. But for most anthropologists this dichotomy has proved faulty. A sufficient number of chieftainship societies in Melanesia, as well as examples of priestly roles, call the bifurcation into question. Nevertheless, religion is appropriate as a heuristic term for all of Oceania's ritual patterns and spiritual outlooks. There is something that may be salvaged from this well-worn regional contrasting, though, in terms of indigenous attitudes towards the character of the world.

If only as a rule of thumb, Melanesians tend to view their worlds more horizontally and the others more vertically. This basically means that, when it comes to comparing beliefs about the relationships between religion and the total environment (or cosmos), Melanesians most often look to the forests, mountains, and waters as abodes of the dead or spirits, whereas Polynesians and Micronesians characteristically envisage the "Earth" between upper and lower worlds. Now, the usual reason given for these different outlooks is a social one: Polynesian and Micronesian societies are stratified to one degree or another. In cases where there is strong hierarchization, as on Hawai'i Tonga and Aotearoa (New Zealand), nobles stand distinct from commoners, and castes of warriors and priests sustain royal or high chiefly houses. The whole economy is made to move toward the social apex, the rulers being engrossed with wealth (even though they bestow much of it on their subjects). Since it is commonly understood that chiefs proceed heavenward at death, often to become stars, we can understand why scholars have deduced that definite social strata in Polynesia and Micronesia have produced vertical images of the cosmos found there, often as the three tiers of heaven, Earth, and an underworld. In Melanesia, in contrast, the more egalitarian struggle between big-men and managers (particularly in highland New Guinea) has been used by ethnographers to explain in ethnography why local cosmoses are more laterally or horizontally conceived, with the spirits of leader and led alike going at death to the same place (whether that be to the mountaintops, for example, as with Wahgi, or at the end or bottom of a river, as in the Bena Bena view, to take two cases from the New Guinea Highlands).

But why should we explain these differing views of the world (or "nature") as the result of social patterns? Might it not be just as easily maintained, perhaps, that spatial relations in the environment have had effects on such contrasting *Weltanschauungen*? The small islands in wider Oceania, whether upthrusted volcanically as typical in Polynesia, or flat coral atolls in Micronesia, sit more starkly between the wide stretch of sky and the mysterious depths of the seas. It hardly seems unfitting, then, that myths should recount how gods drew islands up from the depths – as the Micronesian deity Nareau did, for instance, when ordering the primal eel Riiki to prop up the heavens as if erecting the central post of a house. In a similar vein, one finds myths of cosmic Separation (a Trennung), creation occurring when gods push up the sky from the Earth and give the latter its midway position – as the god Tane did in Maori narratives. Melanesia, by comparison, although showing a fair spread of interest in the sun and moon, and an intriguing small cluster of groups believing in sky-people, is a region better known for "place" deities or spirits. Examples of such place-based beings include volcano gods (as with the Tolai of New Britain), for instance, fearful boundary spirits (such as the Elam Bari who live on the edges of Chimbu country, New Guinea Highlands), who needed placating with pig offerings if the weather was either too wet or too dry, or cave-dwelling beings, some of which became an object of cultic attention (for example, for more than one tribe in Huliland, located in the Southern Highlands of Papua New Guinea).

If in Polynesia such a vertical presence as the coconut tree symbolizes the cosmos, moreover, including the rootedness of a people in its original husk (as held among Rarotongans), in Melanesia wild things in the forest, such as feral pigs, are often emblematic of humans (especially men in a liminal state during initiations), with birds rather than winds (let alone heavenly constellations) most often signaling the presence of spirits (especially the ancestors, because, as the Papuan Orokaiva would say, it is hard to know how or whether birds die). If in Polynesia and Micronesia feasts are more associated with the blessings and protective power of gods, spirits and chiefs from above, in Melanesia the sense of fertility and generation at ground level, albeit with the spirits' help, is more the sense of things. The proposition that preconceived geographical space or the environmental surroundings condition religious worldviews into these differential patterns, though, is less popular at the moment than the view that indigenous approaches to "nature" are predetermined by social power relations and strata (as argued, for example by Daniel de Coppet and Andre Iteanu).

Outlooks specific to the above-mentioned regions may be considered under Melanesia; Micronesia; Polynesia; Papua New Guinea; Hawai'i; New Zealand; etc. In very general terms, to conclude, Pacific islanders considered various places to be sacred or prohibited (tabu) to unauthorized or unprotected humans (not just ancestral sites being meant here, but caves and glades of cultic attention, or swamps, lakes, and dense forests occupied by dangerous beings). Animism as a term to describe all this is inappropriate if it implies that their whole universes were alive with spirit-forces, when it is more typical for islanders to say that spirits inhabit specifiable restingplaces or lairs. Totemism, including the tracing of a tribal lineage to an animal or plant, is common in Melanesia, but not elsewhere in Oceania (where genealogies back to canoe arrivals predominate).

Conservation of flora and fauna on land and in the sea is more a spontaneous than any philosophically intended outcome, the islanders possessing very time-consuming technologies which have been less harm-inducing than techniques later brought by outsiders.

Lineages typically possessed and cultivated ancestral lands (the New Guinea highlands yielding evidence of the earliest known horticultural activity anywhere on Earth), and thus protection and conservation of these lands have been involved in consequence, even if moving from one garden area to another can come into the equation. Symbolic and linguistic life, integral to Oceania's religions, is laden with associations and metaphors drawn from a lively environment – its flying and fast-moving fish, large reptiles, shy possums, many birds (cassowaries, birds of paradise), wild boars – as well as from its arresting topography. Overall, religion and assumptions about the environment ("nature") are utterly intertwined in Pacific Islander understanding, but how differing emphases arose, regionally and in each individual culture, remains a matter for debate. Certainly the spirituality – nature connections in Pacific traditions have been and remain important conservationist impetuses.

Garry W. Trompf

Further Reading
de Coppet, Daniel and Andre Iteanu, eds. *Cosmos and Society in Oceania*. Oxford: Berg, 1995.
Swain, Tony and Garry W. Trompf. *Religions of Oceania*. Library of Religious Beliefs and Practices. New York: Routledge, 1995.

See also: Bouganville (Papua, New Guinea); Hawai'i; Manser, Bruno – and the Penan of Sarawak; New Zealand; Penan Hunter-Gatherers (Borneo); The Philippines; Polynesian Traditional Religions; Surfing.

Pagan Calendar

A calendar evolves as a means for a culture to record its past, plan for the future and determine its holy days. From a religious perspective, the calendar becomes a "Philosopher's Stone" in providing access to spiritual insight and understanding. Incorporating one's basic assumptions concerning nature, spirit and humanity into a calendrical framework of ritual and symbolism, the hidden truths contained therein "will unfold over the years as we integrate them into our own lives" (Crowley 1989: 16). Of the world's major calendars, the Greek, Egyptian and Mexican systems are no longer significantly influential. Hindu and Chinese calendars, however, are still employed for religious determination, while the Hebrew and Islamic continue to function in both civil and theological senses. Nevertheless, the dominant time-reckoning system that the world enjoys today is the modified JulianRoman organization known as the Gregorian calendar.

The neo-pagan "Wheel of the Year" celebration of eight *sabbats* is a mytho-ritual timetable that allows its practitioners to engage in seasonal interaction with nature, cyclical evolution and Pagan spirituality. Nonetheless, its largely Wiccan-inspired contemporary Pagan festivals are located and determined according to the prevailing Gregorian calendar. This last, despite the adjustments made to it through imperial and ecclesiastical authority, is an original formulation credited to the legendary second king of Rome, Numa Pompilius, as a means to keep track of established *feriae* or sacred festivals. But as physical place can often maintain an aura of atavistic attraction, so too might the ancient holiday exert an underlying focal appeal despite whatever historical and cultural overlay. Consequently, the roots of the Roman calendar reveal a complex arrangement and ceaselessly provocative understanding that interface this world with the other. They allegedly constitute a pagan "golden key" to a lost spiritual equilibrium or emancipation embedded in the origins of Western civilization.

Numa's codification integrates the twelve monthly divides or Ides (originally the day of the full moon) with forty-five festival celebrations and the new year's day of March 1st. If this strikes the modern reader as excessive, it should be borne in mind that the Romans had no weekend or regular Sabbath. Of the fixed *feriae*, those of the Saturnalia (December 17th), Lupercalia (February 15th) and Vestalia (June 9th) are perhaps the best known today. The bulk of ritual and celebratory activity concerns the "waxing" half of the year when the sun moves from nadir to apex. Apart from the Latin yule of December, the longest stretch of continuous holiday occurs in the second half of August. Purification rites transpire at various times, but especially in the months of March, April, May, October and February. The Greater Sabbats of Wicca do not appear to receive singular emphasis apart from coinciding with the Kalends (whence our term "calendar") that begin every month and are sacred to Janus and Juno. Most cult activity is focused on the vernal equinox and the two solstices, though the moment of midsummer itself is ritually ignored. All in all, while both the *sabbats* of neo-paganism and the holy days of Christianity are positioned according to the world's secular calendar, the "spiritual radicalism" (Latin *radix* "root") to be found at this calendar's core enshrines the fundamental relationship between nature, religion and society as an organic and holistic dynamic.

Michael York

Further Reading

Crowley, Vivianne. *Wicca: The Old Religion in the New Age.* Wellingborough: Aquarian Press, 1989.

York, Michael. *The Roman Festival Calendar of Numa Pompilius.* New York: Peter Lang, 1986.

See also: Earth First! and the Earth Liberation Front; Pagan Festivals (both); Paganism – Contemporary; Wicca.

Pagan Environmental Ethics

When it comes to actions directed at the preservation and defense of the environment Pagans are often on the front lines. Pagans frequently take leading roles in campaigns to stop what they perceive to be ecologically unsound forestry practices, unnecessary road-building projects, or the desecration of significant environmental landmarks; they actively engage in projects to restore prairies, wetlands, and forests; and many readily embrace renewable energy and support public transportation. At the same time, however, some Pagans also engage in actions not considered to be environmentally friendly: they drive fossil fuel-burning automobiles to their spiritual gatherings, they heat their homes with non-renewable energy, they use natural resources provided through environmentally malignant methods. So, how are we to make sense of the idea of a Pagan environmental ethic?

Given that ethical commitments are not always fully realizable in practice; ethics cannot necessarily be glimpsed via an accounting of the actions of individuals or groups. Since ethics and actions are not the same thing, we must, then, looks elsewhere to uncover Pagan environmental ethics.

Our sense of ethical inclusiveness is a direct function of our sense of social inclusiveness. Our sense of society is part of that which makes up our worldview. We extend direct moral standing and moral consideration to those whom we deem to be part of our social community. The intensity of this ethical commitment corresponds directly to the closeness of this social commitment. Hence, all things being equal, our commitments to human children wins out over our commitment to a goat's kids, and our commitment to our own children wins out over our commitment to someone else's. So, if we can uncover the sense and extent of community expressed by the Pagan worldview then we can more clearly perceive their ethical commitments and their environmental ethics.

In general, even though there are various Pagan traditions, there is a single theme that unifies them: the worship or profound honoring of, and respect for, nature. Surveys by Margot Adler (1986: 415, 445), for example, suggest that environmental concern was one of the most fundamental issues for Pagans, as well as one of the most important catalysts for people entering the religion. Likewise, religion scholar Graham Harvey asserts that "what attracts most people to Paganism now is the stress on honouring Nature" (1997: 43).

Pagans often perceive of themselves as animists, believing that everything in nature – and even perhaps nature itself – possesses an indwelling spirit. Their love of nature and all life, is a natural extension of this animistic catalyst. According to Starhawk, this "love for life in all its forms is the basic ethic of Witchcraft" (1979: 11). More specifically though, that worshipful, even reverential, attitude toward nature prompts a metaphysic of inclusiveness and community, a metaphysic that portrays the human and the nonhuman as unified and conceptually indistinguishable in many ways. There is ample evidence to suggest that Pagans perceive of the nonhuman world as worthy of "personhood," in the full moral sense. Pagans, for instance, often speak of individual animals and plants and environmental wholes as "other-than-human persons." They also refer to environmental entities as "friends" and "neighbors" with whom they share the world. Consequently, actions undertaken involving this other-than-human world assume a friendship or neighborly metaphysic and ethic. This inclusive social and ethical community can be seen, for example in The Wiccan Rede: "And it harm none, do as you will." The Rede resonates ecologically because it calls generally for liberty and freedom, and because it asserts a broad principle of non-harm. More importantly, however, is that the condemnation of harm is applicable to the other-than-human world as well as to the human: "none" also includes the other-than-human. However, a closer and more demanding familial or kinship relationship and social community often emerges as well. This relationship is clearly voiced by the High Priestess of Circle Sanctuary, Selena Fox, when she asserts, "I am Pagan. I am a part of the whole of Nature. The Rocks, the Animals, the Plants, the Elements, and Stars *are my relatives* . . . I am part of this large *family* of Nature" (2001: 110–11, emphasis is mine, but the capitalization of the other-than-human elements is Fox's). Harvey also points out that the Pagan "world view is one in which everything that lives deserves honour and rights not normally given to other-than-human life," and that Pagans insist on "treating all things as alive and in some way *kin* to humanity" (1997: 133, 90).

Such a rendition of Pagan environmental ethics is not wholly uncontested. Catherine Albanese, for example, suggests that, for all of its "radical and cosmic environmentalism," Paganism – and other nature-oriented religions as well – is "intensely pragmatic" (1990: 183). In this sense, one might skeptically view the magical worldview and subsequent rituals of Pagans as engaged in or masking a manipulative relationship with nature. Of course, instrumental valuation can certainly exist alongside intrinsic, and manipulation of and benefit derived from is not the same as a mastery relationship. However, this contestation of Pagan environmental ethics certainly exists and merits mention.

Within the realm of formal philosophical discussions of environmental ethics, this Pagan social community/ethical community relationship, arguably resonates most closely with the Land Ethic of Aldo Leopold. Leopold's theory also prompts ethical obligation on the basis of a shared community. Pagan environmental ethical sensibilities find kinship with the various traditions of American Indians who also express a social and ethical kinship with nature as demonstrated in their myths, legends, and rituals. Both are discussed at length in the work of environmental philosopher J. Baird Callicott.

As a result, for Pagans the sacred rests in daily life, the domestic, this world. Paganism is not other-worldly; Earth and this body are not merely some shoddy way station on the way to transcendental salvation. Humans are full and equal members of this Earth, not resentful of a forced and lesser – but fortunately temporary – inhabitation of this body and this world. The Pagan sense of time, and the celebrations that are based upon it, center on the here and now – planting and harvesting – those things most immediately connected to daily life, life imbued with the sacred, the magical, and the intrinsically valuable and significant. Harvey (1997) nicely captures this fundamental sentiment: "Paganism is a religion at home on Earth."

Given, then, that, in general, our sense of an ethical community and commitment is coextensive with our sense of a social community, and given that Pagans possess a sense of social community inclusive of all of nature, it is evident that they also possess a broadly comprehensive environmental ethic. Pagans, therefore, attribute intrinsic value (i.e., value in addition to instrumental, or use, value) to nonhuman entities, natural processes, and environmental collectives. Their environmental ethic is intentionally holistic, encompassing, and ecocentric.

Because of their commitment to this life, this world, this Earth, and because of their sense of being fully part and parcel of nature, Pagans attempt to radiate respect for life. They deliberately, carefully, and with great humility inhabit the land. They celebrate life and its multifaceted flourishing. Their actions, then, generally reflect this inclusive worldview and powerful ethical commitment.

Michael P. Nelson

Further Reading

Adler, Margot. *Drawing Down the Moon: Witches, Druids, Goddess Worshippers, and Other Pagans in America Today.* New York: Penguin, 1986 (originally published in 1979).

Albanese, Catherine L. *Nature Religion in America: From the Algonkian Indians to the New Age.* Chicago: University of Chicago Press, 1990.

Callicott, J. Baird and Michael P. Nelson. *Ojibwa Environmental Ethics.* Upper Saddle River, NJ: Prentice-Hall, 2004.

Callicott, J. Baird. *Beyond the Land Ethic.* Albany: State University of New York Press, 1999.

Callicott, J. Baird. *In Defense of the Land Ethic*. Albany: State University of New York Press, 1989.

Fox, Selena. "I Am Pagan." In Dennis Carpenter Fox and Theresa Berrie. *Circle Guide to Pagan Groups, 13th Edition*. Mt. Horeb, WI: Circle Publications, 2001.

Harvey, Graham. *Contemporary Paganism: Listening People, Speaking Earth*. New York: New York University Press, 1997.

Starhawk. *The Spiral Dance: A Rebirth of the Ancient Religion of the Great Goddess*. New York: Harper & Row, 1979.

Taylor, Bron. "Resacralizing Earth: Pagan Environmentalism and the Restoration of Turtle Island." In *American Sacred Space*. David Chidester and Edward T. Linenthal, eds. Bloomington: Indiana University Press, 1995, 97–151.

York, Michael. *Pagan Theology*. Washington Square, NY: New York University, 2004.

See also: Bioregionalism; Bioregionalism and the North American Bioregional Congress; Callicott, J. Baird; Druids and Druidry; Earth First! and the Earth Liberation Front; Environmental Ethics; Heathenry – Ásatrú; Hundredth Monkey; Leopold, Aldo; Odinism; Pagan Festivals (both); Paganism and Technology; Paganism – Contemporary; Radical Environmentalism; Reclaiming; Religious Studies and Environmental Concern; Snyder, Gary; Starhawk; Wicca.

Pagan Festivals in North America

Throughout the changing seasons of the year neo-pagans all over North America participate in gatherings and festivals where they share traditions and create rituals together. Some festivals are specific to a single tradition or organization, some are open only to invited participants, while others are eclectic festivals open to the general neo-pagan community and all its sub-groups as well as to interested newcomers. Gatherings for special purposes, such as training new practitioners or organizing events for the year, are different from more open-ended gatherings where the goal is sharing information and networking. Most festivals, however, include rituals and workshops intended to bind participants together in community and to encourage self-exploration. At festivals self-exploration takes place within and alongside group activities: workshops on such diverse topics as astrology, herbal lore, Tibetan chanting, Native American drumming techniques, and large collective rituals. Some of the men, women and children who attend festivals accompany friends and family members and may not identify themselves as neo-pagan. But most festival-goers attend festivals to experience living for a brief time in an entirely neo-pagan community. While neo-pagans attend festivals to engage in workshops and rituals aimed at personal transformation, festivals also provide an opportunity for otherwise isolated individuals to define their place in the North American neo-pagan movement.

Although most neo-pagans consider themselves Earth-based religious practitioners, not all festival activities focus on a direct relationship between humans and nature. Many celebratory or theatrical festival events include references to the elements Earth, air, wind and fire. Evening events such as poetry readings and musical performances make few if any connections to nature. Late-night fires are common at many festivals and typically consist of drumming and dancing around a bonfire into the early hours of the morning. Rituals and late-night drumming and dancing may feature songs and chants that include references to nature, and especially connections between humans and spirits of nature or humans and the elements, such as the popular chants "Air I Am, Fire I Am, Water, Earth and Spirit I Am," and "Earth My Body, Water My Blood, Air My Breath and Fire My Spirit."

The natural world is seen as sacred, but specific spaces in the woods and fields are also made sacred through ritual activity, especially casting a circle. Sacred space is very important at festivals, whether they are held in private nature sanctuaries, at public campgrounds reserved for the occasion, or indoors at a convention center. Many festival announcements actively promote festival sites as enchanted woodlands far removed from ordinary life. They may focus on unique geographical features or the cultural history of an area that was once sacred to indigenous people. Festivals may be geographically isolated, located far from urban areas and their sites hidden over hills or beyond wooded areas, away from prying eyes. The secluded feeling of these sites enhances participants' sense of being close to nature.

Because people who attend festivals are from different backgrounds, arrive with divergent expectations and practice multiple traditions, creating sacred and safe space is a concern for festival communities. Neo-pagan festivals emphasize the sacredness of the natural world and exemplify the belief that spiritual power is immanent. Festival spaces are created in ways that explicitly embody the divine and honor the gods and goddesses that participants believe to live in the woods, fields and streams of the regions where festivals are held. Altars, mounds, shrines and offerings are constructed and left in honor of these regional spirits. Ritual leaders may draw on the belief that spirits surround them by invoking the presence of spirits of the land in their rituals. Sacred space is a method of manifesting "interconnectedness," the belief among neo-pagans that layers of the self, including past lives, are vitally connected to the rest of the planet and its inhabitants.

Most festivals occur in the warmer months and are held outdoors so that participants can make explicit connections to their natural surroundings. Neo-pagan festivals involve anywhere from fifty to a thousand people who come from a broad range of backgrounds and locales. Some live on the private land where festivals occur, but many more live in New York City, San Francisco, Boston, Chicago and other urban areas, so that their journeys to festivals are also pilgrimages to nature. Some festival-goers are nomads living out of vans and renovated school buses or self-employed artists; others are teachers, social workers and computer programmers. Most participants reflect the ethnic and racial characteristics of the North American neo-pagan community in that they are largely of European heritage. Some festivals are designated for men or women only, but most are open to anyone and feature female and male organizers and ritual specialists. African Americans, American Indians and Asian Americans are present at some festivals, though they are in a minority. Neo-pagan festival-goers probably tend to be more middle class than the larger community of North American neo-pagans because they can more easily afford travel and festival admission prices. While not prohibitive, week-long festivals with multiple activities and celebrity performances reflect their overhead costs and in the 1990s charged anywhere from fifty to two hundred dollars for admission.

Festival planning begins months in advance when announcements are sent out and posted on neo-pagan organizations' websites, then circulated via email and word of mouth. Calls are sent out seeking workshop presenters to submit proposals and well-known neo-pagans are invited as guest speakers and performers. Most workshop presenters are not paid, although they receive free or discounted admission. Many festivals require that all participants contribute to the community in some way, from presenting workshops to emptying recycling containers. At some festivals, festival-goers may barter longer work shifts in exchange for free or discounted admission. Volunteer work crews on private nature sanctuaries clear and mark trails through the woods, set up recycling and restroom facilities, rope off and mark ritual and workshop spaces and collect firewood.

Like the larger North American neo-pagan community, neo-pagan festivals do not answer to a national organizing body, and variations between festival locations, workshops topics, festival goals and religious commitment can be striking. Festivals are usually run by a core of people connected to neo-pagan organizations, such as Circle Sanctuary in rural Wisconsin, or a store such as Ancient Ways in Oakland. Many decisions are made by consensus and often incorporate festival participants' feedback through surveys and suggestion boxes. Nevertheless, most festivals follow an ordered pattern of activities that usually includes at least some of the following: opening ceremony, workshops scheduled in the mornings and afternoons, evening rituals and performances, late-night drumming and dancing, fire circles and coffee-houses, a community feast, and a closing ritual.

Festival-goers often travel long distances to festival sites. When they arrive they may be greeted or welcomed in special ways, given amulets or identification tags to wear, handed festival programs and rules, and assigned work shifts and campsites. Campsites are often selected by individual preference, but some festivals group like-minded people or people with special needs together. Festivals designate specific camping areas for families or people in recovery from substance abuse, such as a "twelve-step support camp" as well as quiet areas and camps for late-night music and percussion. First-time festival-goers are immediately aware of one significant difference from the outside world: nudity, or "skyclad," is typically an option at most festivals and costumes are appropriate, as is body paint and other body décor.

Daytime activities at festivals may include nature walks, edible plant workshops, children's craft workshops, and shopping with merchants who sell books, clothing, ritual tools, natural cosmetics and other items – especially handmade items – not available in most stores. Workshops are offered on a range of topics by a variety of festival participants. They are usually held outside or under tents and sometimes focus on the natural environment surrounding the festival. Some workshop presenters simply share an area of expertise – mask making, for example – while others are published authors or nationally known for their drum-making, dancing, ritual or tarot-reading skills and knowledge. Anyone with a certain amount of experience in neo-paganism and a good idea for a discussion topic or a skill to share with a group can run a workshop. Topics include myths and teachings from indigenous and pre-Christian cultures, such as the ancient Celts; healing techniques involving body work, divination or other techniques; Tai Chi, Yoga or other forms of movement; and personal exploration of spirits and deities. Small-scale rituals, such as healing circles, may also take place in workshops. Crafts projects in workshops include making masks and decorations for rituals out of feathers, cloth, clay, pinecones, herbs and other objects found in the woods. Large-scale rituals are often in the evening or even late at night. Opening and closing rituals tend to create bonds between festival-goers and celebrate community, while major rituals in the evenings tend to offer opportunities for personal transformation, such as a ritual modeled on the journey of the ancient Greek goddess Persephone to the underworld.

Festivals are located in specific places and are sometimes connected to participants' home altars and shrines or their region of the country. For some rituals taking place at Circle Sanctuary, for instance, participants were asked to bring stones from their own homes to place in Circle's stone circle. Another festival asked participants to bring a handful of dirt from their homes that was then placed in a large pile near the main ritual area and incorporated into both opening and closing rituals. Neo-pagans emphasize awareness of their surroundings and sensitivity to what they see as the various energies flowing through the land and embedded in festival spaces.

Sarah M. Pike

Further Reading

Berger, Helen A. *A Community of Witches: Contemporary Neo-Paganism and Witchcraft in the United States*. Columbia, SC: University of South Carolina Press, 1999.

Loretta Orion. *Never Again the Burning Times: Paganism Revived*. Prospect Heights, IL: Waveland Press, 1995.

Pike, Sarah M. *Earthly Bodies, Magical Selves: Contemporary Pagans and the Search for Community*. Berkeley and Los Angeles: University of California Press, 2001.

See also: Burning Man; Circle Sanctuary; Indigenous Religions and Cultural Borrowing; Native American Spirituality; Pagan Calendar; Pagan Environmental Ethics; Pagan Festivals (both); Pagan Music; Paganism – Contemporary; Reclaiming; Starhawk; Wicca; Yoga and Ecology.

Pagan Festivals – Contemporary

Contemporary Pagan festivals have largely coalesced around the eight sabbats of Wicca, namely, the solstices, equinoxes and the four Gaelic quarter-day commemorations that, according to Webster, "embody elements of an earlier pastoral society and the later introduction of agriculture" (1986: 31). According to Rees and Rees (1973), the beginning of the Celtic year is uncertain: either Beltane (May 1st) or Samhain (November 1st). Whereas their Indo-European cousins considered the day to start with sunrise, the Celts themselves began the diurnal count with sunset, and likewise it appears more likely that their year too commenced with its dark half. Consequently, and in most standard neo-pagan practice, the New Year is celebrated as Samhain or All-Hallow's Eve. The remaining festival sequence comprises Yule (midwinter), Imbolc (Candlemas), Ostara (vernal equinox), Beltane (May Day), Litha (midsummer), Lughnasad (Lammas), and Mabon (autumn equinox). All together, these are known to contemporary Pagans as the "Wheel of the Year."

Samhain or Hallowe'en is the first of Wicca's four Greater Sabbats. As the Feast of the Dead, it is celebrated on October 31st/November 1st and, according to English Wiccan author Vivianne Crowley, commemorates "when the worlds of matter and spirit draw close to one another and the dead may pass to and fro through the veils" (1989: 190). Because of this, the highly influential Alexandrian Wicca writers Janet and Stewart Farrar speculate that Samhain may derive from the verb "to quiet down, become silent," and provides the occasion for ancestral contact. It is also the commencement of the dark or winter half of the year.

But if Samhain is a major contemporary Pagan celebration, it is followed by one of almost equal significance. Even though the Farrars refer to Yule as a Lesser Sabbat, it celebrates the rebirth of the sun with the winter solstice at the darkest time of the year. In the northern hemisphere, from midwinter forward, days begin to get successively longer, and solar light re-begins its ascent. Many of the Euro-American practices associated with this period for both the Western Pagan and in the wider context of Christmas (gift-giving, costuming, candles, apples, mistletoe, evergreens, holly, yule logs, Old Father Time, the fly agaric mushroom [*Amanita muscaria*] colors of red and white, etc.) derive from original Latin and Germanic yuletide celebrations. The word *yule* has been thought to originate with the Anglo-Saxon word for "yoke" (*geola*). However, in Cornish and Breton, the words for "sun," *hiaul* or *houl*, may also be connected. For contemporary Druids, the winter solstice is known as Alban Arthuan.

Yule is followed by the celebrations of winter purification or Imbolc/Oimelc ("ewes milk") corresponding with either February 1st or 2nd. Another Greater Sabbat, it is associated in particular with the Irish fire and hearth goddess Brigid (Brigantia) – subsequently linked to the Catholic St. Bride. She retains associations as both virgin war-goddess and fertility figure and is connected to the arts of healing, fire making and poetry. This is preeminently a woman's celebration (e.g., the northern European Wives' Feast Day, bride dolls constructed from cereal shafts, and "bride beds"). With light increasing and spring approaching, Imbolc is also associated with straw Brigids or Crosses representing the sun-wheel and used for protection against fire, lightning and tempest.

Ostara (Anglo-Saxon), Alban Eilir (Druid) or the spring equinox on the 20th/21st of March, identified with the cardinal direction of the east, is honored as the moment in which the bright half of the day begins to dominate over the dark, winter ends, and the flowers and burgeoning growth reappear. As Crowley explains:

At the Spring Equinox, "the light equals the darkness" and this can be taken . . . as a representation of . . . equipoise between unconscious animalism and growing conscious awareness. It is at this festival that [the God] impregnates the Goddess but . . . continues roaming the greenwood, as the Horned Hunter (1989: 191).

In the northern hemisphere, the vernal equinox is a major Pagan commemoration among Pagans and Earth religionists of contemporary times.

The Greater Sabbat of Beltane follows Ostara and, as the coming of summer, constitutes another major contemporary Pagan festival. As May Day and the preceding night of Walpurgis Nacht, it marks the beginning of the summer or bright half of the year and once again, in the "crack" between the two annual moieties, communication with the otherworld is deemed most possible. But as this is a time for entering into brightness and warmth, the otherworldly spirit emphasis is directed more toward the world of the fairy, an embodiment of the spirit dimension as it relates to summer rather than to its winter corollary associated with the dead.

Midsummer, the year's longest day in the northern half of the world, marks the culmination of the sun's ascent. As the vernal equinox signifies the mid-point of the spring season from Imbolc to Beltane, Litha occurs at the center of the summer stretch from Beltane to Lammas. In Britain, the geographic/spiritual focus for the year's shortest night is the ancient stone circle of Stonehenge – closed by the government to Druidic ritual and Pagan celebration between 1986 and 2000, but now reopened for public access. Thousands attended in 2000 and 2001. For the Druids, the day is designated Alban Hefin. Since the Julian calendrical reforms, the summer solstice has shifted to June 20th/21st, but both the established ecclesiastical calendar and many folk customs retain the original 24th as the midsummer celebration – what became the feast of St. John the Baptist after the fourth-century triumph of Christianity. Consequently, there are significant aquatic traditions connected with June 24th such as bathing or rolling on the morning dew at sunrise.

Lammas, Lughnassadh or the Anglo-Saxon Hlafmesse ("loaf-bread") falls on or around the first of August. It marks the transition from summer to autumn and is the time for the first grain harvests. The Celtic name of this sabbat is derived from the god Lugh or Lugus, the champion-god and many-skilled deity of brightness. It is followed by Mabon (the Druid Alban Elfed) or commemoration of the autumn equinox. The sun now sets at the cardinal point of west, and the solar decrease that has begun with the summer solstice henceforth leads to night being longer than day. The Lesser Sabbat of Mabon precedes the Greater Sabbat of Samhain marking the end of the old year and beginning of the next.

In Wicca and neo-paganism, the Wheel of the Year is seen as a series of feasts that honor the relationship between the God and the Goddess. The God is born at Yule, grows through Imbolc, mates with the Goddess at Ostara, marries her at Beltane, attains maturity and dominion at Midsummer, is sacrificed at Lammas, returns at Mabon and assumes full godhead at Samhain. The eight sabbats also reveal the turning tides of the natural cycles of birth, life, death, decay and rebirth as well as the seasonal foundations of human civilization in both the animal breeding of husbandry and the sowing, planting, cultivation and harvesting of agriculture. But at the same time, the Wheel is a schematic understanding that is subject to both local astronomical variation and pragmatic shifts in secularized celebration. In other words, equinoxes and solstices could vary as much as a day depending on region and year, while their actual commemoration along with that of the Greater Sabbats may occur on a weekend or some other convenient date.

In the wider Pagan and nature religion community, there are additional variations. While most contemporary traditions invariably celebrate Beltane and Samhain, many overlook the autumn equinox as symbolizing the triumph of darkness over light. There are further differences, emphases and omissions to be found within the reconstructed Pagan traditions. For instance, the Roman festival calendar acknowledges the summer solstice with pre- and post-solstitial fasts, but ritually ignores the culminating conclusion of light's ascent itself. Another consideration arises for those who live south of the Equator. The Farrars express acute awareness of difficulties Australians have in attempting to follow a festival sequence that is rooted in another hemisphere, and they also suggest that those who elsewhere celebrate the largely Celtic-inspired Wheel become mindfully sensitive to local lore and environmental differences. While all nature religionists follow a calendar of celebrations, not all subscribe to the eightfold observation of the Greater and Lesser Sabbats. Ronald Hutton (1991: 303f.) sees this last as largely the fabrication of Margaret Murray. Ancient or not, the Wheel of the Year has emerged as a calendrical tool that allows its practitioners to engage with the changing seasons and perpetual transformations of the natural world.

Michael York

Further Reading

Crowley, Vivianne. *Wicca: The Old Religion in the New Age*. Wellingborough: Aquarian Press, 1989.

Farrar, Janet and Stewart Farrar. *A Witches' Bible: The Complete Witches' Handbook*. Blaine, WA: Phoenix Publishing, 1996.

Farrar, Janet and Stewart Farrar. *Eight Sabbats for Witches*. London: Robert Hale, 1981.

Hutton, Ronald. *The Pagan Religions of the Ancient British Isles: Their Nature and Legacy*. Oxford: Blackwell, 1991.

Pennick, Nigel. *The Pagan Source Book: A Guide to the Festivals, Traditions and Symbols of the Year*. London: Rider, 1992.

Rees, Alwyn and Brinley Rees. *Celtic Heritage*. London: Thames & Hudson, 1961, 1973.

Webster, Graham. *The British Celts and Their Gods under Rome*. London: B.T. Batsford, 1986.

York, Michael. *The Roman Festival Calendar of Numa Pompilius*. New York: Peter Lang, 1986.

See also: Celtic Spirituality; Druids and Druidry; Indigenous Religions and Cultural Borrowing; Native American Spirituality; Pagan Calendar; Pagan Environmental

Ethics; Pagan Music; Pagan Festivals in North America; Paganism – Contemporary; Wicca.

Pagan Music

The term "Pagan music" is of relatively recent coinage. It denotes the music considered key to the emerging culture of nature religions, primarily Wicca but also including other Pagan spiritual paths. Its usage began in the early 1990s, as a part of the emerging Pagan cultural identity. As Pagans began to see their spirituality as equally valid as mainstream religions, it was important to place the music of Pagan spirituality alongside Christian music or Jewish music as a legitimate religious and artistic expression.

Pagan music owes much of its stylistic identity to the British folk revival of the 1960s. Such bands as Fairport Convention and Steeleye Span took traditional folk tunes and added modern rhythms and instrumentation, creating the genre known as folk rock. Today that sound, characterized most simply by acoustic and electric guitar, bass, drums, and fiddle or flute, is found in the vast majority of Pagan bands. In contrast to New Age music, which typically is rich in synthesized aural landscapes, the use of acoustic instruments and hand drums in Pagan music creates a more earthy sound.

One of the more popular musicians, though not explicitly Pagan, is Canadian harpist Loreena McKennitt. Her ethereal voice, combined with the mystical quality of many of her songs, creates an "other-worldly" music that appeals to Pagans' yearning for connection to the spirit realms. With her own musical roots squarely in the folk revival, McKennitt's popularity is a good example of the adoption as Pagan music of mainstream music that speaks to the Pagan experience.

With no central sacred text to the Pagan traditions, Pagans use chants and songs as liturgy. This makes the thematic content of Pagan music all the more important. One of the most widespread themes of all Pagan music is that of human communion and interdependence with all living beings. Other themes include the notion of Summerland, the mythic realm of the spirits where human souls go after death and before their next birth; the constant presence of ancestors and guiding spirits; and humans' ability to call on those spirits in the present day.

Pagan music includes songs by Pagans that reflect the movement's history and identity. Using a wide variety of styles, from Goth to punk to pop and folk, this music speaks of the persecution of Pagans and environmental destruction, and of a time when, many Pagans believe, the balance of nature will be restored. Some of the earliest and most widely known songs of this variety are Charlie Murphy's "The Burning Times" (see below) and Gwyddion Pendderwen's "We Won't Wait Any Longer," both popular since the early 1980s.

Chants in particular have been one of the chief unifying threads among this disparate spiritual community. Chants such as Z. Budapest's "We all come from the Goddess / And to Her we shall return / Like a drop of rain / Flowing to the ocean" create a group state of mind conducive to ritual work, and express one of the chief axioms of Pagan spirituality. Chant and song are used for many different purposes in ritual, including casting a circle, invoking Deity, and raising energy. Pagan chants have historically been spread by traveling musicians and priestesses who teach chants wherever they go. Increasingly, recorded albums of chants are in demand, as more groups form in remote areas and need to learn chants on their own.

Pagan music has also been strongly influenced by world music. It is rare that a ritual with music does not include Middle Eastern drums (doumbeks or tars particularly) as rhythm instruments, and African djembes abound at most drumming circles. Middle Eastern rhythms, particularly the malfouf, underlie most recordings of Pagan chant, as to a lesser degree does African-based clave rhythms. Though Pagan spirituality draws heavily on the Celtic worldview, Celtic rhythms are not as obvious an influence in the chant music.

Though the term "Pagan music" has been useful in galvanizing a movement behind its own musical expression, its usage is not without problems. The music of indigenous Pagan traditions worldwide has generally been referred to as "world music" in the U.S. Traditional music from Africa, India, Australia, Scandinavia, the Caribbean and South America has its roots in a pre-Christian spiritual identity. Because the public face of Paganism has been predominantly European-American, questions of inclusion and ethnocentricity have not often been asked. Yet, as Paganism shifts away from its early identification in opposition to mainstream religions, and particularly as Pagans continue to involve themselves in global interfaith efforts, greater possibilities arise for an identity and terminology reflective of the richness and diversity of Paganism worldwide.

Anne Hill

Further Reading

Magliocco, Sabina and Holly Tannen. "The Real Old-Time Religion: Towards an Aesthetics of Neo-Pagan Song." *Ethnologies* 20:1 (1998), 175–201.

McColeman, Carl. "Music of the Goddess." *New Age Retailer* (July/Aug. 2001).

Pike, Sarah. *Earthly Bodies, Magical Selves: Contemporary Pagans and the Search for Community.* Berkeley, CA: University of California Press, 2001.

See also: Music; Music and Eco-activism; Paganism – Contemporary; Wicca.

Burning Times

The most popular Pagan song ever written is "The Burning Times," by Charlie Murphy (reprinted below). Recorded by literally dozens of different musicians in several countries, it rose to #1 on Ireland's music charts in 1991, with Christy Moore's version. A deeply felt and strongly worded anthem, it evokes powerful emotional reactions in the listener.

The chorus is a recitation of seven goddess names, originally from a poem by Deena Metzger: "Isis, Astarte, Diana, Hecate, Demeter, Kali, Inanna." The repetition of names creates a perception of a unified Mother Goddess from these figures of disparate cultures and time periods, and suggests that goddess-worshipping cultures shared a similar fate.

The first verse describes a "nature people" living in harmony with the seasons, with women as leaders, healers, and teachers "equal with the others, and respected for their worth." These women are explicitly named "witches." The strong positive use of the word "witch" here, coupled with the song's renown, quite probably contributed to the move among witches to publicly identify with the word, in spite of its historical baggage.

The second verse describes the coming of Christianity, and the violent overthrow of nature religions: "And the Pope declared the Inquisition, it was a war against the women whose power they feared." Though one could argue specifics here, the verse does express a famously incorrect statistic, asserting "nine million European women died" in the ensuing "holocaust."

"The earth is a witch, and the men still burn her" in the final stanza equates women with the Earth, implying that both possess a power that is more wild and elemental than human. Woman's power, then, is juxtaposed against the willful slaughtering instincts of men, who rape, strip-mine, and poison both for profit. The song culminates in a powerful invocation of this power to overthrow the forces of destruction.

Anne Hill

Burning Times, by Charlie Murphy
© *Musical Front (BMI)*

In the cool of the evening they used to gather
Neath the stars in the meadow circled near an old oak tree
At the times appointed by the seasons of the earth
And the phases of the moon

In the center stood a woman
Equal with the others and respected for her worth
One of the many we call the witches
The healers and the teachers of the wisdom of the earth
And the people grew through the knowledge she gave them
Herbs to heal their bodies
Spells to make their spirits whole
Can't you hear them chanting healing incantations
Calling forth the wise ones
Celebrating in dance and song

Isis, Astarte, Diana, Hecate, Demeter, Kali, Inanna

There were those who came to power through domination
And they bonded in the worship of a dead man on a cross
They sought control of the common people
By demanding allegiance to the Church of Rome
And the Pope declared an Inquisition
It was a war against the women whose power they feared
In this Holocaust against the nature people
Nine million European women died
And the tale is told of those who by the hundreds
Holding together chose their death in the sea
While chanting the praises of the Mother Goddess
A refusal of betrayal
Women were dying to be free

Isis, Astarte, Diana, Hecate, Demeter, Kali, Inanna

Now the Earth is a witch
And the men still burn her
Stripping her down with mining and the poisons of their war
Still to us, the Earth is a healer
A teacher, a mother
A weaver of a web of life that keeps us all alive
She gives us the vision to see through the chaos
She gives us the courage
It is our will to survive

Isis, Astarte, Diana, Hecate, Demeter, Kali, Inanna

Paganism and Judaism

The Jewish tradition is vitally connected to rituals and practices that could be defined as "pagan" or earth-centered. Nonetheless, it is conventional to describe Judaism as antithetical to paganism and to nature. This oppositional framework has several roots in Jewish intellectual history.

A primary influence is the opposition of the Hebrew prophets to polytheistic worship or the worship of plastic images, often on the grounds that this worship involved ritual sex or human sacrifice. While it is unclear whether prophetic ideas about Ancient Near East worship should be applied to an abstract idea of paganism, there is a visceral aversion in Jewish culture to ritual practices that might be deemed "strange worship," to use the Hebrew term for idolatry. A second source can be found in certain Hasidic and in late medieval Jewish thought, as inflected by neo-Platonism. Form, according to some teachers, was represented by Jewish law and commandments, while matter was equated with nature. Miracles like Israel's crossing through the Reed Sea epitomized the domination of form, *tsurah*, over *chomer*, matter, and were interpreted to mean that God had exalted Jewish destiny above nature. A third source is found in the nineteenth-century interpretation of the evolution of religion, which was strongly influenced by Hegelian idealism. According to this schema, which largely determined the character of modern Jewish attitudes, advanced civilizations were capable of subjugating nature, and were thereby liberated from rituals or mythical beliefs about nature and hence able to impose a moral and historical order on an essentially amoral world.

Modern thinkers have often conflated these sources into a schematic picture of historical religion overcoming nature religion. Ismar Schorsch calls this the "celebration of 'historical monotheism' " and describes it as "a fierce attempt by [modern] Jewish thinkers to distance Judaism from the world of paganism" (1991: 3). Scholars who follow this interpretation define Judaism as the religion that gave birth to the idea of worshipping a God of history who transcended nature, imposed a rigorous moral order, and demanded the purgation of all idolatry of the natural world.

While these ideas are certainly part of Jewish intellectual history, they make for an interpretation of Jewish religion which, as Moshe Sokol writes, is "incoherent" (2000: 262). Works by scholars such as Daniel Boyarin, Theodore Hiebert and Howard Eilberg-Schwartz in recent decades have demonstrated that any assumption of opposition between Judaism and nature leads to an incomplete and inaccurate reading of both biblical and rabbinic culture. Tikvah Frymer-Kensky's book *In the Wake of the Goddesses* has also shown that any categorical picture of "paganism" cannot account for the unique nature of early Israelite opposition to the cultures around it. Furthermore, the usual assumption of those who accept the Pagan–Judaism dichotomy is that all Pagan traditions are lacking, in exactly the same way, a moral or historical perspective on the world – a claim that from a comparative religions perspective is absurd.

The distinction between Judaism and the Pagan is neither as cut-and-dry, nor as fluid, as has been variously claimed. If we define Paganism according to contemporary usage, that is, Earth-centered ritual, the personification of nature as Goddess, and the acceptance of multiple divinities or powers embodied in the natural world, one would be hard-pressed to determine whether Judaism is more "Pagan" or "anti-Pagan." Even a cursory inspection of Jewish ritual will reveal much that can be labeled Pagan. Anthropologists studying Jewish rituals like circumcision discern a layer of primitive meaning that can rightly be called Pagan. There is also no question that a chief element in the Jewish covenant was a close relationship to the land, one which involved giving the land what we would call rights. In the Torah, the Earth is considered a covenantal partner and person; hence from the perspective that any personification of nature is Pagan, Judaism should be considered "Pagan." Likewise, the Psalms assumed a world in which animals, rivers, mountains, etc. are part of the moral order and respond to justice by praising God. The rabbis similarly described a more-than-human world that was characterized by personhood, by praising God, and by moral participation.

Most importantly, as Arthur Waskow argued in *Seasons of Our Joy* (1982), there can be no question that the holiday cycle of Judaism is as much attuned to the cycle of the Earth as any "Pagan" tradition. For example, the Passover festival that celebrates birth always falls on the full moon following the spring equinox. The ritual of waving the lulav or palm branch during Sukkot, beginning on the full moon following the fall equinox, is performed to bring fertility and rains at the beginning of the rainy season. Jews always light Hanukah candles during the new moon closest to the winter solstice, which is in fact the darkest night of year.

Yet there are also fundamental differences between Paganism as commonly defined and Judaism. While Pagan traditions associate these turning points in the calendar with both seasons and with events in the mythical life of the Gods, Jewish tradition insists that each of these dates has a unique meaning in the life and history of the people, in other words, Passover commemorates liberation from Egypt, Sukkot wandering in the desert, and Hanukah the triumph of the Maccabees and the rededication of the Temple. The history of the people in essence took the place of the story of the gods in Israelite religion, while the connection with the cycles of nature remained constant. Another clear difference between Judaism and many of the traditions defined as Pagan is that all divinity in Judaism is focused within a single deity that creates nature and hence is not subject to nature. The Earth in Judaism may have personhood, but it is not a divinity.

Some popular works, emerging from the feminist spirituality movement (Patai 1990, Teubal 1984), have attempted to reclaim Paganism within ancient Judaism by blurring the distinction between Judaism and ancient Canaanite practices. There are many points that may seem to resonate with this approach. For example, most biblical scholars accept that the Torah commanded the worship of one God who created heaven and Earth (monolatry), but accepted the existence of other (lesser) gods. Also, in Kabbalah and more so in Hasidic thought, "Elohim," the name used for the creator God of Genesis 1, is identified with nature or "Hateva" through the process of Gematria or the numerology of Hebrew letters. In one traditional interpretation of this equation, for example, what appears to be nature to "the nations" is revealed to the Jews as God. Finally, there is frequent suggestion in kabbalistic literature of a level of divinity within the Earth, especially under the rubric of the Shekhinah, God's presence in the world. Even with respect to the lives of "the gods," Kabbalah limned a mythical life within the divine realm that was traced through the rituals of Jewish practice.

By way of simplification, one might say that in Jewish culture, the multidimensionality of the divine realm was treated as esoteric knowledge, while the unity of God was treated as common belief. In some Pagan cultures (especially in Greek philosophy), the opposite was true: the lives of the Gods were openly discussed, while the unity of God was known only to the initiated. Thus, even though these approaches to the world of the spirit are profoundly different, they are not necessarily in contradiction. One might nevertheless question what is left that is uniquely Jewish if one erases all of the boundaries that separate it from Paganism.

However one judges these matters, it would be hard to claim that the self-defined Pagans of today are actually Pagan in any ancient sense. What is called Paganism or "neo-paganism" is often closer to a pantheistic version of monotheism than it is to polytheism. Furthermore, the understanding of Pagan or Earth-centered spirituality that is influential in the U.S. and Europe tends to be focused on moral issues, and many neo-pagan communities are politically involved in fighting the oppression of human beings as much as fighting "for nature," in stark contrast to the way Pagan ideas were used once by groups like the Nazis. Thus, even if one accepts the opposition between classical Paganism and Judaism, to apply this to contemporary spirituality is difficult or nonsensical.

For both theologians and anthropologists, the question of the relationship between Judaism and Paganism must not be whether there is similarity or opposition, but rather, how we can redefine the terms so that, as Eilon Schwartz has argued, we are able to read the Jewish tradition on its own terms, and Pagan traditions on their own terms, rather than on polemical grounds. What we find in Judaism is essentially a contradiction of the Pagan–monotheism dichotomy: a tribal tradition in the heart of modernity, intensely connected to nature's cycles and to physical embodiment, while at the same time connected to moral order and philosophical theology. Jewish thought provides grounds for critiquing the naive worship of nature and for rejecting the separation of the natural world from human morality and meaning, but it does so from a position that could equally be described as both Pagan and monotheist.

David Seidenberg

Boyarin, Daniel. *Carnal Israel: Reading Sex in Talmudic Culture.* Berkeley: University of California, 1993.

Boyarin, Daniel. *Intertextuality and the Reading of Midrash.* Bloomington: Indiana University Press, 1990.

Eilberg-Schwartz, Howard. *The Savage in Judaism: An Anthropology of Israelite Religion and Ancient Judaism.* Bloomington: Indiana University Press, 1990.

Frymer-Kensky, Tikva. *In the Wake of the Goddesses: Women, Culture and the Biblical Transformation of Pagan Myth.* New York: Fawcett Books, 1993.

Hiebert, Theodore. *The Yahwist's Landscape: Nature and Religion in Early Israel.* New York: Oxford University Press, 1996.

Patai, Raphael. *The Hebrew Goddess.* Wayne State University Press, 1990.

Schorsch, Ismar. "The Limits of History." *Proceedings of Rabbinical Assembly* 51 (1989), 108–15.

Schwartz, Eilon. "Judaism and Nature: Theological and Moral Issues to Consider while Renegotiating a Jewish Relationship to the Natural World" *Judaism* 44:4 (1985), 437–47; repr. in *Torah of the Earth*, vol. 2, Arthur Waskow, ed. Philadelphia: Jewish Publication Society: 2000, 159–73; and in Martin Yaffe, ed. *Judaism and Environmental Ethics*, Lanham, MD: Lexington Books, 2001, 297–308.

Sokol, Moshe. "Ethical Implications of Jewish Conceptions of the Natural World." In Hava Tirosh-Samuelson, ed. *Judaism and Ecology: Created World and Revealed Word.* Cambridge: Harvard University Press, 2002, 261–82.

Teubal, Savina. *Sarah the Priestess.* Athens, Ohio: Swallow Press, 1984.

Waskow, Arthur. *Seasons of Our Joy: A Modern Guide to the Jewish Holidays.* Boston: Beacon Press, 1982; Woodstock, VT: Jewish Lights, 2000.

See *also*: Animism – A Contemporary Perspective; Judaism; Paganism – A Jewish Perspective; Paganism – Contemporary; Polytheism.

Paganism and Technology

Many contemporary Pagans are reconciling their ideologies of nature and the divine with science and technology in order further to understand the nature of which they are a part. A growing number of Pagans are also working to reverse their own alienation from the natural world, yet not divorce themselves from "civilization" or technology. Instead of eschewing technological advances, many nature-oriented Pagans embrace them and enjoy the benefits of computer-oriented entertainment, kitchen, and leisure technologies: e.g., the internet, CDs, microwave ovens, and cellular phones.

However, this is not always the case: Pagans are becoming more cognizant of and are actively refusing to take part in certain types of technological advances such as certain medical, food, nuclear, and nature-destroying technologies. Due to animal testing, questionable side effects, and other reasons, a growing number of Pagans are limiting their exposure to Western medical advances in favor of herbalism and utilizing remedies from the natural world. In the realm of food technologies, the practices of genetically engineering food and growth hormone supplementation, among others, are leading many Pagans to grow much of their own food or purchase it from organic grocers. Pagan communities often hold nuclear and other technologies believed to harm the Earth and its inhabitants in disdain as well. Additionally, many Pagans work to implement and increase the use of nature-saving or nature-restoring technologies, such as recycling and other scientifically-driven ecological conservation practices.

One of the most important technologies for contemporary Paganism is related to communication: the Internet. Many Pagans, often called Technopagans, work in hi-tech or Internet-related fields, or have grown up with the Internet as a major tool for reaching the outside world and are comfortable with integrating this technology into their religious practice in many ways: communication, community formation and maintenance, research, and ritual performance.

One major aspect of the use of the Internet by practitioners of nature religions is that it allows for contact with like-minded individuals and groups without having to travel long distances for community gatherings or festivals. Use of the Internet also facilitates contact without sacrificing the ideas of personal safety and anonymity that many Pagans feel the need to maintain. From prolonged communication with solitary individuals or established groups, on-line communities can be formed.

Contemporary Pagans and other nature-oriented religious practitioners, as well as some African-derived Santería groups in the United States, were the first religious groups to utilize the Internet for both community growth and ritual practice in the early 1990s. Since that time, the Internet has become a major locus for Pagan networking and is now being utilized as a place for the negotiation of Pagan community ideals. Additionally, there are a rapidly growing number of Pagan-oriented resources (e.g., websites, bulletin boards and mailing lists) aimed at community formation and information dissemination. The preeminent Wiccan website, The Witches' Voice (www.witchvox.com), is one of more than 7000 Pagan-oriented sites on the web and boasts thousands of informative pages, Pagan contacts, and links to other Pagan websites. Additionally, a web search will uncover thousands of Pagan bulletin boards and mailing lists. With all of the positive aspects, one important drawback to the use of the Internet by nature-religion adherents is the propensity to neglect or exclude physical interaction with the "Nature" portions of their religious beliefs.

Even though Paganism professes an adherence to principles of the natural world, many adherents utilize the "non-natural" world of cyberspace and the Internet to learn about Paganism and to supplement their practices by performing online rituals with other Pagans, whom they may or may not have physically met: congregating in chat rooms, dressed in virtual robes, "lighting" candles, and worshipping Deity in a temple created by words typed onto a computer screen. In doing so, these Technopagans are appropriating parts of cyberspace by taking them out of an ambiguous virtual realm into a self-created simulation of real space where the physical elements of ritual are recreated textually and in the minds of the practitioners. This highlights the question of "What is nature?" Some Technopagans argue that nothing is separate from the natural realm; therefore computers and cyberspace are not un-natural. Others believe that "nature" is the realm of nonhuman-made phenomena, therefore computers and cyberspace exist outside of nature and practicing nature-oriented rituals in cyberspace presents a conundrum that must be individually negotiated.

Contemporary Pagan ritual is meant to resacralize diverse aspects of life by solidifying the individual's personal relationships with Deity and nature and by focusing on and celebrating nature. The common Pagan belief that Deity is embodied in all things leads many practitioners to argue that the virtual qualities of cyberspace can be understood as analogous to the Circle, the sacred part of space that is inherent in the natural world, utilized by Pagans for ritual and worship, thus allowing technology to take on aspects of sacredness and the computer to become an extension of one's body and self during Internet-based interaction. In this way, the technological phenomenon of the Internet has begun to include metaphysical associations for Technopagan "cyber-ritual" innovators. As the Internet gains popularity, the number of Pagans who are becoming interested in these applications of technology, especially related to the performance of cyber-rituals and the development of "virtual" communities, is increasing dramatically.

Shawn Arthur

Further Reading
Arthur, Shawn. "Technophilia and Nature Religion: The Growth of a Paradox." *Religion* 32:4 (2002), 305–16.
Davis, Eric. "Technopagans: May the Astral Plane be Reborn in Cyberspace." *Wired* 3:7 (1995).
O'Leary, Stephen D. "Cyberspace as Sacred Space: Communicating Religion on Computer Networks." *Journal of the American Academy of Religion* LXIV:4 (1996), 781–808.
Pearson, Joanne. "Assumed Affinities." In Joanne Pearson, Richard H. Roberts and Geoffrey Samuel, eds. *Nature Religion Today*. Edinburgh: Edinburgh University Press, 1998, 45–56.

Urban, Hugh B. "The Devil at Heaven's Gate: Rethinking the Study of Religion in the Age of Cyber-Space." *Nova Religio* 3:2 (2000), 268–302.

See also: Paganism – Contemporary.

Paganism in Australia

Neo-paganism reached the shores of Australia by at least the 1970s, but was preceded by much earlier interest in all things occult. As British colonization spread throughout the antipodes in the eighteenth and nineteenth centuries, the three major sources of occult revival in England (Spiritualism, Theosophy and the Order of the Golden Dawn) found their way to Australia. Members of these groups co-existed with Druids and Freemasons in an overwhelming Christian population. A focus on Egyptian rituals brought together Freemasonry and Spiritualism and was later incorporated into some of the Pagan rites. In the 1950s more thought was given to ceremony and magic than nature. The emphasis on nature came with concerns for the environment and the feminist movement from the 1960s and 1970s.

Contemporary Australian Pagans have referred to themselves variously as: Pagan, environmental pagan, goddess worshipper, Celtic pagan, shaman, amerindian, runester, fairy, radical fairy, Druid, chaos magician, vodoun, thelemite, occultist, seeker of the light, Church of all Worlds, and as witch or Wiccan. Under witch or Wiccan are other sub-groups such as gardnerian, alexandrian, dianic, seax, hedge, hereditary, eclectic and solitary. Groups such as the Ordo Templi Orientis and Temple of Set have also referred to themselves as Pagan, but there is some dissension in the Pagan community about whether their inclusion is justified. Wiccans or people calling themselves witches are probably the largest single group of Pagans, but there are no reliable statistics available at present to confirm this or to ascertain the extent and spread of Paganism.

Alternative lifestyles abound in Australia and give impetus to increasing interest in Paganism. They are celebrated in various ways through music and art festivals, mind/body/spirit workshops and ConFests (Conference/Festivals), as well as Pagan gatherings and outdoor dance events known as "raves," "doofs" or "bush dances." The latter employ audio-visual technologies to accompany all-night community dancing in natural bush settings. The Woodford Folk Festival is held in Queensland in December each year and attracts more than 10,000 people over several days, culminating in a Celtic fire celebration on the last night. The Mt. Franklin Pagan gathering also attracts large numbers of people and is held in a dormant volcano in central Victoria at Beltaine. The Wiccan Conference is usually held around September each year and the venue changes from one state to another. Environmental consciousness and ecospirituality are the connecting threads in all these festivities. In addition to these major festivals are numerous small local groups of Pagans, linked by word of mouth, newsletters such as *Pagan Times*, and the internet.

The human/land/spirituality triad that is the basis of Aboriginal Australian religion makes Australian Pagans even more aware of environmental concerns and, conversely, some Aboriginal Australians speak of Mother Earth, a concept that did not exist previously in traditional Aboriginal Australia. Pagans tend to become highly conscious of their own involvement with the ecosystem and develop sensitivity to their own regional connections with "place."

Some Pagan environmentalists desirous of maintaining the Earth's ecosystem become politically and actively "green," protesting land mining, excessive timber use, environmental pollution, and supporting Aboriginal land rights. Many intentional communities with an ecological focus (permaculture and eco-villages, alternative communities) exist in rural areas of Australia, and in the 1990s many Australians moved away from cities into the bush in search of a more nature-focused lifestyle.

The regular enactment of rituals heightens Pagans' observations and perceptions of their natural environment. Because of this, the Southern Hemisphere creates problems of cognitive dissonance that do not have to be addressed by Pagans living in the Northern Hemisphere. The cycle of rituals known as the Wheel of the Year requires a reevaluation of the dialectical relationship between practice and myth, nature and ritual.

Australian Pagans are confronted with questions such as: how does the myth cycle relate to the land in Australia, when should one celebrate Samhain, how does the sun appear to move across the sky, and in which direction should a circle be cast? In the Southern Hemisphere, Samhain is in April, winter solstice in June, Imbolc in August, spring equinox in September, Beltaine in October, summer solstice in December, Lugnasadh in February, autumn equinox in March. However, a mere reversal of the Wheel does not address discrepancies that arise when applying the human cycle of birth, fertility and death to the Australian agricultural cycle. Some say that the Wheel and the myth should be kept the same as the Northern Hemisphere, yet others are adamant that adaptations should be made in order to address the realities of nature. The main argument in favor of a Southern Hemisphere adaptation is based on common sense: people feel it is ludicrous to be celebrating winter solstice at the height of a hot Australian summer. But a simple reversal would designate summer as a fertile time according to the myth, when in actuality summer in Australia is a dry, barren time when the fierce southern sun brings drought and bushfires, and depletes human energy – hardly the basis for fertility.

Even within the sacred circle itself, placing the directions of north and south creates some confusion because of their association with the elements. In the Northern Hemisphere, north is regarded as the place of greatest darkness and corresponds to the element of Earth. In the Southern Hemisphere the dark unknown is in the south, and the element of Earth is placed in the south. Conversely, the element of fire is in the south in the Northern Hemisphere and in the north in the Southern Hemisphere. Some have devised a combination mode, using Northern Hemisphere orientations when setting up the circle, celebrating Samhain in October and Beltane in May, but using Southern Hemisphere seasonal cycles for the equinoxes and the solstices. Others completely adapt to the Southern Hemisphere.

Such discrepancies have not resulted in an abandonment of belief. Instead, they have led to a more determined effort to reconsider the myth cycle to coincide with the Australian environment. Differences lead to some heated debates however. To overcome the problem of various groups working according to hemispheric variants, it was suggested at the annual Australian Wiccan Conference in 1988 that ritual circles be cast in either direction (clockwise or anticlockwise) to reflect the different practices used in Australia. It was also suggested that the powers from each of the cardinal directions (north, south, east, west) be invoked in a generic sense so that all present could use their own visualizations and associations. Independent small groups make autonomous decisions about how they will celebrate the Wheel of the Year, but there is sometimes much confusion when different groups converge.

Lynne Hume

Further Reading
Hume, Lynne. "Exporting Nature Religions: Problems in Praxis Down Under." *Nova Religio* 2:2 (1999), 287–98.
Hume, Lynne. *Witchcraft and Paganism in Australia*. Carlton, Victoria: Melbourne University Press, 1997.
St. John, Graham. " 'Heal thy Self – thy Planet': ConFest, Eco-Spirituality and the Self/Earth Nexus." *Australian Religion Studies Review* 14:1 (2001), 97–112.
Tramacchi, Des. "Field Tripping: Psychedelic Communitas and Ritual in the Australian Bush." *Journal of Contemporary Religion* 15:2 (2000), 201–13.
See also: Aboriginal Spirituality and the New Age in Australia; Australia; Paganism (various); Wicca.

SP Paganism – A Jewish Perspective

The idea is currently fashionable that humanity should live "in harmony with nature." Several reasons can be offered for this attitude. As nature is becoming scarcer and the human population is growing, in economic terms this means that the value of nature must increase while that of humanity will decrease.

Another possible reason is that society is becoming increasingly virtual. People suspect that they are being manipulated, without knowing how to prevent or unmask this. Perception influences, and often becomes, reality. One central aspect of contemporary society which is affected by these trends is finance. The development from barter trade through metal coins, paper money, checks and credit cards took a long time, each stage facilitating further the accumulation of wealth. Today, in a cashless society, one's deposits, debentures, shares and other financial instruments may be wiped out by a bank clerk's mistake or an attack by a computer terrorist. The possibility of a meltdown of the insufficiently supervised global monetary system is potentially an even greater threat.

Because humanity is ill at ease with the virtual character of postmodern society, a need is being expressed to find order in a disorderly world and get closer to something real, tangible, and durable. Around long before history began, nature perfectly fills this role. Furthermore, increasing urbanization has cut many people off from nature which has evoked nostalgia for a more "natural" past.

The Image of Nature
Discussions about the image of nature involve truths, half-truths and fallacies. There is a general longing for an imaginary, beautified past which is perceived as "natural." Nature is presented as benign, loving and pure. An extreme form of all this is the self-hatred of those who implicitly claim that nature is good and man is bad. This is not easily recognized for what it is: abstract mythology.

There is neither equality in nature nor anything resembling democracy, two values that the West cherishes. In fact, nature is often fearsome: volcanic eruptions sometimes cause more damage than atom bombs; earthquakes wipe out communities. The expression "forces of nature" carries clear connotations of uncontrolled violence.

Another common saying is that "nature knows best." Many of those who claim this hardly understand what it means. Nature is not benign: it knows neither charity nor any apparent ethical consideration. One never sees a lion hesitate to kill the helpless deer he is pursuing; the bird of prey does not stop midway in its fall, wondering whether to catch a smaller bird. There is no safety-net for marginal beings in nature, no protection for the weak, no consideration for the handicapped and no mercy for the elderly.

No nation in the twentieth century has propagated living in "harmony with nature" so much as Hitler's Germany, where blood and soil became central values in the pseudo-religious world of national socialism. Not surprisingly, the Jews, the people who introduced moral laws in opposition to those of nature, were hated and slated for destruction.

The Resurrection of the Spirits

With the current revival of the importance of nature, the spirits who once were thought to inhabit the forests, lakes and rivers have also been resurrected. Festive days follow nature's rhythms: equinox, solstices and solar eclipses. Neo-paganism has reconstructed rituals for their veneration and that of the sun and moon. Mother Nature and Goddess Earth are riding high again. Ancient elements are often mixed with individual constructs of an invented past which academics respectfully refer to as "alternative religions."

The development of neo-paganism fits in well with postmodern fragmentation of society and the cult of individualism. Increasing worship of nature may partly be seen against the background of this desire to "return" to nature. Neo-pagans are not necessarily implying that everything is permitted. Their main message may well be very different: the perceived failure of all other ideas, including monotheistic religions, totalitarian ideologies, atheism, secular humanism and science.

Neo-paganism is part of a widespread search for both religious roots and unconventional dreams. Its basic philosophy can be interpreted as follows: "Humanity's character has remained the same over the millennia. Let us thus return to the origins of beliefs to which man has adhered from time immemorial, religions intimately connected with sacred nature."

The reasons for the emergence of environmental extremism overlap to some degree with those for neo-paganism. Some analysts claim that, in the distant past, pagans were much more environmentally friendly than monotheists, a statement far too general to be defendable.

Nazism, Paganism and Environmentalism

Among twentieth-century totalitarian movements, Nazism was a semi-religious ideology. One heard more about its racist elements, however, than its Pagan interest in nature. Few people realize that the first significant nature-protection laws in Europe were legislated in Nazi Germany.

Simon Schama comments on how painful it is for ecologically conscientious people to acknowledge that the Reich's passionate protection of trees was totally incompatible with its barbaric, systematic extermination of human beings (1996: 68, 119). Goering put into practice the Reich's Game Law which permitted capital punishment of a person who killed an eagle, and either deportation or confinement in a concentration camp for practitioners of vivisection. He adds that the camp's "medical staff was less fussy about operating on humans than hounds."

Walter Laqueur finds certain affinities between the Nazis and the Greens. The Nazis were strongly opposed to "blind industrialization," "materialist consumerism," the increasingly soulless modern society and its technological excesses. They always stressed the "return to nature, to a simpler and healthier life" (1985: 58).

Robert Pois notes the similarity between some of Hitler's statements and those of some contemporary environmentalists who "with ample reason, proclaim that a sharp-tempered Mother Nature, weary of pitiful man's toying with her inflexible laws, will eventually avenge herself upon those who, at least since the onset of industrialization, have tried her patience" (1986: 37, 42).

Michael Wyschogrod describes the relationship between environmentalism and Nazism, pointing out that Hitler was deeply influenced by such evolutionary concepts as the stronger killing the weaker and the resulting progress of nature (1992). He sees in evolutionary thinking a modern religion of nature, in which the basic conflict between nature and history is no less than the conflict between the moral and the natural. It was in the name of these concepts that the Nazis began to murder the handicapped, considering their lives of no value to society. This policy preceded the murder of the Jews, and helped them to refine their techniques in mass murder.

Michael Gillis highlights the Pagan aspects of environmentalism. For example, the book of Genesis can be read like a polemic against the world of Paganism, with creation as a product of mythical struggles between various gods (personifications of the forces of nature). Power and life are seen as divine, a Pagan view that can give rise to the worship of elements of nature. People are seen as being subject to these divinities, and are supposed to seek harmony with them, a manifestly ecological stand. He considers this to constitute secular Paganism (1992: 6–8).

Justice Opposes Nature's Cruelty

Against this background, one may reflect on the origins of Judaism as described in the Hebrew Bible, Jewish law and tradition. The God who reveals himself to Abraham is non-material; he does not reside in any element of nature. Having created nature, he is above it and can change it at will.

In the revelation to Moses at Sinai, God says that there are no other gods: "You shall not make for yourself a sculptured image, any likeness of what is in the heavens above, or on the earth below, or in the waters below the earth. You shall not bow down to them or serve them" (Deut. 5:8–9). As nature is thus not sacred in itself, it should not be venerated. Coherent with this theocentric worldview, Judaism established justice and social legislation in opposition to the cruel laws of nature.

Of the 613 biblical commandments, only three require the Jew to sacrifice his life rather than transgress them: murder, incest and idolatry. This indicates how central the avoidance of idolatry is in the Jewish worldview. The texts of the prophets are full of admonitions against the Paganism to which the Israelites repeatedly succumb.

For most of the last two millennia, Paganism was no longer of great concern to Judaism. With the establishment in formerly Pagan societies of the two monotheistic religions, Christianity and Islam, the outside challenges to Judaism changed. The paganism which survived in the Diaspora societies was not an explicit religion: it was mainly expressed as syncretism and seemed to have been relegated to the past.

The advent of Nazism in the twentieth century, however, dramatically returned paganism to the Jewish agenda. Neo-Nazi groups continue to propagate environmental theses. There are striking similarities between the Nazis' love of animals and nature combined with their hatred of certain human beings, and the extreme approaches of some environmentalist groups, who claim that the Earth is too heavily populated.

Un-Jewish or Anti-Jewish?

Because both neo-paganism and environmental extremism are fragmented and not highly publicized, few Jewish authors have addressed these subjects. In the early 1970s, Milton Himmelfarb remarked that modern-day Western Pagans may not understand Eastern paganism fully (1973: 290). He reminds us that, as recently as the British Raj in India, widows were still being burned alive, a practise the British had to suppress by force. He also cited a report of the ritual slaying of a 12-year-old boy in Rajasthan state: the boy's neck was slashed by a contractor in an effort to appease the gods when he laid the foundation stone for a new irrigation project.

Various forms of current nature worship are un-Jewish, while several neo-pagan reconstructionists can be considered specifically anti-Jewish. By the early 1990s, the Anti-Defamation League had identified elements of the small Pagan group Odinism with pseudo-religious strains of neo-Nazism and other hate movements. According to the Anti-Defamation League as quoted in Kaplan,

> While there may be Odinists who are not part of a new-Nazi or other hate movement ... Odinism has been a pseudo-religious strain of American neo-Nazi activity and propaganda. These neo-Nazis apparently consider the worship of Odin and other ancient Norse gods as part of their vision of "Aryan" supremacy (Schwartz 1997: 161).

Anti-Semitism is widespread among Russian neo-pagans. Victor A. Shnirelman writes that this phenomenon is rooted in Nazi-style rhetoric which is heavily laced with latent – or even open – anti-Semitism. He adds that militant anti-Semitism was only combined with the myth of Great Slavic prehistory in the 1990s. According to this myth, the Jews emerged as part of an evil conspiracy to dominate the world, trying to seduce the Slav-Aryans in their path (Shnirelman 1998: 1, 7).

Conclusion

It would be wrong, however, to conclude from these critical views of neo-paganism and certain elements of environmentalism that Judaism stands in opposition to nature itself. Moshe Sokol considers that those who speak about a "conflict" between Judaism and nature are wrong, stating that their views relate more to the sociology of Jews who lived in cities than to their beliefs (1998). In fact, Jewish law defines in great detail the Jews' attitude toward nature, which prevents ruthless exploitation and wanton destruction.

The environmental movement has many faces, ranging from fundamentalist ideologists to pragmatists. While their practical approaches often seem to be similar, the values of Jews and fundamental environmentalists differ radically. Norman Lamm, president of Yeshiva University, refused to participate in an important ecology conference because it focused on the concept that "nature is sacred" (1996).

The tension between these two approaches will become increasingly evident with the further development of neo-paganism and environmental extremism. While one should not put neo-Nazis, neo-pagans and environmental extremists together indiscriminately, organized Jewry should be wary of them all to varying degrees.

Manfred Gerstenfeld

Further Reading

Gerstenfeld, Manfred. "Neo-Paganism in the Public Square and Its Relevance to Judaism." *Jewish Political Studies Review* 11:3–4 (1999), 11–38.

Gerstenfeld, Manfred. *Judaism, Environmentalism and the Environment*. Jerusalem: The Jerusalem Institute for Israel Studies/Rubin Mass, 1998.

Gerstenfeld, Manfred. *Environment and Confusion: An Introduction to a Messy Subject*. Jerusalem: Academon, 1994.

Gillis, Michael. "Ecologism: A Jewish Critique." *L'Eylah* 34 (September 1992).

Himmelfarb, Milton. *The Jews of Modernity*. Philadelphia: The Jewish Publication Society, 1973.

Lamm, Norman. "A Jewish View of the Environment and Ecology." Lecture given at the Technion, Haifa, Israel, 7 October 1996.

Laqueur, Walter. *Germany Today: A Personal Report*. London: Weidenfeld & Nicolson, 1985.

Pois, Robert. *National Socialism and the Religion of Nature*. London: Croom Helm, 1986.

Schama, Simon. *Landscape and Memory*. New York: Vintage Books, 1996.

Schwartz, Alan M. Letter from Director of the ADL Research and Evaluation Department to Jeffrey Kaplan, 4 December 1992, as quoted in: Jeffrey Kaplan, *Radical Religion in America: Millenarian*

Movements from the Far Right to the Children of Noah. Syracuse, New York: Syracuse University Press, 1997.

Shnirelman, Victor A. *Russian Neo-pagan Myths and Antisemitism*. Acta No. 13. Jerusalem: The Vidal Sassoon International Center for the Study of Antisemitism, Hebrew University of Jerusalem, 1998.

Sokol, Moshe. "What are the Ethical Implications of Jewish Theological Conceptions of the Natural World?" Background paper, Conference on Judaism and the Natural World, 22–4 February 1998, Harvard University, Center for the Study of World Religions, 4.

Wyschogrod, Michael. "Judaism and the Sanctification of Nature." *The Melton Journal* (Spring 1992), 6–7.

See also: Animism: Humanity's Original Religious Worldview; Ecofascism; Fascism; Israel and Environmentalism; Jewish Environmentalism in North America; Kabbalah and Eco-theology; Neo-paganism and Ethnic Nationalism in Eastern Europe; Odinism; Redwood Rabbis; The Sacred and the Modern World.

Paganism – Contemporary

Paganism labels a set of religions centered on the celebration and veneration of nature that understand and engage it in one way or another as sacred. To fully understand the natural dimension of contemporary Paganism we must apprehend its origins and diversity. Scholars who study such religion generally use "Pagan" or "Paganism" (with a capital P) to denote a religion as identified by its adherents, and "pagan" or "paganism" (lower-case) to refer to more general phenomena such as the pre-Christian religions of ancient Europe.

The origins of the name and of the revival of Paganism in the twentieth century arise from earlier cultural trends and movements. Many Pagans think that "pagan" derives from a Latin word meaning villager or "country-dweller" as opposed to a city-dweller. They associate it not only with rural and traditional values, but also with being close to nature or the land. Of course, this makes it difficult to speak of classical Roman "paganism" since that term must refer to temple-based religious observances in cities and towns. In reality the term originally meant something more like "parishioner," a member of a community living in a particular place – rural or urban – who is therefore obligated to respect sacred places and people in that area. The term "paganism" was created by Christians in the fourth century in order to contrast (negatively) their religion with the religiosity they hoped to replace.

The mere addition of "-ism," however, misdirected attention from cult (the performance or observance of traditionally defined duties toward persons, places and powers worthy of respect) toward beliefs about deities. Despite this, the polemics of the medieval churches against popular religion, including beliefs about anti-Christian activities, maintained a focus on actions rather than ideas, at least as the locus of transgression. With the Enlightenment and Romanticism, the body and its needs and desires became associated not with temptation and sin but with the possibility of good and health. The meaning of "nature" altered from "not yet sanctified" to "as it should really be." Thus "pagan desires" could be valorized as noble and worthy. This exemplifies trends that resulted in the creation of a set of religions, the members of which called themselves Pagans.

In the early to mid-twentieth century Gerald Gardner and companions declared themselves to be members of a Pagan Witchcraft religion. Their ideas were rooted in academic understandings that the alleged witches persecuted in the sixteenth and seventeenth centuries had been continuing ancient pre-Christian fertility religions. However, alongside the theories of Margaret Murray about such witches, and the musings of Robert Graves about the inheritance of Celtic knowledges, were other forms of real but diffuse connections with the ancient religions of Europe. Ronald Hutton has documented four such connections: high ritual magic (ceremonial engagements with "supernatural forces and beings," such as among Hermetic orders and the Rosicrucians), hedge witchcraft (e.g., the low-level folk magic of "cunning men" and Horse Whisperers), the general love affair of the Christian centuries with the art and literature of the ancient world, and folk rites. Thus, Gardner and the Witches that gathered with him blended aspects of previously esoteric ceremonies (e.g., those that invoked elemental beings and guardians of the directions) with the use of herbal remedies, veneration of classical deities (e.g., the Moon and/or Earth as Goddess), and seasonal and lunar festivals. Immediately, therefore, their spirituality focused attention on human relationships with the Earth, places and physical reality.

Witchcraft was not the only form of Paganism to be revived or created. In almost every century since the Roman invasion of Britain there have been claimants to the title "Druid." Until the twentieth century most such Druids were Christians of one sort or another. There were exceptions such as the Gallic-inspired polytheism of Breton Druids since the period of the French Revolution. In the second half of the twentieth century, however, a plethora of mostly Pagan Druid Orders formed. They share with Witches (or Wiccans as some name themselves) a calendar including eight annual seasonal/solar festivals alongside those marking phases of the lunar cycle, a delight in ceremony, and a reverence for nature that sometimes results in environmental activism. Witches and Druids now tend to name deities from ancient Celtic cultures, although some venerate a more eclectic pantheon. It is partially true that Wicca and other Witchcraft traditions are mystery religions enabling the discovery and expression of the individual's higher self in relation to nature, whereas Druidry is a more public or accessible nature religion encouraging a wider population to celebrate.

A third group of Pagans name themselves variously Heathens or Ásatrúar, "those who honor deities." They are inspired by Germanic, Norse, Icelandic and/or Anglo-Saxon cosmologies and literatures. They too engage in magic and ritual, celebrate seasons and venerate deities.

While there has been considerable feminist influence on the various Paganisms, this is most explicit in Pagan branches of Goddess Spirituality and in versions of witchcraft such as that of the Reclaiming covens initiated by Starhawk in San Francisco. Similarly, many Pagans have been influenced by shamanism. Some Heathens, for example, are experimenting with trance techniques and performances rooted in understandings of ancient literary references to "seidr." Both feminism and shamanism have affected the celebratory practices of Pagans and have sometimes encouraged even more direct encounters with nature, including environmental direct action. Paganisms of various other kinds have been revived in different parts of Europe, typically drawing on knowledge of ancestral literatures and traditions and blending them with environmentalism and other contemporary concerns.

Each Pagan tradition, or "path," is divided into myriad local, regional or global affinity groups and networks of various kinds. Sometimes a focus on a particular deity or pantheon distinguishes a group from others. Sometimes a particular teacher or initiator introduces alternative ways of working magic that attract attention and result in the formation of a new lineage of groups. Sometimes a group's stress on a particular sacred place, or the intensity of their commitment to a threatened ecosystem, leads them to identify more strongly together than they do with any previous affiliations. Shifts to different countries, climates, cultures or continents causes significant changes in style or flavor (e.g., "Wicca" refers to a restricted group of covens in the UK, but is a more general term in North America). Only occasionally do such Pagan diversities result in hostilities between groups over morality, politics, and other issues. Generally, Pagans celebrate diversity in self-identity as they do in ecology. Certainly no central authority or hierarchy has emerged that is persuasive to or representative of all Pagans. However, more localized hierarchies can develop when charismatic leaders and powerful inner circles are criticized by others in the community. At such a time small groups may split off and begin their own Pagan communities. In this way the larger Pagan culture remains fluid and malleable, allowing for participants to follow their preferences for community structure and leadership style.

One of the preferences some Pagans exercise is to conduct rituals alone as what are termed "Solitary" Pagans, or to participate in discussions and rituals with other Pagans over the internet as well as, or instead of, in face-to-face groups. The internet has also provided new means of networking and of experimentation with ritual and identity, but generally speaking it simply replicates the modes of affiliation and discourse typical in pre-internet Paganisms.

The common ground among all Paganisms is literally physicality or nature. As ever in religions, it is primarily in relation to engagement with the common ground that diversity is most evident. For Pagans, then, the key questions are about ontologies and epistemologies of other-than-human beings and places and appropriate modes in which humans might relate to them.

It is not irrelevant that the contemporary revival of Paganism has emerged from and is rooted in European cultures and landscapes. Even if Pagans and others are wrong about the origins of the word, it is important that "Pagan" is linked with countryside rather than wilderness. That is, traditional paganisms enabled people to make religious sense of living and working with places and their surrounding community of life. They did not demand pilgrimages that transcended ordinary reality by long treks to distant places less altered by humanity. Indeed, it is doubtful that such true wildernesses have existed anywhere in Europe for a very long time. Even in North America, Africa and everywhere else inhabited or visited by humans, "wilderness" has sometimes been created recently by evicting previous occupants. Everywhere, the Earth is at least partially the result of human interaction with other life and other influences. Thus Paganisms can engage powerfully with the world as it is. Sometimes Pagan celebration of nature takes place in the heart of cities, sometimes it requires confrontation with economic interests transforming ecologically diverse ecosystems, sometimes it encourages organic husbandry, and sometimes results in evocative and playful ceremonies. However, it is certainly true that most Pagan celebrations involve journeys to woodlands, coastal areas or other more "natural" locations. For example, most large Pagan festival gatherings in the U.S. are held in forested areas where the emphasis on getting away from the city to commune with nature is emphasized.

The most obvious sense in which Paganism is centered on the celebration of nature is in its various calendar festivals. The majority of Pagans celebrate a cycle or wheel of eight annual solar/seasonal festivals marked by the two solstices, two equinoxes and the four intervening "quarter days" that mark the beginnings of northwest European seasons. These festivals provide opportunities not only to acknowledge the relationship of Earth and sun, and to celebrate the changing seasons of the natural world, but also to focus attention on individual and communal human life cycles. At summer solstice, for example, Pagans might honor the sun at the height of its (his or her) powers, conduct marriages or other rites of love and commitment, facilitate carnivalesque celebrations of summer, and conduct the energies of the season (and of places) toward the enhancement of the well-being of all life.

The names given these festivals by particular groups of Pagans concomitantly links them to ancestors, reinforcing understandings that challenge modernist individualism, suggesting links with indigenous religions, and reinforcing divergences within the broader religion. The centrality of seasonal celebrations (especially when they require some adjustment to suit local/regional seasonal variations – and temporal ones in the case of the Southern Hemisphere) always insistently roots Paganism in positive engagement with this-worldly rather than transcendent realities.

A focus on this world is true too, however, of Pagan dealings with deities. Although the Christian theological dichotomy transcendent/immanent is referred to by Pagans in discussion with other religionists, their own discourse suggests very different conceptions of the relationship between deity and physicality. Along with many members of polytheistic religions, many Pagans understand that while discrete deities are beings in their own right they may also manifest themselves within various other physical modes. These might include statues or artistic representations, but more commonly deities manifest themselves within particular humans. Thus a central rite of Wicca is "Drawing Down the Moon" when the Goddess, whose reality is incarnated in the moon is invited "into" a priestess, who then speaks words and perform actions taken to be those of the Goddess. (Pagans often speak of "the Goddess" without necessarily meaning that there is only one divinity, or of "the Goddess and the God" without meaning that there are only two.) Again, this fluidity of form and permeability of boundaries is indicative of Pagan notions of the nature of persons. Even while celebrating nature "as it is," Pagans understand that what is visible is not the whole story. The divine is accessible in material, indeed in human, form. Everyday, ordinary life is taken up into divinity and demonstrated to be important and worthy of celebration. Transcendence (the divine) does not transcend the mundane, but rather returns celebrants to their daily lives with renewed insight into the value of ordinary material.

This Pagan polytheism is allied to a pervasive animism, seen in practices that aim to establish respectful communication with a wide range of significant other-than-human living beings. For example, Pagan festivals might include veneration of particular deities, but they will almost certainly acknowledge the importance and invite the participation of other celebrants in the "natural" world. Trees and rocks are commonly understood to be persons in some sense, but Pagans also claim to encounter elemental beings (of Earth, air, fire and water) and those named, by various folk traditions, "faeries" or "elves." Acknowledgement of the priority of the "spirit of place" and other inhabitants of particular places again grounds Pagan environmentalism in engagements with material reality and the everyday world.

Reincarnation has become popular among Pagan and in wider cultural notions of what might happen after death. In the Pagan version reincarnation is not considered to entangle people in the unpleasantness of physicality, animality and sensuality that cannot be escaped. Far from proffering a solution to such "problems" Paganism celebrates embodiment. Physical nature in all its forms is "good" and Pagans rarely speak as if being human were preferable to any other kind of embodiment. In considering environmental threats, some Pagans might actually say the opposite: it would be better not to be human if being human required such assaults on all other life. The Pagan answer to that problematic equation of humanity with eco-pollutant is to encourage respectful action toward the world. No manifesto details what this must mean for all Pagans, let alone all humanity, but inspiration and encouragement is offered toward the pursuit of an adjustment of human control over the world. Many Pagans believe that if Earth were understood to be humanity's permanent home (whether because of the sense of reincarnation as continuous embodiment within Earth's ecosystem or for whatever other this-worldly ontology) and embodiment our eternal state, this should provide a solid foundation for a more respectful and humble participation in the processes of being than is currently typical of humanity.

One of the ways Pagans try to facilitate this kind of participation is through the practice of magic. Various definitions of magic have been inherited from esoteric and traditional sources, but the most common are "the art and science of causing change according to will" and "the art and science of changing consciousness according to will." Both of these indicate that nature (human and beyond) is malleable and that it is, at least sometimes, permissible to manipulate it. Both definitions require ontological similarity between human intention and other purposeful agencies or powers in nature. That is, particular expressions of human will (when sufficiently and appropriately empowered, expressed and performed) can cause changes either in the magical practitioner or in that which they wish to change. For most Pagans, magic's plausibility is rooted in a metaphysics of relationship (inter-influence or inter-dependence between humans and other life). Certainly, Pagans typically hedge the teaching and performance of magic around with ethical injunctions (e.g., the Wiccan Rede) which says that so long as none is harmed it is permissible to enact one's true will (once that is known of course). Warnings are often offered that magic is just like all other actions in that it causes results for the magician as well as beyond them, and that care is required in the statement of intention (uncertainty might lead to chaos). Pagans usually share wider cultural vilification of those who might use magic to harm others (a perspective that underlies most traditional ideas about witchcraft, and thus is somewhat uneasy in this case). The notion that magic is effective also indicates that there are powers in nature that might be controlled, with some effort, for the benefit of others.

Magic and embodiment also invite consideration of sexuality. In the Wiccan "Great Rite" a high priestess and high priest make love as Goddess and God (some do so symbolically rather than "in true," and now always in private). This sacramental sex has roots in the ancient mystery religions of Eleusis and Isis, but also and more importantly in pervasive Pagan understandings of the goodness of sex, desire, bodies, physicality and the natural world. Paganism celebrates life as generated by ordinary sexual processes of evolution, and encourages people to value sexuality positively, and sometimes even as sacred. Pagans do not find religious problems in that which is "natural," nor do they offer a religious solution in denial of desire and embodiment. Instead, its "problems" are perceived threats to the diversity of life, and its "solutions" are the rediscovery of the goodness of the natural.

Tendencies central to Pagan self-understandings might lead to suspect interests. For example, respect for ancestral traditions has led some Pagans toward racist notions of ethnicity and identity. Or perhaps it is that some discourse about ancestors or ancestral tradition dovetails with elements of racist essentialisms that use constructions of the past to claim "authenticity." Such tendencies and temptations are rejected by the majority of Pagans. Many Pagans also reject any belief in a devil or evil-principle, sometimes asserting that Satan is actually part of the monotheistic or specifically Christian pantheon. However, some do find "Satan" useful to symbolize the "dark side" of nature, its forces and processes of death and decay. Even in such discourse, however, these processes are not demonized but reverenced as vital for the continuity of life. Most Pagans find plenty of scope in non-Christian cosmologies for such discussion, some referring to the "dark side of the Goddess" or to Kali as creator and destroyer. It may also be important to note that Satanism is properly considered a self-religion, whereas Paganism is a nature religion.

Paganism is, therefore, the label for a diversity of spiritual movements and practices focused, in a variety of ways, on the celebration of nature. These certainly include festive gatherings and ceremonies, but might also entail eco-activism and ecologically sensitive lifestyles. Few if any of these practices and lifestyles are unique to Pagans, however, and it is the particular accretion of worldviews and lifeways that define something as Pagan rather than something else. Diversity itself is essential to the self-understanding of most Pagans, both when they think about what "nature" means and how it might be encountered and engaged, and when they think about the character of their religion. Even in uses of the internet, fantasy literature, imaginative storytelling and ritualizing, Pagans pursue greater intimacy with the ordinary, physical world. Indeed, even encounters with deities, which in some religions might encourage the transcendence of embodiment and physicality, are experienced as invitations to be more rather than less human and, thereby, natural. Paganism is world-affirming even, or especially, when it confronts what it perceives as threats to ecological diversity or the sanctity of natural life. Its engagement with physicality re-enchants the world not as resource or environment but as community. Its spirituality does not efface or conflict with physicality but finds it not only meaningful but also worthy of celebration and even revelatory of that which is sacred and of lasting value. In these and other ways, Paganism intersects with significant currents in contemporary society (environmentalism, feminism and postmodernism for example). Its self-construction and presentation encourages the perception that nature is more than a context for self-discovery, it is engaged with as a community of co-celebrants.

Graham Harvey

Further Reading
Blain, Jenny. *Nine World of Seid-Magic: Ecstasy and Neo-Shamanism in North European Paganism.* London and New York: Routledge, 2002.
Dowden, Ken. *European Paganism: The Realities of Cult from Antiquity to the Middle Ages.* London and New York: Routledge, 2000.
Harvey, Graham. *Contemporary Paganism: Listening People, Speaking Earth.* New York: New York University Press, 1997.
Harvey, Graham. "Satanism in Britain Today." *Journal of Contemporary Religion* 10 (1995), 283–96.
Hutton, Ronald. *The Triumph of the Moon: A History of Modern Pagan Witchcraft.* Oxford: Oxford University Press, 2000.
Long, Asphodel. *In a Chariot Drawn by Lions.* London: Women's Press, 1992.
Salomonsen, Jone. *Enchanted Feminism: The Reclaiming Witches of San Francisco.* London and New York: Routledge, 2002.
Taylor, Bron. "Bioregionalism: An Ethics of Loyalty to Place." *Landscape Journal* 19 (2000), 50–72.
Taylor, Bron. "Resacralizing Earth: Pagan Environmentalism and the Restoration of Turtle Island." In David Chidester and Edward T. Linenthal, eds. *American Sacred Space.* Bloomington: Indiana University Press, 1995, 97–151.
York, Michael. *Pagan Theology.* Washington Square, NY: New York University, 2004.

See also: Animism (various); Bioregionalism; Druids and Druidry; Earth First! and the Earth Liberation Front; Elves and Land Spirits in Pagan Norse Religion; Gaia; Gimbutas, Marija; Goddesses – History of; Graves, Robert von Ranke; Greco-Roman World; Greece – Classical;

Greek Landscape; Greek Paganism; Green Man; Heathenry – Ásatrú; Koliada Viatichei; Middle Earth; Nature Religion; Odinism; Oshmarii-Chimarii (Mari El Republic, Russia); Neo-paganism and Ethnic Nationalism in Eastern Europe; Neo-paganism in Ukraine; Pagan Calendar; Pagan Environmental Ethics; Pagan Festivals – Contemporary; Pagan Festivals in North America; Paganism and Judaism; Paganism and Technology; Paganism in Australia; Paganism – A Jewish Perspective; Paganism – Mari (Mari El Republic, Russia); Pantheism; Polytheism; Power Animals; Radical Environmentalism; Raves; Reclaiming; Roman Natural Religion; Saami Culture; Satanism; Slavic Neo-Paganism; Snyder, Gary; Starhawk; Trees (Northern and Middle Europe); Wicca.

Paganism – Mari (Mari El Republic, Russia)

Mari El is an autonomous republic of Russia located approximately seven hundred kilometers from Moscow. The ethnic Mari, formerly known as the Chermiss, who speak a Finno-Ugrian language, represent 43.3 percent of the republic's population. Beyond Mari El, the Mari peoples are found also in Bachkorostan, Tatarstan and Udmourtia as well as in the areas of Nijny Novgorod, Kirov and Sverdlovsk.

Upon the rediscovery of its indigenous pagan traditions at the end of the 1980s, the Mari El Republic underwent a nationalist reawakening. By granting legal status to long-standing religious traditions, the 1997 Russian law concerning freedom of religion promoted Mari Paganism as well. Nevertheless, the Mari have encountered difficulties. Despite some Soviet efforts, the Mari pagan tradition had never been suppressed, but at the same time it had also never been officially registered (largely because the Mari do not use houses of worship), and this has made it difficult for the tradition to gain recognition despite the 1997 law.

Mari spirituality is intimately connected to a respect for the natural order. The conception of nature has always been one of alliance rather than domination. Each aspect of the natural world is considered a base for perpetual regeneration. An ecological tradition has emerged for the Mari out of their reverence of nature. Their relationship with the natural manifests in all facets of life. For instance, since the sacredness of water is emphasized, the Mari will not wash their clothing in the rivers. Springs and groves are highly important and constitute places where above all one must behave with dignity. Seasonal considerations play a central role in how the people organize their lives. Though less dependent on hunting today, in former times it was believed that the pursuit of game at inauspicious moments would increase the likelihood that the hunter might be killed by an offended forest spirit. Protective traveling songs insured the vitality and benefit of both the rider and his horse. Overall, animals and humans were considered as equals, and weather was forecast through the appearance of animals. In ritual, animals would have been sacrificed – a practice that appears still to be current.

While the Mari relationship with animals has changed in many respects from what it once was, reverence of vegetation remains much the same as in former times. For the Mari, plant life may be understood as the most direct form of divine incarnation. This is especially true of trees, and tree-worship focuses in particular on the birch, lime and oak – associated, respectively, with women, maidens and men. Understood as divinities, offerings are made directly to trees. They are reputed to be able to heal disease, influence weather and augment the harvest. Tree-worship may also be hierarchical: some trees become commemorative foci to which offerings are made; others are considered to be ancestors. These last, though presents are rarely offered, are appealed to in difficult times. It is forbidden to cut them down. Mari worship is centered on the grove where strict rules apply concerning swearing, spitting and harming trees physically. During festivals, the people don new clothes to come to the grove. Such *loci religiosi* are approached as areas for healing, consolation, comfort, renewal and the solving of domestic problems.

Today, Mari Paganism recognizes approximately three hundred sacred groves. In a country of 23,000 square kilometers and a population of about 700,000, there are around one hundred priests.

Today, the principal opposition to indigenous Mari spirituality comes from the Russian Orthodox Church, which holds Paganism to be dangerous. The Orthodox repression has been mitigated to some extent by the 1997 law that guarantees respect for all religions. Although many Mari are Orthodox, the government supports Paganism and recognizes it as an official religion alongside both Orthodoxy and Islam. While Orthodoxy is understood as part of the hegemonic Russian pervasiveness, Paganism is seen as a cultural factor that supports autonomy against the Russian government. Nevertheless, Mari El nationalism is not activist, but adopts a more passive approach for change to occur naturally and harmoniously. Within the Pagan community itself, however, rivalry between various leaders has caused a degree of friction and difficulty. Despite the "double-faith" situation and predominance of Orthodoxy in Russia, many Christian and Pagan rituals have become associated. By not constructing its edifices directly on the old places of worship but simply near to them, the Church has not engendered the same animosity it has elsewhere in Europe

Consequently, regardless of the difficulties encountered with official registration, there is more tolerance for Paganism in the former USSR republics than in other European states. In Western Europe, with the exception of Iceland and Norway, Paganism is generally ignored and cannot hope at the moment to obtain official recognition.

By contrast, in the republics of Iceland and Norway, it is an offense to criticize Pagan representatives openly. In Eastern Europe, the situation for Paganism becomes even more favorable when it is perceived to augment national identity. From the ethnic perspective within the Mari El Republic, monotheism is seen as non-indigenous and foreign. Since independence, Paganism has come to reinforce ethnic identity. In this regional/ethnic interface between Paganism and local identity, the Mari Republic's evolution may provide some interesting clues as to the future development of European Paganism/neo-paganism.

Anne Ferlat

See also: Neo-paganism and Ethnic Nationalism in Eastern Europe; Paganism and Judaism; Paganism – A Jewish Perspective; Paganism – Contemporary; Russian Mystical Philosophy.

Paiute Culture

The Paiute (meaning "Water Ute") are among the oldest identifiable American Indian cultural groups within North America and are ultimately related through the widely distributed Ute/Aztecan language group to such other groups as the Shoshone, Ute, and even Meso-American groups such as the Aztec. The Ute/Aztecan language and cultural grouping extends from southern Idaho and Oregon to the Valley of Mexico and is thought to comprise the original population of the Great Basin and neighboring areas. Their prehistory has been well-studied and is the subject of numerous monographs and research reports compiled in the "Great Basin" volume of the *Handbook of North American Indians* (Volume 11). Their culture has also been the subject of much theoretical speculation because of their close dependence on a challenging environment and they are sometimes compared to the Eskimo of North America and the Bushmen of Africa in this regard. For example, Julian Steward and other neo-evolutionists within anthropology have attempted to classify them as representative of the earliest examples of human culture due mostly to their hunter-gatherer mode of subsistence, limited population, and patrilocal band organization.

The Paiute are divided by anthropologists into Northern and Southern Branches who together occupy large portions of the western and northern Great Basin, an arid region of about 200,000 square miles in the Western United States ranging from Utah across Nevada's southern tip to the Mojave Desert in California, east to the Wasatch Range, west to the Sierra Nevada, and north into southern Idaho and southern Oregon. Traditional Paiute subsistence is based on seasonal exploitation of riparian, lacustrine, and the oasis-like marshy areas within the Great Basin. For example, the northern-most groups of Paiute in the Great Basin enjoyed access to the aquatic resources of the Columbia and Snake river systems, while the Paiute of the central Great Basin enjoyed access to the resources of such lakes as Pyramid Lake, with the Southern Paiute depending more on oasis and marshy area resources. Traditionally, the Paiute followed a semi-nomadic but very predictable foraging/gathering migratory pattern, moving from temporary settlement to temporary settlement according to a schedule determined by the availability of foods as they ripened and became available for harvest. In spring they depended on roots, seeds, fowl, the spawning runs of fish available at various rivers throughout the northern Great Basin, and various mammalian and avian species. Summer followed with harvesting of other seeds, grasses, berries, roots, small and large mammals, and various bird species. In autumn the pine nut (piñon) harvest was a major focus of both ceremonial and subsistence activity along with the hunting and storage of meat from deer, antelope, mountain sheep, and elk. During the fall and winter, the rabbit drives were especially productive and often resulted in a very productive harvest, in some cases equaling the harvest of anadromous salmon encountered among Northern Paiute. Antelope were also taken through collective activities. The piñon harvest is still a time of great celebration and social interaction with much celebration of this important resource throughout much of the Great Basin including the Ute, Shoshone, and Washoe as well as the Paiute. Proper respect for the piñon is necessary lest the resource itself not be regularly available. Indeed, there is considerable evidence that the piñon harvest is not always available, and that the Paiute have sometimes blamed themselves for having caused such shortfalls through moral infractions and breaking of taboos. The piñon harvest in the Great Basin continues to be accompanied by extensive ceremonialism expressing such necessary respect.

Most traditional Paiute settlements were relatively small, except for a few large ceremonial gatherings associated with harvest of the piñon, anadromous fish, rabbits, and antelope drives. The people spent most of their time in smaller local groups generally limited to several related families whose subsistence needs did not exceed the carrying capacity of the local resource base. Leadership was largely determined by kinship and family position with elders exercising a dominant influence in family affairs. Collective activities such as hunting, gathering, and fishing were cooperative and led by elders. Sometimes shamans were influential in deciding where and when to go for subsistence resources because of their knowledge of the floral and faunal spirit world.

Traditional Paiute religious life focuses on a continuing search for ways of healing and promoting abundance and fertility of the resources on which they depend. Both groups and individuals depend on a number of ceremonies in order to achieve these ends. The vision quest and shamanism along with the sweatbath are principal ceremonies, but the first fruits (thanksgiving), the Sun Dance, and ceremonies associated with various life-crisis events such as birth and death all contribute to the rich religious life of the Paiute people. Spirit power acquired in dreams, visions, and sometimes inherited, is sought by virtually everyone, even though the shaman was a principal specialist in this regard. Illness was traditionally thought to be caused by the breaking of taboos, by sorcery and, in some cases, by soul-loss. Nature is thought to be permeated by a supernatural power or force called puha which is thought to animate all of nature and its creatures. Understanding puha and being able to deal with it constructively is a major concern of shamans. Shamans often visit certain sacred places scattered throughout Northern Paiute territory where they spend several days in prayerful contemplation in order to prepare themselves to deal with their responsibilities. Shamans deal with a variety of supernatural beings routinely addressed in rituals, including such spirits as the Sun and Moon, Thunder, Wind, Clouds, Stars, and other faunal and floral spirits. The peyote plant, although not native to the region, is greatly celebrated as a spiritual teacher who, if followed, will guide its users to moral and productive lives. Prayers to the rainbow and to lightning help the people secure protection, knowledge, and spirit power. The influence of the environment in the worldview and religious life of the Paiute is nowhere more evident than in their rich mythology which routinely stresses the presence and importance of various animal figures such as Coyote, Wolf, Owl, Eagle, Turtle, Insects, Bear, Hawk, Chickade, Bluebird, Antelope, Deer, Elk, Weasel, Porcupine, Bat, Sage Hen, Snake, and Spider. Other environmental features appearing in Paiute mythology include water, rivers, lakes, mountains, roots, piñon nuts, fire, stars, sun, and moon. Spiritually related activities reflected in the mythology include hunting, fishing, gathering, marriage, death, conflicts with such monsters as Cannibal, Rolling Rock, and Water Babies, as well as explanatory stories concerning the origins of the culture, death, birth, pregnancy, and sexuality, all with various references to the natural environment. A major principle in the environmental beliefs of the Northern Pauite is the idea of reciprocity, in which for anything taken from nature there must be a corresponding expression of respect and thanksgiving. Even the smallest environmental resource taken requires a compensatory expression of thanksgiving if the resource is not to be offended and, therefore, make itself unavailable in the future.

Paiute beliefs in an afterlife vary throughout the Great Basin but still reflect the life and environment they have known when living. Some believe that souls journey to an underworld where night is day and day is night but life is otherwise as it is on Earth. Others believe that the soul goes to another world associated with the Milky Way. Certain traditional accounts depict an afterlife in which hunting and gathering are always successful, with much time for dancing, gambling, and other social pursuits. Other accounts are much less clear as to the nature of the afterlife which, among Northern Paiute, is thought to be located in the one of the most important of the cardinal directions.

Deward E. Walker, Jr.

Further Reading

d'Azevedo, Warren L., ed. *Handbook of North American Indians*, vol. 11, Great Basin. Washington, D.C.: Smithsonian Institution, 1986.

Grayson, Donald K. *The Desert's Past: A Natural Prehistory of the Great Basin.* Washington, D.C.: Smithsonian Institution, 1993.

Martineau, LaVan. *Southern Paiutes: Legends, Lore, Language and Lineage.* Las Vegas, NV: KC Publications, 1992.

Maxwell, James A., ed. *America's Fascinating Indian Heritage.* New York: Reader's Digest Association, Inc., 1978.

Walker, Deward E., Jr. *Myths of Idaho Indians.* Moscow: University of Idaho Press, 1980.

Walker, Deward E., Jr. *Indians of Idaho.* Moscow: University of Idaho Press, 1978.

See also: Bison Restoration and Native American Traditions; Harmony in Native North America; Holy Land in Native North America; Lakota; Miwok People; Rock Art – Western United States; Sacred Geography in Native North America; Shamanism – Traditional; Shoshone (Western North America).

Paleolithic Art

It is clear that Paleolithic art – or at least some of it – must be religious, but debate has always raged about what kind of beliefs lay behind its imagery. It is self-evident that these supremely talented artists, who mastered a very wide range of media and techniques, were remarkable observers of animal anatomy and behavior, and could convey a great deal of detail with a few simple strokes. They were a part of the natural world, they lived among the animals which gave them food and raw materials, and therefore one might expect their fellow creatures to loom large in their mythology, their creation tales, and their religious beliefs.

Can one, however, gain any concrete insights into their particular beliefs from their imagery? Unfortunately not, and the never-ending series of interpretations that has been imposed on the same data bears witness to this. For example, there are a small handful of "therianthropes" in Paleolithic art (i.e., figures combining human and animal traits) and they have been seen variously as "horned gods," "sorcerers," and "shamans"; but of course, many historical peoples are known to have a concept in their creation myths of a remote time when animals were people, or vice versa, so it is perfectly possible that these Ice Age depictions may represent mythical ancestors of this type – or simply imaginary beings, or some other concept that escapes us entirely. The fundamental problem is that we are grappling here with the world's oldest art, from a completely alien culture that is so far removed from us in time that we may be completely misinterpreting its art. But archeologists must always cling to the hope that, since these people were fully modern humans identical to ourselves, as far as we can tell, then we can perhaps use this identity as a rough guide to their thoughts and intentions.

Accordingly, a whole series of generalized interpretations has been applied to Paleolithic art, since it became clear that "art for art's sake" was an inadequate explanation for much of it. Far from being a random collection of pretty animal pictures, or an Ice Age bestiary, Paleolithic art comprises – for about 20,000 years – basically the same restricted range of animals, almost always adults drawn in profile, with very few scenes, no groundlines, no landscapes. There are rules involved – some species are often found in association, others never. There are comparatively few human depictions, although they were perfectly capable of drawing them, so their puzzling absence suggests that representing them was forbidden or – more likely – simply irrelevant to what the artists were trying to do. There are scores of human female figurines – the famously misnamed "Venuses" – which Russian archeologists have traditionally interpreted as mother- or ancestor-figures.

The theory of "sympathetic magic," inspired by ethnographic accounts of some Australian Aborigines at the end of the nineteenth century, claimed that artists drew animals that they wanted to kill (sometimes with spears or arrows depicted on them), or animals which they hoped would copulate and reproduce, thus becoming plentiful. These theories of "hunting magic" and "fertility magic" reigned supreme for the first half of the twentieth century, but neither of them holds water – animals marked with supposed "missiles" are found in only a handful of caves, and by and large the artists were not drawing the animals which were their staple foods. There is not a single clear hunting scene in the whole of Paleolithic art, nor a single clear depiction of copulation, among the many thousands of animal images.

Another ever-popular notion has always been that of the caves being used for the initiation of boys into manhood, or of girls into the mysteries of womanhood – an appealing and plausible idea, but there is no hard evidence to support it. We also know that music and sound played a role in certain caves – some contain "lithophones" (i.e., stalactites which were clearly struck repeatedly to make sounds [some are even marked with paint]), while, in others, tests suggest that the best art was placed in the zones with the best acoustics. However, while evocative, the existence of music making in the caves does not necessarily involve religion.

The early decades of the twentieth century also saw the application of notions such as totemism and shamanism to Ice Age art; and since these were hunting peoples closely involved with animals, one cannot deny that some traits of these belief systems might have existed at this remote time; but alas we have absolutely no way of proving it. Rather than impose our own preferences and pet theories on this art, extrapolating wholesale from modern times, it is more honest to let the art speak for itself, and to deduce what one can from its location and content. The prominence of cave art (as opposed to the numerous portable art objects) has often led scholars to see it all as mysterious and religious, but the recent discovery that they were also decorating rocks along rivers and on mountainsides suggests that cave art was not typical of the period – instead caves are merely the places where the art has been best preserved – and open-air art looks inherently less mysterious and sacred than figures in total darkness; yet we know from the ethnography of Australia and elsewhere that open-air art can be just as dangerous, powerful and taboo as anything hidden underground. In the absence of the artists we can never know the precise meaning of Paleolithic art, but we can at least deduce with some certainty from its location and content that much of it sprang directly from religious beliefs that involved animals, either literally or metaphorically.

Paul G. Bahn

Further Reading
Bahn, Paul G. and Jean Vertut. *Journey Through the Ice Age*. London: Weidenfeld & Nicolson / Berkeley: University of California Press, 1997.
Leroi-Gourhan, André. *The Art of Prehistoric Man in Western Europe*. London: Thames and Hudson, 1968.
See also: Art; Paleolithic Religions; Rock Art (various).

Paleolithic Religions

It is impossible to know, from sparse archeological evidence, when the first stirrings of some kind of religious feelings and beliefs arose in our ancestors, but it is probably safe to assume that they involved mysterious or impressive aspects of nature – the heavenly bodies, the weather, earthquakes and fire, echoes, the surrounding fauna and flora. In particular, for hunting peoples, it was likely to involve the large and/or ferocious animals which inspired feelings of awe, such as the mammoth and woolly rhino, the bears and big cats. At the same time, in common with many hunting peoples of the historic period, they may also have felt a special reverence for the species which provided them with the bulk of their food and raw materials – deer, horse, bison and so forth, depending on the environment and climate.

Other than the collection of exotic objects and fossils – which in itself indicates a close observation of nature – there is very little in the archeological record of the first and longest period of humankind's existence, the Lower Paleolithic (ca. 2.5 million to 200,000 years ago), which can plausibly be interpreted as religious in nature, although the earliest possible funerary ritual dates to between 300,000 and 200,000 years ago at Atapuerca. It is only with the arrival of Neanderthals, ca. 200,000 years ago that a few tantalizing clues can be found to some kind of religious feeling – not only the presence of real burials, but also other remarkable phenomena: for example, in 1940 the Middle Paleolithic site of El Guettar, in Tunisia, yielded a carefully made heap of hundreds of spheroid stones mixed with more than 3000 flint tools, 236 mammal teeth and some broken bones. This fully intentional deposit has inevitably been interpreted as "ritual," since it is difficult to envisage a functional purpose for its existence. Recently, a stone and bone "mask," from Neanderthal times, was found in the French site of La Roche-Cotard; clearly intentionally shaped and modified, it is undoubtedly an art object, a "proto-figurine," but it could also be interpreted in religious terms.

Conversely, a great deal of ink has been wasted for decades on a supposed cave-bear cult, mostly associated with Neanderthals, but also sometimes with Cro-Magnons, based on discoveries of bear skulls and bones inside caves in the Alps and elsewhere. The supposed arrangements of the bones led many scholars to see them as evidence for veneration of this species. However, the gradual improvement in knowledge of taphonomic factors (i.e., what can happen to bones between the death of the animal and their unearthing by archeologists) eventually made it clear that most if not all such cases were completely natural, largely produced by the bears themselves blundering about in the dark, and breaking, disturbing and rearranging the bones of their predecessors. One cannot completely rule out the possibility of a Stone Age cave-bear cult, but the basis for its existence has now been virtually reduced to wishful thinking.

It is in the Upper Paleolithic (ca. 40,000 to 10,000 years ago), with fully modern humans, that the evidence for religious beliefs becomes both abundant and crystal clear, particularly through cave art, but also in the number and complexity of human burials, many of which are associated with red ochre, and which often contain beads, seashells, stone or bone tools, or pieces of portable art. The very existence of grave goods is a strong (though by no means infallible) indicator of a belief in an afterlife; Neanderthal burials are sometimes apparently accompanied by animal bones, horns or antlers, which may or may not be meaningful grave goods highlighting the huge importance of animals to these people; but the variety and abundance of goods placed with the Cro-Magnon dead are eloquent testimony to the prominence of religious belief.

How can one be sure that some cave art is religious? Although numerous theories have been put forward about its motivation, there is one fundamental reason why we can be sure that religious beliefs of some kind played a major role in the production of some imagery. The certainty lies in the location of some of the art; for while much of it is "public" (i.e., is easily visible) and even deliberately made accessible to other people, some of it is quite the opposite – hidden away in nooks, crannies, tiny chambers that are only reachable by crawling, or up vertiginous chimneys. These figures were not for public consumption, but were extremely private, made and presumably offered to whatever deities, spirits or ancestors the artist was trying to communicate with. In the French cave of Pergouset, there is an engraved horse head that even the artist never saw, since one cannot insert one's head into the niche where it was drawn – this is the ultimate in private religious art. In certain caves, such as Pergouset or Le Tuc d'Audoubert, it seems to have been the arduous journey into the cave to make the imagery that was important, not perhaps the images themselves, which may have been some kind of offering. And in the Pyrenean cave of Les Trois Frères, a small natural side-chamber is dominated by an engraving of a lioness (the chamber has been dubbed the "lioness chapel") and, in crevices between stalagmites beneath the figure and all around the chamber, very special objects were deposited – animal teeth, flint tools, seashells – which can only be interpreted as votive offerings.

In short, the location of some cave art, together with some extraordinary data like the carefully placed objects in Les Trois Frères, make it very clear that there was a very strong motivation behind some cave art which can plausibly be considered as religious; and in view of the content of the art, it is reasonable to suppose that the religions of the period were directly derived from natural phenomena and certainly involved animals in some way, thus focusing on the relationship between Paleolithic people and the natural world.

Paul G. Bahn

Further Reading

Bahn, Paul G. and Jean Vertut. *Journey Through the Ice Age*. London: Weidenfeld & Nicolson / Berkeley: University of California Press, 1997.

Leroi-Gourhan, André. *The Art of Prehistoric Man in Western Europe*. London: Thames and Hudson, 1968.

Otte, Marcel. *Préhistoire des Religions*. Paris: Masson, 1993.

See also: Hunting and the Origins of Religion; Paleolithic Art; Paleolithic Religions and the Future.

Paleolithic Religions and the Future

All interpretations of Paleolithic religions are conjectural. One reason is the paucity of evidence. The term "Paleolithic religions" is itself questionable, since there is no evidence for systems of belief and practice resembling today's religions. Another problem is imposing interpretive schemes, such as the association of religion with the supernatural, on the deep past. The transition from orality to literacy is a further complication. Today's religions are the creations of literate people who acknowledge nature primarily as an economic resource. Paleoreligion was the creation of primary oral people living in close proximity to and intimate familiarity with nature.

Nevertheless, there are several possibilities for interpreting paleoreligion's implications for the future. These include conjectures grounded in an evolutionary framework, especially the evolutionary environment, those grounded in archeological data, such as prehistoric burials, cave painting, and artifacts such as the Venus of Willendorf, and those grounded in identifying so-called primitive survivals of paleoreligion in contemporary Aboriginal culture.

Interpretive frameworks

Interpreted through the lens of evolutionary biology, paleoreligion appears to have been a powerful if uncertain force mediating interaction between humans and their environment. The gene-shortage problem precludes explaining the complexities of human behavior on a genetic basis. Thus, imaginatively evolved forms of religious belief were almost surely involved in directing practices such as the hunting of game or the burial of the dead.

Other interpretive paradigms, such as ethnography and mythoarcheology, reconstruct Paleolithic "worldviews" on the basis of archeological evidence. Various artifacts including cave paintings are interpreted as manifesting a spiritual awareness of connections between humankind and nature. Through such readings it appears that paleopeople were invested in the myth of the eternal return, maintaining ceremonial cycles and ritual practices believed to ensure the continuing cycle of nature's bounty. Another interpretation is that paleo-people believed in a Great Mother who held humans to her nurturing bosom.

A third interpretive approach studies the religious practices and beliefs of contemporary Aboriginal cultures for clues revealing earlier forms of consciousness. The study of Australian Aborigines, as well as contemporary tribal people of the American Southwest, are particularly suited to such interpretation.

Implications for the future

An interdisciplinary synthesis perhaps mitigates the weakness of single-factor interpretive approaches. If the beliefs of paleoreligionists in the myth of eternal return or the Great Mother weakened the environment so that subsistence was undercut, then the beliefs would be extinguished. Further, the survival of tribal people (e.g., Hopi, Havasupai, Western Apache) in relatively harsh environments such as the desert Southwest appears to confirm the efficacy of some religious beliefs and practices. Apparently some paleoreligions had adaptive value, encouraging harmonious and sustainable relations with the environment. So viewed, paleoreligion has positive implications for a modern world facing pervasive environmental exigencies that elude narrowly technical solution. Given the assumption that paleoreligion encouraged harmony with rather than domination of nature, then its cultural utility appears to lie in what has been termed post-historic primitivism. Paleoreligion thus becomes a source for reweaving a modern cultural fabric that is out of balance with nature. Going back in time is not possible. Rather the effort is to learn from the deep past in ways that inform adaptations to present-day environmental exigencies.

However appealing the idea, a definitive argument does not support this conclusion. An alternative explanation is that paleoreligion had little or no influence in regulating interactions between humans and their environment; indeed, evidence indicates that humans hunted some species to extinction at the boundary of the Paleolithic and Neolithic. Paleoreligion thus appears ecologically inconsequential; the constraining factors on environmental exploitation were not religious beliefs and practices but small populations, primitive technologies, and the absence of permanent human settlement.

The present essay cannot resolve such a division of opinion. Yet given that various interpreters of biblical and other world religions believe their faith has a crucial role to play in shaping the future, then paleoreligion may also play a role. But why? The answer is not intuitively obvious. Partly it lies in the continuing interpretive challenge posed by the discovery of Paleolithic strata in the nineteenth century. And partly it lies in the twentieth-century realization that human beings are language animals. If the pervasive ecological dysfunctions of the modern age are rooted in narratized religious traditions that separate the spiritual and material, then paleoreligion, surely a system of belief more attuned to the connections between humankind and nature, has relevance to the future. Can contemporary people, steeped in textual religiosity now several thousand years old, somehow recover religious sensibilities that connected rather than separated them from the web of life? Only time will tell.

Max Oelschlaeger

Further Reading

Basso, Keith H. *Wisdom Sits in Places: Landscape and Language among the Western Apache.* Albuquerque: University of New Mexico Press, 1996.

Lee, Richard B. and Irven DeVore, eds. *Man the Hunter.* New York: Aldine deGruyter, 1968.

Martin, Calvin. *In the Spirit of the Earth: Rethinking History and Time.* Baltimore: The Johns Hopkins University Press, 1992.

Martin, Calvin. *Keepers of the Game: Indian–Animal Relationships and the Fur Trade.* Berkeley: University of California Press, 1978.

Oelschlaeger, Max. *The Idea of Wilderness: From Prehistory to the Age of Ecology.* New Haven: Yale University Press, 1991.

Shepard, Paul. *Coming Home to the Pleistocene.* Washington, D.C.: Island Press, 1996.

Shepard, Paul. "A Post-Historic Primitivism." In Max Oelschlaeger, ed. *The Wilderness Condition: Essays on Environment and Civilization.* San Francisco: Sierra Club Books, 1992.

Wilson, Edward O. *On Human Nature.* Cambridge: Harvard University Press, 1978.

See also: Animism: Humanity's Original Religious Worldview; Noble Savage; Paganism (various); Paleolithic Art; Paleolithic Religions; Radical Environmentalism; Romanticism and Indigenous People; Shepard, Paul.

Palmer, Martin (1953–)

An Anglican theologian by education, Martin Palmer, director of the International Consultancy on Religion, Education & Culture (ICOREC), has played a leading role in several projects involving religious traditions in environmentalism and conservation. In particular, he has built a close relationship between the World Wide Fund for Nature (WWF) – and its patron Prince Philip – and all the major religious traditions, leading to a series of summit meetings of religious leaders on religion and conservation, and declarations issued by the different religions concerning the environment and respect for nature. Among the outcomes of these activities have been the Network on Religion and Conservation and the Alliance of Religion and Conservation. Martin Palmer is author and editor of several books on religion and conservation.

Tim Jensen

Further Reading

Palmer, Martin. *Holy Ground.* London: Pilkington Press, 1997.

Palmer, Martin. *Living Christianity.* London: Element Books, 1993.

Palmer, Martin. *Christianity and Ecology.* London: Cassell, 1992.

Palmer, Martin. *The Elements of Taoism.* London: Element Books, 1991.

Palmer, Martin. *Worlds of Difference.* London: Blackie and Son, 1989.

Palmer, Martin. *Genesis or Nemesis: Belief, Meaning and Ecology.* London: Dryad Press, 1988.

Palmer, Martin. *Faith and Nature.* London: Rider, 1987.

See also: Alliance of Religion and Conservation; Network on Conservation and Religion; World Wide Fund for Nature.

Panentheism – See Pantheism; Process Philosophy; Process Theology.

Pantheism

Pantheism relates to the question concerning transcendence and the place of deity – whether it is within or beyond space and time. It contrasts essentially with theism that holds that the personality and being of god (God) transcend the universe. For pantheism, the universe as a whole is god or, in feminist "theological" terms, goddess. In this sense, pantheism is to be distinguished both from deism, which still holds a personal god to be creator of the world but neither immanent in nature nor revealed through history or by religious experience, and from atheism as the complete rejection of belief in god's existence. Pantheism is also known as "cosmotheism," which either ascribes divinity to the cosmos or simply identifies god with the world, and as "acosmism," which is the fundamental denial of the existence of the universe as distinct from god. Consequently, pantheism is also to be contrasted with "panentheism" or the doctrine that god/goddess includes the world as a part of his/her being but not the whole of it. In other words, and especially from the acosmic view, god is none other than the combined forces and laws that manifest in the existing universe. In general, the pantheistic position holds that all is god rather than that god is all (theopantism).

Pantheism is often understood as a form of monism, but it may also be either dualistic (as in the ditheism of Zoroastrianism and Manicheism, the bitheism of contemporary Western Paganism or the dyotheism of mind and matter as divine) or pluralistic (as in the polytheism of classical paganism, Shinto, etc.). Monism holds that there is only one kind of metaphysical substance or ultimate reality. Idealistic or spiritual monism explains matter and its phenomena as modifications of mind. This is basically a form of Gnosticism. Materialistic monism, on the other hand, resolves mind into matter, while a third form of monism considers there to be some underlying substance or ultimate reality of which matter, mind and their phenomena become its manifestations or modifications.

One Western philosopher most associated with pantheism is Benedict Spinoza (1632–1677) who employed the terms *natura naturans* and *natura naturata* to express the integral reality of god and the world. Before Spinoza, however, these designations were employed by the Arabian philosopher Averroes (1126–1198), the German cardinal Nicholas of Cusa (1400–1464) and the Dominican monk Giordano Bruno (1548–1600) who was burned at the stake for his conversion to a naturalistic/mystical pantheism. Averroes argued for the co-eternity of a universe created *ex nihilo*. For Bruno, god and the universe were two different names for the same thing. He referred to god – ineffable, whole, transcendent and one – as the *natura naturans*, the creative essence of all things. The infinite division and manifestation of this infinite potentiality are the worlds, orders, objects and events of the *natura naturata*. Bruno saw this world-process as an oscillation between the out-going of divine nature – culminating in the rational human mind in which searching for common denominators represents the turning point – and its return into itself. Before Bruno, another Dominican monk, Meister Johannes Eckhart (ca. 1260–1327), was forced to defend himself against charges of pantheism in his mystical teachings in a famous ecclesiastical trial in 1326. The trial culminated with Eckhart's retraction when the charges were considered proven. He was not executed as were others with similar views, but after his death the following year, Pope John XXII condemned 28 propositions from Eckhart's works.

Spinoza proposes a substance monism in which the physical and mental series are both themselves modes of absolute reality. In his metaphysical system, god and nature are one and the same substance. Spinoza's god, as a being who is not separate or independent from the universe, has no personal qualities. While Spinoza's "god-intoxicated atheistic" monism has been questioned as being truly pantheism, his god contrasts radically with the personal entity of theism by conforming nonetheless to the essential impersonal nature of a pantheistic godhead. In Spinoza's understanding of a god-nature (*natura naturans/natura naturata*) identity, all things interact, universal standards of absolute quality transcend individual sentience and relations, and the infinite order's innate harmony supersedes all rules of morality. He advocates an *amor intellectualis Dei*, the calm contemplation of the changeless within change.

Apart from the various theories of god/goddess/the godhead (theism, deism, pantheism, atheism), the world's major religions themselves are either Abrahamic, dharmic, pagan or secular. Pushed further, the various theological understandings reduce finally to an ethical/metaphysical position that rests on either the immanent perception of paganism or the transcendental one of Gnosticism. The Gnostic position is distinguished by its denial of the ontological and/or axial reality of the physical world – in other words, the viewpoint of idealistic monism. It subscribes to what Catherine Albanese designates as a "nature is illusion" theology rather than to what we could understand as a fundamentally pagan stance, namely, "nature is real." From the dharmic position of Hinduism, the *natura naturans* and *natura naturata* equation becomes a falsity. Instead, all phenomenal reality is an illusion (*māyā*), and the only reality is the inscrutable Brahman, the not-this/not-that. Consequently, while Hinduism advocates a pantheism of sorts, it is a transcendental pantheism even if all is god. But for the individual who perceives reality as absolutely non-differentiated, with no separation of self from the all (*atman* = *Brahman*), the cosmos can be approached only through a type of solipsistic pantheism. This approach necessitates the cultivation of utter detachment from the illusions of apparent existence. All dharmic religions stress the development of emancipation from each and every desire, and even when, as with Buddhism, the tangible world may be accepted as ontologically real, it is still without axial reality or value. From an Abrahamic perspective, by contrast, the impersonal godhead or Brahman is understood as a void of absence, even negativity. With Buddhism, especially inasmuch as it represents what we could assess to be a "Protestant" form of Hinduism, there is no "god" to begin with: it assumes an essentially atheistic theological position. Consequently, especially in its Christian forms, Abrahamic religion posits in response to solipsistic pantheism a transcendental personal god that stands "outside" nature and/or the material world and is its fully autonomous creator. From the theistic perspective, god and nature are ontologically separate and distinct. The Abrahamic religions do not deny the metaphysical reality of the world, but inasmuch as they adopt what is still essentially a Gnostic position, though this world may be the "gift" of the creator god, it is not an end in itself but more an impediment to obtaining or regaining a state of transcendental and/or heavenly grace. This positing of an external god becomes the Christian and Islamic means to break or break through the deadlock of solipsistic isolation. The nullification of the "iron cage" of solipsism is dependent on what the Christian refers to as faith – that is, an absolute faith in its posited god. The ultimate Christian and Islamic rationale is evangelistic: if the entire world were to be "converted" to their particular Abrahamic perspective, the validity of the Christian or Islamic positing of an external creator that ends solipsistic imprisonment would be confirmed and vindicated.

Among the major Abrahamic faiths, Judaism represents a more theologically schizophrenic position. There is no attempt to evangelize the world, for Judaism is essentially an ethnic or tribal identity. In this sense, it is closer to paganism. But secondly, in what is again a pagan position, Judaism accepts the ontological reality of the world. There is no ostensible denial of the tangible until we reach the more esoteric and mystical developments of the Kabbalah. But in mainstream Judaism itself, without the possibility of either reincarnation or an Elysium-type otherworld, all hope is centered on the tribal survival of the Jewish ethnos itself rather than on any kind of personal immortality. As Judaism has historically continued to move away from its pagan origins toward a centering on its god as a transcendental being, its pagan retention of accepting the world as a cherished and acceptably pleasurable tangible reality edges Judaism toward the most schizophrenic theological position, even if it escapes the radical ethical stance between good and evil that unbalance its Christian and Islamic sister or daughter religions.

The contrasting religious ideal-type to both the Abrahamic and dharmic as well as secular (atheist, agnostic and/or mechanical) constructs is, of course, the pagan. Vis-à-vis the supernatural (whether god, gods, the godhead or even goddess), there are both secular pagans and pagan pagans. There are also dharmic pagans – especially people who fuse pagan and Buddhist spirituality and/or practice, while most of vernacular Hinduism is itself pagan in contrast to its "official" theological Gnostic doctrine of Vedantic Brahmanism. And of course, there are even Abrahamic pagans or pagan possibilities and/or elements (e.g. theophagy, veneration of saints, reverence toward an aerolith, worship of Asherah, etc.). But in considering any pantheistic understanding of nature cherished as divine or sacred, we are by default virtually focused on paganism – whether that pantheism includes the supernatural (pagan paganism) or denies it (secular paganism). The distinction between the two lies with the former position entertaining the supernatural as a trans-ontological reality that perhaps operates chiefly through metaphor and synchronicity, if not traditional magic as well. In other words, the supernatural refers to the dimension of autonomous, non-empirical dynamics, though here not one that is considered to be a telluric or cosmic prerequisite. The more secular pagan position tends to follow Spinoza and understand the divine totality, that is, totality as divine, in terms of purely causal relationships, and it approaches the sacred more as a value than as a metaphysic.

Spinoza's philosophy combines immanentism and rational mysticism, and it ultimately represents a methodologically inspired modification of Plotinus. Its pantheism of substance (*natura naturans*) and emanation (*natura naturata*) is an endless series of mechanical diffusion and mutation. More organic forms of pantheism are to be found in the metaphysics of naturalism. Like pantheism, naturalism holds that all experience of temporal and spatial reality occurs within and as a part of nature. Notions of the supernatural are avoided. In other words, all reality is nature, and the ultimate is to be found within the framework of nature and not outside it. To the degree that Spinoza's substance (*natura naturans*) is to be understood as god, he advocates what could be classified as a spiritual or idealistic form of naturalism. His nature is akin to either spirit or mental categories. Materialistic naturalism, in contrast, centers on matter or the matter/energy continuum as the metaphysical fundament. Along with these traditional schools of naturalism, there are also neutral and dynamic understandings – the former sees reality as static entity and relation; the later, as process and energy that are neither mental nor physical. As proponents of descriptive or neutral naturalism, John Dewey (1859–1952), George Santayana (1863–1952) and Justus Buchler (1914–1991) relate the source of potentiality to the material substrate in its very beingness. Numinosity becomes purely a derivative of human projection, and nature is reduced to a series of causal sequences. Its essential humanism in which religious goals derive from social action latently assumes an extra-natural vantage from which to make its judgments on the limits of nature's transformative possibilities and any denial of the unlimited potencies that can emerge from nature's hidden depths.

A more contemporary understanding of naturalism and interpretation of the potencies of *natura naturans* and emerging and emerged orders of *natura naturata* understanding are provided by Robert Corrington. Positing that there can be nothing beyond or outside nature, Corrington argues that notions of an extra-natural, omnipotent, omnipresent, self-conscious creator and sustainer are examples of anthropomorphic projection and hubris. He calls for a categorical foundational analysis to replace traditional theological romanticism and wish fulfillment. From his perspective, the *natura naturans* or what he calls "nature naturing" is the unconscious of nature – one that relates to the orders of the world and universe of astrophysics in the same way that the human unconscious relates to personal consciousness. A fold of nature is an intensified product of nature naturing and not a conscious or superhuman agent of awareness and purpose. Corrington stresses the basic divide that exists between the two halves of an all-encompassing nature that is impossible to define. He is particularly critical of the "militantly self-defensive Western monotheisms" (Corrington 1997: 18) in which a posited linear and self-centered god is thought to bring its own other into existence out of nonexistence and then exercise absolute dominion over it. A creator god has no genuine other. Instead, for Corrington, the sacred is simply nature's most important manifestation, the dimensions of which need to be understood post-anthropomorphically if theology is not to be merely a gender, race or class autobiography. There is "nothing whatsoever outside of nature. The sacred is in and of nature and cannot outstrip nature" (Corrington 1997: 10). Nevertheless, despite human projections that exteriorize elements of the personal and collective unconscious, Corrington's pantheism or what he terms "ecstatic naturalism" recognizes the sacred in the numinous folds of semiotic plenitude that emerge or are ejected from *natura naturans*. Like humanism, Corrington's naturalism rejects any notion of supernaturalism, but unlike humanism, it will not deny but instead affirms "the utter supremacy of the transfiguring potencies of nature" (Corrington 1997: 53). His lexicon is comfortable with such terms as "numinous," "manic," "sacred," "divine," "extra-human," "epiphany" and "transpersonal"; it rejects "magical," "supernatural," "talismanic," "holy" and even "spiritual." Nevertheless, for Corrington, there is the erotic and transordinal spirit – a generic spirit that belongs to nature and not to Christianity. This spirit is "self-othering in the sense that no sign or interpretant can ever envelop it" (Corrington 1997: 161), but it is not a consciousness because it has no center of intentionality. It is always subaltern to nature and located within nature natured. While nature in both its dimensions contains every conceivable type of infinite, spirit for Corrington expresses only one main kind of the non-finite.

The ultimate understanding of pantheism and the relation between the divine and nature rests not only in its distinction from theism but also from the theological framework of panentheism and the process theologies of Alfred North Whitehead (1861–1947) and Charles Hartshorne (1897–2000). Spinoza's monism is usually accepted as the classical form of pantheism: a totally deterministic reality and a god bound by actuality. Panentheism attempts to reassert the godhead as the totality of both actual and potential being. But unlike the "god is all" stance of pantheism, panentheism ("all in god") is closer to the theopantic position of "god is all." In other words, this view asserts that all things are within the being of god, but god is not subsumed or "exhausted" by all things and is additionally something other than the world or cosmos itself. The chief difficulty with the panentheism god is that it appears to be a reversion to theism's timeless and impassible god that simply adopts much of the language of pantheism – especially in its process theology position that sees god as "embracing" the world and lovingly seeking to lure all things toward their maximum aesthetic satisfaction. This notion of god "luring," the idea of god as the ideal which draws things (back) to himself/itself, that is, god as the last cause or goal, was first presented by Aristotle and reintroduced into contemporary thought by Whitehead. But what Whitehead has done is to reject Spinoza's notion of substance and replace it with process (a series of events in space and time). But unlike Spinoza's god who is bounded by actuality, Whitehead accepts that actual occasions provide the fundamental constituents of reality but that the universe at any moment consists of an infinite number of actual occasions. Each occasion is a result of all those that have preceded it but also is something new. For Whitehead, the radically new always exists. Since present newness allows for unpredictability, there is always an open future – bypassing or avoiding Spinoza's deterministic universe. His god is not omnipotent or omniscient in knowing the future but only in knowing all that there is to know. But inasmuch as Whitehead's world is process, it is holistic and organic. And this world/god is, according to Hartshorne, infinitely self-surpassable.

Another thinker within the school of process naturalism is Robert Neville. Like Averroes, he continues the argument of *creatio ex nihilo*, and like Spinoza, he understands the created world as fully determined. But unlike most of the earlier process naturalists, he dismisses the tendency to overly romanticize the human traits within certain orders of nature to the detriment of others. Nevertheless, he is persuaded to affirm the strong link of an independent god to the bound totality of the created world. Unlike the process theologians who privilege creativity itself and have no need for a creator god, Neville sees god and creation unfolding together in the act of world creation – an act in which god overcomes its own transcendence and becomes immanent in the created order as a governing central logos. In traditional process naturalism, the created world (*natura naturata*) becomes part of the divine augmentation process. For Neville's process theology, the world is dependent on god's absolute infinite sovereignty, and this god must become in some sense finite if it is to be involved in the world it has created. On the other hand, in Corrington's ecstatic naturalism, once the *natura naturata* has been ejected or spawned from the unconscious of nature, it is an autonomous foundling with "no direct link to the inaugurating and unruly ground" (Corrington 1997: 119). In place of determination and obligation, there is total independence and availability and, as such, the possibility of perennial renewal.

To summarize, the panentheism of process naturalism wishes to place the divine beyond nature as much as within it. In contrast, the pantheism of ecstatic naturalism asserts simply that there is nothing outside nature/the world/the cosmos. While most naturalisms eschew the notion of a supernatural, they may still hold to an understanding of an immanent preternatural. The opposite of naturalism is not supernaturalism but rather antinaturalism or idealism. However, unlike Corrington's ecstatic naturalism that simply dismisses the magical, in a dynamic pantheistic naturalism, there is the possibility that the supernatural/preternatural might arise as various aporias that open up *within* the natural. To whatever extent the numinous exists or comes to exist within a pantheistic understanding, it is an emergent from nature rather than some antecedent or *a priori* teleological factor. While pantheism *á la* Spinoza may be mechanical, naturalistic understandings of pantheism hold the world or cosmos to be organic, interconnected, in some way monistic and most likely enchanted.

Michael York

Further Reading

Albanese, Catherine. *Nature Religion in America from the Algonkian Indians to the New Age*. Chicago: University of Chicago Press, 1990.

Corrington, Robert S. *Nature's Religion*. Lanham, MD: Rowman & Littlefield, 1997.

Eilberg-Schwartz, Howard. *God's Phallus – and Other Problems for Men and Monotheism*. Boston: Beacon Press, 1994.

Ferm, Vergilius, ed. *An Encyclopedia of Religion*. New York: The Philosophical Library, 1945.

Levine, Michael P. *Pantheism: A Non-Theistic Concept of Deity*. London & New York: Routledge, 1994.

Nelson, William Allan, ed. *Webster's New International Dictionary of the English Language*. Springfield, MA: C. & G. Merriam Co., 1944 (2nd edn, unabridged).

Oman, John. *The Natural and the Supernatural*. Cambridge: Cambridge University Press, 1931 (1950).

Spinoza, Benedictus. *Tractatus Theologico-Politicus* (1670). Samuel Shirley, tr. Leiden: E.J. Brill, 1991.

York, Michael. *Pagan Theology: Paganism as a World Religion*. New York: New York University Press, 2002.

York, Michael. "New Age Commodification and Appropriation of Spirituality." *Journal of Contemporary Religion* 163 (October 2001), 361–72.

See also: Brower, David; Corrington, Robert S.; Gaia; Krutch, Joseph Wood; Leopold, Aldo; Muir, John; Pantheist Association for Nature – PAN; Raphson, Joseph; Spinoza, Baruch; Toland, John; Unitarianism.

Pantheist Association for Nature – PAN

The Pantheist Association for Nature is a religious conservation organization, founded in 1998, to spread Pantheism and encourage environmental action. Members of the small internet-based association "celebrate the wonder, beauty, and divinity of Nature . . ." Premising the sacrality of nature, PAN sees Pantheism as a wellspring of ecological consciousness, and holds that when people view nature as sacred, they may more readily treasure the natural world which sustains all life.

The PAN website posts articles on Pantheism, biographies of individuals animating to the religion, recommended readings, quotations, holidays, suggestions for activism, and links to environmental organizations.

Based in Southern California, PAN conducts local hikes and engages in conservation projects, such as the restoration of endangered native plant habitat in coastal San Diego County. With members spread across the United States and overseas, and free of group infrastructure, PAN seeks mainly to inspire individual belief and action

Inspiration and joy abound in nature, according to the organization's Tenets of Faith, which cite pantheist author and American conservationist Joseph Wood Krutch:

Faith in wildness, or in Nature as a creative force puts our ultimate trust, not in human intelligence, but in whatever it is that created human intelligence . . . By aligning ourselves with Nature, by having faith and trust in its creative energy, we join hands with infinite power and find our greatest peace.

Gary Suttle

Further Reading

Levine, Michael P. *Pantheism: A Non-Theistic Concept of Deity*. London and New York: Routledge, 1994.

See also: Pantheism.

Papua New Guinea

Despite a great diversity in language and other cultural traits, the indigenous population of the Melanesian island nation of Papua New Guinea holds in common ideas that anchor their traditional life-worlds in the land. Mythic knowledge pertains to origins of various environments by actions of deities, or the taking possession of them by the first ancestors – that came from above, or from under, or along the ground, usually providing in the process some means for sustaining life. In the present time, the more recent ancestors play a complementary role in supporting peoples' livelihoods in the closeness of environmental space and in the societal order they share with humans. An envisaged cosmos of such finite attributions entails highly terrestrial values and the common location or habitation of many spiritual powers in the landscape. Only a representative number of cultures can be considered.

Diverse mythic themes concerning primeval events set forth the bonding of life and Earth. According to the traditions of the Chimbu in the highland area of the country, life came out of death, since the pigs, epitomizing social well-being, emerged from the ground where the first slain ancestor was buried. By comparison, the Iatmul on the Sepik River perceive the interrelations of environs and persons mediated through totemic bonds and authenticated by claims to the deeds of mythic ancestors on their primeval overland migrations. Far to the south, the Bedamini and Gebusi of Western Province share in a cosmic geography reflecting their neighborly relations along the Kum River with the image of an upstream power over downstream life. Bedamini mythic ancestors had mortally wounded a lower-world woman because she had intruded on their space; and they utilized her discharges (like urine) for forging features of their landscape (like rivers), and buried her corpse to enhance the fertility of the ground. The Gebusi, on the other hand, recount that their proposed marriage union with people in trees and the sky (as equivalent to the above, the upstream, and, ultimately, the better because more powerful) was rejected with devastating effects for their forebears so that only one primeval couple survived. On the other side of Papua New Guinea, we find that, within their three-tiered world, the Jupna of Madang Province conceive of a deity of the upper plane, who bestowed with the flow of the Jupno River the environs and humans. Ultimately the deity *is* the river, with its potency diminishing from upstream to downstream (where the dead reside).

The landscape itself holds the legacy of the roots and past. The Chimbu know the location of the primeval events to which they relate in the grand pig-killing rites by designating the holy of the holies of the ceremonial grounds as the grave of the slain mythic ancestor. As for the Iatmul, funerals are important occasions for reciting the primeval migrations of their first ancestors, thus asserting their identity with past events on the land. And according to traditions of the Wamira of Milne Bay Province, the early ancestors turned into stone at the end of their time and remain as features of a bygone era in the landscape.

With their conceptions of space people feel integrally connected with their environment. They typically visualize spatial relationships as expanding from the residential area to the entire environs. Going from center to periphery, feelings of security are strongest around the hamlet and ceremonial grounds, slightly less on utilized land, and weak in the bush and other areas of limited control. Such feelings about space express themselves in religious attitudes. A good relationship with one's forebears, for example, apparently often demanded physical proximity and was seen to be essential to human health and economic success. Thus the Binandere of Oro Province buried their dead under the house to secure their cooperation in horticulture and hunting, and they lit a fire there to make them comfortable, which had the added advantage of keeping roaming malevolent spirits and sorcerers away. The Chimbu, interring the dead near the grounds of the ceremonial pig-kill, called on the ghost to share the house fire on the day of a funeral – an expression of bereavement but also the initial step of securing a close relationship. The Wamira went further by imaging a supporting dead sitting at the elbow of a relative.

In contrast, certain sacred places, especially on boundaries or distant from hamlets, were considered dangerous. The spirits inhabiting them could however be dealt with ritually, as for instance, the cyclopean being at the great, upthrust rock of Elim Bari, on the edges of Chimbu and Siane cultures: the belief that he causes too much dryness or wet weather leads these peoples to kill pigs in his vicinity. Such place spirits are called in Tok Pisin: *masalai*, and they are usually dangerous only when you tread on their grounds. Over unknown centuries such beliefs protected many parts of the environment from human interference.

Again, feelings about space are expressed in poetic modes and semantic nuances. It has been shown of a number of cultures that some parts of "nature" are gendered male and others female, and that one responds to the cosmos accordingly. It has been shown of the Eastern Highland Gimi that male and female chants respond to each antiphonally by appealing to these associations in the environment. With the Foi in the Southern Highlands the naming of individual people invokes such preconceptual associations.

People had to redress their ideas of the world from the early colonial times on, and many societies displayed great flexibility in accommodating alien influences on their living space. The newcomers were initially identified in the familiar cosmos and often made welcome, as returning ancestors, or, with the interesting case of Miklouho-Maclay, the Russian naturalist residing in the Madang region in the 1870s, as "the man from the moon." Comparably, Lutheran missionaries into the Yupno Valley in the 1920s as well as explorers into the highlands a decade later were identified with light-skinned sky dwellers. However, the emerging expectation of a partnership that honors reciprocity was never fulfilled in the colonial relationship with administrators, missionaries, and planters, and so people reconceived them as an intrusion into their space and made adjustments. As with others in early contact times, the Binandere found that the ever-so-important proximity of the deceased relatives was severed because of governmental requests to change burial sites – turning one's back on the dead meant diminishing yields of yam and game. But the Wamira ably made qualified adjustments to their Anglican creed; even into the 1980s they still regarded the taro garden as a sacred place, and perceived personal success as resting upon good relationships with one's forebears. In the highlands, a region characterized by competing Christian mission influences, the Chimbu were at first supported by the Catholics (over against the Lutherans and the Seventh-day Adventists) in seeing some continuity between their traditions and the new creed. By signifying the ceremonial grounds with the crucifix and accepting a modified version of the pig-kill, the Church gave way to syncretic meanings of the ritual and its relation to the ground. In various other regions the coming of missionary influence was sacralized with unexpected candor into what became space transformed into modern Christian or sometimes secularized land.

As these processes of change unfolded, there also emerged grassroots movements serving foremost to forge new power relations with their colonial counterparts. Embedded in their discourses was much newly acquired knowledge of the world. In the Madang region it was affirmed, by variously correlating a celebrated myth of the unequal brothers with Christian ideas and foreign lands, that the center of power had shifted to Australia, to Sydney in particular (or Heaven above Sydney), where western commercial goods were made. Manam Islanders saw themselves living on the opposite side of the world from the whites within a rather complex modern cosmos; and they located the "unknown land," which holds the mysteries of life, beyond the German and English abodes. At the same time, highlanders as well as seaboard dwellers reinvested the influential recent ancestors and their abode with new significance in a changed world, and they sought to obtain for themselves the allegedly efficient ways whites had of extracting the riches from indigenous graveyards. With the colonial pacification and community-development programs after World War II, the perception of power centers on Papua New Guinea's own soil grew. Take the Gebusi case: the presence of colonial officialdom induced a change from their previous feeling of dependency on the upstream-living Bedamini to a downstream one, located at the administrative offices. This particular change is supported by visions of a downstream and underground source of wealth.

Inland populations had much of their early experience with the outside world through migrant employment, as did the Huli of Southern Highland Province from the 1950s on. They used the term *nambis* (Tok Pisin for seaboard) as their general spatial metaphor for dealing with all foreign people (including state authority), modern technology, and commodity – these being peripheral to their own power and land. The gold discovery in the 1980s at Mt. Kare gave adjacent landholders like the Huli access to surface and alluvial gold, and the idea emerged that the mythical snake under this mountain sheds her skin as gold. Arising from a high incidence of illness on the gold-fields, the Huli came to connect gold to their all-pervasive idea that pollution was traditionally associated with women, and they now took the handling of gold to be polluting. Mt. Kare as an established sacred site fitted as a microcosm the metaphor of *nambis* because of the Huli's lack of control over access to gold, thus providing evidence for the concept of disempowerment through land development. We see, then, that rapid socio-religious change has produced varied adjustments in Papua New Guinea in terms of approaches to religion, nature, and the environment.

Friedegard Tomasetti

Further Reading

Bergmann, Wilhelm. *The Kumanuku (The Culture of the Chimbu Tribes)*. Harrisville: self-published, 1971 (4 vols).

Burridge, Kenelm. *Mambu: A Melanesian Millennium*. New York: Harper, 1970.

Clark, Jeffrey. "Gold, Sex, and Pollution: Male Illness and Myth at Mt. Kare, Papua New Guinea." *American Ethnologist* 20:4 (1993), 742–57.

Gillison, Gillian. *Between Culture and Fantasy: A New Guinea Highlands Mythology*. Chicago: University of Chicago Press, 1993.

Kahn, Miriam. "Sunday Christians, Monday Sorcerers: Selective Adaptation to Missionization in Wamira." *Journal of Pacific History* 18:2 (1983), 96–112.

Knauft, Bruce. "How the World Turns Upside Down: Changing Geographies of Power and Spiritual Influence among the Gebusi." In Lawrence Goldman and Chris Ballard, eds. *Fluid Ontologies: Myth, Ritual, and Philosophy in the Highlands of Papua New Guinea*. Westport, CN: Bergin and Garvey, 1998, 143–61.

Lawrence, Peter. *Road Belong Cargo: A Study in the Cargo Movement of the Southern Madang District New Guinea*. Melbourne: Melbourne University Press, 1964.

Mantovani, Ennio. "Mipela Simbu! The Pig-Festival and Simbu Identity." In Victor Hayes, ed. *Identity Issues and World Religions*. Bedford Park: Australian Association for the Study of Religion, 1986, 194–203.

Trompf, Garry W. *Melanesian Religion*. Cambridge: Cambridge University Press, 1991.

Waiko, John D. "Na Binandere, Imo Averi? We are Binandere, Who are You?" *Pacific Viewpoint* 26:1 (1985), 9–29.

Wassmann, Jürg. "Worlds in Mind: The Experience of an Outside World in a Community of the Finisterre Range of Papua New Guinea." *Oceania* 64:2 (1993), 117–45.

Weiner, James. *The Empty Place: Poetry, Space and Being among the Foi of Papua New Guinea*. Bloomington, IN: Indiana University Press, 1991.

See also: Manser, Bruno – and the Penan of Sarawak; Melanesian Traditions; Penan Hunter-Gatherers (Borneo).

Parliament of the World's Religions

"We condemn the abuses of the Earth's ecosystems," states the Declaration of a Global Ethic issued by the 1993 Parliament of the World's Religions [POWR]. The Declaration went on to declare respect for "the community of living beings, for people, animals and plants, and for the preservation of Earth, the air, water and soil." Nearly all of the religious leaders present at the POWR endorsed the Declaration, drafted by Catholic theologian Hans Kung. The 1993 Parliament brought spiritual leaders from many traditions to Chicago for nine days of discussion, debate, and rituals designed to address the ethical challenges of a globalizing world. The event was organized by the Council for a Parliament of the World's Religions [CPWR], founded in 1988 by monks from Chicago's Vedanta Society with the purpose of marking the centennial of the 1893 World Parliament of Religions.

The 1893 Parliament is widely recognized as the inaugural event of the modern interfaith movement. An auxiliary congress of the Chicago Columbian Exposition of 1893, the Parliament offered a spectacle of interfaith cooperation as spiritual leaders of many of the world's traditions represented their faiths to a curious audience of

North Americans. Numbering among the speakers were Buddhists and Hindus from abroad as well as Catholics, Jews, and a variety of Protestants from the United States. The Parliament's Anglo-American organizers hoped the event would demonstrate the compatibility of the world's great religions, yet the event was not without conflict. Some Asian delegates used the occasion to denounce Christianity's exclusivist claims and the Church's complicity in colonial and imperial ventures.

The 1993 POWR drew around 7000 delegates interested in exploring spiritual responses to violence, war, economic, and ecological crises. Among the sessions dealing with ecological concerns was "Cosmic Beginnings and Human Ends," a symposium on science and religion that included biologists Lynn Margulis and Michael Dolan on the Gaia hypothesis and theologian Mary Hunt, who offered feminism as a bridge in discussions between theology and science. Other sessions featured Jay McDaniel on the dialogue between Buddhism and Native American traditions; Mary Evelyn Tucker, John Grim, and Stephanie Kaza and McDaniel on Worldviews and Ecology; Charlene Spretnak and Finley Schaef of the North American Conference on Christianity and Ecology, which organized several sessions, on eco-communities; Thomas Berry and Schaef on Ritual in an Ecological Age, as well as sessions on lifestyle and consumption, women and the Earth, theological education, and religious institutions as Creation Awareness Centers.

Organizers of the 1893 Parliament excluded Native Americans and representatives of African tribal traditions, and there were no official delegates from New Thought or other marginalized American religious groups. By contrast, the 1993 Parliament was far more expansive in its embrace of religious diversity. In addition to representatives of the major world religious traditions, there was a large and influential contingent of Earth-centered traditions, including indigenous people and neo-pagans. The Parliament was "the coming-out party for Pagans and Witches into the community of the world's religions," in the words of Andras Corban Arthen, director of the New England EarthSpirit Community. The Church of All Worlds, The Wiccan Covenant of the Goddess, and a variety of Druids played an important role in the Parliament's consideration of ecological issues. Neo-pagans sponsored a Full Moon ritual during the Parliament, attended by over 500 delegates and other observers. The influence of Earth-centered traditions also extended to the "Parliament of the People," a group that met outside the Parliament's formal sessions to discuss strategies for ushering in a new age of harmony and cooperation between spiritual traditions.

The 1993 POWR was not without conflict as Hans Kung and others insisted the Declaration was not an attempt to create a uniform world religion or a moral ideology to be imposed upon the people of the worlds. Rather, it was an effort to discover and identify "a common set of core values" that its signatories believe lie at the heart of every religious tradition. The CPWR plans to reconvene Parliaments of Religion roughly every five years. Subsequent ones were held in Cape Town, South Africa, in 1999 and Barcelona, Spain in 2004. In Barcelona, special attention was focused on water, one of the world's greatest environmental challenges, and strong efforts were made to enlist support for the Earth Charter, in the hopes that CPWR could help to promote it to the United Nations.

J. Terry Todd

Further Reading
Kung, Hans, ed. *Yes to a Global Ethic*. London: SCM Press, 1996.
Matthews, Clifford N. and Roy Abraham Varghese, eds. *Cosmic Beginnings and Human Ends: Where Science and Religion Meet*. Chicago: Open Court Press, 1994.
Teasdale, Wayne and George F. Cairns, eds. *The Community of Religions: Voices and Images of the Parliament of the World's Religions*. New York: Continuum, 1996.

See also: Earth Charter; Gaia; Gaian Pilgrimage; Lovelock, James; North American Conference on Christianity and Ecology [and the] North American Coalition on Religion and Ecology; Paganism (various); Religious Studies and Environmental Concern; United Nations' "Earth Summits"; Wicca.

Pauli, Wolfgang (1900–1958)

Among the most distinguished physicists of the twentieth century, Wolfgang Pauli, winner of the Nobel Prize in 1945, deserves special attention, because his thinking on the interface of natural sciences, philosophy, and psychology very much stimulated later generations. Astonishingly enough, his work is not as appreciated as that of his colleagues, Einstein, Heisenberg, or Bohr. It is only recently – especially in the context of "New Age science" and discussions about holism and religious dimensions of science – that Pauli has been rediscovered.

Quantum mechanics has far-reaching implications on the concept of nature. It refutes the Newtonian paradigm of determinism, causality, and objectivity. Contrasting Bohr and Einstein, who both tended to underrate the revolutionary consequences of quantum mechanics, Pauli was fully aware of the fact that now the observer played a significant role in every experiment. Empirically discernible reality is dependent on the observer's place and subjective condition. Thus, the freedom of the observing person implies that the human psyche cannot be separated from the physical image of the world. Pauli was radical in his conclusions and argued that there is no objective reality. Instead, reality consists of rational and irrational elements. Not everything, therefore, can be explained with rational theories. That the physical world is not fully determined and not even necessarily built on causal relations, Pauli proved with his famous *Pauli Principle*, which says that the distribution of an atom's electrons (i.e., their mutual exclusion) is always *a-causal*. From here it is but one step to today's "chaos theory."

The metaphysical dimension is an integral element of physics itself. In a letter to Markus Fierz, Pauli wrote in 1952 that the singularity of the experiment and its non-determinacy is a return of the *anima mundi* ("soul of the world"), which had been forced away in the seventeenth century. This notion already hints at the intriguing dialogue Pauli had with Carl Gustav Jung. Besides the alchemical connotations of modern science, it was the concept Jung called "synchronicity" that was a major topic of their conversations. It became part of a book they published together in 1952. While the psychologist referred to synchronicity as "a-causal parallels" or "symbolic coincidences," the physicist explained the same phenomena with the doctrines of quantum mechanics. What both scholars shared was the conviction that matter and mind are by no means separate domains.

Pauli's impact on contemporary Western nature discourse has been indirect. His ideas were popularized by C.G. Jung, F. David Peat and others who laid special emphasis on the unity of mind and matter or, subsequently, of the human and the cosmos. In so doing, these ideas have been utilized in order to sacralize both nature and the human soul.

Kocku von Stuckrad

Further Reading

Laurikainen, Kalervo Vihtori and C. Montonen, eds. *The Copenhagen Interpretation and Wolfgang Pauli (Symposia on the Foundations of Modern Physics 1992, Helsinki, Finland June–August 1992)*. Singapore: World Scientific, 1993.

Laurikainen, Kalervo Vihtori. *The Philosophical Thought of Wolfgang Pauli*. Berlin: Springer, 1988.

Pauli, Wolfgang. *Writings on Physics and Philosophy*. Charles P. Enz and Karl von Meyenn, eds. Berlin: Springer, 1994.

See also: Chaos; Complexity Theory; Jung, Carl Gustav; New Age; Peat, F. David.

Payutto, Phra Dhammapitaka (1939–)

Acknowledged to be one of the leading scholar-monks in contemporary Thailand, P.A. Payutto whose current monastic title, Dhammapitaka, was conferred in 1993, was ordained at the age of eleven in 1950. Only one of four novice monks to pass the ninth and highest level of the *sangha* Pali curriculum since its inception, he received higher ordination and the monastic name, Phra Maha Prayudh Payutto in 1961. He graduated with first-class honors from Mahachulalongkorn Buddhist University, and later served as its deputy secretary-general as well as abbot of Phra Phirain monastery in Bangkok. His major contributions to the scholarly study of Buddhism include two Pali dictionaries, editorial leadership in the newest edition of the Thai Pali canon and the Mahidol University CD-ROM Pali canon, and his magnum opus treatise, *Buddhadhamma: Natural Laws and Values for Life*. In addition, he has written extensively on a variety of subjects including Buddhist education, Buddhism and science, Buddhist economics, Buddhism and the environment, as well as Buddhist doctrinal topics. For his outstanding contribution to Buddhist scholarship and education, he has received several honorary doctorates and in 1994 was awarded the UNESCO Peace Education Prize.

In the early 1990s, Payutto addressed the question of the relationship between the Buddhist *sangha* (community of monks) and forests in reaction to what he saw as an excessively political response by some monks to extensive deforestation in northern Thailand and the encroachment by government and private enterprise on traditional village forest management in the northeast. In these talks that were later printed as essays, Payutto makes a case for forest preservation on the grounds of the example of the life and teachings of the Buddha, the traditions of early Buddhist monastic practice, and the development of Buddhism in Thai history. He bases his position on the doctrinal view that overcoming mental defilements (*kilesa*), one of the central teachings of Theravada Buddhism, requires separation (*viveka*) from the confusions, anxieties, and stresses of the getting-and-spending world that typify much of our lives; and, that during the time of the Buddha the forest was the preferred environment for the solitude required for achieving this state of mind. From a historical perspective, he argues that beginning with the thirteenth-century Thai kingdoms, forest monasteries have been essential to the organization and practice of Buddhism in Thailand. Consequently, for the government not to support forest monasteries would contradict a practice that has defined Thai Buddhism from its early beginnings.

Unlike some Buddhists who consider such philosophical concepts as dependent co-arising (*paticca samuppada*) and universal Buddha-nature (*dhammadhatu*) to provide a biocentric ecological argument for the preservation and conservation of nature, Payutto supports a more human-centered position that values the forest, or nature more broadly construed, as the ideal venue for the pursuit of Buddhist spiritual goals and moral values. He offers both doctrinal and historical justifications for his position, arguing that from a Buddhist perspective forest preservation rests on a religious rather than an ecological basis. It is a position that supports conservation on the grounds than an unspoiled natural environment best promotes Buddhist spirituality and has always held a prominent place within monastic traditions. At the same time, however, his position problematizes the activist role of Thai conservation monks who have politicized the role of the *sangha* in Thai society. Implied in Payutto's position, which relies upon a religious and historical justification for conserving natural environments like forests, is a critique of politically active monks who, in his opinion, jeopardize the spiritual goal of Buddhist practice.

In contrast to the close interrelationship between the human community and nature in the Buddhist tradition, Payutto ascribes modern global environmental destruction to the dominant Western worldview – flawed, in his view, by three erroneous beliefs: that humankind is separated from nature, that human beings are masters of nature, and that happiness results from the acquisition of material goods. For Payutto, conservation and preservation of the natural environment cannot be achieved simply by more astute public policy and better enforcement of conservation laws, but only by demanding a paradigm shift: an ethical transformation not only of the prevailing attitude toward nature, but also toward our fellow human beings and our personal life-objective. Advancing the Buddhist position that right view leads to right action, Payutto contends that until the right view prevails and human beings are seen as part of nature, the worldwide trend toward environmental degradation will continue.

Payutto regards three Buddhist ethical values as central to a more positive environmental philosophy. These include the teachings of *gratitude and loving-kindness* which acknowledge all sentient beings as bound together in a mutual and universal process of birth, old age, suffering, and death. This *empathetic sense of mutuality promotes cooperative and helpful actions* rather than competition and hostility. Furthermore, Buddhism teaches that *human happiness depends on the natural environment*. First, nature engenders in us a sense of happiness and well-being; and, second, by carefully observing the processes of nature we are enabled to grow in mental concentration, attentive awareness, and ethical wisdom.

Donald K. Swearer

Further Reading

Payutto, Phra Prayudh. *Buddhadhamma: Natural Laws and Values for Life*. Grant A. Olson, tr. Albany: State University of New York Press, 1995.

Payutto, Phra Prayudh. *Buddhist Solutions for the Twenty-first Century*. Bangkok: Buddhadhamma Foundation, 1995.

Swearer, Donald K. "The Hermeneutics of Buddhist Ecology in Contemporary Thailand: Buddhadasa and Dhammapitaka." In Mary Ellen Tucker and Duncan Williams, eds. *Buddhism and Ecology*. Cambridge: Harvard University Press, 1997.

See also: Buddhism – Engaged; Siam's Forest Monasteries; Sivaraksa, Sulak; Thai Buddhist Monks.

Peat, F. David (1938–)

In many publications, F. David Peat contributed enormously to the popularization of theoretical issues of quantum mechanics and modern science. His thinking is very much influenced by David Bohm, but also reveals the imprint of Ilya Prigogine's and Rupert Sheldrake's holistic theories. Most recognized is his metaphysical expansion of the concept of *synchronicity* that was first introduced by physicist Wolfgang Pauli and psychologist C.G. Jung. This model makes use of the indeterminacy and simultaneity of phenomena as described in quantum mechanics. Peat, for his part, does not restrict himself to the holistic implications of synchronicity but elaborates a full-blown spiritual and metaphysical view of nature and reality, which is both imaginative and speculative. As a result, Peat expects a coming transformation of man and society that will lead to a new integration of matter and mind, of nature and human beings.

Kocku von Stuckrad

Further Reading

Bohm, David and F. David Peat. *Science, Order, and Creativity*. Toronto.: Bantam Books, 1987.

Briggs, John P. and F. David Peat. *Looking Glass Universe: The Emerging Science of Wholeness*. New York: Simon & Schuster, 1984.

Peat, F. David. *Synchronicity: The Bridge between Matter and Mind*. Toronto: Bantam Books, 1987.

See also: Chaos; Complexity Theory; Holism; New Age; Prigogine, Ilya; Sheldrake, Rupert.

Penan Hunter-gatherers of Borneo

The equatorial island of Borneo is characterized by a remarkable degree of cultural and economic diversity – from the material opulence of Brunei Darussalam's royal family to the traditional farming and foraging peoples that occupy much of the island's vast interior. These latter subsistence societies, once infamous for their headhunting raids, are divided roughly between nomadic hunter-gatherers and settled swidden (shifting, slash-and-burn) agriculturalists. Cultivators are mostly concentrated along the main rivers, whereas foraging groups inhabit hilly, interfluvial zones. Forest farmers, such as the Iban, Kayan, Kenyah, and many others, live in traditional longhouses.

Their agriculture focuses on hill rice cultivation supplemented by snare hunting and fishing. Hunter-gathering societies, on the other hand, usually referred to as Penan or Punan, concentrate(d) their efforts on blowpipe and spear hunting of bearded pigs (*Sus barbatus*) and other forest game, as well as the preparation of sago starch from *nangah* (*Eugeissona utilis*), a wild, clump-forming palm. Because both types of subsistence groups collect a variety of non-timber forest products for food, fiber, and medicine, and because some Penan engage in occasional crop cultivation, strict division between one mode of subsistence and another can be arbitrary.

The Penan inhabit the interior regions of the island, reaching to the coast only in East Kalimantan, Indonesia. They are believed to consist of two disjunct populations – the Eastern and Western Penan. Distributed in Sarawak in East Malaysia, Kalimantan in Indonesia, and Brunei Darussalam, these two sub-groups exhibit distinct differences in language, group size, foraging range, nomadic characteristics, and degree of social organization. Both sub-groups of Penan are undergoing many of the sociocultural changes that are affecting other indigenous societies in Borneo, including accepting wage-earning employment, intermarrying with non-Penan cultivating groups, absorbing lexical elements from nearby settled groups, and converting to Islam or Christianity. Many distinctive Penan cultural elements are either being or have already been abandoned, including living in huts, men wearing loincloths, men with distended earlobes, use of penis pins, and plucked eyelashes and brows. There are probably less than 10,000 ethnically distinct Penan remaining, and less than 1000 living as nomadic forest foragers.

The cosmology of the Penan is surprisingly generic and poorly defined, at least compared with that of neighboring, small-scale agriculturalists. Some groups report the existence of a high god named Peselong, as well as a pantheon of lesser deities. For many other Penan, however, the concept of a high god does not exist. Rather, the spiritual universe is perceived to be populated by ill-defined animist spirits, ghost-like entities that constitute the non-material essence of animate and inanimate beings and objects. There is no particular hierarchy or order of importance to the spirit realm. Some entities, however, perhaps by virtue of their inherent salience or perceived power over the lives of the Penan, are afforded more respect. These include, for example, Baléi Liwen, the lightning and thunder spirit. Because bad weather is probably the greatest impediment to hunting success and is perceived to be a source of illness, this entity is the most frequent recipient of offerings, including in the past blood sacrifice. Baléi Tepun, the tiger or leopard spirit, stands out because it represents the fiercest predator in the local forests. Baléi Berungan, the rainbow spirit, is associated with the spirits of the dead. There is also a Baléi Ja'au, the giant or monster spirit, which is not exactly malevolent, but is generally threatening because of its size.

Beyond the named spirits, all natural entities in the Penan's tropical forest world – trees, mammals, birds, physical features, and humans – are believed to possess a spiritual essence. Even the Penan's traditional material possessions, such as blowpipes and sleeping mats, are seen to embody the spirit of the tree or rattan from which they were fashioned. Only recent additions to their material culture, such as longboats, longhouses, and other adopted goods from sedentary farming groups, are lacking a spiritual existence.

Humans are believed to possess three distinct souls (*sahe*) or spirits – one in the pupils of the eyes, one in the hair, and one in the trunk of the body. When a person dies, the three *sahe* make the journey to the afterworld, an unspecified region where the souls of the dead reside. The afterworld is seen as an other-worldly refuge from hunger and sickness, a forager's paradise with the promise of abundant food and reliable hunting. To assist in these activities, the Penan are buried with a few important possessions, including a blowpipe, poison darts, and a small quantity of food.

Like many other traditional societies, the Penan ascribe many of their health problems to disturbed relations with the non-material world. Whether spirits are the harbinger of good or bad luck to the lives of the Penan depends to a certain degree on their ability to maintain a state of equilibrium with the spiritual realm. Although spirits by their nature are neither benevolent nor malevolent, each has the power of retribution if offended or not properly propitiated. Taboo violation, in principle, represents one such spiritual offense. Women, for example, are prohibited from consuming reticulated python during pregnancy, as to do so might lead to health problems. However, the Penan are actually quite flexible in terms of food acceptance, certainly compared to neighboring groups, and very few wild foods are tabooed. In any case, food taboos are neither strictly adhered to nor rigidly enforced.

The Penan, like other Bornean peoples, attribute good and bad luck to the activities of certain omen birds. Species such as *pengiyuh ngereah*, the red-naped trogon, is seen to bring bad luck if it is seen or heard to fly from right to left across a person's path. The person should abandon what he or she is doing and return to the camp immediately. The same is true for good-luck birds, such as *pengiyu buah* (orange-breasted trogon), which portends good fortune when it flies across a person's path from right to left.

Divination and other means of spiritual revelation appear to be poorly developed among the Penan. The use of shamanism and the specialized role of a shaman-healer are not known at present. Neither are trance or spirit possession as a means of communicating with the spiritual realm presently employed. Whether this was true in the past, or is a product of cultural erosion, is not clear. The

Penan do recognize the existence of people with the ability to receive dream messages during sleep. These are not drug-enhanced experiences, as the Penan appear to be wholly ignorant of any mind-altering, psychoactive plants. Rather, these are simply prophetic dreams that suggest to the "dream reader" the nature of a problem, often health or hunting related, and a possible solution. Any person in the group, male or female, might possess this ability. He or she is said to be born with this capacity, having been selected by the spirit world as a conduit of useful information. There is no apprenticeship or initiation into the role; nor is there any particular status associated with the position.

As one of the last surviving tropical forest hunter-gatherer groups, the Penan have been the subject of considerable speculation regarding their relations with nature. For example, the long-held notion that the Penan are descendants of the island's original forest nomads has recently fallen out of favor. The prevailing view is now that foraging societies in these and other moist tropical landscapes have always been culturally and materially dependent on the presence of agricultural groups. Based on the assumption that the carrying capacity of tropical forests was never sufficient to sustain a purely hunting-and-gathering lifestyle, the Penan's foraging mode of subsistence is believed to have developed only after cultivating societies were present on the island.

There have been many anecdotal accounts of the Penan's superlative knowledge of the plant kingdom. Indeed, because the ability to recognize, cognitively classify, utilize, and manipulate plant species was prerequisite to group subsistence and survival, it follows that the Penan, whose livelihoods depend completely on their knowledge of the forest, should maintain a profound knowledge of their primary forest habitats. Nevertheless, it now appears that several factors served to limit the Penan's quantitative knowledge of the plant world. For example, because their migratory way of life allowed for few material possessions, the Penan did not develop a deep lexical understanding of timber species, for which they had little use. Likewise, because their low population density translated to a relatively disease-free environment, the Penan failed to develop the kind of deep understanding of the rainforest pharmacopoeia exhibited by their cultivating neighbors. Overall, the breadth of Penan ethnobotanical knowledge, as indicated by number of named taxa and perceived useful species, is several times less than that of small-scale farming groups. This surprisingly shallow knowledge of most plant species, however, is compensated for by "substantive knowledge" of those few wild resources essential to their foraging mode of subsistence.

The concept that most defines the Penan's relationship with nature is *molong*. This philosophy addresses both the necessity of sharing within the group and the need for conservation of a limited resource base. Indeed, much of the Penan ethic is contained in the often-repeated phrase *mai belabih*, meaning "don't be greedy." For a society whose survival depends so intimately on the providence of the forest, inappropriate means and levels of resource exploitation have obvious direct consequences for all. *Molong* is closely associated with management of the native sago palm, the Penans' starch staple. Although not planted, wild sago is carefully husbanded in order to achieve maximum long-term yield. Older stems are harvested and processed, but the younger stems, *uvud*, are marked and protected for future exploitation. To harvest sago unsustainably would be greedy and reckless, and it would threaten the material survival of the group. It would also represent an offense to the spirits of the forest, upon whose beneficence the Penan likewise depend.

Robert Voeks

Further Reading
Brosius, Peter. "Foraging in Tropical Forests: the Case of the Penan of Sarawak, East Malaysia." *Human Ecology* 19 (1991), 123–50.
Cleary, Mark and Peter Eaton. *Borneo: Change and Development*. Singapore: Oxford University Press, 1992.
Hoffman, Carl. *The Punan: Hunters and Gatherers of Borneo*. Ann Arbor: UMI Research Press, 1983.
Rousseau, Jerome. *Central Borneo: Ethnic Identity and Social Life in a Stratified Society*. Oxford: Clarendon Press, 1990.
Voeks, Robert A. and Peter Sercombe. "The Scope of Hunter-Gatherer Ethnomedicine." *Social Science & Medicine* 50 (2000), 1–12.
Voeks, Robert A. "Environmental Risk and Ethnobotanical Knowledge: Foragers and Farmers in Northern Borneo." In Karl Zimmerer and Kenneth Young eds. *Nature's Geography: New Lessons for Conservation in Developing Countries*. Madison: University of Wisconsin Press, 1998, 307–26.

See also: Ethnobotany; Manser, Bruno – and the Penan of Sarawak; Pacific Islands; Papua New Guinea.

Perelandra

Perelandra is a nature research center in Jeffersonton, Virginia, founded by Machaelle Small Wright in 1977. Named after the book with the same name by C.S. Lewis and similar in spiritual orientation to the Findhorn Community in Scotland, Perelandra is best known for its garden. In maintaining the garden, as well as in developing flower essences and other health aids, Wright practices a "co-creative science" in which she learns from the energetic intelligence of nature how to achieve the natural balance that enables living things to grow and thrive.

Situated within the broad Theosophical lineage, co-creative science involves communicating with the devas, or the "architects," and nature spirits or the "builders," associated with particular plants, animals, and places to discover, for example, what to plant, where and when as well as how to deal with problems such as insect infestations, depleted soil conditions, and other ecological imbalances.

On a larger scale, Wright seeks to make Perelandra a model of environmentally responsible human behavior. In the 1997 edition of her book *Behaving as if the God in All Life Mattered*, Wright wrote that, if humans are to heal the Earth of the damage we have done, we need to be open to "the reality of energy behind form and the consciousness contained in that energy" (1997: 224). The work at Perelandra shows that healing nature does not mean human withdrawal from nature, but rather, conscious pursuit of what Wright calls the Involution/Evolution Balance between what nature provides, on one hand, and human purpose and direction, on the other.

Jan C. Dawson

Further Reading
Nicholson, Shirley and Brenda Rosen. *Gaia's Hidden Life: The Unseen Intelligence of Nature*. Wheaton, IL: Quest Books, 1992.
Wright, Machaelle Small. *Co-Creative Science. A Revolution in Science Providing Real Solutions for Today's Health and Environment*. Warrenton, VA: Perelandra, Ltd., 1997.
Wright, Machaelle Small. *Behaving as if the God in All Life Mattered*. Warrenton, VA: Perelandra, Ltd., 1997.
See also: Findhorn Foundation/Community (Scotland).

Perennial Philosophy

The key idea in perennial philosophy is that behind all the diversity of human thought a perennial truth is discernible and is preserved and transmitted in the various mystical-contemplative teachings and practices that are the energizing core of the several great religious traditions. Perennialist metaphysics claims that behind the seemingly infinite variety of phenomena is one divine spirit that manifests itself hierarchically and over time expresses every possibility. Perennial truth is about that one underlying reality. The human "organ" through which the transcendent truth of the unity of all being in its infinite diversity is discerned is the intellect (what Ken Wilber calls "the eye of Spirit") and is itself divine. Our human consciousness, then, is divine at its source, a source to which we can return with successful training on an esoteric path.

Since there is one underlying sacred, even divine, reality, all of nature is divine, sacred, and holy, manifesting itself in its appropriate position in the hierarchical "great chain of being." Nature's worth infinitely exceeds its monetary or utilitarian values. Modernity denies that perennial truth, which is a spiritual flaw, and our ecological crisis, say perennialists, is the result of that spiritual flaw.

At the level of surface structure, the conceptual frameworks used to articulate perennial philosophy vary. The influence of Platonic or neo-Platonic, Aristotelian or Thomist, Advaita or Madhyamika, or even Hegelian sources is prominent in one or another version. The starting points are revelation and metaphysical insight. The perennial philosopher typically intuits a cosmos emanated into many grades of being or created in multiple ontological levels arranged on a hierarchical scale downward from what might imperfectly be termed the Most Perfect Being (*ens perfectissimum*), or That One (*tad ekam* in the Rig Veda), or simply the One. Perennialists favor mystically grounded metaphysics to articulate perennial wisdom. One task of a perennial philosophy is to understand the immense variety of beings, including nature, in their place in this all-encompassing ontological hierarchy. The counterpoint is to be able to discern the One behind the veils of each phenomenon. Divine intellect grasps the divinity of all beings within all the gradations of being. That is, when our minds have become sufficiently transparent for the One to come through as divine intellect, we can see with that Eye of Spirit, the ultimate One-ness of all being in its graded diversity of manifestation.

Perennialism affirms an originating conscious unity that is prior to all distinctions, to all "saying," and which can be perceived in all of its hierarchically organized levels of being only by intellect. Historian of ideas Arthur Lovejoy reviewed the uses of this kind of cosmogonic model in the West in his classic study *The Great Chain of Being* (1938). This narrative of origins is to be contrasted with the modern scientific notion of a Big Bang which explains the evolution of the physical universe and, finally, results in the emergence of life and awareness on this planet. For perennialists, who reject Darwin's narrative of evolution since more cannot come from less, the purest consciousness is present at the beginning and its pristine truth is transmitted at the origins of human religions. The inherent sacrality of all nature is a key constituent of that truth.

The History of the Idea of a Perennial Philosophy

Three instances of the idea of a perennial philosophy have been particularly influential. The first and earliest known use of the term was in the Latin title (*De perenni philosophia*) of a manuscript edited by Vatican librarian Augustinus Steuchus (1469–1549) and presented to Pope Paul III in about 1540. It was an anthology of extracts from works of Classical thinkers selected to confirm the truth of Christian teachings. The second was in a letter of

1714 from Gottfried Leibniz (1646–1716) to Remond de Montmort. Leibniz aspired to a method of analysis that could distinguish the diamond light of truth from the dross and that would yield something like a perennial philosophy (*perennis quaedam philosophia*). After Leibniz the term fell out of use due to the rise of experimental sciences that proceed from different assumptions about how to obtain reliable knowledge. It reappeared in the twentieth century in another anthology, *The Perennial Philosophy* (1945) edited by Aldous Huxley (1894–1963). This third instance represents the term as referring to the highest common factor among traditional doctrines and as reflecting a set of convergent insights gleaned from the world's great mystics who experienced the ultimate and attempted the impossible – to speak of it.

Perennialism Today
Within the context of the current ecological crisis, contemporary perennial philosophy has much more to say about nature and ecology than earlier sources do. Contemporary perennialism has two tracks, Traditionalist Perennialism represented by Rene Guenon, Frithjof Schuon, Huston Smith, and Seyyed Hossein Nasr, and neo-Perennialism represented most effectively by transpersonal theorist Ken Wilber. All of them agree that modernity in its reductive scientism has blinded us to the inherent sacredness of nature, a belief also held by deep ecologists. Neo-Perennialist Wilber, however, argues that deep ecologists are as reductive as the modernity they criticize.

Contemporary perennial philosophers make clear that the perennial truth is not a concept built up by induction after gathering and comparing the doctrines of the different religious traditions and reports of the experiences of their great mystics. Instead it is intuited directly through divine intellect. This is why the Traditionalist School prefers the specific term perennial wisdom (*sophia perennis*) to the generic term perennial philosophy – in order to place emphasis on the distinctive capacity of the human being for transcendental wisdom. In essence the human is distinguished by intellect which is the presence of divinity within each human being waiting to be uncovered. It is distinct from reason and affords discernment or knowledge of the sacred unity of reality that is attested in all authentic esoteric expressions of tradition.

The historian of religion Huston Smith interprets the world's major religions as great wisdom traditions that preserve both the popular (exoteric) and the virtuoso or spiritual elite (esoteric) versions of a single primordial truth. It is on the revelation of that primordial truth that each tradition is based. The only way for one to approach that single primordial truth is to enter into the orthodox disciplines, practices, and doctrines of one or another of those authentic traditions. Smith was born in China where his parents served as Methodist missionaries, and he first came to the United States for higher education. He remained for a university teaching career during which he also apprenticed himself to a Vedantic Hindu monk, then to a Zen Buddhist roshi, and finally was initiated into the lineage of Sufi Muslim sheikh and perennial philosopher Frithjof Schuon.

Seyyed Hossein Nasr is the most important contemporary representative of the Schuon (or Traditionalist) lineage for issues concerning religion and nature. An Iranian-born Islamic philosopher with Sufi training, he studied at MIT and at Harvard where he received a Ph.D. in the history of science with a thesis on Islamic cosmology in 1958. He recently completed a distinguished career as University Professor at George Washington University where he taught perennial philosophy, history of Islamic science, and philosophy of science. He has produced a number of publications resulting from his concern about the environmental crisis. Notable among them are *The Encounter of Man and Nature* (1968) and *Religion and the Order of Nature* (1996).

Neo-Perennialist Ken Wilber is an independent scholar and a prolific writer who represents an orientation within perennial philosophy that differs from the Traditionalist approach of the Schuon lineage, one that is "evolutionary" rather than "devolutionary." Wilber attributes potentially positive value to scientific, technological, and cultural innovation. Moreover, he agrees with Max Weber that the modern differentiation of the spheres of arts, morality (which includes religion) and science has given conceptual space for the emergence of core modern values of equality, freedom and justice, democracy, gender equality, separation of Church and state, etc.

Traditionalists do not endorse Wilber's assumption that the history of human consciousness is evolutionary but do share the same basic analysis that a spiritual failure is the crucial component of the environmental crisis. For Nasr, modernity renders us insensible to the sacrality of all nature by its exclusive focus on reason to the exclusion of intellect or "the eye of Spirit" which has as its field transpersonal and metaphysical realities. When the transcendent dimensions of being are denied, nature becomes a commodity with only utilitarian worth, no longer a divine manifestation of intrinsic value. Nasr regards the reign of quantity effected by the absolutizing of materialist science as an utter catastrophe. This modern idolatry of science and technology is accompanied by an idolatry of the mind, especially reason, which leads to idolization of everything human, with the unwarranted conclusion that all of the planet exists simply as a set of resources to be used for the fulfillment of any human desire.

For Wilber, who sees the scientific enterprise as a necessary stage in the evolution of consciousness, the extremes of scientism are seen as a distortion of important aspects of modernity that should not divert us from the important gains of modernity in the evolution of consciousness. In psychological terms, scientism is a symptom of a kind of dissociation that is particularly associated with modernity, and the current ecological crisis is its inevitable consequence.

The Perennialist Diagnosis of Modernity and the Ecological Crisis

Traditionalists claim that in the founders and prophets of the great religious traditions we find the full pristine flowering of human consciousness through all levels. Students of esoteric paths within their guardian exoteric traditions may be able to approximate the spiritual level of the founders and prophets, but as time passes the tradition tends to move away from its primordial source; time brings devolution. Modernity is the nadir where reality has become utterly distorted by the removal of spirit from the reality-map. Healing can happen only by a return to a pre-modern orthodoxy that preserves the wisdom born of intellect, a spiritual intuition that is superior to reason and without which reason is blind. Only rare individuals can accomplish this return, and then only from within a vital orthodox tradition. This is how the Traditionalists understand themselves and the larger crisis within which environmental disaster is an obvious symptom.

The Traditionalist picture of the origins of religion is mirrored metaphysically as the cosmos emergent by involution, the eternal One pouring into all levels of reality. The appropriate movement of creation is in the direction of a return to the Absolute. Human consciousness inherently is oriented toward evolution in this sense, in other words, the return to the One. The return has as its final stages the mystical journey that is practiced in the esoteric paths of authentic traditions. The metaphysical suicide, perpetrated by scientism, has resulted in the loss of access to perennial wisdom and has produced the current ecological disaster. Human consciousness, when reduced to reason and disconnected from its spiritual root and source in intellect, is the basis for a scientism that assumes that whatever the senses do not respond to cannot be real. Deep ecology also criticizes modernity and especially its scientism as invalidating the most profound experiences such as love, compassion, and mutual understanding.

Wilber's evolutionary perspective on the development of human consciousness distinguishes him from the Traditionalists. He acknowledges that modernity has brought many important gifts in the process of evolving human corporate consciousness, including our efforts to abolish human slavery, to achieve gender equality, and to break the power of the myths that justify cruelty and the subjugation of one group by another. On the other hand, he agrees with Traditionalists that the spectacular success of technology based on modern science has left us with a cosmology in which only matter really matters, where only what can be measured is regarded as real, where only the exteriors and observable behaviors are valued. Wilber calls this scientistic cosmology Flatland.

Traditionalist Perennialist and Neo-Perennialist Prescriptions

The way out of Flatland-thinking, according to Traditionalists, is to revive traditional religions and regain access to authentic paths to transcendence by recovering, retrieving, or recreating orthodoxies that do not allow a rogue scientific reason to judge and limit them. One thing that is not clear about the Traditionalist prescription is how the genuine gains in freedom, equal justice, etc., would be maintained if their ideological support in modernity were withdrawn. For Wilber the Traditionalist solution represents a regression.

Wilber acknowledges that deep ecologists are in touch with their spiritual hunger and that they correctly understand the ecological crisis as a spiritual crisis. But their resistance to seeing the hierarchical ordering of reality prevents them from understanding the uniqueness of human nature in relation to environments. Once consciousness evolved self-awareness, humans as a species took unprecedented control over their environment. Wilber characterizes eco-philosophies that view humans as just another ingredient in the ecosystem as dangerously naive retrograde romanticism. In a sense, human consciousness contains its ecosphere rather than being contained by it as simply part of the ecosystem. Uniquely, humans are capable of generating alternative conceptions of the ecosphere and then transforming the ecosystem on the basis of them. His assessment of anti-hierarchalism is that it is a dangerous denial of the reality of the cosmic process. It also denies the ultimate goal of humans to attain a return to the One through integration of deeper states of consciousness.

Traditionalists and Wilber would agree that denial of transcendence robs any ecological philosophy, including deep ecology, of sufficient depth. To make the inner transformations that would enable us to stop our self-destructive, even suicidal, corporate behavior would require an understanding of a greater range of ontological dimensions. In addition to what science can tell us about the external dynamics of the natural crisis with the eyes of flesh and mind, according to Wilber, we need to know what can be seen in profound introspection by means of the eye of Spirit.

Traditionalists believe that modernity has devolved rather than evolved, has moved us away from a sacralizing vision of God, humanity and nature that was natural to traditional and primordial cultures. Wilber, on the other hand, criticizes ecological thinkers who look to some earlier culture as the ideal, after which all went wrong. Ecofeminists look back to goddess-centered cultures, before the plow displaced women from their function in horticulture. Ecomasculinists look back to hunter-gatherer cultures. Wilber considers these nostalgias to be instances of the pre/trans fallacy (i.e., to mistake regression toward pre-personal developmental levels for growth toward transpersonal stages). Thus, from his "evolutionary" point of view, the Traditionalist School within perennial philosophy also looks back to less evolved cultures to solve problems of a relatively more evolved culture, and Wilber asserts it is no help to attempt a return to a culture where myth reigns, no matter how it might be symbolically reinterpreted today.

As one step toward the healing of modernity's dissociative consciousness, Wilber advocates a marriage of science and religion. But he means religion denuded of all the myths, dogmas and rituals that fail the truth tests of empiricism. He proposes a "perennial religion" comprised of essential truths held in common by the world's religious traditions. Traditionalists would point out that Wilber's "perennial religion" is limited by its dependence on an empirical search for common beliefs, doctrines, and transformative practices. They would doubt that it could succeed in the absence of discernment that proceeds from intellect and must inform any comparison among traditions that will properly value the distinctive importance of their myths, doctrines and rituals. Traditionalists are convinced that the return to orthodoxy and its esoteric paths is a necessary if not sufficient condition for attaining the level of consciousness at which human behavior could and would change with respect to nature and ecology.

Wilber, who rejects the myths and dogmas of orthodoxies as obstacles to the evolution of consciousness beyond modernity, claims that human consciousness must evolve beyond modernity in the same way that all evolution happens, by transcending and including the prior stages. To transcend modernity would be to include the best of modernity while healing the dissociations. He believes that can happen if humanity is guided by an adequate reality-map, which he claims to provide, and will use tools from traditional paths, which may no longer function as a whole for those who can no longer inhabit a traditional religious worldview, but nevertheless can serve as tools for transformation without the mythic, dogmatic accessories. Tools from transpersonal theory as well as a whole host of therapeutic modalities can be integrated in such a way as to replace the traditional paths that were so interwoven with the metanarratives of the traditions.

Some environmental activists criticize mystical approaches to the environmental crisis as other-worldly and useless, but they have yet to respond to the claim of perennial philosophers that every form of activism is based on metaphysical assumptions and that if the assumptions are inadequate, then the activism will be inadequate. For perennial philosophy, participation on a path of spiritual evolution is an absolute prerequisite to having access to the intellective vision that can enable discernment of the spiritual dimension and significance of the planet.

Shaya Isenberg
Gene Thursby

Further Reading
Bryant, M. Darroll. *Huston Smith: Essays on World Religion*. New York: Paragon House, 1992.
Ferrer, Jorge N. *Revisioning Transpersonal Theory: A Participatory Vision of Human Spirituality*. Albany: State University of New York Press, 2002.
Hahn, Lewis Edwin, Randall E. Auxter and Lucian W. Stone, Jr., eds. *The Philosophy of Seyyed Hossein Nasr*. Chicago: Open Court, 2001.
Huxley, Aldous. *The Perennial Philosophy*. New York: Harper & Row, 1945.
Isenberg, S.R. and G.R. Thursby. "Esoteric Anthropology: 'Devolutionary' and 'Evolutionary' Orientations in Perennial Philosophy." *Religious Traditions* 7–9 (1984–1986), 177–226.
Loemker, Leroy E. "Perennial Philosophy." *Dictionary of the History of Ideas; Studies of Selected Pivotal Ideas*. Philip P. Weiner, ed. New York: Charles Scribner's Sons, 1973:3: 457–63.
Wilber, Ken. *The Collected Works of Ken Wilber*, 8 vols. Boston: Shambhala, 1999–2000.

See also: California Institute of Integral Studies; Huxley, Aldous; Nasr, Seyyed Hossein; Transpersonal Psychology; Wilber, Ken.

Permaculture – *See* The Farm; Findhorn Foundation/Community (Scotland); Genesis Farm; Paganism in Australia; Radical Environmentalism; Re-Earthing; Steiner, Rudolf – and Anthroposophy; Urban Reinhabitation.

Peyote

When the Spanish conquistadors first arrived in what is now Mexico, they discovered that the native inhabitants attributed sacred qualities to three plants: a mushroom (*Teoanacatl*); a vine belonging to the Morning Glory family (*Ololuqui*); and a small, spineless cactus (*peyotl* or *Lophorora williamsii*). The Aztecs referred to the last of these, *peyotl* or peyote, as "the flesh of the gods." This carrot-looking cactus produces small "buttons" that contain at least nine alkaloids known to have psychoactive properties when ingested by humans in either their green or dried state. Together, these alkaloids (of which mescaline appears to have the most profound effects) induce an altered state typically characterized by initial nausea, general stimulation, inability to fix attention, and visual hallucinations – particularly kaleidoscopic displays of color.

Peyote has historically been ingested in structured, ceremonial settings. Although the precise meaning of peyote ceremonies varies from culture to culture, peyotism (the ritual ingestion of peyote) is thought to bring persons in touch with power – both natural and supernatural. First and foremost, peyote is regarded as a potent medicine. Tribal shamans use the power of peyote to divine the causes of illness. Shamans frequently have their patients ingest peyote to bring them the power necessary to effect a cure. Peyote has also been used to obtain visions and the supernatural power that comes from close connection with guardian spirits. Peyote-induced visions are also helpful for various forms of divination such as determining a prey's location, predicting the outcome of a battle, or finding lost objects. And, too, peyote is used to induce a trance that facilitates tribal dancing rites. Although the power obtained through peyote ceremonies can be put to many uses, it invariably reinforces social understandings of the ideal relationships between humans and both the natural and supernatural orders of life.

Peyote use has continued in many parts of Mexico up to the present day, most notably among the Huichol who live in the central Mexican states of Jalisco, Nayarit, Durango, and Zacatecas. The Huichol's ceremonial use of peyote begins with the "peyote hunt" for suitable plants. This is an annual pilgrimage under the strict direction of an experienced *mar'aakame*, or shaman, who has special relations with Hikuri, the Peyote-god. Rituals of confession and purification prepare pilgrims for the hunt. Throughout their quest they must be celibate and form a cohesive and classless community. Pilgrims must renounce all ego, pride, resentment, or hostility. The arduous trek (though in more recent times pilgrims travel in cars) to the ancestral regions where peyote is bountiful further prepares participants for their quest to forge closer relations with the spirit world. Under the *mar'aakame*'s direction, pilgrims collect peyote buttons and ritually ingest them in a fire-lit ceremony. The peyote elicits beautiful lights, vivid colors, and visions of peculiar animals. The meaning of these sensations is provided by the *mar'aakame* who integrates them into the layers of belief that comprise the Huichol worldview. The peyote experience is said to effect a total unification at every level, to kindle communal love, to bond persons to the way of their ancestors, and to give participants a direct experience of a spiritual realm that surrounds the everyday world. In this way Huichol peyote ceremonies structure a return to a mythic past of purity and spiritual power.

Peyote was rarely used north of the Rio Grande prior to 1890. But the forced segregation of Native Americans onto government reservations strained tribal cultures in a way that fostered the rapid spread of peyotism in the United States. Between 1890 and 1920 the use of peyote became more prevalent in the United States, but its meaning varied depending on the tribal context. In the Southwest, with the Mescalero Apache being the prime instance, peyotism remained fairly close to its Mexican roots. Shamans assumed responsibility for directing participants' experience with the powers unleashed through the ceremonial ingestion of peyote. Peyote ceremonies were principally used for ceremonial doctoring, although they might occasionally be used for divination purposes such as locating an enemy, predicting the outcome of some undertaking, or finding lost objects.

Plains Indians in Oklahoma, Kansas, Nebraska, South Dakota, and Wisconsin gradually altered the peyote ceremony in such a way as to shift the focus from the shaman to every participant's quest for power. The peyote ceremonies that continue to this day throughout the western United States typically follow this pattern and seek to help persons establish harmony with supernatural power. These all-night ceremonies are held in a traditional tipi, with the door facing east. Preparation for the ceremony begins with rituals pertaining to the acquisition of peyote, either by sending individuals to Mexico or, in more recent times, by purchase and delivery through the U.S. Postal Service. Once acquired, the peyote is blessed through prayer and consecrated for use in bringing health to all who will ingest it. Any member of the peyote cult may rise to the position of ritual leader, often known as the "roadman." The leader is assisted by a drummer, a fireman, and a cedar man.

The precise order and content of the ceremony varies by tribe and the idiosyncratic preferences of the leader, but invariably begins with the leader's prayer to the power of peyote. The other participants follow the leader's lead and begin praying silently to the "earth-creator" or "earth-lord." Following these initial prayers, participants begin to eat the dried buttons of the peyote plant, followed by drumming and singing. The leader's initial song, chanted in a high nasal tone, implores "may the gods bless me, help me, and give me power and understanding." Throughout the night more peyote buttons are eaten (while most members eat about twelve buttons throughout the night, some may consume as many as thirty) and prayer intensifies. Ceremonial dancing is usually an integral part of the ceremony, particularly in Mexico and the American Southwest. Quiet meditation, prayer, and the quest for personal visions predominate in the Plains.

The principal purpose of the peyote ritual is to obtain power. The use of peyote thus overlaps considerably with other traditional methods of obtaining power such as the medicine dance or the vision quest. The power generated by ingesting peyote is therefore often understood to be capable of curing illness. Typically the leader will offer prayers that petition God to cure participants in need of healing. Cures of almost every kind have been attributed to the power generated in peyote ceremonies. Other participants seek to use the power of peyote to procure a personal vision. Still others eat peyote to increase their powers of concentration and introspection.

Peyote rituals also emphasize preaching and moral instruction. Moral lectures are commonplace. Participants admonish one another to forgo vices, particularly in regard to abstaining from alcoholic beverages. Weston La Barre observed that it is typical for participants to

> pray aloud, with affecting sincerity, often with tears running down their cheeks, their voices choked with emotion, and their bodies swaying with earnestness as they gesture and stretch out their arms to invoke the aid of Peyote. The tone is of a poor and pitiful person humbly asking the aid and pity of a great power, and absolutely no shame whatever is felt by anyone when a grown man breaks down into loud sobbing, during his prayer (1975: 48).

This emphasis upon preaching and moral repentance escalated when Christian elements were incorporated into the peyote ceremony in some tribal settings (particularly among Plains groups). The Bible was introduced to the liturgical format of the peyote "singing" as early as the 1890s. Prayers once made to Indian spirits were redirected to the Christian God. Although most of the formal characteristics of the peyote ceremony persisted, their meaning changed in ways reflecting Native American cultures' progressive accommodation to white Christian culture: the fire in the peyote tipi became associated with the Light of Christ; the water drunk at midnight became associated with Christ's alleged midnight birth; the roadman's gestures to the four directions became a way of announcing the birth of Christ to all the world; and the meal eaten in the early morning became a sacrament for all those who are saved in Christ. In essence, the Christianized peyote rituals synthesized the religious heritages of Native Americans and Europeans. Peyotism thereby fostered the belief that the Great Spirit and the God of Christianity are one and the same. This Great Spirit created the universe and controls the destiny of every person and all events. The Great Spirit put some of his supernatural power into peyote which can have the same redemptive or sacramental power that other Christians avail themselves of when consuming bread and wine. In this way peyotism sustains fundamental Indian concepts about powers, visions, and native modes of doctoring while yet permitting eclectic appropriation of Christian teachings. To be sure, however, many versions of peyotism have eschewed any connection with Christianity. For example, peyote use among the Mesalero Apache has led to an intensification of native values and traditions. And, as many Native Americans have in recent years become more concerned with preserving their cultural heritage, the appeal of Christianized versions of peyotism has weakened somewhat.

Peyotism never lacked for critics. The most persistent opposition came from white officials who viewed it as contrary to the goal of assimilating Native Americans into white, middle-class culture. One major line of argument against peyote use was that it was allegedly injurious. Despite evidence to the contrary, peyote was said to be both physically and morally debilitating. A more important objection was more political in nature. The rapid spread of peyotism reinforced traditional culture and amplified nativistic tendencies among American Indian populations. Both Christian missionaries and officials in the Bureau of Indian Affairs were disturbed by the cultural threat posed by this overt continuation of native tradition (and the pan-Indian solidarity that it celebrated and fostered). By 1907 BIA officials began orchestrated attempts to pass anti-peyote legislation. Native Americans responded by organizing small religious organizations that claimed peyote use should be tolerated as part of America's time-honored commitment to protect the freedom of religious practice. In 1918, the "Native American Church" was incorporated in Oklahoma and soon developed into an intertribal peyote church that stretched throughout the western and central United States. Subsequently reorganized as the "Native American Church of North America," this group has been largely successful at influencing state courts to respect their legal right to use peyote in religious ceremonies.

The Native American Church eventually obtained religious exemption from drug laws in 27 states. In 1990, however, the United States Supreme Court ruled against the exemption of peyote from the government's "war on drugs." By a narrow 5–4 margin, the Court emphasized the need to safeguard society from the chaos that could conceivably erupt if individuals are free to act however they please simply by claiming that these actions are part of their personal religion. Writing for the four dissenting members of the Court, Justice Blackmun noted that there is no evidence that the religious use of peyote has ever harmed anyone. He noted that the Native American Church's use of peyote is so ritually structured that there is no real concern for health and safety. In sum, Blackmun maintained that "peyote simply is not a popular drug; its distribution for use in religious rituals has nothing to do with the vast and violent traffic in illegal narcotics that plagues this country."

In a series of legislative acts including the Religious Freedom Restoration Act of 1993, the federal government has put statues in place that specifically permit the Native American Church to use peyote in its religious ceremonies. This legal protection is not, however, afforded to non-Indian groups. Many Anglo-Americans have sought to emulate Native American spirituality and have consequently come to believe peyote is essential to their spirituality since it helps them establish harmony with nature. The Peyote Way Church of God is an example of a group of approximately eighty (and largely non-Native American) persons who pursue experiences of the Holy Spirit through the sacramental use of peyote. State and federal courts have ruled against such groups, maintaining that their use of peyote does not qualify for an exemption from the government's drug-enforcement laws.

In more recent years, peyotism has been instrumental in reinforcing commitment to environmental activism. Peyotism is a sacrament. The ceremony thus heightens awareness of the spiritual beauty residing within nature and consequently fosters a commitment to protecting nature from human defilement. Furthermore, peyote itself is an endangered species. The popularity of peyotism, particularly among white, Euro-Americans who have harvested large quantities of the cactus, has threatened both Huichol culture in Mexico and the cactus species itself. While there is considerable irony in the fact that a sacrament resulting in greater connection to nature has created an environmental threat, it remains a fact that peyotists are acutely aware of the plant kingdom's precarious situation. It should also be pointed out that while Native American peyotists speak of their sense of connection to nature, they now generally receive their peyote from the United States government. The traditional ritual of gathering peyote has thus been thoroughly severed from the ceremony in which it is ingested. Many Native American peyotists have therefore lost some of their traditional Earth connection. It is thus not uncommon for white, Euro-American "converts" to peyotism to evidence more environmental concern than their Native American counterparts.

In sum, peyotism has performed a variety of religious, cultural, and environmental functions over the past hundred or more years. Religiously, peyotism helped sustain native ritual traditions amidst the encroachments of white Christianity. The peyote cult offered to heal and to protect its members through the worship of a supreme "earth-creator" who for all intents and purposes is identical with the God of Christianity. The peyote button – like sacramental bread and wine – provided a material vehicle for availing oneself of regenerating power. Peyote is understood as a "medicine," a "power," a "protector," and a "teacher." The peyote ceremony deepens subjective feelings of personal relationship to a sacred power, yet does so in a carefully orchestrated ritual that ultimately assists individuals to subordinate their personal desires to group goals and values. And although peyote is combined with almost as many theologies as it has users, it has almost universally fostered such culturally valued ethical traits as love, hope, charity, ambition, and honesty. And, finally, peyotism is frequently a catalyst for intensified concern for the environment. The entire peyote ceremony reinforces a sacramental view of nature, leading participants to care for the healing of Earth.

Robert C. Fuller

Further Reading
Aberle, David and Stewart Omer. *Peyotism in the West*. Salt Lake City: University of Utah Press, 1984.
Fuller, Robert. *Stairways to Heaven: Drugs in American Religious History*. Boulder: Westview Press, 2000.
La Barre, Weston. *The Peyote Cult*. New York: Anchor Books, 1975.
Meyerhoff, Barbara. *Peyote Hunt: The Sacred Journey of the Huichol Indians*. Ithaca: Cornell University Press, 1974.
Schaefer, Stacy B. and Peter T. Furst, eds. *People of the Peyote*. Albuquerque: University of New Mexico Press, 1996.
Shonle, Ruth. "Peyote: The Giver of Visions." *American Anthropologist* 27 (1925): 53–75.
Stewart, Omer. *Peyote Religion: A History*. Norman: University of Oklahoma Press, 1987.
See also: Ayahuasca; Castanada, Carlos; Entheogens; Ethnobotany; Ethnoecology; Psychonauts; Yoeme (Yaqui) Ritual.

The Philippines

There are at least seventy traditional culturo-linguistic groups in the Philippines Islands. Their languages belong to the Malayo-Polynesian group of languages, which have spread from the Indian Ocean right across the Pacific Ocean. Extensive religious change has occurred during modern times in lowland regions, and although the populations there fall into large groupings with customary and language distinctiveness (Tagalong, Cebuanos, Ilocanos, Illongros, etc.), these are now overwhelmingly Catholic Christian (and accepting the label Filipino).

There is a sizable Muslim population in Mindanao composed of three major ethnolinguistic groups – the Maranao in Lanao, the Magindanao in Cotabato and the Tausug in Jolo. The current Christian–Muslim conflict goes right back to the beginning of the Spanish colonization of the Philippines: when Lopez de Legazpi undertook the conquest of Luzon in 1570 his chief opponent then was Rajah Soliman who had settled in Manila.

Mountain peoples apart from the Maranao in Mindanao were little impacted by either the process of Islamization or Christianization. The reason is fairly simple; they lived in inaccessible places both in Northern Luzon and in the forested highlands of Mindanao. Over almost three and a half centuries of conquest Spanish rule was never established in these areas.

Today these tribal people (or *lumads*) usually live in

great poverty on the margins of Philippines society. The cultures of the *lumads* are under tremendous pressure at the beginning of the third millennium. Many anthropologists fear that, within a few decades, many of the *lumad* languages and cultures will disappear because they will have lost their forest lands.

Beginning in the 1930s wave after wave of lowlanders from the central islands and Luzon have migrated to Mindanao and dispossessed the tribal peoples of their lands. Different understandings between lowland Filipinos and tribal people about land and land ownership facilitated this dispossession. Most tribal societies have complex (*adat*) laws governing land use and ownership. None would subscribe to the notion of private property. The lowlanders who were Christians understood the notion of private property and sought legal titles for their newly acquired lands. It is worth pointing out that private property is not a prominent tenet of the Judeo-Christian tradition. Most of the ideas about land and private property came from Roman Law rather than the Bible. The code of Justinian in the fifth century gave people the right to *jus jutendi, jus fruendi et jus abutendi* – the right to use, to enjoy the fruits of and even the right to abuse property. These values in relation to land were taken on board by many lowland Filipinos. When a tribal chieftain gave a lowlander some land in return for a sack of rice the lowlander immediately sought ways to get a legal title to the land which precluded tribal people ever using the land again for hunting or slash-and-burn agriculture (*kaingin*).

Ironically many lowlander Filipinos now realize the *lumads* embody many of their own traditional values in regard to religion and the environment so that by hastening the demise of the *lumads* they put their own culture in jeopardy. For example, the traditional religions are "classically" animistic: all of the environment bears a numinous quality, and all waterways, plants and trees are connected to the spirit order.

Furthermore, one must seek permission from the appropriate spirit before taking anything for human use, as for example, when a tree is cut down. If one contravenes any of these taboos a malign spirit can bring trouble and sickness to the erring person and his or her family. In any case there are malign spirit presences in eerie places, such as cliffs, caves, springs, and the headwaters of springs and rivers. Trespassing in them is to be avoided.

The spirits of both place and ancestry are invoked in group ritual life, as in sowing and harvesting. For some ethno-linguistic groups certain places have a special "sacred" quality. For the T'boli people of South Cotabato Lake Sebu and Silutonn are associated with many of the most important origin myths of the tribe. The *buklug* (or thanksgiving ceremony) is a very important mechanism for uniting disparate groups of the Suban-on people in managing a fragile tropical rainforest environment in the highlands of northwest Mindinao.

The christianization of the Philippines began after Legazpi claimed the islands for Spain from 1564, and over the next 300 years Spanish power consolidated. Christianizing processes involved a superimposition on the underlying primal religious pantheons; but the world remained full of spirit presences. Because the introduced "divine" was a distant, often fear-invoking presence, devotion to saints filled a religious void. Colorful fiestas to the saints picked up from where primal prosperity festivals left off. With such a symbiosis, the effects of religious change on the environment were not considerable. Even into the 1920s the islands' rainforest, which is the Philippines' defining ecosystem, was still intact. Considering it is now down to 10 percent one has to ask what happened.

In 1898 the Philippines were ceded to the United States after the Spanish American War. Population increases soon presented themselves under the new order (the nation's population has risen exponentially from ca. 6 million in Spanish times to ca. 85 million at present). Opening up the forest areas as frontiers of development was an early characteristic of United States' rule: John "Black Jack" Pershing (Brigadier General of the Philippines, 1906–1913) approached the Mindanao rainforest like the "wild west," and his regime treated the inland peoples as if they did not exist. Church programs before the Second World War were also overwhelmingly in favor of helping the Christian lowlanders to cut the forests and open up land, especially for rice growing. In this frontier situation the mountain people and their culture were despised and almost always seen as inferior.

During the years the Philippines were prepared for independence (with a Commonwealth being established by 1935), and after the trauma of World War II (with an independent Republic being declared in 1946), the development myth was heavily promoted and the opening up of Mindanao was received positively throughout the nation. Neither those on the left nor right of politics had time for the environment. The former constantly called for better land distribution, which would mean more pressure on the wilderness; and when the right triumphed under the authoritarian Ferdinand Marcos (President, 1965–1986), foreigners colluded with Filipino magnates to expropriate the islands' resources.

The Catholic Church, which suffered a setback in influence after the collapse of Spanish rule, began to take the plight of the *lumads* more seriously in the wake of the Second Vatican Council, stressing cultural diversity and the championing of downtrodden peoples. By the mid-1980s Columban Father Sean McDonagh, who at that time lived with the T'boli, began a program of activism in an attempt to get the environment on the Church's agenda. Initially most Church personnel were nonplussed by his concerns. However by the late 1980s the country's clerical leadership was persuaded by his arguments concerning the irreversibility of damage to rainforests, including the weakening of the islands' originally high level of biodiversity and the destruction of many species. Indeed, irresponsible human impact of the natural world was now having a noticeable effect – typhoons devastating forested areas and generating uncontrollable floods – as the environmental inroads had gone beyond a point of no return.

This marriage of creation and liberation theology in the Philippines helped stop some so-called development initiatives like the building of a massive hydro-electric dam in the tribal area of Northern Luzon and in the T'boli area of Lake Sebu. It also helped insure that the nuclear power plant which was built at enormous cost at Bataan was never put into production. These were high-profile development projects during the Marcos dictatorship.

With the collapse of the Marcos regime, in 1986, President Cory Aquino picked up the first Pastoral Letter about ecology ever formulated by a Catholic hierarchy entitled *What is happening to our beautiful land?* The Department of Environment received teeth to liaise with local groups about their environmental problems and their solutions. Hard decisions, however, continue to present themselves. Rio Tinto, a multinational mining company, spent a number of years in the 1990s prospecting for gold and copper in the Suban-on area of Zamboanga in Mindanao. Concerted efforts at the local and international level have led to a declaration by Rio Tinto in 1999 that they would not seek mining applications in the Philippines. Other companies like Victoria Gold, operating under the banner of Far South East Gold, took over the effort to gain permits to mine in the tribal areas of Northern Luzon and Mindanao. In most of these situations church groups – Catholic and United Church of Christ – worked actively with tribal peoples to protect their ancestral lands from further degradation through illegal logging or mining. Unfortunately the future does not look too bright from many of the tribal peoples of the Philippines. Much more needs to be done by the local and national government if their unique cultures is to survive and thrive in the twenty-first century. The loss of even one of these ethnolinguistic groups will be a tragedy, not just for that community but for the Philippines and the whole of humanity. We need cultural and linguistic diversity if the human species is to blossom in the future.

Sean McDonagh

Further Reading

Broad, Robin and John Cavanagh. *Plundering Paradise: The Struggle for the Environment in the Philippines.* Berkeley, CA: University of California Press, 1993.

Finlayson, Paul. "Technology, Environment and Ethics." *South Pacific Journal of Mission Studies* 25 (October 2001), 29–43.

Jocano, F. Landa. *Philippines Prehistory.* Manila: Community Publishers Inc., 1975.

Jocano, F. Landa. *The Traditional World of the Malitbog.* Quezon City: University of the Philippines, 1969.

McDonagh, Sean. *To Care for the Earth.* London: Chapman & Sons, 1985.

Schlegel, Stuart. *Tiruray Subsistence: From Shifting Cultivation to Plow Agriculture.* Quezon City: Ateneo de Manila University Press, 1979.

See also: Hawai'i; Melanesian Traditions; Pacific Islands; Polynesian Traditional Religions; Southeast Asia.

Philosophy of Nature

Philosophy of nature, often called in Latin *philosophia naturalis* (already by Seneca, d. 65) or in German *Naturphilosophie*, is the term used for a scrutinization and systematization of the natural world, the processes, dynamics and generative powers of nature, and the relationship between human cognition and "nature." In its long history from antiquity through today, philosophy of nature was closely related to "natural philosophy" (i.e., the exact sciences, on the one hand, and metaphysics on the other). The latter often has far-reaching implications for religious attitudes toward nature, especially when idealistic, transcendental, or pantheistic models are applied. The major and most influential periods of philosophy of nature are the pre-Socratics, the Renaissance, and nineteenth-century German idealism, although this should not dismiss the contributions of other periods as marginal.

From antiquity through the eighteenth century, empirical, "scientific" natural philosophy, and the speculative, metaphysical philosophy of nature, formed a unity. The Ionic philosophers and pre-Socratics (eighth–fifth centuries B.C.E.) were the first to speculate about the four elements, the (atomistic) structure of matter, the mathematical harmony of the cosmos, the relationship between substance and power (energy) and between the organic and the un-organic. Prominent figures were Anaximander (610–546 B.C.E.), Pythagoras (ca. 580–500 B.C.E.), Parmenides (fl. ca. 540–480 B.C.E.), Heraclitus (ca. 544–483 B.C.E.), Anaxagoras (ca. 500–428 B.C.E.), and Empedocles (483/2–424/3 B.C.E.). In this period the terms *physis* (as "nature" or "matter") and *cosmos* (as the order of matter or "world") were coined. Despite disagreements in details most of those early philosophers regarded humans as part of an all-inclusive *physis*. This is true either for the atomists with their analogy of microcosm and macrocosm, for Heraclitus who attacked any kind of anthropocentrism, and for Empedocles who described the differentiation between death and birth as meaningless and ridiculous constructions.

Plato (427–347 B.C.E.) and Aristotle (384/3–322/1 B.C.E.) systematized major earlier currents of thought.

Whereas Plato spoke of *physis* as an effecting (active) and a passive force (*Phaidros*, 270 D), at other times combining it with the idea of ideal being (*ousia*, cf. *Gorgias* 465 A), Aristotle depicts *physis* as the (inner) principle of change (*Physics* III 1, 200b 12). This is the essence of all being. He goes on and speaks of a double nature, one being matter (*hylê*), the other form (*morphê*).

In late antiquity and within the scholastic context of medieval philosophy, influential differentiations were introduced. One of them is the difference between the generative, active power of nature (*natura naturans*) and the "generated" result of that process (i.e., visible nature [*natura naturata*]). This important differentiation was first developed by the Arab philosopher Averroes (Ibn Rushd, 1126–1198), and it found its way into the scholastic philosophy of Albertus Magnus (d. 1280), Thomas Aquinas (d. 1274), and Roger Bacon (d. 1294). *Natura naturans* was described as the divine principle of creation, standing – like God himself – somewhat behind created nature. The "book of nature" (derived from "Holy Scripture") thus was a revelation of transcendental, sacred truths to be deciphered by man. Consequently, the exact sciences were a means to contribute to Christian theological discourse. In this perspective, (created) nature was not itself divine but only a mirror of the divine.

During the Renaissance this model changed markedly. Although there are close relations between them – a fact that is often neglected by scholars of religion and science – two major currents can be differentiated. On the one hand there was a rebirth of the ancient philosophy and religion, resulting in an enthusiastic appraisal of pantheistic and "holistic"-vitalist concepts. Especially within the neo-Platonic milieu of fifteenth-century Italy, esoteric and hermetic doctrines were molded that described nature as a living being connected to humans in various ways of correspondences (one prominent figure was Marsilio Ficino, 1433–1499). On the other hand, a development took place that is often referred to as the "scientific revolution." Two publications can be addressed as the cornerstones of this shift of paradigm. In 1543 Nicolaus Copernicus (1473–1543) published *De revolutionibus orbium caelestium* ("On the Celestial Bodies' Revolution") containing his thesis that the Earth is not the center of the cosmos but revolves around the sun. And in 1687 Isaac Newton (1643–1727) put forward his mechanistic theory of physics and mathematics in his seminal work *Philosophiae naturalis principia mathematica* ("Philosophy of Nature's Mathematical Principles"; note that Newton does not speak of "science"!). Further major contributors to the new paradigm were Tycho Brahe (1546–1601), Johannes Kepler (1571–1630), Galileo Galilei (1564–1642), and the philosophers René Descartes (1596–1650) and Thomas Hobbes (1588–1679). The mechanistic model roughly had four characteristics. Nature was identified as a human artifact; it was described as analogous to a lifeless machine; mechanics was now identified with the whole of physics; the mechanistic model was considered the only valid, "scientific" way of explaining nature and cosmos, hence all disciplines (philosophy, psychology, medicine, law, politics, etc.) had to be adjusted to the new paradigm.

The implications of this development were conceptualized in the eighteenth century. Now a distinction was made between *physica speculativa* and *physica empirica* that led to the modern concept of empiristic science as a separate discipline in contrast to philosophy of nature as mere speculation and metaphysics. It was Immanuel Kant (1724–1804) who worked out the first comprehensive critical theory of nature, which comprised both a mechanistic theory of science and a complementary theory of the organic (i.e., the biological aspect of nature). *Naturphilosophie* in the strict Kantian sense is characterized by a reduction of visible or measurable forces to a small set of general prior forces. Forces that transcend the scope of pure reason are to be excluded from philosophy.

This assumption was harshly refuted by philosophers of the early nineteenth century. A nucleus of the new direction was the University of Jena (Germany), where Friedrich Wilhelm Joseph Schelling (1775–1854) elaborated a full-blown theory of nature. His concept had a considerable impact on later Idealism and Romanticism because it combined a critical rationalistic method with holistic and vitalist explanations of nature as a generative force (*natura naturans*). Biocentric perspectives and pantheistic sacralization of nature – prominent within the European and North American context in the middle of the nineteenth century – cannot be explained without Schelling's strong impact, although the philosophy of Georg Wilhelm Friedrich Hegel (1779–1831), who spoke of nature as the "expression" of the Absolute into material form, superposed it for some time.

Due to the success of empirical science and growing industrialization, the later nineteenth century led to a decline of any speculative philosophy of nature, and a lot of people announced its death, analogous to the "death of metaphysics." But this was a dialectic process, and between 1900 and 1930 there was a rebirth of holistic, monistic and vitalistic concepts. Interestingly, scientists of physics and biology were the driving force in this development. Biologists like Ernst Haeckel (1834–1919) developed a monistic pantheism (he also coined the term "ecology"), and the scientific revolution that was initiated by Albert Einstein's General Theory of Relativity, along with the succeeding Quantum Mechanics, led to a growing suspicion of mechanistic and deterministic explanations of nature. Now a speculative debate emerged on the fringes of physics, philosophy, and psychology – for example, the dialogue between Carl Gustav Jung and Wolfgang Pauli or the "Copenhagen Interpretation" of Quantum physics – which again brought up the issue of "matter and mind," among others.

The so-called "New Age science" is a direct follower of this new philosophy of nature. Speculations related to "Quantum mysticism" as well as to romantic theories were combined in various ways with practical religious attitudes. "Deep Ecology," "Transpersonal Psychology," or nature-based spirituality in general are by no means isolated phenomena of modernity. They are deeply grounded in Western philosophy of nature.

Kocku von Stuckrad

Further Reading

Buchdahl, Gerd. *Metaphysics and the Philosophy of Science: The Classical Origins: Descartes to Kant.* Oxford: Blackwell, 1969.

Coates, Peter A. *Nature: Western Attitudes since Ancient Times.* London: Polity Press, 1998.

Debus, Allen G. *Man and Nature in the Renaissance.* Cambridge: Cambridge University Press, 1978.

Grafton, Anthony, ed. *Natural Particulars: Nature and the Disciplines in Renaissance Europe.* Cambridge, MA: MIT, 1999.

Leclerc, Ivor. *The Philosophy of Nature.* Washington, D.C.: Catholic University Press, 1986.

Vickers, Brian, ed. *Occult and Scientific Mentalities in the Renaissance.* Cambridge: Cambridge University Press, 1984.

See also: Book of Nature; Deep Ecology; Environmental Ethics; New Age; Perennial Philosophy; Southeast Asia; Transpersonal Psychology; Western Esotericism.

Pilgrimage to Sripada (Sri Lanka)

The annual pilgrimage to the sacred mountain Sripada (h. 7415 ft), located in the Sabaragamuva Province of southwest Sri Lanka, is undoubtedly a unique religious experience both for Buddhists and non-Buddhists. Commonly known in Sinhala as Sripada, the mountain pilgrimage site of the historical Buddha's footprint is filled with intense religious piety. For centuries, Sripada has functioned as one of the 16 active ancient pilgrimage sites in Sri Lanka. As a sacred site, it combines the sacred mountain pilgrimage with pious Buddhist practices such as reciting the virtues of the Buddha, while also incorporating religious and mythological beliefs to help the pilgrim understand the relationship that exists between the Buddha and Sri Lanka. It is a place of devotional religiosity combined with nature worship: an important facet of this pilgrimage is having a glimpse of the rising sun from the top of Sripada.

The earliest literary record of Sripada's existence and its religious significance for Buddhists in Sri Lanka comes from the fifth-century Pali chronicle, the *Mahavamsa*, written by Mahanama. The *Mahavamsa* (15:96–7) treats Sripada as a sacred mountain purified by the visits of two Buddhas – Konagamana and Gotama – and in particular, Konagamana's visit as an attempt to save Sri Lanka from drought. The *Mahavamsa* records that during the Buddha's first visit to Mahiyangana, the deity Sumana of Mt. Samanola attained the status of stream winner, the first of the four paths to liberation. Since Sumana desired an object of worship, on that occasion, the Buddha gave him some of his hair to be used as a relic. In his third visit to Kelaniya, accepting Sumana's invitation, the Buddha rested a day at the foot of Mt. Samanola and left his footprint on its peak.

As a pilgrimage site, Sripada has a long history. The thirteenth-century *Pujavaliya* records that Parakramabahu II requested the minister Deva-Patiraja to clear the path to Mt. Samanola (Buddhaputra Thera 1930: 745). The *Culavamsa* (26:27) supports the *Pujavaliya*'s account by maintaining that the minister cleared the path, removing obstructions, building rest-houses, and constructing bridges. The *Pujavaliya*'s account even gives ideas about the nature of pilgrimage by mentioning that pilgrims from 18 provinces visited as groups.

Various episodes suggest Sripada's symbolic importance as a sacred shrine and its visible importance for the practice of many religious communities who dwell in Sri Lanka. While Buddhists consider Sripada the locus of Gotama Buddha's footprint, Hindus regard it as that of Siva, and Muslims as that of Adam, from which it derives one of its names, Adam's Peak.

The annual pilgrimage to Sripada lasts for five months from the full moon of December to the full moon of May. During this pilgrimage season, thousands of Buddhist devotees and non-Buddhists climb this mountain throughout the night with or without religious motivations. While there are two pilgrimage routes to Sripada, most pilgrims prefer the Hatton route which extends for six miles over the longer and more difficult Kuruvita/Ratnapura route.

The night pilgrimage on the Hatton route attracts a large number of pilgrims of various ages and social backgrounds. While some use public transportation to reach Maskeliya, most pilgrims use private coaches since they come as groups, as was the traditional custom in the past.

After dinner, pilgrims start climbing Sripada with the aim of reaching its peak by dawn to see the rising sun. On the pilgrimage route, there are several resting places which devotees use for performing specific rituals. For instance, Sitagangula is a river-crossing station where the pilgrims purify themselves by washing their bodies in the cold water. Crossing the river and cleaning the body with water clearly demarcates the journey from the profane world to the sacred. Indikatupana is another interesting station where devotees do needlework. Traditionally, this station may have been a place where pilgrims mended clothes which were torn during the pilgrimage.

There are certain taboos in this pilgrimage. Senior pilgrims advise novice members to protect themselves against possible dangers caused by abusive words. Unprotected speech may result in people getting lost in the journey. In particular, it is important not to offend the mountain deity. However, the taboos do not prevent the use of positive words. In the Sripada pilgrimage, pilgrims are highly active in making jokes, using good humor, and extending greetings to other pilgrims. One can also observe the devotees who recite devotional quadrants. These activities remove the boredom and make climbing more comfortable. The Sripada pilgrimage is highly entertaining and filled with intense devotional religious activities related to nature.

Mahinda Deegalle

Further Reading
Aksland, Markus. *The Sacred Footprint*. Bangkok: Orchid Press, 2001.
Buddhaputra Thera. *Pujavaliya*. Panadura: P.J. Karunadhara, 1930, 745.
Carpenter, Edward. "Adam's Peak and the Black River." In Edward Carpenter. *Adam's Peak to Elephanta: Sketches in Ceylon and India*. London: Swan Sonnenschein & Co, Ltd, 1903.
Knighton, William. "A Night on Adam's Peak in Ceylon." *India Sporting Review* 6 (1847), 1–20.
Paranavitana, Senarat. *The God of Adam's Peak*. Ascona, Switzerland: Artibus Asiae Publishers, 1957.
Skeen, William. *Adam's Peak*. Colombo: W.L.H. Skeen & Co., 1870.

See also: Sacred Mountains; Sarvodaya Shramadana Movement.

Pinchot, Gifford (1865–1946)

Gifford Pinchot is known primarily as a forester and progressive politician in early twentieth-century America. Generally acknowledged as the first professional forester in the United States, Pinchot also emerged as a major figure in the Progressive and Republican Parties, leading to his election as governor of Pennsylvania in the 1920s. His work in forestry and progressive politics crystallized in his leadership of the movement to conserve natural resources, countering years of unrestrained exploitation of nature. Pinchot, sometimes called the "apostle of conservation," helped to cast conservation as a moral crusade for social reform.

Pinchot was born in 1865 in Connecticut to a wealthy Huguenot family from Pennsylvania with business ties to New York City. As a youth, Pinchot was immersed in the widespread evangelical Protestantism of his time. He read religious classics, attended Presbyterian services, taught

---

Pinchot on Church and Country
Gifford Pinchot expressed practical concerns for rural life and especially country churches in a time of their general decline. He co-authored two books on the country church which were published (1913, 1919) by the Federal Council of Churches, a national group then oriented toward the social gospel. The books were sociological studies of rural areas of New York, Ohio, and Vermont, showing how federated or "progressive" churches could restore the value and care of the land. The following remarks are from Pinchot's opening address to the Conference on Church and Country Life, Columbus, Ohio, December 1915:

> There can be no permanently sound and vigorous life for the Nation unless life in the country is vigorous and sound. Country life cannot be morally sound, physically healthy, attractive in its social opportunities and business returns, and generally satisfying and efficient unless the country church does its full share to make it so. And the country church cannot do its part unless it is sound and vigorous itself. The country church is one of the greatest roots from which spring national integrity, vitality, and intelligence. Its life and power are of nation wide concern.
>
> The permanent strength of any civilization is best measured by the soundness of life on the land. It was the failure of agriculture far more than the decadence of the cities that sapped the power of ancient Rome. The farmer feeds and clothes us all. From the country comes the strong new blood which renews the vigor of the towns. The tenacious spiritual ideals of the open country constitute our most resisting [sic] barrier against the growing laxity and luxury of our social organization. It is the country church rather than the city church which is in fact our best defense against the advance of the evils of our time.

D. Keith Naylor

Further Reading
The Gifford Pinchot Papers, Library of Congress, Manuscript Division. "Address of Gifford Pinchot at the Conference on Church and Country Life." Columbus, Ohio, 11:00 a.m., 8 December 1915.

Sunday School, and was class deacon at Yale, responsible for conducting the religious activities of the class, such as weekday prayer meetings. Upon college graduation, however, Pinchot declined a religiously oriented job with the Young Men's Christian Association and instead cultivated his love of the outdoors, pursuing a career in the not-yet-established profession of forestry.

As an adult, Pinchot was involved with the Episcopal Church, but more important than institutional affiliation was his exposure to the social reform currents of evangelical Protestantism. He may be seen as part of a generational cohort that one historian has called "ministers of reform," who eschewed the Protestant ministry but invoked Protestant values to push for social reform. Pinchot's writings and activities revealed the influence of the then-popular social gospel, sometimes referred to as "the Progressive movement at prayer." Social gospelers, eager to build the kingdom of God on Earth, sought to apply Christian principles to the myriad social problems arising from industrialization. Pinchot's choice of location in setting up his forestry consultancy office disclosed his early conception of forestry (and later, conservation) as part of the broad movement for social reform. He opened his New York forestry office in the United Charities Building, the well-known headquarters in the 1890s for mission and tract societies, organizations fighting to end child labor and poverty, women's rights groups, and consumer rights groups, among others.

Pinchot's pioneering research in the vast woods of the Vanderbilt estate in North Carolina launched his forestry career. His work there formed the basis of his groundbreaking exhibit on scientific forest management at the World's Columbian Exhibition in Chicago in 1893. Pinchot advanced as a national figure in forestry, and was appointed Chief Forester of the U.S. by President McKinley in 1899, a position he held until dismissed by President Taft in 1910. Taking advantage of his close friendship with Theodore Roosevelt, Pinchot combined forestry with issues of irrigation and land reclamation and developed the conservation of natural resources as a primary domestic policy of Roosevelt's presidency. The 1908 White House Conference of Governors on the Conservation of Natural Resources, masterminded by Pinchot, was a high point for conservation as a national movement, and led to historic conservation policies, a national inventory of natural resources, and later, joint conservation agreements with Canada and Mexico.

Pinchot's popularization of the term "conservation of natural resources" revealed his utilitarian approach to nature. While an outdoorsman throughout his life, and a one-time camping companion of John Muir, Pinchot was, nonetheless, wedded to ideas of scientific management, efficiency, and economic benefit in relation to nature. Never an absolute preservationist, he sought to apply scientific principles to the maintenance and use of forests and rivers for the good of humankind. His typically progressive concern for "the greatest good for the greatest number for the longest time" thrust him into battles against monopolistic corporate abusers of the land and cast him as a crusader for the public good.

Pinchot's devotion to the public good was steeped in democratic idealism and was informed by the social gospel emphasis on relieving economic exploitation. Pinchot linked monopolies and economic inequality to the ruinous exploitation of nature and argued for moral reform. His rendering of conservation was a blend of applied science (his forestry background) and applied religion (the social gospel influence) that became a hallmark of the Progressive Era.

Pinchot's autobiography, *Breaking New Ground*, completed shortly before his death in 1946, serves as a significant history of American forestry and conservation. It documents Pinchot's practical, utilitarian approach to nature, and perhaps more important, it registers his religiously based emphasis on the use and care of nature and its resources as a moral issue.

D. Keith Naylor

Further Reading
McGeary, M. Nelson. *Gifford Pinchot Forester-Politician*. Princeton, NJ: Princeton University Press, 1960.
Naylor, D. Keith. "Gifford Pinchot, the Conservation Movement, and the Social Gospel." In Christopher H. Evans, ed. *Perspectives on the Social Gospel*. Lewiston: The Edwin Mellen Press. 1999.
Pinchot, Gifford. *Breaking New Ground*. Washington, D.C.: Island Press, 1998 (commemorative edition).
Pinkett, Harold T. *Gifford Pinchot: Private and Public Forester*. Urbana: University of Illinois Press, 1970.
See also: Conservation Biology; Environmental Ethics; Muir, John; National Parks and Monuments (United States); Wilderness Religion.

Planetary Dance

In April of 1998 and 1999, the Institute for Deep Ecology, in conjunction with the Tamalpa Institute, put on a workshop entitled "Embodying Nature: An Experience in Deep Ecology." The workshop took place at Mountain Home Studio in Kentfield, California, which is located at the home of Anna and Lawrence Halprin on the slopes of Mt. Tamalpais in Marin County, California.

The workshop represented the first collaboration between the Institute for Deep Ecology and Anna Halprin, who is one of the pioneers in Modern Dance as well as a leading figure among those who integrate the expressive and healing arts. The dance workshop, which I attended and here describe, conjoined and culminated in the annual Planetary Dance, which included people not in the original workshop. The Planetary Dance was a separate event from the workshop, with its own history of development, which I describe below.

The two faculty persons for the workshop were Anna Halprin and Ken Otter. Anna Halprin has been a major figure in the world of modern dance for much of the second half of the twentieth century. Ken Otter is one of her students-turned-instructors at the Tamalpa Institute, and he is also active in deep ecology work, and has taught workshops through the Institute for Deep Ecology. Anna Halprin has developed over the course of several decades a movement-based process whereby a person is enabled to experience their personal embodiment of the natural world.

Each day of the workshop began at Mountain Home Studio with warm-ups and movement rituals designed to bring the participants into a deeper awareness and ease with our own movement vocabulary and inner dialogue. The afternoon session involved movement work out on some of the trails on the slopes of Mt. Tamalpais, a short walk from Mountain Home Studio.

On the first day of the workshop, the participants became acquainted with the environment of the dance studio and the environment of the backyard and a trail along one slope of Mt. Tamalpais. Movement exercises in the studio served to move participants from a mode of rational intellectualizing to a mode of physical sensing and feeling. This then set the stage for a hike and blind trust walk along the mountain trail in the afternoon. Participants took turns in pairs leading one another along the trail, and utilizing other sensory modalities in experiencing the trail.

The second day of the workshop moved more deeply into bridging the work done in the studio with the work done on the mountainside. Anna Halprin explained that the work was designed to break down the artificial boundaries between the participants' selves – their bodies – and the natural environment.

The major intention of the third day was to alter our consciousness into a state of pure awareness for its own sake. It was explained that our experiences of being in nature, being with nature rather than against it, involved reconnecting with the state of pure awareness.

The final day of the workshop took place entirely at Mountain Home Studio. There was no afternoon session on the mountain. The focus of the morning work was to provide a structure wherein people could incorporate and integrate the experience of the workshop with their lives and work outside of the workshop. During the afternoon we were shown the score for the Planetary Dance, which was to take place the next day on Mt. Tamalpais.

Halprin understands her work to be about this process of rediscovering the mythical and sacred aspects of dance and community. She also understands human community to be a part of the natural or ecological community, and so all dances for healing of the human community are also dances for healing of the greater natural community of which the human species is a part. Out of this commitment to the sacred and mythical aspects of dance, Halprin developed the Planetary Dance.

The Planetary Dance had its origins in 1981 when Anna and Lawrence Halprin started together with a group of people a project they called "A Search for Living Myths and Rituals through Dance and the Environment." This project occurred at the time that a murderer was stalking the trails of Mt. Tamalpais. They found that the myth that was engaging their community most deeply at that time concerned the feelings of fear, anger and betrayal concerning the presence of the killer on the mountain.

The Halprins worked with members of the community to develop an indoor performance ritual in a theater space at the College of Marin, at the base of Mt. Tamalpais, and an outdoor performance ritual the next day on the slopes and trails of Mt. Tamalpais. The performances enacted a mythic story of the apprehension of the killer and the return of the mountain to a state of safety.

Significantly, a few days later the police received an anonymous tip leading to the apprehension of the alleged killer and the end of the killings. However, upon the advice of Don Jose, a Huichol shaman who was visiting the Tamalpa Institute, the dance ritual was continued for another five years. From that initial project, they decided to hold a community dance ritual focusing upon various environmental and social concerns. Over the years, the ritual has been simplified to the point that it consists primarily of a sunrise walk to the top of Mt. Tamalpais and then a gathering for the dance/run at a clearing somewhere on the slopes.

The dance space itself has evolved over many years to be a large circular space. The dance consists of three concentric circles with drummers located in the center. There are four points around the circle, corresponding to the four cardinal directions, from which people enter the circle. As they enter the circle, they declare their intentions by shouting out for whom or what they were running, and then proceeded to run counterclockwise. At some point, they can move into the next circle, which moves slower and clockwise. The inner circle moves counterclockwise again and the pace is a walk. At some point, people can move out of the inner circle and stand facing the drummers. If a person wants to leave the circle, they need to move up through the concentric circles, in the appropriate direction and at the appropriate speed, and then stand around the space, or at its peripheries.

The power of the Planetary Dance lies in the conjunction of stated intentions, directed physical engagement with the landscape, performative ritual, and communal focus. The Planetary Dance functions as a performed prayer. It is analogous to cultures that dance for healing, or rain, or for bountiful crops. Although there are no specific claims made concerning any particular religious worldview, the strong ritual structure of the Planetary Dance suggests strongly the spiritual underpinnings of the dance. Many scholars of religion have noted the distinction many people make between *religion* as an institution and *spirituality* as being the expression of moral values and deep personal experience. This suggests that the Planetary Dance is a performed expression of the spirituality of the persons involved, many of whom have been associated with Halprin and the Tamalpa Institute. This particularly provides an example of Anna King's description of *spirituality* as being "a term that firmly engages with the feminine, with green issues, with ideas of wholeness, creativity, and interdependence, with the interfusion of the spiritual, the aesthetic and the moral" (King 1996: 345). Halprin has traveled around the world and established Planetary Dances in many different countries, so there will be a number of dances going on simultaneously, often on the weekend closest to the spring equinox. Out of this is developing a global community of persons who share this spirituality with its particular ecological and moral vision and its performed and aesthetic expression.

Craig S. Strobel

Further Reading

Halprin, Anna. "Healing the Mountain." *Context* 5 (Spring 1984), 57–60.

Helminiak, Daniel A. *The Human Core of Spirituality*. Albany: State University of New York Press, 1996.

King, Anna S. "Spirituality: Transformation and Metamorphosis." *Religion* 26 (1996), 343–51.

Roof, Wade Clark. *A Generation of Seekers*. San Francisco: Harper, 1993.

Strobel, Craig. *Performance, Religious Imagination and the Play of the Land in the Study of Deep Ecology and Its Practices*. Unpublished dissertation. Berkeley, CA: Graduate Theological Union, 2000.

Taylor, Bron. "Earth and Nature-Based Spirituality (Part I): From Deep Ecology to Radical Environmentalism." *Religion* 3 (2001), 175–93.

Zinnbauer, Brian J., Kenneth I. Pargament, et al. "Religion and Spirituality: Unfuzzying the Fuzzy." *Journal for the Scientific Study of Religion* 36 (1997), 549–64.

See *also*: Dance; Deep Ecology; Deep Ecology – Institute for.

Plastic Medicine Men

"Plastic medicine men" is a term that refers to people who falsely claim to be indigenous spiritual leaders. Some plastic medicine (wo)men make no claims to be indigenous, but do make false claims about being mentored by a spiritual leader. One prominent example is Lynn Andrews, the author of several books, including, *Medicine Woman*, and *Jaguar Woman*. She claims to have been mentored by a Cree Medicine Woman, Agnes Whistling Elk. However, her book describes a hodgepodge of pan-Indian cultural practices, and no one by the name of Agnes Whistling Elk lives in the community Andrews claims to have visited. Some plastic medicine (wo)men actually claim to be indigenous, such as Brooke Medicine Eagle and Dhayani Yahoo, although the tribes in which they claim membership do not recognize them. And finally, some plastic medicine (wo)men actually are recognized members of a native nation, but they do not have the authority within their tribe to act as a spiritual leader. One of the most famous such figures was Sun Bear, who became famous on the New Age lecture circuit, but whose teachings were generally denounced by native communities.

The appropriation of Native American spiritual/cultural traditions by white society has a long history in the U.S. – from colonists dressing as Indians during the Boston Tea Party, to the YMCA sponsoring "Indian Guide" programs for youth. In contemporary society, this practice of "playing Indian" is particularly notable in the New Age movement in which American Indian spirituality, with its respect for nature and the interconnectedness of all things, is often presented as the panacea for all individual and global problems. An industry has developed around the selling of sweatlodges or sacred pipe ceremonies, which promise to bring individual and global healing. Consequently, it has become economically profitable for peoples to market themselves as spiritual leaders. While there is not a monolithic opinion on this practice or on particular plastic medicine (wo)men, many native nations and organizations, such as the Traditional Circle of Elders, have publicly denounced this phenomenon. Hopi, Cheyenne, and Lakota elders have also issued statements against it. One Oakland-based group named SPIRIT exists only to oppose spiritual appropriation. Indian nations are even using the legal apparatus of intellectual property rights to file lawsuits against those who make a profit by stealing Indian culture. Unfortunately, these attempts have been largely unsuccessful to date because native traditions are considered "public" property under current U.S. intellectual property rights. Ironically, because copyrights are not granted to communities, individuals can actually appropriate native songs, traditional medicines, etc. that are considered part of the public domain, claim intellectual ownership over them, and deny native communities use of these same traditions.

On the surface, it may appear that native spiritual appropriation is based on a respect for Indian spirituality. Consequently, it often comes as a surprise to many non-Indians that native communities have become increasingly vocal in opposing this appropriation. One reason for this conflict between those who appropriate native religious traditions and native communities is that many non-Indians often hold essentially Christian assumptions about how all spiritual practices should operate. One common assumption is that indigenous religious traditions are proselytizing traditions – that is, native spiritual leaders want non-Indians to know about and to practice native spiritual traditions. Unlike Christianity, however, native spiritualities depend upon the land base that gave rise to them; they cannot easily be transplanted to another geographical area. Many ceremonies must be performed at specific locations.

Christian colonizers in the U.S have had a very different relationship with the land than native people. Christians have often regarded the land as something to controlled and subdued. Christian understandings of land are reflected in Genesis 1:28:

> God blessed them, and God said to them, Be fruitful and multiply, and fill the earth and subdue it; and have dominion over the fish of the sea and over the birds of the air and over every living thing that moves upon the earth.

Because Christian traditions have often regarded land simply as something for human use, it generally does not figure prominently in religious practice. By contrast, because native peoples regard the land as their relative, it is critical that land be respected ceremonially. Just as the land provides for the people so that they can live, so must the community care for the land ceremonially so that she can live. As a result, unlike Christianity, native traditions are not proselytizing. Traditions are seen as applying specifically to the land base from which they arise; they do not apply to peoples from other lands.

Because Christianity is a proselytizing religion, its adherents generally attempt to "spread the Word" to as many potential followers as possible. The desire is to inform as many people as possible about the Christian religion so that individuals will want to convert to the faith. Also, because Christianity often emphasizes the individual believer's relationship to God, it is important that every individual understand the doctrines and practices of the faith. Native traditions by contrast, often stress communal rather than individual practice. Consequently, it is not always necessary or even desirable for every member of a nation to engage in every ceremony or to have the same level of knowledge about the spiritual ways of a tribe. The reason is that all the members know that the spiritual leaders are praying for the well-being of the whole tribe. As Supreme Court Justice Brennan once stated in defense of Indian religion: "Although few tribal members actually made medicine at the most powerful sites, the entire tribe's welfare hinges on the success of individual practitioners" (in Smith 1999: 13).

It is not always necessary for all members of a tribe to be equally knowledgeable about all ceremonies, and because, as mentioned previously, the ceremonies only apply to the people of a specific land base, in many cases, ceremonial knowledge must be kept secret. Consequently, many tribes prohibit non-tribal members from coming to their lands when ceremonies are performed. The New Age image of the all-wise shaman going on the lecture circuit to teach indigenous traditions is antithetical to the manner in which native traditions are actually practiced. To make these acts of spiritual appropriation even more problematic, most plastic medicine people charge for their services. True spiritual leaders do not make a profit from their teachings, whether it is through selling books, workshops, sweatlodges, or otherwise. Spiritual leaders teach the people because it is their responsibility to pass what they have learned from their elders to the younger generations. They do not charge for their services. Indeed, they generally do not describe themselves as spiritual leaders at all. They are just simply known as such by the community. To quote one native activist, "if someone tells you they are a spiritual leader, they're not."

Andrea Smith

Further Reading

Smith, Andrea. *Sacred Sites, Sacred Rites*. New York: National Council of Churches, 1999.

See also: Aboriginal Spirituality and the New Age in Australia; Holy Land in Native America; Indian Guides; Indigenous Religions and Cultural Borrowing; Manifest Destiny; Mother Earth; New Age; The Sacred and the Modern World; Scouting; Snyder, Gary.

Pogačnik, Marko (1944–)

Born in Kranj (Slovenia) in 1944, Marko Pogačnik has become one of Europe's most important spiritual teachers in landscape and Earth healing. Schooled as a sculpturist, he became known as an artist, landscape planning adviser, and geomancist. Among other things, he designed Slovenia's coat of arms after the country's independence in 1991. He is a teacher at the School for Geomancy "Hagia Chora," which was founded in Germany in 1994–1995. Since the 1980s, the core of his activities has involved Earth-healing projects and applying the principles of geomancy. Pogačnik has developed his own distinctive methods based on his spiritual experiences, but has sought to make them measurable and replicable for other geomants. He believes that with the turn of the millennium the Earth began a major evolutionary transformation process and he has engaged himself in planetwide actions around this theme.

Pogačnik's basic idea is the multidimensionality of Earth and landscape: the physical forms of Earth phenomena – from individual life forms to landscapes – are intimately connected with different levels of non-material dimensions which are essential for the maintenance and health of the web of life. He distinguishes three such dimensions: a "structural" or "emotional" dimension through which the etheric life-forces nourish all levels and forms of life; the vital-energy dimension which distributes life-power over the Earth's surface to keep it and its beings alive; and the dimension of "planetary consciousness" which imbues the Earth's phenomena with intelligence and through which these phenomena communicate with the universe. All these dimensions are inhabited with a large variety of spiritual beings from angels and archangels in the higher spheres to elemental nature spirits connected to individuals, he believes. By meditating, dreaming, receiving visions (which he says come through his daughters Ajra and Ana as well) and by interpreting experiences such as sickness in his own life, Pogačnik communicates with this spiritual world and receives indications on how to diagnose and restore the Earth where it has suffered from human destruction.

Pogačnik has organized many landscape and Earth healing projects that involve many people. His workshops include meditative practices with color visualization, songs and dances, etc., as well as the placing of art objects, especially *lithopuncture*: the placing of large needle-shaped stones at selected spots to remove energy blockades and restore energy flows. He also applies "cosmograms" – engraved on the stones or cast in bronze plaques – designed to transmit cosmic signals to the place. As his scope gradually expanded from local to planetwide projects, he increasingly emphasised individual and group exercises to maintain the Earth's energy balance during her current transformation process. Such practices are explained in his latest books and on the internet.

Pogačnik's influence has grown through his books, which describe his various projects and perspectives. His project at Thüringen Castle Park in Germany, for example, was reported in *To Heal the Earth* (1989). In *Nature Spirits and Elemental Beings* (1995) he described the elemental beings that he believes inspire plants, animals, and human beings, and are connected with the Earth's higher-level dimensions, especially the so-called "landscape temples," namely, energy patterns transmitting the higher impulses from the universe to the lower dimensions of the Earth. *The Secret of Venice* (1997) and *Healing the Heart of the Earth* (1997) provided detailed accounts of the cosmos – Earth relations and healing work in Venice and elsewhere. In *School of Geomancy* (1996) he described all these views and methods in a more systematic way.

In *The Landscape of the Goddess* (1993) he discussed a major spiritual principle, the "Landscape Goddess," which he discovered in the geomantic structures of landscapes, architecture, and art, and which he considers the long-suppressed mythical Goddess worshiped in the ancient past. He perceives the Goddess in three aspects: the (white) Virgin Goddess representing wholeness; the (red) Mother Goddess standing for creativity; and the Black Goddess instigating transformation. This trinitarian and female goddess is elaborated in *The Daughter of Gaia* (2001), where Pogačnik looks back on three decades of personal, revelatory experiences, describing what he sees as the reemergence of the feminine principle and ways to reconnect with it in human individuals, cultural history, the animal kingdom, and in the sacred dimensions of the landscape.

In *Christ Power and the Earth Goddess: a Fifth Gospel* (1998) Pogačnik claims to discover, using his intuitive powers, heretofore unrevealed messages woven into the texts: a "Fifth Gospel" referring to the Earth's transition to the next stage of evolution. Instead of a doomsayer's prophecy, it offers perspectives of love and nondualistic wholeness between humanity and its spiritual environment. In *Earth Changes, Human Destiny* (2000) he linked the Revelation of St. John to the current transition process. Earth changes are now appearing on the physical level, and human participation (through practical exercises) is essential to facilitate them.

Pogačnik's interpretation of the world has affinity with the one posed by Rudolf Steiner. However, he derives his views largely from his own experience. He aims at art and healing, not at science, not even at spiritual science. His books provide stories not studies. He does not claim that his observations are the ultimate truth but that they are just a new layer of truth destined to be revealed in our epoch. His view is apocalyptic in that the world's future is at stake, but he sets his hope in humanity's choice to accept the message and act by it on its own free will – the primordial gift to us at the beginning of the Christian era. Although Pogačnik's charismatic personality attracts many people to his gatherings, there is as yet no organized movement of followers behind him. But his influence is far-reaching and appealing to those who perceive a connection between their own personal development, the restoration of nature's sacredness, and the spiritual development of the planet as a whole.

Cathrien de Pater

Further Reading
Pogačnik, Marko. *The Daughter of Gaia: Rebirth of the Feminine.* Forres, Scotland: Findhorn Press, 2001.
Pogačnik, Marko. *Earth Changes, Human Destiny: Coping and Attuning with the Help of the Revelation of St John.* Forres, Scotland: Findhorn Press, 2000.
See also: Geomancy; New Age.

Pollution Beliefs in South Africa

Illness and misfortune among all South African Bantu-speakers is traditionally believed to be caused by one of three main agencies – ancestral displeasure, witchcraft/sorcery and, to a much lesser extent, the Supreme Being. In all these cases the causal agent is conceived of as an intelligence. But there is a further possible cause of indisposition, this time working independently of human and spiritual volition, that is the result of individuals' being in a dangerous state, through no fault of their own. These states have strong negative aspects and may be described as pollution. They are all mystical in nature and must be removed as quickly as possible by rituals or medicines. They are typically highly contagious, especially to those close to the sufferer.

The way in which pollution is conceptualized differs somewhat between the four main cultural categories – Venda, Tsonga, Nguni and Sotho – present in South Africa.

Among Venda, certain purifications are performed after the birth of twins, after an abortion and following a homicide or death. There is evidence of a fear of "heat" (see below), as when twins are killed and buried in damp Earth to "cool" them, but generally the removal of pollution consists of the use of medicines and washing, which is suggestive that the condition is thought of as dirty. Among Tsonga, the following are the four main causes of pollution: the menstrual flow, the lochia (vaginal discharge after childbirth), death and the birth of twins. People contaminated by these states are regarded as being temporarily marginal to society and are subjected to various taboos, particularly regarding sexual intercourse. The pollution is removed by a ritual sexual act, performed without seminal emission, or smoking and steaming in medicinal vapors, aspersion and scarification with medicines.

Among the Xhosa-speaking Cape Nguni, pollution is termed *umlaza*, a form of ritual impurity connected with both the sexual functions of women and with death. Among the Mpondo, for instance, a woman has *umlaza* during her periods until she washes after the flow ceases; after a miscarriage, for approximately one month after the death of a husband, or child; and after sexual intercourse until she washes. A man is polluted for a month after the death of a wife or child. *Umlaza* is dangerous to cattle, men and medicines (whose strength they nullify), and also to sick people. A polluted person may not approach a diviner. It thus appears that the Mpondo, like the Venda, think of *umlaza* as dirt that must be washed away. Zulu-speakers, on the other hand, described pollution as "blackness" (*umnyama*). It can occur either in the environment, which can be contaminated by the "undesirable tracks" of people, in elements discarded in healing, by the action of witches, or, much more commonly, it can inhere in people at certain times. *Umnyama* is typically associated with a person who has recently given birth, a menstruating woman, and, in the past, with a girl who became pregnant before marriage. As among Cape Nguni, in all these cases the main danger is to men, whose virility suffers through contact with the woman. "Blackness" can also be caused through contact with a corpse or with a homicide. The *umnyama* caused by the death of a homestead head was removed, in the past, by the ceremony of "washing the spears," at a ritual hunt: that of a widow by washing. But the main technique used by Zulu to expel pollution is the use of enemas and emetics; some state that men should perform, as a prophylactic, the ritual act of vomiting daily if they work at places where many people come together. There is some evidence that "heat" is also a form of pollution among Zulu, but it is a minor one. Such references as there are in the literature merely refer to the smoldering "anger" of men – to the sexual act, which is itself thought to generate a dangerous heat.

But it is among the Sotho-speaking peoples that the concept of pollution has reached its greatest elaboration in South Africa, and here the metaphor used for conceptualizing the condition is heat (*fisa*). Literally translated *fisa* means a state of hotness, but associated with it are certain other states, each with a specific name, caused either by "heat," or through contact with a sinister and contagious force known as "shadow." The application of the term *fisa* clusters round the following areas: death of a close relative, certain types of sexual contact, pregnancy. The connection with menstruation does not seem as strong as with the Nguni, but perhaps the most dreaded cause of *fisa* is a miscarriage for, if the fetus if not ritually buried, it might affect the whole country The ethnologist-missionary H.A. Junod, writing in 1910, describes how his Sotho parishioners told him that when a woman has a miscarriage and conceals it, drought would strike the country. "This woman has committed a great wrong. She has spoiled the country of the chief" (Junod 1910: 140). Other states of *fisa*, also broadly associated with heat, are *makgoma*, a highly contagious state, affecting twins in the womb, which is caused by an abortion or by someone eating of the first-fruits before they are first "bitten" by the chief; *magaba*, especially connected with feverishness in children; and *sefifi* ("darkness"), caused by the "shadow" of dead people that can be picked up while traveling.

It is not surprising that Sotho pollution medicines and rituals should all stress coolness and use cooling media. This includes pouring cooling water on the ancestral shrines, and variations of this theme, such as watered gruel and beer. Anti-*fisa* rituals, in addition, use chyme (the green undigested stomach contents of slaughtered animals) and ash and soot (themselves the "detoxified" result of fire), which can be drunk in infusions, used in washing, poured onto shrines, or used in steaming and aspersions. A possible reason for the difference between Nguni and Sotho practice is that the former live in the eastern, well-watered parts of South Africa, while Sotho inhabit the high inland plateau where precipitation decreases steadily toward the west until the Kalahari desert is reached. The appropriateness of "heat" to symbolize misfortune is thus clear.

William David Hammond-Tooke

Further Reading

Berglund, Axel-Ivar. *Zulu Thought-patterns and Symbolism*. Uppsala: Swedish Institute of Missionary Research and Cape Town: David Phillips, 1976.

Hammond-Tooke, William David. *Boundaries and Belief: The Structure of a Sotho Worldview*. Johannesburg: Witwatersrand University Press. 1981.

Hammond-Tooke, William David. *Patrolling the Herms: Social Structure, Cosmology and Pollution Beliefs in Southern Africa*. 18th Raymond Dart Lecture. Johannesburg: Witwatersrand University Press, 1980.

Junod, H.A. "Les conceptions physiologiques des bantous sud-africains et leurs tabous. Revued." *Ethnographie et de Sociologie* 1 (1910), 126–69.

See *also*: Venda Religion and the Land (Southern Africa); Venda Witch Beliefs (Southern Africa); Xhosa-Speaker's Traditional Concept of God; Zulu (amaZulu) Ancestors and Ritual Exchange; Zulu (amaZulu) Culture, Zulu (amaZulu) Smelting; Zulu (amaZulu) War Rituals.

Polynesian Traditional Religions

Fanning out from the Lau Islands in eastern Fiji to Hawai'i in the northeast, and from Aetoroa (New Zealand) in the southwest in an arc across to Rapanui (Easter Island), Polynesia is well known for its commonalities of Austronesian languages, its hierarchized societies, and its peoples' propensity to image the world vertically from heaven to underworld. Lexical equivalents of nature are usually lacking, but covered by words for "world," which can often denote Earth as distinct from heavens (e.g., Samoan lalala[n]gi [earth/land] *vis-à-vis* la[n]gi [heavens] and lalulela[n]gi [underworld]), while terms to denote what is "beautiful" (e.g., Samoan aulelei) can apply to places as well as humans and artifacts.

Polynesian creation stories reflect an intense interest in the role of "departmental deities" whose province can be sky, Earth, forest, wind, sea, volcanoes and the underworld. Of the creator figures, Ta'roa/Tangaroa/Tane is most renowned; as offspring of sky and Earth, he often draws up the island world from the sea and is involved in a separation of sky from Earth (as, for example, the Maori Tane, who, becoming chief of the gods, is lord of the forests and also creator of humans). The gods typically have ranking and genealogies, and apart from the deities or guardians of the Underworld, one generally looked heavenward for blessings of the departmental gods. The rainbow, as in Hawai'i, could be a sign of answered prayers from above.

District, tribal or place deities, of lesser rank but important for day-to-day dealings, were usually related to local fertility and agricultural productivity, with signals from on high – the rainbow (itself a deity), lightning, even meteorites – betokening group survival in working the land without mishap and fighting off enemies. Special places, including stones, valleys, mountains, ancestral burial sites, and ancient landing-places were revered, and visitors sang their way into them with appropriate chants. These chants not only evoked gods and their associated roles in the cosmos, but also special sites, and features of beauty (flowers, plants, shells, pools, etc.). Ritual pleading would take place at sacred spots where offerings were made (items of a deceased person, for example, would be thrown into the crater of Kilauea, on Hawai'i Island, with a priestly plea made after a pig was killed so that the beloved one should become an ancestor in "volcanic manifestation" [*e lilo i pele*]).

Ancestors, especially those of nobles (or of the chiefly, warrior and priestly castes) mediated between the community of the living and realm of the greater spirits. They were genealogically related to the gods, and their division into male and female applied to the gods as well. All living (as against inert) things were divided into male and female, and primeval Earth (e.g., Papa-tua-Nuku of the Maori, or Vari "the Great Mother" for the Mangaians) was the generatrix of proximate and usable things. This has commensurability with the frequent presence of a powerful queen or female chief at the top of the social scale in Polynesian traditions. Gods and spirits could take on other living and thus human forms, however, which meant that women were vulnerable to being taken by them sexually. Various lesser beings could bear trouble (by causing women to abort) or show protection by appearing as animals, birds, etc.

Concerning land, it was normally possessed by kin groups (e.g., Samoan: 'aiga) rather than individuals, though sometimes senior chiefs or monarchs could lay claim as the head of a territory's ramage (or as descendant of that person who led the first-arriving canoe in the distant past). Land was meant to be distributed to every family, and available resources required everyone's duty of care to support populations in small territories. Exchange of necessities was complemented by gift-giving of ceremonial items (e.g., mats at feasts), and the flow of produce toward the top of the social hierarchy nonetheless meant that at great feasts the pigs killed and foodstuffs arranged in grand festal display were to flow back down even to the less well-off commoners (as the Hawaiian king would announce, for instance, at the Makahiki New Year festival). Land exploited for sustenance and the circulation of produce, moreover, always needed the help of local gods or tutelary deities, and the fertility of animals and gardens was an expression of their *mana* (spirit-power) and those attending to them, just as victory signaled good relations with the war god[s]. Human hunting, however, could put animal species at risk in fragile environments, as is notoriously known in the case of the great, flightless moa birds, killed to extinction for meat and feathers by the prehistoric inhabitants of Aetoroa (New Zealand). In war, moreover, enemies' gardens could be vulnerable, and in one rare and notorious case, that of Rapanui or Easter Island, a tribal (or civil) war resulted in the mass destruction of forests.

Given the sense of environmental expanse, connections between religion and nature were sometimes reflected in a broad geocosmic awareness. The Tongans, for example, forged imperial-looking influences to the west. They recognized the largest of their home islands, Tongatapu, to be very sacred (*tapu* being cognate with *tabu*) and the location of the most powerful (and arbitrating) chiefdom, indeed kingship, while the two other nearby Tongan island groups recurrently fought each other. Tonga's far-flung and fragile empire, which was held together by canoe fleets and lasted from the eleventh to the nineteenth century, came at a cost to the environment, with many large trees, especially from forests on Fiji and Niue, being felled for vessels. The fertile, productive resources of Tongatapu, however, which lay outside the worst conflict zones, were crucial for the survival of Tongans as a whole. The coming and going of the commoners on the face of the Earth, for example, illustrates the connection between religion, upholding the empire, and land. The term *fonua* means the grave of a commoner, the placenta linking a new-born to the Earth, and the nurturing of the Earth itself. The graves of kings and nobles, however, are called *langi* (sky), for only the ruling class proceeded to the heavens at death.

All Polynesians had a sense of arriving originally at their islands from a great distance, and their notions of a far-off "spiritual homeland" (most often called Hawai'iki) betokened much more than localized cosmologies. So did their understanding of the stars – spirit-beings related to sun, moon, etc. – by which they navigated and calculated time (as the Maori held). After all, trading expeditions had to be planned and braved to make exchanges on the far side of huge oceanic stretches.

Myths allow us to infer that those whose canoes arrived first, called anthropologically the first ramage, earned ruling and noble status thereafter.

The known order in Polynesia had its horrific and tragic sides. The Underworld was feared and sometimes associated with volcanoes. In various contexts going to the Underworld rather than to a heavenly beyond could depend on whether you managed to follow the correct procedures on your spirit-journey straight after death, giving the appropriate gifts to demons of the dead (a Marquesan belief), or perching at the last on the right rock (as Raiateans of the Tahitian group held).

Among some groups we hear of the legendary Maui, who in Maori myth takes on the sun, the volcano goddess Mahu'ike, and meets his match with the Ancestress of the Underworld, seeming in his daring to symbolize the need for heroic struggle against environmental dangers. As a sad contrast, we find how all commoners in pre-Christian Tonga were expected at death to become mere vermin – to eat the soil – with only the nobles privileged with escape from such a fate.

Garry W. Trompf

Further Reading
Kirch, Patrick V. *The Evolution of Polynesian Chiefdoms*. Cambridge: Cambridge University Press, 1984.
Siikala, Jukka. *Cult and Conflict in Tropical Melanesia*. (FF Communications, 233) Helsinki: Academia Scientarum Fennica, 1982.
Swain, Tony and Garry W. Trompf. *Religions of Oceania*. New York: Routledge, 1995.

See *also*: Hawai'i; Melanesian Traditions; New Zealand; Pacific Islands; Surfing; Volcanoes.

Polynesia – New Religious Movements

Upon contact with the outside world (especially from 1800 onwards), various adjustment movements arose in the Polynesian islands in response to traders and their new goods, the missionary message, and colonial intrusions. Because of the relative "vertical" orientation of Polynesian traditional cosmologies, the world being universe as sky, Earth, and Underworld, the islander leaders of these movements often presented themselves as mediators between heaven and Earth. European goods and their outsider bearers were commonly thought to have descended from the sky (hence, for example, the Samoan word for the missionaries and all whites after them: papala[n]gi – sky beings). The power these new leaders were alleged to receive, though, was to counter the unwanted influences that accompanied the dramatic changes overtaking smaller-scale societies. In almost every case, the new God taught by the missionaries was accepted as the greatest source of power – and also protection (an important theme in Polynesian indigenous religions). The old deities were powerless to prevent post-contact changes; the new God was turned to ward off the worst consequences of interaction with intruders, these problems including threats to land and environment. Thus even if some movements were pro-traditionalist and anti-missionary, they nonetheless appropriated the new God within a syncretic platform to try ousting the whites (as with the Tahitian Mamaia movement, which was overcome in battle by the pro-Mission monarch Pomare IV in 1833). In virtually all Polynesian movements supreme power from above was sought to protect or recover land from the external settlers' pretensions. Whether they took up arms in this cause or not, and whether some of these movements were more successful than others, religious hopes and ideals to secure the spiritual bases of their homelands were crucial for all of them.

Among various new religious movements, indigenously originated churches have emerged in Polynesia. In Tonga, of central importance in Polynesian history for having forged a widespread maritime empire, we find that the first known independent church in the whole Pacific was born. This was the Free Church of Tonga, initiated by the victorious secular chief Taufa'ahau (King George Tupou I), who used Wesleyan missionary legitimation of his monarchy to ward off threats of British annexation. In 1852 he capped off his skilled defenses with a forced succession to the sacred kingship called the Tu'i Tonga. Being only a "secular" chief, he needed to take over the role of Tonga's most sacral figure, who monitored military conflict and the circulation of produce in the whole island group from Tongatapu Island. The Tu'i Tonga was crucial in controlling ceremonies of fertility and assessing the relative availability of produce, especially on land, and he could impose a taboo on specified foods if any was scarce (with food restrictions also applying at other times, as when the Tu'i Tonga died).

By absorbing the secular and sacred rules, King George preserved the political autonomy and relative religious unity of Tonga, and cultivated the traditional ideology of fonua, that the Earth is sacred like the womb of all. The requirement to care for the Earth is symbolized by the placenta being buried in the land designated for a child or his family, and by graves being built of coral standing above the Earth itself. This ideology, however, could be said to be more a vehicle for continued royal and aristocratic control over most of the land than a group-conscious new religious program of eco-sustainability.

Because of the persisting royal rule, we can take the Tongan case to the present time. The royal family and nobility have been sponsors of new crops advocated by outsiders and in the end were mainly responsible for new styles of land management and its attendant ecological problems. A crisis, having to do with soil quality, arose by 1970 (because of banana plantations). The evident vulnerability of Tongan soil, together with the obvious stranglehold over most land by nobles, has led to much debate. Tonga is a scene of incessant religious debate, in which Christian theology and traditional values have been constantly debated, yet, as exposure to the rest of the world has increased, democratic and more radical Christian ideas about the just distribution of land have begun to subvert old preconceptions. Interestingly, the Catholic Mission had first established itself on Tongatapu, and a line of chiefs always claimed succession as the true Tu'i Tongas. A quiet claimant in recent times (yet a man clashing with the current king over the nobility's unjust wielding of power) was the famous Catholic bishop Patelision Finau (1934–1993), famous for advocating a nuclear-free and ecologically sustainable Pacific. He held that Tonga's inequitable land policies were inappropriate in the democratizing world, and socio-theologically inexcusable. That huge parcels of land are not given out to the people, on the other hand, could be defended as a form of land care, with nobles keeping a great deal of ground fallow or unexploited for produce.

Surveying post-contact religious movements among other Polynesian islands, we find that in Samoa during the 1860s there emerged a series of freelance preachers in different localities of the countryside, often claiming access to God or Jesus from above, and with hopes of an abundance of material blessings. The epithet "Joe Gimlet movement" covers these urgencies. Yet they also preached protection of local lands. The fact that Samoa's chiefly system was characteristically decentralized made it susceptible to outside control (to the Tongans, Germany, New Zealand and the United States in turn). These local impetuses, especially in Western Samoa, warned against selling or relinquishing land and thus in the long run contained the effects of colonialism (at least on West Samoa). Others were not so fortunate and virtual occupancy by outsiders has resulted. The Maori fought two well-known wars with the British (the worst occurred during 1843–1844 and 1864–1865), while the royal Hawaiian house, siding with the Church of England, attempted a last-resort revolt to prevent the takeover of the American White Cartel and their environmentally exploitative sugar plantation schemes in 1894, but failed. Religious leaders in such protests, and most noticeably Maori prophets in and after the wars, were champions of both religious separatism and the shoring up of native land. Their protest activity finds continuity in contemporary movements for independence or autonomy. The Hawaiian Sovereignty Movement combines both these causes, and believes Hawai'i's autonomy will secure a better environmental future and a safeguarding of remaining sacred sites. In expressions of this movement various grassroots activities awaken a sense of the traditional spirits of the land among tourists and the non-indigenous population on the islands.

Much further to the south, we discover a new religious wave less identifiable as a movement, but which has brought currents of neo-traditionalist sentiment and indigenous Christian organizations together. This wave developed over the last half century and is the "cult of Io." In certain Maori traditions Io is represented as a distant Supreme Being far beyond layers of other gods and departmental deities. The long vernacular texts, needed to help scholars decide one way or another about the traditional basis for such claims, are only now being edited. Before their publication views have ranged from accusations that the Theosophical Society had unduly influenced a positive evaluation of the "Io cult," using it to promote its neo-Gnostic emanation theory, on the one hand, to arguments like that of the Dominican Michael Shirres that Io conducts one to the very heart of Maori cosmic mysticism with its intense sensitivity to the beauties and significances of nature. By 2000 the so-called

"Io cult" had spread, and it has been gaining popularity on the Cook Islands. Across the Polynesian region, also, the appropriation of the term *natura* to replace vernacular equivalents is often to make the point that indigenous Polynesians are more attuned to nature and its needs than most outsiders (who are usually doing business there, and commonly hold secular and profiteering attitudes and agendas).

Garry W. Trompf

Further Reading

Shirres, Michael P. *Te Tangata: The Human Person*. Auckland: Accent, 1997.

Siikala, Jukka. *Cult and Conflict in Tropical Polynesia: A Study of Traditional Religion, Christianity and Nativistic Movements*. (FF Communications, 233) Helsinki: Academia Scientiarum Fennica, 1982.

Stevens, Charles. "Taking Over What Belongs to God: The Historical Ecology of Tonga since European Contact." *Pacific Studies* 22:3/4 (1999), 189–219 (Special Issue: Sustainability in the Small Island States of the Pacific).

Swain, Tony and Garry Trompf. *Religions of Oceania*. Library of Religious Beliefs and Practices. New York: Routledge, 1995.

See also: Hawai'i; New Zealand; Polynesian Traditional Religions.

Polytheism

Polytheism is the consideration that there are many gods. It holds that divinity is numerically multiple. In its original or fundamental sense, polytheism represents a celebration of the plurality of nature. Also known as "multitheism," it relates to "myriotheism" (belief in a countless number of gods) and "henotheism" (a term coined by Max Müller to denote either the belief in one god without excluding belief in others or, more precisely, the tendency among some peoples to make different gods in a pantheon supreme one after the other – attributing to each one in turn the attributes of the others). Polytheism is contrasted chiefly with monotheism (belief in only one god) and more broadly with theism itself – especially in its psychotheistic sense that god is pure spirit. Consequently, there is the tendency for polytheism to conform to or include physiotheism that ascribes physical form to deity – especially as the veneration of the physical powers of nature. In many respects, it resembles animism.

There is a prevailing affinity for polytheistic conceptions of divine reality to be grounded in a pantheistic understanding of cosmic actuality, but this need not invariably be the case, and polytheism might in some circumstances be understood as a sub-category of theism itself that posits the godhead to be transcendent. From a social evolutionist perspective, the polytheistic way of thinking is seen as the beginning of reflection that has had two historical results: "One was in the direction of pantheism and absorption in the One; and the other in the direction of monotheism and victory over the many" (Oman 1931/1950: 407). But in a less strictly Eurocentric analysis that accepts polytheism as *sui generis*, it is to be argued that there are two fundamental philosophies of polytheism: the monistic and the radical. The former argues for an underlying unity behind proliferation and differentiation. It holds that behind the plurality of gods, there is a fundamental, singular reality from which the many descend or emanate. Radical polytheism, by contrast, is pluralistic in an ontological sense. It comprehends there to be several if not many ultimate substances. Such a doctrine was held by the Ionian philosophers in their consideration of fire, air, Earth and water as fundamentals. It also appears in Leibniz's hierarchy of monads as well as in the arguments of Johann Friedrich Herbart's realism and William James' pragmatism.

But apart from philosophical metaphysics, polytheism in practice has appeared to be a spontaneous perception that springs from direct or intimate contact with a natural environment. It has traditionally appeared among peoples largely or originally unaffected by Western civilization and industrialization: indigenous tribals of Africa, Asia, Oceania and the Americas; the competing cultures of Hinduism, China and Japan; and in the various Afro-Latin diasporas. Typically understood as nature worship, at least in its seminal appearance, early polytheisms represent appreciations of the blessings produced by the natural environment as well as the fears of its dangerous elements. The gods were almost invariably personifications of direct natural powers, but as they proceeded in time to become increasingly spiritualized, they simultaneously were humanized and their nature origins have often become less apparent. In an overall sense, polytheism in both its naturalistic and humanistic forms tends to resist the rationalism of pantheism but accepts nonetheless the basic understanding of the non-transcendental immanence of deity, while at the same time it retains theism's notion of divine personality (in this case, multiple) whether as a reality, a metaphor or both.

The resurgence in contemporary Western Pagan polytheism is to be seen as part of the personalization that Stewart Guthrie understands as the essence of religion. Against the power imbalance between the macrocosm and microcosm, Guthrie argues that religion is an attempt to humanize the universe. Projecting a personal deity as author or at least as a co-inhabitant of the universe allows humans to perceive an increase in the odds for survival and even prosperity. Even the medieval serf, by addressing the landowner as "lord" or "seignior," was seeking the possibility that a human face remained on the other end of power disparity and hence the hope for concomitant compassion and understanding. In the subsequent dynamic transformations of the West through the rise of capitalism, Max Weber predicted a steady increase of society's bureaucratization. In the resultant situation, the polytheistic response may be understood as a possible reaction to the enormous augmentation of modernity's impersonal bureaucracy and technological depersonalization. In this context, nature becomes the paradigm of successful interaction and interdependence between a plurality of quasi-autonomous forces. Whether for reasons that seek succor against overwhelming odds or simply the emotional comfort to be found in a cooperative multitude, personifying pluralistic cosmic conditions results in polytheism.

Consequently, the multiplicity suggested through a polytheistic perspective is in part a recognition of the ambivalent position of nature *vis-à-vis* humankind. For instance, the core deities of the proto-Indo-Europeans comprise a "heptatheon" (a pantheon of seven figures) that is suggested through such metaphors as the sun, moon, Earth, bright sky, dawn, fire and lightning. In contrast to these divine prototypes, these same peoples posited a range of antithetical entities (anti-gods or *asuras*) whose chief symbols are the volcano, the drought and the tempest. In other words, the proto-Indo-European employed the diverse natural panorama to express theological understandings of the negative and positive sides of divinity as well as a "force" or "forces" opposed to both. The relationship of Indo-European polytheism to pantheism is also ambivalent: expressing on the one hand that divinity is not the all of what is, and yet, on the other, that the "asurian" as the personification of the primordial void does not ontologically exist. It is instead an "operative nonexistent."

But apart from the nexic prototypes of most if not all pantheons being nature, the challenging interface of polytheism revolves around the issues of idolatry, the one versus the many, and enchantment. Some of the greatest minds of the twentieth century (e.g., Max Weber, Aldous Huxley) have engaged the pragmatic values of polytheism as a conceptual framework. While traditional theology tends exclusively to seek the abstraction alleged to be behind concrete manifestation, an organic idolatry is polytheistic and finds the sacred not only in the ethereal but in and as nature throughout. It may be difficult to ascertain fully the historic revulsion to idolatry, but suspicion suggests that it springs, at least in part, from a human fear of impermanence. A beloved grows old and eventually dies. Even a highly revered stone *lingam* will wither over time and crumble. Any tangible embodiment is precarious and vulnerable. But nature (from *natus* "born") comprehends not only birth but the passing as well. Nature is the celebration of the complete cycle as well, when it is time, a letting go. To find the divine in the full natural round is polytheism to its core.

If Isaiah 44 and Galatians 5 as well other biblical passages condemn idolatry because of a preference for a non-spatial being that stands over or beyond all telluric phenomena, Huxley argues nevertheless that there is no conceivable way to demonstrate whether the godhead is one or many. For him, both are true, but he questions whether both are equally useful. For Huxley, monotheism and polytheism are rationalizations of distinct psychological states: people for whom a unifying urge predominates worship one god; those who are consciously aware of diversity within the world and themselves, worship many gods. Ontologically, "though the 'real' existence of the deities of any pantheon may be doubted, the existence of the internal and external diversity of which they are symbolical is undeniable" (Huxley 1936: 16). Huxley sees that polytheists honor instinct, passion, intuition and variety – the very antitheses of abstract knowledge concerning the general and uniform that allows the explanations, predictions, organizations, practicalities and efficiencies upon which modern life depends. All the same, any worship of a perfect One is the worship of an abstraction and the equivalent of worshipping nothing at all. Instead, "To live, the soul must be in intimate contact with the world, must assimilate it through all the channels of sense and desire, thought and feeling, which nature has provided" (Huxley 1936: 35). Yet, as Weber explains in describing the contemporary condition of the hegemony of rationalized structures in a denatured world,

> We live as did the ancients when their world was not yet disenchanted of its gods and demons, only we live in a different sense. As Hellenic man at times sacrificed to Aphrodite and at other times to Apollo, ... so do we still nowadays, only the bearing of man has been disenchanted and denuded of its mystical but inwardly genuine plasticity (1958: 148).

Whereas Karl Marx speaks of alienation and Emile Durkheim of anomie, Weber is concerned with disenchantment: the spiritual wasteland achieved by dogmatic and totalized rationality. "The fate of our times is characterized by rationalization and intellectualization and, above all, by the 'disenchantment of the world'" (Weber 1958: 155).

Influenced by Weber, Huxley claims that out of experiential knowledge of the world's diversity and "of the inner diversity of the human spirit, the poetic imagination of man extracts the deities of polytheism" (1936: 36). A monotheistic perspective or a "maimed version of polytheistic ritual ... represents only a part of the psychological and cosmic reality," while a true pantheon includes "every dionysiac reaction to the world, every corybantic participation of individual energies with the energies of living nature" (1936: 36). As Weber sees it, polytheism encourages an evaluative critique of our mechanical world: the iron cage of disenchanted rationalization. It allows for healthy choice-making, while its nemesis is the dogmatic, one-dimensional and anti-enchantment monopoly of monotheism.

As Weber is arguing optimistically for the receding night of modernity and the dynamics of reenchantment, Huxley calls for a new religion to replace the predominant monotheism of the present age – "either because it feebly believes in a decaying Christianity, or else secularly and irreligiously monotheistic, with the unitarianism of science, of democracy, of international capitalism" (1936: 37). He is considering the plight of the individual and society, whereas today we can include the ecological peril of the planet, the diminishment of its resources and the growing loss of an organic self-sustainability. But Huxley sums up the need for a pluralistic spirituality that "will have to be all, in a word, that human life actually is" (1936: 40). For "even in its worst days," Huxley explains, "polytheism never degenerated, as monotheism has done, into bloodless religious spirituality on the one hand, and an irreligious worship, on the other, of no less bloodless intellectual abstractions and mechanical efficiency" (1936: 38).

Nevertheless, as Alkis Kontos indicates,

> recovery of our essential plasticity does not occur in the bosom of Nature; it takes place in the iron cage of modern culture ... The spirits and gods of the enchanted world of the past, the world of Nature, now surface as impersonal forces, abstractions, ideas and ideals; ultimate values (1994: 240).

This amounts to an evocation of a new polytheism for a reenchanted future. But while for Kontos, "Nature is no longer the horizon upon which the humanly meaningful can be projected, ... for we have lost Nature forever" (1994: 229), and "Dynamic and self-confident, the modern soul stands before a disenchanted world, aware of its inadequacies, ready to seek its amelioration, never intoxicated with the illusion of omnipotence, never paralysed by despair and resignation" (1994: 238), we might still keep in mind Robert Corrington's insistence that there is nothing beyond nature. It is all that is – including the mechanized, dispassionate iron cage of modernity as well as Weber's polytheistic firmament and the organic stabilizing foundation for the primitive, the peasant and the ancient Greek. "Polytheism is only irrational when ... we regard its theology as its essence" (Oman 1931/1950: 401).

What is polytheism's essence is its affirmation of diversity and choice. In today's world the threat to an impoverished, diminishing nature and its elimination *vis-à-vis* urban encroachment and short-sighted management of the environment constitutes a reduction of human choice let alone of healthy sustainability. The current Western emergence of "nature religions," spiritualities that ground in natural metaphor and celebration of whatever is conceived as the "unspoiled," represents a spontaneous challenge to the loss of spiritual democracy within a world without an organic sense of direction. The modern/postmodern polytheisms are reactions to ill-conceived monopolies and are attempts to renegotiate through rituals and social service with long-neglected numinous powers of both nature and human culture. Polytheism *qua* polytheism seeks neither mystical retreat nor conquest of the one over the many but instead the cooperation between different interests and realities. When it grounds itself in a naturalistic pantheism or acosmic polydaemonism, it values both nature and civilization as sacred and worthy of unadulterated protection.

Michael York

Further Reading
Corrington, Robert S. *Nature's Religion*. Lanham, MD: Rowan & Littlefield, 1997.
Guthrie, Stewart Elliott. "Religion: What Is It?" *Journal for the Scientific Study of Religion* 35:4 (December 1996), 412–19.
Huxley, Aldous. "One and Many." *Do What You Will*. London: Watts, 1936, 1–40.
Kontos, Alkis. "The World Disenchanted, and the Return of Gods and Demons." In Asher Horowitz and Terry Maley, eds. *The Barbarism of Reason: Max Weber and the Twilight of Enlightenment*. Toronto: University of Toronto Press, 1994, 223–47.
Oman, John. *The Natural and the Supernatural*. Cambridge: University Press, 1931/1950.
Weber, Max. "Science as Vocation." In H.H. Gerth, tr. and C. Wright Mills, eds. *Max Weber: Essays in Sociology*. New York: Oxford University Press, 1958, 129–56.
York, Michael. *The Divine Versus the Asurian: An Interpretation of Indo-European Cult and Myth*. Bethesda, MD: International Scholars Publications, 1995.
See also: Animism; Paganism (various); Pantheism.

Population and Consumption – Contemporary Religious Responses

Environmental scientists maintain that the chemical balance of the atmosphere is being upset by the introduction of alien chemical species and the increased flow of greenhouse gases. The Intergovernmental Panel on Climate Change predicts a doubling of carbon dioxide and other greenhouse gases late in the twenty-first century drastically altering the Earth's climate. Although the atmosphere is self-cleaning, its self-cleaning is too slow to cope with the excess gases pumped into the atmosphere by our industrial development. As a consequence, we face the greenhouse effect that threatens human, animal and plant welfare. This is a problem we have created for ourselves and which population increase will make worse. Some suggest that the rise of the world's population, together with accompanying increasing levels of consumption, is rapidly outstripping the Earth's carrying capacity so that the very survival of humans, other species, and the quality of our environment are in question. Recently the 58 National Academies of Science from around the world called for zero population growth within the lifetime of our children and for changes in production and consumption patterns. Current demographic projections show a population increase of unprecedented magnitude continuing well into the twenty-first century.

At the 1992 Rio Earth Summit sponsored by the United Nations, the developing countries of the South responded to the developed countries of the North on this issue saying that the problems is not one of overpopulation in the South, but of excessive consumption of the Earth's resources by the well-off few in the North. For example, a baby born in Europe or North America will likely consume thirty times as much of the Earth's resources (and produce thirty times as much pollution) as a baby born in a developing country. But even this generalization is too simple, for there are increasing numbers of well-off people in developing countries such as India and China who consume at the same unsustainable level as those in developed countries. Also, although consuming less per capita, Asia's 3.2 billion people consume more of the Earth's resources than the 0.3 billion people in North America. What religions think about population and consumption is important for it is clear that religions can and do shape people's attitudes to nature, to fertility, and to the just sharing of the Earth's resources.

It is only recently, partly in response to growing concerns regarding population and consumption, that the various religions have had to question their sources with regard to the interaction of humans with nature. For example, the advent of eco-theology in Christianity has made nature and environment new, "cutting-edge" topics. In the Hindu context, Vandana Shiva offers a similar critique. What responses do religions offer?

In the Jewish tradition the mystical thought of the kabbalists suggests that humans must learn to limit themselves – their rate of reproduction, their use of natural resources, and their production of fouling wastes. As humans, we are to pattern our behavior after the example God gives in the creation of the world. If God is omnipresent then, reasoned the kabbalists, the only way God could create the world would be by an act of *tsimtsum* – of voluntary withdrawal or limitation so as to make room for creation. Similarly, we as humans must limit our reproduction and our wants, so as to make room for coexistence with our environment in this and future generations. If we humans are everywhere, our presence would herald the end of the great diversity of nature. The Jewish "exile" metaphor suggests that we humans find ourselves in a difficult diasporic condition in the twenty-first century, one that demands we take seriously the need to limit our population and consumption out of respect for the other communities of plants and animals with which we live as sojourners within nature.

Some scholars judge that Christianity has had a major responsibility for fostering much of the world's excessive consumption and overpopulation. Yet within Christianity there are strong forces at work transforming its mainstream into a self-critical force for justice, peace and the maintenance of the integrity of nature. The ecology of the planet cannot be separated from population and social justice concerns when seen through the lens of Christian feminist theology. In this context, the traditional Christian opposition to fertility control is being critically examined in relation to the looming crisis of overpopulation. Christian thinkers are recognizing, however, that it is overconsumption by the developed countries and classes that is both polluting the environment and depriving the developing countries of the resources they need. This leads to the radical conclusion that well-off Christians should reduce their own reproduction and resource consumption so as to make room for the migrating poor, and out of respect for our balance with nature. This is seen as a responsible practice of fertility in relation to others and nature. It also challenges the traditional patriarchal family patterns basic to many Christian cultures. Such teaching is in line with the teaching of the Hebrew prophets who maintain that humans and nature are required to live together in justice, and with the teaching of Jesus that one must love one's neighbor in need (e.g., as did the Good Samaritan). Christians today are realizing that their neighbor's welfare is strongly affected by the way they treat the environment and by the number of children they produce. The resulting ethic is one of interdependence with the rest of creation.

Some Muslims see natural disasters such as floods, hurricanes, and earthquakes as warnings from God that people are embarked upon a fundamentally wrong course of action, and that the disasters the greenhouse effect threatens might be similarly understood. When seen as a "wake-up" call from God, the greenhouse effect resulting from excessive consumption by humans poses a serious dilemma to Muslims around the world, but particularly to those Muslim countries such as Saudi Arabia, whose economy has come to depend upon the heavy use of oil. For such countries, and for the world at large, Islam's view of humanity as the "custodian of nature" (*Khalifa*) poses critical questions. As Muslim scholar, Nawal Ammar, points out, the Qur'an teaches that humans, as custodians of nature, are free to satisfy their needs *only* with an eye to the welfare of all creation. The harmony and beauty God gave nature must be respected by humans in their stewardship of nature. Thus the use of natural resources must be balanced and not excessive. No one owns nature, therefore humans must share natural resources and population pressure will dictate limits to consumption so that there can be just access to resources by all. While fertility control is generally forbidden in the Qur'an, some Muslims now suggest that fertility control may be acceptable if seen as part of the self-discipline required from humans to avoid upsetting the divinely established balance of nature.

A Buddhist scholar, David Loy, has argued that when a functional definition of religion is adopted, the global market economy is seen to be the most powerful contemporary world religion. Today, he suggests, the market economy is rapidly binding all corners of the globe into a worldview with "consumerism" as its dominant value-system. This new world religion threatens to overwhelm both the value-systems of the traditional religions and the environment that sustains us. Rather than putting a brake on our excessive growth in consumption, the global market appears to do the reverse. More and more natural resources are needed to fuel the ever-expanding global market, leaving less for future generations and producing more climate-altering greenhouse gases. To the religion of the market, the challenge of the population explosion does not pose a problem. It simply creates a larger market to be "developed," which, of course, entails more exploitation of the Earth's already overexploited ecology. The Buddhist response, Loy explains, offers a way in which we may be unhooked from the religion of consumption and gives equal place to the need to discourage excessive reproduction. The key question is what values and practices would convince people to consume and reproduce less when they have the technological capacity to consume and reproduce more? Buddhism has focused on meditational techniques that have the power to transform one's consumerism into "the middle way." Meditational practice allows one to actualize the central Buddhist teaching of the interconnectedness of everything in one's daily life. This doctrine has potential implications for one's response to the ecological challenge of today. It means that our individualistic sense of identity can be expanded, through meditation, until one experiences a "we-self" in which we are connected to everything and everything to us. Reality is seen as composed of a web-like causality in which everything affects everything else in some way; everything (including humans, animals, plants, Earth, air and water) is interdependent.

From such a Buddhist perspective, the urge to consume more and more and the urge to reproduce are both equally serious problems. Both spring from egocentric motivations and produce results that seriously damage nature. Meditation on the interdependence of humans with nature can result in the negating of selfish desires for children or material possessions when having them would harm other persons or the environment. In terms of our language of rights and responsibilities, the rights of other beings (including animals and future generations) must not be infringed upon by our excessive reproduction and consumption; and we are responsible not to harm other beings unnecessarily through our reproduction and consumption. All of this happens when *trishna*, or desire, is renounced through meditation. Happiness, from the Buddhist perspective, comes when the self-centered greed for more of everything, including children, is given up. Then limits to consumption and reproduction, such as our current ecological crises may require, are experienced not as personal loss but as normal and pleasant in the interdependent matrix of nature.

The above is a modern interpretation of Buddhist thought in response to the challenges of population pressure and excess consumption. While this approach has yet to be adopted in many largely Buddhist societies that have historically maintained high birth rates, it does offer a new and hopeful response.

From a Hindu scholar's perspective, Vasudha Narayanan notes the close connections between teachings in the Hindu epics and *puranas* on *dharma* (righteousness, duty, justice) and the ravaging of the Earth. When *dharma* declines, humans take it out on nature. It is in the *dharma* rather that the *moksa* or enlightenment texts that Narayanan finds resources for a Hindu response to the problems of population pressure and excess consumption. She searches out *dharma* texts with helpful teachings and matches up *dharma* practices in which present-day Hindus are engaged. She finds many teachings condemning the cutting down of trees and supporting the planting of trees – even to the goddess Parvati teaching that one tree is equal to ten sons! Hindu temples such as the Tirumala-Tirupati temple in South India are showing great initiative in fostering the *dharma* of tree planting by giving out about 100,000 saplings a day to pilgrims for them to plant when they return home. This practice is more powerful than it may seem, since the Tirumala-Tirupati temple is the richest in India and carries considerable dharmic clout with Hindus at home and in diaspora communities. In Hindu texts trees – like cows – are recognized as preservers and sustainers of life and therefore appropriate symbols of God. Turning from trees to rivers, Narayanan notes that rivers also occur in *dharma* texts as sacred purifiers of pollution, with the Ganges as the prime example. Observing that the rivers of India are rapidly being dammed and fouled by both industrial and human wastes, Narayanan points out that it is the women of India who lead the fight against these practices. Some successes have been achieved such as the protest led by Ms. Medha Patkar resulting in the stopping of the Narmada river dam project. Women have also led the way in pressing Hindu dance into the service of ecology.

Turning to the population problem, Narayanan observes that *dharma* texts that emphasize the duty of procreation were formulated during periods when epidemics and famines kept population levels down, child mortality was high and death came early. Now, with modern medicine, India's population has rapidly increased to levels that are causing serious ecological damage. However, in certain states, such as Kerala, where girls are educated and women are employed at all levels; reproduction is at the replacement rate only. Thus, the key may be the seeking out of texts such as those in the *Upanisads* that set forth the education of girls and women, as well as examples in the epics and *puranas* of women who do not conform to the patriarchal dharmic ideals espoused in those texts. Regarding consumption, Narayanan notes that Hindu texts are replete with the dangers of futility of possessions. Yet consumerism is rapidly taking over India in the name of modernization. Even worse, perhaps is the use of the dowry system as a way of fulfilling greed for consumer luxury items. While the Hindu theological response is showing some success in producing positive ecological practices, it seems to be losing ground to desires for excess consumption.

Regarding their response to the issues of population and consumption, there is much in common between the Aboriginal traditions and Chinese Religions. Aboriginal scholar Daisy Sewid-Smith maintains that although Aboriginal traditions place a high value on the sacredness of life, contraception and abortion have historically been practiced to maintain an ecological balance. Methods employed included birth control by sexual abstinence during periods of war, hunting or spiritual quest, and the knowledge of medicine people who specialized in contraceptive medicines and techniques. Overall guidance in such matters is provided by the Aboriginal sense of needing to live in interdependence with nature – to maintain a state of equilibrium between humans and their natural environment. This ethic also guided the Aboriginal approach to the consumption of material resources – aided by the lack of a notion of private property which seems basic to much contemporary consumerism.

Chinese Religions should be seen as divergent from the traditional pronatal approaches of most religions. As the scholars of Chinese thought, Jordan and Li Chuang Paper, show, during China's early history the concern was with underpopulation, therefore the sources offer little guidance regarding overpopulation. However, during the past three centuries, overpopulation and its negative impact upon the environment have become a matter of serious concern. With the possibility of a doubling of the population every generation, China in 1980 adopted a one child per family policy. This policy is widely practiced and appears to have the support of the people, who see overpopulation as a threat to the future of the globe and to family well-being. The success of this policy in controlling population growth is especially remarkable as it clashes directly with the fundamental imperative of Chinese Religion, namely the continuation of the patrilineal family. If the one child is not a son to conduct the family rituals then, according to traditional Chinese Religion, the parents, the grandparents, etc., will cease to exist upon the last son's death and the family will come to an end. However, changes are occurring which suggest that a gender-neutral family is developing, in which a daughter or a son could perform the rituals required for the continuation of the family and the support of those in the afterlife. This would enable Chinese Religion to support the one-child policy and its goal of preventing overpopulation from disrupting the balance (*tao*) of nature.

Harold Coward

Further Reading

Ammar, N.H. "Islam, Population and the Environment." In Harold Coward, ed. *Population, Consumption and the Environment*. Albany: State University of New York Press, 1995, 123–36.

Coward, Harold, ed. *Population, Consumption and the Environment*. Albany: State University of New York Press, 1995.

Coward, Harold. "Religious Responsibility." In Harold Coward and T. Hurba, eds. *Ethics and Climate Change: The Greenhouse Effect*. Waterloo: Wilfrid Laurier University Press, 1993, 39–60.

Coward, Harold and D.C. Maguire, eds. *Visions of a New Earth: Religious Perspectives on Population, Consumption and Ecology*. Albany: State University of New York Press, 2000.

Hare, E.K. "The Challenge." In Harold Coward and T. Hurka, eds. *Ethics and Climate Change: The Greenhouse Effect*. Waterloo: Wilfrid Laurier University Press, 1993, 11–22.

Houghton, J.T. and IPCC. *Climate Change: The IPCC Scientific Assessment*. Cambridge: Cambridge University Press, 1992.

Keller, Catherine. "A Christian Response to the Population Apocalypse." In Harold Coward, ed. *Population, Consumption and the Environment*. Albany: State University of New York Press, 109–22.

Loy, David R. "The Religion of the Market." In Harold Coward and D.C. Maguire, eds. *Visions of a New Earth*. Albany: State University of New York Press, 2000, 15–28.

McFague, Sallie. *The Body of God: An Ecological Theology*. Minneapolis: Fortress Press, 1993.

Narayanan, Vasudha. "One Tree is Equal to Ten Sons." In Harold Coward and D.C. Maguire, eds. *Visions of a New Earth*. Albany: State University of New York Press, 2000, 111–30.

Paper, Jordan and Li Chuang Paper. "Chinese Religions, Population and the Environment." In Harold Coward, ed. *Population, Consumption and the Environment*.

Albany: State University of New York Press, 1995, 173–94.

Ruether, Rosemary Radford. *Gaia and God: An Ecofeminist Theology of Earth Healing*. San Francisco: HarperSanFrancisco, 1992.

Sewid-Smith, Daisy. "Aboriginal Spirituality, Population and the Environment." In Harold Coward, ed. *Population, Consumption and the Environment*. Albany: State University of New York Press, 1995, 63–72.

Shiva, Vandana. *Staying Alive: Women, Ecology and Development*. London: Zed Books, 1988.

Zoloth, Laurie. "The Promises of Exiles: A Jewish Theology of Responsibility." In Harold Coward and D.C. Maguire, eds. *Visions of a New Earth*. Albany: State University of New York Press, 2000, 95–110.

See also: Abortion; Breeding and Contraception; Fertility and Abortion; Fertility and Secularization; Judaism and the Population Crisis; Population, Consumption, and Christian Ethics; United Nations' "Earth Summits".

Population, Consumption, and Christian Ethics

The United Nations projects that the world's population will grow by 50 percent from approximately six billion in 2000 to nine billion in 2050. Virtually all of that growth will be in the nations of the developing world. Concerns have been expressed that this continued growth in the world's population will further endanger the planet ecologically. Representatives of developing nations, however, have insisted that any attention to population policy be conjoined with examination of ecologically ruinous consumption patterns among citizens of developed nations. This entry summarizes recent Christian ethical reflection on population and consumption issues by Rosemary Radford Ruether, Sallie McFague, John Cobb, Jr., and James Nash.

The area of population policy has gone through some significant changes in recent years. Since the failure of ill-conceived and invasive policies in the 1960s, a narrow focus on population control and contraceptive technologies has been largely rejected in favor of placing population programs within the broader context of development policies, and to a lesser extent, women's reproductive rights and health. In addition, more attention has been given to the ecological impact of population growth and consumption patterns.

In the past, ethicists have evaluated population policies that contain various types of incentives, disincentives, and forms of coercion by considering their impact on four primary human values: freedom, justice, general welfare, and security or survival. While responsible moral evaluation of specific population polices involves reflection on all four of these primary values, ethicists have arranged these values in different orders of priority. For example, some have made the values of general welfare and security/survival subordinate to the more fundamental values of freedom and justice. Others have taken the opposite approach and have emphasized that without a fundamental measure of general welfare and security it is impossible to experience the values of freedom and justice.

This difference in the ordering of primary moral values is reflected in recent Christian ethical reflection on population and consumption issues. Rosemary Radford Ruether has argued that it is vital to ground population issues in a broader context of social and economic justice. Arguing that population growth is rooted in poverty and injustice, Ruether insists that one essential dimension to this task is the need to narrow the gap between the rich and the poor. Linking population and consumption issues, Ruether argues in *Gaia and God* that the "high consumption of the wealthy" and the "low consumption of the many" are not separate but interdependent realities caused by global economic systems that benefit the affluent few and harm the numerous poor (1992: 89). Ruether also insists, however, that another essential dimension of population policies must be the goal to improve the status of women and to empower them in terms of moral agency. She is convinced that population policies that do not place a priority on improving the status of women and their moral agency will be abusive to women and also will not work. Ruether acknowledges that "(h)umanity has no real alternative to population control," but she argues that the best way to avoid a doubling in the world's population is by addressing the twin challenges of poverty and patriarchy (1992: 263–4).

Sallie McFague makes similar arguments in her work, though she has focused more on the ecological challenges posed by rapacious rates of consumption in wealthy, industrialized nations. McFague argues in *The Body of God* that those most responsible for global ecological degradation are "first-world, usually white, usually male, entrepreneur(s) involved in a high-energy, high-profit business" (1993: 4). More recently, McFague argues in *Life Abundant* that the high-consumption lifestyle of North American middle-class Christians is not only sinful, but also evil because it "lies at the root of the systemic structures that make the wealthy richer and the poor more impoverished" (2001: 117). The primary remedy she offers is the virtue of frugality and a theology of sacrifice. She implores Christians with means to live more simply so that others may simply live. McFague acknowledges that these appeals to character formation will be insufficient by themselves to close the gap between the rich and poor, but she believes that cultivation of the virtues of frugality and sacrifice is a necessary part of any solution. Once fundamental attitudes change, then new policies can be conceived that will reduce poverty, population growth, and overconsumption along with their negative ecological impacts.

Another important figure in discussions of population and consumption issues is John Cobb, Jr. On the consumption side, Cobb has worked hard to offer conceptual foundations and workable policies for a more just, peaceful, and sustainable world. Cobb's contributions to population issues have varied quite significantly, however, according to his chosen dialogue partners. For example, *The Liberation of Life*, which Cobb co-authored with Charles Birch in 1981, articulates the moral foundations for a population policy that bears a striking resemblance to the consensus emerging in the international community today. In league with Ruether, Birch and Cobb recommend that population growth must be seen in the larger context of the process of development and that the real key to lower fertility rates rests with improvement in the lives of women. In 1989, however, Herman Daly and John Cobb offered a controversial proposal for population stabilization in *For the Common Good*. In a chapter devoted to population policy, Daly and Cobb consider "transferable birth quota plans" in which governments would issue birth rights certificates to parents to sell or use as they deem fit on an open market. One of the criticisms of their proposal, however, is that on an unequal economic playing field the poor would be faced with the terrible option of having to sell their fundamental right to bear children in order to purchase fundamental necessities like food, clothing, and shelter. Daly and Cobb acknowledge that one of the weaknesses of this plan is its inability to assure "just distribution" of births and they do not think that current demographic circumstances are serious enough to warrant the use of the plan now, but they do believe that the plan should be held in reserve "should present demographic trends reverse themselves" (1989: 251).

Like Cobb, James Nash has offered similar realistic sentiments in his work. In *Loving Nature*, Nash consistently links his treatment of population and consumption issues, referring to both as manifestations of "anthropocentric imperialism" (1991: 211). Nash argues that contraception must serve as the centerpiece of a morally adequate policy aimed at curbing population growth. This would include the fundamental right to information and education about birth control as well as access to various means. In addition, Nash also emphasizes that a morally adequate population policy will need to be part of a broader goal of increasing socio-economic justice and sustainable development. But Nash's concerns about *effectively* lowering the rate of population growth also lead him to propose criteria for evaluating population polices that seek to do more than just inform and enable voluntary family planning. Nash's willingness to consider more coercive means of regulating human fertility flows out of his rights-based approach to a Christian environmental ethic. Cutting against the increasing international emphasis on reproductive rights and the United Nations Declaration of Universal Human Rights, Nash argues that humans do *not* have the right to reproduce, although they may have the right not to be *forced* to reproduce. In his discussion of the relationship of human rights to human environmental rights, Nash argues in *Loving Nature* that "(s)ecurity and subsistence rights always impose limits on other citizen's freedoms of action" (1991: 50). Thus, Nash is able to support the limitation of human reproductive freedoms on the grounds of ecological security and couches such action in terms of ecological justice.

In my own work, I have sided primarily with Ruether and her dual emphasis on social and economic justice as well as the importance of improving the lives of women. I share her confidence that development oriented toward the needs of the poor and social reforms designed to improve the status of women are good in their own right and are also effective means to achieve global population stabilization. A survey of recent demographic data indicates that, when female literacy, education, and reproductive health rates increase, fertility rates decline. I also agree with Cobb, however, that simplistic approaches to development have not worked and will remain "unworkable" until the failed paradigm of development as economic growth is replaced with a new paradigm of sustainable development. Until it becomes clear, however, that this alternative approach has been tried and has failed, I will remain reluctant to abide much discussion of various forms of coercion in population programs, although I do believe there is a place for carefully monitored incentive packages.

James B. Martin-Schramm

Further Reading

Cobb, John B., Jr. *Sustainability: Economics, Ecology, & Justice*. Maryknoll: Orbis Books, 1992.

Cobb, John B., Jr. and Herman E. Daly. *For the Common Good: Redirecting the Economy Toward Community, the Environment, and a Sustainable Future*. Boston: Beacon Press, 1989.

Cobb, John B., Jr. and Charles Birch. *The Liberation of Life: From the Cell to the Community*. Denton: Environmental Ethic Books, 1990.

Martin-Schramm, James B. *Population Perils and the Churches' Response*. Geneva: World Council of Churches Publications, 1997.

McFague, Sallie. *Life Abundant: Rethinking Theology and Economy for a Planet in Peril*. Minneapolis: Fortress Press, 2001.

McFague, Sallie. *The Body of God: An Ecological Theology*. Minneapolis: Fortress Press, 1993.

Nash, James A. *Loving Nature: Ecological Integrity and Christian Responsibility*. Nashville: Abingdon Press, 1991.

Ruether, Rosemary Radford. *Gaia & God: An Ecofeminist Theology of Earth Healing*. San Francisco: HarperSanFrancisco, 1992.

See also: Abortion; Breeding and Contraception; Fertility and Abortion; Fertility and Secularization; Population and Consumption – Contemporary Religious Responses.

Power Animals

The particular consciousness that fosters spiritual experience and religious form evolved through direct and significant experience with the natural world, including a special relationship with what have become known as "animal guides" or "power animals." Of these, first and foremost may have been the bear. The bear cult of the Paleolithic is one of the oldest of human traditions, growing out of the Neanderthals' systemized veneration of the giant cave bears they competed with for shelter and food. Archeological evidence indicates the first human burials coincided with the earliest use of altars and shrines, and the rituals of appeasement, gratitude and wonder that must have attended them. The bear in particular retained its religious significance among the early Celts, the tribes of Siberia, and the surviving traditionalist Ainu of northern Japan.

For most of human existence connection to the realm of spirit, vision and power was commonly believed to come through intimate relationship with plant and animal intermediaries. Totemism can mean a clan or tribe identifying with the ancestors of a certain species, but it can also refer to personal affiliation with a particular "animal of power." In this case the person heeds what he believes to be its instruction and example, and through ritual communion or interpenetration seeks to make its abilities, penchants and wisdom his own. Totemism may have developed not so much out of envy of the superior speed or strength of other creatures, as from a deep and abiding identification with them.

Among many Native American tribes, members wore several names during their lifetime, such as one denoting what clan and lineage they belonged to, another extolling their deeds or skills, and still another proclaiming their personal animal guide. The carved Haida wolf hat, the Kwakiutl totem pole and the costumes of Hopi Deer Dancers are representative of power animals, specifically species the people depend upon on for sustenance or inspiration.

Like our various ethnic animist and pantheist ancestors, a percentage of contemporary environmentalist and Pagan communities look to the more-than-physical world for essential lessons, assistance and alliance. The "New Age" approach often involves picking an animal that the person would most want to be like, either from reading about the habits of animals, or by drawing a card and image from a shuffled "medicine deck." For some Pagans and ecospiritualists one's power animal is not their favorite, but rather that species that seems to call to them from dreams, or manifests itself in their life and actions. Unlike the sky-god religions of "civilized" cultures, these groups draw from terrestrial sources for direction and sense of purpose. It could be said that the animal "spirits," however ephemeral, are both substantive and natural: embodied contextually, organically, energetically and spiritually in nature.

To the "deep" or spiritual ecologist, direct observation of and interaction with other life forms is considered the best way to explore and exploit their valued gifts. Through example if not design, these "others" can encourage a fateful return: to authentic and sentient self, and to intimate reciprocal relationship with place. In this totemic journey one may go beyond unconscious symbiosis with other life forms and enter into a personal and committed relationship with specific advisory totems. To some, the acceptance of "kindred spirits" as guides must include a pledge fully to utilize their gifts and lessons, acting for the good of the whole with all the joy and resolve that could be expected from the honorable totems themselves.

Jesse Wolf Hardin

Further Reading
Campbell, Joseph. *The Way of the Animals (Part 2): Mythologies of The Great Hunt*. New York: Harper & Row, 1988.
Hardin, Jesse Wolf. *Kindred Spirits: Sacred Earth Wisdom*. North Carolina: Swan, Raven & Co. 2001.
See also: Animals; Animism (various); Deep Ecology; New Age; Paganism; Paleolithic Religions; Totemism.

Prairyerth Fellowship

The Chicago-area-based Prairyerth Fellowship is a prime example of the kind of dynamic religious experimentation and entrepreneurship that has found fertile ground within the spiritual ecology movement. Prairyerth was founded in 1998 as a lay-led Unitarian Universalist (UU) fellowship focused on healing and harmonizing with the Earth. The fellowship maintains a special spiritual identification with its local bioregion and gets its name from an old geological term for the soils of North America's central grasslands. "Prairyerth" is essentially the word for the American Prairie ecosystem and, for fellowship founders, this was the perfect image to describe the nature of their nascent spiritual community – "an independent network of plants, animals, people, fire, earth, and sky that forms the richest, most nurturing soil in the world." Prairyerth's descriptive literature, found on its website, explains that like the prairie itself: "We seek renewal through the interdependent web of life. We too spring from the land that nourishes us." Members affirm a special bond of union that states in part: "We pledge ourselves to a fellowship that recognizes the Earth as home, that acknowledges the unity of life while affirming each entity as a unique and irreplaceable resource in the web of all existence" (www.prairyerth.net).

The fellowship itself is governed by four councils each with its own responsibilities: the Council of Wisdom, the Council of Earth, the Council of Healers, and the Seventh Generation Council. Each has two members who represent the council on the Board of Trustees. Rather than hire resident religious specialists and administrators (ministers or priests), the Prairyerth community seeks to empower each individual to play an active role as spiritual leader within the community. Fellowship members rotate responsibilities for planning and facilitating worship and ritual, such as seasonal celebrations or coming-of-age ceremonies. Others organize community programs that reinforce the Prairyerth principle of harmony with nature through children's and adult education workshops and prairie restoration projects. Fellowship members have a special interest, however, in learning about Native American healing traditions and in supporting efforts that support the cultural viability of local tribes and conserve Native American sacred sites and burial grounds.

Because Prairyerth's worship is fundamentally Earth-centered in focus, its members do not congregate on Sunday mornings as do most UU churches. Prairyerth's members instead gather for fellowship and celebration at the new or full moon, in accordance with the cycles of Earth and sun that mark solstices and equinoxes, and also gather to celebrate traditional planting and harvesting festivals. The meeting place for such gatherings is flexible and adapts to the type of worship event, migrating indoors (where space is rented from local Unitarian Universalist churches) or outdoors to special places in nature, depending on climate and ceremonial needs. "Prairie animals too migrate," Prairyerth's website points out, citing the example of the buffalo.

The fellowship accepts members from all different religious traditions and encourages "a free and responsible search for truth and meaning." Inspiration for its basic stated community values (harmony with nature and respect for the interdependent web of life) stems from a variety of sources, but the legacy of Ralph Waldo Emerson and Henry David Thoreau (both associated with the roots of the Unitarian Universalist tradition) has played a significant role, as have a number of historical and contemporary Native American holy people. The membership body of the fellowship extends throughout 12 different states; similar groups within the Midwest have likewise adopted the "Prairyerth" image and operate under Unitarian Universalist Association (UUA) affiliated status. One such fellowship is the "Prairyerth Zen Center" in Topeka, Kansas, which emphasizes spiritual connection to the local bioregion and is also a recognized UUA affiliate.

Sarah McFarland Taylor

Further Reading
Buell, Lawrence. *The Environmental Imagination: Thoreau, Nature Writing, and the Formation of American Culture.* Cambridge, MA: Harvard University Press, 1995.
Buell, Lawrence. *Literary Transcendentalism: Style and Vision in the American Renaissance.* Ithaca: Cornell University Press, 1973.
Engel, J. Ronald. *Sacred Sands: The Struggle for Community in the Indiana Dunes.* Middletown, CT: Wesleyan University Press, 1986.
Least Heat-Moon, William. *PrairyErth*. Boston: Houghton Mifflin Company, 1991.
Wigmore-Beddoes, Dennis. *Yesterday's Radicals: A Study of the Affinity Between Unitarianism and Broad Church Anglicanism in the Nineteenth Century.* Cambridge, England: J. Clarke, 2002.

See also: Back to the Land Movements; Bioregionalism; Emerson, Ralph Waldo; Restoration Ecology and Ritual; Romanticism; Thoreau, Henry David; Transcendentalism; Unitarianism.

Prakriti

Prakriti was the word the speakers of the languages of North India chose to translate the English word "nature," and these days, many English-speaking persons from India perceive the words as synonymous. *Prakriti* was originally a Sanskrit word and it has a range of meanings. It is an important philosophical and theological concept in the Hindu religious tradition.

The meaning of the word *prakriti* in the early Sanskrit texts is "that which precedes," "original form," "the first" and "the model." It means "normal," and "health." *Prakriti* means also "material cause," "the producer of effects." In the plural it means "productive causes," "constituents," and "parts." *Prakriti* is the source from which the things of the world are produced, but it has also come to refer to all the products of *prakriti*, that is, nature as a whole. *Prakriti* is a grammatical feminine. This has purely grammatical reasons (Sanskrit nouns made by adding the ending -ti to the root are generally grammatically feminine). Two common synonyms of *prakriti*, *pradhana* and *avyakta*, are neuter.

As the material cause of the world, *prakriti* is a process having two aspects, dissolution and manifestation. The world dissolves into *prakriti*, but it also becomes manifest from it. These two aspects of *prakriti* were explored by different religious traditions. Among renunciant groups the dissolution of the manifestations of *prakriti* by means of meditation and knowledge was seen as the method for the individual to gain release from rebirth (*moksha*). Later, in other religious groups, *prakriti* as the creative principle became an epithet of the Goddess and *prakriti* was worshipped as a divine feminine principle.

The renunciant view of *prakriti* was systematized by the ancient Samkhya and yoga schools of religious thought. Samkhya and yoga are salvific systems, that is, the goal of their practice is release from rebirth (i.e., to realize the absolute separation of the principle of pure consciousness [*purusha*] from the principle of matter [*prakriti*]). This is attained with the dissolution of the manifestations of *prakriti*. Prakriti is an independent principle. It is also eternal, an object of consciousness, common to all, unconscious, productive and interdependent.

That everything in the world is interdependent does not mean that nature is perceived as harmonious. Nature is filled with incompatible species, that is, what is food for one individual is another living being's death. According to Samkhya and yoga, no enjoyment is possible without causing injury to other beings; suffering is therefore a basic characteristic of existence. As a response to this, Samkhya and yoga emphasize restraint and non-injury. To aim for the dissolution of the manifestations of *prakriti* of the individual into their material cause and the separation of *purusha* from *prakritit*, is the ultimate act of non-injury. Even if the goal of the renunciants is release from the world, the renunciants in India often stay at places of striking natural beauty. Likewise, the centers of the Hindu saints and renunciants often have beautiful gardens and they are described in the classical Hindu texts as earthly paradises. The descriptions of the natural beauty and harmony of these places are meant to convey the ideal of renunciation. As a result of the advanced spiritual state of the humans living there, their presence does not disturb the peace of nature. The views of Samkhya and yoga of the material principle and consciousness as two independent principles and of the principle of consciousness as the ultimate source of freedom from pain, therefore, generate an attitude of renunciation favorable to the non-destruction of nature. Through non-attachment and withdrawal humans minimize their impact on the natural world. Renunciation and non-attachment are not only important to the renunciants, but are also fundamental values of the Hindu culture at large. These traditional values have increasingly been challenged by consumptive attitudes promoted by the modern economic value system. The institution of renunciation has however retained its strength.

Hindu theologians inherited the concept of *prakriti* as the material cause of the world from the Samkhya and yoga systems of religious thought. The principles of matter (*prakriti*) and consciousness (*purusha*) were transformed into cosmological and divine principles. *Prakriti* as the material cause of the world was understood as dependent on the divine principle and was personified as a goddess. In Hinduism ultimate reality is often seen as bipolar, as the union of a male and female divine principle. The dualism of matter and consciousness of Samkhya and yoga was transferred to the divine couple. Only some of the attributes of *prakriti* were transferred to nature as a goddess. Most important were the attributes of being productive, diverse and interdependent. By being personified, consciousness was also transferred to *prakriti*.

According to one Hindu sacred story, at the beginning of creation the highest God divided himself into two, a male and a female half. The female half, called *prakriti*, divided herself further into other goddesses. Women are also said to be incarnations of this divine *prakriti*. In all the modern languages of India derived from Sanskrit, women are called *prakriti* or seen as symbols of *prakriti*.

Prakriti in the senses of goddess and women, and at the same time as a synonym of the English word "nature," has been promoted by feminist environmentalism in India as an alternative to, and a critique of, what is perceived as "the Western concept of nature" and to promote "goddess ecology" and feminist environmentalism. One of the foremost spokespersons for this brand of environmentalism, Vandana Shiva, asserts in her book *Staying Alive* that "feminism as ecology and ecology as the revival of Prakriti, the source of all life ... are the powers of political and economic transformation" (1989: 7). The famous Chipko movement, which has protected traditional use of the forest against industrial interests, is in many respects a women's environmental movement and is seen to exemplify the close relationship between *prakriti* and women. For the women of the Chipko, writes Vandana Shiva, "the nature they protect is the living Prakriti" (1989: xix). This Indian concept of *prakriti*, as a living female power, is by Shiva contrasted to the Cartesian concept of nature as passive, mechanistic, inferior and separate from human beings. Indian women are seen as protecting nature as *prakriti*, a "feminine principle from which all life arises" (1989: xviii) against those who view nature as dead matter and only a resource for industrial use.

Knut A. Jacobsen

Further Reading

Jacobsen, Knut A. *Prakrti in Samkhya-Yoga: Material Principle, Religious Experience, Ethical Implications.* New York: Peter Lang, 1999.

Jacobsen, Knut A. "The Female Pole of the Godhead in Tantrism and the Prakrti of Samkhya." *Numen* 43 (1996), 56–81.

Larson, Gerald James. *Classical Samkhya: An Interpretation of its History and Meaning.* Delhi: Motilal Banarsidass, 1979.

Shiva, Vandana. *Staying Alive: Women, Ecology and Development*. London: Zed Books, 1989.

Vatsyayan, Kapila, ed. *Prakrti: The Integral Vision*. 5 vols. Delhi: Indira Gandhi National Centre for the Arts, 1995.

See also: Ahimsa; Dharma – Hindu; Hinduism; India; Shakti; Shiva, Vandana; Tantra; Yoga and Ecology.

Prayer and the Contemplative Traditions

In the world's religions there are many kinds of prayer. Two general types are "prayers of address" and "contemplative prayer."

Prayers of Address

In prayers of address, the divine reality – understood as a multifaceted mystery in which the whole of the universe is enfolded – is addressed as a subject who is capable of hearing and responding to the petitions, praises, lamentations, questions, and feelings of those who pray. According to Hinduism this divine reality has many names and faces, such that particularized gods and goddesses can be seen as prismatic colors through which its uncreated light shines and becomes visible to human beings. Thus prayers of address can be addressed to the uncreated light itself (God) or to its particularized energies (gods and goddesses). These prayers may be communicated in words, but they can also be communicated through music, dance, ritual, and inner longings or, as the New Testament puts it, "sighs too deep for words." The latter idea suggests that some forms of prayer may not be conscious or focused, but rather dim and preconscious, expressive of deeper aims toward satisfactory survival, of which the one doing the praying is unaware. Prayers of address occur when these deeper aims are given expression, either consciously or unconsciously, and released into a larger divine context. This larger context can be conceived in a variety of ways: pantheistically, supernaturalistically, panentheistically, monistically, and otherwise. Beyond the various conceptions is the more general feeling, felt by many in the act of praying, that someone or something is listening.

This impulse to communicate with something vast and mysterious – a larger yet listening context in which the whole of the universe is nested – is thought in modern times to be restricted to human beings who consciously believe in the divine realities at issue. When the rest of nature is conceived in strictly mechanistic terms, as if devoid of any capacity for the self-expression of interior states, it is assumed that other living beings do not pray in an addressive way. However, in many religions traditions it is believed that other living beings are endowed with psychic properties of one sort or another, and studies in cognitive ethology bear this out. This opens up the possibility that they, too, each in their way, release sighs too deep for words into a divine reality, in which case they, too, "pray" in their ways, albeit without the kinds of explicit intention characteristic of conscious human prayer. This would mean that when the Psalmist speaks of all living beings as praising God in their own way, it is possible that indeed they do so. It would also mean that conscious human praying is an expression of, not an exception to, a kind of activity found throughout much of the natural world. Thus addressive prayer can be seen as adding to a chorus of nonhuman voices, each of whom has already been praying, in its own unique way, for millions of years. It is not an un-natural act or a super-natural act, but an ultra-natural act.

Contemplative Prayer

The phrase "contemplative prayer" comes from the Christian tradition, but it names a kind of praying that occurs in many world religions, sometimes (in Asian contexts) under the rubric meditation. In a Christian context, there are two kinds of contemplative prayer: contemplation of nature and contemplation of God. Contemplation of God can be compared to the state of consciousness one enjoys while sitting beside a person with whom one has been in love for many years. In the sitting together, there is no need to be anywhere else or to say anything, because both partners are already where they want to be. In the case of contemplative prayer, the beloved is the divine reality itself, and this reality is present within the very soul of the one who rests in the silence of the moment. There is no place to go and no need to say anything, because God is in the silence or wordless listening itself, as an embracing and compassionate context.

While this experience may seem distinctively human, it is perhaps not unlike the feelings that are known by mammalian embryos within the womb: a sense of being fully protected and immersed in a safe and wordless whole. It is no accident that, in some traditions, such prayer is understood as a returning to that more innocent and womb-like consciousness that preceded a fall into dualistic consciousness.

This spirit of being present in the moment – of wordless listening – can also occur in ordinary waking consciousness and in relation to the rest of creation. In the Orthodox Christian tradition, as explained by Kallistos Ware, this occurrence is called the contemplation of nature (1995: 90). According to Ware, this way of being present to nature involves two sensibilities simultaneously. One is a wordless attention to what Zen Buddhists call the sheer suchness – the as-it-isness – of each blade of grass, each face, each frog, each pond, each mountain. This attention is both relaxed and aware, and it is often accompanied by a sense of grateful amazement, or pure appreciation, for the pure existence of what is, as it is. In addition, the contemplation of nature involves an awareness that each individual creature is, its own way, a prism through which the divine reality is beheld, not unlike the way (described above) that the gods and goddesses are understood in Hinduism as such prisms. Thus, when a person gazes into the eyes of, for example, a wolf, the uncreated light of the divine shines through those eyes, even as it is not exhausted by those eyes. The wolf is seen as a vessel of holy mystery.

Analogous forms of "nature contemplation" are found in many religious traditions around the world, ranging from indigenous sensitivities to individual living beings being carriers of divine wisdom, to Buddhist emphases on mindful awareness of trees and stars, to Islamic emphases on the whole of creation being a sign (aya) of Allah. These kinds of experiences can also an important part of scientific observation, whether within or apart from accompanying beliefs in God, as exemplified by what one science writer, Ursula Goodenough, calls a willing assent to what presents itself for observation, combined with a more general sense of amazement or appreciation for what is given.

Some speculate that the capacity for relaxed yet alert attention in the present moment – for a contemplation of nature – has parallels in pre-agricultural periods of human history and also in other forms of life. Perhaps the early experiences of hunters and gatherers required wordless alertness in the stalking of prey and the gathering of herbs, and these sensitivities then gave rise to what we now call contemplative prayer. Additionally, capacities for relaxed and alert attention seem to be part of much animal life. The eighteenth-century British poet Christopher Smart wrote a long poem in praise of his cat Jeoffry, who, for Smart, displayed an implicit knowledge of the divine reality while in rest and sleep, leading one interpreter, Edward Hirsch, to speak of Smart's intuition of "divine catfulness" (Hirsch 1999: 68–9). If Smart is right, then, a contemplation of nature, like the prayers of address noted above, is a unique evolutionary expression of, not exception to, states of consciousness that are found throughout nature. And if Hirsch is right, then human appreciation of ways in which God is present in other forms of life, as illustrated in a sense of divine catfulness, is itself one form of contemplative prayer.

Jay McDaniel

Further Reading

Berry, Thomas. *Dream of the Earth*. San Francisco: Sierra Club, 1998.
Goodenough, Ursula. *The Sacred Depths of Nature*. New York: Oxford University Press, 1998.
Hirsch, Edward. *How to Read a Poem: And Fall in Love with Poetry*. New York: Harcourt Brace, 1999.
Kaza, Stephanie. *The Attentive Heart: Conversations with Trees*. New York: Ballantine Books, 1993.
McDaniel, Jay. *Living from the Center: Spirituality in an Age of Consumerism*. St. Louis: Chalice Press, 2000.

McFague, Sallie. *Super, Natural Christians*. Minneapolis: Fortress Press, 1997, 118–49.
Merton, Thomas. *Contemplative Prayer*. New York: Image Books, 1965.
Nasr, Seyyed. *The Spiritual Crisis in Modern Man*. Chicago: Kazi Publications, 1997.
Snyder, Gary. *The Practice of the Wild*. San Francisco: North Point Press, 1990.
Ware, Kallistos. *The Orthodox Way*. New York: St. Vladimir's Press, 1995.

See also: Animals; Cognitive Ethology, Social Morality, and Ethics; Magic; Religious Naturalism.

Prigogine, Ilya (1917–2003)

Ilya Prigogine, a Belgian scientist of Russian descent, has contributed considerably to the contemporary discourse on physics, nature, religion, and the humanities. Although Prigogine, who won the Nobel Prize in 1977 for his work on the thermodynamics of nonequilibrium systems, writes in a very sophisticated scientific style, his books gained enormous influence in a wider New Age context, albeit in a somewhat refined manner.

The starting point to understand Prigogine's theory is his new reading of thermodynamics. Newtonian dynamics are purely mechanical and treat time as reversible, while classical thermodynamics talk of an "arrow of time" that moves to increased entropy and loss of energy. Prigogine refutes both models and proposes his theory of *dissipative structures*. Dynamic and open systems that are far from equilibrium (like organic systems), he argues, bring forth new orders of higher complexity. In so doing, they do not follow universal laws, but develop according to their own systems' dynamics. And what is more, such open systems advance in constant exchange with the environment (dissipation) and are able to repair themselves on their evolutionary path (this process is totally different and much more complex than Darwin's paradigm had suggested). Prigogine's well-accepted discovery was the birth of a new discipline: *Synergetics*. Although living organisms are the most obvious examples of this – contrasting apparently "closed systems" like a clock-work, Prigogine, like other adherents of systems theories, maintains that dissipative structures can also be found in human artifacts that show a considerable capacity for self-organization. Consequently, he applies this model to social systems and human interaction. In this view, the human place is *within* nature, since human culture is a subsystem with countless interrelations to neighboring systems. Hence, humanity's role is neither domination nor stewardship, but involvement and empathy.

It is important to note that dissipative structures do not necessarily tend to gain a state of increased structure, but they just reach higher orders of instability and fluctuation.

Indeed, similar to other philosophies (cf. Schelling or Bergson), it is the *becoming* and not the *being* which is essential for Prigogine's theory. Therefore, he is critical of the belief in cosmic harmony or eternal laws and looks at the universe as always endangered, fragile, and uncertain. This attitude brings Prigogine in opposition both to scientists, who strive for a simple structured "Grand Unified Theory" (Steven W. Hawking, for instance, whom Prigogine sees as clinging to the old paradigm of "being"), and to teleological models prominent in New Age science. There is no "telos," Prigogine argues: instead of being a simple consequence of the present, future must be addressed as a lively process with a cornucopia of possibilities.

The theory of dissipative structures and the interdependence of natural and social subsystems – hence, the entanglement of mind and matter in self-organizing systems – leads to the assumption that small systems are able to influence the overall structure of nature and the universe. Humankind and even the individual are no longer passive objects but acknowledge their responsibility and power to influence the whole system. This in particular has attracted New Age thinkers who at the same time played down the more discontenting features of Prigogine's theory, like his refutation of teleological or causal assumptions, which goes along with his notion of contingency and the possibility of failure. Hence, Prigogine has gained a selective reception by authors like Erich Jantsch, Fritjof Capra, David Bohm, and even Marilyn Ferguson, all of whom brought into his theory a more mystical and teleological understanding.

Kocku von Stuckrad

Further Reading

Prigogine, Ilya (in collaboration with Isabelle Stengers). *The End of Certainty: Time, Chaos, and the New Laws of Nature.* New York: The Free Press, 1997.

Prigogine, Ilya. *From Being to Becoming: Time and Complexity in the Physical Sciences.* San Francisco: Freeman, 1980.

Prigogine, Ilya and Isabelle Stengers. *Order out of Chaos: Man's New Dialogue with Nature.* London: Heinemann, 1984.

See also: Bohm, David; Capra, Fritjof; Chaos; Complexity Theory; New Age.

Primate Spirituality

On 14 July 1960 I arrived, for the first time, on the shores of Gombe national park (it was a game reserve then) to learn about the behavior of wild chimpanzees. Little did I think as I snuggled into my tiny camp-bed on the first night, that I was launching what is today the longest uninterrupted study of any group of animals, anywhere. Or that the chimpanzees would provide me with information that would help us to redefine our relationship with the rest of the animal kingdom and to redefine what it means to be human.

The great apes (chimpanzees, bonobos, gorillas and orang-utans) have brains more like ours than those of any other living creatures. They are capable of intellectual performances that were once thought unique to us, including recognition of the self, abstraction and generalization, and cross-modal transfer of information. They have a sense of humor. They can experience mental as well as physical suffering. They use more objects as tools for a wider variety of purposes than any other creature except ourselves. And they modify objects for specific purposes, thus showing the beginning of tool-*making* – an ability once thought to differentiate humans from the rest of the animal kingdom. Moreover, across their range in Africa, chimpanzee communities show different tool-using behaviors which, as they are passed from one generation to the next through observation and imitation, can be defined as primitive cultures. Chimpanzees form affectionate, supportive and enduring bonds between individuals, especially family members, which may persist through life – they can live more than sixty years. They are capable of true altruism. Sadly, also like us, they have a dark side. They are aggressively territorial, and may perform acts of extreme brutality and even wage a kind of primitive war.

Clearly, then, there is no sharp line dividing humans from the rest of the animal kingdom. It is a very blurred line, and differences are of degree rather than kind. This leads to a new respect for the other amazing animal beings with whom we share Planet Earth. We *are* unique, but we are not as different as we used to think. The main difference is, perhaps, our extraordinarily complex intellect, and our ability to communicate ideas by means of a sophisticated *spoken* language, by the use of *words*. It should, however, be noted that apes in captivity can be taught to understand and use more than 300 signs of the American Sign Language as used by the deaf. They can communicate with these signs not only with their trainers but with each other. They can also learn to communicate using a variety of lexigrams and computer symbols. They can use these language skills in many contexts once they have been acquired.

Many theologians and philosophers argue that only humans have "souls." My years in the forest with the chimpanzees have led me to question this assumption. Day after day I was alone in the wilderness, my companions the animals and the trees and the gurgling streams, the mountains and the awesome electrical storms and the star-studded night skies. I became one with a world in which, apart from the change from day to night, from wet season to dry, time was no longer important. And there were moments of perception that seemed almost mystical so that I became ever more attuned to the great Spiritual Power that I felt around me – the Power that is worshipped as God, Allah, Tao, Brahma, the Great Spirit, the Creator, and so on. I came to believe that all living things possess a spark of that Spiritual Power. We humans, with our uniquely sophisticated minds and our spoken language that enables us to share and discuss ideas, call that spark, in ourselves, a "soul." Is not the same true for a chimpanzee? Or any other sentient, sapient being? It is most unlikely, however, that any animals other than ourselves care – or are capable of caring – as to whether or not they possess immortal souls!

Often I am asked if the chimpanzees show any signs of religious behavior. I think perhaps their "elemental" displays are precursors of religious ritual. Deep in the forest are some spectacular waterfalls. Sometimes as a chimpanzee – most often an adult male – approaches one of these falls his hair bristles slightly, a sign of heightened arousal. As he gets closer, and the roar of falling water gets louder, his pace quickens, his hair becomes fully erect, and upon reaching the stream he may perform a magnificent display close to the foot of the falls. Standing upright, he sways rhythmically from foot to foot, stamping in the shallow, rushing water, picking up and hurling great rocks. Sometimes he climbs up the slender vines that hang down from the trees high above and swings out into the spray of the falling water. This "waterfall dance" may last for ten or fifteen minutes.

It is not only waterfalls that can trigger displays of this sort. Chimpanzees "dance" at the onset of a very heavy rain, reaching up to sway saplings or low branches rhythmically back and forth, back and forth, then moving forward in slow motion loudly slapping the ground with their hands, stamping with their feet, and hurling rock after rock. Twice I have seen them perform thus during the first violent gusts of wind, presaging a storm. And sometimes a chimpanzee charges slowly along a stream-bed, picking up and throwing rocks as he goes.

Is it not possible that these performances are stimulated by feelings akin to wonder and awe? After a waterfall display the performer may sit on a rock, his eyes following the falling water. What is it, this water? It is always coming, always going – yet always there. What unseen strength suddenly produces the great claps of thunder, the torrential downpour, the savage gusts of wind that bend and sway the chimpanzees clinging to their nests at night? If the chimpanzees had a spoken language, if they could discuss these feelings among themselves, might not they lead to an animistic, pagan worship of the elements?

When I arrived at Gombe I had no scientific training beyond A-level biology. Louis Leakey, who had proposed the study, wanted someone whose mind was "unbiased by the reductionist thinking of most ethnologists" of the early 1960s. Thus it was not until I was admitted to a Ph.D. program at Cambridge University that I learned that one could only attribute personalities, minds and emotions to *human* animals. It was acceptable to study similarities in the *biology* of humans and other animals, but comparisons should stop there. How fortunate that I had been taught otherwise, throughout my childhood, by my dog, Rusty! The challenge was to express my findings in ways that would, eventually, change the view of human uniqueness that was held not only by scientists, but also by Western philosophers, theologians – and a vast percentage of the general public.

It has been a hard battle, and it has by no means been won. There are still pockets of resistance – resentment even, mostly from those who exploit animals. Because once we accept that we are not the only beings with personalities, feelings, and minds that can know suffering – that there are other sentient, sapient beings out there – all manner of ethical concerns clamor for our attention. If animals have feelings and can suffer, what about those subjected to intensive farming, trapped for fur, hunted for "sport," experimented on for medical research and the pharmaceutical industry, used in the circus, advertising, and other forms of "entertainment," the pet industry, and so on? That we also inflict massive suffering on other human beings does not lessen the suffering of the animals, nor does it lessen the cruelty of our behavior toward them. Instead it brutalizes us. How did the world come to be this way?

One explanation for cruel behavior is ignorance. So often people simply do not realize the suffering endured by millions of animals. Other people are brainwashed into accepting cruel practices because, they are told, that is the way it has to be. They become numbed, "all pity choked by custom of fell deed." Others try to deny what they suspect is going on because they cannot bear the suffering but they lack the will to try to do anything about it, or feel helpless. Or they are inhibited by social pressure, or they do not want to be classified along with "crazy" animal activists.

There is a deeper and more disturbing reason underlying the prevailing view of animals as "things" rather than as individual beings whose lives have value in and of themselves, beyond their potential value to humans. In the original Hebrew text of Genesis chapter 1 verse 26 God gave man "v'yirdu" over his creation, and this has been translated as "dominion." But many Hebrew scholars believe that the true meaning of the word is to "rule over," as a wise king rules his subjects, "with care and respect." A sense of responsibility and enlightened stewardship is implied. St. Francis understood. But throughout the Judeo-Christian world today animals are typically regarded as mere *things*, to do with as we will so long as it is for, or might be for, human good.

This attitude is so often fostered in our children. I was lucky, for my early fascination with animals, common to most children, was nurtured by a very perceptive mother. When I was 18 months old she found me in bed with a handful of earthworms. Instead of scolding me she just said quietly, "Jane, if you keep them here they'll die. They need the earth." I gathered up the worms and toddled with them into the garden. Thus her gentle wisdom guided my early exploration of the animal world. And I was taught that most important lesson – respect for all forms of life.

Children quickly learn from those around them, especially from those they love, and those they admire. From an early age children are attracted to animals and easily learn to be kind to them. But they can also learn to treat animals with indifference or cruelty. In most Western households children discover that the animals chosen to share their homes are to be loved but that it is acceptable to kill "pests" – such as insects, rats, and mice. They learn that it's okay to kill animals for food or for their skins. Many learn that it is "manly" to shoot them for sport. And children are often told that animals don't have feelings like ours, that they don't feel pain in the same way. This is how teachers persuade sensitive students to kill and dissect an animal. Thus our children typically come to accept the status quo. Only a few have the perspicacity or the courage to protest the system.

Nowhere is our lack of stewardship seen so clearly as in the way in which we are systematically destroying the natural world. The Western materialistic lifestyle is spreading throughout the planet as a result of globalization. In the wealthier sections of society there is terrible over-consumption, which has led to unprecedented, unsustainable demands on decreasing natural resources. More and more forests are cut down and soil erosion and desertification follow. More and more pollutants are released into the environment – synthetic chemicals, fossil-fuel and methane emissions. The protective ozone layer is under attack. Global climate is changing. The ice is melting at the poles. Animal and plant species that took millions of years to evolve are becoming extinct. Floods and draughts, hurricanes and tornadoes, are getting worse. We are tinkering with the genetic make-up of our foods. The threats of nuclear, biological and chemical warfare are horribly real. And environmental destruction and exploitation by the wealthy has led the economically poor people of the developing world into a vicious cycle of overpopulation, poverty, hunger, and disease. Ancient cultures, which allowed people to live in harmony with their environment, are being swept away.

In this frightening world we are losing our old connections with Mother Earth, connections so important for our psychological development and spiritual well-being. When we destroy or pollute areas of wilderness we are harming not only the ecosystem, but also the individual animal beings who live there. From their perspective we are committing acts of terrorism.

I went past a beautiful wooded area just last week and saw a sign board announcing that it had been sold. The trees would soon be gone, replaced by houses and tarmac and lawns spread with pesticides, adding to the urban sprawl. Into my head came the words:

This land has been bought by the Developers.
The small creatures go on with their lives,
Not knowing.

As our numbers increase, and as our technology enables us to destroy and pollute with ever-greater speed, we face losing nature itself. God help us then, for in this world everything is interconnected. We are but one part of a complex web of life, each piece of importance in the scheme of things. And, to our own peril, we are destroying piece after piece. In this changing world, thousands have become spiritually sick, stranded with no sense of meaning or self-worth. They have lost their religion; they have lost God; they have lost hope.

We have indeed come dangerously close to the point of no return. Yet there is still hope. It is only recently that people around the world have admitted and faced up to the terrible environmental and social problems. The human brain has created amazing technology – 100 years ago the idea of people on the moon, for example, would have been considered science fiction. So now, faced with the destruction of life on Earth as we know it, human brains are struggling to find ways in which we can live in greater harmony with the natural world. More and more of us are trying to leave lighter footprints as we move through life – we are beginning to realize the difference it will make if each one of us "walks the talk." And nature is amazingly forgiving: places devastated by us can once more become beautiful if we give them a chance, and animal and plant species on the brink of extinction can, with protection and captive breeding, get another chance. Young people, when they understand the problems and are empowered to help, have enormous energy and enthusiasm as they try to make their world a better place.

There is growing determination to do something to improve the lives of those living in poverty, to rectify the horribly unequal distribution of wealth around the world. More and more young people are questioning the value-system of materialism as they search for meaning in their lives. We have begun to realize that human health, both physical and psychological, is dependent on the health of the planet, that only when we reestablish our connection with the natural world and with the great Spiritual Power, can body and mind, heart and soul, once again function as a whole.

It is good news that the indigenous people are coming into their own. They have endured decades of bitter persecution – they were killed by the hundreds of thousands and their traditions brutally suppressed. Yet against all odds, in spite of the risk of punishment and even death, many of the elders, the spiritual leaders and shamans, the medicine men and women, secretly held onto their cultures and their beliefs. And now they are joining forces around the globe reaffirming the connectedness of all life and the spiritual power of the Creator. They are reminding us that, as St. Francis said, the winged ones and the finned ones and the four-footed ones are indeed our brothers and sisters, that their lives matter too.

As we enter this twenty-first century, theology and science seem to be entering into a new relationship. Some of the latest thinking in physics, quantum mechanics and cosmology are coming together in a new belief that Intelligence is involved in the formation of the universe, that there is a Mind and Purpose underlying our existence. For my own part, the more science has discovered about the mysteries of life on Earth, the more in awe I have felt at the wonder of creation, and the more I have come to believe in the existence of God.

Jane Goodall

See also: Animals; Animism; Cognitive Ethology, Social Morality, and Ethics; Earth Charter; Elephants; Environmental Ethics; Francis of Assisi; Goodall, Jane; Paganism – Contemporary; United Nations' "Earth Summits".

Prince Charles (1948–)

Prince Charles, the Prince of Wales, eldest son of Britain's Queen Elizabeth II and heir to the British throne, is also the future head of the Church of England and thus holds the title "Defender of the Faith." He has been described as a super-ecumenist. His strong friendship with the Afrikaner naturalist Laurens van der Post (1906–1996) resulted in the latter becoming godfather to Charles' eldest son, Prince William. Like van der Post, the Prince of Wales has been influenced by the ideas of Carl Jung. He keeps a dream journal and allows himself to be directed by synchronicity. In March 1977, he visited the tropical jungles of Kenya for three weeks in what has subsequently been described as a period of isolated spiritual initiation.

Prince Charles follows in the tradition of the Royal Family's interest in Spiritualism and spiritual healing. He augments allopathic medicine with homeopathy, and, on 14 December 1982, in his role as President of the British Medical Association, he made a critical noteworthy speech to the society that focused on the sixteenth-century German physician Paracelsus in which he stressed the importance of examining the unorthodox but perhaps divinely inspired consideration of cosmic unity. He lampooned science's estrangement from nature and the allopathic view of the human body as a mere machine. In this talk, he advocated the need to understand illness as a disorder of the total person that involved body, mind and spirit as well as self-image and one's relation to the cosmos. He suggested that "the whole imposing edifice of modern medicine, for all its breath-taking successes is, like the Tower of Pisa, slightly off balance" (in Dale 1986: 206).

Since the early 1980s, Prince Charles has consistently promoted the development of a holistic and sustainable relationship between humanity, ecological preservation, organic and vegetarian or demi-vegetarian diet, architecture, education and spirituality. In his BBC Radio Four address on 10 May 2000, although framing this talk in a more traditional understanding of a "sacred trust between mankind and our Creator," the Prince echoed the salient features of current nature-religion sentiment. He spoke about the need for "a sacred stewardship of the earth," and he deplored "the prevailing approach which seeks to reduce the natural world to a mechanical system." Recognizing that modern science is forced to rule out the existence of the sacred as a nuisance that can be evaded or at least manipulated, the Prince of Wales argued instead that we need, in place of the science of manipulation, a science of understanding – one that sees science as a part of nature and not something opposed to it. He proclaimed, "We need to rediscover a reverence for the natural world and to understand the reciprocity between God, man and creation." This must be founded upon "humility, wonder and awe over our place in the natural order." Since "the earth is unique, and we have a duty to care for it . . . we must restore the balance between the intuitive and the rational scientific mind."

Prince Charles' appeal speaks to the emergent form of popular spirituality that we find not only in nature religion, New Age and goddess spirituality but also in more innovative developments across the Christian mainstream. The central chord in this appeal and the emergent spirituality it reflects is a denial of a civilization and nature opposition. The Prince of Wales has long emphasized that culture is to be situated *within* the natural and not be posited as something antagonistic to it.

Michael York

Further Reading
Dale, John. *The Prince and the Paranormal*. London: W.H. Allen, 1986.
See also: Holism; Jung, Carl Gustav; New Age; van der Post, Laurens; World Wide Fund for Nature (WWF).

The Process

The Process Church of the Final Judgement emerged in London in the 1960s, oriented toward four gods: Jehovah, Lucifer, Satan, and Christ. Each represented a different psychological orientation toward nature. Founded by two former Scientologists, Robert and Mary Anne de Grimston, the Process initially was a psychotherapy intended to realize human potential.

In 1966, two-dozen core members lived in a ruined coconut plantation on the Yucatan coast, which they named Xtul (pronounced *schtool*), gathering food from nature and experiencing unprotected the wrath of Jehovah in the form of a fierce hurricane. Some members who were uncomfortable with Jehovian control sought Luciferian liberation in free love, and they conceptualized nature as a nurturant source of pleasure. Later, Satan joined the pantheon as a dual deity, whose lower aspect represented bestiality and whose higher aspect represented spiritual detachment from the biological realm. Finally, Christ entered in 1971 as the spirit of reconciliation for the other gods, unifying spirit with body and harmonizing humanity with nature.

In the early 1970s, the Process established itself in several North American cities, employing a dazzling array of rituals and spiritual techniques in what proved to be a vain attempt to transcend the limitations of mundane existence. In a schism, the major faction rejected polytheism in favor of Jehovah-worship, becoming the Foundation Faith of the Millennium. At the end of the decade, the Foundation moved to the American Southwest to reestablish roots in nature.

From the beginning the Process was anti-vivisectionist. It possessed several large dogs who peacefully slept through the rituals, and the experience at Xtul had created a special awareness of nature. Today, under another name, the group maintains a large animal sanctuary and promulgates a spiritualized orientation toward nature over the World Wide Web.

William Sims Bainbridge

Further Reading

Bainbridge, William Sims. *The Sociology of Religious Movements*. New York: Routledge, 1997.

Bainbridge, William Sims. "Social Construction from Within." In James T. Richardson, Joel Best and David Bromley, eds. *The Satanism Scare*. New York: Aldine de Gruyter, 1991, 297–310.

Bainbridge, William Sims. *Satan's Power: A Deviant Psychotherapy Cult*. Berkeley: University of California Press, 1978.

See also: New Religious Movements; Scientology.

Process Philosophy

Most Western philosophy, especially since Descartes, has depreciated the natural world. Descartes viewed everything except the human mind as mere matter. Some philosophers, materialists, took this merely material world as the whole of things and understood even human experience to be a part of it. Hume, in contrast, taught that we have no access to any world other than the sensory data that constitute our empirical experience. Kant responded by emphasizing the activity of the human mind in creating its world. To this day most philosophy and much religious thought are deeply influenced by these views. They contributed to providing a context in which the degradation of the Earth was little noted until recently.

Another strand in Western thought has been naturalism. It gained ground through the influence of evolutionary thinking, which implies that human beings, including human experience, have come into being through natural processes and are part of nature. Today it is sometimes called "constructive postmodernism." Whereas materialists took the fact that humanity is part of nature to justify their belief that there is nothing other than mere matter, naturalists argued that a nature that includes human experience is far richer than that.

Process philosophy is a form of philosophical naturalism, to be distinguished from both Humean empiricism and Kantian idealism as well as materialism. Hume and Kant both took the epistemological standpoint and assumed the primacy of sense experience. Accordingly, they separate the human knower from the natural world or even deny independent existence to that world. Naturalism locates human beings in the context of a nature affirmed to be fully actual apart from human knowledge. For naturalistic thinkers, human experience grows out of nature; it does not create or constitute it. Materialism affirms the reality of the natural world but describes it in such a way that it cannot contain the human knower.

Naturalism holds that since nature is inclusive of all things, it is much richer than matter (as described in the Western tradition). Nature includes subjectivity as well. Since evolutionary thinking teaches us to see continuity throughout the whole of nature, many naturalists hold that there is some element of subjectivity in all actual entities.

Process philosophy shares this view, and it further emphasizes that all the ultimate actual entities should be understood as events. Each of these events is something in and for itself, a subject, as well as something for all subsequent events, an object. A sequence of such events constitutes a process. Events and processes make up the world. Since personal experience is a process made up of momentary human experiences, we can gain some notion of what other creatures are like through examining our own experience.

Alfred North Whitehead provides the fullest account of this processive world. To deal with the problems that led to idealism and empiricism, he developed an alternative doctrine of causality and showed how it explained that in fact our experience is not cut off from the natural world in the way both of those schools imply. Whereas Hume had reduced causality to a regular succession of sense data, and Kant taught that it is an inescapable category of thought imposed on sense data by the mind, Whitehead argued that it is immediately felt in all experience. One momentary experience arises out of previous ones. In the moment in which we hear the end of a musical phrase, the earlier chords still resonate. The earlier experiences are taken up into the later ones. This relation Whitehead called a physical feeling or prehension, and he took this inclusion of the past in the present as the key to understand causality in the natural world. The immediately preceding states of the brain are also causally efficacious in informing our present experience. They are causally affected in turn by events in other parts of the body, and these by events in the wider world. Of course, there is a great difference between these events as they are for themselves and the way they are experienced in high-grade human experience. Human experience interprets and organizes the multiplicity of influences into a unified creation. It is creative, as Kant emphasized. But the real initiatory influence of the natural world remains, and there are connections between our experience and the world out of which it arises.

One who understands human life as part of a larger system of natural events should be highly receptive to knowledge about the details of this interconnectedness. Although the ecological crisis was not present to Whitehead's own consciousness, other process thinkers, such as Charles Hartshorne and Bernard Meland, were among the first philosophers to become concerned, and process thinkers continue to be involved at both practical and theoretical levels.

Process philosophy locates intrinsic value entirely in what an actual entity is in and for itself. Because it attributes subjectivity to all actual entities, it attributes value to all as well. But apart from animal experiences, these actual entities are, for the most part, the elementary constituents of natural objects such as waterfalls and forests, not the complex objects that inspire awe in human observers. Their contribution to our enjoyment is their instrumental value for us. Furthermore, viewed in terms of intrinsic value, some actual entities have far more than others. A dog's experience is of greater value than that of a flea, and the flea's, than that of plankton. So far as we know, on this planet, the greatest value is to be found in human experience. On the other hand, plankton may be of greater instrumental importance for life on the planet than dogs or human beings. Instrumental value must be considered very seriously in judging what actions to take.

Because of its high appraisal of human value, and its denial of intrinsic value to complex systems as such, some persons with intense ecological concerns criticize process philosophy. It calls for concern for other creatures quite apart from their instrumental value for human beings, but it recognizes that lesser values must often be sacrificed for greater ones. It seeks synergistic solutions, but often it must engage in efforts to find the best compromise possible among competing interests. It does not lend itself to absolutes.

Whitehead believed that actual entities are not only shaped by influences from the past but also have some ability to constitute themselves. This led Whitehead to reflect on the source of creative novelty, and he called this "God." This God is not the omnipotent creator of all things who predetermines the outcome of events. Instead, God is the lure toward novelty and the reason that there is freedom and responsibility in human life.

God is present in all creatures and all creatures are present in God. This means that all the joy and suffering in the world is also included in the divine life. This heightens the desire to inflict as little suffering as possible and to enhance positive experience, both among human beings and among other creatures.

An experience is more valuable according to the extent of diversity that it can integrate. Therefore, the presence of diversity in the human environment is an important contributor to value in human experience. Biodiversity is needed both within and among ecosystems. Since the divine experience also attains its richness through the contrasts of many diverse elements, love of God undergirds the conviction that human beings have responsibility to avoid further destruction of the complex living systems of the planet. For process thinkers, God rejoices in the multifariousness of the world and the vast diversity of species. This applies also to differences among human individuals and cultures.

John B. Cobb, Jr.

Further Reading
Birch, Charles and John B. Cobb, Jr. *The Liberation of Life: from the Cell to the Community.* Cambridge: Cambridge University Press, 1981.
Ferre, Frederick. *Being and Value: Toward a Postmodern Constructive Metaphysics.* Albany: State University of New York Press, 1996.
Griffin, David Ray, John B. Cobb, Jr.. Marcus P. Ford, Pete A.Y. Gunter and Peter Ochs. *Founders of Constructive Postmodern Philosophy: Peirce, James, Bergson, Whitehead, and Hartshorne.* Albany: State University of New York Press, 1993.
Haught, John. *The Promise of Nature, Ecology and Cosmic Purpose.* New York: Paulist Press, 1993.
Whitehead, Alfred North. *Adventures of Ideas.* New York: The Macmillan Co., 1933.
Whitehead, Alfred North. *Science and the Modern World.* New York: The Macmillan Co., 1925.
See also: Christianity (7f) – Process Theology; Cobb, John; Descartes, René – and the Problem of Cartesian Dualism; Whitehead, Alfred North.

The Protestant Ethic

The Protestant ethic had a profound impact on the emergence of capitalistic societies and the way in which they treated the natural environment. In the first comprehensive study of the significance of this ethic for the growth of capitalism, Max Weber, in *The Protestant Ethic and the Spirit of Capitalism*, sought to establish a relationship between Calvinistic religious beliefs and a capitalistic mentality of which the bourgeoisie from Calvinistic churches were the leading exponents. While there have been various criticisms of his position, what is often missed is that Weber was not claiming that religion was the *only* important factor in the rise of capitalism, but that he was singling out this religious element for examination in *his* explanation.

According to Weber, these religious beliefs produced a certain type of personality with a high motivation to achieve success in worldly terms by working diligently to create and accumulate economic wealth. But this wealth was not to be pursued for its own sake or enjoyed in lavish consumption, because the more possessions one had, the greater was the obligation to hold these possessions undiminished for the glory of God and increase them through relentless effort. A worldly asceticism was at the heart of this ethic, which gave a religious sanction to the acquisition and rational use of wealth to create more wealth.

This notion of the Protestant ethic was of particular importance in American society as capitalism developed. It was an ingenious social and moral invention that offered a moral framework for the early stages of capitalism, emphasizing both the human and capital sources of productivity and growth, and in this sense offering the first supply-side theory. It emphasized the human side of production through hard work and the aspect of the calling, but it also advocated that people should not only work hard, but that the money they earn in the process should also be put to work. Inequality was thus morally justified if the money earned on capital was reinvested in further capital accumulation which would benefit society as a whole by increasing production and creating more economic wealth.

The Protestant ethic proved to be consistent with the need for the accumulation of capital that is necessary during the early stages of industrial development. Money was saved and reinvested to build up a capital base. Consumption was curtailed in the interests of creating capital wealth. People dedicated themselves to hard work at disagreeable tasks and justified the rationalization of life that capitalism required. All of this was a major shift away from the behavior and general type of conceptual frame that informed medieval agrarian society.

Embedded in the Protestant ethic is the moral imperative both for the maximization of production and for the minimization of consumption. The new ethic thus pressured equally toward effective production and efficient consumption, which while sustaining maximum productivity, also maximized savings and potential investment capital. But, of perhaps even deeper significance is the fact that while the Protestant ethic contained a moral limit on consumption in the interests of generating more economic wealth and building up a capital base to increase production, it made the pursuit of wealth an end in itself, and allowed for exploitation of both humans and nature in the interests of increasing economic wealth. In a practical sense, this ethic may have served as a moral cover for behavior motivated by nothing more than greed. While obviously consumption had to increase with the production of more and more goods and services, the emphasis was on the production of wealth rather than consumption.

And, as religious ties were loosened, as the Protestant ethic gave way to the more general work ethic, even a religious justification lost its moorings and with it whatever moral constraints on consumption it may have provided. With the purposes and meanings provided by this moral matrix no longer relevant to a consumer culture that emphasizes instant gratification and increased consumption, not only production but also consumption became ends in themselves divorced from any broader or larger moral purposes. Thus there has been progressively more waste produced needing disposal, more pollution generated, and more resources used, all to support a growing consumer culture.

The Protestant ethic thus constituted a moral framework that informed the development of capitalism and provided a legitimacy for its existence by offering a moral justification for the pursuit of wealth and the distribution of income that were a result of economic activity within this system. This ethic contributed to rapid economic development and exploitation of resources, both human and natural, in the interests of increasing economic production. Weakening of this ethic and its inherent restrictions on consumption resulted in both production and consumption becoming ends in themselves, with little or no thought given to the environmental consequences of such activities. This ethic emphasized the accumulation of material capital and provided no restriction on the depletion of natural capital, and this disregard of natural capital pervaded the consumer culture to which it contributed. Only in recent years, when the consequences of such depletion of natural capital could no longer be ignored, have environmental concerns emerged as important considerations.

However, environmental concerns about resources that are becoming more and more depleted and waste material that is becoming more and more difficult to dispose of run headlong into the cultural values related to increased consumption and immediate gratification. The ethics of production, consumption, and economic growth, with their own self-justifying ends, seem on a collision path with an environmental ethic related to conservation and preservation of the environment. These conflicts take many forms, whether it is the protection of an endangered species versus the logging industry battling over further logging of public lands, or preservationists versus the mining industry over setting aside more public lands in trust for future generations.

Many people are turning to nature itself for self-gratification, finding meaning in closeness to the natural environment and viewing it less in instrumental terms. As a result, more and more people are seeking to preserve parts of nature in something of a pristine state, and use resources in a sustainable manner in order to leave something for future generations. Business organizations themselves are slowly beginning to focus on sustainability concerns and their impacts on resource usage and the natural environment. An environmental ethic tied to the enrichment of human existence in all its fullness and recognizing our ties to nature has the potential to bring both the concerns of individuals seeking less materialistic self-gratification in nature itself, and pressures from the marketplace, to direct production and consumption toward more sustainable paths, into an evolving relationship that can provide a new moral framework for capitalism. The Protestant ethic with its emphasis on material capital and exclusion of natural capital from moral concern is further eroding in the face of growing environmental concern.

Rogene A. Buchholz
Sandra B. Rosenthal

Further Reading

Bell, Daniel. *The Cultural Contradictions of Capitalism*. New York: Basic Books, 1976.
Ditz, Gerhard W. "The Protestant Ethic and the Market Economy." *Kyklos* 33:4 (1980), 625–33.
LaPiere, Richard. *The Freudian Ethic*. New York: Duell, Sloan, and Pearce, 1959.
McCelland, David. *The Achieving Society*. New York: The Free Press, 1961.
Weber, Max. *The Protestant Ethic and the Spirit of Capitalism*. New York: Charles Scribner's Sons, 1958.
Yankelovich, Daniel. *New Rules: The Search for Self-Fulfillment in a World Turned Upside Down*. New York: Random House, 1981.

See also: Christianity (6c) – Reformation Traditions (Lutheranism and Calvinism); Christianity(6c2) – Calvin, John – and the Reformed Tradition; Social Science on Religion and Nature; White, Lynn – Thesis of.

Proto-Indo-Europeans

The focus of contemporary Indo-European Studies is on the proto-Indo-European (PIE) substrate of European and Indian culture. Since the recognition of similarities between Sanskrit, Greek and Latin by two Jesuits working in India (Stephens in 1583; Coeurdoux in 1767) and the final recognition by Sir William Jones in 1796 that the Gothic, Celtic and Persian languages also appeared related to the other three, Western scholars have sought to determine who were the original Indo-Europeans, from where do they come, what was their original lifestyle and what were their earliest beliefs. While the proto-homeland remains to be definitively located, the most convincing argument has been put forward by Marija Gimbutas as the lower Volga steppe of Kazakhstan. She identifies the original PIE culture-bearers with the chalcolithic culture known by its distinctive earthen mound or barrow (Russian *kurgan*). These first appear in approximately the second half of the fifth millennium B.C.E. The Kurgan peoples were semi-nomadic but characterized by small settlements of fortified hilltop villages. They had domesticated the horse, and they practiced at first a mixed farming and herding level of transhumant economy.

In the late eighteenth and early nineteenth centuries, the foundations of the science of philology were established – with Friedrich von Schlegel coining the term "comparative grammar." It was, however, the German linguist Franz Bopp who first considered the designation "Indo-European." Eventually, the Indo-European languages have come to be understood as including the Indo-Iranian, Hellenic, Italic, Celtic, Germanic, Baltic, Slavic, Anatolian and Tocharian branches along with such isolates as Phrygian, Armenian, Thracian, Illyrian and Albanian. Today, approximately half the world's population speaks an Indo-European tongue as its first language. In searching for cognates or words shared between these various languages, the Indo-Europeanist seeks to establish the PIE lexicon. We find here common words for "horse," "cattle," "wolf," "bear," "salmon," "oak," "beech," "birch," "willow," "boat/ship" and "snow," but not for "rain," "sea," "tiger," "lion," "palm," "olive," "cypress" or "vine." Through such matching and eliminating, the Indo-Europeanist endeavors to fuse the disciplines of archeology and comparative linguistics in order to determine where the PIE originated and how she/he lived. Included in this quest is the attempt to understand Aboriginal spiritual perception and religious practice. Agricultural and husbandry terms are also detectable in the proto-vocabulary, and these in turn raise questions for contemporary scholars concerning the impact of the Indo-Europeans on the environment.

Among the major synthesizers behind understanding PIE society and its worldview is Friedrich Max Müller. The foundation for his comparative mythology is the equation of the Vedic Dyaus with the Greek Zeus. Müller argued that without a means by which to express abstract concepts, the PIE resorted to analogies based on nature. For Müller, the central ancestral symbol is the sun. Others who followed in his footsteps posited different mythopoeic foundations. In place of Müller's solarism, for Adalbert Kuhn, it was meteorological; for Georg Hüsing, lunar; for Angelo de Gubernatis, animal allegory; for Johannes Hertel, pyric; for Friedrich L.W. Schwartz, wind symbolism; and for Ludwig Preller, celestial. Together, the consensus suggests the underlying impetus of naturalism. Certainly, the etymology behind Indo-European theonyms derives principally from the phenomena of nature – with the derivatives from the recoverable root of *dyêus (the "daytime or bright sky" – from *dei- "to shine"), the dawn-goddess designation from *awes- ("to shine"), the earth-mother nomen from *ghdem- ("earth") and *sawel- ("sun") being the most ubiquitous.

In the twentieth century, however, it became fashionable to designate the methodology of Müller and his colleagues as the "older comparative mythology" in contrast to the "new comparative mythology" of Georges Dumézil (1898–1986). The French sociologist, a student of Emile Durkheim, successfully managed to restore Indo-European studies as a legitimate area of investigation and research following the demise of Müller's solar mythology. Dumézil, however, repudiated the anthropology of James Frazer and sought a Durkheimian sociological understanding of PIE culture rather than the naturalism of Müller. For Dumézil, PIE society was a tripartite division of three classes: a first or sovereign function of priests and judges, a second or warrior function of the nobility, and a third consisting of farmers and craftsmen. Following Durkheim, Dumézil has sought to identify the various deities as projections or collective representations of the different levels of social organization. In this way, he has divorced the ancestral PIE gods from what otherwise would appear as their naturalistic base of origin.

The Dumézilian hegemony over Indo-European studies has appeared to have passed its peak. At the Sixth UCLA Indo-European Conference in 1994, Bernfried Schleratt (Freie Universität, Berlin) rejected Dumézil on the basis of a selective, manipulative and contradictory methodology. An emergent third approach to Indo-European studies consists of a revaluation and updating of Müller's comparative methods rather than their outright repudiation. Increasingly, a nature-based IE perspective denies many of Dumézil's specific correspondences between Indian, Iranian and European deities. Dumézil ignored underlying hypostases that at some early point must have been recognized and must be accounted for within the proto-society. In general, it would seem the French sociologist has been influenced by Christian or, more broadly, Levantine thought that relegates both the natural and the supernatural to the status of "other." In this, he falls within the gambit of postmodern criticism that seeks to expose intertextual tendencies that marginalize or neglect the excluded other. Inasmuch as contemporary nature religion is an attempt to re-recognize nature and understand the natural within a sacred context, it is a spirituality that follows in essence a postmodern agenda. Resisting Hegel's attempt to reduce all to the logic of the same, contemporary nature-oriented spiritualities incorporate the other through their stress on celebration of difference and multiplicity.

Nevertheless, a central Western paradigm – one rooted in proto-Indo-European and, more specifically, Hellenic understandings – posits the natural as the wild and untamed that surround and perpetually threaten the hard-won yet precarious domain of civilization. Among one of the clearest and most influential contemporary articulations of the culture versus nature construct is the civilization thesis of Freud. One of the questions for today's scholars in this context concerns how much the Indo-Europeans expanded through conquest (Gimbutas' patriarchal warrior theory) and how much through the spread of agriculture (Colin Renfrew's "wave of advance" hypothesis involving the gradual spread of farming). While archeologists are increasingly rejecting the first, the second has so far not received serious consideration by Indo-Europeanists. Implicit in how the West looks today at its prehistoric past is the consideration of environmental change brought about by Neolithic economy. Terms for grain (possibly designating wheat or spelt) have wide distribution. More restricted are such reconstructions for rye and barley – suggesting increased regional differentiation and ecological transformation after the original dispersals. The clearest indication of the intimate connection between Neolithic spirituality and economy remains the Latin verb *colere* which designates both "to till the earth" and "to worship." Its past participle *cultus* gives rise to the English words *agriculture*, *cultivation* and *culture*.

It is obvious that the rise of farming techniques and the production of food surplus radically altered primordial natural conditions. How much the ensuing environmental changes can be attributed to Indo-European migration and how much to a "wave of advance" from the Levant or some other center are still open and unanswered questions. What is clearer, however, is that an unbiased understanding of the PIE spiritual heritage and worldview, one freed from the reductionism of Dumézil and politicizing of Gimbutas alike, has the potential to resituate humanity's rupture from nature with a more holistic perspective. Accordingly, PIE ideology posits a double duality or, more accurately, a dichotomy and a polarity. In the former, creation as the natural and human worlds is perceived as perpetually threatened by the primordial void of chaos. In Indo-European terms, this is mythically depicted as a cosmic contest between divine and asurian (anti-divine) forces. Chaos is considered as that which endeavors to undermine and annihilate the perpetual round of nature, but inasmuch as the cosmic void is itself an empty nothingness, the proto-Indo-European appears to have understood it as ultimately an operative nonexistent. On the other hand, the binary existence to which it is opposed comprehends the continually realigning natural dualities of the positive and negative, dark and light, female and male, and spiritual and material dimensions of reality. This primordial IE paradigm that seeks accord and respect with the world that is, while no less searching for that supernatural other that has enticed humanity since the beginnings of time, is one that frames itself in the rhythms and metaphors of nature. The relevancy of this PIE understanding to today's over-accelerating and viable-horizon-diminishing world suggests a reassessment of the point where the natural and spiritual intersect.

Michael York

Further Reading

Cardona, George, Henry M. Hoenigswald and Alfred Senn, eds. *Indo-European and Indo-Europeans*. Philadelphia: University of Pennsylvania Press, 1970.

Ehrich, Robert W., ed. *Chronologies in Old World Archaeology*. Chicago: University Press, 1965.

Gimbutas, Marija. *The Living Goddesses*. Miriam Robbins Dexter, ed. Berkeley: University of California Press, 1999.

Hencken, Hugh. "Indo-European Language and Archaeology." *American Anthropologist* 57:6 (1955), Pt. 3 Memoir 84.

Mallory, James P. *In Search of the Indo-Europeans: Language, Archaeology and Myth*. London: Thames and Hudson, 1989.

Mallory, James and Douglas Q. Adams, eds. *Encyclopedia of Indo-European Culture*. London/Chicago: Fitzroy Dearborn, 1997.

Renfrew, Colin. *Archaeology and Language: The Puzzle of Indo-European Origins*. London: Jonathan Cape, 1987.

Watkins, Calvert. "Indo-European and the Indo-Europeans" and "Indo-European Roots." In William Morris, ed. *The American Heritage Dictionary*. Boston: Houghton Mifflin, 1969/1980.

York, Michael. *The Divine Versus the Asurian: An Interpretation of Indo-European Cult and Myth*. Bethesda, MD: International Scholars Publications, 1996.

See also: Celtic Spirituality; Gimbutas, Marija; Hinduism; India; Müller, Friedrich Max; Sun Worship.

Psychonauts

Shamans and psychonauts are individuals who choose to embark upon a voyage of discovery into the universe of the mind. Such a journey is initiated via a variety of means by which a perspective shift, an altering of normal consciousness, occurs leading the subject into states of ecstasis. For psychonauts, the vehicles chosen for such an Odyssey are predominantly entheogens (plant sacraments or shamanic inebriants evoking religious ecstasy or vision; literally the term means becoming divine within) and alchemical alkaloids derived from visionary-inducing vegetation that grows throughout the world.

The German chemist, Arthur Heffter, was the first to gain the title of *psychonaut*, a name given to him by Ernst Jünger in his logbook of personal drug experimentation *Annaherungen: Drogen und Rausch* (*Drugs and Inebriation*). Heffter was defined in this way as a result of his self-experimentation with the four pure alkaloids that he had isolated from *peyotl* in the late 1890s. His ingestion of these alkaloids revealed mescaline hydrochloride to be the active entheogenic principle of *Lophora williamsii* (*peyotl*/*peyote*), and his experience marked the world's first "trip" with a purified chemical compound. As a result of this, the Heffter Technique now refers to human self-experimentation with psychoactive compounds otherwise known as the psychonautic bioassay.

Psychonautic bioassays are usually grounded in the sphere of science and attempt to shed light on questions pertaining to pharmacology, posology (the study of drug dosages), cognitive psychology, ethnomedicine and anthropology. However, scientific experimentation with entheogens may also lead into mystical insight and experience thereby facilitating access to the visionary worlds frequently inhabited by shamans, artists and ascetics. In this way *psychonauts* are by no means confined to the methodology of Western science, and their inner voyages may bridge many worlds.

Entheogenic substances such as mescaline, lysergic acid diethylamide (LSD) and psilocybine were all discovered by *psychonauts*, chemists evaluating their chemicals via bioassays. If these had not taken place a great number of valuable psychoactive drugs would have been disregarded or put on the shelf, perhaps not to be reinvestigated for years. A prime example of this was Albert Hoffman's discovery of LSD. On the basis of animal tests in 1938, pharmacologists at the Sandoz laboratory determined that LSD was of little pharmacological interest, and it was due to a peculiar presentiment that Albert Hoffman returned to it five years later. In 1943 he repeated the synthesis of LSD but had to leave the laboratory due to an onset of strange physical and psychological symptoms. Assuming that it may have been the result of the substance he was working on, he conducted a series of self-experiments. The outcome of these led to his discovery of the most potent psychoactive substance known at that time.

Until the U.S. prohibition of LSD and a number of other psychoactive compounds in the late 1960s, scientists, psychoanalysts, artists, writers and musicians alike embarked on psychonautic journeys into the unknown. Many believed and publicly claimed that they were gaining insight into the workings of the mind, the creative process and the spiritual realms previously inhabited only by those capable of having spontaneous mystical experiences. The creative activity of such individuals has contributed to the study of ways in which people may experience transcendence and the effect that this can have on their lives.

One such pioneer, the English novelist and critic Aldous Huxley, wrote about his experience with mescaline in his book entitled *Doors of Perception*. He stated that the entheogenic experience had the potential to "shed light on unsolved riddles such as the place of mind in nature and the relationship between brain and consciousness." He also suggested that such insights might bring one closer to understanding the worlds of the visionary, medium and even the mystic.

However, such a subjective approach to the study of pharmacological, psychological, and religious phenomena is still considered controversial and hotly debated. The question of whether it is ethically and religiously defensible to use mind-altering drugs to help us understand religious, spiritual and artistic phenomena still rages. Yet, despite prohibition and moral arguments, the employment of shamanic inebriants for spiritual purposes is extraordinarily widespread. Ceremonies and rituals that involve the subjects entering an altered state of consciousness can be found both historically and presently throughout the world, with particular prevalence in South America, Siberia, Asia and Central West Africa.

If as Weston La Barre asserts, "there were shamans before there were Gods," then the origins of religion could potentially be explored within the context of shamanism. Thus, psychonautics, while a comparatively new term, is certainly not a new phenomenon; indeed, it could be considered integral to the study of religious phenomena.

In the scientific field, the study of psychoactive compounds has been limited due to the legal steps taken by authorities around the world in the late 1960s and the media attention that has consistently highlighted the abuse of such substances. Such attention has meant that government funding has been difficult if not impossible to obtain and many scientists have not wished to jeopardize their careers by exploring such a controversial area of research. The subjective experience (the psychonautic bioassay) is still largely disqualified and while pharmacological studies on animals may be useful in determining toxicity, they reveal very little of the psychoactive effects of the drug on the central nervous system and the impact the experience has on the subject over time.

Ethical procedures for human testing of psychoactive agents have been admirably established and followed by Alexander T. Shulgin and colleagues, whose self-testing of over 100 novel psychotropic agents is described in his and his wife Anne Shulgin's 1991 book, *PIHKAL: A Chemical Love Story*. Such psychonautic bioassays are carried out to produce a total clinical evaluation of (novel) psychoactive compounds. The subjective experience is recorded and levels of activity carefully monitored with a number of different doses of the drug in question being examined. These experiments are carried out by a team of volunteers who are experienced at entering and being in altered states of consciousness. The experimenters are fully aware of the risks and returns to be expected.

Whatever the motivations for the exploration of mind-altering substances, there are a number of prominent features of the experience commonly shared. Psychonauts report seeing the world brilliantly illuminated, objects seeming to "shine from within" (Huxley). The sensation of seeing the world with fresh eyes, with a "naked intensity" (Huxley), unclouded by everyday abstractions is often described and the intensification of colors and reports of sensing the innate nature of things are experiences shared by shamans, mystics, artists and psychonauts alike.

Following his experiences with LSD, Hoffman wrote that the most valuable spiritual benefit gained was the "experience of the inextricable intertwining of the physical and spiritual." This fundamental fusion of spirit and matter has been upheld by the traditional shamanic worldview throughout history but was undermined by the emergence of Cartesian dualism embodied by Western science.

Psychonauts such as Huxley, Hoffman, Wasson and Ott have reported that the entheogenic experience could enable individuals to transcend the dominant materialistic worldview, breaking down the dualistic notions of body *versus* soul and culture *versus* nature. Through direct experience individuals are describing that which quantum physics is now teaching us – that everything is energy, and matter a hallucination resulting from the mechanisms of our everyday perception.

It has been argued that the assumption that humankind is separate from the rest of nature and superior by way of mind, has led to the subjugation of other life forms and the exploitation and destruction of the Earth. Experiencing and appreciating the unity of life directly and perceiving the life-force and energy of both animate and inanimate things can therefore potentially awaken a greater ecological sensitivity and concern for the survival of the biosphere. Ironically, the subjective experiences resulting from many psychonautic bioassays carried out for Western scientific purposes point towards this unified worldview, thereby building a bridge between science, shamanism, and environmental concern.

Hattie Wells

Further Reading

Hoffman, Albert. *LSD: My Problem Child*. New York: McGraw-Hill, 1980. (Orig. *LSD-Mein Sorgenkind*, 1979).

Huxley, Aldous. *The Doors of Perception*. London: Chatto & Windus Ltd, 1954.
La Barre, Weston. *The Ghost Dance: The Origins of Religion*. Garden City, NJ: Doubleday, 1970.
Ott, Jonathan. *Pharmacotheon: Entheogenic Drugs, Their Plant Sources and History*. Kennewick, WA: Natural Products Co., 1993.
Shulgin, Alexander T. "A Protocol for the Evaluation of New Psychoactive Drugs in Man." *Methods and Findings in Experimental Clinical Pharmacology* 8:5 (1986), 313–20.
Shulgin, Alexander T. and Anne Shulgin. *PIHKAL: A Chemical Love Story*. Berkeley, CA: Transform Press, 1991.
Wasson, R. Gordon. *The Wondrous Mushroom: Mycolotry in Mesoamerica*. Ethnomycological Studies No. 7. New York: McGraw-Hill, 1980.

See also: Alchemy; Ayahuasca; Entheogens; Ethnobotany; Huxley, Aldous; Leary, Timothy; Peyote.

Pure Brethren

The *Ikhwan al-safa*, or "Pure Brethren" were an anonymous group of philosophers who lived and worked in Basra during the tenth century. Among their many treatises is one that gives a lengthy argument for animal rights, entitled *The Case of the Animals versus Man Before the King of the Jinn*. In this unusual work, representatives from the animal kingdom bring a court case against the human race whom they accuse of abusing their position. The animals point out that before the creation of man they roamed the Earth in peace and harmony, in what might be called "natural balance" in contemporary language.

The Brethren's view of the natural world is striking for its exceptionality in the context of tenth-century Muslim society. They were a radical group, as indicated by their choice to remain anonymous, and in subsequent centuries, only the heterodox Sevener-Shi'i or Isma'ili sect, identified today with the Aga Khan, adopted their writings as authoritative.

Richard C. Foltz

Further Reading

Ikhwan al-Safa (Pure Brethren). *The Case of the Animals versus Man Before the King of the Jinn*. Lenn Evan Goodman, tr. Boston: Twayne, 1978.
Nasr, Seyyed Hossein. *An Introduction to Islamic Cosmological Doctrines: Conceptions of Nature and Methods Used for Its Study by the Ikhwan al-Safa', al-Biruni, and Ibn Sina*. Albany: State University of New York Press, 1993.
Netton, Ian Richard. *Muslim Neoplatonists: An Introduction to the Thought of the Brethren of Purity (Ikhwân al-Safâ')*. London & Boston: Allen & Unwin, 1982.

See also: Animals; Animals in the Bible and Qur'an; Council of All Beings; Dogs in the Islamic Tradition; Islam.

Puritans

The English Puritans who arrived in New England in the early seventeenth century brought a complex of beliefs about their purposes in the "New World" and what they would encounter there. They also brought understandings about human physiology and morality – their bodies and souls – that would determine their attitudes toward and interactions with this unfamiliar landscape. Both frightened and exhilarated by anticipated engagement with the environment and inhabitants, the colonists' abstract, often conflicting ideas about New England became concrete realities in their actual exchanges with new terrain, climate, foods, plant and animal life, and humans. By the end of the seventeenth century, these exchanges had produced permanent alterations in Anglo-american bodies and the New England landscape.

Committed to the rigorous theology of Swiss Protestant reformer John Calvin (1509–1564), New England Puritans, like John Winthrop, governor of the Massachusetts Bay Colony, and Boston minister John Cotton, believed themselves to be the "New Israel," divinely chosen to fulfill God's plan for bringing the twin beacons of civilization and Christianity ("culture") to New England's savage, heathen "wilderness" ("nature"). They also believed that God was leading them to America to "possess the land" and harvest its natural resources for profit. Typical of early modern European attitudes about "foreign lands," Puritans viewed the American environment as both dangerous and fertile, threatening and exotically enticing. Employing biblical metaphors, colonists like William Bradford, governor of Plymouth Colony, imagined it as the abode of Satan, a "howling wilderness" containing "wild beasts" and "savage and brutish men." But, according to historians Perry Miller and Peter N. Carroll, when intentionally subdued through the civilizing labor of clearing forests, cultivating fields, and building permanent fences, dwellings, and "godly" communities, it would become an Edenic "garden," producing untold riches. Such biblical rhetoric invested the New England landscape with potent sacred meanings, furthered by the belief that God communicated directly with his people through the natural world. Conflating spiritual morality and worldly economics, Puritans carefully read "divine providences," like a large haul of cod or crop destruction by locust infestation, as indications of God's pleasure or anger toward his chosen ones.

Religious metaphors about the New England landscape were brought to ground when English men and women set foot on American soil and physically engaged its environmental elements – both its remarkable abundance of lumber, game, fish, and furs and its frightening dangers of uncharted forests, wolves, unfamiliar foodstuffs, and native Algonquians, described by travel writers and colonists like Plymouth's Edward Winslow. Puritans held two models of their physical relationship with the environment, derived from the ancient Galenic system of the humors and from a Calvinist theology of the body, that shaped their understandings about how the wilderness might cause alterations in their bodies and souls and how they, in turn, would alter the wilderness landscape.

From Calvin, Puritans had inherited an emphasis on *eupraxia*, or "godly industry," which they understood, in part, to mean hard, physical labor to domesticate the savage wilderness into a civilized landscape. Using organic metaphors of domesticated seedlings, as historian John Canup has noted, they intended to "plant" themselves in the wilderness, that is, to labor in establishing plantations, cultivating and ordering the landscape according to English notions of godly civilization, and exploiting its natural resources for profit. However, the image of planting, of sending roots into the soil and absorbing environmental elements, was more than metaphorical; Puritans understood it literally, as well. According to standard early modern medical theory, based on the humoral system developed by Roman physician-philosopher Galen (ca. 129–210), the human being was a complex moral and organic entity composed of fluids, particles, and qualities – the humors and spirits – in constant, but ideally balanced, flux and flow. The four humors and their related personality temperaments corresponded to the four elements – earth, air, water, and fire – which provided all matter with forms and properties – heat, moisture, cold, and dryness.

Because human bodies were constituted by the same elements and properties as all other material things, the boundaries between soul, body, and the surrounding environment were unstable and permeable. According to historian Carolyn Merchant, through exchanges among elemental, humoral, and spiritual qualities, human physiology and moral character were understood to be continuously and directly influenced and altered by climate, weather, air quality, foods and drinks, and, as in Calvinist *eupraxia*, the amount of physical exercise one pursued. Thus, the colonists believed that living in a new country would inevitably cause their bodies and souls to absorb qualities of that environment; without vigilance, they could become wilderness creatures, their English godliness replaced with a "savage" character, like that of the native inhabitants and those "Indianized" Englishmen who shed the constrictions of civilized society to live among the natives.

Fears that the wilderness would negatively affect English bodies came true during the first years of colonization, when many died for lack of skill in negotiating the new environment. But Puritan leaders like Bradford argued that it was *because* they had experienced threats to their health, like changes in air, food, and drink, that God supported them in those early years and ultimately caused them to prosper; rigorous wilderness life was held up as morally and physiologically superior to the "civilized" lives of those still in England. Eventually, colonists discovered that New England actually offered an exceptionally healthy and prosperous climate, which permanently altered Anglo-american bodies for the better. With regular access to animal protein, unpolluted air, and fresh water, they lived longer and grew taller than their English counterparts, women were more fertile and produced more twins, and there were fewer infant mortalities.

The inherent tension between images of the "savage" wilderness as physically and morally dangerous and images of the wilderness as the land given by God to his people as their "possession" was resolved as Puritans promoted the "godly" body as one that rigorously labored to cultivate and domesticate the environment. Such diligent, civilizing activity was seen as a balancing mechanism, protecting colonists from the detrimental moral effects of life in the "savage" wilderness. Despite Puritan leaders' struggles to maintain close-knit communities and limit expansion into the wilderness, colonists' desires for economic gain pushed the frontier westward, eradicating the "savage" influences of wolves, Indians, and uncharted forests, privatizing wilderness land, and harvesting and commodifying New England's natural resources, as noted by environmental historian William Cronon. Over the course of the seventeenth century, the "wilderness" was transposed into a fruitful "garden" and the New England environment permanently altered.

Martha L. Finch

Further Reading

Albanese, Catherine L. *Nature Religion in America: From the Algonkian Indians to the New Age*. Chicago: University of Chicago Press, 1990.

Bradford, William. *Of Plymouth Plantation, 1620–1647*. Samuel Eliot Morison, ed. New York: Alfred A. Knopf, 1994.

Canup, John. *Out of the Wilderness: The Emergence of an American Identity in Colonial New England*. Middletown: Wesleyan University Press, 1990.

Carroll, Peter N. *Puritanism and the Wilderness: The Intellectual Significance of the New England Frontier, 1620–1700*. New York: Columbia University Press, 1969.

Cotton, John. "God's Promise to His Plantations" (London: 1630). In *Old South Leaflets* 3:53, 1–16. Boston: Directors of the Old South Work, n.d.

Cronon, William. *Changes in the Land: Indians, Colonists, and the Ecology of New England*. New York: Hill and Wang, 1983.

Finch, Martha L. " 'Civilized' Bodies and the 'Savage' Environment of Early New Plymouth." In Janet Moore Lindman and Michele Lise Tartar, eds. *A Centre of Wonders: The Body in Early America*. Ithaca: Cornell University Press, 2001, 43–59.

Merchant, Carolyn. *Ecological Revolutions: Nature, Gender, and Science in New England*. Chapel Hill: University of North Carolina Press, 1989.

Miller, Perry. *Errand into the Wilderness*. Cambridge: Belknap Press, 1956 and 1984.

Nash, Roderick Frazier. *Wilderness and the American Mind*. 2nd edn, 1973. New Haven: Yale University Press, 1973, reprint.

Winslow, Edward. *Mourt's Relation: A Journal of the Pilgrims at Plymouth* (London: 1622), Dwight B. Heath, ed. Bedford, MA: Applewood Books, 1963.

Winthrop, John. "General Considerations for the Plantation in New-England; with an Answer to Several Objections." In *Chronicles of the First Planters of the Colony of Massachusetts Bay, from 1623 to 1636*. Alexander Young, ed. Boston: Charles C. Little and James Brown, 1846.

See also: Christianity (6c1) – Reformation Traditions (Lutheranism and Calvinism); Christianity (6c2) – Calvin, John and the Reformed Tradition; Nature Religion in the United States.

Pygmies (Mbuti foragers) and Bila Farmers of the Ituri Forest (Democratic Republic of the Congo)

The Mbuti hunter-gatherers of the Ituri Forest in the Democratic Republic of Congo consist of perhaps about 30,000 people in all, and are one of the many Forest Peoples throughout the Central African rainforest region, peoples often grouped under the term "Pygmies."

Understandings of the Mbuti have been strongly influenced by the anthropologist Colin Turnbull's classic study of the Mbuti (1961, 1965, 1983). His study is built on the notion of a structural opposition between the Mbuti hunter-gatherers, living in harmony in the world of the forest, and the world of the road, where the Bila village farmers are described by Turnbull as fearing the surrounding forest and – in clearing their fields – are forever battling against their forest environment in order to survive. Turnbull characterizes Mbuti cosmology as being founded on trust in their benevolent forest which is regarded as both mother and father to them; and he characterizes Bila cosmology as being centred in their fear and mistrust of the forest, in fearing and seeking their ancestors' intervention, and in fearing witchcraft and sorcery. In Turnbull's eyes the Mbuti's fragile forest of Eden will inevitably be broken by the intrusion of modern forces.

The Mbuti ("Pygmies") have played an important part in many debates about human nature and the nature of culture. In earlier debates they were often seen as representing the earlier or inner nature of humanity. This is evident in looking at the writing of the diffusionists such as Father Wilhelm Schmidt, who argued that religion has always been central to human existence, and that the idea of God is derived from the Pygmies, who were themselves the original cultural circle. In arguing this, people such as Father Paul Schebesta were reacting against the biologists' assertion that primitive man had no religion. In the preface to Schebesta's *Among Congo Pigmies*, Gerald Griffin stated that "previous explorers" maintained that "they had discovered a race that had no religion and no conception of the soul as a separate entity from the body," and so:

> fastened on this pseudo-discovery as bearing out their contention that primitive man had no religion. Dr Schebesta ... shows how these little African gypsies, who ... are the nearest approach in primitiveness to the wild animals on which they prey, have a definite religious cult and ethical social codes of their own (Griffin in Schebesta 1933: 5).

Schebesta himself later goes on to say that, although "the Christian onlooker gets the impression that the Bambuti are actually a race devoid of any religious cult. This impression [is] an utterly fallacious one" based on "the lack of external demonstrations in the Bambuti religion" (1933: 162). His image of the Mbuti as possessing true religion, totally unlike the "superstitious belief in witchcraft and magic which they have picked up from the negroes" (1933: 162), is an image which is consistently and powerfully reworked by Turnbull, who sharply differentiates between the Mbuti's pure experience of their sacred forest and the Bila villagers superstitious ancestor worship and fear of the forest.

Turnbull dwells on the advantages of Mbuti life over Bila life, and makes an absolute opposition between their cosmologies. The following passage makes clear that to him the contrast between villagers' fear of – and Mbuti respect for – the forest, has nothing to do with historical circumstance and everything to do with the essential nature of these two cultures:

> instead of acceding to the natural, the villagers with their superior technology combat it; and instead of respecting the supernatural in the sense that the Mbuti respect it, the villagers oppose it with fear, mistrust and occasional hate. They people the forest with evil spirits, and they fill their lives with magic, witchcraft and a belief in sorcery. The forest achieves the establishment of two virtually irreconcilable systems of values (Turnbull 1965: 21).

Turnbull's, research, however, coincided with the most effective period of Belgian colonial domination, which treated the villagers and the Mbuti very differently. The Mbuti were allowed to move through the forest freely, while the Bila were forced to move their villages to the roadside and to pay taxes in the form of maintaining the roads, feeding immigrant labourers, and growing cotton to pay as a form of tax. Having to manipulate the Mbuti into working their fields to help produce the required cotton, was the last in a long chain of exploitative extractive relations emanating from commercial decisions made in Europe, and made possible by colonial control. A preoccupation with Turnbull's structural opposition obscures the dynamic movement between forest and village which is central to both Mbuti and Bila identity – prior to the effective imposition of Belgian restrictions, since independence, and even under Belgian control as is evident in Turnbull's own writing.

Current Anthropological Understandings

Anthropologists such as Tim Ingold and Nurit Bird-David have invoked Turnbull's analysis to draw a sharp contrast between hunter-gatherers' and farmers' cosmologies, and to suggest that such hunter-gatherers experience the forest as a sharing partner, their relationship with each other and with the forest being characterized by trust. Clearly the Mbuti do work very hard to establish co-operation and trust in their relationship with each other and the forest; through such practices as demand-sharing, the cooperative nature of the net hunt and child care, and the central *molimo* ritual. However (contra Turnbull) the forest is not seen by the Mbuti as a separate "god-head" from whom they worship and seek blessings. The forest is seen as continuous with human life. There is no division between a transcendent forest and the human realm, rather when they are calling the forest *ema, epa, tata* (mother, father, grandparent) they are calling on their own and all ancestors who have become and are the forest. All that is past is present and is available in relationships entered into through ritual and everyday relations.

Thus there is a continuity between the world of humans and the world of nature which is evident in the nature of the hunt, the *molimo*, and in beliefs about the forest, beliefs which can be summed up in the image that the forest is alive in the form of the ancestors who are themselves the ancestors of all who are alive today – both human and other creatures. There is not; therefore, the division between humans and the rest of nature upon which many in the West base their notion of a universal opposition between culture and nature, with ritual always being seen as the attempt to impose control on nature.

The central *molimo* ritual can take place nightly in Mbuti hunting camps and involves endless singing between the camp and the voice of the forest/ancestors that arrives in the camp in the form of a trumpet, a hollowed-out tree carried into the camp by the youths. The *molimo* tends to either emerge out of a relaxed and abundant state in camp, or be a response to conflict, to someone trying to exert control over others, to a death or disharmony or bad hunting. As it progresses, it gradually tends to draw the camp deeper and deeper into more complex harmonies demanding and echoing the complex cooperation required in the hunt. Rather than being about transcending and controlling the forest or other people, the *molimo* is about restoring cooperative relationships between all members of the camp and between the camp and the forest/ancestors, to ensure both the camp's well-being and that the relationship with the forest is well, which will inevitably lead to a good hunt. However the *molimo* is not in any way an attempt to secure "the transcendental support of the forest" (contra Collier and Rosaldo 1981: 301), for the forest is not experienced as transcendent, as separate from human interaction with it. For both the Bila and the Mbuti there is a continuum, rather than an opposition, between the living and the ancestors, and the ancestors and the forest.

In considering the environment as a living rather than an inert entity, Ichikawa makes the important point that Bird-David's portrayal of a hunter-gatherer "cosmic economy of sharing" with the environment fails to include Mbuti experience of the negative aspects of "nature": "while the forest may sometimes be called 'father' or 'mother' and described as a 'womb,' it is also conceived to be a place 'where dead ancestors roam' " (Ichikawa 1992: 41).

This passage comprehensively highlights the broad range of Mbuti experience of the forest. However, rather than recognize the importance of the "ancestors as forest," Ichikawa instead leaves them to occupy simply a negative intrusive role. On the contrary, for many Bila, as well as for the Mbuti, they address the forest and the ancestors in the same breath because they are, for them, the same being. Thus the Mbuti experience ambivalence in their relationship with the forest, but they generally work within the *molimo* to make the relationship good. For the Mbuti, restoring harmony in their relationship with the forest inevitably means restoring harmony among themselves; for the forest is inhabited by the living and the dead, it is alive with those who are living and those who are now both ancestor and forest. Thus the qualitative distinction and opposition we in the West habitually make between the living elders and the ancestors does not hold for the Bila and the Mbuti. Furthermore, the division we habitually make between people (whether ancestors or living) and their environment (in this case the forest), also does not hold for the Mbuti, nor, to a certain extent, for the Bila either.

Thus, the ancestors should not be understood as being elevated to a place that is outside and opposed to "nature" and the living human community. The full range of negative and positive Mbuti beliefs about the forest, and the full range of their extractive and respectful relations with both it and the Bila, make sense when understood within the context of the forest/ancestor complex. For the Mbuti and the Bila, the aliveness of their environment is experienced and expressed through their interaction with it, and through the awareness of their ancestors inhabiting the forest both in the past and in the present, a form of inhabiting in which they and the forest become indistinguishable. In a key passage describing Mbuti religion, Turnbull himself hints at this interpretation when he describes *keti* as "spirits, human and animal, who are not necessarily the spirits of the dead but may be independent manifestations of the forest, and who are disembodied only in that they are invisible to the Mbuti" (1965: 249). The ambiguity in this passage – about who the *baketi* are – mirrors Ichikawa's insistence on broadening our understanding of Mbuti experience. The implications of Turnbull's ambiguity here are in strong contrast to the sharp and explicit distinction he customarily makes between village ancestor worship and Mbuti forest worship. In this passage the spirits of the forest are *both* human and animal, *both* spirits of the dead and independent manifestations of the forest, *both* invisible and embodied.

The Mbuti listen to the spirits, normally in the form of their own ancestors but also in animal and other forms, who come to them in dreams telling them such things as where to hunt, or that they must not hunt on a certain day but should stay in camp. Ancestors also arrive in a far more disruptive role when they enter one of their living relatives in a form of spirit possession, often angry because their relative has not behaved properly. This happened both to Bila and Mbuti young women during my fieldwork. In both cases the *molimo* trumpet, representing the forest/ancestors, entered the camp to deal with the angry ancestor in the individual. And in both cases male and female Mbuti elders, dialoguing with the *molimo*, linked the need to restore harmony to the individual with the need for the *molimo* to bless and restore good fortune to the hunt: the *molimo* being referred to both as the spirit or animal of the forest, and as a powerful ancestor. One Mbuti elder explained it like this:

Ketyo batata abaano-ba suba ndula . . .
Keti na ndula beko-o kadi, kabakatani, kadi tu.
(The spirits of the ancestors are in the forest.
Spirit and forest are one, inseparable, one always.)

Justin Kenrick

Further Reading

Bird-David, Nurit. "Beyond 'The Original Affluent Society': A Culturalist Reformulation." *Current Anthropology* 33:1 (1992), 25–34.

Brandewie, Ernest. *Wilhelm Schmidt and the Origin of the Idea of God*. Lanham, MD: University Press of America, 1983.

Ichikawa, Mitsuo. Comment on Nurit Bird-David's "Beyond 'The Original Affluent Society': A Culturalist Reformulation." In *Current Anthropology* 33:1 (1992), 40–1.

Ingold, Tim. "Hunting and Gathering as Ways of Perceiving the Environment." In Roy Ellen and Katsuyoshi Fukui, eds. *Redefining Nature: Ecology, Culture and Domestication*. Oxford: Berg, 1996, 117–55.

Kenrick, Justin. "Anthropology and Anthropocentrism: Images of Hunter-Gatherers, Westerners and the Environment." In Alan Barnard and Henry Stewart, eds. *Self- and Other Images of Hunter-Gatherers* (SENRI). Osaka: National Museum of Ethnology, 2002.

Kenrick, Justin. "Reflections in the Molimo Pool: Gender, Ritual, Economics and the Mbuti of Zaire." In Karen Biesbrouck, Stefan Elders and Gerda Rossel, eds. *Challenging Elusiveness: Central African Hunter-Gatherers in a Multidisciplinary Perspective*. Leiden: CNWS, 1999, 153–68.

Köhler, Axel. "The Forest as Home: Baka Environment and Housing." In Karen Biesbrouck, Stefan Elders and Gerda Rossel, eds. *Challenging Elusiveness: Central African Hunter-Gatherers in a Multidisciplinary Perspective*. Leiden: CNWS, 1999, 207–20.

Kopytoff, Igor. "Ancestors as Elders in Africa." *Africa* 41 (1971), 129–42.

Lewis, Jerome. *Forest Hunter-Gatherers and Their World: A Study of the Mbendjele Yaka Pygmies of Congo-Brazzaville and Their Secular and Religious Activities and Representations*. Ph.D. Thesis: University of London, 2002.

Lewis, Jerome. "Forest People or Village People: Whose Voice Will Be Heard?" In Alan Barnard and Justin Kenrick, eds. *Africa's Indigenous Peoples: "First Peoples" or "Marginalised Minorities"?* Edinburgh: CAS, 2001, 61–78.

Ortner, Sherry. "Is Female to Male as Nature Is to Culture?" In M.Z. Rosaldo and L. Lamphere, eds. *Woman, Culture and Society*. Stanford: Stanford University Press, 1974, 67–88.

Schebesta, Paul. *Among Congo Pigmies*. London: Hutchinson & Co., 1933 (reprinted 1977 by New York: AMS Press Inc).

Turnbull, Colin M. *The Mbuti Pygmies: Change and Adaptation*. New York: Holt, Rinehart & Winston, 1983.

Turnbull, Colin M. *Wayward Servants: The Two Worlds of the African Pygmies*. London: Eyre & Spottiswoode, 1965 (1966).

Turnbull, Colin M. *The Forest People*. London: Pimlico, 1961 (1993).

See also: Biodiversity and Religion in Equatorial Africa; Congo River Watershed.

Q

Quaker Writers in Tasmania (Australia)

The island state of Tasmania (previously Van Diemen's Land) is situated 40 degrees south in the path of the Roaring Forties. It was known as Trowenna and Loutrouwitter by its Aboriginal tribes, comprising roughly nine dialect groups, each band having a spiritual affiliation to its own territory. Because of its geographical isolation the island was selected as a penal colony when white settlement to Van Diemen's Land began in 1803. Naming and function created the conceptual debris of a landscape of the damned situated alongside Romantic constructions of the landscape as Paradise. Quaker settlers brought with them a pragmatic Romanticism and Christian stewardship in their concern for indigenous rights and penal reform.

Practical romanticism was evident in The Friends' opposing war, refusing to bear arms, pay tithes, take oaths, and asserting individualism and equality. As a result many Quakers were imprisoned, giving rise to their interest in penal reform. The status of Van Diemen's Land as a penal colony was for them less a deterrent than a missionary opportunity.

"The First Publishers of Truth" as the Quakers or Friends were originally called fostered a vernacular approach to the study of English which included geography and history. The emphasis on the natural sciences and the essay form produced personal and interdisciplinary nature writing. In addition, natural history education served Quakers in their stewardship of the land. Farming was new to many in the colony, and though climate and soil appeared similar to England's, Quakers willingly experimented with rather than replicated agrarian practices.

In 1828 free settlers Francis Cotton (1801–1883) and Anna Tilney (1800–1882) homesteaded on the east coast, then occupied by the Oyster Bay tribe. The social activism and anti-slavery movement of the Evangelical Quakers created ambiguity for the Cottons once situated among convict and indigenous populations. A 5000-acre land grant meant Cotton benefited from convict labor; consequently, his was not a leading voice in the anti-transportation movement. In addition, pastoralist claims conflicted with the hunting claims of indigenes whose geosophical or spiritual links to place were hardly recognized. The scientific view of the land that was a result of Quaker education in natural history did not, however, extend to an anthropological view of Aborigines. Quaker belief in the presence of God within all people led to the foundation of the Aborigines Protection Society (1837) patterned after William Penn's response to the treatment of Native American Indians. Cotton recorded Aboriginal myths, and his attitude toward the indigene influenced his thirteenth child, Joseph (1840–1923), who recalls meeting the last full-blood male Tasmanian Aborigine, William Lanney (d. 1869). Oral accounts of Aboriginal Dreaming were later published in *Touch the Morning: Tasmanian Native Legends* (1979) by Jackson Cotton, Joseph's grandson.

One story, "The Beginning," attributed to Timler ("high priest" of the Big River tribe) is a creation story about the island's Dreamtime inception. The cosmology is anthropomorphized – the sun Moinee is the spirit of Trowenna, an island created out of grief and pain due to the loss of Moinee's wife, Vena, who disappears when the iceberg she is on melts. The myth reveals an ice-age climatology beyond human memory, while ascribing to the island an emotional temperament which will be borne out historically in its white-settler appropriation as a penal colony and in its displacement of the indigenous population.

Woreddy (d. 1842) of the Nuenone (Bruny Island) people, tells the story of Moinee creating the first man. Moinee's brother, Dromerdene, takes pity on man whose tail prevents him from sleeping. Dromerdene cuts off the tail, creating delineation between human and nonhuman. When man stretches the tail, creates a spear "and straight away set off to hunt," hunting becomes a natural extension of human–animal relationships though symbolically the spear exists as a reminder of their interrelatedness.

Jackson Cotton attributes authority to the stories by appealing to Quaker truth-speaking, though the recovery of myths is marked by unconscious reinvention. For instance, Timler's *Genesis* story contains Aboriginal and Greek cosmologies; the title of Woreddy's story "The First Blackman" signals colonial Otherness absent in the complementary story of the first *white* man, Adam.

Quaker presence in the colonies increased after the 1832 visit of missionaries under concernment, James Backhouse (1794–1869) and George Washington Walker (1800–1859). It was while "standing in the nursery ground at Norwich" that Backhouse experienced his calling to Australia. In *A Narrative of a Visit to the Australian Colonies* (1843), an important botanical work, Backhouse describes contacting the government, advocating the return of Aboriginal hunting grounds. After visiting Port Arthur penal settlement Backhouse urged the government to grant garden plots to prisoners as a reward for good behavior and as a deterrent to scurvy. In his dealings with the human and nonhuman, he recorded a moment when nature afforded him an opportunity for reform as soldiers tormented sharks in the spirit of revenge:

> We succeeded in convincing the men that they were wrong in giving way to this spirit, and that it was their duty either to kill the sharks by the most speedy means or to liberate them, as they had as much right to take the baits, as the soldiers had to take the fish; seeing that in so doing, they only followed an instinct given by their Creator (Backhouse 1843: 42).

Quakers' reputation of probity and truth-speaking served them well in business. In 1884 draper William Levitt Wells (1853–1918) and Elisabeth Lidbetter left England to settle in the renamed Tasmania. Published posthumously, *Immense Enjoyment: The Wells Journals 1884–1888* demonstrates how experience of nature conflicts with the literary pastoral as a metaphor for refuge. The chain of economy extends from the resource value of parrots (as pets, and pests, robbing Wells of his peaches) to their being skinned for wallets, or eaten for their flesh which is like "roast beef." Hunting provides a meal, or material for the taxidermist's needle to feed the scientific minds of Wells' children.

Half a century later, the novel *Huon Belle* (1930), by Isabel (Charlotte) Dick (1881–1959) offers an ecofeminist perspective on economic and intrinsic values of the land. Dick's great-grandfather William Shoobridge (1781–1866) pioneered methods of hop growing. Another relative, Louis Shoobridge, campaigned to preserve Russell Falls. As a result, in 1885, Mount Field National Park became one of Australia's first National Parks. The title *Huon Belle* conjoins topography and anatomy in its reference to a local mountain, and character, Virginia Lee. In nineteenth-century terms she is a "natural" child, and homeless. She marries the orchard owner, whose husbandry toward her and the orchard is equally flint-hearted and profit-driven. She secures this material *oikos* because of her use-value as property and labor, but refuses to be cut off from her *genius loci*, the mountain, which becomes symbolic of inviolability. Virginia, a reconstructed Eve, becomes legal owner of the apple orchard. The patriarchal order is replaced by the primacy of feminized and productive nature. The subsequent partnership of Virginia and Simon Peter (God's Rock) is marked by shared reverence for the mountains, and joint ownership of the revered text, Thoreau's *Walden* (1854).

Kelsey Aves' essay collection *Hither and Thither* (1996) discusses conservation and Quakerism. Aves (b. 1907) migrated with his wife, Margaret, in 1940; both became Quakers in 1952. President of the Field Naturalists Club, he published two cassettes about the Tasmanian environment, "Songs and Calls of 64 Tasmanian Birds" and "Under the Blackwood Tree." He credited *The Nature of the Physical World* (1935) by Quaker scientist Sir Arthur Eddington with providing a connection between mysticism and wisdom that helps "to bring us back to Earth." Aves' migrant status initially colored his receptivity to the bioregion: in "On Learning to Love" he had to "learn to love the rainforest."

Fellow migrant Clive Sansom (1910–1981), was born in England, married Ruth Large, and migrated in 1949. His publications include ten poetry collections; four verse dramas, a work of fiction, and educational texts. Although Sansom's mental landscape was informed by the land he left behind, he became a strong advocate for the land in which he now lived. In 1950, he campaigned to stop the reestablishment of sealing on Macquarie Island. The London *Times* printed his letter, and international condemnation halted the sealing ship. He campaigned against the flooding of Lake Pedder (1972), an ancient alpine lake. The campaign failed but gave rise to The United Tasmania Group, the world's first green party. In 1976 Sansom became one of the (then-Tasmanian) Wilderness Society's founding patrons.

The belief that Tasmanian Aboriginals were extinct explains their lack of representation in early to mid-twentieth century Quaker nature writing. Notions of what constituted Tasmanian Aboriginality, along with its impact on Native Title, were being contested by the offspring of nineteenth-century white sealers and abducted Aboriginal women. The Hydro-Electric Commission's plan to flood the Franklin River, and, consequently, Kuti Kina Cave, an Aboriginal sacred site, helped publicize their cause. Sansom spoke against the flooding of this last wild river, but died the year before the successful "Fight for the Franklin" campaign. His final publication *Francis of Assisi* (1981) is fitting given the suggestion that Francis be "patron saint for ecologists" (Lynn White, Jr.). In the section "The Creatures" he wrote, "Our universe is tangled, strand with strand; / And brain-bound man, he little knows how much / That web is trembled by a single touch" (Sansom 1981: 64).

C.A. Cranston

Further Reading

Aves, Kelsey. *Hither and Thither*. Hobart: Kelsey Aves, 1996.

Backhouse, James. *A Narrative of a Visit to the Australian Colonies*. London: Hamilton, Adams, 1843 (1967).

Cotton, Frances. *Kettle on the Hob: A Family in Van Diemen's Land 1828–1885*. Orford, Tasmania: Joan Roberts, 1986.

Cotton, Jackson. *Touch the Morning: Tasmanian Native Legends*. Hobart: O.B.M., 1979.

Dick, Charlotte I. *Huon Belle*. London: Arthur H. Stockwell, 1930.

Gardam, Faye, ed. *Immense Enjoyment: The Illustrated*

Journals and Letters of William L. Wells 1884–1888. Devonport, Tasmania: Devon Historical Society, 1987.
Oats, William Nicolle. *Backhouse and Walker: A Quaker View of the Australian Colonies 1832–1838*. Sandy Bay, Tasmania: Blubber Head Press, 1981.
Sansom, Clive. *Francis of Assisi: The Sun of Umbria*. Hobart: Cat & Fiddle Press, 1981.

See also: Australia; Christian Nature Writing; Francis of Assisi; Friends – Religious Society of (Quakers); White, Lynn – Thesis of.

Quakers – *See* Friends, Religious Society of

The Qur'an

The Qur'anic approach to nature differs from that of two major approaches: the biocentric and the anthropocentric. One can most appropriately designate the Qur'anic approach as theocentric. One Qur'anic verse expresses this: "[God] is the creator of everything" (6:102). Without him the heavens and the Earth will collapse: "Surely, God holds Earth and heaven from collapsing. If they collapse, no one can hold them after Him . . ." (35:41). Being the sole creator God is the center of everything; in the Qur'an all things point to him. Sovereignty belongs to God only (12:67). Among God's creatures, man is the most conscious. Although, man is the most powerful and independent of God's creatures, the Qur'an explicitly states that God is man's creator: "Lo! We create man from a drop of semen to test him; so We make him hearing, knowing" (76:2).

According to the Qur'an, nature is a mirror of God's beautiful names. The whole of creation is the reflection of God's name *al-Khaliq* (The Creator) (13:16, 15:28, 35:3, 38:71, 39:62, 40:62, and 59:24). It is not just randomly created, it is wonderfully designed: "you can see no fault in His creation" (67:3). Concerning this wonderful design, the creation of man is emphasized. According to the Qur'an, God has shaped humanity, nature, and all of his creation in the most beautiful manner (64:3). So perfectly arranged is God's creation, that everything from plants to human beings is a miraculous work of art. Therefore, there is no absurdity in nature.

The Qur'an refers to nature as a sign or verse. There are two types of signs (ayāt) of God. One is the Qur'anic verse. Each verse is considered an "ayah" or a statement from God. The second is nature; each part of nature is also considered an "ayah" or a "sign" of God. According to the Qur'an, there are limitless signs of God. The water which God sends down from the sky, the ordinance of the winds and clouds are signs (2:164). They are not created in vain: "We created not the Heaven and the Earth and all that is between them in vain" (38:27). In the heavens and the Earth are signs for believers; the creation of humans is a sign, likewise the changing from night to day, and the provisions God sends from the sky, and thereby sustains the Earth, are signs, statements, or messages from God (45:3–5). Accordingly, the Qur'an speaks of nature not for the sake of itself but for the sake of its Creator. Thus, the Qur'an indicates that nature has a divine characteristic, as it is a reflection of God. The Qur'an does not detail the physical structure of natural phenomenon, but instead, focuses on the purpose of such phenomenon, which is designated by its creator. When the Qur'an talks about the sun, it does not describe it as a physics book would, but describes it as a "dazzling lamp" for humanity and thus emphasizes that the sun is a sign of God's mercy toward humanity (78:16).

The main purpose of creation, according to the Qur'an, is to serve as a sign of God and to reflect God's beautiful names. In this regard, a fly and an elephant serve the same purpose, shoulder to shoulder, and the fly is worth no less because of its smallness. In the teaching of the Qur'an an atom is no less a sign of God than a mountain, because both are his handiwork. In the Qur'an over 99 names of God are mentioned. Chapter 59 contains over 13 names of God: the Knower of the invisible and visible, the Beneficent, the Merciful, the Sovereign, the Holy, the Peace, the Keeper of Faith, the Guardian, the Majestic, the Compeller, the Superb, the Creator, and the Modeler (59:22–24). All these names at different levels are seen in the mirror of nature. For example, life is very precious in nature. The source of life is one. According to the Qur'an all living creatures reflect God's name al-Hayy (The Living One). (For references to al-Hayy see 2:255, 3:2, 20:111, 25:58, 40:65). The Qur'an frequently expresses the need for humans to recognize the beautiful names of God reflected in nature: "Lo! In the creation of the heavens and the Earth and in the difference of night and day are signs of His sovereignty for men of understanding" (3:190).

Nature is also Sunnat-Allah (The Way of God). The Qur'an indicates that there is consistency in nature, which reflects the unchangeable laws of God (33:62). Only via miracles can the consistency of natural law be interrupted. The Qur'an gives examples of this, such as the miracles of Abraham, Moses, and Jesus (21:69, 27:12, 5:110). Abraham was thrown into fire, but fire did not burn him. According to the Qur'an Abraham was saved because, God said "O fire, be cool and peace to Abraham" (21:64). Moses was able to turn his staff into a snake (27:12). Jesus made birds, by breathing into them to give them life (5:110). Miracles, such as these, are, according to the Qur'an, intended to present evidence of the truthfulness of God's messengers. Despite such miraculous events, which interrupt natural law, there is a consistency of cause and effect which God has enacted. Human beings are, therefore, required to follow the laws of nature. Islamic scholars interpreting the importance of following the laws of nature say that the punishment of disobedience is urgent (it will come in this life), as well as the reward. For example, cold weather will make the person sick if the appropriate measures are not taken.

The Qur'an offers evidence that creation was purposively designed: "And verily we have beautified the world's heaven with lamps" (67:5). "He it is who appointed for you the night that ye should rest therein and the day giving sight. Lo! Herein verily are signs for a folk that heed" (5:67). According to the Qur'an, human beings are to recognize that God's creation is structured for them, and they should therefore be aware of cosmic events, such as the sunrise and the sunset: ". . . celebrate the praises of [their] Lord ere the rising of the sun and ere the going down thereof. And glorify Him some hours of the night and at the two ends of the day . . ." (20:130).

As it is seen in the above verses, humans have great responsibility to see the signs, which are presented in nature – in other words, the meaning of the verses of nature. Accordingly, God has placed humanity at the apex of creation. Humans are to serve as vicegerents of God, and to them nature is subjugated: "He it is who hath placed you as viceroys of the Earth and hath exalted some of you in rank above others . . ." (6:165). The high position of humans gives them great responsibility as the supervisors of nature and as the addressees of God's message. Although in the value pyramid of creation human beings are at the apex, sometimes because of corruption they are considered to be lower than animals (7:179). In the teaching of the Qur'an, animals do not bear the responsibilities that humanity does, because they are not given reason and consciousness. However, they have the right to be protected and are not to be abused.

The Qur'an stresses the importance of animals as a part of the natural environment and the responsibility humanity has toward them. The Qur'an even equates them with humanity in terms of creation. The following Qur'anic verse forms a paradigm as far as the human relationship with animals is concerned: "There is not an animal in the Earth nor a flying creature flying on two wings but they are communities like you" (6:38). This verse indicates that the community of animals is similar to that of people, and therefore places a heavy responsibility on humans to care for animals. Several Qur'anic chapters are named after animals. For example, there are Qur'anic chapters entitled "The Cow" (Chapter 2), "The Cattle" (Chapter 6), "The Bee" (Chapter 16), "The Ant" (Chapter 27), and "The Spider" (Chapter 29). According to the Qur'an, the provisions given by God are to be shared by man and animals (80:32). Animals are intended to benefit humanity and caring for animals is to be viewed as a way of receiving God's bounty. Therefore, the Qur'an asks people to treat animals kindly. In the story of a Qur'anic prophet, Salih, people are required to share their water with the she-camel of the prophet, which is called "the she-camel of God" (nāqat Allah). Salih, the messenger of God, requests that the people allow her to drink, and the people deny this request and send a base man to kill the camel. Having killed an animal, without reason, the people are destroyed by lightning (17:5, 69:59, 91:11–15).

According to the Qur'an, animals have a sophisticated language of communication. One verse speaks of an ant that warns its fellow ants to take shelter in order to avoid being stepped on by the army of Solomon (27:18). Solomon is taught, by God, to understand the language of birds (27:16). According to the Qur'an, Solomon considered this ability to be a blessing from God and a sign of his favor. Animals also serve as the companions and mounts of humans, as the Qur'an says "We have created from them of our handiwork, the cattle . . . so that some of them they have for riding . . ." (36:71–72). This verse illustrates that because animals are also the creation of God, and they benefit humans, humans have a responsibility to care for and protect them. The purpose of animals and that which humans may use them for is specified in the Qur'an. Animals may be used as mounts or for food, but they are not to be abused or wasted. Islamic law, which stems from the Qur'anic teaching, prohibits cruelty toward animals, such as loading animals beyond their capacity. The prophet of Islam is said to have rebuked a person for trying to make a camel carry too heavy a burden. Also, Muhammad, following the revelations of the Qur'an, declared the holy site of Mecca to be a Haram, which can best be understood in modern terms as a National Park, in which it is criminal to kill so much as an insect or to uproot a plant. Some Muslim mystics have even been known to tie bells to their shoes, in order to warn small animals in their paths that might otherwise be crushed underfoot. This tradition is still essential in Islam, during hajj (pilgrimage). For example, Muslims are not allowed to cut grass during this time, in the area of Haram. They are not allowed to kill living creatures, including insects. If they happen to act in such a manner during hajj, they perform penance for this unlawful action.

Just as the Qur'an stresses the importance of protecting animals, it also stresses the importance of respecting other aspects of God's creation of nature. Many Qur'anic chapters take their names from natural elements, such as "Thunder" (Chapter 13), "Light" (Chapter 24), "Star" (Chapter 53), "Iron" (Chapter 57), "Date Trees" (Chapter 16), "Cave" (Chapter 18), "Sun" (Chapter 91), and "Moon" (Chapter 54). Natural elements in the Qur'an are presented in a variety of contexts. There are some natural elements, which are referred in nearly every page of the Qur'an, such as Earth, which is mentioned nearly 500 times in the Qur'an. Water, Sun, Moon, Stars, and Sky are also among the frequently mentioned elements. For example, water is presented as a gift from God or a helper sent by God from the sky to help fruits grow in order to provide sustenance for humans (2:22, 14:32, 16:65, 20:53, 22:63). The Qur'an also refers to water as a tool of cleanliness for humanity (8:11). In a different context, water is the "ground" of God's throne (11:7). Water can also serve as a tool of punishment and destruction, as in the story of Pharaoh (29:40) and of Noah (11:40–44). Although water can be a tool to destroy life, it is also, according to the Qur'an, the source of life (21:30). Pure water is a gift to those in paradise, while contaminated water is a punishment for non-believers: "Hell is before him and he is made to drink a festering water . . ." (14:16). Similarly, Earth is also a "cradle" for humanity (20:25). At the same time, however, it is a tool of punishment that swallows non-believers, such as Korah, a wealthy man who opposed God and was consumed by the Earth because of his non-belief (29:40). Earth glorifies God, and suffers when inappropriate things are attributed to God. For example, the Qur'an indicates, "the heavens are torn and the Earth is split asunder and the mountains fall in ruins, that ye ascribe unto the Beneficent a son . . ." (19:90–91). The Earth is treated as a living creature, when the Qur'an says, "And the heaven and the Earth wept not for them [the non-believers] . . ." (44:29).

The Qur'an gives examples of the bounties of God seen in nature. There are many examples of natures' modification for the benefit of humanity. The Qur'an laments the lack of human understanding, saying,

> Have they not seen how We have created for them of Our handiwork the cattle, so that they are their owners and have subdued them unto them so that some of them they have for riding, some for food? Benefits and diverse drinks have they from them. Will they not then give thanks? (36:71–73).

The following verse wonderfully illustrates the benefits of natural elements for man:

> Let man consider his food. How we pour water in shower. Then split the earth in clefts. And cause the grain to grow therein. And grapes and green fodder and olive-trees and palm-trees and garden-closes of thick foliage and fruits and grasses. Provision for you and your cattle (80:24–32).

Again and again the Qur'an reveals the things that God has created for the benefit of humanity: "And We have given you (mankind) power in the Earth, and appointed for you therein a livelihood . . ." (7:10). Ten verses in chapter 78 are dedicated to listing the things that God has created as a gift for humanity. For example, Earth is to serve as a cradle for humans, the mountains are to serve as protections, sleeping is to provide a rest, night is to be like a covering garment, and day is to be a time of work, and the sun is to be a dazzling lamp (78:6–16). Thus, "clouds heavy with rain" is another phenomenon that the Qur'an mentions as from God's mercy:

> He it is who sends the winds as tidings heralding His mercy, till when they bear a cloud heavy with rain, We lead it to a dead land, and cause water to descend thereon and thereby bring forth fruits of every kind (7:5).

The Qur'an speaks of nature as related to the divine. That is to say, the Qur'an wants to open the veil of nature covering the hands of God, and thus make understood the ultimate reality of God, beyond cause and effect. Humanity, in turn, is expected to reflect and be thankful for all the bounties of God. This thankfulness necessitates that humanity act responsibly as God's viceroys and protect nature. Humans must utilize the bounties of God carefully and without waste, in order to express their thankfulness.

Therefore, all types of pollution are prohibited by the Qur'an. For example, the Qur'an says that "the wasteful are the friends of Satan" (17:27) and "God does not like the wasteful" (10:83). Wasting includes any misuse of natural resources. The Qur'an teaches people to use resources economically; this teaching is so strong that a person may not waste water, even if he or she lives next to the ocean. Also, noise pollution is to be prevented by the Qur'anic command "Don't be arrogant in your walking on Earth. Be humble, lower your voice. The most detestable voice is that of an ass" (31:18–19). Pollution of the body, as well as of the environment, is prohibited by the Qur'an. The Qur'anic teaching of cleanliness is very compatible with the modern hygienic process of preventing disease and promoting healthcare. For example, the Qur'an asks believers to wash their faces and their hands up to the elbows, clean their hair, and to wash their feet before prayers. If people are unclean they are not to approach prayer until they purify themselves (5:6). Muslims are expected to perform the prescribed cleansing before each of the five daily prayers. According to the Qur'an, if someone comes from the water closet, they are asked to clean themselves with water (5:6). A woman at the end of her monthly period is asked to bathe, and she is to refrain from sexual intercourse during this time (2:2). Even the Qur'an itself is not to be touched but by clean people (56:79). God loves those who are clean (200:22, 9:106). The tool of cleanliness is primarily water, thus the natural element of water has a special significance in the Qur'an. The Qur'an also stresses the importance of preserving a clean environment. For example, Abraham and Ishmael are asked to clean the house of God (2:125). Humans are also directed to preserve the cleanliness of their outdoor environment. The Qur'an indicates that the natural world is to be kept from pollution, because God sends rainwater to clean the Earth: "We send water from the sky as a cleaner for you" (25:48). Thus the Qur'an suggests a clean environment.

The Qur'anic paradigm of such environment is found in the description of paradise. The Qur'anic name for Paradise is Jannah (garden); it is filled with trees, rivers of milk, flowers, and fruits. The basic description of Paradise is a place under which rivers run. Therefore, the environment of Paradise is one of water and greenery (2:25, 3:15). Even the fruits of Paradise are eternal (9:21). There are beautiful springs (44:52). The Qur'an, by describing the beauty of Paradise, stresses the importance of environment. This description is intended to serve as a model for earthly abodes. For example, modern Islamic architecture is influenced by the Qur'anic description of Paradise, as being without a sun, or direct source of light, and having only indirect light. Modern Islamic architecture attempts to utilize indirect light, while blocking harsh direct light. The Qur'an does not give any information about the location of Paradise. It does say that Paradise is located in the world of the unseen, a realm parallel to our own. It is understood that this world can be seen after the end of this physical life. It says it is an abode of righteous people; those who do good deeds toward humans and nature. To create a paradise-like environment on Earth complements the Muslim desire for Paradise. The destruction of nature affects the Muslim's entry into the final abode of Paradise. Destruction of nature on Earth is unlawful according to Islamic tradition. This might serve as an obstacle for one's entry into Paradise. Having a paradise-like life on Earth is not an obstacle on the path to Paradise after death; on the contrary, it is a preparation for that future life. People should thus make this Earthly environment as beautiful as possible.

According to the Qur'an, nature is not eternal. The end of nature is a kind of punishment for humankind, but is also an appointed time, which God has promised to bring. The end will be in the form of a natural disaster described in the Qur'an. For example, the Qur'an says, in a chapter entitled "Earthquake," that "the Earth will be shaken with her final earthquake" (100:1). The sky will be torn away and mountains will become like discarded wool (81:11). The hills will move, the sun will cease to shine, and the stars will fall (81:1, 2). The planets will disperse and the moon will split (82:2, 54:1). Seas will be poured forth and will rise (81:6, 82:3). According to the Qur'an, the Earth will be replaced with another "Earth" different from this one (14:48). This will be a transformation from the transient world to the eternal world. It is understood, from Qur'anic verses, that all of these things will occur because of the corruption of humans. By polluting the Earth and wasting the bounties of God, humans hasten the Earth's end. However, another Qur'anic verse offers hope if God's creation is respected and protected by humanity: "If they do right, they will not be punished" (11:117). There is an Islamic tradition (8:33; 17:15) which indicates that as long as people are obedient to God, this system that God created in the universe will continue. In this way there would be no destruction. It is believed that the destruction of pre-Islamic nations resulted from their disobedience toward God. If they had obeyed God, then the result would have been different; there would have been no destruction. This is a general principle, understood from an overall picture of the Qur'an. However, there are also several verses which discuss the appointed time for the end of this worldly life. This is not because it is a terrible fate to expect; it is instead referring to the end of the period of the test. This life is a test, and when this period ends, people will be either rewarded or punished. The reward will come in the afterlife. Muslim traditions, when speaking of the end of this life, say that God will take the lives of all believers in him, in an easy and beautiful way, in order not to destroy the Earth upon them. They will not have to face the destruction of the Earth. When they are resurrected, they will find themselves in a changed, eternal place. The destruction is not a punishment; it simply serves to end one period, while ushering in the beginning of a new, eternal life. To clarify further, according to Qur'anic traditions, the Earth has been created as a house for humanity. Humans are responsible for the upkeep of this house. It is a ship which takes humanity to the land of eternity. Humanity is in a perpetual state of motion and travel. The ship, then, is well protected in the ocean of space. If the Earth is ever destroyed so too will the lives of humans be destroyed. Life on Earth is a test for humanity. The Qur'an mentions a huge earthquake, but it is not meant to be a punishment for humanity. There is an element of irony here. A Qur'anic verse indicates that the end of time will occur during a time of human corruption. Although this happened because of human free will, God knew beforehand that this would occur. There are several matters intertwined, namely human free will, God's destiny and the destruction of the Earth. This change is apparently a punishment which occurs as a result of corruption. For real believers, however, it is symbolic of a change to a better reality. God is thought to act with wisdom, according to various laws and principles. In the world to come, God's name al-Qadir will be dominant. As a result of this, everything will occur simultaneously. According to the Qur'an, there are signs for the final Hour (47:18), as there is prophetic tradition (Muslim, al-Fitan, 39–40). Where ten signs of the Hour are listed, the final of these signs is the rising of the sun from the west. This marks the end of the test, with a positive change occurring for those who pass. The Qur'an describes this end in the following verses: "And the garden (Jannah) will be brought nigh to the righteous and hell (al-Jaheem) will appear plainly to the erring" (26:90–91).

Zeki Saritoprak

Further Reading

Ajmal, M. and M. Rafiq. "Islam and the Present Ecological Crisis." In O.P. Dwivedi, ed. *World Religions and the Environment*. New Delhi: Gitanjali Publishing House, 1989.

Amar, Nawal. "Islam and Deep Ecology." In David Landis Barnhill and Roger S. Gottlieb, eds. *Deep Ecology and World Religions*. Albany: State University of New York Press, 2001, 193–211.

Chittick, William. " 'God Surrounds all Things': An Islamic Perspective on the Environment." *The World and I* 1:6 (June 1986).

Nasar, Seyyed Hossein. "Islam and the Environmental Crisis." In Steven C. Rockefeller and John C. Elder, eds. *Spirit and Nature: Why the Environment is a Religious Issue*. Boston: Beacon Press, 1992, 82–108.

See *also*: Animals in the Bible and Qur'an; Dogs in the Islamic Tradition; Islam (various); Muhammad – The Prophet of Islam; Sufism.

Radical Environmentalism

Radical environmentalism most commonly brings to mind the actions of those who break laws in sometimes dramatic displays of "direct action" in defense of nature. Such action – which may involve civil disobedience and sabotage, some instances of which involve risks to people – have generated criticism and vilification of these movements. Radical environmentalists are sometimes labeled terrorists and believed to harbor, and hope to develop, weapons of mass death. The focus on their tactics, real and imagined, often obscures their religious motivations as well as their ecological, political, and moral claims.

Not all radical environmentalists engage in illegal activities, of course, and many specific tactics are controversial within these movements, especially those which might entail risks to living things, including human adversaries. While the embrace of direct action and support for extra-legal nature defense is an important common denominator in radical environmental sub-cultures, it is even more important to understand radical environmentalism as a cluster of environmental political philosophies, and corresponding social movements, which claim to understand the roots of the environmental crisis and offer effective solutions to it. In this sense radical environmentalism includes not only groups like EARTH FIRST! AND THE EARTH LIBERATION FRONT, but also bioregionalists and green anarchists, deep ecologists and ecopsychologists, ecofeminists and participants in the feminist spirituality movement, Pagans and Wiccans, anti-globalization protestors and some animal-liberation activists.

Radical environmentalists can be recognized by their diagnoses and prescriptions regarding the environmental crisis. Their diagnoses generally involve a critique of the dominant streams of occidental religion and philosophy, which are said to desacralize nature and promote oppressive attitudes toward it, as well as toward people. Prescriptions generally include overturning anthropocentric and hierarchical attitudes (especially capitalist and patriarchal ones). Accomplishing this is generally believed to require "resacralizing" and reconnecting with nature (which is usually gendered as female, as in "mother earth" or "mother nature"), combined with direct-action resistance to oppression in all forms.

Reconnection and consciousness transformation can be facilitated in a number of ways. Most important among these is spending time in nature with a receptive heart, for the central spiritual episteme among radical environmentalists is that people can learn to "listen to the land" and discern its sacred voices. Other means of evoking and deepening a proper spiritual perception include visual art (appearing in tabloids or photography presented in public performances), which appeal to one's intuitive sense of the sacredness of intact ecosystems, and music, dancing, drumming (sometimes combined with sacred herbs or "ENTHEOGENS"), which can erode the everyday sense of ego and independence in favor of feelings of belonging to the universe, or even kindle animistic perceptions of interspecies communication.

Many radical environmentalists can accurately be labeled "nature mystics." And many of them express affinity with religions they generally consider more nature-beneficent than occidental religions, such as those originating in Asia such as Buddhism and Daoism, religious beliefs or practices surviving among the world's remnant indigenous peoples, or being revitalized or invented anew, such as PAGANISM and WICCA. Paganism and Wicca are considered to be (or to be inspired by) the Aboriginal nature religions of the Western world, which have been long suppressed by imperial Christianity and Islam.

Sometimes newly invented nature spiritualities, such as JAMES LOVELOCK's Gaia hypothesis or THOMAS BERRY's Universe Story (and the corresponding EPIC OF EVOLUTION), have become new, free-standing religious movements which promote radical environmental ideas. Other times, stories without an immediately apparent religious theme, such as ALDO LEOPOLD's epiphany about the intrinsic value of all life, including predators, upon seeing the "green fire" die in the eyes of a she-wolf he had shot, have become mythic fables incorporated into poetry, song, and movement ritualizing. Regularly, newly invented songs, myths, or nature-related ritual forms are grafted onto already existing religious forms in the constantly changing religious bricolage that characterizes countercultural spirituality in general, and radical environmentalism in particular. Increasingly, nature-related spiritualities birthed and incubated at the margins of countercultural environmentalism are escaping these enclaves and influencing both mainstream environmentalism and institutional religion, and arguably, even institutions like the United Nations, and the UNITED NATIONS' "EARTH SUMMITS." In such ways radical environmental spirituality has, despite its marginality, become a significant social force.

Whatever the nature of the hybrids and new religious amalgamations, the religious alternatives to occidental monotheisms that characterize radical environmentalism are thought to harbor environmentally friendly values and to promote behaviors that cohere with them. These alternatives promote not only a sacralization of nature but a kinship ethics wherein all life forms are considered family in the journey of evolution. Within this kind of worldview, all life deserves respect and reverent care.

Not all participants in radical environmental movements, of course, consider themselves "religious," and this includes many scientists and CONSERVATION BIOLOGY pioneers who have supported certain radical environmental groups and initiatives. Participants who do not consider themselves religious usually say this is because they equate religion with the Western, institutional forms that they consider authoritarian and anti-nature, and have thus rejected. Nevertheless, such figures rarely object to and almost always rely on metaphors of the sacred to express their conviction that nature has intrinsic value (value apart from its utility for humans). They likewise commonly describe environmental destruction as "desecration" or "defilement." Even though some participants in these movements consider themselves atheists, this generally means they do not believe in other-worldly deities or divine rescue from this world, not that they disbelieve that there is a sacred dimension to the universe and biosphere. And they often characterize as "spiritual" their own connections to nature and ultimate values.

Certainly religious studies scholars can identify features of these movements that are typical of what they call "religion." They have myth, symbol, and ritual, for example. The myths usually delineate how the world came to be (cosmogony), what it is like (cosmology), how people fit in and what they are capable of (moral anthropology), and what the future holds. Whatever the variations may be, radical environmentalists share an evolutionary cosmology and cosmogony – they generally derive their view of the unfolding universe from cosmological and evolutionary science and their understandings of humanity from primatology and anthropology. Their apocalyptic view of the present – namely that human beings are precipitating a massive extinction episode and threatening life on Earth – are gathered from contemporary environmental science. They differ widely over whether, how, and when there might be a reharmonization of life on Earth, based on differing perceptions about human beings and their potential for changing in a positive direction.

Toward the envisioned, needed changes, radical environmentalists have invented new forms of ritualizing, such as the COUNCIL OF ALL BEINGS, to promote proper spiritual perception. Such ritualizing functions in a typically religious way, drawing devotees and intensifying commitment. Moreover, movement stories and rituals express ethical mores and social critiques that are essential to the action repertoires of the movement.

Although such stories and ritualizing promote solidarity and ethical action, radical environmentalism is plural and contested, both politically and religiously; it is characterized by ongoing controversies over strategies and tactics, as well as over who owns, interprets and performs the myths and rites. Nevertheless, certain core beliefs, values, and practices make it possible to speak of "radical environmentalism" in the singular, as a complex and plural family; for there are some critical ideas and beliefs that unify these groups, at the same time that there are penultimate ideas and practices that produce various and different tendencies, priorities, and practices.

Views generally shared by radical environmentalists are depicted in the chart below, "Binary Associations Typical of Radical Environmentalism" (adapted from Taylor 2000: 276).

Shades of Radical Environmentalism

Differing stresses on the relative importance of such elements lead to differing priorities and factions among radical environmentalists. Among the most militant and best-known branches of the radical environmental tree are EARTH FIRST! AND THE EARTH LIBERATION FRONT, which are discussed separately in more detail elsewhere in this

Binary Associations Typical of Radical Environmentalism

Good	Bad
Foraging (or small-scale organic horticultural) societies	Pastoral and agricultural societies
Animistic, Pantheistic, Indigenous, Goddess-Matriarchal, or Asian Religions	Monotheistic, Sky-God, Patriarchal, Western religions
	Anthropocentrism (promotes destruction)
Biocentrism/Ecocentrism/Kinship ethics (promotes conservation)	Reason (especially instrumental)
Intuition	Mechanistic & dualistic worldviews
Holistic worldviews	Centralization
Decentralism	Modern technology
Primitive technology	Globalization and international trade
Regional self-sufficiency	Hierarchy/Nation-states/Corruption/Authoritarianism
Anarchism/Bioregionalism/Participatory democracy	Pragmatism
Radicalism	

encyclopedia. They tend to be among the most apocalyptic in their view of the human role in causing species extinctions and the most insistent that political systems are corrupt, dominated by corporate and nation-state elites, who cannot be reformed and must be resisted. Other branches of radical environmentalism have their own distinctive emphases, but in reviewing these branches it is important to recognize the extent to which they are engaged in a reciprocal process of mutual influence, often sharing religious and ethical ideas, political perceptions, and tactical innovations.

Green Anarchism, Daoism, and Paganism

Green anarchists and social ecologists focus on hierarchy as the chief cause of social and environmental calamity. Anarchists exposed to radical environmental thought rather easily adopt environmental and animal liberationist concerns, as anthropocentrism and "speciesism" are obviously oppressive, hierarchal value systems. (Speciesism is a term coined by Richard Ryder and spread widely by the Animal Liberationist philosopher Peter Singer to liken the oppression of animals to racism or sexism.) Moreover, because small-scale, indigenous societies are viewed as more ecologically sensitive and less- (or non-) hierarchal, they and their supposedly animistic nature religiosity are often held in high esteem. Indigenous societies are therefore viewed, and increasingly so, as religious and ethical models for a post-revolutionary world.

This is a remarkable development given how much anarchist thought was birthed in Europe and has long had a decidedly anti-religious ethos. In European anarchist thought, religions have often been viewed as the instrument of rulers used to legitimate and maintain oppressive regimes. Early in the emergence of radical environmentalism, figures like the social ecologist Murray Bookchin were harshly critical of the nature mysticism he believed typical among radical environmentalists; this was an unsurprising critique given anarchist history.

Increasing numbers of anarchist thinkers, however, such as John Clark, have countered that religions such as Daoism, and many minority sects within larger religions, have promoted environmentally sensitive forms of anarchism. Meanwhile other anarchist thinkers, such as John Zerzan, who promotes a type of anarcho-primitivism, express increasing openness to considering non-hierarchal, nature-spirituality as an important resource for the struggle to overturn industrial civilization (telephone discussion with Zerzan, October 2003). And this kind of anarchism has become increasingly influential within the radical environmental milieu, including within Earth First! and the Earth Liberation Front. Moreover, certain streams of Paganism and Wicca have adopted anarchist ideology or had members promoting it enthusiastically, from the DONGA TRIBE and DRAGON ENVIRONMENTAL NETWORK in the United Kingdom to the CHURCH OF ALL WORLDS in Northern California. Perhaps best known in this regard has been the Wiccan priestess and author STARHAWK, whose RECLAIMING collectives by early in the twenty-first century had spread beyond the San Francisco Bay area, gaining adherents and sponsoring events at a wide variety of locations throughout the United States and Western Europe. Indeed, Starhawk's long-term work within the anti-globalization movement has both drawn Pagans and Wiccans into it while also exposing other anti-globalists to this kind of anarchistic, radical environmental Paganism.

Bioregionalism

BIOREGIONALISM is a rapidly growing green political philosophy that by the turn of the twenty-first century boasted over a hundred regional organizations in the United States, and conservatively, at least several thousand adherents. Jim Dodge, an early proponent, explained in an early treatise that the term comes "from the Greek bios (life) and the French region (region), itself from the Latin regia (territory), and earlier, regere (to rule or govern)." A bioregion, therefore, as "life territory" or "place of life," can mean, "perhaps by reckless extension, government by life" (1981: 7).

The three tributaries to bioregionalism are thus, according to Dodge: "regionalism" (with regions defined by one or another set of ecological criteria), "anarchism" (meaning "political decentralization, self-determination, and a commitment to social equity"), and "spirituality" (with its key sources being, "the primitive animist/Great Spirit tradition, various Eastern and esoteric religious practices, and plain ol' paying attention") (Dodge 1981: 7–9).

Put simply, bioregionalism envisions decentralized community self-rule ("participatory" or "direct" democracy), within political boundaries redrawn to reflect the natural contours of differing ecosystem types. Its goal is the creation (some would say "remembering" or "borrowing") of sustainable human societies in harmony with the natural world and consistent with the flourishing of all native species.

Bioregionalism is animated by two central convictions: 1) people within a given ecological region can, by virtue of "being there" and "learning the land" (its climate patterns, native flora and fauna, water systems, soils, and even its spirits), better care for and build ecologically sustainable lifeways than can people and institutions placed further away; and 2) if local communities are to revision and construct sustainable and just lifeways, a fundamental reorienting of human consciousness is needed – at least this is the case for modern, industrial humans. As with other branches of radical environmentalism, this reformation of consciousness includes a "deep ecological" valuing of the natural world for its own sake. Usually this deep ecological conviction is tied to a perception that the land is sacred and its inhabitants are kin to whom humans owe reverence and care giving. Moreover, we should listen to and learn from the land and its inhabitants. As the bioregionalist poet Gary Lawless put it in *Home: A Bioregional Reader* (1990),

> When the animals come to us,
>   asking for our help
>   will we know what they are saying?
> When the plants speak to us
>   in their delicate, beautiful language,
>   will we be able to answer them?
> When the planet herself
>   sings to us in our dreams,
>   will we be able to wake ourselves and act?
> (in Taylor 2000: 50)

Not only Lawless and Dodge express affinity with animism or Gaian spirituality; so have most of the pioneers of the bioregional movement. Some of them wrote books that convey such spiritual perceptions which, they believe, have affinity with the spirituality of indigenous peoples – for example GARY SNYDER in *Turtle Island* (1969), David Abram in *The Spell of the Sensuous* (1996) and Freeman House in *Totem Salmon* (1999). Snyder's book was especially important, breaking ground by promoting both animistic spirituality and a bioregional sensibility, thereby significantly contributing to another wave of America's countercultural BACK TO THE LAND MOVEMENTS. And *Turtle Island* was one of the first books to use the term "biological diversity" (1969: 108) and to champion its importance, placing Snyder among the earliest proponents of deep ecological and radical environmental thought.

Although bioregionalists share the ecological apocalypticism common within radical environmental subcultures, they tend to be somewhat more hopeful than their more militant brethren that the worst of the suffering brought on by environmental degradation can be avoided. Instead, they generally tend to take a longer view, believing that by working on alternative visions and models for spirituality, livelihoods and politics, they can point the way toward a sustainable future.

Ecopsychology

ECOPSYCHOLOGY is both a distinct enclave within radical environmentalism and a significant contributor to its spirituality and religious practice. Ecopsychology can be traced at least as far back as the publication of *Nature and Madness* (1982) by the influential ecologist and environmental theorist PAUL SHEPARD. Gary Snyder and Shepard are probably the most influential scholars of radical environmental and deep ecology theory in America. In their own ways they both provided critical spadework for bioregionalism, ecopsychology, and neo-animism, all of which are closely related, and reinforce a radical environmental worldview.

Put simply, ecopsychology considers human alienation from nature as a disease born of Western agriculture and its attendant monotheistic religions and dualistic philosophies. It offers as a prescription diverse therapeutic and ritual strategies, including WILDERNESS RITES OF PASSAGE and RE-EARTHING processes, as well as workshops in BREATHWORK and Spiritual Activism.

Interestingly, ecopsychology has had increasing intersections with the psychodynamic therapy of Carl Jung and the therapeutic schools known as Humanistic and Transpersonal Psychology. James Hillman, one of the leading figures in Jungian, archetypal psychology, for example, took a surprising ecological turn with the publication (with Michael Ventura) of *We've Had a Hundred Years of Psychotherapy and the World's Getting Worse* (1993). This complemented a growing number of books (for example by Theodore Roszak, Warwick Fox, David Abram, Roger Walsh, Ralph Metzner, and Andy Fisher) promoting earthen spiritualities, therapies, and ritual processes – pantheistic, Gaian, animistic, indigenous, and shamanistic – as antidotes to human alienation from nature and as a means to foster an environmental renaissance.

On-the-ground evidence of the blending of ecopsychology with a radical environmental-style deep ecology was evident in 1993 and 1995 at two conferences sponsored by the International Transpersonal Association, the first in Ireland, the second in Brazil. Both conferences included an eclectic mix of proponents of New Age spirituality and transpersonal psychology. The Ireland gathering featured figures known for working at the intersection of consciousness, spirituality, and New Age spirituality (Ram Dass, Stanislav Grof, and Roger Walsh), radical environmentalists, especially those who had worked with indigenous peoples (David Abram, Alastair McIntosh, and Erik Van Lennep) and indigenous environmental justice advocates (Winona LaDuke, Millilani Trask, and others) and the Indian ecofeminist and anti-globalization leader Vandana Shiva.

The psychologist Ralph Metzner, who was the driving force behind these two conferences, labored to build bridges between these therapeutic, New Age, and radical environmental sub-cultures. His own nature-spirituality began with his participation with Timothy Leary in some of the earliest LSD experiments at Harvard. But he found in the 1990s that his bridge-building efforts had limits. A number of Transpersonal Association Board members felt he had taken the organization too dramatically in a radical environmental direction. Nevertheless, he continued to work toward the transformation of human consciousness that he considered a prerequisite to environmental sustainability, including helping organize a conference in San Francisco in the year 2000, this time sponsored not by the International Transpersonal Association, but by the California Institute of Integral Studies. Titled "Ayahuasca: Shamanism, Science and Spirituality," the conference was devoted to the use of entheogenic plant medicines (and in particular to the Ayahuasca plant used for spiritual and medicinal purposes by a number of Amazonian peoples). Metzner had come to believe that, if taken in proper spiritual and therapeutic contexts, sacred plants like Ayahuasca can play a positive role in transforming human consciousness in ways that promote deep ecological spirituality and ethics.

The suspicion of some transpersonal psychology advocates (like those on the International Transpersonal Association board) toward radical environmentalists is reciprocated by radical greens who view with suspicion the emphasis on personal experience that is prevalent among ecopsychologists. Many radical environmentalists feel the critical thing, once one understands the environmental crisis and the accelerating rate of species extinction, is to resist the destruction. Such activists may be sympathetic to and even influenced by the nature spirituality in ecopsychology but critical of what they take to be its self-indulgent tendencies. Such mutual suspicion is likely to be long-standing and keep these groups from forming strong strategic alliances. Nevertheless, there is substantial worldview agreement, and significant mutual influence, between ecopsychologists and other radical greens.

Ecofeminism and Feminist Spirituality Movements

This general worldview agreement is true also for ECOFEMINISM, which, like green anarchism and bioregionalism, is especially critically of hierarchy, but stresses a particular kind, patriarchy, as the most fundamental cause of environmental decline and interhuman injustice. Some ecofeminists have been harshly critical of at least some radical environmentalists, particular in the early years of the Earth First! movement, viewing it as led by boorish and sexist men. But generally speaking, these criticisms have come more from individuals outside of these movements than inside of them. Radical environmental groups are so deeply influenced by both anarchist and feminist ideals and individuals that they are vigilant against behavior that appears to be hierarchal or sexist, indeed, to the point that some activists believe this and other anthropocentric concerns have distracted the movement from its biocentric mission.

The basic proposition of ecofeminism, that a "logic of domination" is at work in modern civilizations which subjugates women and nature, is quite widely accepted within radical environmental sub-cultures. This provides a solid ground for collaboration between ecofeminists and other radical environmentalists. It may be that it was the affinity for such ideas within radical environmental sub-cultures that drew ecofeminists to them in the first place. It is certainly true that aggressive environmental campaigns were looked upon favorably by many ecofeminists, drawing many of them and their ideas into the movement. Whatever dynamics were most responsible, ecofeminist perspectives have been influential and sexism has been taken seriously within the radical environmental milieu.

Animal Rights and Animal Liberationism

In their most influential, early articulations, "animal rights" and "animal liberation" philosophies, as articulated by Peter Singer or Tom Regan, were not articulated in religious terms. These ethics have not, generally speaking, been considered close kin to radical environmentalism in the philosophical literature. Yet there are interesting intersections both religiously and ethically between animal-focused and radical environmental activism and ethics, as well as significant differences. As explained in ENVIRONMENTAL ETHICS, the apprehension of the value of animals, and the affective connection to them, can be understood in spiritual terms by participants in these movements and such spirituality sometimes leads to the development of ceremonies to express and deepen such perceptions, as is the case with Tom Regan.

The key to understanding whether animal liberationists fit in a radical environmental camp, of course, depends on how one defines radical environmentalism. One prerequisite seems clear: radical environmentalism must be biocentric or ecocentric; the good of whole ecosystems and well-being of habitats must take precedence over the lives or well-being of individual sentient animals. As unfortunate as it may be, there are many cases where a moral agent cannot have it both ways. With animal rights or liberationist perspectives, there is no reason to value organisms which there is little reason to believe can suffer (plants or amoebas for example), or to prefer the lives of individuals essential to the survival of an endangered species over those who are not. Radical environmentalists but not animal liberationists approve of hunting, for example, in cases where killing is the only effective means to reduce the populations of animals threatening endangered species. These are intractable differences.

Yet in the cross-fertilizing milieu of radical environmental and animal liberationist sub-cultures, there are many causes in which collaboration is not only possible but common. Such encounters rarely if ever cause a narrowing of ethical concern among the radical environmentalists to an exclusive concern for sentient animals, although environmentalists often adopt a vegetarian or vegan lifestyle out of revulsion for the ways animals raised for food are treated. Such encounters more often facilitate the broadening of ethical concern among animal liberationists toward an ecocentric perspective. Moreover, as animal liberationists move toward greater collaboration with radical environmentalists and become engaged with them, those who continue in such collaborations tend to shift their activist priorities toward issues that have more to do with the protection of wild, endangered animals than with protecting domestic animals. Animal activists rarely, however, abandon entirely their activism on behalf of

Rodney Coronado and the Animal Liberation Front

The Animal Liberation Front (ALF), which was founded in the United Kingdom in 1976 and has spread to many other countries in Europe as well as having a strong presence in the United States and Canada, can be considered, in many but not all ways, to be a radical environmental group. One of the ALF's most notorious activists, Rodney Coronado, has worked hard to build bridges between radical environmental, animal liberationist, and anarchist sub-cultures, especially in North America. His activist career illuminates the affinities and limits to the fusion of the Animal Liberation Front and radical environmentalism.

Moved and angered by the suffering he witnessed when viewing a television documentary about the Canadian harp seal hunt when he was 12 years old, Coronado immediately contacted and sent money to Captain Paul Watson of the Sea Shepard Conservation Society, who was featured in the film directly resisting the sealers. Seven years later, in 1985, Coronado volunteered as a crew member, and a year later in a Sea Shepard-supported mission, he helped destroy a whale-processing station and sink two whaling ships in Iceland.

After this Coronado became a spokesperson for the Animal Liberation Front, and in 1988 attended the national Earth First! Rendezvous. There he flew anarchist and ALF flags, which helped to escalate already present political and ethical tensions, which showed the fault line between the animal liberationists, like Coronado, and biocentric activists including meat-eating ones like Earth First! co-founder Dave Foreman, who took pleasure in grilling steaks near these vegan activists.

Coronado would soon launch an aggressive campaign against the fur industry, infiltrating it to capture images of the suffering animals, releasing minks from their cages (with ceremonial blessings from a Blackfoot medicine woman who "smudged them off" as they were sent "into the wild world for the first time"), and beginning in 1991, torching the facilities of a number of industry-affiliated researchers. Coronado eventually served four years in prison for a 1992 arson attack on the office of a Michigan State University researcher for which the ALF had claimed responsibility. After his release from prison Coronado worked periodically for the *Earth First!* journal, contributing significantly to its increasingly militant and anarchistic character, and began to travel regularly to promote radical environmental and animal liberationist activism at university campuses and other venues. He became a visible and charismatic activist working at the intersection of animal liberationist and radical environmental sub-cultures.

Coronado considers himself an indigenous and spiritual natural rights activist, promoting freedom both for domestic and wild animals, as well as indigenous and other oppressed peoples. An activist of Pascua Yaqui Indian ancestry from the Southwestern United States, he believes that the destruction of life comes from the same, dominating mindset of the European conquistadors; consequently the liberation of nature, animals, and human beings, are mutually dependent:

> I never became first an environmental activist, then an animal rights activist and then an indigenous rights activist. I always was a natural rights activist because I believe everything in nature has a right to exist (Wolff 1995: 24).

Moreover, Coronado claims that spiritual power depends on its connection to the power of Earth, its spirits, and animal relations:

> As an indigenous person, I've had to relearn that fighting for the Earth as Earth First! does is a very old, sacred and honorable duty. It's one where I've learned that we can be the most effective when we take advantage of the knowledge and power our enemies know nothing of. They have laughed at this kind of thing for hundreds of years, and I'm glad they don't get it. They never will, but I've seen the Earth spirits. I pray to them and have had them help me carry out successful attacks against the Earth's enemies. I know that when I was out there on the run, it was they who protected me and warned me of danger ... Spirituality [is] ... a kind of road map one uses to successfully navigate through life ... When who you are and what you are is about the Earth, you learn that your own true power can only come from the Earth. That's what Geronimo and other great warriors knew. Only when we believe in our own power more than that of our enemies will we rediscover the kind of power the Earth has available to us as warriors. My power comes from the very things I fight for (interview in *Earth First!* 23:3 (2003), online).

Indeed, "Anarchism" itself, Coronado believes, "is grounded in spirituality, in listening to the Earth and her creatures" (public talk, the University of Florida, March 2003). And thus for Coronado, anarchism, animal activism, and Earth liberation are all grounded in an animistic episteme, a religious thread common to radical environmentalist groups.

Continued next page

> Despite his efforts to fuse animal, anarchist, and Earth activism, Coronado believes that if a choice must be made between an individual animal (*including a human animal*) and the health of an ecosystem or the survival of a species, he would prioritize the latter (author's interview, Fresno, California, February 2003). He would insist, however, that while such a concession might occasionally be a tragic necessity in the short term, the long-term struggle is to make such tragic choices unnecessary and a thing of the past. Even so, Coronado's viewpoint suggests that while radical environmentalists, anarchists, and animal liberationists will often find common cause, the difference between spiritual holism and empathetic individualism will prevent these groups from a thoroughgoing fusion.
>
> *Bron Taylor*

domesticated animals and generally retain their lifestyle choices, such as veganism, even if they become more biocentric in their overall ethical outlook.

In addition to a biocentric outlook, radical environmentalism also involves a political ideology harshly critical of current political arrangements if not of nation-state governance itself. Here, participants in animal liberation movements are as diverse as other radical environmentalists, from those who retain hope that their movement of conscience will precipitate effective political reforms, to anarchists who believe the entire system must be torn down.

Animal rights and liberation movements, then, prompt some radical environmentalists to add to their array of concerns, sentient, domestic animals, and in a reciprocal way, often provide new activists for biodiversity protection campaigns. And they are often influenced by the religious metaphysics of interconnection and kinship ethics often found in the increasingly global environmental milieu. Nevertheless, a philosophical line between individualism and holism limits the extent to which animal liberationist sub-cultures belong to radical environmental ones, despite the efforts of some activists, such as Animal Liberation Front activist Rodney Coronado, to unite these sub-cultures.

Criticisms and Responses

There are as many criticisms of radical environmentalism as there are differing ideas, emphases, factions and priorities within these movements and adversaries to them. Some of the criticisms come, of course, from those who profit from resource extraction of various sorts, who sometimes label vandalism, verbally abusive behavior, or even civil disobedience as "ecoterrorism." But criticisms also come from other environmentalists as well as a wide variety of religious actors, social justice advocates, and political theorists.

Some of the typical arguments are not directly or obviously related to religion. For example, environmentalists and liberal democrats Martin Lewis and Luc Ferry, claim that these movements are atavistic, primitivist, and Luddite; offer no realistic way to live in the modern world; and are anti-democratic, refusing to abide by decisions arrived at through democratic processes. Others argue that these movements are counterproductive to building sustainable societies because they do not value and support science, which is a critical foundation for environment-related public policies, but is already assailed by religious conservatives and hardly needs its credibility further eroded in the public mind by radical greens.

Some in the less developed world, such as Ramachandra Guha, have criticized the effort to protect wilderness and biodiversity as elitist, misanthropic, and callous to the needs of the poor. As radical environmentalism turned its attention to globalization, some multinational corporations piggybacked on such criticisms, arguing that the aversion of radical greens to biotechnology and free trade reflected a pernicious elitism that is callous to the needs of growing human populations.

Meanwhile, religious conservatives from the Abrahamic traditions often view these Pagan or quasi-pagan movements with suspicion or worse, as agents of dark, demonic forces. It is not uncommon for corporations, perhaps especially in rural communities with religiously conservative workers, to fan such fears among them in order to galvanize support during resource-related controversies. Some writers on radical environmental movements contribute to such fears. In *Earth First!: Environmental Apocalypse* and subsequent articles, Martha Lee asserted that some radical environmentalists represent violence-prone forms of religious millenarianism. Gary Ackerman, Deputy Director of the Chemical and Biological Weapons Nonproliferation Program at the Monterey Institute of International Studies, concluded even more chillingly that the likelihood is increasing that one or another radical environmental group will deploy weapons of mass death to promote their cause.

Social scientists and political theorists sympathetic to environmental causes have, more judiciously, focused on radical environmentalism's typical presuppositions, diagnoses, prescriptions, and tactics. They often find these simplistic and counterproductive.

Radical environmentalists widely presume, for example, that a transformation or "resacralization" of consciousness is necessary for radical action to occur. But scholars who have studied grassroots environmental movements globally have found that direct-action resistance to environmental degradation has also been undertaken by those whose religious traditions are Abrahamic or whose value systems are anthropocentric. Moreover, the common radical environmental belief in the importance of consciousness toward a spiritual biocentrism and away from monotheisms does not fully appreciate the extent to which all religions are malleable and change in response to changing and exigent circumstances.

The radical environmental prescription to decentralize political arrangements by abolishing nation-states has also been sharply criticized by a number of political theorists, including Andrew Dobson, Dan Deudney, and Paul Wapner. Another critic, Andrew Bard Schmookler, criticized green anarchism not only in general in *The Parable of the Tribes*, but also right in the pages of the *Earth First!* journal. He asked how good people can prevent being dominated by a ruthless few, and what will prevent hierarchies from emerging if decentralized political self-rule is ever achieved. One does not have to believe all people are bad to recognize that not all people will be good, he argued, and unless bad people all become good, there is no solution to violence other than some kind of government to restrain the evil few; moreover, those who exploit nature gather more power to themselves, and therefore, there must be institutions to restrain that growing power. While Schmookler agreed that political decentralization could be beneficial, it must be accompanied by a "world order sufficient [to thwart] would-be conquerors" and "since the biosphere is a globally interdependent web, that world order should be able to constrain any of the actors from fouling the Earth. This requires laws and means of enforcement" (1986: 22). There is no escaping government or the need to deal with power, Schmookler concluded, because "our emergence out of the natural order makes power an inevitable problem for human affairs, and only power can control power" (1986: 22). Schookler's analysis challenged not only the decentralist social philosophy of radical environmentalism and much green political thought, but also the prevalent hope that a return to small-scale, tribal societies, with their nature-based spiritualities, would solve our environmental predicaments.

Radical environmentalists would or could respond to the battery of criticisms they typically face along the following lines. To environmentalists who assert that they hurt the environmental cause they could point out, accurately, that many mainstream environmentalists, even some who denounce them publicly, share their sense of urgency and feel that radical tactics contribute significantly to the environmental cause, in part by strengthening the negotiating positions of "moderate" environmentalists. To those who call them terrorists they could ask them to produce the bodies or document the injuries that would prove the charge. To those who use anthropocentric and monotheistic environmentalism to dispute their insistence that a wholesale change in the consciousness of Western peoples is needed, they could offer the rejoinder that spiritualities which consider nature sacred and displace humans as the center of moral concern provide more consistent and powerful motivations for environmental action than other religious ethics. And to those who criticize willingness to break laws, they would certainly respond that reformist, politics-as-usual, and centralized nation-state governance have not slowed environmental degradation and species loss, and would accuse their critics of complacency and of promoting anemic responses that promise nothing but more of the same.

The more thoughtful among them acknowledge that they do not have all the answers and that some of the criticisms need to be taken into consideration. But they would nevertheless insist that the primary moral imperative is to halt the human reduction of the Earth's genetic, species, and cultural variety. And they would claim that direct-action resistance is a necessary, permissible, and even morally obligatory means in the sacred quest to preserve life on Earth.

Bron Taylor

Further Reading

Abbey, Edward. *Desert Solitaire*. Tucson, AZ: University of Arizona Press, 1988.

Abram, David. *Spell of the Sensuous: Perception and Language in a More-Than-Human World*. New York: Pantheon, 1996.

Ackerman, Gary. "Beyond Arson? A Threat Assessment of the Earth Liberation Front." *Terrorism and Political Violence* 15:4 (Winter 2004), 143–70.

Andruss, Van, Christopher Plant, Judith Plant and Eleanor Wright. *Home! A Bioregional Reader*. Philadelphia, PA: New Society, 1990.

Barnhill, David Landis. *At Home on Earth: Becoming Native to Our Place*. Berkeley, CA: University of California Press, 1999.

Bender, Frederic. *The Culture of Extinction: Toward a Philosophy of Deep Ecology*. Buffalo, NY: Humanity, 2003.

Berg, Peter, ed. *Reinhabiting a Separate Country: A Bioregional Anthology of Northern California*. San Francisco, CA: Planet Drum, 1978.

Best, Steven and Anthony J. Nocella, eds. *Terrorists or Freedom Fighters? Reflections on the Liberation of Animals*. New York: Lantern, 2004.

Bookchin, Murray and Dave Foreman. *Defending the Earth*. Boston, MA: South End Press, 1991.

Callicott, J. Baird. "Holistic Environmental Ethics and the Problem of Ecofascism." *Beyond the Land Ethic: More Essays in Environmental Philosophy*. Albany, NY: State University of New York Press, 1999.

Clark, John. "The French Take on Environmentalism." *Terra Nova* 1:1 (1996), 112–19.

Clark, John, ed. *Renewing the Earth: The Promise of Social Ecology*. London: Green Print, 1990.

Clark, John. *The Anarchist Moment*. Montréal: Black Rose, 1984.

Coronado, Rod. "Every Tool in the Box: Learning to Live Like the Coyote Nation." *Earth First!* 18:2 (1997), 3, 21.

Diamond, Stanley. *In Search of the Primitive: A Critique of Civilization*. New Brunswick, NJ: Transaction, 1974.

Dobson, Andrew. *Green Political Thought*. London: Unwin Hymen, 1990.

Eckersley, Robyn. *Environmentalism and Political Theory*. Albany, NY: State University of New York Press, 1992.

Eller, Cynthia. *Living in the Lap of the Goddess: The Feminist Spirituality Movement in America*. New York: Crossroad, 1993.

Ferry, Luc. *The New Ecological Order*. Chicago: University of Chicago Press, 1995.

Fisher, Andy. *Radical Ecopsychology: Psychology in the Service of Life*. Albany, NY: State University of New York Press, 2002.

Foreman, Dave. *Confessions of an Eco-Warrior*. New York: Harmony Books, 1991.

Fox, Warwick, ed. *Toward a Transpersonal Psychology*. Albany, NY: State University of New York Press, 1996.

Fox, Warwick. *Toward a Transpersonal Ecology*. Boston, MA: Shambhala, 1990.

Friedmann, John and Haripriya Rangan, eds. *In Defense of Livelihood: Comparative Studies in Environmental Action*. West Hartford, CT: Kumarian Press, 1993.

Glendinning, Chellis. *My Name Is Chellis and I'm in Recovery from Western Civilization*. Boston & London: Shambhala, 1994.

Hillman, James and Michael Ventura. *We've Had a Hundred Years of Psychotherapy and the World's Getting Worse*. San Francisco, CA: HarperCollins, 1993.

House, Freeman. *Totem Salmon: Life Lessons from Another Species*. Boston, MA: Beacon Press, 1999.

Kaplan, Jeffrey. "The Postwar Paths of Occult National Socialism." In Jeffrey Kaplan and Heléne Lööw, eds. *The Cultic Milieu: Oppositional Subcultures in an Age of Globalization*. Walnut Creek/New York/Oxford: Altamira/Rowman and Littlefield, 2002, 225–64.

Keepin, William. "Toward an Ecological Psychology." *Revision: A Journal of Consciousness and Transformation* 14:2 (1991), 90–100.

Lee, Martha F. "Environmental Apocalypse: The Millennial Ideology of 'Earth First!'." In Thomas Robbins and Susan Palmer, eds. *Millennium, Messiahs, and Mayhem*. New York & London: Routledge, 1997, 119–37.

Lee, Martha F. *Earth First!: Environmental Apocalypse*. Syracuse, NY: Syracuse University Press, 1995.

Lewis, Martin W. "Radical Environmental Philosophy and the Assault on Reason." In *The Flight from Science and Reason*. P.R. Gross, N. Levitt and M.W. Lewis, eds. Baltimore, Maryland: John Hopkins University Press, 1996, 209–30.

Lewis, Martin W. *Green Delusions: An Environmentalist Critique of Radical Environmentalism*. Durham, NC: Duke University Press, 1992.

Manes, Christopher. *Green Rage: Radical Environmentalism and the Unmaking of Civilization*. Boston, MA: Little, Brown, 1990.

McGinnis, Michael Vincent, ed. *Bioregionalism*. New York and London: Routledge, 1999.

Metzner, Ralph. *Green Psychology: Cultivating a Spiritual Connection with the Natural World*. Rochester, VT: Inner Traditions International Ltd., 1999.

Metzner, Ralph, ed. *Ayahuasca: Human Consciousness and the Spirits of Nature*. Berkeley and New York: Thunder's Mouth Press, 1999.

Mollison, Bill. *Introduction to Permaculture*. Tyalgum, Australia: Tagari, 1991.

Plant, Christopher and Judith Plant. *Turtle Talk: Voices for a Sustainable Future*. Santa Cruz, CA: New Society Publishers, 1990.

Regan, Tom. *The Case for Animal Rights*. Berkeley, CA: University of California Press, 1983.

Regan, Tom and Peter Singer, eds. *Animal Rights and Human Obligations*. 2nd edn, 1989; reprint, Englewood Cliffs, NJ: Prentice Hall, 1976.

Roszak, Theodore. *The Voice of the Earth: An Exploration of Ecopsychology*. New York: Touchstone, 1992.

Roszak, Theodore, Mary E. Gomes and Allen D. Kanner, eds. *Ecopsychology: Restoring the Earth, Healing the Mind*. San Francisco, CA: Sierra Club, 1995.

Sale, Kirkpatrick. *Dwellers in the Land: The Bioregional Vision*. San Francisco, CA: Sierra Club Books, 1985; reprint, Philadelphia, PA: New Society Publishers, 1991.

Scarce, Rik. *Ecowarriors: Understanding the Radical Environmental Movement*. Chicago, IL: Noble, 1990.

Schmookler, Andrew Bard. *The Parable of the Tribes: The Problem of Power in Social Evolution*. Berkeley, CA: University of California Press, 1984; reprint, Albany, NY: The State University of New York Press, 1995.

Schmookler, Andrew Bard "Schmookler on Anarchy." *Earth First!* 6:5 (1986), 22.

Seed, John, Joanna Macy, Pat Fleming and Arne Naess. *Thinking Like a Mountain: Towards a Council of All Beings*. Philadelphia, PA: New Society, 1988.

Shepard, Paul. *Coming Home to the Pleistocene*. San Francisco, CA: Island Press, 1998.

Shepard, Paul. *Nature and Madness*. San Francisco, CA: Sierra Club Books, 1982.

Singer, Peter, ed. *In Defense of Animals*. New York: Basil Blackwell, 1985.

Smith, Samantha. *Goddess Earth: Exposing the Pagan Agenda of the Environmental Movement*. Lafayette, Louisiana: Huntington House, 1994.

Snyder, Gary. *Turtle Island.* New York: New Directions, 1969.

Starhawk. *Webs of Power: Notes from the Global Uprising.* Gabrioloa Island, British Columbia: New Society Publishers, 2002.

Taylor, Bron. "Threat Assessments and Radical Environmentalism." *Terrorism and Political Violence* 15:4 (Winter 2004), 173–182.

Taylor, Bron, "Deep Ecology as Social Philosophy: A Critique." In Eric Katz, Andrew Light and David Rothenberg, eds. *Beneath the Surface: Critical Essays on Deep Ecology.* Cambridge, MA: MIT Press, 2000, 269–99.

Taylor, Bron. "Green Apocalypticism: Understanding Disaster in the Radical Environmental Worldview." *Society and Natural Resources* 12:4 (1999), 377–86.

Taylor, Bron, ed. *Ecological Resistance Movements: The Global Emergence of Radical and Popular Environmentalism.* Albany, NY: State University of New York Press, 1995.

Tokar, Brian. *Earth for Sale: Reclaiming Ecology in the Age of Corporate Greenwash.* Boston, MA: South End Press, 1997.

Wall, Derek. *Earth First! and the Anti-Roads Movement: Radical Environmentalism and the Anti-Roads Movement.* London: Routledge, 1999.

Walsh, Roger and Francis Vaughan. *Paths beyond Ego: The Transpersonal Vision.* Los Angeles, CA: Tarcher/Perigee, 1993.

Wapner, Paul. *Environmental Activism and World Civic Politics.* Albany, NY: State University of New York Press, 1996.

Watson, Paul. *Seal Wars: Twenty-Five Years on the Front Lines with the Harp Seals.* Buffalo, NY: Firefly Books, 2002.

Watson, Paul. *Ocean Warrior: My Battle to End the Illegal Slaughter on the High Seas.* Toronto: Key Porter, 1994.

Willers, Bill, ed. *Learning to Listen to the Land.* Washington, D.C.: Island Press, 1991.

Wolff, Patricia. "Defender of the Faith: An Interview with Rod Coronado." *Wild Forest Review* 2:4 (1995), 23–27.

Zimmerman, Michael E. *Contesting Earth's Future: Radical Ecology and Postmodernity.* Berkeley and Los Angeles: University of California Press, 1994.

Zimmmerman, Michael E., et al. *Environmental Philosophy: From Animal Rights to Radical Ecology.* Englewood Cliffs, NJ: Prentice-Hall, 1993.

See also: Abbey, Edward; Ananda Marga's Tantric Neo-Humanism; Anarchism; Animism (various); Berry, Thomas; Biocentric Religion – A Call for; Bioregionalism; Bioregionalism and the North American Bioregional Congress; Breathwork; Conservation Biology; Council of All Beings; Deep Ecology; Depth Ecology; Diggers and Levelers; Donga Tribe; Dragon Environmental Network (United Kingdom); Earth First! and the Earth Liberation Front; Ecofeminism – Historic and International Evolution; Ecopsychology; Ecosophy T; Environmental Ethics; Epic of Evolution; Faerie Faith in Scotland; Gaia; Gaian Pilgrimage; Green Politics; Heathenry – Ásatrú; Heidegger, Martin; Hopiland to the Rainforest Action Network; Indigenous Environmental Network; Left Biocentrism; Lovelock, James; Magic, Animism, and the Shaman's Craft; Music and Eco-activism in America; Music of Resistance; Naess, Arne; Pagan Environmental Ethics; Paganism – Contemporary; Re-Earthing; Reclus, Elisée; Religious Environmentalist Paradigm; Romanticism – American; Romanticism – Western toward Asian Religions; Romanticism and Indigenous People; Scotland; Seed, John; Shepard, Paul; Snyder, Gary; Starhawk; Transpersonal Psychology; Wicca; Wilber, Ken.

Raëlian Religion – *See* UFOs and Extraterrestrials.

Rainbow Family

In the summer of 1972, while hippie back-to-nature idealism was still in full bloom, a crowd of some 20,000, mainly young counterculturists, gathered near Granby, Colorado, for a several-days-long "gathering of the tribes" inspired by some of the legendary hip music festivals (especially the Vortex Festival near Portland, Oregon, in 1970), the San Francisco "Be-In" of 1967, rural hip communes, and other such countercultural phenomena. The gathering would have no central stage, no paid or featured entertainers, and no fee for admission. It would be free-form and self-defining, although the original organizers did proclaim that the fourth and last day would feature a silent meditation for world peace. A remote wilderness location was chosen to emphasize close contact with nature and rejection of contemporary urban life.

Although there were no initial plans for a second gathering, one was held rather spontaneously the following year in Wyoming, and by the third year (in Utah) the Rainbow Gathering had become an annual event. In 1976 the Rainbow Family, as participants were by then calling themselves, decided to have the festival always occur on the first seven days of July. That time-period remains the heart of the festival, although participants, including those who volunteer to provide set-up and clean-up, are typically at the site for at least two months.

The Rainbows, whose core principles are egalitarianism and non-hierarchical organization, insist that the Family have no leaders and no formal structure. Decisions, for example, are made at the Gatherings by consensus by a council consisting of anyone who wants to attend. No one is excluded from joining. Some dedicated, long-term participants, however, have devoted considerable energy to perpetuating the Gatherings. Over the years they have published various newsletters and now maintain several Rainbow websites. In the absence of leaders, "focalizers" help provide direction and continuity for Rainbow activities. A Magic Hat passed at gatherings as a collection plate gathers funds that are used for publishing Rainbow manuals and periodicals, providing necessary supplies for the Gatherings (including, in some cases, trucked-in water), and other miscellaneous expenses. Rainbows, however, are generally expected to bring all of their own supplies, including food, to use and to share. Money is disdained at the Gatherings, although a lively barter economy flourishes.

Although there is no official theology or ideology among the Rainbows, many of them espouse neo-pagan or other nature-based spirituality. Admiration and appropriation of American Indian spirituality is widespread. The use of entheogens or natural psychedelics (psychoactive mushrooms, peyote) is common and held to be a natural way to explore ultimate reality. Nature-affirming ceremonies are believed to foster human interdependence and deeper respect for the Earth. Although most Rainbows explicitly disavow political activism, Earth First! and other radical environmental groups are represented and often draw new recruits from those attending.

Rainbow Gatherings are always held on public land, and the Rainbows have steadfastly refused to seek official permission for their events, which attract tens of thousands of participants. That refusal has led to repeated confrontations with public authorities. Colorado Governor John Love ordered that the road to the first gathering be blocked, but a crowd of some 4000 marched up to the roadblock chanting and singing, insisting on their right to gather peacefully on public lands. Finally Love relented and the Rainbows walked several miles to their chosen site. Opposition from local residents and public officials typically precedes each year's Gathering, although some rural towns appreciate the influx of business that 20,000 or more visitors bring. Nudity is common at the Gatherings, and it spawns both denunciations from local residents and crowds of voyeurs.

Nudity is just one facet of the oneness with nature that Rainbows have always considered central to their quest. Although the large Gathering crowds would be expected to take a heavy toll on wilderness resources, elaborate advance preparations seek to minimize any damage. A month or more before the Gathering begins an advance guard shows up to prepare the necessary facilities, including carefully contained latrines. Others remain at the site for several weeks afterwards systematically erasing nearly all traces of human impact. During the gathering participants are exhorted to observe basic rules of cleanliness and sanitation and to protect streams and lakes from contamination. Even the critics of the Rainbows concede that their land stewardship has been exemplary. During the 1994 Gathering near Big Piney, Wyoming, a forest fire broke out nearby, and thousands of Rainbows joined bucket brigades that helped extinguish it.

Some critics, however, maintain that no gathering that large can fail to have a serious adverse impact on the environment, and the open nature of the gatherings means that some who attend will engage in destructive behaviors of various kinds. Although marijuana is the substance of choice at the gatherings, alcohol and other more destructive drugs sometimes lead to problems.

The large, national Gatherings in July have led to a variety of other Rainbow events, mainly Gatherings in other countries and smaller regional Gatherings in the United States. Dozens of such events now take place annually.

Timothy Miller

Further Reading
Adams, Barry "Plunker." *Where Have All the Flower Children Gone?* Self-published, 1988.
John, Michael, et al. *The Rainbow Nation 1982 Cooperative Community Guide V: A Peoples Guide to the Liberation of Planet Earth*. McCall, ID: 1982.
Niman, Michael I. *People of the Rainbow: A Nomadic Utopia*. Knoxville: University of Tennessee Press, 1997.
See also: Entheogens; Hippies; New Religious Movements; Radical Environmentalism.

Rainbow Serpent (North Wellesley Islands, Australia)

The Lardil and Yangkaal people are coastal hunter-fisher-gatherers who occupy the North Wellesley Islands of the southern Gulf of Carpentaria in northern Australia. Their cosmological and cosmogonic belief system has developed and evolved from their dependence upon the sea for their survival. They employ the classical elements of Australian Aboriginal religions combined in a culturally distinctive system of knowledge with a strong marine environmental basis.

A body of Lardil and Yangkaal sacred knowledge deals with the Dreamtime histories that tell of the creation of the North Wellesley environment by Ancestral Beings. *Maarnbil, Jirn Jirn* and *Diwal Diwal* were the human colonizers of the country and seas, and all subsequent Lardil and Yangkaal people descend from this trio. The coastal systems and various offshore features were all physically made by *Maarnbil, Diwaldiwal* and *Jirn Jirn*, and contain a wealth of geography, resource places, campsites and religious sites. The perimeters of the islands although consisting of natural components, are seen from the Lardil and Yangkaal viewpoint to be artificial.

Of the different coastal place types, "Story Places" have

the most complex set of properties. They are marked neither by artifacts nor structures, and even their natural characteristics are not necessarily outstanding visually, yet within local cosmology, their invisible properties are very powerful. The ancestors *Maarnbil*, *Jirn Jirn* and *Diwildiwil* were the original creators of these sacred sites, but further properties have been added by subsequent supernatural beings. Each Story Place is believed to be inhabited by a separate spiritual entity that generates energies at the site. These beings reproduce at these sites, whether they are inside the ground or under sea. Aboriginal people are able to catalyse processes of reproduction or fertility by performing simple ritual actions or songs at these places. Some sites are said to generate plant or animal species, while others produce meteorological phenomena. The energies of the spiritual occupants of each Story Place are supplemented by the energies of *Thuwathu*, the Rainbow Serpent. The domain of the invisible energies of *Thuwathu* and his agents is in the marine and littoral systems. Changes in the health of humans and in environmental activity (cyclones, storms, lightning, waterspouts and strong winds) are believed to be caused by activating energies in this saltwater environment. The spiritual entities act as agents for *Thuwathu* by monitoring the actions of humans and inflict *markirii* sickness upon those who do not adhere to specified behavioural rules.

Story Places are also believed to connect into another time dimension. According to Lardil belief, the Dreamtime is a second spatial universe that somehow split away from the material world of everyday human existence at some time in the remote past. The Dreamtime coexists in time with the material environment, but is situated in a separate space dimension that is not visually accessible under normal circumstances. Although there are believed to be two separate universes, there are places where the properties of one overlap with the properties of the other. Connections between these two universes occur via dreams and Story Places.

The aggregate of Story Places are the geographical sources of Lardil sacred knowledge. By frequenting a Story Place, individuals may receive gifts of knowledge via dreams from unseen people in the Dreamtime dimension. The nature of this knowledge appears to be qualitatively different at each particular Story Place. Knowledge received in a dream at such a place is likely to deal with the nature of the local Story Place inhabitants. The Lardil believe that to maintain a balanced system of communal knowledge, it is essential to have contributions of knowledge imparted in dreams in the vicinity of each and every Story Place. The basis of knowledge, and hence social authority, can be seen to lie in social geography, through the association of patriclan groups to Story Places.

The spiritual inhabitant of each Story Place is regarded as possessing some human qualities, and these entities are also associated with the unseen people of the area (reincarnated ancestral spirits). The local residents of the area (the patriclan) are also said to share the energies of the Story Place being. These energies are also transmitted from the Story Place to humans who are born or conceived near the Story Place, or who preside over and regularly occupy the local area. These humans then possess a close identity with their Story Place and its occupants. The totemic entities thus provide personal subjective links into a coexisting religious world, and render everyday life experience both profound and personalized.

The system of religious knowledge has thus evolved to explain marine environmental changes and transformations. This belief system involves a configuration of human and environmental elements that are believed to be interconnected in a variety of ways, often via systems of environmental signs and indices, as well as through a spatio-temporal model of the universe and notions of visible and invisible phenomena. In addition the model carries with it, codes of behaviour or "laws," providing preferred norms of social and territorial behavior. Identity is defined within a cognitive domain of place-specific knowledge and invisible properties of place.

In Lardil cosmology, people, places and natural species are seen as interdependent, each with a set of beliefs consistent with the other. The Dreamtime universe forms a fourth interdependent domain, and links into this world can be found in the landscape.

In the late 1990s, marine Story Places and their religious properties were presented as evidence in the Federal Court of Australia by the Lardil and Yangkaal in order to win claim of rights to their seas under the *Native Title Act 1993*. This claim stems from their concern about threats to the marine ecology by mining projects and commercial fishing practices and the need to enforce indigenous environmental management practices.

Paul Memmott

Further Reading

McKnight, David. "Systems of Classification among the Lardil of Mornington Island." In *People, Countries and the Rainbow Serpent*. New York: Oxford University Press, 1999.

Memmott, Paul. "Social Structure and Use of Space amongst the Lardil." In N. Peterson and M. Langton, eds. *Aborigines, Land and Land Rights*. Canberra: Australian Institute of Aboriginal Studies, 1983, 33–65.

Memmott, Paul. "Rainbows, Story Places and Malkri Sickness in the North Wellesley Islands." *Oceania* 53:2 (1982), 163–82.

See also: Aboriginal Dreaming (Australia); Australia; Cihuacoatl – Aztec Snakewoman; Serpents and Dragons; Snakes and the Luo of Kenya; Weather Snake.

Rainforest Action Network – *See* Hopiland to the Rainforest Action Network.

Rainforest Information Centre – *See* Radical Environmentalism; Re-Earthing; Seed, John.

Rainforests (Central and South American)

In the neotropics, the interrelationships between religion and nature are appreciated by many people, but especially by indigenes. This entry first surveys the forests including the correlated cultural diversity as the context of indigenous religions, next discusses the Maya as an illustration of spiritual ecology, and concludes by considering the disruption to both indigenous religions and nature from European colonization to globalization.

After four billion years of evolution on Earth, life reached its greatest diversity and complexity in tropical rainforests. Half of all life on the planet is in these rainforests, whether measured by number of species (biodiversity) or sheer weight (biomass). This is remarkable because tropical rainforests are concentrated on only 6 percent of the Earth's terrestrial surface. About half of the world's rainforests are in Central and South America.

Tropical rainforests are the most luxuriant plant communities on Earth. They are found where climatic conditions are ideal for plant growth; that is, high mean monthly temperature (>26°C) and mean annual rainfall (>1,800 mm) throughout or during most of the year. They contain up to ten times as many species in the same area as temperate forest. Beyond the Equator plant communities are susceptible to greater stresses like seasonal drought or cold.

Diversity in its manifold expressions is the single most important characteristic of tropical rainforests. They exhibit diversity in plant structures, such as lianas (vines), epiphytes (plants that grow on top of other plants), and large roots that buttress the trunks of giant trees up to 50 m tall which emerge above the forest canopy (top). Diversity occurs as well along the vertical microclimatic and microenvironmental gradients from the forest floor through the strata (layers) of vegetation into the canopy, as sunlight, temperature, and wind increase upward while humidity decreases. Gaps created by natural tree falls allow the penetration of sunlight which stimulates heavy new plant growth on the ground. Collectively, forests gaps produce a mosaic of patches of vegetation at different stages of succession or development. Thus, tropical rainforests are also dynamic ecosystems that vary through space and time.

In general, in regions where biodiversity is high, so is the diversity of cultures (including religion), and vice versa, something called the diversity principle. This correlation is probably more than coincidental. Diversity within and among tropical rainforests offers more opportunities for niche differentiation; that is, different adaptations to the wide variety of habitats and resources, although the natural environment is not the only factor in cultural and associated linguistic and religious creativity and variation. In the neotropics there is a multitude of local variations in indigenous technology, economy, customs, religion, and language reflecting variations in geography, environment, history, and other factors. It is estimated are that at the time of European contact more than a thousand distinct cultures existed in South America and more than a hundred in Central America. Neotropical countries that contain both large areas of rainforests and unusually large indigenous populations are Belize, Guatemala, Ecuador, Peru, and Bolivia. Many of these indigenes retain at least some elements of their traditional religion.

On the surface the relatively uniform traditional technology of indigenous peoples throughout neotropical rainforests appears simple, principally bow-and-arrow hunting; hand gathering of wild plants and small animals; fishing with bow and arrows, spears, and plant poisons; and swidden horticulture. The latter involves cutting a small section of forests with axes and machetes (large bush knives); burning the debris after it has dried out during the dry season; and then planting crops in holes made with a pointed stick. However, technological sophistication cannot be judged on the basis of tools or material culture alone, but also involves knowledge and skills which can be complex, especially in a natural habitat with such high diversity. With low population density, high mobility of sub-groups, and a rotational system of farming and foraging (including trekking), most of these indigenous societies are sustainable, with any environmental impact allowing natural regeneration to proceed at a normal rate. Furthermore, these highly adaptive techno-economic systems allowed ample free time for the elaboration of complexity in other aspects of culture, especially in ceremonies, rituals, oral literature, arts, and symbolism. Thus, the neotropical rainforests have provided inspiration as well as habitat and refuge for numerous and varied indigenous cultures, including their religion.

In particular, animism, a belief in multiple spiritual beings and forces in nature, is an integral component pervading indigenous daily life as well as the socio-cultural system and its ecology. Moreover, the basic holistic principles of a viable spiritual ecology are apparent in most traditional indigenous societies, including those in neotropical rainforests. These principles variously emphasize that the arenas of humans, nature, and the supernatural comprise a functional, spiritual, and moral unity through their interconnectedness and interdependence. The awesomeness, mysticism, and powers of an enchanted nature require appropriate respect, reverence, and reciprocity. Humans are embedded in nature's kinship and spirituality, and this they affirm and celebrate through cycles of ritual as well as myths and symbols. Accordingly, traditionally for most indigenous societies, religion promotes and maintains the dynamic equilibrium within and between the social and ecological systems. Whenever disequilibrium arises it is treated as much if not more spiritually than otherwise.

These and other sound principles of spiritual ecology are reflected in many traditional indigenous cultures, including those residing in neotropical forests. For instance, collectively the Maya are the second largest indigenous population in the Americas with some 7.5 million people. They live in the northern sections of the lowlands of the Yucatan peninsula and in the central highlands of the state of Chiapas in southern Mexico as well as in portions of the Central American countries of Belize, Guatemala, Honduras, and El Salvador. There is also a Mayan diaspora in North America. Some 28 different Mayan languages are spoken. Mayans range from lowland into the highland wet and dry forests with tremendous variation in their ecology, cultures, languages, and histories. However, the core religious principles which are more or less common to most Maya are outlined in the sacred text called *Popol Vuh* which was written down after initial contact with the Spanish. For the Maya, the natural and supernatural realms are intimately interconnected and interdependent. For instance, animals and plants were created first by the supreme deity, and thereafter the animals helped create humans from the sacred corn plant. Consequently, the relationship between humans, animals, and plants is supposed to be one of respect, caring, and cooperation. Many Mayans demonstrate profound reverence and compassion for animals and plants in their habitat through their daily activities as well as sacred stories, rituals, chants, and prayers. When trees are cut down to clear an area for a swidden, for example, the farmer requests pardon from the guardian spirit of the forest. Spirituality permeates the beings and things in the forests; nature is far more than merely a resource or commodity. However, many Mayans simultaneously embrace the Christian religion, especially Catholicism, blending it with their native religions.

Lacandons of Yucatan remain the most traditional Maya, but in the 1990s in Guatemala and elsewhere a movement arose to revitalize Mayan cultural and religious beliefs, values, and practices, including the use of sacred sites for rituals such as particular caves, hills, or mountains. However, Mayans also have to struggle with the disruptions created by Western influences which are often contrary to their traditions and ecology, including civil wars in most countries of Central America during the 1960s–1980s. The 1994 Chiapas rebellion is just one recent symptom of their continuing struggles.

Indigenes surviving in neotropical rainforests as sanctuaries as well as habitats are descendants of some of the original spiritual ecologists. Many maintained relative balance and harmony within their society and between their society and the ecosystems in their habitat, despite political, economic, and other depredations of up to five centuries of Western colonialism. The neotropical rainforest as a whole was not endangered 500 years ago, but it has progressively become so as a result of Western abuses, especially in the last half of the twentieth century. This is not to assert that all indigenous societies are always in ecological equilibrium. For example, there are some Mayan areas where overpopulation and over-exploitation led to deforestation and other problems prior to European contact. Also some portions of Mayan forests are anthropogenic, with unusual concentrations of useful trees like ramon, breadnut, sapodilla, and avocado. However, the net trend for most indigenous societies has been toward balance and harmony with nature. It is unlikely to be otherwise, given the awesome depth of their environmental knowledge and their intimate daily interaction with their habitat combined with their nature religions. Only when their circumstances change substantially and they have no economic alternatives are they likely to deplete resources and degrade land irreversibly, especially under Western influences. But indigenous spirituality is antithetical to the generally anthropocentric and egocentric environmental ethics of colonial and industrial societies which usually attempt to segregate, objectify, and commodify nature as merely a material resource.

Because of the intimate interconnections among the rainforest ecosystems and the indigenous societies which reside in them, any threat to one is likely to be a threat to the other as well. Moreover, these generally adaptive systems are being endangered by maladaptive ones, first with European colonialism, then after national independence with internal colonialism, and in the most recent decades with economic globalization. Because native religion is often the most crucial factor promoting social as well as ecological harmony and balance, missionization can be most disruptive spiritually, culturally, and ecologically.

Indigenous societies likely to survive colonial contact possess these attributes: geographical and economic marginality; balance between separation and integration (not assimilation); attachment to ancestral lands, self-sufficiency, and self-determination allowed by a democratic state respecting multi-ethnicity; a stable or increasing population; memory of pre-contact and contact history in combination with a conscious countercultural strategy opposing colonials; common identity with meaningful and resilient traditions including their own religion; and political organization and mobilization as well as networking with other indigenous organizations and relevant environmental and human rights non-governmental organizations.

The Kogi provide a case in point. They are descendants of the Tairona culture who survived the incursion of the Spanish in 1514. The Kogi have persisted in the Sierra Nevada de Santa Marta in Colombia because of their tenacious determination to maintain their own cultural autonomy as well as the geographic protection of the rugged terrain of their mountain habitat. This habitat varies ecologically with increasing altitude from tropical rainforest to savannah to alpine meadows and glaciers, a microcosm of the climatic zones of the world in some respects. The Kogi envision themselves as living at the heart of sacred Mother Earth. They practice environmental stewardship through a series of material and ritual cycles of exchange conducted from the sea coast to the mountain top which are supposed to maintain the vitality and fertility of their diverse ecosystems. Much of this exchange is directed by their priests who also determine which elements from the outside world are accepted or rejected. The Kogi are also alarmed by what outsiders, who they call younger brother, are doing to the detriment of the ecology of the planet. For example, they see one result of global warming in the melting of glaciers high in their mountains. They attempt to address these threats through their cosmology and rituals as well as by warning outsiders.

Economic, social, spiritual, and environmental health are all interrelated and interdependent. The indigenous societies remaining in the refuge of the rainforests of Latin America and elsewhere provide alternative heuristic models or adaptive repertoires for others to consider in designing sustainable, green, and ecocentric economies, societies, and spiritualities if they are to have any healthy future.

Leslie E. Sponsel

Further Reading

Abrams, Elliot M., Anncorinne Freter, David J. Rue and John D. Wingard. "The Role of Deforestation in the Collapse of the Late Classic Copan Maya State." In Leslie E. Sponsel, Thomas N. Headland and Robert C. Bailey, eds. *Tropical Deforestation: The Human Dimensions*. New York, NY: Columbia University Press, 1996, 55–75.

Bodley, John. *Victims of Progress*. Mountain View, CA: Mayfield Publishing Co., 1999.

Dow, James W., ed. *Middle America and the Caribbean, Encyclopedia of World Cultures*, vol. 8. New York: G.J. Hall, 1995.

Elsass, Peter. *Strategies for Survival: The Psychology of Cultural Resilience in Ethnic Minorities*. New York: New York University Press, 1992.

Ereira, Alan. *The Heart of the World*. London, England: Jonathan Cape, 1990.

Kinsley, David. *Ecology and Religion: Ecological Spirituality in Cross-Cultural Perspective*. Englewood Cliffs, NJ: Prentice-Hall, 1995.

Maffi, Luisa, ed. *On Biocultural Diversity: Linking Language, Knowledge and the Environment*. Washington, D.C.: Smithsonian Institution Press, 2001.

McGee, R. John. *Life, Ritual and Religion among the Lacandon Maya*. Belmont, CA: Wadsworth, 1990.

Montejo, Victor D. "The Road to Heaven: Jakaltek Maya Beliefs, Religion, and Ecology." In John A. Grim, ed. *Indigenous Traditions and Ecology: The Interbeing of Cosmology and Community*. Cambridge: Harvard University Press, 2001, 175–95.

Sponsel, Leslie E. "Human Impact on Biodiversity: Overview." In Simon Asher Levin, Editor-in-Chief. *Encyclopedia of Biodiversity*. San Diego, CA: Academic Press, 2001, 3:395–409.

Wilbert, Johannes, ed. *South America, Encyclopedia of World Cultures*, vol. 7. New York: G.K. Hall, 1994.

Wilson, David J. *Indigenous South Americans of the Past and Present: An Ecological Perspective*. Boulder, CO: Westview Press, 1999.

See also: Andean Traditions; Ayahuasca; Ethnobotany; Ethnoecology; Huaorani; Incas; Indigenous Activism and Environmentalism in Latin America; Indigenous Environmental Network; Kogi (Northern Colombia); Maya Religion (Central America); Maya Spirituality (Eustanda Highlands); Reichel-Dolmatoff, Gerardo – and Ethnoecology in Colombia; Rubber Tappers; Shamanism – Ecuador; Shamanism – Traditional; Traditional Ecological Knowledge; U'wa Indians (Colombia); World Conference of Indigenous Peoples (Kari Oca, Brazil) Yanomami.

Ralegan Siddhi

Ralegan Siddhi, a village in a drought-prone region of Ahmednagar District in the Indian state of Maharashtra, is the setting of one of the most successful programs of ecological, economic, and social restoration known in India in recent years. It is a key example of the application of Hindu religious teachings to social and ecological reform. The transformation was the result of the leadership of Kishan Baburao Hazare (b. 1940), a local villager known affectionately as Anna (elder brother) Hazare, and the influence upon him of the religious thinker and reformer, Swami Vivekananda (1862–1902).

Before 1975 the village of about 1500 people was stricken with poverty and social disintegration. Sources of irrigation had dried up. Agricultural production was inadequate and drinking water was scarce. Lack of sanitation afflicted villagers with water-born diseases. Villagers borrowed heavily from lenders in neighboring villages. Unable to repay, their debts increased, leading to hopelessness, alcoholism, and violence. Social barriers isolated the 16 Harijan families. The village survived on profits from the sale of illegal alcohol to neighboring villages. Few children attended school. Religious life in the village had lost all meaning. Villagers had removed wooden parts of the temple to fuel the liquor stills.

Anna Hazare came to Ralegan Siddhi as the child of a family whose fortune had been dissipated by relentless economic pressures. As a young man, he joined the army where he began to question the meaning of life. Uncertainty over whether life was worth living eventually drove him to despair. He had fully decided to end his life when in a railway station bookstall he encountered a short collection of the thoughts of Swami Vivekananda. He testified later that here for the first time he discovered the meaning of life: that life is meant for service to God through service to others. While Hazare spent his annual leaves in Ralegan Siddhi and witnessed the continuing degradation of his village, the works of Vivekananda gave new direction to his life. While driving a military truck during the 1965 war with Pakistan, an attack by enemy aircraft left most of his colleagues dead. He believed that God had given him a new life and the opportunity to put the thoughts of Vivekananda into practice. He took a vow not to marry but to remain in the army until he was eligible for a pension. He returned to Ralegan Siddhi on his retirement in 1975.

Because be believed the restoration of the village could not proceed without a moral and spiritual awakening, Anna Hazare began with an effort to renovate the dilapidated Yadavbaba Mandir, the village temple. With Vivekananda, he believed that God is everywhere, but that the temple is crucial to village life because it is here that children first learn the important values of life. Because he used his own retirement fund for the restoration of the temple, his work attracted the attention of villagers. The temple became his venue for teaching the religious ideas of Vivekananda, and the application of these ideas to community problems. Preaching purity of mind, purity of action, and the value of self-sacrifice, Hazare's teaching addressed the hopelessness and apathy that immobilized the village. He also related the villager's received sense of the sacredness of land and water to an understanding of the material benefit these provide when cared for with conscientious effort. Hazare's most influential teaching was that selfless work is worship. Impressed by his initiative, the people gradually began to contribute their labor to the project. As work progressed, Hazare brought singers and storytellers to the temple who supported his teachings with songs and stories from the religious tradition. Such temple meetings became the foundation for the Gram Sabha, or village assembly, that eventually became the principal decision-making body of the village.

By means of the organization of voluntary labor as service to God, the villagers undertook a watershed management plan to restore irrigation and agriculture, and provide drinking water at the village level. During the process, the temple became the focus of the restoration effort. It was at a meeting in the temple that the villagers collectively resolved to close the liquor dens and impose a ban on alcohol consumption in the village. Because the decision of the village had been made in the temple, it had the force of a religious commitment.

The restoration of the moral fabric of the community brought about significant results. With wells viable throughout the year, irrigation dispersed to productive fields, and drinking water distributed to a faucet in every household, the village now exports more agricultural products than it imported in the days before the restoration began.

Following the thoughts of Vivekananda, Anna Hazare holds that nothing has fractured Indian society more than the caste system and the practice of untouchability. With Hazare's leadership, social barriers were removed and people of all castes came together to celebrate community life. Villagers have built houses for the Harijan families, and helped them repay their debts. For the past several years, the honor of leading the procession in the village bullock festival, once the subject of bitter contention, has been given to the Harijan community, integrating them within the religious life of the village.

The restoration of Ralegan Siddhi is now being replicated in other villages in Maharashtra and beyond. Young people selected from these villages undergo training at Ralegan Siddhi to provide leadership for similar programs in their own villages. Hazare challenges them with the analogy of the grain of wheat that has to sacrifice itself to give birth to a swaying field of grain. The transformation of Ralegan Siddhi was the result of the mobilization of a village through a religious and moral awakening that empowered the people to address conditions of material, social, and ecological decay.

George A. James

Further Reading
Agarwal, Anil and Sunita Narain. *Towards Green Villages*. New Delhi: Center for Science and Environment, 1990.
Hazare, Anna. *Ralegan Siddhi: A Veritable Transformation*. B.S. Pendse, tr. Pune: Ralegon Siddhi Pariwar Prakashan, 1997.
Pangare, Ganesh and Vasudha Pangare. *From Poverty to Plenty: The Story of Ralegan Siddhi*. Studies in Ecology and Sustainable Development. New Delhi: INTACH, 1992.
See also: Hinduism; India.

Raphson, Joseph (1648–1715)

Cambridge intellectual Joseph Raphson originated the terms pantheist and pantheism. Historians know little of Raphson's life; not even an obituary has been found. Born in Middlesex, England, he attended Jesus College Cambridge and graduated with a Masters degree in 1692. Raphson gained membership in the prestigious Royal Society in 1691 on the strength of his first book, *Analysis Aequationurn Universalis* (1690). Raphson also wrote a mathematical dictionary (1702), and other works, including *De Spatio Reali seu Ente Infinito* (1697) in which he penned the words "pantheos" and "pantheismus."

Many sources name John Toland as the originator of the word pantheist. But Raphson's citation predates Tolands first recorded use of the term by eight years. Toland had read Raphson's *De Spatio Reali* and commented upon the book, which strongly suggests he picked up the word from Raphson. (Toland still deserves notice for the first use of pantheist in an English-language publication.)

Stephen H. Daniel, Professor of Philosophy at Texas A&M University, discovered Raphson's terms and made the connection between Raphson and Toland in 1994. According to Professor Daniel, "it is now clear that Raphson, not Toland is the person who coined the terms pantheist and pantheism; he just happens to have been writing in Latin at the time" (personal communication with author).

De Spatio Reali delineates two pantheistic outlooks. In one, God comprises nature, the material cosmos, as ultimate reality. Raphson labels adherents of this view panhylists (from the Greek pan = all + hyle = wood, matter) because they believe everything derives from matter. He equates panhylism with atheism. In the other, God comprises space, the overarching element, as ultimate reality. Raphson calls followers of this view pantheists (from the Greek *pan* = all + *theos* = god) because they believe in "a certain universal substance, material as well as intelligent, that fashions all things that exist out of its own essence" (Raphson 1697).

The noted Jewish philosopher Benedict Spinoza (1632–1677), who wrote perhaps the most rigorous exposition of pantheism in all philosophic literature, never employed the terms pantheism and pantheist because they had yet to be conceived. He died just twenty years before Joseph Raphson contributed these valuable and now universally used words to posterity.

Gary Suttle

Further Reading

Copenhaver, Brian P. "Jewish Theologies of Space in the Scientific Revolution: Henry More, Joseph Raphson, Issac Newton, and Their Predecessors." *Annals of Science* 37 (1980), 520–46.

Daniel, Stephen H. "Toland's Semantic Pantheism." In Philip McGuinnes, Alan Harrison and Richard Kearney, eds. *John Toland's Christianity Not Mysterious: Text, Associated Works and Critical Essays*. Dublin: The Lilliput Press, 1997, 303–12.

O'Conner, J.J. and E.F. Robertson. "Joseph Raphson." *Online Biographies*. Scotland: University of St. Andrews, 1996.

Raphson, Joseph. *De Spatio Reali seu Ente Infinito*. London: John Taylor, 1697.

See also: Pantheism; Spinoza, Baruch; Toland, John.

Rappaport, Roy A. ("Skip") (1926–1997)

Roy A. Rappaport, one of the leading ecological anthropologists of the twentieth century, was born in New York City. Known as "Skip" to his friends and colleagues, he earned his undergraduate degree in hotel administration from Cornell University and during the 1950s owned and operated an inn in Lennox, Massachusetts. In 1959 (at the age of 33) Rappaport sold his inn and enrolled at Columbia University where he studied anthropology under Marvin Harris, Harold Conklin, Margaret Mead, Conrad Arensberg, and Andrew P. Vayda. Rappaport always insisted that the anthropologist who most influenced his thought was Gregory Bateson, who he first met in 1968. Bateson introduced Rappaport to systems theory and encouraged him to look at evolution and adaptation as informational processes.

Between 1962 and 1964, Rappaport conducted fieldwork among the Maring of Papua, New Guinea, primarily among the Tsembaga clan cluster. His most important contributions to ecological anthropology are tied to his minute observations and precise measurements of the activities of 204 Maring speakers during 1962 and 1963. In 1964, Rappaport presented a seminal paper "Ritual Regulations of Environmental Relations among a New Guinea People" at the Detroit meeting of the American Anthropological Association. The paper was later published in the journal *Ethnography* and has been widely reprinted. It contains, in abbreviated form, almost all the ideas that were to occupy Rappaport throughout his professional life. Rappaport's 1966 Ph.D. dissertation served as the basis for *Pigs for the Ancestors*, which set new standards for the collection and presentation of anthropological and ecological data. Rappaport's goal in *Pigs* was to transcend cultural materialism and functionalism by focusing on the adaptive value of ritual in maintaining carrying capacity, the persistence of species, human nutritional well-being, and the frequency of warfare in small-scale societies. He identified ritual as *the* major mechanism for regulating peace and warfare among the Tsembaga Maring. *Pigs* is one of the most cited books in the history of anthropology and is required reading for graduate students. It is cited in almost every introductory text.

Pigs for the Ancestors is a wide-ranging work. It covers ritual and its effects, human population and ecosystems, information and meaning, and introduced the use of systems theory to ecological anthropology. Rappaport suggested that ecological systems regulate themselves through feedback – like a thermostat. All parts (pigs, humans, yams) within a system are subject to the regulatory forces of the whole. In the case of warfare among the Maring, the *kaiko* ritual – a ceremonial slaughter of pigs to ancestral guardians – serves as the major regulator. Rappaport postulated that the Maring would not go to war as long as their accumulated debts to the ancestors remained unpaid. Instead, they spent their energies and resources amassing more and more pigs. But eventually the number of pigs (and the labor required to tend them) became intolerable, and a *kaiko* would be held to restore the ratio of pigs to people. *Kaiko* also provided much needed protein and facilitated the distribution of "pig surpluses in the form of pork throughout a large regional population" (Rappaport 1968: 18).

The 1968 edition of *Pigs* generated tremendous controversy among anthropologists, biologists, and ecologists. Some early critics faulted Rappaport for what they saw as his *naive* functionalism, while others accused him of reductionism and/or environmental determinism. A major issue of contention was Rappaport's rejection of "culture" as the primary unit of analysis. Rappaport's model, borrowed from the biological sciences, focused on human populations – not cultures. He saw humans as a part of nature. This did not set well with a number of social anthropologists (notably Marshall Sahlins and Robert F. Murphy) who argued that instead of studying human activities as a part of nature, human activities should be studied apart from nature. Marxist anthropologists (notably Eric Wolf and Jonathan Friedman) accused Rappaport of ignoring cultural change among the Maring. Rappaport's approach, they asserted, could only work for a closed system, but the Maring in 1962 had already been very much influenced by contact with outsiders – including missionaries and anthropologists. Were an anthropologist to observe a *kaiko* ceremony in 1954 or 1968, would he or she have come to the same conclusions as Rappaport (cf. Friedman 1994)?

Rappaport took these criticisms to heart, but never altered his basic systems approach. A second edition of *Pigs* appeared in 1984 to answer critics. It is nearly twice the length of the first edition and includes ten appendices of raw data. Rappaport's goal in the 1984 edition was to allow other scientists to view and critique his observations. He also deposited his personal papers (including his New Guinea field notes from 1962–1963 and 1981–1982) in the Mandeville Special Collections Library at the University of California-San Diego (MSS 0516). *Pigs* introduced one of Rappaport's key findings in human ecology and religion; most notably, what he saw as an occasional contradiction between "operational" and "cognized" environments. By contrasting the "operational" environment – which he saw as being governed by the immutable laws of the physical universe – and the "cognized" environment – which he defined as "the sum of the phenomena ordered into meaningful categories by a population" (Rappaport 1979: 6), Rappaport greatly advanced the study of both rituals and ecology. He emphasized that the "cognized" environment differed from the "operational" environment because "cognized" environments are less bound by physical laws. Rappaport argued passionately that the relationship between culturally constructed meanings and values and organic well-being should be the central concern for all ecological anthropologists.

In 1979, Rappaport published a collection of his papers entitled *Ecology, Meaning, and Religion*. This collection gives an indication of Rappaport's catholic interests and highlights his desire for their integration. He recognized early on that *Pigs for the Ancestors* was only a "beginning" since it represented treatment of the relationship between ritual and ecology from only one of many possible perspectives. An important essay "On Cognized Models" (included in the 1979 collection) attempts to go beyond what Rappaport saw as his earlier, crude attempts to establish the relationship between religion and ecology in *Pigs*. He felt that his earlier efforts had overemphasized organic and ecological functions to the exclusion of cultural understandings. This signaled a dramatic shift in his thought from functional to structural concerns.

Another pivotal essay in *Ecology, Meaning, and Religion*, "The Obvious Aspects of Ritual," outlines the consequences of ritual's outwardly distinctive features; especially, how stereotypical behaviors counter the human potential for lying and deceit. According to Rappaport, two obvious aspects of ritual are that: 1) it constitutes an invariant sequences of acts and utterances; and 2) its participants are required to perform according to these invariant sequences. Ritual thus imposes standards of conduct which go beyond the will of individual participants and demonstrates participants' clear and public acceptance of conventions as they literally "act" them out. For Rappaport, ritual constitutes the foundation of all convention and is the basic "social act." Ritual establishes the possibility of trust and truth, and it provides a place where "the unfalsifiable supported by the undeniable yields the unquestionable, which transforms the dubious, the arbitrary, and the conventional into the correct, the necessary and the natural" (Rappaport 1979: 217).

Rappaport's work articulates a middle ground in which he attempts to give equal weight to evolutionary processes and the constraints of convention. He was not an idealist. But he did not see himself as a cultural materialist either (e.g., Marvin Harris). He situated ritual precisely at the juncture between embodied acts of individual behavior and the disembodied meanings of sacred symbols, but refused to grant priority to either.

In 1965, Rappaport joined the Anthropology Faculty at the University of Michigan where he remained for over thirty years. He served as chair of the Department of Anthropology and was President of the American Anthropological Association from 1987 to 1989. As AAA President, he attempted to bring anthropological findings to bear on social issues of the day. Ecology was always a major focus. Rappaport served as a consultant for the State of Nevada on the advisability of storing nuclear waste at Yucca Mountain and was a member of the National Academy of Sciences Task Force dealing with the leasing of off-shore oil rights.

From 1991 until his death, Rappaport was head of the Program on Studies in Religion (PSIR) at the University of Michigan. He regularly offered the course Anthropology 448/Religion 452: "Anthropology of Religion: Ritual, Sanctity, and Adaptation." Many of his Anthropology 448 students have themselves made important contributions to ecological and anthropological studies of religion; notably, Ellen Messer, Susan Lees, Fran Markowitz, Peter Gluck, Melinda Bollar Wagner, Michael Lambek, Aletta Biersack, and Jim Greenberg.

While heading PSIR, Rappaport embarked on what was to be his last major study published as *Ritual and Religion in the Making of Humanity*. He began writing the book after having been diagnosed with lung cancer. It was published posthumously. In *Ritual and Religion*, he attempted to establish a new set of categories for the study of religion and provided a comprehensive and erudite analysis of ritual forms. *Ritual and Religion* has been favorably compared to Emile Durkheim's classic *The Elementary Forms of Religious Life* published in 1912. Both Durkheim and Rappaport were deeply concerned with the issues of social order and persistence. Critics have pointed out that Rappaport's theory is incomplete because he pays scant attention to religious pluralism or religious conflict. But what sets Rappaport's study apart from other studies is that it is not only "about" religion but is in itself also a profoundly religious book. *Ritual and Religion* makes a strong case for religion's central significance in human evolution and argues convincingly for the reconciliation of religion and science. Rappaport boldly asserted that human survival depends on developing a postmodern science thoroughly grounded in ecology, and concluded that ritual should be the major focus of religious studies because ritual is the "ground" where all religion is made.

Rappaport was not a religious man in the usual sense; indeed, he was distrustful if not hostile toward many forms of organized religion. Nevertheless, he was sympathetic toward religion, perhaps because he so adamantly "believed" his own findings concerning ritual among the Maring. Ultimately for Rappaport, the primary question was not *if* religion is true, but *of what* is religion true?

Stephen D. Glazier

Further Reading

Friedman, Jonathan. *Cultural Identity and Global Process*. London: Sage, 1994.

Harris, Marvin. *Cultural Materialism: The Struggle for a Science of Culture*. New York: Harper & Row, 1979.

Messer, Ellen and Michael Lambek, eds. *Ecology and the Sacred: Engaging the Anthropology of Roy A. Rappaport*. Ann Arbor: University of Michigan Press, 1999.

Rappaport, Roy A. *Ritual and Religion in the Making of Humanity*. New York: Cambridge University Press, 1999.

Rappaport, Roy A. *Ecology, Meaning, and Religion*. Richmond, CA: North Atlantic Books, 1979.

Rappaport, Roy A. *Pigs for the Ancestors: Ritual and Ecology of a New Guinea People*. New Haven: Yale University Press, 1968/1984.

Watanabe, John M. and Barbara B. Smuts. "Explaining Religion Without Explaining It Away: Trust, Truth and the Evolution of Cooperation." *American Anthropologist* 101 (1999), 98–112.

See also: Anthropologists; Bateson, Gregory; Domestication; Ecology and Religion; Ecological Anthropology; Evolutionary Biology, Religion, and Stewardship; Harris, Marvin; A Religio-Ecological Perspective on Religion and Nature; Religious Environmentalist Paradigm; Traditional Ecological Knowledge; Wonder toward Nature.

Rastafari

Rastafari originated in the 1920s and 1930s in Jamaica, especially among poor black men migrating into Kingston from Jamaica's rural regions. From there it expanded into a global movement with a broad spectrum of beliefs and practices. Generally, Rastafari do not identify themselves according to doctrinal positions. Furthermore, the central ritual of the movement is "reasoning" – a process of ongoing talking and thinking out concerns. "Reasoning" is relatively amorphous and lends itself to a fluid range of intellectual positions and practices. Additionally, the social locations and characteristics of Rastafari vary tremendously. Consequently, the relationship of Rastafari and nature is best seen not in doctrines or practices, but rather in a range of themes running through diverse strands of the movement. The themes that best reflect where nature and ecology fit into a typical Rastafari worldview are "Babylon/Zion" and "Ital."

Babylon/Zion

The Rastafari symbols Babylon and Zion express a difference between the world as it is generally experienced and the world as it truly is and could be experienced. At the same time, Babylon and Zion concretize this worldview by symbolizing geographical locations: Babylon is the city, the West, the colonized world, the U.S. and Britain, and other locations of suffering; Zion is the countryside, the forest, Africa, and other places where one is free. Babylon in particular is also used adjectively to refer to problems corrupting the world (e.g., the system of forces in society that conspire to maintain humankind in captivity might be called the "Babylon Shitstem" – that is, the Babylon System).

Babylon is seen to be rife with corruption and injustice, greed, competition, jealousy, racism, war, and death. Babylon chokes out life by killing or blinding us to the "I," the divine within. Zion is a world of promise, the world as it could and will be: harmonious, flourishing, natural. The more concrete connotations of Babylon and Zion remain stamped by the early Rastafari experiences of transition from countryside to city, and the radical revaluations of blackness, African heritage, and colonial oppression that continue to undergird the whole movement.

Life in Babylon disconnects man [sic] from one another and nature through "downpression" (oppression). Thus, nature is invisible in Babylon except as it is reintroduced through positive lifestyle choices that undo "downpression." Life in Babylon is a constant struggle, perhaps best expressed through cultural images, such as the descriptive song titles of the late Jamaican reggae singer and Rastafari, Bob Marley: Babylon is a "Concrete Jungle," a "Rat Race," and a "War." "War" sets to music a speech (dated by some to 1968 and by others to a 1963 speech to the UN) by the late Emperor of Ethiopia Haile Selassie, whom some Rastafari regard as divine. In it, Selassie warns that man's condition will be perpetual war until the time that "the color of a man's skin is of no more significance than the color of his eyes." Racism is endemic in Babylon, and the true horror of racism is that it hides the divine within from all men.

In Zion a man [sic] can be a man, true to the "I" in himself, in others, and in the world. In Zion, interactions are guided by truth, not deception, and they renew and rejuvenate rather than destroy. In Zion, no man suffers because of his skin color, and blackness can be embraced.

For some Rastafari, Zion necessarily implies a return to Africa (or Africa's metonymic representative, Ethiopia), where an Ital life is possible. For others in Babylon, Zion is approached as best as can be through an Ital lifestyle marked loosely by behaviors ranging from vegetarianism to working solely for oneself. For others again, an Ital life is lived by retreat to the bush or forest, or in communes, of varying size, or alone, growing one's own food, organically, in communion with the natural environment. At the furthest extreme, some Rastafari (e.g., "higes knots," "earth men" or "Nomn Te") totally reject anything associated with Babylon, going so far as to refuse to touch money, to wear shoes or Western clothes (wearing grass clothes or sacks instead), to eat anything processed, to step on pavement, or to participate in any way with the world.

Selassie, Haile (1892–1975)

Any exploration of Rastafari inevitably leads to the enigmatic former Emperor of Ethiopia, His Imperial Majesty Haile Selassie, whom many Rastafari venerate as the Supreme Creator (i.e., God or "Jah"). The name Rastafari is a combination of his early title, Ras ("Prince"), plus Selassie's given name (Tafari).

Selassie lived from 1892 to 1975. He was the son of Ethiopian Prince Ras Makonnen, and his lineage is said to be traceable to King Solomon and the Queen of Sheba. Though not directly in line for the throne, in 1930 Ras Tafari took control of the Ethiopian Empire. It was in ascending to the throne that he assumed the title Haile Selassie ("Might of the Trinity"). One consequence of his ornate coronation was a photo essay in National Geographic, which many scholars link to the growth of the Rastafari movement in Jamaica. Many Rastafari saw Selassie's coronation as fulfillment of an apocryphal saying by pan-Africanist, Marcus Garvey, to look to Africa for the crowning of a black king.

Selassie's rule was autocratic, but he was also a modernizer, interested in developing Ethiopia economically. In 1966, Selassie traveled to Jamaica, where he was unexpectedly met at the airport with throngs of Rastafari worshippers. Despite his own disavowals of divinity (he was Ethiopian Orthodox Christian), many Rastafari continued to worship him.

Selassie's death is controversial among Rastafari, some of whom claim that, as Creator, he could not have died.

Richard C. Salter

It is important to note that these ways of experiencing, apprehending or approaching Zion are not necessarily mutually exclusive, and many Rastafari understand and participate in Zion in various ways at different times in their lives.

Ital

The Ital lifestyle can be understood as the ethos of Zion, and it is this ethos that shows the most direct connections of Rastafari to nature and ecology. The basic characteristics of an Ital lifestyle are a reverence for life and a belief that human beings are at their best when connected to nature. For example, an Ital diet is typically vegetarian, grown organically, with minimal processing. Rastafari tend to reject chemical fertilizers, pesticides, or genetically engineered crops because: they destroy life in the long-run, they are ultimately unhealthy for humans, they promote economic dependence on corporations and first-world nations, and they dismantle traditional relations with the land and traditional knowledge of crops, crop cycles, lunar planting and harvest cycles. Rastafari farmers tend to value traditional modes of planting and cooperative farming because they preserve the relationship of the farmer to the land and to tradition.

For similar reasons, many Rastafari primarily use "bush medicine," or traditional herbal cures, when sick. These bush herbs are given by the Creator as food and medicine for humans, a claim supported with biblical references (e.g., Gen. 1:29, giving plants to people for food; Rev. 22:2, suggesting ganja (marijuana) as the "healing of the nations"). Significantly, many Rastafari prefer to grow their own ganja, or buy only from other Rastafari, and reject on principle the extra-potent hybridized varieties, especially when these are understood as having been developed in North America.

The characteristic Rastafari hairstyle, dreadlocks (matted hair), also reflects reverence for life. According to many Rastafari, one ought not cut one's hair or shave one's beard because the growing hair signifies life and strength, and life cannot be stopped and ought not be hidden. Among many Rastafari, contraception and abortion are rejected for similar reasons.

Ecological Ethic

Rastafari frequently read and are influenced by the Bible, especially the Hebrew Bible. Yet the ecological ethic among most Rastafari cannot be said to be based on a dominion theology or a stewardship model of ecology. Moreover, though many Rastafari do long for Zion, and experience profound renewal from sojourns in Zion, the use-value of land for agriculture and the value placed on self-determination among Rastafari, mitigate against an ethic that values land for recreation.

In general, the tendency of Rastafari to see the divine throughout the natural world leads to the strongest affinities between Rastafari and those ecological ethics which see inherent value in all of nature. Yet these ecological affinities will also continue to exist with a certain amount of tension, for Rastafari history tells us of the special value Rastafari place on human self-determination and liberation. Nature is valuable, but the value of nature cannot be imposed on humans from outside or it will ring false; attempts by first-world nations to impose an ecological ethic on Rastafari will be rejected simply because they come from outside, regardless of profound affinities at the level of content.

Richard C. Salter

Rastafarian Activism

Rastafarian beliefs have directly inspired activism within the green movement. Rastafarians have been involved in Green Parties and a range of environmental groups, especially those concerned with animal liberation. In Britain the Rastafarian poet Benjamin Zaphniah has written verse promoting a vegan diet and raised funds for groups such as Friends of the Earth. In the United Kingdom the Jamaican poet Brian Wilson founded Friends of MOVE to support the Philadelphia-based radical group. Friends of MOVE mobilized green activists, anarchists and Rastafarians to campaign for the release of U.S. political prisoner and MOVE supporter Mumia Abu-Jamal. They also took part in direct-action protest with Earth First! on a range of issues including road construction.

Perhaps the best-known Rastafarian green activist is the New Zealand Member of Parliament, Nandor Tanzcos. Elected in 1999 for the Green Party, he has pioneered the campaign for the legalization of cannabis in N.Z., spearheaded the Wild Greens direct-action group who famously raided laboratories growing GM crops and is a leading advocate of multicultural ecology. His activism started in the 1980s in Britain and included a stay at Molesworth peace camp. Nandor's spiritual beliefs are closely linked to his anti-capitalism. Nandor argues that the Rastafarian principle of *Ital* provides an alternative to capitalism,

It begins with private ownership – the idea that people can own the Earth, as if fleas could own a dog... Ital is the opposite of that. Ital is natural livity. I&I say that the land is from the creator, creativity is from the creator, life is from the creator. So how can a person own any of that, in any true sense?

He conceptualizes *Ital* as a means of opposing consumerism, noting, "Capitalism is also built on self-hatred. Consumer society depends on us being unhappy with who we are... Natural hair, natural smell, natural living – that is ital, that is dread. Babylon hates this, because it cannot be commodified." Nandor argues that there is an affinity between his religious beliefs and his activism, "So I am a Rasta. I am also an MP for the Green Party. Both these ways of being are about natural law, about social justice, ecological wisdom, peace and true democracy." Indeed the links between Rastafarianism and green political activism are based on a shared sense of nature as sacred and the pursuit of social justice as morally obligatory.

Derek Wall

Further Reading
Wall, Derek. "Dread, Gold and Green: An Interview with Nandor Tzancos." *Green World* 39 (2003), 10–11.

See also: Earth First! and the Earth Liberation Front; MOVE; Radical Environmentalism.

Further Reading

Chevannes, Barry. *Roots and Ideology*. Syracuse, NY: Syracuse University Press, 1994.

Homiak, John P. "Dub History: Soundings on Rastafari Livity and Language." In Barry Chevannes, ed. *Rastafari and Other African-Caribbean Worldviews*. New Brunswick, NJ: Rutgers University Press, 1995.

Murrell, Nathaniel Samuel, William David Spencer and Adrian Anthony McFarlane, eds. *Chanting Down Babylon: The Rastafari Reader*. Philadelphia, PA: Temple University Press, 1998.

See also: Caribbean Cultures; Entheogens.

Raves

From the late 1980s in Britain and subsequently elsewhere around the globe, youth have danced *en masse* to the syncopated rhythm of electronic "house" or "techno" (or "tekno") musics, which, with the assistance of psychotropic lights, hypnoblobic video and alterants (especially the entheogen MDMA, or "ecstasy," LSD and nitrous oxide), have enabled altered states of consciousness. In what are arguably crucibles of contemporary youth spirituality, all-night endurance dancing within the context of these "raves" is variously claimed to facilitate transcendence of the self, communion between participants and/or a deep somatic relationship with the natural environment.

A clandestine pleasurescape, the rave has been described as "an overwhelming yet depthless barrage of the senses that transforms the dancefloor into a magical megasurface" (Hutson 1999: 58). While consistent with experiences occasioned by traditional underground or even "club" events, the description becomes especially applicable to "raves" celebrating celestial events and seasonal transitions (e.g., moon cycle, solstices) held in outdoor locations (where dance floors are positioned in bushland, forest, beach or desert), facilitated and attended by Pagans, travellers and other practitioners and affiliates of earthen spirituality. This is certainly the case for "Trance Dance" or "psytrance" (psychedelic trance) events, themselves influenced by traveller's full moon parties held in Goa, India, during the 1980s. Trance Dance rituals may incorporate fluorescent décor, fractalized mandala projections, altars, chai tents, totemic installations, sacred geometry, earthworks, large speaker stacks positioned at the cardinal points and "trance" music – a metronomic four-quarter beat overladen with exhilarating arpeggios, infused with "ethnodelic" samples (e.g., didgeridoo, djembe, sitar). Sonorous and sensual, such events are celebrated as "no spectator" style odysseys with a celebrated climax ("rebirth") at sunrise.

While raving and techno-music culture became subject to commercialism and government regulation from the early 1990s, anarcho-spiritualists have consistently advocated the interfacing of *technology, ecology* and *spirituality*. Editor of *Evolution* magazine (originally *Encyclopedia Psychedelica*) and founder of the London dance club Megatripolis, Fraser Clark, was particularly influential in articulating this convergence. Having coined the term "zippie" (Zen Inspired Pagan Professional) to describe "a new kind of hippy who rejected the sixties Luddite pastoralism and embraced the cyberdelic, mind-expanding potential of technology," Clark evangelized rave as "the expression of a new Gaia-worshipping eco-consciousness" (Reynolds 1998: 167). The idea that Britain would be revitalized by a fusion of the House and Green movements was articulated on Clark's compilation album *Shamanarchy in the UK*. Not inconsistent with the view that raves are "programmed" by digital technicians (DJs and other cyber-engineers) possessing "techno-shamanic" qualities, Clarke optimistically viewed the rave as a contemporary form of "tribal shamanism." Similarly, for influential scholar of ethnopharmacology and radical historian Terence McKenna, as shamanic dance ritual, raving was part of the natural psychedelics-led "archaic revival" which will end alienation from the "Gaian supermind" (McKenna 1991).

The work of anarcho-mystic Hakim Bey (aka Peter Lamborn Wilson) has been heavily drawn upon in forging the primitivist–extropian alliance at the heart of such a worldview. Throughout the nineties, Bey's *Temporary Autonomous Zone* (1991), or TAZ, was the poetic benchmark in conceptualizing an appropriate horizontal, non-commodified dancescape for the exploration of psychedelic spirituality. The free outdoor rave-TAZ became a new tech-savvy anarcho-liminal utopia wherein inhabitants claim to achieve that which resembles a peak experience, or union, with co-liminaries *and* nature. Throughout the nineties, numerous inspired *techno-tribes* emerged in Europe, North America and Australia to pursue the desired "revival" through the facilitation of such events. A future-primitivism was early exemplified by London "terra-technic" sound system, Spiral Tribe, who believed they were connected to prehistoric nomadic tribes and that techno was the new "folk music." The Spirals believed free parties were

> shamanic rites, which using the new musical technologies in combination with certain chemicals and long periods of dancing, preferably in settings with spiritual significance, could reconnect urban youth to the Earth with which they had lost contact, thus averting imminent ecological crisis (Collin 1997: 203–4).

These strands impacted upon the development of a global "techno-pagan" or cyber-spirituality movement for whom the rave assemblage would facilitate the return to "forgotten tribal roots." It was well received in San

Francisco, where experimentation into the psychedelic-spirituality-technology interface was particularly advanced. There, Full Moon parties and events operated by the New Moon collective and other rave communities were prevalent throughout the nineties.

In Australia, "bush doofs" were early facilitated by the likes of Electric Tipi on the northern coast of New South Wales, and later GreenAnt in Victoria and Dragonflight in Queensland. In a proactive and reconciliatory atmosphere, Australia has also seen a strengthening alliance between radical environmentalism, ecospirituality and rave culture manifested in *dance activism*. Popularly dubbed "Free NRG," this post-rave movement has seen youth rise to challenge mining and forest industries, and defend sacralized landscape ("country") threatened by natural-resource developers. Emerging in 1995, anarcho-spiritual techno-tribe Ohms not Bombs, became alarmed by current levels of non-renewable energy consumption and patterns of Earth destruction. A key objective of "Free NRG," they argue, is "tuning technology with ecology, DJing our soul-force into the amazing biorhythms of nature" (*www.omsnotbombs.org*). Furthermore, with "co-created magic," they have declared

> this land is returned to the ancient and magical indigenous chain of wisdom. If we unite our purpose a massive healing can be set in motion ... Help institute a sound system for all, join the Earthdream, support Aboriginal sovereignty, and help dance up the country in rave-o-lution (*www.omsnotbombs.org*).

An annual "tech-nomadic" carnival of protest touring through Central Australia, Earthdream (www.beam.to/earthdream) emerged in 2000 as the proactive millenarian event of the techno-spiritual movement. Over a period of four or five months during the winter, a series of free party "teknivals" and intercultural anti-uranium mining protests are held on Aboriginal lands – with the full co-operation of traditional owners – including a major event held on the winter solstice. Exemplifying a contemporary strategy of reenchantment, Earthdreamers actively participate in native landscapes.

Earthdream exemplifies the immanent *communing* potentiated by the geo-dancescapes of the rave/post-rave. Participating in the dancescape – through dancing, through *ecstasis* ("raving") – is a means of temporary inhabitation, rendering possible an enduring relationship with place. Commentators expound upon the spiritual potential of Trance Dance as a ritual of communion. For instance, psy-trance pioneer Ray Castle asserts that outdoor trance events "celebrate an experiential celestial electro-communion – a participation mystique – with the numinous oneness and interconnectivity of all creation" (Castle 2000: 146). According to proponent of Chaos Magick, Kathleen Williamson, while sounds produced by the likes of Castle constitute "the new epic poetry," Trance Dance "is the 'coming of age' ritual which Western culture has long forgotten." According to Williamson, "tekno anarcho-activists" understand "the power of the gnosis of trance," using techniques to "direct the energy of the dance." While music is significant in achieving "transcendence" or "inner-knowledge" in such contexts, trance artists have also "buried crystals under dance areas" and have investigated "the symbology and iconography of ancient magickal and spiritual traditions." Moreover, in "reviving lost traditions," the dance rite constitutes an answer to modern distancing from natural world rhythms:

> Our convenient industrial cultures have practically negated our direct relationship with the earth and its seasons and cycles, and it seems that there is less and less reason to rely on, let alone investigate our instinctual being. Our experiences with sound, psychedelics and the dance ritual are the stirrings of communicating via the ebb and flow of the earth's rhythms and letting it seep into our collective emotions (Williamson 1998).

In tracing the collective paroxysm of Trance Dance to its putative Pagan or "tribal" origins, Australian fluorescent "rainbow warrior" Eugene ENRG (aka DJ Krusty), reveals a chthonic dimensioned dance philosophy. Characteristically, it is believed that "energy," located in and channeled from the Australian landscape, is responsible for the ecstatic states associated with Trance Dance. For Krusty, a dancer's body can "become a conduit for energy":

> I think there's a sense of the spirit of the land. [For instance] this land we now call Australia has a real spirit to being stomped. And if you've ever watched Aboriginal dance, its very much about stomping the earth ... And if you watch techno ... It's very much about stomping the earth ... [It] brings energy into the body, Earth energy into the body (interview with the author, 30 December 1997).

Moreover, within contemporary trance discourse, beyond the "homeopathic" consequences for the individual and the community said to derive from both sound and landscape, it is believed that such dancing performs a somatic connection to, and enables a spiritual relationship with, the natural world.

Graham St John

Further Reading

Bey, Hakim. *TAZ: The Temporary Autonomous Zone – Ontological Anarchy and Poetic Terrorism.* New York: Autonomedia, 1991.

Castle, Ray. "Doof Disco Didges of the Digerati." In Alan Dearling and Brendan Handley, eds. *Alternative Australia: Celebrating Cultural Diversity*. Dorset: Enabler, 2000, 146–51.

Collin, Matthew. *Altered State: The Story of Ecstasy Culture and Acid House*. London: Serpents Tail, 1997.

Hutson, Scot. "Technoshamanism: Spiritual Healing in the Rave Subculture." *Popular Music and Society* 23:3 (1999), 53–77.

McKenna, Terence. *The Archaic Revival*. San Francisco: Harper, 1991.

Reynolds, Simon. *Energy Flash: A Journey Through Rave Music and Dance Culture*. London: Picador, 1998.

St John, Graham. "Techno Millennium: Dance, Ecology and Future Primitives." In Graham St John, ed. *Rave Culture and Religion*. London: Routledge, 2004.

Tramacchi, Des. "Field Tripping: Psychedelic Communitas and Ritual in the Australian Bush." *Journal of Contemporary Religion* 15:2 (1999), 201–13.

Williamson, Kathleen. "Trance Magick." *Octarine* 3 (Solstice 1998), unpaginated.

See also: Anarchism; Dance; Entheogens; Ferality; Radical Environmentalism.

Raymo, Chet (1936–)

Chet Raymo was born 17 September 1936 in Chatanooga, Tennessee, and became Professor of Astronomy at Stonehill College in North Easton, Massachusetts. Beginning in 1985, Raymo wrote a weekly science column for *The Boston Globe*. He has also published more than a half dozen books addressing the connection between spirit and science.

Although Raymo's upbringing was religious, he found himself increasingly drawn to the beauty of science, finding the features of the universe more readily understood in terms scientific than religious. As a child, he was often wakened in the middle of the night by his father. They would go together into the dark yard to study the starry night skies; he would later characterize these midnight excursions as having a profound influence on his life as his youthful scientific curiosity came into conflict with his religious upbringing. Yet while science offered him knowledge and understanding, it did not offer the comfort and tradition he had found in religion. Only through his exposure to such mystics as Julian of Norwich, Thomas Merton, and Teilhard de Chardin was a world revealed that allowed both science and religion a place.

Place is central in Raymo's books, beginning with *The Soul of Night* (1985). By 1999 he had come to understand that the teachings of science could not contradict his religious faith; that faith is based not on dogma but on love; and that "knowledge is a prerequisite for love" (1999: xv). Further, he argues, science allows us "to participate in an evolutionary drama larger and richer than ourselves, in which the human soul awakens in the course of deep time to a new season of consciousness and intelligence" (1999: 46). He notes, for instance, that as a trained astronomer he fully understands the make-up of a comet, can plot its course around the sun, its trajectory across the sky. But none of that knowledge can diminish his spiritual joy in the presence of the comet. "Knowledge and wonder and celebration," he writes, "went hand in hand in hand: the archetypal religious experience" (1998: 239).

Raymo writes of his life as a continual process of "relearning how to pray" (1999: ix). Rejecting the self-centeredness of his childhood prayer – "the vain repetition of 'me, Lord, me' " (1999: xiv) – he prefers to meditate upon natural phenomena as a catalyst for his spirituality. His is not a ritual-bound spirituality, though; Raymo lives well outside the New Age. Nor does he follow Stephen Jay Gould's imperative that science and religion ought always to remain entirely separate realms of understanding. In the world as Raymo understands it, God and nature serve one another; the kind of knowledge offered by science does not impede, but rather enhances, a religious or spiritual experience of nature. Both in his books and in many of his weekly columns, Raymo seeks to show the mystery of the natural world; thus while he does not write explicitly about "the environment," he guides readers into that natural mystery in the understanding that by doing so they will come to value nature for its own sake.

In exchanging the dogma of his childhood religion for a mature vision of spirit as an elemental part of the natural world, Raymo echoes two writers with whom he is most often compared: Loren Eiseley and Annie Dillard. Raymo speaks, though, with a unique voice, one informed by the ancient stars in the night sky, the differently ancient stones of the Irish coast and the long traditions they represent – a voice content in the knowledge that science and religion have equal roles in the cosmos and in his own life.

Richard Hunt

Further Reading

Raymo, Chet. *Natural Prayers*. St. Paul: Hungry Mind Press, 1999.

Raymo, Chet. *Skeptics and True Believers: The Exhilarating Connection between Science and Religion*. New York: Walker, 1998.

Raymo, Chet. *Honey from Stone: A Naturalist's Search for God*. New York: Dodd, Mead, 1987.

Raymo, Chet. *The Soul of the Night: An Astronomical Pilgrimage*. Paramus, NJ: Prentice Hall, 1985.

See also: Dillard, Annie; Eiseley, Loren; Teilhard de Chardin, Pierre.

Reclaiming

"Reclaiming" is an ecofeminist Witchcraft community and spiritual organization. While the Reclaiming *tradition* is a specific feminist branch of contemporary American Pagan Witchcraft, the Reclaiming *community* refers both to the local Witchcraft community in the San Francisco Bay Area of California and to the women and men, primarily in North America and Western Europe, who identify with this tradition. The tradition arose from a teaching collective within the San Francisco community, founded in 1979 by the Jewish author, feminist and activist Starhawk and her circle of friends. In 1980 the collective, which by then ran an ecofeminist "school" in Witchcraft, decided to name its work *Reclaiming – A Center for Feminist Spirituality*. Within a few years Reclaiming became a well-established institution on the Pagan scene in Northern California. Twenty years later, Reclaiming has recruited more than fifty teachers/leaders and probably has adherents in the tens of thousands.

According to Reclaiming Witches, the values of their tradition stem from an age-old "magical consciousness" that sees all of life as sacred and interconnected, and any living being as a dynamic composition of matter, energy and spirit. The natural world is venerated and ultimate spiritual authority is believed to reside within each and every person. Reclaiming works with both female and male images of the divinity, although the goddess symbol is usually preferred. To name life-generating powers "Goddess" is meant to be a continual reminder of what they value the most, namely life brought into the world, and not an act in which gender narrowly is attributed to divine reality.

Reclaiming's deep spiritual commitment to the Earth and to the well-being, justice and equity of all people has attracted people to the community who seek to combine spirituality with political activism – often with a strong ecological mission and a desire to convert Witchcraft into green activism. Although a "metaphysics of interdependence" is manifest in this Witchcraft community, there are aspects of their worldview that also are critical of much green "deep ecology" spirituality and activism. They do, for example, claim a radical notion of power that includes both ecological and social structures: even though all beings have a share in the same life-generating powers and therefore are equally valuable in terms of their "power-from-within," people are valued as having a higher worth than worms. Also, political action is regarded as impossible without rating and choosing one alternative before another. To take the name "Witch" is itself an act of choosing, of ethically separating out from immanent reality an identity more preferable than another. Furthermore, religious devotion involves more than political activism to a Witch: there are mystical and initiatory aspects of practicing Witchcraft that challenge every person to mature and grow.

In 1994 Reclaiming incorporated as a nonprofit religious organization and in 1997 it reorganized to accommodate its membership that had grown by then to several thousand followers in the U.S., Canada and Europe. The San Francisco Reclaiming collective dissolved itself and was replaced with a local "Wheel" and a transnational "Spokes Council." A statement of core values, the "Reclaiming Principles of Unity," guided the process of reformation. A Reclaiming *tradition* was thus defined for the first time, not in terms of a theology, but in terms of a worldview and methodology. By this careful move, Reclaiming came to augment the position that feminist Witchcraft is not necessarily a new religion, but perhaps rather a new spiritual (and magical) practice.

Even though the old Reclaiming community in San Francisco has a new organizational heart, the ideological continuity between 1980 and today is clear. When Reclaiming was founded, Starhawk and friends interpreted Witchcraft in terms similar to those of Z Budapest: as the claiming back (re-claiming) of an ancient, goddess-worshipping religion in which nature was viewed as sacred and women believed to hold honorable and powerful positions. But unlike Budapest's lesbian and separatist *Dianic* interpretation, Starhawk wanted to introduce a feminist version of Witchcraft to both genders and emphasize its environmental and political implications. From the very beginning and in alignment with their brand of feminist-anarchism, the collective decided to organize in independent working cells in order to teach classes or publish a newsletter, and to make all decisions through a consensus process. They also decided to teach within the structure of ritual and always keep at least two teachers in every class. This was meant to give the students an ideal experience of how a small ritual unit, a coven, might function and to make transparent how a community of equals ideally might work.

The primary work of Reclaiming is to empower individuals and communities with visions of a new culture and new magical-practical tools to help bring it forth by means of classes, workshops, summer programs ("Witchcamps") and public rituals. They are announced regularly in the *Reclaiming Quarterly*, Reclaiming's own magazine for Witchcraft and magical action (printed in 2000 copies). Three core classes have been taught since 1980. The first class, "The Elements of Magic," teaches how humans are interconnected with the natural world and how ritualizing basically means interaction with the four elements (air, fire, water and Earth) in terms of moving energy. In the second class, "The Iron Pentacle," the students work with a notion of the human body as a microcosm mirroring a larger macrocosm and how bodily energies can be used for healing purposes. In the third class, "The Rites of Passage," the students learn to see the human life-course as a sacred manifestation of birth, growth, initiation, repose, death and decay. In all Reclaiming classes, students also learn about Goddess spirituality, the ethical foundation for the practice of magic, and how to create their own rituals. The three core classes are a prerequisite to become initiated – an event which in Reclaiming is customized to the individual seeker. A hallmark of the Reclaiming tradition is that initiation does not lead to any sort of entitlement. Neither is it required for teaching, running a coven or officiating at public rituals.

Reclaiming offers public rituals to celebrate the Witches eight high holidays (sabbats) in a so-called Reclaiming-style – ecstatic, improvisational and with many priests and priestesses that take different roles at rituals – and the community has in particular become famous for the annual *Spiral Dance* ritual. Starhawk wrote the ritual script herself to celebrate and promote her first book (with the same title) in November 1979 and the event has, since then, become a permanent institution. The ritual celebrates and mourns the intertwining of life and death, and the ritualists pledge to remember those who have died from violent deaths in order to fight for peace and justice. The *Spiral Dance* is regarded as Reclaiming's annual gift to the larger San Francisco Bay Area Pagan community, and draws 1500–2000 celebrants.

A major reason for the growth of the Reclaiming community both inside and outside of San Francisco has been Starhawk's influential writings – in particular *The Spiral Dance* (1979), which in 2000 had sold more than 300,000 copies – and the spread of "Witchcamps." These have been offered to students outside San Francisco since 1985 and their curriculum is usually a condensed version of the three core classes mentioned above. Issues such as community building and sustainable living may be raised, as well as training for nonviolent direct political action. Reclaiming tradition Witchcamps are today organized throughout the U.S. (Georgia, California, Florida, Michigan, Missouri, Pennsylvania, Texas, Vermont, Virginia), Canada (Vancouver) and Western Europe (Germany and England). Between fifty and a hundred people attend each one of these Reclaiming-identified camps. This means that more than a thousand people go through Reclaiming's "educational system" every year without becoming members of the San Francisco community, being part, rather, of radical environmentalism's diverse sub-cultures.

Jone Salomonsen

Further Reading

Salomonsen, Jone. *Enchanted Feminism: Ritual, Gender and Divinity among the Reclaiming Witches of San Francisco*. London and New York: Routledge, 2001.

Starhawk. *Truth or Dare: Encounters with Power, Authority and Mystery*. San Francisco: Harper & Row, 1987.

Starhawk. *The Spiral Dance: A Rebirth of the Ancient Religion of the Great Goddess*. San Francisco: Harper & Row, 1979 (revised 1989 and 1999).

See also: Anarchism; Earth First! and the Earth Liberation Front; Environmental Ethics; Hundredth Monkey; Magic; Radical Environmentalism; Paganism – Contemporary; Starhawk; Wicca.

Reclus, Elisée (1830–1905)

Elisée Reclus, a leading nineteenth-century French intellectual, was one of the foremost geographers of his age and a major figure in anarchist political thought. He is most widely recognized for his *New Universal Geography* (1876–1894) a massive 19-volume, 17,000-page work that has been called the greatest individual achievement in the history of geography. His final work, *L'Homme et la Terre* (Man and the Earth) (1905–1908), a 5-volume, 3500-page synthesis of geography, history, anthropology, philosophy, and social theory, is perhaps his most enduring contribution to modern thought. Beginning with the statement "Humanity is Nature becoming self-conscious," [my translation] it is a sweeping account – a kind of anarchist "Grand Narrative" – of the history of both humanity and the Earth, and shows Reclus to be one of the most important precursors of contemporary ecological thought, and of social ecology in particular. Reclus is most widely known today for his place in the history of both geography and anarchist theory. However, through his influence on Kropotkin, another famous anarchist geographer, and on later thinkers such as Patrick Geddes and Lewis Mumford, he has remained a significant figure in regionalist, decentralist and communitarian thought.

There are two sides to Reclus' story of humanity and the Earth. One is his depiction of the process of human self-realization in dialectical interaction with nature. He showed how the natural world shaped human development as humanity transformed and contributed to the unfolding of nature. Reclus contended that historical progress has resulted from mutual aid and social cooperation. Accordingly, he believed that the full self-realization of humanity will depend on a social revolution that embodies such practices in a free, egalitarian, anarcho-communist society. Moreover, he held that the fate of the Earth will hinge on humanity's ability to establish social institutions that express a deep concern for the natural world and for all living beings on the planet.

The other side of Reclus' narrative focused on the long history of domination that has impeded human progress, alienated humanity from nature, and increasingly devastated the face of the Earth. Although he devoted much attention to the domination of human beings through such institutions as the centralized state, capitalism, patriarchy, and racism, he was unusual among social theorists of his era in making the human domination of nature one of his central themes. He was an early critic of the ecological devastation resulting from ruthless industrialization and technological rationalization, he decried the destruction of ancient forests as early as the 1860s, and he was a tireless advocate of ethical vegetarianism and of the humane treatment of animals.

Reclus' survey of human history included extensive discussion of religion and its effects both on society and on humanity's relationship to nature. He traced the origins of religion to tribal societies in which the shaman was both a teacher who conveyed knowledge based on observation of the real world and also a priest who expressed fantasies concerning an illusory world. He contended that as a result of this heritage, society's traditional outlook has been a confusion of myth and reality, truth and falsehood. He held that as knowledge of society and nature progressed, science and religion increasingly diverged, and in the modern period entered a period of war with one another. Reclus believed that in this struggle science must ultimately triumph and reveal religion to be a relic of past ignorance and superstition.

Reclus stressed the influence of nature on the development of the great world religions. In his view, the monotheism of the Ancient Near East reflects in part the austere character of that region, with its geographical uniformities, its hot, dry climate and its harsh sunlight. He contrasted this unifying vision to the unity-in-diversity expressed in Indian religion, contending the latter reflects the sub-continent's vast ecological diversity of forests, mountains, and rivers, and its extremes of climate. The history of religion is thus for Reclus a clear expression of the dialectic between humanity and nature.

Reclus believed the founders of the great religions often had metaphysical and moral insights that conflicted starkly with later religious institutions. He argued that throughout history, religion has been transformed into an ideology at the service of forms of domination such as patriarchy, statism, militarism, capitalism, racism, and repressive morality. He saw Buddhism as the classic case of such a transformation. He contended that the Buddhist teaching of compassion for all sentient beings had revolutionary social implications, and that the Buddhist appeal to direct experience was a radical challenge to all ideologies and institutions. These liberatory dimensions of Buddhism were lost, however, when its practice was reduced to a code of personal morality, the Buddha was declared a god, and the dharma became an official state religion. A similar process, he said, was used later by Constantine to "kill" Christianity. He noted an even more extreme conflict between ideology and practice in the case of the Jains, observing that their respect for nature, and indeed for all forms of life (which would today be called "biocentric egalitarianism") did not prevent them from becoming an elite group that exploited the masses.

Despite Reclus' professed atheism and secularism, there is an implicit, but very significant, religious undercurrent in his work. He sometimes wrote in a pantheistic vein of the experience of nature as involving a loss of the ordinary sense of selfhood and a merging with the surrounding environment. In some works (for example, his *History of a River*, 1869), he expressed not only an intense love of nature, but also something close to the experience of union with nature typical of nature mysticism. Furthermore, at times he referred to his own philosophy as a kind of humanistic religion based on the pursuit of the good of the whole. He held that such a commitment to a larger good was the positive core of ancient religions, and that, although it has been largely betrayed by institutionalized religions, it is still put into practice by their more enlightened and compassionate adherents of these traditions.

Reclus thus saw religion as significant in three areas. First, he looked upon institutionalized religion as a negative social force insofar as it has been a powerful ideological support for systems of domination of humanity and nature. Secondly, he held that religions have had a positive dimension to the degree that their founders and some of their followers have expressed values based on feelings of solidarity and a concern for a greater whole. And finally, Reclus himself expressed a certain religious impulse founded both on his ethical concern for the larger good of humanity and nature, and on his immediate experience of a kind of spiritual union with nature.

John P. Clark

Further Reading
Clark, John and Camille Martin. *Anarchy, Geography, Modernity: The Radical Social Thought of Elisée Reclus*. Lanham, MD: Lexington Books, 2004.
Clark, John. "The Dialectical Social Geography of Elisée Reclus." *Philosophy and Geography I: Space, Place, and Environmental Ethics*. Lanham, MD: Rowman & Littlefield Publishers, Inc., 1997, 117–42.
Reclus, Elisée. *The Earth and Its Inhabitants: The Universal Geography*, 19 vols. London: H. Virtue and Co., Ltd., 1876–1894. (Translation of the *Nouvelle géographie universelle*.)

See also: Anarchism; Kropotkin, Peter; Radical Environmentalism; Social Ecology.

Redwood Rabbis

The redwood forest of America's Pacific Northwest is one of the ecological and spiritual treasures of the world. In the 1820s, settlers of European descent encountered two million acres of dense forest and pristine waterways. At the turn of the millennium, only 4 percent of that primeval ecosystem remained, islands of old-growth reserves in a vast sea of second- and third-growth timberland frequently subjected to clear-cutting, burning and herbicide use.

Jewish settlers made their way north from San Francisco to remote Mendocino and Humboldt Counties in the early nineteenth century, and by the 1980s the region had become home to a small progressive Jewish community, culturally predisposed to environmental activism. Many of the region's environmental organizers, scientists and attorneys are of Jewish descent.

In 1985 MAXXAM Corporation of Texas acquired Pacific Lumber, a timber company whose 200,000-acre holdings included nearly 20,000 acres of virgin old-growth, the largest remaining unprotected stands of ancient redwoods, among them the Headwaters Forest. MAXXAM tripled the rate of logging ancient groves, rapidly felling some of the largest and oldest living things on Earth to make luxury products – premium lumber for siding, decking and hot tubs. For nearly twenty years the redwood forest has been the locus of public demonstrations, litigation, legislative initiatives, and direct-action civil disobedience. Public concern extends beyond loss of the majestic trees themselves to degradation of the ecosystem caused by loss of forest canopy and root strength, leading to increased soil erosion, landslides, aggradation and pollution of streams, and destruction of fish habitat. In 1997 a mudslide originating on MAXXAM clear-cuts destroyed several homes downslope and numerous residential wells have been befouled by sediment; lawsuits brought by residents have been settled out of court.

Working together as the Redwood Rabbis, the three Jewish religious leaders in the region invoked the Talmudic principle of *bal tashchit* that forbids destruction of resources. In rabbinic legend Adam is told: "Do not spoil and desolate My world, for if you do, there will be no one after you to repair it" (*Midrash Ecclesiastes Rabbah* 7:28).

In September 1996 Rabbis Lester Scharnberg and Naomi Steinberg addressed approximately 8000 people rallying at the edge of Headwaters Forest; the rabbis were among over 1000 people arrested for acts of nonviolent civil disobedience.

In January 1997 Rabbis Margaret Holub and Naomi Steinberg organized *Tu BiShevat in the Redwoods*, an observance of the midwinter full moon New Year of the Trees. Over 250 people braved rainstorm and flooding to gather at a local Grange Hall to hear environmental presentations and a teaching by eco-theologian Rabbi Arthur Waskow. A break in the storm allowed participants to travel to a nearby park to celebrate the traditional New Year of the Trees *seder* (ritual meal) of tree-borne fruit while seated on the ground beneath ancient trees. As the ritual ended, the rain resumed and more than ninety participants drove to the outskirts of Headwaters Forest for the holiday custom of planting trees; redwood saplings were planted on creekside timber company property as an act of peaceful civil disobedience and effort to stabilize the stream bank.

Through ongoing public speeches, articles, lobbying and direct action, the Redwood Rabbis attempt to inform the public and influence political developments toward the protection and restoration of the redwood forest. The Redwood Rabbis' efforts have been reported in Jewish and non-Jewish press in the United States and Israel.

Jewish ethics include the obligation of *tokhechah*, delivering rebuke to wrongdoers. The Talmud states that the obligation of rebuke extends not only to individuals, but also to the community, and even to the whole world; if one does not fulfill the commandment of rebuke, one accrues the guilt of those that might have been reformed (Shabbat 54b). In this spirit, the Redwood Rabbis have engaged in years of effort to communicate with MAXXAM owner Charles Hurwitz, a generous donor to the Jewish community in his native Houston, Texas. The rabbis have appealed to the timber tycoon through correspondence, telephone, private and public meetings. In an open letter in California and Houston Jewish press, the Redwood Rabbis called on Charles Hurwitz to make a *t'shuvah sh'leymah*, a complete change of direction, and dedicate himself to sustainable forestry practices and restoration efforts. The rabbis added words of encouragement from nineteenth-century Chassidic master Rabbi Nachman of Bratslav: "If you can spoil, you can fix." Although Pacific Lumber has been cited for approximately 400 violations of the Forest Practices Act since 1995, MAXXAM absorbs the minimal fines and has not acknowledged responsibility for environmental damage. In *The Jerusalem Report* columnist Gershom Gorenberg observed,

> ... the Redwood Rabbis are right to treat their cause as a Jewish one. Arguing "I own it," Charles Hurwitz posits the absolute sovereignty of the individual, and the complete license of private ownership, limited at most by the law of the land but not by ethical demands. But in Judaism, the individual is not sovereign. God is. He owns the earth. Human beings have, minimally, the duty of tenants to care for the Landlord's property. More stringently, they bear the obligations of caretakers, put in this world – as is said of Adam and the Garden of Eden – "to till it and guard it." A caretaker doesn't destroy the Landlord's rarest treasures, doesn't stand and watch it happen (*The Jerusalem Report*, 14 November 1996).

In September 1998 an Earth First! activist was killed near Headwaters Forest when an irate logger felled a tree in the young man's direction; one of the Redwood Rabbis delivered a eulogy at the young man's funeral. Two other lives have been lost in "tree-sit" accidents in the bioregion.

In addition to drawing attention to the plight of the forest and streams of northern California, the Redwood Rabbis bring forward the following questions in Jewish and interfaith discussion: are religious communities morally obligated to take an active role in environmental protection and restoration? Are products derived from non-sustainable practices ethically acceptable? Do religious communities and leaders have a responsibility to deliver rebuke to co-religionists who contribute to pollution and environmental destruction? And, how can we acknowledge natural resources as spiritual resources?

Naomi Steinberg

See also: Earth First! and the Earth Liberation Front; Jewish Environmentalism in North America; Judaism; Waskow, Rabbi Arthur.

Regan, Tom – See Environmental Ethics; Radical Environmentalism.

Re-Earthing

Awakening to the Earth

As I look back, I see two waves, spirit and the Earth, that have sculpted my life. Or are they perhaps just two sides of the same wave?

Spirit emerged from a life-transforming LSD session in London in 1972 which blasted me out of the life I had been living up till then, out of a failed marriage and my job as a systems engineer at IBM. Suddenly the life I had been living lost all its meaning and appeal and I followed an overwhelming urge to start afresh with a clean slate. The following year found me on the road in India for the first time, studying Tibetan meditation with Lama Yeshe and Zopa at Kopan monastery in Nepal and vipassana meditation with Goenka at the Burmese Vihar in Bodh Gaya.

I arrived back in Australia in August 1973 after a five-year absence. The 1960s didn't really reach Australia until the early 1970s. Lots of young people went back to the land then, especially around the small town of Nimbin in northern New South Wales and I immediately gravitated there upon my return.

My friends and I started offering meditation retreats to the burgeoning New Age community, and by 1976 we had built the Forest Meditation Centre. Then, twenty of us bought 160 acres of forest nearby, sloping down to Tuntable Creek, and started Bodhi Farm. We dedicated ourselves to caretaking the meditation center, organic gardening, social action, and looking after each other. It was a beautiful time. Before a hole in the sky made us fear the sun, we worked naked in the gardens and bathed in the pure water of our creek. We planted fruit trees, delivered our own babies, and built our dwellings. We shared vehicles. One day a week we sat in silent meditation together, one day we met in council. My son Bodhi was the first born there in 1977, quickly followed by seven or eight others, including two sets of twins, and so we became known in the district as Baby Farm.

My awakening to the Earth took place four or five miles from Bodhi Farm, at Terania Creek, in 1979, when a couple of hundred hippies staged what was, as far as I know, the first direct nonviolent action in defense of the rainforests anywhere in the world. This was the biggest turning point in my life. I think now that we were successful because we were so naive and innocent and unaware of precedents. A film from that period shows a policeman with a happy smile on his face sitting by the forest having his bald head massaged by a young hippie woman. Another shot shows a band of tie-dyed minstrels standing in front of a bulldozer in the rainforest singing songs of love and peace. People climbed high into the trees and lay on the ground in front of the dozers. Hundreds were arrested, but there was not a single incidence of violence.

Perhaps it was all the sitting in meditation. But I felt as if the rainforest could speak to me and was asking me to give it voice. It was as if I had been plucked from my human throne and suddenly found myself a commoner, a plain member of the biota as Aldo Leopold called it, with a burning desire to awaken humanity to the folly of sawing off the branch that we are sitting on, unraveling the biological fabric from which we too are woven. If we enter the rainforest and allow our energies to merge with the energies we find there, I found, a most profound change in consciousness takes place. As I wrote in *Thinking Like a Mountain* (a book I wrote with Joanna Macy, Arne Naess and Pat Fleming in 1986), I realized that our psyche is itself a part of the rainforests. "I am protecting the rain forest" becomes "I am part of the rainforest protecting myself. I am that part of the rainforest recently emerged into thinking."

It took a number of years, countless demonstrations, press conferences, leaflets, and many people willing to sit in front of bulldozers and go to jail. But eventually 70 percent of the people of New South Wales came to agree with us, and the government established a series of national parks. To protect the remaining rainforests in 1981 we formed an organization, the Rainforest Information Centre (RIC).

From the Rainforest Information Centre to Earth First!

In response to our success, however, Australian logging companies began to look offshore, and in 1983, community representatives from the Solomon Islands contacted RIC for aid in resisting the same logging companies we had fought, as well as Malaysian and Japanese companies. In the years that followed, RIC volunteers provided technical, financial, and political support to defend forests and communities in the South Pacific, Asia, South America, and Russia.

In 1981 North American poet Gary Snyder visited Australia and we took him for a walk through Terania Creek.

As he learned about our actions in defense of the rainforests he said he was reminded of a new group that had formed in the United States called "Earth First!" Armed with Gary's introduction I contacted Earth First! Founder Dave Foreman and was soon writing for their journal.

In 1984 I was invited by Earth First! activists to the U.S. With Foreman and another of Earth First!'s founders, Mike Roselle, we spent two months bouncing around in the back of an old Volkswagen bus, conducting "road show" performances made up of music and storytelling, promoting our biocentric vision and direct-action resistance to deforestation. We ended our tour in San Francisco at a venue where Gary Snyder read a poem about Terania Creek and Randy Hayes announced the formation of a new international organization, the Rainforest Action Network.

The years that followed were full of activity: direct action to save forests and wilderness, boycotts of Mitsubishi and other transnationals, support for indigenous people in their struggles. Yet it was clear that the planet could not be saved one forest at a time. For each forest we were able to spare, a hundred were lost. The Earth is not a rock with resources growing on it; the Earth is alive, and to try to protect it by preserving a tiny patch of wilderness here and there is something like trying to keep humans alive by preserving representative samples of skin here and there.

Consciousness Change and Re-Earthing Ritualizing

To protect the Earth, to protect ourselves, we had to change the way we saw both the Earth and ourselves. We had to change our consciousness. Unless we could address our underlying spiritual disease, no forests would be saved for long. But how, I wondered, are we to identify and understand the spiritual malaise that leaves modern humans so lonely and isolated and no longer able to hear the glad tidings of the Earth which is our home? How are we to heal the great loneliness of spirit that finds us unable to feel loyalty and gratitude to the soil, which has fed and nourished and supported us without pause for 4000 million years?

Searching for an answer, I turned to the indigenous people who lived more or less in harmony with the Earth for hundreds of thousands of years. When we look at indigenous cultures, we may notice that without exception ritual affirming and nurturing the sense of interconnectedness between people and nature plays a central role in the lives of these societies. This suggests that the tendency for a split to develop between humans and the rest of nature must be very strong. Why else would the need for such rituals be so universally perceived? It also suggests the direction we must search for the healing of the split: we need to reclaim the ritual and ceremony which were lost from our culture a long time ago, and to our amazement we find that this is incredibly easy to do. Working with the Buddhist activist Joanna Macy, we developed a ritual to address our contemporary situation. The Council of All Beings, as we called it, began with mourning for what has been lost, the acknowledgement of rage and anger. Using guided visualization, movement, and dance, we reexperienced our entire evolutionary journey. We made masks to represent our animal allies and give voice to these voiceless ones, invoking the powers and knowledge of these other lifetimes to guide us in appropriate actions and empower us in our lives. We see that the pain of the Earth is our own pain and the fate of the Earth is our own fate.

The Council of All Beings was just the first of the "re-Earthing" rituals that we developed in the years that followed, searching for processes that resonated for modern humans while fulfilling the function that such ceremonies had done for all indigenous cultures without exception since the beginning of time.

In the Council of All Beings we remember to speak on behalf of the animals and plants and landscapes with whom we share the Earth. In another of our new processes, "The Timeline of Light," we recapitulate our entire evolutionary journey, the five billion years since the Earth was born and before that, the eight or nine billion years since the birth of the universe itself. When we enact this story as our very own creation myth, when we recall that every cell in our bodies is descended in an unbroken chain from the first cell that emerged on the Earth, then a wonderful new perspective opens up in our lives and a fierce loyalty for life may arise that cuts through the conditioning and habits that trap us, and empowerment may blossom to serve the Earth.

Staying Connected

It takes a certain discipline, of course, to stay connected, to continually hear the Earth's voice. For many years, it had been my custom to seek guidance from the Earth. I would lie down in the forest and cover myself in leaves and say, "Mother, I surrender to you," and then I would deliberately allow all my energies to sink into the Earth. In 1992, the instructions I received in response to my prayers and meditations changed, and from that point onward, all that I received went like this: "John, finish what you've started. Don't start anything new. Leave space for me, Gaia," Sometimes this message would come while I was sitting quietly in nature. At other times, at the end of a weekend workshop, the last exercise would be for each of the participants (including myself) to write a letter to themselves which started "dear (your name), this is your mother, Gaia," after that the instructions were just to keep writing without stopping, without thinking and just see what came out. Previously I had received all kinds of practical advice about projects to undertake, or new directions for my work. Now, this was all that came through: "John, finish what you've started. Don't start anything new. Leave space for me. Gaia." I felt that Gaia was telling me to take time to seek deeper answers to my questions about how the perennial spiritual thirst of humanity could be aligned with the need to address the ecological crisis. It was time to purify myself. It was time to visit some of the projects that I had helped initiate and support but had never seen with my own eyes. It was time to visit my beloved India and weave once again the spiritual warp and ecological woof of my life.

With all the projects that were underway, it took me about three years to hand over the last pieces of my work and return to India, my spiritual home, in search of nourishment and vision. Meanwhile, all the psychological aches and pains, which had mysteriously vanished when my Earth service was all-consuming, now returned. I finally had time on my hands again.

So I returned to India in 1995 searching for some resolution to the spiritual crisis that had begun for me a few years earlier. I decided to spend some time with the 86-year-old Advaita teacher, Poonjaji. I was hoping that meditation and *satsang* dialogues with him would help me to understand the connection between my work to save the planet and spiritual work. I felt a great need to join my activist side with my contemplative side, and I hoped Poonjaji could help me. He had found enlightenment fifty years before as a disciple of Sri Ramana Maharshi, perhaps the greatest Hindu sage of his century, on the sacred mountain Arunachala in the southern Indian state of Tamil Nadu.

Poonjaji, or Papaji as he was affectionately known, had many Western devotees who believed that he was also a fully enlightened master. Some 200 of us from all over the world crowded the hall Satsang Bhavan four mornings a week. Behind him on the wall were portraits and photos of Ramana. We handed him letters (his hearing was failing) with our spiritual questions which he would read and answer. I was interested in exploring with Papaji the relationship between the human spiritual quest and the ailing Earth. I had been wondering how, as long as people look on the Earth as *maya*, illusion, and as an obstacle to realization, as is generally the case in religions originating in the East, we could find the intense spiritual will necessary to make the tremendous changes in our values, lifestyles, and institutions, and in our very consciousness, that would prevent the continued destruction of the Earth?

Lucknow seemed an unlikely place to search for enlightenment. Noisy, highly polluted, and hardly conducive to a spiritual quest. Still, some of my closest friends had reported that a great opportunity existed there while this great sage was alive. There I would hang out with the other seekers, listening to stories from people from around the world. Once I visited the sad remnants of a forest nearby and prayed for direction, for renewal, for Gaia to call me once again, but I felt frustrated and full of doubt.

I found myself fascinated by Shiva, the Hindu god of creation and destruction, and tried to find out as much about him as possible. For Shivaratri, the anniversary of Shiva's wedding, I caught the train to Varanasi where that wedding had taken place. Millions of pilgrims crowded the festive city, and I watched the *naga babas* naked, ash-covered, dreadlocked *sadhus* carry their tridents down to the Ganges to purify themselves.

While there I came across an interview with Vandana Shiva, the Indian feminist ecologist and writer, who spoke about the river goddess Ganga and Shiva. She said that the power of the goddess was so strong that if she landed on Earth she would just destroy. It is symbolic of the way we get our monsoon rain. It comes so strong, that if we don't have forest cover, we get landslides and floods. So the god Shiva had to help in getting the Ganges down to Earth. And Shiva laid out his hair, which was very matted, to break the force of the descent of the Ganga. Shiva's hair, Vandana concluded, is seen by many in India as a metaphor for the vegetation and forests of the Himalayas.

When I returned to Lucknow three days later, I wrote to Papaji twice about these concerns. The first time his answer was mostly mysterious to me and left me unsatisfied. So I plucked up my courage and wrote again a couple of weeks later:

Dear Papaji, Lakshmana Swami once said that, since God had chosen to manifest as the world and everything in it, one could worship God by having respect for the world and all the life forms it contains.

For many, many years, Papaji, it has been my privilege and joy to worship God in this manner, to feel the living Earth play my life like a musical instrument. A couple of weeks ago, when I first wrote to you at satsang, you said this: "To the man speaking of Mother Earth I say: To help Mother Earth means you stand and shout at the top of your lungs."

I have shouted long and hard, Papa. I shouted in front of bulldozers and was thrown in jail. I made films and a book, which was translated into 10 languages, and conducted workshops around the world, donating the proceeds to the work, raising hundreds of thousands of dollars for the protection of Nature from the Amazon to New Guinea.

For the last 15 years Papa, the Earth worked through me and I was tireless and full of joy, but eventually the impurities of ego and the conditioned mind began to rise again until a couple of years ago, the Earth asked me to hand over what I had been doing to others and purify myself for the next task that she has for me. And here I am.

This time Papaji looked directly at me and said in his deep voice:

When you take care of your mother then you will get

some prize. When you are helping the Earth, then you are helping everybody who's living on the Earth – plants, animals, and men. And now you have a reward: that the work will carry on. You may now sit quiet, and she will give you something in the way of peace. So, my dear friend your work is very good. I bless you for this task that is in hand, and let me tell you, both sides can happen simultaneously: Work for the good of the Earth and the people. And for your own good do something else. They needn't interfere with each other. Stay for some time before sleep and in the morning and sit quietly for five or 10 minutes. The rest of the time you may give for the world, help those who need your help.

What a blessing it was to feel Papa rekindle the flame inside me which had been wavering and doubtful. I could not yet know how, but I knew that from this turning point it would begin to flare forth once more.

And indeed, over the following years my work was renewed: fundraising on behalf of activists and cutting-edge projects around the world; in Ecuador to protect the Amazon headwaters from the ravages of the oil industry; a film I produced with David Attenborough and Olivia Newton-John to help protect the endangered forest species on New South Wales and the reforestation of Arunachala.

Shiva's Mountain

My retreat with Papaji was drawing to a close, but there was still one place I had to visit: the great mountain Arunachala, in Tiruvanamalai, 18 hours south by train.

Nearly ten years before, in 1987, I had received a letter from Apeetha Arunagiri, an Australian nun residing in the Sri Ramana Ashram at the foot of Arunachala. She wrote that when Ramana had arrived there, the holy mountain was clothed in lush forest and one might even meet a tiger walking on its flanks. Now little grew there but thorns and goats. Terrible erosion trenched Shiva's sides, and torrents of mud attended each monsoon. She had heard about our work for the forests. Could we please help her to reclothe the sacred mountain?

I had composed a reply to Apeetha, encouraging her in her efforts but pleading that we had no competence in reforestation or the rehabilitation of degraded landscapes – our mission was the protection of intact ecosystems. But it was no use, I couldn't send the letter. Ramana's smiling face, which I had first seen smiling from the back of his book *Who Am I?* in London in 1970, kept popping up before me. So we raised some money and sent it to Apeetha. Through her efforts a local NGO was born, the Annamalai Reforestation Society. The following summer solstice I was facilitating a Council of All Beings workshop at John Button's shack at Sundari community in northern New South Wales. John was a permaculture designer and tree-planter who was heading for the deserts of central Australia to become involved in a tree-planting project. For some reason I asked him if he would like to try this in the deserts of Tamil Nadu instead. He asked for details, and when I mentioned Ramana, his face turned pale and he told me that he was a long-time devotee of Ramana.

Since that time, John and his partner, Heather Bache, helped organize the rehabilitation of Arunachala. The space between the inner and outer walls of the vast 23-acre temple complex has been transformed from a wasteland into the largest tree nursery in the south of India. Hundreds of people had received environmental education, and a 12-acre patch of semi-desert was donated to the project and transformed into a lush demonstration of permaculture and the miraculous recuperative powers of the Earth.

Hundreds of Tamil people have now been trained in reforestation skills – tree identification, seed collection, nursery techniques, watershed management, erosion control, sustainable energy systems. Shiva's robes are slowly being rewoven. Furthermore, hundreds more have been trained in the techniques of permaculture, inspired by the Annamalai Reforestation Society's model farm.

The train finally rolled into Tiruvanamalai and I was able to visit Arunachala myself and see the tremendous work that had been done to revegetate the sacred mountain. Upon my arrival I discovered that many people there believe that to walk around the base of Arunachala is the fastest way to enlightenment. Each full moon, tens or hundreds of thousands of devotees and pilgrims do so. It upset me to see the indifference with which most of these folks regarded our work. Most were oblivious, but some even complained that the newly planted trees interfered with their view of the sunset. A great deal had been accomplished by the Annamalai Reforestation Society, but how much more could be achieved if only the pilgrims would realize the unity of the spirit and the Earth!

What if their worship of Shiva included devotion to his physical body, Arunachala? Imagine if they lent a hand to the planting and maintenance of the trees as part of their devotion? The greening of the mountain would be accelerated. I was giving talks and lectures in the town and I began to challenge the ecological indifference I found and to propose to the pilgrims that surely the act of worship and respect of watering the young saplings that were weaving themselves into robes to cover his nakedness was an even faster route to liberation than circumambulating the mountain.

A week later I was stricken with remorse. How could I be so presumptuous as to make such claims without having even asked Shiva? So one morning I climbed the mountain and found a quiet place among the trees to meditate and pray and apologize. After some time I opened my eyes to a noise. Some monkeys had appeared from the young forest. Slowly they filed past and stood guard while scores of their tribe came into view, and then they began to relax.

They groomed each other, they made love, mothers breast-fed their babies, children played and cavorted, utterly unself-consciously living their everyday lives in my astonished and grateful presence. I saw a new-born infant cautiously explore the ground, leaving the safety of her mother's body for what seemed to me the first time, and leaping back and climbing her fur at the slightest noise or disturbance. I had never felt more accepted by the nonhuman world. I knew that Shiva had answered my prayer, had acknowledged my efforts, and was giving me his sign of approval.

It doesn't really matter what symbols we use – Shiva, Gaia, Buddha, God. What we need now is for the followers of all faiths to turn their allegiance to the Earth. What matters is that we refuse to be drawn to one or the other of the great polarities: spirit and Earth. We must neither reduce everything to spirit, from where it appears that the material world is some kind of illusion, nor reduce everything to the material, so that it looks as if spiritual seekers are abdicating responsibility to care for the creation.

John Seed

Further Reading
Badiner, Allan Hunt, ed. *Dharma Gaia*. Berkeley, CA: Parallax Press, 1990.
Berry, Thomas. *The Dream of the Earth*. San Francisco: Sierra Club, 1990.
Devall, Bill. *Simple in Means, Rich in Ends: Practicing Deep Ecology*. Salt Lake City, UT: Peregrine Smith, 1988.
Foreman, Dave. *Confessions of an Eco-Warrior*. New York: Harmony Books, 1991.
Macy, Joanna. *Widening Circles: A Memoir*. Philadelphia: *New Society Publishers*, 2000.
Macy, Joanna. *Coming Back to Life: Practices to Reconnect Our Lives, Our World*. Philadelphia: *New Society Publishers*, 1998.
Macy, Joanna. *World as Lover, World as Self*. Berkeley, CA: Parallax Press, 1991.
Manders, Jerry. *In The Absence of the Sacred*. San Francisco: Sierra Club, 1991.
Naess, Arne. *Ecology, Community and Lifestyle*. New York: Cambridge University Press, 1989.
Roszak, Theodore. *The Voice of the Earth*. New York: Simon & Schuster, 1992.
Shiva, Vandana and Maria Mies. *Ecofeminism*. London: Zed Books, 1994.
Snyder, Gary. *The Practice of the Wild*. San Francisco: North Point Press, 1990.
Swimme, Brian and Thomas Berry. *The Universe Story*. New York: HarperCollins, 1992.

See also: Biocentric Religion – A Call for; Council of All Beings; Deep Ecology; Earth First! and the Earth Liberation Front; Entheogens; Epic of Evolution; Hopiland to the Rainforest Action Network; Macy, Joanna; Paganism – Contemporary; Psychonauts; Radical Environmentalism; Seed, John; Shiva, Vandana; Snyder, Gary.

Reichel-Dolmatoff, Gerardo (1912–1994) – and Ethnoecology in Colombia

Gerardo Reichel-Dolmatoff, anthropologist, ethnographer, archeologist, ethnoecologist, ethnohistorian and ethnoastronomist, carried out extensive research in Colombia (South America) among the Amerindians of the Amazon (Vaupes), Caribbean coast (Uraba, Guajira, Sierra Nevada), Pacific Coast (Choco), Andean and inter-Andean areas, and in the savannah area of the Llanos.

Reichel-Dolmatoff was one of the founders of Colombian anthropology and archeology. As an ethnographer he lived for decades among indigenous peoples and was a staunch defender of Amerindian peoples. The author of over 20 books and 300 articles on prehistoric and contemporary Amerindians, Reichel-Dolmatoff also was a member of scientific institutions such as the National Academy of Sciences of the United States, the Academy of Sciences of Colombia, the Third World Academy of Sciences, and the Linnean Society of London, among others.

Reichel-Dolmatoff's anthropological work contains detailed ethnographies on dozens of Amerindian cultures and contributes significant theories and methodologies. For example, he analyzed indigenous shamanism, cosmologies and worldviews as templates for socio-environmental analysis and conservation, and related these to specific religious systems, modes of subsistence, socio-political structures, medicine, art, philosophies, and ethics that are used by communities to achieve long-term environmental and social well-being. He largely documented this among the Tukano Indians of the Northwest Amazon (Vaupes) and among the Kogi Indians of the Sierra Nevada de Santa Marta on the Caribbean coast.

Reichel-Dolmatoff pioneered archeological research in many Colombian regions and produced the first interpretive overviews of the millenarian cultural evolution of Colombia. He discovered, among others, early formative sites in the Caribbean area, which documented the (then) most ancient pottery of the Americas that was related to the origins of sedentary subsistence and agriculture tribal societies 6000 years ago.

In addition, he analyzed the symbolism of material culture, and particularly of goldwork, crystals, basketry, ceremonial items, and vernacular architecture – such as the Amazon *maloca* communal longhouse or the Kogi temple – advancing new theories on the shamanism and the cosmologies underlying such objects and artifacts of memory. His work emphasized the great values of indigenous cultures for their wise, respectful, and ethical modes of balancing community well-being with socio-environmental sustainability. He contrasted these to ecocidal and ethnocidal non-indigenous cultures and insisted that they halt the destruction of Amerindian societies.

Life and Work

Reichel-Dolmatoff, who became a Colombian citizen in 1941, was one of the founders of Colombian Anthropology in the 1940s under the direction of French ethnologist Paul Rivet. During the 1940s and 1950s Reichel-Dolmatoff was a member of the National Institute of Ethnology, creator and Director of the Magdalena Ethnological Institute, a professor at the University of Cartagena and founding member of the Colombian Institute of Anthropology. During those two decades he carried out ethnographic research among the indigenous groups of the Guahibo, Pijao, Yuko, Chimila, Chami, Kogi, Ika, Sanka, Embera, Noanama, Cuna and Guajiro, among others. He also engaged in archeological excavations in the Andean, Atlantic and Pacific regions and lower Magdalena area.

In his two-volume monograph, published in 1949 and 1951, of the Kogi Indians (Chibcha speakers) of the Sierra Nevada de Santa Marta, and a series of other publications, he investigated Kogi spirituality from an emic (insider/folk/vernacular) perspective through concepts such as "sewa," "yuluka," and "aluna" that indicated the profound indigenous understanding of nature and society in cosmological context and their application for sound socio-ecological management. Because the Kogi hold that their society is part of a world that lies between four skies and a netherworld of four underworlds in a multileveled and interconnected cosmos created by the Great Mother, he analyzed how the use of natural resources involves ritually "asking permission" to the supernatural Guardians, Owners or Lords of the resources, as well as an effective "payment" in "Thought" and in action to restore ecosystem balance. Reichel-Dolmatoff underlined how the "Mama" shaman-priests guided these agricultural mountain individuals and collectivities to reach a "balanced" life within nature, and he described Kogi life as sober, dignified and respectful of the environment and communal conviviality. He studied dozens of other indigenous cultures which shared many of these features, though the struggle of the Kogi to maintain their traditional cultures he found unique.

Linking his archeological, anthropological and ethnohistorical investigations of the Sierra Nevada region, Reichel-Dolmatoff made the first regional and diachronic analysis of the area to investigate biocultural dynamics among indigenous peoples and mestizo (1961) peasant communities. He contrasted the modes by which they conceived, used or abused nature. Indians respected nature, underused resources or replaced them, and balanced resource extraction with population control or sustainable conservation, while making material and spiritual "payments" to the Guardian "Owners" of nature. Non-Indians, he found, generally exploited and destroyed nature and other peoples, and specifically despised Indians and their forms of resource management.

Reichel-Dolmatoff not only made the first stratigraphic excavations in the area, but also established chronologies and typologies and interpreted the cultural dynamics occurring in mountain, desert, rainforest and coastal ecosystems of northern Colombia. He created and directed a museum in Santa Marta where he highlighted the great value of the prehistoric and contemporary Amerindian cultures and their social and ecological wisdom. This was unprecedented in Colombia.

In 1963 he founded and chaired Colombia's first Department of Anthropology (Universidad de Los Andes, Bogota). During the 1960s he engaged in fieldwork in the Vaupes area of the Amazon among the Desana Indians (Eastern Tukano speakers) and other Amazon peoples. His publications on Desana cosmology, shamanism, social organization, ethnoastronomy, ethnobiology, art, narcotics and hallucinogens (or entheogens), vernacular architecture and the symbolism of "maloca" longhouse; and on native concepts of territory and ecosystem, pioneered a new era of Amazonian structuralist anthropology.

In 1973 he became affiliated with the University of California Los Angeles as Adjunct Professor. Between the 1970s and 1990s he continued ethnographic research and developed ethnoecology as a category of interpretive anthropology requiring intercultural and interdisciplinary research. Among the Kogi and the Desana (Tukano) Indians he expanded analyses on socio-environmental management, ethnoecology, shamanism, cosmology, worldview, ethnoastronomy, mythology, art, material culture, ritual, and on neurocognition, ethnopsychology, ethnomedicine, pharmacology, and environmental anthropology. He studied the role of hallucinogens and narcotic plants in shamanism (1978b, 1975) within their social and religious contexts to reinforce ecological decision making, and he analyzed the myths, rituals, and altered states of awareness they engaged. He examined the hallucinatory imagery during the ritual intake of *Banisteriopsis* and indicated how the visualization of phosphenes (universal optical perceptions) were interpreted with shamanic cultural codes to correct socio-ecological malfunctioning. He made exceptional analyses of the modes by which shamans guided communities in their use of narcotics, hallucinogens, altered states of awareness and experience of the sacred in order to reenchant biosocial existence within a grander cosmic context in such a way as to promote respect for all forms of being and sentience.

Based on a paradigm that Reichel-Dolmatoff termed "Cosmology as Ecological Analysis" (1976) in the Huxley Memorial Lecture, he examined Amerindian cosmologies as templates that are used to generate updated ecological analysis and accountability, and which are applied for sustainable resource use. He related cosmologies to subsistence patterns, environmental management strategies, population density, dispute-settlement mechanisms, and to an ethos of shared responsibility among neighboring cultures to control socio-environmental imbalances and lead a peaceful coexistence. Portraying the Desana as pragmatic peoples and profound thinkers who are efficient planners with highly adaptive behavioral rules to manage rainforest ecosystems, and who recreate effective institutions and coherent belief and value systems to do so, Reichel-Dolmatoff explained the importance of their ecological eidos and ethos, indicating the importance of the coherence of their socio-political, economic and religious systems.

Between the 1970s and 1990s Reichel-Dolmatoff developed the field of ethnoecology and demonstrated the importance of indigenous ecological knowledge and traditional ecological skills. He emphasized the importance of apprehending the Indians' own concepts and understanding of their ecological practices and beliefs.

He demonstrated how Amerindians consider their universe or cosmos to be composed of a network of skies, Earth, and underworlds which are interconnected by common forces of energy, "Thought," spirit, or matter, deemed to exist in a finite quantity and which require permanent and careful management. Each of these levels of the universes is believed to have supernatural Guardians who are "Owners" of parts of nature and of resources with whom shamans negotiate human existence by exchanging, or not exchanging, quotas of these finite forces. Thus, for Reichel-Dolmatoff, the conceptual dualism or opposition between nature and society is not extant among Amerindians such as the Kogi and Desana, and this cultural awareness that echoes the laws of nature, he concluded, is common wisdom among other indigenous societies in spite of their threatened cultures and territories.

Reichel-Dolmatoff conducted his research in collaboration with his Colombian wife, anthropologist and archeologist Alicia Dussan. He died in Bogotá in 1994 after dedicating more than fifty years to studying the religious and ecological values of Amerindian peoples, and to disseminating the relevance of the indigenous cultures of Colombia.

Nature and Society among the Kogi and Desana

Reichel-Dolmatoff's research among the Kogi Indians of the Sierra Nevada mountains, and among the Desana and Tukano Indians of the Amazon rainforest, pioneered research methodologies and theories of relevance for ethnoecology, shamanism, cosmology and worldviews, and he indicated how their communities used these to live balanced lives based on sound social and environmental management. While analyzing how these Amerindians consider that their society is embedded within nature, the world, and the cosmos, he explored the relevance of the indigenous ethics of care and respect for all forms of existence. He highlighted that this awareness was the result of acute observations and millenarian experimentation upon the ecosystems and of human activity within these.

Reichel-Dolmatoff held that the Desana's beliefs and practices are grounded in their cosmologies and worldviews. He demonstrated how cosmologies are used by shamans to monitor human activities in particular rainforest ecosystems in the Amazon and he analyzed the indigenous concepts, terms, symbols, principles, practices, and socio-ecological codes to do so. Interpreting how shamans seek to make calibrations between the microcosmos and the macrocosmos in rituals throughout the year and in individual rites of passage, as well as in subsistence practices such as foraging or agriculture, or in medicinal practices and in conflict management, Reichel-Dolmatoff showed how Desana shamanism correlates seasonal socio-ecological dynamics within the larger ecological, climatic, meteorological, astronomical and cosmic referents to monitor the place of human agency within. These cosmic linkages engage a three-leveled universe (sky, world, underworld) composing a closed system that is connected by circuits of limited energy, spirit and matter where the birth or death of one being affects others. In the shamanic geography and topography, these linkages are projected in sacred sites (hills, caves, rapids, spaces demarcating founding acts in cosmogenesis and ethnogenesis), in the borders and centers of ethnic territories, and in sacred spaces in each maloca longhouse.

Desana Indians reiterate their care of and respect for the beings and forces that compose the world and cosmos. Through shamans and elders they "ask permission," and pay the Masters (Jaguar-Shamans) or "Guardian Spirits" of the animals, plants, soils, winds, waters, and of seasons, skies, earths, and underworlds, to use resources and to harmonize their lives with new seasons, years and eras.

Thus before the Desana Indians hunt tapirs or deer, for example, the shaman "asks" the Guardian Spirits or Master of the Animals for "permission" to hunt. The shaman ritually negotiates with the Master in their abodes deliberating how to replace the predatory activity, though it is termed also as a form of courtship and exchange. The shaman, consuming coca, tobacco, or hallucinogens, also "flies" across the different levels of the cosmos and across diverse ecosystems as a bird, or may roam as a jaguar or some other predator to negotiate with the Owners of nature and the universe in order to "retrieve" lost souls of sick or dying people, or to punish other humans for overutilizing resources.

The shamans "repay" the Owners of nature for any resources that are to be exploited, and they seek to replace the "energy" or "spirit" in exchange for human lives of people who are to be sick or die, while promising to prevent the future overutilization of resources by all the people of his community who are held to constitute a single unit of socio-ecological responsibility. The shamans continually induce the community, which lives together in a maloca longhouse, to respect the limited availability of matter, energy and spirit, and they permanently seek to solve conflicts over resource use, while collectively men and women do so along gender lines. According to Reichel-Dolmatoff, the symbolism of the maloca communal longhouse also reflects the architecture of the interconnected three-leveled cosmos to remind each community that it is a sentient part of the world and universe. The Desana thus consider their societies to be a part of nature, and that all ecosystems are embedded within the planet and the cosmos, according to Reichel-Dolmatoff (1971, 1976, 1978a, 1979, 1986, 1989, 1981, 1990, 1996a, 1996b, 1997).

All ecosystems are correlated to grander cycles of the world, skies and underworlds, deemed to be affected not only by the energy of the sun and by climatic and astronomical changes, but by the forces of ancestors and spirits. The territories that belong to ethnic groups are also categorized in cosmological terms, and their rivers, mountains, and sacred sites, have cosmological connections to the skies and underworlds.

The different neighboring groups who share environmental responsibility are likewise inscribed into the symbolism of their territories, and the structure of pan-tribal organization and of marriage alliances and of reciprocal exchange of goods and services are reflected in the symbolism of the landscape to engage kin and allies in joint resource management.

The Desana's own categories and classificatory codes pertaining to ecosystem structure and function are coded according to energy levels and to sensorial categories such as color, smell, shape, or such, and through the imagery of a sexualized polarity, according to Reichel-Dolmatoff. Territorial boundaries that refer to the six phratries (kinship groups) that compose the twenty Tukanoan tribes, and the three exogamic units (one is the Desana) are related to the imagery of hexagonal crystals that correlate to the sky, Earth, and underworld, and to astronomical referents (delimited by Pollux, Procycon, Canopus, Achernar, T3 Eridani, and Capella with Epsilon Orion in the center). Altogether this shamanic topography codifies specific cultural behaviors in demarcated spaces to avoid socio-environmental malfunctioning, though the cosmology implies an enchanted universe. Using these shamanic references, the Desana men and women manage resources at local and pan-regional scales, recreating their semi-sedentary life as foragers and shifting cultivators through the concerted conservation, use or redistribution of goods, services, or marriage partners among allied groups intent on enhancing communal coexistence, restricting the mismanagement of natural resources, reducing social violence and fomenting environmental conservation for future generations.

Among the Kogi of the Sierra Nevada mountains, Reichel-Dolmatoff analyzed how their cosmology and worldview permeates both ceremonial and daily life and their wise and austere use of natural resources. He investigated their concepts of the universe to understand the overall scheme through which they managed biocultural resources within their religious systems, and the symbolism of cosmogenesis and ethnogenesis.

The shape of the Kogi cosmos is believed to be composed of nine layers (four skies above, four underworlds below, and this world in the middle – the latter is the flat disc of the spindle used by the Great Mother to demarcate Kogi territory). The skies, Earth and underworlds are believed to be affected by the path of the sun between solstices and equinoxes, and by the path of the moon and other astronomical phenomena, as well as by meteorological, climatic, hydrological and other environmental dynamics which the Kogi monitor while alluding to their communication with the Lords, Masters, Fathers and Mothers of the universe, resources, and to their ancestors.

This model of the cosmos is reiterated in the symbolism of the Kogi territory, and it is also expressed in the layout of villages, in lithic astronomical observatories, in the architecture of their village temples, as well as in certain objects of material culture and in the symbolism of the human body. These mnemonic devices are used by the Kogi as "polymetaphoric thought patterns," according to Reichel-Dolmatoff (1987: 78), to interpret how to achieve a life of "completeness" or to achieve spiritual depth and high-ranking. "Mama" priests and elders use them as references to counsel individuals and communities to achieve a transcendental existence. With ritual ceremonies, dream analysis, divinatory practices, pilgrimages, confessions and meditation, they guide people toward an austere and balanced life.

Reichel-Dolmatoff analyzed how the model of the Kogi cosmos is projected in the symbolism of the architecture of their temples. The four skies are represented in the four rafters of the roof, and the world is represented in four hearths that indicate a sacred square that is delimited by the path of the sun between solstices and equinoxes (since the temples are also used as astronomical observatories). According to lineage affiliation, each Kogi sits by one of the four hearths to discuss the "laws of the ancestors," changing places throughout the year. A series of invisible and inverted temples are held to exist in the dark underworlds (with a black sun), which represent invisible but important realities.

Reichel-Dolmatoff demonstrated that this symbolism projects the form of the cosmos with key features of astronomy, geography, ecology, and social and political organization, linking past, present and future generations. According to Reichel-Dolmatoff, the symbolism of the

Kogi weaving loom corresponds to that of the temple, linking the structure of the cosmos to that of Kogi territory within the Sierra Nevada mountain environment and to the intermarrying Kogi lineages, and past with present and future generations, reminding the Kogi to reject material accumulation and promote the acquisition of wisdom, and the goal of socio-environmental sustainability in the short, mid- and long term.

The deep religious tradition of the Kogi and their quest to master the "balance" of mind and spirit and a balanced life, and their self-reference as the "Elder Brothers" who are the custodians of the world and universe because the white peoples or "Little Brothers" have forgotten their responsibility toward nature, led Reichel-Dolmatoff to investigate the many lessons the Amerindians have for the contemporary world. He urged Colombians and international forces to respect the cultures, lands, spiritualities, cosmologies, and modes of life of Amerindians such as the Kogi who are truly engaged in sustainable development and in concert with the laws of nature. According to Reichel-Dolmatoff, the "ideological foundations of Kogi culture and society" (1987: 75) are exemplary and he states

> I truly believe that the Kogi, and many other traditional societies, can greatly contribute to a better understanding and handling of some of our modern dilemmas, and that we should consider ourselves fortunate to be the contemporaries of a people, who, perhaps, can teach us to achieve a measure of "balance" (1987: 112).

Reichel-Dolmatoff's last three books, *The Forest Within* (1996a), *Yurupari: Studies of an Amazonian Foundation Myth* (1996b), and *Rainforest Shamans* (1997) offer an overview of his understanding of the Amazon Indians in relation to nature. For the Kogi Indians, this overview appeared previously in his monograph on the Kogi and notably in articles such as "The Loom of Life: A Kogi Principle of Integration"; "Some Kogi Models of the Beyond"; "The Great Mother and the Kogi Universe"; and "Cultural Change and Environmental Awareness."

Conclusion

Reichel-Dolmatoff pioneered anthropological, archeological and ethnoecological research in Colombia. He analyzed the modes by which Amerindian social, political, economic, religious, philosophical, medical, artistic, and ethical systems were used by diverse indigenous societies to sustainably manage biocultural resources and live in community-based bands, tribes and chiefdoms. He indicated how Amerindians planned resource use, demographic density, land and water use, and managed residence and subsistence patterns for sustainable resource conservation, and he indicated that these dynamics could only be understood within their cosmological and shamanic contexts.

According to Reichel-Dolmatoff, Amerindian conservation of resources is calculated within short-, mid- and long-term frameworks, and engages collaboration between local, regional and pan-regional contexts that are sentient of the interdependent linkages among all living beings and forms of existence across humanity, the biosphere, world, and cosmos. The Amerindian calibration of resource-use follows a millenarian shamanic tradition that avoids ecocide and foments communal conviviality, and these practices echo the Amerindian understanding that they form part of nature, and explain why they deem ecosystems to be linked to forces in the skies, Earth, and underworlds in order to foster sustained resource conservation. Reichel-Dolmatoff demonstrated that among traditional contemporary indigenous cultures there is no concept of a separate existence or opposition between nature and society nor motifs to dominate or exploit a subordinate domain of nature and peoples, and he analyzed the role of these lessons of Amerindian shamanism, cosmologies and worldviews in the making of the biological and cultural diversity in Colombia, while defending the indigenous peoples' rights to their cultures and lands.

Reichel-Dolmatoff was one of the first scholars to recognize and interpret what is now called "Traditional Ecological Knowledge," "Indigenous Knowledge Systems" and "Ethnoecology."

Elizabeth Reichel

Further Reading

Reichel-Dolmatoff, Gerardo. *Rainforest Shamans: Essays on the Tukano Indians of the Northwest Amazon.* London: Themis-Green Books, 1997.

Reichel-Dolmatoff, Gerardo. *The Forest Within: The Worldview of the Tukano Amazonian Indians.* London: Themis-Green Books, 1996a.

Reichel-Dolmatoff, Gerardo. *Yurupari : Studies of an Amazonian Foundation Myth.* Cambridge, MA: Harvard University Press, 1996b.

Reichel-Dolmatoff, Gerardo. *A View From the Headwaters: A Colombian Anthropologist Looks at the Amazon and Beyond.* In *Ethnobiology: Implications and Applications: Proceedings of First International Congress of Ethnobiology (Belem 1988).* Belem, Brazil: Museu Parense, 1990, 9–17.

Reichel-Dolmatoff, Gerardo. "Desana Texts and Contexts." *Acta Ethnologica et Linguistica: Series Americana* 12:62 (1989), Vienna-Foehrenau.

Reichel-Dolmatoff, Gerardo. "The Great Mother and the Kogi Universe: A Concise Overview." *Journal of Latin American Lore* 13:1 (1987), 73–113.

Reichel-Dolmatoff, Gerardo. "A Hunter's Tale From the

Colombian Northwest Amazon." *Journal of Latin American Lore* 12:1 (1986), 65–74.

Reichel-Dolmatoff, Gerardo. "Some Kogi Models of the Beyond." *Journal of Latin American Lore* 19:1 (1984), 63–85.

Reichel-Dolmatoff, Gerardo. "The Kogi Indians and the Environment: Impending Disaster." *The Ecologist* 13:1 (1983) 13–18.

Reichel-Dolmatoff, Gerardo. "Cultural Change and Environmental Awareness: A Case Study of the Sierra Nevada de Santa Marta." *Mountain Research and Development* 2:3 (1982), 289–98.

Reichel-Dolmatoff, Gerardo. "Astronomical Models of Social Behavior among some Indians of Colombia." In *Ethnoastronomy and Archaeastronomy in the American Tropics*. Anthony Aveni and Gary Urton, eds. New York: New York Academy of Sciences, 1982, 165–81.

Reichel-Dolmatoff, Gerardo. "Desana Shaman's Rock Crystal and the Hexagonal Universe." *Journal of Latin American Lore* 5:1 (1979), 117–28.

Reichel-Dolmatoff, Gerardo. "Desana Animal Categories, Food Restrictions and the Concept of Color Categories." *Journal of Latin American Lore* 4:2 (1978a), 243–91.

Reichel-Dolmatoff, Gerardo. "The Loom of Life: A Kogi Principle of Integration." *Journal of Latin American Lore* 4:1 (1978b), 5–27.

Reichel-Dolmatoff, Gerardo. "Cosmology as Ecological Analysis: A View from the Rainforest." *Man* 2:3 (1976), 307–18.

Reichel-Dolmatoff, Gerardo. *The Shaman and the Jaguar: A Study of Narcotic Drugs among the Indians of Colombia*. Philadelphia: Temple University Press, 1975.

Reichel-Dolmatoff, Gerardo. *Amazonian Cosmos*. Chicago: University of Chicago Press, 1971.

See also: Amazonia; Anthropologists; Anthropology as a Source of Nature Religion; Ecology and Religion; Entheogens; Ethnobotany; Ethnoecology; Kogi (Northern Colombia); Rainforests (Central and South America); Shamanism – Ecuador; Shamanism – Traditional; Religious Environmentalist Paradigm; Traditional Ecological Knowledge; Tukanoan Indians (Northwest Amazonia); U'wa Indians (Colombia); Yanomami.

A Religio-Ecological Perspective on Religion and Nature

If the study of religion is a science, as the German term *religionswissenschaft* posits, then some of its methods should allow a degree of predictability. One such approach is that of religio-ecology. The method was developed by the Swedish scholar, Åke Hultkrantz, who pioneered a social scientific comparative study of religion. The approach was stimulated by the anthropological method of cultural ecology, developed by William Sanders, as a means to study the evolution of Mesoamerican urbanism from its earliest roots.

In essence, religio-ecology is an approach to the study of religion that considers religion in the context of a culture's ecological *gestalt*, including the various relationships between humans (social, economic, political, etc.), as well as the relationships of humans to animals, plants, climate, terrain, geography, etc. Although religio-ecology was initially used to examine Native American religious traditions, especially those in gathering-hunting and horticultural-hunting situations, if the methodology is valid, then it should be applicable to all cultures in all stages of development, including contemporary societies. To demonstrate this hypothesis, as well as the possibility of generalized predictability, a half-dozen religio-ecological paradigms will be briefly examined with regard to the religious and other understandings of nature, with a focus on animals: gathering-hunting, horticulture-hunting, herding, agricultural, industrial, and post-industrial cultures.

Among contemporary humans maintaining gathering-hunting cultural traditions, the entire cosmos is understood to be numinous (having an aura of sacredness), including animals and plants, particularly those on which human life, in various ways, depends. These understandings may, to a degree, be read back into the earliest human cultures, as they accord with Paleolithic art in their representation of animals and, rarely, humans. Such cultures understand that the world is a family in which humans are inferior members. Every encounter with a nonhuman being is with an entity that is simultaneously a natural and a spiritual being. Sought after animals and plants, gifts of the Earth mother, in various guises, must be supplicated to offer their individual lives so that pitiable humans may live. Every act of hunting larger animals, as well as gathering plants, sea creatures and smaller animals is ritualized. Predatory animals are spiritual models for the human hunters, and the dog is a hunting companion, whose sacrifice, as well as that of the human-like bear, is essentially a substitute for human self-sacrifice to the numinous realm. Shamanistic trance enables humans intimately to interact with theriomorphic spirits (spirits in animal form).

When plants are domesticated with the development of horticulture, the gathering-hunting religious understanding of the cosmos continues. The domesticated plants, however, understood as daughters of Earth, gain ritual preeminence over animals, as do the roles of females, who primarily carry out the gardening. Those animals that are domesticated are no longer understood to be spiritual entities superior to humans, but members of the human community ranging from quasi-children to pets, whose every slaughter is a ritual sacrifice. Hunted animals continue to be supplicated and treated with considerable respect as in the gathering-hunting religio-ecological niche. But the shift from semi-nomadism to semi-settled living-patterns leads to a closer relationship with the matrilineal-matrilocal family and clan dead. This begins a transition from theriomorphic and plant spirits to anthropomorphic spirits (spirits in human form). Outside of the Americas, this led to a shift from shamanism to mediumism, as the living members of the clan sought the advice of the clan dead.

Semi-nomadic gathering-hunting cultures that domesticate migratory herding animals, most recently occurring among reindeer hunters of northern Eurasia, underwent a major shift in the religious conception of the particular animal or animals on which their economy depends. No longer individual numinous entities, the domesticated herds as a whole are understood to be a gift from their female numinous superior. Gifts of sacrificed animals from the herd are in turn offered to her. The human hunter shifts to the role of the "good shepherd." Animal predators are no longer spiritual role models for human hunters but enemies of the herded animals, for whose welfare humans are responsible. As hunting activities shift to herding, those ritual activities associated with shamanism are no longer generalized among the population as an essential aspect of hunting and gathering but become concentrated among ecstatic religious specialists.

The horticultural-hunting religious understanding of animals and plants continues with the rise of agriculture, but there are significant socio-economic transformations. The majority of males shift from hunting-raiding-trading roles to farming, while females continue their gardening-nurturing roles. With the average male no longer expert with hunting weapons, warrior specialists supported by surplus agricultural productivity tend to become the hereditary elite of a stratified social order, and the matrilineal-matrilocal pattern tends to shift toward a patrilineal-patrilocal pattern in consequence of the increased importance of the male roles. When warriors become the rulers, this patrofocal pattern tends toward patriarchy. Warriors also become ritual specialists, or a separate caste of female and male priests develops. The spirit realm now consists of ancestors, divinized ghosts, and/or anthropomorphic deities who were not previously human. These deities are understood in hierarchies modeled on the now-stratified human socio-political structures. An offshoot of this development, which occurred in one culture, becoming the basis for Western civilization, is for the male chief of the divinities to be considered the sole divinity of the culture, the "king of kings."

With a patrofocal social stratification between elite males who use weapons and the majority of males who wield farming implements, hunting of large animals becomes the prerogative of the elite as ritualized practice for warfare, also ritualized. Hence, undomesticated animals are treated as respected human enemies. Domesticated animals continue to be slaughtered solely in sacrificial rituals, but these rituals tend to be carried out by professional ritual specialists who are separated from the raising of the animals, no longer understood as quasi-children. Save for the Religions of the Book (Judaism, Christianity, and Islam), aristocrats play a major role in these sacrifices, which comprised primarily the offering of food and alcoholic beverages to the spirits. But the aristocrats tend to distance themselves from the actual slaughtering of the animals for the meat dishes; the killing and butchering being left to professionals. Remnants of this pattern continue in Western culture in the Jewish and Islamic ritualized slaughter of animals by religious specialists.

The concentration of hunting activities among the elite as an avocation serves to create a disjunction among the general populace from the undomesticated world, leading to the concepts of wilderness and wild animals. Culture distinguishes humans from animals, as well as humans of different cultures, now understood as "wild" humans or barbarians. Humans no longer relate to wild animals as sacred beings but as savage beasts to be tamed and/or killed. Spanish culture maintains a resplendent version of both these archaic perspectives – taming and killing – in the highly ritualized *corrida des toros*, although the modern ritual in itself is not of great antiquity.

With agriculture, the relationship between humans and animals falls into four distinctive categories. For the elite, animals are 1) pets, either playthings or facilitators for human hunting; 2) working domesticants, particularly the horse, used for warfare and hunting, that become romanticized along with warriors toward the ends of these periods; 3) domesticated animals for ritualized consumption; 4) or wild beasts, often found in royal hunting parks, ritually hunted with the same weapons used in warfare. The peasants raise the domesticated animals, ritually slaughtered and eaten by the elite, although peasants rarely have the opportunity to eat these animals themselves. As they are responsible to the elite for their welfare, predatory animals are feared by the peasants for their predations and killed when possible. Game animals (notice our language in this regard) are forbidden to them, being reserved for the elite; peasants who are caught hunting these animals are liable to be executed. The middle class fall somewhere in between, of course, depending on their status.

In the transition from horticulture to agriculture, the understanding of plants changes from revered spiritual relatives to desired entities whose sole purpose is the nourishment or other use of humans, or undesired entities, such as weeds, which hinders the growth of the farmed plants. Similarly, animals also change from revered spiritual relatives to entities whose sole purpose is to feed or be of other use to humans, entities who threaten those animals, or entities that can be killed for practice in preparation for warfare. Of course, there are many cultural variations and moderate exceptions to this pattern.

In India, for example, cows became a special case, due to the unusual, virtually exclusive, dependence on them for animal protein (milk and milk products), edible oil (clarified butter), traction (draft animals) and fuel (dried dung). Hence, the concept of cows in India is closer to the understanding of animals in horticulture-hunting traditions than agricultural societies. But in India, hunting still tends to be reserved for the hereditary aristocracy or the new aristocracy modeled on the former British colonizers, save for remnant pockets of horticultural-hunting villages in the interior mountains.

Further changes in socio-economic structures leads to increasing distance from the earlier human patterns in these relationships. As industrial manufacturing desacralized metals, clay and wood, so the spread of industry over agriculture led to the desacralizing of Earth, plants and animals in every regard. It is to be noted that this process begins in Christian cultures that had long since limited the numinous to the male Sky and understood the female Earth, as well as human females, to be the locus of evil. Industrial manufacturing and the spread of industrial practices to agriculture also led to the increasing urbanization of the population, further distancing the average person from an intimacy with domesticated plants and animals, save for pets, which tend to be understood as quasi-humans rather than animals, and ornamental plants. Agribusiness factory production of meat and grain leads to animals and grain plants no longer understood as beings, let alone as relatives or gifts from the sacred realm. Undomesticated animals now are neither sacred entities nor respected enemies but anthropomorphized, desacralized fantasies: the "Bambi" syndrome.

Only among the anachronistic remnants of the European aristocracy or their industrial-era replacements (factory owners, etc.) does hunting continue combined with respect for and acknowledgment of a special nature of hunted animals (who cannot be accorded numinous status in monotheistic traditions). Non-urbanized Euroamericans, lacking a hereditary aristocracy, maintain hunting as a ritual of Americanism which renews their connections with a mythicized "pioneer" past and wilderness onto which is projected a sacred aura of pristine purity.

In the post-industrial world, where virtual reality is increasingly replacing normative reality, the traditional real world is becoming transformed into a realm of fantasy, and experience in nature *qua* nature is being replaced by actual (e.g., dirt bikes and "personal water craft") and vicarious thrills. Animals become valued with no understanding of their life cycles and ecological situations and are understood to be utterly divorced from food. Cellophane-wrapped meat is not understood, from either the emotional or the religious standpoint, to come from living animals, just as factory-manufactured, cellophane-wrapped bread or pasta is not understood to come from living plants. The various traditional ritual relationships with animals and plants completely disappear to be replaced by concepts of "cuteness"; wild animals are perceived no differently than non-working pets. Hence, campaigns are mounted against hunting in general, regardless of potential disastrous consequences for non-competitive herbivores in terrains where natural predators have been exterminated, and hunters become the epitome of evil.

The distancing of humans from animals, plants, and Earth in post-industrial cultures becomes absolute. Theriomorphic and plant spirits, once replaced by anthropomorphic spirits, are for an increasing number of contemporary Westerners now replaced by alien spirits from cosmically distant sacred realms. The North American spiritual journey into romanticized wilderness has been superseded by fantasized alien abduction.

Jordan Paper

Further Reading

Hultkrantz, Åke. "Ecology of Religion: Its Scope and Methodology." In Lauri Honko, ed. *Studies in Methodology*. The Hague: Mouton, 1979, 221–36.

Hultkrantz, Åke. "An Ecological Approach to Religion." *Ethnos* 31 (1966), 131–50.

Paper, Jordan. *The Spirits are Drunk: Comparative Approaches to Chinese Religion*. Albany: State University of New York Press, 1995.

Sanders, William T. and Barbara J. Price. *Mesoamerica: The Evolution of a Civilization*. New York: Random House, 1968.

See also: Ecological Anthropology; Ecology and Religion; Evolutionary Biology, Religion, and Stewardship; Religious Environmentalist Paradigm; UFOs and Extraterrrestrials.

Religion and Ecology Group, American Academy of Religion – See Religious Studies and Environmental Concern.

Religious Campaign for Forest Conservation

The Religious Campaign for Forest Conservation (RCFC), established in 1998, is a coalition of religious persons primarily identifying themselves as members of Christian or Jewish faith traditions who seek a "right relationship" with forests and the promotion of "religious values" in regard to forest conservation. The campaign is coordinated by Fred Krueger in Santa Rosa, California and is managed by a steering committee of members associated with local congregations in many parts of the United States and with prominent environmental, religious, academic and commercial institutions, such as the Commission on Environment and Jewish Life, Christians Caring for Creation (Los Angeles, CA), the Religion, Environment and Economics Project (London), the Franciscan Environmental Network, Department of Earth Literacy of St. Mary of the Woods College (St. Mary of the Woods, IN) and Larand International, to name a few.

"Right relationships" are said to entail an apprehension of responsibility understood as the exercise of "correct dominion" in regard to forests specifically and the whole of creation generally. "Rightly understood," the RCFC argues, "dominion binds the person back to God and requires justice, humility, stewardship, wisdom and concern for Creation's ultimate end. To understand dominion as an unbridled right to domination is wrong." "Correct dominion" is further appreciated as an embodiment of one's duty to God. As the RCFC summarizes, "The forests belong first to God; we are its stewards" (creationethics.org, 9 January 2002). In this regard, the definition of "correct dominion" follows closely several other elaborations, particularly those offered by James Nash and Eric Katz, among others.

The RCFC argues that the "excessive material and financial focus," which is prevalent in Western society at large and which has promoted forest degradation, corresponds to a "deadening of spiritual sensitivity" that has become embodied as a failure to exercise "correct dominion." It argues that this "deadening of spiritual sensitivity" has become increasingly prominent since the Enlightenment. Further, "commercial activity," primarily logging, is said to be "unraveling the integrity of forest systems."

The RCFC insists that while wood products are clearly needed, harvesting of timber should not occur "at the expense of the integrity of Creation [or] the health of its life support systems." To this end, the RCFC advocates harvesting timber on private property and rejects doing so on federal lands and in state forests. It calls for the reform of management practices on private lands by advocating an end to the cutting and harvesting of old-growth forests, an end to clear-cutting, an end to logging in riparian zones and on "steep or unstable slopes" and an end to practices that convert natural forests to "monoculture plantations." It also calls for the use of 100 percent post consumer recycled paper, a reduction in packaging and modifications in construction methods so as to ease the demand for forest products. Justice is seen as working toward "not only corporate profits, but also decent, health-giving jobs and the long-term survival of our biodiverse forests" (Krueger 2000a: 15) in a manner consistent with "correct dominion."

The RCFC emphasizes and values the role that forests play in regard to the maintenance of clean water, the regulation of carbon dioxide levels and climate, the opportunities forests provide for eco-tourism and the spiritual/psychological benefits that are provided to persons by forests. Moreover, forests are seen as a source of "wisdom" and inspiration.

The RCFC has made significant contributions in regard to forest conservation. It has actively supported various legislative initiatives and has engaged in extensive lobbying campaigns, both in Congress and with senior administration officials particularly at the Departments of Agriculture and Interior. Additionally, the organization coordinates a program titled "Opening the Book of Nature," a series of retreat experiences held at various locations designed to assist participants in experiencing and articulating the spiritual significance of forest conservation. The RCFC also reports that its own intensive work with World Bank officials has resulted in the granting of a significant loan to Mexico for reforestation. As a result of its efforts, the RCFC anticipates additional World Bank reforms that are consistent with forest conservation. Assessments of the reasons for the organization's success are a matter of speculation, but it can be said that its appeal to tradition plays a major role.

While the RCFC affirms a sense of "interconnectedness and interrelatedness" (Krueger 2001: 35) within the whole of creation, the notion of "correct dominion" is nonetheless maintained as an integrating paradigm. Consistent with the conception of "correct dominion," the RCFC emphasizes, "Wilderness is a system of knowledge by which we are led deeper into an understanding of God's truths" (Krueger 2001: 34). Given that forests are then appreciated instrumentally as a vehicle for the apprehension of wisdom by human persons, an affirmation of natural law, in some sense, seems to be implicit in their work. If so, this affirmation suggests a reformulation of how natural law can be conceived, perhaps in a manner akin to that which has been recently suggested by Nash, a reformulation that entails moving away from anthropocentrism and, correspondingly, involves the understanding that "moral responsibilities are discovered by reflecting not only on human nature but also on our interactions with the whole of nature" (Nash 2000: 228).

The RCFC has clearly met with success as an activist organization in regard to the conservation of forests. To this end, its apprehension and articulation of "correct dominion" has played a central role. That conception, however, invites important questions which relate to how "right relationships" can be understood among persons in relation to God, to nonhuman entities in the created realm and to one another. As Elizabeth Johnson suggests, differing paradigms may effectively incorporate an awareness of past understandings within the Christian tradition in both positive *and* negative ways so as to prompt a rejection of hierarchal paradigms that, following Johnson, limit the apprehension of "another kind of godly order structured according to genuine interdependence and mutuality" (2000: 12), a structural understanding that as she suggests, seems more consistent with the certain observations from contemporary science. Johnson's emphasis on "genuine interdependence and mutuality" is consistent with contemporary understandings such as the "partnership ethics" of Caroline Merchant (1995: 217) and ecofeminist philosophical insights such as those expressed by Val Plumwood among others. Differing paradigms of this sort may also provide an effective platform from which to engage in Christian environmental activism and may prompt further investigation in regard to the notion of "right relationships" within the whole created realm as well.

Michael Llewellyn Humphreys

Further Reading

Creation Song, Hymns Celebrating the Lord's Earth. The Religious Campaign for Forest Conservation Publication Service, 2000.

Davidson, Jim, et al., eds. *The Wilderness Handbook: An Introductory Guide to Jewish and Christian Belief about Creation with Emphasis on Wilderness and its Spiritual Values.* Santa Rosa, CA: The Religious Campaign for Forest Conservation Publication Service, 2001.

Johnson, Elizabeth. "Losing and Finding Creation in the Christian Tradition." In Dieter T. Hessel and Rosemary Radford Ruether, eds. *Christianity and Ecology.* Cambridge: Harvard University Press, 2000, 3–21.

Katz, Eric. *Nature as Subject, Human Obligation and Natural Community.* New York: Rowman & Littlefield, 1997.

Kidwell, Clara Sue, Homer Noley and George E. "Tink" Tinker. *A Native American Theology.* Maryknoll: Orbis, 2001, 35–51.

Krueger, Frederick W., ed. *Advisory Statements from the Regional Explorations of the Spiritual Values of Wilderness.* The Religious Campaign for Forest Conservation Publication Service, 2001.

Krueger, Frederick W., ed. *Preserving Our Forest Heritage, A Declaration on Forest Conservation for the 21st Century.* The Religious Campaign for Forest Conservation Publication Service, 2000a.

Krueger, Frederick W. *A Nature Trail through The Bible: An Ecological Tour of Key Passages.* The Religious Campaign for Forest Conservation Publication Service, 2000b.

Krueger, Frederick W. *The Historical Roots of our Ecological Crisis.* Santa Rosa, CA: The Religious Campaign for Forest Conservation Publication Service, 1997.

Merchant, Caroline. *Earthcare, Women and the Environment.* New York: Routledge, 1995.

Nash, James A. "Seeking Moral Norms in Nature: Natural Law and Ecological Responsibility." In Dieter T. Hessel and Rosemary Radford Ruether, eds. *Christianity and Ecology.* Cambridge: Harvard University Press, 2000, 227–50.

Nash, James A. *Loving Nature, Ecological Integrity and Christian Responsibility.* Nashville: Abingdon, 1991, 102–7.

Plumwood, Val. *Environmental Culture: The Ecological Crisis of Reason.* London: Routledge, 2002.

Religious Campaign for Forest Conservation. http://creationethics.org, 9 January 2002.

Ruether, Rosemary Radford. "Ecofeminism: The Challenge to Theology." In Dieter T. Hessel and Rosemary Radford Ruether, eds. *Christianity and Ecology.* Cambridge: Harvard University Press, 2000, 97–112.

See also: Evangelical Environmental Network; Krueger, Fred; National Religious Partnership for the Environment; North American Conference on Christianity and Ecology [and the] North American Coalition on Religion and Ecology; Sierra Treks; Wise Use Movement.

The Religious Environmentalist Paradigm

In environmental studies it has commonly been assumed that there exists a fundamental connection between a society's management of natural resources and its perception of nature. With the publication of "The Historical Roots of Our Ecologic Crisis" (1967) Lynn White was among the first to focus more narrowly on the relationship between the state of the environment and religion, postulating a direct linkage between the two. He blamed mainstream Christianity – in particular Judeo-Christian cosmology of man's mastery of nature – for the environmental ills facing the world today.

Since the publication of White's paper it has become fashionable to read ecological insight into religious dogmas and practices. Within much of the environmental movement there has been a tendency to appeal to traditional, religious ideas and values rather than to ecological science and technology in the face of environmental problems. Religious ideas and values have come to play prominent roles in environmental discourse. The Danish anthropologist Poul Pedersen has termed this approach the "religious environmentalist paradigm" (1995).

One early example of this approach was the meeting held in Assisi (Italy) in 1986 to mark the 25th anniversary of the World Wildlife Fund (later renamed the World Wide Fund for Nature), ending with the Assisi Declaration (WWF 1986). More recent examples are the series of conferences on religion and ecology held at the Center for the Study of World Religions at Harvard University, the associated "Forum on Religion and Ecology" as well as many entries to this encyclopedia.

Two sources have particularly inspired scholars and laymen alike in the construction of the religious environmentalist paradigm, namely East and South Asian cosmologies (particularly those of Daoism, Buddhism and Hinduism) and indigenous traditions (first of all American Indians). These have given fuel to the images of "noble oriental" and "noble savage," respectively. What religious dogma has been to the construction of the former, traditional ecological knowledge (TEK) – alternatively indigenous, folk, local or practical knowledge – has been to the latter. But, unlike a narrow, scientific understanding of "ecology," TEK is intimately connected with religious beliefs and values. For good reasons the human ecologist Fikret Berkes called his book on TEK and indigenous resource management *Sacred Ecology* (1999).

Asian and indigenous concepts of nature are not less complex than their Western counterparts, and it is therefore dangerous to generalize. Nonetheless, whether looking at indigenous traditions or Asian religious creeds, scholars of such worldviews have almost invariably stressed that they are what Christianity allegedly is not, namely, ecocentric and monistic, promoting a sense of harmony between human beings and nature. Christianity in contrast is portrayed as anthropocentric and dualistic, promoting a relation of domination rather than harmony. By focusing on how these traditions are different from Western ones, non-Western religions meet the demand for new ecological paradigms that unite man and the environment as parts of one another.

Everything is Interconnected

One of the most common and enduring stereotypes in environmental literature on non-Western religions is that they are organic-holistic where everything is interconnected through cosmic webs. Human beings are not seen as something outside and above nature but as interconnected and integrated within nature. This preoccupation with interconnectedness is, for example, clearly expressed in the subtitles given to the Harvard volumes on non-Western religions:

Hinduism and Ecology: The intersection of earth, sky, and water
Buddhism and Ecology: The interconnection of dharma and deeds
Confucianism and Ecology: The interrelation of heaven, Earth, and humans
Daoism and Ecology: Ways within a cosmic landscape
Jainism and Ecology: Nonviolence in the Web of Life
Indigenous traditions and ecology: The interbeing of cosmology and community
But...
Christianity and Ecology: The well-being of Earth and Humans
Islam and Ecology: A Bestowed Trust

Judaism and Ecology: Created World and Revealed Word

This idea of interconnectedness is expressed somewhat differently in various non-Western traditions, but they are all claimed to be ecocentric rather than anthropocentric and nondualistic or monistic rather than dualistic. People are seen as intimately united with nature.

Scholars of Indian religions often quote from the Bhagavadgita that the person of knowledge "sees no difference between a learned Brahmin, a cow, an elephant, a dog or an outcaste," and in East-Asian Buddhism the distinction between the animate and inanimate has gradually been erased to the extent that mountains, stones, mist and the sound of blowing winds have become sentient beings, and thus in possession of Buddha-nature (*dharma*). In Japanese Shinto one talks about *kami*, i.e. a divine power or spirit that resides in anything which gives a person a feeling of awe or spiritual experience, a notion shared with many indigenous traditions around the world. As everything may have Buddha-nature or has the potential of harboring divine powers, all creatures, animate and inanimate, are – at least in some contexts – on the same level. There is thus not a sharp line, as in much of Judeo-Christian thinking, between humans and the rest of nature. Here we encounter worldviews where "nature" corresponds to the cosmic whole, i.e. the totality of existing phenomena. In such views nature and the "universal principle" might be inseparable and intrinsically linked.

Jainism tells us that everything possesses *jiva* or life-force, and in Chinese cosmology the notion of *qi* (*chi'i*) or vital force not only permeates everything from rocks to heaven, but may even be seen as the very substance of the universe. *Qi* is thus seen as the cosmological link between all beings and all events, giving rise to the Chinese notion of "cosmic resonance" (*kan-ying*), whereby otherwise independent events are mutually influencing one another.

The interconnectedness has also a temporary aspect, through the laws of cause and effect (*karma*). Common to Buddhism, Hinduism and Jainism is the notion of reincarnation. In Jain thought all are souls entrapped in different states of karmic bondage, a notion that may lead to an ascetic life and a reverence for everything. But whereas Jainism holds that plants and animals must first be reborn as human beings before entering a state of eternal, blessed solitude, *kevala*, Eastern Buddhism holds that even plants can escape the suffering of rebirths and enter directly into *nirvāṇa*. Beliefs in reincarnation can also be found among indigenous hunters, as among the Cree Indians of North America who believe that killed animals will be reincarnated if rituals are properly performed.

Few, if any, of the above claims are controversial. But what many religious environmentalist writers have done is to clothe these observations, and many more, in the language of ecology and environmental ethics. According to some of the participants at the Harvard conferences, the notion of *karma*, for example, is taken to entail an environmental moral responsibility, often seen as binding individuals to the environment. To locate human beings with animals, plants and stones is in this discourse supposed to foster a deep reverence for nature, encouraging us to think "like a mountain," a notion borrowed from the American ecologist Aldo Leopold. And seeing the universe as a dynamic, ongoing process of continual transformation is, according to one of the editors of the Harvard series, precisely the "organic, vitalistic worldview which has special relevance for developing a contemporary ecological perspective" (Tucker 2003: 218).

Critical Voices

However, many observers have questioned the truth of the myths of the ecologically noble Other, whether they are savages or Orientals. The Indian sociologist Ramachandra Guha (1989) objects to attempts to turn Oriental religions into ecocentric religions. He views this Western appropriation of oriental religions as yet another expression of the need of Westerners to universalize their messages and to uphold a false dichotomy between the rational and science-oriented Occidentals and the spiritual and emotional Orientals. Others have argued that the concepts "ecocentric" and "anthropocentric" themselves are creations of the Cartesian worldview with little relevance to non-Western traditions, which may be one or the other depending on the context.

Many skeptics have pointed out that traditional practices are not necessarily benign to the environment. Historical ecology has indicated that indigenous peoples both in Polynesia, Europe and North America may have hunted a number of endemic species to extinction. Native North Americans have been reported to kill indiscriminately, although their environmental values are based on humanistic notions and morality toward nature where animals have intrinsic value. And early agrarian civilizations in, for example, China and Japan experienced serious deforestation and erosion long before industrialization, despite allegedly "environmental-friendly" religions such as Daoism, Buddhism and Shinto. The Chinese and Japanese managed to correct the situation, whereas the prehistoric Maya and Indus civilizations seem to have been unable to halt depletion of their forests. Hence it is certainly far too simplistic to blame all ills in non-Western societies in terms of Westernization and modernization.

We need to tread cautiously when inducing ecological practices from philosophical traditions. Discrepancies between theory and practice are common, as L. Holly and M. Stuchlik argued in 1983 and the geographer Yi-Fu Tuan asserted in his critique of the Lynn White's thesis in 1968. Tuan warned us not to assume *a priori* that people's attitudes and norms toward nature are mirrored in their actual behavior. This is important not only because we, as those before us, often are ignorant of the effects of our practices, but also, as Eugene Hargrove has reminded us, because "moral principles and precepts are normative, not descriptive. They do not, in other words, describe how people actually behave; rather they prescribe how people – again often generally and obliquely – ought to behave" (1989: xx). Moreover, attitudes and norms do not merely serve as guides for our behavior, they serve to rationalize and legitimize behavioral choices already made.

Skeptics have accused religious environmentalist writers for selective readings of religious texts and practices and for ignoring beliefs and practices potentially harmful to the environment. But, writing about the situation in South Asia, Lance Nelson (1998: 5–6) asserted, "the negative outcomes of religious teachings that can be used to rationalize environmental neglect are probably greater than the positive influence of those that encourage conservation and protection." Russel Kirkland made a similar point regarding Daoism. This situation is probably equally true for the whole of East and Southeast Asia, and most likely with all religious teachings. Worldviews and cosmologies are in this perspective not seen as coherent constructions but full of contradictions, making them vulnerable to interpretation and reinterpretations. It might be argued that it is precisely this ambiguity that makes religions versatile and adjustable to changing circumstances.

That worldviews are ambiguous and harbor contradictory views and values on nature, and that there are discrepancies between people's attitudes toward nature and their actual behavior, ought not to surprise anybody. It is probably less trivial that the organic-holistic perspective, where everything is seen to be interconnected and changing, in itself might be part of the problem rather than the solution many advocates of the religious environmentalist paradigm want us to believe. Several arguments have been offered to this effect.

First, it has been argued that an organic-holistic view implies that there is no clear distinction between nature created by gods and artifacts created by people. In other words, artifacts and nature are not opposed, and nature becomes everything around us whether it is a river or teapot, a mountain or heap of garbage. Litter or a vending machine is just as much a part of nature as a crane or a pine tree. They may all harbor Buddha-nature, be potentially the abode for a spirit, be permeated by *qi* or possess *jiva*. Writing about Japan, the French geographer Augustin Berque stated that there "it can be natural to destroy nature" (1997:143). In more general terms, without some distinction between nature and humanity, we can hardly be held responsible for the adverse effects our activities may have on the environment. This does not inhibit human intervention in nature but rather opens the way for a utilitarian approach to it. Thus, an organic worldview that explicitly recognized the unity of the natural and social worlds may fail to give rise to sound environmental practices and may even contribute to the environmental problems.

Second, seeing nature as dynamic implies that it is not regarded as something unchanging or absolute but as a process of something becoming, or entering into, a certain state. Nature is situational or contextual, and this view allows for multiple concepts of nature to coexist: the wild and threatening nature which sometimes plays havoc with people and landscape, or nature in its most cultivated form: a garden, a dwarfed tree (*bonsai*). It is argued that it is in this latter idealized form that nature is most appreciated, at least in East Asia. It is appreciated because it is cultured, which means that it is brought into people's social universe. It has been argued that human assistance is often necessary in order for things to appear in their real "natural" state, and even that the important thing is not the manifestation of nature itself but the idea about nature.

Third, the notion of *karma*, which underlines the dynamic character of many Asian religions, is intimately connected with a search for liberation from an endless cycle of death and rebirth. In viewing nature as a process, where everything decays and dies only to give birth to new lives in an endless cycle, one may arrive at the conclusion that natural objects acquire little value in and of themselves. In Hinduism, Jainism and Buddhism there is a strong tendency to withdraw from the world of suffering (*saṃsāra*) to escape into some kind of blissful void (*kevala*, *nirvāṇa*), and many scholars have therefore stressed the world-denying features of Asian religions that encourage people to turn their backs on the world. In such a perspective nature becomes irrelevant, which is hardly the best starting point to address the issue of environmental destruction.

Finally, it has been argued that when nature is seen as immanently divine, as it is in animism, this leads to a "love of nature" relationship. But the close relationship between people and spirit also enables people to entice spirits to move from their abodes in order to utilize the locations in question for other purposes. Before the construction of a house can commence, for instance, ground-breaking ceremonies can be performed. Moreover, it is recognized that it is the nature of things that one organism feeds upon another, creating relations of indebtedness in the process. Human beings are considered to become indebted to nature when exploiting it, but can "repay" harm that has been inflicted upon nature, animate or inanimate, through offerings. Memorial rites have been reported for Japanese as well as indigenous hunters throughout the world. A divine nature is, therefore, by no means a guarantee against environmental degradation, as has often been claimed.

If its critics are right, why then, one may ask, has the religious environmentalist paradigm acquired such a prominent position within the environmental discourse? There may be several answers to this question. Images of the Other do not only help us define ourselves but also serve as a powerful, internal cultural critique. Kay Milton has even claimed that such images are fundamental to the radical environmentalist critique of industrialism (1996: 109).

The paradigm can, moreover, help people to carve out new roles for old religions. This is true not only for Western eco-theologians who are busy searching the Bible and other Christian texts for ecological insight, but even more so for non-Westerners. Pedersen suggests,

> By offering to the world what they hold to be their traditional, religious values, local peoples acquire cultural significance. When they speak about nature, they speak about themselves. They demonstrate to themselves and to the world that their traditions, far from being obsolete and out of touch with modern reality, express a truth of urgent relevance for the future of the Earth. This achievement, with its foundation in appeals to imagined, traditional religious values, represents a forceful cultural creativity which would not have worked by the invocation of "pure" ecology or environmentalism (1995: 272).

This opportunity to acquire cultural significance should no doubt be applauded and encouraged. Two warnings are nonetheless in place. First, the religious environmentalist paradigm's notion of the ecologically noble Other has occasionally contributed to chauvinism and even nationalism among indigenous peoples themselves. Second, and more important, by using images of the Other in cultural critiques of modernity, it becomes imperative to stress what the Other is not, namely modern. Only by being "authentic" – that is "uncontaminated" by modern ways – are they noble and worth our consideration. Corrupted by modern ways they become fallen angels. In the hands of some environmentalists, as Beth Conklin and Laura Graham concluded in their study of ecological politics and Amazonian Indians, the notion of the ecologically noble Other locked them in an "ethnographic present" of more idyllic pre-modern days.

Arne Kalland

Further Reading

Berkes, Fikret. *Sacred Ecology: Traditional Ecological Knowledge and Resource Management*. Philadelphia: Taylor and Francis, 1999.

Berque, Augustin. *Japan: Nature, Artifice and Japanese Culture* (translated from French by Ros Schwartz). Northamptonshire: Pilkington Press, 1997.

Brightman, Robert A. "Conservation and Resource Depletion: The Case of the Coreal Forest Algonquians." In

Bonnie M. McCay and James M. Acheson, eds. *The Question of the Commons: The Culture and Ecology of Communal Resources*. Tucson, AZ: University of Arizona Press, 1987, 121–41.

Conklin, Beth A. and Laura R. Graham. "The Shifting Middle Ground: Amazonian Indians and Eco-politics." *American Anthropologist* 97 (1995), 695–710.

Edgerton, Robert B. *Sick Societies: Challenging the Myth of Primitive Harmony*. New York: Free Press, 1992.

Guha, Ramachandra. "Radical American Environmentalism and Wilderness Preservation: A Third World Critique." *Environmental Ethics* 11 (1989), 71–83.

Hargrove, Eugene C. "Forward." In J. Baird Callicott and Roger T. Ames, eds. *Nature in Asian Traditions of Thought*, Albany: State University of New York Press, 1989, xiii–xxi.

Harris, Ian. "Buddhism and the Discourse of Environmental Concern: Some Methodological Problems Considered." In Mary Evelyn Tucker and Duncan R. Williams, eds. *Buddhism and Ecology: The Interconnection of Dharma and Deeds*. Cambridge, MA: Harvard University Press, 1997, 377–402.

Headland, Thomas N. "Revisionism in Ecological Anthropology." *Current Anthropology* 38 (1997), 605–30.

Holy, L. and M. Stuchlik. *Actions, Norms and Representations*. Cambridge: Cambridge University Press, 1983.

Kalland, Arne and Pamela Asquith. "Japanese Perceptions of Nature: Ideals and Illusions." In Pamela J. Asquith and Arne Kalland, eds. *Japanese Images of Nature: Cultural Perspectives*. London: Curzon Press, 1997, 1–35.

Kirkland, Russel. " 'Responsible Non-action' in a Natural World: Perspectives from *Neiye, Zhuangzi*, and *Daode jing*". In N.J. Girardot, James Miller and Liu Xiaogan, eds. *Daoism and Ecology: Ways Within a Cosmic Landscape*. Cambridge, MA: Harvard University Press, 2001, 283–304.

Krech, Shepard III. *The Ecological Indian: Myth and History*. New York and London: W.W. Norton and Company, 1999.

Milton, Kay. *Environmentalism and Cultural Theory: Exploring the Role of Anthropology in Environmental Discourse*. London/New York: Routledge, 1996.

Nelson, Lance. "Introduction." In Lance E. Nelson, ed. *Purifying the Earthly Body of God: Religion and Ecology in Hindu India*. Albany: State University of New York, 1998, 1–10.

Pedersen, Poul. "Nature, Religion and Cultural Identity: The Religious Environmentalist Paradigm." In Ole Bruun and Arne Kalland, eds. *Asian Perception of Nature: A Critical Approach*. London: Curzon Press, 1995, 258–76.

Posey, Darrell Addison, ed. *Cultural and Spiritual Values of Biodiversity*. London: Intermediate Technology Publication/UNEP, 1999.

Tuan, Yi-Fu. "Discrepancies Between Environmental Attitude and Behaviour: Examples From Europe and China." *The Canadian Geographer* 12 (1968), 176–91.

Tucker, Mary Evelyn. "Ecological Themes in Taoism and Confucianism." In Richard C. Foltz, ed. *Worldviews, Religion, and the Environment: A Global Anthology*. Belmont, CA: Wadsworth, 2003, 217–23.

White, Lynn Jr. "The Historic Roots of Our Ecologic Crisis." *Science* 155 (1967), 1203–7.

WWF (World Wide Fund for Nature). *The Assisi Declarations: Messages on Man and Nature from Buddhism, Christianity, Hinduism, Islam and Judaism*. Gland, Switzerland: WWF International, 1986.

See also: American Indians as "First Ecologists"; Anthropologists; Bhagavadgita; Buddhism; Buddhism – East Asian; Daoism; Descartes, René; Domestication; Ecological Anthropology; Ecology and Religion; Eden's Ecology; Environmental Ethics; Evolutionary Biology, Religion, and Stewardship; Francis of Assisi; Hinduism; India; Jainism; Japanese Religions; Noble Savage; Radical Environmentalism; Religious Studies and Environmental Concern; Romanticism and Indigenous People; Savages; Social Science on Religion and Nature; Traditional Ecological Knowledge; White, Lynn – Thesis of; World Wide Fund for Nature (WWF).

Religious Naturalism

A working definition of religious naturalism was developed online in 2003 by members of a religious-naturalism internet discussion group on religious naturalism. The statement, a modification of the Campion statement of self-understanding generated by the Institute on Religion in an Age of Science, is as follows:

> We find our sources of meaning within the natural world, where humans are understood to be emergent from and hence a part of nature. Our religious quest is informed and guided by the deepening and evolving understandings fostered by scientific inquiry. It is also informed and guided by the mindful understandings inherent in our human traditions, including art, literature, philosophy, and the religions of the world.
>
> The natural world and its emergent manifestations in human creativity and community are the focus of our immersion, wonder, and reverence. We may describe our religious sensibilities using various words that have various connotations – like the sacred, or the source, or god – but it is our common naturalistic orientation that generates our shared sense of place, gratitude, and joy. We acknowledge as well a shared set of values and concerns pertaining to peace, justice, dignity, cultural and ecological

diversity, and planetary sustainability. We may differ on how these concerns are best addressed, but we are committed to participating in their resolution.

Several of the terms and concepts included in this statement are described in more detail below.

Naturalism
"Naturalism" is most commonly used to describe a philosophical lineage that starts from the framework of materialism – the universe is constructed from matter and energy – and articulates philosophical propositions within that framework. Given that our scientific understanding of the material world has undergone a vast expansion since the naturalism project was launched, and since philosophical responses are framed in cultural contexts, much of the thought that would be included in a historical treatise on naturalism would not resonate well with present-day understandings (this is true as well, of course, of other philosophical traditions). To release the term "naturalism" from its historical constraints is not to release it from the fundamental impulse of the naturalism project, however, which is to perceive and construct meaning systems based on what is known of the natural world.

What is known of the natural world has generated a recent and profound transition, moving from facts-about-physics (quanta) or facts-about-biology (genetics) to a sweeping integrated story – the Epic of Evolution – that deeply informs us about who we are (symbol-manipulating primates, social, mortal, creative, members of ecosystems) and how we got to be here (the Big Bang, nucleosynthesis, biological evolution, brain evolution, emergence). This shift has in turn enlarged the scope of the naturalism project: the challenge is not only to construct meaning systems based on a knowledge of, say, quantum uncertainty or genetic specification, but also to construct meaning systems that emerge from the new meta-narrative itself.

Religious Naturalism
Loyal Rue defines a religious orientation as that which offers personal wholeness and social coherence, and suggests that this is accomplished in traditional religions via metanarratives that indicate how-things-are and which-things-matter. The adjective religious can be said to encompass three spheres of human experience. 1) The *interpretive* sphere (akin to theological) describes responses to the big questions raised by the narrative (e.g., Why is there anything at all rather than nothing? Does the universe have Plan? Purpose? How do we think about death?). 2) The *spiritual* sphere describes inward responses to the narrative, responses such as gratitude, awe, humility, and reverence, responses that for some are best accessed in community with others. 3) The *moral* sphere describes outward, communal responses to the narrative such as compassion and fair-mindedness and respect.

Religious naturalism is best thought of as a generic term for mindful religious approaches to our understandings of the natural world. As such, it does not represent a detailed system of religious beliefs. Instead, the specificity shifts to, and resides within, the religious naturalists themselves.

Religious Naturalist
Religious naturalists are anchored in and dwell within their understandings of the natural world. They find their primary religious orientation within that narrative/perspective and develop mindful religious responses to it – interpretive, spiritual, and moral. These responses are then transfigured into emergent valuations that are called religious orientations and beliefs. Importantly, these valuations and beliefs may deeply overlap with those espoused by existing ethical and religious traditions: the substitution of one meta-narrative for another does not necessarily alter the human impulse toward common spiritual and moral sensibilities; rather, it influences how we get there.

Religious naturalists holding shared orientations and beliefs may go on to associate as more focused communities, albeit this possibility has not yet become widespread. These communities may, for example, develop art and ceremony that honor and celebrate their understandings of the sacred, and may commit to engagements in social and environmental activism. Such communities may coalesce within existing faith traditions, or they may come to stand alone. Examples include the World Pantheist Movement (www.pantheism.net), the Teilhard Association (www.teilhard.cjb.net), and the religious naturalism interest group of the Institute on Religion in an Age of Science.

Ursula Goodenough

Further Reading
Berry, Thomas. *The Great Work: Our Way into the Future.* New York: Bell Tower Press, 1999.
de Waal, Frans B.M. *Good Natured: The Origins of Right and Wrong in Humans and Other Animals.* Cambridge: Harvard University Press, 1996.
Damasio, Anatonio. *Looking for Spinoza: Joy, Sorrow, and the Feeling Brain.* Orlando, FL: Harcourt, 2003.
Deacon, Terrence. *The Symbolic Species: Co-Evolution of Language and the Brain.* New York: W.W. Norton, 1998.
Drees, Willem B. *Creation: From Nothing until Now.* New York: Routledge, 2001.
Foot, Philippa. *Natural Goodness.* New York: Oxford University Press, 2001.
Goodenough, Ursula. *The Sacred Depths of Nature.* New York: Oxford University Press, 1998.
Harrison, Paul. *Elements of Pantheism: Understanding the*

Divinity in Nature and the Universe. London: Element Press, 1999.

Kellert, Stephen R. and Timothy J. Farnham, eds. *The Good in Nature and Humanity: Connecting Science, Religion, and Spirituality with the Natural World.* Washington, D.C.: Island Press, 2002.

Leopold, Aldo. *A Sand County Almanac.* New York: Oxford University Press, 2000 (2nd edn).

Matthews, Clifford, Mary Evelyn Tucker and Philip Hefner, eds. *When Worlds Converge: What Science and Religion Tell Us about the Story of the Universe and Our Place in It.* Chicago, IL: Open Court, 2001.

Peacocke, Arthur. *Paths from Science towards God.* Oxford: Oneworld Publications, 2001.

Peters, Karl. E. *Dancing with the Sacred.* Harrisburg, PA: Trinity Press, 2002.

Rue, Loyal. *Everybody's Story: Wising Up to the Epic of Evolution.* Albany: State University of New York Press, 2000.

Swimme, Brian. *The Universe is a Green Dragon: A Cosmic Creation Story.* Santa Fe, NM: Bear & Co, 1988.

Tucker, Mary Evelyn. *Worldly Wonder: Religions Enter Their Ecological Phase.* Chicago, IL: Open Court, 2003.

Woodruff, Paul. *Reverence: Renewing a Forgotten Virtue.* New York: Oxford University Press, 2001.

See also: Berry, Thomas; Environmental Ethics; Epic of Evolution; (and adjacent, Epic Ritual); Religious Studies and Environmental Concern.

Religious Society of Friends – See Friends, Religious Society of (Quakers).

Religious Studies and Environmental Concern

The establishment and growth of Religion and Ecology as a new area of study can be attributed in part to its instigation by scholars who feel morally and ethically compelled to address serious environmental problems. That religion itself has been implicated as a catalyst of environmental decline has prompted such scholars to examine the relationships among human cultures, religions, and environments. The *Encyclopedia of Religion and Nature* is, of course, one manifestation of the effort to understand such relationships. But it is hardly the first example of interest in religion and ecology among religious studies scholars, and some of this interest is more than analytic, it is itself religious. Indeed, especially since the mid–1960s, there has been intense scholarly interest in the relationships between human cultures, religions and environments, not only among religious studies scholars, but also among philosophers who have been pioneering the field of ENVIRONMENTAL ETHICS. Some ANTHROPOLOGISTS have also focused attention on ECOLOGY AND RELIGION and have been developing a field known as ECOLOGICAL ANTHROPOLOGY. A good starting point for the study of religion and nature is to review the range of scholarly approaches to understanding the relationships between cultures, religions, and environments. Here we focus on the role played by religious studies scholars in religion-related environmental studies and activism.

Religion and Ecology in the American Academy of Religion
In 1989 and 1990 David Barnhill (then a professor of Buddhism and Environmental Studies at Guilford College) and Eugene Bianchi (a professor of Christian Theology and specialist in Roman Catholicism at Emory University) teamed up to propose a religion and ecology "Consultation" to the American Academy of Religion, an important academic association devoted to the study of religion. The consultation was approved and held its initial sessions in 1991. The Christian process theologian Jay McDaniel, and the Buddhist scholar and deep ecology activist Stephanie Kaza were among the group's earliest supporters, both of whom were engaged in their own scholarly and activist work toward environmentally friendly religion. Demonstrating strong interest from Academy members, in 1993 the Consultation became a "Group," a status which it has maintained to this writing.

The religion and ecology initiative represented a concerted effort to focus scholarly attention on the religion variable in human/ecosystem interactions. Some of the scholarly work presented there clung strictly to historical or social scientific analysis. The majority of the group's presentations, while they might have been involved in or taken such work as their starting point, have also had a normative, ethical dimension.

Some participants explored how the world's dominant religions could be "mined" or "reconfigured" to promote environmentally sustainable lifeways. Others, influenced by perspectives articulated during the emergence of ENVIRONMENTAL ETHICS and RADICAL ENVIRONMENTALISM, promoted the revitalization of cultures and religions they considered to be environmentally benign (such as indigenous, pagan and animistic ones), but that had been declining in the face of what the presenters considered the world's dominant, imperial religions (especially the monotheistic ones). Still others proposed or endorsed recent religious innovations (such as the "Universe Story," "EPIC OF EVOLUTION," ECOFEMINISM, and various NEW RELIGIOUS MOVEMENTS including WICCA) as correctives if not antidotes to anthropocentric religions that view the Earth instrumentally and consequently degrade it. Yet others advanced an EARTH CHARTER in order to capture and deploy religious ethics in a way that would promote a new environmental ethics, one that would consider the preservation of biological diversity a sacred duty, while simultaneously valuing cultural and religious diversity.

Within the wider American Academy of Religion, critics of the religion and ecology group have argued that religion and ecology scholars are more engaged in green religion and "missionary" work than in scholarly analysis. Such criticisms are likewise addressed to other ethically or religiously engaged groups in the AAR and reflect a wider fissure within it. For some scholars of religion, religious studies should promote religious tolerance and thus a more humane world, and therefore to promote the "greening" of religion, or to participate in it, would be appropriate modes of academic engagement. For others, such as Donald Wiebe (1999) and Russell McClutcheon (2001), who analyze in complementary ways the religiosity animating much of what is called "religious studies" today, the task of the discipline is properly to analyze religion rather than to defend or engage in it.

The conflicting responses of those in the religion and ecology group reflect this fissure. Some are apparently not involved in religious production or environmental ethics. Others unapologetically defend the normative religious or ethical dimension of their work and the group's attention to it, arguing that the world cannot afford to have scholars sit on the sidelines in the struggle for sustainability.

The differing approaches and tensions reflect the plural identity in the religion and ecology field to date, which has scholars engaged in both analytic and normative work. This said, most participants and observers of the AAR's Religion and Ecology Group would acknowledge that much of the work of its affiliated scholars is animated, at least in part, by environmental concern. And some of the participants would certainly understand themselves to be "engaged scholars" involved, in one way or another, in the struggle to "green" religion and ethics. (The word "green" is now used not only as an adjective but also as verb and adverb in a linguistic innovation that signals environmental action.)

Religion and Ecology Beyond the Academy

Outside of the American Academy of Religion, the contributions of religious studies scholars to the greening of religion is more transparent and less controversial. These contributions have been substantial and driven by a sense of environmental urgency, an impulse which predated the controversy of the LYNN WHITE THESIS. America's premier twentieth-century conservationist Aldo Leopold, for instance, urged the revisioning of ethics and religion toward a biocentric axiology in the 1940s, as Curt Meine, his biographer, reminds us in this encyclopedia. As Leopold asserted in 1947, when it comes to conservation, "philosophy, ethics, and religion have not yet heard of it" (Flader and Callicott 1991: 338).

Philosophy, ethics and religion have now all heard plenty about nature – beginning perhaps with a number of little-known conferences that focused on religion, ethics, and nature during the 1970s and 1980s. Several of these occurred as the disciplines of environmental ethics and CONSERVATION BIOLOGY got off the ground. But two events deserve to be singled out for dramatically increasing public and especially religious attention to environmental ethics.

The first, in 1986, was inspired in part and influenced by religion scholar and Roman Catholic priest THOMAS BERRY, and held at the Basilica di S. Francesco in Assisi, Italy, during the WORLD WIDE FUND FOR NATURE's twenty-fifth anniversary celebrations. Leaders of the five world religions who had been invited issued the "Assisi Declarations on Religion and Nature," which set forth religious obligations to nature and spurred additional discussion and statements among and from other faiths in the subsequent years.

The second was a "Spirit and Nature" conference held at Vermont's Middlebury College in 1990. It featured the Dalai Lama and a number of prominent religious leaders and scholars who had previously focused attention on religious responsibilities toward nature. The conference was followed by a similarly titled American Public Television broadcast and widely distributed video (produced by the well-known journalist Bill Moyers), and a book (Rockefeller and Elder 1992). All three "spirit and nature" manifestations promoted the idea of nature protection as a fundamental religious duty.

The driving force behind this conference was Steven Rockefeller, a Middlebury comparative religion scholar with a Ph.D. from Columbia, who also happened to be a practicing Buddhist born of one of America's wealthiest and most politically prominent families. No doubt Rockefeller's background and connections help explain the success of the conference. More importantly, the conference was successful because it reflected and captured a growing environmental concern among a wide variety of religious individuals and groups, and it evoked and inspired more of the same. The conference was capped by an interfaith religious service that included the voices of whales and other creatures, brought to the congregation through the medium of Paul Winter's music, itself an expression of contemporary nature religion.

In the subsequent years, Rockefeller and a number of other religious studies professors would become even more deeply involved in promoting a fusion of environmental concern and religious ethics.

The "Religions of the World and Ecology" Conferences

The next most significant development along these lines was a series of conferences, hosted by The Center for the Study of World Religions at Harvard University with support from diverse environmental, religious, and animal welfare groups. Entitled "Religions of the World and Ecology," the conferences occurred between 1996 and 1998. Like the "Spirit and Nature" conference, these were followed by publications. Between 1997 and 2004, ten

SP Critical Perspectives on "Religions of the World and Ecology"

Since its inception, the issue of "engaged" scholarship has been a focal point for intense debate within the field of Religion and Ecology. The sharpest criticism has come from those who charge that scholarship incorporating ethical concerns and thus an "environmental agenda" ultimately compromises the critical acumen associated with distanced scholarship. These are not idle concerns, but they were not easily resolved, nor were they foremost in my mind when in 2001 I was asked to evaluate the Harvard book series during a Religion and Ecology Group session at the American Academy of Religion meeting in Denver, Colorado.

After first acknowledging the monumental contribution of the Harvard Series, I expressed a number of reservations about the way it was framed and some of the tendencies found in the published articles. Three of these are worth repeating here, for they reflect some of the concerns that led to this encyclopedia project, which is itself an exercise in religious studies, and was designed to remedy lacunae in the inherited "religion and ecology" field as it had unfolded in its initial decades.

The first criticism was that the "Religions of the World and Ecology" enterprise was not as inclusive as it sounded, for its main conferences and book series focused only on those religions labeled "world religions." To their credit, the series included indigenous religions, which until recent decades had not been studied as a related religious type in venues like this. But the "world religions" category is problematic in itself and any list of religions so labeled will be difficult to maintain against criticisms. Scholars increasingly recognize that the contemporary multi-religious world decreasingly fits into tidy and conventional religious categories such as "world religions." Moreover, the conferences and books drew primarily on scholars and figures closely associated with, if not committed to, the traditions under scrutiny. This left much nature-related religiosity out of sight, including individuals and groups engaged in nature-focused spirituality, such as many environmentalists who are not involved in any formal, established religion but who often consider nature to be sacred in some way, as well as Pagans, Wiccans, and some New Age devotees, who consider a perception of nature's sacredness to constitute the very center of their religious worldview.

Although such lacunae were pointed out to the conference organizers early enough to remedy the oversight, and despite a sympathetic hearing and a recognition by them that there were significant gaps, nothing was done to make the conferences and book series more inclusive. Many scholars and religionists aware of this episode traced it to anti-Pagan bias and/or a desire not to offend mainstream religions, especially the conservative monotheistic ones that have typically ridiculed Earth-based religions and sometimes even repressed their practitioners. Even if a lack of funding made rectifying the oversight difficult, leaving the original decision in force represented a choice, one that reinforced the original omission.

A second criticism was that embedded in the series was not only a clear bias toward mainstream traditions but also one favoring the mainstreams *of* these traditions. The "World Religions" format established a structural and conceptual hurdle that made it made it difficult to attend fully to the critically important dynamic of religious bricolage. On the one hand this obscured the important dynamic of hybridization in the contemporary greening of religion. It also undermined the desire for "creative revisioning" that was set out as a goal in the "Series Foreword" by (Tucker and Grim 1997: xxii) by casting implicit suspicion over such hybridization, seeing it as somehow impure compared to the existing traditions. This kind of tone was present in many of the contributions in the series, largely because so many of them were entrusted to scholars who were experts in their tradition's texts; even when critical, they tended to remain loyal to what they took to be the text's original meanings. Some of the authors ridiculed those engaged in what they considered inauthentic religious innovation, that is, at least, when they did not ignore popular religiosity and social movements altogether in favor of textual and worldview analysis.

In short, the series, by privileging the mainstream in its choice of its speakers and contributors (with a significant exception in the Indigenous conference and book, which paid substantial attention to contemporary grassroots engagements, and a few other notable exceptions) did not consistently look to the margins, where religious innovation tends to be most intense, arguably providing more fertile ground for new religiosities, including greener ones. Even when such religious production was charitably evaluated as possibly of some environmental utility, it was clear that many of the scholar-elites writing in these volumes considered such innovations to be "misunderstandings" and "misappropriations." This may have well served "political correctness" or religious orthodoxy, implying that only people with a certain background can or ought to interpret a tradition, but it was not good religious studies. Critical religious studies recognizes the critical role that hybridity and boundary transgression plays in the history of religion and that for non-devotees, ethical judgments about such transgressions will have to rely on concerns other than faith-based belief regarding what constitutes a "pure" strain of an extant tradition. In summary, assumptions that often accompany textual and worldview analysis often

Continued next page

discount popular, nature-oriented spirituality, making them invisible, and this kind of analysis has been the priority of the Harvard series, and indeed much of the religion and ecology field.

A third criticism was the idealistic (namely idea-focused) premise of the entire enterprise. Tucker and Grim in their series foreword insisted, quoting Lynn White, that "Human ecology is deeply conditioned . . . by religion" (in Tucker and Grim 1997: xvi). But this claim unfortunately assumed that which needs to be a central *conundrum* and subject of a scholarly inquiry into the relationships between religion and nature. It would have provided a better starting point for the religion and ecology series to turn this premise into a question: "*Is* environmental action conditioned by religious attitudes about nature?" Then, if an affirmative action were to follow, we could then push deeper, "If environmental behavior is so conditioned, how does this work within the immensely complex ecological and political systems in which we are all embedded?" Certainly many of the entries in this encyclopedia question the idealistic premise of this series and the majority of the inherited "religion and ecology" field. Some of these suggest, on the contrary, that it is environments which decisively shape religions, not vice versa, and that over the long run, the only religions that will endure will be those proving "adaptive" within their earthly habitats.

In these areas of criticism – undemonstrated idealism combined with a narrow focus and privileging of religious mainstreams – and in a number of other problematic assumptions conveyed by this series and much of the "religion and ecology" field, two differing approaches to the field can be discerned. One is activist in its priorities and chief orientation. It seeks to turn religions green while being careful not to offend religious majorities and mainstreams. For an activist, even a scholar-activist, this is an understandable choice, for to the extent that religious worldviews influence behaviors and thus impact ecosystems, the ones held by more people will be the most important environmentally. Another approach places the priority on simply understanding the relationships between *Homo sapiens*, their religions and other cultural dimensions, and their livelihoods, environments, and so on – which is no simple task! This effort may also be motivated by environmental concern and it is certainly not value-neutral – many of its scholarly practitioners hope that the answers to such critical inquiry can help guide both environmental activism and public policy. But the approach endeavors to bracket value assumptions in an effort to prevent them from occluding understanding of the role of religion in nature.

Although these can be distinct approaches, in the real world these approaches, and those engaged in promoting them, sometimes, inevitably, intersect. Tensions between these approaches can even operate synergistically, helping to illuminate together the religion and nature terrain better than either would in isolation. Nevertheless, it is time for scholars involved in this interesting field of inquiry to exhibit greater self-reflexivity and transparency with regard to the approach they are engaging in, alerting the reader to when they are engaged in this approach, and their rationale for such choices. This would lead to greater clarity and would help guarantee that the inevitable tensions that accompany scholarly inquiry will be creative and productive as the field evolves.

Bron Taylor

Further Reading
Tucker, Mary Evelyn and John Grim. "Series Forward." In Mary Evelyn Tucker and Duncan R. Williams, eds. *Buddhism and Ecology*. Cambridge, MA: Harvard University Press, 1997, xv-xxxi.

See also: Ecological Anthropology; Ecology and Religion; Environmental Ethics; Evolutionary Biology, Religion, and Stewardship; Religious Environmentalist Paradigm; Social on Science, Religion and Nature; White, Lynn – Thesis of.

Harvard University Press books appeared, constituting an impressive series bearing the same title as the conferences. The volumes explored what the series editors decided were the world's major religious traditions: Buddhism, Christianity, Confucianism, Daoism, Hinduism, Indigenous Traditions, Jainism, Judaism, Islam, and Shinto.

The conferences were organized and the book series edited by two Bucknell University Religious Studies Professors, Mary Evelyn Tucker and John Grim, both of whom had been inspired by the work of Roman Catholic theologian PIERRE TEILHARD DE CHARDIN, as well as by Thomas Berry and his protégé [philosopher and mathematician] BRIAN SWIMME, who together became the most influential religionists promoting the consecration of scientific and evolutionary narratives, which they called *The Universe Story* (Swimme and Berry 1992). They and others moved by these narratives have been involved in grafting these new sacred stories onto existing and new religious forms, sometimes monotheistic ones (such as when Christians celebrate the "Universe Story" linking it to creation through ritual performance), sometimes not (such as can be found in ritualizing of the EPIC OF EVOLUTION, and in the COUNCIL OF ALL BEINGS as presented in the work of Buddhism scholar/activist JOANNA MACY and the deep ecologist JOHN SEED).

Tucker and Grim have been instrumental in promoting the Universe Story through their long service as Vice President and President (respectively) of the American

Teilhard Society. The Society was founded in 1964, Thomas Berry himself serving as its president during the 1970s. Grim assumed the presidency in the early 1990s, and continued well into the twenty-first century. Tucker called the Society the "Seedbed for Thomas Berry" in a 2003 interview (31 January in Bucknell, Pennsylvania; this paragraph and its quotes are gleaned from this same interview). Tucker and Grim, her husband, were well placed to know, for they had facilitated the society's role in this regard. For example, Tucker assembled a number of Berry's essays and presented them to a publisher in the early 1970s, which led eventually to the publication of Berry's influential *The Dream of the Earth* (1988), which would sell over 70,000 copies. For another example, the new journal *Teilhard Studies* (winter 1978) devoted its first issue to Berry, entitled "The New Story: Comments on the Origin, Identification, and Transmission of Values." Tucker and Grim were also been active in the AAR's Religion and Ecology Group and instrumental in the development of the journal *Worldviews: Environment, Culture, Religion*, which commenced publishing in 1997, providing additional venues for promoting a sacramental sense of the Universe's evolution. They have worked to draw the broader religion academy's attention to the Earth Charter as well, which also conveys such spirituality.

As important as an inspiring universe or other religious worldviews might have been in fostering the emergence of "religion and ecology" as a sub-field of religious studies, the field was driven as much by an apocalyptic reading of the current state and likely near-future of the planet. Tucker and Grim, for example, began the series foreword of "Religions of the World and Ecology" with a strikingly apocalyptic tone:

> Ours is a period when the human community is in search of new and sustaining relationships to the earth amidst an environmental crisis that threatens the very existence of all life-forms on the planet . . . As Daniel Maguire has succinctly observed, "If current trends continue, *we* will not" (Tucker and Grim 1997: vi).

Although some may think the extinction of *Homo sapiens* is a real, near-term possibility, few scientists share such a view, let alone fear that "all life-forms on the planet" will go extinct. This suggests that the framing of these volumes may be grounded more on an apocalyptic faith than biosphere science. Scientists increasingly do, of course, express alarm about the extent and rate of environmental degradation. It should be no surprise that this would fuel apocalypticism. Indeed, some future scenarios do envision the end of the world as we know it, even suggesting this has already occurred, as Bill McKibben problematically did in his best-selling *The End of Nature*. He did so by conceptually extracting humans from nature, for humans can only end nature if they are not a part of it. This illogical feat McKibben accomplished with little criticism, which was made possible by the apocalypticism of the age. We might, nevertheless, have wished for a more judicious framing of McKibben's book, which had much otherwise to commend it, as well as the Harvard series, which despite such framing, will properly be understood as a benchmark for a certain type of engaged religion and ecology scholarship. And on a human level, the apocalyptic framing is understandable, for soberly presented ecological prognostications are certainly frightening enough to warrant such fears.

What is even more important to the current religion and nature discussion is the claim by Tucker and Grim in the introduction that the environmental crisis is grounded in defective religious perception, "We no longer know who we are as earthlings; we no longer see the earth as sacred" (1997: xvii). This implies not only that the Earth is sacred, but that earlier humans had a different and superior religious sensibility toward nature than modern humans.

Whatever the truth of such assumptions, they certainly make comprehensible why Tucker and Grim, and the other scholars who share such presuppositions, have labored so assiduously in developing the "Religion and Ecology" field. They hope to rekindle a sense of the sacredness of the Earth, which they consider a prerequisite to restoring ecological harmony. Indeed, a fundamental premise of most of the ferment occurring under the "Religion and Ecology" is a global, green-religious reformation.

The introduction to the Harvard series made this clear: Religious studies scholars could contribute significantly to the quest for sustainability by identifying and evaluating

> [t]he *distinctive ecological* attitudes, values, and practices of diverse religious traditions . . . Highlight[ing] the specific religious resources that comprise such fertile ecological ground: within scripture, ritual, myth, symbol, cosmology, sacrament, and so on (Tucker and Grim 1997: xxiii).

The objective of the conference series was thus to establish a common ground among diverse religious cultures for environmentally sustainable societies, while treating individual traditions as resources to be mined for the envisioned religious reformation. Many if not most of the scholars writing for the Harvard Series seemed to share the objective of its editors, striving to uncover and revitalize the green potential of the religions they were analyzing.

This encyclopedia provides many examples of scholars deeply involved in this process. Perhaps one of the more interesting is that of J. Baird Callicott, a protégé of Aldo Leopold, and one of the world's pioneers of the field of environmental ethics. As if taking a cue from Leopold's above-mentioned lament that philosophy, ethics, and religion have had little to do with conservation, Callicott has tramped worldwide pursuing cultural and religious resources for Leopoldian land ethics. Perhaps the foremost expression of Callicott's religion-related work is *Earth's Insights: A Survey of Ecological Ethics From the Mediterranean Basin to the Australian Outback* (1994), a project he pursued although, as he discloses in NATURAL HISTORY AS NATURAL RELIGION in this encyclopedia, he regards most religions as superstitious. He nevertheless hopes they can be made to promote conservation ethics that cohere with ecological science.

"Culminating Conferences" and Targeting the United Nations

After the World Religions and Ecology conferences at Harvard that focused on religious traditions, two "culminating conferences" were held, producing or contributing to three significant trends: 1) the spreading of spiritualities in which the evolution of the universe and life on Earth is considered a sacred story; 2) the wider extension of green forms of mainstream religions; and 3) the greening of international institutions.

The first culminating conference, "Religion, Ethics, and the Environment: An Interdisciplinary Dialogue," occurred on 17–20 September 1998 at Harvard University. The focus of this conference was cosmology, environmental ethics, and the world religions. Speakers included Thomas Berry, the entomologist and biodiversity advocate E.O. WILSON, and J. BAIRD CALLICOTT, all of whom have in their own ways promoted the consecration of scientific narratives. Steven Rockefeller also spoke. Since the Vermont "Spirit and Nature" conference, Rockefeller had become a critically important facilitator of the Earth Charter process. The Charter, intended for United Nations ratification as a sustainability strategy, is a remarkable document claiming that all life has intrinsic value and expressing reverence for the miracle of life, while calling the nations to understand, in one way or another, that preserving the Earth is a "sacred trust."

The second culminating conference took place on 21 and 22 October 1998, and brought the themes of the earlier conferences, including the sense of the sacredness of the universe, right to the United Nations (the second day was held at the American Museum of Natural History). This conference illuminated the role of religious studies scholars in the Earth Charter initiative, and indeed, one of the sessions was devoted specifically to "charting the course" for the Earth Charter.

One of the speakers was Oren Lyons, a professor of Native American Studies at the State University of New York at Buffalo, and the "Faithkeeper" of the Turtle Clan, Onondaga Nation, one of the traditional nations of the HAUDENOSAUNEE CONFEDERACY. In 1991, Lyons himself had participated in another important extension of nature spirituality into the culture's mainstreams, through a Bill Moyers public television program based on a conversation with Lyons. Mary Evelyn Tucker was another speaker at the United Nations, bringing the message she was taking from the overall conferences, that religions were indeed turning green, sometimes in dramatic and decisive ways. Her experiences of this perception she discussed several years later in *Worldly Wonder: Religions Enter Their Ecological Phase* (2003). Thomas Berry and Brian Swimme were also presenters, bringing their reverence for the universe directly to the conference, and kindling substantial interest. The first day at the United Nations drew an overflow crowd including many United Nations employees, and 1000 people attended the sessions at the Natural History Museum.

Perhaps even more importantly, a number of prominent figures associated with the United Nations spoke and endorsed the overall effort to green religion and ethics, including Maurice Strong, who reportedly first hatched the Earth Charter idea while serving as the Secretary-General of the United Nations Conference on Environment and Development. This conference was held in 1992 in Rio de Janeiro and became known simply as the "Earth Summit." Adnan Amin, the Executive Director of the United Nations Environmental Program, also articulated his support for the overall effort to promote a global environmental ethics and politics congruent with it. A few years after this meeting at the United Nations, in 2002, on the occasion of the United Nations' World Summit on Sustainable Development in Johannesburg (which was the official follow-up meeting to the Earth Summit), Steven Rockefeller played the leading role in promoting the Earth Charter. The Charter received respectful mention from a number of world leaders, but no formal attention on that occasion.

This discussion has demonstrated that ideas and initiatives, incubated if not birthed by religious studies scholars, have played important roles in the greening of religion and environmental ethics. They are, moreover, beginning to influence global environmental politics, bringing to them an important and sometimes innovative religious and ethical dimension.

The Forum on Religion and Ecology

Mary Evelyn Tucker and John Grim developed the conferences to encourage scholarly work in the service of greening the world's religions, to promote a sense of the sacredness of the universe and evolutionary narratives, and to support related ethical initiatives including the Earth Charter. To continue such efforts they also used the conferences to spawn a long-term initiative, which they called the "Forum on Religion and Ecology." Known to many by its acronym, FORE, the organization was, according to its website, established to help develop "religion and ecology as an academic area of study and research in universities, colleges, seminaries, and other religiously affiliated institutions."

A number of religiously affiliated colleges and seminaries have been developing religion and ecology as specialties, and in 2003, the University of Florida, a state-sponsored, secular institution, inaugurated the first "Religion and Nature" emphasis as a central part of its new Ph.D. program in Religion. Such developments – occurring both in religious and secular institutions – suggest that the field of religion and ecology began emerging from its infancy in the early years of the twenty-first century. The differing approaches, confessional/ethical on the one hand, and historical/social scientific, on the other, will sometimes be in tension, but this is likely to be a creative one. Sometimes the differing approaches will be blended in creative scholarly hybrids. Taken together, the various approaches will produce diverse kinds of scholarly work as the field is further constructed.

Bron Taylor

Further Reading

Barnhill, David Landis. *Deep Ecology and World Religions: New Essays on Sacred Ground.* Albany, NY: State University of New York Press, 2000.

Barnhill, David Landis. *At Home on Earth: Becoming Native to Our Place.* Berkeley, CA: University of California Press, 1999.

Berman, Morris. *The Reenchantment of the World.* Ithaca, NY: Cornell University Press, 1981.

Berry, Thomas. *The Dream of the Earth.* San Francisco: Sierra Club Books, 1988.

Callicott, J. Baird. *Earth's Insights: A Survey of Ecological Ethics From the Mediterranean Basin to the Australian Outback.* Berkeley: University of California Press, 1994.

Flader, Susan and J. Baird Callicott, eds. *The River of the Mother of God and Other Essays by Aldo Leopold.* Madison, WI: University of Wisconsin Press, 1991.

Goodenough, Ursula. *The Sacred Depths of Nature.* New York & Oxford: Oxford University Press, 1998.

Kaza, Stephanie. *The Attentive Heart: Conversations with Trees.* New York: Fawcett Columbine, 1993.

Leslie, John. *The End of the World: The Science and Ethics of Human Extinction.* London and New York: Routledge, 1996.

McCutcheon, Russell T. *Critics Not Caretakers: Redescribing the Public Study of Religion.* Albany, NY: State University of New York Press, 2001.

McDaniel, Jay B. *Earth, Sky, Gods & Mortals: Developing an Ecological Spirituality.* Mystic, CT: Twenty-Third Publications, 1990.

Lyons, Oren and Bill Moyers. *The Faithkeeper: Oren Lyons with Bill Moyers.* New York: Mystic Fire Video, 1991.

Rockefeller, Steven C. and John C. Elder, eds. *Spirit and Nature: Why the Environment Is a Religious Issue: An Interfaith Dialogue.* Boston: Beacon Press, 1992.

Rue, Loyal. *Everybody's Story: Wising Up to the Epic of Evolution.* Albany, NY: State University of New York Press, 2000.

Swimme, Brian and Thomas Berry. *The Universe Story: From the Primordial Flaring Forth to the Ecozoic Era: A Celebration of the Unfolding of the Cosmos.* San Francisco: Harper Collins, 1992.

Tuan, Yi-Fu. "Discrepancies between Environmental Attitude and Behaviour: Examples From Europe and China." *The Canadian Geographer* 12 (1968), 176–91.

Tucker, Mary Evelyn. *Worldly Wonder: Religions Enter Their Ecological Phase.* LaSalle, IL: Open Court, 2003.

Tucker, Mary Evelyn and John A. Grim. "The Emerging Alliance of World Religions and Ecology" (special issue: M.E. Tucker and J. Grim, eds. "Religion and Ecology: Can the Climate Change?"). *Daedalus: Journal of the American Academy of Arts and Sciences* 130:4 (2001), 1–22.

Tucker, Mary Evelyn and John Grim. "Series Forward." In *Buddhism and Ecology.* Mary Evelyn Tucker and Duncan R. Williams, eds. Cambridge, MA: Harvard University Press, 1997, xv–xxxi.

Wiebe, Donald. *The Politics of Religious Studies: The Continuing Conflict with Theology in the Academy.* New York: St. Martin's Press, 1999.

See also: Anthropology as a Source of Nature Religion; Berry, Thomas; Callicott, J. Baird; Conservation Biology; Earth Charter; Environmental Ethics; Epic of Evolution; Leopold, Aldo; Lyons, Oren; Religious Environmentalist Paradigm; Teilhard de Chardin, Pierre; United Nations' "Earth Summits"; Wilson, Edward O.; Winter, Paul; World Wide Fund for Nature (WWF).

Restoration Ecology and Ritual

Ecological restoration is the active attempt to return a landscape or ecosystem such as a prairie, a wetland or a lake to a previous condition, usually regarded as more "natural." This is done through the alteration of soils, topography, hydrology and other conditions, the introduction of extirpated or otherwise missing species of plants and animals, and the elimination or control of species not present in the historic, or model landscape.

Although restoration has existed in its modern form since early in the twentieth century, for most of that time it was merely a curiosity represented by only a scattering of projects, and playing no significant role in conservation thinking or practice. Only since about the mid-1980s have conservationists begun to take restoration seriously. This development has been accompanied, or perhaps to some extent driven, by the growing recognition of the value of restoration as a conservation strategy, a technique for basic ecological research, a way of experiencing and learning about landscapes and ecosystems.

At the leading edge of this ongoing discovery of

restoration are practitioners who have begun to explore its value as a context for the creation of ceremonies and rituals to explore and celebrate the relationship between humans and the rest of nature. The value of restoration as a basis for performance, ritual and other forms of expressive action arises from its essentially active nature.

Preservation, for example, despite its importance as a conservation objective, entails an essentially non-active relationship with the landscape, and offers few opportunities for expressive action in direct relationship with the land and other species.

Restorationists, in contrast, participate in evocative activities such as the gathering and sowing of seed and the reintroduction of animals, which provide occasions for celebration. They also participate in psychologically problematic activities such as the burning of vegetation and the "control" – that is, usually, the killing – of unwanted species, and in the contamination of "nature" by these and other intentional human activities.

The negative feelings aroused by activities of this kind are no doubt one of the reasons why environmentalists ignored and even resisted restoration for so long. But they are also the reason why restoration is so valuable as a context for exploring and defining the terms of our relationship with the rest of nature in a non-sentimental, psychologically and spiritually comprehensive way.

One way to explore the potential of restoration as a performing art, or as a context, occasion, or basis for ceremony, ritual and other modes of expressive action is to consider parallels between the "act" or "story" of restoration and other performative genres. Of these, perhaps the most obvious is dramatic reenactment. Restoration is, after all, a kind of time travel, which may be undertaken and understood variously as an attempt to reverse, repeat, alter or obliterate history. Thus the practice of restoration has been imaginatively linked with historical reenactments in events such as the annual Trail of History days at Glacial Park, site of a landscape-scale restoration project near Richmond, Illinois.

Another performative genre that parallels the practice of restoration in suggestive ways is pastoral art, which explores the relationship between humans and the rest of nature through action carried out in the field of tension between them. In classic forms of literary or dramatic pastoral, such as Thoreau's *Walden*, or Shakespeare's *A Midsummer Night's Dream*, this usually involves movement across the landscape, typically a double action of withdrawal from civilization (represented by a city, factory, court or the like) in the direction of nature (represented by a garden, or a wilderness, natural area or pastoral landscape) and then an ultimate return. The restorationist, however, performs this pastoral "experiment," in a very different way, not by moving from one place to another, but by attempting, in effect, to remove culture from nature by modifying a single place. This variation on the pastoral

---

New Academy for Nature and Culture

The New Academy for Nature and Culture is a school without walls being developed to provide college-level training for leaders of community-based conservation efforts. Conceived by a consortium of restoration practitioners associated with the Society for Ecological Restoration, the New Academy is taking shape as a network of regional centers each comprising a number of partners, including environmental and civic organizations and at least one college or university, which provides basic courses, leading ultimately to a degree with a certificate from the New Academy.

Based on the idea that most of the resources needed to accomplish its mission already exist, both on and off campus, the New Academy is being developed primarily to identify these resources and to bring them together in behalf of a coherent, mission-driven program of study and reflective experience working with both the human and the biotic communities. Its aim is to help participants develop the skills they need to help others derive full value from conservation efforts in the physical, intellectual, psychological and spiritual as well as the purely ecological dimensions of value. These values, then, can serve as the value-base for the formation of communities, or "congregations" based in watersheds or other ecologically or culturally significant units, and for paying fees, or tithing to support the leadership needed to coordinate the effort.

The first regional center of the New Academy was established in 2001 in the Chicago area in partnership with Loyola University, Northeastern Illinois University and a number of non-academic partners. Development of a related program at the junior-college level, based at Merritt College in Oakland, California, has been underway since the early 1990s, and will probably become a regional center within a year or so, and there are also centers of interest at universities in Texas, Arizona and Michigan.

William R. Jordan III

---

design has important environmental implications, not least because it dramatizes the possibility of the redemption of the city, and also because it provides a constructive alternative to the essentially consumptive use of the natural landscape modeled by "retreatants" such as Thoreau or Edward Abbey.

Restoration also offers close parallels with traditional rituals of initiation. In particular, the task of copying – rather than imaginatively imitating – the model or "given" landscape provides an occasion for the radical self-abnegation or setting aside of the will characteristic of some traditional rituals of initiation (see, for example, Grimes 2000). When properly developed, this may serve as an opportunity for achieving membership in the biotic community, a paradigm of relationship long favored by environmentalists. At an even deeper level of engagement, restoration provides a context for confronting the most problematic aspects of life, including the killing of plants and animals and the exercise of a kind of hegemony over entire ecosystems. Since it opens up the possibility of offering back to nature some recompense in nature's own kind for what we have taken from it, it also opens up the possibility of a kind of redemption in our relationship with nature through a ritual offering back to it, rather in the manner of the institution of ritual sacrifice characteristic of many traditional and pre-modern cultures.

At the present time, restorationists have made some progress toward the realization of these imaginative possibilities. Ritual in the context of restoration efforts currently ranges from the informal and minimally self-conscious bagel breaks and sharing of stories during workdays to more ambitiously conceived forms of ceremony and ritualization. In Lake Forest, a suburb of Chicago for example, the burning of brush piles resulting from the clearing of exotic species in rare oak savannahs has become the occasion for an annual festival featuring a parade of bagpipes, linking the city's cultural history with its biotic past and future. Other restorationists, like the San Francisco practitioner Amy Lambert or the Mt. Horeb, Wisconsin environmental artist Barbara Westfall, have used restoration projects as the occasion for the creation of installations or performances designed to explore and enhance the meanings generated by these projects (see *Restoration & Management Notes* 10:1 [1992], 59).

Others have used restoration projects and events as occasions for special ritual events such as weddings, or seasonal events such as solstices or equinoxes, illustrating ways in which meanings inherent in the task of restoration resonate with those of traditional events such as certain holidays, festivals and occasions of life-crisis and transition.

These developments are of special importance for environmentalism because they represent the value of reflective action rather than deduction and argument in the development of meanings and other environmental values. Since environmentalism, regarded as a religious endeavor, has arguably been rather "top-down," or "theological" in its approach to the formation of values and attitudes, an emphasis on ritual as a source of values and a context for conscience formation may prove to be of fundamental importance in the development of an environmental religion based on values that truly emerge from the experiences of groups of people in particular places.

William R. Jordan III

Further Reading
For articles on ritual in restoration, or the development of restoration as a performing art, see articles in *Ecological Restoration* (formerly *Restoration & Management Notes*), especially:

Bomar, Charles R. Patricia Fitzgerald and Cathy Geist. "Ritual in Restoration: A Model for Building Communities." *Ecological Restoration* 17:1, 2 (1999), 67–74.

Grimes, Ronald L. *Deeply into the Bone: Reinventing Rites of Passage.* Berkeley: University of California Press, 2000.

Holland, Karen. "Restoration Rituals: Transforming Workday Rituals into Inspirational Moments." *Restoration & Management Notes* 12:2 (1994), 121–5.

Lambert, Amy M. and Maya R. Khosla. "Environmental Art and Restoration." *Ecological Restoration* 18:2 (2000), 109–14.

Meekison, Lisa and Eric Higgs. "The Rites of Spring (and Other Seasons): The Ritualization of Restoration." *Restoration & Management Notes* 16:1 (1998), 73–81.

Simpson, Dave. "Picks, Shovels and Musical Comedy: A Note on Restoration Theater." *Restoration & Management Notes* 15:2 (1997), 179–82.

For an extended discussion of the value of restoration as a basis for performance and ritual, see: Jordan, William R., III. *The Sunflower Forest: Ecological Restoration and the New Communion with Nature.* Berkeley: University of California Press, 2003.

See also: Biodiversity; Biophilia; Conservation Biology; Epic of Evolution (and adjacent, Epic Ritual); Ritual.

[P] Restoring Eden

Restoring Eden is a nonprofit organization working to re-establish nature appreciation and environmental stewardship as a core value within the Christian community. Headed by Peter Illyn, an evangelical Christian minister, Restoring Eden creates simple, heartfelt messages that target Christians in churches, universities and communities in an effort to raise up grassroots environmental advocates.

Illyn became an environmentalist during a 1000-mile llama trek through the Cascade Mountains of Oregon and Washington. As he recalls the experience,

> One night, while camping in an alpine meadow, I watched a herd of elk come to graze. As I stood in the moonshadow, I saw a bull elk raise his head, snort and then bellow out a loud rutting call. I was overcome by the primal wildness around me. I finally understood, though dimly, the scripture in Genesis where God, after creating the wild animals, stated that it was "good." But two days later my llamas and I followed the trail into a massive clearcut. There were no trees left standing, no birds flying, no elk rutting. It had the quiet desolation of an abandoned battle field.

According to Illyn, while sitting there on an ancient fir stump, doing his daily Bible reading, he came upon Proverbs 31:8, which states that we should "speak out for those who cannot speak for themselves." Brokenhearted by the devastation he saw from horizon to horizon he prayed, "Lord – who speaks out for your forest, your elk, your salmon?" "It was at that moment," he tells his audiences, "two days after seeing the elk, that I decided to become a voice for creation."

Illyn states that he went into the mountains a minister but four months later came out as an environmentalist, committed to preaching the biblical call to love, serve and protect God's creation. To further that commitment, in 1996, he founded Christians for Environmental Stewardship, to identify and network a church-based grassroots movement. In 2001, the organization's name was changed to Restoring Eden.

A cornerstone of the work is assertive outreach efforts. According to Illyn: "Our goal is to be unapologetic, yet winsome in our advocacy. Our message is simple, 'God is a good God, God made a good Earth, God calls us to be good stewards.'" Illyn and the others drawn to Restoring Eden recognized that the agents of change in the Church are seldom the pastors in the pulpit, but instead are the lay-leaders in the pews, and they focus on their potential.

The goal is to organize these lay-leaders into a grassroots voice willing to speak out about the goodness of creation in Church and in the political arena. Restoring Eden representatives' table at Christian rock festivals, start environmental clubs in Christian colleges, and host student lobby-training events in Washington, D.C. They have come to the defense of protecting endangered species, protecting wild forests from road building, and have lobbied to prevent the U.S. government from permitting oil drilling in the Arctic Refuge.

Through this activism, Restoring Eden has developed important partnerships with indigenous Christians working to protect their tribal land and subsistence economies and cultures. These partnerships have taken Illyn on speaking tours of tribal communities in Papua New Guinea and Alaska. He held workshops there with tribal leaders to confirm that a true biblical land ethic is similar to their traditional tribal land ethic – take only what you need, be thankful for all you have and see the connections and interdependencies. Often referring to themselves as "belly-button" Christians, these tribal communities still see their umbilical cords connected to their "mother," the Earth. This is contrasted with a commonly held land ethic within the modern Church that believes God made the Earth for us, so take as much as you can, as fast as you can.

On these speaking tours, Illyn operates within the Christian tradition as a traveling evangelist. Prior to his mini-crusades, Restoring Eden volunteers and local environmentalists arrange for a meeting hall, contact media, and place posters up throughout the community.

Billed as "The Theology of Wild," Illyn creates a biblical message of nature appreciation, environmental stewardship and political activism. The sermons advocate for native habitats, wild species and the rights of indigenous cultures.

According to Illyn,

Scripture is clear that humans have been given both the privileges and the obligations of stewardship. While we have the right to eat from the fruit of creation, we do not have the right to destroy the fruitfulness thereof. It is our sacred duty to love, serve and protect the rest of God's creation. We are foolish and narcissistic to think this creation was all about us.

Restoring Eden's goal is to establish a three-part strategy to make hearts bigger, hands dirtier and voices stronger. To get the heart involved it uses the traditional, but forgotten, spiritual discipline of nature appreciation to help people see the wonder, wisdom and whimsy of God revealed in nature. It gets hands involved through environmental restoration service projects and inventorying their lifestyle choices. Finally, the organization's voice becomes stronger through public advocacy and political activism.

Illyn finds that getting Restoring Eden's message can be difficult for some. The occasional negative reactions are usually based on differing political and religious understandings. Among the absurd but too common political responses he has heard are assertions that environmentalists are part of a conspiracy by supporters of the United Nations to create a one-world government and take over land in the United States. The religious arguments include claims that Christians need not be concerned with this Earth, because, as Illyn remembers hearing them, "God is unconcerned about the state of nature"; "God made the Earth for humans – he expects us to use the Earth and the sooner we use it up, the sooner Christ will return"; "God can re-create any species that go extinct"; "the Earth is not our home – I'm heaven bound!"; and perhaps most commonly, "Preaching the salvation message is the only important work of Christians – all else is a distraction." Sometimes an apocalyptic expectation plays an important role in devaluing environmental concern, "My Bible predicts that things are going to get worse, no matter what we do." Such assertions are often accompanied by claims that environmentalists "worship the creation instead of the Creator" and promote un-Christian "New Age" or "Pagan" worldviews.

Reflecting on the challenges, in 2003 Illyn stated,

while our work is still controversial and viewed with suspicion by some, we are winning the argument that environmental concern is appropriate for the church. But so far we're losing the argument that such concern for creation should be a high priority.

Many Christians have been taught that evangelism is all that matters. But according to Illyn, "the Great Commission found in the Gospel of Mark is to preach the good news to *all* creation. Habitat destruction and species extinction is not good news for creation." Illyn passionately speaks out for the goodness and integrity of nature and believes that Restoring Eden can help Christians realize that environmental stewardship is an important Christian duty. According to Illyn, "If you love the Creator, you must take care of creation."

Peter Illyn with Bron Taylor

See also: Biblical Foundations for Christian Stewardship; Christianity (7i) – An Evangelical Perspective on Faith and Nature; Evangelical Environmental Network; Stewardship; Wise Use Movement.

Rewilding

The long-term preservation of nature depends on a sustainable shift in the way we perceive and thus act upon the world around us – the return to conscious, authentic being, which I call "rewilding." Wildness could be described as a condition of dynamic wholeness and authentic expression. In our case this means oneness with our bodies, needs, desires, sensations, instincts and dreams . . . and with the natural world of which we are an integral part. Rewilding is the intentional restoration of wholeness: the integrity of entire ecosystems as well as the integrity of our individual beings.

In wilderness restoration we intentionally work to repair the torn ecological fabric, remove the invasive and the artificial, encourage the flourishing of every native form, protect against its dismemberment or destruction, and contribute to a state of continuous flux and balance. In personal rewilding we do much the same, mending our individual ecologies, the connections between our bodies and souls, hearts and minds. We purge any lies our societies may have taught, and those illusions that fear has wrought, while learning to express every aspect of our essential native selves. We do what we can to protect against distraction and dissolution. We strive for balance in our lives, and in our relationships to both the human and more-than-human world.

Alexander Marshack described humanity as a "persistent flowering of an ancient reality." The rewilding of the self is neither a retreat to the past nor transformation into something new. Instead, it is a re-formation, the reinhabitation of original form. It is being who we really are: the act of simply being. It is the uncomplicated if difficult cessation of all pretense, artifice, conditioning, labeling, distraction, manipulation, domination, preoccupation with the future, suppression and repression. Rewilding is both a beauteous flowering and an essential coming into self.

The rewilding of the self begins with the rewilding of the body: reimmersion in the sensorial field, engaging every aspect and element of the world around us – and every experience – with every one of our atrophied senses, refamiliarizing ourselves with the feel and function of our flesh. The senses take us into ourselves, even as they reach out and thereby enlarge us. The wild body is fueled by passion, the passion to experience miraculous, finite life. Its rewilded sexuality is an ally of immediacy, moving us beyond objectification and back into the intensity of the moment, responding directly to fete or foe, task or poem. The rewilding of the psyche involves the reawakening of primal mind, restoring the sense of wonder and awe to its rightful place as a determinant of the human/nature relationship. As such, rewilding is a socio-religious experience as much as a personal epiphany or practice. It results not only in awakened ecocentric spirituality but also in social and political action.

The rewilded person is resonant with, protective of, and responsive to the natural world. Such persons act as activists and advocates for wilderness, which they recognize as our original home, the playground of evolution, and the formative context for a wilder humanity. Only since the 1900s has wilderness been looked at as a place to visit, a sequestered island of undeveloped Nature surrounded by a developed and depleted landscape. For most of our upright existence, humankind has lived with/in the flesh and flux of wilderness. As an extension of inclusive nature, we are a product of it. Our species was shaped by the nourishment and challenges of a wild life, responding to the constantly changing situations of a natural world. The way adrenalin speeds our heart and fuels our muscles when we sense danger, and the way love jerks us around whether we're ready for it or not, are both dynamics developed in our wild past. For several hundred thousand years we were integral rhythmic elements in the wilderness concerto. Judging by the attitudes and behavior of both our primate relatives and many existing "primitive" peoples, humans were likely blissfully engaged in the sensorial field whenever not hungering or actively being preyed upon. And whether we were ecstatic nature mystics or not, we were natural elements of a well-functioning whole – contributing to both the flowering and balance of what remains an incredible, evolving composition. We must bear in mind that the entire world, in all its wholeness, was not so long ago wilderness. And out of that authenticity, vibrancy and wholeness we were born. A wild Earth may yet be a necessary condition for the highest manifestation of human and nonhuman potential. It is the sacred source, the cauldron of creation on whose behalf the "wilder" makes his or her stand.

Like a growing number of anarchists, deep ecologists and indigenous peoples, author Derrick Jensen finds nothing absurd about either the possibility or necessity of dismantling the existing structures and paradigms of our techno-industrial civilization. "It just seems like a lot of hard work, done by a lot of people in a lot of places in a lot of different ways," he tells us. What's absurd is "the possibility of allowing this inhuman system to continue" (Jensen 2002: 588). Certainly, the dichotomy between wilderness and civilization is not a quandary to be solved, but rather, a choice to be made. Everyone, at some point in their lives, makes a deliberate decision to desensitize in a deal for comfort, to live in confinement rather than face the uncertainties of nature, to acquiesce to outside powers in order to avoid the demands of responsibility, to allow the destruction of wilderness and human wildness in exchange for the techno-gratification of our times. It's a matter of how we judge what is truly valuable in life. To determine something's worth a "wilder" asks: Is it freely and gracefully embodying its own nature? Is it real, authentic, and intensely itself? Does it contribute to diversity, wholeness/holiness, interdependence and balance? Does it sing, laugh, resonate? *And can you dance to it?*

Inspirited Gaia whispers in every river and shouts from every granite peak: reclaim and reinhabit! Revere and resacrament! Resist and reshape! Re-member ... and rewild! And we respond, with both our bodies and souls.

For all the difficulties of rewilding in this day and age, it is a shift that provides immediate rewards. Life presents all its flavors only to the wild, only to those who dare. In our reconnection to self and place, Earth and Spirit, we function as will-full conduits for the ancient ways, conscious receptors and transmitters of Gaian consciousness. In this great manifesting and gifting, we become the newest and most grateful members of the wild covenant, the response-able inheritors of the legacy and duties of the sacred wild.

Jesse Wolf Hardin

Further Reading

Hardin, Jesse Wolf. *Kindred Spirits: Sacred Earth Wisdom.* Columbus, NC: Swan, Raven & Co., 2001.

Jensen, Derrick. *The Culture of Make Believe.* New York City: Context, 2002.

Snyder, Gary. *The Practice of The Wild.* New York City: North Point Press, 1990.

See also: Sexuality and EcoSpirituality; Sexuality and Green Consciousness.

Rexroth, Kenneth (1905–1982)

Kenneth Rexroth was an American poet, translator, and cultural critic. Raised in the Midwest, he settled in California where he became a major figure in the San Francisco Renaissance and influenced the development of poets such as Gary Snyder and Allen Ginsberg. Three of his distinctive contributions are his blending of Catholic and Buddhist spirituality, a sweeping knowledge of world literature, and his affirmation of the interrelatedness of nature, mysticism, the erotic, and the political. This complexity resulted in some of the most compelling and socially significant nature poetry in the English language.

Central to his vision of nature is a deep sense of radical interrelatedness within a vast universe. He frequently drew on Huayan Buddhism's image of Indra's Net, in which all phenomena are likened to mirrors reflecting each other. "Doubled Mirrors" concludes with the narrator discovering the source of many tiny points of light: "Under each / Pebble and oak leaf is a / Spider, her eyes shining at / Me with my reflected light / Across immeasurable distance" (1966: 224).

Equally important is his realization of the flux of life. This theme exemplifies both the traditional Buddhist emphasis on impermanence and the Japanese aesthetic of *aware*, a bittersweet realization of the ephemerality of all that is beautiful. This sensitivity is evoked when he exhorts his daughter to "Believe in all the fugitive / Compounds of nature, all doomed / To waste away and go out" (1966: 241).

This ongoing flow of time contains brief eternities. In "May Day," he contrasts his vision to workings of the men of power who "are pushing all this pretty / Planet ... / ... nearer and nearer to / Total death." Despite his apocalyptic view, he can affirm to his daughter that "we have our own / Eternity, so fleeting that they / Can never touch it, or even / Know that it has passed them by" (1966: 331).

Rexroth's nature poetry emanates a this-worldly mysticism in which the natural world is itself sacred, a view reinforced by his interest in Tantric Buddhism. "The holiness of the real / Is always there, accessible / In total immanence" (1966: 248). To apprehend this sacrality, one needs to drop the cravings, aversions, and delusions of the ego and realize the contemplative flame that burns in each of us. His mysticism is also erotic: the body too is sacred and sexual love is one of the principal means of realizing the holiness of the real. Some of his finest nature poems are also intense love poems.

His sense of an interrelated and sacred world was the foundation for a deeply moral vision and engagement in radical social movements. He combined the traditional Buddhist critique of normal consciousness with a condemnation of the devastating power of social structures that manifests and reinforces the distortions of the ego. In particular he denounces the hierarchical, authoritarian politics and acquisitive economic systems of the modern nation-states. The state "lives by killing you and me" (1966: 241) – i.e., by extinguishing our contemplative flame and severing our organic relatedness to the natural and social worlds. In numerous poems he combines exquisite sensitivity to nature and an incisive awareness of human suffering and evil.

Rexroth's ethical mysticism was formed early in life by his commitment to social justice, a Quaker-influenced ideal in a free community of responsible persons, his readings in Christian mysticism, and his view of Christ as a model for feeling "unlimited liability" for the ills of the world. Later in life his social and ecological concerns became increasingly influenced by the Mahayana Buddhist ideal of the bodhisattva, who vows "I will not enter Nirvana / Until all sentient creatures are saved" (1968: 292–3). Unqualified compassion enables the bodhisattva to hear "the crying of all the worlds" (1968: 292) and effortlessly move to help those in distress – an ideal most subtly developed in his masterpiece, *Heart's Garden, Garden's Heart* (1967), a long poem written in Japan.

David Landis Barnhill

Further Reading

Gibson, Morgan. *Revolutionary Rexroth: Poet of East-West Wisdom.* Hamden, CT: Archon Books, 1986.

Gutierrez, Donald. *The Holiness of the Real: The Short Verse of Kenneth Rexroth.* Madison, NJ: Fairleigh Dickinson University Press, 1996.

Morrow, Bradford, ed. *World Outside the Window: The Selected Essays of Kenneth Rexroth.* New York: New Directions, 1987.

Rexroth, Kenneth. *Collected Longer Poems.* New York: New Directions, 1968.

Rexroth, Kenneth. *Collected Shorter Poems.* New York: New Directions, 1966.

See also: Anarchism; Beat Generation Writers; Indra's Net; Snyder, Gary; Tantra; Tantrism in the West; Zen Buddhism.

Ritual

By some accounts ritual behavior is utterly natural, "hard-wired" into the structure of the brain and nervous system, a function of our biological or animal "hardware" rather than of our cultural "software." Even if one tries to escape explicit rites, tacit ritualization nevertheless emerges unbidden. So, for instance, if we do not initiate youths into adulthood, they will, perversely in all likelihood, initiate themselves. By this account, all habitual behavior, perhaps even all social behavior, is ritualized. Ritualizing and dramatizing are universal, givens in human nature. Our very biosocial being is dependent upon these twin foundational activities. Even if people avoid formal rites and refuse to attend stage plays, they cannot escape ritualizing and dramatizing. They permeate human actions the same as they do the mating and aggressive behavior of birds and fish.

By other accounts, however, ritual is a most unnatural activity, not at all the sort of behavior one *cannot help* doing. Ritual is not like eating, sleeping, digesting, and breathing, or even copulating and speaking. Ritual is optional – one can choose *not* to engage in it. Whereas being alive requires eating and sleeping, it does not require ritualizing. Even if one claims that humans and other animals exhibit an inherent urge to ritualize, responding to that urge is optional, and because it is optional, ritual is cultural rather than natural.

The dichotomy, cultural versus natural, is familiar. It is a staple of Western thought, typical of its dualistic tendencies. And ritual is not the only human activity to be hoisted onto the horns of this perennial dilemma. But the dilemma is easy to overstate, thus rendering it a false dualism. There are ways around the problem; a third, less polarized view is possible. For instance, one might argue that it is perfectly natural for humans, given their upright postures and large brains, to be cultural. Or one might observe that cultural activities, when sustained for a sufficient time in the right environmental niche, can have genetic, which is to say, evolutionary, consequences. In other words, even though a noticeable cultural/natural divide characterizes much human behavior, this great divide is not impassable. It is a membrane rather than a wall. The distinction between things cultural and things natural, in this third view, is relative rather than absolute, making it conceptually possible that ritual, like language (but unlike digestion) is both natural and cultural, a cultural edifice, if you will, constructed on a natural foundation.

If this is the case, the question, then, becomes: what is this natural foundation? If brains and tongues and ears lay the groundwork from which human languages sprout and then diversify, what is the bedrock upon which human rites are built? The question is really two: 1) How essential is ritual to being human? and 2) By what basic biosocial means does ritual operate? Is ritualizing just one activity among many others, and doing it or not doing it like the decision to wear green rather than red, or like opting to ride bikes rather than paddle canoes as one's hobby? Is the choice merely aesthetic, a matter of taste or personal preference? Or does something larger, grander, and greater depend on the choice to ritualize or not?

Examined historically and crossculturally, the consensus answer to the question would seem to be that participation in certain specific rites is an indicator of whether one is truly human or not. The view that ritual is merely optional or only decorative is anomalous in human religious and cultural history. It is an attitude mostly recent and largely Western. The questions: Who is truly human? and What is truly natural? have often been answered: the truly human people are those most truly in tune with nature, and those most truly in tune with nature are those who dance this particular rhythm in this particular ritual dance. So the natural, the human, and the ritualistic are, in the final analysis, one.

If one were to allow a minor variation in the nature question – thus, What is truly natural, or supernatural? – the threefold equation would account for almost every religious tradition the world has known. In short, ritual participation (or not) has been utilized as a primary behavioral indicator not just of who "we" (as opposed to "they") are, but of who is truly human and what is truly natural or supernatural.

This equation generates a peculiar torque in our thinking about rites. On the one hand, a rite is a cultural human construction. People make it up, revise it, and evaluate it. Politics and economics swirl about it as they do about any other human activity. On the other hand, the gods delivered it or the ancestors bequeathed it. A rite is not a work of fiction. It has no author, and no one dreamed it up out of his or her imagination. The popular mind-rites, especially religious ones, are above critique and debate. Those who evade the revealed sacred liturgy are unnatural and inhuman. Do it or die.

The contemporary form of the ritual conundrum is slightly different from the more historic form. The older form was: Which rite (thus which tribe, which nation, which tradition, which people) is the right one? The question seldom posed a real option. If you were a so-and-so, you knew your own ritual system was the right one.

The newer form of the ritual question is: To ritualize or not? Being born into a society with a divinely given rite is no longer the norm. Instead, this rite and that one seem equally plausible (or equally implausible). Besides, who wants to fight and die for a way of performing cultural ideals, all of which are relative anyway?

Rites typically (although not always) express associated cultural myths, predications of what is real and not, what is worthy and not. For cultures in which the question is, "To ritualize or not?", the dominant myth is scientific and technocratic. Scientists, it is believed, study nature, things as they really are, not supernature, things as they might, or should, be. So we who are steeped in such cultures look to theory, fact, and evidence to warrant our decisions and evaluations. We resist labeling these "myth" even though they work in much the same way as more obviously mythic myths do.

And what does current scientific myth say about the necessity, or lack of it, to ritualize? First of all, it is seriously out of scientific fashion to talk as if human behavior issues from an urge, instinct, or drive. The current way of speaking of something as built-in is to say it is "encoded" in the genes, the DNA. But, of course, genes and DNA do not account for *everything* any more than the old drives and instincts or the older gods and spirits did.

Environment and natural selection are today's other co-star actors. Together, DNA, environment, and natural selection make us who and what we are. And we are embodied, be-brained, mammalian, bipedal homonoids. Some of us ritualize and some do not. So the question is not 'Do we ritualize?' but 'Should we?' The ritual question is morally and practically driven. The long form of the current existential ritual question, then, is: Should humans ritualize in order to be attuned to nature and thereby avoid planetary destruction?

Why would it ever occur to anyone to pose the question this way? There are two reasons: 1) ethnographic social science is presenting rich traditions in which rites are understood to be the primary means of being attuned to the environment; and 2) psychological and anthropological science is tendering theories which claim that ritual activity synchronizes the halves of the brain, thereby diverting human tendencies to make war on their fellow "conspecifics," thus making us better stewards of the Earth's deep structure.

The import of the ethnographic testimony is that ritual participants the world over believe their rites enable them to live in synchrony with the natural world, especially animals and plants, sometimes even rocks, mountains, bodies of water, and specific places. This ritual sensibility is not characteristic of every ritual system, but it is typical of many of them, especially the local, smaller-scale ones. In these, people behave with humility and receptivity. They are, they confess, not more powerful than other creatures, and the human task in life is not only to use the creatures but also to be receptive to their teachings. In the ritualized world presented by ethnographers, what we in the West think of as nature (as opposed to culture) is peopled. Animals and plants and places are people too. So the nature/culture divide either does not exist or it is much less pronounced. In rites, animals and plants and places are addressed with respect as equals or even superiors.

The ethnographic evidence is that ritual participants believe they attune themselves with rites to the natural-supernatural world. Some non-participants believe this too, and they wish the Western technocratic world were more ritually saturated than it is. But – and this is an important "but" – animals and plants are also treated in ritually rich cultures as food. Albeit with apology, song, and prayer, they are killed or harvested, then distributed and eaten – either that or avoided altogether. Animals, like exceptionally generous people, give themselves to hunters, and hunters are the kin of animals. But hunters also track, stalk, study, and strategize. The ritual attitude, then, does not preclude a pragmatic attitude. Prey are persons, but they are also targets for arrows.

The ethnographic evidence, then, reminds us that rites are not foolproof; the game become angry, which is to say, the game are sometimes shot out and the fields over-harvested. Although rites attune, they do not do so perfectly or completely. Thus, not all native people in every place and time have been "natural ecologists." Rites not only attune participants to nature, they insulate people from nature. Rites can become ends in themselves or tools for wreaking environmental and social havoc. Everything depends on which people at which times in which specific places of nature are engaging in which kind of ritualizing.

In the current Western scientific and technocratic world, true believers, of course, look with some skepticism on the claims of ethnographically presented ritualists. At best, their testimony is soft rather than hard evidence. At best, ethnographic reports present stories, beliefs, descriptions, occasionally even hypotheses, or theories, but not proven facts, which is to say, demonstrated and replicable ones. So the best one can claim, and still honor the sacred tenets of scientism, is that certain ritual practices *may* have survival value. They *may* enhance the adaptability and thus the longevity of the human species on the planet Earth.

We must reiterate the "may" as long as we have not eliminated the alternative, namely, that deeply ritualized human life can become more one-dimensional, stereotyped, and inflexible than non-ritualized human life. In short, rites *may* make us humans maladaptive. If "stereotypy" (to use a term explicitly used in one theorist's definition of ritual) were ever a ritual virtue in some other place and time, it is, in the Darwinian universe that most encyclopedia-readers inhabit, most definitely a vice. Loss of postural and gestural diversity and flexibility would not stand us in good stead with Natural Selection, the reigning deity of the current, almost inescapable Darwinian myth. Loss of bodily flexibility, like loss of cultural and biological diversity, would jeopardize human health and longevity. If ritualizing implies rigidifying, we are courting earthly extinction rather than planetary salvation by engaging in it. So the answer to the question, "To ritualize or not?" depends on how we define ritual, or, if not that, then on which kinds of ritualizing we practice and which kinds we forgo.

Anthropologist Charles Laughlin and psychologist Eugene d'Aquili, along with their colleague John McManus, have articulated some of the strongest theoretical arguments in favor of ritual's adaptive import. If they are right, ritualization is more natural (in the sense of having more survival value) than is non-ritualization. In their view ritual, which emerged evolutionarily along with encephalization, is crucial for both the control and the transformation of consciousness. Rites employ various driving mechanisms such as drumming, chanting, dancing, ingesting, ordeals, and privations as means of retuning, or returning balance, to the autonomic nervous system. Ritual activity facilitates the entrainment (penetration and embodiment) of symbols into the human system.

More specifically, ritual practices facilitate simultaneous discharge of the excitation (ergotropic) and relaxation (trophotropic) systems. Laughlin and company posit a drive toward wholeness in all biological systems, and consider rites a primary means for achieving both social and neuropsychological wholeness. They stop short of claiming that rites are the *only* means. Since they say many of the same things about both play and contemplation as they do about ritual, it seems that ritual is not the exclusive agent of wholeness, unless, of course both play and contemplation are conceptualized as kinds of ritual. In any case, for Laughlin and associates it is neither the "natural" nor the "supernatural" that takes precedence but rather the holistic. In the end, Laughlin, d'Aquili, and McManus espouse a wedding of what they call "mature contemplation" (in my view, a species of ritual activity) and neuroscience as the most holistic (in an older vocabulary, "natural") form of consciousness.

Their claims are less appropriate to some kinds of ritual and more appropriate to others, especially those at the top and bottom end of the scale, for example, trance dance and meditation. These require, respectively, either sustained exertion or else the stilling of physical and mental activity. More than mainline worship and liturgy, these kinds of ritual activity evoke the extremes of the autonomic nervous system, thus facilitating the "crossing over" that these theorists treat as the primary virtue of ritual.

Another anthropologist, Roy Rappaport, is intent to restore ritual's authority, hoping it can close the maws of several great beasts: desertification, ozone depletion, species extinction, and environmental degradation. Against the Goliath of quality-denying, "monetized" epistemologies rooted in cost-benefit analysis, which he clearly considers maladaptive, he marshals the slingshot of ritual, hoping its emphasis on complementarity and reciprocity can displace the forces of disintegration. Rappaport is more willing than most anthropologists to admit that the very idea of ecology is as much a religious conception as it is a scientific hypothesis. Ecological ideas encourage the preservation of the world's wholeness in the face of pervasive fragmenting and dissolving forces. For Rappaport, the idea of an ecosystem, not just as a scientific hypothesis but as an active intervention, is a guide for how to behave in the world. He actively calls for ritual performance grounded in the concept of the ecosystem. For him, ritual performance is not merely a means for humans to illustrate ideas about the world. Rather, ritual is the way the world itself tries to ensure its own persistence.

But much ritual is in the custody of the so-called world religions. They claim to have a repository of wisdom, much of it ritualistic, that can help save the planet from ecological destruction. But the large-scale, multinational faiths have been slow to mobilize, and they are typically saddled with environmentally hostile or indifferent myths, ethics, and rites.

Religious leaders are now scouring the scriptures in

search of images that might inspire ecologically responsible behavior. The big religions are defending their traditions against attacks that blame them for the sorry state of the environment. In self-defense, they launch criticisms of economic greed and human failure to exercise stewardship of the land.

The monotheistic traditions bear a large share of the blame, because of their entanglement in Western ideologies of natural domination and dualistic separation. The truth is that none of the large-scale religions has resources adequate to the crisis. None of the "world" religions is an Earth religion. The non-local religions are in no better shape than the multinational corporations. Because so much pollutes the spiritual environment, cleaning it up is every bit as urgent and challenging as cleaning up the physical environment.

Assuming religious leaders were to take a more creative and critical ritual initiative, what might an eco-rite look like? Clear-cutting in Thailand has become so extensive that monks began preaching about the suffering of trees and land. In the 1970s, after his ordination, Phrakhru Pitak noticed the deforestation around his home and the consequent damage to watersheds and local economies. He started to preach against the destruction but found that the villagers, even those who believed him, went home from temple services only to continue clearing the land. Moral admonition was not enough. So in 1991 he ordained a tree, wrapping it in monk's robes. To down an ordained tree would be to kill a sentient being and incur religious demerit.

At first the monk led people in sprinkling holy water on the trees. Later he upped the ante by requiring village leaders to drink holy water in front of a statue of Buddha by a tree. This way, community leaders ritually enacted their identification with the tree, and thereby pledged themselves to its protection. Sometimes, posted on an ordained tree would be a sign saying, "To destroy the forest is to destroy life, one's rebirth, or the nation." Sincere Buddhists do not want to tamper with their rebirth.

This improvised ritualizing is now attracting upstanding citizens. As a result, the Thai debate is no longer purely political but also moral and religious. The metaphoric act of ordaining trees has made it so. If trees have Buddha-nature, to saw one down is to slice yourself in half. Now, it costs moral and religious capital to lay low the ancestor-teacher trees. Ritual is a primary means of ensuring that moral behavior does not become merely moralistic, that instead, it is embodied and enacted.

Ronald L. Grimes

Further Reading

d'Aquili, Eugene G., Charles D. Laughlin, Jr. and John McManus. *The Spectrum of Ritual*. New York: Columbia University Press, 1979.

Darlington, Susan M. "The Ordination of a Tree: The Buddhist Ecology Movement in Thailand." *Ethnology* 37:1 (1998), 1–15.

Grimes, Ronald L. "Performance is Currency in the Deep World's Gift Economy: An Incantatory Riff for a Global Medicine Show." *Interdisciplinary Studies in Literature and Environment* 9:1 (Winter 2002).

Kinsley, David. *Ecology and Religion: Ecological Spirituality in Cross-Cultural Perspective*. Englewood Cliffs, NJ: Prentice Hall, 1995.

Krech, Shepard, III. *The Ecological Indian: Myth and History*. New York: W.W. Norton, 2000.

Laughlin, Charles D., Jr., John McManus and Eugene G. d'Aquili. *Brain, Symbol & Experience: Toward a Neurophenomenology of Human Consciousness*. Boston: Shambhala, 1990.

Rappaport, Roy A. *Ritual and Religion in the Making of Humanity*. Cambridge: Cambridge University Press, 1999.

Rappaport, Roy A. *Pigs for the Ancestors: Ritual in the Ecology of a New Guinea People*. New Haven, CT: Yale University Press, 1984 (enlarged edition).

Rappaport, Roy A. *Ecology, Meaning, and Religion*. Berkeley, CA: North Atlantic, 1979.

See also: Ecology and Religion; Epic of Evolution (and adjacent, Epic Ritual); Rappaport, Roy; Restoration Ecology and Ritual; Ritualizing and Anthropology.

Ritualizing and Anthropology

Ritual is a term rooted in nineteenth-century Western scholarship on the anthropology of religion that has been used to categorize and describe certain types of religious behavior. There is no single, universally agreed-upon definition of ritual. Nineteenth- and early twentieth-century scholars tended to define ritual as a patterned set of actions intended to bring about changes in the relationship between humans and supernatural agents, such as gods or spirits. In the late twentieth century, scholars began to view ritual more as a process than an object: a formalized response intended to bring about change that religions and cultures apply to a particular situation. Rituals are an important part of cultures and religions, and mark secular as well as sacred occasions.

Types of Rituals

French ethnologist Arnold Van Gennep identified two principal types of rituals, both tied to natural cycles: *rites of passage* and *rites of intensification*. Rites of passage involve transformations in the life cycle of an individual. They typically occur around times of personal transition, such as birth, puberty, marriage and death. Initiation rites for shamans, healers, priests and priestesses are also considered rites of passage. In some religions, rites of passage involve the temporary isolation of initiates from the rest of society. Among the Plains Indians in North America, for example, young men often underwent a period of fasting, physical trials and retreat during which they would seek the guidance of nature spirits, who would appear to them in visions offering wisdom. Since Amerindians generally viewed their relationship to nature as reciprocal and contiguous, obtaining the protection of spirit guides was an important part of attaining maturity. In other indigenous traditions, young people underwent initiation in groups. Among the Mbuti of Central Africa, young initiates were taken away from their villages to a men's house, where elders instructed them on hunting techniques and the ways of the forest spirits. During the period when initiates are isolated and undergoing instruction and testing, they are said to be *liminal*, or in a threshold state betwixt and between social categories. The liminal stage is characterized by social equality and a temporary suspension of everyday norms of behavior, a condition anthropologist Victor Turner called *communitas*. Usually, upon completion of the rite of passage, initiates are reunited with their communities in a ritual of reintegration that celebrates their new status. While rites of passage serve an important function in the life of the individual, they are also important for the community, in that they help groups come to terms with changes in their members' life cycles. This is particularly true of birth and death rites, where the subject cannot participate fully in the ritual.

Rites of intensification mark important transitions in the life of a community. There are two types: *calendrical* or *year-cycle rites* and *rites of crisis*. Year-cycle rites center around important times in a community's seasonal calendar which often coincide with environmental changes – for example, the transition from winter to spring. They often mark crucial agricultural events such as harvest and planting times, or the seasonal migration of herd animals. Calendrical rites repeat yearly, and often involve a prolonged period of celebration which includes secular as well as religious aspects. There may be music, dancing, feasting and dramatic performances that enact myths associated with the seasonal cycle. Often, these celebrations are thought to be necessary for the continuation of the natural cycle. Rites of crisis, in contrast, are held in response to a crisis in the community, such as a drought, plague or other drastic event. In many religions, these events are often understood as being the result of disharmony between humans and nature. Rites of crisis serve to restore the relationship to a state of balance.

All rituals communicate through symbols, and many of these are rooted in the natural world. They act out important stories or ideas, often by bringing together a number of symbolic opposites in culture in a meaningful way. Participation in rituals helps communicate these concepts to the community, and brings the community together in recognition of their shared values. Because rituals enact important values, they can also become points of contention and strife, especially when religions are undergoing rapid change. Some rituals reverse social norms through a process called *symbolic inversion*, in which important symbols are literally turned upside down or mocked. Ultimately, though, even such rites of reversal tend to uphold the existing social system by demonstrating its limits.

Ritual and Nature
Since the early nineteenth century, scholars have recognized a relationship between rituals and the natural world. Among the earliest observers of ritual was the German linguist Max Müller (1823–1900), who theorized that rituals originated as poetic dramatizations of natural and celestial phenomena, especially what appeared to early peoples as the movement of the sun in the sky. Since early humans depended on the sun as a source of light and heat, and feared the darkness, Müller hypothesized that they developed rituals as a way of attempting to control these natural phenomena. Later, anthropologists such as Edward B. Tylor argued that rituals were rooted in the belief that natural objects had a soul and could interact with humans, a notion he called *animism*. Tylor's disciple James G. Frazer (1854–1941) argued that rituals in all cultures enacted the death and resurrection of the divine king, whose life was connected to the fertility of the crops and herds and the prosperity of his people. Frazer's theory led to the emergence of the myth-ritual school, a group of early twentieth-century scholars who applied Frazer's idea of death and rebirth not only to rituals, but also to many forms of folklore such as folktales, myths and legends, folk drama and even children's games, which they thought had derived from rituals. For the myth-ritualists, almost all forms of expressive culture enacted the seasonal cycle of death and rebirth of crops and vegetation. Despite many scholarly criticisms of Frazer and the myth-ritual school, these theories continued to hold sway until well into the mid-twentieth century.

By the 1960s, scholars were becoming more aware of how cultures were uniquely adapted to their environments. This led to the emergence of new ways of interpreting the relationship between rituals and nature. Anthropologist Roy A. Rappaport pioneered the idea that rituals could regulate cultures' relationships to their environment. In his study of the Maring-speaking Tsembaga in New Guinea, he found that a complex ritual cycle involving warfare with neighboring groups, the raising of pigs and the cultivation of gardens helped to maintain ecological balance, ensured a fair distribution of land and protein among people living in a territory, limited the frequency of fighting between neighboring tribes, and helped create alliances between groups. Rappaport's work inspired a generation of scholars to examine rituals' function not only in creating social cohesion, but also in ensuring that human groups did not exceed the carrying capacity of their ecosystems. For example, Gerardo Reichel-Dolmatoff examined the hunting rituals of the Tukano Indians of the northwest Amazon basin, in Colombia and Venezuela. He concluded that many of the prohibitions and rites surrounding hunting actually restricted hunters' activities in a way that ensured that the Tukano would not exhaust the supply of game in their ecosystem, and would be able to continue to survive within their territory without causing environmental degradation. The Tukano did not see themselves as existing apart from nature, and their myths and rituals ensured that humans could maintain a certain quality of life only if other organisms in their natural environment were also permitted to live and develop. In yet another study, O.K. Moore found that the divination practices of the Naskapi of the upper Labrador peninsula served to ensure that these arctic peoples hunted throughout their territory, rather than concentrating their efforts in only a few areas and thus overhunting the herds. These studies and many more like them helped to change anthropological perspectives on the relationship between nature and ritual by examining the ways rituals actually function in the material world. While scientists believe they may not function in the way their practitioners believe they do – namely, by regulating relations between humans and the supernatural world – they may, in some cases, have quite specific ecological and economic functions that maintain the balance between humans and their environment.

It is important to note, however, that not all myths and rituals function to maintain harmony between humans and their ecosystems, nor do all pre-industrial peoples ritually regulate their relationship to their environment. The Bible, in which Yaweh gives human beings "dominion" over nature, has been criticized as justifying the voracious exploitation of nature that has characterized the emergence of colonialism and capitalism in the West. And archeologist Mark Raab has demonstrated that Indians living along the southern coast of California before colonial contact overhunted fish and shellfish to the point of causing their own famine and near-extinction. Therefore, the relationship of each ritual system to nature must be carefully examined before drawing conclusions about ritual's function *vis-à-vis* the natural world.

Sabina Magliocco

Further Reading

Babcock, Barbara, ed. *The Reversible World*. Ithaca: Cornell University Press, 1978.
Bell, Catherine. *Ritual: Perspectives and Dimensions*. New York: Oxford University Press, 1997.
Douglas, Mary. *Natural Symbols*. New York: Pantheon Books, 1970, 1982.
Geertz, Clifford. "Religion as a Cultural System" and "Ritual and Social Change: A Javanese Example." In Clifford Geertz. *The Interpretation of Cultures*. New York: Basic Books, 1973, 87–125 and 142–69.
Gennep, Arnold van. *The Rites of Passage*. Monika B Vizedon and Gabrielle Caffee, trs. London: Routledge, 1909.
Grimes, Ronald L. *Beginnings in Ritual Studies*. Columbia, SC: University of South Carolina Press, 1995 (rev. edn).
Grimes, Ronald L. *Ritual Criticism: Case Studies in its Practice, Essays on its Theory*. Columbia, SC: University of South Carolina Press, 1990.
Harris, Marvin. *Cows, Pigs, Wars and Witches: The Riddles of Culture*. New York: Vintage Books, 1974.
Moore, O.K. "Divination – A New Perspective." *American Anthropologist* 59:1 (1957), 69–74.
Rappaport, Roy A. "Ritual Regulation of Environmental Relations among a New Guinea People." *Ethnology* 6:1 (1967), 17–30.
Reichel-Dolmatoff, Gerardo. "Cosmology as Ecological Analysis: A View from the Rain Forest." *Man* 11 (1976), 307–18.
Turner, Victor. *The Ritual Process*. Ithaca: Cornell University Press, 1969.

See also: Animism; Anthropologists; Ecological Anthropology; Ecology and Religion; Harris, Marvin; Müller, Friedrich Max; Rappaport, Roy A. ("Skip"); Reichel-Domatoff, Gerardo; Ritual.

River Ganga and the Clean Ganga Campaign
– *See* Hinduism and Pollution.

Rock Art – Australian Aboriginal

Aboriginal people of Australia have a rich heritage of carving and painting on rocks, extending back well more than 20,000 years. Rock art, Australia's oldest surviving art form, expresses the Aborigines' social, economic and religious concerns through the centuries. In the form of petroglyphs (carvings) and pictographs (paintings), rock art is found across the continent. It served a variety of functions, and provides the earliest illustration of Aboriginal beliefs, technologies and activities. Australia is a particularly rich region for rock-art research because it is one of the few areas where the art is still being produced, which has facilitated the work of anthropologists in collecting some of the myths and meanings associated with the art. We know that as humans, our relationship with the world is deeply affected by the images we use to understand and express our place in nature and the cosmos. By combining ethnographic field research and archeological findings we can begin to interpret the cultural significance of prehistoric rock art in Australia.

Various regions developed particular styles of art, and Aboriginal rock art is often classified by these main regional types. Continuity of motifs within regions and across time is attributed to the extreme conservatism of Aboriginal religion. Some of the earliest known Aboriginal rock art lies underground, in the limestone caves of the southern portion of the continent. Perhaps the best-known depository of parietal designs is Koonalda Cave, where the markings consist of finger meanders (made by sets of parallel finger strokes executed on the soft and pliable areas of the cave wall) and incised lines scratched into the harder surfaces. The prehistoric use of torches in Koonalda resulted in deposits of charcoal near dense concentrations of the finger flutings. Associational dating with the charcoal indicates that this artistic development in Australia occurred about 20,000 years ago.

Another common type of rock art in South Australia is called Panaramitee after a site containing many petroglyphs of this classification. Panaramitee rock engravings are also found in portions of the Northern Territory, New South Wales, Tasmania, and Queensland. They were made by pecking away the dark, patinated outer surface that forms on exposed rocks, to reveal the lighter, unweathered rock underneath. Circles, tracks, tectiforms, and meanders predominate.

The Kimberly region in northwestern Australia offers interesting examples of the relationship between rock art and mythology. Aborigines claim that some of the paintings in the central Kimberly district contain the spirits of the Ancestral Beings known as *Wandjina*, the preeminent Ancestors in the religion of this region. When a Wandjina completed his Dreamtime actions he turned himself into a picture containing his spirit and power. Each clan in the Kimberly region has a number of totemic species or objects associated with its Wandjina. Hence, in addition to paintings of Wandjina, many of the caves contain representations of kangaroo, eagles, fish, and various plants. A significant component of the Wandjina cult was the duty of each clan to retouch the paintings in its caves, thereby ensuring a supply of the natural species represented there.

The Pilbara region of Western Australia has the largest concentration of petroglyph sites in Australia – perhaps millions of individual figures. The large numbers of human figures at these sites show a highly stylized and developed art form, and a great degree of creativity. Some are fairly accurate representations of humans with well-proportioned bodies, while others are biomorphs; part human and part animal, apparently representing Dreaming beings.

The rock shelters of sub-tropical Arnhem Land hold an abundance of varied and skillfully executed examples of rock art. The two most general pictograph styles in Arnhem Land are the X-ray and Dynamic (sometimes called Mimi) paintings. Both tend to be basically naturalistic, yet their differences in form and subject matter are striking.

The Dynamic style is generally simpler in design than the X-ray art, yet its elegance is remarkable. The anthropomorphs depicted in the Dynamic art are Mimi spirit people, the beings responsible for teaching the Aborigines to paint. Dynamic-phase figures are often slender and shown in action – dancing, fighting, hunting, and running. They are monochrome paintings, and are said to have been made by the small Mimi spirits. X-ray pictographs, generally larger and polychromatic, are usually representations of people and animals, and unlike the Mimi paintings, are essentially static pictures. The X-ray art is so called because it illustrates not only the body of a subject, but some internal organs and skeletal features as well; the heart, lungs, stomach, and backbone of an animal are often depicted. One of the most pervasive and distinctive contexts in which this art was created was through the practice of increase rituals at sacred sites.

The pigments used to create these and other rock paintings throughout Australia were primarily derived from pulverized minerals, often mixed with a natural binder such as tree resin or animal fat. Various shades of red and yellow ochre were utilized, as well as white pipeclay and black manganese. Charcoal was used often, as were brushes, probably made of human hair, bark, feathers, or a twig chewed at one end to loosen the cellulose fibers.

Many of the rock shelters of Arnhem Land contain painted images considered of vital religious importance to the Aborigines. Since it was believed that the act of creating or retouching a painting could release the spirit of the subject, these acts were often considered a necessary component of ritual. The practice ensured the preservation of the paintings, but with the breakdown of many aspects of traditional Aboriginal culture repainting has ceased, and the designs are slowly fading away. There have been some historical examples of rock-art production in the region, and the artists claimed that the placing of clan designs in rock shelters is an assertion of rights over the site, as well as an effort to keep religious tradition alive.

Scattered around the vicinity of Laura in the southeast Cape York Peninsula of far northern Queensland are some of the best-preserved pictograph galleries of the world. Hundreds of adorned shelters and caves are scattered throughout the hills and valleys of this region. The majority of the Cape York rock paintings are human and animal motifs representing totemic animals, mythological beings, game animals, and an assortment of human figures.

In the Carnarvon Ranges of south-central Queensland, the stenciling of hands and cultural material objects was a highly developed rock-art technique. The stencils are often arranged in intricate patterns, which form large murals of a dozen or more paintings within a single composition. They were made by pressing a hand or object against the rock and splattering paint around it to produce a negative imprint. The expression of physical and spiritual connection appears to have been an important feature of this art.

Thousands of petroglyph sites occur near Sydney, where numerous exposures of sandstone form large, horizontal rock pavements. The petroglyphs depict humans and animals, mythical beings, tracks, weapons, and various non-figurative motifs. The most unusual feature of this art is its scale. The large, flat rock surfaces enabled the Aborigines to depict their subjects life-size or larger; there are human figures and kangaroos measuring over seven meters, eels over ten meters long, and full-size whales. The huge scale suggests that some of these engravings may portray mythological Dreaming beings.

Rock art in Australia was once a prolific expression of social and material culture and religious thought. Through rock art, the Aborigines communicated ideas and concepts that were at the center of a complex set of cultural beliefs. While symbolism is inseparable from Aboriginal art, it should be understood that rock art was essentially utilitarian; it was one medium through which the powers of the Dreaming were brought to bear upon everyday affairs.

Paul Faulstich

Further Reading
Layton, Robert. *Australian Rock Art: A New Synthesis.* Cambridge: Cambridge University Press, 1992.
See also: Aboriginal Art; Aboriginal Dreaming (Australia); Art; Rock Art (various).

Rock Art – Batwa/Pygmies (Central Africa)

The central African hunter-gatherer rock-art zone has been termed the "Schematic Art Zone" by J. Desmond Clark. Nearly 3000 hunter-gatherer rock-art sites have been found within this zone and some 90 percent of these comprise superimposed layers of massed, finger-painted, geometric designs. The other 10 percent of sites comprise highly stylized and distorted animal forms plus rows of finger dots. Both seem to have a history extending back many thousands of years.

While the geometric art always dominates, the two traditions go together as a pair: they co-occur across a huge area and are regularly found close by, but in only a handful of cases can they be found together in the same site. They seem to be kept near, but apart. Both are found in the same overall distribution, in an area that encircles the central African rainforests and includes: Angola, Zambia, Malawi, northern Mozambique, the Democratic Republic of Congo, southern and western Tanzania, western Kenya, Uganda, Congo and the Central African Republic. The dominance of geometric rock art makes this area immediately distinctive from the other hunter-gatherer rock-art regions in Africa all of which, by contrast, contain a high percentage of brush-painted animals, humans and human-animal conflations. Little research has been conducted on this art tradition and it is therefore still poorly understood by comparison with hunter-gatherer rock art in other parts of Africa.

Throughout most of central Africa, the pre-farmer hunter-gathering populations have gone and they exist today only in the archeological deposits and in oral traditions. Modern central African Bantu-language speakers remember these people as the Batwa (a word that is used widely in eastern, central and southern Africa to refer to any autochthonous hunter-gatherer people). They are described by many groups, and across a wide geographic area, as "short-statured, dark-skinned and hairy." In those areas close to southern Africa they are remembered as being immediately distinctive from the San (or Bushmen). The rock art supports this division: it is entirely different from San rock art. The dividing line between southern African San rock art and central African Batwa rock art follows the Zambezi River and the Anglo/Namibia border. The archeological remains also show strong divergence along this same line. The later Stone Age lithic technologies vary to such an extent that they have been given different names: those in southern Africa are known as the Wilton/Smithfield whereas those of central Africa are known as Nachikufan. The cultural distinctions between central, southern Africa hunter-gatherers are thus profound.

The only surviving groups of central African Batwa are the so-called forest "Pygmies." Genetic studies appear to confirm the archeological division between the ancestral heritage of these groups and that of the southern African San. Geneticists suggest great antiquity to the division between the San and the Pygmies, perhaps with a divergence in excess of 40,000 years. Pygmy groups are known to have occupied many sections of the central African "Schematic Art Zone" even into historical times, and it is probable that the full former distribution of these groups can be recognized from the distribution of the art. Certainly, elements within recorded Pygmy traditions help us to understand central African rock art.

Pygmy traditions, such as those recorded by Colin Turnbull amongst the Mbuti, are dominated by two major ceremonies. The Mbuti call these *molimo* and *elima*. *Molimo* is organized by men and *elima* by women. Both ceremonies traditionally take place in a clearing in the forest and involve singing around camp fires for night after night, sometimes for as long as a month. *Molimo* is often held after the death of an important member of the group or in the case of a violent argument; *elima* usually marks important women's occasions such as coming of age. Turnbull describes how the songs in both ceremonies seek to bring out the spirit of the forest. In *molimo* the spirit of the forest literally comes out and its unearthly song can often be heard encircling the campfire in the darkness (the song is in fact sung by a boy through a special *molimo* pipe).

Turnbull argues that the purpose of calling out the spirit of the forest in these ceremonies is to restore harmony within the camp and the forest. He argues that the Mbuti see this state of harmony as essential to allowing the dead to be released back to the forest and to giving heath and fertility to the girls. Smith and Blundell argue that it is these same concerns that underlie central African Batwa rock art. The stylized animal depictions mark the symbols and concerns of the ceremony of *molimo* (specifically the calling of the spirit of the forest) and the geometric designs represent the symbols and concerns of *elima* (specifically fertility and rain divination). They argue that this is why the two arts are found locally separated, and yet are together within the landscape. The arts were made by different groups within the same society and, together, they form a conceptual whole.

B.W. Smith

Further Reading

Cavalli-Sforza, Luca L. *Genes, Peoples and Languages.* Berkeley: University of California Press, 2000.

Clark, J. Desmond. "The Rock Paintings of Northern Rhodesia and Nyasaland." In Roger Summers, ed. *Prehistoric Rock Art of the Federation of Rhodesia and Nyasaland.* Glasgow: National Publication Trust, 1959, 163–220.

Smith, Benjamin W. *Zambia's Ancient Rock Art: The Paintings of Kasama.* Livingstone: National Heritage Conservation Commission, 1997.

Smith, Benjamin W. and Geoffrey B. Blundell. *The Art of the Spirit World.* Cape Town: Double Storey Books, 2004.

Turnbull, Colin. *The Forest People.* New York: Simon & Schuster, 1961.

See also: Pygmies (Mbuti foragers) & Bila Farmers (Ituri Forest); Rock Art – Hadzabe/Sandawe; San (Bushmen) Apocalpytic Rock Art; San (Bushmen) Religion (Eastern Africa); San (Bushmen) Rainmaking.

Rock Art – Chewa (Central Africa)

The ancestors of the Chewa and Nyanja peoples of central Africa were among (and adjacent), the most prolific of Africa's Bantu-speaking farmer rock artists. More than 400 Chewa rock-art sites have so far been found spread across central Malawi, eastern Zambia and neighboring areas of Mozambique. Nearly 70 percent of the known sites fall within the Dedza-Chongoni hills of Malawi and it seems that this was a core area for Chewa art.

Chewa rock art divides into two separate art traditions: the art of nyau and the art of chinamwali. As is typical of rock-art traditions made by Bantu-speaking peoples, the primary color used is white and this is applied thickly by daubing. In rare instances where the art is especially well preserved, black finger-painted decoration may be seen executed over the primary white design. The white pigment is a form of powdered clay, which can be dug out of most riverbeds in this area. The same pigment is used in traditional house decoration today. The black pigment is powdered charcoal. Both pigments seem to have been mixed using only water, as neither is tightly bonded to the rock surfaces. Rock engravings (also known as petroglyphs) are unknown in these traditions.

The art of nyau is a tradition belonging to Chewa men. Nyau rock art is comparatively rare and fresh-looking when compared with chinamwali rock art. Only a few dozen sites are known. It depicts a range of masked men and, in particular, larger animal basketwork figures. These are readily recognizable as the elaborate masked characters that still perform in the ceremonies of the nyau closed association. While the subject matter of the art is known, the art is no longer created today nor is the rationale behind it remembered.

It has been argued that the nyau art tradition belonged to the specific historical context of the nineteenth and early twentieth centuries, a time when nyau was forced to become an underground movement because of its suppression by Ngoni invaders, missions and the colonial government. According to this explanation, the art served as a mnemonic device, helping to teach young initiates about the construction and meaning of large nyau structures that could not be made in this troubled time. The art went out of use when the suppression of nyau ended and initiates could once again learn by making and using the real structures. The need for the rock art was thus removed.

The art of chinamwali is far more numerous and, judging by the many layers of superpositions – more than a dozen at some sites – it is a tradition that has a far greater antiquity than nyau art. It seems likely that this tradition of art has been passed down from the time of the earliest ancestors of the Chewa in this region, more than one thousand years ago. This, therefore, is traditional Chewa rock art. This art has been linked to Chewa women and to the girls' coming-of-age ceremony: chinamwali. The painted symbolism is thought to revolve around concepts relating to water and fertility. It contains many instructive messages that teach and remind those attending chinamwali how to behave and conduct themselves.

Similar designs to those in the rock art are modeled in clay and used in chinamwali and similar ceremonies in a number of places within central Africa. These designs each have a name, a dance and an instructive song and the image helps the young girls to remember the varied and complex teaching of the ceremony. The subject matter of these designs and their form suggest close parallels with Chewa rock art. It seems likely that the images in the rock art were also linked to song and to dance. Chinamwali rock art is no longer created today, but some of the shelters containing this art are still used for chinamwali ceremonies. There are indications that the secret meanings of many of the designs are still understood, but there has been no published confirmation of this to date.

B.W. Smith

Further Reading

Lindgren, N.E. and J. Matthew Schoffeleers. *Rock Art and Nyau Symbolism in Malawi*. Department of Antiquities Publication No. 18. Zomba: Malawi Government Printers, 1978.

Phillipson, David W. *The Prehistory of Eastern Zambia*. Nairobo: British Institute in East Africa, 1976.

Smith, Benjamin W. "Forbidden Images: Rock Paintings and the Nyau Secret Society of Central Malawi and Eastern Zambia." *African Archaeological Review* 18:4 (2001), 187–212.

Smith, Benjamin W. *Zambia's Ancient Rock Art: The Paintings of Kasama*. Livingstone: National Heritage Conservation Commission, 1997.

See also: Nyau – A Closed Association; Rock Art – Northern Sotho.

Rock Art – Hadzabe/Sandawe (Eastern Africa)

Within central Tanzania is a localized tradition of brush-painted hunter-gatherer rock art that stands apart from the predominantly finger-painted geometric rock art of other parts of central Africa. The southern boundary of this art follows the southern limits of Kondoa and Singida districts and the northern boundary is Lake Eyasi. The length and breadth of this distribution does not exceed 200 kilometers. This art is by far the most regionally confined of all African hunter-gatherer rock arts. Within this same region is a finger-painted rock-art tradition executed in yellow/white. This art was made by Bantu-speaking farmer groups within boys' initiation ceremonies. (I am concerned here only with the older hunter-gatherer art.)

The brush-painted hunter-gatherer art of this region has been known since the early 1900s, but was made famous by the work of Ludwig Kohl-Larsen, Henry Fosbrooke, Eric Ten Raa and Mary Leakey. The art contains depictions of a wide variety of animals and a few birds and reptiles. It is painted in an unusually varied collection of manners of depiction ranging from outline, through linear, dotted and gridded fills, to partial and fully filled forms. Humans are depicted in these same manners in a range of standing, bending and "floating" postures, sometimes with bows, and often with large and bizarre head forms that may or may not reflect the wearing of headdresses. A few humans are painted with animal heads. Early researchers tried to sequence the manners of depiction, but more detailed recent studies by Fidelis Masao and others have found that the proposed sequences are flawed. There are too many conflicting overlays when one collects together the evidence from a large number of sites. It now appears that variety in manner of depiction is one of the characteristics of this art tradition.

The distribution of this art matches closely the historically known distribution of the only two click-speaking groups in eastern Africa: the Hadzabe and the Sandawe. It is widely believed by researchers and claimed by the groups themselves, that it was the ancestors of the modern Hadzabe and Sandawe that made the rock art. There has been much debate on the relationship between these groups and the southern African click-speakers such as the San (Bushmen). Linguists now see the languages as highly divergent and recent genetic evidence suggests that these groups may have diverged as long ago as 70,000–100,000 years before the present. These are therefore two of the oldest populations on Earth and the fact that they both speak click-languages is suggestive about the nature of the first languages.

As with most African hunter-gatherer rock arts, it appears that the art was part of traditional religious practice. Ten Raa, working among the Sandawe, records three instances in the mid-twentieth century when he witnessed Sandawe people creating rock art. Through this personal experience he connects some of the art with hunting magic and some with an ecstatic cult called simbó. In simbó, dancers use vigorous movement and hallucinogenic beer to attain an ecstatic state. In this state the Sandawe say that people become lions. David Lewis-Williams has argued that many of the bizarre head forms, many of the postures, such as the floating posture, and the depiction of therianthropes (animal-people) link much of the central Tanzanian rock art to this ritual experience of altered states of consciousness.

B.W. Smith

Further Reading

Knight, Alec, et al. "African Y Chromosome and mtDNA Divergence Provides Insights into the History of Click Languages." *Current Biology* 13 (2003), 1–20.

Leakey, Mary. *Africa's Vanishing Art: The Rock Paintings of Tanzania*. London: Hamish Hamilton, 1983.

Lewis-Williams, J. David. "Beyond Style and Portrait: A Comparison of Tanzanian and Southern African Rock Art." In Rainer Vossen and Klaus Keuthmann, eds. *Contemporary Studies on Khoisan* 2. Hamburg: Helmut Buske, 1987, 93–139.

Masao, Fidelis. *The Later Stone Age and the Rock Paintings of Central Tanzania*. Wiesbaden: Frans Steiner, 1979.

Ten Raa, Eric. "Dead Art Living Society: A Study of Rock

Paintings in a Social Context." *Mankind* 8 (1971), 42-58.

See also: Rock Art - Batwa/Pygmies; San (Bushmen) Apocalyptic Rock Art.

Rock Art - Northern Sotho (Southern Africa)

In addition to its celebrated hunter-gatherer rock art made by the San (or Bushmen), southern Africa has a number of later rock-art traditions made by Bantu-speaking farmers. The most extensive of these traditions in terms of area covered and number of sites is the rock art of the Northern Sotho. This art is found spread across the greater part of northern South Africa.

Northern Sotho rock art is easily distinguished from San rock art both by its color and by its form. It is predominantly executed in white and was applied thickly onto the rock by finger (in contrast to the polychrome brushwork paintings of the San). Occasionally, red and black pigments are also used, usually as decoration over the primary white design. The white used is a form of powdered clay found in many riverbeds in the area. The choice of white as the dominant color is characteristic of rock-art traditions belonging to Bantu-speaking agriculturists. Reflecting this, these arts have become colloquially known as the "late whites."

Northern Sotho art is found in its greatest concentration in the more remote hill areas of Limpopo Province, South Africa. Areas particularly rich in this art include the Soutpansberg and Waterberg mountains as well of the Makgabeng plateau. In total, nearly 300 sites with Northern Sotho rock art are currently known.

The art divides into an earlier and a later period. The early art depicts a range of wild animals such as elephant, zebra, lion, rhino, kudu, hyena and hippo, but the dominant subject is the giraffe. Almost all of the art is concealed in large rock shelters in remote and secluded mountain areas. These places are the traditional venues for the secretive Northern Sotho boys' initiation practices. Elders in some areas acknowledge a link between this art and tradition initiation practices, but they state that, while some of the painted sites are still used for initiation ceremonies today, the tradition of creating rock art has ceased.

It seems that each painted animal carried a particular instructive and symbolic message within the boys' initiation ceremony and indications as to how this symbolism operated survive in the continued use of animal symbolism within modern initiation practices. Within the modern initiation lodge, for example, the fire is sometimes referred to as the lion cub, the magic tree as the giraffe, the cairn of stones as the hyena and the structure under which food is placed as the elephant. Many of the instructive songs learnt by the initiates are also concerned with these same animals. The secret teachings in these songs are often unclear to the initiates, but concealed within this complex structure of animal imagery are social messages that become progressively understood through life with age and experience.

In the latter half of the nineteenth century, the rock art underwent a dramatic change. The intrusion of white settlers into the region brought taxes, land clearances and conflict. A series of wars to subdue Northern Sotho traditional leaders left many homeless and destitute. At this time whole communities fled to the hill areas. Many of the old initiation sites became refuge settlements. A new form of rock art developed at this time dominated by depictions of steam trains, soldiers, settlers and guns. The images capture a people's tragedy, but served a more important purpose. They poked fun at the troublesome new intruders and through this pointed humor served to overcome some of the terrible stresses of the times. The art marks the origins of protest art in northern South Africa - ordinary people protesting their right to land and self-determination, and fighting the destruction of their traditional structures and cultural values.

B.W. Smith

Further Reading

Roberts, Noel and C.A.T. Winter. "The Kgoma, or Initiation Rites of the Bapedi of Sekukiniland." *South African Journal of Science* 12 (1916), 561-78.

Pitje, G.M. "Traditional Systems of Male Education among Pedi and Cognate Tribes." *African Studies* 9 (1950), 53-76, 105-24, 194-201.

Smith, Benjamin W. and Johan A. van Schalkwyk. "The White Camel of the Magkabeng." *Journal of African History* 43 (2002), 235-54.

See also: Rock Art - Chewa; San (Bushmen) Apocalyptic Rock Art; San (Bushmen) Religion.

Rock Art - Sintu

Throughout much of south-central and southern Africa there extends a finger-painting tradition associated with Bantu-speaking groups. In the countries of Zaire, Zambia, Malawi, Angola, Botswana, Zimbabwe and South Africa, this art form most often occurs where there are rocky outcrops on boulders and in shelters and caves. An expression of a primal religion, this art form can be considered a cultural complex, which is both religious in character and strongly linked to nature. In this artistic tradition we find highly schematized depictions of abstract zoomorphic and anthropomorphic figures, fantastic beings, abstract symbols, signs and smears which can be linked to human sexuality and procreation. It is also associated with traditional rulers, rainmaking, initiation, diviners, secret societies, and to society in general. The overriding concern, however, is for the fertility of man, beast and land, all of which impinge directly upon human society and welfare.

This artistic tradition differs greatly from Khoisan rock art in execution, intent and meaning, having been painted with a finger, or perhaps a stick, unlike Khoisan brushwork. It also has a much wider distribution extending from East Africa down to the northern South Africa, with isolated examples evident as far south as the Eastern Cape, yet it is less understood and far less researched. Early dates of 1800 BP have been suggested for the oldest depictions, but they may be older.

Sintu rock art is highly symbolic, reflecting and reinforcing ritual action, group structure, beliefs regarding nature and the wider cosmos. The manner in which the motifs and symbols are perceived and manipulated reflect people's attempts to manage natural and supernatural forces that impinge upon their physical and conceptual worlds.

In many parts of Africa caves and shelters are favored by ritual specialists for rainmaking and other religious activities, and many of those shelters given ritual status are decorated with paintings. This is almost certainly linked to widespread beliefs in Bantu-speaking Africa that holes, hollows and rock shelters are entrances to the ancestor-world and that, through these special points, communication with the ancestors and deities is possible. Supernatural beings are held to control the elements, and so it is here that appeals are made and offerings offered. Painted shelters are often used for rainmaking, thus linking sacred points with climatic phenomena.

Naturalistic and abstracted zoomorphic symbols, such as crocodiles and snakes, are associated with concepts of kingship, divinership, initiation and rainfall, but most importantly, with fertility and procreation. Many such motifs not only occur in the finger paintings but are also used as educational diagrams during initiation.

Bantu-speaking groups stress institutionalization of passage in which initiation is an elaborate affair emphasizing fertility. Not only do finger paintings form part of this iconography, but so also do schematic and naturalistic figures, masks and costumes of fantastic beings. In these societies, greater emphasis is placed upon hunting than among patrilineal cattle-complex groups. Here the killing of prey is associated with male sexuality, indicating that wild animals, as a communal concept in finger paintings, are yet another expression of fertility.

As a rule, African worldviews are unified, phenomena within them fading into one another, creating a holistic structure of both the physical and conceptual worlds, so that each becomes indistinguishable from the other.

The art expresses a liminality of interaction among the principles that govern the mundane world. Here, in shelters and caves, fantastic beings live and are represented in the rock art and iconography, often with exaggerated features, such as exceptionally elongated necks, as an expression of their liminal status.

Diviners are prominent figures in finger paintings. They perform the rainmaking and fertility ceremonies and are the masters of initiation. They communicate with the ancestors in caves and shelters. Like the initiation event, and like the shelters, diviners are liminal, and it is their very ambiguity that entitles them to control the elements through the ancestors.

It is significant that the finger-painting tradition is widespread among groups who depend upon hunting and upon the fertility of game. The preeminent threats to hunting-based agrarian economies are drought and other natural disasters that reduce animal and plant populations. The positive expression of fertility may be seen as the ultimate symbol of well-being, and a manifestation that the social and natural order are operating smoothly. These conceptual associations permeate throughout different levels of society, and are believed to be reflected in the fertility of males and females entering adulthood.

Sian Hall

Further Reading
Blacking, J. "Songs, Dances, Mimes and Symbolism of Venda Girls' Initiation Schools, Part 2 Milayo." *African Studies* 28 (1969), 69–118.
Brelsford, V. "Some Reflections on Bemba Geometric Decorative Art." *Bantu Studies* 11 (1937), 37–45.
Lindgren, N.E. and J.M. Schoffeleers. *The Prehistoric Rock Paintings of Malawi*. Lilongwe: Department of Antiquities, 1978.
Phillipson, D.W. *The Prehistory of Eastern Zambia*. Nairobi: British Institute in Eastern Africa, 1976.
Prins, F.E. and S. Hall. "Expressions of Fertility in the Rock Art of Bantu-speaking Agriculturalists." *The African Archaeological Review* 12 (1994), 171–203.
Richards, A.I. *Land, Labour and Diet in Northern Rhodesia*. Oxford: Oxford University Press, 1969.
Richards, A.I. *Chisungu – A Girl's Initiation Ceremony Among the Bemba of Northern Rhodesia*. Oxford: Oxford University Press, 1954.
Stayt, H.A. *The BaVenda*. Oxford: Oxford University Press, 1931.
Turner, V. *The Forest of Symbols: Aspects of Ndembu Ritual*. Ithaca: Cornell University Press, 1967.
Wilcox, A.R. *The Rock Art of Africa*. Johannesburg: Macmillan, 1984.
See also: Xhosa-Speakers' Traditional Concept of God.

Rock Art – Western United States

Scattered across the immense and often empty expanses of the desert southwest in North America is a vast collection of imagery pecked, rubbed, or scratched (commonly referred to as petroglyphs) and sometimes painted on stones: the legacy of a people long gone. These ancient, mystifying images, collectively termed rock art, are the portrayal of a world we can now only faintly imagine, a representation on stone of the experience of America's first human discoverers, the hunter-gatherers of prehistory.

Although the Bering Strait theory of migration is anathema to certain tribes of Native Americans, evidence continues to surface to support this idea; also, the very likely ocean routes by boat must be more strongly considered. The indisputable fact is that people did come, many great waves of them, by land, by sea, from many different origins. The various waves of migration streaming across the land bridge brought with them not only their tools for survival and their meager possessions; they also brought their ideology, their customs and beliefs, and their ancient forms of religion: animism couched within a framework of shamanism. Many of their rock-art images, though not all, were related to shamanistic themes, and images of birds are especially conspicuous; "... birds are the most common and most obvious symbols of shamanic transformation and magical flight" (Hedges 1976: 84). And in this myriad of imagery, if we pause and look closely, we can see the expression of "art and religion, twin mirrors of human thought" (Turpin 1994: 76).

Bird images in particular stand out in the iconography of shamanic rock art, whether in the explosive beginnings of Paleolithic cave art or the prehistoric rock art of the hunter-gatherers of North America. From the "bird-on-a-stick" image in Lascaux cave to the Egyptian ba, to the paintings along the Pecos River, the bird has appeared repeatedly as a metaphor for the human soul, and "There is no other symbol of the shaman's power of flight, his most essential magic capability, as logical and powerful as that of the bird" (Wellman 1976: 101).

These early people wandering across North America were completely immersed in the natural world; it sustained them and it destroyed them, and from its deeper dimensions they acquired their magic and their power. Religion, magic, and spirituality were expressions of the same thing.

> The close relationship between men and animals, and the shaman's ability to share in the occult powers of the animal world is one of the major messages of shamanism in general ... Birds in particular symbolize shamanic flight. Becoming a bird allows one to take the ecstatic journey to sky and beyond, and in many places in the world, bird elements are commonly incorporated into shamans' costumes. In rock art, birds fly over and around the heads and toward and away from the bodies of the anthropomorphic forms (Schaafsma 1994: 53).

Some of the rock-art styles, especially the older, painted ones, are noticeably replete with bird imagery, often in conjunction with snakes. (The overworld and the underworld.) This is especially true of the Barrier Canyon style of south central Utah and the Pecos River paintings of southern Texas and Northern Coahuila, Mexico. Other styles, such as the petroglyph images in the Wind River Range, Wyoming, are noted for their "owl-men" or "bird-men," and the Basketmaker II rock art of the early Anasazi (Colorado plateau, 200 B.C.E.–400 C.E.) has hundreds of images of anthropomorphic figures with ducks on their heads, or, more commonly, ducks as heads.

These bird images can be so prevalent in certain styles that they become the central theme.

> One of the core beliefs of modern shamanism, the "bird-like flight of the soul" (Furst 1977: 2) is a major theme of the Archaic Pecos River pictographic style, an elaborate body of polychrome art painted by hunters and gatherers that occupied the arid lands of southwestern Texas and northern Mexico. Depictions of ascending, descending, and soaring anthropomorphic figures are augmented by a number of flight metaphors, such as birds, wings and feathers ... These many illustrations of magical flight confirm the importance of religious ecstasy in Pecos River ritual ... In fact, it can now be said with some security that magical flight, derived directly from the trance experience, is the dominant theme in Pecos River style art (Turpin 1994: 73, 82).

Among the petroglyphs of Pueblo peoples of New Mexico are numerous portrayals of the roadrunner, and sometimes just its odd, elongated, X-shaped footprint is displayed as a metaphor for the whole bird. "The mere presence of the roadrunner track in prehistoric rock art was strongly indicative that the roadrunner and/or its track had religious significance in the prehistoric southwest" (Schaafsma 1989: 26).

Owls, parrots, cranes, ducks, roadrunners, turkeys, eagles, quail, herons, woodpeckers, hummingbirds, hawks, to name only a few, were part and parcel of the prehistoric pantheon. And while "birds of all kinds were associated with shamans," (Whitley 1994: 25), certain birds held particular significance to specific groups of people. The duck, for example, continues to be revered in the Pueblo world as a messenger to the spirit world. Likewise, the prehistoric Pueblo world held the duck in great esteem, as is evidenced not only in the many images for ducks *per se*, but notably in the Basketmaker II anthropologic images known as "duck heads."

The duck is a magical being and a great shape-shifter (these figures often have distended hands and feet, an indication that shape is being transformed); it can walk on land, lay eggs in the rushes at water's edge, and tend to its nest in an earthly way. It can also fly up into the sky where the cloud-beings live, its power of flight so easy, so natural. And, most magically of all, not only can it swim and float on water, it can also dive under the water – and come back up again! To a people who likely saw puddles and ponds as an entryway to the underworld, this must have seemed the epitome of magic.

Other water birds such as cranes or coots or herons (or their footprints) are also widely represented in the prehistoric rock art of the desert southwest, not surprising in cultures that were trying to eke out an existence in places where the rainfall was often far below the prerequisite 14 inches a year that are considered minimum for human survival. With the idea of supplication for rain, it is no wonder that water birds images are so prevalent, as are those of clouds, frogs, tadpoles, and fish. Images of turkeys were often associated with rain also, as these birds tended to reside in the mountains where there was more water, next to springs and streams, just as they do today.

It is a logical extension of bird imagery that bird feathers and bird parts served as a metaphor for the whole bird, and there is a long tradition brought forward into the present of using bird feathers in connection with sacred ceremonies, altars, prayer bundles, dances and rituals, and shamanic costumes. "Of all life forms found as decorative motifs in Pueblo art, the bird has undoubtedly enjoyed the most widespread use. Bird designs occur abundantly on prehistoric and historic culture materials from the Pueblo region" (Wellman 1976: 97).

Bird imagery in the Rio Grande style rock art is quite often generic (depending on the site); that is, the idea of birds is presented, though no effort has been made to suggest a specific kind of bird. And just as often, a specific bird image may dominate a site, such as raptors in Tenabo, New Mexico, the duck-men of the San Juan River area in southeastern Utah, the star-faced birds of prey in the Galisteo Basin in north central New Mexico, or the owl-men of Dinwoody Lakes, Wyoming.

And there are some sites that are wonderfully and inexplicably anomalous, such as the premier rock-art site of Three Rivers, in southern New Mexico. This remarkable site, with its many thousands of petroglyphs pecked into the basaltic lava along a hogback rising above the desert floor, hosts at least fourteen separate, identifiable species of birds, as well as birds with eggs in their bodies, bird migrations, seasonal portrayals and even a bird embryo, where the oval shape of the rock forms the egg. Most of the images are portrayed alone, and a few seem to have an overt shamanic context, though certainly the wide variety of images has generated numerous, often conflicting interpretations.

Unraveling the mystery of the many different bird species represented at Three Rivers is an appropriate metaphor for the study of the larger world of rock art. Not only by learning to live with the mystery without having to explain it rationally on our own terms, but also by accepting it as the essence of the magic inherent in rock art, and learning, each in our own way, how to celebrate (and protect) that mystery, may we come into a true contact with the many people who left them there so long ago.

Brad Draper

Further Reading

Hedges, Ken. "Southern California Rock Art as Shamanic Art." In *American Indian Rock Art*, vol. 2. El Paso, TX: El Paso Archeological Society, 1976.

Schaafsma, Polly. "Trance and Transformation in the Canyons: Shamanism and Early Rock Art of the Colorado Plateau." In *Shamanism and Rock Art in North America*. San Antonio, TX: Rock Art Foundation, Inc., 1994.

Schaafsma, Polly. "Supper or Symbol: Roadrunner Tracks in Southwest Art and Ritual." In *Animals into Art*. Howard Morphy, ed. London: Unwin Hyman, 1989.

Turpin, Solveig. "On a Wing and a Prayer: Flight Metaphors in Pecos River Art." In *Shamanism and Rock Art in North America*. San Antonio, TX: Rock Art Foundation, Inc., 1994.

Wellman, Klaus F. "Some Observations on the Bird Motif in North American Indian Rock Art." In *American Indian Rock Art*, vol. 2. El Paso, TX: El Paso Archeological Society, 1976.

Whitley, David. "Shamanism, Natural Modeling and the Rock Art of the Western North American Hunter-Gatherers." In *Shamanism and Rock Art in North America*. San Antonio, TX: Rock Art Foundation, Inc., 1994.

See also: Paleolythic Religions; Rock Art (various); Shamanism (various).

Rock Climbing

Can rock climbing be understood as a religion? As a practitioner and a scholar, I think it can. Surely it entails a sensation of transcendence, an experience of raw nature, and calls forth a kind of reverence. Climbing offers a respite from the constraints of the horizontal world, recreating the *axis mundi* with each new ascent. While such sentiments convey aspects of what I feel when I climb, they serve only to obscure what I see as a scholar. As much as I'm prone to romanticizing my choice of leisure pursuits, here I want to approach climbing with a critical eye, still under the broad category of religion. This entails a shift to ritual. If we view climbing as ritualized behavior, we move beyond platitudes and speculations about the "beliefs" of climbers to analyze the social processes and practices they perform.

Climbing is almost wholly ritualized. This will become readily apparent to anyone who attempts to invent the sport *de novo*, as I did in my hapless early teenage years.

Armed with a bike lock, leather gloves, and an old sailing line, my friend Dan and I decided to "go climbing." Before we had much of an opportunity to kill ourselves, Dan and I were approached by some "real climbers" who, while chuckling the we-know-better laugh, took us under their wing and initiated us into the esoterica at the heart of the sport. In language and gestures meant to close the gap between our ignorance and their "reality," we were taught about the acquisition and use of proper ritual paraphernalia (ropes, carabineers, and anchors), appropriate regalia (climbing boots, designer clothes), ritual speech ("on belay"), sacred texts (guide books and various "how to" texts written by "founding fathers"), ongoing revelation (climbing magazines), sacrificial rituals (leisure blood letting by way of cuts and bruises – "badges of honor" – and the occasional involuntary corpse offering), salient ethnic distinctions (sport climbers, traditional climbers, alpine climbers), relevant ancestors and deities (local heroes), heretics (heroes from somewhere else), and most importantly, levels of salvation (grades of difficulty) and ethics (aesthetics – "good style"). More than this, we learned that "real climbing" is established around certain pilgrimage sites (Yosemite being Mecca and Jerusalem both), and only the apostate (independently minded climbers) or the visionary (sponsored climbers) venture beyond the sanctioned and sanctified cathedrals. However, meeting the needs of practitioners who can't always and everywhere engage "pure tradition" (going climbing), climbers have invented traditions to match their late capitalist predilections (climbing gyms with espresso bars and interactive websites that successfully reproduce the social milieu – which is garden-variety, pecking-order calibration – of the "really real").

Now, lest my critical view be taken as cynicism, let me point out the positive attributes of climbing as ritual. There is more *communitas* in climbing circles than there are bad dissertations on liminality – which is to say heaps. Climbing is about bonding, and bonding quite beyond the structures and constraints of everyday life. If there was ever "serious play," this is it. At the level of rope mate, trust is paramount and all ascents are dually authored and doubly experienced. Beyond the sacred duty to one's partner (holding his or her rope), climbing bonds extend like fractals, taking in ever-greater numbers of people yet linking them in the most intimate ways. Moreover, the very ritualism of climbing is so explicit and marked that it constitutes the primary identity of most adherents. This makes climbers remarkably visible and sympathetic to one another (intra-ethnic strife aside). Thus, to speak personally, I am certain that I have more in common – in terms of passions, appetites, ideals – with climbers from, say, Thailand, than I do with my neighbors. So it is that climbers can travel the world and have ready-made communities waiting to accept them. So, while climbers fashion themselves as radicals, independents, and iconoclasts, what I find revealing in our ritual analysis is that it is precisely the sub-cultural homogeneity of climbing – produced and reproduced through ritual practices – that renders climbing the social phenomenon it is.

Turning to the sharper edge of my critical knife, I want to address the relationship of climbers to nature by way of exposing one particular class of rituals to analysis: the first ascent. Climbers most often take the first ascent to be the epitome of the sport. It represents the "best and purest" form of climbing. Adventurous, bold, committed, visionary, self-less: these are common ways first ascentionists fashion themselves, and most climbers endorse this discourse through consumption of it. As a first ascentionist myself, I've participated in this rhetorical economy, and I think many of the claims and aspirations surrounding first ascents are sincere and harmless. However, I would insist that the quest for the perfect route (climbing's Holy Grail) by climbers as a whole and the quest for ego gratification by individuals have caused climbing to manifest itself in rather imperial ways. New climbing areas are sought with the fervor of New World explorers, and the consequences to nature (and sometimes natives, as with disputes between climbers and Indians at Devils Tower and Cave Rock attest) are similar in effect, but certainly not in scale, to those of their symbolic predecessors. Trails are cut, vegetation is removed, machinery bolts are drilled into the rock for anchors, erosion exacerbated, and litter is left by climbers "developing" new climbs.

I would also call attention to symbolic features of first ascents that strike me as dubious and revealing. These are signaled by the metaphor often chosen by climbers to describe establishing a first ascent: authorship. Climbers speak as if the act of climbing a rock somehow brings it into being – and so it does, for a certain social world. Beyond this, authorship is viewed to convey moral possession of the route to those who established it. In other words, subsequent climbers are to repeat the route by way of the standards of the first ascentionists, and any modification of the route (the addition of new anchors, for example) requires consent from its "authors." Moreover, first ascentionists very often understand their act as one that confers entitlement in another sense. Quite literally, climbers have a long tradition of claiming the right to naming based on the first ascent. Even if a rock feature had a name before an ascent, climbers will re-christen the rock upon climbing it. And, in ways reminiscent of the Reformation, climbers will, on occasion, dispute the legitimacy of an ascent, registering their view by climbing it themselves and renaming it upon success. Route names enter climbing discourse swiftly and indelibly, eventually becoming recorded in guidebooks, often along with the "author's" name. In this way, first ascents are perhaps best viewed in terms of apotheosis – human beings reaching for the gods in order to become them. As with so many human projects to transcend our limitations, in the game of climbing nature often becomes a means to our ends – even while we purport to be worshipping it.

Yet, if we grant certain ego needs and failures to our kind, perhaps we can view climbing – and things like it – as simultaneously muddled and miraculous. On the latter side, climbing, for all of my skepticism, still affords the chance to gain a celestial view from a terrestrial perch. Doing so, climbing allows for an oceanic experience that inspires a caring rather than a conquering attitude toward the rock. And it must be said that within the climbing community there has always been a vocal environmentalist element. These climbers – from the very beginning of the sport – have maintained a "clean" ethic, seeking to leave no trace on the rocks they ascend. Moreover, their sensibilities extend to the broader context of public land use. Such climbers and the action groups they form and support have been instrumental in advancing low-impact approaches to nature.

Greg Johnson

See also: Deep Ecology; Mountaineering; Naess, Arne; Surfing.

Rolston III, Holmes (1932–)

Leading environmental philosopher, ethicist, and theologian, Holmes Rolston III is widely recognized as the "father of environmental ethics" for his central role in developing environmental ethics as a modern academic discipline. Throughout his distinguished career, he has helped make explicit the ethics of nature that have been implicit in philosophical and sacred writings since ancient times. Born in the Shenandoah Valley of Virginia on 19 November 1932, Rolston's multidisciplinary educational career included a childhood spent in contact with nature, an undergraduate degree in physics (Davidson College, 1953), a divinity degree (Union Theological Seminary, 1956), a Ph.D. in theology (University of Edinburgh, 1958), and later a masters in philosophy of science (University of Pittsburgh, 1968). He wrote the acclaimed books *Philosophy Gone Wild* (1986), *Environmental Ethics* (1988), *Science and Religion: A Critical Survey* (1987), *Conserving Natural Value* (1994), and *Genes, Genesis and God: Values and their Origins in Natural and Human History* (Gifford Lectures, University of Edinburgh, 1997–1998) (1999). He edited *Biology, Ethics, and the Origins of Life* (1994), and in 1979, helped found the now-refereed professional journal *Environmental Ethics*. Additional works include 80 chapters in other books and over 100 articles, a number of which have been used in college courses and have been translated into at least a dozen languages. A founding member of the International Society for Environmental Ethics (1990) and delegate to the United Nations Conference on Environment and Development (Rio de Janeiro, Brazil, 1992), Rolston has lectured on all seven continents, consulted with dozens of conservation groups, received numerous awards including the 2003 Templeton Prize for Progress Toward Research or Discoveries about Spiritual Realities, and currently serves as University Distinguished Professor of Philosophy at Colorado State University, his professorial post since 1976.

For four centuries following the Enlightenment and the scientific revolution in Europe, Western philosophy promoted an almost exclusively anthropocentric focus, perceiving nature as mechanistic and only having value in relation to human uses and preferences. In the early 1970s, Rolston acknowledged that nature had instrumental or use-values for medicine, agriculture, and industry. He went further, though, recognizing that nature had other values – aesthetic, ecological, educational, historical, recreational, scientific, economic, and religious – as well as intrinsic value. Fundamentally, he argued, organisms (including plants, animals, and humans), species, ecosystems, and the Earth have intrinsic value just for the fact that they have evolved and survived for millions and billions of years. Each level also has systemic value (value associated with processes and capacity to produce) that is interwoven with instrumental and intrinsic values. Rolston posits that for all of these reasons and more, humans have ethical obligations to the environment.

An ordained Presbyterian pastor like his father and grandfather, Rolston frequently draws on the Bible, emphasizing in writing and in lectures its implied guidance on environmental ethics. He likes to think of the "swarms of living creatures" brought forth from land and sea (Gen. 1:20, 24) as early references to biodiversity and notes that when God reviewed the display of life he found it "very good." According to Rolston, the story of Noah's ark illustrates that God wills for species to continue (Gen. 6:19) and the rainbow is God's sign re-establishing "the covenant . . . between me and you and every living creature that is with you, for all future generations" (Gen. 9:12–13). In addition to the ecological, intrinsic, aesthetic, instrumental, and religious values implied in Genesis and Matthew 6, Rolston highlights biblical passages that speak to economic and other values, as well as human responsibilities.

Rolston promotes the idea that ethics are for people, but not only about people. To whom much is given, much is required, and humans have a rich and ancient inheritance, the Earth and biosphere, to steward. Rolston says that perhaps we make our deepest error "forever putting ourselves first, never putting ourselves in place in the fundamental biosphere community in which we reside" (2000: 83). Through his writings and lectures, he attempts to instill a more profound sense of civic and environmental responsibility, calling upon people to live up to their duties as *Homo sapiens*, the so-called wise species.

Paula J. Posas

Further Reading

Rolston III, Holmes. "Intrinsic Values in Nature." In II Congresso Brasileiro de Unidades de Conservaçao, Anais, vol 1. Conferências e Palestras, organizadores Miguel Serediuk Milano e Verônica Theulen (Proceedings of the Second Brazilian Congress on Conservation Areas), 5–9 November 2000, Campo Grande, Brazil, 76–84.

Rolston III, Holmes. *Genes, Genesis and God: Values and their Origins in Natural and Human History*. Cambridge, UK; New York: Cambridge University Press, 1999.

Rolston III, Holmes, ed. *Biology, Ethics, and the Origins of Life*. Boston: Jones and Bartlett, 1995.

Rolston III, Holmes. *Conserving Natural Value*. New York: Columbia University Press, 1994.

Rolston III, Holmes. "Creation: God and Endangered Species." In Ke Chung Kim and Robert D. Weaver, eds. *Biodiversity and Landscape*. New York: Cambridge University Press, 1994, 47–60.

Rolston III, Holmes. *Environmental Ethics: Duties to and Values in the Natural World*. Philadelphia: Temple University Press, 1988.

Rolston III, Holmes. *Science and Religion: A Critical Survey*. Philadelphia: Temple University Press, 1987.

Rolston III, Holmes. *Philosophy Gone Wild*. Buffalo, NY: Prometheus Books, 1986.

Rolston III, Holmes and Andrew Light, eds. *Environmental Ethics: An Anthology*. Malden, MA: Blackwell Publishers, 2003.

See also: Environmental Ethics.

Roman Britain

The inhabitants of Britain at the time of the Roman invasion in the year 43 were Celts. Archeological evidence from temple sites coupled with place-name evidence and inscriptions dating from the Roman period emphasize the importance of features in the landscape such as hills, springs and groves of trees, the last associated with the priestly caste of the Druids whose name is thought to have been derived from the oak tree. Although the art of the pre-Roman period was largely abstract, it included striking images of animals, among them horses, bulls, stags, boars, ravens and waterfowl, all of which were evidently held sacred.

The infusion of Roman ideas did not in any way weaken this empathy with nature, for the Roman cult had long peopled the countryside with its own deities of the wild. Thus the sanctuaries kept holy in the Iron Age often continued to be religious centers even if the deities venerated there were now addressed in Latin and assumed a Graeco-Roman appearance. At Buxton in Derbyshire was a temple dedicated to Arnemetia, whose name derives from the word "nemet" which means a sacred grove. There was another "nemet" at Nympsfield in Gloucestershire, where the word has even been preserved in the modern English name; it may have been attached to an Iron Age and Roman-period sanctuary, recently excavated and located just over the parish boundary at Uley. A final example is preserved in the name of a deity venerated at Nettleham, Lincolnshire called Mars Rigonemetos – Mars, King of the Sacred Grove.

The name of Buxton was formerly Aquae Arnemetiae, showing that Armenitia was a goddess of a spring as well. Even more famous was Sulis Minerva of Bath, Aquae Sulis, who presided over thermal springs. Another goddess-nymph, called Coventina, had a more local cult at Carrawburgh just outside one of the forts on Hadrian's Wall. Sometimes the name of the presiding deity of a spring has been lost but archeology has revealed a complex of temples at Springhead in Kent that attest the same feeling for flowing waters. It is likely that the sources of many rivers had sanctuaries and the actual names of some rivers imply veneration, for instance the River Dee (Deva) in Cheshire, whose name is cognate with the Indo-European word for goddess; the river gave its name to the fortress at Chester.

Many temples lay on hilltops or ridges, including the temple at Uley mentioned above, and those at Lydney, also in Gloucestershire but on the northern side of the River Severn; Maiden Castle, above Dorchester, Dorset; Pagans Hill, Somerset; and Lowbury Hill, Oxfordshire.

Such sites, placing the gods firmly in the natural world, find their reflection in furniture and objects connected with cult, as virtually all deities are connected in some way with the beneficence of nature. Jupiter is often attested by columns that are embellished with scale-like ornament perhaps representing the bark of trees. A capital from one of these, from Cirencester, Gloucestershire, has half-length figures of Bacchus, his consort Ariadne, a Silenus and a figure of Lycurgus with a vine, all emerging from the fronds of the richly embellished Corinthian capital. Another column, represented only by an imbricated shaft from Wroxeter, Shropshire, has inset figures of Bacchus and a cupid. Bacchus was Jupiter's son and seems to have been regarded as a major power in untamed nature. Here, on the two columns cited, he literally supports the majesty of Jupiter himself.

Mercury, god of flocks and herds, was popular among pastoralists. He was venerated at a number of temples including one at Uley, Gloucestershire, where one image shows him as horned, thus in a sense identifying him with the beasts he looked after.

A similar thereomorphic identification is to be seen in

the case of the deity known as Apollo Cunomaglus, the second part of his name being a Celtic word meaning "hound-prince." He is mentioned on an altar from Nettleton Shrub, Wiltshire, but seems to be represented in other reliefs from the Cotwold area including Chedworth, Gloucestershire, as well as on a votive bronze plaque from Gloucester, in both cases accompanied by a hound.

Hounds would appear to have been the familiars of Nodens at Lydney, but instead of being identified with Apollo, Nodens was here assimilated to Mars, generally venerated in Britain (except in the official cults of the Roman army) as a protective, countryside deity rather than as a war god. The marine imagery on a mosaic set in the cella of his temple and on certain pieces of metalwork suggest he may have been connected with the mouth of the Severn below his hill, but he was also closely associated with the iron-rich waters of his healing spring. There may also have been a hunting aspect.

One epithet used for Mars (as on a votive plaque at Barkway, Hertfordshire) is Alator, "huntsman," and it is likely that Mars Cocidius, venerated at Bewcastle, Northumberland, was likewise venerated as a hunting deity.

Silvanus too had a similar function, and one of the most instructive of altars, from moorland near Binchester, County Durham, is dedicated "to unconquerable Silvanus" by a cavalry officer, because the god had helped him "to take a very fine boar which none of his predecessors had been able to bag."

A gentler aspect of nature is represented by so-called mother goddesses (Matres), who in many instances are shown holding fruit or bread rather than actually nurturing children. They are sometimes depicted in triads, thus tripling their power, as is the case of the Matres Suleviae on reliefs from Cirencester, but on occasions a single goddess is shown. A relief at Daglingworth calls her Cuda and it is possible (as suggested by Stephen Yeates) that she was the mother goddess of the Cotswold Hills. On several reliefs she is accompanied by three votaries or minor godlings wearing the distinctive woolen, hooded coat (the birrus britannicus) made in the region. Such representations emphasize the relationship between economy and divine aid.

Some of the most attractive evidence for the veneration and awareness of nature is associated with sophisticated, literate people nurtured on the classics. The villa-owners of Britain loved myth and the themes of many of these were closely associated with the natural world. Not surprisingly the wine god Bacchus with his panther was the theme of a number of mosaics, Bacchus being venerated as a deity who could overcome even death with his life-saving wine. In the Cirencester region, a type of Orpheus mosaic was evolved in which Orpheus accompanied by a hound, or just possibly a fox, occupies a roundel all to himself while animals circulate in friezes around him. The inspiration for these wonderful floors may have come in part from the local hunter god. Venus, water-nymphs and the seasons were also very frequently shown on mosaics.

In one remarkable mosaic found at Hinton St. Mary, Dorset, a bust of Christ occupies a central roundel. Flanked by pomegranates he, like Bacchus, is lord of nature. Four busts representing seasons (?) in the corners, and lunettes with, in one case, a tree of life, and in three others, a hound chasing a stag, present a striking variant on the Orpheus theme.

Perhaps the most successful and integrated expression of a literary, sophisticated approach to nature in religious cult belongs to the gold and silver treasure from a pagan temple at Thetford, Norfolk, dedicated to Faunus. Faunus was an obscure deity of the wild, from the countryside around Rome (Latium) and he was previously known mainly from Roman poets such as Virgil and Horace. Here, at Thetford, he was given local Celtic epithets inscribed on silver spoons dedicated to him such as Medugenus (mead-begotten) or Cranus (guardian of buried treasure). As he had animal-like ears he was called Ausecus (prick-eared), and a representation of his head, goat-like and with little horns and large gem-set ears, ornaments the bezel of a gold ring. Faunus' father was Picus ("the woodpecker"), and it is no surprise that another gold ring has a bezel composed of a pair of woodpeckers, pecking at a wine bowl whose brimming contents are suggested by an inset purple amethyst. The names of the votaries such as Silviola, whose name is derived from "silva," a wood, and Agrestis, whose name means "countryman," remind us of the pervasiveness of the natural world even among the most refined society of the province.

Martin Henig

Further Reading

Alcock, Joan P. "Celtic Water Cults in Roman Britain." *Archaeological Journal* CXII (1965), 1–12.

Blagg, Thomas. "Roman Religious Sites in the British Landscape." *Landscape History* 3 (1986), 15–25.

Henig, Martin. *The Heirs of King Verica: Culture and Politics in Roman Britain*. Stroud: Tempus Publishing Ltd, 2002.

Henig, Martin. *The Art of Roman Britain*. London: B.T. Batsford, 1995.

Henig, Martin. *Religion in Roman Britain*. London: B.T. Batsford, 1984.

Johns, Catherine and Timothy Potter. *The Thetford Treasure: Roman Jewellery and Silver*. London: British Museum Publications, 1983.

Rivet, A.L.F. and Colin Smith. *The Place-Names of Roman Britain*. London: B.T. Batsford Ltd, 1979.

See also: Celtic Spirituality; Druids and Druidry; Roman Natural Religion; Roman Religion and Empire.

Roman Catholic Religious Orders

There are references in the New Testament to unmarried men and women who served the local communities in special ways. Later, this celibate tradition continued as some Christians went into the deserts of Egypt and Syria to live their commitment in solitude. These men and women were variously called "hermits," "anchorites" and "The Desert Fathers." In the wilderness, they found a peace and tranquility that was conducive to prayer, contemplation and reflection. Saint Anthony (d. 350) said that, in creation, he could read the word of God.

Demonic powers also resided in the desert. The anchorites saw their presence in the wilderness as a process of re-creating an earthly paradise, of reestablishing the dominion over all life that existed before the Fall. The stories of encounters with wild animals illustrated their spiritual power. The monk Florentius had a bear as a companion. The animals taught the hermits what was poisonous.

Their spirituality was to encounter a strange territory and move from conflict to harmony, to merge the natural with the supernatural until the two were indistinguishable. This spirituality influenced Celtic spirituality where the theme of voyage or pilgrimage provided a heightened awareness of the natural environment. Celtic spirituality, in turn, influenced Saint Francis of Assisi.

Some men and women of the desert gathered disciples around them and formed communities. These groups became the "cenobites" and their communities came to be characterized by vows of poverty, chastity and obedience. The members choose not to own anything, to live as celibates and to obey their abbot or abbess.

Today, there are several thousand orders and congregations in the Roman Catholic Church. Many use a rule that has been influenced by one of the four largest orders: the Benedictines, Franciscans, Dominicans and Jesuits. Since the 1960s, the Maryknoll family has developed a particularly contemporary response to environmental issues.

The Benedictine Tradition

The Benedictine view of nature is grounded in the monastics' commitment to a specific place, their efforts to be self-sustaining and the rhythm of their daily prayer. Early in the sixth century, Saint Benedict of Norcia wrote a series of guidelines for living together as a religious community. The Rule of Saint Benedict was used by his immediate followers and was also adopted by many existing communities. It became the principle guide for most religious orders before the Middle Ages. Saint Scholastica, Benedict's sister, founded a women's branch.

The Rule is characterized by a commitment to a specific monastery, a daily order that includes chanting psalms and canticles in the chapel seven times a day, manual labor, private prayer, simplicity, frugality, humility, obedience and hospitality. The routine of prayer and the focus on frugality shaped the monastics' view of nature.

The collection of psalms and canticles is called "The Divine Office." The psalms themselves, coming from the Old Testament, contain many images of nature that are meant to express the majesty of God revealed in the grandeur of creation. Chanting the office seven times a day embeds the images of nature in the monastics' minds and gives a rhythm to their lives. The routine places time against the backdrop of eternity. The Office of Lauds, chanted at sunrise, is constructed to view creation and redemption as two aspects of the same divine activity.

Some time each day is to be spent in labor. The things of the house, buckets and spades; and the things of the Earth, trees and plants, are to be respected. Work is seen as an act of co-creation or ongoing cooperation with the Creator.

The view of nature within the Benedictine tradition reflects a basic Christian position. There is both a natural and a supernatural order. The supernatural order is not opposed to, but is above nature. Devotion to the spiritual life does not destroy but perfects and elevates the natural order. Creation will also be delivered from slavery and corruption. God remains distinct from his creation, but the universe has a dynamic structure. It is dependent on God and is constantly being created by God in conjunction with those creatures who cooperate.

There were also other perspectives in Europe between the fifth and thirteenth centuries. A neo-Platonic view exaggerated the distinction between the spiritual and the natural order to a point where the natural was disdained. From the eighth century on, there was also a rationalism that sought explicit explanations for everything. These trends would have influenced individual Benedictines, but did not affect the basics of Benedictine life.

Hildegard of Bingen (1098–1179) was a Benedictine nun who wrote treatises on theology, philosophy, cosmology and medicine and then wrote music to illuminate her vision. She saw human nature as a microcosm that contains the entire creation within it. Because they are so closely interconnected, the natural elements and humanity affect each other. Because of sin, creation turns against humans. In Christ, we can restore the balance. Hildegard saw music as the highest form of praising God. Through music, we integrate body, mind, heart and spirit and thus celebrate heavenly harmony here on Earth.

The Benedictine monasteries were a major means of preserving and spreading Western civilization in the centuries of transition from the Roman Empire into the Middle Ages. Towns grew up around monasteries. The monastic schools provided one of the few means of education and the monks both developed and taught agricultural techniques. The early development of Europe consisted in cutting back forests and reclaiming wetlands for agriculture. The monks were at the forefront of this movement.

As Europe approached the Middle Ages, a need for reform arose. Feudal lords were appropriating monastic revenues. The recitation of the Office had expanded in length, manual work decreased and the rule was interpreted rigidly. Besides monastic reform, several popes called for reforms on a larger scale within the whole Church. One need was a concern for apostolic life, for the care and education of people.

One monastic reform came through Saint Robert of Molesne (d. 1111) and Saint Bernard of Clairvaux (d. 1153). They broke with the mainstream Benedictines and founded the Cistercian Order at Citeaux in France. By this time, much of Europe had become farmland and the Cistercians moved out into wilder country. Their writings expressed a sense of movement from wilderness to paradise. They still followed the Benedictine Rule.

Whereas the Desert Fathers saw beauty in an unspoiled wilderness, Saint Bernard emphasized the beauty of labor in preparing the fields. There should be a profound harmony between the natural beauty of the site and the monastic life set within it. Once nature has become fertile and purposeful, it takes on the utmost significance. Irrigation channels and waterways within the monastery provide sport and food for fish, refreshment for people, nourishment for gardens and a means of cleansing. Humanity and creation achieve perfection together because of human efforts to tend and organize the environment and creation's willing response to humanity's guidance. Creation repays human care by aiding people physically and spiritually. They are partners in a common effort.

Cistercian monastic architecture was medieval and reflected the simplicity and balance of the monks' lifestyle. The floor plan and the monastery's position within the environment were meant to reflect the harmony of creation and the presence of the divine within creation. Light, space, shape and texture were used to reflect this sense.

Because the Cistercians became involved in work away from the monastery, a reform within the Cistercian community began in the sixteenth century and developed until 1892 when a group of Cistercians became independent. The new group was centered at La Trappe in France. This reform revolved around a stronger emphasis on contemplation rather than apostolic activities. The group is known as The Order of Cistercians of the Strict Observance. They are commonly called "The Trappists." Thomas Merton was a Trappist and his writings have greatly influenced contemporary understandings of the relationships between prayer, justice and the environment. Today, there are 1400 communities worldwide who follow the Rule of Saint Benedict.

Over the last thirty years, contemporary currents and attitudes toward nature have influenced monasticism. In an effort to understand present thinking, a survey was sent out to 52 Cistercian and Trappist monasteries in 14 countries. An effort was made to distribute the questionnaire to every third person. 147 questionnaires were returned. What follows is a summary of their responses.

When asked if their sense of the sanctity of creation had grown during their years in the monastery, all but three said it had. Two of the remaining three responded that they had always had a strong sense of nature as sacred.

To the question asking what people or published materials had influenced their view of creation, about half indicated specific books and authors. The Bible was the most frequently mentioned influence, followed by Jesuit Teilhard de Chardin, Trappist Thomas Merton, Franciscan Saint Francis of Assisi, Passionist Thomas Berry, Saint Paul, William Wordsworth, Matthew Fox, Orion Magazine, David Thoreau, Julian of Norwich, Rachel Carson and Trappist Charles Cummings who wrote a book entitled *Eco-Spirituality*.

To the question, "What do you see in the Benedictine and Cistercian tradition that contributes to an ecological perspective?" the strongest response was the Rule of Saint Benedict itself, especially a sentence that says that the monastic should reverence all things as if they were the sacred vessels of the altar. Living in a natural setting, working the land, experiencing the seasons, and loving the place were also frequent answers. In addition, there were many mentions of their lifestyle and a daily order that stresses simplicity, silence, solitude, prayer, the rhythm of the liturgical year and the liturgy itself.

One question asked, "Would you please detail any concrete action that your monastery is taking that would reflect a concern for the environment?" In response, many mentioned recycling. Most made reference to responsible farming methods that include organic gardening, erosion control and the use of environmentally safe chemicals. Some mentioned significant proactive measures. The Trappist Monastery at Conyers, Georgia, converted 700 acres of land from swamp into wetlands. A Trappist monastery in Indonesia has dedicated a quarter of their land as a natural reserve. A monastery in Australia has been replanting five kilometers of river frontage damaged by overgrazing since 1840. The Trappist Monastery at New Melleray, Iowa, publishes a quarterly newsletter with a strong environmental focus. The monks at Vina, California took action against a nuclear power plant and are founding members of Dear Creek Conservancy. The Trappistine monastery at Whitethorn in Northern California was instrumental in stopping a dam on the Mattlole River and preserving 1200 acres of old-growth redwoods as the "Sanctuary Forest." Members of the monastery sit on the board of directors. While most Trappist monasteries are involved in some farming, the sisters at Whitethorn are more focused on preserving a natural environment. Monasteries in Ireland, New Zealand, Hong Kong, Canada, Iowa, Oregon, Nigeria and Eritrea have undertaken extensive reforestation projects. A monastery in Cameroon is replacing eucalyptus they planted fifty years ago because eucalyptus absorbs too much water from the land. The Trappists in Utah have been working for 53 years to preserve 120 acres of rangeland. Several other monasteries reported working with local conservation groups and several have received awards for their work in conservation.

When asked if the environment is one of the major concerns of our times, 98 percent said yes. To the question, "Does the Bible clearly call us to a reverence and respect for the earth?" over 90 percent said that it does.

The Franciscans

The Franciscan view of nature flows out of the nature mysticism of their founder, Saint Francis of Assisi. As Western civilization entered the Middle Ages, a new prosperity created capitalism and a middle class. There was also a universal call for reform within the Catholic Church. A significant mode of that reform came in the person of Saint Francis of Assisi (1182–1226) and his founding of the Franciscan Order. The order was approved by edict of Pope Innocent III on 16 April, 1209.

With the Benedictines, very little is known about the personality of Saint Benedict. It is his written rule that has shaped the order, but with Francis, his personality and charism dominate and is hard to capture in a written rule. The Franciscans became the first of a different type of order. They are friars and mendicants, not monks. Like the monks, they have a distinctive habit (robe) and chant the psalms and canticles of the Bible in common. But unlike the monks, they have a strong emphasis on apostolic work, on preaching and serving people in a variety of ways. They move easily from place to place and are not bound to a particular monastery.

Francis' father was a wealthy cloth merchant who also bought up small farms and expelled the tenants. Francis reacted dramatically to his father's lifestyle and attitude. He saw power, prestige and possessions as leading to violence and so he embraced humility, poverty and the cross. Much of his life was spent alone in nature like the Desert Fathers and the Celtic hermits. In this liminal position, he had a direct and mystical experience of God in creation.

What is unique to Francis is that he is the first known person within the Christian tradition to exhibit a nature mysticism. Previous ascetics were ambivalent. They saw the natural world too much as the realm of demonic powers. For Francis, his union with nature became a mode of God's communication of himself to humanity and humanity's union with God through a perceived presence in the physical world.

There is a charming fresco by Giotto in the Basilica at Assisi. Here, Francis is seen preaching to birds. The famous incident illustrates the Saint's sense of the interdependence he saw in creation, an interdependence that called for respect and obedience. The birds praise God with their song. They each have autonomous worth and beauty and yet are brothers and sisters performing their divinely allotted function. The birds respect Francis because he is also a servant of God. Their response encouraged him to sustain his new perspective and to carry his preaching to people. By implicitly humanizing creation through affective links, Francis made it easier for others to share his bond with creation. It was Francis and the early Franciscans who introduced the use of the crèche, the manger scenes that dramatize the Christmas event.

The legend of the wolf of Gubbio tells of a hungry wolf that was terrorizing a town. Francis went out and preached to the wolf and then preached penance and peace to the villagers. He was thus able to convince the people that the wolf was simply hungry and needed food. He forged a covenant wherein the people agreed to respect the wolf and provide him with food.

Like the monks before him, the psalms and canticles from the Bible shaped Francis' expressions. But unique to Francis, is the influence of the songs and lyrics of the troubadours. The troubadours were wandering musicians who composed and sang love songs. Here, Francis spiritualizes the mistral's interplay of natural setting and human experience, an interplay that elicits love and joy. Francis embraced and expressed the chivalric values of beneficent magnanimity and deference to all.

Like the ascetics before him, Francis also saw nature as allegorical. He had a particular affection for worms because there is a passage in the New Testament where Christ says, "I am a worm and no man." So Francis would carefully pick worms up off the road and place them in safer places. He saw Christ in the worms. The sun is like God because it is beautiful in itself and it gives light.

The clearest illustration of the Franciscan view of creation can be found in Francis' Canticle to Creation. The hymn praises the four elements; fire, air, water, and earth, which were seen as the components of all life forms. In the Canticle, he expresses the intrinsic goodness of the created world, the interdependence of all life, and his passion for beauty and peace. Because we call God "Father," creation becomes our brothers and sisters. He calls for a fraternal model, rather than a model of stewardship. We are to be detached from creatures in order not to possess them. Francis goes so far, at times, as to say that we should even obey animals. The Franciscans were a dynamic argument against the Cathars; a heretical group at the time who held that "the spiritual" had been created by a beneficent divine power and the natural world by an evil one.

Francis forbade his followers to cut down a whole tree. Part needed to be left intact so that new sprouts could bud. Until recently, a Franciscan needed permission from the provincial before cutting down a tree. Francis spent the last years of his life in the wilderness.

Saint Francis represents a watershed in the development of Christian views of nature. Some spiritualities after him flow from him. Others, such as the Rheinland mystics, continue a neo-Platonic tradition.

The Saint of Assisi fulfills Arne Naess' definition of a deep ecologist because he emphasized the diversity and intrinsic value of creation and because he addresses the need to reform behaviors that threaten to destroy entire ecosystems. On Easter Sunday, 1980, Pope John Paul II proclaimed Saint Francis of Assisi the patron saint of ecology, following the suggestion 13 years earlier by Lynn White, Jr., in his seminal article in *Science*.

Today, Franciscan men and women continue their founder's work by focusing on the changes of hearts and minds needed to live in balance. Franciscan Keith Warner trained in geography and worked for a reforestation cooperative in the Pacific Northwest that planted over 600,000 trees. He is on the steering committee of the California Sustainable Agriculture Working Group and has lobbied with The Religious Campaign for Forest Conservation. Warner also campaigns against what he calls "Bird-bath Franciscanism," a superficial and romantic view of Francis depicted in flower-garden statuary. He sees his founder as much more ecologically radical.

Father Richard Rohr, also a Franciscan, founded and is director of The Center for Action and Contemplation in Albuquerque, New Mexico. The center's aim is to seek a balanced life by bringing together the worlds of spirituality, psychology, social action and environmental concerns.

Former Franciscan Leonardo Boff is a Brazilian and a major figure of liberation theology. In *Ecology and Liberation* (1995) and *Cry of the Earth, Cry of the Poor* (1997), he brings together poverty, ecological degradation and liberation. For Boff, the fate of the rainforest and the fate of Amazonian Indians are inseparably linked.

Franciscan sisters run Michaela Farm in Oldenburg, Indiana, where their aim is to seek and teach skills in organic food production and to foster a simple lifestyle in harmony with the Earth. Sister Rita Wienken has similar objectives with her Franciscan Earth Literacy Action Center on 500 acres in Tiffin, Ohio.

The Dominicans

The Dominican view of nature is based on the fact that they were founded to combat a heresy advocating that the natural world was evil. On 17 January 1217, just eight years after Pope Innocent III approved the rule of Saint Francis, Pope Honorius III ratified the constitutions for the Dominican Order. Like the Franciscans, the Dominicans are friars. They work outside the monastery and were founded to combat the Albigensian heresy.

The Albigenses espoused a form of Manicheism, a cosmic dualism, holding that the devil was actually a rival god who created matter. The soul is imprisoned in matter and the objective is to liberate the soul. Therefore, they discouraged marriage and saw death as the final release. For them, Christ was not the Son of God but an angel with a corporate appearance. The first objective of the Dominicans was to restore a Christian view of creation.

The Dominicans call themselves "The Order of Preachers." But "preaching" here is not restricted to a discourse on Sunday morning. They see their charism as closely following the Old Testament definition of a prophet as one called by God to speak for God. They say of themselves that their objective is to contemplate and to share the fruits of their contemplation. Like the Franciscans, the first Dominican priests were friars. They worked outside the monastery and were founded to combat the Albigensian heresy. Today, the Dominican family includes sisters and lay people.

Fra Angelico (1400–1455) was a Dominican and a painter who continued the work of Giotto in giving more natural shape and color to works of art.

Dominican Saint Thomas Aquinas (1225–1274) is considered the greatest of the medieval philosophers and theologians. His *Summa Theologica* is built on Aristotle and provided a synthesis of theology up to that point in time. Saint Thomas presents the knowledge we get from revelation, our experience and our capacity to reason as compatible and complementary ways of knowing. He set the stage for the later development of the scientific method.

A recent movement within the religious orders of women in the United States is to convert the lands that once served as novitiates, mother houses and schools into organic farms and ecological learning centers. The Dominican sisters have been at the forefront of this movement and Genesis Farm is their flagship.

Founded by Sister Miriam Therese MacGillis and the Dominican Sisters of Caldwell, New Jersey, the farm focuses on learning and teaching a new cosmology. They also sponsor a large, community-supported biodynamic garden. Their teaching is build around the works of Thomas Berry, Brian Swimme and a section of Saint Thomas Aquinas' *Summa Theologica*. In Part I, Question 47 of his *Summa*, Aquinas says that God is most fully revealed, not through one species only, but through the whole universe because one creature alone could not adequately represent his goodness.

Genesis Farm uses the structure of a story. The universe is a series of unfolding stories. Humanity needs to listen to the stories and individuals need to see the story of their lives in the context of the universe of which they are a part. MacGillis also uses the image of a punchbowl on a table surrounded by glasses. Each glass is a religious or ethnic tradition that holds some wisdom. When the glasses are emptied into the punchbowl, the wisdom is not lost but enlarged. The families who sponsor the organic garden at Genesis Farm are presently founding a grammar school where their children can progressively learn the stories of the universe.

The Dominican sisters also operate Sophia Garden in Amityville, New York and Siena Spiritual Center in Water Mill, Long Island. They have similar farms and learning centers in Springfield, Illinois; Ponchatoula, Louisiana;

Blacklick, and Bath, Ohio; Houston and Boerne, Texas; Plainville, Massachusetts; St. Catherine, Kentucky; and Pawnee Rock, Kansas. The Dominicans' *EarthLinks* in Denver, Colorado endeavors to link people, especially the economically poor, to each other and nature through hikes, garden projects and school programs. Sister Mary Ellen Leciejewski, based at the Dominican hospital in Santa Cruz, California, works full time on issues related to the impact of health services on the environment. She says, "Our ecological commitment is integral to our healing mission. There is a profound connection that exists between healing the individual and healing the planet." The Dominicans also run an ecological farm in Benin City, Nigeria.

The Jesuits

Saint Ignatius Loyola, the founder of the Jesuits, had a vision, while praying on the banks of the Cardoner River in Eastern Spain, of God's abiding presence in all of creation. He later had a second vision of Christ carrying a cross for the salvation of the world. Putting the two visions together, he developed a series of meditations and contemplations called *The Spiritual Exercises*, in which, a person is guided to enter the vision of God's presence in and love for the world. From there, one moves to a deeper realization of where and how God might be calling that person to serve.

The Jesuit order itself was founded on 15 August, 1534 at Montmartre in Paris. Pope Paul III approved their constitutions in 1540. With the Jesuits, a third type of order comes onto the scene. The Jesuits were to have no special clothing and did not pray the Liturgy of the Hours in common. Their lifestyle and daily order was to focus on what one Jesuit writer called "a mysticism of service."

From their beginning, Jesuits have been involved in education, scholarship and the foreign missions. Early Jesuits were colleagues of Galileo and over thirty lunar formations bear Jesuit names. Athanasius Kircher (d. 1680) was a major link between medieval and modern science. Jirí Kamel, a Czech Jesuit (d. 1706), sent drawings and specimens of insects and plants from Manila to the Royal Society of London. He recognized strychnine in a type of bean and camellia tea is named after him. Christopher Clavius (d. 1612) designed the Gregorian calendar and introduced the decimal point to mathematics. The Jesuits introduced geometry and Western astronomical instruments to China in the seventeenth century.

Teilhard de Chardin (d. 1955) was a French Jesuit paleontologist. He was concerned with the split between his spirituality and what his fellow scientists were saying about the universe's evolution toward entropy. He developed a schema wherein he saw the possibility that the universe was rather evolving toward a deeper spiritual unification.

Gerard Manley Hopkins (d. 1889) was an English Jesuit poet and artist. He was acutely aware of the beauties of creation and coined the word "inscape" for what he saw as the unique and particular quality of each object in nature. The experience of the particular, of the "deep-down" beauty, leads to an experience of the transcendent. He had a Wordsworthian feeling for nature coupled with a sense of nature as an expression of God. The squalor of industrial towns and the oppression of the working class horrified him. His sonnet, "God's Grandeur," begins with the lines; "The world is charged with the grandeur of God. It will flame out, like shining from shook foil; it gathers to a greatness, like the ooze of oil crushed." He then goes on to describe how the Industrial Revolution has damaged the Earth. But he ends the poem by saying,

> And, for all this, nature is never spent. There lives the dearest freshness deep down things. And though the last lights off the black West went – Oh, morning, at the brown brink eastward, springs – Because the Holy Ghost over the bent world broods with warm breast and with ah! bright wings.

He poetically expresses the heart of Jesuit spirituality.

Today, Jesuit John Surette is co-founder of *Spiritearth* in Arlington, Massachusetts. The educational center is built on the principle that an openness and reverence before the universe allows community to form and justice to flourish. The center would like to see humanity enter an ecozoic era. Another Jesuit, Al Fritsch trained as a chemist, worked for Ralph Nader's Center for the Study of Responsive Law and then founded Appalachia Science in the Public Interest in Mt. Vernon, Kentucky. The center is devoted to the notion of sustainability and has developed solar-energy applications, organic gardens, artificial wetlands and dry-composting toilets. Members of the center are helping to develop ginseng as an alternative crop to tobacco and extensive lumbering in Appalachia. The center has conducted over 200 assessments in 34 states and consulted in Haiti, Peru, and the Dominican Republic. Fritsch would like to see a 12-step program addressing people's addiction to material things.

The Jesuits have assisted sixty religious groups in ecological improvements to their property. Jesuits also teach ecology, sustainability and ecospirituality in their many educational institutions.

Maryknoll

The Maryknoll order is a younger group within the Catholic Church and their approach to nature is uniquely modern. They were founded early in the twentieth century as an American foreign missionary society of priests, brothers and sisters. Today, they include lay-people and call themselves the Maryknoll Family.

Working in South America, they experience extensive exposure to liberation theology and as that movement started "turning green" in the early 1990s, so did they. Maryknoll founded Orbis Press, whose publication list includes books on the environment.

Maryknoll lay-people are involved with CEDICAM in Oaxaca, Mexico. The organization works with Indian campesinos and encourages reforestation and crop diversification throughout the Mixteca Alta region. This group has established tree nurseries in 22 farming communities and has planted more than 150,000 trees.

Maryknoll sisters run the Center for the Integrity of Creation in Baguio, The Philippines. The area is threatened by excessive logging. The Center focuses on education for biodiversity and sustainable development.

Maryknoll Father Herb Gappa runs an anti-erosion and tree-planting project in the Shinyanga District of Tanzania. Maryknollers are also working to conserve green space and diversify agriculture in Barquisimeto, Venezuela. In Chile, they develop ecological education units for high schools in Linares, work in the Spirituality and Ecology Center in San Nicolas, provide workshops on spirituality and ecology in Santiago and develop an awareness of the illegal seizure and logging of native trees in Chol Chol. The logging has led to a drop in the water table. Hazardous chemicals and pesticides have also been introduced.

Other Religious Orders

There is a strong movement today to network, to link and affiliate. A project or center might not be staffed exclusively by members of one order. Individual religious from different congregations join local and national conservation groups. The Maryknoll project in Baguio, The Philippines, includes on its staff members of the Redemptorist and Divine Word orders. The Sisters of Charity, Religious of the Sacred Heart and Passionists have projects and centers similar to those run by the Dominicans.

The Global Education Association is an international network and resource for ecologically related issues. Within GEA, The Religious Orders Partnership includes more than 150 orders. Their aim is to cooperate in using their resources of schools, universities, healthcare facilities, community services, retreat centers and churches to further a concern and care for the Earth. Most religious orders include ecology within their programs for social justice.

Thomas Splain, S.J.

Further Reading

Chittister, Joan D. *Wisdom Distilled from the Daily: Living the Rule of St. Benedict Today*. San Francisco: Harper, 1991.

LaChance, Albert J. and John E. Carroll, eds. *Embracing Earth: Catholic Approaches to Ecology*. New York: Orbis Books, 1995.

Merton, Thomas. *When the Trees Say Nothing: Writings on Nature*. Notre Dame, IN: Ave Maria Press, 2003.

Sorrell, Roger D. *St. Francis of Assisi and Nature*. Oxford: Oxford University Press, 1988.

Taylor, Sarah McFarland. *Green Sisters: Catholic Nuns Answering the Call of the Earth*. Cambridge, Massachusetts: Harvard University Press, 2004.

Teilhard de Chardin, Pierre. *The Phenomenon of Man*. New York: HarperCollins Publishers, 1976.

See also: Berry, Thomas; Boff, Leonardo; Christianity (7c) – Liberation Theology; Christianity (7d) – Feminist Theology; Christianity (7e) – Creation Spirituality; Francis of Assisi; Genesis Farm; Hildegard of Bingen; Religious Campaign for Forest Conservation; Teilhard de Chardin, Pierre.

Roman Catholicism in Latin America

Roman Catholicism has long been the religion of peasant farmers in Europe and Latin America, and thus the tradition's ritual practices, annual calendar, and many cognitive and moral beliefs are closely linked to natural cycles and landscapes. The Church does not, however, have a long tradition of explicit theological and moral reflection about the natural world. While this is probably true of most branches of Christianity, the strongly humanistic emphasis of Roman Catholic social thought has arguably slowed the development of debates and theory-building within that tradition in comparison, for example, to Eastern Orthodoxy and some Protestant denominations. In the Roman Catholic tradition, God's work from creation to salvation focuses on human good, and nonhuman nature serves mainly as a backdrop for human action or as a means to human ends. Nature appears to have little intrinsic (non-instrumental) value, but is valuable insofar as it contributes to collective human well-being. This carries the potential risk of justifying almost any exploitation of natural resources that appears to serve human well-being.

Recognizing some of the tensions in the Catholic humanist approach to nature, in recent years Catholic thinkers in the First and Third Worlds have been reworking attitudes toward the natural world. Important differences in perspective and emphasis distinguish Catholic environmental philosophy from different cultures, but they are also united by some overarching themes. First and most important, Catholic thinking about the environment almost invariably contends that God created nature in order to serve human dignity and the common good, not individual profit. Creation is a gift of God, intended for the well-being of all of humanity. Greed, expressed in consumerist culture and unrestrained capitalist economics, leads to overexploitation of both nature and persons, ultimately destroying both human and natural communities. In consequence, people are called to serve as wise and careful stewards of the natural world. Humans are entitled to use natural resources, but this use must be moderate and in the service of the common good rather than individual profit.

These emphases lead to a close link, in most Catholic work on the environment, between environmental and social problems. In Latin America, this means that Catholic thinking about the environment often takes up the themes of social and economic justice. For example, a pastoral letter issued in December 2000 by the Apostolic Vicariate of the department of Petén, Guatemala, titled "The Cry of the Forest in the Jubilee Year: Between Agony and Hope," asserts that "It is not possible to speak of ecology without taking justice into account. It is not possible to defend the conservation of the forest apart from the advancement and life of the poor" (*El Grito de la Selva en el Ano Jubilar*, 9).

Bishops in other parts of Latin America have taken up similar themes. In an April 2000 Pastoral Letter, the Bishops of Northern Mexico denounced the socially and environmentally destructive consequences of forest exploitation, concluding that

> The protection of the forests requires urgent measures . . . The forest is not mere food for industry . . . The forest is a giver of life for its inhabitants. For these reasons we appeal to the conscience of everyone and urge all Christians to take responsibility for preserving the life on this planet that God has entrusted to our care. All of this makes it our obligation to . . . denounce the ecological devastation we are witnessing (http://conservation.catholic.org/bishops_from_around_the_world.htm).

And a statement from the Church in the Dominican Republic asserts that

> Human sins against nature redound always to the detriment of humankind itself . . . It is not right that those who have greater resources, whether countries, cities, groups, or individuals, should lean toward excessive consumption which, in addition to being a provocative insult to the poor, is an evil misappropriation of natural resources necessary for the have-nots of the world (http://conservation.catholic.org/bishops_from_around_the_world.htm).

Similar themes emerge in the environmental writing of Latin American liberationist theologians, such as the Brazilian Leonardo Boff, who gained international prominence in the 1970s and 1980s for his arguments in favor of democratization within the Church, among other themes. In the 1990s, Boff has turned his attention to ecological themes, insisting that, "The very same logic of the prevailing system of accumulation and social organization that leads to the exploitation of workers also leads to the pillaging of whole nations and ultimately the plundering of nature" (Boff 1997: 110–11).

This destructive system must be replaced with "a non-consumeristic type of cultural practice that is respectful of ecosystems, ushers in an economy of what is sufficient for all, and fosters the common good not only of humans but also of the other beings in creation" (Boff 1997: 113). Boff contends that excessive consumption by some harms both the poor and the natural world; the solution requires both more restraint in human use of natural resources and a more equitable distribution of the goods they make possible.

In addition to theological explorations, Catholics in Latin America are addressing environmental problems in grassroots organizations and pastoral projects. Many dioceses and parishes have formed "ecological committees." These take different forms and emphasize different issues, depending on the setting. In many urban areas, primary concern is with issues of "environmental justice," such as waste disposal, sanitation, and air and water quality. In rural areas, attention often focuses on problems related to agriculture, such as soil erosion, reliance on chemical pesticides and fertilizers, and exhaustion of water resources. Latin Americans, Catholic and other, devote less attention to issues such as biodiversity and wilderness protection than do environmentalists in North America and Europe. This emphasis stems both from the urgency of social and economic inequities and also from the dominance of a perspective in which environmental problems are significant in relation to human needs and interests. The Roman Catholic tradition has contributed substantially to this humanistic worldview. There is some evidence of the emergence of more "biocentric" ways of thinking, especially in regions with large wilderness areas remaining, but this remains a minority perspective within Latin American environmentalist thought and activism.

Anna Peterson

Further Reading
Boff, Leonardo. *Cry of the Earth, Cry of the Poor*. Maryknoll, NY: Orbis Books, 1997.
See also: Boff, Leonardo; Christianity (7c) – Liberation Theology; Christianity (7d) – Feminist Theology; Christianity (7e) – Creation Spirituality; Gebara, Ivone; Mayan Protestantism.

Roman Natural Religion

The close association of Roman religion with the natural world is apparent from the various versions of the Roman seasonal calendar ranging from the popular "farmer's calendar" to the much more formal listings of sacrifices and other observances which had to be undertaken by various priestly colleges on behalf of the state. In all cases the purification of the fields, sowing, growth of plants and harvest were central to the pattern of the year, as indeed was the securing of the fecundity of flocks and herds. It is not surprising that this seasonal cycle is so widely celebrated by poets (such as Virgil, Horace, and especially Ovid, who wrote a long poem, the *Fasti*, detailing the festivals month by month); it is also apparent in works of art often described as sacro-idyllic as there is always a religious component, such as representations of shrines and divine images, in Roman portrayals of the countryside.

Many aspects of this religion depended on deities who were the personifications of natural phenomena. Ceres, though later equated with the Greek Demeter, was simply the process of growth; Vesta was the controlled fire of the hearth; Jupiter, with his epithet Fulgur, was the thunderer. The most famous and long-lived of Roman festivals, the Lupercalia, celebrated in February, came to celebrate the myth of Romulus and Remus at the wolf's cave. But the identity of the god to whom the festival was dedicated was no longer really known, though the rites, which included the sacrifice of goats whose skins were put on by otherwise nude runners who would lash out with thongs believed to bring fecundity to the childless, were held in high regard until the end of the fifth century. It was clearly a purification ritual like the April festival of the Parilia, which was concerned with flocks and herds and was symbolized by Pales, a goddess of whom little is known.

Not surprisingly, a grove of trees was often regarded as the dwelling place of a deity, often Mars, who would certainly need to be propitiated if anything were done to it. Cato in his book on agriculture describes the procession and sacrifice that the farmer would have to make if he wished to thin the grove. Evander in Virgil's *Aeneid* (viii, 351–2) describes the woods covering the Capitoline Hill as "the abode of some god." In his *Fasti* (iii, 295–9), Ovid mentions another wood in Rome, a grove by the Aventine, dark with enormous holm-oaks, where the viewer would exclaim, "this is the home of deity." It is not surprising that later Diana, goddess of hunting, had her Roman home here. Ovid, however, associates the spot with more localized rustic deities, saying that Faunus and his father Picus, who was the woodpecker and son of Mars, often came to drink at the spring here. Springs, sacred to major deities such as Neptune or Minerva, or some more localized water deity, or to the nymphs, were widely venerated throughout the Roman world. Typical examples were the springs of the nymph Arethusa at Syracuse in Sicily, and of Sulis, equated with Minerva, at Bath in Britain.

This identity of the divine and the natural worlds meant that nature was frequently employed to interpret the will of the gods. Thus by observing the song and feeding habits of birds, augurs could foretell the future. A related phenomenon is recorded at Tiora near Reate, where according to Dionysius of Halicarnassus (*Roman Antiquities* 1.14.5), at an oracle of Mars, a woodpecker tapped-out on a post responses to questions put by the enquirer. Most important was the study of bird flight across the sky, as this could be divided into sections, each with a meaning. The Etruscan art of haruspicy, in which the haruspex (literally the "gut-gazer") looked at the heart, intestines and liver of sacrificed animals, at first sight could not have been more different from bird-watching but, as is demonstrated by a bronze model liver excavated at Piacenza, carefully marked out in sections, this too could be related to the sky map of the augurs used similarly in divination.

The religious person would look out for omens, which might well be connected with animals, some of which were sacred to specific deities. There are many stories of Jupiter's eagle giving succor and hope to Roman armies; but Juno's peacocks and geese, Apollo's corvine, Minerva's owl, Mercury's cockerel, Diana's deer, the serpent of Aesculapius, the ant of Ceres, the dolphin of Neptune, the panther of Bacchus, and the lions of Cybele, are all familiar in literature and art. Sometimes the animal is so closely associated with the deity that the two are virtually interchangeable, a process known as "theriomorphism." Dea Artio, the bear goddess attested by a figurine from Berne in Switzerland, has a name derived from that of the name for bear. Another goddess originating in the Celtic world was Epona, who can be identified with the horse. In the case of Aesculapius, serpents and hounds lived in his sanctuaries and helped the healing process of the sick by, for example, licking the sores, wounds and swollen limbs of votaries.

In art, this naturalistic religion was prettified and made polite, providing the basis for the idealized view of nature in so much Western Art where fauns (originally godlings of the countryside around Rome) and satyrs gamboled in woods and fields and where Priapus, who developed from a phallic pillar, became a somewhat risqué symbol of sexual activity. The sacro-idyllic landscape was developed, if not invented by a certain Studius who lived in the reign of Augustus. In landscape paintings of this time, as well as in other works of art such as silver plate and gems, we find temples and sacred columns as well as images of Venus or Priapus set in idealized countryside. Venus keeps her place as the garden goddess but is now very much identified with the Greek love-goddess Aphrodite. Both aspects are very much to the fore in the elegant fourth-century poem, Pervigilium Veneris ("Venus' eve"), which celebrates both love and fertility.

Outside the essential domesticity of the estates and gardens celebrated by writers and artists, nature had a darker side, one that needed to be taken by human effort. In myth this is symbolized by the deeds of heroes such as Bellerophon who slew the fire-breathing Chimaera, Perseus who vanquished the sea monster, and, above all, Hercules who killed savage lions, boars, bulls and monsters in a series of Labors. This attitude to a hostile nature beyond the world of humankind, partially at least, explains one of the contradictions in the Roman psyche between the gentle appreciation of the divine in nature, which had such resonance with pantheist eighteenth-century writers, and the savage barbarities of the Roman arena. The venationes (plays) staged at the Roman Coliseum and other amphitheatres celebrated the dominance of Rome over "the other." The "ludi" (games!) were part of the annual cycle of religious festivals in the calendar; they were attended by priests and by the Vestal Virgins. It is clear that despite the obvious dominance of popular entertainment, there was an element of sacrifice here: Rome was offering up the fruits of nature to the gods.

It could be claimed that the introduction of the amphitheatre was relatively late in date, not appearing until the late Republic, but the attitude toward nature as essentially savage is to be found in the Lupercalia. It is also apparent in a famous ritual at the grove of Diana at Aricia beside Lake Nemi. This grove was presided over by a priest, a runaway slave who obtained his office by plucking a bough from a certain tree and then challenging the reigning priest to mortal combat. This curious priesthood was investigated by the famous anthropologist, Sir James Frazer, which started him on his magnum opus, *The Golden Bough*. Although not all of his deductions would now be accepted (for example, his belief that the rites celebrated a single Mediterranean Great Goddess), the cult was almost certainly earlier than its Hellenization and originated in the pattern of death and rebirth which could be observed in nature. The priest, challenged and cut down by his rival, literally died for the goddess, who in classical times was called Diana.

Roman religion cannot be limited to Rome or even Italy, and it is often difficult to decide where Roman religion ends and those of other peoples in the Empire begin. From Britain to Syria the ancient traveler would find many similarities in attitudes to natural features, mountains and mountain passes, rivers, caves and groves, but also local differences. The second-century Greek rhetor, Lucian, describes the superstitions of a Roman senator, Rutilianus, who would only have to see a rock smeared with holy oil or with a wreath laid on it to fall on his face before it. He became the dupe of a charlatan named Alexander, who set up an oracle in which the responses were given by a serpent called Glycon, at Abonoteichos in Asia Minor.

The more or less contemporary guidebook to Greece written by Pausanias was intended for the sophisticated Roman traveler and is full of accounts of a god-filled countryside and rites available to the pilgrim. Nature could be both benign and brutal but it was never regarded as simply secular. At Patras in the sanctuary of Laphrian Artemis, live animals were rounded up and thrown alive onto an enormous bonfire in honor of the deity (Pausanias: VII,18,6). To modern eyes this is incredibly cruel, and a reminder to those who over-idealize the Greeks, that the "Roman" amphitheatre did not signify a unique distinction between the two peoples in this matter. We can also recall that the maenads, servants to Dionysus, tore animals limb from limb in their trances and in doing so were in a sense identified with wild nature. However, other information, for example in Pausanias, has a more gentle charm, describing a countryside of hills, islands and woods peopled with gods who are part of beneficent nature, and which belongs much more to the sacro-idyllic world which we meet in many Latin poets and can observe in depictions on wall paintings, engraved gems, and other works of art.

Religion and Nature in Art

Excavation at Pompeii has found the remains of many gardens, and these, together with frescoes from the Campanian cities and Rome, and engraved gems from throughout the Empire showing the natural world, provide a fascinating body of visual evidence of how ordinary inhabitants of Italy approached the divine around them. It is clear that all landscapes were regarded as having a divine aspect, as does the Christian landscape of southern Europe today with its shrines and churches – everything from the Lararium, which brought the Lares into the front hall, to the garden with its marble figures of Priapus, Venus goddess of gardens, or Mars, associated with Venus in love but also with sacred groves. The peristyle of the House of the Marine Venus, with one painted panel showing the birth of Venus (her physiognomy and coiffure perhaps based on those of the lady of the house) and another a statue of Mars in front of garden plants and birds, was only part playful; these were deities seriously regarded as bringing peace and order to nature.

A panel of landscape on this painting is in fact a "sacro-idyllic landscape," with shrines interspersed with people. Such landscapes, generally with herdsmen, satyrs and nymphs, are highly distinctive and often of high quality, especially in the Augustan period when they were popular as symbols of the return of peace, and are to be found in stuccoes, paintings and marble relief sculpture. One of the carved panels of the screen wall of the Ara Pacis, begun in 13 B.C.E. and completed in 9 B.C.E., shows a figure of Italy suckling two babies in a rich landscape with a stream, a cow and a sheep grazing, and crops ready for harvest. Another depicts Aeneas sacrificing a white sow with her piglets at Lanuvium in a rustic landscape in which there is a temple of his household gods, or Penates. The rich acanthus scrollwork of the pilasters and lower part of the screen inhabited by nesting birds and buzzing insects reinforces the importance of harmony in nature to the Roman ethos. Moreover, on the interior of the screen wall, hanging garlands filled with fruit reinforce the message of the fecundity of a peaceful nature that Augustus and his advisors wished to convey to the Roman people.

In Classical Greek times, Dionysus was, although powerful, a destructive and menacing god. His satyrs often represented untamed nature and were in consequence themselves wild and menacing. There is a tendency, well shown on Roman-period engraved gems, for Roman satyrs to be genial quaffers of wine or players on pan pipes and thus to exemplify the pastoral ideal; they often appear with offspring and if maenads are shown, the sexual relations between male and female tend to be decorous. Frequently these country spirits make offerings on altars in front of little statues of Priapus or Pan, which must have existed in actuality in garden and parkland settings. Dionysus, generally known as Bacchus in Roman times, presided over the vine and the feast and would also be very much at home in a villa setting as is shown by the famous fresco in the Villa of the Mysteries; here the cult scene is shown as taking place in the house, but connections with the great outdoors were to be found in bacchic symbols in the painting, such as the phallus, the organ of generation, which is being uncovered by one maenad, and the nude female maenad-dancer who brings to mind the wild freedom of the god's followers in the myths of the god. Moreover, elsewhere in the house, there were panels depicting sacrifice in a rustic landscape.

The very frequent appearance of such themes on personal objects, such as signet rings, is noteworthy. Satyrs, cupids and countrymen making offerings to the gods of the countryside, doubtless reminded the wearer of his or her obligations to the gods and genii loci, who looked after fields and gardens. Popular themes of animal life, groups of cattle, panthers, goats, eagles, deer, dolphins and ants are equally symbols of the complex relationship, secular and religious, between man and the gods, either as sacrifices or as familiars of deity.

Martin Henig

Further Reading

Farrar, Linda. *Ancient Roman Gardens*. Stroud: Sutton Publishing Ltd, 1998.
Henig, Martin. " 'Et in Arcadia Ego': Satyrs and Maenads in the Ancient World and Beyond." In Clifford Malcolm Brown, ed. *Engraved Gems: Survivals and Revivals*. Washington: National Gallery of Art, (Studies in the History of Art 54), 1997, 22–31.
Ling, Roger. "Studius and the Beginnings of Roman Landscape Painting." *Journal of Roman Studies* 67 (1977), 1–16.
Ogilvie, R.M. *The Romans and their Gods*. London: Chatto and Windus, 2000.
Scullard, Howard H. *Festivals and Ceremonies of the Roman Republic*. London: Thames and Hudson, 1981.

Toynbee, J.M.C. *Animals in Roman Life and Art*. London: Thames and Hudson, 1973.

See also: Animals; Delphic Oracle; Ovid's Metamorphoses; Roman Natural Religion; Roman Religion and Empire.

Roman Religion and Empire

The great ancient Mediterranean empire of Rome provides examples of the ways in which religion determined attitudes to nature, but also of the tendencies of business and politics to circumvent religious sanctions regarding treatment of nature. The amorphous deities of early Roman religion were considered to govern the domestic activities of household and agriculture, but also the wild natural forces they perceived in the forests, waters, weather, and wildlife. The Romans regarded certain features of the landscape, such as springs, groves, and mountains, as sacred. Their rituals and ceremonies were deeply involved in agriculture and the round of the seasons. In the years between 200 B.C.E. and 200 C.E., the Romans were deeply influenced by Greek attitudes to the gods and nature, so that their ideas of the gods became more anthropomorphic. At the same time, a growing Roman orientation toward practicality and desire for profit and control weakened the traditional sanctions that had given a modicum of protection to the natural environment.

Like Greece, Italy was part of the Mediterranean environmental zone, with a hot summer and relatively mild winter, but with more rainfall on average than Greece. The Roman Empire, however, embraced the entire Mediterranean area and extended beyond it into Western Europe. Such a vast area contained a variety of ecosystems from deserts to high forests.

Roman religion followed its own course even though it shared some sources with Greek religion, and in later times eagerly adopted Greek myths and religious practices. Early Roman gods were formless spirits or presences, sensed as *numina*, mysterious presences in the natural world, not as anthropomorphic as the Greek gods, although Romans accepted Greek portrayals of the gods from the late Republic onward. Any natural phenomenon could be seen as the result of a god's operation. Therefore any human activity that affected the environment could be seen as attracting the interest of or provoking the reaction of some god or goddess, and ought to be undertaken with caution.

Since nature was full of gods, natural events could serve as the medium for discerning their intent. To a skilled Roman augur, birds of many kinds, singly or in groups, bearing prey or flying free, on the left or on the right, displayed the plans of gods. In the sound of thunder or the rustling of leaves those who knew how to listen could hear the gods' words.

Roman gods were extremely numerous. Their hierarchy ran from great deities like Jupiter the thunderer to local spirits of springs like Juturna. Roman religion had an agricultural flavor, reflecting the observances of farm families who depended on the orderly cycles of nature for subsistence. The Romans possessed gods of the farmhouse and storehouse (*penates*) and of the fields (*lares*). A god or goddess was the growing spirit of every major crop, such as Ceres of grain and Liber of wine. Every activity of the farm had a deity to be invoked for its success, such as Vervactor for first plowing, Repacator for the second, Imporcitor for harrowing, Insitor for sowing, and even Sterquilinius for manuring. On the margins lurked Silvanus and other wild gods of the forests. Romans were not without reverence for wild places, and personified mountains like "Father Apennine" as gods, but agricultural themes dominated their religion.

Religious worship and appreciation of natural beauty are reasons given for the ascents of high mountains recorded in Roman times. Rome's most famous mountaineer was the Emperor Hadrian, who ascended Mount Casius in Syria by night to see the sunrise and to make an offering to Zeus. He narrowly escaped being struck by a bolt of lightning that killed the sacrificing priest. High mountains were places where the gods could be worshipped.

Sacred groves in Italy were as ancient, numerous, and widespread as in Greece. The Latin words for them were *nemus* (grove), and *templum* (a space marked out). The latter is the root of the word "temple." The Romans never forgot the motive that had created them: religious awe. Virgil said that when they saw the old tree-covered Capitoline Hill, the rural folk who lived around it exclaimed, "Some god has this grove for his dwelling!" (Virgil, *Aeneid* 8:351–52). Seneca remarked,

> If you come upon a grove of old trees that have lifted their crowns up above the common height and shut out the light of the sky by the darkness of their interlacing boughs, you feel that there is a spirit in the place, so lofty is the wood, so lone the spot, so wondrous the thick unbroken shade (Seneca, *Epistles* 4.12.3).

The numerous Roman religious festivals followed the calendar of activities of the ancestral farm, from the hanging of the plow on the boundary marker in the Compitalia in January to festivals of Saturn and Bona Dea, deities of the soil, in December. Sacrifice was usually in the form of the slaughter, cooking, and eating of domestic animals, although wild animals were sometimes offered. Bloodless sacrifices, such as the pouring of wine, oil, milk, or grain, or the presentation of fruit, cakes or cheese, were also made. Sacrifice was a gift to the gods in expectation of benefits, or in thanksgiving for them. The Latin phrase was *do ut des*, "I give (to you) so that you will give (to me)." The animal or substance sacrificed often represented the god. Since the number of victims was sometimes in the hundreds, the effect on the environment through killing animals, consuming fuel, and releasing smoke must have been considerable. Sometimes sacrifice was used as a way to avoid the environmental protections that religion afforded to sacred places. For example, Cato the Elder advised landowners to make a handy prayer "to the god whom it may concern" for permission to cut down trees in a sacred grove (Cato, *On Agriculture* 139–40).

Pliny the Elder, taking a different view, complained that people abuse their mother, the Earth, but should know better. Lucretius had claimed that Earth was growing older and weaker, and therefore less able to reward human labor. The idea that meager crops could be blamed on an aging Earth was attacked by the agriculturist Columella, who placed the blame for nature's infertility not on senescence or changing climate, but on poor husbandry. A good farmer knows how to restore soil to fertility, but those who misuse the land should not be surprised when the result is diminishing crops and sterility. Horace scorned landowners who were neglectful of their land.

To what degree did the religious ideas held by the Greeks and Romans about nature affect their practical treatment of the Earth and its living inhabitants? There is no simple answer. Hunters spared some animals, particularly the young, because gods were thought to punish their killers. Prohibitions against cutting trees saved them in sacred groves. Animism provided an enchantment of nature that made people think twice before harming it. However, the undeniable fact that the natural environment suffered considerable damage at the hands of the Greeks and Romans remains to be explained, and it was more than one would expect from people who worshipped gods of nature and regarded much of the landscape as sacred.

Religion permeated all levels of society, and the beliefs of common folk preserved older practices. The environmental orientation of ancient religion was toward preservation of the natural order. Still, it is characteristic of human beings to evade religious prescriptions when it is in their perceived self-interest. It is possible that tree worshippers might have preserved a few sacred trees while they were cutting down whole forests, if they needed wood for fuel. Some of the mystery religions taught the oneness of human beings with the universe and nonviolence toward other forms of life, but they also stressed purity of soul and escape from the physical world, and therefore neglected the natural environment. Religious doubt increased in later classical times, and Christianity weakened the older nature religion.

Ancient religion could have provided constructive environmental attitudes. But these would not have been effective in conservation without knowledge of the workings of nature and the effects of human actions upon it. There were places where a body of practical knowledge of interactions with the Earth, the result of centuries of trial and error, survived. For example, the practices of subsistence farmers reflected adaptations to the limits of ecosystems they had to live within or perish. They took care of the land as long as their lives were not disrupted by war, which unfortunately they often were. It would have been difficult, however, to decide which practices would bring the best results when an environmental problem first appeared or was exacerbated from a tolerable level to an intolerable one.

It seems, therefore, that the course environmental problems took in the ancient world was not chiefly the result of the religious concepts of the natural world held by the Greeks and Romans. It was also the result of the technology they inherited and developed, the population levels they reached, the agricultural and other economic measures they took to feed, clothe, and shelter themselves, and the patterns of their rural and urban lives. Only through studying the interaction of all these factors will it be possible to gain understanding of the ecological failure that underlies the decline of ancient Mediterranean civilization.

J. Donald Hughes

Further Reading

Coates, Peter. "Ancient Greece and Rome." In Peter Coates. *Nature: Western Attitudes Since Ancient Times*. Berkeley and Los Angeles: University of California Press, 1998, chapter 2.

Dumézil, Georges. *Archaic Roman Religion*. 2 vols. Chicago: University of Chicago Press, 1996.

Ferguson, John. *The Religions of the Roman Empire*. Ithaca, NY: Cornell University Press, 1970.

Glacken, Clarence J. *Traces on the Rhodian Shore*. Berkeley and Los Angeles: University of California Press, 2003.

Grant, Michael and Rachel Kitzinger, eds. *Civilization of the Ancient Mediterranean: Greece and Rome*. 3 vols. New York: Charles Scribner's Sons, 1988.

Hughes, J. Donald. *Pan's Travail: Environmental Problems of the Ancient Greeks and Romans*. Baltimore, MD: Johns Hopkins University Press, 1996.

Hughes, J. Donald. *Ecology in Ancient Civilizations*. Albuquerque: University of New Mexico Press, 1975.

McNeill, J.R. *The Mountains of the Mediterranean World*. Cambridge: Cambridge University Press, 1992.

Palmer, Robert E.A. *Roman Religion and Roman Empire*. Philadelphia: University of Pennsylvania Press, 1974.

White, Kenneth D. *Roman Farming*. Ithaca, NY: Cornell University Press, 1970.

See also: Egypt – Ancient; Greco-Roman World; Greece – Classical; Mesopotamia – Ancient to 2000 B.C.E.

Romanies (Gypsies)

If religion is popularly perceived – as it so often is – to include a place of worship, a clergy and a set of holy scriptures, then it is easy to understand why observers such as Hoyland, Roberts, Morwood, Greenfeld, and others should have reached the conclusions which are quoted below:

> I never could meet with anybody that pretended to say what their private faith and religion may be (Hoyland 1816: 25).

> They have, as a people, no religion (Roberts 1836: xvij).

> The lack of religious ideas, and the want of a peculiar system of worship among the Gipsies, constitute remarkable features in the history of this strange people (Morwood 1885: 281–2).

> They cannot be said to have a religion of their own (Greenfeld 1977: 52).

If, on the other hand the usual dictionary definition is adhered to, such as *Webster's* "belief in a divine or superhuman power or powers to be obeyed and worshiped as the creator(s) and ruler(s) of the universe [and the] expression of this belief in conduct and ritual" (1966: 1228) or *Encarta's* "particular institutionalized or personal system of beliefs or practices relating to the divine" (1999: 1516), then it is clear that they were wrong.

Romanies, often incorrectly referred to as "Gypsies," descend from a migration out of India in the early years of the eleventh century. This exodus was prompted by a succession of raids led by Mohammed of Ghazni between 1000 and 1027 in his attempt to spread Islam into Northern India. The Hindu response was to assemble military forces known as Rajputs, conscripted from various language groups, though ones close enough to share the same genetic descent. The linguistic nature of the Romani language strongly suggests that it began as a composite military lingua franca (under the same circumstances that gave rise to the Urdu language), and for which the name *Rajputic* has been proposed. This only later crystallized into an ethnic mother-tongue when the troops and their camp-followers reached Anatolia and began to marry within the group and produce new generations of children. Because the first written account of the appearance of Romanies in the Byzantine Empire dates from 1054, we can assume that it was reached within fifty years or less of leaving India. If so, it was over two centuries before their descendants finally entered Europe – again because of the spread of Islam, this time toward the West.

It is not difficult to understand why outside observers

were uniformly convinced that Romanies have no religion. Apart from there being no tangible evidence – a sacred text, a temple or a priest for example – Romani society is tightly closed to outsiders, considerably reducing the opportunity to observe cultural behavior at close quarters. Ethnographers attempting to enter Romani households report being kept at arm's length by various means, even by being met at the door with feigned epileptic seizures or frightening explosions of profanity. But it is one of the aspects of Romani religious belief which keeps that barrier in place.

So entrenched is the idea that Romanies lack religion that it has become a part of European folklore: the story that "the gypsies have little or no, if any, religion ... their church was constructed of curds or lard and the dogs ate it" (de Peyster 1887: 58) is widespread. Block repeated it half a century later:

> the gypsies, it is said, once possessed a church of their own built of cream cheese. On one occasion, however, when they were particularly hungry, they ate the church and for this reason are now without a national religion (1938: 234).

Because Romanies come ultimately from India, it is in Hinduism that the roots of their religion are to be found. However, awareness of this has become lost over the centuries and is only now being relearned by Romanies today. Likewise the daily cultural behavior in which Indian-based spiritualism (called *Rromanipen*) manifests itself so clearly is not recognized as such; asked what his religion is, a Romani is likely to say Orthodox or Roman Catholic, Mormon, Muslim or Bahá'í or any one of the non-indigenous faiths acquired, voluntarily or not, since arrival in the West.

Woodcock, like so many others, was wrong when he wrote that

> The gypsies ... are utterly without religious impressions ... they brought with them no Indian idols ... nor indeed Indian rites or observances, for no trace of such are to be discovered amongst them (1865: 84).

While Kounavine claimed to have found Brahma, Indra, Lakshmi and other Hindu deities continuing to be worshipped by name among Romanies in Russia, this has been shown to be fabricated. Nevertheless other connections with Hinduism are in evidence, although the names of only three deities have survived: Sara-Kali, Vayu and Maruthi. Shiva's trident, called *trishula* in Sanskrit, changed its role from Hindu symbol to Christian symbol and has become the Romani word for "cross" (*trušul*). This probably happened when the migration first reached Armenia; in the Lomavren language *trusul* means both "church" and "priest." Similarly, *rašaj* "(Christian) holy man" represents a shift of meaning from Sanskrit *arseya* "of a (Hindu) holy man." The word for "God" is Devel, (from Sanskrit *devata* "divinity," compare Hindu *dev*), while the Devil is known as *o Beng* (from a Munda root meaning a malevolent spirit).

The description here is specifically of beliefs found among the groups of Romanies classified as Vlax (Wallachian), from the dialects of Romani they speak. Vlax Romanies emerged as a distinct group in the Balkans during the five centuries of their enslavement there, where their social and physical isolation enabled them to retain traditions lost elsewhere. While each group maintains more or fewer of these, the present account must not be interpreted as descriptive of all Romani populations everywhere.

Some Romani groups in Europe today appear to maintain elements of Shaktism or goddess-worship; the Rajputs worshipped the warrior-goddess Parvati, another name for the female deity Sati-Sara, who is Saint Sarah, the Romani Goddess of Fate. That she forms part of the yearly pilgrimage to La Camargue at Stes Maries de la Mer in the south of France is of particular significance; here she is carried into the sea just as she is carried into the waters of the Ganges each December in India. Both Sati-Sara and St. Sarah wear a crown, both are also called Kali, and both have shining faces painted black. Sati-Sara is a consort of the god Šiva, and is known by many other names, Bhadrakali, Uma, Durga and Syama among them.

The names of two Indian deities have been preserved in some Romani riddles. Reference to the Vedic god of the wind and the air, Vayu (also called Marut), is retained in a number of these: *Kana hulavel peske bal o Vajo, legenisavol e čar* ("When Vayu combs his hair, the grass sways"), *Amaro Vajo hurjal tela savorrenge podji, aj konik našti t'astarel les* ("Our Vayu flies under everyone's petticoats, and no one can catch him"), *O pharo vurdon e Vajosko cirdajlo ekhe šele grastendar kaj phurden ande'l rrutunja* ("Vayu's heavy wagon is pulled by a hundred horses blowing through their nostrils"); the answer to each *is e balval* "the wind." In Indian theology the task of Vayu's son Maruti (also called Hanuman) is to tear open the clouds and let the rain fall, and in Romani the expression *marutisjol o Devel* means "the sky [*lit.* "God"] is growing overcast." The reference to a hundred horses may also be of Vedic origin; there are several references in the scriptures to the *avamedha yajña* or "horse sacrifice," whereby in ancient India the king would release one hundred horses to roam freely through his kingdom. Stopping them or blocking their path was forbidden.

The female spirits or fates, in Romani called the *vursitorja*, hover in its presence three days after a child is born to determine its destiny and to influence the choice of name the parents will decide upon. They may be compared with the Indian *matrka* or "little mother" spirits who also possess a baby's destiny at the time of its birth. The red thread (the *loli dori*) tied around a new-born's ankle or wrist and worn for two or three years afterwards to guard against the *jakhalo* or "evil eye" reflects the protective properties of that color, which is also worn or painted on the body in India.

The burning of one's possessions after death and even, among some populations at least into the twentieth century, the ritual suicide of the widow has striking parallels with *sati* in India.

Time spent in the non-Romani world (the *jado*) drains spiritual energy or *dji*. Sampson (1926: 257) gives the various meanings of this word as "[s]eat of the emotions, heart, soul; temper, disposition, mood; courage, spirit," comparing it to Sanskrit *jiva*, Hindi *ji*, "life, soul, spirit, mind." In some dialects it has the additional meaning of "stomach." One's spiritual batteries can only be recharged by spending time in an all-Romani environment – in the normal course of events, in family homes. It is in the area of spiritual and physical well-being (*baxt*) that the Indian origin of the Romani people is most clearly seen.

In the preparation of food, and in one's personal hygiene and deportment, it is absolutely essential that a separation between "pure" and "polluted" conditions be maintained. A pure state is achieved by maintaining spiritual "balance" or what is called *karma* in India (and in Romani *kintala*, or in some dialects *kintari* or *kintujmos*) in one's life and avoiding shame (*ladžav* or *ladž*), being declared unclean or, in extreme cases, being shunned by the community. Maintaining balance or harmony pleases the spirits of the ancestors (the *mulé*), and they are there to guard one and help one to do it, but if they are displeased, they will mete out punishment by way of retribution (*prikaza*). Depending upon the nature of the transgression, this may be mild (e.g., stubbing one's toe) or so severe as to involve sickness and even death. The consequences of *prikaza* underlie the universal Romani belief that nothing is an accident; that nothing happens simply by chance.

The penalty for extreme pollution is being banished, or made an outcast, and an out-caste, from the community, which may or may not imply a state of pollution, can be imposed also for other reasons (e.g., disregard for territorial claims). Being in a state of pollution is literally to be "smeared" (i.e., with menstrual blood). This can be contrasted with being "dirty," but only from physical dirt.

Prikaza brings bad luck (*bibaxt*) and illness (*nasvalipe*), and it can be attracted even by socializing with people who are not *vuže* (*vužo* "clean"). Non-Romani people are not seen as *vuže*, which is why Romanies avoid contact that is too intimate. But this is not an inherited condition of non-Romanies, it is because these cultural practices are not maintained. A non-Romani woman who marries into a Romani family is expected to adopt them, and in doing so becomes in that context *vuži*.

The Ayurvedic concept of ritual purity and ritual pollution, so central to Romani belief, existed in the eleventh-century caste system and continues to exist today; thus members of the same *jati* (sub-caste) may eat together without risk of contamination, for example, but will become polluted if they eat with members of other *jati*; and because the jatis of one's associates might not always be known, contact between the mouth and the various utensils shared with others at a meal is avoided, just to be on the safe side. In conservative Romani culture, liquids are poured into the mouth from a container held away from the lips, so that the rim of the vessel (the *kerlo*) is not touched; smoke from a shared tobacco pipe is drawn through the fist clenched around its stem, again to avoid making contact with the mouth. The surest way not to touch utensils used by others is to eat with the fingers, and every one of these habits is to be found among Romanies today.

Like the Rajputs, some Romani groups divide foods into "ordinary" and "auspicious" or "lucky" (*baxtalo*) categories (the Rajputs' terms for these two categories mean "cold" and "hot," though these have nothing to do with either temperature or pepper); this distinction reflects the close relationship between food and health, a particular ingredient being not only beneficial to the physical self but also to the spiritual. "Auspicious foods" include those which are pungent or strongly flavored, such as garlic, lemon, pickles, peppers, sour cream and so on. The use of red pepper in some traditional Romani dishes is typical of Rajput cuisine particularly, and such food is called *ito* or "piquant" in one Romani dialect. Also in common with Indian culinary behavior is the practice of not preparing dishes far in advance of their being eaten, and of not keeping left-over food. Dishes set for the dead at a *pomana* (wake) table or a *slava* (saint's day) table are eventually disposed of by being offered to passers-by, never just thrown away. There are very many customs associated with food and eating: potatoes (*kolompirja*) are not eaten at a *pomana*; there cannot be an even number of chairs at a *pomana* table; greens (*zelenimata*) are not eaten while one is in mourning, or expecting a baby, and so on.

Because access to physicians and hospitals is only sought in extreme cases due to their polluting association, safeguarding the health of the community *within* the community is of special importance. Like groups in northern India such as the Banjara, some Romani populations distinguish illnesses which are natural to the group; these are such things as heart complaints, rashes, vomiting, hiccups, insomnia or irritability, from those which are the result of overfamiliarity with the *jado* or non-Romani world. These latter include, for example, all sexually transmitted diseases. For such afflictions, a non-Romani physician needs to be consulted; but for "Romani afflictions," traditional cures are provided by a *drabarni* or female healer. This is the same as the Hindu *siana*. The root of the word *drabarni* is *drab* which means "medicine" (from Sanskrit *dravya* "medication," compare the Hindi word *darb*). It is also the root of the verb *drabar*, which is usually translated in English as "to tell fortunes," but which from the Romani perspective means "making well." When speaking English, Romanies prefer to call this skill brought from India "advising" rather than "fortune telling," for which another verb, *duriker*, exists.

If it is necessary for a person who has contracted a *gadžikano nasvalipe* to be admitted to hospital, relatives and others will go to him, often in considerable numbers, to provide *dji* and help restore balance. "Relatives, their relatives, and friends of a Gypsy flock around his hospital bed because [of] their culture" (Anderson and Tighe 1973: 282); only recently have hospital administrations begun to recognize this as cultural behavior and to accommodate it. Depending upon the nature of the non-Romani affliction, the individual may be declared defiled; not visited in hospital but instead banished from the community. This is invariably the response when this is, for example, syphilis, AIDS, or other such disease. Infections of this kind are a clear indication of a too-personal involvement in the non-Romani world, since it is assumed that they could never be contracted within the ethnic community.

Romanies and Other Religions

The journey across the Middle East took place too rapidly for Islam to have had an impact on Romani spiritual belief, as well no doubt because it was the religion of an enemy people. There is no linguistic impact at all directly from Arabic, and none from Persian religious vocabulary. Nevertheless there are hundreds of thousands of Romanies throughout the Balkans and Turkey who are Muslim, having converted, or having been converted, during the centuries of Ottoman rule in the area.

Zoroastrianism existed in northwest India at the time of the exodus at the beginning of the eleventh century, and in Persia through which that migration passed, and a number of writers have suggested that Rromanipen has acquired at least some aspects of that religion, particularly its dualism and the significance of fire. It is unlikely that this was the case, however, given the circumstances of early Romani history, the time and location involved, and the fact that these are also characteristics found in Hinduism.

There are numbers of Romanies who profess the Jewish faith, though in each documented case it has been the result of conversion following marriage to a Jewish spouse. Reportedly, during the Second World War several Romani–Jewish marriages took place in a concentration camp (and known as the "marriage camp") close to the Serbian border, though the fate, and religious persuasion, of any survivors is not known.

Christianity was first encountered in Armenian-speaking Anatolia, at the eastern end of the Byzantine Empire. The Romani words for "Easter," "co-father-in-law" and "godfather" are of Armenian origin, all concepts specific to Orthodox Christianity. Whether it was adopted at that time or not is unknown; in the Christian Byzantine Empire professing Christianity clearly brought benefits to the outsider Romani population, and later presenting themselves as Christian penitents and pilgrims in Europe was also a means of distancing themselves from the Muslim threat. But in Ottoman Turkey, being Christian was a liability, and the seriousness with which either religion was embraced is open to question.

In Europe, it was often the Church that was most openly hostile to Romanies. In 1568 Pope Pius V banished them from the entire realm of the Holy Roman Empire, and priests in the Eastern Rite church could be excommunicated for performing Romani marriages. Monasteries in the Romanian principalities were reportedly the cruelest of all toward their slaves, and in Western Europe, Romanies were routinely forbidden from entering churches to worship, and had to listen from outside through the windows. Such incidents are not entirely unheard of today.

Some Romani groups in France relate the story of how Christianity first came to their people. Originally, they say, the woman leader of a group of Romani metalworkers who lived along the Rhône and whose name was Sara saw a boat on the river which was sinking. In it were Saint Mary Salome, Saint Mary Magdalene and Saint Mary Jacobi, the three Marys who comforted Jesus as he died on the cross. Sara was expecting this since she had seen it in a dream, and she waded out into the water and threw out her cloak which became a raft, and which enabled the three Marys to reach the riverbank safely. As a reward, they made her their servant, and converted her to Christianity. This story, however, seems to originate in European, rather than Romani, tradition. Generally speaking, the Romani population of an area will claim to follow the predominant religion of that area: Protestant in Protestant lands, Roman Catholic in Roman Catholic lands and Orthodox in Orthodox lands.

In the early 1950s in northwestern France, a Breton evangelist named Clément le Cossec began preaching Pentecostal Christianity to Romanies in that region, and it spread rapidly through France and Spain, then the rest of Europe, and to North and South America. Today, "Born-Again" Pentecostalism is the fastest growing and most widely found religion among Romanies. It has been suggested that there are two main reasons for this: first, that it is a church that tells its congregants that they are loved, a personal aspect not characteristic of more formal churches, and a message not formerly heard by Romanies. Second, that compared with the Roman or Orthodox churches, it is easy to become a pastor, and to establish a church of one's own. There are today hundreds of Romani churches, with pastors and congregations who are Romani, who preach in Romani and who even have Romani-language evangelical radio programs and who distribute Romani-language sermons on audiocassette tapes. Significantly, the growth of "Born-Again" Christianity has caused a split in the Romani population, some of whom believe it is a major factor in the loss of traditional *Rromanipen*. One successful Pentecostal church in Dallas, Texas, developed a program that has deliberately integrated references to dualism, balance, ancestral spirits and other aspects of Rromanipen, which do not conflict with Christian doctrine, stressing parallels rather than differences.

There are Romanies who have embraced Mormonism, and the Bahá'í religion has acquired numbers of converts, especially in Spain. But with the exception of those completely assimilated to the non-Romani world, whatever religion may be professed, it will exist syncretistically with more or fewer elements retained from the original set of beliefs and practices which find their origins in India.

Ian Hancock

Further Reading
Anderson, Gwen and Bridget Tighe. "Gypsy Culture and Health Care." *American Journal of Nursing* 73:2 (1973), 282–5.
Block, Martin. *Gypsies: Their Life and their Customs.* London: Methuen, 1938.
Clébert, Jean-Paul. *The Gypsies.* London: Vista Books, 1963.
De Peyster, J. Watts. *Gypsies.* Edinburgh: The Aungervyle Society, 1887.
Encarta World English Dictionary. New York: St. Martin's Press, 1999.
Greenfeld, Martin. *Gypsies.* New York: Crown Publishers, 1977.
Hoyland, John. *A Historical Survey of the Customs, Habits and Present State of the Gypsies.* London: Darton, Harvey & Co. 1816.
Morwood, V.S. *Our Gipsies, in City, Tent and Van.* London: Sampson, Low & Co., 1885.
Rishi, Weer R. *Roma: The Punjabi Emigrants in Europe, Central and Middle Asia, the USSR and the Americas.* Patiala: The Punjabi Press, 1976.
Roberts, Samuel. *The Gypsies.* London: Longman & Co., 1836.
Salloway, Jeffrey C. "Medical Care Utilization among Urban Gypsies." *Urban Anthropology* 2:1 (1973), 113–26.
Sampson, John. *The Dialect of the Gypsies of Wales.* Oxford: The Clarendon Press, 1926.
Shields, Marilyn. "Selected Issues in Treating Gypsy Patients." *Hospital Physician* 11 (1981), 85–92.
Thomas, James D. "Gypsies and American Medical Care." *Annals of Internal Medicine* 102:6 (1985), 842–5.
Webster's New World Dictionary of the American Language. Cleveland and New York: The World Publishing Company, 1966.
Wood, Manfri Fred. *In the Life of a Romany Gypsy.* London and Boston: Routledge & Kegan Paul, 1973.
Woodcock, Henry. *The Gipsies.* London: William Lister, 1865.

See also: Hinduism; India; Proto-Indo–Europeans.

Romanticism and Indigenous Peoples

Romanticism with regard to indigenous cultures has its roots in the edenic episode wherein nature and culture were rent apart in the generative moment of the Western narrative. As a taxonomic device, this separation has most often functioned in favor of "culture" and its putative bearers: "culture" defines the "properly human," and it is that which allows humans to claim a certain stewardship over nature. Configured historically by way of imperialism, this taxonomy also distinguishes between people of God (saved) and people given over to nature (fallen). Whether we choose to map this relationship according to the coordinates offered by Augustine, Columbus, or Andrew Jackson, for example, the results will largely be the same. Native peoples – cultural and categorical "others" – become the inverse and absence of "civilization." Lacking spirit, reason, and private property, among other crucial markers, natives are viewed as children of nature. Redeeming them (if indeed they are human and redeemable) entails converting them away from the world, lifting them up, as it were, from their earthly condition.

And yet the very taxonomy put into place by the edenic myth has an historical alter ego. As if unwilling to wait for the apocalypse – the mythological or technological rectification of history – many Westerners have sought to return to the garden by means of a shortcut. Ironically, this path is found precisely through the romantic recoding of the dominant taxonomy. Whether drawn from public discourse or scholarly treatises, we might distill a set of categorical oppositions concerning the relationship between romantic desires and the decidedly less romantic modern condition:

Nature ~ Culture
(source of redemption) ~ (liability, a state of decay)
Past ~ Present
Hunting/agriculture ~ Industry/global economy
Rural ~ Urban
Communal ~ Private

In romantic thought, what is striking about this set of oppositions is the way each term in the right-hand column is understood to be a corruption of the left-hand one. The remedy, then, is to chart a return to the former (if sometimes fictive) state by whatever means available. What is relevant for our purposes are the channels through which this symbolic "return" is navigated. As strong as nostalgic sentiments might be, actually traversing any of these categories is, at turns, impossible, impractical, or frankly undesirable. What is needed is a stand-in: a scapegoat symbolically and metonymically linked to nature who can perform an eternal return to the garden. Enter the native.

Whether in tandem with real political agitation or in place of it, indigenous peoples have been looked to as an environmental and spiritual panacea by people around the globe in their retreat from the perceived failures and implications of modernity. Surely there are positive aspects to this phenomenon, as there is much to be learned from native traditions, particularly in terms of resilience and creativity. And one might add that it is high time that native peoples be celebrated rather than denigrated. It should be noted, however, that the degree to which Indians were "the first ecologists" is a hotly contested issue. Defining, defending, and denying the Earth ethic of Native Americans has become an academic blood sport. Quite beyond the historical and institutional concerns of this debate, I would call attention to several ideological aspects of romanticism that are problematic. First, romanticism is reactionary and escapist: romantic views of indigenous peoples spring from other peoples' needs and desires, not from an appreciation of indigenous people in their own right. Second, romantic tendencies are predicated on a kind of social evolution model, even while its valuations are ostensibly reversed from the imperial pattern. Native peoples are looked to as an antidote to modernity precisely because they are understood – however uncritically – to inhabit the social past, specifically as anachronistic representatives of an imagined natural past (which explains why Native American exhibits are frequently located in natural history museums). The ramifications of such a view are anything but comforting. Third, romanticism reifies the very traditions it exalts, paradoxically suffocating that from which it seeks inspiration. Romantic images portray tradition as fixed, stable, uncontested and, linking us back to our earlier points, anti-modern. To imagine tradition in this way eliminates the prospect that the people romanticized will be heard when they speak in their own voice – even when it comes to speaking about those things which matter to them most, like the land and nature itself.

The narrative I have painted in broad strokes is, of course, distorted in significant ways. Observing this, we want to acknowledge that most people do not imagine or inhabit the world in ways so divided. Most of all, the dichotomy as stated obscures real political efforts of people and groups to heal and sustain nature in ways that neither depend upon the Western narrative nor the burdening of indigenous peoples as surrogate messiahs. That said, the romanticization of native peoples remains – indeed, it seems to escalate with every year and with each new environmental crisis. Complicating the picture, many indigenous people have willfully engaged this discourse, sometimes as authors.

Greg Johnson

Further Reading
Abrahams, Roger. "Phantoms of Romantic Nationalism in Folkloristics." *Journal of American Folklore* 106:3 (1993), 3–37.

Forbes, Jack. "Nature and Culture: Problematic Concepts for Native Americans." In John Grim, ed. *Indigenous Traditions and Ecology*. Cambridge, MA: Harvard University Press, 2001, 103–24.

Gill, Sam. *Mother Earth: An American Story*. Chicago: The University of Chicago Press, 1987.

Greenblatt, Stephen. *Marvelous Possessions: The Wonder of the New World*. Chicago: The University of Chicago Press, 1991.

Krech, Shepard. *Myth and History: The Ecological Indian*. New York and London: W.W. Norton & Company, 1999.

See also: American Indians as "First Ecologists"; Noble Savage; Radical Environmentalism; Religious Environmentalist Paradigm.

Romanticism in European History

Romanticism has long been recognized as a major trope in modern environmental thought and practice. Romanticism, however, was a complex, diverse, changing historical movement. Our present conceptions of Romanticism tend to be defined as much by critics and subsequent commentators as contemporary articulations by Romantic figures. Even the representations of Romanticism within academic studies are the products of different readings from different historical and theoretical positions, and seldom free of polemical overtones. As de Man has noted: "From its inception, the history of romanticism has been one of battles, polemics, and misunderstandings: personal misunderstandings between the poets themselves; between the poets, critics, and the public; between the successive generations" (de Man 1993: 4). Contested are not only the meanings of Romanticism, its very boundaries, origins and influences, and who might be considered a Romantic, but also its conception of nature, its relationship to religion and its relevance to modern environmentalism.

An emblematic text of European Romanticism has long been Wordsworth's *The Prelude*. It is precisely this emblematic status of the poem that gives contestation over its appropriate reading such significance. The poem is an account of the poet's formation as a poet, from his childhood experiences of nature to his mature vision of the sublime. Abrams reads Wordsworth's poem as part of his program for the secularization of inherited theological ideas, for a "natural supernaturalism." The "high argument" of *The Prelude* is that the heights and depths of the mind of man are to replace heaven and hell, and restore the lost paradise; we need only to unite our minds to nature in a holy marriage, and paradise is ours (Abrams 1971: 17–140). Hartman gives central place to the cultivation of the imagination in Wordsworth's poem, attending particularly to the role that "spots of time" – places in nature and time, and in creative time – play in this cultivation. The spirit that lurks in spots of time renews the poet *vis-à-vis* nature; as the *genius loci* or the indwelling spirit of a place, it also acts as spirit inspiring the genial powers of the poet. But for Hartman, the spots of time bring the poet closer to his imagination, not to nature, and the transference of significant experiences to nature acts solely to allow such events, such moments, to reach through time. *The Prelude* is an exercise in soul making, the development of the imagination and the formation of a poet, in which nature takes a secondary role (Hartman 1964: 208–59). McGann, in contrast, sets out to expose the ideology within Wordsworth's poetry, and within such readings of his poetry. McGann is critical of Wordsworth for finding consolation in nature when he should be worrying about the economic realities of the rural life he idealizes. He reads Romantic poetry as an escape from or even suppression of socio-political conditions (McGann 1983: 81–92). These readings of Wordsworth have been highly influential.

Recent critics, however, have found in *The Prelude* both a Romantic ecology and an important religiosity. Bate, for example, argues that Wordsworth's pastoral poetry, highlighting the life and beauty in nature, and finding poetry not only in language but also in nature, has a permanent, enduring power – it is a language that is "evergreen." By fostering an emotional communication between human beings and nature, a love of nature leading to a love of humankind, Bate contends that Wordsworth's poetry offers a political model for modern environmentalism, an "ideology" based on a harmonious relationship with nature that goes beyond, and in many ways deeper, than the neo-Marxist political model to which McGann appeals (Bate 1991: 12–35). Prickett, on the other hand, challenges Abrams' reading, arguing that *The Prelude*, given its historical context, displays not so much the language of secularization as religious revival. Pointing to the relative absence of God from neoclassical literature and critique, and more generally from public life at the end of the eighteenth century, Prickett finds Wordsworth's poem striking for its overtly religious language. Abrams represents Romantic poets as rhetorically adorning the robes of prophets who through the illumination of the mind of man and its communion with nature could restore paradise on Earth. Thus Wordsworth represented himself as the chosen son for his time, the poet now replacing the priest. But Prickett contends that this claim is not simply the poet's retention of the rhetoric of the religious tradition he sought to displace. He argues that we need to take seriously Wordsworth's claims for the religious calling of the poet, and reads *The Prelude* as a pious account of divine election modeled on St. Augustine's *Confessions* (Prickett 1986: 95–104).

The Prelude closes with an image of the poet's ultimate confrontation with nature, the divine and himself; climbing Mount Snowdon, he emerges from a fog to confront a terrifying alpine vista – brooding masses of hills and the dark sea receding into infinity, a chasm of raging waters. The experience of the sublime is the response of the viewer to such a vision that transcends the powers of understanding and imagination, with fear giving way to pleasure as the mind is expanded to encompass what previously seemed beyond comprehension. For Wordsworth, the imagination matured through "spots of time" has the power and autonomy to grasp the whole and dwell in the infinite. An alternative image of such a scene of a wanderer arrested by an infinite alpine landscape is offered by Friedrich's famous 1818 painting "Wanderer above the Sea of Fog." In this image the view remains veiled in part by the fog, which, in addition to heightening the role of the imagination, fragments the visible, eradicates the connecting ground and renders the scene insubstantial. The unusual, distorted perspective only finds its connection in the central figure of the wanderer, which orders and mediates our view of the landscape. This large, central figure with his back to us, viewing the scene, reminds us that the sublime lies not in the object viewed but in the subjective effect on the viewer; it is the experience of nature that is depicted in the painting, how we as viewers participate in what we see. The *Rückenfigur* thus leads us to reflect on our own views of nature. Friedrich's landscapes are natural scenes infused with the divine, yet not explicitly; the divine is both present and absent. His landscapes also represent the alterity of nature, a nature the human subject is not able to appropriate. Indeed, a chasm stands between the wanderer and the landscape before him, a disjunction in the planes of the painting. Whereas in Wordsworth's poem the divine power of the imagination enables the poet to feel at home in the infinite, in Friedrich's image the play between proximity and distance, familiarity and estrangement, revelation and concealment, serves to depict the longing for unity with the infinite rather than its realization.

These images of the experience of the sublime depict on a grandiose and abstract scale what was a concrete and common experience of Romantic figures – a sense of alienation from oneself, from society, from the divine, and from nature. Reflection on this sense of alienation was also a critical consciousness of the limits of all knowledge and experience. Romanticism has often been depicted as a form of idealism in which all is resolved into the human subject. Certainly Romantic thinkers were acutely aware of the role of the mind in knowledge of the world. Yet they were also aware of the impossibility of a full representation of the material world or the divine, of their irreducible otherness. Reflection on the alterity of nature was an acknowledgement of its potent presence, that the material world cannot be wholly abstracted into conceptual knowledge, that nature is at once impenetrable and the ground of all being. Poetic renderings of nature articulated the ultimate indecipherability of nature's script, and hence the need for a continual creative reading and writing, rereading and rewriting, as an unending exploration of its elusive meaning.

Historically, these reflections were not so much a reaction to Enlightenment thought as a development of it. Romanticism has significant continuities with the critical philosophies of the Enlightenment and their radical questioning of social, political and religious institutions, and of traditional systems of thought. Its expression of the impossibility of complete systems of thought or perfect works of art, of the fragmentary nature of all human production, is an extension of Enlightenment critical tendencies. The experience of the French Revolution, in particular, its promise and its failure, was pivotal to its preoccupation with the tensions between illimitable aspiration and actual limitation. The eighteenth century's discrediting of traditional authorities and certainties, its faith in intellectual, moral and material progress, its faith in humanity and earthly happiness, generated an atmosphere of optimism about new freedoms and new possibilities for individuals and society as a whole that was formative for many early Romantics. The failure of this promise, and the violence unleashed by the Revolution and its aftermath both in France and elsewhere in Europe, led to a conception of modernity in which a sense of crisis, a sense of alienation from nature, the self and society, and a sense of the infinite gulf between the ideal and its realization was central. Many poets used the metaphor of the Fall for this crisis, but now figured as a secular history of the individual and humankind, with the current suffering alleviated by the hope of redemption through communion with nature or a strengthened imagination. The celebration of "country" so characteristic of Romanticism was also an eighteenth-century theme – the glorification of the countryside and local places in opposition to the metropolis, of indigenous experiences of nature and culture as opposed to universal truths, of the songs and lore of common folk as opposed to elites or aristocrats. But many Romantic exaltations of country life were written from the distant perspective of privilege rather than direct experience, or ignored the physical and social hardships endured by country folk. Moreover, in the aftermath of the revolutionary wars the love of country often turned into the love of nation and virulent forms of nationalism.

What is not contested is the privileged place of the artist in Romanticism. As the example of Wordsworth shows, Romanticism saw artists cease to be representatives of religious and political powers, and assume the authority in their own right to speak in the name of the concerns of humanity. Bénichou argues that in France the dethronement of former spiritual powers and the elevation of the self to the highest level of critique and edification begun in the eighteenth century led in the Romantic period to the investment of writers with high social function and spiritual power, what he terms the consecration of the writer. In Germany, Schiller gave aesthetics a political role, arguing that an aesthetic education alone is capable of exciting and refining feelings, of cultivating sensibility, so that citizens could take pleasure in the form of things and thus be ready to act according to rational principles rather than out of self-interest. It is through beauty that the human being achieves freedom. Friedrich Schlegel argued that by possessing an element of divinity in his soul, the poeticizing philosopher or the philosophizing poet is the modern prophet. But for all the discussion of artists and their productions, few artists managed to live from their art alone and their aesthetic manifestos did not translate into real political power.

One area where artistic genius and the role of imagination did come to be especially valued was in the study of nature. Kant drew parallels between the judgment of art and the judgment of organic nature in his 1790 *Critique of Judgment*. Schelling developed Kant's philosophy of nature, making a powerful argument for all of nature and each natural product to be conceived as organic, as a complex, dynamic organization of formal and material principles. Schelling held that what is essential to art as well as to the organism is the creative or productive activity of relating matter and form, the real and ideal. It is the *daemon*, the creative spirit or indwelling element of divinity that is part of the nature of all human beings that is alone able to comprehend the productive, synthetic forces of art and nature. But although the study of nature during the Romantic period emphasized the correspondences between the hidden forces of nature, the imaginative genius within human nature and divine creator, it would be oversimplifying their insights to label such philosophies of nature pantheism. Romantics were acutely aware of the gap between infinite aspiration and its actualization, and of the limits of articulation, and often resorted to metaphor when approaching what defied definition, whether it be the absolute or the fundamental forces of nature.

Indeed, the greatest danger in reading Romanticism is confusing the figural with the literal. Perhaps the continued contestation over Romanticism arises from its excessively figurative expressions, from its deceptive play with language, and from its unusually reflexive and ironic critical positioning. Confronting the boundaries of human comprehension and language, even as they had a vision of what exceeded such boundaries, Romantic works are often difficult to engage and hence it is understandable that their significance has been variously construed. As Bate and Oerlemans convincingly demonstrate, however, critical engagement with Romantic works can be an important stimulus for reflection on nature and religion of particular relevance to the concerns of modern environmentalism.

Joan Steigerwald

Further Reading

Abrams, M.H. *Natural Supernaturalism: Tradition and Revolution in Romantic Literature.* New York: W.W. Norton, 1971.

Bate, Jonathon. *Romantic Ecology: Wordsworth and the Environmental Tradition.* New York: Routledge, 1991.

Bénichou, Paul. *The Consecration of the Writer, 1750–1830.* Mark K. Jensen, tr. Lincoln: University of Nebraska Press, 1999 (1996).

Cunningham, Andrew and Nicholas Jardine, eds. *Romanticism and the Sciences.* Cambridge: Cambridge University Press, 1990.

de Man, Paul. "The Contemporary Criticism of Romanticism." In E.S. Burt, K. Newmark and A. Warminski, eds. *Romanticism and Contemporary Criticism: The Gauss Seminar and Other Papers.* Baltimore, MD: Johns Hopkins University Press, 1993.

Hartman, Geoffrey H. *Wordsworth's Poetry: 1787–1814.* New Haven: Yale University Press, 1964.

McGann, Jerome J. *The Romantic Ideology: A Critical Investigation.* Chicago: University of Chicago Press, 1983.

Oerlemans, Onno. *Romanticism and the Materiality of Nature.* Toronto: University of Toronto Press, 2002.

Porter, Roy and Mikuláš Teich, eds. *Romanticism in National Context.* Cambridge: Cambridge University Press, 1988.

Prickett, Stephen. *Words and The Word: Language, Poetics and Biblical Interpretation.* Cambridge: Cambridge University Press, 1986.

See also: Romanticism in European Literature; Western Esotericism.

Romanticism in European Literature

European Romanticism's complex understanding of the word "nature" must be seen against the background of the eighteenth century and the growth of the industrial city, which gave rise to a new understanding of the beauties of nature as these ceased to be a mere backdrop to human activity and became the place where human beings could be closest to themselves and to God. Appreciation of the grander landscape beauties of nature and a fascination for the "sublime," encouraged by the popularity of artists like Salvator Rosa (1615–73), resulted in a new "aesthetics of the infinite" that coincided with changing religious views of nature.

Behind the Latin tags *natura naturans* and *natura naturata* lie roots extending as far back as Classical times, but now revived in complex ways. The latter consists of the "forms of nature," laid out to be investigated and observed. The former, literally "nature naturing," is nature experienced as active, dynamic and constantly changing. It refers to that animating principle that gives life to the objects of nature, which may remain at the disposal of God, or else be regarded as a pantheistic "presence" or a "power of harmony" that in Wordsworth's "Tintern Abbey" "rolls through all things" without God's help. For the Anglican priest John Keble, however, the Book of Nature is precisely to be "read" as an indication of the workings of God. In Keble's poems in *The Christian Year* (1827), nature is a book "which heavenly truth imparts" to the Christian "reader." In a very different Romantic portrayal of Christianity, Chateaubriand's *Genie du Christianisme* (1802), drew his experience of nature from his visit in 1791 to America, where the "cultivated fields" of Europe, which "everywhere meet with the habitations of men," are replaced by virgin forests and the "abysses of cataracts" where alone the unknown "Supreme Being manifests himself to the human heart" and we can find ourselves solely with God. Nature is only truly appreciated where it has escaped the destroying hand of human cultivation.

In the *Lyrical Ballads* (1798), Wordsworth claimed to be writing in the "real language of men," deliberately giving attention to rustic life lived "among the natural abodes of men, Fields with their rural works" (*The Prelude* XIII, 102–3). It was here that the poet sought to recover the roots and affections of human nature. For the young Wordsworth, at least, and certainly for Shelley and Rousseau, human nature is fundamentally good, and most truly discovers itself as it recovers an affinity with nature that the city-dweller has lost. Though their aspirations remained highly idealized, the Romantic poets at least abandoned the classical literary conventions of Theocritus or Virgil, so beloved of the eighteenth century, and donning their walking boots gave minute attention to "the mighty world / Of eye, and ear," and "the beauteous forms / of nature" ("Tintern Abbey"). Yet, at the same time, they were not blind to the heartlessness of nature's creatures, and Keats, even while he celebrates the "flowers gay / Of periwinkle and wild strawberry," laments the "fierce destruction" wrought by the shark, the hawk or even the "gentle robin" as "ravening," as it attacks the worm. For William Blake, this same worm is a canker which destroys the rose by its "dark secret love." Nevertheless, though we live in a fallen world (an acknowledgment which awaited the advent of Darwinian theory later in the nineteenth century), still, for some Romantics the goodness of nature is seen as a proof of the goodness of its creator, while for the pantheistic Wordsworth (Lucy, though her name is not mentioned in the brief lyric of 1799, "A slumber did my spirit seal"), death returns us to an absolute unity with the natural world of rocks, and stones, and trees. Blake, who can "see a World in a Grain of Sand" (a remarkable though probably unconscious echo of Julian of Norwich's hazel nut that is the whole of creation), also sees heaven in a rage at a caged bird ("Auguries of Innocence").

It is typical of the Romantic awareness of the active principle in nature (*natura naturans*) to be conscious also of the universal in the tiny specifics of natural things, a symbolic acknowledgement of what Coleridge calls "the translucence of the Eternal through and in the Temporal" (*The Statesman's Manual*, 1816). At the same time, and concurrently with German Idealist thought, Coleridge and Wordsworth celebrated the shaping spirit of the imagination, recognizing the mind's power to participate in the creation of what we see in a noble interchange of nature and the human. In Coleridge's words, "we receive but what we give / And in our life alone does Nature live" ("Dejection: An Ode"). In an ancient tradition, drawing upon both Greek mythology and Judeo-Christian thought, the German philosopher of Romanticism, Friedrich Schelling, claims a profound kinship between the human spirit and nature. In his *Ideas for a Philosophy of Nature* (1797), Schelling affirms "we do not want that nature only accidentally correspond to the principles of our spirit." Thus for the poet Novalis (1772–1801) the true being of nature and the true being of humans are analogous and one, each revealing the truth of the other. Goethe's young Werther, at the beginning of *The Sorrows of Young Werther* (1774) writes, with absolute truth,

> My whole being is filled with a marvellous gaiety, like the sweet spring mornings that I enjoy with all my heart. I am alone and glad to be alive in surroundings such as these, which were created for a soul like mine.

Even at his death, Werther remains one with nature and the Eternal One: "Through the storm clouds flying by, I can still see a few stars in the eternal sky. No, you will not fall. The Eternal One carries you in his heart as he carries me."

For Goethe and Romanticism there is no final reconciliation between the spirit *in* nature, of which we are a part, and nature *as* spirit, often seen in terms of the ancient Mother-Goddess, and there is a complex, eclectic coming together of Christian theology and mythological references. Later in nineteenth-century literature, the Mother-Goddess may be personified in such figures as Mother Carey in Charles Kingsley's *The Water Babies* (1863), a parable of the purity of nature set against the life-denying city as the chimney sweep Tom becomes conscious of his grimy body, falls into a river and is transformed into a water-baby.

But there is more to Goethe's view of nature than *Werther*. He was also fascinated with scientific observation of plants, animals, rocks, light and color, holding an idea of evolution that, unlike Darwin's later theory, is nonlinear. For Goethe, what evolves in nature is timeless, a spiral development of endless motion, at the heart of which is a central Romantic concept – polarity: the idea that natural processes live by the interaction between opposites. Without this, as Blake said, there can be no progression. The Romantic fascination with science and nature (which often fed a highly mythological viewpoint), finds a later devotee in John Ruskin (1819–1900), who approached art entirely through nature. In some ways a successor to Wordsworth, Ruskin took a far more intelligent interest in nature, and, with his strict religious upbringing, regarded nature, like Keble, as a holy book. He sometimes described himself as nature's priest. As he looked at the minute particulars of nature, Ruskin was both a poet and a scientist, and, like Goethe and the artist Turner, he was fascinated by the quality of light and color. Ruskin regarded nature as a moral being, for both good and ill, objects in nature often "speaking" to us as moral tutors. In *Modern Painters* (vol. 5), the pine tree has "a tremendous unity [which] absorbs and moulds the life of a race. The pine shadows rest upon a nation."

The complex Romantic view of nature has continued to influence our thinking. Aware, long before Darwin or Tennyson's evolutionary version of "Nature red in tooth and claw," of the cruelty in nature, Romanticism nevertheless regarded nature as a primary source of our education and was deeply aware of the dangers of our neglect or destruction of its delicate balance. In the symbiosis between nature and the human spirit, the destruction of the former, symbolized, for example, by the albatross in Coleridge's "Rime of the Ancient Mariner," was also, inevitably the demise of the latter.

David Jasper

Further Reading
Burke, Edmund. *A Philosophical Enquiry into the Origin of our Ideas of the Sublime and Beautiful.* (1756). Philadelphia: J. Watts, 1806.
Halstead, John B., ed. *Romanticism.* London: Macmillan, 1969.
Modiano, Raimondo. *Coleridge and the Concept of Nature.* Tallahassee: Florida State University Press, 1985.
Prickett, Stephen, ed. *The Romantics.* London: Methuen, 1981.
Raimond, Jean and J.R. Watson, eds. *A Handbook to English Romanticism.* London: Macmillan, 1992.
Schelling, Friedrich Wilhelm. *Ideas for a Philosophy of*

Nature, 1797. New York: Cambridge University Press, 1988.

von Goethe, Johann Wolfgang. *Scientific Studies*. The Collected Works, vol. 12. Douglas Miller, tr. Princeton, NJ: Princeton University Press, 1988.

See also: Blake, William; Philosophy of Nature; Romanticism in European History; Romanticism – American; Western Esotericism.

Romanticism – American

American Romanticism is the general term used to encompass the intersections among several philosophical, theological, political, and artistic movements that occurred in the United States during the middle of the nineteenth century, a period characterized by American territorial expansion and industrialization on the one hand, and sweeping religious and social reforms on the other.

Like its earlier European counterparts, American Romanticism represented a reaction to the eighteenth-century Enlightenment values of order, rationality, scientific method and urbanity. While not fully rejecting the gains of the Enlightenment – which included a critique of orthodox Christianity and religious "superstition" that many Romantics shared – Romanticism sought to reinvigorate those aspects of human knowledge and experience that the Enlightenment had pushed aside. These included: attention to mysticism and psychological supernaturalism and a thematic emphasis on the value of the imagination, sentimentalism, natural spiritualism, and pastoralism.

A prominent theme in this intellectual and artistic movement was a renewed attention to nature, not simply as a system of laws to be interpreted (an Enlightenment trope) but as a source of spiritual and psychological renewal. Like the British Romantics (such as Wordsworth and Coleridge), the American Romantics saw experience in nature as a means to return to a childlike state of innocence, unsullied by civilization. Regained innocence, in turn, could lead to a higher level of insight into the nature of the good, the true, and the beautiful (and for some, also, the nature of God). The responsibility of the Romantic artist was not only to advocate for such a return to nature, innocence, and moral purity but also to convey it to others through poetry, essays, paintings, and related arts. Because the American landscape was already steeped in symbolic associations (America as "the new Eden" or "New Canaan"), it is not surprising that the American Romantics would emphasize the uniqueness of American nature in particular. Such emphasis built on the already established symbolic importance of American nature, while also contributing to the Romantic agenda of shaping a new national identity.

American Romanticism is traditionally thought to have begun in the late 1820s and to have ended by the 1860s, the period of the Civil War (1861–1865). Several important historical events and trends were associated with these middle decades of the nineteenth century. Perhaps most importantly, the Romantic era saw a movement away from – and calls for a return to – the Jeffersonian values of agrarian republicanism that had dominated during the preceding Federalist period. Thomas Jefferson had argued that the moral, spiritual, and national integrity of American culture rested upon the citizenry's relationship to the natural landscape and its gentle cultivation, and he had imagined a nation of small farmers. By the 1830s and 1840s, however, industrialization had begun to spread across the American landscape in the form of railroads, steamboats, and agricultural machinery. According to historian Leo Marx, this led to a consciousness of what has been called the "machine in the garden" – the recognition that the utopian and rural values of early American identity were being challenged by industrialism, expansion, and urbanization.

The middle of the nineteenth century also marked a change in American self-perceptions in two important ways. Perhaps most importantly, the question of slavery and abolition became increasingly urgent as the economic and social climates of the urban North and the agricultural South diverged radically and as the opening of the western frontier shifted the balance of political power. At the same time, the territorial expansion of the United States westward also changed the way Americans came to understand and to construct their identity. During this period, characterized by the philosophical imperatives of expansion known as "Manifest Destiny" and shaped by the war with Mexico from 1846–1848, the settlement of the American west was advancing rapidly, so that by 1893 Frederick Jackson Turner could claim that the frontier was closed and that it had irrevocably shaped what it meant to be an American. In the "Frontier thesis," Turner had completed the idealization of the west that had begun during the presidency of Andrew Jackson (1828–1836), and the settlement of the west brought with it new mythologies, stereotypes, and images of progress. American Romanticism may be understood as an alternatively nostalgic and progressive response to these shifting values and as an effort to negotiate the tension between different models of the American relationship to the landscape.

These changing attitudes toward the American landscape and its relationship to national identity are reflected in the art of the Romantic period, particularly in the works of a group of painters known as the Hudson River School. Established during the 1820s and working until about the 1850s in the United States, these painters represented in their images the tensions surrounding American attitudes toward nature and the unsettled wilderness. While earlier paintings of the American landscape had emphasized the aesthetic tradition known as the picturesque, in which the harmonious balance of natural and human elements was central, the Hudson River painters introduced the more complex dynamics associated with the sublime. The sublime had been a central theme of European Romanticism since the 1780s and was used to explore the mind's encounter with objects that overwhelmed the understanding. According to its most important theorist, the English writer Edmund Burke (1729–1797), the sublime was an experience characterized by feelings of fear and anxiety in the face of something awesome – particularly wild and rugged landscapes such as the Swiss Alps, Niagara Falls, or, later, the American west.

While elements of the sublime are present in the work of many painters associated with the Hudson River School, including the works of Asher B. Durand (1796–1886), paintings such as Thomas Cole's (1801–1848) *The Oxbow, the Connecticut River near Northampton* (1836) are considered representative examples of the movement. In this image, Cole captures the contrast between a calm and cultivated pastoral valley and the threat posed by the encroachment of the wilderness, and the painting has been read as symbolizing the Romantic tension between nature and human endeavor. "Luminists" such as John Kensett (1816–1872) continued this tradition of Romantic landscape painting from the 1840s–1880s, focusing on subjects associated with maritime scenery. Most importantly, as the nineteenth century progressed, painters began to create images of the American west that drew upon the visual language of the sublime. Artists such as Albert Bierstadt (1830–1902) and Thomas Moran (1837–1926) helped to mythologize and, therefore, ultimately to preserve areas of the Rockies and the west by helping to create support for the conservationist movement (1850–1920) and for emergence of the National Parks in the 1870s; yet, by representing western America as "virgin" territories, they also reflected the very conditions of "Manifest Destiny" that placed these landscapes in jeopardy of development.

This tension between civilization and wilderness can be seen in the literature of American Romanticism as well, but in these works the dynamic is often internalized. In other words, the contrasting aspects of the landscape often come to symbolize a conflict within the national psyche, which imagined American identity as simultaneously a product of the frontier and of emerging industrial capitalism. Romanticism emphasized the individual encounter with the natural, moral, and spiritual world, and one of its central concerns was the process of self-knowledge. Writers often described this encounter with the self in very different ways, however. Some Romantic writers, such as Edgar Allan Poe (1809–1849), Nathaniel Hawthorne (1804–1864), or Herman Melville (1819–1891), focused on the wild or "savage" drives to power, domination, and cruelty within human nature, and their works often engaged themes of supernaturalism, psychological disturbance, or the Gothic. The classic example of American Romanticism in this vein is Melville's novel *Moby Dick* (1851), which focuses on Ahab's encounter with a natural world that takes on the characteristics of his own mind and its pathologies.

While authors such as Melville emphasized the sublime or Gothic mode of Romanticism, other authors represented the American psyche and the progress toward cultivation of the landscape more positively. Writers such as James Fennimore Cooper (1789–1851), Henry Wadsworth Longfellow (1807–1882), and David "Davy" Crockett (1786–1836) offered images of Anglo settlers and frontiersmen transforming and taming the American wilderness, and these works connected American national identity with the characteristics of the "noble savage." The term "noble savage" was first popularized in the eighteenth century by European philosophers such as Jean-Jacques Rousseau (1712–1788), and it was used as part of the language of colonial encounter to describe indigenous peoples such as the American Indians in ways that idealized them as simple, uncivilized, and close to nature and to natural religion. During the nineteenth century, Anglo writers hoping to create a new literary tradition and to define their own national voice came to assimilate these same "savage" values into an image of American political identity as grounded in a reverence for and personal connection to the landscape, even as individuals participated in its conquest and appropriation. Davy Crockett's *Autobiography* (1834) and the mythology that surrounds him, for example, reveal the powerful legacy of Romanticism on American culture during this formative century.

Finally, the American Romantic period was also associated with a group of writers and philosophers known as the Transcendentalists. This group included writers such as Ralph Waldo Emerson (1803–1882) and Henry David Thoreau (1817–1862), and the movement later influenced or involved important nineteenth-century nature writers such as Margaret Fuller (1810–1850), Oliver Wendell Holmes (1809–1894), or George Perkins Marsh (1801–1882), founder of the conservationist movement. A central theme of Transcendentalism was the idea that complete human experience could only be achieved through harmony with nature and through participation in the universal consciousness ascribed to the living universe. In formulating its ideas, the Transcendentalist movement drew upon several theological and philosophical traditions, including pantheism, Unitarianism, Platonism, and the increasingly available translations of Eastern religious traditions. The literary texts most closely associated with Transcendentalism include Emerson's *Nature* (1836) and Thoreau's *Walden* (1854).

American Romanticism, then, describes a formative period in American cultural history, during which the landscape and its wildness again came to represent a particular source of spiritual, moral, and national vitality. If the previous and first generations of Americans had viewed the wilderness as an obstacle to be overcome in the cultivation of democracy and as a space to be conquered and tamed as one of the conditions of stable nationhood and national identity, the Romantics came to see the matter differently. For the American Romantics, the wilderness came to symbolize an empty space, the very vacancy of which allowed for the projection onto it of an idealized and powerful vision of national identity. Preserving the wild and the mythologies that characterized the wilderness as "empty" allowed the American landscape to become the scene in which the moral, spiritual, and political conflicts of Romanticism were forged and resolved.

Tilar J. Mazzeo

Further Reading

Burke, Edmund. *A Philosophical Enquiry into the Origin of our Ideas of the Sublime and Beautiful.* Adam Phillips, ed. Oxford University Press, 1998. Originally published in 1759.

Marx, Leo. *The Machine in the Garden; Technology and the Pastoral Ideal in America.* New York: Oxford University Press, 1964.

Matthiessen, F.O. *The American Renaissance: Art and Expression in the Age of Emerson and Whitman.* New York: Oxford University Press, 1941.

O'Sullivan, John. "Manifest Destiny." Speech given at Mt. Holyoke College, 1839. http://www.mtholyoke.edu/acad/intrel/osulliva.htm.

Turner, Frederick Jackson. *The Frontier in American History.* New York: Dover Publications, 1996. Originally published in 1893.

See also: Art; American Indians as "First Ecologists"; Emerson, Ralph Waldo; Nature Religion in the United States; Noble Savage; Romanticism and Indigenous Peoples; Romanticism in European History; Rousseau, Jean-Jacques; Savages; Thoreau, Henry David; Transcendentalism.

Romanticism – Western toward Asian Religions

Although some of the pioneers of the environmental movement, notably Henry David Thoreau, were interested in and sympathetic to Asian religious ideas, it was not until the 1960s that the idea that South and East Asian religions are more likely to promote beneficent behavior toward nature became widespread amongst scholars, adherents of those religions, and the public. The idea became popular at a time when environmentalists began to argue that the severity of the environmental crisis demanded a deep and radical change in attitudes rather than scientific or technological fixes.

The perception that scientific and technological intervention in natural processes was a part of the problem, rather than a solution to environmental degradation, was reinforced by the publication of Rachel Carson's *Silent Spring* in 1962. Carson's belief that "whenever we substitute something man-made and artificial for a natural feature of the earth, we have retarded some part of man's spiritual growth" (Carson 1998: 160) found ready acceptance in the counterculture of the period. In 1967, Lynn White argued in an influential article that the roots of the ecological crisis were to be found in Judeo-Christian conceptions of divinely legitimated human mastery of nature. Moreover, White argued that "Marxism, like Islam, is a Judeo-Christian heresy" (White 1996: 189) and that therefore, both shared Christian axioms. Alternative values or an alternative spirituality that could promote a less damaging relationship with the environment had therefore to be sought outside the Western religious tradition in, amongst others, the religions of South and East Asia.

Although each of the major South and East Asian religions has found advocates for the environmentally positive values of the tradition, by far the most significant have been the claims made for Buddhism. White already identified Buddhism as offering the best chance to rethink humanity's relationship to nature, although he remained doubtful of its viability in the West. As Buddhism has attracted more Western converts, the claims made for its environmental credentials have grown. Martine Bachelor and Kerry Brown write, "at its very essence, Buddhism can be described as an ecological religion or a religious ecology" (Bachelor and Brown 1992: viii) and Alan Sponberg makes the claim that "Buddhism is an environmental ethic" (Sponberg 1997). Other prominent Buddhist environmental thinkers and activists, such as Gary Snyder and Joanna Macy, have made comparable claims. Rather more sober estimates have been offered by Ian Harris and Lambert Schmithausen. It is, however, the strength of some of the claims made for Buddhism's environmental credentials, and their similarity to some other Western claims about Buddhism (for example, Rita Gross's claim that "Buddhism is feminism" [Gross 1993: 130]), that may indicate that they owe more to Western interests than to anything that is the case about Buddhism. To demonstrate this, it is worth conceptualizing these claims within the longer history of Western perceptions of Asian religions, and of Buddhism in particular.

Although as early as 1710 the Jesuit writer J.F. Pons had connected the Chinese who revered the Buddha, the monks of Japan and the Lamas of Tibet with the Buddhists reviled as atheists in India, it was not until the 1840s that speculations about the possible African or central Asian origins of Buddhism were finally replaced by a consensus among European scholars that India was the birthplace of Buddhism. Once the question of the relative priority of Buddhism and Brahmanism had been settled in favor of the latter (by about 1850) the idea that Buddhism was to Hinduism as Protestantism was to Roman Catholicism (or, more rarely, as Christianity was to Judaism) became irresistible to northern European authors. The late-nineteenth-century vogue for Buddhism, especially in England, owed much to contemporary revulsion for Hinduism and to anti-Catholic polemic. Philip Almond quotes the Unitarian James Freeman Clarke, who insisted that despite the apparent external resemblance of Buddhist and Catholic ritual, "deeper and more essential relations connect Brahmanism with the Romish Church, and the Buddhist system with Protestantism. . . .. Buddhism in Asia, like Protestantism in Europe, is a revolt of nature against spirit, of humanity against caste, of individual freedom against the despotism of an order, of salvation by faith against salvation by sacraments" (Almond 1988: 74).

Just as the Buddha was represented as the ideal Protestant for a certain northern European, anti-Catholic audience, so he was represented as an agnostic among those doubting Victorians for whom the term was coined in 1869. The idea that the Buddha was an agnostic may be found among both scholars sympathetic to Buddhism, such as T.W. Rhys Davids, and those who were more hostile. That this was another projection arising from intra-European debate may be demonstrated by considering David Snellgrove's comments on the absurdity of applying the term "agnostic" to the Buddha, who is consistently presented in Buddhist sources from the earliest period as omniscient.

The best-known attempt to say something of a general kind about Western perceptions of Asia remains Edward Said's *Orientalism*. For Said, Orientalism is characterized by the conviction that the Orient is above all different, that which the West is not. This gives rise to a series of oppositions that configure Orientalist perceptions of both self and other. Where the West is rational, active, disciplined, masculine and free, the Orient is irrational, passive, degenerate or lascivious, feminine and subjugated – all ideas that can be abundantly documented in relation to early European perceptions of Asia and its religions. Said's work has been subject to extensive correctives – there were always exceptions to the perception of the Orient as entirely "other." For the British, India's "martial races" were masculine, and Buddhism has been seen as a rational, even a scientific, faith. Nevertheless, the best evidence for thinking that ecological concern in the West has simply extended this binary logic by adding another series of oppositions to it (where the West is environmentally destructive and polluting, the Orient – and its religions – are environmentally affirming and beneficent) is the uniformity and vehemence of the claims made on behalf of Asian religions. Indeed, these claims have been made on behalf of all the major South and East Asian traditions and arise not from the overwhelming weight of evidence of practical or doctrinal environmental concern among Asian religions but rather in spite of the (at best) inconclusive nature of such evidence. This strongly suggests that the key reason for the emergence of such claims has been the Orientalist perception of such religions as fundamentally "other." As the West came to perceive itself as environmentally destructive and, following White, to attribute that to its religious formation, this Orientalist logic dictated that Asia – and its religions – being "other," had to be seen as environmentally beneficent. Moreover, as was the case with other Orientalist perceptions, the idea that Asian religions are environmentally beneficent has been readily adopted by adherents of those religions, the more enthusiastically because this perception lacks the derogatory associations of some earlier perceptions of Asian religions despite depending on the same logic of difference.

William Sweetman

Further Reading
Almond, Philip. *The British Discovery of Buddhism*. Cambridge: Cambridge University Press, 1988.
Batchelor, Martine and Kerry Brown. *Buddhism and Ecology*. London: Cassell, 1992.
Carson, Rachel. *Silent Spring*. Boston, MA: Houghton Mifflin, 1962.
Carson, Rachel. *Lost Woods: The Discovered Writing of Rachel Carson*. Boston, MA: Beacon, 1998.
Dwivedi, O.P. "Dharmic Ecology." In Christopher Key Chapple and Mary Evelyn Tucker, eds. *Hinduism and Ecology: the Intersection of Earth, Sky and Water*. Cambridge, MA: Harvard University Press, 2000, 3–22.
Gross, Rita. *Buddhism After Patriarchy*. Albany: State University of New York Press, 1993.
Harris, Ian. "How Environmentalist is Buddhism?" *Religion* 21 (1991), 101–114.
Said, Edward. *Orientalism*. New York: Pantheon Books, 1978.
Schmithausen, Lambert. "The Early Buddhist Tradition and Ecological Ethics." *Journal of Buddhist Ethics* 4 (1997), 1–74.
Sponberg, Alan. "The Buddhist Conception of an Ecological Self." *The Western Buddhist Review* 2 (1997) (http://www.westernbuddhistreview.com/vol2/ecological_self.html).
Tobias, Michael. "Jainism and Ecology." In Mary Evelyn Tucker and John A. Grim, eds. *Worldviews and Ecology: Religion, Philosophy and the Environment*. Maryknoll, NY: Orbis, 1994, 138–49.
Tucker, Mary Evelyn and John Berthrong, eds. *Confucianism and Ecology: the Interrelation of Heaven, Earth and Humans*. Cambridge, MA: Harvard University Press, 1998.
White, Lynn. "The Historic Roots of Our Ecological Crisis." *Science* 155 (1967), 1203–1207; Reprinted: In Roger S.

Gottlieb. *This Sacred Earth: Religion, Nature, Environment*. London: Routledge, 1996, 184–193.

See also: Carson, Rachael; Nobel Savage; Religious Environmentalist Paradigm; Romanticism (various); Thoreau, Henry David.

Rousseau, Jean-Jacques (1712–1778)

Jean-Jacques Rousseau, a leading Enlightenment thinker, was perhaps most famous for his appeal to the "state of nature" as an ideal in whose light the general distortions of modern society could be measured and remedies proposed. Rousseau was a passionate critic of what he perceived to be the artifice, false consciousness, and inequality of modern society, and he advocated strongly the need to recover natural feeling, virtue, natural compassion, freedom, and equality. He placed such trust in "nature" because he trusted nature's God.

Born a Calvinist, Rousseau converted to Catholicism as a young man, and later adopted deist views rejecting revealed religion in favor of "natural religion" based on the evidence of God's existence that reason discerns in the wondrous order and harmony of the system of nature. He elaborated in detail an educational agenda aimed at protecting the natural feelings and growing virtue of young people by having them first engage the challenges and constraints posed by the natural environment, rather than the alienation, prejudice, and competitiveness thrust at them by society. During his last years of life, he turned for comfort to the study of botany and to walking in the countryside. His last book, *Reveries of a Solitary Walker* (1782) described ecstatic periods of direct contemplation of the "great pageant" of creation. This work was widely read and gave impetus to the Romantic Movement's general reverence of the nature and celebration of natural feeling. Rousseau was a watershed figure of the eighteenth century whose writings did much to popularize a growing sense of reverence for nature.

Rousseau followed the lead of classic Christian theologians and deist thinkers in seeing proof of God's existence in the harmony, order and motion of the system of nature. Rousseau drew on Christian and deist views regarding God's providential dominion over the world and on humanity's "fall," combining these into a powerful narrative of original goodness, societal corruption, and proposed paths of recovery and renewal. He broke with the Christian notion of original sin and located the Fall not in human nature, but in human history. Armed with these themes of creation and Fall, Rousseau could launch a harsh indictment against societal alienation and injustice and still affirm hope in humanity's fundamental goodness and potential.

Born and raised in Geneva, Rousseau received no formal education, but his father gave him a love of nature and of books. He was apprenticed to an engraver, but he soon left, and was taken into the home of a Swiss baroness, Madame de Warens, who became his patron and lover. Under her guidance Rousseau converted to Catholicism, enjoyed years of undisturbed study of philosophy and literature, and grew in his appreciation for the beauties of nature. At the age of thirty he moved to Paris, developed a close friendship with Denis Diderot (1713–1784), the pantheistic French philosopher, and met many other philosophers. He achieved notoriety in 1750 with the publication of his essay, *Discourse on the Arts and Sciences*, which sparked controversy by arguing that progress in the arts and sciences distorted human life by pulling us away from the essential goodness, contentment, and virtues found in the "state of nature." This argument clashed with a central assumption of the Enlightenment, namely, that progress in reason and science directly promotes human well-being and moral virtue. After publishing a *Discourse on Inequality* (1755) that developed his account of societal evolution, Rousseau moved out of Paris to the country home of a benefactor. There in rapid succession he wrote his masterworks: *Julie, or the New Heloise* (1761); *Emile, or On Education* (1762), and *The Social Contract* (1762). The first, a novel about romance and love and their conflict with duty, became the most widely read work of fiction in France for a number of years. The second became a recognized classic of educational philosophy. *The Social Contract* became a landmark of political theory. Its stress on popular sovereignty and freedom gave voice to aspirations that anticipated the ideals of revolutionary France. Many critics, however, noted the irony that Rousseau, who could not tolerate the demands of family life and abandoned his five children to a public orphanage, could write so eloquently of love, personal duty, and the importance of children's upbringing.

Rousseau's fullest account of his views on religion is found in *Emile*, in a section titled the "Profession of Faith of the Savoyard Vicar." In it the Vicar explains that when we ponder the marvelous order, harmony, and motion of the physical universe we can only conclude that there exists a rational and benevolent power who wills this universe into existence and sets things in motion. As he says: "I perceive God everywhere in His works. I sense Him in me; I see Him all around me" (Rousseau 1979a: 277). As God is good, so is all God's creation, including humanity itself. Religious belief thus provides Rousseau with basic confidence for trusting nature's goodness and purity. Rousseau thus affirms the essential goodness of humanity even while stressing the history of human corruption. As he put it in the opening of *Emile*: "Everything is good as it leaves the hands of the Author of things; everything degenerates in the hands of man" (Rousseau 1979a: 37). For Rousseau, the path out of societal "sin" lies not in some special divine grace, but rather in recovering our original goodness.

Both *Emile* and *The Social Contract* were condemned in Paris and Geneva by religious and political authorities who viewed the books as subversive. Rousseau fled France and lived for a number of years at the mercy of benefactors. Anxiety ridden and often paranoid, he worked on his *Confessions* and retreated into the solace of the botanical studies and countryside walks. His *Reveries*, published posthumously, describe him as feeling rejected by friends and society and yet experiencing a sense of "peace and contentment" arising from a sustained contact with nature and its simple plant life. Walks in which he observed the "great pageant of nature" gave him a sense of the "unity of all things." Such encounters promote an "expansive soul." "I feel transports of joy and inexpressible raptures in becoming fused as it were with the great system of beings and identifying myself with the whole of nature" (Rousseau 1979b: 108, 111, 112). Walks amidst nature gave him a pure "feeling of existence" (Rousseau 1979b: 89).

Many in Rousseau's lifetime dismissed him as an apostle of "primitivism" and this caricature is alive and well even today. This view arises from readings of Rousseau's *Discourses* where he fails to clarify exactly how we are to recover the "state of nature." In places he does seem to call for a return to the practices of a primordial "golden age." However in *Emile* Rousseau makes clear that such a return is neither possible nor desirable. He states directly that his aim in education is to protect young people's natural feelings and virtues from premature bending under societal pressure so that when they reach adulthood they may join society with their emotional integrity and sense of moral responsibility healthy and uncorrupted. Emile, the boy, is to live in the countryside amidst nature, so he will grow "naturally" and be well prepared to enter marriage and society in adulthood. The "state of nature," for Rousseau, functions less as a claim about historical origins than an assertion about fundamental human capacities to recover natural integrity, simplicity, and virtue.

Rousseau's naturalism anticipates in important ways our ecological understanding of humanity as a part of the natural world. The anthropologist Claude Lévi-Strauss among others admired Rousseau's insights in his attempt to understand humanity's evolutionary history. Rousseau's expansive sense of identification with the rest of creation anticipated a similar emphasis found in today's deep ecology movement. Likewise, while Rousseau followed the general anthropocentrism of classic Western ethics in placing humanity as the crown of the natural world, he extended basic "natural rights" to animals and thus anticipated the core moral principle upheld by today's animal welfare movement. Years before British utilitarian philosopher Jeremy Bentham famously made the same point, Rousseau held that natural compassion urges us both to refrain from harming not just other humans, but also "any other sentient being" except in cases of true necessity. Humans are bound by strict duties toward animals who enjoy "the right not to be needlessly mistreated" (Rousseau 1988: 7).

In addition Rousseau's analysis offers insight into some of the contemporary societal dynamics that increase ecological degradation. For example, his understandings of inequality and how it shapes social structures and psychological dynamics shed light on forces that promote overconsumption and ecological degradation. Similarly, his critique of education anticipated the concerns of ecologically concerned people who fear that modern advertising promotes unsustainable lifestyles. Rousseau's suspicion of socially inflated wants and his affirmation of the simple, virtuous life are as timely now as they were in his day. For all of his eccentricities and faults, Rousseau remains a seminal figure in eighteenth-century Western philosophy and letters challenging many aspects of modernity by an appeal to nature's goodness as it comes from the hands of the divine.

William French

Further Reading

Cooper, Laurence D. *Rousseau, Nature, and the Problem of the Good Life*. University Park, PA: Pennsylvania State University Press, 1999.

Grimsley, Ronald. *Rousseau and the Religious Quest*. Oxford: Clarendon Press, 1968.

Rousseau, Jean-Jacques. "Discourse on the Origin and Foundations of Inequality Among Men." In *Rousseau's Political Writings*. Translated by Julia Conaway Bondanella and edited by Alan Ritter and Julia Conaway Bondanella. New York and London: W.W. Norton & Company, 1988, 3–57.

Rousseau, Jean-Jacques. *Emile or On Education*. Introduction, translation and notes by Allan Bloom. Basic Books, 1979a.

Rousseau, Jean-Jacques. *Reveries of the Solitary Walker*. Translated by Peter France. Middlesex, England, and New York: Penguin Books, 1979b.

Wokler, Robert. *Rousseau: A Very Short Introduction*. Oxford: Oxford University Press, 2001.

See also: Deism; Philosophy of Nature; Romanticism in European History; Romanticism in European Literature.

Rubber and Religion (Belgian Congo)

The Belgian occupation and exploitation of the Congo (1885–1960) was one of the most brutal chapters in world history. At the infamous Berlin Conference of 1884–1885, European powers carved up the African continent into colonial possessions, and the King of the Belgians, Leopold II, was granted sole control of the vast Congo River Basin. A devout Catholic and self-promoting "philanthropist," Leopold founded The Congo Free State (1885–1908) and vowed to bring civilization to its people, which for him meant bringing Christianity to save "pagan" souls. In reality, the Congo Free State was a colonial slave system designed to exploit two of Central Africa's most precious natural resources: its people and its land, first for rubber and ivory and later for minerals. Catholic missions played an integral role in this system, providing moral sanction and local manpower for the plunder, making this form of religion a tremendously destructive influence on the region's environmental and social history. On the other side of the struggle, however, Protestant missionaries brought the horrors of the Congo Free State to the world's attention, while indigenous Congolese religious movements like the Kimbanguist Church rose in staunch resistance to white occupation. Thus religion was a central force in both the establishment of and resistance to Belgian rule in the Congo and its concomitant environmental and social destruction.

Roughly the size of the United States east of the Mississippi River, the Congo Basin is dominated by a network of rivers and tributaries that flow into the one of the world's greatest rivers, the River Congo. This riverine system generously nourishes the immense Central African Rain Forest, which is bordered to the north and south by rolling savannah and to the east by the Ruwenzori Mountains and the great lakes of the Rift Valley, the birthplace of humanity. The original inhabitants of the region, often incorrectly referred to as "Pygmies," count as descendants the baMbuti and the baTwi, who today still live in the Congo's rainforest much like their ancestors did since at least 2000 B.C.E.: living in small kin-based clan units, hunting, gathering, and praising the forest for providing them with the gifts of life. Appreciation of these gifts in the form of dance, song, and prayer remain the ritual emphasis of their religion. One of the most painful ironies of Central African history is, therefore, that a foreign religion, Catholicism, would join forces with Leopold in the massive plunder of this forest and its indigenous peoples who so venerated it.

By around the year 1000, Bantu ethnic groups had migrated from north of the forest to the Congo Basin, eventually becoming the region's dominant peoples, with large and complex centralized kingdoms forming as early as the fourth century. The Bantu brought with them monotheistic religions that were centrally concerned with the dead and local nature spirits, which, for instance, the baKongo call *basimbi*. Certain basimbi reside at local springs or other significant topographical features. A key difference between their worldview and that of the Congo Basin's indigenous peoples was the Bantus' deep-seated fear of sorcery. Bantu religion is in fact largely concerned with the negotiation of sorcery (i.e., with detecting it, combating it, and healing those who are afflicted by it).

Generously funded by Leopold from 1874 to 1877, the Englishman-turned-American Henry Morton Stanley explored the Congo Basin to locate both the source of the River Congo and the famous English Protestant missionary and explorer David Livingstone, from whom no one in Europe had heard in five years. Upon finding Livingstone, Stanley triumphantly returned to Europe, and Leopold promptly hired him to establish commercial relations with local Congolese chiefs and a series of trading stations along the River Congo. Leopold's foray into "The Scramble for Africa" thus began to unfold as European powers looked to the African Continent to provide natural resources for the Industrial Revolution. Like Leopold, most Europeans involved in the Scramble liked to think of themselves as having higher moral purpose, hence the spread of civilization was linked to Christian missions and the abolition of the Afro-Arab slave trade in East Africa.

With the invention of the pneumatic tire, rubber immediately became a key natural resource for a rapidly industrializing Europe. Merely six years after Leopold founded the Congo Free State, his personal colony was producing one-tenth of the world's rubber, upwards to 6000 tons a year. How this was accomplished is one of the most violent and tragic stories in African history. Local chiefs had signed away their lands in treaties that they could not read, while Leopold aggressively sent administrators and missionaries to oversee his plunder of the Congo, ordering them to "neglect no means of exploiting the produce of the forests." To do so, the Belgians enslaved thousands of Congolese, razing their villages and forests to clear land and provide labor for rubber plantations. Symbolic of this great injustice, the *chicotte*, a whip made of strips of dried hippopotamus hide, was liberally used to beat Africans either to work or to death. Along with severed African hands, the *chicotte* would become the symbol of colonial oppression in the Congo.

Resistance to such oppressive and violent domination was of course to be expected. Hence Leopold arranged for the formation in the Congo of *La Force Publique*, a standing army of African mercenaries and forced conscripts under Belgian command. This notoriously brutal force of some 19,000 soldiers served to ensure that Leopold's greed would be satisfied with abundant exports of rubber and ivory. In order to swell the Force's ranks, the King of the Belgians had Catholic missions double as boot camps for thousands of child soldiers. Some were orphans; many others were quite simply slaves. In 1890 Leopold wrote,

> I believe we must set up three children's colonies. One in the Upper Congo near the equator, specifically military, with clergy for religious instruction and for vocational education. One at Leopoldville under clergy with a soldier for military training. One at Boma like that at Leo . . . The aim of these colonies is above all to furnish us with soldiers (Hochschild 1999: 133–4).

In time, many other "children's colonies" were founded by Catholic missionaries, whom Leopold heavily subsidized. Thousands of Congolese became orphans as a result of La Force Publique's brutality. These children were sometimes forced to march hundreds of miles to Catholic missions for military inscription. One priest described the fusion of military and religious symbolism reflective of this horrific arrangement: "the children marched in front, the soldiers following ... During Mass ... at the moment of the elevation of the host, 'present arms!' was sounded by bugles" (Hochschild 1999: 134). Discipline and order were of course maintained by liberal use of the *chicotte*, exacerbating the already inhumane conditions for African children on the Congo Free State's Catholic missions. Between malnutrition, disease, beatings, and long marches, over half of the colonies' children perished. Yet even this was lent a glaze of ecclesial sanction, as seen in the commentary of one mother superior:

> Several of the little girls were so sickly on their arrival that ... our good sisters couldn't save them, but all had the happiness of receiving Holy Baptism; they are now little angels in Heaven who are praying for our great king (Hochschild 1999: 135).

These "little angels" were among some 10 million Congolese who perished in Leopold's Congo Free State, more than half the region's entire population. The Congolese interpreted such oppression in other religious terms, looking to nature to render divine justice, as expressed in their singing:

> O Mother, how unfortunate we are! ...
> But the sun will kill the white man,
> But the moon will kill the white man,
> But the sorcerer will kill the white man,
> But the tiger will kill the white man,
> But the crocodile will kill the white man,
> But the elephant will kill the white man,
> But the river will kill the white man
>   (Hochschild 1999: 139).

Some whites also cried out against the rampant human-rights abuse in the Congo Free State. E.D. Morel was a high-ranking Belgian administrator during the early phase of Leopold's plunder of the Congo. Outraged by the brutality of the occupation, Morel quit the regime and sought to alert the world to the grave injustice of the Congo Free State. His cry was echoed by numerous Protestant missionaries in the Congo Basin, who, unlike Catholic missionaries, were independent of Leopold's regal authoritarianism. In 1904, Morel founded with British Protestant missionaries John and Alice Harris the *West African Mail*, a newsletter that publicized the horrors of Leopold's Congo. Among their more influential readers, Bertrand Russell wrote,

> The only men in the Congo who could not be silenced were Protestant missionaries ... To take one instance out of many, Joseph Clark, of the American Baptist Missionary Union wrote: on March 26, 1896: "This rubber traffic is steeped in blood ... The lake is reserved for the king – no traders allowed – and to collect rubber for him hundreds of men, women, and children have been shot" (Russell 1934: 454).

The world took note, and in 1908 the Congo Free State was annexed from Leopold by the Belgian government and renamed "The Belgian Congo" (1908–1960). Central African prophets (Kikongo: *bangunza*) had by then reinterpreted Christianity to denounce white rule, recasting indigenous notions of sorcery into modes of understanding and denouncing colonialism. The most important of these was Ngunza Simon Kimbangu, whose rapidly blossoming movement was so threatening to the Belgians that he was imprisoned in 1921 and given 120 lashes. Many of his followers were exiled to other parts of the Congo Basin, which only served to spread the movement into an international multi-ethnic religion that today counts some 5 million adherents. After Kimbangu's death in prison in 1950, his son Joseph Diangiende was declared the leader of the Church of Jesus Christ on Earth through the Prophet Simon Kimbangu (*l'Eglise de Jesus Christ sur la Terre par le Prophete Simon Kimbangu*: EJCSK). EJCSK holds that Kimbangu was God's apocalyptic messenger who prophesied the end of white rule, the establishment of the kingdom of God, and the second coming of Christ. The Church was formally recognized by Belgian authorities in 1959, one year before Congolese independence. Since 1970 EJCKSK has been a member of the World Council of Churches.

Terry Rey

Further Reading

Hochschild, Adam. *King's Leopold's Ghost: A Story of Greed, Terror, and Heroism in Colonial Africa*. New York: Houghton Mifflin, 1999.

Russell, Bertrand. *Freedom and Organisation, 1814–1914*. London: Allen & Unwin, 1934.

Wrong, Michela. *In the Footsteps of Mr. Kurtz: Living on the Brink of Disaster in Mobutu's Congo*. New York: HarperCollins, 2001.

See also: African Religions and Nature Conservation; Biodiversity and Religion in Equatorial Africa; Congo River Watershed; Kimbanguism (Central Africa); Pygmies (Mbuti Foragers) and Bila Farmers.

Rubber Tappers

In the year 1839 Charles Goodyear perfected the vulcanization process for rubber, thus creating an immediate worldwide demand for rubber. The Brazilian Amazon, and in particular, the upper Amazon region and the state of Acre, holds the world's largest natural rubber tree stands. In the late 1870s, immigrants from the northeast of Brazil, driven by droughts in the northeast region and drawn by the promise of riches from collecting rubber, provided the labor for extracting, or "tapping" latex. They became known as *seringueiros*, or rubber tappers. The rubber "boom" ended with the domestication of rubber trees in Southeast Asia in the early 1900s. However, another wave of northeastern migrants, known as *soldados do borracha*, or rubber soldiers, came to the region during World War II as the axis powers cut off access to rubber plantation production in Southeast Asia and the upper Amazon once again became the world's source of rubber. This second "boom" ended at war's end, but rubber tappers remained and still ply their trade.

Northeastern migrants brought to the Amazon a strong Catholic faith without indigenous religious influence. The names given to *seringais*, or rubber forest areas, such as São Pedro, São Vicente and São Francisco do Iracema, themselves demonstrate the strength of the Catholic tradition brought by the rubber tappers. However, upon their arrival, the rubber tappers did not wholly impose their religious traditions on the local population, but rather their religious traditions were modified by the new sociocultural and environmental conditions of life in the Amazon. Many of the beliefs of rubber tappers today are of mixed influence, with Catholic traditions influenced by the Amazon folk beliefs held by *caboclos*, or mixed-race river-dwelling populations, and indigenous populations that inhabited the region. Some of these folk beliefs have European origin and were brought by Portuguese settlers in the early seventeenth century. Santo Daime, a religion founded by a rubber tapper in the 1920s which involves the drinking of *ayahuasca* as its sacrament, also reflects this mixing of Christian and indigenous beliefs, as well as African influence. Thus, like the religious beliefs of other Amazon populations, the formation of rubber tapper religious beliefs should be looked upon as a "continuous process" (Galvão 1952: 169), one that retraces their cultural background and adaptation to the Amazon environment for over a century.

The most widespread folk beliefs adapted by many rubber tappers are: *mãe seringueira*, the mother of the rubber tree; *panema*, a hex that prevents rubber tappers from killing game; and *cabloquinho*, father of the forest. Smith (1996) provides an excellent description of *mãe seringueira*, a short, long-haired woman with bleeding arms and legs, that appear to have been cut by a tapper's knife. *Mãe seringueira* appears to those who overexploit her rubber trees. Although regular, measured cuts can be made during the tapping season, "mae de seringa becomes upset when people abuse her children," namely, cut her trees excessively or too deeply, causing the trees to die (Smith 1996: 132). Smith recounts the story of a rubber tapper, in debt to his patron and needing greater rubber production to pay it down. *Mãe seringueira* appeared to him as he was angrily overtapping the trees. Explaining his situation, *mãe seringueira* agreed to provide him the latex he needed if he "would leave her daughters alone" (Smith 1996: 132). He was also told to tell no one about the agreement. However, the following year, unable to keep silent about their accord, the rubber tapper died of a poisonous snakebite, attributed to his broken promise.

Panema is another common belief among Amazon folk peoples. A rubber tapper's "repeated failure" in hunting "that cannot be explained by natural causes" is attributed to *panema*, a hex that contaminates both the individual and their weapon (Galvão 1952: 108). Although *panema* is sometimes referred to as "bad luck," ". . . it is not merely an occasional failure of fortune, but an incapacity," sustained over time (Galvão 1952: 108). Galvão noted that this can occur for various reasons. For example, the consumption of game by a pregnant woman is one common source of *panema*. "Ill feelings or jealousy among friends over food" may cause that friend to experience *panema* (Galvão 1952: 108). A rubber tapper in Acre, Brazil stated that one can get *panema* if one shoots an animal and then cannot find it, thus it dies unconsumed by the hunter (Weigand 1997). A tapper may be stricken with *panema* if his wife sleeps while he is hunting, or if "he hunts with dogs on Thursdays, the day belonging to *Caipora*," the father of the game (Almeida 2002: 123 [our translation]). Methods to cure *panema* may involve the use of plants collected in the forest or grown in home gardens in "smoke" and water baths.

Cabloquinho is described by a rubber tapper in Acre as a "magical boy-like creature, one meter tall and owner of all wild game" (Weigand 1997: 55). *Cabloquinho* punishes hunters who exploit wild game for pleasure or commercial gain. If a rubber tapper hunts every day, beyond consumptive needs, *cabloquinho* may become angry and beat the hunter. Rubber tappers in Acre noted that he may inflict physical pain on both the hunter and their hunting dogs to the point of unconsciousness. One rubber tapper stated that his brother was hunting a peccary when a small boy appeared and touched him on the head before he was able to shoot. The man passed out and when he woke up his ammunition was gone and he felt poorly. The rubber tapper's belief in *cabloquinho* is similar to the more generalized Amazonian belief in the *curupira* legend. Thus, *mãe seringueira*, *panema* and *cabloquinho* illustrate tapper conservation behavior and rationale in using forest resources.

The Santo Daime religion, founded in the 1920s by

Raimundo Irineu Serra, a rubber tapper living in the Southwest Brazilian Amazon state of Acre reflects the melding of Christian, indigenous, and African beliefs. The Santo Daime ritual is centered on the consumption of ayahuasca, a drink made from the psychotropic vine plant *Banisteriopsis caapi*. While drinking ayuahuasca, Serra experienced a series of visions during which he encountered the "Queen of the Forest ... a woman whom he identified with the Virgin Mary" (Mizrach 2003: no page number). It is through these visions that the tenets of Santo Daime, "reincarnation, salvation and protection of the rainforest" were developed (Mizrach 2003: no page number). Hymns and rituals that accompanied the consumption of ayahuasca focused on "enlightenment and healing" (Mizrach 2003: no page number). Today Santo Daime ritual still centers on the drinking of ayahuasca with the chanting of hymns and rhythmic dancing. Although still practiced in small forest communities of southwest Amazonia, it is primarily urban-based, with a growing network of followers in major urban centers in southern Brazil as well as in Europe and the United States.

In addition to its spiritual role, the Catholic Church has also played a critical role in the rubber tapper's struggle for social justice, most notably in the state of Acre. In the 1970s, as the rubber tappers came under increasing pressure from ranchers to abandon their landholdings, the Catholic Church, through the establishment of *Comunidades Eclesiais de Base* and the teaching of liberation theology, became an organizing force for poor landholders in their confrontations with ranchers. The Church supported union organization and educated rubber tappers of their land rights. During *empates*, nonviolent confrontations with workers hired by ranchers to deforest areas where rubber tappers lived, rubber tappers recited prayers, such as *Pai Nosso do Seringueiro* and *Ave Maria do Seringueiro*, to ask God for liberty and justice.

Today, the Catholic Church continues to play an important role in rubber tapper community development in the forest, serving as a base for community organization and social action. In addition, annual festival days celebrating Patron Saints, such as San Sebastion, the Patron Saint of the cities of Rio Branco and Xapuri in Acre, remain important religious holidays to the rubber tapper population. Throughout the 1990s, evangelical churches have also established a growing presence in many forest communities. Future research should examine how different religious beliefs among forest families may be creating new community customs and shaping natural resource use.

In the state of Acre, the state "Forest Government," elected in 1998, is incorporating rubber tapper traditions and beliefs in innovative policies for forest management. These policies are part of a broader state development vision referred to as "neoextractivism," which emphasizes the role of traditional peoples in conserving tropical forests while improving their economic well-being.

Richard H. Wallace
Carlos Valério A. Gomes

Further Reading
Cunha, Manuela Carneiro de and Mario Barbosa de Almeida, eds. *Enciclopédia de Floresta*. Sao Paulo, Brazil, 2002.
Galvão, Eduardo. "The Religion of an Amazon Community: A Study in Culture and Change." Doctoral Dissertation. Columbia University, New York, 1952.
Mizrach, Steven. "Santo Daime." Internet URL: http://www.fiu.edu/~mizrachs/daime.htm. Accessed 28 January 2003.
Smith, Nigel J.H. *The Enchanted Amazon Rain Forest: Stories from a Vanishing World*. Gainesville: University Press of Florida, 1996.
Wagley, Charles. *Amazon Town: A Study of Man in the Tropics*. New York: The Macmillan Company, 1953.
Weigand, Ronaldo. "Conservation Attitudes in Three Rubber Tapper Communities in Acre, Brazil." Doctoral Dissertation. University of Florida, Gainesville, 1997.

See also: Amazonia; Ayahuasca; Brazil and Contemporary Christianity; Christianity (7c) – Liberation Theology; Umbanda.

Ruether, Rosemary Radford (1936–)

Rosemary Radford Ruether is a leading ecofeminist voice. She seamlessly connects feminism, liberationist thought, and concern for the Earth.

Ruether's ecofeminist approach has been a longstanding and vital part of her constructive theological work. Her ecofeminist commitment emerged organically out of her recognition of the connections between human domination of the Earth and human interspecies domination: men over women, "First World" over "Third World" peoples, whites over people of color, rich over poor, Christian over non-Christian, and other forms of oppression. Her influential book *New Woman/New Earth* (1975) made her the first Christian liberation theologian to articulate those relationships explicitly.

Ruether's theology demonstrates thorough historical knowledge. She explores the historical traditions of Jewish and Christian scriptures, Greek philosophy, Ancient Near Eastern worldviews, mainstream as well as marginalized Christian theologies, and more contemporary philosophies of romanticism, liberalism, and Marxism. Her nuanced approach balances incisive critique of elements in these sources that contribute to sexism, racism, and environmental degradation with the reclaiming of liberating aspects of the same sources. *Gaia and God* (1992) expands the sources of her constructive thought to include the new, scientific "creation story."

Ruether's work illuminates the systemic nature of patriarchal, hierarchical, and environmentally destructive attitudes and behaviors. Equality of women with men is not enough if both continue to dominate nature. Bridging the gap between rich and poor countries cannot be accomplished by raising the worldwide consumption rate to the unsustainable levels of northern rich nations. She calls for transformation of religious symbols and cultural values, and also for a radical restructuring of power relationships within societies and globally. To accomplish this restructuring, Ruether builds alliances with others who are struggling for eco-justice and justice in human relationships. The book *Women Healing Earth*, which she edited, includes essays from Third World women about the impact of globally destructive environmental practices and political policies on their lives, their communities, and the natural world around them.

Her far-ranging critique of patriarchal values in Christian thought and in Western social/ecological practice is made more valuable by her concrete pictures of a different way to live. Her books include imaginative portrayals of how life might be different if men and women lived in mutual harmony with each other, in sustainable communities that did not oppress the Earth or privilege one culture over another. In these communities she calls for shared childcare and use of renewable resources, for egalitarian relationships and widely available mass transit. She enticingly describes life in such a place, where people "watch sunsets . . . plant seeds in soil. . . . The sun rises every day. Con Ed sends no bill for sunshine" (1983: 266).

Rosemary Radford Ruether's ground-breaking connections between the human domination of nature and the subjugation of some human groups by other human groups have been a key influence on liberation theology, the feminist movement, and the ecological movement. She untiringly speaks out for the continued struggle for liberation for the Earth and for women and men of all classes and races, cultures and religions.

Barbara Darling-Smith

Further Reading
Ruether, Rosemary Radford. *Gaia and God: An Ecofeminist Theology of Earth Healing*. New York: HarperSanFrancisco, 1992.
Ruether, Rosemary Radford. *Sexism and God-Talk: Toward a Feminist Theology*. Boston: Beacon Press, 1983.
Ruether, Rosemary Radford. *New Woman/New Earth: Sexist Ideologies and Human Liberation*. New York: Seabury Press, 1975.
See also: Christianity (7c) – Liberation Theology; Christianity (7d) – Feminist Theology.

Rumî, Jalaluddin (1207–1273)

Rumî, the greatest Sufi poet of Islam, was born in 1207 in Balkh, Afghanistan. The Muslim world honors him with the title of *Maulana* (Our Master). His uniqueness lies in that he based his anthropocosmic worldview on the principle of love. It is this aspect of his deep vision of the universe, and the place of humanity in it, which attracts environmentalists and provides them with a new perspective to see the deeper dimension of reality.

When Rumî was twelve years old, his family left Balkh to escape the Mongol invasion. For four years, the young Rumî traveled extensively in Muslim lands, encountering majestic mountains and beautiful plains, visiting major cities, and meeting well-known Sufis and scholars of the time. His family performed pilgrimage to Mecca and finally settled in Konya, Anatolia, then part of Seljuk Empire.

Rumî's first teacher was his father, who was an authority in Islamic theology. However, Rumî found theology and classical learning unsatisfyingly occupied with formalism. At this juncture, he had a life-changing meeting with Shams-i Tabrizi, who would become his spiritual mentor. Through his friendship with Shams, Rumî discovered love as the dynamic force of universe. When Rumî died on 17 December 1273, Jews, Christians, and Muslims alike attended his funeral.

God and Creation
For Rumî, God the Cosmic Ego created the material world *ex nihilo* – out of nothing – and never ceases to create new things. Everything has been created with a specific order, duty, purpose, and meaning. There is no lifeless matter in this system; all matter is alive, albeit at various gradations of being. According to Rumî, "earth, and water, fire and air are alive in the view of God, though they appear to be dead to us" (Sharif 1995: 827). He cautions: "never think the earth void or dead; it is aware, it is awake and it is quivering" (Harvey 1994: 56).

Theocentricism is the key concept to understanding Rumî's anthropocosmic worldview. God is the goal of Rumî's thought. For Rumî, God wants to be known, so he manifests himself out of his eternal qualities. Two of God's attributes are especially relevant in this regard: God is the Nourisher of all realms and beings, and as such, he *creates* and *sustains* out of love. Furthermore, God is not a static Absolute, but a perpetually gushing fountain of eternal life, manifesting his Majesty, Wisdom, and Knowledge through the universe. Consequently, in the cosmic system as Rumî sees it, everything happens according to a great plan formulated by Divine Will and Wisdom. Even bees build their houses by inspiration from God. So, a colorful and living world reveals itself in his poetry. While everything is related and connected to each other, everything also has a special space, meaning, duty, and importance.

The cosmos, thus, becomes a meaningful book and precious piece of art which manifests "the attributes and qualities" of its owner. Furthermore, the whole world – fish and moon, atom and sun alike – has been created to worship and love God, and to express its constant adoration in an intoxicated dance. Therefore, Rumi, "teaches his readers to contemplate this aspect of the ever-active God, who shapes the world according to a plan that He alone knows" (Schimmel 1992: 82).

For Rumî, human beings are not outsiders and strangers in a hostile and brutal natural environment. Rather, the whole world is a majestic garden, in which every flower has its function and represents various states and aspects of human life; every leaf on a tree and every bird in a bush offers praise and thanksgiving for God's greatness and sustenance. Every leaf and tree is a messenger from nonexistence, proclaiming the creative power of God, talking with long hands and green, fresh tongues. Not only does Rumî listen to the constant praise uttered by the flowers and all other creatures, but he also visualizes them in the various positions of prayer. A plane-tree, for example, is opening its hand in prayer just like as a believer would do. The clouds, on the other hand, are pregnant from the ocean of love. The morning breeze is a fitting symbol for the life-giving breath of the Beloved that causes twigs and branches to become intoxicated and dance.

Animal symbolism is also prominent in Rumî's poetry. Says Rumî, animals are not at all "machines or automata," as Cartesian philosophy would have us believe. Even the wolf, rooster, and lion know what love is. Therefore, Rumî was very sensitive and kind to animals, as many anecdotes attest. For example, when he was walking, he would not drive a sleeping dog from his path, but rather would wait until the poor creature got up. Moreover, Rumî did not restrict his compassion and love to large animals but embraced every created thing.

The whole of Rumî's poetry can be regarded as admiration of eternal Beauty as reflected in the cosmos. Therefore, he often uses a mirror as a symbol for the created world, which reflects the eternal Beauty of God. Since the natural world is a mirror of divine beauty, God is closer to human beings than their jugular vein. Rumî sees his Loving God's signs everywhere, and he never tires of repeating the marvels of God's creation – the result of the unceasing Divine Will and Power.

Rumî is regarded as an outstanding evolutionary thinker, although not a mechanical or biological evolutionist like Darwin and Spencer. While Darwin presented a biological view of the creation of higher species by blind urges of struggle for existence and life's adaptation with environment, Rumî comprehends the whole process of evolution in a grand system. Instead of explaining it by mechanical dynamics, he resorts to love as the fundamental urge that creates attraction and affinities: "All atoms in the cosmos are attracted to one another like lovers, everyone is drawn towards its mate by the magnetic pull of love" (Sharif 1995: 828–9). The heavenly movements are waves in an infinite ocean of love. If cosmic love were not there, all existence would freeze and shrink into nothingness. The organic would refuse to merge and emerge into vegetation, vegetation would not be lifted into animal life, nor would life ascend toward the mind and spirit. In short, without love, nothing would move. It is clear that Rumî developed a different understanding of evolution as assimilation rather than annihilation, one that is based on love and interdependence instead of conflict and survival of the fittest. His theory of evolution can be compared with Bergson, who also argues the creative and evolutionary dimension of life. But while Bergson views this creative evolutionary process as devoid of goal and meaning, Rumî, on the other hand, regards God as the ground and goal of all existence, thus of evolution (Sharif 1995: 829).

Love as a Dynamic Force

For Rumî, a force – a secret energy – lies beneath the spiritual and material world, informing the invisible, progressive change in the universe (humanity included). This force is love, and it originates in God and moves toward God. According to Rumî, love is the positive energy that is responsible for interaction between particles, thus connecting everything with everything else in the universe. So, everything in the universe is interdependent.

Furthermore, says Rumî, since the love arouses every sense, increases the power of intuition, and leads to insight, love is superior to intellect in human life. In daily social life, for example, love has an important practical function: it solves disputes, eliminates selfishness and egotism, and draws aside all veils from the mind. Thus, not only is love basic and necessary for a religious and ethical life, but also for the sustainability of the cosmic order. In a nutshell, Rumî presents a deep and comprehensive understanding of the interdependence and interrelatedness of humanity and the natural world. In so doing, he affirms the reality of the world and dignity of all life, particularly of human life, which has become self-conscious and conscious of its divine origin and goal.

Humanity

Humanity is the central figure in God's creation and, therefore, is the vicegerent of God on Earth in the sense that it is up to human beings to take care of the whole system. The whole creation is a gift from God and a sign of his creative power. Since God creates and sustains all ecosytems, human beings must interact wisely with the natural world and use its natural resources with care, nurturing a relationship with it founded on love and compassion, which is the essence of all reality.

To conclude, spirituality, rationality, and universal

morality have found a healthy synthesis in Rumî's thought. In his system, God, the universe, and humanity are embraced in a single all-encompassing vision, the vision of creative love. Although six centuries old, Rumî's notions are relevant to present environmental concerns.

Ibrahim Ozdemir

Further Reading
Barks, Coleman. *The Essential Rumi*. San Francisco: Harper, 1995.
Chittick, William. *The Sufi Path of Love: The Spiritual Teaching of Rumi*. New York: State University of New York Press, 1983.
Harvey, Andrew. *The Way of Passion: A Celebration of Rumi*. Berkeley: Frog, Ltd., 1994.
Iqbal, Afzal. *The Life and Thought of Mohammad Jalal-ud-Din Rumi*. Lahore, Pakistan: Bazm-i Iqbal, 1955.
Lewis, Franklin D. *Rumi, Past and Present, East and West: The Life, Teachings and Poetry of Jalal al-din Rumi*. Oxford: Oneworld Publications, 2000.
Schimmel, Annemarie. *The Triumphal Sun: A Study of the Works of Jalaloddin Rumi*. Albany, NY: State University of New York Press, 1993.
Schimmel, Annemarie. *I Am Wind, You Are Fire: The Life and Work of Rumi*. Boston, MA: Shambhala Publications, 1992.
Sharif, M.M., *A History of Muslim Philosophy*. Delhi: Low Price Publications, 1995.
Vitray-Meyerovitch, Eva de. *Rumî and Sufism*. Simone Fattal, tr. Sausalito: The Post-Apollo Press, 1987.
Vitray-Meyerovitch, Eva de. *The Whirling Dervishes: A Commemoration*. London: International Rumi Committee, 1974.

See also: Islam; Sufism.

Russian Mystical Philosophy

Orthodox Christianity had held the official status of state church in pre-revolutionary Russia, but its rivals were numerous and included Christian sects of a Protestant derivation as well as mystical and occult systems of a syncretic religious orientation. Russian esotericism and occultism have given the world such famous names as Theosophy founder Helena Blavatsky (1831–1891), Georgy Gurdjieff (1870s–1949) and his student Pyotr Ouspensky (1878–1947), and Nikolai and Elena Rerikh, all of whom brought Eastern-derived spiritual systems to the West. The mystical element is abundant in the work of many prominent Russian philosophers, such as Vladimir Soloviev, Vassily Rozanov and Nikolai Berdyaev. Less well known in the West but extremely influential in Russia were such mystical and "cosmicist" thinkers and visionaries as Nikolai Fedorov, Dmitry Merezhkovsky, Pavel Florensky, Konstantin Tsiolkovsky, Aleksandr Chizhevsky, Velimir Khlebnikov, Daniil Andreev, and Georgy Gachev. In recent decades, Lev Gumilev, Alexander Dugin, and others have provided an intellectual foundation for the emergence of a variety of strains of Russian ethnonationalism, radical traditionalism, Eurasianism, and right-wing spiritual ecology, most of which are based on ideas regarding the connections between nation or ethnicity, nature, and spiritual or cosmic destiny.

The tradition of Russian mystical philosophy has been characterized by several traits and themes. These include: 1) a propensity for mixing Christian and pre-Christian mythological motifs; 2) a strong social, and often messianic, orientation, evidenced in an intent to inspire the whole nation and to organize it into an ideal societal body; 3) a cosmic dimension, oriented both to a planetary and even extra-planetary future and to the exploration of invisible spiritual worlds; 4) the idea of a global destiny for Russian civilization, based on the premise that its location between Europe and Asia ideally situates it to become the keeper of a universal wisdom combining the best of East and West, and holding forth the promise of Russia becoming the first "post-historical" nation, fated to experience the suffering and illuminations imposed on the world by the struggle of Christ and anti-Christ; and 5) an interest in the notion of a feminine spiritual essence, variously conceived as the Divine Wholeness, Sophia, "the Eternal Feminine" (*Vechnaia Zhenstvennost*), or "The Soul of the World" (*Dusha Mira*).

Cosmism

One of the most popular terms in contemporary Russian philosophical discussions, *cosmism* has come to designate both a particular movement or trend and the principal quality and legacy of Russian philosophy on the whole. Cosmism literally refers to a "cosmic orientation" of thought. The cosmos, in this perspective, is seen as the object of thought, but thought is also considered as a part of the cosmos, both a cognitive reflection of cosmic reality and a constitutive force of cosmic evolution. This philosophy of active evolutionism presupposes the possibility and necessity for the human mind to regulate and transform the laws of nature. Cosmism explains historical, social and psychological processes by the influences of cosmic energies and asserts a reciprocal dependency of the fate of the universe on human consciousness. It is thus a holistic, anthropocentric, teleological and frequently utopian tradition of thought, which sees humanity as in the process of developing a "planetarian consciousness" which could guide the further evolution of the universe and lead to its ultimate perfection.

The roots of cosmism can arguably be found in Eastern Christianity. While Catholicism had a principally historicist and more activist orientation, Orthodoxy is generally considered to be more concerned with the cosmic or vertical dimension of reality. Within the Orthodox tradition, the foremost aspiration of a Christian is seen to be the "deification of the creature," presupposing the transfiguration not of only human flesh but also of the entire substance of the universe and of all living entities. Russian Orthodoxy was built on the foundation of an agrarian economy, and inherited from its pre-Christian substrate both a dualistic worldview of light and darkness and an intense sense of participation in the cyclical processes of nature, contrasting with the linear, historical imagination of the more urbanized West.

Perhaps the first monument of Russian cosmism is the so-called *Golubinaia Kniga*, or the *Book of Depth*. This book presents popular Christian beliefs, as expressed in religious folk songs, as a huge matrix of cosmical elements. For example, it says that human meditations derive from heavenly clouds and draws numerous other parallels between human life and the workings of the universe, thus anticipating the basic presupposition of contemporary cosmism – that humanity and the cosmos are symbiotically joined. In a conventional sense, however, the founder of Russian cosmism is considered to be Nikolai Fedorov (Fyodorov, 1828–1903). The religious thrust of Fedorov's project is the reversal of all natural laws, death being one of them, in order that humanity may manifest God's omniscience and omnipotence. Christianity, for Fedorov, is primarily the religion of resurrection, and the moral task of humanity is not to wait for the Last Judgment, but to follow the example set by Christ and endeavor to make bodily resurrection possible on the Earth, to transform the entirety of human existence into a humanmade and continuous Easter, using whatever technological resources we can muster.

Following in Fedorov's path, Konstantin Tsiolkovsky (1857–1935), commonly honored as the "father" of the Soviet space programs, developed a philosophy according to which all physical matter is animate and sentient, and every atom a living and conscious entity. Two basic ideas of cosmism, the recognition of the universe as a living organism and the active regulation of natural forces through means such as genetics, owe their prominence to Tsiolkovsky. If Fedorov were primarily a religious thinker and Tsiolkovsky a hybrid scientist-visionary, Vladimir Vernadsky (1863–1945) represents the strictly scientific end of the cosmicist spectrum. He originated several new disciplines in the natural sciences – among them biochemistry, geochemistry, and integrative geoscience – and was the first scientist to theorize the geologic role of living matter, and the increasing influence of plant, animal and human life on the evolution of planetary structures. Together with French thinkers Eduard Le Roy and Pierre Teilhard De Chardin, Vernadsky developed the concept of the "noosphere," the collective body of human thought incorporated into the biosphere as an active factor in its transformation. In his view, the geosphere organically overlaps with the biosphere, which in turn grows into the noosphere. Thought is a form of energy and an active factor of geological evolution that allows humanity to cooperate with nature as a complementary part of a living and thinking organism.

Though cosmism, like all other non-Marxist and "idealist" teachings during the Soviet period, was rejected by official ideology, it nevertheless enjoyed a privileged status. Fedorov's project for the resurrection of the dead was implicitly incorporated into some undercurrents of Soviet ideology, as manifested most strikingly in the construction of Lenin's mausoleum, which was designed to preserve his body until technology could resurrect him. In spite of the atheism of Marxism-Leninism and the religiosity of Fedorov, the two systems are compatible inasmuch as both attempt to give immanent realization to transcendental aspirations. The imperative of both ideologies is technological progress that will lead to the mastery by humankind of the blind forces of nature. Both systems criticize capitalist civilization for its social inequality and materialistic obsessions, which appears in Marxism as the greediness of the bourgeoisie and in Fedorov as the dictatorship of fashion, which Fedorov considered to be corrupt and "feminine." Both strive to overcome individualism and egoism, valuing labor instead as the highest moral duty, since the task of humanity is to subordinate nature to teleological and creative reason.

In recent years, Russian cosmism has been reinvigorated by an increased interest in environmental matters, giving rise, in the writings of Svetlana Semyonova (the most prominent follower of Fedorov), Nikita Moiseev, Fyodor Girenok, and others, to a scientific strand that could be considered the Russian equivalent of the environmental holism of James Lovelock, Gregory Bateson, and other "New Paradigm" scientists. Here, cosmism has been influenced by ideas of negentropy, the anthropic principle, and the Gaia hypothesis.

Gumilev's Biocosmic Theory of Ethnogenesis

The son of poets Nikolai Gumilev and Anna Akhmatova, historian and ethnologist Lev Gumilev (Gumilyov, 1912–1990) has been one of the most influential voices in recent popular Russian ecological and cultural thought. Influenced most by the "Eurasianists" of the 1920s–1930s, for whom Russia was a distinct world civilization embodying the combined virtues of Asia and Europe, and by the Earth scientist Vernadsky, Gumilev developed a "theory of living matter," according to which the organic substance of life determines the formation of both inorganic and superorganic (rational) layers of the global ecosystem, including the biosphere and noosphere. In his most important work, *Ethnogenesis and the Earth's Biosphere* (*Etnogenez i biosfera zemli*), Gumilev applies his theoretical model to the development of ethnic groups, or *ethnoi*, proposing that each ethnos undergoes an organic evolution through which it develops a sense of deep connection with its geographic environment. The key factor for development of an ethnos is "passionality," or the "passionate drive." Whereas most people, for Gumilev, are motivated by a desire for self-preservation, a select proportion are "passionaries" who devote their lives to particular goals and charge the larger society with the energy of action. In contrast to this life-affirming energy, necessary for any creative development and associated with the growth of an ethnic group living in harmony with its environment, Gumilev argues that ethnic mixing leads to a dangerous loss of that organic connection with the natural environment, a turn to abstract thinking, and ultimately an entropic degeneration into an inert or "vacuum" state. Another danger, for Gumilev, is represented by the "parasitic ethnos" or "chimera," which develops outside of any environmentally symbiotic context and, when it becomes lodged within the territory of a "benign" ethnos, threatens it with destruction from within. (Gumilev stops short of blaming the Jewish diaspora for the misfortunes of Russian and other ethnoi, but this allusion is implicit in his writings.) Needless to say, Gumilev's assumption of ethnic essences goes against the grain of Western scholarly thinking on nationalism and ethnicity, and his thought bears an obvious resemblance to fascist notions opposing communities of organic solidarity against dangerously rootless "cosmopolitans." Yet he remains an extremely popular cult figure, influential even on elite Russian conceptions of nature and society.

Other Developments

In the post-Soviet context, various streams of nationalist and anti-globalist thought have emerged at the forefront of Russian popular philosophical discourse. Paralleling Western civilizationalist thinkers such as Samuel Huntington, with his argument that global conflicts of the future will be based on the "clash of civilizations," Russian neo-Eurasianists, radical traditionalists, and defenders of "Orthodox civilization" oppose the commercial empire of the "Atlanticist" West, claiming that a Russian-led Eurasia harbors a more proper balance between the spiritual and material worlds. Frequent reference is made to the rather loose notion of "ecology of culture," which draws on Gumilev's ideas about ethnos as a biological phenomenon, as well as the more conventional views of cultural and historical preservationists such as the cultural historian Dmitry Likhachev.

Beyond vague pronouncements about the necessity of environmental protection, however, nature remains muted in most current Russian philosophy, playing second fiddle either to the quest for a Russian national (or civilizational) identity or to a more speculative cosmism. Beliefs in the sacred destiny of Russia and in the power of specific landscapes (such as the Ural mountains), however, have been spread through the work of artist and theosophist Nikolai Rerikh (1874–1947), his wife Elena (1879–1955), and followers of their synthetic spiritual philosophy alternately known as *Agni Yoga* and "Living Ethics" (*Zhivaya Etika*). A mixture of Theosophical occultism, millennial beliefs about Russia's role in a coming world transformation, beliefs in "vital energy" and the power of art to channel this energy, and parareligious revisions of official Soviet ideology, these ideas now inform a broad network of centers and groups, found in every major Russian city today. The teachings of Ukrainian-born nature mystic and ascetic Porphirii Ivanov (1898–1983) have also found a large audience of followers scattered across the former Soviet Union, and have even been incorporated into the official educational curriculum of Kazakhstan. Rejecting materialism, Ivanov advocated a "system" of living in close harmony with nature, including twice-daily cold bathing in natural waters, regular barefoot walking in the outdoors, weekly waterless fasting (from Friday evening to noon Sunday), abstinence from smoking and drinking, and an altruistic demeanor in all activities. With its focus on natural health and rejuvenation and its mixture of personal virtue ethics, rural communitarianism, millenarian optimism, and rejection of worldly power, Ivanov's teaching represents the latest in a long tradition of Russian (and East Slavic) nature religion. Similar ideas and practices have mixed with cosmicist thinking, Asian spiritual trends, occultism, and strands of Orthodox belief, to produce much of the diversity of alternative religion in Russia today.

Mikhail Epstein
Adrian Ivakhiv

Further Reading

Andreev, Daniil. *The Rose of the World*. Hudson, NY: Lindisfarne Books, 1997.

Epstein, Mikhail. "Daniil Andreev and the Mysticism of Femininity." *The Occult in Russian and Soviet Culture*. Bernice Glatzer Rosenthal, ed. Ithaca and London: Cornell University Press, 1997, 325–55.

Epstein, Mikhail. "The Phoenix of Philosophy: On the Meaning and Significance of Contemporary Russian Thought." *Symposion: A Journal of Russian Thought* 1 (1996), 35–74.

Epstein, Mikhail. *The Russian Philosophy of National Spirit: Conservatism and Traditionalism*. Washington D.C.: National Council for Soviet and East European Research, 1994.

Gumilev, Leo. *Ethnogenesis and the Biosphere*. Moscow: Progress Publishers, 1990.

Hagemeister, Michael. "Russian Cosmism in the 1920s and Today." In B.G. Rosenthal, ed. *The Occult in Russian and Soviet Culture*. Ithaca: Cornell University Press, 1997, 185–202.

Shnirelman, Viktor and Sergei Panarin. "Lev Gumilev: His

Pretension as Founder of Ethnology and His Eurasian Theories." *Inner Asia* 3 (2001), 1–18.

Vernadskii, Vladimir. *The Biosphere.* David B. Langmuir, tr. New York: Copernicus Books, 1998.

Young, Jr., George M. *Nikolai F. Fedorov: An Introduction.* Belmont, MA: Nordland, 1979.

See also: Alchemy; Blavatsky, Helena Patrovna; Gurdjieff, G.I.; Neo-Paganism in Ukraine; Ouspensky, Pyotr Demianovich; Slavic Neo-Paganism; Slavic Religion; Western Esotericism.

P Rustlers Valley (South Africa)

Rustlers Valley was established as a community in 1991 under the guidance of Frik Grobbelaar in the eastern highlands of the Free State, South Africa. Rustlers community does not embrace any particular religion but rather draws from religious practices worldwide where they seem appropriate to our world vision. Our world vision is primarily shaped by a belief in the value of diversity and freedom of thought – no method, no guru. This approach derives from the recognition that all religions arose in isolation from one another due to the experience of religious feeling in the individual human breast. We therefore see all religions as garbled human attempts to cater to this feeling. We see this feeling as the only legitimate basis for religion. Living in one of the most beautiful valleys in the world we see the expression of divinity in nature all around us and attempt to enhance this with simple reverence in everyday cultural behavior. By reverence I mean living in the constant awareness of nature's beauty and bounty. To this end we use sweatlodges, ayhuasca ceremonies, drumming circles, traditional healing methods and the upliftment of our surrounding community through the creation of a food-rich environment. We use a permacultural approach which includes organic farming methods but is more like an adaptation of nature by concentrating plants that are useful to the human community while maintaining nature's patterns and strategies.

Rustlers believe society is undergoing a fundamental transformation. A new worldview is being born and whether this birth is to be an easy or difficult one will depend largely upon the individual. It is our aim to assist the individual to cope with and contribute to the birthing process. The goal is to embrace the hopes, transform the fears and discover the magical behind the mundane to encourage the individual to achieve his/her highest level of spiritual awareness.

Rustlers runs permaculture design workshops at the Lodge twice a year and has hosted annual music festivals for the last decade with a view to spreading this awareness. Neighboring Rustlers Valley is Mautse (the valley of the ancestors) which we believe is one of the oldest sacred places in the world, as our valley has had human occupation for a hundred thousand years and this sacred site was inherited by the current indigenous people from the Bushmen who were here before them. Mautse is currently occupied by traditional healers or "Sangomas" who are teaching us about the collection and use of medicinal plants.

Sustainability is our primary value as it applies to the species and to our community and to this end we are creating a model for sustainable African existence, promoting the conservation of all energy including human effort and the use of renewable natural resources. We have a living seed bank of the 280-odd vegetables that are still available on the planet and we use the production of our gardens in our restaurant.

Rustlers Valley works in conjunction with Food and Trees for Africa to promote permaculture in disadvantaged schools and communities throughout South Africa to supplement school feeding schemes and poverty alleviation projects.

Rustlers considers the recognition and integration of nature's bounty to all the people of the planet as a great spiritual healing that will aid the birthing of a new worldview and therefore a new world. The various rituals that we use, such as the sweatlodge at full moon, are meant to assist in the shifting of paradigms through the experience of one's own personal power and sense of well-being in the universal context of one's connectedness to all else.

Frik Grobbelaar

See also: Esalen Institute; Findhorn Foundation/Community; New Age.

Saami Culture

In Sápmi, the traditional settlement area of the Saami (earlier: Lapps) in central and northern Norway and Sweden, northern Finland and northwestern Russia, nature is varied. There are steep coastal mountains and fiords, spruce forests, areas with tundra (a word that originated with the Saami), swampy grounds, the Scandinavian mountain chain, valleys with birchwoods, and many rivers intersect the area. In these different types of biotic communities, the Saami have developed various economies. Fishing in the sea, in lakes and in rivers, hunting for game and game birds, reindeer herding, stock raising and farming have all been traditional Saami means of subsistence.

The different Saami groups in this large area have until the last century lived rather isolated from one another and there are, therefore, great regional differences in culture. Depending on where in Sápmi they live, these differences have made Saamis relate themselves to nature in various ways, but, at the same time, some ideas are and seem also earlier to have been common all over Sápmi. With the help of sources from the western parts of Sápmi during the late seventeenth and early eighteenth centuries and oral traditions collected during the nineteenth and twentieth centuries, it is possible to outline some of the traditional ideas about nature, at least among the reindeer-herding groups that the majority of the sources describe.

Since the landscape is no neutral room, but loaded with meanings, parts of the landscape – mountains, brooks, stone boulders – can function as symbols. Every landscape can be said to consist of both the natural formations and the cultural constructions that add symbolic values to some of these formations. In traditional Saami thought, certain places were regarded as connecting links between our world and the otherworld. These were the lakes where the *noaidi*, the most important ritual specialist, was regarded as being able to travel to the world of the departed, mountains where different types of subterranean beings were regarded as living, burial places of humans and of bears, stones that men smeared with fish fat or the blood of sacrificed reindeer, and the fireplace in the tent or cot (*goahti*) around which women poured out milk or gravy. In all these places rituals were performed. For the nomadic, reindeer-herding groups, there was a concentration of places for rituals and especially sacrificial sites in the area around the tree limit (*orda*) where the reindeer stay during both the mating season in autumn and calving in spring.

The year was traditionally divided into two halves, the dark (when in some areas the sun never rises for two months) and the light (when in some areas the sun never sets for two and a half months). During the dark winter, the Saami navigated with the help of the stars and many had a good knowledge about constellations and movements of the celestial bodies. The importance of nature also permeates Saami language, which is well known for its rich terminology for different types of snow, reindeer, and so on. Attitudes to and interpretations of nature are also embedded in Saami place-names. They are very often descriptive and indicate the physical character of the place or the occurrence of animals there. Also, several of the names of the months convey similar messages: March is "the swan month," April "the month with frozen crust on the snow," and May "the reindeer calf month."

During the era of the indigenous religion, there were ritual ceremonials when several reindeer or other animals were sacrificed, for example during the Great Autumn festival in late September, but those occasions were exceptions. The daily ritual activities and also the *rites de passage* took place in and near the tent, which as the center of the cosmos represented safety in contrast to the wilderness (*meahcci*) in the periphery, where all kinds of dangers – wolves, wolverines as well as evil spirits – threatened herds and humans. One important aspect of nomadic cultures such as the Saami herding groups is their dynamic adaptation to the landscape. Every time the tent was moved to a new site, the center of the cosmos moved as well as the center of ritual life. Therefore, the dynamics of traditional Saami conceptions of the landscape lay in the tension between the sacred places that were stationary in the landscape and the movable sacred places related to the tent.

Saami traditionally also reckoned with another landscape, located beneath and behind the one we can see when awake. It was important to be able to orient oneself also in this invisible landscape (visible only in dreams) where the departed ancestors and different types of spiritual beings were considered to be living. To take one example, the South Saami related, according to sources from the 1720s, that there was a category of beings called *saajvh* that could be inherited, sold, and bought. Status in South Saami society at that time depended on how many *saajvh* a person owned. Many could tell about visits to these beings in the mountains where they lived and about how the *saajvh* had helped them in difficult situations.

Even more important than the *saajvh* were the ancestors. They were socially alive, regarded as members of the family and lived in a world beneath the surface of our world. They could help in hunting, fishing and reindeer herding, they could guard the children and they often gave messages in dreams. For example, when a woman was pregnant, it was ancestors who suggested the name of the child.

For Saami hunters "a respectful attitude to the animal, and the proper treatment of its remains after it has been killed and eaten" was extremely important (Hultkrantz 1994: 357). This meant, for example, that the remains after the meals were placed in special bone deposits. Also, many of the divinities were related to nature. Sun (*Beaivi*) and Moon (*Aske* or *Mánnu*) received sacrifices as well as thunder (*Hovrengaellies*, *Átjá*, or *Dierpmis*) and the divinities for water, snow and ice, migratory birds, etc. A hunting god and a god for the reindeer were responsible for different sources of livelihood. In addition to the rituals directed toward these divinities, there were also rituals for many types of spirits in animal form. The ritual specialists had to relate themselves to spiritual birds, fishes, reindeer bulls, and in the south, every child (or, according to another interpretation, the boys in the families of the ritual specialists) received a special tutelary spirit called name-fish (*nimmeguelie*) in connection with the naming rituals. This fish helped the person through life's difficulties and prayers were directed to it. Another type of spiritual being was the rulers (*hálddit*) who guarded plants and animals and ruled over areas in nature. The most important of the "rulers" was the bear, which was regarded both as an animal and as a spiritual being. It was the bear that was responsible for what we today would call the ecological balance in nature, and in order to safeguard that balance a bear festival was celebrated in springtime. Before, during and after the hunt there were strict rules and the whole hunt was ritualized. When the bear was taken to the settlement, there was a bear feast during which several chants were performed, the most important of which was the bear chant in honor of the animal. The meat was carved from the bones and boiled in a certain order. The men ate some parts of the bear in a tent that had been erected for the occasion, the women and children had other parts in the ordinary tent. During the feast it was important that no bone was broken, because all the bones were to be buried in an accurate order, whereas the skin was used in a game that decided when and by whom the next bear was going to be killed.

To sum up the indigenous religion's relation to nature, one could with Hultcrantz say that even if there were differences between hunters, fishermen and pastoral nomads (and farmers – I would add), indigenous religion in all its forms has been "close to nature in its expression and well adapted to environmental demands" (1994: 367). This is clearly shown by the Saami chants, the yoiks, in which nature and animals are the two most common themes, apart from human individuals. In yoiks about landscape "the localities are always mentioned by name, and by means of their names have an individual quality and power of association; a complex of memories, legends and traditions is linked to each one of them" (Ruong 1969: 17).

After several hundred years of missionary work, animal sacrifices, rituals performed for the indigenous divinities, and many other aspects of the traditional religion were abandoned. In most regions this happened during the eighteenth century, in some areas a century later. However, knowledge about the traditions of the ancestors was transmitted to younger generations and many of the spiritual beings related to nature were more or less integrated into contextualized Saami forms of Christianity. Today, most of the Saami are as secularized as the majority populations in Norway, Sweden, Finland, and Russia, but many young Saamis show a keen interest in the indigenous religion and attend courses to learn more about this important part of their cultural heritage. Some individuals and groups, inspired in some cases by Native American friends, or in others by the neo-shamanism of Michael Harner, have also tried to revitalize parts of the indigenous religion. At the same time, the condemning attitude of the church has changed, opening space for rekindling interest in their indigenous religious traditions. The yoik and the traditional drums, for example, which were heavily condemned by clergymen during the seventeenth and eighteenth centuries, have been used in religious rituals again. This time they are used in Christian contexts and symbolize respect for Saami cultural values. There have also been services of reconciliation where bishops have asked forgiveness from the Saami for how the Church acted during the time of religious confrontation. When it comes to Saami rights to self-determination and as this regards land and water in Sápmi, however, the national churches have not, as of the early twenty-first century, taken clear sides with the Saami.

To use Rochon's words, many Saamis still have "a deep sense of dependency and reliance upon the natural environment," but their concept of nature, based as it is on ecological principles, "has been so drastically manipulated that in many instances this concept is difficult to practice" (1993: 54). The damming of rivers, devastation of forest land, mining, tourism, the use of pasture-lands and hunting-grounds for the European space program or as artillery ranges, and the Chernobyl catastrophe, have all created many problems for the traditional Saami economies and especially for the reindeer breeding which needs large pasture areas for the herds.

The Saami have not been passive onlookers to this process; quite the opposite. The fight against a hydro-electric project in the early 1980s, for example, was decisive for Saami political mobilization. In that case, environmentalist groups and Saami organizations were on the same side of the conflict. In other cases, they have taken opposite stands. This is especially the case in what is usually – because of lack of knowledge about the long Saami cultural history in the area – called "Europe's last wilderness." This "wilderness" is however a cultural landscape, because the Saami have, as Beach put it, "been instrumental in creating their environment which some conservationists wish to label as purely natural" (1994: 183).

Disagreements between the Saami and environmentalists have also occurred over nuisance predators. Environmentalists from the urban regions in the south of Scandinavia and other parts of Europe have in general little understanding for Saami claims for a reduction of the number of predatory animals in the areas used for reindeer herding, even though wolves and wolverines harm the herding economy. The Saami, who base their lives on traditional economies have, through their chosen parliaments, begun to tackle the many environmental issues they face. But since these parliaments have still not been given any authority over land and water in Sápmi, it is difficult for them to get their proposals approved at the level of the nation-states they inhabit.

Håkan Rydving

Further Reading
Beach, Hugh. "The Saami of Lapland." *Polar Peoples: Self-Determination and Development.* London: Minority Rights Group Publications, 1994, 147–205, 228–32.

Gaski, Harald, ed. *Sami Culture in a New Era: The Norwegian Sami Experience.* Karasjok: Davvi Girji OS, 1997.

Hultkrantz, Åke. "Religion and Environment among the Saami: An Ecological Study." In *Circumpolar Religion and Ecology: An Anthropology of the North.* T. Irimoto and T. Yamada, eds. Tokyo: University of Tokyo Press, 1994, 347–74.

Rochon, Timm. *Saami and Dene Concepts of Nature.* Umeå: Center for Arctic Research, Umeå University, 1993.

Ruong, Israel. "Remembering, Feeling and Yoiking." In *Jojk/Yoik.* M Arnberg, I. Ruong and H. Unsgaard. Stockholm: Sveriges Radios förlag, 1969, 7–39.

See also: Aboriginal Environmental Groups in Canada; Harner, Michael – and the Foundation for Shamanic Studies; Inuit; Shamanism – Traditional; Shamanism – and Art.

Sabbath–Jubilee Cycle

Consistent with Ancient Near Eastern practices of debt cancellation and economic renewal during the two millennia prior to the Common Era, the Hebrew Bible records a set of interlocking practices of social and economic redemption. Built into the liturgical calendar of an agricultural society, this Hebraic Sabbath-Jubilee cycle proposed the periodic economic justification of relations among humans and, secondarily, with regard to the land's productivity. Three distinct movements – the Sabbath day of the week, the Sabbatical every seventh year, and the Jubilee every fiftieth year – were built into the cycle. The attempt to proclaim a Jubilee year was revisited by the authors of the Christian gospels as that which occasioned the ministry of Jesus; in these texts, the Sabbath-Jubilee tradition associated the liberty promised by God with redemption from economic injustice and with unburdening the land from Roman and Herodian temple-state constructions. The vision encompassed in the Sabbath-Jubilee cycle was most summarily articulated in the refrain of Isaiah 61:1–2 as good news for the politically and economically oppressed, liberty for enslaved persons, and release for debt prisoners. Poetic elaborations of the same practice envision it as an occasion of "new creation," of a "new earth" (Rev. 21:1).

Historical Context and Hebrew Biblical Background
The Hebraic Sabbath-Jubilee cycle was prefigured in Babylonian and Assyrian "clean slate" legislation. Indeed, edicts announcing the forgiveness of debts extend back to third millennium B.C.E. Sumer. Palaces and temples, often having traders in their employ, were the first major creditors of the ancient world, engaging in forms of corporate enterprise. Agrarian debts – an economic structure secondary to these trade enterprises – accrued most typically when crop failures prevented farmers from delivering the royal and/or temple tithes. Because agrarian debt alienated farmers from the land via land forfeitures, depopulated the countryside, catalyzed wage labor and debt bondage, and therefore occasioned a disruptive economic polarization in a population, rulers periodically restored a basic population distribution pattern of widespread self-support on the land. The Hebrew Bible echoes such a concern in the prophetic complaint of Isaiah against wealthy individuals "adding house to house" and so irresponsibly depopulating the land (Isa. 5:8). Broad-scale debt forgiveness or "clean slate" legislation was probably declared when economic conditions warranted or on such civic occasions as the inauguration of a new ruler or the building of a new temple.

Given "the land" as the primary unit of life in Hebrew thought ("the land" being a collective term inclusive of humans, plants, animals and the terrain), the Sabbath-Jubilee system named for the Israelites a way of living its equitable distribution and its stewardship. Having an allotment of land, the broad space in which bodies take place and the generations of life unfold, grounded the notion of freedom for these people who traced their lineage to former slaves. Once divided according to clan, tribal and household size and need, the family apportionment was made inalienable. Such ties to place theoretically promised human self-sufficiency and sustainable soil management. Further, these laws guaranteeing the distribution of land suggested how God was to be honored as Lord and Liberator. To the extent that human welfare was secured through a subsistence allotment of the land, claiming Yahweh as Sovereign had distributive justice as its socio-ethical consequence.

Hebrew biblical documents suggest some innovation in the ancient pattern of "clean slate" legislation. Removing the control from the king, it placed the practice of "proclaiming liberty . . . the year of the Lord's favor" (Isa. 61:1-2) within the terms of a cyclical liturgical calendar. According to the calendar, the *Sabbath* or *Sabbatical year* (Ex. 23:10-11; Lev. 25:1-7, 18-22; Deut. 15:1-18), which was to be celebrated every seventh year, rested the land by allowing Earth to remain fallow, trees and vines unpruned. Humans were to feed upon the harvest of the sixth year, while allowing the poor and animals to forage volunteer grains and fruits. The removal of the agricultural demarcation between wild and domesticated animal as also between weed and cultivated crop allowed for the freedom of animal and plant, while revitalizing seed stock. Deuteronomy 15 also names this "the year of remission," and Ezekiel "the Year of Liberty" (Ezek. 46:17; see also Ex. 21:2-6). During this year of amnesty, debt and human servitude among the Hebrews themselves would be canceled or redeemed by other family members. Nehemiah 10:31 hints at the continuing practice of this Sabbatical year phenomenon during the fifth century B.C.E.

As a year of liberty throughout all the land, the *Jubilee* or fiftieth year in the cycle was to be a once in a lifetime liberative transformation of all relations (Lev. 25:8-17, 23-55 and Num. 36:4). After every seven sabbatical year cycles, all land reverted to its original pattern of tribal, clan and household distribution. Forgiveness of debt and return to the ancestral land prevented the development of a landed aristocracy, since the sale of land amounted to a lease which could not exceed the life of a generation. The Jubilee also spelled a second year of freedom for the nonhuman constituents of the land community - hence, no cultivating of the soil was to be undertaken, no sowing of seeds was to practiced, neither any pruning nor harvesting. Textual citations averring to the practice of Jubilee range from that of the prophet Jeremiah (34:8-15) in the late seventh century B.C.E. through the work of the prophet Isaiah (61:1-11) to the time of the Maccabees (1 Macc. 10:43, 15:8) in the late second temple period of the first century B.C.E. While these texts do not record direct ecological ramifications from the practice of Jubilee, Ezekiel 47-48 gives poetic and visionary elaboration to such - as does Revelation 21 in the Christian testament.

Historically speaking, the notion of keeping every seventh day as a *Sabbath day* (Lev. 16:31; 23:3; Ex. 23:12; 35:2-3) may have been the last aspect of the cycle to develop and probably should be read in tandem with the Sabbatical year insomuch as it reiterates sabbatical concerns on a more regular, if less extensive scale. Two interrelated traditional memories have been melded into the practice of the Sabbath day - the liberation from slavery via the Exodus from Egypt (Deut. 5:12-15) and the sense of restful, creative fulfillment associated with the seventh day in the priestly creation account (Gen. 1). By suggesting that God's rest was built into the rhythm of the Earth as a law of natural time, this commandment deactivated the obsessive aspects of labor, which as psychic compulsion or economic condition can otherwise become as obsessive as enforced slavery within urban or marginal agricultural situations. Insomuch as rest breaks the instrumental use or objectification of any and all members of the land community (people, animals, slaves, and Earth), keeping the Sabbath day anticipates the Sabbatical and Jubilee years.

Christian Biblical & Theological Considerations

That Rome was the first empire in at least two millennia to refuse debt cancellation may be most significant for understanding the demands for a Jubilee situated at the beginning of the Christian testament. At the time of Mary and Jesus, Jews in Galilee were living at the intersection of several colonizing political institutions - the Pax Romana, the Hasmoneans, and the temple-state of Herod Antipas; how Jews, especially peasants, experienced this Roman-introduced "state of peace" was quite distinct from how Romans themselves thought of their policy. Indeed, Jews of Galilee apparently experienced the Herodian construction of Tiberias along with the Roman architecture of basilicas and aqueducts as, among other things, interfering with the flow or "liberty" of their naturalized sacred cosmology. Consequently what happens to Jesus could be read as the reaction of political, economic, and religious powers to the reintroduction of a demand for a baseline of just relations within the land.

While the celebration of the Sabbath-Jubilee cycle may not have always followed the precise pattern as codified by Israel's priests, the expectations of Jubilee seem close to the surface when reading the Christian gospels. Isaiah (61:1-2) called the Jubilee the "year of the Lord's favor," and this hope for an alternative to the socio-political and economic pattern of empire and temple was taken up by Luke as the framework for Jesus' ministry (4:18-19, but also 1:46-55). While Luke's evocations of Jubilee appear most textually prominent, Matthew as well as Luke transmits this demand in petitionary form in the Lord's Prayer (i.e., "forgive us our debts" [Matt. 6:12]), and in the telling of the parable of the unforgiving servant (Matt. 18:21-35; Lk. 7:40-43). The Hebraic tradition of debt redemption, within which the gospel writers set Jesus' ministry, recognized that "forgive us our debts as we forgive our debtors" had to do with the transaction of properties, with the restitution of peoples to place so as to assure self-sufficiency and more sustainable practices. If the Lord's Prayer carries such a prophetic memory as the Sabbath-Jubilee practice, the ancient baptismal claim from the Pauline tradition (i.e., "In Christ, there is neither [slave, Jew, male] nor [free, Gentile, female]" [Gal. 3:28]), may also recollect the rescinding of structural demarcations in the year of Spirit's amnesty.

In summary, Sabbath-Jubilee suggested an economic practice of the redemption of human livelihood. This restoration of a person to his/her allotment of subsistence sustenance served as a baseline of what was construed as justice. The redemptive cycle periodically interrupted distinctions (e.g., free/slave, rich/poor) which might otherwise be leveraged into enduring systemic oppressions. Unlike later strains of Christianity which articulated the hopes for a "new earth" via apocalyptic cataclysm and the consequent amelioration of all that represented "fallen nature" (e.g., death, transience, temporality, finitude), these cyclical practices recognize that human social and environmental relations do tend to drift towards inequality, but can also be rectified through a change of human social behavior. Suggesting that the Sabbath names what was seen as the equilibrium of shalom or well-being with the Earth, this liturgical cycle oriented one to the nature of work, the goal of human life, the way of living with Earth and other Earth creatures. It suggested a practiced harmony that denied neither the flux nor disequilibrium of systems, but nevertheless took seriously the charge to secure the welfare of the poor. Today we recognize that such a redemption from indebtedness among the poor of the world would also entail ecological redemption of the devastated lands to which the poor have been marginalized. To cite but one example of how economic indebtedness can be related to ecological devastation: the 33 African countries classified as heavily indebted suffered 50 percent more forest loss than non-indebted African countries (Friends of the Earth). Reconsideration of these ancient practices has recently inspired several environmental programs – namely, the UN Environmental Sabbath, Jubilee 2000, and the reclamation of weekly Sabbath as a practice of Earth healing.

Sharon V. Betcher

Further Reading

Canadian Ecumenical Jubilee Initiative (CEJI). *Sacred Earth, Sacred Community: Jubilee, Ecology and Aboriginal Peoples*. Toronto: CEJI, 2000.

Hudson, Michael. "It Shall Be a Jubilee Unto You." *Yes! A Journal of Positive Futures* (Fall 2002), 38–9.

Hudson, Michael. "Reconstructing the Origins of Interest-Bearing Debt and the Logic of Clean Slates." In Michael Hudson and Marc Van De Mieroop, eds. *Debt and Economic Renewal in the Ancient Near East*. International Scholars Conference on Ancient Near Eastern Economies, vol. 3. Bethesda, MD: CDL, 2002, 7–58.

Ringe, Sharon H. *Jesus, Liberation, and the Biblical Jubilee: Images for Ethics and Christology*. Minneapolis: Fortress, 1985.

Ucko, Hans, ed. *The Jubilee Challenge: Utopia or Possibility? Jewish and Christian Insights* Geneva: WCC Publications, 1997.

Wright, Christopher J.H. "Jubilee, Year of." In *The Anchor Bible Dictionary*, vol. 3. New York: Doubleday, 1992, 1025–30.

Yoder, John Howard. *The Politics of Jesus*. Grand Rapids, MI: Eerdmans, 1972.

See also: Environmental Sabbath; Jubilee and Jubilee 2000.

Sacramental Universe

Sacramental moments are experiences of the loving and creative presence of the Spirit. Creation flows from divine vision and is the locus of the human experience of divine presence. People perceive signs of the Spirit in creation, signs that might or might not be acknowledged but which nonetheless link innermost human being with divine Being. People have moments of engagement with the Spirit when they are open to the loving and creative presence of the Spirit in evolutionary creation.

In Christian churches, *sacraments* traditionally have been religious rituals, mediated by a member of the clergy in a dedicated, human-constructed sacred space, which are visible signs or symbols of an invisible experience of God's "grace" – divine presence expressed in relational love – in significant life moments. Recently, pristine places also have come to be viewed as *sacramental* because they reveal the Spirit's loving creativity in their biodiversity, textured topography, and provision of food, water and shelter for the community of life.

The term "sacrament" in the Catholic Church usually is applied to seven church rituals, presided over by a priest in a church building. These rituals, derived from teachings and actions of Jesus, were formalized by the Council of Trent (1547–1563). There have been exceptions to this reserved use of the term. For example, the Vatican II document *Lumen Gentium* called the Church a "sacrament"; and Pope Paul VI stated that "the poor are a sacrament of Christ," a theological expression of the teaching of Jesus in the Last Judgment story in Matthew's Gospel (Matt. 25:31–46).

In 1991 the U.S. bishops, in their national pastoral letter *Renewing the Earth*, said that creation as a whole is sacramental. They declared that "The Christian vision of a *sacramental universe* – a world that discloses the Creator's presence by visible and tangible signs – can contribute to making the Earth a home for the human family once again." The bishops of Alberta, Canada, in their 1998 pastoral letter *Celebrate Life: Care for Creation*, taught

> Catholics see creation in a *sacramental* way. The abundance and beauty of God's creation reveals to us something of the generosity of the Creator. God is present and speaks in the dynamic life forces of our universe and planet as well as in our own lives. Respect for life needs to include all creation.

These church teachings state that the whole of creation can be sacramental for the person of faith, revealing God's grace – offering presence and life – conferring productivity. The sacramental universe teaching has scriptural bases in passages such as Wisdom 13:5: "from the greatness and beauty of created things their original author, by analogy, is seen"; and Acts 17:28: "in God we live and move and have our being."

A sacramental place is naturally a *commons*: a home shared by all the members of the community of life. In it, their food and habitat needs are integrated, their competitive needs are balanced, their relationships are interdependent, and their associations are consciously or unconsciously collaborative. The commons is the locus of engagement of the biotic and abiotic communities, internally in their respective modes of being and engagement and externally in their interaction with each other. The commons is the place in which dynamic natural history evolves, diversifies and complexifies, and the base from which cultural history develops in all its intricacy.

In the Bible, human property in land and goods is part of a human commons (Acts 2:44 describes how the early Christian community "had all things in common"), which is to provide for human needs. In a complementary way, the Earth is a commons: shared space and the source of life-providing goods for all creatures. The Earth commons, then, is not intended solely for humans' use and enjoyment, although as part of the biotic community they share in its benefits; it is being created to provide for all creatures as they live related to and dependent on each other in complex ecosystems.

The *sacramental commons* is creation seen as the locus of the interactive presence and caring compassion of the Spirit. It implies that people are called to integrate the spiritual meaning of "sacramental" and the social meaning of "commons" and engage in concrete efforts to restore and conserve ecosystems: to care about and care for creation as a whole, and to care about and for the members of the biotic community.

The "sacramental universe" becomes localized in the "sacramental commons" when Creator Spirit and created spirits consciously engage each other in sacred space, which is every place in creation. People in their spiritual center experience sacramental moments in sacramental places of a sacramental commons in the sacramental universe. As "sacrament," a place at special moments is revelatory of God-immanent; as "commons," a place at all moments is a sign of the creativity of God-transcendent, while simultaneously providing the natural goods necessary for the well-being of the community of all life. In acknowledging a "sacramental commons," people express an appreciation of the sacredness, integrity, and life-sustaining qualities of creation.

Ethical conduct and ecological consequences flow from sacramental understandings of cosmos and commons. Christians who acknowledge the creative, communicating and community-creating immanence of the Spirit in creation, recognizing thereby the revelatory power of creation as a whole and of the biotic community within it, treat Earth and Earth's inhabitants with reverence and respect. In understanding that the Spirit intends that Earth's goods meet the needs of all Earth's creatures, they avoid consumerism and exploitation. In viewing creation holistically, they act responsibly toward those who are strangers in space, time and species, not solely the human "neighbors" who have the most noticeable claim on their concern, but also otherkind and pristine nature that comprise the variant forms of the community of creation ever emerging from the creative power and loving presence of the Spirit. Within this consciousness, generational and intergenerational responsibility are fostered, the limits on Earth's liveable space, productive places, and available goods are respected, and space, places and goods are shared equitably.

John Hart

Further Reading

Alberta, Canada Catholic Bishops. *Celebrate Life: Care for Creation*. Edmonton, Alberta: Western Catholic Reporter website, online: http://www.wcr.ab.ca/bin/eco-lett.htm, 1998.

Hart, John. "Caring for the Commons: Creation, Church and Community." *New Theology Review* (August 2002).

Hart, John. "A Jubilee for a New Millennium: Justice for Earth and Peoples of the Land." *Catholic Rural Life* 43:2 (Spring 2001), 23–31.

U.S. Catholic Bishops. "Renewing the Earth: An Invitation to Reflection and Action on Environment in Light of Catholic Social Teaching" (1991). In *Renewing the Face of the Earth: A Resource for Parishes*. Washington, D.C.: Department of Social Development and World Peace, United States Catholic Conference, 1994.

See also: Christianity (6a) – Roman Catholicism; Commons and Christian Ethics.

The Sacred and the Modern World

An increasing concern of mine is the use and misuse of the idea of the sacred in the modern world. During the great disaster of the twin towers and Pentagon we constantly heard from the media of many things we "hold sacred," among them our respective freedoms, but other more mundane things. While we certainly needed reassurance that we were the good guys, even when we learned that we had trained most of the terrorists to kill Russians and that we had been a major supporter of the Taliban, the idea of holding things sacred has such a typical American individualist ring that the words now mean very little. We use the phrase to cover all our activities and seem to believe that our attachment to things gives them a sacred validity they would not otherwise have. Contrast this attitude with those of the people of the Middle East, many of whom have no hesitation in sacrificing themselves for beliefs they hold sacred. We can hardly be accused of understanding what the word means in its larger context.

I had previously encountered this flippant American attitude when discussing the sacred nature of the Devils Tower or Bears Lodge to an audience of environmentally conscious people. I explained that several Indian tribes had discovered a feeling of the sacred there and had learned to do ceremonies that enhanced the lives of the people and animals that recognized its power. During the question-and-answer session following my presentation I was, as one might expect, confronted by a husky young man who argued that people should be able to climb the mountain any time they wanted because they held mountain climbing sacred and it was one of the greatest challenges they could face.

In America, religion is easy. We approach it like people at a swap meet, changing and exchanging beliefs to fit our current mood or understanding, seeking a bargain or hoping to find instant reality so that we can confirm the validity of our way of life. It never occurs to us that the way we use religious terminology says much of the depth of our understanding. We act as if we were primarily responsible for the creation and manifestation of the sacred. In other words, in holding things sacred we endow those things with our personal energies, and we believe that we have experienced the same kind of feelings that our ancestors had when they used the same words. Using this logic it is safe to say that we do not believe the sacred exists except for when we call it into being.

I tried, rather unsuccessfully I might add, to distinguish for the young mountaineer the difference between intuiting the sacred in nature and proclaiming a site to be sacred to an individual. Quite obviously if we are able to bestow sacredness then religion in America is a matter of individual choice and not a case of apprehending the mysterious power that seems to be the ground of everything. The Sioux, Cheyenne, and other tribes who perform ceremonies at Bears Lodge do so because they have had experiences so extraordinary that they understand it as a place of reverence.

Many years ago I encountered a book that has been seminal in all my thinking: Rudolf Otto's *The Idea of the Holy*. In it Otto analyzes the constituent elements of the experience of the Holy: *mysterium tremendum fascinans*. The great mystics of all world traditions and the shamans and medicine men of hundreds of smaller groups have testified to the feeling of finitude and helplessness followed by recognitions of compatibility and peacefulness and the absolute emotional certainty created in their beings by this experience. It is mysterious, upsets our intellectual beliefs with a devastating display of energy, and remains with the individual as a fascinating, attractive presence and reminder that there are dimensions to life we cannot possibly imagine.

We need only call to mind Samuel in the Temple hearing a voice, Isaiah confronted with the majesty of a divine throne room, or Black Elk riding with the thunder beings or entering the tipi where the Six Grandfathers gathered to begin to understand that the sacred is a powerful presence when it descends on a human being. The majority of people experiencing this *mysterium tremendum fascinans* report not simply a feeling of insignificance, but their great hesitancy in placing themselves in a situation where they might encounter the sacred. Most people have several preliminary encounters with voices or omens and they pray that they will not be chosen and set aside from their communities to become a holy person. It is unquestionably a burden and it may be an overwhelming burden.

Our popular conception of the sacred can hardly compare with the body of data we have describing the experience of the sacred. In previous decades we used to require of people becoming priests and ministers to have a "call" from God before they enter into the religious life. Anyone describing a call from God in picturesque terms today would certainly be rejected for ordination or employment in our religious institutions since such an experience would be so far outside the mainstream of rational religion as to be threatening to established doctrines and dogmas. We fail to notice that once ordained, whether by an institution or via personal conversion, people representing religion today have no hesitancy in announcing that they have personally talked with God, even as they are measured for the best clothing and ordering an expensive car.

A religious vocation used to imply another realm standing in judgment of our familiar natural world. It had a purpose and direction that guided us in spite of our errors and shortcomings. Those people who received a vocation were destined to become the fulcrum points in a larger historical scenario that was moving toward a celestial conclusion. We were, in a sense, co-creators of the future along with the mysterious presence that provided us with clues and insights into the nature of religion and reassured us that we would ultimately be justified. Revelation was the continuous presence of the sacred to which we were obedient.

Basic religious experiences can be almost anything from the rapid hypnotic heartbeat of fundamentalist hymns to the contemplative moments spent staring onto the Grand Canyon, from ecstasy to a near-comatose state of reflection. Unfortunately we are not inclined in this society to probe any deeper and while we may be properly called aesthetes, I doubt if we have any profound sense of religion in the old classical sense since we stand in awe of nothing and know not of how to contact the truly sacred. A new factor has recently emerged that may invoke substantial changes in the way we view the sacred. For several decades, we have seen the rise of "Near Death Experiences" (NDE) that seem to speak of the continuity of life with data we have not before considered.

In the typical NDE, people facing a severe health crisis, or experiencing a traumatic event such as an automobile accident, find themselves floating above their bodies as the scene unfolds below them. Patients report having unusual powers in this state of being which include being able to walk or fly through physical things, objects, and full command of their thought processes, often wondering what had happened to them. A significant number of people report a tunnel-like landscape in front of them at the end of which is a strong white light, brighter than they have ever seen, and feel an intense desire to move toward it. Often a relative or friend who has passed on earlier greets them.

Most of the literature, and there is an impressive number of books by competent doctors now, concentrates on proving that we have an immortal soul or that there is no judgment placed on our lives, although some people say they were asked to review their lives to that point. Depending on the doctor's range of patients reporting this phenomenon, Jesus greets some people; others see no identifiable religious personality at all. Scientists rejecting NDE experiences have claimed that they can reproduce all the significant elements of these events by probing certain parts of the brain with electrical impulses. No one, however, has been able to reproduce the sequence of the phenomena of NDE. Whether such experiences prove the existence of the soul is irrelevant to me. More important is the fact that people are told they must return to their physical lives because they have not yet accomplished their mission in life.

In religion we often talk about the religious "mission" of the founder and his disciples as if it were something preordained, and NDE seems to validate that concept. Tribal societies were based on a similar idea – that each individual had a specific path to walk – and vision quests were a regular part of seeking this path. One might not be given powers to use in one's daily life, but certainly from all reports no one who made a sincere effort to establish a relationship with the higher powers went unacknowledged. In the NDE case, it seems certain that a predetermined life is the standard for everyone, not just outstanding religious personalities, and the mission may simply be one of caring for family and friends, exercising a certain trade or profession, or acting as a friend to assist others in accomplishing their life's mission.

In Sidney Kirkpatrick's new biography of Edgar Cayce, he reports a dream Cayce had in 1941 while giving a reading. In Kirkpatrick's words, Cayce

> was permitted to visit a great hall of records, which housed bound volumes of recorded events both past and future. The records not only told of what was, but what might have been. According to this dream, had he not married Gertrude Evans, she would have died of tuberculosis in 1906. And Edgar himself would have died, in 1914, from a debilitating stomach condition (Kirkpatrick 2000: 81).

In *Plenty Coups*, the life story of a Crow Indian, Plenty Coups had a vision in which he found himself staring at an old man who was bent, gray and very debilitated, and as the picture became clear in his mind, he realized that this pitiful old man was himself in the far-distant future. Cayce had alternate life scenarios; Plenty Coups saw the result of his life's journey.

We have sometimes involved ourselves in discussions of the omnipotence of God and asked how, if he is all-knowing, we can have free will to choose. Cayce's dream of the bound books suggests that the decisions we make do have profound consequences and that we may be co-creators of the world as it moves into the future. Apparently we can create the future course of events since every decision has some definite alternatives that are realized by our choice. Life, then, has meaning every step of the way.

Everyone with a scientifically bent mind will certainly object to including this kind of data as religious because it cannot be duplicated in a scientific experiment. It is good to get the narrow scientific minds safely on the sidelines when we examine this data because they reject everything that does not fit the materialistic paradigm. There are many things in life that cannot be repeated because they are unique to ourselves or part of a process of growth that cannot be duplicated. There is an old Victor Herbert song "Toyland" that insightfully states that once we pass Toyland's border we cannot return again. Thus our first adolescent crush, our first effort to swim, the time we recited a poem in kindergarten, when we had our first child, when a parent died, almost the whole spectrum of things we experience have a quality all their own and cannot be duplicated by a white-frocked scientist.

How then, do we recapture the sense of the sacred in our lives? If choices are important and, once made, they project particular paths of activities, we can maximize the choices available to us by recognizing that we are helping to create the coming historical scenarios. It seems to me likely that Near Death Experience may be the manner in which the sacred mystery of the universe is reaching out to us. Certainly in a highly urbanized society we cannot be expected to find a place of isolation and open ourselves to this mystery. The sacred may be offering us a new chance to understand the meaning of life. Patients reporting on NDE say their lives and their view of how they were living were permanently changed by the experience.

Today in the study and practice of religion we have abandoned traditional concepts and treat religion like a strange form of sociology. We have very little empirical data to examine so we simply increase our efforts to study obscure points in various traditions. What insights we could gain if we took the phenomena rejected by science and institutional theologians and asked deep and probing questions of it. We would soon learn considerably more about our world.

Vine Deloria, Jr.

Further Reading

Deloria, Vine, Jr. *For This Land: Writings on Religion in America.* New York: Routledge, 1999.

Deloria, Vine, Jr. *Red Earth, White Lies: Native Americans and the Myth Of Scientific Fact.* New York: Scribner, 1995.

Deloria, Vine, Jr. *The Metaphysics of Modern Existence.* San Francisco: Harper & Row, 1979.

Deloria, Vine, Jr. *Behind the Trail of Broken Treaties: An Indian Declaration of Independence.* New York: Dell Publishing 1974.

Deloria, Vine, Jr. *God Is Red.* New York: Grosset & Dunlap, 1973.

Deloria, Vine, Jr. *Of Utmost Good Faith.* San Francisco: Straight Arrow Books, 1971.

Deloria, Vine, Jr. *We Talk, You Listen: New Tribes, New Turf.* New York: Macmillan, 1970.

Deloria, Vine, Jr. *Custer Died For Your Sins: An Indian Manifesto.* New York: Macmillan, 1969.

Deloria, Vine, Jr. and David E. Wilkins. *Tribes, Treaties, and Constitutional Tribulations.* Austin: University of Texas Press, 1999.

Deloria, Vine, Jr. and Clifford M. Lytle. *The Nations Within: The Past and Future of American Indian Sovereignty.* Norman: University of Oklahoma Press, 1985.

Deloria, Vine, Jr. and Clifford M. Lytle. *American Indians, American Justice.* Austin: University of Texas Press, 1983.

Kirkpatrick, Sidney D. *Edgar Cayce: An American Prophet.* New York: Riverhead Books, 2000.

Linderman, Frank B. *Plenty-Coups, Chief of the Crows.* Lincoln: University of Nebraska Press, 1962 (1957). First published in 1930 under the title: *American: The Life Story of a Great Indian, Plenty-Coups, Chief of the Crows.*

See also: Devils Tower, *Mato Tipi*, or Bears Lodge (Wyoming); Holy Land in Native North America; Indigenous Environmental Network; Law, Religion, and Native American Lands; Manifest Destiny; Sacred Geography in Native North America.

Sacred Geography in Native North America

"Portals to the sacred" is an expression I use to convey belief common among Native Americans that there are specific places that possess great sacredness, and this concept illuminates the ritual functions of sacred sites in Native North America. Such "portals" should not be viewed as limited in size or scale. Some may be large in their geographical extent while others are limited in size. Likewise, use of the portals concept must include the understanding that they are not only positioned in geography but also positioned in time, such that they become sacred "time/spaces." Although the concept of the "sacred" is employed widely in recent discussions of sacred geography, no satisfactory definition of this fundamental idea has been offered.

Basic ethnographic research concerning American Indian concepts of sacred geography is sparse. The recent collection of papers edited by Christopher Vecsey (1991), the *Handbook of American Indian Religious Freedom*, stemmed from this absence of research but must be regarded as only a beginning. Research on this topic is abundant for many cultures of Asia, Europe, the Middle East, and Mesoamerica (e.g., Townsend [1982] and Vogt [1965, 1969]), but with few exceptions (e.g., Harrington's 1908 "The Ethnogeography of the Tewa Indians") is a subject largely undeveloped for most regions in North America and northern Mexico. Based on what published sources are available, the following trends seem most common.

In addition to being vital to ritual practice, sacred geography in Native North America is a source of religious meaning in group identity and group cohesion. Sacred sites in Native North America are invested through ritual with complex layers of religious meaning. Tribal religions in Native America differ from most other world religions in their conceptions of the sacred and in their conceptions of sacred geography.

Definitions of the Sacred

In his *Elementary Forms of the Religious Life*, Durkheim defines the sacred as follows:

> A religion is a unified system of beliefs and practices relative to sacred things, that is to say, things set apart and forbidden beliefs and practices which

unite into one single moral community called a Church, all those who adhere to them (Durkheim 1947: 47).

Fundamental to this definition is the distinction Durkheim draws between the sacred and the profane:

> The opposition of [the sacred and the profane] manifests itself outwardly with a visible sign by which we can easily recognize this very special classification, wherever it exists. Since the idea of the sacred is always and everywhere separated from the idea of the profane in the thought of men, and since we picture a sort of logical chasm between the two, the mind irresistibly refuses to allow the two corresponding things to be confounded, or even to be merely put in contact with each other ... The sacred thing is *par excellence* that which the profane should not touch, and cannot touch with impunity. To be sure, this interdiction cannot go so far as to make all communication between the two worlds impossible; for if the profane could in no way enter into relations with the sacred, this latter could be good for nothing ... The two classes cannot even approach each other and keep their own nature at the same time (Durkheim 1947: 40).

This classic distinction does not fit American Indian conceptions of the sacred in Native North America, because the sacred is not viewed as a domain set aside, distinct, and forbidden as Durkheim suggests. Instead, the sacred is an embedded, intrinsic attribute lying behind the external, empirical aspect of all things, but not a domain set aside or forbidden. The situation is both more complex and more subtle. For example, among the Lakota this embedded, intrinsic attribute is *wakan*; among the Algonkians it is *manitou*; among Ute-Aztecans it is *pu'ha*; among the Sahaptians it is *weyekin*; and among the Salishans *su'mesh*. In this large region, accessing the sacred is a primary goal of ritual and entails actually entering into sacredness rather than merely propitiating it. Whereas certain cultures tend to create their own sacred space and sacred time somewhat arbitrarily by special rituals of sacralization, American Indians of North America more often attempt through ritual, visions, and dreams to discover embedded sacredness in nature and to locate geographical points that permit direct access to it in order to experience it on a personal level. Unlike Durkheim, Eliade's view of hierophanies is somewhat more compatible with American Indian views of sacred geography. Citing Eliade, Carrasco says,

> In Eliade's view, all religions are based on hierophanies or dramatic encounters which human beings have with what they consider to be supernatural forces manifesting themselves in natural objects. These manifestations transform those objects into power spots, power objects, wonderful trees, terrifying bends in the river, sacred animals. The stones, trees, animals, or humans through which a hierophany takes place are considered valuable, full of mana, things to be respected and revered. Human beings who feel these transformations in their landscape believe that a power from another plane of reality has interrupted their lives. Usually, they respond with a combination of great attraction and great fear. Their lives are deeply changed as a result of this encounter with *numinous places* (Carrasco 1979: 203).

Sacred Geography in Native North America: General Features

It is the rule rather than the exception that American Indian ritual life is inextricably linked with access to and ritual use of sacred geography. Traditional American Indian spiritual leaders generally assert that the geographical locations of rituals are vital to their efficacy; unless rituals are performed in their proper times at their proper geographical locations they will have little or no effect. Although there are significant differences among American Indian religions, they generally share the following characteristics central to understanding American Indian sacred geography:

1) A body of mythic accounts explaining cultural origins and cultural history, which depend upon the geographical area. These describe a prehuman or precultural time dominated by heros, tricksters, other mythical figures, and animals indigenous to the area.
2) A special sense of the sacred that is centered in natural time and natural geography.
3) A set of critical and calendrical rituals that give social form and expression to religious belief and permit the groups and their members to experience the events of their mythology in various actual geographical ritual settings.
4) A group of individuals normally described as shamans or priests who teach and lead the group in the conduct of their ritual life.
5) A set of ethical guidelines establishing appropriate behavior associated with ritual and extensions of ritual into ordinary life.
6) Reliance on dreams and visions as the primary means of communicating directly with spirits and the sacred. These and oral tradition are the primary sources of sacred knowledge.
7) For individuals, the major goal of ritual is gaining the spiritual power and understanding necessary for a successful life by engaging the sacred at certain special times and in certain special places.

8) For groups, a belief that harmony must be maintained with the sacred through satisfactory performance of rituals and adherence to sacred prescriptions and proscriptions.
9) A belief that while all aspects of nature and culture are potentially sacred, there are specific places that possess great sacredness, which I term "portals to the sacred."
10) In their religious life, American Indian groups of Native North America are rarely hierarchically organized; nor do they favor the tightly constructed hierarchical mythologies or philosophies developed by priestly elites of either the Old or New World agricultural societies; calendrical reckoning of ritual life is somewhat less important among hunting groups of Native North America.
11) The sacred sites of Native North America are more numerous, more diverse, and less geometrically patterned than is seen among religions of Mesoamerica and the Old World. This reflects the diversity of cultural groups in Native North America who are not often unified into only a few major religious systems of the types found in the Old World and Mesoamerica.
12) Mountains and other points of geographical sacredness are not so often at the center of religious life in Native North America as in the Old World or in Mesoamerica. Nor are mountains identified as frequently with the state, with society, or with the group as in Mesoamerica and the Old World. This probably again reflects the diversity of cultural groups in most of Native North America as well as the general absence of large-scale political and religious systems.
13) Generally, hunting groups in Native North America seek the *intrinsic* or embedded sacredness of nature and do not often force their notions of sacredness onto the land in the manner of the pyramid builders and Earth sculptors we see in both the Old World and Mesoamerica.
14) Ritualists in Native North America are generally shamanic unlike the priestly figures encountered in the more complex religious systems of Mesoamerica and the Old World. Priests are more often identified with large-scale political and religious systems that encompass various cultural groups.
15) Sacred sites are numerous and include the following types (see Walker 1991):

   a) Shrines, vision-quest sites, altars, and sweat-bath sites that serve as ritual settings.
   b) Monumental geographical features that have mythic significance in a group's origins or history. Included are mountains, waterfalls, and unusual geographical formations such as Pilot Knob, Kootenai Falls, Celilo Falls, and Mount Adams.
   c) Rock-art sites such as pictograph and petroglyph panels.
   d) Burial sites and cemeteries.
   e) Areas where plants, stones, Earth, animals, and other sacred objects are gathered for ritual purposes or where sacred vegetation such as medicine trees serve as objects or centers of ritual.
   f) Sites of major historical events such as battlefields where group members died. Sites where groups are thought to have originated, emerged, or been created. Pilgrimage or mythic pathways where groups or individuals retrace the journeys and reenact events described in myths and in the lives of mythic and other figures. Lakes, rivers, springs, and water associated with life and the vital forces that sustain it.
   j) Areas or sites associated with prophets and teachers such as Smohalla, Handsome Lake, Sweet Medicine, and others.

Ethnographic investigation of several hundred sacred sites suggests strongly that they are an essential feature of American Indian ritual practice. Without access to them, practice would be infringed or prevented altogether in certain cases. Likewise, all known groups possess a body of beliefs concerning appropriate times and rituals that must be performed at such sites. The more important a sacred site is in the ritual life of a group, the more numerous symbolic representations it will have in art, music, and myth. It has also become clear in this review that sacred sites also have very diverse functions in that they serve to objectify key cultural symbols, illustrate dominant religious metaphors, and sustain patterns of social, economic, and political organization. Sacred sites can also serve as indicators of cultural unity as seen among the various medicine wheels described by the Arapaho and their neighbors of the Northern and Central High Plains. In general, sacred sites lend concreteness to the less visible systems of linkages within and among different cultural groups. Sacred symbol systems, when superimposed on geography, give to geography a significance and intelligibility similar to relatives such as father, mother, or simply kinsmen. Through ritual, sacred sites function to create a conceptual and emotional parallelism between the objective order of the universe, the realm of the spirits, and the intellectual constructs of American Indian cultures. They are portals between the world of humans and the world of spirits through which sacred power can be attained and spirits contacted. Such sites give order to both geographic and social space, and by thus ordering natural space and time they give order to all that exists.

Sacred sites involving a conjunction of geographical, social, seasonal, and other transitions enhance opportunities to access the sacred. In observing these *conjunctions of multiple transitions*, I have been struck by the parallelism of these ideas with those of Arnold Van Gennep concerning rites of passage (1960) and others who have demonstrated that the rites of passage in the human life cycle are ritually celebrated as times of great sacredness in the life of the individual. From this perspective, the sacred may be more easily experienced as individuals go through life-cycle transitions, especially when such transitions are conjoined with other transitions such as "first game" or "first fruits" rituals that may coincide with additional transitions such as equinoxes and solstices. Similar transitions in the lunar cycle in which the first quarter, second quarter, third quarter, and full moon are seen as paralleling the human life cycle in birth, adolescence, marriage, and death are further transitions in nature that may coincide with transitions in the lives of individuals and communities. In Native North America the conjunction of multiple transitions provides heightened opportunities for accessing the sacred, especially at points of geographical and environmental transition such as mountaintops, waterfalls, cliffs, and other breaks in the landscape.

Conclusion

From this view, therefore, sacred sites and sacred geography among cultures of Native North America function as fundamental ingredients of ritual. Points of geographical transition are joined with multiple transitions in the seasons, the sun, the moon, the life cycle of the individual, and the rhythm of community life to form conjunctions of multiple transitions that become especially powerful access points to the sacred or hierophanies. This view of sacredness and sacred geography stresses the embeddedness of the sacred in all phenomena, distinguishes between the general sacredness of all things and the specific sacredness of access points or portals to the sacred. It also notes the importance of conjunctions of multiple transitions in the individual life cycle, in nature, in community, and in tribal life, and how such multiple transitions help establish the times of greatest sacredness and ritual efficacy of sacred sites. It rejects the Durkheimian view that the sacred is a domain set aside or forbidden, and agrees more with the view of Eliade (1964, 1969, 1972) that the sacred can be accessed and experienced directly through ritual practice at appropriate times and in geographical locations.

Deward Walker

Further Reading

Carrasco, David. "Foreword." In Philip P. Arnold. *Eating Landscape.* Boulder: University Press of Colorado, 1999.

Carrasco, David. "A Perspective for a Study of Religious Dimensions in Chicano Experience: *Bless Me Ultima* as a Religious Text." Paper presented to the Chicano Studies Colloquium at the University of California, Santa Barbara, 12 April 1979.

Durkheim, Emile. *The Elementary Forms of the Religious Life.* Glencoe, IL: The Free Press, 1947.

Eliade, Mircea. *Patterns in Comparative Religion.* New York: Meridian Books, 1972.

Eliade, Mircea. *The Quest.* Chicago: University of Chicago Press, 1969.

Eliade, Mircea. *Shamanism: Archaic Techniques of Ecstasy.* New York: Bollingen Foundation, 1964.

Harrington, John Peabody. "The Ethnogeography of the Tewa Indians," in *Twenty-ninth Annual Report of the Bureau of American Ethnology, 1907–1908.* Washington, D.C.: U.S. Government Printing Office, 1908.

Townsend, Richard F. "Pyramid and Sacred Mountain." In Anthony F. Aveni and Gary Urton, eds. *Ethnoastronomy and Archaeoastronomy in the American Tropics.* New York: New York Academy of Sciences, 1982.

Van Gennep, Arnold. *The Rites of Passage.* London: Routledge & Kegan Paul, 1960.

Vecsey, Christopher. *Handbook of American Indian Religious Freedom.* New York: The Crossroads Publishing Co., 1991.

Vogt, Evon Z. *Zinacantan: A Maya Community in the Highlands of Chiapas.* Cambridge, MA: Harvard University Press, 1969.

Vogt, Evon Z. "Structural and Conceptual Replication in Zinacantan Culture." *American Anthropologist* LXVII (1965), 342–53.

Walker, Deward E., Jr. "Protection of American Indian Sacred Geography." In Christopher Vecsey, ed. *Handbook of American Indian Religious Freedom.* New York: The Crossroads Publishing Co., 1991.

See also: Eliade, Mircea; Holy Land in Native North America; Indigenous Environmental Network; Landscapes; The Sacred and the Modern World; Sacred Mountains; Sacred Space/Place.

Sacred Groves of Africa

Sacred groves, which may be forest patches, clusters of trees and even individual trees, are recognized by many African ethnic groups; this recognition often implies that "the community has established a covenant with deities or other sacred entities to refrain from certain uses of the environment" (Lebbie and Freudenberger 1996: 303). Any attempt to do more than list well-known examples of sacred groves, for example, by providing a classification of these sites according to various criteria, runs into many problems. By their very nature, sacred groves are objects of fear and respect, about which people are reluctant to share information with outsiders. In the early years of colonial rule knowledgeable local community members hid much arcane information from colonial officers and missionaries; more recently, many elements of traditional belief systems have been lost, so published sources, of whatever date, are likely to have incomplete information. Even in the post-colonial era, traditional custodians of the groves may deny outsiders the right to enter, as two Nigerian scholars, Okafor and Ladipo, discovered in 1992 when they carried out a study of fetish groves in southern Nigeria. Attempts to analyze unwritten and evolving belief systems also have to cope with the perception that the sacred essence of the groves may be based on several properties, and that some of the groves have multiple functions.

Lebbie and Freudenberger (1996), Michaloud and Dury (1998) and Laird (1999) provide useful short overviews on the significance and function of sacred groves, and readers interested in sacred groves in Africa would also do well to pay attention to some of the extensive literature on Asia. Unlike in Asia, sacred groves in Africa are not typically the site of an actual temple structure; an exception is the sacred grove at Oshogbo (Nigeria), which has over recent decades been the site of considerable architectural and sculptural development, much of it inspired by Suzanne Wenger, a Yoruba priestess of Austrian origin. In Africa, sacred groves may be revered as the residence of a deity, as is the grove of the goddess Numafoa in the Nanhini area of southern Ghana. Another grove particular to a deity is the Pinkwae grove in central Ghana, home of the Afiye god whose powers enabled the Katamanso people to defeat the Ashantis in battle. In Anloga, southern Ghana, the Nyiko grove held the shrine to Nyigbla, the Anlo's war god.

Groves may also be revered as the home of ancestors or other benevolent or malevolent spirits. Rituals in the *kaya* forests of coastal Kenya begin with the erection of small grass houses for the spirits, known as *vitsimbakazi* in the local Mijikenda languages. The Kikuyu believed that trees possessed spirits capable of interfering in human affairs, and when clearing land, people had to leave a large and conspicuous tree at intervals to absorb the spirits from the trees that had been cut down. This tree was not supposed to be cut or allowed to fall without a ceremony transferring the spirits to another tree.

Some groves are burial sites of certain ancestors or revered elders; Kaya Kinondo in Kwale District contains the grave of Nkomboza, a distinguished female rainmaker and clan ancestress. In North Pare, Tanzania, many clans keep their ancestors' skulls in sacred forests, which are also believed to cause rain. In Benin there are graveyard forests where people who have died from accidents or infectious diseases are buried, while in Moyamba District of Sierra Leone there are forests where fetuses removed from the bodies of women who died while pregnant are buried. These forests are controlled by women and their flora and fauna are considered abominable, never to be harvested, particularly by men.

Sacred groves may be located at particular sites, such as mountaintops or ridges (for example among the Kikuyu of central Kenya, as described by Castro and other authors) or along and around bodies of water which themselves may also be sacred. To the west of Anloga in southern Ghana lies the Blolui pond, the home of a powerful goddess, which was formerly surrounded by a thick, dark grove. In such cases the presence of a sacred grove affords protection to the natural vegetation in environmentally sensitive areas such as steep slopes and river banks, contributing to soil and water conservation and reducing the risk of environmental degradation.

While some sacred groves are set apart from human settlements, they can also be located within or close to villages. Trowell and Wachsmann describe Karamoja and Teso villages in northern and eastern Uganda as having an "*Abila*, or central tree, round which are little shrines and stones for sacrificing to the gods and where the hunter places his spears in preparation for the hunt" (1953: 78). In the Oromo region of Ethiopia trees such as *Euphorbia candelabrum* are planted around churches and on graves because "it is believed that trees on a grave look like the flesh of the dead person and serve as statues" (Kelbessa 2001: 44). Every living Oromo has their own *dakkii* tree, which is a symbol of peace and stability, the abode of spirits, and a link between *waaqa* (God) and the individual. In some areas, fences are built around these trees, which may be of a variety of species.

Historic or prehistoric events may explain the sacred nature of certain groves, for example, stories of community origin. The Mijikenda believe that their ancestors originated from a northern homeland and migrated southwards several centuries ago to the areas they presently occupy. Threatened by aggressive enemies, they made their first homes in heavily fortified villages, surrounded by thick forest. Their security was further ensured by the presence of *fingo*, sacred objects essential to community well-being that were buried in the forest. The Mijikenda moved out from these villages as their population increased and security improved, and today the former settlement sites have been reclaimed by forest, but the respect for the groves as the historical homes of each of the nine Mijikenda communities remains. The Asantemanso sacred grove in central Ghana is believed to contain the cave from which the seven clans of the Ashanti tribe originated. Mbewe ya Mitengo in the Lower Shire Valley of southern Malawi is a sacred grove that is said to have been the capital of the Lundu state in the early seventeenth century, and is still used for sacrifices today. Most of the sacred forests in Mpigi (central Uganda) are historical sites, such as the former site of the home of an important leader, the burial site of an important clan member, or the site where an ancient leader had planted a tree. Sacred groves may be former battlegrounds, such as the Pinkwae grove in central Ghana, the site of a battle between the people of Katamanso and the Ashantis in 1826; the spirits of those who died in the battle are believed to dwell there, as well as the Afiye god.

In many pre-colonial African societies, sacred groves had political and economic importance. Among the Kikuyu, the *ituika* ceremonies that marked the handing over of ritual power from one generation to the next were held in the sacred groves. Sacred groves may serve as monuments to the legitimate land tenure of the communities that surround them. Communities make both socio-cultural and material use of sacred groves. Some ethnic groups hold initiation rites for young men and/or women in the groves, which are convenient sites for the periods of seclusion that many such rites involve. The groves may be the meeting places for secret or semi-secret societies, which are responsible for controlling access to the grove and use of its natural resources. The Mende people of Moyamba District, Sierra Leone, have separate groves for the men's (*poro*) and women's (*sande*) secret societies. In some places regular community rituals and celebrations are held in the groves, while elsewhere rituals are only held when particular needs arise, for example, when there is a risk of drought, disease or war. The Mijikenda believe that if appropriate rituals are held in the kaya forests, involving sacrifices, eating of ceremonial food, drumming, dancing and prayers by the kaya elders, rain is sure to follow within a few hours. Rituals may be open to all community members, or restricted by age, gender, ethnicity, menstrual status or other criteria. However, not all members of a kin, ethnic or community-based social group may recognize the sacredness of a particular grove, and certainly neighboring groups may not recognize them as such.

People may visit sacred groves on their own or to consult with healers or spiritual leaders when faced with individual or family problems. In central Kenya women might rub the sap of sacred fig trees on themselves, to increase their chances of having children. At the sacred grove of Edinkra, the goddess of Nkoranza in Ghana, offerings are placed on the roots of a particular large tree and a man may tie a string round the trunk of the tree to remind the goddess to "bear him upon her back as a mother does her child" (Kyeremeh 1996: 3). In July 2001, offerings to the royal ancestors at Mbewe ya Mitengo were made in response to the serious illness of one of the local leaders.

Use of the material resources of a sacred grove may be totally forbidden, as in the sacred groves of central Kenya. Similarly, in northern Ghana,

> The cutting of trees in the sacred grove for any purpose is strictly prohibited except in rare cases whereby prior permission may be sought from the custodians to cut parts of trees for medicinal and other specific purposes. Also the gathering and use of even dry wood from the groves for fuelwood is a taboo (Telly 1998: 2).

No plant material can be collected from the Nkodurom sacred grove in central Ghana, nor can people hunt in the grove. In other cases there is a partial ban, which allows sustainable use of timber, non-timber forest products, wildlife and water resources. Mukamuri describes how the local chiefs responsible for the *rambotemwa* ("refuse to cut") sacred woodlands of the Karanga people of southern and central Zimbabwe made sure that the trees were not cut, but women were allowed to collect deadwood and some hunting was allowed. In coastal Kenya traditional healers, including women, collect medicinal herbs from the kaya forests, though there are particularly sacred areas within these forests, which even they would not normally approach. Some Mijikenda also claim that in the past women were allowed to collect dead wood from the kaya forests for domestic use. As with participation in rituals, entry to the grove to extract resources may be restricted to certain groups, or limited according to a daily, weekly, monthly or seasonal schedule. At Nkodurom nobody is allowed to enter on a Thursday, which is believed to be the day of rest of the original fetish priest of the grove. Visits to Kaya Kinondo are not permitted by the elders during two days at the new moon, on the fourth day ("chipalata") of the Mijikenda four-day week, or early in the morning and after 5 p.m., when the gods and spirits are resting.

Certain plant species may have sacred status, whether or not they are growing in a sacred grove. Falconer names two trees *Okoubaka aubrevillei*, *Chlorophora (Milicia) excelsa* and a liana (*Spiropetalum heterophyllum*) as sacred to many communities in her study area in southern Ghana. In Buganda, central Uganda, individual trees are said to have the ability to prophesy, including one called *Kaindu*, and a forest called *Nakalanga*. Among the Banyoro, also of central Uganda, a sacred tree called *kirikiti* is used to make drums played at the royal court. Among the Kikuyu of central Kenya, the *mugumo* tree (*Ficus natalensis*) is the most significant sacred tree, though other species of *Ficus* may also be sacred. According to Castro "A single tree within a grove often formed the focal point of ceremonies" (1990: 279), but he goes on to say "not every fig tree was sacred, nor were figs always found in the groves." The Shona of Zimbabwe recognize several species of sacred trees; individual ancestral spirits are believed to dwell in large specimens of *Parinari curatellifolia*, which is also used for rainmaking festivals. Another example from Zimbabwe is *Gardenia spatulifolia*, which protects against witchcraft and lightning, and a tree called *muminu* whose removal from a field is said to precipitate fighting between spouses or during a beer and work party. In parts of South Africa, the *marula* (*Sclerocarya birrea*) has sacred status, but also material value, in that its fruits may be stored or made into beer. The Oromo recognize *bokkuu* or scepter trees, under which officials of the traditional courts sit. No branches may be cut from them, and it is not even permitted to collect dry animal dung from around these trees.

However wood can be cut from these trees for roasting meat during certain rituals.

Sanctions on those who break the regulations on entry or use of the grove's resources range from social (often involving payment of a fine to the elders responsible for the grove) to supernatural. Since some groves are seen as repositories of community fertility and power, transgression can lead to disaster for a whole community as well as for individuals. Mijikenda men and women interviewed around Kaya Chonyi, Kilifi District in January 2002 warned that destruction of the kaya would lead to crop failure, disease and poverty. Among the Oromo, it is believed that people who cut the *bokkuu* trees illegally will die soon. Around the sacred groves in northern Ghana, "It is believed that food cooked with firewood from a sacred grove could result in the death of those who eat the food" (Telly 1998: 2). People who enter prohibited forested areas of Mount Mulanje in Malawi are believed to disappear completely, or return after a month or two deaf and dumb. The Karanga of Zimbabwe believe that lion spirits chase people who flout the taboos of the *rambotemwa* sacred woodlands. In Kirinyaga a person who encroaches on a sacred grove has to pay a goat to the elders. People who intrude into the Nkodurom sacred grove are arrested by the traditional guards and sent to the local chief for the imposition of a fine that will pacify the gods and spirits; this may include a cash fine, several bottles of alcohol, and a sheep to be sacrificed. Offending individuals or families may also be subject to social sanctions such as isolation from community members or, as a last resort, curses imposed by particular elders.

The current status of sacred groves varies widely across Africa and even within one country or ethnic group. Groves were powerful metaphors of social, moral and ecological order, and their rituals affirmed orderly meanings of social and ecological interaction. The impact of new belief systems, in particular Islam and Christianity, has been instrumental in weakening the indigenous belief systems that protected sacred groves, and contributing to the chaos of rapid social, political and ecological change in colonial and post-colonial Africa. Greene quotes the German missionary Carl Spiess as rejoicing over school children's apparent loss of respect for a fallen sacred tree, the "Tree of God" in the Anlo region of southern Ghana, in 1927. A comparable event occurred in northern Kenya in January 2002, when a minister of the Assemblies of God church in Laikipia District led his followers in cutting down and burning a sacred fig tree. The tree, locally called *oroteti*, had been the site of offerings and prayers by local elders during recent severe drought years. When the minister refused to make the required payment of a goat and local beer for the elders to cleanse him, they cursed him through traditional chants and threatened to kill him.

In the town of Anloga, the original site of the Nyiko grove is now a police station, erected by the colonial government; the shrine was moved to the outskirts of the town but the trees at the new location were cut down in the early 1960s in order to build a secondary school. Kaya Fungo, the sacred grove of the Giriama sub-group of the Mijikenda of Kenya, was destroyed by British colonial forces on 4 August 1914 in response to Giriama resistance to colonial policies such as taxation and labor recruitment. As vividly described by Brantley,

> The elders watched silently as the main trees and gates were blown up, all the dwellings and trees inside the kaya burned, and the entrance dynamited and barricaded. Next day, it was reported, they went away quietly to their homes. British officials thought the matter was closed ... But despite the outward calm, anger was simmering (1981: 111).

Hostilities escalated, culminating in a one-month military campaign during which the British forces burned at least 5000 houses and killed over 150 Giriama. Kaya Fungo was reopened in 1918 and regained some, although not all, of its traditional power. In recent decades destruction of the kaya forests has been harder to resist, occurring incrementally as the result of pressure for land for settlement and farming and the increasing demand for timber and firewood (Nyamweru 1996). Younger people have moved away from the indigenous belief systems and, driven by joblessness and poverty, are less likely to resist such destruction and may even participate actively in it. However, there have been numerous occasions, quite well documented in the Kenyan press, where elders have, sometimes successfully, resisted attempts to take over the groves and convert them to private property for commercial development. Newspaper stories headed "Elders protest destruction of shrines" (*Daily Nation*, 9 July 1992), "Elders threaten to curse government" (*Daily Nation*, 14 April 1994), "Elders urge Govt to preserve sacred land" (*Daily Nation*, 1 August 1997), and "A sacrifice to thank the gods" (*Daily Nation*, 4 July 2001), testify to the continued activity of some elders' groups and the position of these sacred groves as highly contested resources, as well as to the interest of the Kenyan media in this issue.

Other groves are still largely intact, where pressures are less intense and the traditional belief systems continue to discourage people from entering the groves for destructive purposes. Even though population pressure and competition for land has caused the destruction or drastic reduction of many sacred groves in Kirinyaga, "respect for tradition has caused many landowners, including devout Christians, to preserve some groves" (Castro 1990: 286), and many of the groves referred to in earlier paragraphs are still in existence. In some areas where they survive, sacred groves and the belief systems that sustain them have become the focus of attention, and sometimes material support, from national and international conservation organizations such as the Environmental Protection Agency of Ghana, the National Museums of Kenya, the World Wide Fund for Nature (WWF) and UNESCO. The continued survival of the groves demonstrates the contribution of local management and indigenous knowledge systems to environmental conservation. Examples of successful collaboration between local communities and international agencies include CIPSEG (Co-operative Integrated Project on Savannah Ecosystems in Ghana) which ran from 1992 to 1996, focusing on three sacred groves in Northern Ghana (Schaaf 1998: 146), and CFCU (Coastal Forest Conservation Unit), which began in 1992, located in coastal Kenya and working to conserve the kaya forests (Nyamweru 1996: 20). Optimal strategies for collaborating with local communities to ensure the survival of these culturally and environmentally important sites are still being worked out, though differences of interests between various groups of local, national, and international stake-holders makes this a complex and challenging project. Volumes such as those edited by Ramakrishnan et al. (1998) and Posey (1999) provide an excellent introduction to this dynamic field of debate.

Celia Nyamweru

Further Reading

Beech, Mervyn W.H. "A Ceremony of the Mugumu or Sacred Fig-Tree of the A'kikuyu of East Africa." *Man* 13 (1913), 86–9.

Brantley, Cynthia. *The Giriama and Colonial Resistance in Kenya, 1800–1920*. Berkeley: University of California Press, 1981.

Castro, Alfonso P. *Facing Kirinyaga: A Social History of Forest Commons in Southern Mount Kenya*. London: Intermediate Technology Publications, 1995.

Castro, Alfonso P. "Indigenous Kikuyu Agroforestry: A Case Study of Kirinyaga, Kenya." *Human Ecology* 19:1 (1991), 1–18.

Castro, Peter. "Sacred Groves and Social Change in Kirinyaga, Kenya." In Miriam Chaiken and Anne Fleuret, eds. *Social Change and Applied Anthropology*. Boulder; Westview Press, 1990.

Cousins, Ben. "Invisible Capital: The Contribution of Communal Rangelands to Rural Livelihoods in South Africa." Paper for Symposium on Communal Rangelands, Fort Hare University, South Africa, July 1998.

Daily Nation. "Priest Seeks Police Help Over Sacred Tree Threat." Nairobi, 7 January 2002.

Gombya Sembajwe, William S. "Sacred Forests in Modern Ganda Society." *Uganda Journal* 42 (December 1995) 32–44.

Gonese, Cosmas. "Philosophy & Experiences of AZTREC; Enhancing African Indigenous Cosmovision & Cultural Knowledge in Biodiversity Management." In Xu Jianchu, ed. *Links Between Cultures and Biodiversity*. Yunnan: Yunnan Science and Technology Press, 2000.

Greene, Sandra E. *Sacred Sites and the Colonial Encounter*. Bloomington: Indiana University Press, 2002.

Hobley, Charles W. *Bantu Beliefs and Magic*. London: Frank Cass, 1967 (1st edn 1922).

Kagwa, Apolo. *The Customs of the Baganda*. Ernest B. Kalibala, tr. May Mandlebaum (Edel), ed. New York: Columbia University Press, 1934.

Kelbessa, Workineh. "Traditional Oromo Attitudes Towards the Environment." Social Science Research Report Series 19. Addis Ababa: Organization for Social Science Research in Eastern Africa, 2001.

Kimaru, Elias. "Community Eco-tourism: A Feasibility Study and General Guidelines for Kaya Kinondo Sacred Forest in Kwale District." Ukunda, Kenya: unpublished project proposal, Coastal Forest Conservation Unit, April 2000.

Kyeremeh, Samuel. "The Preservation of Sacred Groves in Ghana: Its Socio-cultural Implications." Talk given in Cape Coast, Ghana, 30 August 1996.

Laird, Sarah. "Forests, Culture and Conservation." In Darrell A. Posey, ed. *Cultural and Spiritual Values of Biodiversity*. London: Intermediate Technology Publications for United Nations Environment Programme, 1999.

Leakey, Louis S.B. *The Southern Kikuyu before 1903*. New York: Academic Press, 1977 (vol. 3).

Lebbie, Aiah R. and Mark S. Freudenberger. "Sacred Groves in Africa; Forest Patches in Transition." In John Schelhas and Russell Greenberg, eds. *Forest Patches in Tropical Landscapes*. Washington, D.C.: Island Press, 1996.

Michaloud, Georges and Sandrine Dury. "Sacred Trees, Groves, Landscapes and Related Cultural Situations May Contribute to Conservation and Management in Africa." In Palayanoor S. Ramakrishnan, Krishna G. Saxena and Uchangi M. Handrashekara, eds. *Conserving the Sacred for Biodiversity Management*. Enfield, NH: Science Publishers, 1998, chapter 9, 129–43.

Mukamuri, Billy B. "Local Environmental Conservation Strategies: Karanga Religion, Politics and Environmental Control." *Environment and History* 1 (1995), 297–311.

Nsiah-Gyabaah, Kwasi and William Oduro. "Creating Green Awareness through Traditional Conservation Practice; The Role of Indigenous Technical Knowledge (ITK) in Protecting Sacred Groves in Ghana." Paper presented at the WAPLEC meeting, University of Ghana, Legon, 2 May 1997.

Ntiamoa-Baidu, Yaa. "Indigenous vs. Introduced Biodiversity Conservation Strategies: The Case of Protected Area Systems in Ghana." *African Biodiversity Series*, 1. Washington, D.C.: World Wildlife Fund, May 1995.

Nyamweru, Celia K. "Sacred Groves Threatened by Development; The Kaya Forests of Kenya." *Cultural Survival Quarterly* (Fall 1996), 19–21.

Okafor, Jonathan C. and Duro O. Ladipo. "Fetish Groves in the Conservation of Threatened Flora in Southern Nigeria." In Leon A. Bennun, Rashid A. Aman and Sally A. Crafter, eds. *Conservation of Biodiversity in Africa*. Nairobi: National Museums of Kenya, 1995.

Posey, Darrell A., ed. *Cultural and Spiritual Values of Biodiversity*. London: Intermediate Technology Publications for United Nations Environment Programme, 1999.

Ramakrishnan, Palayanoor S., Krishna G. Saxena and Uchangi M. Chandrashekara, eds. *Conserving the Sacred for Biodiversity Management*. Enfield, NH: Science Publishers, 1998.

Roscoe, John. *The Bakitara or Banyoro*. Cambridge: Cambridge University Press, 1923.

Schaaf, Thomas. "Sacred Groves in Ghana: Experiences from an Integrated Study Project." In Palayanoor S. Ramakrishnan, Krishna G. Saxena and Uchangi M. Chandrashekara, eds., *Conserving the Sacred for Biodiversity Management*. Enfield, NH: Science Publishers, 1998, chapter 10, 145–50.

Sheridan, Michael J. *The Sacred Forests of North Pare, Tanzania: Indigenous Conservation, Local Politics, and Land Tenure*. Boston University African Studies Center, Working Paper No. 224, 2000.

Spear, Thomas T. *The Kaya Complex*. Nairobi: Kenya Literature Bureau, 1978.

Telly, Edward M. "Tradition and Bio-diversity Conservation: The Case for Sacred Groves in the Northern Region [of Ghana]." Paper delivered at the International Symposium on Natural Sacred Sites, held at UNESCO, Paris, September 1998.

Trowell, Margaret and Klaus P. Wachsmann. *Tribal Crafts of Uganda*. London: Oxford University Press, 1953.

Welling, Menno. "Integrating Narratives of the Past; Challenges of Interdisciplinary Research and the Case of the Maravi States of East-Central Africa, c. 1500–1850 AD." Paper presented at the African Studies Association 44th Conference, Houston, November 2001.

Wilson, Kenneth B. "Trees in Fields in Southern Zimbabwe." *Journal of Southern African Studies* 15 (1989), 369–83.

See also: India's Sacred Groves; Rainforests (Central and South America); Trees – Sacred; Wenger, Susan, Yoruba Art and the Oshogbo Sacred Grove.

Sacred Mountains

As the highest and most impressive features of the landscape, mountains have an extraordinary power to evoke a sense of the sacred. Their imposing peaks, the clouds that gather about their summits, the dramatic play of light on their slopes, the waters that issue from hidden springs, these and other characteristics combine to imbue them with an aura of mystery and sanctity. In that mystery and sanctity, people of diverse backgrounds, both traditional and modern, experience a sense of a deeper reality that gives meaning and vitality to their lives.

As sacred expressions of a deeper reality – however that may be construed – mountains have become associated with the deepest and most central values and beliefs of cultures and traditions throughout the world. Mount Sinai occupies a special place in the Bible as the imposing site where Moses received the Torah and the Ten Commandments, the basis of law and ethics for much of Western civilization. The remote Himalayan peak of Mount Kailas, rising aloof above the Tibetan Plateau directs the minds of millions of Hindus and Buddhists toward the utmost attainments of their spiritual traditions. The Hopi of the American Southwest revere the San Francisco Peaks of Arizona as the abode of the katsinas, ancestral rain deities on whom they depend for their very existence.

The sacredness of mountains manifests itself in three general ways. First, certain peaks are singled out by particular cultures and traditions as places of special sanctity directly linked to their deepest values and aspirations. These mountains – the ones traditionally known as "sacred mountains" – have well-established networks of myths, beliefs, and religious practices such as pilgrimage, meditation, and sacrifice. Primary examples would be Mount Kailas in Tibet and the San Francisco Peaks in Arizona.

Second, mountains that may or may not be revered in themselves are frequently associated with sacred persons or contain sacred sites and objects such as temples, monasteries, hermitages, stones, springs, and groves. Great numbers of people, for example, visit pilgrimage shrines located in mountainous regions, such as the Hindu shrine of Badrinath in the Indian Himalaya or the mountain monastery of Montserrat in Spain. Singling out this role of mountains, a passage in the *Mahabharata*, the religious epic of ancient India, describes a Himalayan peak as a "refuge of hermits, treasury of sacred places" (*Mahabharata* 3.43.21–25).

Third, mountains in general commonly awaken in individuals a sense of wonder and awe that sets them apart as places imbued with evocative beauty and meaning, frequently spiritual in nature. Many tourists, hikers, and climbers today go to the Alps in Europe or the Sierra Nevada in California for aesthetic and spiritual inspiration and renewal, often regarding them as expressions of important cultural values enshrined in works of literature and art. Such peaks function for them as personal sacred mountains.

People of different cultures generally experience the sacredness of mountains through the particular views they have of them, such as the mountain as center of the universe or source of life. These views or themes differentiate the experience of the sacred and provide a framework for exploring the many different ways in which mountains function as sacred places in diverse cultures and traditions around the world. We will examine here ten of the most important and widespread of these themes.

Height
Many people revere mountains as high places. As the highest mountain on Earth, Mount Everest has assumed the status of a sacred mountain in the modern world. Its summit symbolizes for many the highest goal one can strive to attain, whether one's pursuit be material or spiritual. Because of its importance in the West as the ultimate high place, the Tibetan name of Mount Everest, Jomolangma, is almost always mistranslated in Western literature as "Goddess Mother of the World." Foreigners assume that for the Tibetans and Sherpas the highest mountain must be the home of a supremely important deity. In fact, Jomolangma is short for Jomomiyolangsangma, the name of the Tibetan goddess of Mount Everest, one of the Five Sisters of Long Life and a relatively minor deity, invoked for worldly benefits, such as longevity, food, and wealth.

Center
An extremely important and widespread theme is that of the mountain as center – of the cosmos, the world, or a local region. A number of Asian mountains, such as Mount Kailas in Tibet and Gunung Agung in Bali, are patterned on the mythical Mount Meru or Sumeru, which stands as a cosmic axis around which the universe is organized in Hindu and Buddhist cosmology. Meru itself is said to rise from the depths of hell to the heights of heaven.

Many mountains in East Asia, Japan in particular, are viewed as centers of *mandalas* – circular spaces and arrangements of deities used in Buddhist meditation. Some, such as Mounts Koya and Omine, are treated as *mandalas* themselves, their peaks, trees, and other natural features regarded as parts of a sacred circle representing the divine space of a visualized deity with whom a meditator identifies himself or herself.

In North America the highest peak of the Black Hills, known to the Lakota as Paha Sapa, appears as the center of the world in vision quests by religious leaders such as Black Elk. Delphi on the slopes of Mount Parnassus played a central role as the site of the Omphalos or navel of the ancient Greek world.

Power
Many sacred mountains, including those viewed as centers, are places of awe-inspiring, often dangerous, power. The way to the awesome summit of Mount Olympus was blocked by doors of clouds and darkness controlled by the Horae, goddesses of time entrusted with protecting the sacred mountain. Maori warriors crossing the plateau beneath Mount Tongariro in New Zealand used to avert their eyes from its summit for fear of provoking a blinding snowstorm.

The power of mountains can assume various forms. The five principal sacred mountains of China enshrined the political authority of the emperor to rule over the four quarters of his empire, supported by the mandate of Heaven. The earliest annals of Chinese history say that the legendary first emperors of China performed sacrifices on a mountain in each quarter of the empire in order to establish their sovereignty over the princes of the real. Frequent storms made the jagged peaks of Olympus a dramatic setting for vividly displaying the power of Zeus, king of the gods and deity of thunder and lightning. The molten lava of Kilauea in Hawai'i embodies for many Hawaiians today the fiery energy, both destructive and creative, of the volcano goddess Pele.

Deity or Abode of Deity
In many traditions the power of mountains derives from the presence of deities. A poem from the earliest collection of Japanese poetry refers to Mount Fuji as "a god mysterious." In other traditions, a mountain may be regarded as the seat of a divine power. Traditional Kikuyu of Kenya revere Mount Kenya or Kere-Nyaga as the resting place in this world of Ngai or God. Dry paintings used by Navajo singers in healing rituals will sometimes depict the four sacred mountains of the Navajo in the form of hogans, traditional homes of the Navajo people.

As deities or abodes of deities, mountains frequently play important roles as divine guardians or protectors. People invoke their power to protect livestock, crops, religion, the local community or even the state. Like the gods of many other peaks in Tibet and Himalayan border areas, the "country" god of Mount Khumbhila is revered as a warrior deity who watches over the Sherpa region of Khumbu, warding off the forces of evil. Herds of yaks, goats, and sheep fall under his protection. In the Andes, mountain gods are considered protectors of llamas and alpacas as well as wild vicuñas.

Temple or Place of Worship
Deities are frequently associated with the widespread view of the mountain as a temple or place of worship. Members of many traditional societies revere sacred peaks as temples in which their deities reside. Tibetan Buddhists, for example, view Mount Kailas as the pagoda palace of Demchog, the One of Supreme Bliss, a tantric deity embodying the ultimate Buddhist goal of enlightenment. Many temples in India are modeled on the idealized form of the sacred peak and bear the name of Kailasanatha, Lord of Kailas – a reference to Shiva, the Hindu form of the supreme deity who dwells on the mountain.

Mountains may also take the form of places of worship, viewed or imagined as altars, shrines, churches, and cathedrals. Here a deity does not necessarily reside in or on the peak, but rather the mountain provides a special setting for making contact with a divine presence through prayer, ritual, or contemplation. Just as Christians revere churches as sacred places of worship but do not regard them as objects of worship in themselves, so the same applies to mountains for many followers of monotheistic religions.

The view of mountains as places of worship plays an important role even in modern secular societies and is reflected in the names of numerous groves, valleys and peaks. John Muir, the founder of the Sierra Club and a key figure in the genesis of the modern-day environmental movement, wrote of Cathedral Peak in the Sierra Nevada of California that he would climb it "to say my prayers and hear the stone sermons."

Paradise or Garden

Modern societies also share with traditional cultures the view of mountains as gardens and paradises. The Muslim Kirghiz of western China, for example, believe that the snows on the summit of Muztagh Ata, one of the highest peaks in the Pamir, conceal an earthly paradise that goes back to the time of the Garden of Eden. The Buddhist Dai people of southwestern China regard the flora of their Holy Hills as the gardens of the gods. Mount Athos, a mountainous peninsula in northern Greece that serves as the monastic center of Orthodox Christianity, is known as the "Garden of the Mother of God" – a reference to the role of the Virgin Mary as the patron saint of the holy mountain.

Many in the modern world view the untrammeled environment of mountains as a pristine paradise that preserves the purity of creation. Mountain meadows and wildflowers tend to evoke such views: one of the most popular destinations for visitors in Mount Rainier National Park in the United States, for example, is Paradise, a flowering meadow close to the glaciers.

Ancestors and the Dead

A major theme frequently linked to conceptions of paradise as the otherworld is the view of mountains as divine ancestors and places of the dead, often involved in origin myths. Traditional Chinese beliefs hold that the spirits of the dead go to the foot of Tai Shan. Mount Koya, the center of Shingon Buddhism, has one of the most impressive graveyards in Japan. East Africans traditionally bury their dead facing sacred peaks like Kilimanjaro and Mount Kenya.

Many peaks in New Zealand, including Aoraki, or Mount Cook, are revered as the frozen ancestors of the Maori who came to the islands in legendary canoes. According to the origin myth of the Korean people, they are descended from the union of a sky god and a bear woman on the sacred mountain of Paekdu. The natural features of Uluru, or Ayers Rock, in Australia record the formative activities of the Dreamtime Ancestors of the Pitjantjara and Yankunjatjara tribes.

Identity

As divine ancestors and places of origin, mountains provide many societies with their sense of communal identity and cohesiveness. In the Bolivian Andes, the metaphor of Mount Kaata as a human body unites the various communities who live on its slopes into an organic unit that has been able to resist all efforts to break it apart into smaller administrative subdivisions.

At intra-tribal gatherings, Maori ritually identify themselves by first stating their tribal mountain, followed by their river, or lake, and then their chief. One clan of the Yakutat Tlingit has Mount St. Elias, or Washetaca, the second highest peak in Alaska, as its crest or totem. The Armenian people regard Mount Ararat, a volcano in eastern Turkey believed to be the site of Noah's ark in the Bible, as the symbol of their national and cultural identity.

Source

People throughout the world look up to mountains as sources of blessings – most notably, water, life, fertility, healing, and general well-being. Mountains such as Ausangate in Peru, Tlaloc in Mexico, the Himalayan Range, and the San Francisco Peaks in Arizona are revered as abodes of weather deities, places of springs, and sacred sources of rivers and rain-clouds on which societies depend for their very existence.

Sacred mountains also provide the blessings of fertility and healing. Today, great numbers of elderly women climb Tai Shan to make offerings to have grandchildren if their daughters or daughters-in-law have been infertile. Female shamans in Japan and Korea routinely climb sacred mountains to charge themselves with healing powers and conduct rituals for their patients. Traditional singers or medicine men go to the four sacred mountains of the Navajo in the southwestern United States to collect medicinal herbs and pebbles; they also invoke these mountains in rituals and sand paintings intended to restore a sick person to health and harmony. In Europe and North America, there is a tradition of putting sanatoriums, particularly for tuberculosis, on mountains, based on the idea that the mountain air and environment have special curative properties.

Much of the modern appreciation of mountains derives from the perception of them as sources of spiritual and physical well-being. Jean-Jacques Rousseau, the French philosopher who played a major role in transforming European attitudes toward the Alps in the eighteenth century, wrote:

In effect, it is a general impression experienced by

all men, even though they do not all observe it, that on high mountains, where the air is pure and subtle, one feels greater ease in breathing, more lightness in the body, greater serenity in the spirit (Rousseau 1976: 45).

A century later John Muir exhorted Americans to:

> Climb the mountains and get their good tidings. Nature's peace will flow into you as sunshine flows into trees. The winds will blow their own freshness into you, and the storms their energy, while cares will drop off like autumn leaves (Muir 1901: 56).

Revelation, Transformation, Inspiration, and Renewal

The final theme to consider is that of the mountain as place of revelation, transformation, inspiration, and renewal. Mount Sinai plays a prominent role in the Old Testament as the imposing site where God reveals the Torah and the Ten Commandments to Moses. In the New Testament, Jesus is transfigured on a mountain and revealed there as the Son of God. Muhammad received his first revelation of the Qur'an in a cave on Mount Hira.

In China and Japan mountains are regarded as such ideal places for meditation and spiritual transformation that the Chinese expression for embarking on the practice of religion means literally "to enter the mountains." Hua Shan, the most spectacular of the five principal sacred peaks of China, was a favorite haunt of Daoist hermits intent on transforming themselves into immortals. North American Plains Indians, such as the Lakota and the Crow, seek out high places for vision quests that give them spiritual power and determine the course of their lives.

The mountain monasteries and hermitages of Mount Athos in Greece have the primary function of providing an environment conducive to pursuing the Orthodox path of spiritual purification and illumination. The monk or hermit who follows this path to its goal is transformed, in the words of Saint Symeon, the New Theologian, into: "... one who is pure and free of the world / and converses continually with God alone; / He sees Him and is seen, loves Him and is loved, / and becomes light, brilliant beyond words" (Syméon in Bernbaum 1998: 114).

Many people, both traditional and modern, seek out mountains as places of artistic inspiration and spiritual renewal. Kuo Hsi (Guo Xi in Pinyin), one of China's greatest landscape painters, wrote of the reason for painting landscapes: "The din of the dusty world and the confines of human habitations are what human nature habitually abhors; while, on the contrary, haze, mist, and the haunting spirits of the mountains are what human nature seeks (His 1935: 30–1).

Interest in the Alps for scientific, artistic, and mountaineering reasons developed when philosophers and poets such as Rousseau, Goethe, and Shelley began to extol their spiritually uplifting qualities. Inspired by the ideas and sentiments of such writers and their successors, many Europeans today flock to mountains like the Alps and the Pyrenees, seeking spiritual nourishment and inspiration from views imbued with transcendent power and mystery lacking in their everyday lives. In the United States, John Muir, a major figure in the genesis of the modern-day environmental movement, founded the Sierra Club primarily to preserve the natural environment of mountains such as the Sierra Nevada as places where people could go for spiritual and physical renewal.

Each of these themes or views brings together different ideas, images, and associations to evoke the experience of a deeper reality. Tibetan pilgrims, for example, view the peak of Mount Kailas as the pagoda palace of Demchog. The two images fuse in their minds so that the mountain becomes the palace. This fusion of images awakens the experience of something that imbues Mount Kailas with an aura of sanctity. The pilgrim becomes aware of a divine presence emanating from the mountain.

The process works a little like the fusion of two slightly different photographs of a scene in a stereoscopic viewer to trigger a vivid perception of the third dimension inherent in each two-dimensional picture. The scene that looked flat suddenly seems to pop open with depth – in the case of a mountain like Kailas, a luminous depth full of meaning and significance for the pilgrim who reveres it as sacred.

The juxtaposition of images and associations also acts like the resonance of notes in a chord of music. Hearing the different tones resonate together creates a harmony, a sound with a quality that no note can produce by itself. In a similar way, a sense of the sacred issues from the resonance of images and associations in a view of a mountain, not from any single one of them. For followers of religious traditions, however, the fusion or resonance of cultural and spiritual associations in a view of a sacred mountain does not just create an effect: rather, it reveals an underlying reality present but hidden from usual awareness.

For the sake of simplicity, we have examined each theme or view by itself. But in actual practice, they do not appear in isolation. They come in clusters linked to each other in complex ways. The power of a sacred mountain, for example, may come from a deity whose abode lies on a high place at the center of the universe from which life-giving waters flow. The more themes that gather like clouds around a peak, the more associations they bring to bear on it, making the mountain resonate with deeper meaning and significance.

Edwin Bernbaum

Further Reading

Bastien, Joseph. *Mountain of the Condor: Metaphor and Ritual in an Andean Ayllu*. St. Paul: West Publishing Co., 1978.

Bernbaum, Edwin. *Sacred Mountains of the World*. Berkeley & Los Angeles, University of California Press: 1998.

Eck, Diana L. "Mountains." In Mircea Eliade, ed. *The Encyclopedia of Religion*, vol. 10. New York: Macmillan, 1987, 130–4.

Grapard, Allan G. "Flying Mountains and Walkers of Emptiness: Toward a Definition of Sacred Space in Japanese Religions." *History of Religions* 21:3 (1982), 195–221.

Hsi, Kuo. *An Essay on Landscape Painting*. London: John Murray, 1935.

The Mahabharata, 3 vols. J.A.B. van Buitenen, ed. and tr. Chicago: University of Chicago Press, 1975.

Messerli, Bruno and Jack Ives, eds. *Mountains of the World: A Global Priority*. New York & London: Parthenon, 1997.

Muir, John. *Our National Parks*. Boston and New York: Houghton Mifflin, 1901.

Reinhard, Johan. "Sacred Mountains: An Ethnoarchaeological Study of High Andean Ruins." *Mountain Research and Development* 5:4 (1985), 299–317.

Rousseau, Jean-Jacques. *Julie ou la Nouvelle Héloïse*. Paris: Garnier-Flammarion, 1976.

Tobias, Michael Charles and Harold Drasdo, eds. *The Mountain Spirit*. Woodstock, NY: The Overlook Press, 1979.

See also: Devils Tower, *Mato Tipi*, or Bears Lodge (Wyoming); Mountaineering; Mount Nyiro and the Samburu (East Africa); Mountains and Rivers Sutra by Japanese Soto Zen master Dogen Kigen; Mt. Hiei (Japan); Muir, John; Rock Climbing; Rousseau, Jean-Jacques; St. Katherine's Monastery (Mount Sinai, Egypt); Tibet and Central Asia; Venda Religion and the Land (Southern Africa); Volcanoes; Yunnan Region (Southwest China and Montane Mainland Southeast Asia).

Sacred Sites in England

The issue of "sacred sites" links Pagans, Druids and other practitioners of "alternative" religions with heritage management and policy-makers. The issue is of site-preservation versus site-use, and the lines are not clearly drawn. The best-known British prehistoric sites are Avebury and Stonehenge, but sites number in the thousands, and Pagan interests in "using" stones circles, prehistoric barrows or standing stones as sites of worship are increasingly becoming evident not only in traces of "use" expressed through offerings, but in the pressure put on local government and heritage management to recognize the value of even remote sites as contributors to a spiritual as well as an archeological heritage.

In 1998, 16 percent of people visiting Avebury expressed "spiritual motivation" as their reason with a further 11 percent giving "personal meditation" as the purpose of their visit. At the summer solstice in 2002, English Heritage facilitated "managed open access" allowing an estimated 23,500 people into the Stonehenge environs, the third consecutive year such an event has occurred. Such events in Britain and elsewhere display so-called "sacred sites" are a focus of increasing attention and tension, suggesting that such interest warrants serious academic scrutiny.

There are theoretical and pragmatic on-site issues of how British archeological sites (primarily those of prehistoric origin) have been renamed "sacred sites" by contemporary Pagans who engage with them "spiritually" and by heritage management itself, which has had to negotiate these issues. David Miles (Chief Archaeologist, English Heritage) has said that he accepted "Seahenge" was a "sacred site." And Clews Everard, site manager until 2003 at Stonehenge, has referred to the stones as a "sacred site," suggesting this term might be used to develop dialogue between the interest groups involved in summer solstice access negotiations. These issues are of timely concern to the archeologists who excavate and interpret sacred sites, the heritage managers who curate them, anthropologists interested in constructions of identity in contemporary Britain, local communities, the hospitality industry and, of course, Pagans themselves.

To "outsiders," Pagans' interests in the past may initially appear laughable, trivial, inauthentic and romantic: on the latter point at least, some Pagans may indeed romanticize the past in order to "reenchant" their lives in an increasingly secular society. On closer inspection, it is clear that Paganism is far more complex than the tabloid stereotypes imposed on it: Pagans are deeply committed to their religion and take their engagements with "ancestors" very seriously. We consider Pagans' interests in the past must at least be taken seriously and engaged with by those whose professional interests lie with the past and its representation.

Not all Pagans engage with sacred sites, not all sites are perceived to be "sacred," and it is not only Pagans who are interested in them. But for those Pagans who do engage with sites (most famously Druids), they treat such sites as places where the presence of ancestors, gods, goddesses, wights and other nature/spirit beings is felt most strongly, and where communication with these "other than human persons" is particularly effective. Rituals and ceremonies are often conducted at these sites during auspicious times of the year, including at the eight festivals comprising the "wheel of the year," at various phases of the moon, and for Pagans local to sites, on a day-to-day basis. Such rites happen at hundreds of sites across the country, and while some may leave no trace of their occurrence, others may have a significant impact on sites. At an extreme, instances of graffiti and fire damage have been linked by some to Pagans, and a group named "Friends of the Stone" ignited an ersatz napalm-like substance at Men-an-Tol in Penwith, Cornwall. Such incidents are atypical of Pagans generally who tend to have reverence for sacred sites and tend also to respect the "preservation ethic" of heritage discourse. To show their respect for the other-than-human-persons at sites, some Pagans leave votive offerings, increasingly in some places, from flowers and mead to more enduring "ritual litter" such as candles, incense and crystals. Such material remains of Pagan rituals are common in West Kennet long barrow near Avebury, and at a wide variety of other "sacred sites," especially stone circles. In the end, someone has to clear up these remains: until recently, this job fell to National Trust and English Heritage site curators, but whether locally or through such groups such as SOSS (Save Our Sacred Sites) and ASLaN (Ancient Sacred Landscape Network), Pagans are now active in site litter-clearance and the promotion of suitable site etiquette – the maxim encouraging others to "leave only footprints" being borrowed from the U.S. wilderness movement.

Pagan engagements with the past extend beyond the day-to-day use of sites for ceremonies with potentially greater implications for what archeologists do and how sites are curated. Pagans tend to approach sacred sites as part of a wider sacred landscape, and often this sacredness is seen as inherent in the place itself – the genius loci, power spot or wight is not deemed a construction of human imagination, but as extant *a priori* in the landscape. This worldview is in part inspired by indigenous conceptions of landscapes and has implications for archeological theorizing, which tends to take the opposite view, that landscapes are a *tabula rasa* that becomes encultured by humans. There are clear differences of opinion over how sacredness is constituted. The "sacred sites" constitute through a Pagan discourse of a "living landscape" that may be very different for the concept of "sacred site" constructed in the discourse of a heritage manager. At the very least, this indicates it is imperative that a singular meaning of "sacred site" is not set in stone but that sacredness continues to be problematized and theorized. In a further instance of how Pagan and heritage views conflict, Pagans may argue *the sacred site itself* has a view on how it should be managed. Such a point of view grates with rationalist and heritage management, which may write off the idea completely. Yet to do so is short-sighted; the attitudes of Pagans cannot be ignored, as the example of a British reburial issue demonstrates.

The politics of the reburial of prehistoric human remains and associated artifacts is well known as a "hot topic" in, for example, the U.S. and Australia, but, currently, it is also having ramifications in Britain, with the return of not only remains but also artifacts (e.g., a Ghost Dance shirt brought to the U.K. by Buffalo Bill returned to the Lakota by Glasgow's Kelvingrove Museum). British Pagans, drawing on such indigenous claims, have been calling for the reburial of Britain's own "indigenous" prehistoric remains. Many Pagans identify themselves as spiritually allied with the prehistoric peoples who built "sacred sites." Rites at megalithic tombs in particular, involving perceived direct communication with prehistoric "ancestors," prompt these Pagans to feel a responsibility to ancient peoples once interred there, and to the sites themselves. So, not only are contemporary Pagans collaborating with site managers in site welfare (litter collection or removing chalk graffiti) but they have also, more contentiously, begun to address issues of "ancestor welfare"; concerns over the archeological excavation and storage of human remains and artifacts.

British Druid Order member Davies expresses this concern:

Every day in Britain, sacred Druid sites are surveyed and excavated, with associated finds being catalogued and stored for the archaeological record. Many of these sites include the sacred burials of our ancestors. Their places of rest are opened during the excavation; their bones removed and placed in museums for the voyeur to gaze upon, or stored in cardboard boxes in archaeological archives ... I believe we, as Druids, should be saying Stop this now. These actions are disrespectful to our ancestors. When archaeologists desecrate a site through excavation and steal our ancestors and their guardians ... It is a theft ... We should assert our authority as the physical guardians of esoteric lore. We should reclaim our past (Davies 1997: 12–13).

This view clearly has an indigenous-inspired tone to it. Many Pagans, neo-shamans in particular, draw inspiration from indigenous peoples around the world, and in Britain some refer themselves as "new-tribes." More theoretically, we are discussing Pagans as the "new indigenes." Davies outlines how Pagans can get directly involved in this issue:

I speak for the ancestors and guardians of the land, those spirits not currently represented in the archaeological record ... The Druid or Pagan shaman can use their gifts as harmonic bridges to communicate between the realities of archaeology, land developers and Pagan Druids ... Druids should join together and encourage debate between archaeologists and museums in the reburial issue (Davies 1998: 10–12).

At first glance, individual Pagans and Pagan groups do not agree upon core beliefs or practices, let alone centralized spiritual beliefs concerning disposal of the dead. Nonetheless, in "the time of tribes," the reburial issue is gathering momentum and coherency. Stonehenge, within the context of its Management Plan and proposals of a tunnel to replace part of the nearby A303, is currently a focus for Pagan concerns over the excavation of human remains. Druid Philip "Greywolf" Shallcrass, asked a National Trust representative:

> ... if there was any possibility that priests used to working with the spirits of our ancestors ... could make ritual for the spirits of the dead[?] ... He expressed his personal sympathy to the idea. Inspired by this initial contact, I wrote a letter to some appropriate folk in English Heritage and the National Trust. In it, I expressed my concern that any burials found might simply end up in boxes in a museum basement. I asked for access to burials on site when they were uncovered, for permission to make ritual before burials were removed, and also whether it would be possible to re-bury the ancestral remains after a suitable period of study (author interview).

More recently, negotiations have moved forwards. After meetings with the liaison group established to discuss the future of Stonehenge, Greywolf had this to say:

> I've come to focus on respect and reburial as my primary reasons for being involved in the talks ... I have been, and will continue asking for any remains that are found to be treated with respect and then returned to the Earth as near as possible to their original burial sites, preferably with any accompanying grave goods and with suitable ritual (author interview).

While indigenous communities elsewhere can demonstrate genetic or cultural links to satisfy the law, focusing on the extent to which Pagans can claim British prehistoric remains as "theirs" is to miss the point, for two reasons. First, the issue here is one of respect and reburial rather than repatriation: most Pagans do not claim to be exclusively related to the ancestors. And second, the issue here is not one solely of academic discourse versus public understanding, of authenticity versus inauthenticity, or validity/invalidity. Rather, it is of multivocality and forms of knowledge and power within a diverse postmodern or late-modern society. More conservative archeologists may assume they have the power to charge Pagans with inauthenticity because scientific archeological claims are perceived to be more objectively substantive. But positivist dichotomies (authenticity/authenticity, validity/invalidity, etc.) and staunchly empiricist approaches are incompatible with contemporary reflexive archeologies and with current social research methods generally. While it is not required of us that we agree with Pagan claims to the past, in the current post-processual climate of archeology at least, there is need for archeologists, heritage managers and others to be reflexive and transparent, and for them to open up their research/data to external scrutiny. So the issue is really whether archeologists are prepared to address such pluralities and engage with them dialogically, rather than dismiss them as fringe and eccentric.

Robert J. Wallis
Jenny Blain

Further Reading

Blain, Jenni and Robert J. Wallis. "A Living Landscape? Pagans and Archaeological Discourse." *3rd Stone: Archaeology, Folklore and Myth – The Magazine for the New Antiquarian* 43 (2002), 20–7.

Calver, Stephen. "Avebury Visitor Research 1996–1998." *Bournemouth University Report on Behalf of the National Trust*, 1998.

Davies, Paul. "Speaking for the Ancestors: The Reburial Issue in Britain and Ireland." *The Druid's Voice: The Magazine of Contemporary Druidry* 9 (1998), 10–12.

Davies, Paul. "Respect and Reburial." *The Druid's Voice: The Magazine of Contemporary Druidry* 8 (1997), 12–13.

Maffesoli, Michel. *The Time of the Tribes: The Decline of Individualism in Mass Society*. London: Sage, 1996.

Wallis, Robert. J. *Shamans/Neo-Shamans: Ecstasy, Alternative Archaeologies and Contemporary Pagans*. London: Routledge, 2003.

Wallis, Robert J. "Waking the Ancestors: Neo-shamanism and Archaeology." In G. Harvey, ed. *Shamanism: A Reader*. London: Routledge, 2002, 402–23.

See also: Celtic Spirituality; Druids and Druidry; Earth Mysteries; Ireland; Paganism – Contemporary; Sacred Space/Place; Scotland; Shamanism (various); Stone Circles; Stonehenge.

Sacred Space/Place

Landscape, space, and place are three concepts that merge together to create the human experience of the environment. Space is the most basic concept of geography; it is the three-dimensional extent in which objects and events occur. Landscapes and places are both contained within space. Landscape provided the taken-for-granted backdrop for human activity and behavior. It is the most visible but least consciously felt aspect of regional character; it is an assemblage of sensory information, which generates a seen and felt experience of the world. Not only are there practical economic bonds between peoples and landscapes, there are also powerful religious, social, and psychological bonds. It is through these bonds that people develop affinities with particular locales and develop a sense of place.

Part of the human quest for meaning involves the ordering of landscape into places, and all cultures have separate, dedicated, hallowed spaces. Places are discrete units of meaningful space, and are fundamental expressions of human involvement with the world. They are distinguished from landscapes not in their scale, but in their qualitative experiential dimension. Whereas landscape is part of any immediate encounter with the world, place is further distinguished through symbols and affections. Places focus landscapes around human intentions and are sources of inspiration and insight; they are centers of cultural and personal meaning.

A "sense of place" begins with interactions between people and the world and develops out of a symbolic constitution of the environment within which we exist. It involves a blending of intellect, intuition, and imagination. On one hand people feel what it is like to be at a place, and on the other hand people intellectually grasp the meaning of a place. A sense of place unfolds, then, through the application of religious, moral, and aesthetic discernment of specific locations. Place is a universal marker of identity in relation to the landscape, although expressions of this association vary culturally.

Geographical places become sacred or symbolic when they conjoin human social facts with those of nature. A sacred place, then, is a charged meeting ground between person and the other. People in diverse parts of the world have long utilized natural places in their quest to connect with the numinous. Through mythological interpretation of landscape and place, geography is transformed into cosmology. People experience discrete places of power, and these culturally defined sacred places offer a nexus between humans, the physical environment, and deities. Sacred places are symbolic, transcending their immediate physical forms; they are unique parcels of the Earth, which aid in the transformation of self.

Paul Faulstich

Further Reading
Basso, Keith H. *Wisdom Sits in Places: Landscape and Language Among the Western Apache.* Albuquerque: University of New Mexico Press, 1996.
Buttimer, Ann. *Geography and the Human Spirit.* Baltimore, NJ: The Johns Hopkins University Press, 1993.
Faulstich, Paul. "Mapping the Mythological Landscape: An Aboriginal Way of Being-in-the-World." *Ethics, Place and Environment* 1:2 (1998).
Sack, Robert David. *Conceptions of Space in Social Thought: A Geographic Perspective.* London: Macmillan, 1980.
Swan, James A. *Sacred Places.* Santa Fe: Bear and Company, 1990.

See also: Biophilia; Eliade, Mircea; Geophilia; Sacred Geography in Native North America; Sacred Mountains.

Sagan, Carl (1934–1996)

Astronomer, author, educator, and television personality, Sagan was one of the few scientists of the late twentieth century to achieve celebrity status. Through various media, notably his best-selling books and the enormously successful Public Broadcasting Service series *Cosmos* (first aired in 1980), he achieved worldwide fame for his lucid and often entertaining explanations of advanced scientific concepts. A self-proclaimed religious skeptic dedicated to the scientific method and the empirical verification of all truth-claims, Sagan was firmly in the tradition of Western scientism. Nevertheless, he often used religious language to frame his discussions of the aims, methods, and content of modern science. Among other things, Sagan affirmed the role of the imagination in the shaping of scientific inquiry, most conspicuously in his career-long quest to find extraterrestrial life forms. He also eloquently celebrated the sense of awe and wonder evoked by modern views of nature.

Background and Career
Sagan was born in New York City in 1934 to Jewish parents. Although exposed to Judaism as a boy, after his bar mitzvah he largely abandoned normative Jewish thought and practice, including the belief in a personal God, in favor of a career in science. An excellent student, he was voted "Class Brain" in his high school and went on to earn advanced degrees in physics and astronomy at the University of Chicago. As a working scientist, Sagan's projects included studies of the atmospheres of other planets, theoretical works on the possibility of extraterrestrial life, and advisory roles for various NASA missions. From 1968 until his death he was a professor at Cornell University where he served as David Duncan Professor of Astronomy and Space Sciences and director of the Laboratory for Planetary Studies. Politically, Sagan was an unabashed liberal who regularly supported feminist, environmentalist, and arms control causes. No stranger to controversy, he figured prominently in public debates over nuclear weapons policy and missile defense during the Reagan era.

Unlike most of his peers, Sagan had a flair for publicity. His ideas on space science and the origins of life began appearing in newspapers and national magazines when he was still a graduate student. Later, his accessible writing style and media-friendly demeanor helped make him a household name. His first nominal success was a book co-authored with Soviet scientist, I.S. Shklovskii, *Intelligent Life in the Universe* (1966). His real breakthrough, however, came in 1973, when he published *The Cosmic Connection* to wide acclaim, and made the first of 26 guest appearances on The *Tonight Show* with Johnny Carson. Further recognition came in 1977 when his best-seller on the evolution of human intelligence, *Dragons of Eden*, won the Pulitzer Prize for non-fiction. Subsequent books on hominid evolution, space exploration, pseudo-science, and religion also met with critical and popular success. *Cosmos* was the apogee of Sagan's public career and established him as a cultural icon. Estimates suggest that half a billion viewers watched the series during the 1980s, and the book version became the top-selling scientific book of all time. His novel *Contact* (1985), a fictional account of a scientist who successfully communicates with aliens, was made into a movie starring Jodie Foster (released in 1997).

Sagan's rangy interests and high public profile got mixed reviews in the scientific community. He was denied tenure at Harvard in 1967. In 1992, after a rancorous debate, the prestigious National Academy of Science voted against his nomination for membership – in part, because some members felt his scientific work had not been substantive enough to warrant inclusion. Two years later, however, the same body awarded him its Public Welfare Medal for his popular writings.

Scientism and Religion

Sagan was perhaps the leading advocate of scientism of his generation and consistently argued for both the superiority of science to other forms of knowledge and the necessity of greater public understanding of its "delights" and "social consequences" (Sagan 1993: 14). Much influenced by philosopher Karl Popper, he regarded true science as that which could be formulated into testable hypotheses and thus potentially proven wrong, or "falsified." Much of his criticism of traditional religions (as well as pseudo-science and metaphysics) was that they resisted challenge, testing, and revision and thus were not as fully self-corrective as science. Sagan believed that the ethical values that sustained science included "a delicate mix of openness and skepticism," democracy, education, "decency, humility, and community spirit" (Sagan 1996: 431, 434). Because so many religions were "steeped in an absolutist frame of mind," he hailed the strict separation of Church and state as one of the great achievements of the American Constitution and a crucial step in the emergence of free inquiry (Sagan 1996: 432).

Paradoxically, Sagan often enlisted the aesthetic and emotive language associated with religion to make his case for the authority and sufficiency of science. For example, he peppered his popular works with quotations from religious texts ranging from the Bible to the Mayan *Popol Vuh*. In *The Demon-Haunted World: Science as a Candle in the Dark*, he asserted that the very "act of understanding is a celebration of joining [and] merging . . . with the magnificence of the Cosmos." Through science individuals grasped the "intricacy, beauty, and subtlety of life," and the contemplation of scientific ideas produced a "soaring feeling" that combined "elation and humility." Cumulatively, science assumed transcendent qualities, becoming the "transnational, transgenerational metamind" of the modern world. Furthermore, if one defined "spirit" so as not to imply anything immaterial, science was "not only compatible with spirituality," it was "a profound source of spirituality" (this paragraph's quotes from Sagan 1996: 29).

In ethics also, Sagan mingled scientific ideas and traditional religious language. In *The Cosmic Connection*, he argued, given our common evolutionary heritage, that "spiders, salamanders, salmon, and sunflowers are equally our brothers and sisters," and that "the time has come for a respect, a reverence, not just for all human beings, but for all life forms" (Sagan 1973: viii). Conceptually, ethical progress followed the "identification horizon" – the process of extending the Golden Rule to more and more categories of beings. In turn, this ethos supported environmental activism and conservation efforts.

Critique

Perhaps the most common criticism of Sagan was that his optimistic scientism was naive – particularly in light of the persistent social and political strife of the twentieth century. The devastation wrought by modern warfare, genocides, purges, and nuclear proliferation suggested to many that faith in the goodwill and rationality in human nature, even when scientifically informed, was misplaced, even dangerous. One detractor noted that Sagan's dedication to the "spirit of geometry" led to him exclude "non-scientific modes of thought – the very tools needed to understand history and apply its lessons to the present" (Royal 1986: 29). For others, the beneficial effects of scientific knowledge seemed unlikely to mollify what ailed the restless modern spirit. After seeing *Cosmos*, novelist Walker Percy, a Roman Catholic, wrote a wry rejoinder, *Lost in the Cosmos: The Last Self-Help Book*. In it, he jibed, "once everything in the Cosmos . . . is reduced to the sphere of immanence, matter in interaction, there is no one left to talk to except other transcending intelligences from other worlds" (Percy 1983: 173).

As biographer Keay Davidson has noted, Sagan was a man "troubled by grand dichotomies" – a "prophet" who was simultaneously a "hard-boiled skeptic"; a "boyish fantasist" who insisted on "ultrarigorous" analysis; a visionary and cerebral "merchant of awe" whose life was one of hectic schedules and driving ambition (Davidson 1999: 1, 333). His polished persona as a public intellectual belied a complicated personal life, which included two messy divorces, marijuana use, and accusations of arrogance and egotism. With religion too, Sagan was a man of considerable paradoxes. Perhaps the most widely read doubter of received traditions in recent American history, he nonetheless could impress even his critics with encyclopedic knowledge of scriptural traditions, and could forge alliances with religious groups (including the Vatican) who held similar views on environmental issues and arms control.

Overall, Sagan was more than just a genial critic of

supernatural beliefs, he also imagined a world liberated, expanded, inspired and ethically invigorated by scientific knowledge and inquiry. In the words of his wife and collaborator, Ann Druyan, he envisioned humanity "conscious, wise, compassionate, energetically curious, eternally skeptical; [and] immune to the manipulations and intimidations of the powerful." By embracing its "utterly decentralized place in the fabric of nature, space, and time," human culture would be "secure enough at last to embrace the wonder inherent in this reality, [and] awakened to our responsibilities as a link in the generations past and future." In doing so, Sagan advanced nothing less than "a new sense of the sacred" by giving sustained public voice to the "spiritual high that is science's overarching revelation – our oneness with the cosmos" (this paragraph's quotes, Druyan 2000: 25–7).

Lisle Dalton

Further Reading
Davidson, Keay. *Carl Sagan: A Life*. New York: John Wiley and Sons, Inc. 1999.
Druyan, Ann. "A New Sense of the Sacred: Carl Sagan's 'Cosmic Connection.' " *The Humanist* 60:6 (Nov./Dec. 2000), 22–7.
Percy, Walker. *Lost in the Cosmos: The Last Self-Help Book*. New York: Farrar, Straus & Giroux, 1983.
Recinos, Adrian., et al. *Popul Vuh: The Sacred Book of the Ancient Quiche Maya*. Norman: University of Oklahoma Press, 1991.
Royal, Robert. "Carl Sagan in Space." *American Spectator* (June 1986), 29.
Sagan, Carl. *The Demon-Haunted World: Science As a Candle in the Dark*. New York: Random House, 1996.
Sagan, Carl. *Broca's Brain: Reflections on the Romance of Science*. New York: Ballantine Books (reissue edition), 1993.
Sagan, Carl. *Contact*. New York: Pocket Books, 1985.
Sagan, Carl. *Cosmos*. New York: Random House, 1980.
Sagan, Carl. *The Dragons of Eden: Speculations on the Evolution of Human Intelligence*. New York: Random House, 1977.
Sagan, Carl. *The Cosmic Connection*. Garden City, NY: Anchor Press, 1973.
Sagan, Carl and Ann Druyan. *Shadows of Forgotten Ancestors: A Search for Who We Are*. New York: Random House, 1992.
See also: Astronauts; Cathedral of St. John the Divine; Epic of Evolution (and adjacent, Epic Ritual); Motion Pictures; National Religious Partnership for the Environment; Science; Science Fiction; Space Exploration.

Saharan Pastoralists

The territories of Central Saharan pastoral nomads are not bounded spaces, but are a mosaic of water-points, grazing areas, places for social and ritual events, each having symbolic value and chosen to fulfil religious and economic needs within the cultural landscape. The nomadic pastoralists of the Central Sahara today: Tuareg (Kel Tamacheq) and Toubou (Teda, Daza, Zaghawa) are Muslims. Islam, however, is a veneer that overlies an earlier animist belief in spirits, and these pre-Islamic survivals are merged with Islamic rituals. Spirits inhabit pools, trees, mountains and other natural features of the landscape. While the pastoralists move across their exploitation territories, these spirits need to be placated. This can be done by sacrifice, adding a stone to a cairn at the top of a col (a saddle at the head of a valley), refraining from killing the crocodiles (water spirits) that live in the pools (Toubou), or marking the tree, *Maerua crassifolia*, where spirits live (Tuareg). Alternatively, with the latter, stones can be thrown at the tree to scare off the spirits.

A particularly strong belief, which seems pervasive, is in the fire spirits, which are believed to be controlled by endogamous castes of blacksmiths. These smiths practice curing possession rituals among the Tuareg, where the smith becomes the embodiment of the fire spirit. Such rituals may have considerable time depth. In the Tassili n'Ajjer of southeastern Algeria, rock art that is possibly 4000 years old shows a scene with ritual specialists working with fire, observed by "wavy-line" cattle. These "wavy-line" cattle are found in other scenes that appear to be of a narrative nature, depicting pastoral activities.

Rock-art studies elsewhere in the world (e.g., Australia, South Africa, the Americas) indicate that the art is a reflection of deep meaning (i.e., religious beliefs) and has usually been drawn by ritual specialists as part of ceremonial or transcendental experience (shamanism). The art may depict specific events, but is rarely purely narrative in intent. Thus the "wavy-line" cattle may well have been symbols of a more basic religious nature. Cattle are wealth to pastoralists, but they play a much greater role in society than purely economic. Among African pastoralists, cattle are often seen as living representatives of the ancestors, and human/cattle lineages parallel each other in marriage exchanges, with the genealogy of both being well known to all the herders.

Markings on cattle in both paintings and engravings on rock walls are a common theme from the Central Sahara all the way to the Red Sea. Concentrations of these paintings in the main mountain massifs of the Sahara (Tassili n'Ajjer, Hoggar, Aïr, Tibesti, Ennedi) may well have been identity points in the landscape, as would have been (and are) cemeteries where holy men were buried. The tracks connecting rock-art sites, cemeteries and places where spirits lived, along with the water and pasture basic to any herding strategy, would constitute a landscape of belief repeated in stories and myth passed down from generation to generation.

Intentional burial of cattle as part of ritual is first documented in the Western Desert of Egypt at Nabta Playa, dated to between 6500–5500 years ago. This predates the Badarian civilization of the Nile Valley and may well have been a precursor of the later cattle goddess cult of pre-Dynastic Egypt. Such cattle burials are also found in Saharan sites of Niger.

Cultural contact over large distances among pastoralists is well attested today (viz. Fulani and Tuareg distributions across the Sahara and Sahel). Archaeological data suggests that similar connections go back to Neolithic times, more than 7000 years ago. It is across this belt of the Sahara that the pre-Islamic survivals exist. If the rock art and cattle burials are any indication, then these Saharan belief systems predate their appearance in North Africa or the Nile Valley. Rather than seeing the Sahara as a cultural backwater absorbing attributes of more "advanced" people, we might suggest that this was an area of innovation.

Andrew Smith

Further Reading

Holl, Augustin and Stephen A. Dueppen. "Iheren I: Research on Tassilian Pastoral Iconography." *Sahara* 11 (1999), 21–34.

Paris, François. "African Livestock Remains from Saharan Mortuary Contexts." In Roger M. Blench and Kevin C. MacDonald, eds. *The Origins and Development of African Livestock: Archaeology, Genetics, Linguistics and Ethnography*. London: UCL Press, 2000, 111–26.

Rassmussen, Susan J. "Ritual Specialists, Ambiguity and Power in Tuareg Society." *Man* 27 (1992), 105–28.

Smith, Andrew B. "New Approaches to Saharan Rock Art." In G. Calegari, ed. *L'arte e l'Ambiente del Sahara Preistorico: dati e interprettazioni*. Memoria della Societa Italiana di Scienze Naturale. *Milano* 26 (1993), 467–77.

Smith, Andrew B. "The Pastoral Landscape in Saharan Prehistory." In Tilman Lenssen-Erz, et al. *Tides of the Desert – Gezeiten der Wuste: Contributions to the Archeology and Environmental History of Africa in Honor of Rudolph Kuper*. Koln: Heinrich-Barth Institut, 447–57.

See also: Egypt – Ancient; Egypt – Pre-Isamic.

Salmon – *See* Columbia River Watershed Pastoral Letter; Ireland; Fishers; Paiute Culture; Sohappy, David – and Salmon Spirituality; Washat Religion (Drummer-Dreamer Faith); Yakama Nation.

Salvadoran Reflection on Religion, Rights, and Nature

A few decades ago when I was in primary and high school, the Jesuits taught us the importance of becoming God's messengers by defending religion, particularly because of the threat imposed by communism. I remember we were taught about how the devil inspired Martin Luther to attempt to destroy the Church, the saint inquisition and the infallibility of the pope. Of course some stories like Galileo's left some of us confused.

In those days the teachings seemed to be oriented to defend religious rituals – that was the divine duty – and the key idea was that the next life was more important than this one. Genesis stated that all things are here for man's use and man has domination over all things. I remember we, the students, felt the divine obligation to bring flowers to the Virgin Mary in May and take communion every day, and also the need to become crusaders.

A few years after finishing high school, the same Jesuits that warned us about communism were being accused of being communists themselves by the powerful Salvadoran oligarchy. This happened because in their religious teachings these Jesuits were including as a central religious duty the defense of the human being and his or her dignity. New questions were asked such as: Why are people poor? Is it not a social sin when few people in our society have so much and most people have so little, sometimes not even enough to live as a human being? What should a Christian do when we are faced with these circumstances? If all of us were made in the image of God, is it not God who is suffering in the flesh of the poor? Are we not obliged by divine duty to try to change all this?

These human-centered religious teachings, often labeled as theology of liberation, encountered fierce opposition by the ruling economic class, the government, and even by some priests. At this same time the archbishop who had been sympathetic to these new teachings was replaced because of old age, and a new archbishop was appointed in 1977. This new archbishop was "Monseñor" Oscar Romero. Romero was favored by the government and the ruling oligarchy as a religious intellectual. They thought he would get the Jesuits back into teaching the importance of bringing flowers to our Holy Mother, keeping chastity until marriage, and accepting reality as the will of God.

A few weeks after "Monseñor" Romero was appointed, a friend of mine, the Jesuit Rutilio Grande was killed. This was when Monseñor showed who he really was.

I remembered attending Rutilio's funeral and Monseñor Romero's questions were: How can anybody kill a priest? How can anybody kill a person that is helping poor people? How can anybody kill a messenger of God?

Monseñor Romero must have forgotten for a moment that 2000 years ago the same evil forces had killed the Son of God, and what was happening here only showed that not much had changed.

The three following years until Romero's assassination were something unique and exciting in El Salvador. To be at the Sunday masses with Monseñor Romero gave many of us the impression it was Jesus Christ preaching. If for some reason I could not go to a Sunday mass I always had a radio to listen to it.

I remember the day before he was murdered, I attended the Sunday Mass, crowded as usual, and Monseñor Romero was as inspired by the Holy Ghost as ever. I remember I saw the U.S. Ambassador Robert White, attending the Mass also, surrounded by his bodyguards and his car running at one of the church entrances, waiting for him just in case. That day I was scared because the previous Sunday Mass somebody left an attaché case at the church with 72 dynamite candles, which fortunately did not explode. After the Mass, there was the usual press conference given by Monseñor Romero. I then had the chance to talk to him briefly. He asked me for my reaction to what he said during the Mass and also told me that in the middle of his homily the national communications office had blocked the telephone lines so that his homily could not be transmitted outside of the country. The next day Archbishop Romero was killed.

Most of us felt what Ignacio Ellacuria, the president of a Jesuit-run university, said once: the Saint Spirit passed through El Salvador in the figure of Monseñor Romero. A few years later Ellacuría and other Jesuits, my high school teachers, were also killed.

What this experience has taught us is that religion does not need to be the opium of the people, as some religious people have made it seem in the past. I remember during the war in El Salvador, some priests were blessing the army weapons and of course it was very hard to tell poor peasants that the weapons killing them were sacred. What Monseñor Romero taught us is that religion, when rightly interpreted, is a force of liberation. God does not want people to suffer, God wants people to have life and have plenty of it. As Romero said, "There is much of God in the earth and it cries out when some people hoard it unjustly. I raise up my voice to say: do not worship your wealth."

While I am writing this, 23 years after Romero's death, the social conditions, in most places, have not improved. Poverty and violence keep increasing, now aggravated by something else: the destruction of nature.

It is common knowledge that there are environmental problems. Universities and institutes are talking about it and the general public perceives it as the price we have to pay for the good of our civilization. But the problem is that such a price is not paid equitably everywhere and for some people in some regions of the world, it might be unfair and too high a price.

If we compare a southern Country like El Salvador with the northern countries of Europe, USA or Japan, we see that, in the northern countries, the environmental problems are incorrectly perceived by politicians, the general population and sometimes even the scientific establishment. Their discussion of environmental problems remains mostly in the ecological or biological domains, or at the scientific or resource policy levels, since they are not seen as having a considerable impact on the performance of the society. Scientists talk of the disappearance of animal species or the destruction of the ozone layer, activities the impact of which, though affecting the health and well-being of people, is not felt in a direct way and may therefore go unnoticed.

In a country like El Salvador, the situation is rather different. The environmental problems are at the same time social problems in the sense that the average citizen feels them in a direct way. They are becoming political problems because of the violence they generate. When we talk about ecological problems, we are talking about a lack of water to drink. Water with unacceptable levels of pollution leads to the most common causes of childhood death in the country. When we talk about climate change, we are talking about the "El Niño" phenomenon that upsets crop cultivation because of too much or too little water, leading to famine in the country, or we might be talking about Hurricane Mitch that left 12,000 people dead in Central America.

In many countries or regions in the south, the environmental destruction has reached such levels that what were once considered gifts from God, like air, water or food, are now the main sources of death. In El Salvador for example, the leading causes of death are infectious respiratory diseases, coming from air pollution, followed by gastrointestinal diseases coming from water and food pollution. In other words, the most dangerous things that a human being can do in El Salvador is to breathe air, drink water, or eat food.

So the structural violence that Archbishop Romero focused on is not just generated by the social sin of unjust distribution of wealth but also by the mismanagement or lack of natural resources, and their wastes. Water is becoming a source of violence. Sometimes communities fight among themselves over access to a given water spring. Other times the battle is between the local population and the government, when some government agency attempts to take the water away from a rural place to satisfy industry or city demands. This lack of water is even becoming a source of conflict not only in El Salvador but also between many neighboring countries, for example Israel and Jordan.

Environmental destruction in the southern countries is of no surprise, when we realize that the management of natural resources follows the logic of profit and not the logic of the societal well-being or the logic of nature (ecological). Resources are exploited in order to obtain the largest possible profit, irrespective of how much the environment is deteriorated or society is affected.

This state of affairs is something that will be made worse by the current corporate-led globalization. The whole idea behind corporate-led globalization is to remove all possible obstacles or barriers to the "free" flow of capital and goods, so that the corporations can keep up the exploitation of resources. Corporations are interested in profits, and governments, most of the time, follow these corporation guidelines or in the best-case scenario simply do not oppose them.

To facilitate this globalization, the governments of the world, motivated by international capital, have established the World Trade Organization ("WTO") with the objective of facilitating international trade, above any other concerns. There are environmental and social regulations regarding trade that corporations pay lip service to, but according to WTO rules and practices, even if the liberalization of trade brings the displacement of jobs or the pollution of a river, the WTO will favor trade. There is an example in Mexico where a municipality that rejected wastes from a transnational corporation was fined several million dollars by the WTO. The reality is that we live in a social system where the short-term profit of transnational corporations is more important than the medium and long-term benefit of society and nature.

We thus live in a world economic system that intrinsically violates human rights. For example, our system promotes the consumption of goods. Anybody has the legal right to consume as much as he or she wants, limited only by the wealth that he or she possesses. This consumption of goods means, among other things, consumption of resources like oil. Much energy is required for the production of goods and their transportation from the production site to the consumption place. It is scientifically established that the exhaust emissions coming from oil consumption generate carbon dioxide that contributes to climate change, which in turn takes people's lives in other parts of the globe. This means that our present economic system promotes the unlimited consumption of goods by some people, which at the same time damages other people, therefore violating their rights.

The problem is not consumption *per se*, because nature has the capacity to process wastes and transform them into useful products. The problem is overconsumption where wastes, such as gas emissions, exceed the capacity of nature to process them, thus generating problems. In this mode of thinking coming from current societal values, it would be inconceivable to limit the consumption of goods to any sectors of the population, even though such consumption generates suffering to other population sectors.

Some of the most important "rights" in our society are the right to private property, and accumulation of wealth, whether or not that "right" negates other people's most fundamental human rights, like the right to live healthily and in a decent way. The following is article 17 from the Universal Declaration of Human Rights: "(1) Everyone has the right to own property alone as well as in association with others ... (2) No one shall be arbitrarily deprived of his property."

When anybody starts a production unit for example, the law allows the privatization of profits coming from that enterprise, but at the same time the law allows the enterprises to pass some of the costs of production, like the impact generated by garbage or gas emissions, to society, such that many costs are socialized. Why are oil companies allowed to privatize the revenues coming from oil exploitation and consumption and at the same time not required to assume the costs coming from those activities, like pollution of water bodies, destruction of forests or climate change? In the way our society functions, corporations are reaping the benefits of the generation of this socio-ecological debt. Therefore corporations are mostly responsible for the existence of that debt.

The violation of human rights takes many other forms. For example, consider oil again. Every time a new oil well is opened in Colombia, to meet industrial energy demand, there are always people killed, sacred places and forests destroyed and local indigenous populations displaced. A similar situation is developing in the Ogoni land in Nigeria. Thousands of Ogoni people have been killed, many others displaced and tens of thousands live in a pollution nightmare, just to keep the oil running from their wells, motivated by the profit mentality of the transnational oil corporations. The same happens to millions of people displaced by the construction of hydro-electric dams to generate electricity to produce goods, sometimes consumed by people living on the other side of the planet.

Looking at this rationale of our economic system of "privatization of profits and socialization of costs," which has prevailed for centuries and remains to this date, we can deduce that an ecological and social debt has been generated. The people who consume more resources owe this socio-ecological debt to the people who consume fewer resources. In political terms this means a socio-ecological debt owed by people from the overconsumptive North to people from the South. North does not only mean people from the northern countries but also includes upper and middle economic classes from the southern countries that also overconsume. Likewise the South also includes lower economic classes living in the northern countries.

People from urban areas also owe this socio-ecological debt to people from rural areas, because the urban way of life, cities and industries, have always been developed and kept functioning at the expense of rural places. Taking a look at history, starting with the periods of colonization and continuing with interactions between races and sometimes between countries, it can be seen that this socio-ecological debt is also owed by white people to indigenous and colored people all over the planet. Considering our basic gender division and the relationship of exploitation and inequity that has always existed, it must also be realized that men owe this socio-ecological debt to women.

The way our generation and previous ones have misused the resources of the planet means that our generation owes a socio-ecological debt to future generations. Finally, we are just one of the many species that exists and shares the space of the planet. One of the most important differences between human beings and all other living creatures, which amount to between 5 and 30 million species, is that all species take from nature only what they need to survive, except human beings. Humans have developed a social system with a set of values that promotes an ever-increasing consumption of resources and by doing so generates violence to other species that are also part of the creation. Therefore, *Homo sapiens* have a socio-ecological debt to the rest of the creation.

Looking at this social behavior from a religious perspective, there is a basic question that comes to mind. How can human beings claim respect for a Creator and supposedly follow divine laws, when this same human being respects neither the creation nor the creatures that are part of it?

It is unfortunate to realize that there has been little effort by the major religions to consider environmental aspects and the defense of creation with her corresponding creatures as central to religious duty. It is time that a second chapter be written in liberation theology, to include the defense of nature. On one hand, creation is the will of the Creator, and that by itself generates a religious duty, but on the other hand, the destruction of creation also means the destruction of human beings. Polluted water kills people, so does climate change. As the commandments state: Thou shall not kill. It is everyone's responsibility to take that seriously. This means thinking about the consequences of overconsumption, where products come from, and what that means to the people who provide those products. Be a conscious consumer.

Ricardo A. Navarro

See also: Brower, David; A Christian Friend of the Earth; Christianity (7c) – Liberation Theology; Eco-Justice in Theology and Ethics; Globalization; United Nations' "Earth Summits".

Samia Culture (Western Kenya)

For Samia people of western Kenya, like most African peoples, nature is filled with religious significance. The invisible world of god and spirits is symbolized or manifested by natural phenomena, and people see "that invisible universe when they look at, hear or feel the visible and tangible world" (Mbiti 1969: 56–7). Nature, the bountiful source of life, is also unpredictable, dangerous and powerful. It is "wild." For humans to live in their social world, they must – through work and rituals – have appropriate relationships with the natural world and the spirits that inhabit it. Hard work turns wild bush into farmland, producer of food and sustainer of life. Rituals and other religious practices make wild nature more beneficent and orderly.

Samia live around the northeastern shores of Lake Victoria, in a land of steep hills, undulating valleys, and open plains – all lushly green in rainy seasons, rusty brown in dry seasons and droughts. The hills are dotted with trees, roadsides are lined with invasive non-native perennials such as lantana and tithonia, and everywhere there are people, houses and cultivated fields. The Samia in their home area numbered about 75,000 in the 1999 census, though many Samia, especially men, are away as migrant laborers. The Samia are a sub-group of Kenya's second or third largest ethnic community, Abaluyia.

In the late nineteenth century, before colonial rule was imposed, only a small proportion of the land was cultivated. There were few people and many animals such as elephants, crocodiles, hippos, hyenas and leopards. People farmed and herded cattle, fished and hunted. A century later, in post-colonial Kenya, to see elephants and other such animals is rare, hunting is illegal, and with a greatly increased population (more than doubled from 1969 to 1999), the balance between cultivated land and bush has shifted heavily toward cultivation. Today many people do not have enough land to practice the traditional shifting cultivation with bush fallow, a system that renewed soil fertility. Marginal lands are cultivated, deforestation and erosion are growing problems, and, increasingly, farms are too small to be economically viable. Bush that harbors monkeys is cleared because monkeys, great destroyers of crops, may no longer be legally hunted. Fuelwood and thatching grass are scarce. The pre-colonial sustainable subsistence economy and the integrated socio-political-religious-moral system in which it was embedded have been fragmented and, often, replaced by imported ideas and behaviors.

Like their nineteenth-century forebears, contemporary Samia are farmers and cattle herders; unlike their ancestors, they are implicated in the global political economy. But they still wrestle daily with the land and keep an eye on the weather. Because of the tropical climate, many activities take place outdoors all year round. Like Gikuyu in central Kenya, Samia "are daily and hourly in the most intimate contact with Nature" (Kenyatta 1953: 241). The natural world is all around, and the contemporary Samia social and symbolic world is a fabric woven from both human and natural environments, indigenous and Christian cosmologies.

Samia cosmology has a high god, *Were*, creator of the world and everything in it. Were resides in the sky, invisible and all-powerful, the ultimate giver of life and all prosperity. He manifests himself in natural phenomena: sun and moon, rain, rainbows, thunder and lightning. Earthquakes are Were's sign that general bad behavior needs to be corrected. Ancestral spirits (*emisambwa*) are active in their descendants' lives; they are intermediaries between living people and Were. Homesteads had an ancestral shrine of small stones and little mud-houses placed before the senior wife's house. Here people sacrificed meat and beer to their ancestors and prayed for blessings or for help in a crisis. Sometimes the sacrifices were to placate an angry, hence dangerous spirit. Just before sunrise each day, the oldest male in a homestead went outside and, standing by the shrine, spat to the east and asked Were for blessings for the day; at sunset, he spat to the west and asked Were for blessings for the night. Diviners and spirit mediums interpreted events and recommended ritual or practical redress. Rainmakers ritually directed nature's powers to produce rains, destructive or beneficial, and even drought. Sacred trees were meeting places for ancestral spirits; the trees were given names and were not to be cut down; the ground around them was swept clean. Today some huge, old sacred trees are cut down for fuelwood or to make charcoal, and anyone who has an ancestral shrine probably hides it in their house, as most Samia are at least nominal Christians, and some – the born-again "saved" people (in a crossdenominational movement of religious revival) – are adamant that these shrines, rain-making paraphernalia and other such things are Satan's and must be destroyed.

Christian ideology has centered on matters of faith, on sin and salvation. Christian churches in Samia have concentrated on educational and health programs, not environmental issues. A rare exception was the work of Sr. Marianna Hulshof, a Medical Mission Sister who, for nearly thirty years, showed people in Samia how to farm in ecologically more sensitive ways. She did this by practical demonstrations, not by religious rhetoric. Samia have not embraced a "protect the environment" ethos; rather, they deal with their environmental problems individually and pragmatically, sometimes with help from government agriculture and forestry extension agents or in response to directives delivered by government administrators.

Few people follow the old religion in its entirety, yet many aspects persist. Diviners, spirit mediums and herbalists are still consulted – along with priests, doctors and government officials. Ancestral spirits remain active in family life, visiting their kin in dreams or making themselves known through illness. Everyone, saved or not, insists that the dead must be placed in the Earth of their own homes, making generational continuity visible, placating angry spirits and opening oneself to blessings from the spirits. Every Samia person's connections to kin and claims to identity and land are mediated by ancestors' graves, the land itself and the spirits inhabiting it.

Wildness continues to figure in Samia life through everyday experiences, as people move between homestead, farm and bush, and the categorical and symbolic distinctions Samia make between wild and human. The homestead, a physical expression of social life, is a clearly defined moral space, marked by houses, graves, and formerly, ancestral shrines but now by Bibles, crosses and pictures of Jesus. Hedges surround many homesteads, marking off the homestead as "inside" and the land, cultivated and bush, as "outside." Inside is the world of humans, who behave properly, work hard, and are responsible and orderly.

Yet there are interpenetrations, fluid boundaries, ambiguities. Ancestral spirits are betwixt and between, no longer human, yet not wild – except for the bad spirits known as *esikhieno*. Humans go into the bush to make use of its resources such as thatching grass, poles and stones; wild animals such as monkeys, mongooses and snakes come into the homestead. Cattle, sheep and goats who spend the day on grazing lands return to the homestead for night-time security, yet they – like all animals – are wild, even though they are closely implicated in human social life through their ritual roles and use as food, gifts and bridewealth. Thieves, who are humans turned wild, enter homesteads secretly to steal, and the power of witchcraft or an evil ancestral spirit may cross the boundary. Anyone who goes out of the homestead at night runs the risk of meeting a hyena or leopard, or *omulosi*, a person who travels with an animal familiar and creates minor disturbances in homes. Storytellers still tell of the mysterious wild beasts who enter homesteads in human form and then eat the inhabitants. Thus, though the bush and its animal population have been greatly diminished, wild things still enter the homestead, humans go into the wild, and the notion of wildness continues to resonate in Samia thought and ritual action.

Maria G. Cattell

Further Reading
Cattell, Maria G. "Praise the Lord and Say No to Men: Older Samia Women Empowering Themselves." *Journal of Cross-Cultural Gerontology* 7:3 (1992), 307–30.
Kenyatta, Jomo. *Facing Mount Kenya: The Tribal Life of the Gikuyu.* London: Secker and Warburg, 1953 (1938).
Khasiani, Shanyisa A., ed. *Groundwork: African Women as Environmental Managers.* Nairobi: ACTS Press (African Centre for Technology Studies), 1992.
Mbiti, John S. *African Religions and Philosophy.* London: Heinemann, 1969.
Soper, Robert, ed. *Kenya Socio-cultural Profiles: Busia*

District. Nairobi: The Ministry of Planning and National Development & The Institute of African Studies, University of Nairobi, 1986.

Were, Gideon S. *Essays on African Religion in Western Kenya*. Nairobi: East African Literature Bureau, 1977.

See *also*: Christian Environmentalism in Kenya; Kenya Greenbelt Movement; Mount Nyiro and the Samburu (East Africa); Sacred Groves of Africa; Snakes and the Luo of Kenya.

San (Bushmen) Apocalyptic Rock Art

Southern African San or "Bushman" rock art is currently most adequately understood as an outward shamanistic expression of relationships that the San had with each other, with non-San, with an ordinary outer world, and with an extra-ordinary spirit world. For approximately 30,000 years, San rock-engravings and rock-paintings helped connect these co-dependent, parallel, and immanent worlds. San rock-art sites were thus points of breakthrough, and what we call "images" were for the San actual spirit world beings emerging from their home behind the rock. Unlike representational or even symbolic art forms, San rock art represents a radical departure from image making where representation and reality fuse seamlessly.

Similarly, what we call "nature" was for the San a deeply cultural entity that contained the entirety of human experience and that required constant custodianship. Over the last two thousand years, the character of San rock art changed to accommodate immigrant black farmers and KhoeKhoen herders. No longer was the landscape custodial – it became for these immigrants a commodity whose prime function was to provide an economic base for their existence. For a time the landscape's bounty and the San's revered spiritual status allowed the San custodial ethic to cautiously coexist with the imperialistic ethics of KhoeKhoen herders and black farmers. But this uneasy "truce" could not last, and in the last 600 years, images of weapons and scenes of conflict between different groups of people became alarmingly frequent. The arrival of White colonists in the mid-seventeenth century violently increased the hunger for a suddenly finite landscape. When the San realized that "their" land was being taken for granted and that they were being pushed off, it appears that they used rock art as a visible statement of their armed and political resistance by indelibly marking their homes in bright and local pigments. This war lasted 300 years but eventually the superior weaponry and rapacious body politic of the colonists took their toll. In 1875, Dia!kwain, a man who barely survived this war, told the story of *The Broken String* in an attempt verbally to articulate his disbelief at how his unbreakable connection with inner and outer landscapes had, in fact, been broken:

"People were those who broke for me the string. Therefore the place does not feel to me as the place used to feel to me. The place does not feel pleasant to me" (Bleek and Lloyd 1911: 236–7). From physical resistance the San turned, one last time, to a similarly ailing spirit world for deliverance. They tried to coax potent but dangerous spirit world beings into the outer World by painting their grotesque and bizarre likenesses on rock walls. Never-before-imagined frightening phantoms appear in an ephemeral and ghostly white paint, often with enigmatic lines emanating from their misshapen heads. Many marauding dogs representing the powerful trickster god's/Kaggen's "dogs of war" endlessly pursue deformed human figures that represent the Qobé or non-San. These distorted paintings appear to reflect a dislocated self-image and a sense of worldly alienation.

Determined by pigment analyses and study of 645 San rock-painting sites, these paintings date between 1750–1850. In the hotly contested southeastern southern African landscape, this eschatonic or apocalyptic art appears to be an attempt by the San to reclaim their worlds by banishing, by supernatural means, those who did not share their custodial ethos. But the boundaries between inner and outer worlds seem to have become rigid and distant and it appears that not even the most powerful shamans could now bridge this divide. Nor does it seem as if spirit world beings were able to break through the rock and deliver the San from their suffering. Fortunately, the San did survive this Apocalypse. Today about 140,000 San live in Angola, Botswana, Namibia and South Africa. They have remained connected to their spirit world and are helping non-San discover this ancient yet ever-relevant spirituality.

Sven Ouzman

Further Reading

Bleek, Wilhelm H.I. and Lucy C. Lloyd. *Specimens of Bushman Folklore*. London: George Allen, 1911.

Kayser, Wolfgang J. *The Grotesque in Art and Literature*. Bloomington: Indiana University Press, 1963.

Ouzman, Sven and J. Loubser. "Art of the Apocalypse: Southern Africa's Bushmen Left the Agony of Their End Time On Rock Walls." *Discovering Archaeology* 2 (2000), 38–45.

Weber, Eugen J. *Apocalypses: Prophecies, Cults, and Millennial Beliefs through the Ages*. Cambridge: Harvard University Press, 1999.

See *also*: Khoisan Religion; Rock Art (various); San (Bushmen) Religion.

San (Bushmen) Religion

The domain of nature looms large in the lives of the Bushmen (or San). Their natural environment is today primarily the Kalahari of southern Africa, a semi-desert plain with summer rains and winter droughts, and, as recent as a century-and-a-half ago, also included the mountainous grasslands of the northwestern Cape, as well as other regions of southern Africa. As hunters and gatherers, San men and women are intimately involved with their natural environment, its animals, plants, seasons, climatic cycles, wind, weather, and sky. These impact closely on how, when, and where the people forage; they dictate the seasonal cycle of population dispersal and aggregation. Their loose kinship, marriage and leadership institutions, their egalitarian social and gender relations, exchange patterns, notions of territoriality and values of sharing and reciprocity are all affected to varying extent by the people's adaptive lifeways. Religion, too, is intimately linked to nature, so much so that some researchers see in it an "ideology of foraging," that is, a mindset that is congruent with the production mode and social patterns of a foraging people.

Before turning to the nature component of Bushman religion (the main theme of this brief account), it should be noted that San religion addresses itself also to the social domain, in the ways all religions do. Like myths everywhere, Bushman myths, too, explain and validate the social order, while ritual enacts, reinforces or defuses basic social processes, values and conflicts. The Bushman healing dance is a case in point: as the people's central ritual, the trance dance plays out such things as intra- and intergroup sharing, social and gender equality, exchange and kin networking, "ludic" conflict resolution, leveling and cooperation, all of them key structural and ideational elements of Bushman band society. Moreover, the dance becomes an arena for the moral, emotional and creative interplay between the individual and the community, enacting thereby one of the basic structural characteristics of this fluid and loosely organized society – the juxtaposition of the individual to the group and the balance between individualism and communalism.

The element of nature most prominent within Bushman religion is animals. Plants receive far less symbolic elaboration in Bushman myth and ritual, while stellar and meteorological phenomena may be salient features of the myth and lore of some groups (especially the /Xam). An example for the second is the !Kung mystical concept of *n!ow*, the mystical and magical connection of some persons to the wind and rain at their birth, which is dramatically evident also at the person's death, through the unleashing of a mighty wind or rainstorm.

As a hunting people the Bushmen are intellectually and emotionally attuned to animals, especially the game species and the animals that prey on them, the carnivores, in

---

San (Bushmen) Rainmaking

One of the central characteristics of San religion is its fluidity and adaptability. Although all Khoisan people broadly share a similar religious outlook the specifics vary from group to group, and within a group may change according to particular socio-economic circumstances. This is clearly illustrated with reference to the diverse rainmaking practices of the San, which is clearly an expression of their religious outlook. All San ascribed to the Supreme Being, or to a lower and sometimes malevolent deity, the power to create or withhold rain. Among the northern San this deity is frequently prayed to or simply addressed in times of drought. Some healers had the power to know where the rain would fall but the northern San as a rule did not have rainmaker specialists like the southern San. The lower deity among the southern San is, like other forces of nature, zoomorphized and frequently manifests as the rain-animal – a mythological and often dangerous creature with the ability to change its shape.

Southern San healers or shamans have the ability to capture this rain-animal and to create rain where its blood falls on the ground. It is also believed that the spirits of the dead, especially those of previously powerful rain shamans, may cause the rain to fall by riding on the back of the rain-animal. These are often prayed to in times of drought. Whereas many rainmaking rites refer to shamanistic visions and trances, there is substantial evidence that rainmaking became more ritualized where San groups assimilated into the societies of Bantu-speaking farmers. These spirits are often prayed to in times of drought. In addition there is a special relationship between a San girl experiencing her first menses and the rain and it is said that an angry rain may ensue when this girl does not honor the correct customary procedures.

Frans Prins

---

whom the Bushmen see resourceful fellow hunters, one of whom, the lion, they hold in special esteem (so much so that one group, the !Kung, have established a pact of mutual respect and avoidance between themselves and the lions). A sympathetic bond links a hunter to his quarry, which may be palpable, expressing itself through bodily sensations, which the /Xam called "tappings" and experienced in those parts of their body that correspond to the distinctive markings of the prey animal (for instance, on their head, face or eyes, corresponding to the hunted springbok's horns, black facial stripes and back hair). When tracking a wounded animal, the hunter had to refrain from certain actions – such as uttering the animal's name (using its secret name instead), or from drinking and sleeping, lest he invigorate the pursued animal.

Another powerful expression of human-animal identification was the vigorous mimetic "eland dance" a number of Bushman groups performed at the occasion of a girl's first menstruation. It was performed outside the girl's hut, by old men and women, and its steps and choreographed routine were the courtship behavior of the eland, the Bushmen's premier antelope and game animal, because of its bulk, fat and tractability, as well as its mystical association with rain, fertility and health. Inside her menstrual hut, the girl herself, among the /Xam, became a metaphorical eland, drawing the animal toward her, allowing it to be shot by hunters. At male initiation, on the occasion of the young man's "First Buck" ceremony, the eland was once again a portentous presence. Through a variety of acts of contagious magic, a palpable bond was established between the /Xam young hunter and the eland, such as being covered with eland fat and having "eland medicine" – the animal equivalent of *n/om* – rubbed into medicinal cuts.

An especially dramatic and profound expression of animal-human identity is transformation, of a human, metaphorically, spiritually and experientially, into an animal. This happens most elaborately during the trance dance, the universal and principal ritual of the Bushmen. To the women's chanting and rhythmic clapping, one or several healers will dance themselves into a trance state, around a large fire, that is kept lit throughout this nightlong curing ritual. In trance a dancer activates the healing potency (which the !Kung call *n/om*) that resides in his stomach and with it he heals the sick person or persons at the dance (as well as administering, in the spirit of sharing, general palliative treatment to all of the spectators). When he finally collapses, his spirit leaves the dancer's inert body, to fly away, in search of supernatural assistance from the spirits, in his curing task. At one point in their trance experience, some dancers may undergo animal transformation, either into antelopes – ideally elands, that may sprout wings flying heavenward – or into lions. Such "lion experiences" are capable of absorbing a dancer so forcefully that he might feel his "lion-teeth forming and his lion-hair growing."

Therianthropic, man-animal beings also figure prominently in the myths and tales of the Bushmen (while animals are prominent also in Bushman rock art, some of which presents splendid, polychrome depictions of game antelopes, especially elands). The "Early Race" that inhabited the mythic age were, for the most part, such beings – animals who had certain of the anatomical and behavioral patterns peculiar to the species – such as the antbear eating ants and burrowing, or the wasp having a slender waist. Yet, they were also persons; so much so, in fact, that a storyteller will point out that if you came across such beings today, you would not think that they were anything other than people. Yet they could also be a zebra, a lion, a gemsbok, elephant or ostrich; you only need to look more closely and you will see that they are animals. Animals to the Bushmen are evidently more than just bearers of certain anatomical traits – stripes, mane, horns, trunk or long neck. They can be identified by means of non-physical, subcutaneous attributes, drawn from the animal's inner being rather than its exterior form.

There were also humans in the mythic age, as well as animal or human trickster beings, well suited, because of their quixotic and ambiguous nature, to the inchoate conditions of that first order of existence. Other types of being were sun, moon and some stars, who were persons in the mythic past – some of them living on the Earth – before being cast in the sky. The early humans were flawed; they had, so the Nharo storytellers remark, "no customs." Their lives were marred with social and moral transgressions. One common transgression, in /Xam mythology, was the breaking of menarcheal taboos by a girl in seclusion, who was punished by the mysterious rain-divinity *!Khwa*, usually by being transformed, along with all of her hapless band members, into frogs. Their material belongings reverted to their natural state (from digging sticks to shrubs, leather cloaks or jackal tail swats to antelopes or jackal). Thus, the boundary between human and animal and culture and nature was porous in the mythic age and the distinction between ontological realms precarious.

Another problem of the "Early Race" of people (as well as of the animal-people), which is the subject of tales found in all Bushman and Khoe Khoe groups, is in-law tension. One of its manifestations was the murder of the wife of one of the band's men and the eating of her flesh, the perpetrators all the while convincing themselves – and the reluctant husband – that what they were eating was in fact meat, not a person, and that their band member had "married meat." This symbolic equation of women with meat (or game), meat (and fat) with sex, and hunting with sex and marriage, is a pan-Khoisan notion. Beyond its expression of in-law tension, it stands as another forceful expression of human-animal identity.

Through an act of creation, by either a wise animal-person (such as the Anteater-Woman or the Kori Bustard, among the /Xam and !Kung, respectively), or god or the trickster, the early order became transformed. The human component of the therianthropic beings shriveled and they became fully animal (although retaining, in some cases, vestigial humanness within them, to this day). In some cases, the reverse happened, so that the early man-animal, in shedding its animal component, became and remained a person. This, among the /Xam, is what happened to the springboks of the "Early Race."

Through ideas of this kind – humans and animals of today being the animals and humans of the mythic past, women as meat, the ontological fluidity of humans and animals and culture and nature – Bushman mythology provides the symbolic and cosmological basis for an ideology which links humankind closely to nature. That ideology is underscored further by mystical notions and ritual practices of sympathy, between hunter and quarry, a person and the weather, and the transformation of an initiate or shaman into an animal. Bushman religion, being thus informed with the beings and forces of nature, provides the ideological underpinnings for a way of life that is closely attuned to the natural environment.

Mathias Guenther

Further Reading

Biesele, Megan. *Women Like Meat: The Folklore and Foraging Ideology of the Kalahari Ju/'hoansi*. Johannesburg/Bloomington: Witwatersrand University Press/Indiana University Press, 1993.

Guenther, Mathias. *Tricksters and Trancers: Bushman Religion and Society*. Bloomington: Indiana University Press, 1999.

Katz, Richard, Megan Biesele and Verna St. Denis. *Healing Makes our Hearts Happy: Spirituality and Transformation among the Kalahari Ju/'hoansi*. Rochester, Vermont: Inner Traditions, 1997.

Lewis-Williams, David. *Believing and Seeing: Symbolic Meaning in Southern San Rock Art*. New York: Academic Press, 1981.

Marshall, Lorna. *Nyae Nyae !Kung: Beliefs and Rites*. Peabody Museum Monograph No. 8. Cambridge, MA: Peabody Museum of Archaeology and Ethnology, 1999.

See also: Khoisan Religion; Makewana the Rainmaker (Central Malawi); San (Bushmen) Apocalpytic Rock Art.

Sanders, Scott Russell (1945–)

Scott Russell Sanders' religious vision is grounded in Quaker traditions he first encountered as a graduate student in England. "Quakers are mystics," he says in *The Force of Spirit*, "but homely and practical ones, less concerned with escaping to heaven than with living responsibly on Earth" (2000: 155). Sanders' essays and fiction seek ways of living responsibly on an Earth torn by violence, greed, and environmental degradation. In *The Force of Spirit* Sanders says too:

> All the names we use for the fire at the heart of matter are risky – God, Yahweh, Creator, Allah, Manitou, among countless others – for each comes freighted with a long, compromising history. From all the possible names I favor *spirit* because the word seems to catch the lightness, radiance, and windlike subtlety of the power that I seek (2000: 3).

As an essayist and writer of fiction, Sanders explores his relationship with spirit, especially the flashes of illumination it provides him in moments of silence on the mysterious border between nature and civilization.

One can glimpse Sanders' growing preoccupation with matters of the spirit in the titles of his essay collections: *Stone Country* (1985), *The Paradise of Bombs* (1987), *Secrets of the Universe* (1991), *Staying Put: Making a Home in a Restless World* (1993), *Writing from the Center* (1995), *Hunting for Hope: A Father's Journeys* (1998), and *The Force of Spirit* (2000). There is great violence at work in the world Sanders describes. His essay "At Play in the Paradise of Bombs" in the 1987 volume, for example, describes life on a military reservation in northeast Ohio, where he spent some of his formative years. This Ravenna Arsenal becomes a metaphor for our modern predicament. We all live, says Sanders, in a "fenced wilderness devoted to the building and harboring of instruments of death" (1987: 4). His essays, novels, stories, even his children's books, can be read as attempts to understand how we came to inhabit such a grim place and how we might transform it by attending to spirit.

With the exception of a few short stories set in the twentieth century, most of Sanders' fiction takes place before or after our own time. One might expect a writer who almost became a physicist to try science fiction, and Sanders has published three sci-fi novels: *Terrarium* (1985), *The Engineer of Beasts* (1988), and *The Invisible Company* (1989). In *Terrarium* people have moved into fabricated enclosures on the ocean because civilization's toxic by-products were about to destroy wild nature. Like the rebels in Ernest Callenbach's *Ecotopia* novels, the protagonists in *Terrarium* seek to create an alternative to the technocratic, totalitarian society they inhabit. Instead of threatening nuclear blackmail, as Callenbach's characters do, the rebels in *Terrarium* rely on memory of place, sexual love, and ceremonies similar to Quaker worship.

Sanders' historical fiction includes *Wilderness Plots* (1984), *Wonders Hidden: Audubon's Early Years* (1984), and *Bad Man Ballad* (1986). Humanity's troubled relationship with nature is at the heart of all three books. *Wilderness Plots*, for example, is a collection of very brief tales, based on fact, about the people who settled the Ohio Valley. With the stark, unembellished quality of folktales, these brief narratives offer a view of nature that is anything but sentimental. "Embryo Town" tells of a failed attempt to impose civility on a frontier that fosters greed and violence. "Profit and Loss" recounts the story of Daniel Cross, who doubles his wealth in a day by selling a wagonload of oats and then is eaten by wolves.

Sanders' writing is a search for the disciplines at the core of culture and the sacred power at the heart of creation that might allow us to find our way beyond the violence, greed, and destruction that mar our history.

William Nichols

Further Reading

Sanders, Scott Russell. *The Force of Spirit.* Boston: Beacon Press, 2000.

Sanders, Scott Russell. *Hunting for Hope: A Father's Journeys.* Boston: Beacon Press, 1998.

Sanders, Scott Russell. *Writing from the Center.* Bloomington: Indiana University Press, 1995.

Sanders, Scott Russell. *Staying Put: Making a Home in a Restless World.* Boston: Beacon Press, 1993.

Sanders, Scott Russell. *The Paradise of Bombs.* Athens: University of Georgia Press, 1987; Boston: Beacon Press, 1993.

Sanders, Scott Russell. *Secrets of the Universe.* Bloomington: Indiana University Press, 1991.

Sanders, Scott Russell. *Wilderness Plots.* New York: Morrow, 1983; Columbus: Ohio State University, 1988.

Sanders, Scott Russell. *Stone Country.* Bloomington: Indiana University Press, 1985.

See also: Ecotopia; Friends – Religious Society of (Quakers); Quaker Writers in Tasmania (Australia).

Santa Fe, New Mexico

Founded in 1610 by the Spanish, the area surrounding the city of Santa Fe, New Mexico was for centuries the home of the Pueblo Indian tribes of the Rio Grande valley. The city itself was developed on the site of a Pueblo Indian ruin known as *Kaupoge*, or "place of shell beads near the water." The five elements of mystical religions are amply in evidence in the landscape surrounding the city: volcanic, mountainous country forged by *fire*; vast stretches of *earth*, so rich in iron ore that it appears painted; *water*, from the nearby river the Rio Grande; the *cielo grande*, or vast open sky and clear *air*; and *space*, represented by the canyons and ancient standing-stone ruins of the Pueblos that line the Rio Grande to the west of the city. The location of Santa Fe along ancient migration lines from Central America to the north and more modern transportation lines from the eastern United States, situate it as a symbolic crossroads.

The modern era and its union of cultures can be traced to the settlement of the Native American lands by Spanish soldiers, political officials, and Franciscan missionaries. Translated from the Spanish, Santa Fe means "City of the Holy Faith." Like the Mexican ancestors who settled in the area following the Spanish conquest, the contemporary Hispanic Catholic population reveres the Lady of Guadalupe, a manifestation of the Virgin who appeared to the Indian Juan Diego in 1531 at Tepeyac, near Mexico City, and spoke to him in his native language, Nahuatl. The Chapel of Our Lady of Guadalupe in Santa Fe was built in 1795 and her feast day is celebrated annually on December 12.

Another religion to appear in New Mexico was the Brotherhood of Penitents, *Los Hermanos Penitentes*. Primarily composed of men, the Penitentes practice regular flagellation with whips made of local weed and carry heavy wooden crosses to emulate the Passion of Jesus Christ. The religious practices of the Penitentes derive from the landscape, where harsh desert conditions and absence of rain symbolically underscore the ways that human existence can mirror the suffering and privation of Christ. The Brotherhood of Penitents appeared in New Mexico in the early nineteenth century, but in the twentieth century, due to public scrutiny of the rather brutal practices of the group, the society began to hold secret meetings. The group is still active in the region.

Native and Christian beliefs coexist in Santa Fe, making the city and its environs a haven for anthropologists who seek to examine the relationships between native religious practices and Christianity. In the early decades of the twentieth century, the city became a destination for tourists interested in discovering "authentic" and "primitive" cultures in the American West. In the 1920s and 1930s, the Fred Harvey Company drew affluent easterners to New Mexico by combining train travel with motor car excursions through Native American villages. Travelers were escorted by female guides who had been trained in anthropology and literature at Eastern American universities. Tourists were able to learn about the culture and history of the southwest, but were also entertained by native dancers and artisans. The development of US Route 66 in the 1930s meant that more visitors could easily reach the high desert country of northern New Mexico, and the city quickly grew from a religious and trade outpost along the Camino Real and the Santa Fe Trail to the modern capital it is today.

Santa Fe is currently home to many modern nature-based philosophies, metaphysical religions, and spiritual practices. Religious groups holding meetings in Santa Fe today represent Eastern and Western spiritual traditions, and alternative religious groups that emphasize the relationships between mind and body. Vision quests and stone circle meditation retreats are common among women's spiritual groups, some of which are connected to Wicca and some to Eastern religions such as Buddhism. The popularity of the site may be linked to theories of sacred space. As Paul Devereux writes, "We need to go to the moors, deserts, forests and mountains, the remaining wild places of our world [to find] the caves, springs and mountain peaks recognized and selected as natural places of power by traditional peoples" (1992: 15). Places like Santa Fe and its surrounding wild spaces "embody *perennial* knowledge" (Devereux 1992: 15).

This religious history and the ensuing twentieth-century reputation for the city as a place of social tolerance and human rights activism have resulted in the city becoming a spiritual center. The location of Santa Fe in the foothills of the Sangre de Cristo (Blood of Christ) mountains gives it an incredible natural beauty, allows the city to draw from the powerful associations of mountains with spirituality, and engenders an intense sense of responsibility for wild places and natural resources conservation among the local population. While the Navajo ascribe sacred qualities to Blanca Peak in the Sangre de Cristo Mountains to the east of the city, environmental activists fight to restrict the incursion of housing developments and roads into the foothills. Many environmental groups are based in New Mexico, such as the Forest Guardians, the New Mexico Wilderness Alliance, and the Amigos Bravos (Friends of the Wild Rivers) whose special province is the Rio Grande. With its big sky, a visual reminder of divinity, its rivers, the root of life, and its sacred mountains, Santa Fe is the center of a natural religious world, a sacred space on the North American landscape in America.

Marguerite Helmers

Further Reading

Bernbaum, Edwin. *Sacred Mountains of the World.* San Francisco: Sierra Club Books, 1990.

Devereux, Paul. *Earth Memory: Sacred Sites – Doorways into Earth's Mysteries.* St. Paul, MN: Llewellyn, 1992.

Mullin, Molly H. *Culture in the Marketplace: Gender, Art, and Value in the American Southwest.* Durham, NC: Duke University Press, 2001.

Wilson, Chris. *The Myth of Santa Fe: Creating a Modern Regional Tradition.* Albuquerque, NM: University of New Mexico Press, 1997.

See also: Earth Mysteries; Sacred Mountains; Sedona.

Santal Region (India)

India is home to a large number of indigenous tribes known as *adivasi* (early inhabitants), *vanavasi* (inhabitants of the forest), *vanajati* (castes of forest) and *paharia* (hill-dwellers). Among these various tribal groups, the Santals constitute "the largest homogenous scheduled tribe in the country" (Troisi 1978: 24). According to the 1991 census of India, the Santals numbered approximately 4.2 million, largely concentrated in the three Indian states of Bihar, West Bengal, and Orissa. A sizeable number are also found in Assam, Tripura, Meghalaya, Bangladesh, and Nepal. Santal folklore describes the tribe as a wandering race. Although there is no consensus among either scholars or the Santals themselves about their original habitat, by the mid-eighteenth century large numbers of Santals were found in the Chotanagpur tribal belt in central India, who eventually migrated to the Rajmahal hills in the state of Bihar. Reportedly, the British government officials engineered this migration in order to clear the virgin forests and create human habitations as the Santals were renowned for their jungle-clearing skills. Since then the tracts of the Rajmahal hills have been considered the heartland of Santal life.

The Santal religious consciousness and its more concrete expressions (such as myths, rituals, and sacrifices) revolve around a large number of both benevolent and malevolent supernatural beings and spirits called *bongas*, who are believed to conduct the course of nature, human events, and ultimately human destiny itself, and with whom the Santals seek to live in close fellowship. In addition to these spirits, they believe in a number of impersonal powers residing in or connected with natural objects which are not worshipped but controlled through exorcism or magic exercised by the ritual specialist. The *ojha* (diviner) is the minister of white magic since his ministrations are beneficial to society, whereas *dan* (witch or sorcerer) is the minister of black magic. The *ojha* is believed to have the power to deal with the spirits, superior knowledge of common substances and objects, and the ability to diagnose the causes of misfortunes and/or sudden illnesses and prescribe appropriate ritual remedies through magical spells (*mantar*), incantations, and oil divination (*sunum bonga*). In contrast, the *dan* is capable of influencing the evil *bongas* and causing societal misfortune. The office of the *ojah* is reserved for men and a woman claiming to be an *ojah* is suspected to be a witch. Unlike other Indian tribes, the Santals believe that only women practice witchcraft.

The Santal Sacred Grove

The sacred grove and the tree-cult associated with it are widespread among Indian tribal groups. The Santals are no exception. Typically, the Santal sacred grove, known as *jaherthan*, is a cluster of five trees – four sal trees locally known as *sarjom* (*shorea robusta*) and one *mahua* (*bassia latifolia*) tree – believed to be relics of the primeval forest. Each tree in the grove represents one of the five principal spirits of the tribe: *Maran Buru* (great mountain), *Jaher Era* (The Lady of the Sacred Grove), *Moreko-Turuiko* (five-six), *Gosai Era* (a female spirit), and *Pargana Bonga* (boundary spirit). Usually located at the end of the village, the exact location of the *jaherthan* is determined by the first settlers of a Santal village after careful divination in which the principal spirits of the tribe themselves are said to demarcate the site through a human medium.

As the abode of the national spirits and as the locus of community worship, the *jaherthan* is the most auspicious sacred space for various ritual, cultural, and social celebrations. Religiously, it is the preeminent site of interaction between the Santals and the supernatural world. Socially and culturally, the grove also serves as the locus where an individual Santal's identity is constructed, celebrated, and reinforced insofar as major life-cycle ceremonies involve some form of ritual performance at the sacred grove. According to Santal belief, failure to "remember" the spirits (*bongas*) at such occasions would bring disastrous consequences such as epidemics and death.

A number of taboos – gender-specific as well as generic taboos – govern Santals' attitude to the sacred grove. The most important gender-specific taboo concerns women's participation in the ritual activities at the sacred grove. As a rule, women are not permitted to be present when sacrifices are offered nor can they eat the flesh of animals offered to the grove spirits. While women are specifically excluded from ritual activities at the sacred grove, all Santals are forbidden to "cut any of the sacred trees in the *jaherthan* or collect fallen branches" (Troisi 1978: 227). The sacred character attached to the grove and the accompanying taboos instill in the Santals a sense of reverential fear for the spirits and a concomitant respect for the natural environment.

Santal Religious Culture: Seasonal Festivals and Rites

The Santal fellowship with the spirits (*bongas*) is most prominent in their seasonal festivals and calendrical rites that are intimately tied to the agricultural cycle. The Santals observe seven annual community festivals that involve ritual offerings, libations, and blood sacrifices – typically fowls – dedicated to the sacred grove spirits. The *sohrae* (harvest) festival, celebrated in December–January after the harvest is gathered, and the *baha* (flower) festival, held in February–March when the *matkom* trees begin to blossom, are the two most important festivals. The seasonal festivals help to ensure the protection of the benevolent spirits as well as to ward off malevolent spirits. Prior to these festivals, the village priest (*naeke*) is subject to a series of ceremonial taboos and interdictions that typically include purificatory baths, fasts, penance, and abstinence from sexual intercourse intended to ensure the efficacy of the rites and the proper propitiation of the spirits of the sacred grove. Large-scale drinking, singing, drumming, and dancing are characteristic of these seasonal festivals. The seasonal festivals offer important clues to Santal religious culture and its core values. First, they reveal the Santal recognition of the presence of the spirits in the natural order. Second, they demonstrate the Santal dependence on the spirits for societal stability and well-being. Third, they afford an opportunity for the Santals to celebrate the lordship of the spirits over their life, habitat, and fields. This is most evident in the *baha* festival and the offering of the first-fruits of *matkom* flowers to the spirits. Until the spirits are properly propitiated, the flowers can neither be harvested nor eaten. Finally, they reveal the community's desire to live in harmony with nature.

Santal Material Culture

The Santal religious worldview and culture translates into a material culture that values close kinship with nature. As an agricultural community, most Santal villagers grow the rice and vegetables necessary for domestic consumption, procuring other necessary items at the weekly market in the neighboring town several miles away from their homes. Walking is the most conventional way of getting to and from the marketplace (*hatia*), although occasionally bicycles may also be used. In addition to providing a social outlet for intra-village and inter-family fellowship, the custom of walking to the marketplace minimizes Santal dependence on motorized vehicles. Even after walking several miles to the market, Santals are wont to purchase only what is urgently needed. This is due, in part, to their cultural attitude and in part to a lack of storage and refrigeration facilities.

Related to their frugal lifestyle is the Santal tendency to conserve and recycle. Since there are limited industrial resources in the region, the Santals make maximum use of the products they design from raw materials collected from their physical and natural geography. For example, almost every Santal village in West Bengal has bamboo groves from which baskets and other household items are made. Their domestic utensils are generally made of copper, brass, or clay. Furthermore, Santal women tend to reuse old saris and dhotis to tailor children's clothes. Often an entire village shares a single well or pond. Given the limited supply of water, Santals make diligent use of available water. All in all, the Santals demonstrate an ethic of conservation and a certain respect for the land in which they live since their personal and social identity is intimately connected to their physical space.

The third feature of Santal material culture is its reliance on tribal herbal medicinal system. While the Santals view most diseases as unnatural, ascribing them to the agency of certain evil spirits which they believe can be counteracted through religious medicine, they also acknowledge the natural causes of ordinary illnesses. The Santal curative system utilizes medicines made from a large number of plants, herbs, and natural objects. Bodding records a list of 305 Santal prescriptions for various human diseases and 15 veterinary medicines. Whereas the village medicine man (*raranic*) is believed to have good knowledge of roots and herbs and their medicinal power, most adult Santals also have a basic knowledge of this "root medicine" (*rehet ran*). Since they regard nature and vegetation as a valuable resource for cure, Santals are careful not to destroy the vegetation, partly out of self-interest and partly out of reverential fear for the spirits permeating the universe.

Selva J. Raj

Further Reading

Bodding, Paul O. *Traditions and Institutions of the Santals – Horkoren Mare Hapramko Reak Katha*. Oslo: A.W. Broggers Boktrykkeri, 1942.

Bodding, Paul O. "Santal Medicine." *Memoirs of the Asiatic Society of Bengal* 10:2 (1927), 135–426.

Bompas, C.H. *Folklore of the Santal Parganas*. London: David Nutt, 1909.
Mahapatra, A. *Modernization and Ritual: Identity and Change in Santal Society*. Calcutta: Oxford University Press, 1986.
Troisi, Joseph, ed. *Readings in Tribal Life*, vol. 1. Delhi: Indian Social Institute, 1979.
Troisi, Joseph. *Tribal Religion: Religious Beliefs and Practices among the Santals*. Delhi: Manohar, 1978.
See also: Hinduism; India.

Santeria

The mystical worldview of Santeria, like that of its cultural ancestor, the religion of the Yoruba-speaking people of Southwestern Nigeria, is characterized by a highly personalized view of nature. The Yoruba-speaking people, called in Cuba *lucumis*, were brought to that island beginning with the sixteenth century. However, at the end of the eighteenth and throughout the first three-quarters of the nineteenth centuries, due to the expansion of the sugar and coffee plantation enterprise in Cuba, the number of imported slaves grew dramatically. Among them, the Yoruba-speaking were over-represented because it was a time when civil wars were ravaging their homeland, thus turning its inhabitants into easy prey for the slave traders.

In Cuba, Yoruba slaves and their descendants were able to preserve their religion, language, mythology, dances, legends and music. This factor was important in also preserving and transmitting the important relationship between Santeria's beliefs and nature.

In the merging of cultural traditions that took place in the cultural history of Cuba, borrowing and reinterpretation were common in the process that resulted in a new Cuban product. As such, the Yoruba religion in Cuba was placed in contact with other religious beliefs and practices. In the merging process that ensued, the transplanted Yoruba religion borrowed from the Mediterranean Catholic and the European, Kardecian, and Spiritualist beliefs and practices that were prevalent on the island. It also borrowed from beliefs and practices from other African ethnic groups. The Afro-Cuban religion that emerged as a result of these merging processes is commonly called Santeria, or Regla *Lucumi* or Regla de *Ocha*.

Central to the religion of the Yoruba people and of Santeria believers is the belief in supernatural power and energy called *ashe*, and its sources and manifestations. *Ashe* is primarily manifested in important *orishas*, or gods, who are the personification of the generic forces of nature (thunder, lightning, volcanoes, the sea); other *orishas* are patrons of important human activities such as hunting, farming, and smithing. Moreover, *ashe* is manifested in the lesser *orishas* who dwell in rocks, stones, streams, shells and other natural phenomena; it is also manifested in revered ancestors, and in consecrated stones, images, necklaces and all sorts of amulets.

Ashe is power that can be manipulated and controlled by magical means to be used to do good as well as harm. Worship is geared to secure the *ashe* necessary to deal with daily problems, to survive and propagate. Magical and spiritual means are directed to engage the goodwill of gods, who are the sources and manifestation of *ashe*, but who also require human assistance, and so they are constantly demanding to be fed and taken care of. This worldview is in consonance with a value orientation based on an intuitive-sympathy-with-nature stance, rather than the control of nature by scientific and pragmatic means, the value orientation prevalent in Western culture.

Whereas *Ashe* is manifested in all natural phenomena, it is especially present in those related to the Earth. According to McKenzie, "Yoruba religion in the nineteenth century would seem to be a religion of the Earth rather than of the sky" (1997: 38). This statement is validated by Lydia Cabrera's Afro-Cuban informant, "*Los Santos estan mas en el Monte que en el cielo*" ("The saints, or personalized supernatural beings, are in the wilderness rather than in the sky") (in Cabrera, *El Monte*, Havana: Editions Chichirekù, 1954, author's translation). El Monte, the wilderness, is the equivalent of planet Earth, which is inhabited by all kinds of supernatural beings: gods and spirits who constantly intervene in human affairs, thereby causing illness, misfortune, death or conversely good health and fortune.

This Earth-centric stance is reflected in the perception that gods and spirits, the sources or receptacles of magical power or *ashe*, animate most earthly inorganic natural phenomena such as the mountains, volcanoes, rocks, stones, the water in streams, rivers, the sea, and the oceans. Organic natural phenomena are viewed in a similar way. Animals, particularly snakes, snails, lizards, and birds, especially vultures, as well as trees, especially when growing in groves, plants, and herbs are also perceived as receptacles or manifestations of supernatural beings, the *orishas* and spirits, imbued with *ashe*.

On the other hand, atmospheric phenomena, such as lightning, thunder, rain, tornadoes, the wind, which so greatly impact the lives of earthly dwellers, are also perceived as animated by anthropomorphic supernatural spirits, who are also considered important sources of *ashe*. Rainbows are especially admired and revered, though not as much as the more dynamic and destructive atmospheric phenomena. Meanwhile, celestial bodies such as the Sun, the Moon and the Stars, although seen as magnificent manifestations of the greatness of the creation of the Supreme Being, Oludumare, are not objects of religious interest. Finally, *ashe* is also manifested in humanmade symbolic and consecrated objects, such as amulets, which are perceived as receptacles of this power.

Among Afro-Cubans this mystical worldview persists when confronting untamed nature, wild animals, and/or plant life. In Cuba, *la ceiba*, siguaraya, and the royal palm tree are perceived as particularly potent receptacles of the sacred. This belief is evident in the words of Lydia Cabrera's informants and documented in her monumental work *El Monte*. It is in this wilderness where trees, plants, and herbs subjectively interact with humans.

Plants and animals have a distinctive personality and display the whole gamut of human emotions and nature, as demonstrated in the testimony of Florencio Baró. A child of slaves, Baró was born and raised in Carlos Rojas, a town well known in Cuba as one of the cradles of Santeria. He described the magical ambiance of his native town where wild vines and weeds grew, filling the empty lots with mystery and silence. In his own words: "Anything can be *brujo*" (can have supernatural power, can have a spirit) (interview with the author, 1991).

One of the most important functions of Yoruba religion and its cultural descendant, Santeria, is to serve as a health system, providing practitioners the means of diagnosis and treatment for all kinds of ailments. As in traditional Yoruba religion, in Santeria herbalism assures survival and adjustment, which was especially true during the nineteenth century when access to medical care in Cuba was very limited. However, during the last century the role of santeros as pharmacists was deemphasized. Santeros placed greater reliance in medical prescriptions and treatment rather than in their own medicine derived from their knowledge of the healing power of herbs. Consequently, the wilderness in Santeria started to lose importance as a receptacle and source of supernatural power.

In current times there has been a trend for Santeria to flourish in large metropolitan areas where the wilderness is absent and natural phenomena is less threatening than in rural villages and towns. Thus, even though *ashe* remains integral to Santeria's beliefs and practices, the awesome and mystical view of nature in the ambiance of Santeria is being lost.

Mercedes Cros Sandoval

Further Reading
McKenzie, Peter. *Hail Orisha: A Study of Phenomenology of a West African Religion in the Mid-Nineteenth Century*. (Studies of Religion in Africa, 19). Netherlands: Brill Academic Publishers, 1997.

See also: Candomblé of Brazil; Caribbean Cultures; Umbanda; Yoruba Culture (West Africa).

Saro-Wiwa, Kenule Beeson (1941–1995) and the Ogoni of Ogoni

Born in the southern village of Bori, Ken Saro-Wiwa was one of Nigeria's most recognized and accomplished citizens. An Ogoni leader from Ogoni, he was tried and hanged for challenging what he considered to be genocide perpetrated against the indigenous minorities of the Niger River Delta by the petroleum industry and their political allies.

Saro-Wiwa's life was punctuated by careers as a teacher, civil servant, publisher, television producer and dramatist. He is the author of over forty major works, including novels, volumes of poetry, essays, plays, journalism, short stories and children's books. From 1985 to 1990, Saro-Wiwa created, wrote, produced, financed and marketed Nigeria's most popular situation comedy, *Basi & Co.*, watched weekly by 30 million Nigerians. Winner of the Goldman Environmental Prize and the Right Livelihood Award in 1995, he was nominated for the Nobel Peace Prize prior to his execution.

Always environmentally conscious, Saro-Wiwa adopted the plank of environmentalism as a strategic tool to promote the Ogoni cause. "The visit to the United States (1993) sharpened my awareness of the need to organize the Ogoni people to struggle for their environment," Saro-Wiwa wrote. "A bit of research and thinking of my childhood days showed me how conscious of their environment the Ogoni have always been and how far they went in an effort to protect it. I had shown this consciousness all along" (1995: 79).

Jailed under the *Treason and Treasonable Offenses Decree* promulgated in 1993 by President Gen. Ibrahim Babangida, Saro-Wiwa wrote (from prison) poetry that widely echoed the sentiments of the minority delta peoples:

Ogoni is the land
The people, Ogoni
The agony of trees dying
In ancestral farmlands
Streams polluted weeping
Filth into murky rivers
It is the poisoned air
Coursing the luckless lungs
Of dying children
Ogoni is the dream
Breaking the looping chain
Around the drooping neck
of a shell-shocked land
                (widely circulated prison poem).

"The land and the people are one and are expressed as such in our local languages," according to Dr. Owens Wiwa, Ken Saro-Wiwa's brother.

The Ogoni have always respected nature, and this informed the struggle for the environment. There are lots of names for the spiritual trees, sacred rivers and lakes, and the traditions are very important. When people are ill, they revert back to indigenous beliefs and folklore (personal communication, Dr. Owens Wiwa, 2003).

The Ogoni number some 500,000 people today, a minority among a 300 minority and three majority (Yoruba, Igbo/Ibo and Hausa-Fulani) ethnic and religious groups in Nigeria. They live on the coastal plain of the vast mangrove estuary of the Niger River. The floodplain is home to some seven million people, grouped by nation, ethnicity and clan, including: the Ijo, Urhobo, Itsekiri, Isoko, Efık, Etche, Ibibio, Andoni, Ikwere, Ogoni, Isoko, Edo, and Kwale-Igbo. These tribes' relationships to religion and nature are complex and difficult for outsiders to understand.

Like other affiliated linguistic groups in the delta, the Ogoni connection to the environment is defined in spiritual and ritualistic terms, where Earth, soil, water, trees, plants and animals are sacred. (Despite the catastrophic spiritual, ecological and cultural devastation in the delta, this section is written in the present tense to reflect the prevailing attitudes, practices and beliefs.) Certain sacred groves and forests are revered: burial grounds for good and evil people; sacred boundaries between neighboring communities; family heritage forests. Ancient and enormous African oak, Iroko and cotton trees, animals and plants are worshipped. Customary laws have always existed; formal legislation to protect nature proliferated after 1850, and historical accounts of willful or accidental injury to wildlife document punishment by death. Sacrifice and ritual cleansing are daily events used to placate and honor nature spirits and deities. Priests and priestesses hold sway over the delineations and durations of sacred spaces.

Rights of habitation and ownership of communal spaces are intermittently transferred to animals: where the sacred Odumu (royal python) finds a home, it is the legal owner and community law recognizes its rights (until it vacates).

The concept of animal libertarianism has been practiced among the communities of the Niger Delta since antiquity … The people do not hunt animals for sport; rather, they are categorized in accordance with value – religious, ecological, social and economic … Infraction could result in fines, expensive ablution and atonement rites, and ostracism from the age group or the community as a whole … Shell's right to explore and produce hydrocarbon (a right now seriously challenged by all communities of the Niger River Delta) does not preclude the rights recognized to be enjoyed by persons, animals, and other living and nonliving things (Okonto and Douglas 2001: 215–25).

During his final activist years (1989–1995), Ken Saro-Wiwa championed the cause of the Ogoni people in international arenas; toward the end he expressed his indigenous consciousness by addressing Ogoni audiences only in his native Gokana language. In 1991, Saro-Wiwa organized the Movement for the Survival of Ogoni People (MOSOP), and was elected President *in abstentia* in 1993; MOSOP sought to reclaim economic rights and protect the environment against the petroleum ecocide that had already claimed the Ogoni mainstays of fishing, farming, hunting and gathering. In 1992, Saro-Wiwa delivered the *Ogoni Bill of Rights* in person, with his book, *Genocide in Nigeria: The Ogoni Tragedy* (1993) during a speech to the UN Unrepresented Nation's and People's Organization (UNPO) in Geneva, Switzerland. Saro-Wiwa called for an end to the petroleum corporation's occupation of Ogoni, for political autonomy and international attention to the devastation of the delta's ecology.

"The extermination of the Ogoni appears to be policy," Saro-Wiwa stated.

National ideas of national independence, the fact of Africans ruling Africans in nations conceived by and for European economic interests have intensified, not destroyed, the propensity of man to subject weak peoples by force, violence and legal quibbling to slavery and extinction (1995: 98).

After 1992, Saro-Wiwa was relentlessly harassed and prevented from speaking abroad. On 4 January 1993, the first annual Ogoni Day, Saro-Wiwa organized some 300,000 Ogoni in a nonviolent celebration, with music, dance and a rally at each of the seven Ogoni kingdoms. Elaborate masks worn by revelers attested to the indigenous cosmology; "people are supposed to believe what the masks represent" (personal communication, Dr. Owens Wiwa, June 2003). Masks (masquerade) are used as expressions of mysticism and power, and to validate the people's beliefs. "To Shell and the Nigerian government, my brother was a dangerous and irresponsible terrorist" (personal communication, Dr. Owens Wiwa, June 2003).

Saro-Wiwa's detention diary, *A Month and a Day* (1995), expresses his evolution as an Ogoni nationalist: "My worry about the Ogoni has been an article of faith, conceived of in primary school, nurtured through secondary school, actualized in the Nigerian civil war in 1967–1970 and during my tenure as member of the Rivers State Executive council, 1968–1973" (1995: 49). Saro-Wiwa first wrote on the Ogoni as an exploited minority in *The Ogoni Nationality Today and Tomorrow* (1968). In 1970, Ogoni leaders petitioned the Nigerian military government protesting the expropriation of delta life by multinational petroleum corporations. The result at every stage, Ogoni supporters claim, was corruption, deceit, propaganda and violence, against the backdrop of the theft of natural resources (Okonto and Douglas 2001).

Competition between Islam (north) and Christianity (south) fueled by the military government has led to widespread pogroms and communal violence in Nigeria. The persecution of Christians and their churches in the delta provoked an international Christian solidarity movement (1990s). An equally frequent phenomenon is the dogmatic use of religion (Christianity and Islam) to justify punitive and repressive military operations. This phenomenon has been prevalent amongst delta oil communities.

As an example: "Grace be unto you and peace from God our Father and from the Lord Jesus Christ," begins a memo (21 December 1995) from the commander of the Rivers State Internal Security Task Force, charged with "wasting operations" in Ogoni (read: raping, torturing, killing), to Ogoni clergy. "Let us pray for Ogoniland and the Ogonis, even with the following passages in our mind: Luke 18:1; 1 John 5:14, 15; 1 John 8:21, 22."

Raised a protestant, Saro-Wiwa attended church infrequently; but he read the Bible constantly while imprisoned (personal communication, Dr. Owens Wiwa, June 2003). His writings are infused with the symbolism of Islam and Christianity, though he admonished or lampooned these major faiths (and the blind or confused faith of followers) as often as he praised them for attributes in them that he admired. Biblical references were also common, often in the context of biting satire. His writings were equally contradictory about traditional village life, tribal beliefs, indigenous cosmology and paganism; in contradistinction were his confusions about modernity and the "comforts" and "benefits" of Western civilization.

> He wrote: "The Christian church, as I have said, has a powerful hold in Ogoni, and the arrival of the Pentecostal churches at a time of serious economic difficulties had led to even more people seeking solace in religion . . . it was making the people not seek answers to their problems . . . [t]he Pentecostal churches tend to be one-man outfits out to exploit the people. They lack the strength of the organized Churches, which I definitely admire (1995: 152).

On 22 May 1994, Saro-Wiwa was arrested and imprisoned on charges of murder stemming from what was widely regarded as a military frame-up. In an irregular trial convened by a special military tribunal, Royal/Dutch Shell bribed two prosecution witnesses, Ogonis who recanted in exile. Lawyers for Royal Dutch/Shell attended and presented briefs at the hearing. Saro-Wiwa's defense team of high-profile lawyers resigned in refusal to add legitimacy to the proceedings. A posthumous United Nations fact-finding mission documented the extensive irregularities. Amnesty International and Human Rights Watch condemned the trial.

By the time of his death, Saro-Wiwa was a living manifestation of the Ghandian philosophy of *Satyagraha*. Given the opportunity to escape Nigeria, even by the jailers of the cell that held him, Saro-Wiwa refused to abandon his people. "I have devoted my intellectual and material resources, my very life, to a cause in which I have total belief, and from which I cannot be blackmailed or intimidated," he read, from his final defense statement. His last words to the tribunal cited the Quran (Sura 42, verse 41): "All those that fight when oppressed incur no guilt, but Allah shall punish the oppressor." On 10 November 1995, Ken Saro-Wiwa and eight Ogoni men were hanged in a shallow pit at Port Harcourt, Nigeria. His last words were "Lord, take my soul, but the struggle continues."

Protests and repression continued into the twenty-first century, often taking unique spiritual forms. The Ijo Youth Council (1999) initiated "Operation Climate Change" as a vehicle to raise environmental awareness through non-violent protest.

> Tapping the veins of Ijo culture, it sought to bring the pains and travails of the people to national attention through the "Ogele," a traditional Ijo dance where stories, song and mime are deployed to chastise the erring, heal the wounds of the injured, and invoke the spirit of the ancestors to cleanse the land in a festive atmosphere of drink and merriment (Okonto and Douglas 2001: 146).

Keith Harmon Snow

Further Reading

Achebe, Chinua. *Things Fall Apart*. London: Heinemann, 1958.

Alagoa, E.J. "The Niger Delta States and Their Neighbors, 1600–1800." *History of West Africa*, vol. 1. J.F.A. Ajayi and Micheal Crowder, eds. NY: Columbia University Press, 1972.

Biersteker, Thomas. *Multinationals, the State and Control of the Nigerian Economy*. Princeton, NJ: Princeton University Press, 1987.

Madsen, Wayne. *Genocide and Covert Operations in Africa, 1993–1999*. Lewiston, NY: Edwin Mellon Press, 1999.

McLuckie, Craig W. and Aubrey McPhail, eds. *Ken Saro-Wiwa: Writer and Political Activist*. Boulder, CO: Lynne Rienner, 2000.

Ojo-Ade, Femi. *Ken Saro-Wiwa: A Bio-critical Study*. Brooklyn, NY: Africana Legacy Press, 1999.

Okome, Onookome, ed. *Before I Am Hanged: Ken Saro-Wiwa: Literature, Politics and Dissent*. Trenton, NJ: Africa World Press, 2000.

Okonto, Ike and Oronto Douglas. *Where Vultures Feast: Shell, Human Rights and Oil in the Niger River Delta*. San Francisco, CA: Sierra Club Books, 2001.
Robinson, Deborah. *Ogoni: The Struggle Continues*. Geneva, Switzerland: World Council of Churches, 1996.
Saro-Wiwa, Ken. *Similia: Essays on Anomic Nigeria*. Epsom, England: Saros International, 1991; Nigeria: Spectrum Books, 1996.
Saro-Wiwa, Ken. *A Month and A Day: A Detention Diary*. New York, NY: Penguin, 1995.
Saro-Wiwa, Ken. *Sozaboy: A Novel in Rotten English*. White Plains, NY: Longman Group, 1994.
Saro-Wiwa, Ken. *The Singing Anthill: Ogoni Folk Tales*. Epsom, England: Saros International, 1991.
Saro-Wiwa, Ken. *On A Darkling Plain: An Account of the Nigerian Civil War*. Epsom, England: Saros International, 1989.
Snow, Keith Harmon. Personal communications with Dr. Owens Wiwa, June 2003.
Snow, Keith Harmon. "Nigeria: Ogoni: No Safe Haven." *Toward Freedom* (1997).
Snow, Keith Harmon. "Nigeria: State of Occupation, Republic of Shell." *Peacework*. Boston, MA: American Friends Service Committee, September 1996.

See also: Diola (West Africa); Rubber and Religion in the Belgian Congo; West Africa.

Sarvodaya Shramadana Movement

The Sarvodaya Shramadana Movement began in 1958 as a series of youth work camps held to assist depressed villages in Sri Lanka. The work camps, which came to be called *Shramadanas* or "donations of labor," were organized by Dr. A.T. Ariyaratne. Ariyaratne eventually led the volunteers who participated in these Shramadanas to form a new society dedicated to Sarvodaya, or "the awakening of all." Arising in the context of the post-colonial Buddhist renaissance in Sri Lanka, Sarvodaya articulated a vision of a new social order based on Gandhian and Buddhist ideals. From the Gandhian heritage, Sarvodaya adopted the ideal of selfless service and nonviolence as guiding principles of a socio-economic order. Sarvodaya interpreted these Gandhian influences through its Buddhist heritage in Sri Lanka and became one of the first examples of what later came to be called "socially engaged Buddhism." From Buddhism it drew upon the ideal of "awakening" or "liberation," construing this ideal as a process of dual liberation: the liberation of the individual through the liberation of society. Sarvodaya's interpretation of this process of liberation critiqued the image of Buddhism popularized by Weber and other Westerners that regarded it as a world-denying religion. Sarvodaya's description of how liberation takes place through the process of working in society to assist others is expressed through its saying, "We build the road and the road builds us."

Sarvodaya spells out the interdependent nature of awakening and development by specifying six levels of human awakening: personality awakening, family awakening, village or community awakening, urban awakening, national awakening and global awakening. Sarvodaya's view of the awakening of society on these levels constitutes a sweeping reinterpretation of the nature and process of social and economic development. Sarvodaya's model of development is "people-centered" and has as its primary aim "human fulfillment" rather than the creation of material wealth. The economic ideal of the social order Sarvodaya seeks is described as one of "no poverty and no affluence." For Sarvodaya, development is an integrated process involving six elements that reinforce each other to bring about the best society. In this process the reform of the social, economic and political elements of a society should take place in conjunction with the reassertion of its spiritual, moral, and cultural factors. Sarvodaya pursues this program of integrated development and social reform by emphasizing Buddhist spiritual values such as loving kindness (*mettÅ*), compassion (*karuœÅ*), sympathetic joy (*muditÅ*), and equanimity (*upekkhÅ*).

Employing this ideal of an integrated development founded on spiritual values, Sarvodaya has established a program of village development that has sought to provide alternatives to the kind of capitalistic, materialistic development promoted by the government and multinational agencies. In Sri Lanka, Sarvodaya works through a network of district centers and local Sarvodaya societies in over 11,000 villages. Through these groups it seeks to construct from the grassroots up what may be called a form of dharmic civil society that is not driven by the desires of the market but guided by the spiritual values of the Buddhist dharma. As one of the largest non-governmental organizations in Asia, Sarvodaya facilitates a variety of services to empower the people at the village level including programs of village pre-schools, relief and rehabilitation, village banking and micro credit, appropriate technology and sustainable development.

Sarvodaya's integrated approach to development weaves together themes such as economics, spirituality and ecology. Explaining that according to Buddhist teachings all things and all beings are interconnected, Ariyaratne has placed great emphasis on the preservation of nature and the environment. Sarvodaya has sought to promote methods of sustainable agriculture and has established the Sarvodaya Institute for Biodiversity Conservation. Sarvodaya has also opposed government and multinational development plans that endanger the environment. For example, Sarvodaya organized a large demonstration to oppose the government's scheme to build a tourist hotel in an area that was both a semi-wilderness area and a Buddhist sacred area. Sarvodaya argued that such a large hotel would adversely affect the cultural and moral environment of the community, disrupt the ecological balance of the semi-wilderness area where one of the last wild herds of elephants in the country lived, pollute the water supply and infringe on the sanctity of an ancient, sacred Buddhist shrine.

The Sarvodaya Shramadana Movement has also been one of the major voices for peace during the long-running conflict in Sri Lanka. Sarvodaya has organized peace marches and peace meditations since the conflict erupted in 1983. In that year, Sarvodaya organized a massive, Gandhian-styled peace march from the southern tip of Sri Lanka to the north. Although that first march was eventually stopped short by the government, Sarvodaya went on to organize further peace marches and peace meditations. In March, 2002, Sarvodaya held a peace meditation attended by 500,000 people at the ancient Buddhist sacred city of Anuradhapura. Through the peace meditations and marches Sarvodaya has sought to create a critical mass of spiritual consciousness for peace and social transformation.

George D. Bond

Further Reading

Bond, George D. *The Buddhist Revival in Sri Lanka.* Colombia, SC: University of South Carolina Press, 1988.
Kantowsky, Detlef. *Sarvodaya, The Other Development.* New Delhi: Vikas Publishing House, 1980.
Macy, Joanna. *Dharma and Development: Religion as Resource in the Sarvodaya Self-Help Movement.* West Hartford, CT: Kumarian Press, 1983.
See *also*: Ariyaratne, Ahangamage Tudor (A.T.); Buddhism – Engaged; Gandhi, Mohandas; Hinduism; Macy, Joanna.

Satanism

With the foundation of the Church of Satan in 1966, Anton LaVey gave a rational, coherent voice to what had previously existed mainly as a fiction. In prior centuries, the myth of Satanism was used by Christian authorities to control those who might stray from church doctrine. It led to some disgruntled individuals adopting this fictitious adversarial religion in an attempt to resist the hegemony of the self-anointed servitors of Jehovah. These rebels used the tales of the clerics as a template for their practices; hence historians note the emergence of actual Black Masses, as well as the structured debaucheries of the Hellfire clubs. The renegades worshipped God's opponent in an attempt to gain from him what they thought Yahweh had denied them in the here and now. Still, they remained within the Christian paradigm that saw life as transitory, a preparation for either reward or punishment in an afterlife outside of nature.

With the publication of *The Satanic Bible* in 1969, Anton LaVey defined Satanism from the perspective of a practicing Satanist. For the first time, Satanism was presented as a structured philosophy in an above-ground manner via a mass-marketed text. This new religion, rooted in Epicureanism and Nietzschean iconoclasm, rejected Christian definitions, and discarded the dualism that had been a part of Western belief systems since the advent of Zoroastrianism. This Satanism was not "Devil worship." Instead, it embraced the Prince of Darkness, not as God's equal-but-opposite adversary, but as the central archetype of a philosophy promoting personal freedom. Satan, the symbol of the liberated self, is externalized in ritual – a natural behavior of our species – and seen as an extension of the Satanist's psyche or volitional essence. LaVey determined what he called the "unvarnished truth" about the nature of the human animal, and deemed it to be the foundation for this religion that sees nothing sinful in the beast called Man. He understood that beauty and monstrosity are part of the range of our species, and thought that only by accepting these extremes could a final philosophical synthesis be made that is consistent with the normal, healthy state of the human animal. His Satanism attempts to preserve and celebrate, rather than alter or suppress, humankind's natural state of being.

Most significant to this new doctrine is its axiom that man is solely a "carnal" being. To the Satanist, flesh is reality and spirit is fantasy. Satanism thus eschews all spirituality as fiction – rejecting anything posited to be outside of nature as illusion or delusion. There are no gods or devils, angels or demons. Most Satanists thus deny the possibility of any afterlife.

Nature, to the Satanist, is all that exists – the totality of the objective universe. It includes all things organic and inorganic and the processes that govern their existence. Nature exists in and of itself, is inherently self-coherent, and does not require an exterior author. It cycles eternally, from "Big Bang" to "Big Crunch." This recurrent expansion and contraction, emergence and extinction, is accepted by the Satanist, with no need to posit a supernatural "escape clause." Satanists understand that nature is neither benevolent, nor malevolent – it is indifferent. They pragmatically live in harmony with its mechanisms, collectively called "The Law of the Jungle," without trying to impose contrary human idealism over them. To Satanists, these laws must be understood and obeyed if the intent is to move elements of existence in the direction of their will.

Satanists see themselves as their own gods, but they have not deluded themselves that they are or will become actual deity figures. Each individual Satanist is simply the center of his own subjective universe. The Satanist bears the responsibility for creating his own hierarchy of values that determines what he considers to be pleasure and pain. The goal of a Satanist is to enjoy his life to the fullest.

It follows that Satanism offers to each individual his own birthday as his highest holiday. Beyond that, since understanding and embracing the flow of nature is of paramount importance, the days upon which the seasons change – the equinoxes and solstices – as well as the midpoints between these days that are defined as climactic points for the seasons, are celebrated as holidays.

While LaVey's philosophy is man-centered, it does not elevate the human species above the other organisms with whom it shares the globe. Man is just another animal, one small part of the fullness of nature. Satanists appreciate the natural order of the Earth's ecosystem and oppose human activities disruptive to this harmonious structure. Most Satanists strongly empathize with nonhuman animals and thus many choose to support organizations that work toward the preservation of species threatened by humankind. Such pernicious behavior, far worse than any found in those animals who follow their instincts, arises in man because his own instincts have often been warped through the acceptance of unnatural spiritual doctrines.

Satanists condemn such doctrines for inhibiting the instincts of the human animal, perverting these naturally existing mechanisms. Satanists think they are born to their philosophy because they are animals whose instincts remain intact. Individuals with damaged or repressed instincts are seen as being likely to embrace supernatural religions, as they do not feel a part of nature. They are "spiritual," not "carnal," and thus not born Satanists. The conversion of one type to the other is not deemed possible.

In the early 1970s, a small group of members of the Church of Satan began to adopt the idea that a supernatural entity existed, whom they called Set. In 1975, led by Michael Aquino, they left the Church of Satan to found the Temple of Set. Today this remains the only significant offshoot of the Church of Satan, and even though their membership is generally numbered in the hundreds, this organization has developed a consistent philosophy and a body of literature. While these Setians initially saw themselves as "evolved Satanists," their direction from the start was in contradistinction to the philosophy of the Church of Satan. To the Setian, Set exists as a supernatural entity, one with whom members of their Priesthood claim they can "commune." The essence of Setian doctrine states that Set caused the intelligence of the human species to manifest itself, and that this conscious act is counter to the inertia of nature. Set is thus the God of the "non-natural," one who promotes individual consciousness in opposition to the collective blending that is thought to be the mechanism of nature. The followers of Set are named his "elect" and are considered to be special among the human species. Through the process of "Xeper" (pronounced "kheffer" – an Egyptian word meaning "to become") Setian initiates attempt to willfully evolve into a god-like state. Such is not expected to occur in a single lifetime, and so the isolated consciousness of the individual Setian attempts to "Remanifest," essentially to reincarnate, to continue the process of evolution toward a Set-like final state.

Clearly, this is not congruent with the philosophy of the Church of Satan. Setians have recently dropped their claim to being Satanists, and are generally viewed by those who examine fringe religions as being a Thelemic religious organization, derived from the concepts advanced by Aleister Crowley. The Temple of Set considers itself to be part of the Left Hand Path – which Setans define as those religions that seek to isolate individual consciousness from nature, as opposed to the Right Hand Path, which they see as those religions whose adherents seek unity with their deities.

Most recently, the internet has proved to be an avenue for the spread of contemporary Satanism. The Church of Satan itself maintains a presence, as does the Temple of Set. However, primarily because of the use of Satanic imagery by popular musicians, Satanism has recently attracted a diverse group, including many young people who are generally drawn by its imagery, rather than the philosophy itself. This interest is both fueled by and manifested on the internet.

The ease of making a website has led the many fascinated by Satanism to create sites that are an amalgam of materials, including literature from the Church of Satan, the Temple of Set, and numerous other traditions from Eastern and Western occultism that have no relationship with the ideas espoused by these two organizations. Because the authors of these sites are not scholars, and often their research is limited to what they have encountered by chance, these web-based collections of concepts are not necessarily internally consistent. The possibility exists that another philosophy could emerge online, also calling itself "Satanism," which might develop a body of literature and an internally coherent philosophical position.

The philosophy of Satanism as defined by Anton LaVey continues to be embraced by those individuals who agree that man is just another animal, that he is a part of nature, and that being alive, it is his own prerogative to determine his values. To these Satanists, the individual plays the natural role of furthering his species in the niche it has evolved to fill. He decides that he will maximize his pleasures, both intellectual and physical, during that treasured span of his one and only life. In the process, he appreciates his kin, the other living beings with whom he shares the Earth, who are viewed as colleagues in the struggle for exuberant life.

Peter H. Gilmore

Further Reading

Barton, Blanche. *The Church of Satan.* San Francisco: Hell's Kitchen Productions, 1990.

LaVey, Anton Szandor. *Satan Speaks.* San Francisco: Feral House, 1998.

LaVey, Anton Szandor. *The Devil's Notebook.* San Francisco: Feral House, 1992.

LaVey, Anton Szandor. *The Satanic Bible.* New York: Avon Books, 1969.

See also: Paganism – Contemporary; Wicca; Wise Use Movement.

Sauna

Sauna, a Finnish and Sami word for a building in which to bathe for cleansing body and mind, has become somewhat varied, even with commercial meanings in communities without a history of sauna culture. As an inseparable part of Finnish identity, sauna has been part of the Finnish life cycle for thousands of years – and continues to be so, both in Finland with 2.2 million saunas for 5.2 million people – and among expatriate and emigrant Finns.

Sauna as a log building comes from Finnish-related and Slavic peoples living in Northern Eurasian forest territories. Throughout its traditional area it still is a place for ablutions conducive to hygiene and health, but also a part of their ethnic religion and cultural habits. Although the sauna as a building and as a heated construction has undergone various changes, it has been adapted into new milieus. Also, in urban environments, many sauna habits and rituals have shown remarkable strength not only to survive but even to be revived as a part of socially shared group behavior among youth, adults, and environmentalist societies.

There are bathing habits reminiscent of Finnish sauna behavior on other continents (e.g., Roman, Turkish, or Celtic bath; Japanese *furo*; and the Native American sweat-lodge, such as the Lakota *inipi*). What is spiritually common to them is the feeling that bathing in the steam of *löyly* is not only a cleansing experience, but also one touching the very soul. The spirit of *löyly*, greeted in charms, is the main element in the folk belief related to Finnish sauna with birch switches and its healing effects. *Löyly* is a more ancient word than sauna, being a Finno-Ugric word referring not only to the steam issuing forth from the stones, but also to a human soul. The word goes back some 6000 years to the shared ancient vocabulary of the Finno-Ugric peoples.

What the baths of these three continents have had in common with the passing of time has been their connection to human life and their rites. On the other hand, they have also played a part in solving various crises. In *inipi*, *furo* and sauna, the spirit and the body are purified – recreated, as it were, to enable the person to face the challenges life presents. There are religious epics on the sauna in the oral traditions (e.g., in Japanese Buddhist texts, Native American Indian initiation songs, and in the *Kalevala*, the Finnish national epic).

The core of sauna is *kiuas* (i.e., stones in a hot heap), around which, the sauna in a depression in the Earth, and subsequently, the smoke sauna were created. There were numerous stages through which the development passed from mere heaps of stones covered by skin or cloths to the present electrically powered sauna stove in private home apartments or hotels. The public sauna was a part of Finnish city culture before its almost complete disappearance from the Helsinki street scene after World War II. In Tokyo the *furo* is faring better; public facilities for this amount to well over a thousand.

The Finns assumed the task of propagating sauna at an early stage. Around the year 1638, the Delaware New Sweden Colony was established on the eastern seaboard of America, with several hundred Forest Finns among the inhabitants. What was typical of the pioneering tradition of the first habitation was that the settlers built a smoke cabin. The so-called pioneer house on the west coast was no more than a smoke sauna, a log house that served frequently as a model for other inhabitants of the area. The propagation of sauna has continued to this day, with the construction of saunas at their postings being among the first tasks of Finnish UN peacekeeping forces.

Sauna is the Finns' national symbol, just as the *furo* symbolizes the modern Japanese way of life, and the *inipi* the new consciousness of Native American identity. Symbols are important, even more so for the small nations compelled to exist under pressure to change from the major cultures. Sauna is one of the Finnish words recently to be borrowed by other languages. Along with the Finnish, sauna has made its way all around the world, even if not in complete agreement with the rest of the world in the matter of sauna manners.

The sauna has been a sacred place for Finns. According to the weekly routine, there usually was only one visit to sauna, on Saturday evening. Moreover, to heat a smoke sauna for several sessions was a whole day's operation, an operation demanding its own expertise in the selection of kindling, the laying of the kindling, the adding of firewood, and above all an unhurried approach; whoever heated the sauna and bound the birch switches had to have time. The taking of sauna itself entailed a certain ritual which was observed with religious zeal. A proverb has it that one should conduct oneself in sauna as in church – reverently. Going to sauna and partaking of it were social behaviors governed by many rules of conduct: not to be rowdy, curse, gossip, speak evil, break wind or make a noise in sauna.

It is a Finnish custom to greet the *löyly* spirit before entering or mounting the benches. The recipient of this prayer-like salutation was not primarily the sauna building, but rather the spirit of the sauna or the *löyly* itself. Adults and older children were expected to bless themselves as they entered sauna. It was prepared for the sacred space and the delicate nature of the situations; people were naked, the pores of the human body were open and exuding sweat, defenseless against the evil eye and envy. When a sauna was inaugurated, reference was made to the power of Väinämöinen the wise man who is the central figure in the *Kalevala*; the *löyly* itself was said to be "Väinämöinen's sweat."

Löyly, the vapor rising from the water splashed over the stones of the sauna stove, establishes a connection between the sauna or sweat shed and the Hereafter. The steam arising from the stove, like the smoke issuing from the open fire, the door of the smoke sauna, the flue or chimney, established a symbolic connection between the sacred space of the sauna and its people (microcosmos) and the sphere of the Hereafter and its inhabitants (macrocosmos). An individual healing event occurring within the sauna and concerning the health of an individual is linked to the entire universe. It is easier for an individual to recover when he knows that his ailment is part of that universe. Myths are based on a connection to the gods, the departed and to spirits, which are recounted and incanted in the *löyly* of the sauna, or by the campfires. As mentioned above, the word *löyly* is of Finno-Ugric origin. It does not only refer to the steam rising from the sauna stove as it does in Finnish or Estonian (*leil*), but one of a person's souls, linked as it is throughout life to breathing. The Hungarian *lélek* is such a soul. The word encompasses the span of a human life, which in old beliefs was held to last from the first breath to the last. Thus "departure of *henki* 'breath' " (which in Finnish is synonymous with the word for spirit) was thus the end of physical life, the perceptible sign of death.

However, *löyly* is only one of the appellations among the Finno-Ugric languages for "soul." Another is *itse* "self," in Hungarian *iz*, which circumscribes social rather than physical life and death. The "self" of a person has a different lifespan from *löyly*. A person acquires this at a later stage than *löyly*, and it lasts longer. A child acquires the status of "having a self" when s/he acquires a name. He is deemed to have a social existence, his name endows him with a right to inherit, and, among the Saami, with his own reindeer mark of identification. The "self" does not expire when the spirit departs, but only two to three years later. Then the person is dead as an individual. Finnish *henki*, (Estonian *hing*), refers to the third soul, which, according to superstition, is immortal. In the world of shamanhood, the spirit refers to the soul of the shaman traveling outside the human body in various forms, generally as an animal, a fish, a snake, a bear, a reindeer, or a bird to the realm of death.

The sauna was generally the first building a Finnish settler built, thereby also designating the limits of his forest, hunting, fishing and slash-and-burn farming. Building a sauna involves knowledge of timberwork construction, the right type of wood and choice of felling time. As in all buildings with a fireplace of some sort, according to folk belief, there was a spirit watching to see that customs were observed and infringements punished. Thus, the first person to light a fire had to be chosen with care, as it was he who would, according to the superstition, assume the position of *saunatonttu* or spirit of the sauna.

Peaceful heating of the sauna and the correct way of making birch switches was taught by one generation to the next. Expertise in the effects of taking sauna is a special doctrine of traditional Finnish-Karelian folk medicine, of those versed in cupping, bleeding, and healing joints. When a healer was called to sauna or when an injury was being healed in the home circle, very special attention had to be paid to the heating of sauna and to other operations. Alder should be used for the logs. This would ensure greater efficacy of the cures effected in sauna. The familiar proverb encapsulates the effect of sauna: "What tar, alcohol or sauna cannot help is fatal indeed."

Long ago there was a custom in central Finland to lay a table for the spirits of the farmhouse kitchen. While the people of the house bathed, the spirits took to the table. There are many ways in which sauna has been connected to the progress of the agricultural year. Many of the main occupational tasks were performed in it: the softening of flax, the smoking of meat, the brewing of beer and the like in the malt sauna. The annual procedures, lasting for days, were connected to the younger and older family members spending time together with folk poems and songs: erotic songs might be sung in time to the job at hand, yarns were spun, tales told, riddles solved, and the message might well be an erotic one.

For the Finns sauna has been a sacred place to which they go for purification at all crucial points in their existence from birth to laying out of the dead. The rituals at such times are exclusively the women's province. Only in such cases in which the current transition from one state to another is considered by the community to be infelicitous for one reason or another – for example if the child or patient is very sick – would the intercession of a male witch, sage, or folk healer be called for. This is then a crisis situation requiring the most potent religious leader of the locality or family, a woman or man to restore order through remedial procedures.

Until the 1930s, Finnish women mostly gave birth in sauna. The midwife was referred to as the "sauna wife" and the mother-to-be as the "sauna woman." "Sauna time" among the womenfolk might last as much as a week before the child was triumphantly carried into the farmhouse. This marginal situation was associated with precautionary measures against diseases and the evil eye, as a child who was "without self," having no name, and a woman before the churching, six weeks after the birth, was deemed "unclean," both were considered to be in a precarious state.

Upon reaching adulthood, women went to sauna. Girls of marriageable age were bathed and slapped by older women with the birch branches to incantations on procuring love. Traditional Finnish wedding ceremonies involved the bathing of the girl to be given in marriage by her family, the *antilas*. This was done in the sauna by the married women of the family. After the ablutions, the girl's hair, which had so far been worn loose, was plaited and a "wife's cap" placed on her head together with the other symbols of a married woman. In the sauna, in the company of women, the girl was also initiated into how different life would be at her husband's place and what it would be like under the eagle eye of her mother-in-law. She was then completely "away from the paternal home" to which she could only return the August after the birth of a son to visit relatives.

For women, there were more transitions in the sauna than for men: from girl to bride, from bride-to-be to a girl given in marriage, from a girl given in marriage to a wife, from a wife to a "breeding" mother, then to one who suckled an infant. Various functions became attached to various individuals regarding the sauna rituals in the extended family.

Sauna may also be connected to funeral rites. In some rural areas there was a custom that after death the corpse was carried into the sauna on a board where women of the family who specialized in the task washed it. In family-oriented communities it was important that all those with a role in the rituals, those who washed the body, the wailing women, those who spoke the words, and those who made the coffin, should all be family members. If someone was requested to perform such a function, it was tantamount to a last wish, and it would be improper to decline. Once the corpse had been washed with soap reserved for that purpose, it would be dressed and lifted onto a laying-out board in the threshing building.

Ancient Finnish folk tradition indicates consistently that the conception of mixed bathing in sauna, assumed by the rest of the world, is only regionally valid. In most communities men and women had their own turns. Sauna taken in a family group is a more recent phenomenon. Earlier, the farmer would take sauna with his farmhands once the work in the fields was done, while the farmer's wife would go to sauna with the maids after milking. Since the men's turn was first, the women's turn on the eve of the Sabbath might well continue into the Sabbath. Sunset was a delimiting factor until it was superseded by the clock. When the church bells rang at six o'clock in the evening to announce the Sabbath, the women should have left the sauna.

In the Finnish folktales, sauna is a "hard place" and people were afraid to go there alone. Finnish folk beliefs contain many stories about first-hand experiences of encountering the spirit of the sauna in which the spirit has been felt to be "hard." Such an apparition was believed to be a punishment for infringements against the Sabbath. The narrative tradition confirms men's and women's sauna turns. When they had had their sauna, there began a third turn, that of the spirit of the sauna. In most cases, the person experiencing something is a lone woman or a group of women bathing together. Sometimes, it is a question of an obviously erotic dream; the last woman to go to bathe falls asleep on the bench and feels or sees a hairy male creature who comes to throw water on the stones or comes to caress her.

As with the home, the threshing building, the cowhouse or other building with a fireplace, the spirit of the sauna is the first to kindle a fire. Thus, the people of the house would try to find a "nice, mild" person, a kindly old woman or man, to ensure good sauna luck. When the spirit of the sauna is seen, a resemblance is reported with the first person to kindle a fire. This is in accordance with the ancient belief in the playful, blithe child – the most suitable person for a good sauna spirit.

Juha Pentikäinen

Further Reading
Alho, Olli. "Sauna." In Hildi Hawkins and Päivi Vallisaari, eds. *Finland: A Cultural Encyclopedia*. Helsinki: Finnish Literature Society, 1997.
Edelsward, Lisa-Marlene. *Sauna as Symbol: Society and Culture in Finland*. New York: Peter Lang, 1991.
[The] *Finnish Sauna*. Helsinki: Sauna-seura, 1955.
Konya, Allan. *The International Handbook of Finnish Sauna*. Hampshire: The Architectural Press, 1973.
Peltonen, Jarno and Matti Karjanoja, eds. *Sauna: Made in Finland*. Helsinki: Tammi, 1997.
Pentikäinen, Juha, ed. *The Finnish Sauna, the Japanese Furo, the Indian Inipi: Bathing on Three Continents*. Helsinki: Buildin Information, 2001.
"Sauna – A Finnish National Institution." *Finfo* 3. Helsinki: Ministry for Foreign Affairs, 2001.
Sytula, Charles M. *The Finnish Sauna in Manitoba*. Ottawa: National Museums of Canada, 1977.
Teir, Harald, et al., eds. *Sauna Studies*. Papers read at the VI Int. Sauna Congress in Helsinki on 15–17 August 1974. Vammala: The Finnish Sauna Society, 1976.
Viherjuuri, H.J. *Sauna: The Finnish Bath*. Brattleboro, VT: The Stephen Greene Press, 1965.

Savages

Structurally speaking, savages – whether noble or ignoble – are category violators. Ideologically speaking, savagism – again, whether of the noble or ignoble variety – is a discursive device in the service of cultural criticism. In the case of "savages," taxonomic violations – especially imagined cannibalism and incest – are emphasized as a way to mark the differences between "civilization" (proper society: + God and + institutional constraints on human appetites) and "natural man" (– God and – institutions, a veritable Hobbsean war of all against all) and to justify whatever means necessary to redeem the latter category to (the interests of) the former, whether as ends – converted human beings – or as a means to an end (i.e., converted into labor). In the case of the noble savage, cultural criticism is internally leveraged. Here ideological struggles are against "society" itself, with noble savages – à la Montaigne and Rousseau, for example – serving as the counterpart to and antidote for the corruptions of "civilization." While thumbnail, this schema of savage/noble savage holds in some permutation or another from Herodotus to the American novelist Fenimore Cooper. What remains to be specified is how savagism reverberates to the present and with what ramifications for how we understand the intersection between religion and nature.

Here I will limit my comments to the North American context, where savagism persists to the present, particularly in some government policies (continued paternalistic treatment), social practices (Indians facing explicit racism), and media images (one acute example is the character Zach Provo, played by James Coburn in *The Last Hard Men*, who is a particularly smart but depraved "halfbreed"). However, in all of these realms the noble savage has gained ground on the ignoble savage, as reflected in increasingly proactive legislation, softened public sentiment, and romantic Hollywood films, for adults and children alike. The primary characterization of Indians in this mode is as stewards and priests of nature: Indians have become eco-shamans of the contemporary world. This phenomenon has two basic sources: non-Indian and Indian authors.

Historically, non-Indian authors of noble savagism emphasized aspects of native cultures that could be construed as rejoinders to European social constraints, whether at the level of the body, community, property, or the land. Thus, drawing upon native traditions, authors of noble savagism celebrated Indians' putative naturalness, especially as reflected in dress, demeanor and sexuality, "original" democracy, communal property, and connection to the land. In this way, historical noble savagism operated by means of selective interpretation and strategic distortion of existing Indian traditions. Modern noble savagism, by comparison, is less concerned to construct itself in relation to "tradition," and looks instead to already circulating images of "the Indian" that might be refashioned to fit the times. This is particularly true in the representation of Indians as environmentalists. Non-Indian authors of this persona have not, on the whole, worked from the ample resources of Indian traditions concerning care for the Earth. Whether images are cast by way of crying Indians, fictive chiefs' speeches, or new age books, the icon of the noble environmentalist is a product of modernity, even while being a critique of it.

Complicating this picture is that native people are coparticipants in modernity. Not only do they inhabit the present, they shape it. Most significantly, Indians have exerted their voice in the symbolic economy. In particular, Native Americans have gained unprecedented agency in the control of images of themselves. Whether by way of tribal museums, congressional hearings, or mass media, in the last several decades Indians have responded to centuries of savagism (of both varieties) by insisting upon their representational autonomy. One aspect of this has been by way of tremendous cultural revitalization, as tribes and nations have expressed their identities and aspirations in the idiom of local traditions. Here, to be sure, land and nature are emphasized. Land is simultaneously the source of creation (both in the sense of autochthony and as ongoing creation), loss (by way of removal or desecration), and hope (the source and site of future generations). That is, land is frequently spoken of as timeless, in the sense of a geographical synchrony wherein past, present, and future coalesce in and as nature. Maintaining tradition – that which links the generations – is predicated upon maintaining proper relations with the land. It must be said here that such figurations of the land, while building upon ancient religious traditions, constitute an oppositional discourse leveled against the forces and threats of antinative interests. Unlike non-native noble environmentalism, however, here agitation is not a response to abstracted disaffection with the modern condition, but is a response to proximate and concrete impediments to daily life.

Another aspect of Native Americans taking control of self-representations raises new sets of issues. If tradition-centered concern for the land is inwardly focused, we need to describe outwardly focused claims by Indians about the land and nature meant for non-native audiences. This distinction is not in the service of distinguishing between sincere and insincere or authentic and inauthentic claims. Rather, my analysis of inwardly focused and outwardly focused speech is in recognition of the multiple audiences of "tradition." All speakers will modify their speech according to audience in order to achieve desired rhetorical effects. Neither "tradition" nor Indians stand outside of this dynamic; to imagine that they do is to participate in another form of savagism cum essentialism.

When addressing non-native audiences, contemporary Indian orators frequently assume the posture of the noble environmentalist familiar to consumers of the non-native incarnation of the image. In order to reach audiences, Indian speakers often adopt stereotypical images of themselves. This is a lesson native peoples have learned from years of interacting with the dominant society. In the contemporary context this means appearing according to script as eco-shamans. If our analysis ended here, however, we would have failed to see this as a form of resistance to dominant culture, not a capitulation to it (recognizing, however, that "sell-outs" exist). Resistance is waged insofar as adoption of dominant images entails adaptations of them. Specifically, the noble environmentalist takes on a militant edge, appearing as an eco-warrior. This enables native speakers to confront members of the dominant society in forceful and blunt moral terms.

Speaking outwardly as moral warriors, native orators often invoke nature in a schematic way. To paraphrase:

> We are born of nature, our mother. From time immemorial we have had a sacred pact to care for nature. While society has grown away from nature, we have maintained our relationship to her, preserving vital knowledge in the process. Doing so, we have sacrificed self-interest and economic gain. Now we are in crisis because the dominant society has taken advantage of us. Tradition, religion, and language are in decay, and we face cultural extinction as a result. At the same time the world itself is in crisis. The Western ethos has run its course, exhausting nature in the process. The only remedy is for native people to use our knowledge and ritual practices to restore the Earth for the good of all humanity. This situation had been prophesied repeatedly. We are here today to show you that we can heal nature from the damage you have caused her, but only if you first begin to heal the damage you have caused us.

This discourse does a variety of things. Primarily, it signals a desire on the part of Indians to have their moral and political voices registered and seeks to extend the moral authority of the native speaker over the non-native audience. This discourse implicitly – and sometimes explicitly – relies upon feelings of guilt and spiritual inadequacy on the part non-natives, using vulnerable emotional states of the audience as a platform upon which to construct and advance moral claims in a religious idiom. Specifically, moral claims are framed in reciprocal terms: we care for you at the spiritual and cosmic level (by maintaining the Earth); in turn, you must care for us by making sure our political and economic grievances are addressed.

Whether spoken by Hopi representatives to the United Nations, a Ute leader to journalists, a Crow religious leader to museum officials, or by a Lakota political activist to college students, to give some examples, this discourse operates as a kind of strategic essentialism. Insofar as speakers traffic in the dominant culture's stereotypical images, and to the degree that this discourse functions as a modality of cultural criticism, outwardly focused Indian self-representations participate in the rhetorical economy of noble savagism. Recognizing this, we nonetheless want to point out some important respects in which native-produced noble savagism differs from the non-native variety. First, and most importantly, this discourse – however much it is stereotypical and therefore redolent of non-native discourse – is spoken by native people about themselves. Moreover, this version of the noble environmentalist is a form of cultural criticism engaged in by people who are and are not members of the society in question: issues of citizenship and sovereignty pervade this discourse. Finally, even when spoken in the most general and stereotypical terms, this discourse is defined by its concrete sources and sub-texts. One needs to cultivate an ear for how local concerns are made audible to general audiences through this language. For example, in a recent presentation a self-proclaimed "Indian elder" spoke to college students generally about the "desecration of the Earth" and, simultaneously, he gave voice as a Dineh rancher to specific frustrations: his reservation faces regular environmental degradation and so few people seem to care.

Greg Johnson

Further Reading
Berkhoffer, Robert. *The White Man's Indian: Images of the American Indian from Columbus to the Present.* New York: Knopf, 1978.
Ginzburg, Carlo. "Montaigne, Cannibals and Grottoes." *History and Anthropology* 6:2–3 (1993), 125–55.
Pearce, Roy Harvey. *Savagism and Civilization: A Study of the Indian and the American Mind.* Berkeley and Los Angeles: University of California Press, 1988 (rev. edn).
Scott, James C. *Domination and the Arts of Resistance: Hidden Transcripts.* New Haven and London: Yale University Press, 1990.
Taussig, Michael. *Shamanism, Colonialism and the Wild Man: A Study in Terror and Healing.* Chicago and London: University of Chicago Press, 1987.
Weaver, Jace, ed. *Defending Mother Earth: Native American Perspectives on Environmental Justice.* Maryknoll, NY: Orbis Books, 1996.
White, Hayden. *Tropics of Discourse.* Baltimore and London: The Johns Hopkins University Press, 1978.
See also: American Indians as "First Ecologists"; Noble Savage; Noble Savage and the "Ecologically Noble" Savage; Religious Environmentalist Paradigm.

Schelling, Friedrich Wilhelm Joseph (1775–1854)

The work of Friedrich Wilhelm Joseph Schelling is one of the most comprehensive and elaborated philosophies of nature to date. Its influence was enormous, not only on the romantic philosophy of nature, but also on today's nature discourse. Schelling, the colleague of Fichte and Hegel, strove from the beginning to overcome what has been described as the difference between the idea of ontological substance and Transcendental philosophy. Transcendental philosophy asks for the conditions of *cognition* of nature and, consequently, considers the perceiving subject, the active consciousness, as the uniting factor (this was elaborated by Immanuel Kant). In contrast, Schelling defines *Naturphilosophie* (philosophy of nature) as a discipline that asks ontologically for the uniting factor within active nature itself, thus considering nature to be the productive power of its evolution. Nature as an *active category* can only be recognized by transcending its single products – the material world – and looking behind the process of its evolution. To illuminate this, Schelling uses the famous distinction between nature as a mere *product* and object of empiricism (*natura naturata*) on the one hand and nature as *productivity* and subject (*natura naturans*) on the other hand. For Schelling, philosophy of nature deals only with the latter. It tries to find out how nature brings forth its materially given products. The term *natura naturans* designates the aspect of a "living becoming." It contrasts with the study of dead being. The generated, material objects are of importance only insofar as they allow conclusions about the principles of "becoming" that lie beneath them. Hence, Schelling argues against a mechanistic concept of nature that is limited to empiricism, and for an organicist model that has become prominent again in the twentieth century. In this perspective nature is not characterized by stability but by a continuous destruction and reproduction of its products, thus bringing the blind and chaotic productivity into evolutionary form.

With this concept Schelling argues against both Kant and Fichte. In contrast to Kant's contention that the only authority for judging nature lies in the observing subject, Schelling conceptualizes nature as an independent and self-organized entity that can be known by humans through empathy and open-mindedness. This is crucial, because Schelling here overcomes the Cartesian dichotomy of *res extensa* (the extended, material realm) and *res cogita* (the realm of thinking). And in contrast to Johann Gottlieb Fichte, who saw nature as a dead object, Schelling holds the position that the dichotomy between humans and nature has to come to an end. He complains that in his time nature had been (theoretically) reduced to a mere mechanism and (practically) had been forced under human interests, a species that does not shrink from destroying nature. Schelling asserted that this mechanism and exploitation would lead not only to nature's but also to humankind's death.

Against those tendencies, Schelling's philosophy advocates principles of empathy and connectedness, and after 1804 these ideas grew stronger in his work. Schelling argues that the only way truly to recognize nature is to acknowledge nature's familiarity and correspondence with a person's own mind and to approach it with a trait of inner love. To be sure, this aspect of his philosophy mostly influenced Romanticism and Transcendentalism, but it is important to note that Schelling's philosophy did not confine itself to philosophy of nature. Instead, it is integrated in a whole framework of an "absolute system of philosophy," which comprises philosophy of mind (*Geist*) and history, on the one hand, and philosophy of art and religion, on the other. This kind of "meta-philosophy" was the joint project of Schelling and Hegel after 1801. Despite their different approaches and results, both shared an interest in establishing a consistent idea of nature and its formulation in a logical concept.

Kocku von Stuckrad

Further Reading

Bowie, Andrew. *Schelling and Modern European Philosophy: An Introduction.* London and New York: Routledge, 1993.

Esposito, Joseph L. *Schelling's Idealism and Philosophy of Nature.* Lewisburg: Bucknell University Press; London: Associated University Presses, 1977.

See also: Hegel, G.W. Friedrich; Philosophy of Nature; Western Esotericism.

School of Living

Ralph Borsodi, a vigorous critic of industrial civilization, began to advocate a back-to-the-land ethic when he and his wife left Manhattan for a rural acreage in 1920, and his 1933 book *Flight from the City* was a widely read manifesto of decentralist agrarianism. His first large-scale attempt to work out a cluster of small self-sufficient acreages was undertaken at Dayton, Ohio, under government auspices in the 1930s, but he clashed with federal authorities and soon began a similar private project, called Bayard Lane, near Suffern, New York. Borsodi's vision entailed simply-built homes on lots of perhaps two acres (leased, not purchased, to deter speculation) on which residents would engage in subsistence farming and gardening as well as various creative and artistic endeavors. Borsodi called it a School of Living because residents would learn great lessons in life through their mundane activities.

Borsodi's work was outwardly secular in nature, although undergirding it was a quest for individual spiritual fulfillment, moral values, and creativity. His work was part of the larger decentralist movement, a loose grouping of rural idealists who, particularly in response to the economic travails of the depression, sought a return to simple living. Some parts of the decentralist movement, such as the Catholic Rural Life movement, were explicitly religiously oriented, and spiritual seekers of various stripes were represented in many decentralist programs, including Borsodi's.

In the late 1940s, Borsodi's work was revitalized by his disciple Mildred Loomis, who founded a new School of Living in Ohio and then at Heathcote Center in Maryland. Like Borsodi's, Loomis' work was largely secular, but her American Indian-inspired sense of the interrelatedness of all beings provided a spiritual underpinning to it. Several other projects based on Borsodi's thinking emerged as well, and his ideas influenced government depression-era resettlement projects in which clusters of small-acreage tracts were provided for impoverished farmers. Among those influenced by Borsodi's teachings of self-sufficiency and organic gardening were J.I. and Robert Rodale, who visited Bayard Lane and whose magazines, *Prevention* and *Organic Gardening*, spread Borsodi's message much further than he ever had managed to do alone.

Timothy Miller

Further Reading

Borsodi, Ralph. *Flight from the City*. New York: Harper & Row, 1933.

Issel, William H. "Ralph Borsodi and the Agrarian Response to Modern America." *Agricultural History* 41 (April 1967).

Loomis, Mildred. *Alternative Americas*. New York: Universe Books, 1982.

Shi, David E. *The Simple Life: Plain Living and High Thinking in American Culture*. New York: Oxford University Press, 1985.

See also: Back to the Land Movements; New Religious Movements.

Schumacher, Ernest Friedrich (1911–1977)

E.F. Schumacher was a prophet of reverential ecology. His attitude to nature differed from those of utilitarian environmentalists who value the natural world because of its usefulness to humankind: they say, "we need to protect the forests, conserve biodiversity, keep the rivers clean and farm the land organically because these are the necessary 'resources' for the good health of human beings." But such pragmatic proclamations are, according to Schumacher, "metaphysically blind."

Much of the environmental degradation and depletion is caused by the arrogant conviction that human beings are in charge of the Earth, Schumacher argued. He rejected the anthropocentric view that animals, forests, rivers and all the other forms of life are there purely to serve human interest, as well as the belief that there are no constraints upon how far human beings should go to control nature and pursue human desires.

In the context of religious and spiritual understanding of the phenomenal world Schumacher realized that behind the myriad manifestations of life, the creation is a seamless whole. From bacteria and butterflies to mountains and cosmos, including humankind, all are part of an interconnected unity of life. This ever-unfolding, and ever-evolving process of the universe is embedded in the principles of reciprocity, participation and mutuality. Life nourishes life and in return life is nourished by life. There is an everlasting balance of belonging at work. There is a meaningful and intricate relatedness within existence, which maintains the cosmic connectivity and continuity. There is an inbuilt natural justice and ecological ethics, which hold together this symbiotic, systemic, and self-organizing Earth community. Schumacher's vision of wholeness in the cosmic order repudiated the notion of progress based on the human versus nature and spiritual versus material split.

E.F. Schumacher came to ecology from economics. When he was in Burma (now Myanmar), advising the government there on economic development, he came across the Buddhist view of wholeness and spirituality, which he came to believe underpinned the economy of that country. Inspired and enlightened by the Burmese experience he wrote his classic essay "Buddhist Economics" where he questioned the claim that "economic laws are free from metaphysics or values" (1999: 37). Schumacher realized that in Buddhist economics "the maximisation of human well being was dependant on the minimisation of material consumption" (1999: 41).

This encounter with the East was shattering as well as transforming. Schumacher changed from an agnostic intellectual to a spiritual seeker and saw the creation through the eye of the sacred. The Buddhist notion of nature spirituality made him realize that nature is not merely a mine to meet the material needs of human societies obsessed with economic growth. Rather, the natural world is a web of sacred relationships of which human communities are an integral part – endowed with a responsibility to act ethically, nonviolently and reverentially.

Schumacher came to believe that all creatures of the Earth have a right to be and live. He believed that in order to live in harmony with the natural process and to sustain a socially just and economically fair world order our technologies must be appropriate, our organizations small scale, and lifestyles simple. "The essence of civilization," said Schumacher "is not in the multiplication of wants but in the purification of human character" (1999: 39).

E.F. Schumacher was born in Bonn, Germany in 1911. He came to Great Britain in 1930 as a Rhodes Scholar to read economics at New College, Oxford. He went through a variety of careers including, teaching, business and journalism. Eventually he became the head of statistics in the National Coal Board of Britain.

In 1970 Schumacher founded the Intermediate Technology Development Group, which pursued the path of economic development on a human scale leading to spiritual fulfilment. For him technology was a complementary dimension to sustainable agriculture. He became the President of the Soil Association and he campaigned for compassionate and organic methods of farming.

Schumacher published his seminal and best-selling book *Small is Beautiful: Economics as if People Mattered* in 1973. His second book, *A Guide for the Perplexed*, which spelled out more clearly his coherent and spiritual worldview, was published in 1977. In both these books, Schumacher urged his readers to shift their attitudes toward nature from utilitarian and managerial to a reverential and participatory paradigm. Coming from a religious perspective, he saw the natural world not merely as a resource to be mined for human use and managed well for future generations; rather he took a Hindu and Daoist perspective in which humanity is an integral part of the phenomenal world and participates in it as a process of coevolution. This holistic context integrated nature, humanity and religion, and provided a cohesive understanding which underpinned Schumacher's philosophy.

Schumacher died in September 1977 in Switzerland. Immediately after his death the E.F. Schumacher Societies were established in Great Britain and the United States. These two organizations hold prestigious Schumacher Lectures every year.

The speakers and teachers giving Schumacher Lectures and teaching at Schumacher College have included Ivan Illich, Amory Lovins, Fritjof Capra, Hazel Henderson, Wendell Berry, Gary Snyder, Rupert Sheldrake, Vandana Shiva, Dr. A.T. Ariyaratne, Joanna Macy, Arnes Naess, James Lovelock, Kathleen Raine, James Hillman, Thomas Berry, Alastair McIntosh, John Seed, Starhawk, and many others.

Topics and themes covered include deep ecology, ecopsychology, holistic science, care of the soul, politics of compassion, Buddhist economics, nature spirituality, Earth democracy, organic living, sustainable development, bio-diversity and indigenous cultures.

In 1991, Schumacher College was established at Dartington, Devon, UK, in order to carry forward and explore a way of life which is ecologically sustainable, socially just and spiritually fulfilling. *Resurgence* magazine, to which he was a regular contributor, continues to develop and disseminate Schumachian philosophy around the world.

Satish Kumar

Further Reading

Schumacher E.F. "This I Believe." Totnes, Devon: Green Books, 1997.

Schumacher E.F. *Good Work*. London: Jonathan Cape 1979.

Schumacher E.F. *A Guide for the Perplexed*. London: Jonathan Cape, 1977.

Schumacher E.F. *Small is Beautiful: Economics as if People Mattered*. London: Blond and Briggs, 1973; reprinted Abacus: Sphere Books Ltd., 1988; Point Roberts, WA & Vancouver, BC: Hartley & Marks Publishers Inc, 1999 (rev. edn).

See also: Ariyaratne, Ahangamage Tudor (A.T.); Berry, Thomas; Berry, Wendell; Bioregionalism; Buddhism – Engaged; Capra, Fritjof; Ecopsychology; Environmental Ethics; Lovelock, James; Macy, Joanna; Naess, Arne; Radical Environmentalism; Religious Studies and Environmental Concern; Seed, John; Sheldrake, Rupert; Shiva, Vandana; Snyder, Gary – and the Invention of Bioregional Spirituality and Politics; Starhawk; Transpersonal Psychology.

Schweitzer, Albert (1875–1965)

In terms of intellectual achievement and practical morality, Albert Schweitzer has been described as probably the noblest figure of the twentieth century. Born in 1875, he was brought up at Gunsbach in Alsace. His intellectual achievements span four major disciplines. Schweitzer learnt the organ under Charles-Marie Widor in Paris and published *J.S. Bach, le musicien-poete* in 1905. He studied theology and philosophy in Strasbourg, Paris, and Berlin, and published major works of New Testament scholarship, most notably *The Quest of the Historical Jesus* (1906; trans. 1910). In 1896 he made his famous decision to live for science and art until age 30 and then devote his life to serving humanity. Accordingly, despite his international reputation as a musician and theologian, Schweitzer turned to medicine and qualified as a physician. By 1913 he resigned his posts as principal of the theological college in Strasbourg and preacher at St. Nicholas and founded the hospital at Lambaréné, Gabon where he stayed until his death in 1965.

By 1952 Schweitzer had become a legend in his lifetime: his work in Lambaréné captured the public imagination, earning him the Nobel Prize for peace. But Schweitzer considered his most meaningful contribution, the one for which he wished to be remembered, to be his ethic of reverence for life (*Ehrfurcht vor dem Leben*). Although the concept of reverence for life is known, it has been subject to a range of distortions and so it is important to confront these in order to understand what Schweitzer meant by these three words.

The first distorting lens is *legalism*. Contrary to many commentators, Schweitzer does not propound reverence as a moral law, but rather as ethical mysticism. Ethical mysticism begins with a personal reflection on the self in the finite world that binds humans with nonhuman life and God (often referred to as the infinite Will-to-Live). For

Schweitzer, the most immediate and comprehensive fact of consciousness is that "I am life which wills to live, in the midst of life which wills to live." The direct, experiential identification of one's individual will-to-live (life) with other life, and through life with God, is foundational to his ethical mysticism. Though his mysticism starts from the individual subject ("I am life which wills-to-live"), it extends to a generalization on the world (in the midst of other wills-to-live). Crucially, Schweitzer returns to the finite manifestations of life and presents human moral action as the locus of mystical relation: in loving self-devotion to other life we realize our spiritual union with God.

The second distorting lens is *inviolability*. Many commentators have assumed that reverence for life upholds the moral inviolability of all life. It is true that Schweitzer sometimes writes in such a way as to invite this misunderstanding. The ethical person is one who:

> ... tears no leaf from a tree, plucks no flower, and takes care to crush no insect. If in the summer he is working by lamplight, he prefers to keep the window shut and breathe a stuffy atmosphere rather than see one insect after another fall with singed wings upon his table (1987: 310).

At first sight the sheer practical impossibility of these injunctions presents itself. But what Schweitzer offers here are not *rules* but rather *examples* of the type of action expected from one who upholds reverence for life. Indeed, the very word "reverence" (*Ehrfurcht*) indicates that he is not depicting obedience to moral law, it being concerned rather with a new temper of mind.

The third distorting lens is *inconsistency*. Since Schweitzer defines reverence as an absolute ethic which enjoins responsibility without limit toward all that lives, it is perhaps not surprising that reverence is judged to entail inconsistency in practice. Indeed, Schweitzer is not immune from such charges since, for example, he notoriously had fish caught to feed his sick pelicans. Such inconsistencies are made more glaring in the light of his rejection of any moral hierarchy: the ethics of reverence for life makes no distinction between higher and lower, more precious and less precious lives.

Schweitzer is often interpreted at this point as suggesting that no form of life should ever be destroyed and that all creatures, humans to microbes, should have the same moral worth. It is doubtful whether this was his intention. Rather what he is doing is rejecting here the long tradition of hierarchy that places humanity at the top of the pyramid of descending moral worth. Schweitzer readily and regrettably admitted that it is sometimes necessary to make choices between various forms of life. But what he wanted to emphasize was the essentially *subjective* (anthropocentric) nature of these declarations.

Having clarified aspects of Schweitzer's thought, it is now possible to indicate three of his contributions to religio-ethical thought.

The first contribution concerns *service to life as practical mysticism*. In contrast to most mystics, Schweitzer maintains that union with the divine is achieved not through contemplation, but primarily through service to other life: it is through the community of life, not community of thought, that I abide in harmony with the infinite Will. This is the mystical experience of ethics. In short, the phenomenon we call life is not something put here for our use or pleasure; we are part of life and our role is to enhance and serve each and every manifestation of it.

Schweitzer's second contribution concerns his *protest against an anthropocentric view of creation*. In a 1919 sermon he questioned whether humans should be considered the goal of creation: "The purpose of nature, with her thousands of appearances of life, is not understood as merely the presupposition of man's existence ... and humanity may not conceive of itself as the purpose of the infinite world" (1988: 40).

Schweitzer's rejection of the elevation of humans in the universe suggests a transformation of our relationship to other life: we are to perceive each manifestation of life for *itself*, and no longer for *ourselves*.

Building on these insights, Schweitzer challenges the idea that humans' sole responsibility in the world is to take care of their own species. In his exegesis of the parable of the Good Samaritan, he seeks to expand our understanding of neighbor:

> What is the sort of love toward God which compels us to be kind to others? What does love for our neighbour mean? ... The presupposition of morality is to share everything that goes on around us, not only in human life but also in the life of all creatures (1988: 119).

Schweitzer's reading of the parable develops Jesus' refusal to limit the extent of neighbor love by extending the category of neighbor to include all life: reverence does not draw a circle of well-defined tasks around me, but charges each individual with responsibility for all life within his reach and forces him to devote himself to helping that life. Schweitzer reads the parable as a metaphor for moral inclusiveness that corresponds analogically to nonhuman species. Similar to Jesus' rejection of a racially restrictive criterion of neighborly discrimination, Schweitzer counters the limiting structures of communal proximity by highlighting humans' participation in the community of life.

The third contribution concerns *non-injury to life as the central ethical imperative*. A man is truly ethical, Schweitzer writes, only when he obeys the compulsion to help all life which he is able to assist, and shrinks from injuring anything that lives. The time is coming when people will be astonished that humankind needed so long a time to learn to regard thoughtless injury to life as incompatible with ethics (1987: 310).

Schweitzer regarded traditional philosophy which restricted ethics to human-to-human relations as spiritually impoverished. He was deeply critical of animal experimentation, opposed sport hunting, and eventually embraced a vegetarian diet. His hospital at Lambaréné was a model of ecological responsibility: he went out of his way to preserve trees and flora, reused every piece of wood, string, and glass, and rejected modern technological developments which would have resulted in environmental degradation. As he saw it, his life *was* his argument.

To reverence life and to serve it: this is the heart of Schweitzer's commitment. His personal and intellectual legacy continues to hold strong moral appeal and serve as an inspiration for a wider ethic of life. In the words of Rachel Carson: "If during the coming years we are to find our way through the problems that beset us, it will surely be in large part through the wider understanding and application of his principles" (1962: 2).

Ara Barsam

Further Reading

Brabazon, James. *Albert Schweitzer: A Biography*. Syracuse: Syracuse University Press, 2000.
Carson, Rachel. Acceptance Speech for the Albert Schweitzer Medal. Rachel Carson Council, 1962.
Clark, Henry. *The Ethical Mysticism of Albert Schweitzer*. Boston: Beacon Press, 1962.
Ice, Jackson Lee. *Schweitzer: Prophet of Radical Theology*. Philadelphia: The Westminster Press, 1977.
Magnusson, Magnus and Rosemary Gorring, eds. *Chambers Biographical Dictionary*. London: Chambers Harrap Publishers, 1990, 1314.
Schweitzer, Albert. *Out of My Life and Thought: An Autobiography*. A.B. Lemke, tr. New York: Henry and Company, 1990.
Schweitzer, Albert. *A Place for Revelation: Sermons on Reverence for Life*. Martin Strege and Lothar Stiehm, eds. David Larrimore Holland, tr. New York: Macmillan Press, 1988.
Schweitzer, Albert. *The Philosophy of Civilisation*. C.T. Campion, tr. New York: Prometheus Books, 1987, 310.
Schweitzer, Albert. *The Teaching of Reverence for Life*. Richard and Clara Winston, trs. New York: Holt, Rinehart & Winston, 1965.
Seaver, George. *Albert Schweitzer: The Man and His Mind*. London: A. & C. Black, 1947.

See also: Carson, Rachel; Environmental Ethics.

Science

Nature is both a scientific and a religious challenge. Nature must be evaluated within cultures, classically by their religions, currently also by the sciences so eminent in Western culture. Religious persons often find something "beyond," discovering that neither nature nor culture are self-explanatory as phenomena; both point to deeper forces, such as divine presence, or Brahman or Emptiness (*sunyata*) or Tao underlying. Religions often detect supernature immanent in or transcendent to nature, perhaps even more so in human culture, though some religions prefer to think of a deeper account of nature, perhaps enchanted, perhaps sacred.

1. The Physical World: Matter and Energy

Science over the last four hundred years has opened up a vast extent of physical nature in space and time, unavailable to humans when the classical religions were formed. Once only speculative, cosmology has become science – and with mixed religious results, both from the vastness of the universe and from the naturalism, or secularizing, characteristic of science. Earth is lost out there in the stars; humans are dwarfed and shown to be trivial on the cosmic scale, as well as on the microscopic scale, (nothing but) the motion of atoms, molecules, biochemistries. Science seemed progressively to rob both our planet and the humans on it of any special place. But then the physical sciences took an unexpected turn.

Astrophysics and nuclear physics, combining quantum mechanics and relativity theory, have more recently been describing a universe "fine-tuned" for life. Physics has made dramatic discoveries at astronomical and submicroscopic ranges, remote from ordinary, native-range experience. The universe (this universe at least) originated fifteen billion years ago in a "big bang" and has since been expanding. From the primal burst of energy, elementary particles formed, and afterward hydrogen, the simplest element, which serves as fuel for the stars. In the stellar furnaces all the heavier atoms were forged. Some stars subsequently exploded (supernovae). The heavier elements were collected to form, in our case, the solar system and planet Earth.

In the last half-century, physics discovered that startling interrelationships are required for these creative processes to work. Theory interrelates the two levels; astronomical phenomena such as the formation of galaxies, stars, and planets depend critically on the microphysical phenomena. In turn, the mid-range scales, where the known complexity mostly lies (in ecosystems and human brains), depend on the interacting microscopic and astronomical ranges. If the scale of the universe were much reduced, there would not have been enough time for elements to form. If the expansion rate of the universe had been a little faster or slower, then the universe would already have recollapsed or the galaxies and stars would not have formed.

Change slightly the strengths of any of the four forces that hold the world together (the strong nuclear force, the weak nuclear force, electromagnetism, gravitation), change critical particle masses and charges, and the stars would burn too quickly or too slowly, or atoms and molecules, including water, carbon, and oxygen, or amino acids (building blocks of life) would not form or remain stable.

These results have been summarized as the "anthropic principle" (an unfortunately anthropocentric term), which argues that the universe has been programmed from the start and in its fundamental dimensions for the subsequent construction of stars, planets, life, and mind. There are non-theological, naturalistic ways of interpreting these discoveries, but a plausible interpretation is divine design.

Whatever one makes of these anthropic claims, the most complex events known are found on Earth in biological systems, and the most complex of all is the human mind, pursuing its science or its religion. In a handful of humus, which may have in it ten billion organisms encoding a billion years of evolutionary history, there is more coded information (trillions of "bits") than in all of the stars. In the trillion neurons of the three-pound human brain, each capable of hundreds or thousands of connections with the others, there is more operational organization than in the Andromeda galaxy (so far as we know). The number of possible circuits in the brain exceeds the number of atoms in the universe. So we must turn to origins on that Earth, resulting in such a mind.

2. The Biological World: Life

Biology also has developed at two scales, the range of the very small and that of big-scale history. Molecular biology, discovering DNA, has decoded the "secret of life" (once ascribed to the Spirit of God). Evolutionary history has located the secret of life in natural selection operating over incremental variations across enormous timespans, with the fittest selected to survive. At native ranges, life takes place in ecosystem communities, where the competition remains, but also with many interdependencies, and also mixtures of order and disorder.

Over evolutionary time, speciation began with the simple and resulted in the complex, from microbes to persons. As with physics, the two levels have been theoretically interrelated. The genetic level supplies variations, does the coding of life in DNA, and constructs molecular proteins. Organisms cope at their native-range levels, inhabiting ecosystems, and across evolutionary time, species are selected and generated as they track changing environments.

In ecosystems, organisms are both challenged and supported. Every organism is what it is where it is; the "skin-out" environment as vital as "skin-in" metabolisms. Early ecologists favored ideas such as homeostasis and equilibrium. Contemporary ecologists emphasize more of a role for contingency or even chaos. Others incline to emphasize self-organizing systems (autopoiesis), also an ancient idea: "The Earth produces of itself (Greek: *automatically*)" (Luke 4:28). Some find that natural selection operating on the edge of chaos offers the greatest possibility for self-organization and self-transformation.

The process is prolific, but no longer fine-tuned. To the contrary, evolutionary history can seem tinkering and makeshift at the same time that, within structural constraints and mutations available, it optimizes adapted fit. In contrast to the astrophysics and microphysics, in the middle-range earthbound natural history, there is much openness, emergence, surprise, struggle, loss, gain, or wandering. Natural selection is thought to be blind, initially in the genetic variations bubbling up without regard to the needs of the organism, some few of which by chance are beneficial, and also in the evolutionary selective forces, which select for survival, without regard to advance. Many evolutionary theorists insist that nothing in natural selection theory guarantees progress; most doubt that the theory predicts, or even makes probable, the long-term historical innovations that have occurred. Others think that the creative results are inherent in the system.

Though dominant throughout biology, evolutionary theory has proved quite problematic itself (independently of any religious agenda). There are disagreements involving the relative degrees of order and contingency, repeatability, predictability, the role of sexuality, competition and symbiosis, the extent of social construction in evolutionary theory, the evolutionary origins of mind, especially the human mind, differences between nature and culture. The theory is, in many respects, incomplete.

Fundamentalist theology denies (much or any) evolution and sometimes seeks to prevent its teaching in public schools. Others construct an evolutionary theism, emphasizing the continuing vital creative processes over time, the ascent of life from the simple to the complex, the increase of information, the effective and efficient results of genetic creativity and natural selection, producing a quasi-design, the production of more out of less over the millennia. Increasing knowledge of the sophistication of molecular structures has led some to look for intelligent design there. Evolutionary speciation generates and tests novel kinds, a cybernetic process employing open innovation and selection, with analogues in rational thought, including the logic of science, where novel theories are generated and tested.

Asian religious traditions interpret natural history as appearance (*maya*, illusion) spun over Brahman, or as a spinning world (*samsara*) spun over Emptiness, *sunyata*. As with the monotheists troubled by the character of the evolutionary process, Asian traditions too may have difficulties knowing how much of the phenomenal world to embrace, and how much to see through or transcend.

By Buddhist accounts life is suffering, *dukkha*, driven by thirst, *tanha*, which seems biologically compatible; although what becomes of nature in *nirvana*, with desires extinguished (extinction), remains problematic. Taoism is the most naturalistic of the classical faiths, though critics find the ever-oscillating, complementary yang/yin inadequate to explain the historically developing natural history. Native faiths find an enspirited world; they may loosely embrace evolutionary history. They struggle to make their animistic or personalist accounts of animals and plants compatible with those of zoology and botany.

Struggle and suffering, and life renewed in the midst of its death and perishing are central themes in Christianity. In the Psalmist's metaphors, life is lived in green pastures and in the valley of the shadow of death, nourished by eating at a table prepared in the midst of enemies. In the letters of Paul, the creation is groaning in travail, with the labor of giving birth (the original meaning of "nature"). Jesus suffers and dies redemptively. Although non-moral, natural history is "cruciform" even before humans arrive; and in all creating of life there seems to be struggling through to something higher.

Though biologists are typically uncertain whether life has arrived on Earth by divine intention, they are almost unanimous in their respect for life and seek biological conservation on an endangered planet. Earth's impressive and unique biodiversity warrants wonder and care. Anciently, the Hebrews marveled over the "swarms" of creatures Earth brings forth in Genesis 1.

3. Nature and Culture: Human Life

Nature has generated only one species capable of cumulative transmissible cultures. Nature and culture are classical opposites, or complements (as are nature and supernature). By nature humans are "born that way"; by nurture humans learn to become civilized. Humans have a dual inheritance system. In one meaning (recalling Latin etymology, *natura*), "nature" refers to everything generated or produced. For metaphysical naturalists, perhaps for methodological scientists, nature is all that there is, without contrast class. Humans evolved within nature and break no natural laws.

Still, culture differs from nature. Humans are nurtured into an inherited linguistic and symbolic system, a worldview, by which humans communicate, perpetuate, and develop their knowledge. This cultural genius makes possible the deliberate and cumulative, and therefore the extensive, rebuilding of nature. Humans reshape their environments, rather than being themselves morphologically and genetically reshaped to fit their changing environments. Humans come into the world by nature unfinished and become what they become by nurture.

Religious persons find their traditions vital in such nurture, and absent from nature.

Critics may object to distinguishing so sharply nature from culture (too "dualist") on grounds that culture is already present in animals, and also that nature remains a strong determinate in human affairs. If by culture is only meant transfer of acquired (and non-genetic) information from one generation to the next, culture is present in various social animals: chimpanzees (who imitate tool using), even in warblers (who imprint songs or migration routes). In classical anthropological meaning, however, culture requires intentional teaching of language, beliefs, skills, morals, laws, customs, arts, worldviews, religions – all historically transmitted over generations.

In that classical sense, culture remains distinctive to humans and is the dominant determinant in their affairs. Information in nature travels intergenerationally on genes; information in culture travels neurally as persons are educated into transmissible cultures. The determinants of animal and plant behavior are never anthropological, political, economic, technological, scientific, philosophical, ethical, or religious. Animal imprinting and limited transmitting of acquired information notwithstanding, humans gain a deliberated modification of nature that separates humans in their cultures from wild nature, increasingly so in high-technology cultures. Recently decoding our own genome, humans stand at the threshold of rebuilding even their own genetic nature.

Animals are not in this sense nurtured. Without some concept of teaching, of ideas moving from mind to mind, from parent to child, from teacher to pupil, a cumulative transmissible culture is impossible. Though language "comes naturally" to humans, what is learned has been culturally transmitted, using a specific language. The content learned during childhood education is that of an acquired, non-genetic culture. These cultural traditions are the locus of the generation and transmission of religious faith. In that sense religion is a phenomenon of culture, not nature.

4. Worldviews: Causes, Meanings, Values

Humans are only part of the world in biological, evolutionary, and ecological senses, their nature; but *Homo sapiens* is the only part of the world free to orient itself with a view of the whole, to seek wisdom about who we are, where we are, where we are going, what we ought to do. Religious persons claim that, with due admiration for the successes of science discovering causes in nature and culture, science leaves the ultimate value questions still unresolved, those assigning meaning and value. One needs a scientifically informed worldview, but the ultimate value questions remain as acute and painful as ever. There is no scientific guidance of life.

Nor can humans simply follow nature. Nature does not teach us how we ought to behave toward each other. Compassion and charity, justice and honesty, are not virtues found in wild nature. There is no way to derive any of the familiar moral maxims from nature: "One ought to keep promises." "Do to others as you would have them do to you." "Do not cause needless suffering." No natural decalogue endorses the Ten Commandments.

Although nature is not our moral tutor, there may be goods (values) in nature that humans ought to respect and conserve. Animals, plants, and species, integrated into ecosystems, may embody values that, though non-moral, count morally when moral agents encounter these. And, even if one is in doubt about divine creation, or sacred nature, or intrinsic values in nature, there is little doubt that humans and their planet have entwined destinies. Sustainable development has been a recent focus, pleasing economists, developers, and humanists, who find that ecologists and conservation biologists continually caution that what most fundamentally must be sustained is the biosphere.

Humans, if uniquely the wise species, are also uniquely the species that needs redemption. Religions may celebrate creation, or struggle with what to make of evolutionary history. But the real business of religion is salvation, mending the perennial brokenness in human nature. Ultimately such salvation is beyond the natural, perhaps supernatural, by the grace of the monotheist God, perhaps in some realization of depths underlying the natural, such as Brahman or *sunyata*. Meanwhile, whatever the noumenal ultimate, humans reside in a phenomenal world, which they must evaluate, and in which they must live, hopefully redeemed or enlightened by their faiths.

Humans sin, unlike the fauna and flora. Religion is for people, and not for nature, nor does salvation come naturally; even the earthly good life is elusive. Christian and other ethicists can with considerable plausibility make the claim that neither conservation, nor a sustainable biosphere, nor sustainable development, nor any other harmony between humans and nature can be gained until persons learn to use the Earth both justly and charitably. Those twin concepts are not found either in wild nature or in any science that studies nature. They must be grounded in some ethical authority, and this has classically been religious. The Hebrews, for instance, were convinced that they were given a blessing with a mandate. The land flows with milk and honey (assuming good land husbandry) if and only if there is obedience to Torah.

Scientists turning to environmental policy often appeal to ecosystem management. Such management connects with the idea of nature as "natural resources" at the same time that it has a "respect nature" dimension. Christian ethicists note that the secular word "manage" is a stand-in for the earlier theological word "steward." Ethicists have frequently thought of ethics as a social contract; environmentalists add that ethics needs also to be a natural contract, human responsibility for this marvelous planet on which we reside. Humans need a land ethic. Anciently Palestine was a promised land. Today and for the century hence, the call is to see Earth as a planet with promise.

Holmes Rolston, III

Further Reading
Birch, Charles and John B. Cobb, Jr. *The Liberation of Life: From the Cell to the Community*. New York: Cambridge University Press, 1981.
Rasmussen, Larry L. *Earth Community, Earth Ethics*. Maryknoll, NY: Orbis Books, 1996.
Rockefeller, Steven C. and John C. Elder. *Spirit and Nature*. Boston: Beacon Press, 1992.
Rolston, Holmes, III. *Genes, Genesis and God*. New York: Cambridge University Press, 1999.
Sheldon, Joseph K. *Rediscovery of Creation: A Bibliographical Study of the Church's Response to the Environmental Crisis*. Metuchen, NJ: American Theological Library Association and Scarecrow Press, 1992.
Tucker, Mary Evelyn and John A. Grim, eds. *Worldviews and Ecology*. Lewisburg: Bucknell University Press, 1993.

See also: Conservation Biology; Darwin, Charles; Ecological Anthropology; Ecology and Religion; Einstein, Albert; Environmental Ethics; Evolutionary Biology, Religion, and Stewardship; Religious Studies and Environmental Concern; Sagan, Carl; Social Science on Religion and Nature.

Science Fiction

Science fiction is a very diverse category of culture that has explored myriad ways in which religion can relate to nature. Strictly defined, science fiction is the traditional literature that arose around a cluster of magazines, beginning with *Amazing Stories* in 1927 and *Science Wonder Stories* in 1929. More broadly defined, it also includes speculative fiction from any time period or publication source that concerns the human implications of science and technology. Science-fiction movies and television programs are often distinguished by the term "sci-fi," but in an increasingly multimedia culture they also must be considered.

Alien Environments
The Mars novels by Edgar Rice Burroughs and the *Dune* novels by Frank Herbert both concern desert planets with hostile environments. For Burroughs, religion is a parasite, while for Herbert it thrives symbiotically with nature. *A Princess of Mars* and *The Gods of Mars* by Burroughs depict Barsoom, an arid world a million years after the fall of a great civilization, in which life is barely sustained by ancient canals and atmosphere factories that may be

disrupted at any time by warfare between feudal states. The priesthood of the Holy Therns exploits the superstitious Martians, and it does nothing to solve the chronic problems of social and environmental decay. In *The Master Mind of Mars*, an amoral scientist provides immortality to the wicked priestess of an anti-scientific religion, by transplanting her brain into the stolen body of a young woman, in order to get money to carry on his research. Far from promoting harmony with nature, these religions exploit the gullibility of desperate people struggling to survive in a hostile environment.

Frank Herbert's *Dune* novels about the desert planet Arakis also concern religious scheming in a feudal society, but the result is quite different. Centuries ago, a jihad cleansed the galactic empire of computers and artificial biotechnology, so the spirit that would have gone into technological innovation has been diverted into symbiotic experiments with nature. The Bene Gesserit, a women's cult, has been carefully controlling bloodlines for generations to breed a messiah. Human computers, called mentats, accelerate their minds with the spice *melange*, and space navigators employ this psychedelic to guide spaceships between the stars. The spice also prolongs life, so it is the most valuable substance in the universe, and it can be found only on Arakis where it is produced by titanic sand worms. A woman's love for a man causes the Bene Gesserit to lose control of their breeding program, their son launches a fresh jihad, and his son becomes an immortal "god" emperor who is gradually metamorphizing into a mutant worm.

On Barsoom, the people living closest to nature are the Green Martians, exemplified by the character Tar Tarkas, who is too courageous to rely upon religion to assuage fear concerning his own death. But he mourns the death of the woman he loves, so he undertakes a long pilgrimage to the area that the common religion of his planet claims is the land of the dead. There he discovers not his beloved but the unnatural Therns and the monsters they employ to kill deluded pilgrims who enter their realm.

On Arakis, the people living closest to nature are the Fremen, apparently descended from Arabs, who have a demanding faith that helps them survive in the hostile environment. When the perfidious Harkonnens overthrow the Atreides aristocrats who rule the urban areas of Arakis, young Paul Atreides flees into the desert. Bene Gesserit breeding, the psychedic effects of the spice, and a series of ordeals transform him into Muad'dib, the messiah prophesied by Fremen religion. The manipulative religions of Dune are amoral rather than evil, and they possess real supernatural powers derived from their symbiosis with nature.

Alien Messiahs

Extraterrestrials with apparently magical powers abound in science fiction, and some of them are greeted as messiahs when they come to Earth. They seem like gods, in part, because foolish Earthlings cannot rule themselves wisely, and because what is natural on an alien world seems supernatural here.

The Alien, by Raymond F. Jones, imagines a future age in which human society is disintegrating and individuals have lost all hope. A wave of hysteria called the Howling Craze sweeps through the cities, as people mass in the streets and vent their despair by weeping and emitting animal cries of pain. Government leaders last only a few months in office, either quickly impeached or committing suicide, and the populace longs for a superhuman messiah. In the Asteroid Belt between the orbits of Mars and Jupiter, scientists discover a time capsule that has preserved the body of Demarzule, leader of an alien civilization, with instructions on how to restore him to life. A religious movement believing Demarzule to be the divine savior seizes control. When Demarzule awakens, a few scientists realize he is the Hitler rather than the Jesus of his species. They flee across the universe in search of an antidote to this evil faith. On a distant world, a friendly alien must sacrifice his life so a gland that confers supernatural ability can be transplanted into a scientist and he can destroy Demarzule.

Stranger in a Strange Land by Robert A. Heinlein concerns Valentine Michael Smith, a human being who was raised by Martians. First glimpsed in Heinlein's earlier novel, *Red Planet*, the Martians are an ancient and wise race who keep themselves aloof from the first human voyagers to their planet. Therefore, humans do not know that Martians have mental powers that allow them to discorporate any matter, and thus have the power to kill. Valentine Michael Smith is sent to Earth as a spy, unaware of his mission to help the Martians decide whether to destroy humanity. His Martian psychology naturally gives him remarkable powers to gratify people's desires, and a communal religious cult quickly assembles around him. Ultimately he must decide whether to defend himself against fanatics, or become a martyr.

Allegories and Prophecies

Science fiction is a suitable vehicle for religious allegories, of both conventional and radical kinds. For example, *A Canticle for Leibowitz* by Walter M. Miller and *Out of the Silent Planet* by C.S. Lewis are both Christian allegories of humankind's exile from the Garden of Eden. Miller's novel follows a religious order in the centuries after a nuclear holocaust, exploring the difficult question of whether humanity can long survive if it tries to conquer nature by means of atheistic science. Lewis imagines that a Christ rules the planet Mars, where three intelligent species live amicably in an Eden, and Earth is the only planet on which humans have become estranged from God and thus from nature.

The *Star Wars* series created by George Lucas, and the

Babylon 5 series by J. Michael Straczkynski depict fictional cults that have interesting relations with nature, and might in future become real. The Jedi Knights of *Star Wars* are noble warriors with psychic abilities, rather like Knights Templar who have been trained in Zen Buddhism. Their power comes from The Force, which is based in microorganisms found in varying quantities within each living cell, and that spiritually binds the universe together.

Babylon 5 depicts a bewildering variety of cults, some belonging to alien planets and others newly arisen on Earth, but all are primitive reflections of the fundamental reality of nature. God is not a supernatural entity apart from nature. Rather, intelligence evolves from nature as the way in which the universe becomes conscious, and the most advanced intelligent species are in the process of evolving into gods. Billions of years ago, the First Ones evolved in the universe. Most of them departed to seek spiritual destinies on higher planes of existence, leaving the galaxy under the control of two highly advanced but imperfect races, the Vorlons and the Shadows. These two battle over the lesser races for two diametrically opposite principles: order and chaos. Ultimately, humanity must defeat both of these semi-divine influences and proclaim that our species no longer needs gods to rule it.

As allegories, science-fiction stories may shape the reader's subconscious orientation toward both religion and nature. However, it is also possible that the fiction may occasionally become fact. The small Church of All Worlds is partly based on Heinlein's *Stranger in a Strange Land*, and the influential Church of Scientology was founded by a science-fiction author. Many stories, including the *Dune* and the *Star Wars* series, describe religious orders that employ mental training regimes to achieve enlightenment and spiritual power. Science fiction is increasingly shaping popular culture, so real religions patterned on fictional ones may increasingly appear over the coming decades, and science fiction will become a self-fulfilling prophecy. Thus, fiction becomes a realistic venue for exploring the complex relationship between religion and the natural environment.

William Sims Bainbridge

Further Reading

Bainbridge, William Sims. *Dimensions of Science Fiction*. Cambridge, MA: Harvard University Press, 1986.

Clute, John and Peter Nicholls, eds. *The Encyclopedia of Science Fiction*. New York: St. Martin's Griffin, 1995.

Gunn, James E. *The Science of Science-Fiction Writing*. Lanham, MD: Scarecrow Press, 2000.

Reilly, Robert, ed. *The Transcendent Adventure: Studies of Religion in Science Fiction*. Westport, CT: Greenwood Press, 1985.

See also: Church of All Worlds; Motion Pictures; Sagan, Carl; Scientology; Space Exploration.

Scientology – In Two Scholarly Perspectives

In 1950, author and explorer L. Ron Hubbard announced the discovery of Dianetics, which he said was a new science of mental health, and four years later he established Scientology, a new religion dedicated to human spiritual advancement. Although Scientology builds upon some of the same spiritual principles common to traditional religions, it was developed during the scientific era and thus takes advantage of extensive research and technological development.

A clear distinction must be drawn between Hubbard's fiction and his Scientology writings, because his stories are free imaginative explorations rather than religious scriptures. However, two themes connect his science fiction to his work in Scientology: a conception of the Earth as one planet among many in a vast universe of nature, and the conviction that ordinary people can accomplish great things if they seek to gain knowledge and serve humanity. Occasionally the fiction touches upon important environmental issues, such as natural resource depletion in the novel *Battlefield Earth*.

The Church of Scientology considers humans to be spiritual beings, not merely animals, systems of chemical compounds, or stimulus–response mechanisms. Nonetheless, the condition of a person's body is an important factor in that individual's awareness and ability. A body polluted by toxic chemicals, radiation, or other harmful factors can prevent the individual from achieving spiritual betterment. Therefore, an important part of Hubbard's religious research was the discovery of methods for purifying the body.

Scientologists believe that radiation and chemical toxins become lodged in a person's body, chiefly in fatty tissue, and can affect the person adversely even years after the original exposure. The purification program has three chief elements: exercise to stimulate the circulation, sauna to sweat out the accumulated toxins, and a nutritional regimen including specific vitamins, minerals and oils.

The nutritional regimen does not radically alter the individual's usual diet, but supplements it with vegetables and sufficient liquids to offset the loss through exercise and the sauna. Over the course of the program, a precise mixture of vitamins is gradually increased, with close monitoring especially of the niacin ingested. In addition to other minerals, a calcium-magnesium drink called "Cal-Mag" is an important part of the program. The intake of oils is required to replace some of the toxin-ridden fat that the program aims to clear out of the body.

In the view of Scientologists, the use of non-medicinal drugs is unnatural and harmful, and drug addiction is a highly destructive force in contemporary culture. A rehabilitation program called Narconon has been based on Hubbard's purification and communication technology, designed to handle problems of withdrawal and assist people in overcoming the effects of addiction.

Scientologists believe that spirit is potentially superior to material things and can accomplish miraculous changes in the physical universe if freed from the continuing effect of past traumas, transgressions and aberrations. Drugs, radiation, and toxic chemicals not only leave physical traces in the body, in their view, but also affect the individual's mind through powerful memories called mental image pictures that can cause harm when restimulated by later experiences. Thus, the body-oriented purification program is a preparation for a comprehensive series of Scientology processes intended to deal with problems of the mind in order to liberate the spirit.

In its regimen designed to achieve total spiritual freedom, Scientology employs a form of counseling called *auditing* to move the individual up a gradient toward advanced states of *clear* and *Operating Thetan* (OT). A Clear is a person who no longer suffers the ill effects of a reactive mind, that portion of the mind which works on a purely stimulus–response basis. In OT, a Clear becomes refamiliarized with the abilities that belong to his or her fundamental nature.

Scientologists consider psychiatric practices to be unnatural and harmful, especially psychosurgery, electroshock, and drug treatment. Thus, the Church of Scientology has been active in efforts to reform the mental health professions and to make people aware that human beings are not mere biological mechanisms but are by nature spiritual.

Over the half-century of its existence, the Church of Scientology has grown into a worldwide movement, communicating its religious beliefs in more than fifty languages and active in over a hundred countries.

William Sims Bainbridge

Further Reading

Bainbridge, William Sims. "Science and Religion: The Case of Scientology." In David G. Bromley and Phillip E. Hammond, eds. *The Future of New Religious Movements*. Macon, GA: Mercer University Press, 1987, 59–79.

Church of Scientology International. *What is Scientology?* Los Angeles: Bridge Publications, 1998.

Hubbard, L. Ron. *Clear Body, Clear Mind*. Los Angeles: Bridge Publications, 1990.

Hubbard, L. Ron. *All About Radiatio*. Bridge Publications: Los Angeles, 1989.

Hubbard, L. Ron. *Battlefield Earth: A Saga of the Year 3000*. New York: St. Martin's Press, 1982.

Hubbard, L. Ron. *Dianetics: The Modern Science of Mental Health*. New York: Paperback Library, 1950.

Melton, J. Gordon. *The Church of Scientology*. Salt Lake City, UT: Signature Books, 2000.

If one believes comments by Scientology's founder, L. Ron Hubbard (1911–1986), the creation of Scientology's forerunner, Dianetics, related directly to his efforts to improve the success of people who explored nature. The "original goal" of Dianetics, he stated in *The Explorers Journal*, "was to provide expedition commanders and doctors with a therapy tool which would increase the efficiency of personnel and reduce incidence of personnel failure" (Hubbard 1950: 52). Hubbard himself had undertaken several questionable marine explorations, but by 1950 he was claiming that the realm of the human mind was the last great frontier "capable of producing some adventures scarcely rivaled by [African explorer David] Livingston[e]" (Hubbard 1950: 1).

The mind, it seems, replaced nature as an exciting realm for Hubbard's exploration. Nevertheless, in Dianetics and Scientology, Hubbard did develop a set of concepts (called "dynamics") that supposedly identified urges or drives of life. In Dianetics, Hubbard identified the fifth of seven dynamics as being concerned with an individual's affinity for life. By 1956 he refined the dynamics to include eight dimensions, with the fifth one involving "the urge toward existence of the animal kingdom," which includes all flora and fauna (Hubbard 1979: 37). The sixth dynamic involved "the urge toward existence of the physical universe," what Hubbard called "matter, energy, space, and time" (Hubbard 1979: 38). Consequently, in the context of these two dynamics, Scientologists are able to place themselves within an environmental framework.

Throughout his corpus, Hubbard frequently discussed what he called the "environment," but he used the term in the broadest possible sense to refer to "all conditions surrounding the organism from the first moment of present-life existence to death, including physical, emotional, spiritual, social, educational, [and] nutritional" (Hubbard 1951: II, 293). Hubbard rarely discussed the natural world in his major ideological works, unless one includes his lectures and writings about possible radiation poisoning from the environment caused by nuclear bombs. This material reflected widespread fear during the 1950s of nuclear war and contamination, and Hubbard claimed that he had developed a program that would reduce the effects of radiation on the body.

In 1959 and 1960, Hubbard carried out a series of "experiments" (although they were never scientifically published), which "proved" that plants felt pain and feared death. He also experimented with the effects of heated soil on plant growth. For years afterward, media accounts about Scientology carried a picture of a pensive Hubbard looking intently at a vine-ripening tomato that he had hooked up with clamps and wires to the galvonometer (called an E-meter) reputedly used by his organization to identify negative incidents in members' current or past lives. These experiments, however, did not become part of Hubbard's lasting contributions to Scientology.

One of the few lasting images of the natural world in his ideology involved volcanoes, which appeared in Hubbard's 1967 cosmological statement about how soul-like entities (called thetans) forgot previous negative experiences from past lives as they were about to enter new ones. According to Hubbard, 76 million years ago an evil warlord named Xenu (or Xemu) rounded up people on the overpopulated planets that he controlled, sent them to a planet called Teegeeack (which was Earth), placed them in (or near) volcanoes, and exploded hydrogen bombs in craters. Their souls (thetans) survived, but out of fear these thetans grouped together as clusters and continue to attach themselves to bodies. Upper-level Scientology courses supposedly allow people to detach these "body clusters" and thetans from themselves, which is supposed to advance their own developmental progress.

As environmental awareness grew in society-at-large, Scientologists received media attention for their clean-up efforts on beaches, along roadsides, and in urban centers – activities that the Church of Scientology International praises on its own website. In 1998, for example, one special Scientology project in Clearwater, Florida, involved relocating a 100-year-old oak tree. Moreover, in September 2001, The Church of Scientology was among approximately 65 "customers" named by the Los Angeles Department of Water and Power for having made "green power" purchases from renewable energy sources (Los Angeles Department of Water and Power 2001).

While acknowledging that Scientologists share concerns about nature and the natural environment with the wider society, it remains true that the organization attempts to use members' environmental efforts to extend Scientology's "technology" into society. For example, in a secular booklet of moral aphorisms that Hubbard wrote in an attempt to gain recognition of his name, Hubbard instructed his readers to "Safeguard and Improve Your Environment." Yet the unsophisticated level of his thinking about the environment and the natural world resulted in simplistic advice: "There are many things people can do to help take care of the planet. They begin with the idea that one should. They progress by suggesting to others that they should" (Hubbard 1981: 38, 45). Nevertheless, Scientologists hope that non-Scientology organizations will reprint this booklet and distribute it widely, thereby attracting attention to its author (i.e., Hubbard) and stimulating interest in Scientology and his other works. Along these same lines, Scientologists and a Scientology organization had close connections with an environmental group named "Cry Out," and the principal of a Los Angeles-area elementary school canceled the group's planned activities for her students when she realized that its booklet was printed by Hubbard's literary agency, Author Services, Inc., and contained a song that Hubbard wrote.

It seems unlikely that "nature" or "the natural environment" ever will be a significant aspect of Scientology's ideology. A stated purpose of the organization ostensibly is to remove the impact of negative experiences (called engrams) from people, and in many instances their removal (so the group claims) has medical benefit. Concerns, therefore, about nature are secondary (at best), since they are far outweighed by counseling and health issues.

Stephen A. Kent

Further Reading
Atack, Jon. *A Piece of Blue Sky: Scientology, Dianetics and L. Ron Hubbard Exposed*. New York: Lyle Stuart, 1990.
Corydon, Bent. *L. Ron Hubbard, Messiah or Madman?* Fort Lee, NJ: Barricade Books Inc., 1992.
Hubbard, L. Ron. *The Way to Happiness*. Los Angeles, CA: Bridge Publications, 1981 (1984).
Hubbard, L. Ron. *Scientology: The Fundamentals of Thought*. Los Angeles: The Church of Scientology of California, 1979 (1956).
Hubbard, L. Ron. *All About Radiation*. London: The Hubbard Scientology Organization, 1957 (1967).
Hubbard, L. Ron. *Science of Survival: Simplified, Faster Dianetic Techniques*. Silver Spring, MD: Center of Dianetics and Scientology, 1951.
Hubbard, L. Ron. "Terra Incognita: The Mind." *The Explorers Journal* (Winter–Spring, 1950), 1–4, 52.
Kent, Stephen A. "The Globalization of Scientology: Influence, Control and Opposition in Transnational Markets." *Religion* 29 (1999), 147–69.
Miller, Russell. *Bare-Faced Messiah: The True Story of L. Ron Hubbard*. Toronto: Key Porter Books, 1987.
See also: New Religious Movements; Science Fiction.

Scopes Trial

In 1925, Tennessee passed legislation against teaching in state-supported schools "any theory that denies the story of the Divine creation of man as taught in the Bible, and the teaching instead that man has descended from a lower order of animals." The American Civil Liberties Union announced that it would defend any teacher prosecuted under it. George Rappleya saw this as an opportunity to both test the statute and bring national publicity to Dayton. He found support among local school officials and attorneys and science teacher John Scopes agreed to be prosecuted.

Efforts to ban teaching evolution began in the early 1920s. The rise of Christian fundamentalism in the early twentieth century was a reaction against religious modernism, including the "higher criticism" that asserted the Bible is the product of human experience and that God works through history rather than revelation. Some fundamentalists were appalled by modernist efforts to reinterpret the scriptures to conform with scientific understanding. The rapid growth in public school attendance and the exposure of children to rationalism and science, especially Darwinism, seemed a threat to the religious influence of families.

Tennesseans were not uniformly opposed to teaching evolution; many found the statute an embarrassment. At its annual meeting held in Memphis shortly before the trial began, the Southern Baptist Convention voted down an anti-evolution proposal offered by its fundamentalist wing. Even the chief prosecutor questioned the wisdom of the law under which Scopes was charged.

The trial received a major public relations boost when William Jennings Bryan and Clarence Darrow volunteered their services. Bryan, a well-known populist and former U.S. Secretary of State, was a social progressive, religious conservative, and anti-evolution leader. However, he had not tried a case in decades and contributed relatively little to the prosecution's legal work. Darrow was one of the most famous trial lawyers of his day and an outspoken agnostic. He and Bryan had cooperated in progressive social causes, but were bitter opponents on religious matters. Although he did not lead the defense, Darrow played a major role in the trial.

Scopes admitted that he broke the law, but argued that evolution did not conflict with the biblical account of creation. The presiding judge, however, would not allow the jury to hear expert testimony to this effect. The prosecution argued that the only relevant issue was that Scopes broke the law. There were, though, larger issues. Politically, the prosecution argued that majority views should determine what is taught in public schools. The defense supported academic freedom and the authority of science. On a religious level the case embodied the ongoing conflict between fundamentalism and religious modernism.

Each day's session was opened with a prayer delivered by fundamentalist clergy. The judge overruled the defense's objection to this practice and the defense presented a petition from modernist clergy requesting that some prayers be delivered by non-fundamentalists. The defense argued that "we have an opportunity to hear prayer by men who think that God has shown His divinity in the wonders of the world, in the book of nature, quite as well as in the book of the revealed word." This eventually became the practice as fundamentalist and modernist clergy alternated in delivering the prayer.

Darrow called Bryan as an expert witness on the Bible. Eager to defend his faith before the staunch agnostic, Bryan endured a grilling on his belief in the unerring literalness of the Scripture. Darrow questioned him on such points as whether Jonah was actually swallowed by a fish, Joshua made the sun stand still, and the days of creation were 24 hours long. Bryan made a poor showing and eventually agreed that the days could have been periods of indeterminate length, thus opening the door to interpretation beyond biblical literalism.

The following day the judge struck Bryan's testimony from the record. At this point, the defense recommended a verdict of guilty and Scopes was fined $100.00. On appeal, the Tennessee Supreme Court found the statute to be constitutional, but overturned the conviction on a technicality. The statute was not repealed until 1967.

The Scopes trial captured the nation's attention and highlighted the issues, but it did not slow fundamentalist anti-evolution efforts. Other states passed similar legislation and fundamentalists later developed new strategies to introduce "creation-science" and intelligent design arguments into classrooms. Although these efforts have been rebuffed, the conflict continues.

Ernst Myer pointed out that the Darwinian Revolution actually involves a complex collection of social and intellectual changes. These include accepting the geological concept of time, that the Earth has undergone great change, and that evolution is not linear and progressive but adaptive to present circumstances. It took nearly 250 years for these views to be incorporated into biological theory and the process is still underway within the lay public. The Scopes trial was part of this ongoing process.

Many religious people, organizations and denominations have found ways to reconcile scripture and the book of nature. However, the anti-evolution fundamentalists' efforts to reinterpret nature to conform it to their understanding of the Bible promotes a distorted understanding of nature, ecological processes and biological diversity. In addition to retarding environmental understanding, they also promote the unfortunate belief that there is an essential conflict between religion and the vision of nature provided by science. Those who believe that God speaks through nature, as well as scripture, find this notion short-sighted.

Ralph H. Lutts

Further Reading

Larson, Edward J. *Summer for the Gods: The Scopes Trial and America's Continuing Debate Over Science and Religion.* New York: Basic Books, 1997.

Myer, Ernst. "The Nature of the Darwinian Revolution." *Science* 176 (1972), 981–9.

Numbers, Ronald L. *The Creationists: The Evolution of Scientific Creationism.* New York: Knopf, 1992.

The World's Most Famous Court Trial, Tennessee Evolution Case: A Complete Stenographic Report of the Famous Court Test of the Tennessee Anti-Evolution Act, At Dayton, July 10–21, 1925, Including Speeches and Arguments of Attorneys. 1925; Union, NJ: Lawbook Exchange, 1999.

See also: Creationism and Creation Science; Darwin, Charles; Nature Fakers Controversy.

Scotland

As the glaciers of the last ice age finally left Scotland as a bare and empty landscape about 10,000 years ago, pioneer species such as hazel and birch started to recolonize the land, the now-extinct wolf, bear and lynx returned, and people resettled (Edwards and Ralston 2003). These people left their mark in megalithic structures typically erected some 5000 years ago, such as the lunar-aligned Calanais Standing Stones on the Isle of Lewis. Such monuments are often found in beautiful places. Some probably had astronomical and ritual functions. Little can be said about this with certainty, but one claim that can be made without question is that they represent art. As such, the ancient sites have been described as "the longest show running"; a doorway to the imaginal realm where nature and the imagination intersect. The standing stones accordingly testify to a tripartite link between community, spirit and place and, as such, in all probability, to the early presence of nature religion – namely, the understanding that the spiritual realm interpenetrates and animates the natural world.

Scotland's original Pictish inhabitants may have had a matrilineal structure, but little is confidently known about them. The Romans were largely kept out of Scotland; they built two defensive walls to keep the Picts back. According to Tacitus' *Agricola* (ca. 98), the Pictish chieftain Calgacus said of the Romans:

> Harriers of the world . . . they make a desolation and they call it peace . . . We, the noblest souls in all Britain, the dwellers in its inner shrine, had never seen the shores of slavery and had preserved our very eyes from the desecration and the contamination of tyranny: here at the world's end, on its last inch of liberty . . . Then let us fight as men untamed, men who have never fallen from freedom.

During the second half of the first millennium the Scots of Dalriada, originating from Ireland and speaking Gaelic, subsumed whatever had gone before with patriarchal chieftain structures based around the extended family or "clan." Irish-Scots' Celtic monasticism, resting on a Druidic "Celtic Old Testament" base, embodied a rich nature spirituality.

These Irish roots were later used to assert, before the Pope, Scotland's claim of right to be a nation free of Anglo-Norman suzerainty. English invaders based their claim to control Scotland on Geoffrey of Monmouth's "translation" of the *Historia Regum Britanniae* of 1135 – parts of which were probably Geoffrey's own creation, as he later claimed to have lost the original manuscript. The *Historia* maintained that Britain was named after Brutus of Troy who had arrived in the twelfth century B.C.E. after pillaging France and Africa, inspired by an oracular mandate to dominate "the round circle of the whole Earth." Geoffrey claimed Brutus had cleared Scotland or "Albany" of Picts and giants, giving it to his youngest son, Albanactus.

During the Wars of Independence (1296–1424) with England, Edward I used this myth to legitimatize his colonizing conquest of Scotland. As embellished in the Hollywood movie, *Braveheart*, William Wallace and King Robert the Bruce drove the English out. However, to consolidate Scotland's free status they required papal recognition. This was achieved through the Declaration of Arbroath, 1320, a remarkable document that drew on Irish charter texts to trounce Geoffrey's Brutus myth (Ferguson 1998).

The Declaration links Scottish origins to ancient Scythia by the Black Sea, as described, for example, in the *Irish Book of Invasions* (ca. 1168 in final form). This portrays the Scots coming from Scythia to assist Nimrod with building the Tower of Babel, their leader learning all 72 languages of the world after its fall, his being summoned as Pharaoh's linguist while the Israelites were still in slavery, his marrying Pharaoh's daughter ("Scota," hence "Scotland," implying that the Mother of the Nation was black), his reconstructing Gaelic from the 72 languages (hence Gaelic's sometime designation, "the language of Eden"), his people providing the Israelites with bread and wine on the eve of their Red Sea departure, and then later, having received Moses' blessing, completing a 440-year-long migration via Spain to Ireland, and from there, according to the *Scotichronicon's* account (ca. 1449), on to Scotland, bringing as proof of their peregrinations the Stone of Destiny – Jacob's pillow from the original Genesis 28 version of Stairway to Heaven. Scottish nationhood is thereby symbolized by a holy stone, returned in 1996 from Westminster Abbey to Edinburgh Castle. This *axis mundi* stone, we might note, originally symbolized the connection between heaven and the land that Jacob was given; and that in a context where God pronounced blessing on all the world's peoples.

Revealingly, the Declaration of Arbroath locates sovereignty of the Scottish people not in the sovereign, but in the "Community of the Realm" which is "the community of Scotland." As such, and consistent with the principle that only God can own the land (Leviticus 25), Scotland had a King or "Queen of Scots" as distinct from a "Queen of Scotland." Resonant with the spirit of Calgacus, the Declaration asserts, "It is in truth not for glory, nor riches, nor honors that we are fighting, but for freedom – for that alone, which no honest man gives up but with life itself" (Scottish Records Office, 1320). And while Scotland might have had its "Auld Enemy" in the English, the importance of loving the enemy was constitutionally embedded in the Declaration's modification of Galatians 3:28 ("There is neither Jew nor Greek, slave nor free, male nor female, for you are all one in Christ Jesus"), asserting that under "the

Church of God," there is "neither weighting nor distinction of Jew and Greek, Scotsman or Englishman." Thus Scottish identity is generally considered to be civic rather than ethnic: at its best, a person belongs inasmuch as they are willing to cherish, and be cherished, by a place and its peoples.

While the nobles of Scotland as the medieval signatories to the Declaration looked to Rome (and successfully so) for recognition of national sovereignty, the Scots Reformation parliament of 1560 repudiated Rome. Protestants saw late medieval Catholicism as having been lax to the point of almost being "pagan." It is perhaps to the imperative of asserting narrow puritanical rectitude in order to give boundary and faith-based justification to spiritual revolution that we can trace the origins of the neglect, and even fear, of both nature religion and mysticism that has characterized much mainstream Reformed Church religious discourse in Scotland through until the late twentieth century.

That said, John Calvin, the benchmark of Scots Presbyterian Protestantism, was not averse to the love of nature. His *Institutes* (III:XIV:20) speak of the Creation as that "beautiful theatre" in which we might do well "to take pious delight." Similarly, the formative 1647 *Westminster Shorter Catechism* affirms that "God executeth His decrees in the works of Creation and Providence."

However, the seventeenth century, under James VI, who became James I of a "United Kingdom" with England in 1603, saw organized religion applied as an instrument of inner (psychological) and internal (within the British Isles) colonization. As with James' policy in Ulster, muscular Protestantism was indoctrinated through, for example, his 1609 Statutes of Iona and in the 1616 education act. These helped to propagate a Protestant ethic of transcendental deferred gratification such as Max Weber would have recognized as the hallmark of the early-modern mindset.

In Ulster, James' policies wronged the indigenous Catholics and wrong-footed the poor Scots Protestants who he "planted" there. In Scotland, the underlying imperial and mercantile ethic of his polices attacked indigenous bardic politics and laid the ground for the 1707 Union of Parliaments, by which Great Britain emerged as the world's foremost exemplar of neo-Roman presumptions of Empire. Following the Jacobite uprising of 1745, British forces in the Battle of Culloden near Inverness (1746) crushed clan power, and key markers of indigenous culture such as the wearing of the tartan kilt were proscribed. Robert Burns, the national bard, was to say of this era in his poem, *Strathallan's Lament* written in 1787: "The wide world is all before us / but a world without a friend."

With the indigenous leadership now either compulsorily Anglicised or crushed in the remote Highland centers of resistance, land became valued as a commodity rather than for the number of people it could support. Improved breeds of sheep, and demand for wool from the Napoleonic wars, triggered the "Highland Clearances" in which perhaps some half-a-million people were directly, or indirectly from economic pressure, forced off their native territories until the passing of the Crofters Act in 1886. Ironically, displaced indigenous Scots often colonized other native people's territories, the oppressed in some cases becoming oppressor. Much of rural Scotland became, in effect, one of the world's first casualties of what would now be called "globalization."

As with the famine in Ireland, many ordinary pious peasants internalized their oppression as punishment from God. At Croick, a congregation huddled in the churchyard awaiting the arrival of their emigrant ship scratched on a windowpane, "The people of Glen Calvie, the sinful generation." The 1712 Patronage Act had permitted landlords to appoint clergy within the established Church of Scotland. Some of these preached a gospel focused only on a transcendent pie-in-the-sky-when-you-die salvation. As if in antithesis to nature religion, the Earth was portrayed as a realm that had been corrupted with the sin of Adam. It was portrayed as fallen in its own right, rather than merely enduring the consequences of Adam's Fall. The Earth as Christ's "footstool" (Matthew 5:35), the very seat of the immanent presence of God, was overlooked. It was too often presumed that when Jesus condemned "the world" he included nature, rather than, merely, the corrupted human sociological order known as 'worldliness."

Accordingly, the oppressed were, to the landlord's convenience, encouraged to write the world off rather than to discern and seek to redeem it. In any case, Calvin's double-predestination suggested that, ultimately, destiny fell outside of human control. It was mainly to break with patronage under the influence of an emerging liberation theology that the Church of Scotland split in the 1843 "Disruption." In an effort, not always successful, to embody spiritual freedom, the Free Church of Scotland emerged as a more truly Presbyterian or grassroots alternative that recognized the authority of "Christ as Lord" unmediated by any landlord. One of the Disruption's practical consequences was to give spiritual legitimatization to the land reforms that took place at the cusp of the nineteenth–twentieth centuries, and which preserved agrarian "crofting" communities.

Amongst the peasantry a strong nature religion – expressed as awareness of the immanence of God and through supernatural belief and totemistic animism – is continuously evident. However, much of this has been caricatured as residually "Papist," (as with most of Carmichael's great nineteenth-century collection, the *Carmina Gadelica*), or of the faerie faith, and therefore merely superstitious (as with the Rev. Robert Kirk's seventeenth-century *Secret Commonwealth*). Recent work, such as that of the American Gaelic scholar, Michael Newton, and the Scots historian, James Hunter, reflects a continuous close engagement between people and nature expressed in the bardic tradition often outside of or on the margins of the mainstream church. As a generalization, this represents human society as resting on the bedrock of ecological community under the Providence of God. Nature transfigures humankind in a grounded transcendence, thus the motto of Stornoway in the Outer Hebrides is "God's Providence is our inheritance," and the great twentieth-century Gaelic poet, Sorley MacLean, writes in *An Cuilithionn* (The Cuillin): "Beyond the lochs of the blood of the children of men / beyond the frailty of plain and the labor of the mountain . . . / beyond guilt and defilement; watchful / heroic, the Cuillin is seen / rising on the other side of sorrow" (in Hunter 1995: 175).

In the late twentieth century, a few activists, including the present author, used the above analysis of history in an effort to reintegrate nature, spirituality and a bardic politics in the public life of a Scotland developing a "devolved" or semi-detached relationship with the rest of the "United Kingdom." The Isle of Eigg Trust, established in 1991, successfully enabled the residents of a Hebridean island to revolt and rid itself of its landlord and establish a democratic community land trust. This in turn helped stimulate flagship land-reform legislation in the Scottish Parliament, which was reestablished in 1999.

Similarly, when the Isle of Harris was threatened by multinationals wanting to make it a center for European production of roadstone with perhaps two massive "superquarries," theological testimony against violating the integrity of the creation was made by a panel that included Scotland's leading Calvinist, the Rev. Professor Donald Macleod, and the then-warrior chief of the Mi'Kmaq First Nation in Nova Scotia, a Sacred Pipe Carrier.

Attention was drawn in the public inquiry through the Mi'Kmaq testimony to the need for "defense of Mother Earth." Scripture passages such as Genesis 2:15, Proverbs 8, Job 38 and Romans 8 were invoked to argue that it is not creation that is fallen (and therefore treated as fit to have its national scenic areas ravished), but humankind. Professor Macleod noted that the function of the creation is to reflect the majesty of God and that "to spoil the creation is to disable it from performing this function [giving rise to] the consideration that rape of the environment is rape of the community itself" (Macleod in McIntosh 2001: 234). Accordingly, the present writer concluded, an appropriate relationship with nature is one of *reverence*. This is not *pantheism* – God as nature – but it should be understood as, *panentheism* – God being present in the creation as, for example, in Job or Hebrews 1:3.

The Scottish Government that, in the previous year, had abolished feudalism, rejected the superquarry in 2000. The "harriers of the world" may hover yet in the guise of globalization, but the spirit of Calgacus, increasingly expressed through nonviolent direct action, remains strong in fighting, as Tacitus described it, "desecration and the contamination of tyranny: here at the world's end."

Alastair McIntosh

Further Reading
Carmichael, Alexander. *Carmina Gadelica*. Edinburgh: Floris Books, 1994 (1900).
Edwards, Kevin J. and Ian B.M. Ralston, eds. *Scotland After the Ice Age: Environment, Archaeology and History, 8000 BC–AD 1000*. Edinburgh: Edinburgh University Press, 2003.
Ferguson, William. *The Identity of the Scottish Nation*. Edinburgh: Edinburgh University Press, 1998.
Hunter, James. *On the Other Side of Sorrow: Nature and People in the Scottish Highlands*. Edinburgh: Mainstream, 1995.
Hutton, Ronald. *The Pagan Religions of the Ancient British Isles*. Oxford: Blackwell, 1991.
Jackson, Kenneth H. *A Celtic Miscellany*. Harmondsworth: Penguin Classics, 1971.
McIntosh, Alastair. *Soil and Soul: People versus Corporate Power*. London: Aurum Press, 2001.
Newton, Michael. *A Handbook of the Scottish Gaelic World*. Dublin: Four Courts Press, 2000.
Tacitus. *The Agricola and The Germania*. London: Penguin Classics, 1970.
See also: Celtic Christianity; Celtic Spirituality; Christianity (6c) – ReformationTraditions (Lutheranism and Calvinism); Christianity (6c2) – Calvin, John and the Reformed Tradition; Christianity (7c) – Liberation Theology; Christianity in Europe; Faerie Faith in Scotland; Ireland; The Protestant Ethic.

Scouting

Founded during the Progressive Era, the early Scouting movement in the United States embraced the era's widespread beliefs in Darwinism, in the restorative power of nature, and (for the boys) in the spiritual dimensions of physical activity ("muscular Christianity"). Lord Robert Baden-Powell founded the Boy Scouts in England in 1908, and in 1910 a group of men already active in youth work in the United States gathered in New York City to found the Boy Scouts of America (BSA). Juliette Gordon Low created the first troop of Girl Scouts in 1912, and by 1915 the Girl Scouts of America (GSA) was incorporated. Although technically not part of the "Scouting" movement, the Camp Fire Girls, founded by Luther and Charlotte Gulick in 1910 and incorporated in 1912, shared Scouting's ideas and approaches to building nature-based recreational programs for children and adolescents.

Ernest Thompson Seton (1860–1946) played a central role in bringing into the BSA ideas about the relationship between nature and religion. Seton had been experimenting since 1903 with his own youth program, "Woodcraft Indians," based on American Indian lore, and he brought that experience to the BSA in 1910. Seton wrote a good many sections of the first *Handbook for Boys* (1911), including sections on "woodcraft," and he held the title "Chief Scout" until his falling out with the BSA in 1915.

By the turn of the century, Seton had already established strong credentials as both a naturalist and an artist. Although Seton wrote scientifically sound and well-respected books on North American wildlife, he was best known as the author of a number of books of animal stories, such as *Wild Animals I Have Known* (1888). In his stories, Seton gave his animal characters intelligence, emotions, and even a sense of ethics. Although he was sometimes criticized for these stories, Seton defended them as based on scientific observation of animal behavior in the wild. Seton was a committed Darwinist, but his Social Darwinism resembled Peter Kropotkin's view of cooperation and "mutual aid" in nature, rather than the Spencerian view that brutal competition was the natural state of things. Accordingly, Seton's stories are full of animal cooperation and altruism. Although Seton had been developing these ideas over decades, he finally summed up his case for the moral lessons of nature in his 1907 book, *The Ten Commandments in the Animal World*, where he argues (using numerous examples from his observations of animals) that the Ten Commandments are "fundamental laws of all highly developed animals" (Seton 1925: 4).

When Seton turned to creating programs for young people, he brought into this work these same Social Darwinist ideas also found in the Social Gospel movement. Seton and other Darwinist reformers believed that they could intervene in the process of evolution and steer society toward more just and more spiritual (as opposed to material) ways. He read and agreed with G. Stanley Hall's (1844–1924) Darwinist approach to the evolutionary psychology of the race and of the individual child and, like Hall, Seton believed that male early adolescence was a particularly magical period when the boy's natural instincts could be turned to spiritual matters and to selfless service to others.

Seton held up the American Indian as a model for American character, spirituality, and physical fitness. He built his original youth program around Indian lore, and when he resigned as Chief Scout in 1915 (in a dispute with the leadership) he reestablished the Woodcraft Indians as a co-educational group in competition with Scouting. Seton thought that American Indian religions were the perfect model for human spirituality and ethics. Seton had moved from the East to settle in Santa Fe, New Mexico, in the early 1930s to create The College of Indian Wisdom, a training institute for leaders in the Woodcraft Indians and other youth organizations. During these years Seton continued publishing the Woodcraft League's monthly *Totem Board*, where Seton tried out the ideas he finally condensed into one book – *The Gospel of the Redman* (1937) – where the Christ-like qualities of the great Shawnee Chief, Tecumseh, come to represent the merging of American Indian religions and those qualities Seton thought best in Christianity. Not surprisingly, the American Indian's religion in Seton's account relied heavily upon ideas about nature, so Seton was thoughtfully weaving together ideas about male adolescence, spirituality, American Indian religions, and the ethical lessons from the animal world.

Many of Seton's ideas about nature and spirituality survived in the BSA handbooks and programs after his departure, but some of the other founders also had their own ideas about the ways religion and nature came together in Scouting. Three of the founders – Edgar M. Robinson, John L. Alexander, and James E. West – had extensive experience in the Young Men's Christian Association (YMCA), and they brought from those experiences a firm faith in the power of "muscular Christianity." While that philosophy energized the late nineteenth-century commitment to athletics as a means to socialize young men in ethics and morality, Scouting went even further than the YMCA in viewing nature as the playground for the spiritual and ethical training of young men. The "Acadian myth" in the United States is the long-standing narrative that a "return to nature" will save Americans from the debilitating, polluting, and demoralizing effects of urbanization and (later) modernization, and we see in the handbooks and other literature of Scouting this enduring mythological idea of "going into the woods" for spiritual renewal (Schmitt 1990).

The founders and authors of the early BSA handbooks included religion as an important ingredient in the Scouting program. The Twelfth Point (and last) of the Scout Law is that "A Scout is Reverent," and in the 1950s the BSA created a special category of Religious Awards so that the boy could learn more about his own religion and provide service to the congregation as an extension of his service to the community through Scouting. All mention of religion in the BSA materials, however, addresses more traditional understandings of religion. The BSA never formulated explicit ideas of a "nature religion" in these materials; those ideas appear far more often in the BSA publications about nature and in oral comments by Scout leaders (e.g., Scoutmaster's "sermon" in Mechling 2001: 18).

Under the rubric "woodcraft," the study of nature has always been a part of the Scouting program. In the Boy Scouts, boys must learn about nature for a range of badges, beginning at the lowest ranks and extending to Eagle Scout, the highest rank. Boys earn merit badges on topics running from the most general, such as "Nature" and "Environmental Science," to specialized merit badges in such fields as bird study and reptile study. The pamphlets for these badges are usually written by experts in science, but even these publications convey the sense of awe humans have in the presence of nature. If the modern "ecological consciousness" has a religious or spiritual dimension to it, then we see evidence of this in the BSA publications.

The religious or spiritual dimensions of the study of nature in Scouting are subtle but unmistakable. The notion of "stewardship," an idea borrowed from religion by conservationists in the Progressive Era, pervades Scouting's ideas about nature. These are the "conservationist" ideas of people like Gifford Pinchot, Teddy Roosevelt's Secretary of the Interior, rather than the "preservationist" ideas of John Muir in the same period. William Temple Hornaday (1854–1937), who directed the New York Zoological Park from 1896 to 1926 and who was in the circle of Seton's friends, is remembered in the BSA with the William T. Hornaday badge and medals for boys who undertake projects representing "distinguished service in natural resource conservation," evidence of responsible stewardship over nature.

Although the social and cultural impetus for Scouting came from the pervasive sense of a "crisis" in white masculinity in turn-of-the-century Great Britain and the United States, some reformers thought that the ideas of the movement, including ideas about nature and religion, were also applicable to girls. Like Seton, the Gulicks created the Camp Fire program around American Indian lore and took care in designing campfire rituals meant to impart to girls the spiritual and service aspects of their lives as young women. Crafts and camping were part of the Camp Fire program from the beginning, sharing in the "Acadian myth" of the beneficial effects of having girls experience nature. Juliette Gordon Low's ideas for the Girl Scouts (1912) did not rely upon American Indian lore for their program, but Low and her colleagues were just as committed to the view that teaching girls self-reliance for the twentieth century should include woodcraft skills. Seton created still another opportunity for girls with his Woodcraft Girls, an organization paralleling his Woodcraft Boys, with its own handbook, *The Woodcraft Manual for Girls* (1916). All three of these organizations – the Camp Fire Girls, the Girl Scouts of America, and the Woodcraft Girls – were feminist organizations in their cultural context, as they aimed to take young women beyond the domestic sphere and give them knowledge and skills, including campcraft and woodcraft. In these movements' requirements, rituals, and excursions into the wilderness we see the same wedding of nature and spirituality so prominent in the boys' movements.

Jay Mechling

Further Reading

Keller, Betty. *Black Wolf: The Life of Ernest Thompson Seton*. Vancouver: Douglas and McIntyre, 1984.

Macleod, David I. *Building Character in the American Boy: The Boy Scouts, YMCA, and Their Forerunners, 1870–1920*. Madison: University of Wisconsin Press, 1983.

Mechling, Jay. *On My Honor: Boy Scouts and the Making of American Youth*. Chicago: University of Chicago Press, 2001.

Ross, Dorothy. *G. Stanley Hall: The Psychologist as Prophet*. Chicago: University of Chicago Press, 1972.

Schmitt, Peter J. *Back to Nature: The Acadian Myth in Urban America*. Baltimore, NJ: Johns Hopkins University Press, 1990 (1962).

Seton, Ernest Thompson. *The Ten Commandments in the Animal World*. Garden City, NY: Doubleday, Page & Company, 1925.

Wadland, John Henry. *Ernest Thompson Seton: Man in Nature and the Progressive Era, 1880–1915*. New York: Arno Press, 1978.

See also: Indian Guides; Muir, John; Nature Religion in the United States; Pinchot, Gifford.

Scything and Erotic Fulfillment

Ivan Illich has drawn attention to the "vernacular" as those practices and values that, like our vernacular (or native) tongue, are learned in family and community by oft-unconscious processes of social osmosis rather than through formal schooling. It is striking that vernacular activity in the satisfaction of fundamental human needs is typically rich in synergistic layers of meaning. Indeed, as development practitioners and "modernizers" have discovered to their cost, it is often the case in vernacular communities that "implicit meanings of local practices" will outweigh the superficially presented reason for doing things in a particular way. For example, stories abound in Africa of newly installed water pumps being broken by young men. Only then was it realized that having the young women walk to the distant well was an implicit but unspoken opportunity for courtship.

One of the most striking characteristics of much vernacular work is its relationship to rhythm – both as an outcome (for example, in work song), and as an organizing principle aiding the process. This emerges, for example, in walking, rowing, riding, cycling, milking, weaving, spinning, pounding corn, hauling on anchor chains, ropes and fishing lines, casting with a fishing rod, making music, repartee in discourse, varying forms of intercourse, rocking the baby, and in reaping with sickle or scythe.

The ability to "enter into the swing of things" in work, as in sport, is commonly the touchstone of right technique. Chant, song or dance, often in unison with co-workers, may be concomitant to such an extent that some cultures have built up considerable bodies of work-related folk songs. These are songs not necessarily about work, but rather, embodying the rhythm of work. Thus, for example, the American-born Scottish ethnomusicologist, Margaret Fay Shaw, says of the weaving of Harris Tweed fabric in the 1930s: "Those were the days when a wearer could regard his homespun from the Hebrides with the thought of the songs and gaiety that went into the making of it" (Shaw 1986:7).

The wielding of a scythe – a sickle mounted on a frame to allow full-body engagement in harvesting grass and grain crops – is a paramount example of rhythmic vernacular work, and one that is currently generating fresh interest for its Zen-like meditative nature. In his seminal work, *The Scythe Book*, David Tresemer refers to the obviating effect of rhythm and resultant work song on the passing of time, maintaining that, "The main function of these chants and charms and songs was to coordinate the breath and scythe stroke and to 'deceive the tedious time. And steal unfelt the sultry hours away'" (Tresemer 2002: 60).

He sees this phenomenon as being spiritually transcendent, thus concluding his treatise with the paragraph:

> It is my desire on this land, in the context of this small farm, to know the best use of my body, and to move with the scythe as an extension of my body – in relationship with the grass, and in a team of mowers – in the process of developing my own communion with the divinity that creates the task and all its parts (Tresemer 2002: 103).

In *The Scythe Must Dance*, a technical addendum to the second edition of Tresemer's work and widely cited on the internet, Peter Vido likens the correct swing of the scythe to "The practice of T'ai-Chi Chuan, with its emphasis on the executing of smooth motions and while in a reflective state of mind, it is a beautiful – even if idealistic – model" (Tresemer 2002: 169). He too, in his closing paragraph, transcendentally elevates the art, quoting a school essay by eighteen-year-old Hannah Sawyer of Kingfield, Maine. She writes:

> Scything is simple; it is relaxing too. It is no wonder the people of yesteryear had very little problem with stress. The quiet rhythm melts away tension; swish, cut, swish, cut, swish … If I close my eyes it is easy to imagine myself back in time – a bird singing to the sky, the wind whispering to the trees, the splash of a horse pawing the water, the lowing of a cow calling her calf. Would you like to time-travel? I'll teach you how (Tresemer 2002: 181).

I myself grew up on the Isle of Lewis off Scotland, knowing how to hone and handle a scythe for the making of hay and silage to feed our cow. I observe that, today, it has become a near-extinct and hard-to-get tool, driven out by the hegemony of the "strimmer" – the name given in Britain to pernicious petroleum-powered pestilences with rotating nylon whiplashes that brash the grass. Walk a meadow or woodland path that has been strimmed, and you step among the scrappy carnage of flayed vegetation and scuffed ground. By contrast, tread a scythed path, and the vegetation is cleanly cut and laid to the side in pleasing swathes that avoid messing one's footwear. Rarely is the turf damaged because, as the Thai Buddhist Monk Ticht Nhat Hanh puts it in a quotation at the leading website dedicated to the art, "Whenever I see anyone cutting grass with a scythe, I know he is practicing awareness." Indeed, it was a personal meditation on strimmed versus scythed meadow paths in Scotland that inspired me with "The Scyther's Prayer": *May my death be the clean cut of an honest scythe, and never the thousand lashes of an accursed strimmer!*

Time and death wield a scythe because harvesting is both the fulfillment, and the transcendence, of them both. As Sir James Frazer suggested in *The Golden Bough* (1994), the practice of reaping connects humankind with the Corn God or the King of the Woods, and with the Earth Goddess. It is back into her sacred body, the Earth, that the sky god or King seasonally meets his nemesis, as at Diana's Grove of Nemi. To consciously reap the life-force (which can be symbolized by mistletoe or the "Golden Bough") with a hand sickle or scythe is therefore to participate in the perpetual archetypal cycle of life, death and rebirth.

To Frazer, this insight connected the Christian story with a much wider body of world mythology. As he concludes his seminal if professionally controversial and much-disputed yet remarkable work:

> Our long voyage of discovery is over [and] once more we take the road to Nemi. It is evening, and as we climb the long slope of the Appian Way up to the Alban Hills, we look back and see the sky aflame with sunset … over Rome and touching with a crest of fire the dome of St. Peter's … The place has changed but little since Diana received the homage of her worshippers at the sacred grove. The temple of the sylvan goddess, indeed, has vanished and the King of the Wood no longer stands sentinel over the Golden Bough. But Nemi's woods are still green, and as the sunset fades above them in the west, there comes to us, borne on the swell of the wind, the sound of the church bells of Aricia ringing the Angelus. *Ave Maria!* Sweet and solemn they chime out from the distant town and die lingeringly away across the wide Campagnan marshes. *Le roi est mort, vive le roi! Ave Maria*! (Frazer 1994: 714; translatable as, "The king is dead, long live the king! Praise be the Mother of God!").

Frazer's work may have fallen on stony ground when the relationship between Christianity and fertility became a shunned field of study. Nonetheless, it cannot escape notice that in the Last Supper before his "Passion," Christ, the Mahavatan embodiment of God incarnate (and so carnal), offers bread – risen from reaped corn – in memory of eternal communion with his body. The spirituality implicit in the biblical Song of Solomon, Proverbs 8, Luke 7 and Matthew 11 thereby finds conjugal fulfillment in this "feast of love," this "communion of the saints," that realizes heaven as the fulfillment of the erotic.

Alastair McIntosh

Further Reading

Frazer, James. *The Golden Bough: A History of Myth and Religion.* London: Chancellor Press, 1994 (originally 1890).

Illich, Ivan. *Shadow Work: Vernacular Values Examined.* UK: Open Forum, 1981.

Max-Neef, Manfred. "Development and Human Needs". In Paul Ekins and Manfred Max-Neef, eds. *Real-Life Economics: Understanding Wealth Creation.* London: Routledge, 1992, 197–214.

Shaw, Margaret Fay. *Folksongs and Folklore of South Uist.* Aberdeen: Aberdeen University Press, 1986.

Tresemer, David. *The Scythe Book (With an Addendum on the Practical Use of the Scythe by Peter Vido).* Chambersburg, PA: Alan C. Hood & Co. Inc, 2002 (2nd edn).

See also: Aesthetics of Nature and the Sacred; Anthropologists; Nhat Hanh, Thich.

Sea Goddesses and Female Water Spirits

Water is not just regarded as a resource to be managed or exploited or as the source of natural metaphors, but as having an identity on its own. Such an identity has been, in many cultures, personified in the figures of female water deities.

Images of transcendental women surface worldwide – in the lakes, seas, rivers and springs of every continent. Nearly always of great beauty and ambivalence, they are seen as both seductive and threatening; as bringers of salvation and – at the same time – damnation; and – just like their element, water – as life-giving and life-taking, too.

Deities of the water, water spirits and mermaids cannot be seen only as a projection of attitudes toward women or just as a metaphor for male desire for and fear of the female. The following suggest the multiplicity of meanings inherent in a wide range of conceptualizations of sea goddesses in specific local and historical contexts and in connection with particular social practices.

Examples drawn from Europe, Africa, Brazil and Indonesia will focus on rites that are performed at present and which seem to be of growing significance. This reveals local strategies for dealing with the extraordinary, unpredictable and challenging element, water.

Europe – Sirens, Sprites, Melusine and Undine

Each epoch in Europe constructed its own characteristic version of women in the waters. Aphrodite or Venus, the goddess of beauty, unbridled love and creative fecundity, can be linked to pre-patriarchal social structures. In contrast to her, sirens – half-bird, half-woman – seem like dark, strange and uncanny creatures who are full of sensual temptation for Odysseus, whom they try to deflect from his road home. In the post-Homeric era, the sirens lose their threatening characteristics, although in the Middle Ages they come to embody a direct threat to the male, Christian mode of being because they distract from the word of God and promise carnal desires and earthly pleasures. The sprite with her fish's tail moves to the front of the stage. While she is also a seductive creature she is a split being: Her form is human above and animal below. She is wild, but unreachable because of her sexual inadequacy, however in the course of time she is depicted in an increasingly harmless fashion. In early modern times, mermaids with one or two tails – the latter classified as Melusines – frequently appear in churches as well as in book illustrations and decorative folk art. This leads to the gradual supplanting of the wild, sexualized and demonized Melusine by the diminished child-woman Undine. The Undine is never a mixed form, but rather a different one in the sense of embodying a living, immediate naturalism.

The Romantic period sees a multitude of gushing literary variations on this figure. The Undine shares the Melusine's neediness. She needs a man, not only to make her human, but also, through marriage, to gain a Christian soul. After getting it, she is characterized by submission and humility and is similar to the figure of the little mermaid in Andersen's fairytale. Desexualization, devotion and silent sacrifice are central to the tale's bourgeois ideal of motherhood, because the little mermaid dies before she has a chance to seduce the prince.

The death of females by drowning, especially that of Ophelia, takes on a great fascination around the end of the nineteenth century. The lifeless, floating female body represents an increasing deindividualization, while, at the same time, the Undine becomes merely an "art nouveau" ornament. Today, we have Barbie dolls with fishtails and the Lorelei on T-shirts as examples of mass consumer products. Just as nature has been turned into a useful but lifeless object lacking the divine, so the mermaid has degenerated into a commercial sex object and a "harmless" piece of kitsch.

But, simultaneously, the sea even nowadays can provoke impressions of open space, power, eternity, movement, metamorphosis, change of shape and color, and orgasmic waves.

Africa: Mami Wata (Mammy Water)

In Africa water and floods are unpredictable forces, potentially benevolent, but also harmful. The widespread polymorphous figure of Mami Wata (Mammy Water, oscillating between spirit and goddess) is actively worshipped in many African countries between Senegal and Tanzania. In West African cosmology the Mami Wata spirits (there is also Mami Wishnu, Mami Lakshmi or Mami Gabriel) are among the most popular and they are said to possess great mystical powers and authority. They are also known to extend their wrath and anger in the form of torrential rain, floods or lightning. These powerful spirits are usually depicted as mermaids of exceptional beauty or as snakes. Their history seems to be closely connected with colonialism. As there is a definite influx of prints from Europe and India, in the 1980s and early 1990s foreign influences in the iconography of Mammy Water were seen as central in the scientific interpretations of this figure. Mami Wata has many traits of a white woman or fashionable lady of Western style and, as offerings for her mainly consist of things associated with foreigners (a means of symbolic appropriation of their world), her followers appear to be selecting fragments from experiences of foreign cultures and investing them with new meanings. Today Mami Wata religious practice is interpreted as concerned predominantly with the articulation and expression of African social realities and in particular with social change. Other authors observe hybridity in the mixtures of African, European, Hindu and occult elements. Thus, Mami Wata is connected with colonialism, migration, globalization, with literacy, education and increasingly with new media (cf. the Mami Wata websites in the internet). Strangely enough, there are no interpretations of Mami Wata as an icon for environmental protection or as a guard for aquatic ecosystems.

In any case, the idea of an underwater world with splendid palaces and immense riches is a counterimage to the real world. Mami Wata includes aspects of ancient water – and snake spirits: In the Igbo context, in south-eastern Nigeria, the royal python companion refers to the rainbow deity that controls the waters of the sky and unites them with the waters on Earth. Hence Mami Wata and the rainbow serpent are an inseparable pair. In West and Central Africa the river deity Mami Wata is linked with notions of irresistible female sexuality and with modernity in urban life.

Women make up the majority of her adherents, both as priestesses and as adepts of the cults. Her worshippers attest to the goddess' healing powers, benevolence, beauty, mystery and local origins. She can enter people through possession. Possession cults have often been modes of cultural resistance and means to domesticate male and alien powers. Therefore possession by water spirits can be interpreted as an embodied critique of colonial, national, global or religious hegemonies.

But the local meanings differ. For instance, in Igbo religion Mami Wata has a particular significance as a local strategy for dealing with the extraordinary, unpredictable, abnormal, nonconformist, challenging and/or innovative elements and events in nature. Another example is Zaire, where Mami Wata gradually lost her sacred aura and became a symbol for the prostitute. Association with her is seen as immoral because the wealth she provides is not shared. Thus, we can see her as a complex concept of multidimensional divinity and appropriation of nature.

Brazil: Iemanjá

In the Afro-Brazilian religion of Cancomblé, the Sea Goddess Iemanjá (Yemanjá), brought by the slaves from West Africa to South America, is the revered mother of all the gods (Orixás, personifications of the forces of nature). According to the legends, Iemanjá (the waters) married Aganju (dry land). From this marriage Orungan (the air and the heights) was born, but, in the absence of his father, Orungan had sex with his mother, Iemanjá. From this, Iemanjá died and from her womb all the other Orixás were born. Therefore she is considered the mother of all of them.

During the era of slavery, Iemanjá was a source of resistance and part of black cultural identity. Under the cloak of Catholicism, she was venerated as the Virgin Mary. But she also took on some aspects of the Indian Yara. As mother of the fishes, she guarantees fertility, and at the same time, there is a notion that she becomes the devouring mother and lover of fishermen killed at sea. Thus fishermen's wives beg Iemanjá to look after their husbands, whereas their husbands are more likely to ask for a beautiful woman or a new boat. The place where petitions are made can be a temple, the beach or the sea. As gifts, Iemanjá, like Mami Wata in Africa, receives cosmetics, combs, clothing, embroidered cushions, rice powder, flowers, jewels, perfumes, honey – donations toward her beauty and erotic seductive power.

In Candomblé, more and more people of all colors and social classes come to the priestess for help and advice on general questions, relationships, family problems and health matters. People pay homage to Iemanjá in great public feasts, especially in the cities of Rio de Janeiro (8 December), Salvador de Bahia (2 February) and Porto Alegre. Celebrating the beginning of a new year the faithful take their offerings to the goddess, asking that their wishes be fulfilled.

Alaska: Sedna

According to the peoples of northern Canada and Greenland, known as Inuit, the Sea Spirit and mythical Goddess of the Sea, Sedna, on the bottom of the ocean, is the mother of all animals. According to one of the many versions of her legend, Sedna was a young girl who did not want to marry. Finally her father forced her to marry a dog, but afterwards he felt sorry for her and drowned the dog. After her husband died, Sedna was unable to support her children and herself. She had to send her children away and returned to live with her parents. One day, a bird, disguised as a man, sought Sedna in marriage. She accepted and went to live with him. But soon Sedna discovered that her new husband was not a man but only a fulmar. When Sedna's father visited her, he convinced Sedna to leave with him in his boat. Unfortunately the fulmar caught them, and with his wings created an enormous storm, which threatened to overturn the boat. Terrified, Sedna's father tried to throw the girl overboard to her husband, but she grasped the boat's side. In fear, the father cut off Sedna's fingers until she fell into the sea. It is said that Sedna resides at the bottom of the sea with the seals and other sea animals that were created from her fingers.

In contrast to the other sea goddesses, Sedna is not depicted as beautiful. Her hair and body gets dirty and ugly when humans break taboos or behave in bad ways. Then she holds the animals back and sends storms or diseases. Therefore a shaman will undertake an underwater journey to comb her hair and wash her after he has defeated her in a fight. This causes her to let the animals go. More recent research revealed that this shaman can also be a woman. In this case, the interpretation of symbolical sexual subjugation of women (by male shamans) (Zumwalt 1984) becomes obsolete, and the fertility as well as the moralistic aspect of Sedna comes more to the fore. In her image, the behavior of people and the cycles of nature, the weather and the fertility of the animals, are closely connected.

Indonesia: Ratu Kidul

Ratu Kidul is the Queen or Goddess of Java's Southern Ocean. She is the ruler of all spirits, and she appears in the old texts and in the oral traditions of both the Javanese courts and ordinary people. In contrast to the above-mentioned figures, she is not first and foremost a mother goddess in connection with fertility but her central characteristic is the legitimization of political power. From the early seventeenth century onward, she has always been regarded as the consort of the Sultan (from the eighteenth century onward, of the Sultans of both Surakarta and Yogyakarta), supporting him and defending his realm. Implicitly the marriage meant that the ruler was approved and sanctioned by the primordial powers of the Sea. The significance of this relationship has been waning along with the declining positions of these courts in present-day Java. On the other hand, at present, ordinary people can and do ask her for help with all kinds of troubles. Spiritual and material goals become inseparable. Ratu Kidul is an ambiguous figure too: she can be the source of luck, welfare and healing as well as of illness, death and destruction. There are manifold adaptations to both modern life and Islam in imaginations of her, and the quality of her persona depends on the context in which it is presented.

Nevertheless Javanese popular belief in Ratu Kidul is still very vivid.

Judith Schlehe

Further Reading
Drewal, Henry John. "Mermaids, Mirrors, and Snake Charmers: Igbo Mami Wata Shrines." *African Arts* 21 (1988), 38–45.
Jell-Bahlsen, Sabine. "Eze Mmiri Di Egwu, The Water Monarch is Awesome: Reconsidering the Mammy Water Myths." In F. Kaplan, ed. *Queens, Queen Mothers, Priestesses, and Power*. New York: New York Academy of Sciences, 1997, 103–34.
Zumwalt, Rosemary. "The Sea Spirit of the Central Eskimo and Her Relationship to the Living: A Delicate Balance." In Genevieve Calame-Griaule, et al., eds. *Le Conte, Pourquoi? Comment?* Paris: Centre National de la Recherche Scientifique, 1984, 277–93.

See also: Candomblé of Brazil; Divine Waters of the Oru-Igbo (Southeastern Nigeria); Inuit; Rainbow Serpent (North Wellesley Islands, Australia); Serpents and Dragons; Umbanda; Water Spirits and Indigenous Ecological Management (South Africa).

Sea Shepherd Conservation Society – *See* Biocentric Religion – A Call For; Watson, Paul – and the Sea Shepherd Conservation Society.

Seattle (Sealth), Chief (ca. 1790–1866)

Chief Sealth (or Seattle as he is commonly called today) was an influential chief of the Salish-speaking indigenous peoples whose lands included the Puget Sound region of what is now Washington State. Born sometime around 1790 from a Duwamish mother and a Suquamish father, and dying in 1866, this namesake of present-day Seattle was chief during the coming of the "Boston Men" (American-European settlers from the east coast of the United States), and maintained mostly cordial relations with them throughout his life. By nearly all early accounts, Sealth was an able chief and spokesman for the Salish, whose existence centered on the rich tidelands and estuaries that surrounded Puget Sound.

However, his fame today – especially in popular culture – is due mainly to the modern environmental movement, specifically to their appropriation and revision of a speech Sealth allegedly gave along the Seattle waterfront, probably in 1854. The earliest account of the speech, recorded by Henry Smith in the *Seattle Sunday Star* in 1887, comes from Smith's recollections and diary fragments – the latter never found. In Smith's account, Sealth contrasts the white culture with his own: the former apparently favored by God, the latter rejected, with the white religion given by an "angry God" and hence incomprehensible to his and other tribes.

Most pointedly, the speech records Sealth as contrasting the Christianity of the whites (with its stark separation of Heaven from Earth) with his tradition's reverence for the land, hallowed by the very real presence of his people's ancestors. Regarding these sacred ties between the ancestors and the tribe's land, the chief warns: "the dead are not altogether powerless."

The modern legend of Chief Seattle and his "Speech," however, is not primarily due to Smith's account – with its authentic Salish ties between Earth and religion – but due to significant embellishments added by whites more than a century later, most notably from the pens of poets and screenwriters. In the past thirty years or so, in fact, many revisionist versions of Sealth's speech have appeared: quoted at Earth Day celebrations, highlighted at a World's Fair, used by political parties and "Green" political candidates, appearing in a Smithsonian exhibit, and penned even into children's books. Thanks to the massive information-exchange capabilities of the Internet, Sealth's speech – in seemingly infinite variations – is everywhere, from websites touting survivalist themes, to the home web pages of indigenous peoples.

In most of these accounts, Sealth is portrayed as fundamentally questioning not only an upcoming treaty with the U.S. government, but the very notion of private property itself: "How can we buy or sell the sky?" He also bemoans witnessing the "slaughter of the buffalo," despite the fact that bison are not indigenous to the Pacific Northwest, and the great slaughter of buffalo would not occur until a decade or more after Sealth's death. Thus, most scholars acknowledge that much of the text of "Chief Seattle's Speech" was in all probability not uttered by Sealth along the Puget Sound waterfront in 1854. Smith himself was known as something of a poet, and in the Victorian era it was common for writers to add rhetorical flourishes as they saw fit; but unless authentic documents are forthcoming, we are likely never to learn what exactly Chief Sealth uttered that so impressed Henry Smith.

Despite the difficulties in determining where Sealth's words stop and modern embellishments begin, Chief Sealth and his "speech" remain powerful and influential for two significant reasons. First, the authentic core of his speech points toward a land ethic and religious tradition which refuse to objectify nature, and which count ecological respect as a matter of course.

Second, the appropriation and adaptation of Sealth's powerful words, and the linkage of this text to the modern environmental movement, are reminders of the ever-present human impulse toward religious syncretism, the combination or synthesis of different elements from two or more seemingly disparate traditions. Many Native Americans are angry at how some groups of the majority culture have employed Sealth's speech, lifting it out of the specific Duwamish and Salish cultures from which it came. They view this appropriation as yet another example of theft. Others, however, look at the resultant text, not primarily in terms of historical accuracy, but of whether it expresses the truth of the results of persistent environmental degradation.

Michael McKenzie

Further Reading
Bierwert, Crisca. "Remembering Chief Seattle." *American Indian Quarterly* 22:3 (1998), 280.
Furtwangler, Albert. *Answering Chief Seattle*. Seattle: University of Washington Press, 1997.

See also: Indigenous Environmental Network; Indigenous Religions and Cultural Borrowing; Manifest Destiny; Mother Earth; Radical Environmentalism; Religious Environmentalist Paradigm.

Sedona

One of the most celebrated of New Age "power spots," this small town in scenic north-central Arizona has been a hub of New Age and metaphysical activities since at least the late 1970s, when California-based psychic and self-help guru Dick Sutphen began touting it as a power center and psychic Page Bryant identified seven specific "energy vortexes" in the area. Stories about extraordinary phenomena and about the area's healing energies circulated rapidly through the 1980s, and by the early 1990s the number of healing centers, New Age bookstores, crystal shops, and psychic channelers had multiplied far out of proportion to the town's population of ten thousand or so. Groups based in the area have included ECKankar, the Rainbow Ray Focus Group, the Aquarian Concepts Community, the Center for Advanced Energy Healing, and the Aquarian Educational Foundation.

Cradled in its other-worldly red rock surroundings, the town has become a spiritual melting pot of New Age millenarianism, neo-shamanic Earth spirituality, and post-traditional metaphysical and Theosophical occultism. Some of Sedona's channelers regularly contribute to the journal *Sedona: Journal of Emergence*, which has become the flagship of the American channeling community, with its millenarian beliefs in extraterrestrial contact, interdimensional portals, light-bodies and stargates. For some of Sedona's psychics and ecospiritualists, the colorful rock formations, steep-walled canyons, and piñon pine-juniper forests that surround the town are an energetically active and psychically catalytic wilderness rich with mysterious energy "portals" and spiritual presences. At the same time, the rate of real estate and tourist development has turned Sedona into one of the prime tourist sites of the U.S.

Southwest, attracting close to five million visitors annually, and into one of the most expensive places to live in the country, with several environmental conflicts resulting from pressures of development, sewage, land use, and related issues. Sedona's New Age popularity may ultimately not save it from the "Aspenization" or "Californication" that has become the trap of many a picturesque town in the American "new west."

Adrian Ivakhiv

Further Reading

Ivakhiv, Adrian. *Claiming Sacred Ground: Pilgrims and Politics at Glastonbury and Sedona*. Bloomingham and Indianapolis: Indiana University Press, 2001.

See also: Delphic Oracle; Earth Mysteries; Glastonbury; New Age; Santa Fe, New Mexico.

Seed, John (1945–)

John Seed is an Australian environmental activist who, along with Joanna Macy, has done more than any other figure to spread globally deep ecology spirituality and ritual. Motivated in part by long-standing Buddhist practice, in his native Australia he founded the Rainforest Information Centre in 1979 (and by 1984 the World Rainforest Report). In subsequent years, while he has continued political work to protect forests and forest peoples, he has increasingly prioritized his spiritual work. He believes that the environmental crisis is so grave that only a miracle can save the Earth and that a prerequisite for this is the complete transformation of human consciousness along deep ecological lines. Given this conviction, he has put a high priority on creating and teaching ritual forms that evoke in participants a perception of the sacredness of the Earth and feelings of kinship and moral responsibility toward the entire community of life.

Born in 1945 in Budapest Hungary, Seed arrived in Australia at the age of five and recollects that the bushland and coastline around Sydney laid the foundations for his later love of nature. From 1973 to 1979 he steeped himself in Buddhist meditation and helped build a meditation center and community in the bush of northern New South Wales. After withdrawing to the forest, however, the deforestation sweeping the world found him, and he participated in direct-action campaigns in the Nightcap Range NSW (1979–1981), Franklin River Tasmania (1983–1984) and Cape Tribulation Queensland (1985–1986). Each of these campaigns led to the protection of rainforests and the creation of national parks that eventually received World Heritage listing.

In 1980 Seed met bioregionalist Gary Snyder who was reading poetry in Australia. Snyder mentioned to him the recently formed Earth First! movement in the United States, which was also involved in civil disobedience to save forests. Seed hooked up with these activists and during the summers of 1984 and 1985 started doing "road show" performances with Earth First! co-founders Dave Forman and Mike Roselle in the U.S. These performances used songs, slide shows, and lectures, to spread deep ecology spirituality and build direct-action ecological resistance in the U.S. (Seed is an accomplished song writer who has produced several albums of environmental and children's songs.) Seed and Roselle would help Randy Hayes invent the Rainforest Action Network in 1984, which quickly established itself as one of the world's most important environmental non-governmental organizations.

In 1987 Seed co-produced a television documentary for Australian national television about the struggle for the rainforests, which was subsequently shown in many countries around the world. Shortly thereafter he pioneered a number of important projects to protect rainforests in South America, Asia and the Pacific. One of the earliest and most innovative was in Papua New Guinea, providing portable "Wokabout sawmills" to indigenous peoples as a means to conduct sustainable tree harvesting. This was seen as a way to resist deforestation by showing forest peoples an alternative to industrial forestry, which destroys cultural and natural diversity. By the turn of the century he was investing a great deal of time in Ecuador, helping to establish and demarcate forest reserves there, both to protect their ecological integrity and the forest peoples who depend on them. Religious and spiritual organizations, including The Australian Council of Churches and the Foundation for Deep Ecology, have supported his work.

Seed is the source of an aphorism now commonly expressed in radical environmental circles, "I am the forest, recently emerged into consciousness, defending myself," a perception that first came to him while engaged in direct-action resistance to logging, when he felt himself "no longer acting on behalf of myself or my human ideas, but on behalf of the Earth ... I was literally part of the rainforest defending herself" (Seed, et al. 1998: 6). But Seed is probably best known for helping create and widely disseminating the Council of All Beings. He has also developed "Re-Earthing" and other workshops that can be considered Earth-revering rituals. The Re-earthing workshops draw on breathwork practices grounded in Yoga and other religious traditions originating in India. Other rituals, including some that are often used as preliminary exercises in the Council of All Beings, consecrate cosmological and evolutionary narratives; such ritualizing has affinities with the Epic of Evolution and draws on the work of Thomas Berry.

Seed has conducted such rituals and trained others to do so widely, not only in his native Australia and the U.S., but also throughout Western Europe, Poland, Russia,

Slovakia, Mongolia, India, Thailand, Japan, Chile, Ecuador, and Canada. This work has spawned environmental protection groups and projects including the Anammalai Reforestation Society in Tamil Nadu, India which has been engaged since the late 1980s in the reforestation of the sacred mountain Arunachala.

Seed often teaches at countercultural enclaves or spiritual retreat centers such as the California Institute of Integral Studies, the Esalen Institute and Omega Institute (Rhinebeck, New York), Findhorn, Naropa University, and Schumacher College. He also lectures widely at mainstream universities in the U.S., Australia, Europe, and Asia. Awarded the Order of Australia Medal in 1985 by the Australian Government for his conservation efforts, in 2003 he has been writing and producing videos, including *On the Brink*, which captures well the apocalyptic expectation which, combined with his deep ecological spirituality, fuels his passionate Earth activism.

Bron Taylor

Further Reading

Seed, John, Joanna Macy, Pat Fleming and Arne Naess. *Thinking Like a Mountain: Towards a Council of All Beings*. Philadelphia, PA: New Society, 1988.

See also: Berry, Thomas; California Institute of Integral Studies; Council of All Beings; Deep Ecology; Earth First! and the Earth Liberation Front; Epic of Evolution (and adjacent, Epic Ritual); Esalen Institute; Findhorn Foundation/Community (Scotland); Hopiland to the Rainforest Action Network; Hundredth Monkey; Macy, Joanna; Naess, Arne; Naropa University; Radical Environmentalism; Schumacher, Ernest Friedrich; Snyder, Gary.

Seeds in South Asia

In South Asia's predominantly agricultural society, seeds as the source of food and life are generative not only of economic and nutritional value, but also of multiple poetic and religious meanings. Seed imagery is pervasive in Hinduism's earliest sacred texts, and retains its importance into the current era. Actual seeds are present as auspicious offerings in numerous rituals of varied purpose; moreover, ritual actions surround farmers' practices of saving and planting seeds. In the late twentieth and early twenty-first century, conflicts have swirled around the production and marketing of seeds. These include issues of biodiversity versus monoculture; of local control versus multinational corporate production; and most recently of the economic and environmental benefits and hazards of genetically engineered seeds. Seeds thus retain potent symbolic value in multiple and changing contexts through millennia of South Asian history.

The common word for seed in Hindi and Sanskrit is *bij* (or *bija*). From its earliest uses in ancient India this term encompassed a semantic domain similar to that of seed in English: its meanings range from the actual germ of plant life to human or animal semen, and expand to include any primary cause. Particular to Sanskrit usage, however, is the association of seed with the power of sound. *Bij mantra* denotes the mystical letter or syllable essential to an oral spell used to evoke a particular deity.

Hinduism's oldest scriptures, the *Vedas*, pose homologies among seed, milk and other potent substances including butter, and the nectar of immortality – homologies that persevere throughout later Sanskrit literature as well as in vernacular sources. In popular devotional oral traditions, a seed planted and sprouting is a common metaphor for religious knowledge that may come from a guru or the lord, and take root in the human heart.

Because of its close association with semen, seed as male is sometimes identified as part of a cultural complex that disadvantages women. Women may be likened to fields – giving nourishment and growth to seed, but having no great part to play in the final product – whether determining its form or possessing its fruits. However, some South Asian esoteric traditions, such as those of the Bengali Bauls, describe women's menstrual blood as "female seed" whose potency is equal to or greater than that of males. Both male and female seed may be ritually conserved to increase spiritual power and knowledge, or depleted through ordinary sexual intercourse to produce children.

A Sanskrit agricultural treatise called *Krishi-Parashara* prescribes a procedure for prayerfully sowing seeds in which, "The farmer with a pure and concentrated mind and after meditating upon Indra [the god of rain]," sows three handfuls of moist seeds on an auspicious day – thus ensuring prosperity in the future year (Bhattacharya 1976: 293–4). Farmers throughout India have traditionally performed similar rituals to initiate the planting season, before it is time to sow actual crops. In the wake of technological change in recent decades, these practices have waned.

Besides rituals explicitly incorporated into the agricultural work cycle, many other Hindu rites involve seeds. For example, in Rajasthan, the worship of the goddess Sitala Mother (who presides not only over rash and fever disease but over fertility of humans and farms), precedes the monsoon planting season by at least two months. All the women who participate in Sitala's worship on her festival day will go behind her shrine and plough miniature fields in the dirt with their fingers. In these fields they plant seeds for each of the coming season's crops, seeds that have been offered to, and blessed by, the goddess.

Folktales also associate seeds with divine female beings. In Bengali folklore, Lakshmi, the goddess of prosperity, comes disguised as an old woman and gives rice seeds to a poor widow, thus blessing her household with abundance. Throughout India, Lakshmi is associated with grain and grain seeds in iconography and folklore.

Vandana Shiva, one visible and vocal spokeswoman in India's environmentalist movement, explicitly compares the seed today to the spinning wheel during India's Independence movement, declaring that seeds today have become the "site and symbol of freedom." According to Shiva, seeds offer a unique conjunction for issues of cultural and biological diversity (Shiva 1999: 67). In 1999 the "seed satyagraha" movement (echoing Gandhi and nationalism) successfully opposed Monsanto's proposed introduction of seeds with genetically engineered sterility (known as "terminator" or "suicide") to the Indian market. Meera Dewan's *Eternal Seed*, a documentary film released in 1996, unites both ancient religious significance and modern activist politics to present the ongoing potency of seeds in South Asian rituals and lives.

Ann Grodzins Gold

Further Reading
Bhattacharya, Swapan Kumar. *Farmers Rituals and Modernization: A Sociological Study*. Calcutta: Minerva Associates Publications, 1976.
Dube, Leela. "Seed and Earth: The Symbolism of Biological Reproduction and Sexual Relations of Production." In Leela Dube, Eleanor Leacock and Shirley Ardener, eds. *Visibility and Power*. Delhi: Oxford University Press, 1986, 22–53.
Gold, Ann Grodzins. "Abandoned Rituals: Knowledge, Time, and Rhetorics of Modernity in Rural India." In N.K. Singhi and Rajendra Joshi, eds. *Religion, Ritual and Royalty*. Jaipur: Rawat Publications, 1999, 262–75.
Gold, Daniel. "Clan and Lineage Among the Sants: Seed, Substance, Service." In Karine Schomer and W.H. McLeod, eds. *The Sants: Studies in a Devotional Tradition of India*. Berkeley: Berkeley Religious Studies Series, 1987, 305–28.
Hanssen, Kristin. *Seeds in Motion: Thoughts, Feelings and the Significance of Social Ties as Invoked by a Family of Vaishnava Mendicant Renouncers in Bengal*. Doctor Rerum Politicarum dissertation, Department of Social Anthropology, University of Oslo, 2002.
Shiva, Vandana. "Ecological Balance in an Era of Globalization." In Nicholas Low, ed. *Global Ethics and Environment*. London: Routledge, 1999, 47–69.
See also: Globalization; Hinduism; India; Radical Environmentalism; Shiva, Vandana.

Senoi (Malayan Penisula)

Senoi refers to a cluster of Aboriginal or hill-tribe peoples of the Malayan Peninsula (including the Semai, Temiar and Jah Hut). They have long been classified as Negrito (being dark-skinned and with relatively crinkly hair) and they share a linguistic affinity within the Austro-Asiatic family of languages. They received worldwide attention in the 1950s when crosscultural psychologist Kilton Stewart projected the Senoi (more particularly the Ple-Temiar people) as the most socially stable or "hygienic" society on earth, because their lives were governed by day-to-day attention to dreams. In the following decade anthropologist Robert Dentan reported on the Semai as a remarkable "Non-Violent People of Malaya." The question at issue here is whether the absence of violent crime in Senoi cultures, and the ideal of avoiding anger and hostile actions as the mark of group identity, translates into non-violent approaches to nature.

It was Stewart's point that the Senoi recognized threats in the external world both socially and environmentally. They formed semi-nomadic groups constantly struggling to establish garden land against the inroads of bamboo jungle, fearful fauna (such as tigers), and meteorological phenomena violating the normal order of things (such as thunder squalls). As for the socio-spiritual world, there was always the danger of quarrels, of causing offenses (by breaking taboos, for example), or disturbing what may be called "nature spirits." Outer events were coped with through victories achieved in the inner world of dreams: children were taught that humans reproduce the fears and tensions of "the socio-physical environment" inside themselves, and that settling problems in their dream states (conquering "fearful emotions," overcoming "hostile images") allows "powers of the other world" to be harnessed for achieving a cooperative and trouble-free life when awake.

Stewart's idealizations of the Senoi, however, proved premature, and some have even questioned her claims about regular dream "classes" in Senoi family life as a hoax. Whatever the extent of exaggeration, reassessments must be made. Although the Senoi were not in any technological position to harm their environment and never adopted any patterns of fixed routines of labor to modify its influence over them to any great extent, they were highly anxious within it about spirit-related diseases and death, and, despite assumptions about "familiar and regularly recurring phenomena" – even certain claims at rainmaking – they showed themselves more genuinely frightened about unpredictable weather changes than possessing confidence and organizing ability to handle nature's forces. One might concede that they were in a better position to cope through fostering dream-sharing sessions, but in no way more extraordinary than most other small-scale traditional cultures that invest in the instructive power of oneiric life. It has turned out that their dreaming has not made them less susceptible to the enticements of modern technology and consumer products in more recent years, and, during the communist insurgency of the 1950s, "the dream people" were not averse to taking up modern arms in their own defense against outsiders (or against each other, when the fighting generated intertribal hostilities).

Garry W. Trompf

Further Reading

Dentan, Robert Knox. "Senoi Dream Praxis." *Dream Network Bulletin* 2:5 (1983), 1–3, 12.

Dentan, Robert Knox. *The Semai: A Nonviolent People of Malaya* (Case Studies in Cultural Anthroplogy). New York: Holt, Rinehart and Winston, 1979.

Leary, John D. *Violence and the Dream People: The Orang Asli in the Malayan Emergency, 1948–1960.* Monographs in International Studies, Southeast Asia Series 95. Athens, OH: Ohio University Center for International Studies, 1995.

Lisitzky, Genevieve H. *Four Ways of Being Human: An Introduction to Anthropology.* New York: Viking, 1976.

Noone, Richard. *The Rape of the Dream People.* London: Hutchinson, 1972.

Stewart, Kilton. "Dream Theory in Malaya." In Charles T. Tart, ed. *Altered States of Consciousness: A Book of Readings.* New York: John Wiley & Sons, 1969, 159–67.

Stewart, Kilton. "The Dream Comes of Age." *Mental Hygiene* 46 (1962), 230–7.

Stewart, Kilton. "Mental Hygiene and World Piece." *Mental Hygiene* 38 (1954), 387–403.

See also: Aboriginal Dreaming.

Serpents and Dragons

From time immemorial humankind has been fascinated but also frightened by snakes. Their quick locomotion in spite of lack of legs, their poisonous bite, and their way of catching their prey by alleged hypnotization set them apart from men and animals. In all continents they are treated with fear and awe. In Western countries they are regarded as the enemies of humankind and, according to the order of the Lord (Gen. 3:15), man shall bruise the serpent's head while serpents shall bruise man's heel. In Genesis the snake is the tempter and representative of evil; in Matthew 10:16, however, it is an epitome of wisdom: "So be wise as serpents!" This ambivalence has governed the human relation to snakes: hatred and destruction on the one hand, admiration and deification on the other.

Qualities and habits of snakes probably gave rise to some of the snake beliefs and cults. The sloughing of skin by snakes was taken as an ability to rejuvenate and a sign of eternal life. The Gilgamesh epic in the Babylonian version of about 1200 B.C.E. explains the origin of this skill: the hero went to the underworld to obtain the plant of immortality. On the way back to Uruk the snake stole and ate it. Gilgamesh could not revive his friend, but the snake turned young again and again. In folk belief and folktales we meet snakes which possess medicines to restore life and health. First of all, they know the antidotes to snake bites. The Lord advised Moses to make a bronze serpent and set it on a pole, and whoever was bitten by a snake could look at it to be restored (Num. 21:9). Similar places of snake shrines were frequent in antiquity. In Greece they were devoted to Aesculapius, the god of medicine. He was portrayed as a bearded man with a staff; around which a snake coiled. This staff of Aesculapius has remained the emblem of the medical profession until today. In Southern Africa, the healer received his potencies of healing from a (mythical) snake during his initiation, and he led this to a patient to "lick" him. Until recently certain snakes were believed to have a stone in their forehead. This so-called snake-stone was regarded as a safe remedy against a snake bite. You only had to apply it to the puncture and the stone would draw out all the poison. As these cannot in fact be found in snake heads, clever businessmen have sold manmade imitations.

Another characteristic of snakes is their sudden disappearance into the ground. Therefore it is believed that they have connections to the underworld and the world of the dead from which they gain extraordinary knowledge. They were consulted as oracles. Delphi, the most important oracle of early Greece, was inhabited by the dragon Python. The priestess Pythia sat at a crevice from which rose an overpowering steam and told what she learned during a state of altered consciousness. In many countries, particularly among the Bantu-speaking peoples of Africa, a snake which comes to the house is a reincarnated ancestor who inspects his family. He may help or he may punish. Because of similar ideas, some people in Central and Northern Europe fed house snakes as protectors of the welfare of the family. The clash of these ancient concepts and modern ideas is illustrated by a widely known story. A little child used to share his food with a snake that crawled out of the basement of the house. When the parents happened to watch it they thought that the child would be bitten and killed the snake. Within a short period of time the child lost its strength and died.

In West and Central Africa kings lived in a mythical relationship to snakes, mainly pythons. At their residence they had temples in which pythons were kept. These serpents were served by a special priestess who was at the same time the serpents' wife and the king's wife. The peace in the region, the prosperity, the health of cattle, the regularity of seasons and the abundance of game in the country depended upon the pythons' well-being. After the king's death he was believed to turn into a python. The poisonous cobra at the crown of the kings of Lower Egypt was venerated in prehistoric times as the attribute of the goddess Uto in her temple in the Nile Delta. Later it became the Uraeus snake, a symbol of sovereignty, but originally it was a guard of the king which defended him and destroyed his enemies merely with its poisonous breath. Similarly the Nâga snake king protected Buddha and spread his seven heads over him because in deep meditation he had not noticed the approaching thunderstorm. Generally it was believed that snakes guarded treasures, therefore their representations served to guard vessels and buildings. They possess gold. The snake of the folktales, particularly the snake king, has a golden crown. He may give it as a present to the kind maid, but whoever tries to steal it is vehemently persecuted. This tradition is blended with belief in the snake stone. Frequently the snake stone is thought to be a very precious stone, like a diamond. Typically, the thief is killed by the furious snake, but sometimes he succeeds in escaping; as with the Counts of Lynar in Northern Germany, who explain their heraldic animal by this event. A Nigerian story tells how the shining stone of the snake became the moon.

Snakes are closely related to water, for they can live in water as well as on the ground, and creeks and rivers resemble their shape. Snakes found in water are regarded as its personification, and even little ones are frequently not killed, in case the water should disappear. Water also should not be polluted or the snake will leave and the fountain dry up. In the urban cemented water basins in Nepal symbolical snakes of stone take their place. On the other hand, the snake of the river or pond might cause floods. People who drown are said to be pulled into the water by the snake. It either punishes their wrongdoings and breaking of taboos, or it catches them by trickery. First of all, women have to be careful when approaching water. The snake of the river is in close connection to rain and rain-clouds. It might go up to the sky or come down with heavy rains. In various parts of the world, especially Australia and Africa, the rainbow was regarded as its representation and thunder and storm were said to be caused by the snake. As the water supply depended on the goodwill of the serpent, drought-stricken countries made sacrifices; in extreme droughts they sacrificed young girls who were driven into the water until they either drowned or were killed by crocodiles. This was euphemistically called their "marriage" to the snake.

The memory of such sacrifices lived on in Southeast Africa until the twentieth century in reports of girls' initiation ceremonies as well as in Mexican legends about the wells of Chichén Itza being hardened by the skeletons of youths found in the big cenote.

The legend of St. George is a Western example of the concept. St. George fought against a dragon and saved a princess who had been delivered to it so that the country might get water.

Snakes were representations of venom, treachery and evil, but also of eternity and rejuvenation, of healing and wisdom, of ancestors and the underworld, of riches and royalty, of protection and, according to their phallic shape and their connection to water, of fertility of individuals and of countries. In most cases they combined several aspects. Therefore it is difficult for present generations to comprehend the full meaning of ancient snake cults. In addition, we have to take into consideration a continuous development over the millennia.

Snake cults flourished among American Indians, Northern Africa and Southern Asia. They were connected with living snakes like those of the Hopi pueblos. Poisonous snakes are used in twentieth-century fundamentalist churches of the southern U.S. by "snake handlers" to prove their faith.

The female figures of ancient Crete who hold snakes in their hands (1500 B.C.E.) are generally regarded as snake priestesses or goddesses. In Burmese cults, girls danced with living cobras and "kissed" them at the climax of the rite. West African snake cults were exported to the Americas by slaves and kept on in Vodou traditions. In India, many snake cults are still alive, some turned into tourist attractions: the snake-charmer allegedly lets his snake dance to the tunes of his pipe, though the deaf snake only obeys his movements. Such snake-charmers were already known in biblical times. Psalm 58:4–5 warns that the wicked have venom "like the deaf adder that stops its ear, so that it does not hear the voice of charmers or of the cunning enchanter." Snake-charmers in Europe who freed the country of snakes either turned into the sinister exorcists of legends similar to the Pied Piper of Hamlin or venerated saints of the Roman Catholic church (St. Dominicus at Cocullo, Italy; St. Aper at Krautersgersheim, France).

Next to natural snakes, and often blended in the traditions, are mythical snakes of gigantic size, such as the snake of the river (Loch Ness monster) and the rainbow snake. The most famous American example is the Mexican Quetzalkoatl, the Feathered Snake, which, besides many further aspects, is related to weather and storm. In cosmogonic imagery, a giant snake surrounds the Earth. According to the Eddic tradition of Iceland, Thor will battle this Midgard Serpent at the end of the world. The Indian God Vishnu rested on the Naga ananta snake and while dreaming created the world. Mythical serpents frequently have additional attributes: they may have seven heads or the head of another animal or of a human being. Such mixed beings probably were amalgamations of related concepts; for instance the giant snakes of the Namibian Brandberg paintings with the head of another local rain animal, the giraffe (2000–4000 years old). On the Celtic silver kettle found in Gundestrup, Denmark, the god Cernunnos is represented holding a big snake with a ram-head in his left hand. Closely related to the serpent is the dragon, an intensification of the gloomy aspects of snakes. It combines characteristics of crocodiles and further animals but first of all is imagined as a snake. St. Michael fought against "the great dragon, that ancient serpent" (Rev.

12:9). Viking ships had dragon heads at their bows to scare their enemies; the name of St. Olaf's ship was, however, "urmr lange," "long snake." On the other hand, medieval depictions of the temptation of Eve might show the snake in the shape of a dragon, thereby stressing that it is not a natural snake that is purported but the symbolic associations, the imagery of Satan and evil.

From a contemporary point of view, man should not bruise the heads of all snakes. Some, like the python, are legally protected and the trade with their skin is prohibited.

Sigrid Schmidt

Further Reading
Buchler, Ira R. "The Rainbow Serpent: A Chromatic Piece." *World Anthropology*. The Hague: Mouton, 1978.
Hambly, Wilfrid D. *Serpent Worship in Africa*. Chicago: Field Museum of Natural History Publication 289, Anthropological Series 21/1, 1931.
Leach, Maria, ed. *Funk & Wagnalls Dictionary of Folklore, Mythology and Legend*. 2 vols. New York: Funk & Wagnalls, 1949–1950.
Schmidt, Sigrid. "Mythical Snakes in Namibia." In Andrew Banks, Hans Heese and Chris Loff, eds. *Proceedings of the Khoisan Identities and Cultural Heritage Conference Cape Town 12–16 July 1997*. Cape Town: Info-Source, 1998, 269–80.
Vogel, Jean Philippe. *Indian Serpent-Lore or the Nagas in Hindu Legend and Art*. London: A. Probsthain, 1926.

See also: Cihuacoatl – Aztec Snakewoman; Divine Waters of the Oru-Igbo (Southeastern Nigeria); Hinduism; Rainbow Serpent (North Wellesley Islands, Australia); Sea Goddesses and Female Water Spirits; Snakes and the Luo of Kenya; Water Spirits and Indigenous Ecological Management (South Africa); Weather Snake.

P Sexuality and Ecospirituality

The Earth is not only a living world but a sexual one as well, making love to itself through its diverse constituent parts from the autoerotica of single-cell beings to libertine bonobos to monogamous birds. There is an implied sexuality in the way mountain flowers attract the piercing beaks of hummingbirds, and the opening of hardened rock by probing river waters. It is perhaps this intercoursing that weaves together so-called opposites into a single, contiguous whole: male and female, desert and rain. The cooing of mated rock doves and the cries of a mountain lion in heat, give voice to an imperative that is the very fuel of evolution.

The essential connection between humankind and nature was held to be self-evident, and holy, throughout most of our history and prehistory. It was a bond essential to our survival, and was therefore ritually celebrated, as evidenced from the carving of voluptuous "Venus" figurines by early *Homo sapiens* to the revels of Dionysus' Greece and the phallic maypoles of ancient Britain. The eroticized Diana and Artemis find their counterpart in Pan, the lusting, hoofed god of nature and his American Southwest counterpart Kokopelli, the sexually non-ambiguous "hump-backed flute player" found carved in rocks at ceremonial sites.

As I write this I am part of a society that tends to glamorize and commercialize sex, while different elements simultaneously suppress and pervert it. Contemporary civilized populations, regardless of the country, seem to be increasingly divorced from both the intimacies of nature and their own natural sexuality. Contributing factors may include the ascension of religions unnaturally denouncing sexual desires during the Middle Ages, the demographic shift from agrarian and frontier communities to urban centers that continued accelerating throughout the nineteenth century, and now the trend toward virtual reality (erotic video, internet "fantasy" rooms, etc.).

Some contemporary Pagans, practitioners of Tantra and students of the Goddess movement, believe that sexual ecstasy (from the Greek *ekstasis*: to be taken beyond the narrowly defined self) can lead them beyond the fears and preconceptions of the rational mind, and open them to the experience of the sacred. They see sacred sexuality as a means for healing the rift between humans and nature, between the hungering body and the fearful mind. More obviously, they believe, sexual experiences have the ability to reseat one back in present time, in the immediacy of life and the primacy of the sensual and emotional self. In this way, reclaiming a connection to one's sexual being, and to this sexually enlivened Earth, may be seen as an element of both an environmental mission and spiritual assignment.

During the counterculture movement of the 1960s, sexuality was again celebrated, and at times, reconsecrated, even viewed as a sacrament. This was continued to a degree in the 1980s and 1990s by some adherents of deep ecology and ecospirituality. Like the global alternative movement the Rainbow Tribe, the radical environmental group Earth First! was known for its erotic exchanges, especially during the annual get-together known as the "Round River Rendezvous." In this context sexual sensibility and activity aided the suspension of conventional psychological, moral, and societal restraint, and often served the participants' personal rewilding and sensory immersion in the body-nature.

Reacting to what they see as alienation from the Earth, harmful serial monogamy, prudery and sexual dysfunction, some social and environmental activists are experimenting with new forms of relationship. These include "polyamory," a term coined by Morning Glory Zell in 1992 to describe being consciously, carnally involved with more than one other person at a time. "Polyfidelity" has since been used in print to refer to sexually exclusive groupings of three or more. In the literature on contemporary alternative sexuality, authors including Oberon RavenHeart regularly refer to recreating a more natural, nature-oriented sexual dynamic as part of the process of ecological and interpersonal healing.

A correlation has been repeatedly made between the rape of women or boys and that taking-by-force we call environmental destruction, in texts as diverse as Derrick Jensen's *The Culture of Make Believe* and Susan Griffin's *Woman and Nature*. On the other hand, ecosopher (in other words, ecological philosopher) David Abram has written that a new environmental ethic will result from "a rejuvenation of our carnal, sensorial empathy with the living land that sustains us," and that it is only through "our direct, sensory interactions with the land around us that we can appropriately notice and respond to the immediate needs of the living world." Author Terry Tempest Williams has called for an "erotics of place," a purposeful interpenetration of the sensate landscape, as have I. In our own ways we have asserted that a deep sensual and spiritual intimacy with a specific area of land is the cure for both psychological estrangement and the desecration of the natural world.

Jesse Wolf Hardin

Further Reading

Abram, David. *The Spell of the Sensuous*. New York: Pantheon Books, 1996.

Griffin, Susan. *Woman and Nature: The Roaring Inside Her*. New York: Harper & Row, 1978

Jensen, Derrick. *The Culture of Make Believe*. New York: Context Books, 2002.

LaChapelle, Dolores. *Sacred Land, Sacred Sex*. Silverton, Colorado: Finn Hill Arts, 1988.

Williams, Terry Tempest. *An Unspoken Hunger*. New York: Vintage, 1994.

See also: Deep Ecology; Dirt; Earth First! and the Earth Liberation Front; Sexuality and Green Consciousness; Tantra; Tantrism in the West; Wicca.

[SP] Sexuality and Green Consciousness

The confluence of religion, sexuality, and nature is virtually universal though diverse. Ecofeminist theory contends that the shape this confluence assumes under the dominant patriarchal and monotheistic mode is at the heart of the environmental crisis. Here I will explore this argument and outline an alternative "Green consciousness," spirituality and cosmology – in the sense of the 'green' put forth by the twelfth-century revolutionary mystic Hildegard of Bingen – the elemental, implicitly sexual, and divine source energy of life, causing action, fructification, flowering, growth, creativity, healing, and moistness. Green consciousness resists the linked degradations of sex, women, racialized and/or sexualized others, animals, and elemental nature and puts forth an *earthy*, that is, an explicitly sexual, deliberately dirty and immodest spirituality.

Environmental perspectives have emerged from all major religions. Yet, arguably, their hegemonic beliefs support environmental abuse, beginning with the notion of the all-powerful, immutable, human-identified and celibate male god, "The Omnipotent" in Roman Catholic terminology. This notion not only legitimates the dominion of those who claim to be his representatives, but fragments underlying unities. In the social version of this theology, an omnipotent "master" is placed on top, with degraded "others" defined by their supposedly negative qualities, forming a succession of oppositional and hierarchical dualisms including: male/female, culture/nature, light/dark, rationality/desire, civilization/savagery, high/low, spirituality/sexuality, thought/feelings, work/sensuality, immutability/change.

The "master" denies and represses the second part of the dualism, projecting these attributes onto "others" – the wild, animals, tribal peoples, women, lesbians and gays, a working class, a racialized people, and denies his dependency on those he strives to subordinate (e.g., wives, slaves, nature) (Plumwood 1993: 41–8). "He" (this is a masculine subjectivity but the role can be played by women) demonizes and even seeks to destroy those "others" who evoke in him simultaneous feelings of recognition and alienation, desire and fear, worship and hatred. This pattern underlies racial and sexual slaveries, heterosexual normativity, imperialism, and environmental devastation.

Fear – of "nature" and its inherent commonality, diversity, and flux, experienced externally but also internally in the body, particularly through experiences of sex and death – is one cause of this projection. A master consciousness only feels comfortable in monocultures (sexual, religious, ethnic, biological). The ideal human environment becomes a sterile one, dominated by plastic, concrete, steel. The ideal human becomes one made in the image of the artifact or machine.

Though Old Testament-based religions (Christianity, Judaism, and Islam) sometimes celebrate nature as reflecting the divinity of God, nature is not generally understood as itself divine, or even intelligent and active. In Genesis, humanity is granted dominion over nature, man is granted dominion over women and animals. God is transcendent over, not immanent in the world. As nature is degraded, reason must rule over desire, and those aspects of human beings that seem the most natural, our sexual organs, become a locus of shame, seen as "dirty" (like the Earth), hairy, smelly, instinctual (like animals) and wild, not susceptible to will and reason (something that particularly riled St. Augustine). Characteristically, the elite stigmatize the oppressed as more sexual and animalistic than they. Womankind is viewed as the incarnation of sexual desire and disorder and in need of subordination. For much science and many religions, animals are no longer magical, numinous and divine, but soulless and inferior. Of course, in Hinduism as well as many indigenous religions human beings have no special authority over creatures, but, rather, ethical obligations to them.

Writing from a Native American and gynocentric perspective, essayist, poet and novelist Paula Gunn Allen cautions: "A society based on body hate destroys itself and causes harm to all of Grandmother's grandchildren" (1990: 53). Loathing of the body and attendant sex-negativity also cuts us off from knowledges and revelations otherwise inaccessible. Mircea Eliade understands that sexuality's "primary and perhaps supreme valency is the cosmological function ... [E]xcept in the modern world, sexuality has everywhere and always been a hierophany, and the sexual act an integral action (therefore also a means of knowledge)" (1969: 14). For example, in the Tantric tradition bodily desire, pleasure, and sexuality lead to enlightenment.

One of the knowledges that sexuality can bring is a loss of ego and a sense of communion. In many religious traditions, nature – the vast forces and beings not made by humans and outside of our control – is the divine transforming other with whom we connect, paradigmatically sexually. The *hieros gamos*, Greek for "sacred marriage" or "sacred sexual intercourse," refers to a ritual sexual union between deities, an interchange with parallels in such cosmic meetings as sky and Earth, north and south. The *hieros gamos* also can happen between a divinity and a human. In Sovereignty Goddess stories from pre-Christian Ireland, an ugly hag guarding a well requests sexual intercourse from a group of brothers. Only one accepts her invitation. As they copulate, she transforms into a fertile beauty and bestows upon him blessings and the right to rule. In the sacred stories of Southwestern American Indians, wilderness is associated with sexuality and embodied in a spirit being (female or male) who seduces a human into sexual interaction. This intercourse is understood as directing

> the awesome power and energy of our human sexuality – the preserve of wilderness in human beings – into socially useful channels. The coming together of person and spirit may lead to the birth of magical children, the discovery of rich sources of food or water, or the gift of a specific ceremony (Smith 1987: 178).

Such stories recall the Garden of Eden tale and suggest the need for a positive reevaluation of Eve's interchange with the Old Serpent.

Contemporary feminist thinkers reclaim orgasm as a conduit to knowledge of the sacred. Mary Pellauer writes that orgasm allows her to

> melt into existence [as] it melts into me. I am most fully embodied in this explosion of nerves and also broken open into the cosmos. I am rent open; I am cleaved/joined not only to my partner, but to everything, everything-as-my-beloved (or vice versa), who has also become me (1994: 156).

Beverly Clack sensibly realizes that this account is of "particular importance to a world facing an ecological disaster which has arisen precisely through human unwillingness to be identified with the natural world" (2000: 129).

Mary Daly's "elemental philosophy" is based in an identification with the natural world and elemental spirits. In her view, a continuing patriarchal warfare against elemental spirits takes modern forms in technological depredations (e.g., nuclear weapons threaten the final burning of the Earth anticipated in the gospel of Peter). Daly recognizes elementals as "spirits, angels, and demons ... manifesting the essential unity and intelligence of spirit/matter" (1984: 11).

Pagans and or/tribal people generally respect non-human "persons" (including animals, plants, waters, the sun, moon and stars and even objects) as well as *daemons* (energies animating elemental phenomena). These beings – commonly known as gnomes, fairies, trolls, nymphs, and so on – are neither phantasmal nor "supernatural" but an intrinsic part of nature who interrelate with and influence human life (sometimes for good, sometimes for bad) and to whom humans have obligations. In patriarchal religious traditions, daemons are seen as invariably wicked. In 1967 Lynn White called attention to the ecological benefit of animist systems: "By destroying pagan animism, Christianity made it possible to exploit nature in a mood of indifference to the feelings of natural objects" (1996: 189). However apt the criticism, White misses the intersection of sexuality into this meeting of religion and nature, for nature *daemons* along with sex/fecundity goddesses were associated particularly with the sin of lust. Worship of "filthy" *daemons* and "immodest" goddesses was deplored (as in Augustine) and "the celebration of fertility as a dimension of the sacred was identified in the Christian mind with obscenity and evil" (Power 1996: 53). Islam similarly linked goddesses of desire, fecundity, generation, and sexual reproduction with wicked demons. When Mohammed received a revelation naming three local goddesses as intercessors for humans with Allah, he soon attributed this revelation to Satan.

The pagan nature god with his horns, green and sometimes even grassy flesh, protruding tongue (as if in the midst of orgasm), and serpentine and goaty nature is recast as Satan. Misogyny, sex-loathing, demonization of the *daemons*, and nature-hating converged in the fifteenth-century religious/pornographic imagination of female witchcraft based in an insatiable "carnal lust" which led them to sexual trysts with Satan. Contemporary Wiccans affirm green values and celebrate sexuality as participation in the life-giving force of the goddess.

An early banner of the environmental movement is a photograph of the Earth as seen from space. "Love Your Mother" is the accompanying text. Historically, the image of the Earth as a nurturing mother has worked to forestall abuse of the Earth (Merchant 1980). The word "nature" is from the Latin word *nasci*, to be born. The soil of the Earth is understood as the goddess's flesh; its depths or "bowels" her vulva/womb. Female deities represent the Earth and the teeming life of nature. *Yoni* symbols (shells, fruits, caves), the Milky Way, mountains, ocean, and fruit-bearing trees also are seen as re-presenting the body of goddess. This divinity is understood sometimes as a mother but more frequently as a lover.

Masculine sacrality is understood through symbols of a fertilizing sky god, through fire and digging sticks, and through natural symbols (*lingam*), recalling the penis as generative. The basic processes of fructification in nature are understood as akin to human coitus, as the meeting of female soil with masculine heavens or the inverse (the Egyptian sky-goddess Nut and the male Earth Geb). Of course, a green sexual cosmology does not incorporate solely heterosexual and procreative meanings but recognizes homosexuality and gender diversity as utterly natural and necessary to cosmic processes. The biologist Bruce Bagemihl (1999) documents animal homosexuality and explores the ways that non-heterosexual and non-procreative human and animal sexualities have been respected by many indigenous peoples for embodying exuberance, essential to forces of fertility. Sacred homosexual meetings also can be found in nature: In ancient Babylon the most powerful water for purification purposes was found where the mouths of the Tigris and Euphrates met (Johns 1926: 467). In Babylonian, Eliade tells us, the same word means both "source of a river" and "vagina" (1969: 41); the potent meeting of these sacred rivers at their source can be understood as a veritable Lesbian *hieros gamos*.

Currently, the greediest and ontologically neediest societies demand ever-greater infusions of oil, coal, nuclear power and resources from the rest of the world. Monica Sjöö and Barbara Mor find religious significance in the energy crisis: "The patriarchal West cannot solve its energy problems because our minds and spirits were long ago cut off from the real source of energy, or creative power ... the sexual-spiritual source of cosmic ecstasy" (1991: 412). Desire is the force that is most akin to divine powers. In Sumerian myth, the "sex goddess" Inanna gives forth the "desire that generates the energy of the Universe." This energy is known in Hindu cosmology as *Shakti*, the feminine primordial energy, which is the substance of everything, pervading everything, vivifying everything. The manifestation of this power, this energy, is called nature (*Prakriti*). Humans participate in erotic energy through sexual desire as well as creativity, prophecy, intellection, political activism, growth, love, and transformation.

Religious traditions more ancient than the patriarchal often do not hold to a duality between man and woman or between person and nature. They often recognize a primal feminine principle, the inexhaustible source of fruitfulness or greenness, the cosmic matrix from which all are born and to which all return at death. This principle – that of activity, diversity, and creativity exists "in nature and women, as well as men" (Shiva 1988: 48). Patriarchal cultures still recognize this feminine principle (e.g., as Mother Nature or Mother Earth), but degrade it. Ecofeminism finds important parallels between the conceptualizations and treatments of women, racialized groups, and the underclass and conceptualizations and treatments of the non-human world. "Mother Nature," for example, is cast as the all-forgiving dark mother or "mammy," perpetually willing to provide unpaid service and clean-up after oppressive children; the sexual slave, forced and reproducing against her will; a nagging and even mad mother whose warnings and rages can be ignored. The Sovereignty/Earth Goddess becomes the pornographic object to be spread, surveyed, mapped and even snuffed. The Sex/Love Goddess becomes the whore to be had, the spicy/dark other to be eaten (Hooks 1992); the virgin to be raped, the slut to be used; the witch or *femme fatale* to be chastened; the exotic primitive to function as "unnamed presence of difference, body which awakens within a space of exotic fauna and flora," upon whose flesh "the conqueror will write the body of the other and trace his own history" (deCertau 1988: xxv).

Along with imperial conquest, scientific knowledge gravitates toward the language of sexual violation. Merchant traces the characteristic metaphors of the scientific revolution: mastering, interrogating, disrobing, and penetrating nature as a female form. The twentieth-century language of nuclear physicists similarly relied upon rapist images, seeing themselves as investigating the "most intimate properties of matter," tearing away "the veils," and so on. As that technology reached apocalyptic capacities, popular nuclear metaphors emerged centering on father–daughter incest and serial sex murder (Caputi 1993: 117–40).

Arguably, the colonization and exploitation of natural resources begins with the enslavement and exploitation of the erotic force. As H.A. Williams understands it, this mind/body split and subsequent enslavement of the genitals is at the root of environmental disaster:

> Being in hell, the place of undead, they are always somehow planning and threatening their revenge,

they may in the end catapult us into nuclear catastrophe ... The body deprived of Eros inevitably becomes the champion of thanatos (1972: 33).

Williams, however astute, does not take into account the ways that patriarchal cultures construct men as violence objects, and women and those identified as feminine (including some men) as targets for that apocalyptic sexuality. Mary Daly describes this sexuality as "phallic lust," the

> deadly dis-passion that prevails in patriarchy – the life-hating lechery that rapes and kills the objects of its obsession/aggression ... dismembering spirit/matter, attempting annihilation ... Its goal is the obliteration of natural knowing and willing, of the deep purposefulness which philosophers have called final causality (1984: 2).

Its undoing can be found in the release of "Pure Lust," the force of vigor and fertility in nature, the Green source of natural knowing: "pure Passion: unadulterated, absolute, simple sheer striving for abundance of be-ing. It is unlimited, unlimiting desire/fire ... intense longing/craving for the cosmic concrescence that is creation" (Daly 1984: 3).

Many thinkers call for a renewal of an Earth-based religion. Roger Gottlieb outlines a spirituality based in deep ecology that emerges in resistance to environmental destruction, one that is both passionate and spiritually orientated, one that seeks mystical communion with the Earth and its many beings, and recognizes not dominion over but kinship with those beings. Of course, once we recognize environmental devastation as a form of sexualized violence, we must add to this project by calling for an explicitly sexual/animalistic/and elemental cosmology; in short, one that gets down, one that is *earthy*.

Green consciousness/cosmology celebrates erotic expressions based in sexual sovereignty (consensual and non-exploitative, based in the equality of lovers and a context of social justice), revels in our animal souls and our sexual flesh, both female and male. Carol Christ (1997: 91) has claimed that "In the language of the Goddess, the female body is an important metaphor for the creative powers of the earth body." But what of the male body?

Currently, a distorted and objectified notion of the male body is the hidden metaphor for God ("The Omnipotent"). Peeking beneath the robes of the familiar fatherly and most high god (that is, the most removed from the Earth), we find him to be modeled upon a fragmented and fantastical organ – the phallus (a permanently erect/potent penis) – to signify supreme dominance. Of course, the phallus is not a true reflection of the male body. The real, fleshy penis is sometimes hard but more often soft. When the fantastical phallus becomes the metaphor for divine power, power becomes synonymous with weapon-like power over, separation and not connection. But when the actual penis, with capacities for both hardness and softness and its knowledge of and respect for receptivity, darkness, and quiescence, becomes a metaphor for sacred power, James Nelson argues, we arrive at a model of relational power, a "generative power the power of an open energy system" (1994: 206).

In Lacanian psychoanalytic theory, the phallus represents power, authority, the ability to hold rational sway over desire, to control. It ordains individuation and separation from the mother, which we can understand not only as the actual mother, but also as the matrix, the source, the cosmic yoni, the mother/nature. Human separation from the matrix has produced some technological marvels and consumer goods, but also is responsible for ontological loneliness, alienation, an obsessive orientation toward sex, fear of death, and an appetite for destruction.

Rather than the phallic imaginary of omnipotence, green consciousness proposes *cunctipotence*. Cunctipotence is an archaic English word that means "all-powerful" (*Oxford English Dictionary*) and one that some linguists etymologically link to the ancient, but now "obscene" word *cunt*. The "cunt" is obscene to patriarchal religion most particularly because it recalls the outlawed feminine principle, the matrix and source of all life. The Sanskrit word for cunt is *yoni*, with various related meanings, including "vagina, uterus, source, origin, spring, home." *Yoni* is derived from *yu* (join, unite); *yoni* is "what joins or unites." A cunctipotent imaginary connects; it reattaches the disembodied phallus to the biological body, where it becomes the fulsome, relational penis. It recognizes the kinship, not the opposition, of the cunt and penis. Cunctipotence connects the genitals to the mind, the body to the land, and human to nonhuman being. The "*all-powerful*" defining cunctipotence bespeaks not "power over," but participation in the interconnecting power of the all, the commonplace, the whole.

The Yoruban concept of *Aché* refers to "the power to make things happen, the breath that bestows life" (Monroe 1993: 127). *Aché* is power that "passes through us, is used by us, and must be replenished by ritualistic means" (Teish 1985: 63). Green consciousness recognizes that we must nurture the Earth, feed the green as it feeds us. We do this through prayer, creativity, exuberance, and desire, and through respecting the sacredness of our bodily processes including orgasm, eating, excretion, respiration and finally death. The patriarchal Christian tradition, spearheaded by Augustine, deems both sexual desire and death to be essentially "unnatural," the consequences of original sin. Yet, life and death are "twin beings, gifts of our mother" (Allen 1990: 52). Through death we return to the matrix and become once again dirt/earth, a fate or purpose that green consciousness embraces.

The teleology of the religious condemnation of fertility/

desire/lust is a sterile world, marked by pornographic objectification, sensory deprivation, contamination, and extinction. Hildegard of Bingen knew that the "fertile Earth is symbolized by the sex organs, which display the power of generation as well as an indecent boldness" (Bingen 1987: 114). Green consciousness reclaims what patriarchal morality has branded as indecent and boldly affirms the sacredness of lustful, safe, just, and sovereign eroticism, humanity's kinship with the elemental world, and the divinity of nature.

Jane Caputi

Further Reading

Allen, Paula Gunn. "The Woman I Love Is a Planet, The Planet I Love Is a Tree." I. Diamond and G.F. Orenstein, eds. *Reweaving the World: The Emergence of Ecofeminism.* San Francisco: Sierra Club Books, 1990, 52–7.

Bagemihl, Bruce. *Biological Exuberance: Animal Homosexuality and Natural Diversity.* New York: St. Martin's Press, 1999.

Bingen, Hildegaard. *Book of Divine Works with Letters and Song.* Ed. Matthew Fox. Santa Fe, NM: Bear & Company, 1987.

Caputi, Jane. *Gossips, Gorgons, and Crones: The Fates of the Earth.* Santa Fe: Bear and Company, 1993.

Christ, Carol. *Rebirth of the Goddess: Finding Meaning in Feminist Spirituality.* New York: Routledge, 1997.

Clack, Beverly. "Human Sexuality and the Concept of the God/ess." Lisa Isherwood, ed. *The Good News of the Body: Sexual Theology and Feminism.* New York: New York University Press, 2000, 115–35.

Daly, Mary. *Pure Lust: Elemental Feminist Philosophy.* Boston: Beacon Press, 1984.

deCertau, Michel. *The Writing of History.* T. Conley, tr. New York: Columbia University Press, 1988.

Eliade, Mircea. *Images and Symbols: Studies in Religious Symbolism.* P. Mairet, tr. New York: Sheed and Ward, 1969.

Gottlieb, Roger. S. "The Transcendence of Justice and the Justice of Transcendence: Mysticism, Deep Ecology, and Political Life." *Journal of the American Academy of Religion* 67:1 (1999), 149–66.

Hildegard of Bingen. *Book of Divine Works with Letters and Songs.* Matthew Fox, ed. Santa Fe, NM: Bear & Co., 1986.

Hooks, Bell. *Black Looks: Race and Representation.* Boston: South End Press, 1992.

Johns, C.H.W. "Purification (Babylonian)." In James Hastings, ed. *Encyclopedia of Religion and Ethics.* New York: Scribner's, 1926, 10:466–8.

Merchant, Carolyn. *The Death of Nature: Women, Ecology and the Scientific Revolution.* San Francisco: Harper & Row, 1980.

Monroe, Irene. "The Aché Sisters: Discovering the Power of the Erotic in Ritual." In Marjorie Procter-Smith and Janet R. Walton, eds. *Women at Worship.* Louisville, KT: Westminster John Knox Press, 1993, 127–36.

Nelson, James B. "Embracing Masculinity." In James B. Nelson and Sandra P. Longfellow, eds. *Sexuality and the Sacred.* Louisville: Westminster/John Knox Press, 1994, 195–215.

Pellauer, Mary. "The Moral Significance of Female Orgasm." In James B. Nelson and Sandra P. Longfellow, eds. *Sexuality and the Sacred.* Louisville: Westminster/John Knox Press, 1994, 149–68.

Plumwood, Val. *Feminism and the Mastery of Nature.* New York: Routledge, 1993.

Power, Kim. *Veiled Desire: Augustine on Women.* New York: Continuum, 1996.

Shiva, Vandana. *Staying Alive: Women, Ecology and Survival in India.* London: Zed Books, 1988.

Smith, Patricia C. and Paula Gunn Allen. "Earthy Relations, Carnal Knowledge: Southwestern American Indian Women Writers and Landscape." In Vera Norwood and Janice Monk, eds. *The Desert Is No Lady: Southwestern Landscapes in Women's Writing and Art.* New Haven: Yale University Press, 1987, 174–96.

Sjöö, Monica and Barbara Mor. *The Great Cosmic Mother: Rediscovering the Religion of the Earth.* San Francisco: HarperSanFrancisco, 1991.

Teish, Luisah. *Jambalaya: The Natural Woman's Book.* San Francisco: HarperSanFrancisco, 1985.

White, Lynn. "This Historical Roots of Our Ecological Crisis." In *This Sacred Earth: Religion, Nature, Environment.* Roger S. Gottlieb, ed. New York: Routledge, 1996, 184–93.

Williams, H.A. *True Resurrection.* New York: Hold, Rinehart and Winston, 1972.

See also: Daly, Mary; Dirt; Ecofeminism; Eliade, Mircea; Feminist Spirituality Movement; Hildegard of Bingen; Homosexuality; Pagan Festivals in North America; Pagan Festivals – Contemporary; Paganism – Contemporary; Rewilding; Sexuality and EcoSpirituality; Tantra; Tantrism in the West; Virtues and Ecology in World Religions; Wicca.

Shakti

In the religions of the Indian sub-continent, shakti is a cosmological principle of power, the life-force of the universe, specifically denoting cosmic creation and divine procreation, and more generally any form of power or energy. The development of this concept is quite complicated, as it is found in a variety of philosophical, grammatical, mythological, and ritual texts beginning with the earliest literature. Shakti develops as the link between a cause and an effect, such as in the order sustained by the fire sacrifice; it is also conceived of as a dynamic force inherent in nature. Shakti comes to be seen as the female force that acts together with the male force to create and sustain the cosmos. Sometimes shakti is associated with the principle of materiality or nature (prakriti) in opposition to the male principle of pure consciousness (purusha). When personified, shakti is always embodied as a goddess: she is the consort of the male god who needs his shakti to act in the world, as in the interdependent pair Shiva–Shakti, wherein Shiva without Shakti is a *shava* or corpse. Shakti is also seen as the independent, supreme divinity, the complete Absolute, the ultimate source as well as the cause of creation, elaborated most explicitly in the literature of certain Hindu and Buddhist Tantric schools.

The highly influential sixth-century Sanskrit text the Devi-Mahatmya is the earliest exposition of the theology of the goddess as the Great Goddess, or Devi. In this text the Goddess, or Shakti, gathers up the powers of all the gods to kill the demons and protect the world. She is portrayed as the eternal, ultimate reality, the power that creates, maintains, and destroys the universe. She is greater than the male gods and beyond all attributes, but she is also embodied as the Goddess who responds to people and events in concrete, specific ways. Shakti is the basic material from which all creation is manifested, and the universe itself; she is also the active force present in all things, including human beings. It is widely held that women, because they are female like the Goddess, contain more shakti than men. Shakti is a power that can be increased, such as through devotion to a chosen deity.

In various versions of a central myth, a grief-stricken Shiva wanders the Earth with the dead body of his beloved wife on his shoulder, until the gods relieve him of his burden by dispersing pieces of the Goddess' body throughout India. In this system of *shakti pithas*, or places of power, certain geographical places enshrine parts of the body of Shakti, especially mountains, caves, rivers, and other bodies of water. People make pilgrimages to these sacred places, which are seen as *tirthas*, or "crossings" between the human and divine realms. In this way local goddess shrines are integrated into the body of the Great Goddess, Shakti, and the Earth, particularly the Indian subcontinent, is unified as a repository of sacred power.

Elaine Craddock

Further Reading

Erndl, Kathleen M. *Victory to the Mother: The Hindu Goddess of Northwest India in Myth, Ritual, and Symbol.* New York: Oxford University Press, 1993.

Narayanan, Vasudha. "Brimming with Bhakti, Embodiments of Shakti: Devotees, Deities, Performers, Reformers and Other Women of Power in the Hindu Tradition." In Arvind Sharma and Katherine K. Young, eds. *Feminism and World Religions*. Albany: State University of New York, 1999, 25–77.

Pintchman, Tracy. *The Rise of the Goddess in the Hindu Tradition.* Albany: State University of New York, 1994.

See also: Goddesses – History of; Hinduism; India.

Shamanism – and Art

Shamanism is a complex construct. It is a religious approach of personal orientation and personal authority, or self-autonomy. In shamanic worldviews, the Earth is a place, a source of power, reality, and supra-reality above and below this ground of being. The Earth is itself sacralized. Shamanism is therefore "Earth-centered." In this context, Earth, nature, and world are often used interchangeably.

Strictly speaking, shamans do not make art. They make the tools of their trade and they record the maps and imagery of their visions in various permanent or impermanent ways. Thus, the shaman makes masks (or directs others in the making of masks), drums and whistles (to obtain and control trance state), and clothing, containers, and other examples of material culture. The objects are all made for non-ordinary reasons and each object is in itself a container of sacred powers. The shaman also inscribes imagery on rocks, on skin, on wood, metals, shells, and other materials in public or hidden places. The imagery and the objects are all documents, maps, and facilitators of non-ordinary realities for the shaman and the shaman's community.

In Australia today, one may find ancient images of *Wandjina*, the ancestral beings, upon rock walls. The images look as fresh as if they were painted only last month, which is quite possible. It is the practice of the Aboriginal peoples of Australia to repaint ceremoniously and correctly the ancient images of their Wandjina. Not only are their Ancestral Beings sacred and powerful, they are actually alive inside the paintings. The paintings are not representations; they are powers transfigured. What are the Wandjina doing inside those paintings? Perhaps, say the people, the Wandjina are resting from their primordial Dreamtime work.

Use of Visual Patterns

No typology yet exists for so-called "shamanic" art, nor is there likely to be one. The use of radiances, skeletal motifs, or polka dots (to indicate gateways) are not sure indicators of shamanic art. They are simply motifs. Symbolic context is required. For example, the motifs found in the art of the Tukano, a people of the Amazon forest, are very like the neurological visual patterns, or phosphenes, they see after the ritual ingestion of a local hallucinogenic substance. The meaning of these motifs, and the meaning of the visions is, however, culturally controlled and specific to the Tukano. The same phosphenes could be "seen" by non-Tukanos ingesting the same drink, but the motifs would be essentially meaningless. Exhaustion, stress, hunger, pain, illness are all well-known mundane sources of intense neurological visual patterns. "Seeing stars" is one thing, and it is another. Neither meaning excludes yet another meaning.

The heart of the shamanic experience is its originality and its personal authority. Its content is culture-bound only in that something is said or done about the experience. In order to understand the shamanic vision, then, one must use the cultural categories at hand. Each image is the mapped solution of a problem, a question asked. For example, the designs used on the *huilpil* – the embroidered blouses of the Mayan women – are owned by the woman who initially dreams the design. Huilpils made by copying the designs of another woman, even to preserve the design against tropic rot, are locally recognized as uninspired, unsuccessful work no matter how finely the garments have been stitched. The dream authenticates the art.

The Romanian historian Mircea Eliade ably described the shaman as a "specialist in the sacred . . . pre-eminently an ecstatic." In a small-scale, traditional society the shaman is dancer, poet, artist, storyteller, healer – psychically and physically – and, perhaps most importantly, mediator. The shaman mediates – between this world and other worlds, between one person and another, between here and now, and then and what will be. The shaman's talents are considerable and the responsibilities heavy.

As a "specialist in the sacred," the shaman's knowledge of sacred realities is not knowledge of a reality *out there*. The shaman's sacred reality is better thought of as a hyper-reality, or a supra-reality, even as a sur-reality. The sacred reality the shaman knows is a reality located in this world. It is an ecstatic experience of place, of nature, of realms of being – of an upper world and lower world. These worlds are always accessible from this world, this plane of reality. In the traditional societies where shamanism is found, afterlife beliefs do not predominate as they do in societies with belief systems emphasizing creator gods and stories of personal salvation.

Cosmological designs and function

The shaman's moral task is one of rebalancing and harmonizing imbalances. To do this, the shaman uses controlled trance states in order to create a unitary way of seeing the world. The shaman knows any part of the world seen clearly, seen clearly enough, reveals the whole. Thus, the drum is often an important tool that the shaman will use to obtain a controlled trance state in order to travel to another hidden reality.

Among the Saami of northern Scandinavia, the shaman's use of a drum to induce a trance state for both himself (or sometimes, among the Saami, *herself*) is well documented. Typically, the drum is painted with a centered sun motif and depicts a tripartite arrangement of the universe. The Saami do not worship the sun. Their cosmological universe is one with three levels. The figures on the shaman's drum are a cognitive map reminding the shaman's ego-soul which way to travel; in addition, the drum is inscribed in such a way that it can be used as a seasonal calendar. Thus, for those observing the shaman's trance state, the drum's imagery interprets the time and place of the vision for the shaman's public.

The Haida nation of the northwestern coast of Canada value "coppers" as cognitive maps of the ego-soul's journeying. The coppers are, indeed, made of copper, can be quite large, are collected, and are publicly displayed as wealth. They appear to be shields of a sort, axially oriented. The coppers are interpreted as forms symbolizing the human being facing the sun, thus, the copper creates an axis joining three levels of the universe.

The hunting masks of the Inuit of the Bering Sea are renowned for their inventive, expressive character. Each one is a form first visualized by the shaman before it is translated into a carved mask under the supervision of the shaman, who also supervises the mask's ritual destruction after it has been danced. The masks are not carved in duplicate. They are, however, stylized according to local understanding. How else could the shaman's unique vision be communicated to the carver and the community? Thus, the use of holes, polka dots, and hoops on the masks is readily understood by members of the community to represent openings. The openings allow the shaman and food to flow between levels of the universe. The shaman has petitions to make to Tungh'ak. The shaman wants to be fed on behalf of the community. Tungh'ak must release the seafood through an opening.

The visionary experience of the shaman *always* includes the place upon which the shaman stands, the Earth. Often the sun's position matters, too. The Navaho world, for example, is bounded by four sacred mountains. In the sacred geography of the Navaho, the names of the mountains are known; it is not known which geological chunks of terrain carry the sacred names. It does not matter, either, because the world itself *is* known, and the world is home to the Navaho whose nation today is found in the American southwest.

Similarly, among the Saulteaux of north-central Saskatchewan, Canada, there was once a custom of erecting small wooden figures, called *Manitokanac*, on the prairie landscape. Not much is known about them, but it is obvious each of the particular placements serves to orient and center the otherwise endlessly flat landscape. One famous Saulteaux shaman explained, "they can make a home out of the world. This is their power."

On the whole there is little literature on the material culture of shamanism and less on the shaman as artist. The sad state of scholarship in this area is perhaps explicable only if we realize that few anthropologists have been trained in the analysis of material culture as visual documents and few art historians have been trained in cultural anthropology. The objects on display in museum exhibition cases are silent. The stories they once told to the shamans who fashioned them are unknown.

Maureen Korp

Further Reading

Abbot, Donald N., ed. *The World is as Sharp as a Knife: An Anthology in Honour of Wilson Duff*. Victoria: British Columbia Museum, 1981.

Ahlback, Tore, ed. *Saami Religion*. Uppsala: Doner Institute for Research in Religions and Cultural History, 1987.

Barry, P.S. *Mystical Themes in Milk River Rock Art*. Edmonton, Alberta: University of Alberta Press, 1991.

Elkin, A.P. *Aboriginal Men of High Degree*. New York: St. Martin's Press, 1978.

Furst, Peter T. "The Roots and Continuities of Shamanism." *Artscanada* 184–7 (December 1973/January 1974).

Grim, John A. *Patterns of Siberian and Ojibway Healing*. Norman: University of Oklahoma Press, 1983.

Johnson, Ronald. *The Art of the Shaman*. Iowa City, IA: Iowa University Museum of Art Publications, 1973.

Reichel-Dolmatoff, G. *Shamanism and Art of the Eastern Tukanoan Indians*. Leiden: E.J. Brill, 1987.

Seguin, Margaret, ed. *Tshimshian Images of the Past, Views of the Present*. Vancouver: University of British Columbia Press, 1984.

Siikala, Anna-Leena. *The Rite Technique of the Siberian Shaman*. Helsinki: Academia Scientarium Fennica, 1978.

See also: Art; Eliade, Mircea; Inuit; Maya Religion (Central America); Maya Spirituality (Guatemala Highlands); Rock Art (various); Saami Culture; Shamanism – Traditional.

Shamanism – Ecuador

In Ecuador, the most common terms that people use to refer to local shamans are the Spanish words, *curandero*, meaning healer, or *brujo*, meaning witch. However, there are many other words, which vary according to ethnic group and language, which can also be used to describe traditional religious practitioners. A significant number of native Ecuadorians in the Amazon and Andes speak some dialect of Quichua and, accordingly, use the Quichua word, *yachaj*, for medicine person or religious specialist meaning "he who knows" derived from *yachana* "to know or learn." Since Quichua has historically functioned as the primary indigenous trade language throughout highland and lowland Ecuador, we will employ *yachaj*, rather than "shaman," as the general term to refer to native tradition's specialists. Throughout Ecuador it is the *yachaj's* responsibility to forge a network of alliances with the souls of the ancestors and the living forces of nature of the Sierra, Costa and Oriente regions on behalf of his or her home community.

Ecuador is a country characterized by extremes. Approximately the size of the state of Colorado, Ecuador is located on the western-most bulge of the South American continent and is divided into three distinct climactic regions – Costa, Sierra, and Oriente – by the Western and Eastern Andean Cordilleras. The tropical effects of the Equatorial belt, combined with extremes in altitude from sea level to the frozen peaks of the active volcanoes (which rise to 20,700 feet on Mt. Chimborazo) and radical variations in rainfall, result in an extraordinary multiplicity of plant and animal life. Across this rugged and varied country, highland and lowland indigenous ethnic groups have created overlapping religious responses to the diverse geographic realities that confront them. In each community it is the *yachaj's* role to form crosscultural and cross-creatural alliances in order to attract or repel energies that support or impede the circulatory flow of natural resources in and out of their home place.

In the Sierra, *yachajs* may form primary alliances with the spirits of the living mountains known as *cerros* or *urcus*, living and dead *yachajs* throughout the country, and Catholic saints. The mountain usually courts the potential *yachaj*, drawing the person to bathe in springs, which act as eyes, mouths, or doors to the inner mountain world. Once inside the *cerro*, the *yachaj* encounters parallel cities filled with Andean plants, animals, and minerals along with the human dead and the unborn. His role as *yachaj* works to bridge his community on the outside with this world inside the mountain. All creatures are born out of the mountain and return to the mountain upon death. The *yachaj* draws on his alliance to the *cerro* in order to direct the flow of life-giving and life-taking energies. The *yachaj* persuades the mountain to feed and care for its people properly by singing to it and feeding the mountain offerings of *chichi* (beer made from maize or manioc), cigarettes, rum, flowers, guinea pigs (*cuy*), and sometimes, llamas or sheep. If this relationship of exchange falls out of balance, the mountain may grow hungry, jealous or angry and may "eat" the people in landslides, earthquakes, or floods, through drowning or falling accidents, or may erode their energies through illness.

In order to draw the mountain energy toward his own community, the *yachaj* must secure the *cerro's* attention away from rival *yachajs* and neighboring communities. Within this closed circulatory system of limited resources, *envidia*, or envy, becomes the primary cause of illness and misfortune as *yachajs* effectively attempt to wrest *suerte*, luck or energy, from one powerful person or place in order to redistribute it to another. The way that the *yachaj* accesses and then distributes these mountain energies determines whether he becomes known as a healing or killing *yachaj*: a *curandero* or a *brujo*.

The competitive relationship between *yachajs* can become deadly. Because of this, in the Oriente, *yachajs* must learn how to fend off spiritual darts – known to the Quichua as *biruti* and to the Shuara as *tsentsak* – which are sent by rival *yachajs*. He must know how to guide counterattacks and remove *biruti* or *tsentsak* from the bodies of his clients. In order to specialize in spiritual weaponry, *yachajs* from the Napo Runa in northeastern Ecuador go to "school" inside the Colaurcu hills, which they say are made up of many rooms. Inside the hills the *yachaj* chooses his *biruti*, his own personalized spiritual weapon that might be a *chonta* dart, razors, needles or syringes.

For the Napo Runa and the Canelos Quichua, a *yachaj's* training also includes fasting, sexual abstinence and drinking *ayahuasca*, a bitter drink prepared from a hallucinogenic vine of the *banisteriopsis* genus. The ayahuasca enables the *yachaj* to journey into the spirit world where he engages the powerful *supai* or spirits of the mountain, rivers and forest. These may include *Amasanga*, the spirit master of all souls who appears as a black jaguar or *Sungui huarmi* (also known as *Yacu mama*), and water spirit woman who guides the *yachaj* through her fish-, dolphin- and anaconda-filled world. Ranked according to the length of their training and the proven strength of their power, the *sinchi yachaj* works with many spirits and has the power to draw on their help at crucial moments. The most powerful *yachaj*, a *bancu*, literally the seat of spirits, has trained since childhood and has formed extensive alliances with mountain and river *supai* and with living and dead *yachajs* throughout the region.

Once a *yachaj* has established strong alliances with the spirits of his home place he may periodically leave home to fortify his power by training with neighboring *yachajs*. Alternately, he may travel to regional healing centers that emerge from clusters of renowned *yachajs* working in tandem with powerful natural sites. In the Sierra the most famous healing centers in the north include the Otavalo Runa near Imbabura Mountain and the Quito Runa near Carapungo on the outskirts of Quito; in the west, the Tsachila on the coastal Andean slopes near the city of Sto. Domingo de los Colorados; in the east, the Salasacas near the Volcano Tunghurahua, and in the far south, the Cañaris near the city of Cuenca. In the Oriente powerful healers abound in the Native Amazonian communities of the Napo Runa, the Canelos Quichua, the Achuar, Shuar, Cofán, and Siona-Secoya, among others.

Yachajs who want to extend their power to others can exchange stones as a sign of their mutual alliance. Throughout Ecuador the *yachaj's herramientas*, or curing tools, include shaped stones, such as pre-Colombian axheads, or unusually formed stones or crystals that hold spiritual power. In the Sierra the stones form direct, metonymic links to specific mountains and, like a wedding ring, serve as iconic proof of the marriage between *yachaj* and mountain. As the basis of the *yachaj's mesa*, the stones serve as homing devices for the spirits traveling to assist the *yachaj* in curing sessions. In the wet decaying jungle of the Oriente, stones represent permanence and function as attractive homes for spirits and ancient souls. The Napo Runa refer to these stones as *rumi* that may project light or contain suggestive figures of horses or saints. The Canelos Quichua say that these stones are like living soldiers and that the *yachaj* "with his phalanx of animated shaman's class stones is like the center of a military formation."

An experienced *yachaj* possesses an extensive collection of these stones acquired in the course of his travels as gifts from other *yachajs*, the *cerros*, and various spirits (including Catholic saints). The initial acquisition of a stone can serve as a calling to the vocation. The number of stones in a *yachaj's* bundle offers concrete proof of the network of connections at his or her disposal. So too, the sudden loss of a stone signals the loss of the alliance that the stone represents and a drastic diminishing of the *yachaj's* power.

Lisa Maria Madera

Further Reading

Descola, Philippe. *In the Society of Nature: A Native Ecology in Amazonia*. N. Scott, tr. Cambridge: Cambridge University Press, 1994.

Muratorio, Blanca. *The Life and Times of Grandfather Alonso*. New Jersey: Rutgers University Press, 1991.

Robinson, Scott S. *Toward an Understanding of Kofan Shamanism*. Ph.D. dissertation, Cornell University. Ithaca, New York. Ann Arbor, MI: University Microfilms, 1979.

Rubenstein, Steven. *Alejandro Tsakimp: A Shuar Healer in the Margins of History (Fourth World Rising)*. Lincoln: University of Nebraska Press, 2002.

Salomon, Frank. "Killing the Yumbo: A Ritual Drama of Northern Quito." In Norman E. Whitten, Jr., ed. *Cultural Transformations and Ethnicity in Modern Ecuador*. Urbana: University of Illinois Press, 1981, 162–208.

Whitten, Norman E. *Sicuanga Runa: The Other Side of Development in Amazonian Ecuador*. Chicago: University of Illinois Press, 1985.

Whitten, Norman E. *Sacha Runa: Ethnicity and Adaptation of Ecuadorian Quichua*. Chicago: University of Illinois Press, 1976.

See also: Amazonia; Ayahuasca; Ethnobotany; Ethnoecology; Shamanism – Traditional.

Shamanism – Neo

"Shamanic discourse" in North America made a decisive new step in the 1960s. Within the context of the so-called "New Age" movement, the figure of the shaman as a religious specialist became an indication of a new understanding in humanity's relation to nature and the ability to access spiritual levels of reality. Shamanism was no longer regarded as a spiritual path limited only to "classical shamanic cultures." Instead, the Western rationalistic and mechanistic attitude toward reality and nature was increasingly replaced by a holistic and animated one. This led to a "sacramental view of reality" in which shamanism, like Buddhism, became something considered available to everyone – even to those in urban contexts in which people are largely estranged from nature.

Both practitioners and scholars alike refer to this emergent phenomenon as "neo-shamanism," to be differentiated from the revitalization of traditional shamanism that has taken place in countries like Mongolia, Tuva, or Korea. Despite its complexity, several characteristics are discernible:

1) With the seminal work of Carlos Castaneda, the popularization of academic knowledge became an important feature of neo-shamanism. Most major shamanic protagonists hold a degree in anthropology, which they try to combine with their spiritual practice outside academia (e.g., Michael Harner, Joan Halifax, Nevill Drury, Steven Foster, Jonathan Horwitz, Felicitas Goodman, Gala Naumova). Furthermore, this interaction between academic research and religious practice began to affect "classical, indigenous shamanism" inasmuch as native people could read ethnographic accounts and react to anthropological systematization.

2) Neo-shamanism is closely related to Western concepts of nature and religion. Although Euro-American conceptualizations of what we now call "shamanism" are indebted to Western discourses from the seventeenth century, new developments allowed for a new description of shamanism. Among these are the Deep Ecology movement, transpersonal psychology and so-called "New Age science." While neo-shamans tend to refer to deep ecology as "spiritual ecology," transpersonal psychology places emphasis on the "higher self" and altered states of consciousness. "New Age science" builds on earlier philosophy of nature themes such as holism, non-determinism and pantheism.

3) From both religious and sociological points of view, neo-shamanism often shares its concepts and practices with various neo-pagan groups. Much of the spiritual background of neo-shamanic ritual practice, including Wiccan chants and rituals of natural magic, have developed from Native American traditions, on the one hand, and from Celtic and other North European religions, on the other.

4) Neo-shamanism, in its more New Age emphasis, tends to deny the reality of intrinsically nefarious spirits. Jonathan Horwitz expresses a perspective similar to New Age when he proclaims that the spirits of cancer and AIDS might be encountered as revoltingly ugly, but are not evil and can be appealed to as respectable entities in the process of extrication. By contrast, in their environments of origin, shamanic practices tend to approach a spirit of illness as something to be killed and destroyed or at least boomeranged back for the destruction of its sender.

5) Neo-shamanism, in general, is oriented toward personal and spiritual empowerment among practitioners. It is less likely to be community-oriented and community-grounded than traditional shamanism.

6) Comparing neo-shamanism with indigenous shamanisms, we can note that in the former there is little attempt to master the spirits. In fact, the aim is to give power directly back to the people and thereby eliminate the specialist altogether. In Horwitz's explanation, the "new shamanism" is a spiritual discipline that enables one directly to contact and use the spiritual dimension of the universe – one which is based on the animistic understanding that everything that exists in the physical plane contains spirit power. But Horwitz prefers to see this process as a shamanic revival rather than as "neo-shamanism." Still, he recognizes that there is much confusion of the peak experience as the goal rather than simply the doorway. Consequently, an important difference between traditional shamanism and neo-shamanism is the acceptance of negative realities by the former and its engagement in forms of spiritual warfare, and the denial of evil and the need to fight it rather than love and transform it by the latter.

Nevertheless, *vis-à-vis* contemporary Western paganism, the shared overlaps that do occur make it difficult to draw a clear line between neo-shamanism and other phenomena of contemporary nature-based spirituality. In this light, it might be more appropriate to speak of a neo-shamanic field of discourse, in which definitions, identities and concepts are negotiated among different groups. People like Michael Harner describe shamanism as "technique" rather than religion; Wiccans, witches, or crystal therapists may refer to themselves as shamans because of this term's more positive connotation; Native Americans might attack neo-shamans as attempting to colonize indigenous culture. "Authenticity" becomes a major issue not only with respect to "indigenous wisdom" (can a "Caucasian" urbanite partake in a native spiritual tradition?), but also concerning academic authority (can specialists discriminate "real shamanism" from its "hybrid" forms, or can neo-shaman academics "know both sides," etc.?).

While different neo-shamanic groups may exhibit a detectable "family resemblance," it is possible – and perhaps advisable – to discern between both wider and narrower senses of neo-shamanism. For the latter, Carlos Castaneda's books served for many as a primary reference tool. Another major figure is Michael Harner who coined the term *core shamanism* and initiated the "Foundation for Shamanic Studies."

Kocku von Stuckrad

Further Reading
Cruden, Loren. *Coyote's Council Fire: Contemporary Shamans on Race, Gender & Community.* Rochester, Vermont: Destiny Books, 1995.
Drury, Nevill. *The Elements of Shamanism.* Longmead, Shaftesbury, Dorset: Element Books, 1989.
Jakobsen, Merete Demant. *Shamanism: Traditional and Contemporary Approaches to the Mastery of Spirits and Healing.* New York and Oxford: Berghahn Books, 1999.
Lindquist, Galina. *Shamanic Performances on the Urban Scene: Neo-Shamanism in Contemporary Sweden.* Stockholm: Stockholm University Press, 1997.
Nicholson, Shirley, ed. *Shamanism: An Expanded View of Reality.* Wheaton: Theosophical Publishing House, 1996.

See also: Castaneda, Carlos; Entheogens; Harner, Michael – and the Foundation for Shamanic Studies; Huxley, Aldous; Nature Religion; New Age; Peyote; Shamanism (various); Paganism – Contemporary; Wicca.

Shamanism – Neo (Eastern Europe)

Neo-shamanism has emerged since the early 1970s following the publication of Mircea Eliade's book on shamanism, a milestone that received either full anthropological and historical support or, on the contrary, outright rejection. Coupled with Carlos Castaneda's vision quest, the "archaic technique of ecstasy" has become the solid ground based on which many seekers and supporters all over the world have begun to rejoice and celebrate their newly found spirituality. Thus, it has much to do with New Spirituality and New Age religious phenomena connected to Eliade and Castaneda and a host of anthropological studies on the subject (P. Furst, A. Wallace, I.M. Lewis, and A. Hultkranz), but especially the work and activity of Michael Harner. The latter has been more influential than others by introducing the possibility of the collage of neo-shamanic practices to Eastern Europe – often emphasizing South American tribal worldviews and their close relationship to Eurasia – and initiating several individuals and small groups into the secrets of shamanic power.

Shamanism, however, is different from neo-shamanism, for the latter term is reserved here for only those religious and psychic practices that are part of the New Age phenomena and may or may not trace their roots to classical shamanism. However, as many neo-shamanic practitioners argue, Eurasian tribal shamanism, its culturally diverse definitions notwithstanding, is a precursor of their art, a practice of syncretism revitalized by poets, painters, musicians and even scientists. This may be one of the reasons why the following terms are often evoked for neo-shamanism: urban shamanism or shamanizing, shamanic trancing, crosscultural shamanism, shamanic spirituality, world shamanism, and even techno or cyber-shamanism. It also freely combines regional or cultural aspects such as Celtic, Norse, Berserk, Siberian, Amazonian, and European. (Beserker is a regional form of present-day shamanism that utilizes archaic Nordic techniques, especially trancing, that is connected to nature and wildlife preservation.) Interestingly, the scholarly world has also responded to this challenge: European witches (Carlo Ginzburg's *benandanti* for instance), ancient Greek magicians, werewolves and positive vampires are also known to possess shamanic attributes.

Neo-shamanism in Eastern Europe
In Eastern Europe, neo-shamanistic phenomena may be connected to the collapse of the Iron Curtain, and with it, the dismantling of Soviet domination throughout the former East bloc. This was followed by an instant reemergence of religiosity along with new forms of spirituality. It should be mentioned, however, that in certain instances rural practices, with some shamanistic elements, managed to survive Soviet atheistic ideology. Soviet atheistic Marxist-Leninist ideology, aside from a few state religions, did not tolerate overt religiosity or communitarian church affairs. In the vacuum created by the dismantled state institutions, religions emerged with vehemence. From North Asia and Siberia, to East Central Europe, from the Baltic republics, to the Balkan Peninsula, traditional folkways have been utilized to establish cultural continuity and national preeminence. Coupled with the neo-shamanic world are national myths of Pan-Slavic unity, the pagan-Slavdom, the remembrance of prehistoric empires and ruling dynasties (Dacians for Romanians, Scythians for Hungarians), and homogeneous peasant traditions that bespeak of cultural longevity and the existence of an ancestral terrain that are all coupled with elements from nationalist imagery.

Although neo-shamanism varies from country to country – and Siberia and parts of Russia are especially unique in that there is a conscious attempt to rely on previous (i.e., traditional tribal, shamanic practices – there is a fairly homogeneous ideology and symbolism. In Hungary, Romania and Bulgaria, for instance, historical and folkloric sources serve as sources of inspiration. More often than not, neo-shamanic séances are not so much re-created as imagined and created by the practitioners. Often, late nineteenth- and early twentieth-century folkloric elements (songs, dance steps, pieces of clothing, etc.)

are utilized as substitutes to create "authentic" versions of native shamanistic performances. Yet, the core doctrine holds that nature is sacred and that shamanism must create harmony with nature, people and the universe. Moreover, neo-shamanic believers do not negate other religions and gods, but seek to find common elements for unity. In their practices they often use the water from natural springs, ignite sacred fires, and drink libations made of herbs and medicinal plants; they also locate sacred groves and previously utilized religious sites for their shamanizing rituals.

In Lithuania, for instance, the remaking of Lithuanian identity is oriented toward neo-paganism – *Romuva* as it is called – with its re-creation of pre-Christian rituals and faith. In Hungary, a former electronic engineer has registered his own shamanic church and school (Táltos iskola), an educational camp where one can gain first-hand knowledge of holistic healing, fortune telling, and supernatural phenomena. Such formal schooling is also coupled with the explanation of an alternative national history not readily taught in formal schools. Compulsory state education, for instance, does not allow for alternative views of ancient history, an area the neo-shamanic practitioners take for granted. For instance, the Scythian and Hunnish archeological remains and historical sources are viewed as direct evidences of Hungarian connections. Novices are required to pass through several stages, or levels, to advance in their spiritual training. Folklore, songs, and knowledge of Hungarian peasant art, runic writing and history are essential constituents of the shamanic training.

In post-Soviet Siberia, new shamans emerge among the elites, mostly those with university and college education, bringing back long-lost spirituality, lifeways and practices. Among the Buryat-Mongols a specific shamanistic institution (the Golomt Center for Shamanist Studies) serves this quest; in Tuva and Udmurtia, practicing shamans are commonly featured in local media. In Sakha-Yakutia, artists openly declare their shamanic family heritage or their quest to attain shamanic powers. Well-known Siberian artists with shamanic powers are often featured attractions in European festivals and artistic shows. The Sakha (Yakut) dancing and singing ensemble, known as Katylyk, or alternately the Udmurt (Votiak) artist Olga Alexandrova, performing in various Hungarian, Baltic or Western cities, provide not only a lively context to connect neo-shamanism to its traditional precursor, but also reinvigorate interest in shamanistic consciousness and knowledge. Because of the linguistic connection to the Finno-Ugric peoples and languages, Siberian artists and performing groups – Hanty, Mansy, Mari and Udmurt – are frequently featured events in Hungary.

No other explanation serves better the fundamental connection that exists between neo-shamanism and the natural environment than the Buryat Mongolian credo quoted on the Buryat homepage:

From the traditional Buryat point of view, the world is not a dead place, but vibrantly alive with spirits and souls in every thing and in every place, also that all animals and plants have sentient souls much like ourselves. For that reason respect for the spirits of nature and living things shaped a religion and life ethics that minimizes negative impact on the earth. For that reason also, for the many thousands of years that man has lived in Siberia there was minimal negative impact on the environment until the current time. This is a way of life which is radically different from that of European peoples, whose philosophy considers most of the world to be lacking sentience and useful only for exploitation (http://www.buryatmongol.com).

In this sense traditional and late twentieth- and early twenty-first-century shamanists are wholly similar. They see, as well as reveal, the fundamental unity of nature and culture. Neo-shamanism differs fundamentally, however, from classical (tribal and prehistoric) shamanism in that it is anchored not to a single culture, people or time and space. It can be found today in milieus where it never existed before; it can possess complexes that never have been previously utilized. Another major difference is the social environment from which novices are selected and into which they are initiated. A collage of symbolic paraphernalia is also symptomatic of neo-shamanists. Urban shamans often use incantations with no real songs or words. As the claim goes, the feeling, rhythm and spirituality are what matters. Rock musicians, however, often invoke images and texts imitating tribal lore or those that are considered by them to be shamanistic. Similarly, in dancing – which could reflect some borrowed steps and figures from tribal dances – connection to indigenous dance forms is neither a requirement nor an important aspect. The neo-shamanic world borrows elements from European folkways, mysticism, Buddhism, Judeo-Christian beliefs, Yoga, Wicca, Daoism, the occult and Paganism. However, as neo-shamanic intellectuals themselves argue, these religious ways could also trace their roots to the more archaic shamanism(s). Neo-shamanists are also concerned with present-day affairs. Specifically, to them all current evils – breakdown of societal values, unbridled capitalism, industrialization and modernization, pollution and the degradation of the natural environment, consumerism, Westernization, poverty crime, and loss of morals as well as peaceful existence – must be fought with new spiritual strength and vigor. This is based on "traditional values," love of nature and animals, and a holistic way of living. In the neo-shamanic worldview, practitioners find both explanations for the past and solutions for the present ills of the world.

As practiced in Eastern Europe, neo-shamanistic belief is mildly anarchist. It is predicated upon the belief that the post-communist and postmodern era is fraught with increasing injustices and inequalities. Their worldview is both liberal and communitarian in that it places the individual – the shaman with powers – at the center to assist the community and work for its welfare. Believers also claim that the present world is out of balance; there is no central harmony any more and political regimes and states are natural enemies of groups with alternative views and marginal positions in society. Neo-shamanic ideology is also based on utopian consciousness for it argues that the present-day realities are harsher than ever before and that paradise on Earth can only be experienced, or achieved, in a magical world of our own creation. Consequently, the neo-shamanic constitutes a cultic milieu that readily accepts magic, science and half-belief at its base.

Regardless of the claims to authenticity, the specific features of neo-shamanism include four important components: 1) spirit mediation or communication to reach the desired aims; 2) healing and initiation rites to conduct various services; 3) the healthy symbiosis between nature and the biosphere; and 4) a culture of rejuvenation that concerns both the individual, the collective, and the Earth. Neo-shamanistic belief is separated from its more archaic form by the very fact that neo-shamanic rituals are now everyday occurrences that do not necessarily require sacred sites, secrecy of affairs or blood-letting through animal sacrifice. In fact, most neo-shamanic rites avoid "hurting the natural world." Neo-shamanists in Eastern Europe may perform in artistic clubs, university surroundings, corporate offices or urban tenement houses. Neo-shamanic religion is also highly diffuse so it may be extended into rural revitalized neo-pagan events, healing rites and syncretic nationalist revival movements. In its more extreme forms neo-shamanic ways may be utilized for nationalistic or political propaganda. Aside from Western and Northern Europe, in the Ukraine, Russia, and Hungary such extremist versions have been recorded recently.

László Kürti

Further Reading

Balzer, Marjoria Mandelstam. "Two Urban Shamans: Unmasking Leadership in Fin-de-Soviet Siberia." In George E. Marcus, ed. *Perilous States: Conversations on Culture, Politics, and Nation*. Chicago and London: The University of Chicago Press, 1993, 131–64.

Balzer, Marjorie Mandelstam, ed. *Shamanism: Soviet Studies of Traditional Religion in Siberia and Central Asia*. Armonk: M.E. Sharpe, 1990.

Coubrinskas, Vytis. "Identity and the Revival of Tradition in Lithuania: An Insider's View." *Folk* 42 (2000), 19–40.

Dymerskaya-Tsigelman and Leonid Finberg. "Antisemitism of the Ukrainian Radical Nationalists: Ideology and Policy." Acta no. 14. The Vidal Sassoon International Center for the Study of Antisemitism. Jerusalem: The Hebrew University, 1999.

Humphrey, Caroline. "Shamans in the City." *Anthropology Today* 15:3 (1999), 3–10.

Krumina-Konkova, Solveiga. "New Religious Minorities in the Baltic States." *Nova Religio* 4:2 (2001), 289–97.

Kürti, László. "Psychic Phenomena, Neoshamanism, and the Cultic Milieu in Hungary." *Nova Religio* 4:2 (2001), 322–50.

Shnirelman, Victor A. "Russian Neo-pagan Myths and Antisemitism." Acta no. 13. The Vidal Sassoon International Center for the Study of Antisemitism. Jerusalem: The Hebrew University, 1998.

Thomas, Nicholas and Caroline Humphrey, eds. *Shamanism, History, and the State*. Ann Arbor: The University of Michigan Press, 1997.

Znamenski, Andrei A. *Shamanism and Christianity: Native Encounters with Russian Orthodox Missions in Siberia and Alaska, 1820–1917*. Westport: Greenwood, 1999.

See also: Harner, Michael – and the Foundation for Shamanic Studies; Neo-paganism and Ethnic Nationalism in Eastern Europe; Psychonauts; Raves.

Shamanism – Southern Peruvian Andes

In the southern Peruvian Andes, at an average height of 4500 meters above the sea, live small groups of shepherds who raise large herds of alpacas (*Llama pacos*), llamas (*Llama glama*) and sheep. Their traditional religious life is centered on the charismatic figure of the *altomisayoq*, a practitioner who plays the role of a mediator between humans and supernatural beings, and is capable of influencing the course of events. Generally speaking, he may be called, according to anthropological categorization, a shaman.

There appears to be several popular religions rather than a unique and distinctive one in these traditional societies. Depending on the informant, or on the circumstances, one can be referred to one cosmology or another in order to explain natural or social phenomena. Beyond Christian and syncretic explanations (such as for instance the myth of the "three ages of humanity"), lies a coherent group of beliefs, centered on the spirits of mountains, called *apu*. According to the people, these *apu* are the genuine "creators" of the Andean world. Many myths explain the way fauna and flora species were "created" and scattered in the valleys by the *apu*. Mountains are natural borderlines in the Andean space, and species distribution may be different according to valley geographical features. *Apu* control, in the day-to-day life, natural and social phenomena – they are godfathers of recently born children, and a myth says they taught women the art of weaving. Thus, *apu* are the ultimate explanation of natural and social features, and, at the same time, they are part of this world. The "creators" fully belong to their "creation." Within this immanence, shamanic dialogue is possible.

Apu, though, are not the only spiritual entities in this cosmological view: they are rather situated at the top of a hierarchy of spirits, which do not hold any supernatural power by themselves. Generally speaking, traditional Andean shepherds consider that everything in the world owns an *animo*. The word *animo* itself is derived from the Latin "*animus*," which came to their ears through Spanish colonization, but it has a much broader meaning. *Animo* apparently refers to both the vital strength and what we could call the essence of all beings, whether they are humans, animals, vegetables, or even minerals. Each being has a different, particular, *animo*, which is also related to the *apu*, whose *animo* stand at the top of the hierarchy. The term *animo* reflects, therefore, the interdependency of all beings, as well as their specificity.

In order for these societies to communicate with the *apu* and other supernatural beings, an intermediate is needed. This is the role of the *altomisayoq*, who appears to be mainly a priest, a medicine man and a fortune teller. He directs collective propitiatory ceremonies, offered up to the *apu* or the *pachamama*, the goddess-earth, cures sicknesses and tells the future. Although he can communicate with all beings, natural or supernatural, through their *animo*, his interlocutor is, above all, the *apu*. In order to become a shaman, one needs to be selected by one *apu*, and survive a strike by lightning. Novices then go through a long process of initiation, conducted by elder shamans. At one point of this initiation period, they often find, in wild places, the tools of their trade, like small copper bells, which they use to call the *apu*, or strange anthropomorphic or zoomorphic stones, full of supernatural powers. These are gifts of the *apu* itself. Apprentices learn the healing powers of plants, and conjuring tricks. This initiation process culminates with the ritual bath in a *qocha* (a mountain lake), where the shaman-to-be calls his tutelary *apu*, who answers in a guttural voice that seems to come straight out of the mountain's heart. Therefore, the shaman's legitimacy eventually relies on the will of the *apu*.

Direct communication with supernatural beings is scarcely deemed necessary. Collective propitiatory ceremonies do not need such communication powers and can be directed by a *pampamisayoq* (a practitioner of an inferior rank). The same stands for fortune telling, which many perform by observing the features and distribution of coca leaves, poured over a small patch of *wachala*, a traditional piece of clothing. Even when it comes to healing, direct communication with supernatural beings such as *apu* or *soq'a machu* may not be considered compulsory: in that case, the healing treatment will consist of offerings to the spirits responsible for the disease as a means of appeasing them. The traditional healer, be he *altomisayoq* or *pampamisayoq*, brings together these offerings on a square cloth, ties it up from its angles, and burns this bundle, called a *despacho*, on some neighboring hill.

Nevertheless, in some cases, direct communication with spirits may be considered necessary. This communication is not the result of extrasensory perception faculties held by the shaman. On the contrary, the communication process always occurs in the world of day-to-day perception. Since spirits are part of this world as well, a conjunction between them and human beings is possible *here and now*. The *altomisayoq* are the only practitioners capable of such direct communication, because of the tools inherited from the *apu*. Shamanic communication flows from the *apu*, to the shaman. Shamans call for the *apu*, using, as a call sign, their small copper bells: thereafter, it is the *apu* which comes to answer the shaman's questions, in the form of a dove or condor, getting into the room through an open window, and then speaking freely, in a low-pitched or high-pitched voice. Those in attendance hear the sayings of the *apu* as clearly as the shaman does.

One can say traditional shepherd societies in the southern Peruvian Andes still share one coherent cosmology, centered on the *apu*, which for this reason we may call an *apu*-logy. It refers us to very ancient beliefs and practices. It determines the relationship that these societies still hold with natural phenomena, for the *apu* are ultimately responsible for the course of events in the natural world. For instance, the good health of domestic animals depends on the will of the *apu*, and needs retribution in the form of a *despacho*.

Finally, one can say that part of this *apu*-logy is a sort of theory of knowledge (an epistemology in the broad sense), within which the shaman's performance is legitimate. We can shed light upon this theory of knowledge through a patient analysis of beliefs and religious practices of these societies.

Xavier Ricard Lanata

Further Reading
Randall, Robert. "Qoyllur rit'i, an Inca Fiesta of the Pleiades: Reflections on Time and Space in the Andean World." *Bulletin de l'Institut Français d'Etudes Andines* 11:1–2 (1982).

See also: Andean Traditions; Shamanism – Ecuador.

Shamanism – Traditional

Shamanism is the art and science by which one purposely shifts perspective. There are different means by which perspective-shift is achieved (meditative/contemplative techniques, use of entheogens, abstinences, fasting, sleep-deprivation, other austerities, and/or utilizing an illness or fever), but the initial impulse is auto-induced rather than imposed upon the individual by others. Shamanism refers primarily to the techniques employed for achieving changes in consciousness – especially ecstatic consciousness – and secondarily to the body of religious thought and practice in which the personage of the shaman plays a central role.

The terms "shaman" and "shamanism" have increasingly developed into three fundamental applications. The first and most narrow understanding applies the designations to specific institutions among the Tungusic peoples of Siberia. This would be the original import of the terms. Secondly, the label of the "shaman" has become extended to practices among other peoples that reveal similar animistic or quasi-animistic understandings of nature – whether these peoples are indigenous (American Indian, African), national entities (Japan, Korea, Mongolia) or contemporary (New Age, modern Western Paganism). In this wider and more generally used sense, shamanism designates any religious system centered on "a religious specialist who has great powers derived from ecstatic experiences in which he or she has contact with sacred forces" (Smart 1989: 38). Consequently, the term "shaman" as a generic is applied alike to the North American "medicine person," the Latin American *curañdero*, the Japanese *miko* and the practitioner of Michael Harner's "core" shamanism. Lastly, the expression of "shaman" has come to refer to various New Age and neo-pagan practices in general in which the individual seeks to shift his/her conscious perspective for purposes of health, deeper understanding, ecstasy and social concern – including increase in environmental sensitivities. Consequently, shamanism in the context of its relationship to religion and nature may be loosely classified as traditional, New Age, urban and psychonautic. As distinguishable sub-sets of traditional shamanisms, we have individual geographic expressions ranging from Ecuador, Alaska and Lapland to Nepal and Mongolia.

Possibly Immanuel Velikovsky was the first to use the term "shaman" in the more contemporary sense. The German *Schamane* had been adopted from the Russian *shaman* which, in turn, had been received from the Tungus-speaking peoples' *šaman*. However, the designation appears among the now-extinct Tocharian peoples of Central Asia as *ṣamāne* as well as the Indian Prakrit vernacular as *samaṇe*. These are to be traced to the Sanskrit term for "ascetic," namely, *śramaṇás*. In other words, the term is not originally indigenous to the peoples to whom it retains its primary association.

Pivotal roles in the development of the West's understanding of shamanism have been played by the Russian Sergei M. Shirogokorov and the Romanian Mircea Eliade. Shirogokorov's seminal work is the *Psychomental Complex of the Tungus* (1935). Earlier, in 1923, he published his *General Theory of Shamanism among the Tungus*. Another important early work is Knud Rasmussen's *The Intellectual Culture of Iglulik Eskimos* (1929). Eliade's classic originally appeared as *Le Chamanisme et les techniques archaiques de l'extase* in 1951. This was subsequently translated by W.R. Trask in 1972 as *Shamanism: Archaic Techniques of Ecstasy*.

In Siberia, shamanic spiritualism is found among approximately thirty different ethnic groups – with the Yakuts being the largest numerically. The traditional economy is based on reindeer herding. The spirit of the immediate location is believed to enter the stove. Here, with the lighting of the stove, the fire-spirit is offered the first mouthful of food. Recognized spirit places in Siberia include graves, umbilical markers (burial sites of umbilical cords), rivers and mountains. Most shamans were liquidated by the Soviet authorities, and today the resurgence of shamanist elements among the local people is facilitated more by ethnologists, film-makers and the like than by the few surviving traditional shamans in an area roughly the size of the Republic of India and holding a population of approximately one million.

There are countless variations between individual and particular tribal shamanic practices. Nevertheless, there are also certain universal features or patterns that allow it to be considered an identifiable and independent phenomenon in itself. Its basic idea appears to be the institutionalization of a socially recognized intermediary who liaisens between the world of pragmatic realities and the more subtle realm of spirit. From a religious perspective, shamanism is a loose federation of cosmologies. But it is always strictly contextual – relating to the religion and society in which it occurs. Yet despite its many forms and the variety of roles it serves, a certain range of cosmology, religion and society is recognizably conducive to belief in the shaman as someone who specializes in trance techniques during which (one of) his/her soul(s) leave(s) the shaman's body to enter the otherworld. Whether among indigenous peoples of Australia, Siberia, South America, Central and Southeast Asia, sub-Saharan Africa or elsewhere, there appears to be remarkable similarities between particular elements of shamanic mythologies and techniques.

In traditional shamanisms, the shaman's entire endeavor is shaped by his or her role *vis-à-vis* the community. Deliberately sending forth one's free-soul, exploring the spiritual realms of the otherworld, being beyond the boundaries of the norm and of normal behavior is, in a Western cultural context, to be mad, insane or schizoid. And in the indigenous understanding of soul-duality, if a person's dream-soul does not "return" to the waking body, the person's deranged state is a form of mental illness – one that invariably is followed by physical disability as well. For the ordinary person, soul-loss is considered an accident or misfortune. For the shaman, by contrast, the very propensity for entering an altered state of consciousness is his or her trade. But it is still not the *raison d'être*. The purpose instead is the community welfare.

In navigating the dangers of the world of spirit, within the condition of an altered state of consciousness, even for the experienced shaman there is the risk of soul-loss. It is the very social function of the shaman that provides his or her way back to this world. Community service becomes the anchor that prevents the shaman from becoming permanently lost in the otherworld. So while the mediumship of the shaman is what allows a community an access to the spiritual without which there is the danger of collective madness, it is the community itself and the shaman's duty to serve it which provides the shamanic safeguard against the specialist becoming imprisoned perpetually in the world of purely analogical and magical effervescence. It is this aspect that is essential in all indigenous forms of shamanism.

Following Shirogokorov's seminal work in the 1930s, Russian scholars tend to associate shamanism with spiritual healing as its most salient feature. The West, by contrast, under the influence of Eliade, considers the key aspect of shamanism to be its "techniques of ecstasy." This last is more conducive to the wider application of the term to various magico-religious elements found among many non-literate peoples as well as in some world religions. Nevertheless, the healing aspect of the shamanic vision quest is virtually an inevitable feature all the same.

The shaman, therefore is someone who participates directly in spiritual dimensions in the roles of healer, diviner, clairvoyant and/or pyschopomp. For example, the role of the Chinese traditional shaman, designated *wu*, whether male or female, is typically that of seer, healer and keeper of justice in Chinese villages in the context of the popular traditions and/or Daoism. In an induced trance state, the shaman is believed to leave the body and visit other worlds. The purpose of shamanic journeying, therefore, is to convey sacrifices to the gods, to escort the dead to their next destination, to acquire knowledge to heal illnesses, and to return with prophecies. The shaman's duty is both to instruct people on a proper course of action and to cause good things to happen. The shaman's overall function is to ensure, maintain and/or restore his/her people's proper relationship with the natural environment and with the spiritual realm as it manifests itself through that environment. The shaman may also bestow fetishes or sacred objects in the form of feathers, ritual rattles, special drums or ceremonial pipes. These, in turn, are venerated and employed to ensure harmony. Their pragmatic import is to assist their users to be mindful and vigilant concerning the preservation of holistic equilibrium.

The principal means of communicating with the spirit world by the shaman is through the utterance of special words and by rhythmically beating a sacred drum. With the help of healing spirits, the shaman is believed to overcome malignant powers. Shamanism only exists when communication between this world and the spirit world is not deemed to be possible on the part of ordinary persons. Since the shaman's role is one of intermediary, he or she is often found in cultures in which a high god is believed to have receded and become inactive in the affairs of this world. This relates to the "loss of communication" mythology between human beings and spirits at the close of the primal era. In the void which ensues with the high god's absence, numerous ancestor spirits and spirits of nature come to intervene, and it is these beings with whom the shaman becomes an adept in communicating and controlling.

In the traditional context, the would-be shaman responds to a call. In some cases, the profession is hereditary. Normally, however, there is a reluctance to assume the shamanic mantel. While he or she is often highly respected and revered, there is also great fear attached to the shaman who usually lives a relatively isolated life. At first, the candidate undergoes a powerful but spontaneous spiritual experience – one that generally coincides with sexual maturity. This is usually an illness, often mental, which is nevertheless an empowering experience. In many tribal societies, it is not uncommon for many people to suffer an episode of schizophrenic-type illness lasting perhaps six to nine months. Unlike in the West where the mentally ill are sequestered and institutionalized, in the indigenous environment, these people are comforted and integrated as much as is possible into the social framework. Most people eventually recover and assume normal lives thereafter. But those who are deemed to have extra insight and dream-capacity may instead be selected for shamanic training. When viewing contemporary Western forms of shamanism, it is important to keep in mind that traditional shamanic training is often a prolonged and difficult ordeal which, if the candidate succeeds, is followed by an initiation that incorporates themes of death, dismemberment and reconstitution.

Consequently, in the traditional context, there is almost invariably a discernible shamanic trajectory beginning with the call, crisis or initial illness and followed by the training and culminating in initiation and transformation. The shaman then acquires a "spirit-animal" or familiar, demonstrates the shamanic performance and experience of trance, and eventually returns or "re-incorporates" and dispenses knowledge. He or she may finally bequeath implements and information to apprentices. For Western neo-shamans, however, this trajectory is much less rigorous if it exists at all in the first place. While traditional shamans are often initially reluctant to assume the shamanic mantel, for neo-shamans the choice to pursue this path is almost invariably a personal and private preference. Moreover, this decision is rarely made in connection to a supportive social community but reflects the atomization of Western society. Much of the training is self-training, though this can be augmented for some New Age shamans who participate in various eco-tourist opportunities and pursue occasional ecstatic experience through South American *curañderos* in the Amazonian rainforest or the mountains and jungles of Peru, Bolivia and Ecuador. For those who do not pursue this psychonautic route, there are the augmentative options of New Age workshops. However, among the more controversial issues to arise for Western would-be shamans is the question of appropriation of cultural property. Many Lakota Indians, for instance, condemn the theft of Amerindian artifacts (e.g., dream-catchers) and practices (e.g., participation in sweat-lodge ceremonies) as threats to the identity and precarious survival of Native Americans.

Russian scholars have argued that the traditional shaman is an individual who suffers from certain nervous disorders or forms of hysteria – especially in the severe Arctic environment. Others see shamanism as the development of skill in epilepsy. The training and initiation that the shaman receives constitutes in effect a cure. For the traditional shaman, the distinctive feature becomes an ability to control ecstasy and enter trance at will. The shaman is deemed by his or her community to have achieved a great mastery of the natural and psychological dimensions. Typical signs of the traditional shaman's extraordinary superhuman powers include the ability to walk on red-hot coals or even swallow them, to remain unscathed by boiling water, to undergo physical mutilation – including the cutting open of their stomachs which then heal instantly – to release themselves from bonds, and to exercise kinesis.

Nevertheless, despite the various demonstrative signs of the shaman's abilities, it is the ability of certain individuals to communicate with spirits that is the core aspect of traditional shamanism. This feature is closely linked to hunter-gatherer societies and therefore probably of great antiquity. This near universality of shamanism allowed Ninian Smart to surmise that it is ancestral to both the magical or numinous (*bhakti*) and the contemplative or mystical (*dhyâna*) forms of most subsequent religious formation. For Smart, shamanism is an early phenomenon which stretches back deep into prehistory. The shaman is one who encounters numinous beings and the *mysterium tremendum*. He or she is also one who prepares for inner vision and the development of inward narrative through solitude and asceticism. Among its other offshoots are the practice of magic, the development of healing techniques and possibly the creation of epic and lyric poetry. Consequently, the shaman's traditional roles are those of healer-physician, psychopomp, animal-charmer, prophet, sacrificial priest, lawyer, mythologue, epic singer, and keeper of the tribal calendar.

Michael York

Further Reading
Baldick, Julian. *Animal and Shaman: Ancient Religions of Central Asia*. New York: New York University Press, 2000.
Nicholson, Shirley, (compiler). *Shamanism: An Expanded View of Reality*. Wheaton, IL: Theosophical Publishing House, 1987.
Noel, Daniel C. *The Soul of Shamanism: Western Fantasies, Imaginal Realities*. New York: Continuum, 1997.
Smart, Ninian. *Dimensions of the Sacred: An Anatomy of the World's Beliefs*. Berkeley: University of California Press, 1996.
Smart, Ninian. *The World's Religions*. Cambridge: University Press, 1989.
Vitebsky, Piers. *The Shaman: Voyages of the Soul Trance, Ecstasy and Healing from Siberia to the Amazon*. London: Macmillan, 1995.

See also: Amazonia; Animism; Animism – A Contemporary Perspective; Ayahuasca; Breathwork; Entheogens; Ethnobotany; Ethnoecology; Harner, Michael – and the Foundation for Shamanic Studies; Huaorani; Inuit; Magic, Animism, and the Shaman's Craft; Maya Religion (Central America); Maya Spirituality (Guatemala Highlands); Reichel-Dolmatoff, Gerardo – and Ethnoecology in Colombia; Peyote; Psychonauts; Raves; Re-Earthing; Saami Culture; Shamanism – and Art; Shamanism – Ecuador; Shamanism – Neo; Shamanism – Neo (Eastern Europe); Shamanism – Southern Peruvian Andes; Shamanism – Urban; Traditional Ecological Knowledge; Tukanoan Indians (Northwest Amazonia); U'wa Indians (Colombia); Yoga and Ecology; Yanomami; Zulu (amaZulu) Culture, Plants and Spirit Worlds (South Africa).

Shamanism – Urban

Urban shamanism represents the practice of perspective shift within an urban environment and with the purpose of regaining a pantheistic perception. Varieties include New Age, new Pagan, techno-cyber, rave, psychonautic and environmental warrior forms. The underlying question for the urban shaman concerns locating or constructing the sacred from the profane and determining how and when objects and places become charged with holy power. In the urban context, the shaman attempts to implement what Max Weber referred to as the reenchantment of the world. Enchantment is magic, and the urban shaman endeavors either to re-see the world as innately sacred or, actively, to imbue the world with a ubiquitous magical spell. In a sense, urban shamanism represents the attempt to look at one's home turf as if a visiting foreigner.

All urban shamans, whether New Age or new Pagan, access or relate to at least some aspect of nature, the rural and/or the untamed wild, and their task then becomes one of extending the inherent enchantment of the natural to the urban, to see and feel the urban as also natural. The urban shaman may learn to view the teeming life of a metropolitan center as a municipal jungle, a human beehive or ant colony and/or a restructuring akin to the reshaping work of a beaver. In principle, the construction of human habitation differs little from avian fabrication of a nest or an animal's burrowing its shelter. But whereas the bird tends to install its nest *in* the tree, the human might create his/her home by *destroying* the living tree. Because of these extreme differences and the consequential environmental impact, the urban shaman attempts to develop vigilant consciousness and readdress the balance of natural production and formation, on the one hand, and the impinging costs of metropolitan transformation, on the other.

As with the traditional shaman, the urban counterpart is involved with a perpetual practice of divination in the form of interpreting by signs and wonders. The shaman may resort to such technologies of augury as reading the tarot, consulting the *I-Ching*, casting cowry shells or lots, constructing a horoscope or deciphering the supernatural as it presents itself in the intensely reshaped human environment of the city. Instead of the emblems and vehicles of the divine that are more readily found in the natural or rural setting, in "reading the spontaneous," the urban shaman may be forced to resort to the employment of icons from the cultural mythological register that adorn corporate/governmental buildings and public spaces. The miraculous is no less sought in the cosmopolitan locale than it is in the woodlands through the synchronistic and the unexpected and unpredictable coincidence.

Unlike the traditional shaman, the urban counterpart in today's metropolitan world is less apt to have a supportive community behind his or her practice. At best, today's Western shaman may form confederative associations with other shamans in the pursuit of his trade. To remain a shaman, shamans form tribes rather than institutions. Nevertheless, even without conscious community support, the urban shaman seeks to serve his or her wider neighborhood through channeling or opening awareness of the numinous and by inseminating greater sensitivity to the need for sustainable holistic balance. The urban shaman is no less a guardian of the gateway, and in this function, he or she serves the wider community as an educator *par excellence*, one who leads others out from ignorance. While New Age or core-shamans may be more involved with personal growth and enlightenment, the Pagan shaman's principal concern lies instead in combating the "demons" of societal imprisonment, industrial pollution and environmental insensitivity. Even the psychonaut, while pursuing entheogenic and psychotropic changes in awareness, more often than not grounds this pursuit in holistic concern and the further aim of social reform. As with shamans worldwide, the contemporary urban shaman serves the wider community as a vehicle to wider perspectives and as an inspirer toward increased imagination for people in general. He/she also endeavors, in general, to remain sensitive to issues of appropriation. As Dan Noel argued, with its emphasis on the "imaginal" (as opposed both to the imaginary and to Jung's archetypal), the power and process of imagining becomes a workable way *not* to appropriate from other cultures.

In its more nuanced general sense, urban shamanism is to be distinguished from New Age neo-shamanic expressions ranging from the "Higher Self" orientation of Patricia Telesco, the adoptive Hawaiian shamanism of Serge Kahili King, the guided imagery of Michael Harner's "core-shamanism" and the "we must love the spirit of AIDS" approach of Jonathan Horwitz and/or the Native American transplantation of Leo Rutherford. The urban shaman is more independent and individualistic, unconcerned with "lineage" labels, less apt to employ New Age jargon, and more directly preoccupied with "earth-revelations" and "nature-connections" within the metropolitan environment. Practice tends to center on the "arts" of invisibility and flight as well as the cultivation of vigilance and service.

Urban shamanism is also intimately connected to the various forms of techno-shamanism (viz., rave trance-dance, cyberspace ritual, online gender-swapping, techno-mysticism, multi-media/high-tech multi-sensory celebration, emergent artificial intelligence). In this sense, it is part of the growth in the West of non-institutionalized, individually constructed varieties of spirituality or what Thomas Luckmann (1967) calls "invisible religion." For the techno-shaman, "the postmodern world of digital simulacra is [considered] ripe for the premodern skills of the witch and magician" (Davis 1998: 188). The indigenous understanding of a natural world infused with animistic forms of life has been transferred to the "alive" technological world of the metropolitan environment. This fundamental notion of the spontaneous *deus ex machina* or the emergent organism – whether biological or technological – is increasingly underpinned by explanations based on "complexity theory" being developed at such think-tanks as the Santa Fe Institute. Organisms of digital technology, such as computer viruses and "bots," suggest a technical world that lies steadily beyond human control as, in many essentials, does the natural world. The contemporary techno-shaman approaches such possibilities more often than not as akin to magical effervescence. The techno-shaman or techno-pagan, along with zippies (Zen Inspired Professional Pagans), cyber-crusties and techno-hippies tends to integrate shamanic and technical thought processes as ways to encounter and incorporate the spontaneous natural with the fruits of techno-urban development.

It is nevertheless important to keep in mind that the urban shaman invariably grounds his or her practice in the natural world – whether the rave's conclusion with greeting the rising sun, whether the development of ecological awareness and recycling practice, or whether through timing according to lunar or other natural cycles. The urban shaman has become more often than not an eco-warrior in one form or another. He/she may participate in road protest movements, in campaigns to save woodlands and/or other natural sites, or in demonstrations against multi-national corporations and international agencies perceived as heedless contributors to environmental destruction. The emphasis in urban shamanism is no longer upon the healing aspect of traditional shamanism as it applies to individuals, it is instead upon healing as it pertains to a community as a whole. While individual curing still persists, the contemporary urban shaman is primarily concerned with healing the estrangement between his/her society and the natural environment.

Michael York

Further Reading
Davis, Erik. *Techgnosis: Myth, Magic and Mysticism in the Age of Information.* London: Serpent's Tail, 1998.
King, Serge Kahili. *Urban Shaman: A Handbook for Personal And Planetary Transformation Based on the Hawaiian Way of the Adventurer.* New York: Fireside, 1990.
Luckmann, Thomas. *The Invisible Religion: The Problem of Religion in Modern Society.* New York/London: Macmillan, 1967.
Noel, Daniel C. *The Soul of Shamanism: Western Fantasies, Imaginal Realities.* New York: Continuum, 1997.
Telesco, Patricia. *Shaman in a 9 to 5 World.* Freedom, CA: The Crossing Press, 2000.

See also: Donga Tribe; Dragon Environmental Network (United Kingdom); Earth First! and the Earth Liberation Front; Entheogens; Harner, Michael – and the Foundation for Shamanic Studies; Psychonauts; Radical Environmentalism; Raves; Shamanism – Neo.

Sheldrake, Rupert (1942–)

Biologist Rupert Sheldrake has become a famous author of "New Age science," since he proposed his controversial theory of "morphogenetic fields" in the early 1980s. The "hypothesis of formative causation" postulates the existence of invisible organizing fields that are able to transmit information to seemingly independent parts of reality (e.g., to the genes of other members of the species on another continent). This is made possible by what Sheldrake terms "morphic resonance." Although his theory has been refuted by the majority of empirical scientists, a set of independent experiments show it to be at least not improbable. Like Wolfgang Pauli's doctrine of "synchronicity," the concept of morphogenetic fields is able to explain phenomena that seem to be mysterious to traditional physics and biology. If the theory's propositions were accepted, the consequences would totally change our view of nature and the cosmos. Therefore, Sheldrake elaborates a neovitalist, holistic theory that is empirical at the start and purely metaphysical in its implications. In the end, the universe for Sheldrake is a conscious and creative power, which brings forth morphogenetic fields. All single, yet resonating, entities take part in this cosmic "dance" of creativity, including the human mind.

As can easily be imagined, this proposition enthralled environmentalists and theorists of ecological concerns. First, it provides an explanation for the mutual dependency of all levels of nature; second, it places the human in a cosmos of encompassing energy and the vitality of cosmic intelligence; third, it appreciates all forms of life – humans, animals, and plants – as equally intelligent and therefore as carrying intrinsic value. All three conclusions are crucial elements of "deep ecology."

Kocku von Stuckrad

Further Reading
Sheldrake, Rupert. *The Rebirth of Nature. The Greening of Science and God.* New York: Bantam Books, 1991.
Sheldrake, Rupert. *The Presence of the Past: Morphic Resonance and the Habits of Nature.* New York: Vintage Books (Random House), 1989 (1988).
Sheldrake, Rupert. *A New Science of Life: The Hypothesis of Formative Causation.* London: Paladin Grafton Books, 1987 (1981).

See also: Complexity Theory; Deep Ecology; Holism; New Age; Pauli, Wolfgang; Science.

Shepard, Paul (1925–1996)

Paul Shepard was an ecological thinker and father of the field of human ecology. Until his death in 1996, he was Avery Professor Emeritus of Human Ecology at Pitzer College and Claremont Graduate School in southern California. Shepard should be considered one of the most original thinkers in contemporary history insofar as his work explored the primordial relationships between being human in a more-than-human world of animals, plants, and insects. Shepard's work influences the thinking of deep ecologists, bioregionalists, wild-lands advocates, and environmental philosophers.

Shepard's exploration of the path toward a more intimate and compassionate treatment of the living world we inhabit can be found in his books *The Tender Carnivore and the Sacred Game, Thinking Animals, Nature and Madness, The Others: How Animals Made Us Human,* and his final book *Coming Home to the Pleistocene*. In this last book Shepard wrote,

> Everything I have written since [the early 1970s] was influenced by what I uncovered in my research on *The Tender Carnivore*: our perception of animals as the language of nature in *Thinking Animals and The Others*; the "natural" way of childrearing in *Nature and Madness*; and the bear as a dominant sacred animal connecting people ceremonially to the earth in *The Sacred Paw* (Shepard 1998: 2–3).

Shepard's work was founded on the theme of the bioecology of early and present-day hunter-gatherer societies, and the cultural dynamics, religious practice, and psychology of mythmaking, ceremonial dance and storytelling of tribal peoples. At one time, nature spoke and a detailed knowledge of place and ecology was passed on from generation to generation by oral tradition through myths – each myth of a particular place and a people frames human belief structures and religious practice in a context of ancestors and intergenerational communion. Human beings lived within a "sacred geography" of place and political understanding that consisted of a deep and shared vision of place, terrain, and the sacred plants, animals, and insects that are embedded in "a phenology of seasonal cycles." "During prehistory," Shepard believed,

> which is most of the time that humans have been on earth, the dead and their burial places were venerated and mythic ancestors were part of the living present, the dreamtime ones whose world was also the ground of present being. Ignore them as we will, they are with us still (1998: 8).

In examining the lifeways and ecological knowledge of tribal societies, Shepard informed us that the best expressions of our humanity can be found in the prehistorical cultures that precede industrialization and globalization. We can recover a shared ecological identity, Shepard argued, if we recover the sense of wonder and delight that comes with being human in a greater circle of animals, plants and insects.

Shepard's emphasis on the link to our more Pleistocene ecological roots has drawn a mixed response from intellectuals and philosophers. Shepard explored the foundation of human interaction with the natural world. His central thesis was that our relationship with the greater circle of animals, plants and insects – in short, the landscape – is a product of our shared genetic heritage, which has been formed by various religious, animistic, sacred, and institutional practices. Since the dawn of the Pleistocene period, being human has always been shaped by a shared ecology of identity, which is reflected in an array of mimetic dances, rituals, songs, ceremonies, and chants that celebrate the interdependence and relationship with others. For the many he influenced, Shepard provides the foundation for a new (old) way of interacting with the more-than-human world; his scholarship places human beings with nature as an equal participant. Nature is more than a mere simulation of industrial production, something more than an "environment" to behold, being a wondrous world of interconnections that cannot be forgotten. For others more critical of Shepard's work, the return or renewal of the hunter-primitive cultural identification and worldview is impossible, given our technological and scientific understandings of the world. Moreover, critics of Shepard's central thesis believe that it is based on a form of ecological determinism, as if the natural laws of ecology and genetics are the sole determinants of our way of being in the world.

The influence of his ecological thinking continues to shape new ways of relating to the natural world and human beings. As Shepard put it,

> In the face of predominant anthropocentric values, the vision of natural humankind seems eccentric, regressive, even perverse. Our idea of ourselves embedded in the context of the shibboleth of growth places us at odds with the notion of kinship with nature. When we grasp fully that the best expressions of our humanity were not invented by civilization but by cultures that preceded it, that the natural world is not only a set of constraints but of contexts within which we can more fully realize our dreams; we will be on the way to a long overdue reconciliation between opposites that are of our own making (1998: 5–6).

Michael Vincent McGinnis

Further Reading

Shepard, Paul. *Encounters with Nature: Essays by Paul Shepard*. Florence R. Shepard, ed. Washington, D.C.: Island Press, 1999.

Shepard, Paul. *The Tender Carnivore and the Sacred Game*. Athens: University of Georgia Press, 1973.

Shepard, Paul. *Nature and Madness*. Athens: University of Georgia Press, 1982.

Shepard, Paul. *Coming Home to the Pleistocene*. Florence R. Shepard, ed. Washington, D.C. Island Press, 1998.

Shepard, Paul. *The Only World We've Got: A Paul Shepard Reader*. San Francisco: Sierra Club Books, 1996.

Shepard, Paul. *The Others: How Animals Made Us Human*. Washington, D.C.: Island Press, 1996.

Shepard, Paul. *Man in the Landscape: A Historic View of the Esthetics of Nature*. New York: Knopf, 1967.

Shepard, Paul, and Barry Sanders. *The Sacred Paw: The*

Bear in Nature, Myth, and Literature. New York: Viking, 1985.

Shepard, Paul and Daniel McKinley, eds. *Environmental: Essays on the Planet as a Home.* Boston: Houghton-Mifflin, 1971.

Shepard, Paul and Daniel McKinley, eds. *The Subversive Science: Essays Toward an Ecology of Man.* Boston: Houghton Mifflin, 1969.

Shepard, Paul and Melinda Blau. *Thinking Animals.* New York: Viking Press, 1978.

See also: Berman, Morris; Bioregionalism; Bioregionalism and the North American Bioregional Congress; Deep Ecology; Earth First! and the Earth Liberation Front; Environmental Ethics; Paleolithic Religions; Paleolithic Religions and the Future; Quinn, Daniel; Radical Environmentalism; Religious Studies and Environmental Concern; Snyder, Gary.

Shinto – *See* Japanese Religions.

Shiva, Vandana (1952–)

A prominent Indian physicist turned environmental thinker and activist, Vandana Shiva criticizes the dominant Western model of science and development and details its social, ecological, economic, and political impacts. She claims that, since the Enlightenment, the sanctity of this model of scientific knowledge and economic development has replaced the sanctity of life. The current development paradigm, which Shiva refers to as "maldevelopment," effects an epistemological colonization by denying the value of other traditions of knowledge. In contrast to the exclusion and exploitation of the anti-life "maldevelopment," Shiva highlights the knowledge and productivity of indigenous people and Indian cosmology as sources of renewal and sustenance of life.

In *Staying Alive: Women, Ecology and Survival in India* (1988), Shiva details the difference between the goals of Western development and the productivity of Indian women. Western development treats nature and women as a resource to be used for the accumulation of capital; whereas women in sustenance economies share in partnership with nature, using their holistic and ecological knowledge for social benefits and sustenance needs.

The recovery of the feminine that Shiva recommends in *Staying Alive* includes both the knowledge inherent to women's activities of producing life and providing sustenance and the productive feminine force of Indian cosmology. According to this cosmology, nature is an expression of a creative feminine principle (Shakti) and a masculine principle (Purusha). A dialectic of the two allows the creation and renewal of life. Maldevelopment "ruptures the co-operative unity of masculine and feminine" and renders nature and women as passive objects (1988: 6). According to Shiva, cosmological harmony provides a basis for ecological thought and action in India.

In her other writings, Shiva explores more fully the various forms of violence effected by Western science and technology. She argues in *The Violence of the Green Revolution: Ecological Degradation and Political Conflict in Punjab* (1989) that modern science and technology is the source of violence in politics and ethics. To dispute the assumption that science and technology inhabit an objective, value-free domain, Shiva details the connection between political instability and agricultural practices which deplete genetic diversity, soil fertility and water supplies.

Most recently, Shiva has explored the challenges of globalization and increasingly centralized agriculture and natural resource control. *Stolen Harvest: The Hijacking of the Global Food Supply* (2000) chronicles the effects on food production of seed patent laws and genetically engineered food. She sees the dwindling biodiversity in food production as a threat to a global food supply and as a means of further disenfranchising indigenous people and the poor. Similarly, in *Water Wars: Privatization, Pollution, and Profit* (2002), Shiva argues that greater democratization of water and other natural resources is necessary to promote sustainability and to address the causes of inter-ethnic and inter-religious hostilities and violence.

Shiva frames the issues of globalization and natural resource rights within the context of Indian religious and spiritual traditions. Water, for example, is sacred in India. She explains in *Water Wars*, "[R]ivers are seen as extensions and partial manifestation of divine gods" and that Rigvedic cosmology associates the possibility of earthly life with the release of the heavenly waters of India, god of rain.

Some of her critics counter that globalization and technologically advanced agriculture can promote expanded economic opportunities for many of the world's poor. Others believe her feminist religious ethics is grounded on an untenable view that women are inherently closer to nature than men. Nevertheless, she has become an influential and sought-after spokesperson for the international anti-globalization movement in particular, and for green politics in general. Her influence was recognized in 1993 when she was awarded the Right Livelihood Award, known by some as the Alternative Nobel Peace Prize. In addition to contributing regularly to the work of the International Forum on Globalization (formed and funded in part by activists with the San Francisco-based Foundation for Deep Ecology) she is the Director of the India-based Research Foundation for Science, Technology and Natural Resource Policy.

Molly Jensen

Further Reading

Shiva, Vandana. *Water Wars: Privatization, Pollution, and Profit.* Cambridge, MA: South End Press, 2002.

Shiva, Vandana. *Stolen Harvest: The Hijacking of the Global Food Supply.* Cambridge, MA: South End Press, 2000.

Shiva, Vandana. *Tomorrow's Biodiversity.* London: Thames and Hudson, 2000.

Shiva, Vandana, et al. *Campaign Against Biopiracy.* New Delhi: Research Foundation for Science, Technology and Ecology, 1999.

Shiva, Vandana, et al. *The Enclosure and Recovery of the Commons: Biodiversity, Indigenous Knowledge and Intellectual Property Rights.* New Delhi: Research Foundation for Science, Technology and Ecology, 1997.

Shiva, Vandana. *Captive Minds, Captive Lives.* Dehra Dun: Research for Science, Technology and Nature Resource Policy, 1995.

Shiva, Vandana, ed. *Close to Home: Women Reconnect Ecology, Health and Development Worldwide.* Philadelphia: New Society, 1994.

Shiva, Vandana, ed. *Minding Our Lives: Women from the South and North Reconnect Ecology and Health.* Philadelphia: New Society, 1993.

Shiva, Vandana. *Monocultures of the Mind: Perspective on Biodiversity and Biotechnology.* London: Zed Books, 1993.

Shiva, Vandana. *The Violence of the Green Revolution: Ecological Degradation and Political Conflict in Punjab.* Dehra Dun: Research Foundation for Science and Technology, 1989.

Shiva, Vandana. *Staying Alive: Women, Ecology and Survival in India.* London: Zed Books, 1988.

Shiva, Vandana and Maria Mies. *Ecofeminism.* London: Zed Books, 1993.

See also: Ecofeminism, Gaia Foundation and Earth Community Network; Globalization; Hinduism; Hinduism and Pollution (and adjacent), River Ganga and the Clean Ganga Campaign; India; Population and Consumption – Contemporary Religious Responses; Prakriti; Radical Environmentalism; Re-Earthing; Seeds in South Asia; United Nations' "Earth Summits".

Shomrei Adamah

Shomrei Adamah – *See* Jewish Environmentalism in North America.

Shona Women and the Mutupo Principle

When the British entered the territory of present-day Zimbabwe around the turn of the nineteenth century, the Shona and Ndebele viewed and experienced the world through the Mutupo principle. The foundational basis for the Mutupo principle is the relationality of all of existence. The principle focuses on fostering the primary relationships between animals and humans, animals and the deity, humans and humans, nature and humans, deity and humans, women and men, the dead and the living. It attempts to enumerate and approximate the ideal mode of life, which assures a sustainable future for all of existence. In this worldview women and nature are prominent participants who are viewed as equals in all matters concerned with shaping the future destiny of a people. Shona praise poetry is an example of oral sacred literature deriving out of the Mutupo worldview. It shows that, at the turn of the nineteenth century, women were givers and receivers at every level of their society.

The relationship between the clan and its Mutupo is axiomatic in the Shona worldview. This relationship is not only understood as the vantage point from which one experiences and comes to know the world, but it is also the source of a moral code that governs the nature of relationships in existence. In its myth, the Mutupo principle creates a cosmology that is non-anthropocentric, but at the same time celebrates as unique the experience of being human, female, and male in the universe. To the Shona, the mention of one's Mutupo evokes sacral meaning. It resonates with every dimension of human experience, such as worship, security, justice, love, community life, romance, praise, dance, learning, motherhood, beauty, the living, the dead, and the yet-to-be-born.

The substance of Shona praise poetry is the recitation or celebration of an individual's commendable acts. Using classical, bold, flattering, metaphoric language, one's heroic acts are described. Designed to affirm and sanction the tenets of egalitarian relationships in human living, the giving and receiving of Shona praise poetry is not an exclusive male preserve/privilege. Neither is it only for the strong and powerful. In this tradition women are givers and receivers of praise poetry, so are the weak and the powerless. An overriding theme in this wisdom literature is that the web of life is sustained by a reciprocal balance of giving and receiving. Acts of self-giving became heroic acts, symbolizing beauty, truth, joy, freedom.

The function of praise poetry is not only social but also psychological. For Shona women the social function is critical in that it is an affirmation of gender equality in the politics of bonding and solidarity. At the psychological level, praise poetry inspires and affirms the personal worth of the individual. The bold flattery and metaphorical language of Shona praise poetry celebrates commendable acts done by an individual for others. This exercise is also meant to invoke from deep within the individual an awareness of their potential and capacity to shape personal and communal destiny. Praise poetry places an individual's personal accomplishments and triumphs in a historical scheme of a people's destiny in the universe.

It is important to realize that the recitation of praise poetry does something to the poet and the receiver. Highly charged with diction, with powerful, startling metaphors, its effect is reciprocal. It confers status on both the individual who uses it and the one who receives it. It raises the individual to the level of the victor one celebrates. Praise poetry does not merely say something, it does something, psychologically and socially.

At the individual level it serves to build the self-esteem of its object, creating a sense of identity and worth in that person. Mutupo praise poetry is used to excite, delight and affirm. Shona women as agents shaping personal and communal destinies were subjects of this sacred literature. They were expected to give of self, as much as they expected to receive in the web of existence. Even in matters of intimacy, they celebrated the art of giving as they did of receiving. For example, excerpts from love praise poems for the Tembo Mazvimbakupa (Zebra/Lion) celebrate giving and receiving equally for both woman and man:

Hekani Matendera
Maita VaMupanedende
Zvaitwa Mupiyaniswa
Muuya wangu munakunaku
Anenge muvsisivi wouchi
Kagwedu kenyama kanosara pasi
Maita VaMuroro
Hakani VaNyemba, Mubvana wa Chivazve.

Well done Zebra!
Hail, you who gives permission.
Thank you, Your Highness, generous giver.
My deepest gratitude, to you the interlaced one,
My elegant, exceedingly beautiful woman,
Who is like distilled, liquid honey.
Even my little piece of juicy steak is surpassed!
Thank you You Muroro,
Hail, you who belongs to the Nyemba Dynasty,
You mother of my child, yet forever daughter of Chivazve clan.

Male Tembo Mazimbakupa

VaChipanegombe, mombe njuma,
Mukanditi, "Siya amai,
Tizoswera tichirezvana"
Nanhasi nyama tinongodya,
Nehorwe zvose zviripo,
Uchi tinongotamba nahwo,
Maita Matendera.

You who give by the big ladle, you hornless bull,
You invited me, "Leave your mother,
So that we can spend our days in each other's arms."

To this very day we are feasting on meat.
Francolins we have aplenty.
As for honey, we are swimming in it.
You have performed wonderfully, Matendera.
(Pongweni 1996: 126–34)

Mutupo praise poetry as a source among many encapsulates the Shona views on women in society. In this blueprint, women are to be givers and receivers at all levels of social experience. In this worldview all existing entities – women, men, nature, deity, animals – attain freedom and bliss through giving and receiving.

Tumani Nyajeka

Further Reading
Chigwedere, Aeneas. *The Karanga Empire*. London: Macmillan, 1985.
Pongweni, Alec. *Shona Praise Poetry as Role Negotiation*. Gweru: Mambo Press, 1996.
Ruether, Rosemary Radford. *Gaia and God*. San Francisco: Harper, 1992.
See also: African Religions and Nature Conservation; Animals.

Shoshone (Western North America)

Western Shoshone territory extends from what is now northern Wyoming into eastern Nevada and central Idaho, part of the North American cultural area known as the Great Basin. Great Basin cultures were based on water, the most vital component in a primarily desert region. The traditional Western Shoshone were also a nomadic people acclimatized to this diverse environment, seasonally harvesting such foodstuffs as seeds, berries, roots, piñon nuts, and other plant foods growing at known locations. Group names were commonly derived from geographic features and especially predominant local food resources.

Bighorn sheep were the most important hoofed mammal in the economy. Hunters monitored bighorn movements to determine the best spots in which to construct hunting blinds. The Western Shoshone also hunted dove, mockingbird, sage hen, quail, waterfowl, and rabbits, another important source of food and fur harvested seasonally. Black-tailed jackrabbits were found throughout Western Shoshone territory; white-tailed rabbits were scarcer. Two species of cottontail were also taken, as well as pocket gophers and ground squirrels. Antelope were generally hunted by communal driving. The Western Shoshone hunted both antelope and rabbits in an alternating schedule, giving them time to recover. The drives were one of the few occasions during which large groups of people gathered for festivals. Festivals, which generally included the Round Dance, were held whenever food was abundant. Although primarily performed for pleasure, the Round Dance afforded opportunity for courtship and, in various localities, was thought to produce rain. During drives headmen, referred to as chiefs or directors, served only as long as their expertise was needed. To help with the drive a shaman could magically entice the animals along a V-shaped runway to the center of a corral constructed of brush, stone, and poles.

Western Shoshone spirituality is interwoven throughout their lives and culture. Their spirituality provides them with a direct link with the supernatural, and spiritual power is gained through visions and dreams. There are three kinds of Shoshone shamans: specialists who cure specific ailments; individuals whose powers only benefit themselves; and those with general curing ability. There are also two types of dreamed power: one involving a spirit helper, an animal or bird or natural object; another power acquired in dreams carried the ability to be expert in other conventional roles such as hunter, gatherer, warrior, etc.

Dr. Richard Stoffle has completed some of the best and most recent ethnography on Great Basin peoples that focuses on the principles underlying their cultures. A primary foundation of Western Shoshone culture is the concept of power, how it flows in the world, and what humans should do to maintain a balance with it. Supernatural power is viewed as the best explanation for the cultural significance of all things, how these things relate to one another, and how they are intellectually integrated. The Western Shoshone employ the concept of a living universe, a universe that is alive in the same way that humans are alive. It has physically discrete elements as well as power. A few general statements can be made about power:

1) Power exists throughout the universe, but like differences in human strength, it varies in intensity from element to element.
2) Power varies in its uses; it determines what different elements can do.
3) Power is networked. Different elements are connected, disconnected, and reconnected in different ways, occurring largely at the will of the elements with the power.
4) Power derives from the moment of creation and permeates the universe like spiderwebs ramifying power relationships between humans and the environment into one spiritual conformity.
5) Power exists and can move between three levels of the universe: upper (where powerful anthropomorphic beings live); middle (where people now live); and lower, where monsters reside.

Power disperses through networks of relationships among the elements of the universe, including types of air, water, rocks, minerals, topographic features, plants, and animals. Each element and its types make their own relationships, much like people do and for similar reasons of purpose and attraction. Elements have different personalities, intensities, and relationships with people and other elements, relationships that resemble spiderwebs. At various points in the web power gathers, producing powerful places which humans recognize and employ in rituals. Power flows like water and often follows water, yet they two are not identical. Human intervention can alter these networks of power; thus, the Western Shoshone are very concerned about the proper uses of natural resources (elements) of their environments. Improper uses can result in loss of access to such resources. Therefore, the Western Shoshone believe they must establish respectful relations with their environment and its resources in order to survive and maintain the balance of the universe. Every Western Shoshone child is admonished to explain his or her actions before touching, picking, hunting, or otherwise disrupting the element's balance: "do not move a stone without asking its permission"; "a plant will not give medicine or nourishment unless you explain why it will be picked"; "animals killed without their permission will not give themselves to a hunter again"; "never speak loud on the mountain or throw rocks in the water"; and "think of why things are as they are before you change them for personal needs." Rituals accompany all changes in relations between humans and elements of the universe in order that an essential balance be preserved.

For the Western Shoshone the physical and spiritual interactions among people, places, and resources create a phenomenon which anthropologists now call the cultural landscape, an idea that people, through repeated interactions with their surroundings, develop images or ideas of the land and share an understanding of its form and content that is transferred over generations. In the cultural landscape of the Great Basin of the Western Shoshone, power moved over the open deserts, along a web of waterways and connected the mountains to the sky and the depths of the Earth. Establishing and maintaining spiritual relationships between the elements in the Basin enabled the Western Shoshone to develop a nomadic lifestyle able to follow the waxing and waning of resources, to utilize their diverse landscape, and to maintain an essential balance of respect for the resources that enabled survival in a very challenging environment.

Deward E. Walker, Jr.

Further Reading

Azevedo, D. and L. Warren, ed. *Handbook of North American Indians*, vol. 11, "Great Basin." Washington, D.C.: Smithsonian Institution, 1986.

"Basin-Plateau Aboriginal Sociopolitical Groups." *Bureau of American Ethnology Bulletin* 120. Washington,

1938. (Reprinted: University of Utah Press, Salt Lake City, 1970.)
Culture Element Distributions, XXIII: "Northern and Gosiute Shoshone." *University of California Anthropological Records* 8:3 (Berkeley, 1943), 263–392.
Culture Element Distributions, XIII: "Nevada Shoshone." *University of California Anthropological Records* 4:2 (Berkeley, 1941), 209–360.
Steward, Julian H. "Ethnological Reconnaissance among the Desert Shoshoni." In *Exploration and Field Work of the Smithsonian Institution in 1936*. Washington, 1937.
Stoffle, Richard. "The Concept of 'Power' in Numic and Yuman Epistemology." *High Plains Applied Anthropologist* 23:2 (2002), 172–93.
See also: Bison Restoration and Native American Traditions; Lakota; Paiute Culture; Spirit of Sage Council.

Siam's Forest Monasteries

Forest monasticism has been established in Siam, currently called Thailand, for at least eight centuries. According to the historical record, this tradition was transmitted from Sri Lanka in the thirteenth century. Since then the Siamese *Sangha* (monastic order) has been categorized into village dwelling (*gamavasi*) and forest dwelling (*araññavasi*). While the former were entrusted with the task of studying scriptures, the latter were concerned primarily with practicing meditation.

The tradition of forest monasticism can be traced back to the time of the Buddha, who regularly admonished the monks to live in seclusion and practice meditation for the sake of enlightenment. Many monks developed the custom of forest wandering and living in caves for intensive periods of practice. Although permanent monasteries were eventually established where monks could settle for long periods, many of them were built in the forests, far from the villages and towns. Over time, these forest dwellings developed into a distinct tradition, one quite different from village dwelling.

In forest monasteries, monks are expected to live austerely and to observe the monastic code (*Vinaya*) strictly. Contact with the outer world is discouraged, except for daily alms rounds in nearby villages and occasional teachings, while periodic wandering in remote forests is an important part of the spiritual training of such monks. The forest is conducive to meditation practice because its solitude not only brings calmness to the mind but also helps develop insight into the profound nature of life and the world. According to the Buddha, the external nature or environment is inseparable from the inner nature of mind. Contemplating the true characteristics of the former can lead to the realization of the latter's true nature, and thus enlightenment.

Forest monasticism in Siam faded into obscurity 200 years ago for various reasons, including the attempt to rationalize Buddhism in response to modernity. It was not until the 1960s that forest monks drew the attention of and won respect from modern, urban, educated elites. This was due to the growth of the forest monk movement led by Ajaan Man Phuurithatto (1870–1949). Throughout his monastic life Ajaan Man, along with his disciples, wandered extensively in the forests and penetrated into remote areas, many of which were never visited by Buddhist monks before. Many of his disciples later built forest monasteries in various parts of the country. With their strict practice and spiritual achievement, respect toward forest monks spread extensively through the villages, then into the cities and eventually even Bangkok.

Buddhadasa Bhikkhu (1906–1993) is another major contributor to the revival of Siamese forest monasticism. His monastery, Suan Mokkh, in the south of Thailand, has been a distinguished attempt to restore monasticism as practiced in the Buddha's time when monks were close to nature, meditated amidst nature, and developed insight from nature. He also combined scripture study and social awareness with meditation practice, instead of the sole focus on meditation followed by most forest monks.

During the past few decades, forest monasteries have increased in number. They are frequented by people from all walks of life who come with different purposes ranging from practicing meditation to merit making and seeking amulets and sacred objects from the forest monks who are believed to possess supernormal powers.

Apart from their spiritual value, forest monasteries in Siam nowadays play a significant role in ecology. Amidst the widespread deforestation, forest monasteries are rare places where forests have been preserved. Many forest monks not only conserve forests in their own temples, but have also become leaders in protecting community forests in various parts of the country.

Phra Paisal Visalo

Further Reading

Tambiah, Stanley J. *The Buddhist Saints of the Forest and the Cult of Amulets*. Cambridge: Cambridge University Press, 1984.
Taylor, James L. *Forest Monks and the Nation-State*. Singapore: Institute of Southeast Asian Studies, 1993.
Tiyavanich, Kamala. *Forest Recollections*. Honolulu: University of Hawai'i Press, 1999.

See also: Buddhadása Bhikkhu; Buddhism – Engaged; Nhat Hanh, Thich; Payutto, Phra Dhammapitaka; Southeast Asia; Sivaraksa, Sulak; Thai Buddhist Monks.

Sierra Club

Founded in 1892, largely through the labor of John Muir in order to protect the wildlands of California's Sierra Nevada Mountains, the Sierra Club has become a recognized name worldwide for its efforts in conservation. Though steering a course free of any formal religious affiliation, the organization has nonetheless been influenced in its decisions and bolstered by the strength of its founders' and members' religious perceptions, beliefs and identities.

It was Muir's mix of sacred metaphor, along with a perception of the aesthetic, spiritual and intrinsic value of wilderness, which served as a fundamental inspiration for the Club. The mountains were the "cathedral" that John Muir trafficked, and nature was forever his house of worship, as he described in *My First Summer in the Sierra* (1911): "In our best times everything turns into religion, all the world seems a church and the mountains altars" (Muir 1987: 250). His pilgrimages in the Sierra Nevada Mountains led him to champion their protection, for they were his place of revelation, where God became visible:

> Every hidden cell is throbbing with music and life, every fibre thrilling like harp strings, while incense is ever flowing for the balsam bells and leaves. No wonder the hills and groves were God's first temples, and the more they are cut down and hewn into cathedrals and churches, the farther off and dimmer seems the Lord himself (Muir 1987: 146).

Remnants of Muir's Protestant upbringing are still evident in such passages and he continued to use metaphors borrowed from Christianity throughout his life. Recent scholarship, however, has found his religious beliefs had more affinity with pantheism, animism, and Daoism, although during his time, Muir's religious sentiments remained largely unknown, leading Stephen Fox to conclude:

> Muir lived in a Christian society and wrote for a Christian readership. Not wishing to offend, he generally kept the precise nature of his religious ideas to himself, confining them to journals, letters, and private discussions (Fox 1981: 80).

This may help to explain why for Muir and later generations of the Sierra Club, the spirituality of the movement has been complicated and often obscure, perhaps especially to outsiders, more the subject of conversation around campfires during wilderness outings than in Club publications and position papers.

Muir was, of course, a fervent evangelist for what has been called the "out-of-doors gospel of wilderness." Attentive readers of his writings have long perceived something other than orthodox Christianity animating them. Muir trekked through what he called a "terrestrial eternity" in the California hills, urging those who shared his vision to join him in proclaiming, not a kingdom in heaven, but a kingdom of Earth. For Muir, the sacred was woven into earthly life, and he expressed this famously in his metaphysics of interdependence:

> When we try to pick out anything by itself we find that it is bound fast by a thousand invisible cords that cannot be broken to everything else in the universe. I fancy I can hear a heart beating in every crystal, in every grain of sand and see a wise plan in the making and shaping and placing of every one of them. All seems to be dancing to divine music . . . (John Muir Papers, University of the Pacific: Journal, 27 July 1869, in Fox 1981: 291).

This worldview was echoed a century later in *The Sierra Club: A Guide*:

> The history of the Sierra Club is the history of an idea . . . Wild places are not just inconvenient parcels of land to be exploited for human use; they are – along with humans themselves – integral parts of a universe in which everything is hitched to everything else. That was John Muir's creed, and it is what we believe today (Carr and Foster 1989: 48).

While such metaphysics of interdependence have animated the Club for generations, its mission statement evolved with the times, along with new challenges and perceptions. The Sierra Club's mission, as signaled in its incorporation documents, was:

> to explore, enjoy, and render accessible the mountain regions of the Pacific Coast; to publish authentic information concerning them [and] to enlist the support and cooperation of the people and the government in preserving the forests and other natural features of the Sierra Nevada Mountains (in Cohen 1988: 9).

At the time, the notions of "rendering accessible" and "preserving" worked in tandem, and the primary interest of the Club was to create and maintain national parks as "scenic resources" as opposed to economic properties. More importantly, the parks were to be sites of spiritual insight. As Muir once put it, "The clearest way into the Universe is through a forest wilderness" (Muir 1954: 312), and this sort of perception undergirds his and much of the Club's subsequent spiritual epistemology: to hear the divine music, one must pilgrimage into wilderness.

The Sierra Club therefore became famous for its "outings" (also known as High Trips) – backcountry excursions into the stunning wilderness areas of California – trailblazing, mountaineering, and seeking direct communion with nature. The outings functioned not only to bind together the community of faith but also to evoke a reverence for wildlands and empower members to ethical action, namely, the defense of wild places. Indeed, for Muir, domestication of sheep, humans, and other animals was a form of desecration. When describing wild mountain sheep Muir glowed; but tamed sheep he dismissed as "hooved locusts." Likewise, he passionately believed that the "the gross heathenism of civilization," which destroys "nature, and poetry, and all that is spiritual," could be purged from the body by "a good hard trip" (in Fox 1981: 13–14), for what both men and sheep need is "a little pure wildness" (in Oelschlaeger 1991: 200).

The outings thus offered not only adventure but also spiritual therapy for humans who had become spiritually impoverished by domesticated lives in oppressive, profane cities. "Service trips" were later added to help clean up or restore wildlands desecrated by those who visited them without the proper wilderness reverence and ethics. Empowered by the wilderness, Muir and his progeny returned to the city and struggled to influence government land-management practices.

The Sierra Club's first major public battle, led by Muir, involved plans to dam Hetch Hetchy valley in Yosemite National Park in order to provide water for the city of San Francisco. The United States Forest Service Chief, Gifford Pinchot, and other "progressive conservationists" favored the dam, which they considered a "wise use" of public land for the benefit of all. Muir viewed the dam as a sacrilege and its proponents as "temple destroyers" (in Cohen 1988: 28). Muir died a year after losing the battle to save the valley from inundation, but the Sierra Club gained a reputation as a strong voice contesting the unrestrained rush toward economic development by asserting that the nonmaterial benefits of nature outweigh the social benefits that might result from such desecration.

Many ironies inhere to the Club's preservationist philosophy and spirituality. Fighting to keep the National Parks immune from ski resorts, dams and timber interests has often involved compromises in which the Club agreed not to contest the projects outside of park boundaries, oftentimes sacrificing these areas before realizing the consequences. The rise of automobile use in post-war America, which brought more visitors to the Parks to experience these scenic wonderlands, delivered a different type of tourist who demanded new roads and amenities that compromised the terrain. In 1951, partly in response to these trends, the Club mission statement was altered: "rendering accessible" became "preserve." This reflected anxiety about the impacts of the growing number of tourists, as well as the long-standing ambivalence of mountaineers and wilderness lovers toward those outside of the wilderness church. As Linda Graber observed, "wilderness purists," including Sierra Club members, "resent the outsider's presence in sacred space because his 'inferior' mode of perception" leads such a person to "desecrate wilderness" (Graber 1976: 28, 81).

Throughout the 1950s in the United States the very idea of wilderness management was being reformulated, and the Club was instrumental in this process. In 1949 Aldo Leopold's classic, *A Sand County Almanac*, was published and reviewed in the Sierra Club *Bulletin*. Dave Brower, who would go on to be a crucial and controversial figure in the Club, attributed his change in outlook from recreational ideas of wilderness to ecological ideas of wilderness directly to his reading of this book (Cohen 1988: 117). The *Bulletin* itself, under Brower's leadership, also changed its emphasis, from articles about outings to issues of wilderness policy. Biennial wilderness conferences, beginning in 1949, were hosted by the Sierra Club and brought together several conservation groups and government organizations to hammer out common strategies and goals. Bestor Robinson, a Sierra Club member and member of the advisory committee to the secretary of the interior at the time, recognized two different philosophies emerging among participants at these conferences. For some, "the sole function of wilderness is to contribute to the inspiration and wellbeing of people," while for those more in synch with Muir himself, "wilderness itself has a personality – a soul – and should be preserved for its own sake" (in Cohen 1988: 128).

Brower, whose term as executive director began in 1952, and Richard Leonard, a long-time member and Club President in 1953, spearheaded another campaign reminiscent of the Hetch Hetchy battle, calling for the protection of Dinosaur National Monument in Utah in the face of another dam proposal. While the Club argued that the dam was not the only economic alternative, a central aspect of the campaign was to portray Dinosaur as a sacred place. The religious nature of the language used is evident in Brower's plea to Congress:

The axiom for protecting the Park System is to consider that it is dedicated country, hallowed ground to leave as beautiful as we have found it, and not country in which man should be so impressed with himself that he tries to improve God's handiwork (in Cohen 1988: 182).

Wallace Stegner was successfully recruited to edit a photographic book about the site to sway popular support and advertisements were placed in newspapers. These sorts of publications would become a powerful tool of persuasion for the Sierra Club in the future – particularly notable was the stunning landscape photography of Ansel Adams, who was himself motivated by his spiritual connection to the land. The victory at Dinosaur was considered a "David over Goliath" event (Cohen 1988: 160), and the Club achieved recognition as a political force to be reckoned with. However, because the Club did not oppose projects outside of National Parks or Monuments at the time, it did not fight the proposal to build a dam at Glen Canyon on the Colorado River. This decision was later lamented by Brower, who vowed never again to restrict his concern in such a way, thus marking a further broadening of the mission of the Club.

Many of the disagreements between the Sierra Club and the government, including a decisive break with the United States Forest Service in 1960, had much to do with nature-as-sacred religion. Sierra Club members such as Brower, among others, believed that in saving the wilderness, they were protecting the only thing that, in the final analysis, could save humankind (Cohen 1988: 257). According to Nancy Newhall – who wrote the text to complement Ansel Adams' breathtaking photography in the Sierra Club's *This is the American Earth* (1960) – America still held Edenic possibilities and in the freedom of wildness there were "answers to more questions than we yet know how to ask" (Newhall in Cohen 1988: 258). Club publications began to attract critical acclaim and some reviewers recognized their religious dimensions. John B. Oakes of the *New York Times*, for example, wrote about *This is the American Earth* that, "Essentially it is a song of praise to the Earth, a prayer and supplication for its endurance. We can use such songs and prayers" (in Cohen 1988: 259).

The Glen Canyon Dam taught difficult lessons. When proposals for further dams in the Grand Canyon were submitted, the Club responded with a barrage of advertising, both in the form of new books and newspaper ads taken out in the *Washington Post*, the *Wall Street Journal* and the *New York Times*. Responding to the supposed recreational benefits of lakes for Canyon tourism, one memorable Sierra Club advertisement in the summer of 1966 asked: "Should We Also Flood The Sistine Chapel So Tourists Can Get Nearer The Ceiling?" (poster reproduced in *The Sierra Club: A Guide* (1989: graphics insert). This kind of publicity resulted in the rapid growth of club membership and enhanced the Club's reputation for challenging commercial interests and government policy. The Sierra Club's publishing program continued to play an important role in the latter decades of the twentieth century by publishing not only ecological texts but also works by prominent figures promoting nature spirituality of one form or another, including books by Thomas Berry, Wendell Berry, Jerry Mander, Theodore Roszak, and Paul Shepard.

As Club membership became more geographically diverse, advocacy efforts expanded to include a wide variety of environmental issues, such as population growth, energy use, pollution, and human rights. In the late 1990s, the Club began to recognize the potential alliance between religious institutions – particularly Christian ones, whom Club leaders had previously written off as unimportant – and environmental protection. In 1997, for example, Carl Pope, who was then the executive director of the Sierra Club, attended a symposium at the University of California campus in Santa Barbara. On this occasion, Bartholomew I, the patriarch of the Orthodox Christian Church, broke new ground in labeling environmental degradation a sin. In his address to those gathered, Pope apologized for the failure of environmental activists to reach out to the religious community. He later wrote,

> After all, many of the environmental challenges we face today are moral ones. The sin of pride tempts us to imagine that the world exists for our use alone, and Mammon, the god of greed, leads us down the path to environmental destruction (Pope 1998: 14).

Pope also compared environmental issues to the social changes brought about during the civil rights era in which religious organizations led the way. "Yet," he stated,

> for almost 30 years most professional environmentalists stubbornly, almost proudly, denied the need to reach out to the religious community . . . We failed to realize – as some eminent scientists now tell us – that science and religion offer two distinct approaches to knowledge, and that neither has a monopoly on the truth . . . We acted as if we could save life on Earth without the same institutions through which we save ourselves (1998: 14).

Indeed, some Club members have joined their activism and their faith, as is evidenced by various collaborations on urban sprawl, calls for ending commercial logging, political lobbying, and promotion of renewable energy. One example of such collaboration, from a recent article in the Sierra Club Newsletter, noted that priest and Sierra Club member Father Charles Morris conducted a dedication and prayer ceremony for the installation of solar panels and a wind turbine (Heim-Jonson 2001).

No group is immune from criticism, and the Sierra Club has often been criticized sharply from within the environmental movement and from without, and internal debates are likewise often fierce. One long-standing external critique applies not only to the Sierra Club but to the wilderness ideal itself: that the notion of a pristine wilderness absent of humans inappropriately separates human beings from nature. This separation occurs not merely in an abstract, philosophical sense. It separates some humans physically, as with the National Parks model that the Sierra Club helped to spawn, which facilitated the removal (sometimes by murder) of Aboriginal peoples from their land. Moreover, critics argue, with the globalization of the National Park's wilderness ideal and model, deracination from the land and cultural genocide has often followed the development of wilderness-oriented National Parks. Many contemporary Sierra Club and National Park advocates, however, recognize the validity of such criticisms and are now promoting community-based models of environmental protection that promote both biological and cultural diversity. The United Nations' biosphere reserve model, which endeavors to incorporate rather than exile people while protecting biologically sensitive areas, suggests that the criticisms of the inherited wilderness ideal have been undergoing their own globalization.

Other criticisms are explicitly or implicitly religious. Some critics of the Club argue its members care more for nature than people and even promote an irrational if not pagan spirituality that is an affront to God. Meanwhile some avowedly Pagan environmentalists believe the Club has strayed from Muir's spirituality and uncompromising passion to preserve wilderness. Such perceptions have contributed to the emergence and proliferation of radical environmental groups, such as Earth First! and the Earth Liberation Front. This has also served to inspire internal reform movements in the Club that endeavor to return to and revitalize the original charismatic vision of the Club's founder.

The most important of these revitalization movements has been the "John Muir Sierrans," which was founded in 1993 and funded in part by David Brower through organizations he launched after being ousted from the Sierra Club. Led by Chad Hanson (who eventually served on the Sierra Club board) and David Orr, the John Muir Sierrans ran a slate that helped turn the Club in a more radical, biocentric direction. They won membership approval for a strong position against commercial logging on public land in 1996, despite strong opposition from figures they considered the conservative "old guard" of the Club. And trying to reverse the earlier, much lamented capitulation over Glen Canyon, they even urged the draining of Lake Powell, which had been created by the Dam. Moreover, they pushed strong, uncompromising positions across the environmental spectrum, in ways considered misguided, divisive, and counterproductive by more pragmatic Club members. By the turn of the twenty-first century, however, the Sierrans and other biocentric activists, such as David Foreman (co-founder of Earth First!) and Captain Paul Watson (of the Sea Shepherd Conservation Society) had come close to controlling the Sierra Club board. This reflected a large increase in membership support for strong if not radical positions, and arguably, for biocentric spirituality.

In the early twenty-first century internal Club politics continued to be divided largely along the lines of those who considered themselves pragmatic (some of whom were more theistic in their religious sensibilities and anthropocentric in their axiology) and those who confessed that nature is sacred and believed that compromise is cowardly and taboo. Another fault line persisted between environmentalists with a strong social justice agenda, who considered morally wrong many approaches to population stabilization and reduction, including anti-immigration policies, and more biocentric activists, such as Paul Watson, who argued that nonhuman life should not suffer because anthropocentric social justice agendas hinder strong advocacy for policies that would reduce human numbers.

Criticisms from environmental radicals both inside and outside of the Club have helped push it to take increasingly strong positions in defense of the Earth's biodiversity. Left unclear is whether the Club's new-found interest in building bridges to religious communities – many of which have strong anthropocentric, social justice-oriented concerns – will broaden the Club's appeal and influence or exacerbate internal tensions, some of which are religion-related. If the latter dynamic proves decisive, nature-related religion could, ironically, weaken the Club's environmental protection efforts.

Gavin Van Horn
Bron Taylor

Further Reading

Adams, Ansel and Nancy Newhall. *This Is the American Earth*. San Francisco: Sierra Club Books, 1960.

Berry, Thomas. *The Dream of the Earth*. San Francisco: Sierra Club Books, 1988.

Berry, Wendell. *The Unsettling of America: Culture and Agriculture*. San Francisco: Sierra Club, 1977.

Carr, Patrick and Lynn Foster. "Coming into the Club." In Patrick Carr, ed. *The Sierra Club: A Guide*. San Francisco: Sierra Club, 1989.

Cohen, Michael P. *The History of the Sierra Club, 1892–1970*. San Francisco: Sierra Club Books, 1988.

Fox, Stephen. *John Muir and His Legacy: The American Conservation Movement*. Boston: Little, Brown and Co., 1981.

Graber, Linda. *Wilderness as Sacred Space*. Washington, D.C.: Association of American Geographers, 1976.

Heim-Jonson, Sarah W. "In Good Faith." *The Planet Newsletter* (September 2001), www.sierraclub.org/planet/200109/commonground.asp.

Holmes, Steven J. *The Young John Muir: An Environmental Biography*. Madison: University of Wisconsin Press, 1999.

Johnson, Trebbe and Vitale Stefano. "The Second Creation Story." *Sierra* 83:6 (1998), 50–6.

Mander, Jerry. *In the Absence of the Sacred: The Failure of Technology and the Survival of the Indian Nations*. San Francisco: Sierra Club, 1991.

Muir, John. *My First Summer in the Sierra*. New York: Penguin Books, 1987 (1911).

Muir, John. *The Wilderness World of John Muir*. Edwin Way Teal, ed. Boston: Houghton Mifflin, 1954.

Nash, Roderick Frazier. *Wilderness and the American*

Mind. 2nd edn. 1967; reprint, New Haven: Yale University Press, 1973.
Oelschlaeger, Max. *The Idea of Wilderness: From Prehistory to the Age of Ecology*. New Haven: Yale University Press, 1991.
Pope, Carl. "Reaching Beyond Ourselves." *Sierra* 83:6 (November/December 1998), 14–15.
Roszak, Theodore, Mary E. Gomes and Allen D. Kanner, eds. *Ecopsychology: Restoring the Earth, Healing the Mind*. San Francisco: Sierra Club, 1995.
Sears, John. *Sacred Places: American Tourist Attractions in the Nineteenth Century*. New York and Oxford: Oxford University Press, 1989.
Shepard, Paul. *Nature and Madness*. San Francisco: Sierra Club Books, 1982.
Spence, Mark David. *Dispossessing the Wilderness: Indian Removal and the Making of the National Parks*. New York: Oxford University Press, 1999.
Turner, Frederick. *Rediscovering America: John Muir in His Time and Ours*. New York: Viking, 1985.

See also: Adams, Ansel; Bartholomew, Ecumenical Patriarch; Berry, Thomas; Berry, Wendell; Biocentric Religion – A Call for; Biosphere Reserves and World Heritage Sites; Brower, David; Leopold, Aldo; Manifest Destiny; Muir, John; National Parks and Monuments (United States); Shepard, Paul; Watson, Paul – and the Sea Shepherd Conservation Society; Wilderness Religion; Wilderness Society.

Sierra Treks

Begun in the late 1960s, Sierra Treks exemplifies a new form of environmental concern within evangelical Christianity. The letterhead of Sierra Treks' parent organization, Wild Hope, proclaims Wild Hope's Sierra Treks and Littlefoot Expeditions' programs to be "Wilderness Trips for People" and "People Trips for Wilderness." Combining environmental concern with Christian faith, this small outdoor/public lands advocacy group combines strong belief in the value of wilderness with the idea of God as Creator/Redeemer.

Started in 1968 by Robin Wainwright for the Mount Hermon Association, an evangelical camp and conference center in California, Sierra Treks initially combined wilderness camping/fishing trips with evangelistic Bible studies. Given Wainwright's Boy Scout background and Mount Hermon's conservative Christian ideology, trips until 1973 were open only to boys. Sierra Treks expanded and developed its more advocacy-oriented environmental mission under the leadership of Dave Willis, hired as the program's director in 1972. Willis brought a Sierra Club and Outward Bound approach to Sierra Treks, as well as a developing Christian faith that led him to a Bible-based theology that recognizes God's love for all creation.

In 1973, Sierra Treks expanded to include both girls and coed wilderness trips. The activities of all Sierra Treks continued to be modeled after Outward Bound courses. Greater expansion occurred in 1974 when Willis began hiring staff shaped by the environmental movement and progressive evangelical Christianity. Sierra Treks began offering winter mountain courses in 1976 and winter desert treks in 1980. Over the years Sierra Treks has offered courses for colleges, seminaries, churches, women's groups, couples' groups, high school and junior high students, youth-at-risk, seminars for rock climbers, trips for the hearing-impaired, and others. Trips have been in the Sierra Nevada Range in California, the Cascade Mountains in Oregon and Washington, Joshua Tree National Monument in California, the Oregon/California Siskiyou Mountains, and elsewhere.

Sierra Treks and Dave Willis left Mount Hermon in 1983. By 1985 Sierra Treks added a sister organization, Littlefoot Expeditions, that offers custom trips for targeted individuals to endangered wildlands. Politicians, government officials, environmental leaders, media representatives, and foundation staff have all participated in Littlefoot Expeditions, becoming allies in ongoing efforts to protect the areas they visit by experiencing those areas personally. Many years of Littlefoot trips in southwestern Oregon's Soda Mountain backcountry led to President William Jefferson Clinton's June 2000 proclamation of the Cascade-Siskiyou National Monument.

The nonprofit organization Wild Hope was formed in 1988 to incorporate both Sierra Treks and Littlefoot Expeditions. Sierra Treks remains the "Wilderness Trips for People" branch in which students participate in Outward-Bound-type wilderness trips encouraging Christian faith development. According to Dave Willis, Sierra Treks believes in the "value of a wilderness experience for its own sake, while attempting to point to a God who is faithful to all creation." Littlefoot Expeditions remain the "People Trips for Wilderness" branch, emphasizing public lands advocacy. During the late 1970s and early 1980s, Sierra Treks ran up to thirty wilderness trips per year. As Willis has become more involved in wildlands advocacy, more Littlefoot Expeditions (and fewer Sierra Treks) have been offered.

The environmental concern common to both the trip program and the advocacy branch combines a deep belief in the value of wilderness with an all-creation theology. This theology proclaims hope in a Creator/Redeemer God whose faithfulness to humanity is inseparable from faithfulness to all creation.

Lois Ann Lorentzen

Further Reading
Abbey, Edward. *Desert Solitaire: A Season in the Wilderness*. New York: Ballantine, 1968.

The Bible. Genesis 1–9, Job 38–42, Psalm 24, John 1:1–18, Romans 8:18–25, Colossians 1:15–20.

Leopold, Aldo. *A Sand County Almanac*. Oxford University Press, 1949.

Lorentzen, Lois Ann. "Paradise Paved." *Sojourners* 29:6 (2000), 28–36.

Nash, Roderick. *Wilderness and the American Mind*. New Haven, CT: Yale University Press, 1982.

Wilkinson, Loren, ed. *Earthkeeping: Christian Stewardship of Natural Resources*. Grand Rapids, MI: William B. Eerdmans Publishing, 1980.

See also: Au Sable Institute; Biblical Foundations for Christian Stewardship; Christianity (7i) – An Evangelical Perspective on Faith and Nature; Evangelical Environmental Network; Kreuger, Fred; Religious Campaign for Forest Conservation; Restoring Eden; Stewardship; Wilderness Religion; Wilderness Rites of Passage.

Sikhism

According to Sikh tradition, after many years of traveling throughout India and preaching Sikh doctrine, Guru Nanak, the first Sikh Guru, founded and settled in the town of Kartarpur in modern-day Pakistan. Here he put into practice his teachings about honest labor, truthfulness, and charity by taking up a life of tending land. The Guru's first disciples followed their master's teachings and example and like him many became farmers. Though one discerns in these traditions no overt statements about nature itself, clearly there are implications which have become manifest in today's Sikhism. Nature (*qudrat*) and all of its manifest glory is one of the most obvious creations of Akal Purakh (God) and as such must be responsibly tended with care and respect.

Over the centuries land and nature have directly provided many Sikhs their livelihood. Such reverential attitudes toward these thus require no concise positions or statements as these are familiar enough to be taken for granted. Indeed, within the normative Sikh Code of Conduct finalized in 1945 and published in 1950, the *Sikh Rahit Maryada*, as well as within earlier, eighteenth- and nineteenth-century Sikh *rahit* literature from which the *Rahit Maryada* derives, such statements are altogether absent. This is worth pointing out as even today congregations of Sikhs throughout the world often refer to the *Rahit* literature to position themselves *vis à vis* other Sikh congregations or the state on such controversial issues as Sikh identity and abortion among others.

Sikh thoughts toward nature may nevertheless be distinguished from within the principal source of Sikh theology, the Adi Granth, the Sikh scripture, in which we find the hymns of the Sikh Gurus. I do not mean to reduce Sikhism to its scripture, of course, but an "ecological exegesis" of the Adi Granth has nevertheless provided many Sikhs a number of ways with which to begin addressing the dawning environmental crisis. This is logical from the Sikh perspective as it is a firm Sikh belief that the scripture is not merely a book bound with the wisdom of the Sikh Gurus but that within its pages one can discover the mystical presence of Akal Purakh. In many symbolic ways in other words the scripture is alive and must be treated with the respect accorded to both living, human gurus as well as that bestowed upon the eternal Guru or God. Its more popular title therefore is the *Guru* Granth Sahib, the Granth as the eternal Guru. And so it comes as no surprise that every pamphlet or article delineating Sikh attitudes toward ecology begins here.

As a farmer in his later years, Guru Nanak's hymns abound with scenes from the agricultural rhythm of the year, particularly scenes reminiscent of seeding and harvest times. Sensitive to natural beauty Guru Nanak speaks of deer living and eating in the forest, of swimming fish, birds singing in the mango trees, and of snakes slithering along the ground (*Guru Nanak, gauri bairagan* 19; Adi Granth 157) all of which contribute to the wonderful ecological balance established by Akal Purakh. The eternal Guru is himself described in ecological terms:

"He is the Master Blossomer, He who has made the world bloom; He makes the Universe blossom forth, fresh and green. He binds together [and separates] both water and land. Great is [the glory of] the Lord Creator" (Guru Nanak, *Siri Rag* 28:1; Adi Granth 24).

In this light it is thus logical that natural scenes illuminate the first Guru's theology and are deployed as more than just symbols. It is through nature that one may discover the mystical presence of Akal Purakh who is not just the Creator but is also immanent throughout creation. Human beings are intimately connected to nature and the entire cosmos in this cycle as within them too the pious Sikh may experience the presence of the eternal Guru. Guru Nanak's hymn in *rag dhanasari*, for example, implies as much in its symbolic ritual of *aarti*, the waving of lamps in the presence of a divine image. Here the natural universe participates in the worship of Akal Purakh:

The skies are the dish; lamps are the sun and the moon. The stars are pearls; the breeze, incense. All the world's vegetation form the flowers offered [to the divine]. What a wonderful *aarti* ceremony! O You who eliminate all fear. This is Your *aarti*. The unstruck melody is the sounding of the temple drum (Guru Nanak, *Dhanasari aarti* 9; Adi Granth 663).

The unstruck melody refers to the "celestial music" that resounds throughout both humanity and nature. It is often compared to the *shabad*, the "word" or the divine self expression of Akal Purakh which is "heard" at the height of the Sikh spiritual discipline, nam simran. Nature therefore is not just valued for its worth to humans but has intrinsic value unto itself. As such nature must be revered and protected. Failure to do so in Guru Nanak's thought is tantamount to sin and ignorance of the true nature of reality.

How these ideas influence everyday Sikh practice toward the environment should be straightforward but it is not. On the one hand, human beings have a moral responsibility to protect and nurture the environment. As Guru Nanak claims in one of his most famous hymns, "Truth is indeed the highest of virtues. Higher still is living truthfully" (*Siri Rag Ashtapadian* 14:5; Adi Granth 62). As Akal Purakh, the ultimate Truth, permeates the natural world, which is his creation, it is incumbent upon all Sikhs to strive toward maintaining and preserving this Truth. Yet, on the other hand, Sikh farmers have perhaps benefited the most of all Indians from the large-scale introduction of harmful pesticides and chemical fertilizers which engendered the Green Revolution of the 1960s and 1970s, a clear contravention of the Adi Granth's insistence on the preservation of nature. Indeed, to this day it is very common to see the use of such chemicals in the fields of the Punjab.

Even during the Green Revolution, however, a number of Sikh and non-Sikh voices rose in protest against the chemical introduction and the so-called benefits of the Green Revolution. Of these none were louder than that of Puran Singh (1904–1992). A Sikh, Bhagat Puran Singh was often discovered outside the entrance to the Golden Temple in Amritsar handing out literature dealing with a number of contemporary, interrelated issues. The one for which he is today legendary is the care of India's disabled, destitute, poor, and sick. To support his concern for these marginalized groups he founded the All-India Pingalwara Charitable Society in 1947 against the backdrop of the horrors of Partition. Today this institution and Puran Singh (often referred to as India's Mother Theresa – though technically Mother Theresa was an Indian!) are both internationally recognized.

Puran Singh's interest in saving the environment began, according to his own admission, in the 1920s in light of India's increasing deforestation. It was at this time that he recognized, in part through the hymns of the Gurus and his own interests, the interconnectedness of all life and the harmony of the universe. A self-professed Gandhian Sikh, especially in his rejection of harmful technology (i.e., motor cars, etc.) and a prolific writer, many of Puran Singh's pamphlets deal with the environment and its degradation and offer solutions to its restoration. One solution which is outlined in his pamphlet *Apane Viah* (Our Marriages) is celibacy. It must be noted however that celibacy was promoted not within the Gandhian program of purity and bodily control leading to national control but rather because celibacy would eliminate an increase in the population which would therefore lessen the strain on natural resources.

Among his better-known works is *Khatre di Ghanti* (The Death Knell). This pamphlet of just over sixty pages informs Sikhs of the harm engendered by modern technology, soil erosion, pollution hazards, and deforestation. In this he often makes reference to the hymns of the Gurus underscoring Guru Nanak's dictum in his famous composition Japji that "the Earth was created as a dharamsala, an abode of righteousness" (Guru Nanak, Japji 34; Adi Granth 7) which must remain undefiled, in order to persuade Sikhs particularly and people in general to protect the environment and adopt less harmful technologies (bicycles as opposed to automobiles or scooters, for example, and home-spun khadi cloth for clothing as opposed to textiles manufactured with harmful dyes). Pollution in these pamphlets is thus equated with sacrilege and waste tantamount to disrespecting the eternal Guru and his creation (Khatre di Ghanti, 11).

After his death in 1992, the All-India Pingalwara Society has continued to champion Puran Singh's views and thus easily leads the way amongst Sikh institutions in broadcasting concerns about environmental degradation. It does this through conferences and seminars, which take place both within the Amritsar institution and within surrounding villages; through the celebration of Environment Day during which members of Pingalwara visit village schools to instruct children on environmental protection; and through the printing of numerous pamphlets by leading Indian and European environmentalists in Punjabi, Hindi, and English. The works of Sunder Lal Bahuguna who began the protest against the construction of the Tehri Dam in the Indian state of Uttar Pradesh may be cited as example.

The pioneering work of Puran Singh and Pingalwara and the clear message of the Adi Granth notwithstanding, little has been done from the Sikh perspective regarding environmental protection nor as yet has a formal Sikh position, one sanctioned and mandated by the principal Sikh religious institution, the Shiromani Gurdwara Prabhandak Committee, been enunciated. Yet all the sources for such a policy and the lifestyle to which it gives voice are very much available.

Louis E. Fenech

Further Readings

All references to the Adi Granth are from: Singh, Teja. *Shabadarath Sri Guru Granth Sahib ji*, 4 vols. Delhi: Delhi Sikh Gurdwara Prabandhak Committee, 1992 (this text follows the standard 1430-page pagination of the Sikh scripture).

McLeod, W.H. *Guru Nanak and the Sikh Tradition*. Oxford: Clarendon Press, 1968.

Singh, Puran. *Khatre di Ghanti*. Amritsar: All-India Pingalwara Society, 2002.
Singh, Patwant and Harinder Kaur Sekhon. *Garland Around My Neck: The Story of Puran Singh of Pingalwara*. Delhi: UBSPD, 2001.
Singh, Bhagat Puran. *Protector of the Environment – An Anthology of Tributes*. Amritsar: All India Pingalwara Society, 1998.

See also: India.

Silko, Leslie Marmon (1948–)

A key figure of the Native American literary renaissance of the 1970s, Leslie Marmon Silko was born in 1948 in Laguna Pueblo, New Mexico, of Laguna, Mexican, and EuroAmerican heritage. Silko grew up in the storytelling tradition of the Pueblos and writes from a worldview based in communal values and a belief in the sacredness and interdependence of all life forms. In her essay collection *Yellow Woman and a Beauty of the Spirit* (1996), Silko observes that her writing "begins with the land." The Earth, she says, is "the center of a spider's web," and "[h]uman identity, imagination and storytelling" radiate from that center (1996: 21).

Silko's early poetry and fiction, collected in *Laguna Woman* (1974) and *Storyteller* (1981), and her first novel *Ceremony* (1977) are centered in Laguna and reflect the inseparability of Pueblo people, stories, and land. *Ceremony*, now a classic of twentieth-century American literature, tells the story of Tayo, a mixed-blood World War II veteran who returns to Laguna spiritually fragmented and culturally alienated. Through a ceremonial reimmersion in the land and the sacred stories and beings that inhabit it, Tayo is restored to wholeness and heals his community, which had been devastated by the effects of uranium mining and the creation of the atomic bomb.

Silko's subsequent novels address themes of global dislocation. The apocalyptic epic *Almanac of the Dead* (1991) retells the 500-year history of the conquest of the Americas, the dispossession of its native peoples, and their continuing resistance. *Almanac* traces the roots of that violent history to the philosophical, religious, and scientific discourses of Western patriarchy that split human from nature, body from spirit, and dismember the world to produce consumer goods and atomic bombs. The novel ends as armies of indigenous people gather to retake the stolen land, prophesying the "end of all things European." However, as Silko tells interviewers, the retaking of the Americas is a metaphor for a global spiritual awakening already underway that will reconnect humans to the Earth.

If *Almanac of the Dead* diagnoses Western culture's ills, Silko's 1999 novel *Gardens in the Dunes* offers a cure. A historical novel set at the turn of the twentieth century, *Gardens in the Dunes* suggests how humans may participate in Earth's recovery from the devastation of colonial and capitalist greed. Seen through the eyes of a young Indian girl, the gardens cultivated in the desert by her Colorado River tribe and those she experiences on a European tour with the white couple who foster her constitute an extended metaphor for the reverent, reciprocal relationships between humans and nature that can restore human contiguity with the world. The novel also heals breaches between EuroAmerican and native cultures, drawing parallels between the indigenous spiritual traditions of the Americas and those of pre-Christian Europe and Gnostic Christianity. Dissolving boundaries between spirit and matter, nature and culture, Silko's work calls for humans to reinvent their relationships with nature and to participate in the creation of a new, more balanced world.

Ellen L. Arnold

Further Reading
Allen, Paul Gunn. *The Sacred Hoop: Recovering the Feminine in American Indian Traditions*. Boston: Beacon Press, 1986.
Arnold, Ellen L. *Conversations with Leslie Marmon Silko*. Jackson: University Press of Mississippi, 2000.
Nelson, Robert. *Place and Vision: The Function of Landscape in Native American Fiction*. New York: P. Lang, 1992.

See also: Harmony in Native North America; Hogan, Linda; Indigenous Religions and Cultural Borrowing; Snyder, Gary.

Sisters of Earth – *See* Genesis Farm; Green Sisters Movement.

Singer, Peter – *See* Environmental Ethics; Radical Environmentalism (and adjacent, Rodney Coronado and the Animal Liberation Front).

Sittler, Joseph A., Jr. (1904–1987)

Joseph Sittler, an American Lutheran theologian, was a pioneer in relating Christian theology to environmental concerns, giving an ecological reinterpretation of the traditional theological language of "nature and grace."

Born in Upper Sandusky, Ohio, in 1904, Sittler served as a Lutheran pastor before embarking on a teaching career which brought him in 1957 to the University of Chicago Divinity School, where he taught until his retirement in 1973. At the time of his death in 1987 he was

Distinguished Professor in Residence at the Lutheran School of Theology, which now houses the Sittler archives.

Sittler's 1954 article, "A Theology for Earth," and his 1961 address to the World Council of Churches Assembly in New Delhi, "Called to Unity," are both landmarks in the history of ecological theology. In the former, he argues that the theology of his time had "repudiated" the Earth, and that a theology that acknowledges the significance of the nonhuman world is needed if we are to care for the Earth rather than "use [it] as a godless warehouse or to rape [it] as a tyrant." In the latter, he calls for a "Christology of nature" that would overcome the Western dualism of nature and grace and bring the material universe itself into the sphere of redemption.

He carried forward and developed these themes in later writings. His sermon "The Care of the Earth" (1964) asserts that "abuse is use without grace" and contrasts an "economics of use only" which destroys the Earth and degrades human life, and an "economics of joy," in which receiving the world "sacramentally" makes possible also its intelligent use. "Ecological Commitment as Theological Responsibility" (1970) proposes an ecological understanding of grace as "built into the whole constitution of the world" of nature and society as the basis for an environmental ethic. That essay also contains his provocative assertion that environmental degradation is "blasphemy," because it denigrates the grace inherent in creation.

His most comprehensive statement is found in *Essays in Nature and Grace* (1972), which traces the theme of nature and grace through the Bible, the theology of the Eastern and Western churches, the Enlightenment, and into the modern period and the environmental crisis. The impact of Eastern Orthodox theology on Sittler, and his attentiveness to the artist's "unaccredited witness" to creation as a "theater of grace," are evident in this book.

Although he was not a "systematic" thinker, and his published output consists of a few slim volumes and numerous articles scattered among scholarly journals and church publications, Sittler had a profound influence on the following generation of "eco-theologians" (e.g., H. Paul Santmire and John B. Cobb, Jr.). While theological interest in ecology has perhaps to some degree "caught up" to Sittler, his focus on the doctrine of grace remains distinctive and illuminating, and his writings continue to be fresh and evocative invitations to explore the depth and breadth of the relationships between nature and grace.

Peter W. Bakken

Further Reading

Sittler, Joseph. *Evocations of Grace: Writings on Ecology, Theology and Ethics*. Steven Bouma-Prediger and Peter Bakken, eds. Grand Rapids: Eerdmans, 2000.

See also: Cobb, John (and adjacent, The Making of an Earthist Christian); Christianity (6b1) – Christian Orthodoxy; Christianity (7a) – Theology and Ecology; Christianity (9) – Christianity's Ecological Reformation.

Sivaraksa, Sulak (1933–)

Sulak Sivaraksa, Thailand's prominent lay Buddhist social activist and author, is widely known as a major figure in the international engaged Buddhist movement. In 1961, upon his return to Thailand from England where he completed university and law degrees, he became a publisher, university lecturer, and founding editor of the *Social Science Review*, Thailand's leading intellectual journal until 1976 when it was suppressed by the government. In 1971 he organized the Komol Keemthong Foundation with the help and support of Sanya Dhammasakti, chief justice of the supreme court, and Dr. Puey Ungaphakorn, rector of Thammasat University and governor of the Bank of Thailand. Its purpose was to inspire young Thais to dedicate their lives to social justice and the common good rather than solely the pursuit of their own personal gain. The Foundation was the first of many non-governmental organizations (NGOs) Sivaraksa has inaugurated. Prominent among them are the Thai Inter-religious Commission for Development (TICD) and the International Network of Engaged Buddhists (INEB), sponsors of the tri-annual publication, *Seeds of Peace*; the Santi Pracha Dhamma Institute (Institute of Peace, Democratic Participation, and Justice); and the Spirit in Education Movement. Through these and other organizations and networks, Sivaraksa has devoted his life to the pursuit of economic and educational reform, social and environmental justice, human and civil rights. He also founded the Sathirakoses-Nagapradipa Foundation, which promotes cultural, educational, and artistic projects, and numerous publications including the *Pracharayasara* journal, the intellectual successor to the *Social Science Review*. Sivaraksa has authored hundreds of essays and articles in Thai and several collections of essays in English, most notable among them are: *Seeds of Peace: A Buddhist Vision for Renewing Society, A Socially Engaged Buddhism, Religion and Development*, and *Siamese Resurgence: A Thai Buddhist Voice on Asia and a World of Change*. An abbreviated version of his Thai autobiography was published under the title, *Loyalty Demands Dissent: Autobiography of an Engaged Buddhist*. The American Friends Service Committee nominated him for the Nobel Peace Prize and he is the recipient of the Right Livelihood Award, regarded internationally as the "alternative Nobel."

In numerous writings, Sivaraksa has spoken forcefully on the issue of environmental destruction, especially in his own country. Equally important are organizations and movements he has created to promote environmental preservation and environmental justice. Most of the NGOs founded by Sivaraksa include an environmental agenda but for one, in particular, the preservation of the natural environment is uppermost. *Sekhiyadhamma* (Students of the Dhamma), is a network of Buddhist monks working in their communities to preserve local environments, principally forests that are essential to village economies. Their efforts are both educational, teaching villagers better ways to conserve natural resources, as well as political, protecting local social, cultural, and natural environments from the encroachment of commercial, industrial, and urban development. On the outskirts of Bangkok, Sivaraksa has established a conference center, the Wongsanit Ashram, to exemplify the ideal of simple living close to nature or, as he fondly quotes Gandhi, "living simply so that others may simply live." The Ashram serves as a center for the practice of a mindful, non-consumerist, other-regarding way of life.

Like one of his spiritual mentors, the noted Thai monk, Buddhadása Bhikkhu, Sivaraksa grounds his environmental ethic on a holistic understanding of the Buddhist principle of interdependent co-arising conducive to a deep respect for nature. This knowledge of inter-becoming, a term he borrows from Thich Nhat Hanh, is achieved through the development of mindful awareness and leads naturally to an empathetic identification with and compassionate action toward all life forms. On this foundation, Sivaraksa builds a guide for compassionate action using traditional Buddhist teachings – the Four Sublime Abodes (love, compassion, sympathetic joy, equanimity), the four Bases of Sympathy (generosity, kindly speech, life of service, impartiality), and the five precepts (*sila*). For example, he applies the first precept against killing to the structural violence engendered against the poor and the natural environment by global corporate power.

Sivaraksa brings to his environmental agenda a sharp critique of governmental and commercial exploitation of nature at both global and Thai national levels. Applying the principle that power corrupts and absolute power corrupts absolutely, he believes that the global economic structures of free-market capitalism facilitate the concentration of wealth and power at the expense of the poor and the environment, a scenario that he characterizes as structural violence. Free-market capitalism also creates a culture of consumption driven by greed, selfishness, and acquisitiveness rather than promoting the qualities of simplicity, responsibility, and care that are essential to the preservation and conservation of nature. He finds in the culture of consumerism the illusion of autonomous, individualized selves undermining both human community and the mindful-awareness of the interdependence of human beings and nature.

Sivaraksa idealizes the rural Thai environment of relatively small self-sustaining communities living in harmony with the natural environment, not in a naive, antique sense, but as a practical example of a more humane, caring, and harmonious society. Rather than unrealistically advocating a return to a pre-modern, less complex era, he forges alliances and networks among people from many walks of life – academics, laborers, farmers, activists, civil servants, and even the business community – dedicated to the building of a more democratic, egalitarian, inclusive, and compassionate society. He strongly supports the Assembly of the Poor that emerged as a nonviolent, grassroots democratic force in Southeast Asia in the mid–1990s with nearly as half-million members in Thailand. At the core of the Assembly are urban and rural agriculturists and manual laborers with support from the middle-classes. In recent years he has challenged numerous government and private projects that have dislocated villages or undermined traditional ways of life and the communities that support them. These projects include hundreds of dams constructed without prior consultation with local populations geared mainly toward making abundant water supplies for industries at the expense of small-scale agriculture; the destruction of local forests in north and northeastern Thailand for the promotion of commercial enterprises, especially wood-pulp eucalyptus plantations; and land loss around followed by subsequent pollution of Songkhla Lake, Thailand's largest inland body of water.

Sivaraksa's Buddhist environmental philosophy owes a special debt to the thought of Buddhadása Bhikkhu and Thich Nhat Hanh. Yet, in contrast to their more reflective and contemplative styles, he aggressively fights in the trenches for the cause of human and environmental justice. On 6 March 1998, he was arrested during a sit-in protest against the construction of the Burma–Thailand Yadana pipeline in Kanjanaburi province, south Thailand. Typical of Sivaraksa's style as an engaged Buddhist, he was putting his life on the line to protest both human rights abuses and the pipeline's potential for ecological damage.

Donald K. Swearer

Further Reading

Sivaraksa, Sulak. *Loyalty Demands Dissent: An Autobiography of an Engaged Buddhist.* Berkeley, CA: Parallax Press, 1998.

Sivaraksa, Sulak. *Seeds of Peace: A Buddhist Vision for Renewing Society.* Berkeley, CA: Parallax Press, 1992.

Swearer, Donald K. "Sulak Sivaraksa's Buddhist Vision for Renewing Society." In Christopher Queen and Sallie B. King. *Engaged Buddhism: Buddhist Liberation Movements in Asia.* Albany: State University of New York Press, 1998.

See also: Buddhism; Buddhism – Engaged; Caves – Sacred (Thailand); Payutto, Phra Dhammapitaka; Siam's Forest Monasteries; Thai Buddhist Monks.

Sjöö, Monica (1938–)

Monica Sjöö is a Swedish ecofeminist, political activist, author and visual artist. She is known as one of the foremost thinkers of the reemerging Goddess religion. Her most influential publication, co-authored with Barbara Mor, *The Great Cosmic Mother: Rediscovering the Religion of the Earth*, traces the historical roots of Earth-based Goddess religions and the violent oppression of these traditions by patriarchal cultural forces. The book includes 44 of her paintings. Sjöö's research draws on archeological, cultural and religious sources in a global perspective.

Sjöö's journeys to Neolithic sacred sites provide inspiration for her work. These journeys took her to southwest England's ancient sites where she has lived since the late 1950s. Involved in the feminist, anarchist and anti-Vietnam War movements in Sweden and Britain in the 1960s, Sjöö states that her "political activism always grew out of my spiritual understandings of the Earth as the living Mother because the Goddess is injured wherever there is injustice, wanton cruelty, poverty, and pollution" (1987: xix).

Some of her earliest images, "God Giving Birth" (1968) and "Women's Mysteries" (1971), led to the publication of her first pamphlet in 1975, in which she begins to explain her concepts of the Great Mother as the generative force of the universe. Sjöö's work is also influenced by the deaths of her two sons – one from cancer, one killed by a car.

During the 1990s Sjöö's writing critiqued the gurus of New Age religion. In *Return of the Dark/Light Mother or New Age Armageddon?*, she contrasted the New Age focus on transcending Earth and ignoring political activism, which exacerbates Earth's destruction and exploits indigenous spiritualities, with ancient and reemerging Goddess cultures. Sjöö's visual art has been exhibited throughout the United States and Europe; she has contributed to myriad journals, and has led workshops at conferences and festivals throughout the world.

Laura Hobgood-Oster

Further Reading

Sjöö, Monica. *Return of the Dark/Light Mother or New Age Armageddon? Towards a Feminist Vision of the Future*. Austin, TX: Plain View Press, 1999.

Sjöö, Monica and Barbara Mor. *The Great Cosmic Mother: Rediscovering the Religion of the Earth*. San Francisco: Harper & Row, 1987.

See also: Ecofeminism; Feminist Spirituality Movement; Goddesses – History of.

Sky

This entry considers 1) the position of the sky in our perceptual environment and its religious symbolism, 2) sky-gods, 3) the personification of celestial objects, and 4) the disenchantment of the sky in the modern era.

1) The sky is a rich source of religious meanings and symbols. In our perceptual environment it is "the above," a realm of infinity, brightness and purity, something "other" than humanity's environment on Earth. It is a source of water and thus fertility and life. Not only does the Bible mention a sphere of water beyond the heavens (e.g., in Gen. 1:77, Job 38:37), but in many cultures sky-dwelling deities have been propitiated for rain. The sky is a source of wind, thunder and lightning. These are symbols of power and death. Thus, Odin, the Germanic god of storms and tempests was said to reside in the sky. In the daytime, the sky may be shrouded in clouds or may radiate a gleaming blue light. In Hinduism and in Mahayana Buddhism this blue was understood as a symbol of purity of mind and spiritual enlightenment. At sunrise and sunset the sky often abounds in warm, red hues. Greek mythology linked these colors to Iris, the goddess of dawn and twilight.

In the day and at night, the sky is the arena for celestial bodies and phenomena: sun and moon, stars, Milky Way and the planets are commonly seen. These were often regarded as divine or mythical beings (particularly sun and moon) or even the spirits of deceased humans (e.g., among sea-nomads in Southeast Asia). East and west, being the directions of sunrise and sunset, are often imbued with particular meanings. In India, east is considered as an auspicious direction, west as inauspicious. These meanings have influenced sacral and domestic architecture. Rainbows, eclipses, comets, meteor showers, auroras and supernovae are rare and have been impossible or difficult to predict. They are the subjects of a rich mythology and have often been regarded as harbingers of extraordinary events, misfortune or droughts. While the sky's cloud covering may seem to change at random, the motion of sun and moon, and the apparently perpetual revolution of the starry night sky are manifestations of regularity. These seasonal changes in the appearance of the starry night sky parallel annual climatic change.

When brought into relation to the human body, the sky, in being "up" or "above," may be linked to the head as the center of consciousness and mind. Similarly, it may express ideas of hierarchy: divinity as being distinct from, and usually superior to, humans. If deities in a pantheon can be localized in the environment, the superior ones tend to be in the sky. Earthly rulers may claim to derive their power from these sky-gods. Examples are the Inca (Peru) and the Mongolian ruler Genghis Khan. But even in monotheistic religions, God may be thought to reside "above" in the sky. In Christianity, for example, this is where the Bible (Gen. 11:5) and the Lord's prayer locate God.

The sacrality of the Earth has been often understood to derive from the sacrality of the sky. Meteorites in particular, which have literally fallen from the sky, may become centers on Earth where sacrality is manifest, which may otherwise be peculiar to the sky. The Qa'bah in Mecca (Saudi Arabia) is probably the most famous example. According to a ninth-century text, this particular meteorite fell through a hole in the sky. As such, the Qa'bah symbolizes the permeability of sacrality at this place.

2) The belief in sky-gods is, or has been, common to many cultures. These beliefs vary from conceptions that are impersonal or barely personal to anthropomorphic ones. While the material sky has been claimed to be identical with these deities (e.g., in ancient Babylonia, among the Ewe of Ghana or in old China), in other cultures the sky has been considered a space in which the sky-gods reside (e.g., Zeus in Greek mythology). Foucart (1920) considers the universality of sky-gods and the uniformity of their essential characteristics as the "logical consequence of the constant uniformity of the primitive system of cosmogony" (1920: 581). He notes that in many cultures sky-gods have been considered as the creators of the world. If considered the sole agent of creation, the sky-god is usually understood as being male (as in many pastoral societies), but sometimes as female (e.g., the Egyptian goddess Hathor). In other (often agrarian) cultures the world is created in the union of a (male) sky-god and a (female) Earth-goddess. Examples are the Polynesian myth of Rangi and Pepe, and the Greek myth of Ouranos and Gaia. The separation of sky and Earth after the act of creation is a common mythological subject. For example, a myth of the Ewe (Ghana) relates that a cooking fire lit by their ancestors caused the sky-god Mavu to feel a burning sensation in the eye and to withdraw thereupon.

Historians of religion have advanced a variety of ideas about the role of sky-gods in belief systems. Wilhelm Schmidt argued that primitive monotheism stems from the idea of a supreme sky-god. This hypothesis has resulted in a long-lasting debate that remains unresolved. Mircea Eliade notes the tendency of sky-gods to disappear from cults. In general, they become less and less important in ritual and sacrifice. In some cultures, the sky-gods are pleased with their creation and perhaps even tired of the hard work involved (cf. the mythology of the god Puluga on the Andaman islands in the Indian Ocean). While sky-gods may sometimes remain at the head of a pantheon (e.g., the Zoroastrian Ahura Mazda), in other cases they have been replaced by a sun-god. In general, Eliade remarks, sky-gods show little interest in the concern of humans and thus they are often replaced by active deities with more proximity to human life. He also notes, however, that the sacredness of the sky and the stars usually remains unchallenged.

3) The attribution of religious, mythical or symbolic meanings to the visible sky or objects discernible therein is known in virtually all cultures. In an abstract way, the blueness of the sky has been related to the skin color or the dresses worn by sky-gods. Examples are the blue-skinned Tengri (Mongolia) and Mavu of the Ewe (Ghana), who was claimed to wear a blue robe adorned by white clouds. In a number of cultures, sun and moon are imbued with an amazing variety of meaning. They often appear as husband and wife or as siblings and are linked to myths of creation. Among the planets, Venus has been commonly linked to divine or mythical beings. The Pleiades (a conspicuous cluster of bright stars in the constellation Taurus) is probably the most widely identified constellation around the world. Their first visibility in the eastern evening sky (October) marks the beginning of the rainy season in many equatorial regions. At first sight, the night sky may seem like an arbitrary distribution of stars. However, akin to a projective Rorschach test used by psychologists, the patterns discerned in the sky may be considered as projections of symbols which are, or have been, important to a culture. Thus, the symbolism of Greek mythology and everyday life is still inscribed into the sky as seen through (knowledgeable) Western eyes.

4) The disenchantment of the world in the modern era has been debated at least since Max Weber first published *The Protestant Ethic and the Spirit of Capitalism* in 1905. Not only have the physical sciences progressively restricted the realm of divine influence. Celestial phenomena and objects could also now be understood by a unified physical theory. Scientific progress has affected the perception of the sky in a profound way. It came to be looked at as a wasteland, a mute witness to human doings and wrongdoings (e.g., in expressionist poetry). The twentieth century has brought human appropriation of the sky into focus. In the 1920s, a British engineer used diesel fumes to inscribe advertisements into the blue sky (first for the *Daily Mail*, then for "Lucky Strike"). Already in 1893, at the Chicago World Exhibition, slides had been projected onto clouds. Then came the jet trails. In the 1960s, air pollution emerged as a global problem. The discoveries of the Antarctic ozone hole and of global warming have left no doubt about our influence on the sky. Once the abode of deities, it has come apparently under human control. Such a viewpoint is enforced by international law: up to an elevation of 83 kilometers the sky has been declared the territory of any sovereign state.

Götz Hoeppe

Further Reading

Chemeny, Peter. "Sky: Myths and Symbolism". In *Encyclopedia of Religion*, vol. 13. Mircea Eliade, ed. New York: Macmillan, 1993, 345–53.

Eliade, Mircea. *Patterns in Comparative Religion*. New York: Macmillan, 1958.
Foucart, George. "Sky-gods." In *Encyclopedia of Religion and Ethics*, vol. 11. New York: Charles Scribner's Sons, 1920, 580–5.
Frazer, James. *The Worship of Nature*, vol. 1. London: Macmillan, 1926, 19–315.
Lévi-Strauss, Claude. *Mythologiques I: Le Cru et le Cuit*. Paris: Librairie Plon, 1964.

See also: Astronauts; Eliade, Mircea; Ecology and Religion; Greek Paganism; Hinduism; Odinism; Roman Natural Religion; Space Exploration; Sun Worship; UFOs and Extraterrestrials; Zoroastrianism.

Slavic Neo-Paganism

Slavic neo-paganism is a scholarly term for a very broad category of religious groups that see themselves as the legitimate continuation of the pre-Christian religious beliefs of their Slavic ancestors. This legitimacy is largely based on perceived "natural" ways of being for Slavs as a whole or as separate historical nations, which include concepts of intimate ties with certain landscapes and geographical areas as well as broader notions of humanity's place in the natural environment.

Although most Slavic neo-pagan groups are familiar with the scholarly category of "neo-pagan," very few are quick to use it about themselves. They often prefer labels such as "the native faith" (Czech: *rodná víra*, Polish: *rodzima wiara*, Ukrainian: *ridna vira*) or "Slavism" (Russian: *Slavianstvo*). Unlike neo-pagan groups in English-speaking countries, neither magic nor feminism are important parts of Slavic neo-paganism, although they may be present.

Belarus, the Czech Republic, Poland, Russia, Serbia, Slovakia, Slovenia and Ukraine all have documented Slavic neo-pagan movements of larger or smaller sizes. In all of these countries, neo-paganism remains a small minority of the population (under 0.5 percent) and is usually marginalized as a New Religious Movement by the dominant churches and the population at large, regardless of claims of ancient traditions. Some of these countries may also contain even smaller autochthonic non-Slavic neo-paganisms (vigorous Finno-Ugric neo-paganisms in Russia, Baltic Prussian neo-paganism in Poland) as well as a few scattered representatives of imported Western neo-paganisms (Asatru, Wicca and Druidism). Slavic neo-paganism may also be found amongst Slavic émigrés, especially from Ukraine and Russia.

A number of neo-pagan groups were founded throughout Central and Eastern Europe in the 1920s and 1930s. They typically built on a base of nineteenth- and early twentieth-century Romanticism which, along with colorful speculation about the primordial religions of Europe, made influential assumptions about the "noble savage" and the primacy of nature. Although this burst of activity was not limited to the Slavic peoples (important Germanic and Baltic groups were founded at this same time), one of the first organized and explicitly religious groups to appear was the Polish "Święte Koło Czcicieli Światowida" (The Holy Circle of Worshippers of Swiatowid) in 1921. Many of these groups did not find favor with the communist authorities after the Second World War and their leaders either fled their home countries (as did Volodimir Shaian from Ukraine) or were sent off for lengthy prison terms (as was Jan Stachniuk of Poland).

Elements of Slavic neo-paganism were echoed under communism, including nationally televised (non-Christian) seasonal holidays and the encouragement of Slavic rituals among the scouting movements. With the "fall" of communism after 1989, Slavic neo-paganism blossomed again, drawing into its ranks a new generation. Although surviving members of the pre-war organizations often returned from exile, Slavic neo-pagan groups have retained a younger demographic than similar groups in Western Europe.

The radical immanentalism of Slavic neo-paganism (as opposed to the transcendentalism of the dominant Christian Churches) is a key factor in understanding its complex assumptions about what are "natural" ways of being. Explicit worship of divine beings that correspond to natural phenomena, such as the god of thunder, Perun, or the goddess of Earth, Mokosh, are only part of their return to an immanent Sacrum. The blood-ties of families, the Nation (and sometimes the Race), the sovereignty of the State, traditional folkways, traditional language, the seasonal turn of the calendar and biodiversity are all examples of things that may be considered sacred. It is interesting to note that the god Rod (literally: "birth" or "kin"; related to concepts of "native" and "nation") is considered the highest of the gods, the "God of gods" by some Ukrainian neo-pagans, and the goddess Slava, the eponymous mother of the Slavs, is accorded vast importance by the controversial *Book of Veles*.

This has led some outside observers to argue that all Slavic neo-paganisms are fundamentally nationalistic or based on ethnic chauvinism. Such authors assume that all other concerns are secondary or insincere smokescreens for their true goals. Other authors have emphasized the strong current of environmentalism, while discounting the nationalists as a minority radical fringe. The reality lies somewhere between the two, as the Slavic neo-pagan celebration of the physical world can take on many different overtones even in close proximity. Typical is a Slovak neo-pagan magazine that contains an article on dwindling wolf populations, a tutorial on how to sew a traditional Slovak shirt, and a political protest against EU membership as dangerous to Slovak sovereignty, all on the same two-page spread.

The immanent-environmental current in Slavic neo-paganism often sets itself explicitly in conflict with the emphasis put on transcendence in Christianity, blaming it for the degradation of the environment and humanity's alienation from nature. Jan Stachniuk and Volodymyr Shaian were particularly vehement in the 1930s in their condemnations of Christianity as a dangerous distraction from the realities of this world. By the end of the twentieth century, many Slavic neo-pagans were also familiar with Nouvelle Droite spokesman Alain de Benoist's arguments that Christianity was "unnatural", even if they were not familiar with similar lines of thought from the more left-oriented neo-paganisms in the English-speaking world.

In some cases, Slavic neo-pagans seem to prescribe a sort of turning back of the clock as the cure to modern ecological ills. Many Slavic neo-pagans are ardent medieval reconstructionists, meeting for festivals in which they dress in medieval clothes and demonstrate pre-Christian handicrafts. Many are also keenly interested in archeology, history and folklore survivals. "Do-it-yourself" is often preferred to "store-bought," as is the homemade wine produced by the congregation in Kaluga, Russia, for ritual purposes. The legacy of nineteent-century Romanticism is felt strongly in the assumption that modern consumerism and technology is decadent and meaningless when compared with the ancient Slavic arcadia. Extreme Luddite variants, however, are rare and the comfort that many Slavic neo-pagans have with modern technology is visible in websites dedicated to their interests.

Slavic neo-pagans may be found as staunch supporters of the "secular" ecological movement, and the ecological movement often returns the favor by borrowing neo-pagan imagery in their publications and neo-pagan ritual in their events. However, neither side of this equation could be said to hold a controlling interest in the other's activities. Notably, other than some small-scale organic farming, there have been no attempts to create exclusively neo-pagan environmental initiatives such as sustainable housing, recycling programs or nature preserves outside of the framework of the broader environmental movements of the various Slavic countries.

Scott Simpson

Further Reading

Jones, Prudence and Nigel Pennick. *A History of Pagan Europe*. Routledge: London, 1995.

Shnirelman, Victor A. "Christians Go Home: A Revival of Neo-Paganism between the Baltic Sea and Transcaucasia (An Overview)." *Journal of Contemporary Religion* 17:2 (2002).

Simpson, Scott. *Native Faith: Polish Neo-Paganism at the Brink of the 21st Century*. Krakow: Nomos, 2000.

Wiench, Piotr. "Neo-Paganism in Central-Eastern European Countries." In I. Borowik. *New Religious Phenomena in Central and Eastern Europe*. Krakow: Nomos, 1997.

See also: Heathenry–Ásatrú; Koliada Viatichei; Neo-Paganism in Ukraine; Odinism; Oshmarii-Chimarii (Mari El Republic, Russia); Paganism – Contemporary; Russian Mystical Philosophy; Slavic Religion.

Slavic Religion

"The Slavs," like "the Celts," are a modern construct. Since languages spread not only vertically, through ancestry, but also laterally, through conquest, diffusion, assimilation, and other means, "Slavic religion" refers not to the religion of a single transhistorical community of "Slavs," but to the multiple religious practices of Slavic speakers. That caveat aside, archeologists generally consider Slavic-speaking cultures to have emerged in the territory between the Dnieper and Vistula rivers in Eastern Europe sometime in the first millennium B.C.E. Over the course of the mid- to late first millennium and early second millennium, accompanied by territorial migrations to the north, east, and southwest, Slavic-speaking tribal groups combined, transformed, and differentiated into the peoples known today, commonly distinguished into three language groups: East Slavs (Russians, Ukrainians, Belarusans), West Slavs (Poles, Czechs, Slovaks), and South Slavs (Slovenes, Serbs, Croats, Macedonians, Bulgarians).

The reconstruction of pre-Christian Slavic religion draws on three primary types of sources. Written sources include classical writings, Arab travel accounts, Christian teachings (generally aimed at discouraging pagan practices), and medieval chronicles. Archeological sources are plentiful, though debates continue over the identification of Slavic and non-Slavic cultures, the extent of migration and diffusion as opposed to autochthonous development, and so on. Finally, folklore and ethnography, drawing on a wealth of oral and folk traditions, including epic poems, fairytales, ritual songs and dances, have provided scholars with plentiful material from which to reconstruct pre-Christian beliefs, since many of these are thought to have continued in modified and fragmentary forms as late as the beginning of the twentieth century.

The earliest known beliefs of the Slavs reveal strong affinities with neighboring linguistic groups, especially Balts, Indo-Iranians, and Thracians. Linguistic and structuralist approaches (such as those of Vyacheslav Ivanov and Vladimir Toporov) have convincingly identified an Indo-European substrate underlying Slavic beliefs. Following from the work of philologist Georges Dumézil, this includes a tripartite conception of the social order (priests, warriors, and farmers-commoners), the duality of a sky god and his adversary, and worship of the sun, fire and light, and ancestors. More controversially, archeologist Marija Gimbutas has argued that Slavic pre-Christian beliefs represent a mixture of Indo-European patriarchal ideas and an earlier, "Old European" stratum of matrifocal, Earth-centered imagery and practice, the latter reflected in a widespread reverence toward the Earth, sometimes personified as *Maty Syra Zemlia* (Russian/Ukrainian: "Mother moist Earth"). Other scholars, such as Boris Rybakov, emphasize the slow evolution of Slavic religion from simple animistic beliefs in life-giving spirits (Ukr. *berehyni*, or protectresses) and life-threatening ones (*upyri*, or vampires), ancestral cults, and personifications of fertility and communal order (*Lada, Kupala, Rod*, and others), to the "higher mythological" pantheons of the late pre-Christian era.

Slavic peoples considered the world to be animated by a wide variety of spirits, ranging from those that inhabited the rivers and waters (such as *mavkas, vilas*, and *rusalkas*), forests (Russian: *leshy*, Ukrainian: *lisovyk*, or "he of the forest"), fields, and households, to personifications of illness, climatic forces, abstract principles (such as fate, bad luck, and the community or *Rod*), and souls of the dead. Typically, springs and wells, rivers, groves of oaks and other trees, the rounded tops of hills, and raised flat areas overlooking rivers, seem to have been held with particular reverence. Some scholars have sought to explain fairytale characters, such as the East Slavic *Baba Yaga* (the Old Hag) or *Koshchei* the Eternal, as relics of ancient gods or goddesses, but these can perhaps more parsimoniously be explained as products of the folk imagination.

Calendrical rituals were commonly connected to the periodic return of the ancestors, the comings and goings of nature spirits, and the agrarian fertility cycle. Seasonal festivals display a rich semiotics of agricultural and ancestral symbolism: decorations of greenery to welcome the return of the ancestors or nature spirits in springtime, food set aside for the souls of the dead and sheaves of grain and bundles of straw representing ancestors during winter rites, and so on. Late nineteenth and early twentieth-century calendar customs show a synthesis of pagan and Christian elements, typical of the peasant religiosity that scholars have called "double-faith" (Russian: *dvoievierie*). The Christmas period is marked by *Koliada* rites: the lighting of fires, processions of masked carolers performing ritual theatre and offering greetings and wishes for a bountiful harvest, offerings of food and drink to the "visitors" (representing the ancestors). Fire and water figure most prominently in springtime and midsummer rites, often centered around such figures as Yaryla (or Yarovit), Kupalo, and Marena. (The names vary among different ethnic groups.) Kupala's festival, celebrated at midsummer (St. John's Day in its Christian incarnation), included ritual lighting of fires, bathing, divination, songs, dances, and, traditionally, the dressing and sacrifice (by burning or sinking in water) of an effigy representing the deity.

Analysis of Slavic folklore has allowed researchers to reconstruct the archaic mythological image of the Slavic World Tree, a three-tiered vertical structure whose levels correspond to a heavenly world, represented by birds, sun and moon; an earthly world represented by bees and humans; and an underworld represented by chthonic creatures such as snakes and beavers. This structure is arguably preserved in late-pagan statuary; for instance, a four-sided temple statue found near Zbruch in western Ukraine includes, in its top level, representations of distinct deities facing the four cardinal directions, a human *khorovod* or ritual community in its middle level, and a three-headed underworld figure (most likely Veles) holding up the world.

Numerous remains have been found throughout Slav-occupied territories of temples with upraised platforms, frequently located on hills, with wooden or, less frequently, stone statues of deities: some with three or four heads facing the cardinal directions, some holding a drinking horn or decorated with emblems such as sun symbols, incised horse figures, and the like. Twelfth-century chronicles name several deities as having been worshipped in Prince Volodymyr's (Vladimir's) late tenth-century imperial capital, Kyïv (Kiev). The most prominent of these was Perun, god of thunder, law and war, associated with oak trees and groves, and commonly identified with the Germanic Thor. Veles, or Volos, god of horned livestock, wealth, and the underworld, is thought by some to have been his adversary (the duality being analogous to the Indian gods Mitra and Varuna, locked in an eternal combat between sky and underworld). This is attested perhaps by the fact that he was excluded from Volodymyr's temple atop the Kyivan hills, but worshipped in the lower merchant's town of Podol below. Other deities reflect an unmistakable Iranian (Scythian or Sarmatian) influence, while the female Mokosh was likely a fertility goddess. Svarog and Dazhbog both clearly contain elements of sky and sun gods known from other Indo-European speaking peoples. Most of these deities can be traced back to earlier forms as personifications of natural forces.

It seems probable that Volodymyr's pantheon was established in the decades preceding Christianization in an attempt to cement together a religion appropriate to a growing empire. By 988, Volodymyr himself rejected that religion in favor of Byzantine Christianity. Late pagan practices continued in isolated and more northerly areas, most notably at the temple-stronghold at Arkona on the island of Rügen (now in Germany), destroyed by the Christian Danes in 1168. Despite intense efforts, however, beliefs and practices changed slowly in rural areas. Gods were replaced by saints (Perun by St. Elijah, Veles by St. Blasius, Yarylo by St. George), pagan festivals by Christian feast days, sacred sites by churches, and magical and divinatory practices were accommodated to new understandings.

Adrian Ivakhiv

Further Reading

Curta, Florin. *The Making of the Slavs: History and Archaeology of the Lower Danube Region, c. 500–700.* Cambridge: Cambridge University Press, 2001.

Gimbutas, Marija. *The Slavs.* New York: Praeger, 1971.

Ivakhiv, Adrian. "Scholarship on the Ancient Eastern Slavs: A Bibliographic Overview." *Ethnic Forum* 15: 1–2 (1995), 162–75.

Ivakhiv, Adrian. "The Cosmos of the Ancient Slavs." *Gnosis* 31 (Spring 1994), 28–35.

Ivanits, Linda J. *Russian Folk Belief.* London: M.E. Sharpe, 1988.

Jakobson, Roman. "Slavic Mythology." In M. Leach, ed. *Funk and Wagnalls Standard Dictionary of Folklore, Mythology, and Legend,* vol. 2. New York: HarperCollins, 1972, 1025–8.

Kulikowski, Mark. *Bibliography of Slavic Mythology.* Columbus, OH: Slavica, 1989.

Ryan, W.F. *The Bathhouse at Midnight: An Historical Survey of Magic and Divination in Russia.* University Park: Pennsylvania University Press, 1999.

Zaroff, Roman. "Organised Pagan Cult in Kievan Rus: The Invention of Foreign Elite or Evolution of Local Tradition?" In *Studia-Mythologica-Slavica.* Slovenia, 1995, 47–76.

Znayenko, Myroslava T. *The Gods of the Ancient Slavs: Tatishchev and the Beginnings of Slavic Mythology.* Columbus, OH: Slavica, 1980.

See also: Neo-paganism in Ukraine; Russian Mystical Philosophy; Slavic Neo-Paganism.

Smuts, Jan Christiaan (1870–1950)

Jan Smuts served as Attorney-General of the Zuid Afrikaansche Republiek, Boer General, South African Prime Minister, international statesman, scientist (botanist), President of the South African Association for the Advancement of Science, Fellow of the Royal Society (and its President), Rector (St. Andrew's, Scotland), Chancellor (Cambridge University), and philosopher. He was born in the Cape hamlet of Riebeek West on 24 May 1870, and it was here that he acquired his deep, mystical love of nature and, in particular, mountains.

He came from a devout Dutch Reformed Church family deeply influenced by the evangelistic piety of Dr. Andrew Murray. His mystical appreciation for nature he traced to a mystical experience he had when he climbed the peak of Riebeek Kasteel and later, in 1923, he related the significance of "The Spirit of the Mountain" at Maclear's Beacon on Table Mountain. Such was his love for Table Mountain that one of the paths to the summit of Table Mountain that he often climbed is named for him. In later life he was influenced both by the teachings of the Society of Friends (Quakers) and the mystical theories of Evelyn Underhill.

A brilliant student, he spent only four years at school before being awarded the Ebden Scholarship to attend Cambridge University. He was deeply influenced there by the philosophical and sociological thought of the German professor H.J. Wolstenholme, and in addition completed a manuscript on the American Walt Whitman (unpublished, entitled "A Study in the Evolution of Personality"). His studies and especially his reading and study of Walt Whitman, moved him from his earlier pessimistic Calvinism to a more optimistic view of humanity, to conceiving of human personality as a process of becoming, and as the supreme part of nature.

Arising out of his own war experiences of personal and national conciliation and his scientific work in biology, he developed a philosophy of the relatedness of all things, and coined for it the term holism. The kernel of the idea of holism came from his earlier study of Walt Whitman and it developed in the light of Darwin's understanding of evolution. Smuts rejected mechanist and materialist views and held that through a holistic evolutionary process, cosmic individuation was in process, extending from the inorganic through to the spiritual level. Thus he held that the whole of being was moving toward greater freedom, recognition of its relatedness, and personalism. Holism influenced his politics, in that he was an internationalist, rather than a nationalistic leader – a unifier of Afrikaans and English-speaking South Africans; a founder of the Union of South Africa, the League of Nations, the British Commonwealth, and the United Nations. His United Party lost to the Afrikaner Nationalist Party in 1948 and, leaving politics, he died on his farm Irene at Doornkloof, on 11 September 1950.

Iain S. Maclean

Further Reading

Beukes, P. *The Holistic Smuts: A Study in Personality.* Cape Town: Human & Rousseau, 1989.

Friedman, Bernard. *Smuts: A Reappraisal.* Johannesburg: Keartland, 1975.

Hancock, W.K. *Smuts.* Cambridge: Cambridge University Press, 1962 (1968).

See also: Afrikaner Theology; Christianity (6c2) – Calvin, John and the Reformed Tradition; Darwin, Charles; Friends Religious Society of (Quakers); Holism.

Snakes and the Luo of Kenya

Influenced by Western Christianity's diabolization and Freudian phallicization of snakes, many Westerners otherwise concerned with animals, animal rights, endangered species, ecology, and ecofeminism have not expressed similar interest in or impassioned concern for snakes. Joluo (Luo people) of Kenya, in contrast, display keen interest in snakes, particularly pythons. Luo are one of the largest ethnic groups in Kenya, with a population of over 3 million. They are related to Lwoo (Nilotic) people of Uganda and the Sudan, with whom they share some batrachian, piscatorial, and serpentine symbolism. Luo are now predominantly Christian, with affiliations divided among Roman Catholicism, various Western Protestant groups, and membership in African-instituted churches. Several thousand are Muslim. Movement between various denominations is not uncommon and commitment to some indigenous spiritual beliefs coexists with these other affiliations. Historically Luo have been an "agro-pastoral-fishing people." Their homeland since their migration from the Sudan, which followed along the Nile and its tributaries for much of the time, has been around Lake Victoria. One of their auto-appellations for themselves is Jonam, "the people of lakes and rivers." Their interest in snakes who flow their footless forms through several elements can be linked to their history, ecology, and cultural background.

The type of poisonous snakes found among Luo include rhinoceros vipers, Gabon vipers, puff adders, several types of cobras, boomslangs, mambas, hissing sand snakes, and blind snakes. Non-poisonous snakes include African rock pythons, egg eaters, brown house snakes, wolf snakes, green grass snakes, and file snakes. Some people will use *buya*, a word for weeds and *tond bungu* (rope of the forest), as euphemisms for snakes (*thuol, thuonde*), hoping to avoid calling snakes other than the python to them. Snakes tend to keep their distance from humans but occasionally venture onto paths, fields, termite mounds, pit latrines, and other places where snakes and humans meet.

In the past, big snakes, sometimes said to be cobras, were held to have control of wells. Neglect of the big snakes was believed to lead to drought. Some Luo placed offerings to the snakes by dry wells so that the wells would produce again. It was said that snakes had occasionally even demanded the sacrifice of a virgin (or an old woman substitute) in exchange for water. Cobras, along with hyenas and leopards, are clearly associated in Luo thought with night-runners ("night-witches") who are said to cast spells to harm neighbors under the cover of darkness. Black mambas are believed to dislike having humans look at them. Before becoming Christian or Muslim, some Luo made sacrifices to mambas as compensation for disturbing them. The ashes of mambas are still used in medicines made by some doctor-diviners for clients involved in bitter disputes with others. Cobras and mambas are male symbols in Luo thought because of their shared capacity for being dangerous, poisonous, and bitter. If a pregnant woman has a dream with a cobra or black mamba in it, indigenous beliefs hold that this predicts she will give birth to a son.

Luo tend to distinguish pythons from other snakes and to want to have pythons nearby. Prohibitions on humans killing pythons are widespread in Africa, and found among Luo. Pythons' preferred habitat is savannah but they can also be found in or close to water. Pythons are the largest and most aquatic of Africa's snakes. Bodies of water are a female symbol for many ethnic groups around the world, including Luo. Pythons are highly dimorphic; females are much longer and heavier than males. While the saying "power is eaten whole" has been applied to men involved in African politics, the trope has applicability to pythons. Male and female pythons have structural features which enable them to consume animals larger than themselves. Their food includes hare, baboons, jackals, antelopes, porcupines, wild and domesticated pigs, calves, sheep, goats, dogs, doves, water fowl, fish, chickens, rodents, and snakes of other species. Since rodents are responsible for high annual loss of stored grain which is used to make the Luo staple, *kuon* (stiff porridge), pythons feeding on rodents counterbalance predation on domestic livestock. Pythons have the "maximum internal capacity" of all of Africa's snakes. A male python slowly digesting a large meal can resemble a pregnant human female.

Female pythons are highly prolific in the number of eggs they produce each pregnancy. They brood over their eggs protectively. They are not receptive to males while doing this. Their greater size and the position of their cloaca makes forced insemination impossible. While their maternal care is not lengthy, female pythons show the greatest parental care of all snakes. Luo have some interest in male pythons but more in females. This can be linked to beliefs about women's reproductive, healing, and spiritual powers. One Luo term for the uterus (*nyiseche*) is the plural of a word for the Supreme Being (*Nyasaye*). The womb can also be called *nyasach dhako* (the "godliness" of a woman). The Luo inflection of patriliny, polygyny, and the house-property complex makes each mother the head of her own house and of the matricentric segment that comes from her womb. Polygyny enables a long post-partum taboo and period in which women, like their python counterparts, are not receptive to males.

Luo make a distinction between people and animals, but this anti-Linnaean line can waver. Some Luo contend that the prohibition on killing pythons, which is still largely observed, exists because of the Luo belief that pythons were once people. It is said that some women had sought out doctor-diviners for medicine so that the women could be transformed into female pythons. In the present when a python is seen encircling flora, it is said to be signaling to humans that "the best" healing medicine is there. Before they became largely Christian, Luo built shrines at places where pythons stayed and made offerings concerned with increase. Men would pray at the site for a productive wife, women for children. Both would ask for rain and good yield for crops. Milk, which was something commonly offered to pythons, is a word in Luo homophonous with their word for creation and creative powers. Today, Luo no longer build python shrines but continue to respect pythons. Pythons are still linked to the old boons as well as success in business and elective politics. The prohibition on killing pythons is still honored by most Luo. Respect for pythons, like that for ancestors, persists along with belief in imported religions. The effort of clerics to link pythons with the diabolic still meets resistance.

Certain pythons are believed to be larger and to have greater spiritual powers than other pythons. *Kit Mikayi* (Stone of the First Wife), a "natural" megalithic formation of several rocks located about 17 miles from the city of Kisumu, is believed to have sacred python protection. Luo oral narratives recount that Kit Mikayi came into being during a storm and earthquake that occurred where a first wife had gone to reflect, after her husband had rejected her for their child's nursemaid, whom he had taken as a second wife. The first wife, her husband, the second wife, and her child are believed to have been turned into the megalithic formation. One or two pythons are said to guard it. Of those who believe there are two pythons, some speak of a male–female pair. More Luo believe there is a pair of females or one female python, regarding "all snakes responsible for blessings" as female. The python stays in a large pool in the interior of the rock formation. Some say its waters, like those that drip from the rocks, have healing properties. A few hold that the python guards both water and new wealth, contending there is also a pool of petrol inside the rocks protected by the python. People still leave offerings at the site for the python. Nyamgondho and Lwanda Magere, two Luo men who are the subjects of Luo oral narratives, and who met unhappy deaths because they did not treat a first wife well, are said to have come to the python-protected monument as unhappy ghosts, hoping to make redress for their errors. Luo political leaders have visited Kit Mikayi and its environs into the late twentieth and even the twenty-first century, recognizing that the multiple powerful images attached to the site remain central in Luo consciousness, and are a resource to be drawn upon for each generation. Members of several churches including Legio Maria, an African-instituted Catholic church, visit Kit Mikayi. Some Legios contend that Mary, a protector of women, provider of healing, and proponent of the use of holy water ("Mary's medicine") came to Kit Mikayi and increased the healing properties of its waters, making them holy. Some Luo contend that the pool of water in which the python lives goes all the way to Lake Victoria, where the python goes to drink and to visit other snakes. People say the python sometimes flies through the air to get to Lake Victoria accompanied by bats, the flying mammal.

In indigenous spirituality, Lake Victoria is seen as the home of powerful possession spirits who can take the form of pythons or, as is found elsewhere with snake symbolism, rainbows. When they rise from the lake to pierce the sky, their activity is believed to bring rain. Unlike ordinary rainbows, those of the python-rainbow spirits are held to be visible to devotees from dusk into deep night. Three of these python-rainbow spirits, Mumbo, Sumba (Sumba Adongo), and Rabudi, had devotees who came together in early anti-colonial political-religious movements. They grew their hair into long, "wild" or "snake-like" locks. Mumbo was gendered as male; Sumba and Rabudi as female. One of Mumbo's titles was *Min Rech*, "the Mother of Fish." Maternity is so highly valorized by Luo that *Min* (Mother of) is an honorific that can be applied to that which is deemed "the best, biggest, most important, or preeminent," regardless of gender. While all three movements died out before colonialism's end, possession by Mumbo and Sumba has persisted. Sometimes called a consort of Mumbo, Sumba has been seen as a powerful python-rainbow spirit in her own right. She is regarded as the leader of other female possessive spirits. Her female devotees carry flywhisks, symbols of leadership throughout Africa. Ideally, bristles for Sumba's flywhisks come from the tail of a waterbuck. Nyawigoluwe, who dwells above Lake Victoria, is a spirit whose rainbow character is more developed than her snake-side. Nyalkoi is a snake-spirit with an affinity for water spouts.

Nyang'idi, the "daughter-messenger of God," is a python-spirit whose home is Lake Kanyaboli, the largest of the three Yala swamp lakes. Luo have believed she periodically leaves her lake to visit families in the area. If properly welcomed, she will let people touch her. She is said to bless those who present her with food such as hens, cocks, and milk with rain and good yield. One origin legend states Nyang'idi is the mistreated elder wife of a Luo leader who had left her behind on his migration into Yimbo. She turned into a python whose peregrinations took her from Lake Kanyaboli to her husband's Yimbo home as well as other areas of "Luoland." While there have been periodic accounts of her being stoned and killed as she moves around the countryside, Nyang'idi has reappeared over the decades. As with the python who guards Kit Mikayi, Nyang'idi can be seen to embody the understanding that the "outsider" women upon whom Luo patrilineal homes and the female-headed farming system are so dependent can be transformed rather than crushed by abuse. Luo women who find powers and resources within themselves have proven themselves capable of casting off husbands and unhappy lives for new opportunities, much as pythons periodically shed their skins.

Omieri (also called Omweri) is yet another prominent python in Luo life. She is associated with Nyakach location, and in 1987 she was accidentally burned by men who had been clearing land. She was brought to the Kisumu Museum, whose animal specialists tried to save the burned python. Omieri finally died from her injuries. She was given a funeral and coffin as though a person had died. In

1999, the National Museums of Kenya exhumed Omieri and built a special display for her at the Nairobi Snake Park attached to the National Museum. This exhibit was part of the Museum Society's 1999 Arts Festival. Stories of Omieri's "fantastic divine powers" were recounted at the display's opening, and subsequently reported in Kenya's press. In March 2003, after the advent of full multiparty democracy in Kenya with the election of Mwai Kibaki as President on the National Alliance Rainbow Coalition ticket, Omieri was sighted in Nyakach brooding over her eggs. The election, which brought Luo out of the political cold after long-standing political opposition to the Daniel Arap Moi and Jomo Kenyatta regimes, and the return of Omieri shortly thereafter, were linked in the minds of Luo. The NARC Minister for the Environment made a promise in Kenya's Parliament that Omieri would be protected by the new government through the efforts of a committee guided by officials of the Kenya Wildlife Service and National Museums. Omieri again received extensive coverage in the Kenyan press. This time she also made her way into internet discussion lists for Kenyans, online sites devoted to snakes and spirituality, the BBC, and American and other international newspapers. For many Luo, this python who has fascinated so many is not the "daughter" of the old Omieri who "died" of her 1987 injuries, but the same snake as the old Omieri, who was herself the same as the python of Kit Mikayi, Lake Kanyaboli, and the female pythons of Lake Victoria. Snakes are a perduring symbol for Luo.

Nancy Schwartz

Further Reading

Hambly, Wilfrid. *Serpent Worship in Africa.* Chicago: Field Museum of Natural History, 1931.

Kokwaro, John and Timothy Johns. *Luo Biological Dictionary.* Nairobi: East African Publishing House, 1998.

Ocholla-Ayayo, A.B.C. *Traditional Ideology and Ethics Among the Southern Luo.* Uppsala: Scandinavian Institute of African Studies, 1976.

Onyango-Ogutu, Benedict A.A. Roscoe. *Keep My Words: Luo Oral Literature.* Nairobi: East African Publishing House, 1974.

Pope, Clifford. *The Giant Snakes: The Natural History of the Boa Constrictor, the Anaconda, and the Largest Pythons.* New York: Alfred A. Knopf, 1961.

Schwartz, Nancy. "Active Dead or Alive: Some Kenyan Views About the Agency of Luo and Luyia Women Pre- and Post-Mortem." *Journal of Religion in Africa* XXX: 4 (2000), 433–67.

Skinner, H.A. *Snakes and Us: An Introduction to East African Herpetology.* Nairobi: East African Literature Bureau, 1973.

See also: African Religions and Nature Conservation; Biodiversity and Religion in Equatorial Africa; Cihuacoatl – Aztec Snakewoman; Rainbow Serpent (North Wellesley Islands, Australia); Serpents and Dragons; Weather Snake.

Snyder, Gary (1930–) – and the Invention of Bioregional Spirituality and Politics

Gary Snyder is one of the most influential green poets and prose writers of the second half of the twentieth century. He became one of the leading intellectual architects of several green religious movements, including bioregionalism and green anarchism, deep ecology, ecopsychology, radical environmentalism, and what could be called neo-animism. Yet for some he will always be most known as one of the "beat poets" during the second wave of the San Francisco Poetry Renaissance of the 1950s and 1960s. What distinguished him and fellow poets Michael McClure and Kenneth Rexroth from the rest of the beat movement was a deep sensitivity to nature, a perception of its sacredness and "intrinsic value." In those and the following years, Snyder's influence grew throughout environmentalist sub-cultures and the counterculture more widely.

Born in San Francisco and raised on a farm in Washington near Mt. St. Helens and Mt. Rainer, three long streams of his life may be traced to his early years. First, his childhood experiences encouraged both a profound reverence for wild nature and a concern about its destruction:

> From a very early age I found myself standing in an indefinable awe before the natural world. An attitude of gratitude, wonder, and a sense of protection especially as I began to see the hills being bulldozed down for roads, and the forests of the Pacific Northwest magically float away on logging trucks (1977: 15).

And this wonder involved what for Snyder has been an enduring perception.

> I was born a natural animist. It wasn't a moral or intellectual thing, from early childhood, I felt the presence of other beings, and I enjoyed being out in the woods right back of our farm ... I think most kids are natural animists (unless otherwise cited, all quotations are from author's interview with Snyder in Davis, California, June 1993).

Second, Snyder had friends with the left-anarchist Industrial Workers of the World and a grandfather who "soapboxed for the Wobblies" when he was a young adult (1990: 124), and such ideology left an imprint that would emerge in his political writings. Third, he graduated from Reed College with a degree in literature and anthropology, which undergirded much of his future poetry, prose, and activism. Snyder worked a variety of outdoor jobs as a young man, including one as a logger and another briefly with the United States Forest Service after college, a position from which he was dismissed due to his association with leftists during the anti-communist purges of the time.

A New (Old?) Religion and Politics

Snyder's anthropological studies helped draw him to both Native American and East Asian religions, leading him to once contend that they constitute "one teaching" (1980: 67). But finding American Indian cultures inaccessible to non-Indians, "its content, perhaps, is universal, but you must be Hopi to follow the Hopi way" (1980: 94), he chose to study Buddhism intensively, which he did for twelve years beginning in 1955, especially focusing on Zen Buddhism in Japan. In Buddhism he found metaphysics of interdependence and kinship ethics with the nonhuman world that resonated with his own animistic perceptions. But while he also found teachers of "Buddhist anarchism" and formed a commune with fellow anarchist Nanao Sakaki while in Japan, he was disappointed with the more prevalent martial and bureaucratic Buddhism that he encountered there, concluding that world religions primarily function to "reinforce the societies they are in" (1980: 2).

Upon his return to the United States his lifework really began, as he sought to integrate religion and politics into a new, bioregional spirituality that he hoped would, over time, reconnect humans to nature and nudge them to develop ecologically sustainable spiritualities and political arrangements. Snyder first came to public attention as a beat poet, and to those in the know, as the model for the character Jaffe Ryder in Jack Kerouac's *Dharma Bums* (1958). He was deeply influenced by these enclaves, which he described later as rich "with anarchist and Wobblie connections and full of anti-authoritarian leftists." Yet Snyder's influence soon began to extend beyond those enclaves and into environmentalist sub-cultures and the counterculture at large. This was in part because he was offering something innovative, both spiritually (an earthen spirituality to a culture feeling alienated from nature and anxiety about this) and politically (an alternative to an impersonal, technocratic, centralized nation-state).

Buddhist-Animist Spirituality and Deep Ecology

Once back in the United States, fed by and feeding the countercultural ferment of the time, Snyder began to develop and promote a distinct religious perspective and became a major contributor to the "deep ecology" movement, which also expresses a reverence for the Earth's living systems and asserts that nature has inherent value. He concluded that in Western cultures it is probably more politically astute to promote "deep ecology" rather than Paganism (or perhaps even Zen Buddhism). Yet he nevertheless contended in discussions with deep ecology proponents that Zen expressed deep ecological ethics with unsurpassed philosophical sophistication. This is certainly one reason that Buddhism has remained central to his identity. In 1973, he called himself "a practicing Buddhist, or Buddhist-shamanist" (1980: 33), and twenty years later, after first indicating that he considered himself a "fairly orthodox Buddhist," he also labeled himself a "Buddhist-Animist."

Clearly, his enduring animist identity is as central to his nature spirituality as is his Buddhism. When asked in 1993 about interspecies communication, which he had periodically alluded to, he told a story about a woman named Ella, an Irish Mystic he knew in the 1950s, who once accompanied him on a walk in Muir Redwoods, north of San Francisco. Hearing the song of a yellow crown warbler, Ella turned to him and reported that this song was a special gift to her from that bird. Reflecting on this and my follow-up questions about what animism meant to him and what an animistic perception was like, Snyder answered

> Its not that animals come up and say something in English in your ear. You know, it's that things come into your mind ... Most people think that everything that comes into their mind is their own, their own mind, that it comes from within. It may come from someplace deep within or less deep, but everybody thinks it comes from within. That's modern psychology. Well, some of those things that you think are from within are given to you from outside, and part of the trick is knowing which was which – being alert to the one that you know was a gift, and not think, "I thought that." Say [instead], "Ah, that was a gift!" ... I have a poem about a magpie giving me a song (Magpie's song). That's just one [example] ...

And like many environmentalist proponents of animism and Buddhism, Snyder criticizes monotheistic religions. Reflecting on the metaphysics of interrelatedness, which permeates his writing, Snyder said

> Interrelatedness is a commonsense observation. We should remind ourselves that ordinary working people, traditional people ... notice that things are connected. What's not common is the mind–body dualism that begins to come in with monotheism. And the alliance of monotheism with the formation of centralized governance and the national state, that's what's unnatural, and statistically in a minority on Earth. The [most common] human experience has been an experience of animism. Only a small proportion of people on Earth have been monotheists.

Snyder's spirituality and politics are thus linked in his dual critique of monotheism and nationalism. Arguing that these "do seem to go together" he concluded,

> Jews and Muslims are the only pure monotheists, Christians hold to it in a very qualified and tricky way ... Everybody else in the world is a multifaceted polytheist, animist or Buddhist, who sees things in the world [as alive].

It easy to understand why Snyder liked the influential article and book by Christopher Stone, "Should Trees Have Standing?" (1972, 1974), which argued that trees should be represented in the courts and other democratic processes. Reflecting on Stone's argument, Snyder noted that he had long resonated with the "animistic idea that you can hear voices from trees" and commented that this makes it easy to move from the idea that trees should have standing to "nonhuman nature has rights." Snyder came to understand that his own role as a poet was to promote such rights and to speak for the nonhuman world, "to speak for these things, to carry their voice into the human realm" (1980: 74).

For Snyder, these are sacred voices, although he periodically has cautioned against overuse of the word "sacred," noting that this term can devalue what it signifies. Yet his work unambiguously conveys his reverence for life. Indeed, a central theme in Snyder's writings is the sacramental nature of life itself, even the process of eating, and eventually, being eaten.

> Eating is a sacrament. The grace we say clears our hearts and guides the children and welcomes the guest, all at the same time ... (1990:184). To acknowledge that each of us at the table will eventually be part of the meal is not just being "realistic." It is allowing the sacred to enter and accepting the sacramental aspect of our shaky temporary personal being ... (1990: 19). And if we do eat meat it is the life, the bounce, the swish, of a great alert being with keen ears and lovely eyes, with foursquare feet and a huge beating heart that we eat, let us not deceive ourselves ... (1990: 184).

Such a reverence he brought forcefully into poetic movements and the counterculture in general, first in the western United States, then much more broadly.

Anarchism, Bioregionalism, and Radical Environmentalism

While Snyder's spirituality resonated with many in the environmental movement and Western countercultures, he has been equally influential in promoting radical environmental ideas and decentralism in green social philosophy. Specifically, he helped pioneer the green social philosophy now known as "bioregionalism," which promotes decentralized participatory democracy within the contours of different (reconfigured) ecosystem types. Bioregionalism, for Snyder, represents an "exercise of ignoring the presence of the national state" if not an effort to overturn it outright, although he views this not as a violent, short-term revolutionary ideal, but as an evolutionary hope dependent on a transformation of consciousness.

As with his spirituality, Snyder's bioregional perspective was deeply influenced by his understanding of Native American cultures. His reading in the 1950s of the studies of Anthropologist A.L. Krober, who concluded that Native American cultural zones paralleled regional ones, was especially influential on his thinking. Equally so was the anarchist writer Peter Kropotkin, whose thinking Snyder was introduced to in the early 1950s "as part of the poetry and political circles of San Francisco culture."

Reflecting on such tributaries, bioregionalism drew, according to Snyder,

> on the history of anarchist thought ... [on the conviction] that we do not need a state, and that the state or government is *not* necessarily synonymous with the social order and organization inherent in society. By *anarchism* I mean a nonviolent political philosophy that finds order in the possibilities of a free society, and not in the imposed order of a state structure operating with a monopoly on violence ... not ... wild-eyed bomb throwers ... So North American bioregionalism is an extension of anarchist thought, combined with much appreciation of American Indian culture areas, the recognition of the virtues of decentralization, and the insights of "field ecology" (Woods and Schoonmaker 1985: 115–16).

From such sources and many discussions occurring within the cultural underground of the United States, Snyder and other bioregionalists surmised that small-scale societies, which live for a long time close to the land in specific ecoregions, can best figure out how to live there properly, both culturally and ecologically, listening to the land itself, and learning good environmental manners. Fairly rapidly, such ideas grew into the bioregional ideal, especially once a now-obscure figure, Allen Van Newkirk, invented the term in 1975. Snyder and the actor Peter Coyote, as well as Freeman House and Peter Berg (both of whom founded bioregional organizations and wrote widely in support of such ideals), for example, brainstormed together many of the ideas and tropes of the emerging movement – such as "reinhabitation," the idea of reinhabiting land after being away and estranged by it in order to learn to live there sustainably. Snyder and McClure may also have coined the slogan "Back to the Pleistocene," believed to have first appeared in print in an interview republished in *The Real Work* (1980: 57), which would later be adopted by Paul Shepard, one of the premier theorists of both ecopsychology and radical environmentalism. In the early 1980s, the slogan was used by Dave Foreman, one of Earth First!'s co-founders, and in a new kind of primitive marketing, it soon adorned T-Shirts and bumper-stickers. That Snyder also put the Australian Buddhist and rainforest activist John Seed in contact with Foreman in the early 1980s further illustrates Snyder's influence on the evolution of radical environmentalism. Seed became one of the world's leading proponents of deep ecology spirituality and radical environmental action. Indeed, close reading of Snyder's *Turtle Island* (1969), which was awarded a Pulitzer prize in 1975, reveals nearly every idea and theme that would later erupt and find expression in the 1980s in the radical environmental movement, including the idea that industrial civilization is like "a cancer . . . eating away at the breast of mother Earth" (1969: 104–5). The radical environmental novelist Edward Abbey, who was familiar with Snyder's writings, would further promote this metaphor, proclaiming through one of his characters in *The Monkeywrench Gang* that modern society's obsession with growth represented "the ideology of the cancer cell" (1975: 186).

Criticisms and Rejoinders

Despite Snyder's respect for Native Americans and what he believes are their nature-sympathetic cultures, some Indians have criticized him. In *The Remembered Earth* (1979) the Cherokee critic, Geary Hobson, criticized Snyder for "inadvertently" starting a "white shaman fad" with some poems "in which the poet speaks through the persona of an Indian shaman" (Hobson 1979: 105). Hobson was easier on Snyder than many others in his article, acknowledging Snyder's appreciation for Indian culture and that he was "one of the finest poets in America . . . when he is not pontificating about Indian things" (Hobson 1979: 107). But he clearly felt that Snyder and others should leave Indian things alone, so that "contemporary Indian writers" could speak for themselves, and certainly not assume the persona of a shaman. One of his contributors, the American Indian novelist Leslie Marmon Silko, was harsher, arguing that Snyder was a willing participant in a "two-part" attack on Indians, first by assuming in a racist way, along with many other white poets, that he could understand the mind of an Indian and express it in poetry; and secondly, by borrowing widely from Indians in his book *Turtle Island*, even its title, while failing properly to acknowledge "this land he is occupying . . . is *not* his land" (Silko 1979: 215). Silko takes offense that ethnographers and artists, including Snyder, then collect royalties on what she considers "plagiarized materials" (1979: 212).

While Snyder received some of the earliest criticisms of cultural theft from indigenous voices, by the mid-1980s, most of such criticism shifted to those in the New Age movement who fabricated an Indian identity to sell books or profited financially by selling "Native American" ceremonies or other experiences.

But Snyder had understood his spirituality in shamanic terms, so the criticisms cannot be considered off-target, even for those who do not find them compelling. Snyder himself did not duck the issue or distance himself from his worldview, which he saw as cohering with shamanism. In a 1979 interview that brought up the criticisms in Hobson's book, Snyder responded directly. Shamanism comes from powerful experiences and wisdom that flow from making contact "with a totally nonhuman other" (1980: 154), he contended, "that is what I'm talking about when I talk about shamanism, which is a worldwide phenomenon and not limited in a proprietary sense to any one culture" (1980: 155). No one bothers Native American writers who speak in genres derived from European culture, Snyder continued, concluding,

> As artists we are all free to write about anything we like. And if it is inauthentic it will show up sooner or later. If it really works, then people will trust it (1980: 155) . . . The practice of shamanism . . . at its very center is a teaching from the nonhuman, not a teaching from an Indian medicine man, or a Buddhist master. The question of culture does not enter into it. It's a naked experience that some people have out in the woods (1980: 156).

For Snyder, then, authenticity resides in the experience; and the value of ritual rests in its power and efficacy. The emergence of new truths and practices are possible because they can be learned from the dynamic, changing, multivocal Earth, and time will judge their authenticity.

Gary Snyder's work has also been criticized for its anarchistic, bioregional social philosophy. Some consider such ideology naive and utopian or devoid of a concrete strategy for bridling either corporate power or nation-states themselves. Others assert such social philosophy cannot adequately address global issues, such as the destruction of marine fisheries or atmospheric pollution. The political theorist Robyn Eckersley, in *Environmentalism and Political Theory* (1992), criticized anarchistic and bioregional thinking for assuming humans should take their cues from nature, arguing this would actually produce a world where the strong dominate the weak. Eckersley also argued that local communities often oppose ecological flourishing, so promoting regional autonomy often makes little ecological sense. Another political theorist, Dan Deudney, agrees that vesting political autonomy in a bioregion will often not serve either equity nor environmental well-being, arguing that bioregionalism has not explained how it could keep resource-rich bioregions from dominating those less well endowed.

Snyder views such criticisms as based on a misunderstanding of what anarchism means and on a *caricature* of bioregionalism:

> Nobody ever said that anything was going to be autonomous, or that we were going to live [exclusively according to] bioregions. We're talking about theatre. Everybody has to get this into their heads. This is theatre, mythology, visionary praxis. This is forming a new society on the shell of the old. It doesn't mean the old society goes away, but it means you have some alternatives with which to act on the old. And nobody is thinking literally – aha! bioregions! autonomous nations! – or anything like that. There is a whole fluid way of looking at community relationships and jurisdictions. None of that is a useful discussion in terms of twenty-first-century politics.

Here and elsewhere Snyder's rejoinders indicate that he is not a naive utopian who is expecting to see the nation-state fall in the near future, ushering in an ecological new age. Yet he remains hopeful that bioregional spirituality and politics might, "nullify some things or lead to joint management committees between government managers and local people," and that such developments could provide valuable models for an environmentally sustainable and socially just future.

Snyder complains that critics intend "to demolish something that was never created, a theory or proposal that doesn't exist" and fail to apprehend that "bioregionalism is an educational proposal to see where we are." But if people could begin to see bioregional spirituality and politics in this way, Snyder thinks, "we might begin to see some cultural effects [and] then, we might see political effects."

Conclusion

For decades Snyder has been traveling widely from his home in the Sierra Nevada foothills to deliver lectures and poetry readings around the world, sometimes upon the occasion of receiving one of the numerous literary awards he has won. Since 1985, he has also influenced many college students as a professor in the English Department and Nature and Culture program at the University of California, Davis. Meanwhile, in no small measure because of his influence, watershed protection groups have swept across America and local green coalitions in a number of instances have taken over regional governments, including in Snyder's home county.

If Snyder is correct that the proof is in the pudding, then it appears there is something ecologically and socially salutary to be found in the emergence of bioregional politics in America. And if he is correct metaphysically, then there will always be hope because the land and its creatures will always be speaking their truths, and all humans have to do is learn to listen.

I'm not really worried about what white people are going to do on this continent. If anybody lives here long enough, the spirits will begin to speak to them. It's the power of the spirits coming up from the land ... That's what taught us, and it would teach everybody, if they'd just stay here. The old spirits and the old powers aren't lost; people just need to be around long enough to begin to [let them] influence them.

Snyder recalled this "elegant ... if overly optimistic" view from a Crow Indian Elder during a 1985 interview (Woods and Schoonmaker 1985:116). In doing so he showed his ability to temper hope with cautionary realism and a sense that living long and attentively in place will be needed if humans are to reharmonize their lives with the wider natural world.

Bron Taylor

Further Reading

Abbey, Edward. *The Monkeywrench Gang*. New York City, NY: Avon, 1975.

Aldred, Lisa. "Plastic Shamans and Astroturf Sun Dances: New Age Commercialization of Native American Spirituality." *American Indian Quarterly* 24:3 (2000), 329–52.

Barnhill, David Landis. "Great Earth Sangha: Gary Snyder's View of Nature as Community." In M.E. Tucker and D. Williams, eds. *Buddhism and Ecology*. Cambridge, MA: Harvard University Press, 1997, 187–217.

Davidson, Michael. *The San Francisco Renaissance: Poetics and Community at Mid-century*. Cambridge: Cambridge University Press, 1989.

Deudney, Daniel. "Global Village Sovereignty: Intergenerational Sovereign Publics, Federal-Republican Earth Constitutions, and Planetary Identities." In Karen Litfin, ed. *The Greening of Sovereignty in World Politics*. Boston, MA: MIT Press, 1998, 299–323.

Deudney, Daniel. "In Search of Gaian Politics: Earth Religion's Challenge to Modern Western Civilization." In Bron Taylor, ed. *Ecological Resistance Movements: The Global Emergence of Radical and Popular Environmentalism*. Albany, NY: State University of New York Press, 1995, 282–99.

Eckersley, Robyn. *Environmentalism and Political Theory: Toward an Ecocentric Approach*. Albany, NY: State University of New York Press, 1992.

Hobson, Geary. "The Rise of the White Shaman as a New Version of Cultural Imperialism.' In Geary Hobson, ed. *The Remembered Earth*. Albuquerque, NM: Red Earth, 1979, 100–8.

Kerouac, Jack. *Dharma Bums*. Cutchogue, NY: Buccaneer, 1958.

Kroeber, A.L. *Cultural and Natural Areas of Native North*

America. Berkeley, CA: University of California Press, 1947 (1939).

Kropotkin, Peter. *Mutual Aid: A Factor of Evolution*. Montreal: Black Rose, 1914.

McClure, Michael. *Scratching the Beat Surface*. San Francisco, CA: North Point Press, 1982.

Newkirk, Allen Van. "Bioregions: Towards Bioregional Strategy for Human Cultures." *Environmental Conservation* 2 (1975), 108.

Phillips, Rod. *"Forest Beatniks" and Urban Thoreaus": Gary Snyder, Jack Kerouac, Lew Welch, and Michael McClure*. New York: Peter Lang, 2000.

Rose, Wendy. "The Great Pretenders: Further Reflections on Whiteshamanism." In Annette M. Jaimes, ed. *The State of Native America: Genocide, Colonization, and Resistance*. Boston, MA: South End, 1992, 403–21.

Silko, Leslie Marmon. "An Old-Time Indian Attack Conducted in Two Parts: Part One, Imitation 'Indian' Poems; Part Two, Gary Snyder's *Turtle Island*." In Geary Hobson, ed. *The Remembered Earth*. Albuquerque, NM: Red Earth, 1979, 211–16.

Stone, Christopher D. *Should Trees Have Standing – Toward Legal Rights for Natural Objects*. Los Altos, CA: William Kaufmann, 1974.

Stone, Christopher D. "Should Trees Have Standing – Toward Legal Rights for Natural Objects." *So. California Law Review* 45 (1972), 450–501.

Snyder, Gary. *Mountains and Rivers Without End*. Washington, D.C.: Counterpoint, 1996.

Snyder, Gary. *A Place in Space: Ethics, Aesthetics, and Watersheds*. Washington, D.C.: Counterpoint, 1995.

Snyder, Gary. *No Nature: New and Selected Poems*. New York: Pantheon Books, 1992.

Snyder, Gary. *The Practice of the Wild*. San Francisco, CA: North Point Press, 1990.

Snyder, Gary. *The Real Work: Interviews and Talks 1964–1976*. New York: New Directions, 1980 (1969).

Snyder, Gary. *The Old Ways*. San Francisco, CA: City Lights, 1977.

Snyder, Gary. *Turtle Island*. New York: New Directions, 1969.

Snyder, Gary. *The Back Country*. New York: New Directions, 1968.

Snyder, Gary. *Earth House Hold: Technical Notes and Queries to Fellow Dharma Revolutionaries*. New York: New Directions, 1957.

Taylor, Bron. "Bioregionalism: An Ethics of Loyalty to Place." *Landscape Journal* 19:1&2 (2000), 50–72.

Taylor, Bron. "Deep Ecology and Its Social Philosophy: A Critique." In Eric Katz, Andrew Light and David Rothenberg, eds. *Beneath the Surface: Critical Essays on Deep Ecology*. Cambridge, MA: MIT Press, 2000, 269–99.

Taylor, Bron. "Earthen Spirituality or Cultural Genocide: Radical Environmentalism's Appropriation of Native American Spirituality." *Religion* 17:2 (1997), 183–215.

Taylor, Bron. "Resacralizing Earth: Pagan Environmentalism and the Restoration of Turtle Island." In David Chidester and Edward T. Linenthal, eds. *American Sacred Space*. Bloomington, IN: Indiana University Press, 1995, 97–151.

Woods, Bruce and Dane Schoonmaker. "Gary Snyder Talks about Bioregionalism." *Utne Reader* 2:1 (Feb./March 1985), 115–17.

See also: Aboriginal Spirituality and the New Age in Australia; Animism (various); Anarchism; Beat Generation Writers; Bioregionalism; Bioregionalism and the North American Bioregional Congress; Black Mesa; Buddhism – Engaged; Buddhism – North America; Death and Afterlife in Robinson Jeffers and Edward Abbey; Deep Ecology; Earth First! and the Earth Liberation Front; Environmental Ethics; Hopiland to the Rainforest Action Network; Indigenous Religions and Cultural Borrowing; Indra's Net; Kropotkin, Peter; Paleolithic Religions and the Future; Plastic Medicine Men; Radical Environmentalism; Re-Earthing; Seed, John; Zen Buddhism.

Social Construction of Nature and Environmental Ethics

Recent scholarly arguments about the "social construction" of various elements of human experience build on long-standing debates in Western philosophy, with roots in William of Ockham's nominalist claim that there is no intrinsic link between words and what they signify. Nominalism makes clear the disjuncture between things and the terms we use to describe them, and thus provides the crucial insight for theories of the social construction of nature: there is no intrinsic, universal quality that is captured in the terms we use. Instead, those terms are conventions of particular cultures and times, intelligible because of the meanings and values of those cultures. Developing this insight in relation to social institutions and meanings, Peter Berger and Thomas Luckmann argue in *The Social Construction of Reality* (1966) that society is built up by activities that express meaning, such as language and ritual.

Theories of social construction have influenced religious studies in many ways, particularly through the appropriation of sociological approaches, such as that of Berger and Luckmann, which perceive religious rituals, symbols, practices, and texts as key elements in a culture's creation and maintenance of social meaning and legitimation. In the study of religion and nature, the idea that nature is socially constructed has been important in light of debates among theologians and philosophers who believe that nature has objective, even divinely ordained, value prior to any human activity, on the one hand, and those who argue that the significance of natural processes and entities arises from human, rather than "natural" or sacred, processes.

Contemporary scholarship includes a wide range of social constructionist approaches, including Marxian, Foucauldian, deconstructionist, and feminist perspectives. Most of these contend that categories such as sex or race are not universal or natural, but instead depend on particular cultural contexts for their power and significance (Haraway 1991; Peterson 1999). Scholars in various disciplines have also applied this insight to the natural environment. They suggest that, not only are such clearly human phenomena as race socially constructed, but that this is true also for the wild or nonhuman. In this view, cultural contexts influence the ways people interpret and value nature and the diversity that results in understandings of moral responsibilities toward nature.

In the growing literature on the social construction of nature, it is possible to identify two distinct, though not necessarily contradictory, ways in which nature can be viewed as socially constructed. First, different individuals, times, and societies "construct" particular versions of nature insofar as they interpret it in different ways in and through cultural categories and values. Many scholars insist that this type of construction is universal and unavoidable: we cannot experience nature except through the lens of meanings assigned to it by particular cultures and periods. As English literary critic Raymond Williams has noted, "the idea of nature contains, though often unnoticed, an extraordinary amount of human history" (1980: 67). Conceptions of nonhuman nature are historically and culturally determined, and there is no single, essential "nature" that people in all places and times recognize as such. This insight has been elaborated in contemporary ethnographic work, which shows that dominant Western ideas of nature and wilderness often make no sense in different cultural contexts. This meaning of the social construction of nature might more accurately be described as *construals* or interpretations rather than actual "constructions" of nature. What is "constructed" in this sense is not natural entities or objects but rather their meanings in particular contexts.

There is a second sense of the social construction of nature, however, in which nature is seen as being literally, physically created or changed by human activity. Some social constructionists argue that most of what is called natural, from city parks to rainforests, has been shaped by human actions. Very little of the world remains "natural," of course, if natural means free of human intervention. Such intervention includes not only the obviously inhabited areas but also many places commonly viewed as wilderness. For example, Europeans have sometimes viewed lands occupied by indigenous people, especially in the Americas, as untouched by humans, even though hundreds of generations of human inhabitants have helped shape forests, fields, and waterways. Modern industrial cultures, of course, have had much more far-reaching effects on the nonhuman world. This leads British philosopher Kate Soper to assert, "In our own time the human impact on the environment has been so extensive that there is an important sense in which it is correct to speak of 'nature' as itself a cultural product or construction" (1995: 152).

This view of the social construction of nature can inform an evaluation of the varying environmental impacts of different forms of life, from those that remain invisible to outsiders, like the hunting, gathering, agriculture, and forestry practiced by pre-Columbian peoples in much of North America, to those with obvious, and undeniably negative, consequences for both humans and nonhumans, such as the paving, clear-cutting, and burning of modern industrial societies. This perspective also challenges the erasure of native peoples, whose "invisibility," evidenced by the apparent absence of marks of their habitation, has helped justify exploitation of the lands they occupied. Further, awareness of human impacts on the environment is an important step toward critical analysis of those impacts and possible solutions.

Just as awareness of the ways that nature is physically shaped by human cultures enriches environmental ethics, so does an understanding of the symbolic construction of nature. The recognition that interpretations of nature are culturally mediated can challenge established ways of thinking about the nonhuman world and human relations to it. Understanding the diverse ways that nature is humanly shaped in both physical and symbolic ways can help avoid dualistic visions of an eternal, universal, and unmediated nature as the realm of physical relations counterposed to a human realm ruled by symbols. Most importantly, perhaps, both versions of social constructionism remind us that nature, culture, and religion, in their myriad forms, interact with each other, in our minds and also in the physical world.

Despite their benefits, social constructionist interpretations of nature carry certain risks. These are most notable in writings that suggest that the nonhuman has been "invented" by humans and human culture. If all nature is constituted by human interpretation or intervention, for example, then there is no basis for evaluating one environment as better or worse or for resisting certain forms of human intervention in nature. Against this "hard" version of social constructionism regarding nature, several writers have offered a qualified or "soft" realism. Soper argues that while it is true that any distinction we make between the reality of nature and its cultural representation is itself conceptual, it does not follow that "there is no ontological distinction between the ideas we have of nature and what the ideas are about" (1995: 151). Soper argues that there is a nature out there, although she remains agnostic about our capacity to "know" this nature. Holmes Rolston III, one of the earliest philosophers to focus attention on environmental ethics, defends a "harder" realism regarding nature. While acknowledging that "All human knowing colours whatever people see, through our percepts and concepts" (1997: 38), Rolston believes that we can still know nature "out there" in a (relatively and locally) accurate manner. Thus, commenting on Neil Evernden's description of nature as "a category, a conceptual container" (Evernden 1992: 89), Rolston contends that we invent the category nature and put things into it because "there is a realm out there, labeled nature, into which things have been put before we arrive" (Rolston 1997: 42). The word "nature" thus emerged in response to the need for a "container" to match the non-human "forces and processes" that exist prior to and apart from human intervention. Even if terms like "nature" are not universal, they may still have real referents, which we can come to know in a meaningful way.

For many religious thinkers and practitioners, nature has objective reality because it reflects divine powers and processes. To believe that creation has value or meaning only as a result of human activities, in such religious perspective, is thought to entail arrogance about the power and significance of humans in relation not only to nature but also to transcendent or sacred dimensions of life. Thus for the study of religion and nature, strong versions of social constructionism might need correction not only from naturalistic perspectives but also from theological ones. The goal might be to appreciate but not overestimate the significance of human symbolic and discursive activity in regard to nature.

Anna Peterson

Further Reading

Berger, Peter and Thomas Luckmann. *The Social Construction of Reality: A Treatise in the Sociology of Knowledge.* New York: Doubleday/Anchor Books, 1966.
Evernden, Neil. *The Social Creation of Nature.* Baltimore and London: Johns Hopkins University Press, 1992.
Haraway, Donna J. *Simians, Cyborgs, and Women: The Reinvention of Nature.* New York: Routledge, 1991.
Moran, Emilio. "Nurturing the Forest: Strategies of Native Amazonians." In Roy Ellen and Katsuyoshi Fukui, eds. *Redefining Nature: Ecology, Culture, and Domestication.* Oxford and Washington: Berg, 1996.
Peterson, Anna L. "Environmental Ethics and the Social Construction of Nature." *Environmental Ethics* 21:4 (Winter 1999), 339–57.
Rolston, Holmes III. "Nature for Real: Is Nature a Social Construct?" In Timothy Chappell, ed. *The Philosophy of the Environment.* Edinburgh: Edinburgh University Press, 1997.
Soper, Kate. *What is Nature?* Cambridge: Blackwell, 1995.
Soulé, Michael and Gary Lease, eds. *Reinventing Nature? Responses to Postmodern Deconstruction.* Washington, D.C.: Island Press, 1995.
Williams, Raymond. "Ideas of Nature." In *Problems in Materialism and Culture.* London: Verso, 1980.

See also: Callicott, J. Baird; Environmental Ethics; Rolston III, Holmes; Wilderness Religion.

Social Ecology

Social ecology is a contemporary social theory that investigates the interrelationship between social institutions and the natural world. A major project of social ecological analysis has been its attempt to demonstrate that local, regional and global ecological problems are created by authoritarian, hierarchical and exploitative social institutions. As a political ecology, social ecology has been concerned with promoting social changes that could end exploitation and domination within human society and establish an ecologically sound relationship between humanity and the natural world.

Philosophically, social ecology has adopted a holistic and dialectical position, while its politics have tended toward communitarianism, decentralism, anarchism and libertarian socialism. Its dialectical roots can be found in the tradition of Hegel, Marx and critical social theory, while its holistic and organicist dimension is in the tradition of thinkers such as Elisée Reclus and Lewis Mumford. Political theorist Murray Bookchin is its best-known contemporary proponent. Although some have used the term generically to describe all leftist political ecology, and there is also a rather eclectic interdisciplinary academic field of social ecology, the present discussion focuses on social ecology as a political ecology with a libertarian and communitarian social perspective.

Social ecology has gained widest recognition through the writings of Bookchin. Although Bookchin once expressed sympathy with various forms of spirituality, he and his collaborator Janet Biehl have over the past decade developed a strongly anti-spiritual and anti-religious position. On the other hand, some commentators (such as David Watson, Joel Kovel, and John Clark) have argued that various forms of ecological spirituality are not only compatible with the values of social ecology, but also can make an important contribution to its further theoretical development.

In his earlier work, Bookchin emphasized the ecological dimensions of many spiritual and religious traditions. He praised the nondualistic worldview of tribal societies (and specifically their concept of the "way") for uniting custom, morality, sensibility and nature. He suggested that animistic imagination offered modern society an outlook that is not only complementary to that of science but also more "organic" than the latter, and looked forward to a "new animism" based on a respect for and symbiotic relationship with other living beings. He also praised the libertarian, communitarian and ecological values of various radical Christian sects from the Middle Ages and early modern periods. And he wrote of a *telos* and a "latent subjectivity" in substance that led it to develop in the direction of mind and intellect, concepts that from the standpoint of mainstream philosophy have obvious connections with idealist metaphysics and spirituality.

Beginning in 1987, Bookchin began to attack what he saw as irrationalist, anti-human, regressive tendencies in the Deep Ecology movement. His criticism soon broadened into a general indictment of what he typified as "mystical" and "spiritual" ecology. For example, he characterized ecofeminist Goddess spirituality as an attempt to depict women as naturally superior to men and to replace male chauvinism with female chauvinism. In addition, he condemned "mystical ecologists" for a multitude of evils, including rejecting political activity, fostering passivity and fatalism, promoting neo-Malthusianism, encouraging anti-immigrant feelings, exalting irrationality, opposing civilization and technology, devaluing humanity, and believing in an illusory "pristine" nature unaffected by human beings.

Some have questioned the objectivity of such attacks. It has been pointed out that in dismissing ecological thinker Thomas Berry as "misanthropic," Bookchin cites Berry's reference to humanity as a "demonic presence" while failing to note that this depiction of human destructiveness was part of a larger discussion recognizing humanity's capacities for joy, wonder, and celebration of the universe. Boookchin's use of such selective quotation and the kind of sweeping generalities mentioned above have led critics to charge that his attacks on spirituality and religious thought are without scholarly merit.

Bookchin's collaborator Janet Biehl is also a harsh critic of spiritual and religious thought. Biehl contends that theistic spirituality places people in a condition of dependence and subservience and turns ecological politics into a form of "therapy" that makes meaningful political action impossible. However, she focuses her attention heavily on non-theistic feminist, and especially ecofeminist, spirituality. She maintains that many ecofeminists idealize Neolithic Goddess religions and the cultures that produced them, thus promoting irrational beliefs and distorting the history of societies that were in many ways repressive and hierarchical. More generally, she criticizes ecofeminist spirituality (which she characterizes, even in its pantheistic and panentheistic versions, as "theism") as a form of superstition with politically reactionary implications. Thus, she has attacked spiritual ecofeminists, including the well-known writer and political activist Starhawk and ecofeminist theologian Carol Christ, for adopting a spirituality that rejects any idea of historical progress, denies the possibility of development in nature, uses obfuscatory metaphors, and fosters fatalism and political passivity.

Despite the campaign by Bookchin and Biehl against spirituality and religion, a number of theorists who are sympathetic to social ecology as a general perspective have argued that it is compatible with certain spiritual and religious traditions. Joel Kovel, for example, argues that social ecology should pay attention to what can be learned from mysticism, which he holds to be in touch with a primary, pre-linguistic relationship to nature that is unavailable through ordinary consciousness. Kovel rejects what he sees as an overly simplistic ecological outlook that conceives of the relationship between nature and humanity purely in terms of "unity in diversity." He contends that such an outlook, which has been advocated by Bookchin, overlooks the irreducible negativity within human experience and the necessary tension between humanity and the larger natural world. Kovel distinguishes between an *ego* that is associated with domination of the other, rationalization of experience, and dualistic splitting of the self, and *spirit*, which refers to the individual's experience of relatedness to larger and deeper realities, including the whole of humanity and the whole of nature. The concept of spirit, according to Kovel's formulation, expresses a negation of the dominance of the ego and connects the problem of human emancipation to the question of humanity's relationship to larger realms of being. In Kovel's view, an awareness of this connection was at the core of the insights of Lao Tzu, Jesus and Gandhi.

In making a case for a "deep social ecology," David Watson argues that the spirituality of many tribal societies has embodied a view of reality that is more social and more ecological than that of civilization. Watson contends that social ecology must pay more careful attention to the voice of nature as expressed in the myths, rituals and shamanistic practices of tribal peoples. He sees tribal spirituality as an integral part of the egalitarian, cooperative nature of these societies. Watson cites examples, including the Hopi salt expedition, of rituals that are not mere practical or instrumental activities, but are also an expression of the quest for a harmonious relationship with nature and the sacred. According to Watson, animistic religion contained greater truth than the classic modern scientific and technological worldview. He notes that contemporary science has confirmed the animistic view that humans are physically and psychologically continuous with nature.

In arguing for a radically dialectical social ecology, John Clark argues that part of the task of a social ecology is to investigate the physical, psychological and ontological aspects of humanity that link it to other living beings, to the Earth, and to a primordial ground of being. He contends that some concepts of "spirit" have been a means of expressing humanity's relationship to the constantly changing, non-objectifiable reality of nature and to its deeper ontological matrix. He argues that social ecology is compatible with a spirituality that expresses wonder and awe at the unfolding of the universe's potentiality for realized being, goodness, truth and beauty. Furthermore, he finds in such spirituality an implicit critique of the abstract conception of selfhood and dogmatic rationalism found in some versions of social ecology.

Social ecology is at present associated strongly with Bookchin's theoretical position. Consequently, some who have explored the affinities between social ecology and spiritual and religious thought have subsequently gone so far as to disassociate themselves entirely from social ecology as a theoretical and political tendency. Thus, the future relationship of "social ecology" to spirituality and religion will depend in large part on whether the term will primarily connote adherence to Bookchin's system of "dialectical naturalism," or whether it will increasingly refer to a theoretically more diverse tradition founded on a common problematic for inquiry.

John Clark

Further Reading
Biehl, Janet. *Rethinking Ecofeminist Politics*. Boston: South End Press, 1991.
Bookchin, Murray. *Re-enchanting Humanity: A Defense of the Human Spirit Against Anti-humanism, Misanthropy, Mysticism and Primitivism*. London: Cassell, 1995.
Bookchin, Murray. *The Ecology of Freedom: The Emergence and Dissolution of Hierarchy*. Palo Alto, CA: Cheshire Books, 1982.
Clark, John. "A Social Ecology." In *Capitalism Nature Socialism* 8:3 (1997), 3–33.
Kovel, Joel. "Human Nature, Freedom, and Spirit." In John Clark, ed. *Renewing the Earth: The Promise of Social Ecology*. London: Green Print, 1990, 137–52.
Light, Andrew. *Social Ecology After Bookchin*. New York and London: The Guilford Press, 1998.
Watson, David. *Beyond Bookchin: Preface for a Future Social Ecology*. Brooklyn, NY: Autonomedia, 1996.

See also: Anarchism; Berry, Thomas; Earth First! and the Earth Liberation Front; Ecofeminism; Environmental Ethics; Green Politics; Radical Environmentalism.

Social Philosophy – See Environmental Ethics.

Social Science on Religion and Nature

Religion: Good or Bad for the Environment?
"We shall continue to have a worsening ecologic crisis until we reject the Christian axiom that nature has no reason for existence save to serve man." So argued historian of technology and medieval/Renaissance scholar Lynn White, Jr. (1967: 1207), who effectively set the terms of debate over religion and environmental concern for the last three and a half decades. White did not mince words – "Christianity is the most anthropocentric religion the world has seen" (1967: 1205) – and his powerful condemnation of Christianity as the ultimate cause of Western environmental crisis prompted the coming out of allies, as well as the inevitably countervailing response as believers, sympathizers, and reformers scrambled to bring out Christianity's greener hues.

Most scholarly commentaries on Lynn White's bald thesis have fallen somewhere between the two poles of attributing either outright guilt or utter innocence to religion – scholars generally prefer, rightly or wrongly, to complexify such matters – yet none has come close to the stature of White's 1967 publication. An early collection of top scholars of the era included arguments running parallel in some ways to White's thesis, qualified rejections of White's equation of Christian theology solely with dominion over nature, and a prototypical complexification argument claiming that capitalism, democracy, technology, urbanization, wealth, population growth, and resource tenure have all had environmental impacts on the Earth, with religion (in particular Judeo-Christianity) bearing only tenuous connections to this suite of causes. More recent responses have included philosophical and theological developments of the connection between religion and environment, attempts to bring science, religion, and environmental concern into closer dialogue, and inquiries into the ecological dimensions of a broad array of world religions and spiritual traditions.

Enter social scientists into the fray – after all, White's argument, and the counterarguments of White's opponents, are empirical claims concerning social and cultural reality, and thus could in theory be tested by means of rigorous, often quantitative, social science methods. Perhaps the debate over religion and environment would be settled by means of controlled empirical studies, or analysis of data from existing studies, using the powerful statistical methods social scientists routinely deploy. Perhaps science can help us decide whether White's thesis is correct.

This is the aura of science, but not the reality. Social science has done a tremendous service to the study of religion and environmental concern, but it has failed to deliver the conclusive chapter to the story. To understand why, we must first consider how social science approaches this topic, then examine applications of social science to the environmental dimensions of organized religion as well as the religious dimensions of environmentalism.

The Social Science Approach
The world sketched by White is one in which what he termed the "marriage" of Western science and technology,

not entirely consummated until the mid-nineteenth century, has wreaked environmental havoc in recent generations at a hitherto-unknown scale. The roots of these two institutions in Christian thought are deep: White traces the development of a distinctly scientific form of natural theology back to the thirteenth century, and large-scale technology back to the eleventh century, though with much earlier ties to the Christian doctrine of mastery over nature. By way of a causal model, then, White's argument moves from culturally-diffuse *ideas* inherent in Christianity to the powerful *institutions* of science and technology to the environmental *impacts* so obvious today.

The world sketched by a good deal of quantitative social science is rather stark in comparison to White's world. Not only is the timescale reduced to that for which data can be generated – in the case of surveys, the last several decades at most – but the societal complex of differentially powerful persons, ensconced in and carrying forth a wide realm of cultural and political institutions, often turns into a relatively undifferentiated mass of individuals. Virtually all social science tests of the White thesis operate in a world of self-reporting minds, participating – willingly or reluctantly, self-aware, self-deceived, or intentionally deceptive – in surveys designed to capture salient individual-scale characteristics. This rather ubiquitous doctrine of methodological individualism thus leads to a quite different causal model, which statistically aggregates patterns between the self-reported religious and environmental characteristics of *individuals*. *Ideas* are culturally diffuse only to the extent that a certain number of individuals claim to share them; *institutions* do not effectively exist; and *impacts* are assumed to follow based on expressed intent or concern of individuals – a not altogether convincing surrogate.

The challenges faced by social scientists, who wander this depauperate world in hopes of illuminating the much richer, though far less quantitatively tractable, world to which White referred, are understandably immense. Their strategies have been ingenious, and their accomplishments impressive. At the heart of their project have been three methodological questions concerning how to measure individual religiosity, environmental concern, and the relationship between the two. Though the common assumption is that individual religiosity is well described in terms of theological beliefs, religious scholars running from Otto (1923) to Eliade (1959) to the present have emphasized that religious experience and practice are equally if not more relevant. Thus have followed innovative means of characterizing religiosity as a function of individual beliefs, belonging, and behaviors. More directly relevant has been the desire adequately to capture the religiously based idea White blames for environmental destruction: examples have included notions central to White's thesis, such as dominion-over-nature, or related religious characteristics such as fundamentalism, and conservative eschatology. Similarly, individual environmental concern is best captured by a variety of measures, including attitudes and beliefs, policy concerns, and behaviors, though these items do not necessarily produce a consistent picture. Yet many of these factors are omitted in social science analyses due to data restrictions or the view that not all are relevant.

Once the measurement of religiosity and environmental concern has been addressed, the question remains as to how to characterize their relationship. The obvious point of departure is correlation: do individuals who score higher in certain religious characteristics also score higher in certain environmental characteristics, and vice versa? Yet correlation is not causation: if A (in this case, a religious characteristic) and B (an environmental characteristic) are correlated, perhaps A caused B, but perhaps B caused A, or perhaps C (possibly a demographic characteristic such as income or education) caused A and B. Most social scientists translate the White thesis into their world as A (religiously based attitudes toward nature) causes B (lack of environmental concern). Few social scientists are concerned that perhaps B causes A (since A is arguably more general than, and thus includes B); yet there are two exceptions. If one means not "environmental concern" but "the natural environment," the latter certainly has been assigned causal properties in socio-biological and related accounts. Additionally, if one considers A and B in at the institutional scale of organized religion and environmentalism, there is some evidence for the "greening" impact of the latter on the former in recent decades. Nonetheless, a remaining concern is that A and B may jointly derive from C. Thus most studies proceed from simple correlations to regression analyses in which demographic and other factors are added as "controls" – a method of effectively holding C constant to determine whether A has any independent effect on B. This method appears to be much more rigorous than the simple correlation, and has revealed a number of very important complications to the White thesis. But it should be remembered that, given the effective disappearance of institutions (not just science and technology, but, for instance, language and politics) and the reliance upon sample surveys, religion and environmental concern are understood as dimensions of individual human thought and action, alongside potentially complicating demographic and other dimensions of individuals. Even if, in the social science world, A does not seem to cause B, White's world may remain relatively unexamined.

Religion and Environment

There have been many empirical social science studies of the White thesis, but a small number of themes emerges from this literature. The first is that the connection between religion and environmental concern – as evidenced in surveys of sampled individuals – may be statistically evident, but it is substantially weak, especially when demographic (e.g., age, education, gender, social class) and other controls are taken into consideration. The weakness of the religion-environmental concern association has led some of these social scientists to declare the White thesis null and void, and others to reserve judgment until further studies sort out currently unsolved puzzles – as but one example among many, religiosity as defined by behavior appears negatively to influence environmental attitudes, but it positively influences environmental behavior. What is unarguable, however, is that not one single social science study has provided powerful and unqualified vindication of the Lynn White thesis.

The second theme is the theoretical point that, in regards to the relationship between religion and environmental concern among individuals, things are more complicated than they seem; or, put less generously, White's thesis is conceptually simplistic. For instance, several studies have called for some form of denominational disaggregation of Christianity, arguing that religiously based ideas of nature are by no means uniform across the spectrum, and some social scientists have joined other scholars who have argued that there are more ideological options available to Christians than the stark opposites of dominion over nature versus unity with nature.

A third, and quite provocative, theme is that ideas of dominion, and even related attributes of theological fundamentalism, may not be fundamentally religious – or, more broadly, religious affiliation may not itself be strictly religious. If so, White may be barking up the wrong tree in placing sole blame on Christian theology. As just noted, a whole suite of ideas of nature may be theologically available to Christians; perhaps, as these social scientists argue, certain ideas are mobilized by certain religious groups as a part of broader political agendas, and individuals accept these ideas as a part of their political – not merely religious – commitments. This in part explains why political orientation is often a stronger predictor of environmental concern than religiosity. Religious identity may thus play an important role in providing individual support (or opposition) to the larger political-economic project of the domination of nature.

Environment as Religion

The above has assumed that religion and environmental concern are, as A and B, separable entities. Yet what if A and B are coextensive? Rather than consider whether religion has implications for environmental concern, some social scientists have taken a different tack in examining religious dimensions of environmentalism itself, or even more broadly, to explore whether something like nature religion exists. To many people, this phenomenon should be called nature spirituality, since the very term "religion" denotes organized religion, yet characteristic features of religion are indeed found among those for whom nature, not God, serves as sacred locus. Catherine Albanese notes four varieties of nature religion in American history: the Transcendentalist legacy inherited by contemporary environmentalism, metaphysical forms of spiritualism (e.g., Theosophy) reaching to contemporary New Age practices, a revitalized emphasis on bodily healing and well-being grounded in nature, and Enlightenment-style natural religion and natural theology, expressed in peculiarly American forms such as pragmatism. The broad concept of nature religion thus includes, but moves far beyond, environmentalism *per se*.

Empirical work in environment as religion is relatively scarce, however. Most exists in the form of qualitative interviews, which have revealed strong religious dimensions of environmental thought and practice. One major study of American environmental values suggested significant and diverse connections with religion, ranging from nature as "God's creation" to a source of spiritual experience.

But how widespread is this phenomenon? Some indication comes from a question on nature sacredness included in the 1993 International Social Survey Programme (ISSP) environment module, which asked respondents to state whether to them nature is sacred as created by God, inherently sacred, or important but not sacred. Given these three options of transcendent sacredness, immanent sacredness, and non-sacredness, nearly one in four U.S. respondents agreed with immanent sacredness, a strong support of nature religion which raises to nearly two in five (a plurality) among members of environmental groups.

One quantitative study of British responses to the ISSP question discovered that those supporting immanent sacredness in nature scored highest in questions of environmental and scientific knowledge. This finding runs contrary to allegations that nature religion threatens to rob environmentalism of its grounding in scientific rationality. Using other variables from British responses, two scales were constructed, one representing a respondent's "romantic" (anti-scientific, spiritual) inclination, and the other representing a "materialist" (pro-science and economy) stance. Though a negative correlation would be expected there was actually little correlation between the two, and in fact those who scored high on the materialist scale also tended to score high on the romantic scale.

Further social science research on environment as religion may offer a new set of perspectives on the White thesis. Preliminary results from a nationwide survey we administered during spring and early summer 2002 to slightly over 1000 adult Americans suggest that attitudes toward nature sacredness may be a defining feature of American environmental concern. Fifteen candidate statements on nature sacredness were narrowed down to six in a pilot survey. These six statements were included in the final survey, which together with extended respondent interviews indicate that transcendent sacredness and non-sacredness are opposing positions (i.e., two poles on the same underlying factor), but immanent sacredness is a relatively separate factor: those who believe that nature is inherently sacred thus may or may not (despite possible logical contradictions) ascribe to transcendent sacredness or non-sacredness.

Of these three positions on nature, responses regarding immanent sacredness proved to be quite strongly associated with environmental concern among adult Americans. We measured environmental concern in three ways: self-identification as environmentalist, average concern for a suite of six environmental issues, and average participation in six sets of pro-environmental behaviors. Correlations between immanent sacredness (as measured by a factor score of three related variables) and these three measures of environmentalism are given in Table 1. The table gives results of both zero-order (i.e., uncontrolled) and partial correlations controlled for demographic characteristics, political orientation, and theological fundamentalism. For demographic background, we included age, gender, income, and educational level; political orientation was indicated by self-rating on a liberal-conservative scale, and theological fundamentalism involved belief regarding the Bible as the literal word of God. Zero-order correlations are somewhat stronger in all cases, but the reduction following correction for demographic, political, and theological characteristics is minor. The strong association between belief in nature as sacred locus and environmental concern thus cannot be explained in terms of underlying demographic, political, or theological characteristics. In short, nature religion is a phenomenon in its own right, and closely linked with contemporary American environmental concern.

These correlation results are corroborated by a regression analysis, in which demographic, political, and theological characteristics were entered in successive blocks prior to the inclusion of the immanent sacredness factor. Results, using each of the three measures of environmental concern as dependent variable, are given in Table 2. Even following introduction of these other candidate explanatory characteristics, immanent sacredness alone accounted for between 41 and 59 percent of total variance explained in environmental concern. The closest runner-up, political orientation, explained between 29 and 43 percent, and much of this is due to its inclusion in the model before theological fundamentalism, which is highly correlated with political orientation and thus would have absorbed more of the variance if it were included first. (It is worth noting that, even in the strongest case, only about 20 percent of total variance in environmental concern was explained by all of these characteristics combined; environmentalism is thus by no means fully explained by them.) Beta weights (standardized measures of relative importance) of immanent sacredness also were much higher than political orientation, theological fundamentalism, and demographic characteristics.

These preliminary results admittedly suffer from the same limitations of social science analysis noted above. Yet they suggest that American environmental concern is more closely tied to nature religion, in which nature serves as sacred locus, than demographic background, political orientation, or degree of theological fundamentalism. Religion and environment are connected in broadly the manner White suggested, but not necessarily in the manner explored by most social science studies. It is thus possible that environmental concern will ultimately be aided both by the progressive greening of institutional Christianity, *and* the growth of religious expressions rooted primarily in nature and not Judeo-Christian theism. White's preferred "patron saint," Saint Francis of Assisi, may well have felt at home in both camps.

Conclusion

The social science literature on the relationship between religion and environment has concentrated preponderantly on the "Does religion influence environmental concern?" interpretation of the White thesis as noted above, and primarily in the context of Christianity in the United States. While this literature has suggested important complications and elaborations of the White thesis, it has generally been inconclusive. A second interpretation, where environmentalism itself is a form of religion, is promising as suggested by the results of our study and others, yet requires further social science elaboration. And other interpretations have scarcely been explored: as but one example, it is quite possible that Protestantism has played a decisive role in nature–society relations in the West, though whether that role has been religious or more broadly cultural, and positive, negative, or both is open to debate.

One of the great limitations in social science research in

Table 1. Zero-Order and Partial Correlations

Immanent Sacredness	Environmental Self-Identification	Environmental Issues Concern	Proenvironmental Behavior
Zero-Order	0.303	0.395	0.333
Partial	0.274	0.362	0.303

–All correlations significant at $p < 0.001$
–Partial correlations controlled for demographics (age, education, gender, income), political orientation, and theological fundamentalism

Table 2. Linear Regression Results

	Environmental Self-Identification			Environmental Issues Concern			Proenvironmental Behavior		
	Beta	R^2	R^2 Total	Beta	R^2	R^2 Total	Beta	R^2	R^2 Total
1. Demographic Characteristics		0.016			0.023			0.020	
Age	0.112**			0.128***			—		
Education	—			—			—		
Gender	—			—			−0.062*		
Income	0.058*			—			—		
2. Political Orientation		0.072			0.058			0.073	
Conservative vs. liberal	−0.194***			−0.169***			−0.208***		
3. Theological Fundamentalism		0.010			0.002			0.003	
Biblical literalism	−0.097**			—			—		
4. Nature Sacredness		0.068			0.120			0.083	
Immanent sacredness	0.267***			0.357***			0.296***		
			0.166			0.197			0.179

–* p < .05; ** p < .01; *** p< .001; results omitted where p ≥ .05
–Independent variables entered as blocks in sequence as above. Note: Political orientation and theological fundamentalism highly correlated (R = 0.343), thus order of entry into regression reduces explanatory power of fundamentalism

this area has been not only the relative paucity of qualitative studies, but also the virtual absence of coordination between quantitative and qualitative research. Both are important, and play complementary roles: quantitative research tends to be *extensive* in that it seeks generalities across populations, whereas qualitative research tends to be *intensive* in that it seeks depth of understanding in particular groups or individuals. Qualitative studies are also well suited for analysis of institutional forces, and not simply individual attitudes and behaviors. Our recent study mentioned above involved a dual, extensive-intensive methodological approach, in which approximately ten percent of all survey respondents were contacted afterward for open-ended interviews. The principal advantage of this dual methodology is that quantitative and qualitative data are linked by respondent; each component can thus directly shed interpretive light on the other.

What is needed is for social scientists to recognize in their analyses that the world of religion and environment is more than one populated by sampled individual survey respondents. Social science has brought great rigor to the religion-environment question, but at the expense of a highly simplified domain. It could well be, as social scientists have generally argued, that the Lynn White thesis is limited; whether or not this is true, social scientists have not yet offered a conclusive indictment nor a compelling alternative. In their absence, popular culture is deluged with right-sounding proclamations on religion and environment; bookstores are overflowing with new titles. Lots of sweeping theories are being advanced. Many have rather naively suggested that the solution lies in non-Western religious traditions, despite the evidence of serious ecological problems faced in non-Western parts of the world. Social science offers an important empirical check on these notions, but only if it remains mindful of its current limitations and works harder to develop a fuller theoretical and methodological base.

The task is huge, as huge as the scope of religion and nature–society relations. No wonder social science has not yet offered the conclusive word on White's argument! As White himself admitted, "There are many calls to action, but specific proposals ... seem too partial, palliative, negative ... What shall we do? No one yet knows" (White 1967: 1204). Though some have ventured that, given this confusion, "It would probably have been better if the Lynn White debate had never occurred" (Hargrove 1986: xvii), academic research on the relations between religion and environment has surely been enriched. The "ecologic crisis" that so concerned White is still a concern for many of us today; we all want solutions. Yet, to the extent that any solution lays claim on the empirical reality of humans and their relations with the nonhuman world, social science will play an indispensable role.

James D. Proctor
Evan Berry

Further Reading

Albanese, Catherine L. *Reconsidering Nature Religion*. Harrisburg, PA: Trinity Press International, 2002.

Albanese, Catherine L. *Nature Religion in America: From the Algonkian Indians to the New Age*. Chicago History of American Religion. Chicago: University of Chicago Press, 1990.

Barbour, Ian G., ed. *Western Man and Environmental Ethics: Attitudes toward Nature and Technology*. Reading, MA: Addison-Wesley, 1973.

Bartowski, John P. and W. Scott Swearingen. "God Meets Gaia in Austin, Texas: A Case Study of Environmentalism as Implicit Religion." *Review of Religious Research* 38:4 (1997), 308–24.

Berry, Wendell. "A Secular Pilgrimage." In Ian G. Barbour, ed. *Western Man and Environmental Ethics: Attitudes Toward Nature and Technology*. Reading, MA: Addison-Wesley, 1973, 132–55.

Bloch, Jon P. "Alternative Spirituality and Environmentalism." *Review of Religious Research* 40:1 (1998), 55–73.

Boyd, Heather Hartwig. "Christianity and the Environment in the American Public." *Journal for the Scientific Study of Religion* 38:1 (1999), 36–44.

Brockelman, Paul T., Mary Westfall and John E. Carroll, eds. *The Greening of Faith: God, the Environment, and the Good Life*. Hanover: University Press of New England, 1997.

Butigan, Ken and Philip N. Joranson. *Cry of the Environment: Rebuilding the Christian Creation Tradition*. Santa Fe, NM: Bear, 1984.

Cooper, David Edward and Joy Palmer, eds. *Spirit of the Environment: Religion, Value, and Environmental Concern*. London, New York: Routledge, 1998.

Crosby, Donald A. *A Religion of Nature*. Albany, NY: State University of New York Press, 2002.

Dekker, Paul, Peter Ester and Masja Nas. "Religion, Culture, and Environmental Concern: An Empirical Cross-national Analysis." *Social Compass* 44:3 (1997), 443–58.

Dubos, René. *The Wooing of Earth*. New York: Charles Scribner's Sons, 1980.

Dubos, René. "A Theology of Earth." In *Western Man and Environmental Ethics: Attitudes Toward Nature and Technology*. Ian G. Barbour, ed. Reading, MA: Addison-Wesley, 1973, 43–54.

Dunlap, Riley E. and Robert Emmett Jones. "Environmental Concern: Conceptual and Measurement Issues." In Riley E. Dunlap and William M. Michelson, eds. *Handbook of Environmental Sociology*. Westport, CT: Greenwood Press, 2002, 482–524.

Eckberg, Douglas Lee and T. Jean Blocker. "Christianity, Environmentalism, and the Theoretical Problem of Fundamentalism." *Journal for the Scientific Study of Religion* (Dec. 1996), 343–55.

Eckberg, Douglas Lee and T. Jean Blocker. "Varieties of Religious Involvement and Environmental Concerns: Testing the Lynn White Thesis." *Journal for the Scientific Study of Religion* 28:4 (1989), 509–17.

Ehrlich, Paul R. and Anne H. Ehrlich. *Betrayal of Science and Reason: How Anti-environmental Rhetoric Threatens our Future*. Washington, D.C.: Island Press, 1996.

Eliade, Mircea. *The Sacred and the Profane: The Nature of Religion*. New York: Harcourt Brace, 1959 (1st American edn).

Fackre, Gabriel. "Ecology and Theology." In Ian G. Barbour, ed. *Western Man and Environmental Ethics: Attitudes toward Nature and Technology*. Reading, MA: Addison-Wesley, 1973, 116–31.

Gottlieb, Roger S., ed. *This Sacred Earth: Religion, Nature, Environment*. New York: Routledge, 1996.

Greeley, Andrew M. "Religion and Attitudes toward the Environment." *Journal for the Scientific Study of Religion* 32:1 (1993), 19–28.

Guth, James L., et al. "Faith and the Environment: Religious Beliefs and Attitudes on Environmental Policy." *American Journal of Political Science* 39:2 (1995), 364–82.

Hand, Carl M. and Kent D. Van Liere. "Religion, Mastery-over-nature, and Environmental Concern." *Social Forces* 63:2 (1984), 555–70.

Hargrove, Eugene C. "Religion and Environmental Ethics: Beyond the Lynn White Debate." In Eugene C. Hargrove, ed. *Religion and Environmental Crisis*. Athens: University of Georgia Press, 1986, ix–xix.

Horkheimer, Max. *Eclipse of Reason*. New York: Oxford University Press, 1947.

Kanagy, Conrad L. and Fern K. Willits. "A Greening of Religion? Some Evidence from a Pennsylvania Sample." *Social Science Quarterly* 74:3 (1993), 674–83.

Kanagy, Conrad L. and Hart M. Nelson. "Religion and Environmental Concern: Challenging the Dominant Assumptions." *Review of Religious Research* 37:1 (1995), 33–45.

Kellert, Stephen R. and Timothy J. Farnham, eds. *The Good in Nature and Humanity: Connecting Science, Religion, and Spirituality with the Natural World*. Washington, D.C.: Island Press, 2002.

Kempton, Willett, James S. Boster and Jennifer A. Hartley. *Environmental Values in American Culture*. Cambridge, MA: The MIT Press, 1995.

Leiss, W. *The Domination of Nature*. New York: George Braziller, 1972.

Lewis, Martin W. "Radical Environmental Philosophy and the Assault on Reason." In Paul R. Gross, Norman Levitt and Martin W. Lewis. *The Flight from Science and Reason*. Baltimore, NJ: The Johns Hopkins University Press, 1996, 209–30.

Lukes, Steven. "Individualism." In William Outhwaite and Tom Bottomore. *The Blackwell Dictionary of Twentieth-century Social Thought*. Oxford: Blackwell Publishers, 1993, 277–8.

Matthews, Clifford N., Mary Evelyn Tucker and Philip J. Hefner, eds. *When Worlds Converge: What Science and Religion Tell Us about the Story of the Universe and Our Place in It*. Chicago, IL: Open Court, 2002.

McHarg, Ian. "The Place of Nature in the City of Man." In Ian G. Barbour. *Western Man and Environmental Ethics: Attitudes toward Nature and Technology*. Reading, MA: Addison-Wesley, 1973, 171–86.

Mockabee, Stephen T., Joseph Quin Monson and J. Tobin Grant. "Measuring Religious Commitment among Catholics and Protestants: A New Approach." *Journal for the Scientific Study of Religion* 40:4 (2001), 675–90.

Moncrief, Lewis W. "The Cultural Basis of our Environmental Crisis." In Ian G. Barbour, ed. *Western Man and Environmental Ethics: Attitudes toward Nature and Technology*. Reading, MA: Addison-Wesley, 1973, 31–42.

Nelson, Robert H. "Environmental Calvinism: The Judeo-Christian Roots of Eco-theology." In Roger E. Meiners and Bruce Yandle, eds. *Taking the Environment Seriously*. Lanham, MD: Rowman & Littlefield Publishers, Inc., 1993, 233–55.

Oelschlaeger, Max. *Caring for Creation: An Ecumenical Approach to the Environmental Crisis*. New Haven: Yale University Press, 1994.

Otto, Rudolf. *The Idea of the Holy: An Inquiry into the Non-rational Factor in the Idea of the Divine and its Relation to the Rational*. London: H. Milford, 1923.

Sayer, Andrew. *Method in Social Science: A Realist Approach*. London: Hutchinson, 1992 (2nd edn).

Scott, Peter. *A Political Theology of Nature*. Cambridge: Cambridge University Press, 2003.

Shaiko, Ronald G. "Religion, Politics, and Environmental Concern: A Powerful Mix of Passions." *Social Science Quarterly* 68:2 (1987), 243–62.

Shibley, Mark A. and Jonathon L. Wiggins. "The Greening of Mainline American Religion: A Sociological Analysis of the Environmental Ethics of the National Religious Partnership for the Environment." *Social Compass* 44:3 (1997), 333–48.

Stern, Paul C., et al. "Values, Beliefs, and Proenvironmental Action: Attitude Formation Toward Emergent Attitude Objects." *Journal of Applied Social Psychology* 25 (1995), 1611–36.

Stoll, Mark. *Protestantism, Capitalism, and Nature in America*. Albuquerque: University of New Mexico Press, 1997.

Taylor, Bron. "Earth and Nature-based Spirituality (Part I): From Deep Ecology to Radical Environmentalism." *Religion* 31:1 (2001), 175–93.

Taylor, Bron. "Earth and Nature-based Spirituality (Part II): From Earth First! and Bioregionalism to Scientific Paradigm and the New Age." *Religion* 31:2 (2001), 225–45.

Tucker, Mary Evelyn and John A. Grim. "Introduction: The Emerging Alliance of World Religions and Ecology." *Daedalus: Proceedings of the American Academy of Arts and Sciences* 130:4 (2001), 1–22.

van Liere, Kent and Riley Dunlap. "Environmental Concern: Does It Make a Difference How It is Measured?" *Environment and Behavior* 13:6 (1981), 651–76.

Vogel, David. "The Protestant Ethic and the Spirit of Environmentalism: The Cultural Roots of Green Politics and Polities." *Zeitschrift fuer Umweltpolitik und Umweltrecht* 3 (2002), 297–322.

White, Lynn, Jr. "The Historic Roots of Our Ecologic Crisis." *Science* 155 (March 1967), 1203–7.

Witherspoon, Sharon. "The Greening of Britain: Romance and Rationality." In Roger Jowell, ed. *British Social Attitudes: The 11th Report*. Aldershot: Dartmouth, 1994, 107–39.

Wolkomir, Michelle, et al. "Denominational Subcultures of Environmentalism." *Review of Religious Research* 38:4 (1997), 325–43.

Woodrum, Eric and Thomas Hoban. "Theology and Religiosity Effects on Environmentalism." *Review of Religious Research* 35:3 (1994), 193–206.

Zinnbauer, Brian J., et al. "Religion and Spirituality: Unfuzzying the Fuzzy." *Journal for the Scientific Study of Religion* 36:4 (1997), 549–64.

See also: Ecology and Religion; Environmental Ethics; Nature Religion; Nature Religion in the United States; Religious Environmentalist Paradigm; Religious Studies and Environmental Concern; White, Lynn – Thesis of.

Soelle, Dorothee (1929–2003)

Dorothee Soelle is a pioneering figure in German Lutheran theology. She has made significant contributions to post-Holocaust, feminist, and liberation theology from the 1970s to the present. Ecological concerns are reflected throughout her theology, poetry and political activism on behalf of anti-nuclear, anti-war, and anti-capitalist causes. Soelle criticizes traditional Christian theology for conceiving of God as the transcendent ruler of the world who subordinates weak, sinful human beings to "his" omnipotent will, and for conceiving human beings as dependent on God for salvation which implies human passivity in the face of global injustice.

In contrast, Soelle develops the idea of God's suffering with creation. Her panentheistic theism conceives God as immanent wherever sharing and community, rather than domination, occur among living beings. God is a transcendent force enabling persons to heal, forgive and move toward freedom from ideologies of self-interest and profit. She defines sin as a social, not purely individual, phenomenon. Influenced by Karl Marx, Soelle identifies the remedy for sin as the salvation of creation from exploitation, alienation and injustice. She rejects Christian otherworldly understandings of salvation centering on heaven and the immortality of the soul. All of creation can manifest the reality of God's presence, including the beauty of nature, human actions and political action against the exploitation of the human body and nature. Salvation entails the survival and flourishing of all life forms and the ethical awareness that human beings are co-creators with God. Nature is the site of a mystical I–You relation reflecting the non-personal dimension of the divine in beauty, form, and radiant light. Combining an aesthetic and political perspective on nature, Soelle equates faith with resistance against exploitation, and stresses a mystical participation in reality that binds together nature, humanity and God.

Sarah Pinnock

Further Reading

Soelle, Dorothee. *The Silent Cry: Mysticism and Resistance.* Minneapolis: Augsburg Fortress Press, 2001.

Soelle, Dorothee. *On Earth as in Heaven: A Liberation Theology of Sharing.* Louisville: Westminster/John Knox Press, 1996.

Soelle, Dorothee and Shirley A. Cloyes. *To Work and to Love: A Theology of Creation.* Philadelphia: Augsburg Fortress Press, 1984.

See also: Christianity (6c) – Reformation Traditions (Lutheranism and Calvinism); Christianity (7d) – Feminist Theology; Christianity in Europe.

Sohappy, David (1925–1991) – and Salmon Spirituality

The relationship between religion and nature, and the quest for justice that links them, is exemplified in the story of David Sohappy, Sr., a spiritual leader and healer who fought for human and treaty rights in the Northwestern U.S. and beyond. While Martin Luther King, Jr., marched for civil rights for African Americans, and Cesar Chavez fought for Mexican American farmworkers' rights, David Sohappy led the Indian ("Native American") fishing rights struggle. He was a Wanapum ("River People," after "*Che Wana*," the "Great River" as the Columbia was first known) seeking to restore rights guaranteed by the 1855 Fort Yakima Treaty. In the treaty, the region's native peoples were forced to cede some nine million of their ten million acres of land to the federal government, but reserved exclusive fishing rights on their reservations, as well as rights to hunt, to gather roots and berries, and to fish at "all usual and accustomed places." David Sohappy noted that in the treaty, "We gave to non-Indians the *privilege* to fish for salmon to feed their families, while we retained the *right* to fish. A privilege can be regulated, a right cannot" (interview by author, 1988). Reflecting on his people's longevity on the river, he observed that, unlike archeologists, the Wanapum did not have to dig in the ground to know their history: it was preserved in their ceremonies. He declared that it has been evident through history that "fishing is our way of life" (interview by author, 1988). The salmon were special to the Wanapum. The first catch of the season was celebrated with a great feast of thanksgiving in which the whole community shared, and all subsequent catches ensured fresh and smoked fish for subsistence purposes and trade with other peoples.

Native peoples' fishing-rights struggles initially attracted little attention outside of the Columbia River region, until David Sohappy's successful suit against the Oregon Fish Commission and the Oregon Game Commission was upheld by the U.S. Supreme Court in "Sohappy vs. Smith" in 1968. A complementary ruling by federal judge George Boldt in 1974 in "U.S. vs. Washington" stated that native fishers were entitled to 50 percent of the catch on the Columbia.

Populations of fish species and sub-species had continually increased over the approximately ten thousand years that native peoples had lived and fished on the Columbia River. Scientists estimate that some 16 million salmon swam upriver in the 1880s. But in the twentieth century, overfishing by the fish factory industry severely depleted migrating salmon populations in the Pacific Ocean, while mining, logging, other industrial operations and the construction of hydro-electric dams eliminated spawning grounds and habitat for the fish; the dams also impeded the flow of salmon smolts downriver toward the Pacific Ocean, and the return of mature salmon upriver to spawn at their birthplaces. In the past quarter-century in particular, more than a hundred species and sub-species of salmon were rendered extinct. In this context, David Sohappy sought to save the salmon and his people.

David Sohappy was born near Harrah, Washington on 25 April 1925 and raised in a traditional Wanapum family. He attended a few years of elementary school until he was taken out so that he would not lose his native heritage and way of thinking. He grew up in the pacifist Washat or "Seven Drums" religion, some of whose members became "dreamers," visionaries who lived at times alone along the Columbia and were sought out for spiritual guidance and sometimes for practical advice on where to fish for salmon or hunt for deer. He worked to support his birth family, did military service, married Myra and had several children, and worked at different jobs. When he was in his thirties, he had fallen into the Columbia and felt a hand pull him out. A voice told him that his work was not yet finished. On another occasion, he heard a voice tell him that he was to be a spiritual leader. He would say later of these and similar experiences:

> If the Creator wants you to know something he'll tell you. We never see the Creator, only hear him. I was asleep at one time and I heard this voice tell me, "Listen to this, here is a chant you have to repeat all the time" (Sohappy letter to Hart, 1987).

He and his wife, Myra, joined the Feather Religion, a stricter version of Washat, and become healers. He observed that

> When we go to our services to help heal people we pull down the power of the universe. People that can see, can see it coming. You've got to go the way you're supposed to all through your life. If your worst enemy comes over and asks you for help, you've got to help him. As long as you're asked to help, then you've got to help (interview by author, 1988).

David became recognized as a Dreamer who had been called by the Creator to teach, to heal and to struggle for justice. He was following the ways of his great uncle Smohalla, a Washat prophet who had led a resurgence of native spirituality in the late 1800s. During David's healing ceremonies, his patients felt a magnetic force coming from his hands; it was said of him also that he had power to control storms and other natural forces. Referring to his role as a Dreamer, he said "We're told in a dream what's going to happen. You hold services and tell people, 'Here's what I dreamt, here's what we have to do next'" (interview by author, 1988).

During World War II, the River People were forcibly relocated from some of their lands, with little warning by the federal government, so that the Hanford Nuclear Reservation could be established for nuclear weapons development. Today Hanford is known as the most polluted place in North America because of its radioactive sectors and the chemical toxins that are seeping into the Columbia River from its storage sites.

When the Dalles Dam was constructed in 1957, its backed-up waters covered over Celilo Falls, the largest native fishing site in North America. The Dalles and other dams covered native villages, burial sites and petroglyphs. The federal government promised "in lieu" sites to replace the flooded villages and fishing places, but the sites were never constructed. Native fishing was restricted to Zone 6, some 113 miles between the Bonneville and McNary dams: the amount of fish Indians might catch was reduced by ocean factory fishing and by non-native fishers (commercial and sport) in the five zones downriver. David Sohappy and other River People occupied Cook's Landing as their "in lieu" site, and sought to have a permanent fishing village there. He observed wryly later: "They keep trying to tell me that we were only supposed to stay there temporarily. I told them that I'm on this Earth only temporarily, and so is everything else." He noted further, "We're supposed to have our own community, our own beliefs, our own longhouses, the traditions that have come to us" (interview by author, 1988). When federal and state governments tried to restrict the rights of the River People even after his successful court cases, David Sohappy used civil disobedience to fight for those rights. He fished openly and sold fish at the site of an old riverboat dock, Cook's Landing in Washington, which he and other Wanapum had occupied in the 1960s.

In 1982, David Sohappy, Sr., his son, David Jr., and other native fishers were arrested for fishing illegally and selling their fish to undercover agents in an operation the federal government called "Salmonscam." Initially, they were indicted for catching 40,000 fish. The fish were missing from Zone 6, based on the first fish count at Bonneville Dam and the second upriver at McNary Dam. It was discovered later that most of the fish had gone up different rivers to spawn because of effluents from aluminum plants along the Columbia, and were not missing after all, but David and the others still went to trial. They were prosecuted under the Lacey Act Amendments, introduced into the U.S. Senate by Washington's Senator Slade Gorton, whose family owned a major seafood company, while "Salmonscam" was already underway. David was accused ultimately of selling 317 fish to the federal agents, convicted in federal court in 1983 and sentenced to five years in prison. In his trial and appeal, David was not allowed to invoke provisions of the 1855 Fort Yakima Treaty or of the 1978 Indian Religious Freedom Act to justify his activities. The Ninth Circuit Court of Appeals turned down his appeal in 1985.

David and the other fishers were tried and acquitted in Tribal Court in 1986, but the federal government demanded that they remain in federal prison. In his trials, and throughout his appeals, David declared that his people's ancient religious laws, which included teachings about fishing responsibly for salmon, took precedence over the federal and state laws that denied him his fishing rights:

> Lots of people couldn't understand what I was talking about when I told them that I follow Unwritten Laws. They didn't understand. I told them I follow a law that is higher than any written law. So they told me, "So you're above the laws!" I said, "I didn't say that, I follow a law that is higher than any written

law." Their laws can't stop me. Their laws can't stop the storm (interview by author, 1988).

When he taught Washat traditions, David Sohappy spoke about honoring all creation: "Water, the Mother Earth, the Sun and the Wind: without any of these there would be no life on Earth . . . The belief is that if we don't honor these things we will have no more; everything will fade away" (interview by author, 1987). His major focus was on his people's responsibilities to be faithful to their religious beliefs. The Wanapum were to respect the salmon, pray to the salmon spirits, act responsibly toward the salmon, and express gratitude to the salmon for providing food for the people. "The salmon was created for the people to have for their own food . . . We are taught that if we honor our food, it will come back. If we stop, it won't come back" (interview by author, 1988).

While in prison, David Sohappy suffered a stroke (an event initially denied by prison officials, who declared that he was suffering from the "hysterical paralysis" which native peoples sometimes have when confined), and his physical condition deteriorated. Human rights groups around the world urged his release, including at United Nations International Human Rights Commission meetings in Geneva, Switzerland through interventions by Myra Sohappy. Then Senator Daniel Inouye, Chair of the U.S. Senate Select Committee on Indian Affairs, used his political influence to secure David's release in May 1988 after he had been imprisoned for twenty months. On his release, he said, "My life is for the salmon. After my work is done, I will move on" (*Treaty Council News*). His health was poor, and after resuming life at Cook's Landing with limited activity, he suffered another stroke and was hospitalized in Toppenish, Washington. He died there when struck by a third stroke on 6 May 1991.

His people and other natives of the Americas remember David Sohappy as a powerful spiritual leader and healer, as well as a courageous champion of natural rights and the rights of nature.

John Hart

Further Reading

Clark, Robert. *River of the West: A Chronicle of the Columbia.* New York, NY: Picador USA, 1997.

Cone, Joseph. *A Common Fate: Endangered Salmon and the People of the Pacific Northwest.* Corvallis, OR: Oregon State University Press, 1996.

Harden, Blaine. *A River Lost: The Life and Death of the Columbia.* New York, NY: W.W. Norton & Company, 1997.

Hart, John. "Salmon and Social Ethics: Relational Consciousness in the Web of Life." In *Journal of the Society of Christian Ethics* 22 (Fall 2002), 67–93.

Relander, Click. *Drummers and Dreamers.* Seattle, WA: Northwest Interpretive Association, 1986.

Sohappy, Sr., David. Letters from Geiger Prison to John Hart, 1986–1988; Prison interviews with John Hart, 1988.

"Sohappy's Released From Prison; Columbia River Fishing Rights Struggle Continues." In the *Treaty Council News* 8:1 (June 1988), 1.

See also: Columbia River Watershed Pastoral Letter; Washat Religion (Drummer-Dreamer Faith); Yakama Nation.

Soka Gakkai and the Earth Charter

Soka Gakkai is a lay Buddhist organization founded in Japan in 1930 as an educational reform movement by school principal Tsunesaburo Makiguchi (1871–1944) and inspired by the teachings of Nichiren Buddhism. Makiguchi was committed to the development and happiness of each individual student and affirmed the symbiotic relationship between the individual and the environment in his 1903 book, *Jinsei Chirigaku* (The Geography of Human Life). Key principles of Nichiren Buddhism and the Lotus Scripture that guide Soka Gakkai practice are *engi* (the dependent co-origination of all things), *esho funi* (the oneness of life and its environment), and striving to fulfill one's Buddha-nature in this life on Earth.

While all Buddhists teach the balance of wisdom and compassion, Nichiren (1222–1282) is famous for adding the virtue of courage that inspires members of Soka Gakkai to be socially active. Makiguchi died in prison for not cooperating with the military government, and in the 1960s Soka Gakkai formed a political party that became the third largest in Japan by the year 2000. But SG activism and growth has been controversial among established religious groups.

Soka Gakkai spread worldwide in the 1960s and formed Soka Gakkai International (SGI) in 1975. SGI grew to 12 million members in 180 countries and territories by 2002. The emergence of the Earth Charter was seen by SGI as a modern expression of the Buddhist teaching of the interconnectedness of all life. As a result, SGI members have globally sponsored discussion of the Earth Charter, and ecological consciousness has become an integral part of SGI teaching.

SGI has an affiliated research center in Brazil, the Amazon Ecological Research Center, which undertakes tree planting and agroforestry as well as environmental education. SGI also co-sponsored an Earth Council video, *A Quiet Revolution*, which illustrates the importance of grassroots action to rehabilitate the natural environment. SGI organizations are involved in numerous practical initiatives such as energy-saving campaigns, tree-planting activities, environmental exhibitions, and recycling projects. In addition, SGI members in several countries undertake regular "clean-up" campaigns in their local areas.

When SGI-USA built a retreat center, most of its acreage was designated as a permanent nature reserve and it was named the Florida Nature and Culture Center. Because of the role of corporations in damaging nature, an educational Round Table seminar was organized by SGI at the World Bank in Washington, D.C. in April 1998, followed by regular Earth Charter Dinner Dialogues in Washington since March 2001. SGI-USA has presented the Earth Charter at interfaith activities as a common ground that can be shared by all spiritual traditions, and organized a presentation at the World Parliament of Religions held in South Africa in 1999. SGI-USA also sponsored Earth Charter Community Summits in 12 locations in 2001, and by 2002 over 60 local SGI-USA district meetings had discussed the Earth Charter.

In 2000 SGI co-sponsored an "Earth Charter Asia Tour" with exhibitions, panels, and youth forums in the Philippines, Thailand, Singapore, Malaysia, Hong Kong, Korea, and Japan. In response, SGI-Philippines held a Waste Management Seminar on Earth Day, 2001, and in 2002 their women's peace forum discussed the relevance of the Charter to peace. In Thailand, the "Before It's Too Late" environmental exhibit toured nine cities and was seen by 180,000 people. In Malaysia a recycling project was cosponsored, and SGI has developed an Earth Charter exhibition. Beginning in 2002 a regular column called "Love the Earth" was started in Hong Kong SGI's magazine to give information on the Earth Charter. In Korea the Charter was promoted in seminars and photo exhibitions were organized by the SGI student division. In Japan, an environmental group was formed by SGI members in Osaka called KEEP. SGI members in the Netherlands, Australia, France, South Africa and Belgium are also actively promoting the Earth Charter.

Institutionally, SGI has developed several specialized organizations to develop further its mission to promote peace, culture, and education. The Boston Research Center for the 21st Century (BRC) was founded in 1993 by SGI as an affiliate organization. In 1997 the BRC began a program of environmental awareness focused on the Earth Charter that resulted in a series of conferences and several booklets, namely, *Buddhist Perspectives on the Earth Charter* (1997), *Women's Views On the Earth Charter* (1997), and *Human Rights, Environmental Law, and the Earth Charter* (1998). Also, in 2001 Soka University of America was opened in California on a site surrounded on three sides by a 4000-acre nature preserve.

"Soka" means "to create value," and Daisaku Ikeda, president of SGI, emphasizes the value of nature in his writings and in his photographic exhibits. He emphasizes that education at its best involves an inner transformation of values to enable people to recognize their kinship with the environment and build a lasting peace.

At the World Summit on Sustainable Development in Johannesburg in August/September 2002, SGI's proposal for a decade of education for sustainable development was included in the Summit's agreed-upon Plan of Implementation, SGI co-produced the video *A Quiet Revolution* on local ecological initiatives, and SGI linked with the Earth Charter Initiative for "Educating for Sustainable Living with the Earth Charter." By 2002 study of the Earth Charter and ecological responsibility had become important elements of SGI practice worldwide.

David W. Chappell

Further Reading
Boston Research Center, ed. *Human Rights, Environmental Law, and the Earth Charter*. Boston: Boston Research Center, 1998.
Boston Research Center, ed. *Women's Views On the Earth Charter*. Boston: Boston Research Center, 1997.
Boston Research Center, ed. *Buddhist Perspectives on the Earth Charter*. Boston: Boston Research Center, 1997.
Chappell, David W., ed. *Buddhist Peacework*. Boston: Wisdom and Boston Research Center, 1999.
See also: Boston Research Center for the 21st Century; Buddhism – Engaged; Earth Charter; United Nations' "Earth Summits".

Somé, Malidoma Patrice (1956–)

Acknowledging the sanctity of nature is the centerpiece of Malidoma Patrice Somé's message. In his own words, "[n]ature is the foundation of indigenous life" (1998: 37) and

> [i]f you peek long enough into the natural world – the trees, the hills, the rivers, and all natural things – you start to realize that their spirit is much bigger than what can be seen, that the visible part of nature is only a small portion of what nature is (1998: 47).

Malidoma Somé is a shaman of the Dagara culture of West Africa, a former college professor with two doctorates, the founder of the nonprofit organization, Echoes of the Ancestors, and an active voice in the Men's Movement. According to Somé, opening one's sensitivity to the intricacies of nature allows one to experience the natural environment in a more intimate way, ultimately allowing one to utilize its placid, powerful and healing traits. Proper rituals and communal support bolster the power and healing that nature provides to the enlightened individual. It leads the adherent to reunite with the vast forces of the universe that were unleashed during one's birth, or as a Dagara elder once said, to return to one's own center.

Somé's message challenges the machine, monetary, and textual culture of the West. He presents the indigenous culture as fit to embrace the salubrious power of nature, because it recognizes the spirit behind nature. The reliance on modern technology for spiritual fulfillment fosters an internal struggle within the Western spirit. To the Dagara, this type of chasm needs to be mended. A ritual is the typical procedure to reconnect the individual with his or her self, ancestors, and the spirit world, in order to realize one's own life purpose.

The *Baor* ritual – initiation – is the essential step for a Dagara male to reunite his spirit with his corporeal body. The neophytes are required to perform particular exercises that strengthen their awareness and adjust their sensitivity to the natural environment of the bush. These tasks are performed dividually and individually under the auspices and guidelines of the elders and their ancestors, and typically lead to the participants entering into a transcendental state. Out-of-the-body experiences allow the spirit to have the necessary maneuverability to connect to the individual soul. The ability to *sense* and *feel* one's environment is central to success in the Dagara world because it enables one to enter into the sacred realm of the spirit.

Somé was an atypical participant in *Baor*, because at the age of four, he was taken away by French missionaries and sent to a Jesuit school and seminary for 15 years. He walked back to his village at age 20, indoctrinated with colonial Christianity. *Baor* is a dangerous undertaking in which all aspects of the body are vigorously challenged – every year there are participants that never return to their families. Somé was especially disadvantaged because he was considered "initiated" into the white man's world, therefore his ancestral spirit had withdrawn from his body. Analytical thought, especially literacy, suppresses the ability to access certain traditional knowledge, because it occupies a space within one's psyche that is reserved for something else (Somé 1994: 178). Of particular importance to Somé was his experience during the "tree exercise." This event enlivened his ability to *feel* his surroundings in an animated way, rather than just see them in a mundane level. After two tedious days of staring at a *yila* tree, he eventually came to realize its sacrosanct character as he saw a vision of a green lady composed of a green fluid, from the inside out, whom, in her embrace overcame his body with an immeasurable amount of love. This green lady is symbolic of Mother Nature, a conscious embodiment; Somé believes that the relationship between Earth and humans is represented in an intimate mother/child bond of nurturing and love. Thus, humans have a natural spiritual link to the Earth.

These apertures into the otherworld are commonplace in the Dagara experience; there is little distinction between the physical and metaphysical. Going into the other realm is a conduit to understanding, and entering these other realms is ritualized in a communal setting, yet all participants have their own personal experiences, from which they can draw their own personal meaning.

Somé's is a crucial voice to describe to Westerners the relationship between religion and nature in Dagara culture because of his dual citizenship in the modern and traditional worlds. His popularity is evidenced by the diverse circuits that embrace his work. At "spiritual" retreats he promotes the need for elders in the industrial society. Grief ceremonies, ritual initiations for boys and girls, connecting with the ancestors training, and anger-management courses, are among the activities that he encourages under the theme of finding identity and balance.

Somé speaks out to the gay audience by comparing their secondary position in the West with their primary position as "gatekeepers" of the Dagara tribe's relationship with the gods and the spirits. Some women's conferences and groups have placed him among their speakers or added him to their required reading lists. Somé's wife, Sobonfu, also conducts seminars and workshops on the relevance of indigenous ideas and practices to modern problems.

According to Somé, the indigenous cultures of Africa are ideal places to seek pacification and restoration with nature because they are formatted to coordinate with their natural environment. The Dagara rely on each other to survive in the harsh environments of certain places. Somé extends this reciprocal relationship through his work in the Western world. He shares the wisdom of the Dagara, in exchange for the supply of necessary resources like the construction of water reservoirs and the means to fight extreme poverty and sickness to preserve indigenous culture. Moreover, he asserts that indigenous African spirituality can provide a necessary model for people of industrial cultures to develop their own spiritual awakening and healing in their own ritual, communal, and natural environments.

Rosalind Hackett

Further Reading

Somé, Malidoma Patrice. *The Healing Wisdom of Africa: Finding Life Purpose Through Nature, Ritual, and Community*. New York: Penguin Putnam, 1998.

Somé, Malidoma Patrice. *Of Water and the Spirit: Ritual, Magic, and Initiation in the Life of an African Shaman*. New York: Putnam, 1994.

Somé, Malidoma Patrice. *Ritual: Power, Healing and Community*. New York: Penguin, 1993.

See also: Men's Movement; Mutwa, Credo.

Southeast Asia

Southeast Asia is a vast, diverse, complex, and dynamic mosaic of interacting religions and ecologies. Geopolitically, the region encompasses all of the countries East of India and south of China. The region is usually divided into two major parts: the mainland or continental parts include Vietnam, Laos, Cambodia, Thailand, Burma (Myanmar), and peninsular Malaysia; and insular (island) parts include the Philippines, Singapore, Brunei, Indonesia, and parts of Malaysia.

Southeast Asia is extraordinarily rich in biodiversity as a result of being a crossroads, the prevalence of tropical forests, and insularity. Biologists refer to Southeast Asia as the Oriental realm, but it is heavily influenced by the adjacent biogeographic realms of the Palaearctic (mostly East Asia), Ethiopia (northern Africa into the Middle East), and Australia. Each of these three realms has a distinctive natural history including a combination of plant and animal species. The three realms overlap in Southeast Asia. The natural vegetation cover of Southeast Asia is composed mostly of varieties of tropical forest. (Cambodia is the only country in the region with extensive savannahs or grasslands.) Insularity is another important factor. For example, Indonesia is composed of 13,677 islands, and the Philippines of 7100 islands. Geographical isolation, a prime characteristic of islands, stimulates speciation through adaptive radiation as populations competing for limited resources develop distinctive niches. Thus, it is no coincidence that within Southeast Asia, the country with the highest biodiversity is Indonesia. It contains over 20,000 species of plants, 515 mammals, 1519 birds, 270 amphibians, and 600 reptiles. A significant number of these species are endemic; that is, limited in distribution to parts of Indonesia and not found elsewhere.

Cultural diversity refers to the number of cultures in an area and is often estimated by the number of associated languages. Religion, as part of the socio-cultural system, is also part of cultural diversity. In general, there is a correlation between cultural and biological diversity. In areas where cultural diversity is high, so is biodiversity (number of species). In areas where cultural diversity is low, so is biodiversity. Exceptions occur, but this diversity principle reflects a general tendency. As a related generalization, diversity is highest in equatorial regions (especially tropical rainforests), and lowest in polar regions. Indonesia illustrates the diversity principle. It has not only the highest biodiversity in Southeast Asia, but also the highest ethnic, linguistic, and religious diversity. No less than 672 different languages are spoken in Indonesia, most associated with a different ethnic group, and many of these with their own distinct religion.

In Southeast Asia, cultural identity is usually closely related to a particular geographic place and one or more biomes. (A biome is a category of similar ecosystems, such as lowland tropical rainforests.) Indeed, to some degree each culture is a distinctive adaptive strategy for relating humans to their natural environment. Technology, economy, religion, and other components of culture as an adaptive system are all intimately related to the ecosystems in the habitat of a society. Accordingly, in characterizing cultures in Southeast Asia these general types are often recognized – coastal fishers and traders, lowland wet-rice agriculturalists along river floodplains and valley bottoms, and swidden (shifting) horticulturalists and foragers (hunter-gatherers) in the hill and mountain forests. The great rivers of mainland Southeast Asia are the Irrawaddy, Salween, Chao Phraya, Mekong, and Red. These rivers not only supply water to rice paddies, but together with land and sea routes also link the different regions within Southeast Asia and beyond through extensive networks of trade and commerce. The distinctive systems of food production in Southeast Asia are correlated with sharply contrasting levels of population density (individuals/square kilometers): foragers (less than 1), swidden horticulture (dozens to a hundred), and wet-rice agriculture (hundreds to over two thousand). The highest population densities are associated with rice farming on the rich soils of volcanic islands like Java in Indonesia. The higher the population density, the greater the complexity of social, political, and religious institutions as well as other aspects of culture. Furthermore, higher levels of population density cause greater environmental impact through more natural resource extraction and consumption with resulting waste and pollution.

As societies deplete their own natural resources, they must extend their reach to those of other areas through trade or conquest, and states do this far more than any other kind of society. The state, or civilization, is a variety of culture which includes some combination of a centralized government, bureaucratic administration, police and military, cities, monumental architecture, writing, craft and other specialists, and social stratification (socio-economic classes). The earliest states in Southeast Asia began around 500–1 B.C.E. However, only later, starting around the eleventh century, did the famous theocratic cities develop such as Borobudor, Angkor Wat, and Pagan, located respectively in Java, Cambodia, and Burma of the present day. They were among the societies heavily influenced by the spread of the Hindu religion and other aspects of culture from India.

Throughout insular Southeast Asia, the most important form of political organization was often connected with controlling trade and commerce, and the independent harbor principalities headed by chiefs, rajas, or sultans with small territories focused on river estuaries or seaports along the coasts. International commerce developed in Southeast Asia by the first year of the Common Era and flourished from the fifteenth century onward. China was the main market, until European colonialism began to change the dynamics of the political economy in the sixteenth century. For millennia, sporadic wars were fought for the control of routes of trade and commerce, such as the many conflicts between Burma and Thailand.

Religious conversion often accompanied the expansion of trade and commerce from South Asia, with Hinduism and later Buddhism spreading into most parts of mainland

Southeast Asia, and Islam into much of insular Southeast Asia. The introduction of a new religion may have influenced local and regional ecology significantly, but this possibility requires further research.

It is noteworthy that rapid population growth did not begin in Southeast Asia until the eighteenth century or even later. For example, in Thailand, as late as 1825, the population was less than one million, whereas today it is more than 60 million. In the past, the fact that traditionally most Thai males became monks for some period of time, ranging from a few months to years or even a lifetime, combined with the fact that monks are supposed to be celibate, must have helped reduce population growth. However, future population growth in Thailand, and elsewhere in Southeast Asia, is likely to continue well into the next century before it stabilizes, thus putting increasing pressure on the land and resource base, on the ability of the environment to absorb waste and pollution, and on economic, social, political, and religious institutions.

In many parts of Southeast Asia, there have long been occasional tensions and conflicts between the highlanders and lowlanders, the former marginalized in almost every way, and the latter more powerful economically, politically, and militarily. Throughout the region today with increasing population, the need for agricultural expansion, and national security concerns, the highlanders, who usually live in border areas between countries, are often victimized, including through military attacks, involuntary labor, forced relocation, and pressure for conversion to Theravada Buddhism as the dominant state religion, such as in the case of the Karen along the border between Burma and Thailand. For instance, in Thailand the highlanders compose only about 1 percent of the national population, but occupy nearly 20 percent of the national territory. Accordingly, they are destined to continue coming under increasing pressure from lowlanders and the state in the future. As another example, in contemporary Vietnam, economic development in the highlands is controlled by the lowlanders, often with negative impact on highland societies and their environments.

Religion is an extremely ancient, pervasive, and powerful force in society, politics, and history. Furthermore, traditionally religion is usually the primary means whereby the individual and society as a whole orient to the world, find meaning in life, and are guided and motivated. There is a remarkably rich diversity of religions in Southeast Asia.

The mainland is predominantly Buddhist and mostly of the Theravada sect, while the insular portion is mainly Muslim, except for the Philippines which is 80 percent Catholic, a reflection of its long Spanish colonial history. Underlying these mainstream religions, however, are elements of the prior indigenous religions of animism, a belief in multiple spiritual beings and forces in nature. Hinduism has flourished mainly in Bali, and Hindu influences remain in the popular religion of many in Java, southern Sumatra, Cambodia, southern Vietnam, and Thailand. People of Chinese ancestry in Southeast Asia may practice aspects of Confucianism, Daoism, and/or ancestor worship in addition to, or instead of, other religions like Buddhism. Thus, whereas in Western societies an individual usually ascribes exclusively to only one religion, in Asian societies an individual may actually practice more than one religion without any sense of incongruity.

The Indonesian island of Java illustrates the complexity of religion in Southeast Asia. Islam is the main religion of Indonesia. However, on Java, orthodox Islam is mainly practiced by the merchant class, urban bureaucrats emphasize forms of Buddhism and/or Hinduism, and animism is common among farmers and others in rural areas. Furthermore, in Southeast Asia there are enclaves of Muslims in countries that are otherwise dominated by another religion, as is the case for the Malays in southern Thailand and the Cham in Cambodia.

The impact of European colonialism has been more economic and political than religious in Southeast Asia. Christianity has not been as influential there as it has elsewhere in places like Latin America. Nevertheless, today there are millions of Christians in Indonesia and Vietnam as well as in the Philippines. In addition, new religions have developed, or old ones have been revived and revised. For instance, Cao Dai emerged in Vietnam in the early twentieth century as a mixture of Confucianism, Daoism, Buddhism, and Christianity. In part it was a reaction against French colonialism and was outlawed, although now it is an officially accepted religion. Because religions are different in the way they relate to nature, these changes in religion may have ecological consequences, and this possibility needs to be researched.

Religious differences may allow different ethnic groups to coexist in the same environment by promoting niche separation rather than resource competition. For instance, in southernmost Thailand, it is common to find adjacent Buddhist and Muslim communities who use the same environment differently mainly because of their religion. As an illustration, Buddhists exploit a far wider spectrum of wildlife species than do Muslims who consider many species to be unclean and taboo.

Religion can also contribute to nature conservation. For instance, in many parts of Southeast Asia there are individual trees, groves, and forests that are believed to be sacred. Consequently, resource exploitation in such sites may be significantly reduced or even avoided or prohibited entirely. Whether intentionally or inadvertently, sacred places in nature may serve as conservation areas that protect some species as well as portions of ecosystems and landscapes. As a case in point, caves associated with Buddhist monks are considered sacred. Bats which roost in these caves during the day fly far beyond them in feeding at night and are important agents in pollination, seed dispersal, and insect population control. The sacred status of caves may help protect the bats in them and thereby the ecological functions of the bats. However, in many regions Christian and Islamic missionization has threatened or even destroyed sacred places in nature as pagan, and therefore diminished or eliminated any value they might have had in conservation.

The people on the island of Bali in Indonesia remain mainly Hindus, but practice a syncretic religion that also includes elements of animism and Buddhism. Temple priests function through rituals as regulators of the flow of water for irrigating wet-rice paddies. The water is derived from a sacred lake in the volcanic mountain at the center of the island. Also temples in Bali, Thailand, and other places in Southeast Asia often provide sanctuaries for macaque monkeys and/or other species. The animals and plants in temple yards are protected by virtue of their association with the sacred space.

The subject of the relationships between religion and nature has barely started to gain attention in the last two decades in Southeast Asia. However, there have been some significant public initiatives. One is the Siam Society international symposium in Chiang Mai on culture and environment in Thailand. The main conclusion reached by the Thai and foreign participants was that Thailand is experiencing serious environmental degradation because of a decline in adherence to its culture and religion through uncritically and unselectively embracing so-called modernization. In another regional symposium, international participants at the Buddhist Institute in Phnom Penh, Cambodia, explored the environmental crisis and environmental ethics from the perspectives of the Buddhist, indigenous, and Islamic religions. Such initiatives may be indicative of an emerging realization that spiritual ecology has some practical potential to contribute to the reduction of environmental problems in Southeast Asia.

While "modernization" has contributed to the secularization of societies in many ways, religion still remains important in the lives of most Southeast Asians. It is really quite amazing that religions have persisted for millennia under such very different circumstances, yet they have obviously provided meaning and useful guidance in the lives of many people to this day.

At the same time, however, there is the perennial obstacle of the discrepancy between ideals and actions. The core principles of Buddhism and Hinduism can be applied in ways that are environmentally friendly. For instance, both share the ideal of *ahimsa* or avoidance of harming other beings. However, in practice there is natural resource depletion and environmental degradation or even destruction throughout most parts of Southeast Asia. Such discrepancies are nothing new, but have intensified with the pressures of the accelerated growth both in population and materialist consumerism, especially in recent decades with economic development and now globalization. Accordingly, today one of the greatest challenges is for individuals, communities, and nations to identify and more closely follow the ideals in their religion in ways that are most conducive to developing more sustainable and greener societies that conserve, promote, and enhance biodiversity and ecosystem vitality instead of degrading them.

Leslie E. Sponsel

Further Reading
Brookfield, Harold and Yvonne Byron, eds. *South-East Asia's Environmental Future: The Search for Sustainability.* Tokyo: United Nations University Press, 1993.
Chapple, Christopher Key. *Nonviolence to Animals, Earth, and Self in Asian Traditions.* Albany: State University of New York Press, 1993.
Dutt, Ashok, ed. *Southeast Asia: Realm of Contrasts.* Boulder: Westview Press, 1985.
Gyallay-Pap, Peter and Ruth Bottomley, eds. *Towards an Environmental Ethic in Southeast Asia.* Phnom Penh: The Buddhist Institute, 1998.
Keyes, Charles F. *The Golden Peninsula: Culture and Adaptation in Mainland Southeast Asia.* Honolulu: University of Hawai'i Press, 1995.
Lansing, J. Stephen. *Priests and Programmers: Technologies of Power in the Engineered Landscape of Bali.* Princeton; NJ: Princeton University Press, 1991.
McNeely, Jeffrey A. and Paul Spencer Sochaczewski. *Soul of the Tiger: Searching for Nature's Answers in Southeast Asia.* Honolulu: University of Hawai'i Press, 1995.
Siam Society. *Culture and Environment in Thailand.* Bangkok: Siam Society, 1989.
Sponsel, Leslie E., Poranee Natadecha-Sponsel, Nukul Ruttanadakul and Somporn Juntadach. "Sacred and/or Secular Approaches to Biodiversity Conservation in Thailand." *Worldviews: Environment, Culture, Religion* 2:2 (1998), 155–67.
Swearer, Donald K. *The Buddhist World of Southeast Asia.* Albany: State University of New York Press, 1995.
Wheatley, Bruce P. *The Sacred Monkeys of Bali.* Prospect Heights: Waveland Press, 1999.

See also: Ahimsa; Buddhism – Engaged; Caves – Sacred; Elephants; Hinduism; Payutto, Phra Dhammapitaka; The Philippines; Siam's Forest Monasteries; Sivaraksa, Sulak; Thai Buddhist Monks; Yunnan Region (Southwest China and Montane Mainland Southeast Asia).

Space Exploration

Loren Eiseley called the return to Earth from space "the last miracle" in his book *The Invisible Pyramid* (Eiseley was a renowned paleontologist at the University of

Pennsylvania; the most well received of his eloquent popular writings on evolution was *The Immense Journey*). But that is not the first thing that needs to be said in a discussion of space exploration, religion, and nature. So let me return to Eiseley's important insight later on. I want to begin, instead, with astronaut Michael Collins' comment about the Apollo program: he said it was all about leaving.

It is hard to avoid the conclusion that space exploration entails the abandonment of the Earth and its nature, leaving them behind in a technological thrust onward and upward. Surely technology, not nature, has been the emphasis of space exploration, and arguably technology has always been about surmounting nature. Of course, an other-worldly religious orientation in the West has helped to generate such an Earth-denying agenda on the part of technology, so that a film with a fast cut from Gothic cathedral spires to Cape Canaveral gantries would not lack semantic continuity. And Loren Eiseley's book title suggests an even longer history for our superhuman drive to be up, up, and away.

To be sure, the technological mission was eventually meant to *supplant* the spiritual priorities that fueled it, based as it was on scientific perspectives that scarcely allowed for gods in heaven above, let alone in Earth's sacred groves. Thus it was entirely consistent with such perspectives when a Soviet cosmonaut derisively observed the lack of angels visible along his flight path transcending terrestrial skies. By the same token, the U.S. astronauts' Christmas reading from lunar orbit sounded sincere but sentimental – and seriously out of keeping with the mechanistic attitudes they were triumphantly embodying. In spiritual terms their accomplishments were rather a defilement of whatever sacred attributes either the Earth or the moon were thought to possess by more traditionally religious cultures.

Even the mediating image of the garden, representing a more gentle technology in relative attunement with nature, is jettisoned by our recent rocket launches into space. Buckminster Fuller's "Spaceship Earth" idea – described in the inventor and philosopher's 1969 work *Operating Manual for Spaceship Earth* but made public by Fuller even earlier – had already imagined our home planet as a totally technological environment, and a mechanistic vision was no less dominant in dreams of a future in space: gardens completely surrounded and tightly controlled in floating biospheres; space colonies on the moon or Mars, allowing only a life-sustaining minimum of neo-nature, purged of all wildness; "terraforming" fantasies in which heavenly bodies would be scarified in an engineer's caricature of earthly ecology. A 1979 article by George Woodcock summed up these technohorticultural visions as "the garden in the machine," reversing Leo Marx's earlier notion of American environmental history as "the machine in the garden."

Surely, however, venerable American archetypes of

Institute of Noetic Sciences

In 1974, within two years of his flight on Apollo 14, Navy Captain Edgar Mitchell founded the Institute of Noetic Sciences. Approaching Earth at the conclusion of his mission he had envisioned that our home planet and the universe as a whole were involved in a living system, and that we could come to understand this system through other ways of knowing – the ancient Greek sense of the adjective "noetic" – than science presently allowed for. Trained as an engineer and scientist, Mitchell wanted to expand rather than circumvent science, and he felt the human mind, human consciousness, had powers which science, rigorously applied, could yet uncover. His Institute attempts to achieve this and related aims through publications, conferences, and a website (www.noetic.org), plus sponsoring community groups, networking opportunities, and a travel program.

In its *Noetic Sciences Review* and its members' newsletter, there are articles on ecology and environmental ethics, transpersonal psychology and its attempt to explicate various mystical spiritualities scientifically, "new paradigm" physics, alternative or "complementary" healing modalities, and testimonies about altruistic efforts to realize human potentials while supporting peaceful attempts at social change toward ecological sustainability. Reflecting these interests is the Institute's alliance with popular author-researchers such as physicians Deepak Chopra, Dean Ornish, Herbert Benson, and Larry Dossey, scientists Rupert Sheldrake, Amit Goswami, and Peter Russell, and humanistic psychologist Jean Houston. Its current membership numbers around 50,000 worldwide.

Thus has Captain Mitchell implemented in an adventurously scientific and ambitiously institutional way his spiritual vision of the Earth in space.

Daniel C. Noel

---

advancing frontiers and Manifest Destiny continued to shape the efforts of NASA as well as the eloquence of John F. Kennedy in pursuing the space race with the Soviet Union, which propelled us to the moon. Woodcock's essay appeared in a special issue of the *Michigan Quarterly Review* commemorating the tenth anniversary of the first lunar landing. Most of the articles and poems in the issue noted the emphatically technological auspices of the space venture, along with the unreflective if not robot-like behavior of the astronauts, trained to a technical perfection which excluded, with rare exceptions, any philosophical or poetic, let alone religious, musing on their unique experiences in space.

Several contributors to the issue decried this response to space exploration as dehumanizing, but all noted the focus of NASA and its astronauts on finding the factual information and acting on it efficiently, with seldom a thought given to the romance of the journey. The exceptions were indeed rare: Edgar Mitchell returned from space a spiritual seeker with transpersonal psychology interests and founded the Institute of Noetic Sciences; James Irwin splashed down as a Christian evangelical who started a "High Frontier" ministry. These two responses were in stark contrast to the military overtones of the "New Frontier" competition with the Soviets or the later "Star Wars" dreams of missile defense. Mitchell and Irwin saw something sacred in space but also turned back to look at the Earth. And, through the media, so did we.

Certainly it was the view of Earth afforded us by space exploration that led to Loren Eiseley's "last miracle." Of course, this view suggested different things to different onlookers. Some, like President Carter, saw its message as laudably pacific but largely political: no national boundaries were visible on the Earth from space. Others found this an incitement to mystical dreams of Oneness. Some were struck aesthetically by the beauty of a blue-and-white planet that looked like a precious jewel or Christmas tree ornament. May Swenson, in her poem "Orbiter Five Shows How Earth Looks from the Moon," found a dancing woman, a temple celebrant, in the outlines of clouds and continents.

In this poetic perception we begin to get intimations of archaic spirituality, Earth-oriented rituals, myths, and ceremonial sites which once involved reverence for the immanently sacred that aligned us with nature and its cycles. Even popular films with space themes hinted at this deep sense of terrestrial reconnection, as I pointed out in my 1986 book, *Approaching Earth*. The black monolith, modeled on Stonehenge, in *2001: A Space Odyssey*; a Mayan temple that provided the rebel base in the first *Star Wars*; and the Native American sacred mountain serving as the rendezvous point for earthlings and aliens in *Close Encounters of the Third Kind* all bespoke earthly imperatives which counterbalanced the spacefaring quests of the films' main characters and the Space-Age culture they represented. In each case, through these ancient religious rallying sites, a closeness to terrestrial nature seemed the surprising accompaniment to an ostensibly outward-bound focus.

It is fair to say that a renewed connection to nature did not occur in any specific and full-blown way to the Earth's outer-space onlookers until the *Whole Earth Catalog* emerged with the famous photograph on its cover and a message of ecologically sustainable living in its pages. Here a green consciousness was blended with a techie sensibility: technology can yet return to heal the Earth it has sought to abandon.

Still, the whole-Earth photo was pivotal, even miraculous, in reorienting our attention toward the terrestrial environment. When the first Earth Day was proclaimed in 1970 following a decade of manned space flight and the first lunar landing, Earth and its nature became the most significant discovery – or rediscovery – of the Space Age. It seems more than a coincidence that 1970 was also the year that *The Invisible Pyramid* was published.

Loren Eiseley's post-Apollo vision, set forth in this text with the same eloquence he had displayed in *The Immense Journey*, involved his having been shown Halley's comet in the night sky when he was a small boy in 1910. He knew that Halley's would be returning in 1985, and he saw that return – which he did not live to witness – as a metaphor for the conscious and caring re-entry he felt a technological culture in the Age of Space needed to make into the green world, the "sunflower forest," of nature's processes. With characteristic evocative power, *The Invisible Pyramid* set forth his hope for this "last miracle" of technology, the realization of earthly nature and its tending as the first priority of space exploration.

The attitudes of the 1970s in many ways followed the lead of Earth Day and Eiseley's hopes, replacing the attitudes of Earth-denial in the 1960s. In 1974 Lewis Thomas' *The Lives of a Cell* envisioned the Earth as a fragile one-celled organism within which human beings are a kind of nervous system. A year later English geochemist James Lovelock presented his "Gaia Hypothesis," a more scientifically grounded version of Thomas' metaphor, in an article that was succeeded in 1979 by his book with the arresting subtitle *Gaia: A New Look at Life on Earth*.

Lovelock, with biologist Lynn Margulis, had taken his inferences from observing the surface of Mars in work with NASA and applied them to the Earth. He proposed that the latter was an autonomous being creating and adjusting the organic conditions, from the atmosphere to human life, for its own continued existence as a global biosphere. Lovelock got the name for his hypothesis, the pre-Olympian Earth goddess of ancient Greece, from his neighbor in England, the novelist William Golding.

And it has to be said that, at least initially, the Gaia Hypothesis resonated more positively (if often vaguely) with aesthetics and spirituality than with strict science. In fact, Lovelock was taken aback by the outpouring of agreement from those who knew little or nothing about ecology as a science.

Nevertheless, this proposal further underscored the terrestrial reconnection that space exploration had quite amazingly begun to foster: not only was this a redirection of our attention, but also, for many, a reenergized reverence for nature. Sally Ride, the first U.S. woman in space, may have had the extraction of "natural resources" more in mind than a Gaian spirituality, but it was evocative for her to speak in favor of a "Mission to Earth" a few years after the last lunar landing in 1972. The testimony of contemporary literature, too, was for the most part supportive of earthward rather than of spaceward ideals, as Ronald Weber concluded in 1985 in his *Seeing Earth: Literary Responses to Space Exploration*.

By 1986, on the other hand, several reassessments tempered any totally upbeat view of our Space-Age rebirth as eco-earthlings. In the papers from a conference on ecofeminism, Yaakov Jerome Garb raised questions about whether our vantage point from outer space represented "perspective" or, after all, "escape." He deconstructed the whole-Earth photograph to find an alienating distance, a literalistic image, and a disturbingly univocal sign of the "one-true-story." Peter Bishop weighed in with a Jungian critique of "the shadows of the holistic Earth," fears of immensity, loss, and fragmentation hidden in our Space-Age fantasies of environmental harmony and order. I contributed a milder warning with a piece called "Getting Back to Gaia," a prelude to my *Approaching Earth* book, in which I pointed out Lovelock's ignorance of the implications of the name he borrowed for his hypothesis – and the consequent need for a non-scientific sophistication about the myths and metaphors at play in our Space-Age reconsiderations of Earth lest these be lost in exclusively cybernetic strategems.

The explosion of the *Challenger* space shuttle that same year was another disquieting factor, turning us away from space exploration and toward earthly agendas, to be sure, but offering a reminder that our reconnection could be tinged with tragedy.

In the end, though, as appraised from the dawn of a new millennium, when millionaire Dennis Tito has just returned from orbit with an "ordinary citizen's" reiteration of the inspiration the whole-Earth view gave him to be a born-again earthling, the most striking lesson to retain from our first forays into space is clear. They eventually provided the angle of vision that galvanized a new environmentalism, including an emergent ecofeminism, which "greened" most religious expressions, while perhaps as well specifically promoting a resurgent neo-paganism. Admittedly these movements have not swept aside the arguably patriarchal politics of pollution and exploitation. But space exploration provided a new start, and new hope, for the forces seeking ecological sanity and spirituality in a technological future.

Or perhaps it was Earth herself who was calling us back, teaching us that at the height of our highest technological leap beyond her bounds, our humanness required a seemingly outmoded grounding in the dark wet soil of home, Eiseley's ancient sunflower forest. A miracle indeed – a last one, we are well-advised to imagine, in that it is, finally, a remarkably positive legacy from the end of the troubled century when we first ventured into space.

Daniel C. Noel

Further Reading

Eiseley, Loren. *The Invisible Pyramid*. New York: Charles Scribner's Sons, 1970.
Fuller, R. Buckminster. *Operating Manual for Spaceship Earth*. New York: Simon & Schuster Clarion Books, 1969.
Lovelock, James. *Gaia: A New Look at Life on Earth*. Oxford and New York: Oxford University Press, 1979.
"The Moon Landing and its Aftermath" (special issue). *Michigan Quarterly Review* 18:2 (Spring 1979).
Noel, Daniel C. *Approaching Earth: A Search for the Mythic Significance of the Space Age*. Warwick, NY: Amity House, 1986.
Weber, Ronald. *Seeing Earth: Literary Responses to Space Exploration*. Athens, OH: Ohio University Press, 1985.

See also: Astronauts; Eiseley, Loren; Fuller, Buckminster; Lovelock, James; UFOs and Extraterrestrials.

Spinoza, Baruch (1632–1677)

Few thinkers have been as controversial, both in their lifetime and long after, as the philosopher, theologian, and Torah scholar Baruch (or Benedict) de Spinoza, usually referred to simply as Spinoza. At the age of 23 (on 27 July 1656) Spinoza was excommunicated from his synagogue in Amsterdam, in the ceremony known as the cherem, for his denial of the personal immortality of the soul and his doubts about the divine origin of the Torah. He was put under a ban that forbade any member of the congregation from communicating with him or reading any of his future publications. During his subsequent years as a self-supporting lens craftsman living in the southern part of the Netherlands, Spinoza experienced a more subtle form of censorship and was often accused of being an atheist for his anti-supernaturalism and his affirmation of the power of reason to disclose the nature of God. While he was able to get one of his works published in Latin, he had to modify his main work, *Ethics* (published posthumously in 1677) to get it ready for a Dutch language edition. Specifically, whereas in the Latin version Spinoza equated God and nature (*Deus sive natura*), in the sense of power but not in the sense of materiality, in the intended Dutch version he felt that he would have to drop out this correlation with nature. In his political and hermeneutic text *Theological-Political Treatise* (published in 1670) the correlation of God and nature is more boldly asserted, but again, in the sense that each is the power and the manifestation of being as infinite substance.

In the eighteenth and nineteenth centuries, the charge of Spinozism, which carried the taint of pantheism and even atheism, would appear when thinkers of the Protestant left struggled to articulate a more naturalistic conception of the divine. A famous instance occurred when the German Reformed theologian Frederick Schleiermacher (known as the grandfather of liberalism) was accused of importing this dangerous non-biblical and heretical doctrine into the church in his 1799 *On Religion: Speeches to Its Cultured Despisers*. Schleiermacher, while publicly affirming the influence of Spinoza on his thinking, was able to deflect this charge and get his early work past the censor. Yet decades later Schleiermacher's colleague at the University of Berlin, G.W.F. Hegel, strongly criticized any hint of Spinozism in religion – going so far as to say that Eastern religion was actually a form of Spinoza's pantheism because of its alleged corollary belief in one substance. For Hegel, Spinoza's substance was devoid of spirit or self-consciousness and thus could not be a worthy religious object. Even in the twentieth century both Jewish and Christian theologians have often had to tread lightly around any affirmation of the clear pantheism in Spinoza's *Ethics*. Yet Spinoza's positive impact on the Enlightenment, with its quest for a universal religion, and Romanticism, with its hunger for the hidden abyss of nature, can be measured by the courageous ways in which a few major thinkers of this period revivified the study of nature as a religious theme in its own right.

It is often assumed that Spinoza lived an isolated life that was cut off from contact with the creative minds of his time. In fact, he frequently entertained visitors of distinction in his home and was fully aware of what was taking place in the major universities of the Netherlands and beyond. He engaged in lengthy correspondence with noted philosophers and scientists and was able to answer some of the first criticisms of the pre-published manuscript version of his *Ethics*. He was an early champion of the ideas of René Descartes, and continued to teach the Cartesian philosophy to private students who visited him from Leiden University during the period in which such thought was effectively banned from Dutch universities – further damaging his reputation in the eyes of both Jewish and Christian theologians. Yet his championing of Descartes was not unquestioning, especially concerning the ideas of soul and substance.

For Descartes, the world is constituted by two fundamentally different modes of substance, whose interaction is somewhat shrouded in mystery even though he held that there may be a link between them through the pituitary gland in the brain. On one side is extended substance, which exists in three spatial dimensions and can be plotted on a three-axis (x,y,z) coordinate system. This is the realm of matter that can be analyzed using the principles of a mechanistic physics. On the other side is non-extended substance, the realm of mind, which has no spatial traits and is not located within any type of coordinate system. Non-extended or thinking substance provides direct evidence of its own existence through a process of introspection and self-conquering doubt of external reality. From a self-evident foundation of pure internal intuition consciousness can establish both its own immortality and the existence of a perfect deity.

For Spinoza, this dualism produced severe problems that he set out to resolve in his own metaphysics of substance. Unlike any manifest order within the world, substance is that which bears traits, while not having traits of its own; that is, "A substance is prior in nature to its affections (*Ethics*)." Yet for Spinoza there could only be one substance, not two or more. The one infinite substance has an infinite number of affections or modes, only two of which are immediately knowable by us; namely, the physical and the mental modes. Consequently, contra Descartes, there is one substance with two known modes, not two separate substances with a dubious connection. Mind and matter were simple, different modalities of the one nature or God. Further, Spinoza distanced himself from the atomism implicit in Descartes' vision of nature and affirmed a deeper unity that he denoted by the Latin and medieval term "*natura naturans*" or nature naturing – somewhat akin to his use of the Latin concept of *conatus* or striving. Given the principle of unity in his fundamental ontology, Spinoza argued that the most basic value of life, and the foundation of ethics, was the intellectual contemplation of the divine infinite substance. Spinoza did not have any personal or social religious practices that pointed to an experience of the holy as a part of nature, but he did articulate a kind of liturgy of the mind that sought a deep parallelism between the human understanding of the infinite (via two of its modes) and the infinite substance itself. By rejecting supernaturalism and any notion of a personal immortal soul, Spinoza came very close to a kind of nature mysticism in which the distance between the human individual and the divine is overcome through the human instrument of reason. This model provides no place for special historical revelation or for the sacredness of any text, as neither is necessary for the intellectual contemplation of God as nature.

Specifically, Spinoza argued that God (as nature) was unique, a necessary existent, the necessary cause of all things, and was devoid of will or intellect. Further, all things, no matter what their attributes, have their being in and are sustained by God. Again, the distinction between a creator and its creation is denied since both dimensions of nature are part of the same infinity. Interestingly, Spinoza's form of pantheism is necessitarian and denies anything like free will (both in God and in human beings). One implication of this is that, "... all final causes are nothing but human fictions (*Ethics*)." God as nature has no lack in its infinite reality and hence can neither have nor hold forth any unfulfilled goals. This view of the divine puts Spinoza on the opposite side of the divide from contemporary process perspectives, which affirm teleology and incompletion in the divine and in the human order as it relates to the divine.

For centuries the epithet "Spinozism" has been a term of rebuke, yet very few thinkers have actually probed into the meaning of so-called Spinozism and into its key role in the evolution of our understanding of nature. While Spinoza has had little impact on contemporary ecofeminism, he has had a strong influence in two areas of thought that are of growing importance. In the French postmodern milieu he has appeared as a crucial dialogue partner and goad to the reflections of Giles Deleuze who developed a non-linguistically centered ontology of nature and its inner dynamisms. This has opened up an avenue of reflection that is not ensnared in the stultifying debate between French structuralism and deconstruction. In the revival of classical Euro-American pragmatism, which rethinks the late nineteenth- and early twentieth-century texts of Charles Sanders Peirce, John Dewey, and William James, there is now a movement to unfold a metaphysics of nature that has clear and conscious ties to Spinoza. Among thinkers who have acknowledged this tie are Justus Buchler, Don Crosby, Jerome Stone, and this author. Process metaphysics is less open to a dialogue with Spinoza because of the latter's perceived eternalism and static view of the one infinite substance. However, insofar as process thought focuses on the extensive continuum, creativity, or the Platonic container, it may find itself more open to an appreciation of the power of Spinoza's key concept of *nature naturing*. By compelling us to take the concept of immnanentism with the utmost seriousness, Spinoza makes it possible for us to unfold a fully radical and consistent naturalism that neither romanticizes nature nor leaves it in the hands of an alien creator God.

Robert S. Corrington

Further Reading

Curley, Edwin. *A Spinoza Reader*. Princeton, NJ: Princeton University Press, 1994.
Grene, Marjorie. *Spinoza: A Collection of Critical Essays*. New York: Anchor Books, 1973.
Lamm, Julia A. *The Living God: Schleiermacher's Theological Appropriation of Spinoza*. University Park, PA: The Pennsylvania State University Press, 1994.
Mason, Richard. *The God of Spinoza: A Philosophical Study*. Cambridge: Cambridge University Press, 1997.
Nadler, Steven. *Spinoza: A Life*. Cambridge: Cambridge University Press, 1999.

See also: Corrington, Robert S.; Deep Ecology; Environmental Ethics; Naess, Arne; Pantheism; Religious Naturalism.

Spirit and Nature

A theological term analogically borrowed from early natural sciences – namely, stoicism and Platonism – Spirit remains intimately correlated to a culture's philosophy of nature. Insomuch as the philosopher William James once observed that "[r]eligion is our manner of acceptance of the universe" (Goodenough 1998: 47), a given culture's sense of embeddedness or, conversely, self-exclusion from ecological systems may be deduced from its articulation of spirit. Despite the affiliation of dust and spirit in the creation stories of the Hebrew Bible, predominant correlations of Spirit and nature in the twenty centuries of Western Christianity have tended to legitimate an aversion of the Earth through the evocation of Spirit's transcendence.

Early Semitic stories, like many indigenous cosmologies, employed the concept "spirit" (in Hebrew, *ruach*, translated as "breath" or "spirit") without substantively pulling the sacred out of the ecological matrix. Spirit, rather than forcing the value of life to stand away from or against nature, conspired with the physical: quite simply as the air is indivisible, so the breath (spirit) of life that God breathes into the first human is indistinguishable from the human's own breath (Gen. 2:7). Among the Jesus movements of the first century, "Spirit" was a predominant name for the experience of the immanent power and presence of God, that which promised the renewal of creation.

During the first centuries, Christian theologians, philosophically girded with Platonic and Stoic dynamic materialism, capitalized upon Spirit as causal agent or efficacy of the sacred. Yet, two significant tidal turns in Spirit's affiliation with nature transpired during these transitional centuries: 1) Spirit was, given its later Semitic affiliation with prophetic word and textual inscription, increasingly construed as a human, rational phenomenon; and 2) the apocalyptic cosmology of communities politically resisting the Roman empire, which had seemingly returned the Earth to "waste and void" (see Gen. 1:1–2), construed Spirit as another viable life region to which they might immigrate. Later Christian theologians read "the fall" of the Earth not as Earth's conscription by empire, but as an ontological devolution of matter itself. Quite simply, nature, having once been a paradise, wasn't itself any more, but had taken on qualities averse to life in the Spirit – namely, transience, temporality, and suffering.

While Stoicism and Platonism considered Spirit to be the most refined, purified form of matter, with the onset of neo-Platonism in the fourth century, "spirit" (*pneuma*, in Greek, affiliated with "air" or "wind," and "*spiritus*," in Latin, meaning "breath") came rather to designate that which was by definition immaterial. To invoke Spirit as the causal agent of a "new Earth" (Rev. 21) henceforth signaled Christianity's revulsion toward the conditions of finitude, spoilation and mortality. These psychic aversions were simultaneously visited as the occasion of women's subjugation, since (according to Aristotelean sensibilities) while man rationally ensouled, the human woman bequeathed to it its flesh-body. Consequently Spirit, Western Christian theologians up to this twenty-first century have claimed, liberates nature from its "bondage to transience" (Rom. 8:21), its temporal and finite constitution. Spirit's promised "second birth" through baptism lifted "man" out of the history of the animal, organic body, a conviction which has consequently legitimated Western culture's ignorance of and indifference to ecological limits.

Where Spirit was affiliated with human reason, as it has been in Cartesian rationalism, the concept of Spirit can hide humanity's tendencies toward ideological control of nature. Christianity's primary distinction between the sacred and the world, typically invoked as the distinction between "the Creator" and "the created," easily led to Descartes' distinction between the thinking mind and objective bodies of matter. As Divine Spirit was absolutely transcendent over the creation, so the human mind or "spirit" assumed its governance over the material world. This rationalistic aversion to the Earth, carried forward as modernity's cosmological spirit–matter dualism, was accompanied by the fifteenth- to eighteenth-century persecution of those who practiced a vitalistic worldview – herbalists and witches, but also so-called pagans and heathens.

This early modern dualism was countered by the late modern immanent Spirit of Hegelian Idealism in which Spirit dynamically catalyzed cosmic becoming – as evidenced in the modern notions of history, progress, evolution, and development. Nevertheless, Hegel's idealist philosophy – because Spirit was still platonically configured as the inverse of gravity – has had a similar history to that of Cartesian dualism. Both philosophical postures effectively open a psychic fault line between humanity and Earth. To be sure, some twentieth-century theologians have defended this as a necessary distinction between the Creator and the creation. Indeed some theologians like Nicholas Berdyaev have affirmed Western technology for instrumentally interrupting humanity's temptation to commune with elemental spirits, and other theologians have affirmed technology's capacity for rehabilitating "fallen" or devolved nature, for alleviating suffering, death and toil, and for reclaiming the Earth as paradisiacal garden. Still others, like French philosopher Luce Irigaray, critique this stance, asserting that two life economies are thereby created – a metaphysical and capitalist superstructure of immaterial spirit that disregards the Earth, including the human body, and a material substrate to which this superstructure denies spiritual value. In such an assessment, spirit–matter dualism, like its idealist parallel, constitutes a social technology – namely, ways of relating to the Earth that legitimate androcentrism and the commodification of natural resources, at the same time occasioning ecocide, genocide, and the suppression of Earthkeeping peoples.

If neither the Cartesian dualism nor philosophical idealism encouraged humanity to live well with the Earth, modernity has – from another perspective – been viewed as a time of "disenchantment" or "despiritualization." Phenomenologically speaking, belief in a "supernatural" world of Spirit forms when humanity's sense relations have been psychically truncated, such that belief comes to be seen as replacing direct or immediate experience. Modern commitments to instrumental rationalism and methodological objectivity presume that human consciousness is neither organically given nor emergent from sensuous participation in the field of life relations. Neither allows room for sacred value within the material world. Because mechanistic materialism assumed Spirit to be superordinate to nature – or, "supernatural" – and because rationalist empiricism dismissed claims to supernatural phenomenon, Spirit itself seemed during modernity to become irrelevant.

Nevertheless, given twentieth-century physics and revised cosmologies based upon them, it has become possible to think about Spirit without recourse to supernaturalism and therefore without abandoning care for the Earth. Given its valence as a term of energy and vitality, Christian theologians, like Jürgen Moltmann, Mark Wallace and Elizabeth Johnson, have been reconstructing the notion of Spirit with the goal of greening Christianity. Philosophical theologians, like Thomas Berry, consider Spirit to be an emergent order of nature – as the Transcendentalists also seem to have contended. Process theology's relational ontology allows theologians to think an immanental order of Spirit, which, while active in cosmic becoming, is nevertheless distinct from and respectful of the world's own creativity. In yet other suggestive proposals, Spirit, analogically like the quantum vacuum or the vessel of the Tao, pours forth the rare, fragile and wonderful flowering of a material universe, such that – now inverting Platonism – we experience the material world as privilege.

Sharon V. Betcher

Further Reading
Abram, David. *The Spell of the Sensuous: Perception and Language in a More-Than-Human World*. New York: Vintage/Random House, 1997.
Berman, Morris. *The Reenchantment of the World*. Ithaca: Cornell University Press, 1981.
Berry, Wendell. "Christianity and the Survival of Creation." In Michael Katakis, ed. *Sacred Trusts: Essays on Stewardship and Responsibility*. San Francisco: Mercury House, 1993.
Goodenough, Ursula. *The Sacred Depths of Nature*. New York: Oxford, 1998.
Griffin, David Ray. *Reenchantment without Supernaturalism: A Process Philosophy of Religion*. Ithaca: Cornell University Press, 2001.
Griffin, Susan. "Split Culture." In Judith Plant, ed. *Healing the Wounds: The Promise of Ecofeminism*. Philadelphia: New Society Publishers, 1989.
Hiebert, Theodore. *The Yahwist's Landscape: Nature & Religion in Early Israel*. New York: Oxford, 1996.
Johnson, Elizabeth A. *She Who Is: The Mystery of God in*

Feminist Theological Discourse. New York: Crossroad, 1992.

Keller, Catherine. "Postmodern 'Nature,' Feminism and Community." In Dieter T. Hessel, ed. *Theology for Earth Community: A Field Guide.* Maryknoll: Orbis, 1996.

Moltmann, Jürgen. *The Spirit of Life: A Universal Affirmation.* Minneapolis: Fortress Press, 1992.

Wallace, Mark I. *Fragments of the Spirit: Nature, Violence, and the Renewal of Creation.* New York: Continuum, 1996.

See also: Berry, Thomas; Berry, Wendell; Descartes, René; Griffin, Susan; Moltmann, Jürgen; Religious Naturalism; Spirit and Nature Walking Paths.

Spirit and Nature Walking Paths

Early in 1998, a group of central Vermont environmentalists, activists, and naturalists from a variety of faith backgrounds, began planning a series of woodland paths that they called "Spirit in Nature." The trails, eventually located on the spine of the Green Mountains just a few hundred yards from the poet Robert Frost's summer home in Ripton, Vermont, wind through the forest past intermittently spaced "sayings" of various religious traditions, designed to foster reflection and insight for visitors. Inspired by the success of the nearly eight miles of Vermont trails, other groups in different parts of the country have begun to adopt the idea, building permanent or temporary versions of the paths.

Paul Bortz, a Unitarian Universalist minister, left his pulpit in 1996 and began pursuing his vision of a union between faith and environmentalism. Bortz, an accomplished organizer, moved to the Middlebury area where he married Catherine Nichols, pastor of the local Episcopal church. Together they began forming the initial nucleus of the group, drawing on local church members and also students and faculty from nearby Middlebury College, which boasts the nation's oldest environmental studies department. The college eventually leased the group the land it needed to proceed with construction of the trails.

There are now nine trails winding through the beaver meadows, abandoned apple orchards, and riverbanks that mark the site. They represent the Bahá'í, Quaker, Jewish, Muslim, Pagan, Unitarian Universalist, Christian, Hindu, and Buddhist traditions; there is also an interfaith path. All end at a common "sacred circle" furnished with benches and used for occasional ceremonies.

Bill McKibben

See also: Labyrinth.

P Spirit of the Sage Council

Unique in its origin and inspiration, Spirit of the Sage Council was brought together by the ancient whisperings of a most sacred plant of indigenous people of the Americas – White Sage (*salvia apiana*). Operating from a small office in Pasadena, California and a historic farmhouse in Carthage, North Carolina, it seeks to preserve sage scrub habitats wherever they occur, and the indigenous cultures and religions that depend on them.

Endemic to portions of Southern California and Baja, Mexico, the sacred White Sage dominates the less than 2 percent remaining of the Riversidean Alluvial Fan Sage Scrub natural community in the United States. Globally imperiled, this habitat continues to be greatly threatened by human settlement and commercial enterprise. As a nurse, student of natural medicine and indigenous healing methods, I first became "familiar" with the ethnobotanical use of native sage in Lakota Inipi ceremonies conducted by Wesley Black Elk and his father Wallace and cousin Stephen Red Buffalo in the 1980s. As a participant in the ceremony, the sacred sage is not only for cleansing of the bodies of "two-legged" people but also for healing the mind and spirit.

The spiritual connection I made with the sage led me to other indigenous people. I felt as though, whether in waking hours or during sleep, that the Sage spirit took over my life and led me from one person to another who would help protect its areas of residence. Through my connection to the sage, I became extremely sensitive, feeling threats to the sage's existence like a threat to my very own.

In 1986 a commercial harvester, Alfred "Red Sky" Saverilli came into my life and showed me where to find and how to recognize the White Sage. I felt intoxicated and delighted any time I was with the White Sage in the wild. As I began to recognize the plant from miles away, the internal dialog with my sage familiar became stronger.

I sought out the remaining descendants of the indigenous Shoshone "Gabrielino" people to discuss the threats to the White Sage habitats and eventually was steered to Vera Rocha, who some considered Chief. Meeting with her and her husband – the tribe's spiritual leader – Manuel Rocha, we decided quickly to form a group to protect the sage. When I asked them what the conservation group should be named, Manual Rocha said, "It is the Spirit of the Sage that has asked for our help and we have heard it." Vera Rocha added,

> There has been too much destruction – of the Sage, of our Land and the people keep taking till the Sage can give no more. It is time now for us to give back to the Sage. We need to get people to come together that want to help protect the Sage. We can have our own council meetings for the Sage.

Over the years as the health of the Gabrielino elders diminished and Manuel Rocha passed on, I assumed much of the work in consultation with Vera Rocha. We have worked through diverse venues, and in alliance with a variety of groups (including the American Indian Movement, Earth First!, The Green Party, the Rainforest Action Network, the Nation of Islam, and the Azteca Mexica's) to convince decision-makers of the cultural and biological significance of sage habitat. Tactics used have included direct-action blockades against destructive practices and survey stake removal, public education, and lawsuits.

The Spirit of Sage Council has been recognized for its cutting-edge work based on the Endangered Species Act, especially in Southern California, where, in part in response to the Council's work since 1990, the U.S. Fish & Wildlife Service and California Department of Fish & Game began to give the conservation of Coastal Sage Scrub natural communities their highest priority. Coming from the place of respect and reverence for the Earth, the work of Spirit of the Sage Council has directly led to the preservation of over 2000 acres of Coastal Sage Scrub habitat in Southern California, and has set up a nonprofit land trust to receive and manage lands protected through lawsuits.

Part of the argument the Spirit of Sage Council has made is that development that destroys the sage habitats also endangers the culture and religion of the Shoshone Gabrielino Band and other indigenous peoples. We also believe that our connection to Earth and Spirit guides our decisions. The sage even led us to challenge plans by the Los Angeles Catholic Archdiocese to build the largest cathedral in the United States on a site that had indigenous burial remains.

Leeona Klippstein

Further Reading

Hayden, Tom. *The Lost Gospel of the Earth*. San Francisco: Sierra Club Books, 1997.

Miller, Bruce W. *The Gabrielino*. Los Osos, CA: Sand River Press, 1991.

Reid, Hugo. *Letters on the Los Angeles County Indians*. Berkeley, CA: University of California Press, 1939.

See also: Earth First! and the Earth Liberation Front; Ethnobotany; Hopiland to the Rainforest Action Network; Radical Environmentalism.

Spretnak, Charlene (1946–)

Charlene Spretnak's work, as a writer, a teacher, and an activist, flourishes at the meeting place of feminism, green politics, spirituality, and ecological postmodernism. Spretnak suggests that the modern worldview, shaped by the Enlightenment, is giving way to an emergent worldview that connects bodies and nature, a view she refers to as "the real." Her work is groundbreaking as it moves to connect spirituality and activism in pursuit of this paradigm shift.

Born 30 June 1946 in Pittsburgh, Pennsylvania and educated at St. Louis University and the University of California, Berkeley, she was inducted into the Ohio Women's Hall of Fame in 1989 and teaches at the California Institute of Integral Studies. Her earliest works focused on women and religion. *Lost Goddesses of Early Greece* explored pre-Hellenic Goddess mythology, and provided creative, feminist retellings of these myths. With *The Politics of Women's Spirituality* she brought together a collection of writings addressing the intersection of feminism, religion, and politics, including works by many of the most influential feminist theologians, such as Carol Christ, Mary Daly, Naomi Goldenberg, and Starhawk.

Perhaps her best-known book, *Green Politics*, co-authored with Fritjof Capra, explored the holistic, non-exploitative ideology of the German Greens and how such politics could be brought to the United States. With this holistic approach in mind and with the goal of carrying on the vision of the German Greens, Spretnak co-founded in 1984 the Committees of Correspondence, named after grassroots groups that existed in the United States during the Revolutionary War.

The Spiritual Dimension of Green Politics and *States of Grace* returned Spretnak's writing to a more overtly spiritual focus. Her call to the reader is not to any new or even specific religion. She herself has practiced Vipassana mediation, and has appeared in the Canadian film *Full Circle*, which showcases environmental concerns and women's spirituality. Spretnak urges others to turn to the resources within one's own existing tradition that mesh with a post-humanist, postmodern, and post-patriarchal worldview. She devotes considerable attention to all three of these theoretical constructs, in both these books and later writing, to clarify her unique understanding of their meaning and practice.

More recently her essay "Radical Nonduality in Ecofeminist Philosophy" and *Resurgence of the Real* examined the importance of paying attention to body, nature and place. She suggested a move beyond modernism, not to deconstructionist postmodernism, but to what she calls ecological postmodernism. In "Radical Nonduality" Spretnak questioned the tendency of deconstructionist postmodernism to deny any "unitive dimensions of being." She then presented a theory of ecological postmodernism that includes a relational ontology, thus questioning the deconstructionist idea that there is "nothing but social construction in human experience" (1997: 427).

Her scholarly analysis in *Resurgence of the Real* is supplemented at the end by a fictionalized account of how her visions for the future are no mere flights of fancy, but concrete possibilities for an integrated world honoring the significance of nature, gender, and spirituality in sustainability.

Sarah Whedon

Further Reading

Spretnak, Charlene. *The Resurgence of the Real: Body, Nature, and Place in a Hypermodern World*. New York: Routledge, 1999.

Spretnak, Charlene. "Radical Nonduality in Ecofeminist Philosophy." In *Ecofeminism: Women, Culture, Nature*. Karen J. Warren, ed. Bloomington: Indiana University Press, 1997.

Spretnak, Charlene. *The Politics of Women's Spirituality: Essays by Founding Mothers of the Movement*. New York: Anchor Books/Doubleday, 1994.

Spretnak, Charlene. *Lost Goddesses of Early Greece: A Collection of Pre-Hellenic Myths*. Boston: Beacon Press, 1992.

Spretnak, Charlene. *States of Grace: The Recovery of Meaning in the Postmodern Age*. New York: HarperCollins, 1991.

Spretnak, Charlene. *The Spiritual Dimension of Green Politics*. Santa Fe: Bear & Co., 1986.

Spretnak, Charlene and Fritjof Capra. *Green Politics: The Global Promise*. New York: Dutton, 1984.

See also: Capra, Fritjof; Christ, Carol; Daly, Mary; Ecofeminism; Starhawk.

St. Katherine's Monastery (Mt. Sinai, Egypt)

The spectacular fortified monastery of St. Katherine, often described as "the most perfect relic of the 4th century left in the world," still looks much as it did on completion in 565. It is located at the foot of Mt. Sinai in the central Sinai desert, Egypt, has been continuously inhabited since the fourth century and is the oldest Christian monastery in the world in continuous existence. The monastery derives its name from the third-century Christian martyr St. Katherine (or Catherine) whose relics were found on the nearby summit of Mount Katherine (Gebel Katherine). The monastery itself is believed to be built on the site of the Burning Bush, where God spoke to the prophet Moses, in the shadow of Gebel Musa (Mount Sinai) where Moses received the Ten Commandments. Its construction started in the year 337 when the Empress Helena, mother of Emperor Constantine (under whom Christianity became the official religion of the Roman Empire in 313), decreed that a monastery was to be built on the site. The original building became a refuge for increasing numbers of hermits and pilgrims, and between 537–562 the Emperor Justinian expanded its site by adding two churches and building the great walls and fortifications that still stand today. The monastery walls, built of dressed granite, rise to a height of 20 meters in places and are 2–3 meters thick. Inside them, the monastery covers an area less than 70 × 80 meters with a multilevel labyrinth of living quarters, twelve chapels, an icon gallery, hospice, ancillary buildings and the famous library, second in historical significance only to that of the Vatican in Rome. Famous sites within the monastery include Jacob's Well, which never dries up and is supposedly where the prophet Jacob met his future life, as well as the descendant of the original Burning Bush (much vandalized for cuttings) and St. Catherine's Church, built between 542–551 in memory of Justinian's wife, and famous for its wonderful sixth-century doors and 12 enormous pillars covered in icons.

The monastery has survived for centuries as a Christian oasis in an Islamic state as a result of a legend which said that the Prophet Mohammed himself was once kindly received there. In return he issued a letter protecting the monastery for ever, a copy of which can still be seen in the gatehouse entrance. Continuous protection by Roman emperors, Islamic conquerors, Napoleon and various middle-eastern governments account for the survival, unlooted, of the great treasures of the monastery including its spectacular collection of 2000 of the most important icons in the world. The 5000 books and 300 valuable manuscripts in the library have steadily accumulated since the sixth century and are written in Greek, Arabic, Syrian, Georgian, Armenian and Slavonic languages and are now housed in the spacious new concrete library building, constructed between 1930–1942 and occupying most of the southern side of the monastery. Until its removal in 1859 by Constantin von Tischendorf, the library also included the *Codex Siniaticus*, the oldest and most complete Greek manuscript of the Bible ever found, now in the British Museum in London.

During the Crusader period (eleventh–twelfth centuries) the site became a major pilgrimage center, but since medieval times the size of its monastic community has steadily declined. However, it is still a working monastery whose community of around 25 monks start their day of prayer and devotional work with matins at 4 a.m. and liturgy until 7:30 a.m., finishing with evening prayer between 3–5. The Sinai monastic order, independent since the sixth century, observes the Canons of the Eastern Orthodox church under the control of an archbishop of Sinai. The community works in partnership with local Gebaliya Bedouin communities, the descendents of workers of Slavic origin imported in the sixth century by Justinian to construct and protect the monastery. The monastery still operates a guesthouse, offering simple accommodation for pilgrims and those on retreat, but it has now also become a major leisure tourist destination.

During the period 1600–1920, both people and supplies entered the monastery only via a basket drawn up on a ten-meter-long rope over the north wall. Until the 1960s, it probably received less than fifty visitors a year. By the year 2017, it is thought that this may reach half a million a year. The development of St. Katherine's as a tourist destination postdates the Israeli occupation of southern Sinai which took place between 1967–1979, and is related to the rapid expansion of beach resorts such as Sharm el-Sheik on the nearby Red Sea coast. In 1996, mindful of concerns over the lack of protection for the environment and buildings of St. Katherine's, the European Community made a grant of 6. 5million *ecus* which financed a study of the area, and helped create the 4300-square-kilometer St. Katherine's Protectorate, forming an integral part of the southern Sinai protected area system. The St. Katherine's Protectorate includes not only Mt. Sinai itself but many other religious cultural and archeological sites in the surrounding landscape, such as the valley of Wadi Hebran, supposedly the place where the Israelites camped to wait for Moses to return from Mount Sinai with the Ten Commandments. The development of this system of protected areas was instrumental in getting World Heritage status for the monastery and surrounding landscape, finally achieved in 2002.

Concerns for the future revolve around the issue of managing the growth of tourism to the site. Currently, the monastery is open without charge five days per week (except weekends and church festivals) and it now receives nearly 100,000 tourists each year, 80 percent of whom are day-trip visitors and many of whom stay less than half an hour. This is projected to rise to 500,000 visitors by 2017, placing severe pressure on the fabric of the monastery and the ability of its inhabitants to maintain their normal routines. In addition, the area around the monastery is increasingly popular with hikers, many of whom climb Mt. Sinai (Gebel Musa) which, at 2285 meters overlooks the entire area. St. Katherine's still remains a center for pilgrimage, a place of retreat and a combination of working monastery, museum and art gallery – much as it has been for 1500 years – but unless visitor numbers can be controlled it is difficult to see which of these functions will remain in the future.

Myra Shackley

Further Reading

Shackley, Myra. *Managing Sacred Sites; Service Provision and Visitor Experience.* London: Continuum, 2002.

Shackley, Myra. "A Golden Calf in Sacred Space?: The Future of St Katherine's Monastery, Mount Sinai, Egypt." *International Journal of Heritage Studies* 4:3–4 (1998), 123–34.

See *also*: Christianity (6b1) – Christian Orthodoxy; Roman Catholic Religious Orders; Sacred Mountains; Sacred Space/Place.

St. Francis of Assisi – *See* Francis of Assisi.

Starhawk (1951–)

Starhawk is an ecofeminist activist, author and Witch, and a founding mother of the Reclaiming Witchcraft tradition in San Francisco. Starhawk, who was born in 1951 of Russian Jewish descent with the given name Miriam Simos, met Witchcraft in the early 1970s. She was first introduced to Z. Budapest's *Dianic* Witchcraft tradition and later (in 1975) initiated into the Faery tradition by Victor Anderson. The Witches' magical view of the world as a living being made a profound impact on her. Her feeling was not that of hearing something new but of finally being given names and interpretive frameworks for experiences she already had. She also felt empowered by the concept of a religion that worshipped a goddess – the immanent life-force. This hermeneutic distinction between direct experience and cultural symbol has been fundamental to her theological and political thinking ever since, and guided her major work as leader for a new non-dogmatic version of neo-pagan Witchcraft and as a political activist.

The inauguration of her work manifested textually in 1979, when *The Spiral Dance: A Rebirth of the Ancient Religion of the Great Goddess* was first published. It manifested practically in 1980, when she and her coven-sisters founded *Reclaiming*, a center for feminist spirituality and a "school" in Witchcraft. Both in *The Spiral Dance* as well as in other publications such as *Dreaming the Dark* (1982), *Truth or Dare* (1987), *The Fifth Sacred Thing* (1993), *Walking to Mercury* (1997), *A Pagan Book of Living and Dying* (1997), *Circle Round: Raising Children in Goddess Traditions* (1999), and *The Twelve Wild Swans: A Journey into Magic, Healing and Action* (2000), Starhawk interprets neo-pagan Witchcraft as "earth religion," argues for its environmental and countercultural potentials, presents a manual of ritual and magical action and establishes a historical horizon for the practice of contemporary goddess worship.

According to Starhawk, all modern Witchcraft traditions have their spiritual roots in the tribal religions of Europe some 10,000 years ago. Therefore, in spirit, they are related to the surviving shamanic "Earth religions" of the contemporary West, including those of Native Americans, African Americans, the Sami and the Inuits. She has also adopted Marija Gimbutas' disputed thesis that the old Europeans originally worshipped a Great Goddess as divine giver of life, death and fertility, and her son-lover, the Horned God. The fall and regeneration of this Old Religion is comprised by Starhawk as follows: Neolithic Europeans celebrated the immanent life-force and the cycles of the seasons, and their religion provided tools to establish bonds between individuals, the community and the Earth. Just as religion was goddess-centered, society was woman-centered and organized around the mother and her kin as a basic social principle. These matrifocal and matrilineal cultures were egalitarian, peaceful, just and creative, and laid the foundation of our civilization. In time, patriarchal warriors corrupted the cultures, either by internal warfare or through invasion. This long-lasting event conquered or drove out the matrilineal goddess-worshippers and laid the foundation for oppressive societies and patriarchal religions in Europe. But goddess religions continued to live in folk customs, esoteric traditions and among those persecuted as Witches. Finally, in the twentieth century, the Witches' Craft has again emerged from hiding.

Even though scholars have criticized Starhawk for having invented an erroneous historical lineage to contemporary Witchcraft, the narrative has been important in the building of (Reclaiming) Witches' identity. It also gave a platform from which feminist Witches or goddess-worshippers could perceive themselves as freedom fighters from any patriarchal religion, and reach out to other oppressed people, such as Native Americans, without necessarily being accused of having colonialist intentions: by claiming heritage to a common symbol system, such as the four directions/elements, the concept of the circle and reverence for the Earth, they could create bridges based on commonality, not just difference.

Yet, Starhawk's approach to tradition is fundamentally eclectic and anchored in a radical analysis of power: she insists on the freedom of thought, belief and style of organizing to any Pagan group or person and believes that non-hierarchy is the only ethical leadership structure that may support a view of the world that sees the Earth and everything living as interconnected and interdependent. Her version of Witchcraft is also famous for having reduced the role of the Horned God in favor of the Goddess – the argument being, that to value Goddess above God is not narrowly to define or rank gender, but a means to continually be reminded that what is of value is life brought into the world.

In addition to doing the "work of the Goddess" as teacher, writer and ritualist, Starhawk is a community builder, perma-culturer, political organizer and activist, campaigning in particular for environmental, feminist and anti-war issues. In the 1980s she participated in and trained people for large anti-nuclear actions and was arrested several times as a civil disobedient, both in the Diablo Canyon and Livermore Lab actions in California. During the 1990s she has been active in the anti-deforestation campaigns, especially in the redwood biome of California. In 2000 and 2001 she joined the anti-globalization movement, both as organizer and activist, and was at the forefront in the large demonstrations against a neo-liberalist world economy in Seattle, Washington and Genova (Italy). Through all these activities she has had a major influence on groups such as Earth First! and those whose primary work is nature protection. She has also been important for the growth of goddess spiritualities and neo-paganisms in general and for the cross-fertilization between feminist and non-feminist Witchcraft traditions; by 2001, *The Spiral Dance* had sold more than 300,000 copies.

Jone Salomonsen

Further Reading
Eller, Cynthia. *Living in the Lap of the Goddess: The Feminist Spirituality Movement in America*. Boston: Beacon Press, 1993.
Salomonsen, Jone. *Enchanted Feminism: Ritual, Gender and Divinity among the Reclaiming Witches of San Francisco*. London and New York Routledge, 2001.
Starhawk. *Truth or Dare: Encounters with Power, Authority and Mystery*. San Francisco: Harper & Row, 1987.
Starhawk. *Dreaming the Dark: Magic, Sex and Politics*. Boston: Beacon Press, 1982.
Starhawk. *The Spiral Dance: A Rebirth of the Ancient Religion of the Great Goddess*. San Francisco: Harper & Row, 1979 (revised 1989 and 1999).
See also: Anarchism; Earth First! and the Earth Liberation Front; Ecofeminism; Feminist Spirituality Movement; Paganism – Contemporary; Radical Environmentalism; Reclaiming; Wicca.

Steiner, Rudolf (1861–1925) – and Anthroposophy

The relationship between nature and the spiritual side of humanity occurs increasingly within an arena dominated by a rationalistic objectivity based on sense perceptions and critical thinking. The religious dimension can vary from the Cathari view that nature is evil to that of animism, which sees spirit in all aspects of nature. Rudolf Steiner argued for a distinction between religion resting on dogma or belief and spirituality founded on a complementary perception that augments the physical senses. Steiner claimed to have this direct apprehension superseding received revelation, dogma or even simple belief. Born in Kraljevec, Lower Austria, now Croatia, at an early age he became extraordinarily aware of the non-obvious energies within vegetable and animal life describing an insight into nature beyond the normal purview of the senses. He came increasingly to perceive two worlds: an outer, ever more technical one, and a subtle world of formative forces. He was interested in both, and his quest was to bridge the two. The results of his initial efforts of inquiry culminated with the publication of *The Philosophy of Freedom* in 1895. In this work, he stresses the possibility of experiencing thinking as a spiritual activity rather than as an epiphenomenon of the brain. Upon this basis, he subsequently developed his "spiritual science" as the scientific investigation of spiritual worlds.

As Steiner matured he became ever more involved in

the social, artistic, educational and scientific issues of his time and, in particular, the potential contribution spiritual science could make. Having graduated in mathematics, chemistry, and natural history he earned a Ph.D. in philosophy and acquired considerable academic respect by the end of the nineteenth century. However, knowing that the academic establishment would shun him, he nevertheless decided in 1902 to begin speaking openly about his spiritual observations. He became General Secretary of the German Branch of the Theosophical Society until 1912 when he independently founded the Anthroposophical Society dedicated to developing a scientifically based esotericism. He also developed what he termed *eurythmy* – a system of rhythmical body movements and silent gestures portraying poetic speech, song and music. Deeply affected by the First World War and the social/spiritual questions it raised, he re-founded the Anthroposophical Society in 1923 on the basis of his spiritual science and sought to bridge the inner and outer worlds as a means toward finding an authentic humanity.

Steiner's spiritual science endeavors to cultivate additional forms of perception beyond those based solely on the senses. He wanted to treat non-ordinary perception in a scientific manner and hoped to revolutionize humanity's relation to nature. Steiner's spiritual science, instead of constituting a religious approach to spiritual affairs, is meant to be a scientific method that compliments the spiritual. The mission of the Anthroposophical Society is to promote spiritual science and facilitate its application to various practical fields of endeavor. Its worldwide membership is now over 50,000, and it sponsors approximately 10,000 institutions such as schools, colleges, artistic groups, homes for those with special needs, clinics, medical practices, farms, research institutes, etc.

Highly influenced by Goethe, Steiner edited the German poet's nature writings. His own nature-inspired research attempted to delineate a spiritual coevolution of humanity, Earth, nature and what Steiner designated the nine hierarchies of angels and archangels. Steiner proposed a symbiosis between the spirituality of both nature and humanity and felt that angels are not only instrumental in the development of the Earth but also in our evolving along with it. On a practical level, there are consequences for agricultural practice, and, foreseeing the results of a purely materialistic approach, Steiner founded "bio-dynamic agriculture" in 1925. This is a non-chemical organic method of farming that enlists spiritual agencies (or beings) claimed to be active in nature and cooperates with these health-giving forces to improve food and, consequently, the health and spiritual potential of consumers.

Steiner's methodological approach to nature as a spiritual manifestation seeks cooperation in exchange for exploitation. Its goal is a spiritually based ecology founded on natural interdependencies and the spiritual interworking of creative beings.

N.C. Thomas

Further Reading
Bockemühl, Jochen. *In Partnership with Nature.* Wyoming, RI: Bio-Dynamic Literature, 1981.
Hauschka, Rudolf. At the Dawn of a New Age, Memoirs of a Scientist. North Vancouver: Steiner Book Centre, 1985.
Holdrege, Craig. *A Question of Genes, Understanding Life in Context.* Edinburgh: Floris Books, 1996.
Steiner, Rudolf. *Autobiography, Chapters in the Course of my Life: 1861–1907.* Hudson, NY: Anthroposophic Press, 1999.
Steiner, Rudolf. *Knowledge of the Higher Worlds, How is it Achieved?* London: Rudolf Steiner Press, 1969.
Steiner, Rudolf. *The Philosophy of Freedom.* London: Rudolf Steiner Press, 1964 (1895).
See also: New Age; Theosophy; Western Esotericism.

Stevens, Wallace (1879–1955)

Nature, for the great American poet Wallace Stevens, is variously that which Is, that which is constructed by imagination, at times consoling, at times impersonal and remote, sunny south or frozen north, a "firecat" in one of his first lyrics, "Earthy Anecdote," and a bird's "scrawny cry" in one of his last poems, "Not Ideas about the Thing but the Thing Itself." Stevens' entire literary production might be thought of as a poet's circling of the object of attention, noting the changes that occur as one moves each degree of the circle, changes colored also by the passage of time and the shifting qualities of consciousness.

In these kaleidoscopic exercises, Stevens is at his most intense when considering the extremes, nature as given and nature as construct. One of Stevens' most celebrated poems, "The Idea of Order at Key West," is at base a singing contest between a woman and the ocean. In the end, the woman's song proves not simply superior to the monotonous song of the sea, but winds up consuming nature altogether:

And when she sang, the sea,
Whatever self it had, became the self
That was her song, for she was the maker. Then we,
As we beheld her striding there alone,
Knew that there never was a world for her
Except the one she sang, and singing, made (Stevens 1997: 106).

Here, and in many other poems, including the often-anthologized "Anecdote of the Jar," Stevens echoes Oscar

Wilde's cynical Vivian in "The Decay of Lying" who wittily observes that the more he knows of art, the less he cares for nature. Nature is always sending ants to picnics whereas art can selectively remove such nuisances. If anything, Stevens is even more outrageous than Wilde, suggesting that nature is not simply a nuisance but a vanished memory, that which is utterly consumed by imagination and then forgotten.

Equally intense is the Stevens who attempts to possess nature without interference by the imagination and its attendant illusions. As the poet moves to this "green apogee" (1997: 323) of the circle, he supposes it possible to capture the elusive prize, the world seen rather than the world *as* seen. With the icy mind of the snow man who sees "nothing that is not there" as well as the "the nothing that is" (1997: 8), the poet seeks to "trace the gold sun about the whitened sky / Without evasion by a single metaphor" (1997: 322).

The poet's victory, however, is soon seen as an achievement in rhetoric rather than reality: "... the absence of imagination," he discovers, "had itself to be imagined" (1997: 428). And so the poet begins his movement down from the apogee, through each measured degree, in the "ambiguous undulations" (1997: 56) of intricate and endless circling. The poet's function is to articulate these oscillations and, if prodigiously gifted, "help people to live their lives" (1997: 661).

In the end, the poet becomes something of a secular priest who constructs a new religious reality watched over not by the old angels who, it turned out, came to nothing, but new, necessary angels of "reality," completely understood as fictional creations, and in whose sight we "see the Earth again" (1997: 423) as it is, changing, imperfect, tragic and lovely, the site and source of all pleasures and all pains, and all of paradise that any of us will ever know.

Michael Sexson

Further Reading
Bloom, Harold. *Wallace Stevens: The Poems of Our Climate*. Ithaca: Cornell University Press, 1976.
Miller, J. Hillis. *Poets of Reality: Six Twentieth-Century Writers*. Cambridge: Harvard University Press, 1965.
Stevens, Wallace. *Stevens: Collected Poetry and Prose*. New York: The Library of America, 1997.
Vendler, Helen. *On Extended Wings: Wallace Stevens' Longer Poems*. Cambridge: Harvard University Press, 1969.
Voros, Gyorgi. *Notations of the Wild: Ecology in the Poems of Wallace Stevens*. Iowa City: University of Iowa Press, 1997.

See also: Cowboy Spirituality; Memoir and Nature Writing; Nature Religion in the United States; Wilderness Religion.

Stewardship

The term "stewardship" derives from "steward," one who looks after property belonging to another, such as a household or estate. It has been increasingly used in Judaism, Christianity, and Islam as a basis for a religious environmental ethic. (It is, however, generally considered to be alien to Eastern and indigenous traditions.) In this usage, human beings (individually or collectively) are the "stewards," God is the "owner," and the "property" is the created world (or that part of it which humans can affect). Humans are thus responsible for rightly using and conserving natural resources as gifts from God, or for caring for creation on behalf of its Creator.

How typical such a view has been in past Western religious thought has been a matter of some dispute. The idea that humans are stewards of the Earth is not stated explicitly in the Bible, but can be supported by the injunctions to "have dominion" (Gen. 1:26) and to "serve and keep" the Garden of Eden (Gen. 2:15), and in the example of Noah (Gen. 6–9). Scriptural warrants are also found in the recurring themes of God's "ownership" of creation (e.g., Ps. 24:1) and Providential care for it (e.g., Ps. 104), as well as human accountability in the covenantal relationship binding God, the Hebrew people, and the land (e.g., Lev. 25:1–7). Similar grounding can be found in Sura 2:30 of the Qur'an, where Allah says to the angels, "I am placing on the Earth one that shall rule as my deputy."

The explicit use of the concept finds historical precedent in the Protestant reformer John Calvin's interpretation of Genesis 2:15: "... Let everyone regard himself as the steward of God in all things which he possesses. Then he will neither conduct himself dissolutely, nor corrupt by abuse those things which God requires to be preserved" (Calvin in DeWitt 1998: 32). According to the English Chief Justice Matthew Hale,

> In relation therefore to this inferior world of Brutes and Vegetables, the End of Man's Creation was, that he should be the VICE-ROY of the great God of Heaven and Earth in this inferior world; his Steward, Villicus, Bayliff, or Farmer of this goodly Farm of the lower World whose charge is "to preserve the face of the Earth in beauty, usefulness, and fruitfulness" (Hale in Glacken 1967: 481).

In recent usage, stewardship terminology has served a hortatory function, urging believers to environmental concern and engagement, and an apologetic function, countering claims that the biblical idea of human dominion over nature sanctions environmental rapacity. It has also had a polemical function, in controversy with those who hold more ecocentric views of the human–nature relationship as well as with those who continue to assert a more aggressively anthropocentric understanding of human "dominion."

Ecocentric critics argue that stewardship implies an "absentee God" and a desacralized creation; it separates human beings from the rest of nature, inflates their importance in creation, and exaggerates their competence to manage or improve the biosphere. Defenders of the concept of stewardship have replied that environmental concern only makes sense on the assumption that humans have a unique kind of power and responsibility. Some appeal to the moral conviction that human beings are of greater value than other species, and affirm the transformation of nature as part of humanity's divine calling. Some share many of the ecocentric critics' concerns, but believe that the concept of stewardship is flexible enough to accommodate them. They affirm the nonhuman creation's independent (though not necessarily equal) value for God, and define stewardship as loving service to the creation, rather than as simply the management of resources for long-term human benefit. They understand stewardship primarily as the protection of the Earth rather than as its improvement, and as deepening humans' involvement with nature rather than detaching them from it.

Others, while using the language of stewardship, believe that the views of stewardship presented by religious environmentalists are inimical to human interests, a threat to economic freedom and individual property rights, and overly pessimistic about technological and market-based solutions to environmental concerns. It is possible, however, to minimize the need for moral or legal constraints on the human use of nature to such an extent that "stewardship" becomes a mere euphemism for exploitive domination in pursuit of short-term economic gain.

Stewardship is likely to remain a persistent but contested concept within theological environmental ethics. The simplicity and familiarity of stewardship make it both understandable and appealing to many religious people outside the environmental movement. At the same time, it is both adaptable and elusive, subject to contrasting interpretations. Critics sometimes concede that it is at least an improvement over irresponsible exploitation and that it may have its uses; proponents may allow that it needs to be complemented by other understandings of the human–nature relationship.

Peter W. Bakken

Further Reading

Alpert, Peter. "Stewardship, Concept of." In *Encyclopedia of Biodiversity*, vol. 5. San Diego, CA: Academic Press, 2001, 481–94.

Attfield, Robin. *The Ethics of Environmental Concern*. Athens, GA: University of Georgia Press, 1991 (2nd edn).

DeWitt, Calvin B. *Caring for Creation: Responsible Stewardship of God's Handiwork*. Grand Rapids: Baker Books, 1998.

Fowler, Robert Booth. "Stewardship." *The Greening of Protestant Thought*. Chapel Hill, NC: University of North Carolina Press, 1995, 76–90.

Glacken, Clarence J. *Traces on the Rhodian Shore: Nature and Culture in Western Thought from Ancient Times to the End of the Eighteenth Century*. Berkeley: University of California Press, 1967.

Wilkinson, Loren, ed., with Peter DeVos, Calvin DeWitt, Eugene Dykema, Vernon Ehlers. *Earthkeeping in the Nineties: Stewardship of Creation*. Grand Rapids, MI: Eerdmans, 1991.

See also: Biblical Foundations for Christian Stewardship; Environmental Ethics; The Qur'an.

Stone Circles

Stone circles are a special manifestation of raised or upright stones (*menhir, peulvan, orthostats*) in contrast to isolated standing stones as well as those aligned along a straight axis. They are associated in particular with the British Isles but may be found elsewhere, such as the two stone circles forming a figure eight on the island of Erlanic off Brittany near Carnac or the sepulchre circles of Sine-Ngayene in southern Senegal. This last is a necropolis, and the idea of the British stone circle is sometimes conjectured to be a derivative of the stone kerb surrounding various megalithic collective tombs. However, the British structure is clearly related to the henge monument: a special type of stone or timber ceremonial circular edifice enclosed by earthen banks with one or more entrances and sometimes a ditch or ritual pits inside or outside the bank. The earth-banked henge is found only within the British Isles. Those containing stone circles are known as circle-henges. Archeologically, "stone circles" proper have no ditches. They evolved as separate from the henge in the late Neolithic times (ca. 3200–2200 B.C.E.), some associated with stone rows or avenues and some appearing in group-clusters (Stanton Drew and Avebury being perhaps the foremost examples). Avebury, for instance, "consists of a huge bank and inner ditch, with four entrances, enclosing a stone circle round the ditch, with inside it two smaller circles and a 'setting' at the north entrance" (Wood 1963: 131). There are 702 extant stone circles in Britain and 261 in Ireland. An identifiable type is known as the recumbent stone circle. These are found in northeast Scotland (Aberdeenshire, etc.) and consist of two tall standing stones flanking a recumbent "altar" stone in the southern arc with the remaining stones progressively diminishing in size.

The purpose of stone circles for their builders is not known. Some are obviously funerary, but most are described as ritualistic in the sense that, while often involving much organization and labor in their construction, they reveal no apparent purpose or logical function. Many are aligned to natural features and were possibly used for solar, lunar and astral observation. In contemporary times, the conjectured calendrical function of the stone circle has given rise to a field of study known as archeoastronomy, which nevertheless retains a dubious status within the branches of the more established sciences. As Hutton points out, none of the late Neolithic and early Bronze Age monuments "displays any synchronization of the Earth with heaven as stunning as that at Newgrange" (1991: 118).

Some of the more renowned circles include the cross circle of Callanish in the Scottish Hebrides, the Ring of Brodgar at Stenness in the Orkneys, the Abor Low henge of approximately fifty recumbent stones in Derbyshire, Keswick Carles of Castlerigg in Cumberland, the Rollright Stones of Oxfordshire and the Nine Maidens of Boskednan in Cornwall. Unique, however, is the complex of Stonehenge, built in several stages from possibly 2600 to 1800 B.C.E. and culminating with the horseshoe arrangement employing the trilithon (two orthostats capped by a horizontal lintel). Following the Druidic renaissance first promoted by antiquarian William Stuckeley (1687–1765) and Edward Williams, a.k.a., Iolo Morgannwg (1747–1826), the Albion Lodge of the Ancient Order of Druids first met at Stonehenge on 24 August 1905 for a mass initiation. Stonehenge has been ever since associated with the contemporary Druid movement – particularly in association with the summer solstice.

The modern-day use of stone circles relates to the discipline of geomancy that Pennick defines as "The detection of various subtle qualities of the land and place, and the modification of those qualities so as to harmonize human activity there with the inherent natural character of the place" (1990: 189). For Hutton, while the circle might be an obvious unit of sacred space mirroring the sun, full moon and bounds of the horizon, "Earth mysteries" adherents tend non-critically to reflect "an intense sense of the romance and beauty of the prehistoric past and an equally profound impulse to identify personally with it" (1991: 118). This usually translates as an intense distaste for the present world and its ecological shortcomings. But whether the stone circle provides or not an access to redeeming ancient gnosis, to a connection with the "golden age of the Goddess" or one with ley-line "Earth energies," its "sacred space" encapsulates what Van Gennep refers to as liminality – here as a tangible place of transition in which the contemporary spiritual seeker might contemplate and/or incorporate the numinous dimension that refreshes humanity's ultimate link with mystery and nature.

Michael York

Further Reading

Bord, Janet and Colin Bord. *Mysterious Britain*. London: Paladin/Granada, 1974/1978.

Hawkes, Jacquetta. *The Shell Guide to British Archaeology*. London: Michael Joseph, 1986.

Hutton, Ronald. *The Pagan Religions of the Ancient British Isles: Their Nature and Legacy* Oxford: Blackwell, 1991.

Pennick, Nigel. *Mazes and Labyrinths*. London, Robert Hale, 1990.

Van Gennep, Arnold. *The Rites of Passage*. London: Routledge & Kegan Paul, 1909 (1960).

Wood, Eric S. *Archaeology in Britain*. London: Collins, 1963 (1979).

See also: Druids and Druidry; Earth Mysteries; Neo-Wessex Archeology; Paganism – Contemporary; Ritual; Stonehenge; Sun Worship.

Stonehenge

Stonehenge is an arrangement of large standing stones within a circular enclosure located on Salisbury Plain in southern England. It is one of the most visited ancient or historical monuments in Europe, and is recognized by UNESCO as part of a World Heritage site. Among the visitors are many with "spiritual" reasons for being there, although there is considerable variation in what this might mean.

While ancient arrangements of stones are far from rare in Western Europe, Stonehenge is unique in being the only megalithic circle with lintel stones above its standing stones. This makes Stonehenge instantly recognizable, even iconographic of ancestral and sacred places, and perhaps contributes to its immense popularity.

Visitors currently approach Stonehenge from a busy road and find it on chalk grassland. An interested visitor would have to walk around neighbouring sheep-pastures to see it against the skyline. The best place to do so is from within an embanked processional avenue leading to and from the enclosing circular bank and ditch around Stonehenge. From within the circles of stones themselves that avenue is a key part of the site's orientation toward midsummer sunrise.

Most visitors to Stonehenge devote almost all their attention to the stones rather than to the many other interesting features of the surrounding landscape (including burial mounds, and linear, circular and monumental earthworks). There are heated debates and tense rivalries about how to interpret Stonehenge. Almost all that is agreed upon is descriptive facts about the origin of the stones (most were brought from near another circle at Avebury, some twenty miles away, while others came from southwest Wales) and the order in which they were arranged and rearranged over a lengthy period over four thousand years ago. For some interpreters Stonehenge is solely an ancient monument of archeological importance, for others it is primarily a sacred temple that should be devoted largely to spiritual activities. But there are many alternative positions between these polarized positions. For insight into the contested debates about Stonehenge's interpretation and usage see Chippendale, et al. (1990), Bender (1998), and Wallis and Lymer (2001). For a fine example of interpretation rooted in the disciplines of sacred geometry, sacred geography and archeo-astronomy see Dames (1992).

John Michell has said that Stonehenge is a model of the cosmos and therefore, just like the cosmos, it can provide evidence for any theory one might hold. Certainly there is common ground in the understanding that Stonehenge has something to do with the summer solstice sunrise. What this meant to those who erected and re-erected the stones may not be certain, but it is a key to many current visions of the place. For many centuries (and perhaps without a break since it was constructed) people have found Stonehenge to be a significant place from which to observe and celebrate that sunrise. Arguments have been offered for observations of other significant sunrises and sunsets, moonrises and moonsets, various planetary and stellar phenomena, and eclipses.

Archeological excavation has revealed further dimensions of the monument, including cremation burials and offerings within mounds and holes within the site. When the visitors' car-park was being improved a series of postholes were uncovered that proved to be evidence of the earliest human change in the landscape, long pre-dating the construction of the stone circle. Three white painted blobs now mark the location of enormous wooden posts erected in what was then a clearing in a forest. Only rarely is attention directed to this earliest ancestral engagement with the natural environment, one that swiftly led to the clearing of the forest and the evolution of extensive grasslands. In short, Stonehenge has been and continues to be a prime location for considering human relationships with the cosmos and the immediate environment.

By way of example, Stonehenge is the focus of considerable interest for Pagans and other nature-celebrants. Gatherings at each of the eight festivals vary in size, now reaching tens of thousands at midsummer. Access to the center of the site has been a matter of conflict, but seems now to be negotiable. In 1973 Wally Hope and companions initiated the first Peoples Free Festival at Stonehenge, seemingly reviving Stonehenge's medieval fairs and carnivalesque games. For weeks surrounding successive summer solstices increasing numbers of people gathered. Many came principally to hear music, some to experience the last flowering of 1960s "flower-power." But Wally's vision of a tribal gathering to reestablish respectful relationships with the Earth and the land affected many. After his somewhat mysterious death, and especially after his ashes were scattered in the center of Stonehenge in 1976, Wally's name has frequently been invoked reverently. Wally became ancestor to many who had never met him in life but had found the festival to be conducive to engagement with liberative, socializing and environmentalist lifeways. Some of Wally's possessions (e.g., a flag) and the box that once contained his ashes have been part of many ceremonies. Statements he issued that encouraged everyone to act respectfully toward the Earth are reprinted and repeated by many within the festival and countercultural movements.

The banning of the midsummer gathering between 1985 and 2000 effectively diffused a large gathering across Britain and generated many smaller seasonal festivals elsewhere. It has also resulted in much wider popular knowledge about solstices and equinoxes. Meanwhile, various direct, action groups concerned with ecological issues (e.g., those protesting new roads and quarries) benefited from experiences gained in campaigns to regain access to Stonehenge for festivals. With a return to a more tolerant approach to the summer gathering, it is clear that what might once have been a hippy gathering is now more diverse and popular. Stonehenge continues to be the location for rites of passage (including child-namings, weddings, and the scattering of ashes) as Druids, other Pagans, and many diverse celebrants continue to engage with a diffuse popular spirituality that variously honors cosmic and environmental connections. Debates about the concerns of the tourism and heritage industry and of religious visitors continue to demonstrate that perceptions of sacrality, and appropriate responses toward it, are problematic.

Graham Harvey

Further Reading

Bender, Barbara. *Stonehenge: Making Space*. Oxford: Berg, 1998.

Chippendale, Christopher, Paul Devereux, Peter Fowler and Tim Sebastion. *Who Owns Stonehenge?* Manchester: Batsford, 1990.

Dames, Michael. *Secrets of Ancient and Sacred Places: The World's Mysterious Heritage*. London: Blandford, 1992.

Wallis, Robert J. and Kenneth Lymer, eds. *A Permeability of Boundaries?* British Archaeological Reports, International Series, 2001, 936.

See also: Druids and Druidry; Earth Mysteries; Neo-Wessex Archeology; Paganism – Contemporary; Ritual; Stone Circles; Sun Worship.

Storytelling and Wonder

In the prosperous land where I live, at this dangerous and delicious moment on the cusp of this new millennium, a mysterious task is underway to invigorate the minds of the populace, and to vitalize the spirits of our children. In a strange and curious initiative, parents and politicians and educators of all forms are raising funds to bring computers into every household in the realm, and into every classroom from kindergarten on up through college. With the new technology, it is hoped, children will learn to read much more efficiently, and will exercise their intelligence in rich new ways. Interacting with the wealth of information available online, children's minds will be able to develop and explore much more vigorously than was possible in earlier eras – and so, we hope, they will be well prepared for the technological wonders of the coming century.

How can any child resist such a glad initiative? Indeed, few *adults* can resist the dazzle of the digital screen, with its instantaneous access to everywhere, its treasure-trove of virtual amusements, and its swift capacity to locate any piece of knowledge we desire. And why *should* we resist? Digital technology is transforming every field of human endeavor, and it promises to broaden the capabilities of the human intellect far beyond its current reach. Small wonder that we wish to open and extend this dazzling dream to all our children!

It is possible, however, that we are making a grave mistake in our rush to wire every classroom, and to bring our children online as soon as possible. Our excitement about the internet should not blind us to the fact that the astonishing linguistic and intellectual capacity of the human brain did not evolve in relation to the computer! Nor, of course, did it evolve in relation to the written word. Rather it evolved in relation to orally told stories. Indeed, we humans were telling each other stories for many, many millennia before we ever began writing our words down – whether on the page or on the screen.

Spoken stories were the living encyclopedias of our oral ancestors, dynamic and lyrical compendiums of practical knowledge. Oral tales told on special occasions carried the secrets of how to orient in the local cosmos. Hidden in the magic adventures of their characters were precise instructions for the hunting of various animals, and for enacting the appropriate rituals of respect and gratitude if a hunt was successful, as well as information regarding which plants were good to eat and which were poisonous, and how to prepare certain herbs to heal cramps, or sleeplessness, or a fever. The stories carried instructions about how to construct a winter shelter, and what to do during a drought, and – more generally – how to live well in this land without destroying the land's wild vitality.

So much earthly savvy was carried in the old tales! And since there was no written medium in which to record and preserve the stories – since there were no written books – the surrounding landscape, itself, functioned as the primary *mnemonic*, or memory trigger, for preserving the oral tales. To this end, diverse animals common to the local Earth figured as prominent characters within the oral stories – whether as teachers or tricksters, as buffoons or as bearers of wisdom. A chance encounter with a particular creature as you went about your daily business (an encounter with a coyote, perhaps, or a magpie) would likely stir the memory of one or another story in which that animal played a decisive role. Moreover, crucial events in the stories were commonly associated with particular *places* in the local terrain where those events were assumed to have happened, and whenever you noticed that place in the course of your wanderings – when you came upon that particular cluster of boulders, or that sharp bend in the river – the encounter would spark the memory of the storied events that had unfolded there.

Thus, while the accumulated knowledge of our oral ancestors was carried in stories, the stories themselves were carried by the surrounding Earth. The local landscape was alive with stories! Traveling through the terrain, one felt teachings and secrets sprouting from every nook and knoll, lurking under the rocks and waiting to swoop down from the trees. The wooden planks of one's old house would laugh and whine, now and then, when the wind leaned hard against them, and whispered wishes would pour from the windswept grasses. To the members of a traditionally oral culture, all things had the power of speech . . .

Indeed, when we consult indigenous, oral peoples from around the world, we commonly discover that for them there is no phenomenon – no stone, no mountain, no human artifact – that is definitively inert or inanimate. Each thing has its own pulse, its own interior animation, its own life! Rivers *feel* the presence of the fish that swim within them. A large boulder, its surface spreading with crinkly red and gray lichens, is able to influence the events around it, and even to influence the thoughts of those persons who lean against it – lending their thoughts a certain gravity, and a kind of stony wisdom. Particular fish, as well, are bearers of wisdom, gifting their insights to those who catch them. Everything is alive – even the stories themselves are animate beings! Among the Cree of Manitoba, for instance, it is said that the stories, when they are not being told, live off in their own villages, where they go about their own lives. Every now and then, however, a story will leave its village and go hunting for a person to inhabit. That person will abruptly be possessed by the story, and soon will find herself telling the tale out into the world, singing it back into active circulation . . .

There is something about this storied way of speaking – this acknowledgement of a world all alive, awake, and aware – that brings us close to our senses, and to the palpable, sensuous world that materially surrounds us. Our animal senses know nothing of the objective, mechanical, quantifiable world to which most of our civilized discourse refers. Wild and gregarious organs, our senses spontaneously experience the world not as a conglomeration of inert objects but as a field of animate presences that actively *call* our attention, that *grab* our focus or *capture* our gaze. Whenever we slip beneath the abstract assumptions of the modern world, we find ourselves drawn into relationship with a diversity of beings as inscrutable and unfathomable as ourselves. Direct, sensory perception is inherently animistic, disclosing a world wherein every phenomenon has its own active agency and power.

When we speak of the earthly things around us as quantifiable objects or passive "natural resources," we contradict our spontaneous sensory experience of the world, and hence our senses begin to wither and grow dim. We find ourselves living more and more in our heads, adrift in a set of abstractions, unable to feel at home in an objectified landscape that seems alien to our own dreams and emotions. But when we begin to tell stories, our imagination begins to flow out through our eyes and our ears to inhabit the breathing Earth once again. Suddenly, the trees along the street are looking at us, and the clouds crouch low over the city as though they are trying to hatch something wondrous. We find ourselves back inside the same world that the squirrels and the spiders inhabit, along with the deer stealthily munching the last plants in our garden, and the wild geese honking overhead as they flap south for the winter. Linear time falls away, and we find ourselves held, once again, in the vast cycles of the cosmos – the round dance of the seasons, the sun climbing out of the ground each morning and slipping down into the Earth every evening, the opening and closing of the lunar eye whose full gaze attracts the tidal waters within and all around us.

For we are born of this animate Earth, and our sensitive flesh is simply our part of the dreaming body of the world. However much we may obscure this ancestral affinity, we cannot erase it, and the persistence of the old stories is the continuance of a way of speaking that blesses the sentience of things, binding our thoughts back into the depths of an imagination much vaster than our own. To live in a storied world is to know that intelligence is not an exclusively human faculty located somewhere inside our skulls, but is rather a power of the animate Earth itself, in which we humans, along with the hawks and the thrumming frogs, all participate. It is to know, further, that each land, each watershed, each community of plants and animals and soils, has its particular *style* of intelligence, its unique mind or imagination evident in the particular patterns that play out there, in the living stories that unfold in that valley, and that are told and retold by the people of that place. Each ecology has its own psyche, and the local people bind their imaginations to the psyche of the place by letting the land dream its tales through them.

How basic and instinctive is the imaginative craft of telling a tale! And yet how little we exercise these skills in the modern era. Of course, we'll read a story to a child before sleep, but we won't take the time to really learn to tell the story ourselves (without reading it), or to improvise a fresh version of an old tale for our neighbors and friends. We have too little time for such frivolities: a world of factual information beckons, a universe of spreadsheets and stock comparisons. If we crave entertainment, we have only to click on the television or the computer, and straightaway we can synapse ourselves to any one of the rapidly multiplying video games and virtual worlds now accessible through the glowing screen. Surely this rich and rapidly shifting realm of technological pleasures is the niftiest magic of all!

Perhaps. Yet for all their dash and dazzle, the inventions of humankind can never match the complexity and nuance of the sensuous Earth, this breathing cosmos that *invented us*. The many-voiced Earth remains the secret source and inspiration for all the fabricated realms that now beckon to us through the screen. Let us indeed celebrate the powers of technology, and introduce our children to the digital delights of our era. But not before we have acquainted them with the gifts of the living land, and enabled its palpable mysteries to ignite their imaginations and their thoughts. Not before we have stepped outside with our children, late at night, to gaze up at those countless lights scattered haphazard through the fathomless dark, and sharing a story about how the stars came to be there. Not before they've glimpsed the tracks of coyote in the mud by the supermarket, or have sat alongside us on the banks of a local stream, dangling a line in the water and pondering an old tale about the salmon of wisdom . . .

Spoken stories, when we listen to them, or when we make them our own and tell them ourselves, wake us up to our immersion in a dreaming universe – to the vast and enigmatic story deliciously unfolding all around us. They induce us to taste the icicles dangling from the roof, and to smell the breeze, and to wonder: what's going to happen next?

David Abram

Further Reading

Abram, David. *The Spell of the Sensuous: Perception and Language in a More-than-Human World.* New York: Vintage, 1997.

Basso, Keith. *Wisdom Sits in Places: Landscape and Language Among the Western Apache.* Albuquerque: University of New Mexico Press, 1996.

Berndt, Ronald M. and Catherine H. Berndt. *The Speaking Land: Myth and Story in Aboriginal Australia.* London: Penguin Books, 1989.

Bringhurst, Robert, ed., tr. *Being in Being: The Collected*

Works of Skaay of the Qquuna Qiighawaay. Lincoln: University of Nebraska Press, 2002.
Bringhurst, Robert. *A Story as Sharp as a Knife: The Classical Haida Mythtellers and Their World*. Lincoln: University of Nebraska Press, 2000.
Bringhurst, Robert, ed., tr. *Nine Visits to the Mythworld: Ghandl of the Qayahl Llaanas*. Lincoln: University of Nebraska Press, 2000.
Chatwin, Bruce. *The Songlines*. London: Penguin Books, 1987.
Kane, Sean. *Wisdom of the Mythtellers*. Peterborough, Ontario: Broadview Press, 1994.
Phillippi, Donald L. *Songs of Gods, Songs of Humans*. San Francisco: North Point Press, 1982.
Prechtel, Martin. *The Disobedience of the Daughter of the Sun: Ecstasy and Time*. Cambridge, MA: Yellow Moon Press, 2001.

See also: Animism; Animism – A Contemporary Perspective; James Bay Cree and Hydro-Quebec; Magic, Animism, and the Shaman's Craft; Wonder toward Nature.

Sufism

Sufism (Arabic: *Tasawwuf*) deals with the inward, esoteric, mystical, and spiritual dimensions of Islamic beliefs and practices. Historically, this aspect of Islam has given rise to diverse traditions of spiritual techniques, individual and collective rituals, metaphysical and Theosophical expositions, hagiographic writings, and mystical love poetry, as well as institutionalized forms of discipline, education, and mentoring – all of which have been collectively called Sufism.

The environmental movement in its present form is often perceived in the Muslim world as essentially Western in its form and origin, and is therefore linked with the bitter memory and continuing legacy of colonialism or with a perceived conspiracy to keep the Muslim world backward in the fields of industry and technology. In order to be effective in Muslim societies and communities, an indigenous Islamic environmentalism will have to be built on the basis of an eco-theology and environmental ethics that are recognizably Islamic. The rich traditions of Sufism offer invaluable resources that may be actualized for achieving this authenticity. However, Sufism's own legitimacy is often debated and contested by Muslims.

Contemporary Islamic revivalists and Muslim modernists share a tendency with early Orientalists that views Sufism with great suspicion. Revivalists find Sufism otherworldly and therefore incompatible with political activism; modernists find Sufism irrational and therefore unscientific; both agree with early Orientalists who maintained that Sufism was a foreign introduction to Islam. It has often been noted that Sufism arose in the eighth and ninth centuries in part as a reaction against the worldliness and materialism of imperial Islam on the one hand, and against an overemphasis on ritual and legal formalism on the other hand. The followers and sympathizers of Sufism contend that it represents the very soul of Islam; bereft of Sufism's vitalizing energy, Islam would be reduced to a bland set of rational propositions and legal rulings. Without denying that socio-historical circumstances and influences from Greek and neo-Platonic sources played important roles in its development, they insist that Sufism in its essence, inspiration, and goals is derived from the very foundations of Islam (i.e., the Qur'anic revelation and the Sunnah [or practice] of Prophet Muhammad [570–632]) and is therefore intrinsic to Islam.

It can be argued that Sufism in its essential sense – as the spiritual dimension of Islamic beliefs and practices – has always been an integral part of religious life in Muslim societies. The spiritual aspects of Islam were neither absent before the twelfth century, when organized Sufi orders started to play a major role in Muslim societies, nor were they ever confined within such orders. In other words, whatever Muslims believe, experience, or perform as religious beings almost always has a spiritual dimension, even though this dimension is not always labeled or institutionalized in a distinctly identifiable "Sufi" form. It is the manifestation of this spiritual dimension of Islam in the beliefs and practices of Sufism as a more or less specialized discipline that represents, in some ways, a contested area. This is hardly surprising, for Sufism is not a simple and monolithic entity but a collection of rich and diverse traditions with numerous currents that sometimes compete with each other.

Distrust for Sufism among some Muslim jurists and theologians was originally provoked by certain varieties of Sufism that they saw as deviations from Islamic norms. In most cases, however, Sufis themselves have been the first to oppose such tendencies, thereby generating a tradition of self-criticism and internal reform within Sufism. For their part, Sufis have criticized what they viewed as the narrow perspectives of theologians and jurists in general, who, according to the Sufis, were unable to gain a personal apprehension of ultimate reality because of the limited reach of their exoteric disciplines. At the same time, many prominent theologians and jurists in Islamic history have been practicing Sufis as well. Perhaps the most influential of them was Abu Hamid Muhammad Al-Ghazali (1058–1111) who was among the first to defend the Islamic authenticity of Sufism.

Traditionally, a proper knowledge of Islam's exoteric disciplines has been considered a prerequisite for embarking upon the Sufi path; this requirement, however, was not always followed in practice. According to the self-understanding of Sufism, its esoteric framework does not stand in opposition to Islam's exoteric teachings but represents a stronger and more intensified inner experience of their truth. Such a personal apprehension of the nature of reality (*tahqiq*) is opposed to naive faith in ascribed beliefs (*taqlid*), and provides the vital energy for sincere and creative religiosity. Al-Ghazali notes that what is most distinctive about Sufism cannot be grasped by study, but only through immediate experience and personal transformation: "What a difference there is between knowing the definition of health and satiety, together with their causes and presuppositions, and being healthy and satisfied!"

At least part of the opposition to Sufism in Muslim societies has come from governments. Muslim (and later colonial) rulers often recognized that the strong bond of loyalty and commitment that typically develops between master and disciples in institutionalized Sufism, as well as the strong organization and motivation of Sufi orders, could be threatening to their political power. Institutionalized Sufism suffered some setbacks in recent centuries due to Islam's encounter with Western modernity and consequent social transformations, as well as due to its patronage and control by colonial and post-colonial bureaucracies for political reasons; both have led to numerous adjustments and adaptations, or, according to critics, to Sufism's degeneration in many cases into superstitious and exploitative forms of popular religion. Despite its contested nature, however, Sufism in its myriad forms continues to thrive in the contemporary world among Muslims belonging to diverse socio-cultural backgrounds. Perhaps an important reason for Sufism's continuing influence and attraction lies in its ability to address religious yearnings at a deeper existential level and to affirm and channel certain emotional states, a need that receives minimal attention in more rationalized Islamic disciplines like Sharicah (Islamic law) or Kalam (theology).

Like most forms of human religiosity, Sufism has the potential both to serve and hinder the cause of the environmental movement. Optimistically speaking, Sufism's hold on the lives and imaginations of a large number of Muslims could very possibly make it one of the most powerful allies of the environmental movement. The realization of this potential will require the fostering of an ecological consciousness among those traditionally trained scholars and Sufi mentors who represent the best aspects of the Sufi tradition and who enjoy a widespread following. The development of an authentic "eco-Sufism" will also require an environmentally informed critical evaluation of classical Sufi teachings and practices. A deliberate effort will have to be made in order to identify those themes in Sufism that may contribute positively to Islamic environmentalism as well as those that might obstruct its development.

Sufi asceticism (*zuhd*) is a theme that can have both positive and negative consequences for the natural environment. In its extreme manifestation, asceticism can lead to an excessive otherworldliness and withdrawal from the world – an attitude that could lead to a disregard for the concrete social and ecological reality in favor of personal union with the divine. In its mild and moderate forms, however, asceticism can be an asset for Islamic environmentalism, with its potential for fostering spiritual discipline and combating the temptations of consumerism.

Typically, most Sufi teachers would not recommend actually renouncing the world – which is seen as contrary to the vision of Islam – but would encourage the cultivation of a state of mind in which one is only outwardly involved with material possessions and concerns while focusing one's inner attention solely on God. This kind of asceticism often involves living at a subsistence level, taking from the material world only that which is unavoidable for living a life of spiritual and moral purity. Ideally, Sufis would be actively involved in family and community lives, in accordance with Islam's normative ideals, yet they would avoid acquisition of material possessions or enjoyment of material comforts for their own sake. This happy balance, if self-consciously cultivated at a mass level, can have far-reaching economic and ecological consequences.

The attitude of Sufism toward nature may be explored through several themes, one of which is the doctrine of *Wahdat Al-Wujud*, or Unity of Being. Because of the complex nature of this doctrine, brief descriptions are inherently imprecise and potentially misleading. Nevertheless, Sufi ontology based on Unity of Being has important implications for an Islamic eco-theology, as it cultivates the sanctity and intrinsic worth of nature, irrespective of its utilitarian or instrumental value. A Sufi perspective informed by Unity of Being would approach nature with the knowledge that all things and phenomena are interrelated at the deepest ontological level, for they are nothing but the loci of the self-disclosure and self-revelation of the same Ultimate Reality. In Sufism, nature is often seen as being imbued with immense spiritual significance. According to the Persian poet Sacdi (d. 1292): "I love the whole cosmos, for the cosmos is from God." This approach can inculcate an extraordinary love and fascination, as well as awe and reverence, for nature. Since everything in nature is a theophany, service to God's creatures is service to God and crimes against them are sins against God. At the same time, however, certain other – and perhaps less sophisticated – interpretations of the Unity of Being have led to the conclusion that the material world is a mere illusion with which enlightened human beings need not concern themselves. An ecologically conscious Sufism would have to guard itself against such tendencies.

The ecologically beneficial attitudes present in much of Sufism are yet to be translated into heightened environmental consciousness and activism. Even when recognized as environmentally relevant, such attitudes are likely to remain abstract ideals so long as they are neither supported by contemporary culture nor actualized in social institutions, both of which tend to inculcate environmentally destructive behaviors. Hostility against Sufism and the penetration of Muslim societies with

Western capitalism further restrict the effectiveness of such ideals in shaping concrete reality. The classical age of Sufism did not encounter the environmental crisis as it is being experienced now; at best, Sufism's approach to nature can be effective at an individual level, but the power of the collective order to shape individual consciousness and behavior has tremendously increased in the meantime, so much so that it even influences the hopes, fears, desires, and dreams of individuals living under its sway. Consequently, Sufism cannot contribute toward an Islamic environmentalism without making certain adjustments in its theoretical and practical focus, so that it becomes able to direct the spiritual and moral energy generated at an individual level into socially transformative channels.

Achieving a living experience of divine presence is both the goal of Sufism and a prelude to its higher aspiration, which is to find spiritual intimacy (*qurb*) with the divine beloved. The Islamic tradition identifies two ways of achieving this spiritual intimacy, which are by no means mutually exclusive. The first (*taqarrub bil-fara'id*, achieving intimacy through obligations) has a strong social dimension, for it emphasizes the fulfillment of one's duties toward God (*huquq* Allah) and God's human and nonhuman creatures (*huquq al-cibad*). The second (*taqarrub bil-nawafil*, achieving intimacy through supererogatory acts) has a strong individualistic element, for it emphasizes contemplation and private rituals of meditation, devotion, and worship. In general, Sufi thought and practice has shown a marked predilection for the latter way, sometimes at the cost of the former. In order for Sufism to become relevant to the environmental movement, and to movements for social justice in general, a shift of emphasis is needed in the direction *taqarrub bil-fara'id*.

This implies that Sufis, as real or would-be friends and lovers of God, will have to pay greater attention to alleviating the suffering of the creatures of their divine beloved. In other words, Sufism will have to focus its attention on the attainment of spiritual intimacy with God primarily through service to God's creatures – who constitute "God's family" according to a famous *hadith* – without devaluing individual worship. According to the Qur'an, the experience of divine presence can be sought in the world of nature as well as within the human spirit; a shift of emphasis from the latter to the former may also help raise an ecological consciousness among followers of the Sufi path.

While Sufism has been criticized for its tendency to produce passivity, fatalism, and political quietism, its history simultaneously displays a remarkable engagement with social and political reality. For instance, virtually all nineteenth-century anti-colonial movements in the Muslim world revolved around Sufi orders and were led by Sufi masters. While Sufism is certainly not without its problematic aspects, it does contain significant resources that can be actualized for organized activism and movements for social change – a potential that needs to find worthwhile, authentic, and indigenous causes, an eco-Sufism being one very important possibility.

Ahmed Afzaal

Further Reading
Chittick, William C. *Sufism: A Short Introduction*. Oxford, U.K.: Oneworld Publications, 2000.
Ernst, Carl W. *The Shambhala Guide to Sufism*. Boston & London: Shambhala, 1997.
Ghazali, Abu Hamid. *Deliverance from Error: An Annotated Translation of Al-Munqidh Min Al Dalal and Other Relevant Works of Al-Ghazali*. Richard M. McCarthy, tr. Louisville, KY: Fons Vitae, 2000.
Nasr, Seyyed Hossein. *The Need for a Sacred Science*. Albany, NY: State University of New York Press, 1993.
Nasr, Seyyed Hossein. *Sufi Essays*. Albany, NY: State University of New York Press, 1991.
Schimmel, Annemarie. *Mystical Dimension of Islam*. Chapel Hill: The University of North Carolina Press, 1975.

See *also*: Islam; The Qur'an; Rumi, Jalaluddin.

Sun Worship

Worship of the sun as god, goddess or spirit has been a regular feature of indigenous and pagan religions from ancient to contemporary times. Solar deities appear among the peoples of Siberia, Africa and North America. Solar worship is also strongly associated with the ancient Egyptians, Japanese Shinto and Vedic Indians. The sun is still worshipped by Hindus today – either as Surya or under the later identity of Vishnu in the *Puranas*, especially his manifestation as Satya Narayan. In the pre-Christian and pre-Islamic Levant, we also find sun-gods as regular features of various worships. The Romans imported the cult of the Nubian sun-god Mandulis. Another import was Sol Invictus ("the invincible sun"), a Near Eastern sun-god brought to Rome during the Punic wars. In late imperial times, under Elagabalus, he was identified with Mithras and later became important for Julian. The Christian festival of Christmas represents a transformation of the original solstitial festival of Mithras/Sol Invictus. For the earliest Roman, however, the sun was honored under the names of Vediovis and Sol Indiges (the indigenous sun of the Quirinal Hill).

As an Indo-European people, the Romans reflect the persistent sun worship found also among their linguistic cousins, namely, the Greeks, Hittites, Armenians, Slavs, Balts, Norse and Celts. As a male figure, the sun is usually considered a god of judgment. But the sun could equally be recognized as a goddess and progenitrix. In his *Masks of God*, mythologist Joseph Campbell argues that the rise of the solar metaphor in worship reflects the development of consciousness as an emergence from the uroboric and lunar matriarchal matrix of Neolithic times (see further, Neumann 1954). A similar argument is put forward by Julian Jaynes (1977).

If the position of Amaterasu-O-Mi-Kami among Japanese Shinto represents the most developed solar cult in the world today, for the Mahayana Buddhists the name of the central *dhyanibuddha*, Vairocana, is also suggestive and signifies "coming from the sun." Among contemporary Western nature religionists, the sun is likewise emerging as an increasingly important focus. But this development faces the onus of associations and abuses in the name of solar worship committed under the Third Reich. Based on the philological studies of Max Müller and Ernest Renan, the German *Volkstumbewegung* developed a practice of sun worship that included nude sun-bathing and celebration of the solstices. It had been prompted by a popular sense of estrangement from nature in the face of early nineteenth-century urban industrialization and machine-based civilization. The *Völkische* movement turned toward pre-Christian beliefs in which ancient sun worship was considered more consistent with scientific modernism than were the prevailing Christian and Jewish theologies. The contemporary Western Pagan solar focus and solstitial/equinoctial celebrations are based on similar reactions, but, unlike German "folk" paganism, the more liberal and/or left-wing spiritual bias of nature-centered religiosity rejects any notions of ethnic purity or eugenics. But whereas Wicca and Craft manifestations honor the Neolithic totality of light and darkness, Druidic and other reconstructed forms of Paganism, despite their use of stone circles, are decidedly post-Neolithic in their preference for solar orientation and metaphor. This last, similar to what occurs in Shinto worship, often involves ritually witnessing the rising sun. In the milieu of Pagan affinities and contemporary youth culture, all-night dance parties typically culminate at daybreak with ravers greeting the emerging solar orb. This suggests the possibility of convergence between traditional indigenous practice and spontaneous sun-worship developments in the Western world.

Michael York

Further Reading

Campbell, Joseph. *The Masks of God*, 4 vols. New York: Viking Penguin, 1959–1968.

Hutton, Ronald. *The Pagan Religions of the Ancient British Isles: Their Nature and Legacy*. Oxford, Blackwell, 1991.

Jaynes, Julian. *The Origins of Consciousness in the Breakdown of the Bi-Cameral Mind*. Boston: Houghton Mifflin, 1977.

Neumann, Erich. *The Origins and History of Consciousness*. R.F.C. Hull, tr. New York: Bollingen, 1954.

Noll, Richard. *The Aryan Christ: The Secret Life of Carl Jung*. New York: Random House, 1997.

Sutherland, Stewart, Leslie Houlden, Peter Clarke and Friedhelm Hardy, eds. *The World's Religions*. London: Routledge, 1988.

Wedeck, Harry E. and Wade Baskin. *Dictionary of Pagan Religions: The Cults, Rites and Rituals Associated with Polytheistic Religions, from the Stone Age to the Present*. Secaucus, NJ: Citadel, 1973.

See also: Hinduism; Jung, Carl Gustav; Müller, Friedrich Max; Odinism; Proto-Indo-Europeans; Roman Natural Religion; Stone Circles; Stonehenge.

P | Surfing

To the casual observer surfing is an adventure sport not a religion. Such observers would certainly not expect that surfing might promote a veneration of life and a corresponding environmental activism. For many surfers, however, surfing is a ritual, a practice; a way of life that evokes experiences akin to what some scholars have labeled "oceanic" or mystical feelings of oneness with the cosmos. The perceptual alterations that come with surfing, many of its devotees confess, leads them to recognize their obligations toward the Earth's living systems, especially "mother ocean."

Certainly this is not the experience and ethics of all surfers, and popular culture often accurately portrays surfing not as a religious quest producing environmental sensitivity, but as a hedonistic sport sometimes so charged with ego that territorialism leads to brutal fights over the best waves. Meanwhile most religious studies scholars have largely ignored the practice. The popular image and scholarly disinterest has produced a widespread lack of understanding of surfing's history, spirituality, and transformative power. Here two surfers, one religion scholar (Bron Taylor) and a founder of two nonprofit surfing organizations (Glenn Hening), go tandem in an effort to explain what surfing has to do with religion and nature.

Editor's note: This co-authored entry is unusual because Glenn Hening is both a contributing expert as well as an important figure in the contemporary evolution of modern surfing and thus a subject of the analysis. It proved best to draw on his first-person writing in the first two sections, to co-author the third section, and for Bron Taylor to lead-write and quote Hening during the last three sections. The role of the writers in each segment is signaled in the subheadings themselves, and it should be understood that Taylor worked up this introduction and the entry's framework.

The Endless Energy of Surf "Stoke" [Hening]

When I first wanted to be a surfer in the early 1960s, Mom and Dad said, "No way – you'll just end up a beach bum." And at the time, their fears were well founded, given the public image of surfing driven by the Beach Boys and the popular American television program *Gidget*. Now, four decades later, we've come a long way from the motion picture *Beach Blanket Bingo* to a discussion of surfing in this *Encyclopedia of Religion and Nature*. Or have we? Wild rites of passage, zealots wandering in the emptiness of nature, sacred objects and icons, vestments for holy rites, cloistered believers versus the great unwashed – sounds like surfing to me! And why? Because from beginners experiencing the effortless motion of their first ride to those who've ridden thousands of waves around the world, the fundamental experience of surfing is inner joy, leading to a transformation and, for many, a transcendent or religious dimension. (In surf cultures worldwide, "stoked" is the verb most often used to capture the joyful and sometimes ecstatic experience of surfing.)

Of course, it is always a high-wire act when talking about what is "religious" in our lives outside of our church, synagogue, temple or other formal places of worship. One misstep and next thing you know even brushing your teeth could qualify as a religious experience. However, with surfing, we can make some statements that are wholly unique, and from them these threads of truth that are unbreakable no matter where waves break or who is riding them.

The first locus and center point for surfing is, of course, surf. Each wave is born in the marriage of wind and water, but exactly how that birthing occurs is still not fully understood. Every wave is unique, and no two can ever be exactly the same. And wave events, or swells, cannot be predicted with complete accuracy.

It must be remembered that waves are all around us all the time: sound, electricity, light, emotions, are all understood in terms of waves. So waves are not a foreign concept in the real world: there are light waves bouncing off this page and stimulating your eyes, for example.

But the waves of a surfer are a unique energy form in that we can ride them. They occur only where ocean and land combine to transform energy into entities that will exist momentarily before they are gone forever. A surfer's waves exist first in wind-shaped infinitesimal patterns that coalesce into groups, then as walls of water that often march across thousands of miles of ocean. When we witness the final moments of a wave's journey, or participate in its death throes by transforming the energy into personal motion through time and space, we are in contact with the initial center of the surfing "religion."

Surf and Ancient Peruvian Culture [Hening]

In the late 1980s I was invited to an ocean festival in Northern Peru dedicated to honoring the traditions of coastal fishermen and their connection to modern surfing. Because they still use small craft made from bundles of reeds to push out through some of the longest rideable waves in the world, I was very interested in the possibility that a new version of surfing could be found that would pre-date the first accounts of surfing from Hawai'i.

Well, not only did I have a chance to ride waves using craft essentially unchanged since 1000 B.C.E., but I also visited archeological sites where incontrovertible evidence of "surf stoke" can be observed. I have since returned to Northern Peru several times to study the Moche and Chimu societies whose temples, cities, and lifestyles provide a fascinating insight into ancient human relationships with the power of the ocean, breaking waves, and possibly even surfriding itself. Based on this research I have concluded that the pre-Columbian coastal cultures of Northern Peru provide the earliest example of how surf can affect a civilized society.

This may be a bold statement to some. Given that humankind has inhabited coastlines around the world for millennia, how can we talk about a "first" in such a context? Quite easily, I think. The Southern Hemisphere is more water than land, and the storms of the "roaring 40s" (the southern ocean from latitude 40 degrees south to latitude 60 degrees south) circle the planet unimpeded by land masses. This zone of energy is the spawning grounds of more waves than any other oceanic area on the planet. Those waves sweep primarily from west to east as well as northward toward the coast of Peru. Along that coast flows the Humboldt Current, a cold water "river" in the ocean that is one of the richest fishing grounds in the world, a source of protein easily accessible to coastal inhabitants using fishing craft made from reeds, and there is evidence of this going back three thousand years before the Spanish arrived. The ancient Peruvians lived in one of the rare places on Earth where food and waves were omnipresent.

I do not find it surprising, therefore, that sea life and sea energy resonate through the belief systems, architecture, jewelry, weavings, and ceramics of ancient Peruvian coastal cultures. Temple walls, ceremonial courtyards, deities in reed boats gliding through the heavens, even the iconography of specific priesthoods and theocracies suggest a fascination and veneration for what must have been, to them, the unlimited sources of food and sheer power of waves.

The ancient Peruvians didn't know about the causes of storms or big waves. They didn't have satellites or weather buoys. All they knew was that the power of waves was beyond anything else in their world – and that a hundred waves, a thousand waves, a million waves, an infinite number of waves – were coming toward them throughout their lives from a source that was unknown.

To the best of my knowledge, it is in Northern Peru that we find the earliest known graphic design that consistently depicts oceanic waves in their two most easily visible forms: long walls of water moving across the open ocean, and curved, liquid forms that arc forward and explode when the ocean's energy meets terra firma. As Thor Heyerdahl, the famous Norwegian adventurer best known for his kon-tiki and ra expeditions, said during an interview I had with him in 1990,

> Here in Northern Peru we find the earliest examples of large societies living in close proximity to consistently big waves. Of course, the Egyptians and Babylonians also developed the reed boats. However, there is no surf on the Nile, and you'll never see groundswells marching from the horizon in the Mediterranean or the Persian Gulf.

Thus the ancient Peruvians may have been the first to formally consecrate a human connection to waves, a fundamental connection that exists to this day. All this suggests, I think, that a primal constant lies at the center of surfing: endless and immense power formed into beautiful patterns constantly moving towards us.

There is a second fundamental reality of surf: the breaking wave itself. The physics and geometry of how waves break present observers with a striking fact: depending on the underwater topography and the character of the incoming swell, the curves of a breaking wave are the same curves of a nautilus shell, the pattern of seeds in a sunflower, the arms of a storm, the spiraling of a galaxy. And not only does the water spiral over in a beautiful curve, but that curve continues to form as the wave moves along the coast, thus providing a continuous view *inside* nature for as long as the wave is alive. And when its energy is finally expelled, there is another wave right behind it providing the same vision.

On my expeditions to Peru, most recently in 2002 as a tour guide for "thinking surfers" interested in new perspectives on the sport, I focused on possible origins of surfing spirituality in ancient Peruvian depictions of the curves of breaking waves in their art and architecture. There is a temple complex 500 miles north of Lima, for example, built on a promontory overlooking a corner of the coastline where incoming waves bend into the beach and tube over perfectly. Along one wall of the temple a frieze depicts the arcs of breaking waves connected one to another. Further to the north a Pre-Incan society was ruled by kings who would ring their crowns and their raiment with waves as if to suggest that they drew their royal power from the waves themselves, the most endless source of energy they knew.

Endless energy in motion culminating in perfect natural curves – the ancient Peruvians seemingly had a unique vision of the natural world, perhaps as rich and even earlier than was had in the better-known case of Hawai'i, where there is greater documentation of a culture's deep connection if not veneration of the surf, where riding waves was a significant part of the daily lives and rituals of a people.

Surfing in Hawai'i [Hening with Taylor]

There are those such as former world surfing champion Felipe Pomar who would like to trace the reed craft rituals of the Peruvians through Easter Island and then throughout Polynesia and all the way to Hawai'i. Given the available evidence this is a tenuous connection at best, although Thor Heyerdahl's investigations in the early 1950s did turn up stone carvings of reed craft on Rapa Nui (Easter Island). Moreover, we know that ancient Polynesian wayfinders were able to sail across great distances. We also have an early account from the missionary William Ellis, first published in 1836, who reported that in 1823 the Tahitians had a god of the surf called *Huaouri*. But moving beyond curiosity and speculation regarding the possibility of a Peruvian diffusion of reed craft into the Pacific, the recorded history of surfing certainly begins with the Hawaiians, and dates to the 1600s.

Hawai'i is unique in that it is exposed to swells from all directions, and there are literally hundreds of places to surf on all the islands. Ellis mentioned that the surfing he saw in Tahiti in 1823 was nowhere near as developed as what he witnessed in Hawai'i. This is supported by the recorded references to surfing and evidence of a strong connection between the Hawaiian islanders and the waves around them in the reports from the earlier expeditions to Hawai'i by Captain Cook and by subsequent accounts from Europeans and Americans arriving in Hawai'i throughout the nineteenth century.

In Hawai'i, however, as James Houston and Ben Finney explain in *Surfing: A History of the Ancient Hawaiian Sport*, there was no god of the surf, as there was in Tahiti. Nor was surfing specifically a religious observance. It was, however, like other aspects of Hawaiian life, integrally involved with the culture's gods, spirits, and rituals. There may not have been a special god for surfing, but making a surfboard was very much a ritualized process, starting with offerings to the soul of the tree to be cut down.

Houston and Finney also discuss a stone temple *heiau*, apparently dedicated to surfing, which is located directly in front of a good surfing break. They also note the existence of a surf chant:

> Arise, arise ye great surfs from Kahiki
> The powerful curling waves
> Arise with pohuehue
> Well up, long ranging surf
> (in Fournlander 1916–1920: vol. 6, 206–7).

It would be tempting to conclude, in the light of such evidence, that Hawai'i provides an example of surfing's religious presence in a culture. But if this is true, then why did the practice plummet and nearly go extinct there? It is commonly believed that missionaries were responsible for the near death of surfing in the 1800s. Houston and Finney, however, argue that the missionaries did not see surfing as the problem, but objected to the betting and sexual freedom that accompanied the pastime. They believe that when the betting and mixing of the sexes was prohibited, the Hawaiians lost interest in surfing, which if true, seems to cast doubt on the idea that surfing was religiously important to the Hawaiians.

Consequently, it appears we are on shaky ground if we would ascribe to the Hawaiians any sort of deeply held religious beliefs when it came to breaking waves or the act of riding them. Indeed, we have less evidence of such beliefs in Hawai'i than we do from Northern Peru.

But what we do have emerging from Hawai'i is the beginning of a continuum that we can stretch to the present day, where surfing comes to dominate the lives of many people in ways that exemplify certain forms of worship and ritual, providing some of them meaningful, liminal experiences. The aloha spirit of giving, personified by the father of modern surfing, Duke Kahanamoku, is one of the touchstones of surfing's soul. The Duke promoted surfing around the world, and modern surfers see him as the embodiment of an ethical spirituality that may be just this side of a religious belief system.

Surfing Spirituality and Experience [Taylor with Hening]

The key to understanding surfing as a religious experience, of course, is to understand the experience itself.

The archetypal experience in modern surfing, made possible only in recent decades with the advent of relatively lightweight surfboards, is riding inside a perfect wave. The first lightweight surfboards were crafted of balsawood in the early 1950s and by the end of the decade, boards built with foam cores and resin shells were invented. But it was not until the mid-1960s that boards under 10 foot long became popular, and only in the late 1960s that they shrunk in such a way as to provide an entirely new experience. Suddenly the best surfers could visit a space on the planet never before experienced by humankind: the spinning interior of a perfect wave, a place where time actually seems to stand still. This experience was first depicted in a 1970 film called *The Innermost Limits of Pure Fun*. In it one sees the vision that previously only a skilled surfer would have: that of flying through a liquid cylinder – an experience surely outside the boundaries of ordinary reality.

Glenn Hening, who has had extensive experience inside the tubes of perfectly shaped waves, described during our "surf writing" collaboration, how riding inside the tube can alter one's experience of time:

> In the tube one has no frame of reference except the cylinder of water spinning above, around, and below you. The only thing in your vision that provides a sense of place is the opening, or mouth of the wave in front of you. What can happen next is truly remarkable: if the wave starts peeling faster than you are surfing, the illusion is created that you are either not moving at all, or are moving backwards. And in relation to your only visual frame of reference, you are. So you can be going at top speed forward, but the sensation can be that you are going backward.

As 70s surfing explorer Kevin Lovett wrote after discovering and surfing one of the most perfect waves in the world in Indonesia, "One of the most amazing aspects of the surfing experience is the view of life looking out from inside a breaking wave. These unique, intense, timeless, moments help shape consciousness and are carried with you forever" (Lovett 1998).

Commenting on such experience, Hening finds a corollary in how worship can be thought of in ways outside many traditional connotations associated with the word. In this quote from *The Urantia Book*, a text purportedly given through a dream to a Chicago Psychiatrist in the 1930s that Hening considers a guide to enlightened Christianity, Hening found an apt description of the peak surfing experience. For Hening the book suggests that we think of worship as

> the act of a part identifying itself with the whole, the assumption of refreshing, creative, fraternal and romantic attitudes by the human spirit. It is self-forgetting, it is superthinking. It is effortless attention, true and ideal soul rest, and yet a form of restful spiritual exertion . . . It is the yardstick which measures the extent of the soul's detachment from the material universe and its simultaneous and secure attachment to the spiritual realities of all creation. Worship is identifying . . . the finite with the infinite, time in the act of striking step with eternity (Urantia Foundation 1955: 1616).

Indeed, "From the unique and extraordinary vision while riding inside a perfect wave," Hening believes, "the mystic kernel of the religious in surfing grows." And he thinks this is the "first source and center of surfing's spiritual power" even for many of those without the requisite skill to directly experience this vision. This certainly seems plausible, for indeed, in surf film, art, and music, this archetypal experience is presented as somewhat of an experiential holy grail.

Many surfers, such as former world champion Shaun Tomson, report that "time is expanded inside the tube," a place where one can experience space/time relativity, where time seems literally to stand still. Hening's description of the physical reality of a tube ride (above) allowed him to find in Albert Einstein's relativity theory a scientific explanation for the experience. Other well-read surfers find that authors such as Fritjof Capra (*The Tao of Physics*) help them understand their heightened sense of perception while inside a breaking wave. It is remarkably common for surfers to reflect on experiences that for them are satori-like, that resemble the spiritual awakening sought in Zen Buddhism, whereby the practitioner feels as though the universe is flowing through her or his body as the self of self dissolves into that universal, eternal energy.

Although no great surfer, I (Taylor) have had a few hints at such experience. One particularly memorable one was while surfing a southern hemisphere groundswell (waves created by storms thousands of miles away) in northern Malibu. Taking off on a steep wave in an unfamiliar area and making the bottom turn, the wave suddenly pitched up, revealing a rocky reef immediately below the intended, liquid pathway. Suddenly "making it" appeared clearly as the one way to survive the ride, but at the same time I realized that the wave breaking immediately behind me was so fast that survival seemed unlikely. Just as this realization came into consciousness, I had an experience as though I was surfing by automatic pilot – time seemed to stand still and I somehow made the break – then in slow motion, perfectly, I emerged safely out the other side to the hoots of nearby friends. It occurred to me then, as it does now, that the experience was kindred to that which John Muir once had on the North Face of Mt. Ritter, where temporarily frozen in fear and stuck, unable to climb up or down, he suddenly felt the universe take over and flow, climbing, through him, enabling his escape to the mountaintop. It occurs to me that without religious studies lenses, few surfers would interpret such experiences in metaphysical ways. But nevertheless, some do.

It is not difficult on many levels to apply religious categories to an analysis of surfing sub-cultures. Surfers do, for example, engage in elaborate and ritualized pilgrimages all over the Earth, as *The Endless Summer* (1964) and countless other surf films depict – as they go "in search of the perfect wave." The places where spiritual epiphanies occur are constructed in the minds of some surfers as sacred places – self-consciously in some cases and implicitly in others. These places are venerated in many of the same ways that other sacred places are today: they are named, written about, photographed, and fought over. Battles over them are sometimes among surfers coveting the experience and at other times between surfers and those engaged in commercial enterprises that threaten them. These latter types of disputes can be framed as battles between agents of desecration and those having a proper humility and spiritual appreciation of them. Thus are surfing spots, and the surfing experience, made sacred by human action. Two examples of this can, perhaps, be found in the organizations that Glenn Hening has played a major role in inventing, which he describes in the next section.

The Surfrider Foundation and Groundswell Society [Hening and Taylor]

Given the experiential power of surfing and the history of religion it should not be surprising that many would try to exploit the practice commercially. Surfing has become a multi-billion dollar business, extending globally in many manifestations, from surf contests and promotions, to apparel, to the media, music and more. A number of surfing organizations have formed, however, to resist these trends and focus attention on the reasons surfing took off in the first place, the value and power of the oceans.

In 1984 Glenn Hening founded the Surfrider Foundation by forming a team of surfers that included Lance Carson, Tom Pratte, Steve Merrill, Chris Blakely, and Dan Young. Their mission was to create a new respect for the wave and beach environments and to protect them from polluters and developers. The organization chose, fittingly enough, a logo designed by David Moeller, a Huntington Beach (California) graphic artist and Surfrider board member, that depicts the vision from inside a perfect wave. Twenty years later, Surfrider has over fifty chapters in the U.S. and affiliates around the world.

In the late 1990s Hening co-founded the Groundswell Society with Jericho Poppler and Matt Meyerson. "With Surfrider, the problem was surfers getting sick from the ocean. But now, given surfing's explosive growth, the problem is surfers getting sick of each other." Formally incorporated in 2001, the Groundswell Society adds two dimensions to Surfrider's original mission. First, a peace-making mission, seeking to reduce the violent territorialism that had come to characterize the sport as it became more popular. Second, frustrated by Surfrider's identity as an increasingly mainstream environmental organization, Hening has shaped the Society's annual publication to serve as a "voice of conscience" that highlights individuals and groups that contribute to a positive future for surfing while forthrightly identifying elements in modern surfing that profit from surfing's energy and growth while failing to nurture and protect the oceans and surfing communities from which they ultimately draw their substance. Surfrider and the Groundswell Society, along with others such as Europe's Surfers Against Sewage and the Surf Education Committee, represent a nonprofit, nascent and fledgling institutionalization of the spirituality and ethics that characterize surfers and surfing at their best.

One of the best examples of this is the Clean Water Classic, an event held annually at Rincon in California beginning in 1997, which raises funds to fight ocean pollution, and tries to promote a more cooperative and non-commercial surfing culture. Rincon is a place where you can ride inside a perfect wave, and usually the place is very crowded and the attitude in the water very aggressive and intense. But the Clean Water Classic combines environmental *and* social ideals into a memorable experience unique in the world of modern surfing.

Surfing into the Future? [Taylor]
There is much in surfing and its sub-cultures that, if anything, works against the kind of spirituality and ethics that we have suggested is sometimes involved. As Hening has insightfully written, there are aspects of surfing that can work against a spirituality that connects people with each other and the wider natural world:

> The fundamental problem with surfing will always be how powerfully it drives the ego. There is nothing inherently social in surfing's purest moments, because riding a wave is 100% personal. There is nothing "team" about it. So cooperation and humility takes a back seat to aggression and arrogance... As with every powerful experience that involves self-inflation amongst individuals in a crowd, surfing can go from the sublime to the ridiculous in an instant... from a generous free natural environment to a monstrous example of human greed and enmity. Surfers are the blessed sons and daughters of Kahuna gliding through Neptune's kingdom, until they start acting like troops of baboons defending territory against outsiders while engaged in internecine conflicts typical of lower order primate communities (Hening in Young 2000: 137).

This critique is found in an article Hening titled "The Stain on the Soul of Surfing," and it reminds me of the Western prophetic tradition, suggesting that surfing may have its first prophet. In it Hening reminds surfers of their unique blessing, that they are privileged to ride "aqua blue energy in warm water along beautiful coastlines, where the power and the visions provided by our mother ocean combine to make surfing an almost religious experience." But he chastises his fellow surfers for forgetting "that waves are living magic" and argues that the internecine violence they too often engage in will "ruin our heaven on Earth." He continues with, essentially, a call to repentance, suggesting that sharing and generosity must become definitive characteristics of surf culture.

> Until these instincts become definitive of our surfing culture, starting with the surf industry and those making a living off the sport, surfing will suffer from a cancerous sore that won't go away. The pro tours, contests, magazines, videos, surf star reunions, big-wave exploits, and guided trips to remote perfection will all mean very little until the leaders of our sport/art publicly make a commitment that says, "Enough! We leave our egos on the beach, and we enter the ocean with humility and a true sense of brotherhood."

In a way, Hening is calling surfers back to their roots, or at least to those of the patron saint of modern surfing, Duke Kahanamoku, who more than any other figure was responsible for the globalization of the sport, and its original aloha spirit. *Longboard Magazine* has commented, "Groundswell Society's idealism could be surfing's new voice of conscience" (Holmes 2002: 73). Its founders and members, along with Surfrider Foundation, are inventing a surfing style that blends surfing's nature spirituality with environmental and social conscience to create a positive legacy for future generations of surfers.

Glenn Hening
Bron Taylor

Further Reading
Carroll, Nick. *The Next Wave*. Sidney: Agnus and Robertson, 1991.
Ellis, William. *Polynesian Researches*. London: Fisher, Son & Jackson, 1836.
Fournlander, Abraham. *Abraham Fournlander's Fournlander Collection of Hawaiian Antiquities and Folklore*. Thomas G. Thrum, ed., tr. Honolulu: Memoirs of the Bernice P. Bishop Museum, vols. 4–6, 1916–1920.
Holmes, Paul. "Future Surf." *Longboard Magazine* (March 2002), 54–73.
Houston, James D. and Ben Finney. *Surfing: A History of the Ancient Hawaiian Sport*. Rohnert Pomegranate Art Books, 1996 (1966).
Kampion, Drew. *Stoked! A History of Surf Culture*. Salt Lake City, UT: Gibbs Smith, 2003.
Leuras, Leonard. *Surfing: The Ultimate Pleasure*. New York: Workman International, 1984.
Lovett, Kevin. "The Story of Lagundi Bay, Nias." *Surfers Journal* 7:1 (Spring 1998).
Noll, Greg and Andrea Gabbard. *Da Bull: Life Over the Edge*. Missoula, Montana: Bangtail, 1989.
Urantia Foundation. *The Urantia Book*. Chicago, Illinois: Urantia Foundation, 1955.
Wardlaw, Lee. *Cowabunga*. New York: Avon, 1991.
Young, Nat. *Surf Rage*. Angourie, Australia: Nymbodia Press, 2000.
Young, Nat. *A History of Surfing*. Sidney, Australia: Palm Beach Press, 1983.
See also: Hawai'i; Mountaineering; Polynesian Traditional Religions; Rock Climbing.

Sustainability and the World Council of Churches

The word "sustainable" has been a normal part of the English language for a long time. It has had obvious applicability to agriculture, forestry, and fishing, and other human activities that use natural resources. It means that the activity is conducted in such a way that the resource is not exhausted and its use can continue indefinitely. However, the word did not become prominent in the literature until 1975. The event that lifted it to centrality in the discussion was its use by the World Council of Churches Assembly in Nairobi.

The preoccupation of the churches had long been with issues of justice. Many of the member churches were located in Third World countries that were struggling to overcome the legacy of colonialism. They needed assistance in economic development, but they found the economic and political structures of the world arranged to benefit the First World powers. The World Council was sensitive to their concerns, and called for a "just and participatory society." When, around 1970, the ecological crisis became a focus of attention in the First World, many in the Third World saw this as another distraction from the really urgent problems of the Third World. The World Council stood aloof from the 1992 United Nations meeting on the environment in Stockholm.

Nevertheless, many in the World Council were convinced that failure to consider the destructive impact of human actions on the natural world was unacceptable. They made their case at Nairobi. Justice and participation are certainly important, but if a society destroys its natural base so that it cannot survive, these virtues by themselves are radically insufficient. A society must live in a way that is sustainable. The Council added "sustainable" to its slogan, which now called for a "just, participatory, and sustainable society."

In the following seven years the Council organized meetings all over the world to discuss the meaning of "sustainability." These discussions heightened consciousness on the part of many participants as to the destructiveness of many current practices. On the whole it was recognized that the requirement of sustainability imposes limits on economic growth and that the First World might already have exceeded those limits. There was often a strong sense that recognition of the requirements of sustainability pointed to the need to redistribute access to natural resources so that the Third World would have a chance to develop economically. There was some recognition that population increase was also a threat to sustainability, but this topic has always been difficult to discuss in the churches.

Despite seven years of emphasis on sustainability, the next World Council Assembly, in Vancouver in 1982, turned its attention to the topic of peace. Fear of war between the First and Second Worlds had long informed the WCC agenda, and it returned to dominance at this session. Third World delegates saw that this directed attention away from their concerns for justice. The debates centered on peace and justice. Relations to the natural world faded from consideration. However, they were kept alive in the new slogan that emerged from this Assembly: "peace, justice, and the integrity of creation." This led to further conferences all over the world and to less anthropocentric reflection about nature, but it removed "sustainability" from the focus of attention in the churches.

Meanwhile, the term had been adopted widely in the international community. This became apparent especially at the United Nations "Earth Summit" at Rio de Janeiro in 1992. Out of that meeting, the idea of "sustainable development" has taken hold as the overall rubric under which policy is to be formulated.

In this context, however, the implications are quite different from those drawn by the World Council of Churches. "Development" means global economic "development," and economic development means economic growth. Instead of suggesting a society should live within limits, the term "sustainable" now calls for evading limits, making economic growth sustainable. This puts the focus on technology as the instrument through which limits can be pushed back again and again. This approach also sets aside the question of redistribution of resources, since the problems of the Third World are to be solved by overall global growth, which takes place best when the great economic actors are given free reign.

In some contexts, the quest for sustainability still functions to discourage excessive use of resources. An interest in the sustainable use of forests and oceans, for example, sometimes leads to the acknowledgment of limits and to attempts to stay within them. Unfortunately, the origin of the current use of the term in an anthropocentric context restricts its usefulness even in these cases.

John B. Cobb, Jr.

Further Reading
Best, Thomas F., ed. *Vancouver to Canberra, 1983–1990: Report of the Central Committee of the World Council of Churches to the Seventh Assembly.* Geneva: WCC Publications, 1990.
Cobb, John B. *Sustainability: Economics, Ecology, and Justice.* Maryknoll, New York: Orbis, 1992.
See also: Abortion; Breeding and Contraception; Cobb, John B., Jr.; Environmental Ethics; Fertility and Abortion; Fertility and Secularization; Population and Consumption – Contemporary Religious Responses; Population, Consumption, and Christian Ethics; United Nations' "Earth Summits"; World Council of Churches and Ecumenical Thought.

Swadhyaya

Swadhyaya is a spiritual and social movement centering upon the teachings of Rev. Pandurang Shastri Athavale, known to his followers as Dada, or Dadaji, meaning elder brother. Teaching over the past five decades from a center in Mumbai (India) called Shrimad Bhagavad Geeta Pathshala, his purpose is the recovery of the insights and values of India's cultural heritage. Because he recognizes that ancient Indian civilization placed a high value upon nature, the activities of Swadhyaya that address ecological issues are of interest to contemporary environmental theory.

To most specialists in Vedic literature, the term Swadhyaya refers to the recitation of Vedic texts to oneself. For the adherents of the movement known by that name it has the more literal connotation of the examination or study of oneself. Based on ancient Indian religious texts, and the Bhagavadgita in particular, Swadhyaya, invites one to recognize the divinity within oneself and within all persons, giving rise to self-respect, esteem for others, and grateful devotion to God. The teaching that God dwells within every person, and that all persons are spiritual brothers and sisters in the family of God, has been spread by means of devotional tours (*Bhaktipheri*), which Athavale initiated in 1957, wherein adherents visit villages to share the teachings of the ancient tradition with the local people. Without hierarchy or paid workers, Swadhyaya has spread to roughly 100,000 villages in India.

While Athavale accepts no funding from any source, his teaching is that labor is devotion (*Shrambhakti*) and his recommendation of offering one's time, talent, and expertise for one day a month as devotion (*Bhakti*) to God has supported a wide variety of experiments in farming, forestry, fishing, water-resource management, sanitation, education and other areas. Endorsing neither fundamentalism nor politics, Athavale teaches that devotion (*Bhakti*) is a social force that can be effective in solving any human problem.

In 1979, Athavale initiated a phase in the restoration of India's classical heritage that addressed the depletion of the forest cover that had supported Indian civilization from ancient times. He pointed out that the ancient sages of India saw trees as the dwelling of the Lord who pervades the universe. The ancients enjoined the people to see God in trees because of the capacity of trees to instill noble qualities of selflessness and magnanimity. Athavale established Tree Temples (*Vruksha Mandir*) to cultivate the perception of trees as the dwelling and image of divinity. At the establishment of the first Tree Temple, he invited local farmers to offer their expertise to plant and care for the new trees as a devotional activity, and to perceive their tools as sacred implements. People from various villages within a region spend 24 hours at a time in the temple not as workers but priests (*Pujaris*) of the temple of trees. Without the use of chemical fertilizers or pesticides, the participants enter the temple with an attitude of worship, and feel the presence of God in their activities of watering, weeding, and caring for the seedlings, and the growing trees. Coming from differing castes and classes of society, they visit, sing hymns, and eat together, breaking down traditional barriers between sectors of society. The tree temple program now extends to thousands of villages across India.

The initiative known as the Farm of God (*Yogeshwar Krushi*) is a village-based agricultural enterprise in which participants cultivate land leased or purchased with the purpose of recognizing the presence of divinity in the Earth as well as in other aspects of nature. Activity on the Farm of God is understood as worship, and the produce of the soil is distributed anonymously to those in need not as charity but as benediction (*Prasad*) from God, obviating the distinction between donor and recipient. An analogous program called Floating Temples (*Matsya Gandha*) has addressed the depressed material and social conditions of many fishing villages. Capital that enterprises such as the Floating Temples generate is understood to be the outcome of active community devotion, and is acknowledged to belong to God alone. It is called Impersonal Wealth (*Apaurusheya Laxmi*), to be employed for the uplift of the whole community as the family of God. Offering one day a month as active devotion, Swadhyaya communities have undertaken projects of ecological restoration that have produced extraordinary results. In the arid regions of the state of Gujarat, the Pure Water (*Nirmal Neer*) program has recharged abandoned wells and impounded run-off water in ponds, achieving a 300 percent increase in farming productivity at a tenth of the cost of government programs.

Swadhyaya is the revival of an ancient way of life, in which an ancient attitude toward nature is embedded. While the accomplishments of Swadhyaya in the area of environmental concern is a living example of the relevance of Indian religious traditions in the care of nature, ecological restoration is but one manifestation of this religious movement that has had significant positive economic and social implications at the village level and beyond.

George A. James

Further Reading

Athavale, Pandurangshastri. *Light That Leads: Lectures Delivered by Rev. Pandurang Shastri Athavale in the United States*. Mumbai: Vallabhdas J. Jhavera for Sat Vichar Darshan, 1998.

Paranjape, Makarand. "Non-Violent Social Transformation: Lessons from Swadhyaya." *The Eye: A Written Word Movement* 5:1 (October–December 1997), 88–96.

Sat Vichar Darshan Trust. *The Systems: The Way and the Work*. Mumbai: Vallabhdas J. Jhavera for Sat Vichar Darshan, 2000.

See also: Athavale, Pandurang Shastri; Bhagavadgita; Hinduism; India; India's Sacred Groves.

Swedenborg, Emanuel (1688–1772)

Next to the botanist Carl Linnaeus (1707–1778), Emanuel Swedenborg is perhaps Sweden's most famous son. He was a multifaceted genius who made a name for himself in the first half of his life as an inventor, scientist, philosopher and mining expert. He served on Sweden's College of Mines from 1724 to 1747. His first major work focused on mineralogy and cosmology. He published the three-volume work entitled *Opera Mineralia* in 1734 in Leipzig and Dresden. The first volume contained his cosmology and the other two volumes were scientific studies of iron and steel, copper and brass. His last major work of this period was an exploration of the human body entitled *Regnum Animale*. Two volumes were published in The Hague in 1744 and the third volume was published in London in 1745. In this work he had hoped to demonstrate the reality of the soul to the very senses.

A religious crisis in mid-life was the defining experience of his life and created his place in history. His reputation and influence rest on the 18 religious works he published during the second half of his life between 1749–1771. His works claim to reveal the inner meaning of the Bible and the true nature of reality – spiritual and natural. In number 68 of his first work *Arcana Coelestia* (1749), he states he was able to do this because he had had direct experience of the spiritual world, "I have seen, I have heard, I have felt" (1998a: 45). He believed that he was only called to write and publish these revelations and he never attempted to organize a religion based upon them. After his death, others, however, did and today there are a variety of Swedenborgian or New Church (from Rev. 21:2) organizations worldwide.

Despite their relative obscurity currently, Swedenborg's religious teachings have had considerable impact on modern Western culture. He was read by philosophers such as Kant and Emerson, painters like Gauguin, Inness and Keith (a friend of John Muir), poets as diverse as Blake, Baudelaire, Whitman and Borges, founders of new religions like Joseph Smith, Eddy, and Moon, and commentators on religion such as Corbin and Suzuki.

His new Christian religion provides an integrated and complementary view of the relationship between spirit and nature. In a work entitled *Interaction between Soul and Body* (1769), Swedenborg states that the universe is both spiritual and natural and that there are two things that produce all the effects in it, life and nature. In the divine design, they were created so that there would be a perfect correspondence between life and nature, from first to last, from inmost to the ultimate. Mutual love is the organizing principle of life. Space and time are the fundamental features of nature. Nature is a theater representative of the spiritual world and it is from this that all things in nature subsist. In the order of creation, only human beings are a microcosm of the universe, being both spiritual and natural, and therefore they are created to serve as the medium of conjunction between heaven and Earth. In order to fulfill this role, human beings are endowed with freedom and rationality. Conjunction with heaven is theirs to choose. The more spiritual and motivated by mutual love they are, the more they treat Earth as the perfect correspondent of spiritual affections. Thus, the more it is infilled with life. The more natural they are and the more they choose to abuse the heavenly principle of mutual love, the more the Earth is treated as an object for domination.

While nature is not in itself sacred in the teachings of Swedenborg, it plays an essential role in his understanding of the divine design, and therefore it must be preserved and cherished, so that the canvas of correspondences is available for all future generations.

The human race is enjoined in Swedenborg's religious writings to participate in the preservation of the created world. In a work entitled *Conjugial Love* (1768), Swedenborg states that two principles emanate from the Lord for the conservation of the universe. In number 386 he writes that "one is the principle of procreating and the other is the principle of protecting what is procreated" (1998b: 465–6). The desire to protect what has been created is implanted in humans and animals, according to Swedenborg, and can even be seen in the vegetable and mineral kingdoms. This is elaborated in number 389, which states "that seeds are protected by shells, like swaddlings . . . and that there is something like this among minerals appears from the matrices and coverings, wherein noble gems and metals are concealed and guarded" (1998b: 468). He continues in number 391 that it is part of the plan of creation "that the things created must be preserved, guarded, protected, and sustained" (1998b: 468).

This idea is also discussed in his work *Divine Providence* (1764) in number 3:3 where it is written that the preservation of all created things "depends upon the conjunction of the Creator with the human race" (1996a: 4). This number makes it clear that human beings are invited by the Lord to help preserve the universe. According to Swedenborg, this is best done by shunning as sins the evils enumerated in the Decalogue.

Swedenborg's concern for the environment is witnessed by his view that human beings, who genuinely seek spiritual life, will treat everything created by the Lord with honor and respect.

Jane Williams-Hogan

Further Reading

Swedenborg, Emanuel. *Heaven and Hell*. West Chester, PA: Swedenborg Foundation, 2000 (1758).

Swedenborg, Emanuel. *Arcana Coelestia*. 12 vols. West Chester, PA: Swedenborg Foundation, 1998a (1749–1756).

Swedenborg, Emanuel. *Conjugal Love*. West Chester, PA: Swedenborg Foundation, 1998b (1768).
Swedenborg, Emanuel. *Divine Providence*. West Chester, PA: Swedenborg Foundation, 1996a (1764).
Swedenborg, Emanuel. *Interaction between Soul and Body*. In *Miscellaneous Theological Works*. West Chester, PA: Swedenborg Foundation, 1996b (1769), 345–85.
Williams-Hogan, Jane. "The Place of Emanuel Swedenborg in Modern Western Esotericism." In Antoine Faivre and Wouter J. Hanegraaff, eds. *Western Esotericism and the Science of Religion*. Leuven: Peeters, 1998, 201–52.
See also: Gurdjieff, Georges Ivanovitch; Linnaeus, Carl; New Age; Ouspensky, Pyotr Demianovich; Russian Mystical Philosophy; Western Esotericism.

Swimme, Brian (1950–)

Brian Swimme, a mathematical cosmologist, is one of the prime articulators of "the new cosmology," a scientifically informed, mythic, religious narrative of the provenance and progression of the universe and the role of the human within it. An educator noted for his dynamic, energetic presentation style, Swimme holds a Ph.D. in gravitational dynamics from the University of Oregon (1978) and serves on the graduate faculty for the California Institute of Integral Studies in San Francisco. Dr. Swimme's ideas have been featured at conferences sponsored by the American Association for the Advancement of Science, the United Nations, The World Bank, UNESCO, and the International Montessori Association, and have been very influential among secular and religious groups in fostering an ecological awareness, especially among Roman Catholic women's religious communities.

Swimme's research centers on the evolutionary dynamics of the universe, the relationship between scientific cosmology and more traditional religious cosmological perspectives, and the role of the human in the unfolding of the cosmos. In 1990, he established the Centre for the Story of the Universe, an international forum for scientists, artists, ecologists, ecofeminists, educators, and religious thinkers interested in pursuing the new cosmology.

In exploring the new cosmology, sometimes referred to as "the New Story," Swimme has brought his expertise in gravitational dynamics to bear on the relationship of scientific cosmology with more traditional religious cosmological understandings. Informed by an ecological awareness and concern, Swimme has helped interpret the work of cultural historian and "geologian" Thomas Berry, as well as collaborate with him, as evinced by their co-written book, *The Universe Story*. This book attempts to tell the story of the universe – from the "primordial flaring forth," the Big Bang, to its present development – as a dramatic narrative, purporting the universe is a primordial source of human inspiration and religious imagination.

Unlike Berry, however, Swimme concentrates on scientific data surrounding the unfolding of the universe. Whereas Berry endeavors, in part, to lead religious traditions into a scientifically informed cosmological perspective, Swimme attempts, through his writings, public lectures, and video presentations, to deepen this process by reaching a broad, educated public.

For Swimme, the universe is not a calculable puzzle, but a wondrous mystery, manifesting the presence of the divine in each moment of its emergence. Swimme depicts the emergence of the universe as a spellbinding drama, replete with suspense, valor, tragedy, and celebration that took place eons before humans ever stood erect to behold an evening sky. As an undergraduate at Santa Clara University, a Catholic university in California, Swimme encountered the work of Jesuit paleontologist and theologian Pierre Teilhard de Chardin (1881–1955), whose theology addresses a universal, evolutionary perspective, and is also foundational for Thomas Berry.

For Swimme, the divine is not extrinsic to the scientific study of the universe. On the contrary, the divine is what both sustains and transforms the universe, the energy that supports as well as shapes all emerging reality. He equates the quantum vacuum of space with the "all-nourishing abyss," (Swimme 1996), a term which echoes other descriptions of the divine, such as Paul Tillich's "ground of our being." Wellsprings of Swimme's insights continue to be a sense of awe and wonder engendered by mystery of the universe, and a sense of horror at the human destruction of the Earth.

In addressing the role of the human, Swimme cites two poles that must be eschewed. On the one hand, there is the status quo idea that all creation is here solely for humans as resource and playground that Swimme claims we need to avoid. On the other hand, there is the view that says that the human is just one species among others, which Swimme terms overcompensation. Accepting such a view would cause the rest of the Earth community to suffer immensely, since other species seem incapable of cleaning up our mess. We must somehow, Swimme argues, retain humility in regard to our particular status while at the same time be responsible concerning our unique power as a species.

For Swimme, the human is the locus where the universe becomes conscious of itself. No other species, he contends, that we know of, can reflect on all that is and its place in the universe. The human role, then, becomes accepting our task as the self-consciousness of the universe, with a responsibility for learning and perpetuating the principles of the universe, as we perceive them.

Moreover, Swimme trenchantly uses the new cosmology to critique the culture of consumerism, the economic and cultural system that suggests, in Thomas Berry's words, that the "universe is a collection of objects rather than a communion of subjects," and is according to

Swimme the world's most pervasive faith system. Swimme argues that such a consumerist worldview, promulgated by global and ubiquitous advertising, seals off conscious contact with the powers at work in the universe and the Earth, leaving us deeply unsatisfied and turning to other stimulants to deal with our sense of alienation.

Some critics, including Gregory Baum, have suggested that the work of Swimme and Berry lacks a place for social-justice concerns and a plan for social action (Baum 1987). In addition, the "universe story" appears as a supreme metanarrative, one decontextualized from specific social, moral, political, economic, and cultural factors. Swimme and Berry in their more recent work appear to be incorporating such concerns, and the creative integrations of social-justice outreach and cosmological themes in the communities they have influenced, especially women religious involved in ecological ministries, suggests a growing nexus between the new cosmology and social-justice advocacy.

Stephen Bede Scharper

Further Reading

Baum, Gregory. "The Great Work: It Needs Social Action." In Stephen Dunn and Anne Lonergan, eds. *Thomas Berry and the New Cosmology*. Mystic, CT: Twenty-Third Publications, 1987.

Berry, Thomas. *The Great Work: Our Way into the Future*. New York: Bell Tower, 2002.

Scharper, Stephen. *Redeeming the Time: A Political Theology of the Environment*. London and New York: Continuum, 1997.

Swimme, Brian. *The Hidden Heart of the Cosmos* (book and video). Maryknoll, NY: Orbis Books, 1999.

Swimme, Brian. *Canticle to the Cosmos* (audio cassette). Louisville, CO: Sounds True, 1996.

Swimme, Brian and Thomas Berry. *The Universe Story*. San Francisco, CA: HarperCollins, 1992.

Swimme, Brian. *The Universe Is a Green Dragon*. Santa Fe, NM: Bear and Company, 1984.

Swimme, Brian and Matthew Fox. *Manifesto for a Global Civilization*. Sante Fe, NM: Bear and Company, 1983.

See also: Berry, Thomas; Boff, Leonardo; California Institute of Integral Studies; Con-spirando Women's Collective (Santiago, Chile); Council of All Beings; Earth Charter; Epic of Evolution; Epic Ritual; Gaia Foundation and Earth Community Network; Genesis Farm; Re-Earthing; Religious Studies and Environmental Concern; Roman Catholic Religious Orders; Teilhard de Chardin, Pierre; United Nations' "Earth Summits".

T

Tantra

Tantra, a current of religious doctrine and practice found mainly within Hinduism and Buddhism, emerged in India in about the sixth century. It evolved greatly over the subsequent one thousand years, changing in form and content as it spread outward into every Asian region into which Buddhism was practiced including China, Japan, Tibet, Nepal, and Indonesia. While later forms of Tantra tend to be abstract soteriologies (understandings regarding salvation) grounded in internal, meditative identification of the self with some form of the absolute, Tantra emerged in India out of the worship cults of local deities often identified with natural phenomena and the forces of nature. In India, these Tantric deities were very often (but not exclusively) female spirits of the land – mountains, forests, rivers, and pools – and were often identified with or depicted as wild animals, birds, trees, and flowers. Furthermore, when Tantra was exported into other parts of Asia, local deities of those countries were often transformed into the guardians of the mandalas of the Tantric high gods, and into semi-divine intermediaries between the worshipper and those gods. In Japan, for example, the *sanrinjin* (literally, "three bodies with discs") theory, which divided the Buddha's appearances in the phenomenal world into three types, allowed for the transformation and appropriation of the indigenous Japanese *kami* deities into so many "propagators of Buddhism." In this way, deified aspects of the Japanese natural landscape became both Buddhist and Tantric, even as they remained Japanese. Parallel to this was the "translation" of certain Indian Tantric deities into their foreign homologues. So, for example, the *dakini*s of Indian Buddhist Tantra – who were at once semi-divine female intermediaries and human "witches," and who were sometimes identified in India with jackals – were qualified as "fox spirits" in Chinese and Japanese Tantric traditions.

Natural vegetation plays a prominent role in Tantra, beginning with the use of the term "seed" (*bija* in Sanskrit) for the most powerful class of mantras, the sound formulas used in Tantric ritual: the practitioner actually generates the divinity with which he will identify himself by "planting" its seed through his mantric utterance. This image is expanded in the circa tenth-century *Kaulajñananiraya*, a foundational Hindu Tantric text, in which Siva, the supreme deity and creator god states that "Just as there is in an individual seed the origins of a tree possessed of flowers, roots, fruit, leaves, and branches, so it is as well with the other beings that are generated within my body" (16:42). The coeval *Netra Tantra* (12:11–12) assigns this role to a class of female deities called the Mothers, who hold the world inside of themselves, in the form of seeds that they will sow again at the beginning of a new world age, in order that creatures might reappear. Vindhyavasini, the "Goddess Who Dwells in the Vindhya Mountains," one of the earliest and most important Hindu Tantric goddesses, is described in terms of her habitat, which is an extension of herself: a vast forest teeming with plant and animal life. Similarly, the energy of the Hindu goddess Kubjika is described in a twelfth-century Tantric text as flowing outward through the transmission of her teachings, whose conduits are represented as living plants: trees, creepers, roots and vines. A number of later Kubjika texts depict her as a tree with orange or red-colored blossoms – either a tamarind (*ciñca*), a *kimsuka*, or a *kadamba*. This identification, of the female principal, with a flower, is extended to the female consort in numerous Tantric sexual rites, in which she is often called "Lotus Maiden," and whose vulva is called "lotus" (*padma*).

It would be a mistake, however, to qualify the Tantric view of nature, or indeed of the feminine, as a static and passive source of life. In the early medieval Indian context, wild nature was, like feminine sexuality, threatening and antinomian, the polar opposite of the security and order of male-dominated human society. Here, nature was not a peaceable kingdom, but rather an alien wilderness, a place of savage energy, at once alluring and terrifying, nurturing and deadly to anyone who would venture into it, and populated by ravening female entities in the form of predatory animals and rapacious or carrion-feeding birds. In this context, the male practitioner of Tantra *par excellence* was termed a "hero" (*vira*), because he alone dared to confront and master wild feminine nature, energy, and sexuality. So it was that on specific nights of the lunar month, male Tantric practitioners would assemble on lonely mountaintops (*pitha*s) or in forest clearings (*ksetra*s) to await the coming of Tantric *yogini*s or *dakini*s, who would descend on them in the form of lionesses, she-jackals, she-wolves, vultures, crows, cobras, etc. The non-initiates who stumbled into these gatherings (*melakas*) faced certain death: they would be torn apart by these Tantric animal-goddesses or their human counterparts. The Tantric hero, however, empowered by his controlling mantras and ritual knowledge, could control these dread feminine entities and, more than this, actually appropriate their multiple energies – the forces of nature – for himself, in order to have a share in their *super*natural powers. This was, in fact, the principal aim of early Tantric practice: to dominate nature by subjugating wild feminine sexuality as a means to gaining supernatural powers. The most important of these was flight, a "natural" capacity for bird-goddesses whose energy was said to come from their consumption of human flesh.

This Tantric goal lay at the foundation of the most important monumental edifices of early Hindu Tantra in India. These were the Yogini temples, of which approximately 15 ruins remain extant today on lonely hilltops or remote forest tracts, mainly in the Vindhya Mountain belt of central India where Hindu Tantra emerged. These temples were circular and roofless constructions: open to the heavens, they served as landing fields and launching pads for the airborne Yoginis. Carved into niches on the inner wall of these temples and facing an image of Siva or Bhairava at the center were images of the Yoginis, whose near-naked, sexually alluring bodies were crowned by the heads of predatory birds, wild animals, or fanged, terrible human "witches." It was these dread man-eaters that the heroic male Tantric practitioner called down and sought to bend to his will by transforming them into his lovers, in imitation of the Siva or Bhairava at the center of their mandalas.

Over the centuries that followed its South Asian origins, Tantra was exported into Nepal, Tibet, China, Japan, and Mongolia; and in the past several decades it has made its entrance into Europe and the United States. In certain of these export settings, and most particularly in the post-industrial societies of Japan and the West, Tantra has been appropriated by a variety of New Age movements that have adapted the original tradition to respond to their own concerns. Such is natural in these contexts, in which the world of nature is no longer threatening, but rather under threat.

David Gordon White

Further Reading

Samuel, Geoffrey. *Civilized Shamans, Buddhism in Tibetan Societies*. Washington, D.C.: Smithsonian Institution Press, 1993.

Slusser, Mary Sheperd. *Nepal Mandala: A Cultural Study of the Kathmandu Valley*, 2 vols. Princeton, NJ: Princeton University Press, 1982.

White, David Gordon. *Kiss of the Yogini: Tantric Sex in its South Asian Contexts*. Chicago: University of Chicago Press, 2003.

White, David Gordon, ed. *Tantra in Practice*. Princeton, NJ: Princeton University Press, 2000.

See also: Hinduism; India; New Age; Sexuality and Ecospirituality; Sexuality and Green Consciousness; Tantrism in the West.

Tantrism in the West

Since at least the second half of the twentieth century, the Asian tradition known as Tantra or Tantrism has had a powerful impact on Western spirituality and on the relationship between religion and nature in the West. A vast and complex body of traditions that spread throughout the Hindu, Buddhist and Jain religions since at least the fifth century, Tantrism has long held a profoundly ambivalent place in the Western imagination. When it was first discovered by European orientalist scholars in the nineteenth century, Tantrism was typically singled out as the very worst example of all the licentiousness and idolatry believed to have corrupted Indian religions in modern times. Yet in our own generation, Tantrism has often been celebrated as a much-needed affirmation of the human body, sexuality and the sacrality of the natural environment itself.

Although it has been defined in a wide variety of different ways, Tantrism might be said to center first and foremost around the concept of Shakti – the divine "power" or "energy" that circulates through all levels of the universe, from the individual human body, to the social body, to the vast body of the cosmos itself. Typically identified with the great Goddess in her most aggressive forms, such as Kali or Durga, Shakti is the divine feminine power that creates, sustains and destroys all things. In practice, Tantrism is essentially a complex body of spiritual techniques that aim to harness and direct this power, both toward this-worldly goals of material enjoyment and toward the ultimate goal of spiritual liberation. In their spiritual practice, Tantrikas seek to awaken this power as it lies concealed in the most seemingly mundane, even profane, natural acts and physical objects – including normally impure substances and forbidden acts, such as meat, wine and sexual intercourse in violation of class laws.

Not surprisingly, the first Christian missionaries and European scholars to come upon Tantrism during the colonial era were quite horrified at this seeming confusion of religion and sensuality. As the Baptist missionary William Ward described it, Tantrism is "a most shocking mode of worship" involving rites "too abominable to enter the ears of man and impossible to be revealed to a Christian public." However, toward the end of the nineteenth century, a few more courageous scholars such as Sir John Woodroffe made a bold attempt to rescue and defend the Tantric tradition. In Woodroffe's view, Tantrism is not only a sophisticated philosophical tradition, but also a profound vision of the physical cosmos that is basically in agreement with the findings of modern Western science. While modern science had only recently discovered that all matter is simply a form of energy, the Tantrikas had long known that the natural universe is simply a manifestation of Shakti, the Goddess as power.

But it was not until the first decades of the twentieth

century that Tantrism began to enter the Western world in a significant way, with the foundation of the first "Tantrik Order in America" in New York City by Dr. Pierre Arnold Bernard in 1906. A contemporary of Sigmund Freud, Bernard saw modern Western society as terribly repressed in its attitudes toward the human body, sexuality and the natural environment. Tantrism, he believed, offered the most effective means to liberate these oppressed powers of sexuality and nature.

Beginning in the 1960s, Tantrism entered in full force into Western popular culture, first with the early Beat movement, and then finding a welcome home among the sexual revolutions of the 1960s and 1970s. In the words of Alan Watts – the ex-Anglican priest turned Zen master and psychedelic guru of the Beat generation – Tantrism is "a marvelous and welcome corrective to certain excesses of Western civilization." In contrast to Western society, with its patriarchal domination of nature and its separation of spirit from matter, Tantrism can bring us an "understanding the creative power of the female" and an appreciation of the inherent goodness of the natural world. Perhaps the first great high priest of "Neo-Tantrism" was the infamous "Sex Guru" known in his early years as Bhagwan Shree Rajneesh and in his later life as "Osho." Redefining Tantra as a kind of "religionless religion" based on the rejection of all fixed institutions and the celebration of sexuality and material nature, Rajneesh offered a new ideal for human existence – the ideal of "Zorba the Buddha," who combines the sensuality of Zorba the Greek with the spiritual insight of the Buddha.

By the 1980s and 1990s, Tantrism had become a basic part of the amorphous movement known as the "New Age," and increasingly identified with a wide variety of religious traditions believed to honor the forces of nature, sexuality and femininity. Thus, as *Tantra: The Magazine* defines it, Tantrism is no longer a tradition confined to certain forms of Hinduism and Buddhism in Asia, but is in fact a universal tradition of nature-, goddess-, and sex-worship followed by peoples of all cultures, from pre-historic shamans to modern neo-pagans:

> Tantra is life in balance ... Tantra is practiced by Native Peoples the world over, through profound respect for All that Is. It is also practiced through the respect of the divine feminine worshipped in her physical form through attending the needs of Mother Earth as our own body (1991: 3).

Now reconceived as an ancient global tradition centering on the reverence of nature and sexuality, Tantrism has been increasingly embraced by many of the various "green" movements and other environmentalist groups that have emerged in the last three decades. As we see in a wide array of movements such as GreenSpirit, Creation Spirituality, and various Wiccan and Pagan groups, Tantrism is welcomed as a unifying vision that brings together spirituality and physical nature. In contrast to the life-denying, other-worldly and male-dominated Abrahamic traditions, Tantrism represents for many a positive expression of human sexuality and spirituality, with the power to unite people to the sacred energies of the Earth, even empowering them for her defense. According to one popular Australian website,

> TANTRA is part of a broad evolutionary process in consciousness, which is moving toward an integration with the Natural World, the physical body and the many sexual expressions of human behavior. All of Nature is then perceived as a sacred manifestation of the Divine, where there is no separation between Spirit and Nature (www.tantra.co.nz).

For many neo-pagans, this discovery of Tantra by the West is really only a rediscovery of the long-forgotten divinity of nature that lies at the core of Western traditions, as well. In the words of the one of the most prominent figures in the early Wiccan revival, Doreen Valiente, it is only fitting that modern Western witches should rediscover Eastern Tantric techniques; this is simply the great spiral dance of Shakti, the Great Goddess Earth herself, coming round full circle. It follows naturally,

> in accordance with the evolving trends of the Aquarian Age, that modern witches should adapt the Tantric sexual magic for use in their own magic circles ... Everything in this world is flowing. Nothing stands still, nor does time go back upon itself; but it proceeds in a spiral ... The spiral has come round again, to its ancient place (Valiente 1988: 151).

In the course of its transmission to the modern West, Tantrism has undergone a profound transformation and reinterpretation. Once a highly esoteric tradition focused on secret ritual and acquisition of power, Tantrism has today become a popular form of spirituality focused on the celebration of nature and the liberation of sensual pleasure. There are various conflicting opinions as to how we ought to judge this transformation. More skeptical critics tend to view it as a tragic misinterpretation of an ancient religious tradition, which has been mistakenly appropriated for modern Western interests and hopelessly confused with Western sexual obsessions. More sympathetic observers, conversely, see this as just one more example of the changing nature of religious traditions in new historical contexts, as a much-needed corrective to the destructive attitudes of modern Western society, and as a powerful affirmation of the inherent sacrality of the natural environment.

Hugh B. Urban

Further Reading

Anand, Margo. *The Art of Sexual Ecstasy: The Path of Sacred Sexuality for Western Lovers.* Los Angeles: Jeremy P. Tarcher, Inc., 1989.

Bernard, Pierre Arnold, ed. *International Journal of the Tantrik Order* 5:1 (1906).

Douglas, Nik. *Spiritual Sex: Secrets of Tantra from the Ice Age to the New Millennium.* New York: Pocket Books, 1997.

Eliade, Mircea. *Yoga: Immortality and Freedom.* Princeton, NJ: Princeton University Press, 1971.

Evola, Julius. *The Yoga of Power: Tantra, Shakti and the Secret Way,* G. Stucco, tr. Rochester: Inner Traditions, 1992.

Feuerstein, Georg. *Tantra: The Path of Ecstasy.* Boston: Shambhala, 1998.

Garrison, Omar. *Tantra: The Yoga of Sex.* New York: Julian Press, 1964.

Lysebeth, Andre van. *Tantra: The Cult of the Feminine.* York Beach, ME: Samuel Weiser, 1995.

Rajneesh, Bhagwan Shree. *Tantra Spirituality and Sex.* Rajneeshpuram: Rajneesh Foundation International, 1983.

Rawson, Philip. *Tantra: The Cult of Ecstasy.* Greenwich, CT: New York Graphics Society, 1973.

Tantra: The Magazine. Torreon, NM, Tara issue, no.1 (1991).

Tantra: The Supreme Understanding. Poona: Rajneesh Foundation, 1975.

Taylor, Kathleen. *Sir John Woodroffe, Tantra and Bengal: "An Indian Soul in a European Body?"* London: Curzon Press, 2001.

Urban, Hugh B. *Tantra: Sex, Secrecy, Politics and Power in the Study of Religion.* Berkeley: University of California Press, 2003.

Valiente, Doreen. *Witchcraft for Tomorrow.* Blaine, WA: Phoenix Publishing, 1988.

Watts, Alan. "Tantra." *Loka: A Journal from Naropa Institute* 1 (1976), 55–7.

White, David Gordon, ed. *Tantra in Practice.* Princeton, NJ: Princeton University Press, 2000.

Woodroffe, Sir John. *Shakti and Shakta.* New York: Dover, 1978.

Zimmer, Heinrich. *Philosophies of India.* New York: Meridian Books, 1956.

See also: Hinduism; India; New Age; Sexuality and Ecospirituality; Sexuality and Green Consciousness; Tantra; Yoga and Ecology.

Taoism – *See* Chinese Traditional Concepts of Nature; Daoism.

Target Earth

Target Earth is an international Christian Environmental organization founded in 1986 by Roy and D'Aun Goble, who were inspired to begin a retreat center after taking a course together at Westmont College, a small Christian College located in Santa Barbara, California. Target Earth started simply as the Hidden Lakes Retreat Center in the Sierra Nevada Mountains of California and it remained the Goble's sole project for many years. In 1992 the Gobles encountered a writer from *Christianity Today* magazine and the result of that meeting and collaboration was Target Earth International, and the beginning of a global outreach program.

Target Earth is a response to the biblical mandate found in Genesis, which states that humans have dominion over the Earth. Target Earth sees this not as encouragement to plunder the Earth, but as a call to be caring stewards of God's creation. It is a partner of the Evangelical Environmental Network and offers a Campus Programs Division, including 45 campus chapters across the United States, which assists students with lobby training, student conferences and alternative spring breaks. It also publishes a Magazine entitled *Target Earth.*

In addition to maintaining the Hidden Lakes Retreat Center, Target Earth offers numerous international educational opportunities. Students can participate in short seven- to fourteen-day missions or eight-week internships in Belize, Honduras, Mexico, Russia, and South Africa. Target Earth offers a Global Stewardship Study Program at its Environmental Research and Education Center at Jaguar Creek in Belize. It also works with conservation groups to select areas of the rainforest for preservation. One such property is the 8000-acre area of Jaguar Creek in Belize. Target Earth also maintains the Lasting Impressions Wilderness in Zimbabwe, Africa; and in North America, it has focused on preserving land in the Soda Mountain Wilderness in Oregon.

The Target Earth website expresses the mission of "Serving the Earth, Serving the Poor." In this sense, Target Earth is like many other Christian environmental organizations with a presence on the internet, which indicate that they are involved in human rights advocacy, spreading of the gospel, and preservation the environment. Such a multiple mission avoids elevating the Earth to a position of importance above humanity. The Earth is not preserved for the Earth's sake alone, but because it is God's creation.

While sharing these views and attributes, Target Earth International is noteworthy in part because, unlike some other Christian environmental organizations, it is attractive to students and others who may not otherwise join a Christian group. Target Earth maintains a liberal and educational approach, offering a resources page outlining environmental justice, recycling, simple lifestyles and biblical references supporting each activity. This combination of practical projects and faith-based environmentalism makes Target Earth appealing to a wide variety of people.

Andrea A. Kresge

See also: Evangelical Environmental Network; Restoring Eden; Sierra Treks.

Tattoos

Tattooing (from the Tahitian word *tatau*) is an art form of body modification that has been practiced throughout history in many regions of the world. Modifying the body, according to some anthropologists, is one of the simplest ways that human beings become social beings. The human body is the place where the natural world, social worlds, and personal experiences join. The practice of tattooing and body modification, which often has strict, gender-dependent rules, thus situates the human body within a particular visible context for community members.

Tattoos have often been used to construct identity: by marking criminals, denoting social status and rank, symbolizing fighting ability, showing community membership, and as symbols of successful initiation. Initiation tattoos symbolize the wearer's willingness and ability to accept social responsibility and established socio-cultural values. Other, more voluntary, tattooing practices mark the body for aesthetic or erotic purposes, in rebellion against societal norms, or as medical therapy. Tattoos have also been used as symbols of religious affiliation and community membership. Many Coptic, Syrian, and Russian Christians returning from the Holy Land often acquired "cross" tattoos on their hands, and even though proscribed in the Qur'an, many Turkish Muslims returning from the *hajj* to Mecca have received tattoos to commemorate their completed pilgrimage.

In societies where spiritual forces are understood to be present in the natural world, objects, and living creatures, the human body becomes an avenue for relations between the spiritual and physical realms; the blood of the tattooing process symbolizes manipulation of the life-force. For example, tattooing was performed to bring prosperity and fertility to the wearer among many traditional African communities. Thus the physical body, having more than functional meaning, can become a unique magical talisman that integrates the spiritual, physical, and social aspects of life. For example, the North American Cree not only had tattoos for luck, beauty, and protection of health, but men also received tattoos, derived from dream-images, to help them communicate with nature spirits. Also, the complex designs found among Polynesian tattoos represented aspects of their lives within the natural world (e.g., centipedes and water symbols), tribal status, strength of character, and esoteric religious teachings.

In Middle Kingdom Egypt the tattoo functioned as a bridge between the physical body and the afterworld. In order to activate their procreative powers after death and assure their immortal salvation and resurrection into the realm of Osiris, some women were incised with special lines and dots related to the Goddess Hathor. Also, Native American Eskimo women traditionally tattooed their faces and breasts in order to assure a happy afterlife.

Tattoos as marks of protection from evil forces and chaos were believed to make the wearer invisible or unrecognizable to malignant spirits or forces (e.g., among the African Nuba and Butwa). Nineteenth-century Alaskans utilized tattoos as protection from the spirits of animals and people that they had killed. Additionally, Thai Buddhist monks inscribe Buddhist sayings and symbols onto the bodies of male lay practitioners for protection purposes and to create embodied mantras.

The Edo period in Japan saw a rise in the practice of tattooing (called *horimono* – dug things) among urban lower-class social groups such as firemen and theater workers. Japanese tattooing utilizes figures from Buddhism, mythology, and literature (such as the *Suikoden*, a translation of the fourteenth-century Chinese classic about tattooed bandits that fought against injustice). Additionally, many of the most important Japanese tattoo motifs are based on folk beliefs about the powers of flora and fauna of the Earth and sea. These motifs are important because of the belief that tattoos are able to transfer to the wearer the power inherent in the meaning of the symbol. Personality traits such as loyalty and fierceness are embodied in the symbol of the lion-dog, strength and restraint (the dragon); religious elements such as devotion (Buddha, Kannon, and Fudo the Guardian), a Buddhist-inspired understanding of impermanence (cherry blossoms); as well as material aims such as longevity (the tortoise) are common themes among Japanese tattoos.

Almost all societies have seen traditional forms of body modification disappear. Only the West, especially in America where tattoos often function as markers for ideals of individualism, is witnessing a growth in tattooing practices at the beginning of the twenty-first century. Tattoos in America have begun to symbolize the ideals of self-actualization, spiritual growth, social and personal transformation, and ecological awareness. The New Age Movement, Women's and Men's movements, the ecology movement, and the Paganism and Goddess movements of the late twentieth century have promoted an understanding of the body as sacred. Individuals within these movements often understand tattooing as a means of decorating the sacred temple of their body.

For some wearers, tattoos symbolize spiritual ideals, for others the process itself is considered a spiritual transformation. For example, common tattoo narratives of women relate themes of self-healing, empowerment, and reclaiming control of their lives and bodies. Additionally, an emergent sub-set of Americans practice tattooing and body modification as a means of reconnecting their minds with their physical bodies and the natural world while aligning themselves with non-Western religious ideals thought to be more spiritually and ecologically aware than those provided by the consumer-driven Western society (e.g., idealized visions of Irish Celtic Pagan and Native American relationships with the spirits of nature, or Buddhist and Daoist notions of the interconnectedness of all life). Valorizing non-Western ideals, these "modern primitives" not only work to provide ecologically oriented ethics but they also promote awareness of the spiritual aspects of traditional forms of body modification and their potential value in modern contexts.

Shawn Arthur

Further Reading

DeMello, Margo. *Bodies of Inscription: A Cultural History of the Modern Tattoo Community*. Durham, NC: Duke University Press, 2000.

Richie, Donald and Ian Buruma. *The Japanese Tattoo*. New York, NY: Weatherhill Inc., 1980.

Rubin, Arnold, ed. *Marks of Civilization: Artistic Transformations of the Human Body*. Los Angeles: Museum of Cultural History, University of California, 1988.

Taylor, Alan. *Polynesian Tattooing*. Laie, HI: Institute for Polynesian Studies, 1981.

Vale, V. and Andrea Juno. *Modern Primitives: An Investigation of Contemporary Adornment and Ritual*. San Francisco, CA: RE/Search Publications, 1989.

See also: Feminist Spirituality Movement; Men's Movement; New Age; Polynesian Traditional Religions.

Tawhid (Oneness of God)

Tawhid literally means "making one" or "unifying," and generally refers to the Islamic doctrine of the oneness of God. In the Qur'an, *Tawhid* implies both belief in God's unity as well as the corresponding conduct demanded by such belief. *Tawhid* therefore has a doctrinal as well as an ethical dimension.

As the most basic premise of Islam, *Tawhid* finds its expression in the first half of the testimony of faith: "There is no god but God." The meanings and implications of this deceptively simple statement are far-reaching and manifold. *Tawhid* can be seen as the very life-force of Islam, for all aspects of Islamic belief, thought, and practice are rooted in its unifying and integrating vision. In any epistemology based on *Tawhid*, for instance, knowledge of nature cannot be divorced from knowledge of God's oneness.

Lynn White's critique of Christianity has been taken as an indictment of the entire Abrahamic tradition, including monotheism's Islamic manifestation in *Tawhid*. A single transcendent God is necessarily outside of nature, making the latter appear as a profane object, fit for human manipulation and domination. The description of God in the Qur'an and its reception and development in the subsequent Islamic tradition present a more complex picture. To begin with, the God of the Qur'an is both transcendent and immanent. In the Islamic tradition, the proponents of classical theology and jurisprudence typically emphasized the former aspects of the divine due to their reliance on discursive reason and concern with the maintenance of social order. The proponents of the sapiential and mystical traditions, on the other hand, often emphasized the latter aspects of the divine because of their interest in inculcating a close personal relationship between God and the human individual.

In short, *Tawhid* embraces divine transcendence from and incomparability with creation (*tanzih*), as well as divine immanence in and similarity to creation (*tashbih*). Consequently, the God of the Qur'an, while not identical with nature in any simplistic or pantheistic way, is not far removed or separate from it either. While the former perspective opens up the possibility of legitimately making use of nature, the latter perspective sets ethical limits on such use. In the vision of *Tawhid*, nature is anything but a profane object.

The key Qur'anic term that must be emphasized in order to apprehend the relationship between God and nature is *ayah*, or sign. The word appears in the Qur'an as referring to miracles of prophets, to the beings and phenomena of nature, to the realities found in the human soul, to major historical events, and to the verses of the Qur'an itself – all of these are signs of God. The Qur'anic position seems to be that even though there may not be any adequate rational proof for the existence of God, there are more than enough signs that point or allude to the Ultimate Reality. According to the vision of *Tawhid*, everything other than God is a portent or pointer that signifies God. In this context, the Qur'an puts particular emphasis on directing the reader's attention to the innumerable and easily accessible beings and phenomena of nature as so many signs through which God may be known.

By positing all existing things as signs of God, the Qur'an brings sacredness back into nature. By using the same word for the verses of the scripture and the beings and phenomena of nature, the Qur'an indicates that the book of nature is as sacred as the scripture itself, each representing a modality of divine speech. For those who forget God, both the Qur'an and nature can serve as reminders. The supernatural revelation of the Qur'an and the natural phenomena of the universe disclose and unveil the same truth, indicating the unity of Ultimate Reality. The ordinary distinction between natural and supernatural becomes irrelevant in this context.

How is the relationship between the signs and the Signified understood? From one perspective, the beings and phenomena of nature point toward God just as a work of music or painting indicates the qualities of the artist who created it. From another perspective, God's being forms the very essence or reality of everything that exists. According to Indian philosopher-poet Muhammad Iqbal (1877–1938), the universe does not confront God as its other; time, space, and matter are not independent realities but only interpretations or intellectual modes for apprehending the creative energy or life of God. What mind perceives as a plurality of things in nature is actually one continuous and dynamic divine act. Nature, in Qur'anic parlance, is the habit of God. By observing nature in the *Tawhidic* frame of mind, human beings come in close contact with the behavior of Ultimate Reality, thereby sharpening their inner perception for its more direct and deeper vision.

The ethical attitude demanded by *Tawhid* may be understood in terms of *cibadah* and *khilafah*, two central Qur'anic terms that define the consequences of accepting the oneness of God. The first can be translated as servanthood, or the attitude of loving obedience and humility that human beings ought to display toward God. The second may be translated as vicegerency, or the privileged capacity for exercising God-like authority with respect to the world. In the *Tawhidic* framework, vicegerency presupposes servanthood; human beings cannot become partners in God's creative work without first humbling themselves before their Creator-Lord. While the ethic of dominion is inherent in the notion of vicegerency, the Qur'an views the exercise of human powers without genuine servanthood toward God as illegitimate. The Qur'anic notion of vicegerency includes the understanding that human powers are not their own but have been delegated to them from a higher authority, for a limited time and for a specific purpose. Human beings must exercise these powers within the limits set by the Real Sovereign, or they will be seen as criminals and rebels (*taghut*), no longer acting in accordance with the demands of *Tawhid*.

Tawhid implies that everything in the universe belongs to God – a frequently repeated Qur'anic theme. Consequently, the idea of material possessions and natural resources as constituting a sacred trust (*amanah*) from God is also built into the notion of vicegerency. Human beings have been temporarily bestowed with certain "possessions" through which they are being tested; this is true of individuals as well as communities and humankind as a whole. Ultimately, there is no such thing as human property. This understanding calls for an attitude of careful and vigilant restraint (*taqwa*) on the part of human beings vis-à-vis nature, which is divine property under temporary, partial, and conditional human stewardship.

These ethical implications of *Tawhid* are not limited to individual morality but extend to the dynamics of the collective order as well. In addition to religious beliefs and ethical norms, the Qur'an provides the outlines of a social order through which these beliefs and norms can be actualized in concrete human reality; the social order established by the Prophet Muhammad in seventh-century Arabia constitutes a paradigmatic model for Muslims in this regard. The Qur'an recognizes that human beings are rarely able to act in accordance with their professed beliefs and norms if these are not simultaneously supported by social structures and institutions. Consequently, the actualization of *Tawhid* in a given community remains incomplete and precarious if it is confined to the individual's consciousness as a doctrine but does not shape the collective order.

The present-day ecological situation in the Muslim world is a forceful reminder that the chasm between ideal and reality will exist whenever professed beliefs and norms are not embodied in the collective order. *Tawhid* is no longer the central principle in the various social orders prevailing in the Muslim world, where the role of Islam in shaping public policy is itself a fiercely contested area. Moreover, any secularizing trend in the Muslim world further weakens Islam's ability to be ecologically relevant at a collective level. It is hardly surprising that the ecologically beneficial imperatives of *Tawhid* have only a limited impact in everyday reality. *Tawhid's* great potential in this regard, however, may be tapped through Islam-based environmental movements at the grassroots level.

Ahmed Afzaal

Further Reading
Chittick, William C. "God Surrounds All Things: An Islamic Perspective on the Environment." *The World and I* (June 1986), 671–8.
Iqbal, Muhammad. *The Reconstruction of Religious Thought in Islam.* Lahore, Pakistan: The Institute of Islamic Culture, 1996.
Manzoor, S. Parvez. "Environment and Values: The Islamic Perspective." In Ziauddin Sardar, ed. *The Touch of Midas: Science, Values and Environment in Islam and the West.* Manchester, UK: Manchester University Press, 1984, 150–69.
Murata, Sachiko and William C. Chittick. *The Vision of Islam.* St. Paul, MN: Paragon House, 1995.
Nasr, Seyyed Hossein. *Religion & the Order of Nature.* New York: Oxford University Press. 1996.
See also: Islam; The Qur'an; Sufism.

Technological Immortality

Suffering death is the price that humans pay for their intelligence, yet through intelligence humans have long sought to overcome death, by means either of religion or technology. A single-celled animal such as the amoeba is in a sense immortal. While it can die, every living amoeba is many millions of years old, because it reproduces by splitting, whereas multi-celled creatures such as ourselves die of old age after a short life. Many animals suffer when they die, but probably only humans are fully aware of the meaning of death and know from early childhood that they are mortal. From the time of the ancient Egyptians, some cultures and individuals have sought partially technological solutions, but only in recent decades have fully non-supernatural alternatives become plausible.

Cryonics

Probably inspired by science-fiction stories and the success of the frozen food industry, in the 1960s, Robert C.W. Ettinger launched the cryonics movement to freeze dying human beings. The original idea was that cryopreservation could halt death for years until medical science had developed a remedy for the individual's fatal illness, at which point he or she would be thawed out, cured, and restored to a normal life.

A number of organizations set up laboratories to develop methods of cryopreservation, and a few dozen bodies were actually frozen. Ettinger and some other members of his movement began to think that future technologies could not only restore life but also improve it, giving people saved by cryonics a chance to become superhuman and even possibly god-like. A number of technical problems would need to be overcome, however, especially the extensive chemical and mechanical damage caused to large, slow-cooling human bodies by the freezing process itself.

More recently, rapid progress in gene analysis and genetic engineering has led to the idea that much of an individual's character might be preserved in a sample of DNA. For example, the Center for Reproduction of Endangered Species at the San Diego Zoo has established a collection of cryopreserved animal cells. The Coriell Institute for Medical Research has established a research repository of cells from human beings with inherited diseases, and a sufficient sample is four teaspoons of blood.

Frozen DNA samples can be stored indefinitely without deterioration, and in future centuries they might be used to create a clone of the deceased individual, or the individual's genetic code could be employed in some other method of technological resurrection. However, DNA does not contain information about anything the person experienced or learned, so this approach would have to be combined with some method to preserve the individual's personality and memories.

Cybersurvival

In his 1953 novel, *The City and the Stars*, Arthur C. Clarke imagined that people could be archived inside an advanced computer, for technological resurrection thousands of years after their deaths. Many recent developments in computation, information storage, and cognitive science have provided both hope that this dream actually could be realized and some hint of how this could be done.

In his influential book, *The Age of Spiritual Machines*, computer entrepreneur Ray Kurzweil predicted that human beings and their computers will gradually merge over the next century, and that we will thereby become god-like spirits inhabiting cyberspace as well as the material universe. Specifically, Kurzweil suggests that magnetic resonance imaging (MRI) or some even more advanced technique could be used to read out the neural structure of a person's brain, which then could be simulated inside a computer.

A second approach is to videotape extensive interviews, then use computer graphics and artificial intelligence technology to create a virtual human. A virtual copy of a person is called an *avatar*. This term traditionally refers to a manifestation of a Hindu deity, including incarnation in human form. But it is used currently in computer engineering to refer to a software embodiment of a human personality.

The most impressive project to preserve interviews digitally is Steven Spielberg's Survivors of the Shoah Visual History Foundation which has recorded interviews with over 52,000 survivors of the European Holocaust at a cost of $175,000,000. The same effort devoted to a single individual could preserve enough to make a convincing avatar, and the needed digital library and graphics technology is progressing rapidly.

A third approach is to employ the full range of psychological tests and sociological questionnaires to archive opinions, attitudes, beliefs, and other aspects of a personality. Even a relatively simple computerized database permits a kind of conversation with such a corpus of personal data, querying it for information in the form of questions and answers. Existing scientific measures of personality are designed to compare individuals along a few standard dimensions. Researchers working on personality preservation have recognized the need to develop new approaches designed to capture an individual's unique characteristics.

Thus, several rapidly developing technologies are making it possible to record aspects of a person, and it seems likely that the technology will permit recordings of increasingly higher fidelity over the coming decades. The problem then becomes how to integrate the different kinds of data (genetic, neuro-structural, audio-visual, linguistic, and social-psychological), and there is much room for debate whether even a highly advanced computer system could accomplish this.

Conclusion

Death is a natural phase of human existence, but it is also part of our nature to seek solutions to problems, even the most challenging ones. For thousands of years, the preferred responses to mortality depended upon belief in a supernatural realm that transcended the limitations of material existence. Science, the systematic quest for the secrets of nature, now offers the possibility of technical solutions that conceivably could obviate the need for religion.

It may prove difficult to develop the technology, either requiring many decades or ultimately succeeding only partially. If science can preserve and reanimate only portions of the human personality, then future centuries may develop a hybrid approach to death that blends the technical with the sacramental, thereby building a bridge between the natural and the supernatural.

William Sims Bainbridge

Further Reading

Bainbridge, William Sims. "Religious Ethnography on the World Wide Web." In Jeffrey K. Hadden and Douglas E. Cowan, eds. *Religion on the Internet* (volume 8 of *Religion and the Social Order*). New York: Elsevier/JAI, 2000, 55–80.

Chidester, David. *Patterns of Transcendence: Religion, Death, and Dying.* Belmont, CA: Wadsworth, 1990.

Ettinger, Robert C.W. *Man into Superman.* New York: St. Martin's Press, 1972.

Kurzweil, Ray. *The Age of Spiritual Machines: When Computers Exceed Human Intelligence.* New York: Viking, 1999.

Stark, Rodney and William Sims Bainbridge. *A Theory of Religion.* New York: Toronto/Lang, 1987.

See also: Paganism and Technology.

Tehri Dam

Tehri Dam, a hydro-electric power project on the principal upper tributary of the Ganges River, will, if completed, be the fifth highest in the world, and the highest in Asia. Located just below the confluence of the Bhagirathi and the Bhilangana Rivers in the Indian state of Uttar Pradesh, the Earth and rockfill dam of 260.5 meters will flood 45 kilometers of the Bhagirathi Valley and 35 kilometers of the Bhilangana Valley, impounding 3.22 million cubic meters of water spread over 42.5 square kilometers. The reservoir will submerge the town of Tehri, and 5200 hectares of land. It will displace an estimated 70,000 to 100,000 people. Promising 2400 megawatts of electric power to such cities as Allahabad and Kanpur, it is expected to irrigate 270,000 hectares in the western districts of Uttar Pradesh, providing 500 cubic feet per second of drinking water to Delhi.

Since its inauguration, public protest against the project has centered upon the interrelated issues of ecology, economic and environmental justice, and religion. At a meeting in Brazil in 1997, J.P. Raturi, the representative of the Tehri Dam Resistance Struggle Committee (*Tehri Bandh Virodhi Sangharsh Samiti*), stated Indian culture sees divinity in nature. He observes that to the rulers, the Ganges is megawatts of power and hectares of irrigated land. To the local people, she is a life-giving goddess. Sunderlal Bahuguna, one of the most visible leaders of the movement against the dam, recalls that the goddess Ganga (the Ganges river) answered the prayers of King Bagiratha to descend to the Earth only after Lord Shiva permitted her to descend into his matted locks, preventing her from becoming a destructive torrent. Bahuguna states that the locks of Shiva are the natural forests of the Himalayas which protect the land from floods. But the catchment area of the Bhagirathi River is the victim of massive deforestation by commercial forestry, and has turned the Ganges into the destructive force of which the ancient story told. For him, the dam is a further desecration of a sacred environment.

The religious significance of the Bhagirathi and Ganges rivers pertains to objections raised on grounds of ecology and environmental justice. The Himalayan region is seismically active, and the dam site is located only 15 kilometers from the boundary of two plates of the Earth's crust. Local people, however, have worked this land productively for many generations. Upstream from the dam site is a scenic valley, the heart of an ancient village culture. The proposed reservoir will fill this valley, with its 23 villages, and their terraced fields, sculpted over centuries of painstaking work. In 1978, when officers of the Uttar Pradesh government arrived to inaugurate construction on the first diversion tunnel for the dam, thousands of men, women, and children blocked their way and shouted: "You love electricity, we love our soil." J.P. Raturi has argued that while the project will provide electric power and irrigation to the affluent, to the local people it will bring displacement and disaster. Bahuguna states that when the Ganges flows in her natural course she benefits all, irrespective of caste, creed, color, poverty or wealth. When she is dammed, she becomes the possession of the privileged and powerful who can dispense her blessings on a partisan basis.

Bahuguna argues that religion traditionally played a vital role in the regulation of natural resource use. As the industrial revolution began to see nature as a commodity, this crucial feature of religion came to be covered over with rituals. When development was identified with economic growth, a new religion was born: the temple of this religion is the market, technocrats and experts are its priests, and the dollar is the new god. Our political leaders, he says, are prepared to make the highest sacrifices to this god to bring it home. With his frail body, his white beard, and his simple Kadi apparel, Bahuguna appears as a prophet standing against an idolatrous faith. The dam, he argues, is a project to realize a false hope. It is based on a view of reality that equates progress with the affluence of the few. We should not kill our sacred river, he says, on the promises of a false vision of reality.

Bahuguna's idiom of resistance supports his credibility. Personifying the traditional ideals of nonviolence (*ahimsa*), renunciation of possessions (*aparigraha*), and devotion to God (*Ishvar-pranidhana*), Bahuguna states that the method of *satyagraha*, or standing courageously for the truth, is the only form of protest that can be effective. In the course of this struggle, Bahuguna has undertaken several fasts that have received much media attention. Ranging from 11 to 74 days, they have repeatedly brought him close to death. Early in 1996 the Tehri Hydroelectric Development Corporation ordered the people and businesses to vacate the town of Tehri and move to the New Tehri town located on a hillside above the dam site. The town was to be submerged by the end of June 1996. Local activists argued that the call was intended to convince the people that a review of the project was no longer possible. Again in June of 1999 all government offices, educational institutions and businesses were asked to vacate the town by the end of the month, but the plan was again postponed. In December 2001 with the rising waters behind the dam, the Ganga Kuti or hut on the bank of the river in which Sunderlal Bahuguna had been residing in *satyagraha* for the past fifteen years was the first dwelling to be submerged.

George A. James

Further Reading

Bahadur, Jagdish. *Environmental Hotspots: Tehri Hydro-Electric Project, Narmada Valley Project*. New Delhi: Vigyan Prasar, 1998.

Pearce, Fred. "Building a Disaster: The Monumental Folly of India's Tehri Dam." *The Ecologist* 21:3 (May/June 1991).

Paranjpye, Vijay. *Evaluating the Tehri Dam: An Extended Cost-Benefit Appraisal*. Studies in Ecology and Sustainable Development 1. New Delhi: INTACH, 1988.

Rigzin, Tinzen, ed. *Firewood in the Heart, Firewood on the Back: Writings on and by Himalayan Crusader Sunderlal Bahuguna*. Tehri (UP), India: Parvatiya Navjeevan Mandal, 1997.

See also: Ahimsa; Bahuguna, Sunderlal; Hinduism; Hinduism and Pollution (and adjacent, River Ganga and the Clean Ganga Campaign; Sarvodaya Shramadana Movement (Sri Lanka).

Teilhard de Chardin, Pierre (1881–1955)

Pierre Teilhard de Chardin was born on 1 May 1881 to Emmanuel and Berthe-Adele Teilhard de Chardin. His birthplace in Auvergne in southern France had a lasting effect on his experiences of love for the natural world. In 1899 he entered the Jesuit order where he launched into his lifelong effort to unify science and religion through the study of evolution and the role of the human as part of evolutionary processes. Three years later the novitiate was moved to the island of Jersey in England due to anti-clericalism in France. It was also at this time that his eldest brother died, his younger sister became seriously ill and two years later another sister passed away. These experiences had a profound effect on Teilhard who considered engaging only in theological studies and turning away from science.

Instead he was sent to teach at the Jesuit College in Cairo from 1905–1908. It was here that he developed his naturalist's inclinations by studying Egypt's flora and fauna as well as the fossil record. Teilhard spent from 1908–1912 in Hastings, England, where he continued his theological studies but also pursued his interest in evolution. He encountered Henri Bergson's newly published *Creative Evolution*. This had a profound effect on his ideas regarding the spirit and direction of the evolving universe. It was also during this period that the attack on modernism and evolution arose under the papacy of Pius X. From 1912–1915 Teilhard studied geology and paleontology in Paris eventually earning his doctorate in 1922 from the Sorbonne.

The war years interrupted his studies as Europe was plunged into bloody trench warfare. Teilhard served as a stretcher bearer and was awarded the Legion of Honor for his heroic service. The experience of war had a profound effect on him as he wrote of his growing sense that even in the midst of such turmoil there emerges a feeling for a purpose and direction to life more hidden and mysterious than history generally reveals. It was shortly after the war when he was recuperating in Jersey that he wrote his essay on "The Spiritual Power of Matter." For Teilhard all of matter has a psychic/spiritual component and it is this interiority of matter that helps to move evolution toward greater complexity and consciousness.

In 1923, at the invitation of the Jesuit Emile Licent, Teilhard sailed for China to undertake paleontological research. Together they traveled numerous times to the Ordos desert on the border with Inner Mongolia to study Paleolithic remains as well as the natural terrain. Teilhard returned to France a year later to resume teaching at the Institute Catholique, but the conservative climate perpetuated by the Vatican created a difficult atmosphere for him to develop his thinking on evolution. This conservative climate was due in part to the anti-modernist movement spearheaded by the Vatican before World War I. Rome sought to thwart the efforts of Catholic intellectuals who were interested in introducing broader elements of biblical criticism as well as reconciling aspects of religion and science, especially around the theory of evolution. In response, Rome tried to preserve orthodox Catholic teaching by requiring all clerics to take an anti-modernist oath.

Teilhard returned to China and settled in Beijing where he continued his scientific studies, interacted with a broad circle of intellectuals, and wrote *The Divine Milieu*. This work eventually caused his Jesuit Superior General to insist that Teilhard confine himself to his scientific work and not publish any of his theological writings. This was in large part because his vision of an immanental evolving cosmos appeared to more conservative minds to have pantheistic elements not in line with strict interpretations of the doctrine of creation. There were some who were concerned about Teilhard's profound immanental sensibilities regarding the infusion of the divine in nature. This was seen to be in contrast to the more orthodox position that God was transcendent or beyond nature. Teilhard was thus encouraged to stay in China where he remained until after World War II except for brief visits to France.

Teilhard engaged in several key research projects including the discovery of Peking Man in 1929–1930, the Mongolian Expedition sponsored by the American Museum of Natural History, the Yellow Expedition sponsored by Citroen, as well as expeditions to India, Burma, and Java. In 1931 he traveled across the United States, which inspired him to write *The Spirit of the Earth*. This work situates the human within evolutionary emergence and suggests that recognizing our deep embeddedness in nature is crucial to the future of all life. Teilhard voices his concern that humans embrace their common destiny as members of the Earth community and help to create a viable future by activating, not stifling, the larger spirit of the Earth within each human.

It was in 1940 that he completed his most important work, *The Human Phenomenon* (originally translated as *The Phenomenon of Man*). After the war when he was able to return to France his Jesuit superior would still not allow this work to be published. He spent the last years of his life in New York City with a research position at the Wenner-Gren Foundation. *The Human Phenomenon* was not published until after his death in 1955. It was first translated into English in 1960 and a new, more accurate translation by Sarah Weber was published in 1999.

In *The Human Phenomenon* Teilhard outlined the fourfold sequence of the evolution of galaxies, Earth, life, and consciousness. Teilhard presented his vision of the emergence of the human as the unifying dimension of the evolutionary process. For Teilhard the awakening of humans to the idea of evolution since Darwin is unique in history and he likens this to the moment when a child becomes aware of perspective. He felt that for humans to realize that they participate in cosmogenesis, namely that they are part of evolutionary developmental time, results in a major change in knowledge and beliefs. Absorbing this perspective, he felt, was a critical juncture for the growth of human awareness.

Teilhard sees consciousness as intrinsic to the process of evolution, not as an extrinsic addition to matter. For him all reality consists of simultaneously a within and a without. Matter and spirit are thus joined in this vast evolutionary unfolding toward a final Omega Point. The universe in this context is a *divine milieu*, a center that has the possibilities of uniting and drawing all things to itself. For Teilhard the evolutionary process is characterized by increasing complexity and consciousness and the divine is seen as part of the process, not simply transcendent to it.

Humans are the self-conscious mode of the universe in whom complexity and consciousness has come to its fullest expression. One of Teilhard's greatest hopes was that this large perspective of a purposeful universe would help to inspire human action for building the human community. In contrast to a resigned or fatalistic perspective, he spoke of the need to reignite in the human community a joy for action and a zest for life. Human suffering he saw not as due to original sin but as a form of potential energy which if transformed could change the face of the Earth in positive ways.

Teilhard's optimistic perspective has led to critiques from theologians who grapple with the problem of evil and feel that Teilhard may gloss over this pervasive reality in the human community. It has also resulted in criticisms from deep ecologists who view him as highly anthropocentric and his vision of "building the Earth" as lacking in awareness of the need for environmental restraints. Many are thus wary of Teilhard's apparent faith in technology and in progress. Moreover, Teilhard was a product of his times in having a rather limited understanding of religions outside of Christianity. His strong Christocentric approach and language infuse his writings.

Nonetheless, conscious of these critiques and aware of Teilhard's limitations, Thomas Berry and Brian Swimme have drawn on Teilhard's evolutionary perspective in developing their idea of *The Universe Story* as a comprehensive context for an expanded ecological sensibility. Like Teilhard, they see cosmogenesis as critical to understanding the role of humans as intrinsic to evolution and as responsible for its continuity. Teilhard's ideas continue to inspire appreciation and critique in the search for sustaining human–Earth relations.

Mary Evelyn Tucker

Further Reading

Teilhard de Chardin, Pierre. *The Human Phenomenon* (New translation by Sarah Appleton Weber). Brighton: Sussex Academic Press, 1999.

Teilhard de Chardin, Pierre. *Toward the Future*. New York: Harcourt, Brace, Jovanovich, 1975.

Teilhard de Chardin, Pierre. *Human Energy*. New York: Harcourt, Brace, Jovanovich, 1971.

Teilhard de Chardin, Pierre. *Hymn of the Universe*. New York: Harper's, 1965.

Teilhard de Chardin, Pierre. *The Divine Milieu*. New York: Harper's, 1960.

See also: Berry, Thomas; Earth Charter; Environmental Ethics; Epic of Evolution; Religious Studies and Environmental Concern; Roman Catholic Religious Orders; Swimme, Brian; United Nations' "Earth Summits".

Thai Buddhist Monks

In 1986, the ecclesiastical council of the Thai Sangha, the order of Buddhist monks, recommended to the Thai government that the Departments of Forestry and Religious Affairs work together on conservation and rural development projects. This recommendation foreshadowed the currently popular environmental movement in Thailand and the growing number of projects throughout the nation involving monks and the use of Buddhism in development and conservation. In the face of severe problems of deforestation and damaged watersheds across Thailand, several monks are advocating forest conservation, along with rural development schemes, based on their interpretations of Buddhist notions of respect for and balance with nature.

The work of these self-proclaimed "environmentalist monks" (Thai, *phra nak anuraksa thammachaat*) raises controversial issues concerning the relationship between Buddhism and environmentalism. The debate goes beyond equating the religion with nature, a simplistic interpretation often made by both these activist monks and environmentalists throughout the Buddhist world. (For example, the Buddha's birth, enlightenment, teaching and death all occurred in forests, providing evidence in this line of thinking for the importance of the forest for spiritual development and environmental conservation.) The Buddhist environmental movement, amorphous as it is in Thailand, raises questions about both the appropriateness of monks' involvement in such "this-worldly" affairs as environmentalism and the philosophical grounding of their interpretations of Theravada scriptures and ritual practices.

Although making up only a small percentage of the total Sangha in Thailand, environmentalist monks became prominent in the 1990s. Controversies involving some well-known monks, such as the arrest of Phra Prajak Khuttajitto for allegedly trespassing in a national park while documenting illegal logging, and a sex scandal surrounding the environmental activist Phra Yantra (in which he was accused of fathering a child with one of his followers), heightened the debate and put all activist monks under increased public scrutiny. The controversies and public image of environmentalist monks also tend to keep most "forest monks" – meditation masters who remove themselves from society to emphasize religious practice and asceticism – away from involvement in environmental activities.

Nevertheless, environmentalist monks maintain that their actions follow the Buddhist invocation to end suffering (Pali, *dukkha*). They are critical of changes wrought in Thai society as a result of the capitalist economic development promoted by the government since the 1950s. The consumerism that has swept across the nation and the accompanying debt and environmental degradation, these monks argue, are based on greed, one of the three root causes of suffering in Buddhist thought. They see it as their responsibility *as monks*, therefore, to engage in changing people's attitudes and behavior toward the natural environment and the economy. By promoting environmental conservation and sustainable development (by which they primarily mean growing one's own food through organic agriculture), they aim to help people recognize their responsibilities toward nature and avoid the desire that underlies capitalist development. Environmental degradation, economic development, and the abandonment of religious principles and practice are all intertwined in environmentalist monks' assessments of the major problems Thailand faces today.

In their efforts to deal with these problems, environmentalist monks focus on three main types of activities: reinterpreting traditional rituals, education, and activism. The interplay between these approaches highlights the cultural creativity of these monks as they draw on local, national and Theravada Buddhist beliefs and practices in response to the environmental crisis in Thailand. Their more activist approach is supported by teachings of prominent scholar monks such as Buddhadása Bhikkhu and Phra Prayudh Payutto (current monastic title, Dhammapitaka).

Environmentalist monks reinterpret a range of traditional rituals to promote conservation and engender laypeople's participation in conservation projects. These rites include symbolically ordaining trees in endangered forests, drawing people's attention to their mutual dependence on the forest. They also incorporate tree seedlings for reforestation with the traditional lay donations of robes to monks. Some monks perform "long-life" ceremonies for bodies of water, such as rivers and reservoirs, to highlight the urgency of protecting water supplies from drought (often caused by deforestation) and pollution. One monk even modified the monks' daily practice of alms-rounds to ask people in his village to donate land to the temple, thereby gaining religious merit, to use in a model integrated agriculture farm. Through reinterpreting a familiar practice, the monk aimed to get villagers to rethink how they lived from the land.

Education is a major component of environmentalist monks' activities. They teach both laity and the larger Sangha about ecology, appropriate technology and organic agriculture to provide tools to live in an ecologically sensitive manner. The monks emphasize meditation and Buddhist teachings, seeing the religion as the basis for positive change in society. They use principles such as dependent origination or the interdependence of all things (Pali, *paticca-samuppada*) to teach people responsibility toward the natural environment.

The most controversial activity of some environmentalist monks is their activism. Many of these monks have initiated local conservation projects or protested ecologically harmful policies and actions by the government, military and big business. Together with local people and non-governmental organizations, monks have protested both the construction of a dam in northeast Thailand and a natural gas pipeline coming from Burma through a Thai national park for both their negative ecological effects and their impact on the livelihoods of local people. Monks have established sanctified, protected community forests and fish, bird and wildlife sanctuaries, and organized Dhamma walks in which monks, environmentalists and other lay people walk and meditate mindfully for several days or weeks, engaging with local people to draw attention to endangered areas such as lakes and forests (see Bhikkhu 2000). In northern Thailand, one young monk runs a model organic farm and provides seeds, seedlings and knowledge to farmers as they shift from cash cropping to integrated, organic agricultural techniques.

The actions and religious interpretations by environmentalist monks are diverse and controversial. They are also genuine efforts to make Buddhism relevant in a changing society. Despite – or perhaps because of – the debates surrounding these monks, they are contributing to rethinking the religion and religious practice in light of the urgency of the environmental crisis. The result is a form of cultural creativity that, while grounded in an ancient tradition, has the potential radically to change the way Thai Buddhists think about their religion and their natural environment.

Susan M. Darlington

Further Reading

Bhikkhu, Santikaro. "Dhamma Walk around Songkla Lake." In Stephanie Kaza and Kenneth Kraft, eds. *Dharma Rain: Sources of Buddhist Environmentalism*. Boston: Shambhala Publications, Inc., 2000, 206–15.

Darlington, Susan M. "Rethinking Buddhism and Development: The Emergence of Environmentalist Monks in Thailand." In Christopher S. Queen, Charles S. Prebish and Damien V. Keown, eds. *Action Dharma: New Studies in Engaged Buddhism*. Surrey, UK: Curzon Press, 2003.

Darlington, Susan M. "Practical Spirituality and Community Forests: Monks, Ritual and Radical Conservatism in Thailand." In Anna L. Tsing and Paul Greenough, eds. *Imagination and Distress in Southern Environmental Projects*. Raleigh, NC: Duke University Press, 2003.

Swearer, Donald K. "The Hermeneutics of Buddhist Ecology in Contemporary Thailand: Buddhadasa and Dhammapitaka." In Mary Evelyn Tucker and Duncan Ryuken Williams, eds. *Buddhism and Ecology: The Interconnection of Dharma and Deeds*. Cambridge, MA: Harvard University Center for the Study of World Religions and Harvard University Press, 1997, 21–44.

Taylor, Jim. " 'Thamma-chaat': Activist Monks and Competing Discourses of Nature and Nation in Northeastern Thailand." In Philip Hirsch, ed. *Seeing Forests for Trees: Environment and Environmentalism in Thailand*. Chiang Mai: Silkworm Books, 1996, 37–52.

See also: Buddhism – Engaged; Nhat Hanh, Thich; Payutto, Phra Dhammapitaka; Siam's Forest Monasteries; Southeast Asia; Sivaraksa, Sulak.

Theme Parks

The term "Theme Park" has been used to describe everything from small amusement attractions, such as family entertainment centers with a few rides, to the massive Walt Disney World entertainment complex outside Orlando, Florida. Theme parks are not to be confused with fairs, carnivals, or amusement parks. The relationship between theme parks and their predecessors – both medieval carnivals, festivals and fairs, and nineteenth-century amusement parks and World's Fairs – is well documented. What is of interest here is the way the more than 225 major theme parks in the United States (as at the turn of the 21st century), and unknown numbers of others around the world, have evolved to present a new cultural intersection of religion and nature. We can identify several prominent religious possibilities for presentations of nature in contemporary theme parks.

In the 1950s, theme parks began to embody what has been called "civil religion" (Bellah 1967), central tenets of which were: capitalism, nuclear family and domesticity, scientific and technological progress (leading to utopian community living), wealth and leisure provided through national supremacy, and triumph over nature.

Themes of progress and domination of all things natural have also been prominent in a "frontier religion" common in theme parks, including such places as Disneyland and Disney World, Southern California's Knott's Berry Farm, and Silver Dollar City in the Missouri Ozarks. A prominent narrative in such locales as Disney's Frontierland, Knott's Berry's Ghost Town, and Silver Dollar City in its entirety is the rejuvenating value of an anti-modern experience with a romanticized, simpler period of American exploration, conquest, and new settlement.

Finally, what can be called a religion of "nature celebration" has been made possible by the more recent, steady increase in the use of natural themes in park design. What Disneyland started with exotic recreations of flora and fauna has increasingly developed into a more overt role at such parks as Busch Gardens: Africa: The Dark Continent, the Sea World parks, and Disney's Animal Kingdom. Now nature is no longer presented as mere backdrop for entertainment and practical landscape manipulation. It *is* the point (and source) of the experience.

Critics have called these parks to task in recent years for encouraging visitors to feel that their attendance amounts to environmental action since their messages are often intensely scientific and environmentally sound, focusing upon the veterinary and conservationist activities that may go on there. The parks are often built on fragile habitats and clearly encourage unsustainable consumption. Some critical scholars portray the success of nature-focused theme parks as especially problematic for their influence on American tourist culture in general. There is concern that zoos, museums, and even national parks will be remodeled to mimic theme parks (Davis 1997; Wilson 1991).

It is one thing to say that theme parks present visitors with a particular view of nature, to worry, for instance, that Sea World's oceans, Busch Garden's African landscape, and Disney's multiple geographies narrate a particular version of nature as exhibited by each corporate interest. It is quite another thing to consider what people are *doing* with those presentations of nature. Scholars need to ask why Sea World attendees have been known to strip off their clothes and jump into the dolphin tank (an unsanctioned activity). Do they seek only to cool off? Do they simply find swimming with dolphins entertaining? Or is there a more fundamental desire for an authentic experience that has a religious dimension?

Some have argued that theme park visitors desire a particular set of experiences that in many ways can be considered sacred. Margaret J. King (1981) joined a growing scholarly focus on Disney parks, calling them the "popular culture capitals" of the country, noting that more so than Washington, D.C., families are motivated to go on a double pilgrimage to Disneyland and Walt Disney World – first as children and later with children. For King, this notion evokes community, communal experience, shared values, ritual motion, and perhaps additional traditionally religious language and imagery. This is not to say that theme parks have become traditionally religious for their visitors. Instead, visitors value community and the feeling of shared, ritual experience on a broad cultural level – rituals of a civil religion (King 1981).

Anthropologist Alexander Moore (1980) compared theme parks with traditional baroque pilgrimage centers. Though he argues that Walt Disney World's form replicates that of a pilgrimage center, behavior in the Magic Kingdom, he says, is not traditionally religious. Instead, ritualized play seems to be gaining importance over both organized religion and obligatory rituals. Theme parks are isolated and enclosed. There are ritualized barriers separating them from the outside world (e.g., private highways, toll booths, parking lots, and ticket counters). Like traditional pilgrimage centers, theme parks evoke the supernatural (with its emphasis on magic, fantasy and make-believe), or at least a mytho-heroic past. Moore discusses the cultic and symbolic dimensions of the park, arguing that going to theme parks is not only about playing but bearing witness to the metaphors they evoke and pay homage to. Increasingly, those metaphors highlight nature and its religious significance. He concludes that the social and spatial order of a place like Disney World is the genuflection – ritual motion – of mass industrial society.

Much more research is needed to explore the roles of religious experience of nature presentations in theme parks, but that audiences have transcendent experiences in theme parks is unquestioned. For example, a 33-year-old father in New Hampshire wrote to *The Unofficial Guide to Walt Disney World*,

It was on this trip that I experienced what can only be described as . . . an epiphany. I was on the ferry boat that runs between the Magic Kingdom and the TTC, waiting for it to fill up and cast off. The rain had cooled things off comfortably, and a rainbow had formed behind the Contemporary Resort, disappearing over the rooftops of the Wilderness Lodge that poked from behind the treeline. It was beautiful, and I just felt so relaxed, peaceful and happy. I also felt a little silly – here I am, a 33-year-old guy, alone in Walt Disney World, and I'm feeling like there's not a problem in the world. But that's the effect this place can have on you. Sure it can be hot, crowded, muggy, and it'll suck your wallet dry . . . but that's a small price to pay for those moments when the "Disney Magic" takes over and all seems right with the world.

In the passage we see references to human creation: the ferry boat, the Magic Kingdom, the crowds, etc. But we see references to nature: the rain, a rainbow, the treeline. As Van Maanen (1992) pointed out, there are important cultural contrasts that intensify the meaning potential of theme park nature. Mugginess, crowds, waiting, and spending money are offset by beauty, relaxation, peace, happiness, and contentment. Religion sociologist Wade Clark Roof (1993) has argued that, increasingly, late modern Americans engage in similar quests to seek new symbols and meanings – incorporating such experiences with prior beliefs to cobble together their own belief systems. Is it possible that such popular cultural (and for profit!) corporate creations as theme parks provide at least some of the meaningful material? Are the creators and operators of these parks able successfully to present a crafted "nature" that transforms their commercial endeavors into profoundly moving, even religious, experiences for paying customers? And is it worth the cost? By positioning theme park nature as entertainment, information, and even transcendent inspiration, are we denying our own threat to its authenticity?

We can only be certain that theme parks will continue to draw visitors, providing an experience that will undoubtedly carry on a contribution to the ongoing evolution of the story of transcendent nature.

Joseph G. Champ
Rebecca Self Hill

Further Reading
Bellah, R. "Civil Religion in America." *Daedalus* 96(1) (1967), 1–21.
Davis, Susan. *Spectacular Nature: Corporate Culture and the Sea World Experience*. Berkeley: University of California Press, 1997.
Isozaki, Arata. "Theme Park." *South Atlantic Quarterly* 92:1 (1993), 175–82.
Johnson, David M. "Disney World as Structure and Symbol: Re-Creation of the American Experience." *Journal of Popular Culture* 15:1 (1981), 157–65.
Kasson, John F. *Amusing the Millions: Coney Island at the Turn of the Century*. New York: Hill and Wang, 1978.
King, Margaret J. "The Audience in the Wilderness: The Disney Nature Films." *Journal of Popular Film and Television* 24:2 (1996), 60–8.
King, Margaret J. "The New American Muse: Notes on the Amusement/Theme Park." *Journal of Popular Culture* 15:1 (1981), 56–75.
Moore, Alexander. "Walt Disney World: Bounded Ritual Space And the Playful Pilgrimage Center." *Anthropological Quarterly* (1980), 207–17.
Roof, Wade Clark. *A Generation of Seekers: The Spiritual Journeys of the Baby Boom Generation*. New York: HarperCollins, 1993.
Van Maanen, John. "Displacing Disney: Some Notes on the Flow of Culture." *Qualitative Sociology* 13:1 (1992), 5–35.
Wilson, Alexander. *The Culture of Nature: North American Landscape from Disney to the Exxon Valdez*. Toronto: Between the Lines, 1991.

See also: Disney; Disney Worlds at War.

Theosophy

The modern Theosophical movement, which commenced in 1875 with the founding of the Theosophical Society by Helena P. Blavatsky, Henry Steel Olcott, and others, has had a role in the emergence of recent spiritualities of nature and ecology. The new movement was viewed by its founders as a middle way between what they perceived as the twin dogmatisms of the nineteenth century, science and theology. Theosophy represented, they believed, a path based on the profounder perspective of the "ancient wisdom," the vision of nature and humanity held by premoderns who, to judge from those most often cited in the literature, tended broadly to be in the tradition of Vedantins, Mahayana Buddhists, and Platonists together with their neo-Platonic, Gnostic and Cabalistic progeny.

In respect to nature, nineteenth- and twentieth-century Theosophy has contributed to nature spirituality insofar as it: a) presented quasi-religious images and concepts to embody the romantic view of nature as vibrant with life and meaning, both visible and invisible; b) popularized in the West monistic and pantheistic Eastern experiences of nature, humanity, and the divine; and c) expanded evolution (known best in its controversial Darwinian form at the time of the Society's founding) to embrace all of nature, together with humanity, in immense cosmic evolutionary schemes. Such ideas are certainly not unique to Theosophy, but in the late nineteenth and early twentieth centuries Theosophists were pioneers in presenting them in popular as well as academic and literary venues. In lodge meetings, publications, and such centers as the Pt. Loma community in San Diego, started by Katherine Tingley in 1897, or Krotona, established in Hollywood in 1912 and moved to Ojai, California, in 1924, the idea of evolutionary kinship with nature deeply felt by many Theosophists took such concrete forms as vegetarianism, humanitarianism toward animals, progressive farming, and appreciation of the salutary spiritual effect of an inspiring natural environment.

The core Theosophical idea is usually said to be oneness: that the unity of all being is more fundamental than any apparent separateness and diversity. Oneness therefore overrides all dualism, whether of the One and the many, the human and the divine, consciousness and matter, or humanity and nature. A corollary of this perspective is the assumption that consciousness, though perhaps in rudimentary or radically nonhuman form, is found consistently throughout all levels of the universe. Some modern Theosophists (as well as some scientists) have seen evidence of universal consciousness underlying matter in the phenomena described in quantum theory.

Recent Theosophical writers and teachers like Joy Mills, Shirley Nicholson, Amit Goswami, and Ravi Ravindra have emphasized the congruity of the Theosophical worldview with what seems to be emerging on the frontiers of physics and cosmology, especially as interpreted by such sympathetic writers as David Bohm, Rupert Sheldrake, Ken Wilber, and Gary Zukov. The Theosophical stress on oneness, the consistent interaction of consciousness and matter, and the coexistence of many planes or dimensions are particularly mentioned. Out of such conceptions has come a recent Theosophical environmental ethic like that of Shirley Nicholson in *Ancient Wisdom, Modern Insight*, particularly Chapter 3, "Holism and

Hierarchy." Nicholson here views nature as a series of increasingly large "interlocking wholes," in which a prime imperative in any ethical choice involving nature – as do nearly all choices, ultimately – is taking into account its "reverberations" up and down the interlinked system.

Theosophy regards nature as alive, conscious on various levels, continuous with humanity both immanently and in evolutionary process, and so legitimately entitled to personification. Theosophical writers like Blavatsky, Annie Besant, C.W. Leadbeater, and Geoffrey Hodson, have not hesitated to personify powers of nature with names generally derived from venerable mythologies regarded as vehicles of the Ancient Wisdom. Out of theosophy's classic texts emerge creative Dhyan Chohans (cosmic buddhas or, in Western parlance, archangels), Sanat Kumara the world-spirit and Kwanyin or Mary as world-mother, devas who serve as guardians of particular places or phenomena of nature, on down to "elementals" and the elves or dryads of garden and field. Some of these identifications have become more and more commonplace as part of the New Age attempt at reenchantment of the world through recovery of enlivening perceptions of nature recalled from childhood or folklore. As Leadbeater put it, "It is one of the most beautiful characteristics of Theosophy that it gives back to people in a more rational form everything which was really useful and helpful to them in the religions which they have outgrown" (Leadbeater 1928: 1).

In both the personification of natural entities and its efforts toward reconciling science and spirituality, Theosophy's distinctive attitude toward nature has had an impact on recent nature spirituality generally.

Robert Ellwood

Further Reading
Goswami, Amit. *The Self-Aware Universe*. New York: Tarcher/Putnam, 1995.
Greenwalt, Emmett A. *California Utopia: Point Loma, 1897–1942*. San Diego: Point Loma Publications, 1978 (2nd rev. edn).
Hodson, Geoffrey. *The Kingdom of the Gods*. Adyar, Madras, India: Theosophical Publishing House, 1972.
Leadbeater C.W. *Invisible Helpers*. Madras, India: Theosophical Publishing House, 1928.
Nicholson, Shirley. *Ancient Wisdom, Modern Insight*. Wheaton, IL: Theosophical Publishing House, 1985.
See also: Blavatsky, Helena Patrovna; Bohm, David; Hinduism; Krishnamurti, Jiddhu; Sheldrake, Rupert; Swimme, Brian; Theosophy and Ecofeminism; Wilber, Ken.

Theosophy and Ecofeminism

The international Theosophical movement founded by Helena Petrovna Blavatsky in the 1870s has kept alive in the West the ancient belief that meaningful relationships can occur between human beings and other animals and plants. Some ecofeminisms posit a special bond between women and nature other than that based on shared or interdependent patriarchal oppression; while many ecofeminists celebrate the special connections between women and nonhuman nature. Ecofeminism and feminist spirituality have, however, lacked compelling cosmologies, whereas the core Theosophical idea is of a cosmos permeated by energetic relations that manifest themselves as different forms of consciousness. Theosophy, on the other hand, has not been interested in the question of under what conditions one gender is better able than another to have special relationships with animals or plants or places. Ecofeminism and feminist spirituality, however, have had this concern.

Connecting Theosophy and ecofeminism is the pioneering work done by women Theosophical leaders to restore ecological health to the movement's various communities. Madame Blavatsky's famous garden in England; what historian Emmett Greenwalt has called Katherine Tingley's "agricultural Eden" at Point Loma, California; and the grounds at the Theosophical Society's international headquarters at Adyar, India in which Annie Besant took considerable interest, were all early twentieth-century efforts to infuse ecology with concepts from Theosophy's cosmology. Findhorn, Scotland, and Perelandra, Virginia, are related recent examples of communities sustained largely, although not exclusively, by communication between women and nonhuman nature (by Eileen Caddy and Dorothy Maclean and by Machaelle Small Wright, respectively).

Jan C. Dawson

Further Reading
Gaard, Greta, ed. *Ecofeminism: Women, Animals, Nature*. Philadelphia: Temple University Press, 1993.
Nicholson, Shirley and Brenda Rosen, eds. *Gaia's Hidden Life: The Unseen Intelligence of Nature*. Wheaton, IL: Quest Books, 1992.
Tompkins, Peter and Christopher Bird. *The Secret Life of Plants*. New York: Harper & Row, 1973.
See also: Ecofeminism (various); Findhorn Foundation/Community (Scotland); Krishnamurti, Jiddhu; Theosophy.

Thoreau, Henry David (1817–1862)

Henry David Thoreau was an author, naturalist and leading member of the nineteenth-century literary, social and religious movement that came to be known as Transcendentalism. Thoreau is best remembered for his two-year venture in "living deliberately" on the shores of Walden Pond in his hometown of Concord, Massachusetts from 4 July 1845 to 6 September 1847, an experiment which led to the publication of *Walden* in 1854. Though few of his writings were widely known at mid-century, his work became increasingly sought after in the late nineteenth and twentieth centuries. His other well-known published writings include: *A Week on the Concord and Merrimack Rivers* (1849), *Cape Cod* (1865) and *The Maine Woods* (1864).

Even in his own time, local responses to Thoreau's experiment at Walden helped to shape two competing portraits of Thoreau that have persisted into the present: Thoreau as "wilderness man" *par excellence*, living self-sufficiently in the wild woods and, to a lesser extent, Thoreau as hypocritical crank, grinding his literary ax to chop at society and its conventions, while regularly going into town and dipping into the maternal cookie jar. While both of these portraits contain some truths, they are caricatures of a man and his work that often miss the complexity of his vision and the multifaceted dimensions of his legacy.

Thoreau's sojourn at Walden was never intended to be an attempt at perfect self-sufficiency or wilderness living. In terms of setting alone, Thoreau's retreat to Walden cannot be considered a wilderness venture, as Concord in the mid-nineteenth century had been a settled village for two centuries. Thoreau's purpose in going to Walden should be understood as practical, spiritual and symbolic, none of which demanded a lifelong retreat to the woods or absolute purity in his practice of self-reliance.

Practically, Thoreau sought a means of making a living which would preserve the time he desired in order to cultivate his craft as a writer, while maintaining a mode of life that permitted generous swaths of time for outdoor walks, leisure and meticulous nature study. The retreat to Walden was, at a fundamental level, a first step in solving the practical problem of livelihood that all writers face.

The spiritual dimensions of Thoreau's decision were tied to the practical impetus behind his choice, but also went beyond them. While Thoreau sought to reduce his needs (of food, clothing, shelter and leisure) to a minimum in order to maximize time to write, this pursuit of simplicity was itself a form of spiritual practice. With Emerson and other New England Transcendentalists, Thoreau subscribed to principles of plain living: a simple, often vegetarian diet; avoidance of tea, coffee and alcohol; regular excursions in the fresh air, frequent intellectual interchange and a complementary pursuit of solitary contemplation. All of these practices were understood to be means of cultivating the self and, more particularly, "Reason" (knowledge through intuition) and imagination. In addition, Thoreau (like other Transcendentalists) assumed that nature had particular lessons to teach and that simple, "natural" ways of living would help to cultivate his moral sense. The spiritual practice of "self-culture" (which began when the young Thoreau changed his name from David Henry to Henry David) was an essential aspect of the retreat to Walden.

The experiment at Walden was also intended to resonate symbolically, both in Concord and beyond. While living at Walden enabled Thoreau to develop inwardly (to learn about himself in a natural context, to practice his craft as a writer, and also to grieve the early death of his brother), his life at Walden was also intended to be an outwardly directed comment about (and against) prevailing social norms. While he farmed beans for part of his livelihood, he denigrated the commercial aspects of farming and praised instead the educational and spiritual benefits of tilling the soil. While he made trips to the village almost daily, Thoreau constantly criticized village life, particularly the idle conversation and status-seeking mores he felt dominated the town.

Although he cultivated a sometimes biting and misanthropic persona in his texts, Thoreau's reputation as a misanthrope is inaccurate. Thoreau was no hermit. He enjoyed frequent visitors from among family, friends and laborers near the pond and went into town frequently, especially in the winter months when he supported himself with odd jobs as a handyman and surveyor. During his time at Walden, he maintained an active correspondence, regularly attended lectures and often appeared at gatherings at the homes of Ralph Waldo Emerson, Bronson Alcott and other Concord friends. Through the symbolic act of withdrawing to the woods, Thoreau intended not to recommend such a withdrawal for everyone, but rather to symbolize through deed (and then word) the virtues of independent thought and action, rather than behaving in line with social convention.

Walden (1854) is Thoreau's most celebrated text, a carefully crafted manuscript that went through eight drafts before publication. Thoreau's ambitious reworking of the material from his journals included the adoption of a seasonal structure (summer to spring) and the collapsing of two actual years into a single narrative one, a model nature writers have followed to this day. The text stands as the most complex fusion of his post-Christian, Transcendentalist religious orientation with his detailed and scientifically informed observation of a particular natural surround. *A Week on the Concord and Merrimack Rivers* (1849), which preceded Walden (and was a publishing failure) is more obviously metaphorical. While a travel narrative in some respects, it is interspersed with philosophical departures, essays, poems and fragments from

Thoreau's reading, while also intending to serve as an elegy to his brother, John. Throughout the text, attention to natural detail appears and recedes, but ultimately takes a back seat to Transcendentalist philosophy and the workings of Thoreau's young literary and religious imagination. Thoreau's late writings lean in the other direction, his unpublished manuscripts on seed dispersion and the development of flora in Concord (recently collected and published posthumously as *Faith in a Seed* [1993] and *Wild Fruits* [1999]) contain still accurate and scientific useful documentation of the growth, development and distribution of plants in New England.

When traced through the corpus of his writing, Thoreau's view of nature is clearly a dynamic one, shifting and changing in response to Thoreau's own growth as a writer and his synthesis of naturalistic observations accumulated over the years. In general terms, Thoreau's interpretive stance toward nature is a view shaped by his European and New England, Protestant heritage, yet defying easy categorization. It is neither Christian, nor secular; neither wholly scientific, nor traditionally religious. With the European Romantics, and older Transcendentalists, Thoreau saw nature as something other than simply God's creation (the traditional Christian view and one that was itself comparatively neglected by Christians of his day, who placed more emphasis on personal salvation).

Thoreau was a lifelong critic of the Church, even the liberal Unitarian church attended by the majority of his family. His vision of nature was pursued outside the boundaries of both Christian orthodoxy and liberalism and his contemporaries therefore often criticized his writing (or expurgated it) because of its "paganistic" tendencies. Even Thoreau's Aunt Maria worried that portions of *A Week* sounded like "blasphemy" both because of Thoreau's approving nods toward Buddhism and Hinduism, as well as his claims that the divine could be found *within* both nature and humanity. While *Walden* was a comparative success, the same kinds of criticisms came from more theologically conservative circles, who praised the examples of detailed "nature study" in the text, but not the more radical philosophical and religious themes.

Thoreau's approach to the natural world was particularly informed by his reading of the Romantics, who saw nature as the ultimate source of insight and a means of return to childhood innocence untainted by "civilization's" expectations and failings. Thoreau's sense of ethics and aesthetics emerged from the Romantic (and later, Transcendentalist) presumption that nature is the ideal teacher. His purpose was to cultivate himself, in return, as an ideal pupil. Yet such an embrace of nature was not wholly positive, nor was his construction of nature exclusively beneficent, though it was prevailingly so. The "Higher Laws" section of *Walden* show a Thoreau who is sometimes ill at ease with the unseemly, violent, or lowly aspects of nature (including his own body) and reveal a typical Transcendentalist and post-Christian preoccupation with purity: nature in her ideal, good and "higher" aspect. His writings of travels in the Maine woods also display an unexpected fear of the wilderness in its most rugged form. Overall, however, nature is a source of goodness and a model for humanity in Thoreau's view.

Nature occupied a space in Thoreau's imagination that his Christian neighbors reserved for God. Thoreau enjoyed needling others with this unorthodox, but increasingly popular, approach, commenting toward the end of his life that "a snowstorm was more to him than Christ" (Harding 1965: 464). Thoreau was also influenced by the newly (and sometimes inaccurately) translated Eastern religious and philosophical texts becoming available in America, which gave testimony to the sacredness of particular aspects of the physical world (mountains, rivers, etc.) Thoreau welcomed the *Vedas, The Laws of Manu* and purported sayings of the Buddha into his literary repertoire (using them often to support his own Transcendentalist assertions) and argued for the equal legitimacy of the religions of the world. In addition, he drew deeply – though perhaps less consciously – on a broader legacy of Christian and especially Protestant, New England interpretations of nature as a book to be read, the so-called "Book of Nature." While leaving Christian theology behind, Thoreau retained the Christian – and particularly, American – legacy of finding in nature lessons and morals for leading an ethical life. While rejecting traditional Christian typology, Thoreau maintained a "typological stance" toward nature, seeing lessons for humanity in battles between ants, the lure of the woodchuck and the play of the loon.

Thoreau's daily practice of attentiveness toward nature, however, enabled him to go beyond a "reading" of nature only for moral and spiritual guidance. His daily walks became a means for gathering precise naturalistic data within the limited boundaries of a particular watershed over several decades, an invaluable contribution – before its time – that leaves us with a thick ecological portrait of a particular bioregion. His "amateur" conclusions regarding the succession of trees, his identification of rare plants and his innovations in everything from pencil-making to predicting ways to lengthen the cranberry harvest were all discoveries that were independently supported or produced by professionals in later years.

While Thoreau's Transcendentalism always led him to see "more" in nature than a scientist would discern, his unflagging curiosity and rigorous record-keeping also helped him to become a self-taught naturalist and to establish literary naturalism as an American genre. More than any other Transcendentalist, Thoreau wove together contemporary scientific knowledge and liberal, post-Christian interpretations of nature's symbolic capacity. On the other hand, Thoreau's criticism of Christian institutions, his insistence on seeing the divine *in* nature (and in the self) and his respect for other religious traditions of the world opened his writing up to charges of paganism and pantheism that persist in conservative, evangelical circles. Yet a close reading of Thoreau's work clearly reveals its intellectual and spiritual debt to New England Protestantism. His thinking and writing is "post-Christian" more than it is anti-Christian, pantheistic or pagan. Like Emerson, but going beyond him, Thoreau knitted together a Protestant heritage, a philosophical interest in idealism and a passion for observation and study of natural phenomena in the field.

Today, Thoreau's legacy is less felt in religious circles than it is in environmental ones. Hand in hand with the growth of the environmental movement from the 1960s forward has been an ever-increasing enthusiasm for Thoreau's work, though few read more than portions of *Walden*. Thoreau's relative self-sufficiency, his concerns about the marketplace and emerging capitalism, and his view of nature as a beneficent source of spiritual transformation all contributed to the dominant themes of contemporary environmentalism: a growing interest in simple, sustainable living, a critique of consumer culture and a view of nature as the source for personal (often spiritual) renewal.

Though prone to misrepresentation, Thoreau's writing and his example continue to speak to both religious and non-religious audiences, to scientists and to humanists, to those who read nature symbolically and to those who simply admire the vast records of this "self-appointed inspector" of snowstorms.

Rebecca Kneale Gould

Further Reading

Buell, Lawrence. *The Environmental Imagination: Thoreau, Nature Writing and American Culture.* Cambridge, MA: The Belknap Press of Harvard University Press, 1995.

Cameron, Sharon. *Writing Nature: Henry Thoreau's "Journal."* New York: Oxford University Press, 1985.

Cavell, Stanley. *The Senses of Walden.* New York: Viking, 1972.

Harding, Walter. *The Days of Henry Thoreau: A Biography.* New York: Knopf, 1965.

Peck, Daniel. *Thoreau's Morning Work.* New Haven: Yale University Press, 1990.

Richardson, Robert D., Jr. *Henry David Thoreau: A Life of the Mind.* Berkeley: University of California Press, 1986.

Shanley, James Lyndon. *The Making of Walden.* Chicago: University of Chicago Press, 1957.

See also: Back to the Land Movements; Book of Nature; Emerson, Ralph Waldo; Radical Environmentalism; Transcendentalism; Unitarianism.

Tibet and Central Asia

The Tibetan form of Buddhism is the dominant religious system throughout the Tibetan plateau, and is also widespread in surrounding areas, particularly Mongolia, northern Nepal, Bhutan, areas of Central Asia and Russia, and the northern Indian regions of Sikkim and Ladakh. Buddhism was first introduced to Tibet during the early dynastic period from the seventh to ninth centuries. Following the demise of the Yarlung dynasty (so called because its power base was the Yarlung Valley of central Tibet), Buddhism's influence declined until it was reintroduced in the twelfth century. In the following centuries it became increasingly popular throughout the Tibetan plateau as well as neighboring states.

The main sources of Tibetan Buddhism were the great north Indian monastic universities and charismatic Tantric lineages that were centered in Bengal and Bihar. The Buddhism of the monastic universities emphasized scholasticism along with meditative practice, and the Tantric lineages taught a more meditation-oriented form of practice based on visualization and ritual practices. The present-day forms of Tibetan Buddhism are mainly derived from these two sources.

From the mid-seventeenth century until 1959, Tibet was ruled by the Dalai Lamas or their regents. The Dalai Lamas are believed to be physical manifestations of the Buddha Avalokiteŷvara (Tibetan: Chenrezi), and the present one, Tenzin Gyatso (b. 1935), is the fourteenth incarnation. In 1950 China invaded and annexed Tibet, and in 1959, following an abortive popular uprising against Chinese rule, he fled to India, where he established a government-in-exile headquartered in Dharamsala in the north Indian state of Himachal Predesh.

In many ways, Buddhism might seem to be an unpromising religion for someone seeking conceptual resources for an environmental ethic. According to Buddhist doctrine, all sentient beings are reborn over and over as a result of their actions (*karma*), and the world is conceived as a place of suffering. The ultimate goal of Buddhist practice is liberation from the world and the cycle of rebirth, and cyclic existence is conceived as irredeemably unsatisfactory. There is no way to fix it up and make it bearable, but despite these attitudes, Buddhists have traditionally asserted the importance of avoiding harm to the environment. In the Indian text Dhammapada, for example, one of the distinguishing features of an awakened being (buddha) is that he or she avoids harming plants and animals and lives in harmony with the surrounding environment.

In recent decades, a number of Tibetan Buddhist thinkers have developed a Buddhist approach to environmentalism based on the doctrine of interdependence (*pratitya-samutpada*), which holds that all things come into being in dependence upon causes and conditions and change in every moment as a result of causes and conditions. The world is conceived as an infinitely complex causal network in which each individual part acts on all other parts while simultaneously being influenced by its surrounding environment. These notions are connected with the Buddhist doctrine of no-self (*anatman*), which holds that there is no enduring "self" or "soul" and that living beings are instead individual continuums composed of various constituent elements that are changing with every moment. This process operates in intimate connection with the surrounding environment, and there is said to be no real dividing line between oneself and the world. Thus, concern for oneself naturally extends to concern for the environment. The fourteenth Dalai Lama has become one of the leading proponents of this idea, and he claims that prior to the Chinese invasion Tibetans did in fact live in harmony with the environment.

Some contemporary commentators dismiss this idea, claiming that prior to the mid-twentieth century Tibet was an agrarian society in which most people subsisted on low-technology agriculture and animal husbandry. Prior to the Chinese invasion, the utilization of biomass was closely related to the physical conditions of Tibet, which had a stable population and little change in agricultural or animal husbandry techniques for centuries. Furthermore, in vast areas of the Tibetan plateau the poor soil and sparse vegetation required that people avoid overgrazing and overfarming. Most of what people consumed came directly from the Earth, and their waste products were mainly biodegradable and were returned to the environment. Thus the fact that they maintained a sustainable approach to the environment was non-reflective and merely a direct result of their technological backwardness and the physical limitations of their environment.

There is some merit to this idea, and it is doubtful that most Tibetans had (or have) a consciously articulated environmental ethic that guided their approach to the environment, but there were also significant conceptual factors influencing the Tibetan approach to the natural world. In addition to Buddhist doctrines of nonviolence and interdependence, there were also pre-Buddhist animistic ideas about the Tibetan plateau, which was seen as the abode of innumerable forces that owned the land. Among these were the *sadak* ("lords of the Earth"), and *lu* (water spirits), which respectively guarded the soil and water. Ethnographic studies of contemporary Tibetans have demonstrated that belief in these natural forces is widespread and that Tibetans commonly assert that people who cause harm to the environment draw the wrath of these beings, who can cause great harm to humans. Any building or construction is commonly preceded by a ceremony that asks their permission, and great care is taken to avoid angering them by causing unnecessary damage to the Earth. In addition, mining was almost unknown in Tibet, because it was thought that digging up the Earth to extract resources was effectively robbing the "lords of the Earth," who would inflict punishment on the offenders.

Similarly, polluting water causes the *lu* to harm offenders, and prior to the Chinese takeover, Tibet's rivers and lakes had some of the most unpolluted water in the world. In addition, exile Tibetans often point with pride to the fact that hunting was outlawed by the fifth Dalai Lama in 1642. According to his official decree, all birds, fish, and non-predatory animals were protected by law. Since at least that time, Tibetans have generally avoided killing wild animals and fishing for sport, and travelers in Tibet prior to the Chinese invasion often remarked at the large herds of grazing antelopes, wild ass, and deer that were found throughout the region. Moreover, because Tibetans generally avoided cutting down trees there were extensive old-growth forests in the lower regions of the Tibetan plateau.

Although environmental concern has become an important theme in publications by the Tibetan government-in-exile, there is little evidence of this concern prior to the mid-1980s, when the Dalai Lama first began articulating the notion that Tibetans have for centuries consciously protected the environment. The first exile government statements on the environment followed the publication of reports of widespread environmental damage to the Tibetan plateau by the Chinese, and the exiles' environmental awakening was at least partly reflexive and political. Particularly during the chaotic period of the Cultural Revolution (1966–1976), when marginal land was taken over for agriculture and forests were clear-cut, many animal species were hunted to extinction, and significant – and in many cases probably irreversible – damage was done to Tibet's fragile ecosystem. Thus the exile government's newly pro-environment stance was part of a larger polemical attack on China's annexation of their country and its subsequent record in administering it.

Several commentators have also noted that even the language used in Tibetan publications on the environment indicates that conscious concern with environmental issues is part of the discourse of modernism, in which Tibetans and other indigenous people have been constructed as "naturally green" by Westerners seeking to construct an idealized primitive "other" whose practices implicitly critique those of technologically advanced societies. It should also be noted that much of the vocabulary used in Tibetan exile publications on the environment is derived not from Buddhist doctrine but instead employs contemporary Western notions and language. The "greening" of Tibet and Tibetan Buddhism is also connected with the discourse of Buddhist modernism, which portrays Buddhism as essentially "rational" and "scientific" and represents Buddhism as the conceptual basis of social movements like environmentalism, human rights activism, social reform, and feminism.

There is no reason to believe that the widespread

influence of Buddhism contributed significantly to the general practice of sustainable agriculture and animal husbandry in Tibet, nor that the exile government's pronouncements and publications on the environment have significantly affected either attitudes or practices toward the environment. These publications are the work of a small, educated elite, and the massive accumulation of garbage along the roadways of Dharamsala – along with the common practices of spitting, urinating, and defecating into public water supplies – is ample demonstration of this. It should be noted, however, that although Tibetans have only recently begun to articulate environmental concerns, and the leading figures are a small elite group, there is some evidence that their message is gaining ground at least among the Tibetan exile community, and there have been several grassroots campaigns to clean up their environment in recent years.

John Powers

Further Reading
Atisha, Tenzin P. "The Tibetan Approach to Ecology." *Tibetan Review* 25:2 (1991), 9–14.
Clarke, Graham E. "Tradition, Modernity, and Environmental Change in Tibet." In Thierry Dodin and Heinz Räther, eds. *Imagining Tibet: Perceptions, Projections, and Fantasies.* Boston: Wisdom Publications, 2001, 339–56.
Geshe Damdul Namgyal. "Buddhist Ecology – Its Theoretical Base." In *Tibet Environment and Development News.* Dharamsala: Department of Information and International Relations, 1994, 27–30.
Gyatso, Tenzin (Dalai Lama XIV). "His Holiness the XIV Dalai Lama on the Environment: Collected Statements." Dharamsala: Department of Information and International Relations Publications, 1994.
Huber, Toni. "Green Tibetans: A Brief Social History." In Frank J. Korom, ed. *Tibetan Culture in the Diaspora.* Wien: Verlag der Österreichischen Akademie der Wissenschaften, 1997, 103–19.
Räther, Heinz. "Views on Ecology among Tibetan Intellectuals." In Per Kvaerne, ed. *Tibetan Studies. Proceedings of the 6th Seminar of the International Association for Tibetan Studies.* Fagernes 1992, vol. 2. Oslo: Institute for Comparative Research in Human Culture, 1994, 670–5.
Schmithausen, Lambert. *Buddhism and Nature.* Tokyo: International Institute for Buddhist Studies, 1991.
Tucker, Mary Evelyn and Duncan Williams, eds. *Buddhism and Ecology: The Interconnection of Dharma and Deeds.* Cambridge, MA: Harvard University Center for the Study of World Religions, 1997.
See also: Bon (Tibet); Buddhism – Tibetan; Dalai Lama; Nepal; Sacred Mountains; Yunnan Region (Southwest China and Montane Mainland Southeast Asia).

P Tikkun Olam – A Jewish Imperative

At a time when there are almost daily reports about disturbing developments – global climate change; the destruction of tropical rainforests, coral reefs, and other habitats; soil erosion and depletion; air, water, and land pollution; desertification; droughts, severe storms; widening water shortages; and other threats – it is essential that Jews engage in *tikkun olam*, the mandate to repair, heal, and transform the world.

One of the main reasons that the world faces so many critical problems is that there are sharp deviations between its values and methods and basic Jewish teachings. Among the many Jewish teachings that should be applied as part of *tikkun olam* are the following:

- "The Earth is the Lord's and the fullness thereof" (Ps. 24:1) – we are to be partners and co-workers with God in protecting the environment (Talmud: *Shabbat* 10a).
- *Bal tashchit* – based on a torah teaching that we are not to destroy fruit-bearing trees, even in times of war (Deut. 20:19–20), the talmudic sages made a general ruling that we are not to waste or unnecessarily destroy anything of value.
- We are to imitate God in his attributes of compassion, justice, and mercy (Talmud: *Sotah* 14a) – since God is concerned about the Earth and its creatures, we should be as well.
- We are to "work the land and to guard it" (Gen. 2:15) This Torah teaching indicates that the dominion that people are given is not one of domination, but rather of responsible stewardship.
- "Justice, justice shall you pursue" (Deut. 16:20) The repetition of the word "justice" indicates that we are to practice justice, whether to our profit or loss, in word and action, and to Jew and non-Jew (Hertz 1957: 820).

As co-workers with God, charged with the task of being a light unto the nations and accomplishing *tikkun olam*, it is essential that Jews apply these and other teachings to the struggles to reduce pollution and the wasteful use of natural resources. We must proclaim that it is contrary to religious values to pollute the air and water, to slash and burn forests, and to wantonly destroy the abundant resources that God has so generously provided.

To reduce potential threats to the world, we must adopt simpler lifestyles. Religious institutions, schools, and private and governmental organizations must all play a role. We must redirect some of our industrial capacity toward recycling, solar energy, and mass transit. We must design products for long-term durability and ease of repair. We must revise our agricultural and industrial methods so that they are less wasteful of resources and energy. Perhaps there should be a Presidential Commission appointed solely to consider how we can stop being such a wasteful society.

We should make *tikkun olam* a major focus of our synagogues, Jewish schools, and other Jewish groups and institutions in order to help move our precious planet to a path that is more just, humane, and sustainable. Changing will not be easy, since our society and economy are based on consumption and convenience, using and discarding. But it is essential that we make supreme efforts, for the survival of humanity may be at stake.

Richard Schwartz

Further Reading

Amsel, Nachum. *The Jewish Encyclopedia of Moral and Ethical Issues*. Northvale, NJ: Jason Aronson, 1996.

Hertz, J.H. *The Pentateuch and Haftorahs*. London: Soncino, 1957.

Regenstein, Lewis. *Replenish the Earth: The Teachings of the World's Religions on Protecting Animals and the Environment*. New York: Crossroads, 1991.

Rose, Aubrey, ed. *Judaism and Ecology*. New York and London: Cassell, 1992.

Schwartz, Richard H. *Judaism and Global Survival*. New York: Lantern, 2002.

Shatz, H., Chaim I. Waxman and Nathan J. Diament, eds. *Tikkun Olam: Social Responsibility in Jewish Thought and Law*. Northvale, NJ: Jason Aronson, 1997.

Waskow, Arthur I., ed. *Torah of the Earth: Exploring 4,000 Years of Ecology in Jewish Thought*. Woodstock, VT: Jewish Lights, 2000 (2 vols).

See also: Eco-kabbalah; Hasidism and Nature Mysticism; Hebrew Bible; Israel and Environmentalism; Jewish Environmentalism in North America; Judaism; Kabbalah and Eco-theology; Vegetarianism and Judaism; Waskow, Rabbi Arthur.

Toland, John (1670–1722)

Historians describe John Toland as a multifaceted man – a philosopher, a writer, a linguist, a polemicist, a diplomat, a biblical scholar, a deist, and ultimately a proponent of pantheism. Lexicographers credit Toland with the first English-language usage of the term pantheist.

Born near Londonderry, Ireland on 30 November 1670, and christened in the Catholic Church, Toland converted to Protestantism around age 15. Subsequent higher education and an inquiring mind led him to extensive questioning of accepted religious doctrines. Toland acquired a degree from the University of Edinburgh in 1690, and studied further in England, Germany, and Holland.

A friend described Toland as "a free-spirited, ingenious man" (in Berman 1997: 223). But his unorthodox views forced him to move from place to place to avoid prosecution, and made it hard to earn a living. Toland penned political pamphlets and biographies for aristocratic patrons. He wrote prolifically on a wide range of subjects, including religious tolerance and civil liberty.

A large bibliography lists almost two hundred works authored or ascribed to him. He claimed to know ten languages and often published anonymously or in a foreign tongue to keep critics at bay. An important early book, *Christianity Not Mysterious*, provoked controversy because it claimed that human reason could explain biblical mysteries. Clerics burned the book and one official requested, "that Mr. Toland himself should be burnt" (in Berman 1997: 226). But Toland's work garnered fame as well as fusillades. He discussed philosophy with notables like the German thinker Wilhelm von Leibniz, and the Queen of Prussia, Sophia Charlotte.

Despite ill health and financial woes, Toland remained productive to the end of his life. He wrote *Physic without Physicians* shortly before he died, decrying his doctor's inept treatment: "They learn their Art at the hazard of our lives, and make experiments by our deaths" (Toland in Mossner 1967: 141). Toland's self-written epitaph concluded, "If you would know more of him Search his Writings" (in Berman 1997: 229).

A book Toland wrote in 1705 entitled *Socinianism truly stated . . . recommended by a Pantheist to an orthodox friend* contains the first known use of the term "pantheist" in an English-language publication. (Earlier, in 1697, Cambridge mathematician Joseph Raphson coined the words "pantheist" and "pantheism" in a theological work written in Latin; Toland had read and commented upon Raphson's book). In 1709, a Toland critic named J. Fay used the term "pantheism" in English, and both terms quickly became common. Toland's use of the term appears to derive from the pantheization of his religious outlook, as reflected in his later works, although some scholars question his committal to any particular religion.

Toland had previously expressed pantheistic theory in *Clito* (1700) and in *Letters to Serena* (1704), but had not employed the term. He thought "All things were full of God," and pronounced that "The sun is my father, the Earth my mother, the world is my brother and all men are my family" (members.aol.com/pantheism0/toland.htm).

The Roman materialist Lucritius and especially the Italian philosopher Giordano Bruno (martyred for his pantheistic beliefs in 1600) greatly influenced Toland's perspective.

Toland detailed his own pantheism in *Pantheisticon: sive Formula celebrandae Sodalitatis Socraticae/Pantheisticon: or, the Form of Celebrating the Socratic Society* (1720, anonymous English translation, 1751). He believed in a boundless universe. He visualized the unity of all matter and the ceaseless motion of atoms. He spurned personal immortality yet averred that "Nothing dies totally, the death of one thing brings the birth of another, by a universally reciprocal exchange, and everything contributes necessarily to the preservation and welfare of the Whole" (members.aol.com/pantheism0/toland.htm).

John Toland had a significant impact on his generation during the Age of Enlightenment. And he brought the concept of pantheism as well as the word "pantheist" into wider circulation, a term now commonly used by philosophers, theologians, and nature religionists throughout the world.

Gary Suttle

Further Reading

(Most of John Toland's works remain out of print and are available only in rare library collections.)

Berman, David. "The Irish Freethinker." In Philip McGuinness, Alan Harrison and Richard Kearney, eds. *John Toland's Christianity Not Mysterious: Text, Associated Works and Critical Essays*. Dublin, Ireland: The Lilliput Press, 1997.

Berman, David. "John Toland." In Gordon Stein, ed. *The Encyclopedia of Unbelief*. Buffalo: Prometheus Press, 1985, 668–70.

Daniel, Stephen H. "Toland's Semantic Pantheism." In Philip McGuinnes, Alan Harrison and Richard Kearney, eds. *John Toland's Christianity Not Mysterious: Text, Associated Works and Critical Essays*. Dublin: The Lilliput Press, 1997, 303–12.

Daniel, Stephen H. *John Toland: His Method, Manners, and Mind*. Kingston and Montreal: McGill-Queen's University Press, 1984.

Mossner, Ernest Campbell. "John Toland." In Paul Edwards, ed. *The Encyclopedia of Philosophy*. New York: Macmillan Publishing Company Inc. and The Free Press, 1967.

Oxford English Dictionary. Second Edition, 1989.

See also: Corrington, Robert S.; Pantheism; Raphson, Joseph; Spinoza, Baruch.

Tolstoy Farm

Huw "Piper" Williams was a peace activist who founded an open-land community on some of his family's farm property in eastern Washington State in 1963, seeking to promote a Christian lifestyle of simplicity, self-reliance, and cooperation. His inspiration came from some of the religious essays of Tolstoy and from the nonviolent philosophy and activism of Gandhi. Friends from the peace movement and the Catholic Worker movement soon joined him. The sole rule at Tolstoy Farm was that no one could be asked to leave, which meant that all differences would have to be worked out directly and peacefully.

The poverty at Tolstoy in its early years was striking, with dozens of residents trying to eke out survival with antiquated farm equipment and a cash income of only a few dollars per person per month. Over time, however, the community managed to acquire 240 acres of land in two tracts and, as the counterculture became more popular and Tolstoy's reputation spread, it attracted large numbers of visitors, some of whom stayed and built their own houses. The farm's lack of rules meant that social life tended to consist of a rather freewheeling anarchy. Williams, who eventually married and had children, finally left and later founded another organic, self-sufficient farming community, Earth Cycle Farm, 25 miles away. Tolstoy endured, however, becoming more stable as the permanent residents improved their homes (some have installed off-the-grid power systems) and continued to strive for rural self-sufficiency. In recent years, many members have embraced Earth-centered religions, holding an annual all-night Corn Dance, full moon rituals, and community sweats. In 2000, Tolstoy reported about fifty members.

Timothy Miller

Further Reading

Davidson, Sara. "Open Land: Getting Back to the Communal Garden." *Harper's* (June 1970).

Fairfield, Richard. *Communes USA: A Personal Tour*. Baltimore: Penguin, 1972.

Miller, Timothy. *The 60s Communes*. Syracuse: Syracuse University Press, 1999.

See also: Anarchism; Back to the Land Movements; Hippies; New Religious Movements.

Torres Strait Islanders (Australia)

Torres Strait Islanders, who are, with Aborigines, one of two peoples indigenous to Australia, are grounded in continuous exchanges between people, kin groups, and the natural and numinous worlds. Of the 100 or so islands strewn over the 150km-wide, 10–15-meter-deep seas that lie between the Western Province of Papua New Guinea and the Cape York tip of the Australian mainland, 16 support communities. The current geography of Torres Strait has been in existence since approximately 6500 BP. Islander society is generally regarded as Melanesian, particularly on the northern islands, although those living in the southwest of the Strait share cultural characteristics with Cape York Aborigines. While Torres Strait Islanders originate in the Strait, over 80 percent of people who identify as Islanders in Australia (around 29,000), are resident on the Australian mainland where they cherish their island of origin, family history, totemic, wind and star affiliations. The enduring attachment of Islanders to their land was made evident in the historical Murray Island Land Case of 1992, the most significant legal acknowledgement of indigenous rights and interests in Australia. The High Court of Australia recognized the Meriam peoples ownership, occupation and possession of their Mer (Murray Island) land, overturning the concept of *terra nullius* (land belonging to no one) that had guided Australian courts and governments on questions of indigenous rights to their lands since settlement in 1788.

Torres Strait Islanders were traditionally a maritime people who combined small-scale agriculture (growing yams, taro, cassava, sweet potato, bananas and coconuts) with marine and land foraging to meet their subsistence needs. By the turn of the twentieth century colonization had impacted on the elaborate horticultural and marine rituals that ensured the continuation of the seasonal calendar and increased the produce of the sea and land. Despite colonization a great deal of the worldview that encompassed these rituals continues to inform the experience of Islanders today. Religious rituals were transitional points that substantiated relations of responsibility and care between Islanders, the natural and the numinous. Thus, the ceremonial display and feasting of harvested yams publicly expressed appropriate uses of land through an exchange of energies between gardeners and soil resulting in the yield and the recognition of various social relationships by sharing the produce through a feast. The numinous dimension resided in a complex interaction between moral behavior, environmental care, and environmental behavior. In a worldview that understands the environment to express the actions of the people to which it is related, including Ancestors, uses of land through gardening and the sea through fishing or marine hunting (turtle and dugong [sea cow]) are relationships of nurturance and responsibility.

On the island of Mabuiag, it is said that a person is constantly connected to key sites in their family and clan lands through an imperceptible umbilical link. The smell of a person who has tended a food garden is recognized by plants in that garden and quickens their growth. Prosperous gardeners, healthy bodies and the plentiful provision of foodstuffs reflect a mutually constituting exchange and resource ceremonies gave regular public expression to these relationships. In contrast a person who does not care for the places they attain responsibility for, which can simultaneously include reefs, foreshores, cays, rivers, waterholes, stars, winds and lands, either through lack of visitation and resource use or morally objectionable behavior, can have an adverse effect on these locations and social relationships that are integral to relationships of place.

While colonialism has had great impact on Islander society, the rich cultural meanings and beliefs that inspired lapsed horticultural and marine ceremonies continued or transformed to emerge in new forms. The display of garden produce found a place in the church calendar of the Anglican (Episcopalian) church for roughly the first half of the twentieth century as Torres Strait Islanders gathered harvests and piled them for show on important days of yearly church commemoration. Harvests are no longer publicly displayed through the religious calendar, but prestige is still accorded to men who provide turtle, dugong and ceremonial yams of long length and succulence, and to women who provide crabs and fish for church-based feasts. Also, the migration of many Islanders away from their traditional places of residence in the last half-century has led to the development of new relationships of care that transcend the inability to be present and active at particular places. Islanders maintain these connections by reciting memories, creating songs and dances that evoke significant associations to land and sea, and writing genealogies, seasonal and cosmological information, and agricultural and marine practices in family-owned manuscripts. These compositions sustain relationships to place by recording and making available the intricate connections between people, place and the numinous to family members physically separated from their terrestrial and marine territories.

The sea and landscapes of Torres Strait are permeated with individual, collective and cosmological histories in which personal experience and movement has constant reference to Ancestral activities and totemic affiliations. The mythical narratives in which Ancestral Beings construct the sacred geography of the region (*adhiad*) provide an important schema for relating individual identity, relationships to place and relationships between peoples and groups. Alongside mythical narratives of Ancestors who rarely participate in daily affairs exist active family-oriented Ancestral Beings that share responsibility for the nurturance of territories particular to their family or clan group. On the island of Saibai the identification of people with their terrestrial territories is given fullest expression through relationships with family Ancestral Beings called *muruyg*, who take the shape of snakes. *Muruyg* are recognized as being high-status Ancestors who have gardened at a particular area as humans and have over a long period of time transformed into snakes with special powers. Their presence around garden beds that they were associated with in human life is propitious for cultivated crops and if a fire has devastated a garden they help bring it back to good health. They also act in a protective manner for their descendants' lands and sometimes extend the range of their activities to include monitoring other lands within a clan estate.

At present, Islanders in the Strait face significant issues of environmental care. High levels of trace metals in marine biota, some of which may originate in the Ok Tedi outflow (located in the headwaters of the Ok Tedi, a tributary of the Fly River) may render some marine foods inedible for Islanders. Also, Islanders are unable to support the high cost of licenses and infrastructure needed to take advantage of lucrative local commercial fisheries.

Accessing the wealth from this industry would help establish independent economic security, resource management and sustainability and continue long-established affinities to the marine environment.

Richard Davis

Further Reading
Beckett, Jeremy. *Torres Strait Islanders: Custom and Colonialism.* Cambridge: Cambridge University Press, 1989.
Lawrie, Margaret. *Myths and Legends of Torres Strait.* St. Lucia, Queensland: University of Queensland Press, 1970.
Mosby, Tom and Brian Robinson. *Ilan Pasin (This is Our Way): Torres Strait Art.* Cairns: Cairns Regional Gallery, 1988.
Sharp, Nonie. *No Ordinary Judgement: Mabo, The Murray Islanders Land Case.* Canberra: Aboriginal Studies Press, 1996.
Sharp, Nonie. *Stars of Tagai: The Torres Strait Islanders.* Canberra: Aboriginal Studies Press, 1993.

See also: Australia; Pacific Islands.

Totemic Practices in Borgu (West Africa)

Borgu straddles present-day Republic of Benin and Nigeria in West Africa. Before its partition by the British and the French in 1898, Borgu covered a vast expanse of land, stretching from the Atakora mountains in the west to the River Niger in the east, with three main kingdoms (Bussa, Illo, and Nikki) and several chiefdoms. The major towns included Bussa, Illo, Kaiama, and Nikki. The Borgu people spoke several languages, but the major ones were Batonu and Boko. In spite of the partition and linguistic differences, the people practised similar religious belief systems. Before the penetration of Islam and Christianity, the Borgu people associated religion with nature by worshipping the sun, moon, rocks, and rivers. They demonstrated the intersection of nature and religion by venerating animal, reptile, bird, and plant totems. Thus, the forces of nature brought spiritual attraction.

A British colonial officer described Borgu religion as "a fumble of superstitions, with strong indications of totemism," but this religious belief system was not unique to the Borgu society because the veneration of natural phenomena was a common concept in West Africa. A mystic relationship existed between an individual or clan and an animal, bird, or plant totem whereby the totem could not be killed or eaten. This practice was common among individuals of both sexes and clans. The people believed in the existence of spirits who were invoked or appeased by particular rites. In the Batonu language, totems are referred to as *shesheru*.

The most prominent animal totems were the leopard and the red antelope but others included the weaverbird, monitor lizard, rabbit, and crab. Reptiles, such as the python and cobra were also revered. Mostly, the sacred animals and birds were from non-domestic species because as hunters the people related more to animals in the bush than domestic ones.

The leopard, known as *musuku* or *musu*, was a royal animal totem of Mora and Kenu clans. Members of the Mako, Sawe, Yari-Ateuwa, and Yo clans, who were mostly farmers and hunters, adopted the leopard as a totem. The spiritual relationship has been explained in the tradition, which claims that the leopard embodied the soul of their ancestors. A live leopard was accorded respect in human fashion, but if found dead, members of the clans would bury it with two cowries and mourn it seven days. Sacrifices of appeasement were often offered and the adherents of the totem believed that the leopard usually ate up the food that was put at a shrine located within the courtyard of the palaces.

As hunters, the people believed that if they were lost in the bush, the leopard would lead them back to the town safely. If somebody accidentally killed a leopard, a propitiatory sacrifice would be offered. Failure to perform the sacrifice would evoke the leopard's wrath in form of widespread sickness among the clan members. The Mako clan referred to the leopard as "father," which accentuates the close relationship between the animal and the people. A surviving oral tradition indicated that a leopard protected the clan ancestors by attacking and killing their enemies during a battle. Hence, in appreciation of the animal, the ancestors gave great respect to the leopard and preserved the act of revering it in their clan tradition and history.

The veneration of the leopard in Borgu was closely related to that of the Jukun (Kwararafa) and the Nupe in central Nigeria. The Kisra legend, which was popular among many West African societies, referred to Kisra as the founder of the dynasties of the Borgu, Hausa, Jukun, Nupe, and Yoruba polities. The familial relationship has been supported by the similarity in the treatment of dead leopards among the Jukun and Borgu peoples. If a Wukari Jukun killed a leopard, he would parade the dead animal around the town mounted on a mat. The people would salute the animal with uplifted arms as they would a chief. However, the slayer was required to perform propitiatory rites and three days' solitude in the bush. To kill a leopard among the Igara of Nupe was tantamount to committing an offence against the living and dead chiefs. A dead leopard was often brought to the chief, dressed up in white, and carried around the town with singing and beating of drums. The royal mausoleum of the Ata (the king) of Nupe was known as "The Grave of the Leopard."

The *gbero* (red antelope) was the animal totem of several clans, such as the Bare, Kabo, Kpai, Kpasi, Mako, Mora, Mori, Sawe, Yari-Ateuwa, and Yo clans. These clans may have had a common ancestry or they migrated from the same place. While on a hunting expedition, an ancestor of the Mora clan entered the warren of an animal to rest, but he could not find his way out. Fortuitously, a *gbero* made a hole through which the ancestor came out. As an expression of gratitude, the ancestor declared the *gbero* a totem for members of his clan.

Reptiles constituted another form of totem in the Borgu society. The Tosu royal clan of Okuta revered the python, which inhabited the Kuroboko hill. Pythons (*mleda* in the Boko language) lived in two shrines located at *Kabami* rocky hill in Gurai town. Bare, Kabo, Wanro, and Yari Wanro clans also revered *shurokoru* (cobra). The reverence of pythons and cobras might have developed from snake worship, which was commonplace in pre-colonial West Africa. People kept serpents in their homes and allowed them to wander about the village without being attacked by members of the community. Among the Mako, Kenu, Sawe, and Yo clans, both *gunusemu* (rabbit) and *shekuro* (weaverbird) were accorded human burial. One cowry would be buried with it and mourning would last only a day.

Animal totems were more common than plant totems but spirits lived in sacred trees. The Lesaworu clan at Ilesha revered the *Besigondo* tree but *Baatoko* tree was the plant totem of the Yari at Okuta. The Laru-speaking people of Lashibe in Wawa District regarded *Kanya* tree as the abode of *Zarami*, an important spirit who provided security for members of the community in times of sickness or epidemics. The chief priest of *Lashi*, an important Earth spirit represented by a stone in a hut, could not be circumcised, and was not allowed to farm. The chief of Sabon Gari could not eat new yam until he made a sacrifice of a sheep and corn to *Lashi*. The *Kani* spirit lived in *Kawo* tree and often accepted a sacrifice of a white cock, a libation of honey, milk, and flour for appeasement. *Antsa*, represented by a small piece of iron, could be invoked in case of sterility. The spirit of *Fu* lived in a *Rimi* tree. In addition, the spirit of *Dauda* at Kagogi near Bussa lived in *Duki* tree. Furthermore, the spirit of *Doguwa Fara* in Illo lived in the sacred *tamarind* tree.

Unlike the others, the Dandawa (Muslim) clans, such as the Taruwere, Ture, Mane, and the Wangara merchants, did not adopt any animal totem. But like other clans, the Muslims observed food taboos, which do not fall within the category of totemism. For a long time, the Borgu people refused to be Islamized and the veneration of animal and plant totems could be seen as one of the devices of resisting the Islamic religion. Mohammed Bello, the Sultan of Sokoto, once described the Borgu people as "devils and of stubborn nature" because of their refusal to accept Islam.

The people of Borgu worshipped other natural phenomena, such as rocks, hills, and rivers. Jekanna, a rocky hill in Bussa, was invoked for childbirth, sickness, and wealth, and its chief priest was called the Bamaso. Another rocky hill, Kuroboko, served a natural barrier against external military attacks, but it was also a symbol of religious practice. A newly installed chief of Okuta would visit the Kuroboko hill for prayers and to offer a sacrifice for a peaceful and prosperous reign. Before and after a war, sacrifices were offered at the Kuroboko hill. The Ozera hill in Kaiama served both political and religious functions. During the annual Gani festival, the traditional shaving of the royal family took place at the Ozera hill. The people of Ilesha chiefdom used to offer sacrifices to Tutuku hill, especially during epidemics.

The River Niger with its tributaries, including Alibori, Makrou, Minni, Moshi, Oli, and Teshi were worshipped and sacrificed to for successful fishing and peace. Daraku was the only river that the people of Okuta worshipped. The spirits of the river inhabited a hole in a big tree and the chief priest was called Shina Wosho.

The centrality of nature and religion cannot be undermined in the Borgu society. As deeply religious, farming, hunting, and fishing communities, the Borgu people placed high emphasis on the interplay of nature and religion. Whether adopted as primary or secondary totems, animals, birds, rocks, and rivers have been employed as instruments of religion to consolidate socio-cultural cohesion and cross-clan relations. They served as symbols of unity within the society. The breaking of a totemic practice could imperil the unity of the clan. Determined to remain traditionalists and nature worshippers, the Borgu people did not adopt Islam or Christianity until the colonial period. Traditional religion still exists, an example of which is Bionkuro, whose shrine is represented by a collection of fine stones in Kenu and the priest attends to patrons who come to ask for improved health, wealth, or childbirth. Although Islam and Christianity are gaining ground in contemporary times, they have not completely obliterated the practice of totemism and nature worship.

Julius O. Adekunle

Further Reading

Adekunle, Julius O. "On Oral Tradition and History: Studies on Nigerian Borgu." *Anthropos* 89 (1994), 543–51.

Frazer, J.G. *Totemism and Exogamy: A Treatise on Certain Early Forms of Superstition and Society*, 4 vols. London: Macmillan, 1910.

Meek, C.K. *The Northern Tribes of Nigeria*, vol. 1. London: Frank Cass, 1971.

Stewart, Marjorie Helen. *Borgu and Its Kingdoms: A Reconstruction of a Western Sudanese Polity*. Lewiston: The Edwin Mellen Press, 1993.

Weissenborn, Johannes. "Animal-worship in Africa." *African Affairs: Journal of the Royal African Society* 5 (1905–1906).

See also: African Religions and Nature Conservation; Totemism; West Africa; Yoruba Culture (West Africa).

Totemism

The word totem comes from the Algonquin language of the Chippewa (or Ojibwe) people of the American mid-West. It first came to prominence in the late eighteenth century, when trader James Long wrote:

> The religious superstition of the Savages consists in each of them having his *totam*, or favourite spirit, which he believes watches over him. This *totam* they conceive assumes the shape of some beast or other, and therefore they never kill, hunt or eat the animal whose form they think this totam bears (Long 1791: 86).

Long also told the story of a Chippewa man whose "*totam*" was bear. The man one day killed a bear, thereby angering the Master of Life. So he was punished by a second bear, who admonished him and struck his face. As it turned out, Long had confused the Chippewa's idea of a personal guardian spirit (or *manitoo*) with their idea of a collective clan spirit (or *totam*), but the words "totem," "totemic," and "totemism" developed and gelled in the English language from that time on.

Totems are usually defined as objects or beings that are emblematic of individual or group identities. Typically, the totem is an animal; less typically a plant or some other natural feature (like fire, rain, the sun, or the moon). In Long's time, and for more than a hundred years afterwards, anthropologists usually interpreted totemism as the classical type of "primitive" religion – religion that belonged to such a low level of human social development that it was inextricably tied to nature, whose forces were seen to dominate primitive worlds. Some even argued that it was a kind of "pre-religion" or magic found among people who had yet to take any significant steps toward civilization and the rational control of natural forces. Spiritual beliefs from throughout the Americas, Australia, the Pacific Islands, and Africa, as well as large parts of Asia, all came to be lumped together under the category "totemism."

These speculations more or less came to a definitive end when Claude Lévi-Strauss published *Le Totémisme Aujourd'hui* in 1962. Lévi-Strauss drew attention to the incredible variation that existed in the ethnographic record, suggesting that no single form of totemism could be identified as characteristic of the phenomenon as a whole. Totems could symbolize individual, lineage, or sexual identities, to name only a few, and have been found in all kinds of combinations in a single society. However, Lévi-Strauss did make one positive observation about this variety, saying that each type of totemism had to be understood as an example of a universal human propensity to utilize metaphor in the negotiation of identity. From that moment on, Aboriginal and other tribal people's use of totemic emblems became no more remarkable than Americans identifying with the bald eagle, an army regiment identifying with its mascot, or the American prisoner Robert Stroud becoming "the Birdman of Alcatraz." Recent attempts to enlist ostensibly tribal forms of totemism to environmentalist or New Age agendas, so that pandas, dolphins, salmon, or wolves, for example, come to symbolize particular human identities, such as conservation organizations or neo-tribal shamans, build on firm traditions long embedded in modern as well as pre-modern thought.

The extensibility of totemism is a key question in its ethnographic definition. For example, W.E.H. Stanner once described the local selection of Australian Aboriginal totems as "irreducibly arbitrary" (1979: 130). His account is worth quoting more fully.

> A totem is in the first place a thing; an entity, an event, or a condition – what I have called an existent. Virtually anything perceivable can serve: plants and animals of all kinds – anything in the entire floral and faunal realms; wind, rain, storms, thunder, lightning, stars, sun, moon and clouds – anything of the heaven; tools and weapons, food and cosmetics, fire and smoke, mist and spume, fresh water and salt – anything of the Earth; the human exuviae and genitals – almost anything of the body ... Sexual desire, cold weather, sweethearts, vomiting, runaway wives, mother's milk and innumerable pests have all been recorded as totems. A part of an object can serve – the handle of a spear-thrower, or the bowels of an animal; so can a disease – diarrhoea or colds; so can flood-wrack swirling down a river, or tide marks on a beach. Living persons evidently cannot be totems, but a mythical person can be – for example, the Warramunga "laughing boy" (1979: 129–30).

The totemic impulse is similarly protean in Western societies, where, for example, sports teams have totems that include not only animals, but also colors, peoples, professions, mythical beings and abstract energies, to name but a few. Such versatility is found in totemic systems worldwide, both modern and pre-modern.

Yet totemic systems do tend to be dominated by animals, probably because humans are also animals – hence a strongly perceived similarity between "us" and "them." But at the same time humans are more diverse within the species, so that differences between nonhuman animals are readily employed to symbolize differences between people. Paradoxically, totemic species then appear closer to their equivalent groups of people than other humans and, in common parlance, the totemic species often comes to be referred to as a friend or relative. Indeed, "totem" is actually taken from the Algonquin expression *ototeman*, which translates as "he is a relative of mine." In societies similar to that of the Chippewa, it is common to call totemic species "brother," "mother," "grandfather," and so on, so that totems, or any of the objects or spirit beings which instance them, are fully regarded as kin or extensions of the self. Totemic relationships, be they religious or secular, are invariably marked by familiarity and special intimacy.

In recent centuries the contrast between humans and other animals has been heavily compromised by the idea that humans are somehow beyond animality, or cultural rather than natural. Hence totemism has come to be perceived as "kinship with nature," "nature worship" or "analogy between nature and culture" – this even though the Chippewa and other classically totemic societies did not originally possess a concept of nature in opposition to a concept of human society. Neo-totemic characterizations are usually strongly wedded to the romantic critique of civilization, which tends to claim that the West has lost touch with nature and needs to reinstate a reciprocal relationship with it. In this mindset, totemism tends to take on a distinctly New Age feel in terms of the ability of people to communicate with nature and comes to be strongly connected with the wisdom of "primitive peoples," particularly insofar as they are exponents of shamanism and spiritual journeys to commune with other species. The extent to which this romantic vision accurately reflects past ethnographic reality remains problematic, but it is certainly now part of the contemporary ethnographic landscape.

Take, for example, the contemporary image of the wolf. This creature has a long history in the totemic folklore of a large part of the Northern Hemisphere. In Europe, the wolf is most famously associated with the stories of Little Red Riding Hood and the Three Little Pigs, where he is the personification of the forest and a symbol of the potential destruction and transformation of childhood. He also appears in a related unkindly guise as the werewolf. But the wolf also figures in the totemic mythology of Native North America, where the associated symbolism, often more benign, is rapidly hybridizing with the ongoing romantic backlash against the modern world. For example, Jungian works like Clarissa Pinkola Estes' *Women Who Run with the Wolves* invert classical European imagery to make a statement about modernity.

> Within every woman there lives a powerful force, filled with good instincts, passionate creativity, and ageless knowing. She is the Wild Woman, who represents the instinctual nature of women. But she is an endangered species. For though the gifts of wildish nature belong to us at birth, society's attempt to "civilize" us into rigid roles has muffled the deep, life-giving messages of our own souls (1992: 1).

Hence, loss of kinship with the wolf, which is lack of contact with nature, is also detachment from one's own nature – one's true self. Neo-totemism preaching this kind of "back-to-nature" scenario inevitably establishes links with tribal regimes.

The reference to the Wild Woman/wolf as "endangered species" is telling, for in recent years the "originators" of totemism, the Chippewa people, have organized with other Native American groups (Nez Perce and Dakota Sioux) to protect wolves in their local areas. Chippewa spokespeople have stated in relation to their campaign that they are "concerned citizens that are worried for the protection of the wolf" and they have claimed the right to participate in "decisions that will affect our brother the wolf." They back their claims with mythological precedent, saying that, at the beginning of time, Anishinable (the first Chippewa man) walked the Earth alone "naming all creation, lands and waters." Because he was alone, the wolf was created to walk with him and share his fate. What would happen to one would also happen to the other. And this is how the Chippewa see their dispossession in the modern world. Just as they have had their lands taken, and been hunted and pushed to near extinction, so too has the wolf become endangered. If, as the Chippewa and others intend, the wolf returns in numbers to the land and gains in strength, then this will show how Chippewa life, culture and spirituality will also return and gain strength in those places where they were once destroyed. And perhaps, they say, "the wolf will lead the way to a more natural living" and teach the new Americans to respect "Mother Earth" (Bob Shimek and Jean Brave Heart. "Native Americans Enter Wolf Controversy." http://nnic.com/mnwolves/nap.html, visited 3 July 2001).

These ideas are at once old and new, a recasting of totemic traditions in hypermodern circumstances. They also mark a tense conjunction of interests expressed by indigenous peoples, environmentalist groups and New Age spiritualists. These interests often help to form strong alliances, but they also often lead to accusations of neo-colonialism and the wrongful appropriation of indigenous knowledge. Some ethnographers have argued that classical totemic systems, in effecting ritual control of human movement and foraging, have long played a part in environmental resource management in pre-modern societies. In turn, successful environmental management is reflected in spiritual beliefs about maintaining harmony and balance in the cosmos. Yet violent hunting practices and other pragmatic issues in indigenous communities do not always sit easily with contemporary environmentalist or New Age sensibilities. Consequently, neo-totemic solidarity across the indigenous/non-indigenous divide cannot be taken for granted, but is rather a matter for negotiation. In recent decades, environmentalists and New Age spiritualists have been on steep learning curves in relation to totemic sensibilities in indigenous communities; but, equally, indigenous peoples have been keen to discover what the West's disenchanted have to offer in their struggle against neo-colonial domination.

When Lévi-Strauss penned *Le Totémisme Aujourd'hui* his intention was to dissolve the phenomenon into something different and far broader. While his intention has been supported by examination of the fuller content of totemic systems, the core problematic relationships between "nature" and "culture" (animality and humanity, "primitive thought" and "modern thought") have remained ideologically to the fore. Indeed, the British anthropologist Roy Willis recently observed that, thanks to the ongoing twinning of primitivism and ecological concern, the period after *Le Totémisme Aujourd'hui* has been marked by a kind of "totemic revival" (1990: 5). The Chippewa situation described above can be taken as symptomatic of this neo-totemic environment in which the contrast between indigenous and non-indigenous peoples has become synonymous with the opposition between human nature ("the soul") and its corruption by technocratic rationality. But Lévi-Strauss's words still strike a note of caution; totemic emblems have never been restricted to natural species, any more than they have been exclusively religious in the conventional sense. We live in a world dense with personal and corporate emblems, only some of which resonate with the juxtaposition of religion and nature.

John Morton

Further Reading

Estés, Clarissa Pinkola. *Women Who Run with the Wolves: Contacting the Power of the Wild Woman*. London: Rider, 1992.

House, Freeman. *Totem Salmon*. Boston: Beacon Press, 1999.

Knudtson, Peter and David Suzuki. *Wisdom of the Elders*. London: Allen and Unwin, 1992.

Lévi-Strauss, Claude. *Le Totémisme Aujourd'hui*. Paris: Presses Universitaires de France, 1962.

Long, James. *Voyages and Travels of an Indian Interpreter and Trader, Describing the Manners and Customs of the North American Indians*. Toronto: Coles, 1791.

Stanner, W.E.H. *White Man Got No Dreaming: Essays 1938–1973*. Canberra: ANU Press, 1979.

Willis, Roy, ed. *Signifying Animals: Human Meaning in the Natural World*. London: Routledge, 1990.

Willis, Roy. *Man and Beast*. St. Albans: Paladin, 1975.

See also: Anthropology as a Source of Nature Religion; Ecology and Religion; Estés, Clarissa Pinkola; Indigenous Religions and Cultural Borrowing; Religious Environmentalist Paradigm; Totemic Practices in Borgu (West Africa).

Traditional Ecological Knowledge

The theme of traditional ecological knowledge is important for the consideration of a broad range of questions related to nature–human relations. Different groups of people in various parts of the world perceive and interact with nature differently, and have different traditions of environmental knowledge. Their perceptions and knowledge are in part shaped by their values, worldviews, and environmental ethics – religion in the broader sense. In the exploration of environmental ethics and religion toward an ecologically sustainable society, indigenous peoples and traditional ecological knowledge have attracted considerable attention from both scholars and popular movements. Traditional ecological knowledge may be defined as "a cumulative body of knowledge, practice and belief, evolving by adaptive processes and handed down through generations by cultural transmission, about the relationship of living beings (including humans) with one another and with their environment." As a knowledge-practice-belief complex, traditional ecological knowledge includes the worldview or religious traditions of a society. It is both cumulative and dynamic, building on experience and adapting to change, as societies constantly redefine what is considered "traditional." It is an attribute of societies with historical continuity in making a living in a particular place.

Many discussions of traditional ecological knowledge and indigenous knowledge focus on North American Indian peoples. However, there are traditions of ecological knowledge in various indigenous societies in South America, Australia, and parts of Africa and Asia. Culturally transmitted, cumulative, multigenerational knowledge is held also by some groups that have European backgrounds, such as Newfoundland fishers and Swiss Alpine people.

TEK in *Our Common Future*

Tribal and indigenous peoples' ... lifestyles can offer modern societies many lessons in the management of resources in complex forest, mountain and dryland ecosystems ... These communities are the repositories of vast accumulations of traditional knowledge and experience that link humanity with its ancient origins. Their disappearance is a loss for the larger society, which could learn a great deal from their traditional skills in sustainably managing very complex ecological systems (*Our Common Future* 1937: 12, 114–15).

Fikret Berkes

Traditional ecological knowledge may be considered as a sub-set of indigenous knowledge, defined as local knowledge held by indigenous peoples or local knowledge unique to a given culture or society. There is controversy over the term, traditional. Some scholars consider that the term implies backwardness, and instead favor "indigenous" or "local." Others point out that many indigenous peoples themselves see "tradition" in a positive light. They do not take it to mean inflexible adherence to the past but rather to mean time-tested and wise.

These considerations make it difficult to generalize about traditional ecological knowledge. But in any case, one cannot generalize about "the Amerindian (or African) view of nature." Every cultural group has within it a range of environmental values and ethics, and a range of practices. Environmental relations of a group are not uniform; they are shaped by the day-to-day contingencies, as well as their worldview and ethics. Environmental ethics do not describe how people actually behave, but indicate how they *ought to* behave. Human–nature relations tend to be ambivalent; there often is a discrepancy between belief and practice.

Origins of Traditional Ecological Knowledge and its Development as a Field

The intellectual roots of traditional ecological knowledge are in ethnoscience (mainly ethnobotany) and human ecology. The field started with the documentation of lists of species used by different indigenous groups, and elaborated a science of folk taxonomies of plants and animals, and later, of other environmental features such as soils. Early ethnobotany goes back at least to Barrows' 1900 work on Coahuila Indians of southern California who made a living in a seemingly barren desert environment by harvesting no less than 60 kinds of edible plants and 28 kinds of medicinal plants. The science of folk taxonomies is often associated with the name of Harold Conklin who documented in the 1950s the extensive plant knowledge and classification systems of traditional groups such as the Hanunoo of the Philippines.

There is a technical literature on various kinds of indigenous environmental knowledge. For example, traditional agricultural practice is a major field of indigenous knowledge; others include traditional medicine and architecture. Much of the indigenous knowledge literature is not about ecological relationships but about other kinds of ethnoscience, including agriculture, ethnobiology, ethnopharmacology, ethnoveterinary medicine, and ethnopedology (soils). Some of these areas, for example, traditional practices of water conservation and erosion control, are directly related to ecological knowledge, but others (e.g., ethnoastronomy) are less so.

The shift of emphasis from the documentation of species used by indigenous groups and their taxonomy, to a consideration of functional relationships and mechanisms, gave rise to the field of traditional ecological knowledge. The field borrows from the cultural ecology tradition of the anthropologist Julian Steward who emphasized the study of *adaptive processes*, and argued that social organization itself may be considered an ecological adaptation of a group to its local environment. This emphasis on adaptive processes in human–nature relations may be seen in some of the key volumes on traditional ecological knowledge. As defined in this literature, traditional ecological literature overlaps with cultural ecology, ecological anthropology or anthropological ecology but is not a sub-set of these fields because it often goes beyond the discipline of anthropology.

The rapid development of traditional ecological knowledge as a field in its own right started with the documentation of a tremendously rich body of environmental knowledge, not just of species but also their ecological relations, among a diversity of groups outside the mainstream Western world. These included studies of shifting cultivation and biodiversity conservation in tropical ecosystems, and traditional knowledge and management systems in coastal fisheries and lagoons, semi-arid areas, and the Arctic. These studies showed that a variety of traditional peoples, in diverse geographical areas from the Arctic to the Amazon, had their own understandings of ecological relationships and distinct traditions of resource management.

By the mid-1980s, the rapidly growing literature on traditional ecological knowledge led to a recognition in the international arena of its potential applications to contemporary resource and environmental problems. This recognition is reflected in *Our Common Future*, the 1987 report of the World Commission on Environment and Development. The report pointed out that indigenous peoples hold a wealth of knowledge based on thousands of years of experience, and that their practices can offer modern societies lessons in the management of resources in complex forest, mountain and arid land ecosystems.

Traditional Ecological Knowledge and Science

Even though the importance of traditional ecological knowledge is recognized in the international arena and the number of publications has grown rapidly since the 1980s, the relationship between Western science and traditional knowledge has remained controversial. There are both similarities and differences between traditional science and Western science. Both kinds of knowledge are ultimately based on observations of the environment, and both result from the same intellectual process of creating order out of disorder. But they are different in a number of substantive ways. Traditional ecological knowledge is often an integral part of a culture, and tends to have a large social context. Different kinds of traditional knowledge have their own rules, but they are different from science regarding rules of evidence and repeatability.

Some of the conflict between science and traditional knowledge is related to claims of authority over knowledge. In the modernist tradition, Western science is seen as having a monopoly on truth. Hence, knowledge and insights that originate outside institutionalized Western science are not easily accepted. Scientists tend to dismiss understandings that do not fit their own (and this often includes understandings of *other* scientists using different paradigms). Scientists tend to be skeptical, demanding evidence when confronted with traditional knowledge that may not easily lend itself to scientific verification.

Some traditional knowledge may include elements, such as the religious dimensions of the environment, which do not make sense to science. For example, many of the Dene (Athapascan) peoples of the North American subarctic consider that some non-living parts of the environment (including rivers and mountains), as well as all living beings, have spirit. Science has no tools for the study of the spiritual dimensions of the environment, but nevertheless such beliefs are important for understanding Dene traditional ecological knowledge.

For their own part, traditional knowledge holders are skeptical of book learning, and tend to dismiss scientists who do not have extensive first-hand knowledge of a specific land area. As well, they are often baffled by the preoccupation of scientists to measure and quantify everything. Power relations become an issue when Western experts and Aboriginal experts have different political agendas. Traditional ecological knowledge has frequently been used to assert indigenous land and resource rights and to fight government-imposed development projects on native land. In turn, science may be used to justify the very same projects.

Hence the issue is complex, even if one agrees with postmodern philosophers of science that Western scientific methodology is merely one way, and not the only way, to acquire knowledge. However, it is the one that happens to be the dominant knowledge system by far, and the one used as the basis of environmental decision-making by centralized bureaucracies throughout the world.

Significance of Traditional Ecological Knowledge

Traditional knowledge and Western science need not be thought of as opposites. Rather, it may be useful to emphasize the potential complementarities of the two, and to look for points of agreement rather than disagreement. The use of traditional knowledge contributes to conceptual pluralism, and expands the range of approaches and information needed to solve environmental problems.

The explosion of interest in traditional ecological knowledge since the 1980s is in part related to its practical significance. However, the interests of different parties are quite different. For many indigenous groups, the broader social and cultural aspects of traditional knowledge are very significant, and this is one of the reasons why dealing with traditional ecological knowledge has become politically volatile. In many indigenous areas, researchers no longer have a free hand to conduct their work independently from the people themselves.

Politically organized groups of indigenous peoples are beginning to assert control over their knowledge systems for at least two reasons. First, some indigenous groups have seen their knowledge and biological resources (for example, medicinal plants) turned by others into profit-making commodities. Thus, they have started to ask the question of who benefits from the recording of their knowledge, and to investigate how they themselves can control their knowledge and products.

Second, indigenous knowledge has become a symbol for many groups to regain control over their cultural information. Reclaiming their indigenous knowledge has become a major strategy in many parts of the world for movements of cultural revitalization. For example, many of the Aboriginal groups in Alaska and Northern Canada have been carrying out their own traditional knowledge studies as part of an effort to strengthen their culture, educate their young people, prepare land and resource claims, and assert their rights. Such revitalization is not merely a cultural exercise; it is about empowerment and political control.

The need for indigenous groups to control their knowledge has to be balanced against the importance of traditional ecological knowledge as the common heritage of humankind. There are tangible and practical reasons why traditional ecological knowledge is important for the rest of the world's people. I have identified seven areas in which traditional ecological knowledge is significant. First, it is a source of biological knowledge and ecological insights. Second, indigenous knowledge is important for the sustainability of difficult-to-manage ecosystems such as tropical forests. Third, it is important for community-based conservation by connecting human values with conservation values. Fourth, some traditional systems are of special interest for biodiversity conservation because they are based on multiple-use principles that distribute resource-use pressures in space and time. Fifth, in-depth local environmental knowledge and trends over time for a given site are important for environmental assessment. Sixth, traditional knowledge is essential for development, especially for "bottom-up" (as opposed to top-down) development planning with people.

Finally, traditional ecological wisdom is a source of inspiration for environmental ethics. Belief systems of many indigenous groups incorporate the idea that humans are part of the natural environment, and their relationship with nature may be characterized as peaceful coexistence. Callicott points out that some traditional ecology sees humans and nature in a symbiotic relationship, with mutual obligations leading to "respect," a central idea in the relations of many Amerindian groups with nature.

These observations are significant. The explosion of interest in traditional ecological knowledge in recent years reflects in part the need to derive ecological insights from indigenous practice, and the need to develop a new ecological ethic based in part on indigenous wisdom.

Fikret Berkes

Further Reading

Berkes, Fikret. *Sacred Ecology: Traditional Ecological Knowledge and Resource Management.* Philadelphia: Taylor & Francis, 1999.

Callicott, J.Baird. *Earth's Insights. A Multicultural Survey of Ecological Ethics from the Mediterranean Basin to the Australian Outback.* Berkeley: University of California Press, 1994.

Ford, Jesse and Dennis Martinez, eds. "Traditional Ecological Knowledge, Ecosystem Science and Environmental Management." (Special issue) *Ecological Applications* 10:5 (2000).

Posey, Darrell A. and Graham Dutfield. *Beyond Intellectual Property: Towards Traditional Resource Rights for Indigenous Peoples and Local Communities.* Ottawa: International Development Research Centre, 1996.

Posey, Darrell A. and William L. Balee, eds. *Resource Management in Amazonia: Indigenous and Folk Strategies.* New York: New York Botanical Gardens, 1989.

Warren, D. Michael, Jan Slikkerveer and David Brokensha, eds. *The Cultural Dimension of Development: Indigenous Knowledge Systems.* London: Intermediate Technology Publications, 1995.

Williams, Nancy M. and Graham Baines, eds. *Traditional Ecological Knowledge: Wisdom for Sustainable Development.* Canberra: Centre for Resource and Environmental Studies, Australian National University, 1993.

See also: American Indians as "First Ecologists"; Domestication; Ecological Anthropology; Ecology and Religion; Environmental Ethics; Ethnobotany; Ethnoecology; Evolutionary Biology, Religion, and Stewardship; Harris, Marvin; Indigenous Environmental Network; Native American Languages (North America); Rappaport, Roy A. ("Skip"); Religious Environmentalist Paradigm; A Religio-Ecological Perspective on Religion and Nature; Traditional Ecological Knowledge among Aboriginal Peoples in Canada; Water Spirits and Indigenous Ecological Management (South Africa); Yunnan Region (Southwest China and Montane Mainland Southeast Asia).

Traditional Ecological Knowledge among Aboriginal Peoples in Canada

Each contracting Party shall, as far as possible and as appropriate: Subject to national legislation, respect, preserve and maintain knowledge, innovations and practices of indigenous and local communities embodying traditional lifestyles relevant for the conservation and sustainable use of biological diversity and promote their wider application with the approval and involvement of the holders of such knowledge, innovations and practices and encourage the equitable sharing of the benefits arising from the utilization of such knowledge innovations and practices (from www.biodiv.org – the Convention on Biological Diversity's website).

For generations, indigenous peoples in what is now known as Canada have been using their own knowledge systems to live sustainably with the land. Indigenous knowledge systems are unique systems of generating, storing and transmitting knowledge completely separate and independent from Western science and Western epistemologies. Rooted in relations with the spirit-world, indigenous knowledge continues to provide Aboriginal peoples with unique worldviews, languages that are constructed to reflect those worldviews, systems of governance, values, and processes and ways of knowing and interacting with the land. Aboriginal philosophies and values reflect worldviews that are based on interrelationships and interdependency with the natural world and all other elements of the cosmos. Traditional teachings, stories, songs, dances and ceremonies reinforce the importance of relationships and process in the lives of individuals, communities and nations. Indigenous knowledge is dynamic and creative and, although it varies from nation to nation, has certain common elements and themes. Indigenous knowledge is at once ancient and contemporary knowledge, recording through the oral tradition the collective knowledge of a people in addition to documenting the impacts of colonization, colonialism and environmental destruction. Experts in indigenous knowledge are not academics or researchers who study TEK, but they are the Elders and knowledge-holders who not only hold the knowledge, but who have lived the knowledge and the teachings over the course of their lives. It is these experts who are best equipped to provide leadership around this topic, and it is these experts that need to be included in an effective way in discussions regarding the many potential applications of Traditional Ecological Knowledge (TEK).

During the initial stages of colonization, Europeans were dependent upon indigenous peoples and their knowledge for their survival. The colonizers relied upon technology in the areas of transportation, hunting, fishing, food gathering, nutrition, healthcare and navigation. They relied upon Aboriginal peoples for their most basic needs and in turn had great respect for indigenous knowledge. However, as the settler economy developed and the infrastructure needed to support the colonizers way of life was realized, they no longer relied on Aboriginal peoples and

Aboriginal knowledge for their continuance and survival. Subsequently, over that next five centuries, indigenous knowledge was disrespected, undermined and assimilated into Canadian society with no recognition or acknowledgement for Aboriginal peoples. Many of the modern symbols of Canadian culture, such as maple syrup, canoes, kayaks, snow shoes, wild rice and wild meat, represent appropriated Aboriginal knowledge. The systemic dispossession of Aboriginal nations from their territories along with the assimilative policies of the Canadian government through the Indian Act would have come close to destroying indigenous knowledge if it were not for the resistance and commitment of past generations of Aboriginal peoples.

In recent times, non-Aboriginal researchers, academics, environmentalists, industry and government personnel have once again become interested in what has become known as Traditional Ecological Knowledge. Many environmentalists believe that TEK holds answers to the pending ecological crises and provides Euro-Canadian society with a blueprint toward sustainable living. The pharmaceutical and natural health products industries are interested in the Aboriginal knowledge and use of traditional medicines and medicinal plants so that these might be commercially exploited for profit. Natural resource managers at the federal and provincial levels are interested in TEK in hopes that it can contribute to the management of renewable and non-renewable resources in a positive way. These interests in the knowledge of Aboriginal peoples have unfortunately caused researchers to separate out "ecological" or "environmental" knowledge from other kinds of knowledge, because it is the component of the knowledge system that outside researchers are currently most interested in learning. Existing academic literature regarding TEK continues along this line of thinking, privileging the components of indigenous knowledge that conform well to Western ideals over the spiritual basis of indigenous knowledge. Aboriginal spiritual traditions, beliefs and values form the foundation of traditional knowledge, and are completely integrated into every aspect of TEK and indigenous thought. Much of the TEK literature published in applied scientific journals and publications is written by non-Aboriginal scientists and academics and has focused on introducing TEK to scientists. Works written by Fikret Berkes, for instance, attempt to gain acceptance for TEK and Aboriginal peoples in disciplines that have traditionally ignored the contribution and knowledge of indigenous peoples. Publications in scientific journals generally ignore contemporary impacts of colonization and colonialism on indigenous peoples, the land, and their knowledge, marginalize indigenous elders and knowledge-holders, and undermine the oral tradition, thereby constructing "TEK" in a manner that is often not meaningful to the very people who hold the knowledge. These criticisms, long observed by indigenous elders and knowledge-holders are making their way into the academic literature articulated by indigenous scholars such as Marie Battiste, James Sa'ke'j Youngblood Henderson, Leanne Simpson and Deborah McGregor.

Aboriginal peoples have approached these outside interests with caution, concerned that their knowledge could be taken out of context, misused and appropriated. Indeed, there have been several examples of this kind of exploitation increasingly occurring, and indigenous peoples continue to take special precautions when sharing knowledge with people from outside their communities and nations. Many communities have developed information-sharing policies and guidelines for researchers entering their territories in addition to their traditional protocols for sharing and transmitting knowledge. Some communities and organizations, like the Pauktuutit Inuit Women's Organization are investigating the possibility of using Canadian Intellectual Property law to protect aspects of their knowledge, despite current deficiencies in the laws in terms of indigenous knowledge.

Internationally, TEK has most recently been recognized in the United Nations Convention on Biological Diversity. Article 8j (see the epigraph) of the Convention outlines the importance of indigenous knowledge and indigenous peoples in the protection of biodiversity. Canada, as a signatory to the Convention, is slowly working toward implementing Article 8j in its domestic legislation. As a result, environmental impact assessments, co-management agreements, and certain pieces of legislation such as the proposed Species at Risk Act are beginning to include certain aspects of indigenous knowledge within them. Despite these initiatives, there are many barriers to including TEK in environmental management in ways that respect Aboriginal peoples and bring about meaningful change to these processes. Scientists and resource managers have little opportunity to learn about Aboriginal peoples and their TEK first-hand. This can create misunderstandings regarding the nature of TEK. Governments often require their bureaucrats to include TEK in policy and legislation without proper consultation with Aboriginal peoples, in unrealistic timeframes, and without appropriate financial support. Governments also regularly require TEK to be written down or documented before it is considered useful. Documented TEK is then integrated into processes and frameworks that remain strongly rooted in Western science, and much of the transformative potential of indigenous knowledge is assimilated in the process. Many Elders are concerned that once their knowledge is removed from the oral tradition and the knowledge-holders, translated into English and textualized, it is removed from its context and all of the relationships that give the knowledge its meaning. Aboriginal advocates have challenged this approach and Aboriginal peoples are monitoring these initiatives with concern. It is critical that Aboriginal people, not just isolated components of their knowledge, are included in a meaningful and respectful way in environmental management in Canada, and it is important to realize that including the knowledge of Aboriginal peoples in environmental decision making ultimately means that different decisions will be made.

Contemporary Aboriginal peoples in Canada are concerned about protecting their territories from environmental destruction not only as a way of protecting their relations with the natural world, the health of their communities and their cultures, but also as a way of protecting their knowledge systems. Indigenous knowledge comes from the land. Without these relationships, it is difficult to strengthen, promote and preserve the knowledge of Aboriginal peoples for the coming generations and it is difficult to envision healthy, sustainable Aboriginal nations in the future. TEK has much to offer Aboriginal and non-Aboriginal societies if it is accessed and used in a way that is respectful and fair from the perspective of the people who hold the knowledge. As interest in TEK grows, and Aboriginal voices are listened to, so does the potential for using both indigenous and Western forms of knowledge together to address some of the many local, national and global environmental issues facing the world.

Leanne Simpson (Anishnaabe Kwe)

Further Reading

Battiste, Marie and James (Sa'ke'j) Youngblood Henderson. *Protecting Indigenous Knowledge and Heritage: A Global Challenge*. Saskatoon, SK: Purich Publishing, 2000.

Good Striker, Duane. "The TEK Wars." In J. Weaver, ed. *Defending Mother Earth: Native American Perspective on Environmental Justice*. Maryknoll, NY: Orbis Books, 1997, 144–53.

LaDuke, Winona. "Voices from White Earth." In H. Hannum, ed. *People, Land and Community: Collected E.F. Schumacher Society Lectures*. Barrington, MA: E.F. Schumacher Society, 1997, 22–37.

LaDuke, Winona. "Traditional Ecological Knowledge and Environmental Futures." *Colorado Journal of International Environmental Law and Policy* 5 (1994), 127–48.

McGregor, Deborah. "Indigenous Knowledge in Canada: Shifting Paradigms and the Influence of First Nation Advocates." *Conference Proceedings of Science and Practice: Sustaining the Boreal Forest*. Edmonton, AB: Sustainable Forest Management Network, 14–17 February 1999, 192–8.

Simpson, Leanne, R. "Decolonizing Our Processes: Indigenous Knowledge and Ways of Knowing." *Canadian Journal of Native Studies* 21 (2001), 137–48.

Thorpe, D., ed. *People of the Seventh Fire*. Ithaca, NY: Akwekon Press, 1996.

Youngblood Henderson, James. *Sa'k'ej Ayukpachi: Empowering Aboriginal Thought*. In Marie Battiste, ed. *Reclaiming Indigenous Voice and Vision*. Vancouver, BC: UBC Press, 2000, 248–79.

See also: American Indians as "First Ecologists"; Ecological Anthropology; Ecology and Religion; Ethnobotany; Ethnoecology; Evolutionary Biology, Religion, and Stewardship; Indigenous Environmental Network; Native American Languages (North America); Religious Environmentalist Paradigm; Traditional Ecological Knowledge; Water Spirits and Indigenous Ecological Management (South Africa).

Transcendental Meditation

Transcendental Meditation is a spiritual movement organized by Maharishi Mahesh Yogi, an Indian who came to the U.S. in 1959 to utilize modern media and communications to spread his teachings. These teachings are based on monistic Advaita-Vedanta, a Hindu tradition that describes the universe as diverse manifestations of a single, underlying Absolute, called Brahman. The goal of meditation is personally to experience direct knowledge of Brahman, and realize that the essence of one's own self is this same Brahman. In the 1970s, Maharishi rephrased his teachings to use Western scientific terminology and described his meditation program as the Science of Creative Intelligence (SCI) with Creative Intelligence being the all-pervasive, organizing principle of the universe. Nature appears in two areas of SCI, first as Brahman and second in the context of environmentalism.

In writings from the 1980s, Maharishi often used "Nature" instead of "Brahman" when describing the underlying foundation of the cosmos. In this context, nature is described as the basis of all order and the goal of meditation is to become aware of it. TM uses the language of physics, mathematics, and chemistry to explain the order of the universe and show that modern science is describing a unified cosmos that coincides with the ancient Indian scriptures, the Vedas. Maharishi makes effective use of the Grand Unification Theories of physics to communicate the idea of the basic unity of all material existence to a Western audience. This emphasis on science also allows TM to define itself as a practical technique for improving modern life rather than a religion with a creed. Referring to the Absolute as "nature" rather than God or Brahman facilitates the movement's non-religious identity.

Nature is not, however, completely passive. It is the Creative Intelligence that organizes the cosmos and is said to have "moved Maharishi" to begin his life of teaching. This teaching is necessary for "nature to work out its divine plan for the spiritual regeneration of mankind" (Maharishi 1986: 2). From such statements, it is clear that nature is an active, conscious force in Maharishi's philosophy. And the divine plan requires that people learn to meditate so that they can realize their inherent oneness with the cosmos and be brought into harmony with the natural order of the universe. This, in turn, transforms one's life and leads to the full realization of "human potential." A person who is attuned to nature will be confident and content, able to handle the pace of modern life without succumbing to stress. Such a person is in harmony with the cosmic order. Maharishi attributes his success and his movement's growth to "the natural expression of the force of evolution, silently reshaping the destiny of the world through the thought and action of one moving in perfect attunement with the infinite intelligence of nature" (Maharishi 1986: 1). If his followers meditate, they too will be successful at life because they are in accord with the natural order.

TM's description of nature concerns the cosmic whole, not specific phenomena such as the sun or mountains. The same is true of the movement's approach to the earthly environment. One of TM's stated goals is "To maximize the intelligent use of the environment" (Forem 1974: 10). However, TM writings do not have specific aims such as stopping global warming or requiring that all members be vegetarian. Rather, there is a general belief that those who practice TM will find themselves naturally living a more harmonious life. This will include better human relationships, reduced stress, greater clarity of thought, and better choices about how to live. Among these will be environmental awareness, because polluting the world is selfish and places short-sighted gratification before long-term well-being.

Although TM does not champion specific causes, Maharishi describes two ways in which it can have an effect on the world beyond its membership. First, he suggests that the "custodians of this knowledge" should serve in governments where they will create "problem-free" nations and raise life to the level of a "Heaven on Earth." Second is the "Maharishi Effect," the theory that the mental states of a few people can influence the behavior of others at a distance. According to TM, if the square root of one percent of a population meditates regularly, the higher consciousness of the meditators will affect the whole area and social problems will be alleviated. Thus, their efforts will bring the society into harmony with nature.

Cybelle Shattuck

Further Reading

Forem, Jack. *Transcendental Meditation*. New York: E.P. Dutton, 1974.

Maharishi Mahesh Yogi. *The Science of Being and Art of Living: Transcendental Meditation*. New York: New America Library, 1988 (1963).

Maharishi Mahesh Yogi. *Thirty Years Around the World – Dawn of the Age of Enlightenment*, vol. 1, 1957–1964. Vlodrop, The Netherlands: MVU Press, 1986.

Rothstein, Mikael. *Belief Transformations*. Aarhus, Denmark: Aarhus University Press, 1996.

See also: Hundredth Monkey; Natural Law Party; New Age.

Transcendentalism

Transcendentalism refers to the intellectual and social movement that emerged primarily in Boston and surrounding areas during the mid-nineteenth century and included such familiar figures as Henry David Thoreau, Ralph Waldo Emerson and Margaret Fuller, as well as Fredric Henry Hedge, George Ripley, James Clark, Orestes Brownson, Bronson Alcott, Elizabeth Peabody, and Theodore Parker, among others. Already known to each other through intellectual and social circles, the Transcendentalists formalized their relationship (to the extent that they ever did so) through a regular symposium – sometimes dubbed "the Transcendental Club" – that gathered at participants' homes from 1836 to 1840. The group analyzed such topics as "the essence of religion as distinct from morality," "American Genius," "Pantheism" and "the nature of Poetry." As these titles indicate, the preoccupations of this group were flexible and wide-ranging (as was its informal membership).

Participants in the club were interested in expanding the latest trends in German philosophy, developing original – recognizably American – literary contributions and experimenting with new forms of religious life and thought. Often, they were referred to as the "New School" by their critics and even the term "Transcendentalist" was more often a term of criticism leveled by opponents than a term used by its participants. While regular meetings of the club waned after 1840, the Transcendentalists continued to communicate and exert their influence through their publication, *The Dial* (1840–1844), which was edited first by Fuller and then by Emerson.

The Transcendentalists were highly individualistic in both character and philosophical outlook, resisting any common doctrinal or intellectual stance. They shared, however, a highly optimistic vision of humanity and a confidence in the future of American intellectual life and thought, freed from the bonds of intellectual precedent or religious superstition. These young writers also shared an intellectual affection for various forms of idealism, from neo-Platonic thought to the increasingly influential work of Immanuel Kant, whose use of the term "transcendental" – mediated through the writings of Samuel Taylor Coleridge – these thinkers both borrowed and transformed for their own purposes. What was "transcendental" for the Transcendentalists was a preference for spiritual (or "intuitional") over material (sense-based) forms of knowledge. Similarly, they expressed a commitment to shaping life according to individually discerned aesthetic and spiritual priorities, rather than those of social convention or the marketplace. Their intellectual stance was the starting place from which they developed their ideas of nature, as well as their moral and religious views.

The intellectual agenda of the Transcendentalists was broad, eclectic and not always consistent, consistency itself not being an ideal toward which the Transcendentalists strove. In the most general sense, however, the Transcendentalists embraced a new theory of knowledge. This theory refuted the, then prevailing, Lockean view of the process of human knowing. At the same time, the Transcendentalists put forward new theories of morality that countered more conservative religious approaches, while also opposing the skepticism of David Hume and other Enlightenment figures. In a general sense, the Transcendentalists can be said to have welcomed the Enlightenment critique of religion, while resisting recourse to forms of rationalism that overlooked human emotions and disenchanted the natural world.

In terms of epistemology, the Transcendentalists resisted Locke's empiricist approach, which proposed that knowledge comes from sense experiences which are impressed on the waiting mind just as words are written on a blank slate. While Locke's own view was more complex than that of his followers, Lockean psychology was generally accepted by the intellectuals of the eighteenth and early nineteenth century, particularly the New England Unitarians. Taking cues from the writings of Kant and Coleridge, the Transcendentalists responded against Locke by articulating a distinction between "understanding" (rational reflection on sense experience) and Reason (the use of intuition and one's innate, divinely created capacities to discern the good, the true and the beautiful). While accepting Locke's confidence in the rational capacities of humanity, the Transcendentalists argued that Reason was also an innate human gift which each individual should cultivate.

The Transcendentalist's view of the moral life followed from this epistemological premise. While rejecting orthodox religion and even the comparatively liberal Christian Unitarianism that was culturally dominant in nineteenth-century Boston, the Transcendentalists also rejected Hume's skepticism with respect to religion and morality. Most Transcendentalists affirmed their belief in a divine Creator, while rejecting the notion of divine revelation of miracles. Many also became increasingly interested in the religions of China and India as these became available to them through newly available European translations of Eastern texts. Moreover, Transcendentalists' vision of human nature was indefatigably optimistic, resting on the assumption that all individuals carry the divine within them and must dedicate their lives to nurturing this divine potential, particularly through education and artistic expression.

The Transcendentalists' view of nature rests on the important epistemological and moral assumptions described above. As with particular philosophical, literary and political preferences, the Transcendentalists' reading of nature also varied among individuals. In general, however, the Transcendentalists borrowed from the European Romantics the notion that a regular contact with nature (by which was generally meant: living in or visiting rural and pastoral settings) was essential for regaining human innocence and originality that was corrupted by civilization. Intimacy with nature could return the individual (especially the writer) to a state of childlike openness and wonder. Such a state was crucial to developing what Emerson famously termed an "original response to the universe."

The quest for originality and authenticity both in spiritual experience and in literary expression was a central preoccupation of the Transcendentalists. While the foundations of their ideas were, belatedly, shaped in response to European Romanticism, the Transcendentalists worked to create literature, educational theory and, more broadly, "culture" that was distinctly American. Because such work was dependent on the experience of and response to a particular natural landscape (primarily, pastoral New England), it is no surprise that much Transcendentalist literature concerns itself with "nature" both as an abstract concept and as a particular physical context for spiritual experience.

When considering the Transcendentalists' views of nature, it is important to recognize the complexity of what the term "nature" could signify. In its broadest sense, it represented what was not the self. "Nature" then was equivalent to the Kantian "not-Me." More particularly, nature might refer to a particular biophysical context for the experiences of insight and intuition that were sought after by the Transcendentalists: the "bare common" upon which Emerson experienced himself as a "Transparent Eyeball," Thoreau's Walden or the communal Brook Farm in West Roxbury. Even in these instances, however, the reading of nature offered by the Transcendentalists was not one of appreciating nature for what today we might call its "intrinsic value." While theologically departing firmly from their Puritan heritage, the Transcendentalists continued, while altering, the Puritan view of nature as a "book" to be read for spiritual lessons. They also carried forward Unitarian interests in natural theology, particularly the study of nature to comprehend the character of the divine. The Transcendentalists reworked and re-imagined these Puritan and Unitarian legacies, ultimately asserting the presence of the divine *in* nature (as well as in humanity), while also not limiting their understanding of the divine to the Christian tradition. They incorporated spiritualism, Emmanuel Swedenborg's theory of correspondences and Eastern concepts of sacred geography into their cultural repertoire.

Nevertheless, nature remained in what we might call a "spiritually utilitarian" position. Nature was most often understood to be something which was "read" by the individual artist (the Poet, as Emerson conceived him), whose job it was to decipher and interpret the moral lessons hidden in nature. Nature was valued, then, for what it could teach the attentive student and its function was that of moral formation. The ultimate emphasis remained on the ideal Transcendentalist (which each Transcendentalist saw latent within) whose practice of self-cultivation would enable him or her to "read" nature correctly and to share that reading with a wider audience. Nature, in the Transcendentalists' view, was primarily *symbolic*, representing moral truths and aesthetic insights that lay "behind" or "inside" external, natural phenomena. The pursuit of nature was most often a pursuit of the self, or of knowledge of the divine, without and within.

At the same time, pastoral and wilderness environments remained vital as the ideal *contexts* for Transcendentalist self-cultivation, as was the case in Thoreau's experiment at Walden. Thus, paying close attention to the natural world as a symbolic "book" for spiritual insight also led many Transcendentalists to acquire a large body of scientific knowledge of their surroundings. Many kept detailed records of flora, fauna, weather patterns and natural events in the places where they lived or traveled. Emerson, for instance, was an amateur orchardist and early conservationist of threatened woodlands, while Thoreau's work in natural history and studies of plant succession were consulted by professional scientists of his day.

Rebecca Kneale Gould

Further Reading
Buell, Lawrence. *The Environmental Imagination: Thoreau, Nature Writing and American Culture*. Cambridge, MA: The Belknap Press of Harvard University Press, 1995.
Buell, Lawrence. *Literary Transcendentalism: Style and Vision in the American Renaissance*. Ithaca: Cornell University Press, 1973.
Howe, Daniel Walker. *Making the American Self*. Cambridge, MA: Harvard University Press, 1997.
Miller, Perry, ed. *The Transcendentalists: An Anthology*. Cambridge, MA: Harvard University Press, 1950.
Myerson, Joel, ed. *Transcendentalism: A Reader*. Oxford: Oxford University Press, 2000.
Myerson, Joel, ed. *The Transcendentalists: A Review of Research and Criticism*. New York: Modern Language Association of America, 1984.
See also: Adams, Ansel; Emerson, Ralph Waldo; Muir, John; Pantheism; Romanticism in European Literature; Romanticism – American; Swedenborg, Emmanuel; Thoreau, Henry David; Unitarianism.

Transpersonal Psychology

Transpersonal psychology is the branch of psychology which integrates psychological concepts, theories, and methods with the subject matter and practices of the spiritual disciplines. Its interests include spiritual and mystical experiences, meditative practices, ritual, shamanism, and the connections between spiritual experiences with disturbed states such as psychosis, mania, and depression. Transpersonal psychologists apply their work in clinical and counseling psychology, spiritual guidance and pastoral counseling, organizational and community development, healthcare and healing, the transpersonal dimensions of interpersonal relationships, cultural diversity, gender studies, business, ecopsychology, and other areas.

The root of the term transpersonal, or literally "beyond the mask," refers to self-transcendence, the development of the self from a sense of identity which is exclusively individual to one that is deeper, broader, more inclusive, and more unified with the whole. The core concept in transpersonal psychology is nonduality, the recognition that each part or person is fundamentally and ultimately a part of a larger, more comprehensive whole. From this insight come two other central insights: the intrinsic health and basic goodness of the whole and each of its parts, and the validity of self-transcendence.

Transpersonal psychology is phenomenological, inclusive, and optimistic. It values and integrates the personal with the transpersonal, the psychological with the spiritual, exceptional mental health with psychological disturbance, and analytical intellect with contemplative ways of knowing. It finds wisdom in Western psychology and philosophy, Eastern spirituality, postmodern insights, and worldviews of indigenous traditions. Such overlaps between psychology and spirituality have been present in both psychology (e.g., the work of William James, Carl Jung, and Abraham Maslow) and in the spiritual traditions (which have their own rich views of development, cognition, social interactions, emotional and behavioral suffering, and methods of healing). The work of Ken Wilber (Integral Psychology) and Stanislav Grof are at the forefront of transpersonal psychology today. Among its important projects are describing the stages and processes of transpersonal development, researching the psychological effects of meditation, exploring spiritual emergencies (those mystical or spiritual experiences which also create acute debilitating psychological suffering), and identifying the transpersonal dimensions of nature experiences.

Transpersonal psychology is a field of inquiry which includes theory, research, and practice, offering insights and applications based on research and experience and methods for evaluating and confirming or disconfirming its findings. It is scientific in the broad sense of the phenomenological or "human" sciences. Research in transpersonal psychology uses both qualitative-phenomenological methods and quantitative methods such as experimental designs. In recent years, the *Journal of Transpersonal Psychology* has published reviews of research on psychospiritual problems, mystical experiences, meditation, and measures of transpersonal development. Still, most of the work and practice of transpersonal psychology concerns psychotherapy and self-development.

Meditation, contemplative prayer, and similar forms of open-ended phenomenological inquiry are core practices for transpersonal psychology. These practices lead to an expanded awareness, a greater sense of presence, and a greater degree of self-integration or self-transcendence. While such practices have been successfully used for self-regulation, relaxation, and pain control and for self-exploration and psychotherapy, they have traditionally been used for self-transcendence and self-liberation. Despite their many surface forms, meditation and contemplative practices can be a means of disidentifying from our "masks" or personalities and realizing our fundamental nonduality.

Ritual is another core practice for transpersonal psychology. For many individuals and in many cultures and spiritual systems, ritual is the central means of discovering connections with each other, with communities, with the Earth, and with the cosmos. Other practices that are associated with transpersonal psychology include shamanism, lucid dreaming, visualization, chanting, transpersonal uses of music and art, and religious uses of psychedelic drugs.

Transpersonal psychology arose in the 1960s out of work by Abraham Maslow, Stanislav Grof, Anthony Sutich, and others in humanistic psychology. The work of William James on mysticism, Carl Jung on the collective unconscious, and Roberto Assagioli on psychosynthesis anticipated the development of transpersonal psychology. Interest in the psychological implications of Buddhism, Yoga, shamanism, psychedelic states, and holistic medicine fueled its development. At the present time, transpersonal psychology is gaining acceptance by many psychologists, and a number of professional organizations have been established worldwide. The Association for Transpersonal Psychology has published the *Journal of Transpersonal Psychology* since 1969. Its influences are found in a number of other psychological and psychiatric journals and books, both scientific and popular. Conferences and training programs sponsored by professional organizations such as the Association for Transpersonal Psychology and the International Transpersonal Association also provide training in transpersonal psychology and contribute to developments in the field.

Most transpersonal psychologists are involved in counseling and psychotherapy. Transpersonal psychotherapists may deal with spiritual crises or other explicitly transpersonal content, or they may bring a transpersonal context and processes to a broader range of psychological issues such as addictions, emotional distress, relationships, and life transitions. Art therapists, music therapists, dance therapists, and body-centered psychotherapists often use transpersonal principles in their work as well.

Transpersonal studies are arising in a number of fields, including medicine, education, anthropology, and organizational development. There are also strong connections between transpersonal psychology, ecopsychology, and deep ecology. Many people find transpersonal experiences in contact with nature, and many nature-based personal growth practices such as wilderness retreats, rites of passage, and other Earth-centered rituals have transpersonal dimensions. Similarly, some environmental activists bring a transpersonal perspective into their work. Deep ecologists such as Arne Naess, Warwick Fox, and John Seed and ecopsychologists such as Theodore Roszak and Ralph Metzner have promoted a kind of self-transcendence or transpersonal identity as a basis for environmental action. They argue that when one's identity expands or deepens beyond the individual self to include the Earth (i.e., a kind of self-transcendence), environmental action is more likely to be based on love, joy, and caring than on fear, shame, or sacrifice and that such a transpersonal attitude leads to action which is more effective and more sustainable.

Transpersonal psychology proponents believe that the practices they are developing benefit both psychology and the spiritual disciplines. Psychology can expand toward a fuller and richer accounting of the full range of human experience and potential and incorporate practices that develop this potential. The spiritual disciplines can incorporate insights and skills related to human development and healing to deal more skillfully with the psychological issues that arise with spiritual development. They can more effectively use these issues as gateways, rather than obstacles, to self-realization and authentic service.

John Davis

Further Reading

Cortright, Brant. *Psychotherapy and Spirit: Theory and Practice in Transpersonal Psychotherapy.* Albany, NY: State University of New York Press, 1997.

Davis, John V. "The Transpersonal Dimensions of Ecopsychology: Nature, Nonduality, and Spiritual Practice." *The Humanistic Psychologist* 26:1-3 (Spring/Summer/Autumn 1998), 69-100.

Grof, Stanislav. *Psychology of the Future: Lessons from Modern Consciousness Research.* Albany, NY: State University of New York Press, 2000.

Roszak, Theodore. *The Voice of the Earth: An Exploration of Ecopsychology.* New York: Touchstone, 1992.

Roszak, Theodore, Mary E. Gomes and Allen D. Kanner, eds. *Ecopsychology: Restoring the Earth, Healing the Mind*. San Francisco: Sierra Club, 1995.
Scotton, Bruce W., Allan B. Chinen and John R. Battista, eds. *Textbook of Transpersonal Psychiatry and Psychology*. New York: Basic Books, 1996.
Walsh, Roger and Francis Vaughn, eds. *Paths Beyond Ego: The Transpersonal Vision*. New York: Putnam, 1993.
Wilber, Ken. *Integral Psychology: Consciousness, Spirit, Psychology, Therapy*. Boston: Shambhala, 2000.
See also: Deep Ecology; Depth Ecology; Ecopsychology; Esalen Institute; Jung, Carl Gustav; Naess, Arne; Naropa University; Re-Earthing; Seed, John; Wilber, Ken; Wilderness Rites of Passage.

Tree Music

When I was 26, needing to rest after injuring my back while landscaping, I realized that I would much rather relax in the forest of Washington's Olympic Peninsula than in Seattle. So I drove out to Graves Creek Campground on the Quinalt River, and spent four days reading and playing my guitar next to a giant Douglas Fir tree. At the end of the four days, right before I left to return home, the song "The Tree" came flowing out. I looked up at the big Douglas Fir and said "I bet this is your song."

For years after that I'd sing "The Tree" and mention that I thought it was the big Douglas Fir's song. It seemed like a nice thought, and as the concept of a tree having "a song" had never come up in my scientifically oriented Western education, I only light-heartedly believed it.

A few years later I was invited to a celebration on Orcas Island, where the Lummi Indians and their allies had succeeded in saving a place called Madrona Point, where a developer had hoped to build condominiums on top of a Lummi Indian burial ground. After a 10-year battle, the United States Congress appropriated money to buy the land and give it back to the Lummi people.

The celebration was held at the Oddfellows hall on Madrona Point near Eastsound. Several hundred people gathered from the Lummi Reservation and Orcas Island. There was a huge potluck feast with salmon and berry pies and salads and fried bread. Spirits were high and children ran around everywhere.

The man who invited me to the celebration then told me that the chief wanted me to sing "The Tree." I expressed reluctance, however, unsure whether this quiet song could be heard over the clanking dishes and spirited children. My friend simply restated, "The chief would like to hear 'The Tree.'"

After I was introduced, the place quieted down and I began to sing, noticing immediately something that had never happened before at one of my concerts. While everyone seemed to be enjoying the tune, the elder Lummis were riveted, holding on to every note, every word. I felt honored that they would care so much about this song.

Afterwards I spoke with the chief and several elders. I told them the story of spending four days with the old Douglas Fir tree by the Quinalt River and how I had always thought it was the Tree's song.

"It is," said the chief, "I recognize the tune. It is a song from a tree in our region. In Lummi tradition, and for many of the peoples of this region, we get our music from trees. Each tree has its own song. We go out and spend three or four days next to a tree where we fast and pray and listen for that tree's song. We take the song and sing it or play it on the flute. In this era when so many of our ancient trees are being cut down, we go out and learn their songs before they die, as a way of honoring the great trees. We are working to save the last remaining ancient groves on our territory."

I have never looked at a tree in the same way since then. I have never looked at any creature in the same way since then.

Dana Lyons

Further Reading

Lyons, Dana. *The Tree*. Bellevue, WA: Illumination Arts, 2002.
See also: Animism (various); Earth First! and the Earth Liberation Front; Heathenry – Ásatrú; Music; Music and Eco-activism in America; Music of Resistance; Pagan Music.

Trees – as Religious Architecture

It goes without saying that trees are essential to many architectural creations. Not only do they serve structural functions, but they are often also imbued with symbolic meaning as well. This is seen quite clearly in religious contexts. Examples are found around the world from ancient to present times. Shinto shrines, Egyptian and Greek temples, Celtic groves, the Lakota Sun Dance, Pacific Northwest coast totem poles, Buddhist stupas, and Christian churches – along with associated "Green Man" imagery – are briefly examined here as a sample of the great variety of places that exist.

We begin with Japan and Shinto beliefs. Some of the oldest Shinto shrines sites are groves or forested hillsides where rituals were performed in relation to *kami*. The idea, and thus the definition, of *kami* has changed over the millennia as influences from China, Korea, and India, among other places, participated in the shaping of Japanese thought on the subject. In general, however, *kami* can perhaps be best understood within a polytheistic context, where powerful spiritual forces are conceived as embodied through human, animal, tree, river, rock, wind, sun, or other natural forms. In early Shintoism trees themselves were shrines to *kami*. Later, human-built shrines were erected. The natural and the built overlapped in meaning. The same characters that today are interpreted as *jinga*, or shrine, were understood in ancient texts as *kamu-tsu-yahshiro*, or *mori*, two terms meaning "kami grove." Close relationships between trees and architecture are visible in the *torii* gates and in the cylindrical wooden columns supporting shrine floors and ridge poles. At Ise Shrine, unique in that it is rebuilt every twenty years, rituals pertaining to the protection, burial, re-use, and adornment of the heart-pillar (*shin no mihashira*) hearken back to early Shintoism.

Similarly, trees played functional and symbolic roles in Egyptian temples. Columns were shaped to reflect lotus, papyrus, and palms. These were intentionally suggestive of the connections between religious beliefs, the fertility of the land, and the well-being of people. Other columns were shaped to represent Osiris. In addition to vegetative abundance, the myths and rituals associated with him revolve around themes of death and resurrection. A link between religious belief and trees is also indicated by the story of how he was murdered, set adrift down the Nile in a sarcophagus, incorporated into a growing tree along the river's banks, and installed within a temple as a pillar.

Greek temples also manifest relationships between trees, architecture, and belief. Doric columns are reminiscent of organic forms. Their girth, taper, and overall appearance is quite tree-like. Architectural historians point out that logs could have been easily sculpted into a series of planar surfaces amenable to fluting. Peg features, triglyphs at the end of what would have been beams, and mutules imitative of rafters all support claims of the column's wooden derivation. A number of Doric traits were replicated in Ionic and Corinthian forms. Greek temple architecture also suggests the physical appearance of sacred groves. The manner in which temple space was divided into spaces was intended to mimic the sense of multiple spaces within groves.

Sacred groves were also central to Celtic traditions, found across a vast area spreading from Asia Minor through continental Western Europe and into Britain and Ireland. While beech and various conifers figured prominently in the rituals and beliefs of some groups, oak appears to have the most widespread symbolic significance. The word "Druid," in fact, is closely associated with a Celtic term for oak. In some cases altars were constructed for use in these groves. Tree motifs are commonly carved upon them. Additionally, trees themselves served as religious architecture. Miranda Green, author of *Symbol & Image in Celtic Religious Art*, speaks of archeological finds in Germany at places like the Goloring and the Goldberg where a large tree-like pillar was set in the center of an enclosure. There are many instances in the archeological record where Celtic groups dug pits and left offerings in association with living trees and pillars.

Trees are important in Native American beliefs, and there are many circumstances where trees serve as architecture. It is not romantic to say that participation in traditional ceremonies helps root contemporary native peoples in their heritage. Trees can play very important roles. Lakota Sun Dance ceremonies, for instance, revolve around a central pole that is understood to be a sacred tree. It is ceremonially harvested from the forest and erected in the center of a Sun Dance site. Dancers attach themselves to the pole with long cords as they pray and engage in acts of self-sacrifice. As symbol, the sacred tree links the elements of the larger universe with the dancers, and through them to the entire community gathered for the ritual.

Totem poles are associated with native peoples of the Pacific Northwest, and are especially common in the coastal regions of British Columbia and southeastern Alaska. Coast Salish, Nuu-chah-nulth, Kwakiutl, Nuxalk, Tsimshian, Haida, and Tlingit are representative groups. Great diversity of language and religious practices exists among them. Diversity is found in the poles as well. Some serve memorial purposes, while others have mortuary uses. There are also frontal poles and house posts; both are incorporated into the structure of traditional homes. All poles are made of red cedar. Preferences for one or another type vary among groups. Carvings are not actually totems. Rather, they symbolize crests and signs of a given family or clan. Pole-raisings were, and today typically are, attended by the narration of stories, prayer, singing, drumming, dancing, feasting, and the gift exchange known as potlatching. In contemporary times a fifth type of pole – the commercial pole – is often carved for non-natives and erected in non-traditional settings. More important than merely generating revenue, these intentionally communicate the vitality of indigenous groups and indicate that their ties to the land remain.

Buddhist architecture, such as that found in stupas, also features a central pole with strong tree associations. Originally a type of pre-Buddhist Indian burial mound, stupas were tumuli with a wooden post in their center. The pole may have symbolized Aryan traditions where community leaders met under a tree for discussions, and it may have symbolized their beliefs about sacred or cosmic trees. In Hindu contexts, the tree and umbrellas under which royalty were shaded, and ideas of Mt. Meru, were all combined in stupa architecture. Buddhists adopted and embedded these notions into places like Sanchi, where a central axle-pole at the top of the stupa symbolizes the process of enlightenment. The vertically arranged series of disks on the pole represent levels of enlightenment; they are in essence stylized branches of the cosmic tree.

Tree motifs, some of which refer to a cosmic tree, are integral to the architecture of churches and cathedrals. Not only are representations of the Tree of Knowledge and the Fall highly significant, but in many places carved foliage and even the Green Man is seen. The Green Man appears in church architecture as a male face encompassed by leaves. Sometimes leaves are shown sprouting from his mouth. Common across much of Western Europe, the Green Man evidently predates the spread of Christianity, and very well may have Celtic associations with fertility. The Church incorporated the Green Man as an expression of death and resurrection. In a similar way the cross, symbolizing resurrection and the promise of salvation, is often understood to be a tree or tree-like. One example is found in the architecture of St. Andrews in Ellensburg, Washington. On the interior wall behind the altar hangs a large wooden cross. Behind it a series of tightly clustered beams stretch toward the ceiling, spreading ever-further apart as they go. The overall effect is that of a tree emerging from the cross.

In the sites described here, as in many more from all around the world – Africa, Oceania, Australia, Europe, Asia, and the Americas – trees are a significant element of religious architecture. While the particular symbolic meaning of a tree or trees may differ from one culture to another, they are all reminders of the organic connection between humans and the world they inhabit.

Joel Geffen

Further Reading

Green, Miranda. *Symbol & Image in Celtic Religious Art*. London: Routledge, 1989.

Minoru, Sonoda. "Shinto and the Natural Environment." In John Breen and Mark Teeuwen, eds. *Shinto in History: Ways of the Kami*. Richmond, Surrey: Curzon Press, 2000, 32–46.

Norberg-Schulz. *Meaning in Western Architecture*. New York: Rizzoli International Publications, Inc., 1980.

Stewart, Hilary. *Looking At Totem Poles*. Vancouver: University of Washington Press, 1993.

Stover, Dale. "Postcolonial Sun Dancing at Wakpimni Lake." *Journal of the American Academy of Religion* 69:4 (December 2001), 815–36.

Volwahsen, Andreas. *Living Architecture: Indian*. New York: Grosset & Dunlap, 1969.

See also: Cathedral Forests and the Felling of Sacred Groves; Druids and Druidry; Heathenry – Ásatrú; India's Sacred Groves; Japanese Religions; Lakota Sun Dance; Sacred Groves of Africa; Tree Music; Trees in Haitian Vodou; Trees (Northern & Middle Europe); Trees – Sacred; Wenger, Susan, Yoruba Art & the Oshogbo Sacred Grove.

Trees in Haitian Vodou

Vodou crystallized as a religion among African and African-descended slaves in the French colony of Saint-Domingue (1697–1804), whose massive sugar production made it Europe's most lucrative colonial enterprise. With the most dynamic early Vodou communities springing up in settlements of escaped slaves from diverse African ethnic groups in the colony (which became the independent Republic of Haiti in 1804), since its inception the religion has demonstrated significant variety. Certain traditions are primarily ancestor cults, while others focus on particular spirits brought from West Africa or others revealed in the New World. Because of the clandestine and variegated nature of colonial-era Vodou, moreover, the religion has no founder, no unifying doctrine, and no formal organizational network. Neither any of these, nor a Vodou scripture, has ever developed.

Slaves brought to the colony were baptized Catholic upon arrival and given minimal religious instruction by Dominicans, Capuchins, and Jesuits. Syncretism thus immediately resulted, as slaves identified Catholic saints as new manifestations of African spirits, and adopted crosses, holy water, and incense as powerful religious trinkets to be used in conjunction with the amulets that they reconstructed from African religious memory. The Catholic "pantheon" – with its single high creator God, Virgin Mary, and host of dead individuals (the saints) who intervene in the world of the living – lent itself quite fluently to assimilation with the traditional African community of spiritual beings, which likewise has a single distant creator God (called *Bondyè* in Vodou) and numerous spirits and ancestors, who, much like the Catholic saints, are perceived of as accessible and with whom the greatest amount of human/divine commerce transpires.

Spirit possession and divination are the main forms of communication with the dead (*lemò*) and the spirits (*lwa yo*) in Vodou, and together form its ritual focus. Put simply, when our relationship with *lemo* and/or *lwa yo* is in harmony, life is full and pleasurable, whereas when this relationship is discordant, sickness, some other hardship, or even death may result. Upon the occurrence of such misfortune, ritual specialists (female: *manbo*; male: *oungan*) are consulted. Either through divination or the orchestration of ceremonies aiming to provoke spirit possession (which most often take place either in temples [*ounfò*], family burial compounds, or public cemeteries), the *manbo* or *oungan* effects communication with the *lemò* or *lwa yo* in order to discover the cause of the illness or discord and to determine a means of reestablishing harmony or effecting healing. Both the maintenance and the reconstitution of this harmony rely primarily on sacrifice in various forms, while healing often involves herbalism and ritual baths.

Haitian Vodou thus combines a variety of traditional African (e.g., Fon, Yoruba, and Kongo) and Catholic elements. While decidedly more akin in ritual and belief to African traditional religion than to Catholicism, Vodou is not an African religion but a product of the Haitian experience of and response to the social and natural worlds. Its understanding of nature is thus more rooted in

West African spirit and ancestor cults than in Catholic theology, which is especially reflected in the religion's great reverence for trees and forests. In Vodou, spirits and the ancestors abide in nature. Together they are spoken of as the mysteries (*myste yo*), and, as in Africa, trees (called in Haitian Creole *pyè bwa*; lit.: "wood foot") are among their most cherished homes.

Vodou is deeply rooted in and sensitive to nature, with many *lwas* being associated with natural phenomenon. The serpent-rainbow lwa Dambalah Wedo, for example, lives in waterfalls, while other spirits are embodied by natural forces, such as Ogun, the *lwa* of the iron. The dead are likewise deeply enmeshed in nature and conceived of as residing either under the ground, across the water, or in the forest. Trees and the forest, though increasingly scarce in the impoverished nation, have thus always featured prominently in Haitian Vodou's rich symbolism and mythology.

Trees gain their great religious significance in Vodou for a number of reasons, such as being the source of sacred drums and the gourd out of which is made the Vodou priest's sacred rattle (*asson*). The most important reason is that trees are believed to be the residence and the "preferred avenue of divine approach," in Maya Deren's terms, of the *lwas*. Because of this, certain species of trees considered especially sacred are planted around Vodou temples, or temple sites are determined by the presence of such trees. These trees, called in French *arbres-reposoirs* (lit.: resting-place trees; altar trees), are recognizable by the straw sacks and strips of cloth that often hang on their branches. Since the *lwas* are thus considered to live in these trees, the *arbres-reposoirs* are themselves rendered cult in Vodou, and thus the straw sacks sometimes contain offerings for these trees and/or the spirits who reside in them, candles are lighted at their trunks, and pottery is broken against them. As the home of the *lwas*, these sacred trees are also addressed by candidates during initiation rituals in rural Haiti.

Whereas virtually all of the *lwas* may live in trees, and most *lwas* prefer certain species of trees, four *lwas* in particular are most closely associated with trees: Legba, Gede, Gran Bwa (Great Forest) and Loko. As the guardian of the crossroads where intersect the sacred and the profane, and as the gatekeeper who holds the keys to the doors of communication between spirits and humans, Legba is in a true sense the most important member of the *lwa* pantheon. Every Vodou temple has a post at its center that runs from the floor to the roof, down which are believed to arrive the *lwas* during communal ceremonies. Commonly known as the *poto-mitan* (center post), this essential feature is also called the *poto-Legba*, reflective of Legba's authority over all use of the pole by spirits or humans. As the gatekeeper, moreover, Legba's sacred tree is the most important in or around the temple yard, and it invariably stands near the entryway. And as the *lwa* of the crossroads, any tree standing near the intersection of paths or roads may be a site of devotion to Legba.

The most venerated tree in Haitian Vodou is the mapou (alt.: mapou africain; mapou zonbi), or *ceiba pentenda*, one of the most majestic trees in the Caribbean. In West Africa, especially in Benin, the homeland of an important segment of Saint-Domingue's slave population, the spirits of the ancestors are believed to reside in *ceiba pentenda*. The mapou, which appears in many Haitian proverbs and is revered in other parts of the Afro-Caribbean, is the preferred home of the Gede family of spirits, the *lwas* of death and the dead (and, dialectically, of life and the living) who collectively represent Vodou's trickster spirit. Being the moments when the veil between the living and the dead is most permeable, noon and midnight are times when the mapou is reserved for the Gede, hence Vodou practitioners know to stay clear of mapous at 12:00 a.m. or p.m. Given the power of the mapou at noon and midnight, on occasion secret religious societies in Haiti have been known to hold ceremonies then and there.

The *lwa* who is most associated with trees generally is Loko, the spirit of vegetation and the life-force within all plants and trees. As such, Loko provides the healing power manifest in Vodou's rich herbalism and is thus the patron *lwa* of the religion's "leaf doctors" (*medsin fey*). There is consequently a tradition in Haitian Vodou reminiscent of many Native American ritual preparations for the hunt, wherein the Vodou practitioner makes offerings to Loko to secure his blessing before cutting down any tree.

However pervasive is this spirit of reverence for trees in Haiti, it has been overwhelmed by the nation's grueling poverty and overpopulation, which has resulted in, among many other catastrophes, Haiti's almost total deforestation: 95 percent of the country's forest has been lost, and each year 15,000 acres of fertile topsoil is washed away as a result. With an annual per capita income of roughly $250, Haitian peasants cut trees for charcoal as a means of income, while electricity-deprived urban Haitians also rely on charcoal for cooking. The result is desertification and a litany of related ecological problems. Thanks to Vodou, at least, in some of the countries most desertified regions there are at least a few mapou trees and *arbres-reposoirs* that remain standing.

Terry Rey

Further Reading

Deren, Maya. *Divine Horsemen: The Living Gods of Haiti*. New York: McPherson, 1991 (1953).

Métraux, Alfred. *Voodoo in Haiti*. New York: Schoken, 1972 (1959).

See also: Caribbean Cultures; West Africa; Yoruba Culture (West Africa).

Trees (Northern and Middle Europe)

Apart from the arctic prairies and deserts on the northern fringes, Europe is a continent of trees. The dark, evergreen conifers of spruce and fir characterize the northernmost part, the light conifers with its larches and pines are to be found where the sunlight is more generous the year around. The forests reign in Middle Europe where the seasons are even and the rainfall bountiful. The deciduous forests, with their oaks and beeches, show much more diversity of trees than the boreal conifers.

The Teutonic, Celtic, Baltic and Slavic tribes who inhabited Northern and Middle Europe from at least 900 B.C.E. were of Indo-European origin, akin to tribes in Southern Europe. Their languages were and are related, and many of the surviving myths and legends are similar. The Finnish-Ugrians who inhabited the northeast of Europe form a special group within the family of European cultures. The religious history of the continent is multilayered and complex, because the settlements of the ancient tribes were scattered or they were nomadic, and their ideas diverse. Moreover, the extant sources of information are often colored by the worldviews of the commentators.

Julius Caesar described the religious, sacrificial practices of the Druids, the religious class of the Celts, in his *Gallic Wars* (VI.13, composed ca. 50 B.C.E.). Caesar pictured the Druids weaving immense figures out of twigs, which were filled with living people and set on fire. The funeral rites, according to Caesar, were also connected with great bonfires. A century later, Pliny the Elder spoke in his *Natural History* about the Druids as the "people of the oak," a name derived from the Greek "drouios" which means "oaken" or "from the oak," and stated that their magic potions consisted primarily of oak-bark (XVI). Pliny also described the sacredness of the mistletoe for the Druids. According to Pliny, mistletoe grows rarely on a hard oak, and when it occurs, it is collected with a great ceremony, which takes place around the oak tree.

According to *Edda* (a collection of poetry from ca. 300–800 and preserved in fourteenth-century Icelandic manuscripts), the mythical tree of Nordic mythology is the Ash of Yggdrasill, the largest tree in the world, stretching its branches over the skies. Yggdrasill has three roots and each is stretched over a well. The first root is in heaven, over a well where the gods have their sanctuary. Three Fates who represent past, present, and future guard the well and decide the fate of humans. Human ancestry is thought to have come from the twigs of Ash and Elm that floated to shore and were given spirit, breath, and life. The second root reaches over a well filled with water of wisdom, where the primal, yawning void of the Nordic creation story used to be. In exchange for the water in the well, Odin had to be hanged on the tree for nine nights. The name of the tree means "the stallion of Odin" (one of Odin's names is Ygg) and is derived from this ordeal. The third root ranges over hot-spring Hvergelmir, filled with snakes. Yggdrasill constantly suffers a great hardship, as four stags bite the trunk from above, and below the snakes gnaw its root. The Fates wash the tree every day with white clay, which keeps Yggdrasill green, in this balance of destruction and preservation, until the day of doom.

The hanging of Odin may bear shamanistic traits of connections with and travel to the underworld and point to an influence from the Finnish-Ugrians on the Teutonics. *Kalevala* (the epic poem of the Finns, collected in 1835–1849), tells the story of Väinämöinen, who goes to the underworld in search of a magic formula which he needs to finish his oak-boat. He walks for three weeks, through a stand of saplings, bird-cherry and, at last, through junipers (Poem 16). In the end he meets the giant Vipunen (Poem 17), who is fast asleep under the ground. An aspen grows on his shoulders, birch from the brows, alders spread from the jaws, willows from the beard, firs from the forehead, and the pines from the teeth. Väinämöinen is swallowed by Vipunen, but the former tortures the tree-monster from within the belly until Vipunen sings the magic rhyme of the creation of the world.

Bonaventure (1217–1274) was a Franciscan teacher at the University of Paris. His book, *The Tree of Life*, is an important Christian source on trees and spirituality in medieval Europe. *The Tree of Life* is based on tree metaphors in the Bible, framed by the trees of the first and the last books of the Bible, the trees of knowledge and life in Eden and Revelation 22. The tree of Revelation bears twelve kinds of fruits and the leaves of the trees are for the healing of the nations. For Bonaventure the twelve fruits are symbols of twelve virtues, which all show aspects of the life and ministry of Jesus as described in the gospels. According to Bonaventure, one can avoid the fallacy of Adam, who chose the tree of knowledge instead of the tree of life, by meditating on the fruits of the tree of life in Revelation, each of which symbolizes the life of Jesus from his conception in eternity to resurrection. The goal of meditating on the tree and its fruit is to be one with the body of Christ in ecstatic unity.

The popularity of *The Tree of Life*, miracle plays, and old Roman traditions of using evergreens as decorations, may have inspired the Christmas tree. This tradition became popular in Germany after the Reformation, especially at the end of the eighteenth century. It was expanded to Britain, America, and throughout the world in the nineteenth century, under the strong influence of Victorian family values, where the tree became the center of family and home rituals during Christmas. The tradition of celebrating spring with a dance around the maypole in Northern Europe is another example of a European tree ritual.

Sigridur Gudmarsdottir

Further Reading

Bonaventure, Saint. *The Soul's Journey into God; The Tree of Life; The Life of St. Francis*. Evert Cousins, ed., tr. New York: Paulist Press, 1978.

Bonnefoy, Yves. *Mythologies*. A restructured translation of *Dictionnaire des Mytho-logies et des Religions des Sociétés Traditionelles et du Monde Antique*. Prepared under the direction of Wendy Doniger. Gerald Honigsblum, tr. Chicago: University of Chicago Press, 1981.

Caesar, Julius. *The Gallic War*. H.J. Edwards, tr. Cambridge, MA: Cambridge University Press, 1958.

The Elder Edda: A Selection. P. Taylor and W.H. Auden, trs. New York: Vintage, 1967.

The Kalevala or Poems of the Kaleva District. Elias Lönnrot, comp. Francis Peabody Magoun Jr., tr. Cambridge, MA: Harvard University Press, 1963.

Pliny, the Elder. *Natural History IV*. H. Rackman, tr. Cambridge, MA/London: Harvard University Press/W. Heinemann, 1962.

See also: Cathedral Forests and the Felling of Sacred Groves; Druids and Druidry; Heathenry – Ásatrú; Odinism; Sacred Groves of Africa; Trees as Religious Architecture; Trees – Sacred.

Trees – Sacred

A tree is a tall, single-stemmed, woody plant which bears branches some distance from the ground. Trees are the oldest and largest living organisms on planet Earth. The bristle cone pine (*Pinus longaeva*) in the White Mountains of California can live to be over 4000 years old. The species with the largest individual trees is the giant sequoia (*Sequoiadendron giganteum*), averaging at maturity 300 feet tall and 15 feet in diameter.

In many ways trees are a primary source for life on our apparently unique planet Earth. A leaf is a miniature food-making factory – sunlight, air, and water interact with chlorophyll cells in the leaf through photosynthesis and with nutrients from the soil to produce food which allows the tree to grow. In turn, the tree produces food and shelter for other plants (epiphytes), animals, fungi, and microorganisms that visit or reside somewhere on it. Trees influence other life far more than any other kind of plant by their wood, leaves, and fruit, as well as by the special kinds of environments they create (shelter, shade, microclimatic zones).

For humans, trees provide oxygen, food, fuel, building and craft materials, paper products, shade, and soil-erosion and flood control. The monetary value of the environmental services provided by a single tree that lives for fifty years has been calculated at nearly $200,000.

There are also whole cultures, sub-cultures, industries, and occupations focused on trees of a particular kind such as logging redwoods (*Sequoia sempervirens* and *Sequoiadendron giganteum*) in the Pacific coast forests of the northwest United States; maple sugar (*Acer* spp.) in New England; rubber trees (*Hevea brasiliensis*) in the Amazon and rubber tree plantations in South and Southeast Asia; mulberry (*Morus alba*) for the cultivation of silk worms in China; olive (*Olea europea*) in the Mediterranean and Middle East; and coconut (*Cocos nucifera*) in the Pacific islands and other tropical areas. In addition, special arts have developed around trees like topiary, tree sculpturing in eighteenth-century England, and bonsai, the cultivation of miniature or dwarf trees in Japan. Trees can have physiological and psychological impacts on individual humans as well, such as relaxing heart rate, blood pressure, and brain waves. Research has shown that hospital patients recover faster than otherwise if they can see a tree outside their window.

From observations such as the above it is little wonder that trees may also be considered sacred. The common characteristics of sacred trees are described by Nathaniel Altman:

> A tree becomes sacred through recognition of the power that it expresses. This power may be manifested as the food, shelter, fuel, materials used to build boats, or medicine that the tree provides. How a tree is used will vary according to geography, species of tree, and the particular needs (and ingenuity) of the human culture involved. Sacred trees have also provided beauty, hope, comfort, and inspiration, nurturing and healing the mental, emotional, and spiritual levels of our being. They are symbols of life, abundance, creativity, generosity, permanence, energy, and strength (1994: 9).

I first discovered the existence of sacred trees while conducting field research in Thailand. From Bangkok to the remotest rural villages, one often sees colorful cloth wrapped around the lower trunk of a tree. A small spirit house with offerings such as candles, incense, food, and water may be placed near the base of the tree. Local people believe that the tree is the residence of a spirit. Anyone who harms such a tree might experience misfortune, sickness, or even death as the spirit takes revenge. Consequently, because of their special status sacred trees are usually protected in effect.

Sacred trees are usually extraordinary in age, size, shape, or some other attribute. For example, in one village in Thailand that I visited, a giant ironwood tree or Malacca teak (*Afzelia bakeri*) is considered sacred. Its secretions resemble blood. Also residents in the area mentioned that twice lightning struck and burned other trees nearby, but did not touch this tree because of its extraordinary power. In addition, some residents have seen an unusual light near the tree in the early evening.

Certain species of trees are sacred because of their

relation to a religion. The banyan (*Ficus bengalensis*) and bodhi (*F. religiosa*) have been associated with Buddhism since its inception. The Buddha is believed to have been previously incarnated as a tree spirit and later during his reincarnation in human form he reached enlightenment under a bodhi. Also in Hinduism the bodhi is supposed to be the home of the gods Krishna, Brahma, Vishnu, and Shiva. Thus, the bodhi is the most sacred of trees for both Hindus and Buddhists, and this is reflected in its species name. The banyan tree is also considered sacred by Hindus. Moreover, in the Buddhist country of Bhutan, it is actually illegal to cut down any living tree.

In many Asian countries, some monks wander in forests where they shelter and meditate under trees, emulating the life and teachings of the Buddha. Furthermore, in Thailand, a number of monks have symbolically ordained trees by ceremonially wrapping the saffron robes around giants in the forest to protect them from loggers. By mere association, the surrounding trees may also be protected. Tree ordination as a conservation technique has usually proven successful in Thailand.

Throughout the world, diverse cultures recognize sacred trees. For instance, the Celts, Druids and many other tribes in ancient Europe venerated single trees, groves, and forests, especially of oak (*Quercus* spp.). Oaks seem more prone to being struck by lightning than other tree species, and this may have contributed to their sacred status. Oak and spruce (*Picea* spp.) were of special significance in ancient Germanic rituals, and this is the origin of the modern tradition of the Christmas tree. Yew trees (*Taxus* spp.) were especially important in ancient Britain, and churchyards were built around or close to them. To this day there are several hundred shrines throughout Europe associated with individual trees.

In the United States, the Mormon religious faith was born near the town of Palmyra in New York. There today it is still possible to visit the Sacred Grove where the Mormon prophet Joseph Smith first had divine visions. Also in the United States and elsewhere, some families plant trees as a living memorial when a relative or friend dies. A tree that survived the bombing of the federal building in Oklahoma City became a symbol of renewal and a sacred tree of sorts.

At first glance a single sacred tree may not appear to have much if any significance for environmental and biodiversity conservation. However, a single tree is part of a hierarchy of progressively larger ecological systems. A large tree can host dozens or more of other species such as lianas (vines), epiphytes, mosses, and fungi. In turn there may be dozens to hundreds of species of resident and transient animals. Millions of microorganisms may also inhabit a single tree. Interacting with these species are others as predators, parasites, competitors, and so on. In addition, birds, bats, insects, and other animals pollinate flowers of the tree and those of other members of its species in the surrounding environment. Such animals may eat fruit from the tree and disperse the seeds elsewhere, thereby stimulating growth of other individuals of that species. In such ways, diverse animals link individual trees of the same species into wider networks of reproduction and production.

A large tree also creates microclimates and microenvironments for plants, mosses, fungi, and other organisms which grow on its leaves, branches, trunk, and roots as well as on the adjacent ground. The leaf-fall and other litter from the tree yields nutrients for plants and animals below on the ground through decomposition by decomposer species. A large tree may also act like a water pump, its deeper tap roots pulling water toward the surface. Some of this water may become available for surrounding plants as well. The roots of the tree may pump nutrients to the surface too. Acting something like a sponge, the tree captures and slowly releases some rainwater which might otherwise contribute to more soil erosion. Thus, trees are a very important component of the composition, structure, and function of many ecosystems.

From this systems perspective a single tree can contribute to environmental and biodiversity conservation. When a large tree is considered sacred, and thus afforded special protection from harm, it may help conserve a multitude of other species and their symbiotic relationships as well as specific microclimates, microenvironments, soil, and water resources. Of course, these manifold ecological functions of a single tree are multiplied many times over in groves and forests which are even more important for conservation.

If more people appreciated the numerous diverse meanings and significances of trees, then they might appreciate even more the groves and forests, and consequently be more concerned about their wise use and conservation.

Leslie E. Sponsel

Further Reading

Altman, Nathaniel. *Sacred Trees*. San Francisco, CA: Sierra Club Books, 1994.

Darlington, Susan M. "The Ordination of a Tree: The Buddhist Ecology Movement in Thailand." *Ethnology* 37:1 (1998), 1–15.

Guha, Gita. "A Culture of Trees." *Resurgence* 168 (1995), 31–5.

Jones, Owain and Paul Cloke. *Tree Cultures: The Place of Trees and Trees in Their Place*. New York, NY: Berg, 2002.

Kaza, Stephanie. *The Attentive Heart: Conversations with Trees*. Boston, MA: Shambhala Press, 1996.

Perlman, Michael. *The Power of Trees: The Reforesting of the Soul*. Dallas, TX: Spring Publications, 1994.

Rival, Laura, ed. *The Social Life of Trees: Anthropological*

Perspectives on Tree Symbolism. New York, NY: Berg, 1998.

Thomas, Peter. *Trees: Their Natural History.* New York, NY: Cambridge University Press, 2000.

See also: Animism (various); Buddha; Cathedral Forests and the Felling of Sacred Groves; Donga Tribe; Druids and Druidry; Earth First! and the Earth Liberation Front; Heathenry – Ásatrú; India's Sacred Groves; Japanese Religions; Lakota Sun Dance; Middle Earth; Odinism; Sacred Groves of Africa; Tree Music; Trees in Haitian Vodou; Trees as Religious Architecture; Trees (Northern and Middle Europe); Wenger, Susan, Yoruba Art & the Oshogbo Sacred Grove.

The Trickster

The trickster is a virtually universal figure in world mythology, especially that of hunter-gatherers, on whose mythological landscape he holds center stage. Trickery and deceit, frequently exercised in the form of coarse and hurtful practical jokes on a duped party, and excessive biological drives, are the trickster's characteristic traits. He is usually a solitary figure who roams the landscape, playing pranks and getting into scrapes, as his deceit and cunning (due to the stupidity with which they are usually performed) may backfire on him. In the context of his prankish and foolish antics, he may, more or less inadvertently and haphazardly, find himself in the role of culture hero and transformer, bringing such things as fire, cooking, curing, weapons, carnal knowledge, conception by sex and painful childbirth, death to humans, setting the sun in the sky, or pulling the fished-up islands of Polynesia into the ocean. He may transform food plants into stars, mud into the Earth, clay into humans, ogres into animals or, in the manner very much of the trickster, create the waterholes and river-beds of the Kalahari with his hugely swollen testicles that he drags behind him through a hitherto featureless landscape, or, with one mighty, cosmic fart, scatter all living creatures to the various places on the Earth (as did the Nharo Bushman Pate and the Winnebago trickster Wakdjunkaga, respectively). His exploits and misadventures are the stuff of many tales, or tale cycles, that provide entertainment to an audience both of children and adults, as well as act as cultural mechanisms for venting social frustration and for reaffirming social values and beliefs.

Trickster figures are particularly prominent in the folklore of America and Africa. They appear in the former continent in such personas as Raven (along the northwest coast), the stealer of the sun and bringer of light to the world, or as Hare, Beaver or the anthropomorphic Nanabusho or Wiseakjak (both variously spelled) among the Algonkians and Athapaskans, who are variously tricksters, teachers and transformers. The most widespread and clearly delineated North American trickster being is Coyote. His African counterpart, Jackal, is a trickster figure also in southern Africa, along with /Kaggen (Mantis), as well as numerous others. For Hare, too, we find an African counterpart, in the folklore of a number of Bantu-speaking peoples. Spider – Ananse and Tore, among the Ashanti and Azande – and the "Pale Fox" – Ogo (Yurugu, among the Dogon) – are two of Western and central Africa's better-known tricksters. West Africa's most complex trickster figure is the messenger god and god of divination Elegba (or Eshu, or, as he is known among the Fon and Aflateke, a name meaning "I have tricked you"), who is prominent also in the folklore and belief systems of New World Afro-Americans in Surinam, Brazil, Trinidad and Cuba.

He is reminiscent of the Greek figure of Hermes, another messenger god, as well as god of thieves, for which role he is suited through his qualities of cunning, fraud and perjury. Another European trickster god was Loki of Nordic mythology, the *enfant terrible* of the teutonic pantheon who was a comic trickster and transformer in the early myths, but who became progressively evil and destructive in the later cycles, having been the chief force to bring about the *Raganrök* – the twilight of the gods – and the end of their realm and world. Other European tricksters are the medieval figures of Renart (Reynard) the fox and Till Eulenspiegel, both anti-establishment figures whose dupes were the temporal and clerical power holders of the day, as well as the towns' burghers. Finally, there is the figure of Robin Goodfellow (alias Puck, of "Midsummer Night's Dream"), the mischievous fairy being of English folklore, a trickster *par excellence*. As a shape-shifter – "sometimes a horse, sometimes a hound, a hog, a headless bear, or sometimes a fire" – who played a seductive pipe, this "shrewd and knavish sprite" lured forest travelers into swamps, "laughing at their harm." He delighted in watching the follies of humans and – as is the trickster's wont – in "frightening the maidens of the villagery."

As is evident from this brief and quite incomplete survey of the world's rogues' gallery of tricksters, we have here a figure of great diversity and complexity. In his role and being, the trickster is an ambiguous blend of things: prankster-protagonist, culture hero and transformer and, in some instances, also god. Ambiguity is evident also in his ontological make-up, which is that either of an animal – usually one sly, agile and elusive – or of a human. However, neither guise is unequivocally "animalian" or humanoid. As animal – Coyote, Spider, Mantis, Hare, Raven – trickster, the storytellers insist, is also "a person." As for the humanoid tricksters, these figures may be of misshapen bizarre appearance, such as the Nharo Bushmen's Pate, a one-legged manikin who was covered with cocoon fibers and had big toes sticking out from all over his body, or the Canadian Micmac's Kuloscap, who was a giant. Humanoid tricksters may have trouble with their limbs and body parts, which may work at cross-purposes with each other or may become unfastened from their owner's body, running off on their own. The body parts that are especially active in the trickster are those that contain orifices, especially those of the alimentary canal and nether regions; they – anus, penis, along with buttocks, testicles, and entrails – may sever themselves, to fly off on some mischievous pranks that blend scatology with lasciviousness (two examples of tricksters with such errant body parts are Wakdjunkaga and Kauha, of Winnebago and !Kung folklore). In refastening themselves to his body, the trickster's parts may be haphazardly reordered, such that his head may be fastened to his bottom or his penis to his back. His anatomy is thus quite fluid and unstable; its inconstancy is heightened whenever he undergoes one of his shape-shifting transformations to animal, tree, rock, or water body. The trickster delights in transformation, both of himself and of beings and states around him; as a result, he and the world around him are a-quiver with inchoate, liminal ambiguity.

Ambiguity also marks the trickster's sexual and social disposition. While usually male – with often voracious heterosexual appetites – he may also assume a female guise, usually in the context of some sexual escapade. While generally solitary, the trickster may wander with a companion, who may be the butt of his pranks, or who may turn tables on the trickster and outwit him; the classic example is Coyote and Wolf (or, in the southern African variant, Jackal and Hyena). In Amazonia, the trickster may be one of a pair of mythical twins, while the Chippewan Wenebojo's sibling companion was Nekajiweizik – one of his two younger brothers (after he had killed the second brother). Some tricksters – such as the /Xam and !Kung Bushmen's /Kaggen and Kaoxa (or Kauha) – have wives and live in extended families, permanently or for a while. The family members provide a foil to the trickster's moral and social failings, of food greed, failure to share or provide properly, sexual lusts and jealousies (frequently incestuous in bent), which all conspire against the trickster's ever being a solid family man.

While the moral qualities of this vindictive and destructive prankster and boaster, vulgarian and libertine, may seem to be unequivocal, once again we note ambiguity. The trickster may also be seen in the role of *Heilbringer*, extending help, generosity, compassion and protection to those he deals with, especially weak or oppressed beings who are threatened by danger or monsters. An example is the Athapaskan-speaking Tagish people's "Smart Beaver" who, in a cycle of myths that chronicle his heroic voyage down what is probably the Yukon river, "cleaned out" all the giants and animals (and scaled down the latter to their current size, as well as changing their diet to foods that excluded human flesh).

The ambiguity that surrounds the trickster also has a temporal dimension. While his world is usually the inchoate, mythic age back in the mythological past, he may also enter the historic and recent past; thus, we find the Khoisan tricksters Heiseb or Jackal roaming the farms of the pioneer trek Boers and working for, and duping the *baas*, or the Zande Tore, who was arrested by the British colonists who, among other things, taught him to drive an automobile. Life and death are poles that the trickster confounds as well. Many a tale tells of his death or murder, sometimes in a gruesome manner, through burning, drowning, dismembering, being devoured and swallowed up, only to be revivified anew (or revivifying himself). He may do so by healing himself, as did the !Kung trickster Kauha (introducing thereby the trance curing dance to humankind).

The fact that this being, of deceit, moral turpitude and stupidity, may also be a being that is god-like in his power and acts, and the reverential attitudes he may invoke in the people, who, at other times, would laugh at his antics and express outrage at his moral perversities, is perhaps the most striking manifestation of the ambiguity that envelop the trickster figure. Among the Navaho, Coyote was both a holy being and a buffoon, and to the Bushmen, the tricksters /Kaggen or //Gãuwa were, in addition to pranksters and vulgarian, both also gods, who protected game animals and were a numinous presence at initiation and curing rites. Among some of the Bushman groups, the curing shaman had to seek out the help of trickster god, who was a bit of a curer himself, when he went on his trance-induced outer-body, spirit journeys. As among the North American Indians, there is a similarity between some of a trickster's exploits and adventures and shamans' journeys to the spirit world.

Combining in his being the traits of animal, human and god, the trickster points out the unity of such universally separated realms as culture and nature, sacred and profane, natural and supernatural. Among hunter-gatherers, whose trickster figure is especially prominent, well delineated and universal, and whose guise is usually animalian – yet, at the same time also human – the inseparableness of nature and culture is perhaps the main symbolic message of the trickster. That humans and animals are kindred beings, that the ontological and conceptual boundaries that separate them are fluid or even illusory, is a message that resonates with the lifeways and worldviews of hunter-gatherers, which are embedded within nature. Among other societies, with states and food production and complex pantheons and charter myths, the trickster is more likely to be a god – such as Loki, Hermes, Legba, or Maui, respectively of the Scandinavians, Greeks, West Africans and Polynesians – with his own divine profile and purpose, as creator or destroyer, demiurge, messenger, translator, diviner, protector or fertility god. Through the constraints of his human and animal side, such a trickster-god displays a sacred quality that is different from that of other gods. It is a sacrality that is both more and less accessible than that of the other divine mortals. Through his foolishness and carnality, his lies and moral failings, he is akin to mortals and their own follies and failings. Yet the trickster-god is capable also of dumbfounding the gods, of stealing from them, outsmarting and out-talking them, through witty double-talk that contains depth of wisdom that may surpass their own divine understanding.

As a wanderer, an outsider, a "marginal man," the trickster, in each of the places and domains he enters, causes both havoc and consternation. The reason is that he shocks its inhabitants – humans, animals, gods – into recognizing the relativity and fragility of the world of order and structure they have created for themselves and live by unself-consciously. Puck's exclamation – "Lord, what fools these mortals be" – is the message of the trickster everywhere, presented by the outsider looking in on the insiders' ways of doing things, living their lives, thinking their thoughts, which to him, the outsider, seem antic and contestable. In upsetting and challenging them, he reminds humans – or gods, or animal-humans of the mythic age – of the arbitrariness and limitations of a set and seemingly given cultural, sacral and biological order. As such, the trickster becomes an agent of creativity who challenges a culture's monocultural ways and univocal thoughts; he brings a "more than this" dimensionality to existence, alerting humans to the "unquenchable fecundity of all that truly is and can be" (Hynes 1993: 212, 216).

Mathias Guenther

Further Reading
Evans-Pritchard, E.E. *The Zande Trickster*. Oxford: Oxford University Press, 1967.
Guenther, Mathias. *Tricksters and Trancers: Bushman Religion and Society*. Bloomington: Indiana University Press, 1999.
Hynes, William J. "Inconclusive Conclusions: Tricksters – Metaplayers and Revealers." In W.J. Hynes and W.G. Doty, eds. *Mythical Trickster Figures*. Tuscaloosa: The University of Alabama Press, 1993, 202–17.
Pelton, Robert D. *The Trickster in West Africa: A Study of Mythic Irony and Sacred Delight*. Berkeley: University of California Press, 1980.
Lopez, Barry H. *Giving Birth to Thunder, Sleeping with his Daughter: Coyote Builds North America*. New York: Avon, 1977.
Norman, Howard, ed. *Northern Tales*. New York: Pantheon Books, 2000, 101–40.
Radin, Paul. *The Trickster*. New York: Schocken Books, 1956 (1972).
Sullivan, Lawrence E., Robert D. Pelton and Marc Linscott Ricketts. "Tricksters." In Mircea Eliade, ed. *The Encyclopedia of Religion*, vol. 15. New York: MacMillan Publishing Company, 1997, 45–53.
See also: West Africa.

Tucker, Mary Evelyn – *See* Religious Studies and Environmental Concern.

Tu B'Shvat – *See* Jewish Environmentalism in North America; Waskow, Rabbi Arthur.

Tukanoan Indians (Northwest Amazonia)

The Tukanoan Indians form a linguistic macro-unit divided into two geographically separated populations in Northwest Amazonia, the Western and Eastern Tukanoans. Straddling the borders between Colombia, Ecuador and Peru, the Western Tukanoans (including principally the Secoya, May Huna, Siona and the Koreguaje ethnic groups) comprise some 1500 individuals living on the upper Putumayo and Caquetá rivers and the lower Napo river. The considerably larger population of Eastern Tukanoans, amounting to some 20,000 people, inhabit the Vaupés and Apaporis drainages in the Colombian Amazon and the upper Rio Negro region of Eastern Brazil. Though related closely linguistically, the two populations are socially and culturally distinct.

The habitat of the Eastern Tukanoan Indians (henceforth Tukanoans) is interfluvial (*terra firme*) tropical lowland forest. The Vaupés region is ecologically described as a blackwater ecosystem with nutrient poor soils and rivers (Moran 1993). Biological diversity is high while the productivity of terrestrial and riverine fauna is low, even by Amazonian standards. In these harsh surroundings the native populations make a satisfying living by means of shifting cultivation (bitter manioc being the staple), fishing, hunting and gathering. Population density is low, and settlements widely dispersed along rivers and streams. The traditional settlement is the multifamily longhouse or *maloca* comprising a patrilineally extended family. Today settlements are increasingly concentrated around schools, shops and other facilities, and the traditional *maloca* is largely replaced by smaller, single-family houses grouped into villages. Though the traditional livelihood system still provides the basis for sustenance, petty trade, mining and contract labor are increasingly important in the local economy.

The Tukanoan social universe is composed of some twenty named exogamous groups (including the Tukano proper, the Desana, Cubeo, Wananao, Bara, Barasana and Makuna), each identified with a distinct language and a proper river territory. Each group reckons descent in the male line from a putative, mythical ancestor, conceived of as an Anaconda. The exogamous group also holds what may be described as corporate sacred property, including tangible ritual goods (musical instruments and dance ornaments), sacred substances (blessed coca, tobacco, red paint and beeswax), and intangible, spiritual wealth, such as chants, songs and a specific set of personal names which circulate among its members in alternate generations. The most important material symbol of the group is the set of sacred palm-wood flutes, the Yurupary instruments, which are said to embody the ancestors. This sacred property is described as the "weapons" and "defenses" of the group.

Different exogamous groups relate to each other as putative kin (between which marriage is avoided) or affines (between which marriage is prescribed). Tukanoan society is economically undifferentiated, and there is little evidence of political cohesion beyond the local group of adjacent settlements. Leadership is confined to settlement headmen and occasional charismatic local leaders. However, this equality in the economic and political field goes with a conspicuous differentiation in the religious and ritual domain. Shamans and other ritual specialists (dancers and chanters) of varying and complementary skills play an important role in society. Large-scale public rituals are frequent and considered essential for survival and prosperity.

Tukanoan religion is conveniently described under three general headings: the Yurupary cult, animism and shamanism. Of these, the Yurupary cult does not (and probably never did) form part of the Western Tukanoan religious universe, while the essential features of animism and shamanism appear to apply to both the Eastern and Western groups.

Environmental understanding is constitutive of Tukanoan religion. Social and religious imagery draws on, and is fundamentally inspired by, indigenous knowledge of biological and ecological processes. The Tukanoan environmental understanding is encoded in an animistic ontology-cosmology. Animism, as understood here, implies a fundamentally monistic, participatory orientation to the world, transcending the Western ontological divide between nature and culture, the animate and the inanimate. The human–environment relationship is one of relatedness, inter-subjectivity and inter-agentivity; it is fundamentally social and dialogical in nature. This is the ontological basis for Tukanoan shamanism.

It can be argued that such a participatory stance is conducive to environmental sustainability and the conservation biological diversity. The traditional Tukanoan notion of reciprocity, which guides their interaction with the environment, and the mythologically grounded ritual regulation of resource use, provide strong behavioral sanctions against the overexploitation of forest and river resources. In the Tukanoan view, human life is ultimately geared toward the overall goal of sustaining the cosmos. This life-sustaining responsibility is epitomized in the role of the shaman. Fundamentally concerned with human survival and the continuous fertility of nature, shamanism is the dominant mode of religious practice among the Tukanoan Indians.

The Yurupary Cult

The Yurupary cult is the fullest expression of (Eastern) Tukanoan religious life. Misunderstood as a "devil's cult" by early missionaries, the Yurupary complex involves the ritual use and display of sacred palm-wood flutes and trumpets (the Yurupary instruments) representing the deified ancestors of the clan and exogamous group. The cult, which is common to the Tukanoan and Arrawakan groups of the Vaupes-Icana region of Northwest Amazonia, has therefore been described as an ancestor cult with features of a male secret cult. The Yurupary instruments are handled by adult men only, and the ritual display of the most sacred instruments is the key event in the process of male initiation. The Yurupary complex is thus intimately connected to the patrilineal descent system – the establishment of gender difference and the formation of male personhood and collective identity. However, beyond their patrilineal connotations, the sacred instruments are associated with the fertility of nature and the regeneration of life at large. The ancestors, embodied in the Yurupary instruments, are the generative source of all life.

There are two types of Yurupary rituals: the principal ritual, involving the display of the most ancient and sacred instruments, and the Tree Fruit ritual. The latter is a weaker version of the main ritual, involving less sacred instruments and the ritual redistribution of forest fruits. The main ritual, which does not feature any ritual redistribution of fruits, is held at the beginning of the rainy season, which is also the season of the ripening of the wild forest fruits. In Tukanoan thinking, this is the beginning of the annual cycle. The Yurupary ritual heralds the new year, and is seen as instrumental in bringing about the renewal of nature and the spiritual revitalization of the community.

Just as it inaugurates the annual cycle, the Yurupary ritual initiates male adulthood and conveys full membership in the descent group. As the key event in the male initiation process, it marks a new stage in the life cycle of men. Indeed, the annual ritual cycle, beginning with the Yurupary ritual and ending with the Peach Palm festival, a food feast celebrating the peach palm harvest and the final departure of the recently dead, symbolically reproduces the male life cycle from initiation to death. Also pubescent women are ritually initiated. However, in contrast to the male ritual, which is a collective and public affair, female initiation is a private and discrete event following upon first menstruation.

At male initiation, a group of pubescent boys are made to see the Yurupary instruments. Under the effect of hallucinogenic *yagé* (*Banisteriopsis* sp.), and supervised by elders and the officiating shaman, the initiates are brought into direct contact with the ancestors (in the form of the sacred instruments). Women and children are excluded from the central events of the ritual. The ritual sequence follows the familiar pattern of a passage ritual: the initiates are symbolically killed (immersed in a cold forest stream) at the eve of the ritual, and brought back to life as new-born beings at the end (as they are again made to immerse themselves in the river, now together with the instruments, and subsequently led back into the house). At the height of the ritual, the initiates sit in fetal position inside the house, as the instruments are played over their heads and motionless bodies. Thus, they are impregnated with the vital force of the living ancestors. The boys are then whipped to become hard and strong. The Yurupary instruments are imaged as fierce predators (jaguars and anacondas), swallowing and regurgitating the initiates and thereby reconstituting them as full social and spiritual beings. Infused with regenerative, patrilineal essence, the pubescent boys are reborn as fertile, adult men.

Animism

Tukanoans inhabit an animated landscape where everything created has the capacity to become alive and to actively intervene in the course of events. Hills, mountains, rocks and rivers are infused with the forces of creation; they are seen as consubstantial with the creators and incorporate their powers. Every place and feature of the landscape has a name and tells a story about the deeds of the ancestors. These mythical events, encoded in names and places, confer particular powers to the local landscape. The beings – plants, fishes, land animals and humans – inhabiting this empowered landscape share in its potency; they are charged with creative as well as destructive powers which must be ritually handled to ensure human survival and well-being. Everything made and crafted from natural materials is also believed to contain this ancestral potency; baskets, tools and weapons, houses and canoes situationally obtain agency and become alive. Objects are fundamentally subjects; subjectivity is their natural condition. Crafted things are thus doubly potent; they contain not only the powers of the materials from which they were made but also the agency and creative intentionality of their makers.

In Tukanoan metaphysical discourse, nonhuman animals and plants are generally described as "people" or "humans." The term, which in ordinary discourse is used to denote an (unspecified) exogamous group and to distinguish human beings from other living kinds, is thus contextually expanded to include all living kinds. In the religious ontology of Tukanoan peoples there is no absolute distinction between human and nonhuman beings. Social groups and natural species are categorically fused; exogamous groups are natural kinds, and different species are "distinct peoples." Nonhuman animals and plants are attributed with human agency, will and intention. Animals and plants have houses, are organized into communities, have headmen and ritual specialists. Game animals, in particular, are said to live like human beings: they cultivate the land, harvest their crop and prepare their food, make their proper ritual dances and drink their beer. They have their own ritual attire and, most significantly, their proper Yurupary instruments. Like all people, they have "culture." Humanity, the human life form, is the model for all living kinds. Culture is what all mortal beings, human and non-human, have in common.

What distinguish different species or "peoples" from one another are their distinctive "bodies," their shape, coloring, sound and corporeal habits which are all associated with their different mythical origins and the specific metaphysical roles assigned to them in the cosmic scheme of things. In the case of animal species, difference is conceived of in "cultural" terms – as distinctive "clothing," body paint, language, food habits and ritual property ("weapons" and "defenses"). Natural differences are, as it were, culturalized. Conversely, in the case of humans, cultural difference is essentialized and naturalized: differences in language, food habits and ritual goods are perceived as natural – innate and corporeal, constitutive of group identity. To Tukanoans, culture is nature – timeless and unchanging, created along with the rest of nature and handed down to present generations from the first ancestors.

A wholly socialized or humanized cosmos such as that of the Tukanoans, in which the Western nature–culture divide is abolished and where all beings and things are construed as actual or potential subjects-persons, is conveniently called animistic. Animism, in this precise (and revised) sense, refers to a participatory (monistic) type of ontology which is extremely widespread among indigenous peoples around the world, and one which is fundamentally distinct from, or opposed to, the naturalistic (dualistic) ontology characteristic of Western modernity.

Shamanism

Tukanoan social and religious practice is situated in this ontological-cosmological space. Survival, reproduction and the pursuit of well-being take place in a perceived reality where every life form (species) is seen as a "people," and every being a person – a sentient, intelligent subject. Natural objects, artifacts and features of the landscape have a subjective side and, thus, a potential for intentionality and agency. What is generally referred to as shamanism should be understood against this animistic background. Tukanoan shamans, invariably male, are part-time ritual specialists possessing expert knowledge of the ultimate powers. Their function is to mediate between humanity and the nonhuman agencies that surround them in order to make human life possible and to oversee the proper working of the cosmos.

Shamanic knowledge is essential for making a living in

this animated world, made possible by the creative and destructive powers of the ancestral beings. By shamanic means – incantations, spells and blessings – the world is made safe, food is blessed and human beings protected from spiritual dangers. Shamans are, quite literally, gods on Earth; they cure and prevent disease, but may also send sickness and death; they supervise and metaphysically control the events at birth, initiation and death, literally constructing, deconstructing and reconstructing human persons; they ensure, by ritual means, the continuing fertility of nature and, thus, the availability of game and fish for human consumption; and they transform beings of nature (game, fish and forest fruits) from potentially perilous subjects and vehicles of death and disease to life-giving and strengthening food (Arhem 1996).

Tukanoans distinguish between two kinds of shamans, one intimately associated with curing but also with causing death and disease, the other associated with protective, preventive and life-sustaining shamanism in connection with life-cycle rituals and public rituals more generally (Hugh-Jones 1996). The former, usually referred to as payé in the literature, is feared and perceived as a morally ambiguous figure of comparatively low social status. The source of his power is highly inspirational and idiosyncratic. As curer and sorcerer, he operates as an individual, often at the margins of society. In many respects he is the prototypical shaman.

The other, life-sustaining and protective shaman, by contrast, has attributes usually associated with priesthood: his role is entirely benevolent and thoroughly social. Directed toward the good of the community, the life-sustaining shaman is morally unambiguous. Consequently, his social standing is high, usually merging secular and ritual authority. The source of his authority is his knowledge of the mythical canon of the group. The office tends to be inherited from a senior patrilineal relative and invariably involves many years of apprenticeship, from initiation to mature age. Recognition as a true life-sustaining shaman comes only with advanced age and demonstrated expertise.

All initiated, mature men are attributed with some amount of shamanic knowledge. All men know how to bless food and, thus, to render it safe for consumption, and all men are capable of sustaining themselves in the local environment: they know the spiritual dangers and assets of their territory and the ritual acts that necessarily accompany the everyday chores in the forest and on the river. However, only the curing shaman is capable of treating the seriously ill, and only the life-sustaining shaman possesses the expertise to direct the major life-cycle rituals and the public ritual events aimed at ensuring the fecundity in nature.

Yet, even among the shamans, knowledge and skills are differentiated and graded. Thus, only the most reputed and knowledgeable of life-sustaining shamans are entrusted with the supervision of the annual Yurupary ritual, when the ancestors come alive and enter into direct contact with the living community members. At this ritual, the officiating shaman turn into a primordial being himself; he embodies the Yurupary, the omnipotent Ancestor-Creator. Among the Makuna, one of the Tukanoan groups in the Pirá-Paraná region of the Colombian Amazon the principal Yurupary is identified as the Ancestral Bumble-Bee, the Primordial Pollinator. The imagery is revealing: feeding on flowery plants, the Pollinator enables the plants to reproduce and multiply. Impersonating the Primordial Pollinator, the shaman fecundates nature and renews the world.

In the 1970s and 1980s, the indigenous population in the Vaupés region was heavily affected, in close succession, by the booming Colombian coca trade and the Amazonian gold rush. Both events implied dramatic upheavals in the regional economy. For many indigenous communities they provided much needed cash income but also caused social disruptions and local environmental depletion. Nevertheless, the Eastern Tukanoan homeland has, on the whole, been spared large-scale forest destruction and settler penetration. In 1982, the main part of the Colombian Vaupés (some 3.5 million hectares) was declared Protected Indigenous Land (*resguardo*). Within this legal framework, Tukanoan Indians have largely been successful in defending their heritage and homeland against external intrusion. Indigenous interests have been effectively promoted by the Regional Indigenous Organization (CRIVA), founded in 1973, and by its several local offshoots.

Missionary influence is strong along major waterways and in the vicinity of frontier towns and trading settlements. In more remote areas, however, indigenous beliefs and practices remain strong. Partly in response to the threats posed by the cocaine boom and the subsequent gold rush, partly as a result of the activities of the regional indigenous movement, there are today signs of indigenous cultural revival in the region (Arhem 1998b). Traditional rituals are performed with renewed vigor, and shamans and other local authorities are assuming a new role in the emerging Tukanoan leadership, now efficiently interacting with state institutions, the church, and pro-indigenous international organizations.

Kaj Århem

Further Reading

Arhem, Kaj. *Makuna: Portrait of an Amazonian People.* Washington, D.C.: Smithsonian Institution Press, 1998a.

Arhem, Kaj. "Powers of Place: Landscape, Territory and Local Belonging in Northwest Amazonia." In N. Lovell, ed. *Locality and Belonging.* London: Routledge, 1998b, 78–102.

Arhem, Kaj. "The Cosmic Food-web: Human–nature Relatedness in the Northwest Amazon." In P. Descola and G. Pálsson, eds. *Nature and Society: Anthropological Perspectives.* London: Routledge, 1996, 185–204.

Bird-David, Nurit. " 'Animism' Revisited: Personhood, Environment, and Relational Epistemology." *Current Anthropology* 40 (Supplement 1999), 67–91.

Descola, Philippe. "Constructing Natures: Symbolic Ecology and Social Practice." In P. Descola and G. Pálsson, eds. *Nature and Society: Anthropological Perspectives.* London: Routledge, 1996, 82–102.

Goldman, Irvin. *The Cubeo: Indians of the Northwest Amazon.* Urbana: The University of Illinois Press, 1963.

Hugh-Jones, Stephen. "Shamans, Prophets, Priests and Pastors." In N. Thomas and C. Humphrey, eds. *Shamanism, History, and the State.* Ann Arbor: The University of Michigan Press, 1996, 32–75.

Hugh-Jones, Stephen. *The Palm and the Pleiades: Initiation and Cosmology in Northwest Amazonia.* Cambridge: Cambridge University Press, 1979.

Langdon, E. Jean Matteson. "Shamanic Power in Siona Religion and Medicine." In E.J. Matteson Langdon and G. Baer, eds. *Portals of Power: Shamanism in South America.* Albuquerque: University of New Mexico Press, 1992, 41–62.

Moran, Emilio. *Through Amazonian Eyes: The Human Ecology of Amazonian Populations.* Iowa: University of Iowa Press, 1993.

Reichel-Dolmatoff, Gerardo. "Cosmology as Ecological Analysis: A View from the Rain Forest." *Man* 11 (NS 1976), 307–18.

Reichel-Dolmatoff, Gerardo. *Amazonian Cosmos: The Sexual and Religious Symbolism of the Tukano Indians.* Chicago: University of Chicago Press, 1971.

Viveiros de Castro, Eduardo. "Cosmological Deixis and Amerindian Perspectivism." *The Journal of the Royal Anthropological Institute* 4 (NS 1998), 469–88.

See also: Amazonia; Animism (various); Ethnobotany; Ethnoecology; Rainforests (Central and South America); Reichel-Dolmatoff, Gerardo – and Ethnoecology in Colombia; Rubber Tappers; Shamanism – Traditional; Traditional Ecological Knowledge; U'wa Indians (Colombia); Yanomami.

U

U'wa Indians (Colombia)

The U'wa Indians live on the slopes of the Andes in northeastern Colombia, along the eastern side of the range called Sierra Nevada del Cocuy. Brutally reduced in numbers and in territory by the Spanish conquest, the U'wa remained somewhat isolated in the Andes until the 1940s and 1950s when a road was constructed by the government opening their lands to white peasants and to Catholic mission settlements. At the turn of the twenty-first century the U'wa numbered about 5000, and the Colombian government acknowledged only a small portion of their original territory. Much of this land has been affected by ongoing civil war, by illegal drug trafficking, and by the government's policy of promoting oil exploitation. A large number of U'wa, and the governing authority of the tribe itself, adhere to their traditional ways while they struggle to keep these outside forces from invading their culture. Their struggle is carried on by political and legal means, but at bottom it is a religious one, for the U'wa world is essentially constructed of spiritual beliefs.

The U'wa believe that they are descended from deities of an upper world and a lower world. They occupy a middle world that is delicately balanced between the upper and lower worlds, and believe it is their duty to maintain this balance through chants and by living in harmony with the processes of the universe. If the balance is upset, the universe will come to an end. Thus, for example, in certain ceremonies the U'wa chant myths all night to assure that the sun and other natural processes continue along their proper courses, and they chant at different times of the year to keep the cycle of seasons moving. There are pathways connecting the three worlds, along which the deities travel. The paths of the upper world are those of certain stars, sun and moon, while the paths of the lower world are rivers, and all paths meet in lakes. By these paths, various good and bad qualities enter the middle world, and the master shaman chanters, under hallucinogens, travel the paths in order to shut out bad qualities or allow good ones to enter the middle world. Nature serves as a central symbol in this cosmology, as it does in the simpler metaphor that the U'wa sometimes use, namely, that the world is a body with its head in the highlands, caves are mouths, mountain ranges the spinal cord, and the forest the pubic hair of lower world deities.

This religious view of nature guides the way the U'wa live in their environment. As agriculturalists, hunters, gatherers and fishers, they change their place of residence several times a year, from tropical lowlands, to foothills, to high mountain rainforest. The moves, at set times, appear not to be related to agricultural or climatic advantage, but rather to maintaining the balance of upper and lower worlds. Maize is not sown in optimal planting conditions, but rather at the times and locations that assure its harvest will be available for scheduled religious ceremonies in which maize plays an important role. The U'wa do not enter certain high mountain areas, and do not fish, bathe or drink from certain lakes and rivers. In clearing fields for cultivation, they do not touch trees that provide fruits or nuts for animals or humans, and they leave a great deal of vegetational cover and mulch. Fields are left fallow for a period of years before replanting. Animals are to be caught only by trapping and the spilling of their blood is to be avoided. Many of the U'wa's chanted myths (they have no written language) are about forest foods, cultivated foods, and animals. They believe these things will disappear if they stop chanting about them. Indeed, they are disappearing as white settlers and others encroach on the U'wa traditional territory. One U'wa response is to increase the chants in order to re-create them.

The U'wa have no known tradition of violence to settle conflicts among themselves or with outsiders. Animosities do arise within the tribe and with outsiders, but the U'wa eschew use of knives or firearms in disputes, and say their weapons consist of thoughts and words. Today, they strive to be left alone, aligning themselves with neither side in the civil war and resisting foreign encroachments that affect their land or environment. Through political stances and legal actions, they accuse white colonization and the Colombian government in general of taking their territory, introducing diseases, exhausting natural resources, causing hunger, preventing them from living materially on their land in the traditional way, and refusing to acknowledge their beliefs that all the natural world is sacred and the U'wa are its keepers. They view the government's current opening of their territory to international oil companies in apocalyptic terms. In actions from lawsuits to civil disobedience to an international media campaign, the U'wa insist upon recognition of their belief that oil was distributed throughout this world and the lower world by the deities when they created the universe, that it is a living resource as if it were the blood of Mother Earth doing its sacred work just where it is, and that to exploit it would be a sacrilege destroying the balance of the universe and provoking the collapse of U'wa culture. A network of international activists has formed to aid the U'wa in their struggle against oil companies and the government. Struck by the poignancy of this small, spiritual tribe resisting oil exploitation because it believes oil is the blood of Mother Earth, human rights and environmental activists from Colombia, the United States and Europe have publicized the natives' plight, helped them in litigation, brought U'wa tribal leaders on foreign tours, and pressed their own governments to protect the U'wa. Colombian anthropologists and lawyers, the Italian Green Party, a coalition of several groups operating as The U'wa Defense Project, Earth Justice Legal Defense Fund, and Harvard Unversity's Program on Nonviolent Sanctions and Cultural Survival, among others, have all played key roles. Amazon Watch several times brought tribal leaders to address the annual shareholders' meeting of a California oil company threatening U'wa land. A young American environmentalist, impressed by the naturalistic religion of the U'wa, was in U'wa territory in the late 1990s together with two native American Indian women leaders to build international solidarity when the three were sequestered and assassinated by gunmen of the Fuerzas Armadas Revolucionarias de Colombia (FARC), demonstrating further that the U'wa world has turned chaotic.

If the oil drilling goes ahead, the council of elders – the most respected tribal authority – has recommended that the U'wa follow a precedent said to be known in their oral history from the sixteenth century: with the Spanish in pursuit, the U'wa men, women and children jumped from a high cliff in a mass suicide.

Robert W. Benson

Further Reading

Osborn, Ann. "Mythology and Social Structure Among the U'wa of Colombia." Thesis submitted for the degree of Ph.D., University of Oxford, 1982.

Project Underground. *Blood of Our Mother: The U'wa People, Occidental Petroleum and the Colombian Oil Industry.* Oakland, California: Project Underground, 1998.

See also: Amazonia; Andean Traditions; Ayahuasca; Ethnobotany; Ethnoecology; Huaorani; Incas; Indigenous Activism and Environmentalism in Latin America; Kogi (Northern Colombia); Mother Earth; Reichel-Dolmatoff, Gerardo – and Ethnoecology in Colombia; Rubber Tappers; Shamanism–Ecuador; Shamanism–Traditional; Traditional Ecological Knowledge; Tukanoan Indians; World Conference of Indigenous Peoples; Yanomami.

UFOs and Extraterrestrials

Flying saucer cults and the broader UFO movement work in general within a galactian theological framework that ranges between gnostic and astral worldviews. From the transcendental orientation of gnosticism in which the material is either denied reality or significant value, nature is dismissed as a foil to spiritual meaning. The astral view is of course closer to the pagan inasmuch as both ground themselves in the tangible. Where it differs, however, is in crossing the "death of God" threshold to deny any ontological validity to the supernatural. Astral galactianism replaces the supernatural with the extraterrestrial and technological in order to demystify and demythologize primarily the Abrahamic religions, simultaneously (if unconsciously) mythologizing and ideologizing science and technology. Inasmuch as galactian spirituality centers on the cosmos as its all-encompassing structural reference and tends often to employ an Enochian narrative concerning "fallen angels" and their revolt against the divine hierarchy, nature religion becomes largely incidental. Nevertheless, UFO groups are highly individualistic, and must be examined on an ad hoc basis to discern whatever nature-spiritual dynamic may inform their particular outlooks. These range from James Jacob Hurtak's writings (*The Keys of Enoch*), those of Elizabeth Clare Prophet (Church Universal and Triumphant) and the Urantia Foundation to such groups as George King's Aetherius Society and Claude Vorilhon's Raëlians.

The galactian inspiration of New Age UFO thought derives from Theosophy and the concomitant notion of the Great White Brotherhood of Ascended Masters who have become reinterpreted as extraterrestrial space beings. In a language reminiscent of science-fiction and scientific conceptualization, the galactian matrix includes an emphasis on cosmic law, engineering codes, electromagnetism, wave-form harmonization and/or "faulty genetic circuits" as well as such notions as pyramid power, Atlantis, Lemuria, extraterrestrials or space brethren, and the Pleiades as a command center of higher forms of consciousness. Such groups as Guy and Edna Ballard's I AM Religious Activity or Mark and Elizabeth Clare Prophet's Summit Lighthouse/Church Universal and Triumphant (CUT) concentrate on the principle of cosmic law alone, whereas Hurtak, the Raëlian Movement, Urantia, Ron Hubbard's Church of Scientology, and Marshall Applewhite's Heaven's Gate all express a typical and fully galactian cosmology of absolute and material immanence in which life is not the result of a process of natural evolution, but one of extraterrestrial biotechnological fabrication. At the same time, while spiritual seeking through galactian frameworks often intersects with ufology, not all flying saucer cults are necessarily galactian or can even be considered as New Age. Closer to the gnostic galactianism position that considers supersensuous possibilities that transcend the natural might be King's Aetherius Society and Ernest and Ruth Norman's Unarius. But like New Age's lack of clearly articulated differentiation between its gnostic and pagan elements, the same fluid confusion exists between galactianism's gnostic and astral formulations. Elements of both appear throughout the various UFO or flying saucer groups as well as in José Argüelles' *Surfers of the Zuvuya* or Benjamin Creme's teachings on Maitreya.

At the center of the galactian theological world is a single ultimate God. In other words, the galactian worldview extends the gnostic and medieval chain of being into an infinite plenum of multiple dimensions. This divine source of all being is usually presented in masculine terms (e.g., Urantia's Fatherhood of God and Brotherhood of Man). Nevertheless, although the heavenly bureaucracy is also portrayed as male, Urantia does speak of a Mother Spirit. A different galactian understanding is encountered with the Universal Faithists of Kosmon (headquartered in Salt Lake City). For the Faithists, the godhead is both masculine and feminine, and half the heavenly host is female.

In galactian spiritual history, the central rupture is the Luciferian rebellion considered as the free will breaking on higher dimensions with the even higher law of cosmic harmonics and its plan for intergalactic evolution. The story of the segment of heavenly hosts who broke away under the leadership of Lucifer and came to Earth is recorded in the Genesis 6:2 tale of the "sons of God." The fuller version is found in the apocryphic Book of Enoch's narrative of the Watcher Angels who, in violation of their assigned role, had intercourse on Earth with female humans. Their giant offspring, consisting of "genetic aberrations," are accordingly the corruptive elements within the human race. In CUT's understanding, these descendants of the Watcher Angels are now those who head the world's governments, financial institutions, multinational corporations and the underworld drug cartels.

In galactian expectation, the rebels are eventually to be defeated by the archangel Michael. They will be imprisoned and secluded in permanent torment. This notion of eternal damnation is a prominent feature of most galactian theology. There are, however, exceptions. For both the Aetherius Society and the Faithists, as recorded in their central work *Oahspe*, there is no ultimate annihilation and all souls are finally cleansed. There is no hell of everlasting punishment. But what is common to all forms of galactian mystic theology is the belief that the purpose of existence is the continual progression of the human soul toward perfection. The idea of *nirvana* or the attainment of supreme oblivion is considered a delusion and replaced with the notion of eternal evolution.

Consequently, there are different understandings of space brethren and the role of the flying saucer or space ship. Following a more Theosophical gnostic orientation, former CUT leader, Elizabeth Clare Prophet considered the visiting extraterrestrial as a dangerous Luciferian agent. On the other hand, in the non-Theosophical astral framework such as we find in Raëlianism, Heaven's Gate and possibly Urantia, it is the advanced knowledge of the "more advanced" races from other spheres or dimensions who, through their superior technical skills concerning genetic manipulation, are responsible for life on Earth in the first place. The Raëlian Movement International began in December 1973 when French race-car driver, Claude Vorilhon, while walking in the Clermont-Ferrand region of France, encountered and boarded a flying saucer. Over a six-day period, the extraterrestrials taught to Vorilhon the "true" purport of the Bible concerning the biotechnological origins of humanity. Henceforth known as Raël ("messenger of the Elohim"), Vorilhon is accepted by his followers as the last of forty prophets. In Raël's reinterpretation of the Old Testament, the alternate designation of Yahweh, namely, Elohim, becomes a reference to the extraterrestrials ("our fathers from space") who, through their perfect mastery of DNA, created humanity in their own image. While in the past, the Elohim have subsequently spoken to their creations through Moses, Buddha, Jesus, Mohammed and others, their mission is now to convey through Vorilhon/Raël the imminent danger to the human race through self-annihilation. So while CUT considers that we are entering the New Age of Aquarius in which the central spiritual master is the Comte de Saint Germain rather than the Piscean Jesus Christ, Raëlains consider instead that the foremost prophet for the present "Age of the Apocalypse" that began with the nuclear detonation of 1945 is Raël.

Typical of galactian thinking is the concern with "interdimensional reality." Its spiritual hierarchy often exists on multiple levels or dimensions of cosmic reality. However, in the Urantian understanding of the cosmos, allegedly channeled and recorded during 1934 and 1935 to assist humanity in our local galaxy's evolution toward perfection, the elaborate polytheism presented in its *Urantia Book* is not outside our space-time, but one in which its higher beings live on various spheres found within our universe. This more corporeal notion of the heavenly hosts may reflect Mormon theology in which God has a material body. Usually, however, galactian theology comprehends its enormous hierarchical bureaucracy of spiritual beings (angels, deities, evolved souls and ascended masters) in a plenitude of realms that extend not only throughout our own three-dimensional world but beyond it as well – a perspective closer to contemporary cosmological theory that envisions there to be an eleven-dimensional multiverse containing an infinite number of parallel universes. For the Raëlians, our galaxy is simply a tiny particle of an atom of a living being on a planet revolving around a sun in some super-galaxy. Likewise, the sub-atomic particles of atoms in our own world are seen by Raëlians as galaxies in themselves. The Raëlian mystical union between the sub-universes and super-universes within and beyond the individual is accomplished through the practice of Sensual Meditation, a set of contemplation techniques that aim for individual communication with the Elohim in order to regain control over and happiness in all areas of life

(body discovery, sexuality, enjoyment through the senses, cosmic organism, etc.)

When the multiple cosmos is conceived along Theosophical gnostic lines, it will entertain an understanding of the supernatural as an operative factor. But if galactian thought formulates itself along a strictly astral horizon, there is no spiritual, and the universe has no beginning. For the Raëlians, for example, matter is purely mechanical. There is no *anima mundi* to the world or the cosmos. Consequently, while the "astral" realm is a Theosophical concept developed to describe a supersensible substance supposed to pervade all space and bodies and one that provides a bridge between the spiritual and physical planes, in the astral school of galactian interpretation, there is no spiritual dimension, and the astral is essentially an extension of matter. The final contrast between the two forms of galactian theology is in the gnostic understanding of the spiritual as *a priori*, while the astral recognizes instead the centrality and permanence of matter. This last is similar to Paganism and the general emphasis of nature religions which also centralize matter, but it differs from these by not regarding the mental, spiritual and supernatural as emerging from the tangible and at best achieving an ultimate co-validity with it. With astral galactianism, in place of evolution, there is simply engineering of the eternally pre-given physical reality.

Unlike the more atheistic astralism of the Raëlian movement, the Aetherius Society founded in 1955 by George King (1919–1997), is both gnostic and astral. This "saucer cult" reveres a Cosmic Hierarchy, engages in a battle with evil forces, and expects that everyone will eventually become a Master and continue to evolve. As a regular practitioner of yoga, King claims to have attained *samadhi* in which he has gained access to many cosmic secrets. In 1954, the Venusian Cosmic Master who had assumed the name "Aetherius" reputedly told King that he was to become the voice of the Interplanetary Parliament that is headquartered on the planet Saturn. The following year the Aetherius Society was established in London, and King allegedly receives "Cosmic transmissions" from Aetherius and other Cosmic Masters while in his yogic trance state.

The Aetherius Society holds belief in both reincarnation and the Great White Brotherhood of Ascended or Cosmic Masters that includes Jesus, Krishna, Buddha and others. Inasmuch as everyone will eventually become a Master, the Brotherhood consists of members from both genders. Like CUT, the Society's belief system is essentially both Christian and Buddhist (both Jesus and Buddha are said to come from Venus), but unlike CUT's distrust of flying saucers as containing negative entities, King teaches that saucers have played an important role for humanity and have saved the planet on several occasions from atmospheric damage caused by human civilization – specifically from experimental nuclear fallout. His movement considers that the Earth is regularly orbited by space ships, and, in particular, Satellite Three distributes special Prayer Hours of spiritual energies or *prana* that members of the Society can then channel toward specific concerns through King's invention of Spiritual Energy Radiators. The periods during which this distribution occurs, usually lasting three to four weeks, are called "spiritual pushes." One, designated Operation Bluewater, ended in 1976 and involved charging a specific Spiritual Energy Battery, a "radionic" storing device that can be used in times of crisis to alleviate the Earth's magnetic field warp caused by both atomic experimentation and negative human thought. Another "spiritual push," Operation Starlight, lasted for just over three years (1958–1961) during which King and others climbed eighteen mountains around the world that had been selected through a vision of the Master Jesus. The purpose of this push was to charge these mountains permanently with spiritual power. Regular pilgrimages to these sites now allow members to use the holy energies through prayer for terrestrial benefit such as the relief of physical suffering, diminishment of belligerent tensions, the aversion or reduction of such catastrophes as earthquakes or famine, and individual and environmental healing.

While the Aetherius Society's Interplanetary Parliament (or Cosmic Hierarchy) is responsible to the Lords of the Sun, it argues that each planet functions as a learning stage that must be completed before one progresses to the next. Many reincarnations are necessary on each planet before one learns to live according to God's Laws. Some Masters already live on the Earth, but the coming Master, whose magic powers exceed all terrestrial military might, will appear in a flying saucer and launch a millennium of planetary peace. Before this, however, the Great White Brotherhood is engaged in a cosmic battle with an organization of black magicians who seek to enslave humanity. The Society assists in this warfare by training its members in what is known as Operation Prayer Power: redirecting or channeling *prana* (energy) through mantras and prayers in order to heal disease. Apart from spiritual healing and the use of yoga, the Aetherius Society is also concerned with alternative medicine, dowsing and most of the practices characteristic of New Age and Human Potential. It has remained at the forefront of ecological anxieties relating to nuclear radiation pollution and industrial contamination.

Similar concerns with planetary well-being are shared by the Raëlian movement. While Raël communicates with the Elohim and Yahweh, his personal teacher and Elohim president, primarily through telepathy, he has been instructed that a major enterprise for the Raëlians is to construct an international embassy to which the Elohim can return once more to Earth to welcome the planet into a technological world of choice, infinity and pleasure. Following instructions from the Elohim, the movement would hope to establish this embassy near Jerusalem.

World government is then to be established as a form of "geniocracy" or rule by geniuses. Along with this, a universal humanitarian economy will eliminate the need for inheritance. The movement's mission as well as difficulties involved in establishing its Elohim embassy, however, is similar to the delays and opposition to the construction of the Pyramid Temple of the Unity of God's Faces by the Religion of Aumism at its monastery of Mandarom Shambhasalem in Castellane, France. The followers of Hamsah Manarah likewise believe that such an "anchoring bridge" is required for the inauguration of a Golden Age of Unity but, following a more Theosophical and Hindu framework, the Aumists understand their Temple as a "Spiritual Pole" that will link God to the material realm, whereas for Raëlians, the embassy will serve as a landing station for the spaceships of the Elohim. Nevertheless, the Aumist temple is expected to facilitate the rapprochement of science and spirituality and allow nature to recover its proper position by returning to ecological equilibrium.

Unlike the more typical gnostic-idealist aversion to the joys of the physical universe, with the Raëlians there is no rejection but rather an endorsement of worldly pleasure. Some of the methods of its central practice of Sensual Meditation are to be used by two people of the opposite sex, and this involves nudity, sensory awareness exercises and sexual experimentation with the aim of achieving a mystical experience of oneness. Nevertheless, the movement stresses complete choice in the selection of sexual partners as well as in all other aspects of life. As long as no one else is harmed, Raëlians are encouraged to be free of social mores and inhibitions. With its astral rejection of the supernatural and/or spiritual, the immortality of reincarnation is instead to be achieved through the process of serial cloning. Consequently, and in view of the Raëlian belief that all earthly life originated artificially, Raëlians support biotechnological developments – whether concerning genetically altered foods, increased mechanization, robotized automation, space exploration, use of computers or reproduction of animal and human life through cellular cloning. The Raëlian belief that all life is synthetic "grounds an empathy for all organisms, vegetable and animal" in appreciation of the biotechnological artist's abilities: "This approach to nature and the advocacy of the use of reproductive technology are the religion's primary points of engagement with ecological concerns" (Sentes and Palmer 2000: 101). It is through the steady advances of science as well as the assistance of the Elohim that the Raëlians expect the world will enter its golden age.

Whether pursued by organized groups and movements, or whether individual UFO sightings made by pilots of aircraft or by people of all occupations, the UFO myth remains "one of the world's most powerful religious or semi-religious narratives" (Rothstein 2001: 134). It relates to the "crop circles" of Britain, and while many of both flying saucer sightings and crop circle constructions are clearly hoaxes, some are not as readily established as such but persist as unexplained paranormal paradoxes. Psychologically, the UFO would appear to be a product of counter-intuitive beliefs that include what we normally relate to the supernatural but are not necessarily restricted to this. But as a phenomenon in and of itself, contact with spaceships and extraterrestrials tends to interlink with the ideas of evolution that derive from Theosophy and have entered the general New Age vocabulary. For Rothstein, the UFO is "elusive, flexible and versatile and therefore an obvious candidate to become a global cultural representation distributed along the ever-expanding means for easy international communication" (2001: 147). As twenty-first-century Earth continues to face ever-increasing environmental threats, and while the possible perception of extraterrestrial technology is nothing new (e.g., the experiences of the biblical prophets Elijah and Ezekiel), the UFO encounter and corpus of belief are now more focused on both spiritual and ecological progress.

In this light, the studies conducted by Harvard psychiatrist John Mack on UFO abductees have shown that while little is reliably gained concerning knowledge of extraterrestrial life, abduction reports tell us much about our own culture and psychology and an emerging ecological sensitivity. Mack finds that the chief reasons given for UFO abduction are either to develop offspring between humans and aliens or to increase human consciousness toward preventing the destruction of the planet's ecosystems. By linking ufology and ecology, Mack is possibly founding a new religion based on the "green politics" of star people. He has at least uncovered within the U.S. alien-abduction mythology that has developed since the 1960s the link between an alleged encounter with extraterrestrial beings and both spiritual transformation and environmental awareness.

Michael York

Further Reading
Curran, Douglas. *In Advance of the Landing: Folk Concepts of Outer Space.* New York: Abbeville, 1985.
Eberhardt, George M. *UFOs and the Extraterrestrial Contact Movement: A Bibliography.* Metuchen, NJ: Scarecrow, 1986.
Mack, John E. *Passport to the Cosmos: Human Transformation and Alien Encounters.* New York: Crown, 1999.
Rothstein, Mikael. "The Myth of the UFO in Global Perspective." In M. Rothstein, ed. *New Age Religion and Globalization.* Aarhus: University Press, 2001, 133–49.
Sachs, Margaret. *The UFO Encyclopedia.* London: Corgi/Transworld Publishers, 1981.
Sentes, Bryan and Susan Palmer. "Presumed Innocent: The Raelians, UFO Religions, and the Postmodern Condition." *Nova Religio* 4:1 (2000), 86–105.

Thompson, Richard L. *Alien Identities: Ancient Insights into a Modern UFO Phenomenon*. San Diego: Govardhan Hill, 1993.
Vallee, Jacques. *Messengers of Deception: UFO Contacts and Cults*. Berkeley, CA: And Or Press, 1979.
York, Michael. "The Church Universal and Triumphant." *Journal of Contemporary Religion* 10:1 (1995), 71–82.

See also: Astronauts; Crop Circles; New Age; Scientology; Space Exploration; Yoga and Ecology.

Umbanda

Umbanda is a syncretic religion *par excellence*, creatively blending African religions, particularly from Yorubaland and Congo, with Native American traditions, folk healing, Iberian Catholicism, spiritism, "Oriental" esoterism, and popular culture. This complex and often contradictory mixture emerged in Brazil in the early 1900s, as the country was making the transition from empire to republic. This period also marked Brazil's entry to modernity, with incipient processes of industrialization and urbanization. Umbanda reflects these social dynamics, originating in the increasingly cosmopolitan cities of Rio de Janeiro and São Paulo. Today, Umbanda is present throughout Brazil and sustains relations of competition, accommodation, and cross-fertilization with other Afro-Brazilian religions such as Candomblé, Xangô, Batuque, and Tambor de Minas. Umbanda has also spread in South America, with thriving centers in Uruguay, Argentina, Peru, and Venezuela. Not surprisingly, it has also traveled to the United States, to New York, Boston, and Miami, with the waves of immigrants who have come from Brazil since the late 1970s.

Umbanda holds ambivalent attitudes toward nature. As a "cult of affliction," to draw from anthropologist Victor Turner, this religion takes an instrumental view of the environment, seeing it as a set of forces that can be carefully manipulated to produce physical and spiritual healing and well-being. Nevertheless, Umbanda has at its core a relational ethos that tightly links humans, spirits, and the natural world. This ethos challenges notions of a sovereign, detached, and purely calculating self, standing over against nature.

As an African-based religion, Umbanda shares many elements with Candomblé. Like Candomblé, Umbanda adheres to a monistic and panentheistic worldview. All entities – animate and inanimate, mineral, vegetable, animal, human, and spiritual – are informed by and are ultimately expressions of a sacred vital force called *axé*. Because this elán vital flows unevenly across the Umbanda cosmos, a central concern in the religion is to provide practitioners with the right knowledge and proper ritual practices to place themselves strategically in the changing grid of energy generated by *axé*. Umbanda's aim is thus unabashedly practical: to help the practitioner negotiate a favorable position *vis-à-vis* other entities, particularly humans and spirits, through strategic exchanges of energy (for example, special foods offered to one's head spirit in exchange for health, good fortune, or happiness in love). The aim is to establish a reciprocal balance of forces that will allow the practitioner's own *axé* to fulfill its destiny.

As in Candomblé, Umbanda locates high concentrations of *axé* in the *orixás*, the ancestral spirits that are part of the African pantheon of gods. *Orixás*, which are associated with specific natural forces or domains like thunder (*Xangô*), the sea (*Iemanjá*), and sweet water (*Oxum*), and their iconic representations serve as powerful openings to and conduits for *axé*. This explains why the religion is organized around *terreiros*, territorially based extended spiritual families headed by specialists (*pais and mães de santos*) who train initiates in the correct ritual etiquette to relate to *terreiro's* and the practitioner's head spirits. An essential component of this relation is the incorporation of *orixás* by practitioners in trances that are often accompanied and supported by drumming and the use of liquor and tobacco. In these trances, the *orixá* descends on the head of the medium, "riding" him or her, that is, controlling his or her body movements and speech. In this way, *orixás* become publicly present and can receive the respect and loyalty of their devotees.

In contrast to more Africanized Candomblés, however, Umbanda tend to privilege interaction with what we may call intermediate or lower spirits. It is not that *orixás* disappear altogether; they continue to be displayed prominently in *terreiro* altars albeit through their Catholic correlates (the saints). However, Umbanda mediums prefer to work with spirits native to Brazil, rather than with the African royalties represented by the *orixás*. This is where Umbanda demonstrates a high degree of syncretism and adaptability to the local environment, for the central spiritual characters in Umbanda are indigenous Brazilians and backwoodsmen (*caboclos*), old African slaves of colonial Brazil (*pretos velhos*), and rogues and prostitutes (*exus*). These are characters that are salient in the way in which Brazilians, particularly at the grassroots, imagine their nation.

Caboclos play a key role in Umbanda's attitudes and relations toward nature. In the Umbandista imagination, *caboclos* are associated with Brazil as it existed prior to the conquest, an exuberant mythical land without manmade social hierarchies. *Caboclos* represent the untamed spirit of the wilderness, the undifferentiated jungle prior to domestication by the Portuguese. This idealized wilderness is often connected with the land of Aruanda, the mythical home of *caboclo* spirits said to be located in the Congo-Angola region of Africa. *Caboclos* belong to a wild, pristine place where all species are closely interconnected and where distinctions between animals and humans are tenuous. Thus, *caboclos* are seen as rugged, proud, and rebellious characters, always capable of transgression. As part of this transgressive personality, they are quick to smoke cigars and drink *jurema*, a drink with mild hallucinogenic properties made out of a mixture of the sacred plant *Pithecolobium diversifolium Bent*, herbs, honey, and alcohol.

Pretos velhos contrast sharply with *caboclos*. They represent post-conquest Brazil, a Brazil marked by violence and deep social inequalities. Whereas the initiate who incorporates a *caboclos* becomes brash and struts around whooping and beating his/her chest, the medium who receives a *preto velho* will behave meekly, speaking softly and haltingly and walking with his/her back bent to represent the fact that s/he is carrying the whole weight of slavery. Their humble condition allows *pretos velhos* to have great empathy for those in trouble and to be great healers. Like the *caboclos*, they also carry a wealth of ethnobotanical knowledge (from the forest in *caboclo*'s case and from the ancestors in the case of *preto velho*), which they can use to cure ailments ranging from persistent headaches to nervous breakdowns.

Besides contributing to the therapeutic dimension of Umbanda, the *caboclo-preto velho* dyad serves a commentary on what the religion sees as the contradictions in Brazil's entry to modernity – tensions such as servitude versus autonomy, hierarchy versus equality, and domination versus resistance. The dyad is a way to narrativize, and thus legitimize, the civilizing process in Brazil. Yet this civilizing process is incomplete, subject to the destabilizing power of nature as represented in the transgressive, almost carnivalesque figure of the *caboclo*. The *caboclo-preto velho* dialectic, thus, offers a view of nature as "savage and primitive" forces periodically irrupting in the midst of a precarious and contradictory humanmade world.

Transgression is also preeminent for *exus*, spirits commonly associated with the underworld. In West African traditions the *exu* is a single trickster figure linked to sexuality and fertility. In Brazilian Umbanda, the *exu* assumes multiple identities, coming to stand for marginal social groups like thugs, thieves, prostitutes, and other "devils," figures which local lore and the national mass media alternatively vilify and celebrate for their resourcefulness. The centrality of *exus* in Umbanda reflects its adaptation to the modern urban environment, where the tough streets of the city become the stage for sacred dramas. The *exus* are, in fact, a vehicle to sacralize the profane, to cosmicize the everyday life of poor Brazilians, who are the country's vast majority. Extending Karen Brown's argument about Vodou in Brooklyn, it be can argued that Umbanda's emphasis on protean *exus* is a way to solve the "cosmological problem": the ecological dissonance produced by the need to practice a religion that is tied to natural places and entities in the heavily humanmade context of the city. If *caboclos* are the transgressor of the originative jungle, harkening back to pristine origins, *exus* are the border-crossers of the new concrete and asphalt jungles, subverting bourgeois morality. *Exus* help Brazilians negotiate the tension between the city's built environment and the "natural" environment. It is common to find food offerings to the *exus* at street corners near Umbanda centers. After all, because they are lower spirits, very close to matter, *exus* are considered masters of the crossroads. They literally have one foot in the spiritual world and another in the all-too-human world, which is the reason why they limp when they walk. Because of their hard life and street smarts, *exus* are considered excellent problem solvers. They can be very loyal and effective when accorded the proper recognition and properly fed, but they can rapidly turn vengeful and destructive if disrespected or ignored.

Umbanda also distinguishes itself from Candomblé by its closer relation with Spiritism. Spiritism originated in France in the mid-1800s, with the prolific writings of Hyppolyte Léon Denizard Rivail (1804–1869), a Parisian educator and translator of scientific books, who took the name of Allan Kardec from his previous incarnations. Spiritism is itself a highly syncretic philosophy, blending "Eastern" notions such as karma and reincarnation with parapsychology (construed as the science of the soul), Enlightenment ideas of progress and education, and a secularized version of Christianity stripped of supernatural content and stressing heavily a humanist ethic of charity. Borrowing piecemeal from Hinduism and Buddhism, Kardec held the existence of disembodied spirits closely connected with the material world. Sensitive to the effects of good and bad actions (the karmic law), these spirits seek to purify themselves through multiple reincarnations. As part of their education and progress toward becoming pure light (gaining release from the constraints of material world), the spirits may communicate with us through mediums to guide us in our own spiritual development or to request our help.

Spiritism's belief in the close interaction between the spiritual and material world dovetails with Umbanda's monistic panentheism. Spiritism's therapeutic system is partly based on the notion that all animate beings contain a spiritual fluid, a kind of electro-magnetic energy, that can be transferred. Spirit centers train *passistas*, literally "hand passers or hand layers," who hold periodic cleansing clinics where they help discharge negative energies, often produced by *espíritos obsediados* (obsessing or perturbing spirits), by passing their hands over the bodies of those afflicted by physical or psychological problems. Positive spiritual fluids can also be concentrated in water that has been prayed over by the religious specialists. This "sacred water" (*água fluidificada*) is imbibed by the practitioners. Along with fluidified water, clients may also receive homeopathic prescriptions. Umbanda also recognizes Spiritism's concern with disincarnate spirits seeking perfection by giving place to *eguns* (the wandering souls of dead people) and more evolved spirits in its pantheon.

The latter are considered spirits of light or guide spirits (*babas/espíritos guías ou de luz*), who like Socrates, Buddha, and Francisco Cândido Xavier (a.k.a. Chico Xavier, a famous Brazilian Spiritist and interpreter of Kardec), stand in sharp contrast to the "baser" spirits, the *exus*. Whereas *exus* are summoned through drumming and relish the pleasures of the flesh, the wild dancing, drinking, and smoking involved in many Umbanda public celebrations, spirits of light prefer to engage in quiet learned conversation. This tension has led scholars such as Roger Bastide to argue that Spiritism "whitens" or "europeanizes" Umbanda, distorting its African roots. Umbandistas, for their part, see the confluence of European, Eastern, African, and Brazilians strands as proof of the universal nature of their religion and as a reflection of the hybrid culture that is Brazil.

In terms of attitudes toward nature, Spiritism's influence on Umbanda is ambivalent. On the one hand, Spiritism's religious humanism reinforces Umbanda's anthropocentric tendencies – the stress on the instrumental manipulation of natural forces to produce personal well-being and success. Moreover, Kardec affirms that, from the moral point of view, there is a clear hierarchy in the universe, with human beings being able to rise above their instincts and have full consciousness of their spiritual nature. On the other hand, this anthropocentrism is counterbalanced by Spiritism's recognition that there is an underlying order in the universe in which all entities are interconnected in a progressive evolutionary scale. Thus, it is essential to overcome egotism and behave charitably toward the whole of creation. For instance, in his popular psychographed book *Nosso Lar* (Our Home), Chico Xavier offers a utopian vision of a celestial colony in which spirits hold basic goods in common and are governed by benevolent philosopher kings, the most evolved spirits. Leaving aside Diana Brown's and David Hess' discussion as to whether Umbanda and Spiritism reproduce the clientelism that has typified Brazilian politics, in Xavier's spiritual home there is not only peace and moral happiness – since everybody knows his/her place – but also harmony with nature. The spirits are presented as carrying their intellectual discussions in a tropical paradise of inexhaustible resources which the inhabitants exploit with rational moderation. This tropical paradise is suspiciously similar to an idealized version of Rio de Janeiro. This perfect society is said to exist directly above the city.

Spiritism's contradictory impact on Umbanda highlights the latter's complex character. Umbanda reflects Brazilians' ambivalent relations with their local environments, both natural and humanly constructed. On the one hand, Umbanda offers a pragmatic ethics of individual self-improvement adjusted to the demands of Western, urban modernity. On the other, it holds a relational ethos more in tune with traditional, "rural" lifeways which stress interdependence and reciprocity. Umbanda's hybridity, its power to syncretize, adapt, and even present itself as an all-encompassing religion, is in large part the result of this capacity to bridge between individuality and collectivity, and between matter and spirit.

Manuel Vasquez

Further Reading
Bastide, Roger. *African Religions of Brazil: Toward a Sociology of the Interpenetration of Civilizations*. Baltimore, NJ: Johns Hopkins University Press, 1978.
Brown, Diana DeG. *Umbanda: Religion and Politics in Urban Brazil*. New York: Columbia University Press, 1994.
Brown, Karen McCarthy. "Staying Grounded in a High-Rise Building: Ecological Dissonance and Ritual Accommodation in Haitian Vodou." In Robert Orsi, ed. *Gods of the City*. Bloomington: Indiana University Press, 1999.
Brumana, Fernando Giobellina and Elda Gonzales Martinez. *Spirits from the Margins: Umbanda in São Paulo*. Uppsala: Acta Universitatis Upsaliensis, 1989.
Hess, David J. *Spiritists and Scientists: Ideology, Spiritism, and Brazilian Culture*. University Park, PA: The Pennsylvania State University Press.
See also: Candomblé of Brazil; Caribbean Cultures; Santería; Trickster; West Africa; Yoruba Culture (West Africa).

Umehara, Takeshi (1925–)

Takeshi Umehara, a Japanese philosopher, has published many works on philosophy, religion and literature. His unique approach to the deep strata of Japanese culture and religions through archeological and mythological studies is known as "Umehara's Japanology." His numerous lectures and writings, which have drawn people from various academic fields and sections of society, are given considerable credit for the recent rise of interest in rediscovering Buddhism, Shintoism and earlier Japanese spiritual traits, as well as so-called "Joomon (Japanese neolithic) period studies" in general. His insight has also proved to be a particular inspiration for environmental educators and conservationists calling for the revitalization of forests, rivers, wetlands and indigenous lifestyles harmonious with the natural environment of each region.

Umehara was born in Sendai, Miyagi Prefecture in 1925. He grew up in Aichi Prefecture and graduated from Kyoto University, where he majored in European philosophy. Immediately after World War II, haunted by the specter of the nuclear holocaust in Hiroshima and Nagasaki, he became absorbed in the writings of Frederich Nietzsche and Martin Heidegger. Umehara was acutely conscious of the void left by a collapse of values following the introduction of European modernism. Influenced also by such thinkers as Kitaroo Nishida (author of *Zen no kenkyuu* Studies on Goodness, 1911) and Tetsuroo Watsuji (author of *Fuudo*, Climate and Culture, 1935), he began studying Japanese Buddhism and then Shintoism, the indigenous religion of Japan. He assumes religious imagination to be the key to the rise and fall of civilizations. Thus, from the outset, Umehara's thought attempted to bridge the gap between East and West in order to lift Japan and the world itself from the ruins of modernity.

Umehara's studies of Japanese culture, developed in such works as *Jigoku no shisoo* (*The Concept of Hell*, 1967), *Kamigami no ruzan* (*The Exiling of the Gods*, 1985) and *Nihonjin no anoyo kan* (*The Japanese View of the Other World*, 1989), culminated in *Mori no shisoo ga jinrui o sukuu* (*The Worldview of Forest-dwellers Will Save Human Beings*, 1991), which addresses the relationship of religion to nature. In this book he rejects the traditional assumption that the Japanese come from a homogeneous race of rice-growing farmers – first by noting that 67 percent of the land in Japan has been preserved as forest, thereby reflecting widespread worship of trees, and then by proposing an alternative view that the original culture of the Japanese is retained in the minority Ainu and Okinawan cultures. He points out various elements common to Ainu and Okinawan religious rites and mythologies, and to Japanese Shintoism and Buddhism. He interprets the well-known Japanese Mahayana Buddhist phrase "Mountains, rivers, grass, and trees, all can become Buddha" as advocating the equality of all living beings. All can go to the other world (*anoyo*) where there is neither distinction of heaven and hell, nor final judgment, and eventually all will return to this world. Today, after many stages of transformation and syncretism, Buddhist temples take care of the rites for the dead, while Shinto shrines celebrate the birth and growth of all beings in nature. Belief in reincarnation can be found in the Ainu rites of sending bears and other animals back to the world of the gods above and in the Okinawan rites of communing with the eternal otherworld of ancestors beyond the sea.

Umehara reinforces his assumption by referring to the findings of archeologists and physical anthropologists, which suggest that an early type of Mongoloid people, of whom Ainu and Okinawans are the remnants, had lived throughout the archipelago as hunters or fishers and gatherers during the Joomon period (ca. 12,000–300 B.C.E.) with a highly developed pre-agricultural forest culture, exemplified by their sophisticated earthenware. Then, around the third century B.C.E., a newer type of Mongoloid people arrived on the Japanese islands with a rice-growing culture. They expelled some of the indigenous people, and mixed with others to build the Yayoi culture (ca. 300 B.C.E.–300 C.E.). Umehara asserts that the natural religion born in the ancient forests survived the transition of cultures and even the introduction of such a powerful world religion as Buddhism in the sixth century. He believes that human beings today should revaluate the polytheistic natural religions of the forest and view the cyclic movements of life as a whole beyond individuals, races and species. It is an ecological and practical necessity for human beings to stop conquering nature and to live harmoniously with others in order to survive in the postmodern world.

Umehara has headed archeological expeditions to the sites of ancient civilizations in China and the Middle East as well as within Japan. He served as president of Kyoto Municipal University of Arts, was the first Director General of the International Research Center for Japanese Studies in Kyoto, and has been president of the Japan Pen Club since 1997. He is also a Kabuki playwright. He has won major literary awards and was honored with the Order of Culture in 1999.

Sadamichi Kato

Further Reading

Umehara, Takeshi. *Lotus and Other Tales of Medieval Japan*. Paul McCarthy, tr. Tokyo: Tuttle Publishing, 1998.

Umehara, Takeshi. *The Concept of Hell*. Robert Wargo, tr. Tokyo: Shueisha Publishing, 1996 (1967).

See also: Heidegger, Martin; Japanese Religions.

Unitarianism

The Unitarian movement can be defined as a radical tradition that emerged into self-consciousness during the European Reformation in the sixteenth century as an alternative to the authoritarian traditions of Luther and Calvin. Like their Anabaptist cousins, the Unitarians were suspicious of the misuse of ecclesial power to enforce such non-biblical teachings as the eternal Trinity, infant baptism, the exclusivity of revelation, and the doctrinal method of establishing worthiness for salvation. On the positive side, Unitarians affirmed a more immanent deity closely bound to nature, universal salvation, and the necessity of religious tolerance and freedom of the pulpit. Because of these beliefs, many Unitarians lived under religious persecution from both the Protestant and the Roman Catholic authorities until well into the eighteenth century. The most infamous case of this occurred when the Spanish Unitarian theologian Michael Servetus was burned at the stake by Calvinist forces in 1553. Servetus' crime was to have published a treatise, *Christianismi Restitutio* in 1552 in which he attacked the Trinity, orthodox Christology as it was determined by the Council of Nicaea in 325 – which affirmed the co-equality of Christ and God while rejecting the proto-Unitarian view of Bishop Arius who denied this equality – and the doctrine of infant baptism. Implicit in his views was a pantheism that found God to be co-extensive with nature. This early Unitarian laid the groundwork for a universalist pantheism, which rejected a transcendent, sovereign, deterministic and punitive God.

Unitarianism's most readily identifiable form emerged in 1805, when radical professors at Harvard won the Hollis Chair of Divinity for their Unitarian candidate Henry Ware, thus marking the end of Congregational power at that institution. Soon Unitarianism was rocked by the even more radical religious movement of Transcendentalism initiated by the former Unitarian minister Ralph Waldo Emerson when he threw down the gauntlet to the church establishment in his 1838 *Divinity School Address*, in which he went so far as to divinize the self, deny the centrality of Jesus, make nature holy, and posit a form of purely personal revelation that was self-validating outside of any form of ecclesial community. Three years later the Unitarian minister Theodore Parker delivered an equally controversial ordination address, *The Transient and Permanent in Christianity*. While more Christian in tone than Emerson's address, it rejected the importance of dogma, liturgy, and anything other than ethics and a gospel of love.

Theologically, contemporary Unitarianism is diverse in expression and often even questions the need for theological reflection insofar as there is no agreement as to the real or alleged object of such reflection. However, there are identifiable philosophical commitments that mark Unitarianism as a decidedly nature-oriented perspective. Historically the distinction between liberal and conservative Protestant traditions was expressed by the difference between positive and natural religion. In the context of the post-Kantian milieu in which this distinction came to the fore, positive religion stressed a unique historical revelation, a unique textual record of that revelation, the centrality of a founder whose eternal word was embodied in a spirit-guided church, and the superiority of Christianity to any other religion. Natural religion denied any special revelation while placing a great deal of value on universalizable reason. It rejected the importance of texts in favor of a renewed understanding of the book of nature. The power of autonomous natural and atemporal reason replaced the role of the historical founder. Reason operated within the framework of a radically open experience of the whole or the infinite. Further, Christianity was often seen as a religion that had begun to exhaust its resources, thus paving the way for an honest exploration of other religions. Unitarianism has long embraced the basic commitments of natural religion, but has moved them more directly into a post-mechanistic view of a growing, infinitely complex, and fecund nature.

Insofar as Unitarianism would affirm a metaphysics it would deny the doctrine of *creatio ex nihilo*, while asserting that nature has neither beginning nor end, with the stipulation that the world of astrophysics, which affirms the Big Bang creation, is but one world within the infinity of nature which has its own subaltern conception of creation, perhaps out of imaginary time. Transforming the eighteenth- and nineteenth-century distinction between positive and natural religions, it is perhaps preferable to speak of anti-naturalist and naturalist religions. The anti-naturalist forms embrace supernaturalism, miracles, a sovereign and external Creator, and a devaluation of creation over its Creator. Naturalist religions, which can be either panentheistic or pantheist, but not theistic or personalistic, are not only immanentist, but also affirm that nature is the genus of which the object of religion is the species. Nature is the all-encompassing category, and actually transcends the genera (classes) of all orders that occur within and as nature. Hence the term "nature" functions as both the highest category and a pre-category, that is, there is no opposition term to nature precisely because nature is all that there is, both actual and potential. For many Unitarians all-encompassing nature is itself holy while for others nature is neither holy nor unholy *per se*; it simply obtains in its infinite unfolding.

Panentheist naturalism retains some remnants of the Christian traditions insofar as it affirms that a dimension of the divine is discontinuous with the orders of nature (the dimension of *nature natured*), even though fully relevant to them. Pantheist naturalism is more radical in that it decisively moves beyond the Christian traditions by asserting that the dimension of the divine in nature can in no way be discontinuous from any or all orders of *nature natured*. This deeper dimension of the one nature is often denoted by the term "*nature naturing*," a term used by Emerson in this sense.

Within the Unitarian movement this tension is expressed as the difference between a more optimistic somewhat Christian progressivism tied to the evolutionary advance of the divine (panentheism) and a more quietist post-Christian meliorism correlated to a less optimistic view of human prospects within infinite nature (pantheism). In either case, Unitarianism affirms that supernaturalist religion remains a destructive force in culture insofar as it masks our deeper relationship to the eternal self-creating nature.

This underlying, and not always self-conscious, naturalism is manifest in both the liturgy and practice of the contemporary Unitarian Universalist Church. In 1961 the-then separate but theological similar movements of Unitarianism and Universalism joined to form a common Fellowship that is now call the Unitarian Universalist Association. Since 1961 the liturgy of the Fellowship has been shaped in ways that mark the transition to a more nature-centered worldview. Services are now dedicated to solar and lunar events as well as to the inner rhythm of the seasons. Generally the liturgy celebrates cyclical rather than historically unique events, although traditional world religious holidays are often celebrated as well, and the services use texts from all of the major religious and secular traditions.

Native American and pagan traditions are often used to transform religious consciousness by returning to the pre-monotheistic world, a world held to be friendlier to nature than that of the supernatural monotheisms. Among the more important yearly events is the Flower Communion in which each member of the congregation is asked to bring a flower that is placed in a common vase at the front of the meeting room or sanctuary. At the end of the service, each member takes a different flower home. The Czech Unitarian minister Norbert Capek created this service before the Second World War. Capek also created the symbol of the flaming chalice, which combines the naturalistic symbols of enlightening fire and the wisdom-holding cup, which is now the central liturgical object in the Unitarian Universalist movement. Capek was executed in a Nazi concentration camp in 1942 for his resistance work in which the symbol of the flaming chalice was used as a code to help escaping Jews.

Along with a strong social gospel tradition, Unitarian Universalists today fully participate in the worldwide movement of the greening of the Church. There is a direct involvement in local issues of justice and the use of resources in a way that distributes them equitably and does minimal harm to the environment. Each member of the congregation is asked to use ecologically friendly practices in all dimensions of personal and social life. In the national realm, the Association works to create laws that will bring these practices into being. On the international level, the Association has long fought for forms of just trade and reduced First World consumption. One particular focus of this concern is with critiquing the growing power of international corporations as they control the yearly sale and distribution of hybrid seeds for which they have the patents. Given that Unitarian Universalism denies the reality of a potentially salvific deity who could create an apocalypse that would rescue a few of us from our abuse of nature, congregation members feel compelled by conscience to work toward the reversal of the natural degradation partially caused by the monotheisms.

Robert S. Corrington

Further Reading
Bumbaugh, David E. *Unitarian Universalism: A Narrative History*. Chicago: Meadville Lombard Press, 2000.
Dorrian, Gary. *The Making of American Liberal Theology: Imagining Progressive Religion 1805–1900*. Louisville: Westminster John Knox, 2001.
Parke, David B. *The Epic of Unitarianism: Original Writings from the History of Liberal Religion*. Boston: Skinner House Books, 1985.
Robinson, David. *The Unitarians and the Universalists*. Westport, CT: Greenwood Press, 1985.

Wright, Conrad. *The Prophets of Religious Liberalism: Channing, Emerson, Parker*. Boston: Unitarian Universalist Association, 1986 (2nd edn).
See also: Corrington, Robert S.; Emerson, Ralph Waldo; Nature Religion in the United States; Pantheism; Spinoza, Baruch; Transcendentalism.

United Nations – See Bahá'í Faith and the United Nations; Earth Charter; Religious Studies and Environmental Concern; United Nations' "Earth Summits."

United Nations' "Earth Summits"

The first international United Nations' "Earth Summit," formally known as the United Nations Conference on Environment and Development, was held in Rio de Janeiro, Brazil from the 3rd to the 14th June, 1992. It included 172 national representatives (of which 108 were heads of state) and over 2400 representatives of non-governmental organizations (NGOs), and addressed the threat of global environmental degradation as nations seek economic development. The gathered national leaders signed the Convention on Climate Change and the Convention on Biological Diversity and the conference itself adopted The Rio Declaration on Environment and Development, The Forest Principles, and Agenda 21, a plan for coordinating environmental and national development by the next century. The Commission on Sustainable Development was formed to monitor and report on the implementation of these declarations and principles.

The 1992 Earth Summit emerged from an earlier United Nations Conference on the Human Environment, held at Stockholm in 1972, which for the first time placed environmental issues before the international community, and led to the formation of the United Nations Environment Program. By 1983 the relationship between environmental degradation and economic and social development had led to the formation of the United Nations World Commission on Environment and Development, known as the Brundtland Commission. This issued the 1989 report entitled *Our Common Future*, which defined sustainable development as "that which meets the needs of the present without compromising the ability of future generations to meet their needs" and called for international strategies combining both environmental protection and development. Significantly, the envisioned programs include action not only at the international, but also at regional, national and local levels, and involving state and non-state actors. The United Nations General Assembly voted in 1989 to hold the first United Nations Conference on Environment and Development (UNCED) in 1992.

UNCED was a watershed, but not only for the obvious environmental reasons. The United Nations moved toward the Rio meeting by hosting several preparation committee meetings in New York. Those who attended these meetings included not only government officials but also representatives of non-governmental organizations who could apply for official NGO status with the UN and provide input into the process. Each country could solicit contributions from numerous organizations and individuals, including that of both organized religious bodies and other groups motivated by nature-related spirituality whose main identity was not religious. These official conversations involved intense debates and disagreements about what was to be included and excluded from the agenda. Many compromises were made prior to and at UNCED.

Running parallel to the UNCED was an "Earth Summit" – a people's conference – an exclusively NGO event that coexisted with UNCED also in Rio. Although sponsored by the UN, this event drew environmental and political activists from all over the world. Seventeen thousand or more people (or their organizations) paid their own way (or their organizations did) to discuss the social and environmental situation around the world. Here a radical environmental and social agenda emerged and alternative treaties were written. The Earth Summit represented the critical social politics that had been emerging over decades, such as international feminism, indigenous peoples' rights, post-Marxist and post-colonial analyses, peace, human rights, and environmental agendas. The crucial presence of these groups pressured the UNCED's official governmental representatives to strengthen their environmental commitments, with particular attention to marginalized peoples. One result of UNCED and the Earth Summit was that it was now evident that citizens groups had developed their own analyses and viewpoints, were no longer going to accept their government's positions, and would be very active in planning and presenting alternatives. One of the most dynamic conversations took place at the Women's Tent – Planeta Femea – with speakers such as Wangari Matthai, Peggy Antrobus, Bella Abzug, Vandana Shiva, and over a hundred other engaging radical feminists, all of whom asserted strongly that the environmental crisis is connected to the oppression of women. The women's caucus worked hard to make the negotiators respond to the world's most disadvantaged peoples, especially women, who make up the majority of the world's poor in every country and are critical to sustainable agriculture and poverty eradication.

Others, such as the Canadian Scientist and television documentarian David Suzuki, North American Indian Faithkeeper Chief Oren Lyon of the Onondaga, economist Hazel Henderson, and world-famous television oceanographer-documentarian Jacques Cousteau, and many more, brought a sharp and multidisciplinary focus on the complexity and urgency of the environmental crises around the world. Religious voices were woven throughout these presentations. Oftentimes there was an open speaker forum, such that the conversation was participatory, democratic and lively. Music from indigenous drummers, the Earth musician Paul Winter, and the North American popular singer John Denver, brought home the need to connected together spirituality, music and politics.

Thousands of journalists reported on Rio 1992. This event showed clearly the signs of a global citizens movement, which continued on to Rio+10 and is manifested in the World Social Forum.

A strong religious voice promoting environmental sustainability and social justice emerged at Rio and continued to develop through subsequent United Nations environmental events. The World Council of Churches, the Vatican, and representatives of other world religions, notably Judaism, Islam, Buddhism, Bahá'i for example were represented at the 1992 Earth Summit. The Dalai Lama played a significant role as a spokesperson for religious sensitivities. He spoke at UNCED and especially the Earth Summit, offering a sunrise ceremony for participants at the latter venue. Given his respect for diversity and reputation for moral and spiritual integrity the Dalai Lama was able to call to awareness the many religious traditions that teach the sacredness of the Earth. Reverence for the Earth was a dimension added to intense environmental and social analysis, which strengthened both. His presence also brought a certain spiritual authority to the NGO community at the Earth Summit, as it pressured the UNCED delegates to take action. In addition, hundred of indigenous peoples gathered nearby at Altimura and brought both indigenous teachings and a powerful political presence to the events. They focused attention on the importance of protecting "Mother Earth" and helped contribute to the growing appreciation among some United Nations officials and delegates of the value of their cultures and "traditional ecological knowledge."

Although many religious traditions were present in Rio, the overall effect was an interreligious cooperation on social and environmental issues. The fact that religious leaders from around the world, representing many faiths, symbols and customs, could join as one voice in claiming the religion is an integral aspect of any viable solution. Rituals occurred at many times, and most often in a combining of rituals, teachings and wisdom. This multi-religious presence registered the need for religions to work together, and initiated a host of public and political collaboration on environmental issues. As well, religious leaders were often on panels where economics, human rights, gender equity and biodiversity were discussed, which led to an understanding that religion is an integrated voice in the conversation and solutions.

A proposal for an "Earth Charter" may prove to be the most significant religion-related development at the UNCED. This initiative mimics the strategy that guided the

United Nations Declaration on Human Rights, in which ratification by member-states is sought as a means to leverage better environmental behavior among individuals, institutions, and nation-states. Although not officially embraced at the UNCED the idea was soon championed and developed by influential actors in the non-governmental community.

The Earth Charter was initially brought forward by Maurice Strong, the Canadian who was the main organizer of the Earth Summit. In subsequent years Strong laced his speeches promoting the Charter with Gaian spirituality. The Charter's most famous early proponent was Mikhail Gorbechev, the former leader of the Soviet Union, who promoted Glasnost and presided over the Soviet Union's rejection of communism, before going on to serve as the President of Green Cross International, which is devoted to turning international institutions green. Less well known is that Gorbechev's environmentalism was grounded in a biocentric axiology in which "life has value in itself" (Gorbechev 1997:14), and a pantheistic, earthen spirituality, as he put it, "I believe in the cosmos ... *nature is my god*. To me, *nature is sacred*. Trees are my temples and forests are my cathedrals" (1997: 15). It is not uncommon for actors engaged with the United Nations' sustainability efforts to express such spirituality.

After the UNCED at Rio, the next United Nations Conference on environment and development was labeled the World Summit on Sustainable Development (WSSD) and held in Johannesburg, South Africa from 26 August to 4 September 2002. This summit was the largest UN conference ever held, with 65,000 participants, including 104 heads of state, and with representatives from over 8000 NGOs and voluntary associations. There were, however, fewer heads of state than at Rio; in contrast, there were many more NGO representatives and other citizens. The conference was contentious as it spotlighted the growing imbalance in living standards between developed and less developed nations. According to most observers, the progress that was made on a number of issues was insignificant when compared to the scale of the problems, and overall the conference failed to gain a comprehensive implementation plan for Agenda 21, a chief conference objective.

There was, however, significant evolution in the religious, ethical challenge to business as usual by the nation-states. A "Sacred Space" was designated at Ubuntu Village, for example, the main exhibition venue, where interfaith ritualizing and prayer for the well-being of the Earth's community of life was a regular occurrence. The primatologist Jane Goodall, for example, spoke widely from the official venue as well as at the venue devoted to non-governmental organizations representing "civil society" and at a conference organized by the International Union for the Conservation of Nature. She brought her own biocentric ethics and animistic spirituality to a wide audience, including during one session devoted to promoting the Earth Charter, which by 2002 had been through many drafts and had been officially brought before the United Nations. At this Earth Charter celebration, an "Arc of Hope" was present, which was on its own pilgrimage around the world, taken by those promoting this initiative. Its outside was adorned with Earth-related symbols from the world's major religious traditions, and inside of it, in addition to messages of hope from children around the world, was the Earth Charter itself, as a new sacred text, painstakingly scribed on papyrus. The Charter was mentioned favorably by a number of heads of states, or their representatives, during the WSSD, and in the conference's political declaration, a phrase from it urging respect for the wider "community of life" remained in the final text, which was the first such reference in a United Nations International Law document, according to Stephen Rockefeller, one of the Charter's most influential proponents (email correspondence after the conference).

Jane Goodall and some other important figures who had promoted Earth-focused spirituality at the official WSSD venues also appeared at the so-called "People's Earth Summit," held nearby at an Anglican school, which became during the WSSD the epicenter of anti-globalization resistance. At that venue, spiritualities of connection and belonging to an Earth considered sacred were often expressed, even being included in declarations protesting the failure of the WSSD itself to take decisive action to protect the environment and promote social justice. African traditional religions and religious leaders (*Sangomas*) were given a special place of honor. Among the well-known activists and scholars speaking at that venue, in addition to Goodall, were the ecofeminist Vandana Shiva and the anti-globalization leader Helena Norberg-Hodge. For them and others at the venue, "disconnection" with nature was viewed as a fundamental cause of environmental decline and "reconnecting with nature" as the antidote. African Sangomas led rituals to connect people to the ancestors and solicit their guidance and power for the present environmental struggle, explaining that in African traditional religion the ancestors live in a corporeal world connected to this one, and that the well-being of the Earth and the worlds inhabited by the ancestors are connected, and that environmental protection is necessary for our well-being not only in this world, but also in the one to come.

But it was not only at the WSSD's margins that Earth-related spirituality appeared, and was evolving. In addition, the Japanese power industry ran expensive advertising in the *International Herald Tribune* under the headline "Let's Be Grateful to Mother Earth", then defending nuclear power as an energy source. Less commercially, the major institutional religious actors who had been present at the Rio Summit were represented again, issuing position papers, and endeavoring to influence delegates toward strong positions in defense of ecosystems and for greater equity in the distribution of the world's natural resources. Perhaps even more significant were developments in Earth-related spiritualities beyond the sphere of institutional religions, some of which may presage the emergence of a kind of non-sectarian global civic Earth religion.

Jane Goodall, South African President Thabo Mbeki, and the Secretary-General of the UN, Kofi Annan, for example, along with many other dignitaries, led a pilgrimage on 1 September to Sterkfontein, which was located near the WSSD site, and had been inaugurated in 2001 by the United Nations Educational, Scientific and Cultural Organization as as World Heritage Site. There the *Australopithecus*, an extinct form of pre-humans dating to 4 million years ago, had been found in the 1930s, leading the place to be called the "Cradle of Humanity." Mbeki himself gave a speech there (and during his comments during the WSSD's opening ceremony) and although not overtly religious, his words were in many ways reminiscent of the Epic of Evolution, expressing a reverence for the natural world as the habitat of humanity. He asserted that this site in particular, and evolution in general, shows the kinship of all humanity, and the interconnection of all life forms. The pilgrimage to and celebration of this site was remarkable, as was the way in which it was repeatedly mentioned at the WSSD and viewed as relevant to the conference's mission, given that so many, on religious grounds, reject a Darwinian understanding of human origins, and because politicians generally avoid making pronouncements that might give offense. Even the pageantry of the conference's opening ceremony assumed an evolutionary understanding, implied a reverence for life, and envisioned an (at least) quasi-religious utopian hope for the reharmonization of all life on Earth. Such events suggest that the consecration of evolutionary narratives is making progress beyond the figures and religious enclaves that have birthed and nurtured such religious production.

The United Nations has thus become a venue where the world's religions and newer forms of religiosity increasingly press an environmental agenda upon nation-states and international institutions. Increasingly these diverse voices express the conviction that all is interconnected and that the Earth and its living systems are inherently valuable and sacred in some way, understood either as divine themselves, or as divinely imparted gifts from a beneficent Creator.

Bron Taylor
Iain S. Maclean
Heather Eaton

Further Reading

Clifford, Anne M. et al. *And God Saw That It Was Good: Catholic Theology and the Environment*. Washington, DC: National Catholic Bishops Conference, 1996.

Fowler, Robert Booth. *The Greening of Protestant Thought*. Chapel Hill, NC: University of North Carolina Press, 1995.

Gransberg-Michaelson, Wesley. *Redeeming the Creation: The Rio Earth Summit: Challenges for the Churches*. Geneva: WCC Press, 1992.

Hessel, Dieter and Larry Rasmussen, eds. *Earth Habitat: Eco-Justice and the Church's Response*. Minneapolis, MN: Fortress Press, 2001.

Keenan, Marjorie, Sr. *From Stockholm to Johannesburg: An Historical Overview of the Concern of the Holy See for the Environment*. Vatican: The Pontifical Council for Justice and Peace, 2003.

Posey, Darrell Addison. *Cultural and Spiritual Values of Biodiversity*. Nairobi, Kenya: United Nations Environmental Programme, 1999.

Rasmussen, Larry. *Earth Community: Earth Ethics*. Maryknoll, NY: Orbis Books, 1996.

UNESCO (Man and the Biosphere Program). *Man Belongs to the Earth*. Paris: UNESCO-MAB, 1988.

See also: Bahá'í Faith and the United Nations; Biosphere Reserves and World Heritage Sites; Earth Charter; Epic of Evolution; Environmental Ethics; Environmental Sabbath; Globalization; Goodall, Jane; Indigenous Environmental Network; Primate Spirituality; Religious Studies and Environmental Concern; Shiva, Vandana; Sustainability and the World Council of Churches; World Conference of Indigenous Peoples (Kari Oca, Brazil); World Council of Churches and Ecumenical Thought.

Universal Pantheist Society

Founded in 1975, the Universal Pantheist Society (UPS) is the world's oldest membership organization dedicated to the advancement of modern pantheism. The Society's stated purposes are

> to unite Pantheists everywhere into a common fellowship, to undertake the conveyance of information about Pantheism to the interested public, to encourage discussion and communication among Pantheists, to provide mutual aid and defense of Pantheists everywhere, to stimulate a revision of social attitudes away from anthropocentrism and toward reverence for the Earth and a vision of Nature as the ultimate context for human existence, and to take appropriate action toward the protection and restoration of the Earth.

The Society's name underscores its "universal" outlook, not tied to any single view of pantheism, but rather recognizing a diversity of viewpoints within it. UPS accepts and explores various interpretations of pantheism, stressing the importance of each member's personal pantheistic beliefs. Recognizing that freedom of belief is inherent in the Pantheist tradition, the UPS's bylaws prohibit any particular interpretation of Pantheism or imposition of any particular dogma.

Comments by members on what Pantheism means to them reveals the insights that are our collective faith. One member stated simply: "Being one with all life and nature." Another said, "All are one – I am a part of nature not above nature." Similarly, another wrote, "I am somewhat surprised, but delighted to learn that there are other Pantheists . . . I find a grand Unity, a wonderful Oneness with the Universe."

This last statement shows Pantheism is not usually something that someone hears from others and then decides to become. Instead, our members typically say they already know how they feel and what they believe about religion and nature, and rejoice when they find the name "Pantheism," which they find an apt term for what they already believe. One new member wrote: "I feel a strange feeling of relief – because for many years I felt the forces of nature were 'God' – without ever hearing about Pantheists."

Such statements testify that despite the diversity of viewpoints, members share one consistent direction in looking toward the natural world for our source of spiritual enrichment. Pantheism is an ancient faith experiencing a modern renaissance. Out of this understanding the UPS was born.

Accordingly the overall vision of the Society is more attuned to promoting reverence for nature and an ethical pantheism of responsible action and life-affirming practices than philosophical debate regarding the nuances of religion or philosophy. Persons joining the UPS may engage in seeking freedom and nourishment of religious experience from fellow pantheists and through the practice of the spiritual path of Pantheism in ways meaningful to themselves.

UPS publishes a quarterly journal *Pantheist Vision* and maintains a website offering an array of material on pantheism, including articles, reading lists, and members reflections on their beliefs. An online forum addresses questions about pantheism, lifeways, and other issues. UPS hosts an Ecological Community Preservation Fund that encourages donations from members to protect natural habitats.

Harold Wood

Further Reading
Wood, Jr., Harold. "Modern Pantheism as an Approach to Environmental Ethics." *Environmental Ethics* (Summer 1985), 151–63.
See also: Pantheism.

Universe Story – *See* Berry, Thomas; Epic of Evolution; Religious Studies and Environmental Concern; Swimme, Brian; United Nations' "Earth Summits".

University of Creation Spirituality – *See* Christianity (7e) – Creation Spirituality.

Urban Reinhabitation – CERES as Case Study (Australia)

How do we treat the ground beneath our feet? What is the attitude of Western civilization to the ground on which we walk and live? This ground is always, of course, part of land, and the approach of Western civilization to land has been to treat it as a *tabula rasa* on which individuals and societies are free to impose their own designs. This is true in every society which has been subjected to regimes of Westernization/modernization: land, in all its ecological, topographical and geological particularity, has been reduced to a neutral substrate to be divided up in accordance with abstract geometrical principles.

This approach has been described as a Euclidean one: it imposes a conceptual grid of straight lines on land, and land is then parceled up into the discrete, usually rectangular "blocks" of the surveyor's plan. The blocks are treated as separate entities, generally leveled or otherwise physically modified to constitute the "blank sheet" that can then accommodate the designs of its subsequent "owners." In this process little if any account is taken of the contents even of adjoining blocks, let alone of the character of the region at large. The bumps and curves of actual things, the particularity of the actual ground on which we stand, is regarded as incidental, contingent; the world as it is given to us is mere "scenery," a manifold of "appearances" which can be replaced and rearranged, like theatrical backdrops, to suit our purposes. All the world is indeed, from this point of view, a stage.

Why has the West opted for this approach and why is it wrong to do so? Suffice it to say here in answer to this very large question that the Euclidean approach follows from a worldview according to which the fundamental metaphysical datum is not land, in all its particularity, but matter, conceived as neutral substrate. From this point of view, the objects that we see around us and the ground beneath our feet are just the forms that this neutral substrate, this essentially undifferentiated matter, happens to take at a particular point in space and time. Neither objects nor ground possess integrity of their own or intrinsic significance. There is thus no reason why we should not rearrange this matter to suit our convenience. The Euclidean grid is a correlate of this view and serves as a conceptual tool for optimizing our use of matter.

If we are to respect the world as it is given to us however, if we are to adapt our thinking and our practice to the "lie of the land," following the original contours of the environment rather than imposing our Euclidean grid, then we need a metaphysics which affirms that the world as it is given to us does indeed possess a certain integrity. Such metaphysics will involve an ascription of *life* to the world: the things around us and the ground beneath our feet will harbor ends and meanings of their own, ends and meanings which they can moreover share with us. Such a view of the world, as alive with a life of its own and potentially communicatively open and responsive to us, of course suggests the possibility of new forms of praxis and a new poetics to match.

Does environmentalism hold the key to such a praxis and such a poetics? In its traditional forms, hardly. As Aboriginal philosopher, Mary Graham, says, environmentalism is just another Western "ism." It is just another grid that we impose on the world, failing to notice the contours of the given. In this sense it is as decontextualized as the rest of Western praxis. Consider, for instance, how environmental organizations are typically housed in ordinary offices – neutralized, decontextualized spaces – which environmentalists themselves treat in as instrumental a fashion as real-estate agents treat other "property." More generally, environmentalists tend to ignore the world as currently given, urbanized and industrialized and ecologically "fallen," in favor of a dream, a "mise-en-scene," of restored forests and eco-villages.

We can begin truly to respect the world as it is given to us, to regard it as a thing with ends and meanings of its own which it can in principle communicate to us and in which we can participate, by simply honoring and cherishing the place in which we find ourselves, whether that place happens to fall in the degraded heartlands of the inner city or the pristine expanses of the outback. To affirm the life and integrity of the world is to *reinhabit* it just as it is, via the local modality of place. To reinhabit the places in which we live is not to raze the smokestacks and freeways that we might find there but to fit them back into larger unfoldings of land and planet and cosmos. It is to embrace our own role in those unfoldings, both at the level of sustainable practices and at the level of communicative exchange: by engaging with place communicatively, by singing it up, as indigenous people say, we encourage it in its unfolding and become implicated in its ends. In this way a dialogical poetics begins to evolve out of a praxis which turns around engagement with the given. Indeed, praxis and poetics become inseparable, because all the praxes of everyday life constitute interactions with world, and hence in a reawakened world all these interactions will have a dialogical, and hence a poetic, potential.

One example of such an integrated praxis-and-poetics of reinhabitation in an urban context is CERES (Centre for Education and Research in Environmental Strategies), an environment park in the inner city of Melbourne. CERES differs from most environmental organizations in that it is first and foremost a *site*. That is to say, it is not merely *housed* on a site; its identity is inextricable from the site itself.

CERES started out twenty years ago on a degraded ten-acre lot on the banks of the Merri Creek. In its early days it was used by a number of community groups for small environmental projects. As these groups had few resources, they had no alternative but to work with the site as it was, adapting their plans to the contours of the land and to the materials at hand. No "master" plan prevailed. In consequence, the site developed *organically*, taking shape by a kind of natural selection of appropriate initiatives rather than by any premeditated design. Since the site was "in charge" of its own regeneration in this way, it soon assumed a life of its own, emanating a palpable presence. Attuning to this presence, people developed a sense of loyalty to the site, a loyalty which also generally translated into loyalty to CERES' organizational aims. By inducing this custodial sentiment in people, the site enabled CERES, as an organization, largely to transcend ideologies of the political left or right, and to attract a true community to itself on its own account.

CERES then represents an instance of environmentalism in a custodial and dialogical mode. The role that *naming* has played in the "singing up" or "en-chanting" of place in this instance is notable. "Ceres" is, of course, the Roman name for the Greek grain goddess, or goddess of fertility, Demeter. The original choice of this name – on the one hand an allusion to an ancient fertility goddess of the settler peoples and on the other an acronym for a thoroughly technical exercise in scientific intervention – accurately portended the unique blend of techno-environmentalism and reenchantment that would in time give rise to this now blossoming locus of reinhabitation. But the name functioned not only descriptively and predictively in this way, but also as an *invocation*, a *call* to the sacred forces of renewal in the land. In this sense CERES' intent was dialogical from the start. Though the call was drawn from the mythic memory of a colonizing culture, it was nevertheless addressed to *this* land, as it now is; it was thus less a homage to a foreign past than an attempt, in an only dimly remembered idiom, at dedication to an indigenous presence. The resacralization of this degraded site via its dedication to Demeter has in any case been uncannily successful: Demeter's myth is being played out with extraordinary appositeness in its present antipodean setting.

What is this myth? It is, of course, a myth of descent and return. Demeter loses her beloved daughter, Persephone, to the god of the underworld. In her desolation she withdraws the life-force from the land; plants wither, animals cease to thrive or give birth. The goddess retreats, in her grief, to Eleusis. Eventually Persephone, who has become Queen of the Underworld, is restored to Demeter, but only for part of each year. Reunited with her daughter, Demeter renders the land fruitful again, and thereafter Persephone's descent marks the onset of winter, her return the arrival of spring.

The CERES site itself started out as a quarry, a hole in the ground, a gateway to the underworld. Subsequently, it was a tip – the very image of waste, desolation, blight. Then, twenty years ago, when the goddess Demeter was invoked, the process of renewal began. The soil, originally compacted and barren, gradually became fertile again. The ground sprouted with gardens and groves; animals (particularly pigs, the creatures sacred to Demeter) made their home there; and people – especially schoolchildren – came from far and wide to visit the site and learn about the ways of renewal, exemplified in windmills and solar generators, methane digesters and grey water systems, worm farms and native permaculture. There was music and dancing and art, as the devotees of Demeter understood the need for celebration as much as for work. There were many festivals, notably the annual Kingfisher Festival.

In classical times, the cult of Demeter and Persephone gave rise to the most revered and hallowed event in the religious calendar of the ancient world: the initiation rites at Eleusis. There, where Demeter was believed to have grieved for her daughter, a large-scale enactment of the descent of the goddess was conducted each spring, for the purpose of revealing to initiates the promise of regeneration hidden within the mystery of death.

In an almost eerie resurrection of the Eleusinian Mysteries, adapted to the present place and time, the Return of the Sacred Kingfisher Festival is held at CERES each spring. The recent return of this little azure bird, the sacred kingfisher, to its homelands along the Merri creek, after the long "winter" of colonization/development/modernization, affords an appropriate indigenous Australian expression of the sacred daughter's return.

The festival brings hundreds of local performers of different ethnicity and cultural provenance – schoolchildren, dancers and artists – together with thousands of local residents, environmentalists and activists, in a cathartic, high-energy celebration of place. Its dramatic reenactment of the retreat of the kingfisher in the face of ecological holocaust and its return in response to the efforts of local people to regenerate their "country" through revegetation and restoration, symbolizes the beginning of a new "season" of peaceful coexistence between people and land in this locality. Mythic elements from Aboriginal culture are woven into the proceedings, and the Aboriginal custodians who lead the entire performance "initate" nonindigenous Australians into ancient local rituals of place, thereby inducing a more custodial consciousness in the new peoples, and inviting all, indigenous and nonindigenous alike, to become "reconciled" as one people through their common commitment to homeplace. With a blend of forms faithful to the land and its first and later peoples then, but also to the archetypal meaning of its eponymous goddess, CERES both celebrates and powerfully invokes, via this festival, the return of life, of fertility, to our blighted planet.

The Kingfisher festival is an instance of a participatory poetics, an event conceived and presented wholly *in place*. It is an event which could not be "staged" anywhere but at CERES. Each year, moreover, the "festival" comes closer to being a *ceremonial* event, with "audience" being invited to process along the creek, light tapers and perform other ritual actions in the context of the kingfisher story. Each year too the site joins in, adding cicada choirs and rainbows, for instance, with dazzling appositeness, at strategic junctures.

In so greatly expanding the meaning of its original environmental brief, so that it encompasses the mythopoetic in addition to the technological, and takes as its starting point the actual ground beneath our feet, CERES is perhaps pointing the way, not only for environmentalism but also for something larger than environmentalism. As churches are being closed down and sold off throughout the Western world, perhaps it is time to see "centers" like CERES, which answer to the increasingly ecological tenor of contemporary spiritual sensibilities, taking their place. In such centers people could come together to experiment collectively, both practically and poetically, with new, locally specific ways of being in the world, negotiating a new covenant with reality that would not only sustain "the environment" but would also reconnect us to the sources of meaning in life.

Freya Mathews

Further Reading

Carter, Paul. *The Lie of the Land*. London: Faber & Faber, 1996.

Graham, Mary. Interview on Aboriginal Perspectives, Caroline Jones and Stephen Godley, ABC Radio National (1992).

Mathews, Freya. "CERES: Singing Up the City." *PAN (Philosophy Activism Nature)* 1 (2000).

Mathews, Freya. "Becoming Native: An Ethcs of Countermodernity II." *Worldviews* 3:3 (1999).

Mathews, Freya. "Letting the World Grow Old: An Ethos of Countermodernity." *Worldviews* 3:2 (1999).

See also: Australia; Bioregionalism; Greece – Classical; Snyder, Gary.

Utopian Communities

Many religions around the world have an ancient myth that people once lived in harmony with nature, but sin expelled humanity from this Edenic environment. Similarly, inhabitants of industrial societies have often longed to recapture the lost bliss they imagine that people enjoyed in traditional agricultural society, marked by brotherhood and communal sharing. On the basis of such myths, utopian experiments have sought to revive harmony between humans and between humanity and nature. These are worldwide phenomena, but the utopian communities of the United States have been especially well documented.

Sects and Cults

Some of the most successful communes have been Protestant sects in the German Anabaptist tradition that migrated to North America: notably Amana, Harmony, Zoar and the Hutterites. A sect is a religious movement that broke away via schism from a larger and less intense denomination, and that seeks to create a more perfect version of the religious tradition in which it arose. The members of such sects tend to have long-standing social bonds with each other, and their internal group cohesion is so strong they often lose bonds to the surrounding society and thus are well prepared to establish their community in a new land.

Because utopian sects try to return to ancient forms of agricultural community, they live close to the land. This means that in many respects they live in harmony with nature, but they also dominate and exploit nature, so their relation to the natural world is fundamentally ambivalent. This can be seen, for example, in the great variation in birth rates across these groups, Harmony producing no children and the Hutterites having among the highest fertility rates of any group in the world. Similarly, they tend to be ambivalent toward technology, often accepting innovations that improve agricultural productivity while resisting innovations that would increase their contacts with secular society.

Other communal groups are sometimes called cults, although this term has such negative connotations that many scholars call them "new religious movements" instead. Technically, a cult is a religious movement that departs significantly from the dominant religious tradition, and cults tend to be founded by individuals, couples, and very small groups of friends. Two extremely well documented examples are the Shakers and Oneida. Both of these have some affinities with conventional Protestantism, but they innovated significantly in both beliefs and practices. Oneida was born in America, whereas the Shakers developed their distinctive way of life in America from a loosely knit group of less than a dozen people that came from England. Because they tend to begin very small, cults must recruit rapidly if they are to survive, and most of them die out very quickly.

Because of their innovativeness, cults are culturally diverse and thus have many different relationships with nature. Some of them, including both the Shakers and Oneida, are very articulate about their philosophies and contradictions. In an 1823 Shaker treatise, *A Summary View of the Millennial Church*, Calvin Green and Seth Wells argued that communal life was "contrary to the partial, aspiring and selfish nature of man." Thus, they believed, only actual divine intervention could overcome this sinful nature. John Humphrey Noyes, founder of Oneida, developed techniques for controlling natural erotic urges that would allow men to have sexual intercourse without ejaculating. While ambivalence about human nature runs throughout all major religious traditions, these communal cults take it to an extreme.

Principles of Religious Communes

Scholarly research on utopian societies, both modern and historical, has provided evidence to support a number of scientific hypotheses about these phenomena. First of all, Green and Wells seem to have been right, in a sense, because religious communes tend to last far longer than secular communes, although communes of all kinds tend to die within a generation or two after formation. Second, erotic relations between individual members challenge the social integrity of communes, so successful groups tend to regulate them strictly, sometimes going to the extremes either of celibacy or of organized multipartner sexuality. Sexual tensions among members, and the tension of separation from the surrounding society, may be among the strongest factors causing ambivalence toward nature in general.

During the twentieth century, the proportion of the general population involved in agriculture declined rapidly, and society became heavily urban. This profound shift may have reduced the opportunities for new communal sects that try to re-create essentially medieval agrarian communities, without necessarily reducing the opportunities for more radical communal cults. This suggests that utopian ambivalence toward nature is increasing, with some groups embracing the Earth while others try to escape it. The sect–cult distinction is only a matter of degree, however, and either kind of group can evolve back toward conventional society. For example, the Amana sect became a household appliance corporation, and the Oneida cult became a silverware corporation.

Acknowledging the instability that comes from their experimental character, we can learn much from utopian religious communes about building sustainable society in harmony with the environment. Their transcendent ideals and social cohesion allow them to work cooperatively for shared goals. The material lifestyle of successful communes tends to emphasize efficiency rather than luxury, and their need for social harmony causes many of them to develop effective means for controlling the birth rate. Humanity needs brotherhood and harmony with nature, so utopian religious communes can provide valuable myths for the twenty-first century and beyond.

William Sims Bainbridge

Further Reading

Bainbridge, William Sims. *The Sociology of Religious Movements*. New York: Routledge, 1997.

Bainbridge, William Sims. "Utopian Communities: Theoretical Issues." In Phillip E. Hammond, ed. *The Sacred in a Secular Age*. Berkeley: University of California Press, 1985, 21–35.

Barthel, Diane L. *Amana: From Pietist Sect to American Community*. Lincoln: University of Nebraska Press, 1984.

Carden, Maren Lockwood. *Oneida: Utopian Community to Modern Corporation*. Baltimore, NJ: Johns Hopkins University Press, 1969.

Kanter, Rosabeth Moss. *Commitment and Community*. Cambridge: Harvard University Press, 1972.

Lévi-Strauss, Claude. *The Raw and the Cooked*. New York: Harper, 1970.

Stark, Rodney and William Sims Bainbridge. "Social Control in Utopian Communities." In *Religion, Deviance and Social Control*. New York: Routledge, 1996, 157–82.

Stein, Stephen J. *The Shaker Experience in America*. New Haven, CT: Yale University Press, 1992.

See also: *Ecotopia*; Ecotopia – The European Experience; Ecotopian Reflections; Eden and Other Gardens; Hippies; New Religious Movements; New Age; Science Fiction.

V

Valuing Nature

In a provocative 1997 article for the journal *Nature*, Robert Costanza and 12 colleagues calculated that the Earth's ecological systems and natural resources contributed "ecological services" valued at an average of U.S. $33 trillion per year. The calculations included all renewable ecosystem services but excluded non-renewable resources, such as fuels and minerals. In their valuing of nature, Costanza et al. attempted to be comprehensive, estimating and including values for ecological services that are excluded by market processes but nonetheless provide important benefits. Their estimations of value even included "aesthetic" and "spiritual" services provided by nature. In their article, the Costanza group admitted "there are many conceptual and empirical problems inherent in producing such an estimate" (253). However, they also noted that whenever humans make decisions about ecosystems, we are inevitably making decisions about the value of nature, even if only implicitly. Thus, for Costanza et al., it is important to determine explicitly the monetary value of nature for public policy making, despite the difficulties with such financial calculations.

Most contemporary religions also affirm the importance of valuing nature. Such perspectives from religions could also validate the work of Costanza et al. to ascertain financial values for public policy making. Yet, from the perspective of contemporary religions, the assignment of financial worth cannot adequately capture the full value of nature. For example, how is it possible to assign a financial value for spiritual ecoservices provided by nature? Rather, financial valuing of nature would be subsumed under a broader, overarching valuation.

In the creation story of Genesis 1 – which is shared as sacred scripture by the three Abrahamic traditions of Judaism, Christianity, and Islam – God follows a pattern of creating, then seeing and judging that what has been created is good. The chapter concludes with God's final evaluation: "God saw everything that he had made, and indeed, it was very good. And there was evening and there was morning, the sixth day" (Gen. 1:31, NRSV) Thus, from the perspective of the Abrahamic traditions, creation is valued because God has judged it good.

Despite this scriptural warrant that nature is to be valued, Christianity – especially the Western Christianity of Roman Catholicism and Protestantism – has been harshly criticized for devaluing nature. Representative of this critical view is the essay, "The Historical Roots of Our Ecologic Crisis," by Lynn White, Jr. In this 1967 essay, White acknowledges that, historically, humans have always modified their environment for their own benefit. While this power was limited in the past, White argues that twentieth-century humans now have the scientific and technological power radically to transform ecological systems. This profound power appears to be out of control, and "Christianity bears a huge burden of guilt" for the ecological damage incurred, since it has been the dominant cultural paradigm where science and technology have experienced rapid advances.

White bases his contention on the foundational assumption that humans' attitudes toward nature derive from their religious beliefs and perspective. He observes: "What people do about their ecology depends on what they think about themselves in relation to things around them . . . that is, by religion" (19). As we have seen, the creation story in Genesis 1 appears to value nature highly. Yet, White observes that this creation story also elevates humans above the rest of creation in a monarchical role, when it claims that humans are created in the image of God.

> Then God said, "Let us make humankind in our image, according to our likeness; and let them have dominion over the fish of the sea, and over the birds of the air, and over the cattle, and over all the wild animals of the Earth, and over every creeping thing that creeps upon the Earth" (Gen. 1:26, NRSV).

White claims that this elevation of humanity serves to devalue the rest of creation, thus giving humans an implicit permission to degrade the environment as they please. As White observes, "Christianity . . . not only established a dualism of man and nature but also insisted that it is God's will that man exploit nature for his proper ends" (18).

There are some obvious flaws in the harsh critique of Christianity represented by White. For instance, if Western Christianity is the principal factor creating attitudes that devalue nature and lead to its degradation, then logically we would not expect ecological crises to occur in areas informed by other cultural paradigms. Unfortunately, this is not the case and other areas that are not predominantly Christian have also had ecological crises. Despite such flaws in the position represented by White, many Christian thinkers have taken the broad criticism seriously.

In his book, *The Travail of Nature*, Paul Santmire

provides one of the most thoughtful treatments of White's thesis. Santmire argues that there are two competing theological motifs present throughout the historical development of Christian thought. On the one hand, Santmire finds an ecological motif that grounds a strong stewardship ethic calling upon Christians to care for God's creation. Yet, on the other hand, Santmire also finds evidence for a spiritual motif that emphasizes a spiritual salvation in such a manner that the physical environment becomes significantly less important. If not properly balanced by the ecological motif, the spiritual motif could indeed justify a boundless exploitation and degradation of the environment as White claims for Western Christianity. Santmire argues that both of these theological motifs are present throughout the historical development of Christianity, and that they may even be simultaneously present in the same theologian or theological concept.

Our rather close examination of Western Christianity suggests that there is a diversity of perspectives on the value of nature. Whereas most religions would affirm the importance of the ecological services provided by nature, many religions would assert that the value of nature extends beyond – and subsumes – a mere financial accounting. For Christianity, the value of nature occurs because God created and saw that it was good. Yet within Western Christianity, there can be profound disagreement as to what the implications of valuing nature mean for faith and life.

Richard O. Randolph

Further Reading

Costanza, Robert, et al. "The Value of the World's Ecosystem Service and Natural Capital." *Nature* 387 (15 May 1997), 253–60.

Santmire, Paul. *The Travail of Nature, The Ambiguous Ecological Promise of Christian Theology.* Minneapolis: Fortress Press, 1985.

White, Jr., Lynn, "The Historical Roots of Our Ecologic Crisis." *Science* 155 (1967), 1203–7. Reprinted in Louis P. Pojman, ed., *Environmental Ethics, Readings in Theory and Application* (2nd edn). Belmont, California: Wadsworth Publishing Company, 1998.

See also: Christianity (various); Economics; Environmental Ethics; White, Lynn – Thesis of.

van der Post, Laurens (1906–1996)

Sir Laurens Jan van der Post was born in the Orange Free State of South Africa on 13 December 1906 and he died shortly after his 90th birthday in London. His was a life of travel to the far reaches of the Earth, an Earth he loved and fought hard to preserve: his long and creative life as a soldier, journalist, author, explorer and conservationist earned him a knighthood and the honor of Commander of the British Empire.

Sir Laurens spent the 1930s writing and farming in England and his first book, *In a Province*, was pioneering in its dealing with the tragedy of apartheid. After the outbreak of World War II, he enlisted in the British Army and served until 1942 in Abyssinia, Syria and Southeast Asia, where he was then captured by the Japanese Army on the island of Java. During the ensuing three and a half years in a prisoner-of-war camp, he was instrumental in organizing extensive educational efforts among his fellow prisoners. The experiences of this camp were described in his two books, *The Seed and the Sower* (later made into the film, "Merry Christmas, Mr. Lawrence") and *The Night of the New Moon*.

All told, Sir Laurens wrote more than two dozen novels, along with countless short stories, memoirs and essays dealing with psychology, the nature of prejudice and good and evil, the environment and the importance of story in our lives. One of his many talents was the ability to weave these themes together into one and the same character or work, for example in his telling of the Bushmen stories in ways that illustrate basic human psychology and inspire a love for nature. The best known of his books are *The Lost World of the Kalahari* and *The Heart of the Hunter*. He also made numerous films for the BBC, including *All Africa Within Us* and *Jung and the Story of our Time*.

His encounter and ensuing friendship with the Swiss psychiatrist Carl Gustav Jung shortly after his return from the war was decisive and marked the beginning of his striving to understand outer and inner nature, macrocosm and microcosm. He combined Jung's philosophy with his own that had been formed from his African and Asian jungle experiences, and shared it widely with readers, viewers and friends for the rest of his life.

As a result of talking to Jung about the Africa I had within myself, I was re-confirmed into a new area of the human spirit which had been singularly mine intuitively ever since I was born. Nothing seemed to me more wonderful than the prophetic observation by Sir Thomas Browne, the intuitive alchemist figure of Norwich in the Elizabethan age: "We seek the wonders without that we carry within – we have all Africa and its wonders within us" (van der Post 1998: 311).

Sir Laurens lived his life with passion, and one of his greatest passions was the preservation of the Earth, our environment. Gifted storyteller that he was, he spent much of his time and energy in the last years of his life telling stories about the creatures of the Earth and pleading that more attention be given to our environment. He freely shared his views with gatherings of people large and small, in interviews and in his books and other writings. In an interview conducted for Earth Day in 1990, he responded to a question about why it is more important today than ever for people to experience nature and wildlife first-hand, a primary goal of an organization he championed, The Wilderness Foundation:

> We are trying to conserve the spirit of the conservationist in people ... If you keep the Earth as close to the initial blueprint of creation as you can, and you bring a person into contact with it, a person who is not whole, from a lopsided society, poof, that person changes. I've never known it to fail. Problem children, all sorts of people who have lost their way in life, once they've had this experience, they're different (van der Post 1998: 311).

In his 1985 essay entitled, "Wilderness – A Way of Truth," he wrote:

> Some of our scientists talk about "managing wilderness" and this worries me a bit. It is like saying they want to control revelation. But the moment you try to control it, there is no revelation ... We try to give it elaborate definitions, but we all know what wilderness really is, because we have it inside ourselves. We know it is a world in which every bit of nature counts and is important to us, and we know when it is not there (van der Post 1985: 47).

Sir Laurens spent the final decades of his life not only continuing to write both fiction and historical pieces, but also speaking widely throughout the world promoting the importance of nature and our environment.

Robert Hinshaw

Further Reading
van der Post, Laurens. "Introduction: A Word from Laurens van der Post." In Robert Hinshaw, ed. *The Rock Rabbit and the Rainbow: Laurens van der Post Among Friends*. Einsiedeln: Daimon, 1998.
van der Post, Laurens. "Wilderness – A Way of Truth." In Robert Hinshaw, ed. *A Testament to the Wilderness*. Zurich: Daimon, 1985, 47.

See also: Prince Charles; Wilderness Religion; World Wide Fund for Nature (WWF).

Vegetarianism and Buddhism

Buddhist outlooks toward the eating of meat vary by historical periods and traditions, and they often reflect the influence of local cultural practices and social ethoses. Generally speaking, Buddhist attitudes toward animals are shaped by the ethical principle of non-injury to others (*ahimsa*), and by the virtues of compassion, respect, and love that extend toward all beings. The principle of non-injury was shared by Buddhism and other religious traditions in ancient India, and is a core ethical virtue of Indian religions. Its importance in Buddhism can be seen from the fact that the first of the Five Precepts – which define the ethical foundation of Buddhist life and serve as the basis for other forms of spiritual cultivation – is the injunction not to kill any living creatures. While Buddhist texts and leaders often try to discourage the killing of animals, in actual practice there is a wide range of attitudes toward the practice of vegetarianism among different Buddhist groups and traditions, ranging from strict adherence to vegetarian diets to conspicuous consumption of meat by the clergy.

The texts of the monastic code of discipline, the *Vinaya*, indicate that the early monastic order did not adopt a strictly vegetarian diet. According to these sources Buddhist monks were allowed to eat meat provided it was "pure" by fulfilling three requirements: that a monk who is given a meat dish has not heard, seen, or become suspicious that the animal was specifically killed for him. Monks were of course prohibited from killing animals, or even small creatures that might reside in water used by them. Because for their food they relied on alms received from the faithful, monks were supposed to eat whatever they were offered while practicing detachment from the sensual pleasures associated with eating. In the *Vinaya* there is also the story of the Buddha's refusal to make vegetarianism compulsory for all monks, when that was proposed by his evil cousin Devadatta as part of a request to institute a range of new rules initiated by him in order to create schism within the monastic community.

While monks were absolved from any transgression if they consumed meat that fulfilled the three requirements, in early Buddhism, killing of animals was regarded as an unwholesome act and was proscribed by Buddhist moral values. It was believed that for lay people the killing of animals brought about negative karmic consequences, while the sparing of animal lives became a cherished Buddhist ideal. The positive regard of animals was reinforced by Jataka stories, which depict previous lives of the Buddha. In a number of these stories the Buddha is depicted as being reborn in a previous lifetime as an animal, and noble feelings and actions are attributed to wild animals such as elephants. A similar point of view was adopted by the famous Buddhist monarch Aśoka (r. ca. 265–238 B.C.E.), who recognized the sanctity of animal lives and instituted official days when animals were not to be killed. In one of his inscriptions the Emperor states that he has conferred many boons to animals, birds, and fish, including the saving of their lives. Aśoka himself abandoned hunting and eventually prohibited the killing of animals in order to supply food for the court and the imperial household. Aśoka's example was followed by a number of Buddhist monarchs, such as Sri Lankan kings who prohibited the slaughter of animals, and Emperor Wu of the Liang dynasty (r. 502–549) in China, who practiced vegetarianism and issued decrees that restricted the killing of animals.

Adoption of vegetarianism became more prevalent with the emergence of the Mahayana tradition. That was largely motivated by an increased emphasis on compassion as a prime Buddhist virtue, although external criticisms of Buddhist meat eating might have also played some part. Mahayana promoted universalistic ethics that was predicated on the notion that the pursuit of the bodhisattva path is to be undertaken for the sake of benefiting all beings. Since animals, like all other creatures, were objects of the bodhisattvas' compassionate regard and selfless salvific acts, it was deemed improper for Mahayana practitioners to consume their flesh. Explicit critiques of meat eating appear in a number of Mahayana scriptures and other texts composed by leading figures of the movement. Arguably the most trenchant critiques can be found in the Lankavatara Scripture, which presents a series of arguments that highlight the evils of meat eating and includes a call to disallow the practice. According to the scripture, eating of animal flesh is disgusting, creates hindrances to spiritual progress, contributes to bad health, and leads to unpleasant rebirth. Conversely, in addition to being healthy, the adoption of a vegetarian diet accords with Buddhist values and ideals, aids spiritual cultivation, and helps one to avoid the negative karmic consequences of meat eating. The scripture also takes to task the permissive attitudes of earlier Buddhist texts and traditions, proclaiming that arguments made in support of meat eating, including the notion that meat is pure if it fulfills the three requirements, are spurious. The text also states that the Buddha never permitted the eating of meat, and for good measure it also explicitly prohibits the eating of meat by all disciples of the Buddha under all circumstances.

With the transmission of Mahayana forms of Buddhism to China, vegetarianism became a characteristic feature of Chinese Buddhism. From the medieval period onward meat eating was prohibited in Buddhist monasteries, and Chinese monks and nuns adopted a strict vegetarian diet that also precluded the consumption of eggs, diary products, and certain types of leeks (which more or less amounted to veganism). Vegetarianism was given additional canonical legitimacy by the Brahma Net Scripture, an apocryphal text composed in China, which contains a series of bodhisattva precepts that became accepted as normative by Chinese Buddhists. Since this text prohibits the eating of meat, abstinence became binding for all monks and nuns who received bodhisattva ordinations as part of their entry into the monastic order. Vegetarianism was, and still is, practiced by lay Buddhists as well. Vegetarian feasts are a common feature of Chinese Buddhist festivals, and lay devotees who have not adopted a vegetarian diet often abstain from meat eating on certain observance days, such as festivals dedicated to popular bodhisattvas. Vegetarianism also had a broad effect on traditional Chinese society. Under Buddhist influence, during the medieval period the imperial government issued decrees that restricted or prohibited the slaughter of animals on certain dates, and vegetarianism was also adopted by Daoist monastic orders. Vegetarianism continues to be a basic feature of Chinese Buddhism, which remains distinct among the Buddhist traditions by its stress on the injunction against the eating of meat.

The practice of vegetarianism was also transmitted to other areas of Asia that adopted Chinese forms of Buddhism, viz. Korea, Japan, and Vietnam. In Japan that influence extended until the onset of the modern period, as by and large in traditional Japanese society most people lived on a largely vegetarian diet (although they consumed fish). Meat eating became more prevalent from the late nineteenth century onward with the greater emphasis on modernization and the acceptance of Western mores. With the increased secularization of the Buddhist clergy, the various Buddhist sects abandoned the age-old prohibitions against meat eating, although training monasteries, especially ones belonging to the Zen sects, formally retain vegetarian diets for priests undergoing formal training. Among other Mahayana traditions, vegetarianism is not widely practiced in Tibetan Buddhism. Although compassion and love for all beings are regarded as cardinal virtues by the Tibetans, the widespread meat eating by the clergy is largely explained by the difficulty of practicing a vegetarian diet in Tibet's harsh climate.

Although the prohibition against killing and the call to adopt attitudes of kindness toward animals are accepted as normative by the contemporary Theravada traditions, the practice of vegetarianism is a rare occurrence in all Theravadin countries. In Sri Lanka most Buddhists avoid killing animals (which often does not extend to fish), and most butchers are Muslims. The Buddhist concern with killing is also reflected in the relatively low consumption of meat and the rarity of making offerings of red meat to the monks, although few Buddhists identify themselves as vegetarians. Meat eating is much more prevalent in other Theravada countries such as Thailand, where the vast majority of monks engage in conspicuous consumption of large quantities of meat. There vegetarianism is often frowned upon, although there are a few monks who are trying to promote the idea of vegetarianism. Vegetarianism is much more widespread among Western Buddhists. That seems to be influenced by a number of disparate factors, including increased interest in vegetarianism by the general society, adoption of specific views about Buddhist values and lifestyles, and adherence of ethical principles informed by ecological concerns.

Mario Poceski

Further Reading

Harvey, Peter. *An Introduction to Buddhist Ethics*. Cambridge: Cambridge University Press, 2000, 156–70.

Walters, Kerry S. and Lisa Portmess, eds. *Religious Vegetarianism: From Hesiod to the Dalai Lama*. Albany: State University of New York Press, 2000, 61–91.

See also: Animals; Buddha; Islam, Animals, and Vegetarianism; Jataka Tales; Vegetarianism and Judaism.

Vegetarianism and Judaism

In traditional Jewish thinking, not only are normative laws regarded as binding solely upon the authority of divine revelation, but ethical principles as well are regarded as endowed with validity and commended as goals of human aspiration only if they, too, are divinely revealed. Accordingly, the value of vegetarianism as a moral *desideratum* can be acknowledged only if support is found within the corpus of the Written or Oral Law.

A proof-text often cited in support of vegetarianism as an ideal to which humans should aspire is a statement recorded in the Talmud (BT *Sanhedrin* 59b):

> Rav Judah stated in the name of Rav, "Adam was not permitted meat for purposes of eating as it is written, 'for you shall it be for food and to all beasts of the Earth' (Gen. 1:29), but not beasts of the Earth for you. But when the sons of Noah came [He] permitted them [the beasts of the Earth] as it is said, 'as the green grass I have given you everything'" (Gen. 9:3).

Some writers have regarded this statement as reflecting the notion that primeval humanity was denied the flesh of animals because of its enhanced moral status. Permission to eat the flesh of animals was granted only to Noah because, subsequent to Adam's sin, mankind could no longer be held to such lofty moral standards. Nevertheless, they argue, people ought to aspire to the highest levels of moral conduct and eschew the flesh of animals.

In point of fact, this talmudic dictum is simply a terse statement of the relevant law prior to the time of Noah, but is silent with regard to any validating rationale. The classic biblical commentators found entirely divergent explanations for the change that occurred with regard to dietary regulations.

An examination of the writings of rabbinic scholars reveals three distinct attitudes with regard to vegetarianism:

1) The Gemara (BT *Pesachim* 49b) declares that an ignoramus ought not to partake of meat:

> "This is the law of the animal . . . and the fowl" (Lev. 11:46): whoever engages in [the study of] the Law is permitted to eat the flesh of animals and fowl, but whoever does not engage in [the study of] the Law may not eat the flesh of animals and fowl.

This text should certainly not be construed as declaring that meat is permitted only to the scholar as a reward for his erudition or diligence. *Maharsha* (Rav Shmuel Eliezer Halevi Eidels, fifteenth century) indicates that this text simply reflects a concern for scrupulous observance of the minutiae of the dietary code. The ignoramus is not proficient in the myriad rules and regulations governing the eating of meat, including the differentiation between kosher and non-kosher species, the purging of forbidden fat and veins, the soaking and salting of meat, etc.

2) A number of medieval scholars, including R. Isaac Abravanel (also spelled "Abarbanel," 1437–1508) in his commentary to Genesis 9:3 and Isaiah 11:7, and R. Joseph Albo (c.1380–1444) in *Sefer ha'Ikarim*, Book III, chapter 15, regard vegetarianism as a moral ideal, not because of a concern for the welfare of animals, but because of the fact that slaughter of animals might cause the individual who performs such acts to develop negative character traits, viz., meanness and cruelty. Their concern was with regard to possible untoward effect upon human character rather than with animal welfare.

Indeed, R. Joseph Albo maintains that renunciation of the consumption of meat for reasons of concern for animal welfare is not only morally erroneous but even repugnant. Albo asserts that this was the intellectual error committed by Cain and that it was this error that was the root cause of Cain's act of fratricide. Albo opines that Cain did not offer an animal sacrifice because he regarded humans and animals as equals and, accordingly, felt that he had no right to take the life of an animal, even as an act of divine worship. Abel maintained that humans were superior to animals in that they possessed reason as demonstrated by his ability to use intellect in cultivating fields and in shepherding flocks. This, Abel believed, gave human beings limited rights over animals, including the right to use animals in the service of God, but it did not confer upon him the right to kill animals for his own needs. Abel's error was not as profound as that of Cain, but it was an error nonetheless. And, declares Albo, because Abel shared the error of his brother, he was punished by being permitted to die at the hands of Cain. Cain's error was egregious in the extreme. Hence he was so lacking in favor in the eyes of God that his sacrifice was rejected. Although he was also guilty of error, Abel's sacrifice was accepted by God because his error was not as serious as that of his brother.

According to Albo, Cain failed to understand the reason for the rejection of his sacrifice and assumed that, in the eyes of God, animal sacrifice was intrinsically superior to the offering of produce. Since Cain remained confirmed in his opinion that humans and animals are inherently equal, he was led to the even more grievous conclusion that just

Vegetarianism and Kabbalah

Abstinence from the flesh of animals is also the subject of scattered comments in kabbalistic writings. R. Moses Cordovero, *Shi'ur Komah* (Warsaw 1883: 84b), advises that a person seeking spiritual perfection should "distance" himself from eating meat. Accepting the principle of transmigration of souls, R. Moses Cordovero expresses the concern that the soul of a wicked human being may be present in a slaughtered animal and exert a deleterious influence over the person who consumes its flesh. In a footnote appended to that text, the editor remarks that, according to this thesis, one who is imbued with the Divine Spirit, and hence capable of determining that no such soul is incarnated in the animal he is about to eat, has no reason to refrain from eating meat.

A similar position is attributed to R. Eliyahu de Vidas' *Reishit Chokhmah* (sixteenth century) in *S'dei Chemed* (an encyclopedia of Jewish Law by R. Chayyim Chizkiyahu Medini, nineteenth century), "Ma'arekhet Akhilah" sec. 1. *Reishit Chokhmah* is cited as stating that one should not eat the flesh of any living creature. The reference appears to be to the Amsterdam, 1908 edition of *Reishit Chokhmah*. However, an examination of pp. 129b–30a of that edition reveals that, rather than advising total abstinence from the flesh of living creatures, *Reishit Chokhmah* offers counsel with regard to the time of day most suitable for the partaking of meat.

Opposition to the consumption of meat appears to be a narrowly held view even within the kabbalistic tradition. A number of kabbalistic sources indicate that, quite to the contrary, the doctrine of transmigration yields a positive view regarding the eating of meat. According to these sources, transmigrated souls present in the flesh of animals may secure their release only when the meat of the animal has been consumed by a man. The *mitzvot* performed in preparation and partaking of the meat and the blessings pronounced upon its consumption serve to "perfect" the transmigrated soul so that it may be released to enjoy eternal reward. See, for example, *Shevet Musar* (by R. Eliyahu Hakohen of Izmir, d. 1729), ch. 36 and R. Tzvi Elimelekh of Dinov (1783–1841, also spelled "Elimelech"), *B'nei Yissaskhar, Ma'amarei haShabbatot, Ma'amar* 10 sec. 4, and *Sivan, Ma'amar* 5, sec. 18. Scripture speaks of fish as "gathered" rather than as slaughtered and similarly speaks of the righteous as being "gathered" to their forebears rather than experiencing the throes of death. Righteous individuals who must undergo transmigration in expiation of minor infractions are incarnated in fish in order to spare them the pain of slaughter. See also R. Moshe Teitelbaum (1759–1841), *Yismach Mosheh, Parshat Vayeira, s.v. vayikach chem'ah v'chalav* [Gen. 18:8]. R. Yechiel Mikhel Halevi Epstein (1829–1908), *Kitzur Sh'lah* (Jerusalem, 1960: 161) advises that particular effort be made to eat fish on *Shabbat* so that the souls of the righteous which may be incarnated in the fish be "perfected" through consumption of the fish by a righteous and observant Jew.

R. Menachem Mendel Schneerson (the Lubavitcher rebbe, 1902–1994) is quoted as having expressed opposition to vegetarianism, at least tentatively, on kabbalistic grounds. He is reported by R. Shear-Yashuv Cohen (chief rabbi of Haifa and lifelong vegetarian) to have voiced the concern that refraining from consumption of meat will prevent the "elevation of sparks," a goal that is central to the kabbalists' view of the human purpose in life (Slae, *Min hattai*, Jerusalem, 1988).

J. David Bleich

---

as one is entitled to take the life of an animal so also he was entitled to take the life of a fellow human being. This position, Albo asserts, was adopted by succeeding generations as well. It was precisely the notion that humans and animals are equal that led, not to the renunciation of causing harm to animals and to concern for their welfare, but rather to the notion that violence against one's fellows was equally acceptable. The inevitable result was a total breakdown of the social order, which ultimately culminated in punishment by means of the Flood. Subsequent to the Flood, meat was permitted to Noah, Albo asserts, in order to impress upon humankind the superiority of human beings over members of the animal kingdom.

Albo does not explain why the generations after the Flood drew the correct conclusion and were not prone again to commit the error of Cain. There is, however, a rabbinic text that effectively resolves the issue. Genesis 7:23 declares that during the period of the Flood God destroyed not only humans but also every living creature. The Gemara, BT *Sanhedrin* 108a, queries,

> If man sinned, what was the sin of the animals? Rabbi Joshua the son of Korchah answered the question with a parable: A man made a nuptial canopy for his son and prepared elaborate foods for the wedding feast. In the interim his son died. The father arose and took apart the nuptial canopy declaring, "I did nothing other than on behalf of my son. Now that he has died for what purpose do I need the nuptial canopy?" Similarly, the Holy One, blessed be He, said, "I did not create animals and beasts other than for man. Now that man has sinned for what purpose do I need animals and beasts?"

Those comments serve to indicate that the extermination of innocent animals in the course of the Deluge must be regarded as proof positive of the superiority of human beings over members of the animal kingdom. Animals could be destroyed by a righteous God only because the sole purpose of those creatures was to serve humanity. Hence, if humankind is to be destroyed, the continued existence of animal species is purposeless. Thus the basic principle (i.e., the superiority of humans over members of the animal kingdom) was amply demonstrated by the destruction of animals during the course of the flood.

3) One modern-day scholar who is often cited as looking upon vegetarianism with extreme favor is the late Rabbi Abraham Isaac Kook. It is indeed the case that in his writings Rabbi Kook speaks of vegetarianism as an ideal and points out that Adam did not partake of the flesh of animals. In context, however, Rabbi Kook makes those comments in his portrayal of the eschatological era. He regards man's moral state in that period as being akin to that of Adam before his sin and does indeed view renunciation of enjoyment of animal flesh as part of the heightened moral awareness which will be manifest at that time. But Rabbi Kook is emphatic, nay, vehement, in admonishing that vegetarianism dare not be adopted as a norm of human conduct prior to the advent of the eschatological era. Rabbi Kook advances what are, in effect, four distinct arguments in renunciation of vegetarianism as a goal toward which contemporary man ought to aspire:

i) Rabbi Kook remarks almost facetiously that one might surmise that all problems of human welfare have been resolved and the sole remaining area of concern is animal welfare. In effect, his argument is that there ought to be a proper order of priorities. Rabbi Kook is quite explicit in stating that enmity between nations and racial discrimination should be of greater moral concern to humankind than the well-being of animals and that only when such matters have been rectified should attention be turned to questions of animal welfare.
ii) Given the present nature of the human condition, maintains Rabbi Kook, it is impossible for humans to sublimate their desire for meat. The inevitable result of promoting vegetarianism as a normative standard of human conduct, argues Rabbi Kook, will be that humans will violate this norm in seeking self-gratification. Once taking the life of animals is regarded as being equal in abhorrence to taking the life of human beings, it will transpire, contends Rabbi Kook, that in pursuit of meat, people will regard cannibalism as no more heinous that the consumption of the flesh of animals. The result will be, not enhanced respect for the life of animals, but rather debasement of human life.
iii) Human beings were granted dominion over animals, including the right to take animal lives for their own benefit, in order to impress upon human beings their spiritual superiority and heightened moral obligations. Were they to accord animals the same rights as human beings they would rapidly degenerate to the level of animals in assuming that humans are bound by standards of morality no different from those acted out by brute animals.
iv) In an insightful psychological observation, Rabbi Kook remarks that even individuals who are morally degenerate seek to channel their natural moral instincts in some direction. Frequently, they seek to give expression to moral drives by becoming particularly scrupulous with regard to some specific aspect of moral behavior. With almost prescient knowledge of future events, Rabbi Kook argues that, were vegetarianism to become the norm, people might become quite callous with regard to human welfare and human life and express their instinctive moral feelings in an exaggerated concern for animal welfare. These comments summon to mind the spectacle of Germans watching with equanimity while their Jewish neighbors were dispatched to crematoria and immediately thereafter turning their attention to the welfare of the household pets that had been left behind.

Despite the foregoing, vegetarianism is not rejected by Judaism as a valid lifestyle for at least some individuals. There are, to be sure, individuals who are repulsed by the prospect of consuming the flesh of a living creature. It is not the case that an individual who declines to partake of meat is *ipso facto* guilty of violation of the moral code. On the contrary, Scripture states, "and you will say: 'I will eat meat,' because your soul desires to eat meat; with all the desire of your soul may you eat meat" (Deut. 12:20). The implication is that meat may be consumed when there is desire and appetite for it as food, but may be eschewed when there is no desire and, *a fortiori*, when it is found to be repugnant. The question is one of perspective. Concern arises only when such conduct is elevated to the level of a moral norm.

J. David Bleich

Further Reading

Bleich, J. David. *Contemporary Halachic Problems*, v. 3. New York: Ktav Publishing/Yeshiva University Press, 1989.

Cohen, Alfred S. "Vegetarianism from a Jewish Perspective." *Journal of Halacha and Contemporary Society* 1:2 (1981), 38–63.

Rosner, Fred. *Biomedical Ethics and Jewish Law*. Hoboken, NJ: Keav Publishing House, 2001.

See also: Animal Rights in the Jewish Tradition; Judaism; Kabbalah and Eco-theology; Vegetarianism and Rabbi Abraham Isaac Kook; Vegetarianism, Judaism, and God's Intention.

Vegetarianism and Rabbi Abraham Isaac Kook (1865–1935)

Rabbi Abraham Isaac Kook, often referred to by the Hebrew title *Rav Kook*, was the leading Orthodox Jewish thinker of the Zionist movement. Born in Griva, Latvia, Kook was a leading Talmudic scholar and expert in Jewish law, while also deeply influenced by Jewish mysticism and Hasidism. After serving as rabbi to two Eastern European towns, in 1904 Kook immigrated to Palestine to serve as rabbi of Jaffa. While attending a convention in Europe in 1914, Kook found his return route to Palestine cut off by the outbreak of World War I. He spent the duration of the war in a temporary rabbinical position in London, and afterwards returned to Palestine to serve as Chief Rabbi of Jerusalem. In 1921 he was elected first Ashkenazi (European) Chief Rabbi of Palestine.

Kook's prolific writings meld traditional Jewish philosophical and mystical ideas with elements of modern European philosophy to create a comprehensive Jewish worldview. He viewed history as the dialectical unfolding of a cosmic drama of redemption, encompassing processes ranging from biological evolution to the spiritual advancement of humanity. At the center of this drama stands the Jewish people, whose own historical development serves as a catalyst for, and harbinger of, the perfection of humanity as a whole, bringing about, ultimately, the perfection of the entire universe both in its material and spiritual aspects.

In this context, the return of the Jewish People to Palestine may be seen as aimed at achieving its *rapprochement* with physical nature. Kook taught that an unbalanced attachment to nature invites the dangers of idolatry and pantheism. The Jewish people had been exiled from their land in order to distance Judaism from nature and purify Jewish monotheism of idolatrous and pantheistic tendencies. Now that those dangers had been dealt with, the time had come for the Jewish People to return to its land. Immunized against idolatry and reestablished in its home soil, Judaism can safely engage with the physical world in order to perfect and bring to light the holiness implicit in all of reality, including inorganic matter. Building upon earlier traditions, Kook claimed that the Land of Israel (Palestine) is peculiarly endowed with a unique spiritual quality whose influence is necessary for the Jewish People to fulfill their spiritual quest.

Reflecting his belief that every part of the Jewish people plays an essential role in the redemptive process, Kook sought ties with people from all sections of the Jewish population, from the radically anti-religious socialist-Zionists, to the Ultra-orthodox anti-Zionist pietists of Jerusalem. He was something of a controversial figure, antagonizing modernists with his insistence on the absolute centrality of religion in Jewish life, and scandalizing traditionalists by embracing Zionism. True to his belief in the inherent goodness within all phenomena, he viewed secular atheism as a spiritually profound and ultimately beneficial challenge to traditional religiosity. Modernist atheism would catalyze monotheism's final purification. Similarly, Kook found in the theory of evolution an expression of the cosmic drive toward perfection that informs all created beings.

Kook's writings on vegetarianism, collected in a pamphlet entitled *Hazon HaTzimchonut v'haShalom miV'khinah Toranit* (*The Vision of Vegetarianism and Peace from a Torah Perspective*), have been the subject of great interest and misunderstanding. On the one hand, Kook addressed the morality of human/animal relations in remarkably radical terms. Judaism has traditionally objected to unnecessary animal suffering and to the wanton destruction of nonhuman life. However, these are often regarded within Judaism as spiritually damaging to the human perpetrator, rather than genuinely evil in themselves. Kook went beyond such considerations to speak of human *injustice* toward animals. Not only is the slaughter of animals for food wrong, but also even the nonviolent exploitation of animal products such as wool and milk constitutes a form of theft!

Kook was careful to explain that full moral consideration for animals should only be implemented when humanity achieves its highest spiritual development in the messianic era. His view is rooted in the ancient Jewish notion that while God originally forbade humans to eat meat ("Behold I have given you every seed-bearing plant upon all the Earth, and every tree that has seed-bearing fruit; they shall be yours for food" [Gen. 1:29]), after the Deluge God permitted it as a concession to human weakness ("Every creature that lives shall be yours to eat; as with the green grasses, I give you all these" [Gen. 9:3]). Kook claimed that while the earlier ban on meat would be reinstated in messianic times, a premature demand for vegetarianism and full justice toward animals would be spiritually destructive. In their present fallen state, people would understand such a demand as implying the essential equality of humans and animals. They would forget humanity's unique spiritual vocation and lapse into a brutish and purely corporeal existence. Tyrannical governments would use radical campaigns for animal protection as tools for the oppression of humans, and as a propagandistic distraction from the injustices they perpetrate against people. Kook argued that absolute justice for animals should be demanded only after *inter-human* relations are free of violence, oppression and injustice.

For the time being, Kook taught, many biblical commandments serve to remind us of the present imperfect state of human attitudes toward animals. Jewish laws including careful ritual guidelines for humane slaughter, and the prohibition against eating blood (Deut. 13:23) serve to prepare us for the day when vegetarianism will be required of humans. The law stating, "You shall not boil a kid in its mother's milk" (Ex. 23:19) reminds us that by right the milk belongs to the kid. The prohibition against wearing "cloth combining wool and linen" (Deut. 22:11) reminds us that, in terms of absolute justice, each sheep is the genuinely legitimate owner of its own wool.

Berel Dov Lerner

Further Reading

Agus, Jacob B. *Banner of Jerusalem*. New York: Bloch Publishers, 1949. Reprinted in 1972 under the title *High Priest of Rebirth*.

Ben Shlomo, Yosef. *Poetry of Being: Lectures on the Philosophy of Rabbi Kook*. Shmuel Himelstein, tr. Tel-Aviv: MOD Books, 1990.

Ish-Shalom, Benjamin. *Rav Avraham Itzhak HaCohen Kook: Between Rationalism and Mysticism*. Ora Wiskind-Elper, tr. Albany: SUNY Press, 1993.

Kook, Abraham Isaac. *Rav A.Y. Kook: Selected Letters*. Tzvi Feldman, tr., ed. Ma'aleh Adumim, Israel: Ma'aliot Publications of Yeshivat Birkat Moshe, 1986.

Kook, Abraham Isaac. *Hazon HaTzimhonut v'HaShalom miVekhina Toranit* (*The Vision of Vegetarianism and Peace from a Torah Perspective*, Hebrew). Rabbi David Cohen, ed. Jerusalem: Nezer David Publications, 1983.

Kook, Abraham Isaac. *Abraham Isaac Kook: The Lights of Penitence, The Moral Principle, Lights of Holiness, Essay, Letters, and Poems*. Ben Zion Bokser, tr. New York: Paulist Press, 1978. This book includes the essay "Fragments of Light," which constitutes the final section of *Hazon HaTzimhonut*, and which summarizes much of its content.

See also: Animal Rights in the Jewish Tradition; Judaism; Kabbalah and Eco-theology; Paganism and Judaism; Paganism – A Jewish Perspective; Vegetarianism and Judaism (and adjacent, Vegetarianism and Kabbalah); Vegetarianism, Judaism, and God's Intention.

[SP] Vegetarianism, Judaism, and God's Intention

And God said: "Behold, I have given you every herb yielding seed which is upon the face of all the Earth, and every tree that has seed-yielding fruit – to you it shall be for food" (Gen. 1:29).

God's initial intention was that people be vegetarians. The foremost Jewish Torah commentator Rashi states the following about God's first dietary regime: "God did not permit Adam and his wife to kill a creature to eat its flesh. Only every green herb were they to all eat together" (Rashi's commentary on Gen. 1:29). Most Torah commentators, including Rabbi Abraham Ibn Ezra, Maimonides, Nachmanides, and Rabbi Joseph Albo, agree with Rashi.

The Talmud also asserts that people were initially vegetarians: "Adam was not permitted meat for purposes of eating" (BT *Sanhedrin* 59b).

The great thirteenth-century Jewish commentator Nachmanides indicates that one reason behind this initial human diet is the kinship between all sentient beings:

> Living creatures possess a soul and a certain spiritual superiority [to non-human creation] which in this respect make them similar to the possessors of intellect [human beings] and they have the power of affecting their own welfare and their food, and they flee from pain and death (commentary on Gen. 1:29).

God's original dietary plan represents a unique statement in humanity's spiritual history. It is a divine blueprint for a vegetarian world order. Yet millions of people have read this Torah verse and passed it by without considering its meaning.

After indicating that people should consume only plant-based foods, God saw everything that he had made and "behold, it was very good" (Gen. 1:31). Everything in the universe was as God wanted it, in complete harmony, with nothing superfluous or lacking. The vegetarian diet was a central part of God's initial plan.

The strongest support for vegetarianism as a positive ideal in Torah literature is in the writing of Rabbi Abraham Isaac HaKohen Kook (1865–1935). Rav Kook was the first Ashkenazic Chief Rabbi (Rav) of pre-state Israel and a highly respected and beloved Jewish spiritual leader and thinker. He was a writer on Jewish mysticism and an outstanding scholar of Jewish law. In the early twentieth century he spoke powerfully for vegetarianism, as eventually recorded in *A Vision of Vegetarianism and Peace* (1961).

Rav Kook believed that the permission to eat meat was only a temporary concession to the practices of the times, because a God who is merciful to his creatures would not institute an everlasting law permitting the killing of animals for food.

People are not always ready to live up to God's will. By the time of Noah, humanity had morally degenerated. "And God saw the Earth, and behold it was corrupt, for all flesh had corrupted their way upon the Earth" (Gen. 6:12). People had degenerated to such an extent that they would eat a limb torn from a living animal. So, as a concession to people's weakness, God granted permission for people to eat meat: "Every moving thing that lives shall be food for you; as the green herb have I given you all" (Gen. 9:3).

According to Rav Kook, because people had descended to such an extremely low spiritual level, it was necessary that they be taught to value human life above that of animals, and that they concentrate their efforts on first working to improve relations between people. He writes that if people had been denied the right to eat meat some might eat the flesh of human beings instead, due to their inability to control their lust for flesh. Rav Kook regards the permission to slaughter animals for food as a "transitional tax," or temporary dispensation, until a "brighter era" can be reached, when people will return to vegetarian diets. Just prior to granting Noah and his family permission to eat meat, God states:

> And the fear of you and the dread of you shall be upon every beast of the Earth, and upon every fowl of the air, and upon all wherewith the ground teems, and upon all the fish of the sea; into your hands are they delivered (Gen. 9:2).

Now that there is permission to eat animals, the previous harmony between people and animals no longer exists. Rabbi Samson Raphael Hirsch argues that the attachment between people and animals was broken after the flood, which led to a change in the relationship of people to the world.

The permission given to Noah to eat meat is not unconditional. There is an immediate prohibition against eating blood: "Only flesh with the life thereof, which is the blood thereof, shall you not eat" (Gen. 9:4). Similar commands are given in Leviticus 19:26, 17:10 and 12, and Deuteronomy 12:16, 23 and 25, and 15:23. The Torah identifies blood with life: "for the blood is the life" (Deut. 12:23). Life must be removed from the animal before it can be eaten, and the Talmud details an elaborate process for doing so.

When the Israelites were in the wilderness, animals could only be slaughtered and eaten as part of the sacrificial service in the sanctuary (Lev. 17:3–5). The eating of "unconsecrated meat," meat from animals slaughtered for private consumption, was not permitted. All meat which was permitted to be eaten had to be an integral part of a sacrificial rite. Maimonides states that the biblical sacrifices were a concession to the primitive practices of the nations at that time: people (including the Israelites) were not then ready for forms of divine service which did not include sacrifice and death (as did those of all the heathens); at least the Torah, as a major advance, prohibited *human* sacrifice. God later permitted people to eat meat even if it was not part of a sacrificial offering:

> When the Lord your God shall enlarge your border as He has promised you, and you shall say: "I will eat flesh," because your soul desires to eat flesh; you may eat flesh, after all the desire of your soul (Deut. 12:20).

This newly permitted meat was called *basar ta'avah*, "meat of lust," so named because rabbinic teachings indicate that meat is not considered a necessity for life.

The above verse does not *command* people to eat meat.

Rabbinic tradition understands the Torah as acknowledging people's desire to eat flesh and permitting it under proper circumstances, but not as requiring the consumption of meat. Even while arguing against vegetarianism as a moral cause, Rabbi Elijah Judah Schocher, author of *Animal Life in Jewish Tradition*, concedes that "Scripture does not command the Israelite to eat meat, but rather permits this diet as a concession to lust" (1984: 300). Similarly, another critic of vegetarian activism, Rabbi J. David Bleich, a noted contemporary Torah scholar and professor at Yeshiva University, states, "The implication is that meat may be consumed when there is desire and appetite for it as food, but it may be eschewed when there is not desire and, *a fortiori*, when it is found to be repugnant" (1987: 245). According to Bleich, "Jewish tradition does not command carnivorous behavior..." (1987: 245).

The Talmud expresses this negative connotation associated with the consumption of meat:

> The Torah teaches a lesson in moral conduct, that man shall not eat meat unless he has a special craving for it... and shall eat it only occasionally and sparingly. The sages also felt that eating meat was not for everyone: Only a scholar of Torah may eat meat, but one who is ignorant of Torah is forbidden to eat meat (BT Pesachim 49b).

Some authorities explain this restriction in practical terms: only a Torah scholar can properly observe all the laws of animal slaughter and meat preparation. While there are few conditions on the consumption of vegetarian foods, only a diligent Torah scholar can fully comprehend the many regulations governing the preparation and consumption of meat. However, master kabbalist Rabbi Isaac Luria explains it in spiritual terms: only a Torah scholar can elevate the "holy sparks" trapped in the animal.

How many Jews today can consider themselves so scholarly and spiritually advanced to be able to eat meat? Those who do diligently study the Torah and are aware of conditions related to the production and slaughter of meat would, I believe, reject meat eating.

Rav Kook writes that the permission to eat meat "after all the desire of your soul" contains a concealed reproach and an implied reprimand. He states that a day will come (the Messianic Period) when people will detest the eating of the flesh of animals because of a moral loathing, and then people will not eat meat because their soul will not have the urge to eat it.

In contrast to the lust associated with flesh foods, the Torah looks favorably on plant foods. In the Song of Songs, the divine bounty is poetically described in references to fruits, vegetables, nuts, and vines. There is no special *b'rakhah* (blessing) recited before eating meat or fish, as there is for other foods such as bread, cake, wine, fruits, and vegetables. The blessing for meat is a general one, the same as that over water or any other undifferentiated food.

Typical of the Torah's positive depiction of many non-flesh foods is the following evocation of the produce of the Land of Israel:

> For the Lord your God brings you into a good land, a land of brooks of water, of fountains and depths, springing forth in valleys and hills; a land of wheat and barley, of vines and fig trees and pomegranates; a land of olive oil and date honey; a land wherein you shall eat bread without scarceness, you shall not lack anything in it. ... And you shall eat and be satisfied, and bless the Lord your God for the good land that He has given you (Deut. 8: 7–10).

Rav Kook believes that there is a reprimand implicit in the many laws and restrictions over the preparing, combining, and eating of animal products (the laws of *kashrut*), because they are meant to provide an elaborate apparatus designed to keep alive a sense of reverence for life, with the aim of eventually leading people away from meat eating. He also believes that the high moral level involved in the vegetarianism of the generations before Noah was a virtue of such great value that it cannot be lost forever. In the future ideal time (the Messianic age), people and animals will again not eat each other's flesh. People's lives will not be supported at the expense of animals' lives. Rav Kook based these views on the prophecy of Isaiah:

> And the wolf shall dwell with the lamb,
> And the leopard shall lie down with the kid;
> And the calf and the young lion and the fatling together;
> And a little child shall lead them
> And the cow and the bear shall feed;
> Their young ones shall lie down together,
> And the lion shall eat straw like the ox ...
> They shall not hurt nor destroy in all My holy mountain ... (Isaiah 11:6–9).

In a booklet which summarizes many of Rav Kook's teachings, Joseph Green, a twentieth-century South African Jewish vegetarian writer, concluded that Jewish religious ethical vegetarians are pioneers of the Messianic era; they are leading lives that prepare for and potentially hasten the coming of the Messiah.

Although most Jews eat meat today, God's high ideal – the initial vegetarian dietary law – stands supreme in the Torah for Jews and the whole world to see.

Based on the above Torah teachings, and because animal-centered diets violate and contradict important Jewish mandates to preserve human health, attend to the welfare of animals, protect the environment, conserve resources, help feed hungry people, and pursue peace, Jewish vegetarians believe that Jews (and others) should sharply reduce or eliminate their consumption of animal products.

Richard Schwartz

Further Reading
Berman, Louis. *Vegetarianism and the Jewish Tradition*. New York: K'tav, 1982.
Bleich, Rabbi J. David. "Vegetarianism and Judaism." *Contemporary Halakhic Problems*. Volume III. Ktav/Yeshiva University: New York 1987, 237–50.
Cohen, Alfred S. "Vegetarianism from a Jewish Perspective." In Alfred S. Cohen, ed. *Halacha and Contemporary Society*. New York: Ktav, 1984, 292–317.
Cohen, Noah J. *Tsa'ar Ba'alei Chayim – The Prevention of Cruelty to Animals, Its Bases, Development, and Legislation in Hebrew Literature*. New York: Feldheim, 1979.
Kalechofsky, Roberta. *Vegetarian Judaism*. Marblehead, Massachusetts: Micah Publications, 1998.
Kalechofsky, Roberta, ed. *Rabbis and Vegetarianism: An Evolving Tradition*. Marblehead, Massachusetts: Micah Publications, 1995.
Kook, Abraham Isaac HaKohen. "A Vision of Vegetarianism and Peace." In David Cohen, ed. *Lachai Ro'i*. Jerusalem: Merkaz HaRav, 1961.
Robbins, John. *Diet for a New America*. Walpole, New Hampshire: Stillpoint, 1987.
Schochet, Elijah J. *Animal Life in Jewish Tradition*. New York: K'tav, 1984.
Schwartz, Richard H. *Judaism and Vegetarianism*. New York: Lantern Books, 2001.
Sears, Dovid. *The Vision of Eden: Animal Welfare and Vegetarianism in Jewish Law and Mysticism*. Spring Valley, NY: Orot, Inc., 2003.
See also: Animal Rights in the Jewish Tradition; Animals in the Bible and Qur'an; Judaism; Kabbalah and Ecotheology; Jewish Environmentalism in North America; Maimonides; Vegetarianism and Judaism; Vegetarianism and Rabbi Abraham Isaac Kook.

Venda Religion and the Land (Southern Africa)

By the combined use of oral traditions and archeology, the oldest Venda clans (mitupo) of the Soutpansberg Mountains area between South Africa and Zimbabwe can be traced back roughly 600 years. More recent clans from Zimbabwe settled in the Soutpansberg area roughly 500 years ago and again some 250 years ago. As settled agriculturists and specialized long-distance traders ruled by powerful chiefs, the various Venda clans were intimately tied to the land and its features. Chiefs enjoyed both political control over decision making and access to high status ancestral spirits. These dual powers of a chief were metaphorically expressed by reference to prominent features on the landscape. The Venda likened a chief's political power to a mountain, whereas they likened his spiritual abilities, such as being responsible for soil fertility and rain, as a pool.

The organization of royal Venda living space also expressed this dichotomy between politics and religion. Stone-walled royal settlements were divided between a low-lying assembly area, or "pool," and a higher royal living area, or "mountain." The assembly area was the venue for various fertility rituals, including rainmaking, renewal of the Earth, and pre-marital rites. Various Venda clans recall that they originally came from a fertile pool in a mountain, so the rituals within the assembly area actually reenact the creation stories.

The royal living area inhabited by the chief, his councilors, and wives, was the arena of political decision making and maneuvering. Reference to this area as a mountain is metaphorically expressed in oral traditions as a conquering chief stepping from mountain to mountain. In the same vein, when a chief dies, it is said, "The Mountain has fallen."

Medicines buried at the entrance to the assembly area, or "pool," were intended to protect the royal settlement from invaders. Venda people believed that if invaders crossed this protective threshold, then the assembly area turned into an actual pool. This pool returns to normal once the enemy has been frightened away or drowned. However, if the invaders' medicines proved too strong, then the assembly area permanently turned into a pool, inundating the royal mountain portion of the settlement. As mentioned above, this is a metaphorical expression of the demise of the chief's political power.

It is abundantly clear from various oral traditions, however, that a new chief respected or even feared a subjugated chief's intricate spiritual link to the land and its associated ancestors. Accordingly, the new chief almost invariably recognized the spiritual potency, or pool status, of his predecessor. Even though the subjugated chief lost his political power, or mountain status, he normally retained his spiritual potency to make rain and influence soil fertility, or pool status. In some instances the subjugated chief actually became a ritual specialist to the incoming chief and so increased his prestige as ritual rainmaker. But shifting political fortunes did not end here as subsequent chiefs in turn established their hegemony. A new chief became the mountain, his immediate predecessor became the pool, and the original chief became a so-called "dry-one" (i.e., his pool status has "dried up"). The "dry-one" label applies to those chiefs who came from a line that formerly had great powers, but due to repeated political misfortunes were eventually ostracized from the recognized political system. Those in power viewed the formerly influential chiefs on the periphery of the status quo as a threat and conveniently branded them as witches.

Yet, since the most current chiefs and their ritual functionaries respected the intimate and long-lasting spiritual connection of the first chiefly dynasty to the land, they did not kill their descendants. It was believed that elimination of these ancient people might upset the original spirits of the land. Instead of elimination, the most recent ruling dynasty normally avoided contact with descendants of the original rulers. This process explains the historic distinction between the Singo rulers with their mountain status, the Mbedzi with their pool status, and the Dzhivhani "dry-ones."

According to oral traditions and radiocarbon dates from associated settlements, we know that the Dzhivhani lived in the Soutpansberg at least 600 years ago when they enjoyed mountain status, but possibly also enjoyed prestige as being responsible for fertility and rain. Mbedzi immigrants from southern Zimbabwe subjugated the Dzhivhani chiefs some 500 years ago. The Mbedzi immigrants stripped the Dzhivhani of their political powers, but respected their abilities as pool people, particularly as rainmakers. Approximately 250 years ago the Singo from central Zimbabwe in turn conquered the Soutpansberg. Since that time, the Mbedzi became the official rainmakers, while the Dzhivhani lost their pool status.

The different status categories are expressed by the distinctive burial practices of the various clans. Typically, Singo chiefs are buried in mountains, Mbedzi chiefs in pools, whereas Dzhivhani chiefs have no particular burial mode any more. But the importance of the original rulers, such as the Dzhivhani, still resonates in the Soutpansberg Mountains. Various noticeable locations on the landscape, in particular old stone-walled ruins of royal settlements, pools, mountains, caves, and boulders, are either avoided or treated with respect. These are the locations believed to be portals to the underworld where ancestral spirits reside. Venda people believe that ancestors send messengers, in the form of dangerous animals and/or distorted mountain and water creatures, to scare disrespectful trespassers. At certain unusual locations, including San rock-art sites, Venda still leave trinkets to appease the original spirits of the land. Another reason for leaving gifts at sacred spots is to obtain fertility from the very old spirits.

Although the political clout of the ancient Venda dynasties is long gone, their religious legacy lives on in unusual landscape features and in the old ruins. This legacy prohibits Venda people from altering the landscape too much. Very old rock art, for instance, is not to be tampered with. Unlike their Sotho-speaking neighbors to the south, Venda people tend not to repaint or scratch the rock paintings of their San predecessors, to cite one example. Also, "traditional" Venda farm laborers discourage their European masters from installing mechanical pumps at sacred pools in fear that such alterations might anger the spirits and make them "hot." Sheet metal roofs and fences are similarly believed to cause spirits to become "hot" and vengeful. In other words, there is a deeply felt and widely shared belief among Venda people that any alterations or modifications at sacred locales would upset the spirits of the land and result in misfortune.

Supernatural sanction against killing animals residing in old ruins or in sacred pools can also be linked to respect for the original occupants of the land. In this sense then, the Venda-speaking people from the Soutpansberg can be considered to be conserving the land, irrespective of the fact that their intensive farming and overgrazing practices have resulted in damaging soil erosion. Even those Venda clans that were specialist copper miners or elephant hunters did not exploit the available copper ore deposits or elephant herds to their fullest. Whereas technological inability to exhaust such resources no doubt was a contributing factor, supernatural sanction against overexploitation might have been another. For example, abandoned copper mine shafts in the Limpopo River valley were supposedly haunted by spirits of the Musina clan and considered off-limits to trespassers. Whereas conservation among the Venda was almost certainly not an end in itself, their worldview contributed to the preservation of unusual cultural and natural features of the Soutpansberg.

Johannes Loubser

Further Reading

Beach, D.N. *The Shona and Zimbabwe 1900–1850*. Gwelo: Mambo Press, 1980.

Blacking, J. "Songs, Dances, Mimes and Symbolism of Venda Girls' Initiation Schools: Part 1, Vhushsa; Part 2, Milayo; Part 3, Domba; Part 4, The Great Domba Song." *African Studies* 28 (1969), 28–35, 69–118, 149–99, 215–66.

Loubser, J.H.N. "Oral Traditions, Archaeology and the History of the Venda Mitupo." *African Studies* (1990), 13–42.

Ralushai, V.N.M.N. and J.R. Gray. "Ruins and Traditions of the Ngona and Mbedzi among the Venda of the Northern Transvaal." *Rhodesian History* 9 (1977), 1–12.

Stayt, H. *The Bavenda*. London: Oxford University Press, 1931.

Van Warmelo, N.J. *The Copper Miners of Musina and the Early History of the Soutpansberg*. Ethnological Publication 8. Pretoria: Government Printer, 1940.

See also: San (Bushmen) Apocalyptic Rock Art; San (Bushmen) Religion (and adjacent, San (Bushmen) Rainmaking); Venda Witch Beliefs (Southern Africa).

Venda Witch Beliefs (Southern Africa)

The Venda people inhabit the far northern area of the Republic of South Africa as well as the extreme south of Zimbabwe, bordering on either side of the Limpopo River. In South Africa, they occupy the fertile Soutpansberg mountain range where they were traditionally horticulturalists and pastoral cattle-keepers, until the discovery of diamonds and gold in the nineteenth century introduced migrant labor as a way of life for the menfolk.

The Soutpansberg mountain range is a richly forested area whose trees provide wood for ritual, ceremonial, and utilitarian purposes, as well as fruits that are an important source of food. The rivers of Vendaland and especially the sacred lake Fundudzi have a religious and mystical significance for the Venda people. Rivers flowing through forested areas, such as the famous Phiphidi falls, are associated with the spirits of the VhaNgona, the original inhabitants of Venda at the time of the early Iron Age, ca. 200. To propitiate these spirits, everyone crossing the falls must contribute an offering: a bracelet or piece of broken pot for a woman, a tuft of hair for a man. Cattle are not excluded and some cow hairs must be offered if the animal is not to incur misfortune.

The Venda people are made up of various tribal clusters who migrated to the area at different times; some came from Zimbabwe to the north and others from the Sotho-speaking areas to the south and east. The Venda language is unique among South African languages in having links to the early Iron Age (200–800) inhabitants of Southern Africa. Among the important migrations from the Karanga area of southern Zimbabwe were the Vhathavhatsinde people, so called because many families in this group were great medicine men (diviners) who supplied a powerful antidote to evil from the mutavhatsinde tree. The name is said to derive from the word muta, referring to the small enclosure surrounding women's huts and tsinde, meaning the stem or trunk of a tree. Medicine men or diviners from the Vhathavatsinde still erect poles in the yards of their homesteads to indicate their avocation. I was able to photograph the pole erected by well-known diviner and herbalist, Mr. Nelson Shonisani, at his home in Kubvhi, central Venda in 1988.

Much of the work of herbalists (*nanga*) and diviners (*maine*, pl. *mingoma*) among the Venda has to do with protecting people from the machinations of witches (sg. *muloi*, pl. *vhaloi*) who seek to kill or harm their fellows, as well as providing charms to protect people against misfortune. A simple charm might be a piece of wood taken from a branch of a tree overhanging a well-used pathway. The charm is believed to contain strength given to it by travelers who trod that path without coming to any harm.

Most medicine people among the Venda are herbalists who specialize in curing diseases and who are consulted often about ordinary ailments. The *mungoma* or diviner is believed to have occult powers and is always consulted after someone has died so that the family of the deceased can discover who the evil person was who caused the death. Like many other African peoples, the Venda believe that death (except in the case of the very old) is not a natural occurrence. Most diviners are *maine vha lufhali*, diviners who discover the identity of witches who are responsible for most misfortunes and deaths, which are often believed due to the use of sorcery in the form of poisons obtained from plants and added to the victim's food.

Among the Venda, a diviner or herbalist may be male or female. A man inherits his knowledge from his father and a woman from her mother. Witches (*vhaloi*) are believed to be of either gender but are more generally women. They operate at night, sometimes traveling long distances on the back of a hyena or other animal, and they may send snakes, owls or, particularly, a *turi* (stoat) into the victim's home to bite him or her and cause disease or death. Wild animals such as snakes, owls, hyenas, and stoats are creatures of dark places or the night, like witches, and are known to cause harm either by biting humans and animals as snakes do, or by attacking small stock, like hyenas, or sucking the udders of cows, as stoats are believed to do. Stayt comments that the *turi* is especially feared, as it is believed the animal can become invisible and in that way enter the body of its human victim and cause a mortal illness (Stayt 1931: 278).

There are two distinct types of witch in Venda that correspond to the famous distinction made by E.E. Evans-Pritchard for the Azande of Central Africa. The first type are witches who act unconsciously. They are unaware of their evil-doing. The second type corresponds to the sorcerer among the Azande. This witch uses material means such as spells made from powdered roots and bark or magic, to cause harm. The first type of witch is believed to act during sleep. It is at this time that the witch spirit leaves the body of its innocent human victim and goes out on its evil mission. Other persons sleeping with the muloi are believed to be put into a deep sleep so the witch is never seen, except by the herbalist or diviner. Apart from killing people, the witch also is believed to be very fond of milk and may force a cattle owner, while asleep, to go into his cattle enclosure, milk his animals, and give the milk to the witch. Alternatively, the *muloi* may send a *turi* (stoat), well known as a witch familiar, a creature that carries out the bidding of a witch and operates usually at night, to suck the milk from the cows. Protection against witches comes from the mother's ancestors, and if these spirits are angry with the victim, they may withdraw their protection and allow the witches evil work to proceed.

Remedies against the work of witches consist of charms, made, for instance, from the powdered root of the mukundulela tree (Niebuhria triphylla) which translates as "the way of force," mixed with the powdered bones of a snake, owl, bat's wing, and stoat. As this mixture is made up of parts of all the witch's familiars, it is considered especially powerful in making the wearer invulnerable to attack by witches.

The second type of witch, the sorcerer, uses black magic to kill her or his enemies. This magic is known as *madambi*. Herbalists (*nanga*) are sometimes suspected of assisting a *muloi* to work harm in this way. *Madambi* usually works by the witch getting hold of an object belonging to her/his enemy and using it to destroy the person. Thus, nail and hair clippings are carefully hidden. Stayt notes that the most popular *madambi* is made of sand from an enemy's footprint, which is mixed with poisonous herbs and through sympathetic magic the owner of the footprint dies from poisoning. Sometimes the evil powder will be blown on, or toward, a hare. The animal will run to the intended victim and look him or her in the eyes and then vanish. The victim is believed to die soon after while the hare vanishes.

The herbalist can provide a protective charm against this sorcery, a magic powder mixed with fat, which, when rubbed over the body, envelopes the wearer in a kind of magic coat. Herbalists provide many other charms made from powdered roots or bark that act as antidotes to evil, as spells, or as protective amulets. For instance, the powdered roots of the *mpeta* (Royena pallens) protect against ordinary diseases and keep the ancestral spirits from worrying the wearer.

Witch beliefs in Venda are similar to those in other Bantu-speaking societies in Africa, especially those of their neighbors, the Lovedu, who live in a deeply forested area to the southeast of the Venda, and who are famous for their rain-queen, Modjadji. These witch beliefs tend to reflect social strains in predominantly kin-based cultures. That is, those most likely to be accused of being witches are often neighbors or co-wives, in polygamous homesteads.

Nowadays, a successful business entrepreneur may find himself the target of malicious accusations, as happened to Isaac Ramakulukusha, a Zionist bishop who owned numerous business enterprises, including butcheries and filling stations in Venda. In 1975, he sued the Commander of the Venda National Force for wrongful arrest and defamation. He was accused of being a ritual murderer (*mavia vhatu* – slaughterer of human beings) after the body of a four year-old girl was found in the Nzehele River in Venda. Forensic science came to the aid of the bishop when the child was found to have drowned and crabs had eaten part of her body.

Accusations of witchcraft also have increased in recent years with the change to a democratic majority rule in South Africa. With the power of chiefs and headmen waning, some have resorted to devices like the murder of young children (so-called "muti" [medicine] murders) to prop up their waning influence.

Gina Buijs

Further Reading

Evans-Pritchard, Edward. *Witchcraft, Oracles and Magic among the Azande*. Oxford: Clarendon Press, 1937.

Krige, Eileen Jensen and J.D Krige. *The Realm of a Rain Queen*. Cape Town: Juta & Co., 1980.

Stayt, Hugh. *The BaVenda*. London: Oxford University Press, 1931.

See also: Muti and African Healing; Muti Killings; Venda Religion and the Land (Southern Africa).

Virgin of Guadalupe

On 8 December 1531, the legend goes, the apparition of the Virgin of Guadalupe appeared to Juan Diego on the hill of Tepeyac north of Mexico City. In 1999, Pope John Paul II proclaimed Our Lady of Guadalupe the Patron Saint of the Americas. Devotion to the tradition of Guadalupe has been sustained for nearly 500 years and has played a significant role in Mexican history, whether as a symbol for independence, the Church's resistance to political intervention, the rights of native populations, or for social conservatism and control. Although contentious debates over the historical credibility of the apparition-narrative mark the Guadalupan tradition, the image and legend of the Virgin of Guadalupe has provided a powerful symbol for Mexican nationalism, and by the twentieth century, a symbol of freedom for oppressed native peoples and agrarian reform. As a symbol fusing religion and politics, native and Christian images, the Virgin of Guadalupe, patron saint of the Americas, remains a complicated symbol embodying conquest, pre-Colombian Earth goddesses, nature, the modern nation, and various, complicated social relations.

The first account of the appearance of the Virgin of Guadalupe was not published until the mid-seventeenth century. This account tells the story of Guadalupe's appearance in December 1531 to Juan Diego, a poor Christianized native. Speaking to him in the Aztec language of Nahuatl, she asks Juan Diego to tell the bishop of Mexico, Juan de Zumárraga, to build a chapel in her honor at Tepeyac. After two unsuccessful visits, Zumárraga instructs Juan Diego to return with signs from the apparition. Disconsolate, Juan Diego meets the apparition of the Virgin of Guadalupe for the third time. Guadalupe tells Juan Diego to climb the hill of Tepeyac and gather roses and flowers as signs for the bishop. When Juan Diego opens his cloak in front of the bishop, the roses tumble out, revealing a life-size image of Guadalupe found miraculously imprinted on the cactus-fiber cloth of his cloak. Realizing that a miracle had taken place, the bishop places the image in the cathedral for public devotion and later brings it to Tepeyac. The painted icon on what is alleged to be Juan Diego's cloak remains the heart of the cult and tradition of the Virgin of Guadalupe, on display today in the twentieth-century basilica in Mexico City that serves as the central locus for Guadalupan devotion.

Scholars find it significant that the Guadalupan tradition was introduced 35 years after the conquest. Native peoples understandably resisted domination, sometimes overtly through resistance, but more commonly through ongoing practice of traditional religious beliefs and lifeways. Syncretic practices that merged Christian images and ideas with local beliefs and rituals were employed as methods of proselytizing native peoples. In the case of Guadalupe, cults of Mary imported by the Spaniards merged with pre-Colombian Earth deities. Tepeyac had long served as a pilgrimage site for various Earth goddesses referred to collectively as Tonantzin, our "revered mother." Early veneration of Guadalupe and pilgrimages to Tepeyac, some sixteenth-century priests complained, only continued pre-Christian practices since native worshipers still associated her with sacred space and power coming from the Earth.

Although Guadalupe may have had an early following among native peoples and been used as a means of evangelization by the Catholic Church, by the seventeenth century Guadalupe became associated with the interests of Mexican-born Spaniards or Creoles. Guadalupe became championed as the American Mary, thus serving Mexican patriotism and nationalism, but also justifying the conquest. After Mexico City and Puebla were devastated by the plague in 1737, Mexico City claimed the Virgin of Guadalupe as its patron saint, and by 1754 the Pope named her patroness of Mexico. In 1895 the Virgin of Guadalupe was crowned Queen of the Americas. During these centuries of merging religion and patriotism, it should be noted that the image of Guadalupe was not explicitly employed to champion native peoples. The Virgin of Guadalupe was important for the Catholic Church and its position in Mexican society, as well as for patriots who employed it to champion Mexican identity. In relation to policies and practices concerning native peoples and their lands however, the cult of Guadalupe was used primarily as a conservative, paternalistic, and exclusionary mechanism.

It was not until the twentieth century that the image and tradition of the Virgin of Guadalupe became explicitly associated with the rights of native peoples, disenfranchised populations, and the land. Pancho Villa and Emiliano Zapata both used the symbol of Guadalupe during their revolutionary struggles, thus associating Guadalupe with social and agrarian reform. Peasant followers of Emiliano Zapata carried banners of Guadalupe through Mexico City following the defeat of General Victoriano Huerta in 1914. These indigenous peasants also visited Tepeyac to venerate Guadalupe who, as both Earth goddess and patron saint, came to symbolize the protector of damaged land and oppressed peoples. Banners of Guadalupe regularly appeared in marches organized by Cesar

Chavez and the United Farm Workers beginning in the 1960s. Numerous contemporary Chicana artists now depict Guadalupe in ways that link her to pre-Colombian Earth goddesses, thus championing both native peoples and the land. Contemporary Latina/o theologians claim that both images and fiestas demonstrate Guadalupe's clear connection to nature. In popular religious images, the sun, stars, moon, and nature surround Guadalupe. Daybreak on December 12, "the time of new beginnings and the rebirth of the sun" is the time of Guadalupe's feast and celebration and a dawn song, *Las Mañanitas* is sung to her (Rodriguez 1994: 147).

Our Lady of Guadalupe remains a contested symbol – standing at different points in history for conquest as well as indigenous rights; for Earth goddesses and nature as well as the power of the nation-state.

Lois Ann Lorentzen

Further Reading
Brading, D.A. *Mexican Phoenix: Our Lady of Guadalupe: Image and Tradition Across Five Centuries*. Cambridge, UK: Cambridge University Press, 2001.
Poole, Stafford. *Our Lady of Guadalupe: The Origins and Sources of a Mexican National Symbol, 1531–1797*. Tucson, AZ: University of Arizona Press, 1995.
Rodriguez, Jeanette. *Our Lady of Guadalupe: Faith and Empowerment among Mexican-American Women*. Austin, TX: University of Texas Press, 1994.
See also: Ecofeminism (various); Goddesses – History of; Mary in Latin America; Maya Religion (Central America); Mayan Catholicism; Mayan Protestantism; Mesoamerican Deities.

Virtues and Ecology in World Religions

Virtues (commonly understood as *excellences of character acquired through self-cultivation*) play a role in all major world religions – even as ideals of personal cultivation differ significantly from tradition to tradition. Recent adaptations in religious attitudes toward nature to a large degree involve changes in the perception and cultivation of virtues as well. Across the board, religious environmentalists highlight the ecological import of traditional traits of character, such as moderation, humility, and compassion. However, to speak of a uniform "green" religious virtue ethic would be to deny the varied contexts of religious belief and practice that continue to give these virtues their full meaning. By examining relationships between the virtues and ecological awareness in Christianity, Judaism, Islam, Hinduism, Buddhism, and Confucianism we can see the various types of green virtue ethics.

Frugality

Under a number of names, frugality has been a prominent moral norm and practice in all the great religious traditions, including Buddhism, Christianity, Confucianism, Hinduism, Islam, Judaism, and Daoism. These traditions often have interpreted frugality as an expression of love or its equivalent – that is, seeking the good of others in response to their needs.

Frugality is the virtue of economic constraint – a standard of excellence for both character formation and social transformation in necessary interaction. It connotes moderation, thrift, sufficiency, and temperance. It demands careful conservation, comprehensive recycling, minimal harm, material efficiency, and product durability. Frugality is a middle way that struggles against both overconsumption by the affluent and underconsumption by the poor.

Frugality, according to its advocates, is an antidote to a cardinal vice of the age, prodigality – or excess in the goods humans take from the Earth, and excess in the wastes and contaminants we return to it. These excesses are unfair and unsustainable. The profligate take more than their due, and thereby deprive others – poor people, other species, and future generations – of their due. In this setting, frugality is a necessary condition of justice and sustainability, seeking a greater thriving of all life together by sparing and sharing global goods.

Contrary to some stereotypes, frugality is not generally a world-denying asceticism. On the contrary, the word's Latin root, *frux*, defines its essential character: fruitfulness and joyfulness. Frugality is an Earth-affirming and enriching norm that delights in the less-consumptive joys of the mind and flesh, especially the enhanced lives for human communities and other creatures that only constrained production and consumption can make possible on a finite planet.

Frugality is regularly defended as a universal norm, not bound to particular religious confessions. Interpreters argue that it can be ethically justified, apart from appeals to privileged revelations, as a rational response to economic maldistribution and ecological degradation. For its fans, frugality is the subversive virtue in rebellion against the ethos of excess.

James A. Nash

Further Reading
Nash, James. A. "Toward the Revival and Reform of the Subversive Virtue: Frugality." *The Annual of the Society of Christian Ethics* (1995).
Westra, Laura and Patricia H. Werhan, eds. *The Business of Consumption: Environmental Ethics and the Global Economy*. Lanham, MD: Rowman and Littlefield, 1998.
See also: Dirt.

Virtue and Ecology in Christianity

In 1976, historian Lynn White charged that the environmental crisis will only be reverted if Christians exchange their arrogant attitudes toward nature for St. Francis' model of humility. Since then, virtues have played a major role in the greening of Christianity. From qualities of character marking a person's journey to an other-worldly salvation, they changed into qualities of character fitting the flourishing of persons-within-ecocommunities in which the immanent Spirit of God is made manifest. As a result, a thoroughly reinterpreted and reshuffled catalogue of desirable traits is emerging.

Changes range from simple extensions to radical innovations of meaning. Rather than hope for the salvation of human souls only, Christians may now hope (even against all odds) for the liberation of all creation. Rather than humbly consider themselves at the bottom of an ontological ladder, they may humbly accept their place in the web of earthly relations. Rather than practice vigilant control of emotions, they may try to relearn spontaneity. And rather than divert their attention away from the physical details of this world (*contemptus mundi*), they may practice sensuousness in order to attend properly to this world – following a recast model of Jesus as a teacher with an eye for illustrations drawn from animal and plant life.

Some observers doubt whether such attitudinal changes go far enough in addressing ecological problems. They stress the need for complementary social analysis and organized efforts to transform institutions (e.g., Dieter Hessel). Others question whether personal transformation can be thorough enough as long as Christians continue to see themselves as managers of creation (e.g., Elizabeth Dodson Gray). The most radical critics suggest that Christians look outside their tradition toward Eastern and indigenous religions for alternative models of ecological self-cultivation (e.g., Joanna Macy). Christian scholars typically respond to this last charge with a warning against the vice of romanticism.

Virtue and Ecology in Judaism

From the rich array of Jewish scripture, legal traditions, stories, rituals, and cultural practices, virtues emerge as those personal character traits that renew and sustain the chosen people's covenant relationship with God. The Jewish community has received many blessings from the transcendent Creator of the universe; in return, it must look after creation, following the commandments of the *Torah*. This covenant bond is especially served by gratitude, responsibility, and repentance for failure. Today, those who interpret the environmental crisis as a sign of covenantal breakdown find new significance in these traditional virtues (e.g., Eric Katz).

Ancient blessings for food, natural beauty, and seasonal renewal continue to express appropriate gratitude for the gifts of creation. Entrusted with those gifts, responsible stewards will be caring and compassionate, keeping in mind the suffering of all living beings (*tza'ar ba'alei chayim*). They will also be in the habit of exercising personal restraint, demonstrated every Sabbath by refraining from nature-altering activities. Following the commandment not to destroy (*bal tashchit*), they will be averse to vandalism (including specifically the wanton destruction of fruit trees), cruelty (including animal abuse), and wastefulness. Conflicts of interest they will approach with prudence, new environmental challenges with love of learning. Even responsible stewards may fail, however. They must be able to admit mistakes and repent for their shortcomings.

Like Christianity, Judaism has been charged with promoting arrogance by putting humans in charge of the Earth. Critics also say that Jewish anti-paganism prevents appropriate reverence for nature. Jewish scholars typically respond that a covenantal life actually inspires humility and awe before God's marvelous works. Some go further and draw on Jewish mystical traditions (*Kabbalah*) that do allow full-blown reverence for the Divine Presence in creation (e.g., Arthur Green).

Virtue and Ecology in Islam

Although Islamic ethics is especially known for its tradition of law (*Shari 'ah*), the life of a Muslim should in all aspects be marked by the cultivation of one main virtue: surrender (*islam*) to God (*Allah*). Each other virtue (*fadilah*), either leads up to, belongs to, follows from, or is perfected by the Muslim's singular commitment to the transcendent Creator and Sustainer of the universe. While largely remaining within this traditional framework, which is based on scripture (*Qur'an*), the example and teachings of the Prophet Mohammed (*Hadith*), and the work of great thinkers such as Al-Ghazali (1058–1111), modern scholars of Islam have begun to identify ecologically relevant virtues.

Muslims look upon creation as the extended family of God, in which each species forms a community designed to live harmoniously with all other communities. Thus, beneficence toward any creature takes on meaning as an act of devotion by which the believer treats God's family well. Planting and sowing, insofar as they benefit human and nonhuman communities, are concrete instances of such charity. Respect for the basic needs of others requires vigilant control (*jihad*) over destructive "lower" desires, especially greed, aggression, and jealousy. The willingness to make such personal sacrifices for the common good, strengthened annually during the fasting month of *Ramadan*, again ultimately underscores the believer's respect for God.

Ecofeminists and those who follow Lynn White's line of reasoning have leveled the same criticism against Islam as against Christianity and Judaism: its belief in a transcendent God and its elevation of humans as the viceregents of creation are likely to engender exploitative attitudes toward nature. Two types of Islamic responses are emerging. Most scholars stress that a viceregent (*khalifa*) should be responsible. They also qualify the implications of divine transcendence (e.g., Al-Hafiz Masri). For example, they highlight scriptural texts that depict creation as a mosque, or as bearing many signs (*ayat*) of divine grace, and argue that such a sacramental world demands human respect. Some scholars, however, contend that an other-worldly focus on a transcendent and all-powerful God should in fact benefit the environment, insofar as it encourages frugality and deep humility (e.g., Seyyed Nasr).

Virtue and Ecology in Hinduism

Within the multifaceted spectrum of Hindu traditions, the ideal of living in mental and bodily harmony with all beings, seen as a divine unity (*Vasudeva/Brahman*), stands in creative tension with the ideal of self-transcendence. Both ideals require self-cultivation through various forms of meditation and discipline (*yoga*). However, Hindus seeking self-transcendence must ultimately renounce all aspects of the natural world as illusory (*maya*) to attain an entirely other-wordly liberation (*moksha*) from the cycle of life and death. Because of these distinct (though complexly intertwined) foci, Hindu traditions offer both rich resources and significant challenges for a this-worldly, ecological virtue ethic.

Ancient Hindu texts, such as the *Gautama Dharmasutra*, already stress the importance of compassion for all creatures. Today, against the backdrop of India's serious environmental problems, other traditional virtues are reinterpreted within an expanded doctrine of *dharma* as the duty to act for the entire ecological community (e.g., Christopher Chapple). Those who practice universal veneration (mindful of the interconnectedness and divinity of all things, as well as the transmigration of souls) will tend to cultivate an attitude of non-injury (*ahimsa*) toward other living beings, indeed toward all species, ecosystems, and elements that adorn the divine Mother Earth (*Devi Vasundhara*). Living a life of nonviolence in turn requires simplicity (restraint of greed), tranquility (restraint of anger and envy), and truthfulness (*satyagraha*). Through such personal sacrifice (*yajna*) the environment can be purified – just as, conversely, the vices of selfishness and willful ignorance cause (*karma*) environmental ravage (e.g., Seshagiri Rao).

Despite Lynn White's doubt whether Eastern traditions could change Western attitudes toward nature, Hindu teachings have helped to shape ecological consciousness in the first industrialized nations. Virtues such as universal respect and *ahimsa*, as well as the ideal of self-realization (*atman moksha*) within the context of the oneness of all beings, now also guide many Western people of non-Indian descent.

Virtue and Ecology in Buddhism

Buddhist virtue ethics takes its shape from the earliest teachings of the Buddhist monastic community: the universality and inevitability of suffering (*dukkha*), the impermanence of everything (*anitya*), the dependence of everything on everything else (*pratitya-samutpada*), and the absence of an enduring self or soul (*anatman*). Insofar as Buddhists deny the existence of a self, their efforts at being virtuous cannot be understood in any strict sense as self-cultivation. Yet Buddhist practitioners do cultivate their minds and seek emotional equanimity. Theravada Buddhists tend to do so primarily in expectation of personal release from the suffering inherent in the cycle of life and death (*nirvana*). Mahayana Buddhists may also focus on relieving the suffering of others, an aim perfected in the life of the *bodhisattva*. In either case, however, mind and emotions are channeled to enable adaptability to change (impermanence) and awareness of mutual dependence (dependent arising). Many observers have noted the remarkable fit between these basic Buddhist attitudes and an ecological worldview (e.g., Stephanie Kaza).

Buddhists have long held that those who are mindful of the suffering around them will see the appropriateness of showing compassion to human and nonhuman alike. The Indian emperor Asoka (270–232 B.C.E.), for example, is famous for constructing hospitals for both people and animals. In addition to seeking relief of suffering, Buddhists also teach the need for prevention through an attitude of non-injury (*pranatipata-virmana*). The effects (*karma*) of a nonviolent lifestyle again extend beyond the human community. For example, one will as far as possible avoid slaughtering animals and cutting trees. Moreover, by overcoming one's greed, anger, and delusions through understanding their source in self-clinging, one can avoid the ecologically harmful effects of these vices.

Both external and internal critics find a relative neglect of social ethics in some or all Buddhist traditions. However, Buddhism does offer an explicit and scientifically compatible theory of how the personal practice of virtues affects social and indeed ecological systems. According to the doctrine of dependent arising, each person's way of being and acting in the world affects every other aspect of the world. Thus, the cumulative effects of human virtuous agency should be understood not as a matter of simple addition, but rather as following the mathematics of complexity (cf. Stuart Kauffman). Beyond a certain threshold of virtuous people, a *web* of new social and ecological connections will emerge.

Virtue and Ecology in Confucianism

Virtue (*de*), understood as self-cultivation following the *dao* (the Way), is the main pillar of Confucian ethics. From the days of classical Confucianism, character formation has been understood in relation to the natural world as an attempt to live in harmony with the ever-changing dynamism (*qi*) of Heaven and Earth. Mountains, plants and animals provide helpful analogies for self-cultivation, and the four main human virtues of humaneness (*ren*), righteousness (*yi*), propriety (*li*), and wisdom (*zhi*) all have cosmological components. Accordingly, various modern scholars (e.g., Tu Weiming, Mary Evelyn Tucker) have identified Confucian tradition as a rich resource for environmental ethics.

While the four main virtues and their derivatives are first and foremost understood to guide five spheres of human relationships (parent–child, husband–wife, older–younger siblings, friend–friend, ruler–minister), their implications reach into the nonhuman world as well. Neo-Confucian thinkers of the Song and Ming dynasties already suggested that humaneness (*ren*) includes consideration (*shu*) for animals, plants and even stones, as all are one body sharing the vitality of *qi*. And insofar as people are children of Heaven and Earth, it is fitting for them to show filiality and self-restraint toward nature. All in all, the exercise of proper reciprocal relations with "the myriad things" is central to the Confucian conception of the exemplary person (*junzi*), who seeks to live in accordance with the Mandate of Heaven (*tian-ming*).

Critical observers have wondered whether Confucian virtue ethics (like any other religious virtue ethics) may be greener on paper than in practice – a question complicated by the current absence of recognizable institutions to facilitate and represent such practice. Some note the many uneasy compromises within Confucianism between general teachings and specific (often pre-Confucian ritual) cultural practices (e.g., Donald Blakeley). Confucian hierarchalism may also conflict with ecologically attuned self-cultivation. However, many observers agree that, considering the tradition's deep-seated holism, the dynamism of *yin-yang* cosmology, and the appreciation for spontaneity, deference, and adeptness in living, it contains significant potential for guiding people toward more ecological ways of being.

Concluding Observations

The following general patterns characterize the relationship between the cultivation of virtue and ecological awareness in Judaism, Christianity, Islam, Hinduism, Buddhism, and Confucianism. 1) Across the spectrum, the ecological import of traditional virtues is assessed and highlighted. 2) Adjustments often involve extending the reach of virtuous acts to nonhuman entities. 3) Radical changes (e.g., a traditional vice, such as sensuousness, being reassessed as a virtue, and vice versa) are rare and most likely to occur in Christian circles. 4) Certain virtues emerge so frequently and universally that they may be considered part of a crosscultural catalogue of ecological virtues, namely: gratitude, respect, humility, caring, compassion, generosity, gentleness, frugality, and wisdom. 5) Across the world religions, these virtues are more similar in their outward effects on the environment than in their broader significance, which depends heavily on specific contexts of belief.

Louke van Wensveen

Further Reading
Blakeley, Donald N. "Neo-Confucian Cosmology, Virtue Ethics, and Environmental Philosophy." *Philosophy in the Contemporary World* 8:2 (Fall–Winter 2001), 37–49.

Bretzke, James T. *Bibliography on East Asian Religion and Philosophy*. Lewiston, NY: Edwin Mellen Press, 2001.

Nash, James A. *Loving Nature: Ecological Integrity and Christian Responsibility*. Nashville, TN: Abingdon Press, 1991.

Pedersen, Kusumita P. "Environmental Ethics in Inter-religious Perspective." In Sumner B. Twiss and Bruce Grelle, eds. *Explorations in Global Ethics: Comparative Religious Ethics and Interreligious Dialogue*. Boulder, CO: Westview Press, 1998.

Swearer, Donald K. "Buddhist Virtue, Voluntary Poverty, and Extensive Benevolence." *Journal of Religious Ethics* 26:1 (1998), 71–103.

Tucker, Mary Evelyn and John Grim, eds. *Religions of the World and Ecology [Series]*. Cambridge, MA: Harvard University Press, 1997–2004.

World Wide Fund for Nature. *World Religions and Ecology Series*. Cassell Publishers, 1992.

See also: Environmental Ethics; Religious Environmentalist Paradigm; Religious Studies and Environmental Concern; White, Lynn – Thesis of.

Vodou – See Drumming; Indigenous Religious and Cultural Borrowing; Trees in Haitian Vodou; Umbanda.

Volcanoes

One aspect of the cultural appropriation of nature is the religious appropriation of volcanoes. As part of nature, volcanoes provide various metaphors for religion. The colossal threats and blessings emerging from volcanic activities are made meaningful through cognition and active processes of practical engagement, often by ritual means and sacrifices. Ideas that attribute sacred qualities to mountains, and especially to the peaks of volcanoes, are familiar to many cultures worldwide. This is illustrated in textual and visual imagery; it can be traced in myths and oral traditions and can be observed in ritual practices. Frequently the (cosmic, mythological) mountain is the chosen image of analogy between the macro and the micro perspective. Volcanoes are believed to be the foci of magical power and supernatural forces. They are considered spiritually endowed as they are seen as sites where gods and ancestor spirits dwell. These gods and spirits take active part in human affairs. Either they give blessing and fertility or they destroy by volcanic eruptions. This expresses ambivalent experiences as people feel life-giving qualities in volcanoes as well as powerful, awe-inspiring and destructive forces.

In most studies of contemporary natural disasters, research includes neither the interpretations of the affected people nor the symbolic and religious meanings in the context of their lives and worldviews. But disasters like volcanic eruptions must also be seen in terms of how they are perceived and estimated by those affected, including the symbolic basis of human perceptions of nature and natural disasters.

Although it is important to note that volcanic eruptions are conceptualized, structured and negotiated in multiple, changeable contexts, there are certain similarities in the ways in which nature is constructed as parallel to human society. Frequently volcanoes are anthropomorphized, and there are close associations between cosmos, morality and social conduct. Due to such analogies of nature and societies, seen as mutually constitutive, in Africa, Asia and Latin America, natural disasters often are not explained by natural causes alone but are traced back to incorrect conduct of human beings. Thus, in many regions of the world volcanoes are seen, among other things, as natural seismographs for social harmony or disharmony. They are sometimes considered as a sign of dissent or conflict between the native people or particular clans that provoke the tempers of the ancestors or of the gods. Based on the idea that the structure of the cosmos is mirrored in the religio-political realm, rulers of ancient Southeast Asian kingdoms constructed their legitimization through mystical connections with volcanoes. The mandate for political authority was connected with the role of the ruler as divine mediator with the whole living universe. But once there were calamities, these were seen as signs for social injustice and connected to political revolts and upheavals, and as a consequence the ruler lost his power. In this context it is important to note that supernatural explanations of natural events do not only legitimize but can also delegitimize political power.

In the Vesuv region, the Roman people celebrated every year on 23 August a festival called Volcania, where they threw living fish caught in the river Tiber in the fire to calm down Vulcanus, the god of the fire, who was later treated as equivalent to Hephaistos, the god of the smiths. Fish sacrifices are still today a usual practice at the volcano Lewotobi perempuan on the Island Flores in Indonesia. In general, the more active and dangerous a volcano is, the more elaborate are the sacrificial ceremonies. The offerings sacrificed vary from region to region and are often accompanied by local dances, prayers and all kinds of ritual activities. In some regions human sacrifice was practiced, such as in Nigeria or Indonesia where some clans sacrificed boys or girls aged around 15 to the mountain spirits. Their blood was poured into the volcanoes, whilst their corpses were buried normally. In Tanzania the Maasai at Oldonyo Lengai worship the god Engai (the last elaborate ceremony with about 100 participants took place during an eruption in 1983) in offering him sheep and goats. At the volcano Lewotobi laki-laki (the last extensive ceremony took place during the eruption in 1992), a small goat is ripped apart with bare hands. The Chagga in Tanzania used to hold great ceremonies on the top of the mountain Kifunika, close to Kilimanjaro, during which they offered some pieces of meat and the blood of a cow, goat or sheep, mixed with mbege (local beer) and sale (holy yukka plant leaf) for the mizimu (spirits). Like in many other regions, the practice of sacrifice did not disappear completely after Christianization, but occurs rarely and only in secret.

Beyond that, volcanoes are, in almost all regions, considered in gender categories. Sometimes they are determined, either male or female, according to the kinship and political organization of the local population. Occasionally women or witches are treated as equivalent to volcanoes and are seen as responsible for an eruption. There are many stories in the large collection of Icelandic folktales concerning volcanoes. One story in the Icelandic Eyrbyggja Saga tells of Katla, a volcano located in Southern Iceland, and a wicked female cook in the monastery of þykkvabæjarklaustur. After killing a shepherd who had stolen some of her magic trousers, she flung herself into a dark crevasse in the ice cap. Ever since, according to tales, she avenges her fate by pouring fire and water onto the nearby regions.

If there are two or more volcanoes located next to each other, the mythology of their origin is often connected with love or war stories, such as the myth about Popocatepetl and Iztaccihuatl in Mexico. Popocatepetl was an Aztec warrior who was in love with Iztaccihuatl, the emperor's daughter. While Popocatepetl was at war, Iztaccihuatl was mistakenly informed that Popocatepetl had been killed. In despair she killed herself. When Popocatepetl returned and found Itzaccihuatl dead, he was overcome with grief. He built a mound and laid her body on it and vowed that he would never leave her again. Examining the two volcanoes one will notice in Iztaccihuatl the shape of a woman, lying on her back, covered with a white sheet of snow. At her feet stands Popocatepetl, eternally watching over her. Today the people of Pueblo worship the saint San Gregoria Chino by bringing their offerings such as flowers and fruits to the slopes of Popocatepetl.

At times, there are almost exactly the same stories told by people in different parts of the globe that create parallel worlds. This is the case for reports about giants or ghosts, sitting inside the volcano and cooking meals for the neighbor mountains, their lovers or husbands, as in Indonesia on the Island Flores at the volcano Inerie, and in Iceland on the Island Heimaey at the volcano Hekla.

There are numerous stories about Pele who has long been the fire-goddess of the Hawaiians. Her home was in the great fire-pit of the volcano of Kilauea on the island of Hawai'i. The word "Pele" has been used with three distinct definitions by the old Hawaiians: Pele, the fire goddess; Pele, a volcano or fire-pit in any land; Pele, an eruption of lava.

The Kelimutu in East Indonesia is a complex volcano with three crater lakes of different colors. The frequent color changes of the crater lakes are caused by mineral reactions, primarily by iron oxidization. Schooling throughout Indonesia – including the outer islands – has disseminated a knowledge of volcanoes that is indeed limited, yet comparable in part to the European standard. Old Indonesian religious concepts remain nonetheless extremely significant. For inhabitants of the volcano's vicinity, the Kelimutu is the home of the *ebu nusi* (ancestral spirits) and *nitu* (natural spirits). The ruler of the Kelimutu is the volcanic spirit *Konde*, who is the grandchild of *Rongge* and *Ranggo* the ancient ancestors of the village Moni. This explanation of their descent – from "spirits of the volcano" – is common to inhabitants of many regions in the world. *Konde* lives on Kelimutu in a village that looks like Moni. He regularly holds big parties there and tries to take human women as prisoners. The first lake of Kelimutu is called *tiwu ata polo* (lake of the evil demon) and is the lake in which the "souls" of thieves, murderers and practitioners of "black magic" land after their death, also sometimes called *api nereka* (fires of damnation). The second lake *tiwu koö fai* (lake in perpetual motion) is the lake in which the "souls" of deceased children land, and the third lake *tiwu ata bupu* (lake of very old men) is the lake in which the "souls" of elderly people land after their death. The "reactions" of the volcanoes – be these eruptions or color changes – are interpreted by the Florinese as emotional gestures – as expressions of sadness or anger about social events – and as a coded symbolism which is of social interest.

Occasions of political and social conflict in Indonesia are often accompanied by debates about volcanic activity. This religio-political meaning is well known for the very active "high risk volcano" Mount Merapi in Central Java. Every year a ceremony is conducted by the members of the Sultan's palace in order to pacify the destructive power of the spirits residing in the crater. The ceremony acts as a reminder about a mythological promise that the country will always be protected against Merapi's eruptions because the ruler of the volcano realm will never send the lava toward the Sultan's palace in the nearby city of Yogyakarta. But in 1994 for the first time an eruption turned to the south, in the direction of Yogyakarta. Many people saw this as a sign that the spirits disapproved of the behavior of Indonesia's ruling elite. Thus, the symbolic discourse on the Merapi can be instrumentalized not only by the rulers to justify themselves, but also by the oppressed.

Judith Schlehe
Urte Undine Frömming

Further Reading

Forth, Gregory L. *Beneath the Volcano: Religion, Cosmology and Spirit Classification Among the Nage of Eastern Indonesia.* Leiden: KITLV Press 1998.

Frömming, Urte Undine. "Volcanoes: Symbolic Places of Resistance. Political Appropriation of Nature in Flores, Indonesia." In Ingrid Wessel and Georgia Wimhöfer, eds. *Violence in Indonesia.* Hamburg: Abera, 2001, 270–81.

Schlehe, Judith. "Reinterpretations of Mystical Traditions: Explanations of a Volcanic Eruption in Java." *Anthropos* 91 (1996), 391–409.

Trausti, Ari. *Volcanoes in Iceland.* Reykjavik: Vaka-Helgafell, 1996.

Westervelt, William D. *Hawaiian Legends of Volcanoes.* Rutland, VT: C.E. Tuttle, 1963.

See also: Aztec Religion – pre-Colombian; Delphic Oracle; Hawai'i; Maasai (Tanzania); Mayan Spirituality and Conservation; Sacred Mountains.

Walker, Alice (1944–)

Alice Malsenior Walker was born in Eatonton, Georgia in 1944. She attended Spelman College in Atlanta, Georgia for two years and completed her B.A. at Sarah Lawrence College in New York in 1965. She is the author of over twenty-five works including novels, volumes of poetry, essays, short stories and children's books. She has written and spoken out for human rights and ecological justice globally.

Walker is a "womanist" – a black feminist or feminist of color, committed to "the healing and wholeness of entire communities, male and female." A womanist "loves the Spirit" and to love the Spirit is to love creation (Walker 1983: xi–xii). It is in Walker's Pulitzer prize-winning novel *The Color Purple* (1982) that the healing power of creation becomes explicit. The sexually and physically abused Celie learns from blues-singer Shug that God is not an old white man: "it pisses God off if you walk by the color purple in a field somewhere and don't notice it." Celie finds salvation in creation – first trees, then air, then birds, then feels "being part of everything, not separate at all." She "knows" that if she "cut a tree" her "arm would bleed" (Walker 1982: 167). "Creation" is more than "nature"; it also means creativity. Celie finds economic freedom by making pants instead of cutting "Mister's" throat. Moreover, creation includes the erotic. God pleasures in Celie's relationship with Shug. Walker's novel, *Possessing the Secret of Joy* emphasizes the sacredness of women's natural bodies and holistic experience of the erotic. A minor character in the novel is pansexual and makes love with trees, a boulder, the Earth, or a waterfall (Walker 1992: 175–76). Creation is imbued with love and invites loving response.

Walker describes herself as a "pagan" who worships nature. Baptized at age 7, she was fascinated by the leaves in the muddy creek.

> I was unable to send my mind off into space in search of a God who never noticed mud, leaves, or bullfrogs. Or the innocent hearts of my tender, loving people ... It is fatal to love a God who doesn't love you (Walker 1997: 24–25).

It is not "Jesus" that Walker has a problem with but the *Christian tradition's* alienation of Jesus from the folk and from nature. Jesus "coexists quite easily with pagan indigenous peoples," she writes, because they have already learned the love that he preached (Walker 1997: 25). Feminists and womanists from a diversity of faith perspectives employ Walker's writings. Such diversity is possible because Walker's spiritual starting point is everyone's common ground – the Earth. In *The Same River Twice*, Walker refers to her own Trinity: the Earth, Nature, and the Universe. She writes of Nature sustaining her happiness and as opening her "to love, intimacy, and trust" (Walker 1996: 43). She often cites the following poem in essays and public talks:

We Have A Beautiful Mother
We have a beautiful
mother
Her hills
are buffaloes
Her buffaloes
hills.

We have a beautiful
mother
Her oceans
are wombs
Her wombs
oceans.

We have a beautiful
mother
Her teeth
the white stones
at the edge
of the water
the summer grasses
her plentiful hair.

We have a beautiful
mother
Her green lap
immense
Her brown embrace
eternal
Her blue body
Everything
We know (Walker 1997: 106–7).

The poem captures Walker's admiration for the planet in the context of a larger universe, speaking from the heart of her Pagan spirituality. For Walker, the Earth is our mother. She observes that the relationship is not always easy. In "Everything We Love is a Human Being," she struggles with human destructiveness toward an alienated Earth. "I *love* trees," she says to the trees. The trees respond, "Human, *please*," ignoring her protest that it is the lumber company who mutilates them, ". . . we find you without grace, without dignity, without serenity, and there is no generosity in you either – just ask any tree" (Walker 1988: 141–2). The trees associate Walker with all humans, denying her claims to individual innocence. Walker has come to refer to herself as "earthling." The term "earthling" represents a sharing of power, resistance to human supremacy, and places all individuals, animate and inanimate in mutual relationship.

Spirituality is not grounded in a father god for Walker, but in Mother Earth, who sends the "grandmother spirit" to teach wisdom.

Karen Baker-Fletcher

Further Reading

Walker, Alice. *Sent By Earth: A Message from the Grandmother Spirit after the Bombing of the World Trade Center and the Pentagon.* Berkeley: Publishers Group West, 2001.

Walker, Alice. *Anything We Love Can be Saved: A Writer's Activism.* New York: Random House, 1997.

Walker, Alice. *The Same River Twice: Honoring the Difficult.* New York: Scribner, 1996.

Walker, Alice. *Possessing the Secret of Joy.* New York: Harcourt, Brace, Jovanovich, 1992.

Walker, Alice. *Living By the Word.* New York: Harcourt, Brace, Jovanovich, 1988.

Walker, Alice. *In Search of Our Mothers' Gardens: Womanist Prose.* New York: Harcourt, Brace, Jovanovich, 1983.

Walker, Alice. *The Color Purple.* New York: Harcourt, Brace, Jovanovich, 1982.

See also: Christianity (7g) – Womanism; Ecofeminism (various); Environmental Justice and Environmental Racism; Memoir and Nature Writing; Paganism – Contemporary; Williams, Delores S.

Wallace, Alfred Russel (1823–1913)

Alfred Russel Wallace was among the leading English field naturalists of the nineteenth century who also wrote widely on non-scientific topics such as politics, social reform, and alternative religion. His best scientific works, including *The Geographical Distribution of Animals* (1876) and *Island Life* (1880), were highly regarded and contributed substantively to the emergence of modern biology. Perhaps his most noteworthy scientific achievement was his formulation of a novel evolutionary theory in the late 1850s. Although independently conceived, Wallace's views were remarkably similar to the ideas that Charles Darwin had been working on (and largely keeping to himself) since the late 1830s. Both theorists emphasized variation among the members of a species, environmental pressures that led to competition, and the concept of natural selection. Wallace first proposed his ideas to Darwin in an essay and letter sent in 1858. Darwin, shocked to find that someone else had developed similar views, nonetheless made sure that Wallace shared credit when their ideas were first presented to the scientific community. Darwin was also prompted to write up a more comprehensive version of the theory, *On the Origin of Species*, first published in 1859. This work became the starting point for all subsequent discussions of evolutionary theory and thus largely eclipsed Wallace's contributions. In their latter careers, the two men kept up a regular correspondence and often joined forces to defend the concept of natural selection against its various critics. However, they disagreed on some issues, notably the relevance of natural selection to the human mind and human destiny.

Although Wallace was raised in the Anglican tradition, he largely abandoned traditional religion as a young man. In the 1840s he began exploring alternative belief systems, including the burgeoning spiritualist movement, which emphasized communication with spirits that were thought to dwell in higher planes of existence that surrounded the Earth. Typical practices involved ritual séances presided over by mediums who claimed to contact the spirits and relay messages. Although skeptics (which included many of Wallace's scientific colleagues) dismissed the movement as trickery or delusion, Wallace insisted that spiritualism could be studied experimentally, and had, to his satisfaction, passed numerous tests. During his latter career, he wrote numerous articles, books, and pamphlets that defended spiritualist phenomena.

Like other advocates, Wallace believed that spiritualism was entirely compatible with a scientific worldview and reform activism. For example, he supported women's rights, the utopian experiments of Robert Owen, and various land reform movements. He also opposed what he felt were reactionary or cruel applications of science, such as the eugenics movement and vivisection. Linking these disparate activities was a master narrative of progress that spiritualists believed was at once natural (organic evolution), socio-political (progressive reform), and spiritual (survival and improvement of the soul after death).

How did Wallace's spiritualism square with his views of nature? Most significantly, while he staunchly defended evolution by natural selection for nonhuman organic systems, Wallace eventually came to believe that the higher mental functions of human beings (the "moral and intellectual faculties") could not be fully accounted for by natural selection. Instead, he invoked an "Overarching Intelligence" that guided the process of variation and accumulation of beneficial changes and that ultimately produced brains capable of mental and moral progress.

In this he implicitly argues for a separation between humanity from other animals that many (including Darwin) felt was no longer viable. Ironically, it may well have been an overdependence on natural selection (what some call Wallace's "hyper-adaptationism") that led to his distinction from Darwin. Wallace felt that natural selection acted exclusively in response to environmental conditions and eventually created perfect adaptations to those conditions. When considering humans in a "primitive" or "savage" state, Wallace could imagine no conditions that would require such a large, complex, and versatile organ as the human brain, hence his recourse to supernatural guidance. Darwin, on the other hand, employed the principle of correlation to deal with this problem. He felt that the higher functions of the human mind, including self-consciousness and abstraction, could have emerged in connection with the advantages conferred by language development.

Outside of biology, however, Wallace's attempts to situate organic evolution in a more comprehensive worldview that embraced progress, reform, immortality, spiritual belief, and ritual practice paralleled the efforts of much of the religious left of the late nineteenth century. Akin to various liberal theologies that developed in that era, Wallace yearned for a new synthesis of science and religion that would be consonant with various political and humanitarian reforms. In contrast to conventional liberalism, however, Wallace worked in an eclectic intellectual milieu that thrived largely outside of traditional religious institutions. Similar attempts to "spiritualize" science continue, most notably within the contemporary New Age movement. However, akin to Wallace, some resist what is arguably the major religio-ethical implication of evolutionary theory – that human beings are not exceptional to the natural process. Thus in spite of his obvious love of the natural world and his willingness to think boldly, Wallace's legacy was a religiosity that continued the traditional Western pattern of looking to the transcendence of nature. A religious vision that combined evolutionary theory and was spirituality oriented toward powers and processes within nature would have to emerge from other thinkers.

Lisle Dalton

Further Reading

George, Wilma. *Biologist Philosopher: A Study of the Life and Writings of Alfred Russel Wallace.* New York: Abelard-Schuman, 1964.

Kottler, Malcolm J. "Charles Darwin and Alfred Russel Wallace: Two Decades of Debate Over Natural Selection." In David Kohn, ed. *The Darwinian Heritage.* Princeton, NJ: Princeton University Press, 1985.

Wallace, Alfred Russel. *The World of Life: A Manifestation of Creative Power, Directive Mind and Ultimate Purpose.* London: Chapman & Hall, Ltd., 1910.

Wallace, Alfred Russel. *Miracles and Modern Spiritualism.* London: George Redway, 1896 (rev. edn of 1874 original).

See also: Darwin, Charles; New Age; Transcendentalism; Western Esotericism.

Washat Religion (Drummer-Dreamer Faith)

The *washat* is the name for what was commonly called the "Drummer-Dreamer religion," a Native American religious revitalization movement that began in the early part of the nineteenth century. The religion took its earlier name from the drums used in its rituals and celebrations, and from the belief that its leaders had died, obtained visions from the afterlife (and hence had been "dreaming"), then returned from the dead to lead their people. The movement began in the American Northwest and spread eastward, spawning other tribal religions with various specific rituals, but the emphasis on the discovery of tribal identity through religious practices was retained.

The precise roots of the *washat* are notoriously difficult to pin down, but the religion owes much of its origin to the Wanapum prophet Smohalla who lived on the Columbia Plateau in what is now central Washington State. Smohalla, whose name means "dreamer" or "preacher," was born sometime between 1815 and 1820. After a vision quest on a nearby desert mountain, Smohalla moved to the isolated village of *P'Na* on the Columbia River (now Priest Rapids), where he refined his religion, rejecting the "gospel and plow" message of the missionaries, and embracing the ancient traditions of the elders. The faith was strongly animistic, believing that all creation was capable of being imbued with spirit, and hence deserving of respect. Thus, it is hardly surprising that Smohalla rejected what he saw as agriculture's destruction of the Earth, and insisted that his followers return to traditional means of food gathering, social customs, and most of all, religion. Since many natives looked with alarm at the increasing encroachment of the whites, the *washat* found a ready audience.

The religion was steeped in symbolism that called the worshipper back to a foundational relationship with nature. Smohalla began the weekly ceremony with a meal that reminded some visitors of the Christian Eucharist, with the sipping of water from the Columbia, taken with bits of salmon. In addition, the religion's calendar celebrated salmon runs and root harvesting; the flags over the lodges contained the nature symbols of sun, moon, and star; and a tall pole adjacent to the prophet's tule mat lodge held a small wooden bird, carved by Smohalla himself that represented the Bullock's Oriole, the bird that had revealed the religion to the prophet when he was on his vision quest.

As Smohalla's fame spread during the 1860s and 1870s, other prophets, most notably Skolaskin, Haslo, and Wovoka took the religion's basic message back to their tribes, where the latter's refinements were the genesis of the famous "Ghost Dance" of the peoples of the Northern Plains.

Today at Priest Rapids, there is something of a resurgence of the *washat*, with the religion's innate respect for the environment finding a receptive audience among both natives and whites. Gone is the insistence that natives reject agriculture and other devices of European-Americans. Instead, the modern *washat* stresses an attitude of thankfulness to the Creator, which in turn prompts worshippers toward looking at nature with care and respect. Men and women still worship apart in the lodge; the drums still beat for much of the ceremony; the dancers' movements are much the same as they were in the days of Smohalla; and all participants continue to partake of the ritual meal of salmon and river water. But the *washat*'s move away from outward societal rejection reveals a religion that works through transformation of society.

Many Wanapums today carry this transformist spirit with them, working in local industries, orchards, and farms, with some actually employed on the Priest Rapids Dam, the dam that flooded some of the Wanapum's prime fishing grounds. This evolution of the *washat* points to the relationship that the tribe enjoys with the Grant County Public Utility District (PUD), the organization that owns the dam. The District strongly supports tribal religious identity, and works with the tribe to assist its environmental efforts along the "Hanford Reach," the last free-flowing stretch of the Columbia River in the United States. This part of the river is one of the few sites in the Pacific Northwest that still supports strong runs of Chinook Salmon, and the partnership between the Wanapums and the Grant County PUD is a significant reason for the health of the salmon population. Thus, despite the religion's changes since its rebirth in the 1800s, the *washat*'s influence on the ecosystem of the Columbia Plateau remains profound.

Michael McKenzie

Further Reading

Relander, Click. *Drummers and Dreamers*. Seattle: Pacific Northwest Parks & Forests Association, 1986.

Ruby, Robert H. and John A. Brown. *Dreamer-Prophets of the Columbia Plateau*. Norman: University of Oklahoma Press, 1989.

See also: Columbia River Watershed Pastoral Letter; Ghost Dance; Indian Shaker Religion; Seattle (Sealth), Chief; Yakama Nation.

Waskow, Rabbi Arthur (1933–)

One of the recognized prophets of eco-Judaism in the United States, Rabbi Arthur Waskow has been a principal and energetic proponent of such things as: "eco-kosher" practice, the "greening" of Jewish liturgy, reclaiming the ecological wisdom found in the Torah, and marrying ecological sustainability with daily spiritual practice. A lifelong political activist, Waskow began reinterpreting and opening up Jewish traditions to the concerns of the day after a pivotal Passover he spent in Washington, D.C. The year was 1968, Martin Luther King, Jr. had recently been assassinated, and Federal troops had been called out to control rioting within the District's African-American community. Waskow's visceral experience of African-American neighborhoods under "lock-down" conditions imposed by government troops prompted him to reexamine the traditional sacred narrative of Passover in light of current events. Waskow felt a need for the "haggadah," the booklet that tells the liberation story of the Jews moving out of slavery from Egypt (a story read during the Passover Seder service or ritual meal) to address the dynamics of racial oppression and violence he witnessed that day. In 1969, Waskow wrote and published a "Freedom Seder Haggadah" that adapted the traditional story of Exodus to address the realities of contemporary racism within a narrative framework of Jewish and African-American liberation. Many adaptations of the haggadah have followed Waskow's innovation, including feminist-based and eventually environmentally focused haggadot.

Since then, Rabbi Arthur Waskow's name has become synonymous with "Jewish Renewal," a trans-denominational movement that seeks to reclaim, renew, and reinterpret traditions of Judaism that it views as having been lost or regrettably "sanitized" in the face of the historical pressures imposed by cultural assimilation and anti-Semitism. In response, Jewish Renewal embraces and incorporates spiritual elements from Hasidism, as introduced by two of Jewish Renewal's founding leaders, Rabbi Shlomo Carlebach and Rabbi Zalman Schachter-Shalomi, who left the Lubavitch Hasidic movement but retained its daily spiritual rhythms and mystical components. In addressing environmental concerns in particular, Waskow explores what wisdom might be gleaned from the daily prayer and spiritual mindfulness observed in Hasidic tradition and the powerful importance placed on Shabbat (a time of sacred rest) for transforming patterns of consumption, "workaholism," and globalization, which he believes threatens the entire web of life.

In 1983, at the invitation of the Reconstructionist Rabbinical College, Waskow founded The Shalom Center in Philadelphia. The center is a self-described "network of Jews who draw on Jewish tradition and spirituality to seek peace, pursue justice, heal the Earth, and build community." Later, Waskow distanced the center from its

Reconstructionist affiliation and embraced instead the trans-denominationalism of the Jewish Renewal Movement. His encounters and exchanges with Rabbi Schachter-Shalomi in 1993 were especially formative for this shift and ultimately helped to catalyze Waskow's ordination as a rabbi in 1995.

The Shalom Center implements both social and environmental justice projects. Its members helped produce the *Trees, Earth, and Torah* anthology, a collection of resources for understanding and conducting the "Tu biSh'vat" ceremony, a midwinter holiday that celebrates the "Jewish New Year of Trees," and *Torah of the Earth*, an anthology that explores ecological wisdom in the history of Jewish thought.

Center programs and publications also encourage "eco-kosher" practice, which takes into account not only food choices but also other consumption choices and their effects on the well-being of the planetary community. For example, Waskow asks the pointed question, "Are tomatoes that have been grown by drenching the Earth in pesticides "eco-kosher" to eat at a wedding reception?" (Waskow 1996b: 297). For Waskow, such questions extend to other lifestyle choices such as what bank one chooses to do business with or whether one chooses to consume renewable or non-renewable energy sources. "If what we sow is poison," warns Waskow, "what we reap is poison" (Waskow 1996b: 299).

In 1996, the United Nations named Waskow a "Wisdom Keeper," a designation given to honor forty religious and intellectual leaders around the world who are actively working on environmental issues. Together with his wife Phyllis Berman, who is no less an activist than her husband, Waskow travels to universities, synagogues, and community centers to lead Torah study groups, conduct ritual observances, and lead services in the style of Jewish Renewal. Berman is co-director of Elat Chayyim, a Jewish retreat center for healing and renewal near Woodstock, New York, where visitors eat an organic diet, study Torah, pray, and meditate. Berman is also the co-author of *Tales of Tikkun: New Jewish Stories to Heal the Wounded World* (Aronson and Berman 1996) and specializes in new liturgies for women.

Sarah McFarland Taylor

Further Reading

Berman, Phyllis Ocean. *Tales of Tikkun: New Jewish Stories to Heal the Wounded World*. Northvale, NJ: Jason Aronson, 1996.

Elon, Ari, Naomi Hyman and Arthur Waskow, eds. *Trees, Earth, Torah: A Tu B'Shvat Anthology*. Philadelphia: Jewish Publication Society, 1999.

Goldberg, J.J. "Seasons of Reinterpretation: How a Radical Demonstration 32 Years Ago Changed the Culture of Passover." *The Jewish Journal of Greater Los Angeles* (21 April 2002), 16.

Waskow, Arthur, ed. *Torah of the Earth: Exploring 4,000 Years of Ecology in Jewish Thought*. Woodstock, VT: Jewish Lights Publications, 2000.

Waskow, Arthur. *Godwrestling – Round 2: Ancient Wisdom, Future Paths*. Woodstock, VT: Jewish Lights Publication, 1996a.

Waskow, Arthur. "What Is Eco-Kosher?" In Roger Gottlieb, ed. *This Sacred Earth: Religion, Nature, and Environment*. New York: Routledge, 1996b, 297–300.

Waskow, Arthur. *Down to Earth Judaism: Food, Money, Sex, and the Rest of Life*. New York: William Morrow & Co., 1995.

Waskow, Arthur and Phyllis Berman. *A Time For Every Purpose Under Heaven: The Jewish Life-Spiral as a Spiritual Path*. New York: Farrar, Straus, and Giroux, 2002.

See also: Hasidism and Nature Mysticism; Hebrew Bible; Jewish Environmentalism in North America; Judaism; Judaism and Sustainability; Kabbalah and Eco-theology; Redwood Rabbis.

Water in Islam

The religion of Islam, as revealed in the Qur'an, which Muslims believe to be the word of God (Allah), emerged in the western part of the Arabian peninsula – a dry, mountainous region similar in many ways to the Iranian plateau. The Qur'an mentions water on more than sixty separate occasions, and rivers more than fifty times. There are also frequent references to the sea, to rain and hail, fountains and springs. It is not surprising that the Qur'an, and for that matter pre-Islamic Arab tradition, place enormous emphasis on the importance of managing scant water resources sustainably and equitably.

Consistent with contemporary scientific understanding, the Qur'an states that water is the very source and origin of life: "We made from water every living thing" (Qur'an 21:30). Water is also the source of nourishment and sustenance, a gift from God: "Behold! . . . In the rain which Allah sends down from the skies, and the life which he gives therewith to an Earth that is dead . . ." (2:164); "It is He who sendeth down rain from the skies; and with it we produce vegetation of all kinds" (6:99); "It is He who sendeth down water fom the sky in due measure and thereby We quicken the dead land" (43:11); "And We send the water from the sky and give it to you to drink" (15:22); "We send down pure water from the sky, that We may thereby give life to a dead land and provide drink for what we have created" (25:48–49); and "We provided you with fresh water" (77:27). The Qur'an also makes reference to groundwater and springs: "He leads it through springs in the Earth" (39:21); "From it also channels flow, each according to its measure (13:17); and "Say: 'Think: if all the water that you have were to sink down into the Earth, who would give running water its place?" (67:30). Finally, water, with which Muslims must perform ablutions before praying and after sex, has the religious function of purifying the believer: "... and He caused rain to descend on you from heaven to clean you therewith" (8:11).

It is noteworthy that the Arabic term *shari'a*, which later came to be the term for Islamic law, originally designated "the path which leads to the watering hole." Qur'anic descriptions of heaven, furthermore, depict it as being watered with flowing rivers (5:119, 87:17). The abundance of water imagery in the Qur'an leads M.A.S. Abdel Haleem, a contemporary Islamic scholar, to assert that water has greater religious significance to Muslims than to followers of any other tradition.

The notion of community (*umma*) is of central importance in Islam, and social justice is one of the most prominent themes in the divine revelation. According to the Qur'an, water is community property: "And tell them that the water is to be divided between them" (54:28). The traditions of the Prophet Muhammad (*hadiths* – which following the Qur'an constitute the second source of Islamic law) report him as saying, "People share three things: water, pasture and fire." The *hadiths* also prohibit the withholding of water from those who need it, and from using it wastefully: "Excess in the use of water is forbidden, even if you have the resources of a whole river."

Classical Islamic jurisprudence was formulated mainly during the eighth and ninth centuries of the Common Era and set down in the texts of four schools recognized by Sunni Muslims (the Shafi'i, the Maliki, the Hanafi, and the Hanbali), plus a fifth school, the Jaf'ari, which is accepted only by Shi'ites. The latter are a minority within the Muslim world as a whole, but in Iran they constitute a majority of perhaps 90 per cent. For the most part Islamic jurisprudence has remained a theoretical construct, an ideal toward which Muslim societies should strive, rather than a system actually practiced. Even in the Islamic Republic of Iran today, the official view is that the country is "working toward" an Islamic state; it does not yet claim to be one.

Within the classical legal system, water rights are determined first and foremost by the need to quench thirst. This primary right was accorded not only to humans, but to animals as well. Thus, irrigation systems must be available to all who are in need, and must not be polluted so as to protect the rights of downstream users. Furthermore, according to John C. Wilkinson, "New upstream appropriations may only take place if they do not affect . . . prior rights" (1990: 61). According to the *hadiths*, the Prophet stipulated that "no more than an ankle's depth" of water could be taken – that is, providing adequate moisture storage in the soil for a seasonal crop. Wilkinson notes that the terms of the Prophet's restriction arise from the Arabian context, where water-flows typically result from flash floods. Classical jurisprudence, seeking "the spirit of the law," therefore determined that the intent was to prevent accumulation of excess water for purposes of speculation.

The *hadiths* also establish the principle of protected zones (*harim*), which include watercourses, rivers, and, significantly, their adjoining lands, including lands adjacent to wells. The *harim* is "the buffer zone surrounding a water body within which human activities, apart from the lawful use of water, are prohibited. The cardinal rule of harims adjoining waters is that they must remain undeveloped."

Islamic criteria for water purity, which perhaps reflect ritual more than health concerns, state that water is polluted (*najis*) if it has undergone noticeable changes in color, taste, or smell as compared to its "clean" (*tahir*) state at the source. In short, as Wilkinson summarizes, the norms for managing water which are found in classical Islamic legal sources are comprehensive, sustainable and just:

> The existence of both surface and groundwater flows are recognized and the *harim* rules ensure that tapping does not occur, nor that a new irrigation system or well are constructed too close to an existing one. The existence of problems of water quality and pollution, as well as of water quantity, are also treated in the Islamic code (1990: 63).

Water distribution systems in traditional Muslim societies, whether irrigation networks in rural areas or urban water supplies for public use, often fell under the classification of *waqfs*, which are pious endowments for the public good, protected from both taxation and government seizure. Those who made *waqf* endowments – usually wealthy families – were not only able to protect their wealth by investing it in this way, but could also exercise enormous power within their communities by controlling systems vital to the community's survival. In Esfahan (Iran) province a system of regulating the distribution of water from the Zayandeh river was stipulated by an early sixteenth-century document, popularly but anachronistically attributed to the Safavid minister Shaykh Baha'i. Much of the traditional canal system still exists, although throughout the recent drought the channels have remained dry.

Throughout Iran and Central Asia the traditional qanat systems, which provided water both for irrigation and domestic uses for three millennia, have now largely been abandoned in favor of "modern" practices such as the damming of rivers and the pumping of groundwater. Likewise, control of water resources has been transferred from pious endowments to government bodies. These changes have been brought about as a result of the application of development models imported from the West.

Richard C. Foltz

Further Reading

Abdel Haleem, M.A.S. "Water in the Qur'an." In Harfiyah Abdel Haleem, ed. *Islam and the Environment.* London: Ta-Ha Publishers, 1998.

Ahmad, Ali. "Islamic Water Law as an Antidote for Maintaining Water Quality." *Water Law Review* (1999), 170–88.

Lambton, A.K.S. "The Regulation of Water of the Zayandeh Rud." *Bulletin of the School of Oriental and African Studies* 9 (1937–1939), 663–73.

Wescoat, Jr., James L. "The 'Right of Thirst' for Animals in Islamic Law: A Comparative Approach." *Environment and Planning D: Society and Space* 13 (1995), 637–54.

Wilkinson, John C. "Muslim Land and Water Law." *Journal of Islamic Studies* 1 (1990), 54–72.

See also: Water in Zoroastrianism; Zoroastrianism.

Water in Zoroastrianism

From ancient times, Iranian civilization has possessed an ethical system that recognized both the ecological realities of the plateau's desert climate and the social imperative of conserving and distributing water in a way that ensures its availability to all. In Zoroastrianism, the original pre-Islamic religion of the Iranians, which is still practiced by a small minority today, each of the four elements is represented by a deity (*izad*) and revered through special invocations (*yasht*). Water is associated with the goddess Anahita (Nahid), whom Herodotus identified with Aphrodite. Another deity, Patet Apam, is described as guardian of rivers, springs, and the sea.

According to the Zoroastrian sacred text known as the Avesta, water must be kept pure and unpolluted. When Zoroastrians approach a stream, waterfall or spring, they should recite an invocation called the Ardvisura Banu (or Abzavar), from the Aban yasht in the Avesta. The ritual calendar of the Zoroastrians marks the fall harvest, Paitishahem, by commemorating the primordial creation of water.

Traveling through Iran in the fifth century B.C.E., Herodotus reported that Iranians did not defile water by spitting in it, did not wash their hands with it and could not stand seeing anyone pollute it. Strabo (ca. 63 B.C.E.–24 C.E.) corroborates this by observing that Iranians do not bathe in water, and will not throw anything unclean in it.

Most of Iran's Zoroastrians today live in the central desert regions of Yazd and Kerman. For them, the daily sprinkling of courtyards and alleyways (performed throughout Asia as a means of keeping down dust) is accompanied by the diffusing of fragrant herbs such as wild rue, frankincense, aloe and marjoram, and still has a religious significance.

Richard C. Foltz

See also: Water in Islam; Water Spirits and Indigenous Ecological Management (South Africa); Zoroastrianism.

Water Spirits and Indigenous Ecological Management (South Africa)

Many international organizations, such as the Convention of Biodiversity, the United Nations Working Group on Indigenous Populations (WGIP), and the Working Group on Traditional Resource Rights (WGTRR), are calling for the recognition of indigenous peoples' rights to self-determination, the value of their knowledge, and the need for strategies to protect and preserve this knowledge. This has largely been precipitated by the global environmental crisis, which has revealed the shortcomings of an exclusively scientific approach, often within the Western economic development paradigm, in solving the multitude of environmental problems facing present and future generations. There has been a corresponding awareness of the need to revisit how indigenous people have managed to live sustainably within their environments, both in the past and the present. The religious worldviews (cosmologies) and knowledge systems of many indigenous peoples are intimately embedded within their physical, spiritual and social landscapes and can only be understood within these contexts.

There is an intimate connection that exists between the physical, spiritual and social dimensions of southern African spiritual healers' knowledge and practice particularly with reference to water resources. There is a common corpus of knowledge linking the African healing traditions with water spirits over a wide area in southern Africa. Although there are regional variations, the recurrence of common themes and key symbols remain the same throughout and form the cornerstone of the spiritual healing traditions.

Among many of the southern African indigenous peoples, there exists a set of complex beliefs regarding water, river systems and riparian zones. The spirit world is regarded as the ultimate source of such life-sustaining resources, as well as the source of knowledge of healing and fertility. Integral to such beliefs are various zoomorphic spirit manifestations, primarily the snake and the mermaid, which reside in or beyond the water and which interact with humans in a variety of ways. The rivers and the sea are the dwelling places of such manifestations and are of fundamental importance to many of the African healing traditions and their practitioners (termed *amagqirha* by the amaXhosa, or *izangoma* by the amaZulu). The snake and the spirits of the water are specifically associated with the calling of individuals to become diviners and are seen as the providers of wisdom, knowledge and medicines, which are given to chosen individuals. This usually involves the physical submersion of the candidate under the water of a certain river, pool, or the sea (for a few hours, to days or even years) after which it is alleged that the individual emerges wearing the full regalia of a healer: a symbolic snake wrapped around his/her body and medicines. It is the spirits that choose the client, not the other way around, and resistance to the "calling" usually leads to misfortune. Relatives are not allowed to display any grief at the disappearance of one who has gone under the water or he/she may never be returned to the living. Anyone who enters these water sources without the calling of the ancestors will disappear, never to return. Messenger animals that summon the "chosen" one to meet the spirits are remarkably similar within all the cultural groups, namely, the snake or python, the water monitor, the hippopotamus, the dolphin, the otter, the crab, and various insects.

Certain places are more favored by the river spirits than others. They are believed to live in deep pools of certain rivers, often below waterfalls or fast moving "living" water or in the sea. The occurrence of certain plants near pools, such as the reed, wild tobacco or water buchu, indicate the presence of the water spirits.

Among the amaZulu of KwaZulu-Natal the water spirits in the form of the snake are referred to as the *amakhosi* (the great ancestors). Local informants suggest that they distinguish between the snake(s) that is/are a manifestation of the "family" (shade snakes) and the big one, "The one which is the Lord," representing the Supreme Deity. For example, one informant describes the python as *iNkosi yamadlozi* ("the lord of the shades") who resides in the pool.

The amaZulu also recognize the existence of another category of nonhuman water spirits or semi-daemons, that are half-human/half-fish (mermaids) and have stated that this is one of the forms the heavenly princess, *iNkosazana*, can take. These creatures very often have transformative powers. For instance *iNkosazana* can manifest as the mermaid, the snake, the rainbow and gentle soft rain. This link with the rainmaking forces and fertility is a common theme throughout southern Africa. *Inkosazana*, the Zulu heavenly princess, as the bringer of soft soaking rains, is responsible for both agricultural and human fertility. She has all the qualities of the archetypal Fertility Goddess. Propitiation and appeals are made to her by virgins at the beginning of spring each year, appealing to her to bestow her gifts of fertility and to help them select a suitable husband.

There are many other rituals that are performed for the water spirits at rivers throughout southern Africa. The purposes for conducting them and the ritual process may vary from group to group. They are mainly conducted for diviners at various stages of their training, but some households will propitiate periodically to appeal to the spirits to bestow them with wealth, rain, good harvests and fertility. Caves that are in close proximity to pools, especially those with rock art, are often used by healers as sites for rituals, and are viewed as very sacred. Archeologist Frans Prins has argued there is a close association between the San rainmaking trance rituals that are held in caves near deep pools, and the amaZulu and amaXhosa beliefs surrounding the water. Much of the rock art in the eastern Free State, northeast Cape and Transkei feature snakes and water animals such as hippos. These rain animals have been linked to experiences healers have of the spirit world while in trance.

As a result of the profound sacred status that the many rivers, pools and water sources hold for southern African indigenous communities, there existed in the past, and among certain communities today, a range of taboos surrounding their access and utilization. Certain pools are held with a mixture of awe, fear and reverence. Only healers associated with the water are allowed to approach such areas. It is strictly taboo for anyone to extract plants or resources from the water's edge. This can only be done by healers who are allowed plants for medicinal use. Common people are forbidden to go near sacred pools where the snake, mermaids and spirits are known to exist. This injunction is reinforced with the fear that uninvited people will be taken under the water never to return. Many groups limit the distance within which residential units can be erected near rivers and where cultivation can take place. Many of these beliefs and practices have been abandoned over the last century, with devastating environmental effects. In certain places there has been a resurgence of interest in these beliefs and practices. Recently in the Mvoti river area of KwaZulu Natal certain rural communities have reinstituted the ancient day of rest (*lesuku lweNkosazana*) for the heavenly princess, in response to claims made by a number of individuals who say she has visited them and complained that she needs the rivers to be left alone on certain days so that she can enjoy them and renew them without any disturbance. Collecting water, washing or utilizing any water directly from the river on her day (Mondays and Saturdays), is strictly prohibited.

The water spirits are generally believed to live in pools and swamps that never dry out. It is said that their role is to protect water sources and keep them alive. They are the guardians of the river and the providers of rain. They can however be chased away from their pools, which results in the drying up of water sources and the infliction of drought. This is precipitated by lack of respect demonstrated by people toward each other and the Earth's resources. Pollution, noise, the use of cement in rivers and dam building can all negatively affect the spirits. Killing or injuring any of the messengers of the water (such as crabs, snakes, frogs or water birds) is also regarded as a great offence. Social conflict and disrespect at both the local and national level can offend these spirits, resulting in catastrophic floods or droughts. Scholars have demonstrated how people harness the idiom of the water spirits to mount powerful community opposition to social, political and developmental projects (e.g., the Ambuya Juliana movement in southern Zimbabwe in the early 1990s).

Spiritual healers (diviners) are regarded as the repository and custodians of much valuable knowledge and wisdom accumulated from the past. This knowledge is by no means static as it is continually being revived and renewed through communication with the ancestors. However their access to such knowledge is under sustained threat by the forces of modernity: globalization, capitalism and religious intolerance. Ensuring indigenous people access to these sites is essential since such features are integral aspects of the nature, formation and transmission of knowledge. Changes in land distribution and ownership patterns in South Africa over the last 150 years have profoundly affected healers' access to certain sacred features of their landscape that are necessary to perpetuate their living heritage. Protection of such resources from the ravages of modernization is also crucial, as the presence of these spirits is believed to be dependent on healthy river systems. Rivers are under sustained threat in southern Africa as a result of commercial development, farming operations, large-scale agroforestry, dam building and toxic overflow. State and private landowners may also decide to install dams or draw off large amounts of water, which may negatively affect inflow requirements to sacred pools or submerge them altogether. Sacred sites, including pools and cave rock-art sites, are also threatened by tourism (and recreational fishing), which may damage them in both physical and spiritual terms. All these factors pose great threats to the resources and knowledge base of spiritual healing in southern Africa, and mechanisms are urgently needed to protect the rights of indigenous healers, their environments, and their communities from such intrusions.

Penelope S. Bernard

Further Reading

Aschwanden, Herbert. *Karanga Mythology: An Analysis of the Consciousness of the Karanga in Zimbabwe*. Gweru: Mambo Press, 1989.

Berglund, Axel-Ivor. *Zulu Thought Patterns and Symbolism*. London: C. Hurst & Company, 1976.

Bernard, Penelope. "Guérisseurs Traditionnels du Natal: Une Authenticité Négociée." Veronique Faure, ed. *Dynamiques Religieuses en Afrique Australe*. Paris: Karthala, 2000.

Bernard, Penelope. "Water Spirits – Indigenous People's Knowledge Programme: The Relevance of Indigenous Beliefs for River Health and Wetland Conservation in Southern Africa." *South African Wetlands* 11 (November 2000), 12–16.

Bowie, Fiona. *The Anthropology of Religion*. Oxford: Blackwell, 2000.

Callicott, J. Baird. *Earth's Insights: A Survey of Ecological Ethics from the Mediterranean Basin to the Australian Outback*. Berkeley: University of California Press, 1994.

Gottlieb, Roger. *This Sacred Earth: Religion, Nature and Environment*. New York: Routledge, 1996.

Gray, Andrew. *Indigenous Rights and Development: Self-determination in an Amazon Community*. Providence: Berghahn Books, 1997.

Hirsch, Eric and Michael O'Hanlon. *The Anthropology of Landscape: Perspectives on Place and Space*. Oxford: Clarendon Press, 1995.

Lewis-Williams, J. David. *Discovering Southern African Rock Art*. Cape Town: David Philip, 1990.

Mawere, Abraham and Ken Wilson. "Socio-religious Movements, the State and Community Change: Some Reflections on the Ambuya Juliana Cult of Southern Zimbabwe." *Journal of Religion in Africa* XXV:3 (1995), 252–87.

Metzner, Ralph. *Green Psychology: Transforming our Relationship to the Earth*. Rochester: Park Street Press, 1999.

Posey, Darrell Addison and Graham Dutfield. *Beyond Intellectual Property: Toward Traditional Resource Rights for Indigenous Peoples and Local Communities*. Ottawa: International Development Research Centre, 1996.

Prins, Frans. "Praise to the Bushmen Ancestors of the Water." In Pippa Skotness, ed. *Miscast: Negotiating the Presence of the Bushmen*. Cape Town: University of Cape Town Press, 1996.

Tilley, Christopher. *A Phenomenology of Landscape: Places, Paths and Monuments*. Oxford/Providence: Berg, 1994.

Woodhouse, Bert. *The Rain and its Creatures: As the Bushmen Painted Them*. Rivonia: William Waterman Publications, 1992.

See also: Serpents and Dragons; Traditional Ecological Knowledge; Traditional Ecological Knowledge Among Aboriginal Peoples in Canada; Weather Snake; Xhosa-Speakers' Traditional Concept of God; Zulu (amaZulu) Culture, Plants and Spirit Worlds (South Africa).

Watkins, T.H. (1936–2000)

T.H. Watkins was an impassioned environmentalist and author of twenty-eight books and hundreds of articles and reviews. Watkins exemplified the American sensibility of devotion to place that re-places an institutionally and historically centered sacrality with a commitment to, and awe before, the splendor of untamed and unspoiled land. Best known as editor of *Wilderness*, 1982–1997, the magazine of the Wilderness Society, from which in 1988 he received the Robert Marshall Award for his "devoted long-term service to and notable influence upon conservation and the fostering of an American land ethic," he was also a historian of the West and depression-era America. Watkins's 1991 book, *Righteous Pilgrim: The Life and Times of Harold L. Ickes, 1874–1952*, was a finalist for the National Book Award.

As a nature writer and land-ethic activist, Tom Watkins was devoted to the idea and experience of wilderness. His last book exemplified his call for the preservation of public lands and his celebration of place, written and photographic – from geology to political disputes – for the sheer wonder of the redrock canyons of southern Utah. The first Wallace Stegner Distinguished Professor for Western American Literature at Montana State University, Watkins was a tireless advocate for western lands and good writing about those lands. In the conservationist tradition, Watkins believed that wilderness would teach humans how to live: "For in wilderness," he wrote,

> as in the eyes of the wild creatures that inhabit it, we find something that binds us firmly to the long history of life on Earth, something that can teach us how to live in this place, how to accept our limitations, how to celebrate the love we feel when we let ourselves feel it for all other living creatures (Watkins 1994: 104).

In *Stone Time* Watkins reveals his attachment to wilderness rather like a young Wordsworth of the *Prelude*:

> I have two important landscape memories from my childhood – that of the seashore and that of the desert ... The sundown sea of my childhood gave me abundant joy, a sense of freedom and possibility, but it was an easy place, generous and forgiving; even the sea itself, its waves eternally flowing toward security, promised salvation. But this contrary landscape, this desert place of rock and sky, sere and implacable and forever challenging, gave up nothing easily (Watkins 1994: 5–6).

His romanticism was anchored to meticulous geological, historical, and legal information and insights. And as with many nature writers, he thought what was needed to save this land was to look upon it and reflect. As an environmental ethicist, he worked to affect legislation that would preserve the place for a walk, a look, a reflection. He loved the desert, and there his ashes were scattered.

Lynda Sexson

Further Reading
Watkins, T.H. *The Redrock Chronicles: Saving Wild Utah*. Baltimore: Johns Hopkins University Press, 2000.
Watkins, T.H. *The Hungry Years: A Narrative History of the Great Depression in America*. New York: Henry Holt & Company, Inc., 1999.
Watkins, T.H. *Stone Time, Southern Utah: A Portrait & a Meditation*. Preface by Terry Tempest Williams. Santa Fe: Clear Light Publishers, 1994.
Watkins, T.H. *On the Shore of the Sundown Sea*. Earl Thollander, illus. American Land Classics. Baltimore: Johns Hopkins University Press, 1990 (reprint edition).

See also: Autobiography; Marshall, Robert; Memoir and Nature Writing; Wilderness Religion; Wilderness Society.

Watson, Paul (1950–) and the Sea Shepherd Conservation Society

Terrorist to some, ecowarrior to others, Captain Paul Watson has been a looming presence over the animal rights and environmental movements for the last three decades. Since the 1970s, Watson has been a founding member of Greenpeace, a medic in the 1973 Wounded Knee face-off between the American Indian Movement and the U.S. government, and the founder and president of the Sea Shepherd Conservation Society. Although he has tracked elephant poachers in East Africa, saved wolves in the Yukon, liberated monkeys from zoos in Grenada, defended bison in Montana, and campaigned for the rainforests in Brazil, Watson is best known for his dramatic efforts to halt the slaughter of whales, dolphins, seals, and fish of the sea.

Watson's militancy is fueled by his intense sense of connectedness to the living Earth as expressed in his biocentric philosophy that all life is rich, beautiful, intrinsically valuable, and sacred. Watson had a number of startling epiphanies that spoke of his destiny to protect animals, such as in 1975 when a mortally wounded whale looked him directly in the eye, expressing pity for humankind, and communicating that he knew Watson was trying to help. Watson's biocentrism is conjoined to a scientific understanding of the laws of ecology that dictate how human beings must live on the Earth if they are to live at all. Watson condemns the anthropocentric hubris that presumes the laws of society can override the laws of nature. He decries the violence human primates have long inflicted on the Earth, other species, and one another, and warns of an impeding species extinction crisis the like of which has not been seen since the age of the dinosaurs. Echoing Aldo Leopold, Watson believes the human species is doomed so long as it sees itself as conqueror of the biocommunity rather than a respectful citizen within it. More explicitly than Leopold, however, Watson calls for "Biocentric Religion" (including in volume one of this encyclopedia).

Born in Toronto, Ontario, Canada in 1950, Watson's love and protective instincts for animals and nature were manifested early. Living in southern New Brunswick, he fell in love with the water and marine life. A "kindred spirit" to all animals, Watson protested any abuse he witnessed and destroyed snares and traps. His Earth-consciousness was so intense that by age 15 he had "pledged allegiance not to Canada, the Church, or humanity, but to nature" (2002: 49).

In 1968, Watson signed up as a merchant seaman and found his true home at sea. He joined the Don't Make a Wave Committee that protested nuclear testing by sailing activist crews into target areas. In 1972, with Watson as a co-founder, the group renamed itself the Greenpeace Foundation and cruised into French and American nuclear testing zones. During this time, Watson also did freelance writing and studied linguistic and interspecies communication at Simon Frasier University, thereby adding scientific weight to his belief that animals such as whales and dolphins have highly evolved brains and communicative capacities.

From 1972–1977, Watson emerged as the most militant member of Greenpeace. At his urging, the organization expanded its focus to include wildlife preservation issues and in 1975 launched the world's first sea-going expedition to protect the whales. In 1976, Watson led the first Greenpeace expedition to the ice floes off the Labrador Front to rescue seals and document the killing. He returned the next year with a larger crew that included French actress Brigitte Bardot, whose presence drew unprecedented international publicity to the seal slaughters. Watson's plan was to spray the seals with a harmless green dye to render their beautiful coats valueless to sealers, but the Canadian government quickly outlawed the tactic leading Greenpeace to renounce it. Saving the dye tactic for future campaigns, Watson instead shielded seals with his body, moved them to safety, and threw sealers' clubs into the sea.

By breaking Canada's "Seal Protection Act" Watson saved many seal lives and helped to inaugurate a new era of direct action for animals, but the Greenpeace board voted him out in 1975 after concluding that he violated their direct-action guidelines which stress nonviolence and bearing witness. Stung by the betrayal, Watson berated Greenpeace as the "Avon ladies of the environmental movement" because of their focus on fundraising over action. They in turn denounced him as a "terrorist" and interfered with his subsequent campaigns.

Watson started his own group, first named Earthforce and then the Sea Shepherd Conservation Society, which he calls "the most aggressive, no-nonsense, and determined conservation organization in the world" (1994: xv). With the help of Cleveland Amory and the Fund for Animals, Watson purchased the first of many Sea Shepherd ships in December 1978. In a series of bold, notorious actions, Watson and crew rammed pirate whaling ships at sea and sunk others at dock, sprayed thousands of seals with dye, intervened to halt dolphin kills, and destroyed miles of driftnets that environmentalists denounced as "curtains of death."

Influenced by Marshall McLuhan's theories of electronic media, Watson argues that nothing is real or believable for the public until it becomes a media event. Through sensationalist tactics, celebrity supporters, videotaped evidence, and dramatic press conferences, Watson aimed to galvanize a sleeping global village to help protect marine mammals.

Unlike many activists who resort to sabotage in defense of animals and the Earth, Watson accepts that property destruction tactics can be called "violence," but he argues sabotage is necessary to thwart a much greater violence and to capture media attention. As he explains it,

> To remain nonviolent totally is to allow the perpetuation of violence against people, animals, and the environment. The Catch-22 of it – the damned-if-you-do-damned-if-you-don't dilemma – is that, if we eschew violence for ourselves, we often thereby tacitly allow violence for others, who are then free to settle issues violently until they are resisted, necessarily with violence ... sometimes, to dramatize a point so that effective steps may follow, it is necessary to perform a violent act. But such violence must never be directed against a living thing. Against property, yes. But never against a life (1982: 26–7).

Watson's strategies and rationales place him squarely in the radical environmental camp, where illegal tactics are considered morally permissible if not obligatory to thwart the destruction of a sacred and intrinsically valuable natural world. Indeed, he made strong connections during the 1980s with the Earth First! movement, which musingly considered the Sea Shepherd Conservation Society its Navy, as they were his Army. Indeed, at Earth First! gatherings, Watson's heroism is often celebrated in poetry and song, and individuals who have served as crew for the Sea Shepherd have recruited there with some success.

Watson's champions credit him with inventing a powerful new mode of activism and bringing bold warrior tactics and values to the defense of the Earth. His critics berate him as an arrogant vigilante and violent pirate, an "eco-terrorist" who recklessly destroys property and endangers human life. Like most radical environmentalists, Watson insists that he explored the "proper channels" for appeal, protest, and change, but found only corrupt governments that either ignore or defend immoral and unsustainable killing. He argues, moreover, that he has proposed credible alternatives to industries such as sealing only to be rebuffed without a hearing. Where laws such as the 1986 International Whaling Commission ban on whaling are flouted without consequence, Watson insists he is upholding, not breaking, the laws. He freely admits to violating statutes such as the "Seal Protection Act," while reminding us that Gandhi and King also disobeyed laws in contradiction with the just and the right. Watson feels the charge of terrorism carries little weight coming from those who profit from killing, and he finds no credible comparison between damaging property to save life and slaughtering life for profit. For Watson, the true violence and real terrorism lies with those who massacre animals and devastate the Earth.

Critics also accuse Watson of being a misanthrope, a Eurocentric imperialist, and a dictator on his ship. Watson is unapologetic about the kind of discipline and command required to run a ship in high-risk conditions. He unflinchingly affirms that his primary allegiance is to life itself, and especially sea life, as he openly expresses contempt for a human species plundering the planet and exterminating species. Privileging animals over humans, Watson repudiates claims advanced by some members of indigenous societies, such as a number of the Inuit and Makah, who assert they have a right to kill seals or whales in order to preserve their cultures and identities. Watson believes that when marine species are at risk of extinction further killing cannot be justified, no matter what group of people is involved or rationale they articulate. Watson thus epitomizes "no compromise" radical environmentalism as he calls others to such activist, biocentric religion. Despite such radicalism, he continues to work with mainstream environmental and animal liberation organizations including the Sierra Club, whose members elected him to serve on its national board of directors in 2003.

Steven Best

Further Reading

McLuhan, Marshall. *The Medium is the Message.* New York: Bantam, 1967.

Watson, Paul. *Seal Wars: Twenty-five Years on the Front Lines with the Harp Seals.* Toronto: Key Porter Books Limited, 2002

Watson, Paul. *Ocean Warriors: My Battle to End the Illegal Slaughter on the High Seas.* Toronto: Key Porter Books Limited, 1994.

Watson, Paul. *Earthforce! An Earth Warrior's Guide to Strategy.* La Canada: Chaco Press Publications, 1993.

Watson, Paul. *Sea Shepherd: My Fight for Whales and Seals.* New York, Norton, 1982.

See also: Animals; Biocentric Religion – A Call for; Animism (various); Dolphins and New Age Religion; Earth First! and the Earth Liberation Front; Greenpeace; Radical Environmentalism (and adjacent, Rodney Coronado and the Animal Liberation Front); Sierra Club; Whales and Whaling; Whales and Japanese Cultures.

Watsuji, Tetsuro (1889–1960)

Tetsuro Watsuji played an important role as a major twentieth-century nativist philosopher in the Japanese response to modernization and Westernization. The 1867 Meiji Restoration ended a 250-year seclusion to reestablish the imperial throne to power and to survey Western models and train abroad to construct a new Japan as the best defense against Western colonization and commercial exploitation. By the 1890s, many knowledgeable Japanese who had gone abroad despaired at the great gaps between the West and Japan, some reacting by reexamining the values of the Japanese cultural past.

Tetsuro Watsuji trained under several famed nineteenth-century nativists (such as the novelist Natsume Soseki and the imperial ideologist philosophy professor Inoue Tetsujiro). In 1927 he spent a year in Germany studying Western philosophy; in direct response to the publication of Martin Heidegger's *Existence and Time*, Watsuji developed his theory of "natural environment" (*fudo* in Japanese), which he would subtitle "Considerations about Human Ecology" (*Ningengaku-teki kosatsu*). While others before him had considered the Japanese sense of nature, Watsuji was the first to do so in a modern Western philosophical style.

His starting point was Heidegger's emphasis on "beingness" (*sein*) as the singular foundation of human existence. Watsuji felt this to be incomplete because it stressed individual self-discovery in a temporal context; his Japanese experience of a communal society anchored in a unique awareness of nature led him to incorporate a spatial (i.e., natural environment) foundation to human self-discovery, which he termed *fudo*. It is usually translated as "climate, scenery, geologic conditions, weather" and so on, but is better rendered the "natural environment," and includes as well the nuances of the French *milieux* ("surroundings, social sphere"). Watsuji's starting point for developing the concept of "natural environment" was the human awareness of cold – that cold is much more than a characteristic of surroundings external to the human or a sensation or an interior mental event, it is actually a human subjectively experiencing an objective awareness. The context of the experience as well as the process itself is *fudo*, "natural environment." He interpreted Heideggerian self-awareness to involve both beingness and *fudo*, for the latter makes any objective self-discovery possible (Watsuji 1988: 12–13); since it enables humans to stand outside themselves, *fudo* is the "self-active physical principle of the human spirit objectifying itself" (1988: 10). This natural environment provides the opportunity or turning point (*keiki*) for concrete human activity. Humans face the challenge of survival because of the natural environment (the "tyranny of nature" [1988: 6]), so that all basic elements of survival such as food, shelter, and clothing, are inevitably tied to it. Tool making and the invention of all material products and all cultural acts occur within this natural environment; thus culture and the natural environment are interrelated.

Watsuji did several things with *fudo*. 1) He rejected any standard Western deterministic relating of culture and natural environment. 2) He applied the traditional Japanese sense of a natural world populated by indigenous spirits or *kami* (as described in archaic times in the Japanese myth cycles in the seventh-century *Kojiki* and eighth-century *Nihon-shoki*) that was subsequently refined by the worldview of the Buddhist Kegon (Chinese: *Hua-yen* or "Wreath of Flowers") school which posited a thoroughly integrated holistic cosmology of beings, contexts, and processes. 3) Noting that human awareness occurs existentially (Watsuji's Japanese natural environment consists of immanent *kami* as an interrelated holism) he thus conceptualized an ontological relationship between natural environment and culture – this is *fudo*.

But this was only the first half of an essentially nativist project. In his travels during the 1920s, Watsuji noted great variations in vegetation, landscape, natural light, architecture, urban design, transportation, etc., across Asia, Europe and the Middle East, so he proposed three basic kinds of *fudo*: desert (Arabia), meadow (Europe), monsoon (South and southern East Asia). Since *fudo* structures all human activity as culture, he saw humans developing distinctive material lifestyles in each of these natural environments, but also social structure, cultural acts, and national temperaments. Desert *fudo* is the most intense human struggle with nature – echoed in a nomadic survival with fierce possession of essential resources, intra-human resistance and conflict, religions of stark ethics and a totally dominant, all-powerful one god. Meadow *fudo* began with classical Greece and Rome in a brilliant Mediterranean light and comfortable nature, making possible much contemplation about order and structure – thus Greek philosophy and science and recent European civilization leaps across the globe. Monsoon *fudo* is an over-intense nature – from the archaic deification of nature phenomena in Vedic India through a common trend toward seeking either a single powerful unity underlying such lush and ever-changing life (*brahman* in Hinduism) or the universe as the unity itself (*dharmadhatu* in Buddhism). (Thus humans master nature in the meadow environment, but at best struggle and respect nature in the desert and monsoon environments.) Japan is part of this monsoon *fudo*, so his challenge next became how to clearly distinguish Japanese culture in relationship to its natural environment in contrast to the giants India and China, but also to the contiguous cultures of southeast Asian, Korea, and the Pacific.

Japan's environment is unique among monsoon *fudo* in Watsuji's eyes because 1) it is an island off the east coast of the Asian continent, 2) it lies on a geographical north/south axis, 3) unlike any other East Asian nation, its northern half receives cold Arctic air from Siberia and the Japan Sea, while 4) its southern half is both mainland monsoon belt-influenced but also Pacific island-related.

In his earliest writings in 1918, Watsuji had already linked Japanese culture to its natural environment, and soon did not limit this relationship to the development of material culture, but extended it deeply into the development of national character and ethos. With broad cultural sweeps, he linked such institutions as the Japanese corporate family, for example, to the traditional layout of the Japanese house, compared Buddhist temples to gothic cathedrals, Western gardens to Japanese, and so on. In parallel with such other well-known twentieth-century nativists as Okakura Tenshin and Suzuki Daisetsu, Watsuji also labored to isolate a uniquely Japanese national temperament as evidenced by its material culture. Here Watsuji built off of the Meiji imperial government's advocacy of a new national religion/ideology of *kokutai* ("nation-as-corporate body," the Japanese people as individual cells, and the imperial government as the head). As the Japanese began to establish the first modern Asian empire, the Greater East Asian Co-Prosperity Sphere (*Dai-toa-kyoeiken,* 1940–1945), Watsuji expanded *fudo* to legitimate the role of the state in integrating "territorial opportunities" (*keiki*) as human ecology. He became best known for his *Ethics*, his life's work about collective relationships and responsibilities in Japanese society. He would never see the Japanese state, its nation-as-corporate body ideology, or its martial spirit as reasons for Japan's World War II defeat, his nativism always sending him back in Japanese history to moments of foreign contact – so Watsuji could only find the reason for Japan's downfall to have been its two and a half centuries of seclusion (1508–1867) which denied it long-range access to and mastery of modern Western technology.

Dennis Lishka

Further Reading
Befu, Harumi. "Watsuji Tetsuro's Ecological Approach: Its Philosophical Foundation." In *Japanese Images of Nature: Cultural Perspectives*. Pamela J. Asquith and Arne Kalland, eds. Surrey, England: Curzon Press, 1997, 106–120.
Watsuji, Tetsuro. *Climate and Culture: A Philosophical Study*. Geoffrey Bownas, tr. New York: Greenwood Press, 1988.

See also: Heidegger, Martin; Japanese Gardens; Japanese Love of Nature; Japanese Religions.

Weather Snake

Among the Zulu-speakers of KwaZulu Natal, Southern Africa, there is a myth of an immense snake that rides upon storms, wreaking havoc and destruction. Greatly feared, this sinuous goliath is kaleidoscopic in appearance, able to change its form, carnivorous, irate and itinerant. In the Midlands its abodes are the many dams and rivers that run from the heights of the Drakensburg mountains some 70 kilometers to the northwest.

This creature is both a monster and a deity, associated with the negative power of the ancestors and the destructive forces of weather and nature. It is also associated with major landmarks such as Mpendle Mountain, some 10 kilometers outside of the town of Howick. From the summit of this mountain this brilliant creature is said to fling its full length upon the back of the storm, although some would say that it is the very storm itself.

As he races across the landscape upon the high winds, the glitter of corrugated roofing, so typical of shacks in southern Africa, attract his attention, leading him to mistake this for the shimmer of water. He drops from the sky and hits the roof, only to realize his mistake. Frustrated and furious, he throws himself back upon the storm, flicks his tongue of lightning and growls his rumble of thunder, twists his torso into a tornado and takes revenge upon the domestic landscape below. His tortured path rages from Mpendle Mountain through the scenic softness of white-owned farms, toward the expanse of Midmar Dam and on toward the Howick Falls.

This waterfall is regarded by Zulu *sangomas* (diviners) as a sacred place of power. Here for innumerable years, during the training of initiates, they have offered sacrifices to the ancestors and to the inkanyamba who are associated one with the other, and have even become each other in a blurring of boundaries. To awaken the snake from its watery sleep here is to invite its wrath in the form of storms, tornadoes and flooding.

The water-snake myth appears to have been introduced into southern Africa with the Bantu-speaking people some 2000 years ago, for the concept is prevalent throughout the southern sub-continent. But while this concept has taken the form of a water-snake among Bantu-speaker's, among San hunter-gatherers it was regarded as the rain-animal who could take many forms, and was a creature associated with the otherworld and responsible for weather and rain. The San were the great rainmakers, the controllers of weather and nature. For these abilities, and for their magical qualities, the Nguni feared them, yet sought their services.

In the Drakensberg region, the San were present until relatively late, having been driven out by various fugitive African groups, by the expanding Sotho and by white colonial groups, from about 1838 onwards. The last raid in the Midlands took place at Kamberg in 1872. The descendants of the San continue to linger on in these their old hunting-grounds. Here, in the rock shelters of these mountains, they left an immense lithic, or stone, gallery of rock art – a celebration of superb paintings. Among these are depictions of the rain-animal in the forms of the rain-bull and rain-herds of cattle, or presented as snakes, some of supernatural appearance. Among these are the rain-snakes.

Descriptions of the inkanyamba are similar to those for lake and water serpents the world over. Some of the features shared in such cases are the sinuous serpentine form, a mane, or integument of long hair or scales down the elongated neck, and sometimes an equine head. A creature resembling the inkanyamba is evident in a number of San rock paintings in the Drakensberg range. These serpents sometimes have a hogged mane like that of a zebra, horns, and either the head of a serpent, an equine head, or that of an Nguni cow or wildebeest. Whiskers occasionally adorn its face.

It appears that the Nguni and San engaged in a borrowing and merging of beliefs manifesting in the bovine or equine-headed serpent of the rock art, and with the weather-whipping inkanyamba of the Zulu-speakers, which flies along the old raiding routes of the San during its celestial journeys.

A giant mythical snake is not so far from European tradition. European descendants in this area have interpreted this mythical creature for themselves as a water-monster similar to that of Loch Ness in Scotland. Indeed, residents of this small town have reported sightings of a plesiosaur-type creature, or snake-like creature; sightings that have caught the attention of both national and local media. Part of the sensationalism surrounding the creature includes fake photographs of the monster and its young – published in a local newspaper – and crocodile eggs obviously imported into this area and said to be the eggs of the monster found at the pool at the base of the falls.

Clearly the water-monster is a means by which English-speaking European descendants have appropriated a local legend and presented it in a form to which they can better relate. The taming of the Howick Falls monster is just one way in which they have re-created an aspect of British culture and landscaped the African environment into a familiar domestic and cultural setting. Indeed, they are just one of three diverse groups, all of whom have manipulated a concept, to be found in many cultures worldwide – that of the dragon. Here, in the Midlands of KwaZulu Natal, European descendants have tamed the dragon, while the Zulu-speakers' inkanyamba is clearly a manifestation of the dark side of nature. Among the San, the creature is simply an expression of their magical qualities and mastery over a biddable nature – indeed, an expression of their mystical selves.

Sian Hall

Further Reading

Meurger, Michel. *Lake Monster Traditions.* London: Fortean Tomes, 1988.

Vinnicombe, Patricia. *People of the Eland.* Pietermaritzburg: Natal University Press, 1976.

Woodhouse, B. *The Rain and its Creatures: As the Bushmen Painted Them.* Rivonia: William Waterman, 1992.

See *also*: Divine Waters of the Oru-Igbo (Southeastern Nigeria); Sea Goddesses and Female Water Spirits; Serpents and Dragons; Water Spirits and Indigenous Ecological Management (South Africa); Zulu (amaZulu) Ancestors and Ritual Exchange; Zulu (amaZulu) Culture, Plants and Spirit Worlds (South Africa).

Wenger, Susan (1916–), Yoruba Art, and the Oshogbo Sacred Grove

Susanne Wenger was born in 1916 at Graz, Austria. She arrived in Nigeria in 1950 and this marked the beginning of her involvement with Yoruba religion. Before coming to Nigeria, she had exhibited her works in Paris, Zurich, Austria, and other parts of Europe. Ajagemo, a high priest of Obatala (god of whiteness), introduced her to Yoruba religion in Ede and there she began her artistic works for the gods. The first of such works was the reconstruction of the Soponna cult at Ede and subsequently the renovations of the shrines of other gods in the Osun groves at Oshogbo. Her main work over the years has been the constant reconstruction, renovation, and conservation of the shrines in the Osun Oshogbo groves. The fusion of art and religion is at the core of Susan Wenger's art, and she says the singular purpose of her work is to protect the sacredness of nature. Her works present a mixture of architecture, religion, and art.

Works of art consist of two elements, the inner and the outer, as well as two levels of knowledge, esoteric and exoteric. The esoteric knowledge level usually informs the inner element of art through knowledge, which is informed by the artist's intended meaning(s) for the work of art. This knowledge is accessible to a few people, the artist and/or cultic functionaries in the case of religious art. The outer element of art gives expression to the inner element and manifests at the exoteric knowledge level, for it is accessible to all. It is expressed in aesthetic values and decorations. The outer element gives the work of art its visible and audible qualities. Both elements are significant and affect the performance/presentation of any work of art.

The site where Wegner carries on her art is the Osun grove. The Osun grove is located at the outskirts of Oshogbo town in Nigeria. It is an expanse of land fenced round, within which one finds the Osun River, Osun shrine, shrines for other Yoruba deities, and sculptures for the deities by Wenger and her assistants. The grove is a blend of fauna and flora and is usually a quiet and serene place. The art of Susan Wenger at the Osun grove in Nigeria exhibit the influence of both the inner and outer elements of art in Yoruba religion. The sculptures, put in place by Wegner and her assistants, are expressions of and means of conservation in Yoruba religion. The forms of the sculptures are wholly organic, with components used in proportions determined by religious injunctions. The cement is mixed with a prescribed amount of the grove's red Earth. To ensure the conservation of nature in the grove, Wenger has been able to get the Osun grove onto the list of the Nigerian Antiquity conservation areas. Understandably, farmers who perceive these areas as a means of livelihood opposed the move vehemently, but with adequate information on the usefulness of such a stance, harmony has been achieved. Because Susan Wenger is a Yoruba by conversion/calling and not by birth/origin, her art presents some paradigms that may proffer significant import for existing relations between nature and religion.

The Yoruba hold that a combination of art and ritual remains indispensable to communication between humans and the divine. Further, nature is perceived as being sacred. Consequently, the Yoruba are more apt to think of art as an act of creative imagination (*oju ona*), executed with skill and an understanding of the subject, rather than see art as an object. For the Yoruba then, artistry is the exploration and imaginative re-creation of received ideas and forms, usually from the divine. Art is a vital part of being, and creativity is associated with the divine. This stance informed the state and significance of the Osun grove prior to Wenger's work. Emphasis was on verbal art and recitations rather than a prevailing need to erect sculptures for the Yoruba gods, as done by Wenger and others. While it is true that figures of Yoruba gods existed prior to Wenger's artwork, this was more at the level of individual worshippers – an example is the twin figures (*ere Ibeji*).

The shrines of the gods are for them a ceremonial home, while the sculptures embody their myths. Embedded in these myths are characteristics and taboos of each god. The main features of Susan Wenger's sculptures are life-size or larger figures and bulging eyes. Both features are known characteristics of Yoruba art, in pre-colonial times and presently. In addition, the bulging eyes are signs of spiritual power in mythology and religious experiences, depicting a higher consciousness. Her figures are usually larger than human figures, but these sculptures are representations of deities and records of mythology. She sometimes works with assistants in the restoration of these shrines within the grove. Most of these assistants are artists and adherents of Yoruba religion. Some of the sculptures produced by Wenger and her assistants in the Osun grove at Oshogbo include: Ontotoo (a senior deity in the heavenly abode), Obatala (the deity of purity and whiteness), and Iya moopo (protector of all women's crafts and trade). These figures are characterized by a blend of fauna and flora. Natural vegetation can be seen clinging to the shrine while monkeys, birds and other animals visit at their pleasure. Wenger's sculptures for the gods and goddesses are therefore at home in nature. These sculptures enhance the vividness of the deities to observers and worshippers alike.

The cooperation between religion, nature and culture in the Osun shrine could best be described as a collaborative phenomenon. Features of the sculptures emanate through myths from the people's religion and cultural ethos. Whereas nature nurtures the sculptures, religion and culture manifest themselves through them. Wegner and her assistants further collaborate in the Osun grove by combining their intellectual endeavors.

The resilience of Yoruba religion is being manifested continually within and outside Nigeria. The sacred grove of Osun Oshogbo is a big monument where the intertwining of the flora and fauna with the aesthetic presence of ritual artwork coexist. The grove serves as a conservation matrix and, at the same time, proclaims the record of Yoruba myths and deities; in so doing, it contributes to the vitality of Yoruba religion worldwide.

Oyeronke Olajubu

Further Reading

Apostolos-Cappadona, Diane, ed. *Art, Creativity and the Sacred.* New York: Crossroad, 1988.

Lawal, Babatunde. *The Gelede Spectacle.* Seattle: University of Washington Press, 1996.

See also: Sacred Groves of Africa; Yoruba Culture (West Africa); West Africa.

West Africa

West Africa is a vast region, encompassing a land mass of 2.4 million square miles, bounded on the north by the Sahara Desert, on the west and south by the Atlantic Ocean, and in the east by the mountain ranges along the Nigerian–Camerounian border. It is Africa's most populous and diverse region, with nearly a third of Africa's 800 million inhabitants. Its northern limit, the Sahel, receives less than 500 mm of rain per year, concentrated in a short dry season, but it is traversed by two major rivers, the Senegal and the Niger, which bring life-giving water for human settlement and irrigated or flood-plain agriculture. As one moves south, rainfall increases and becomes more regular. In the Sudanic region, rainfall ranges from 500–1100 mm, the rainy season is longer, and vegetation is lusher. It was in this region that major African kingdoms developed, centered on control of the trans-Saharan commerce. Still further south, are Guinean forests which receive rainfall from 1100–3000 mm, whose lush vegetation sheltered tsetse flies and African Sleeping Sickness, which protected its inhabitants from the Sudanic kingdoms and their cavalry-focused military power.

These climate zones tend to correspond with religious affiliations. Today, the Sahel is overwhelmingly Muslim; some areas have been Muslim for over a thousand years. The Sudanic region is predominantly Muslim, but includes notable communities of followers of traditional African religions, most notably the Dogon of Mali, and also Christians, most notably the Mossi of Burkina Faso. Islamic communities are much newer in the Guinean forest areas and remain distinct minorities behind substantial Christian and traditionalist communities along both the Upper and Lower Guinea coasts. Islam tended to follow trade across the Sahara to the trading centers of the Sahel and Sudanic regions, and was a weaker influence in forest areas that relied on human porterage to transport goods through forest zones where African Sleeping Sickness was endemic. Nature is a critical aspect of African traditional religions in the Sudanic region and forest zones of Upper and Lower Guinea.

West African traditional religions are monocentric; that is, they focus on a supreme being who created the universe and is the source of all life-enhancing powers. They also emphasize the role of lesser gods or lesser spirits and ancestors. Particularly in the Sudanic region and along the Upper Guinea coast, the supreme being tends to be associated with the sky and with rain. For example, the Diola of Senegal address their supreme being as Emitai or Ata-Emit, which means "of the sky," and call rain "Emitai ehlahl," "falling from God." Given climates where plants wither and die during the long dry season and return to life overnight after the first rains of the year, it is no wonder that the supreme being as giver of life is closely linked to the sky and to life-giving rainfall. This is particularly true in the Sudanic region and the northern part of Upper Guinea. In Lower Guinea, where rainfall is less of an issue, Earth goddesses attain greater prominence. Lesser gods and spirits may also be associated with rain, the ocean, particular rivers or springs, forests, fire, or with the forces of procreation.

Creation myths associated with particular religious traditions provide important insights into their representations of nature. For example, Dogon religious traditions describe various ways in which the Earth was created, but in all of them, an initially androgynous creator god becomes a predominantly male god in the process of creating the universe. As creation continues, this supreme being, Amma, becomes identified with the sky and the life-giving properties of rain. Amma rapes a passive and voiceless Mother Earth and fathers a solitary trickster figure, the jackal, which wanders the Earth seeking a partner. It is Amma's breath, *nyama*, which is seen as a dynamic, life-enhancing power that flows throughout the universe.

It is embodied in the moist, serpent-like Nummo, who purify Earth with the power of the First Word, which is identified with cloth made out of natural vegetation, twisted into coils in a primordial loin-cloth. As other disruptions in the creative process occur, the Nummo bring new, more sophisticated Words to restore order. The last and most complex is associated with the powers of the forge and of agriculture, which work in tandem restoring the Earth's life-giving powers and bringing order out of chaos. In Dogon cosmogonic traditions, one finds a common dichotomy between the settled areas of villages and towns and the dangerous, solitary chaos of the bush. Among the Bambara, the supreme being is initially seen as a seed and agriculture is central to their religious life. As part of their transition to adulthood, Bambara boys are initiated into the tyiwara society, which celebrates the role of an antelope deity, Tyiwara, in introducing agriculture to the Bambara, and the necessity of performing agricultural rituals to ensure the fertility of the land.

Other myths describe agriculture in more disruptive terms, seeing the act of planting seed and pounding harvested grain as the reason why the supreme being withdrew from a place just above the world, to a safer place high up in the heavens. Other myths describe creation in terms of their observations of the natural order. Thus, the Yoruba describe how the supreme being, Olodumare, gave a lesser god, Obatala, a chicken and a shell filled with sand and told him to create a world. Obatala poured the sand on the primordial waters and placed the chicken on it. It began to scratch in its constant search for food, and quickly spread the sand out, creating the dry Earth. Then Obatala began to create other living things from clay and did so in an orderly fashion, until he became drunk on palm wine and began to create deformed people and animals.

The gods and lesser spirits themselves reveal important ideas about West African representations of the natural order. The Fon and Ewe of Lower Guinea group their deities in three pantheons corresponding to the three most important realms of the universe. Mawu-Lesa, a complex god that is both female and male, heads the sky pantheon. Their children and grandchildren are associated with the pantheon of earth gods and the pantheon of ocean gods.

In many West African societies, the Earth is seen as a goddess. This is not only true of the Dogon, but is equally true for the Igbo of southeastern Nigeria and the Ashanti of Ghana. Ala, the Igbo earth goddess, guards the fertility of the land and is closely associated with the enforcement of moral codes. The Igbo term for morality, *omenani*, refers to "what happens on our land." Prohibited actions can render the location of such acts barren and incapable of producing crops. This is true of the Diola as well. Asase Ya, the Ashanti earth goddess, is also linked to the maintenance of the moral order and of fertility.

Similarly, the Yoruba's Ogboni Society, associated with a male Earth god, is responsible for conducting the judicial investigations into violent crimes; the shedding of blood is regarded as a profanation of the Earth. "The Beng of the Ivory Coast also have a male Earth god, whose priests, the Masters of the Earth, play an important role in reconciling the social order of humanity and the life-enhancing powers of the Earth. To the Beng, the Earth is all-knowing, able to distinguish between lies and truth and with a long memory as to the ritual obligations pledged to him when seeking his assistance. As Beng establish villages, the Master of the Earth ritually plants a Kapok tree, marking the space as one of human habitation, as opposed to the forest. This planting also permits the development of family life, especially sexual relations without the danger of conceiving a forest creature, a problem if sexual relations occur in lands unseparated from the bush. The Beng also worship lesser earths, refractions of the earth god, but capable of assisting them with more local tasks and punishing them for neglecting their obligations. The Earth is seen as so powerful that one day of each six-day week is set aside for his worship.

Many gods are associated with bodies of water. Thus, the Bambara of Mali link a stretch of the Niger River with the water spirit, Faro, who is a guardian of fertility. Yemoja, Oshun, and Oya, three Yoruba goddesses, are all associated with rivers, whose apparent stillness and depth mask powerful currents that can overcome human initiatives. The Igbo's goddess of wealth, Idemili, is associated with a river of the same name. These goddesses can bestow riches in children and in economic power to their devotees. The Diola identify a whole category of spirits, the *ammahl*, with water. They are often linked to some of the most powerful Diola shrines or can remain independent, revealing themselves only to a chosen few. Powerful gods of thunder, like the Yoruba's Shango and the Igbo's Amadioha, demonstrate the destructive power associated with rainfall.

Other gods are associated with diseases. Afflictions can either be a source of punishment for wrongdoing or neglect of one's responsibilities or a summons to take on ritual responsibility. Thus, the Diola's family shrine of Hupila seizes men with a disease that makes their body feel like it is bound with rope. Part of the healing process involves building a shrine; it may require learning to become a priest as well. The Diola fire spirit, Gilaite, associated with blacksmithing, punishes thieves or their families with leprosy. The Yoruba deity, Shopona, and the related Fon and Ewe Sakpata, used to be associated with smallpox, seizing those who survived it as its priests and killing those who had violated its edicts. Since the elimination of smallpox, however, this deity has found a new disease to manifest its power, HIV-AIDS.

Finally, trickster gods are common in much of West Africa where they are closely associated with particular animals who are regarded as extremely wily and outside of human control. Thus, the Akan's Ananse is identified as a spider. The Dogon's tricksters are identified with foxes and jackals, who speak in crude, highly symbolic language, the language of divination. These deities are not evil, but forces of disorder that disrupt human attempts to impose order on the world. They introduce diseases, natural disasters, animal pests, and powers of the bush against the people of settled townships. In the case of the Fon's trickster, Legba, and the Yoruba's Eshu, they portray the disruptive power of unsocialized, that is, natural, sexual powers and the disorder that they engender. All of these tricksters provide vivid evidence of the persistent ability of natural forces to disrupt humanity's attempts to construct a world order. They provide powerful explanations of human suffering in a universe where humans exert little control.

In many West African religions, human beings are also linked to a variety of non-domesticated animals. In much of West Africa, there is a complex theory of the soul, which is created from aspects associated with one's patrilineage, one's mother's patrilineage, and one's grandparents' patrilineages. Each of these parts of the soul is symbolized by a particular type of animal, with whom that person shares a portion of his or her soul. When the human is born, so is the animal. These animals suffer whatever pain the human suffers and vice versa. The death of one threatens the life of the other. Lineages respect the type of animal associated with them, as well as those animals associated with their paternal and maternal ancestors. In Diola society, these animals are said to live in sacred forests or other special places associated with a lineage. They are not normally hunted or eaten, even by people outside the lineage. These animals may range from mamba snakes, to hyenas, to hippopotami. In Dogon traditions, kinship with particular animals reflects the descent of all animals, plants, and people from the heavens to the Earth and the special ties that people shared in the particular portion of the celestial granary that descended to Earth carrying the necessities of Dogon civilization. This type of totemic connection is primarily a reflection of one's patrilineage. This emphasis on spiritual ties between humans and wild animals transcends the dichotomy between settled land and the bush, which is so central to many West African religions.

Animal sacrifice is central to most West African rituals. Spoken prayer is seen as containing a spiritual power in itself. This can be added to through offerings of water, milk, palm wine, millet beer, or even gin, all of which are seen as containing a life-force that can enhance prayer. The offering of the life-force of an animal, represented by the blood which is poured on the shrine, however, gives still greater power to the prayer, enhancing its ability to pass into the world of spirits or divinities. The cooking of certain meats which are consumed by the human congregants, and the blood, which is consumed by the spirits that are invoked, creates a type of ceremonial meal in which divinities and humans both partake.

West African oral traditions include a number of anecdotes about African rulers who were unable to end droughts through the offerings of sacrifices at royal shrines. In each of these accounts Muslim scholars offered successful prayers to bring rainfall and led the rulers to conversion to Islam. For example, the ruler of eleventh-century Ghana converted because a Muslim teacher was able to pray for rain, when he had failed. More recent testimony by traditional religious leaders tends to emphasize the idea that the frequent droughts of the last quarter of the twentieth century were caused by peoples' abandonment of their religious obligations and their embracing of Christianity or Islam, which have had little to say about environmental issues. Among the Diola of southern Senegal, this has led to the intensification of a prophetic tradition, focused on the performance of rain rituals. The most famous of these prophets, a woman named Alinesitoué Diatta, also rejected French agricultural schemes which would have shifted the emphasis of Diola agriculture from rice to peanuts, and led to the cutting down of the forest areas within Diola territory, which she saw as linked to the persistent droughts. She also criticized those Diola who converted to Islam and Christianity and refused to participate in Diola rituals or observe a Diola day of rest for the land, every sixth day. The rapid growth of Islam and Christianity, coupled with their relative neglect of rituals focused on nature, occurred at a time when droughts and desertification became increasingly severe. Whether or not the perception that religions indigenous to West Africa can more effectively supplicate the powers that govern nature will affect the continued growth of these newer religions remains to be seen. Conversely, one might predict that the instrumental aspects of Christianity and Islam that are focused on links to the powers of nature may become accentuated by African spiritual concerns brought by their converts and the growing ecological crisis affecting so much of West Africa.

Robert M. Baum

Further Reading

Akyeampong, Emmanuel. *Between the Sea & the Lagoon: An Eco-Social History of the Anlo of Southeastern Ghana c. 1850 until Recent Times.* Oxford: James Currey, 2001.

Bascom, William. *The Yoruba of Southwestern Nigeria.* Prospect Heights, IL: Waveland Press, 1984.

Baum, Robert M. "Alinesitoué: A Diola Woman Prophet in West Africa." In Nancy A. Falk and Rita M. Gross, eds. *Unspoken Worlds: Women's Religious Lives.* Belmont, CA: Wadsworth, 2001.

Gottlieb, Alma. *Under the Kapok Tree: Identity and Difference in Beng Thought.* Bloomington: Indiana University Press, 1992.

Ilogu, Edmond. *Christianity and Igbo Culture.* New York: 1974.

Sapir, J. David. "Fecal Animals: An Example of Complementary Totemism." *Man* 12 (1977), 1-21.

See also: Diola (West Africa); Saro-Wiwa, Kenule Beenson – and the Ogoni of Ogoni; The Trickster; Yoruba Culture (West Africa).

Western Esotericism

"Esotericism" has become a highly popular term during the last three decades. Like "New Age," it is a catchword for a lot of quite disparate religious or cultural phenomena, and its usage in the wider public differs considerably from its usage in academic contexts. Since its first appearance in the nineteenth century, a definition of "esotericism" often refers to the meaning of the Greek *esôteros* ("inwardly," "secretly," "restricted to an inner circle") and lays the main emphasis on secrecy and concealment of religious, spiritual, and philosophical truths. This characterization turned out to be not very helpful, given the fact that a lot of "esoteric" knowledge has been published and openly discussed – especially (but not only!) in the twentieth century. Therefore, other definitions have been proposed. Among the most influential is the concept of Antoine Faivre, who became the mentor for "history of esotericism" as a new branch of religious studies.

Systematic Definition

Faivre argued that esotericism should be defined systematically as a certain *worldview* or as a means to conceptualize cosmos, nature, and humankind. He distinguishes six characteristics, four of them being crucial for esotericism and two being indicative only in certain contexts. 1) The most important characteristic is the *doctrine of correspondences*. In this view, each part of the visible and invisible universe is connected and every single part mirrors one of the others in a symbolic way. The correspondences take the form of two different approaches to reality: following the well-known principle of "Microcosm-Macrocosm," there exist obvious or veiled correspondences between different layers of the material and immaterial world (e.g., between the planets on the one hand and metals, the human body, or plants on the other). But correspondences may also exist between nature (or cosmos), history, and revealed texts. Nature and scripture are believed to be in harmony, which is the key to understand medieval and early modern talk of the "book of nature" being revealed like the Bible itself. 2) The doctrine of *living nature* conceptualizes the universe as a dynamic system, in which all interconnected parts are animated. This is also an essential assumption of a particular branch of the Western philosophy of nature, as it is of magic since ancient and Renaissance times. 3) *Imagination and Mediations* is a characteristic that follows the doctrine of correspondences, insofar as it implies the possibility of mediation between the higher and lower world(s), by way of ritual and symbolic performance or through revelatory agents like angels and intermediate spirits. Imagination is not only a form of clear concentration necessary for magical rituals but was also depicted in early modern times as a particular "organ of the soul" that can establish a cognitive and visionary relationship with an intermediate world. 4) Borrowing a term from alchemy, the fourth characteristic is called *experience of transmutation*. It denotes the process of personal initiation on a spiritual path, either through a social event (like in freemasonry) or as a private change of status. Transmutation also means that the old person is entirely left behind, providing room for a new birth into wholeness and illumination, a process of regeneration and purification.

In addition to these four "intrinsic characteristics" – meaning that all of them have to be present to qualify a cultural setting as "esoteric" – there are two relative or non-intrinsic features that often occur. One (point 5) is called the *praxis of concordance*, which alludes to the frequent attempt to display the commonalities between two or more – ideally even all – different traditions. Prominent examples are the belief in a *prisca theologia* ("old theology") or a *philosophia perennis* ("eternal philosophy") that captured the imagination of medieval and Renaissance scholars. Another example is the seminal work of Helena Petrovna Blavatsky and the Theosophical Society; Blavatsky searched for a common denominator of all spiritual traditions and presented her Theosophy as the revelation of the secret key to true (and universal) knowledge. A final component (point 6) can be seen in the *transmission* of esoteric teachings from master to disciple. This is either a sociological characteristic indicating the necessity of being introduced to a spiritual tradition or the legitimization of authority and "authenticity" by means of an "age old" chain of masters. For instance, Freemasons present King Solomon as the founder of their tradition; Rosicrucians refer to the mythic figure of Christian Rosenkreutz; in contemporary parlance the notion of "avatars," "ascended masters," or the "Great White Brotherhood" plays a decisive role in securing authenticity and spiritual identity.

Esoteric "Disciplines" and Their Historical Development

Applying the systematic characterization of esotericism mentioned above to the Western history of science and religion, several cultural phenomena show their obvious relation to esotericism. Furthermore, there were times of thought in Western history that appear crucial for the evolution of esoteric thinking. To begin with the esoteric "disciplines," it might be argued that *astrology* provides a key to all other esoteric explanations of the cosmos. It directly follows the doctrine of correspondences to search for the symbolic – rather than the causal – relation between the astral world on the one hand and mundane or human events and dispositions on the other. Astrologers try to translate the all-encompassing dynamics of the world's visible and invisible features into the symbolic language of planetary energies, thus creating a fundamental tool for esoteric interpretation. *Magic*, then, can be described as the practical application of astrological symbolism. If one wants to perform a ritual, it will be advisable to assemble those components that are likely to support one another because they belong to the same cosmic principle; for a "Venus ritual" one might burn incense of Mugwort (*Artemisia vulgaris*), use an Aventurine stone, put up the Tarot card "III – The Empress," light green candles, chant the vocal "a," and so on. Those features are thought to "invite" the cosmic energy of Venus and help the magician to focus her or his concentration (imagination) on the ritual's goal.

Magic and astrology share a lot with the third esoteric discipline – *alchemy*. Using astrological symbolism and magical ritualizing, alchemy is focused on the interrelationship between mind and matter. But rather than being interested in the mere transformation of lower material into higher material – to turn lead into gold – the alchemists regard this process as mirroring the purification of the adept's soul, thus connecting the alchemist to the hidden levels of nature. It is important to note that both alchemy and magic are not opposed to "science." Until the eighteenth century, they were inseparably linked to the scientific disciplines. Although alchemy and magic build on a holistic model of the cosmos, their relation to nature was by no means a "sacramental" or devotional one. Alchemy and *magia naturalis* in many respects aimed at subordination and control of nature (through nature's "purification" and "improvement"), even when animistic or pantheistic perspectives were involved.

From a historical point of view, the origins of esotericism unquestionably are to be found in antiquity and can be regarded as a confluence of philosophical and religious assumptions. The Stoic philosophy conceptualized the universe as a dynamic system of interrelated and animated parts, whereas Middle and neo-Platonism contributed to esoteric thinking with its idea that the material world is only a very insufficient mirror of the "real" world lying hidden in the transcendent or – as Christian Gnostics would have it – in man's "sacred core," which is undefiled by "nature." The Greco-Egyptian tradition attributed to Hermes Trismegistus (the "Thrice-Greatest Hermes") as the divine revelator of universal truths contributed significantly to the formation of esotericism, especially with its macrocosm-microcosm doctrine and the enthronement of Hermes Trismegistus as the "founder" of the occult sciences. In late antiquity, astrology, magic, and alchemy were fully developed and enjoyed a high reputation, despite the fact that Roman and Christian emperors periodically tried to punish experts who exercised those disciplines. In medieval times, the Islamic world showed considerable interest in the esoteric disciplines. Due to their sophisticated knowledge of Greek philosophy and science, Muslims and Jews were famed for their alchemical and astrological skills, and it was only in Renaissance times that the Christian West opened itself to that tradition.

For Islamic, Jewish, and Christian esotericism alike, the fifteenth century was a decisive turning point. A central figure in this development was Marsilio Ficino (1433–1499); the Florentine Medici chose to build up a Platonic Academy in 1450. But before Ficino could translate Plato's works, he had to translate the newly discovered *Corpus Hermeticum* for a highly interested audience. Although Isaac Casaubon in 1614 proved that the *Corpus* could not be older than the early Christian documents, it was continuously honored as a text preceding Plato and Moses. Until 1641 it had been published and translated 25 times. The Renaissance discovered the *philosophia perennis*, and Ficino was among those highly educated scholars who described humanity's new place within the cosmic orders and a new attitude toward nature. The human soul was – neo-Platonically – thought of as resembling and mirroring the *anima mundi* ("world soul"), and nature itself was considered part of that all-encompassing spiritual dimension of the universe. Although Renaissance esotericism shared the contemporary model of nature as a "great machine," that machine was considered alive and dynamically intertwined with the human body, mind, and soul – today we call this concept holistic. That esotericism was exercised on the interface of magic, science, and religion becomes obvious when one considers the important works of Henricus Cornelius Agrippa (*De occulta philosophia*, 1533), John Dee (1527–1608), and Giordano Bruno (1548–1600). Furthermore, an important contribution to esotericism was the Jewish Kabbalah, a mystic tradition going back into the twelfth century. It was widely appreciated in Western esotericism, although not in its original form but assimilated to the Christian tradition. Decisive here were Pico della Mirandola (1463–1494) and Knorr von Rosenroth, who translated (large parts of) the Jewish "Zohar" into Latin. The kabbalistic "Tree of the Sephirot" became a standard model for describing the dynamic interrelation between the several spheres of the universe, the revelatory aspects of divine knowledge, and the sanctification of nature as a reflection of God's holiness (to be sure, this was not the main interest of the Jewish kabbalists). The impact of Christian adaptations of kabbalistic models on the Western philosophy of nature can hardly be overestimated. One example is F.W.J. Schelling, who in the nineteenth century used the kabbalistic doctrine of "Tsimtsum" to explain the continuous destruction and reproduction of nature in its historical development.

This connection can also be found in the eighteenth century, when esoteric doctrines were confronted with – and often integrated in – Enlightenment positions. To name but a few important protagonists of that time: Emmanuel Swedenborg (1688–1772) was among those arguing for a presence of spiritual dimensions in the material world, for which Immanuel Kant attacked him; the mysticism of Jakob Böhme (1575–1624) was adopted by philosopher of nature and alchemist Friedrich Christoph Oetinger (1702–1782). The tension between a holistic esoteric worldview and the dualistic or mechanistic model established by Isaac Newton (who nevertheless wrote alchemical treatises and a commentary on the *Tabula Smaragdina*, which was attributed to Hermes Trismegistus himself!) became even more imperative in the nineteenth century, when increased rationalization and mechanization of science, religion, and nature provoked a counter-reaction. What Max Weber called the "disenchantment" of the world was answered by romantic authors in Europe and North America with an intensified focus on the wholeness and sanctity of nature. In doing so, these philosophers, scientists, and artists built on esoteric doctrines of "living nature" and "correspondences," not to mention the revelatory aspects of divine knowledge now being "experienced" in nature. Although there had been trends of pantheism and nature's admiration before, it was Romanticism that fully brought about a religious dimension of esotericism's attitude toward nature. Like in today's "deep ecology" – which is a follower of nineteenth-century thought – for Romantic authors, nature was not the mere object of study, but an object of adoration.

When in 1875 H.P. Blavatsky and others founded the *Theosophical Society*, a movement took on institutional form that must be regarded as a kind of turntable between nineteenth- and twentieth-century esotericism. Blavatsky's works – especially her *Secret Doctrine* – remained standard reference-books for people searching for a *philosophia perennis*, now including even Buddhist and Hindu traditions that have been popularized by the Theosophical Society. In accordance with the esoteric tradition – and to some degree contrasting pantheistic Romanticism and Transcendentalism – Blavatsky and her followers described nature as a revelation of the primordial truths, still containing in essence the symbolic formula of the cosmos. In doing so, nature does not necessarily have intrinsic value, but it serves as a means for humans to understand the universe and their place within it. What counts is the perfection of humankind and the transformation of the spiritual self into a cosmic consciousness. This basic attitude is still discernable in those areas within the "New Age movement" where Theosophical traditions have been adopted.

In sum, one could say that esotericism is an integral part of the Western history of thought, influencing both science and religion. It employs a holistic model for interpreting the universe and focuses on the refinement and accomplishment of humans. As can be seen in alchemy, this also implies an "improvement" of nature (i.e., a transformation of impure matter into a state of pure essence). Hence, esotericism does not lead to any kind of environmental ethics, in which nature would have intrinsic value and rights. When nature is adored, it is adored for being a mirror of humankind's primordial (and utopian) state of sacredness and perfection.

Kocku von Stuckrad

Further Reading
Amir-Moezzi, Mohammad Ali. *The Divine Guide in Early Shiism: The Sources of Esotericism in Islam*. Albany: State University of New York Press, 1994.
Broek, Roelof van den and Wouter J. Hanegraaff, eds. *Gnosis and Hermeticism from Antiquity to Modern Times*. Albany: State University of New York Press, 1997.
Debus, Allen G. *Man and Nature in the Renaissance*. Cambridge: Cambridge University Press, 1978.
Faivre, Antoine. *The Eternal Hermes: From Greek God to Alchemical Magus*. Grand Rapids: Phanes Press, 1995.
Faivre, Antoine. *Access to Western Esotericism*. Albany: State University of New York Press, 1994.
Hanegraaff, Wouter J. *New Age Religion and Western Culture: Esotericism in the Mirror of Secular Thought*. Leiden: E.J. Brill, 1996.
Lindberg, David C. and Robert S. Westman, eds. *Reappraisals of the Scientific Revolution*. Cambridge and New York: Cambridge University Press, 1990.
Tuveson, Ernest Lee. *The Avatars of Thrice Great Hermes: An Approach to Romanticism*. Lewisburg: Bucknell University Press, et al., 1982.
Vickers, Brian, ed. *Occult and Scientific Mentalities in the Renaissance*. Cambridge and New York: Cambridge University Press, 1984.

See also: Alchemy; Astrology; New Age; New Religious Movements; Paganism – Contemporary; Theosophy; Transcendentalism; Wicca.

Whales and Japanese Culture

Whales have for centuries been hunted and eaten by the Japanese, and whaling activities are intimately bound up with religious beliefs and practices. According to a widespread Japanese view, which stresses the interdependence of supernatural, human, and animal worlds, the whale is seen as a manifestation of Ebisu, the patron deity of fishing, who often disguises himself in this way when on festival days he approaches shrines to pray. Whales are believed to sacrifice themselves for the benefit of humans, and in return the whalers ought to utilize the carcass to the fullest – wastes are seen as an insult to the whale – and to take care of their immortal souls. Failure to do this may cause the whales to turn into "hungry ghosts" that can cause illness, accidents and other misfortunes.

The souls of whales have in many whaling communities therefore been treated in ways similar to the souls of deceased human beings. Tombs and memorial stones can be found on at least 48 places, from Hokkaido in the north to Kyushu in the south, and annually at least 25 festivals (*matsuri*) and memorial rites (*kuyô*) are held in honor of whales. A tomb at Koganji (an old temple dedicated to whales) has been designated a national historical monument and marks the burial of 75 whale fetuses. In late April, the temple hosts elaborate memorial ceremonies with Buddhist priests reciting sutras for several days in order to help the souls of deceased whales to be reborn in a higher existence. Such services have a number of meanings. The temple priest may perform the memorial service in the belief that the whale will reach enlightenment and thus be released from rebirth into this world and enter Paradise as "Buddha." Some villagers may believe that the whale will be reborn as another whale to be hunted. Finally, memorial services are held to ensure that the whalers, and the gunners in particular, are forgiven for the sin involved in taking life. Memorial services therefore carry special meanings to the gunners, and they frequently go directly to the temple upon returning home in order to conduct memorial services for the whales they have killed.

A number of lesser ceremonies and rituals are performed in order to repay whales for their personal sacrifice and thus secure safe voyages and rich catches. Whaling companies gather whalers and their wives for ceremonies before, as well as after, the commencement of the seasons, and in some places the wives go on pilgrimages to local shrines. Daily religious observations are conducted in front of the family Shinto altar, praying for the husband's safety and good catches. Similar rituals are performed on the boats, where a piece of the whale's tail may be offered to the Shinto altar. Rituals tie whalers to each other, to their families, and to the whales, thus giving the local residents both a feeling of the common heritage and meaning to their lives. This common cultural heritage is expressed and reinforced in festivals, songs, dances and local dishes of whale meat. Rituals give the community its distinct character: the set of Shinto deities is unique to each community and the festivals are different as well. But they are all variations of common themes based on a conception of the whale as a creature with an immortal soul and a worldview stressing the interdependence of supernatural, human, and animal worlds.

Successes as well as failures are explained in relation to the divine. Accidents may be caused by failure to repay the whale's sacrifice through ritual neglect, but can also be caused by breaking taboos. There are several stories about the malevolent spirits of whales, some of them known throughout Japan. The most famous is the disaster that struck Taiji in 1878 when whalers broke an old taboo and attacked a right whale with calf. More than one hundred whalers lost their lives in the following gale. Such accidents, which have become part of the communities' cultural heritage, and thus help in giving them their peculiar identities, have reinforced the validity of the taboo, a taboo that, incidentally, might carry some value in the conservation of the stocks.

Today many people, particularly in the Western world, see whaling as barbaric and eating whale meat as close to cannibalism. Anti-whaling groups have been especially critical of Japan, and their anti-whaling campaigns have ranged from ecotage and consumer boycotts to attempts to change Japanese views. At first sight, it seems they have had some success. Images of "cute" whales and dolphins adorn bridges, gateways, post offices, fire stations, manholes, and *pachinko* parlors. The number of Japanese who go whale-watching has soared, and visitors to "Whaleland" – a museum located in a whaling town – are invited to listen to "the messages of the whales." Certainly, the Japanese have not been immune to Western discourses on whales.

At the same time, there is considerable resentment against Western environmentalists as well as the International Whaling Commission for what many Japanese see as a double standard. When the United States goes to great lengths to secure quotas of endangered bowhead whales to its Alaskan population while denying Japanese whalers the right to hunt the non-endangered minke whales, this triggers a national discourse that asserts the Japanese are victims of Western racial prejudices. It is felt that not only whaling but Japanese culture and its most important symbol, food, is under attack. In response, eating whale meat has acquired new significance: to some it has become a ritual act through which the partakers express their belonging to the Japanese nation. Moreover, whaling festivals, music and dances – most of which underscore the interdependence of the supernatural, human and whale worlds – have been strengthened and even reinvented to foster feelings of local identities in the name of cultural diversity.

Two global discourses on the uniqueness of whales and on the value of cultural diversity meet in Japan without creating contradictions. While "Whaleland" asks people to "feel like a whale," its souvenir shop sells whale meat and other whale products. Compassion does not rule out consumptive use, and their coexistence is made possible by the holistic and contextual approach to nature found both in Buddhism and Shinto.

Arne Kalland

Further Reading

Akimichi T., P.J. Asquith, H. Befu, T.C. Bestor, S.R. Braund, M.M.R. Freeman, H. Hardacre, M. Iwasaki, A. Kalland, L. Manderson, B.D. Moeran and J. Takahashi. *Small-*

type *Coastal Whaling in Japan*. Edmonton: Boreal Institute for Northern Studies, Occasional Paper No. 27, 1988.

Japan, Government of. *Papers on Japanese Small-type Coastal Whaling Submitted by the Government of Japan to the International Whaling Commission, 1986–1996*. Tokyo: The Government of Japan, 1997.

Kalland, Arne. "Japanese Perceptions of Whales and Dolphins." In J. Knight, ed. *Wildlife in Asia*. London: Curzon Press, 2002.

Kalland, Arne and Brian Moeran. *Japanese Whaling: End of an Era?* London: Curzon Press, 1992.

Manderson, Lenore and Haruko Akatsu. "Whale Meat in the Diet of Ayukawa Villagers." *Ecology of Food and Nutrition* 30 (1993), 207–20.

Naumann, Nelly. "Whale and Fish Cult in Japan: A Basic Feature of Ebisu Worship." *Asian Folklore Studies* 33:1 (1974), 1–15.

See also: Animals; Buddhism – East Asian; Cetacean Spirituality; Dolphins and New Age Religion; Fishers; Japanese Love of Nature; Japanese Religions; Radical Environmentalism (and adjacent, Rodney Coronado and the Animal Liberation Front); Watson, Paul – and the Sea Shepherd Conservation Society; Zen Buddhism.

Whales and Whaling

Whales (or cetaceans, a term that also include dolphins and porpoises) have fascinated people all over the world and figure prominently in myths from the Greeks of antiquity to contemporary Amazonians and Californian New Age adherents. The best-known myth in Western societies is probably the biblical story of Jonah who was swallowed by a huge "fish" (usually believed to be a whale). The myth may symbolically represent Christ's crucifixion, entombment and resurrection on the third day, with the darkness of the whale's womb representing Hell. This is a very different perspective than that in an Inuit myth where the interior of the whale – its soul and heart – is a young and beautiful maiden who demands only one thing from her guests: never to touch the oil-lamp. But a raven cannot resist touching the sacred flame, the heart of the whale, whereupon the maiden dies. In this myth the whale's interior may represent a Garden of Eden destroyed by human greed and curiosity. The myths disclose very different views on the human–nature relationship, but we should be careful not to draw premature conclusions about their impact on management ethics.

Several themes can be recognized in many of the myths. Some of them are trivial: whales assist people to catch fish, save them from drowning or engage playfully with human beings. Others are more spiritual. In many cultures whales are seen as embodied deities. In Greek mythology, Apollo turned himself into a dolphin to rescue people lost in a gale; in Japan whales might be regarded as the embodiment of the patron deity of fishing; and in Vietnam cetaceans receive human-like funerals to become "Angels of the Sea." In most cases the whale is beneficial, but on Tikopia in the Solomon Islands stranded whales represent manifestations of potentially harmful spirits that must be appeased.

Another common theme is metamorphosis, particularly between dolphins and human beings. Both in the Amazon and in Micronesia, dolphins are believed to take human form to attend village celebrations, but the metamorphosis may also go the other way. According to Greek mythology, the first dolphins came into existence once the wine god Dionysus traveled between the Greek islands. Discovering that the crew plotted to sell him as a slave, he transformed the oars into snakes and filled the ship with vines. In panic the crew jumped into the sea where Poseidon, the god of the seas, took pity and turned them into the first dolphins. In many Pacific societies people are believed to transform into dolphins when they die, particularly if they have drowned, and the Haida in British Columbia believed that in such cases they would take the form of a killer whale. From here it was but a short step to regard whales as ancestors and guardians.

A related theme is anthropomorphism; whales live in societies remarkably similar to those of human beings. In Oceania, in the Amazon and on the American Northwest Coast, whales live in underworld societies where they behave and live much like human beings. People and whales live in parallel worlds; the whales may even be known as "underwater people." The parallel marine and terrestrial worlds may also create a pairing of land and sea creatures, a common phenomenon in much of the Pacific. The ritual pairing of taro and whales seems to be particularly common in Micronesia, as on the Woleai atoll in the western Caroline Islands. One interpretation is that whales and taro constitute important binary oppositions symbolizing the dualities of land versus sea and male versus female. Similar pairing has been reported for killer whales and wolves among the Siberian Chukchee and American Northwest Coast Indians. In some cases each marine species has a counterpart on land.

Whale-related myths are not found only among whalers, but it is among whalers that we find the most elaborate beliefs and practices. Most whalers share with hunter-gatherers throughout the world the belief that the prey voluntarily gives itself to the hunter. This notion is strong among the Inuit and Japanese as well as in Micronesia. The exception are whalers in Western societies where, for example, Icelanders and Norwegians may rather regard whales as a gift from God. In either case, the whalers become tied in relationships of indebtedness. Svend Foyn, the Norwegian inventor of modern whaling and a very pious man, felt the same obligation to utilize all parts of the carcass as has been reported from Alaska and Japan, and among the Faroese it may be regarded not only as laziness but also as a sinful act *not* to catch and accept this gift from God.

However, the notion of indebtedness is much stronger and more all-encompassing in non-Western societies, where whaling typically is seen as a sacred act that unites animals and human beings in webs of reciprocity. This is particularly noteworthy among the Iñupiat in northern Alaska where people and bowhead whales are believed to communicate in subtle ways. In order to attract a whale, the hunter and his family must prove that they are worthy of the whale's sacrifice. The whales are believed to be very knowledgeable and able to hear, see and smell over long distances and can immediately tell a good and generous person from a bad and stingy one. Great care must therefore be taken not to displease the whale, or else the animal will evade the hunter. Conflicts, noise, quick movements, dirt, blood, and death are all believed to be offensive to the whale and must be avoided.

A number of taboos have to be observed during the preparation for the whaling season, during the hunts as well as during butchering and distribution of the meat. Some of these are shared with other whaling cultures. Boats and equipment must be repaired, painted and cleaned before the season can commence, and new clothing prepared. During hunts, whalers may observe taboos pertaining to food, clothes, shelter and behavior. Among the Inuit, as well as in Norway, one should keep land clearly separated from the sea: the Inuit may refrain from eating caribou and berries during the whaling seasons, and in the past did not bring dogs to the ice at this time. Most Norwegian whalers will not bring waffles, goat cheese or rucksacks aboard the vessel. Nor should they mention terrestrial animals by their proper names. In Lamalera, Indonesia, this prohibition extends to places, whales, and persons as well.

In times of poor catches, whalers may perform magic rites. The Lamalera whaler may "turn the luck" by washing his mouth with holy water, formerly with blood. Sometimes the magic may involve deliberate breaking of taboos. A Norwegian whaler, who for a long period of time had been stuck in port due to adverse weather conditions, smeared horse excrement (doubly defiling because the dung came from a farm animal) on the cannon, the most sacred place on board. The storm calmed and the crew caught a minke whale just outside the harbor.

Most such beliefs and practices are shared with fishermen, as is the commonly found taboos against women in whaling. There are Norwegian whalers who still feel uneasy when women are on board, as they are believed to bring bad luck. But women have also more positive roles to play. One wife used to spit on the cannon at her husband's departure, and intercourse shortly before the voyage is held to be beneficial to the hunt. The ambiguous position of women in whaling is very evident among many Inuit, and formerly, among the Northwest Coast Indian whalers as well. Although women are not allowed on the ice during whaling, the wives of whaling captains play crucial roles, to the extent that captains may say that "I'm not the great hunter, my wife is." Before the season she may perform a ceremony directed to the moon asking for whales, and in another rite she may represent a whale symbolically being harpooned – it has even been suggested that she *is* the whale. The close association between the wife and whale is also expressed during the hunt. Details vary, but women have been, and some still are, severely restricted in their movements while their husbands are out whaling. Wives of Alaskan whalers sometimes remain quiet and move cautiously during the hunt. Researchers are divided whether to interpret this behavior as imitative magic acts meant to calm or to attract the whale. It is certainly a way to underline gender roles.

If everything is right (i.e., all preparations have been properly done, taboos have been observed, appropriate charms and songs have been used, and the captain's generous wife is quietly at home and at peace with the community), the whale is believed to come and give itself as food to the people. In the past, this meant that the whale should be handled with respect. In northern Alaska, a successful catch initiated a ritual period during which time no sharp implement should be used for fear of hurting the whale's shade. However, recently much of the respect has given way to merrymaking and a festive mood. But the captain's wife is still given the flipper to keep for the whaling festival, and she may make the first ritual cuts and offer the whale a drink of water in a ceremony to welcome the whale to the community. The head is, at times with great ceremony, returned to sea so that the spirit can reincarnate and return as a whale.

Similar beliefs and practices have been reported elsewhere. On the Woleai atoll in the Caroline Islands, for example, an eight-day period of taboos and rituals was imposed after a pod of dolphins was caught, and during this time many of the gender roles were reversed. And in Japan, the tip of the tail is presented to the Shinto altar on board the whaling boat, and on shore people pay respect to the whales in Buddhist memorial rites.

In return for giving themselves to the hunters, people are morally obliged not only to make the fullest possible utilization of the carcasses but also to share them with others. Generosity and sharing are among the highest values in most hunting societies. And the whales will know to reward the generous. Among the Inuit in particular, there is a notion that the more one gives away, the more will come – a notion that, together with a belief in whale reincarnation, does not easily promote sustainable use of the resources. The whaling captain and his wife will feast the people several times during the year. The most important event is the whaling festival, *nalukataq*, held in

June after the end of the bowhead whaling season. Held inside a sacred ring, this three-day feast is a major social event among the Iñupiat. But the feast is also held in gratitude and honor to the whales caught, and as a reenactment of the hunt itself. The meals mark a communion with the whale's soul, thus uniting people and whales spatially and temporally. Hence, the feast not only marks the end of one whaling season, but begins the preparations for the next. The ritual distribution of meat is an invitation for the whales to come again the following year.

Since the 1960s, there has been a marked shift in many people's perceptions of whales, particularly in the industrialized Western world. Several whale stocks had by that time become severely depleted and whaling became a symbol of environmental destruction. A new image of the whale was created and this was endowed with all the qualities we would like to see in our fellow human beings: kindness, caring, playfulness. An important element of this new image is the notion that whales are extraordinarily intelligent. This is widely believed, although the cetacean brain according to Dr. Margaret Klinowska – mammalian researcher at the University of Cambridge and a member to IUCN Cetacean Specialist Group – is quite primitive. In an article in *New Scientist*, she suggests that when the whales returned to live in the oceans some 20 to 40 million years ago, their brains were stuck at a stage today only found among the most primitive terrestrial mammals such as hedgehogs and bats. Another widely held notion is that whales, particularly small toothed whales like dolphins and porpoises, are spiritual beings.

At first sight these perceptions seem to resemble those held by many non-Western whalers. This is, however, to ignore one fundamental difference. According to the worldviews of Inuit and Japanese whalers, among others, the spirituality of the whales creates webs of reciprocity linking whales and whalers. Whereas their view helps to bridge the divide between animal and human realms, Western environmentalists tend to do the opposite. This is particularly the case with animal rights advocates, such as Tom Regan, who claims that whales have rights not to be disturbed in any way, whether for commerce, research or recreation.

The final connection between human and animal worlds is thereby broken. Not even beached whales may be utilized. The Maori, the indigenous people of New Zealand, have recently been denied access to stranded whales, which they regard as theirs by treaty rights. Seen as gifts from Tangaroa – God of the Ocean – beached whales have been utilized for their meat, oil, teeth, and bones, and access to them has become a symbol in the Maori struggle to safeguard their rights as indigenous people. The Maori, hosting the 3rd General Assembly of the World Council of Whalers, in 2001, underlined the importance of this issue.

Other native peoples see whaling practices as part of their cultural revival. In 1999, the Makah in Washington State took their first gray whale in about seventy years amid a storm of protests from animal rights groups. One of the leaders of the campaign against Makah whale hunting was Paul Watson of the Sea Shepherd Conservation Society. In a 1973 dream at Wounded Knee, Watson allegedly received an instruction from a bison to save all marine mammals, particularly whales. Whereas the U.S. Government defended the rights of the Makah, it reacted strongly against Canada when the Inuit there resumed bowhead whaling in the 1990s. In retaliation the United States has vetoed all discussions of marine mammal issues at the Arctic Council.

The International Whaling Commission has authorized "aboriginal subsistence whaling" that shows strong cultural ties related to whaling and the use of whales. The Japanese have long argued that they have strong cultural ties to whaling, but Norway did so only after resuming commercial whaling in 1993. Japan had not resumed commercial whaling as of 2004. Whale protectionists have tended to divide humankind into two opposing categories: those who care for the Earth versus those who seek short-term profit. As long as native peoples do not engage in trade (i.e., "live close to nature"), their takes of whales may not upset this dichotomy. In this worldview, whales serve as totem for "nature-loving" people: whales are not only used as an emblem by protectionists who care about nature, but protectionists also claim a ritual and spiritual relationship between themselves and whales. But the totem system of the protectionists is different from those reported from non-Western societies. In combination with a missionary zeal, it is more than a system of classification; it can be argued that it has unleashed a crusade against those with other perceptions and ideas. To whalers around the world the protectionists and their governments are therefore little better than fanatical fundamentalists, again in plain contrast to the importance of context found in many non-Western creeds.

Arne Kalland

Further Reading

Alkire, William H. "Porpoises and Taro." *Ethnology* 7 (1968), 280–89.

Alpers, Antony. *The Book of Dolphins*. London: John Murray, 1960.

Kalland, Arne. "Management by Totemization: Whale Symbolism and the Anti-whaling Campaign." *Arctic* 46:2 (1993), 124–33.

Lantis, Margaret. "The Alaskan Whale Cult and its Affinities." *American Anthropologist* (n.s.) 40 (1938), 438–64.

Slater, Candace. *Dance of the Dolphin: Transformation and Disenchantment in the Amazonian Imagination*. Chicago: The University of Chicago Press, 1994.

Taylor, J. Garth. "The Arctic Whale Cult in Labrador." *Études/Inuit/Studies* 9:2 (1985), 121–32.

Turner, Edith. "American Eskimos Celebrate the Whale: Structural Dichotomies and Spirit Identities among the Inupiat of Alaska." *The Drama Review* 37:1 (1993), 98–114.

See also: Animals; Biocentric Religion – A Call for; Cetacean Spirituality; Dolphins and New Age Religion; Elephants; Hyenas; Nile Perch; Primate Spirituality; Radical Environmentalism (and adjacent, Rodney Coronado and the Animal Liberation Front); Watson, Paul – and the Sea Shepherd Conservation Society; Whales and Japanese Culture.

White, Lynn (1907–1987) – Thesis of

The "Lynn White thesis," articulated in its most well-known form in White's "The Historical Roots of Our Ecologic Crisis," (1967) was one of the most important interpretations of history to come out of medieval studies in the second half of the twentieth century. Linking the ethos of medieval Christianity to the emergence of what White called an "exploitative" attitude toward nature in the Western world during the Middle Ages, White's ideas set off an extended debate about the role of religion in creating and sustaining the West's increasingly successful control of the natural world through technology. The explosiveness of this debate, which still reverberates, was touched off by a confluence of factors: urgency in the late 1960s and 1970s over the newly discovered environmental crisis, White's ability to reach an audience beyond that of professional historians, and the perception that White's ideas constituted an "attack" on Christianity which needed to be answered before additional damage was done to the value of conventional religious beliefs. Alongside and to some extent at odds with this debate, were the responses to White's work by medieval historians and historians of technology. These historians, concerned with specific issues raised by historical evidence and methods, found much to criticize about White's arguments, yet acknowledged White as the founder and shaper of the new field to which they themselves now belonged. White's ideas, and the range of responses to them, constitute an essential chapter in contemporary discussion about the relationship of religion and attitudes toward nature.

Lynn Townsend White, Jr. was the first American historian seriously to examine the role of technological invention in the Middle Ages. Although best known in the larger world for his ideas on the causes of contemporary environmental problems, within the scholarly community he was regarded first and foremost as a pioneer in the field of medieval technology. After receiving his Ph.D. from Harvard in 1938, he taught briefly at Princeton and Stanford until becoming president of Mills College in 1943. In 1958 he left Mills and until his retirement in 1974 was Professor of History at the University of California at Los Angeles, where he published *Medieval Technology and Social Change* (1962), demonstrating the profound effects of technological innovation on medieval society, and *Medieval Technology and Religion: Collected Essays* (1978). He continued to write and engage in intellectual debate until his death in 1987.

White's work was informed by his view that not only were the Middle Ages the decisive period in the genesis of Western technological supremacy but that the uniquely activist character of medieval Christianity provided the "psychic foundations" of modern technological inventiveness. White was hardly the first scholar to associate Christianity with the birth of Western science and technology. Max Weber, Robert Forbes, and Ernst Benz, among others, had earlier suggested general causal links. However, White refined these arguments by pointing not only to broad elements within the Judeo-Christian tradition (the biblical mandate of Genesis 1:28 giving humankind "dominion over the Earth," Christian compassion, the destruction of pagan animism, and the notion of matter as inert material) but also to the specific characteristics of Western monasticism as the fundamental cause of Western technological development. European monks, White argued, believed work to be an essential form of worship and embodied this assertion not only in the *Rules* governing their lives but also in their practice of their faith. Monastic communities spearheaded new technological techniques. Their cathedrals, in marked contrast to Byzantine churches, were typically equipped with mechanical clocks and organs, two of the most complex machines known prior to the early modern period. Additional evidence that medieval Christianity sanctioned technological advance can be found in manuscript illuminations, among them a ninth-century illustration of David's army using a rotary grindstone driven by a mechanical crank to sharpen their swords while the heathen enemy uses an old-fashioned whetstone, and a fifteenth-century illustration of a personification of the virtue of Temperance, standing on a windmill, a bridle and bit in her mouth, spurs on her feet, holding eyeglasses and wearing a clock on her head. This kind of evidence, taken together with the record of medieval technological invention, White argued, demonstrated that deep-seated values embedded within Latin Christianity made the pursuit of technology appear morally virtuous, leading ultimately not only to Western technological dominance but also to the continuing impact on the environment of an aggressive stance toward nature.

White's ideas on the relationship of Christian values, technological dynamism and environmental decline can only properly be understood within the context of his overall approach to the study of history. White believed that religion was perhaps the most important force shaping human societies and, furthermore, that religious values often operated below the level of conscious expression yet had direct effects on human behavior. As a medievalist, he was inclined to see the Middle Ages as the wellspring of Western culture. He also thought that the study of history was not a merely antiquarian enterprise but held meaningful lessons for the present. Finally, despite his negative assessment in "Roots," elsewhere he frequently asserted that technology was a fundamentally humane and liberating force, and he implicitly suggests an image of an inherently dynamic, progressive and Christian West in which "values" rather than politics or economics determine history. These underlying views informed his work, giving it a power and resonance beyond narrower historical interpretations.

The impact of White's thesis on the community of environmentalists, philosophers of technology, and religion scholars concerned with environmental issues was immediate and long lasting. In the twenty years following the publication of "The Historical Roots of Our Ecologic Crisis," over two hundred books and articles used White's ideas as a focal point. His ideas penetrated the popular press, appearing in *Time Magazine, Horizon, The New York Times, The Boy Scout Handbook* and *The Sierra Club Bulletin*. The great bulk of these responses were to one particular aspect of White's argument, his claim in "Roots" that Christianity inculcated a specifically "exploitative" attitude toward nature and consequently that Christianity bore "a great burden of guilt" for the current environmental crisis. Biblical scholars and eco-theologians, among them James Barr, Carl Braaten, John Cobb, and Joseph Sittler, argued instead that the Judeo-Christian tradition could more accurately be described as mandating a care-taking or stewardship relationship to the natural world; Christianity therefore was not part of the problem, but part of the solution to environmental issues. Guidance should be sought from those many elements within the Judeo-Christian tradition that mandated that humans should be the guardians of nature, not its despoilers. Paradoxically, although many eco-theologians argued vociferously against White, they could use his thesis to reinforce the view that environmentalism was at bottom a religious and ethical movement. Like White, they believed that religious values were the most effective antidote to environmental degradation and, like White, who had suggested that St. Francis be made the patron saint of ecologists, they believed that Christianity was a sufficient repository of environmentally sensitive attitudes.

Among historians and philosophers of technology, however, White's thesis stimulated a rather different debate. These scholars called for a closer look at the history of Western attitudes toward nature, labor and the environment and questioned whether White's characterization of medieval values might be overdrawn. In company with the eco-theologians – scholars such as Susan Power Bratton, Paul Santmire, Roger D. Sorrel, and Clarence Glacken – White found an appreciation for nature on its own terms and a sense that human use of nature and animals should be governed by spiritual and moral obligations found to be normative within medieval theology. A detailed study by Jeremy Cohen of the medieval exegesis of Genesis 1:28 showed that medieval commentators typically dealt with questions of God's covenant and human sexuality, bypassing the issue of technological dominion of nature altogether. George Ovitt, Jr. argued, against White, that by the thirteenth century most monastic orders no longer directly performed work with their hands and, far from elevating manual labor in and of itself, consistently subordinated it to spiritual ends. A number of scholars provided evidence that non-Western and pre-Christian cultures also had records of environmental damage. Other scholars, including Carl Mitcham, John Passmore, Robin Attfield and others, found a sympathetic attitude toward human control of the natural environment in Classical, chiefly Stoic, writers, similarly cutting into White's argument that Christianity had a uniquely aggressive approach to nature. Finally, some writers questioned whether White had done more than show an association between Christianity and technology in an age in which a religious perspective permeated every dimension of human life. Had White shown that religion was a cause of technological development, or simply that technological development taking place for economic and political reasons was framed in Christian terms by medieval and later people?

This broad range of responses demonstrated that the links between religion, technology and environmental decline were hardly as direct or straightforward as White had made them appear. Nevertheless, White's powerful and original reading of history, which has shaped a generation of scholarship, remains the touchstone for current and future discussion.

Elspeth Whitney

Further Reading

Hargrove, Eugene C., ed. *Religion and Environmental Crisis*. Athens, GA and London: University of Georgia Press, 1986.

Livingstone, David N. "The Historical Roots of Our Ecological Crisis: A Reassessment." *Fides et Historia* 26 (1994), 38–55.

Ovitt, George, Jr. *The Restoration of Perfection: Labor and Technology in Medieval Culture*. New Brunswick, NJ: Rutgers University Press, 1987.

White, Lynn, Jr. *Medieval Religion and Technology: Collected Essays*. Berkeley and Los Angeles: University of California Press, 1978.

White, Lynn, Jr. "The Historical Roots of Our Ecologic Crisis." *Science* 155: 3767 (10 March 1967), 1203–1207.

White, Lynn, Jr. *Medieval Technology and Social Change.* London: Oxford University Press, 1962.

Whitney, Elspeth. "Lynn White, Ecotheology, and History." *Environmental Ethics* 15 (1993), 151–69.

See also: Ecology and Religion; Radical Environmentalism; Religious Environmentalist Paradigm; Religious Studies and Environmental Concern; Sittler, Joseph A., Jr.

Whitehead, Alfred North (1861–1947)

Alfred North Whithead's life and work can be divided into three relatively distinct phases: an early period of mathematics and logic (1885–1913), a middle period of epistemology and philosophy of science, (1914–1924) and a later period of constructive metaphysics (1924ff.).

In 1885 Whitehead became a fellow of Trinity College in Cambridge where he remained until 1910. His *Treatise on Universal Algebra* in 1898 won him election to the Royal Society in 1903, but the mathematical period was epitomized by *Principia Mathematica* I–III (1910–1913), co-authored with Bertrand Russell, Whitehead's earlier student. *Principia Mathematica* argued that mathematical symbols are derived from intuitive schemes of logical reasoning. This rooting of abstract mathematical concepts in basic human activities anticipated a tenet in his later constructive metaphysics, as did his distinction between pure and applied mathematics, laid out in *An Introduction to Mathematics* (1911), which can be seen as a forerunner of the later distinction between eternal objects (EOs), or mere possibilities, and the actual occasions (AOs), which embody specific configurations of order.

In his middle period Whitehead worked mostly in London, where he taught mathematics at University College (1910–1914), and held a professorship in Applied Mathematics at the Imperial College of Science and Technology (1914–1924). Already in *The Concept of Nature* (1920) Whitehead aimed to overcome the "bifurcation of nature," which is the result of a mind–body dualism but also follows from the epistemic dichotomy between "real" nature and "mere" phenomena. Whitehead's way here departed from Russell's. Since the apprehension of the world is part of the way the world is, "knowledge is ultimate" (Whitehead 1920: 22). Whitehead here laid the ground for his later doctrine of panpsychism (the view that mental properties apply to all things, including atoms).

In 1924 Whitehead moved to Harvard University where he remained Professor of Philosophy until his retirement in 1937. In *Science and the Modern World* (1925) he set out to account philosophically for the new physics of relativity and quantum theory. With relativity he argued that there is no simple location of things as assumed by Newtonian physics; space-time-matter makes up a unified field of internally related energies-and-events. With quantum theory he argued for a temporal atomicity, according to which the constituents of matter are not solid substances but ephemeral events (cf. Planck's Constant). This view was later developed in his main work, *Process and Reality* (1929). In contrast to a mechanical view of nature, however, Whitehead endorsed a panexperientialist position. Actual occasions "prehend" their immediate past environment and possess a freedom in the process of their becoming; immediately after their actualization they perish and become the stuff for future processes of emergence, or "concrescence."

Since *Religion in the Making* (1926), Whitehead assumed three ultimate principles, 1) creativity, or the chaotic energy presupposed by all actual occasions, 2) eternal objects as the source of information or possibility, and 3) actual occasions which combine creativity with some specific combination of eternal objects. Neither creativity nor eternal objects "exist" on their own, but only as ingredients in actual occasions. God is the chief example of these metaphysical principles. Just as anything else, God is an actual entity with both physical and mental aspects. God's "consequent nature" is derived from the past occasions of the world, while God's "primordial nature" is derived from the divine envisagement of eternal possibilities.

As said in *Process and Reality*, God is both a creature of the world, and the world's creator (Whitehead 1978: 348). Accordingly, God is not the creative source of all that is (as in the Abrahamic traditions), but the formative source of order and novelty in the universe (as in Plato). God is therefore not omnipotent, but has the consistent will of stimulating the growth of complexity in the universe by offering divine "lures" to each actual occasion. God is only one agent among others, but is a formative cause in all worldly events. Moreover, God is one actuality among others, but God is unique by being an everlasting actual entity who never perishes. As everlasting, God encompasses all past reality, which achieves "objective immortality" by being preserved and evaluated in the "consequent nature" of God.

Whitehead considered his own thought as an "inversion of Kant's philosophy." The world cannot be construed on the basis of a perceiving subject; rather, mind and subjectivity are "superjects" which are co-determined by their environment and immediate past. Whitehead termed his own philosophy "organicism," but his metaphysical scheme seems to be influenced by mathematics and physics more than by evolutionary thought. It has been up to later process thinkers such as Charles Hartshorne, John B. Cobb, David Ray Griffin and Charles Birch to develop the evolutionary and ecological aspects of process thought. In the science–religion discussion, Whitehead's philosophy has been carried forward by Ian Barbour.

Niels Henrik Gregersen

Further Reading

Barbour, Ian G. *Religion and Science: Historical and Contemporary Issues.* San Francisco: Harper, 1997.

Ford, Lewis S. *The Emergence of Whitehead's Metaphysics 1925–1929.* Albany: State University of New York Press, 1984.

Hartshorne, Charles. *Whitehead's Philosophy: Selected Essays 1935–1970.* Lincoln and London: Nebraska University Press, 1972.

Lowe, Victor. *Alfred North Whitehead: The Man and his Work*, vols 1–2. Baltimore: Johns Hopkins University Press, 1985/1990.

Schilpp, Paul Arthur, ed. *The Philosophy of Alfred North Whitehead* (The Library of Living Philosophers vol. III). Evanston-Chicago: Northwestern University Press, 1941.

Whitehead, Alfred North. *Process and Reality: An Essay in Cosmology* (1929). Corrected edition by David Ray Griffin and Donald W. Sherburne. New York: Free Press, 1978.

Whitehead, Alfred North. *Religion in the Making.* New York: MacMillan, 1926.

Whitehead, Alfred North. *The Concept of Nature.* Cambridge: Cambridge University Press, 1920 (reprinted 1986).

See also: Christianity (7f) – Process Theology; Cobb, John; Process Philosophy.

Whitman, Walt (1819–1892)

Walt Whitman, the self-professed bard of the people, was born on Long Island in 1819. Whitman spent much of his life in Brooklyn, where he worked as a printer, school teacher, and journeyman. These experiences and the myriad people of New York who Whitman met as a result would later frame the ideas of democracy and equality at the heart of so many of his poems.

Whitman's best-known collection of poems, *Leaves of Grass*, probably would have – like its author – fallen into utter obscurity had it not been for a letter of praise for the volume written by New England Transcendentalist Ralph Waldo Emerson. Emerson extolled the volume for its unadorned language and bold treatment of nature in a letter written to Whitman, which the latter published in well-read papers for all to see. Whitman's decision to do so was a successful marketing ploy: following the publication of this letter, the poet and his volume were vaulted into the literary public eye. It ought to come as no surprise that Emerson was taken by Whitman's poetry: influenced by Eastern texts such as the Bhagavadgita, Whitman articulated many of the beliefs held and articulated by Emerson and other Transcendentalists, such as Thoreau, who was a welcome visitor at Whitman's home in Brooklyn.

Whitman's writing also demonstrates his affinity for the works of long-time friend, John Burroughs, and his talents as a naturalist. Readers of his *Specimen Days* will find detailed descriptions of the Midwestern prairie and the geology of the American West. The work also contains extensive lists of wildflowers and animals as well as keen observations concerning migration patterns of many bird species and panegyric praise for the immense power of the Mississippi River.

Walt Whitman was raised in a family with long-standing ties to the Quaker Church; however, any influence he might have received from the Society of Friends is eclipsed by his Eastern and Transcendent cosmology. Whitman, like Emerson and others, held that any idea of God is best understood in terms of a universal energy that manifests itself in every living creature. Although Whitman's later writings do suggest a turn toward Christian theology, much of his *oeuvre* is marked by this sense of universal connection and ecstasy.

Whitman worshipped the physical: the blade of grass that revealed the oneness of the Earth and the cosmos, the prostitutes in Philadelphia, the odor of an armpit after a day of work. He saw a clear division between the soul and the body and contended that the fault of many religions is that they reject the physical while privileging the spiritual. In place of this ideology, Whitman suggested that we view the two aspects as married to one another, and he set about celebrating the divine within the maligned physical existence. To this end, he contended that the universe and all its transcendental splendor could best be found in the common elements of the natural world. Our willingness to step outside the constructs of society and self in order to revel in these elements allows us to actualize these ideas of universal connection in our own lives. This idea of universal connection is often expressed by Whitman in highly sexualized terms. In "Song of Myself," Whitman depicts spiritual rapture through sexual union. This connection, he held, makes manifest the unity between individuals, their environment, and the divine.

Whitman's belief that sexual union – both metaphoric and literal – grants access to the eternal was the cause of much controversy surrounding his work. His homoerotic overtones along with his unconventional and often explicit marriage of sexuality, nature, and God caused him to fall out of favor with Emerson, his initial champion. He was also fired from his governmental job at the Bureau of Indian Affairs in the U.S. Department of the Interior for the "obscene" nature of these beliefs. The controversy surrounding Whitman was heightened by his self-described role as a messianic figure. Convinced of the verity of his beliefs, Whitman saw himself as a sort of savior or oracle for the people, and he held that his "democratic literature" articulating this universal connection could help Americans fully actualize their spiritual imaginations.

These same elements of Whitman's poetry are what

have allowed for his continued popularity. Whitman's willingness to break out of hegemonic culture and its mores in order to celebrate the mundane and unconventional has ensured his relevance today. His belief in the organic connection of all things, coupled with his organic development of a poetic style that breaks with many formal conventions have caused many scholars and critics to celebrate him for his innovation. His idea of universal connection and belief in the spirituality present in a blade of grass succeeded in transmitting a popularized version of Eastern theology and Whitman's own brand of environmentalism for generations of readers.

Kathryn Miles

Further Reading

Greenspan, Ezra, ed. *The Cambridge Companion to Whitman*. New York: Cambridge University Press, 1995.

Maslan, Mark. *Whitman Possessed*. Baltimore, MD: Johns Hopkins University Press, 2001.

Reynolds, David. *Walt Whitman's America*. New York: Knopf, 1995.

See also: Bhagavadgita; Emerson, Ralph Waldo; Friends – Religious Society of (Quakers); Nature Religion in the United States; Religious Environmentalist Paradigm; Romanticism – American; Romanticism – Western toward Asian Religions; Transcendentalism.

Wicca

Wicca emerged in 1940s' England as a highly ritualistic, nature-venerating, polytheistic, magical and religious system, which made use of Asian religious techniques, but operated within a predominantly Western framework. It arose from cultural impulses of the nineteenth century, in particular from the occult revival of the 1880s onwards and Romantic literary rediscovery of Classical ideas of nature and deity. Various threads were gathered together and woven into Wicca by Gerald B. Gardner (1884–1964), a British civil servant who retired in 1936 and lived in Highcliffe and London, England before moving to the Isle of Man in 1954. He visited archeological sites in the Near East, and joined esoteric groups like the Folklore Society, the Co-Masons, the Rosicrucian Fellowship of Crotona, and the Druid Order. Gardner claimed that the Fellowship of Crotona contained a hidden inner group of hereditary witches who initiated him in 1939 and whose rituals he wrote about in fictional form in the novel *High Magic's Aid* (1949) under the pseudonym Scire. Gardner's writing borrowed from many sources, including the work of magician Aleister Crowley (1875–1947), writer D.H. Lawrence (1885–1930), a ritual magic group called The Golden Dawn, Freemasonry, spiritualism, and archeology, to name a few.

According to Gardner, witchcraft had survived the persecutions of early modern Europe and persisted in secret, following the thesis of British folklorist and Egyptologist Margaret Murray (1862–1963). Murray argued in her book, *The Witch Cult in Western Europe* (1921), that an old religion involving a horned god who represented the fertility of nature had survived the persecutions and existed throughout Western Europe. Murray wrote that the religion was divided into covens that held regular meetings based on the phases of the moon and the changes of the seasons. Their rituals included feasting, dancing, sacrifices, ritualized sexual intercourse, and worship of the horned god. In *The God of the Witches* (1933) Murray traced the development of this god and connected the witch cult to fairy tales and Robin Hood legends. She used images from art and architecture to support her view that an ancient vegetation god and a fertility goddess formed the basis of worship for the witch cult.

From the 1940s on many Wiccans believed, based on Murray's work, that they were continuing this ancient tradition of witchcraft. However, since the first appearance of Murray's thesis, historians and other scholars have refuted her evidence and, over time, dismissed most of it. Most, though not all, Wiccans today acknowledge that there is little evidence for a continuous witchcraft tradition, but claim that their religion is a revitalization and re-invention of ancient folk practices that existed in pre-Christian Britain, even if they were not part of any organized tradition. Some Wiccans today continue to identify "The Burning Times," as they call the witch persecutions, as their "holocaust," even though historians have shown that the so-called witches of early modern Europe existed in the imaginations of their persecutors, though many may have participated in folk practices such as herbal healing that were prevalent at the time in the general population.

After the repeal of the 1736 Witchcraft Act in England (an act that made the practice of witchcraft a crime) in 1951, Gardner was able openly to publish accounts of Wicca under his real name in *Witchcraft Today* (1954) and *The Meaning of Witchcraft* (1959). *Witchcraft Today* brought public attention to Gardner and he made numerous media appearances promoting Wicca. Both books contained information on Wicca as it existed at the time and in the following years Gardner initiated many new witches. Covens also sprang up and operated according to the outlines provided by Gardner's books. By the mid-1950s, Wicca had become relatively popular, at least in part because of Gardner's love of publicity, which drew public attention to it. In the early 1960s it was exported to the United States by Raymond Buckland. Gardner died in 1964, but by that time his tradition of Gardnerian Wicca was firmly established.

The religion described in Gardner's books and spread by his students takes nature as a central aspect of devotional life. Gardner's ideas about god and goddess drew from British literature and occult circles that promoted Romanticism's fascination with the gods and goddesses of the ancient world. Over time specific deities such as Demeter and Pan were transformed into an archetypal mother goddess and an archetypal fertility god. According to historian Ronald Hutton this process was complete by the 1940s and represented post-war Britain's desire for and fear of wildness: "the domains that civilized humans had traditionally found most alien and frightening; they were those of the two deities to whom the modern imagination, frightened, jaded, and constricted by aspects of civilized living, had turned" (Hutton 1999: 50). The attraction of urban dwellers to deities that embody nature and rituals associated with seasonal changes that many modern people have lost touch with continues to be an important aspect of Wicca and among the reasons for its growth throughout the twentieth and into the twenty-first century. Gardner's rituals also offered an alternative to the modern world in that participants were nude and sexuality and the body were seen as sacred.

Four main rituals were celebrated on the four seasonal festivals described by Murray as the witches' sabbats (Candlemas, May Day, Lammas, and All-Hallows Eve). Most Wiccans today also celebrate four other festivals: winter solstice, summer solstice, spring equinox and autumn equinox. These eight festivals make up the Wiccan "Wheel of the Year." At each of these seasonal rituals the god and goddess are addressed in their aspects appropriate to the season, and they are embodied by the priest and priestess leading the rituals. For instance, on May Day the goddess/priestess as embodiment of giver of life and nurturer of new seeds is most prominent. Many contemporary Wiccans call this festival Beltain, an Irish name for "Bright Fire," and weddings or "handfastings" are often performed at this time. A midwinter ceremony or Yule ritual might celebrate the return of the sun during the longest night and the rebirth of the sun god. Wiccan festivals are intended to remind participants of the cycle of life, of human death and rebirth, and the changes evident around them in the natural world.

Gardner's Wicca was initially described as a fertility cult rather than a "nature religion," although Wiccan perceptions of both male and female deities are linked to nature and regarded as empowering forces for both men and women. One of Wicca's most well-known ritual texts – *The Great Charge*, written by Gardner's one-time High Priestess and collaborator Doreen Valiente (1922–1999) from earlier versions – concentrates specifically on the Wiccan perception of the goddess as the world of nature. The "Charge" describes her as "the beauty of the green Earth," "the white moon among the stars," "the mystery of the waters," and "the soul of nature who gives life to the universe." The goddess' male counterpart is also connected to nature and moves through The Wheel of the Year. He is The Lord of the Greenwood, Sun King, Corn King, Lord of Life and Death, and Leader of the Wild Hunt.

Wicca is a religion in which the divine is immanent; its goddess and god live in the Earth, the moon, the stars, the bodies of men and women. Humans, nature and gods are all interconnected and sacred. The basic ritual form of Wicca – the circle casting – illustrates another way in which the divine is in the world, not outside it. While different variations on circle casting exist, most circles are oriented with the four cardinal directions and these directions are typically associated with forces of nature: fire, air, water and Earth. Some Wiccans address the "powers" of a particular direction while others address the "winds" while casting their circles. In preparation for ritual work Wiccans shed their clothes or don special robes, then someone marks the perimeter of the circle with a knife or wand and the four directions are greeted and invoked, as a way of asking for the powers that they represent to be present. For Wiccans ritual space is thus oriented in relation to the natural forces identified with each direction, in order to remind participants of their relationship to the world around them.

Since Gardner's first covens, Wicca has spread across North America, northern Europe, Australia, New Zealand and South Africa, evolving, and at times mutating quite dramatically. Wiccans have only a few beliefs that most of them adhere to, and these include "The Witches Rede: An it harm none, do what you will," and "The Law of Threefold Effect," the belief that any action a person commits will return to that person threefold. As Wicca has spread to different parts of the world, debates about belief and practice have surfaced. For instance, in the Southern Hemisphere Wiccans disagree as to how the seasonal rituals of the Wheel of the Year should be celebrated, given that winter solstice/Yule in the Northern Hemisphere is midsummer in the Southern. In the United States and Canada, practices borrowed from North American Indians have been adopted by Wiccans and this cultural appropriation has been criticized by other Wiccans as well as by native people. But this debate means little to some Europeans who turn to Celtic, Saxon or Germanic traditions for inspiration, making links to the supposed indigenous traditions of northern Europe. Likewise, feminist Witchcraft, which was shaped by the American feminist movement, has had a profound impact on Wicca in the United States, and is in part responsible for the fact that many Wiccans have dispensed with the god and focus on one great goddess. In the United States in particular a multitude of derivations have developed, including Reclaiming, Faery Wicca, Dianic Wicca and Seax Wicca, all of which have in turn crossed back to Europe.

Both Gardner and Murray emphasized the importance of polarity, of goddess and god, and identified men with masculine qualities and the god, and women with feminine energy and the goddess. However with the influence of feminism and gay rights movements many Wiccans today believe that same sex couples can work effective rituals together and that men can embody goddess energy just as women can embody the god. Within Wicca there is much diversity of opinion concerning whether or not masculinity and femininity are essential qualities each sex is born with, and these issues remain controversial in some Wiccan communities.

The increase in Wicca's popularity is partly due to the parallel rise in environmental awareness since the 1970s. Vivianne Crowley, a Wiccan priestess and author of *Wicca: The Old Religion in the New Age* (1989), notes the changing emphasis within Wicca from nature veneration to nature preservation: "Wicca . . . moved out of the darkness, the occult world of witchery, to occupy the moral high ground – environmentalism" (Crowley 1998: 177). Crowley asserts the centrality of the veneration of nature, which is "considered to be ensouled, alive, 'divine' . . . The divine [being seen] as a 'force' or 'energy' and as manifest in the world of nature" (1998: 170). She further points out that the processes of nature, such as "conception, birth, mating, parenthood, maturation, death" are portrayed in The Wheel of the Year.

However, Wiccans demonstrate a wide range of attitudes toward protecting the natural world. Some are radical environmentalists while others view nature more abstractly. The development of Wicca was influenced by idealized views of nature in the writings of English Romantics as well as more recent works of literature such as J.R.R. Tolkien's description of the woods of Lothlorien in *The Fellowship of the Ring* (1954). Understandings of nature in Wicca also derive from Western esotericism, particularly as transmitted by nineteenth-century Romanticism. Nature, in esoteric thought, is a reflection of a greater divine reality or part of a greater magical totality, and as such it requires a different level of engagement. The esoteric theory of correspondences portrays the cosmos as complex, plural and hierarchical, with living nature occupying an essential place within it. Nature is at once both an intermediary between humanity and divinity, and imbued with divinity itself. "Nature" is often perceived by Wiccans as something different from "the environment." For those Wiccan groups which retain a link to their heritage in high ritual magic and hence the Western esoteric tradition, there is every reason for a focus on inner nature due to the basic law of magical correspondence: humanity is a part of the cosmos, and therefore any operation performed on or in a person will affect the entire universe. In treating the self as well as nature as sacred center, Wicca follows in the wake of esoteric and occult philosophy, in which these are one and the same. While there may be a spiritual and/or magical engagement with nature, this does not necessarily translate into environmental action.

For some urban-dwelling Wiccans, imaginative descriptions of the natural world may provide a more "real" experience than an actual walk in the woods. Anthropologist Susan Greenwood observed that some Wiccans show no interest in nature other than as a backdrop for rituals, with celebrations held in the woods becoming in effect a celebration of the liberation of the inner self from the domination of the everyday world. "One Wiccan, when invited to go for a walk, cried off because it was raining and he might get his feet wet: 'Can't we just visualize it?' he said" (Greenwood 2000: 113). The Wiccan response to nature is thus often confused, revealing both intimacy and distance as nature is shaped by the Wheel of the Year, sacred circles, and ritual to suit people's needs for relationship with the Earth. There is a turn to nature as a source of revitalization, an attempt to reengage with a nature from which participants feel estranged, to reenchant the natural world which they feel has been exploited and dominated. The veneration of nature, the concern for the Earth, and the pantheism of seeing the divine in all of nature has led to an attitude of reverence for a romanticized wild, untamed landscape on the one hand, and to sadness or revulsion at human estrangement from this ideal, living in towns and cities away from the land, on the other. For some Wiccans veneration of nature and identification as "Wiccan" or "Pagan" manifests as a romantic attachment to the countryside, a dream of living away from towns and nurturing a closer relationship with nature. Some Wiccans do live in rural areas, but most continue to live urban lives and very few depend on the land for their living. Nature and Wiccans' understanding of it are extraordinarily complex, and this is exacerbated by the diversity of contexts in which an examination of Wicca's engagement with nature must occur.

Some Wiccans have become involved in environmental struggles as a way of putting their beliefs into practice. One of the most vocal of these is the American Starhawk, whose writings have been heavily influenced by feminist and environmentalist movements. Starhawk's popular book *The Spiral Dance: A Rebirth of the Ancient Religion of the Great Goddess* (1979) is largely responsible for spreading feminist Wicca in the United States. Starhawk has also been the most vocal American Wiccan in promoting activism of all kinds and has involved herself in numerous protests that range from anti-nuclear demonstrations, to forest activism blocking logging in old-growth redwood groves in northern California, to anti-globalization resistance. Although much of her environmental activism has been in high-profile protests, she has also organized workshops combining watershed conservation and forest ecology with magic and ritual. Other environmentalists also hold Wiccan beliefs and practice "eco-magic," such as organizations like the Dragon Environmental Group in England and both British and American Earth First! radical environmentalists. While Wicca and environmentalism do not automatically go hand in hand, although some Wiccans argue that they should, in practice Wiccans live their relationship to nature in different ways.

Wicca has become a global phenomenon and significant Wiccan communities can be found in most countries inhabited by significant populations of people of European descent, including Great Britain, the United States, Australia, New Zealand, Canada and South Africa, but Wicca has also spread to countries such as Japan that are closely linked to Western cultures by the global economy and media. Gardner's original prototype of a coven meeting in the woods and dancing naked under the trees retains its attraction as a fertility religion that allowed men and women to feel closer to the natural world and to pass on their knowledge by secret initiation, but today it is as likely to be spread through internet sites and how-to books that can be ordered from online stores, even while it maintains a focus on nature.

Joanne Pearson
Sarah M. Pike

Further Reading

Adler, Margot. *Drawing Down the Moon: Witches, Druids, Goddess-Worshippers, and Other Pagans in America Today*. Boston: Beacon Press, 1986 (1979).
Crowley, Vivianne. "Wicca as Nature Religion." In Joanne Pearson, Richard H. Roberts and Geoffrey Samuel, eds. *Nature Religion Today: Paganism in the Modern World*. Edinburgh: Edinburgh University Press, 1998, 170–9.
Gardner, Gerald B. *The Meaning of Witchcraft*. London: Aquarian Press, 1959.
Gardner, Gerald B. *Witchcraft Today*. London: Rider, 1954.
Gibbons, B.J. *Spirituality and the Occult from the Renaissance to the Modern Age*. London: Routledge, 2001.
Greenwood, Susan. *Witchcraft, Magic and the Otherworld: An Anthropology*. Oxford: Berg, 2000.
Harvey, Graham. *Contemporary Paganism: Listening People, Speaking Earth*. New York: New York University Press, 1997.
Hutton, Ronald. *The Triumph of the Moon: A History of Modern Pagan Witchcraft*. Oxford: Oxford University Press, 1999.
Murray, Margaret A. *The Witch Cult in Western Europe: A Study in Anthropology*. Oxford: Clarendon Press, 1921.
Pearson, Joanne. *Wicca: Magic, Spirituality and the "Mystic Other."* London: Routledge, 2005.
Starhawk. *The Spiral Dance: A Rebirth of the Ancient Religion of the Great Goddess*. New York: Harper & Row, 1979.

See also: Animism; Animism – A Contemporary Perspective; Aradia; Astrology; Circle Sanctuary; Donga Tribe; Dragon Environmental Network (United Kingdom); Druids and Druidry; Earth First! and the Earth Liberation Front; Ecofeminism (various); Eisler, Riane; Feminist Spirituality Movement; Freemasonry; Gimbutas, Marija; Goddesses – History of; Golden Dawn; Indigenous Religions and Cultural Borrowing; Middle Earth; New Age; Pagan Calendar; Pagan Festivals; Paganism – Contemporary; Pantheism; Polytheism; Radical Environmentalism; Reclaiming; Shamanism (various); Starhawk; Wicca – Dianic; Z Budapest.

Wicca – Dianic

Dianic Wicca, sometimes called feminist Witchcraft, began in Southern California in 1971, when Z Budapest and five friends met to celebrate the Winter Solstice. The time was ripe for a meeting of Wicca and feminism. Both were gaining in visibility. By 1969, "Marion's Cauldron" was being broadcast over the airwaves regularly in New York City, and Central Park was the site of a 1970 "Witch-In" attended by over 1000. In the same year, some 50,000 people marched down Fifth Avenue in support of the Women's Liberation Movement. A few years earlier, a small group of radical feminists calling themselves W.I.T.C.H. had publicly and theatrically linked the image of the witch to women's empowerment. Arguing that all oppression, including the abuse of nature, was due to male domination, they saw themselves as resistance fighters, and proceeded to use Halloween costumes and guerilla street theater to get their message across with drama and humor. Their success led to autonomous covens of W.I.T.C.H. springing up in major cities across the country.

W.I.T.C.H. was decidedly political, not spiritual. Like other feminists critical of religion, Budapest argued that the spiritual *was* political. She claimed that patriarchal religions had colonized women's souls and her unique contribution was to embrace the image of the witch as a symbol of women's empowerment and use it to create a feminist version of Wicca. Building on the then-popular belief in ancient Goddess-worshipping matriarchies, she called her new tradition Dianic Witchcraft after the Goddess of the Witches in Charles Leland's *Aradia*. That the Goddess Diana was independent of men added to the attraction of the name. Presented as a new religion with ancient roots, the Dianic Craft incorporated many elements of Gardnerian Wicca, so many that it is considered a Wiccan tradition.

Dianic Witches do a radical feminist analysis of gender and power, seeing women's oppression and environmental abuse as intimately linked and firmly rooted in patriarchal religions, in hierarchies that privilege the spiritual over the material, the mind over the body, and men over women. Like other Wiccans, they celebrate the Earth and the turning of the seasons. Unlike them, Dianics also celebrate women's "blood mysteries" – birth, menstruation, birth/lactation, menopause and death – which are understood as women's ability to create life, sustain it, and return it to the Source. In doing this they attempt to link what they believe is the sacred within them to the sacred around them in the natural world.

Divinity is envisioned as an autonomous female goddess. Some Dianics believe she is an entity, others see her as a metaphor for the Earth. Almost all agree that it is not necessary to believe in Goddess in order to experience her, as she is also understood to be immanent in nature as well as the interconnection between every living thing. The dynamic cycle of birth, life and death is represented in Goddess' three aspects of Maiden, Mother and Crone and mirrored in the phases of the moon. This image of the Triple Goddess represents major stages of women's lived experience, and provides a symbol with which they may identify throughout their lives. She is seen as the Original Creatrix, drawing all life out of herself in an act of divine parthenogenesis. She is the matrix from which all else arises. Acknowledging Goddess, the Divine Self, within themselves allows Dianics to spiritually give birth to themselves as they leave behind male-dominated and sometimes misogynist religious conditioning.

Unlike other Wiccans, Dianics do not incorporate concepts of male divinity into their practice and reject the belief in the need for sexual polarity in order to practice magic. Men are traditionally not allowed to participate in Dianic rituals nor become members of Dianic covens.

Hierarchy is seen as a patriarchal "thought form," and most Dianic covens attempt to govern themselves by consensus or through a circle of elders, rather than incorporate the more familiar Wiccan role of high priestess. An exception to this is the McFarland Dianic tradition out of Texas. Developing independently from Budapest's lineage, this feminist group functions with high priestesses and includes men. However its impact has been limited and the name Dianic usually refers to those whose spiritual roots can be traced back to that first winter solstice in Los Angeles.

At least two Dianic groups in the United States do a great deal of teaching, and welcome to their classes any women who are open to "Goddess consciousness," whether or not they are or become Dianics. These are the Reformed Congregation of the Goddess (RCG) out of Madison, Wisconsin, and its affiliate, the Circle of Aradia (CoA) in Los Angeles. Literally thousands of women have passed through their training classes, making their influence felt far beyond their numbers would suggest. Although Starhawk – Witch, theologian and widely read author – is not Dianic, she has also had a significant impact upon the Dianic Craft, especially in the strong commitments to the environment and peace that are present in the practice today.

Wendy Griffin

Further Reading
Barrett, Ruth Rhiannon. "The Power of Ritual." In Wendy Griffin, ed. *Daughters of the Goddess: Studies of Healing, Identity and Empowerment*. Walnut Creek, CA: AltaMira Press, 2000.
Budapest, Z. *The Holy Book of Women's Mysteries, Part II*. Berkley: Susan B. Anthony Books, 1980.
Eller, Cynthia. *Living in the Lap of the Goddess: The Feminist Spirituality Movement in America*. New York: Crossroad Publishing Co., 1993.
Griffin, Wendy. "The Embodied Goddess: Feminist Witchcraft and Female Divinity." *Sociology of Religion* 56:1 (1995), 35–49.

See also: Aradia; Astrology; Circle Sanctuary; Ecofeminism (various); Eisler, Riane; Feminist Spirituality Movement; Gimbutas, Marija; Goddesses – History of; Pagan Festivals; Paganism – Contemporary; Reclaiming; Starhawk; Wicca; Z Budapest.

Wilber, Ken (1949–)

Drawing on thinkers ranging from Plotinus and Aurobindo to Hegel and Piaget, and grounding his own thought in extensive meditation practices, Ken Wilber synthesizes modern science and traditional spirituality to provide a progressive understanding of cosmic, biotic, human, and divine evolution. In *Up From Eden: A Transpersonal View of Human Evolution* (1981), Wilber describes the three basic modes of human development: prepersonal, personal, and transpersonal. The prepersonal characterizes societies oriented by magical and mythical modes of consciousness. Personal consciousness emerges in a few elite persons thousands of years ago and eventually culminated in the mental-egoic consciousness of Enlightenment modernity. Unfortunately, mental-egoic or personal consciousness often (but not always) involves dissociation of ego-mind from body, emotions, nature, female, and God. Mental-egoic consciousness entails heightened death-anxiety, which people (especially men) have sought to assuage through Atman projects that seek to make the mortal ego immortal. The technological domination of nature may be understood in part as such an Atman project. Although alienated and dissociated both from nature and from God, mental-egoic consciousness may continue its evolutionary trajectory toward the centauric stage, which reintegrates mind/body while recognizing the perspectival and thus partial character of worldviews. In subsequent transpersonal stages, humankind would experience the divine presence in all phenomena, thereby generating compassion for all sentient beings. According to Wilber, all phenomena are manifestations of the divine, the Alpha and Omega of cosmic history.

Despite the drawbacks of mental-egoic consciousness, Wilber maintains that worldwide achievement of it and the institutions related to it (including constitutional democratic government, freedom of inquiry, sustainable economic development) could have a dramatic positive impact on humanity's treatment of nature. Rational-democratic societies do not make war on one another; moreover, they can alter their practices in ways that avoid environmental catastrophe, thereby making possible the continuing evolution of consciousness needed for the long-term well-being of the Earth and humankind.

In *Sex, Ecology, Spirituality* (*SES*) (1995) and *A Brief History of Everything* (1996), Wilber lays the groundwork for "integral" thinking. Deemphasizing his earlier emphasis on death anxiety and Atman projects, Wilber now seeks to unite the perennial idea of the Great Chain of Being, as informed by spiritual, cultural, social, and natural scientific evolutionary concepts, with a four-fold set of distinctions allegedly capable of analyzing all phenomena. Drawing on the notion of holons developed by Jan Smuts and Arthur Koestler, Wilber maintains that virtually all phenomena are wholes from one perspective and parts from another. A cell in an organism, for example, is a whole that includes parts, but is also a part of the organism. Emphasizing that holonic evolution generates emergent qualities, Wilber divides the Kosmos into four grand domains: physiosphere, biosphere, noosphere and theosphere. The physiosphere includes the non-biological features of the universe, including the stars and planets that arose in the billions of years following the Big Bang. The biosphere, the domain of life, depends upon the much older and much vaster physiosphere, but involves features that transcend the physiosphere. Finally, the biosphere gives rise to the noosphere, which includes complex sentient life such as mammals and humans. Again, the noosphere both depends on physiosphere and biosphere, but also transcends them, by exhibiting emergent characteristics, including self-consciousness, language, and rationality. The theosphere, which both includes and transcends the other three domains, refers to dimensions of consciousness that include what is traditionally understood by the notion of God.

In a controversial move, Wilber argues that just as the biosphere contains the physiosphere in the sense of comprising all its basic features (although plainly *not* its material expanse), so too the noosphere contains the biosphere in the sense of comprising all its basic features (although not its biotic mass), while adding new ones. Affirming that neither biosphere nor noosphere were "destined" to emerge on Earth, Wilber joins proponents of the anthropic principle in arguing that the cosmos is ordered such that biosphere and noosphere would eventually emerge *somewhere*.

To this vision of cosmic evolution, Wilber adds his four-quadrant analysis. The four quadrants are: Upper Left (UL), individual as experience internally; Upper Right (UR), individual as experienced externally; Lower Left (LL), collective as experienced internally; Lower Right (LR), collective as experienced externally. Consider how the four quadrants may be used to analyze someone purchasing tickets for a figure-skating competition. Seen from UL, the activity is the first-person experience of someone eager to witness athletic and artistic prowess; seen from LL, the person shares certain cultural views about sport, artistic expression, and so on; seen from the UR, the object of investigation is an organism whose constituent parts obey natural laws and whose behavior accords with predictable patterns; from LR, the individual's actions are interpreted in terms of social, political, and economic categories. In *SES*, Wilber reduces the four quadrants to the Big Three: UR/LR, LL, and UL, which correspond to the topics of Kant's critiques of pure reason, practical reason, and judgment. According to Kant, Weber, and Habermas, modernity's triumph was to differentiate among domains (for example, religion, politics, art) that are collapsed together in pre-modern societies. Although the Big Three originally distinguished three legitimate modes of inquiry and behavior (natural science, politics/morality, and personal experience and aesthetic expression), eventually the UR/LR quadrants (natural and social sciences) marginalized the UL and LL quadrants, which take into account domains that can be understood only from the inside.

Wilber argues that a constructive, integral postmodernity will restore legitimacy to all four quadrants. Instead of viewing sentience as an accidental feature of the cosmos, integral thinking adheres to Whiteheadian panpsychism, according to which all phenomena – even atoms – have at least some meager interiority. Greater interior complexity confers higher moral status on entities. Because a cow screams louder than a carrot, many people have fewer moral qualms about eating the latter than the former.

Although endorsing the valid ecological concerns of deep ecologists, Wilber criticizes them for holding "retro-romantic" views involving worship of nature, especially when that "nature" in fact involves the same reductionistic materialism and systems theory that forms what Wilber calls "industrial ontology." Authentic nature worship, as described by nature mystics such as Emerson, involves discerning that material nature is but the lowest-level manifestation of nature, understood as creative Spirit. A vigorous opponent of naïve yearning for pre-modern social formations, while simultaneously a critic of heedless technological exploitation of nature, Wilber affirms the dignity of modernity while acknowledging the crucial contributions of pre-modern peoples. Although his views are at times sharply contested, he is widely admired for his ambitious effort to integrate nature, humankind, and Spirit in order to form a constructive postmodernism that re-enchants the world without inviting personal and social regression.

Michael E Zimmerman

Further Reading

Rothberg, Donald and Sean Kelly, eds. *Ken Wilber in Dialogue*. Wheaton, IL: Quest Books, 1998.

Wilber, Ken. *Collected Works*, 8 vols. Boston: Shambhala, 1999.

Wilber, Ken. *The Marriage of Sense and Soul: Integrating Science and Religion*. New York: Random House, 1998.

Wilber, Ken. *The Eye of Spirit*. Boston: Shambhala, 1997.

Wilber, Ken. *A Brief History of Everything*. Boston: Shambhala, 1996.

Wilber, Ken. *Sex, Ecology, Spirituality: The Spirit of Evolution*. Boston: Shambhala, 1995.

Wilber, Ken. *Up From Eden: A Transpersonal View of Human Evolution*. Boulder: Shambhala, 1981.

Zimmerman, Michael E. "Ken Wilber's Critique of Ecological Spirituality." In David Barnhill and Roger Gottlieb, eds. *Deep Ecology and World Religions*. Albany: SUNY Press, 2001.

See also: Deep Ecology; Ecopsychology; New Age; Perennial Philosophy; Transpersonal Psychology; Whitehead, Alfred North.

Wilderness Religion

The conceptual associations of religion with wilderness, and religion with nature, are enormously complicated, whether considered semantically, historically, epistemologically, metaphysically, scientifically, or ethically. The challenges of definition alone are daunting. "Nature" is one of the most semantically confused words in English. Definitions for "religion" abound, yet none is universally accepted. "Wilderness" offers no respite from confusion. Such semantic and conceptual tangles frame the account here, beginning with the apparent antagonism between the spiritual domain of religion and the material domain of nature.

If wilderness is conventionally associated with *the natural*, that is, the evolved composition, structures, and functions of the world, and religion is conventionally associated with *the supernatural*, that is, phenomena such as God outside the evolutionary pale, then how conceivably can religion be meaningfully conjoined with notions of wilderness? Heaven and all things godly – the supernatural – are sacred. And the Earth and all things wild – the natural – appear profane. Thus religion appears to be antithetical to wilderness and nature.

There is considerable evidence to support such a conclusion. Religion has long been associated with the cultural legitimation of the economic exploitation of the natural world. Although preservationists associate wilderness with those areas of the Earth that are "untrammeled," that is, landscapes free of economic utilization where humans are visitors only, the religious mainstream tends to position nature as a resource provided by a supreme being to serve human needs. The natural world is conceptualized as "fallen," as a material domain that, despite its fallen nature, offers redemptive possibilities. Through economic utilization and technological control the faithful might recover in part from the Fall, thus restoring the human spirit – which is associated not with the natural and material world but the supernatural and spiritual world.

On this account, relatively wild places, such as mountains, deserts, forests, and bogs, are conceptualized as the "ruined Earth." Thus domestication, whether harnessing a wild river, mining gold from a mountain, logging an ancient forest, or draining a wetland, is religiously warranted as part of the recovery from the Fall. Apparently, with perhaps exceptions such as Native American and other Earth-friendly religions (e.g., Wiccans, goddess feminists), religion legitimates an assault on the wild Earth. So viewed, the metaphysical divide between the natural and the supernatural is insuperable.

Nevertheless there are strategies, especially for the religiously faithful who believe in the possibilities of a continuing revelation, by which wilderness, religion, and nature can be related. Lynn White, Jr.'s famous essay, "The Historical Roots of Our Ecologic Crisis" (1967), can be interpreted as the beginning of a continuing reconsideration of the relationships between wilderness, religion, and nature. If we think of religious narrative as simultaneously describing a reality that is and prescribing a reality that ought to be, then the world's religions can be influential in rethinking humankind's place in, actions upon, and obligations to the Earth's remaining wild and natural places. Such an analysis begins by attempting to uncover the religious sources of contemporary beliefs about nature and wilderness.

The idea of wilderness does not easily equate with the idea of nature. One conventional meaning of "wilderness" is that part of nature which is untrammeled or free (for example, as reflected in the language of the Wilderness Act in the United States of America). Wilderness connotes those lands which are part of the "pristine biosphere," a term used by ecologists to denote natural systems continuing on evolutionary trajectories largely free of human influence. (Some analysts believe that such a notion of wilderness is a "received idea" that is scientifically untenable.) Many scientists, including conservation biologists and ecological restorationists, believe that the conservation and restoration of extensive core wilderness areas are essential to the future of life.

But "wilderness" does not have the same connotation as "nature." Clearly, the former connotes habitat whose conservation is a necessary condition for continuing the evolved composition, structure and function of natural systems. As the history of science makes clear, the latter connotes an epistemic object for scientific study. Wilderness draws our attention to the world beyond ourselves. Nature draws our attention to the world that can be known scientifically. Ironically, this distinction is grounded in a religious history of effects that is clearly evident in the writings of Frances Bacon and René Descartes at the advent of the scientific revolution. For them nature became an object of science, for it was through inquiry that humankind would be able to turn the natural world to our will, thus recovering from the Fall.

The distinction of the ideas of wilderness and nature does not imply that wilderness cannot be known scientifically. Scientists, such as wildlife ecologists, conservation biologists, and ecological restorationists, actively study wilderness ecosystems. The point of these activities, however, is not to achieve control over the object of study through theoretical knowledge. Rather the end in view is the comprehension of the many circumstances and processes (from genetic to ecosystemic levels of organization) that created the natural system, many of which remain essential to its continued functioning. Such knowledge also articulates the consequences of our actions on the web of life – in religious terms, the creation itself. Contemporaneous ecological science makes clear that the human dominion of nature, despite its religious warrant, is an impossibility.

If "nature" connotes a theoretic object of study through which humans hope to gain causal control over the world, and "wild nature" connotes places which humans affect (to a greater or lesser extent) but do not control, then it follows that wilderness is more natural than nature. Ecologists use the term "anthropogenic biosphere" to denote nature in this sense. Nature is increasingly trammeled by humans, exploited through commerce, and polluted by industry. Wilderness advocates argue, with some justification, that "wilderness management" is an oxymoron, a self-contradictory notion since the essential quality that defines the wild (self-direction or natural agency rather than human control) is lost. Wilderness, then, is by definition on a self-willing or self-organizing trajectory rather than one controlled by human beings.

As the twenty-first century begins, there are few if any true terrestrial wildernesses – lands unaffected by, let alone devoid of, human influence. A number of prominent scientists argue that the wild world hangs on the precipice of catastrophe. The language used to describe the so-called biodiversity crisis is often religiously resonant. "An Armageddon," Edward O. Wilson writes, "is approaching at the beginning of the third millennium. But it is not the cosmic war and fiery collapse of mankind foretold in sacred scripture. It is the wreckage of the planet by an exuberantly plentiful and ingenious humanity" (Wilson 2002: xxiii).

Given the contrast between a naturally evolved and untrammeled world continuing on an evolutionary trajectory and the increasingly trammeled and declining anthropogenic biosphere, the idea of wilderness carries two prescriptive ideals. One is the idea that some considerable portion of the evolved world – the flora and fauna and their habitat – should remain wild and free. While this ideal is conventionally associated with the wilderness preservation movement, it increasingly finds religious warrant. The other ideal is that those areas of the Earth and the associated flora and fauna whose continued existence has been jeopardized by human activities should be restored to a relatively wild trajectory. Again, this ideal finds religious justification, since restoration is as much about normative human self-conceptualizations as it is about actions on the world.

Arguably, given the hold of narrative traditions on human consciousness, the continuing articulation and later realization of these prescriptive ideals has been argued by many as necessitating the commitment of religionists. Some have argued that only through the engagement of religiously faithful communities can culturally dominant notions of nature and wilderness be reconsidered, and a turn toward sustainability be made.

How then do world religions figure in such reconsideration? While no comprehensive account can be attempted here, there are many possibilities. Indigenous, Eastern, and so-called nature religions offer various points of departure for challenging sedimented beliefs that the natural world is nothing but an economic resource. Or that nature is merely material. Some of these sources are ancient, with origins before the onset of literacy, as with the Vedas in the Upanishads. The notion that Atman is Brahman implies that the ever-increasing hold of egoic-consumerist consciousness within the new world order is a contingency rather than a necessity imposed by human nature. Such an ancient insight clearly resonates with the contemporary ecological realization that interconnection within systems is a more fundamental reality than individuation. Likewise, Native American traditions, such as those of the desert Southwest in the United States, position the natural world as one which is spiritually alive rather than dead matter moving mechanically.

The Forum on Religion and Ecology, a continuing academic project involving dozens of scholars, is actively exploring the potential of the world's religions for ecological reform, including the preservation and conservation of wild species and their habitat. The Forum website contains essays exploring the ecological possibilities of most of the world's religions, including Buddhism, Christianity, Confucianism, Hinduism, Indigenous, Islam, Jainism, Judaism, Shinto, and Daoism.

There can be little doubt that the world's religions provide narrative sources that serve as the basis for reconsidering human relations and obligations to the naturally evolved world. However, because industrialized European and North American nations are the world's most prolific consumers and polluters, and thus impose the heaviest load on wilderness areas such as the Amazon, because the sources of the governing attitudes toward wilderness and nature in the West are grounded in biblical sources, and because the global political economy is largely dominated by nations whose religious roots are in Judaism and Christianity, the biblical religions are crucially important.

Biblical sources of Western attitudes toward wilderness and nature reflect a lingering consciousness of what was lost in the ecological transition from the Paleolithic to the Neolithic. Just as the "3K" background radiation is interpreted as evidence of primordial cosmological events, so biblical texts, such as the Garden narrative in Genesis, can be interpreted as evidence of a recent (ca. 15,000 B.C.E.) yet receding past, that is, the transition from a 200,000-year era of nomadic hunting and gathering to sedentarism and agriculture. This epochal ecological transition arguably leads to a psychic sense of the loss of connection with the natural world which in turn underlies the mythic narrative of expulsion from the Garden of Eden. Expelled from the Garden, humankind falls into agricultural drudgery and a perpetual longing for return. Some argue that ecological dysfunction will not be resolved until environmentalists escape this dream.

Likewise, Psalm 104 can be read as remembrances of things past, when humans lived in close association with and possessed an intimate knowledge of the natural world – its seasons and cycles, flora and fauna. Psalm 104 is interpreted by some as the textual underpinning of natural theology and, finally, the ecological sciences themselves. Such biblical themes are also clearly resonant in the Romantic poets, such as William Wordsworth and Percy Bysshe Shelley. Their poetry celebrates the created world and mourns the loss of our connection to it. The Romantics, in this sense, see a further fall from grace in the industrialization of the world.

These streams of thought from Genesis to the Romantics constitute the narrative sources for nineteenth- and twentieth-century ideas of wilderness. Conditioned in part by the Romantics, nineteenth-century writers often saw the wilderness and nature through a biblical lens. George Perkins Marsh, considered by many as the first environmentalist in a modern sense, exemplifies this idea. Recognizing the pervasive and deleterious consequences of the actions of humankind on the natural Earth, he argued that these changes were the consequence of the failure to heed the created order.

Wilderness was viewed also through a biblical lens by Henry David Thoreau and John Muir (less obviously in Thoreau than Muir). Thoreau, read as critically responding to Ralph Waldo Emerson's transcendentalist notion that nature was made for Man by God, came to the realization that the wild Earth needed no purpose other than its own. In wildness alone, he argued, was the preservation of the world. He equated the walker with a pilgrim in search of holy ground, and characterized wild nature as a sanctum sanctorum. John Muir, read as one of the first evolutionary thinkers, believed that he saw the Creator still at work in the mountains of California. Wild nature, the flora and fauna, the mountains and valleys, the forests and the rivers were sacred ground to Muir. Their value exceeded any economic utilization. Every day in the mountains, Muir proclaimed, was a resurrection day for the human spirit.

Biblical sources continue to influence the late twentieth and early twenty-first century. Aldo Leopold, a seminal wilderness thinker and staunch defender of wilderness, critiqued a biblically based Abrahamic ethic that saw the land community as nothing but an economic resource. He argued that only by superseding such an ethic for a land ethic could humans live on the land without spoiling it. Lynn White's later critique (1967) set in motion a continuing theological reassessment of humankind's relations to nature. Religious conservatives such as Francis Schaefer and liberals such John Cobb, Jr. were among the first to respond to White's arguments in the early 1970s. Today there are literally thousands of biblically based and religiously inspired reassessments of humankind's place in and obligations to the natural world. And scholars from the scientific community, such as E.O. Wilson, now recognize new ecological possibilities in biblical sources. "For the Abrahamic religions, Judaism, Christianity, and Islam, the environmental ethic is compatible with belief in the holiness of the Earth and the perception of nature as God's handiwork" (Wilson 2002: 157).

As the new millennium begins there is a growing energy among the religiously faithful to engage themselves with the questions of their faith-based relations to the wild Earth and nature more generally. While there is enormous theological diversity, there is also a convergence on a central idea. Roughly, the notion that there is an order to the created and still evolving world that transcends and in many but not all cases takes precedence over humanly created orders.

What conclusions, if any, can be drawn from this study of the complicated interrelations of wilderness, religion, and nature? Clearly, religion figures significantly in reinterpreting our place in nature, and especially our relations to those few habitats and species that remain relatively wild. Religion must play such a role, since humans cannot reinvent themselves *ex nihilo* but only move on from the culturally accumulated experiences of the past into an imaginative future. Charles Taylor argues in his monumental *Sources of the Self* that

> It would greatly help in staving off ecological disaster if we could recover a sense of the demand that our natural surroundings and wilderness make on us ... The world is not simply an ensemble of objects for our use, but makes a further claim on us ... This demand, though connected with what we are as language beings, is not simply one of self-fulfillment. It emanates from the world (Taylor 1989: 513).

Many religious sources embody these demands, requiring only that the religiously faithful identify such interpretations therein.

There are some, of course, who deny the possibilities for tomorrow existing at the convergence of wilderness, religion, and nature. And clearly there remains antipathy among some religionists toward the natural (and thus fallen) world. Yet religion, in all its diversity and whatever its insufficiencies, is one of the richest and potentially most promising sources for discovering and articulating the claims the world makes upon us.

Max Oelschlaeger

Further Reading

Albanese, Catherine L. *Nature Religion in America: From the Algonkian Indians to the New Age.* Chicago: University of Chicago Press, 1990.

Callicott, J. Baird. *Earth's Insights: A Multicultural Survey of Ecological Ethics from the Mediterranean Basin to the Australian Outback.* Berkeley: University of California Press, 1994.

Glacken, Clarence. *Traces on the Rhodian Shore: Nature and Culture in Western Thought from Ancient Times to the End of the Eighteenth Century.* Berkeley: University of California Press, 1967.

Levin, Simon A. *Fragile Dominion: Complexity and the Commons.* Reading, MA: Perseus Books, 1999.

Merchant, Carolyn. *Reinventing Eden: The Fate of Nature in Western Culture.* New York: Routledge, 2003.

Oelschlaeger, Max. *Caring for Creation: An Ecumenical Approach to the Environmental Crisis.* New Haven, CT: Yale University Press, 1994.

Oelschlaeger, Max. *The Idea of Wilderness: From Prehistory to the Age of Ecology.* New Haven: Yale University Press, 1991.

Petersen, Anna L. *Being Human: Ethics, Environment, and Our Place in the World.* Berkeley: University of California Press, 2001.

Schneidau, Herbert N. *Sacred Discontent: The Bible and Western Tradition.* Baton Rouge: Louisiana State University Press, 1976.

Shepard, Paul. *Nature and Madness.* San Francisco: Sierra Club Books, 1982.

Taylor, Charles. *Sources of the Self: The Making of Modern Identity.* Cambridge: Harvard University Press, 1989.

White, Lynn, Jr. "The Historical Roots of Our Ecologic Crisis." *Science* 155 (1967), 1203–1207.

Wilson, Edward O. *The Future of Life.* New York: Alfred A. Knopf, 2002.

See also: Biocentric Religion; Callicott, J. Baird; Cobb, John; Conservation Biology; Earth First! and the Earth Liberation Front; Ecopsychology; Leopold, Aldo; Marshall, Robert; Muir, John; National Parks and Monuments (United States); Paleolithic Religions and the Future; Romanticism – American; Religious Environmentalist Paradigm; Religious Studies and Environmental Concern; Restoration Ecology and Ritual; Shepard, Paul; Social Construction of Nature and Environmental Ethics; Thoreau, Henry David; White, Lynn – Thesis of; Wilderness Religion; Wilderness Society; Wilson, Edward O.

Wilderness Rites of Passage

Across time and in countless ways, people of many cultures have gone into the wilderness to mark life transitions and seek guidance. They sought closeness with God, the Mystery, or a higher self. They found a time alone, exposure to the elements in an unfamiliar place, a radical shift in self and world, a trial and a gift, and a ritual death and rebirth. The core of the form was clear: leaving the ordinary world, crossing a threshold, and returning with a gift and a task. It was an initiation, a rite of passage, a new birth in the womb of the natural world.

Modern cultures seem to have forgotten most of what our ancestors knew about the importance of initiatory rites for sustaining individuals and their communities. Instead, we find ourselves strangers in our own lives, unsure of our status and value, and hungry for a connection with the abiding rhythms of the Earth and an enduring spirit.

Yet, the roots of this search remain alive. Recently, a growing number of people have created wilderness-based rites of passage for a modern context. Stephen Foster and Meredith Little, authors of *The Book of the Vision Quest* and *The Four Shields*, are among those most influential in developing and articulating a form appropriate to our time and place, the vision fast. Since the 1960s, they have trained vision fast guides through their School of Lost Borders and spearheaded the development of professional groups such as the Wilderness Guides Council. Recent developments in this field include greater collaboration among those doing such work in North America, Europe, Africa, and Australia and the development of programs and training in academic settings.

In general, people seek wilderness rites of passage in times of significant life transition or to complete life transitions begun earlier but not completed. The transition from adolescence to adulthood is an important time for initiation. Adolescents need the chance to confirm their fitness and willingness to step toward adulthood. Mid-life, marriage, divorce, loss, or simply a time of confusion and disillusionment are also common calls to a wilderness rite of passage.

These practices facilitate ego-transcendence and an opening to spirit. In doing so, they also bring healing and renewed connections with lost or abandoned capacities for guidance, vitality, and joy. Their goals include bringing back to one's people and place something of value:

personal power, stability, energy, wisdom, or a maturity that is expressed in service to others and to the Earth.

Structure of a Typical Wilderness Passage Rite

While there are many specific forms these quests can take, they all express a common deep structure. The anthropologist, van Gennep, used this deep structure to describe traditional rites of passage, and Carl Jung and Joseph Campbell use it as the basis for the archetype of the Hero's Journey. Despite variations in surface structures, this pattern is broadly crosscultural. Here, I will describe a form currently being used by many wilderness rites of passage guides. It is built around a one- or two-week wilderness trip.

Preparation

This is a time for participants to identify their reasons, inner resources, and commitment for this undertaking. More mundane issues of logistics, equipment, and safety are equally important.

Severance

Participants travel to a wilderness setting and set up a base camp where they become accustomed to living close to the land, opening their senses to the features of that place, and tuning in to the rhythms of the Earth. Wilderness is a relative term, and many vision fast groups without ready access to wilderness have found that more cultivated lands can support this work. Processes for life review are helpful here. They use council-style group discussions and simple Earth-centered ceremonies along with walks, journaling, and contemplative practices such as meditation and sensory awareness.

Threshold

This phase usually comprises three or four days of solitude and fasting from food (with water, a buddy system, and other safeguards). Participants may engage in awareness practices and self-generated ceremonies, but aside from safety considerations, there are few rules. The threshold is the doorway into sacred time and space and the edge between the old, which is no longer, and the new, which is not yet. In many ways, the threshold time represents a symbolic death and facilitates an ego-death.

The wilderness (or wilder) setting is an important part of the threshold phase, providing both challenge and support for the inner work of disidentifying from old psychic structures, creating deeper integration both within one's psyche and with the world, and discovering deeper sources of relating to the world.

Return

The return, or reincorporation, phase is a symbolic rebirth. This begins upon the return to base camp with quiet celebration and reflection and continues as we rejoin our communities. Sharing stories and reflecting on them, participants begin to integrate their insights and visions. The goal is to help participants discover their own meaning in their experiences and apply their own belief systems, not to impose meaning.

Implementation

After the wilderness trip, participants are supported in bringing their experiences into their lives more fully. However, it is necessary that the work of this phase belongs to each participant. This is the phase in which the gifts of the initiation are shared. Essentially it is the rest of one's life.

Elements of Wilderness Passage Rites

Key elements of these trips are the stages of the rites of passage model, a ritual or ceremonial attitude, and the wilderness environment. Underlying them is exposure. Participants are exposed to new terrain, weather, and wildlife, large and small. They are exposed to their own vulnerability, boredom, frustration, strength, contentment, delight, and curiosity – all the states that can emerge from being alone in a living place with an authentic intention of openness. The patterns and meanings of personal history, self-concepts, ideals, and shadows are exposed as well.

Changes in sensory and cognitive input from living closer to nature lead to changes in ego structures. Familiar ego structures are no longer supported, leading to changes in self-images and less fixated conceptual structures. The natural world mirrors, evokes, and develops those inner qualities usually assigned to the realm of religion and spirituality – unconditional love, joy, power, peace, support, grace, and guidance.

Making intimate contact with the wild world brings us into contact with our "wild selves," the parts of us that have not been conditioned by familial and cultural forces. Wild places are those not under our control and not subject to our wills, walls, or arbitrary boundaries. On wilderness rites of passage, as in all forms of deep psychological or spiritual work, we are going into wild places. We are entering realms where the artificial structures and demands of the ego and society have not restricted or walled off our innate guidance, aliveness, generosity, or fascination with the world. At the same time, wilderness rites of passage cultivate and refine those qualities necessary for living in the world in a full and engaged way, knowing our own hearts and minds, tolerating ambiguity and discomfort, being autonomous, searching deeply, and staying open to new answers.

Sometimes, the "visions" of a vision fast resemble shamanic experiences with unusual sensory or psychospiritual manifestations. More often, however, the most transforming and longest lasting changes are prompted by subtle, more ordinary experiences. It is the totality of the rite rather than a specific experience that usually carries the deepest impact.

In most modern wilderness rites of passage trips, participants discover a renewed relationship with the natural world, a sacred relationship. To the detriment of this relationship, participants can idealize and romanticize wild nature and the ceremony, causing a split between the wild and their familiar worlds. Such a split tends to foster dissatisfaction and depression as well as rejection of the needs of one's home community and its natural setting. One of the goals of wilderness rites of passage is to support participants in returning home with a new or renewed commitment to living in a more sustainable way and caring for the Earth as well as a new sense of self.

Such responsible environmental action arises not from a sense of imposed obligation or coercion, but from the deep psycho-emotional bond arising from spending such ceremonial time alone in nature. Environmental action, whatever form it takes, becomes an expression of love, joy, and caring rather than a product of shame, guilt, or fear. The world becomes less a collection of commodities to be used or exploited, and more the embodiments of an alive, enchanted, sacred world. Many of these trips conclude with specific practices, often ritualized to deepen their meaning, which support participants in articulating and accepting a sacred task related to environmental responsibility. A lesson of modern wilderness rites of passage is that living authentically means living here and now, in this place, embodied, and part of the environment. Sacred ("heaven") and profane ("Earth") are not divorced.

This is not easy work, nor does it promise a quick fix. However, wilderness rites of passage and Earth-centered initiatory practices do develop confidence, trust, wholeness, a sense of enchantment and home in the wilder parts of our selves, and a natural impulse to contribute to our world. These are the foundations for maturity, inner freedom, and service.

John Davis

Further Reading

Foster, Steven and Merideth Little. *The Four Shields: The Initiatory Seasons of Human Nature.* Big Pine, CA: Lost Borders Press, 1998.

Foster, Steven and Merideth Little. *The Roaring of the Sacred River: The Wilderness Quest for Vision and Self-Healing.* Big Pine, CA: Lost Borders Press, 1989.

Foster, Steven and Merideth Little. *The Book of the Vision Quest: Personal Transformation in the Wilderness.* New York: Prentice Hall Press, 1988.

Greenway, Robert. "The Wilderness Effect and Ecopsychology." In Theodore Roszak, Mary Gomes, and Allen Kanner, eds. *Ecopsychology: Restoring the Earth, Healing the Mind.* San Francisco: Sierra Club Books, 1995.

Mahdi, Louise, Nancy Christopher and Michael Meade. *Crossroads: The Quest for Contemporary Rites of Passage.* Chicago: Open Court Publishing Company, 1996.

See also: Breathwork; Ecopsychology; ECOtherapy; Naropa University; Native American Spirituality; Re-Earthing; Transpersonal Psychology; Wilderness Religion.

Wilderness Society

Founded in 1935, The Wilderness Society is a nonprofit organization devoted to the protection of wilderness in the United States and to the development of a network of wild lands through public education, scientific analysis, and political advocacy. Headquartered in Washington, D.C., by the early twenty-first century it had eight regional offices, a membership of 200,000, and an annual budget of $14 million. While it would be misleading to describe The Wilderness Society as a religious organization, some of its founders were motivated by spiritual perceptions or religious worldviews that led them to view wilderness as sacred and worth preserving. And certainly the zeal and devotion with which its founders, leaders, and members have pursued the Society's mission demonstrates the ways in which the concept of wilderness has functioned as a significant center of material and symbolic value in the late twentieth-century United States.

Like the idea of nature, wilderness is a concept with a long intellectual pedigree, which the founders of The Wilderness Society inherited and also helped to shape. The idea of wilderness arose with the advent of herding and agriculture some 15,000 years ago, when humans first began to distinguish domesticated animals from wild ones and civilization from the surrounding wilderness. Until the rise of romantic aesthetics and cultural nationalism in the early nineteenth century, wilderness was primarily perceived as hostile wasteland to be conquered in the name of human progress. In the United States, the rapid loss of wild lands that accompanied the nation's urbanization and industrialization – popularly symbolized by the "closing of the frontier" in 1890 – had a particularly strong effect on the growth of wilderness appreciation.

The founders of The Wilderness Society extended the cultural critique of modernity advanced by early advocates of wilderness, but they did so with a singular opponent in mind: the automobile tourist, whose professed love of the wilderness ultimately threatened to destroy it. The eight founding members – including Robert Marshall, Benton MacKaye, Robert Sterling Yard, and Aldo Leopold – differed in their justifications for the significance of wilderness, but all of them agreed with Marshall's desire to keep the American wilderness "*sound-proof* as well as *sight-proof* from our increasingly mechanized life" by preventing the construction of roads in the national forests. They sought to preserve these roadless areas as sacred spaces whose aesthetic, cultural, and spiritual values could best be appreciated through more "primitive" forms of outdoor recreation.

In the post-war years, The Wilderness Society broadened its arguments for wilderness preservation, particularly in response to new threats posed by increased timber harvesting and dam building by the federal government and new developments in the biological sciences. Led by Executive Secretary Howard Zahniser and Director Olaus Murie, the Society played an instrumental role in the passage of the Wilderness Act of 1964, which defined a wilderness as "an area where the Earth and its community of life are untrammeled by man, where man himself is a visitor who does not remain." Since then, The Wilderness Society has helped to add 104 million acres to the National Wilderness Preservation System, often in collaboration with other environmental organizations that share its worldview. Despite the growth of its membership and the evolution of its arguments, The Wilderness Society remains committed to its founders' emphasis on preserving wilderness for the recreational and spiritual renewal of future generations.

Daniel J. Philippon

Further Reading

Fox, Stephen. *John Muir and His Legacy: The American Conservation Movement.* Boston: Little, Brown, 1981.

Glover, James M. *A Wilderness Original: The Life of Bob Marshall.* Seattle: The Mountaineers, 1986.

Meine, Curt. *Aldo Leopold: His Life and Work.* Madison: University of Wisconsin Press, 1988.

Sutter, Paul. *Driven Wild: How the Fight against Automobiles Launched the Modern Wilderness Movement.* Seattle: University of Washington Press, 2002.

See also: Leopold, Aldo; Marshall, Robert; Muir, John; Murie, Olaus J.; National Parks and Monuments (United States); Sierra Club; Wilderness Religion.

Williams, Delores S. (1937–)

Delores Williams is an African-American Presbyterian theologian who has played a formative role in the development of womanist theology, centering on historical and present testimonies of black women. Like other types of feminist and liberation theology, Williams' womanist theology rejects traditional dichotomies between body/spirit and humanity/nature that pervade mainstream Christian thought. Williams offers a theological response to the defilement of black women's bodies and identities in antebellum and postbellum America. She analyzes the surrogacy roles that were imposed on black women's bodies, raped and forced to substitute for white women sexually and economically and used to breed slave offspring. She makes parallels between such surrogacy and the exploitative rape of nature perpetrated by strip-mining the land and clear-cutting forests – both cases represent sin involving efforts to exploit and control the productive and reproductive capacities of nature.

Williams argues that these types of sin have been nearly invisible in Christian theology. Along with her expansion of the notion of sin, she also proposes a non-anthropocentric concept of salvation, indicating her hope for the end of violence and the liberation of creation from oppression. Using the biblical story of Hagar, the concubine of Abraham banished to the wilderness with her son Ishmael, Williams represents black women as "sisters in the wilderness." The metaphor of wilderness symbolizes a place of danger, fear and vulnerability, but also a place where God is present and strength is discovered. However, her theology lacks reflection on "wilderness" in itself as threatened. Wilderness is viewed as a projection of the human fear of exile. Given the strategic need to articulate black women's voices and theological responses to racism and sexism, Williams has made major strides toward an "ecowomanist" theology that exposes exploitative sins against black women's bodies and nature and points toward salvation.

Sarah Pinnock

Further Reading

Williams, Delores S. *Sisters in the Wilderness: The Challenge of Womanist God-Talk.* Maryknoll, NY: Orbis Books, 1993.

Williams, Delores S. "Sin, Nature and Black Women's Bodies." In Carol J. Adams, ed. *Ecofeminism and the Sacred.* New York: Continuum, 1993.

Williams, Delores S. "Black Women's Surrogacy Experience and the Christian Notion of Redemption." In Paula Cooey, et al., eds. *After Patriarchy.* Maryknoll, NY: Orbis Books, 1991.

See also: Christianity (7g) – Womanism; Walker, Alice.

Williams, Terry Tempest (1955–)

Author, activist, naturalist, desert mystic, poet, and green prophet, Terry Tempest Williams is made up of nearly as many layers as the geological cross-sections of Utah's canyon country she brings to life in her writing. Steeped in the Mormon culture of her upbringing, Williams is also a feminist, environmentalist, and outspoken anti-war activist. A descendant of Brigham Young and able to trace her heritage back through five generations of Latter-Day Saints, Williams possesses an intense passion for the sacred landscape of her Utah home and for the larger American West – a landscape she experiences as inspirited by wildness and grace. Her sojourns in the desert assume a revealing quality that leaves her heart open and exposed, vulnerable to her readers. This is precisely the point and in this respect Williams leads by example. For instance, she writes,

It is time for us to take off our masks, to step out from behind our personas – whatever they may be: educators, activists, biologists, geologists, writers, farmers, ranchers, and bureaucrats – and admit we are lovers, engaged in an erotics of place. Loving the land. Honoring its mysteries. Acknowledging, embracing the spirit of place – there is nothing more legitimate and there is nothing more true (Williams 1994: 84).

Williams is best known for *Refuge: An Unnatural History of Family and Place* (1991), which interweaves natural history and personal family narrative. In this work, she juxtaposes her experiences "midwifing" her mother through her ovarian cancer death to the simultaneous destruction of the Bear River Migratory Bird Refuge from human-produced flooding. Williams' grief over both is palpable. More than anything, she witnesses to the environmental cancer that is upon the Earth and the continuity between the earthbody and the human body. In "Clan of the One-Breasted Women," the epilogue to *Refuge*, Williams recites the list of (clean-living, non-smoking, non-drinking) Mormon mothers, aunts, and grandmothers in her family who have all been stricken with breast cancer and who have died or been rendered unlikely Amazons through mastectomies. She also links these cancers to the years that the U.S. Government bombed the American West, conducting atmospheric testing of atomic weapons in Nevada and exposing other western states as well to radioactive fallout drifting on wind currents. Williams rails at this injustice and deems the cancers a price far too high to be paid for obedience – the unquestioning acceptance of authority instilled and reinforced in Mormon culture. She writes,

> as a Mormon woman of the fifth generation of Latter-day Saints, I must question everything, even if it means losing my faith, even if it means becoming a border tribe among my own people. Tolerating blind obedience in the name of patriotism or religion ultimately takes our lives (Williams 1991: 286).

Williams is a self-described "edge-walker," who travels the narrow space between the religious tradition she credits for having "forged her soul," and her direct and very personal experiences in nature that have revealed a truth of their own. Throughout her work, she negotiates this edge by embracing themes that resonate for both Mormons and environmentalists – the importance of community, home, family, heritage, and commitment. Her co-edited anthology, *New Genesis: A Mormon Reader on Land and Community* (1998), carefully presents essays from a variety of Mormon writers who promote principles of ecological care and conservation as grounded in Mormon scriptural sources. The ideal of the nineteenth-century Mormon village is revisited as a model of self-sufficiency and sustainability, and Brigham Young's advocacy of water conservation is repeatedly invoked. The anthology ultimately succeeds in marrying Mormon and environmental perspectives in a way that is inviting rather than threatening to more conservative readers.

If Williams is an "edge-walker," then her "edgiest" book is *Desert Quartet: An Erotic Landscape* (1995). In this work, she explores the land as mystical lover and embodies a kind of "eco-eroticism" that blurs boundaries between skin and rock, wind and breath, blood and water, and fire and flesh. Williams leads the reader on a poetic journey through the desert and into intimate encounters with the Earth's four basic elements (Earth, air, fire, water). In so doing, she engages the Earth's "body" in a primal mystical union that pulses with pleasure and erotic intensity.

Williams sounds similar "eco-erotic" themes in her collections of essays, *An Unspoken Hunger* (1994) and *Leap* (2000), a book dedicated to her obsession with painter Hieronymus Bosch's medieval triptych "The Garden of Delights." The burning question within Williams while she was writing *An Unspoken Hunger* was "How do we make love to the land?" (1995), a question she confesses intrigues her in part because eroticism is so taboo in Mormon culture (Jensen 1995: 312). In *Leap*, Williams explicitly draws parallels between a fear of intimacy and eros within Mormon culture and the narrow valuing of nature solely for its practical human utility. She observes, "I see my community's fear of homosexuality, even wilderness, as a failure of imagination. Sex is like land. It must be used for something" (Williams 2000: 195).

Issues of land use and wilderness preservation are indeed central to Williams' activism. She has testified to protect Utah's wild lands before a U.S. Senate subcommittee hearing on the Utah Public Land Management Act and has spoken before Congress on behalf of "America's Redrock Wilderness Act." She has also compiled and presented to Congress a volume of writers' witness to the historical and spiritual importance of preserving America's public lands. At a time when the idea of "wilderness" has been exhaustively deconstructed and its use aggressively critiqued within academia, Williams continues to "buck this trend," boldly making the case for the spiritual, psychological, and ecological importance of protecting wild places. "I choose to err on the side of preservation," writes Williams,

> and stand shoulder to shoulder with brothers and sisters in our shared desire to protect the last large expanses of wilderness we have left . . . I want to speak the language of grasses, rooted yet supple in the presence of wind before a storm. I want to write in the form of migrating geese like an arrow pointing south toward a direction of safety. I want to keep

my words wild so that even if the land and everything we hold dear is destroyed by shortsightedness and greed, there is a record of beauty and passionate participation by those who saw it coming (Williams 2001: 19).

In 1995, the *Utne Reader* named Terry Tempest Williams one of its "100 visionaries." She is a Rachel Carson Institute Inductee in recognition of her work as an environmental leader; she is also the winner of a Guggenheim Fellowship and a Lannan Literary Fellowship for her creative non-fiction.

Sarah McFarland Taylor

Further Reading

Jensen, Derrick. "Interview with Terry Tempest Williams." In *Listening to the Land: Conversations about Nature, Culture, and Eros*. San Francisco: Sierra Club Books, 1995, 310–26.

London, Scott. "The Politics of Place: An Interview With Terry Tempest Williams." [Radio Broadcast Transcript] "Insight and Outlook Radio Series." Santa Barbara, CA (22 May 1995).

Williams, Terry Tempest. *Red*. New York: Pantheon Books, 2001.

Williams, Terry Tempest. *Leap*. New York: Pantheon Books, 2000.

Williams, Terry Tempest. *Desert Quartet: An Erotic Landscape*. New York: Pantheon Books, 1995.

Williams, Terry Tempest. *An Unspoken Hunger: Stories from the Field*. New York: Pantheon Books, 1994.

Williams, Terry Tempest. *Refuge: An Unnatural History of Family and Place*. New York: Vintage, 1991.

Williams, Terry Tempest, William Smart and Gibbs Smith, eds. *New Genesis: A Mormon Reader on Land and Community*. Layton, UT: Gibbs Smith, 1998.

See also: Autobiography; Church of Jesus Christ, Latter Day Saints; Memoir and Nature Writing; Sexuality and Green Consciousness.

Wilson, Edward O. (1929–)

An entomologist by training, E.O. Wilson's hypotheses have had far-reaching influence not only in the biological sciences, but in the humanities and social sciences as well. Wilson's ideas connect religion and nature on two levels. First, he argues that religion, like social behavior in general, is subject to natural selection. Second, Wilson's primary intellectual endeavor has been to demonstrate the religiosity implicit in the natural sciences. His litany of publications includes several well-respected contributions to the field of ecology, but he is most widely known for his theory of sociobiology, and for his championship of environmental issues. This hypothesis established a scientific field devoted to finding the biological origins of animal social behavior at both the genetic and the environmental levels. Sociobiology presents challenges to current conceptualizations in the biological sciences as well as the social sciences. Sociobiological studies seek to understand the evolutionary foundations of social behaviors in animals, and to apply an ecological model to the social sciences. At the heart of E.O. Wilson's ideas is the assertion that scientific investigation can radically improve the production of knowledge, and can be synthesized with other disciplinary systems.

Due to a boyhood fishing accident, Wilson's vision is good in only one eye; and he has subsequently trained himself for close observation. His career in insect biology supplied him with many resources for the extension of scientific study into other fields. He is renowned for his work on the behavior of social insects, but has branched out tremendously into studies of ecology, gene-culture co-evolution, sociobiology, biogeography, environmental ethics, environmentalism, and environmental policy. He is the recipient of two Pulitzer prizes: one for his work in *On Human Nature*, and the other for his co-authorship of the definitive entomological work *The Ants*. Following his fieldwork in Cuba and New Guinea, Wilson joined the Harvard faculty of biology. He remains active there as a professor in the Department of Organismic and Evolutionary Biology, and as the honorary curator in entomology at the Museum of Comparative Zoology.

As a part of his larger project to understand human social life scientifically, Wilson has argued that religion is a product of natural selection. Beyond Wilson's sentiments that religion is biological in origin, he also believes that traditional religions are ill-equipped to deal with the environmental and social problems of the modern world. In *Consilience*, one of his most accessible works, Wilson seeks to renew the enlightenment project of finding ultimate meaning through science. As a voice of twentieth-century biology, Wilson presents a continued call for an empirically grounded metaphysics, a religion based in fact, sounded a century earlier by such thinkers as Auguste Comte. Such a worldview would invalidate anthropocentric conceptualizations of the universe, and seek to create social harmony based on a coordinated effort between biology and the social sciences. His quest is lofty; not only does he advocate a massive research endeavor to establish scientific consensus on moral issues, he further believes that this new faith in facts needs to be created in poetic form, as an epic cultural narrative. He is a board member of the Epic of Evolution Society, and collaborates with those engaged in the consecration of scientific narratives in this way. His call for such a scientific undertaking has, however, been refuted directly by Wendell Berry in *Life is a Miracle*, and many non-scientists look at sociobiology as a highly controversial theory. Feminists, cultural anthropologists, and many religious leaders present serious challenges to the legitimacy of Wilson's scientific ideology, arguing respectively that such a position reinforces a patriarchal, scientistic, and one-sided view of moral and cultural issues.

Wilson's call for a scientific ethic in relation to environmental issues, specifically biodiversity, is espoused in *Biophilia*. His call for a conservation ethic grounded in scientific understanding parallels Aldo Leopold's ideology, and harkens back to Thoreau's idea of nature as the refuge of the spirit. Wilson's version of environmental ethics adds a new dimension to these older ones: he situates it amid the knowledge of a more mature ecology, and focuses on the complex dynamics of both genetic coevolution and biodiversity. Wilson shares the straightforward understanding of humanity as dependent upon nature for survival with his predecessors, but comes armed with a more sophisticated understanding of the fundamentally intertwined existence of humans and their environment. Biophilia is the innate human tendency to affiliate with other organisms. From a biological point of view, humanity is an interdependent member of the complex energy cycles of the world ecosystem. To study this system, and to further our understanding of ourselves as a part of it, is for Wilson, the central task not only of the sciences, but also of human moral and religious activity. *Biophilia* posits that true meaning can only come from science. This is not an epistemological claim for the superiority of scientific knowledge. Wilson is setting forth the idea that as humans are biological organisms, what they find meaningful should itself be biological. This suggestion is at the core of Wilson's thinking; scientific understanding of the biological world allows humanity to renew its entire mode of being, in essence to invent a new religion.

Evan Berry

Further Reading

Berry, Wendell. *Life is a Miracle: An Essay Against Modern Superstition*. Washington, D.C.: Counterpoint, 2000.

Hunter, Anne E., ed. *On Peace, War, and Gender: A Challenge to Genetic Explanations*. New York: Feminist Press, 1991.

Lumsden, Charles. *Genes, Mind, and Culture: The Coevolutionary Process*. Cambridge, MA: Harvard University Press, 1981.

Wilson, Edward O. *Sociobiology: The New Synthesis*. Cambridge, MA: Belknap Press of Harvard University Press, 2000.

Wilson, Edward O. *Consilience: The Unity of Knowledge*. New York: Knopf, distributed by Random House, 1998.

Wilson, Edward O. *Biophilia*. Cambridge, MA: Harvard University Press, 1984.

See also: Berry, Wendell; Biocentric Religion – A Call for; Biodiversity; Biophilia; Conservation Biology; Ecology and Religion; Environmental Ethics; Epic of Evolution (and adjacent, Epic Ritual); Evolutionary Biology, Religion, and Stewardship; Geophilia; Natural History as Natural Religion.

Winter, Paul (1939–)

The music of Paul Winter defies easy categorization. A recent characterization of his work is "ecological jazz," but his music has also garnered such titles as "chamber jazz" and even "symphony world beat." Winter credits his fusion of styles to a combination of his background playing jazz and bee-bop in Chicago, his time living in Brazil, his frequent ocean trips with zoologist-friend Roger Payne to record the complex songs of whales, and his annual pilgrimages to visit famously self-sufficient Maine homesteaders Helen and Scott Nearing. Considering this eclectic and quintessentially postmodern blending of influences, it is not surprising that Winter has often been described as a "musical shapeshifter" (Oliver 1992: 76). Not only does his music cross music genres: jazz, bossa nova, world music, chamber music and, more recently, Celtic music, it also crosses artistic media so that his songs are often referred to as "sound paintings" or alternately "tone poems."

Indeed, in his own personal life, raised a Presbyterian as a boy growing up in Altoona, Pennsylvania, and now a world traveler and longtime Zen meditator, Winter is no stranger to crossing genres in the combined realms of music and religion. Not unlike the prevailing patterns in American spirituality, Winter's artistic and spiritual leanings are both energetically and unapologetically combinatory. A self-identified "Earth musician," Winter explicitly and negatively compares singularity in sound to the environmentally detrimental practice of "monocropping" (Parmalee 1990: 17). Instead, Winter and his "Paul Winter Consort" of world musicians cultivate a kind of ecospiritual polyphony that brings together the voices of endangered species, as well as the voices of "endangered" musical instruments – symphonic instruments that are rarely heard in favor of the much more popular electronic and synthetic sounds that dominate today's music sales. It is this commitment to what Winter calls "natural music" that helped give rise to the creation of Winter's famed "Owlegy" – a composition dedicated to the preservation of owls and ancient forests, as played by "endangered" instruments.

For his CD *Prayer for the Wild Things*, Winter embedded the voices of 27 indigenous birds and animals into his music, creating a virtual "soundscape" of the Northwestern Rockies. Each participating creature is considered by Winter to be a "musician from the symphony of wildlife," and each is brought to the foreground of the piece, then recedes into the mountain landscape. Not only do instruments represent animals in classic "Peter and the Wolf" style, but Winter goes one step further, allowing the animals to vocalize for themselves, as his human "Earth Band" echo these voices with their own humanmade sounds.

Winter's most famous work, the "Gaian Mass," was composed and recorded in alternate locations: in the Cathedral of St. John the Divine in New York, with its forest of gigantic stone columns, and also in the Grand Canyon, dubbed by Winter "the Earth cathedral." In both places, Winter has been fascinated by the dynamics of echo and the similarity and degree of "reverb" caused by both cavernous spaces as multiple voices come in contact with multiple surfaces. It so happens that both the Cathedral in New York and the cathedral of the Grand Canyon have the same eight-second reverb. This acoustic similarity carries both symbolic and artistic significance within Winter's work. The parallel acoustics unite the more institutional space of the Cathedral (connected with the history of the Church and more structured, formal forms of worship) with the freer, nature-identified spirituality inspired by the canyon space. This kind of nature-inspired spirituality has permeated American philosophical and cultural movements from the Transcendentalists, to twentieth-century back-to-the-landers like Helen and Scott Nearing, to contemporary New Age forms of worship (Albanese 1990).

By including actual echo and by using "echo" as trope in his music, Winter conjures a sacred antiphonal relationship with the land. This call and response and Winter's play of surfaces and sound evoke a sense of intimacy, a reciprocal love affair between the human and nonhuman world that imbues Winter's composition and performance. In many respects, Winter's commitment to the importance of so-called "natural music" or "Earth music" echoes David Abram's argument in *Spell of the Sensuous* that in modernity cultures ultimately end up losing "a common discourse that opens directly onto the evocative sounds, shapes, and gestures of the surrounding ecology" (Abram 1996: 139). For Abram, it is the move from oral performance to the written word that goes hand in hand with a discourse that becomes closed off to the "voices" of nature. In contrast to the kind of tone deafness Abram describes and a silencing of the natural world, Winter's inclusion of whales, loons, wolves, and wind effectively demonstrates an attempt to compose or rather *re-compose* a spiritual soundscape that is intrinsically "alive, aware, and expressive" in its planetary diversity.

Sarah McFarland Taylor

Further Reading
Abram, David. *The Spell of the Sensuous*. New York: Pantheon Books, 1996.
Albanese, Catherine. *Nature Religion in America: From the Algonkian Indians to the New Age*. Chicago: University of Chicago Press, 1990.
Oliver, Joan Duncan. "Earth Sounds: Paul Winter's Music Celebrates All of Earth's Creatures." *Wildlife Conservation* (July/August 1992), 76–91.
Parmalee, Patty Lee. "Interview: A Conversation With Paul Winter." *The Saxophone Symposium* (Summer 1990), 7–19.
Taylor, Sarah M. Interview with Paul Winter. Litchfield, CT, 26 June 2000.

See also: Back to the Land Movements; Cathedral of St. John the Divine; Gaian Mass; Music; Nature Religion; Nature Religion in the United States.

Wise Use Movement

The term "wise use" was used by the first forester and chief of the United States Forest Service (USFS), Gifford Pinchot. It can refer to the "multiple use" doctrine that is supposed to guide the management of public forests, allowing recreation and resource extraction compatible with ecosystem health. But the more common contemporary usage of the term as the name of a movement, first applied by Ronald Arnold, a former Sierra Club activist and a major figure in the wise use movement, implies that the wise use of land overrides environmental constraints. This understanding owes much to James Watt, Secretary of the Interior under the U.S. Reagan administration, and founder of an early wise use group, the Mountain States Legal Foundation (MSLF). Although the wise use movement (called the share movement in Canada) has a diversity of groups and priorities, participants in the wise use movement agree that natural resources are here for human use and that immediate concerns hold priority in the "use" of land and resources. Some of the individuals and groups involved in the movement are motivated by religious concerns.

The "wise use movement" emerged first in the 1980s in the western United States as an alliance of disgruntled ranchers, loggers, hunters, off-road vehicle owners, gun owners, outdoor sports enthusiasts, farmers, land developers, and extractive industries united to fight a common enemy – environmentalism. The movement, which now reaches beyond its U.S. origins, includes those who desire more access to public lands, resent government regulation against the use of their lands, oppose environmental restrictions on free-market economies, dispute consensus scientific understandings of environmental threats such as global warming, and oppose environmentalism by claiming it is Pagan, a religion in itself, or anti-Christian. According to Richard Wright (1995) some even see environmentalism replacing communism as the next, great threat to liberty and claim that environmentalists are trying to establish a "one world" government. An early articulation of the movement's goals was Alan M. Gottleib's *The Wise Use Agenda* (1989). The Cornwall Declaration on Environmental Stewardship (2000) provides an example of the ways in which conservative religionists support the movement.

The wide range of interests involved in these movements often pits "wise users" against the National Parks, the Environmental Protection Agency, the U.S. Forest Service and other federal and state agencies, as well as major environmental, religious and scientific organizations. From the perspective of environmentalists, however, state and federal enforcement and land management agencies are frequently viewed as supportive of wise use and corporate interests. Similar conflicts are seen around the globe. In addition to trying to influence public opinion, media representation and legislation, gain members and protest current polices, other more intimidating tactics are sometimes used. Corporations involved in conflicts often request that media access and coverage be blocked or censored, as in the anti-old-growth forest logging campaigns in Victoria, Australia. Frequently lawsuits are filed. These range from money- and energy-draining "SLAPP suits" (strategic litigation against public participation) to lawsuits against environmental regulations. Wise use groups have argued in the courts, for example, that the U.S. Clean Air Act is unconstitutional and that Forest Service decisions to protect lands sacred to indigenous people for ritual use amounts to the establishment of religion and are therefore unconstitutional. Going beyond legal means, some participants in wise use groups have been engaged in the desecration of sacred sites, illegal logging and hunting, character defamation, harassment, death threats, and violence against environmental activists, as detailed in David Helvarg's *War Against the Greens*. Public Employees for Environmental Responsibility (PEER) documents harassment, threats and violence on their website and publications.

Wise use groups are sometimes named in ways that seem to support environmental values. The Evergreen Foundation, the Wetlands Coalition and the British Columbia Forest Alliance, for example, are all industry fronts. The anti-environmental agenda of the movement can more clearly be seen in the titles of the books written by its proponents, such as *Ecology Wars* or *Undue Influence: Wealthy Foundations, Grant Driven Environmental Groups and Zealous Bureaucrats That Control Your Future*, by Ronald Arnold. Arnold is well known for two statements: "Our goal is to destroy, to eradicate the environmental movement," and "Environmentalism is the new paganism. Trees are worshipped and humans sacrificed at its' altar. It is evil" (*Boston Globe*, 1/13/1992). Arnold also claimed that there is a green conspiracy to eradicate rural America. In the aftermath of 9/11, he and other wise use advocates intensified efforts to have civil disobedience such as tree sitting and blockading logging roads declared "ecoterrorism" and urged stronger laws against such activities.

Arnold and Gottleib (who also promotes gun ownership rights) are both associated with the Center for the Defense of Free Enterprise (CDFE). The title of this organization, like that of Citizen's for a Sound Economy (CSE), the American Freedom Coalition, or the Acton Institute of Religion and Liberty, illustrates the centrality of the defense of free enterprise and economic liberty, the links between wise use ideology and libertarianism, and the way conservative religion sometimes becomes intertwined with these efforts. The Competitive Enterprise Institute (CEI) proclaimed that its mission is "advancing liberty from ecology to the economy," while the Cato Institute (called the most important environmental thinktank by the Wall Street journal) advertises its own with a banner reading, "Individual Liberty, Limited Government, Free Markets and Peace." The Cato Institute focuses in part on "environment and climate change" (the term climate change is used to imply that it is just a natural part of the Earth's history) and its staff includes a vocal opponent of global warming theory, Patrick Michaels, co-author with Robert Balling, of *The Satanic Gases: Clearing the Air about Global Warming*. Cato, and others who frequently deny or downplay the existence of environmental problems, promote themselves as "eco-realists." Wise-use groups and institutes, such as CATO's and CSE, are funded in part by multinational corporations, including extractive industries and biotechnology. The Reverend Sun Myung Moon's Unification Church, motivated by his enthusiasm for free enterprise capitalism, is a backer of groups such as the American Freedom Coalition which had ties to Arnold's CDFE. Many of these organizations have close ties with various U.S. Republican presidential administrations, for example: U.S. Secretaries of the Interior James Watt and Gale Norton were both closely associated with MLDF, and the back cover of The Wise Use Agenda pictures author Alan Gottleib with President George Bush.

These close connections are evident in the religiously oriented Acton Institute, whose website claims to be a "leading voice in the national environmental and social policy debate," while also saying that environmental activists want companies to "commit suicide" and stifle their rights to "economic initiative." At a 2003 Exxon-Mobil shareholders' meeting, Acton's president, Catholic priest Robert Sirico (a former director of the LA Gay and Lesbian Community Center) spoke against interfaith activists, such as CERES (the Coalition for Environmentally Responsible Economies), who file shareholder initiatives urging corporations to improve their human rights and environmental records. Reverend Jerry Zandstra, director of Acton's Center for Entrepreneurial Stewardship, praised the company on its "excellent" record in human rights and the environment. Acton also helped found the Interfaith Council for Environmental Stewardship (ICES), made up of

Jews, Catholics and Protestants, as a way to counter what it views as wrong and misleading religious environmentalism. ICES board members E. Calvin Beisner and Robert Royal have published influential books, *Where Garden Meets Wilderness* (Beisner 1997) and *The Virgin and the Dynamo*, which warn of "the use and abuse of religion in environmental debates" (Royal 1999, book subtitle). Beisner is a board member of the Committee for a Constructive Tomorrow (CFACT), whose website "boldly proclaims that the Western values of competition, progress, freedom, and stewardship can and do offer the best hope for protecting not only the Earth and its wildlife, but even more importantly, its people." Both CFACT and Acton produce hundreds of radio spots on environmental issues. Many of the major groups, such as CDFE and Acton, fund conferences and have active publishing programs.

Acton, ICES, Sirico and Beisner are well known within conservative Jewish and Christian circles for the "Cornwall Declaration on Environmental Stewardship" (CDES), signed by two prominent evangelical Christians, Focus on the Family president Dr. James Dobson and Campus Crusade for Christ founder Bill Bright. The declaration was produced in order to respond to the Evangelical Environmental Network's "Evangelical Declaration of Creation Care" (EDCC) (signed by other high-profile evangelicals as Cal Dewitt and the directors of World Vision and Inter-Varsity Christian Fellowship). The differences in the two documents are instructive: the Cornwall Declaration affirmed private property ownership and market economies, while the Evangelical Declaration (1994) promoted "lifestyle choices that express humility, forbearance, self restraint and frugality" and "godly, just and sustainable choices." The CDES prioritizes the needs of humans over nature, argues that free-market forces can resolve environmental problems and denounces the environmental movement for embracing faulty science and a gloom-and-doom approach. In contrast, the EDCC encourages Christians to become ecologically aware creation care-takers. Other differences revolve around the place and privileges of humans relative to nature, issues of biblical interpretation, the definition of stewardship, God's sovereignty, and the worry that saving the Earth is replacing the central Christian emphasis on saving souls.

These disagreements reflect more than internal Christian conflict; the Cornwall Declaration reinforced the wise use emphasis on the ongoing improvement of the environment through human technology, the abundance of resources put here for human use, the privileged place of humans, and the opposition to seeing more-than-human nature as an idyllic, harmonious state that must be preserved. Other major targets by conservative religious opponents are environmentalists' concern over overpopulation and animal rights ("pro-abortionists and animal rights advocates" are often presented as synonymous with environmentalism). Mainstream environmental and religious groups are viewed as radical. Acton staff member, Phillip DeVous, (2002) called the collaboration, between the Sierra Club (a "radical" group) and the National Council of Churches, to try to prevent oil drilling in the Arctic National Wildlife Refuge an "unholy alliance." Other opponents charged that the EDCC held Christian doctrine hostage to an environmental agenda.

Richard Wright, a Harvard-trained scientist and evangelical Christian who wrote a widely used environmental textbook, responded directly to the wise use movement's attack on the Evangelical Declaration in "Tearing Down the Green." He argued that those who attack environmentalists use poor science and falsely accuse environmentalists of nefarious conspiracies, including of serving the anti-Christ by trying to bring about a global, totalitarian government. Rush Limbaugh, who in the 1990s and early twenty-first century had become the most widely listened to right-wing radio commentator in the United States, frequently has claimed that environmentalists are leftist or religious fanatics, and enemies of liberty. Such claims are common to both secularist and religious anti-environmentalists. The Former Idaho Republican U.S. Representative Helen Chenoweth, for example, in a speech delivered to the U.S. House of Representatives on 31 January 1996, attacked "environmental policies [that] are driven by a kind of emotional spiritualism that threatens the very foundation of our society." She added,

> there is increasing evidence of a government sponsored religion in America. This religion, a cloudy mixture of new age mysticism, Native American folklore, and primitive Earth worship (Pantheism), is being promoted and enforced . . . in violation of our rights and freedoms.

This conflation of some of the religious and philosophical sources of environmental concern leads some conservative Christians to label deep ecologists George Sessions and Arne Naess "eco theologians" (CFACT) and to warn Christians not to "let the trees do the talking," as they think Native Americans and Pagans do. Environmentalists are frequently accused of "worshipping Creation" rather than the Creator.

Despite significant diversity within the movement, which includes both avowedly secular and explicitly religious voices, participants in the movement see environmentalists as threatening sacred values: either that of the American nation-state, the world's guarantor of freedom, of free-market economics, or of true religion, or all three.

Laurel Kearns

Further Reading

Arnold, Ron. *Undue Influence: Wealthy Foundations, Grant Driven Environmental Groups and Zealous Bureaucrats That Control Your Future*. New York: Free Enterprise Press/Merrill Press, 1999.

Arnold, Ron. *Ecology Wars: Environmentalism as if People Mattered*. New York: Free Enterprise Press/Merrill Press, 1997.

Ball, Jim. "The Use of Ecology in the Evangelical Protestant Response to the Ecological Crisis." *Perspectives on Science and Christian Faith* 50 (March, 1998), 32–40.

Beisner, E. Calvin. *Where Garden meets Wilderness: Evangelical Entry into the Environmental Debate*. Grand Rapids, MI: Acton Institute/Eerdmans Publishing Co., 1997.

Boston Globe. "New, Militant Anti-environmentalists Fight to Return Nature to a Back Seat." 13 January 1992.

Bratton, Susan Power. "The Eco-theology of James Watt." *Environmental Ethics* 5 (1983), 225–36.

"Cornwall Declaration on Environmental Stewardship." In Michael Barkey, ed. *Environmental Stewardship in the Judeo-Christian Tradition: Jewish, Catholic and Protestant Wisdom on the Environment*. Grand Rapids, MI: Acton Institute, 2000, xi–xv.

DeVous, Phillip. "Unholy Alliance: Radical Environmentalists and the Churches." *Acton Commentary*, 10 April 2002.

Diamond, Sara. *Roads to Dominion: Right-Wing Movement and Political Power in the United States*. New York: Guilford, 1995.

"Evangelical Declaration of Creation Care." In R.J. Berry, ed. *The Care of Creation: Focusing Concern and Action*. Downers Grove, IL: InterVarsity Press, 2000.

Gottlieb, Alan M. *The Wise Use Agenda: A Task Force Report Sponsored by the Wise Use Movement*. Bellevue, WA: Free Enterprise Press, 1989.

Helvarg, David. *The War Against the Greens: The Wise-Use Movement, the New Right, and Anti-Environmental Violence*. San Francisco, CA: Sierra Club Books, 1994.

Mazza, Dave. *God, Land and Politics: The Wise Use and Christian Right Connection in 1992 Oregon Politics*. Portland, OR: Western States Center, Helena, MT: Montana AFL/CIO, 1993.

Michaels, Patrick J. and Robert C. Balling, Jr. *The Satanic Gases: Clearing the Air about Global Warming*. Washington, D.C.: Cato Institute, 2000.

Rowell, Andrew. *Green Backlash: Global Subversion of the Environmental Movement*. New York & London: Routledge, 1996.

Royal, Robert. *The Virgin and the Dynamo: The Use and Abuse of Religion in Environmental Debates*. Grand Rapids, MI: Ethics and Public Policy Institute/Wm. B. Eerdmans Publishing Co., 1999.

Smith, Samantha. *Goddess Earth: Exposing the Pagan Agenda of the Environmental Movement*. Lafayette: Huntington House, 1994.

Switzer, Jacqueline Vaughn. *Green Backlash: The History and Politics of Environmental Opposition in the United States*. Boulder: Lynne Rienner, 1997.

Taylor, Bron and Joel Geffen. "Battling Religions in Parks and Forest Reserves: Facing Religion in Conflicts Over Protected Places." In David Harmon and Allen Putney, eds. *The Full Value of Parks and Protected Areas: From Economics to the Intangible*. Lanham: Rowman & Littlefield, 2003, 281–93.

Wright, Richard. "Tearing Down the Green: Environmental Backlash in the Evangelical Sub-Culture." *Perspectives on Science and Christian Faith* 47 (June 1995), 80–91.

Wright, Richard. *Environmental Science: Toward A Sustainable Future*. New York: Prentice Hall, 2002 (8th edn).

See also: Au Sable Institute; Cathedral Forests and the Felling of Sacred Groves; Christianity; (2) – Jesus (and adjacent, What Would Jesus Drive?); Christianity (7i) – An Evangelical Perspective on Faith and Nature; Earth First! and the Earth Liberation Front; Evangelical Environmental Network; North American Conference on Christianity and Ecology [and the] North American Coalition on Religion and Ecology; Religious Campaign for Forest Conservation; Stewardship.

Women and Animals

Western cultures have theoretically equated women, children, animals, and "the natural" with one another and with the body. This constructed connection served and continues to serve as a means of oppression in patriarchal cultures. Why did this begin and where?

Historically, women's seemingly more obvious reproductive functions resulted in women being identified as more animal-like in their bodily functions than men. Therefore, many cultures functioned under the assumption that women's bodies supposedly intruded upon their rationality. Since most Western theorists construed rationality as the defining requirement for membership in the moral community, women – along with men of color and animals – who were seen as less able to transcend their bodies, were long excluded.

We cannot know precisely when and where this began, though a few argue that a matriarchy preceded patriarchy and that its overthrow – due in part to a change in human's relationships with the other animals – enabled both women's and animals' oppression. Others argue against this interpretation. Some believe that through the domestication of animals, the role of the male in inseminating the female was discovered, and from this arose the idea of controlling women's reproductivity. Rosemary Radford Ruether sees a connection between the domestication of animals, the development of urban centers, the creation of slavery, and the creation of the inequality of the sexes. Lori Gruen suggests various cultural and historical frameworks for these connections, including the shift from nomadic cultures to stationary agrarian communities with the accompanying increased demand for laborers; thus women became "breeders of a workforce."

In response to the historical alignment of women and the other animals, feminist analysis at first chose to sever the woman–animal identification, asserting that women are not animals and must be seen as equally human as men. Since the 1970s, an alternative analysis has been proposed by feminists, primarily in the U.S. and U.K., that women's oppression must be seen as a part of an understanding of the interlocking systems of oppression that organize the world (and the oppressed) by gender, race, class, and species, and that feminism, as a transformative philosophy, must embrace the amelioration of life on Earth for all life forms.

From this analysis, rich scholarly insights have arisen. This entry can only briefly summarize some of them.

- The association of women, animals, and body manifests itself in violence on a personal level (domestic and sexual violence), and a cultural level (for instance, depiction of "meat" animals as sexualized bodies).
- The recent development of anthropornography ("depicting animals as whores") takes place in a context of women's sexual inequality, and illustrates the construction of inequality.
- Anti-violence interventions and theories will be inadequate if they ignore the control perpetrators gain by violence toward animals loved by the victims. In fact, by analyzing violence to the animals in the household, the deliberate nature of this violence is clearly established.
- Species, like gender, race, and class, is socially constructed, and should not be the basis upon which ethical decisions rest.
- Patriarchal science fosters biological determinism not only regarding women, but also regarding other animals.
- The defense of hunting by some environmentalists arises from its association with male self-identity.
- Falsely generic words (such as man and mankind) that elevate men to full human status must be analyzed alongside animal pejoratives for women (catty, bitch, sow, shrew, dog, chick, cow).
- A patriarchal culture feminizes animal victims; this explains the low status of animals confined for food.

The role of religion in maintaining these oppressions or as a source for liberation is much debated. Myriad questions are being posed within the ongoing dialogue. Is the resistance to examining the treatment of the other animals in religions a way of avoiding a recognition of the animality of human beings? Is the result of anthropomorphizing God that God and humans, especially male humans, are seen as more alike than humans and animals? Is it the case that the more theology moves from being androcentric, the less likely it is to be anthropocentric? Would a body-affirming theology justify the exploitation of animals for food, clothing, or entertainment? Can religious concepts of alienation, brokenness, and separation address the treatment of devalued bodies? *Could* theologies of relinquishment, for men in their control over women, and for humans in their control over the other animals, *emerge as sources for embodied transformations?*

As ecofeminist philosophies and theologies continue to engage these issues, the links between women and animals, and the reality of human beings as animals, is poised to remain in the forefront of ideological discussions and practical applications.

Carol J. Adams

Further Reading

Adams, Carol J. *The Pornography of Meat*. New York: Continuum, 2003.

Adams, Carol J. *The Sexual Politics of Meat: A Feminist-Vegetarian Critical Theory*. New York: Continuum, Oxford: Polity Press, 1990.

Adams, Carol J. and Josephine Donovan, eds. *Animals and Women: Feminist Theoretical Explorations*. Durham, NC: Duke University Press, 1995.

Corea, Gena. *The Mother Machine*. New York: Harper & Row, 1985.

Gruen, Lori. "Dismantling Oppression: An Analysis of the Connection between Women and Animals." In *Ecofeminism: Women, Animals and Nature*. Greta Gaard, ed. Philadelphia: Temple University Press, 1993.

Mason, Jim. *An Unnatural Order*. New York: Simon & Schuster, 1993.

See also: Animals; Ecofeminism (various); Environmental Ethics; Hunting Spirituality; Radical Environmentalism (and adjacent, Rodney Coronado and the Animal Liberation Front); Vegetarianism (various).

Wonder toward Nature

Broadly conceived, wonder toward nature includes awe and dread in relation to the cosmos, a sense not only of transfixion but also of the numinous in specific locations, a marveling over something remarkable or some "first moment," and a felt loss of explanation before the unusual or mysterious. Wonder, then, is a crucial psychological state for bringing nature and religion together (though in this state nature will often be taken as more than ordinary and thus super-natural). Wonder is a matter affecting

Western theories of religion, and has been crucial in the construction of constituting modern motions of "primitivity."

The acclaimed founder of capitalism, the Scotsman Adam Smith (1723–90), was first to devote a third of a treatise – his *History of Astronomy* – to the sentiment of wonder. Wonder, by his definition, is the response to "extraordinary and uncommon objects" (meteors, comets, and eclipses being of obvious singularity among them), and in humanity's earliest state, "every object of nature . . . considerable enough to attract his attention" will be enough to imbue wonder in the "savage's" mind (Smith 1982: 48–9). To anything quite overawing, such as lightning, simple people will respond with a reverence that approaches fear, being totally without the rational explanations known to men and women of the Enlightenment.

Smith imagined that "primitives" were very anxious lest they offend the gods. This was a position more famously accentuated by his near-contemporary Giambattista Vico of Naples (1668–1744). Vico speculated that both morality and religion first began when "Jove's lightning bolt" struck with horrendous surprise while promiscuous couples were having sex, this happening at an early stage when humans were almost like beasts. The brilliant Vico, who could be said to have founded the theory of animism in a few brief passages in his New Science of 1744, did not stop with negatives, for he conceived the primitive mind to be one of "prodigious imagination" (*vigorosissima fantasia*), everything bearing a wondrous aspect because of an "ignorance of causes" (*ignoranza di cagioni*) (Vico [1744] 1959: 412). Smith would have agreed. He assessed many phenomena we now see as "perfectly beautiful and agreeable" what were in earliest times "the proper objects of reverence and gratitude," inspiring wonder as proceeding "from some intelligent beings" (1982: 40–2, 48–9). And the Scot saw the absence of causal thinking as a key factor in this complex. The sentiment of wonder behind either "consternation" and "complacency" had arisen very early, as philosopher David Hume (1711–1776) doubtless influenced Smith to conclude that early humans were not able to make a connecting, "imaginal" bridge between events. This could have occurred in much the same way as an eighteenth-century European rustic would wonder, given no explanation, over the peculiar movements of iron before a loadstone.

For the titular founder of the discipline of comparative religion, Anglo-German Friedrich Max Müller (1823–1900), a century later, wonder was a wellspring of religiosity, but in his approach the Enlightenment outlook tended to be replaced by Romanticism. What he described as the natural "appreciation of the infinite" was the naive, childlike freshness with which the most ancient poets continually experienced their worlds. "A new life flashed by every morning before their eyes, and the fresh breezes of dawn [that] reached them like greetings wafted across the golden threshold of the sky." Such new life was from "the rainer, the thunderer, the measurer," or especially from those "bright beings, the Sun, the Sky, the Day, the Dawn . . . opposed to the powers of night and darkness," this "contrast of light with dark being of very ancient date" (Müller 1899: 618).

Müller inferred what he took to be the earliest textual evidence of humanity's spiritual life; namely, the signs of reverence behind the most ancient body of Sanskrit texts, the *Rig Veda* or Vedic hymns. Müller trusted little else but texts for revealing the nature of religions in the distant past, yet he was reacting against a more popular trend. For, by the late eighteenth century, the amount of ethnographic reporting on indigenous peoples had expanded exponentially, and the new fashion of evolutionism tempted many intellectuals to extrapolate from the most apparently primitive among contemporary indigenes back to the prehistoric origins of religion. Müller, however, was a decided "historist," and he took a different tack by giving such priority to the Vedic hymns and what could be inferred behind them. On the other hand, he held the intriguing view that, long after the more-aware stage reflected in these hymns, many dispersed human groups lapsed into a confusion of thought – through a "disease of language" – that brought about the enormous, "curious array of belief systems . . . too often called savage," found in the "anthropological religions" of tribal Africans, Australians, Pacific Islanders and the like (in Trompf 2002: 42). A true son of Romanticism, Müller placed the primordial impetus of an authentic wonder first, as response to a primal revelation, and the peoples his contemporaries were calling primitives and savages came only later.

Out of Müller's views arose the common assumption that primitives, while they may be struggling with the connections of things, may also be very curious or wondering – but only "to get it wrong" (1962: 49).

This did not square, however, with the theory of Herbert Spencer (1820–1904), the English inventor and social evolutionist, arguably the first sociologist of comparative religion. Wonder, or even curiosity, he had decided by 1856, were not properties of the savage mind. That could be safely inferred even from the behavior of village rustics he observed while on his holidays, who, because they showed little interest in Spencer's makeshift scientific demonstrations, led him to comparative insights about the reception of newly created goods. He likened the reactions of rural folk to the relative "indifference which low savages display, when shown looking-glasses, watches, or other remarkable products of civilized life," as missionary accounts had allegedly shown. "Surprise or curiosity are not the traits of the utterly ignorant," Spencer argued (1904: 476–7). By the act of his imagination, or an extrapolation from an alleged relic in the English countryside both across to the inexperienced modern primitive and then backwards to a supposed "original" one, we find

Spencer representing "first peoples," or the members of most small-scale, traditional societies, as duller of wit or as often lacking in curiosity and a sense of wonder – being the very opposite to Spencer's ideal scientist, who is a person more naturally prepared for surprise and educated by higher religion to marvel in a civilized way.

Spencer's social evolutionism, influential in the capitalist West, bears comparison with the theories of the founder-figure of communism Karl Marx (1818–1883), who was a protagonist of historical evolution (or development) in his own manner. Apropos wonder, Marx's *The German Ideology* has history begin with a primal fear of overwhelming elements in the environment and end with complete mastery over both technology and sociality. Although Marx thought there were some reasons to admire the earliest societies – especially because they had not dissolved "their relations to the Earth" (1973: 497) – primitives are nonetheless in utter awe of external forces and inevitably create the gods out of them because they are at the mercy of the not-yet-controllable. Through fear, humans are naturally driven to a mutual (his friend Engels would add "classless") dependence on each other, and from then on history is a story of lessened uncertainty and wonder, and increasing control over the environment.

With the turn into the twentieth century, the European projection of the "wondering savage" had taken on more various aspects. By then Oceania had come into the picture. What early field researcher R.H. Codrington told of central Melanesian notions of *mana* – that "power or influence, not physical," belonging "to the region of the unseen" (1891: 118–19) – had been construed as an apprehension of the "supernatural" that surprised "the natives" in their daily round. Thus, while English religious thinker F.B. Jevons (1858–1936) felt compelled by the new ethnographic data to reject the (Müllerian) thesis that "primitive man lived in a state of perpetual surprise," he thought it fair to assume that "at any rate occasionally" any unexpected, "startling frustration" in calculations during the "natural" routine of life would make primitives realize that they were "in the hands of a mysterious and supernatural power" (Jevons [1896] 1927: 18, 20).

The Scot James George Frazer (1854–1941) was having some effect here, because he had given back to the primitive (in spite of Smith and Spencer) a sense of "the experimental." The attempt to work magic, for all the mistaken assumptions involved, was the predecessor to modern science (and was also prior to religion). For Jevons, though, it was implicitly the failure of expectations in a world of magic that induced wonder, and thus religiosity.

A famous English theorist of religion, R.R. Marett (1866–1943), paid homage to Jevons' approach when he argued, almost a decade before Rudolf Otto in Germany, that the word "awe" is "the one that expresses the fundamental religious feeling most nearly," that sense of "thrill . . . whereof the component 'moments' are fear, admiration, wonder, and the like, whilst its object is, broadly speaking, the supernatural" (Marett 1914: 8, 10, 13). The Melanesians' *mana* was invoked – and, too, the comparably vague (and for Marett pre-animistic) conception of the supernatural among the African Masai, who not only took mysterious steaming holes as *ngai*, but also the white man Joseph Thompson, and his lamp as a sign of interest in indigenes' wonder upon contact with outsiders. Marett was influenced by Scotsman Andrew Lang (1844–1912) and what he had written about primitive actions to the unexpected – and to the spooky. Marett consequently played down talk of magical experimentation and heightened his emphases instead on psychological states – on feeling and states of uncertainty before the supernatural.

The story of such European imaging has further developments in Continental and Anglophone theory. Austrian Sigmund Freud (1856–1939) speculated about the "omnipotence of thought" as common to both infants and savages (in his *Totem and Taboo*). Essentially he argued that one could infer "latent" psychological states in primitive peoples that were generated from the surprises of life "present to the senses and the consciousness" (Freud [1913] 1946: 122). The phenomenologist of religion, Dutchman Gerardus van der Leeuw (1890–1950), picked up on the inheritance of scholarship and stressed the primacy of wonder in religious consciousness; yet, like Freud, he pronounced on the greater suggestibility of primitives. For him, as a child of his times, "the natives" had a habit of over-exaggerating and letting their thoughts run away, as little-known expeditions to Melanesia – one by Anglo-American psychologist William McDougall to the Torres Strait in 1898, and another by psychological anthropologist Richard Thurnwald to German Neuguinea in 1906–1909 – had already been designed to confirm.

Less denigrating models were canvassed by the German theologian Rudolf Otto (1869–1937) and the Swiss psychologist Carl Jung (1875–1961). For Otto the feeling of "something 'uncanny,' 'eerie' or 'weird' . . . emerging in the mind of the primitive human being forms the starting-point for the entirety of religious development in history" (Otto [1917] 1959: 29). Of this shuddering before the numinous, however, apprehension of "the 'supernatural' has nothing to do with the case," according to Otto. In qualifying Marett, Otto contended that this was "much too imposing an expression" for the primitive case. What he called "the vestibule of religion" was the product of "naive, rudimentary fancies" paying "homage to natural objects that were frightening or extraordinary" (Otto 1959: 134–5). Otto, however, wrote of this incipience of holy dread less out of empirical interests than out of a desire to solve a philosophical problem, that of giving the religious sense a status *sui generis*; and thus the primitive mind, embodied above all in the savage wonderer, was constituted as preface to high theological insights.

As for Jung, what Otto conceives more in terms of outer

relations, with primitives responding to shadows and lakes, and eventually theological minds to the "Wholly Other," comes to be transformed in analytical psychology into interior events. Primitives operate in a world affected by "unconscious regulators-dominants" that invade the inner numinosum, generating astonishment, awe and fear. This view, however, entailed Jung's problematic subscription to Frenchman Lévy-Bruhl's theory of the indigenes' "mystical participation" with nonhuman agencies in this cosmos, or pre-logical mentalities that conditioned the fearful images and phantasms erupting as interior astonishments in dreams.

The goal-posts for the better understanding of *les sauvages*, in any case, tended to be shifted in accordance with specialist games played in European academic disciplines. That earthier English soul D.H. Lawrence (1885–1930), for one, who was a theorist of religion in his own right, and who knew some Jung but surprisingly never read Freud, wondered where bodies had gone in all this. He apparently wanted primal wonder to be relocated in the close encounter with or near touch of nakedness, when "blood," not just mind, was thinking (Lawrence [1923] 1971: 102–16). When blood did come into it further down the track, the interest in awe and wonder took on sinister-looking undertones, and the Dionysians' cultivations of fascination for the lost pagan *mysterium* led on to the sacred Teutonic grottos of the Nazis, and the tragic misappropriations of Otto's *Das Heilige*. Concern for wonder, on this account, began to lose what momentum it had left. If the *unheimlich* (uncanny) could metamorphose into the *grausig* (horrible) politically, that had to be reckoned with experientially. Awe, dread and curiosity became in psychological texts "mixed emotions" – of surprise and fear, fear and expectancy, surprise and acceptance respectively – sometimes indistinguishable from other mixed emotions, and wonder hardly coming into view at all.

The American psychologist B.F. Skinner was quick to categorize wondering under "superstition," when, in consolidating earlier work by fellow countryman Thorndike and the Russian Pavlov, he found animals were "startled" to find reinforcement (food availability) by performing some action "totally irrelevant" to the norm (of pressing a bar), and so by experiencing what in the language of Jevons and Marett "defeats reasonable expectation" (Marett 1909: 12).

The Western intellectual community was losing its own sense of wonder – symptomatically perhaps, considering the Era of Violence – and from Durkheimian talk about collective excitations or effervescence to fancy new language about "cognitive engrossment" and "effortless dissociation," wonder was obscured behind other categories rather tangential to it. It apparently was being "dis-spelled" by hundreds of a hundred-and-one photographic books, by the exponentially quickened appearance rate of new inventions, and by an ethos combining smart technology with the blasé. It has just managed to hold on with the naive delights of children; and it somehow remains as a sense of "political correctness" when a person realizes that he/she should not dupe others with "tall stories" or play on their susceptibilities for too long.

Reckoning that the culture of high technology has subtly and tragically suppressed our older sense of wonder, Rollo May holds that social psychological health in the West is under threat. The disenchanting of the world, another way of describing the decline of wonder, seems symptomatic of the decay of religion itself. Paradoxically, the globalized access to new consumer goods from Western-originated markets has produced reactions of religious wonder among First Peoples and in other quarters. "Cargo cults" of various kinds come to mind, these not only being confined to Melanesia; and one contemplates the recently emergent Indian goddess, Santoshi Mata, to whom one prays for new commodity items. In all such reactions, however, nature portends to be the sufferer and the nexus between wonder and nature is impoverished.

In this light, it is no wonder there are religious voices calling us to attune our attentions afresh to the wonders of creation (e.g., Matthew Fox), depth ecologists persuading us that we should treat planet Earth as a living being (J.E. Lovelock), and philosophers encouraging us to "re-enchant" nature (e.g., Morris Berman).

Garry W. Trompf

Further Reading

Berman, Morris. *The Re-enchantment of the World*. Ithaca, NY: Cornell University Press, 1981.
Codrington, Robert. *The Melanesians*. Oxford: Clarendon Press, 1891.
Freud, Sigmund. *Totem and Taboo*. A.A. Brill, tr. New York: Vintage, 1946 (1913).
Jevons, Frank Byron. *An Introduction to the History of Religion*. London: Methuen, 1927 (1896).
Lawrence, D.H. *Fantasia of the Unconscious, and Psychoanalysis and the Unconscious*. London: William Heinemann, 1971 (1923).
Marett, R.R. *The Threshold of Religion*. London: Routledge/Thoemmes, 1997 (1909).
Marx, Karl. *Grundrisse* (trans. M. Nicolaus). Harmondsworth: Penguin, 1973.
Müller, Friedrich Max. *Introduction to the Science of Religion*. New York: Arno, 1978 (1899).
Otto, Rudolph. *The Idea of the Holy*. J.W. Harvey, tr. Harmondsworth: Penguin, 1959 (1917).
Sharpe, Eric J. *Comparative Religion: A History*. London: Duckworth, 1986 (2nd edn).
Smart, Ninian, John Clayton and Stephen Katz, eds. *Nineteenth Century Religious Thought in the West*. 3 vols. Cambridge: Cambridge University Press, 1985.
Smith, Adam. *Essays on Philosophical Subjects* [1795] in

Works and Correspondence, vol. 3. W.P.D. Wightman and J.C. Bryce, eds. Indianapolis: Liberty Fund, 1982.

Spencer, Herbert. *An Autobiography*, 2 vols. London: Williams & Norgate, 1904.

Spencer, Herbert. *The Principles of Sociology*, vol. 1. Westport, CT: Greenwood, 1975 (1882).

Trompf, Garry W. *In Search of Origins*. Studies in World Religions, 1. Delhi: Sterling, 2002 (2nd edn).

Vico, Giambattista. "La Scienza Nuova." In *Giambattista Vico. Opere*. Paolo Rossi, ed. Milan: Rizzoli Editore, 1959 (1744).

See also: Animism; Anthropologists; Berman, Morris; Conservation Biology; Earth Charter; Ecology and Religion; Fox, Matthew; Hunting and the Origins of Religion; Jung, Carl Gustav; Lovelock, James; Müller, Friedrich Max; Religious Naturalism; Storytelling and Wonder; Sun Worship.

World Conference of Indigenous Peoples (Kari Oca, Brazil)

The religious traditions of indigenous peoples of the world weave together religion and nature. The extent to which these traditions are still observed today depends both on the political and economic contexts in which they are now situated, and the degree of dedication of regional spiritual leaders to conserving a traditional heritage at variance with contemporary cultural ideas and practices from the dominant societies in which they are located. In the Americas, for example, after centuries of efforts by Euro-American religious and political leaders to eradicate American Indian rituals and erase Indian culture; centuries of taking away Indian lands whose boundaries had been guaranteed by signed treaties; and more than a century of government and business control over economic development on those lands, the people in many Indian communities live in poverty and suffer the ravages of unemployment, family destabilization, alcoholism, dilapidated housing and dependence on government assistance granted at the whims of political authorities. Federal government statistics on employment and poverty witness to the state of Indian lands and communities. The casual traveler through "Indian Country" in parts of the United States, and non-Indians living on or near reservations, often note the poverty and environmental degradation of such areas – but often without probing their underlying causes. Despoiled terrain and depressed people in these contexts do not mean that native cultures reject rather than retain traditional values; rather, they reveal the chasm between those values – sometimes maintained by only a few, often termed "traditionalists" – and perspectives and practices absorbed from or imposed by the wider social milieu.

In this situation, Indian peoples in the Americas (and in

Indigenous Voices from Kari Oca

Why do we call animals, birds, fish, trees, and plants our relatives? Because we believe we are intrinsically related. And by calling them our relatives, we show respect for our environment and the world in which we live. Life is community.

Joaqquisho (Chief Oren Lyons), Haudenosaunee Nation (Six Nations), United States

In the spiritual life, what we see and what we follow are the instructions that were given to us when the Peacemaker came. He came to this world and he instructed us in the things we must follow... The Creator created the world, the universe, and put things here for our benefit. We must give thanks to the Creator for all the things he has given us... We need to seek a balance between the spiritual and the political. There should be no separation of spirituality from political or social life. Americans have two houses, one for government and one for prayer. Our people keep them together.

Leon Shenandoah, Tadadaho (Chief of Chiefs), Haudenosaunee Nation

The forests, which are still preserved as a common reserve for the people of the world, are mostly in indigenous territories. Because we live in the natural world, we treat the natural world as our Mother. In Panama, in the last ten years, the desertification has been great. The forests that remain are on indigenous lands.

Atencio López, Cuna Nation, Panama

We, the children of the Earth, have come to share with the world and the United Nations our way of thinking, our visions, our way of life, an alternative. We do not speak of the "environment"; we speak of the spiritual and physical world in which we live, a territory in which people and nature are interrelated. "Land" is only the soil, but a "territory" is land in cosmic relation with nature, with rivers and animals and air and people, a place in which all are related. "Territory" means also our language and our values. We indigenous people are protectors and keepers of the territory, the "environment," because we are part of it.

Valerio Grefa, Ecuador

If we have no water, we have no life. We are responsible for seeing that the lives of generations to come will be possible. Our individual lives are a part in time of the longer life of the people. If men create an environment that harms us, the life of the community will end.

Pauline Tangora, Maori, Aotearoa (New Zealand)

John Hart

other parts of the world) began in the twentieth century to reaffirm their history and their environment-related spirituality. This took various forms. Some activists have used language as a means of social transformation, cultural affirmation and political regeneration: recovery of their native tongue, and teaching it in native schools; using "nation," rather than "tribe," to refer to their people, focusing thereby on treaties as agreements between sovereign entities; and transforming the word "Indian" into a transnational reference to native nations and individuals, although usually replaced by a specific reference to their own ethnic identity (Lakota, Hopi, Haudenosaunee, Muskogee, for example) in describing their particular origins. Others have focused on renegotiating treaties and economic contracts, using Indian lawyers rather than depending on advice from the Bureau of Indian Affairs and the benevolence of corporate attorneys; and on filing successful lawsuits against federal and state governments. Numerous American Indians (including Hopi, Haudenosaunee, Lakota and Dine') have used their own national passports when traveling abroad, beginning in the 1980s, rather than U.S. passports; these have been accepted by foreign governments as official credentials.

Concerns and efforts such as these led to the organization of the "World Conference of Indigenous Peoples on Territory, Environment and Development" which was held in 1992 at Kari Oca, a site on the outskirts of Rio de Janeiro, Brazil, during the week immediately preceding the United Nations Conference on Environment and Development (UNCED, otherwise known as the "Earth Summit"). Indigenous leaders from throughout the world, concerned about devastation of Earth, which peoples from North America referred to as a sacred "Mother Earth," and peoples from South America called "Pacha Mama," met to address issues of sovereignty, conservation and restoration of their lands, intellectual property, racism, and cooperation with non-Indian peoples to care for the Earth environment and promote concern for the human rights and cultural identity of native peoples.

During preparations for Rio, indigenous representatives had urged the UN to speak not of "indigenous people" but of "indigenous peoples," thereby acknowledging the diversity of peoples throughout the world and the responsibilities of nations to respect their lives and culture – including their traditional nature-based spirituality – and the territorial and ecological integrity of their land bases.

At the Kari Oca site, some 650 indigenous representatives celebrated their cultures from 25–30 May 1992. Through diverse religious ceremonies incorporating elements of pristine creation, they offered prayers to the Creator and Mother Earth, and pleaded for help on behalf of animal, plant and bird life; some sought the healing power of herbs and natural forces. They spoke of seeking freedom to conserve and express their spiritual beliefs and engage in their religious rituals. In a nod to contemporary conservation efforts, solar-powered lights illuminated the dirt roads at night with their stored energy.

Marcos Terena, a leader from the Terena people of Matto Grosso, Brazil, was a conference organizer, the Coordinator of the Brazilian Intertribal Committee, and the elected spokesperson to address the Earth Summit on behalf of the World Conference of Indigenous Peoples. In an interview after the Kari Oca meeting, he emphasized the relation between religion and nature:

We have organized this global conference because we did not have space within the United Nations, or in the debates of the NGOs [non-governmental organizations], and because we, as indigenous peoples, wanted to be treated in a specific manner, in a special manner, as peoples who know nature . . . We, the indigenous peoples, for many years, have always had a harmonious relationship with nature, from which we have taken our sustenance – not only material sustenance, but also our spiritual resistance and sustenance. Many people, including religious people, do not understand what we mean when indigenous peoples speak in this way. What we mean is that we do not have a "religion." We do not have a "church." We have only our spiritual power. Everyone has their spiritual power. But now [non-indigenous peoples] are far from their spiritual power. They are much closer to their technological and scientific powers. Because of this, they cannot know what nature and Mother Earth want to say. But we, the indigenous peoples, have tried to show that in daily practice we the indigenous peoples are knowers of nature and also that our resistance, our strength comes from a spiritual relationship with nature.

The indigenous peoples have suffered a great rejection, a great genocide . . . The indigenous culture previously was treated as folklore, but now we have been able to demonstrate that our cultural force represents our own dignity as a people. If we can demonstrate this day after day, we can also demonstrate that indigenous culture is something very alive, very strong, that has sustained us in this time. We are always joined in a perfect relationship of harmony with nature and with Mother Earth (Interview with and translated by author 30 May 1992, Kari Oca village, on the last evening of the event).

On the final day of the conference, the indigenous peoples from around the Earth issued the "Kari Oca Declaration." The declaration expressed the intergenerational consciousness of traditional cultures when it declared that indigenous peoples "walk to the future in the footprints of our ancestors." The document affirmed cultural and historical continuity, and a claim on native territories, by stating that those footprints are "permanently etched upon the lands of our peoples."

Indigenous peoples' human, territorial and civil rights, even when supposedly guaranteed by treaties, often have been violated by national governments in which native lands are situated. The Kari Oca Declaration condemns rights violations by asserting that indigenous peoples "maintain our inherent rights to self-determination," despite "centuries of deprivation, assimilation and genocide." On their lands and territories, they maintain "inalienable rights" to their waters and to all resources, and profess their "ongoing responsibility to pass these on to the future generations."

Earth Summit organizers had sought in vain to have the United Nations delegates approve an "Earth Charter" that would promote ecological integrity and the well-being of the biotic community. At Kari Oca, the assembled delegates were successful in promulgating a 109-point "Indigenous Peoples' Earth Charter." In it, they asserted their rights to their traditional manner of life and their spiritual way of life, beginning with a forceful demand to "the right to life." They noted that their territories are "living totalities in permanent vital relation between human beings and nature." They stated that the UN Convention on Genocide must specifically include genocide against indigenous peoples. The "Indigenous Peoples' Earth Charter" recalled the link between land, spirituality and self-determination by asserting, "Indigenous peoples were placed upon our Mother, the Earth, by the Creator. We belong to the land. We cannot be separated from our lands and territories." The charter called for the establishment of an indigenous peoples' environmental network; condemned the dumping of toxic wastes and nuclear wastes on native lands; called for the return of indigenous peoples' human remains and artifacts to the original peoples from which they had been taken; asserted that "traditional knowledge of herbs and plants must be protected and passed on to future generations"; and stated that indigenous peoples should be free to use their own development strategies, ones which would promote "economic and ecological viability." (In the U.S., ideas from the "Indigenous Peoples' Earth Charter" have been put into practice by such organizations as the International Indian Treaty Council NGO, founded in 1974 and with offices now in San Francisco, California, New York City, and Palmer, Alaska; and the Indigenous Environmental Network, founded in 1991 and headquartered in Bemidji, Minnesota.)

The Kari Oca gathering was important for six significant accomplishments. It provided a forum for indigenous peoples to exchange particular and universal spiritual insights and to integrate them with diverse social-political-ecological-economic perspectives; it established a foundation for and inspired ongoing collaborative work; it reinforced an ongoing pan-Indian sharing of religious perspectives and ethical values; it strengthened international indigenous cooperative efforts to promote the material well-being of native peoples, particularly through rights to natural resources and territorial sovereignty; it affirmed global native efforts to weave together nature-oriented spiritual values, environment-related religious ethics, and indigenous communities' efforts to conserve and control natural resource use and to retain religious traditions; and it taught peoples of non-native cultures about indigenous concerns for territorial and spiritual integrity, both linked to a profound respect for Mother Earth. Although the Kari Oca ideals are still, for the most part, visions of what the future might bring, Indian traditional spiritual leaders, social activists, NGOs, and local grassroots organizations are planning and working to make those visions a concrete reality in the lives of their peoples.

John Hart

Further Reading

Josephy, Alvin M., Jr. *Now That the Buffalo's Gone – A Study of Today's American Indians*. New York: Alfred A. Knopf, 1982.

Lyons, Oren, John Mohawk, Vine Deloria, Jr., Laurence Hauptman, Howard Berman, Donald Grinde, Jr., Curtis Berkey and Robert Venables. *Exiled in the Land of the Free – Democracy, Indian Nations, and the U.S. Constitution*. Santa Fe, NM: Clear Light Publishers, 1992.

Suzuki, David and Peter Knudtson, eds. *Wisdom of the Elders: Honoring Sacred Native Visions of Nature*. New York, NY: Bantam Books, 1992.

Vecsey, Christopher and Robert W. Venables, eds. *American Indian Environments: Ecological Issues in Native American History*. Syracuse, NY: Syracuse University Press, 1980.

See also: Indigenous Activism and Environmentalism in Latin America; Indigenous Environmental Network; Mother Earth; Native American Languages (North America); United Nations' "Earth Summits".

World Council of Churches and Ecumenical Thought

The institutional center of ethical thought about environmental issues inside the World Council of Churches is the working group on Justice, Peace and Creation. Theological and ethical ecumenical thought relevant to environmental concerns has a wide base and a long history, which is embedded in the ecumenical thought of the twentieth century. One can trace the history of ecumenical thought through the various conferences sponsored by the WCC in the decades since World War II, key discussions and decisions taken at Central Committee meetings or assemblies of the WCC in the last decades, and through publications of the WCC and of the people related to it. One can similarly trace ecumenical environmental thought in this way and also through the participation of WCC staff and those of member churches in such events as the United Nations environmental conferences in Rio de Janeiro in 1992, and Johannesburg 2002.

The environmental thought of the WCC is closely related to, and in close conversation with, long-standing concerns of the WCC. It reflects the ongoing attempt of the WCC to develop overarching ethical themes which encompass in different ways the almost 400 member churches of the WCC, and thus reflect the global reach of the organization, as well as reflecting the centrality of its often-stated ethical commitment to justice, especially for the poor and the weak around the world.

While its ethical concerns have varied according to the issues of the times, one finds in the ethical thought of the WCC an ongoing interest in global economics and an often-stated concern for the uneven and unjust effects of capitalism on communities and individuals. This concern has changed shape according to the times, so that what was once an ethical critique of colonialism and Northern domination of Southern economies currently takes the form of a thoroughgoing critique of economic globalization, and corporations and international financial institutions which impose their logic and their will and demonstrate little or no concern either for the life of local communities or for their natural environments.

Another ongoing concern of the social thought of the WCC directly related to issues of the environment is that of science and technology. As was made clear in the well-known conference, "Faith, Science and the Future," sponsored by the WCC which took place at M.I.T in July in 1979, ecumenical thought is concerned about the many ways in which both science and technology can escape community controls and aims, thus achieving a kind of autonomy that can result in the undermining of central values and practices relating both to the human social world and the natural environment.

In contrast to those who would let science and technology develop autonomously, ecumenical thought has stressed the inescapable moral responsibility human beings have for the social world in which they live, including the responsibility over the developments of science and technology. Such developments often largely determine human social relationships and relationships with the natural world, and cannot be left to develop on their own.

While members of the WCC work closely with other religious and secular groups, it is clear that the root of concern for the environment in ecumenical thought is a shared Christian conviction that nature is God's creation, and is therefore sacred, possessing its own worth which cannot be determined by humanity. The sacredness of nature means above all that it is to be cared for and not ruined by human beings, who themselves are of course a part of nature. Thus faith communities can be and should be sources of values that are alternative to those that see nature as simply a resource to be exploited for human ends of pleasure and commerce. The Orthodox Churches have contributed considerably to this ecumenical theology of nature.

While the WCC member churches and staff often work with others to actualize their values, the WCC has also established several programs of its own which deal directly with issues of the environment, such as the WCC Climate Change Program, which started in 1988. The WCC has also sponsored programs and research on mobility, and on biotechnology, nuclear arms and genetic engineering.

The title of various programs and conferences of the WCC in the last several decades demonstrate both the continuity and the change in ongoing ecumenical environmental thought and action. In the 1970s the WCC developed the ethical goal of a "Just, Participatory and Sustainable Society." In the 1980s it talked about "Justice, Peace and the Integrity of Creation." In the 1990s the phrase "The Theology of Life" described a decentralized, contextual, community-based approach to the integration of these same basic elements which are critical for what ecumenical thought calls sustainable communities.

One strength of ecumenical environmental thought is clearly this long-standing insistence on keeping the values of justice, sustainability, peace and environmental responsibility together, and relating them to other issues such as science and technology, capitalist development, and globalization. Another unique strength is the incredible diversity of the experiences of its member churches around the world which require ecumenical social thought, including ecumenical environmental thought, to be methodologically both very general and very specific and contextual simultaneously.

The diversity of experiences and contexts as well as theologies and interests contained in the ecumenical movement which make it so rich can also make it difficult for substantive ecumenical environmental ethics to move ahead. It is difficult to achieve ethical consensus across the many kinds of diversity of member churches. It is also difficult to hold member churches accountable to each other in concrete efforts to achieve in their own contexts and communions some of the goals to which they have agreed in voting for general statements of the ruling bodies of the WCC.

Heidi Hadsell

Further Reading

Faith and Science in an Unjust World. Roger Shinn, ed. Report of the WCC Conference on Faith, Science and the Future. Vol. 1 Plenary Presentations. Cambridge, MA, 12–24 July 1979. WCC, 1980.

Faith and Science in an Unjust World. Paul Abrecht, ed. Report of the WCC Conference on Faith, Science and the Future. Vol. 2 Reports and Recommendations. Cambridge, MA, 12–24 July 1979. WCC, 1980.

Hallman, David G. *Spiritual Values for Earth Community.* Geneva: WCC Publications, 2000.

Rasmussen, Larry. *Earth Community, Earth Ethics.* Maryknoll: Orbis Books, 1996.

See also: Christianity (8) – Ecumenical Movement International; Christianity (9) – Christianity's Ecological Reformation; Christianity and Sustainable Communities; Eco-Justice in Theology and Ethics; Environmental Justice and Environmental Racism; United Nations' "Earth Summits".

World Heritage Sites and Religion in Japan

Adopted in 1972 for the protection and preservation of precious natural and cultural sites; the World Heritage Convention of the United Nations Education, Science and Cultural Organization (UNESCO), thirty years after its founding, had inscribed 730 properties (563 cultural, 144 natural, and 23 mixed "cultural landscapes") from 125 countries on the World Heritage List. Nominations for World Heritage designation require well-documented governmental commitment to protect a site in perpetuity, clear and undisputed boundary surveys, and unambiguous arguments for the "outstanding uniqueness" of sites representing certain historical, aesthetic, or scientific genres.

Though in its formative years World Heritage selections were largely informed by Western aesthetic notions favoring monumental architecture and national parks, more recently UNESCO has worked to counterbalance this Euro-American bias by including "intangible" heritage such as sacred mountains, ritual performance traditions, and prayer (UNESCO 2001:2).

Japan's World Heritage sites

By 2003 the World Heritage Convention had recognized eleven Japanese sites, including Hiroshima's Peace Dome, Okinawa's Ryukyu castles (gusuku) and Yakushima's ancient cryptomeria forests. The sacred Kii mountain range running through Mie, Nara and Wakayama prefectures, with its unique combination of ascetic training grounds and lush forests, was nominated for consideration as Japan's twelfth designation.

Shugendô Mountain Asceticism

Asceticism as practiced in Japan's Kii mountains, known as Shugendô ("The Way of Acquiring Supernatural Power"), is a marginalized tradition that borrows selectively from Buddhist, Daoist, and Shintô sources. None of these borrowings is "final or authoritative" – when cosmology does not fit natural mountain formations, writes Paul Swanson, "so much the worse for cosmology" (Swanson 1981: 79). Denying themselves adequate food and sleep during long, treacherous climbs, Shugendô practitioners perform extreme austerities to access patron deities' spiritual power for worldly benefits.

Though Shugendô has no founder or formal doctrine, the basic procedure for achieving catharsis and healing is explained by priest-guide Gojô Kakugyô like this:

> You must discover the Buddha or deity within each of you. Weep for all the words left unspoken, the acts unfulfilled. Recognize your smallness in the face of the beauty and grandeur of great nature. This is the essential meaning of *sange* (repentance, recognition). If you cannot apologize face to face, apologize to the mountains, stones and rivers. But above all you must weep (*naku*). Only by shedding tears will you re-emerge whole (interview, Yoshino Japan, July 2002).

Humankind, animals, supernatural beings, and great nature exist in mutual interdependence, connected by the ability to weep. Because the individuals from whom practitioners sought forgiveness are no longer living or else their relationships are too chaotic, practitioners welcome the empathy and contemplation nature affords. Joblessness, infertility, alienated family relationships, and disquieted ancestors are common motivations for participating.

Mythmaking Potential of World Heritage

Throughout history, Shugendô has reinvented itself in response to proscription, ideological attack, and followers' changing needs. Priests at Kimpusen-ji temple (Nara prefecture) cleverly sought UNESCO's aid to imbue its sacred mountain Mount Omine with the aura of World Heritage. If successful, the designation will have honored and protected a pilgrimage trail (the Okukake) that neither the Bureau of Cultural Affairs or Nara Prefectural Government planned on designating as National or Prefectural Cultural Properties. UNESCO designation, said Tanaka Riten-san, the priest who initiated the nomination, is a critical step toward reclaiming Japan's religious consciousness "thrown out" (tsuterareta) by American Occupational forces' separation of Church and state (interview, Yoshino Japan, July 2003). Terence Hay-Edie's analysis of a Tibetan minority in Nepal finding opportunities for "new mythmaking exercises in world heritage ordered space," illustrates a similar convergence between UNESCO and marginalized communities' interests in heritage protection. In both cases, claims for uniqueness and authenticity rested upon stewardship of sacred mountains (Hay-Edie 2001:3).

Prior to the Kii peninsula's World Heritage nomination, an active community-based campaign promoted pride of place, cleanliness, and keeping its festivals well attended. Other voices from within and outside the community, however, questioned UNESCO's rhetoric of "promoting peace and security in the world through collaboration among nations" while ostensibly appropriating Japan's sacred sites for a global consumer market. Though UNESCO strives to help local and international organizations convert its ideals into effective "instruments for action," as in the case of Biosphere Reserves which Ron Engel discusses in these volumes, critics such as McGuire have charged that Japan's World Heritage designations have strayed from UNESCO's founding principles of protecting endangered sites and degenerated into a system of elite cultural prizes. Far from being endangered, Japan's World Heritage sites have long been protected by the domestic cultural property system and have been designated to boost sagging tourist markets. The resultant tourist deluge has been so great that some sites actually became endangered after UNESCO designation. On Yakushima, for example, hordes of mainland day-trippers have trampled sacred cryptomeria trees' exposed roots, forcing caretakers' to construct unsightly wooden rampways around the trees.

Wakayama's Environmental Crisis

Tateishi Kôshô-san, another Kimpusen-ji priest, has been successful manipulating the forces of World Heritage designation to protect the natural environment in nearby Wakayama. Among his devotees are individuals diagnosed with terminal lung cancer and heart failure who recovered completely after performing austerities under Kôshô-san's guidance. Kôshô-san is frequently described as "wild" (yasei-teki), "aboriginal" (senjumin-teki), and an "authentic mountain ascetic" (honmono no yamabushi). He established his own sect called "Shizendô" ("The Way of Nature") blending Shugendô with yoga, environmentalism, and dance. His spiritual practices are grounded in criticisms of Japan's environmental exploitation, cultural chauvinism, and floundering national education system. The Shugendô "boom" that began in the late 1990s, occasioned partly by UNESCO designation, has given Kôshô-san the ear of a growing international clientele who discovered Shugendô on the internet.

Kôshô gives greatest priority to protecting Wakayama's natural environment. He has been a strident critic of the Bureau of Cultural Affairs and prefectural government's declaring prominent religious sites "Important Cultural Properties," but then creating special laws and funds to protect only individual sites. This has left a mess of the overall environmental scene in surrounding areas. Former sacred peaks and riverbanks have been smashed into gravel pits. Over 50,000 used *tatami* mats were dumped into a ravine, creating a thirty meter high "*tatami* mountain." Junked buses and cars protrude from sacred waterfalls. Meanwhile government officials congratulate each other about forthcoming World Heritage designations to protect sacred peaks.

A major problem Kôshô-san and Wakayama residents face occurs when corporations buy land in the countryside promising to compost tatami mats or build dairy farms but instead carve gravel or dump illegally. Locals upset by these practices have been too weak, frightened, or poor to respond effectively.

Enlisting the Help of Local Bureaucrats and the Media

Kôshô-san has been successful working with local public officials, television and print media to raise awareness about Wakayama's environmental problems. In 1996 he first confronted the Japanese mafia who created these dumping grounds – a single man standing against wealthy corporations. Blowing his conch shell, reciting sutra, and with the force of Shugendô's patron deities Zao Gongen and Fudô-myô-ô behind him, he tried to stop them. At first his adversaries were amused and simply continued. But after getting the public officers and reporters behind him his movement gained traction. The tatami mountain was relocated to a legal dumpsite in 1996; by 1998, Kôshô'san and his environmental team bankrupted three corporations' gravel production ventures.

Spiritual Eco-tourism

Kôshô-san has kept meticulous records of media reports documenting his activities and shows practitioners damaged sites where trucks and machinery remain. He asks, "Is *this* World Heritage?" Seeing ascetics perform ablutions in a sacred waterfall with a protruding Toyota Land Cruiser provokes a direct, spiritual impression that statistics cannot convey. He hopes clients will appreciate the area's natural beauty and help protect it. Kôshô-san's efforts are a type of spiritual eco-tourism. He encourages university students who participate to choose environmentally responsible careers. After performing austerities in Wakayama's ancient forests to gain self-knowledge and overcome depression, students develop a sense of environmental stewardship. He appeals to their desires for rigorous exercise and communion with wild nature, but then gives them spiritual and ecological guidance which helps "green" their worldviews and consumer habits. Kôshô-san has also seized upon foreigners' interests in protecting Kumano's natural environment to motivate Japanese people who might not otherwise recognize its value.

Conclusions

In his role as ascetic mediator between environmentally destructive corporations and concerned locals, Kôshô-san has raised questions and confronted practices ignored by others. Fortified by austerities performed in the local mountains and waterfalls, Kôshô-san appears to be uniquely qualified to assess and respond to Wakayama's environmental crises. He leverages the potency and prestige of local and national media outlets, divinities, and foreign clients to protect Wakayama's natural environment. Kôshô-san is in spiritual kinship with similar charismatic reformers in Japanese religious history such as Ippen and Kukai, as well as with contemporary spiritual leaders in global environmental resistance movements, such as the Dalai Lama and Chief Oren Lyons. Local individuals with global vision and savvy media skills, like Kôshô-san and to a lesser extent Tanaka Riten-san, have mobilized UNESCO's universal vision of World Heritage to advance their own political agendas and inspire a generation of spiritually inclined environmentalists in Japan and abroad to protect their ascetic training grounds in the Kii Mountains.

Mark McGuire

Further Readings

McGuire, Mark. "What's at Stake in Designating Japan's Sacred Peaks UNESCO World Heritage Sites." In Rupert Cox and Christoph Brumann, eds. *Making Heritage in Japan*. London: Berg Press, 2004.

Miyake, Hitoshi. *Shugendô: Essays on the Structure of Japanese Folk Religion*. Ann Arbor, MI: University of Michigan Press, 2001.

Swanson, Paul L. "Shugendô and the Yoshino-Kumano Pilgrimage: An Example of Mountain Pilgrimage." *Monumenta Nipponica* 36:1 (1981), 55–84.

UNESCO. *First Proclamation of Masterpieces of the Oral and Intangible Heritage of Humanity*. Paris: UNESCO Publications, 2001.

See also: Biosphere Reserves and World Heritage Sites; Dalai Lama; Japanese Love of Nature; Japanese Religions; Lyons, Oren; Sacred Mountains; United Nations' "Earth Summits".

P | World Pantheist Movement

The World Pantheist Movement is an international grassroots membership organization promoting a completely naturalistic religious response to nature and the universe, with nature as the central focus of beliefs, practices, activities and ethics.

The WPM emerged from public interest generated by the pantheism website of its founder and president, United Kingdom environmentalist Dr. Paul Harrison. It was incorporated in the U.S. in 1998, and opened for membership in 1999. Its core beliefs are incorporated in the Pantheist Credo, a statement drawn up democratically by a group of 15 volunteers and revised at intervals.

The pantheist credo begins with a statement of reverence for the self-organizing universe's overwhelming power, beauty and fundamental mystery. It views all matter, energy, and life as an interconnected unity. It asserts that humans are an integral part of nature, which we should cherish and preserve in all its magnificent beauty and diversity, living in harmony with nature locally and globally. Acknowledging the inherent value of all life, human and nonhuman, it urges that all living beings should be treated with compassion and respect.

The credo's "social clause" asserts that all humans deserve a life of equal dignity and respect, and actively endorses freedom, democracy, justice, and non-discrimination, in a world focused on peace, sustainable ways of life, full respect for human rights and an end to poverty. It supports religious freedom and the separation of religion and state.

The WPM credo has a strongly naturalistic base. Nature, the entire living and non-living universe, is all that exists. There are no supernatural entities and no separate spirit realms. There is a single kind of substance, energy/matter, which is vibrant and infinitely creative. Consciousness and mind are emergent qualities of energy/matter. The senses and science are our best means of developing our ongoing knowledge of the universe, and the most solid basis for aesthetic and religious feelings about reality. Nature is seen as the only real basis on which religious feeling can be built.

Death is also viewed naturalistically, as a return to nature through the natural recycling of our elements, which should be facilitated by cremation or natural burial in simple linen shrouds or wicker baskets. There is no afterlife for the individual consciousness, but we live on through our actions, our ideas and memories of us, giving us a powerful incentive to do good.

The credo is not a requirement of membership, it is a "notice on the door," a guide to core WPM tenets for people who are thinking of joining. These beliefs are closely related to those of deep ecology, religious humanism, religious naturalism, Unitarian Universalism, and modern Western versions of Stoicism, Daoism and Zen Buddhism, and the WPM welcomes membership by anyone who self-describes as one of these.

Ritual is optional in the WPM and there are no prescribed practices. Ceremony is seen not as magical placation of a supernatural being or beings, but essentially as self-expression of reverence and belonging. Members enjoy complete freedom of expression, and this may vary from nature walks, through individual meditation within nature, to shared organic meals or even pagan-like rites of a purely symbolic character. Some members are comfortable using religious terms in pantheistic ways, while others avoid them. The WPM aims eventually to provide a network of civil celebrants for nature-oriented weddings and funerals. As of 2003 this was limited to authorizing members to celebrate weddings and funerals on behalf of friends and relatives.

Many of the WPM's members are active environmentalists, but the organization also directly facilitates nature-related activities. It encourages members to join its group, saving wildlife habitat by daily clicking at the Ecology Fund's website. By summer 2003 this group had saved 25 acres. This activity is funded by sponsors. The World Pantheist Movement itself sponsors this aspect of Ecology Fund and of Care2's Save Rainforest sites, and by summer 2003 had saved an additional 62 acres in this way. Finally, in association with the National Wildlife Federation in the United States, the WPM encourages its members to set aside land (even small amounts) for wildlife, through wildlife-friendly gardening and sustainable management in the interests of native wildlife. So far 42 acres have been dedicated to wildlife.

The WPM also encourages direct contact among members and other pantheists. Local groups tend to meet in natural settings for walks, picnics, star watching and so on. The WPM set up the first generic pantheist mailing lists, the pantheist Usenet list, as well as almost sixty mailing lists and bulletin boards of its own devoted to discussion, local activities, specific topic areas, and organizational development.

Paul Harrison

Further Reading

Harrison, Paul. *Elements of Pantheism*. New York: HarperCollins/Element Books, 1999.

See also: Corrington, Robert; Daoism; Deep Ecology; Epic of Evolution; Pantheism; Religious Naturalism; Wilson, Edward O.; Zen Buddhism.

World Wildlife Fund – *See* World Wide Fund for Nature (WWF).

World Wide Fund for Nature (WWF)

The World Wide Fund for Nature (World Wildlife Fund in the U.S.) has organized and supported a series of initiatives on religions and conservation, to build new partnerships with the world's faiths in the struggle to save the natural world. The first event was an Interfaith Ceremony in the Basilica di S. Francesco in Assisi, Italy, organized as part of WWF's 25th anniversary celebrations in September 1986. Five major religions were invited to make declarations on Religion and Nature. These declarations, addressed by religious leaders to the faithful in the Buddhist, Christian, Hindu, Jewish and Muslim worlds, describe the values and ethics that lead them to the conservation of nature. In the years following that event, other religions joined in making similar declarations, including the Bahá'ís (1987), the Sikhs (1989), the Jains (1991), and the Daoists of China (1995).

WWF, in collaboration with Martin Palmer of the International Consultancy on Religion, Education & Culture (ICOREC), built on the Assisi event to establish a Network on Conservation and Religion to link faiths worldwide working on conservation projects. As a result, in the first nine years, an estimated 100,000 religious communities became involved in conservation activities The faiths launched programs of work, education and instruction based around their teachings on nature. Undamaged native forests on monastery land on Mount Athos, Greece, were protected from logging. A Hindu Environment Center was established in the pilgrimage town of Vrindavan, India.

In 1995, after nine years of activity, WWF invited the religions to review progress and plan for the future at the Summit on Religions and Conservation which it organized in two parts. The first session of activists and thinkers within the faiths was held in Japan on 3–9 April 1995. It took stock of what had been achieved since Assisi, and drafted Faith Reviews and Future Plans. This was followed by the second session, a summit meeting of top religious leaders in England, 29 April–3 May 1995. The event was hosted by Prince Philip at Windsor Castle, meeting in the room where William Shakespeare first performed the Merry Wives of Windsor. Participants included Madame Rabbani, leading Bahá'í dignitary; Venerable Kushok Bakula, twentieth incarnation of the Arhat Bakula, for the Buddhists; The Ecumenical Patriarch Bartholomew (Orthodox); Rev. Bernard J. Przewozny, Pontifical Adviser on environmental issues (Catholic); Rev. Dr. Samuel Kobia, World Council of Churches, and the Archbishop of Canterbury (Anglican) for the Christians; Swami Vibudhesha Teertha, Acharya of the Madhva Sect for the Hindus; Dr. L.M. Singhvi for the Jains; Rabbi Arthur Hertzberg, Vice President Emeritus, World Jewish Congress Dr. Adnan Bakhit, President of the University of Al al-Bayt, Jordan, representing Crown Prince El Hassan bin Talal, for the Muslims; Sri Singh Sahib Jathedar Manjit Singh, Jathedar of Akaal Takhat (Throne of Timeless Being) for the Sikhs; and Mr Xie Zongxing, Vice President, China Taoist Association; all accompanied by supporting staff. Each of the nine religions presented a paper on ecology and faith describing their accomplishments, commitments, initiatives and future prospects.

At the summit, four experts were invited to present the issues to the religious leaders for discussion: Andrew Steer, Director of the Environment Department at the World Bank; Dr. Arthur Dahl, Deputy Assistant Executive Director of the United Nations Environment Programme; Dr. Susan George, author and Associate Director of the Transnational Institute; and Sam Younger Managing Director, BBC World Service. Various themes were discussed over the four days of the summit. The harmony among the distinguished participants demonstrated how much their spiritual principles in this area converged.

At the beginning of the summit, an ecumenical celebration was held in the St. George's Chapel in Windsor Castle, with each religion presenting something of particular significance to their tradition. The summit was followed by a procession of the leaders in London from Westminster Abbey to Westminster Cathedral.

One result of the summit was the formation of an Alliance of Religions and Conservation as the successor to the WWF Network on Conservation and Religion to follow up on the commitments made. The Alliance assembled a series of projects relevant to ecology and faith for which it sought outside support. The summit also increased the engagement of the faiths with secular organizations such as the World Bank, which led to a continuing dialogue.

Another step in this WWF initiative was the preparation by the faiths of sacred gifts for the living Earth which they announced at an interfaith celebration in Kathmandu, Nepal in November 2000 during WWF's annual conference. Two additional religions, the Zoroastrian and the Shinto, joined the Alliance of Religions and Conservation at that time. The initiative continues to spread, with WWF France organizing an interfaith colloquium in 2003. WWF has also published various books on world religions and ecology.

Arthur Dahl

Further Reading

Edwards, Jo and Martin Palmer, eds. *Holy Ground: The Guide to Faith and Ecology*. Yelvertoft Manor, Northamptonshire: Pilkington Press, 1997.

See also: Alliance of Religion and Conservation; Indigenous Environmental Network; Network on Conservation and Religion; Palmer, Martin; Prince Charles; Religious Environmentalist Paradigm; van der Post, Laurens.

Wright, Judith (1915–2000)

Judith Wright (b. Armidale, Australia; d. Canberra, Australia) was one of Australia's best-known poets, twice nominated for the Nobel Prize. One of the generation of poets who emerged from World War II – about which she wrote so passionately in early poems like "The Company Of Lovers" – she brought a new note to a tradition which, largely secular and patriarchal, had ignored the erotic and religious. Writing the "feminine" into it, she brought it closer to the culture of the land's First Peoples with whom she had a lifelong affinity – the Aboriginal poet and activist Oodgeroo Noonuccal was one of her closest friends.

Her feeling for nature was essential to this. Born into a pioneering pastoral family she grew up not only on the land, "my blood's country" (Wright 1994: 20), but also with it, ". . . riding the cleared hills, / plucking blue leaves for their eucalypt scent, / hearing the call of the plover / in a land I thought was mine for life" (316).

As she grew older, however, she began to realize how destructive her colonial inheritance had been: "What swells over us now is a logical spread / from the small horizons we made – / the heave of great corporations / whose bellies are never full" (407).

The task was to make amends, to live with the Earth, not to exploit it. Poetry, the voice of feeling and empathy, became her way of doing this. But she also became an environmental activist and champion of Aboriginal Australians.

Her experience as a woman of love, pregnancy, and birth also drew her into the life of the cosmos. In "Woman To Child," for instance, mother and child are part of the unfolding story of creation: "Then all a world I made in me; / all the world you hear and see / hung upon my dreaming blood. / There moved the multitudinous stars, / and coloured birds and fishes moved. / There swam the sliding continents" (28).

This moved her beyond the merely anthropocentric into the dimension of the sacred. Another poem is addressed to Ishtar, goddess of childbirth: "You neither know nor care for the truth of my heart; / but the truth of my body has all to do with you. / You have no need of my thoughts or hopes, / living in the realm of the absolute event" (102).

Her religious sense was thus essentially sensuous and bodily, immanent and transcendent, as the sequence "Flesh" makes this clear:

God walked through all my ages. He set in me
the key that fits the keyhole; use it right
and eternity's lightning splits the rock of time.
And there I was begun and so begotten
in that unspeakable heart of flame (146).

Significantly this cosmic and mythic perspective echoes that of Aboriginal culture: "Earth watches through our eyes, and as we stare / she greets, by us, her far compatriots there, / the wild-haired Suns and the calm Wanderers. / Her ancient thought is marked in every name; / hero and creature mingle in her dream" (203).

But it also led her to grieve over the land's sufferings at our hands: "I am what land has made / and land's myself, I said. / And therefore when land dies? / opened by whips of greed / these plains lie torn and scarred. / Then I erode; my blood / reddens the stream in flood" (279).

In this way, too, she shared the feelings of the land's First Peoples, "the night ghosts of a land / only by day possessed" (354) who represented the other side of the triumphalist story of settlement.

This identification combined with physical frailty as

she grew older made her increasingly angry and she identified with the darker energies of the cosmos. In this poem to the moon, "ruler of women / and singler-out of poets," for instance, she claimed the powers of a crone:

> . . . To you, chill Domina,
> I make the prayer of age. In my last quarter
> let me be hag, but poet.
> The lyric note may vanish from my verse
> but you have also found acceptable
> the witch's spell –
> even the witch's curse (341–2).

To the end she insisted on involvement: ". . . who wants to be a mere onlooker? every cell of me / has been pierced through with intergalactic messages" (422).

Her sense of self has become truly cosmic here, attuned to the language and energies of creation beyond good and evil as we know them, energies she glimpsed hanging over a rockpool's "wild embroideries." Admiring it, ". . . the devouring and mating, / ridges of coloured tracery, occupants, all the living, / the stretching of toothed claws to food, the breeding / on the ocean's edge" (419).

But there was also the deep sense of belonging, of being attuned to the language of the world, expressed in "Rainforest," for instance: "We with our quick dividing eyes / measure, distinguish and are gone. / The forest burns, the tree-frog dies, / yet one is all and all are one" (412).

That is perhaps why after the age of seventy she wrote no more poetry. But the world would continue to speak. Self, nature, poetry and the sacred are one. In one sense, that involved a return to a more "primitive" sense of reality. But in another, it pointed a way out of the crisis posed by our present technological culture. So her *Collected Poems* conclude:

> All's fire, said Herclitus; measures of it
> kindle as others fade. All changes yet all's one.
> We are born of ethereal fire and we return there.
> Understand the Logos; reconcile opposing principles.
>
> Perhaps the dark itself is the source of meaning,
> the fires of the galaxy its visible destruction . . .
>
> . . . "Twisted are the hearts of men – dark powers posses them.
> Burn the distant evil-doer, the unseen sinner."
> That prayer to Agni, fire-god, cannot be prayed.
> We are all of us born of fire, possessed by darkness (426).

Veronica Brady

Further Reading
Brady, Veronica. *South Of My Days: A Biography of Judith Wright*. Sydney: Angus and Robertson, 1998.
Turner, Ian, ed. *The Australian Dream*. Melbourne: Sun Books, 1968, 102.
Walker, Shirley. *Australian Bibliographies: Judith Wright*. Melbourne: Oxford University Press, 1981.
Wright, Judith. *Collected Poems: 1942–1985*. Sydney: Angus and Robertson, 1994.
See also: Aboriginal Dreaming; Aboriginal Spirituality and the New Age in Australia; Australia; Australian Poetry.

Xhosa-Speakers' Traditional Concept of God

The Xhosa-speaking peoples of South Africa, living along the eastern seaboard between the Great Fish River in the south and the KwaZulu-Natal border in the north, were the first Bantu-speakers to engage with the expanding white colonists in the late eighteenth century. Their traditional religion, like that of all Southern Bantu, comprised four main elements: the belief in a Supreme Being, the veneration of the ancestors, the manipulation of medicines and the fear of witchcraft. Of these, the belief in God was the least developed, although there is evidence that it was early influenced, to some extent, by concepts derived from neighboring San (Bushmen) and Khoekhoen ("Hottentots"). Later, under the teachings of missionaries, the concept was greatly modified.

The belief in a supreme creator being can be traced at least to 1100, when Late Iron Age agropastoralist Bantu-speakers moved out of the coastal plains of the Transvaal Lowveld onto the interior plateau or, as among Nguni, down the fertile corridor between the Drakensberg range and the Indian Ocean. Belief in a Supreme Being may, indeed, go back to the first settlement of Early Iron Age peoples south of the Limpopo River, dated to ca. 600. The Xhosa-speakers (or Cape Nguni) over the centuries split up into a number of chiefdom clusters, such as Thembu, Xesibe and Mpondo; the Xhosa proper, discussed here, were the southernmost group, living in what was formerly the Ciskei and southwestern Transkei.

The Xhosa had a number of names for the Supreme Being. Some obviously derived from the pre-Khoesan contact period, as both Xhosa and Zulu share them. These comprise distinct sets of reference. One set perceives God as a craftsman – the Maker, the Molder or, by extension, as *uHlanga*, referring, in Xhosa, to a mystical cave and, in Zulu, to a bed of reeds, from which all beings came forth by God's command. Another set of concepts conceived him as a nature god, seeing him in the natural phenomena of lightning, thunder and rainbow, and in the all-important rain. Thus God was called the Lord of the Sky, iNkosi yeZulu. He acted by his powerful will; his actions – good or evil were beyond question, whether he struck human or beast with lightning or withheld rain. No sacrifice was offered to him: only prayer or entreaty could propitiate him. He was different from and beyond the ancestors, and his actions would never be confused with witchcraft, even though it was believed that God sometimes sent the "lightning bird."

The pre-Khoesan period also undoubtedly employed a kinship-related metaphor in its theology. The association of God with uHlanga and the emergence of humans and animals was as the creator of the world, the First-in-Time, Mvelatangi or Mvelanqangi. But he seems to have been likened also to a firstborn son (imvelanqangi), forever identified as the First Authority, on the model of a homestead head, autonomous over his family and expressing the vitally important principle of agnatic authority characteristic, particularly, of Nguni. But he was not in any way a type of super-ancestor, for he was utterly outside the realm of ancestorhood. An authoritative explanation of misfortune, evil, ill-health and death is an important function of all religions. Here the explanations of choice among Xhosa (as in all South African groups) were ancestral wrath, witchcraft and pollution. Explanation in terms of God was more in the nature of an ultimate residual category when these failed – rather like the exasperated statement "God only knows!" In this sense, God was peripheral to the everyday, practical religion of the common man or woman. The ever-present, brooding, spiritual influences resided in the ancestors.

Among Xhosa, however, there appears to have been a new elaboration of the God concept, related to the institution of chieftainship, and possibly influenced by Khoe culture. This change is expressed by the introduction of two new names for God, uQamata and uThixo, the most typical Xhosa names for God today. Both derived from San (or from Khoe) sources, possibly after Xhosa began to intermarry with San and Khoekhoen.

The term *uQamata* first appears in the literature only in the 1870s, but Xhosa oral tradition holds that it is the most ancient of the two San (Khoe) terms. L.F. Maingard speculated that *uQamata* was perhaps the name of a Khoe culture hero. Tentative reconstruction of the *uQamata* cult suggests that it only operated in times of national crises, was orchestrated by the chiefs and held on mountaintops – unlike the ancestral rituals, which always took place in the cattle byre. If all the rainmakers' medicine had failed, then the chief prayed to uQamata on behalf of the people for rain, or the warding off of storms. This cult contrasted strongly with the kin-based ancestral blood sacrifice, officiated over by clan elders. It, significantly, consisted of prayer only. With one exception, none of the old records mention sacrificial killings or libations in uQamata's honor. It thus reflected God's role in the interface between society and nature, not, typically, the relationships between kinsmen – the essence of the ancestor religion. It also had a national, political dimension.

Probably due to Christian practice, the name of God most widely used today is uThixo, deriving from Khoe *Tsui//Goab*, meaning "Wounded Knee," the name of the divinized hero and Rain God of the Khoekhoen. It was adapted in this form by the missionaries, to clearly distinguish traditional concepts from that of the new, universal deity that they proclaimed.

Heinz Kuckertz

Further Reading

Hammond-Tooke, W.D. "World-view: A System of Beliefs, a System of Action." In W.D. Hammond-Tooke, ed. *The Bantu-speaking Peoples of Southern Africa*. London: Routledge & Kegan Paul, 1974, 318–63.

Harinck, Gerrit. "Interaction between Xhosa and Khoi: Emphasis on the Period 1620–1750." In L. Thompson, ed. *African Societies in Southern Africa*. London: Heinemann, 1969, 145–70.

Hodgson, Janet. *The God of the Xhosa*. Cape Town: Oxford University Press, 1982.

Junod, Henri. *The Life of a South African Tribe*. London: Macmillan & Co., 1927.

Maingard, L.F. "The Linguistic Approach to South African Prehistory and Ethnology." *South African Journal of Science* XXXI (1934), 117–43.

Peires, J.B. "Visions and Interpretations." In *The House of Phalo*. Johannesburg: Ravan Press, 1981, 64–78.

Schapera, I. *The Khoisan Peoples of South Africa: Bushmen and Hottentots*. London: Routledge & Kegan Paul, 1930.

Wilson, Monica. "The Shades, Medicines, Witchcraft and God." In *Religion and the Transformation of Society: A Study in Social Change in Africa*. Cambridge: Cambridge University Press, 1971, 26–51.

See also: Khoisan Religion; Pollution Beliefs in South Africa; Venda Religion and the Land; Zulu (amaZulu) Culture, Plants, and Spirit Worlds.

Yakama Nation

The peoples now commonly called the Yakamas traditionally lived in much of what is now central and eastern Washington State. Under provisions of the Walla Walla Treaty of 1855, the tribes ceded over 10 million acres to the United States government, and what is called the Yakama Indian Reservation was created. The Yakamas, who now number nearly 9000 tribal members, actually comprise 14 different bands and tribes, sharing a Sahaptin linguistic base, and a similar social history involving a migratory hunter-gatherer existence.

The Yakama Reservation itself is the largest in the Pacific Northwest, comprising nearly 1.4 million acres, nearly half again as large as Rhode Island. It stretches from the summit of the Cascade Mountains east to the irrigated farmlands and native range lands of the Yakima Valley (the Yakamas changed their own name to reflect original spellings). The Reservation has significant natural resources, with extensive farming and grazing lands, proximity to both the Yakima and Columbia Rivers, and healthy stands of commercially viable timber, including both Ponderosa Pine and Douglas Fir.

This biological diversity and richness is connected to the present religious diversity of the Yakamas, and how the various spiritual traditions view the environment. It is essential, however, to note that all three religious traditions – despite different theological orientations – have made room for a significant amount of agreement on the importance of environmental respect. This agreement often translates into a significant power base in deciding questions of environmental policy on the Reservation.

There are three major spiritual traditions on the Reservation: the traditional *washat* (sometimes called the Seven Drum Religion or Longhouse Religion), more traditional expressions of Christianity as brought by missionaries in the nineteenth century, and the Indian Shaker Faith. The *washat* was founded along the Columbia River by the "Dreamer Prophet" Smohalla in the mid-nineteenth century, and represents a native revitalization movement that combines certain religious elements from Western Christianity with native spirituality. At the outset the religion was adamant in its stand against agriculture and mining, believing such practices to be antithetical to the proper attitude toward the Creator and toward the Earth. Today, the faith no longer rejects these practices, but the *washat* still takes environmental respect as one of its cornerstones.

Its modern strongholds also reflect the environmental tenets of the religion, which mirror the Yakamas' ties between Creator and nature. The modern *washat* is celebrated at a number of locations both on and off the reservation, including the traditional fishing villages of Priest Rapids and Rock Creek, both on the Columbia River. That the *washat* is celebrated along the banks of what was once the greatest salmon fishery in the world is no accident. This connection between religion and geography emphasizes the fact that the *washat* celebrates the salmon as one of the Creator's principal gifts to his people.

Much of traditional Yakama mythology centers on the Columbia River and the salmon, and often spotlights "*Spil-yay*" the trickster (portrayed by the coyote) acting on the people's behalf. In the Yakama story "Spil-yay Breaks the Dam," Coyote acts to save his people when the greedy Swallow Sisters dam the Columbia, preventing the salmon from reaching the traditional fishing sites. In "Legend of the Lost Salmon," even Coyote is ineffectual in reviving the salmon when the people disregard the Creator's rules about the proper way to fish. Only through the miraculous intervention of an elder are the salmon restored, reminding the people that greed and disrespect for the Creator have no place in their lives. Such stories are an essential part of the *washat* heritage, and reflect the intense love and respect for the environment that is at the heart of the religion.

The *washat* enjoys certain cultural and historical advantages due to its being interwoven into the very fabric of traditional native social life, and its beliefs on nature are disseminated far more often than at formal times of worship. For example, at times of crisis such as the death of the tribal member, Yakama storytellers are still retained to relate traditional stories about nature's creatures, the connections between worship toward the Creator and tribal morality, and sacred places on the reservation. The stories function both as explanation for cultural and tribal morality, and distraction for the grieving family. Thus, the recent surge in the *washat*'s popularity among the Yakamas has been accompanied by an increased focus on encouraging traditional ways of looking at social structures.

There are also Yakamas who worship in traditional Christian denominations, represented in mainline and Pentecostal churches. These churches are mostly situated in the most populated areas of the reservation, from the middle Yakima Valley northwest to the border of the Reservation at the city of Yakima itself.

Most Yakamas who attend traditional Christian services

do so at churches started fairly recently, and aimed specifically at reaching native populations. Some, however, attend churches started by missionaries during the nineteenth century, during the days of federal policy that gave priority to one religious group for each reservation.

For the Yakama Reservation, the Methodist-Episcopal denomination was selected by the administration of President Ulysses Grant as the religion that would be responsible for the "moral and spiritual education" of the Yakamas, and in the formative years of the Reservation, Methodism's popularity was boosted by this governmental sponsorship. During this time period, Methodism's opposition to traditional native spirituality – especially toward Smohalla and the *washat* – was personified in the person of James Harvey Wilbur, Indian Agent from 1864–1882. Wilbur did everything in his power to defeat the *washat*'s influence, believing that traditional native religious views toward nature were the single biggest barrier to "Indian civilization," and his promotion of native agriculture was second to none in the entire Indian service of that time.

Today, Christian churches on the reservation do not attempt to change traditional Yakama attitudes and beliefs toward the environment, preferring to focus more on evangelism. To be sure, since traditional Yakama spirituality knows little or no separation between theology and morality, and since many of the traditional spiritual beliefs contain animistic elements that are more directly confrontational with traditional Christianity, some conflict is unavoidable. Nonetheless, the Christian churches' otherworldly focus results in many Yakama worshippers retaining traditional views toward nature, at least in part. Thus, Yakamas who consider themselves as Christians are free to side with *washat* attendees on environmental issues – despite a different spiritual orientation.

The Shaker religion in the Pacific Northwest was founded by John Slocum near Olympia, Washington, in the late 1800s, and represents a third religious option on the Yakama Reservation. Shaker beliefs have always been centered more on individual piety and morality, rather than the rejection of any particular culture's practices (e.g., agriculture), and the churches' present location reflects this concern. The three Indian Shaker Churches are located not at traditional villages (as is often the case with the *washat*), nor close to populations centers (like more traditional Christian churches), but in the heart of the Reservation's prime agricultural lands. Historically, many Yakama Shakers have been employed in the agriculture industry, and Shaker teachings have never equated modern technology with impropriety.

The religion itself combines ritualistic elements from both Protestantism and Catholicism, and considers itself a type of Christianity reserved for Native Americans. The Shaker faith does not focus on extensive doctrinal subtleties, however, and hence there is a great deal of latitude amongst individual worshippers on beliefs considered tangential to individual holiness. Thus, many believers have not rejected the traditional Yakama views on nature, and, on many key issues such as water rights or salmon restocking, both *washat* attendees and Shakers often present a united front.

Thus, despite three very different religious traditions amongst the Yakamas today, there is a growing voice on the need to respect the environment – a voice not lost by the very real religious diversity on the reservation. Certainly not rejecting agriculture or logging, but insisting on wisdom as a foundational value for environmental policy, this voice serves in many ways as a counter-voice to the surrounding voice of the majority culture. To cite just one example, despite the mostly dismal picture on the state of the northwest salmon, the Yakamas have been at the forefront of an intense program of stream revitalization and salmon stocking, and there have been a number of local successes in terms of fish returns. Thus, when focusing on the connections between religion and nature, the Yakama Nation is serving as an important example to other native peoples. Large in size, rich in resources, the Yakama Reservation and its peoples have demonstrated that religious diversity need not be a barrier to environmental progress.

Michael McKenzie

Further Reading
Beavert, Virginia, ed. *The Way it Was*. Seattle: The Consortium of Johnson O'Malley Committees of the State of Washington, 1974.
Castile, George. "The 'Half-Catholic' Movement: Edwin and Myron Eells and the Rise of the Indian Shaker Church." *Pacific Northwest Quarterly* (October 1982), 165–74.
Hunn, Eugene. *Nch'I-Wána ("The Big River"): Mid-Columbia Indians and Their Land*. Seattle: University of Washington Press, 1990.
Moses, L.G. "James Mooney and Wovoka: An Ethnologist's Visit with the Ghost Dance Prophet." *Nevada Historical Society Quarterly* 23:2 (Summer 1980), 71–86.
Ramsey, Jarold ed. *Coyote Was Going There: Indian Literature of the Oregon Country*. Seattle: University of Washington Press, 1987.
Ruby, Robert H. and John A. Brown. *Dreamer-Prophets of the Columbia Plateau: Smohalla and Sko'askin*. Norman, OK: University of Oklahoma Press, 1989.
Whitner, Robert Lee. "The Methodist Episcopal Church and Grant's Peace Policy: A Study of the Methodist Agencies, 1870–1882." Dissertation, The University of Minnesota, 1959.

See also: Columbia River Watershed Pastoral Letter; Washat Religion (Drummer-Dreamer Faith).

Yamuna

The Yamuna is a river that flows from its source of Yamunotri high in the central Himalayas for about 826 miles to its confluence with the Ganges on the plains at Allahabad. It has long been considered one of the holiest rivers of northern India, and for centuries has been worshipped as an aquatic goddess. Today, however, much of the river has become polluted, causing a variety of responses from the religious community that is associated with the worship of the Yamuna.

The Yamuna originates from the Yamunotri glacier at an elevation near 20,000 feet above sea level. This glacier is nestled on a steep slope just below the crest of Mount Kalinda, located about six miles west of the Bandarpunch peak (20,735 feet), the dominant mountain in the central Himalayan region of Garhwal that divides the watershed of the Yamuna and Ganges. The Yamuna gushes out of the morainic snout of the glacier to fill the pond Saptarishikund, named after seven sages who called the river down from heaven for the benefit of Earth, and from here cascades down the southern face of Mount Kalinda. Accordingly, the Yamuna is also called "Kalindi." The cold water stream drops into a canyon where it joins the other recognized source of the Yamuna: a hot spring that flows from a stone wall of the canyon. Here, at an elevation of about 10,500 feet, is located the Yamunotri complex, an important temple site and destination of a popular pilgrimage. Pilgrims have been coming to this site for centuries to worship Yamuna and seek her blessings.

Yamuna is depicted at her Himalayan source in her Puranic form as a goddess having a dark complexion, clothed in red garments, holding in her hand a pot filled with good fortune, and sitting on the back of a turtle. Because the goddess Yamuna brings life-giving water from the mountains, and is associated with the creative powers that animate all life, she is often addressed as "Mother." Yamuna is considered to be the sister of the goddess Ganges, who sits by her side in the Yamunotri temple. Yamuna is also considered to be the daughter of Surya, god of the sun, and the twin sister of Yama, the god of death, and as such the priests who attend the Yamunotri pilgrimage complex regard her as an auspicious goddess who blesses the lives of her pilgrims and protects them from death. Pilgrims visiting the Yamunotri complex cook food in the hot spring's boiling water, which is considered to be a gift of the sun to his daughter, and bathe in a tank filled with its hot water to be blessed, purified, and freed from sins.

The Yamuna descends rapidly from the Yamunotri pilgrimage complex to carve a valley through the beautiful Garhwali Mountains before forcing its way through the Shivalik foothills and emerging onto the Indo-gangetic plains at the town of Dakpathar. Here where the Yamuna leaves the wild mountains and enters the "civilized" plains a great change takes place: Dakpathar marks a transition from the natural to the industrial, from river worship to river management, and from the Yamuna as a majestically unimpeded river to Yamuna as a greatly reduced stream, for here a huge barrage (a dam-like structure comprised of a long series of gates that regulate water flow for irrigation and hydro-electric power) has been built across the entire river and the great majority of the water is removed from the riverbed to be channeled off into utility canals. A little further downstream, the Yamuna reaches Tajewala, site of another massive barrage that blocks the river for irrigation and channels its water into the Western and Eastern Canals. The Yamuna then flows through the industrial towns of Yamunanagar, Karnal, Panipat, and Sonepat before arriving in the huge metropolis of Delhi, capital of the modern nation of India. Only 10 percent of the volume of water leaving the mountains reaches Delhi; almost all of the water remaining in the riverbed is extracted for domestic and commercial use in the capital city, which has borne the major weight of the rapid development that has occurred in India since the late 1980s. Although Delhi was built on the bank of the Yamuna long ago because of the river's bounty and beauty, today the city dumps millions of gallons of untreated sewage and industrial effluents into the Yamuna, making the stretch of the river downstream one of the most polluted in India.

What remains of the Yamuna, after Delhi, flows past the ornate temples and magnificent sandstone bathing platforms of the pilgrimage centers of Vrindaban, Mathura, and Gokul in Braj, the important cultural region associated with the Hindu god of love, Krishna. This is also the area in which Yamuna is most celebrated as a goddess and her theology has been most fully developed, for here she is regarded as a goddess of supreme love. Consequently, there are more temples dedicated to Yamuna in this region than anywhere else along her course. Much of the theological tradition associated with Yamuna is the lasting result of a cultural efflorescence that took place in this region in the sixteenth century.

Although the river is becoming increasingly polluted, religious practices directed to Yamuna are still common: her devotees bathe in her daily, they sip her water reverently, make special offerings to her liquid form, and honor her presence in the many temples of Braj. Her water is also an essential ingredient in many of the temple rituals conducted in this region. For her Braj devotees, Yamuna is a goddess of exquisite love and compassion who initiates souls into the divine love affair. Among the pantheon of Hindu goddesses it would be difficult to find one more representative of divine love than Yamuna. In Braj, she is considered to be a chief lover of the youthful god Krishna. So great is her eagerness to join Krishna that, rather than being pictured on the back of a slow turtle, Yamuna is portrayed in this region running to offer her beloved a flower garland. Moreover, she experiences the deepest of all loves, and yet rather than selfishly holding onto the joy of that love for herself, she shares its life-enhancing bliss with all who approach her with an open heart. The theme of Yamuna's loving generosity is thus fundamental to her theology in Braj.

The Yamuna leaves the pilgrimage towns of Braj and winds her way through dry arroyos to reach Agra, site of the celebrated Taj Mahal that stands on a high bank overlooking the river. Downstream the Yamuna is joined by some important tributaries, most significantly the Chambal River, which drains the eastern slopes of the Aravalli Mountain range in southeastern Rajasthan. After receiving fresh water from these tributaries, the Yamuna is somewhat restored. By the time the Yamuna arrives at the confluence with her sister the Ganges at Allahabad she is clearly the bigger of the two rivers. The confluence of these riverine sisters offers a remarkable sight: water from the Yamuna is deep blue in color, whereas water from the Ganges is chalky white; the two meet to form a wide expanse of water that is divided by a clearly distinguishable line.

This is site of the famous Kumba Mela, the largest religious gathering of human beings on the planet, and another favorite bathing spot for the many pilgrims who come here for a life-blessing "holy dip." Although the Yamuna nominally ends at Allahabad, devotees of this river insist that the resulting confluence is "Ganges in name, but Yamuna in form." Since about two-thirds of the water flowing past the confluence comes from the Yamuna riverbed, the "Ganges River" that flows past the holy city of Benares and empties into the Bay of Bengal is to a large degree the Yamuna.

Religious responses to the increasing environmental degradation of the river move in two different directions: religious practices are declining as a result of the pollution, and religious sentiment is being marshaled to check the contamination. Although religious beliefs and practices related to the Yamuna are still common, they are being weakened by the declining health of the river. For example, many people who used to bathe regularly in the river for religious purposes are no longer doing so, and Yamuna water is no longer being used in many of the temple rituals in Braj. People are beginning to recognize that the life-giving river goddess is "sick"; some of her devotees even suggest that Yamuna is "dying." Clearly the pollution of the river has a great impact not only on the physical health of the people who inhabit her banks, but also on the religious culture that has thrived along her course for centuries.

Devotees of Yamuna are not only lamenting her declining health; some are taking direct action to save her. Although the Indian government has attempted to remedy some of the problems of Yamuna pollution through the Yamuna Action Plan inaugurated in 1993, most of the inspiration for cleaning the river has come from the religious community. In the past, "loving service" (*seva*) to Yamuna typically has been expressed through a variety of acts of worship; today the idea is emerging that the proper form of loving service is environmental activism. Motivated by a deep love for the goddess Yamuna, some of her devotees have initiated political demonstrations and environmental education programs, and have taken polluters and the government to court in an effort to halt the pollution of the river. Their actions provide instructive examples of how religious sentiment has been enlisted to save rivers, and how river worshippers express their devotion through environmental activism.

David L. Haberman

See also: Hinduism; India; Mammy Water; Water in Islam; Water in Zoroastrianism; Water Spirits and Indigenous Ecological Management (South Africa).

Yanomami

The Yanomami are indigenes who live on either side of the border between northern Brazil and southern Venezuela in the Amazon rainforest near rivers in the lowlands and streams in the Guyana Highlands. Some 20,000 Yanomami reside in up to three hundred or more separate communities, which range in size from a few dozen to a hundred or more individuals. Their subsistence economy is characterized by a sustainable rotational system of bow-and-arrow hunting, fishing, gathering, and swidden farming. This economy is associated with low population density and high mobility. Sub-groups or a whole community forage from camps in the forest, on treks of days to months in duration, several times a year. Thus, Yanomami interact daily in intimate ways with each other and their natural habitat.

The Yanomami do not rigidly distinguish between the natural and supernatural realms. Religion permeates their daily life, society, culture, and ecology. Their variety of animism or nature religion focuses on numerous and diverse spiritual beings which inhabit the forests, streams, mountains, and other physical features in their habitat. Some of these spirits are contacted and manipulated by shamans, part-time ritual specialists. Several men in each community may practice shamanism. One or more shamans dramatically chant and dance ritually almost every afternoon or evening in the communal house, frequently combining their complementary powers as a team. A shaman usually employs a hallucinogenic snuff powder developed from psychoactive plants to contact helper spirits. Through spirit possession the shaman helps fellow villagers cope with practical problems like fostering success in hunting, avoiding danger in the forest, healing the sick, and taking revenge on enemies in other villages. If, for example, an individual's spirit counterpart or alter-ego which dwells in the forest is lost, then the person becomes sick and may even die. A shaman can find and restore this spirit for the individual. Shamans are the most highly respected individuals in society and the reputation of exceptional ones extends to distant villages.

Yanomami may also employ a wide variety of numerous plants for medicinal purposes. However, their religion, including the associated oral literature, focuses overwhelmingly on animal spirits. Indeed, the Yanomami believe that humans and animals may be transformed into one another. A shaman, for example, may not only imitate the behavior of an animal like a jaguar when possessed by its spirit, but even be physically transformed into the animal and roam the forest.

Up to a year or more is required for an apprentice to learn the mysteries, ritual chants, dances, and practices of shamanism. The apprentice is supposed to abstain from sex, certain foods, and various kinds of hunting and other activities. There are food taboos for menstruating, pregnant, and lactating women as well. Fathers of new babies must also follow certain food prohibitions. Such taboos, in conjunction with a multitude of various other practices like regular trekking, reduce the environmental impact of the Yanomami and usually allow the normal regeneration of nature.

Yanomami interact with animals in their habitat on a daily basis both physically and spiritually. Ornamental body-paint designs usually symbolize animals and certain ones are believed to protect an individual from dangers like poisonous snakes. Even personal names, which are essentially considered sacred as well as private, are usually those of animals. Every Yanomami has an animal spirit counterpart in the forest. Accordingly, the hunter cannot kill members of that species without potentially endangering himself.

When an individual dies, his or her soul travels to a paradise above Earth. However, if the corpse is not treated with proper mourning, respect, and ritual by relatives, then the deceased's spirit may return to the village and cause harm. Also after death, the spirits who reside in an individual's body become spirits or animals in the forest. A wild animal that strangely appears in a village may be interpreted as a bad omen or evil spirit.

Reciprocity is the pivotal principle that underlies the worldview, attitudes, values, and behavior of the Yanomami. The natural, social, and spiritual components of the Yanomami world influence each other in many different ways. The unity, interconnectedness, and interdependence of all life from the perspective of Yanomami philosophy and religion permeates their rich oral literature as well.

While Yanomami religion has yet to be thoroughly studied, let alone its ecological meaning and significance, it is quite probable that their worldview tends to promote respect and reverence for nature in general. Whether in natural or social relations, harmony prevails on a daily basis in Yanomami life, in spite of occasional eruptions of disharmony. Part of the role of the shaman is to monitor and adjust these relations.

The survival and welfare as well as harmony of the Yanomami are, however, increasingly threatened by the encroachment of external forces. Most devastating have been introduced Western diseases, which often become raging epidemics, especially in areas where alien wildcat goldminers have intruded into Yanomami territory. In the matter of religion, Christian missionaries have had only nominal success in converting Yanomami, even though they have worked in several areas since the 1950s. Consequently, missionaries have precipitated relatively little disruption of traditional shamanistic animism which remains a vital part of Yanomami life. However, missionaries have introduced substantial changes in other aspects of Yanomami culture which could eventually impact on their traditional religion and ecology as well. At the same time, missionaries usually provide regular and long-term medical, educational, and other types of sorely needed assistance, given the dismal failure of state governments to fulfill its responsibilities to all citizens in Brazil and Venezuela. The Yanomami, including their spiritual ecology, will continue to face many serious challenges in the future.

Leslie E. Sponsel

Further Reading
Lizot, Jacques. *Tales of the Yanomami: Daily Life in the Venezuelan Forest.* New York: Cambridge University Press, 1985.
Peters, John F. *Life among the Yanomami: The Story of Change Among the Xilixana on the Mucajai River in Brazil.* Orchard Park, NY: Broadview Press, Inc., 1998.
Ramos, Alcida Rita. *Sanuma Memories: Yanomami Ethnography in Times of Crisis.* Madison: University of Wisconsin Press, 1995.
Tierney, Patrick. *Darkness in El Dorado: How Scientists and Journalists Devastated the Amazon.* New York, NY: W.W. Norton & Co., 2001.
Wilbert, Johannes and Karin Simoneau, eds. *Folk Literature of the Yanomami Indians.* Los Angeles: UCLA Latin American Center Publications, 1990.

See also: Amazonia; Ayahuasca; Cosmology; Entheogens; Ethnobotany; Reichel-Dolmatoff, Gerardo – and Ethnoecology in Colombia; Religious Environmentalist Paradigm; Shamanism (various).

Yoeme (Yaqui) Ritual

The Río Yaqui is the northernmost of five Mexican rivers that drain the mountains of what was once called New Spain and which is now called the state of Sonora. Sitting within this land, alongside the Yaqui River, are the Yoeme Pueblos, often referred to as the original Eight Pueblos. (The term "original" marks a distinction between these communities in Sonora and those created much later on the other side of the U.S.–Mexico border.) Within these villages live the Yoeme Indians, often called the Yaquis. Based on the direct translation "Yoemem" = "People," and joining a recent cross-tribal move to reference tribes by names in their respective languages, I retain the use of "Yaqui/s" in the contexts of proper place-names, previously published quotes, and titles, while using "Yoeme/m" within the following descriptions.

Yoeme oral tradition places their homeland in northwest Mexico long before European contact and sometime earlier than human existence as we know it today. Any research into aboriginal Yoeme lifeways will undoubtedly lead to the world of the Surem, small proto-Yoemem who lived in complete unity with their environment. These ancestors of the Yoemem are said to have communicated telepathically with all living beings and were the original inhabitants of the hiakim, or Yoeme homeland. Oral histories of this primary era recount the presence of a tree that was making an unintelligible humming sound. After much confusion, a young woman was able to translate the tree's prophecies that a group of people were coming over the ocean from the west and that some of them would try to take the land, and others would bring new technologies, baptism, and subsequently a whole new way of living. The prophecy leads to some of the Surem leaving to the hills and the ocean, to remain enchanted beings. The other half of the Surem decided to stay in the *hiakim*, Yoeme "homeland," preparing to fight the Conquistadors and welcome the Jesuits. According to some Yoeme historians, the Konkista (the real "conquest") took place as the people responded in factions to the prophecy, before the Europeans ever arrived.

Having defeated Spanish armies three times between 1533 and 1609, Yoemem were able to invite two Jesuit missionaries to their pueblos in 1617, while simultaneously keeping the Spanish conquistadors at bay. Military strength provided Yoemem control over their own combining of pre-contact traditions and Catholicism. We are immediately faced, therefore, with a different colonial situation than that confronted by most Native Americans and many indigenous peoples elsewhere. Yoemem powerfully enforced and strategically maintained their territorial and cultural boundaries, allowing for self-management from pre-Columbian time up through Jesuit collaboration. Thus, the Yoeme clearly cannot be quickly included within popular scholarly imaginings of "The" indigenous colonial experience. Primarily, in contrast to forced "conversions," we know from both Yoeme and Spanish sources that the Yoeme invited the Jesuits into their territory. Both Jesuit documents and Yoeme oral traditions record that the Yoemem were eager to learn new approaches to civil planning, including farming and ranching. According to the primary Yoeme myth, The Singing Tree, the people had already received prophetic knowledge that such changes were coming.

The Singing Tree, many Yoemem claim, also prophesied that outsiders to the tribe would seek to push Yoemem off their homeland. The relationship between history and myth is nowhere more important than in these issues of boundary maintenance. In the early nineteenth century, approximately fifty years after Spain expelled the Jesuits, the emerging Mexican administrators began instituting an *encomienda* system of land tenure which slowly and steadily led to the more familiar colonial relations we see across the globe between indigenous peoples and colonizers. Throughout most of the next century, Yoeme people were deported, massacred, and driven off their homelands. Perhaps the crux of this disregard for Yoeme sovereignty came in the early twentieth century, when Angostura Dam was being built to direct water to larger Mexican cities and away from the original Eight Pueblos. The remaining half of the twentieth century framed Yoemem rebuilding villages, reinvigorating religious societies, and developing ways to regain control of their Aboriginal homeland. The control of land and the continuation of indigenous identity are co-dependent for most Yoemem.

One movement toward environmental sovereignty includes working with Mexican banking institutions to develop credit relations using the land as collateral. However, a widespread concern among the Yoeme is that the land has become a means of exchange with the banks. In order to support themselves and accumulate collective wealth for such things as education programs and ceremonial performances, Yoemem in the Río Yaqui are repeatedly forced to borrow money to work their own land, the profits of which are distributed so thinly that they are in constant debt. Essentially, they are working their own land, but only earning enough for the most basic level of sustenance, always in fear of losing that land to the banks. Another option some community members want to explore includes selling land outright to the banks or non-Yoeme individuals, thereby avoiding the long process of slow debt accumulation and possible loss of land. Either of these two maneuvers put the tribe in a disadvantageous position: living in debt, or selling their tribal inheritance. So although Mexican President Lazaro Cárdenas in 1937 decreed a *Zona Yaqui*, members of the Eight Pueblos still struggle for complete control over their *hiakim*. Understandably, the struggle is fueled by a collective sense of belonging to a native community and is secured by a landscape and religious tradition that reaches beyond the times of Spaniards and Jesuit missionaries.

Still, most of the ethnographers of Yoeme culture have struggled to make sense of Yoeme religious identity since the cultural performances suggest that they converted; and most Yoemem themselves claim to be Catholics. For example, almost every village performs a season-length passion play of the life of Jesus (a man who walked through the hiakim) while simultaneously bringing to life masked beings, deer dancers, and their related dimensions. But scholars have previously been looking for preconceived categories of sacred or profane, Christian or pagan, ritual or art, pre- or post-contact; all of which fail to characterize Yoeme notions of religious action. Thus, some of the most well-versed ethnographers of Yoeme culture understood the deer dance as a folk art left over from a pre-Christian culture (Painter 1986: 271; Spicer 1984: 289–99). How do we make sense of rituals that clearly signify a previous mode of sustenance when those relationships with "nature" are no longer available or feasible? As of recently, very few Yoemem continue to hunt deer in the Eight Pueblos. Yet, few scholars have been attentive to the ways that Yoeme rituals utilize Christian symbols or characters within an indigenous logic, a conceptual framework that is inseparable from the geography, landscape and dimensionality that many might call "nature."

Many Yoemem understand their world as dimensionally composed of overlapping, yet distinct worlds or realms, called "*aniam.*" The literature suggests as many as nine different *aniam: tenku ania*: a dream world, *tuka ania*: night world, *huya ania*: wilderness world, *yo ania*: enchanted world, *nao ania*: corncob world, heaven, hell, purgatory, and *sea ania*: flower world. Each of these worlds provides a home for powerful beings or forces, and Yoeme relate deer dancing with three specifically, since the deer emerges from an enchanted home, *yo ania*, into the wilderness world, *huya ania*, and dances for us in the flower world, *sea ania*. Understanding the importance of the *sea ania* in Yoeme religion is fundamental, since flowers, *seewam*, are the actualization of sacrifice and the nurturing acts of giving. The most nurturing aspects of nature are found in *the sea ania*: streams, lakes, clouds, rain. The deer lives in the *sea ania* and when he is killed, he is laid atop a bed of flowers. Hunters must have *sea taka*, or flower power, to hunt deer successfully. Flowers adorn the deer dancer's antlers and skirt, as well as the necklaces and hair of the *pahko'olam*. In their extensive study of deer songs, Larry Evers and Felipe Molina write that the most common words found in the songs are Yoeme terms for flowers. For Molina, a well-respected scholar and Deer Singer, the main purpose of the songs is to bring Deer's voice from the *sea ania* to the ceremony. He adds that, "almost every piece of regalia and every instrument used in deer dancing and deer singing may be called '*seewa*' or '*sea*' as well" (Evers and Molina 1987: 52).

The deer dance always entails the dancing of the *pahko'ola* (fiestero). Wearing black masks in either the shape of a humanoid face or of a goat's head, *pahko'olam* lead the deer dancer into the performance area where he will spend the evening dancing with him, the two clowning around with each other, and entertaining the guests. When not dancing with the deer, *pahko'olam* wear their masks backwards or hang them from the left side of the head, since the devil is said to come from the left. Common mask designs include the elongated goat-face style with ears and horns. Small insects or desert animals are often painted on the masks. Typical Yoeme *pahko'ola* masks feature a band of small triangles pointing inward around the outside circumference, considered to be goat's teeth, sun rays, or mountains. Additionally, many masks have cross-like paintings which some relate to Christianity, although I have also heard in various conversations that this was a pre-contact, sand-painting symbol for the sun. Both the elongated and face-shaped masks have horse hair dangling over the eyes and from the chin. There is a strong connection in the ethnographic literature between *pahko'olam*, goats and the *yo ania*. Their pre-colonial beginnings are referenced by their often used title, "old men of the fiesta." Since they also are sometimes called "sons of the devil," we should again be conscious of the tendency to relate the *yo ania* to concepts of evil and the devil. When attending an all-night *pahko*, the banter and antics of the *pahko'olam* help elevate the moods and energy of the crowd. The dancers are charged with passing out cigarettes to the audience members and more often than not create quite a stir by attempting to humiliate the deer dancer, musicians, the female societies to their right, and even the spectators.

Undoubtedly, the most well-known and most often described Yoeme rituals are those within the ceremonial season associated with Lent. From January 3rd to May 5th, the pueblos are governed by the religious society authorities. During these months, the atmosphere changes as both indigenous and Christian dimensions come together in a fantastic spectacle on Easter Saturday. On the morning of Holy Saturday, the *Fariseos* (pharisees, religious soldier group) and masked beings use a series of processional formations and building and staccato rhythms to rush the church repeatedly. As protectors of the church and the saints inside, *anhelitom* ("our angels," children dressed as beautiful angels) whip these "evil" aggressors with willow twigs and chase them out of the church. After the last assault, the black curtain – which had dissected the front quarter from the rest of the church – is thrown wide open to reveal all the *anhelitom* and saints. Christ has risen, the tomb is empty, and the *anhelitom* chase the defeated aggressors out of the church for the last time. The ceremonial society of Mary, the *matachinis*, play their music and dance flowers for her, holding flower wands and wearing flower hats. First in the church and then moving outside the front doors, the *pahko'olam* dance around the flower patio. Simultaneously, the deer dancer is bringing his cosmic dimension, the *sea ania*, into presence. The *sea ania*, or flower world, is another realm of the Yoeme cosmos where the deer live, often conceived as under the dawn, and wherever the *huya ania* (wilderness world) opens up into the blossoms of complete being. Thus, through this ritual sacrifice the various Yoeme dimensions coexist: the pueblo, the church, the *huya ania*, the *sea ania*, and since these latter two are pre-Christian derivatives, they also signify the enchanted world of Yoeme ancestry, the *yo ania*. Here at the place where these worlds come together, the onlookers throw confetti flowers at the attacking soldiers (*Fariseos*). For what seems like hours, the community is showered by multicolored flowers drifting on the wind and upon a sea of swirling being. After the whole community defeats evil, fireworks shoot into the sky, heralding Saint Michael's return to heaven since he has collected everyone's sacrifice in the form of the flower. Everyone who has come and given of themselves during the previous season (performers, family members, observers) are considered to be sharing in this flower, this grace that originates not from God on high but through collective sacrifice.

As other contributors have noted in this volume, the word "nature" has no direct translation in Yoeme; nor can we directly translate "religion." I quickly learned in my work in Yoeme villages that to talk about religion, I would use the word "*kohtumbre*" (a Spanish loan word for "custom" but used also for "society"), which most closely approximates the idea of religion. To ethnographically unpack the concept of "nature" entails the discussion of all seven or eight *aniam*, or possible states of being, which roughly relate to geographical/cosmological spaces. Perhaps the best term to draw all this material together is *lutu'uria*, which translates as "truth" but entails a socially performative component, a sharing of ritual knowledge. Thus, references to the *aniam*, as well as experiential knowledge of cultural traditions and religious practices, are expressed in performances that socially assert and test truth claims. These dances and speeches are religious obligations and ways of representing core aspects of Yoeme identity. Thus, *lutu'uria* provides a means by which Yoemem share their sense of the "real" world, namely, "nature."

David Shorter

Further Reading

Evers, Larry and Felipe Molina. *Yaqui Deer Songs, Maso Bwikam*. Tucson: Sun Tracks and University of Arizona Press, 1987.

Kaczkurkin, Mini Valenzuela. *Yoeme: Lore of the Arizona Yaqui People*. Tucson: University of Arizona Press, 1977.

Kelly, Jane Holden. *Yaqui Women: Contemporary Life Histories*. Lincoln: University of Nebraska Press, 1978.

Maaso, Miki, Felipe Molina and Larry Evers. "The Elders' Truth: A Yaqui Sermon." *Journal of the Southwest* 35:3 (1993), 225–317.

Painter, Muriel Thayer. *With Good Heart: Yaqui Beliefs and Ceremonies in Pascua Village*. Tucson: University of Arizona Press, 1986.

Shorter, David. "Binary Thinking and the Study of Yoeme Indian 'Lutu'uria/truth.' " *Anthropological Forum* 13:2 (November 2003).

Spicer, Edward H. *Pascua: A Yaqui Village in Arizona*. Tucson: University of Arizona Press, 1984 (1940).

Spicer, Edward H. *The Yaquis: A Cultural History*. Tucson: University of Arizona Press, 1980.

Steward, Julian H. *Contemporary Change in Traditional Societies 3: Mexican and Peruvian Communities*. Urbana: University of Illinois Press, 1967.

See also: Castaneda, Carlos; Radical Environmentalism (and adjacent, Rodney Coronado and the Animal Liberation Front).

Yoga and Ecology

The Yoga tradition originated several thousand years ago in India. Early evidence of Yoga practice can be found in Indus Valley seals unearthed in Mohenjodaro and other cities that date from 3500 B.C.E. Textual references to Yoga appear in the middle Upanisads and the Mahabharata, dating from about 600 B.C.E. The Buddha and the Jina (ca. 500 B.C.E.) both taught yogic styles of meditation. By around 200, Patanjali summarized Yoga practices in a classic text known as the *Yoga Sutra*. Sanskrit texts such as the *Yogavasistha* (ca. 1000) and the *Hatha Yoga Pradipika* (ca. 1500) describe various forms of Vedantic and esoteric Yoga. Haribhadra's *Yogadrstiscmuccya* (ca. 750) and Hemacandra's *Yogasastra* (ca. 1250) discuss the adaptation of the tradition to the Jaina faith, while the later texts of Kabir and Guru Nanak allude to Yoga meditation from universalist and Sikh perspectives. Yoga continues to be practiced throughout India and has become increasingly popular worldwide.

In its various manifestations, Yoga includes practices and philosophical positions that accord with values espoused by modern ecologists. Unlike many other schools of thought in India, Yoga is thoroughly realistic. It builds upon the Samkhya school of philosophy, first espoused by a near-mythical sage named Kapila who perhaps lived in northeastern India around 900 B.C.E. Kapila's teachings were later systematized by a philosopher known as Isvarakrishna, who composed the *Samkhya Karika* in the early centuries of the Common Era. In this seminal text, the author exerts great care to articulate the existence and importance of the natural world. He posits that the world is known to us through its effects, and the effects stem from a common cause, *prakriti*, a term that many scholars choose to translated as "nature." Nature provides experience and liberation for her silent observer, the spiritual consciousness or *purusa*. According to the *Samkhya Karika*, all things exist for the purpose of serving and liberating this consciousness. Through understanding the nature of the creative force known as nature, one advances toward a state of freedom. To understand the structures and purposes of things one is able to cultivate a state of nonattachment that, from the perspective of this philosophy, entails a state of appreciation and respect, not disdain and abnegation for nature.

The earliest depictions of Yoga, found on sculptures that date from 5500 years ago, show persons imitating various aspects of the animal domain. An early statue from Mohenjadaro shows a man with his jaw wide open and his eyes bulging, approximating the roar of a lion. This pose later earns the name of *simhasana*, lion's pose. A tableau first found in Indus Valley steatite seals and then repeated thousands of years later etched into the pillars of countless temples, shows a meditating deity, now known as Pasupati or Lord of the Animals. This imposing figure sits cross-legged and austere, surrounded by devoted and attentive animals such as goats, cattle, and what today seem to be make-believe creatures. This genre of representation exudes a sense of being in harmony and perhaps communion with the animal realm, and convey a sense of comfort in the company of nonhuman realities.

In the middle, Upanisadic period of Yoga, we find speculative discourses and dialogues about the nature and function of the human body and mind. By reflecting on the functions of the body, particularly the breath, and by seeking to still the mind, the Upanisads state that one can establish a connection with one's inner self or Atman, often translated as soul. Passages from the early Upanisads such as the *Chandogya* and *Brhadaranyaka Upanisads* emphasize the primacy of breath and the relationship between the microphase and the macrophase aspects of reality. By getting to know oneself through focusing on the power of the breath, one feels an intimacy with the larger aspects of the Earth and heavens, perhaps most aptly conveyed in the first section of the *Brhadaranyaka Upanisad*, which first correlates the various functions and regions of the universe with the cosmic horse, and then makes a similar series of correspondences with the human body. By understanding one's desires and impulses, as well as the structures and functions of one's body and mind, one gains an understanding of the cosmos.

The later Upanisads and the Bhagavadgita speak directly of Yoga as the technique to be utilized in order to feel that intimate connection with the flow of life and one's place within reality. The *Svetasvatara* and *Maitri Upanisads* state that by drawing the senses inward and controlling the breath, one can reach a state of equipoise. The Bhagavadgita comes to describe the Yogi as one who comprehends the relationship between the "field" or nature (*prakriti*) and the "knower of the field" or spirit (*purusa*). Within the body of Krishna, the entire world, in its splendor and terror, can be seen, appreciated, and embraced. The metaphor of the human body becomes extended in the *Gita* to include all aspects of the universe.

The *Yoga Sutra* of Patanjali outlines an eightfold practice to ascend toward the state of self-realization through which one realizes one's connection with the universe. The underlying philosophy of Yoga places great value on feeling the connection between one's self and the larger world of nature. This continuity becomes celebrated in the term *samadhi*, the goal of Yoga, which describes an experience of non-difference between oneself, one's sensory and mental processes, and the world. As described by Patanjali, the practitioner of Yoga becomes like a clear jewel, with "unity among grasper, grasping, and grasped" (*Yoga Sutra* I: 41). This state of consciousness allows one to melt into one's surrounding and in the process diminish and eventually reverse past tendencies (*samskara*) bringing one to a state of clarity and immediacy.

The eight practices identified by Patanjali can be seen in light of environmental ethics. The beginning stage of Yoga includes five ethical practices (*yama*), held in common with the Jain tradition. First and foremost, Patanjali discusses nonviolence (*ahimsa*), which entails not harming any living being by thought, action, or assent to harmfulness. This precept advocates the protection of all forms of life, and certainly can be applied to cultivating an attitude of respect toward individual creatures as well as ecosystems. To support this discipline, Patanjali includes four additional vows. Truthfulness (*satya*) can be used to inspire acknowledgement of wrongdoing to the living realm. Not stealing (*asteya*) can be applied to remedy the imbalance of resource consumption in modern times. Sexual restraint (*brahamacarya*) can be used as a corrective to the crass commercialization of sex as well for population control. Non-possession (*aparigraha*) allows one to minimize the greed and hoarding that has plundered the planet. These five practices entail holding back, disciplining oneself, saying no to such behaviors as violence, lying, stealing, lust, and possessiveness.

The second stage of Patanjali's Yoga seeks to cultivate positive behaviors that can similarly be interpreted through the prism of heightened ecological awareness. Five practices are listed. Purity (*sauca*) can be seen in terms of keeping one's body, thoughts, and intentions clean in regard to one's surroundings. Contentment (*santosha*) encourages a philosophy of accepting what is "enough" and not striving to gather more than one truly needs. Austerity (*tapas*) entails putting oneself in difficult situations for the purposes of purification and the building of strong character. Self-study (*svadhyaya*) generally entails reading and reflecting on philosophical texts and in the case of environmental applications might include reading the nature poets. Devotion to god (*isvara pranidhana*) for an environmentalist might encourage regular forays into the wilderness to feel that important connection with the awe that nature inspires. Each of these serves as a touchstone for self-exploration and appreciation of one's place within the world.

The third phase of Patanjali's eightfold system, the practice of yoga postures (*asana*) receives relatively scant mention in the *Yoga Sutra*. Patanjali states that the purpose of performing the physical exercise of Yoga is to gain "steadiness and ease, resulting in relaxation of effort and endless unity" (*YS* II: 46–47). In later centuries, this aspect of Yoga was adumbrated and expanded by later writers, who draw extensive parallels between the practice of physical Yoga and the ability to see one's relationship with the animal realm.

In order to understand the significance of animals as it develops in later Yoga traditions, we need to discuss briefly the nature of shamanism. Mircea Eliade describes the importance of shamanic rituals that display intimacy with specific animals as follows:

> Imitating the gait of an animal or putting on its skin was acquiring a superhuman mode of being ... by becoming this mythic animal, man becomes something far greater and stronger than himself ... He who, forgetting the limitations and false measurements of humanity, could rightly imitate the behavior of animals – their gait, breathing, cries, and so on – found a new dimension in life: spontaneity, freedom, "sympathy" with all the cosmic rhythms and hence bliss and immortality (Eliade 1963: 460).

These remarks by Eliade underscore the important relationship cultivated between humans and animals from prehistoric times. Animals were noted for their particular abilities and accomplishments. To imitate these fine qualities was considered a sign of spiritual attainment.

In the later Yoga texts, animals play an important role. Many postures (*asanas*) carry the names of animals. The *Hatha Yoga Pradipika*, written by Svatmarama in the fifteenth century, lists several poses named for animals. Some examples are the Cow Head's Pose (*Gomukhaasana*) [HYP 20], the Tortoise Pose (*Kurma asana*) [HYP 24], the Rooster Pose (*Kukkuta asana*) [HYP 25], the Peacock Pose (*Mayur asana*) [HYP 32], and the Lion's Pose (*Simha asana*) [HYP 52–54].

Additionally, later Yoga manuals such as the *Gheranda Samhita* include several additional poses named for animals, including the Serpent Pose (*Naga asana*), the Rabbit Pose, the Cobra Pose (*Bhujanga asana*), the Locust Pose (*Salabha asana*), the Crow Pose (*Kakasana*), the Eagle Pose (*Gauruda asana*), the Frog Pose (*Manduka asana*), and the Scorpion Pose (*Vrischika asana*), to name a few.

Yoga practice does have an emotional effect that goes beyond mere strength or flexibility of the body. In the performance of the Peacock pose, one feels a sense of balance, a sense of pride, an affirmation of one's ability to move competently in the world. In the Eagle pose, one feels a sense of entwinedness and focus, a honing of one's vision and purpose. In the Cobra pose, one feels both a tremendous gravity and a rising up, a sense of being weighted and glued to the Earth, yet yearning and stretching to rise above. In the Lion pose one feels positively regal, refreshed and energized. At the close of a Yoga session one feels renewed and in a sense redefined, prepared to encounter the world with greater agility and balance.

In India, animals are part of one's everyday reality, even in the cities. One encounters cows, goats, cats, dogs, and numerous other animals on a daily, sometimes continuous basis. People often feed birds before taking their own meal, birds that fly into the home at dinner time, expecting acknowledgement. Gurani Anjali, a contemporary teacher of Yoga, has urged her students to observe animals, to learn from animals. One has a sense that the attention required to move into and sustain a Yoga pose carries a connection with the ancient shamanic tradition of animal imitation.

However, it could also be argued that a danger lies in over-romanticizing the mysterious or shamanic aspects of animal mimesis. For instance, Denise Kaufman, a prominent Yoga teacher in Los Angeles, suggests that one adapt a largely empirical attitude toward doing Yoga and relating with animals. In an interview she commented:

> Animals move; people can learn about movement from animals. House pets stretch all day long, creating space in their joints. Animals sit in different kinds of positions. Monkeys and apes do things with their hands. Perhaps as humans we need to reclaim our four leggedness. Getting down on all fours stimulates the pranic flow. Sitting in chairs tightens the hamstrings and the lower back. Animals don't sit on furniture; they have not built things contrary to their nature (personal communication, February 1999).

From her perspective, Yoga involves recapturing our animal physicality, reconditioning the body to establish itself within a non-technologically enhanced environment.

The relationship between sacred power and the human cannot be divorced from the harnessing of the deep images evoked by intimacy with the animal world. Early peoples of India revered animals. They depicted animals in tableaus of adornment. They surrounded their early sacred meditating Yogi with animals. Animals find prominence in classical literature. The later medieval Yoga texts explicitly prescribe animal poses as integral to mystical attainment.

We learn to be empathetic and connected from our experience of and relationship with animals. As Thomas Berry has noted, our consciousness as humans, our development and affectivity, radically depend upon our openness and sensitivity to the natural order. To the extent that Yoga heightens our senses and brings us into visceral relationship with the nonhuman realm, our own sense of worth, well-being and connectedness becomes enhanced.

Following the mastery of the physical realm through Yoga postures, one reaches the capacity to effectively control the breath (*pranayama*), the fourth phase of Yoga. As noted earlier, the breath plays an important role in the philosophy of the Upanisads, and in the *Yoga Sutra* the mastery of the inbreath and outbreath leads to "dissolving the covering of light" (*YS* II: 52). The *Hatha Yoga Pradipika* and the *Gheranda Samhita* describe intricate techniques for manipulating the breath. Through this process, one reaches into the core of one's life-force, sees the relationship between breathing and thinking, and cultivates an inwardness and stability, leading to Patanjali's fifth phase, the command of the senses (*pratyahara*). This ability to draw one's energy into oneself opens one to the higher "inner" practices of Yoga: concentration, meditation, and *Samadhi*, collectively known as *samyama*. Construed through an ecological prism, the inner work from the controlling the breath to *Samadhi* can be seen as enhancing one's sensitivity to nature, an increase in empathy, and a willingness to stand to protect the beauty of the Earth. In a sense, the culmination of Yoga leads one to the very beginning point of nonviolence, a sense that no harm must be allowed.

The beginning of this inner threefold process requires sustained exercises of concentration (*dharana*). A standard concentration practice entails attention given first to the great elements (*mahabhutas*), then to the sensory operations (*tanmatras*), the sense and action organs (*buddhindriyas* and *karmendiryas*) and finally to the threefold operation of the mind (*manas, ahamkara, buddhi*). By concentrating on the Earth (*prthivi*) one gains a sense of groundedness and a heightened sense of fragrance. By reflecting on water (*jal*), one develops familiarity with fluidity and sensitivity to the vehicle of taste. Through attention to light and heat (*tejas, agni*), one arrives at a deep appreciation for the ability to see. Awareness of the breath and wind (*prana, vayu*) brings a sense of quiet and tactile receptivity. All these specific manifestations occur within the context of space (*akasha*), the womb or container of all that can be perceived or heard.

Intimacy with the sensory process allows one to maintain focus on the operations of the mind. Thoughts (*citta-vrtti*) generated in the mind lead one to question and investigate the source of one's identity and ego (*ahamkara*). Probing more deeply into the constituent parts of one's personality, one begins to uncover the maze and mire of karmic accretions housed in the deep memory structures (*buddhi*), lightened and released gently through reflective and meditative processes. However, in order for any of these purifications to arise, an intimate familiarity with the body and collection of habits must occur, an intimacy that takes place through an understanding of time and place. Yoga enables a person to embrace and understand the close connection between the body and the world. By understanding each, one attains a state of clarity.

From an ecological perspective, the practice of Yoga can prove beneficial. Through Yoga one can begin to see the importance of the food we eat in constructing our bodies. One can find a calmness of mind through which to appreciate the stunning beauty of landscape and sunset and sunrise. Through Yoga, one can understand that all things within the universe rely on the creative expression of the five great elements and that we gain access to all experience and all knowledge through our own sensuality and intuition. The practice of Yoga provides rich resources for persons to reconnect with the body and with the world. Through the insights and applications of Yoga, one can begin to live with the sensitivity, sensibility, and frugality required to uphold the dignity of life, stemming from a vision of the interconnectedness of all things.

Christopher Key Chapple

Further Reading

Chapple, Christopher Key. *Nonviolence to Animals, Earth, and Self in Asian Traditions*. Albany: State University of New York Press, 1993.

Chapple, Christopher and Eugene P. Kelly, Jr. *The Yoga Sutras of Patanjali: An English Translation with Accompanying Sanskrit Grammatical Analysis*. Delhi: Sri Satguru Publications, 1991.

Eliade, Mircea. *Shamanism: Archaic Techniques of Ecstasy*. Willard R. Trask, tr. Princeton, NJ: Princeton University Press, 1963.

Gheranda. *The Gheranda Samhita*. Rai Bahadur Srisa Chandra Vasu, tr. Delhi: Sri Satguru Publications, 1979 (First published, 1914–1915).

HansrajYadav, Yogacharya. *Yoga Course for All*. Bombay: Bharatiya Vidya Bhavan, 1977.

Kenoyer, Jonathan Mark. *Ancient Cities of the Indus Valley Civilization*. Karachi: Oxford University Press, 1998.

Muzumdar, S. *Yogic Exercises for the Fit and the Ailing*. Bombay: Orient Longmans, 1949.

Saraswati, Swami Muktibodhananda, tr. *Hatha Yoga Pradipika: Light on Hatha Yoga*. Munger, India: Bihar School of Yoga, 1985.

Saraswati, Swami Muktibodhananda. *Asana Pranayama Mudra Bandha*. Munger, India: Bihar Yoga Bharati, 1966.

Svatmarama. *The Hatha Yoga Pradipika*. Pancham Sinh, tr. New Delhi: Munshiram Manoharlal, 1997.

Tobias, Michael, ed. *The Soul of Nature: Visions of a Living Earth*. New York: Continuum, 1994.

Vishnudevananda, Swami. *The Complete Illustrated Book of Yoga*. New York: Bell Publishing Company, 1960.

Vithaldas, Yogi. *The Yoga System of Health and Relief from Tension*. New York: Bell Publishing Company, 1957.

See also: Ahimsa; Art of Living Foundation; Breathwork; Hinduism; Jainism; Martial Arts; Prakriti; Re-Earthing.

Yolngu Ceremonial Architecture (Australia)

The religious beliefs and practices of the Yolngu people of northeast Arnhem Land in the Northern Territory of Australia are manifest in, and expressed through, their ceremonial or religious architecture.

As for other Aboriginal Australians, the world of the Yolngu was created by the travels of their ancient Ancestors imbuing sacred powers within the landscapes, flora, fauna, and people that they created. Through their activities the Ancestors marked the landscape: with their digging sticks they created waterholes and springs; where they swam they created rivers; when they rested they left permanent marks and tracks on the ground; and when they left objects behind on their journey such things were transformed into natural landscape features. As the Ancestors travelled, they also passed on knowledge and law to the Yolngu people, encompassing all aspects of their social and physical environments. This knowledge, and the actions and power of the Ancestors, are maintained and continuously reinforced through the process of ceremony. Yolngu ceremonies not only reenact ancestral events at places, but they create a temporal and spatial reference in which the people, places and actions "become" those of the Ancestors. Hence, Yolngu Ancestors are not considered part of the past, they are "ever present" in the places, things, people and marks they made in the landscape. The social identity of Yolngu people is partly constructed through their connection to particular Ancestors and places.

Yolngu ceremony grounds are places of worship that allow Yolngu to connect with their Ancestors, and although they are "unroofed," the combination of place, structures and symbols constitute an indigenous ceremonial architecture. Structures that can be called "ceremonial architecture" are not shelters or dwellings *per se*, but are important religious symbols and spatial/architectural tools that are employed during ceremony. Although a number of these structures may be similar to those employed in everyday domiciliary life, their meanings change and are enhanced when used in ceremonial contexts. For example, in certain Yolngu sacred histories, flaming dwellings act as "vehicle for change" in which Ancestral Beings are burnt and metamorphosed into another state following the breaking of a moral code, and then continue their respective journeys.

During the process of Yolngu mortuary ceremonies the deceased's soul is transported back to their ancestral homeland through the invocations of song and actions of dance, incorporating sacred objects, structures and sculpted landforms. The sculpted landforms can be either representations of Ancestors themselves, the remnant marks of ancestral actions left on the landscape, or maps of the places they created. The sculpted landforms, which are low Earth ridges creating a diagram when viewed from above, are particular to the deceased's social identity. They are also a metaphor for the ancestral homeland to which the soul of the deceased will be transported through the process of the ceremony. Around and within the sculpted land forms, the Yolngu "dance" the actions characteristic of the Ancestors and undertake purification rituals in circular pits or wells by washing and cleansing themselves, as well as burning items that have had direct contact with the deceased's body.

Accompanying the sculpted landforms may be specially constructed shelters to hold the body of the deceased until the burial stage of the ceremony. Each shelter is specific to each mortuary ceremony and is given the name of the ancestral resting place that it symbolizes. The shelters are often decorated with feathers, shells, string and applied patterns, every detail of which relates to the social identity of different kin who are aiding the deceased on their journey. Mortuary shelters can be laden with symbolism and religious knowledge about the deceased that can only be interpreted by initiated members of the group. The form of the shelter may represent both the Ancestor, a geographical place that was the resting place of the Ancestor, and other physical manifestations of the ancestor.

Other objects representing particular characteristics of the Ancestor or ancestral homeland may also be incorporated into mortuary ceremonies. Externally, these objects may be present as upright forked posts and a ridge-pole (sometimes symbolic of a dwelling of the Ancestor), a rock, a dead tree trunk positioned vertically in the ground with suspended paperbark parcels of bones, or a line of decorated string (symbolic of all the Yolngu groups associated with the Ancestor and linked through country and ceremony). Such objects act as spatial and semiotic markers for the ceremonial participants.

Hollow logs and mortuary flags are other elements of Yolngu mortuary ceremonies. Hollow log coffins were traditionally used to store the deceased's clean and crushed bone remains and were placed in a vertical position on the ground. Such log coffins are highly decorated with Yolngu symbols and have been transformed into a contemporary art form. Mortuary flag poles are used to denote or bring news of death, and were erected in the ground near a customary camp, or outside houses in contemporary settlements, or on special mortuary grounds. Mortuary flags of the Yolngu come in a variety of colors, each associated with a particular group of people and their traditional country.

The forked post and ridge-pole are esteemed as religious objects, rich in meaning, and are used across both the profane and sacred spectrum of Yolngu life. They are employed in a variety of ways depending on the nature and ancestral origin of the ceremony. Traditionally they were often used as a storage place for the deceased's bones (wrapped in bark) as well having a role in ritual dance. Their significance originates in the mythology of the Wagilag sisters who built the first dwelling in the region. In the Wagilag sacred history for Yolngu of the mainland in northeast Arnhem Land, a vaulted shelter supported on forked posts is built by two sisters as they camp beside a sacred waterhole where an Olive Python Ancestor resides. In this story, which is regularly depicted in Yolngu paintings, the shelter plays an important role in the protection of the women from both the Python and the environment. The archetypal shelter of the Wagilag takes on further sacred meanings in other ceremonies where male initiates are placed inside the shelter and emerge as part of a "re-birthing" ritual. The shelter represents the womb and its regenerative qualities. A more general interpretation of the forked post and ridge-pole, taken together, is that they symbolize the themes of the intersection of male and female principles, the theme of swallowing and enclosing, and the interrelated themes of support, nurturance and protection.

Shaneen Fantin
Paul Memmott

Further Reading

Keen, Ian. *Knowledge and Secrecy in Aboriginal Religion.* Oxford, UK: Oxford University Press, 1994.

Memmott, Paul and Shaneen Fantin. "Donald Thomson's Contribution to the Study of Indigenous Ethno-Architecture in Australia." In B. Rigsby and N. Peterson, eds. *Donald Thomson's Contribution to Anthropology.* Canberra: Academy of the Social Sciences, 2002.

Morphy, Howard. *Aboriginal Art.* London: Phaidon Press, 1998.

Reser, Joseph. "Values in Bark: Traditional Aboriginal Dwellings." *Hemisphere* (1978), 27–36.

Tamisari, Francesca. "Body, Names & Movement, Images of Identity among the Yolngu of North-east Arnhem Land." Ph.D. Thesis in Social Anthropology. London School of Economics and Political Science, University of London, 1995.

See also: Aboriginal Art; Aboriginal Dreaming (Australia); Australia; Rock Art – Australian Aboriginal; Trees – as Religious Architecture.

Yolngu Waters of Being (Australia)

In northeast Arnhem Land, Australia, the Yolngu people have a sensory awareness of the land and waters in which their personal and group identities and essences reside. All human, animal, vegetable, mineral, and atmospheric elements are placed in a complex, interwoven web of social and spiritual connections and significations. This web of belonging is determined by affiliation to one or other of two exogamous patrilineal moieties, or halves of the cosmos, called Dhuwa and Yirritja. These ties bind all things together and underpin the Ancestral Law – a set of social, moral and spiritual rules laid down in the distant past by ancestral beings. Ancestral beings were simultaneously human and animal and left human essences in the landscape as they transformed country by making rivers, carving out headlands, creating waterholes and leaving ancestral power in the environment. The first Ancestors birthed people at different waterholes and then returned inside, marking the land and the waters where their spiritual essence remains today.

So, when Yolngu look at waters they do not just see a clear liquid substance, but they perceive the embodiment of living and deceased relations as well as Ancestral Beings. These waters hold the memories of loved ones while reflecting images of their own bodies and spiritual essences that will one day come to be subsumed in water at death. Different waters resonate, meander, bubble, gurgle and change color as they tell of family members, their personalities and influence upon others. When freshwater and saltwater merge, they communicate processes of conception and birth, while particular water movements depict the consummation of marriage in the mingling and swirling of waves. A senior Wangurri man commented to me:

> There's a good relationship there – for marriage. It shows how we are related to other people because the water forms that relationship for us. The freshwater and the land have overlapping stories with the sea as they form the basis of close relationships (Mathulu, personal communication).

Currents are always viewed in relation to river sources where freshwater and saltwater mix in swirling streams at particular points, generally at the mouth of a river. These confluences occur most commonly between mother, *ngändi*, and child, *waku*, currents or between grandmother, *märi*, and granddaughter, *gutharra*, watercourses. When waters come together the Yolngu call it *ganma* and say the water tastes brackish, *dhäkay-murrkthuna* (a term that provokes much amusement from those singing or talking about it) as it can imply the mixing of bodily fluids in sexual intercourse. In particular, the frothy bubbling of major water courses is known as *gapu-djulk*, also the term for the breaking of waters at birth and the placenta.

The topography of ancestral waters further embodies human anatomical parts: the fresh waterholes are referred to as the eye, *mangutji*; a stream is the neck, *mayang*. Adjoining tributaries are the arms, *wana*; and the points of confluence of two tributaries are known as the elbows, *likan*. The lower reaches of the river are referred to as a tail or leg, *yangara*, and are referred to more generally as the bottom, *dhudi*; while close to the shoreline coastal waters are known as chest waters, *gumurr gapu*. Bundurr ritual group surnames identify freshwater and saltwater people with the upper or lower reaches of rivers. For example, in the Yirritja moiety, the "bottom" *Gumatj, Gumatj-dhä lukulili*, are known by one surname, *Munungguritj*, and come from *Bawaka*. Their surname is synonymous with the tail portion of their ancestral crocodile in the saltwater. The two other sub-groups, Burrarrwangga from Matamata and Yunupinggu from Biranybirany are aligned with the headwaters of the crocodile in the form of a spring that joins with the lower reaches of the river.

Personal and group affiliations to and authority in water can only be fully accessed through ritual language as Rev. Dr. Djiniyini Gondarra, leader of the Golumala clan and Aboriginal representative for the Australian Church Congress, told me, "The relationship between these identities can only be known as you sing." Songs tell of waters washing upon the land, reflecting the genealogical ties of individuals and groups through their movements, colors and sounds while simultaneously marking those who do not belong to an area. Performing identities from the sea and land, then, becomes a way of knowing the self and others as waves of song invoke ancestral power through musical experience, combining movements of the ancestral past in the landscape and seascape with Yolngu identities in the present.

Fiona Magowan

Further Reading

Bagshaw, Geoff. " 'Gapu Dhulway, Gapu Maramba': Conceptualisation and Ownership of Saltwater Among the Burarra and Yan-Nhangu Peoples of North East Arnhem Land." In N. Peterson and B. Rigsby, eds. *Customary Marine Tenure in Australia*. Sydney: University of Sydney, 1998.

Gurruwiwi, Djalu. "The Gälpu Story." In W. Caruana and N. Lendon, eds. *The Painters of the Wawilak Sisters Story 1937–1997*. Canberra: National Gallery of Australia, 1997.

Keen, Ian. *Contemporary Significance of Coastal Waters in the Spiritual and Economic Life of the Aborigines*. Submission to the Australian Parliamentary Joint Select Committee on Land Rights in the Northern Territory. Official Hansard Report, 1977.

See also: Aboriginal Dreaming (Australia); Australia; Mammy Water; Water in Islam; Water in Zoroastrianism; Water Spirits and Indigenous Ecological Management.

Yoruba Culture (West Africa)

The Yoruba constitute a linguistic, cultural, and political entity in West Africa. They claim common ancestry in Oduduwa and they developed the concept of *ebi* (kinship) as a symbol of unity. The Yoruba established kingdoms, many of which survived until the nineteenth century when the imposition of colonial administration engendered a new geopolitical configuration in Nigeria. The political rearrangement affected the Yoruba because while the majority of them are in Nigeria, others found themselves in what later became the present-day Republic of Benin and Togo. People of Yoruba ancestry also constitute a sizeable portion of the African Diaspora, the result of the trans-continental migration occasioned by the Atlantic slave trade. Wherever the Yoruba people exist, their interlocking concept of religion and nature remains with them. Their emphasis on the sacredness of life underscores the importance they place on religion and nature as well as their political and socio-cultural institutions. For example, *Ori* ("head," signifying the origin of life), land (that produces food and supports the living and the dead), kingship, marriage, naming, death, places of worship and religious rituals are held sacred. The Yoruba worship many deities, revere and deify ancestors, and use natural phenomena to personify deities. In the past, Yoruba religion contributed to the preservation of the natural flora and fauna in that virtually all settlements were surrounded by green belts in addition to numerous groves, which harboured various species of shrubs and trees as well as animals. Until the assault of Islam, Christianity, and Western civilization, Yoruba religion not only attached sacredness to nature, it also helped to preserve physical environment from human encroachment. Clearly, nature plays a prominent role in Yoruba religious beliefs and practices.

The Yoruba refer to the beginning of life as *orirun* or *orisun* (the source of the stream of life) therefore every household worshipped Ori, the god of fate. The Yoruba, however, possess the concept of a Supreme Being. In Yoruba religion, there are no temples, no sacrifices, no regular prayers, and no priests to the Supreme Deity because he is assumed to reside in the remote sky called *Orun* (Heaven). According to their cosmogony, Olodumare (the Creator), also known as Olorun (the Owner of Heaven), designated divinities to create the Earth. One strand of their tradition states that the Earth existed as a watery, marshy waste and divinities, possibly human beings, used to descend from heaven on a spider's web to hunt on the vast expanse of water. To create solid Earth, Olodumare gave Obatala (or Orisa-nla), one of the divinities, a handful of sand, a pigeon, and sixteen palm kernels. Obatala let loose the pigeon to spread the sand in order to create dry land. Obatala planted the palm kernels to explain how trees came into being. The spot on which these events took place is called Ile-Ife (that which is wide).

A variant tradition believes that although Obatala was originally designated, it was Oduduwa, another divinity, who carried out the assignment of creating dry land and all living things. Oduduwa supposedly supplanted Obatala and descended to the Earth through a gold chain, equipped with a snail's shell filled with sand, a white hen, a black cat, five pieces of iron, and a palm nut. Oduduwa led the delegation to the world and landed on a hill called Oke-Oramfe (the hill of expansion) in Ile-Ife. The hen spread the sand and farmland appeared. Hence, the Yoruba regard Ile-Ife as the nucleus of life and their "Garden of Eden." The Yoruba creation story accentuates the importance of nature and why it constitutes a major part of their religion. They conceptualize religion and nature as intricately interwoven because all natural phenomena originated from Olodumare, as indicated in the attribute *Oba a s'eda aye* (King, the creator of the Earth).

The Yoruba worship many *Orisas* (gods and goddesses), which Bolaji Idowu referred to as the ministers of Olodumare. They act as intermediaries between humans and Olodumare and the leading ones include Ela, Esu, Obatala (Orisa-nla), Ogun, Orunmila, Osun, Sango, and Yemoja. The places of worship, which are approached with an aura of sacrosanctity, include the grave of ancestors, shrines and temples, groves, hills and mountains, trees, banks of rivers, and markets. Land, on which these places of worship are erected, is also held sacred. D.O. Fagunwa, a prominent Yoruba novelist, became popular through one of his books *Igbo Olodumare* (The Forest of the Almighty). Although the Yoruba claim that they have 401 divinities, there seem to be more when several other local deities are added. The worship of numerous gods and natural phenomena is not unique to the Yoruba people, for their pantheon compares with other African peoples. The slave trade, which forced many Yoruba people to North and South America, and the European partition, which arbitrarily divided the Yoruba, helped the spread of these divinities. For example, some of the divinities are worshipped in the Republic of Benin, Brazil, Cuba, and Trinidad and Tobago.

Most of the divinities personify nature and spirit. Orunmila, the oracle divinity and second in rank to Olodumare, posseses a vast knowledge of heaven. Orunmila communicates with other divinities through *Ifa* (divination). Ifa is a literary and divination system, which is found especially among the Yoruba-speaking people but also among other peoples of West Africa. Samuel Johnson, the father of Yoruba history and culture, contended that the Yoruba met Ifa at Ile-Ife but it became an official religion during the reign of Alaafin Ofinran, which coincides with the period of exile. The Yoruba use natural objects such as a palm kernel in the *opele*, or chain, the carved wooden tray, and the tapping staff or *iroke*. The Yoruba believe that Olodumare empowered Esu, the trickster divinity, to mediate between the forces of good and evil and convey the secret power of rituals and sacrifices to other divinities, in order to reduce evil exploits on humans. Wande Abimbola, a distinguished scholar of Yoruba religions, asserts that Esu changes his appearance and is capable of assuming 256 different forms of existence. Represented by a block of ironstone upon which worshippers pour palm oil, and by a wooden carved staff, Esu favors those who sacrifice to him. Hence the Yoruba say *eni o rubo ni Esu u gbe* (Esu supports he who offers sacrifice). Esu, in Yoruba belief, is therefore different from the Christian concept of the devil. Yemoja is known as the goddess of waters and motherhood because the lagoons, oceans, rivers, and seas flow out of her body. Because of Ogun's nature, he is variously referred to as a violent god, the forest god, master of iron, and god of war, and is widely worshipped by hunters, blacksmiths, or people whose occupations deal with iron. Other sobriquets associate Ogun with wealth for he is called *Onile owo, Onile ola, Onile kangunkangun ode orun* (the owner of the house of money, the owner of the house of riches, the owner of the innumerable houses of heaven). Sango, a historical figure as the fourth Alaafin (King) of the Oyo Empire, was deified after his death. Owing to his violent disposition and ability to emit fire from his mouth, Sango is known as the god of thunder and lightning while Oya, his wife, is the goddess of thunderstorms. One of the songs devotees render during the worship of Sango partly states: *A so 'gi d'eniyan; bi o soro, a s'eniyan d'eranko* (He turns a tree into a man; when he chooses to be ferocious, he turns a man into an animal). Sacrifice is an indispensable aspect of worship in Yoruba religion and every divinity has its favorite food items for sacrifice as well as taboos. For example, food items such as *egbo* (mashed maize), pounded yam, goats, and fish are offered to Oya but dog is her taboo. While Esu accepts grains of maize, fowls, he-goats, and dogs, he despises *adin* (oil extracted from palm-kernels).

Like the Borgu people, the Yoruba also venerate animals and reptiles as totems. According to Yoruba belief, animals and plants have souls. The land, hills, rivers, rocks, and trees, which spirits inhabit, are held sacred. Samuel Johnson referred to totems as denoting the origin of a family. There are *Erin* (Elephant), *Oni* (Crocodile), *Agbo* (Ram), and *Okin* (the Lovebird), *Ojo* (Rain), Lion, Python, and Cobra families. Clan or lineage members recognize these animals and reptiles as members of their families and their assistance can be sought from time to time for various reasons. *Oni* (Crocodile) families observe an elaborate burial ceremony for a dead crocodile. The crocodile is wrapped in a white piece of cloth and buried like a human being in a grave. During the ceremony, three fowls are sacrificed, drums are beaten, guns are shot, and clan members entertain their friends with food and drinks.

Secret societies formed part of the Yoruba religious belief system. The societies were secret because membership was restricted and they often engaged in mysterious activities (only the initiates having knowledge of these activities). Secret societies with a religious background are mainly concerned with the cult of the dead and they wield enormous power over their communities. The cults include the Aje (Witches), Ogboni, Oro, Egungun, Agemo, and Eluku. Some of these cults also performed social and political functions. The Ogboni, a political society, held the symbol of metal images of human figurines (*Edon*), which the uninitiated could not see. The society is known as *Imole* in Ile-Ife and *Oshugbo* in Ijebu. Robert Smith, a historian of the Yoruba people, described the Ogboni society as "a semi-cult devoted to the worship of the Earth, which wielded both religious and political sanctions" (1988: 93–4). The religious activities of the Ogboni included the worship of the Earth spirit (*ile*) and members wore beads on their necks and wrist, tied a wrapper across the left shoulder, and wore a sash (*Itagbe*) over their right shoulder.

The *Egbe Awo* (Association of Diviners) is often misconstrued as having maleficent purposes and activities. The training of an Ifa student lasts about ten years with a complex initiation process. During this time, the individual acquires knowledge and skills in the field of divination, medicine, pharmacy, psychiatry, psychology, and philosophy. There is a great deal of interaction between religion and nature in these branches of religious and healing practice.

The concept of life after death predominates in Yoruba religion. The Ifa corpus clearly states that the soul does not die but transposes to a new world. Thus the Yoruba regard the Earth as a marketplace, or as a journey, and heaven is their permanent home. It is believed that the ancestors watch over and influence the affairs of the living. To maintain a good relationship and to receive blessings from the ancestors, regular or annual visits and sacrifices are offered at the *oju ibo* ("the place of worship" that is, the gravesites of ancestors), often located within the compound. The different types of sacrifice include thanksgiving, votive, propitiatory, and preventive. Sacrifices also occur during the laying of the foundation of a house or at the beginning of a business venture. Requests for childbirth, improved health, and success at work are made to the ancestors. The concept of an afterlife also calls for good behavior on Earth because people will reap in heaven what they sow on Earth. *Egungun* (masquerades), believed to embody the spirits of the ancestors, appear during funeral ceremonies.

The Yoruba express their religious beliefs in names, epithets, proverbs, and songs. Proverbs such as "good character is a god; the better the worship, the more the blessings"; "there is no god like the throat; it accepts sacrifices everyday"; "no god favors a lazy person; he can prosper only by using his hands to work"; and "nothing can be done to the Ifa oracle to prevent it from behaving like palm kernels" (palm kernels are used in the consultation of the Ifa Oracle) illustrate the extent of the intersection of Yoruba religion and nature.

Many rivers, hills, and trees in Yorubaland are also objects of veneration. Notable among the rivers are: the Niger (Oya), Ogun, Owena, Oni, and Osun. River-spirits are appeased to prevent flooding and disaster during the rainy season. Yemoja (the deity mother of all rivers and fishes) is believed to be a generous giver of children. Prominent hills such as Iyamopo in Igbeti, Oke-Ibadan in Ibadan, Olumo Rock in Abeokuta, Oke Ila in Igbomina, and Asabari in Saki are worshipped. Iyamopo's appellation, "The hill of protection, the mighty hill that flatters its back to carry its children," indicates its protective role in Yoruba warfare. Sacrifices are offered to the Orosun hill at Idanre and the Ajo and Okelota hills at Ado-Ekiti on an annual basis for their protective values. The Yoruba respond to their forest environment by venerating the deities who live in trees such as *iroko* (*Chlorophora excelsa*) cotton tree (*Eriodendron orientale*), baobab (*Andansonia digitata*), and *ayan* (African satinwood where the god of drums resides).

The Yoruba apply their artistic skillfulness to express their religious beliefs. Wood carving, drawing, and painting found in shrines depict their high level of artistic imagery. The style and features of an image more often than not portray the religious emotions of the artist. Carved images are mere symbols and not the real objects of worship. But because Olodumare is supreme and remote, there are no images, no liturgies, and no shrines dedicated to him.

Religion and nature are almost inseparable elements in Yoruba history and culture. The deifying of people, the worshipping of deities, and the reverencing of animals, reptiles, and trees prevail in Yoruba religious practices. Nature has been so ingrained in Yoruba religion that food items are offered to the gods and leaves and roots are used for charms, and treatment of illnesses. Severing nature from religion is tantamount to rendering the Yoruba culture and belief system worthless.

The introduction of Christianity through the European missionaries and Islam through Muslim merchants has not detached Yoruba religion from nature. Christianity made significant inroads among the Yoruba, most especially because of its attractive elements of Western education and medicine, and Islam is fast growing. Christianity and Islam have drawn their adherents from and have denigrated the Yoruba religion. Each opposed its closeness to nature. The impacts of Islam and Christianity have been crushing on Yoruba religion, particularly since both of them received encouragement during the colonial period, and subsequent political administrations after independence have promoted them.

The number of adherents of the Yoruba religion is dwindling in the face of competition from Christianity and Islam, but the religion has not been completely displaced in the society. Although still struggling to survive, the most persistent attempts at revitilization come from Africans in diaspora who see a commitment to Yoruba religion as an identity or a key in the search for their roots. The preservation and revitalization of the Yoruba religion is carried on at the Oyotunji village, outside Beaufort in South Carolina, where the religion is practiced. The frequent pilgrimages to Yorubaland, such as during the Osun festival at Osogbo and the Ifa festival at Ile Ife, have become pointers to the greater global dimension that Yoruba religion has assumed. There is also the quasi-academic attempt to preserve knowledge of Yoruba religion in the World Orisa Congress, which seems to be of some attraction in the Americas. However, contemporary economic problems faced by people on the African continent have had negative effects, giving rise to charlatans, just as attempts to modernize have resulted in bastardization. Divination and traditional healing system, which are intricately interwoven with Yoruba religion and nature, are still carried out in modern times. This shows that Yoruba religion continues to exist in spite of the challenges it faces from other religions.

Julius O. Adekunle

Further Reading

Abimbola, Wande. *Ifa: An Exposition of Ifa Literary Corpus*. Ibadan: Oxford University Press, 1976.

Awolalu, Omisade J. *Yoruba Beliefs and Sacrificial Rites*. London: Longman, 1979.

Bailey, James A. *The Yoruba of Southwestern Nigeria and Santeria in the Southeastern United States: History, Culture, Rituals, and Ceremonies of an Afro-Cuban Cult*. New Bern, NC: Godolphin House, 1991.

Bascom, W.R. *The Yoruba of Southern Nigeria*. New York: Holt, Rinehart and Winston, 1969.

Biobaku, S.O., ed. *Sources of Yoruba History*. Oxford: Clarendon Press, 1973.

Eades, J.S. *The Yoruba Today*. New York: Cambridge University Press, 1978.

Fadipe, N.A. *The Sociology of the Yoruba*. Ibadan, Nigeria: Ibadan University Press, 1970.

Forde, C. Daryll. *The Yoruba-speaking Peoples of Southwestern Nigeria*. London: International African Institute, 1962.

Idowu, E. Bolaji. *Olodumare: God in Yoruba Belief*. London: Longmans, 1962.

Johnson, Samuel. *The History of the Yorubas: From the Earliest Times to the Beginning of the British Protectorate*. London: Routledge & Kegan Paul, 1969 (reprint).

Ojo, G.J. Afolabi. *Yoruba Culture*. London: University of London Press, 1966.

Pemberton III, John and Funso S. Afolayan. *Yoruba Sacred Kinship: A Power Like that of the Gods*. Washington, D.C.: Smithsonian Institution Press, 1996.

Smith, Robert, S. *Kingdoms of the Yoruba*. London: James Currey, 1988.

See also: Candomblé of Brazil; Caribbean Cultures; Congo River Watershed; Diola (West Africa); Santería; Saro-Wiwa, Kenule Beeson – and the Ogoni of Ogoni; Umbanda; Wenger, Susan, Yoruba Art, and the Oshogbo Sacred Grove; West Africa.

Yuchi Culture and the Euchee (Yuchi) Language Project (Southeastern United States)

The struggle of the Yuchi (also spelled Euchee) community to pass forward its ancient language to younger generations is representative of challenges facing the majority of indigenous nations bounded by elaborated colonial economic and social structures. As of this writing there are only six remaining elders out of perhaps 2400 Yuchis who are available to help teach the language to younger members of the Yuchi community. The Yuchi nation arrived at this point of extreme urgency in the life of its language only after exhibiting extraordinary resiliency across many generations. Yuchi people were accosted by successive and overlapping waves of physical genocide, brutal dislocation, and forced assimilation.

In ancient times Yuchi people were found in the area now known as Tennessee and lived primarily in the areas that became known as Georgia and Alabama throughout the colonial and early American periods. They had established towns along the ample rivers in the region, living primarily from corn and other crops, with seasonal celebrations for the gifts that sustained their society. During the decade of the 1830s they, along with other nations in the region, suffered deadly dislocation under President Andrew Jackson with many Yuchis taken in chains a thousand miles to what became known as Oklahoma.

Although the displaced peoples brought their sacred ceremonial fires as centers of their social, economic and political lives to their new locations, they were faced with an enormous and accelerating shift in their subsistence patterns and traditional ethos with dramatic implications for ceremonial life and their understanding of the world. In the old homelands the major ceremonial traditions and daily ritual activities related rather directly to the long-standing subsistence patterns and lifestyle of the society. They mediated a fit between the regular requirements of hunting and planting and the broad understanding of how the world worked, both reinforcing proper behavior and reflecting this larger worldview.

The central ceremonial cycle focused on what has been

discussed in scholarly literature as Green Corn ceremonialism. The annual ceremonies celebrated the beginning of a new year with fresh crops and was marked by a new fire rite. Community members were forbidden to partake of fresh corn until these ceremonies of purification and thanksgiving had been completed. This was a time of renewal and cleansing for the community as members carried out their founding instructions, reenacting ancient primal events. The timing was based on the seasonal movements of the sun and moon and required careful observation of plant life for gathering all the proper medicines. The special use of certain animals, such as garfish and terrapins, also required an intimate engagement with the animal world.

All these ceremonial traditions are still followed by those community members who remain active in one or more of the three ongoing Yuchi ceremonial grounds. The "clean ground," as it is referred to in the language, where the ceremonies are carried out, becomes a sacred space where expressions of strife between members is forbidden. The central ceremonial area, often referred to as the "big house" in the language, is carefully oriented within the cosmos along the four directions and founded with sacred medicines in the fireplace at the center point. This ritual space is where the entire family of the Yuchi community is welcomed with their friends and where ceremonial ground members, from both the present day and earlier times, gather to carry out their ceremonial responsibilities for another year. The longer cycle of four ritual ball games and four dances culminates in a structured time of ritual separation between men and women, fasting, taking medicines, and purification rites. Only after the sacred ground itself has been fed medicine can the fast be broken and a time of communal feasting begun. These ceremonies hinge explicitly upon using the gifts of particular medicine plants and on the special songs given long ago by a specific large bird. It is through a set of special dances (misleadingly referred to as social dances by some scholars) that relations are renewed and maintained with specified plants and animals.

These traditions now face great challenges. The process of physical displacement in the nineteenth century had created an extremely difficult transition period for keeping proper relations with the new living environment. Community members increasingly came under the influence of the material arrangements and social values of the larger society. There was a broad shift in such areas as the traditional family, clan relations, residency patterns, medicinal practices, and reliance on traditional agriculture. These mounting pressures combined with corrosive influences from both native and non-native churches through the late twentieth century, from Euro-American education, and "allotment," the breaking up of communal lands into small individual holdings by the federal government.

All of this created pressure on the ceremonial traditions and challenged the underlying worldview. The displacement of traditional foods by store-supplied items had perhaps the greatest impact on the underpinnings and practices of traditional society as many of the daily ritual activities and traditional arts fell into disuse. The ceremonial calendar was adapted to fit modern work schedules. Current community members no longer live by farming and do not normally raise traditional crops of corn, beans, squash or tobacco. The strong link between the celebrations of the main ceremonies and this form of livelihood is no longer so apparent. The natural environment around the community was subjected to degradation and modern waterway management techniques instituted by the U.S. Army Corps of Engineers resulted in the flooding of ecological niches where many of the important plants were previously collected, making it harder to find plant sources for traditional foods and medicines. The relationship with animals was greatly attenuated as many species were driven to near-extinction.

Against these imposed difficulties Yuchis still perform the buffalo dance at their annual ceremonies despite having virtually no contact with the animals since the mid-nineteenth century, whereas they were once common in the original homeland areas of the Yuchi in what is now referred to as the southeastern United States. Responding to the rhythms of the Earth, many within the Yuchi nation continue to maintain their ancient ceremonies as the center of community life, with its implicit ethic teaching a life of balance and harmony. The health of the Yuchi nation in proper relation to the larger community of life depends on these vital ancient activities. Indeed, in traditional perspective the continuity of the cosmos itself is tied to the successful completion of these ceremonial duties. In turn, the ceremonies themselves rest on the use of the Yuchi language. While the language has always been an essential bearer of Yuchi culture, the role of the language is now further heightened. As the ethos in the community continues to tilt in the direction of the enormous weight applied by Euro-American society, the value of the language becomes even more critical for passing forward a tradition-rich view of the world.

In the case of the Yuchi – like many other nations – the long-term processes of physical genocide and cultural assault were coupled with a kind of intellectual erasure in which the very existence of the Yuchi nation and language were denied for over a century and a half in government reports and published authoritative sources. The published denials continue into the present and now include internet sources and current reference publications. The community was again denied formal recognition by the federal government in 1995. The language itself is spoken by few, has no known cousins from which to borrow or learn, and has no standard orthography.

Despite these many obstacles, the Yuchi people remain as bearers of a unique language, even as they maintain their traditional ceremonies. Yuchi has been identified as a language isolate, standing apart from groups of related languages in what are termed language families. As such, the language transmitted by today's elders represents one of the world's cultural treasures from an immemorial human past. With only a handful of fluent speakers the community has launched into an aggressive revitalization effort led by the Euchee (Yuchi) Language Project with the goal of passing their ancient language forward from current speakers (whose average age is over 80 years) to a new line of younger speakers who will be enabled to carry forward the language for the benefit of coming generations. Even as there were those who carried the coals from our ancient ceremonial places a thousand miles to unknown lands so that the fires of our traditions could be rekindled and spread again among the people, so we now pursue the goal of developing a second handful of competent speakers who can carry forward the language to later generations.

This goal has necessitated a focus on immersion learning in small clusters of master and apprentice teams. The most valuable and essential asset to the project has been the support and knowledge of the gifted speakers of the language, as we rely on elders who grew up in the 1920s—the last generation with a large percentage of first-language speakers of Yuchi. Various arms of the Euchee (Yuchi) Language Project (ELP) include community outreach through a newsletter and Yuchi language radio and a Yuchi language page in the Muscogee Nation News. Weekly language classes for children and beginners have been conducted since 1993 building off of several earlier community classes. These classes not only seek to address in an appropriate manner the language needs for the ceremonial ways but have also sought to pass forward through hands-on methodologies traditional arts, agricultural practices, and older lifeways built around identifying, gathering, and preparing traditional foods. Perhaps the greatest challenge for second-language learners is to develop enough competence in the language to absorb the fullness of the underlying worldview reflected in the language. Another arm of the ELP deals with documentation and archiving of extant recordings. The purpose of creating and maintaining these recordings is to expand the memories of the Yuchi learners, as an aid that will allow them more time in which to absorb the rhythms and words that are their natural heritage. That is, the cohesive focus of these various aspects of the project is on finding potential dedicated learners and developing new speakers as quickly as possible.

While this approach specifically addresses the most urgent needs of the community it also serves to highlight the divergence between community needs and the interests of the academic enterprise (see Grounds 2003). Given the context of the extremely fragile status of the language, with so few fluent speakers the community is forced to decide between meeting the agenda of the academy with its focus on textual production or addressing the challenge of passing forward the oral language to a new generation of speakers with its time-consuming requirement of immersion in the spoken language.

The urgency and importance of the language revitalization work is of utmost value to the Yuchi community and, indeed, to the diversity of global humanity. As a linguistic isolate the Yuchi language provides a unique and direct link to an ancient human past. The language is the vehicle for intimate knowledge of medicine plants, local ecosystems, and hidden histories of the Yuchi people, and remains vital to the traditional ceremonies. The richness of the community life, as reflective of a unique worldview, is born by the language – a world that remains inaccessible through the English language, a world in which men and women speak different forms of the language. This is a world in which the people referred to as Yuchis in history texts are known by a different name in their language, as the offspring of [the] Sun, who is recognized as female. There is an exceedingly musical and lyrical quality to the spoken rhythms of fluent Yuchi. This quality is bound up with the meaning of the language and effectively prevents first-language speakers from understanding the staccato delivery of English speakers in their early attempts to learn the Yuchi language.

The Yuchi cosmos is one that has no general term for animals and one whose grammar does not separate humans from animals. All living beings are recognized as part of the greater living world. Every Yuchi sentence that refers to an individual person (including animals) or to any non-person necessarily speaks in terms of their physical form in relationship to the Earth. In the evocative Yuchi language the place where one lives is where one habitually sits upon the Earth. The deepest beliefs of the most important rituals are mediated through the language. The healing process using powerful medicinal plants does not rely solely on their pharmaceutical properties but is traditionally administered with specific songs or chants that are essential for effecting a cure. Yuchi words are not empty symbols but are understood to have power and efficacy. The passage from this world to the next is mediated through ritual words in the language.

This extremely compelling understanding of the world – a beautiful and profound grasp of it – is at the same time fragile and precious due to its orality. Like other indigenous languages it can become all-but-lost in the span of a single generation. The Yuchi language is now making its last call to a younger generation to get in the dance, to join the ancient spiral of Yuchi culture bearers and learn the language, the depth of its melodies and the richness of its rhythms, so that a new generation will understand their place within the cosmos in the fullness of their primordial relation to the created world.

Richard A. Grounds

Further Reading

Grounds, Richard A. "Yuchi Travels: Up and Down the Academic 'Road to Disappearance.'" In Richard A. Grounds, David E. Wilkins, and George E. Tinker, eds. *Native Voices: American Indian Identity and Resistance.* Lawrence: University Press of Kansas, 2003, 290–317.

Wagner, Gunter. *Yuchi Tales.* Publications of the American Ethnological Society, vol. 13. Franz Boas, ed., New York: G.E. Stechert, 1931.

See also: Bison Restoration and Native American Traditions; Indigenous Environmental Network; Native American Languages (North America); Traditional Ecological Knowledge.

Yunnan Region (Southwest China and Montane Mainland Southeast Asia)

Yunnan, meaning "south of the clouds," is located in Southwest China bordered by the Tibet Autonomous Region and Sichuan, Guizhou, and Guangxi provinces of China on the west, north and east, and the countries of Vietnam, Laos, and Myanmar to the south and southwest. Geophysically, Yunnan serves as the roof of Mainland Southeast Asia due to its location on the headwaters of all the major rivers within this montane region. The ecological health of this "roof" of southwest China and Southeast Asia is the concern of many stakeholders in all the surrounding countries and provinces. A planned increase in regional development will bring new and vast construction of communication and transportation infrastructure along the Mekong and other river systems. Yunnan, with a total area of 394,000 square kilometers, consists of 128 counties in 16 districts or prefectures and has a population of 42.9 million people, including 14.6 million ethnic minority peoples with diverse indigenous cultures and livelihoods. The ethnic minorities of the Yunnan uplands include Tibeto-Burman peoples, such as Tibetan, Naxi, Yi, Hani (Akha), Jingpo, Lisu, Lahu, Nu, Derung, Primi, and Jinuo; Mon-khmer, such as Wa, Bulang, and Deang; and Miao-Yao including the Miao and Yao. The ethnic minorities in Yunnan are characterized by complex dialects within groups and distinctive socio-economic systems because of the region's biological complexity.

Sacred Knowledge

Many activists and scholars fear the loss of local knowledge in the region. Despite the dynamic cultural practices of indigenous people, their knowledge systems or indigenous knowledge, as they are called by outsiders, are rapidly fading away. Due to market penetration, out-migration and external education, the local languages, sacred knowledge and religious practices linked to worship of sacred space and maintenance of biodiversity has already been extinguished in some places. Although the indigenous people have been living in the mountain regions for thousands of years as hunters-gatherers, pastoralists, and agriculturalists, they are viewed by outsiders as objects to be managed rather than citizens in the mountain ecosystems. As managed objects, the political-administrative structures they are located in systematically marginalize their aspirations and the knowledge they apply to achieving them.

Sacred knowledge, as part of indigenous knowledge systems, is locally rooted in the culture of a particular geographical territory. Sacred knowledge refers to the nature (both geophysical and ecological environments), mythical cosmology, cultural beliefs, religious rituals and stories of a place assigned by people to their space. Sacred knowledge is mostly culturally or religiously transmitted, with the help of collective memory encoded in stories, myths, legends, songs, dances, rituals, and systems of classification of resources. Sacred knowledge constitutes a significant part of the identity of each cultural group and is a specialized knowledge often held by persons with special experiences, such as religious leaders within local communities. Some individuals in the local culture achieve a degree of coherence in rituals and other symbolic behavior and act as intermediaries between the material and spiritual world. They are persons who possess sacred knowledge like the Bimo in Akha and Yi societies, or the Dongba in Naxi society or the Lama among the Tibetans. As young people are not taking over these roles and no longer know many practices recalled by elders, large gaps in knowledge are emerging between generations.

Sacred Space

Sacred space refers to sacred places (mountains, hills, lakes, rivers, temples, shrines, etc.), sacred objects (religious sculpture, stone, painting, hierogram, costumes and other sacred objects), and their associated life (animal, plants, trees, forest) and imaged super-nature (e.g., kylin, an imaged totem animal, with a deer-like body, covered scute, single horn, cattle tail. Chinese believe the kylin always bring good luck). Therefore sacred spaces are "contextualized" by the way they are expressed through "material culture," such as any religious objects or any product of human expression in the geophysical landscape. The sacred space can vary from a few square meters to hundreds of square kilometers in the geophysical scale, and from household, community, multiple communities to multiple ethnic groups in the socio-cultural scale. Sacred spaces are maintained through practicing religious rituals, ceremonies and sanctions and participating within a specific cultural group. The sacred places or sites are the sources of powerful forces or energy; sacred objects are revelatory and powerful instruments in religious rituals; the associated life are either reincarnated human beings or communicators between humans and nature; the imaged super-nature represents the soul of nature, which formulates the sacred ecological system for the natural landscape in the mountain region. Cultural identity is the vehicle to direct experience of the sacred. The sacred ecology refers to non-productive and non-reproductive, and the cultural dimension of interactions between human and nature in the particular terrain. The concepts of "connectivity" between humans and nature, existing in this and the next life, and the "spirituality" of nature and human behaviors and decision making are key principles for sacred ecology. The sacred ecology emphasizes that human beings are only part of the ecosystem and all life is equal in terms of power, skill, and moral responsibility.

Sacred Ecology: Indigenous Perceptions of the Nature

Spirit of nature "shu": The Naxi people's perception
Dongba is a term for a Naxi priest meaning "wise man" or "sage." According to the mythological records in the manuscripts of Dongba religion, Dongba priests could communicate between humans and the spiritual world, and they advised clan chieftains. They are considered by the Naxi people to be wise men since they have sacred knowledge about the supernatural and natural worlds. They know how to pray for good luck, blessings and happiness and prevent bad luck and evil, and they know how to deal with relations between humans and nature. Various rituals are performed in different occasions for harmonizing relations with nature, such as worshipping the gods of grains and animal husbandry, the hunting spirits, the mountain god, the god for protection of villages, the spirits for the fireplace in the house, the god of blacksmith, the god for war and victory, the god for herb medicine, etc.

Shu is worshipped by the Naxi as a spirit of super-nature or god for governing nature. Shu has the shape of a human body with a snake tail, wearing a *wubao* hat (a hat with five treasures). In Naxi oral history, Shu and human beings used to be stepbrothers from the same father. When the two brothers split family property, humans got valleys, crops, and domestic animals, while Shu got mountains, rivers, forests, birds, and wild animals. Ever since, humans kept invading the property of Shu, and the latter became very angry and decided to take revenge by making it difficult for humans to survive. Humans appealed to Dongba to control Shu. Shiluo sent a rock warrior to conquer Shu. Under the mediation of Shiluo, humans and Shu made an agreement that they would never harm each other again. Humans could obtain the necessities of life from nature, but they had to pay Shu at certain times by worshipping it. This is the origin of the Shu Worshipping Ritual. Each year, on either the day of the dragon or the day of the snake in the second month of the lunar calendar, people get together in order to worship Shu and pray for blessings for their offspring, favorable weather for agriculture, prosperity, and longevity of the community. People usually choose a water source or pond near the village as the site for the Shu Worshipping Ritual. The ritual consists of two rites: to repel evil and to worship Shu. The rituals take place on the sacred altar, Shu's place, and the evil spirits' place.

The first ritual is the rite to repel evils. In Dongba belief, evils (*hui*) have two meanings, one is the dirt in nature and the other is human misbehavior or behavior against moral codes. A Dongba blows a white shell, beats the gong and drum, burns incenses to heaven, and lights the sacred lamp while another Dongba lights an azalea torch and smokes the evils on the sacred altar and in Shu's place. Usually the Dongba will chant scriptures, such as "setting up the sacred altar," "offering food to gods," "inviting gods," and "worshipping gods" to invite the gods in. Then, the Dongba will dance at the evil spirits' place as one of them chants verses from "The Origin of Evils" and some other scriptures. Later they will feed the Dan, which are three puppies, the nonhuman descendants of the human ancestor Congrenli'en and the straight-eyed girl from heaven. After being fed, the Dan are separated from the evil spirits. Then the participating villagers and Dongba cleanse the evil spirits' place with water and torches. They also kill a chicken to feed the dirty spirits with its blood and feathers and to drive the spirits to where they belong. At the same time, the Dongba begin the dance of the gods to destroy the evil spirits' place. The Dongba also fell the tree of evil spirits until all the spirits are suppressed.

The Shu worshipping rite follows the evil repelling rite. Shu's place is characterized by wood: plates representing heaven, Earth, and the five Shu kings, and the so-called repayment wood consisting of plates with drawings of different animals, the tower of Shu, and mountain bamboos. Shu's place; consists of three parts: the first is heaven, Earth, and the five Shu kings; the second is the guard of Shu's palace and the third is the foolish Shu's place. One Dongba will chant scriptures in front of Shu's place: "The Origin of Shu," "Inviting Shu," "Burning Incenses," "Offering Food," and "Locking Shu's Door." This chanting indicates that they have invited heaven and Earth and all the Shu kings to stay in the village and enjoy the offerings of the humans. The Dongba will also chant "Wake Up Shu When The Rooster Crows," "Offering Food," "The Fight Between the Rock and Shu," and stories about how human ancestors offended Shu and how Shu took its revenge, as well as how humans and Shu fought and were reconciled. Then they offer and serve Shu with medicine as they chant "The Origin of Medicine," "Using Medicine," and other scriptures to heal Shu's wound from the bite of the rock, thereby repaying all the debts. They set free a chicken whose neck is tied with a ribbon of five strips of cloth which symbolize five dimensions as a promise to sacrifice another chicken the next year. The Dongba chant "Praying For Longevity" and "Praying For Blessings Befalling on

Offspring," give gifts to all the Shu from different places, and then send them all back whence they came, accompanied by a chant of "Sending Off Shu." Finally, they burn incense on the sacred altar, dance the godly dance, and send the gods up to the eighteenth layer of heaven with the chant "Sending Off Gods." The Shu Worshipping Ritual is a solution that the Naxi ancestors found to the reconciliation of humans and nature in history. It is a means of reminding humans of their agreement with Shu. Only by disciplining themselves and living in harmony with Shu can humans ensure a good living environment and sustainable social development.

Dai people's "Holy Hills"
The Dai people can be found in Northwest Vietnam, Upper Laos, Shan Hills of eastern Myanmar, Northern Thailand, and Southern Yunnan in southwest China. The valley-based Dai People in Xishuangbanna have practiced a predominantly Buddhist religion since the middle of the Tang Dynasty (618–907). Before the introduction of Hinayana Buddhism, the Dai people appear to have practiced a polytheistic religion bound heavily to the natural world. Like many early groups, the Dai associated forests, animals, and plants that inhabited them and the forces of nature with the spiritual realm. Proper actions and respect for the gods were believed to result in peace and well-being. Improper activities and disrespect incurred the wrath of the gods who punished the Dai villagers with a variety of misfortunes. Thus, the early Dai were encouraged to live in harmony with their surroundings, such as cultivating fuel wood (*Cassia siamea*) in the foothills and planting religious plants in the temple yard. In the traditional concepts of the Dai, the gods reside on the forested Holy Hills, or *Nong* in their own language. All the plants and animals that inhabit the Holy Hills are either companions of the gods or sacred living things in the gods' garden. In addition, the Dai believe that the spirits of great and revered chieftains go to the Holy Hills to live, following their departure from the world of the living.

Holy Hills are an important visual landscape with good forest cover nearby the Dai village. They are a key component of the local ecosystems, which consists of paddy fields, home gardens, and cultivated fuel-wood forest. There appear to be two types of Holy Hills. The first, *Nong Man*, refers to a naturally forested hill, usually 10 to 100 hectares, worshipped by a natural village (called *Man*); the second, *Nong Meng*, refers to much larger forested hill, often hundreds of hectares, worshipped by the traditional administrative village or a governed area (called *Meng*). The traditional Dai people's practice of the Holy Hills has made a significant contribution to environmental goods and service the local and regional landscapes. Studies show a high concentration of endemic and endangered species in the Holy Hill forests.

The Hani concepts of village and nature
The Hani people, with a population of 1.25 million in Yunnan, are originally from the Tibetan Plateau. *Ha* meaning snow, strong and brave, combines with *ni*, meaning the people who live in mountains, to create the strong, brave mountain-dwelling Hani. The Hani people migrated from the Hong He, the Red River region of central Yunnan, where they are believed to have practiced irrigated agriculture toward what is now Xishaungbanna more than a thousand years ago. Other members of the same group migrated south, reaching northern Thailand and Myanmar early in the eighteenth century. Finding the river valleys of the warm, humid, sub-tropical regions already occupied by other groups, the Hani learned to practice shifting cultivation in the still vacant uplands.

During a long history of migration and readaptation to their new environment, a group of people, including *zoema*, *biemo* and *nipa*, who hold sacred and ecological knowledge about nature, have played a key role for cultural identity and continuity. The Hani are a patrilineal clan. The village chief (*zoema*) is normally a hereditary position but may be selected by a group of knowledgeable and well-to-do village men. The role of the village chief was traditionally imbued with legal authority and religious functions, but never as an absolute ruler.

The *biemo* is the natural encyclopedia of Akha society. He is the knowledge keeper of the genealogy tree, or all male ancestors of the clans, generally committing over sixty generations to memory. He recites all the ancient oral traditions about the origin of the Hani or Akha, the history, the migrations, the plant and animal cycles, etc. He is in charge of precisely establishing in the Akha calendar the date of every festival. He plays the role of an intermediary between the spiritual world of the ancestors (the past) and this world (the present). The Biemo also holds ceremonies for funerals. Every village has a *zoema* village head but not necessarily a *biemo*. Sometimes several villages share one *biemo*, or there are several *biemos* in a village.

Another knowledgeable person is the *nipa* or shaman. Most are women who have been designated by the spirits to fulfill this role. She learns from her dreams and can easily communicate with the spirit world. If somebody gets sick, *nipa* is asked to diagnose the illness and communicate with spirits for treatment, often combining rituals, dancing and medicinal plants. The *Nipa* and *biemo* have a close relationship. If somebody is sick because they have broken a natural law, or taboo, the *nipa* will identify whose spirit the person has violated. As she does not have the power to ask for pardon from the spirit, the *biemo* performs the rituals for facilitating dialogue with the spirit.

The Hani village is surrounded by a village protection forest (*pucang*) of several hundred meters divided into a human lived place (*pucang*) and nature (nonhuman) world (*baolcang*), with a village gate entrance (*lanlkang*). There is another gate to the ancestors living area (*laoqbiml*), the cemetery forest. The super-nature, mother of the Earth, governs all gods related to agriculture, who live in the village sacred forest (*milsanl-sanqqu*) and is often represented by a big, strong and long-living tree (such as oak, *Castanopsis mekongensis* or *Ficus religiosa*), called dragon trees by some Hani people. In a lucky day every June, a big ritual is held by *zoema* with participation of an adult male representative from each family. Hani people believe that different spirits have their own habitats, such as wetlands, lakes, strange stones, and particular trees (e.g., *Terminalia myriocarpa*).

The Hani people in Yunnan have a tradition of preserving forests in the mountainous areas where they live. As an ethnic group primarily living in southern Yunnan and bordering northern parts of Myanmar, Lao, Vietnam and Thailand, the Hani have kept harmonious relations with their natural surroundings for many centuries. According to their cultural beliefs, humans are a part of the natural world in which everything has its own spirit, and most of the spirits reside in certain forests. Human activities, like collecting forest products, hunting, and cutting trees in these forests are taboo for the villagers.

Tibetan sacred mountains and concepts of space

As high mountain dwellers, mountain worship is the most characteristic cultural belief and practice of Tibetan peoples. The spread of Buddhism on the Qinghai-Tibetan Plateau imbued their sacred mountains with new or even greater significance. There are different kinds of sacred mountains for Tibetan people. *Songre* is a little peak designated for the spirit, with small shrines but no residential houses, worshipped only by a small village or even one or two families. *Nieda/Reda* (some use them interchangeably) is a whole mountain body, bigger than *Songre*, and shared by larger village communities within a small region. People may live on it, though some Tibetan communities view such a mountain as very spiritually sensitive, believing that it is especially propitious to supplicate such a sacred location with prayers. *Nieqian/Niere* is a holy mountain highly regarded by the Tibetan community at large. It refers to the whole mountain from bottom to top. *Nieqian* is a respectful term such as Nieqian Qumalangma (Mt. Everest) and Khabadkapo. Reincarnated Buddhist Lamas purposely make sacred mountains cover a very large area because they believe that the bigger the area, the less likely it is that spirits will be disturbed. There is also evidence of concern among some Lamas that a rapid opening of pristine nature to tourism development might result in destruction of such sacred places. Some even go as far as designating religious names to new sites in an attempt to prevent their being disturbed.

In Deqen Tibetan Prefecture of northwest Yunnan, local Tibetans believe that the land, animals and people are governed by mountain gods residing on the peaks. There are over 15 sacred mountains found in the region of different sizes and religious power. Among them, the Meli Snow Mountain (Khabadkapo), the highest peak in Yunnan, is considered sacred by not only local Tibetans but all believers of Mizong (Kagyupa, one of the most important branches of Tibetan Buddhism). The Khabadkapo, with a height of 6740 meters above sea level and a total area of over 200 square kilometers, is ranked as one of the eight most important sacred mountains in the Tibetan Plateau. Each year, thousands of believers from Yunnan and other parts of the Tibetan region make pilgrimage to the mountain.

The Tibetan people have named and classified space into internal and external worlds. The internal world or human community is the permanent residence and village, including each named piece of land, each named house built on the named piece of land. The people adopt the name of the house as the family name. The external world, outside of the house or house walls, consists of arable lands, wild lands, lakes and forestlands with plants, trees, fish, rocks, wildlife, etc. The sacred objects, such as incense burning stands, pagodas, and *mani* stone piles, function as sacred places for Tibetans to have dialogue with life and spirits in the external world. The graveyard is considered a transitional place between earthly life and transcending into the "world of the death," the external world controlled by spirits. Those spirits associate with each other to form a group of mountain gods represented by mountain ranges centered on Mt. Khabadkarpo. Tibetans believe that these mountains can transform into human beings and vice versa. The concept of reincarnation pervades the Tibetan worldview. The key to good reincarnation into the next life is to undertake pilgrimages to commonly recognized sacred spaces; Mt. Khabadkarpo is considered the most holy in northwest Yunnan.

Yi people's polytheistic beliefs

The Yi people have a large population living traditionally in the provinces of Yunnan, Sichuan, Guizhou and Guangxi of southwest China. They believe that human beings and wildlife are offspring of the snow clan. The offspring of the snow clan had twelve categories, including six categories with blood (frog, snake, eagle, bear, monkey and human) and another six without blood (grass, trees, firs, etc.). Everything is divided into male and female: big trees are female, small trees male, big stones female and small stones male, big mountains female and small mountains male. All beings, human and non-human, have a soul or spirit. These communicate with and respect each other. In the Chuxing Yi Prefecture of central Yunnan, local people believe that humans survived through calamities with the help of these plants, while others are associated with gods or spirits. Recent surveys conducted in this prefecture by Liu and others have indicated that at least 21 plant species are generally worshipped and protected by local Yi communities due to various cultural beliefs. Historically, the Yi people evolved and practiced a polytheistic religion, which is an integration of Shamanism, Daoism, Buddhism and Confucianism. In their practice, 1) everything has a soul, whether it is tree, water, stone, wind, star or animal; 2) nature is worshipped and there is a super-nature of those gods (as of land, mountain, and tree) that have power to control human beings; 3) the tiger is considered to be the original totem for Yi people; 4) reproductive fertility is also worshipped, for example, in the alder tree (*Alnus nepalensis*) due to its plentiful seeds; 5) ancestors are worshipped, as is the god of Earth (which is next to ancestors in terms of importance), and sacred places and sacred forests.

Most rituals are held by the *biemo*, the Yi priests. The mosaic of sacred sites of Yi people forms an important cultural landscape, which contributes to local environmental goods and services.

Conclusion

Sacred spaces are found in different geographical scales and are worshipped and protected by different social groups, households, villages, religious sub-groups, ethnic groups and regions. The designation of sacred mountains has profound cultural and political implications while it also serves an important ecological function. Sacred mountains, besides serving as locations of deities connecting the human with the spiritual world, this life and the next, deliver products and perform ecological functions and services. The most obvious to local people as well as to outsiders is as sources of streams, benefiting both humans and wildlife. Old people often recall seeing collections of wildlife, such as deer and parrots, gathering along the streams. Therefore, good water-source forests, even when located outside of sacred forests, still receive extra protection from nearby villages and are usually designated as sacred sites closed to fuel-wood harvesting.

The relationship between natural resources and people has been forged within religious, moral, cultural, political, economic, and ecological boundaries. Respect for these boundaries by different communities and social groups resulted from historically accepted formal and informal rules and norms. For the Dai people of Xishuangbanna, their forest-oriented philosophy and the religious basis of traditional life have instilled a respect for forests, plants, animals, and their own ecological niche and imbued them with the formal and informal norms and rules of their society. The traditional worldviews or cultural beliefs of the Naxi, Dai, Hani, Tibetan, Yi and other minorities in Yunnan, combined with indigenous management strategies for natural resources for productive purposes, have succeeded in maintaining the forests of this region, and have effectively managed biological diversity in their environment over a long period of time. These factors can be seen as an example of the positive impact of the interaction of human culture with the environment and the conservation of biological diversity that existed in many earlier societies.

Indigenous people have drawn on their own sources of knowledge about biodiversity and environment, which features its diversity and adaptation in mediating their relationship with the local environment and ecosystems. Indigenous knowledge of this kind is a pluralistic approach to conservation and management of resources in the mountain region. It is a subjective understanding and social construction process, which incorporates a distinct corpus of understanding of the cosmos (worldviews), a praxis, and institutions to guide human action by adaptive processes. Indigenous knowledge about biodiversity and environment in mountain regions is composite and diverse, and yet it remains also holistic due to its gradation in altitude and latitude, as well as ethnic diversity in the mountain ecosystems. This knowledge comes from different sources – from one generation to the next, by way of indigenous experts and religious leaders. Both indigenous and conventional scientific knowledge are always imperfect and incomplete, and using one does not necessarily mean rejecting another. Conservation and resource management thus requires mutual respect and involves an iterative learning process. Indigenous knowledge systems bring a cognitive diversity to the scientific learning process. Just as biodiversity is essential to nature and invaluable for human beings, so too is cognitive diversity. Among the many things we can learn from indigenous knowledge and indigenous people is how to shift from a reductionist to a systemic view of the world, which includes ourselves, as living beings, in the ecosystem, and how to shift from expert-based environmental management to a participatory-based ecosystem stewardship.

Xu Jianchu

Further Reading

Cox, Paul Alan. "Will Tribal Knowledge Survive the Millennium?" *Science* 287:5450 (2000), 44–5.

Guo, Jing A. "Mountain of Nature, A Mountain of Divinity: Indigenous Knowledge about the Space of Mt. Khabadkarpo." In Xu Jianchu, ed. *Links between Cultures and Biodiversity: Proceedings of the Cultures and Biodiversity Congress 2000, 20–30 July Yunnan, China*. Yunnan Sciences and Technology Press, 2000, 230–39.

Liu, Aizhong, Pei Shengji and Chen Sanyang. "An Investigation and Study on the Plant Worship in Chuxiong, Yunnan." *Chinese Biodiversity* 8:1 (2000), 130–6 (in Chinese with English Abstract).

Liu, Hongmao, Xu Zaifu and Xu Youkai. "The Role of the Traditional Beliefs in Conservation Plant Diversity: A Case Study in Xishuangbanna, Southwest China." In

Xu Jianchu, ed. *Links between Cultures and Biodiversity: Proceedings of the Cultures and Biodiversity Congress 2000, 20–30 July, Yunnan, China*. Yunnan Sciences and Technology Press, 2000, 812–18.

Pei, Shengji. "Some Effects of the Dai People's Cultural Beliefs and Practices on the Plant Environment of Xishuangbanna, Yunnan Province, Southwest China." In K.L. Hutterer, A.T. Rambo and G. Lovelace, eds. *Cultural Values and Human Ecology in Southeast Asia*. Paper No. 27. Ann Arbor: University of Michigan, 1985, 321–39.

Pei, Shengji and Luo Peng. "Traditional Culture and Biodiversity Conservation in Yunnan." In Xu Jianchu, ed. *Links between Cultures and Biodiversity: Proceedings of the Cultures and Biodiversity Congress 2000, 20–30 July, Yunnan, China*. Yunnan Sciences and Technology Press, 2000, 230–9.

Pei, S.J. "Conservation of Biodiversity in Temple Yards and Holy Hills by the Dai Ethnic Minorities of China." *Ethnobotany* 3 (1991), 27–35.

Sutherland, William. "Parallel Extinction Risk and Global Distribution of Languages and Species." *Nature* 423 (15 May 2003), 276–9.

Xu, J.C., Jefferson Fox, et al. "Effects of Swidden Cultivation, State Policies and Customary Institutions on Land Cover in a Hani Village, Yunnan." *Mountain Research and Development* 19:2 (1999), 123–32.

Yang, Wanzhi. "Jingping: Home of Ethnic Minorities." *Shacha Human Geography* 4 (1999), 10–33.

See also: Chinese Traditional Concepts of Nature; Confucianism; Daoism; Mongolian Buddhism and Taimen Conservation; Polytheism; Sacred Mountains; Sacred Space/Place; Southeast Asia; Tibet and Central Asia; Traditional Ecological Knowledge; Traditional Ecological Knowledge among Aboriginal Peoples in Canada.

Z

Z Budapest (1940–)

Known simply as Z Budapest, Zsuzsuanna Emese Mokcsay was born in 1940 and was only 16 when she fled to Austria escaping the Soviet crackdown on the Hungarian Revolution. By 1958, she had immigrated to Chicago and married. An aspiring actor/director, Budapest took drama classes in Chicago and then in New York, where she moved with her husband and their two sons. At the age of thirty, Budapest left for a three-week vacation in Southern California. She never went back.

Almost immediately she became involved with the women's liberation movement in Los Angeles, but feminist politics failed to meet her spiritual needs or address her growing belief that women needed to reclaim their souls from male-dominated religions. On the winter solstice of 1971, Budapest and five friends created the Susan B. Anthony Coven Number 1, a circle of feminist separatist Witches. With Budapest as High Priestess, the group began to do religious rituals and call their practice Dianic Witchcraft. Members opened a small occult supply store called Feminist Wicca that became a gathering place for a growing spiritual community.

An arrest in 1975 for reading Tarot made Budapest a national figure and a hero to many who found her "wimmin's religion" (a popular spelling among radical feminists that signified men were not included) empowering and even transformative. But for over a decade, this charismatic leader known as the Mother of Dianic Witchcraft was a controversial figure among other feminists who saw Dianic Witchcraft as an embarrassment, and among other Wiccans who objected to its highly improvisational nature and female-only focus.

The primary focus of Budapest's message has always been women's empowerment, but a secondary element of nature religiosity has become more visible over time. Although she always preferred to hold her rituals in wilderness areas, her earliest writing said simply that the Dianic Craft was rooted in paganism and that practitioners worked in harmony with "Mother Nature." As in other Wiccan traditions, the major ritual celebrations were on the days that mark the changing of the seasons, and the Earth was understood to be the body of the Goddess. But so was the greater universe.

By 1986, Budapest called the Dianic Craft an "Earth Religion," writing that the Goddess was life on Earth. By the end of the decade, the concept had changed slightly. The Earth was now a living, breathing, conscious being and the Goddess present in all living beings. The increasing emphasis on the environment and growing understanding of the divine in and through nature present in the Dianic Craft today are largely due to the priestesses who came after Budapest. But there is no doubt that it was she who planted the seeds when she first picked the Goddess Diana as the representation of the numinous and called her the "Soul of the Wild."

Z Budapest lives in Oakland, California, where she continues to mentor, teach, organize rituals and conferences, and publish books that attempt to provide women with tools for spiritual empowerment.

Wendy Griffin

Further Reading

Budapest, Zsuzsanna. *The Grandmother of Time*. San Francisco: Harper & Row, 1989.

Budapest, Zsuzsanna. *The Holy Book of Women's Mysteries*, vol. 1. Oakland, CA: Susan B. Anthony Coven No. 1, 1979 (revised 1986).

See also: Ecofeminism (various); Goddesses – History of; Feminist Spirituality Movement; Mother Earth; Mother Nature Imagery; Wicca; Wicca – Dianic.

Zen Buddhism

Zen (*Chan* in Chinese, *Son* in Korean) is a form of Buddhist practice that developed and flourished in East Asia, and, since the latter part of the twentieth century, has become part of the spiritual landscape in North America and Europe. Tracing its fundamental inspiration to the enlightenment experience of Gautama the Buddha (ca. fifth century B.C.E., India), Zen presents as its model the Buddha seated cross-legged in a state of yogic contemplation (*dhyāna*). Seated meditation (*zazen* in Japanese) enables a practitioner to cultivate inner stillness leading to illuminative insight, which in turn enhances clarity of vision and spiritual discernment. Zen can be a transformative factor for one's entire way of life, as it opens the practitioner to an experiential realization of oneness with nature, bringing about a heightened ecological awareness.

The philosophy and practice of Zen can be situated in the wider context of the Buddhist tradition. As such, it derives features of its cosmology from the Hindu tradition. Hence we must first look at this wider picture in attempting to understand the view of nature implied in Zen.

There is a notion stemming from the Hindu tradition assimilated into Buddhism, as articulated by Indian commentators beginning with Vasubandhu (fourth century), to the effect that the universe exists within a cyclic pattern of origination, maintenance, and annihilation. The physical world, undergoing this cyclic pattern, is taken simply as the objective environment in which sentient beings, conceived of as belonging to six distinguishable modes, including the hell-dwellers, hungry ghosts, malignant spirits, animals, humans, and heavenly beings, live out their spans of existence. Sentient beings are born into the universe in one of the six modes, and upon death, depending on the karmic merit or demerit accumulated by one's actions in this life or previous spans of life, are reborn as one of the six, again to repeat the cycle.

The basic message of Buddhism in such a context revolves around the liberation of sentient beings from the cycle of birth and death and further rebirth within the six modes of existence, and entry into a realm called nirvana, described as "the other shore." Early Buddhist texts suggest that nirvana was understood as a state attainable in this life by one who has extinguished one's defilements and has freed oneself from inordinate attachments, thus arriving at a place of inner peace. However, later developments led to a view of this attainment as pertaining to an afterlife, or after multiple lifetimes of continued striving.

This aspiration for liberation from cyclic existence, or *samsara*, is the dynamism underlying the central Buddhist doctrine of the Four Ennobling Truths. The way to this liberation is spelled out in the Ennobling Eightfold Path, culminating in the seventh and eighth, Right Mindfulness and Right Concentration.

Buddhist meditative practice thus pertains to the cultivation of attitudes and habits that are conducive to personal liberation and transformation. As such, strictly speaking, in Indian Buddhism, there arises no specific interest in or concern for the natural world, regarded merely as the "environment" or stage wherein sentient beings live out their lives, a provisional reality that is itself subject to the cyclic pattern of origination, maintenance, and annihilation.

As Buddhism developed and flourished in Chinese, Korean, and Japanese soil, however, the meditative practice encouraged in the tradition that came to be known as Chan/Son/Zen took on elements from these East Asian cultures that became constitutive aspects of its worldview. Daoist perspectives on nature in particular came to inform the way practitioners articulated their understanding of the world in the light of their Zen experience. This Daoist influence on Buddhism as it was transmitted into Chinese soil is the crucial factor that made East Asian Buddhism distinctive and different from Indian Buddhism with regard to views on nature.

A key dictum underlying the entire Zen tradition is the affirmation that "all sentient beings are endowed with Buddha-nature" (*fo-xing* in Chinese, *bussho* in Japanese). The notion of "sentient being" came to be expanded beyond the framework presented in Indian culture. In the latter, sentient beings referred to the six modes of being, from the hell-dwellers up to the heavenly beings. Vegetative life as a whole did not belong to this circle of sentients, and together with mountains and rivers and "the natural world," plants were considered as belonging to the objective environment. In China however, it came to be asked whether plants were also endowed with Buddha-nature, and this question was given an affirmative answer.

This principle of Buddha-nature inherent in all sentient beings, conjoined with a maxim of Zen, namely, of "seeing into one's nature (Chinese: *xing*; Japanese: *Shō*) and thereby becoming a Buddha" (Dumoulin 1988: 85), brought new dimensions in the understanding of nature and of reality as a whole.

The following verbal exchange between a Zen master and student, included in a collection known as the *Wu Men Guan* (No. 37) serves as an illustration of this new dimension of understanding.

> A monk asked Chao-chu: "What is the meaning of the Bodhidharma's coming from the West?"
> Chao-chou answered, "The oak tree in the courtyard" (Aitken 1990: 226).

Such verbal exchanges in the context of Zen practice, called *gong-an* (Chinese) or *kōan* (Japanese), contain veiled allusions to that realm of one's true "nature." The opening question about the Bodhidharma's coming from the West is a standard gambit that sets the tone of the exchange, asking: what is the quintessence of the practice of Zen? In other words, "In what consists that true nature, the seeing of which one becomes a Buddha?" Or more succinctly, "Who am I, really?" The answer given in this case, "The oak tree in the courtyard," is the key that can open the practitioner's eyes to that realm whereby one becomes enlightened, that is, becomes a Buddha. In short, truly to "see" the oak tree in the courtyard, with the inner eye of the mind, is what the verbal exchange enjoins a practitioner. And this experience of truly seeing can occur in the context of seated meditation, as one is able to overcome the wall of separation that divides what is seen and the subject that sees. In this context, "seeing" is no-other than "becoming." The oak tree in the courtyard is the locus of the revelation of one's true nature.

With Dogen (thirteenth-century Japan), the scope of sentient beings expands further, to include not only the vegetative realm, but also the whole universe of ten thousand myriad things, such as mountains and rivers, rocks and stones, the great wide Earth, the sun, the moon, the stars. And what is important in this context is that mountains and rivers are not "things" in the objective world "out there," but are precisely manifestations of one's true nature. *Zazen* is the locus in which this comes to be realized.

In short, this experience of "seeing into one's true nature" is the entry into a continuum, a realm whereby the barrier that separates one (as a human subject) from the natural world, the myriad things of the universe (as things "out there," objects of my perception) is overcome. The view of nature that comes to the fore in the context of Zen practice is the view from within, whereby one sees "mountains and rivers, the great wide Earth," no longer as objects of the physical world, but as the very manifestation of one's true nature, one's true self.

The historical track record of Zen presents an ambivalent answer as to whether Zen practice can foster an ecologically oriented vision and way of life. Many individuals are led to Zen practice in search for answers to existential questions, or in search for inner peace, in search for healing, or in search for a community of spiritual support. The practice of *zazen* can be and has been indeed a powerful way of seeing through and coming to a resolution of big existential questions in life. It can be and has been an effective way for individuals to find a source of inner peace, to find healing for psychological and other kinds of woundedness, as well as to connect with a community of kindred spirits. But these effects of Zen practice, beneficial as they may be toward the integration of the individual's personality, are *as such* not yet necessarily connected with an ecological awareness and way of life.

A phase of Zen practice involves an "inward turn" wherein an individual focuses one's energy and attention upon spiritual pursuits, in a way that can diminish concern with the events of the everyday world. To engage in this practice can thus initially deflect one from concerns of ecological import. For a viable ecological awareness to arise and become a prominent element in a practitioner's life, another dimension may need to enter, namely, an actual exposure to the Earth's woundedness in its many forms, that would call forth a response of com-passion (that is, "suffering-with").

With such an exposure to the reality of the natural world in a state of woundedness in the background, and as individuals commit themselves to Zen practice and experience the fruits thereof, something *may* happen that may awaken, enhance, or reconfirm an ecological awareness and commitment. In brief, as one deepens the experience of inner stillness, one comes to an illuminative insight into one's true nature as inseparable from the trees and the flowers, the mountains and rivers, the great wide Earth. One experiences these as the manifestation of one's own self, one's own "home" (*oikos* in Greek, from which "ecology" is derived). From this vantage point, the pain of the denuded mountains and the polluted rivers and oceans become one's very own pain, and to care for the Earth is nothing other than to care for one's own home. A renewed vision and strengthened resolve toward healing the Earth's wounds can arise as an outflow of the inner stillness that is the hallmark of Zen practice.

Ruben Habito

Further Reading
Aitken, Robert. *The Gateless Barrier: The Wu-men Kuan (Mumonkan)*. San Francisco: North Point Press, 1990.
Dumoulin, Heinrich. *Zen Buddhism: A History*, 2 vols. New York: MacMillan & Co., 1988, 1990.
Habito, Ruben. *Healing Breath: Zen Spirituality for a Wounded Earth*. Dallas: MKZC Publications, 2001.
Habito, Ruben. "Mountains and Rivers and the Great Earth: Zen and Ecology." In Mary Evelyn Tucker and Duncan Ryuken Williams, eds. *Buddhism and Ecology*. Cambridge: Harvard University Center for the Study of Religions, 1997, 165–75.
Harris, Ian. "Attitudes to Nature." In Peter Harvey, ed. *Buddhism*. London: Continuum, 2001.
See also: Buddhism – East Asian; Japanese Gardens; Japanese Love of Nature; Japanese Religions; Mountains and Rivers Sutra by Japanese Soto Zen Master Dogen Kigen.

Zhuangzi

"Fish thrive in water; humans thrive in the *dao*. Those who thrive in water dart about in the pond and find nourishment there; those who thrive in the *dao* work 'without doing' and their nature is realized" (*Zhuangzi* Chapter 6). For over two millennia, this "second master" in the Lao-Zhuang or "Early Philosophical Daoist" tradition has provided Chinese religion with provocative images of the human within its environment, using such rhetorical devices as fable, fantasy, dialogue, debate, and models of practice.

The superb ambiguity in which the Chinese character often grounds major religious terms has stimulated numerous interpretations in Asian and Western languages about the relationship between Zhuangzi's ideal Daoist and "nature" itself. Formidable philosophical and aesthetic issues arise with translation from the original Chinese – such as the unarticulated assumptions and prejudices of several generations of Western Romantic individualist translators (that determine the incalculable choices of meaning made at each fork of ambiguity along the textual road). Likewise, additional issues of interpretation occur in target language translations as readers introduce their own preconceived notions and values to supply meaning to the translator's choices.

Zhuangzi contains no literal Chinese equivalent to the Western term "nature" ("nature" commonly understood as the material, nonhumanmade elements on Earth). Yet the text makes constant lyrical use of actual plant, animal, meteorological, and geographical phenomena, sometimes as virtual beings, often as metaphorical devices. Usually the obvious linkage or equivalence is made by the reader between Western "nature" and Zhuangzi's concept of *dao* (the "Way" or "flow" of reality). Many readers also "read into" Zhuangzi's *dao* the entire conceptual structure of Laozi's *Daode-jing* (*dao*, *de* [individual spiritual capacity], *wuwei* ["without doing"], *ziran* ["naturalness"], etc.). The resulting image is a vibrant anti-anthropocentrism that resets the human within nature. Yet "nature" is only accessible in *Zhuangzi* once the Daoist context for the human and its capacities are understood, because Daoism pushes the ramifications of a true anthropomorphism to a far greater extent than does any Western worldview.

First, in terms of scope, the *dao* refers to the entire universe as the context for human living – rather than simply the natural Earth as the site of human habitation. Second, given the archaic Chinese acceptance of change (as the neutral basis of reality – rather than as a negative or positive characteristic of it), the entire universe is in constant flux. The appropriate Daoist term is "in transformation" (*hua*) or what is commonly appropriated from the text's water imagery, the "flow." Third, throughout its 33 chapters, the text builds a Daoist ideal, a practitioner or sage who develops a combination of attitudes, actions, and responses. The important attributes of a sage are to be calm (Chapter 32), to see all things equivocally and not to discriminate (2), not to quantify (17), not to think in terms of cause and effect (4), not to make value judgments (17), thus not to separate oneself from the totality of the universe (19), and to be in continual awe at the mystery and sacrality of all things in this totality. (These attitudes are of course those of the purely non-anthropocentric sage who realizes his participation within the universe and so cannot differentiate in any way among all creatures and things in terms of quantity, causality, values, or varied emotional responses.) These attitudes allow the sage: to respond unthinkingly and to develop only fluid, temporarily emerging goals (13), to adapt to the flow (20), to harmonize the *yin* and *yang* energies within oneself (22), to act spontaneously, and to "know how" (rather than to "know what") by means of one's intuition (22). Just as a person sits on the bank of a stream and sees the stream flowing by, so a human experiences *dao* as a flow from one's own fixed reference point as a single creature. Likewise each anthropocentric human being understands dao as flow because each socially references a universe in which the human is believed to naturally be the center. But from the standpoint of totality and of all the creatures and things that comprise it, a sage experiences the dao by such attitudes and behavior as relaxed fluidity, adaptability, spontaneity, harmonizing, and intuiting, both to participate in the never-ending transformation (of the universe as totality) and to respond to the distinct transformations (of each individual participant).

The goal of the text is to enable the Daoist practitioner to decentralize oneself from ones privileged position as anthropocentric observer and to begin to act in this totality as a "willing, equal" participant. Thus the concept of nature that indirectly pervades much of *Zhuangzi* serves a number of important purposes instrumental to the Daoist practitioner's spiritual transformation: 1) it provides many observable everyday examples of the life cycle (birth, growth, aging, death), the seasons, and processes of transformation; 2) it provides the immediate environment of change/flow in which the human must live and act; 3) it continually reveals the sheer complexity and depth of the transformations of creatures and things in this environment that is far beyond the rational comprehension of any human; 4) it provides specific materials or environments that are worked by craftsmen, artists, and athletes who exemplify discovering and acting within the flow of the *dao* (butcher Ding [3], woodcarver Jing [19], wheelwright Pian [13], carpenter Qiu [19], the tiger trainer [4], etc.); and 5) specific natural phenomena serve as metaphors or examples for Daoist attitudes or "values" – such as unobstructed living [the pheasant, 3], consistency [pine and cypress trees, 5], balance [still waters, 5], the aesthetic appreciation of the "earth's music" [2], etc.

A surprisingly effective way of discovering how the human relates to nature in *Zhuangzi* is to examine what the text says and implies about the modern Western issue of ecological activism. *Zhuangzi* mentions no literal concept of ecology and does not allude to ecological problems (this occurs only in the Confucian text roughly contemporary with *Zhuangzi*, the *Mencius*, with its well-known story of the deforestation of Ox Mountain [Book VI, Part 8, Section 8]). Yet it does contain a number of positions and issues both supportive and critical of such activism.

Sympathetic are its general strategies for abandoning anthropocentrism ("within the compass of Heaven and Earth, I am no more than a pebble or a bush on a great mountain" [17]). As an abridgement created by Guo Xiang (who died in 312), the current text is divided by scholars into the philosophically and stylistically consistent "Inner Chapters" (1 through 7) and mixed and fragmentary "Outer Chapters" (8 through 33). The homogeneous sense of nature of the Inner Chapters does not fit well with the more sporadic emphasis of the Outer Chapters that contain textual fragments of contemporary Primitivist (8 through 10) and Agrarianist movements. (The Primitivists advocated an archaic tribal social and political utopianism of humans living by a pre-moral consciousness in accord with nature, while the Agrarianists or "School of the Tillers" [*Nong-jia*] promoted an archaic utopian classless agrarian economy of fixed prices with minimal or no political leadership). Specific natural phenomena (such as a "tree-of-Heaven" [1], a "sacred" gigantic chestnut-leaved oak [4], and a mountain tree [20]) function as examples of a major metaphor running throughout the text that suggests the adaptable, ambitionless, non-evaluative Daoist practitioner:

> The trees in the mountains ask to be chopped down. Fat added to the fire consumes itself. The cinnamon tree is edible, so it is cut down. The lacquer tree is useful, so it is slashed. Everyone knows the usefulness of the useful, but no one knows the usefulness of the useless (Chapter 4).

An object created from nature is occasionally discredited (how both the libation vessel and the scraps of wood at its making have lost the "nature of wood" [8]); the accretion of wealth that is one great motive for despoiling nature is also condemned [29].

On the other hand, because *Zhuangzi's* basic purpose is an advocacy of Daoist practice, it contains much that is antithetical to ecological activism. The aforementioned attitudes that maintain the Daoist's equilibrium within the *dao* (both as corporate totality and dynamic flow) repeatedly emphasize that no single perspective or fixed goal is useful (these always lead to value judgments), that trying to mentally process reality by means of discrimination and opposites is absurd [the entire Chapter 2], that attempting to "pattern" or arrange the infinite *dao* into finite separate entities as responsible agents or to sort them into causes and results is "a mistake" [4]. The life cycle of any species or entity is a process of transformation ("between cohering and dissolving, each has its form" [25]); the Daoist is to accept such changes (the frequent mention of the crippled, mutilated criminals, and misshapen humans who not only accept such transformations but also live with them prosperously) because no human can comprehend the "patterns" of living and dying ("It is not that death and life are far away, but the patterns of them cannot be perceived" [25]). *Zhuangzi* is by-and-large neutral about technology (other than Primitivist and Agarianist comments). It is precisely nature's raw materials that are used by those exemplary craftsman who have discovered how to act within the flow of the *dao* (including the hunchback whose techniques of catching cicadas teach even Confucius [19]). Consistently, the spiritual, the indescribable (beyond forms), and the intuitively comprehended are advocated over the material, the written-down and the rationally organized [13], because nurturing one's spiritual capacity (*de*) is always the primary goal. Daoist "without doing" (*wuwei*) involves letting things alone, refraining from deliberate action, never attempting to freeze the flow by means of discrimination [2] or by substituting the illusion of the certainty of reason for the flexibility of response that is spontaneity [2]. In his denunciation of swordsmanship to King Wen of Zhao, Zhuangzi dismisses the typical human recourse to any physical solution to a problem as "the (useless) sword of the common person" (in contrast to the cosmos as the sword of the Son of Heaven and the harmonious community of warriors as the sword of a prince of state [30]).

Issues concerning ecological activism raised by these ideas in *Zhuangzi* are the following. 1) Is a destroyer of a natural ecology actually part of some kind of transformation within the *dao* – or is such action a disruption or dysfunction of it? 2) Can there be a "Daoist" activist attempting to stop such destruction – because the required motivation and decision-making process uses such intellectual discrimination as isolating specific events, quantification, and cause-effect reasoning, to affect value-laden, fixed-goal-driven acts? 3) Is not the activist just as anthropocentric and selfish-will-imposing toward reality as is the destroyer (and thus is not an activist incapable of acting in a Daoist manner?) 4) Is the living and dying of any species not a "natural" transformation of the *dao* – or are there "natural" and "unnatural" (i.e., human-initiated exterminatory) livings and dyings? 5) Is the use of nature as raw material only justifiable for the Daoist craftsperson, artist or athlete as spiritual practice? 6) Is there enough ambiguity in *Zhuangzi* to support some directed action toward nature?

The answers can perhaps be found among the craftsmen and artisans who engage the *dao* in action – the best example furnished by Cook Ding, when he is asked about his technique by the surprised Prince Wen Hui who is touring his kitchen on the morning of a diplomatic banquet.

> Cook Ding laid down his cleaver and said, "Technique?" What I really care about is the *dao* – which is much more important than any technique! When I first began to butcher oxen, I could see only the entire ox before me. But then after three years I no longer saw an entire ox. At present, it is my spirit that apprehends – I do not use my eyes to see; my senses are idle, but my spirit moves where it wants. Guided by the natural grain, I slip through great hollows and travel in broad spaces, making use of things just as they are. Thus I miss the large sinews and I hack into no great bones ... There are spaces between the joints [of the bones] and this blade is very thin and sharp, so there is more room than anyone ever needs to get through! This is why after nineteen years the blade of this cleaver is as good as when it was brand new and sharpened for the first time.
>
> Yet sometimes there are very tough joints. When I begin to feel difficulty, I slow down and barely move the blade until suddenly there is a plop! and the pieces fall apart as easily as a clump of Earth dropping to the ground. Whenever this happens, I withdraw the blade and I stand still, just letting the joy of the work sink in. Then I wipe the blade and put it away (Chapter 3).

Cook Ding summarizes how he discovered the *dao* as a practice – early struggles as a beginner ("I could see only the entire ox"), gradual acceptance of the work situation ("after three years I no longer saw an entire ox"), mastery of technique such that his perceptions relaxed ("I do not use my eyes to see; my senses are idle") and his movements not labored ("guided by the natural grain I slip through ... and travel ... making use of things just as they are"). He intuits ("it is my spirit that apprehends") the situation and where to move moment-by-moment ("my spirit moves where it wants"). His intuition does not involve premeditation, rational choice, or directed awareness – instead it is related to mastery of technique, much learned experience, and relaxed awareness, always open for response ("When I begin to feel difficulty, I slow down and barely move the blade").

In *Zhuangzi*, the Daoist discovers the *dao* and acts within it in four broad stages: 1) to relax and empty the heart ("emptiness, stillness, calmness, serenity" [13]); 2) to be illumined by Heaven (which is responsible for all things beyond human will) to be able to reflect the total situation; 3) to be filled with this "unpatterned or unsorted" totality ("he does not escort things as they go or welcome them as they come, he responds but does not retain" [7]); and 4) spontaneously to respond as the situation moves one ("he responds like an echo [to a sound]" [33]). One surrenders any need to shape or control the situation or even one's own action – this is the spontaneity of all creatures but the human. One empties the heart of ambition, of discrimination, rationality, causality, and fixed goals. One cannot perceive by surveying with the senses or by processing within one's mind a stream of information sequentially because the situation (the flow of the *dao*) is an immediacy, a totality, a *gestalt*. The only way this can be done is that one's heart must be as empty of all such "objects" as is a mirror which does not present things but instead reflects what is illuminated ("He is the reflector of Heaven and Earth, the mirror of the myriad things" [13]). What is reflected makes the relationships of its constituents apparent ("and *what fills him sorts itself out*" [13]). The more minimal one's self-assertion is while the greater one's reflecting awareness is, the brighter will be Heaven's illumination of all things and the more subtle will be the transformations one is aware of and can respond to without obstruction. Thus one spontaneously responds – being inevitably "caused" to act by what fills one instead of choosing what to do oneself; this is termed "Heaven working through the sage" (7). One's action is successful because one's own spiritual capacity (*de*) accommodates the *de* of all other participants in the flow of totality.

The traditional Chinese term equivalent to the English "nature" is *ziran*, variously translated by Western scholars of Daoism as "unmediated by rule or principle," "spontaneity," "spontaneous activity," "to follow one's own *de*," "self-expressing," "self-creating," "self-actualization," "self-evidencing," "self-so-ing," "to be party to transforming things," "to assist the self-so-ing of each and all things" (*Daodejing* 64), "naturalness" (*Daodejing* 25), "natural flourishing." At first glance, such interpretations seem to span a range of focusing on an individual at one end through that of totality at the other. The individual orientation emphasizes direct and immediate action unique to a person's qualities, as expression (communication) and as creativity (craft and art), literally producing one's particularity as action unique, specific and "natural" only to oneself. It is one's own behavior that establishes one as a participant in totality – it reveals and authenticates oneself in terms of one's uniqueness. This action can only occur within the ever-changing totality comprised by always-transforming participants, so at the other totality – or holistic end of the spectrum – an individual's behavior not only occurs simultaneously among the actions of other participants and witnesses what all others do, but is also thoroughly integrated (or "interrelated") and thus enables the flow. However, no polar model can readily depict how a Daoist sage understands reality, precisely because the Daoist acts within totality and among the actions of all participants. Any emphasis upon only one of its major characteristics of 1) individual participant, 2) totality, 3) all participants, or 4) flow [transforming participants and changing reality] over-emphasizes one at the expense of the others.

The term *ziran* (which appears earliest in the *Zhuangzi* and the *Daodejing*) suggests that these dimensions comprise the *dao* itself. If the Daoist sense of nature involves a withdrawal of such attendant Western concepts and values as anthropomorphism, separate individuality, linear causality, human capacity to shape, control and dominate, etc., and it emphasizes a cosmological dynamic inherent in the written Chinese character and in Chinese religions in general, then the term could be more accurately translated into English as "naturing".

Dennis Lishka

Further Reading

Callicott, J. Baird and Roger T. Ames, eds. *Nature in Asian Traditions of Thought: Essays in Environmental Philosophy*. Albany: State University of New York Press, 1989.

Chuang-tzu. *The Seven Inner Chapters and Other Writings from the Book Chuang-tzu*. A.C. Graham, tr. London: George Allen & Unwin, 1981.

Giradot, Norman, James Miller and Liu Xiaogan, eds. *Daoism and Ecology: Ways within a Cosmic Landscape*. Cambridge: Harvard University Press, 2001.

Graham, A.C. "Taoist Spontaneity and the Dichotomy of 'Is' and 'Ought.' In Victor H. Mair, ed. *Experimental Essays on Chuang-tzu*. Honolulu: University of Hawai'i Press, 1983, 3–23.

See also: Chinese Traditional Concepts of Nature; Confucianism; Daoism; Religious Environmentalist Paradigm.

Zimbabwe Spirit Mediums, Guerrillas, and Nature

In Zimbabwe, a loosely interacting and overlapping series of rain-cult networks have existed for centuries. The Portuguese mentioned some of these during the sixteenth and seventeenth centuries. At the other end of the colonial period, the Rhodesia Front paid a great deal of attention to Zimbabwean African Religion. In the mid-1970s one of its ethnographers, C.J.K. Latham, compiled a "Spirit Index" that listed and numbered every major spirit, every medium, every shrine and every sacred place throughout the country. Latham also compiled *The Shamanism Book*, which described in detail the five major cultic systems. Most of the spirits recorded by the Portuguese reappear in the "Spirit Index" or *The Shamanism Book*. The reason that both the Portuguese and the Rhodesians felt the need to make these reports was that they believed the cults were crucial to African politics and to African consciousness.

Some of the major spirits are supra-human figures, embodying the forces of nature; others represent founding ancestors, chiefs and kings. It is often hard to separate the two categories. Myths of founding chiefs, "princesses" and "grandmothers" often describe them as creating natural phenomena such as salt-pans or even rivers. Even more often they describe them as being able to control nature: "princesses" are described as having the power to draw wild animals to the hunter or to divide the Zambezi River so that the people could migrate. The possessed spirit mediums, which are their living incarnations, are believed to possess the same powers, enabling them to make rain, cause drought, or strike down enemies with lightning.

In the nineteenth century, white hunters respected the spirit mediums' control over nature, especially over game. The famous hunter, Frederick Courtney Selous, described how he had paid tribute to the medium of the great spirit of Chaminuka, in order to be able to hunt elephant successfully. African kings paid a similar respect. King Lobengula of the Ndebele state sent tribute to rainmaking mediums to the northeast of his kingdom.

After the colonial conquest in the 1890s, however, the powers of the mediums were curtailed or ignored. Africans were forbidden to hunt and white hunters no longer needed to seek permission from anyone. Chiefs were chosen by the Native Department without the endorsement of the mediums. In the early colonial years, there were direct assaults on the most powerful mediums and shrines. During the African uprising of 1896, one of the priests of the High God, Mwali, was shot dead and other officials of the cult were arrested and put on trial. The female medium of the great rain-spirit, "princess" Nehanda, was arrested, tried and hanged in 1897. The rainmaking cult of Musikavanhu on the eastern border with Mozambique was turned into a secular chieftancy, and when the possessed medium drove out the new chief, the Native Commissioner marched with a small army to reinstate the chief and expel the medium. In the 1920s, the Dzivaguru shrine in the northeast, which had figured largely in Portuguese accounts, was closed down in what was called "The Mount Darwin Ritual Murder Case."

Gradually these repressions gave way to constant government supervision of the major mediums. It came to be believed that the mediums and their cults were mostly concerned, after all, with nature, with rainmaking, the fertility of crops, etc. Now that nature and political authority had been separated, they were no longer thought to be politically dangerous.

In reality, nature and political authority had not been separated. A major component of white ideology was that they had taken over the land. By this, they not only meant that they had evicted the Africans and created their own farms, they also meant that the whites had become "the people of the land" in the most intimate and essential way. Rhodesians prided themselves on "bushcraft," and the myth of the "Great White Hunter" and, later, the Game Conserver flourished in Rhodesia, as well as in Kenya.

By contrast, African hunting was stigmatized as cowardly and cruel. In her recent writings, the novelist Doris Lessing powerfully expressed the feeling that white farm children grew up with the idea that the land was theirs. Whites believed that they alone appreciated landscape, and quite often they deliberately set out to create spectacular views. In these senses, not only the physical but also the imaginative ownership of nature was being taken over from Africans.

Missionaries played a major role in these processes. Some of them were critical of colonial evictions and disliked the commercial growing of crops like tobacco, or the bad conditions on the tea plantations. But all of them were involved in the creation of a Christian landscape in the African areas – a landscape of villages, clustered around their church and cemetery, which was very different from huts perched on the hill-tops or the burial of chiefs in the rocks.

For a long time spirit mediums could do little about this. They were still consulted for rain. When possessed, they often articulated with the voice of the spirit its dislike of new methods of tilling the land, or of damming and diverting rivers. But such protest was ineffective. Then there came the rise of mass nationalism; the rediscovery of a heroic past; the invocation of the Nehanda spirit at nationalist meetings; the visits paid by nationalist leaders to senior spirit mediums. By the 1960s, both African nationalists and Rhodesian administrators began to take the mediums much more seriously.

The climax of this new importance was the guerrilla war of the late 1960s and 1970s. There were several reasons why young guerrillas took mediums seriously. They needed legitimacy in the eyes of the people and they needed spiritual protection. The mediums represented traditional claims to the land. Guerrillas who had been trained by Chinese advisers in Tanzania had been taught the Maoist doctrine that they must respect the beliefs of the peasants. But their needs were a more powerful incentive. It was the mediums of the Dzivaguru "circle," which overlapped the boundary between Zimbabwe and Mozambique, who made the first contact with Zimbabwe African National Liberation Army guerrillas on Mozambican soil. Mediums from inside Zimbabwe were called to a meeting across the border and they agreed to give spiritual support to the young fighters. Gradually, numbers of mediums settled in special quarters of the guerrilla camps inside Mozambique; these exercised some sort of control over sexual relations, and tried to predict and warn of Rhodesian raids.

As the guerrillas crossed into Rhodesia they came into contact with the mediums of other "circles." The best-known account of these interactions is given by the anthropologist, David Lan, who describes how the mediums of the Dande Valley gave legitimacy to the guerrillas. Where Rhodesian propaganda described them as animal-like beings with tails, who prowled the evil bush, the Dande mediums depicted the guerrillas as the descendants of the heroes who had founded kingdoms and chiefdoms and human society itself in the past. The mediums imposed prohibitions and taboos on the young fighters. They revealed to the guerrillas the caves and hiding places and even permitted them to make use of the burial caves of chiefs or the rainmaking shrines sacred to the High God.

Above all, the mediums gave back to the guerrillas and took away from the whites the "ownership" of nature. David Maxwell has described in his study of the northern Nyanga disctrict how it came to be believed that all of nature was mobilized on the side of ZANLA. Eagles flying overhead showed them safe routes; snakes slithered out of their way, only to return to lie in wait for Rhodesian soldiers; lions appeared to convey the support of the senior ancestral lion-spirits; talking baboons carried messages; rivers flooded to prevent Rhodesian soldiers from reaching guerrilla strongholds. During the 1970s, the whites began to realize that they did not after all possess superior "bushcraft." By contrast, the guerrillas came to believe that they were in every sense "sons of the soil."

On their side, the Rhodesians tried everything they could to win mediums over and to use them to denounce the spilling of blood on the soil. It became very dangerous to be a medium, the guerrillas killing "sell-outs" and the Rhodesian forces eliminating those who worked with ZANLA. Nevertheless, the mediums emerged from the war with their reputations and influence greatly enhanced. In independent Zimbabwe, their power over nature has been recognized in various ways. In the so-called Campfire schemes, in which African communities receive cash returns from safaris, white hunters once again give gifts to mediums to ensure good hunting. Many mediums in the south of the country have been recruited into schemes for a "second independence" struggle, this time to rescue the environment. A Prophetess, Mbuya Juliana, has endlessly traversed southern Zimbabwe during the last ten years, bearing the message that the water spirits in the streams must be propitiated in order to end drought. The struggle over nature in Zimbabwe continues.

Terence Ranger

Further Reading
Lan, David. *Guns and Rain: Guerrillas and Spirit Mediums in Zimbabwe.* London: James Currey, 1985.
Maxwell, David. *Christians and Chiefs in Zimbabwe.* Edinburgh: International African Institute, 1999.
McLaughlin, Janice. *On the Front-Line.* Harare: Baobab Books, 1996.
Nhongo-Simbanegavi, Josephine. *For Better or Worse: Women and Zanla.* Harare: Weaver, 2001.
See also: San Rainmaking (adjacent to San [Bushmen] Religion); Zimbabwe's Matopo Hills.

Zimbabwe's Matopo Hills

The Matopo Hills of western Zimbabwe lie south of the Matabeleland city of Bulawayo and about an hour's drive away from it. They take the form of a very extensive granite mass, throwing up great domed hills and kopjes fantastically decorated with eroded rock pinnacles. The hills, which today stretch across the borders of three administrative districts, are the source of most of the rivers of southern Matabeleland, and there are many rock pools with perennial water.

Most tourists visiting the hills go to the National Park, an area in the center of the Matopos set aside in 1962 when all its African occupants were evicted. The National Park contains the grave of the founder of the white Rhodesian state, Cecil Rhodes, after whom the country was named. It also contains a Game Park into which giraffe and rhino were imported after 1962. There is a "wilderness" area, which can only be entered on foot, and where one can still see the bases of huts and granaries. But though the Park itself has so recently been made "wild," the Matopo Hills are still occupied by African farmers to the south and east of it. In the Communal Areas of Kumalo, Gulati, and Matopo, one can still see people living among the rocks, cultivating the alluvials, grazing cattle in the grassy valleys and collecting wild fruits as they have done for centuries.

The successive inhabitants of the hills have all developed contrasting cults of "Nature." The Matopos have been occupied by humans for some 40,000 years. For most of this time foraging peoples moved in and out of the hills on a seasonal basis. But some 9000 years ago permanent populations built up at favored sites in the Matopos. These "San" peoples (Khoisan-speaking nomadic tribes in Southern Africa) used grassland and riverine environments, but hunted rock-rabbits on the granite hills and gathered fruit and roots in the woods. There is no doubt that their religious specialists conducted rituals in the great caves of the Matopos which were intended to give success in hunting and to make rain. Rock-art specialists have interpreted many of the thousands of paintings from this period as depicting rainmakers in a state of trance. These paintings did not portray "Nature" but were designed to give control over it. Caves filled with San paintings have continued to be ritual and rainmaking centers ever since.

Sheep and pottery appear in the archeological record some 2200 years ago. It was thought by early Rhodesian students of the Matopos that the "San" hunter-gatherers withdrew when these "Bantu" farmers arrived. Archeologists today believe that there was considerable interaction between the Late Stone Age "San" communities and the Early Iron Age "Bantu" settlements. Some of the later rock paintings were done by the farmers and their uses of the environment and patterns of residence were very similar to those of their predecessors, with the addition of livestock and cereals. Studies of the interaction of "San" groups with black farming peoples in South Africa and Namibia have shown that the cultivators paid "San" experts to make rain; and that their own rainmakers performed in the painted caves and used the pigments for powerful medicines. It is likely that something like this happened in the Matopos and that there were substantial continuities in the rituals practiced there. It is clear, at any rate, that over the last few centuries, at least, the farming communities living in the hills have used the painted caves for rainmaking. Pre- and post-pubertal women danced in them and threw water in the air.

At an unknown date, however, a more elaborate religion of "Nature" emerged among the farming communities of the Matopos. This religion has become known in the literature as "the Mwali cult." Mwali is the Bantu name for the Creator God. It implies female fertility – elsewhere in Central Africa, "Mwali" is used to describe a female initiate or a rain divinity. One of the shrines at which the Voice of Mwali was heard was situated in the eastern Matopos. It was called the Zame shrine, Zame meaning "breast," and people came to it to drink rain just as a baby drinks milk. When there was a particularly heavy drought, old women would enter a cave where a remote female ancestress lay buried and give her water to "drink." At Zame, shrine priestesses inherited power matrilineally. It seems likely that this female version of creative power represents the earliest form of the Mwali cult.

By the time we have evidence about it, however – in the late nineteenth century – there had built up around the shrines, as at the Apollo shrines in classical antiquity, an apparatus of male control. Male priests interpreted the gnomic utterances of women possessed by Mwali. The various oracular shrines had come to represent the combined spiritual power of men and women. The perennial pools in the caves were thought of as the amniotic fluid; lightning was thought of as the manifestation of male virility. The Matopos, containing as they did these powerful shrines, were regarded far and wide as the very site of creation. Hundreds of miles to the southeast of the hills, creation myths have been collected which hold that the granite rocks were originally rain-clouds come down to Earth at the beginning of the world, and that the rivers had poured forth from the rocks when they were penetrated by the "needle" of lightning.

The Mwali shrines represented "Nature." No iron tool was used to clear away the bush around the cave. The priest-custodian of the shrine was believed to be instructed in his duties by snakes and leopards, and climbed the mountainside naked but for a leopard skin. This concept of bare "Nature" might have represented – as the first missionaries thought it did – a mere submission to the environment. But for the adepts of the Mwali Cult it was out of "Nature" that culture and cultivation sprang. Cattle were taken to the shrines to be sacrificed; millet seeds were taken to the shrines to be soaked in the water of the caves and then brought back to be planted. Newly selected chiefs were endorsed and blessed at the shrines. At one shrine, Dula, warriors were blessed and later cleansed. The ideology of the shrine was that 'Nature" and culture were interdependent. Later colonial environmentalists demanded that everybody be cleared out of the Matopos so that the rivers would not silt up. The priests of the shrine believed that the waters would dry up without people. Rivers were there because people were there – and this was true, too, of animals and fruits and roots.

We can construct this picture of the Mwali Cult from the nineteenth-century evidence. The shrines continued to control agriculture in the Matopos deep into the twentieth century. The shrine priests told their congregations where and when cattle could be grazed; when planting should begin; when the first green crops could be eaten; when harvesting should start; and which groves and streams should be set aside as sacred to Mwali. The Matopos were a ritually controlled environment. The Mwali agricultural cycle was very different from the practices recommended by colonial experts, and, in particular, it allowed controlled use of the sponges and wet places that were fenced off and prohibited by colonial agricultural officers. In the eastern Matopos, the people have continued to use the sponges and to observe the Mwali injunctions to this day.

This was the religious situation in the Matopos when

whites began to arrive in the second half of the nineteenth century. White traders and hunters ignored the Mwali cult. Missionaries regarded it as diabolical. Catholics and Protestants alike believed that the Mwali adepts were terrified "children of Nature," living out their lives in fear of natural forces and unable to control or exploit them. As the Jesuits passed through the Matopos in the 1870s, they held a Mass in one of the caves, proclaiming that Christianity would liberate humanity and redeem "Nature." The very hills trembled when the Mass was performed, they claimed.

But traders and missionaries passed through the Matopos. They were not claimed by whites until 1896. In that year there was a great uprising against the recent, but brutal, rule of Cecil Rhodes' British South Africa Company. African warriors fell back into the Matopos and there was fierce fighting from rock to rock, in which many whites died. In this way whites came to know the hills and to feel that they had purchased them with their blood. It was in 1896, too, that Cecil Rhodes stumbled upon the hill where he now lies buried. He at once realized that it was ideal as a pilgrimage site for future white Rhodesians. "World's View," as it is now called, was easy to ascend but commanded a huge vista. Rhodes at once ordered that he should be buried there when he died; he also ordered that the site should become a "Rhodesian Valhalla," where white heroes should be laid to rest. The proper context for the bones of heroes and of his own bones was wilderness, the "grandeur" of the Matopos.

Rhodes died in 1902; his body was brought by train and ox-wagon from Cape Town; on 10 April 1902, he was buried in the Matopos. Little doubt was left that in death Rhodes had taken command of "Nature." The Bishop of Mashonaland recited by the graveside Rudyard Kipling's funeral ode, which ended with the lines: "The immense and brooding Spirit still Shall quicken and control. Living he was the land, and dead His soul shall be her soul." After 1902, white Rhodesians went to Rhodes' Grave on pilgrimage, just as African pilgrims from all over southern Africa were still going to the Mwali shrines.

Rhodes' Grave symbolized the dominant white theory of the relation between religion and "Nature" in the Matopos. The hills were thought of as "wilderness." They were exempt from the general colonial view that "Nature" should be exploited, even though some missionaries taught their converts how to use ploughs to farm in the hills. The general white view was that the Matopos should be reserved as a place for whites to wander and to have solemn religious thoughts. Over the decades after Rhodes' death, white conservationists argued for the preservation of the hills. In their eyes, this meant getting rid of their black inhabitants. The only humanity that could be tolerated in the Matopos – except for the tourists – were the long-dead "San" hunter-gatherers, who had created the thousands of rock paintings. These men and women, it was held, had coexisted with "Nature," living in the environment without impacting on it. But cattle grazing and cultivation, though practiced in the Matopos for two thousand years, were held to be destructive and eroding. When the people-less National Park was created in 1962, a sign was erected at one of the painted caves saying: "Agriculture should never be practiced in these hills." Nor was the present National Park the only area which conservationists wanted to be cleared of people. From the 1940s onwards, there were demands that the inhabitants of the eastern Matopo Reserve, who cultivated the sponges as the Mwali cult had long taught them to do, should be removed from the hills. The several Mwali shrines in Matopo Reserve – Dula, Zame and the rest – were to be closed down. And if conservation meant a triumph over African religion, it also involved a victory over mission Christianity. When the National Park was created, the London Mission Society church at Whitewaters – a center of Christian agriculture – was torn down and its stones used to make the entrance to the Game Park.

There was, then, a "San" ideology of "Nature" in the Matopos, a "Bantu" ideology, and a Rhodesian ideology. In protest against this last, and drawing upon some features of the first, there also arose an African nationalist ideology. At first nationalist opposition to evictions in the Matopos was led by the "progressive" Christians of Whitewaters. But when they failed, nationalists began to turn to the still functioning Mwali shrines, and especially to the senior shrine of Njelele in the southwestern Matopos and to the "war" shrine at Dula in the east.

Before looking at the nationalist alliance with the shrines from the 1950s onwards, it is important to realize that the shrines were not just "traditional survivals." The priests had lain low under early colonialism. But the shrines had continued to operate and to adapt. They developed their agrarian ideology, extending their support not only to subsistence cultivators but to small peasants, striving to produce a surplus for the colonial market. They absorbed and adapted Christian ideas – Njelele is today widely described as Mount Sinai: the late priestess, Gogo Ncube, used to take her Bible with her into the cave. The priests' children, and future successors, attended Christian schools and achieved literacy. The Mwali cult has proved to be a dynamic religion.

When the nationalists approached the shrines in the 1950s, the priests were also able to extend their theory of history. The Mwali cult had possessed for several centuries not only a theology of *place* – of the Matopos as the navel (the soft spot on a baby's head) of the world – but a theology of *time*. It taught a theocratic history, narrating how the successive rulers of southwestern Zimbabwe had flourished when they were blessed by Mwali, but also narrating how they had been cursed and overthrown when they defied Mwali's commands. Legitimacy could only be gained by submission to the Voice from the Rock. "Nature" itself condemned the illegitimate ruler with drought and locusts. This had happened to all previous African kingdoms and it would now happen to the whites. Thus when Joshua Nkomo, who was to become the leader of mass nationalism in the late 1950s and early 1960s, paid his now famous visit to Dula shrine in 1953, the Voice spent the whole night telling him "history"; the history of how to replace an illegitimate regime and how to establish a legitimate one.

Thereafter, Nkomo came to be thought of as the chosen one of Mwali. At Dula, so it was believed, he had been promised that "Nature" itself would protect him, and that while people died around him in the war that was to come he would be safe. His nationalist pseudonym – little slippery rock – was given to him by the cult. The nationalist claim was that the land belonged to its indigenous people. Such a claim was given a particular resonance at the Mwali shrines where religion and culture and the land were inseparable.

This closeness to the Mwali cult persisted until Nkomo's death in 1999. During the guerrilla war of the 1970s, his fighting men drew legitimacy and protection from the shrines. When the war ended and Nkomo returned to campaign in the 1980 election, he held his first election rally in the Matopos, at Njelele. "Nature" itself seemed to endorse him as the legitimate leader, as thunder rolled, lightning flashed and rain came down in torrents. Robert Mugabe became the leader of the new Zimbabwe, however. Mugabe is a man who did not come to the Matopos shrines and was thus denied legitimacy by them. Nkomo found himself and his party harassed and threatened by the Mugabe regime. He himself fled the country – disguised, according to myth, in the black robes of a Mwali priest. His closest supporters went secretly to the shrines to seek consolation. After 1987 when Nkomo signed the Unity Accord and rejoined Mugabe's government, his greatest ambition was to develop Njelele into a great international religious site, like Westminister Abbey or Mecca. During his last years Nkomo used to retreat to one of the smaller Mwali shrines in the southeastern Matopos, Kozi. His son tells a story about "Nature's" respect for Nkomo in his old age. The old man sat in his chair under a tree; a dust-devil sprang up and leaves and dust piled up all around him; the tree bowed down and with its leaves swept away the mess; when Nkomo died, the tree died.

Yet the Mwali cult has never been captured by kings or presidents or politicians. It has remained constant to its own vision of "Nature." Local people never warmed to Nkomo's vision of motels and lavatories and mass pilgrimages. Today, as throughout their history, the shrines remain caves and rocks in the bush.

Terence Ranger

Further Reading
Daneel, Martin. *African Earthkeepers*, vol. 1. Pretoria: UNISA, 1998.
Daneel, Martinus. *The God of the Matopo Hills*. The Hague: Mouton, 1970.
Ranger, Terence. *Voices from the Rocks: Nature, Culture and History in the Matopos Hills*. Oxford: James Currey, 1999.
See also: Masowe Wilderness Apostles; San (Bushmen) Religion; Zimbabwe Spirit Mediums, Guerillas, and Nature.

Zion Christian Church (South Africa)

The Zion Christian Church (ZCC), based in the Pietersburg district, Northern Province, has become the largest of the Zionist independent African Churches in South Africa. Founded about 1910 by a Pedi Christian convert, Engenasi (Ignatius) Lekganyane (born ca. 1885 in Thabakgone, Pietersburg district – died in Moria, 31 May 1948), who had previously experienced healing in the Zion Apostolic Church and membership in the Zion Apostolic Faith Mission, it rapidly evolved into a church appealing across ethnic lines to the rapidly urbanizing African poor. In the 1940s the ZCC bought two farms in the Boyne district, McClean and Kleinfontein, and these, after merging into one parcel of land, were renamed Moria after the biblical Mount Moriah or Jerusalem, and became the administrative and cultic center for the church. Under the founder's son Edward (born ca. 1923, in Thabakgone, died in Moria, 1967) and then grandson, Barnabas, the church grew from about 25,000 adherents in 1925 to about a quarter million by 1970 to a million in 1990 to a striking five million according to the 1995 census.

In 1928 Lekganyane introduced a badge as a token of membership, the silver star on a black cloth backdrop. His son, Edward was to change this to a five-pointed Star of David with the initials ZCC in the center. This badge still serves as a unifying symbol, as well as an amulet for protection against crime in urban areas. The church is organized on traditional tribal lines with Lekganyane as chief and ministers appointed, ordained, and responsible to him alone. The church emphasizes teaching on purity and thus prohibits pork, tobacco, and alcohol as well as use of African traditional medicines and Western medicines, seeking rather to trust in spiritual healing. There is thus great focus on personal and communal purity that enjoins a strict personal morality, a rigorous code of ethics, abstention from specific foodstuffs, and the avoidance of party politics.

Addressing a different context than other traditional Zionist churches, the ZCC has largely avoided the divisions that rent these other groups and has preserved its membership through a powerful hierarchy that continues to offer its members a sense of meaning, purpose, and spiritual healing, as well as a strong code for daily living. A significant feature of the ZCC is its emphasis on sacred land. It should be noted that the years of its founding happened to be the years when the Union of South Africa was created and the Native Land Act passed (1913), which forbade individual black ownership of land, though churches were exempt from this law.

The ZCC, like the Zulu Ama Nazariti, have a highly developed sacred geography that combines biblical, traditional, and nature themes. Thus, 25 miles north of Pietersburg, lies Mount Moria where Edward Lekganyane laid out the church headquarters in the midst of vast agricultural holdings, symbolizing the power of black land ownership, until recently restricted by law. Mount Moria serves also as a center for three annual pilgrimages, the most notable being the Easter festival when, over the past twenty years, attendance figures have reached over the three million mark. ZCC members believe that at these Easter celebrations they experience in part the New Jerusalem when the Messiah builds his kingdom. The emphasis on a sacred and thus purified geographic center, as well as personal purity, has also led in the last decade to a greater awareness of environmental degradation, and has evoked a variety of initiatives involving sacred water, treeplanting, and land conservation. All these are understood as flowing from the sacred Mount Moriah and ushering in personal and social peace, healing, and blessing.

Iain S. Maclean

Further Reading

Comaroff, Jean. *Body of Power, Spirit of Resistance: The Culture and History of a South African People*. Chicago: University of Chicago Press, 1985.

Naude, Piet. *The Zionist Christian Church in South Africa: A Case-Study in Oral Theology*. Lewiston, NY: Edwin Mellen Press, 1995.

Schoffeleers, Matthew. "The Zion Christian Church and the Apartheid Regime." *Leidschrift* 3 (1988), 42–57.

Sundkler, Bengt. *Bantu Prophets in South Africa*. Oxford: Oxford University Press, 1965.

See also: African Independent Churches (South Africa); Masowe Wilderness Apostles; Sacred Mountains.

Zoroastrianism

Much is unclear about the origin and earliest developments of Zoroastrianism and its community of believers. Religious tradition ascribes the faith's tenets to Zarathushtra, later called Zoroaster by the Greeks. Members of the faith customarily referred to themselves as Mazda-yasna (later Mazdesn) or Mazda worshipper (Mazdean), with the designations Zarathushtri (later Zarathoshti, Zartoshti, Zardoshti) or Zoroastrian and Majus or Magian being subsequent categorizations based on referring to members of the community in terms of their founder – Zarathushtra – or their priesthood – the magi.

Zarathushtra himself appears to have been a devotional poet, trained in the recitations and rites – centered around fire and water (much later noted in the Iranian context by Strabo [lived ca. 64 B.C.E.–25 C.E.], *Geography* XV, 3:14) – of Indo-Iranian religion. When and where he lived are not definitely known, but linguistic and archeological data suggest a time framework of between the eighteenth and sixteenth centuries B.C.E. (i.e., the late Bronze Age), somewhere in Central Asia. As a community of followers developed around him and his words, Zarathushtra gradually attained the status of a prophet – possibly several centuries after his demise and when Zoroastrians and other Proto-Iranians had resettled on the Iranian plateau.

Gradually Zoroastrianism was spread among the peoples of the Iranian plateau, becoming a widespread faith there from the fifth century B.C.E. onward until it was elevated to the position of state religion under the Sasanians (224–651). By late antiquity, Zoroastrianism also had become a popular faith in Central Asia at cities such as Bukhara and Balkh. The demographic decline of Zoroastrianism in Iran and Central Asia occurred after the Arab Muslim conquest of those regions in the seventh century. Some Zoroastrians migrated from Iran to the Indian sub-continent around the tenth century, to avoid conversion to Islam, and their descendants came to be called Parsis or Persians by other Indians. A smaller group relocated to China but their descendants did not survive past the Middle Ages. In modern times, Zoroastrian diasporas have sprung up in many nations through immigration for religious freedom and economic opportunity. The current demographical distribution of the community, based on national censuses and membership in community organizations, is approximately: 45,000 in Iran; 76,400 in India; 10,000 in Canada; 10,000 in the U.S.; 4000 in England and Scotland; 2000 elsewhere in Europe; 2800 in Pakistan; 1000 in Australia; 1000 in Tajikistan and Uzbekistan; 150 in Hong Kong; 130 in Bahrain; less than 100 per country in South Africa, Sri Lanka, and Zaire; and even smaller groups in other nations. The faith is still practiced mainly by descendants of the original Iranian Zoroastrians, with very few converts – conversion is discouraged by many contemporary Parsis, occasionally accepted by some contemporary Iranians, and periodically encouraged without much success to date by a few Zoroastrian settlers in North America and Europe.

Nature-related Doctrines

Drawing upon the semi-pastoral, semi-agrarian social setting of his community, and reacting to aggression upon the settled people and the environment by nomads, Zarathushtra grounded his words in the concept of Asha or universal Order which was equated to righteousness:

"Order is good, it is best. According to (our) wish it is, according to (our) wish it shall be. Order belongs to best order" (*Ashem Vohu prayer, Yasna* 27:14).

Order, personified by the masculine spiritual entity Ahura Mazda (later Ohrmazd) or Wise Lord, the creator deity of Zoroastrianism, and his generative hypostasis called Spanta Mainyu (later Spenta Mainyu, Spenog Menog) or Beneficent Spirit, was thought to permeate every aspect of existence. Order was believed to ensure harmony and completeness, connecting the spiritual world to the corporeal one, linking life to afterlife, and leading from creation to eschaton. Disrupting order was Drug or Confusion. Confusion, supposedly emanating from an independent spiritual locus termed Angra Mainyu (later Ahreman, Ganag Menog) or Destructive Spirit, the devil of Zoroastrianism, was believed to disturb, deceive, and defile the harmony of nature – and therefore was regarded as sinful. Thus, Zarathushtra, perceiving conflicts as upsetting natural order, is said to have chanted in the Old Avestan language: "When, O Mazda, will right mindedness come with order to provide good dwelling and pasture through (correct) authority?" (*Spenta Mainiiu Gatha, Yezidha Haiti, Yasna* 48:11). Likewise, speaking on behalf of all animals, especially domesticated species, Zarathushtra is believed to have asked of Ahura Mazda: "The soul of the cow complains to you, 'For whom did you craft me? Who created me? Wrath, force, oppression, bondage, and violence hold me shackled'" (*Ahunauuaiti Gatha, Xshmauuoiia Haiti, Yasna* 29:1). Decrying violence against all aspects of the natural world – which was held to have been created in a perfectly ordered manner by Ahura Mazda – Zarathushtra supposedly censured everyone who "ravages the pastures and wields a weapon against the follower(s) of order" (*Ahunauuaiti Gatha, Xvaetumaiti Haiti, Yasna* 32:10). Moreover, he would entreat: "May Mazda, who remembers precisely, note deeds perpetrated now and in the future by demonic beings and (evil) mortals" (*Ahunauuaiti Gatha, Xshmauuoiia Haiti, Yasna* 29:4).

Pronouncements on human interaction with the environment by early Mazda worshippers who followed Zarathushtra, and also lived prior to or around the fifteenth century B.C.E., echoed the founder's concern with all aspects of nature. They praised "Ahura Mazda who created the cow and order, who created water and good plants, who created light, Earth, and all good things" (*Yasna Haptanghaiti, Yasna* 37:1). They also venerated Ahura Mazda's creations including "this Earth" and "the waters" (*Yasna Haptanghaiti, Yasna* 38:1, 3) plus "the souls of harmless wild animals" (*Yasna Haptanghaiti, Yasna* 39:2). Most of all, they wished:

> Through these best endeavors, we exhort those who listen as well as those who do not listen, those who wield authority as well as those who do not wield authority, to establish peace and (to provide) pasture for cattle (*Yasna Haptanghaiti, Yasna* 35:4).

A devotional poem in the Young or Standard Avestan language (based on early, pre-Zoroastrian religiosity, but revised ca. 900–300 B.C.E. for incorporation into the Zoroastrian scripture or Avesta) to the male Yazata or praiseworthy spiritual entity Mithra (later Mihr) further stressed the beneficial links between deity, lesser divinities, humanity, and nature: "I shall audibly worship him, Mithra of the wide pastures, who grants peaceful and good dwellings in Iranian territories" (*Mihr Yasht, Yasht* 10:4). Another devotional poem, this one to the female Yazata named Aredwi Sura Anahita (later Ardwisur Anahid), commented on that spiritual entity's major role as Ahura Mazda's proxy in safeguarding a vital natural resource: "She purifies the waters" (*Ardwisur Yasht, Yasht* 5:5).

Human Mythology Involving Nature

Myths gradually developed to connect humans, from their very first corporeal existence, to nature. The Zoroastrian story of creation, finally codified in the Pahlavi or Middle Persian language, claimed that when Gayo Maretan (later Gayomard) the primordial androgyne was slain by Angra Mainyu and his demonic forces,

> his seed was purified by sunlight . . . (then) remained in the Earth for forty years, after which time Mashya and Mashyana (the first human couple) grew out of the Earth in the form of a rhubarb plant . . . (and) developed from plant form into human form (*Greater Bundahishn* 14:5–6, 10, compiled ninth to thirteenth centuries).

Gradually, Zoroastrian theology in antiquity and medieval times united all beneficial aspects of the world, producing a nexus between corporeality – both animate and inanimate – and spirituality – both ritual and supernatural. So, aspects of material existence such as water, Earth, fire, metals, plants, animals, and human beings were connected symbolically to spiritual beings and through those entities to god. The six interconnecting spirits are called Amesha Spentas or Holy Immortals (Ahura Mazda is regarded as the seventh, in addition to his role as Creator) and are thought to represent various categories of material creation: Vohu Manah (later Wahman) or Good Thought represents animals, Asha Vahishta (later Ardwahisht) or Best Righteousness represents fire, Xshathra Vairya (later Shahrewar) or Desirable Dominion represents metal, Spenta Armaiti (later Spendarmad) or Good Disposition (later said to be Holy Devotion) represents Earth; Haurvatat (later Hordad) or Integrity/Wholeness (later thought of as Perfection) represents water, and Ameretat (later Amurdad) or Immortality represents plants.

Humans are believed to oversee this belief structure in

the corporeal world. This theological structure bestowed upon humanity a central role – Zoroastrianism holds that humans were created by Ahura Mazda as allies in his cosmic struggle against Angra Mainyu. So it was written, later, in the *Greater Bundahishn* (3:23–24) that Ahura Mazda deliberated with the immortal souls of humans who realized that the Destructive Spirit would be vanquished forever if they entered the corporal world. Ahura Mazda, in turn, promised to resurrect all humans and grant them immortality once Angra Mainyu had been defeated. As a result of this covenant, the religious function of each person is thought to lay in aiding the increase of righteousness and combating the forces of evil through every action performed during his or her lifetime. Essentially, Zoroastrians concluded that good deeds – like prevention of pollution, performance of ritual, and reverence for aspects of nature – by people in the material state further individual and cosmic triumph of righteous order over chaotic confusion on the spiritual level and that this maintains harmony in nature. Parthian or Arsacid-era poems lauded the appropriate and full utilization of nature, without waste of natural resources:

That lofty (date palm) tree said . . . "They make ships of me that sail the seas. They make brooms of me to clean houses. They make pestles of me to pound grain . . . Kings stop here for shade in summer. People eat my fruit to fill their stomachs. Small birds nest here and scatter my seeds" (*Draxt i Asurig*, ll 7–16, compiled ca. first century B.C.E.).

Purity and Pollution in Relation to Nature

Word of Zoroastrian concern for nature, not surprisingly, reached members of other cultures. The Greek historian Herodotus (ca. 484–430 B.C.E.) remarked, regarding Iranians living during the Achaemenian dynasty: "They greatly revere rivers. They will not urinate, spit, or wash their hands therein, nor allow anyone else to do so" (*History* I: 138). Yet, Zoroastrians have always felt that they could not safeguard nature without spiritual assistance. So, even the Achaemenian king of kings Darius or Darayavahush I (ruled 522–486 B.C.E.) implored: "Ahura Mazda is a great god who created this Earth, who created that sky, who created humans . . . May Ahura Mazda protect this land . . . from harm" (*Naqsh-e Rostam Inscription A* 1–3:51–53).

Zoroastrian concern that nature not be polluted, even in symbolic and ritual ways, resulted in a notion that decaying flesh should not come into contact with soil, water, crops, domestic animals, and humans. So the magian practice of exposing human corpses became popular (Herodotus, *History* I:140). The original Old Iranian term for a grave or tomb, *daxma*, came to designate another type of funerary locale – places where corpses could be exposed. At first daxmas were established in areas away from settlements such as on mountaintops, but later as population density increased they became walled enclosures or funerary towers. After exposure of a corpse and desiccation of its flesh – often aided by mangling of corpses by wild animals – the bones would be collected and placed within an *astodan* or ossuary in the belief that rock could prevent any residual religious impurity from spreading through nature. Archeological remains of Parthian-era (ca. 238 B.C.E.–224) and Sasanian-era funerary towers and ossuaries, large and small, ornate and simple, are found throughout the Iranian plateau and Central Asia occasionally together with inscriptions and minor reliefs. Ritual exposure of corpses is still practiced by the Parsis in cities like Mumbai or Bombay (India) and Karachi (Pakistan), where daxmas often are referred to as towers of silence. Such funerary towers attract vultures who strip the flesh off corpses. During the past few years, as urban density transformed cities in the Indian subcontinent into metropolises, the population of vultures has declined – leading to attempts by Parsis in Mumbai to breed those birds and to seek alternate means of speeding up desiccation. Moreover, in India and Pakistan for the past few centuries, bones are no longer collected and entombed but are swept into a lime pit at the center for each tower to dissolve over time. In Iranian daxmas, the bones remained on site, slowly disintegrating. The practice of exposing corpses in funerary towers was phased out by the Zoroastrians of Iran during the 1960s under modernist pressure from the Pahlavi dynasty and so the funerary towers at traditional Zoroastrian settlements such as Sharifabad near Yazd fell into disuse. Zoroastrians in Iran began to wrap each corpse in a white shroud and bury it following Muslim practice. Zoroastrians who have migrated to other countries from Iran and India during the past two hundred years also independently adopted inhumation. Cremation is now gaining popularity among Zoroastrians in Western countries as a means of preventing symbolic pollution of the Earth by decaying, buried, corpses – although cremation leaves unresolved, for many practitioners, the issue of a brief pollution of fire in the crematorium. In most circumstances, whether in Iran, India, or elsewhere, corpses are cleansed prior to exposure, burial, or cremation – again an attempt to limit ritual pollution of the environment. Zoroastrian notions of purity and pollution, and the impacts of those ideas on the world, were assimilated into Shi'i Islam shaping the parameters of *najes* or uncleanness that structure the religious lives and the relationship to nature for the majority of Iranians.

Historically, however, corpses of ancient Iranian monarchs were embalmed and then entombed (Herodotus, *History* I:140). There are the archeological remains of the Greek-style tomb of Cyrus or Kurush II (ruled 549–530 B.C.E.) at Pasargadae (also mentioned by Arrian, lived ca. 95–175, *Anabasis Alexandri* VI, 29, following an account by Aristobulus; Strabo, *Geography XV*, 3:7–8, following accounts by Aristobulus and Onesicritus; and Plutarch [lived ca. 45–120], *Lives: Alexander* 69:4) and the seven rock-cliff tombs of Darius I and his successors at Naqsh-e Rostam and Persepolis (also mentioned by Photius [lived ninth century], *Bibliotheca* 72:38a–b, following Ctesias [lived mid-fifth to early fourth century B.C.E.], *Persica*), from Achaemenian times. The tombs of Parthian or Arsacid rulers at Nisa (mentioned by Isidorus Characenus [lived ca. first century B.C.E.–first century C.E.], *Mansiones Parthicae* 12) and Arbela (mentioned by Dio Cassius [lived ca. 155–235], *History of Rome* 78:1) were well known. The Sasanian elite praxis of using *aspanuran* (*haspanwaran*) or tombs is documented in medieval texts (*Kar namag i Ardashir Papakan* 14; 17; and *Pahlavi Texts* 55:1–5; both surviving in post-ninth-century redactions). Again, the underlying notion was a religious attempt to safeguard nature from symbolical harm thought to be produced by demonic forces that supposedly cause death and decay.

As safeguarding nature became increasingly important, with the augmentation of ritual purity concerns in medieval times under the Sasanian dynasty and later under the Umayyad and Abbasid Muslim regimes, probably in reaction to increased contact between Zoroastrians and members of other faiths living in Iran, the Zoroastrian clergy or magi issued numerous injunctions to guide the laity. For example, devotees were cautioned: "Do not sin against (i.e., pollute) water, fire, and beneficent creatures ... so that heaven may not be barred (to you)" (*Pahlavi Texts*, p. 151, ll 7–9, compiled third to ninth centuries). By the late Middle Ages, magi were counseling: "Whoever teaches cares for all these seven creations (Earth, water, fire, metal, plants, animals, and humans) does well and pleases (Ahura Mazda)" (*Supplementary Texts to the Shayest ne Shayest* 15:6, compiled ninth through fourteenth centuries). Such advice was not simply religious. It reflected a pragmatic view of the world. Zoroastrian commentators had pointed out that water had to be protected from pollution because impure water could not be used for drinking, cooking, cultivation, or rituals (*Denkard*, p. 452, ll. 17–21, compiled ninth century).

Opinions, pertaining to religious and practical views of nature, continued into pre-modern times, when Iranian Zoroastrians advised their Indian counterparts, the Parsis, that fire, water, land, and crops should be kept free from pollutants (*Persian Revayats*, 81–87, compiled fifteenth though eighteenth centuries). Likewise, more recently in 1869, a high magus wrote in a Paris Gujarati language catechism: "Water is one of the finest gifts given by god to humans. We must keep it clean and use it. If we do not keep it clean and use impure water, then it will harm the health of people" (*Rehbar-e Din-e Jarthushti*, 108). The tanka system of harvesting rainwater, devised by early Parsi farmers in Gujarat, India, and still utilized at rural locales – as documented by the UNESCO-assisted PARZOR Project – plus the far more ancient quant system of water distribution, still employed by the villagers (now Muslims and Zoroastrians) of Iran, have both been regarded by Zoroastrians as not only serving practical functions but also continuing to be tangible manifestations of the religion's approach to utilizing natural resources appropriately. Moreover, Zoroastrian concepts have periodically been drawn upon by Muslim regimes in Iran to support environmental causes. So, for example, a publication issued in 1968 by the Iranian Ministry of Information at Tehran during the regime of Mohammed Reza Shah Pahlavi (ruled 1941–1979) justified conservation of forests by claiming:

> The national religion of the Persian Empire until the coming of Islam was firmly based on agriculture. The desert was seen as a work of Evil; God was manifest in the crops, in the fruit and nut-bearing trees, in the abundance of game, in the multiplying herds of cattle and sheep (*12 Points for Progress*, 35–6).

Thus in the task of safeguarding Iran's forests from development, that country's most recent monarch was presented as adhering to divine will, indirectly the wishes of Ahura Mazda. More recently, in the decades following the Islamic Revolution of 1979, Muslim Iranian intellectuals have turned nostalgically to their country's heritage, seeking in their national, ancient, past relevant themes of natural harmony and coexistence as counterbalances to theocracy.

Worship and Celebration Connected to Nature

The days of each month of the Zoroastrian calendar are dedicated to Ahura Mazda, the Amesha Spentas, and the Yazatas – thereby uniting spiritual entities and nature to time. Because worship and praise are directed by Zoroastrians through their rituals to the righteous entities that are believed to inhabit the spiritual realm, calendrical-based devotional ceremonies include overt references to the categories of nature associated with those spirits.

Most Zoroastrian rituals are conducted within complexes known as fire temples. Fire, as the aspect of nature considered absolutely pure, became the icon of the Zoroastrian faith. Ritual fires burn in altars at Zoroastrian temples – permanently at some temples in Iran and India, temporarily in other temples in Iran, India the United States of America, and elsewhere. The central devotional ceremony performed in major fire temples is the Yasna or Worship (originally Sacrifice) where, among other rites, the haoma or ephedra plant is pounded, mixed with water and milk to make a libation, and then symbolically offered by participating priests to Ahura Mazda and other divine spirits. Jashan or Thanksgiving services are performed at fire temples on days such as Nav Ruz or the New Year's festival (at the vernal equinox), Mihragan or the Feast in honor of Mithra (at the autumnal equinox), and the Gahanbars (also Gahambars) or Communal Feasts. On those occasions fruits, flowers, and cooked foods made from plants – and now less frequently animals – are consecrated to the divinities and then consumed by the community. Although its origins are not completely clear but may ultimately derive from variations on Sasanian practice, contemporary Iranians of the Zoroastrian and Muslim faiths continue to set up an arrangement of seven items – whose Persian terms begin with the letter *sin* or *s* such as garlic, apples, dried fruits, vinegar, vegetables, hyacinth, and coins (plus an oil lamp, prayer book, mirror, and other symbolic items) – called the *haft sin* on a table in each home. Again, the purpose of those offerings is to unite various aspects of the corporeal world during acts of worship and celebration. Originally, animals were sacrificed by Zoroastrians in both Iran and India on religious and communal festivals. But Hindu vegetarian influences on the Parsis led to the gradual phasing out of animal sacrifice, and Parsi praxis spread from India to Iranian Zoroastrians in the twentieth century as the training of magi came to be conducted in seminaries in India.

Between the ages of seven and fifteen each Zoroastrian boy and girl undergoes initiation into the religion. The ceremony is termed the *Navjote* or new birth by Parsi Zoroastrians and *Sedra-Pushun* (also *Sedra-Pushi*) or donning the sacred undershirt by Iranian Zoroastrians. It symbolizes a spiritual rebirth. After initiation each believer becomes fully responsible for his or her own religious, moral, and communal life. During the ceremony, the initiate – having learned the basic prayers of the religion – dons a white cotton undershirt called the *sudra* (also *sedra*), and ties a lamb's wool cord known as the *kusti* (also *koshti*) around the waist and so is yet again linked to other creatures. Flowers, fruits – such as coconuts among the Parsis and pomegranates among Iranians – and rice are incorporated into the ritual actions of the initiation. The same general array of items are present during wedding ceremonies. As with most other aspects of Zoroastrianism, the function of each item is to unite the officiating priest, the devotee undergoing initiation or couple entering into marriage, and the members of the audience with nature and so reaffirm humanity's central role in the religious universe.

Jamsheed K. Choksy

Further Reading

Boyce, Mary. *A History of Zoroastrianism*, vol. 1. Leiden: E.J. Brill, 1989 (2nd edn).
Boyce, Mary. *A Persian Stronghold of Zoroastrianism*. Oxford: Claredon Press, 1977.
Choksy, Jamsheed K. *Purity and Pollution in Zoroastrianism: Triumph over Evil*. Austin: University of Texas Press, 1989.

Kotwal, Firoze M. and James W. Boyd. *A Persian Offering, The Yasna: A Zoroastrian High Liturgy*. Studia Iranica cahier 8. Paris: Association pour l'avancement des études iraniennes, 1991.
Modi, Jivanji J. *The Religious Ceremonies and Customs of the Parsees*. Bombay: British India Press, 1937; reprint Bombay: Society for the Promotion of Zoroastrian Religious Knowledge and Education, 1986.
Williams, Ron G. and James W. Boyd. *Ritual Art and Knowledge: Aesthetic Theory and Zoroastrian Ritual*. Columbia: University of South Carolina Press, 1993.
Windfuhr, Gernot L. "The Logic of the Holy Immortals in Zoroastrianism." In S.J.H. Manekshaw and P.R. Ichaporia, eds. *Proceedings of the Second North American Gatha Conference*. Womelsdorf, PA: Federation of Zoroastrian Associations of North America, 1996, 237–74.

See also: Creation Myths of the Ancient World; Islam and Environmentalism in Iran; Water in Islam; Water in Zoroastrianism.

Zulu (amaZulu) Ancestors and Ritual Exchange

One of the fundamental ideas in ancestral-based religions, such as that of the Zulu, or amaZulu (a more accurate term), is that of the life-force, essence or energy which exists in all animate and inanimate phenomenon, including animals, plants, and various geographical or even atmospheric features. This life-force is in constant circulation and although it is indestructible it may be converted, exchanged and utilized in different ways by humans, for good or bad intent. The following account describes these dynamics in the context of Zulu notions of the ancestral and spirit worlds. These are, however, broadly representative of many other African groups' ideas and concepts on the subject, especially the Nguni-speaking peoples of southern Africa.

According to Harriet Ngubane, the Zulu collective term for all the departed spirits is *amathongo*. Zulus believe that when a person dies the life-force exits the body in the form of a shadow, or spirit, known as *isithunzi*. The spirit enters a liminal phase where it is "betwixt and between" the living and the ancestral worlds. Among the Zulu, certain tasks have to be performed by living members of the agnatic (male) kin group to help get these spirits empowered, purified and "cleaned," in order that they may join the benevolent ancestral body (*amadlozi*) that has an important role in protecting and guiding descendants. This usually involves a series of sacrificial rituals that should be performed after a certain lapse of time (usually within a year) after physical death. The final ritual of incorporation of a departed spirit, known as *ukubuyisa*, signifies the return of the ancestor (*idlozi*) to the home. Departed individuals who have lived good moral lives and attained the status of elder are regarded as the most active of the *amadlozi*, as they are the most concerned with the well-being of the living. Typically it is believed that a person's deceased parents, grandparents, and great-grandparents are more interested in their descendants, although the more remotely distant ancestors are regarded as participating at rituals held in their honor and can still influence and have interest in the affairs of the living. The ancestors are regarded as being present in the homestead and should be treated with respect befitting that of elders. They should be kept informed of any events and changes that have occurred within the homestead, such as a change of family residence, work or fortunes. They should be actively informed of all the "life crisis" stages that require "rites of passage," such as the birth of children, attainment of adolescence and adulthood, marriage and death. They can be consulted for advice and guidance on any problem facing the family and they are seen to act as a protective force against evil. In their purified state they are seen as being close to God and in the context of Christianity they are often equated with the angels, who have the power to directly appeal to God on behalf of the living. When they are forgotten they are regarded as no longer having adequate strength to protect the living and they withdraw their support, leaving the family vulnerable to attack by hostile forces. However they do not disappear and their potential to intervene always exists, should the appropriate steps be taken by the living to empower them.

The intensified presence of the ancestors is to be found in a number of regions in the domestic domain. These include the cattle byre (*isibaya*), especially around the central post, and in the sacred ancestral hut (the *indlu enkulu* or "the great house"). In the latter they are thought to reside in the rafters above the shrine (*umsamo*) found opposite the doorway of the round hut. These are the sites where sacrificial offerings are placed.

However when questioning Zulu diviner-healers (*izangoma*) about the locality of the ancestral body (the *amadlozi*) one gets a more complex response than these spatial domains suggest: they reside in one's body, they can manifest themselves in animals and plants, and they also exist in the air, under water, and under the Earth (*abaphanzi* = those down below). In other words they are omnipresent. Regarding the presence of the ancestors within a person's body, it is believed that they commonly reside in the regions of the reproductive organs. The aim of *izangoma* training is to activate the *amadlozi* by bringing them to the head and shoulders so that the healer can hear and see the messages they bring. In addition to the drinking of special herbal medicine (*ubulawu*), an important aspect of diviner-healer training is to spend long hours dancing and singing to the rhythmic beating of drums, usually in the early hours of the morning (after midnight). It is believed that this helps activate the *amadlozi* and "brings them up"

from the lower reproductive regions to those of higher consciousness, associated with the brain, throat, eyes, ears and heart. In this way the ancestors can empower one with knowledge and foresight by communicating through means of visual (clairvoyant), auditory (clairaudient), mental (dreams and visions) or vocal (glossalia) messages. Another area of the body vulnerable to their presence is in the supra-scapular region at the top of the shoulders and at the base of the neck. This is the area the ancestors stimulate with sharp or scratching pains when they are said to be trying to attract the attention of an individual to be a healer.

The Zulu also identify a more powerful category of ancestral spirits. These are the "great ancestors" or the *amakhosi*. These are powerful spirit beings that are often associated with those healers that are taken "under water" for their training. The *amakhosi* communicate directly with such healers via high-pitched whistles that emanate from the rafters of the sacred hut. These whistles are audible to all present, and the healer who has been taken "under water" for training has the ability to translate the messages in this form. In explaining the difference between the *amakhosi* and *amadlozi*, diviner-healers say that the *amakhosi* are powerful *amadlozi*, but not all *amadlozi* attain the rank of *amakhosi*. According to Ngubane, whistling spirit divination is regarded as the most powerful and accurate of all the types of divination found among the Zulu.

The ancestral spirits are also capable of manifesting as animals, birds, reptiles and even insects (such as bees). For the Zulu the snake, in the form of the python (*inhlwati*), is the most potent manifestation of the great ancestors and is often respectfully referred to as "lord" (*inkosi*). The "great spirits," or *amakhosi*, described above, are often said to visit the living in python form. This variety of fauna may manifest in people's houses, often behaving in ways different to that expected of their species. Their presence serves to alert the living to the fact that the ancestors are trying to draw their attention and acknowledge their presence, usually to perform certain tasks or to call an individual to become a diviner-healer. These are regarded as spirit animals and are viewed as distinct from ordinary creatures and they should never be harmed. The clue to their ancestral/spirit nature lies in their "abnormal" behaviour. Such animals may also appear in a person's dreams and are regarded as very significant in the training process of healers.

The character, or essence, of all living creatures is believed to adhere to their flesh, especially in fatty tissue. Thus many medicinal mixtures incorporate wild animal fats and these are used to achieve the natural characteristics possessed by the animal. It is also believed that wild plants and animals are imbued with the essence of potential ancestral power. This power is referred to as *amandla*, and at decomposition, after death, this potential is absorbed into the soil and is taken in by plants and animals. Certain plants (e.g., various *ubulawu* species) are regarded as having an affinity to this potential ancestral power, and these are used in *izangoma* training to connect them with the ancestors via dreams. Animals concentrate this power/essence in certain parts of their bodies when they consume vegetation and/or other animal flesh. The liver, and its by-product, bile, is regarded as possessing especially high concentrations of this power/essence, and hence these both feature strongly in sacrificial rituals. Wild animals and plants are thus seen as a manifestation or a medium to convey the power of the ancestral world to that of the living, and they form part of the complex system of exchange that takes place between the living and the dead. This becomes most obvious in sacrificial ritual.

The Importance of Ritual Exchange in Zulu Sacrifice

Fundamental to the benefits that the living seek from the spirit world, be they for good or bad intent, is the notion of reciprocity and exchange. Benefits can only flow in exchange for something else, invariably another life. Diviner-healers are regarded as having been called from the benevolent ancestral world to help ease the suffering of humankind, and to restore and heal the physical individual as well as the social body, and to overcome the evil forces that prey upon humankind. Usually the healing of the individual is dependent on the healing of the whole kin group. In order to do this they have to clean and feed the ancestors through regular ritual, often involving animal sacrifice, and during such rituals emphasis is placed on resolving any interpersonal conflicts that may be besetting the home. In addition to *izangoma* developing healing and divinatory abilities, they gain certain personal benefits from the ancestors, especially in the form of mystical protection and warnings about those who may wish to harm them, as well as a certain amount of material comfort for the healer, the living kin, and their descendants in later generations.

The process of Zulu sacrifice demonstrates the immersion of the human body in the natural world. The system of symbolic associations in the exchange is complex and there are multiple meanings attached to the movement of gifts during sacrifice that reveal the cosmological order regarding the division between nature/culture, animal/human, wild/domesticated, female/male, corporeality/non-corporeality, and raw/cooked, as has been noted by scholars such as Lévi-Strauss and Hammond-Tooke. Sacrificial exchange is associated with consumption. In order to gather the energy needed to send messages to the living the spirit world requires sustenance and "food." The food that is given requires a high level of investment and value for the living. One cannot sacrifice wild animals, but only that which has been reared or cared for by humans. Thus, transformed domesticated plants (sorghum/millet beer) and the blood, bile and flesh of domesticated animals (chickens, goats, sheep and cows) provide the necessary food for the ancestors. These domesticated or transformed products represent the wealth of the supplicant, even if they have to be purchased. As in any system of exchange the means are as important as the end. Gifts have to be transmitted through a form of energy, or a channel of communication. The living open up the channels of communication to the spirit world through the products of culture: domesticated animals and plants, as well as speech, dance and music, while the spirit world opens up the communication channels to the living through nature, the bodies of wild plants (*egubulawu*) and animals (*isilwane*).

Zulu ritual sacrifice is a very public, socially affirming event where the bonds of kinship are constantly emphasized. All family members are expected to participate and the event is open to any member of the general public who wishes to attend and consume the beer and meat that is prepared for the occasion. It is overall a celebration of the positive unity that exists between the living and the ancestral world, and the benefits that flow from such a union. It is this that sets it apart from other more secretive and negative forms of mystical empowerment that are associated with commodity exchange and the evils of individual material accumulation and greed.

Obtaining Mystical Power through Commodity Exchange

Diviner-healers are expected to reveal and counteract the activities of evil forces, which ally themselves to those humans who seek power and wealth, and exhibit it through greed, arrogance, malice and envy. It is believed that some spirits that still possess their corporeal identity and character, may linger in the environment for a period of time, especially if they harbor any grudges, had unfinished business to complete, or were too grasping of the material riches in this life. Both the benevolent ancestral forces and the lesser, more negative, spirit forces can influence the way a person thinks or behaves and can affect his/her fortunes. This means that a certain amount of what we would see as individual motivation and self-directed behaviour is sometimes attributed to external forces (although free will is still recognized). The less developed spirits or spirits of malicious people, particularly those who exhibited a vindictiveness or lack of control of desires while alive, or those who were aggrieved by a violence done to them, can also be employed by the living to assist them to do harm to rivals, and to help enrich and empower their benefactors. These spirits are thought to linger around graveyards or the environs that they frequented during their lifetime. They are believed to be able to give people a certain amount of foresight and advanced knowledge, but they are capricious and demanding, and can be dangerous to work with, often taking, in exchange for their services, the life of a close kinsman or child. It is asserted that some *izangoma* may resort to engaging the power of these spirits, especially if they have failed to establish or maintain contact with their own ancestors. There are many reasons for this failure: sometimes novice healers, who cannot afford to continue the long and often expensive training that is needed to access their benevolent ancestral power, resort to this less expensive and demanding form of empowerment. Some fail to empower the ancestors because they are weak, while others have been abandoned by their ancestors for transgressing the strict moral norms of spiritual and social behavior, largely through embracing the morals of individuality associated with greed and desire for power. Engaging the power of these lesser spirits is called *izizwe nesizwana*, and such powers are gathered by working with medicines in the graveyard, which entrap these "lost" spirits and get them to work for their captors. All the representations associated with this form of empowerment are negative. It is done in secret and in the dark, and the spirits are not from the body of ancestral kin. All these serve to threaten the requirements for sociality and healing. Supernatural and mythical animal familiars, such as the *ithikoloshe*, *mamlambo*, *imfene* and *inyoni* (*impundulo*) can also be harnessed for these purposes, and it is believed that these can be created and nurtured by witches and sorcerers. *Ithikoloshe* (the highly sexed dwarf with an enormous penis) and *mamlambo* (the snake), are veritable shape-shifters, and are used to pursue the pleasures of the flesh, particularly of a sexual nature, but they are also associated with gaining wealth. The *imfene* is the baboon, on whom the sorcerer rides backwards when he goes on his nightly evil errands, while *inyoni* (*impundulo*) is the evil "lightning bird" which is sent to attack those whom a witch or sorcerer bears grudges against. It kicks the victim on his chest, causing haemoptysis (i.e., tuberculosis), or strikes him on his back and head, causing a paralyzing stroke.

Izangoma assert that there are a number of "healers" who engage the services of such familiars. It is believed that these creatures can be manufactured and activated by plant and animal medicines, as well as human body parts, and can be purchased through a Westernized form of commodity exchange. Those individuals that use medicines and familiars to gain immediate wealth are engaging in what is termed *ukuthwala*, while *ukuthwesa* (or *ukuthwalisa*) refers to those "healers" who engage in the sale of such medicines. It is generally believed that herbalists are more prone to enter into such business enterprises than *izangoma*, as the latter run the risk of losing ancestral support if they engage in such activities.

Summary

The ancestors are a positive force in the Zulu traditional worldview. They integrate both the natural and the social worlds, provide benefits for the living, and offer an effective means to enforce the moral order. However they are not completely autonomous and they rely as much on the living for their well-being as the living do on them. This relationship is based on a reciprocal flow of goods and services, represented most vividly during ritual sacrifice, and this has strong moral and social binding. As commodity exchange systems and desire for individual accumulation penetrate this relationship, the cosmic and moral basis of the exchange changes, and the spirit power shifts from that of the positive and life-giving *amadlozi* to the more negative and vindictive lesser or evil spirits.

Underlying these notions is the spiritual potential of the natural world of which the ancestors are an integral part. It is through the natural world that they can manifest and their power can be accessed or activated. Their manifestation may take different forms, be they through plant-induced dreams or via visitations to the living in animal form. Thus the natural world provides more than just resources for consumptive or functional use; it carries potential ancestral power and knowledge that, if used in a socially moral context, is vital for harmonious and balanced living.

Penny Bernard

Further Reading
Berglund, Axel-Ivor. *Zulu Thought-patterns and Symbolism*. London: C. Hurst & Company, 1976.
Hammond-Tooke, W. David. "The Symbolic Structure of Cape Nguni Cosmology." M.G. Whisson and M. West, eds. *Religion and Social Change in Southern Africa*. Cape Town: David Philip, 1975.
Lévi-Strauss, Claude. *Structural Anthropology*. Garden City, NY: Doubleday, 1967.
Ngubane, Harriet. *Body and Mind in Zulu Medicine: An Ethnography of Health and Disease in Nyuswa-Zulu Thought and Practice*. London, New York and San Francisco: Academic Press, 1977.

See also: Mutwa, Credo; Water Spirits and Indigenous Ecological Management; Weather Snake; Zulu (amaZulu) Culture, Plants, and Spirit Worlds (South Africa).

Zulu (amaZulu) Culture, Plants, and Spirit Worlds (South Africa)

Imithi or herbal medicines play an important role among the Zulu or amaZulu (a more accurate term for the Zulu-speaking people) of southeastern Africa. An examination of the use of *imithi* among Zulu *izangoma* (diviner-healers, often called *sangoma* in pan-African discourse) suggests a fundamentally different conceptual framework regarding the boundaries and relationship between the social, natural and spiritual worlds compared to those paradigms embraced by Western philosophical and scientific thought. In Zulu thought, the physical and social well-being of both individuals and groups are a result of the dynamic interplay between the social, the spiritual and the natural worlds. Ill health results when the balance between these dimensions is disrupted or undermined, or when individuals with evil intentions manipulate the spiritual and natural forces in order to bring about social disorder and misfortune on victims. The Zulu are a sub-category of the larger linguistic group known as the Nguni-speaking peoples. These include the Xhosa-speaking groups (such as Xhosa, Gcaleka, Mpondomise, Mfengu, Thembu), the Swazi, the Shangaan and the Ndebele. They share many common cultural features, and have similar concepts to what is described below for the Zulu peoples.

Plants, whose potencies are often enhanced through combination with wild animal products, provide the medium whereby cures can be achieved, and the power of the spirit world can be accessed, enhanced and modified to suit social and personal needs and desires (be they for good or bad purposes). While some plants have potency in themselves that may help or harm individuals, many require ritual activation through symbolic actions and verbal empowerment. Thus plants are seen as essentially neutral in moral terms, but ultimately become extensions of their users and their ambivalent power is dependent on the purposes to which they are put and the "heart" of the person using them. *Izangoma* emphasize that they may only use medicines for good purposes. Their powers of divination and healing, and the identification of plant remedies, come to them directly from the benevolent ancestral world that has strict sanctions on the way medicines may be used. A diviner who fails to adhere to these strict moral guidelines runs the risk of losing further ancestral guidance and help. They are aware, however, that there may be practitioners (mainly herbalists who do not rely on ancestral guidance) who have strayed from these moral norms and provide medicines that are used for harming others, and/or for self-enrichment. Social commentary against such forms of accumulation and practice is pervasive among diviner-healers in contemporary South Africa. Those suspected in engaging in such enterprises are seen as engaging in witchcraft and sorcery (*ubuthakathi*). The forces that have resulted from globalization and modernity, particularly the pressure for individual gain and success within the context of poverty and social fragmentation, have exacerbated these suspicions and have had a profound influence on the ways to which plant-based medicines are used in the present context.

Thus, although the Zulu have a wide range of plants that are used for their physically therapeutic effects on diseased bodies, their understanding of the processes that lead to physical disorder are more complex than the way Western science understands pathogenesis. They must, therefore, be understood within the context of a rapidly changing society.

Zulu knowledge of healing plants is extensive. Hutchings and others in *Zulu Medicinal Plants* (1996) documented some 1032 species of plants that are known and used by healers in KwaZulu Natal. This figure represents approximately 25 percent of the flora that occurs in this province in South Africa, suggesting that there could well be many more species that are used that have not been documented. Moreover, for any one plant identified there are multiple uses, ranging from symptomatic therapies that may cure the physical ailment (with demonstrable pharmacological activities) to mystical and magical uses.

The multiple uses to which plant-based medicines are put can be categorized into three main areas: for physiological curing purposes, for spiritual purposes and for social purposes. This knowledge is flexible and adaptive to changing needs and demands encountered in contemporary society. The following discussion focuses on the conceptual elements of plant-use in Zulu cosmology and on the spiritual and social uses of plant-based medicines.

Plant-use in Training and Healing Activities

Plants are extensively used in both the training and healing activities of *izangoma*, who believe they are called to their profession by the ancestors through dreams or illness. The spiritual uses of plants fall under three broad categories. They are used as connectors to the spirit world, as spiritual cleansers of both the living and the dead, and for protection against evil forces, including crime and violence. The connecting and cleansing function of plants often overlaps, as do the cleansing and protecting functions. The cleansing and connecting functions are most prominently seen in the use of a certain group of plants collectively known as *ubulawu*. The primary aim of training for *izangoma* is to enhance awareness of the various forms of communication received from the ancestral world. Dreams are of particular importance and a variety of plant species are imbibed to enhance the clarity and reception of powerful message dreams. These are collectively referred to as *ubulawu* and include a range of trees, shrubs, climbers, grasses and small flowering plants from a variety of habitats. Different parts of the plant (roots, stems, bark, bulbs and leaves) are used depending on the species. They are combined into specific mixtures, depending on the individual's progress and the nature of his/her dreams. A mixture or combination of *ubulawu* species is used at the commencement of training, during the training process and after the healer has qualified. They are often administered during group rituals, or may be taken daily by novices, when it is accompanied by prayer, invocation and/or singing. Certain species of *ubulawu* are also associated with different clans and are used as a form of identity during collective clan rituals.

The efficacy of *ubulawu* is largely dependent on the ritual and cultural context in which it is used. The *ubulawu* are soaked in cold water and beaten to a thick foam with a forked stick (again made of a certain plant species), which is then imbibed. The ritual is often performed at pools, rivers or in forests where the ancestors are thought to reside. This is usually accompanied by singing. The foam is regarded as having a special cleansing ability, in both a physical and a spiritual sense. The *ubulawu* are also said to "clean" the ancestors. The power of a healer is ultimately dependent on the power of the ancestors, and by "cleaning" with *ubulawu* and the periodic sacrifices of goats, chickens and cattle, the ancestors are strengthened, thus enabling the healer to do his or her tasks more effectively. *Ubulawu* is also an important element in ritual animal sacrifice, as it forms a connecting thread between the sacrament, the initiate and the ancestors. The use of such plants without spiritual calling and sanction renders them ineffective. *Izangoma* are insistent that if a person has done wrong and offended the ancestors, or if the timing is not right, or the initiate is in a temporary state of pollution (female menstruation), then the *ubulawu* will not foam despite vigorous beating. The ancestors are thought to be actually present in the foam, and lack of foam signifies their refusal to manifest themselves. It is preferable that healers collect their own *ubulawu* as there is less chance of pollution occurring this way. Although many of the *ubulawu* species are sold on the street markets, these are usually only used when it is not possible to gather them personally. Cultivated species are also regarded as losing much of their spiritual potency and are not a viable alternative.

Imphepho (*helichrysum sp.*) is another important connecting plant used in all rituals performed for the ancestors. This is burnt and allowed to smoke profusely as a form of incense, and is used whenever an individual wishes to draw the attention of the ancestors close to hear prayers and appeals, or to receive offerings such as in sacrifice. In addition to its connecting or summoning function it is thought to have a purifying effect as well. *Umphafa* or *umlahlankosi* (*ziziphus mucronata*) is the connecting plant *par excellence* for the Zulu and its importance cannot be underestimated especially within the context of the social and kin fragmentation that have resulted from the migrant labor system and increasing urbanization in South Africa over the last century. After death, the spirit of the deceased enters a form of limbo, a transitional phase between the world of the living and that of the ancestors. Traditionally it was vital that the living kin perform the *ukubuyisa* ritual a year after the death of an individual, to incorporate him or her into the body of the active benevolent ancestors. Ideally the body of the deceased should be buried at the homestead. However this is a difficult task for families when members have died far away from home, such as in the cities and the mines. A branch from the *umphafa* tree helps resolve this problem since it can be used by the chief mourners to convey the spirit of the deceased back to the homestead where it can then become incorporated with the ancestors at the ancestral shrine or hut. The tree is characterized by branches that have small sharply hooked thorns on their stem, and during the ritual to transport the spirit back home, the chief mourner has to clutch a branch of *umphafa*. With the help of other kin members, or a ritual officiant, they approach the gravesite or the place where the death occurred, be it a hospital or elsewhere, and sweep the branch over the ground or the place where the victim died. For instance, if the victim died in a car accident they would visit the accident site and sweep the branch on the road at the point of the accident. If the person died in hospital they would go to the bed in which the person died. Singing and praying, the ritual party plead with the spirit to grasp hold of the branch and to hold on to it while they convey him/her back to the ancestral home (this may entail covering long distances by car or bus). The chief mourner who holds the branch is forbidden to speak for the whole journey for fear of confusing the spirit, but the accompanying supporters can talk to the spirit constantly informing him/her as to the progress of the journey. Upon reaching the homestead the branch is fed to two goats that are tethered outside the entrance. One is expected to eat the leaves while the other should refuse it, and if this does not happen, then the whole procedure has to be repeated as it indicates that the spirit had failed to grasp hold of the branch. The goat that refuses to eat the leaves on the branch is slaughtered at the gate and its chyme (undigested food) is used to cleanse all the family present, while the one that eats it is now believed to be carrying the spirit within it, and is led into the ancestral hut where it is sacrificed in the name of the ancestors and the meat is placed at the *umsamo*, the place where the ancestors are thought to reside (opposite the main doorway to the round hut). In this way the spirit is reunited with the ancestors.

Plant-use and Witchcraft

The cleansing and protecting functions of plants are often employed together in the ritual removal of witchcraft or *umnyama* (darkness). Harriet Ngubane has noted the fundamental importance of Zulu color symbolism (black, red and white) in the way medicines are used for spiritual purposes. The order in which different color medicines are administered in these rituals are connected to the cosmic order of night (black), dawn/sunset (red) and daylight (white) and they must be strictly adhered to. The process must always go from black medicine (representing darkness – *umnyama* – and heat), to red (a transition color between darkness and light – warm), to white (openness, clarity and purity – associated with daylight and coolness). The thermal qualities of the medicines are also observed. Hence dark medicines that are administered to remove *umnyama* from a victim are usually boiled or steamed, while white medicines are always administered as a cold solution.

Plants that are used to protect against evil, or to deflect evil away from one, are widely used in South Africa. Michelle Cocks and others documented that the most popular category of medicine purchased from amaXhosa (a more accurate term for the Xhosa-speaking people) traditional medicine (*amayeza*) stores is for protection against evil spirits. These are usually applied to the body as a wash or as an unguent, or worn as a charm around the waist or neck. They can also be used to sprinkle around ones property and possessions. The category of plants known as *intelezi* refers to a wide variety of plants (usually bulbs and tubers) that are used to protect against evil. A mixture of *intelezi* species are usually chopped up and soaked in cold water (they are categorized as white medicines) and this is sprinkled around the perimeter of the homestead before any important rituals are performed. This is to minimize any negative mystical interference by those who harbor witchcraft (*umthakathi*) or darkness (*umnyama*) in their hearts. Protection of one's property against criminals is in high demand in contemporary South Africa where crime has escalated alarmingly in the post-apartheid era. The services of *izangoma* are frequently sought to provide such protection. Known as *ukubetela* this usually involves a complex series of rituals over several days at the homestead of the client where family members are medicated with protective herbs. In some instances river stones that have been heated and medicated with a variety of plant- and animal-based solutions and substances are buried at strategic places (such as gates and entrances) of the homestead, and the air is stabbed in the four cardinal directions. This is believed to chase away anyone who approaches the homestead with evil or criminal intentions in their heart.

Umgcabo is a prophylactic procedure employed whereby complex mixtures of protective medicines that are stored in an oil (animal fat) base are applied to incisions that have been made at points over the clients body (i.e., joints) that are believed to be vulnerable to the entry of evil forces. *Ukutshoba* is a curative therapy used against mystical invasions of the body. In the latter case the medicines are introduced into the skin through a puncture made with a porcupine quill or a bicycle spoke, according to Frank and Stephen Jolles.

Some plant tubers are used as a decoy to deflect sorcery and witchcraft. A mixture of medicines with the blood or saliva of the potential victim is inserted into the tuber (*inkomfe*) and it is then buried in a remote place. The person must leave without looking back. In this way anyone wishing to do harm on the person will fail as the evil familiar will be confused and go to the tuber rather than the potential victim for whom it is intended. Its potential can be further refined with a few more symbolic actions whereby the evil that is being sent to the intended victim actually rebounds and returns to afflict the sender (known as *ukucupha*). This practice, that is still followed today, was first recorded by Callaway in 1870 and demonstrates the enduring nature of some of this knowledge.

There are a number of other plant-based protective devices that are currently used. A notable example is the use of a special tree, the bark of which is soaked and then ritually thrown over the person's shoulder. It is believed that this will fool aspiring robbers or criminals who approach a treated household. As they approach they will hallucinate and "see" the household members standing at the door of the house. It is hoped that the "presence" of family members will deter the criminals from attempting to rob the house. In addition there are plants and medicines that are believed to make the user become invisible and thus avoid detection by those wishing to harm him/her. This medicine has an ambivalent value, however, as it can also be used by criminals to help them escape detection from the police.

The Social Uses of Plants

The ambivalent nature of plant-based medicines (*imithi*) is most evident when examining the social uses of plants. (Muti is the pan-African term most commonly used to refer to plant and animals used in potions for healing or other purposes; even human parts can be used, which helps account for the term's sometimes negative connotation in Zulu culture.) Plants that fall under such a category are mainly used for luck, be it in education, business, competitions (i.e., sport), court cases, or, most importantly, love. In the research in the Eastern Cape led by Michelle Cocks and reported in 2000 and 2002, it was found that the second most popular category of plants purchased at *amayeza* stores were those to achieve luck. The most common profile of the customers for luck-enhancing medicines was young, educated and upwardly mobile individuals. *Umayime* (*clivia sp.*) and *umlomo mnandi* (lit. "mouth that is nice") are plants that are used when one wants to be able to speak with conviction and persuasion, for instance when one is pleading in a court case. There are a number of plants that can be used to attract a lover by making one appear "nice." These can also be used in beauty competitions to ensure success. Some plants are used to keep a lover faithful or stop him/her from straying to others. Aggrieved women who suspect that their lovers or spouses are seeking sexual favors from others have recourse to a plant-based medicine (*typha capensis*) that will make the competing lover (female) excessively moist and undesirable. These ideas suggest that achievement is not about individual ability, hard work, or personal attributes, but is something that can be obtained by external interventions via the spirit world or through magical manipulation.

Plants, Wealth, and Power

Although it may be argued that these examples present moral ambiguities, there is one category of medicine that is regarded by most *izangoma* as unacceptable and morally reprehensible. These are the medicines used to achieve financial wealth and political power. Those individuals who use such medicines to gain immediate wealth are engaging in what is termed *ukuthwala*, while *ukuthwesa* (or *ukuthwalisa*) refers to those "healers" that engage in the sale of such medicines. Human body parts may be used in the creation of such medicines. This accounts for antagonistic responses toward those who engage in such trade. Moreover, the use of such medicines always comes at a cost, the death of those who are closest to the purchaser. The literal "consumption of others" (i.e., human body parts and deaths of closest kin) is an appropriate representation of such practices and is a powerful commentary against the disruptive effects of excessive accumulation of wealth and power.

Plants and the Fluid Boundaries between Spiritual and Natural Worlds

It is quite evident that Zulu notions of the boundaries between the social, natural and spiritual worlds are more complex and fluid than those found in the Cartesian worldview. Plants and animals are seen as the manifestation and medium of the spirit world and they are influenced by the intentions of the user. Together, the plant, the spirit and the user occupy a common moral universe. This idea of tapping into the positive healing power of the natural world through right and good moral intentions is illustrated in the way medicines are collected and used by diviners. These should always be collected in a respectful way. Plants are approached in a humble manner with the clapping of the hands, while the gatherer requests permission from the ancestors to be allowed to remove the plant. Thanks offerings, usually in the form of white beads, should always be made after collection. This will ensure the right potency of the plant as well as offer assurance that more plants will always be made available by the ancestral world. The ancestors show the healers the correct plants to use for healing in their dreams and even indicate to them the most suitable places for collection. This is important since plants vary in their potency depending on their habitat and the timing of their collection (diurnally and seasonally). Moreover it is strongly believed that plant-based medicines will be rendered useless (or may become dangerous) if there is lack of harmony in the household. Unfortunately many of these principles and practices have been abandoned in the modern era and plants are now gathered indiscriminately and without ritual observance by entrepreneurs, who have little regard for, and knowledge of the ancestral world.

Despite these problems, the spiritual and social uses of plants by the Zulu *izangoma* are both enduring and dynamic. They provide a mechanism through which social and spiritual order can be maintained and the means by which the pressures associated with contemporary lifestyles can be commented on and managed.

Fenny Bernard

Further Reading
Callaway, Henry. *The Religious System of the amaZulu*. Cape Town: C.Struik (Pty) Ltd, 1970.

Cocks, Michelle and Anthony Dold. "The Role of 'African Chemists' in the Health Care System of the Eastern Cape Province of South Africa." *Social Science and Medicine* 51:10 (November 2000), 1505–515.

Cocks, Michelle and Valerie Møller. "Use of Indigenous and Indigenised Medicines to Enhance Personal Well-being: A South African Case Study." *Social Science and Medicine* 54:3 (February 2002), 387–97.

Hutchings, Anne, Alan Scott, Gillian Lewis and Anthony Cunningham. *Zulu Medicinal Plants: An Inventory*. Pietermaritzburg: University of Natal Press, 1996.

Jolles, Frank and Stephen Jolles. "Zulu Ritual Immunization in Perspective." *Africa* 70:2 (2000), 229–48.

Ngubane, Harriet. *Body and Mind in Zulu Medicine: An Ethnography of Health and Disease in Nyuswa-Zulu Thought and Practice*. London: Academic Press, 1977.

Prins, Frans. "Prohibitions and Pollution at a Medicinal Plant Nursery: Customary Implications Associated with Ethnobotanical Reserves in Conservative Areas of KwaZulu-Natal." *Natal Museum Journal of Humanities* (8 December 1996), 81–93.

See also: African Religions and Nature Conservation; Descartes, René; Ethnobotany; Muti and African Healing; Mutwa, Credo; Weather Snake; Xhosa-Speakers' Traditional Concept of God.

Zulu (amaZulu) Smelting

Adulphe Delegorgue provides the only detailed eyewitness account of iron-ore smelting in what is now KwaZulu-Natal, South Africa. In 1842 he visited a place he called Zimpy (*insimbi* = iron) while hunting in the Zulu Kingdom. He described an enclosure of 25 by 12 paces in which three parallel oval "pits," the furnaces, were situated. At either end of each pit, pipes of sun-dried clay carried air expelled from twin bellows into the furnace. Four relays of six men operated the bellows continuously throughout the smelt, which lasted four hours from eight till midnight. The following day, the team removed pieces of iron bloom from the still-hot furnaces and amalgamated them into a rough ingot with heat and hammer. Tools such as hoes and spears were later forged from the ingots. With the exception of some details, Delegorgue's account is consistent with the picture provided by archaeological evidence dating to the eighteenth century.

Smelting was not simply a technical skill but a process

rich in symbolic content. This is because smelting involves the transformation of material from one form (ore) to another (metal). People order and make sense of the world around them by creating discrete classificatory categories. Classifications are arbitrary, however, and the world is chaotic. Aspects of it defy classification, being neither one thing nor another. These anomalies cause anxiety because they threaten order and are consequently considered powerful and dangerous. Similarly, things and beings associated with overlapping boundaries, or the transition from one category to another, may become saturated with danger.

In Zulu belief, this danger is conceptualized as *umnyama*, meaning darkness. As part of the natural order of things, *umnyama* is a mystical condition or state of being that is unavoidable in the course of normal living. It opens afflicted people to misfortune and affects cattle and crops, causing milk to dry and plants to shrivel. *Umnyama* is most strongly associated with birth and death, which involve transitions from one world to another. For instance, in giving birth, women act as a channel between this and a pre-birth world (in fact, the ancestral world). They enter a dangerous state of darkness (*umnyama*) that threatens both their own health and, when most intense, the health of people and things around them. Through their reproductive capacity, signified not only by pregnancy and birth but also by menstruation, women move constantly toward and away from the margins of this world, into and out of darkness.

Smelting among the Zulu, as throughout much of sub-Saharan Africa, was homologous with procreation. The furnace, its penetrating clay pipes, and the act of its operation were symbolically equivalent to genitalia and the sexual act, ending with the "birth" of iron. A twentieth-century smith worked at his smithy for a few days each month, just after the full moon. He explicitly linked his timing to women's menstrual cycles, noting that this was when "the iron flows out nicely" (Berglund 1976: 360). Red earth and red iron ore, he said, are the Earth's blood, specifically her menstrual blood, and the "earth is the mother of iron." Outcrops of iron ore, as representations of the Earth's capacity to give birth, were likely charged with *umnyama*, forcing miners to protect themselves through ritual practice.

Red ochre (*ibomvu*), a form of iron ore, is associated with the color red (*-bomvu*) just as darkness (*umnyama*) is associated with the color black (*-mnyama*). Black is opposed to white (*-mhlophe*) in the Zulu color system, and with red they form a color triad. Red is a liminal color, signaling transformation at dusk and dawn. Red's liminality extends beyond the diurnal rhythm to other areas of transformation and transition. Blood from the fatal wound of an animal sacrificed for the ancestors is referred to as the "wound" (*inxeba*), and distinguished from the rest of the animal's blood. The "wound" provides a point of access or bridge to the ancestral world, making it a liminal construct of special significance. Menstrual blood is conceptually similar to the "wound" because it provides evidence of a woman's reproductive capacity, and reproduction is the domain of the ancestors. Thus, men who worked with the Earth's blood and delivered her child (the iron bloom), entered a liminal zone where they made contact with the ancestral world. Not surprisingly, smelting was as intensely shrouded with *umnyama* as the birth of a child; when smelting, men exposed themselves to the same danger faced by parturient women. For this reason, furnaces were generally sited away from homesteads.

If the Earth was the bloom's mother, then she was also the smelters' (or head smelter's) wife, and it was appropriate that they *hlonipha* (respect) her. This was also true for the ancestors invoked at the furnace. *Hlonipha* behavior involves the use of ritualized language and action to honor and respect spouses, in-laws, people of seniority and ancestors. Improper and disrespectful behavior can disrupt family harmony so severely that a sacrifice may be required to restore peace. Such behavior at the furnace would have angered the ancestors and resulted in the failure of the smelt. Smelters therefore, acted in formal ritualized ways during the smelt and used *hlonipha* words for the furnace and their tools. Respect for the ancestors was also manifested in a prohibition on sex before and during a smelt. Men are affected by *umnyama* after sexual intercourse, and although this weakened condition does not last long, they should not approach their ancestors in a state of impurity. Smelters who ignored the sanction risked the displeasure of ancestors, who caused the smelt to fail.

The site of the furnace was a place dark with *umnyama*, a place of transformation where worlds and categories overlapped and intersected. When smelting, men invoked their ancestors, had sex with the Earth, and were both father to her child and midwives during its birth. The men at Zimpy worked at night, when no ordinary work occurs. As a result, a dangerously contagious *umnyama* settled on the smelters from which they needed release, both for their own protection and in order to reenter society. This involved washing, treatment with medicines, and in at least some cases, the slaughter of cattle. These rites released smelters from their liminality back into normal daily life.

Gavin Whitelaw

Further Reading

Berglund, Axel-Ivar. *Zulu Thought Patterns and Symbolism*. Cape Town: David Phillip, 1976.

Hall, Martin. "An Iron-smelting Site in the Hluhluwe Game Reserve, Zululand." *Annals of the Natal Museum* 24:1 (1980), 165–75.

Maggs, Tim. "'My Father's Hammer Never Ceased Its Song Day and Night': The Zulu Ferrous Metalworking

Industry." *Natal Museum Journal of Humanities* 4 (1992), 65–87.

Maggs, Tim. "Hloma Mathonsi, the Zulu Blacksmith: A Record by the Reverend H.F.O. Dedekind in 1929." *Annals of the Natal Museum* 27:2 (1986), 481–9.

Maggs, Tim. "Mabhija: Pre-colonial Industrial Development in the Tugela Basin." *Annals of the Natal Museum* 25:1 (1982), 123–41.

Ngubane, Harriet. *Body and Mind in Zulu Medicine: An Ethnography of Health and Disease in Nyuswa-Zulu Thought and Practice.* London: Academic Press, 1977.

Raum, O.F. *The Social Functions of Avoidances and Taboos among the Zulu.* Berlin: Walter de Gruyter, 1973.

Whitelaw, Gavin. "Precolonial Iron Production around Durban and in Southern Natal." *Natal Museum Journal of Humanities* 3 (1991), 29–39.

See also: Mutwa, Credo; Zulu (amaZulu) Ancestors and Ritual Exchange; Zulu (amaZulu) Culture, Plants, and Spirit Worlds; Zulu (amaZulu) War Rituals.

Zulu (amaZulu) War Rituals

The Zulu believed in an overlap that existed between this world and the world of the spirits. This was expressed by a mystical force, *umnyama*, which was darkness or evil influence, and was represented by the color black. It could be contagious in its most virulent forms. Because such pollution was a mystical rather than organic illness, it could be cured only by symbolic medicines. Death by violence, expressed as *umkhoka*, was an especially powerful form of *umnyama*, as the killer himself was polluted. Thus warriors of the nineteenth-century Zulu kingdom, when about to go to war, were in especial spiritual danger, and needed to be ritually purified of evil influences and strengthened against them.

Members of an *ibutho* (age-grade regiment) caught and killed bare-handed a black bull from the royal herds upon which all the evil influences in the land had been ritually cast. *Izangoma* – who were not herbalists but diviners, possessed by the spirits of the ancestors (*amadlozi*), which made them a link between this and the spirit world – cut strips of meat from the bull, and treated them with black medicines to strengthen the warriors and bind them together in loyalty to their king. The strips of meat were then roasted on a fire of wood collected by the warriors the previous day. The *izangoma* threw the strips up into the air and the warriors, who were drawn up in a great circle, caught and sucked them. Meanwhile the *izangoma* burned more medicines and the warriors breathed in the smoke and were sprinkled with the cinders. Then, in order finally to expel all evil influences, each warrior drank a pot of medicine, and a few at a time took turns to vomit into a great pit. The ritual vomiting was also intended to bind the warriors in their loyalty to their king. Some of the vomit was added to the great *inkatha* of the Zulu nation, the sacred grass coil that was the symbol of the nation's unity and strength. The following day the warriors went down to any running stream to wash, but not to rub off the medicines with which they had been sprinkled.

With the completion of these rituals the warriors (who had undergone a symbolic death) could no longer sleep at home nor have anything to do with girls or women since they themselves had now taken on a dangerous state of *umynama*.

While the warriors were thus setting themselves apart from ordinary life and dedicating themselves to war, the king called pairs of favored *amabutho* (age-grade regiments) into the royal cattle enclosure to boast of their courage and to issue ritual challenges to outdo one another in the coming campaign.

For the Zulu, good fortune in an enterprise depended on the approval of the *amadlozi* who lived under the ground and were interested in every aspect of their descendants' lives. Because the spirits maintained the status they had enjoyed while alive, it was particularly necessary before proceeding on campaign to secure the favor of the *amadlozi* of the king's royal forebears since they were necessarily concerned with the welfare of the entire Zulu nation. The way the living propitiated the *amadlozi* was through cattle sacrifice when the spirits partook of the burnt offerings and "licked" the meat set aside for them. The Zulu were essentially pastoralists, living in a land of mixed grazing ideally suited to raising livestock. Cattle were especially prized as the prime indicator of wealth and also for their ritual importance in communicating with the *amadlozi*. Before it marched away to war, therefore, it was vital that the army satisfy the royal *amadlozi* with a generous sacrifice from the royal herds so that the spirits were induced to accompany the warriors and deploy their powers against the enemy.

In battle a ritual the Zulu followed was to *hlomula*, or for many warriors to stab an enemy who had already died courageously. This practice was connected with the hunt, and was observed only when a fierce and dangerous animal like a lion had been overcome. Killing a foe in battle, as well as participating in the *hlomula* ritual, severely contaminated the warrior with *umnyama*. It was thus necessary to undertake many ceremonies to achieve ritual purification. One was to slit open the belly of a slain foe so that *umnyama* would not affect the killer and make him swell up like the dead. The killer would also put on items of the dead man's apparel in place of his own – which would have been contaminated by the harmful influences of the victim's blood – in order that he might *zila*, or observe the customary abstentions after a death until ritually cleansed.

Ritually contaminated warriors returning from campaign could not immediately report to the king, nor resume normal domestic life because they were highly contagious. They were separated for four days from their companions in special homesteads and fed on cattle captured in battle. Daily, they washed ritually in a river and returned to *ncinda*, or to suck medicine from their fingertips and spit it in the direction of their enemies in order to gain occult ascendancy over the vengeful spirits of their victims, the blood from whose fatal wounds formed a dangerous bridge between the living and the spirit world. On the final day the *izangoma* completed the warriors' ritual purification by sprinkling them with medicines before they presented themselves in the royal cattle enclosure before the king. There they exchanged accounts of the fighting, and repeated the ritual challenges made before setting out to war. The king duly praised some individuals for bravery, humiliated others for cowardice and honored and rewarded the *ibutho* that had most distinguished itself.

John Laband

Further Reading

Calloway, Rev. Canon Henry. *The Religious System of the Amazulu. Izinyanga Zokubula; or Divination, as Existing among the Amazulu, in Their Own Words, with a Translation into English, and Notes.* Natal: John A. Blair, Springvale; Cape Town: J.C. Juta; London: Trubner & Co, 1870.

Laband, John. *The Rise and Fall of the Zulu Nation.* London: Arms and Armour Press, 1997.

Ngubane, Harriet. *Body and Mind in Zulu Medicine: An Ethnography of Health and Disease in Nyuswa-Zulu Thought and Practice.* London: Academic Press, 1977.

Webb, Colin and John Wright, eds. *The James Stuart Archive of Recorded Oral Evidence Relating to the History of the Zulu and Neighbouring Peoples*, vol. III. Pietermaritzburg and Durban: University of Natal Press, 1982. Testimony in 1912 of Mpatshana kaSodondo.

Webb, Colin and John Wright, eds. *A Zulu King Speaks: Statements Made by Cetshwayo kaMpande on the History and Customs of His People.* Pietermaritzburg and Durban: University of Natal Press, 1978. Cetshwayo's evidence in 1883 to the Cape Government Commission on Native Laws and Customs.

See also: Mutwa, Credo; Zulu (amaZulu) Ancestors and Ritual Exchange; Zulu (amaZulu) Culture, Plants, and Spirit Worlds; Zulu (amaZulu) Smelting.

Index

Due to the unique organization of this encyclopedia the index begins with a list of all the "practitioner" and "scholarly perspectives" articles, as described in the "Reader's Guide" (pp. xix), which is a good place for readers to learn effective ways to use this reference work. The alphabetized index follows these two lists.

In the index entry titles are in bold font wherever they appear. The entry titles appear both alphabetically and where they provide information pertinent to other indexed subjects. The words "see also" refer to other items in the index itself, unless they are in bold font and thus refer to an entry. When "see also" refers to an entry, readers should also consult the cross-references under the alphabetized encyclopedia entry. The word "see" directs readers to another term under which the indicated subject matter will be found.

A special feature of this index is its regional categories, where readers can find a comprehensive list of items that relate to a specific area of the world. Some items in the regional groupings are not indexed elsewhere. Countries and topics related to individual nations have been organized according to the United Nations' system of categorization used when reporting global statistics. The regional categories illustrate the interrelationships found among many of the people and topics discussed in the encyclopedia. These relationships demonstrate both the encyclopedia's interdisciplinary scholarship and reflect the exchange of ideas occurring through processes currently labeled "globalization." The regions organized and alphabetized are: Africa, Asia, Caribbean, Europe, Meso-America, North America, Oceania, South America. This encyclopedia has 520 contributors from around the world. The name of each contributor is indexed alphabetically, and their contributions are listed below their names.

Practitioner Entries

Animism: Humanity's Original Religious Worldview 83–91
Biocentric Religion – A Call for 176–179
Bioregionalism 188–189
Black Mesa 199–202
Breathwork 214–217
Cetacean Spirituality 285–286
Christianity (7i) – An Evangelical Perspective on Faith and 369–371
Circle Sanctuary 392
Council of All Beings 425–429
Depth Ecology 469–471
Dragon Environmental Network (United Kingdom) 506–507
Ecotopian Reflections 566–568
Epic Ritual 612–613
Gardening and Nature Spirituality 687
Harmonic Convergence and the Spiritualization of the Biosphere 738–741
Holy Land in Native North America 785–788
Hunting Spirituality and Animism 811–812
Mongolian Buddhism and Taimen Conservation 1099–1100
Music of Resistance 1135–1137
Orixa Iroko 261–262
Pagan Music 1238

Pantheist Association for Nature – PAN 1261
Planetary Dance 1281–1283
Qur'an, The 1321–1324
Re-Earthing 1354–1358
Redwood Rabbis 1352–1354
Rewilding 1383–1384
Rotting Tree Fairie 634
Rustlers Valley (South Africa) 1439
Satanism 1483–1484
Sexuality and Eco-spirituality 1518–1519
Spirit of the Sage Council 1592
What would Jesus Drive? 318
Wilderness Rites of Passage 1748–1750
World Pantheist Movement 1769–1770

Scholarly Perspective Entries

Abortion 13–14
Aesthetics of Nature and the Sacred 18–21
Animism – A Contemporary Perspective 81–82
Anthropologists 94–96
Ayahuasca 141–142
Bahá'í Faith 151–152
Biblical Foundations for Christian Stewardship 173–174
Biophilia 183–188

Christianity and Nature Symbolism 377–379
Cognitive Ethology, Social Morality, and Ethics 397–399
Critical Perspectives on "Religions of the World and Ecology" 1375–1376
Dharma – Hindu 479–481
Dirt 486–487
Dualism – A Perspective 511
Earth Bible 515–516
Eco-justice in Theology and Ethics 539–542
Ecojustice Hermeneutics 515
Fascism 531
Fauna Cabala 644–647
Gaian Pilgrimage 683–685
Geophilia 693–694
Globalization 698–700
Harmony in Native North American Spiritual Traditions 741–742
Heavenism 516
Holocaust and the Environmental Crisis, The 783–785
Homosexuality and Science 789–790
India's Sacred Groves 831–833
Islam and Eco-Justice 862–866
Islamic Basis for Environmental Protection 879–883
Jung, Carl – A Perspective 941–943
Kabbalah and Ecotheology 945–950
Ladakh Buddhism 976–977

1828 Index

Lakota Sun Dance 985–987
Magic, Animism, and the Shaman's Craft 1023–1026
Making of an Earthist Christian 394–396
Native American Languages 1160–1162
Natural History as Natural Religion 1164–1169
Natural Law and Natural Rights 1169–1171
New Academy for Nature and Culture 1380
Orthodox Spirituality 336–337
Paganism: a Jewish Perspective 1244–1246
Paleolithic Religions and the Future 1256
Plastic Medicine Men 1283–1284
Population and Consumption – Contemporary Religious Responses 1292–1295
Primate Spirituality 1303–1306
Religious Naturalism 1371–1372
Restoring Eden 1381–1383
Restoration Ecology and Ritual 1379–1381
Ritual 1385–1388
Sacramental Universe 1444–1445
Sacred and the Modern World, The 1446–1448
Sacred Sites in England 1460–1462
Scientology 1499–1501
Scything and Erotic Fulfillment 1507–1509
Sexuality and Green Consciousness 1519–1523
Space Exploration 1585–1588
Tawhid (Oneness of God) 1623–1624
Thomas Berry on Religion and Nature 166–168
Urban Reinhabitation – CERES as Case Study (Australia) 1684–1686
Vegetarianism and Judaism 1693–1695
Wilderness Religion 1745–1748

A

Abbey, Edward 1–3
  anarchism 3 (see also Anarchism)
  Earth First! 519 (see also Earth First! and the Earth Liberation Front)
  death 2 (see also Death and Afterlife in Robinson Jeffers and Edward Abbey)
  desert 474–475
  sabotage (and ecotage), ethics of 538
  radical environmentalism 1565 (see also Radical Environmentalism)
Abel 85, 87, 482, 755, 1693
Aboriginal Art 4–5, 1392
Aboriginal Dreaming (Australia) 5–7, 375
Aboriginal Environmental Groups in Canada 9–10
Aboriginal Spirituality and the New Age in Australia 10–12
Abortion 13–14, 689, 865, 1286, 1295, 1346, 1549, 1757 (see also Breeding and Contraception; Fertility and Abortion)
Abou El Fadl, Khaled
  contribution in this encyclopedia, see Dogs in the Islamic Tradition
Abraham 177, 431, 434, 755, 756, 874, 937, 938, 939, 1125, 1321, 1751
Abram, David 190–191, 635, 687, 946, 1329, 1519, 1755
  contributions in this encyclopedia, see Depth Ecology; Storytelling and Wonder; Magic, Animism, and the Shaman's Craft
Abravanel, R. Isaac 65, 1693
Achebe, Chinua see Africa – Western
acropolis see Europe – Southern
Adams, Ansel 14–15, 107, 490, 615, 1545–1546
Adams, Carol 16, 536
  contribution in this encyclopedia, see Women and Animals
Adams, John Quincy see North America – United States
Adekunle, Julius O.
  contribution in this encyclopedia, see Totemic Practices in Borgu; Yoruba Culture
Advaita Vedanta see Hinduism
adventure see Climbing; Mountaineering; Surfing
Aesthetics and Nature in China and Japan 16–18
Aesthetics of Nature and the Sacred 18–21
Afrasiabi, Kaveh L
  contribution in this encyclopedia, see Islam and Post-Anthropocentrism
Africa
  African traditional religions (ATR) 26, 28, 73, 118, 1682, 1725
  agriculture 575, 1808
  animals see Animals in African Legend and Ethiopian Scriptures
  Central Africa
    art see Rock Art – Batwa/Pygmies; Rock Art – Chewa; Rock Art – Sintu; Wenger, Susan, Yoruba Art, and the Oshogbo Sacred Grove
    Congo see Congo River Watershed
    cradle of humanity 413, 707, 1683
    Kaphirintiwa see Kaphirintiwa – The Place of Creation
    Ndembu religion see Ndembu Religion
    Nyau see Nyau – A Closed Assocation
    Pygmies 163, 413, 954, 1047, 1211, 1392, 1430, 1431 (see also Pygmies (Mbuti Foragers) and Bila Farmers of the Ituri Forest)
  Christianity in Africa
    Afrikaner Theology see Afrikaner Theology
    animals see Animals in African Legend and Ethiopian Scriptures
    churches
      Church of Nazareth see Church of Nazareth, KwaZulu – Natal (South Africa)
      Earthkeeping Churches see African Earthkeeping Churches – Association of (Zimbabwe)
      Zion Church see Zion Christian Church (South Africa)
    environmentalism see Christian Environmentalism in Kenya
    Kimbanguism see Kimbanguism (Central Africa)
    Masowe see Masowe Wilderness Apostles
    Samia Culture see Samia Culture – Western Kenya
    Schweitzer, Albert see Schweitzer, Albert
    St. Katherine's Monastery see St. Katherine's Monastery (Mount Sinai, Egypt)
  Eastern Africa
    art see Rock Art – Hadzabe/Sandawe
    greenbelt movement see Kenya Greenbelt Movement (and adjacent, Wangari Maathai on Reforesting Kenya)
    International Tree Foundation see Men of the Trees
    Lake Victoria 1206–1207, 1469, 1561
    Luo people see Snakes and the Luo of Kenya
    Maasai see Maasai
    Matopos Hills see Zimbabwe's Matopos Hills
    Mugabe, Robert 1810
    Nkomo, Joshua 1810
    Rhodes, Cecil 1807, 1809
    rain see Makewanta the Rainmaker (and adjacent, Mbiriwiri – The Sacred Rainmaking Drum)
    Samburu see Mount Nyiro and the Samburu
    Selassie, Haile see Selassie Haile (adjacent to Rastafari
    spirit sites see Kasama Spirit Sites
    spirits see Zimbabwe Spirit Mediums, Guerillas and Nature
    gods and goddesses see gods, goddesses, deities and nature spirits
    nature conservation see African

Index

Religions and Nature Conservation;
African Earthkeeping Churches
Northern Africa
creation myths *see* Creation Myths of
the Ancient World
Egypt
ancient *see* Egypt – Ancient
pre-Islamic *see* Egypt – Pre-Islamic
pastoralism *see* Saharan Pastoralists
sacred groves *see* Sacred Groves in Africa
Southern Africa
AIDS *see* AIDS
apartheid 29, 30, 371, 404, 700
art *see* Makapansgat Cobble; Rock Art
 – Northern Sotho; San (Bushmen)
Apocalpytic Rock Art
Khoisan religion *see* Khoisan Religion
Matopo principle *see* Shona Women
and the Mutopo Principle
Mbeki, President Thabo 1683
Muti *see* Muti and African Healing;
Muti Killings
Mutwa, Credo *see* Mutwa, Credo
Native Land Act 1811
pollution *see* Pollution Beliefs in South
Africa
Rustlers Valley *see* Rustlers Valley
sacred stones *see* Etsheni Sacred Stones
San people *see* San (Bushmen)
Aocalpytic Rock Art; San (Bushmen)
Religion; San Bushmen Rainmaking
Van der Post, Laurens *see* Van der Post,
Laurens
Venda religion *see* Venda Witch
Beliefs; Venda Religion and the Land
water management *see* Water Spirits
and Indigenous Ecological
Management
Zulu *see* Zulu (amaZulu) Ancestors
and Ritual Exchange; Zulu
(amaZulu) Culture, Plants and
Spirit Worlds; Zulu (amaZulu)
Smelting; Zulu (amaZulu) War
Rituals
Western Africa *see* West Africa
1725–1727
Achebe, Chinua 1034–1035
Asante Religion *see* Asante Religion
Diola *see* Diola
divination *see* Ifa Divination
Mammy Water *see* Mammy Water
Ogoni *see* Saro-Wiwa, Kenule Beeson
and the Ogoni of Ogoni
Oru-Igbo *see* Divine Waters of the
Oru-Igbo
totems *see* totems; Totemic Practices in
Borgu
Yoruba culture *see* Yoruba Culture
African Earthkeeping Churches –
Association of 22

African Independent Churches 24–26,
388
African Religions and Nature
Conservation 26–28
Afrikaner Theology 29–30
Afzaal, Ahmed
contributions in this encyclopedia, *see*
Ibn Al-cArabi, Shakyh Muhyiddin;
Sufism; Tawhid (Oneness of God)
Aggarwal, Safia
contribution in this encyclopedia, *see*
India's Sacred Groves
agriculture
Africa *see* Africa
agricultural revolution 84, 217
and animals 1364
and religion
Amish 349
Confucianism 409, 412
Judaism 708
monotheism 552
origins of and religious revolution 503
Darré, Walther 450
decentralist agrarianism 1490
environmental decline 518, 1070, 1637,
1712
India *see* Asia – Southern
land value 1346
pesticides 270, 277, 291, 309, 310, 399,
491, 598, 687, 722, 784, 1065, 1129,
1206, 1345, 1550, 1614, 1714
Rome *see* Europe – Southern
types
agribusiness 797
bio-dynamic farming 451, 1597
community supported *see* Community
Supported Agriculture
industrial
factory farms 243, 309, 875
technology 1539
irrigation agriculture 550, 571
organic farming 118, 133, 451, 491,
559, 643, 691, 726, 884, 1629
permaculture 691, 1272, 1357, 1439
plantation 750
state-run 834
subsistence 349, 1191
sustainable agriculture 540, 610, 964,
1492
agroforestry revolving loan fund
(ARLF) 666
forestry 667
land institute (Natural Systems
Agriculture) 892, 988
sustainable agricultural working
group 1406
Ahimsa 30–31
abortion 654
as an ideal 1585, 1627, 1783
as non-violence 53, 194, 767, 824, 907

Buddhism 242
Deep Ecology 31
Gandhi, Mohandas 31
Hinduism 824–827
Jainism 894, 895
vegetarianism 824, 1192, 1691, 1706
Ahmad, Ali
contribution in this encyclopedia, *see*
Islamic Law
Ahura Mazda *see* gods, goddesses, deities
and nature spirits
AIDS 26, 566, 955, 1139, 1144, 1216,
1528, 1536, 1726
Aitken, Robert *see* Buddhism – Engaged
Albanese, Catherine x, 1173–1174, 1233,
1258, 1573
contribution in this encyclopedia, *see*
Nature Religion in the United States
Albert the Great 31
Albo, R. Joseph 1693–1694, 1697
Alexander, Thomas G.
contribution in this encyclopedia, *see*
Church of Jesus Christ of Latter-day
Saints
Aliens 1012, 1140, 1464, 1587, 1674 (*see
also* Mutwa, Credo)
Alchemy 32–33, 55, 123, 124, 163,
448–449, 706, 932, 940–942,
1729–1730
Allen, Paula Gunn 33–34, 1520
Alley, Kelly D.
contributions in this encyclopedia, *see*
River Ganga and the Clean Ganga
Campaign (and adjacent, Hinduism
and Pollution); Alliance of Religion
and Conservation 34, 1193, 1257
Alpha Farm 35
Altars and Shrines 36–37
Africa 414, 485, 496, 819, 1452, 1561
Armenian cosmology 62
Asante 119
Buddhist 219
burial 1298
China 295
Christian 157
England 221
fire 1814
Greece 661, 717, 719, 755
Hawai'i 953
India 768–769
Indonesia 549
Maya 1065, 1069–1070
Native American 201, 794, 990
North America 1450
Pagan festivals 1234
pilgrimage 1458
rain shrine *see* Makewana the
Rainmaker
Rome 1410
Shinto 438, 902, 1656–1657

Altner, Gunter 37, 381
Amazonia *see* South America
Amazonian Folktales 40–41
American Indians as "First Ecologists" 42–45
Ammar, Nawal
 contribution in this encyclopedia, *see* Islam and Eco-Justice
Ammons, A.R. 45–46
Amte, Baba 46–47, 826
Ananda Marga's Tantric Neo-Humanism 47–49
Anarchism 49–56
 Abbey, Edward *see* Abbey, Edward
 and Buddhism 1563
 and paganism 54
 and social ecology 603
 Bakunin, Mikhail 3
 Bari, Judy 520, 1003, 1136
 contemporary 55
 Earth First! and the Earth Liberation Front 519–521,
 green 58, 603, 642, 971, 1328, 1330, 1333, 1562
 radical environmentalism *see* Radical Environmentalism
 Snyder, Gary *see* Snyder, Gary and the Invention of Bioregional Spirituality and Politics
Analects *see* Confucianism
Anarcho-primitivism and the Bible 56–58 (*see also* Ferality)
Anatman (no self) *see* Buddhism
Andean Traditions 59–62
Andrews, Lynn 11, 1283
Angkor Wat *see* Asia – Southeastern
Anglo-Saxons *see* Europe – Northern
Anima Mundi – The World Soul 63, 325, 1265, 1673, 1729
Animals (*see also* organisms – fauna)
 Africa 1216 (*see also* Animals in African Legend and Ethiopian Scriptures; Snakes and the Luo of Kenya)
 Animal Liberation Front (ALF) 64, 420, 1332 (*see also* Rodney Coronado and the Animal Liberation Front adjacent to Radical Environmentalism)
 Aquinas, Thomas *see* Aquinas, Thomas
 agriculture 1364
 art 1254, 1392, 1394–1395
 and Maimonides *see* Maimonides
 animal taming 570, 1364
 as pets 78, 497, 570, 1123, 1320, 1364–1365, 1695, 1784
 behavior *see* Fauna Cabala
 Buddhism *see* Creatures' Release in Chinese Buddhism; Jataka Tales
 Center for Reproduction of Endangered Species 1625

Christianity 1403, 1405, **Christianity and Animals; Animals in the Bible and Qur'an**
endangered species act 174, 309, 370, 625, 935, 954, 1159, 1593
experimentation 1242, 1494 (*see also* **Jewish Law and Animal Experimentation**)
hunting 1364 (*see also* **Hunting and the Origins of Religion; Hunting Spirituality; Hunting Spirituality and Animism**)
Islam 1214–1215, 1322, 1435 (*see also* **Animals in the Bible and Qur'an; Dogs in the Islamic Traditions**)
Japan *see* **Whales and Japanese Cultures**
Judaism *see* **Animal Rights in the Jewish Tradition; Jewish Law and Animal Experimentation**
locomotion 1074
monotheistic traditions *see* **Dogs in the Abrahamic Traditions**
paganism 1251
Paleolithic religion *see* **Paleolithic religion**
sacrifices *see* sacrifices
symbolism 67, 819 (*see also* **Power Animals**)
women *see* **Adams, Carol; Women and Animals**
Animals in African Legend and Ethiopian Scriptures 73–76
Animals in the Bible and Qu'ran 76–78
Animal Rights in the Jewish Tradition 64–66
Animism 78–81
 and aboriginal worldviews *see* **Animism: Humanity's Original Religious Worldview**
 and anthropology *see* **Anthropology as a Source of Nature Religion**
 and God 281
 and indigenous peoples 799, 1338, 1584, 1666–1667, 1778
 contemporary *see* **Animism: A Contemporary Perspective**
 hunting *see* **Hunting Spirituality and Animism**
 Nepal 1191
 original worldview *see* **Animism: Humanity's Original Religious Worldview**
 paganism 1231, 1249
 shamanism *see* **Magic, Animism and the Shaman's Craft**
 totemism *see* **Totemism**
 Tylor, Edward B. 94, 618, 1389
Animism: Humanity's Original Religious Worldview 83–91

Animism: A Contemporary Perspective 81–83
Anishnabeg Culture 91–93, 979
American Indians *see* North America – Native Americans
Amish *see* Christianity (6c3) – Anabaptist/Mennonite Traditions
amulets 103, 156, 223, 1017, 1235, 1478, 1543, 1658, 1702
androcracy 584
Anthropic Principle 94, 1435, 1744
anthropocentricism
 affinity with
  Descartes 473
  Guha, Ramachandra 1150
  Inuit 851
  Krutch, Joseph Wood 974
  natural laws 1170
  Oikos 1220
  Umbanda 1676
 antagonism toward
  anarchist critique 50
  Confucianism 408, 410, 411
  Dragon Environmental Network 506
  environmental ethics 598, 600
  Gebara, Ivone 689
  Heidegger, Martin *see* Heidegger, Martin
  Moltman, Jürgen 1098
  Nash, James 1297
  radical environmentalism 518, 1326, 1719
  Schumacher, Ernest Friedrich 1491
  Schweitzer, Albert 1493
  Shepard, Paul 1538
  Williams, Delores S. 1751
 bias of, western religious 63, 1400
 Christianity 68, 316, 329, 331, 332, 342, 354, 356, 357, 368, 372, 379, 394, 397, 511, 697, 1165, 1571
  Eastern Orthodox 334
 contrasted with ecocentrism 416, 456, 458, 518, 519, 567, 598, 600, 848, 886, 1339, 1368
 contrasted with biocentrism 176–179, 436, 936, 1149, 1330, 1547, 1753
 contrasted with cosmocentricism 356, 1540
 Earth Bible 515
 Fascism 641
 Islam 818, 886, 1321 (*see also* Islam and Post-Anthropocentrism)
 Teilhard de Chardin, Pierre 1628
Anti-defamation league 1245
Anthropologists 94–96, 1373
Anthropology as a Source of Nature Religion 96–98 (*see also* Animism; Ecological Anthropology; Ecology and Religion; Ethnobotany; Ethnoecology, Ritual and Anthropology)

anthropology, postmodern environmental *see* Ecological Anthropology
Anglicanism *see* Christianity (6c4) – Anglicanism (Reformation Traditions)
Apache *see* North America – United States, Native Americans
Appiko Movement 101
apocalypticism
  apocalyptic literature 917, 928, 929
  Christianity *see* Apocalypticism in Medieval Christianity
  environmental 804, 1132–1133, 1329, 1377
  feminist theology 362
Aquinas, Thomas 102–103
  abortion 13, 653, 655
  animals 356, 376
  homosexuality 791
  natural theology 210, 327, 329, 381, 1177, 1406
Aradia 103–104
Archambault, JoAllyn
  contribution in this encyclopedia, *see* Bison Restoration and Native American Traditions
archeomythology 696
Architecture 104–105
  Aztec 144
  Buddhist 1667
  Center for Maximum Potential Building Systems 665–666
  Christian 325, 335, 724, 725
  Confucianism 410
  Egypt 579
  geodesic dome 568, 676–677
  Greek 274, 467
  green 275, 665
  green man *see* Green Man
  Incas 822
  Islamic 866, 868, 1324,
  monastic 335, 1404
  Roman 1443
  temple 274, 467
  Trees *see* Trees – as Religious Architecture
  Yolunga *see* Yolunga Ceremonial Architecture
Argüelles, José *see* New Age
  contribution in this encyclopedia, *see* Harmonic Convergence and the Spiritualization of the Biosphere
Århem, Kaj
  contribution in this encyclopedia, *see* Tukanoan Indians
Aristotle *see* philosophy
Ariyaratne, Ahangamage Turdor (A.T.) 105–106, 240, 1482, 1492
Arnold, Ellen L
  contributions in this encyclopedia, *see* Hogan, Linda; Silko, Leslie Marmon

Arnold, Phillip P.
  contributions in this encyclopedia, *see* Haudenosaunee Confederacy; Lyons, Oren
Arnold, Ronald 1755–1756
Arrernte Increase Ceremonies (Central Australia) 106–107
Art 107–114
  American 490
    Cole, Thomas 303, 1153, 1425
    Franck, Frederick 276
    Hudson River School 303, 490, 1425
    Romanticism *see* Romanticism – American
  and science 113
  Asian art 303 (*see also* Aesthetics in Nature in China and Japan)
  Buddhism 232, 235
  Confucianism 297, 410
  Daoist 51
  Hindu 446, 586, 766, 776
  Australia *see* Aboriginal Art; Rock Art – Australian Aboriginal
  Baltic indigenous 156, 157
  burning man 246, 247
  Celtic 282–285, 302
  Christian 157, 168, 301–303, 363, 585 (*see also* Christian Art)
  Egyptian 576
  golden section 109–110
  mandalas 109, 327, 771, 773, 898, 1457, 1619
  Paleolithic *see* Paleolithic Art; Paleolithic Religions
  photography
    Adams, Ansel *see* Adams, Ansel
  rock art *see* Rock Art – Australian Aboriginal; Rock Art – Batwa; Pygmies; Rock Art – Chewa; Rock Art – Hadzabe/Sandawe; Rock Art – Northern Sotho; Rock Art – Sintu; Rock Art – Western United States; San Apocalyptic Rock Art
  Roman 1411–1412
  Shamanism *see* Shamanism – and Art
  Yoruba *see* Wenger, Susan, Yoruba Art and the Oshogbo Sacred Grove
Art of Living Foundation 115–118 (*see also* adjacent, Shankar, Sri Ravi on Consciousness, Nature and the Art of Living)
Arthur, Shawn
  contribution in this encyclopedia, *see* Paganism and Technology; Tattoos
Asante Religion (Ghana) 118–121
Ásatrú *see* Heathenry – Ásatrú
Asceticism 121–122
  Christianity 45, 99, 315, 1309
  Eastern Orthodox 335, 336
  Hinduism/Buddhism 31, 301, 828, 1150

Islam 867, 1605
Maimonides 938
Shugendo 1767
Asia
  Eastern Asia
    aesthetics and nature *see* Aesthetics and Nature in China and Japan
    Buddhism *see* Buddhism – East Asia; Mongolian Buddhism and Taimen Conservation; Thai Buddhist Monks; Zen Buddhism
  China
    animals *see* Creatures' Release in Chinese Buddhism
    environmentalism *see* Chinese Environmentalism
    fengshui *see* Fengshui
    nature *see* Chinese Traditional Concepts of Nature
    religions
      Daoism *see* Daoism
      Confucianism *see* Confucianism; Confucianism and Environmental Ethics
    Three Gorges Dam 293
    Ziran 296–297, 447, 1803, 1805
  Japan
    gardens *see* Japanese Gardens
    historical sites *see* World Heritage Sites and Religion in Japan
    mountains *see* Mt. Hiei
    nature *see* Japanese Love of Nature
    religions (*see also* Japanese Religions)
      Buddhism
        Zen *see* Zen
      Shinto
        altars 1733
        Amaterasu 1607
        dance 444–445
        homosexuality 792
        kami *see* gods, goddesses, deities and nature spirits
        nature 17, 289
        rituals 1607, 1731
        shrines *see* Altars and Shrines
      Shugendo 1767–1768
      whales *see* Whales and Japanese Culture
      writers
        Kawabata, Yasunari *see* Kawabata, Yasunari
        Matsuo Bashô *see* Matsuo Bashô
        Michiko, Ishimure *see* Ishimure, Michiko
        Minakata, Kumagusu *see* Minakata, Kumagusu
        Miyazawa, Kenji *see* Miyazawa, Kenji
        Umehara, Takeshi *see* Umehara, Takeshi

Korea
  creation myth 1458
  Earth Charter 1581
  religion (see also **Buddhism – East Asia**)
    Confucianism, influence of 408, 411
    Shamanism see **Neo-Shamanism; Shamanism – Traditional**
  landscape see **Korean Mountains**
  Lee-Park, Sun Ai 313
Mongolia see **Mongolian Buddhism and Taiman Conservation; Teilhard de Chardin, Pierre; Tibet and Central Asia**
  Yunnan Region see **Yunnan Region**
Central Asia see **Asia – Tibet and Central Asia**
gods and goddesses see **gods, goddesses, deities and nature spirits**
Islam see **Islam**
martial arts see **Martial Arts**
Southern Asia
  ahimsa see **ahimsa**
  Gandhi, Mohandas see **Gandhi, Mohandas**
  gods and goddesses see **gods, goddesses, deities and nature spirits**
  India 823–827
    Bhagwan Jambeshwar (Jambaji) 194–195
    cows see **organisms – fauna**
    dance see **Indian Classical Dance**
    environmental activists see **Amte, Baba; Bahuguna, Sundarlal; Shiva, Vandana**
    Environmental movements see **Appiko Movement; Auroville; Chipko Movement; Ralegon Siddhi**
      Narmada Bachao Andolan 47, 827, 1150
      Sankat Mochan Foundation 778
    Guha, Ramachandra 301, 1150, 1332, 1369
    Kabir 217, 1782
    Laws of Manu 69, 480, 774, 1635
    literature
      Ramayana 101, 445, 480, 765–777, 778
      Mahabharata 101, 172, 480, 765–777, 1456, 1782
      Bhagavadgita see **Bhagavad Gita**
    Pantanjali 1782–1785
    peoples of India see **Bishnoi; Maldharis of Gujarat; Santal Region**
    rivers
      Ganga see **Hinduism and Pollution** (and adjacent, **River Ganga and the Clean Ganga Campaign**)

Yamuna see **Yamuna**
Ramanuju 172, 765, 768, 772–774
Shankara 772, 774
Sikhism see **Sikhism**
  Adi Granth (Guru Granth Sahib) 1549–1550
  Guru Nanak 1549–1550, 1782
spiritual leaders see **Aurobindo, Sri**
trees see **India's Sacred Groves; Santal Region**
Varanasi 778, 826, 1356
villages see **Ragelon Siddhi**
Vishwa Hindu Parishad (VHP) 709
Vivekananda, Swami 1150, 1340–1341
Jainism see **Jainism**
Nepal 241, 586, 709, 768, 858, 1058, **1190–1192**, 1517, 1771
Pakistan 658, 859, 861–862, 1341, 1811, 1813
  Kalash see **Kalash Culture**
  seeds see **Seeds in South Asia**
Sri Lanka 105, 240, 404, 586, 858, 1692
  Sarvodaya Shramadana movement see **Sarvodaya Shramadana Movement**
  Ariyaratne, Ahangamage Turdor (A.T.) see **Ariyaratne, Ahangamage Turdor (A.T.)**
  pilgrimage see **Pilgrimage to Sripada**
Tantra see **Tantra**
Rajneesh, Bhagwan Shree 1197, 1620
Southeastern Asia see **Southeast Asia** 1582–1585
Angkor Wat 769, 770, 771, 1583
Indonesia
  Freeport see **Freeport (West Papua, Indonesia)**
  Gunung Mulu National Park (Borneo) 1046
  Mandailing people see **Mandailing People**
  Penan see **Manser, Bruno and the Penan of Sarawak; Penan Hunter-Gatherers**
  Senoi see **Senoi**
Philippines 105, 537, 1041–1042, 1071, **1275–1277**, 1408, 1583–1584
  Philippine Department of the Environmental and Natural Resources (DENR) 1071
Thailand
  caves see **Caves – Sacred**
  Dai people 1796
  monasteries see **Siam's Forest Monasteries**
  monks see **Thai Buddhist Monks; Trees – Sacred**

Payutto, Phra Dhammapitaka see **Payutto, Phra Dhammapitaka**
Sivaralsa, Sulak see **Sivaralsa, Sulak**
Yantra, Phra 1629
Tibet and Central Asia 1636–1638
Iran
  Bahai'i see **Bahai'i Faith; Bahai'i Faith and the United Nations**
  birth control 861
  environmentalism see **Islam and Eco-justice; Islam and Environmentalism in Iran**
  Nasr, Seyyed Hossein see **Nasr, Seyyed Hossein**
  Zoroastrianism see **Zoroastrianism**
  water see **Water in Zoroastrianism**
  Zarathushtra 510–511
  Zohar 543–544, 1729 (see also **Kabbalah and Eco-theology**)
Tibet
  Bon see **Bon**
  Buddhism 704 see also **Buddhism – Tibetan; Ladakh Buddhism**
  Dalai Lama 1100 see **Dalai Lama**
  sacred mountains 1797
  Mount Everest 1457
  Mount Kailas 1457
Western Asia
  Attrahasis Epic 653
  Babylon 99, 123, 431, 570, 653, 724, 755, 1344–1346, 1521
  Enuma Elish 431, 534
  fertile crescent 84, 85, 287, 552
  Israel
    anarcho-primitivism see **Anarcho-Primitivism and the Bible**
    environmentalism see **Israel and Environmentalism**
    Israelites 74, 88, 176, 304, 434, 573, 661, 662, 791, 927, 937, 938, 1442, 1503 (see also **Hebrew Bible**)
    Gordon, Aharon David see **Gordon, Aharon David**
    Gush Emunim see **Gush Emunim**
    Jerusalem 56, 74, 99, 434, 571, 733, 889–890, 989, 1021, 1091, 1811
    Judaism see **Judaism**
    six-day war 732–733
    Zionism 25–26, 177, 890, 912, 934, 1696
  Mesopotamia see **Mesopotamia – Ancient to 2000 B.C.E.**
    agriculture 573, 635
    Gilgamesh 431–433, 618, 1090, 1516
    gods and goddesses see **gods, goddesses, deities and nature spirits**
    myths see **Creation Myths of the Ancient World**
    plants 621
Asoka, emperor see **Buddhism**

Association for Holotropic Breathwork 214 (*see also* **Breathwork**)
Association of Diviners 1790
Astrology 123–124, 144, 295, 636, 706, 771, 932, 940, 1728–1729
Astronauts 125–126, 684, 1210, 1586
astrophysics *see* **Science**
Astroshamanism *see* **Shamanism**
Athavale, Pandurang Shastri 126–127, 1613–1614
Attenborough, David 1074, 1357
ATWA (Air, Trees, Water and Animals) 127–128
Atwood, Margaret 256, 260
Au Sable Institute 129, 370, 589, 1213
Aurobindo, Sri 130–131, 132, 615
Augustine, Saint *see* **Christianity**
Auroville 131, 132–133
Auschwitz *see* **Europe – Western**
Australia *see* **Oceania**
Australian Poetry 137–138
Autobiography 138–140, 249, 858
Avebury *see* **Europe – Northern**
Averroes 1258, 1260, 1278
Ayahuasca 39, 141–142, 597, 620–621, 743, 1432–1433, 1527
axis mundi 57, 491, 590, 635, 989, 1398, 1503
Aztecs *see* **MesoAmerica**
Aztec Religion – Pre-Colombian 143–147 (*see also* adjacent, Flower Song – Xochicuicatl; A Song of Sorrow – Icnocuicatl; The Fall of Tenochtitlan; Tlatelolco)

B

Babylon *see* **Asia – Western**
Backes, David
 contribution in this encyclopedia, *see* Olson, Sigurd F.
Bacon, Frances *see* **Science**
Bacon, Roger 1209, 1278
Back to the Land Movements 148–151, 1329
Baha' i Faith (apocalypticism) 151–152
Baha' i Faith and the United Nations 153–154
Bahn, Paul G.
 contributions in this encyclopedia, *see* Burial Practices – Prehistoric; Cannibalism – Paleolithic; Makapansgat Cobble; Paleolithic Art; Paleolithic Religions
Bahuguna, Sunderalal 101, 154–155, 300–301, 775, 826, 1550, 1626–1627
Bainbridge, William
 contributions in this encyclopedia, *see* Family, The (Children of God); Fertility and Secularization; Process, The; Science Fiction; Scientology; Technological Immortality; Utopian Communities
Baker, Don
 contribution in this encyclopedia, *see* Korean Mountains
Baker-Fletcher, Karen 367, 610
 contributions in this encyclopedia, *see* Christianity (7g) –Womanism; Walker, Alice
Bakken, Peter
 contributions in this encyclopedia, *see* Sittler, Joseph A. Jr.; Stewardship
Bakunin, Mikhail 49–50
Balaam 75, 756–757
Balée, William L.
 contribution in this encyclopedia, *see* Ethnobotany (with Merideth Dudley)
Baltic Indigenous Religions 155–158
Banda, Dr. Hastings Kamazu 1216–1217
Banda, Mangadzi 1028–1029
Banyacya, Thomas 200–201, 796
Barbe Baker, St. Richard 152, 1081
Bari, Judi *see* **Anarchism**
Barlow, Connie 613, 630
 contribution in this encyclopedia, *see* Evolutionary Evangelism (with Michael Dowd)
Barnhill, David Landis 1373
 contributions in this encyclopedia, *see* Aesthetics in Nature in China and Japan; Buddhism – East Asia; Japanese Gardens; Kawabata, Yasunari; Le Guin, Ursula K.; Matsuo Bashô; Matthiessen, Peter; Rexroth, Kenneth
Barsam, Ara
 contribution in this encyclopedia, *see* Schweitzer, Albert
Bartlett, Brian
 contributions in this encyclopedia, *see* Domanski, Don; Lilburn, Tim
Barth, Karl 342–343, 347, 382
Bartholomew I, Ecumenical Patriarch 158, 307, 338, 339–340, 973, 1546, 1770 (*see also* Bartholomew in His Own Words)
Bartholomew in His Own Words 159
Bassett, Libby
 contribution in this encyclopedia, *see* Environmental Sabbath
Bateson, Gregory 160, 266, 558, 615, 1342, 1437
Baugh, Tom
 contribution in this encyclopedia, *see* Friends – Religious Society of (Quakers)
Baum, Robert 789
 contributions in this encyclopedia, *see* Diola (West Africa); West Africa
Baumann, John
 contribution in this encyclopedia, *see* Alpha Farm
Beat Generation Writers 161–162 (*see also* Snyder, Gary – and the Invention of Bioregional Spirituality)
Behn, Sarja 155, 826
Bekoff, Marc 72, 165
 contribution in this encyclopedia, *see* Cognitive Ethology, Social Morality, and Ethics
Bellah, Robert 488–489, 1173, 1630
Bellarsi, Franca
 contribution in this encyclopedia, *see* Beat Generation Writers
Benavides, Gustavo
 contribution in this encyclopedia, *see* Ecology and Religion
Benedict, Saint *see* **Christianity**
Benedictines *see* **Roman Catholic Religious Orders**
Bennett, David
 contribution in this encyclopedia, *see* Birch, Charles
Bennett, John G. 162, 546–547, 731
Benson, Robert W.
 contribution in this encyclopedia, *see* U'wa Indians (Columbia)
Bentham, Jeremy 601, 1429
Berdnyk, Oles 1189
Berg, David Brandt *see* **Moses David**
Berger, Helen
 contribution in this encyclopedia, *see* EarthSpirit Community
Bergmann, Sigurd 382, 407
 contributions in this encyclopedia, *see* Altner, Gunter; Architecture; Christianity in Europe; Composting
Berkes, Fikret 1368, 1650
 contributions in this encyclopedia, *see* James Bay Cree and Hydro-Quebec (and adjacent, TEK In Our Common Future)
Berman, Morris 163–164, 1762
Berman, Phyllis 1714
Bernard, Penelope S.
 contributions in this encyclopedia, *see* Watkins, T.H.; Zulu Ancestors and Ritual Exchange; Zulu Culture, Plants and Spirit Worlds
Bernbaum, Edwin
 contribution in this encyclopedia, *see* Sacred Mountains
Berry, Evan
 contributions in this encyclopedia, *see* Social Science on Religion and Nature

(with James D. Proctor); Wilson, Edward O.
Berry, Thomas 164–166
　American Teilhard Society 1377
　contribution in this encyclopedia, see Thomas Berry on Religion and Nature 166–168
　creation-centered theology 332, 680–681, 1406, 1591, 1616, 1785
　criticisms of 1212–1213, 1570
　Genesis Farm see Genesis Farm
　Green Sisters Movement see Green Sisters Movement
　Miriam McGillis and Genesis Farm 612, 691
　shamanic personality 428
　universe story 426, 630, 681, 1326, 1378
Berry, Wendell 151, 169–170, 249, 310, 540, 811, 988, 1080, 1753
Best, Steven
　contribution in this encyclopedia, see Watson, Paul – and the Sea Shepherd Conservation Society
Bestiary 170–172, 1254
Betcher, Sharon V.
　contributions in this encyclopedia, see Commons and Christian Ethics; Sabbath-Jubilee Cycle; Spirit and Nature
Bey, Hakim (Wilson, Lamborn) 55, 1347
Bhagavadgita (Bhagavad Gita) 127, 172, 300, 481, 765, 772, 774, 780, 1149, 1368, 1614, 1783
Bhatt, Chandi Prasad 300–301, 827
Bhikku, Santikaro
　contribution in this encyclopedia, see Buddhadasa Bhikku
Bible, The
　abortion 654, 661, 668
　Anarcho-primitivism see Anarcho Primitivism and the Bible
　animals see Animals in the Bible and Qu'ran; Dogs in the Abrahamic Traditions
　Catholic religious orders see Roman Catholic Religious Orders
　Cowboy Spirituality 430–431
　creation see Creation Story in the Hebrew Bible; Creationism and Creation Science
　Earth Bible see Earth Bible
　Ecofeminism see Ecofeminism and Biblical Interpretation
　Evangenicalism see Christianity (7i) – An Evangelical Perspective on Faith and Nature
　genetic engineering see Jewish Law and Genetic Engineering
　Hebrew Bible see Hebrew Bible; Judaism

Holy Spirit 378, 704
literalism 435–436, 1575
Muir, John 1127
Scopes Trial see Scopes Trial
stewardship see Biblical Foundations for Christian Stewardship
trees 1660
use in Israel 889
Women's Bible 361
Biblical Foundations for Christian Stewardship 173
Biehl, Janet 13, 50, 55, 1569–1570
Bigfoot 174–175
Binet, Rene 735
Bingham, Reverend Sally 309
Biocentrism (see also Biocentric Religion, A Call For)
　and abortion 13–14
　and Christianity 366, 378
　contrasted with anthropocentrism 598, 936
　deep ecology see Deep Ecology
　Gaia Mass 682
　Goodall, Jane see Goodall, Jane
　Gorbachev, Mikhail 1682
　Jackson, Wesley S. 892
　left biocentrism see Left Biocentrism
　Muir, John 1127
　Qur'an, The 1321
　radical environmentalism 1327, 1330–1333, 1355, 1719 (see also Radical Environmentalism)
　Sierra Club 1547
　song writers 1134
Biocentric Religion, A Call For 176–179
biocosmic theory of ethnogenesis 1437
biogenetic law 735
Biodiversity 179–181
　Africa 49, 958–959 (see also Biodiversity and Religion in Equatorial Africa)
　Amazon 208
　cultural diversity 1338
　Christianity 353, 373, 377, 542, 1308, 1444
　Confucianism 412
　conservation of 193, 521, 774–775, 831, 869–170, 938, 1171, 1482, 1491, 1647, 1662, 1798 (see also Conservation Biology; Biophilia)
　criticisms of 1332
　decline 133, 699, 1169, 1277, 1539
　Ecofeminism 534
　Iran 869–870
　Radical Environmentalism 521
　sacred sites 1069
　seeds see Seeds in South Asia
　Southeast Asia 1583
　Wilson, Edward O. 546, 1746
Biodiversity and Religion in Equatorial Africa 182–183

biodynamic garden 692, 1406
Bioneers Conference 183
Biophilia 180, 183–188, 605
　and conservation biology 415, 1754
　advocates 436
　Daly, Mary 444
　Geophilia 693
Bioregionalism 188–189
　and environmental ethics 1328–1329
　Berg, Peter 188, 190, 1564, 1567
　biodiversity, conservation of see Biodiversity
　compared with Geophilia 693
　deep ecology 457–458, 1174 (see also Deep Ecology)
　globalization, opposition to see Globalization
　House, Freeman 188, 1329, 1564
　indigenous peoples, principles of see Indigenous Environmental Network; Indigenous Religions and Cultural Borrowing; Indigenous Activism and Environmentalism in Latin America; Natural History and Indigenous Worldviews; World Conference of Indigenous People
　industrialism, opposition to 54, 569, 846, 1002, 1370
　knowledge, local see Traditional Ecological Knowledge; Traditional Ecological Knowledge among Aboriginal Peoples in Canada
　natural law see Natural Law and Natural Rights; Natural Law Party
　North America see Bioregionalism and the North American Bioregional Congress
　Radical Environmentalism 458, 521
　reinhabitation 691, 726
　Snyder, Gary see Snyder, Gary – and the Invention of Bioregional Spirituality and Politics
　social movement see Back to the Land Movements
　watersheds 133, 202, 244, 1201, 1380 (see also Columbia River Watershed Pastoral Letter)
Bioregionalism and the North American Bioregional Congress 190–191
Biosphere Reserves and World Heritage Sites 192–193
Birch, Charles 194
Bishnoi 101, 194–195, 300, 774, 826
Bison Restoration and Native American Traditions 196–197
Black Elk 44, 72, 197–199, 795, 826
Black Mesa 199–202, 519, 787, 794, 796
Blackwelder, Brent
　contributions in this encyclopedia, see

Brower, David (with Gavin van Horn);
    A Christian Friend of the Earth
  Blackfoot Cosmos as Natural Philosophy
    202–205
Blackfoot confederacy *see* North America
    – United States
Blain, Jenny
  contributions in this encyclopedia, *see*
    Heathenry – Ásatrú (and adjacent
    Seidr); Sacred Sites in England (with
    Wallis, Robert J.)
Blair, John
  contribution in this encyclopedia, *see*
    Britain (400–1100)
Blake, William 51, **205–206**, 316, 482,
    596, 641, 1146, 1422–1423, 1611, 1615
Blavatsky, Helen Patrovna **206–207**,
    287, 1012, 1180, 1632–1633, 1728,
    1730
Bleich, Rabbi J. David *see* Judaism
Bly, Robert 1081, 1134
Bodhi Farm 1354
Boff, Leonardo 48, **207–208**, 213–214,
    332, 358–359, 404, 512, 783, 1406,
    1409
Bohane, Ben
  contribution in this encyclopedia, *see*
    Moro Movement (Guadalcanal,
    Solomon Islands)
Bohm, David **208–209**, 582, 946, 1266,
    1303, 1632
Bols, Rijk *see* ECOtherapy
Bon (Tibet) 209
Bonaventure *see* Christianity
Bond, George
  contribution in this encyclopedia, *see*
    Sarvodaya Shramanada Movement
Book of Changes see Confucianism
Book of Nature 137, **210–211**, 256, 400,
    463, 595, 1215, 1278, 1422, 1502, 1623,
    1635, 1679, 1728 *see also* Christianity
    (7h) – Natural Theology; Religious
    Naturalism
Bookchin, Murray 50, 55, 191, **457–458**,
    473, 580, 603, 725, 1328, 1569,
    1570–1571
Boniface, Saint *see* Christianity
Boone, Daniel *see* North America – United
    States
Borsodi, Ralph 150, 1490–1491
Boston Research Center for the 21st
    Century **211–212**, 243, 1581
botanical dimensions 1072
Bougainville (Papua New Guinea) **212**,
    1077
Bowman, Marion 658
  contributions in this encyclopedia, *see*
    Celtic Spirituality; Druids and
    Druidry
Boy Scouts *see* Scouting

Brady, Veronica
  contributions in this encyclopedia, *see*
    Australian Poetry; Wright, Judith
Brahman *see* Hinduism
Bramwell, Anna 451, 643
Bratton, Susan Power
  contribution in this encyclopedia, *see*
    Christian Art
Brazil *see* South America
Brazil and Contemporary Christianity
    213–214
Breathwork **214–217**, 1329, 1513
Breeding and Contraception **217–219**
    (*see also* population)
  abortion *see* Abortion
  abstinence 26, 99, 121, 122, 513, 549,
    864
  fertility *see* Fertility and Abortion;
    Fertility and Secularization
  Malthus, Thomas Robert *see* Malthus,
    Thomas Robert
Brent, Morgan
  contribution in this encyclopedia, *see*
    Ayahuasca
Brigit, Saint (Brigid or Brigantia) 351,
    219–220, 392, 854, 856
Britain *see* Europe – Northern
Britain (400–1100) 221–224
Broch, Harald Beyer
  contribution in this encyclopedia, *see*
    Fishers
Brook Farm 148, **224–225**, 1653
Brower, David 3, 140, 200, **225–226**, 310,
    906, 1545–1547
Brown, Lester 540
Brown, Vinson 227
Bruno, Giordano 32, 736, 1258, 1639,
    1729
Bryan, William Jennings 436, 454, 1502
Bryant, Page 528, 1512
Bryce National Park 387
Bube, Paul Custodio
  contributions in this encyclopedia, *see*
    Abortion; Cobb, John B. Jr; Jackson,
    S. Wesley "Wes"; Land Institute
Buber, Martin 52, **227**, 746
Buchholz, Rogene A
  contribution in this encyclopedia, *see*
    The Protestant Ethic (with Sandra
    B. Rosenthal)
Bucko, Raymond A.
  contribution in this encyclopedia, *see*
    Lakota
Buddha, The 227–229
  and anarchism 50–51
  and elephants 586
  footprint *see* Pilgrimage to Sripada
  nature 232–233, 1265, 1662
  on poverty 90
  statues 277

Buddha Amitabha *see* gods, goddesses,
    deities and nature spirits
Buddha Mahavairocana *see* gods,
    goddesses, deities and nature spirits
Buddhadasa Bhikkhu 230–231, 1543
Buddhahood of Grasses and Trees
    231–232
Buddhism
  animals 69–70, 814, 824 (*see also*
    Creatures' Release in Chinese
    Buddhism)
  anarchism 50–55, 519
  art 16–18, 111
  and Beat Writers 161 (*see also* Snyder,
    Gary – and the Invention of
    Bioregional Politics and Spirituality)
  Asoka, emperor 234, 480, 767, 770,
    1706
  beliefs
    anatman (no self) 241, 443, 1122, 1637,
      1706
    asceticism 227
    Buddha nature 231, 237–238
    compassion 238–239, 438, 972, 978,
      1121–1122, 1192, 1352, 1553, 1580,
      1692
    dependent co-arising 1019
    dharma 53, 231, 232, 237, 242, 680,
      1352, 1482
    emptiness 17, 46, 161, 229, 231, 848,
      898, 976, 1495
    enlightenment, (philosophical) 116,
      161, 231, 237, 240, 858, 900, 933,
      1049–1050, 1121–1122, 1192, 1657
    impermanence 18, 234, 377, 581
    interconnectedness 364, 847, 899 (*see
      also* Indra's Net)
    karma 219, 228, 233, 235, 438, 654,
      1706
    mindfulness 51, 52, 111, 234, 239, 242,
      244
    non-dualism 237
    reincarnation 443, 654, 1797
  Bon *see* Bon
  Buddha *see* Buddha
  Buddhadasa Bhikkhu *see* Buddhadasa
    Bhikkhu
  East Asian *see* Buddhism – East-Asian
  aesthetics *see* Aesthetics and Nature in
    China and Japan
  Mahayana 235, 848
  monasticism *see* Thai Buddhist Monks;
    Siam's Forest Monasteries
  scriptures and texts
    Heart Sutra 17, 898
    Lotus Sutra 1057, 1097, 1123
    Shingon Buddhism 898, 1458
  economics *see* Economics
  engaged *see* Buddhism – Engaged
  Aitken, Robert 240, 243, 519, 1801

1836 Index

Buddhist Alliance for Social Engagement (BASE) 240
Buddhist Peace Fellowship 240–241, 243
  international network of engaged Buddhists 240, 243
  Macy, Joanna see Macy, Joanna
  Nhat Han, Thich see Nhat Han, Thich
  Seed, John see Seed, John
  Soka Gakkai 211, 240, 243, 1199 (see also Soka Gakkai and the Earth Charter)
gardens 898
goddess worship 704
Hinayana 235
Huayan 237
issues
  abortion 14, 652, 654
  breeding 217, 219
  homosexuality 789, 792
  vegetarianism see Vegetarianism and Buddhism
Jataka tales see Jataka Tales (and adjacent, Great Monkey Jataka)
meditation see meditation
metaphysics see metaphysics
monasticism see Buddhism – East Asia
Mongolian Buddhism see Mongolian Buddhism and Taimen Conservation
nature, perspectives on 233, 253, 292, 900 (see also Buddhahood of Grasses and Trees)
North America see Buddhism – North America
  Naropa University see Naropa University
  Sakyamuni see Buddha
  Shingon Buddhism see Buddhism – East Asia
Tantric practices 236
tension with Islam 874
Tibetan 209, 249, 704, 978, 1636–1637, 1692, 1797 (see also Buddhism – Tibetan)
  Dalai Lama see Dalai Lama
  Ladakh Buddhism see Ladakh Buddhism
worldview 90, 289, 680
Zen see Zen Buddhism
  Kigen, Dogen see Kigen, Dogen; Dogen Kigen's Mountains and Rivers Sutra (excerpts); Mountains and Rivers Sutra by Zen master Dogen Kigen
  zazen 900, 1800, 1802
Buddhism – East Asian 231, 236–239
Buddhism – Engaged 239–241
Buddhism – North America 242–244
Buddhism – Tibetan 244–245
buffalo see organisms – fauna

Buijs, Gina
  contribution in this encyclopedia, see Venda Witch Beliefs
burial practices see death
Burial Practices (Prehistoric) 246
Burning Man 246–247
Burning Times 1239 (adjacent to Pagan Music)
Burroughs, Edgar Rice 1497
Burroughs, John 247–249, 595, 1172–1173
Burton-Christie, Douglas
  contributions in this encyclopedia, see Christian Nature Writing; Contemptus Mundi (adjacent to Christianity (4) – Early Church (Fathers and Councils)); Christianity (4) – Early Church (Fathers and Councils)
Butala, Sharon 249–250, 1080
butterfly effect 288
Byers, James H.
  contribution in this encyclopedia, see Ethics and Sustainability Dialogue Group (with James Nash)
Byrne, Peter 175, 660

C

caboclos see South America – Amazonia
Caddy, Eileen and Peter 288, 658–659, 1633
Caesar, Julius see Europe – Southern
Cain 85, 87, 222, 256, 482, 497, 591, 635, 755, 937, 1693–1694
California Institute of Integral Studies 131, 251, 1329, 1514, 1593, 1616
Callenbach, Ernest 252, 564–566, 1474
  contribution in this encyclopedia, see Ecotopian Reflections
Callicott, J. Baird 252–254, 458, 599–600, 604–605, 1103, 1233, 1377–1378, 1648
  contribution in this encyclopedia, see Natural History as Natural Religion
Campbell, Heidi
  contribution in this encyclopedia, see Motion Pictures (with Heather Elmatti)
Campbell, Joseph 254–255, 510, 615, 616, 942, 1607, 1749
Canaanites 176, 573, 756
Canada see North America
Canada Nature Writing 258–260
Candomblé of Brazil 260–265 (see also adjacent, Orixa Iroko)
Cannibalism 745, 1088, 1113, 1488, 1695 (see also Cannibalism (Paleolithic))
Cannibalism (Paleolithic) 265–266

Capra, Fritjof 266–267, 289, 641, 1002, 1303, 1593, 1611
capitalism see Economics
Caputi, Jane 532, 1521
  contributions in this encyclopedia, see Dirt; Sexuality and Green Consciousness
cargo cults 212, 846, 847, 1076–1077, 1762
Caribbean
  Cuba
    Santeria see Santeria
  culture see Caribbean Cultures
  Haiti
    Iwa Dambalah Wedo (Serpent Rainbow) 268, 1659
    Vodou see Trees in Haitian Vodou
  Jamaica
    Rastafarianism see Rastafarianism; Rastafarian Activism; Selassie, Haile (see also Cuero, Delfina)
  Trinidad see Mother Earth and the Earth People
Caribbean Cultures 267–269, 819, 1052, 1058, 1105, 1659
Carson, Rachel 269–271, 291, 595, 598, 1494 (see also adjacent, Carson on Sea Spirituality)
Carson on Sea Spirituality 270
Casas, Bartolomé de las 271–272, 991
Castaneda, Carlos 98, 272–273, 1528
Castro, Adrian
  contribution in this encyclopedia, see Ifa Divination
Cathars 513–514, 1405
cathedral forests see forests
Cathedral Forest Action Group 520
Cathedral of St. John the Divine 165, 166, 273–274, 352, 682, 683, 1158, 1755
Cato Institute 1756
Cattell, Maria
  contributions in this encyclopedia, see Gardening and Nature Spirituality; Samia Culture
Caves – Sacred (Thailand) 276–277
Celestine Prophecy 278–280, 804
Celtic calendar 283
Celtic Christianity 222, 280–281, 351, 509, 853–854, 857
Celtic Spirituality 282–283, 1403
Central Arizona Project see North America – United States
Center for Action and Contemplation 1406
Center for Ecotherapy 563
Center for Education and Research in Environmental Strategies (CERES) 1685
Center for Health, Environment and Justice 541

Center for Human Ecology (Edinburgh, Scotland) 284–285
Center for Maximum Potential Building 655–656
Cetacean Spirituality 285–286
Champ, Joseph
  contributions in this encyclopedia, see Disney (with Rebecca Self Hill); Media (with Stewart M. Hoover); Theme Parks (with Rebecca Self Hill)
Channeling 287–288, 428, 446, 636, 637, 657, 1012, 1193, 1195, 1199, 1536, 1605, 1673, 1817
Chaos 288–289 (see also Chaos, Creation, and the Winter Garden; Complexity Theory)
Chaos, Creation, and the Winter Garden 289–290
Chappel, Christopher Key
  contributions in this encyclopedia, see Buddha; Jainism; Yoga and Ecology
Chappell, David W.
  contribution in this encyclopedia, see Soka Gakkai and the Earth Charter
Chartres Cathedral see Europe – Western
Chávez, César Estrada – and the United Farm Workers 290–292, 1578, 1703–1704
Chidester, David 460
  contributions in this encyclopedia, see Animism; Mutwa, Credo
Children of God see Family, The
Chinese Environmentalism 292–293
Chinese Religions see Confucianism; Taoism
China see Asia – Eastern
Chinese Traditional Concepts of Nature 294–299
Chipko 101, 154, 155, 195, 300–301, 535, 686, 774, 775, 776, 826, 827, 1136, 1300
Chidester, David 460
  contributions in this encyclopedia, see Animism; Mutwa, Credo
Chouinard, Yvonne 1119
Christ, Carol 301, 534, 648, 1522, 1570, 1593
Christian Art 157, 301–303
Christian Camp Meetings 304
Christian Environmentalism in Kenya 305–306
Christian Fellowship Church (Soloman Islands) 306, 1076–1077
Christian Friend of the Earth, A 307–310
Christian Nature Writing 310–312
Christian Theology and the Fall 312–314

Editors' Note: the main entries on Christianity are organized historically and by a numbered outline, and these begin after the first indexed Christianity entry, "Eastern versus Western", which appears immediately below this note. After this outline of the main entries is indexed, a subsequent index section beginning with "Christianity" provides details.

Christianity – Eastern versus Western 314–315
Christianity (1) – Introduction 316–317
Christianity (2) – Jesus 317–319 (see also adjacent, What Would Jesus Drive?)
Christianity (3) – New Testament 319–323
Christianity (4) – Early Church (Fathers & Councils) 324–326 (see also adjacent, Contemptus Mundi)
Christianity (5) – Medieval Period 326–328
Christianity (6a) – Roman Catholicism 328–332
Christianity (6b1) – Christian Orthodoxy 333–337 (see also adjacent, Eastern Orthodox Monasticism; Orthodox Spirituality; Common Declaration on the Environment: Common Declaration of John Paul II and the Ecumenical Patriarch His Holiness Bartholomew I)
Christianity (6b2) – Greek Orthodox 338–340
Christianity (6c1) – Reformation Traditions (Lutheranism and Calvinism) 340–343
Christianity (6c2) – Calvin, John – and the Reformed Tradition 344–348 (see also adjacent entry Reformed Tradition it its Own Words, The)
Christianity (6c3) – Anabaptist/Mennonite Traditions (Reformation Traditions) 348–351 (see also adjacent, David Kline on Amish Agriculture)
Christianity (6c4) – Anglicanism (Reformation Traditions) 351–352
Christianity (6c5) – Methodism (Reformation Traditions) 352–353
Christianity (7a) – Theology and Ecology (contemporary introduction) 354–355
Christianity (7b) – Political Theology 355–357
Christianity (7c) – Liberation Theology 357–360
Christianity (7d) – Feminist Theology 360–362
Christianity (7e) – Creation Spirituality 363
Christianity (7f) – Process Theology 364–365

Christianity (7g) – Womanism 367
Christianity (7h) – Natural Theology 368–369
Christianity (7i) – An Evangelical Perspective on Faith and Nature 369–371
Christianity (8) – Ecumenical Movement International 371–372
Christianity (9) – Christianity's Ecological Reformation 372–375
Christianity (index details)
  Africa see Africa – Christianity
  Anabaptist/Mennonite see Christianity (6c3) – Anabaptist/Mennonite Traditions
  Anglicanism see Christianity (6c4) – Anglicanism
  animals see Christianity and Animals (see also Cathedral of St. John the Divine; Christianity and Animals; Elephants; Nile Perch; Hyenas; Vegetarianism – Christian)
  antagonism toward 372, 350, 489, 518, 589, 735, 1183, 1247, 1636, 1755
  anti-materialism see Contemptus Mundi; Dualism; Dualist Heresies
  Aquinas, Thomas see Aquinas, Thomas
  art see Christian Art
  Augustine
    abortion 655
    apocalypse 99
    book of nature 210
    city metaphor 104
    fall, the 312
    medieval Christianity 327–328
    on animals 68, 77
    sexuality 1520, 1522
  Australia see Australia
  Benedict, Saint 274, 329, 1403–1404, 1405
  Bible, the see Bible, the
  Book of Nature see Book of Nature
  Bonaventure, Saint 167, 327, 670, 1660
  Calvin and the Reformed Tradition see Christianity (6c1) – Reformation Traditions (Lutheranism and Calvinism); Christianity (6c2) – Calvin, John and the Reformed Tradition
  Catholicism, Roman see Christianity (6a) – Roman Catholicism
  Benedict, Saint 274, 329, 725, 1403, 1405
  bishop's Conferences 331, 655 (see also Columbia River Watershed Pastoral Letter)
  nuns see Genesis Farm; Green Sisters Movement; Roman Catholic Religious Orders

Index

Pope, John Paul II 156, 159, 307, 329–332, 354, 400, 671, 1159, 1406, 1703 (*see also* Common Declaration on the Environment: Common Declaration of John Paul II and the Ecumenical Patriarch His Holiness Bartholomew I, adjacent to Christianity (6b1) – Christian Orthodoxy)
purgatory 157, 662, 1224, 1781
religious orders *see* Roman Catholic Religious Orders
Vatican 13, 193, 331, 363, 586, 670, 689, 788, 998, 1094, 1464, 1627
Celtic *see* Celtic Christianity; Celtic Spirituality
Church of Jesus Christ of Latter-Day Saints *see* Church of Jesus Christ of Latter-Day Saints
Clement of Alexandria 73, 325, 402, 814
contemplative traditions *see* Prayer and Contemplative Traditions
creation *see* Christianity (7e) – Creation Spirituality; Creationism and Creation Science; Creation's Fate in the New Testament
  dominion over 71, 76, 259, 308, 313, 319, 322–323, 328, 331, 341–342, 393, 454, 473, 502, 570, 915–917, 1068, 1168, 1201, 1284, 1390, 1428, 1519, 1689, 1695, 1735
  ex nihilo 28, 281, 348, 385, 928, 1258, 1260, 1679, 1747
  criticisms of *see* White, Lynn – Thesis of
Early Church *see* Christianity (4) – Early Church (Fathers and Councils)
Eastern *see* Christianity (6ba) – Christian Orthodoxy
ecotheology *see* Christianity – theology
ecumenics *see* Christianity (8) – Ecumenical Movement International; Eco-justice in Theology and Ethics; Eleventh Commandment Fellowship; Floresta; Gaian Mass; Moltman, Jürgen; World Council of Churches and Ecumenical Thought
Eden, Garden of *see* Eden and Other Gardens; Eden's Ecology; Restoring Eden
environmental groups, influence upon *see* Au Sable Institute; A Christian Friend of the Earth; Earth Ministry; Sierra Treks; Target Earth
Climbers for Christ 1042
environmental justice *see* Eco-justice in Theology and Ethics; Eco-justice Hermeneutics; Environmental Justice and Environmental Racism

Episcopalian Christianity *see* Christianity (64c) – Anglicanism (Reformed Traditions)
Episcopal Ecological Network 352
Episcopal Power and Light 309, 352, 541
eschatology 323, 342, 354–355, 783, 1572 (*see also* Creation's Fate in the New Testament)
ethics *see* Commons and Christian Ethics; Population, Consumption and Christian Ethics
Europe *see* Europe – Christianity
Evangelicalism *see* Au Sable Institute; Biblical Foundations for Environmental Stewardship; Christianity (7i) – An Evangelical Perspective on Faith and Nature; Evangelical Environmental Network; Restoring Eden; Sierra Treks; Stewardship; Target Earth
Fall, The *see* Fall, The
Feminist Theology *see* Christianity (7d) – Feminist Theology; Christianity (8g) – Womanism
Francis of Assisi *see* Francis of Assisi
gospels, synoptic 320
holy grail 33, 514
Holy Spirit 320–322, 345–346, 352, 354–355, 378, 382, 674, 759, 1054–155, 1067, 1098, 1207–1208, 1275 (*see also* Christianity and Nature Symbolism)
Image of God (*imago Dei*) 70–71, 76, 327, 333–334, 353–354, 356, 366, 375, 381, 454, 716, 939, 1167–1168, 1466, 1689
Interfaith organizations *see* Interfaith Center on Corporate Responsibility; Interfaith Council for Environmental Stewardship
Irenaeus 312, 324–325, 336, 513, 1045
Jesus (Christ) *see* Christianity (2) – Jesus (and adjacent, What Would Jesus Drive?); Jesus and Empire
Cosmic Christology
  Cosmic Christ 89, 123, 354, 356, 363, 670, 854
  cosmic cross 325
  cosmic redemption 342–343
  incarnation 217, 310–311, 317, 319–321, 324, 327, 329, 333, 354, 377, 437, 759, 1008, 1072, 1558
Mary 108 (*see also* Mary in Latin America; Virgin of Guadalupe)
Medieval *see* Christianity (5) – Medieval Period
Mesoamerica *see* Meso-America – Christianity
Methodism *see* Christianity (6c5) – Methodism (Reformation Traditions)

(*see also* Christian Fellowship Church (Solomon Islands))
Middle Ages *see* Christianity – Medieval
miracles 319–321, 437, 463, 928, 933, 1180, 1240, 1321
monasticism *see* Eastern Orthodox Monasticism (adjacent to Christianity (6b1) – Christian Orthodoxy; Religious Orders in the Roman Catholic Tradition (*see also* Christianity (4) – Early Church)
Mormons *see* Church of Jesus Christ, Latter-Day Saints
nature mysticism *see* nature mystics; nature mysticism (*see also* Christianity's Contemplative Traditions)
nature writing *see* Christian Nature Writing
New Testament 56–57, 77, 103, 308, 375, 791, 907, 1301, 1403, 1459, 1492 (*see also* Christianity (3) – New Testament; Creation's Fate in the New Testament)
North America *see* North America – Christianity
Oceania *see* Oceania – Christianity
Orthodoxy *see* Christianity (6b1) – Christian Orthodoxy
  Greek Orthodox *see* Christianity (6b2) – Greek Orthodoxy
    Bartholomew I *see* Bartholomew I, Green Patriarch; Common Declaration of John Paul II and the Ecumenical Patriarch his Holiness Bartholomew (adjacent to Christianity (6b1) – Christian Orthodoxy)
  Icons 61, 109, 336, 577, 1536, 1594
Protestant ethic *see* Protestant Ethic
Reformation Traditions *see* Christianity(6c1) – Reformation Traditions (Lutherism and Calvinism); Christianity (6c2) – Calvin, John – and the Reformed Tradition
Roman Catholicism *see* Catholicism – Roman
South America *see* South America (*see also* Christianity (7c) – Liberation Theology)
statements of environmental concern *see* Columbia River Watershed Pastoral Letter; Common Declaration of John Paul II and the Ecumenical Patriarch his Holiness Bartholomew (adjacent to Christianity (6b1) – Christian Orthodoxy)
stewardship *see* Stewardship

theology
  ecotheology see Christianity (7a) – Theology and Ecology (Contemporary Introduction); Christianity (9) – Christianity's Ecological Reformation; McDonagh, Sean
  feminist theology see Christianity (7d) – Feminist Theology; Christianity (8g) – Womanism
  liberation theology see Christianity (7c) – Liberation Theology
  natural theology see Book of Nature; Christianity (7h) – Natural Theology
  Pauline theology 77, 314, 511, 513, 1444
  political theology see Christianity (7b) – Political Theology; Christianity (7c) – Liberation Theology
  process theology see Christianity (7f) – Process Theology; Cobb, John B. Jr. (and adjacent, The Making of an Earthist Christian); Schweitzer, Albert
  Unitarianism see Unitarianism
  United Church of Christ 318, 540, 630, 791, 1152, 1277
  womanism see Christianity (7d) – Feminist Theology; Christianity (7g) – Womanism
Christianity and Animals 375–377
Christianity and Nature Symbolism 377–379
Christianity and Sustainable Communities 379–381
Christianity in Europe 381–383
Chryssavgis, John
  contributions in this encyclopedia, see Bartholomew I, Ecumenical Patriarch; Orthodox Spirituality; Christianity (6b1) – Christian Orthodoxy
Church of All Worlds 383–384, 520, 1174, 1243, 1264, 1328, 1499
Church of Euthanasia 384–385
Church of Jesus Christ of Latter Day Saints 383–388
Church of Nazareth Baptists (KwaZulu Natal, South Africa) 388–390
Church of Satan 1484
Cicero see Europe – Southern
Cihuacoatl – Aztec Snakewoman 390–391, 1052
Circle Sanctuary 392–393, 1235
Circles, Lone Wolf see Hardin, Jesse
Cistercians see Roman Catholic Religious Orders
Civilian Conservation Corp see North America – United States
Clark, John 55, 603, 1328, 1570

contributions in this encyclopedia, see Anarchism; Social Ecology
Clement of Alexandria see Christianity
Clemmer, Richard
  contribution in this encyclopedia, see Hopi-Navajo Land Disputes
Clifton, Chas
  contributions in this encyclopedia, see Aradia; Bigfoot; Entheogens
climate change 540–541, 869–870, 1159, 1214, 1292, 1647–1648
Climate Change Program 1152, 1766
Clinton, Bill see North America – United States
Coalition for Environmentally Responsible Economics 393
Cobb, John 343, 353, 364, 372, 393–397, 555–556, 601, 892, 1297, 1747
  contributions in this encyclopedia, see The Making of an Earthist Christian (adjacent to Cobb, John); Process Philosophy; Sustainability and the World Council of Churches)
coca see organisms – flora
coffee see organisms – flora
Coffey, Jane
  contribution in this encyclopedia, see Orixa Iroko
Cognitive Ethology, Social Morality, and Ethics 397–399
Coldwater Springs see North America – United States
Cole, Juan
  contribution in this encyclopedia, see Baha'i Faith
Cole, Thomas see Art
Coleridge, Samuel Tyler see Europe
Colligan-Taylor, Karen
  contribution in this encyclopedia, see Miyazawa, Kenji
Columbia River Watershed Pastoral Letter 399–401, 540
Committee for a Constructive Tomorrow (CFACT) 1757
Common Declaration on the Environment: Common Declaration of John Paul II and the Ecumenical Patriarch His Holiness Bartholomew I 339–340 (adjacent to Christianity (6b2) – Greek Orthodox)
Commons and Christian Ethics 410–404
compassion
  Buddhism see Buddhism
  toward nature 818,
  toward animals 1027, 1062, 1339, 1429, 1435, 1692, 1705
  Islam 860, 873–875
  Jataka tales 903
  Judaism 919, 1638
  communalism 306, 1472

Community Education Technical Advocates 48
Community Supported Agriculture 404–405, 525
Complexity Theory 288, 405–407, 1020, 1536
Composting 407, 525, 634, 691,726, 1407
Confucianism 407–411
  Analects 408
  agriculture 409, 412
  anthropocentrism 253
  Berry, Thomas 164
  Book of Changes 410, 412, 650
  dance 445
  environmental ethics see Confucianism and Environmental Ethics
  Fei, Han 655
  Homosexuality 792
  influence on art 16, 238
  Mengzi (Mencius) 297, 408–410, 1803
  Neo-confucianism 969
  virtue and ecology 1706–1707
Confucianism and Environmental Ethics 411–413
Congo River Watershed 413–415
Conradie, Ernst
  contribution in this encyclopedia, see Afrikaner Theology
Conroy, Dan 589, 1213
Conservation Biology 45, 415–417, 521, 580, 600, 1327, 1374
Con-spirando Women's Collective 418–420, 537, 689
Constant, Alhonse-Louis see Levi, Eliphas
Consumerism see Economics
Cook, Captain James 953, 1200
Cook, Jonathan
  contributions in this encyclopedia, see Ammons, A.R.; Desert Writers (Western United States)
Cooper, James Fenmore 42, 43, 139, 1153, 1211, 1425, 1488
Contemptus Mundi 324, 1705 (adjacent to Christianity (4) – Early Church (Fathers and Councils))
Corbett, Jim 685
Cornelius, Agrippa 933, 1729
Cornwall Declaration 849–850, 1756–1757
Coronado, Rodney – and the Animal Liberation Front 1331–1332
Corpus Christi 61, 348
Corrington, Robert 420, 1259–1260, 1292
  contribution in this encyclopedia, see Unitarianism
Cosmology 420–424
  Africa
    Central Africa 414
    Mbuti 1316
    West Africa 1510

and Ecosophy T 560–563
and Sri Ravi Shankar 116
Aymaran 62
Aztec 147
Bishnoi 195
Calvinistic 29
Candomblé 261
Chinese 164, 412, 649, 1368
Christian 325, 1367
ecology-based 208
economic 56
gift 57
Gurdjieff, Georges Ivanovitch 731
Hildegard of Bingen 762
Hindu 643, 1521, 1539
holistic 1722
Inuit 851–852
Kabbalistic 948
Laguna Pueblo 33
Lardil 1337
Maasai 1017
Maya 1060
medieval 931
New *see* Swimme, Brian
Norse 592
Odinist 1218
Penan 1047, 1267
Samia 1470
transcendent 1738
cosmetics 66, 921, 1235, 1510, 1644
Cosmic Christ *see* Christianity (2) – Jesus
Council of All Beings 191, 243, 417, 425–429, 457, 460, 521, 558, 612, 803, 1019, 1327, 1355, 1357, 1376
Cousteau, Jacques 1074, 1681
Covenant of the Unitarian Universalist Pagans 429–430
Coward, Harold
contribution in this encyclopedia, *see* Population and Consumption
Cowboy Spirituality 430–431
cows *see* organisms
Craddock, Elaine
contributions in this encyclopedia, *see* Chipko Movement (with Vinay Lai); Shakti
Cradle of Humanity *see* Africa – Central
Cranston, C.A.
contribution in this encyclopedia, *see* Quaker Writers in Tasmania (Australia)
Crawford, Harriet
contribution in this encyclopedia, *see* Mesopotamia – Ancient to 2000 B.C.E
Creation Myths of the Ancient World 431–434
Creation Story in the Hebrew Bible 434–435

creationism *see* Christianity
Creationism and Creation Science 435–437
Creation's Fate in the New Testament 437–438
Creatures' Release in Chinese Buddhism 438–439
cremation *see* death
Critical Perspectives on "Religions of the World and Ecology" 1375–1376
Croce, Paul Jerome
contributions in this encyclopedia, *see* Creationism and Creation Science; James, William
Crockett, Davey *see* Motion Pictures
Cronon, William 438, 1315
Crop Circles 439–440, 525, 1113, 1674, (*see also* Earth Mysteries)
Crovetto, Helen
contribution in this encyclopedia, *see* Ananda Marga's Tantric Neo-Humanism
Crowley, Aleister 706, 1021, 1231, 1484, 1739
cryonics 1625
Cuero, Delfina 440–441
cults 178, 217, 221, 267–268, 466, 503, 577, 585, 782, 846–847, 1076, 1499, 1510, 1517, 1658, 1671, **1686**, 1703, 1762, 1790, 1806–1807 (*see also* Utopian Communities)
Currier, Mary
contribution in this encyclopedia, *see* Anima Mundi – The World Soul
Curry, Patrick
contribution in this encyclopedia, *see* Middle Earth
Cusa, Nicolas of **441**, 1258
cultural materialism 96, 545, 744, 1342
Cyborgism 441–442

D

Dahl, Arthur 152, 1770
contributions in this encyclopedia, *see* Baha'i Faith and the United Nations; Brown, Vinson; Klingenthal Symposia; Men of Trees (East Africa); World Wide Fund for Nature
Dalai Lama (Tenzin Gyatso) **443**
Earth Summits 1681
environmental concern 243, 1769
government in exile 240, 978, 1636
Mongolia 1100
on population 122
peace plan in Tibet 241, 243, 1637
Dalton, Lisle
contributions in this encyclopedia, *see* Darwin, Charles; Linnaeus, Carl;

Malthus, Thomas Robert; Sagan, Carl; Wallace, Alfred Russel
Daly, Mary 361, **444**, 534, 1520, 1522
Daly, Herman *see* Economics
Dance
and bees 646–647
bear dance 717, 1096
cosmic dance 290
deer dance 1298, 1781–1782
Donga 1795
Gaian Mass 682
ghost dance *see* Ghost Dance
Indian dance *see* Bharata Natyam; Masai; Indian Classical Dance
Indian folk dance 1031
Nyau 1216
planetary *see* Planetary Dance
round dance 1541–1542
Shiva *see* Dance of Shiva
spiral 976, 1351, 1620
sun dance 795, 1253, 1657 *see also* Lakota Sun Dance)
trance dance 1347–1348, 1473
white deerskin dance 701
Daneel, Inus (M.L.) 21, 1055
contribution in this encyclopedia, *see* African Earthkeeping Churches
Daoism 447–450
Anarchism 50, 51, 54, 519, 1328
Art 16, 111, 238
criticisms of 1496
dancing 445
dao 16, 295–297, 410, 902, 989, 1169, 1706, 1802–1805
Daode jing 447, 448, 1803
deep ecology 456
Homosexuality 792
Lao Tzu (Laozi) 1, 50, 289 447, 448, 1050
nature 292, 901–902, 1169, 1803 (*see also* Chinese Traditional Concepts of Nature)
qi 16, 17, 295, 296, 411, 412, 417, 448–449, 649–650, 1050, 1057, 1368–1369, 1707
Radical Environmentalism 519, 1328
reproduction 655
Way of Celestial Masters 443
Yin/yang 50, 289, 295–296, 410, 447, 449, 649, 792, 901, 1001, 1021, 1121, 1496, 1707, 1803
Zhuangzi *see* Zhuangzi
Darling-Smith, Barbara
contribution in this encyclopedia, *see* Ruether, Rosemary Radford
Darlington, Susan M.
contribution in this encyclopedia, *see* Thai Buddhist Monks
Darré, Walther 450–451, 643
Darrow, Clarence 1502
Darwin, Charles 451–454

and creationism 435
and religion 79
and Wallace, Alfred 1711–1712
Darwinism *see* Creationism and
Creation Science; Darwin, Charles;
Haekel, Ernst; Scopes Trial
ethics 1166–1167
evolution 83, 397, 583, 628, 1435
opposition to 1269, 1302
science and technology 1209
Social Darwinism 531, 641, 1506
David, Moses 636
Davis, Andrew Jackson 287, 1180
Davis, John 190
contributions in this encyclopedia, *see*
Naropa University; Transpersonal
Psychology; Wilderness Rites of
Passage
Davis, Mark 520
contribution in this encyclopedia, *see*
Freeport (West Papua, Indonesia)
(with Alexandra Szalay)
Davis, Richard
contribution in this encyclopedia, *see*
Torres Straight Islanders
Davy, Barbara Jane
contributions in this encyclopedia, *see*
Cyborgism; Nature Religion
Dawson, Jan
contributions in this encyclopedia, *see*
Perelandra; Theosophy and
Ecofeminism
**Death and Afterlife in Robinson Jeffers
and Edward Abbey**
death (*see also* Church of Euthanasia)
animals in Judaism 921–922
Buddhism 978, 1706, 1801
burial practices 455, 719, 1107, 1700 (*see
also* Burial Practices (Prehistoric);
Green Death Movement)
cremation 134, 549, 720, 723, 779, 905,
1089, 1601, 1813
Dominicans 1406
Fall, The 916–917
funerals 296, 510, 672, 722
Hinduism 779, 1777
holocaust 784
hunting 806–807
Hyenas 814–815
in MesoAmerica 1087
Marshall, Robert 1048
Natural Death Centre 722
near death experiences 527, 1447
Pantheism 1749
pollution 1286
practices regarding *see* Burial Practices;
Green Death Movement
Romanies 1416
Sun Dance 986
symbolic 1749

technology *see* Technological
Immortality
Wicca *see* Wicca; Wicca – Dianic
Zoroastrianism 1814
Zulu 1815–1816, 1820, 1822–1824
Death and Afterlife in Robinson Jeffers
and Edward Abbey 455
De Boeck, Filip
contribution in this encyclopedia, *see*
Neo-Paganism and Ethnic
Nationalism
DDT *see* pesticides
Deegalle, Mahinda
contributions in this encyclopedia, *see*
Mt. Hiei (Japan); Pilgrimage to
Sripada (Sri Lanka)
Deep Ecology 456–459
ahimsa 31
and social ecology 725
anima mundi (world soul) 63
Bioregionalism 190–191, 1174
Buddhism 244, 1004, 1019
Church of All Worlds 383
conflict with Judaism 936
Conservation Biology 415–417
Council of All Beings 558, 612 (*see also*
Council of All Beings)
depth ecology *see* Depth Ecology
Devall, Bill 456, 457, 460, 600, 601,
675
Earth First! 416, 519, 1136
ecofeminism *see* Ecofeminism – Historic
and International Evolution
Ecopsychology 558
environmental ethics 473 (*see also*
Environmental Ethics)
Findhorn Foundation/Community 659
Fox, Warwick 458, 538, 558, 1329, 1655
Friluftsliv *see* Friluftsliv
indigenous practices 846
influence on ecopsychology 558
Institute *see* Deep Ecology, Institute for
Ireland 857
Jung, Carl 942
Left Biocentrism *see* Left Biocentrism
Mountaineering 1119
Naess, Arne *see* Naess, Arne
platform *see* Deep Ecology Platform
Sessions, George *see* Deep Ecology
Platform; Environmental Ethics
Spinoza, Baruch 933
Deep Ecology – Institute for 460–461,
1019, 1281–1282
Deep Ecology Platform 457, 458,
601, 1003, 1149 (adjacent to Deep
Ecology)
Deere, Phillip 461–462
deforestation *see* forests
Deism 210, 287, 394, 453, 462–464,
1176, 1178, 1257

deities *see* gods, goddesses, deities and
nature spirits
Deloria, Vine 198, **464–465**, 600
contribution in this encyclopedia, *see*
Sacred and the Modern World, The
Delphic Oracle 465–468
Delumeau, Jean 551
DeMallie, Raymond J.
contribution in this encyclopedia, *see*
Black Elk
Demons 43, 48, 49, 74, 209, 221, 223, 228,
259, 321, **468–469**, 590, 621, 721, 829,
1288, 1520
dependent co-arising *see* Buddhism;
Buddhism – Engaged
Depth Ecology 469–471
Descartes, René 168, 601,1307, 1589,
1591, 1746 (*see also* Descartes, René –
and the Problem of Cartesian Dualism)
Descartes, René – and the Problem of
Cartesian Dualism 471–474
desert fathers 316, 474, **1403–1405**
Desert Writers (Western United States)
474–475
Devall, Bill *see* Deep Ecology
Devas *see* gods, goddesses, deities and
nature spirits
Devereaux, Paul 527, 1475
Devi, Savitri 475–477
devil *see* Satanism
Devil's Tower (*Mato Tipi*, Bear's Lodge)
477–479
DeMallie, Raymond J.
contribution in this encyclopedia, *see*
Black Elk
DeWitt, Calvin 211, 1158, 1213, 1757
contributions in this encyclopedia, *see*
Au Sable Institute; Biblical
Foundation for Christian
Stewardship; Christianity (7i) – An
Evangelical Perspective on Faith and
Nature
Dharma – Hindu 69, 105, 172, **479–481**,
654, 763, 765, 823, 827, 829, 1294,
1706 (*see also* Hinduism)
Dharma – Buddhist *see* Buddhism
Diana 103, **481–482**, 1410–1411, 1508,
1742, 1800
Dianetics 1499–1500
Diatta, Alinesitoue 485, 1727
Dickens, Charles 1209
Diggers and Levellers 482–483 (*see also*
adjacent, Diggers' Song)
Diggers' Song 483
Dillard, Annie 249, 310, 311, **483–484**,
1079–1080
Diola (West Africa) 484–486 (*see also*
West Africa)
Dirt 486–487, 769
disequilibrium societies 546

Disney, Walt, and Companies 487–488, 814, 1074, 1157 (see also Theme Parks)
  Epcot 488, 490, 491
  Eisner, Michael 491
  motion pictures see Motion Pictures
Disney Worlds at War 489–493
Divine Waters of the Oru-Igbo (Southeastern Nigeria) 494–496
divination 123, 141, 144, 268, 295, 296, 297, 414, 422, 466, 619, 620, 621, 692, 753, 821, 940
  (see also Ifa Divination)
Dodge, Jim 188, 1328–1329
Dogen 239, 745, 1801 (see also Mountains and Rivers Sutra by Japanese Soto Zen Master Dogen Kigen (and adjacent, Dogen Kigen's Mountains and Rivers Sutra (excerpts))
Dogs in the Abrahamic Traditions 497–498
Dogs in the Islamic Tradition 498–500
dolphins see organisms
Dolphins and New Age Religion 500–501
Domanski, Don 502
Domestication 56, 67, 85, 133, 365, 502–504, 635, 651, 660, 673, 1043, 1758
Dominicans see Roman Catholic Religious Orders
Donaldson, Laura
  contribution in this encyclopedia, see Harmony in Native North America
Donga Tribe 504–506, 521, 557, 603, 1328
Doniger, Wendy 597, 1661
Dorothy Maclean 659 (adjacent to Findhorn Foundation/Community)
Doty, William G.
  contributions in this encyclopedia, see Campbell, Joseph; Jung, Carl – A Perspective
Douglas, Mary 95, 421, 468, 486, 664, 1021
Dowd, Michael 613, 630,
  contribution in this encyclopedia, see Evolutionary Evangelism (with Connie Barlow)
dowsing 113, 527, 563, 692, 1180, 1673
dowsers 527
Dragon Environmental Network (United Kingdom) 506–507, 521, 554, 556, 1328
Dragon Reclaiming Eco-magic (DREM) 554
Draper, Brad
  contribution in this encyclopedia, see Rock Art – Western United States

Droogan, Julian
  contribution in this encyclopedia, see Neo-Wessex Archeology
Druids and Druidry 274, 282, 283, 507–509, 661, 710, 754, 853–854, 1236–1237, 1247, 1264, 1461, 1660
Drums and Drumming 268, 509–510, 1037, 1816 (see also Pagan Music; Washat Religion)
Duncan, Isadora 444, 735
Dualism 510–512, 765, 772, 841, 941, 948, 1035, 1210, 1360, 1406, 1519, 1563, 1589, 1591, 1689
  (see also Descartes, René – and the Problem of Cartesian Dualism)
Dualist Heresies 512–514
Duncan, David James 667, 668, 1080
Duchrow, Ulrich
  contribution in this encyclopedia, see Globalization
Dudley, Meredith
  contribution in this encyclopedia, see Ethnobotony (with William Balée)
Dundzila, Vilius Rudra
  contribution in this encyclopedia, see Baltic Indigenous Religions
Dunn, Meghan
  contribution in this encyclopedia, see Fuller, Buckminster
Durkheim, Emile 95, 548, 852, 989, 1020, 1311, 1344, 1449
dwarves 592, 1092, 1218, 1224–1225
Dwyer, Jim
  contributions in this encyclopedia, see Callenbach, Ernest

E

earth acupuncture 527
Earth Bible 515–516, 532, 533
Earth Charter 193, 212, 243, 365, 516–517, 542, 707, 843, 959, 1213–1214, 1373, 1378, 1681–1682, 1765
  (see also Soka Gakai and the Earth Charter)
earth citizenship 681
Earth Community Network see Gaia Foundation and Earth Community Network
Earth Day 43, 44, 117, 243, 307, 394, 530, 542, 598, 599, 601, 602, 780, 909, 935, 1512, 1587, 1691
Earthdream 1348
Earth First! see Radical Environmentalism
Earth First! and the Earth Liberation Front 518–523
Earth Island Institute 225
Earth Liberation Front 54, 603, 651, 1326–1328, 1547 (see also Earth First! and the Earth Liberation Front; Radical Environmentalism)
Earth literacy 530, 691, 726, 1366
Earth Ministry 524–525, 540
Earth Mysteries 525–528, 556, 693, 1091–1092, 1600
EarthSpirit Community 529–530, 1264
Eastern Orthodox Monasticism 334 (adjacent to Christianity (6b1) – Christian Orthodoxy)
Eaton, Heather 532–533
  contribution in this encyclopedia, see United Nations' "Earth Summits" (with Bron Taylor and Iain S. Maclean)
Eckhart, Meister Johannes 363, 806, 813, 1258
Eco-apocalypticism 1132–1133
Ecocentrism see Left Biocentrism
Eco-church 530–531, 1213
Ecofascism 458, 531–532, 603, 641
Ecofeminism
  Adams, Carol see Adams, Carol
  bioregionalism 190
  Bible see Ecofeminism and Biblical Interpretation
  Center for Human Ecology 284
  Christianity see Christianity (7d) – Feminist Theology; Christianity (8g) – Womanism
  Con-spirando Women's Collective 418–419
  critique 1109
  Cyborgism 442
  Deep Ecology 457
  Environmental Ethics 599 602
  feminist spirituality 1330–1331
  Gebara, Ivone 689
  gender assumptions 473
  Greenham women's peace camp 536
  Griffin, Susan 251
  Hildegaard of Bingen 361
  history see Ecofeminism – Historic and International Evolution
  in Europe 382
  Judaism 912, 945
  Merchant, Carolyn see Merchant, Carolyn
  on nature 1521 (see also Merchant, Carolyn)
  Plaskow, Judith 532, 536
  Plumwood, Val 458, 538, 1367, 1519
  Ruether, Rosemary Radford see Ruether, Rosemary Radford
  Starhawk 54
  Theosophy see Theosophy and Ecofeminism
  urban 689
Ecofeminism and Biblical Interpretation 532–533
Ecofeminism – Historic and International Evolution 533–538

ecocide 384, 784
eco-crisis 371
Eco-justice in Theology and Ethics 539–543
Eco-justice Hermeneutics 515
Eco-kabbalah 543–544, 947
eco-kosher movement 568
Ecological Anthropology 544–547, 605, 1373, 1647 (*see also* Ecology and Religion; Rappaport, Roy A.; Harris, Marvin)
ecological footprint 275, 436, 666
eco-navy 728
eco-praxis 382
Eco-village Training Center 639
Ecological Buddhism *see* Buddhism – Engaged
Ecological Indian *see* American Indians as "First Ecologists"
ecological poetics 6, 7, 134–135, 1084 (*see also* Aboriginal Dreaming)
ecological reformation 316–317 (*see also* Christianity (9) – Christianity's Ecological Reformation; A Manifesto for North American Middle-Class Christians)
Ecology and Religion 251, 548–553, 605, 1373
Eco-magic 506–507, 554, 556–557, 1741
Economics 555–556
  alternative models 511, 591, 1004, 1317, 1336, 1408, 1150, 1221, 1674, 1736
  and eco-justice 539, 609
  and oil 1293
  Buddhist 555, 599, 1004, 1491
  capitalism
    criticisms of 48, 51, 858, 1003–1004, 1133, 1346, 1553,
    effects of 1776
    greening global 380 (*see also* Green Politics)
    religion 1309–1310
      Christianity 170, 329–330, 403, 436, 555 (*see also* Christianity and Sustainable Communities)
      support of 454
  community based 725
  consumerism 22, 30, 35, 128, 148, 151, 241–243, 315, 546, 555, 556, 568, 588, 774, 846, 895, 938
  consumption *see* Population and Consumption – Contemporary Religious Responses; Population, Consumption and Christian Ethics
  corporate responsibility *see* Interfaith Center on Corporate Responsibility
  criticism of 501, 988, 1031, 1639
  Daly, Herman 372, 396, 397, 555, 599, 602, 1297
  dominance in world affairs 396, 1294, 1766
  globalization 698 (*see also* Globalization)
  human development index 699
  Index of sustainable ecological welfare 396–397
  International Monetary Fund (IMF) 371
  Judaism *see* Sabbath-Jubilee Cycle
  Malthus, Thomas Robert *see* Malthus, Thomas Robert
  poverty 105, 117, 122, 269, 358–359, 404, 415, 666, 823, 870, 939, 957, 1150, 1296, 1305, 1454, 1763, 1769
  Roman Empire *see* Europe – Southern
  Smith, Adam *see* Economics
  subsistence 810, 1778, 1803
  sustainable 589, 988, 1409 1469 (*see also* Christianity and Sustainable Communities)
  Trade Related International Property rights (TRIPS) 699
  World Bank 34, 314, 371, 396, 415, 699, 836, 837, 869, 973, 1071, 1099, 1366, 1581, 1616, 1771
Eco-paganism 507, 556–557 (*see also* Donga Tribe; Dragon Environmental Network; Eco-magic; Earth First! and the Earth Liberation Front; Neo-Paganism and Ethnic Nationalism in Eastern Europe; Neo-Paganism in the Ukraine)
Eco-pagan anarchists 591
Ecopsychology 63, 457, 460, 557–559, 945, 1329–1330
eco-ritual 557
Ecosophy T 560–563, 600, 1149–1150
eco-terrorists 3, 1720
Ecotherapy (by Hans Andeweg and Rijk Bols) 563–564
Eco-Thomism 102, 331
Ecotopia 252, 564–566 (*see also* Ecotopian Reflections; Ecotopia – The European Experience; Utopian Literature)
Ecotopian Reflections 566–568
Ecotopia – The European Experience 568–569
ecotourism 457, 597, 1116
Eco-womanists 537 (*see also* Christianity (7g) – Womanism)
Ecumenical Movement *see* Christianity
Eden *see* gardens
Eden and Other Gardens 569–572
Eden's Ecology 572–575
Edwards, Felicity
  contributions in this encyclopedia, *see* Aurobindo, Sri; Knowledge, Knowing and Nature
Edwards, Jonathon *see* North America – Christianity
Egypt *see* Africa – Northern
Egypt – Ancient 575–577
Egypt – Pre-Islamic 577–580
Ehrenfeld, David 416, 580–581, 910
Ehrlich, Gretel 249, 581
Ehrlich, Paul 84, 394, 599
Einstein, Albert 94, 406, 582, 681, 1278, 1611
Eisenberg, Evan 635, 910
Eiseley, Loren 582–584
Eisenberg, Evan 635, 910
  contribution in this encyclopedia, *see* Eden's Ecology
Eisler, Riane 584
Eisner, Michael *see* Disney
El niño 615
Elat Chayyim *see* Judaism
Elephants 140, 176, 182, 415, 457, 584–588, 768, 814, 815, 824, 1483
Eleusis 433, 597, 717, 1250, 1686
Eleventh Commandment Fellowship 588–589, 973, 1213
Eliade, Mircea xiii–xiv, 108, 137, 164, 464, 486, 589–590, 989, 1103, 1449, 1520–1521, 1525, 1529, 1533–1534, 1555, 1784
Ellul, Jacques 56, 590–591, 1020
Ellwood, Robert
  contributions in this encyclopedia, *see* Blavatsky, Helen Patrovna; Eliade, Mircea; Theosophy
Elmatti, Heather
  contribution in this encyclopedia, *see* Motion Pictures (with Heidi Campbell)
Elohim 574, 746, 926, 948, 1240, 1672–1674
elves 82, 221, 637, 752, 1092, 1113, 1218, 1224, 1249, 1633
Elves and Land Spirits in Pagan Norse Religion 592–593
Elvey, Anne
  contributions in this encyclopedia, *see* Ecofeminism and Biblical Interpretation; Geneology and Spiritualities of Place (Australia)
Emenhiser, JeDon A.
  contribution in this encyclopedia, *see* G-O Road (Northern California)
Emerson, Joseph 1039
Emerson, Ralph Waldo 594–595 (*see also* Natural History as Natural Religion; Nature Religion in the United States; Thoreau, Henry David; Transcendentalism; Whitman, Walt)
  American romanticism 1425
  Christianity 1679
  manifest destiny 1040
  mountains 1119

Native Americans 1179
Pantheism 15, 248
slavery 1179, 1180
Transcendentalism 148, 1176, 1179, 1182, 1744, 1747
vanishing landscapes 1152, 1153
Emissaries of Divine Light 595, 1199
emptiness *see* Buddhism
endangered species act *see* animals
Engel, J. Ronald 1768
 contribution in this encyclopedia, *see* Biosphere Reserves and World Heritage Sites
Engels, Frederick *see* philosophy
Enlightenment, the *see* Europe
Enlightment (philosophical) *see* Buddhism
Engaged Buddhism *see* Buddhism – Engaged
England *see* Europe – Northern
Entheogens 33, **596–597**, 619, 751, 813, 1072, 1312, 1326, 1336, 1532 (*see also* Leary, Timothy; McKenna, Terrence)
Environmental Ethics **597–606**
 asceticism 122
 Buddhism *see* Buddhism – North America
 Callicott, J. Baird *see* Callicot, J. Baird
 Christianity
  emerging ethics 314 –375
  problem with *see* White, Lynn – Thesis of
 Confucianism *see* Confucianism and Environmental Ethics
 Cronon, William 438, 1315
 deep ecology *see* Deep Ecology
 Descartes, René *see* Descartes, René and the Problem of Cartesian Dualism
 history *see* Natural History as Natural Religion
 Indigenous people *see* Traditional Ecological Knowledge
 Islam *see* Islam and Environmental Ethics; Islam and Environmentalism in Iran
 Judaism *see* Tikkun Olam – A Jewish Imperative
 Leopold, Aldo 1180
 Naess, Arne *see* Naess, Arne
 nonduality 774
 Pagan *see* Pagan Environmental Ethics
 Radical Environmentalism *see* Radical Environmentalism
 Rolston III, Holmes *see* Rolston III, Holmes
 scholarship *see* Religious Studies and Environmental Concern
 Venice Declaration of Environmental Ethics 159
environmental justice 189, 290, 291, 309, 367, 400, 541, 674, 781, 840, 858, 877, 935, 1213, 1329, 1409, 1714 (*see also* Environmental Justice and Environmental Racism; National Council of Churches, Eco-Justice Working Group (USA))
Environmental Justice and Environmental Racism 165, 367, 603, 608–610
Environmental Protection Agency (EPA) 525, 609, 666, 1014, 1214, 1756
environmental racism 242, 367, 537 (*see also* Environmental Justice and Environmental Racism)
Environmental Sabbath 611, 1444
Environmentalism (and nature religion) 97, 98, 258, 279, 638
Epcot *see* Disney
Epic of Evolution 165, 491, **612–616**, 691, 707, 1326, 1372, 1376, 1683 (*see also* adjacent, Epic Ritual)
Epic Ritual 612–613
Epstein, Mikhail 1694
 contribution in this encyclopedia, *see* Russian Mystical Philosophy (with Adrian Ivakhiv)
equinoxes 123, 158, 167, 283, 422, 445, 510, 649, 721, 781, 853, 1237, 1244, 1248, 1299, 1361, 1381, 1601
Erhlich, Paul and Anne 1034
Esalen Institute 215, **615–616**, 1194, 1514
essentialism, gender 441, 705
Estes, Clarissa Pinkola 616, 1645
Ethics and Sustainability Dialogue Group 616–617
Ethnobotany **617–621**, 1647
Ethnoecology 547, **622–623** (*see also* Reichel-Dolmatoff, Gerardo – and Ethnoecology in Colombia)
ethnography 95, 97, 1230
Etsheni Sacred Stones 623–624
Europe
 Celtic Spirituality *see* Celtic Spirituality
 Christianity *see* Christianity in Europe
  Anglicanism *see* Christianity (6c4) – Anglicanism
  Annabaptist/Mennonite Traditions *see* Christianity (6c3) –Anabaptist/Mennonite Traditions; Book of Nature
  architecture *see* Green Man
  ecumenical movement *see* Christianity (8) – Ecumenical Movement International; Sustainability and the World Council of Churches; World Council of Churches and Ecumenical Thought
  globalization *see* Globalization
  Ireland *see* Northern Europe – Ireland
  Medieval Christianity *see* Apocalypticism in Medieval Christianity; Christianity (5) – Medieval Period
  Natural Theology *see* Christianity (7h) – Natural Theology
  organizations *see* Centre for Human Ecology
  orthodoxy *see* Christianity (6b1) – Christian Orthodoxy; Christianity (6b2) – Greek Orthodox Christianity; (6a) – Roman Catholicism
 people, influential
  Albert the Great *see* Albert the Great
  Altner, Günter *see* Altner, Günter
  Aquinas, Thomas *see* Aquinas, Thomas
  Bartholomew I, Ecumenical Patriarch 158–159, 307, 338, 339–340, 973, 1546, 1770
  Bridget *see* Bridget
  Cusa, Nicholas of *see* Cusa, Nicholas of
  Francis of Assisi *see* Francis of Assisi
  Hildegard of Bingen *see* Hildegard of Bingen
  McDonagh, Sean *see* McDonagh, Sean
  Moltmann, Jürgen *see* Moltmann, Jürgen
  Palmer, Martin *see* Palmer, Martin
  Schweitzer, Albert *see* Schweitzer, Albert
  Steiner, Rudolf *see* Steiner, Rudolf – and Anthroposophy
  Teilhard de Chardin, Pierre *see* Teilhard de Chardin, Pierre
 politics and political theology *see* Diggers and Levelers; Christianity (7b) – Political Theology
 Protestant Reformation *see* Christianity (6c1) – Reformation Traditions: Christianity (6c2) – Calvin, John and the Reformed Tradition
 Scotland *see* Northern Europe – Scotland
Coleridge, Samuel Tyler 43, 351, 1423, 1652
Eastern Europe
 Baltic religion *see* Baltic Indigenous Religions
 Blavatsky, Helen Petrovna *see* Blavatsky, Helen Petrovna
 Fedorov, Nikolai *see* Russian Mystical Philosophy
 Gorbachev, Mikhail 516, 1188
 Ivanov, Porfyrii Korniiovych 1189, 1438
 Koliada Viatichei *see* Koliada Viatichei
 Kropotkin, Peter *see* Kropotkin, Peter
 paganism *see* Neo-Paganism and Ethnic Nationalism in Eastern Europe; Neo-Paganism in Ukraine; Slavic Neo-Paganism
 philosophy *see* Russian Mystical Philosophy; Gurdjieff, Georges

Ivanovitch; Ouspensky, Pyotr Demianovich
Pravoslavia movement 1188
Ridnovira (Ukraine Native Faith) 1188
Romania
  gypsies *see* Romanies
  shamanism *see* Shamanism – Neo
Slavokia
  religion *see* Slavic Religion; Slavic Neo-Paganism
Pogacnik, Marko *see* Pogacnik, Marko
Soviet Union 298, 562, 1003, 1586, 1682
Stalin, Joseph 298, 1100
Tolstoy, Leo 52, 1640
Vernadsky, Vladimir I 679, 730, 739–740, 1437
Enlightenment, the 63, 211, 228, 328, 351, 368, 369, 453, 462–464, 471, 512, 580, 641, 670, 1033, 1053–1054, 1176, 1181–1184, 1421, 1424, 1428, 1539, 1653, 1676
European Parliament for the Green Party 1120
European Youth For(est) Action 568
gods/goddesses *see* gods, goddesses, deities and nature spirits
Holocaust 477, 934–935, 1103, 1625
Indo-Europeans *see* Proto-Indo Europeans
Northern Europe
  Druidry *see* Druids and Druidry
  Heathenry *see* Heathenry – Ásatrú
  Iceland 593, 728, 751–753, 1218–1220, 1708–1709
  Norway
    Frilufsliv *see* Frilufsliv
    Naess, Arne *see* Naess, Arne
    Norse Religions *see* Elves and Land Spirits in Pagan Norse Religion
  Saami *see* Saami Culture
  trees *see* Trees – Northern and Middle Europe
United Kingdom
  Britain
    anarchy 54
    Anglo-Saxons 221, 222, 991, 1041
    archaeology *see* Neo-Wessex Archaeology
    Avebury 283, 508, 1460–1461, 1599–1600
    Beowulf 174, 221–222, 751
    environmental organizations *see* Douga Tribe; Dragon Environmental Network
    middle ages *see* Britain **400–1100**
    politics *see* Diggers and Levelers (and adjacent, Diggers' Song)
    Prince Charles *see* Prince Charles
    raves *see* Raves
    roman influence *see* Roman Britain

sacred sites *see* Earth Mysteries; Glastonbury; Sacred Sites in England; Stone Circles; Stonehenge
Wallace, Alfred Russel *see* Wallace, Alfred Russel
Wicca *see* Wicca
Scotland 1503–1506
  faerie faith *see* Faerie Faith in Scotland; Rotting Tree Faerie
  Findhorn Community *see* Findhorn Foundation/Community
  human potential organizations *see* Centre for Human Ecology; Findhorn Foundation/Community
  stone circles *see* Stone Circles
Ireland 853–857 (*see also* Brigit)
  Celtic Religion *see* Celtic Christianity; Celtic Spirituality
  Ecotopias *see* Ecotopia – the European Experience
  music *see* Burning Times (adjacent to Pagan Music)
Renaissance, the 467, 526, 571, 697, 933, 949, 972, 990, 1021, 1277, 1278, 1728–1729
Romanticism *see* Romanticism in European History; Romanticism in European Literature
Southern Europe
  Greece
    acropolis 717–718
    Cicero 715, 1169
    classical *see* Greece – Classical; Greco-Roman World
    creation myths *see* Creation Myths of the Ancient World
    Delphi *see* Delphic Oracle
    landscape *see* Greece – Landscape
    mountains
      Olympus, Mount 716, 717, 719, 721, 738, 1457
      Parnassus, Mount 466, 717, 1457
    myths *see* Myths of the Ancient World
    Odysseus 433, 1050, 1509
    paganism *see* Greek Paganism
    philosophers *see* philosophy
    Ptolemy, Claudius 123, 715
    Pythagoras 110, 288, 814
    Sophists 711–712
    Virgil 1402, 1413, 1422
  Italy
    art *see* Art
    geography *see* Lake Pergusa
    Roman empire
      agriculture 1280, 1412
      Caesar, Julius 908, 1660
      Jesus *see* Jesus and Empire

religion *see* Roman Natural Religion; Roman Religion and Empire
Vatican *see* Christianity (6a) – Roman Catholicism
Western Europe
France
  Chartres Cathedral 274, 975
  Rousseau, Jean-Jacques *see* Rousseau, Jean-Jacques
  Teilhard de Chardin, Pierre *see* Tielhard de Chardin, Pierre
  van Gennep, Arnold 1388, 1451, 1600, 1749
Germany
  Auschwitz 193, 355, 642, 653 783–784
  Devi, Savitri *see* Devi, Savitri
  Himmler, Reichsfuhrer Heinrich 476, 526, 641
  Hitler, Adolf 355, 450, 451, 476, 477, 562, 640, 642, 1245, 1498
  National Socialism *see* National Socialism
  Nazism *see* National Socialism
  Odinism *see* Odinism
  Odinist Fellowhip 1219
  Trier's Cathedral *see* Green Man
  Inquisition 513–514, 1239
  Spanish conquest 61, 391, 1059, 1085, 1088, 1475, 1670
  Spanish revolution 50
  Wordsworth, William 139, 453, 813, 1404, 1419–1420, 1422–1424, 1747
  Yeats, William Butler 508, 633, 706, 710, 1224
Evangelical Environmental Network 275, 318, 370, 624–625, **624**, 850, 973, 1152, 1158, 1621, 1757
Everest, Mount 34, 683, 805, 1457, 1797 (*see also* Messner on Everest and Cosmos, adjacent to Mountaineering)
Evola, Julius **625–627**, 1187
evolution and evolutionary biology *see* Science
Evolutionary Biology, Religion, and Stewardship 627–629
Evolutionary Evangelism 629–631
Explorer Petroglyphs (Western United States) 632
Exxon 309, 310, 491, 849, 1756
Ezekiel 309, 434, 516, 571, 724, 757, 947, 1443, 1674

F

Faarlund, Nils 675
factory farms *see* agriculture
Faerie Faith in Scotland 633, 1504 (*see also* adjacent, **Rotting Tree Faerie**)
Fall, The 634–636
  Annabaptists and Mennonites *see*

1846 Index

Christianity (6c3) – Annabaptist and Mennonite Traditions
garden of Eden see Eden and Other Gardens; Eden's Ecology
Judaism 932 see Jewish Intertestamental Literature
nature 1174 (see also Christianity and Nature Symbolism; Wilderness Religion)
New Testament see Christianity (3) – New Testament
Reformed Traditions see Christianity (6c1) – Reformation Traditions (Lutherism and Calvinism)
Rousseau, René 1428
science 1209
theology see Christian Theology and the Fall; Christianity (7a) – Theology and Ecology (Contemporary Introduction); Christianity (7d) – Feminist Theology
Fall of Tenochtitlan; Tlatelolco, The 146 (adjacent to Aztec Religion – Pre-Colombian)
Family, the (Children of God) 636–637, 1197
Fantin, Shaneen
contribution in this encyclopedia, see Yolngu Ceremonial Architecture (Australia) (with Paul Memmott)
Fantasy Literature 637–638, 1250
Farrar, Janet and Stewart 1236–1237
Farm, The 149, 639, 1199
Fascism 603, 626, 639–643 (see also Ecofacism)
political, religion as a see Ecofascism; Fascism
Faulkner, William see North America – United States
Faulstich, Paul
contributions in this encyclopedia, see Aboriginal Art – Warlpiri; Ethnoecology; Geophilia; Natural History and Indigenous Worldviews; Rock Art – Australian Aboriginal; Sacred Space/Place
Fauna see Animals; organisms
Fauna Cabala 644–647
Feast of the Dead 1236
feminism (see also Feminist Spirituality Movement)
Christianity see Christianity (7d) – Feminist Theology; Christianity (7g) – Womanism
Daly, Mary see Daly, Mary
Ecofeminism see Ecofeminism
Feminist Spirituality Movement see Feminist Spirituality Movement
Goddess worship see Goddesses – History of

LeGuin, Ursula K. see LeGuin, Ursula K.
Pinkola, Clarissa see Pinkola, Clarissa
Spretnek, Charlene see Spretnek, Charlene
Walker, Alice see Walker, Alice
Wicca see Wicca – Dianic
Feminist Spirituality Movement 647–649
Con-spirando Women's Collective see Con-spirando Women's Collective
Cyborgism see Cyborgism
Feminine Principle of Creation 103
goddess spirituality 703
Starhawk see Starhawk
feminist theology see Christianity (7d) – Feminist Theology
Fenech, Louis E.
contribution in this encyclopedia, see Sikhism
Fengshui 292, 293, 296, 649–650, 692, 1091
Ferality 650–652
Ferguson, Marilyn 804, 943, 1195, 1303
Ferlat, Anne
contributions in this encyclopedia, see Kalash Culture (Northwestern Pakistan); Paganism – Mari (Mari El Republic, Russia)
fertility see Abortion; Breeding and Contraception; Fertility and Abortion; Fertility and Secularization; Judaism and the Population Crisis; Population and Consumption – Contemporary Religious Responses; Population, Consumption, and Christian Ethics
Fertility and Abortion 652–656
Fertility and Secularization 657–658
Fiala, Andrew
contributions in this encyclopedia, see Creation Myths of the Ancient World; Ovid's Metamorphoses
Ficino, Marsilio 63, 933, 1130, 1278, 1729
fiction see Apocalyptic Literature; Fantasy Fiction; Utopic Literature
Field, David N.
contribution in this encyclopedia, see Christianity (6c2) – Calvin, John and the Reformed Tradition
Field, Steven
contribution in this encyclopedia, see Fengshui
fig tree see organisms – flora
Figueroa, Robert Melchior
contributions in this encyclopedia, see Chávez, César – and the United Farm Workers; Environmental Justice and Environmental Racism

Finch, Martha
contribution in this encyclopedia, see Puritans
Findhorn Foundation/Community 658–660 (see also adjacent, Dorothy Maclean)
Fire 660–663
and Promethius 89, 433
Anishnabeg Culture 91–92
Aztecs 144–145
ceremonial 158, 1065, 1243, 1273, 1473, 1486, 1523, 1811, 1814
divine/celestial 63, 206, 714, 755, 1087, 1465
domestic 57
Hinduism 763, 764, 766, 767, 770, 1191
internal 721, 1050, 1522
Jainism 893, 894
Yellowstone 1157
Fisher, Andy 1329
contributions in this encyclopedia, see Ecopsychology
Fishers 120, 663–665, 749, 1583, 1646 (see also Fly Fishing; Sohappy, David – and Salmon Spirituality)
fishing 41, 120, 213, 267, 438, 718, 953, 1206, 1560, 1578 (see also Fishers; Fly Fishing)
Fisk, Pliny 665–666
flora see organisms – flora
Floresta 666–667
Flower song – xochicuicatl 144, 146 (adjacent to Aztec Religion – Pre-Colombian)
Fly Fishing 667–669
Foltz, Richard C.
contributions in this encyclopedia, see Islam; Islam and Environmentalism in Iran; Islam, Animals and Vegetarianism; Izzi Dier; Nasr, Seyyed Hossein; Pure Brethren; Water in Islam; Water in Zoroastrianism
foraging societies 112, 144, 313, 456, 664, 801, 835 (see also Huaorani; Penan Hunter-Gatherers; Pygmies (Mbuti Foragers) and Bila Farmers of the Hari Forest; San (Bushmen) Religion)
Foreman, Dave see Radical Environmentalism
forests
cathedral 274, 278, 518 (see also Cathedral Forests and the Felling of Sacred Groves)
deforestation 30, 38, 44, 274, 314, 546, 624
and Confucianism 410
and Neo-Humanism 48
Athonite peninsula 335

collapse of Maya civilization 835
 in Africa/biodiversity 180, 576, 820
 in the Amazon 41, 213, 836
 in the Caribbean 269
 in Hawai'i 749
 in India 101, 300
  chipko 768, 775, 823, 827
 smudging ceremony 569
 environmental protection
  Africa see Kenya's Greenbelt Movement; Sacred Groves of Africa
  California see G-O Road; Redwood Rabbis
  India see Appiko; Chipko Movement; India's Sacred Groves
  Iran 1814
  Israel see Israel and Environmentalism
  Latin America 1409
  Thailand 1629 (see also Siam's Forest Monasteries)
 national parks 1152–1153
 nature spirits 819
 rainforests 28, 38, 182, 238, 840 (see also Rainforests)
 reforestation 894, 909, 1357, 1366, 1408, 1514, 1629 (see also Kenya Greenbelt Movement; Men of the Trees; Restoration Ecology and Ritual)
 religion see Religious Campaign for Forest Conservation; Trees – as Religious Architecture
 Seed, John see Seed, John
 slash and burn 666, 835
 trees
  Europe see Trees – Northern and Middle Europe
  Haiti see Trees in Haitian Vodou 1658–1659
  music see Tree Music
  ordaining 1388, 1629 (see also Trees – as Religious Architecture)
 organizations
  Tree of Peace Society 748
  Trees for Life 658, 660
 sacred 95, 119, 157, 261, 273–274, 434, 590, 619, 718, 724, 768, 800, 963, 986, 1115, 1413, 1453–1454, 1470, 1477, 1643, 1657, 1659, 1682 (see also Trees – Sacred)
 Wise Use Movement see Wise Use Movement
Forum on Religion and Ecology 1367, 1378–1379, 1746
Foundation for Shamanic Studies see Harner, Michael – and the Foundation for Shamanic Studies
Fox, George 674
Fox, Matthew 89, 165, 332, 363, 456, 512, 669–670, 857, 1213, 1762

Fox, Selena see Wicca
Fox, Stephen 417, 1544
Fox, Warwick see Deep Ecology
Foyn, Svend 1732
Francis of Assisi, Saint 670–672 (see also Gaian Mass)
 animals 77, 122, 377, 570
 festival 276, 352, 682
 Franciscans 1405–1406
 mysticism 329
 nature 327
 White, Lynn 1168
Franciscans see Roman Catholic Religious Orders
Franck, Frederick see Art
Franklin, Benjamin 352, 463, 707, 748, 1015
Frazer, James xiii, xvii–xix, 94–95, 672, 744, 1020–1021, 1311, 1389, 1411, 1508
Freeman, Nick
 contribution in this encyclopedia, see Graves, Robert von Ranke
Freemasons 489, 1022, 1243, 1728 (see also Masons, Fraternal Order of)
Freeport (West Papua, Indonesia) 672
French, William
 contributions in this encyclopedia, see Christianity (6a) – Roman Catholicism; Frances of Assisi; Moltmann, Jürgen; Rousseau, Jean-Jacques
Freud, Sigmund 163, 673, 808, 989, 1034, 1229, 1311 (see also Jung, Carl – A Perspective; Magic; Wonder Toward Nature)
Friends Committee on Unity with Nature (FCUN) 674
Friends of the Earth 225, 226, 307, 507, 675, 906, 1346 (see also A Christian Friend of the Earth; A Salvadorian Reflection on Religion, Rights, and Nature)
Friends – Religious Society of (Quakers) 361, 674–675, 727, 1178, 1198, 1474 (see also Quaker Writings in Tasmania)
Friluftsliv 675
Frömming, Urte Undine
 contribution in this encyclopedia, see Volcanoes (with Judith Schlehe)
Frugality 122, 316, 374, 487, 1296, 1403, 1704, 1785 (adjacent to Virtues and Ecology in World Religions)
Fruitlands 148, 675–676
Frye, Northrop see North America – Canada
Fuller, Buckminster 109, 665, 676–678, 1586
Fuller, Margaret 224, 676, 1425

Fuller, Robert
 contribution in this encyclopedia, see Peyote
funerals see death

G

Gaard, Greta 533, 538
Gabriel, Angel 862, 929, 1200
Gaia 679–680
 Church of All Worlds see Church of All Worlds
 environmental movement 1013
 foundation see Gaia Foundation and Earth Community Network
 Gaia Liberation Front 385
 hypothesis 33, 63, 383, 1587
 Institute 275
 Lovelock, James see Lovelock, James
 mass 1755 (see also Gaian Mass)
 pilgrimage see Gaian Pilgrimage
 raves 1347
 re-earthing 1355–1356
Gaia Foundation and Earth Community Network 680–682
Gaian Mass 682–683, 1755
Gaian Pilgrimage 683–685
Gaines, Betsy
 contribution in this encyclopedia, see Mongolian Buddhism and Taiman Conservation
Galeano, Juan Carlos
 contribution in this encyclopedia, see Amazonian Folktales (and adjacent, Mapinguari)
Gandhi, Mohandas 685–686
 ahimsa 31, 53, 894
 autobiography 139
 Bhagavadgita 172, 1149
 Ecosophy T 1149–1150
 environmentalism 826, 1150
 Greenpeace 727–728
 Sarvodaya 53, 105 (see also Sarvodaya Sramadana Movement)
 satyagraha 53, 139, 155, 826, 1046, 1481, 1515, 1627
 Singh, Puran 1550
Ganga (Ganges) River see Asia – Southern
Gardner, Gerald B. 1247, 1739–1740, 1742
Gardening and Nature Spirituality 687
gardens
 Chinese 297
 Eden see Eden and Other Gardens; Eden's Ecology; Restoring Eden
 floating 143
 gardening see Gardening and Nature Spirituality
 in art 110–111

Islam *see* Gardens in Islam
Japan 955, *see* Japanese Gardens
landscapes, sacred 1080, 1458
Gardens in Islam 688
Garrard-Burnett, Virginia
  contributions in this encyclopedia, *see*
    Mayan Catholicism; Mayan
    Protestanism
Gaskin, Stephen 639, 1199
Gebara, Ivone 213, 313, 359, 419, 512, 532, 533, **689–690**
Geertz, Clifford 549, 989
Genealogy and Spiritualities of Place (Australia) 690
General Systems Theory *see* Science
Genesis Farm 165, 404, **691–692**, 1406
genetic engineering *see* Science
genius loci 104, 554, 557, 687, 1320, 1420, 1461
geodesic dome *see* Architecture
Geomancy 104, 295, 296, 525–526, 576, 626, **692**, 771, 969, 1091, 1284, 1600
geomorphology *see* Delphic Oracle
Geophilia 693–694
Gerstenfeld, Manfred
  contributions in this encyclopedia, *see*
    Hebrew Bible; Judaism and
    Sustainability; Paganism – A Jewish
    Perspective
Gestalt therapy 615, 1194
Ghost Dance 198, 199, 510, **695–695**, 785, 1096, 1713
Gilmore, Peter H.
  contribution in this encyclopedia, *see*
    Satanism
Gimbutas, Marija 301, 527, 528, 534, 584, 593, 635, **696**, 981, 1310–1311, 1557, 1595
Ginsberg, Allen 55, 160–161, 1384
Gitau, Samson
  contribution in this encyclopedia, *see*
    Christian Environmentalism in
    Kenya
Glacken, Clarence James 274, **696–697**, 1108, 1598, 1736
Glass, Matthew
  contributions in this encyclopedia, *see*
    Deloria, Vine Jr.; Devil's Tower (*Mato Tipi* or Bear's Lodge); Law, Religion
    and Native American Lands;
    Manifest Destiny; Mother Earth;
    Mount Rushmore; National Parks and
    Monuments
Glassman, Bernard 243–244
Glastonbury 697–698
Glazier, Stephen D.
  contribution in this encyclopedia, *see*
    Rappaport, Roy A.
Glen Canyon Dam 226, 1546
Glen Canyon Institute 226

Global Education Association 1408
global ethics 411, 517, 542, 1170 (*see also* Earth Charter)
Globalization 698–700
  and nature 299, 374
  effects of 181, 360, 461, 840, 841
  International Forum on Globalization 1539
  opposition to 54, 380, 459, 700, 912 (*see also* Anarchism; Earth First! and the Earth Liberation Front; Economics)
  Transnational Corporations (TNC) 309, 699, 841, 1468
  World Trade Organization (WTO) 380, 699, 1198, 1468
global warming 44, 212, 227, 309, 318, 541, 728, 740, 839, 958, 1044, 1340
Glock, Charles 1198
Glover, James M 1048, 1129
  contributions in this encyclopedia, *see*
    Marshall, Robert; Murie, Olaus J.
Gnosticism 512–513, 704, 724, 1257–1258, 1671
G-O Road (Northern California) 701–702
gods, goddesses, deities and nature spirits
  devas 35, 288, 554, 659, 771, 1136, 1269, 1633
  originating in Africa
    Apep/Apophi 432, 1205
    Eng'ai (Ng'ai, Nkai, Enkai) 1016–1018
    Inkosi yeZulu 1773
    Isis 575, 704, 1239, 1250
    Makewana *see* Makewana the Rainmaker
    Mammy Water *see* Mammy Water
    Mwari 1055
    Neith/Nit 1205–1206
    Nyang' idi 1561
    Omieri 1561–1562
    Osiris 432, 578–579, 704, 724, 1206, 1622, 1657
    Re/Ra 575, 1206
    Sobek/Sebak 576, 1205–1206
    Thunga 1029–1030
    Yoruba gods/goddesses 1780
  originating in Asia
    originating in East Asia
      Buddha Amitabha 236
      Buddha Mahavairocana 232
      Ebisu 1730
      Kami 36, 113, 899–903, 1121, 1368, 1656–1657, 1722
      Shu 1795–1796
    originating in South Asia
      AvalokiteYvara 1636
      Bhu-devi 766
      Ganesh 69, 586, 768, 824
      Kali 704, 142, 1250, 1619
      Lakshmi 586, 765, 766, 768, 773, 1514–1515

Parvati 480, 486, 767–769, 1294, 1415
Red Machchendranath 1192
Sarasvati 704, 763–764
Shiva 36, 586, 642, 766, 767, 769, 824, 826, 1031, 1356–1357, 1524, 1626
Vac 764
Vayu 1191, 1415
Vishnu 194, 195, 709, 765–766, 767–768, 770, 772–774, 824, 826, 829, 1191, 1517, 1606
originating in Western Asia
  Ahura Mazda 661, 1555, 1812–1814
  Amesha Spentras (6 interconnected spirits) 1812, 1814
  Anahita (Nahid) 1716, 1812
  Innana (Ishtar) 704, 1090, 1771
  Marduk 431, 1090
  Patet Apam (guardians of the river) 1716
originating in Europe
  originating in Greece and Italy
    Aphrodite 704, 714, 1251, 1410, 1509, 1716
    Apollo 466–468, 619, 716–719, **1227–1228**, 1291, 1402, 1410, 1732, 1808
    Artemis 481, 704, 716–717, 719, 810, 1411, 1518
    Athena 619, 704, 716–719
    Cinyras 1228
    Daphne 1227–1228
    Demeter (Ceres) 433, 619, 704, 717, 981, 1107, 1685–1686, 1740
    Diana *see* Diana
    Dionysus (Bacchus) 302 444, 719, 724, 1227, 1411–1412, 1518
    Echo 1228
    Europa 1228
    Ge (earth) 466, 679, 716
    Hyacinthus 1228
    Io 1228, 1289
    Jupiter (Jove) 433, 1227–1229, 1401, 1410, 1412
    Mars 1410–1411
    Myrrha 1228
    Narcissus 1227–1228
    Persephone 433, 687, 704, 980–982, 1285, 1685–1686
    Prometheus 89, 433
    Pygmalion 1228
    Semele 1227
    Venus 575, 1227–1228, 1410–1411, 1509
    Zeus 433, 717, 719, 1415, 1457, 1555
  originating in Germany
    Midgard 752, 1218, 1517
    Odin 593, 1554, 1660 *see also* Odinism
    Yggdrasil 751–752, 754, 1218, 1660

originating in Norway
  elves and land spirits *see* **Elves and Land Spirits in Pagan Norse Religions**
  Freyja 592, 752, 1218
  Freyr 592, 752
  Thor 592, 1517, 1558
  Vanir 592, 752–754, 1218
originating in Meso-America *see* **Mesoamerican Deities**
originating in North America
  Hawaii
    Kanaloa 748–749, 953
    Lono 748, 750, 953
    Pele 1709
  Native American tribes
    Great Spirit 43, 200, 796, 830, 851, 987, 1274
originating in Oceania
  Tane 1200, 1231, 1287
sea goddesses *see* **Sea Goddesses and Female Water Spirits**
sky gods 534, 1077 (*see also* Sky)
Goddesses – History of 702–705
goddess spirituality 288, 301, 696, 1248, 1351, 1570 (*see also* **Christ, Carol; Gimbutas, Marija**)
Goethe 641, 735, 1423, 1459
Gold, Ann Grodzins
  contribution in this encyclopedia, *see* **Seeds in South Asia**
Golden Dawn 706, 1021–1022, 1054, 1243, **1739**
golden section *see* Art
Golding, William 679, 1587
Goldtooth, Tom 838
  contribution in this encyclopedia, *see* **Indigenous Environmental Network**
Gombe Stream Research Center 707
Gomes, Carolos Valerio A.
  contribution in this encyclopedia, *see* **Rubber Tappers** (with Richard H. Wallace)
Goodall, Jane 72, 139, 140, 398, 602, **706–708**, 1682–1683
  contribution in this encyclopedia, *see* **Primate Spirituality**
Goodenough, Ursula 165, 1302, 1590
  contribution in this encyclopedia, *see* **Religious Naturalism**
Gorbachev, Mikhail *see* Europe – Eastern
Gordon, Aharon David 708, 909, 934
Goshalas (Home for Aged Cattle) 709, 825
gospels, synoptic *see* Christianity
Gottleib, Alan M. 1756
Gottleib, Roger 1522
  contribution in this encyclopedia, *see* **The Holocaust and the Environmental Crisis**

Gould, Rebecca Kneale
  contributions in this encyclopedia, *see* **Back to the Land Movements; Berry, Wendell; Book of Nature; Burroughs, John; Christianity (7h) – Natural Theology; Deism; Emerson, Ralph Waldo; Thoreau, Henry David; Transcendentalism**
Grand Canyon 200, 225, 794, 796, 1129, 1546, 1755
Grau, Marion
  contributions in this encyclopedia, *see* **Christianity (6c4) – Anglicanism; Jubilee and Jubilee 2000; Oikos**
Graves, Robert von Ranke 596, 637, **710**, 1247
Great Chain of Being 328, 339–342, 352, 376, 940, 1010, 1269, 1744
great cosmic liturgy 166–168
Great Monkey Jataka, The (Mahakapijataka) 904–905
Great Spirit *see* gods, goddesses, deities and nature spirits – North America
Great White Brotherhood of Ascended Masters 1671
Greco-Roman World 711–716
Greece – Classical 716–718
Greek Landscape 719–720
Greek Paganism 720–722
Green, Arthur 544, 1705
  contributions in this encyclopedia, *see* **Eco-Kabbalah; Hasidism and Nature Mysticism**
Green Cross International 516, 1682
Green Death Movement 407, **722–723** (*see also* death)
Green Gulch Zen Center 243, 244
Green Man 506, 557, 637, **723–724**, 1134, 1656–1658
Green Politics 725–726
green revolution *see* Asia – Southern
Green Sisters Movement 691, **726–727**
greenhouse gases 309, 839, 843, 958, 1292, 1294
greening of religion *see* Environmental Ethics; Religious Environmentalist Paradigm; Religious Studies and Environmental Concern (and adjacent, Critical Perspectives on "Religions of the World and Ecology"); United Nations' "Earth Summits"; White, Lynn – Thesis of
Greenpeace 44, 227, **727–728**, 780, 1075, 1132, 1720
Greenway, Robert 558
Gregersen, Niels Henrik
  contribution in this encyclopedia, *see* **Whitehead, Alfred North**

Griffin, Roger
  contribution in this encyclopedia, *see* **Fascism**
Griffin, Susan 54, 251, 534, 535, 729, 1109
Griffin, Wendy
  contributions in this encyclopedia, *see* **Wicca–Dianic; Z-Budapest**
Grim, John 96, 1264, 1376–1378
Grimes, Ronald L.
  contribution in this encyclopedia, *see* **Ritual**
Grobbelaar, Frik 1439
  contribution in this encyclopedia, *see* **Rustlers Valley (South Africa)**
Groff, Stanislav 214–216, 729, 1654–1655
Gross, Rita M.
  contributions in this encyclopedia, *see* **Buddhism – Tibetan; Feminist Spirituality Movement; Goddesses – History of**
Grounds, Richard A.
  contributions in this encyclopedia, *see* **Native American Languages; Yuchee Culture and the Euchee Language Project (Southeastern United States)**
Gruenschloss, Andreas
  contributions in this encyclopedia, *see* **Aztec Religion – Pre-Colombian; Lost Worlds**
Gudmarsdottir, Sigridur
  contributions in this encyclopedia, *see* **Corrington, Robert S.; Trees (Northern and Middle Europe)**
Gudorf, Christine E
  contribution in this encyclopedia, *see* **Breeding and Contraception**
Guenther, Mathias
  contributions in this encyclopedia, *see* **Khoisan Religion; San (Bushman) Religion; The Trickster**
Guha, Ramachandra *see* Asia – Southern
Gulen, Fethullah 729–730
Gumilev, Lev 1437–1438
Gupta, Roxanne Kamayani
  contributions in this encyclopedia, *see* **Indian Classical Dance**
Gurdjieff, George Ivanovitch 162, **730–732**, 1225
Guru Nanak *see* Asia – Southern
Gush Emunim 732–734
Gutierrez, Gustavo 358
Gypsies *see* Romanies

H

Habel, Norman
  contributions in this encyclopedia, *see* **Eco-Justice Hermeneutics** (adjacent to **Earth Bible**); **Heavenism**

1850 Index

(adjacent to Earth Bible); Earth Bible
Haberman, David
  contribution in this encyclopedia, see Yamuna
Habito, Ruben L.F.
  contribution in this encyclopedia, see Zen Buddhism
Hackett, Rosalind
  contribution in this encyclopedia, see Somé, Malidome Patrice
Hadith see Islam
Hadith and Shari'a on Man and Nature 876
Hadsell, Heidi
  contributions in this encyclopedia, see Brazil and Contemporary Christianity; World Council of Churches
Haeckel, Ernst 358, 359, 643, **735–736**, 1278
Hagelin, John 1171–1172
Hahn, Eduard 503
Hahne, Harry
  contributions in this encyclopedia, see Christianity (2) – Jesus; Christianity (3) – New Testament; Jewish Intertestamental Literature; Types of Intertestamental Literature (adjacent to Jewish Intertestamental Literature)
hair 223, 391, 445, 724, 1028, 1034–1036, 1279, 1346, 1356, 1511
Hale, John R.
  contribution in this encyclopedia, see Delphic Oracle
Hall, Sian
  contributions in this encyclopedia, see Etsheni Sacred Stones; Rock Art – Sintu; Weather Snake
Hallman, David 541
Hallman, Max O.
  contribution in this encyclopedia, see Nietzsche, Friedrich
hallucinogens 33, 423, 619–620, 1359–1360, 1370 (see also Ethnobotany; Ethnoecology; Entheogens; Huxley, Aldous; Leary, Timothy; Peyote)
Halprin, Anna 444, 1281–1282
Hammond-Tooke, William David
  contribution in this encyclopedia, see Pollution Beliefs in South Africa
Hancock, Ian
  contribution in this encyclopedia, see Romanies (Gypsies)
Hardin, Garrett 599–600, 602–603, 1034
Hardin "Wolf", Jesse 1134
  contributions in this encyclopedia, see Bioneers Conference; Drums, Drumming, and Nature; Music and Its Origins; Music of Resistance; Power Animals; Rewilding; Sexuality and Eco-spirituality
Hardy, Thomas 736–737
Harjo, Joy 737, 994
Harmonic Convergence 11, **738**, 804 (see also Harmonic Convergence and the Spiritualization of the Biosphere)
Harmonic Convergence and the Spiritualization of the Biosphere **738–741**
Harmony in Native North American Spiritual Traditions **741–742**
Harner, Michael 620, 1441, 1528–1529 (see also Harner, Michael – and the Foundation for Shamanic Studies)
Harner, Michael – and the Foundation for Shamanic Studies **743–744**
Harris, Adrian 557
  contributions in this encyclopedia, see Dragon Environmental Network (United Kingdom); Eco-Magic
Harris, Marvin 95, 96, 545, 709, **744–745**, 1342
Harrison, Paul 1769
  contributions in this encyclopedia, see World Pantheist Movement
Hart, John
  contributions in this encyclopedia, see Columbia River Watershed Pastoral Letter; Deere, Phillip; Fisk, Pliny; Indigenous Voices from Kari Oca (adjacent to World Conferences on Indigenous People); Sacramental Universel; Sohappy, David and Salmon Spirituality; World Conference of Indigenous Peoples (Kari Oca, Brazil)
Harvey, Graham
  contributions in this encyclopedia, see Animism – A Contemporary Perspective; Michell, John; Otherworlds; Paganism – Contemporary; Stonehenge
Hasidism see Judaism
Hasidism and Nature Mysticism **745–746**
Hatutasi, Veronica
  contribution in this encyclopedia, see Bougainville (Papua New Guinea) (with Elizabeth Johnson and Gary W. Trompf)
Haudenosaunee see North America
Haudenosaunee Confederacy **746–748**, 1378
Hawai'i 528, 739, **748–750**, 952–954, 1230, 1287, 1457, 1609–1610
Hayes, Randy 1355, 1513
  contribution in this encyclopedia, see Hopiland to the Rainforest Action Network

Hazare, Anna 1341
healing
  Africa 264 (see also Muti and African Healing; Muti Killings)
  Ayurvedic medicine 586
  herbal medicine 261, 485, 819, 1144, 1793, 1816, 1181 (see also Ethnobotany; Zulu (amaZulu) Culture, Plants, and Spirit Worlds)
  sauna see Sauna
Heath, Jennifer
  contributions in this encyclopedia, see Chaos, Creation and the Winter Garden; Eden and Other Gardens
Heathenry – Ásatrú **751–754** (see also adjacent, Seidr)
Heavenism 516 (adjacent to Earth Bible)
Hebrew Bible 539, 661, **754–757**, 907–908, 915, 926, 1169, 1245, 1346, 1442, 1590
Hegel, G.W. Friedrich 403, 453, **758–759**, 1005, 1174, 1278, 1589
Heidegger, Martin 138, 420, 457, **759–761**, 1677
Helenistic literature see Roman Religion and Empire
Helmers, Marguerite
  contributions in this encyclopedia, see Diana; Labyrinth; Sante Fe, New Mexico
Henig, Martin
  contributions in this encyclopedia, see Roman Britain; Roman Natural Religion
Henning, Glen 1607–1612
  contribution in this encyclopedia, see Surfing (with Bron Taylor)
Heraclitus see philosophy
Hernandez, Nimachia
  contribution in this encyclopedia, see Blackfoot Cosmos as Natural Philosophy
Hessel, Dieter T. 369, 1705
  contribution in this encyclopedia, see Eco-Justice in Theology and Ethics
Hetch Hetchy Dam see North America – United States (see also Muir, John)
Hill, Anne
  contributions in this encyclopedia, see Pagan Music (and adjacent, Burning Times)
Hillman, James 942, 1329
Hilltop youth 734
Hildegard of Bingen 99, 329, 361, 363, **761–762**, 1403, 1519, 1523
Hillary, Sir Edmond 34
Himmler, Reichsfuhrer Heinrich see Europe – Western
Hinduism **762–776**
  abortion 219, 654

Advaita Vedanta *see* Vedanta
animals 68–69 (*see also* Goshalas)
atman 774, 826, 1258, 1706
beliefs
 ahimsa see Ahimsa
 dharma see Dharma-Hindu
 karma 68–69, 90, 824–825, 1191, 1193, 1370
 maya 772, 1356, 1495, 1706
 moksa 779, 1294
 reincarnation 68
 Bhagavadgita *see* Bhagavadgita
Brahman 772, 774, 824, 1179, 1191, 1258, 1497, 1651, 1746
Ganesh *see* gods, goddesses, deities and nature spirits
goddess worship 704 (*see also* Goddesses – History of)
gods/goddesses *see* gods, goddesses, deities and nature spirits – originating in South Asia
homosexuality 792
nagas 36, 768–769
pollution *see* Hinduism and Pollution (and adjacent, River Ganga and the Clean Ganga Campaign)
Polytheism *see* Polytheism
prakriti see Prakriti
purusha 116, 764, 771, 773, 824, 1300, 1524, 1539
Ramakrishna 813, 1455
renunciation 31, 774, 825, 828, 1300
Rig Veda 69, 619, 764, 1269, 1760
Shakti see Shakti
Shiva *see* gods, goddesses, deities and nature spirits
soma 141–142, 208, 596, 619, 764
Tantra *see* Tantra
Vedanta 172, 772–774, 1181, 1651
Vedas 69, 476, 480, 596, 654, 823, 1191, 1514
Vishnu *see* gods, goddesses, deities and nature spirits
worship practices 36
yoga *see* yoga; **Yoga and Ecology**
Hinduism and Pollution 777–779 (*see also* adjacent, River Ganga and the Clean Ganga Campaign)
Hinshaw, Robert
 contribution in this encyclopedia, *see* van der Post, Laurens
Hippies 247, 636, 639, **779–780**, 1354, 1536
Hippocratic tradition 712, 715
Hirsch, Rabbi Samson Raphael *see* Judaism
Hitler, Adolf *see* Europe – Western
Hobbes, Thomas *see* philosophy
Hobgood-Oster, Laura
 contributions in this encyclopedia, *see*

Adams, Carol; Christianity (7d) – Feminist Theology; Ecofeminism – Historic and International Evolution; Estés, Clarissa Pinkola; McFague, Sallie; Merchant, Carolyn; Sjöö, Monica
Hodgson, Dorothy L.
 contribution in this encyclopedia, *see* Maasai
Hoeppe, Götz
 contributions in this encyclopedia, *see* Sky
Holmes, Steven J.
 contributions in this encyclopedia, *see* Autobiography; Muir, John
Hogan, Linda 311, 487, **781**, 794–795
Holidays 30, 158, 649, 721, **781–782**, 1351, 1679
Holism 208, 238, 282, 359, 411–412, 638, 689, **782–783**, 946, 1007, 1559
Holocaust *see* Europe
Holocaust and the Environmental Crisis, The 783–785
Holy Grail *see* Christianity
Holy Land
 Abrahamic Religions 785
 Israel 887–888, 930–931 (*see also* Israel and Environmentalism)
 Mormons 149
 North America *see* Holy Land in Native North America
 pilgrimage *see* pilgrimage
Holy Land in Native North America 785–789
Homosexuality 789–793, 814 (*see also* adjacent, **Homosexuality and Science**)
Homosexuality and Science 789–790
Hooks, Bell 367
Hoover, Stewart
 contribution in this encyclopedia, *see* Media (wth Joseph G. Champ)
Hopi *see* North America – United States
Hopi–Navajo Land Dispute 793–795
Hopiland to the Rainforest Action Network 795–798
Hopkins, Samuel Taylor 1039
Hopkins, Gerard Manley 310, 316, **798–799**, 1008, 1407
horoscopes *see* New Age
Hosken, Liz
 contribution in this encyclopedia, *see* **Gaia Foundation and Earth Community Network** (with Fiona Worthington)
Hoskins, Richard
 contributions in this encyclopedia, *see* **African Religions and Nature Conservation** (with Faith Warner); **Biodiversity and Religion in Equatorial Africa** (with Faith Warner);

Kimbanguism (Central Africa) (with Faith Warner); Muti and African Healing; Muti Killings
Huaorani 509, **799–802**
Hubbard, L. Ron 177, **1499–1501** (*see also* Scientology – In Two Scholarly Perspectives)
Hudson, Nancy
 contributions in this encyclopedia, *see* Christianity (5) – Medieval; Cusa, Nicholas of
Hudson River Valley School *see* Art
Huffman, Kirk
 contribution in this encyclopedia, *see* Kogi (Northern Colombia)
Hughes, J. Donald 601
 contributions in this encyclopedia, *see* Egypt – Ancient; Greece – Classical; Roman Religion and Empire
Hultkrantz, Ake 1301, 1363, 1441
Human Potential Movements *see* New Age
human rights 701, 788, 797, 836–837, 839, 841–842, 846, 913, 933, 998, 1171, 1178, 1297, 1468, 1580, 1682 (*see also* United Nations Declaration of Human Rights)
humanism 177, 259, 271, 272, 580, 760, 886, 1183, 1259, 1677 (*see also* Ananda Marga's Tantric Neo-Humanism)
Hume, Lynne
 contribution in this encyclopedia, *see* Paganism in Australia
Humphreys, Michael Llewellyn
 contribution in this encyclopedia, *see* Religious Campaign for Forest Conservation
Hundredth Monkey 802–805 (*see also* adjacent, **Monkeys in the Field**)
Hunt, Richard
 contribution in this encyclopedia, *see* Raymo, Chet
hunter/gatherer cultures *see* foraging societies
hunting
 and indigenous people 891
 ethics 891
 predators 185, 186, 585, 800, 801, 808, 813, 1129, 1157, 1364, 1365, 1667
 prey 28, 39, 45, 196, 313, 348, 366, 806–808, 852, 1472, 1516
 religion *see* Hunting and the Origins of Religion
 shamanism 800
 spirituality *see* Hunting Spirituality; Hunting Spirituality and Animism
Hunting and the Origins of Religion 805–808
Hunting Spirituality 809–810
Hunting Spirituality and Animism 811–812

husbandry 403, 422, 437, 443, 1248, 1310
Hutton, Ronald 1237–1247, 1600, 1740
Huxley, Aldous 475, 596, 601, 812–813, 1291–1292, 1313
Hviding, Edvard
  contribution in this encyclopedia, see Christian Fellowship Church (Solomon Islands)
hydro-electric power 38, 155, 200, 836, 1277, 1468, 1578 (see also Tehri Dam)
Hyenas – Spotted 266, 813–816, 1560

I

Ibn Al-cArabi, Shaykh Muhyiddin 817–818, 859
Iceland see Europe – Northern
icons see Christianity – Orthodoxy
Ifá Divination 818–820
Illich, Ivan 1492, 1507
Illyn, Peter 1381–1383
  contribution in this encyclopedia, see Restoring Eden (with Bron Taylor)
Immergut, Matthew
  contributions in this encyclopedia, see Church of Euthanasia; Krueger, Fred (with Laurel Kearns)
Imperialism, European 29, 207, 298–299, 1179
impermanence see Buddhism
incarnation see Christianity
Incas 820–823
India see Asia – Southern
Indian Classical Dance 776, 828–830
Indian Guides 830
Indian Shaker Religion 831, 1776
India's Sacred Groves 831–833
Indigenous Activism and Environmentalism in Latin America 833–838
Indigenous Environmental Network 838–844, 1765
Indigenous Knowledge Systems see Ethnoecology; Traditional Ecological Knowledge
Indigenous Religions and Cultural Borrowing 845–847
Indigenous Societies
  Colombia see Reichel-Dolmatoff, Gerardo – and Ethnoecology in Colombia
  conferences 748 (see also Indigenous Voices from Kari Oca; World Summit of Indigenous People)
  environmental organizations see Aboriginal Environmental Groups in Canada; Indigenous Activism and Environmentalism; Indigenous Environmental Network

environmental justice 609–610
environmental sustainability 39, 97, 180, 421, 422, 545, 600, 835, 837 (see also Water Spirits and Indigenous Ecological Management (South Africa)
Haudenosaunee see Haudenosaunee
Hogan, Linda see Hogan, Linda
Indigenous Peoples' Earth Charter 1765
Maori see Oceania – New Zealand
Latin America see Indigenous Activism and Environmentalism in Latin America
Native Americans see North America – United States
on nature 629, 700, 1059 (see also Mayan Spirituality and Conservation)
Penan see Penan; Manser, Bruno and the Penan of Sarawak
religious beliefs see Animism; Animism – a Contemporary Perspective; Indigenous Religions and Cultural Borrowing Magic, Animism and the Shaman's Craft; Mayan Spirituality
romanticism see Romanticism and Indigenous People
Shiva, Vandana see Shiva, Vandana
traditional ecological knowledge see Traditional Ecological Knowledge; Traditional Ecological Knowledge Among Aboriginal Peoples in Canada; Yunnan Region (Southwest China and Montane Mainland Southeast Asia)
Indigenous Voices from Kari Oca 1763 (adjacent to World Conference of Indigenous Peoples)
Indra's Net 237, 847–848, 1384
industrialization 218, 299, 449, 769, 862, 1245, 1278, 1424, 1750
Ingalsbee, Timothy
  contribution in this encyclopedia, see Fire
Intelligent Design see Creationism
Interfaith Center on Corporate Responsibility 393, 848
Interfaith Council for Environmental Stewardship 625, 849–850, 1756
International Consultancy of Religion, Education and Culture (ICOREC) 1193, 1257, 1770
International Monetary Fund (IMF) see Economics
International Network of Engaged Buddhists see Buddhism – Engaged
International Society for Environmental Ethics 1400
International Whaling Commission 1720, 1731–1732, 1734

Institute for the Harmonious Development of Man 731
Institute of Noetic Sciences 849–850, 1586, 1587 (adjacent to Space Exploration)
Internet 385, 501, 517, 547, 612, 690, 804, 1003, 1141, 1143, 1147, 1242, 1248, 1371, 1484, 1602
Intertestamental Literature, Types of 402, 913–918
Inuit 850–852, 896, 1103, 1510, 1525, 1732–1734
Ireland see Europe – Northern
Irenaeus see Christianity
Isaiah 99–100, 223, 303, 309, 434, 662, 755–757, 1154, 1442, 1699
Isenberg, Shaya
  contribution in this encyclopedia, see Perennial Philosophy (with Gene Thursby)
Ishimure, Michiko 857–858
Islam 858–862
  animals see Animals in the Bible and Qur'an; Islam, Animals and Vegetarianism
  anthropocentrism see Islam and Post-Athropocentrism
  environmentalism see Islam and Environmental Ethics; Islam and Environmentalism in Iran
  environmental justice see Islam and Eco-Justice
  environmental leaders see Izzi Dien, Mawil Y.
  environmental protection see Islamic Basis for Environmental Protection
  foundations see Islamic Foundation for Ecology and Environmental Sciences; Islamic Foundation for Science and Environment
  Gabriel, Angel 862
  gardens see gardens
  Hadith 71, 858–861, 862, 864, 890, 1606, 1715 (see also Islam, Animals and Vegetarianism; Islam and Environmental Ethics)
  homosexuality 792
  Ibn Al-cArabi, Shaykh Muhyiddin see Ibn Al-cArabi, Shaykh Muhyiddin
  law see Islamic Law
  Mecca 75, 178, 584, 730, 878, 1115, 1124, 1334, 1555, 1622
  Muhammad see Muhammad, The Prophet of Islam
  mysticism see Rumî, Jalaluddin; Sufism
  oneness of God see Tawid
  perspectives on nature see Islam on Man and Nature; Hadith and Shari'a on Man and Nature
  Qur'an, The see Qur'an, The

science *see* Islamic Foundation for Science and Environment
vegetarianism *see* Islam, Animals, and Vegetarianism
water *see* Water in Islam
Islam and Eco-Justice 862–866
Islam and Environmental Ethics 866–868
Islam and Environmentalism in Iran 869–872
Islam and Post-Antropocentrism 872–873
Islam, Animals and Vegetarianism 873–875
Islam on Man and Nature 875–879 (*see also* adjacent, Hadith and Shari'a on Man and Nature)
Islamic Basis for Environmental Protection 879–893
Islam Foundation for Ecology and Environmental Sciences 884
Islam Foundation for Science and Environment 884–885
Islamic Law 500, 603, 792, 858, 860, 885–886, 1322
Israel and Environmentalism 887–890
Israel *see* Asia – Western
Ital lifestyle 1345–1346
Ivakhiv, Adrian
 contributions in this encyclopedia, *see* Crop Circles; Earth Mysteries; Glastonbury; Harmonic Convergence; Neo-paganism in Ukraine; Russian Mystical Philosophy (with Mikhail Epstein); Sedona; Slavic Religion
Ivanov, Porfyrii Korniiovych *see* Europe – Eastern
Ives, Christopher
 contribution in this encyclopedia, *see* Japanese Love of Nature
Iwa Dambalah Wedo (Serpent rainbow) *see* Caribbean – Haiti
Izzi Dien, Mawil Y. 890

J

Jackson, President Andrew *see* North America – United States
Jackson, S. Wesley "Wes" 313, 540, 892
Jackson, William Henry 303, 1042, 1154
Jacobsen, Knut A
 contributions in this encyclopedia, *see* Ahimsa; Bhagavadgita (and adjacent, Great Monkey Jataka, The Mahakapijataka); India; Jataka Tales; Naess, Arne; Prakriti
Jain, Anrudh 653

Jainism 654, 823–826, 892–895, 1368 (*see also* India)
Jambho-ji 774
James Bay Cree and Hydro-Quebec 895–896
James, George A.
 contributions in this encyclopedia, *see* Amte, Baba; Appiko Movement (India); Athavale, Pandurang; Shastri; Auroville; Bahuguna, Sundarlal; Ralegon Siddhi; Swadhyaya; Tehri Dam
James, William 484, 596, 679, **897–898**, 1183, 1290, 1590, 1655
James, William Closson
 contributions in this encyclopedia, *see* Canada; Canadian Nature Writing
Jansdotter, Maria
 contributions in this encyclopedia, *see* Christ, Carol P.; Eisler, Riane
Japan *see* Asia – Eastern
Japanese Gardens 898–899, 955
Japanese Love of Nature 899–900
Japanese Religions 900–903, 1124
Jasper, David
 contributions in this encyclopedia, *see* Romanticism in European Literature
Jataka Tales 227, 229, **903–905** (*see also* adjacent, Great Monkey Jataka, The Mahakapijataka)
Jeffers, John Robinson 15, 417, **906** (*see also* Death and Afterlife in Robinson Jeffers and Edward Abbey)
Jeffreys, David
 contributions in this encyclopedia, *see* Egypt – Pre-Islamic
Jell-Bahlsen, Sabine
 contributions in this encyclopedia, *see* Divine Waters of the Oru-Igbo; Mammy Water
Jensen, Molly
 contributions in this encyclopedia, *see* Allen, Paula Gunn; Griffin, Susan; Shiva, Vandana
Jensen, Tim
 contributions in this encyclopedia, *see* Alliance of Religion and Conservation (ARC); Network on Conservation and Religion; Palmer, Martin
Jesuits *see* Roman Catholic Religious Orders
Jesus *see* Christianity
Jesus and Empire 907–908
Jerusalem *see* Asia – Western
Jewish Environmentalism in North America 909–913
Jewish Intertestamental Literature

913–918 (*see also* adjacent entry Types of Intertestamental Literature)
Jewish Law and Animal Experimentation 918–921
Jewish Law and Environmental Protection 921–923
Jewish Law and Genetic Engineering 923–925
Jewish Renewal *see* Judaism
Jianchu, Xu
 contribution in this encyclopedia, *see* Yunnan Region
Johns, David 803
 contributions in this encyclopedia, *see* Berman, Morris; Ehrenfeld, David; Noble, David F.
Johnson, Elizabeth 1076, 1366, 1591
 contribution in this encyclopedia, *see* Bougainville (Papua New Guinea) (with Veronica Hatutasi and Garry W. Trompf)
Johnson, Greg
 contributions in this encyclopedia, *see* Ghost Dance; Rock Climbing; Romanticism and Indigenous Peoples; Savages
Jordan III, William R.
 contributions in this encyclopedia, *see* Restoration Ecology and Ritual (and adjacent, New Academy for Nature Culture)
Jubilee and Jubilee 2000 925 (*see also* Sabbath-Jubilee Cycle)
Judaism
 animals *see* Animal Rights in the Jewish Tradition; Jewish Law and Animal Experimentation
 Bleich, Rabbi J. David 65, 922, 1698
 contributions in this encyclopedia, *see* Jewish Law and Animal Experimentation; Vegetarianism and Kabbalah; Vegetarianism and Rabbi Abraham Isaac Kook
 creation stories *see* Creation Stories in the Hebrew Bible
 Elat Chayyim 1714
 environmentalism *see* Israel and Environmentalism; Jewish Environmentalism in North America; Jewish Law and Environmental Protection
 environmental leaders *see* Redwood Rabbis
 genetic engineering *see* Jewish Law and Genetic Engineering
 haNasi, Rabbi Yehudaha 65
 Hasidism *see* Judaism – mysticism
 Hebrew Bible *see* Hebrew Bible
 Hirsch, Rabbi Samson Raphael 924, 1698

Holocaust *see* Holocaust and the Environmental Crisis
Intertestamental literature *see* Jewish Intertestamental Literature; Types of Intertestamental Literature
Jubilee *see* Jubilee and Jubilee 2000; Sabbath-Jubilee Cycle
Kook, Rabbi Abraham Isaac 66, 544, 733, 887, 909 (*see also* Vegetarianism and Rabbi Abraham Isaac Kook)
kosher *see* Eco-Kosher
Maimonides *see* Maimonides
mysticism *see* Eco-Kabbalah; Hassidism and Nature Mysticism; Kabbalah and Ecotheology
paganism *see* Paganism and Judaism; Paganism: A Jewish Perspective
Passover 497, 909, 1240, 1713
population *see* Judaism and the Population Crisis
sabbath *see* Sabbath-Jubilee Cycle
Schachter-Shalomi, Rabbi Zalman 544, 912, 1713–1714
sects
  reconstructionist 791, 908, 1714
  reform 177, 219, 791, 911
  renewal 708, 910, 934, 1713–1714
Sharnberg, Rabbi Lester 911, 1353
Steinberg, Rabbi Naomi 911, 1353
  contributions in this encyclopedia, *see* Redwood Rabbis
sustainability *see* Judaism and Sustainability
Tikkun Olam *see* Tikkun Olam – A Jewish Perspective
Torah 57–58, 64–65, 791, 926, 928, 931–933, 939, 1240, 1459, 1638, 1713–1714 (*see also* Vegetarianism, Judaism, and God's Intention)
Tu bi sh'vat 544, **909**, 911, 946, 1081, 1714
vegetarianism *see* Vegetarianism and Judaism; Vegetarianism and Kabbalah; Vegetarianism and Rabbi Abraham Isaac Kook
Judaism and Sustainability 937–938
Judaism and the Population Crisis 938–939
Julian of Norwich 363, 484, 1249, 1404
Jung, Carl – A Perspective 940–943
Jung, Carl Gustav 32–33, 160, 164, 263, 1265, 1329, 1655, 1690 (*see also* Jung, Carl – A Perspective)

K

Kabbalah *see* Judaism – Mysticism
Kabbalah and Eco-theology 945–950
Kabir *see* Asia – Southern
Kalash Culture (Northwestern Pakistan) 950–951
Kalland, Arne 902
  contributions in this encyclopedia, *see* Dolphins and New Age Religion; The Religious Environmentalist Paradigm; Whales and Japanese Culture; Whales and Whaling
Kami *see* gods, goddesses, deities and nature spirits
Kant, Immanuel *see* philosophy
Kaphirintiwa – The Place of Creation (Central Africa) 951–952, 1028–1029
Kaplan, Jeffery 1246
  contribution in this encyclopedia, *see* Devi, Savitri
Kapu in Early Hawaiian Society 952–954
Karamanolis, George
  contribution in this encyclopedia, *see* Greco-Roman World
Karman, James
  contribution in this encyclopedia, *see* Jeffers, John Robinson
Kasama Spirit Sites (Northern Zambia) 954–955
Kasof, Joseph
  contribution in this encyclopedia, *see* Leary, Timothy
Kato, Sadamichi 1093
  contribution in this encyclopedia, *see* Umehara, Takeshi
Kawabata, Yasunari 955–956
Kaza, Stephanie 1264, 1373, 1706
  contribution in this encyclopedia, *see* Buddhism – North America
Kearns, Laurel
  contributions in this encyclopedia, *see* Earth Ministry; Krueger, Fred (with Matthew Immergut); North American Coalition on Religion and Ecology; Wise Use Movement
Keepers of Lake Eyre (South Australia) 956–957
Keepin, Will
  contribution in this encyclopedia, *see* Breathwork
Keller, Catherine 355, 362
Kellert, Stephen R. 605, 810
  contribution in this encyclopedia, *see* Biophilia
Kenrick, Justin
  contribution in this encyclopedia, *see* Pygmies (Mbuti Foragers) and Bila Farmers
Kent, Stephen A.
  contribution in this encyclopedia, *see* Scientology – In Two Scholarly Perspectives
Kenya Green Belt Movement 957–961
(*see also* adjacent, Wangari Maathai on Reforesting Kenya)
Kerouac, Jack 160–162
Kerridge, Richard
  contribution in this encyclopedia, *see* Hardy, Thomas
Keyes, Ken 804
Keyfitz, Nathan 656–657
Khalid, Fazlun M. 884,
  contribution in this encyclopedia, *see* Islamic Basis for Environmental Protection; Islamic Foundation for Ecology and Environmental Sciences
Khoisan Religion 961–962
Khuttajitto, Phra Prajak 1629
Kierkegaard, Soren *see* philosophy
Kiernan, James P.
  contribution in this encyclopedia, *see* African Independent Churches
Kigen, Dogen *see* Mountains and Rivers Sutra by Japanese Soto Zen Master Dogen Kigen (and adjacent, Kigen, Dogen Mountains and Rivers Sutra (excerpts)) 1121
Kimbanguism (Central Africa) 962–963
King, Sallie B.
  contribution in this encyclopedia, *see* Nhat Hahn, Thich
kinship
  biological or ecological 373–374, 492, 517, 533, 559, 668, 711
  kinship ethics 986, 1327, 1332, 1563
Kirn, Marda
  contribution in this encyclopedia, *see* Dance
Kline, David 963–964 (*see also* David Kline on Amish Agriculture, adjacent to Christianity (6c3) – Anabaptist Mennonite Tradition)
Klingenthal Symposia 964
Klippstein, Leeona
  contribution in this encyclopedia, *see* Spirit of the Sage Council
Knights Templar 1021, 1053, 1499 (*see also* Magic)
Knowledge, Knowing and Nature 965–966
Kogi (Northern Columbia) 966–967
Koliada Viatichei 967–968 (*see also* Neo-Paganism and Ethnic Nationalism in Eastern Europe)
Kontos, Alkis 1292
Koran *see* Qur'an
Korean Mountains 968–969
Korp, Maureen
  contributions in this encyclopedia, *see* Art; Shamanism – and Art
Kraft, Kenneth
  contribution in this encyclopedia, *see* Buddhism – Engaged

Kraus, James
  contribution in this encyclopedia, see Merwin, W.S. (William Stanley)
Kratophany 108, 112
Krech III, Shepard
  contribution in this encyclopedia, see American Indians as "First Ecologists"
Kresge, Anrea A.
  contribution in this encyclopedia, see Fox, Matthew; Target Earth
Krishna, P.
  contribution in this encyclopedia, see Krishnamurti, Jiddhu
Krishnamurti, Jiddhu 813, 970–971
Kropotkin, Peter 52, 453, 971–972, 1564
Krueger, Fred 972–973, 1212–1213, 1365
Krutch, Joseph Wood 973–974, 1261
Kuckertz, Heinz
  contribution in this encyclopedia, see Xhosa – Speakers' Traditional Concept of God
Kumar, Satish
  contribution in this encyclopedia, see Schumacher, Ernest Friedrich
Kumba Mela 1778
Kundali Yoga see Yoga
Kürti, László
  contribution in this encyclopedia, see Shamanism (Neo) – Eastern Europe

L

La Barre, Weston 807, 1274, 1313
Laband, John
  contribution in this encyclopedia, see Zulu (amaZulu) War Rituals
La Bella Farm 674
Labyrinth 113, 571, 975–976
Ladakh Buddhism 976–979 (see also adjacent, Ladakh Project)
Ladakh Project 977
LaDuke, Winona 536, 609, 979–980
  contribution in this encyclopedia, see Holy Land in Native North America
LaFleur, William 14, 654
Lake Havasu 200
Lake Pergusa (Sicily) 980–982
Lake Victoria see Africa – Eastern
Lakota 196–197, 445, 464, 478, 695, 785, 786, 787, 983–985, 997, 1104–1105, 1118, 1535, 1592 (see also Black Elk; Lakota Sun Dance)
Lakota Sun Dance 985–987, 1657
Lal, Vinay 1550
  contributions in this encyclopedia, see Bishnoi (Rajasthan, India); Chipko Movement (with Elaine Craddock); Gandhi, Mohandas
Lamarck, Jean Baptiste 452
land ethics 600, 138 (see also Back to the Land Movements; Environmental Ethics; Leopold, Aldo)
land
  Back to the Land Movements see Back to the Land Movements; Thoreau, Henry David
  Land Institute 892, 988 (see also Land Institute)
  landscape see Landscape
  Native Americans see Holy Land in Native North America; Law, Religion, and Native American Lands; Hopi-Navajo Land Dispute open land movement see Open Land Movement
  sacred space/place see Sacred Space/Place
Landscapes 988–990 (see also Art; Geophilia; Greek Landscape)
Langton, Katherine
  contribution in this encyclopedia, see Findhorn Foundation/Community
language see Gimbutas, Marija; Indigenous Environmental Network; Native American Languages; Yuchee Culture and the Euchee Language Project
Lao Tzu (Laozi) see Daoism
Larsen, David K.
  contributions in this encyclopedia, see Evangelical Environmental Network; Interfaith Council for Environmental Stewardship
Laubach, Marty
  contribution in this encyclopedia, see Covenant of the Unitarian Universalist Pagans
Laugrand, Frédéric
  contribution in this encyclopedia, see Inuit
laws of ecology 178–179, 1538, 1719
Laws of Manu see Asia – Southern
law of octaves 731
Law, Religion, and Native American Lands 990–999
LeGuin, Ursula 566, 637, 638, 1000–1001
Leakey, Louis 139, 707, 1304
Leary, Timothy 738, 1002–1003, 1329
Lease, Gary
  contribution in this encyclopedia, see Hunting and the Origins of Religion
Left Biocentrism 1003–1004
legio maria 1207, 1561
Leibniz, Gottfried Wilhelm 1005
Leopold, Aldo 1005–1007 (see also Environmental Ethics; Natural History as Natural Region; Nature Religion in the United States)
  autobiography 139
  conservation 1226
  environmental ethics 598, 1167, 1374
  hunting 811
  intrinsic value theory 1326
  Land Ethic 252, 253, 456, 458, 598, 600, 1167, 1180, 1204
  National Parks 1157
  nature spirituality 180, 519, 1354, 1369
  religion 1166, 1168, 1169, 1179, 1374, 1377
Leopold II, King 1429–1431
Lerner, Berel Dov
  contributions in this encyclopedia, see Gordon, Aharon David; Jewish Law and Environmental Protection; Vegetarianism and Rabbi Abraham Isaac Kook
Letcher, Andy
  contribution in this encyclopedia, see Eco-Paganism
Levertov, Denise 351, 1008
Levi, Eliphas 1021–1022
Lévi-Strauss, Claude 95, 421, 618, 1211, 1429, 1644, 1646, 1817
Levinger, Rabbi Moshe 732–733
Lewis, C.S. 260, 1268, 1498
liberalism see neo-liberalism; Schleiermacher, Frederick
Liberation Theology see Christianity (7c) – Liberation Theology
Liddy, Mags
  contribution in this encyclopedia, see Ecotopia – the European Experience
Light, Andrew
  contribution in this encyclopedia, see Buber, Martin
Lilburn, Tim 1008–1009
Limbaugh, Rush 1757
Lincoln, Abraham 489–490, 1042
Lindisfarne Association 680, 1158
Linnaeus, Carl 368, 1009–1010, 1084
Lion King see Motion Pictures; Disney Worlds at War
Lishka, Dennis
  contributions in this encyclopedia, see Mountains and Rivers Sutra by Japanese Soto Zen Master Dogen Kigen (and adjacent, Dogen Kigen's Mountains and Rivers Sutra (Excerpts)); Watsuji, Tetsuro; Zhuangzi
Littlewood, Roland
  contribution in this encyclopedia, see Mother Earth and the Earth People
Livingston, David 1430, 1500

Locke, John *see* philosophy
Lodahl, Michael
  contribution in this encyclopedia, *see* Christianity (6c5) – Methodism
Lodrick, Deryck O.
  contributions in this encyclopedia, *see* Domestication; Goshalas
Loeffler, Jack 519
  contributions in this encyclopedia, *see* Abbey, Edward; Black Mesa (New Mexico)
Loomis, Mildred 150, 1491
Lomer, Beverley
  contribution in this encyclopedia, *see* Hildegard of Bingen
Long, Mark C.
  contribution in this encyclopedia, *see* Levertov, Denise
Lopez, Barry 311, 1010–1011, 1080
Lorentzen, Lois Ann
  contribution in this encyclopedia, *see* Boff, Leonardo (with Iain S. Maclean); Gebara, Ivone; Sierra Treks; Virgin of Guadalupe
Lost Worlds 1011–1013
Lotus Sutra *see* Buddhism
Loubser, Johannes
  contribution in this encyclopedia, *see* Venda Religion and the Land
Lovelock, James 33, 63, 275, 383, 406, 505, 528, 637, 679, 721, 730, 1013, 1587 (*see also* Gaia; Gaia Foundation and Earth Community Network)
  contribution in this encyclopedia, *see* Gaian Pilgrimage
Low, Juliette Gordon 1505, 1507
LSD *see* Entheogens; Leary, Timothy
Lubis, Abdur-Razzaq
  contribution in this encyclopedia, *see* Mandailing People (Sumatra)
Lucas, George *see* Motion Pictures
Lucas, Phillip Charles
  contribution in this encyclopedia, *see* Eleventh Commandment Fellowship
Lucifer 469, 633, 1672 (*see also* Satanism)
Luo, Kenya 816, 1207
Lutts, Ralph H.
  contributions in this encyclopedia, *see* Nature Fakers Controversy; Scopes Trial
Lyons, Dana 521, 1136
  contribution in this encyclopedia, *see* Tree Music
Lyons, Oren 747–748, 1014–1015, 1378–1379
  contribution in this encyclopedia, *see* Haudenosaunee Confederacy

M

Maasai (Tanzania) 1016–1018, 1208, 1708
Maathai, Wangari 305–306, 538, 815, 961 (*see also* Kenya Green Belt Movement and adjacent, Maathai, Wangari on Reforesting Kenya)
  contribution in this encyclopedia, *see* Maathai, Wangari on Reforesting Kenya
MacGillis, Miriam 165, 426, 612, 1406 (*see also* Genesis Farm)
Mack, John 1146–1147, 1674 (*see also* UFOs and Extraterrestrials)
Maclean, Dorothy *see* Dorothy Maclean (adjacent to Findhorn Foundation/Community)
Maclean, Iain S.
  contributions in this encyclopedia, *see* Boff, Leonardo; Christianity (7c) – Liberation Theology; Holism; Smuts, Jan Christiaan; United Nations' "Earth Summits" (with Bron Taylor and Heather Eaton); Zion Christian Church (South Africa)
Maclean, Norman 311, 668, 1080
Macy, Joanna 1019 (*see also* Sarvodaya Shramadana Movement; Buddhism – Engaged; Deep Ecology; Seed, John)
  contribution in this encyclopedia, *see* Council of All Beings
Council of all Beings 457, 558, 612, 1355, 1376
  despair and empowerment work 558
  Institute for Deep Ecology 460
  meditation 243
  nuclear weapons 241
  science and spirituality 251, 1426
Madera, Lisa Marie
  contributions in this encyclopedia, *see* Andean Traditions; Mary in Latin America; Shamanism – Ecuador
Magic 1020–1022
  Age of Magic 384
  and astrology 1729
  black 263, 841, 1476, 1673, 1702, 1709
  Eco-magic 507, 556, 557 (*see also* Eco-Magic; Golden Dawn)
  Kabbalah 932–933
  Knights Templar 1021, 1053, 1499
  shamanism *see* Magic, Animism, and the Shaman's Craft
  sympathetic magic 505, 1254, 1702
  thelemic 1021, 1022, 1484
  use of plants 619–620

Magic, Animism, and the Shaman's Craft 1023–1026
Magliocco, Sabina
  contributions in this encyclopedia, *see* Altars and Shrines; Ritualizing and Anthropology
Magowan, Fiona
  contribution in this encyclopedia, *see* Yolungu Waters of Being (Australia)
Maguire, Daniel C. 13–14, 1377
  contribution in this encyclopedia, *see* Fertility and Abortion
Maier, Harry O.
  contribution in this encyclopedia, *see* Jesus and Empire
Maimonides 1026–1027
  and neighbors 922
  and use of resources 937–938
  animals 65, 66, 68, 71, 919, 1698
  on religion and science 931–932
Makapansgat Cobble 1027–1028
Makewana the Rainmaker (Central Malawi) 1028–1030 (*see also* adjacent, Mbiriwiri – The Sacred Rainmaking Drum)
Making of an Earthist Christian 394 (adjacent to Cobb, John)
Makrides, Vasilios N.
  contributions in this encyclopedia, *see* Christianity – Eastern versus Western; Christianity (6b2) – Greek Orthodox; Greek Paganism
Maldharis of Gujarat (India) 1030–1032
Malinowski, Bronislaw 95, 663–664, 1020
Malthus, Thomas Robert 453, 653, 1032–1034
Mammy Water 495, 1034–1036, 1510
Mandailing People (Sumatra) 1037–1038
Mandalas *see* Art
Manicheans 314, 325, 511, 513, 679, 968, 1257, 1406
Manifesto to North American Christians 1044–1045
Manser, Bruno and the Penan of Sarawak 1045–1048; (*see also* Penan Hunter-Gatherers (Borneo))
Manson, Charles *see* ATWA (Air, Trees, Water, and Air)
Maori *see* Oceania – New Zealand
Mapinguari 40
Margiis, Ananda 48–49
Marshall, Robert 1048–1049, 1156, 1719, 1750
Martial Arts 412, 1049–1051
Martens, Susan
  contribution in this encyclopedia, *see* Chinese Environmentalism

Martin-Schramm, James B.
  contribution in this encyclopedia, see
    Population, Consumption and
    Christian Ethics
Marx, Karl see philosophy
Mathews, Freya
  contribution in this encyclopedia, see
    Urban Reinhabitation – CERES as
    Case Study
Mary see Christianity
Mary in Latin America 1051–1053
Maryknoll see Roman Catholic Religious
  Orders
masks 1216, 1235, 1393, 1396, 1480,
  1524–1525, 1558, 1781
Maslow, Abraham 615, 1654–1655
Masons, Fraternal Order of
  1053–1054
Masowe Wilderness Apostles
  1054–1056
master units 49
Mather, Cotton 210, 1178
Matsuo Bashô 20, 956, 1056–1057
Matthiessen, Peter 1058–1059, 1080
Mauss, Marcel 1020
maya see Hinduism
Maya see Meso-America
Maya Religion (Central America)
  1059–1062
Maya Spirituality (Guatemala
  Highlands) 1062–1065
Mayan Catholicism 1066–1067
Mayan Protestantism 1067–1068
Mayan Spirituality and Conservation
  (Western Highlands, Guatemala)
  1068–1070
Mazzeo, Tilar J.
  contribution in this encyclopedia, see
    Romanticism – American
Mbiriwiri – The Sacred Rainmaking
  Drum 1029 (adjacent to Makewana the
  Rainmaker)
McDaniel, Jay 313, 353, 364, 1264, 1373
  contributions in this encyclopedia, see
    Christianity (7f) – Process Theology;
    Prayer and the Contemplative
    Traditions
Mburu, Gathuru
  contribution in this encyclopedia, see
    Kenya Green Belt Movement
McAllister, Judy
  contribution in this encyclopedia, see
    Dorothy Maclean (adjacent to
    Findhorn Community/Foundation)
McCarthy, Kate
  contribution in this encyclopedia, see
    Daly, Mary
McCay, Mary A.
  contribution in this encyclopedia, see
    Carson, Rachel

McDaniel, Jay 353, 364, 1264, 1373
  contributions in this encyclopedia, see
    Christianity (7f) – Process Theology;
    Prayer and the Contemplative
    Traditions; Prigogine, Ilya
McDonagh, Sean 856, 1070–1071,
  1276
  contribution in this encyclopedia, see
    Philippines, The
McFague, Sally 343, 361, 362, 368, 377,
  533, 535, 555, 610, 1071–1072, 1296
  contribution in this encyclopedia, see
    Manifesto for North American
    Christians
McGinnis, Michael Vincent
  contributions in this encyclopedia, see
    Bioregionalism; Shepard, Paul
McGregor, Davianna Pomaika`i
  contribution in this encyclopedia, see
    Hawai'i
McGuane, Tom 668–669
McGuire, Mark
  contribution in this encyclopedia, see
    World Heritage Sites and Religion in
    Japan
McIntosh, Alastair 284–285, 634
  contributions in this encyclopedia,
    see Faerie Faith in Scotland (and
    adjacent, Rotting Tree Fairie);
    Scything and Erotic Fulfillment;
    Scotland
McKenna, Terence 1072–1073, 1225,
  1347
McKenzie, Michael
  contributions in this encyclopedia, see
    Explorer Petroglyphs (Western
    United States); Indian Shaker
    Religion; Seattle (Sealth), Chief;
    Washat Religion (Drummer-Dreamer
    Faith); Yakama Nation
McKibben, Bill 318, 1377
  contributions in this encyclopedia, see
    What Would Jesus Drive? (adjacent to
    Christianity (2) – Jesus); Spirit and
    Nature Walking Paths
Mechling, Jay
  contributions in this encyclopedia, see
    Indian Guides; Scouting
Meeker, Lloyd (Uranda) 595
Media 1073–1075
meditation
  Art of Living Foundation *see* Art of
    Living Foundation; Shankar, Sri Ravi
    on Consciousness, Nature and the Art
    of Living
  breathwork *see* Breathwork;
    Re-Earthing
  Buddhism 18, 51, 161, 232–233, 239,
    241–242, 1202, 1457, 1513, 1543,
    1629, 1800

Hinduism 1706 (see also yoga; Yoga and
  Ecology)
peace 1483
prayer see Prayer and the
  Contemplative Traditions
transcendental see Transcendental
  Meditation
Meine, Curt 416–417, 1374
  contribution in this encyclopedia, see
    Leopold, Aldo
Melanesia see Oceania
Melanesia – Eco-Missiological Issues
  1075–1076
Melanesia – New Religious Movements
  1076–1077
Melanesian Traditions 1077–1078
Memoir and Nature Writing
  1079–1080
Memmott, Paul
  contributions in this encyclopedia, see
    Arrernte Increase Ceremonies
    (Central Australia); Rainbow Serpent
    (North Wesley Islands, Australia);
    Yolngu Ceremonial Architecture
    (Australia) (with Shaneen Fantin)
Men of the Trees (East Africa) 152, 1081
Menache, Sophia
  contributions in this encyclopedia, see
    Animals in the Bible and Qur'an;
    Dogs in the Abrahamic Traditions
Men's Movement 1081–1082
Mendieta, Eduardo
  contribution in this encyclopedia, see
    Casas, Bartolomé de las
Menelik 74
Mengzi (Mencius) see Confucianism
Merchant, Carolyn 473, 532, 534–536,
  1083, 1108–1109, 1315, 1367, 1521
Merleau-Ponty, Maurice 1023
Merwin, W.S. (William Stanley) 1084
Meso-America
  Associación de Agricultores Ecológicos
    (ASAECO) 1070
  environmentalism see Indigenous
    Activism and Environmentalism in
    Latin America
  Incas see Incas
  Mexico
    Tenochtitlan 143, 147, 390–391, 1052,
      1085 (see also adjacent, The Fall of
      Tenochtitlan/Tlatelolco)
    Yoeme ritual see Yoeme (Yaqui) Ritual
    Zapata, Emiliano 1703
    Zapatista movement 1067
  rainforests see Rainforests
  religion
    Aztec see Aztec Religion –
      Pre-Colombian; Flower Songoo –
      Xochicuicatl; A Song of Sorrow –
      Icnocuicatl

1858   Index

Christianity in Meso-America
  Casas, Bartolomé de las *see* Casas, Bartolomé de las
  Catholicism *see* Mayan Catholicism; Roman Catholicism in Latin America
  Liberation Theology *see* **Christianity (7c) – Liberation Theology**
  nature and religion in El Salvador *see* **Salvadoran Reflection on Religion, Rights, and Nature**
  Quakers *see* **Friends – Religious Society of (Quakers)**
  Protestantism *see* Mayan Protestantism
  deities *see* gods, goddesses, deities and nature spirits
  sacrifice *see* Mesoamerican Sacrifices
Mesoamerican Deities 1084–1087
Mesoamerican Sacrifice 1087–1088
Mesopotamia – Ancient to 2,000 B.C.E. 503, 573, 621, 635, **1088–1091** (*see also* **Creation Myths of the Ancient World**)
Messner, Reinhold 1119 (*see also* adjacent **Messner on Everest and Cosmos**)
Messner on Everest and Cosmos 1120 (*see also* **Rock Climbing**)
Metaphysics
  American Metaphysical Movement 288
  Buddhist 237–238
  Deep Ecology 458
  Fascism 640
  Monist 859
  Nursi, Said 1215
  of interconnection 491, 804, 1112, 1249, 1332, 1350, 1544, 1563,
  of nature *see* Kawabata, Yasunari
  Perennial Philosophy 1269
  process 1590
  Spinoza, Baruch 1589
  Thomist 330
  Whitehead, Alfred 465, 1737
Metz, Baptist 358, 783
Metzner, Ralph *see* psychology
Mexico *see* Meso-America
Michael, Archangel 469, 642, 1672
Michell, John 526–527, **1091–1092**, 1601
Middle Earth 637, 752, **1092–1093**, 1225
Miles, Kathryn
  contributions in this encyclopedia, *see* **Blake, William; Whitman, Walt**
Miller, James
  contribution in this encyclopedia, *see* **Daoism**
Miller, Timothy
  contributions in this encyclopedia, *see* Brook Farm; Emissaries of Divine Light; Farm, The; Fruitlands; Hippies; MOVE; Open Land Movement; Rainbow Family; School of Living; Tolstoy Farm
Minakata, Kumagusu 1093–1094
mindfulness *see* Buddhism
miracles *see* Christianity
Mirsky, Seth
  contribution in this encyclopedia, *see* **Men's Movement**
Mitchell, Edgar 125, 1586, 1587
Mitchell, Elyne 1094
Mitchell, Joni 1132
Miwok People 1094–1096
Miyamoto, Yotaro
  contribution in this encyclopedia, *see* **Japanese Religions**
Miyazawa, Kenji 1097–1098
moksa see Hinduism
Molesky-Poz, Jean
  contributions in this encyclopedia, *see* **Cuero, Delfina; Maya Spirituality**
Moltmann, Jürgen 342–343, 347, 358, 382, 783, **1098–1099**
  contribution in this encyclopedia, *see* **Christianity (7b) – Political Theology**
Monaghan, Patricia
  contributions in this encyclopedia, *see* **Brigit; Chaos; Gaia**
Mongolian Buddhism and Taimen Conservation 1099–1100
monism 161, 735, 817, 933, 1188, 1257–1258, 1260
Monkeys in the Field 803 (adjacent to **Hundredth Monkey**)
monkeywrenching 128, 519 (*see also* Abbey, Edward – sabotage)
Monserud, Bruce
  contribution in this encyclopedia, *see* **Bennett, John G.**
Montejo, Victor 834
  contribution in this encyclopedia, *see* **Maya Religion**
Moore, Michael D.
  contribution in this encyclopedia, *see* **Hopkins, Gerard Manley**
Mora, Pat 1100–1101
Morton, John
  contribution in this encyclopedia, *see* **Totemism**
Mormonism *see* Church of Jesus Christ, Latter Day Saints
Moro Movement (Guadalcanal, Solomon Islands) 1077, **1101–1102**
Moses 21, 226, 257, 434, 661, 755–756, 787, 907, 939, 1245, 1321, 1456, 1516, 1594–1595
Mother Earth 9–10, 93, 156, 200, 216, 228, 283, 290, 300, 407, 442, 461–462, 610, 670, 742, 804, 805, 834, 838–839, **1102–1105** (*see also* Deism; Indigenous Environmental Network)
Mother Earth and the Earth People (Trinidad) 1105–1107
Mother Nature Imagery 1107–1110
Motion Pictures 489, 1074, **1111–1113**
  actors
    Wayne, John 44, 1042–1043
  directors and writers
    Lucas, George 1498
    Speilberg, Steven 478, 1625
  movies
    Disney 491
    Bambi 491, 1365
    Davy Crockett 488, 490, 1043, 1425
    Pocahontas 492, 1112
    The Lion King 488, 491, 314, 1112
    martial arts 1049
    Star Wars 1012, 1498–1499, 1587
Mount Nyiro and the Samburu (East Africa) 1114–1117
Mount Rushmore 1042, **1017–1018**
Mountaineering 1046, **1119–1120**, 1192, 1545 (*see also* adjacent, **Messner on Everest and Cosmos**)
Mountains and Rivers Sutra by Japanese Soto Zen Master Dogen Kigen 1120–1122 (*see also* adjacent, **Dogen Kigen's Mountain and Rivers Sutra (excerpts)**)
MOVE 1122–1123, 1346
Moyers, Bill 254, 811, 1014, 1374, 1378
Moyniham, Michael
  contributions in this encyclopedia, *see* **ATWA; Darre, Walther; Evola, Julius; Odinism**
Mpoke, Leina
  contribution in this encyclopedia, *see* **Mount Nyiro and the Samburu** (with Jacob Wanyama and Asenath Omwega)
Mt. Hiei (Japan) 113, 1121, **1123–1124**
Mt. Olympus *see* Europe – Southern
Mt. Parnassus *see* Europe – Southern
Mt. Shasta *see* North America – United States
Muhammad, The Prophet of Islam 1124–1125 (*see also* Islam)
Muir, John 1126–1127
  Autobiography 139
  environmentalism 1507 *see* Environmental Ethics; Sierra Club
  John Muir Institute for Environmental Studies 601
  National Parks *see* **National Parks and Monuments**
  on wilderness xi–xii, 20–21. 168, 178, 225, 595, 1459

religion 1154, 1747 (*see also* Nature Religion in the United States)
Mukonyora, Isabel
  contribution in this encyclopedia, *see* Masowe Wilderness Apostles
Mulcock, Jane 12
  contribution in this encyclopedia, *see* Indigenous Religions and Cultural Borrowing
Müller, Friedrich Max 1128, 1310, 1760
Murie, Olaus J. 1128–1129, 1751
Murphy, Patrick D.
  contributions in this encyclopedia, *see* Harjo, Joy; Ishimure, Michiko; Minakata, Kumagusu; Mora, Pat; Ortiz, Simon J.
Murray, Margaret 1237, 1247, 1739
Music 1129–1130
  drums *see* Drums and Drumming; Mbiriwiri – The Sacred Rainmaking Drum (adjacent to Makewana the Rainmaker)
  Grateful Dead 1132
  environmental activism *see* Music and Eco-activism in America; Lyons, Dana; Winters, Paul; Music of Resistance; Tree Music
  origins *see* Music and Its Origins
  paganism *see* Pagan Music
  songs *see* Diggers' Song (adjacent to Diggers and Levelers); Flower Song and Song of Sorrow (both entries located adjacent to Aztec Religion)
Music and Eco-activism in America 1131–1133
Music and Its Origins 1133–1135
Music of Resistance 1135–1137
Muti and African Healing 182, 1137–1138
Muti Killings 1138–1139
Mutwa, Credo 1139–1147
Myers, Ched
  contributions in this encyclopedia, *see* Anarcho-Primitivism and the Bible; Fall, The

N

Nachmanides 65–66, 925, 1697
Naess, Arne 1149–1150
  and Gandhi, Mohandas 686, 1149–1150
  Bhagavadgita 173
  conservation biology *see* Conservation Biology
  contribution in this encyclopedia, *see* Ecosophy T
  Deep Ecology *see* Deep Ecology
  Ecosophy T *see* Ecosophy T
  mountaineering 1119

Nagas *see* Hinduism
Narmada Bachao Andolan *see* Asia – Southern
Narayanan, Vasudha 1294–1295
  contributions in this encyclopedia, *see* Dharma – Hindu; Hinduism
Naropa University 1150–1151
Nash, Kate 537
Nash, James 343, 353, 368, 377, 1297
  contributions in this encyclopedia, *see* Christianity (1) Introduction; Christianity (9) – Christianity's Ecological Reformation; Ethics and Sustainability Dialogue Group (with H. James Byers); Natural Law and Natural Rights; Frugality (adjacent to Virtues and Ecology in World Religions)
Nasr, Seyyed Hossein 859, 867, 868, 1125, 1151, 1270, 1706
Natadecha-Sponsel, Poranee
  contribution in this encyclopedia, *see* Caves – Sacred (Thailand) (with Leslie E. Sponsel)
National Council of Churches, Eco-Justice Working Group (USA) 1152
National Parks and Monuments (United States) 1152–1157
National Religious Partnership for the Environment 275, 276, 307, 352, 541–542, 624, 849, 850, 911, 1152, 1158–1159
National Socialism (*see also* ATWA; Fascism; Nationalism)
  as political religion 642, 1244
  criticisms of 967
  Darre, Walter *see* Darre, Walter
  Devi, Savitri *see* Devi, Savitri
  EcoFascism *see* EcoFascism
  Haeckel, Ernst 735 (*see also* Haeckel, Ernst)
  Heidegger, Martin *see* Heidegger, Martin
  Himmler, Reichsfuhrer Heinrich *see* Europe – Western – Germany
  Hitler, Adolf *see* Europe – Western – Germany
  holocaust *see* The Holocaust and the Environmental Crisis
  misperceptions of 1219
  neo-Nazism 1187, 1246
  paganism and environmentalism 1241, 1245
  romanticism 211
Nationalism (*see also* Fascism; Neo-Paganism and Ethnic Nationalism in Eastern Europe)
  Afrikaaner 29
  American 1117
  Christian 489
  Eco-nationalism 134

European 211
Hindu 792, 829
Latin America 833
Mexican 1703
Russian 968
Zulu 1141
Native American Languages 1160–1162 (*see also* Yuchi Culture and the Euchee Language Project)
Native American Spirituality 737, 1144, 1162–1163, 1274
Native Faith Association (ORU) 1188
natural death movement *see* Green Death Movement
Natural History and Indigenous Worldviews 1163–1164
Natural History as Natural Religion 1164–1169
Natural Laws (laws of ecology) 461–462, 1166, 1538
Natural Law Party 1171–1172
nature mystics 671, 679, 1326, 1383, 1744
natural philosophy *see* philosophy
naturalism, ecstatic 420, 1259–1260
natural theology 210, 311, 327, 341–343, 349–350, 356, 368, 381, 394, 452, 462–463, 512, 914, 945, 947, 1653 (*see also* Book of Nature; Christianity (7h) – Natural Theology; Religious Naturalism)
Nature Fakers Controversy 1172–1173
Nature Religion xiii, x, xii–xiii, xv, xvii–xviii, xx, 1173–1175
  Alpha Farm 35
  anthropology *see* Anthropology as a Source of Nature Religion
  Britain 221–222
  Celtic 282, 284
  Circle Sanctuary *see* Circle Sanctuary
  Disney 493
  Druidry *see* Druids and Druidry
  Earth First 519, 521
  Graves, Robert Von Ranke *see* Graves, Robert Von Ranke
  Heathenry *see* Heathenry – Ásatrú
  Leary, Timothy *see* Leary, Timothy
  Muir, John *see* Muir, John
  Neo-paganism *see* Neo-Paganism
  Scottland *see* Faerie Faith in Scotland
  United States *see* Nature Religion in the United States
Nature Religion in the United States 1175–1184
nature mysticism (*see also* Pantheism)
  criticisms of 603, 1328
  Emerson, Ralph Waldo 484 (*see also* Transcendentalism)
  Hassidism *see* Hassidism and Nature Mysticism

numinous 3, 20, 51, 91–93, 165–166, 168, 232, 292, 295, 298, 299, 634, 641, 732–733, 1080, 1759
Perennial Philosophy 601
Reclus, Elisée 52, 1352
Saint Francis 1405 (*see also* Francis of Assisi)
Spinoza, Baruch *see* Spinoza, Baruch
Zaehner, R.C. 640
nature spirituality 49, 50, 54, 392, 415, 417, 490–493, 519, 522, 598, 603, 674 (*see also* Gardening and Nature Spirituality)
Hundredth Monkey 804
nature writing 139, 188, 248–249, 271, 484, 582, 730, 736, 1058 (*see also* Canadian Nature Writing; Christian Nature Writing; Hardy, Thomas; Memoir and Nature Writing; Williams, Terry Tempest)
Navajo *see* North America – United States
Navarro, Ricardo A.
  contribution in this encyclopedia, *see* Salvadorian Reflection
Naylor, D. Keith
  contributions in this encyclopedia, *see* Pinchot, Gifford (and adjacent, Pinchot on Church and Country)
Nazism *see* National Socialism
Ndembu Religion (South-Central Africa) 1185–1186
near death experiences *see* death
Nearing, Helen and Scott 150–151, 1754–1755
Nelson, Lance 772, 1369
Nelson, Michael
  contributions in this encyclopedia, *see* Callicott, J. Baird; Pagan Environmental Ethics
Nelson, Richard 96, 260, 809, 811–812
Neo-liberalism 698–699
Neo-paganism
  compared with Nazism 531
  Ethnic Nationalism *see* Neo-paganism and Ethnic Nationalism in Eastern Europe
  Judaism 1245–1246
  Slavokia *see* Slavic Neo-Paganism
  Ukraine *see* Neo-Paganism in Ukraine
Neo-paganism and Ethnic Nationalism in Eastern Europe 1186–1188
Neo-paganism in Ukraine 1188–1189
Neo-Platonism *see* philosophy
Neo-Wessex Archeology 1189–1190
Nepal *see* Asia – Southern
Network on Conservation and Religion 34, 1193, 1771
New Academy for Nature and Culture 1380 (adjacent to Restoration Ecology and Ritual)

New Age 1193–1197 (*see also* New Religious Movements)
  Argüelles, Jose 60, 739, 804, 1672
  astrology *see* Astrology
  Australia *see* Aboriginal Spirituality and the New Age in Australia
  Campbell, Joseph *see* Campbell, Joseph
  Castaneda, Carlos *see* Castaneda, Carlos
  channeling *see* Channeling
  criticism 1554
  dolphins *see* Dolphins and New Age Religion
  Emissaries of the Divine Light *see* Emissaries of the Divine Light
  Esalen Center *see* Esalen Center
  faerie faith *see* Faerie Faith in Scotland
  Findhorn Foundation *see* Findhorn Foundation/Community
  Gestalt Therapy 615, 1194
  Gurdjieff, Georges Ivanovitch *see* Gurdjieff, Georges Ivanovitch
  Harmonic Convergence *see* Argüelles, Jose; Harmonic Convergence
  horoscopes 124, 771
  human potential movements 279, 615, 804, 1194
  Hundredth Monkey *see* Hundredth Monkey
  Jung, Carl *see* Jung, Carl
  labryinth *see* Labryinth
  Leary, Timothy *see* Leary, Timothy
  literature *see* Celestine Prophecy; Fantasy Literature
  medicine men *see* Plastic Medicine Men
  Mutwa, Credo *see* Mutwa, Credo
  power spots 738, 1449, 1512
  re-earthing *see* Re-Earthing
  science 160, 266, 1279, 1303, 1528, 1537
  Shamanism *see* Shamanism
  Tantra *see* Tantrism in the West
  Tarot 1021–1022, 1235, 1536, 1729, 1800
  UFOs *see* UFOs and Extraterrestrials
Newbury Bypass Campaign 556
New Findhorn Association (NFA) *see* Findhorn Foundation/Community
New Religious Movements 36, 648, 656, 1197–1199, 1200, 1373, 1687 (*see also* Melanesia – New Religious Movements; New Age; Polynesia – New Religious Movements)
Newton, Isaac *see* Science
New Zealand *see* Oceania
Non-governmental Organizations (NGO's) 153, 292, 379, 541, 998, 1482, 1552, 1681
Nhat Hanh, Thich 243, 1175, 1202–1203, 1508, 1553 (*see also* Buddhism – Engaged)

Nichols, William
  contributions in this encyclopedia, *see* Kline, David; Sanders, Scott Russell
Nicholson, Shirley 680, 1632–1633
Nietzsche, Friedrich 137, 255, 472, 625, 643, 760, 1203–1205, 1677
Nihilism 289, 315
Nile Perch 1205–1208 (*see also* organisms)
Nkomo, Joshua *see* Africa – East
Noah 64–65, 172, 302–303, 304, 309, 357, 434, 436, 585–536, 756, 886, 916, 919, 938–939, 1400, 1458, 1693, 1698
Noble Savage 10, 42, 741, 968, 998, 1105, 1208–1209, 1425, 1488, 1556 (*see also* Noble Savage and the "Ecologically Noble" Savage)
Noble Savage and the "Ecologically Noble" Savage 1210–1212
Noble, David F. 1209–1210
Noel, Daniel C. 255
  contributions in this encyclopedia, *see* Space Exploration (and adjacent, Institute of Noetic Sciences)
Noll, Richard 942
  contributions in this encyclopedia, *see* Haeckel, Ernst; Jung, Carl Gustav
non-anthropocentrism *see* biocentrism, eco-centrism, deep ecology
non-dualism 130, 237–238, 242, 670, 772 (*see also* Hinduism – Vedanta)
Norberg-Hodge, Helen 977, 1682
  contributions in this encyclopedia, *see* Ladakh Buddhism; Ladakh Project
North America
  Bioregionalism *see* Bioregionalism and the North American Bioregional Congress
  Buddhism *see* Buddhism – North America
  Canada 255–258
    environmental organizations *see* Aboriginal Environmental Groups in Canada
    Akwesasne Task Force on the Environment (ATFE) 9
    Assembly of First Nations (AFN) 9
    Frye, Northrop 255, 256, 260
    hydro-electric power *see* James Bay Cree and Hydro-Quebec
    nature writing *see* Canadian Nature Writing
    traditional ecological knowledge *see* Traditional Ecological Knowledge among Aboriginal Peoples in Canada
  Christianity in North America
    Cathedral of St. John the Divine *see* Cathedral of St. John the Divine

Christian Friend of the Earth, A *see* **Christian Friend of the Earth, A**
Creation Spirituality *see* **Christianity (7e) – Creation Spirituality**
Evangelical Christianity *see* **Christianity (7i) – An Evangelical Perspective on Faith and Nature**
Ecological Reformation *see* **Christianity (9) – Christianity's Ecological Reformation**
Eco-justice *see* **Eco-justice in Theology and Ethics**
Eco-feminism *see* **Ecofeminism – Historic and International Evolution**
people, influential
  Berry, Thomas *see* **Berry, Thomas** (and adjacent, **Thomas Berry on Religion and Nature**)
  Berry, Wendell *see* **Berry, Wendell**
  Christ, Carol *see* **Christ, Carol**
  Cobb, John *see* **Cobb, John**
  Edwards, Jonathon 139, 210, 346–347, 1039, 1178
  Fox, Matthew *see* **Fox, Matthew**
  Kline, David *see* **Kline, David; David Kline on Amish Agriculture** (adjacent to Christianity (6c3) **Anabaptist/Mennonite Traditions**)
  Krueger, Fred *see* **Krueger, Fred**
  Muir, John *see* **Muir, John**
  Pinchot, Gifford *see* **Pinchot, Gifford** (and adjacent, **Pinchot on Church and Country**)
  Ruether, Rosemary Radford *see* **Ruether, Rosemary Radford**
  Sittler, Joseph A. Jr. *see* **Sittler, Joseph A. Jr**
  White, Lynn – Thesis of *see* **White, Lynn – Thesis of**
  Williams, Delores S. *see* **Williams, Delores S.**
Process Philosophy *see* **Process Philosophy**
Process theology *see* **Christianity (7f) – Process Theology**
Puritans *see* **Puritans**
Restoring Eden *see* **Restoring Eden**
Unitarianism *see* **Unitarianism**
Womanism *see* **Christianity (7g) – Womanism**
Christianity in practice (institutes, movements, and organizations)
  Au Sable Institute *see* **Au Sable Institute**
  Christian Camp Meetings *see* **Christian Camp Meetings**
  Columbia River Watershed Pastoral Letter *see* **Columbia River Watershed astoral Letter**
  Earth Ministry *see* **Earth Ministry**

Eco-Church Movement *see* **Eco-Church Movement**
Eleventh Commandment Fellowship *see* **Eleventh Commandment Fellowship**
Evangelical Environmental Network *see* **Evangelical Environmental Network**
Genesis Farm *see* **Genesis Farm**
Green Sisters Movement *see* **Green Sisters Movement**
Interfaith Council for Environmental Stewardship *see* **Interfaith Council for Environmental Stewardship**
National Council of Churches, Eco-Justice Working Group *see* **National Council of Churches, Eco-Justice Working Group (USA)**
National Religious Partnership for the Environment *see* **National Religious Partnership for the Environment**
North American Conference (Coalition) on Christianity and Ecology *see* **North American Conference (Coalition) on Christianity and Ecology**
Religious Campaign for Forest Conservation *see* **Religious Campaign for Forest Conservation**
Stewardship *see* **Stewardship**
Target Earth *see* **Target Earth**
Tolstoy Farm *see* **Tolstoy Farm**
What Would Jesus Drive? *see* **What Would Jesus Drive?** adjacent to **Christianity (2) – Jesus**)
Wise Use Movement *see* **Wise Use Movement**
Haudenosaunee 9, 1014–1015 (*see also* **Haudenosaunee Confederacy**)
pagan festivals *see* **Paganism Festivals in North America**
United States
  American Renaissance 594
  American Spiritualism 287
  art *see* **Art**
  bison *see* **organisms – fauna**
  Boone, Daniel 1042
  Civilian Conservation Corp 1081
  cowboys *see* **Cowboy Spirituality**
  Declaration of Independence 641, 1039, 1155
  environmental organizations (*see also* North America – Christianity – Christianity in practice)
    Alliance of Religion and Conservation *see* **Alliance of Religion and Conservation**
    Don't Make a Wave Committee (DMWC) 727, 1720
    Earth First! *see* **Earth First! and the Earth Liberation Front**
    Greenpeace *see* **Greenpeace**

Network on Conservation and Religion *see* **Network on Conservation and Religion**
Sea Shepherd Conservation Society *see* **Watson, Paul – and the Sea Shepherd Conservation Society**
Sierra Club *see* **Sierra Club**
Wilderness Society *see* **Wilderness Society**
World Wide Fund for Nature *see* **World Wide Fund for Nature**
frontier myth 256, 430, 488
Hawai'i *see* **Hawai'i**
gods/goddesses *see* **gods, goddesses, deities and nature spirits**
Hawaiian Sovereignty Movement 1289
Kapu *see* **Kapu in Early Hawaiian Society**
surfing *see* **Surfing**
manifest destiny *see* **Manifest Destiny**
Native Americans
  American Indian Movement 93, 461, 492, 522, 830, 998, 1014, 1163, 1719
  American Indian Religious Freedom Act 465, 478, 701, 785, 990, 996
  Apache
    Apache Survival Coalition 998
    language 1161
    music 1134
    peyote 1273–1274
    spiritual practices 788
  as symbols *see* **Noble Savage; Savages**
  crying Indian 44, 1488
  Blackfoot confederacy 202, 205
  Bureau of Indian Affairs 464, 747–748
  environmental organizations *see* **Indigenous Environmental Network**
  ghost dance *see* **Ghost Dance**
  guides *see* **Indian Guides**
  influential figures, *see* **Black Elk; Deere, Phillip; Deloria, Vine Jr; Harjo, Joy; LaDuke, Winona; Lyons, Oren; Ortiz, Simon; Seattle (Sealth), Chief**
  land
    disputes *see* **Hopi-Navajo Land Dispute**
    sacred sites *see* **Sacred Geography in Native North America**
  languages *see* **Native American Languages**
  National Congress of American Indians (NCAI) 464, 788
  peoples
    Anishnabeg *see* **Anishnabeg Culture**
    Hopi 44, 445, 474, 520, 738, 787, 975, 993. 996, 1298, 1496, 1563,

1862   Index

(see also Black Mesa, New Mexico; Hopi-Navajo Land Dispute; Hopiland to the Rainforest Action Network)
Inuit see Inuit
Lakota see Lakota; Lakota Sun Dance
Miwok see Miwok People
Najavo 520, 787, 1161, 1457–1458, 1476 (see also Black Mesa (New Mexico); Hopi-Navajo Land Dispute; Law, Religion and Native American Lands)
Paiute see Paiute Culture
Shosone see Shosone
Yakama nation see Yakama Nation
Zuni 785–787, 790, 998
perspectives on nature see American Indians as "First Ecologists"; Blackfoot Cosmos as Natural Philosophy
peyote see Peyote
Peyote Way Church of God 1275
religion see Indian Shaker Religion; Washat Religion
Smohalla 1102–1103, 1108, 1579, 1712–1713, 1775–1776
spirituality see Harmony in Native North American Spiritual Traditions; Native American Spirituality
Swamp, Jake 748
sweat lodge 92, 1485
National Parks 43, 107, 192, 387, 415, 444, 490, 693, 782, 869, 1425, 1544–1546 (see also National Parks and Monuments)
Nature Religion 1173–1175 (see also Nature Religion in the United States)
Northeastern United States
Haudenosaunee Confederacy see Haudenosaunee Confederacy
Northwestern United States
Coldwater Springs 788
Seattle, Chief see Seattle (Sealth), Chief
Watershed Protection see Columbia River Watershed Pastoral Letter
Presidents
Adams, John Quincy 1040
Clinton, Bill 748, 786, 1144
Jackson, Andrew 992–993, 1424, 1791
Lincoln, Abraham 489–490, 1042
Reagan, Ronald 601, 1330, 1734
Roosevelt, Theodore 247, 248, 386, 477, 998, 1041, 1042, 1118, 1127, 1156, 1173, 1281, 1507
Romanticism see Romanticism – American; Romanticism – Western toward Asian Religions

Southwestern United States
Central Arizona Project 200–201
Sante Fe see Santa Fe, New Mexico
Sedona see Sedona
Tantra see Tantrism in the West
Western United States
art see Rock Art – Western United States
education programs and institutes see California Institute of Integral Studies; Esalen Institute
environmental issues see G-O road; Redwood Rabbis
Headwaters Forest (California) 243, 1353
Hetch Hetchy Dam 386, 1127, 1545
John Muir Institute for Environmental Studies 601
petroglyphs see Explorer Petroglyphs
social justice movements see Chávez, César – and the United Farm Workers
historical sites see Devils Tower; Mt. Rushmore
Mountain States Legal Foundation 478, 518, 1755
Mt. Shasta 288, 528, 738, 739
Rocky Mountain Institute 275, 541
von Humboldt, Alexander 1040, 1126
writers see Desert Writers
Yellowstone National Park 168, 193
Yosemite National Park 15, 107, 168, 444, 1096, 1126–1127, 1399, 1545 (see also National Parks and Monuments)
Southern United States
Perelandra see Perelandra
writers
Faulkner, William 1043
Twain, Mark 474, 1154
Yuchi culture see Yuchi Culture and the Euchee (Yuchi) Language Project
Wildlands project 416, 521, 803
North American Conference on Christianity and Ecology [and the] North American Coalition on Religion and Ecology 1212–1214
Norway see Europe – Northern
Norwich, Julian of 351, 363, 484, 1349, 1404, 1423
nuclear weapons 241, 519–520, 532, 565, 727, 803, 804, 910, 1463, 1520, 1579
nudity 648, 780, 1235, 1336, 1674
numinous (in nature) see Nature Mysticism
Nursi, Said 1214–1215 (see also adjacent, Nursi on Nature and God)
Nursi on Nature and God 1214

Nyajeka, Tumani
contribution in this encyclopedia, see Shona Women and the Mutupo Principle
Nyamweru, Celia
contribution in this encyclopedia, see Sacred Groves of Africa
Nyau – A Closed Association (Central Africa) 1216–1217

O

Oceania
Australia 255–258
Aboriginal spirituality see Aboriginal Spirituality and the New Age in Australia
Alawa 88
ancestors 4–7, 106, 134, 690
animism see Animism – Humanity's Original Religious Worldview
architecture see Yolngu Ceremonial Architecture
Arrernte see Arrernte Increase Ceremonies
art see Aboriginal Art; Rock Art – Australian Aboriginal
Birch, Charles see Birch, Charles
CERES see Urban Reinhabitation CERES as a Case Study
Dolphin People see Dolphins and New Age Religion
dreaming see Aboriginal Dreaming
Lake Eyre see Keepers of Lake Eyre
Mount Field National Park 1320
paganism see Paganism in Australia
poetry see Australian Poetry
Rainbow Serpent see Rainbow Serpent
rock art see Rock Art – Australian Aboriginal
sacred space see Genealogy and Spiritualities of Place
Seed, John see Council of All Beings; Seed, John
Torres Strait Islanders see Torres Strait Islanders
Yolngu see Yolngu Waters of Being
Christianity in Oceania
Liberation Theology see Christianity (7c) – Liberation Theology
Eco-missiological issues see Melanesia – Eco-Missiological issues
McDonagh, Sean see McDonagh, Sean
Philippines, The see Philippines, The
Quakers see Friends – Religious Society of (Quakers); Quaker Writers in Tasmania (Australia)
Melanesia
Melanesian Traditions see Melanesian Traditions

Moro Movements *see* Moro Movement
New Religious Movements *see* Melanesia – New Religious Movements
Papua New Guinea 1230, 1261–1263, 1342, 1382, 1513
Bougainville *see* Bougainville
Organisasi papua merdeka (OPM) 672
Solomon Islands *see* Christian Fellowship Church; Melanesia – New Religious Movements
traditions *see* Melanesian Traditions
New Zealand 1200–1201
Maori 1200–1201, 1289, 1457–1458, 1734
Pacific Islands 1230–1231
Polynesia
religion
new *see* Polynesia – New Religious Movements
traditional *see* Polynesian Traditional Religions
O'Connor, Sandra Day 701, 996–997
Odinism 476, 642, 1218–1220, 1246 (*see also* Heathenry – Ásatrú)
Odysseus *see* Europe – Southern
Oelschlaeger, Max 14, 811, 1545
contributions in this encyclopedia, *see* Paleolithic Religions and the Future; Wilderness Religion
Oikos 23, 1220–1221, 1320, 1802
Olcott, Henry Steel 206, 1180, 1632
Olson, Sigurd F. 1221–1222
Olympic Games 661, 722
Olympus, Mount *see* Europe – Southern
Omwega, Asenath
contribution in this encyclopedia, *see* Mt. Nyiro and the Samburu (with Leina Mpoke and Jacob Wanyama)
Open Land Movement 1222
Order of the Golden and Rosy Cross 1054
organic farming *see* agriculture
organisms
fauna (*see also* Fauna Cabala)
antelope 623, 807, 824, 961, 1473, 1541
bats 276–277, 1584–1585
bear 717, 790, 808, 851, 896, 1298, 1403, 1441, 1644
buffalo 786, 983, 1512 (*see also* Bison Restoration and Native American Traditions; Lakota Sun Dance)
bulls 67, 73–74, 389, 1017
chimpanzees 706–708, 1028, 1496 (*see also* Primate Spirituality)
cows 69, 73–74, 390, 430, 768, 824–825, 951, 978, 1365 (*see also* Goshalas)
dolphins 41, 285–286, 724, 1720, 1731 (*see also* Dolphins and New Age Religion; Whales and Whaling)

dung beetle 644–645
elephants *see* Elephants
fish 120, 963
anemone fish 645–646
as a symbol 77, 220, 267, 741
as food 1578, 1668, 1692, 1694
behavior 896
carp 113
conservation of 297, 496,
decline of 177, 257, 309, 857, 871, 1579
in bible 319–320
in Egypt 576, 579
in myths 235, 741–742, 766
perch *see* Nile Perch
release of 438
salmon 188, 399, 525, 661, 668, 742, 785–786 (*see also* Sohappy, David – and Salmon Spirituality)
sustainable fishing 213 (*see also* Fishers; Fly Fishing; Creatures' Release in Chinese Buddhism)
kingfisher 135, 1686
lions 76, 491, 768, 808, 1018, 1473, 1807
mongoose 647
pigs 77, 305, 309, 499, 545, 548, 672, 1078, 1231, 1261–1262, 1287, 1343
goats 210, 951, 1018, 1064, 1410, 1820
jaguar 800–801, 1360, 1527, 1779
reindeer 156, 619, 752, 1364, 1440–1441, 1553
snails 120, 645, 788
snakes 157, 389, 645, 796, 1018, 1034, 1396, 1516–1517, 1641 (*see also* Snakes and the Luo of Kenya)
python 466, 496, 1029, 1034–1035, 1516, 1642, 1787, 1816
tigers 685, 768, 808, 886, 969
vultures 1813
whales 285–286, 500, 637, 852, 1011, 1143, 1168, 1720, 1754 (*see also* Whales and Japanese Culture; Whales and Whaling)
wolves 87, 616, 1442, 1645
flora (*see also* Ethnobotany; Ethnoecology; Entheogens)
Ayahuasca *see* Ayahuasca
coca 60, 62, 620–621, 820, 966–967
coffee 525, 1037, 1106, 1478
fig trees 319, 437, 1017, 1453, 1699
peyote *see* Peyote
tobacco 39, 41, 169
trees *see* forests
Orixa Iroko 261–263 (adjacent to Candomblé of Brazil)
Orthodox Spirituality 336–337 (adjacent to Christianity (6b1) – Christian Orthodoxy)

Ortiz, Beverly
contribution in this encyclopedia, *see* Miwok People
Ortiz, Simon J. 609, 1223–1224
Orton, David
contribution in this encyclopedia, *see* Left Biocentrism
Oru-Igbo *see* Divine Waters of the Oru-Igbo (Southeastern Nigeria)
Osborne, John
contribution in this encyclopedia, *see* Art of the Living Foundation
Oshmarii-Chimarii (Mari El Republic, Russia) 1223–1224
O'Sullivan, John 1038–1040
Otherworlds 144, 157, 764, 1224–1225
Ott, Jonathon 596, 1313
Otto, Rudolf 484, 1761
Ouspensky, Pyotr Demianovich 730–732, 1006–1007, 1225–1227
Ouzman, Sven
contribution in this encyclopedia, *see* San Apocalpytic Rock Art
overconsumption 122, 331, 506, 1293, 1468
overpopulation *see* population
Ovid 289, 433, 570, 814, 981, 1410 (*see also* Ovid's Metamorphoses)
Ovid's Metamorphoses 570, 814, 1227–1229
Oyeronke, Olajubu
contributions in this encyclopedia, *see* Wenger, Susan, Yoruba Art and the Oshogbo Sacred Grove
Ozdemir, Ibrahim
contributions in this encyclopedia, *see* Muhammad, The Prophet of Islam; Nursi on Nature and God (and adjacent, Nursi, Said); Rumî, Jalaluddin

P

Pacific Islands *see* Oceania
pacifism 271
Pagan Calendar 519, 1231–1232
Pagan Environmental Ethics 1232–1233
Pagan festivals 510, 557, 1189, 1558 (*see also* Pagan Festivals in North America; Pagan Festivals – Contemporary)
Pagan Festivals in North America 1234–1236
Pagan Festivals – Contemporary 1236–1237
Pagan Music 1238 (*see also* adjacent, Burning Times)
Paganism
Aradia *see* Aradia
Australia *see* Paganism in Australia

calendar *see* Pagan Calendar
contemporary *see* Paganism –
  Contemporary; Nature Religion
Donga Tribe *see* Donga Tribe
Eastern Europe *see* Neo-Paganism and
  Ethnic Nationalism in Eastern
  Europe; Neo-Paganism in the
  Ukraine; Oshmarii-Chimarii; Slavic
  Neo-Paganism
ecological *see* Eco-Paganism; Pagan
  Environmental Ethics
Eco-Magic *see* Eco-Magic
festivals *see* Pagan Festivals –
  Contemporary; Pagan Festivals in
  North America
Greece *see* Greek Paganism
Heathenism *see* Heathenry – Ásatrú
Influential figures *see* Darré, Walther;
  Eisler, Riane; Gimbutas, Marija;
  Graves, Robert von Ranke;
  Starhawk; Z Budapest
Judaism *see* Paganism and Judaism;
  Paganism: A Jewish Perspective
music *see* Pagan Music; Burning
  Times
Neo-paganism *see* Neo-Paganism Pagan
  Church of all Worlds 520
Norse Paganism *see* Elves and Land
  Spirits in Pagan Norse Religion
Odinism *see* Odinism
organizations *see* Church of All Worlds;
  Circle Sanctuary; Covenant of
  Unitarian Universalist Pagans;
  Dragon Environmental Network;
  Koliada Viatichei; Reclaiming
Otherworlds *see* Otherworlds
Pakistan *see* Kalish Culture (Northwest
  Pakistan)
Radical Environmentalism 1326, 1328
Raves *see* Raves
Russia *see* Oshmaril – Chimari;
  Paganism – Mari
Shamanism *see* Shamanism – Neo;
  Shamanism – Neo (Eastern Europe);
  Shamanism – Urban
technology *see* Paganism and
  Technology
Wicca *see* Wicca
Paganism and Judaism 1239–1241
Paganism and Technology 1241–1242
Paganism in Australia 1243–1244
Paganism: A Jewish Perspective
  1244–1246
Paganism – Contemporary 1247–1250
Paganism – Mari (Mari El Republic,
  Russia) 1251–1252
Pahnke, Walter M.D. 596
Paiute Culture 198, 1252–1253
Paleolithic Art 1253–1254, 1363
Paleolithic Religions 1254–1255

Paleolithic Religions and the Future
  1256–1257
Palmer, Martin 34–35, 1193, **1257**, 1770
Pantanjali *see* Asia – Southern
Pantheism 1257–1260 (*see also* Nature
  Mysticism)
  Abbey, Edward 3
  Adams, Ansel 15
  and animism 90
  Diggers and Levelers 482
  Einstein, Albert 582
  Emerson, Ralph Waldo 248
  Fox, Matthew 670
  Haeckel, Earnst 736
  Jeffers, John Robinson 906 (*see also*
    Death and Afterlife in Robinson
    Jeffers and Edward Abbey)
  Kalish polytheism 951
  Spinoza, Baruch 600
  Whitman, Walt *see* Whitman, Walt
Pantheist Association for Nature – PAN
  1261
Paper, Jordan 1103
  contributions in this encyclopedia, *see*
    Anishnabeg Culture; Chinese
    Traditional Concepts of Nature; A
    Religio-Ecological Perspective
Papini, Robert
  contribution in this encyclopedia, *see*
    Church of Nazareth Baptists
Papua New Guinea *see* Oceania –
  Melanesia
Parliament of the World's Religions
  1263–1264, 1581
Parvaiz, Mohammad Aslam
  contributions in this encyclopedia, *see*
    Islam on Man and Nature (and
    adjacent, The Hadith and Shari'a on
    Man and Nature); Islamic Foundation
    for Science and Environment
Passover *see* Judaism
Pater, Cathrien de
  contributions in this encyclopedia, *see*
    ECOtheraphy (by Hans Andeweg and
    Rijk Bois); Pogacnik, Marko
Pastoralism 56, 98, 148, 163, 211, 247,
  302, 570, 1018, 1031, 1040, 1114, 1116,
  1347, 1424–1425, 1824 (*see also*
  Saharan Pastoralists)
Paton, Joseph Noel 633
Patterson, John 808
Pauli, Wolfgang 582, **1264–1265**, 1266,
  1278, 1537
Payne, Roger 285, 1754
Payutto, Phra Dhammapitaka
  1265–1266, 1629
Pearson, Joanne
  contribution in this encyclopedia, *see*
    Wicca (with Sarah M. Pike)
Peat, F. David 289, 1266

Pecotic, David
  contributions in this encyclopedia,
    see Gurdjieff, Georges
    Ivonovitch; Ouspensky, Pyotr
    Demianovich
Pedersen, Kusumita P.
  contribution in this encyclopedia, *see*
    Asceticism
Pederson, Poul 1367, 1370
Pennick, Nigel 526, 692, 1600
Penan Hunter-Gatherers (Borneo)
  1266–1268 (*see also* Manser, Bruno –
  and the Penan of Sarawak)
Pentikäinen, Juha
  contribution in this encyclopedia, *see*
    Sauna
Perelandra 660, 1268–1269
Perennial Philosophy 601, **1269–1272**
  (*see also* Huxley, Aldous)
permaculture *see* agriculture
Persinger, Michael 527, 806
personalism 330, 353, 591, 783
pesticides *see* agriculture
Peters, Chris 785
Peterson, Anna 605
  contributions in this encyclopedia,
    see David Kline on Amish
    Agriculture (adjacent to Christianity
    (6c3) – Anabaptist/Mennonite
    Traditions); Roman Catholicism in
    Latin America; Social Construction
    of Nature and Environmental
    Ethics
Peterson, Brandt Gustav
  contribution in this encyclopedia, *see*
    Indigenous Activism and
    Environmentalism
Peterson, David 810
  contribution in this encyclopedia, *see*
    Hunting Spirituality and Animism
Peterson, Mark C.E.
  contributions in this encyclopedia, *see*
    Descartes, René – and the Problem of
    Cartesian Dualism; Heidegger,
    Martin; Martial Arts
Petroglyphs 108, 444, 584, 1390–1393,
  1397, 1398, 1579 (*see also* Explorer
  Petroglyphs)
pets *see* animals
Peyote 199, 596–597, 780, 1253,
  1272–1275, 1312, 1336 (*see also*
  Ethnobotany)
Philippines, The *see* Asia – Southeastern
Philippon, Daniel J.
  contribution in this encyclopedia, *see*
    Wilderness Society
Philo of Alexandria 544, 928
philosophy
  anarchy *see* Abbey, Edward;
    Anarchism; Reclus, Elisée

Buddhist philosophy 976 (*see also* Buddhism; Dalai Lama)
environmental philosophy *see* Bioregionalism; Deep Ecology; Environmental Ethics; Leopold, Aldo; Naess, Arne; Sarvodaya Shramadan Movement; Snyder, Gary
Esoterism *see* Western Esoterism
Indian 771–774, 828, 892 (*see also* Gandhi, Mohandas; Yoga and Ecology)
natural philosophy 352, 452, 454, 467, 714, 1165–1166, 1227 (*see also* Lopez, Barry; Blackfoot Cosmos and Natural Philosophy; Natural History as Natural Religion; Philosophy of Nature)
Neo-humanism *see* Ananda Marga's Tantric Neo-Humanism
perennial philosophy *see* Perennial Philosophy
philosophers
  Aristotle 65, 653, 698, 713–716, 814, 1166, 1260, 1277–1278
  Cusa, Nicholas of *see* Cusa, Nicholas of
  Descartes, René *see* Descartes, René and the Problem of Cartesian Dualism
  Engels, Frederick 403–404, 1033, 1761
  Gurdjieff, Georges Ivanovitch *see* Gurdjieff, Georges Ivanovitch
  Hegel, G.W. Friedrich *see* Hegel, G.W. Friedrich
  Heidegger, Martin *see* Heidegger, Martin
  Heraclitus 63, 712, 1277
  Hobbes, Thomas 56, 698, 1166, 1211, 1278
  James, William *see* James, William
  Kant, Immanuel 394–395, 463, 1174, 1278, 1307–1308, 1421, 1490, 1652–1653, 1730
  Kierkegaard, Soren 759
  Leibnez, Gottfried Willhelm *see* Leibnez, Gottfried Willhelm
  Locke, John 463, 698–699, 991–992, 1653
  Marx, Karl 80, 230, 473, 566, 591, 699, 759, 1033, 1291, 1761
  Nietzsche, Friedrich *see* Nietzsche, Friedrich
  Ouspensky, Pyotr Demianovich *see* Ouspensky, Pyotr Demianovich
  Plato 63, 99, 210, 312, 324–330, 433, 561, 570, 712–716, 859, 928, 941, 1012, 1107, 1183, 1227, 1278, 1403, 1590–1591, 1729
    Neo-platonism 99, 328, 330, 671, 1278, 1403, 1729
  Reclus, Elisée *see* Reclus, Elisée

Rousseau, Jean-Jacques *see* Rousseau, Jean-Jacques
Rumî, Jalaluddin *see* Rumî, Jalaluddin
Schelling, Friedrich Willhelm Joseph *see* Schelling, Friedrich Willhelm Joseph
Schlegel, Friedrich 1174, 1310, 1421
Smuts, Jan Christiaan *see* Smuts, Jan Christiaan
Spinoza, Baruch *see* Spinoza, Baruch
Umehara, Takeshi *see* Umehara, Takeshi
Watsuji, Tetsuro *see* Watsuji, Tetsuro
personalism *see* 330, 353, 783, 1559
political *see* 190, 297, 1001, 1165, 1328, 1564
Process *see* Christianity (7f) – Process Theology; Cobb, John; Process Philosophy; Whitehead, Alfred
Russian Mystical Philosophy *see* Russian Mystical Philosophy
Social Philosophy *see* Environmental Ethics
Transcendentalism *see* Transcendentalism
Philosophy of Nature 208, 237, 266, 758, 928, 1005, 1009–1010, 1122, **1277–1279**, 1490, 1528, 1590, 1728–1729 (*see also* Process Philosophy; Whitehead, Alfred; Cobb, John)
photography *see* Art
phylogenetic tree 735
phylogeny 735, 812
Physicians for Social Responsibility 461
Pike, Sarah M.
  contributions in this encyclopedia, *see* Burning Man; Pagan Festivals in North America; Wicca (with Joanne Pearson)
pilgrimage (*see also* sacred geography)
Africa
  Egypt (St. Katherine's monastery) 1594–1595
  Zimbabwe 1809–1810
Asia
  China 295
  Japan 902, 1123, 1731
  India
    Hindu 34, 101, 763, 766, 769, 774–775, 826, 1777–1778
    Jain 894
  sacred forests 770
  Sri Lanka *see* Pilgrimage to Sripada
Europe
  Baltic indigenous religions 156–157
  Delphic oracle 466–467
  England 697 (*see also* Sacred Sites in England)
  Ireland 854

Italy 981–982
Gaia *see* Gaian Pilgrimage
goddess worship 301
Meso-America
  Andes 62
  Aztec 1052
  Maya 1060
  Virgin Guadalupe 1703
North America
  César, Chávez 291
  Genesis Farm 692
  Hopi-Navajo 794
  theme park 1631
  UNESCO sites 193
Pilgrimage to Sripada (Sri Lanka) 1279–1280
Pinchot, Gifford 602, 1041, 1127, 1280–1281, 1545, 1755 (*see also* adjacent, Pinchot on Church and Country)
Pinchot on Church and Country 1280
Pinnock, Sarah
  contributions in this encyclopedia, *see* Soelle, Dorothee; Williams, Delores S.
Planetary Dance 444, 1281–1283
plants *see* organisms – flora
plant-inspired religion *see* Ayahuasca; Entheogens; Ethnobotany; Peyote
Plaskow, Judith *see* Ecofeminism
Plastic Medicine Men 1061, 1283–1284
Plato *see* philosophy
Plows, Alexandra
  contribution in this encyclopedia, *see* Donga Tribe
Plumwood, Val *see* Ecofeminism
Pocahontas *see* Motion Pictures
Poceski, Mario
  contributions in this encyclopedia, *see* Buddhahood of Grasses and Trees; Creatures' Release in Chinese Buddhism; Indra's Net; Vegetarianism and Buddhism
Pogacnik, Marko 1284–1285
political theology *see* Christianity (7b) – Political Theology
pollution
  air 318, 578, 888, 890, 1467
  industrial 253, 299, 305, 310, 387, 401, 531, 696, 823, 987 (*see also* Pollution Beliefs in South Africa)
  noise 757, 923
  water 30, 212, 718, 723, 755, 871, 1468, 1611, 1778 (*see also* Hinduism and Pollution and adjacent, River Ganga and the Clean Ganga Campaign)
Pollution Beliefs in South Africa 1285–1286
Polynesian Traditional Religions 1287–1288

Polynesia – New Religious Movements 1288–1290
Polytheism 77, 680, 720, 752, 951, 1249, 1290–1292, 1307, 1672
population
  consumption see Population and Consumption – Contemporary Religious Responses; Population, Consumption, and Christian Ethics
  control see Abortion; Breeding and Contraception; Fertility and Abortion; Fertility and Secularization
  Gebara, Ivone see Gebara, Ivone
  growth 122, 149, 177, 297–298, 387, 550, 749, 823, 865, 888, 939, 985
  Judaism see Judaism and the Population Crisis
  Malthus, Thomas Robert see Malthus, Thomas Robert
  overpopulation 13, 384, 458, 626, 653, 689, 769, 860, 865, 1293, 1339, 1659
Population and Consumption – Contemporary Religious Responses 1292–1295
Population, Consumption, and Christian Ethics 1296–1297
Porterfield, Amanda
  contributions in this encyclopedia, see Cowboy Spirituality; Native American Spirituality
Posas, Paula J.
  contributions in this encyclopedia, see Astronauts; Goodall, Jane (with Bron Taylor); Rolston III, Holmes
Potts, Grant
  contributions in this encyclopedia, see Church of All Worlds; Golden Dawn; Lovelock, James; Masons – Fraternal Order of
Power Animals 743, 816, 1298
Powers, John
  contributions in this encyclopedia, see Dalai Lama; Tibet and Central Asia
poverty see Economics
Prairyerth Fellowship 1298–1299
Prakriti 1299–1300, 1521, 1524, 1783
Pravoslavia movement see Europe – Eastern
prayer 159, 167, 201, 311, 329, 498–499, 847, 873, 931, 966, 1172, 1727
Prayer and the Contemplative Traditions 1301–1302
predators see hunting
prey see hunting
Prigogine, Ilya 266, 1266, 1302–1303
primates see organisms
Primate Spirituality 1303–1306
Primavesi, Anne 354, 532, 534
Prince Charles 1306

Prins, Frans 1717
  contribution in this encyclopedia, see San Rainmaking (adjacent to San (Bushmen) Religion)
Process, The 1306–1307
Process Philosophy 343, 1307–1308 (see also Whitehead, Alfred North)
Process Theology see Christianity (7f) – Process Theology; Cobb, John; Process Philosophy
Proctor, James D.
  contribution in this encyclopedia, see Social Science on Religion and Nature (with Evan Berry)
progress, myth of 164, 535, 636
Protestant Ethic, The 1155, 1309–1310, 1504
Protestant Reformation see Christianity
Proto-Indo-Europeans 1128, 1291, 1310–1312
PROUT (progressive utilization theory) 48
psychology
  animal 79, 1173
  ecopsychology see Deep Ecology; Ecopsychology; Radical Environmentalism; Transpersonal Psychology
  ecotherapy see Ecotherapy by Hans Andewag and Rijk Bols
parapsychololgy 287, 364
psychologists
  Aurobindo, Sri see Aurobindo, Sri
  Bateson, Gregory see Bateson, Gregory
  Freud, Sigmund see Freud, Sigmund
  Jung, Carl see Jung, Carl Gustav (and adjacent, Jung, Carl – A Perspective)
  Metzner, Ralph 251, 811, 1329–1330, 1665
  Skinner, B.F. 1762
  Wilber, Ken see Wilber, Ken
  wilderness therapies see Wilderness Rites of Passage
  Transpersonal Psychology see New Age; Transpersonal Psychology
Psychonauts 1312–1313
Ptolemy, Claudius see Europe – Southern
Purack, Akal 1549–1550
Pure Brethren 859, 874, 1314
purgatory see Christianity – Catholicism, Roman
Puritans 148, 316, 474, 518, 1039, 1178, 1314–1315
purity
  moral 71, 586, 880, 927, 1121, 1413, 1424, 1605, 1823 (see also Hinduism and Pollution (and adjacent, The River Ganga and the Clean Ganga Campaign))

  physical 531, 549, 661, 951, 1187, 1715, 1810
  ritual 499, 549, 769, 779, 1286, 1416, 1813–1814
  symbols of 77, 468, 498, 516, 956, 1163, 1178, 1554, 1724 (see also Dirt)
purusha see Hinduism
Pygmies see Africa – Central
Pygmies (Mbuti Foragers) and Bila Farmers of the Ituri Forest (Democratic Republic of the Congo) 1316–1318
Pythagoras see Greece

Q

Qi see Daoism
Quaker eco-witness 674
Quaker Environmental Action Network 674
Quakers see Religious Society of Friends
Quaker Writers in Tasmania (Australia) 1319–1321
quantum theory (mechanics) see Science
quietism 289, 514, 1606
Quimby, Phineas 1182
Quinn, Daniel 635, 812
  contribution in this encyclopedia, see Animism: Humanity's Original Religious Worldview
Quorum of the Twelve Apostles 386–387
Qur'an, The 71–72, 74–75, 571, 791, 1321–1325

R

racism 165, 371, 536–538 (see also Environmental Justice and Environmental Racism)
Radical Environmentalism 1326–1323 (see also adjacent, Rodney Coronoado and the Animal Liberation Front)
  Abbey, Edward see Abbey, Edward
  anarchism see Anarchism
  Animal Liberation Front see Rodney Coronado and the Animal Liberation Front (adjacent to Radical Environmentalism)
  bioregionalism see Bioregionalism; Bioregionalism and the North American Bioregional Conference; Snyder, Gary – and the Invention of Bioregional Spirituality and Politics
  Coronado, Rodney see Coronado, Rodney and the Animal Liberation Front (adjacent to Radical Environmentalism)
  Deep Ecology see Deep Ecology
  Earth First! see Earth First! and the Earth Liberation Front

ecotage (see sabotage, below)
Ecofascism see Ecofacism
environmental concern 1373
Foreman, Dave 1136, 1331, 1355, 1547, 1565 (see also Monkeys in the Field adjacent to Hundredth Monkey)
biocentric activism 1331
Earth First! 600, 1136, 1355, 1565 (see also Earth First! and the Earth Liberation Front)
monkeywrenching 128
on population 457–458
wildlands project 416
music see Music and Eco-activism in America
National Socialism 476 (see also National Socialism)
radical faeries 792
reclaiming see Reclaiming
Regan, Tom 601–602, 1330, 1734 (see also Environmental Ethics; Environmental Racism)
sabotage 3, 54, 416, 518, 520, 522–523, 556–557, 1326, 1720
Shepard, Paul see Shepard, Paul
Singer, Peter 580, 601, 1328, 1330
Snyder, Gary see Snyder, Gary – and the Invention of Bioregional Spirituality and Politics
Watson, Paul see Watson, Paul – and the Sea Shepherd Conservation Society
Raglan, Lady 723–724
rain (see also Makewana the Rainmaker (and adjacent, Mbiriwiri – The Sacred Rainmaking Drum; San Rainmaking, adjacent to San (Bushmen) Religion))
importance of 26, 1114
interdependence 7
Machendranath 1192
rain animals 1723
rain dancing 445–446, 1282
rain-making 485, 1063, 1069, 1396, 1470, 1806, 1808
Rainbow Family 1335–1336
Rainbow Serpent (North Wellesley Islands, Australia) 1336–1337, 1510
Rainbow Warrior 227, 728
rainbows 755, 1400, 1478, 1510, 1561
sacredness 180, 1055, 1456, 1539, 1717, 1773
Rainforest Action Network 1355, 1513, 1593 (see also Hopiland to the Rainforest Action Network)
Rainforests (Central and South America) 1338–1340
Raj, Selva A.
contribution in this encyclopedia, see Santal Region

Rajneesh, Bhagwan Shree see Asia – Southern
Ralegon Siddhi 1340–1341
Ramakrishna see Hinduism
Ramayana see Asia – Southern
Ramirez, Susan Elizabeth
contribution in this encyclopedia, see Incas
Randolph, Richard O.
contributions in this encyclopedia, see Christianity and Animals; Valuing Nature
Ranger, Shelagh
contribution in this encyclopedia, see Animals in African Legend and Ethiopian Scriptures
Ranger Terence
contribution in this encyclopedia, see Zimbabwe Spirit Mediums, Guerillas, and Nature
Raphson, Joseph 1341–1342, 1639
Rappaport, Roy A. ("Skip") xvi, 95–96, 744, 1342–1344, 1387–1389 (see also Ecological Anthropology; Ecology and Religion)
Rasmussen, Larry 343, 369, 404, 555
contributions in this encyclopedia, see Christianity (8) – Ecumenical Movement, International; Christianity and Sustainable Communities
Rastafari 269, 1106–1107, 1344–1346 (and adjacent, Rastafarian Activism; Selassie, Haile)
Rastafarian Activism 1346
rationalism 463, 471, 582, 637–638, 641, 942, 1173, 1290, 1403, 1502, 1571, 1591, 1653
Raval, Shishir R.
contribution in this encyclopedia, see Maldaharis of Gujarat (India)
Raves 135, 1243, 1347–1348
Raymo, Chet 1349
Read, Kay A.
contributions in this encyclopedia, see Cihuacoatl – Aztec Snakewoman; Mesoamerican Deities; Mesoamerican Sacrifice
Reader's Guide to the Encyclopedia of Religion and Nature xix
Reagan, President Ronald see North America – United States
realism 248, 561, 627–628, 1568–1569
Reclaiming 1248, 1328, 1350–1351, 1596
Reclus, Elisée 50, 52, 1351–1352, 1569
Redekop, Calvin
contribution in this encyclopedia, see Christianity (6c3) – Anabaptist/Mennonite Traditions

Redfield, James 278–280, 804 (see also Celestine Prophesy)
Redwood Rabbis 911, 1352–1354
Re-Earthing 1329, 1354–1358
reforestation see forests
Reformed Tradition in its Own Words see Calvin, John – and the Reformed Tradition
Regan, Tom see Radical Environmentalism
Reichel, Elizabeth
contributions in this encyclopedia, see Cosmology; Reichel-Dolmatoff, Gerardo – and Ethnoecology in Colombia
Reichel-Dolmatoff, Gerardo – and Ethnoecology in Columbia 96, 549, 801, 1211, 1358–1362, 1390
Religio-Ecological Perspective on Religion and Nature 1363–1365
Religious Campaign for Forest Conservation 211, 274, 973, 1213, 1365–1367, 1406
Religious Environmentalist Paradigm 1367–1371
Religious Naturalism 615, 1371–1372, 1769 (see also Evolutionary Evangelism; Book of Nature)
religious studies
critical perspectives on see Critical Perspectives on "Religions of the World and Ecology" (adjacent to Religious Studies and Environmental Concern
ecology see Religions of the World and Ecology
environmental concerns see Religious Studies and Environmental Concern
Religious Society of Friends see Friends – Religious Society of (Quakers)
Religious Studies and Environmental Concern 1373–1379 (and adjacent, Critical Perspectives on "Religions of the World and Ecology")
remembering, the 426–427
Renaissance, the see Europe
reproduction, sexual see sexuality (see also Breeding; Population and Consumption)
Reser, Joseph 559
Ress, Mary Judith
contribution in this encyclopedia, see Con-spirando Women's Collective
Restoration Ecology and Ritual 1379–1381 (and adjacent, New Academy for Nature and Culture)
Restoring Eden 1381–1383
revelation 323, 437, 926

Rewilding 1383–1384, 1518
Rexroth, Kenneth 160, 1384–1385, 1562
Rey, Terry
  contributions in this encyclopedia, see
    Caribbean Cultures; Congo River
    Basin; Rubber and Religion (Belgian
    Congo); Trees in Haitian Vodou
Ricard Lanata, Xavier
  contribution in this encyclopedia, see
    Shamanism – Southern Peruvian
    Andes
Richmond, Keith
  contribution in this encyclopedia, see
    Bon (Tibet); Nepal
Ride, Sally 1587
Riding, Laura 710
Ridnovira (Ukraine native faith) see
  Europe – Eastern
Rieger, Joerg
  contributions in this encyclopedia, see
    Dualism – A Perspective (adjacent to
    Dualism); Dualist Heresies;
    Economics
right-wing ecology see ATWA;
  Ecofacism; Facism
Rig Veda see Hinduism
Rigoglioso, Marguerite 982
  contributions in this encyclopedia, see
    California Institute of Integral
    Studies; Lake Pergusa (Sicily)
Ringing Rocks Foundation 1142, 1144
Rio Earth Summit see United Nations'
  "Earth Summits"
rites of spring 223, 529
Ritual 1385–1388
Ritualizing and Anthropology
  1388–1390
Rival, Laura
  contribution in this encyclopedia, see
    Huaoroni
River Ganga and the Clean Ganga
  Campaign 778
Roach, Catherine M.
  contribution in this encyclopedia, see
    Mother Nature Imagery
Roberts, Richard H.
  contribution in this encyclopedia, see
    Centre for Human Ecology
    (Edinburgh, Scotland)
Rock Art – Australian Aboriginal
  1390–1392
Rock Art – Batwa/Pygmies (Central
  Africa) 1392–1393
Rock Art – Chewa (Central Africa)
  1393–1394
Rock Art – Hadzabe/Sandawe (Eastern
  Africa) 1394
Rock Art – Northern Sotho (Southern
  Africa) 1395
Rock Art – Sintu 1395–1396

Rock Art – Western United States
  1396–1398
Rock Climbing 225, 1398–1400
Rockefeller, Steven 1374, 1378
  contribution in this encyclopedia, see
    Earth Charter
Rocky Mountain Institute see North
  America – United States
Rodman, John 600
Rolston III, Holmes 1400–1401
  contributions in this encyclopedia, see
    Aesthetics of Nature and the Sacred;
    Science
Romaine, Suzanne 1161–1162
Roman Britain 221–222, 1401–1402
Roman Catholic Religious Orders
  1403–1408
Roman Catholicism in Latin America
  1408–1409
Roman Natural Religion 1409–1412
Roman Religion and Empire
  1412–1414
Romanies (Gypsies) 1414–1418
Romanticism and Indigenous People
  1418–1419
Romanticism in European History
  1419–1422
Romanticism in European Literature
  1422–1423
Romanticism – American 1424–1426
Romanticism – Western toward Asian
  Religions 1426–1427
Roosevelt, Theodore see North America –
  United States
Rose, Deborah Bird 690
  contribution in this encyclopedia, see
    Aboriginal Dreaming
Roselle, Mike 797, 1136, 1355, 1513
Rosenfeld, Jean E.
  contribution in this encyclopedia, see
    New Zealand
Rosenthal, Sandra B.
  contributions in this encyclopedia, see
    The Protestant Ethic (with Rogene A.
    Buchholz)
Rosicrucians 1021–1022, 1247, 1728
Roskos, Nicole
  contributions in this encyclopedia, see
    Cathedral Forests and the Felling of
    Sacred Groves; Christian Theology
    and the Fall
Ross, Eric B.
  contribution in this encyclopedia, see
    Harris, Marvin
Ross-Bryant, Lynn
  contributions in this encyclopedia, see
    Ehrlich, Gretel; Lopez, Barry
Rossi, Vincent 588, 973
Roszak, Theodore 559, 1329, 1546, 1655
Rothenberg, David 457

contributions in this encyclopedia, see
  Friluftsliv; Music
Rotting Tree Faerie 634 (adjacent to
  Faerie Faith in Scotland)
Rousseau, Jean-Jacques 10, 42, 463,
  1079, 1166, 1208–1210, 1422, 1425,
  1428–1429, 1459, 1488
Rubber and Religion (Belgian Congo)
  1429–1431
Rubber Tappers 213, 836, 1432–1433
Ruck, Carl A.P. 596–597
Rue, Loyal 1372
  contribution in this encyclopedia, see
    Epic of Evolution
Ruether, Rosemary Radford 313, 332,
  361, 539, 610, 680, 1296–1297,
  1433–1434, 1758
  (see also Ecofeminism and Biblical
  Interpretation)
Rumî, Jalaluddin 1214, 1434–1436
Ruskin, John 1423
Russell, Bertrand 1431, 1737
Russian Mystical Philosophy 730,
  1436–1438
Rustlers Valley (South Africa) 1439
Rydving, Håkan
  contribution in this encyclopedia, see
    Saami Culture

S

Saami Culture 1440–1442
Sabbath 41, 57, 73, 99, 126, 174, 309–310,
  354, 543, 919, 927, 1099, 1177,
  1444, 1487, 1705 (see also
  Environmental Sabbath; Sabbath-
  Jubilee Cycle; Jubilee and Jubilee 2000)
Sabbath-Jubilee Cycle 1442–1444
Sabin, Scott C.
  contribution in this encyclopedia, see
    Floresta
sabotage see Radical Environmentalism
sacrifices
  animal 65, 69, 71, 209, 233, 389, 756,
    1017, 1115, 1441, 1477, 1708, 1820
  fire 770
  human 145, 229, 661, 1139, 1517
  ritual offerings 36, 60, 119–120, 295,
    432–433, 592, 718, 721, 764, 820, 926,
    938, 1088, 1115–1117, 1364, 1413,
    1452–1453, 1470, 1434, 1626, 1643,
    1790
Sacramental Universe 331, 351, 400,
  1444–1445
Sacred and the Modern World, The
  1446–1448
sacred geography (see also pilgrimage)
  groves see Sacred Groves of Africa;
    Trees – as Religious Architecture;
    India's Sacred Groves

mountains *see* Sacred Mountains
North America *see* Holy Land in Native North America; Sacred Geography in Native North America
sites *see* Sacred Place/Space; Sacred Sites in England
Sacred Geography in Native North America 1448–1451
Sacred Groves of Africa 1451–1455
Sacred Mountains 1456–1459
  Africa 27
  Andes (South America) 60
  Australia 6–8, 11
  Celtic 283
  Central America
    Guatamala 837
    Maya 1059, 1061, 1068–1069
  China 1798
  England *see* Sacred Sites in England
  India 769, 777, 785, 826, 998,
  Japan 113, 902, 1123, 1768
  North America 528, 786, 797, 1155, 1299, 1525 (*see also* Sacred Geography in Native North America)
  Hawaii 1289
  Tibet 1797–1798
Sacred Sites in England 1460–1462
Sacred Space/Place 1462–1463
Sagan, Carl 275, 613, 735, 1113, 1158, 1463–1465
Saharan Pastoralists 1465–1466
Sallnow, Michael 61
salmon *see* organisms
Salomonsen, Jone
  contributions in this encyclopedia, *see* Reclaiming; Starhawk
Salter, Richard C.
  contributions in this encyclopedia, *see* Selassie, Haile (adjacent to Rastafari); Rastafari
Salvadoran Reflection on Religion, Rights, and Nature 1466–1469
Samhain (Hallowe'en) 283, 508, 1236–1237, 1243–1244
Samia Culture – Western Kenya 1469–1470
Samkhya yoga *see* yoga
San (Bushmen) Apocalyptic Rock Art 1471
San (Bushmen) Rainmaking 1472
San (Bushmen) Religion 1472–1474 (*see also* adjacent, San (Bushmen) Rainmaking)
Sanders, Scott Russell 1474–1475
Sandoval, Mercedes Cros
  contribution in this encyclopedia, *see* Santeria
Sankat Mochan Foundation *see* Asia – Southern

Santa Fe, New Mexico 1475–1476, 1506, 1536
Santal Region (India) 1476–1477
Santeria 260, 1478–1479
Santmire, Paul 316, 343, 376, 377, 1552, 1689–1690
  contribution in this encyclopedia, *see* Christianity (6c1) – Reformation Traditions
Santo Daime *see* South America – Brazil
Sarasvati *see* gods, goddesses, deities and nature spirits – originating in Southern Asia
Saritoprak, Zeki
  contributions in this encyclopedia, *see* Gullen, Fethullah; Qur'an, The
Saro-Wiwa, Kenule Beeson and the Ogoni of Ogoni 1479–1481
Sarpong, Most Rev. Peter K.
  contribution in this encyclopedia, *see* Asante Religion
Sarvodaya Shramadana Movement (Sri Lanka) 105, 240, 1019, 1482–1483
Sasquatch *see* Bigfoot
Satyagraha see Gandhi, Mohandes
Satanism 1250, 1483–1484
Sauna 1485–1487, 1499
Savages 42, 79, 80, 89, 518, 741, 833, 840, 992, 1041, 1144, 1211, 1487–1489, 1644, 1760 (*see also* Noble Savage and the "Ecologically Noble" Savage)
Schaefer, Jame
  contribution in this encyclopedia, *see* Aquinas, Thomas
Scharper, Stephen Bede
  contribution in this encyclopedia, *see* Swimme, Brian
Schlegel, Friedrich *see* philosophy
Schelling, Friedrich Wilhelm Joseph 940, 1174, 1278, 1421, 1423, 1489–1490, 1729
Schipper, Kristopher 448
Schlehe, Judith
  contributions in this encyclopedia, *see* Sea Goddesses and Female Water Spirits; Volcanoes (with Urte Undine Fromming)
Schmidt, Sigrid 961
  contribution in this encyclopedia, *see* Serpents and Dragons
Schmithausen, Lambert 1426
  contribution in this encyclopedia, *see* Buddhism
Schmookler, Andrew Bard 1333
Schoffeleers, Matthew 952, 1028, 1056
scholars, of religion and nature
  Abram, David 190–191, 635, 687, 946, 1329, 1519, 1755
  Barth, Karl 342–343, 347, 382
  Bellah, Robert 488–489, 1173, 1630

Callicott, J. Baird *see* Callicott, J. Baird
Campbell, Joseph *see* Campbell, Joseph
Cobb, John *see* Cobb, John
Doniger, Wendy 597, 1661
Douglas, Mary 95, 421, 468, 486, 664, 1021
Durkheim, Emile 95, 548, 852, 989, 1020, 1311, 1344, 1449
Eliade, Mircea *see* Eliade, Mircea
Fox, Matthew *see* Fox, Matthew
Frazer, James xiii, xvii–xix, 94–95, 672, 744, 1020–1021, 1311, 1389, 1411, 1508
Geertz, Clifford 549, 989
Goodall, Jane *see* Goodall, Jane
Grim, John 96, 1264, 1376–1378
Harris, Marvin *see* Harris, Marvin
James, William *see* James, William
Kaza, Stephanie 1264, 1373, 1706
Leakey, Louis 139, 707, 1304
Lévi-Strauss, Claude 95, 421, 618, 1211, 1429, 1644, 1646, 1817
McDaniel, Jay 313, 353, 364, 1264, 1373
McFague, Sally *see* McFague, Sally
Müller, Friedrich Max *see* Müller, Friedrich Max
Nash, James 343, 353, 368, 377, 1297
Otto, Rudolf 484, 1761
Rappaport, Roy A. ("Skip") *see* Rappaport, Roy A. ("Skip")
Reichel-Dolmatoff, Geraldo *see* Reichel-Dolmatoff, Gerardo – and Ethnoecology in Columbia
Ruether, Rosemary Radford *see* Ruether, Rosemary Radford
Santmire, Paul 316, 343, 376, 377, 1552, 1689–1690
Schweitzer, Albert *see* Schweitzer, Albert
Smart, Ninian 74, 1535
Smith, Huston 596, 1270
Spinoza, Baruch *see* Spinoza, Baruch
Taylor, Bron 668, 1174, 1607
Teilhard de Chardin, Pierre *see* Teilhard de Chardin, Pierre
Tillich, Paul 108, 342–343, 543, 615, 1616
Tucker, Mary Evelyn 1376–1378, 1707
Turnbull, Colin 1211, 1392–1393 (*see also* Pygmies (Mbuti Foragers) and Bila Farmers)
Turner, Victor 95, 1185, 1389, 1675
Tylor, E.B. 78–80, 94–95, 989, 1103, 1389
Weber, Max 1270, 1291, 1309, 1504, 1535, 1555, 1730, 1735

Whitehead, Alfred North *see*
  Whitehead, Alfred North
Scholasticism 327, 346, 1177, 1636
School of Living 1490–1491
Schultes, Richard 596, 619
Schumacher, Ernest Friedrich 105, 555, 564, 599, 731, 988, 1004, **1491–1492**
Schuon, Frithjoj 1151, 1270
Schwab, Jim 541
Schwartz, Nancy
  contributions in this encyclopedia, *see* Elephants; Hyenas – Spotted; Nile Perch; Snakes and the Luo of Kenya
Schwartz, Richard 66, 909
  contributions in this encyclopedia, *see* Tikkun Olam – A Jewish Imperative; Vegetarianism, Judaism, and God's Intention
Schwartz, Steven 492
Schweitzer, Albert 37, 68, 181, 356, 381, 601, **1492–1494**
Science **1494–1497** (*see also* Conservation Biology)
  affirming science 332, 338–340, 372, 381, 383
  and magic 902, 1021–1022
  art 108, 113–114
  astrophysics 420, 643, 1259, 1494–1495, 1679
  criticisms of 165, 313, 342, 1539 (*see also* Merchant, Carolyn)
  creationism *see* Creationism and Creation Science; Scopes Trial
  ecology 95, 359, 381–382, 1746
  evolution and evolutionary biology *see* Darwin, Charles; Epic of Evolution; Evolutionary Biology, Religion, and Stewardship; Evolutionary Evangelism; Scopes Trial
  fiction *see* Science Fiction
  genetic engineering 66, 728, 1071, 1210, 1625 (*see also* Jewish Law and Genetic Engineering)
  homosexuality *see* Homosexuality and Science
  indigenous people *see* Traditional Ecological Knowledge; Traditional Ecological Knowledge among Aboriginal Peoples in Canada
  natural science 210, 715
  nature 20–21 (*see also* Fauna Cabala)
  new age science *see* New Age
  religion and science 338, 363, 373, 392, 394, 473, 685, 1113, 1627, 1633, 1712 (*see also* Western Esotericism; Wilber, Ken)
    Hinduism *see* River Ganga and the Clean Ganga Campaign
    Islam *see* Islamic Foundation for Ecology and Environmental Sciences; Nasr, Seyyed Hossein
    Judaism *see* Judaism
  revolution 163, 535, 1054, 1108, 1166, 1278
  scientific materialism 207
  scientific realism 248
  scientists (biologists, ecologists and physicists)
    Bacon, Frances 313, 473, 535, 583, 598, 698, 759, 1012, 1083, 1108, 1209, 1226, 1746
    Darwin, Charles *see* Darwin, Charles
    Einstein, Albert *see* Einstein, Albert
    Haeckel, Ernst *see* Haeckel, Ernst
    Linnaeus, Carl *see* Linnaeus, Carl
    Lovelock, James *see* Lovelock, James
    Newton, Isaac 266, 288, 342, 406, 1005, 1053, 1278, 1302, 1730, 1737
    Pauli, Wolfgang *see* Pauli, Wolfgang
    Peat, F. David *see* Peat, F. David
    Prigogine, Ilya *see* Prigogine, Ilya
    Raymo, Chet *see* Raymo, Chet
    Sagan, Carl *see* Sagan, Carl
    Sheldrake, Rupert *see* Sheldrake, Rupert
    Swimme, Brian *see* Swimme, Brian
    Wilson, Edward O. *see* Wilson, Edward O.
  social science *see* Social Science on Religion and Nature
  theories and principles
    anthropic principle *see* Anthropic Principle
    chaos *see* Chaos
    complexity theory *see* Complexity Theory
    General Systems Theory 267, 1019
    quantum theory (mechanics) 364, 406, 683, 1632, 1737
    theory of relativity 582, 1278
  technology 338, 363, 423, 442, 1209, 1651, 1766 (*see also* Fuller, Buckminster; Technological Immortality)
    appropriate technologies 105, 131, 540, 665, 797, 869, 1482, 1629
Science Fiction 383, 501, 520, 566, 638, 1001, 1012, 1474, **1497–1499**, 1625, 1671
scientific revolution *see* Science
Scientology 177, **1499–1501**, 1671
Scopes, John 436, 1501
Scopes Trial 436, 454, **1501–1502**
Scotland *see* Europe – Northern
Scott, Kim 690
Scott, Susan L.
  contributions in this encyclopedia, *see* Butala, Sharon; Memoir and Nature Writing
Scouting 43, 211, 830, 1173, **1505–1507**
Scything and Erotic Fulfillment **1507–1508**
Sea Goddesses and Female Water Spirits **1509–1511**
Sea Shepherd Conservation Society *see* Watson, Paul – and the Sea Shepherd Conservation Society
Seattle (Sealth), Chief 44–45, 492, 846, **1511–1512**
Secaira, Estuardo
  contribution in this encyclopedia, *see* Mayan Spirituality and Conservation
secret societies 587, 1453, 1790
sects *see* Utopian Communities
Sedona 527, 1196, **1512–1513**
Seed, John 162, 165, 214, 238, 243, 425, 426, 457, 558, 612, 634, 659, 675, 803, 857, 1019, 1136, 1376, **1513–1514**
  contribution in this encyclopedia, *see* Re-Earthing
Seeds in South Asia **1514–1515**
Seidenberg, David 910
  contributions in this encyclopedia, *see* Animal Rights in the Jewish Tradition; Jewish Environmentalism in North America; Kabbalah and Eco-Theology; Maimonides; Paganism and Judaism
Seidr 744, **751–752**, 753, 754 (adjacent to Heathenry – Ásatrú)
Selassie, Haile 269, 1345 (adjacent to Rastafari)
Self Hill, Rebecca 493
  contributions in this encyclopedia, *see* Disney (with Joseph G. Champ); Theme Parks (with Joseph G. Champ)
Selling, Kim
  contribution in this encyclopedia, *see* Fantasy Literature
Senior, John
  contribution in this encyclopedia, *see* Noble Savage
Senoi (Malayan Peninsula) **1515–1516**
Serpents and Dragons **1516–1518**
Servetus, Michael 1678
Seton, Ernest Thompson 43, 830, 1156, **1172–1173** (*see also* Scouting)
Sexson, Lynda
  contributions in this encyclopedia, *see* Bestiary; Dillard, Annie; Watkins, T.H.
sexuality (*see also* Tantra; Tantrism in the West)
  as sacred 584, 1740
  Christianity
    Augustine 325
    reproduction 550–551

ecospirituality *see* Sexuality and Ecospirituality
environmental consciousness *see* Sexuality and Green Consciousness
erotic fulfillment *see* Scything and Erotic Fulfillment
fertility *see* Fertility and Secularization
homosexuality *see* Homosexuality; Homosexuality and Science
reproduction, sexual 374, 550, 567, 614, 644, 654–655, 673, 719, 1032, 1083, 1520
utopias 564, 1687
Whitman, Walt 1738
Sexuality and Ecospirituality 1518–1519
Sexuality and Green Consciousness 1519–1523
Shackley, Myra
  contribution in this encyclopedia, *see* St. Katherine's Monastery (Egypt)
Shaker religion *see* Indian Shaker Religion
Shakti 586, 773, 776, 824, 828, 1521, **1523–1524**, 1619–1620
Shamanism (*see also* Castaneda, Carlos)
  art *see* Rock Art – Western United States; Shamanism – and Art
  astroshamanism 124
  Druidry 508
  Foundation for Shamanic Studies *see* Harner, Michael – and the Foundation for Shamanic Studies
  indigenous peoples 422, 801, 852, 1267, 1358, 1364, 1565, 1667
  magic *see* Magic, Animism and the Shaman's Craft
  Mayan 1068
  Neo-Shamanism *see* Shamanism – Neo; Shamanism – Neo (Eastern Europe)
  South America *see* Shamanism – Ecuador; Shamanism – Southern Peruvian Andes
  Totemism 1645
  traditional *see* Shamanism – Traditional
  urban *see* Shamanism – Urban
  Yachajs 61, 1052, **1526–1527**
Shamanism – and Art 1524–1526
Shamanism – Ecuador 1526–1527
Shamanism – Neo 1528–1529
Shamanism – Neo (Eastern Europe) 1529–1531
Shamanism – Southern Peruvian Andes 1531–1532
Shamanism – Traditional 1532–1535
Shamanism – Urban 1535–1537
Shankar, Sri Ravi on Consciousness, Nature and the Art of Living 116 (adjacent to Art of Living Foundation)
Shankara *see* Asia – Southern

Shaolin masters *see* Asia – Eastern
Sharma, Arvind 792
Shattuck, Cybelle
  contributions in this encyclopedia, *see* Natural Law Party; Transcendental Meditation
Sheba, Queen of 74–75, 1345
Sheldrake, Rupert 563, 804, 1266, 1492, **1537**, 1586, 1632
Shepard, Paul 395, 456, 519, 558, 581, 600, 635, 810, 812, 1329, **1537–1538**, 1565
Shinto *see* Asia – Eastern
Shirogokorov, Sergei M. 1533–1534
Shiva, Vandana 535, 680, 775, 1293, 1300, 1329, 1356, 1515, **1539**, 1682
Shnirelman, Victor A. 1246
  contributions in this encyclopedia, *see* Koliada Viatchel; Neo-Paganism and Ethnic Nationalism; Oshmarii-Chimarii (Mari-El Republic, Russia)
Shona Women and the Mutopo Principle 1540–1541
Shorter, David
  contribution in this encyclopedia, *see* Yoeme (Yaqui) Ritual
Shoshone (Western North America) 1541–1542
Shugendo *see* Asia – Eastern
shrines *see* Altars and Shrines
Siam's Forest Monasteries 1543
Sierra Club 178, 200, 225–226, 240, 625, 870, 998, 1099, 1123, 1179–1180, 11210, 1459, **1544–1547**, 1757
Sierra Treks 1548
Sikhism 823, **1549–1550**
Silko, Leslie Marmon 475, **1551**, 1565
Simoons, Frederick 503, 709
Simpson, Leanne
  contributions in this encyclopedia, *see* Aboriginal Environmental Groups in Canada; Traditional Ecological Knowledge Among Aboriginal Peoples in Canada
Sinai, Mt. *see* St. Katherine's Monastery
Singer, Peter *see* Radical Environmentalism
Sittler, Joseph A. Jr. 316, 342, 539, 599, **1551–1552**, 1736
Siva *see* gods, goddesses, deities, and nature spirits
Sivaraksa, Sulak 240, 243, **1552–1553**
Six-day War *see* Asia – Western
Sjöö, Monica 1521, **1554**
Skinker, Mary 270
Sky 1554–1555
Slater, Peter 257–258
Slavic Neo-Paganism 1556–1557

Slavic Religion 1557–1558
Slocum, John 831
Smart, Ninian 74, 1535
Smith, Adam *see* Economics
Smith, Andrea
  contribution in this encyclopedia, *see* Plastic Medicine Men
Smith III, J. Andy
  contributions in this encyclopedia, *see* Coalition for Environmentally Responsible Economics; Interfaith Center on Corporate Responsibility; National Council of Churches Eco-Justice Working Group (USA)
Smith, B.W.
  contributions in this encyclopedia, *see* Kaphirintiwa – The Place of Creation (Central Africa); Kasama Spirit Sites (Northern Zambia); Makewana the Rainmaker (and adjacent, Mbiriwiri – The Sacred Rainmaking Drum); Nyau – A Closed Association (Central Africa); Rock Art – Batwa Pygmies (Central Africa); Rock Art – Chewa (Central Africa); Rock Art – Hazabe/Sandawe (Eastern Africa); Rock Art – Northern Sotho (Southern Africa)
Smith, Huston 596, 1270
Smohalla *see* North America – United States
Smuts, Jan Christiaan 208, 359, 782–783, **1559**, 1774
Snakes and the Luo of Kenya 1559–1562
Snow, Keith Harmon
  contributions in this encyclopedia, *see* Manser, Bruno – and the Penan of Sarawak; Saro-Wiwa, Kenule Beeson – and the Ogoni of Ogoni
Snyder, Gary *see* Snyder, Gary – and the Invention of Bioregional Spirituality and Politics; Anarchism 53, 1564–1566
  animistic perception 1024
  Bioregionalism 188, 599, 603, 1329
  Buddhism 243
  Cosmology 456
  hunting 810
  influence on ecopsychology 1329
  nature 161, 519, 848
Snyder, Gary – and the Invention of Bioregional Spirituality and Politics 1562–1565
Snyder, Samuel D.
  contribution in this encyclopedia, *see* Fly Fishing
Social Construction of Nature and Environmental Ethics 1567–1569
Social Darwinism *see* Darwin, Charles
Social Ecology 1569–1571
social justice *see* Chávez, César and the

United Farm Workers; Eco-justice in Theology and Ethics; Environmental Justice and Environmental Racism; Eco-justice in Theology and Ethics; Eco-Justice Working Group; Social Ecology
Social Science on Religion and Nature 605, 1571–1576
Soelle, Dorothee 1577–1578
Sohappy, David – and Salmon Spirituality 1578–1580
Soka Gakkai see Buddhism – Engaged
Soka Gakkai and the Earth Charter 1580–1581 (see also Earth Charter)
Sokol, Moshe 1240, 1246
Solomon, King 74–75, 269, 307, 908, 1053, 1141, 1153, 1322, 1345, 1728
Solomon Islands see Oceania
solstices 156, 276, 283, 721,1236, 1237, 1244–1245, 1248, 1361, 1451, 1484, 1601, 1607
Soma see Hinduism
Somé, Malidome Patrice 1581–1582
Song of Songs 326, 533, 1698
Song of Sorrow – Icnocuicatl 146 (adjacent to Aztec Religion)
Sophists see Europe – Southern
Sotiriu, Eleni
 contribution in this encyclopedia, see Greek Landscape
South America
 Amazonia 37–39, 82, 141, 178, 180, 597, 621, 680, 799, 801, 837
 ancestors 618, 620
 caboclos 38–39, 1432, 1675–1676
 deforestation 1406
 economic exploitation 38–39 (see also Boff, Leonardo)
 folktales see Amazonian Folktales (and adjacent, Mapinguari)
 Tukanoan Indians see Tukanoan Indians
 Andes see Andean Traditions; Shamanism – Southern Peruvian Andes
 Brazil
 Boff, Leonardo see Boff, Leonardo
 Gebara, Ivone see Gebara, Ivone
 Kari Oca see World Conference of Indigenous Peoples
 indigenous peoples see Indigenous Activism and Environmentalism
 religion
 Candomblé see Candomblé of Brazil; Orixa Iroko
 Christianity see South America – Christianity
 plant-inspired religion see Ayahuasca
 Santo Daime 142, 597, 620, 1432–1433
 Umbanda see Umbanda
 Rubber Tappers see Rubber Tappers
 water spirits see Sea Goddesses and Female Water Spirits
 Yanomani see Yanomani
 Christianity in South America
 Catholicism see Roman Catholicism in Latin America
 Contemporary Christianity see Brazil and Contemporary Christianity
 Liberation Theology see Christianity (7c) – Liberation Theology
 organizations
 Con-spirando Women's Collective see Con-spirando Women's Collective
 Floresta see Floresta
 people, influential
 Boff, Leonardo see Boff, Leonardo
 Gebara, Ivone see Gebara, Ivone
 Colombia
 ethnoecology see Reichel-Dolmatoff, Gerardo and Ethoecology in Colombia
 Kogi see Kogi
 U'wa Indians see U'wa Indians
 Ecuador
 Shamanism see Shamanism – Ecuador
 rainforests see Rainforests
Southard, Mary 726
Southeast Asia see Asia – Southeastern
Soviet Union see Europe – Eastern
sports 565, 830, 1201, 1644 (see also Fly Fishing; Mountaineering; Rock Climbing; Surfing)
Space Exploration 254, 1585–1588 (see also adjacent, Institute of Noetic Sciences; Astronauts; Sagan, Carl)
Speilberg, Steven see Motion Pictures
Spencer, Daniel T.
 contributions in this encyclopedia, see Community Supported Agriculture; Homosexuality (and adjacent, Homosexuality and Science)
Spencer, Herbert 1183, 1760
Spinoza, Baruch 456, 582, 601, 736, 933, 1027, 1150, 1342, 1588–1590 (see also Pantheism)
Spirit and Nature 829, 1423, 1590–1591, 1615, 1620
Spirit and Nature Conferences 243, 1374 1378
Spirit and Nature Walking Paths 1592
Spirit of the Sage Council 1592–1593
spirit mountain 787
spiritualism 80, 287, 1180–1181, 1196, 1199,1711,1757 (see also Theosophy)
spiritual warrior 273
spirit writing see Ziran
Splain, Thomas
 contributions in this encyclopedia, see Dualist Heresies; Esalen Institute; Roman Catholic Religious Orders
Sponsel, Leslie E.
 contributions in this encyclopedia, see Amazonia; Anthropologists; Anthropology as a Source of Nature Religion; Biodiversity; Caves – Sacred (Thailand); Ecological Anthropology; Noble Savage and the "Ecologically Noble" Savage; Rainforests (Central and South America); Southeast Asia; Trees – Sacred; Yanomani
Spretnak, Charlene 251, 419, 538, 725, 1264, 1593–1594
Sri Lanka see Asia – Southern
St. Bernard of Clairvaux 100, 167, 1404
St. John, Graham
 contribution in this encyclopedia, see Australia
St. Katherine's Monastery (Mount Sinai, Egypt) 1594–1595
Stalin, Joseph see Europe – Eastern
Stange, Mary Zeiss
 contribution in this encyclopedia, see Hunting Spirituality
Starhawk 54, 442, 507, 510, 537, 554, 662, 680, 975–976, 1233, 1248, 1328, 1350, 1570, 1595, 1741, 1743
Stark, Rodney 657, 1198, 1200
Steigerwald, Joan
 contribution in this encyclopedia, see Romanticism in European History
Steinberg, Rabbi Naomi see Judaism
Steiner, Rudolf – and Anthroposophy 451, 563, 692, 1285, 1596–1597
Steiner, William
 contribution in this encyclopedia, see Kapu in Early Hawaiian Society
Stevens, Wallace 46, 259, 502, 1597–1598
Stewardship 23, 30, 83, 129 169, 319, 347, 370, 1598–1599 (see also Biblical Foundations for Christian Stewardship; Christian Friend of the Earth, A; Interfaith Council for Environmental Stewardship)
Stone Circles 283, 392, 508, 526–528, 692, 1235, 1237, 1460–1461, 1475, 1599–1600
Stonehenge 283, 508, 510, 526,624, 738, 989, 1237, 1460–1462, 1587, 1600–1601
story place 1336–1337
Storytelling and Wonder 1602–1603
Stover, Dale
 contribution in this encyclopedia, see Lakota Sun Dance